Caribbean
Slavery
in the
Atlantic World

This page intentionally left blank

Caribbean Slavery in the Atlantic World

A Student Reader

Verene A. Shepherd

Hilary McD. Beckles

Ian Randle Publishers
Kingston

James Currey Publishers
Oxford

Marcus Wiener Publishers
Princeton

First published in Jamaica, 2000 by
Ian Randle Publishers Limited
206 Old Hope Road, Box 686
Kingston 6, Jamaica

ISBN 976-8123-61-3 (paperback)

This is a revised and expanded edition of the work previously published as
Caribbean Slave Society and Economy.

A catalogue record for this book is available from the National Library of Jamaica

First published in the United States of America by
Markus Wiener Publishers
231 Nassau Street
Princeton, NJ 08540

Library of Congress Cataloging-in-Publication Data

Caribbean slavery in the Atlantic world / Hilary McD. Beckles and Verene A. Shepherd.
    p.cm.
    "This is a revised and expanded edition of the work previously published as
Caribbean slave society and economy" – T.p. verso.
    ISBN 1-55876-185-3 (pbk.: alk. paper)
    1. Slavery – Caribbean Area – History. 2. Slave-trade – Caribbean Area – History.
    3. Plantation life – Caribbean Area – History. 4. Sugar workers – Caribbean Area – History.
    5. Slaves – Emancipation – Caribbean Area – History. 6. Caribbean Area – Race relations –
History. I. Beckles, Hilary, 1955- II. Shepherd, Verene.
    HT1071. C343 1999
    305.5'67'09729 – dc21

First published in the United Kingdom by
James Currey Publishers
73 Botley Road
Oxford OX2 0BS

ISBN 0-85255-767-1 (paperback)

British Library Cataloguing in Publication Data

Caribbean slavery in the Atlantic world. – 2nd ed.
    1. Slavery – Caribbean Area – History 2. Sugar workers
    Caribbean Area – History 3. Plantation life – Caribbean Area – History 4.
    Slaves – Emancipation – Caribbean Area – History
    I. Beckles, Hilary McD. II. Shepherd, Verene III. Caribbean slave society and economy
    305.5'67'09729

Cover and book design by Robert Harris
Set in Times New Roman 10/12 x 16
Printed and bound in the U.S.A. by Data Reproductions Corporation

Cover painting: *Sonthonax distributes arms to the freed slaves* by Eddy Jacques, 1991.
Collection: Afrique en Créations

Dedicated to the memory of
Elsa Goveia,
C.L.R. James and
Eric Williams

This page intentionally left blank

Contents

Introduction

In 1944, Eric Williams published *Capitalism and Slavery* and placed Caribbean slavery within the context of Atlantic modernity. Chattel slavery was an integral part of North Atlantic capitalist accumulation, and subject to the forces of the market economy. Capitalism promoted slavery as part of its primitive accumulation and removed it subsequently as part of a systemic rationalization in search of efficiency gains. Colonialism, slavery, and capitalism since then have been represented by scholars of the Caribbean as expressions of a materialist age, represented conceptually in terms of individualist rationality and race interests. The Caribbean was at the centre of an imperialist policy that saw modernity taking its clearest form as a network of contradictory and unstable forces. Caribbean slavery was a place of new beginnings.

Colonization, the process of territorial acquisition and settlement, was effected by six European nations in the Caribbean between 1492 and the end of the eighteenth century. The most important of these nations, from the point of view of impact upon the region's socio-economic development, were Spain, England, France and Holland. The other nations, Denmark and Sweden, were minor powers whose presence did little to shape the direction and nature of the colonial enterprise. These imperial powers all attempted to carve out spheres of influence in space formerly occupied and under the control of a heterogeneous but well-entrenched indigenous people. European colonization was based on racist assumptions about the indigenous Caribbean and led to a process of "othering" which generated an opposing struggle for freedom and dignity.

The European colonization of the Caribbean, then, neither remained uncontested, nor proceeded unproblematically. There was, for example, an on-going struggle between the Kalinago of the Eastern Caribbean islands and their English and French colonizers which was not settled until late in the 18th century. The Kalinago repulsed attempts to take over their land entirely and reduce them to the status of servile labourers. Despite their brave struggles against subjugation and domination, the indigenous populations, for the most part, were decimated. Where they survived, [as in Guyana and sections of the Eastern Caribbean islands], they were placed in conditions of dishonorable social and economic marginalization. The decimation of large numbers of indigenous peoples and the reluctance or inability of Europeans to reduce the survivors to the status of servile labourers, created the context within which thousands of white indentured servants and millions of Africans were imported to the region to form a labour force. The plantation was considered to be the most efficient basis of the agrarian export economy and large-scale slavery the most efficient means of labour exploitation on the large plantation. Thus what the imperial powers all held in common by the middle of the eighteenth century, was an overwhelming dependence upon enslaved African labour to sustain expansion and economic viability.

Since the colonial period, the historiography of these slave systems depicted not only the interests and sensibilities of imperialist groups, but has increasingly reflected the consciousness of activities of the 'insider' Creole community. In recent years, the volume of published work has reached such large proportions that scholars now speak in terms of an historiographic revolution. Michael Craton, a leading historian of Caribbean slave systems, has suggested, for example, that slave studies are now more than a *vogue*, but *nouvelle vague*.

One result of this historiographical development is that scholars who shoulder the additional responsibility of conducting large-scale student seminars, now find the task of comprehensively assimilating the literature rather immense. The process of systematically searching through dozens of journals, not to mention the financial strain of purchasing increasingly expensive monographs, poses a range of special problems for students and tutors alike.

The preparation of this volume of essays constitutes a modest attempt to redress at least two of these difficulties. It is conceived and designed as a student/tutor companion, and has as its target, the debate environment of the University and College seminar on Comparative Slave Systems. The wide range of coverage reflects the main themes of recent research and publication. Essays are selected in order to provide macro-perspectives on the slave mode of production (its internal and external dimensions) as well as its constituent parts along with their socio-economic and ideological expression.

They cover the sociology and economics of slavery, illustrating the dynamic relations between modes of production and social life. The superstructures of slave systems have fascinated scholars perhaps to a greater degree than their economic substructures; as such the debates on race and colour relations, health and mortality, religion, recreational culture, women, family organization and kinship patterns, as well as the endemic problems of social reproduction are represented in a number of essays. Also, the fundamental and unifying characteristics of these slave societies – maturing anti-slavery consciousness and politics – are addressed as one central element to the discourse on social control and resistance. This theme provides part of the general background to investigations of the disintegration of the slave systems, from Haitian Revolution to Spanish Caribbean emancipation towards the end of the nineteenth century.

The general guiding principle of tracing the evolution of slavery in Atlantic modernity shaped the selection of essays, but two important objectives were kept firmly in mind: (i) to provide a pan-Caribbean, trans-imperial thematic focus, sensitive to the formation of Creole culture and identity that imposed a binding socioculture trajectory on the region; (ii) to illustrate the many patterns and forms of socio-economic life and activity that shaped the region's heterogeneous slave societies and to account for their uneven pace and diversity of development.

It took over 100 years for the system of slavery to sink and spread its roots deeply into the social, institutional and market responses of Caribbean inhabitants. It also took over 100 years of organized constitutional efforts, by revolution and reform to remove them in their entirety. The complex, and dialectical relations between these two sets of historical processes are central to the thematic flow of this collection. We hope that it makes a contribution, no matter how small, to students' understanding of Caribbean-Atlantic history and society, and that it acts as an energy source for scholars in their search for new evidence and interpretations.

Verene A. Shepherd
Hilary McD. Beckles

Acknowledgments

The Editors and Publishers are grateful to the authors and original publishers for permission to reproduce their work in this volume. Listed below are the original publication details.

The Atlantic Slavery Project

Walter Rodney, "How Europe Became the Dominant Section of a World-wide Trade System", from *How Europe Underdeveloped Africa* (Bogle-L'Overture, London 1972), pp. 84-101.

A. Russell-Wood, "Before Columbus: Portugal's African Prelude to the Middle Passage and Contribution to Discourse on Race and Slavery", in Vera Hyatt and Rex Nettleford, eds, *Race Discourse and the Origins of the Americas* (Smithsonian, Washington, 1995), pp. 134-169.

Orlando Patterson, "The Constituent Elements of Slavery" [extract from *Slavery and social death*]. (Harvard University Press: Cambridge, Mass. 1982, pp. 1-14.)

Sidney Greenfield, "Madeira and the Beginnings of New World Sugar Cane Cultivation and Plantation Slavery: A Study in Institution Building", *Annals of the New York Academy of Sciences*, 292, 1977, pp. 610-628.

John Thornton, "The Birth of an Atlantic World", in *Africa and Africans in the Making of the Atlantic World*, 1400-1680, [Cambridge University Press, 1992] pp. 13-42

The Indigenous Peoples: Conquest, Resistance and Representation

David Henige, "On the Contact Population of Hispaniola: History as Higher Mathematics" *Hispanic American Historical Review*, Vol. 58, No. 2, 1978, pp. 217-37.

Alvin Thompson, "Amerindian-European Relations in Dutch Guyana" in *Colonialism and Underdevelopment in Guyana, 1580-1803*, Caribbean Research and Publications, Bridgetown, 1987 00191-213.

Phillip Boucher, "First Impressions: Europeans and Island Caribs in the Pre-Columbian Era", in Phillip Boucher, *Cannibal Encounters*, (Johns Hopkins, 1992) pp. 13-30.

Hilary McD Beckles, "Kalinago (Carib) Resistance to European Colonization of the Caribbean", *Caribbean Quarterly*, Vol.21:1 (1987) pp. 55-77.

Paul Thomas, "The Caribs of St. Vincent: A Study in Imperial Maladministration, 1763-73" *Journal of Caribbean History*, Vol. 18, No. 2, 1984, pp. 60-73.

Imperialism and Colonial Slavery

David Watts, "Early Hispanic New World Agriculture, 1492 to the end of the 16th Century", in Watts, *The West Indies: Patterns of Development, Culture and Environmental Change since 1492* (Cambridge University Press, 1987)

Franklin Knight, "Imperialism and slavery", in Knight, *The Caribbean: the genesis of a fragmented nationalism* (Oxford University Press: New York), pp. 67-92.

Paul Kopperman, "Ambivalent Allies: Anglo-Dutch relations and the struggle against the Spanish Empire in the Caribbean, 1621-1641", *Journal of Caribbean History* Vol. 21:1, 1987 pp. 55-77

Nuala Zahedieh, "Trade, Plunder and Economic Developments in Early English Jamaica", *Economic History Review*, 39, 1989, pp. 205-222.

Paul Butel, "France, the Antilles, and Europe in the 17th and 18th Century: Renewals of Foreign Trade", in James D. Tracy, *The Rise of Merchant Empires: Long Distance Trade in the Early Modern World* (Cambridge University Press, 1990), pp. 153-174.

Servitude, Slavery and New Economic Orders

Robert C. Batie, "Why Sugar? Economic Cycles and the Changing of Staples on the English and French Antilles, 1624-54" *Journal of Caribbean History*, Vols 8-9, 1976, pp. 1-41.

Hilary McD. Beckles, "A 'riotous and unruly lot': Irish Indentured servants and freemen in the English WI, 1644-1713". (*The William & Mary Quarterly* 3rd series, vol. XLVII October 1990, pp. 505-522)

Hilary McD Beckles, & Andrew Downes, "The Economics of the Transition to the Black Labour System in Barbados, 1630-1680", *Journal of Interdisciplinary History*, XVIII (1987), 225-47.

Verene Shepherd, "Livestock and sugar: aspects of Jamaica's agricultural development from the late seventeenth to the early 19th century", *The Historical Journal* 34:3 (1991), 627-643.

Franklin Knight, "The Transformation of Cuban Agriculture, 1763-1838" in *Slave Society in Cuba During the 19th Century* (Madison, 1970), pp. 3-24. University of Wisconsin Press, 114 North, Murray St., Madison, Wisconsin, 53715, U.S.A.

Francisco Scarano, "The Origins of Plantation Growth in Puerto Rico" in *Sugar and Slavery in Puerto Rico*, (Madison, 1984), pp.16-34, University of Wisconsin Press, 114 North, Murray St., Madison, Wisconsin, 53715, U.S.A.

Slavery, Finance and Trade

Joseph E. Inikori, "The slave trade and the Atlantic economies, 1451-1870", pp. 56-85. *The African slave trade from the 15th to the 19th century*. Reports and papers of the meeting of experts organised by UNESCO at Port-au-Prince, Haiti, 31 January - 4 February 1978. Pub. 1979 by UNESCO, the United Nations.

Carlos Marichal & Matilde Souto Mantecón, "Silver and Situados: New Spain and the financing of the Spanish Empire in the Caribbean in the 18th century". *Hispanic American Historical Review*, Vol. 74 no. 4 (Nov. 1994), Duke University Press, Durham NC pp. 587-614.

K.G. Davies, "The Origins of the Commission System in the West India Trade." Royal Historical Society, University College, London, Gower St. London WC1 6BT.

Robert Stein, "The French West Indian Sugar Business" in *The French Sugar Business in the 18th Century*, Louisiana State University Press, Baton Rouge, 70893, Louisiana, USA, 1988, pp. 74-89.

Selwyn Carrington, "The United States and the British West Indian trade, 1783-1807". In *West Indies Accounts*, Roderick McDonald, ed. [The Press, UWI, 1996], pp. 149-167.

Verene Shepherd, "Trade and Exchange in Jamaica in the Period of Slavery" Unpublished.

The Work Culture of the Enslaved

Barry Higman, "Physical and Economic Environments". Chapter. 3 of *Slave populations of the British Caribbean* (Johns Hopkins, 1984; The Press, UWI, 1996)

Lucille Mathurin Mair, *Women Field Workers in Jamaica During Slavery* (1986 Elsa Goveia Lecture, Department of History, University of the West Indies, Mona)

Franklin Knight, "Slavery in a Plantation Society". From Knight, *Slave society in Cuba during the Nineteenth Century* (The University of Wisconsin Press: Madison, 1970) pp. 59-84.

Dale Tomich, "Slavery in Martinique in the French Caribbean" in Tomich, *Slavery in the Circuit of Sugar*, pp. 214-248; 321-325. (Johns Hopkins: Baltimore, 1990).

N.A.T. Hall, "Slavery in three West Indian towns", in Barry Higman, ed., *Trade, Government and Society* (Heineman, Kingston, 1983), pp. 17-38.

Slavery and Capitalist Globalization: The First Phase

Eric Williams, "*Capitalism and Slavery*", Andre Deutsch, London.

C.L.R. James, "French Capitalism and Caribbean Slavery", in *The Black Jacobins: Toussaint L'Ouverture and the San Domingo Revolution* (Vintage Books, 1963) pp. 47-61.

Franklin Knight, "Slavery and Lagging Capitalism in the Spanish and Portuguese American Empire", in Barbara Solow, *Slavery and the Rise of the Atlantic System* (Cambridge, 1991).

William Darity, "Mercantilism, Slavery and the Industrial Revolution", in Paul Zarembka, ed. *Research in Political Economy* (Jai Press, Greenwich, Conn. 1982), pp. 1-21. Jai Press INC, 36 Sherwood Place, Greenwich, Conn., 06830.

Slavery and Capitalist Globalization: The Second Phase

Manuel Moreno Fraginals, "Plantations in the Caribbean: Cuba, Puerto Rico, and the Dominican Republic in the late 19th century", in Fraginals, et. al, eds., *Between slavery and free labor: the Spanish-speaking Caribbean in the 19th century* (Johns Hopkins: Baltimore, 1985), pp. 3-20.

Luis Fernandez-Martinez, "The Sweet and Bitter: Cuban and Puerto Rican Response to the mid-19th Century Sugar Challenge", *New West Indian Guide*, vol. 67, 1993, pp. 47-69.

Veront Satchell, "The early use of steam power in the Jamaican sugar industry, 1768-1810". [repub. from The Newcomen Society for the study of the history of engineering and technology. *Transactions*, Vol. 67 (1995-96), pp. 221-231.

Laird Bergrad, "Slave prices in Cuba, 1840-1875", *Hispanic American Historical Review* 67: 4 (Nov. 1987), pp. 631-655.

Race, Class, Colour and the Power Order

Gordon Lewis, "Pro-Slavery Ideology", in *Main Currents in Caribbean Thought* (Johns Hopkins, 1983) pp. 94-136.

Elsa Goveia, "The West Indian Slave Laws of the Eighteenth Century" Originally published in *Revista de Ciencias Sociales*, IV, No. 1 (1960), pp. 75-105. Editorial de al Universidad de Costa Rica, Apdo. 75, 2050 San Pedro de Montes se Oca, Costa Rica. Also in Laura Foner and Eugene Genovese (eds), *Slavery in the New World: A Reader in Comparative History* (New Jersey, 1969).

Carl Campbell, "Trinidad's Free Coloureds in Comparative Caribbean Perspectives", in his *Cedulants and Capitulants* (Paria Pub. Co. Ltd. Port of Spain, 1992), chap. 2 (pp. 52-83; 350-57 of notes).

Verene Shepherd, "Livestock Farmers and Marginality", *Social and Economic Studies*, 41, 2 (1991), 183-201.

Anton L. Allahar, "The Cuban Sugar Planters, 1790-1820: "The Most Solid and Brilliant Bourgeoisie Class in all of Latin America", *Americas*, 41, 1984, pp 37-58.

Sex, Race and the Gender Order

Joseph Dorsey, "Women Without History": Slavery and the International Politics of Partis Sequiter Ventrem in the Spanish Caribbean", *Journal of Caribbean History*, 28:2, 1995, pp. 165-208

Hilary Beckles, "White Women and Slavery in the Caribbean", *History Workshop Journal*, vol. 36, 1993.

Marrietta Morrissey, "Women's Work, Family Formation , and Reproduction Among Caribbean Slaves" University Press of Virginia, Box 3608, University Sta., Charlottesville, VA 22903, U.S.A. *Review*, IX, 3 (Winter 1986), pp. 339-67.

Digna Castañeda, "The Female Slave in Cuba During the First Half of the 19th Century", in Shepherd, *et al.*, (eds.) *Engendering History* (Ian Randle Publishers, 1995), pp. 141-155.

Hilary McD Beckles, "Property Rights in Pleasure: The Marketing of Slave Women's Sexuality in the West Indies", in Roderick McDonald (ed) *West Indies Accounts* (UWI Press, 1996), pp. 169-188.

Verene Shepherd, "Gender and Representation" [unpub. Paper]

Subaltern Social Autonomy: Social and Economic Culture

Humphrey Lamur, "Slave Religion on the Vossenburg Plantation (Suriname) and Missionaries' Reactions" Vinson H. Sutlive *et al.* editors Studies in Third World Societies, Dept. Anthropology, College of William and Mary, Williamsburg, Virginia, 23185, U.S.A.

Neville Hall, "Slaves use of their 'free time' in the Danish Virgin Islands in the later 18th and early 19th century", *Journal of Caribbean History*, 1980

Hilary McD Beckles, "An Economic Life of Their Own: Slaves as Commodity Producers and Distributors in Barbados", *Slavery and Abolition*, vol. 12, no. 1, 1991

Dale Tomich, "The Other Face of Slave Labour: Provision Grounds and Internal Marketing in Martinique" The Johns Hopkins University Press. As above.

Sidney Mintz & Douglas Hall, "The Origins of the Jamaican Internal Marketing System"in Mintz (ed) *Papers in Caribbean Anthropology*, No. 57 (New Haven, 1970), pp.3-26

Mary Turner, "Chattel Slaves into Wage Slaves: a Jamaican Case Study", in Turner. ed., *From Chattel Slaves to Wage Slaves* (Ian Randle Publishers), pp. 33-47.

Deadly Business: Mortality, Health, Nutrition and the Crisis of Social Reproduction

Kenneth Kiple & Virginia Kiple, "Deficiency Diseases in the Caribbean", I.T. Press Journals, 55 Hayward Street, Cambridge, MA 02142-9949, U.S.A. *Journal of Interdisciplinary History*, Vol. 11, No. 2 (1980), pp. 197-215.

Michael Craton, "Death, Disease and Medicine on Jamaican Slave Plantations: The Example of Worthy Park, 1767-1838" The editor, *Histoire Sociale/Social History*, c/o Dept. of History, Univ. of Ottawa, Ottawa, Ontario, Canada K1N 6N5

Humphrey Lamur, "Demographic Performance of Two Slave Plantations of the Dutch Speaking Caribbean" CEDLA, Keizers-gracht, 395-397, 1016 EK, Amsterdam, the Netherlands.

Rejecting Slavery: Blacks Speak Back

Olaudah Equiano, *The Life of Olaudah Equiano* (ed). Paul Edwards, Addison Wesley Longman Ltd, Essex, England., pp. 15-28

Esteban Montejo, *The Autobiography of a Runaway Slave* (eds), Miguel Barnet and Alistair Hennessey (McMillan, 1993), pp. 65-80

Mary Prince, *The History of Mary Prince: A West Indian Slave Related by Herself*, (ed), Moira Ferguson (Pandora, 1987), pp. 47-71

Touissaint L'Overture, Speeches and Letters, extracts from George Tyson, Jr. *Touissaint L'Overture* (Prentice Hall, 1973), pp. 27-45.

Caribbean Wars: Marronage and Rebellion

Hilary McD Beckles, "Caribbean Anti-Slavery: The Self Liberation Ethos of Enslaved Blacks' *Journal of Caribbean History*, Vol, 22, Nos. 1-2 1988, pp. 1-19.

Kamau Brathwaite, "Caliban, Ariel and Unprospero in the conflict of creolisation: a study of the slave revolt in Jamaica in 1831-32", in Rubin and Tuden eds., *Comparative Perspectives on Slavery in New World Plantation Societies*, New York Academy of Sciences, New York, pp. 45-69.

Verene Shepherd, "Liberation Struggles on Livestock Farms in Jamaica During Slavery" (unpub. paper)

N.A.T. Hall, "Maritime Maroons: *Grand Marronage* from the Danish West Indies" Editors, William and Mary Quarterly, Box 220, Williamsburg, Virginia, 23187, U.S.A. *William and Mary Quarterly*, 3rd series, Vol. XLII, October 1985, pp. 476-97.

Bernard Moitt, "Slave Resistance in Guadeloupe and Martinique, 1791-1848", *Journal of Caribbean History*, vol. 25: 1 & 2, 1992, pp. 136-160

The Haitian Revolution

John K Thornton, "African Soldiers in the Haitian Revolution", *Journal of Caribbean History* vol. 25: 1 & 2, 1992, pp. 58-81.

C.L.R. James, "The San Domingo, Masses Begin", in *The Black Jacobins: Toussaint L'Ouverture and the San Domingo Revolution* (Vintage Books, 1963).

Carolyn Fick, "The St. Domingue Slave Insurrection of 1791: A socio-Political and Cultural Analysis", in *Journal of Caribbean History*, vol. 25: 1 & 2, 1992, pp. 1-41

Rebel Women: Anti-Slavery Feminist Vanguard

Lucille Mathurin Mair, *The Rebel Woman in the British West Indies during Slavery*, (Institute of Jamaica, 1975) pp 1-37.

Hilary Beckles, "Persistent rebels: Women and Anti-slavery Activity", from Beckles, *Natural Rebels* (Rutgers, 1989) pp. 152-174.

Bernard Moitt, "Women, Work and Resistance in the French Caribbean during Slavery", in Shepherd, et al, eds., *Engendering History*, (Ian Randle Publishers, 1995), pp. 155-175.

Capitalism, Ideology and Emancipation Processes

Selwyn Carrington, "The State of the Debate on the Role of Capitalism in the Ending of the Slave System", *Journal of Caribbean History*, Vol, 22, 1-2 (1988), pp. 20-41.

Seymour Drescher, Review of The Antislavery Debate: Capitalism and Abolitionism as a Problem in Historical Interpretation. Thomas Bender (ed) (Berkeley: University of California Press, 1992), in *History & Theory: Studies in the Philosophy of History* 32:3 (1993), 311-329 [Wesleyan University, Middletown, Conn 06459, USA]

Seymour Drescher, "The Decline Thesis of British Slavery since *Econocide*" Frank Cass Co. Ltd., Gainsborough House, 11 Gainsborough Rd., London E11 1RS. *Slavery and Abolition*, Vol. 7, No. 1 (1986), pp. 3-23.

Andre Midas, "Victor Schoelcher and Emancipation in the French West Indies" *Caribbean Historical Review*, Vol. 1 (1950) pp.110-30

Ivan Schulman, "The portrait of the slave: ideology and aesthetics in the Cuban anti-slavery novel" in Rubin and Tuden eds., *Comparative Perspectives on Slavery in New World Plantation Societies*, New York Academy of Sciences, New York, pp. 410-422.

Rebecca Scott, "Explaining Abolition: Contradiction, Adaptation, and Challenge in Cuban Slave Society, 1860-86" The Johns Hopkins University Press, 701 West 40th St., Baltimore, Maryland 21211, U.S.A.

This page intentionally left blank

SECTION ONE
The Atlantic Slavery Project

The westward movement of African slavery within the Atlantic basin preceded the Columbus mission, and was a noticeable trend as early as the mid-fifteenth century. Madeira, an island in the Atlantic Ocean off the northwest coast of Africa, provided the link between sugar production by European Christians in the Mediterranean and the plantations of the New World. In the second and third quarters of the fifteenth century plantations and plantation slavery were established in Madeira. In one sense, argues Greenfield in this section, Madeira might be considered the link between Mediterranean sugar production and plantation slavery and the system that was to dominate Caribbean history and society into the nineteenth century.

The birth of the Atlantic World as an integrated economy characterized by an enormous movement of Africans and Europeans into the Americas hinged on the infrastructural development of chattel slavery as a specific category. As a system of socio-economic exploitation, chattel slavery was familiar to both Europeans and Africans, though both had little experience with it until the post-Columbian era. What was common to the experiences of all groups, however, was deep involvement in transnational trade and finance. The making of an integrated market culture in the Atlantic may have been associated with international warfare, political tensions, and the social degradation associated with slave trading and slave owning, but perceptions of profitability was the central focus of all participants.

The Atlantic slavery project, therefore, was not suddenly conceived and implemented. It evolved slowly at first, but gained rapid momentum during the second half of the fifteenth century. By the mid-sixteenth century its principal elements were in place. States and entrepreneurs drove their interests as aggressively as they could, and the mechanisms and logic of expansionism and long-distance trade generated a distinct socio-cultural order. African, European, and their Mediterranean cultural experiences, created a Creole vision that ultimately became the symbols of an Atlantic identity. In this section, Rodney and Russell-Wood examine the background to burgeoning imperialist mentality as it relates to the Atlantic project. Patterson places slavery within its wider historical context, while Greenfield and Thornton illustrate the specific steps taken and ideas formulated along the way in the making of the Atlantic World.

1

How Europe Became the Dominant Section of a World-wide Trade System

WALTER RODNEY

Because of the superficiality of many of the approaches to 'underdevelopment', and because of resulting misconceptions, it is necessary to re-emphasise that development and underdevelopment are not only comparative terms, but that they also have a dialectical relationship one to the other: that is to say, the two help produce each other by interaction. Western Europe and Africa had a relationship which ensured the transfer of wealth from Africa to Europe. The transfer was possible only after trade became truly international; and that takes one back to the late 15th century when Africa and Europe were drawn into common relations for the first time - along with Asia and the Americas. The developed and underdeveloped parts of the present capitalist section of the world have been in continuous contact for four and a half centuries. The contention here is that over that period Africa helped to develop Western Europe in the same proportion as Western Europe helped to underdevelop Africa.

The first significant thing about the internationalisation of trade in the 15th century was that Europeans took the initiative and went to other parts of the world. No Chinese boats reached Europe, and if any African canoes reached the Americas (as is sometimes maintained) they did not establish two-way links. What was called international trade was nothing but the extension overseas of European interests. The strategy behind international trade and the production that supported it was firmly in European hands, and specifically in the hands of the sea-going nations from the North Sea to the Mediterranean. They owned and directed the great majority of the world's sea-going vessels, and they controlled the financing of the trade between four conti-

nents. Africans had little clue as to the tri-continental links between Africa, Europe and the Americas. Europe had a monopoly of knowledge about the international exchange system seen as a whole, for Western Europe was the only sector capable of viewing the system as a whole.

Europeans used the superiority of their ships and cannon to gain control of all the world's waterways, starting with the western Mediterranean and the Atlantic coast of North Africa. From 1415, when the Portuguese captured Ceuta near Gibraltar, they maintained the offensive against the Maghreb. Within the next sixty years, they seized ports such as Arzila, El-Ksar-es-Seghir and Tangier, and fortified them. By the second half of the 15th century, the Portuguese controlled the Atlantic coast of Morocco and used its economic and strategic advantages to prepare for further navigations which eventually carried their ships round the Cape of Good Hope in 1495. After reaching the Indian Ocean, the Portuguese sought with some success to replace Arabs as the merchants who tied East Africa to India and the rest of Asia. In the 17th and 18th centuries, the Portuguese carried most of the East African ivory which was marketed in India; while Indian cloth and beads were sold in East and West Africa by the Portuguese, Dutch, English and French. The same applied to cowry shells from the East Indies. Therefore, by control of the seas, Europe took the first steps towards transforming the several parts of Africa and Asia into economic satellites.

When the Portuguese and the Spanish were still in command of a major sector of world trade in the first half of the seventeenth century, they engaged in buying cotton cloth in India to exchange for slaves in Africa to mine gold in

Central and South America. Part of the gold in the Americas would then be used to purchase spices and silks from the Far East. The concept of metropole and dependency automatically came into existence when parts of Africa were caught up in the web of international commerce. On the one hand, there were the European countries who decided on the role to be played by the African economy; and on the other hand, Africa formed an extension to the European capitalist market. As far as foreign trade was concerned, Africa was dependent on what Europeans were prepared to buy and sell.

Europe exported to Africa goods which were already being produced and used in Europe itself - Dutch linen, Spanish iron, English pewter, Portuguese wines, French brandy, Venetian glass beads, German muskets, etc. Europeans were also able to unload on the African continent goods which had become unsaleable in Europe. Thus, items like old sheets, cast-off uniforms, technologically outdated firearms, and lots of odds and ends found guaranteed markets in Africa. Africans slowly became aware of the possibility of demanding and obtaining better imported goods, and pressure was exerted on the captains of European ships; but the overall range of trade goods which left the European ports of Hamburg, Copenhagen and Liverpool was determined almost exclusively by the pattern of production and consumption within Europe.

From the beginning, Europe assumed the power to make decisions within the international trading system. An excellent illustration of that is the fact that the so-called international law which governed the conduct of nations on the high seas was nothing else but European law. Africans did not participate in its making, and in many instances African people were simply the victims, for the law recognised them only as transportable merchandise. If the African slave was thrown overboard at sea, the only legal problem that arose was whether or not the slave ship could claim compensation from the insurers! Above all, European decision-making power was exercised in selecting what Africa should export – in accordance with European needs.

The ships of the Portuguese gave the search for gold the highest priority, partly on the basis of well-known information that West African gold reached Europe across the Sahara and partly on the basis of guesswork. The Portuguese were successful in obtaining gold in parts of West Africa and in eastern Central Africa; and it was the 'Gold Coast' which attracted the greatest attention from Europeans in the 16th and 17th centuries. The number of forts built there was proof to that effect, and the nations involved included the Scandinavians and the Prussians (Germans) apart from other colonial stalwarts like the British, Dutch and Portuguese.

Europeans were anxious to acquire gold in Africa because there was a pressing need for gold coin within the growing capitalist money economy. Since gold was limited to very small areas of Africa as far as Europeans were then aware, the principal export was human beings. Only in a very few places at given times was the export of another commodity of equal or greater importance. For instance, in the Senegal there was gum, in Sierra Leone camwood, and in Mozambique ivory. However, even after taking those things into account, one can say that Europe allocated to Africa the role of supplier of human captives to be used as slaves in various parts of the world.

When Europeans reached the Americas, they recognised its enormous potential in gold and silver and tropical produce. But that potential could not be made a reality without adequate labour supplies. The indigenous Indian population could not withstand new European diseases such as smallpox, nor could they bear the organised toil of slave plantations and slave mines, having barely emerged from the hunting stage. That is why in islands like Cuba and Hispaniola, the local Indian population was virtually wiped out by the white invaders. At the same time, Europe itself had a very small population and could not afford to release the labour required to tap the wealth of the Americas. Therefore, they turned to the nearest continent, Africa, which incidentally had a population accustomed to settled agriculture and disciplined labour in many spheres. Those were the objective conditions lying behind the start of the European slave trade, and those are the reasons why the capitalist class in Europe used their control of international trade to ensure that Africa specialised in exporting captives.

Obviously, if Europe could tell Africans what to export that was an expression of European power. However, it would be a mistake to believe that it was an overwhelming military power. Europeans found it impossible to conquer Africans during the early centuries of trade, except in isolated spots on the coast. European power resided in their system of production which was at a somewhat higher level than Africa's at that time. European society was leaving feudalism and was moving towards capitalism; African society was then entering a phase comparable to feudalism.

The fact that Europe was the first part of the world to move from feudalism towards capitalism gave Europeans a head start over humanity elsewhere in the scientific understanding of the universe, the making of tools and the efficient organisation of labour. *European technical superiority did not apply to all aspects of production, but the advantage which they possessed in a few key areas proved decisive.* For example, African canoes on the river Nile and the Senegal coast were of a high standard, but the relevant sphere of operations was the ocean, where European ships could take command. West Africans had developed metal casting to a fine artistic perfection in many parts of Nigeria, but when it came to the meeting with Europe, beautiful bronzes were far less relevant than the crudest cannon. African wooden utensils were sometimes works of great beauty, but Europe produced pots and pans that had many practical advantages. Literacy, organisational experience, and the capacity to produce on an ever-expanding scale also counted in the European favour.

European manufactures in the early years of trade with Africa were often of poor quality, but they were of new varieties and were found attractive. Estaban Montejo, an African who ran away from a Cuban slave plantation in the 19th century, recalled that his people were enticed into slavery by the colour red. He said:

It was the scarlet which did for the Africans; both the kings and the rest surrendered without a struggle. When the kings saw that the whites were taking out these scarlet handkerchiefs as if they were waving, they told the blacks, 'Go on then, go and get a scarlet handkerchief', and the blacks were so excited by the scarlet they ran down to the ships like sheep and there they were captured.

That version by one of the victims of slavery is very poetic. What it means is that some African rulers found European goods sufficiently desirable to hand over captives which they had taken in warfare. Soon, war began to be fought between one community and another for the sole purpose of getting prisoners for sale to Europeans, and even inside a given community a ruler might be tempted to exploit his own subjects and capture them for sale. A chain reaction was started by European demand for slaves (and only slaves) and by their offer of consumer goods - this process being connected with divisions within African society.

It is often said for the colonial period that vertical political divisions in Africa made conquest easy. This is even more true of the way that Africa succumbed to the slave trade. National unification was a product of mature feudalism and of capitalism. Inside of Europe, there were far fewer political divisions than in Africa where communalism meant political fragmentation with the family as the nucleus, and there were only a few states that had real territorial solidity. Furthermore, when one European nation challenged another to obtain captives from an African ruler, Europe benefitted from whichever of the two nations won the conflict. Any European trader could arrive on the coast of West Africa and exploit the political differences which he found there. For example, in the small territory that the Portuguese later claimed as Guinea-Bissau, there were more than a dozen ethnic groups. It was so easy to set one off against another that Europeans called it a 'slave trader's paradise'.

Although class divisions were not pronounced in African society, they too contributed to the ease with which Europe imposed itself commercially on large parts of the African continent. The rulers had a certain status and authority, and when bamboozled by European goods they began to use that position to raid outside their societies as well as to exploit internally by victimizing some of their own subjects. In the simplest of societies where there were no kings, it proved impossible for Europeans to strike up the alliance which was necessary to carry on a trade in captives on the coast. In those societies with ruling groups, the association with Europeans was easily established; and afterwards Europe hardened the existing internal class divisions and created new ones.

In effect, particular aspects of African society became weaknesses when Europeans arrived as representatives of a different phase of development. And yet the subjugation of the African economy through slave trade was a slow process at the outset, and in some instances African opposition or disinterest had to be overcome. In the Congo, the slave trade did not get underway without grave doubts and opposition from the king of the state of Kongo at the beginning of the 16th century. He asked for masons, priests, clerks, physicians, etc.; but instead he was overwhelmed by slave ships sent from Portugal, and a vicious trade was opened up by playing off one part of the Kongo Kingdom against another. The king of the Kongo had conceived of possibilities of mutually beneficial interchange between his people and the European state, but the latter forced him to specialise in the export of human cargo. It is also interesting to note that whilst the *Oba* (king) of Benin was willing to sell a few female captives, it took a great deal of persuasion and pressure from Europeans to get him to sell male African prisoners of war, who would otherwise have been brought into the ranks of Benin society.

Once trade in slaves had been started in any given part of Africa, it soon became clear that it was beyond the capacity of any single African state to change the situation. In Angola, the Portuguese employed an unusual number of their own troops and tried to seize political power from Africans. The Angolan state of Matamba on the river Kwango was founded around 1630 as a direct reaction against the Portuguese. With Queen Nzinga at its head, Matamba tried to co-ordinate resistance against the Portuguese in Angola. However, Portugal gained the upper hand in 1648, and this left Matamba isolated. Matamba could not forever stand aside. So long as it opposed trade with the Portuguese, it was an object of hostility from neighbouring African states which had compromised with Europeans and slave-trading. So in 1656 Queen Nzinga resumed business with the Portuguese - a major concession to the decision-making role of Europeans within the Angolan economy.

Another example of African resistance during the course of the slave trade comes from the Baga people in what is now the Republic of Guinea. The Baga lived in small states, and about 1720 one of their leaders (Tomba by name) aimed at securing an alliance to stop the slave traffic. He was defeated by local European resident, traders, mulattoes and other slave-trading Africans. It is not difficult to understand why Europeans should have taken immediate steps to see that Tomba and his Baga followers did not opt out of the role allocated to them by Europe. A parallel which presents itself is the manner in which Europeans got together to wage the 'Opium War' against China in the 19th century to ensure that Western capitalists would make profit while the Chinese were turned into dope addicts.

Of course, it is only as a last resort that the capitalist metropoles need to use armed force to ensure the pursuit of favourable policies in the dependent areas. Normally, economic weapons are sufficient. In the 1720s, Dahomey opposed European slave traders, and was deprived of European imports – some of which had become necessary by that time. Agaja Trudo, Dahomey's greatest king, appreciated that European demand for slaves and the pursuit of slaving in and around Dahomey was in conflict with Dahomey's development. Between 1724 and 1726, he looted and burnt European forts and slave camps; and he reduced the trade from the 'Slave Coast' to a mere trickle, by blocking the paths leading to sources of supply in the interior. European slave dealers were very bitter, and they tried to sponsor some African collaborators against Agaja Trudo. They failed to unseat him or to crush the Dahomian state, but in turn Agaja failed to persuade them to develop new lines of economic activity, such as local plantation agriculture; and, being anxious to acquire firearms and cowries through the Europeans, he had to agree to the resumption of slave trading in 1730.

After 1730, Dahomian slaving was placed under royal control and was much more restricted than previously. Yet, the failure of this determined effort demonstrated that a single African state at that time could not emancipate itself from European control. The small size of African states and the numerous political divisions made it so much easier for Europe to make the decisions as to Africa's role in world production and trade.

Many guilty consciences have been created by the slave trade. Europeans know that they carried on the slave trade, and Africans are aware that the trade would have been impossible if certain Africans did not cooperate with the slave ships. To ease their guilty conscience, Europeans try to throw the major responsibility for the slave trade on to the Africans. One European author of a book on the slave trade (appropriately entitled *Sins of Our Fathers*) explained how many other white people urged him to state that the trade was the responsibility of African chiefs, and that Europeans merely turned up to buy the captives - as though without European demand there would have been captives sitting on the beach by the millions! Issues such as those are not the principal concern of this study, but they can be correctly approached only after understanding that Europe became the centre of a world-wide system and that it was European capitalism which set slavery and the Atlantic slave trade in motion.

The trade in human beings from Africa was a response to *external* factors. At first, the labour was needed in Portugal, Spain and in Atlantic islands such as São Tome, Cape Verde and the Canaries; then came the period when the Greater Antilles and the Spanish American mainland needed replacements for the Indians who were victims of genocide; and then the demands of Caribbean and mainland plantation societies had to be met. The records show direct connections between levels of exports from Africa and European demand for slave labour in some part of the American plantation economy. When the Dutch took Pernambuco in Brazil in 1634, the Director of the Dutch West Indian Company immediately informed their agents on the 'Gold Coast' that they were to take the necessary steps to pursue the trade in slaves on the adjacent coast east of the Volta - thus creating for that area the infamous name of the 'Slave Coast'. When the British West Indian islands took to growing sugar cane, the Gambia was one of the first places to respond. Examples of this kind of external control can be instanced right up to the end of the trade, and this embraces Eastern Africa also, since European markets in the Indian Ocean islands became important in the 18th and 19th centuries, and since demand in places like Brazil caused Mozambicans to be shipped round the Cape of Good Hope.

Africa's contribution to the economy and beliefs of early capitalist Europe

The kinds of benefits which Europe derived from its control of world commerce are fairly well-known, although it is curious that the recognition of Africa's major contribution to European development is usually made in works devoted specifically to that subject; while European scholars of Europe often treat the European economy as if it were entirely independent. European economists of the 19th century certainly had no illusions abut the interconnections

between their national economies and the world at large. J.S. Mill, as spokesman for British capitalism, said that as far as England was concerned, 'the trade of the West Indies is hardly to be considered as external trade, but more resembles the traffic between town and country'. By the phrase 'trade of the West Indies' Mill meant the commerce between Africa, England and the West Indies, because without African labour the West Indies were valueless. Karl Marx also commented on the way that European capitalists tied Africa, the West Indies and Latin America into the capitalist system; and (being the most bitter critic of capitalism) Marx went on to point out that what was good for Europeans was obtained at the expense of untold suffering by Africans and American Indians. Marx noted that 'the discovery of gold and silver in America, the extirpation, enslavement and entombment in mines of the aboriginal population, the turning of Africa into a commercial warren for the hunting of black skins signalised the rosy dawn of the era of capitalist production'.

Some attempts have been made to try and quantify the actual monetary profits made by Europeans from engaging in the slave trade. The actual dimensions are not easy to fix, but the profits were fabulous. John Hawkins made three trips to West Africa in the 1560s, and stole Africans whom he sold to the Spanish in America. On returning to England after the first trip, his profit was so handsome that Queen Elizabeth I became interested in directly participating in his next venture; and she provided for that purpose a ship named the *Jesus*. Hawkins left with the *Jesus* to steal some more Africans, and he returned to England with such dividends that Queen Elizabeth made him a knight. Hawkins chose as his coat of arms the representation of an African in chains.

Of course, there were inevitably voyages that failed, slave ships that were lost at sea, etc. Sometimes trade in Africa did well, while at other times it was the profit in the Americas that was really substantial. When all the ups and downs are ironed out, the level of profit had to be enough to justify continued participation in that particular form of trade for centuries. A few bourgeois scholars have tried to suggest that the trade in slaves did not have worthwhile monetary returns. They would have us believe that the same entrepreneurs whom they praise in other

(1862) the principal port of the world for this infamous commerce; although the cities of Portland and Boston are only second to her in that distribution.

American economic development up to mid-19th century rested squarely on foreign commerce, of which slavery was a pivot. In the 1830s, slave-grown cotton accounted for about half the value of all exports from the United States of America. Furthermore, in the case of the American colonies of the 18th century, it can again be observed that Africa contributed in a variety of ways - one thing leading to another. For instance, in New England, trade with Africa, Europe and the West Indies in slaves and slave-grown products supplied cargo for their merchant marine, stimulated the growth of their ship-building industry, built up their towns and their cities, and enabled them to utilise their forests, fisheries and soil more effectively. Finally, it was the carrying trade between the West Indian slave colonies and Europe which lay behind the emancipation of the American colonies from British rule, and it was no accident that the struggle for American independence started in the leading New England town of Boston. In the 19th century, the connection with Africa continued to play an indirect role in American political growth. In the first place, profits from the slave activities went into the coffers of political parties, and even more important the African stimulation and black labour played a vital role in extending European control over the present territory of the U.S.A. - notably in the South, but including also the so-called 'Wild West' where black cowboys were active.

Slavery is useful for early accumulation of capital, but it is too rigid for industrial development. Slaves had to be given crude non-breakable tools which held back the capitalist development of agriculture and industry. That explains the fact that the northern portions of the U.S.A. gained far more industrial benefits from slavery than the South which actually had slave institutions on its soil; and ultimately the stage was reached during the American Civil War when the Northern capitalists fought to end slavery within the boundaries of the U.S.A., so that the country as a whole could advance to a higher level of capitalism.

In effect, one can say that within the U.S.A. the slave relations in the South had by the second half of the 19th century come into conflict with the further expansion of the productive base inside the U.S.A. as a whole, and a violent clash ensued before the capitalist relations of legally free labour became generalised. Europe maintained slavery in places that were physically remote from European society; and therefore inside Europe itself, capitalist relations were elaborated without being adversely affected by slavery in the Americas. However, even in Europe there came a moment when the leading capitalist states found that the trade in slaves and the use of slave labour in the Americas was no longer in the interest of their further development. Britain made this decision early in the 19th century, to be followed later by France.

Since capitalism, like any other mode of production, is a total system which involves an ideological aspect, it is also necessary to focus on the effects of the ties with Africa on the development of ideas within the superstructure of European capitalist society. In that sphere, the most striking feature is undoubtedly the rise of racism as a widespread and deeply rooted element in European thought. The role of slavery in promoting racist prejudice and ideology has been carefully studied in certain situations, especially in the U.S.A. The simple fact is that no people can enslave another for centuries without coming out with a notion of superiority, and when the colour and other physical traits of those peoples were quite different it was inevitable that the prejudice should take a racist form. Within Africa itself, the same can be said for the situation in the Cape Province of South Africa where white men were establishing military and social superiority over non-whites ever since 1650.

It would be much too sweeping a statement to say that all racial and colour prejudice in Europe derived from the enslavement of Africans and the exploitation of non-white peoples in the early centuries of international trade. There was also anti-Semitism at an even earlier date inside Europe and there is always an element of suspicion and incomprehension when peoples of different cultures come together. However, it can be affirmed without reservations that the white racism which came to pervade the world was an integral part of the capitalist mode of production. Nor was it merely a question of how the individual white person treated a black person. The racism of Europe was a set of generalisations and assumptions, which had no scientific basis, but were rationalised in every sphere from theology to biology.

Occasionally, it is mistakenly held that Europeans enslaved Africans for racist reasons. European planters and miners enslaved Africans for *economic* reasons, so that their labour power could be exploited. Indeed, it would have been impossible to open up the New World and to use it as a constant generator of wealth, had it not been for African labour. There were no other alternatives: the American (Indian) population was virtually wiped out and Europe's population was too small for settlement overseas at that time. Then, having become utterly dependent on African labour, Europeans at home and abroad found it necessary to rationalise that exploitation in racist terms as well. Oppression follows logically from exploitation, so as to guarantee the latter. Oppression of African people on purely racial grounds accompanied, strengthened and became indistinguishable from oppression for economic reasons.

C.L.R. James, noted Pan-Africanist and Marxist, once remarked that:

The race question is subsidiary to the class question in politics, and to think of imperialism in terms of race is disastrous. But to neglect the racial factor as merely incidental is an error only less grave than to make it fundamental.

It can further be argued that by the 19th century white racism had become so institutionalised in the capitalist world (and notably in the U.S.A.) that it sometimes ranked above the maximisation of profit as a motive for oppressing black people.

In the short run, European racism seemed to have done Europeans no harm, and they used those erroneous ideas to justify their further domination of non-European peoples in the colonial epoch. But the international proliferation of bigoted and unscientific racist ideas was bound to have its negative consequences in the long run. When Europeans put millions of their brothers (Jews) into ovens under the Nazis, the chickens were coming home to roost. Such behaviour inside of 'democratic' Europe was not as strange as it is sometimes made out to be. There was always a contradiction between the elaboration of democratic ideas inside Europe and the elaboration of authoritarian and thuggis practices by Europeans with respect to Africans. When the French Revolution was made in the name of 'Liberty, Equality and Fraternity', it did not extend to black Africans who were enslaved by France in the West Indies and the Indian Ocean. Indeed, France fought against the efforts of those people to emancipate themselves, and the leaders of their bourgeois revolution said plainly that they did not make it on behalf of black humanity.

It is not even true to say that capitalism developed democracy at home in Europe and not abroad. At home, it was responsible for a talk or certain rhetoric of freedom, but it was never extended from the bourgeoisie to the oppressed workers; and the treatment of Africans must surely have made such hypocrisy a habit of European life, especially within the ruling class. How else can one explain the fact that the Christian church participated fully in the maintenance of slavery and still talked about saving souls! The hypocrisy reached its highest levels inside the U.S.A. The first martyr in the American national war of liberation against the British colonialists in the 18th century was an African descendant, Crispus Attucks; and both slave and free Africans played a key role in Washington's armies. And yet, the American Constitution with its famous preamble that 'all men are created equal' sanctioned the continued enslavement of Africans. In recent times, it has become an object of concern to some liberals that the U.S.A. is capable of war crimes of the order of My Lai in Vietnam. But the fact of the matter is that the My Lais began with the enslavement of Africans and American Indians. Racism, violence and brutality were the concomitants of the capitalist system when it extended itself abroad in the early centuries of international trade.

References

Oliver Cox, *Capitalism as a System* (New York: Monthly Review Press, 1964).

W. E. B. DuBois, *The Suppression of the Atlantic Slave Trade to the United States of America. 1638-1870* (New York: Social Science Press, 1954).

F. Clairemonte, *Economic Liberalism and Undedrdevelopment*

Philip D. Curtin, *The Image of Africa* (Madison: The University of Wisconsin Press, 1964)

Leo Huberman, *Man's Worldly Goods: the story of the wealth of nations* (New York and London: Harper Bros., 1936)

Winthrop Jordan, *White Over Black: American attitudestowards the negro* (Chapel Hill: Published for the Institute of Early American History and Culture at Williamsburg, 1968)

Richard Pares, *Yankees and Creoles: the trade between North America and the West Indies before the American Revolution* (London: Longmans Green, 1956)

Eric Williams, *Capitalism and Slavery* (Chapel Hill: University of North Carolina Press, 1944)

2

Before Columbus: Portugal's African Prelude to the Middle Passage and Contribution to Discourse on Race and Slavery

A.J.R. RUSSELL-WOOD

In 1992, from China to Peru, exhibits, lectures, and symposia were held in connection with the quincentennial of the first voyage of Christopher Columbus and his 'discovery' of America. For some, this was an occasion for celebration – of the epoch-making voyage of an exceptional navigator who returned to tell the story, of the European crossing of the Atlantic, and of the revelation of a continent hitherto unknown to Europeans, with subsequent migration, settlement, colonization, and exploitation of the new land's mineral resources and agricultural and commercial potential. Native Americans, however, found no cause for celebration. For them, 1492 marked the beginning of their decimation, through disease, conquest, forced relocation, forced labour, the seizure of their tribal lands, and the destruction or erosion of their cultures. Nor was it a happy occasion for Africans and persons of African descent. One scholar has referred to half a millennium of humiliation, which they have suffered in the Americas dating back to Columbus's landfall on October 12, 1492, in the island group that came to be called the Bahamas (see Van Sertima 1976:27, 28).

My purpose in this chapter is to take 1492 not as the beginning of an era, but as the end. The half-century preceding 1492 witnessed the inauguration of an exclusively seaborne slave trade from sub-Saharan Africa to Europe. The addition of an American dimension resulted in modifications to what had become institutionalized before 1492. In mid-fifteenth-century Por-

tugal, points of reference were established for future discourse on race and slavery and for debates that were to tax theologians, jurists, and statesmen in the sixteenth century, preoccupy thinkers of the Enlightenment, and take on nationalistic tones in the nineteenth-century polemic over the abolition of slavery and the slave trade.

To fully understand the situation, it is necessary to examine the background to the pre-Columbian slave trade from West and Central Africa to Portugal. The first European intrusion into Africa in the early modern period occurred in 1415 when a Portuguese force took Ceuta. This was prompted, among other considerations, by military and religious motivations to exert additional pressure on the Moors in Granada, the need for a secure base from which to attack Moorish shipping, internal domestic pressures on the Portuguese king, the hope of tapping into routes – or, preferably, reaching the sources - of African gold, and a desire for booty, access to Moroccan grain harvests, and for acquisition of fertile lands to expand revenues from agriculture (see Livermore 1965:3-13; Beazley 1911:11-23; Ricard 1955:3-78; also Boxer 1969:15-38). If Dom Henrique (known erroneously to the English-speaking world as 'the Navigator') had hitherto only heard rumours about the trans-Saharan gold trade, in Ceuta he learned details not only of the trade but also of the importance of Timbuktu. He set his sights on reaching West Africa by sea, and thereby hoped to circumvent

Muslim domination of North Africa. With a checkered record in Morocco, notably the disastrous expedition against Tangiers (1437), and later success at Alcàcer-Seguer (1458), Portugal pursued a policy of exploration, settlement, and trade. Between the discovery, or rediscovery, of Madeira (1419) and 1492, the Portuguese voyaged extensively in the African Atlantic, beneficiaries of the current and wind systems. By the later 1420s, they had reached the Canaries and the Azores. The following decade saw Portuguese settlements on Madeira and the Azores. Crucial was Gil Eanes's passage (1434) beyond Cape Bojador. Caravels reached Senegal and Cape Verde by 1445 and Sierra Leone by 1460, explored the Gulf of Guinea and its islands (notably São Tomé and Príncipe) in the 1470s, and crossed the equator in 1474-75. Diogo Cão (1482-84) reached the Congo and as far south as Walvis Bay in modern Namibia.[1] With the exception of Diogo Cão, such voyages were privately financed, albeit under the aegis of the Crown or as royal concessionaires. In 1488 Bartolomeu Dias rounded the Cape of Good Hope and the seaway had been opened to the Indian Ocean. Although Africa, unlike the American continent before 1492, did not live in mutual isolation from Europe or Asia, that Central Africa should have become better known beyond the African continent was attributable mainly to the Portuguese.

By 1492 the Portuguese had an excellent knowledge of the African coast as far south as northern Angola.[2] In this, they were not alone among Europeans, nor indeed was this exercise limited to the sons of the Iberian peninsula. One such person was a Genoese named Cristoforo Colombo. Shipwrecked off southern Portugal en route to England in the late 1470s, Cristoforo had joined his brother Bartolomeo in Lisbon in his cartography and bookselling business and married the daughter of the donatory of Porto Santo. There he learned firsthand about the ocean surrounding the archipelago of Madeira, and in Lisbon he studied charts and books. Columbus became acutely conscious of the importance of the Canaries to any potential oceanic crossing and the likelihood of other archipelagoes. In the early 1480s he sailed to the Gulf of Guinea on a Portuguese caravel and learned that to return to Portugal vessels had to tack south to pick up the equatorial currents that would carry them north-

west to the Gulf Stream, which, together with the North Atlantic westerlies, would bring them to Europe. This knowledge enabled him to sail westward in 1492 confident of an easy return. While in Portugal, Columbus learned of a letter written by Paolo dal Pozzo Toscanelli in 1474 postulating a western route to the Spice Islands (Diffie and Winius 1977:166-72).

Overland routes permitted trade and exchange between sub-Saharan Africa and the lands bordering the Mediterranean. The problem was that the Muslims dominated these routes, as well as North Africa, and thus blocked Christian Europe from access to regions south of the Sahara known through the reports of Jewish merchants to have commercial potential. Rumours circulated of great rivers, especially of a western Nile, of gold, of a land called Bilad Ghana inhabited by blacks, and of a commercial emporium called Timbuktu. Also rumoured was the existence of Christian monarchs, notably a powerful monarch named Prester John who lived in "the Indies" and who, in the fifteenth century, was identified with Ethiopia (Blake 1937:4; Curtin 1990:29-38; Rogers 1962:103-4). Believing that some of the major rivers of West Africa were extensions of the Nile, the Portuguese assumed that the West African coast was closer to Ethiopia than was the case. The potent mixture of fiction, fallacy, and fixation stimulated Portuguese exploration of the lands and peoples previously unknown to Europeans (Pereira 1937:bk. I, chs. 4, 5, 27; bk. 2, ch. 7).[3]

According to historians, it was not the quest for a labour pool that first stimulated this exploration. Rather, Dom Henrique hoped to spread the Christian gospel and to defeat the Muslim strongholds in North Africa. He also hoped eventually to make contact with the fabled Prester John as a prelude to a joint military expedition against Islam and to disrupt Islam trade. Then, too, there was the lure of exploration for exploration's sake, trade, expansion of fishing areas, the search for a sea route to bring West African gold to Portugal or to find revenues to meet his household expenses. Whether Dom Henrique or any other Portuguese were aware of the full commercial potential of such ventures is open to question, but experience would reveal that for a comparatively modest capital outlay, the revenues were such that they would not only cover the initial investment but provide a reasonable profit. Black Africans brought to Portugal on board the exploratory caravels were not viewed in Portugal as forerunners of a trade in slaves, but were transported to Europe as examples of human exotica, a practice later to become widespread - be they Native Americans, Indians, or Chinese.

Twenty-five years were to elapse between the initial Portuguese voyages along the northwest coast of Africa and the first taking of captives at Rio do Ouro (modern Río de Oro) by Antão Gonçalves and Nuno Tristão on their voyage of 1441. Once it was recognized that such voyages could not only be self-financing but revenue-generating, the rate of exploration accelerated, landfalls on the West African coast and islands increased, and Portuguese activities took on a markedly aggressive commercial and political tenor. By the 1450s and 1460s trade in goods and people had become commonplace. In 1448 a trading post (*feitoria*) was established on Arguim. The Treaty of Alcàçovas (1479) marked the end of Castilian-Portuguese rivalry, with Castilian renunciation of claims to West Africa (Blake 1937:41-56; de Barros 1945-46:I:bks. 1-3). In 1482 the Portuguese established a permanent presence in the Gulf of Guinea by constructing the stone fort of São Jorge da Mina, which they held until the Dutch conquest of 1638. Elmina was the first of a series of Portuguese 'strong houses'. A fort was also constructed in Sierra Leone but later had to be abandoned. The fort at Byhurt in Senegambia had not been completed by the end of the reign of Dom João II in 1495. During the early sixteenth century, forts were constructed at Axem (1503), Samma, and Accra; the fort of Santa Marta was built on Santiago in the Cape Verdes, and by 1506 there was a small fort on São Tomé (Blake 1937:98-105; Lawrence 1963). For much of the fifteenth century, Portuguese activities in West and Central Africa were confined to such trading posts and forts. It was not until the opening of the southeast passage to the Indian Ocean that the Portuguese embarked on what has been called a 'policy of expansion'. Hitherto the Portuguese had acted as explorers and entrepreneurs moving into new regions and seeking to consolidate political, diplomatic, or commercial gains, before proceeding further along the coast.

Prior to 1454 and from 1480 until 1530 the Portuguese held a virtual monopoly on European trade with Upper and Lower Guinea. This trade was built around exchange of gold, ivory, malaguetta pepper, hides, ambergris, wax, gum, mats, cloths, and slaves for goods from northern Europe, Portugal and Morocco. The demand for the European imports appears to have been driven by African consumer preferences, vanity, changing tastes and the prestige associated with possessing such imports, and not by inadequate technology, production shortfalls, poor quality, or the need for products that could not be met from African sources (Thornton 1992:43-53). Portuguese forts and trading stations in West Africa, the Atlantic islands, and Gulf of Guinea became part of a trade diaspora that included Portuguese trading centres in Morocco and Portuguese commercial agents in Andalucia, London, Antwerp, and Venice, and as far north as Danzig. The revelation of a 'New World' by Columbus and his successors, Vasco da Gama's opening of the cape route to India in 1498, and Pedro Álvares Cabral's arrival on the coast of Brazil in 1500 had little immediate impact on this lucrative exchange between Africa and Europe, nor were values of commodities undermined or inflated by early landfalls on the American continent. Actually, the profitability of this African trade was to inspire French and English incursions into Upper Guinea after 1530. Rising costs incurred by the Portuguese in trying to hold interlopers at bay, rather than the side effects of Columbus's voyage, were to lead to waning Portuguese investment in Guinea by the late sixteenth century.

The half-century prior to 1492 can be viewed from five perspectives: the Portuguese encounters with Africans in Africa, Portuguese trade in slaves from Africa, the African presence in Portugal, attitudes towards Africans and persons of African descent in Portugal, and the legacy of the fifteenth century to colonial Brazil.

Portuguese Encounters with Africans in Africa

During the fifteenth century, Portuguese contacts with Africa, from Mauretania to Kongo, were primarily in the context of commerce. In the aftermath of razzias on villages on the Saharan littoral, the Portuguese entered a half-century of peace and friendship with leaders in sub-Saharan Africa or established cooperative working relationships with African intermediaries and suppliers of slaves and other goods. Negotiation was an essential precondition to exchange. Much in the same way as potential traders to West Africa had to obtain licenses before setting sail from Portugal, so too did they have to secure the permission of local rulers before beginning their exchanges with African entrepreneurs. The German Martin Behaim and the Venetian Alvise da Cà da Mosto described accords in the 1450s between Portuguese and local leaders in Senegambia, such as the *mansa* Niumi. Later, accords were reached with the king of Benin (Tinhorão 1988:66-70; Ryder 1969:24-41).

Be it tacit recognition of their dearth of manpower, military vulnerability, or lack of familiarity with local mores and trading networks (or a combination of all three), the Portuguese made every effort to collaborate with local traders and leaders. A first step in this direction was to teach Africans Portuguese so they could act as interpreters. Another was to use *lançados* or *tangosmãos*, white convicts who were put ashore in the expectation they would become Africanized and serve as intermediaries for later Portuguese commercial or diplomatic overtures. In many cases, however, they became illegal traders and operators beyond the control of Portuguese authorities. When referring to Portuguese commercial ventures in West Africa, a distinction must be made between illegal traders, those operating under the aegis of the Crown, and private traders from Cabo Verde. During this West and Central African phase of their history, the Portuguese were not interlopers in already existing trading networks (as was later to be the case in the Indian Ocean), nor did they assert themselves territorially. Neither did they seek to suppress fluvial trade or navigation by Africans, nor was there a sustained effort to convert Africans to Catholicism or to eradicate what were - to the Portuguese – 'barbarous' customs and practices.[4]

In 1490 there was a brief move away from this predominantly commercial framework. The Portuguese had reached the kingdom of Kongo in the 1480s, and in 1490 a mission was dispatched from Portugal in response to the interest shown by King Nzinga Nkuwu in other than commercial matters. The proposed exchange now included technical assistance, military operations, evangelization, and political ties between Kongo and Portugal. Initially, there was a great deal of misinformation and misunderstanding on both sides. From the outset, the driving force was the Kongo king who envisaged a king-to-king relationship. A few years earlier, expectations of such a personal relationship had led the ousted Prince Bemoim (as he was known to the Portuguese) to leave Senegal and set sail for Setúbal to ask Dom João II in person for assistance. After his formal entry into Lisbon, and instruction and baptism, he was granted aid in the form of an expeditionary force of twenty caravels (Pina 1950:cap. 37).

In the case of Kongo, the African king hoped to expand trade and obtain military and technical assistance through this new relationship. It is unclear whether the apparent interest in Christianity, which was enthusiastically embraced at least by the ruling cadres, was sincere, or whether it represented a shrewd assessment that this was a means of drawing the Portuguese into the relationship, or was seen as yet another factor that could only enhance their own religious beliefs and relations with the divine or supernatural. That the Portuguese arrived by sea suggested a supernatural quality to the intensely religious African peoples, who saw them as possessors of occult powers. King Nzinga Nkuwu was baptized in 1491 and took the name of João I. His son and heir was also baptized, changed his name, and ruled as Afonso I (1506-43). In the late fifteenth century the seeds were sown that led Kongo to adopt Portuguese names, manners, dress, laws, religion, court manners, insignia of sovereignty, domestic and military architecture, and even a European model of urban planning, and to send young Kongo men to Portugal to become students and in exchange allow Portuguese men of the cloth, traders, administrators, and technical consultants to reside in the capital of São Salvador do Congo. By the 1520s, the pressures and profits of the slave trade had begun to erode this relationship. It also was an exercise in mutual disillusion: the Kongo hopes of European military and technical assistance were not realized; Portuguese dreams of finding Prester John in Kongo soon dissipated and the initial assessments of the riches of the kingdom proved to be overblown. Kongo is an example of the Europeanization of an African people and the Africanization of Europeans and the emergence of powerful mulatto traders (Pina 1952:caps.

57-63; Randles 1968:87-96, 183-95; Balandier 1968; Birmingham 1966).

Portuguese Trade with Africa

A long-standing European practice – exemplified by the slave trades established by the republics of Venice and Genoa – had been for outlying territories to supply slaves to the core (Verlinden 1955).[5] Portugal, too far removed from the Mediterranean supply-and-demand cycle to obtain slaves from the Black Sea, Crimea, or Caucasus, was on the lookout for alternative sources for labour. Attacks on Moorish vessels in the Straits of Gibraltar or in transit between Morocco and Granada and raids on Guanches, indigenous to the Canaries, provided the Portuguese with labour. Blatant acts of piracy were carried out under the guise of armed offensives against non-Christians, thereby bestowing honour on the noble participants. Such activities first exposed the Portuguese to sub-Saharan blacks in transit from the Maghreb to Granada. Guanches were regarded as fair game by Portuguese, Catalans, and Andalusians in that they were considered 'pagans', but they continued to be enslaved even after Christian settlement of some islands in the Canaries. It has been estimated that 50,000 Guanches, about two-thirds of the archipelago's population, were forcibly relocated to the Iberian peninsula and to Madeira before 1450. During the time of the first slave raids in West Africa in the 1440s, the Portuguese were also raiding the Canaries for Guanches as slaves. A third method of securing labour was to conduct raids on coastal villages of the Maghreb from Portuguese bases in Morocco and the Algarve. From 1441 on, raids were also made on Idzagen villages of the Saharan littoral. Twelve dark-skinned Idzagen captured in raids on coastal Mauretania were transported to Portugal by Antão Gonçalves and Nuno Tristão. In 1444, 235 blacks and Idzagen were landed in Lagos. Between 1444 and 1446 captures were made at Río de Oro, Arguim, and islands just south of Arguim (Godinho 1963, 1965:2:520-23; Zurara 1960:caps. 12-14).[6]

During the late 1440s the Portuguese began changing their method of operation. Raids were replaced by exchange or purchase. Militarism gave way to trade with Muslim and black suppliers. Notions of a crusade or 'just war' were replaced by unbridled commercialism. A trading station was established on Arguim island and a ten-year monopolistic contract entered into by Prince Henry and a consortium. The trading station was replaced in 1461 by a fort and the commercial contract by a crown monopoly, which was farmed out. This marked the genesis of bilateral Afro-Portuguese relations rather than European intrusion. These relations evolved in three phases during the fifteenth century (Tinhorao 1988:43-70).

Camel-based Moorish nomads of the Sahara, operating out of oases in North Africa, had traded with the Sudan long before the arrival of Portuguese. From Uadam, three major routes had led to the Maghreb, Tunis, and Cyrenaica. Camel-based nomads had bartered with Sudanese traders, exchanging horses, silks, silver, and salt for gold dust and black slaves. With the arrival of the Portuguese in West Africa, the nomads began losing their monopoly on trade between Mediterranean Africa and Granada and sub-Saharan Africa. Although the only significant overlap of commodities between those offered by Portuguese and nomads was Moroccan horses, the Portuguese offered black traders alternative goods, such as Moroccan cloths, garments and blankets, wheat (initially from Madeira and later from Morocco), and even treacle. This shopping list was soon to include articles from northern Europe as well as North Africa: stirrups, saddles, copper bracelets and bowls, iron bars, knives, steel swords, silver, cloth, red coral, and glass beads.

In the seventeenth century, caravans still carried gold from south of the Sahara to Fez and Marrakech, but by then the Portuguese had diverted much of the trade otherwise in the hands of trans-Saharan camel caravans to themselves with a sea route, which afforded a speedier alternative to routes across the Sahara to the Mediterranean.[7] The Africans were unable to meet the Portuguese challenge. Current systems that facilitated maritime passage from Europe to West Africa effectively blocked access to the Mediterranean by mariners from West Africa, although they did possess vessels capable of making such a voyage.

Another important development in this region was the arrival of Europeans between 1444 and 1460 along the Guinea coast as far south as modern Sierra Leone who began trading in slaves and gold.[8] African rulers and traders collaborated with the Portuguese. By the mid-1450s, the trade in slaves had moved into Senegal and Cape Verde. Wolof, who occupied the interior as well as part of the coast south of the Senegal, signed treaties with the Portuguese agreeing to supply them with Africans.[9] Up to the turn of the century, between 200 and 400 slaves a year were traded from the Senegal River. The Wolof were receptive to exchanging Africans for items brought by Portuguese caravels that sailed up river to the trading fair at Tucuror. From Cape Verde to the Gambia, however, the reception Africans gave the Portuguese was mixed. Trading relations were established around the Salum River. Throughout the second half of the fifteenth century slaves were exported from the ports of Andam and Ale. In the 1450s, Mandinga of the Gambia signed agreements of 'peace and friendship' with Diogo Gomes and Cà da Mosto. The king (*mansa*) of Bati provided slaves for European traders and this source flourished for the remainder of the century.

On the coast, African merchants traded slaves for horses. Traders at the fairs at Cantor exchanged commodities brought up the Gambia by Portuguese caravels for gold, ivory, and slaves. By the end of the fifteenth century, Mandingas and Hulufs of the Casamance River were also trading slaves, indigenous cotton, and civet cats for Portuguese imports: horses, red cloth, and the highly coveted and valued iron. So flourishing was this trade, and so cordial the relations, that Portuguese merchants resided in the royal court. Also in the 1450s, Mandingas and Banyun on the Cacheu River began trading with the Portuguese, and Europeans were invited to reside in the court of the *farim* of Braço, Guoguolii and Beafar of the Geba River, along with traders on the Geba, Buguba, and Nuno rivers, established commercial relations with Africans, exchanging slaves, ivory, skins, musk, cotton, and other commodities for brass bracelets, Alentejan blankets, cotton cloths, and horses. From here southward to Sierra Leone, local traders provided Europeans with slaves, gold, and ivory in exchange for metal utensils, beads, and red cloth.

The 1470s marked the opening of a third phase in slave exports. This centred on the Gulf of Guinea, explored by Fernão Gomes, who came into contact with gold from the Gold Coast and capsicums from Benin. In 1482 the Portu-guese established their major port and entrepôt in West Africa, São Jorge da Mina. São Jorge siphoned off slaves from as far west as the Costa da Malagueta (at that time designating the coast from Sierra Leone to Cape Palmas) and as far east as Rio dos Escarvos. São Tomé and Príncipe were tapped for slaves who were transported to Elmina. São Tomé became a way station for slaves from Kongo and Benin.

In 1485 the Portuguese reached the kingdom of Benin. They established a trading post at Ughoton in 1486 (but abandoned it before 1495 because of its unhealthy location) on the Formoso River, and had trading agents in Benin (Ryder 1969:30-41). The data on slaves arriving at Elmina in the fifteenth century are incomplete, but it appears that from August 1504 to January 1507, 440 slaves arrived at Elmina. As for the Portuguese interaction with Kongo, the 1490 mission had had a broad agenda but by the early sixteenth century Portuguese interest in Kongo centred almost exclusively on slaves. Objects for which such slaves were traded differed little from those found acceptable further west: copper bracelets and utensils, cloth, coral, cowries, and even silver. There were also objects of African origin, acquired by Portuguese in return for commodities from Europe or Morocco, and for which there was a demand elsewhere in Africa. These included kolanuts from Sierra Leone in demand in Senegambia, Kongo bark cloth carried to Benin for sale, beads (*coris*) fashioned from a blue stone veined with red, or yellow and grey, available in Benin and carried to Elmina, and yellow beads (*alaquequas*) carried from North Africa to Senegambia (Thornton 1992:48-9, 52). In addition to slaves, the Portuguese acquired ivory, red pepper, gold dust and bangles, cotton, skins, and parrots.

Elmina marked a significant departure from previous practices. Not only was it the point of convergence for slaves drawn from west and east along the coast and for slaves from islands of the Gulf of Guinea, who were then re-exported to Cape Verde and Madeira as well as Portugal, but there was also re-export from Elmina of slaves needed to meet the African demand for labour in gold-bearing forest regions and for porters to transport gold and other goods from the interior to the coast and loads of cloth, brass, and other trade goods from the coast to inland. Duarte Pacheco Pereira visited Benin city several times and described how prisoners of war were sold at low prices to the Portuguese, who transported them to Elmina, where they were sold to local traders for gold. Allegedly, African traders at Elmina would pay twice the price such slaves would fetch in Portugal (Pereira 1937:2:chs. 7, 8; Blake 1937:93; Barros 1945-46:1:3:3). In the fifteenth century, because of the additional distance and time involved in transporting slaves from the Gulf of Guinea to Portugal, most remained in that region. Thus the slaves that went to Portugal and the Atlantic islands were more likely to be drawn from Senegambia and Rios de Guiné. Although they started out as raiders and challengers to African traders, in the course of the fifteenth century the Portuguese developed working relationships with sub-Saharan traders and leaders and became intermediaries in a supply-and-demand network whereby Africans supplied fellow Africans as slaves to the Portuguese, who then supplied them to other Africans to meet an African demand for labour. The slave trade could no longer be justified as a crusade or noble enterprise. There was the anomalous situation of Portuguese supplying to persons whom they regarded as Gentiles slaves ostensibly converted to Christianity.

In addition to the trade to Portugal, the economic development of Madeira (primarily sugar) and the Cape Verdes (sugar, cotton) siphoned off slaves from West Africa. The prosperity of both archipelagoes was linked to the supply of labour from West Africa. For the Cape Verdes, numbers remained small in the fifteenth century, but already Santiago was taking on a new role as a distribution point for slaves imported from Guinea specifically for re-export, a role curbed, however, by a royal order of 1518.

One of the prominent features of these encounters in the half-century before 1492 was the low level of conflict and absence of warfare between Europeans and sub-Saharan Africans. This was quite different from the earlier tense relations in North Africa and Mauretania and the naval engagements in the Straits of Gibraltar. Cynics might attribute the absence of a Portuguese military agenda to a realistic assessment of the shortage of manpower that Portugal could bring to bear in African theatres. Closer to the truth was that Portugal realized that blacks of West and Central Africa could muster enough force and firepower by land or by sea to repulse

Portuguese landing parties but not enough to capture Portuguese vessels (Thornton 1992:36-40). Another significant factor in fifteenth-century West and Central Africa was that little effort had been made to establish Portuguese settlements other than those ancillary to trading posts or forts. The Portuguese did not need to conquer or settle the region to achieve their commercial goals, and this policy of non-intervention removed a source of potential conflict. It was not until the Kongo-Angolan phase of the sixteenth century that conflict developed, as a result of Africa's internal dynastic crises and tensions created by an increasingly aggressive Portuguese pursuit of the slave trade and by evangelization efforts, which eventually led to Portuguese military expeditions.

The era of 'encounter' in West Africa lasted more than half a century and ranged from Río de Oro to Kongo and brought a diversity of African peoples in contact with the Portuguese. In general, relations between Africans and Europeans were cordial, although sometimes coercive. A factor contributing to this state of affairs may have been that European commerce in Upper and Lower Guinea, other than in trading stations and forts, was constrained by navigational problems and climate and thus limited to the months from September to April. As one African chief pointed out, the irregularity of such contacts reduced the likelihood of tensions that might occur with everyday contact and may also have kept sexual relations between Portuguese males and African women at a low level in fifteenth-century Guinea (Blake 1937:13).[10]

In seeking treaties of 'peace and friendship' with the Africans, the Portuguese appreciated early on that they lacked not only the manpower necessary for war, but also the requisite linguistic and bartering skills, were unfamiliar with commercial practices, were ignorant of the terrain and supply routes, and could not gain access to local suppliers without African assistance. Thus they recognized the importance of training black interpreters - Africans captured and brought to Portugal to learn the language. By the 1450s a corps of such interpreters was available in Portugal (Saunders 1982:12). That the Portuguese did gain a commercial footing was as much attributable to African intermediaries as to their own skills as diplomats or traders and to the fact they could tap into existing networks.

The cordial relations that prevailed in this early period extended to the highest levels of African leadership, as shown not only by treaties of friendship but by the many gifts that local leaders sent to Portuguese kings. At times, the gifts included slaves. In 1487 the Wolof prince Bemoim sent Dom João II gold and 100 young slaves. In response to initial Portuguese overtures, the king of Kongo sent Dom João II elephants' teeth, ivory objects, and mats woven from palm fibres. In 1515 the king of Kongo sent 78 slaves to Dom Manuel and suggested that Portuguese send more vessels from São Tomé to engage in trade with Kongo rather than with his rivals (Pina 1950:caps. 37, 58; Resende n.d.:88 *apud* Almeida 1922-29:3:218-220).[11] Further indication of Luso-African cooperation was that local leaders allowed the Portuguese to establish trading posts and forts. These examples do not mean that Africans were passive participants in trade with Europeans. On the contrary, Africans and not Europeans called the plays, and trade within Africa remained firmly in the hands of African rulers and elites.

Through their contacts with the diverse populations of Africa, the Portuguese came to be aware of the regional and ethnic differences among sub-Saharan peoples. Generic designations - *Negro, Etíope, Guineú* - of earlier periods gave way to greater ethnic precision, notably in the *Esmeraldo de Situ Orbis* (ca. 1505-8) of Duarte Pacheco Pereira. African peoples are referred to by their own names or Portuguese versions thereof: Idzagen, Jalofo, Barbacini, Serreri, Mandinga, Beafar, Guoguolii, Nalun, Teymen, Bouloe, Jaalungua, Souzo, Felupe, Banhun, Sape, Tiapi Ijo, Huela, Subou, and Urhobo. Some can be identified, whereas others - especially of traders at Elmina - defy identification, and others show an etymology that confused titles of individuals with names of peoples or states. Whereas some, such as the Wolof and Mandinga, were clearly familiar to the Portuguese as the result of repeated and intensive contacts, others were probably no more than names based on hearsay. Writers also noted chromatic variations, significant departures from what was for Europeans the somatic norm for blacks. These encounters also gave the Portuguese a glimpse of vastly different ways of life - different mores and styles of dress, and prac-

tices such as tattooing, piercing, scarification, circumcision, and the filing of teeth.[12]

In some cases - for example the commerce in slaves by Saharan traders - the Portuguese provided an alternative to already established slaving networks. In other cases - for example, the supply of labour to gold-bearing regions of the interior - Portuguese acted as intermediaries between African suppliers and African buyers. They easily filled this role in part because there was little oceanic (as opposed to fluvial or coastal) shipping in the Gulf of Guinea before the arrival of the Portuguese, it was impractical to transport slaves overland for long distances such as those from Kongo to Benin, and their caravels - albeit small - were capable of carrying substantial cargoes. The Portuguese presence made it possible to meet the demand for slaves in the gold-bearing regions of Benin by expanding the pool of potential labour to regions that would otherwise not have been tapped.

Nevertheless, it must be emphasized that slavery was already an established institution in West and Central Africa before the Europeans arrived, and there was already an active trade in slaves and slave markets. European involvement did not alter the fact that all phases of the trade in slaves within Africa - from initial procurement to sale to Europeans or their representatives in the ports - were controlled by Africans: rulers, elites, middlemen. However, a large gap existed at this time between the concept and practice of slavery as accepted in Africa and the concept of slavery and the position of slaves in society as embodied in Christian theology and civil laws. It was only in the Atlantic theatre that Europeans were to dominate blue-water trade and were to establish colonial economies based on black slave labour. Long before the voyage of Vasco da Gama, Madagascar had provided slaves for East African coastal settlements as far north as the Red Sea and to the west coast of India. Ethiopia had been a source of slaves for the Levant and as far east as India or as far west as Greece. Outside the Atlantic basin, the Portuguese were to engage in slavery and the slave trade within the bounds of the conventions already established by indigenous traders (Godinho 1963, 1965:2:545-6).[13]

That Africans were keenly aware of factors governing supply and demand and the European markets for their goods was demonstrated by increased prices, as measured by the number of copper bracelets or horses demanded by Africans. Over this half-century, the price exacted by local merchants, as measured in the number of slaves per house, doubled: for example, from the Senegal to the Gambia, a horse had initially bought twenty-five to thirty slaves, but this number was reduced by half by 1460, and was cut in half again by the beginning of the sixteenth century. On the Rio dos Cestos the price of a slave rose from two shaving basins to four or five. The few data that are available suggest that, although the purchase price of a slave (regardless of gender) remained at twelve or thirteen *cruzados* throughout the half-century from 1450 to 1500, in terms of disposable income there had been an increase from about 3,000 *rs* to 5,000 *rs* (Godinho 1963, 1965:2:527-28; Blake 1937:86-87; Saunders 1982:25-27; Vogt 1973:10-11).[14] It is erroneous to assume a chicken-and-egg relationship between the acquisition of slaves alone and motivation for further Portuguese exploration. Although Portuguese kings placed a high priority on Guinea gold, revenues from slaves and capsicums were more lucrative in the fifteenth century. What can be said is that before 1492 slaves were one of several exports from West Africa whose transportation and sale in Europe afforded profits enough to encourage the search for new theatres of trade in sub-Saharan Africa, and that profits derived from the slave trade came to occupy an increasingly prominent place in overall profits derived from Portuguese trade with sub-West and Central Africa (Saunders 1982:31-32).[15]

The international dimension of trading diasporas extended to rivalry on the African coast and in the Atlantic. Castilians had been as active as Portuguese in piracy in the Straits of Gibraltar, raids on the Canaries, and plundering villages of the Maghreb and Mauretania. At various times, the Canaries attracted Catalans, Castilians, Normans, Genoese, and Aragonese, in addition to Portuguese. Other rivals included French, Flemish, and English raiders. The Genoese were prominent in West African trade. At no time were the Portuguese authorities totally successful in enforcing the royal monopoly with respect to their own nationals, let alone other Europeans. Some participated legally in Portuguese enterprises. In 1486-87 Bartolomeu Marchioni, a Florentine merchant residing in Lisbon, held the licence to trade to the Rio dos Escravos. Castilian rivalry ended with the treaty of Alcácovas (1479), whereby Castile renounced claims to trading rights in West Africa and recognized Portuguese possession of the Azores, Madeira, and Cape Verdes in return for Portuguese recognition of Castilian dominion over the Canaries. After 1530, English and French rivalry posed a severe threat to the monopoly the Portuguese had enjoyed for the previous fifty years. This international dimension was not always adversarial. Much of the financing for Portuguese commercial ventures was of Italian, Flemish, and German provenance.[16] African leaders were doubtless conscious of the rivalries between different European nationals, but how far they were able to turn such hostilities to their own advantage or even incite them (in order to safeguard themselves against exploitation by any single European nation) is not clear.

Once it became apparent that Africa was growing in commercial importance for Portugal, a Casa de Ceuta was created in Lisbon. This reflected the still-limited geographical interest of Portugal in Africa and emphasis on commerce, conquest, and crusade, and predated exploration and trade south of Morocco. West African trade was initially a monopoly granted to Dom Henrique and after his death (1460) was held by the Crown. During his lifetime, Dom Henrique kept a tight hold on the administration and the purse strings of the trade through his own treasurer (*vedor*). Administration of the Arguim and Guinea trades was moved from Lagos to Lisbon, and all West and Central African interests were consolidated (1486) in the Casa de Guiné e Mina, also known as Casa da Mina. By 1501, the Casa de Guiné e da India - known as the Casa de Guiné, Mina e Indias, or simply Casa da India - was established. The Portuguese Crown consolidated its prerogatives (already set out in a royal decree of 1474) on all aspects of the Guinea trade as a crown monopoly after 1481. Only royal officials, contractors, and licencees were permitted to trade with Guinea. Centralization was a key component of Portuguese commercial policy and practice, as indicated by royal initiatives in exploratory and commercial voyages; in the establishment of trading posts and forts; in appointments; in the impositon of levies, dues, and fees; in regulations; and in an official policy of secrecy, espionage, and disinformation. During the reign of Dom Manuel (1495-1521), standards were to be established for accommodation, provisions, and conditions on slave boats. In the period under discussion, substantial numbers of slaves were imported through Setúbal and ports of the Algarve, notably Lagos, although Lisbon was gaining in importance. In 1512 Lisbon was officially designated as the sole point of entry.[17]

By 1492, the Portuguese had established a series of commercial networks in the African Atlantic. These were coastal (Arguim, São Jorge da Mina, Axem) and insular. The Cape Verdes and São Tomé (to a lesser extent Príncipe) became import/export way stations for slaves whose final destinations lay elsewhere in Africa and Europe. A large maritime network of trading routes had been established that had not hitherto existed in West or Central Africa. It included the Cape Verdes and nearby African coast; the Kongo and Benin with São Tomé; Benin and Elmina; São Tomé and Príncipe with Elmina; Arguim and Portugal; Cape Verdes and Portugal; Elmina and Portugal.

In fifteenth-century Africa, the Portuguese initiated the practice of establishing trading stations and forts. Eventually they had forty such establishments ranging from the Maghreb to the Moluccas and Japan. This was to be both the strength and weakness of their seaborne empire. During the fifteenth century, the Madeiras and the Azores were already settlement colonies, exhibiting many of the institutional characteristics of continental Portugal but also with other features that would come to typify the pattern of social and economic development in Portuguese America (Vieira 1984, 1987). The Cape Verdes and São Tomé were slower to develop. In short, many aspects that were to become hallmarks of a global seaborne empire were already present in Portuguese enclaves in Africa and the African Atlantic before 1492.

The African Presence in Portugal

Estimates of the numbers of Africans transported to Europe in the fifteenth century are based on informed guesswork. Unfortunately, a good deal of information was lost in the 1755 earthquake that destroyed the Casa dos Escravos de Lisboa (founded 1486) which had been the section of the Casa de Guiné responsible for the administration of the slave trade from West and Central Africa, the collection of duties, and the farming out of royal contracts. The evidence that is available suggests that the number of slaves exported from Upper Guinea in the latter part of the century varied from year to year, but declined over the period as a whole. According to the Portuguese historian Vitorino Magalhães Godinho, between 1,000 and 2,000 slaves were exported from Mauritania and the Sahel in the period 1441-48. With Portugal's establishment of a *feitoria* at Arguim and trading relations, initially with Sudanese traders and later with traders between Senegal and Cape Verde, these numbers increased. For the decade 1450-60, there were between 800 and 1,000 exports annually through Arguim. Exports through Arguim for the period 1450-1505 were certainly no less than 25,000 and possibly as high as 40,000. As Europeans reached southward, slave exports increased. Some 5,000 slaves were estimated to have been exported from between Senegal and Sierra Leone in the decade 1450-60, and this number doubled in the following decade. In the 1480s, some 3,500 slaves from that region may have been exported annually, with the number declining in the 1490s. Runs are not available for slaves arriving in, and exported from, Elmina in the decade following its founding, but it appears unlikely that these exceeded 200 a year. A rough estimate of slave exports from Africa prior to 1492 might be 1,500 for coastal Sahara; 25,000 through Arguim; 55,000 for Senegal-Sierra Leone (Guiné de Cabo Verde); and 2,000 for Elmira. This gives a figure of some 80,000 persons exported as slaves from the area between the Saharan littoral and Kongo in the half-century preceding Columbus's landfall in the Americas.[18] Their destinations included islands in the Gulf of Guinea and the Atlantic (especially Madeira), and Europe. Of these, probably less than a third, or about 25,000, had European destinations and most of these originated in Upper Guinea (see Curtin 1969:17-21).

Portugal was the major European recipient, acting both as the final destination and point of re-export to Castile, Andalucia, Valencia, and Barcelona and, in the early sixteenth century, to the Antilles. In 1510, 250 black slaves were purchased in Lisbon for shipment to the Spanish West Indies. Some twenty years were to elapse before Dom João III authorized direct sales from São Tomé and the Cape Verdes to America, but even after this date slaves continued to be shipped from Africa to Europe before being sent to America. In 1466 the Bohemian baron Leo of Rozmital commented on the extraordinary number of 'Ethiopians' in Portugal, especially in Oporto, and this was echoed by Hieronymus Munzer in 1494 (*Travels of Leo of Rozmital* 1957:106-7, 110, 118; Pfandl 1920:87). Such comments should be taken with a grain of salt, however, because neither traveler had much prior exposure to blacks or to slaves. By the end of the fifteenth century, there were already significant numbers of blacks in Portugal but several decades were to elapse before blacks outnumbered Moors as slaves. As in Brazil - where the dependence on Native Americans for labour would give way to the use of blacks and Amerindians and finally to a preponderance of slaves of African origin - so, too, in Portugal Moorish slaves were gradually supplanted by black slaves. Portugal was the first European country to have a significant black population.

This is not the place for a detailed discussion of black slaves and free blacks in Portugal in the fifteenth century. The Canadian historian Alistair Saunders has shown that the long-held thesis that slaves were imported to compensate for the siphoning off of manpower overseas must be qualified for the sixteenth century. For the fifteenth century, Portuguese going to West Africa were too few to constitute a drain on metropolitan resources. Although information on the number and distribution of slaves in fifteenth-century Portugal is sporadic, it is safe to say that there were nuclei of black slaves in Oporto and Lisbon, lesser numbers in Evora and Lagos, some few in coastal towns between Estremadura and the Minho, and even fewer inland. In the fifteenth century, the term 'slave market' applied only to Lisbon, Oporto, and Lagos. Probably most of the black slave population of fifteenth-century Portugal was in Estremadura (which included the region later designated the Beira) and south of the Tagus. Most worked in urban areas. For the years 1527-31, Saunders suggests a total of some 35,000 blacks in Portugal (32,370 slaves; 2,580 freedmen), in other words, about 2.5 to 3 per cent of the population. For the period prior to 1492, it would be surprising if half this number had been present. Males probably predominated slightly. Slaves were engaged in agriculture, clearing forests, draining marshes, and

public works, and worked as vendors, fishermen, ferrymen, artisans, and porters. Some earned money for their owners. Still others were not engaged in revenue-generating activities, in that they were personal servants and lackeys whose prime purpose was to demonstrate the social standing and wealth of their owners (Saunders 1982: 47-88; Tinhorão 1988:82-110).[19]

This raises the question of whether a community of Africans as such existed in fifteenth-century Portugal. Certainly, language(s) alone set them apart. There are fifteenth-century references to African songs and dances such as the *mangana*. Blacks were invited by civic authorities to perform pageants and music. In 1451, 'blacks and Moors' performed in Lisbon in celebrating the marriage of the infanta Dona Leonor to Frederick III of Germany, who was crowned Holy Roman Emperor in 1452. In Santarém, blacks were given permission to hold their own festivals on Sundays, but these became so popular that permission was rescinded. The only reference to corporate activity concerned the lay brotherhood dedicated to Our Lady of the Rosary, a veneration particularly dear to blacks and already in existence by the 1490s. Although there were free blacks in fifteenth-century Portugal, they were too few to constitute a separate group (Pereira 1972:4:9-47; Saunders 1982:105-6, 150-52; Tinhorão 1988:114-16, 122-34).

As for Portuguese attitudes towards blacks, these were shaped in part by ideas dating back to the early Christian era and the Middle Ages. One such notion was that the region from Mauretania to Egypt should be named Ethiopia, for since ancient times the term had been used to signify those with dark skins who lived far to the south. Another such notion was that Africa was part of a southern or lower hemisphere (in contrast to the upper, or European and circum-Mediterranean) that was associated with infernal regions or regions populated by monsters (see Kapler 1980; Wright 1925; Horta 1991:233, n. 57, 60 pp. 244-45). These legacies were to play a crucial role in setting the framework for Portuguese discourse about, and attitudes toward, blacks from West and Central Africa.

Before the first Portuguese probings down the African coast, let alone their first encounters with blacks, slavery was a well-established institution in Europe. By the fifteenth century, Portugal's labour force included Guanches and

Moors, the latter seized from vessels and from the coastal regions of Mauretania and the Sahara. Whereas the former were considered Gentiles (*gentios*), the latter were 'infidels,' a term that in civil and canon law was broadly applied to all non-Christians. *Jose da Silva Horta* (1991:258) has observed that the adjective 'infidel' was most frequently applied to Muslims as the true enemies of Christianity and Christendom, but that in the context of discourse on 'just war' the term encompassed Muslims, Jews, and Gentiles. In both cases, in accordance with the principles of 'just war,' resistance to capture by Christians made their enslavement justifiable. In Portugal, Moors were referred to as *escravos brancos* (literally, 'white slaves'), and there was a saying, 'Work is for Moors.' As for Africa, a distinction was made between Terra dos Mouros and Terra dos Negros. The slave labour force in the former included both *mouros* and *negros*. Even before black slaves arrived on Portuguese soil in the 1440s, the condition of enslavement had become associated with a lack of religious orthodoxy, or deviance from what the Portuguese regarded as such, or paganism. Physical labour had come to be regarded as belittling. Only 'others' - namely, non-Catholics and non-Portuguese - engaged in physical labour. By so doing, they debased themselves still further from the already vilified position to which their religious affiliation or lack of it had condemned them. Unlike Catalonia, Aragon, and the Balearics, where black slaves had been present since the thirteenth century, only in the 1440s were the Portuguese exposed to blacks transported from Mauretania and West Africa specifically to be slaves. To the geography of 'otherness' based on religious and social differences was added a racial component.

In the latter half of the fifteenth century, discussion about blacks, slavery, and the slave trade - insofar as there was any - was still couched in the language of discourse inherited from an earlier age, namely, that of crusade and 'just war' (Saraiva 1950:566-97). The nomenclature that evolved during the fifteenth century had both religious and racial components. At the opening of the century, the term *mouro* was still applied to slaves, although it was not synonymous with slave. If a Moor were free, the adjective designating this status

would be added, namely *mouro forro*. Initial Portuguese contacts with blacks used *mouro* to denote slave and *negro* to describe pigmentation, hence *mouro negro*. This was the terminology used by Zurara in his *Chronicle of the Discovery and Conquest of Guinea* to describe the cargo of 235 slaves landed at Lagos in 1444.

This practice presented a problem. As Muslims, *mouros* were infidels and not eligible for redemption, whereas blacks, given their uncommitted status, were still eligible for salvation by conversion to Christianity. Some few blacks in fifteenth-century Portugal may have been Muslims who refused baptism. They were required to wear a red crescent on the shoulder of outer garments, as was the case for white Muslims. The solution (from ca. 1459 onward) was to use the term *escravo* to describe a slave. If pigmentation were a factor, the adjectives *prêto* or *negro* were added; if religious affiliation, *mouro* or *branco* were added. *Cativo* could be substituted for *escravo* but connoted a technical distinction within servitude, namely, a slave totally subject to an owner's authority in contrast to an *escravo forro* who had negotiated a degree of freedom (see Saunders 1982:xii, 42, 140; Horta 1991:260). Slaves who obtained their freedom received *cartas de alforria*. In 1501 Dom Manuel granted a *carta de alforria* to Francisco Lourenço from Benin, who had also been the slave of Dom João II (Almeida 1925:235-39). All freedmen were called *forros*, regardless of how they had acquired their freedom. The designation *forro* did not distinguish between a black person born free in Portugal and a black who had been manumitted, either by self-purchase or by an owner in return for services.

No publications critical of the slave trade or of the conditions of black slaves appeared in Portugal during the fifteenth century. The first attack on the legality of the trade appeared in Fernão de Oliveira's *Arte da Cuerra no Mar* (1555). It was not until the latter part of the sixteenth century that moral theologians began to express concern about the cruelty of the trade and inequities inherent in slavery, but not about the institution itself. Slavery as an institution raised few eyebrows in fifteenth-century Portugal. Neither the princes of the church nor kings had qualms of conscience as to the morality or practice of slavery and the trade in humans. No less authorities than the Bible and Aristotle, civil and canon laws, had sanctioned the institution.

Medieval commentators agreed that prisoners of war (excluding Christians captured by Christians) could be legally enslaved, that offspring of slaves took their parents' status, and that slaves were chattels whose sale was governed by commercial law. This view was further refined in the doctrine of 'just war,' whereby not only infidels but pagans resisting the forces of Christianity or rejecting Christianity could justifiably be reduced to slavery provided such hostilities met criteria of appropriate authority (royal or papal), sufficient cause, and right intention (absence of ambition, hatred, vengeance). Territorial conquest, not merely subjugation of peoples, was justified on the ground that the Portuguese were reclaiming for Christ lands that had at one time been consecrated by Him but had subsequently fallen into non-Christian hands and been profaned. Early articulation of this doctrine in Portugal is attributed to the Franciscan Alvaro Pais, who lived in the fourteenth century; had studied in Bologna and Paris, was assistant to Pope John XXII in Avignon, and authored a treatise on clerical immorality. Dating from the late 1530s or early 1540s is the closely argued but anonymous document titled 'Por que causas se pode mover guerra justa contra infieis' (Russell-Wood 1978:esp. 23-28; Perrone-Moises 1989-90; 5-10).

Two aspects of African slavery marked a significant change from previous practices: overt commercialism and enslavement of peoples who had not been offered the benefit (or the opportunity for rejection) of Christianity. Official justification for this new departure focussed on the trade rather than on slaves or the institution and was made on religious grounds, namely that the Portuguese were acting on behalf of Christianity. Traffic in slaves and enslavement were but vehicles that would bring additional souls into the Christian fold. Before attacking Ceuta, Dom João I had consulted theologians and been advised that attacks against *mouros* and *gentios* were justified because they had denied articles of faith of Catholicism. Dom Duarte (1433-38), whose reign witnessed not only the disastrous attack on Tangier but the rounding of Cape Bojador, had

also consulted jurists and been advised that, in the absence of reconquering for Christianity lands that had subsequently fallen into the hands of *infiéis*, the only justification for Christian offensives against lands that had never occupied by Christians was if their inhabitants attacked Christians. If offensives against Ceuta and Moorish strongholds in North Africa had been been justifiable in the spirit of crusade and 'just war,' subsequent razzias on the Mauretanian coast were only questionably so, and Portuguese offensives into Central and West Africa were not justifiable because there had not been any prior occupation by Christians of lands between Senegal and Sierra Leone nor had their inhabitants been exposed to Catholicism. In the absence of actions by Africans that were clearly detrimental to Catholicism or to Catholics, or interpretable as such, no Portuguese action was justifiable. The only other case that could be made to justify Portuguese actions was the assertion that, although not recorded by history, the body of presumption supported the claim that Christianity had indeed been introduced into these regions. Thus the inhabitants would not be *gentios* but *cristãos incertos*. Such claims could be legitimized by the pope, as could rights of conquest and domain. The Crown took immediate steps to secure approval through papal bulls, of which the first was *Illius qui* (1442). *Dum Diversas* and *Divino Amore Communiti* (1452) authorized the Portuguese to attack, conquer, subdue, and enslave all enemies of Christ and pagans in West Africa and take possession of their territories and property. *Romanus Pontifex* (1454) justified Portuguese claims to territorial acquisitions, legitimated Portuguese offensives against hostile peoples, legitimated the denial of sovereignty to African chiefs and failure to acknowledge sovereign states, justified taking prisoners on the grounds of the Portuguese record of conversions - past and anticipated - to Christianity, and granted Portugal a commercial monopoly from the Maghreb to 'the Indies.' *Inter Caetera* (1456) asserted the spiritual jurisdiction of the governor of the Order of Christ over peoples coming under Portuguese control (Saunders 1982:35-46).[20] The slave trade was legitimized on the ground that slaves would be converted. Commerce was justified because, by diverting revenues to Christian hands, not only were the Portuguese providing financial support for crusading forces but also depriving infidels or pagans of revenues that might be used militarily against the armies of Christ. The goal of reasserting Christian control over lands, consecrated by Christ but subsequently lost, imbued with even greater significance myths and vestiges of Christianity - be they Prester John, religious symbols associated with Christianity, communities such as the Nestorians in Ceylon and Malabar, or communities in southern India converted to Christianity by Thomas the Apostle.

There was also the inference that slaves would benefit from contact with Portuguese 'civilization.' The term *bárbaro* referred not only to non-Christian peoples, but to persons whose mode of behaviour and belief systems were too divergent from those of the Portuguese to be considered 'civilized'. Conversion to Christianity was not only conversion to a revealed faith, but also to 'civilization'. It was suggested that civilised people not only conformed in their behaviour to norms acceptable to Europeans, but also lived according to codes of morality. If this was the official line, others - depending on their education and positions in Portuguese society - expressed more personal assessments. These included charges of barbarism, a designation embracing all practices held by Portuguese to be abhorrent or deviant: cannibalism, bestiality, sodomy, and incest. Such practices were regarded as violations of natural law and were punishable by the pope or his agents. The term *bestial* also embraced intemperate and unrestrained eating and drinking habits, the use of primitive weapons made of stone and wood, hunting and gathering and fishing as modes of subsistence, nudity, impermanent dwellings, the absence of bread and wine, and sloth and ignorance.

Portuguese Attitudes toward Africans and Persons of African Descent

So far the discussion has made little reference to race or blackness. This is not an oversight, for race was not a major concern in fifteenth-century Portugal, nor had a link been established between blackness and slavery. As mentioned earlier, there was a medieval legend linking blackness with Ethiopia, but the Portuguese had already encountered persons of darker skin, such

as the Berbers of North Africa and the dark-skinned Idzagen of Mauretania, before they encountered the Wolof south of the Senegal, their first contact with blacks of an identifiable kingdom. The characterization *negro* had been generic in that, unless accompanied by more specific identifiers such as 'da Etiópia' or 'de Guiné' or the adjectives *etíopes* and *guinéus*, it referred to a person of dark skin but not necessarily negroid.

The association of blackness with slavery derived from the Biblical story of Ham. Ham had sinned by observing his father Noah naked, while the latter was drunk. Noah had cursed Canaan, Ham's son, and condemned him and his descendants to eternal slavery. (Genesis 9:21-27). The link between sin and perpetual slavery, the view that servitude was divine punishment, and the link between sin and bestiality had no racial component. But the absence of a specific racial component did not mean that the ancient Hebrews had not thought that some ethnic groups were more suitable for enslavement than others. To be a 'Canaanite slave' had been to suffer the ultimate debasement ethnically and in terms of exploitation. Although Hebrews could be slaves, their lot had been infinitely superior to that of Canaanites, damned by the inferiority of birth. As the criteria used to identify a 'Canaanite' in the early Christian era became relaxed, and were further stretched in the Middle Ages, with examples drawn from the racial poles of African blacks and white Slavs, a much broader sample of people came to be referred to generically as 'Canaanites'.

Rather, that enslavement and debasement became linked with blacks has been attributed to Mishradic and Talmudic sources of the fourth to sixth centuries A.D. Although the Koran makes no such association, it occurred repeatedly and unambiguously in Muslim literature of the eighth century. Thus the racial component - that is, blackness - was not of Christian or European genesis. It was the ever-increasing presence of sub-Saharan slaves in Egypt and the Near East and, after the establishment of Islam, in Muslim territories, that led blacks to be equated with slavery and 'otherness.' William Evans noted that the rise of Islam as a unifying force eliminated much of the disorder in the Near East that had hitherto provided captives and that, with the elimination of sources of lighter-skinned persons for slave markets, 'Muslim slavery became Negro slavery'. In Arabic, the word *mamluk* referred to a high-status, white, European, slave in contrast to '*abd*,' which referred to a black slave who was not only cheaper and less favoured, but was of the lowest status and used for more menial labour. Black slaves ('*abid'*) came to be associated less with their legal status than their race. Emancipation rarely meant other than a continuation of tasks they had performed as slaves. This racial stereotyping and racial stratification – the equating of blacks with debasement – had been part of the Muslim legacy to Iberia. Onto this were grafted European stereotypes associating slaves (regardless of colour) with moral shortcomings such as laziness, promiscuity, and stealing. Portuguese exploration and commerce in Upper Guinea brought to Portugal black 'Slavs,' whose position in Portuguese society was predetermined by myths, stereotyping, and associations. An interesting question raised by José da Silva Horta is the extent to which Christian attitudes toward blacks may have been influenced by antecedents in Arabic literature and culture (Evans 1980:15-43; also Saunders 1982:38-40, 190, n. 18; Horta 1991:210, n. 8 and pp. 244-55).[21]

There was an attitude – popularly accepted, but without justification in Roman or canon law – that blacks were inherently associated with servile positions. There was no comprehension in fifteenth-century Portugal of the divergence between slavery in Europe and slavery in Africa, its very different legal and institutional roots in African societies, different concepts of ownership and what could be owned, or how private ownership of labour was tantamount to possession of wealth that had the potential to generate more wealth, that such labour was heritable, and that right to labour was an acceptable mode of taxation imposed by kings or states. Slavery in Africa did not carry the connotations of degradation, debasement, and 'otherness' that were associated with the institution in early modern Portugal (for discussion, see Miers and Kopytoff (1977:3-81; Thornton 1991:72-97).

In fifteenth-century Portugal, the royal chronicler Gomes Eanes de Zurara brought together these different inherited notions in his *Crónica dos feitos de Guiné*. He established the link between black Africans and the cursed descendants of Ham. He also subscribed (via Aqui-nas) to the notion of sin placing a constraint on freedom, thereby reducing persons to slavery. Zurara set out criteria distinguishing mankind from animals: food, clothing, speech, and living by social laws. By failing to meet such criteria, Africans were sinful, bestial, and thus by nature condemned to slavery. Unlike Islamic peoples of North Africa, who were 'enemies of the Faith,' persons of West and Central Africa were *gentios*, whose contact with Islam – if any – was regarded as too superficial to have corrupted them. All was not lost. Conversion to Christianity and baptism and exposure to 'civilization,' which might take the form of covering their nakedness, could redeem them from their inherited state of bestiality and immorality. Although Zurara was aware of the stereotypical medieval image of blacks, in his chronicle he did not attribute to all black Africans a position of inferiority based on skin colour alone (Horta 1991:251-52).

Zurara was writing during the first phase of Portuguese slaving activity in Africa and even he attributed to Africans physical qualities associated with warrior leaders. Further contacts in the fifteenth century revealed that sub-Saharan peoples – notably in Senegambia, Benin, and Kongo – did meet criteria for 'civilization': they had rulers, social hierarchies and organizations, established courts, states, cities and towns, laws, order and stability in personal relationships, sophisticated eating habits, complex language groups, technical skills as demonstrated in cloth weaving and ivory carving, fighting strategies and iron weapons, and what might be termed a work ethic. The Portuguese came to acknowledge that reason, and not instinct or disorder, governed the policies and practices of some Africans with whom they came into contact. Chronicler Rui de Pina, commenting on the public speech at the Portuguese court by the Senegalese prince Bemoim, observed that such was his command of language and expression that 'they did not appear as from the mouth of a black barbarian but of a Grecian prince raised in Athens'. [22] Although references to bestiality and barbarity did not disappear in sixteenth-century Portuguese discourse, they were few. Nor was the argument developed in fifteenth- or sixteenth-century Portugal linking divine punishment to perpetual natural slavery. Nor was the discussion of Hamitic origin and slavery sustained other than to explain why blacks were black, not why they were slaves.

Allowed to slumber were claims that exposure to 'civilization' improved the material conditions of slaves. The official line was that the slave trade and slavery were effective vehicles for converting and catechizing persons who would not otherwise have been exposed to the Gospel. João de Barros was later (1539) to refer to São Jorge da Mina as the 'cornerstone of the Catholic Church in the East' (*primeira pedra da Igrega oriental*). While this was the rhetoric, not before the second decade of the sixteenth century did actions match these words. Somewhat tardily (1513, 1514), Dom Manuel issued orders for the administration of sacraments to slaves dying on vessels, and baptism and catechism of slaves, but there remained a gap between the rhetoric of evangelization and the reality of a slave population largely unversed in tenets and practices of Christianity.

One yardstick for measuring at least official attitudes lies in the laws of a community. The *Ordenaçòes Afonsinas* (1446), a compilation of canon and Roman law, had addressed the issue of slavery but it was the *Ordenaçòes Manuelinas* (definitive edition, 1521) that included a slave code. This asserted the dependence of slaves on owners and their right to life, albeit as chattels. Aggression against an owner was a serious act of insubordination. Slaves could be manumitted, be it by self-purchase or gift, conditionally or unconditionally. Slaves (like foreigners) were forbidden to carry arms, although this rule was relaxed if they had their owner's permission or were acting in defence of an owner. Two points should be emphasized. First, such laws were discriminatory. All lower classes had few rights. The application and enforcement of criminal law depended on the status of the victim and of the protagonist. Slaves received the same trials and punishments as lower-class free white commoners (and quite often the same ending, namely a collective grave if they were fortunate, or a dunghill if they were not). Second, in a society in which not only blacks but also Jews and Moors were slaves, Moors were viewed as the greatest potential threat and subject to more severe penalties and constraints. Not being Christians, Moors could not achieve integration into Portuguese society. They were characterized as capable of violence, whereas blacks were associated more with petty crime and theft. A 1469 municipal edict by the city council of Lisbon forbade the sale of wine in taverns to slaves, regardless of their colour. Blacks were favoured over Moors in legislation concerning carrying arms, curfews, or assisting runaway slaves. They were not regarded as insurrection material. These attitudes were reflected in legislation concerning fees for capturing runaways. A 1459 law set fees for capturing blacks at a third of those for Moors, and the *Ordenaçòes Manuelinas* set lower fees for the recapture of blacks than for Jews, Moors, or even Indians (Almeida 1925:3:135, 231; Serrão 1977:2:194-97; esp. Saunders 1982:113-33, 138-47). In short, neither blackness nor place of origin militated against blacks from West or Central Africa as revealed in laws couched in the language, and reflecting attitudes, of a seigneurial society in which religious deviance was more harshly condemned than racial 'otherness'.

Contacts with blacks from West and Central Africa forced the Portuguese to reassess the attitudes inherited from a precontact era. Categories and classifications had to be redefined to be applicable to the new reality. These were reflected in considerations as to the appropriateness of applying certain terms to sub-Saharan peoples: gentios, inimigos da Fé, infiéis, idólatras, feiticeiros. In the course of the fifteenth century, the Portuguese came to appreciate that, where faith was concerned the equation between blacks and *gentios* could not be universally applied. Blacks in the Terra dos Mouros were Muslims (*inimigos da Fé*) and thus not capable of conversion. But blacks of West and Central Africa had either had no exposure to any revealed religion and thus were *gentios* whose salvation could be achieved through baptism, or had only superficially been converted to Islam (*infiéis*) but were descendants of *gentios* and thus susceptible to conversion to Catholicism. The term *mouro* had to be qualified to reflect the distinction between Moors of the Iberian peninsula and the 'new' Moors of the south, namely of the Sahara and circum-Saharan regions. *Mouro* was replaced by the terms *negro* or *guinéu* to refer to peoples of West and Central Africa. At this early stage, the Portuguese had yet to learn that the region they knew as Terra dos Negros did indeed contain substantial Muslim populations, and hopes as to the effectiveness of dialogue as a prelude to conversion had not yet given way to lowered expectations or even disenchantment.[23]

In fifteenth-century Portugal there was substantial religious and national diversity. Merchants and businessmen from Italy, England, France, and Germany resided in its major cities. Slaves were accepted as journeymen, although nonracial factors could militate against their admission into certain guilds. As for the church, although it condoned slavery and regarded slaves as chattels, it granted communion and the sacraments to slaves. In the 1490s, anti-Semitism began to rear its ugly head, and in 1503 and 1506 there were riots against Jews, leading to deaths. There were no such attacks on blacks.[24]

Other sources for Portuguese attitudes toward blacks are iconography, popular culture, and literature. Catalonian and Castilian iconography of the thirteenth century contains stereotypical depictions of the black Moor, but it is not until the sixteenth century that such depictions or commentary on blacks appear in Portuguese art and literature. They include blacks in scenes of the Epiphany and Adoration of the Magi. Secular art, such as Books of Hours, depicted blacks in different walks of life: pages, musicians, servants, women carrying baskets. The cloister of the monastery of the Hieronymites in Belím contains the sculpted head of a black. Such depictions did not distort the physical appearance of their subjects, nor are there indications of negative attitudes by artists to the aesthetic appearance of blacks. Silva Horta has observed that such depictions of blacks are not portraits but generic representations.[25] As for literary references, of sixteen sources between about 1453 and about 1508 that treat West and Central Africa, only six preceded 1492, and only three (in comparison with nine by Germans and four by Italians) were penned by Portuguese: Zurara's *Crónica dos feitos de Guiné* (ca. 1453-60), the anonymous *Este livro he de rotear* (ca. 1480-85), and Duarte Pacheco Pereira's *Esmeraldo de Situ Orbis* (ca. 1505-8). Zurara had been the first to comment on the physical appearance of blacks. 'For amongst them there were some white enough, fair to look upon, and well proportioned; others were less white than mulattoes; others again were as black as Ethiops, and so ugly, both in features and in body, as almost to appear (to those who saw them) the images of a lower hemisphere.' This stark contrast in Zurara

between positive and negative aesthetic appraisals of blacks of West and Central Africa is not characteristic of subsequent writings. Literary sources of the fifteenth century noted physical features of blacks, notably colour (*negro; prêto*) and hair (*crespo*), and emphasized their well-formed and strong bodies.

Silva Horta has noted that references to lips, eyes, and noses occur for the most part only in cases of physical deformity and were based on hearsay and thus linked to a fantasy world of monsters, satyrs, and zoomorphic beings. Writing at the turn of the century (ca. 1497-1504), Rui de Pina commented favourably on the physical appearance of the Wolof prince: 'Bemoim was a man of some forty years, large of body, very black, with a very long beard, whose limbs were well proportioned, and of pleasing appearance' (Beazley and Prestage 1896, 1899:cap. 25; Pina 1950:chap. 37, p. 91); Horta 1991:242-48).

With rare exception some depending on textual interpretation fifteenth-century physical descriptions by Portuguese of blacks of West and Central Africa were not negative and blackness and beauty were not incompatible. Sixteenth-century literary works were more judgmental. An example of 'língua de Guiné' was included in Garcia de Resende's *Cancioneiro Geral* (1516), which incorporated *trovas* of the late fifteenth century and perpetuated the theme of the *diabo negro*. Blacks, and their speech patterns, are present in plays of Gil Vicente (*Auto dos Reis Magos*, 1503; *Frágoa d'Amor*, 1524; *Nao d'Amores*, 1527; *Clérigo da Beira*, 1529/1530) and often subject to ridicule. In *Frágoa d'Amor*, Vicente included the black who wished to 'become as white as a hen's egg,' with well-shaped nose and thinner lips. Earlier, there had been the perception that black women were less attractive than Moorish. Mulattoes were also preferred over blacks. But fifteenth-century Portuguese were not as conscious of chromatic variations as their Genoese predecessors and contemporaries, who noted nuances of colour, especially of young women whom they offered for sale. Only in late sixteenth-century Portugal were blacks from different regions distinguished on aesthetic grounds. References to blacks in *vilancicos* only appear to date from the late sixteenth or seventeenth centuries (Gioffrè 1971:13-61, esp. 33-36 on blacks; Scammell

1981:174; Saunders 1982:102-3, 167; Tin-horao:1988:202-5, 233-47).[26]

The Legacy of the Fifteenth Century to Colonial Brazil

Although Pedro Álvares Cabral made his landfall in what was to be known as Brazil in 1500, only in 1549 was a crown government established in Portuguese America. Native American labour prevailed. This continued to be the case even after the introduction of Africans. As early as 1511 vessels had returned to Portugal from Brazil with small numbers of Amerindians as potential labourers. To the donataries Martim Afonso de Sousa and Duarte Coelho was granted the right to send annual shipments of small numbers of Amerindians to Portugal. Any notion that there might have been of using Native Americans as labour in Portugal soon evaporated. In Portuguese America, despite laws (1570, 1595, 1605, 1609) forbidding the practice, de facto Indians were enslaved or 'reduced' to circumstances akin to forced labour (Godinho 1963, 1965:536-37; Marchant 1942; Schwartz 1978:43-79). Only tardily did Africa come to be regarded as a source for slave labour in Brazil. A few Africans were imported in the 1530s and 1540s. By the 1570s there were some 2,000-3,000 black slaves in Brazil. In the early 1580s, Fernão Cardim, S.J., placed at 2,000 the number of Guinea slaves in Pernambuco (on a par with Europeans) and 3,000-4,000 in Bahia (also equal to the European population but less than the 8,000 Indians converted to Christianity). The last fifteen years of the century witnessed significant increases: in 1587 Gabriel Soares suggested 4,000-5,000 black slaves in Pernambuco and at least 4,000 in Bahia. By 1600, Magalhães Godinho posits that black slaves from Guinea and Angola made up about 50 per cent of the slave population in Brazil, namely about 60,000 (Goulart 1949:98-101; Godinho 1963, 1965:2:544-45). Except for Pernambuco and Bahia, Portuguese America had few African slaves before 1600. In the sixteenth century, the slave trade was still focussed not on Africa but on Brazil and on Native Americans.

Some features of the fifteenth-century African slave trade and black slavery in Portugal carried over into the Middle Passage and Brazilian experience, despite differences of scale. The acquisition and supply of slaves remained in African hands, among slaves transported to Brazil males predominated over females, and the Gulf of Guinea and Angola developed as major sources. The Portuguese Crown lost its monopoly on the trade but continued to derive substantial revenues at all stages. Slaves were sold as chattels. The church did not condemn either the trade or the institution of slavery. Despite royal orders that slaves be baptized prior to embarkation and given spiritual guidance, and be granted the right to communion and the sacraments, the responsibility for enforcing such rights was placed on owners rather than on civil or ecclesiastical authorities. Slaves enjoyed some protection under the law, but authorities were not disposed to intervene in domestic disputes between owners and slaves, unless the conduct of the owner was flagrantly cruel or immoral. There was no separate slave code for Brazil. The *Ordenações filipinas* (1603), which incorporated earlier codifications, were in force throughout the colonial period. Rare was the person who did not own a slave in the colony, and there were no constraints on blacks or mulattoes owning slaves. In Portuguese America there was greater social permeability and mobility for persons of African descent than had been the case in the stratified Muslim circum-Mediterranean. The numbers of mulattoes and of manumissions increased, notably in the eighteenth century. Some slaves were worked to death in mines or on plantations, others were hired out as *escravos de ganho* and had considerable freedom of movement, and others were domestic slaves. Slaves continued to be indicators of an owner's financial and social standing. The incidence of literacy and of church marriages among all persons of African descent remained low in the colony.

There were notable differences between colonial Brazil and fifteenth-century Portugal. Crown laws, gubernatorial decrees, and municipal edicts constrained the movement and behaviour of slaves in Brazil. Municipal and gubernatorial edicts and orders echoed white fears of slave revolts. Such fears were reflected in the severity of punishments for infractions by slaves. In the colony, slaves did form their own communities, had their own brotherhoods, and took individual and collective decisions. They performed at civic festivities, practiced their own religions clandestinely, and preserved African cultural traditions and languages.27

Two aspects in Brazil reflected both continuation and change from European antecedents. That such attitudes were irradicably part of the colonial mentality may be illustrated by examples taken from the third century of Portuguese colonization in America. The first lay in the equating of slavery with the absence of social standing. To be a slave was to be a 'base person' (*pessoa vil*). In the 1720s a black slave was accused of murder. Despite lack of evidence, he was sentenced to 'judicial torture to arrive at the truth.' In justifying this measure, a judge of the highest court of appeals in Brazil, ruled as follows:

Circumstantial evidence based on even fewer facts than those presented in this case would constitute more than adequate grounds for torture when the accused is a slave or base person [*pessoa vil*] because in such cases, no matter how few clues there may be, torture is justified. And, because in this case the defendant is a base person and a slave as he himself confesses, in my judgment the weight of proof is overwhelming.[28]

The second concerned the concept of 'purity of blood.' In fifteenth-century Portugal this had referred to religious purity, namely a Catholic 'untainted' by Jewish or Moorish ancestry. This concept travelled with the Portuguese to the Americas. Whereas the Islamic component became obscured but did not entirely disappear, the generic term 'forbidden races' was expanded to include persons of African descent. Persons who did not meet such racial as well as religious criteria were not normally eligible for office in state, church, or municipal government. As late as 1749 an applicant to the Third Order of St. Francis in Bahia sought five witnesses to testify on his behalf that he was 'of undoubted whiteness and unquestionably an Old Christian, pure of blood and of descent without any blood of Jew, Moor, Morisco, mulatto, or of any other infected nation of those prohibited by our Holy Catholic Faith.' Subsequently, the candidate requested the judge of the ecclesiastical court of appeals to issue a 'justification of purity of blood' (*justifiçãcao de limpeza de sangue*) (Russell-Wood 1989:esp. 68). A 1773 law abolished the distinction between Old and New Christians, but old habits died hard. Documents of the 1790s still referred to Old and New Christians. As for racial 'purity,' this remained a pre-occupation for committees of enquiry of Third Orders throughout the eighteenth century.

In this essay I have viewed the Columbus landfall and its aftermath in the context of events preceding 1492. Those events took place on the stage of West and Central Africa and the African Atlantic and the central actors were the Portuguese. It was during this phase of their seaborne empire that they practiced and honed the monopolistic system that was to be a characteristic of the Crown's control of the meatier or more strategically sensitive sectors of their commerce overseas. This phase also represents the first attempt to circumvent indigenous intermediaries to reach sources of commercial commodities. As such, it was the precursor to a policy leading to the cape route to India.

The West and Central African phase provides examples of the policy that was to be both the strength and the Achilles heel of Portuguese activities overseas: namely, the establishment of forts and trading stations, which were too few to provide effective protection of Portuguese interests over long stretches of coast, but numerous enough to be a drain on the exchequer and on limited human resources. In Upper and Lower Guinea and the Atlantic islands, the Portuguese came to appreciate the diversity of geography, soil conditions, climates, and the importance of selecting crops in accordance with these conditions, if there was to be successful cultivation of crops of European or Asian provenance in the Atlantic basin. In Upper Guinea, the Portuguese came to realize that there was as much heterogeneity among Africans as among Europeans and that what now is termed multiculturalism was an African characteristic. Although the Portuguese at various times designated as 'Guinea' regions from Senegal to Sierra Leone, from Senegal to northern Angola, or even from Senegal to the Cape of Good Hope, they were acutely conscious of distinctions between peoples. This awareness of ethnic distinctions continued in Brazil in reference to Africans of different 'nations' (*naçôes*). Exposure to the physical face of sub-Saharan Africa, be it by contact with peoples or observation of their customs, behaviours, and religious practices, did lead the Portuguese to modify some stereotypes and classifications inherited from a precontact era and to engage in a continual learning process between the 1440s and 1490s. Increased understanding and sensitivity were not such as to lead them fully to abandon perspectives that were Europacentric and heavily imbued with conviction as to the mission of Portuguese as propagators of the faith and of 'civilization.'

The first significant shipment (ca. 250) of black slaves to Spanish America was from Seville in 1510. Only in 1518 did Charles V authorize unlimited slave imports to the Spanish Antilles. Such slaves had already been cleared through Lisbon and Seville, a practice that continued until the 1530s, when Dom João III of Portugal authorized direct passage from São Tome and Príncipe to America. Even in the 1550s many slaves who had left Africa and whose final destination was America, touched at Lisbon and Seville. These were still early days in a trade that would transport between 3.6 and 5 million slaves to Brazil, somewhere between 38 and 52 pe rcent of all slaves from Africa imported into Europe, the Atlantic islands, and the Americas. In 1818, persons of African descent constituted a majority (Africans 2,515,000; Europeans 1,040,000; Amerindians ca. 250,000) in Portuguese America.[29] Brazil had become the wealthiest of Portugal's overseas territories, was on the verge of independence, and enjoyed an intellectual life attuned to current ideas in Western Europe and the United States. In the post-Englightement era, it is remarkable that discourse on race and slavery in Brazil should still have exhibited vestiges of perceptions and attitudes present in Portugal before Columbus's voyage in 1492.

Notes

1. An excellent overview of this phase is in Serrão (1977:119-202). See also the essay by Meneses (1989:79-114).
2. An exemplar is Pereira's "book of cosmography and navigation" (1937:vol. 79). The most comprehensive study is by Carvalho (1983).
3. Two works of synthesis for this period are Fernandez-Armesto (1987) and Phillips, Jr. (1985).
   Whereas the former suggests that the voyages of Columbus and his successors were the outcome of exploration and trade in the Mediterranean of the late Middle Ages, the latter traces the trajectory from slavery in Rome through to medieval and Renaissance Europe, Islamicized regions, the Atlantic islands, sub-Saharan Africa, and to America.
4. Only after 1510 did Dom Manuel evince concern about the spiritual side of slaves' existence and the shortcomings of whatever religious instruction they did receive. See Saunders (1982:40-42).
5. On slavery in medieval Portugal, see Heleno (1933).
6. For discussion of discrepancies in numbers, see the definitive edition by Bourdon (1960:17, n. 3 and p. 108, n. 3).
7. For the struggle of caravans versus caravels, see Godinho (1963:1:153-202, and end map on commercial routes in northeast Africa at the end of the fifteenth century in vol. 2).
8. This and the following is based on Godinho (1963, 1965:2:525-35; see also Blake (1937:26-40).
9. "Neste tempo o negócio de Guiné andava já mui corrente entre os nossos e os moradores daquelas partes, e uns com os outros se comunicavam em as cousas do comercio com paz e amor" (Barros 1945-46:1:2:2).
10. "Porque os amigos que se viam de tarde em tarde com mais amor se tratavam, que quando se vezinham" (Barros 1945-46:1:3:2). See also Boxer (1969:32).
11. The Oba of Benin sent presents to officials at Elmina. See Ryder (1969:36).
12. State boundaries in precolonial West and Central Africa are discussed in Thornton (1991:xii-xxxviii). For modern names and identifications, see S.W. Koelle's linguistic inventory reproduced in Curtin (1969:291-98 and figures 20-24).
13. For discussion of African maritime capabilities, see Van Sertima (1976:50-70) and Thornton (1991:36-40). On the Indian Ocean trade, see Beachey (1976) and Harris (1971).
14. A factor that contributed to price increases was Castilian competition, which ended with the Treaty of Alcáçovas. See Russell (1971:5-33).
15. See Godinho (1963, 1965:1:164-93) for sporadic figures on imports into Portugal of West African gold in the fifteenth century.
16. The best survey of this rivalry remains Blake (1937; 1942:vols. 86, 87). See also Vogt (1973:4-5).
17. For an introduction to these administrative entities, see Saunders (1982:8-11); Vogt (1973:1-16); Peres (1947).
18. Godinho (1963, 1965:2:524-26, 529-30) suggests between 140,000 and 170,000 for the period 1450-1505 from Arguim to Sierra Leone inclusive. Boxer (1969:31) suggests about 150,000 slaves acquired by the Portuguese between 1450 and 1500. Saunders (1982:19-25) is more conservative, especially for the period 1470-90; he considers these data inadequate as a base for conclusions, and offers a few data prior to 1499. Vogt (1973:7-8) notes recorded entries into Portugal of 3,589 slaves between 1486 and 1493. Tinhorão (1988:80) suggests between 117,000 and 131,000 between 1441 and 1495. My estimates are lower than Magalhàes Godinho's figures, but substantially exceed Curtin's (1969:115-16) estimate of 33,500 slaves imported into Europe, Atlantic islands, and São Tomé for 1451-1500, and Lovejoy's (1983) estimate of about 41,000. Elbl (1986) suggests the volume of Portuguese trade in slaves to Europe at about 77,000 for the fifteenth century. See also Azevedo (1929:73).

19. For the proposition that the population of Portugal fluctuated little between 1495 and 1527, see Lobo (1903:27-62).

20. English translations are in Davenport (1917-34:1: 13-26, 28-32). Summary in Boxer (1969:20-23). See also Horta (1991:255-58) and sources cited therein; de Witte (1958); and Rogers's (1962:64-66) interpretation of the word "Indians."

21. Use of the adjective *prêto* referring to blacks from sub-Saharan Africa appears to date only from the beginning of the sixteenth century, see Tinhorão (1988:75-76).

22. "O qual com grande repouso, descriçam, e muita gravidade, fez huma falla pubrica, que durou per grande espaço, em que pera seo caso meteo palavras, e sentenças tam notavees, que nom pareciam de Negro barbaro, mas de Principe Grego criado em Athenas" (Pina 1950:cap. 37); see also Horta (1991:247-48, 251). Also Barros's (1945-46:1:3:2) characterization of Caramansa at Elmina illustrated this changed attitude: "Caramansa, peró que fosse homem barbaro, assi per sua natureza como pela communicação que tinha a gente dos navios que vinham ao resgate, era de bom entendimento e tinha o juízo claro pera receber qualquer cousa que estivesse em boa razão."

23. On beliefs, language and attitudes, see Horta (1991:255-84), on which the above is based, and personal correspondence.

24. Despite few references to slaves or blacks, or to Jewish and Morisco communities, the best history of privacy and society in fifteenth-century Portugal is Oliveira Marques (1971).

25. An exception is a black depicted in the Lisbon Beatus MS. of 1189, Saunders (1982:181, introduction, n. 2). See also Horta (1991:209). For reproduction of sixteenth-century Portuguese art depicting blacks, see Bugner (1976-:2:2:figs. 185-87, 195-200).

26. A comprehensive survey of representation of blacks in travel literature from ca. 1453-1508 - but of which there only three examples of Portuguese authorship out of sixteen - is Horta (1991:209-339, esp. 221-55 on physical characteristics).

27. For extensive discussion of slaves and freedmen, see Russell-Wood ([1982] 1993).

28. Cited in Russell-Wood (1987-88).

29. The figures presented by Curtin (1969:table 77) are probably on the low side. Numbers may have exceeded 5,000,000. For a full discussion, see Conrad (1986:25-34).

References

Almeida, Fortunato de, *História de Portugal*. 6 vols. Coimbra:Atlântida. 1922-29

Azevedo, João Lùcio de, *Epocas de Portugal económico: esboços de história*. Lisbon: Livraria Clássica Editora. 1929

Balandier, Georges, *Daily Life in the Kingdom of the Kongo from the Sixteenth to the Eighteenth Century*. Translated by Helen Weaver. New York: Pantheon Books. 1958

Barros, João de, *Asia*. 4 vols. 6th ed. Annotated by Hernani Cidade. Lisbon: Agência Geral das Colónias. 1945-46

Beachey, R.W., *The Slave Trade of Eastern Africa*. London: Rex Collings. 1976

Beazley, C.R., "Prince Henry of Portugal and the African Crusade of the Fifteenth Century." *American Historical Review* 16:11-23. 1911.

Beazley R., and E. Prestage, *The Chronicle of the Discovery and Conquest of Guinea*. 2 vols. London: Hakluyt Society. 1896, 1899

Birmingham, David, *Trade and Conflict in Angola: the Mbunda and their Neighbours under the Influence of the Portuguese, 1483-1790*. Oxford: Clarendon Press. 1966

Blake, John W., *European Beginnings in West Africa, 1454-1578*. New York: Longman, Green. Reprinted Westport: Greenwood Press, 1969. 1937

———. Europeans in West Africa (1450-1560). 2 vols. London: Hakluyt Society. 1942

Bourdon, Léon, *Chronique de Guineé*. Ifan-Dakar: Memoires de l'Institut Français de l'Afrique Noire, no. 60. 1960

Boxer, C.R., *The Portuguese Seaborne Empire, 1415-1825*. London: Hutchinson. 1969

Bugner, Ladislas, *The Image of the Black Western Art*. 4 vols. New York: William Morrow. 1976

Burns, Bradford, *A History of Brazil*, New York: Columbia University Press. 1970

Carvalho, J.B. de, *A la recherche de la spécifité de la renaissance portugaise*. 2 vols. Paris: Calouste Gulbenkian Foundation.

Conrad, Robert Edgar, *World of Sorrow. The African Slave Trade to Brazil*. Baton Rouge: Louisiana State University Press. 1986

Curtin, Phillip D., *The Atlantic Slave Trade: A Census*. University of Wisconsin Press: Madison. 1969

———. The Rise and Fall of the Plantation Complex. Essays in Atlantic History. Cambridge: Cambridge University Press. 1990

Davenport, F.G., *European Treaties Bearing on the History of the United States and Its Dependencies*. 3 vols. Washington D.C. 1917-1934

de Witte, Charles-Martial O.S.B., *Les bulles pontificales et l'expansion portugaise au XVe siècle*. Louvain. Reprinted from articles in the Revue d'histoire ecclésiastique, vols. 48, 49,51,53. 1958

Diffie, Bailey W., and George D. Winius, *Foundations of the Portuguese Empire, 1415-1580*. Minneapolis: Univeristy of Minnesota Press, 1977

Elbl, Martina, 'Portuguese Trade with West Africa 1440-1520'. Unpublished Ph.D. diss., University of Toronto, Toronto, Ontario. 1986

Evans, William McKee, "From the Land of Canaan to the Land of the Guinea: The Strange Odyssey of the "Sons of Ham." *American Historical Review* 85(1):15-43. 1980

Fernández-Armesto, Felipe, *Before Columbus: Exploration and Colonization from the Mmediterranean to the Atlantic, 1229-1492*. Philadelphia: University of Pennsylvania Press. 1987

Gioffrè, Domenico, *Il mercato degli schiavi a Genova nel secolo XV*. Genoa: Fratelli bozzi. 1971

Godinho, Vitorino Maglhães, *Os descobrimentos e a econimia mundial*. 2 vols. Lisbon: Editora Arcádia. 1963-1965

Goulart, Murico, *Escravidão Africana no Brasil*. São Paulo: Livraria Martins Editora. 1949

Harris, Joseph E., *The African Presence in Asia. Consequences of the East African Slave Trade*. Evanston: University of Illinois Press. 1971

Heleno, Manuel, *Os escravos em Portugal*. Vol. I. Lisbon: Emprêsa do Anuário Comerical. 1933

Kappler, Claude, *Monstres, demons, et merveilles à la fin du Moyen Age*. Paris: Payot. 1980

Continued on page 1120

3

The Constituent Elements of Slavery

ORLANDO PATTERSON

All human relationships are structured and defined by the relative power of the interacting persons. Power, in Max Weber's terms, is 'that opportunity existing within a social relationship which permits one to carry out one's will even against resistance and regardless of the basis on which this opportunity rests.'[1] Relations of inequality or domination, which exist whenever one person has more power than another, range on a continuum from those of marginal asymmetry to those in which one person is capable of exercising, with impunity, total power over another. Power relationships differ from one another not only in degree, but in kind. Qualitative differences result from the fact that power is a complex human faculty, although perhaps not as 'sociologically amorphous' as Weber thought.

Slavery is one of the most extreme forms of the relation of domination, approaching the limits of total power from the viewpoint of the master, and of total powerlessness from the viewpoint of the slave. Yet it differs from other forms of extreme domination in very special ways. If we are to understand how slavery is distinctive, we must first clarify the concept of power.

The power relation has three facets.[2] The first is social and involves the use or threat of violence in the control of one person by another. The second is the psychological facet of influence, the capacity to persuade another person to change the way he perceives his interests and his circumstances. And third is the cultural facet of authority, 'the means of transforming force into right, and obedience into duty' which, according to Jean Jacques Rousseau, the powerful find

necessary 'to ensure them continual mastership.' Rousseau felt that the source of 'legitimate powers' lay in those 'conventions' which today we would call culture.[3] But he did not specify the area of this vast human domain in which the source of authority was to be found. Nor, for that matter, did Weber, the leading modern student of the subject.[4] I show that authority rests on the control of those private and public symbols and ritual processes that induce (and seduce) people to obey because they feel satisfied and dutiful when they do so.

With this brief anatomy of power in mind we may now ask how slavery is distinctive as a relation of domination. The relation has three sets of constituent features corresponding to the three facets of power. It is unusual, first, both in the extremity of power involved, and all that immediately implies, and in the qualities of coercion that brought the relation into being and sustained it. As Georg Hegel realized, total personal power taken to its extreme contradicts itself by its very existence, for total domination can become a form of extreme dependence on the object of one's power, and total powerlessness can become the secret path to control of the subject that attempts to exercise such power.[5] Even though such a sublation is usually only a potential, the possibility of its realization influences the normal course of the relation in profound ways. An empirical exploration of this unique dimension of the dialectic of power in the master-slave relationship will be one of the major tasks of this work.

The coercion underlying the relation of slavery is also distinctive in its etiology and its composition. In one of the liveliest passages of the *Grundrisse*, Karl Marx, while discussing the attitudes of former masters and slaves in post-emancipation Jamaica, not only shows clearly that he understood slavery to be first and foremost 'a relation of domination' (his term and a point worth emphasizing in view of what has been written by some recent 'Marxists' on the subject) but identifies the peculiar role of violence in creating and maintaining that domination. Commenting on the fact that the Jamaican ex-slaves refused to work beyond what was necessary for their own subsistence, he notes: "They have ceased to be slaves, . . . not in order to become wage labourers, but, instead, self-sustaining peasants working for their own consumption. As far as they are concerned, capital does not exist as capital, because autonomous wealth as such can exist only either on the basis of *direct* forced labour, slavery, or *indirect* forced labour, *wage labour*. Wealth confronts direct forced labour not as capital, but rather as *relation of domination*' (emphasis in original).[6] It is important to stress that Marx was not saying that the master interprets the relationship this way, that the master is in any way necessarily precapitalist. Indeed, the comment was provoked by a November 1857 letter to the *Times* of London from a West Indian planter who, in what Marx calls 'an utterly delightful cry of outrage,' was advocating the reimposition of slavery in Jamaica as the only means of getting the Jamaicans to generate surplus in a capitalistic manner once again.[7]

Elizabeth Welskopf, the late East German scholar who was one of the leading Marxists students of slavery, discussed at great length the critical role of direct violence in creating and maintaining slavery.[8] Force, she argued, is essential for all class societies. Naked might - violence, in Georges Sorel's terminology[9] – is essential for the creation of all such systems. However, organized force and authority – what Welskopf calls 'spiritual force' – usually obviated the need to use violence in most developed class societies where non-slaves made up the dominated class. The problem in a slaveholding society, however, was that it was usually necessary to introduce new persons to the status of slaves because the former slaves either died out or were manumitted. The worker who is fired remains a worker, to be hired elsewhere. The slave who was freed was no longer a slave. Thus it was necessary continually to repeat the original, violent act of transforming free man into slave. This act of violence constitutes the prehistory of all stratified societies, Welskopf argued, but it determines both 'the prehistory and (concurrent) history of slavery.' To be sure, there is the exceptional case of the Old South in the United States, where the low incidence of manumission and the high rate of reproduction, obviated the need continually to repeat the violent 'original accumulation' of slaves. While Welskopf does not consider this case (her concern is primarily with the ancient world), her analysis is nonetheless relevant, for she goes on to note that the continuous use of violence in the slave order was also made necessary by the low motivation of the slave to work – by the need to reinforce reward with the threat and actuality of punishment. Thus George P. Rawick has written of the antebellum South: 'Whipping was not only a method of punishment. It was a conscious device to impress upon the slaves that they were slaves: it was a crucial form of social control particularly if we remember that it was very difficult for slaves to run away successfully.'[10]

But Marx and the Marxists were not the first to recognize fully the necessity or the threat of naked force as the basis of the master-slave relationship. It was a North Carolina judge, Thomas Ruffin, who in his 1829 decision that the intentional wounding of a hired slave by his hirer did not constitute a crime, articulated better than any other commentator before or after, the view that the master-slave relationship originated in and was maintained by brute force. He wrote:

With slavery . . . the end is the profit of the master, his security and the public safety; the subject, one doomed in his own person, and his posterity, to live without knowledge, and without the capacity to make anything his own, and to toil that another may reap his fruits. What moral considerations such as a father might give to a son shall be addressed to such a being, to convince him what it is impossible but that the most stupid must feel and know can never be true - that he is thus to labour upon a principle of natural duty, or for the sake of his own personal happiness. Such services can only be expected from one who has no will of his own; who surrenders his will in implicit obedience in the consequence only of uncontrolled authority over the body. There is nothing else which can operate to produce the effect. The power of the master must be absolute, to render the submission of the slave perfect.[11]

Justice Ruffin may have gone a little too far in what Robert M. Cover describes as 'his eagerness to confront the reality of the unpleasant iron fist beneath the law's polite, neutral language.'[12] He certainly underestimated the role of 'moral considerations,' to use his term, in the relationship. But his opinion did penetrate to the heart of what was most fundamental in the relation of slavery. There is no known slaveholding society where the whip was not considered an indispensable instrument.

Another feature of the coercive aspect of slavery is its individualized condition: the slave was usually powerless in relation to another individual. We may conveniently neglect those cases where the slave formally belonged to a corporation such as a temple, since there was always an agent in the form of a specific individual who effectively exercised the power of a master.[13] In his powerlessness the slave became an extension of his master's power. He was a human surrogate, recreated by his master with god-like power in his behalf. Nothing in Hegel or Friedrich Nietzsche more frighteningly captures the audacity of power and ego expansion than the view of the Ahaggar Tuaregs of the Sahara that 'without the master the slave does not exist, and he is socializable only through his master.'[14] And they came as close to blasphemy as their Islamic creed allowed in the popular saying of the Kel Gress group: 'All persons are created by God, the slave is created by the Tuareg.'[15]

These Tuareg sayings are not only extraordinarily reminiscent of Ruffin's opinion but of what Henri Wallon, in his classic study, wrote of the meaning of slavery in ancient Greece:

The slave was a dominated thing, an animated instrument, a body with natural movements, but without its own reason, an existence entirely absorbed in another. The proprietor of this thing, the mover of this instrument, the soul and the reason of this body, the source of this life, was the master. The master was everything for him: his father and his god, which is to say, his authority and his duty . . . Thus, god, fatherland, family, existence, are all, for the slave, identified with the same being; there was nothing which made for the social person, nothing which made for the moral person, that was not the same as his personality and his individuality.[16]

Perhaps the most distinctive attribute of the slave's powerlessness was that it always originated (or was conceived of as having originated) as a substitute for death, usually violent death. Ali Abd Elwahed, in an unjustly neglected comparative work, found that 'all the situations which created slavery were those which commonly would have resulted, either from natural or social laws, in the death of the individual.'[17] Archetypically, slavery was a substitute for death in war. But almost as frequently, the death commuted was punishment for some capital offence, or death from exposure or starvation.

The condition of slavery did not absolve or erase the prospect of death. Slavery was not a pardon; it was, peculiarly, a conditional commutation. The execution was suspended only as long as the slave acquiesced in his powerlessness. The master was essentially a ransomer. What he bought or acquired was the slave's life, and restraints on the master's capacity wantonly to destroy his slave did not undermine his claim on that life. Because the slave had no socially recognized existence outside of his master, he became a social non-person.

This brings us to the second constituent element of the slave relation: the slave's natal alienation. Here we move to the cultural aspect of the relation, to that aspect of it which rests on authority, on the control of symbolic instruments. This is achieved in a unique way in the relation of slavery: the definition of the slave, however recruited, as a socially dead person. Alienated from all 'rights' or claims of birth, he ceased to belong in his own right to any legitimate social order. All slaves experienced, at the very least, a secular excommunication.

Not only was the slave denied all claims on, and obligations to, his parents and living blood relations but, by extension, all such claims and obligations on his more remote ancestors and on his descendants. He was truly a genealogical isolate. Formally isolated in his social relations with those who lived, he also was culturally isolated from the social heritage of his ancestors. He had a past, to be sure. But a past is not a heritage. Everything has a history, including sticks and stones. Slaves differed from other human beings in that they were not allowed freely to integrate the experience of their ancestors into their lives, to inform their understanding of social reality with the inherited meanings of their natural forebears, or to anchor the living present in any conscious community of memory. That they reached back for the past, as they reached out for the related living, there can be no doubt. Unlike other persons, doing so meant struggling with and penetrating the iron curtain of the master, his community, his laws, his policemen or patrollers, and his heritage.

In the struggle to reclaim the past the odds were stacked even more heavily in favour of the master than in the attempt to maintain links with living relatives. One of the most significant findings of Michael Craton's study of the oral history of the descendants of the Worthy Park plantation slaves of Jamaica was the extraordinary shallowness of their genealogical and historical memory.[18] The same is attested by the recorded interviews with American ex-slaves.

When we say that the slave was natally alienated and ceased to belong independently to any formally recognized community, this does not mean that he or she did not experience or share informal social relations. A large number of works have demonstrated that slaves in both ancient and modern times had strong social ties among themselves. The important point, however, is that these relationships were never recognized as legitimate or binding. Thus American slaves, like their ancient Greco-Roman counterparts, had regular sexual unions, but such unions were never recognized as marriages; both groups were attached to their local communities, but such attachments had no binding force; both sets of parents were deeply attached to their children, but the parental bond had no social support.

The refusal formally to recognize the social relations of the slave had profound emotional and social implications. In all slaveholding societies slave couples could be and were forcibly separated and the consensual 'wives' of slaves were obliged to submit sexually to their masters; slaves had no custodial claims or powers over their children, and children inherited no claims or obligations to their parents. And the master had the power to remove a slave from the local community in which he or she was brought up.

Even if such forcible separations occurred only infrequently, the fact that they were possible and that from time to time they did take place was enough to strike terror in the hearts of all slaves and to transform significantly the way they behaved and conceived of themselves. Nothing comes across more dramatically from the hundreds of interviews with American ex-slaves than the fear of separation. Peter Clifton, an eighty-nine-year-old ex-slave from South Carolina, was typical when he said: 'Master

Biggers believe in whippin' and workin' his slaves long and hard; then a man was scared all de time of being sold away from his wife and chillun. His bark was worse than his bite tho', for I never knowed him to do a wicked thing lak dat.'[19]

Isaiah Butler, another South Carolina ex-slave, observed: 'Dey didn't have a jail in dem times. Dey'd whip em, and dey'd sell 'em. Every slave know what I'll put you in my pocket, Sir' mean.'[20]

The independent constituent role of natal alienation in the emergence of slavery is vividly illustrated by the early history of slavery in America. Winthrop D. Jordan has shown that in the early decades of the seventeenth century there were few marked differences in the conception of black and white servitude, the terms 'slave' and 'servant' being used synonymously. The power of the master over both black and white servants was near total: both could be whipped and sold.[21]

Gradually there emerged, however, something new in the conception of the black servant: the view that he did not belong to the same community of Christian, civilized Europeans. The focus of this 'we-they' distinction was at first religious, later racial. 'Enslavement was captivity, the loser's lot in a contest of power. Slaves were infidels or heathens.'[22] But as Jordan argues, although the focus may have changed, there was really a fusion of race, religion, and nationality in a generalized conception of 'us' – white, English, free – and 'them' – black, heathen, slave. 'From the first, then, vis-à-vis the Negro the concept embedded in the term Christian seems to have conveyed much of the idea and feeling of we as against they: to be Christian was to be civilized rather than barbarous, English rather than African, white rather than black.'[23] The strangeness and seeming savagery of the Africans, reinforced by traditional attitudes and the context of early contact, 'were major components in that sense of difference which provided the mental margin absolutely requisite for placing the European on the deck of the slave ship and the Negro in the hold.'[24]

Although using different symbolic tools, much the same sense of apartness, of not belonging, emerged in other cultures to differentiate the genuine slave from other forms of involuntary servants over whom almost total power was exercised. Yet the natal alienation of the slave was not necessarily expressed in religious, racial, or even ethnic terms. Among primitives, as we shall see, alienation from one's natal ties was all that was necessary. Sometimes law alone, superimposed on the slave's sense of not belonging, was sufficient. Indeed, it was Moses Finley, drawing on the Greco-Roman experience, who was among the first to emphasize what he called the 'outsider' status of the race as a critical attribute of his condition.[25] He did not make the mistake that Henri Lévi-Bruhl had earlier made, of generalizing from the Roman experience to the conclusion that the social alienation of the slave was necessarily an ethnic one.[26] Insofar as Roman slaves were foreigners, Finley argued, they were outsiders twice over, clearly allowing for the reduction of locally recruited slaves to the status of outsiders.

I prefer the term 'natal alienation,' because it goes directly to the heart of what is critical in the slave's forced alienation, the loss of ties of birth in both ascending and descending generations. It also has the important nuance of a loss of native status, of deracination. It was this alienation of the slave from all formal, legally enforceable ties of 'blood,' and from any attachment to groups or localities other than those chosen for him by the master, that gave the relation of slavery its peculiar value to the master. The slave was the ultimate human tool, as imprintable and as disposable as the master wished. And this is true, at least in theory, of all slaves, no matter how elevated. Paul Rycaut's classic description of the Janissaries as men whom their master, the sultan, 'can raise without Envy and destroy without Danger'[27] holds true for all slaves in all times.

The incapacity to make any claims of birth or to pass on such claims is considered a natural injustice among all peoples, so that those who were obliged to suffer it had to be regarded as somehow socially dead. Callicles in Plato's *Gorgias* goes to the heart of the matter when he says:

By the rule of nature, to suffer injustice is the greater disgrace because the greater evil; but conventionally to do evil is the more disgraceful. For the suffering of injustice is not the part of a man, but of a slave, who indeed had better die than live; since when he is wronged and trampled upon, he is unable to help himself, or any other about whom he cares.[28]

All slaves of all times and places were forced to suffer the natural injustice of which Callicles spoke. But nowhere in the annals of slavery has their condition been more poignantly expressed than by an American ex-slave, a Mr. Reed, who was interviewed by Ophelia Settle Egypt of Fisk University in about 1930.

The most barbarous thing I saw with these eyes - I lay on my bed and study about it now - I had a sister, my older sister, she was fooling with the clock and broke it, and my old master taken her and tied a rope around her neck - just enough to keep it from choking her - and tied her up in the back yard and whipped her I don't know how long. There stood mother, there stood father, and there stood all the children and none could come to her rescue.[29]

How, we may ask, could persons be made to accept such natural injustice? The question applies not only to the victims but to those third parties not directly involved in the slave relation who stood by and accepted it. Denying the slave's humanity, his independent social existence, begins to explain this acceptance. Yet it is only a beginning, for it immediately poses the further question: how was the slave's social death, the outward conception of his natal alienation, articulated and reinforced?

There it will be shown that the master's authority was derived from his control over symbolic instruments, which effectively persuaded both slave and others that the master was the only mediator between the living community to which he belonged and the living death that his slave experienced.

The symbolic instruments may be seen as the cultural counterpart to the physical instruments used to control the slave's body. In much the same way that the literal whips were fashioned from different materials, the symbolic whips of slavery were woven from many areas of culture. Masters all over the world used special rituals of enslavement upon first acquiring slaves: the symbolism of naming, of clothing, of hairstyle, and of body marks. And they used, especially in the more advanced slave systems, the sacred symbols of religion.

Natal alienation has one critical corollary that is an important feature of slavery, so important indeed that many scholars have seen it as the distinguishing element of the relation. This is the fact that the relation was perpetual and inheritable. James Curtis Ballagh's assessment sums this up for many scholars: "The distinguishing mark of the state of slavery is not the loss of liberty, political or civil, but the perpetuity and almost absolute character of that loss, whether voluntary or involuntary.'[30] He then showed, from the case of Virginia, how in legal terms the crucial emerging difference between indentured servants and slaves during the seventeenth century was the consolidation of the view that 'all negroes and other slaves shall serve *durante via,*' beginning with the passage of the 1661 act of the Assembly, which stated that blacks, unlike white indentured servants, 'are incapable of making satisfaction [for the time lost in running away] by addition of time.'[31]

Ballagh was wrong, however, in his assumption that the inheritability of slavery was the 'natural consequence' of the life bondage of the slave, although in fairness we should point out that he was shrewd enough not to commit the easy error of deriving inheritability from the totality of the master's power. It is easy to show in purely empirical terms that neither absolute power nor lifetime subjection to such power necessarily imply the inheritability of such status. The most obvious case is that of prisoners serving life sentences. Some oriental societies, especially China, did reduce the children of such convicts to slavery, but they were the exceptions.[32] More telling perhaps is the case of debt-bondage. In many societies the masters of debt-servants had as complete control over them as they did over slaves, including the right to sell them. The distinction, often made, between selling their labour as opposed to selling their persons makes no sense what ever in real human terms. Debt-servitude was, for all practical purposes, usually lifelong in societies where it was found, since the debtor's labour only repaid the interest. Still, despite the totality of the master's power and the expected lifelong servitude of the debtor, this status was almost never inherited by the debtor's children, even those born after servitude began.[33] Clearly then, there was no 'natural' development from total power and lifelong subjection to hereditary servitude.

The hereditary factor only entered in when the servant lost his natal claims to his own parents and community. Having no natal claims and powers of his own, he had none to pass on to his children. And because no one else had any claim or interest in such children, the master could claim them as his own essentially on the grounds that whatever the parents of such children expended in their upbringing incurred a debt to him. Not by virtue, then, of his lifetime power over the slave did the master claim the latter's issue, but by virtue of the absence of any third party's interest in the child, the absence of the child's capacity to assert a claim on any such third parties, and the claim that necessarily accrued to the master with the parent's expenditures for childrearing.

The peculiar character of violence and the natal alienation of the slave generates the third constituent element of slavery: the fact that slaves were always persons who had been dishonoured in a generalized way. Here we move to the socio-psychological aspect of this unusual power relationship. The slave could have no honour because of the origin of his status, the indignity and all-pervasiveness of his indebtedness, his absence of any independent social existence, but most of all because he was without power except through another.

Honour and power are intimately linked. No one understood this more than Thomas Hobbes. In the chapter of *Leviathan* in which he sets out to define his central concept - power - and related conditions, Hobbes devotes more than two-thirds of his effort to a detailed disquisition on the nature of honour. Fully recognizing that honour is a social-psychological issue, Hobbes wrote: 'The manifestation of the Value we set on one another, is that which is commonly called *Honouring,* and *Dishonouring.* To Value a man at a high rate, is to *Honour* him; at a low rate, is to *Dishonour* him. But high, and low, in this case, is to be understood by comparison to the rate that each man setteth on himself.'[34] The link between honour and power is direct: 'To obey, is to Honour, because no man obeys them, whom they think have no power to help, or hurt them. And consequently to disobey, is to Dishonour.' Somewhat cynically, Hobbes observes that it really does not matter 'whether an action . . . be just or unjust: for Honour consisteth onely in the opinion of Power.'[35]

As usual, Hobbes overstates his case: and his materialism prevents him from recognizing important dimensions of honour which, if anything, might have strengthened his argument. Hobbes, however, gives us a useful starting point, for he was basically right in recognizing the significance of honour as a critical aspect of the psychology of power. Furthermore, his emphasis on the concept as a social-psychological process, as distinct from a purely psychological one, is still far in advance of, say, the reductionist utilitarianism of John Stuart Mill, who speaks of 'the sense of honour' as 'that feeling of personal exaltation and degradation which acts independently of other people's opinion, or even in defiance of it.'[36] Nor does Mill ever make the critical connection between honour and power that came so easily to the more incisive mind of Hobbes.

The slave, as we have already indicated, could have no honour because he had no power and no independent social existence, hence no public worth. He had no name of his own to defend. He could only defend his master's worth and his master's name. That the dishonour was a generalized condition must be emphasized, since the free and honourable person, ever alive to slights and insults, occasionally experiences specific acts of dishonour to which, of course, he or she responds by taking appropriate action. The slave, as we shall see, usually stood outside the game of honour.

The honouring of the master and the dishonouring of the slave were the outward product of their interaction. We can say little or nothing about the private lives of the members of either group. Certainly we know next to nothing about the individual personalities of slaves, or of the way they felt about one another. The data are just not there, and it is the height of arrogance, not to mention intellectual irresponsibility, to generalize about the inner psychology of any group, be they medieval Jewish merchants, New England Puritan farmers, or Scythian slave policemen in Athens.

What we do know a great deal about, however, is the political psychology of the everyday life of masters and slaves in their relationships with one another. The interaction was complex and fascinating, fraught with conflict and perversity. It was Hegel who first explored in depth the dialectics of this political psychology.[37] Eugene Genovese, paraphrasing Hegel, has argued that 'the slaveholder, as distinct from the farmer, had a private source of character making and myth-making - his slave. Most obviously, he had the habit of command, but there was more than despotic authority in this master-slave relationship'[38] I disagree with Genovese on what is

critical in the interaction, just as I do with Hegel on his stance that the slave stood interposed between his master and the object his master desired (that which was produced).[39] This may have been partly true of the capitalistic antebellum U.S. South, but as the comparative data will show, in a great many slaveholding societies masters were not interested in what their slaves produced. Indeed, in many of the most important slaveholding societies, especially those of the Islamic world, slaves produced nothing and were economically dependent on their masters or their master's non-slave dependents.

What was universal in the master-slave relationship was the strong sense of honour the experience of mastership generated, and conversely, the dishonouring of the slave condition. Many masters, especially among primitives, acquired slaves solely for this purpose. But even if the motivation was chiefly materialistic, the sense of honour was still enhanced. The traits Genovese attributed to the southern slaveholder- 'his strength, graciousness, and gentility; his impulsiveness, violence, and unsteadiness the sense of independence and the habit of command [which] developed his poise, grace and dignity'[40] - hold for the way in which all slave masters conceived of themselves, whether they were Toradja tribesmen in the central Celebes, ancient Greek intellectuals, or Islamic sultans. What they actually were is a matter on which I do not feel qualified to comment.

The counterpart of the master's sense of honour is the slave's experience of its loss. The so-called servile personality is merely the outward expression of this loss of honour.[41] And it is truly remarkable how consistent are the attributes of the expression of generalized dishonour not only among all slaves but among all oppressed peoples. There is, for example, the crushing and pervasive sense of knowing that one is considered a person without honour and that there simply is nothing that can be done about it. As Sosia observes in Plautus' *Amphitryo*, 'It's not just the work, but knowing you're a slave, and nothing can alter it.'[42] There is, too, the outward expression of self-blame. 'You know,' observes Phaniscus in Plautus' *The Ghost*, 'slaves get the masters they deserve.'[43] One finds this view repeated constantly by American ex-slaves in their interviews. 'De Massa and Missus was good to me but sometime I was so bad they had to whip me,' said Victoria Adams.[44] 'It was always for something, sir, I needed the whippin',' recalled Millier Barber.[45]

More tragic than the victim's outward acceptance of blame as part of the dynamics of interaction with the master was his tendency to express psychological violence against himself: the outward show of self-hatred in the presence of the master, which was prompted by the pervasive indignity and underlying physical violence of the relationship. In Plautus' most mature play, *The Rope*, Palaestra, a slave anticipating escape from her condition, begins to cry, exclaiming, 'Oh life and hope.' She is roguishly comforted by Trachalio, who tells her, 'Just leave it all to me.' To this Palaestra retorts, 'I could if I had no force to fear, force which forces me to do violence to myself.'[46] It does not matter whether these were Plautus' words or the words of the Greek playwright he was adapting. Whoever wrote them knew, in a profound way, what slavery really meant: the direct and insidious violence, the namelessness and invisibility, the endless personal violation, and the chronic inalienable dishonour.

It was in the interaction between master and slave that such feelings were expressed and played out. Clearly, no authentic human relationship was possible where violence was the ultimate sanction. There could have been no trust, no genuine sympathy; and while a kind of love may sometimes have triumphed over this most perverse form of interaction, intimacy was usually calculating and sadomasochistic.

Occasionally we get a glimpse of the relationship in action from incidents recalled by American ex-slaves. This is how Grace Gibson from South Carolina described the moment when she was given as a present to her young mistress:

I was called up on one of her [Miss Ada's] birthdays, and Marster Bob sorta looked out of de corner of his eyes, first at me and then at Miss Ada, and then he make a little speech. He took my hand, put it in Miss Ada's hand, and say: "Dis your birthday present, darlin'." I make a curtsy and Miss Ada's eyes twinkle like a star and she take me in her room and took on powerful over me."[47]

Frederick Douglass, undoubtedly the most articulate former slave who ever lived, repeatedly emphasized as the central feature of slavery the loss of honour and its relation to the loss of power. After physically resisting a brutal white who had been hired by his exasperated master to break him, Douglass, whose spirit had nearly broken and who had run the risk of being executed for his resistance, recalls that he felt 'a sense of my own manhood . . . I was nothing before, I was a man now.'[48] And he adds in a passage for which this chapter may be read as an extended exegesis: "A man without force is without the essential dignity of humanity. Human nature is so constituted that it cannot honour a helpless man, although it can pity him; and even that it cannot do long, if the signs of power do not arise."[49]

At this point we may offer a preliminary definition of slavery on the level of personal relations: *slavery is the permanent, violent domination of natally alienated and generally dishonoured persons.*

Even at this most elementary level of personal relations it should be clear that we are dealing not with a static entity but with a complex interactional process, one laden with tension and contradiction in the dynamics of each of its constituent elements. The power of the master, in its very extremity, tended to become sublative; the slave's natural love for and attachment to kinsmen worked against the master's attempt to deny him all formal claims of natality; and the master's need for honour and recognition was both enhanced and undermined by the dishonouring of the slave and the latter's own effort to eke out some measure of pride and dignity in the face of the master.

However, it is not solely on the level of personal relations that we should examine slavery. Like all enduring social processes, the relation became institutionalized. Patterned modes of resolving the inherent contradictions of the relation were developed. Such modes were no less dynamic in their operation than were the constituent elements. On the institutional level the modes of recruitment, enslavement, and manumission were all intimately interrelated. The desocialized new slave somehow had to be incorporated; but the process of incorporation created new contradictions, which usually made necessary the process of manumission. One of the major tasks of this work will be to disclose the dynamics of this institutional process.

Notes

1. *Basic Concepts in Sociology,* trans. H.P. Secher (Secaucus, N.J.: Citadel Press, 1972), p. 117. This translation is a much better rendering of the original than that of Parsons and Henderson, which converts Weber's definition into a probabilistic expression of action theory: Max Weber, *The Theory of Social and Economic Organization,* ed. Talcott Parsons and A.M. Henderson (New York: Free Press, 1947), p. 152.

2. See David V.I. Bell, *Power, Influence, and Authority* (New York: Oxford University Press, 1975), p. 26. Bell's work is extremely enlightening, especially his discussion of influence.

3. *The Social Contract,* ed. Charles Frankel (New York: Hafner Publishing Co., 1947), bk. 1, chap. 3, p. 8. Note how Rousseau's formulation of the concept of authority and its relation to power anticipates Weber's almost identical position.

4. *Basic Concepts in Sociology,* pp. 71-83. See also Weber's *Theory of Social and Economic Organization,* pp. 324-400.

5. *The Phenomenology of Mind,* trans. J.B. Baillie (London: Swan Sonnenschein, 1910), pp. 228-240.

6. *Grundrisse,* trans. Martin Nicolaus (London: Penguin and New Left Books, 1973) , pp. 325-326.

7. Ibid.

8. *Die Produktionsverhältnisse im alten Orient und in der griechisch-römischen Antike* (Berlin: Deutsche Akademie der Wissenchaften, 1957), pp. 158-177.

9. See the useful distinction between violence and organized force in Sorel, *Reflections on Violence,* trans. T.E. Hulme (New York: Collier Books, 1961), p. 175.

10. 'From Sundown to Sunup: The Making of the Black Community' in George P. Rawick, ed., *The American Slave: A composite Autobiography* (Westport, Conn.: Greenwood Publishing Co., 1972), vol. 1, p. 59. Stephen Crawford arrives at the same conclusion in his quantitative analysis of the slave narratives: 'Quantified Memory: A Study of the WPA and Fisk University Slave Narrative Collections' (Ph.D. diss., University of Chicago, 1980), chap. 3.

11. Cited in John S. Bassett, *Slavery in the State of North Carolina* (Baltimore: Johns Hopkins University Press, 1899), pp. 23-24.

12. Cover, *Justice Accused: Antislavery and Judicial Process* (New Haven: Yale University Press, 1975), p. 78.

13. The Romans, it is true, were unique in promoting the idea that it was possible for a slave to exist without a master. The idea of a masterless slave was a legal concept, one that provided a means for getting around a few tricky legal problems - for example, those related to abandoned or unlawfully manumitted slaves and to the fraudulent sale of freemen (often with their own complicity) - but difficult to make sense of sociologically. As the legal historian Alan Watson, observed, 'The idea of a slave without a master is not an easy concept.' In reality, all that being a *servus sine domino* meant was either that a potential relation of slavery existed, although the person in question – for example, the abandoned slave - was not at the time actually in a slave relationship or in a position to claim free status, or that the person was actually in a relation of slavery but was potentially a free person and could legally claim such a status. Legal technicalities aside, in actual practice all Roman slaves had at least one master. The technicalities referred to very temporary situations. Those who were illegally enslaved and could prove it had their illegal masters quickly removed (there was always a presumption in favour of freedom) and therefore ceased to be slaves; those who were corporately owned by the state (such as the *servi poenae*) would not only have been very surprised to learn that they had no masters but, had they been privy to such legal niceties, would have considered the fiction of their masterless status a grim piece of judicial humour. See W.W. Buckland, *The Roman Law of Slavery* (Cambridge: Cambridge University Press, 1908), p. 2; and Watson, *The Law of Persons in the Later Roman Republic* (Oxford: Clarendon Press, 1967), chap. 14.

14. André Bourgeot, 'Rapports esclavagistes et conditions d'affranchissement chez les Imuhag,' in Claude Meillassoux, ed., *L'esclavage en Afrique précoloniale* (Paris: François Maspero, 1975), p. 91.

15. Pierre Bonte, 'Esclavage et relations de dépendence chez les Touareg Kel Gress,' in Meillassoux, *L'esclavage en Afrique précoloniale,* p. 55.

16. *Histoire de l'esclavage dans l'antiquité* (Paris: Hachette, 1879), p. 408.

17. *Contribution à une théorie sociologique de l'esclavage* (Paris: Mechelinck, 1931), p. 243.

18. *Searching for the Invisible Man: Slaves and Plantation Life in Jamaica* (Cambridge, Mass.: Harvard University Press, 1978), pp. 367-384. Craton, much to his own disappointment, found that 'references to external events dating back beyond present lifetimes were, in fact, remarkably absent' and that 'the attempt to trace precise lineage . . . led to disappointment in nearly every case. At best the information was inaccurate; at worst there was ignorance or even indifference' (pp. 374-375).

19. Rawick, *The American Slave,* vol. 2, pt. 1, p. 207.

20. Ibid., p. 58.

21. Winthrop D. Jordan, *White over Black: American Attitudes toward the Negro, 1550-1812* (Baltimore: Penguin Books, 1969), pp. 45-48. Jordan observes that the distinction between owning and selling someone's labour as opposed to their person 'was neither important nor obvious at the time' (p. 48).

22. Ibid., p. 56.

23. Ibid., p. 94

24. Ibid., p. 57

25. Finley, 'Slavery,' *Encyclopedia of the Social Sciences* (New York: Macmillan Co. And Free Press, 1968), vol. 14, pp. 307-313.

26. Lévy-Bruhl, 'Théorie de l'esclavage,' in M.I. Finley, ed., *Slavery in Classical Antiquity* (Cambridge: W. Heffer and Sons, 1960) pp. 151-170.

27. *The Present State of the Ottoman Empire*, 1668 (London: Arno Press, 1971), p. 25.

28. Plato, *Gorgias*, in Benjamin Jowett, ed. and trans., *The Dialogues of Plato* (New York: Random House, 1937), vol. 2. p. 543.

29. Rawick, *The American Slave*, vol. 18, p. 44.

30. *History of Slavery in Virginia* (Baltimore: Johns Hopkins University Press, 1902), p. 28.

31. Ibid., p. 34. See also Jordan, *White over Black*, pp. 52-91.

32. See E.G. Pulleyblank, 'The Origins and Nature of Chattel Slavery in China,' *Journal of the Economic and Social History of the Orient* I (1958): pp. 204-211.

33. For the classic comparative study of debt-servitude see Bruno Lasker, *Human Bondage in Southeast Asia* (Chapel Hill, University of North Carolina Press, 1950), esp. Chap. 3. On the ancient world see M.I. Finley, 'La servitude pour dettes,' *Revue historique de droit francais et étranger* 43 (1965): 159-184 (ser. 4).

34. *Leviathan* (London: J.M. Dent & Sons, 1914), p. 44.

35. Ibid., pp. 44, 47.

36. 'Bentham,' in J.S. Mill, Utilitarianism (and Other Essays), ed. Mary Warnock (London: Collins, 1962), pp. 100-101.

37. *The Phenomenology of Mind*, pp. 228-240.

38. Genovese, *The Political Economy of Slavery* (London: MacGibbon & Kee, 1966), p. 32. Cf. David Brion Davis, *The Problem of Slavery in an Age of Revolution, 1770-1823* (Ithaca, N.Y.: Cornell University Press, 1975), pp. 561-564.

39. Genovese, *The Political Economy of Slavery*, p. 32. This is a paraphrase of the more radical but untenable section of Hegel's thesis.

40. Ibid., p. 33. See Genovese's more recent discussion of the psychology of master and slave in his *The World the Slaveholders Made* (New York: Vintage Books, 1971) pt. 1, pp. 5-8, and pt. 2.

41. I deliberately avoid getting involved with the thesis of Stanley Elkins regarding the personality of American slaves as set forth in his *Slavery: A Problem in American Institutional and Intellectual Life* (Chicago: University of Chicago Press, 1962). As already indicated, I am concerned with discussing the problem of honour relative to the political psychology of slavery, not with problems of human personality on which I can offer neither theoretical expertise nor relevant data. See Ann J. Lane, ed., *The Debate over Slavery: Stanley Elkins and His Critics* (Urbana: University of Illinois Press, 1971).

42. *Amphitryo*, in Plautus, *The Rope and Other Plays*, ed. and trans. E.F. Watling (New York: Penguin Books, 1964), p. 234.

43. *The Ghost*, in Plautus, *The Rope and Other Plays*, pp. 67-68.

44. Rawick, *The American Slave*, vol. 2, pt. 1, p. 11.

45. Ibid., pp. 39-40.

46. Plautus, *The Rope and Other Plays*, pp. 116-117.

47. Rawick, *The American Slave*, vol. 2, pt. 2, p. 113.

48. *Life and Times of Frederick Douglass* (1892; reprint ed., New York: Bonanza Books, 1972), p. 143.

49. Ibid.

4

Madeira and the Beginnings of New World Sugar Cane Cultivation and Plantation Slavery: A Study in Institution Building*

SIDNEY M. GREENFIELD

Although the tropical New World is generally taken as the context for the comparative and historical study of plantation systems and of slavery, the institutional complex of the slave plantation[1] did not have its origins in the Western Hemisphere. Instead, as Charles Verlinden[2] and others have demonstrated so ably, the culture complex can be traced back to the European colonies established in Palestine following the First Crusade. There sugar was grown by a mixed force of free and slave workers. The sugar then was exported, with some of it reaching the developing markets of Western Europe.

Sugar cane had been known to Europe at least as far back as antiquity, although its distribution was limited. The cultivation of the crop, and its increased availability and wider distribution, came to Mediterranean Europe in the wake of the expansion of Islam. Sugar cane, most probably first domesticated in India, had been grown in Asia Minor and was carried along with the spread of Islam to the coastal regions of North Africa, the islands of the Mediterranean, and eventually to the Moorish kingdoms in the Iberian peninsula.[3]

Given the intensity of the conflict between Christianity and Islam during the Middle Ages, trade between the areas controlled by the rival religions tended to be minimal. Hence sugars produced in areas under Moslem control went, for the most part, to supply markets in the Near East and North Africa, while the markets of Europe had to be supplied from areas under Christian control.

Christian production in the eastern Mediterranean moved to the island of Cyprus at the end of the thirteenth century when the colony in the Holy Land fell to the expanding Turks. Another colony was established in Sicily after the Norman conquest of the island. The Moors had set up sugar estates when they first took the island. The Normans took over the estates and Sicily remained an important producer of sugar into the sixteenth century.

In Cyprus Venetian and Genoese entrepreneurs financed and traded sugar produced on lands owned by French conquerors and Italians that was grown and processed by a labour force composed of Arabs and Syrians taken as slaves, local free workers and emigrants from Palestine.[4] In Sicily free labour was used primarily in sugar,[5] although the taking of slaves was far from unknown.[6]

As Moslem strength in the eastern Mediterranean increased, the European Christians were driven from the subtropical colonies they were using to raise sugar. The major expansion of the Ottoman Turks in the fifteenth century, however, coincided with the expansion of Europe into the Atlantic, and then to Africa and the New World.

The island of Madeira in the Atlantic Ocean off the northwest coast of Africa (Figure 1) provided the link between sugar production by

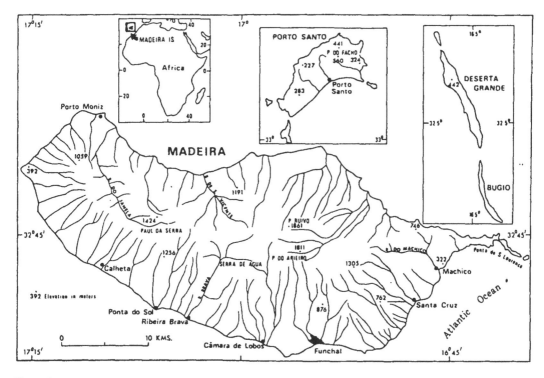

Figure 1

European Christians in the Mediterranean and the plantations of the New World. In the second and third quarters of the fifteenth century sugar plantations and plantation slavery were established in Madeira. Madeira, however, was settled by colonists from Portugal, a nation that had gained its independence just a few centuries earlier and was in the process of expanding overseas as perhaps the first true nation-state in Western Europe.

The appearance of the nation-state was to change the nature of colonies and of plantations. Madeira is the first place in which sugar-cane plantations were incorporated as part of an expanding national society. Also, in Madeira the exclusive use of slave labour on plantations is established, the pattern that then is to dominate the New World.

In one sense Madeira might be considered the link between Mediterranean sugar production and plantation slavery and the system that was to dominate New World history and society into the nineteenth century. In another sense, however, Madeira may be thought of as marking the transition from the plantation system and slavery of

the Middle Ages to the modern system that was the basis of what Curtin has referred to as the South Atlantic system.[7]

The following pages examine what happened in Madeira in the half-century or so following its rediscovery and settlement. My specific concern is with the emergence of the cultural pattern that combined plantations and slavery in an overseas colony within the context of an expanding nation-state.[8]

The Island of Madeira

The island group referred to as the Madeira Islands (see inset of Figure 1), composed of Madeira, Porto Santo, Deserta and the Selvagens, is located in the Atlantic Ocean off the northwest coast of Africa between Parallels 32o 7'50" and 33° 7'50" north latitude and between meridians 16° 16'30" and 17° 16'38" west longitude. They occupy a deep trough in the ocean between isothermals 64° and 68°.

Madeira is the largest island in the group, measuring 57.9 kilometres in length and 22.9 kilometres in width, with an area of 728 square kilometres. Since Deserta and the Selvagens proved to be uninhabitable, and Porto Santo never was able to develop plantations and a plantation society, I shall limit the following discussion to the single island of Madeira.

The island is of volcanic origin and extremely rugged. Its soils are generally very fertile, especially along the coast-although, (See figure 1), irrigation is needed to make them productive.

The mountains rise precipitously out of the sea to heights of almost two thousand metres. The landscape is broken and there are but few relatively flat areas, mostly along the coast. The interior of the island is dominated by sharply rising mountains that are difficult to ascend and of limited agricultural value.

Madeira lies in the path of the trade winds emanating from the Azorean anticyclone. This high pressure causes marked regularity in force, direction and temperature of the winds blowing over the north side of the island. Precipitation on the north side as a result is more evenly distributed annually than it is on the south side of the island.

The mountains shelter the south side from the northerly winds; but peripheral winds, moving clockwise away from the Azorean anticyclone, and passing over parts of the western African desert, return to Madeira from the southeast. These *lestes*, as they are called, are hot and dry and often cause sudden rises in temperature as well as decreases in humidity.

The winds from the south-southwest are humid, but do not condense until they have reached the higher elevations on the south side of the island. Hence precipitation is heaviest above 1,300 metres. Some rain, however, may be falling in Monte, a town at 545 metres, while the sun continues to shine in Funchal on the south coast.

The winds, on the whole, play a very important part in shaping the climate of the island. However, their influence is modified by the Gulf Stream, which descends from the north-northwest, bathing the island on all sides. Its warming effect, though, is limited to a small coastal strip, characterized on the south side of the island by steep bluffs.[9]

The Discovery and Colonization of Madeira

Although certainly known about earlier, Madeira remained uninhabited and unexplored by Europeans until its discovery, or rediscovery, by the Portuguese in 1419. In that year, as the chroniclers tell the story, two squires of Prince Henry the Navigator were blown off course by a storm. Good fortune carried them to the island of Porto Santo, which they named in gratitude for being saved. While repairing their ship, they sighted Madeira beneath a dense cloud and also explored it.10

On their return home the squires, impressed by what they had seen, are reported to have asked their lord for permission to settle and establish a colony. Permission was granted and in May of 1420 a party led by João Gonçalvez Zarco and Tristão Vaz Teixeira (the two squires), along with Bartolomeu Perestrelo, another squire, left to found a settlement.[11]

Ships, supplies and provisions are reported to have been provided by Prince Henry. Zarco, Tristão and Perestrelo, however, had to recruit on their own those who would accompany them. This was to prove no simple matter. Not only were the legitimate fears of sailing off to some unknown island in the dangerous Atlantic to be overcome, but also conditions at the time in Portugal, especially for the lower classes, were not such as to encourage their emigration.

The country as yet had not recovered from the ravaging effects of the Black Death in the previous century.[12] One consequence of the decline in population caused by the plagues and epidemics of the fourteenth century was that the lot of the labouring classes had improved.[13] The nobles, likewise, as Johnson[14] recently has demonstrated, also were not suffering. Economic conditions in Portugal were good and there were opportunities on the mainland for ambitious, enterprising people of all classes and sectors. Who then, we might ask, responded to the appeals of Zarco, Tristão and Perestrelo, and who accompanied them in their colonizing venture?

According to Oliveira Marques, 'Less than a hundred people, under the leadership of the three presumed 'discoverers' . . . , landed in the two lands of Madeira and Porto Santo . . . . They were probably recruited,' he continues, 'in the islands which belonged to Prince Henry and the order of Christ. The majority seem to have come from the Algarve . . .'[15] All three leaders,' he then adds, 'belonged to the lower ranks of the nobility . . . and the same was true of about fourteen others. The rest were plebeians (including some outcasts), socially and economically dependent upon them . . .'[16]

Little in fact is known about these early colonists. Some, as Oliveira Marques reports, are believed to have been from impoverished noble families. But their claims, made in almost all cases decades if not centuries later by descendants after the latter had acquired wealth and position, must be accepted with more than a degree of skepticism. Most of the settlers, probably more than half excluding the convicts, were labourers and artisans.[17] The only reasonable explanation for their volunteering would attribute to them aspirations for social mobility. In the context of the rigid hierarchy of Portuguese society in the early fifteenth century this would mean specifically that they aspired to noble status and its privileges.

Had the colonists who went to settle Madeira been satisfied with the 'drudgerous,' uneventful life of agricultural labourers and artisans, they could have remained on the continent where land and jobs were more than available and conditions were far from onerous. There would have been no need for them to undertake the hardships and uncertainties of a fifteenth-century voyage into the Atlantic in search of islands where establishing a settlement could be expected to be significantly more difficult than would have been a comparable undertaking in the Minho or the Algarve.

Instead, I would maintain, the most likely motivation for their volunteering is a strong desire for social mobility. In the context of early fifteenth-century Portuguese society this is to say that they aspired to noble status. In turn, this implies that they hoped, either consciously or implicitly, to escape the tilling of the soil and working with their hands and backs, the stigma of the lower classes. By contrast, it may be assumed that from the beginning they dreamed of a life in which their material needs would be provided and they could devote themselves to worthy causes other than mundane physical labour.

As we shall see, they and their descendants, for the most part, were to achieve this goal. But someone had to perform the roles of the lower classes if the settlers were to be able to assume those of the nobility.

From later documents[18] we may reconstruct that the captains had been empowered to distribute land grants in the islands to their followers. The records containing the names of the recipients of these first *sesmarias*, as the grants were called, no longer exist. Likewise we do not know who received what lands. However the general pattern appears to have been for the captain, starting from the centres of the original settlements-Funchal, Machico and Porto Santo-to move along the sea coast, bestowing lands on the eligible household heads. The properties given out then ran from the coast, extending inland to some unspecified point in the mountains. Natural boundary markers, such as rivers and streams, set the remaining borders of each holding (see Figure 1). The recipients of land grants then held parcels that ran from the coast up into the mountains, and from a river or hillock on one side that set the boundaries between his estate and that of his neighbour to a river or stream on the other.

We have no idea as to how large the actual grants were. We do know, however, that each recipient came to hold a variety of ecological niches within his grant, only some of which were considered to be of value to him.

Prince Henry, as we have seen, had provided supplies for the colony. Included were seeds for crops such as wheat, plus domestic animals. But before anything could be planted, the thickly forested island first had to be cleared. This was done with the aid of fire,[19] which appears to have gotten out of hand. Gaspar Frutuoso, for example, reports that at one point the flames burned so fiercely that the settlers were driven into the sea.[20] The ash resulting, however, when added to the virgin soil, produced a land of considerable agricultural potential. But before it could be put in crops, one additional problem had to be resolved.

Although water was more abundant on the island, rainfall was irregular, especially in the lower warmer and relatively flatter areas where agriculture could be assumed to have been first undertaken. In their natural state the lands potentially best suited for planting did not obtain sufficient moisture for agriculture. The remedy was to be technically simple, but difficult to implement.

Irrigation had long been practiced in continental Portugal. And as Dias and Galhano[21] tell us, the irrigation system established in Madeira required no new technology. The long-known principle of redirecting the flow of water carried by gravitational force to another point at a lower elevation was applied. But the topography of the island was more extreme than anything the Portuguese had known on the continent; and when combined with the absence of a labouring class to construct the system, a problem was created whose resolution was to contribute directly to the creation of the slave plantation and plantation slavery.

As Lamas succinctly has summarized the problem:

When the settlers arrived (in Madeira) they soon realized that the land would be difficult to conquer. The island was marvelous, ... But it was densely forested and mountainous.

With the aid of fire and their muscles the trees were felled and the lands put in crops. But without water the enterprise would be in vain. And the water came from inaccessible summits and ran where it could not be put to use.

Consequently the settlers had to devise a way of irrigating their crops. It is difficult to imagine, especially when one is not familiar with the unlikely relief of the island, the obstacles that had to be surmounted to accomplish this gigantic undertaking.

Suffice it to say that the water had to be diverted, almost always at distant points of difficult access. The task therefore not only was exhausting but dangerous, taking many lives and was not completed for many years . . .[22]

From later sources we know that not long after the initial settlement the rivers and streams in the mountains were being diverted and irrigation canals called *levadas* were being constructed.[23]

The first document referring specifically to irrigation in the island is dated 1461.[24] In it the Infante D. Fernado, Prince Henry's heir and the new lord proprietor, charged two men to be responsible for the fair allocation of water for irrigation.[25]

The second reference is found in a letter by King D. João II dated 1493.[26] But in it he refers to a document by his great grandfather, D. João I, regulating the use of water in the island. The king had declared it illegal for anyone to cut off and stop the flow of water from above to lands at lower elevations. The obvious implication is that already during the reign of D. João I (1385-1433) irrigation works had been constructed in Madeira and regulations had been laid out for their use. But it is to the construction of the irrigation works that we must now return.

The thesis I wish to propose is that the European colonists in Madeira did not themselves build the irrigation works. Instead, as the result of events unrelated to the internal problems of the island and its development, they participated in the capture of pagan natives in the Canary Islands. It was the Canarians, as slaves captured in a 'just war,' who built the *levadas*; and in this way slave labour was introduced to perform the onerous and difficult physical activities that on the continent had been performed by the lower, but free classes. Later, with the introduction of sugar cane and its commercial success, we shall see that Canary Islanders and Moors-followed by Africans-as slaves, performed the necessary physical labour that enabled the upwardly mobile settlers of Madeira to develop a life style, derived from the tradition of the continental nobility but based upon the physical efforts of slaves producing commercial crops for sale on the markets of the continent, that characterized the emerging social institution of the slave plantation.

The Canary Islands

The Canary Islands probably had been known to Europe since the time of the Roman empire and most probably had been visited on occasion during the Middle Ages. At the end of the thirteenth century Genoese mariners are reported to have landed on one of the islands and to have built a fort.[27] Between 1326 and 1334 Norman ships landed and shortly thereafter a Castilian nobleman, D. Luis de la Cerda, 'procured a grant . . ., with the title of King, from Pope Clement VI, upon condition that he would cause the Gospel to be preached to the natives.'[28]

Two points of importance must be stressed. First, title to the Canary Islands had been given to a Castilian. Second, the legitimacy for the grant came from the Pope on the condition that the natives (and in contrast with Madeira the Canaries were inhabited) be converted to Christianity.

By the first quarter of the fifteenth century, however, these conditions had not been satisfied. Therefore, after Portugal conquered Ceuta and settled a colony in Madeira, she tried to claim jurisdiction to the Canaries by meeting the conditions Castile had been unable to satisfy.[29]

The natives of the Canary Islands had resisted the efforts of the European Christians to subjugate and convert them. To make matters worse they fought off the European intruders who, in their eyes, were attacking their homeland. But to the Europeans, resistance to the advance of the 'true faith' was the equivalent of a declaration of war against all of Christendom. Consequently, all future relationships between Europeans and Canary Islanders, in the eyes of the Europeans, were placed in the legal framework of parties engaged in war. Furthermore, for the Europeans the war was of a special kind referred to as a 'just war.'[30] Roman law (the law of the Roman church, that is) had laid down that persons captured in a just war became the slaves of their captor and their goods the property of the victor.[31]

The immediate consequence of this was that all Canary Islanders taken as captive by Europeans, no matter how they were captured, became the legal slaves of the Europeans.

The periodic raids that had been made by the various Europeans in the fourteenth and fifteenth centuries included sacking, pillaging and the taking of slaves, with most of the latter sold.[32]

Although this is not the place to discuss the Canary Islands and their aboriginal population, several points are essential to our story. First, the islands themselves are similar in formation and appearance to Madeira, only more so. They are volcanic and rise precipitously out of the sea to heights that in the case of Tenerife, for example, exceed 4,000 metres. Also, like Madeira, the landscape is ruggedly mountainous and dominated by peaks with narrow and difficult passes and deep gorges and ravines, with relatively little flat land away from the coast.

The native population was remarkably well adapted to this mountainous habitat. Father Galindo, for example, describes them as being well built, strong and very nimble, and as taking 'great delight in leaping and jumping, which is their principal diversion. . . .'[33] They were well adapted in strength and physical dexterity to conditions very much like the ones in which the Portuguese settlers in Madeira had to build irrigation works as a prerequisite to the development of the island.

Portugal, as we have seen, however, had designs on the Canary Islands. The initiative in the implementation of the Portuguese pretensions had been taken by Prince Henry, whose role in Madeira and its colonization has been discussed.

In 1415 an unsuccessful Portuguese attack had been launched on Grand Canary. In 1424 a fleet of 2,500 infantry men and 120 horses under the command of Fernando de Castro embarked in the hopes of taking the as yet unconquered islands of Grand Canary, Palma and Tenerife. This was just four years after the colony had been established in Madeira.

Although there is no direct documentation in support of the assertion, it is more than probable that from the beginnings of its settlement, and perhaps one of the reasons justifying the investment of resources in the island, Madeira was a port of call for ships outward bound on voyages from Portugal. There repairs were made, while fresh water and supplies were taken on.[34]

Also, although again there are no documents to confirm it, it is more than likely that at least some of the former heroes of the Ceuta campaign to have settled in Madeira[35] joined with de Castro's forces in the attack on the Canaries.

The attempt failed, but as was common practice by the beginning of the fifteenth century, when unable to conquer the islanders, captives were taken, usually to be sold in the slave markets of the Mediterranean.[36]

The Canary Islanders, however, were ideally suited to the task of cutting irrigation ditches across the rugged mountains of Madeira. I would venture to suggest that the warrior-adventurers to have settled Madeira aspiring to noble status and who participated in the attack on the Canary Islands were aware of this. And as a result, some of the captives enslaved in the unsuccessful effort at conquest were taken back to Madeira, where they were impressed into service in the construction of *lavedas*.[37]

Between 1420 and 1446 there were at least four major and several minor assaults by Portuguese forces on the Canary Islands. All stopped first in Madeira where they were joined by some of the settlers, many of whom had served with Prince Henry in the conquest of Ceuta. All were unsuccessful, but captives were taken, some of whom were brought back to Madeira.

The unrecorded details of what most probably happened in Madeira can be summarized in Ramsey's statement, made several centuries later, on the construction of irrigation ditches in Madeira. He writes:

Slaves and convicts alike were all forced to labour, and the first and most important work on which they were employed was the construction of the levadas. As before stated, these water-courses were carved out of the solid face of the rock by means of primitive implements and tools. The slaves were lowered over the mountain precipices by ropes from above; and when the gigantic nature of the undertaking is considered, it is not surprising to learn that hundreds of them perished by crashing onto the rocks below.[38]

Upon completion of the first irrigation works, Madeira was transformed into a veritable agricultural paradise.

Cereal Production in Madeira

The first crops to be sown on the island were those brought by the settlers from the European mainland. Within a short time then the island was producing cereals in abundance of the needs of the settlers. The harvests were such that surpluses soon were being exported and sold commercially on the continent.[39] Portuguese agriculture at the time had still not recovered from the decline of the previous century and shortages of wheat and other grains were serious.[40] The cereals from Madeira, needless to say, were more than welcome on the continent.

To both reward and further encourage the islanders in grain production, privileges were granted them under the regency of the Infante D. Pedro,[41] and by mid-century the chroniclers were reporting the production and export of large quantities of cereals, with shipments from the island going to Africa to supply the Portuguese forces there.

We now have two of the three basic elements of the slave plantation present and operational in the developing social system of Madeira: (1) slaves from the Canary Islands (and later North Africa); and (2) large properties with subtropical soils given to aspiring elites as land grants. Still missing is a commercial crop for which there is a demand in the emerging European world market which cannot be produced on the continent. The crop to be introduced into Madeira that was to complete the transformation of the island, and establish on a firm footing the institutions of the plantation and plantation slavery on a societal level, was sugar cane.

Introduction of Sugar Cane into Madeira

Sugar cane most probably was introduced into Madeira from Sicily under the initiative and direction of Prince Henry.[42] Some authorities, however, doubt this since at the time the crop

already was being grown in Portugal and in the Moorish Kingdoms in southern Spain. Alternatively, Duarte Leite believes that Italian merchants brought the crop to Madeira on their own from the eastern Mediterranean.[43]

According to Gaspar Frutuoso, although he does not provide us with the dates, the first sugar sold in Madeira came from the *vila* (town) of Machico on the northern side of the island.[44] But legend has it that when Prince Henry had the plant introduced, it first was grown on lands in what today is the city of Funchal on the south side of the island. Those lands are referred to as the 'Campo do Duque,' perhaps in commemoration, as Lúcio de Azevedo[45] notes, of the role played by Henry, who held the title of Duke of Viseu.[46]

The juice was first squeezed from the plants in hand-operated presses of limited efficiency called *alçapremas*. The producers were required to pay the lord proprietor one and one-half *arrobas*[47] of sugar per year for each *alçaprema*. The extant documents refer to the canes being ground and processed into sugar in the *lagar* of the Infante (Henry). Since the word *lagar* also was used to refer to an olive press, some authorities have inferred the presence of a press, perhaps like the ones used to squeeze olives, and possibly moved by animal power, as a second step in the development of the processing of the cane.

By the middle of the fifteenth century enough cane was being grown in Madeira to justify the construction of a water-driven mill, or *engenho*. In 1452, therefore, Henry contracted with Diogo de Tieve, another squire and loyal servant, to build the mill. According to the contract, Henry assigned to his servant the monopoly for the grinding of cane in the island.[48] In return, those to use the mill were to pay to Henry one-third of the sugar ground from their plants. Those who preferred to continue with the less efficient hand mills were permitted to do so, paying the same rate as before.

The *Cartas de Doação* (grants) given to Zarco, Tristão and Perestrelo make no reference to sugar cane, although taxes are specified for other crops. Since the formal documents are dated after the actual establishment of the colony, we may conclude that sugar-cane cultivation in Madeira first came to be important in the early 1450s. Then the tax on the hand presses was established, followed by the one-third tax levied at the mill. These seemingly stiff charges, however, did not deter the colonists from rapidly expanding the production of the crop.

Zurara, the first of the chroniclers, who wrote in 1452, said almost nothing about the value of the sugar being produced. By 1455, however, Cadamosto reported an annual production in excess of 6,000 *arrobas*.[49] The following year the first Madeiran sugars were exported to Bristol.[50] A document of 1468 referred to by Oliveira Marques indicates that by then there already was a regular sugar trade between Madeira and Flanders.[51] By 1472 more than 15,000 *arrobas* were being produced, and two decades later the figure surpassed 80,000 *arrobas*.[52]

The population of the island meanwhile also is increasing. Zurara reports 150 settlers whose numbers have been increased by merchants and later immigrants: single men and women and servants (*mancebos*) of both sexes.[53] Three decades after the founding of the colony Cadamosto speaks of 800 men, of whom 100 have horses - which is to say that they have qualified as *cavalheiros* in the social hierarchy.[54] Shortly thereafter the numbers increase significantly so that by the end of the century there are more than 15,000 people, including several thousand slaves.

The production and processing of sugar for export is the primary stimulus to the growth and development of the island, both economically and demographically. However, external political and economic factors provide the conditions that make the development possible.[55] As already noted, by the middle years of the fifteenth century the Ottoman Turks had succeeded in cutting off European access to commerce in the eastern Mediterranean, the Near East and in Asia. As a result the markets of western Europe were without commodities like sugar, formerly supplied by Genoese and Venetian middlemen-traders. As the supply dwindled, prices rose. Madeiran sugars appeared in the markets of western Europe just at the time prices were high and the demand was unsatisfied. The profits earned stimulated further production.

With the trees felled, the lands distributed in *sesmarias*, and water now available for irrigation thanks to the construction of the *levadas*, the single factor remaining to determine the amount of sugar that could be produced on the island was labour. But from where was the labour to plant and process the canes in Madeira to come? As Cadamosto has noted, one-eighth of the male household heads already had qualified as *fidalgos* (nobles) by 1455.[56] Furthermore, with Madeira as a stopping off point on the way to Africa, where fame, fortune and recognition were to be won, the residents of Madeira were not about to spend their time dirtying their hands in the back-breaking job of raising, harvesting and processing sugar cane. Instead, as Sarmento concludes, they participated in the conquests and discoveries, further increasing the fame of the island and its settlers.[57] But without someone to work the cane fields and *engenhos,* neither sugar nor the fortunes to be made from it would have been possible. Who then was planting, harvesting and processing the cane while the recipients of *sesmarias* and their descendants were off distinguishing themselves as warriors, conquerors, merchants, statesmen and heroes of the expansions and discoveries?

Although the early documents are conspicuously silent, later evidence makes it more than clear that the labour force used in the growing and processing of sugar was composed in more than considerable part of the Canary Islanders, Moors and later blacks taken as slaves. In the *Regimento do Infante D. Fernando,* Henry's nephew and heir, dated 1466, mention finally is made of the Canarian, Moorish and Negro slaves brought to the island to work in the sugar industry.[58] Then, between 1470 and 1490, the references to slaves in the documents increase, while after 1490 when the slave population began to create problems, full recognition was given to the presence of slaves in the island.

Sugar Production in Madeira in the Fifteenth Century

For a picture of the sugar industry and sugar production in the last quarter of the fifteenth century we can turn to the reconstruction and analysis by Rau and Macedo based upon the text of the *Livro do Almoxarifado dos Açuqarres do Funchal,* dated 1494.[59]

To collect their share of the revenues (at first one-third and later reduced to one-fourth and eventually one-fifth), the lord proprietors quite early established the practice of appointing individuals in the island to estimate the size of the crop growing on the lands of each producer prior to the harvest.[60] Then, when the canes were cut and processed, the amount of sugar accruing to the lord of the island would be taken. Unfortunately, the document on which the reconstruction is based is the work of a tax collector interested in the sugar cane growing in the fields. As a result, much information of interest to the social scientist and historian is not included. No data are available on land tenure, for example, and we do not learn of the actual size of the parcels of land owned by proprietors. Instead, all that we have is a record of the amount of cane on which each producer is to be taxed.

The list of producers recorded in the book included names identified as nobles and merchants, but also contained carpenters, shoemakers, bakers, tax collectors, scribes and other public employees, plus widows and servants of the elite. The conclusion to be drawn is that persons from all walks of life were among the producers of sugar cane by the end of the fifteenth century.

Although we lack data on the ownership of the land, we may conclude that a free population of artisans and labourers had been established and that at least some of these non-elites had gained access to the land. Whether this represents the purchase of plots from the recipients of *sesmarias* - and there were some - or a practice of renting or sharecropping we are not sure. Since all were present in the Portuguese agrarian tradition, we may conjecture that a system not unlike that found in Brazil the following century may have been operating.[61]

There were 16 *engenhos* in Funchal in 1494, half the number reported by Gaspar Frutuoso for the end of the sixteenth century[62] and significantly fewer than the 150 *engenhos* reported by Lippmann for the beginning of the sixteenth century.[63] Together they processed a little over 5,700 *arrobas* of sugar belonging to their owners. The remainder of their production, almost 75,000 *arrobas*, was for other cane producers who may well have been like the *lavradores de cana* described by Schwartz.[65]

The overall picture is not one of large *fazendas* with thousands of slaves known in Brazil in the seventeenth and eighteenth centuries. Instead, it is one of managerial separation and subdivision, with the *engenho* as one operation and the land as another. The land, although perhaps owned by a small number of elites, was administered and worked by renters and/or sharecroppers who raised the canes ground by the mills.[66]

What is significant about the development of Madeiran sugar production is that it soon came to be a source of great profit and wealth. At first, as has been noted, sugar from the island was shipped to markets in northwestern Europe - to replace supplies no longer available from areas controlled by the Ottoman Turks. However, as relations between Christian Europe and Islam deteriorated further, Madeira was soon supplying most of the continent with sugar. The 120,000 *arrobas* produced in 1498, for example, were exported not only to England, Flanders, France and Brittany, but also to Rome, Genoa, Venice, and as far east as Constantinope.[67] In short, sugar production in Madeira had become a big business able to return huge profits to those engaged in its production and distribution.

The turning point had long been reached. As the second half of the fifteenth century drew to a close, Madeira had become a major commercial producer and exporter of sugar with an economy earning great wealth.[68]

The Sugar Cane Plantation and Plantation Slavery

The distinctiveness of Madeira in the development of the world economy was that the uninhabited island was settled by what I have referred to as aspiring Portuguese nobles who found themselves without the lower classes to perform the manual labour that made possible society in the stratified way it was known on the European continent at the time. One might hypothesize that the settlers of Madeira could have cleared the land and irrigated it so as to have made subsistence agriculture possible. If perhaps the island had been discovered and settled by farmers of English, Scots, Irish or Scandinavian background, such as those who later settled in parts of North America, this might have been the case. But the early colonists in Madeira were not of these cultural backgrounds; hence they did not behave in this way. Instead, consistent with the tradition to which they, as upwardly mobile Portuguese, aspired, they created the conditions that would enable them to live the life of an Iberian noble. Consequently, they participated as fully as possible in the campaigns that constituted what we refer to now as the expansion and discovery. And when labour was needed to develop their island society, as in the building of irrigation works, rather than staying home and using their hands and backs, as a northern European farmer might have, they took Canary Islanders and Moors in the conduct of a just war, and put them to work.

The slaves then were incorporated into the labour force, first in the difficult and dangerous activity of building irrigation works, and then most probably in preparing and planting the land in cereals; then when sugar cane was introduced, they were used to plant and to harvest it and to mill it into sugar. Their use then freed the colonists to participate in the socially valued and rewarding activities of discovering new lands and conquering the heathen in the name of king and church. But as the years went by and profits to be earned from sugar increased, the place of slavery in the developing society was rapidly transformed. From a primarily religiously justified status associated with the fighting of a just war against the infidel, slavery soon was to become an essentially economic activity.

By the late fifteenth century the natives of the Canary Islands were just about extinct and Moors had become more difficult to obtain as slaves, especially since the Iberians had come to expend their major energy discovering and conquering the world rather than concentrating on the Islamic foe. By the end of the fifteenth century, therefore, Africa came to be the primary source of supply for slaves. But by then, rather than the slavery of the late Middle Ages, commercial-industrial slavery had been born, thanks specifically to the events that had taken place the century before in the island of Madeira.

But Madeira was not for long to be the sole beneficiary of the prosperity derived from sugar and slavery. By the 1470s sugar cane, and the institutionalized arrangements for the organization of its production, had been introduced and was being experimented with in the Azores and in the Cape Verde Islands. By the 1490s the crop had been introduced into the Canaries, where Africans were brought as slaves to raise sugar in the former home of the first peoples to be used by the Europeans in the Atlantic islands in the commercial production of tropical crops. And in the same decade the crop was introduced into São Tomé in the Gulf of Guinea. Then, before the turn of the century, it was carried to the New

World by its discoverer, who had spent more than a decade in Madeira and had married the daughter of Bartolomeu Perestrelo, captain of Porto Santo. And within a few more decades the Portuguese, stimulated at least in part by residents of Madeira, were introducing the crop into Brazil. And then from Brazil, where the system brought from Madeira was modified and elaborated, the sugar-producing slave plantation was carried to the Dutch, English, and French West Indies from where it diffuses, producing other crops, to parts of lowland Central America and to the southern United States.

Although the system of the slave plantation is modified and expanded over the course of the next four centuries by each of the European nations is to establish colonies and to participate in the slave trade, the activities of the fifteenth-century Portuguese settlers of Madeira and the social system they established are critical to understanding the origins of the institution and to comprehending the range and diversity it was to develop in later years.

Acknowledgments

I wish to thank Dr. António Aragão Mendes Correia, director of the Archives in Funchal, Madeira, Dr. Fernando Alberto Jasmins Pereira Rodrigues, Dr. António H. De Oliveira Marques, and María de Lourdes Freitas Ferraz for their kindness and assistance during my stay in Portugal and Madeira.

Notes

*This research was supported financially by the National Science Foundation and by the Graduate School of the University of Wisconsin-Milwaukee.

1. For our present purposes the slave plantation may be defined as a territorial unit producing a commercial crop for sale on the markets of Europe, owned by Europeans, but located in tropical or subtropical regions outside Europe, and worked primarily by slave labour of non-European origin. The first crop to be raised on plantations and which was to become the standard for all later slave plantations was sugar cane.

2. Verlinden, Charles. 1970. *The Beginnings of Modern Colonization.* Cornell University Press. Ithaca and London; Verlinden Charles. 1966. *Les origines de la civilisation atlantique.* Paris and Neuchâtel; Verlinden, Charles. 1954. *Précédents médiévaux de la colonie en Amérique.* Mexico City; Verlinden, Charles.

1953. Les origines coloniales de la civilisation atlan-tique: Antécédents et types de structure. *Journal of World History* I: 378-398.

3. For a survey of the history of sugar see: Amorim Par-reira, Henrique Gomes de. 1952. *História do Açucar em Portugal. Estudos de História da Geografia da Expansão Portuguesa.* Anais, Vol. VIL, Tomo I. *Junta das Missoes Geograficas e de Investigacoes do Ultramar. Lisbon*; Deerr, Noel. 1949-50. *The His-tory of Sugar* (2 vols.). Chapman and Hall. London; Leite, Duarte. 1941. *Os primeiros acucares portugue-ses. Coisas de Varia História. Lisbon*; and Lippmann, Edmund von. 1941-2. *História do Açucar* (2 vols.). Instituto do Açucar e do Alcool. Rio de Janeiro.

4. Verlinden, Charles. 1970. *op. cit.* :19

5. Rebora, Giovanni. 1968. *Un 'impresa zuccheriera del cinquecento.*:11. Universita' Degli Studi di Napoli. Napoli.

6. Verlinden, Charles. 1958. *Esclaves alains en Italie et dans les colonies italiennes au XIV siècle. Revue belge de philogie et d'histoire XXXVI:451-57;* Ver-linden, Charles. 1963. *L'esclavage en Sicile au bas moyen age. Bulletin de l'Institut Historique Belge de Rome XXXV: 13-113;* Verlinden, Charles. 1965. *L'es-clavage en Sicile sous Frédéric II d'Aragon* (1296-1337). Homenaje a Jaime Vicens Vives. Vol. I:675-90. Barcelona.

7. Curtin, Philip D. 1969. *The Atlantic Slave Trade.* The University of Wisconsin Press. Madison, Wisc.

8. The theoretical framework I have adopted for the presentation is that of the evolutionist, but with the focus on specific rather than general evolution (see Sahlins, Marshall & Elman Service, Eds. 1960. *Evo-lution and Culture.* University of Michigan Press, Ann Arbor). Consequently, I shall treat culture as an adaptive system with an emphasis on ecology. Criti-cal variables will be the cultural heritage of the set-tlers of the island and the habitat to which they were adapting. The presentation shall be couched implic-itly in terms of the decisions and choices of the ac-tors in terms of the broadest arena in which they were operating. In this way I propose to make ex-plicit some of the values and motives that led a small group of settlers from mainland Portugal to combine elements in their culture while adapting to a new setting so as to establish the institution of the slave plantation.

9. Ferreira. 1955. *O Clima do Portugal.* Lisbon; Norrl, Elof a Ostman. [n.d.] On Irrigation in Madeira. Manuscript in the Arquivo da Câmara Municipal do Funchal. Funchal, Madeira.

10. Zurara, Gomes Eanes da. 1973. *Crónica de Guiné.* Segundo o ms. de Paris, Chapt. LXXXIII. Livraria Civilízação-Editora. Lisbon; Barros, João de. 1932. *Asia. Primeira Decada,* Livro I, chapts. 2 and 3. Impresna da Universidade. Coimbra; Goes, Damiao de. 1724. *Crónica do Principe D. João,* chapt. VIII. Lisbon.

11. Royal authority with respect to the islands, and dele-gation of jurisdiction to them in the form of a char-ter, or *foral,* was not granted to Prince Henry until

September of 1433, after the death of his father, King D. João I (see Magalhães Godinho, Vitorino. 1943. *Documentos Sobre a Expansão Portugues.* Vol. 1. Edições Cosmos, Lisbon). Then after as-suming the throne, D. Duarte, Henry's brother, granted him *senhorio* (overlordship) as *donatário* (lord proprietor) of the Madeira Islands (*ibid.*). ac-cording to the chroniclers, who wrote a quarter of a century or more after the fact, Prince Henry di-vided the island of Madeira in half, giving the southern part, called Funchal, to João Goncalves Zarco as captain, and the northern half, called Ma-chico, to Tristão Vaz Teixeira. The captaincy of Porto Santo was given to Bartolomeu Perestrelo. The dates of the official grants (*doaçoes*) contain-ing the rights and responsibilities of the parties were 1440 for Texeira's captaincy, 1446 for Per-estrelo's and 1450 for Zarco's (*ibid.*). All are after the death of D. Duarte.

12. Oliveira Marques, António H. De. 1968. *Introducão a Histíria da Agricultura em Portugal. A Questao Ceralifera durante a Idade Media,* 2nd ed.:50-60. Ediçoes Cosmos. Lisbon.

13. See Rau Virginia. 1946. *Sesmarias Medievais Portuguesas.* Lisbon; and Cortesao, Jaime. 1964. *Os Factores Democráticos na Formaçao de Portugal.* Lisbon.

14. Johnson, Harold B. 1973. *A Portuguese estate in the late fourteenth century. Luso-Brazilian Review* X(2): 149-62.

15. Historians are generally agreed that the early settlers of Madeira came from the Algarve in southern Portu-gal. However, basing his conclusions on ethno-graphic data and analysis, Jorge Dias believes that they probably came from the north of the country, most probably the Minho (Dias, Jorge. 1952. *Notulas de etnografia Madeirense* Contribuição para o es-tudo das orignes etnicos-culturais da populacao da Ilha da Madeira. Biblos 28: 179-201).

16. Oliveira Marques, António H. De. 1972. *History of Portugal.* Vol. 1: *From Lusitania to Empire.* :152. Columbia University Press. New York, N.Y.

17. Zarco, Tristão and Perestrelo were granted royal per-mission to take with them condemned prisoners, which they are reported to have done. We have no idea as to how many they took and what percentage of the total group they were. It is interesting to ob-serve that the chroniclers, again writing at least three decades after the fact, after the colony is contributing to the wealth and prestige of the expanding King-dom, state that the captains took only criminals who had committed minor offences and who had not been accused of religious crimes.

Portuguese society at the time was hierarchical and rigidly stratified. Three broad categories, or estates could be distinguished, each performing a distinctive role in the division of societal labour and each receiv-ing differing rewards.

The numerically largest category performed agricul-tural labour in a society that was primarily agrarian. The nobility, by contrast, defended the land, per-formed administrative tasks, and protected the labourers and the clergy, whose spiritual functions rounded out the three primary activities of late medieval society.

Although surpluses were minimal, the nobility (including the royal family), along with the clergy, received more proportionately for performing their roles than did the labourers for performing theirs, enabling them to live better than those involved in the tilling of the land. The latter, for what usually was bare subsistence, performed the difficult, dirty and 'drudgerous' activities on the land. The nobility, by contrast, did not labour on the land. Instead, as often exaggerated in song and story, and as perceived and perhaps fantasized by the labourers reacting to the drudgery of their own lives, participated in adventures, fought for noble causes, and performed administrative tasks; they did not dirty their hands nor break their backs with such mundane matters as ploughing, planting and harvesting crops.

18. Jasmins Pereira, Fernando. 1961. *Indices dos Documentos do Século XV Transcritos do Tombo Primeiro do Registro Geral da Cámara do Funchal.* Casa Figueira. Funchal, Madeira.

19. Barros, João de, *op. cit.*, Livro I, Chapt. 3.

20. *Op. cit.* :64.

21. Dias, Jorge & Fernando Galhano. 1953. *Aparelhos de Elevar a Agua de Rega. Contribuição para o Estudo de Regadio em Portugal.*:26. Junta da Provincia de Douro-Litoral. Porto, Portugal.

22. Lamas, Maria. 1956. *Arquipelago da Madeira.* :104. Editora Eco. Funchal, Madeira.

23. Silva, Padre Fernando Augusto da. 1965. Levadas. *Elucidario Madeirense.* 3rd ed. Vol. II. Padre Fernando Augusto da Silva and Carlos Azevedo de Menenzes, Eds. Tipografia Esperanca. Funchal, Madeira; Frutuoso, Gaspar, *op. cit.*

24. *Ibid.*:677.

25. Arquivo da Câmara Muncipal do Funchal. Tomo I :207. Funchal, Madeira.

26. Frutuoso, Gaspar, op. cit. :673-4.

27. Serra y Rafols, Elias. 1941. *Los Portugueses en Canarias.* :215-6. Imprenta y Libraria "Curbelo." La Laguna, Canary Islands.

28. Galindo, Juan de Abreu de. 1764. *The History of the Discovery of the Canary Islands.* :1-2. London.

29. Silva Marques, João Martins da. 1944. *Descobrimentos Portugueses-Documentos para a Sua História.* Vol. 1 :291-346. Instituto para a Alta Cultura. Lisbon.

30. Keen, Maurice. 1965. *The Laws of War in the Late Middle Ages.* Routlege and Kegan Paul. London. 'Given their sins,' writes Keen (p. 13) referring to the acts of those who opposed and resisted the spread of the faith and God's order, 'it was reasonable and legitimate to reduce those taken in war against the infidel to slavery, and, provided it had the Church's sanction, a war of conquest waged against them might even be said to be naturally just.' Zavala observes that 'this attitude may be noted in the Leyes de Partidas' (of thirteenth-century Castile) ''which lists among the just cause of war: 'the first,

in order that the peoples shall increase their faith and that those who would combat it shall be destroyed . . .''' (Zavala, Silvio. 1964. *The Defence of Human Rights in Latin America.'*15. UNESCO. Paris.)

31. Keen, Maurice, *op. cit.* :137, 156.

32. Galindo, J., *op. cit.*, Introduction :1-3; Verlinden, Charles. 1955. *L'esclavage dans L'Europe Medieval.* Tome I. Peninsule Iberique-France. University of Ghent. Bruges.

33. Galindo, J. *op. cit.* :6.

34. In support of this position is a document in the *Arquivo da Câmara Muncipal do Funchal* dated 1425 (cited in Sarmento, Alberto Arthur. 1935. Madeira e Canarias. *Fasquias da Madeira.* Diaria de Noticias. Funchal, Madeira) in which King D. João I thanks the settlers of the island for the help they have given to the Portuguese forces. The date is significant in that there was no other undertaking by Portuguese forces at the time other than the attack on the Canary Islands that could have been aided by the settlers in Madeira that could have earned them the formal gratitude of their sovereign.

35. Barros, J. *op. cit.*, Livro I, Chapt. 3; Sarmento, Alberto Arthur. 1932. *Madeira e as Praças de Africa.* Funchal, Madeira.

36. Wölfel, D.J. 1930. La Curia Romana e la Corona de España en la defensa de los aborígenes Canarios. Anthropos 25: 1011-1083.

37. What I am suggesting as the probable beginnings of the use of slave labour in Madeira is consistent with the division of labour and the reward and value structures implicit in the highly stratified social system of the period. I have referred to the settlers of Madeira as would-be nobles not possessed of the means requisite for the status they desired. I also have suggested that the most adequate explanation for their undertaking the settlement of the island related to the opportunities it offered for social mobility.
Zarco, Tristão and Perestrelo had served in the households of members of the Portuguese royal family. Other settlers also had served, and amongst other things had participated in the attack on Ceuta in 1415. From this we may conclude that they had received training in seamanship and in the waging of war, and had learned that acts of daring and bravery in support of the causes of their lord brought rewards.

38. Ramsey, L.F. 1920. *Levada Walking in Madeira.* : 408-416. National Review. London.

39. Serrão, Joel. 1950. Sobre o Trigo das Ilhas nos Séculos XV e XVI. Das Artes e da História da Madeira 1(2): 1-6; Freitas Ferraz, Maria de Lourdes de. 1971. A Ilha da Madeira e o Problema de Trigo no Século XV. Geographica 28: 46-52.

40. Magalhães Codinho, Vitorino. 1971. *Os descobrimentos e a Economia Mundial.* Vol. 2, Part III, chapt. 1. Editorial Arcadia. Lisbon; Oliveira Marques, A., *op. cit.*; Serrão, J., *op. cit.*

41. Silva Marques, J. *op. cit.* :400.

42. Cadamosto, Luis de. 1944. Le Navigazioni Atlantiche de Luis de Cadamosto. In Silva Marques, J., *op. cit.* :173; Dias Leite, Jeronimo. 1947. *Descobrimento da*

Ilha da Madeira e Discurso da Vida e Feitos Dos Capitães da dita Illba. :19. Coimbra; Frutuoso, G., *op. cit.* :431.

43. Leite, Duarte. 1941. Os primeiros acucares portugueses. *Coisas de Varia História.* Lisbon. This interpretation is consistent with the general picture presented by Verlinden above (see Reference 2).

44. Frutuoso, G. *op. cit.* :113.

45. Azevedo, J. Lúcio de. 1947. *Epocas de Portugal Económico: Esboços de Historia.* Livraria Classica Editora. Lisbon.

46. Dias Leite, J. *op. cit.* :27.

47. One *arroba* equals 14.686 kilograms or 32.37 pounds.

48. Frutuoso, G. *op. cit.* :665-6; Silva Marques, J. *op. cit.* Supplement to Vol. 1: 343.

49. Cadamosto actually writes of 400 cântaros. Lucio de Azevedo (*op, cit.*: 221 footnote 1), basing his findings on Sombart, says that a cântaro equals 228 or 250 kilograms. Hence, we may calculate Cadamosto's figure as either 6,080 or 6,666 *arrobas.*

50. Freitas Ferraz, Maria de Lourdes de. 1971. O Açucar e a sua Importância na Economic Madeirense. Geographica. 25: 30-38, 78-88.

51. Oliveira Marques, António H. De. 1965. Notas para a História da Feitoria Portuguesa na Flandres no seculo XV. Ensaios de Historia Medieval. :240. Portugalia Editora. Lisbon.

52. Frutuoso, G. *op, cit.* :637-8; Rau, Virginia & Jorge de Macedo. 1962. *O Açucar da Madeira Nos Fins do Século XV: Problemas de Produção e Comerico.*: 130. Junta Geral do Distrito Autonimo de Funchal. Funchal, Madeira.

53. Zurara, G., *op, cit.* :348.

54. Cadamosto, L. *op, cit.* :172.

55. As Rogers summarizes the situation, by the later fourteenth century, "A series of events terminated Western travel to the Orient via the Eastern Mediterranean. The conversion of the Il-Khans of Persia to Islam, the waxing might of the Ottoman Turks, and the xenophobic Ming dynasty in China brought about an isolation of India and Cathay at precisely the moment the dynasty of Avis acceded to power in Portugal. Increasing Mamluk fear, both of belated Christian crusades and Moslem Ottoman challenge, blocked access to Ethiopia via Egypt or the Red Sea area at the time when sporadic embassies from Ethiopia were exciting the curiosity of the West." (Rogers, Francis M. 1961. *The Travels of the Infante Dom Pedro of Portugal.*: 107. Harvard University Press. Cambridge, Mass.)

56. Cadamosto, L. *op, cit.*

57. Sarmento, A. 1932. *op, cit.*

58. Freitas Ferraz, M. *O Açucar e a Sua Importância na Economia Madeirense. op, cit.* :79.

59. Rau, V. & J. Macedo. *op, cit.*; see also Rau, Virginia. 1964. *The Settlement of Madeira and the Sugar Cane Plantations.* Afdeling Agrariche Geschiedens. A.A.G. Bijdragen. No. 11, Wageningen.

60. Jasmins Pereira Rodrigues, Fernando A. 1959. Alguns Elementos Para o Estudo da História Economica da Madeira (Capitania de Funchal-Seculo XV). Dissertação de Licenciatura em Ciencias Historico-Filosóficas, apresentada a Faculdade de Letras da Universidade de Coimbra, Portugal.

61. In describing the lavradores de cana (cane growers) in Bahia in the following century, Schwartz outlines a variety of tenure situations, all derived from the relationship between the cane grower and the *engenho*. The mill owners, for example, leased lands received by them in sesmaria. Other lands owned by them were awarded to dependents on a sharecropping basis. In addition, the mills ground the canes of freeholders who had purchased their plots, but were unable to afford their own mill. Each engenho ground the canes it planted on its own, plus those of its renters and sharecroppers, along with those of freeholders with fields nearby. The records of the Engenho Sergipe do Conde in Bahia reveal that the mill took 50 per cent of the sugar made from "free cane", that is, the plants raised on freeholds. It took an additional third or quarter from the renters and the sharecroppers (Schwartz, Stuart B. 1973. *Free labour in a slave economy: The lavradores de cana of colonial Bahia. Colonial Roots of Modern Brazil.* Dauril Alden, Ed. The University of California Press. Berkeley, Calif.)

62. Frutuoso, G. *op, cit.*

63. Lippmann, E. *op, cit.*

64. Rau, V. & J. Macedo. *op, cit.*

65. Schwartz, S. *op, cit.* Rodrigues de Azevedo, for example, speaks of free colonos who supervised slaves on land, "sob a inspecção delles" (Frutuoso, G. *op, cit.* :680).

66. A possible exception was the famous Lombado dos Esmeraldos, a fazenda reportedly rented by João Esmeraldo, a Genoese and friend of Christopher Columbus from Rui Conçalves da Câmara, son of João Gonçalves Zarco. Rui, who was to gain fame as a warrior in Morocco and on the African coast, was the second captain of Funchal. In the late fifteenth century the Lombada is reported to have produced 20,000 *arrobas* of sugar annually and to have been worked by 80 slaves - Moors, Canary islanders, mulattoes and Negroes. (Frutuoso, G. *op, cit.*; see also Silva, Padre Fernando Augusto de. 1933. *A Lombada dos Esmeraldos na Ilha de Madeira.* Funchal, Madeira).

68. Rau, V. & J. Macedo, *op, cit.* :14-15.

69. Deerr, N. *op, cit.*, Vol. I: 100, for example, writes: "The large quantity of sugar made in Madeira was sufficient to influence the course of European trade, and to cause the distribution of sugar more freely over the whole of Europe than had ever happened when the Mediterranean was the only supplier. . . ."

5

The Birth of an Atlantic World

JOHN THORNTON

The shape of the Atlantic zone

The European navigations of the fifteenth century in the Atlantic opened up a new and virtually unprecedented chapter in human history. Not only did European sailors provide direct ocean routes to areas that had been in contact with Europe through more expensive and difficult overland routes (such as West Africa and East Asia), but the ships reached areas that had had no previous sustained and reciprocal contact with the outside world. Of course, this was obviously true of the American continents, and historians have rightly focussed their attention on this immense new world in their discussions of the period. But it was not just the Americans who came into outside contact, for virtually the entire region of west central Africa, south of modern Cameroon, was also without outside contacts, in spite of the fact that it was geographically a part of the land mass whose eastern and western parts had long-standing connections to the Mediterranean and Indian Ocean.[1] Thus, in addition to easing and intensifying relations between various parts of the Old World (which in this case also included West Africa), the European navigations opened up connections between the Old World and two new worlds-the two sections of the American continent and the western part of central Africa.

The French historian Pierre Chaunu has argued that perhaps the most significant consequence of European navigation was what he calls "disenclavement" the ending of isolation for some areas and the increase in intersocietal contacts in most areas. This allowed an increased flow of ideas as well as trade throughout the world, ultimately leading to a unified world economy and potentially, at least, to higher levels of economic development.[2] As such then, the opening of the Atlantic was crucial in this process, all the more so because it was only here that true isolation was broken.

More than this, however, the birth of an Atlantic world also involved a gigantic international migration of people, certainly without precedent in the Old World and undertaken nowhere else in the field of European expansion. Not only did thousands of Europeans move to the Atlantic islands and the Americas, but literally millions of Africans crossed to the Atlantic and Caribbean islands and the Americas, becoming the dominant population in some areas. This demographic fact was not lost on early residents and visitors: Gonzalo Fernández Oviedo y Valdez described Hispaniola as a "New Guinea"[3] in the mid-sixteenth century when slave imports for its burgeoning sugar industry had changed its demography; Ambrósio Fernandes Brandão used exactly the same term to describe Brazil's sugar-rich northeast in 1618.[4] In the Atlantic, disenclavement meant much more than it did elsewhere in the world; it was not just increased communication but a reshaping of whole societies and the literal creation of a "New World." Moreover, it was a reshaping that involved Africa quite directly, for by 1650 in any case, Africans were the majority of new settlers in the new Atlantic world.

Understanding the origin and direction of this gigantic episode in intersocial relations requires a knowledge of the basic geography of the areas involved-areas in which transport by water defined for most purposes the entire region. One must always remember that in the age before rail and air travel, waterborne travel was immensely cheaper and more practical-despite the risks of storm and shipwreck-than overland travel. Not only could boats and ships average fairly good time, but they were energy efficient in an era that had few energy resources, and they could, moreover, carry heavy and bulky goods easily. Thus, creating a geography of the Atlantic area must take areas accessible by water transport as its first dimension, for use of the water would greatly alter other considerations of space and distance, linking regions that were apparently distant more easily than regions that apparently lay close to each other.

The first of these great water routes was the Atlantic itself, opened for practical use in the fifteenth and early sixteenth centuries. But the Atlantic was also linked to riverine routes in both Africa and the Americas, which formed a vital supplement to the ocean, bringing societies and states that often lay hundreds of kilometres from the coast into contact with the ocean and, thus, with other societies and states. Even the rivers that did not allow ocean-going vessels to pass into interior regions (because of falls, narrows, or sandbanks) served as connections to extensive travel and commercial networks in the interior. The combination of ocean and river routes defined the shape of the Atlantic zone.

But one must not simply look at a map of the Atlantic and imagine that it was equally penetrable and that those who sailed it had equal access to all parts of the zone. In many ways, in the days of wooden sailing ships, the ocean was as much channeled as were rivers, whose direction of flow is clearly defined. No sailor could ignore the patterns of prevailing winds and currents on the ocean. This was crucial for the development of Atlantic navigation, for the winds and currents created barriers to traffic for thousands of years. They limited contact between the Mediterranean and Africa for a very long time and thwarted whatever potential Africans might have had for effective navigation into the Atlantic beyond their coastal waters, just as it would act as a brake on American ventures to Africa and Europe.

Raymond Mauny has shown that the constant north-to-south flow of the Canary Current along the Saharan coast made it possible for ships from the Mediterranean to sail southward as far as West Africa but prevented a return voyage.[5] For Mediterranean sailors, Cape Bojador, just south of the Canary Islands, represented a point of no return, and even if voyages, intentional and unintentional, went beyond it, they did not pioneer any route with practical significance. Arabic accounts cite several voyages made by accident beyond this point. al-Idrisi (1154) cites one that left from Lisbon,[6] ibn Sa'id heard from a Moroccan traveller named Ibn Fatima of a similar voyage sometime before 1270,[7] and al-'Umari heard of another one from Almeira in Spain made by Muhammad b. Raghanuh in the early fourteenth century - all were forced to return to the Mediterranean area by overland routes.[8] It was only in the fifteenth century, and then using routes leading back through the Canaries, Madeira, and the Azores and risking a high-seas voyage, that Europeans were able to finally conquer the difficulties of the Bojador on a regular basis.

If the problems with the winds and currents off the Saharan coast checked Mediterraneans from entering the African portion of the Atlantic, a similar problem hampered African navigators. Of course, Africans would have been just as interested in going to North Africa and Iberia by sea as the Mediterranean people were interested in reaching Africa, given the knowledge that each area had of the other through the overland trade,[9] but the constant current that prevented return trips to the Mediterranean also frustrated African efforts to go to the Mediterranean from the very start. The extent of northward sailing by African vessels seems to have been the salt works of Ijil on the Mauretanian coast, at least according to al-Idrisi's twelfth-century account.[10]

On the other hand, Africans faced the strongly prevailing westward-flowing Equatorial Current from the Senegambian region into the Caribbean basin. Although this current may have made African voyages to the Americas possible, it required fairly well developed techniques for high-seas navigation to even begin, and Africans could not develop such technology on short voyages in calm seas. Thus, Ivan van Sertima, who has championed the idea that Africans made frequent voyages to the Americas since around 800 B.C., has had to acknowledge that these voyages, if they occurred at all, were accidental and initiated no transatlantic commerce. However well such African navigators may have fared in long crossings in craft not designed to sail in the high seas, they faced insuperable barriers to making return trips to any familiar point on the African coast.[11]

Of course, some of the Caribbean peoples developed sufficiently large craft to sail regularly in the Caribbean, and such ships might well have travelled to the Old World. Historian Aurelio Tió has shown how important the native people of the Caribbean were in guiding early European voyages from Florida to the Orinoco, and how they knew the regime of wind and current throughout the basin well. He suggests that they also knew a good deal of the oceanic geography of the western Atlantic.[12] But for them, as well, the problem of a return voyage was similar to that the Europeans faced in their own early Atlantic navigations. Indeed, not until the late fifteenth century, when the entire system of Atlantic winds and currents was understood and European sailors knew all the potential landfalls on either side of the Atlantic, was a truly practical round-trip navigation achieved.

But even when the system was understood and European ships could travel (at least in theory) to every point in the Atlantic, they were nevertheless forced to respect the wind and currents. Pierre and Hugette Chaunu, examining the usual voyages of Spanish ships from Seville into the Atlantic, and Frédéric Mauro, considering Portuguese navigation in the same area, have shown that the habitual routes of commerce, stopping points, and even commerciall developments were strongly conditioned by these winds.[13]

The regime of wind and current explains a number of developments not immediately apparent to modern travellers. One of the strongest motives for the establishment of an English colony in Barbados in 1624 was that its upwind position relative to Caribbean navigation made it difficult to access for Spanish fleets-fleets that had defeated earlier English attempts in the area. At the same time, British colonies in North America were bound more strongly to their Caribbean counterparts by the fact that return navigation from the Caribbean on the Gulf Stream naturally brought Caribbean settlers and traders to the North American coast. Thus navigational considerations joined economic ones to link the two regions.[14]

If water routes were the earliest form of travel, then the streams of the ocean must be joined to land streams if we are to see the full dimensions of the Atlantic world. This is abundantly demonstrated by the connections of the western Sudan to the Atlantic. Riverine routes going deep into West Africa connected points quite distant from the coast to the Atlantic. Although narrows and sandbars blocking the mouths often obstructed the travel of large, sea-going vessels on African rivers, smaller craft designed for river travel navigated them easily, and portages reduced the obstructions caused by falls.

Michal Tymowski has shown convincingly how important the Niger River was to the economic life of the central portions of the western Sudan, where very large craft were constructed and carried bulky cargoes along the river. Although there were falls from time to time that interrupted the navigations, each segment of the Niger divided by the falls was a veritable highway, and fairly short overland routes around the falls did not form an insurmountable barrier to long-range navigation.[15]

One could make an equally good case for the Senegal River, even if the falls at Felu made inland voyages from the ocean difficult. Certainly there was substantial traffic on the Senegal above and below the falls from medieval times onward, for it was probably on this river that the "strongly made boats" of the people of Ghana travelled in al-Idrisi's account of the Sudan of the twelfth century.[16] Moreover, items were transshipped through overland routes from the Senegal to the Niger or from these two rivers to the Gambia River, which formed the third member in a triad of much-used West African rivers. An overland route that took approximately twenty-five days to complete connected the Niger and the Senegal, and a portage of about 250 kilometres connected the Senegal and the Gambia rivers.[17]

The empire of Mali remained the heart of political power in the western part of the Sudan from the thirteenth century until well into the seventeenth century largely because of its central position at the headwaters of these three river systems. Philip Curtin has demonstrated how merchants based on the upper courses of these rivers could switch exports to the Atlantic from one of the systems to another to make the best of market opportunities in the seventeenth and eighteenth centuries.[18] Some of the earliest accounts of Senegambia speak of "Jaga" (probably the town of Diakha on the Senegal or Dia on the Niger, both near the headwaters of the river systems) as both the capital of Mali (which it may never have been) and a source for all the gold in Senegambia and the Gold Coast, indicating the crucial position that such a central location could play in the shifting gold trade.[19] Even in the early sixteenth century, merchants based that far away were capable of diverting the trade from the Gambia to the Gold Coast or back should it suit their interests.[20]

An indication of the significance of the river system to the geography of the western Sudan is revealed by the fact that many Moslem writers regarded the rivers as forming a single complex system- the "Nile of the Sudan"- a view that was shared not just by amateurs living in North Africa but by West African merchants themselves.[21] Not only did the Niger-Senegal-Gambia complex unite a considerable portion of West Africa, but the Niger provided a corridor that ultimately added the Hausa kingdoms, the Yoruba states, and the Nupe, Igala, and Benin kingdoms to a hydrographic system that was ultimately connected to the Atlantic. When one considers the Benue River as an extension, then one can get an idea of how deeply the riverine system penetrated into West Africa. Geographical ideas held by Africans and outsiders alike in the sixteenth century conflated all these rivers- the Senegal, Gambia, Niger, and Benue- into a single "Nile of the Blacks" ultimately connected to the Nile of Egypt.[22] Although it is mistaken geography, it is a real reflection of the transport possibilities of river routes.

West central Africa was also oriented by its rivers, especially the Zaire and the Kwanza. Likewise, António de Oliveira de Cadornega used rivers to orient his geography of central Africa (and his knowledge extended far into the interior) and combined it with a lengthy paean to the Kwanza River.[23] These rivers bore substantial commerce. Not only was the Kwanza used by the Portuguese in their conquest of Angola, but it was a major artery of commerce for Africans as well, as Paulo Dias de Novais, the first Portuguese to describe the region, made clear in the mid-sixteenth century. Riverine commerce was connected with coastal commerce and African craft plied the coastal waters between the Zaire and the Kwanza.[24]

For many Africans elsewhere as well, the coast was like a river system that connected distant points; it nourished a trade that predated and often complemented that of the Europeans operating on the high seas. Jean-Pierre Chauveau has examined the role of coastal societies and navigation in West Africa and shows that maritime navigation provided coastwise communication between substantial regions, which has often been overlooked in earlier assessments. In Loango, Senegambia, Sierra Leone, and Liberia, coastal estuaries, creeks, and lagoons form an inter-connected, protected system of waterways facilitating the large-scale movement of goods. Such coastal waterways also allow easy communication between the mouths of the Senegal and the Gambia. Likewise, the coast of modern Ivory Coast possessed a system of lagoons and coastal lakes; however, it was less active in Atlantic commerce and thus less well-known to modern scholarship.[25] Finally, of course, was the network of waterways that stretched from the mouth of the Volta River across the Niger delta to modern Cameroon, which is beginning to be understood as both a political and an economic axis.[26] Here, as in the Senegambian case, the coastal stretch linked up with rivers flowing into the interior. The Niger, of course, was one such river, but there were others as well. Capuchin priests who visited Allada in West Africa in 1660-62 observed that the several rivers that flowed into the coastal lagoon were navigated by large locally built canoes that permitted the people to travel far into the interior.[27]

American rivers also extended the Atlantic zone. Thus, geographers of North American settlements have noted that major rivers such as the Saint Lawrence, the watershed of the Chesapeake Bay, the Connecticut, and the Hudson formed major roads deep into the interior largely because these rivers were easily navigable for small sea-going vessels and were used heavily by Europeans as an axis for settlement. The Amazon, which is navigable from the Atlantic to the Andes, and the Orinoco, which also is navigable far into the interior, were also connected to Atlantic commerce. Control of both river systems lay in the hands of Native American societies, whose cultural sophistication has only recently been appreciated. From the earliest days of European contact, visitors on the Amazon and Orinoco noted extensive local traffic, and traders at the mouths of the rivers were the end points of riverine trade routes equivalent to the Senegal-Niger corridor of West Africa, where European metal goods were traded for gold, slaves, and cotton hammocks, which were exported by the thousands.[28] Because the natives of these regions (like the inhabitants of the Mississippi valley in North America)[29] controlled commerce and held the Europeans at bay, we know much less about these areas than we do of those that formed arteries of communication for Old World settlers.

Thus, water routes defined the Atlantic zone, and rivers extended the zone far beyond the shores of the ocean itself. The mastery of the sea, however, made it possible for all these continental routes to be in communication. There were considerable problems to be overcome before the connections could be made, in spite of the occasional transatlantic voyages that may have preceded Columbus's voyages and the Portuguese voyages along the African coast. Such problems had proved practically insurmountable to Africans, Americans, and Mediterranean people before 1400. It is therefore worth exploring the circumstances that enabled the Europeans to make transatlantic voyages practicable.

Origins of Atlantic navigation

Europeans' experience with waterborne travel was probably the most significant factor in allowing them to be the ones who finally conquered the Atlantic. The difficulties of tackling South Atlantic navigation may explain why Africans, for their part, seem to have focussed their boatbuilding talents on craft designed for coastal and riverine navigation[30] and as a result had engaged in little deliberate oceanic navigation, leaving even fairly close islands, such as the Cape Verdes and São Tomé, uncolonized and uninhabited. Indeed, they had even eschewed long-range navigation in the Gulf of Guinea (beyond the colonization of Bioko Island, visible from the mainland), which might have proved economically feasible, though hampered by the same problems of currents that prevented transatlantic navigation.

The people of the Americas had a slightly better chance than the Africans, for the Caribbean was fully navigable by them long before the Europeans arrived. Thus, the boats of the Caribs and Arawaks were often seen at sea and, unlike African craft, could undertake long sea voyages.[31] But just as the predictability of the monsoons in Asia may have inhibited certain breakthroughs in shipbuilding technology by presenting few challenges, perhaps also navigation of the Caribbean, with its long chain of islands, was too easy.

Europeans had two large inland seas, however: the Mediterranean in the south and the North and Baltic seas in the north, along with a difficult, but passable, stretch of coast between them. Thus, separate navigation traditions could develop to solve the specific problems in each area and then merge through intercommunication to present solutions to further problems. By the fourteenth or fifteenth century, these major seas were regularly navigated, and seagoing vessels were a standard part of every European inventory. Thus, as Pierre Chaunu has argued, it was the opening (or reopening, for such connections were frequent in Classical times) of regular commerce between the Mediterranean Sea and the northern seas in the late thirteenth century that ultimately would lead to European navigation in the Atlantic as well. This trade, signalled by the first recorded voyage of a Genoese ship to northern Europe in 1277, was largely connected with the grain trade and movement of other bulk commodities that could not stand the cost of overland trade.[32]

These early voyages not only helped to start, as we shall see, the Europeans on their conquest of the Atlantic, they linked the various European seas and ultimately helped shape the European boundaries of the Atlantic world. Fernand Braudel has argued strongly in favour of the significance of the connection between the northern seas and the Mediterranean, and it was sailors familiar with each of these two great bodies of water and with the attached riverine areas (such as Germany along the Rhine and even Poland along the Vistula) who came to participate in the larger oceanic economy of the Atlantic.[33]

Although the northern Europeans were late in entering the South Atlantic commerce that linked Africa to the Americas, the Vikings had long pioneered the northern routes westward, colonizing Greenland at the least and providing the first strong links between the northern seas and the Mediterranean. The English and the Dutch were fairly early and frequent in the Atlantic; the Swedes settled in North American early in the seventeenth century and had posts on the African coast as well, and in Africa they were joined by the Danes and by Baltic countries like Kurland and Brandenburg.

Not only did the needs of this seaborne trade between the Mediterranean and northern Europe serve as a stimulus to Iberian shipbuilding and interest in the inter-regional trade, but the fairly large number of ships involved increased the potential for accidental voyages of discovery. The career of Lanzaroto Malocello is a case in point. Malocello was a Genoese merchant who had commercial connections with Cherbourg in northern France and Ceuta in Morocco and thus had frequent recourse to travel in the Atlantic both north and south of Gibraltar. On one of these voyages he discovered (or rediscovered, for they were known in Classical times), probably by accident, the Canaries in about 1312. The Canaries were the first Atlantic islands rediscovered by Europeans, and their colonization by Malocello around 1335, represented an early and important step into the Atlantic.[34]

In addition to multiplying the opportunities for accidental voyages of discovery, maritime travel between the Mediterranean and North Atlantic, especially because it involved bulk shipping, allowed the diffusion of shipbuilding techniques. Thus, the sturdy round ships of the North Sea and Baltic were blended with the long and maneuverable galleys of the Mediterranean. This eventually resulted in the creation of ships capable of carrying more cargo and sailing under a wider variety of conditions than could be found in either the Mediterranean or the North Atlantic. To these discoveries were added techniques in sailing and navigation borrowed from the Muslim world, with which the Genoese and Iberians had constant commerce.[35]

Possessing the means to make oceanic voyages and to discover new lands did not necessarily mean that extensive oceanic travel or exploration would be undertaken, however. There also had to be a reasonable set of motives, and financial backers had to have some confidence that such voyages would be worth the considerable risks that their undertaking entailed.

European motives: long-range geopolitical and economic goals

A number of technical and geographical factors combined to make Europeans the most likely people to explore the Atlantic and develop its commerce. But the task also required strong political or economic motives before it would be undertaken. An older, romantic school of historians maintained that Europeans undertook this exploration for the pure joy of discovery or to break the Moslem stranglehold on the eastern trade. These motives were enough, in this interpretation, to allow visionaries like Infante Henrique (Prince Henry the Navigator) of Portugal or Queen Isabella of Spain to finance the voyages.[36]

This romantic vision has been reduced to more mundane dimensions by the work of Portuguese historians, especially Duarte Leite and Vitorino Magalhães-Godinho. They have stressed that exploration and voyages proceeded step-by-step, over a long period of time, and were fueled by the prospect of immediate profits that were readily attainable using existing (or only slightly modified) technology.[37] Under such conditions the capital costs were small, profits and returns were all but certain, and the potential for dramatic discoveries was limited. Even the greatest leaps - Columbus's transatlantic voyage of 1492 and da Gama's circumnavigation of Africa in 1498 - were built on many years of profitable exploitation of the Atlantic and excellent intelligence of the prospects (in da Gama's case) or potentially profitable fallbacks such as the hope of finding new Atlantic islands (in Columbus's case).

In this scenario, it is possible to see the technological breakthroughs in sailing methods as following rather than leading the discoveries. People developed the technology once they knew for sure that they could profit by improving their techniques.

There is evidence, however, to support both cases, and it is dangerous to accept more quickly the research of the recent scholars with their less romantic interpretations. After all, many of those who described voyages wrote of the romantic vision themselves. For example, the fifteenth-century chronicler Gomes Eannes de Zurara stresses principally geopolitical motives when he gives a list of reasons that compelled Infante Henrique to send out the ships that pioneered direct sea travel between West Africa and Europe. These motives derived from the centuries-long struggle between Christians and Moslems for control of the Mediterranean world. Henrique's principal desire, according to Zurara, was his wish to defeat the North African Moslems, and economic considerations were secondary. He hoped that his mariners would contact a Christian power south of Morocco with whom to form an anti-Moslem alliance or establish trade with non-Moslem southern neighbours who might be converted to Christianity and agree to such an alliance or who at least might be persuaded to cease trade with Morocco.[38]

Zurara was expressing a long-held hope of Christians in Iberia. Writers and visionaries living in the period before the voyages sponsored by Infante Henrique had proposed several schemes to outflank the Moslems in one way or another. In 1285, for example, a Mallorcan theologian named Ramon Llull dreamed of converting the king of Ghana to Christianity, thus creating a Christian state in the hinterland of Moslem North Africa.[39] Since 1306, when an Ethiopian delegation had arrived in Europe seeking a Christian alliance with the "King of the Spains," to "offer him aid against infidels,"[40] the idea of an Iberian-Ethiopian connection had been considered. Indeed, King Anfós IV of Aragon came close to arranging a double marriage with the negus of Ethiopia in 1428,[41] and the Portuguese Crown sent Pedro de Corvilhão to Ethiopia in 1487 to prepare similar alliances.[42]

Modern scholars have been less convinced by grand geopolitical schemes of a religious and military nature than they have been by economic motives, and consequently some emphasize the fabulous wealth to be had through oceanic trade, with the spice-rich islands of India and Southeast Asia or with West Africa, mainly for its gold. Such an interpretation is supported by the correlation between Atlantic exploration and the fall of Acre, the last outpost of direct European commercial relations with the eastern Mediterranean, which passed into Moslem hands in 1291. Thus, in the same year that Acre fell, the Vivaldi

brothers set sail from Venice to find an Atlantic route to the Indies; they never returned.[43] The cartography of the age, admittedly very speculative, encouraged such attempts by representing Africa in a form that suggested an easy circumnavigation.[44] A Franciscan friar from Castile reported his own circumnavigation of Africa in 1360, but his book was fictional, being based on speculation and the kind of knowledge that well-connected Franciscans might glean from contemporary maps, cosmographies, and commercial gossip in the western Mediterranean.[45]

Of all the economic possibilities that might provide motives for Atlantic navigation, however, the prospect of a short route to the West African goldfields seems the most likely. The Indies, after all, were far away in anyone's conception of world geography, whereas West Africa, known to be wealthy in gold, was much closer and clearly accessible by a sea route. West Africa had been a source of gold for Mediterranean countries for centuries, perhaps since Byzantine times.[46] Moslem writers since the ninth century at least were aware of the gold-producing areas, and a steady stream of Arabic-language descriptions of West Africa resulted, including one made by the famed North African al-Idrisi for the Christian king Roger II of Sicily in 1154.[47] These were joined by Christian accounts, especially those generated by the Catalan and Italian merchant communities of North Africa, who had been dealing in the gold (called the "gold of Palolus" in these sources) since the twelfth century.[48]

A sea route to the goldfields seemed relatively practical, because it did not involve the circumnavigation of Africa. Many maps of the period showed the "River of Gold" (probably the Senegal) and, according to the legend on the map of Mecia de Villadestes (1413), where one could "obtain the gold of Palolus." Although the actual field lay upstream, the "mouth of the river is large and deep enough for the biggest ship in the river."[49] Christians believed that Moslems regularly sailed to the river - the anonymous Franciscan friar even claimed (falsely) to have sailed there himself around 1360 on a Moslem ship,[50] and as early as 1346 Jacme Ferrer, a Catalan merchant, actually attempted to reach it.[51]

European motives: the prevalence of short-range goals

Whatever their dreams or fantasies, whether it was encircling and isolating the Moslems or reaching the spices of Asia or the gold of West Africa, these long-range plans were largely restricted to kings and intellectuals, and neither group proved particularly willing to actually finance the voyages they considered, and private or small-scale ventures (such as those of the Vivaldis and Ferrer) failed. Thus, whatever contemporary writers may have said about motives, or how much rulers may have desired the results of such schemes, the progress of Atlantic exploration ultimately depended on financial considerations. Financial considerations must ultimately force us to agree with the Portuguese historians on the prevalence of short-range, unromantic, step-by-step exploration as the principal method of European expansion.

It is also important to note that another romantic fantasy - that the Iberians were the sole leaders of the exploration - is untrue. The exploration of the Atlantic was a truly international exercise, even if many of the dramatic discoveries were made under the sponsorship of the Iberian monarchs. The people who undertook the voyages gathered the human and material resources from wherever they were available. English, French, Polish, Italian people, ships and capital joined Iberians in this effort. If the Iberians were pioneers in anything, it was that monarchs of these countries were quick to claim sovereignty (or to offer their protection to the earliest colonists) and to make the effort necessary to enforce these claims, usually after the economic benefits were clearly revealed by an international group of pioneers.

We can conveniently divide the expansion into two "wings," or two directions. The first of these was an African wing, which sought mainland products such as slaves and then gold as the means to finance short voyages along the coast, and whose leaders expected to find people to raid or to trade with all along the route. The second was an Atlantic wing, which sought exploitable but not necessarily inhabited land in which to collect valuable wild products or to begin agricultural production of cultivated products in high demand in Europe. The colonization of these lands began with cutting timber or gathering wild honey, but its real profitability was ultimately realized by producing wheat, sugar, or wine in rich tropical and volcanic soils.

In many respects, the Canary Islands, rediscovered by Malocello in the early fourteenth century, provided the common starting point for both wings and combined in itself both sources of profit. The islands were inhabited and could thus be raided or support commerce, they possessed wild products of interest, and ultimately they became a centre for the production of both wine and sugar. Moreover, because travelling to them was fairly easy and profitable, they provided financial security to those who sought more profits on the adjacent Saharan coast or the uninhabited Atlantic islands farther out.

Malocello and those who followed him in the early to mid-fourteenth century rapidly discovered that the Canaries produced a number of useful products. Perhaps the most useful were orchil (a dyestuff derived from lichens that grew on the rocks of the islands) and "dragon's blood," a resin also used as a dyestuff. The islands could also be profitably raided for cattle and people; slaves were always in demand in the Mediterranean world.[52]

An early voyage to the Canaries (under Portuguese auspices, but with a mixed crew and an Italian captain) in 1341 went both to trade and to raid, buying hides, dyestuffs and wood products, but also carrying weapons for raiding, and King Afonso IV of Portugal reported that slave raiding was under way at least as early as 1346.[53] Catalan merchants joined the Portuguese at an early date in both raiding and trading with the Canarians.[54] Attempts to colonize grew out of these ventures. The earliest colonization in various parts of the islands, by Malocello around 1339, an Aragonese group in 1342, and a group under French auspices in 1344, were all probably simply attempts to set up a trading factory and slave-raiding fort, and none brought any long-term and productive settlement. Castilians always seemed to have favoured simply raiding and trading from Spain itself.[55]

Castille, however, sponsored the first permanent colonization, though it was Norman nobles Gadifer de la Salle and Jean de Bethencourt who actually organized and carried it out, in 1402-5. Like their predecessors, they seem to have been most interested in dyestuffs (they both came from textile-producing areas), organizing the

Canarians to gather it. They also brought in Norman colonists and made a land division, although the export of profitable crops seems to have required a century.[56] Later Castilian-Spanish colonization continued agricultural expansion, and by 1520 the islands were producing sugar, wines, and sheep and cattle products.[57]

But whether visited for conquest and raiding or trade, the islands were seen as a source of profit, and much attention was paid to navigation to them throughout the fourteenth century. This activity brought more shipping into the area south of the Straits of Gibraltar, extending Christian raiding and commercial activity farther south and acquainting them with the area and the nearby regions of the African coast. In this way the Canaries, whether as colonies or simply as convenient landfalls, served as bases for further operations along the African coast or to the uninhabited islands farther out in the Atlantic, such as Madeira and the Azores, which were probably known to Europeans since the voyages of da Recco in 1341.

The African wing of expansion

The raiding and commerce of the Canaries provided the base and the motives for European activities farther down the Atlantic coast of Africa. Thus, Jacme Ferrer began his ill-fated voyage to the 'River of Gold' in 1346 with a stop at the Canaries.[58] Likewise, Jean de Bethencourt, conqueror of the eastern group of islands, took some time off from his efforts to raid the Atlantic coast of Africa, although he attempted no voyages beyond the customary limits of navigation.[59]

When Bethencourt did homage to the king of Castille in 1405, Portugal found its claim to the islands, vigorously pressed since at least 1341, and its commercial connections there weakened. In this context, Infante Henrique of Portugal pressed hard for conquering the remaining islands and launched an expedition against them in 1415. In 1424 he sent a much larger expedition, involving some 2,500 infantry and 120 cavalry.[60] This increase in Portuguese activity in the Canaries resulted in the papal bull *Romanus Pontifex* of 1436 renewing Portuguese claims on the still-unconquered islands[61] and a corresponding increase in activity along the Saharan coast.

These renewed attacks on the remaining Canaries and the Saharan shore resulted in the doubling of Cape Bojador (though he proceeded little farther) by the Portuguese sailor Gil Eannes in 1434.[62] The year before this feat Eannes had led a slave-raiding expedition against Gran Canaria Island, and the Bojador expedition was a natural excursion in the same vein. Indeed, the sailing craft of the time could avoid some of the difficulties of the currents by sailing out to the Canaries, thus alleviating the age-long problem of return navigation from beyond Bojador.

In spite of the potential for this breakthrough, however, the Portuguese did not immediately reach the Senegal, although expeditions to the "River of Gold" were sent out almost immediately, they did not actually sail so far. Some of these expeditions brought back commodities such as oils and skins (as did one in 1436),[63] but most were simply slave raids, in the tradition of the attacks on the Canaries or southern Morocco, and rarely ventured farther along the coast than was necessary to secure a profitable cargo. It was only in 1444 that the Portuguese actually reached the Senegal, although they had attacked and intercepted caravans bound from there northward in previous years.[64]

Thus, the actual motivation for European expansion and for navigational breakthroughs was little more than to exploit the opportunity for immediate profits made by raiding and the seizure or purchase of trade commodities. It was these more limited objectives that ultimately made possible the voyage to the Senegal that geographers and thinkers contemplating longer-range commercial or geopolitical schemes had dreamed of since at least the fourteenth century. It was more or less an extension of these same sorts of motives that eventually allowed the Portuguese to attain that even more distant long-range goal - so important both to commercial and to geopolitical thinking – the rounding of Africa and the discovery of a sea route to India and Ethiopia.[65] The predominance of limited aims in the voyages of reconnaissance and expansion explains why the necessary exploration took so long – from 1434, when the major navigational obstacle was overcome, until 1488, when Dias showed that the Cape of Good Hope was the end of the African continent.

In the Senegal region the profits were made from gold and slaves (first captured in raids, later purchased). Gold was available from many points along the coast, and sailors expanded rapidly southward until they reached the coast of modern Sierra Leone around 1460. Much of the energy of travelling even during those years, however, was spent on commercial or military voyages intended to consolidate and explore the possibilities of the areas already known[66] or to establish bases. The uninhabited archipelago of Cape Verde Islands was crucial to further expansion and was colonized in the 1460s.[67]

But there were other commercial possibilities to be found further on, and perhaps the prospects of the next stretch of coast to produce the pepper known as malaguetta pepper[68] were known to Fernão Gomes when he petitioned the Crown for exclusive rights to the trade of West Africa exclusive of the areas earlier granted to the settlers of Cape Verde in 1469.[69] In any case, his grant included a provision that he explore further sections of the coast, and his expeditions rapidly began exporting the pepper. Shortly afterward (perhaps about 1471), to his infinite good luck, Gomes's sailors reached the gold-producing region of the Gold Coast (modern Ghana), an unexpected find that paid off handsomely for both Gomes and eventually for the Crown.[70] His sailors located another pepper-producing region at Benin the next year, although it was only in 1485-6 that regular trade began there.[71] They also discovered, on the island of São Tomé, another potential base for operations in the region.

Thus, for a long stretch of time, between about 1340 and 1470, European expansion proceeded slowly along the African coast. It paid off handsomely for the private parties who had sponsored most of it, and in 1482, for the first time, the Portuguese Crown decided to sponsor its own expedition into the Atlantic rather than to charter other people, who raised their own capital.[72] Unlike the earlier voyages, the royal voyages of Diogo Cão had a clearly geopolitical goal. According to João de Barros, intelligence received from Benin suggested to the court that Portuguese sailors were near the lands of Prester John and a circumnavigation of Africa was now possible.[73] Thus, Cão made the first attempt at expansion cast in the romantic mold, but he discovered only that the African continent turned south and ran thousands more kilometres before eventually turning. But fortunately for the Crown, Cão did come to the kingdom of Kongo, whose export products helped recoup the cost of the voyages and contributed to the success of the colony on São Tomé.[74] Undeterred by the length of Africa, the Portuguese Crown continued sponsoring exploration, first by Bartolomeu Dias and finally by Vasco da Gama, whose voyages have generally replaced the more prosaic earlier travels in textbook and romantic history as the search for the Indies.

The Atlantic wing and the discovery of America

Like the African wing, the Atlantic wing of exploration began from the Canaries, but it was fueled by the potential for collecting wild products and colonizing otherwise uninhabited areas. Because its results were less impressive, it was slower. Madeira, for example, was probably known (as a result of exploration of the Canary Islands, no doubt) as early as 1339,[75] but its colonization was not undertaken until about 1425.[76] However, its colonization set a strong precedent, because the Azores, reached by Diogo de Silves only in 1427,[77] were already being colonized in 1440.[78]

Because they were uninhabited, islands such as Madeira and the Azores offered no commercial prospects for trading, but they could still be exploited for wild products. In all probability, its early settlers (João Gonçalves Zarco, Tristão Vaz Teixeira, and Bartolomeu Perestrello) relied heavily on the export of available wild products such as wax, honey,[79] wood,[80] and dyestuffs or they raised cattle, which could be easily maintained on the unwooded islands of Porto Santo and Ilha Deserta.[81] Early colonization of the Azores was similar. The order for colonization, given in 1439, already mentioned such products,[82] and Zurara, referring to 1446, indicates that some were already being exported.[83] On the other hand, the Azores were never particularly rich and served more as a base for operations in the Atlantic than as a major centre of production.

The process was repeated on all the other uninhabited Atlantic islands. The royal charter giving the Cape Verde Islands to Infante D. Fernando in 1462 clearly indicates that he expected early earnings to be from wild products or those that required little investment to obtain.[84] Likewise, the earliest settlers of São Tomé in 1485 had a charter that also specified duties for export of wild products expected for that tropical island.[85] In each case, the king, in granting the charter, specified easy terms for the export of a variety of products, both wild and cultivated, that were expected to thrive in the tropics.

The gathering of wild products, the first incentive to visit these islands, gave way to cultivation of readily exportable agricultural products once soil and climate conditions were reasonably well known. In Madeira, clearing land and planting wheat, the first cultivated export, required extra labour; some workers were brought as dependent workers from Europe,[86] and others were probably obtained in attacks on the Canaries.[87] Indeed, the Madeira settlers assisted in the 1424 attack on the Canaries on the very eve of the colonization, so that the two operations went hand in hand.[88]

Madeira and the Canaries rapidly began to export wheat in large quantities, and the virgin soil produced, according to the enthusiastic testimony of Zurara in 1446, 50 for 1;[89] a more sober da Mosto said initial yield of 60-70 for 1 had declined to 30-40 for 1 in 1455,[90] still a boon by the standards of the time. The wheat was exported to Portugal and to Portuguese forces in Morocco, on the Saharan coast, and in West Africa, much of it already baked into bread.[91] But the real earnings came from wine, already described as an excellent product in 1455 by da Mosto,[92] and especially from sugar, which flourished and for which slaves, especially Canarians, provided the labour.[93] Exports of sugar were substantial by 1455 and grew rapidly until Madeira was one of the leading producers of sugar in the European economy.[94]

The success of the Madeira venture encouraged others and showed that even uninhabited islands, especially if they lay in tropical or subtropical zones, could be of economic value and could fairly quickly repay the efforts of populating them.

Not all the islands were as successfully exploited as Madeira was, although some, such as Saã Tomé, became very profitable indeed. But they did serve as bases for ventures along the African coast (such as the Cape Verdes and Saã Tomé) or for further Atlantic navigation (as the Azores would for the Brazil and India fleets). More than that, however, the prospect of finding uncharted and uninhabited islands in an Atlantic seemingly full of them encouraged sailors to look west into the Atlantic as well as south to Africa for their fortune. Indeed, just a few years before Columbus's journey, in 1486, the Crown granted Fernão Dulmo, the captain of the island of Terceira (in the Azores group), title to all lands he might discover in the Atlantic, including "a great island or islands, or coastal parts of a mainland."[95]

It was the combination of the prospect of finding new islands and the dream of reaching India that inspired Christopher Columbus's voyage of 1492 - for though he may well have thought his trip would take him to the lands of the Great Khan, his charter specified islands as well.[96] Columbus, of course, discovered many islands and, shortly afterward, a great continent, which (even though Columbus died believing he was in Asia) was soon recognized as being an entirely new and completely unexpected land mass.

In short, then, European navigation in the South Atlantic was not the product of long-range visionary schemes, an explosion of pent-up commercial energy, or even the response to new technology. Instead it was the cautious advance of a new frontier, using or slightly modifying existing technology and relying on relatively small amounts of private capital. Only in the last, dramatic voyages to round Africa or cross the Atlantic did royal patronage, substantial capital, and geopolitical thinking come to dominate the activity. For example, only when Portuguese sailors visiting Benin reported the possibility of contacts with Prester John (in Ethiopia) did the Portuguese Crown decide to fund its own voyage, Diogo Cão's attempt to circumnavigate Africa.[97] All the previous century of expansion had been privately funded though royally sponsored. Likewise, only the conquest of the last of the Canaries and Columbus's voyages received Spanish funding.[98]

It was a pattern that would continue to dominate European activity. The wealthier merchants, government officials, and grand schemes would be saved until politically weaker people had demonstrated the certainty of success, and then the wealthy and powerful would follow up, absorb the activities and profits of the pioneers, and turn the exploitation of the new discoveries over to those who dominated all society.

Thus, by the late fifteenth century the pioneers had fully tested the regime of wind and currents that dominated Atlantic navigation.[99] By discovering this key, Europeans were able to unlock the commerce of the Atlantic, and because they had single-handedly developed the routes, their domination of the high seas in the Atlantic was ensured in a way that was not possible in any other extra-European area of navigation. In neither techniques nor experience did they dominate the Indian Ocean and South China Sea with the completeness that they dominated the Atlantic.[100]

Oceanic navigation and political domination

Scholars have argued that this domination of the seas gave Europeans insuperable political and commercial advantages over local people in Africa and the Americas.[101] This claim, although possessing some merit, overlooks the complexity of the situation, especially on the coasts of the continents, and when studied in detail is not as persuasive as it first appears. Although Europeans did make some conquests in both Africa and the Americas, it was not naval power that secured the conquests. Their failure to dominate local coastal commerce or overwhelm coastal societies, most pronounced in Africa but also the case in some parts of the Americas, means that we must amplify our estimation of the role played by these societies in the shaping of the Atlantic world. Domination of high-seas commerce is significant, to be sure, but perhaps not as significant as domination of the mainlands.

Naval encounters and Afro-European commerce. Europeans clearly hoped that their maritime abilities would give them military advantages that would result in large profits and perhaps conquests. They were prepared to take over territory and enslave people, and their actions in the Canary Islands bore witness to that desire. However much some visitors to the Canaries might have wanted to engage in peaceful trade, it was ultimately the slave raiders and conquerors who won out. Control of the seas allowed Europeans to land freely on the islands, resupply their forces when necessary, and concentrate large forces for their final battles - and thus maritime superiority could arguably have been the cause of their success.

The earliest sailors who reached the African coast in the fifteenth century naturally hoped to continue this tradition, as apparently did the Spanish sailors who began the conquest of the larger Caribbean islands in the late fifteenth and early sixteenth centuries. But in Africa at least, their confident approach was rebuffed. Unlike the Canarians, who possessed no boats at all, the West Africans had a well-developed specialized maritime culture that was fully capable of protecting its own waters.

One of the first expeditions to the Senegal River, led by Lançarote de Lagos in 1444, brutally seized the residents of several off-shore islands. The inhabitants, although they managed to inflict some casualties, had little other recourse than to try to flee to areas of difficult access. Other expeditions that followed did more or less the same, but it was not long before African naval forces were alerted to the new dangers, and the Portuguese ships began to meet strong and effective resistance. For example, in 1446 a ship under Nuno Tristão attempting to land an armed force in the Senegambian region was attacked by African vessels, and the Africans succeeded in killing nearly all the raiders. Likewise, in 1447 Valarte, a Danish sailor in Portuguese service, was killed along with most of his crew when local craft attacked him near the island of Gorée.[102]

Although African vessels were not designed for high-seas navigation, they were capable of repelling attacks on the coast. They were specialized craft, designed specifically for the navigational problems of the West African coast and the associated river systems. From the Angolan coast up to Senegal, African military and commercial craft tended to be built similarly. Generally, they were carved from single logs of tropical trees and only occasionally had their sides built up. Consequently, they tended to be long and very low in the water. They were almost always powered by oars or paddles and thus were manoeuverable independent of the wind. They drew little water and could operate on the coast and in rivers, creeks, and inland estuaries and lagoons. Craft that were designed to carry soldiers could, according to contemporary witnesses, carry from fifty to one hundred men.[103]

These specialized craft presented a small, fast, and difficult target for European weapons, and they carried substantial firepower in their archers and javelin men. However, they could not go far out to sea, and the larger, high-sided Portuguese vessels were difficult for them to storm. Alvise da Mosto, a Venetian trading in Africa with a Portuguese licence, records an encounter he had with an African flotilla in the Gambia in 1456. Da Mosto was mistaken, with justice, for being another raiding party from Portugal and was immediately attacked by seventeen large craft carrying about 150 armed men. They showered his ships with arrows as they approached, and da Mosto fired his artillery (bombards) at them, without, however, hitting anything. Although the attackers were temporarily stunned by this unexpected weapon, they nevertheless pressed the attack, at which point crossbow men in the upper rigging of the Venetian ship opened fire, inflicting some casualties. Again, although impressed by the weaponry, the Africans continued fighting until da Mosto eventually made it known he did not mean to attack them, and a cease-fire ensued.[104]

The Africans were unable, in most circumstances, to take a European ship by storm, and the Europeans had little success in their seaborne attacks on the mainland. As a result, the Europeans had to abandon the time-honoured tradition of trading and raiding and substitute a relationship based more or less completely on peaceful regulated trade. Da Mosto attempted this in his voyage, and the Portuguese Crown eventually dispatched Diogo Gomes in 1456 to negotiate treaties of peace and commerce with the African rulers of the coast.[105] As a result, Portugal established and maintained diplomatic relations with a host of African states. Already in 1494, Hieronymous Münzer, a German visitor to Lisbon, noted that the king sent frequent presents to the rulers of African states to win their favour, and as a result Portuguese could travel freely in Africa under the protection of these rulers.[106] These diplomatic and commercial relations easily replaced the raid-and-trade or raid-and-conquer patterns of other parts of the Atlantic, especially because the Portuguese soon discovered to their pleasure that there was also a well-developed commercial economy in Africa that maritime commerce could tap into without engaging in hostilities.

The presence of African naval craft along most of the coast seems to have deterred a recurrence of a raid-and-trade pattern by most subsequent Portuguese voyages to Africa, although, of course, the policy of refraining from attacks on Africans was not always followed. Newcomers or less established powers might still go for the short-term advantages of raiding, as did a Castilian expedition that was sent in 1475 to trade for gold on the Gold Coast but that also raided fairly extensively.[107] Likewise, early English voyages, in the late sixteenth century, especially those to volatile areas like Sierra Leone with its many states, also raided or at least let violence and seizure of people predominate over peaceful trade.[108] But such violence "spoiled" trade in an area, and most countries that had a long-term stake in trade took steps to prevent hostilities. Indeed, one of the earliest North American voyages, made from Boston in 1645, was involved in raiding, and the city officials actually returned the slaves seized by the ship with an apologetic note, probably to retain or regain good relations with their potential trade partners.[109]

Even the Portuguese Crown sometimes had to relearn these lessons. In 1535 the Portuguese attempted to conquer the Bissagos Islands, home of some of the most renowned sailors and raiders on the Guinea coast, but with disastrous results.[110] For the most part, however, such exceptions were sporadic, and peaceful trade became the rule all along the African coast, and given the large number of participants and the somewhat uncertain nature of virtually all long-distance trade in the pre-industrial period, it is not surprising that some breaches occurred.

Not only did African naval power make raiding difficult, it also allowed Africans to conduct trade with the Europeans on their own terms, collecting customs and other duties as they liked. For example, Afonso I, king of Kongo, seized a French ship and its crew in 1525 because it was trading illegally on his coast.[111] It was perhaps because of incidents such as this that João Afonso, a Portuguese sailor in French service, writing at about the same time, advised potential travellers from France to Kongo to take care to conduct trade properly, explaining that when a ship enters the Zaire, it should wait until the officials on shore send one of their boats and do nothing without royal permission from the king of Kongo.[112]

Portugal's one sustained military excursion into Atlantic Africa, the conquest of Angola, was the result of economic controversy rather than territorial aspirations. The colony was originally intended to be a commercial factory to regulate the trade from Ndongo and for four years functioned as such.[113] When a trade dispute led to war in 1579, the Portuguese position was saved only by the intervention of a Kongo army, and even though Kongo itself joined an anti-Portuguese coalition in 1591, Portugal had acquired a foothold and local allies sufficient to maintain itself.[114]

Naval conflict and conquest in the Americas. Although our purpose is principally to reveal the African role in shaping the Atlantic world, it is worth noting, at least briefly, that in some parts of the Americas European naval superiority was not particularly decisive. Most of the spectacular conquests by Europeans in America involved inland empires, in which naval power was relatively unimportant (with the possible well-known exception of the role played by Spanish brigantines in the siege of Tenochtitlan by Cortes).[115]

It was the Spanish failure in the Caribbean that is most dramatic, however. The Spanish did, of course, conquer (with considerable local help) the larger islands. But in some ways they simply forestalled their conquest by the militaristic inhabitants of the southern and eastern Caribbean. The Kulinago of the Lesser Antilles and the Carib and Arawak people of the mainland of Venezuela and the Guianas (often, though not always accurately, designated "Caribs" in Spanish documents)[116] not only proved capable of resisting Spanish attempts to attack their homes but managed to raid the Spanish possessions of the Caribbean throughout the sixteenth and seventeenth centuries. The people of the eastern Caribbean basin possessed sufficient naval technology (on African lines, composed of fairly small, manoeuvrable craft)[117] to defeat Spanish ships, for they did actually take ships on the high seas.[118] The French, English, and Dutch who eventually settled in the West Indies and the mainland were forced into first a co-dominion and then a long-lasting military struggle, which was really only decided by the superior numeric strength of the settlers.

Even in the mainland areas, the European conquest of the Americas was far from complete. Outside the central areas of Mexico and Peru there were many Native American peoples who resisted European incursions or yielded to them only slowly after long-standing military pressure. Among these one might mention the indigenous inhabitants of Florida, who not only defeated Ponce de Leon's celebrated attack on them but pursued his men out to sea in canoes, capturing several of his ships.[119] Even on land, Europeans were unable to easily defeat either the Araucanians of Chile[120] or the "Chichimecas" of Mexico,[121] each of whom resisted European settlers and conquerors with such success that settlement was slowed and undertaken either with their concurrence and assistance or only after long struggle. The Tupinámba and Tapuya of Brazil gave ground to Portuguese settlement very slowly, and by 1680 many regions in South America were either entirely in the hands of natives or were jointly ruled by Native Americans with European settlers in an uneasy co-dominion.[122]

One should not therefore imagine the Americas as simply lying securely under European sovereignty. In many places a long struggle for control ensued; in other places frontier conditions without secure European sovereignty continued for a long time. When Africans were brought to the Americas as slaves, they found this situation often worked to their advantage, and for them, the unsettled nature of the Americas provided the opportunity to escape, to play off the contending parties, or to use the potential for defection or escape to improve their situation.

By the middle of the sixteenth century, then, the Atlantic world had begun to take shape. European sailors, who had come to understand the winds and currents of the Atlantic, had established a system of navigation that bound Europe, Africa, and the Americas into a single system of commerce. European rulers and the more powerful of their subjects had come to see the system as being of great significance and holding potential for wealth and were well on their way to wresting political and economic control away from the pioneers who had created it. But if the powerful of Europe controlled the commerce of the seas, in Africa they were unable to dominate either the coast or coastal navigation, and in the Americas the subdued regions were surrounded by hostile and sometimes aggressive unconquered people. Thus the African role in the development of the Atlantic would not simply be a secondary one, on either side of the Atlantic. In Africa, it was they who would determine their commercial role, and in America they were often the most important group among the early colonists. Even when they played no particular political role, they often could capitalize on the incompleteness of European domination.

Notes

1. The paradox of west central Africa is that its isolation in commercial and intersocietal relations was not matched by a uniquely different culture. Indeed, west central Africa was in many ways culturally similar to parts of West Africa and even more so to East Africa, especially in language and basic world outlook. The most common explanation for the linguistic situation is the "Bantu migration" hypothesis, which connects all African languages north of South Africa and south of the equator into a single family. But the separation between the western Bantu and eastern Bantu sections is ancient, reflecting, perhaps, an ancient isolation. See the general discussion F. van Noten with Pierre de Maret and D. Cohen, "L'Afrique centrale," in UNESCO histoire générale de l'Afrique (Paris, 1980-), 2:673-93.

2. Pierre Chaunu, L'expansion européen du XIIIe à XVe siècles (Paris, 1969), pp. 54-8.

3. Gonzalo Fernández Oviedo y Valdez. Historia general y natural de las Indias, ed. Juan Pérez de Tudela Bueso, 5 vols. (Madrid, 1959), bk. 4, chap. 8.

4. Ambrósio Fernandes Brandão, Diálogos das Grandezas do Brasil, 2d integral ed., edited by José Antonio Gonçalves de Mello (Recife, 1968), dialogue 2, p. 44.

5. Raymond Mauny, Les navigations medievales sur les cotes sahariennes anterieures a la decouverte portugaise (1434) (Lisbon, 1960).

6. Abu 'Abd Allah Muhammad b. Muhammad al-Sharif al-Idrisi, "Nuzhat al-mushtaq fi iktiraq al-afaq" (1154), in Nehemia Levtzion and J.F.P. Hopkins, eds., Corpus of Early Arabic Sources for West African History (Cambridge, 1981), pp. 130-1.

7   'Ali b. Musa ibn Sa'id al-Maghribi, "Kitab Bast al-ard fi 'l-tul wa-'l-'ard" (ca. 1270), in ibid., pp. 190-1.

8   ibn Fadl Allah al-'Umari, "Masalik al-absar fi mamalik al-masar," in ibid., pp. 272-3.

9   See Jean Devisse with S. Labib, "Africa in Intercontinental Relations," in UNESCO General History of Africa 4:635-6.

10 al-Idrisi, "Nuzhat," pp. 106-7.

11 Ivan van Sertima, They Came before Columbus: The African Presence in Ancient America (New York, 197), pp. 37-109.

12 Aurelio Tio, "Relaciones iniciales Hispano-Araguacas," Boletin de la Academia Puertoriquena de la Historia 9 (1985): 33-61; van Sertima, Before Columbus, pp. 253-6, cites some classical references to suggest that a Isot canoe of Arawaks may have visited Gaul during Roman times.

13 Chaunu and Chaunu, Seville et l'Atlantique, vol. 7 and atlas attached; Mauro, Portugal et l'Atlantique, pp. 71-3.

14 Richard S. Dunn, Sugar and Slaves: The Rise of the Planter Class in the English West Indies, 1624-1713 (Chapel Hill, N.C., 1972), pp. 815.

15 Michal Tymowski, "Le Niger, voie de communication des grands etats du Soudan Occidental jusqu'a la findu XVIe siecle," Africana Bulletin 6 (1967): 73-98.

16 al-Idrisi, "Nuzhat," p. 110.

17 Philip Curtin, Economic Change in Precolonial Africa: Senegambia in the Era of the Slave Trade, 2 vols. (Madison, 1975), 1:278-86.

18 Ibid., 1:83-91.

19 E.g., Jean Fonteneau dit Alfonse de Saintogne [Joao Afonso], La cosmographie (1544), fols. 122v, 124 (the edition of Georges Musset [Paris, 1904] marks the original foliation); Martin Fernandez de Enciso, Suma de geographia q trata de todas las partidas & provincias del mundo . . . (Seville, 1519), p. 107 (original has no pagination, pagination given here written in pencil on the edition I consulted, Biblioteca Nacional de Lisboa, Reservados, 717 V). These tow accounts were probably based on the same material; see Paul E.H. Hair, "Some Minor Sources for Guinea, 1519-1559; Enciso and Alfonse/Fonteneau," History in Africa 3 (1976): 19-46, which gives a partial English translation and comparison.

20 See documents and analysis in Avelino Teixeira da Mota, "The Mande Trade in Coast da Mina according to Portuguese Documents until the Mid-sixteenth Century," paper presented at the Conference on Manding Studies, School of Oriental and African Studies, London, 1972.

21 E.g., ibn Sa'id, "Kitab Bast," pp. 184-5; al-'Umari, "Masalik al-absar," pp. 156-7. For the same ideas presented to early European travellers by West Africans themselves, see Diogo Gomes, "De prima inuentione Gujnee" (composed ca. 1490), in Valentim Fernandes, "Descrica da cepta e sua costa" (1507), in Antonio Baiao, ed., O manuscrito "Valentin Fernandes" (Lisbon, 1940), fols. 276v-7; Andre Donelha, Descricao da Serra Leoa e dos Rios de Guine do Capo Verde (1625) (modern ed. Avelino Teixeira da Mota, Leon Bourbon, and Paul Hair [Lisbon, 1977]), fols. 29v-30. Europeans often knew of the deep interior of West Africa from sources on the Niger, or near Benin, and sometimes oriented their geography by the river; see Alan F.C. Ryder, Benin and the Europeans, 1485-1897 (London, 1969), pp. 32-3, 126-34; for political units on the river, see John Thornton, "Traditions, Documents, and the Ife-Benin Relationship," History in Africa 15 (1988); 351-62.

22 Thornton, "Ife-Benin Relationship."

23 Antonio de Oliveira de Cadornega, Historia geral das guerras angolanas (1680-81) (modern ed. Jose Delgado and Matias da Cunha, 3 vols. [Lisbon, 1972]), 3:58-61 (on the Kwanza), 219 (with notices of the Kasai River and the first mention of the Lunda of central Africa.

24 Antonio Mendes to Jesuit Father General, 9 May 1563, MMA 2:499, 503.

25   Jean-Pierre Chauveau, "Une histoire maritime africaine est-elle possible? Historiographie et histoire de la navigation et de la peche africaines a la cote occidentale depuis le Xve siecle," *Cahiers d'etudes africaines* 36 (1986): 173-235.

26   Robin Law, "Trade and Politics behind the Slave Coast: The Lagoon Traffic and the Rise of Lagos, 1500-1800, "*Journal of African History 24* (1983): 321-48.

27   Biblioteca Provincial de Toledo, Colecion de MSS Bourbon-Lorenzana, MS. 244, Basilio de Zamora, "Cosmografia o descripcion del mundo" (1675), fol. 53.

28   For an early account of the Orinoco, see "Memoria y relacion que hizo Martin Lopez de su viaje desde la Margarita hasta el Rio Coretin" (1550), in Antonio Arellano Moreno, *Relaciones geograficas de Venezuela* (Caracas, 1964), pp. 45-7. The significance of Amazonian and Orinoco societies is highlighted by the work of Anna Curtenius Roosevelt; see among others, "Chiefdoms in the Amazon and Orinoco," in Robert Drennan and Carlos Uribe, eds., *Chiefdoms in the Americas* (Washington, D.C., 1987), pp. 153-84.

29   The strength and commerce of the Mississippi societies is well documented archeologically. For an attempt to link this with the Atlantic and European activities, see the paper presented by William Swaggerty at the American Historical Association, 102d Annual Meeting, Washington, D.C., 28 December 1987.

30   van Sertima, *Before Columbus*, pp. 52-3, though here emphasizing the possibility of standing up to long-distance travel as well. See also Stewart C. Malloy, "Traditional African Watercraft: A New Look," in Ivan van Sertima, ed., *Blacks in Science: Ancient and Modern* (New Brunswick and London, 1983), pp. 163-76, which makes the same point but still shows clearly the focus on riverine and coastal navigation.

31   Desmond Nicholson, "Precolumbian Seafaring Capabilities in the Lesser Antilles," *Proceedings of the International Congress for Study of Pre-Columbian Culture of the Lesser Antilles 6* (Pointe a Pitre, 1976), pp. 98-105.

32   Pierre Chaunu, *Expansion europeen*, pp. 92-3.

33   For an illuminating discussion of the boundaries of the Mediterranean, see Braudel, *Mediterranean*, 1:168-230. For the significance of the Mediterranean connection to the northern seas, see idem, *Civilization and Capitalism, Fifteenth to Eighteenth Centuries*, 3 vols., trans. Sian Reynolds (New York, 1982-4), 3:92-173.

34   See the discussion in Charles de la Ronciere, *La decouverte de l'Afrique au moyen age: Cartographes et explorateurs*, 3 vols. (Cairo, 1925-6), 2:3-4. Much of the material on Malocello's activity comes from a now lost genealogy of 1453 cited in a polemical work of 1632 to counter claims made by the eventual conquerors, the family of Jean de Bethencourt, and must be viewed with suspicion. On the other hand, the map of Angelino Dulcert, drawn in 1339, clearly shows the Genoese in possession of the island that still bears the Malocello's name. According to the genealogy, Malocello ruled the island for twenty years before being expelled by the local habitants (ibid., p. 3, n. 2, and documents quoted).

35   See the summary of an extensive literature in Pierre Chaunu, *Expansion europeen*, pp. 273-308.

36   Summarized in ibid., pp. 233-40.

37   Summarized in ibid., pp. 243-5.

38   Gomes Eannes de Zurara, *Cronica dos feitos de Guine*, chap. 8. Thee are many editions, the best being that of Torquado de Sousa Soares (2 vols.; Lisbon, 1978). The French translation (Leon Bourbon, *Chronique de Guinee* [Dakar, 1960]) contains a valuable introduction to the history and discussion of textual problems. An English translation, from a less thorough edition and with dated notes, is by C.R. Beazley and E. Prestage (2 vols.; London, 1896-9).

39   Ramon Llull, "Libre d'Evast e d'Aloma e de Blanquerna" (ca. 1283-5), chap. 84 (ed. Joan Pons I Marques), in Ramon Llull, *Obres essencials*, 2 vols. (Barcelona, 1957), 1:241-2. On Llull's geopolitical philosophy, see Armand Llinares, *Raymond Lulle, philosophe de l'action* (Paris, 1963).

40   Recorded in Jacopo Filippo Foresti da Bergamo, "Supplementum Chronicarum" (1483), from notes taken by Giovanni da Carignano at the time the mission passed through Genoa. Published (from the 1492 edition) in Youssouf Kamal, *Monumenta Cartographica Africae et Egypti* (Leiden, 1926-53), vol. 4, fol. 1139. A translation (from the 1483 edition) and discussion by R.A. Skelton appears in O.G.S. Crawford, *Ethiopian Itineraries*, circa 1400-1524 (Cambridge, 1958), pp. 212-15. As a result of this visit, the geographer Giovanni da Carignano concluded that Ethiopia was the home of the legendary "Prester John," more or less permanently displacing an Asian location. See Enrico Cerulli, "Giovanni de Carignano e la cartografia dei paesi a Sud dell'Egitto agli inizi del secolo XIV," *Atti del XIV Congresso geografico italiano* (Bologna, 1949), p. 507.

41   See a discussion in the light of Catalan activity and plans in the eastern Mediterranean in Lluis Nicolau d'Olwer, *L'expansio de Catalunya en la Mediterrania oriental*, 3d ed. (Barcelona, 1974), pp. 171-5.

42   Mordechai Abir, *Ethiopia and the Red Sea: The Rise and Decline of the Solomonic Dynasty and Muslim-European Rivalry in the Region* (London, 1980), pp. 19-40.

43   De la Ronciere, *Decouverte* 1:50-1.

44   See Jaime Cortesao, *Os descobrimentos portugueses*, 2 vols. (Lisbon, 1960), 1:304-5.

45   "Libro del conscimiento de todas las tierras y senorios que son por el mundo y de las senales y armas que han cada tierra y senorio," in Kamal, *Monumenta* 4: fol. 1259-9v (note that folios are numbered consecutively from volume to volume). This includes an English translation.

46   Timothy Garrad, "Myth and Metrology: Trans Saharan Gold Trade," *Journal of African History 23* (1982): 443-61.

47 For example, the early descriptions of Abu al-'Qasim ibn Hawqal, "Kitab Surat al-ard," in Levtzion and Hopkins, *Corpus*, p. 49; Abu 'Ubayd 'Abd Allah b. 'Abd al-'Aziz al-Bakri, "Kitab al-masalik wa-'l-mamalik," in ibid., pp. 77-85; and al-Idrisi, "Nuzhat," in ibid., pp. 110-11.

48 These sources are often reflected in the maps of the era; see the discussion in de la Ronciere, *Decouverte* 1:121-41. Most of these maps are reproduced in Kamal, *Monumenta*. For a detailed discussion of the sources of the Malloracan group, see Yoro K. Fall, *L'Afrique a la naissance de la cartographie moderne: Les cartes majorquines, XIVe-XVe siecles* (Paris, 1982), pp. 55-120. The problem of "Palolus" has been discussed in detail in Susan K. MacIntosh, " A Reconstruction of Wangara (Palolus, Island of Gold)," *Journal of African History* 22 (1981): 145-58. This gold was sufficiently common in Barcelona that a public ordinance of that city in 1271 simply refers to gold as "gold of Palolus" (de la Ronciere, Decouverte 1:114).

49 Kamal, *Monumenta* 4: fol. 1370.

50 "Libro del conscimiento" in ibid., fol. 1258v.

51 *Monumenta* 4: fol. 1235.

52 An excellent recent survey of Mediterranean slavery at this time is Jacques Heers, *Esclaves et domestiques dans le monde mediterranean* (Paris, 1981), esp. pp. 23-64, on the long Mediterranean background of slave raiding and its Atlantic extensions.

53 Chronicle attributed to Giovanni Boccaccio, "De Canaria et insulla reliquis, ultra Ispaniam, in occeano nouiter repertis," *Monumenta Henricina*, 14 vols. (Lisbon, 1960-74), 1:202-6, on the 1341 expedition; Afonso IV to Clement VI, 12 February 1345, *Monumenta Henricina* 1: 230.

54 Charles Verlinden, *L'esclavage dans l'Europe medieval: 1. Peninsule iberique-france* (Bruges, 1955), pp. 628.

55 On Malocello and the Aragonese, see Charles Verlinden, "Lanzarotto Malocello et la decouverte portugaise des Canaries," *Revue belge de philologie et d'histoire* (1958): 1173-90; on the French attempt, Clement VI, "Tue deuotionis sinceritas," 15 November 1344, *Monumenta Henricina* 1:207-14; and on Castillian tactics, B. Bonnet Reveron, "Las expediciones a las Canarias en el siglo XIV," *Revista de Indias* 6 (1945): 215-18.

56 Pierre Boutier and Jean le Verrier, *Le Canarien* (modern ed. Elias Serra Rafuls and A. Cloranescu, 2 vols. [Teneriffe, 1959]) vol. 1, chap. 87.

57 Described in detail in Fernandez-Armesto, *The Canaries after the Conquest* (London, 1982).

58 See the legends to various maps in Kamal, *Monumenta* 4: fol. 1235.

59 Boutier, *Le Canarien*, vol. 1, chap. 00.

60 Recounted in Zurara, *Cronica*, chap. 79; see additional details in de Barros, *Decadas de Asia* I, bk. 1, chap. 12; de Barros was a sixteenth-century writer who saw documents on this expedition in the archives of Portugal. On the general situation, see Florentino Perez Embid, *Los descubrimientos en el Atlantico y la rivalidad castellano-portuguesa hasta el Tratado de Tordesillas* (Seville, 1948).

61 See Luiz Suarez Fernandez, *Relaciones entre Portugal y Castilla en la epoca del Infante D. Henrique* (Valladolid, 1960), pp. 244-72.

62 Zurara, *Cronica*, chap. 8.

63 *Ibid.*, chap. 11.

64 *Ibid.*, chaps. 8-16.

65 Several Portuguese historians, such as Duarte Leite and Vitorino Magalhaes-Godinho, have stressed the short-range plans and immediate profits of expansion, although their specific arguments differ from the one presented here; see the historiographical discussion in Chaunu, *Expansion europeen*, pp. 243-51.

66 The exact timing of these trips is difficult to ascertain; a good survey and new argumentation are found in Joaquim Verissimo Serrao, *Historia de Portugal*, (Lisbon, 1977), 2:164-70.

67 Cf. Orlando Ribeiro, "Primordios da ocupacao das ilhas de Cabo Verde," in *Aspectos e problemas da expansao portuguesa* (Lisbon, 1962), pp. 130-8. See also, on the general use of the Cape Verdes as a base, T. Bentley Duncan, *Atlantic Islands: Madeira, the Azores and the Cape Verdes in Seventeenth-Century Commerce and Navigation* (Chicago and London, 1972), pp. 166-9.

68 An early description of the pepper trade can be found in Eustace de la Fosse, "Voyage a la cote occidentale d'Afrique," 1479-80, MMA2 1:473-4. Pepper was bieng exported from the Gambia region and northern Sierra Leone by the mid-1450s (Magalhaes-Godinho, *Descobrimentos* 1:476-8.

69 The terms are known only from their citation in de Barros, *Decadas de Asia* I, bk. 2, chap. 2.

70 See the discussion in Cortesao, *Os descobrimentos portugueses*, 2:416.

71 If one accepts Rui de Siqueira, in 1472, as the first European visitor; see Ryder, *Benin and the Europeans*, pp. 30-2.

72 Martin Behaim, *Liber Cronicarum cum figuris et ymaginibus ab inica mundi usa nunc temporis*, 1497, fol. 326v, MMA 1:30.

73 de Barros, *Decadas de Asia*, bk. 3, chap. 3.

74 Rui de Pina, "Chronica del Rei Dom Joao II," chap. 57, MMA 1:32-5; de Barros, *Decadas de Asia* I, bk. 3, chap. 3. On Kongo's export trade see Duarte Pacheco Pereira, *Esmeraldo de Situ Orbis* (ca. 1506), bk. 2, chap. 2 (modern variorum ed., Augusto Epiphanio da Silva Dias [Lisbon, 1905; reprint, 1975]), p. 134; and legend on the Cantion Atlas (1502), reproduced in Armando Cortesao and Avelino Teixeira da Mota, eds., *Portvgalliae monumenta cartographica*, 6 vols. (Lisbon, 1960), 1:12.

75 It appear on Dulcert's map or 1339, as well as the Atlas Mediceo of 13521 (Kamal, *Monumenta* 4: fols. 1222 and 1248).

76 A date favoured, with good reason, by Duncan, *Atlantic Islands*, pp. 7-8.

77 See Damiao Peres, *Historia dos descobrimentos*, 2d ed. (Coimbra, 1960), pp. 78-87, citing a map of Gabriel Valseca dated 1439.

78 Duncan, *Atlantic Islands*, p. 12. Colonization at the "seven newly discovered islands" was begun in

1439 (Authorization of Infante Henrique, 2 July 1439, *Monumenta* Henricina 6:334).

79 Alvise da Mosto, "Mondo Novo" (title from one of four recensions) (modern ed. Tullia Gasparrini-Leporace, *Le navigazione atlantiche de Alvise da Mosto* [Milan, 1966], p. 17.

80 Zurara, *Cronica*, chap. 5, lists wood, wax, honey, dyestuffs, and other products. Several documents of the fifteenth century also refer to water-powered saws, evidently for cutting the wood.

81 *Ibid.*, chap. 83, from circa 1446; similar observations can be found in da Mosto, "Mondo Novo," pp. 14-15.

82 Order of Infante Henrique, 6 July 1439, *Monumenta Henricina*, vol. 6.

83 Zurara, *Cronica*, chap. 83.

84 Donation to D. Fernando, 29 October 1462, MMA2 1:423-4.

85 Letter of privilege to Sao Tome settlers, 24 September 1485, MMA 1:50-1.

86 Alberto Iria, *O Algarve e a Ilha da Madeira no seculo XV* (Lisbon, 1974).

87 An argument cogently made by Sidney Greenfield, "Madeira and the Beginnings of New World Sugar Cane Cultivation and Plantation Slavery: A Study in Institution Building," *Annals of the New York Academy of Sciences*, 292 (1977): 541-3.

88 See document cited in ibid., p. 550, n. 34, thanking them for their participation in the attack, dated 1425.

89 Zurara, *Cronica*, chap. 83.

90 da Mosto, "Mondo Novo" (ed. Gasparrini-Leporace), p. 16.

91 Magalhaes-Godinho, *Descobrimentos* 1:282-6.

92 da Mosto, "Mondo Novo" (ed. Gasparrini-Leporace), p. 17

93 *Ibid.*, p. 22; Greenfield, "Madeira."

94 Magalhaes-Godinho, *Descobrimentos* 1:426-50.

95 Donation to Fernao Dulmo, 3 March 1486, in Jose Ramos Coelho, ed., *Alguns documentos do Archivo Nacional da Torre do Tombo acerca das navagacoes e conquistas portuguezas* (Lisbon, 1892), pp. 58-9.

96 See the remarks of Samuel Elliot Morrison, *Journals and Other Documents on the Life of Admiral Christopher Columbus* (New York,1963), pp. 26-30; idem, *Admiral of the Ocean Sea: A Life of Christopher Columbus* (Boston, 1942), pp. 138-45.

97 de Barros, *Decadas de Asia* I, bk. 3, chap. 4.

98 Rumeu de Armas, *Espana en el Africa Atlantida* (Madrid, 1956).

99 Avelino Teixeira da Mota, "As rotas maritimas portuguesas no Atlantico de meados do seculo XV ao penultimo quartal do seculo XVI," *Do Tempo e da Historia* 3 (1970): 13-33.

100 See the important work of K.N. Chaudhuri, *Trade and Civilization in the Indian Ocean: An Economic History from the Rise of Islam to 1750* (London, 1985), pp. 138-59.

101 This discussion has been summarized and examined in Chauveau, "Histoire maritime africaine," pp. 176-90.

102 Zurara, *Cronica*, chaps. 24-5, 30-6, 86, and 94.

103 On West African boats and especially their military characteristics, see Chauveau, "Histoire maritime africaine," pp. 191-7.

104 da Mosto, "Mondo Novo" (ed. Gasparrini-Leporace), p. 82-4.

105 Gomes related his mission in "De prima inuentione Gujnee," in Fernandes, "Descrica," fols. 272-83 (this is the foliation of the original text).

106 Hieronymous Munzer, "Itinerrium," 23 November 1494, MMA² 1:247-8. Some of these diplomats are known: Records exist for missions from Kongo, Benin, Labida, and Jolof, all to Lisbon.

107 Alonso Fernandez de Palencia, *Cronica de Enrique IV*, 5 vols. (Madrid, 1904-9), 4:127.

108 For example, Cavendish's attack in August 1586 and Cumberland's in October 1586, of which various accounts have been gathered and edited in P.E.H. Hair, "Early European Sources for Sierra Leone," *Africana Research Bulletin* 13 (1974): 71-2, 76-7.

109 Richard Saltonstall to Massachusetts General Court, 7 October 1645, in Robert Moody, ed., *The Saltonstall Papers, 1607-1815*, 2 vols. (Boston, 1972-4), 1:138-9; Boston Council meeting minutes, sessions of 1 and 14 October 1645, 4 September, 1 October, and 4 November 1646, in Nathaniel B. Shurtleff, ed., *Records of the Governor and Company of the Massachusetts Bay in New England*, 5 vols. (Boston, 1853-4; reprint, New York, 1968), 2:84, 129, 136, and 168.

110 See the retrospective account of Andre Alvares de Almada, "Tratado breve dos Rios da Guine," 1594, MMA² 3:319; and contemporary documentation. Donation to Infante Luis, 27 March 1532 and 5 September 1534, MMA² 2:226-9 and 263-5.

111 Alvara of Afonso I to Officials of Sao Tome, 27 December 1525, MMA 1:455-6.

112 Jean Alfonse de Saintogne, *Les voyages advantureux* (Paris, 1559), fol. 55. Although published in 1559, this text was probably written around 1530 - Afonso died, in any case, around 1544.

113 See the 1571 contract between Paulo Dias de Novais and the Crown, which stipulated commercial relations, although it did allow Dias de Novais to conquer a section of the barren southern coast, then outside of Ndongo's jurisdiction (Carta de Doacao a Paulo Dias de Novais, 19 September 1571, MMA 3:36-51.

114 Detailed in Beatrix Heintze, "Die portugiesische Besiedlungs-und Wirtschaftpolitik in Angola, 1570-1607," *Aufsatze zur portugiesischen Kulturgeschichte* 17 (1981-2): 200-19.

115 There are several surveys of the period, the best, perhaps being Carl Sauer, *The Early Spanish Main* (Berkeley and Los Angeles, 1966); and Troy Floyd, *The Columbus Dynasty in the Caribbean, 1492-1526* (Albuquerque, 1973).

116 On the complexities of the ethnological, historical, and archaeological situation in the southern Caribbean basin (including the Guianas and the Orinoco basin), see Marc de Civrieux, "Los Caribes y la conquista de la Guyana espanola," *Montalban* 5 (1976): 875-1021.

117 For an account of naval war between Carib canoes and European vessels that is equivalent in some ways to da Mosto's account for Africa, see the eyewitness account of Jean Baptiste du Terte, *Histoire*

generale des Antilles habitees par les Francois, 4 vols. (Paris, 1667), 1:508-12.

118 For a good survey of Spanish relations with the inhabitants of Dominica and for Carib military prowess in general, see Joseph Barome, "Spain and Dominica, 1493-1647," *Caribbean Quarterly* 12 (1966): 30-47.

119 Antonio Herrera y Tordesillas, *Historia general de los hechos de los castellanos* . . . (1724) (several modern eds.), decade 7, bk. 7, chaps. 5, 8-10.

120 Louis de Armond, "Frontier Warfare in Colonial Chile," *Pacific Historical Review* 23 (1954): 125-32; Robert C. Padden, "Cultural Change and Military Resistance in Araucanian Chile, 1550-1730," *Southwestern Journal of Anthropology* (1957): 103-21.

121 See the admirable discussion in Phillip Powell, *Soldiers, Indians and Silver: The Northward Advance of New Spain, 1550-1600* (Berkeley, 1952).

122 John Hemming, *Red Gold: The Conquest of the Brazilian Indians, 1500-1760* (Cambridge, Mass. 1978), is the best survey; for other regions, such as Paraguay, see James Lockhart and Stuart Schwartz, *Early Latin America: A History of Colonial Spanish America and Brazil* (Cambridge, 1983), pp. 253-304.

SECTION TWO

The Indigenous Peoples: Conquest, Resistance and Representation

European social design of Atlantic modernity was centred around notions of military conquest, slavery, and cultural domination. The control of people was not differentiated from the possession of lands and other economic resources. The people who occupied this space now called the Caribbean encountered the European, therefore, as carrier of mass destructive weapons, new viruses, cultural ideas, and economic principles. In many ways the formulation of these attitudes and opinions preceded the contact, and suggest a measure of inevitability in the social outcome.

Caribbean slave societies were established in space occupied and formerly under the control of a heterogeneous, but well-entrenched native people. All European colonists arriving in the region, following the Columbus mission of 1492, considered it necessary to use their more developed military technology in an effort to subjugate the autochthon as a prerequisite to successful colonization. The indigenous Caribbean people, as Beckles and Thomas show, fought wars of resistance, but were ultimately defeated and reduced to a range of servile relations. Many were enslaved in the way Africans

were, and others forced into dishonourable socio-economic conditions of marginalization and servitude. The results of these developments were extremely tragic demographically.

In this section, Henige revisits the quantitative dimensions of the 'genocidal' consequences of colonization, while Thompson examines the complex commercial, political and social relations established between Amerindians and Europeans.

Boucher's focus is slightly different and has been informed by the fact that a fundamental aspect of European colonization was the 'othering' of the indigenous peoples as justification for atrocities committed in the name of 'civilization'. He explains the abysmally negative images which the Spaniards constructed about the island 'Caribs' who, despite evidence to the contrary, persisted in the European accounts as 'savages' and 'cannibals'. Dominant Spanish images received extensive attention in France and England and had some impact on North-West European activities in the Eastern Caribbean. Such misrepresentations had a lot to do with the Kalinagos' fierce resistance to colonization.

6

On the Contact Population of Hispaniola: History as Higher Mathematics

DAVID HENIGE*

But is it certain that antiquity was so much more populous, as it is pretended?[1]

The most dramatic recent development in Latin American historical demography has been the changing interpretation of the size of the population of the New World at the arrival of the Europeans.[2] Figures as much as ten times greater than those most commonly advanced only a few decades ago are widely accepted today. In this trend the work of Sherburne Cook and Woodrow Borah, particularly for central Mexico, has been exceptionally influential, as shown by the incorporation of their postulated figures into works of a general nature.[3] Willingness to accept extremely high population figures (75 million or more) for the aboriginal New World appears to have reached a point where proponents of middle-range figures (35–75 million) often seem to be functioning as devil's advocates, while those favoring even lower figures are voices crying in the proverbial wilderness. Why such a consensus is developing is not at all clear, but it would seem to be attributable in part to the tenacity of the advocates of a high population and in part to bedazzlement by their extensive use of quantitative tools. In any case, it is not principally the result of any signal increase in data directly and unambiguously supporting arguments for a large precontact population.

Since confidence in these high estimates (or in any estimates) can be no greater than confidence in the means by which they were generated, I propose to discuss in this paper certain aspects of the methods used by proponents of high population estimates. 'Method', in this essay, will include the handling of sources; the assumptions implicit in their statistical procedures (rather, I hasten to add, than the procedures themselves); their explicit and implicit argumentation; and problems of *petitio principii*. Let me emphasize that I will confine myself here to an examination of the attempt by Cook and Borah to estimate the population of Hispaniola in 1492.[4] However, since the authors have brought some of the methods they used in studying central Mexico to their essay on Hispaniola, it is possible that some of the comments offered here may be of use to those attempting to evaluate their more important Mexican work. Angel Rosenblat has covered some of the same ground, but with differing purposes and emphases.[5]

Briefly, Cook and Borah conclude that about 8 million Indians were probably living on Hispaniola when Columbus landed there; that this population was halved during the next four years; that it was reduced to some 30,000 Indians by 1514; and that there were almost no Indians alive by the middle of the sixteenth century.[6] The last two points are well documented and enter into the present discussion only marginally. The earlier figures (for 1492 and 1496) result partly from a logarithmic projection based on a series of later figures, and partly from a series of assumptions whose validity it is one of the purposes of this paper to test.

From all appearances the Cook and Borah

*The author is African Studies Bibliographer at the University of Wisconsin, Madison. He would like to thank John Smail and Mary Braun for their help and comments on an earlier draft of this paper.

Hispanic American Historical Review, Vol. 58, No. 2, 1978, pp. 217–37.

microstudy has thus far been received with approval, even enthusiasm, and its conclusions accepted as reasonable and valid.[7] This ready acceptance is rather puzzling, particularly in view of the fact that previous modern estimates of Hispaniola's contact population ranged between 60,000 and 600,000.[8] It seems that many reviewers, while granting that the essay is provocative, have been persuaded by the authors' handling of their sources and their imaginative statistical procedures. It is to the first of these aspects of their argument that I now turn.

Every truth has two sides; it is well to look at both before we commit ourselves to either.[9]

Borah has recently asserted that his and Cook's work on Hispaniola was characterized by 'careful textual criticism' using the methods developed by the Bollandists and others.[10] Given the importance of a very few sources to any discussion of Hispaniola's aboriginal population, this assertion deserves to be tested rigorously. In their discussion Cook and Borah concentrate on three groups of sources: the reports of Columbus recorded in the journal of his first voyage; the figures adduced by Bartolomé de las Casas in some of his major works; and the evidence for a repartimiento of Indians reportedly undertaken in or about 1496. I would like to examine each of these in turn, discussing both the nature of their evidence and the ways in which the authors used these data.

Columbus' Testimony

Quite properly Cook and Borah begin by citing several passages from Columbus' journal for December 1492 and January 1493, since this is the only available eyewitness account of Hispaniola at that time. However, there are several problems in using this material. Columbus saw and described only a portion of the northern coast, and offered occasional observations of conditions in the near hinterland. Then, too, the only extant manuscript copy of the journal is in the handwriting of Las Casas, who was himself working from a second-hand copy.[11] Inevitably this introduces imponderables regarding the accuracy of the transcription. Finally, there is the crucial matter of Columbus' well-known and long-documented penchant for the metaphor and hyperbole, an appreciation of which is fundamental to any precise interpretation of his 'initial impressions'.[12] Cook and Borah discuss none of these problems.

Turning to their appraisal of Columbus' data,

the analysis consists of little more than selecting those passages in which Columbus rhapsodized on the beauty and populousness of the island, transcribing his original language, and juxtaposing their own translations which are sometimes debatable in themselves.[13] In addition to Columbus' assertions about the charms of Hispaniola, which were usually expressed in grandiloquent but opaque language, his journal contains many passages suggesting in more concrete and realistic terms the existence of a sparse population in many parts of the island which fell within his purview. Apparently few people lived along the coast, perhaps from fear of Carib attacks. But even efforts to locate towns and large numbers of people in the interior were usually unfruitful.[14] The authors do not mention these passages.

Viewed in toto, then, Columbus hardly offers a coherent and unambiguous picture of the island's population, although on balance it seems to me to suggest a relatively small population. Nor is it very difficult to account for Columbus' exaggerations. He had hoped to reach the Far East, the land of 'the Great Khan'. He believed he had done so when compiling his journal (and perhaps until his death) and was convinced that Hispaniola was actually Marco Polo's Cipangu.[15] In these circumstances it was all too easy to fall victim to, as one writer has aptly phrased it, 'psychological illusions', which justified and sustained this hope.[16] So it was that, after sailing along the coast for some 75 miles, Columbus was already believing that Hispaniola was larger than England when it was only half its size.[17] He was also able, after seeing by his own estimation fewer than 10,000 Indians, to predict that the remainder of the island contained twice as many people as Portugal.[18]

In sum, Cook and Borah's use of Columbus' testimony to support their contention of a large and 'dense' population can be faulted on two grounds: the selection and analysis of only those passages which might support that view, and the failure to come to grips in any way with the probable validity of that testimony. By culling this source so discriminatingly, the authors cultivate an impression which they seek to reinforce by arguing that there was 'unanimity' as to the existence of a dense population. This claim — and its corollary that 'none of the earliest testimony reported an exiguous population' — is both incorrect and misleading.[19] And this would be true even if every statement of Columbus they cite, however extravagant on its face, could be taken seriously, even literally.[20]

The Estimates of Las Casas

As the only sources to offer comprehensive estimates of early Indian demographic decline under Spanish rule, the works of Bartolomé de las Casas inevitably serve as points of departure for modern investigators seeking to do the same in whole or part. For Cook and Borah, though, Las Casas' figures for Hispaniola serve as constant justification for their own arguments. Where others have seen these figures as inflated, the authors regard them as internally consistent and uncharacteristically conservative.

It need hardly be emphasized that the writings of Las Casas, insofar as they dealt with Spanish treatment of the Indians, were relentlessly and unabashedly polemical. As it relates to the size of the Indian population of Hispaniola, his work can be shown to be curiously dichotomous as well. In order to document and buttress his claims of harsh treatment — scarcely deniable in any case — Las Casas brought to bear a formidable arsenal of numbers, particularly in his *Brevísima relación de la destrucción de las Indias*, representing his view of the enormity of this treatment.[21] Some of his estimates of Indian population appeared in his major works, *Brevísima relación, Apologética historia*, and *Historia de las Indias*, but even more can be found in his many letters, memorials, and lesser tracts. Since Cook and Borah overlooked these materials, I have arranged them in chronological order to illustrate the point I wish to make about Las Casas' values:

1516 'se han disminuidos de un cuento [million] de ánimas que había en la isla Española...'[22]

1518 'un cuento y cient mil ánimas que había en la isla Española...'[23]

1531 'el cuento e cient mill *de toda esta isla* [Española]...'[24]

1535 '...y mataron un cuento y cient mill ánimas *que yo ví en ella por mis ojos*.'[25]

1542 '...que habiendo en la isla Española sobre tres cuentos de ánimas *que vimos*.'[26]

1542 '...y es la cuenta que han dado de tres cuentos de ánimas que había en sola la isla Española.'[27]

1543 '...perdidos que están de los muchos cuentos de ánimas *que vimos por nuestros ojos* en la isla Española, San Juan y Cuba.'[28]

1555 '...la grande isla Española donde...sobre tres cuentos de ánimas.'[29]

1552/1560 'Yo creo cierto que [Española] pasaban de tres y de cuatro cuentos los que hallamos vivos.'[30]

The *Historia de las Indias* was begun in 1527 but not completed until the early 1560s and hence cannot be fitted into this schema. In it Las Casas presented three more estimates of this population. In one of these he accepted the figure of 1.1 million while his other estimates were about 3 million.[31]

Viewed in this way, a clear pattern emerges from Las Casas' various attempts to estimate the Indian population on Hispaniola. Obviously, sometime between 1535 and 1542 he tripled his early estimate, without ever accounting plausibly for the change. Thus Las Casas' figures, long regarded as prima facie unlikely, are even less reasonable when viewed *en ensemble*. For not only are his two groups of figures widely different, but he repeatedly contradicted himself in advancing his ocular 'proofs'.[32]

Why this abrupt change? We can only speculate. From all indications the figure of 1.1 million regularly offered by Las Casas in his first twenty years of writing sprang from information obtained from the Archbishop of Seville and from Bernardo de Santo Domingo, who apparently prepared a legal opinion for the Hieronymites on their arrival in 1517.[33] These estimates in turn referred to reports of a repartimiento allegedly carried out by Bartolomé Colón.[34] Before 1535, Las Casas always presented this figure without qualification and we must presume that he accepted it as accurate. Later, though, he would argue, rather unconvincingly, that this count *must* have included only parts of the island, despite his earlier explicit statement to the contrary.[35]

Influenced by his reading of certain classical authors' estimates of population in antiquity, Las Casas came to believe that Hispaniola was capable of supporting 'a much greater number' even than the 3 million he was by then attributing to it.[36] Perhaps, too, the passions aroused during the compilation of *Brevísima relación* made it easier for him to accept this reasoning. Or perhaps it was merely the result of becoming further removed in time and space from Hispaniola.[37] But whatever the stimuli may have been, the disconcerting fact of his abrupt and unaccounted change remains.

It has generally been held that his population estimates speak more to the depth of Las Casas' outrage than to his skills as a demographer; that is, it is impossible to distinguish Las Casas the historian from Las Casas the Defender of the Indians. In contrast, by arguing that Las Casas was consistent in his citations and that he actually erred on the low side in his estimates for

Hispaniola, Cook and Borah create a symbiosis in which certain of Las Casas' data are used to support their own high figures, which in turn are used to exonerate him from charges of pardonable exaggeration. It is important to try to appreciate Las Casas' purposes in offering his figures, to explore as far as possible his sources for them, and to relate the various arguments he adduced to an analytical and temporal framework. Ignoring the vast interpretative literature on Las Casas as well as much of his own work, Cook and Borah fail to do any of these.

The Repartimiento of ca. 1496

Two allotments of Indians loom large in the authors' calculations. One of them, carried out in 1514, is not at issue here.[38] The other, which, following Carl Sauer, they date to 1496, is not well documented, even though they are able to cite several references to it, all dating from 20–50 years later.

In constructing their population decline curve, Cook and Borah first mention three estimates made between 1519 and the mid-1540s. All three suggest that there had been 2 million Indians when Columbus arrived.[39] One of these sources suggested that this figure resulted from an actual census while the others presented the figure without comment. The authors then proceed to the information in Peter Martyr who, in his De Orbe Novo, spoke of reports of a population of 1,200,000.[40] Martyr was exceptionally well informed, but there are risks in citing him for details about the condition of Indian society on the arrival of the Spanish. Martyr was a charter member of the school of historical and philosophical thought which idealized the native cultures of the New World, saw the Indians as having existed in a kind of golden age, and contrasted this idyll with the depravity and corruption of Europe.[41] In fact, the chapter in which Martyr cited this figure is, perhaps not inappropriately, principally a catalog of wonders and marvels.[42] All things considered, his attribution of any particular population does not induce easy acceptance.

Cook and Borah next cite several other sources, each hovering around a figure of 1 million Indians. They concentrate on four of these and the relevant information in them is schematized in Table 1.[43] Some of these sources mentioned a count by Columbus or his brother Bartolomé; some merely alleged that the Indians had been counted; and others maintained only that about 1 million Indians had been living on the island when it was discovered.[44] Later I will discuss the uses to which Cook and Borah put these data; for the moment I propose to mention a few interpretative problems in accepting them.

The authors give pride of place to the figure of 1,130,000 Indians mentioned by the licenciado, Alonso de Zuazo.[45] First, on the basis of their own problematic translation, they argue that Zuazo had access to documentary evidence for his figure.[46] Then, too, they are impressed with 'the exactness' of Zuazo's number, in much the same way as biblical scholars of long ago sought to justify belief in antediluvian longevity because of the precise life-spans attributed to many of the biblical patriarchs. We do not really know from where his information came. It could easily have resulted from inferences of his own based on rumor, oral testimony or incomplete data.[47]

In fact the tenor of most of the allusions to a reported count (and Cook and Borah are not unaware of this) is one of hearsay. Obviously there was a popular belief in such a repartimiento. But rumor does not constitute evidence of any event — only of a subsequent belief in it. Cook and Borah recognize the ambiguous and contradictory nature of later accounts and the variety of the numbers cited and attempt to make a virtue of this deficiency by asserting that this very disparity is 'very strong evidence' of such a count and that rounding off is common to oral transmission.[48] While admitting the force of the latter argument, students of oral tradition and oral testimony would, I am sure, be chagrined at this example of the desire to know fabricating its own rationale. In effect, the authors

Table 1: Early Estimates of Aboriginal Population of Hispaniola

Source/Date	Figure cited	Unit described	Area encompassed
Anonymous (1516–17)	1,000,000	Souls	Entire island
Dominicans (1519)**	1,100,000	Persons	Not stated
Bernardo de Santo Domingo (1517)**	1,100,000	Vecinos	Entire island
Alonso de Zuazo (1518)	1,130,000	Indians	Entire island

**Those sources marked (**) referred to a count as well as an allotment. The two should not be thought to be necessarily synonymous.

like exact figures *because* they are exact; and they like inexact figures as well, *because* they are inexact!

What evidence is there against a repartimiento in or around 1496? We cannot reasonably expect to find sources from the time explicitly denying its occurrence, so we must argue by indirection. While any *argumentum e silentio* is at worst foolish and at best inconclusive, I propose a modest exercise of it here.[49] There were two occasions which are reasonably well documented and in which mention of any count would have been appropriate, though by no means necessary. When Nicolás de Ovando was sent to govern Hispaniola in 1501 he was issued a long set of instructions, several of which referred to relations with the Indians. This would seem to have been a good opportunity to allude to any formal arrangements that may already have existed. In the instructions the Indians were regarded as tributary (they were, of course, never thought of in any other way), but there was no mention of an earlier allotment. In fact, one of Ovando's charges was to institutionalize Spanish–Indian relations.[50]

In 1516, the Hieronymites went to Hispaniola to inquire into ways and means of alleviating the maltreatment and depopulation of the Indians there. A commission established soon after their arrival elicited testimony from several long-time settlers. The verbatim record of the testimony has survived in the form of a series of standard questions and the replies to them.[51] Several of the witnesses had resided in Hispaniola continuously since 1494 and some of these mentioned previous allotments in passing, but always referred only to those carried out under Ovando and later.[52] Apparently they knew of no earlier repartimiento, referring most often to Ovando's because it established a precedent in their minds.

All in all, the documentary evidence for a repartimiento under Columbus is far from convincing; it can be argued either way. We can reach only a slightly more satisfying conclusion by asking whether the Spanish had the capability to undertake such an allotment. The accounts of Las Casas and others picture Bartolomé Colón scurrying about the island trying to tamp down incipient Spanish disaffection on the one hand and growing Indian hostility on the other.[53] A chain of small outposts had been established to secure control of the auriferous areas but, despite the defeat of the cacique Caonabo and his allies the previous year, the Spanish were in a position only to try to establish their authority in most of the island through terrorism, since they could no longer

rely on friendly caciques for support. Cook and Borah follow Sauer in choosing 1496 as the year of the count and Sauer's choice was based merely on eliminating all other times during the regime of Bartolomé.[54] However, the chroniclers' record of Spanish activities does not lead one to accept effective Spanish control much beyond the immediate area of their main settlement at Isabela. However much they may have wished to do so, they were simply not yet able to enforce a large-scale formal allotment of Indians.[55]

The Evidence of Other Early Sources

In several cases the same sources which mention a million or more Indians when speaking abstractly about Hispaniola leave a very different impression when describing specific events. In addition to imputing an extremely dense population to the small island of Saona (which, perhaps not coincidentally, he thought his own), Michele de Cuneo described the capture of 1,600 Indians. Five hundred of these dispatched to Spain, some were distributed among the settlers, and the remaining 400 were allowed to return to their homes. However, the latter fled to the mountains, causing Cuneo to lament that 'from [then] on scarcely any [slaves] will be had.'[56] In other words, the dispersal of 1,600 Indians apparently resulted in the virtual depopulation of the area around Isabela.

For the years after 1494, we have several references to the size of Indian armies which from time to time attempted to stem the Spanish tide. By far the largest of these figures was Columbus' claim to have defeated an army of 100,000 Indians at La Vega Real in 1495.[57] This Indian force was a coalition of several major caciques, but Columbus' figures were, as usual, certainly much inflated. In this case the exaggeration was part of an attempt to claim that the victory resulted from divine intervention.[58] Cuneo, writing about the time of the battle, reckoned that Caonabo, the major Indian leader in the battle, could field 50,000 men, but when the Spanish moved to occupy the Cibao, where he ruled, they were opposed by an army of no more than 5,000 men.[59] Later Guarionex and several other caciques made a concerted attempt to resist Spanish encroachment, hoping, we are told, to raise an army of 15,000. This mobilization never occurred because the Spanish learned of the preparations, so we cannot know if even this small number of men could have been assembled.[60] Yet, the Spaniards regarded Caonabo and Guarionex as the most powerful caciques on the island.[61] All these figures, even those cited by Columbus for La Vega Real, are remarkably modest under the circumstances hypothesized by Cook and Borah.[62] Certainly they do not suggest an island teeming with 5 or 6 million people.[63]

In sum, it is difficult to share Cook and Borah's enthusiasm for their sources. The documentary evidence they marshal does not provide the consensus on which they so meticulously insist, and they have failed to weigh critically even those data which at first glance might seem to support their argument. Despite chiding Rosenblat for failing to attempt 'the massive critical examination of sources customary in medieval and ancient European studies', Cook and Borah resolutely ignore their own advice.[64] The choices they make are not random, but systematic — designed always to support arguments for a high population. Sound scholarly procedure, it seems to me, requires that research be approached with questions in hand rather than answers in mind and that the more the data seem to fit a hypothesis, the more they demand the closest scrutiny before they can be accepted. But Cook and Borah seem not to agree with this.[65]

I began this discussion by referring to Borah's belief that he and Cook had adopted the methods of the Bollandists in their source analysis. For comparison, let me close by citing the opinion of an early Bollandist leader regarding that exegetical method. He emphasized that it was predicated on 'the duty to explain their view concerning the degree of veracity and the circumspection of the witnesses on whose testimony they support their preference . . . and no one should imagine that the obligation of providing original texts eases the burden. [Rather] it occasions additional studies and work, obliged as they are to collate minutely several manuscripts . . . and there is no place for adroit reticences and oversights.'[66]

When I use a word it means just what I choose it to mean — neither more nor less.[67]

Leaving the subject of source credibility temporarily aside, I intend now to concentrate on method. Having found the information they needed in the sources they used, Cook and Borah proceed to give precision to ambiguity, providing numbers where they had been lacking and offering new numbers in place of earlier estimates. Their method involves developing a population curve for the documented period and then projecting it backwards to 1492. There are three crucial points on this curve: reports of a vestigial population in the 1540s; the repartimiento of 1514 for which figures survive; and the reported repartimiento of 1496. Here we can grant that by the 1540s the Indians were nearly extinct, and that the count of 1514 might have represented as many as 30,000 Indians (even though only about 23,000 were actually recorded).[68] For the years 1508–10, the authors postulate a decline from about 92,000 to 66,000. These figures are modest enough but they are uniquely theirs, and they represent an increase of about 50 per cent above those cited in the sources.

This augmentative aptitude is most clearly manifested in their discussion of the reported 1496 count. Remember that the citations used by Cook and Borah ranged from less than 1 million to 2 million, but clustered around the 1,000,000–1,200,000 level. Table 1 shows that three of the four major sources specified that about 1 million human beings were involved, and three of them stated explicitly that their figures encompassed the entire island. It is at this point that the authors do engage in questioning their sources and conclude that the figures are much too low to indicate the total population. As a result 'persons' and 'Indians' become 'human units', enabling them to argue that this count included only 'able-bodied adults of 14 and above' on the grounds that in later usage the term 'indio' came to have this connotation among others.[69]

Once accepting this assumption, the rest of the argument flows swiftly and easily. Relying on Sauer's conclusion that 'a scant half' of Hispaniola was then under Spanish control, Cook and Borah double Zuazo's figures and attempt to convince the reader that to do so is in reality a conservative procedure. At this point, then, they argue, there were actually about 2,250,000 able-bodied adults on Hispaniola. The remainder of the population is calculated at 40 per cent, yielding a total of 3,770,000, as 'the most probable single figure with which to operate'.[70] It is the figure they employ to infer the size of the population four years previously.

A towering edifice constructed entirely of non-load-bearing 'possible to probable' assumptions may seem risky to the occupants of the top floor. Cook and Borah's 'most probable' figure can be no more likely than the product of the probability of each inference. At this point, in any event, they have reached the limit of the numerical sources; beyond 1496, they are left with the vague observations of Columbus. Undismayed, they look to mathematics in the hope that where historical evidence fails, statistical procedures will not.

They begin by attempting to eliminate any awkward imponderables (ecological constraints, epidemiology, warfare, for example) by boldly arguing that population decline may be 'a logarithmic function of time', and support this startling suggestion by asserting that such a decline in the early sixteenth century 'conforms entirely [sic] to our knowledge' for that period.[71] Having closed the circle of their argumentation in this fashion, they find it easy to project their population curve backwards — a procedure which elicits a population figure of about 8 million for 1492.

Cook and Borah are well aware that this extraordinarily large figure requires a net decline of over 20 per cent per year between mid-1493 and mid-1496 (their chosen parameters). They *do not hesitate, however, to try to explain it.* Ignoring the rugged terrain of much of the island, they characterize Hispaniola as 'predominantly low-lying tropical coast' capable of supporting dense populations.[72] In modern times, though, it is estimated that only about one-third of Haiti and one-half of the Dominican Republic is arable.[73] The authors rely, of necessity, on the capacity of the agricultural resources of Hispaniola and the agricultural sophistication of the Indians and speak of 'unusually favorable food resources', including maize, cassava, fish, and local fauna.[74] Inevitably this brings us to the matter of the explicatory powers of the 'carrying capacity' argument. Carrying capacity is, of course, an optimal concept — what *could* be if all constituent factors operated optimally. Sauer emphasized the nutritive value of the food crops native to Hispaniola, their quick and easy harvesting, and the advanced agricultural techniques of the Taino.[75] Yet, despite the development of the *conuco* field systems, they had apparently just begun to discover means of fertilizing the soil artificially, and their practices in this regard were still characterized more by magic than method when the Spanish arrived.[76]

Even more important, we know very little about the ethnography of the Hispaniola Indians. Yet, in order to know the efficiency of an agricultural system (that is, actual production measured against hypothesized carrying capacity), we need to know a great deal about those social and cultural factors such as marriage patterns, age of marriage, kinship relationships, and land tenure practices which help to determine the growth and density of a particular population.[77] None of the little we know about

these aspects of fifteenth-century Taino society leads us to believe that they put any emphasis on building up population. As a ceiling concept, carrying capacity can directly support an argument against a large population, but it is not useful in supporting an argument for such a population.[78]

Sauer also characterized the Taino as living in 'peace and amity', but from all indications Carib attacks on the Arawak inhabitants of the Greater Antilles were at their height during the fifteenth century.[79] At the same time, Carib occupation of the Lesser Antilles prevented fresh immigration from northern South America, hitherto the major source of Arawak expansion.[80] It is possible, then, that the population of Hispaniola actually may have been declining during the period just before the arrival of the Spanish.

Having argued, though, that Hispaniola could (and did) support a huge contact population, Cook and Borah are left with the task of explaining an equally large decline in so short a time. Unlike Sauer, who emphasized societal disruption with resulting social and psychological malaise, they place primary emphasis, in a process of a priori reasoning, on epidemics which, they argue, must have ravaged the island almost from the day Columbus first anchored.[81] An early epidemiological catastrophe would indeed provide both explication of the decline and some justification for arguing large pre-contact populations, but the complete silence of the sources with regard to epidemics of any kind before the introduction of smallpox in 1518–19 somewhat vitiates the case for it.[82]

Could the death of more than 1 million Indians each year have escaped the notice of the Spanish who were, by Cook and Borah's own argument, in effective control ('occupation') of half the island during the mid-1490s? Could they, in their preoccupation with securing adequate manpower, have failed to mention the effects of disease and taken some sort of precautions against them? Would Columbus' host Guacanacarí have maintained his hospitable attitude in the face of such tragedy? Despite the authors' suggestions to the contrary, the most reasonable answer to these questions is no.

It is unfortunate that the very sources in whose reliability Cook and Borah repose such faith have failed them in accounting for such a decline. While it is bold to argue that something did not happen, it is even more so in the absence of any mention of that occurrence. That so overwhelming a decimation of a huge population could have happened within the purview of sources which resolutely ignored it is difficult to accept.

Although it would be unfair to argue that the arrival of the Spaniards could not have had immediate epidemiological effects, the only disease specifically identified in our sources is 'the French disease' or syphilis.[83] However communicable syphilis was, it was seldom immediately lethal — especially, we are told by Las Casas, among the Indians of Hispaniola where it had long been endemic.[84] In short, the early arrival of epidemics needs to be argued on the basis of some sort of evidence. To produce the specter of epidemiological disaster merely as a deus ex machina to explain the otherwise unaccountable results of a chosen statistical procedure simply fails to persuade.

He had been for Eight Years upon a Project to extract Sun-Beams out of Cucumbers.[85]

Historians like to believe that they approach the record of the past with due regard for the data and free of inhibiting predispositions. Cook and Borah have, I think, given evidence in the essay under review how very difficult it is to subordinate theory to evidence. But if one cannot agree with their methods or their conclusions, one may still be grateful to them for prompting us to ask questions about just what historians are, or ought to be. The authors frame two of the several alternatives clearly: should we approach a problem such as determining the size of the contact population of Hispaniola by a thorough and judicious scrutiny of all the evidence we can muster, or should we use conventional evidence only selectively and for illustration and rely on, say, mathematical techniques for our conclusions? Put another way, should we think of processes such as population decline as responding to a great number of variables — disease patterns, ecological changes, and cross-cultural impact — or should we consider them as completely susceptible to statistical analysis? Can a chapter of human experience really be 'a logarithmic function of time'?

An interest in numbers and a knowledge of statistical method can be useful tools in historical reconstruction and explanation, but they should never become an infatuation which blinds the ardent suitor to the defects of his inamorata. Historians who will become quantifiers must realize what statisticians already know — that, although sophistication of technique might temporarily disguise the weaknesses of the data, it can never really transcend them. All too often numbers have become

will o' the wisps, in the frantic search for which the hunter seems to feel obliged to shed one layer of caution after another in hopes of becoming as protean as his elusive quarry.

If there is a correlation between density of population and level of culture, however defined, then it would undeniably be useful to gain some fairly precise understanding of the magnitude of the populations of various parts of the New World at the time of contact. Nor should the meagerness of the data by itself deter investigation. But the investigation must involve carefully structured hypotheses which, if not demonstrably true, at least represent the most reasonable interpretation of the available evidence. Or, as is to be greatly preferred from the historian's point of view, it must produce new evidence.

The intent of this paper has not been to offer yet another estimate of the population of Hispaniola in 1492, nor even to comment extensively on the many different estimates which have already been propounded. On the contrary, I would argue that it is futile to offer any numerical estimates at all on the basis of the evidence now before us. It can readily be granted and, indeed, hardly doubted, that whatever the population of Hispaniola and the rest of the New World was in 1492, there was a tragically precipitate decline during the first several decades of Spanish rule which in some cases led to extinction. But for the moment it is not possible to measure the rate of this decline for the earliest period of colonial rule, as is convincingly demonstrated by the attempt of Cook and Borah to do just that.

Notes

1. David Hume, *On the Populousness of Ancient Nations*.
2. For the extent of the literature see William M. Denevan (ed.), *Native Population of the Americas in 1492* (Madison, 1976), pp. 299–331, and Henry F. Dobyns, *Native American Historical Demography* (Bloomington, 1976).
3. See, for example, John H. Parry, *The Spanish Seaborne Empire* (New York, 1966), pp. 215–16; Thomas H. Hollingsworth, *Historical Demography* (Ithaca, NY, 1969), pp. 135–36; Ralph Davis, *The Rise of the Atlantic Economies* (London, 1973), p. 54; William H. McNeill, *Plagues and People* (Garden City, 1976), p. 203.
4. Sherburne F. Cook and Woodrow Borah, 'The Aboriginal Population of Hispaniola', *Essays in Population History*, 2 vols (Berkeley, 1971–74), I, 376–410.
5. Angel Rosenblat, 'The Population of Hispaniola at the Time of Columbus' in Denevan (ed.), *Native Population*, pp. 43–66. This is a translation of parts of his *La población de América en 1492: Viejos y neuvos cálculos* (México, 1967) and, although there is an addendum, Rosenblat does not comment specifically on Cook and Borah's essay.

6. Cook and Borah suggest a range from 4,070,000 to 14,560,000 but, not surprisingly, the figure most often cited in reviews is their mid-point figure of 8,000,000 and this figure, if any, is that most likely to be subsumed into the literature.

7. See the following reviews of the first volume of *Essays: Historical Methods Newsletter*, no. 5 (June 1972), 120–22 [Sims]; *American Historical Review*, 78 (April 1973), 512–13 [Cooper]; *Ibero-Americana Pragensia*, 6 (1972) 204 [Vebr]; *Ethnohistory*, 20 (Summer 1973), 292–96 [Dobyns]; *HAHR*, 53 (February 1973), 109–12 [Mörner]; *American Studies*, 5 (November 1973), 1809–810 [Crawford]; *Journal of Latin American Studies*, 5 (November 1973), 289–90 [Denevan]; *Rivista Storica Italiana*, 85 (September 1973), 795–98 [Carmagnani]; *Historia Mexicana*, No. 98 (October–December 1975), 316–18 [Gerhard]; *Geographical Review*, 66 (January 1976), 106–08 [Veblen]; *Annals of the Association of American Geographers*, 66 (September 1976), 464–96 [Robinson/Licate]. Only Mörner and Denevan express doubts about Cook and Borah's conclusions.

8. Charles Verlinden, 'La population de l'Amérique précolumbienne: Une question de méthode' in *Méthodologie de l'historie et des sciences humaines: Mélanges en honneur de Fernand Braudel* (Paris, 1973), pp. 453–62 [60,000]; Rosenblat, 'Population', pp. 43–66 [100,000]; Manuel A. Amiama, 'La población de Santo Domingo', *Clío*, no. 115 (1959), 118–19, 132–33 [100,000]; Alejandro Lipschutz, 'La despoblación de los indios después de la conquista', *América Indígena*, 26 (July 1966), 238–40 [100,000–500,000]; Samuel E. Morison, *Admiral of the Ocean Sea* (Boston, 1948), p. 393 [300,000]; Efrén Córdova, 'La encomienda y la desaparición de los indios en las Antillas mayores', *Caribbean Studies*, 8 (October 1968), 23 [500,000]; Frank Moya Pons, *Española en el siglo XVI, 1493-1520* (Santiago, 1971), pp. 66–7 [600,000]. Moya Pons' estimate seems to result from a misreading of Las Casas' account of a population of 60,000 in 1508. Las Casas did not state that this represented 'a tenth part' of the contact population, but that it showed that during the preceding seven or eight years, the Indian population had declined 'more than nine-tenths'. Las Casas, *Historia de las Indias*, II, xiv, in his *Obras escogidas* (hereafter cited as *OE*), 5 vols. (Madrid, 1957–58), II, 43. Others, like Carol O. Sauer, *The Early Spanish Main* (Berkeley, 1966, p. 66, and Pierre Chaunu, 'Las Casas et la première crise structurelle de la colonization espagnole', *Revue Historique*, 299 (January–March 1963), 76–77, accept the repartimiento count of *ca.* 1496 discussed below but do not offer their own estimates.

9. Aesop, *Fables*, 'The Mule'.

10. Borah, 'The Historical Demography of Aboriginal and Colonial America: An Attempt at Perspective', in Denevan (ed.), *Native Population*, p. 33.

11. Morison, 'Texts and Translations of the Journal of Columbus' First Voyage', *HAHR*, 19 (August 1939), 237–38.

12. Cook and Borah, 'Aboriginal Population', p. 376.

13. For example the authors translate 'mayor que' in the phrase 'toda la gente de aquella isla, que estimaba ya por mayor que Inglaterra' as 'more populous', *ibid.*, p. 378. Cf. Cristoforo Colombo, *Diário de Colón* (Madrid, 1968), p. 128. It is just possible that Columbus meant this, but it is more likely that he was comparing the size of 'isla' with 'Inglaterra' rather than its population — the position taken by all previous translators of the journal. Cook and Borah offer no explanation for their innovation.

14. Colombo, *Diário*, pp. 100–17. Rosenblat, 'Population', pp. 59–61, discusses these entries at some length. I mention them only to emphasize the unduly selective nature of Cook and Borah's examples.

15. See, for instance, Colombo, *Diário*, pp. 103, 129–130, 136–37. For a discussion of the importance of the chimera of the Great Khan to Columbus, see Antonio Ballesteros y Baretta, *Cristóbal Colón y el descubrimiento de América*, 2 vols (Buenos Aires, 1945), I, 83–91, and Henry Wagner, 'Marco Polo's Narrative Becomes Propaganda to Inspire Columbus', *Imago Mundi* [London], 6 (1949), 3–13. More generally see Wilcomb E. Washburn, 'The Meaning of "Discovery" in the Fifteenth and Sixteenth Centuries', *American Historical Review*, 68 (October 1962), 1–21.

16. Leonardo Olschki, 'What Columbus Saw on Landing in the West Indies', *Proceedings of the American Philosophical Society*, 84 (July 1941), 633–59, discusses this and related points. Later Hispaniola grew in Columbus' mind until he remembered it as comparable in size to Spain. Columbus to Luís de Santagel, February 1493, in Morison (ed.), *Journals and Other Documents on the Life and Voyages of Christopher Columbus* (New York, 1963), p. 185. Columbus' attitudes toward numbers of Amerindians is illustrated by the transformation in his accounts of an effort to locate large populations on Cuba in 1492. Two men were sent out for this purpose and, according to Columbus' journal, they reported that they had found only a single large village of about 1,000 inhabitants and several small clusters of houses. Colombo, *Diário*, p. 61. A few months later, when writing to Santangel to plead his case for royal support, he stated that these scouts had found 'an infinite number of small villages and people without number'. Morison (ed.), *Journals*, p. 182.

17. Throughout his first voyage Columbus overstated sailing distances, sometimes by two or three times. Among others see Morison, 'The Route of Columbus Along the North Coast of Haiti and the Site of Navidad', *Transactions of the American Philosophical Society*, 31 (December 1940), 239–44 *passim*.

18. Colombo, *Diário*, p. 138.

19. Cook and Borah, 'Aboriginal Population', p. 380. In this assessment they include the testimony of Michele de Cuneo discussed below.

20. As late as 1502, Columbus thought that Hispaniola was 'Tarsis, Scythia, Ophir, Ophaz, and Cipango' rolled into one — an impressive triumph of credulity over disappointment. Columbus to Alexander VI, [Febuary], 1502, in Colombo, trans. by Rinaldo Caddeo, *Relazioni di viaggio e lettere di Cristoforo Colombo, 1493-1506* (Milan, 1941), pp. 244–45.

21. On this see André Saint-Lu, 'Acerca de algunas "contradicciones" lascasianas' in *Estudios sobre Fray Bartolomé de las Casas* (Seville, 1974), pp. 1–3; Charles Bayle, 'Valor histórico de la *Destrucción de las Indias*', *Razón y Fé*, no. 147 (April 1953), 379–91.

22. Memorial of Las Casas to Cardinal Ximénez de Cisneros, in *Colección de documentos inéditos relativos al descubrimiento, conquista y organización de las antiguas posesiones españolas* de América y Oceania (hereafter cited as *CDI*), 42 vols (Madrid, 1864–84, I, 225.

23. Petition to Charles V, *ibid.*, VII, 106.

24. Letter to the Council of the Indies in Las Casas, *Opúsculos, cartas y memoriales, OE*, V, 48, with emphasis added.

25. Letter to Charles V, October 15, 1535, Benno M. Biermann, 'Zwei Briefen von Fray Bartolomé de las Casas, 1534–1535', *Archivum Fratrum Praedicatorum* 4 (1934), 213, with emphasis added.

26. *Brevísima relación de la destrucción de las Indias* (Buenos Aires, 1973), p. 25, with emphasis added. Though published in 1552, the original draft of this work was presented in 1542.

27. *Entre los remedios*, likewise written in 1542, but published only ten years later. Las Casas, *Opúsculos*, p. 75.

28. Las Casas and Fray Rodrigo de Andrada or [Ladrada] to Council of the Indies, 1543. Lewis Hanke, 'Un festón de documentos lascasianos', *Revista Cubana*, 16 (July–December 1941), 169, with emphasis added.

29. Las Casas to Fray Bartolomé Carranza de Miranda, August 1555. *CDI*, VII, 302, Elsewhere in this letter Las Casas claimed that the contact population had been greater than that of 'all Spain' and that each of the five major *cacicazgos* on Hispaniola was larger than Portugal. *Ibid.*, 297, 302.

30. *Apologética historia*, xx, *OE*, III, 65.

31. *Historia de las Indias*, iii, 94, *OE*, II, 397; ii, 18, *OE*, II, 51–52; iii, 19, *OE*, II, 217.

32. Cf. Sancho Panza's observation: 'He that told me the story said that it was so certain and true that when I told it to others I could affirm and swear that I had seen it all myself.'

33. *Historia de las Indias*, iii, 94, *OE*, II, 396–97. Las Casas resided in Hispaniola for many years and may have had other, unidentified, sources for his earlier estimates.

34. We know of this *parecer* only from Las Casas' allusions to it. Another *parecer* prepared at the same time and for the same purpose, and signed by nine other Dominican friars, mentioned neither a repartimiento nor a population estimate. 'Parcecer de los religiosos de Santo Domingo sobre los indios', *CDI*, XI, 211–15. For the repartimiento see below.

35. *Historia de las Indias*, ii, 18, *OE*, II, 51–52.

36. *Apologética historia*, xx, *OE*, III, 65.

37. Note that as Las Casas' numbers increased, so too did his explicit accusation of direct Spanish responsibility for this population decline.

38. For the repartimiento of 1514 see Cook and Borah, 'Aboriginal Population', pp. 380–85, and the sources cited there. In addition see Emilio Rodríguez Demorizi, *Los Domínicos y las encomiendas de indios de la Isla Española* (Santo Domingo, 1971), pp. 73–248.

39. Cook and Borah, 'Aboriginal Population', p. 387.

40. *Ibid.* Pietro Martire de Anghiera, *Décadas del Nuevo Mundo* (ed.) by Edmundo o'Gorman, 2 vols (México, 1964), I, 363. This part of Martyr's work was published in 1516. His principal informants for Hispaniola seem to have been Columbus and Andrés de Morales, cited in Sauer, *Early Spanish Main*, pp. 41–42.

41. This aspect of Martyr is discussed by María Olmedillas de Péreiras, *Pedro Mártir de Angleria y la mentalidad exotística* (Madrid, 1974), and Alberto Salas, 'Pedro Mártir y Oviedo ante el hombre y las culturas americanas', *Imago Mundi* [Buenos Aires], No. 1 (December 1953), 16–25. More generally, John B. Lynch, 'Apocalyptic, Utopian, and Aesthetic Conceptions of Amerindian Culture in the Sixteenth Century', *Comparative Literature Studies*, 4:3 (1967), 363–70.

42. Anghiera, *Décadas*, I, 359–68.

43. To their list add the letter of Pedro de Córdova, the Dominican Vice Provincial, to the Spanish King, May 28, 1517, *CDI*, XI, 217. Córdova spoke of 'more than a million' Indians 'destroyed or dead' but did not relate this figure to any count. It seems more likely that he was referring to a cumulative total.

44. Cook and Borah, 'Aboriginal Population', pp. 388–91.

45. Zuazo, Santo Domingo, to Guillaume de Croy, Comte de Chièvres [Xev(b)res], January 22, 1518, *CDI*, I, 310.

46. Zuazo wrote: 'Digo que a lo que se alcanza de los re-

partimientos pasados' which Cook and Borah translate as 'I say that according to what may be found in the records of past allotments of Indians for service'. 'Aboriginal Population', p. 388, whereas a more reasonable rendering would be: 'I say that from what may be gleaned from past allotments.' As it happens, they follow this with a series of qualifications that in effect swallow the original statement but the aftertaste remains — that Zuazo's statement is certain evidence that records of a Columbian repartimiento existed in his time.

47. An even more exact figure was cited in the middle of the seventeenth century when Juan Melgarejo Ponce de León stated that there had been 1,006,000 Indians when Columbus 'occupied' Hispaniola. Rodríguez Demorizi, (ed.), 'Relaciones históricas de Santo Domingo,' *Boletín del Archivo General de la Nación* [Santo Domingo], No. 20–21 (January–April. 1942), 117. Ponce de León had been governor of Hispaniola and presumably would have had access to any records. Why, then, the discrepancy, if Zuazo was citing the same records?

48. Cook and Borah, 'Aboriginal Population'. p. 393.

49. Rosenblat, 'Population', pp. 47–55, presents his views on the quality of the evidence for this repartimiento.

50. Instructions to Ovando, September 16, 1501, *CDI*, XXXI, 13–25. Nor did the instructions to Bobadilla in 1499 mention an allotment, but this is less surprising since his mission was to settle disputes among the Spanish. J. Marino Inchaústegui Cabral, *Francisco de Bobadilla* (Madrid, 1964), pp. 505–11.

51. Rodríguez Demorizi, *Dominicos*, pp. 273–354 passim.

52. *Ibid.*, pp. 276–78, 293–96, 330–32. Manuel Giménez Fernández, *Bartolomé de las Casas*, 2 vols (Seville, 1953–60), I, 309–18, discusses what is known about these informants.

53. Las Casas, *Historia de las Indias*, i, 113–17, *OE*, I, 306–18. For discussions of Bartolomé Colón's administration see Gustavo Mejía Ricart, *Historia de Santo Domingo*, 8 vols (Ciudad Trujillo, 1949–56), III, 179–207, and Troy S. Floyd, *The Columbus Dynasty in the Caribbean, 1492–1526* (Albuquerque, 1973), pp. 33–38.

54. Sauer, *Early Spanish Main*, p. 66.

55. It seems inexplicable that none of the chroniclers mentioned a repartimiento in their accounts of Spanish activities during this period. Given Las Casas' close attention to all Spanish mistreatment of the Indians, including the encomienda system, and that his father was a settler on the island at the time, this omission (if omission it was), is strange.

56. Cuneo's letter, October 15/28, 1495, in Morison, *Journals*, p. 226. See also Cuneo, 'De novitatibus insularum Oceani Hesperii repertorum a Don Christoforo Colombo Genuensi', *Revista de Historia* [Caracas], 4 (January 1965), 54. Cuneo also mentioned the short lifespan of the Indians, declaring that he had seen none he thought older than fifty. *Ibid.*, p. 61.

57. Ferdinand Colón, *Vida del Almirante Don Cristóbal Colón* (Buenos Aires, 1947), pp. 180–81.

58. For the miraculous aspects of the tradition of the battle see Apolinar Tejera, 'La cruz del Santo Cerro y la batalla de la Vega Real', *Boletín del Archivo General de la nación*, no. 40–41 (May–August 1945), 101–119.

59. Cuneo, 'De novitatibus', p. 48; Anghiera, *Décadas*, I, 148.

60. *Ibid.*, p. 155; Gonzalo Fernández de Oviedo y Valdés, *Historia general y natural de las Indias*, 14 vols (Madrid, 1851–55), II, 60; Antonio de Herrera y Tordesillas, *Historia general de los hechos de los castellanos en las*

islas y tierrafirme del mar océano, 17 vols (Madrid, 1934–57), I, 314.

61. Tejera, 'Caonabo y Manicaotex', *Boletín del Archivo General de la Nación*, No. 52-53 (May–August 1947), 103-22 for early views of Caonabo.

62. In conditions of full mobilization it is usually reckoned that one-quarter to one-fifth of the populace bears arms. Stanislas Andreski, *Military Organization and Society* (Berkeley, 1968), pp. 33-74; Hollingsworth, *Historical Demography*, pp. 227-32. For New World applications see Cook and Lesley B. Simpson, *The Population of Central Mexico in the Sixteenth Century* (Berkeley, 1948), pp. 26-30; Robert C. Eidt, 'Aboriginal Chibcha Settlement in Colombia', *Annals of the Association of American Geographers*, 49 (December 1959), 379-91; Juan Friede, *Los Quimbayas bajo la dominiación española* (Bogotá, 1963), pp. 20-21; Horacio A. Difrieri, 'Población indígena y colonial' in *La Argentina: Suma de geografía*, 9 vols (Buenos Aires, 1958-63), VII, 25-28.

63. That is, a figure midway between 8 million in 1492 and 4 million in 1496. Peter Martyr mentioned a famine about this time which he thought had resulted in the death of 50,000 men. Anghiera, *Décadas*, I, 145.

64. Cook and Borah, 'Aboriginal Population', p. 376.

65. From time to time the authors have spoken of the need for such scrutiny but have not put principle into practice, at least for Hispaniola.

66. *Acta Sanctorum, Martii*, 3 vols (Antwerp, 1668), I, xx, quoted in H. Delehaye, *L'oeuvre des Bollandistes, 1615-1915* (Brussels, 1920), pp. 100-01.

67. Humpty-Dumpty in *Through the Looking-Glass*.

68. Cook and Borah, 'Aboriginal Population', pp. 397-99, 401. The authors attribute repartimiento counts to 1508, 1509, and 1510, but one of the witnesses at the Hieronymite inquiry specified that there had been but three allotments during his fifteen years (1502-17) on Hispaniola. Rodriguez Demorizi, *Dominicos*, p. 282. There may have been counts without allotments, but this would have been a wasteful and unlikely procedure.

69. Cook and Borah, 'Aboriginal Population', p. 394.

70. *Ibid.*, p. 397.

71. *Ibid.*, p. 403.

72. Cook and Borah, *Essays*, I, xii; and 'Aboriginal Population', p. 408.

73. Marc A. Holly, *Agriculture in Haiti* (New York, 1955), p. 31; Gérard Pierre-Charles, 'Haiti: Esencia y realidad del desarrollo', *Revista Mexicana de Sociología*, 31 (July-September 1969), 595-97; *Area Handbook for the Dominican Republic*, 2d edn (Washington, 1973),

pp. 7-8, 12-14, 180. Each of these estimates assumes a wider practice of irrigation than seems to have existed among the Taino.

74. Cook and Borah, 'Aboriginal Population', p. 408.

75. Sauer, *Early Spanish Rule*, pp. 51-59, 68-69.

76. Adolfo de Hostos, 'Plant Fertilization by Magic in the Taino Area of the Greater Antilles', *Caribbean Studies*, 5 (April 1965), pp. 3-5. William G. Sturtevant, 'Taino Agriculture' in Johannes Wilbert (ed.), *The Evolution of Horticultural Systems in Native South America* (Caracas, 1961), pp. 69-82, demonstrates that some early estimates of Taino field size were impossibly large.

77. Direct knowledge of Taino ethnography on Hispaniola derives almost entirely from the account of Taino cosmology and religious practices by Fr. Ramón Pane in Ferdinand Colón's life of his father. See Colón, *Vida*, pp. 183-208, and Edward G. Bourne, 'Columbus, Ramón Pane, and the Beginnings of American Anthropology', *Proceedings of the American Antiquarian Society*, 17 (April 1908), 310-48. For Taino culture generally see Sven Lovén, *Origins of Tainan Culture* (Göteborg, 1935).

78. Recent discussions of the problems in determining and applying carrying capacity are Brain Hayden, 'The Carrying Capacity Dilemma: An Alternative Approach' in Alan C. Swendlund (ed.), *Population Studies in Archaeology and Biological Anthropology: A Symposium* (Washington, 1975), pp. 11-12, and Stephen B. Brush, 'The Concept of Carrying Capacity for Systems of Shifting Agriculture', *American Anthropologist*, 77 (December 1975), pp. 799-811.

79. Sauer, *Early Spanish Main*, p. 69.

80. Marcio Veloz Maggiolo, 'Las Antillas precolombinas: Ecologia y población', *Revista Dominicana de Arqueología y Antropología*, 2 (July 1971–June 1972), 165-69.

81. Cook and Borah, 'Aboriginal Population', pp. 409-10. Cf. Sauer, *Early Spanish Main*, p. 203.

82. On the epidemiological consequences of the discovery of the New World see, among others, Alfred W. Crosby, *The Columbian Exchange* (Westport, Conn., 1972), pp. 35-63; Wilbur R. Jacobs, 'The Tip of the Iceberg: Pre-Columbian Indian Demography and Some Implications for Revisionism', *William and Mary Quarterly*, 2nd ser., 31 (January 1974), 123-32; Crosby, 'Virgin Soil Epidemics as a Factor in the Aboriginal Depopulation of America', *William and Mary Quarterly*, 2nd ser., 33 (April 1976), 289-99.

83. Colón, *Vida*, p. 230.

84. Las Casas, *Apologética historia*, xix, *OE*, III, 58-60.

85. Jonathan Swift, *Gulliver's Travels*, Pt. 3, chap. 5.

7

Amerindian-European Relations in Dutch Guyana

ALVIN O. THOMPSON

In the book from which this article has been taken we have dealt peripherally with the ways in which European, largely Dutch, contacts with the Amerindian communites affected the lives of the latter. At this point it is necessary to focus attention more closely on this subject. All the Amerindian societies were affected to a greater or lesser extent by their contacts with the Europeans. These contacts had to do mainly with trade and military assistance, but the Dutch were able to exploit Amerindian manpower in a variety of other ways, such as in cultivating provision grounds and acting as boat hands, messengers, timber cutters, baggage carriers and guides. The Dutch would have found it impossible to trade, reconnoiter and carry on their other activities in the hinterland without the Indians' assistance. These people influenced the material culture of the Dutch in Guyana in several minor ways, but the Dutch influenced their life more deeply. Still, taken as a whole, the Indian culture-systems remained substantially intact. This was due to some extent to the fact that the Dutch did not generally try to impose their way of life on the Indians, so that their political and social systems embraced very few Indians. In one area, however, the European contact was traumatic.

In Guyana, as in other parts of the Americas, the European advent and colonization had a catastrophic effect upon the demography of the Indian communities. A number of factors account for this situation, such as European diseases, the development of the Indian slave trade, intense warfare often relating to questions of trade, and forced migration resulting from the military and social pressures exerted by the other factors just identified. Warfare and forced migration tended to cause the Indian groups to split into even smaller units than before. Fission led to further vulnerability and further fissioning and so the process of decimation unfolded, as both cause and effect of these fissiparous tendencies. The impression gained from the Dutch contemporary records and from more recent documents is that there was excessive fragmentation of Amerindian political and ethnic groups. In few instances during the period under consideration was the process of aggregation noticeable, and certainly no Amerindian group increased significantly its territorial or political control. The military mastery of the Dutch in the more northerly areas was underscored by the continual expansion of the plantation system there. On the other hand, they had very little jurisdiction over the areas beyond the plantations.

Two kinds of Indian migration are discernible in the context of Guyana during this period: interior migration, that is, from one area to another within Guyana; and inward migration, chiefly from Spanish and Portuguese territories into Guyana. It is difficult at present to trace any pattern or sequence of migration; all that will be attempted here is to give some indication of the general and specific factors relating to such migrations and the groups involved in the same.

The European presence is the obvious factor with which to begin the discussion. As Sheridan points out:

Not only were the Europeans accompanied to the New World by invisible microparasites, but these conquerors and colonists were themselves macroparasites.[1]

The early Dutch pushed the Indians out of their homelands, and those whom they could not push out they attempted to wipe out with

Colonialism and Underdevelopment in Guyana, 1580–1803 (Caribbean Research and Publications, Bridgetown, 1987), pp. 191–213.

superior military technology and strategy. In some instances the Indians offered physical resistance, but at other times they quietly retreated to areas less accessible to the new invaders. This pattern of migration was noticed in Berbice in the 1670s, and in Demerara in the second half of the eighteenth century. Hartsinck notes that in the early days it was possible to find relatively large villages of sixteen to eighteen households in the lower (most northern) parts of the colonies, but that the situation was quite different by 1770. The villages were now located much further inland, while only two or three households could be found living together in the lower areas.[2]

The Dutch presence in Guyana resulted mainly in the interior rather than the outward migration of the Indians. This was due to two main factors. Firstly, the upper reaches of the rivers and some other areas of the hinterland were never occupied or controlled by the Dutch and in several instances they had nothing more than a trading presence there. Secondly, the Spanish and Portuguese presence had created similar pressures on several Indian groups in those localities, so that there was strong disincentive to migrate to those areas.

Spanish presence and activities in the northwest district and the Cuyuni area during the second half of the eighteenth century led to fissile multiplication and migration of the Indians further east. Thus in 1758 and 1762, as a result of Spanish activities around the Dutch post in Cuyuni, many Caribs fled the area and sought new homes in upper Essequibo. As late as 1769–70 the Dutch were reporting the continual withdrawal of these people from Cuyuni.[3] In the northwest, too, Spanish attacks on Post Moruka in 1769 and 1744 led to extensive dislocation of the Indians living there. According to the Dutch authorities, before the Spanish attacks some 700 Indians could be found around the post, but by 1772 most of them had disappeared from the area. In 1774 they were said to be seeking refuge in Corentyne. The Pomeroon Indians were also greatly dislocated at this time by the Spanish activities.[4] The Spanish had earlier been responsible for the retreat of many Indians from Orinoco into Moruka in fairly large numbers, though actual statistics are unavailable.

As early as 1685 the Caribs are recorded as migrating from the Spanish to the Dutch zone in face of reprisals for an attack (along with some Frenchmen) on Santo Thomé in the previous year. They sought refuge in Amacura, Barima and Waini in northwest Essequibo. In 1752–54

the Dutch records noted the retreat of the Caribs from Orinoco to the Dutch side as a result of continual Spanish harassment. In 1755 these records mentioned that a Spanish priest had recently come to claim some Indians of the Chima (Shiamacotte) nation, who had deserted the Spanish missions for Post Moruka some ten years previously. In 1767 and 1769 some Warraus were also recorded as retreating from Orinoco to Barima; while in the latter year a large number of Caribs were also said to have migrated from the Spanish missions to Mahaicony, some of them clad in priestly garments and ornaments.[5]

Northwest Essequibo witnessed the greatest incidence of inward migration and also the greatest degree of dislocation. But inward migration also took place occasionally from the Spanish zone into the Cuyuni-Mazaruni district. Thus in 1755 Gravesande reported that the chiefs of the Panacay people in upper Cuyuni had paid him a visit recently. They were at loggerheads with the Spanish and were offering their assistance to the Dutch against possible Spanish encroachment on territory which the Dutch held as their own. The Panacays even promised to settle down around the Cuyuni post, but we do not know whether they made good this promise. In 1769, again, it was rumored that a group known as the Cerekous (Cerekon) had moved from Spanish territory into the area just below Post Arinda and were annoying the Akawois. Finally, in 1790 four Indian chiefs along with their followers migrated from the Spanish missions into Dutch territory in Mazaruni.[6]

More to the south and southwest of Guyana, the migrants came from the area of modern Brazil, specifically the Rio Branco–Rio Negro district. The factors leading to migration from this area are less certain, but the most general one was again the European (this time mainly the Portuguese) presence and activities. These activities may be summarized as slave raiding, founding mission stations by the use of force, and establishing a politico-military administration. Dutch activities in the Rio Branco area also played some part in the migration of Indians. The obvious factor was the trade, and especially the slave trade, which the Dutch traders and their cohorts pursued here, as in Orinoco. Groups, perhaps seeking refuge from the Portuguese, Dutch, Carib and other slave raiders, crossed the Ireng and Takutu rivers and made their way into secluded areas within the vast expanse of virtually uninhabited territory in the Rupununi district. This was true of the Macusis, as we shall see shortly.

Another factor which might have accounted for inward migration was the attraction or pull of Dutch trade on one or two groups in the Rio Branco. For instance, the Manaos, a people inhabiting the middle-upper reaches of the Rio Negro, who wanted to establish direct and regular trading contact with the Dutch, found that their efforts were being thwarted by the Caribs and Akawois who occupied strategic areas along the established trade routes. The Akawois feared that their own trading interests might be compromised by their more southern neighbours, but they seem also to have feared that the Manaos would use any opportunity to enslave them and lord it over them.

Actually, the first reference to the Manaos in connection with the Dutch trade occurred in 1719, when they were mentioned in Portuguese records as trafficking with the Dutch in the headwaters of the Rio Branco, though their residence appears to have been on the Rio Negro. They are referred to in a Portuguese source of a later period as being the nation of greatest renown throughout the Rio Negro, on account of their numbers, valor, language and customs. In the 1720s they were the most notorious slave dealers of that district.[7] Their first appearance in Essequibo seems to have been in 1722. In the following year they paid another visit to the area, arriving in three boats carrying about thirty persons, including some slaves whom they hoped to sell to the Dutch. However, their advent produced quite a stir among the Caribs and Akawois there, who warned the Dutch officials that they had come with hostile intentions. The colonial government reacted swiftly to this supposed threat by sending a party to apprehend the Manaos and take them to the fort for questioning. Most of them escaped but about eight or nine of them were caught. This incident shook them quite a bit. Later investigations revealed that they had in fact come with amicable intentions and mainly to improve trade relations with the Dutch. In 1724, no doubt because of the incident mentioned above, they were attacking the Akawois and Caribs in upper Essequibo and threatening to kill all the Dutch. The colonial government resolved to send a force comprising Europeans and Indians to drive them away.

The Manaos were not heard of again in Guyana for some time and virtually disappeared from the Dutch records until 1751, when they were reported by the postholder of Arinda to be harassing the Indian inhabitants of upper Essequibo. This is somewhat surprising, for the Portuguese records in 1727 mentioned their Paramount Chief, Ajuricaba, as being in alliance with the Dutch, and even flying their flag. He had become the scourge of the Rio Negro and Rio Branco, enslaving the inhabitants of those places and selling them to the Dutch. Even after the Portuguese got rid of Ajuricaba in the following year, the Manaos remained a powerful slave-raiding group, obviously in close association with the Dutch traders. But curiously enough, in 1754 Gravesande referred to them as being in alliance with the Portuguese, while in reality they were often at each other's throats.[8] In 1763 Gravesande was thinking of forming an alliance with them, which he believed would further Dutch trading interests in the Rio Branco, while holding the ring politically against the Portuguese, who wanted to promote their interests there. On the other hand, he did not want to antagonize the Caribs, useful allies and, in fact, the most redoubtable military auxiliaries of the Dutch. The Caribs were trying to oppose the alliance; the postholder of Arinda reported that an attempt made in the previous year by the Manaos to send an embassy to the Dutch government in Essequibo had been hindered by them. A sharp encounter had actually taken place between the two groups and the Caribs had been defeated, but the losses sustained by the Manaos had been sufficiently heavy to force them to postpone their visit until the following year. Meanwhile, the Caribs were rallying their forces for the expected confrontation, so that Gravesande feared that the largest Indian war during his administration was imminent. In order to avoid this he send word to the Manaos that they should send only a small force to Arinda, from where they would be escorted to headquarters.[9] As it turned out, the alliance never came about, nor were the Manaos able to establish their own corridor of trade with the Dutch, a circumstance which Gravesande attributed to 'a political dodge of the Carib nation'.[10] Instead, the Manaos had to be content to allow the Dutch and their Indian auxiliaries to come and purchase their slaves from the Rio Branco.

The events outlined above show clearly the pull that Dutch trade had on groups even in the far interior, and also the conflicts which the trade could and did generate among interested parties. This was seen on a much smaller scale in relation to the Wapisianas. In 1753 it was reported that they had killed three white traders who had gone to upper Essequibo to trade with the Portuguese. The incident probably took place somewhere close to the lower-middle Rupununi river, which was the normal route for access into the Portuguese zone. We are not aware of what transpired as a result of the attack, but we know that Gravesande contemplated employing the Caribs who, along with the Macusis, had also been attacked by them, to drive them away from the route they were obstructing or, as he put it, 'away inland far from the River Essequibo'.[11] It is possible that he either made good this threat or that the Indians migrated from fear of reprisals. When the postholder met them some years later, in 1769, he reported that they were occupying both banks of the Ireng river and that they had not seen a white man for sixteen years. He also stated that they lived in the plains during the day but slept in inaccessible rocks and cliffs during the night, and heavily palisaded and defended their nocturnal dwellings for fear of the Manaos, with whom they were always in conflict.[12] They seem to have been divided into a number of families, living apart from each other and shifting their dwellings periodically. In 1739 Horstman had found them south of the Takutu and Uraracuera rivers in what is today modern Brazil. The eighteenth- and nineteenth-century descriptions of them located them roughly between the Rupununi on the east and the Ireng, Takutu and Rio Branco on the west. Schomburgk estimated the number of those living in Guyana around 1840 at 500 souls.[13] From all appearances they were a predatory group (or groups) who found themselves frequently in conflict with their neighbours. It is thought that they forced the Macusis to move further north, and that they absorbed the Atorais.

The Macusis themselves were another group of migrants who entered Guyana at a relatively early period. Iris Myers suggests that a reference on Du Val d'Abbeville's map of 1654 to the Muchikeriens (a people inhabiting the area around Lake Parima), might be applicable to them.[14] The first Dutch document available to us on the subject was written in 1753. It mentions them specifically and strongly implies that they were already well known to the Dutch. This is not surprising for they appear to have been among the chief victims of the Caribs, Manaos and others who sold them as slaves to the Dutch. They were regarded as the least warlike of the groups in the Rio Branco.[15] Their main homeland was probably the Rio Negro area, from where a number of them migrated to Guyana towards the middle of the eighteenth century. The Dutch source just referred to mentions them as the neighbours of the Wapisianas. One view is that they occupied the southern Rupununi savanna first and that they were forced northward by the Wapisianas. Around 1840

Schomburgk declared that their occupation sites included the savannas of the Rupununi and Rio Branco, and the mountain chains of the Pakaraima and Kanuku. He estimated their total number at 3,000, and those living in Guyana at 1,500,[16] a figure which made them one of the largest groups in the country at that time (if his figures are reasonably accurate). By 1786, according to the Portuguese Commandant of the Rio Branco district, they were one of two groups there who were very attached to the Dutch.

The Paravilhanos (Paravianas) were another group originally inhabiting the Brazilian area who migrated in small numbers into Guyana, possibly in the eighteenth century. They are mentioned in Portuguese records as occupying several sites along the Rio Branco and Takutu rivers, and by 1770 they had become the dominant group in that region. Their presence in Guyana is barely mentioned in Dutch records. In 1739 Horstman seems to have found some of them on the Essequibo, about a day's journey above its confluence with the Siparuni. According to Gravesande in 1769, during his early administration they used to live 'up in Essequibo', but because the Caribs repeatedly harassed them they were forced to move to the Ireng river, in close proximity to the Wapisianas.[17] In 1788 they were mentioned in Portuguese records as dwelling close to the headwaters of the Takutu, along the ranges between that river and the Rupununi. They had gained notoriety as dealers in human flesh. According to Farabee, they had become extinct by 1914.

Finally, we must mention the Tarumas in connection with inward migration. We do not know the date of their migration but it is generally thought that they entered the country sometime in the eighteenth century. In 1764 Gravesande mentioned them as a 'numerous and powerful nation' living in upper Essequibo.[18] In the 1720s some of them were living along the Takutu river, from where they probably migrated to the area close to the sources of the Essequibo river.

The migrations into southern Guyana did little to people that region, which throughout the eighteenth century remained largely uninhabited. The main occupation sites were located in the region between the Rupununi in the east and the Takutu and Ireng in the west. Virtually no inhabitants could be found to the east of the upper reaches of the Essequibo river. On the other hand, Indian groups in the north spread out over a much wider area than formerly. Refugee groups found their way as far east as the Corentyne, while others sought asylum along the middle reaches of the Essequibo and Berbice rivers, and in upper Demerara.

A factor which ought not to be overlooked in this discussion as a probable cause of fission and migration is the warfare carried on by groups traditionally residing in Guyana. The problem here, however, is that the records available to us have little to say about these wars, and even less about their effects on Indian migration. Therefore, all that can be attempted here is a summary of the wars to which the records attest. These wars involved mainly the Caribs and to a lesser extent the Akawois, the two groups that the Dutch generally regarded as the most warlike of those dwelling in Guyana.

In 1673 the Dutch records reported that the Caribs and Arawaks of Barima had just concluded a peace agreement. In 1680 the Caribs and Akawois of the Cuyuni-Mazaruni-Essequibo area were engaged in a relatively large-scale war which had not been resolved up to 1683. In 1684 the Barima–Orinoco area was the scene of petty warfare, while in 1686 the Akawois and Caribs of Mazaruni were locked in a power struggle leading to the loss of several families. Conflicts also occurred between the Caribs and Warraus of the Barima–Orinoco area in 1748. But the most sustained war seems to have taken place from 1765 to 1768, between the Akawois and Caribs in upper Demerara and the middle Essequibo–Mazaruni areas. At one stage it even threatened to merge with a conflict between similar groups in the Corentyne.

The conflicts between the various Amerindian groups upset the balance of life among them and caused considerable anxiety. They led on several occasions to the stoppage of trade with the Europeans. Indeed, the hinterland trade depended to a large extent on the goodwill of the Indians and their ability to maintain amicable relations among themselves and also with the Europeans, particularly the Dutch. This was an important reason why the Dutch officials always attempted to keep the peace with them and on several occasions to act as intermediaries between belligerent groups. Thus they intervened in Indian disputes in 1680, 1683, 1686, 1765 and 1766, but they were not always able to bring about peace. In 1680, for example, the Akawois in Cuyuni refused to accept bribes from them or allow them to act as peacemakers in their war with the Caribs.

One of the main problems which the Dutch officials faced in this respect was their limited political authority over the hinterland. Of course, several contemporary and modern writers have asserted that by the late eighteenth century the Dutch had established a kind of protectorate over the Indians. For instance, in the arguments put forward in 1898 by the British authorities in their boundary dispute with Venezuela they asserted that the Amerindian chiefs became 'formally accredited officers of the Dutch Colony, and exercised their authority with the sanction of the West India Company'.[19] A more recent writer declared in 1977 that the Indians had 'unquestionably recognized the protectorate of the Dutch, and the Dutch had assumed the responsibilities of a protecting power'.[20] The British authorities had made virtually the same statement earlier, specifically in relation to the Caribs,[21] while Rodway had said much the same thing in 1896.[22] These views demonstrate a complete misunderstanding of the relations between the two parties during the period under discussion. In general, it was the Dutch and not the Indians who needed to be protected — from threatened Spanish invasion, maroons and even the ravages of hunger. They were the ones who were dependent on the Indians, and not the latter on them. Nevertheless, they were to some extent responsible for fostering the myth of their role as protectors of the Indians. Especially in their boundary disputes with the Spanish, they were bent upon demonstrating their political, military and commercial hegemony over the region under dispute. The rights of the Indians were never considered by them when it came to the question of territorial jurisdiction, any more than they were considered by the Spanish, British, French or Portuguese. The Europeans simply viewed them as having no territorial rights (and very few other rights). According to the so-called 'law of nations' of that period, which was completely Eurocentric, their lands were open to expropriation and colonization, provided they were not already under the jurisdiction of some Christian (European) power. But since effective occupation was regarded by the Europeans as the clearest expression of sovereignty, the Dutch tried hard to create the impression that they were the effective occupants of a much wider area than they actually administered.

One must also distinguish between the language sometimes used in official correspondence between the WIC and the local Dutch administrators, and the reality of the situation on the ground. Sometimes this official correspondence seems to imply that the Indians were under Dutch control but in moments of greater lucidity and honesty Dutch dependence on the goodwill and substantial assistance of the Indians becomes manifest. On balance, the sources indicate a delicate alliance between the so-called 'colonizer' and the 'colonized'.

It is obvious that from the point of view of the vast majority of the Indians in Guyana the Dutch did not exercise the slightest jurisdiction over them. Without doubt, Dutch influence was felt over a wide area, as we have seen already. However, we must not confuse influence with jurisdiction, alliance with allegiance, fraternalism with paternalism. No formal empire of any significant territorial size was established by the Dutch and it is quite doubtful whether we should even regard the degree of Dutch influence as constituting an informal empire. It should perhaps be said here that the same argument holds good in relation to Spanish jurisdiction over the sprawling provinces of Guayana, Barcelona, Cumaná, Santa Fé, etc.

Effective Dutch jurisdiction touched relatively few Indians, chiefly the Arawaks and Warraus, who came to reside either around the Dutch hinterland posts or on the peripheries of the estates, and who underwent the most extensive acculturation. It is true that the Indians were sometimes required by the Dutch to obtain passes to go beyond the posts, but these appear to have been Indians living below the posts. In 1763 the Commander of Demerara issued a permit allowing a Carib chief to go to Berbice. Similar passes were issued to Indians by other Dutch officials in 1778 and 1779.[23] Dutch merchants had to pay a small sum of money to obtain such passes, but this does not appear to have been the case with the Indians.[24] What is clear is that official Dutch policy — in contrast to that of the Spanish and Portuguese — was to eschew the use of force to restrict the movement and way of life of the Indians. The Dutch tried to use persuasion rather than coercion to keep the Indians in alliance with them and in close proximity to their settlements. This was the rationale behind the postholdership system and the periodic distribution of gifts to the Indians. It is necessary to stress here that this distribution was not an act of patronage but rather one of friendship. Dutch records leave us in no doubt that without these gifts the friendship and services of the Indians could not be assured.

The custom of regular distribution of gifts to the Indians seems to have originated in the late seventeenth century. According to Van Berkel, each Indian captain or chief at that time received biennially from the Dutch in Berbice (and perhaps also in Essequibo) a red worsted dress and a hat, with which he appeared at the fort.[25] Another source of the same period makes it clear that such gifts were necessary 'to keep on friendly terms with the Chiefs'.[26] As time went by the practice embraced a large number of chiefs from an increasingly wider area, and was put on a more official footing in 1778 when a number of chiefs were invited to the Dutch headquarters in Essequibo and presented with hats having broad silver rims, and staves with silver knobs. At the same time the Indians were encouraged to show fidelity to the Dutch government at all times, to give their assistance whenever requested to do so, and to refer their disputes to the Dutch authorities. They were told that the instruments they had just received were indicative of the Dutch government's recognition of them as chiefs, and that whenever they wanted to appoint new chiefs they should choose those proposed by the Dutch government. It is also said that the chiefs and their followers were elaborately entertained at Duinenburg, the Company's plantation, and that they expressed loyalty and friendship to the Dutch government.[27]

In the following year similar gifts were distributed to a large number of chiefs of the Carib, Arawak and Warrau peoples. The staves were engraved with the WIC's seal, a practice which soon became customary. In 1784 the WIC approved an elaborate plan put forward by the colonial authorities in Essequibo and Demerara to honor the chiefs, especially those of the Caribs. They were to be invited to come to the fort in Essequibo from the various districts of the country, and were to be offered lands on which to settle permanently, close to the Dutch settlements. In addition, they were to be given the staves, as mentioned above, and also silver ring-collars and rum. In return, they were to pledge themselves to return to the fort once annually to give a list of the men under their command, and to renew their pledge to assist the Dutch in times of military need. In order to induce them to do so, they were to be given gifts on such occasions.[28] Here, then, is the system which several writers have regarded as tantamount to a recognition by the Indians of the paramountcy of Dutch authority, a view strengthened by Hartsinck's statement in 1770, some years before the system was elaborated fully, that the chiefs were being appointed by the Dutch Governors.[29]

On the contrary, a close look at the situation reveals that for three important reasons the Dutch cannot really be said to have exercised paramountcy over the Indians in general. In the first place it must be realized that the reason for putting forward the scheme was because the Indians were withdrawing from the neighbourhood of the Dutch settlements. The scheme was therefore designed to attract them once again to the lower reaches of the rivers, where their services would be more readily available in times of need, particularly against runaways and maroons. This was actually stated in the document of 1784 which set out the scheme, while it is implied in those relating to the convocation of 1778.

Secondly, the minutes of the Court of Policy of 1778, which recorded the actual visit of the chiefs in that year, declare that the presents were given to them as 'a token of friendship', not to make vassals of them.[30] In 1785, also, when three chiefs and 105 of their followers from upper Essequibo visited the fort, the chiefs were given silver ring-collars as 'tokens of friendship'.[31] While it is possible that a few of the chiefs were raised to the office or had their power enhanced by the Dutch, in general their power emanated solely from their kinsmen, to whom they were ultimately responsible. This point was made by Hilhouse, who was well-acquainted with the Indians. He indicated in 1825 that the chief's authority was still subject to that of his people, and that the Akawois elected their own captains (chiefs), acknowledged no white protector, and rejected any interference in their domestic affairs.[32] Several years earlier, in 1769, Gravesande had stated that when the principal chiefs visited him they immediately took a chair, sat down, and refused to eat and drink anything but what he himself had. They referred to him only as 'mate' and 'brother'.[33] It was only during the governorship of Sir Henry Light (1838–48) that the colonial government really began to appoint chiefs, and only then can they be said to have become the accredited agents of the colonial government.[34]

The third major reason relates to the land grants. It appears that few if any Indians accepted the offer of such grants. They preferred to retain their independence and mobility, rather than come under the thumb of the Dutch, as would certainly have been the result if they had accepted the land grants. It was only under the British that the system of creating Indian reservations, first mooted by the Dutch, came into operation.

The tendency of the Indians to withdraw a fair distance from the seat of Dutch power was one of the clearest expressions of their independence. The Dutch continued to coax them to return, or at least not to move farther afield. Thus in 1803, in their instructions to their postholders, they enjoined strict application of the regulations concerning the humane treatment of the Indians. When the British occupied the colony later in the same year they showed a similar concern about the Indian question. They felt that their earlier occupation (1796–1802) had led to the withdrawal of a considerable number of Indians to more remote districts in the country, a circumstance which might have had grave consequences for their colonies. They therefore reintroduced the system of annual presents that thad lapsed temporarily. Gradually, however, they extricated themselves from this system as they felt more confident of their control over the colonies and the hinterland. In 1831 they made the presents triennial, and on the eve of the final abolition of slavery in 1838 they discontinued the practice altogether. The result was a significant withdrawal of the Indians from the main colonial areas to more remote positions.[35] This circumstance reinforces the view that the presents were the nuts and bolts of the alliance between the Europeans and the Indians. The British, like the Dutch, saw the alliance mainly as a security in times of slave uprisings; while the Indians were only prepared to stay close to the Europeans as long as they were willing to give them gifts, allowances and rewards for military service against the slaves. The friendship between the two parties was no love relationship but rather a business arrangement. During the Dutch regime giving presents to the Indians was an ineluctable necessity for the colonial administrations. In fact, by the nineteenth century the Indians had even begun to view the presents and allowances as a form of tribute. In 1813 Colonel Edward Codd, Acting Governor of Demerara, had this to say:

It is obvious that our Colonies are tributaries to the Indians; whilst the proper system of policy would be to make them allies, looking to us for protection.[36]

He had good reason to be apprehensive about this arrangement. In 1810 Mahanarva, a Carib chief, had moved into the capital with his men, threatening to use physical force unless the customary presents and allowances withheld from him by the British were paid. The government decided to appease the chief rather than risk his taking umbrage on this occasion. The presents were given but the government reserved the right — at least so the Governor wrote — to decide whether it would make presents in future. As noted above, the presents continued for another two decades.

It is sometimes asserted that even if the Indians were not politically, they were at least militarily, subordinate to the Dutch, that they could be summoned in times of military need, and that they were committed to placing their forces under Dutch officers. There is some ambiguity in the Dutch records on this matter. Sometimes these records convey the impression that the Indians were under some compulsion to respond to the Dutch call for assistance, and indeed the Dutch records at times contain such words as *summoned* and *ordered* when referring to the call for assistance. However, the term *requested* or an analogous term is used as commonly. On each occasion when military assistance was rendered, material rewards had to be given to the Indians, apart from the annual presents. In 1763, for instance, when the assistance of the Caribs was being sought by the Director-General of Essequibo to quarantine the colony from the slave uprising in Berbice, this is what he had to say to the WIC:

I shall write to Post Arinda as soon as possible to instruct the Postholder to induce the Carib nation, by the promise of a recompense, to take up arms in this matter.[37]

Such requests and rewards were quite common. In one sense, therefore, the Indian military auxiliaries may be viewed as mercenaries rather than allies.

It is also somewhat inaccurate to say that the Indians generally fought under Dutch officers. Again, there are instances when the Dutch records state that Dutch officers were being sent to head the Indian contingents. In 1769 the Commander of Demerara stated that he had appointed a persom whom the Arawaks respected as commander over them in order to prevent them from migrating to Berbice. The person was almost certainly a white burgher officer.[38] A few years later, in 1744, an Essequibo burgher officer, Stephanuṣ Gerardus van der Heyden (Heijden), was appointed by the Dutch authorities there as colonel over the Indians of that territory, while his sons were appointed captains.[39] Though the evidence on the subject is at present rather scanty, it appears that during the second half of the eighteenth century the Dutch began to appoint officers to act on their behalf in their military dealings with the Indians. These officers, however, were only liaisons between the Dutch and Indian forces, and were not commanders superimposed by the Dutch over the Indians. They attempted with varying degrees of success to coordinate the efforts of the whites and Indians in bush expeditions. But they were never recognized by the Indians as their superiors, and on some occasions it proved virtually impossible to achieve coordination between the two forces. Thus in 1769 when Backer, the Dutch Commandant, attempted to get a Carib chief to put his forces under Dutch command, he replied: 'No, I am master of the Caribs. You can be master of the whites and of the other nations, and then we can together become masters of everything.'[40] Hilhouse indicated in 1825 that when expeditions were composed of whites and Indians there was 'always considerable confusion and insubordination', and that this could only be avoided by dividing the forces along racial lines.[41]

The Indians were never formally recruited and constituted by the Dutch into a military corps. The nearest they came to this was to attract several of them to the most important posts established in the hinterland. In the late eighteenth century about twenty-five of them were receiving small monthly stipends as military auxiliaries attached to Post Moruka. Even so, no attempt was made to train them in European combat tactics. It is certainly untrue, then, to state that the Indians were generally militarily subordinate to the Europeans.

Some writers regard the fact that on several occasions the Indians sought redress from the Dutch government for wrongs they had suffered at the hands of the colonists as evidence that they were amenable to Dutch law. However, we must also challenge this view on the basis that the referral of such disputes was the result of a clear understanding between the Dutch colonial authorities and the Indians that the two parties would eschew the use of force, as far as possible, in their relations with each other. Thus the Indians complained, not from a position of subordination, but from one of alliance. It hardly needs to be said that the fact that a complaint has been lodged by someone against another person to a third party does not necessarily mean that the complainant is under the jurisdiction of the third party, but rather that the accused is under such jurisdiction. This was the situation between the Dutch and the Indians. The latter always reserved the right to resort to the arbitrament of force if they should fail to obtain redress through the Dutch judicial process. In fact, when grave offenses were committed against them they sought immediate retribution by appeal to arms, rather than referring the matter to the colonial authorities. Thus Amerindian–Dutch relations were often punctuated by physical conflicts, as happened in 1747, 1750 and 1755–56.

The colonial authorities were quite sensitive to the need to court the favor of the Indians and therefore published laws periodically prohibiting the colonists from ill-treating them. As early as 1627 Abraham van Pere, the proprietor and founder of the colony of Berbice, had agreed as one of the conditions of his proprietary grant to treat the Indians justly and honestly.[42] Similar instructions were given to Abraham Beekman, Commander of Essequibo, in 1768, and to the postholders. Laws were actually published on this matter for the information of the colonists in 1729 and around 1760. According to the edict of 1729 delinquents were to be fined f.50 for the first offense and f.100 for the second, while a third offense was to meet with a much heavier penalty.[43] In spite of these laws the Indians were often abused by the colonists.

An important reason for this was that even when the Indians lodged complaints against the miscreants the Dutch courts rarely dispensed justice impartially. For one thing, Indians, like Africans, were considered as an inferior and untrustworthy species of humanity whose testimony could not be admitted against whites in Dutch law courts. The result was that even when the colonists were obviously guilty they usually got off very lightly, as we can see from two cases brought before the colonial judiciary in 1750. The first was against Pieter Marchal, a planter in Mazaruni, whom the Caribs accused of refusal to pay them for services rendered him over a period of four months. Although the Court of Justice found the evidence heavily weighted against him, it simply admonished rather than compelled him to keep the peace with the Indians and pay them their dues. The other case concerned the ill-treatment of another group of Caribs by the colonist Pieter de Bakker. This time the Indians' testimony was corroborated by that of another white person. Nonetheless, the court simply reprimanded him.[44] Again, in 1752 the actions of one Christian Tonsel in seizing the children and friends of some Caribs of Barima met with only reprimand and an order to restore the persons seized to their relatives.[45]

Generally, the colonial judiciaries were not interested in dealing out even-handed justice in cases involving Europeans and Indians. But there were a few occasions on which *raisons d'état* made it imperative to rule in favour of the Indians, as can be illustrated by reference to two incidents which took place in 1760 and 1772. The first concerned Nicolas Stedevelt, a trader who had put a Carib from Cuyuni in fetters and taken away his wife for allegedly stealing his goods. Though he had a white witness who confirmed that the Indian had confessed to com-

mitting the crime, the Court passed judgement against him. He was fined f.250 and cautioned that he would be banished from the colony for a similar offense in future.[46] Two probable reasons account for this unusual judgement. A law had recently been passed prohibiting the whites from mistreating the Indians and Stedevelt's actions seemed a flagrant disavowal of the authority of the government. More importantly, Spanish activities in Cuyuni were a constant source of bother to the Dutch. They were therefore sparing no efforts to maintain friendly relations with the Indians in that area, whom they hoped to use as a counterfoil to the Spanish. Stedevelt's actions threatened to embroil the Dutch in a conflict with the Indians at a time when the former could least afford it.

The second instance concerned one F. W. Gerds, who was imprisoned for twenty-four hours, heavily fined, and ordered to pay f.50 as compensation to an Indian whom he had whipped. Again, in this case Dutch 'humanitarianism' and 'sense of fair play' must have been mixed with the leaven of enlightened self-interest. It is interesting to note that the same dispatch that carried the story about Gerds also mentioned that a slave revolt was taking place on the sea coast and that the assistance of the Indians was being sought; hence the need to ensure that the Indians did not have fresh cause for umbrage against the Dutch.[47]

Apart from cases where the Indians brought complaints against the colonists, there were a few instances when the Dutch courts tried Indians for wrongs committed by them. In 1765 an Indian was charged with committing murder in the Moruka district; in 1783 a similar event took place.

A third incident involving the Carib chief Aritanna in 1755 became a *cause celèbre* some years after the event, for the British (in their main argument concerning their boundary dispute with Venezuela in 1898) used it as evidence-in-chief of Dutch jurisdiction over the Indians. They alleged that the chief had been *summoned* by the Dutch authorities to appear before the Court of Justice, because he had killed certain Akawois in the Mazaruni district. But this allegation was not completely correct.[48] In the first place, the person on trail was not Aritanna but rather the colonist Pieter Marchal who had incited him to commit the act. He confessed to having killed the Indians at Marchal's instigation, but no action was taken against him. Moreover, although Gravesande wrote to the WIC on January 5, 1765, that the Court of Justice had sent someone to *summon* the chief

(*Indiaen op te ontbieden*), in an earlier dispatch of November 24, 1755, he had stated that the Court had decided to invite (*te versoeken hier te weesen*) the chief to testify at the trial.[49] This incident cannot therefore be used as conclusive evidence of Dutch jurisdiction over the Indians in Mazaruni.

The entire rationale behind Dutch claims that they were offering the Indians protection against the whites can be gathered from Gravesande's candid statement in 1769:

There is no one, Your Honours, who is more convinced how advantageous and necessary the friendship of the Indians is to this Colony . . . I therefore neglect no possible opportunity of cultivating the friendship of the same and of protecting them from all the ill-treatment and tyranny of the whites as far as it is expedient to do.[50]

This was it. For a brief moment the Director-General exposed the naked truth: the cause of the Indians was only espoused as long as it was expedient for the Dutch to do so. Expediency, however, sometimes made the colonial officials consider playing off one group of Indians against the other. Thus in the Dutch–Akawois conflict of 1755-56 Gravesande contemplated requesting the assistance of the Caribs to fight the Dutch cause, but we have no evidence that he actually had recourse to this measure. In 1763 he expressed the hope that his Carib allies would 'get a good hiding' from the Manaos because he felt that they were obstructing the latter from making direct contact and permanent alliance with the Dutch. Later in the same year an expedition comprising Dutchmen and Caribs, *en route* to assisting the whites to put down the Berbice slave uprising, killed several Indians on the contention that they had come to kill an Akawois chief. It was often the colonists, rather than the colonial authorities, who played off the Indians against each other for their unscrupulous ends and who were also responsible for instances of impassioned invective and armed hostilities between the Dutch and the Indians. Up to the end of the Dutch period there were still several instances of festering grievances between the two parties.

On a few occasions the Dutch offered military assistance or gave moral support to their Indian allies against outsiders, but on each occasion that we have come across a particular Dutch interest was at stake. In 1724 they decided to assist the Caribs of upper Essequibo to repel the Manaos, but this was done because they had received a report that the latter had threatened to kill all Dutchmen, and also because their attacks on the Caribs and Akawois might have led to the migration of these people to other areas, to the detriment of the Dutch fisheries there.[51] In 1746 the Dutch offered military assistance to the Indians in Waini who had been attacked by other Indians from Orinoco. This was the time when the boundary problem with the Spanish in Orinoco was becoming a major issue and the Dutch suspected that the attacks had been instigated by the Spanish in Cumaná. The Dutch were therefore hoping, in effect, to use the Indians of Waini and the other rivers in the northwest to hold the ring against the Spanish, instead of shielding the Indians from attacks. Again, in 1769 they gave their blessings to a Carib expedition which was about to attack some Cerekous Indians in upper Essequibo, who were alleged to have arrived from Orinoco under Spanish instructions to harass those Indians in alliance with the Dutch. Needless to say, important Dutch territorial and trading interests were at stake. Curiously enough, however, when in 1757 the Caribs were preparing to attack a new Spanish religious mission in Cuyuni in an area which the Dutch claimed as belonging to them, the government in Essequibo not only refused to provide them with arms but sent an emissary to Orinoco to apprize the colonial government there of the intended attack. The Dutch reasoned on this occasion that their action would secure the goodwill of the Spaniards.[52] This proves once again that it was narrow self-interest which was the crucial variable in Dutch relations with the Indians. The latter were often used as pawns in the game of diplomatic and military chess between the various European colonial powers. As far as the Dutch were concerned, once their own interests were not at stake the Indians could kill themselves or each other without their batting an eye at what was taking place.

While issues relating to war and trade dominated Amerindian–Dutch relations, the exigencies of life forced the Dutch to forge links with the Indians at other levels. As already indicated, one of the vital ways in which the Indians assisted the Dutch in the daily running of the plantations was by providing bread and fish for them, or more precisely for their slaves. Indian methods of preparing cassava and fish were also commonly employed on the plantations. The Indians affected the culture of Dutch plantation society in these and several other ways, such as through the use of hammocks in place of European-style beds; Indian boats, which were admirably suited to riverine navigation; and the local palms for thatching roofs. The *troolie* palm was particularly widely used. When laid properly, it forms thatching which is very durable and quite resistant to rain. It was used by the Dutch to thatch their boiler rooms, slave huts and other buildings.

Although contact between the two parties was regularly maintained, most Indians, even those who gave some service to the plantations and the posts, preferred to live some distance away from the Dutch establishments. Nonetheless, some of them found it convenient to live on or close to the Dutch settlements — especially the Arawaks and Warraus. The Dutch considered the former to be the most docile, sedentary and civilized of all the Indians. They were certainly the ones who underwent the greatest degree of acculturation to European values, a circumstance which must have had a lot to do with the European view of them. On the other hand, the Caribs and Akawois, who rarely gave any but military service,[53] were vilified as the most barbarous and incorrigible groups, to whom raid and rapine were the normal way of life. The Dutch, of course, never bothered to address the question of the impact of their own presence and activities on the escalation of Indian warfare.

As a rule, the Indians were sensitive about their rights, as we gather from both Van Berkel and Hartsinck. They refused to be coerced into doing a job or to be ordered about, and allowed no impairment of their rights as freemen.[54]

In return for their services they received a wide assortment of European manufactured goods — cloth, hats, mirrors, beads, fish hooks, pins, needles, scissors, pots, basins, cutlasses, axes, adzes, firearms, powder, shot, etc.[55] Iron tools were the most important of these commodities, from the point of view of the economic improvements they were capable of bringing about in Indian societies. The iron axes made it easier to clear the dense forest, while the cutlasses were quite handy for light cutting purposes. These tools therefore were in great demand; nevertheless, it would be a gross exageration to suggest, as Seggar does, that these tools revolutionized the economic life of the Indians.[56] The fact is that they had a surprisingly limited impact on Indian agriculture. They were not introduced in sufficiently large quantities to make them commonly available throughout the country during the Dutch period. Stone tools therefore survived for a long time after the introduction of the new tools, as was also the case in West Africa for over a thousand years after iron technology had been introduced there. The iron tools which the Dutch sold the Indians were also quite shoddy and anything but durable,[57]

nor did the Dutch make their knowledge of iron smelting available to the Indians. While iron ore has not been discovered in large quantities in Guyana, the knowledge of iron smelting might have enhanced Indian societies appreciably.

The Dutch also failed to influence Indian agricultural technology, apart from the use of iron tools. We must record a series of negatives on this score: no animal manure or artificial fertilizers, no wheel and plow, no rotation of crops, no soil conservation methods. Instead, they continued to use their old methods well into the nineteenth century: slashing and burning, planting a variety of crops in a single field, and leaving the land fallow after three or four years.[58]

Even in relation to new crops the Dutch had little to offer. The sugar cane was the only exotic crop of note which they introduced, and, even so, the Indians made very limited use of it. They cultivated it as a secondary crop alongside their other crops. In fact, nineteenth-century sources dealing with Indian domestic crops generally do not mention sugar cane, but only crops of local origin. Cassava remained by far the most important Indian crop.

Apart from European agricultural tools, there were other tools (especially the adze) which were used to manufacture boats and other wooden items. The European contribution in this area was quite significant, mainly in lightening the various tasks and providing a better finish. However, once again we notice the absence of any substantial modifications in either shapes, sizes or methods of construction of Indian boats.

Iron was used for a wide variety of other purposes. It often replaced the bone or wooden points at the tip of javelins and arrows, thus giving these implements sharper and more durable points. Sometimes, also, iron hunting and fishing tools were used side by side with the traditional tools. For fishing, of course, the Indians utilized the metal fish hooks which were imported in seemingly large quantities. (Among the items which the British distributed to the Indians in 1827 were 11,972 fish hooks.)[59] But for a long time fishing with hooks did not displace the traditional method of fishing, which entailed damming and poisoning the rivers and using nets and arrows to obtain large catches.[60]

Firearms were perhaps the most significant innovation and certainly the most coveted implement introduced by the Dutch, even though their impact was largely negative. Of course, up to at least the last years of the eighteenth century gun technology was still not highly advanced.

Moreover, the 'trade guns' exported from Europe were usually the worst of their kind, as was certainly the case with the majority of Dutch trade guns introduced into Guyana.[61] Even in the late nineteenth century, under the British regime, the Indians were receiving guns which are said by Im Thurn to have been of 'a most trumpety kind'.[62] Occasionally, more efficient weapons found their way through illicit trade into Indian hands, but even these often became rusty and defective in the tropics because of the climate and, more importantly, neglect to service them regularly. There must also have been problems in repairing them and obtaining adequate supplies of gunpowder and ammunition. In spite of these limitations, guns gave their users a certain military advantage over opponents using such traditional weapons as spears, bows and arrows. Consequently, the Indians made every effort to acquire them. In practice, however, the supply of guns was always limited, even for European personnel in the colonies. Relatively few Indians therefore acquired them, so that they never completely displaced the traditional weapons. The Caribs seem to have obtained more than their neighbours, which increased their striking power considerably and allowed them to prosecute the slave trade virtually with impunity. Both Spanish and Portuguese documents attest to this fact.

After a while the Dutch authorities began to show some uneasiness over the trade in guns to the Indians or even putting such weapons in their hands to assist the whites in their military undertakings. In 1755 Gravesande expressed fears that the possession of such weapons would considerably increase the difficulty of keeping the Indians in check and that one day they might turn the guns against the whites. They were not trustworthy, since their friendship with the whites was based upon 'fear or by reason of the profit they make out of trading with us than from inclination'.[63] A few years earlier, in 1750, he complained to the Zeeland Chamber that occasionally they obtained good guns, and that their acquisition of firearms made them lose their awe of these weapons, which he obviously saw as the ultimate security of the whites. He suggested that the surest way to eliminate this overarching threat was to abolish the gun trade completely, under stiff penalties against delinquents.[64]

Actually, the Chamber prohibited the trade on at least two occasions, in 1735 and again in 1752, no doubt acting on the Director-General's suggestion. However, these embargoes did little

to stop the flow of arms to the Indians, especially since the suppression of the trade was likely to lead to a rupture of the alliance between the Indians and the Dutch. In fact, in 1762 the Caribs laid the cards on the table: they were not prepared to fight the white man's wars without firepower. Thus the authorities were forced to equip the Indians with firearms to fight for them in 1762, 1763, 1778 and 1785, and no doubt on other occasions.[65]

Firearms added a new and significant factor to Indian warfare during the eighteenth century, though this did not mean that they invariably ensured success by their possessors against groups using mainly traditional weapons. They remained a prized possession for a long time, as Seggar noted in 1965: 'The shot-gun eventually became, and still is the greatest prestige or status possession [among the Indians].'[66]

European manufacturers also modified Amerindian societies in areas of dress and ornamentation, mainly in relation to the use of new materials. Glass beads commonly replaced seeds, shells, bark, etc, as the basic material for making women's aprons, especially among the groups in regular contact with the Dutch; the notable exceptions were the Warraus.[67] Imported beads were also used to make necklaces, but traditional materials held their own for a much longer time in the manufacture of these ornaments. Blue cloth was now used to make men's laps, but we do not know how common this practice had become by the end of the Dutch period. What we know is that cloth formed an increasingly important item of the trade. Bolingbroke, writing around the end of the period, indicated that the Indians used their cloth laps when visiting the European headquarters. On such occasions the chiefs were more 'elaborately' clad, in full European garb.[68] We also learn from Im Thurn, who wrote about three-quarters of a century later, that only the Warraus retained the use of bark cloths at that time instead of imported cloths.[69]

The Europeans were much less successful in introducing domesticated animals into the Indian societies in Guyana. This is quite surprising when we note that the introduction of such animals constituted a major input into many Indian societies in the Americas. The introduction of the horse, for example, revolutionized Indian warfare in several parts of the Americas. However, in the case of Guyana, it was not the horse but the dog which was the major innovation, and its impact was in respect of hunting rather than warfare. Even so, the Indians owed the introduction of this animal more to the

Spanish and the Portuguese than to the Dutch. The small breeds of hunting dogs formerly possessed by the Indians were increasingly displaced by dogs imported from Spanish and Portuguese territories. Schomburgk stated that the Akawois went to Colombia and Brazil to obtain these animals.[70] The Tarumas in upper Essequibo had become breeders of these dogs by the late nineteenth century,[71] by which time they were equal in value to a good gun or a large canoe.

Apart from dogs, no other animal had a major impact on Indian societies in Guyana. Horses were expensive and suffered a high mortality rate, at least in the plantation area. Their limited utility was also due to their unsuitability to the terrain in which the majority of the Indians lived. They simply could not compete with the canoe and the Indian's bare feet in mobility and versatility along the rivers and over the paths. The animals which the Europeans used for food were considered by the Indians well into the nineteenth century as unclean.[72] It is only in more recent times that they — mainly those in the Rupununi savanna — have taken to raising cattle, pigs, sheep and goats.

Speaking more generally, the Indian-European contact led to a much more highly developed barter economy among the former. By the end of the Dutch period this had led, if not to the emergence of a specialized trading class, at least to certain groups taking the leading role in trade. These came mainly from the Akawois and to some extent the Carib communities.

Outside of the purely material aspects of Indian life, contact with the Dutch affected the Indians in a few other ways. From the early days the Dutch cohabited with Indian women and produced a small mixed group. In the early nineteenth century they were living mainly at Bartica, at the junction of the Mazaruni and Essequibo rivers, by which time they had become considerably mixed with African blood. They were chiefly engaged in cutting timber and salting fish for the Europeans. They often spoke a hybrid language known as Creole Dutch, which had become the lingua franca of the slaves and several Indians by the late eighteenth century.[73] Dutch lexical items had also found their way into the Amerindian languages, for instance, *negotiae* for 'trade' and *kleine flinte* for 'small arms'.[74]

In the field of religion, almost nothing was done to Christianize the Indians. The Moravians and Roman Catholics were the only groups which showed some interest in them. The Moravians turned to them after encountering planter opposition to their efforts at converting the slaves. They turned to the Arawaks in Berbice, where they founded a mission in 1738. They established their headquarters at a place called Pilgerruh (Pilgerhuth), at the junction of the Wiruni (Wironje) and Berbice rivers, and lived a simple life, fishing, hunting and engaging in tailoring and shoemaking to obtain a livelihood. In time they learnt the Arawak language and began to translate the Bible into it, and also to compile a dictionary. By 1759 they had about 300 Indians under their spiritual charge, but shortly afterwards a number of their followers died of an epidemic which swept the colony at that time. The mission survived until 1763, when it was destroyed by the slaves during the uprising in that year. The missionaries moved to Corentyne (Ephraim), where their coreligionists had established another mission in 1757; this survived until 1806 when it was destroyed by fire and eventually abandoned. After the Moravians departed the Indians quickly forgot most of the missionaries' teachings, though some memories survived for a long time.[75]

The Indians in Essequibo and Demerara did not undergo any Christian instruction. In 1729 A Roman Catholic priest from Orinoco visited Essequibo and requested permission to start work among them, but the Commander turned down the request.[76] This seems to have been the only attempt to start a mission among the Indians there.

On the whole, it can be said that the Amerindians were as much in the mainstream of developments in Guyana, both positive and negative, as the Africans and the Europeans. The advent of the Europeans had quite a negative impact on their political structures. Many Indian communities became fragmented and some were destroyed, a situation which reflected in vivid miniature what had taken place and what was still going on throughout the continent of North and South America where whole civilizations were destroyed. This was all part of the process of underdevelopment characteristic of the European impact on autochthonous societies. New communities sprang up from the devastation and destruction, but these were small and perhaps less cohesive than their predecessors, and were sometimes pitted against each other in an interlocking struggle for survival. This is certainly the picture which emerges of the Caribs and Arawaks around the mid-eighteenth century. Without doubt, the European advent multiplied the incidence of warfare within

Indian communities, while Indian-European wars, and animosities bred between Indians and Africans due to the use of Indians as slave catchers, added further dimensions to the military factor. Our preliminary investigations strongly suggest that in several instances relatively peaceful zones in the pre-European period, such as the middle Essequibo-Mazaruni area, became battlegrounds in which the use of firearms escalated the conflicts. More peaceful pursuits also took place. A more sophisticated network of trade developed, with the Indians exchanging a variety of local goods for exotic products. But even here the military factor was intrusive, especially in relation to the slave trade, the repercussions of which were felt over a wide area.

The Dutch needed the Indians, as they needed the Africans, in order to develop viable colonies. They needed them for trade, military purposes, manpower availability, and a variety of other purposes. Indian initiative and response to the new groups did much to determine the pattern of plantation and hinterland development. In time the Dutch found it possible to arrange a *modus vivendi* with several Indian groups, but only relatively few of them came under effective Dutch jurisdiction. What the Dutch hoped to do, and what they actually did in a number of instances, was to establish a sphere of influence over various groups in the hinterland. This allowed them to further their commercial objectives, and also gave them some claims vis-à-vis their European neighbours to possession of territories, particularly in those areas where their postholders and Indian allies resided.

Notes

1. R. Sheridan, *Doctors and Slaves: a Medical and Demographic History of Slavery in the British West Indies 1680-1834*, (Cambridge, 1985), p. 40.
2. Jan J. Hartsinck, *Beschrijving van Guiana of de Wildekust in Zuid-America* (Amsterdam, 1770), pp. 290-91, 293.
3. British Guiana Boundary Arbitration with the United States of Venezuela. The case on behalf of the Government of Her Britannic Majesty (London, 1898), hereafter BGBV, Appendix ii, pp. 143, 214, 217; British Guiana Boundary Arbitration with the United States of Brazil. The case on behalf of the Government of Her Britannic Majesty (London, 1903), hereafter VGB, Appendix, i, p. 83; United States Commission on Boundary between Venezuela and British Guiana; Report and Accompanying Papers of the Mission Appointed by the President of the Unites States . . . (Washington, 1897), hereafter USC, i, p. 340.
4. *BGBV*, App. ii, pp. 8-9, 12; App. iv, pp. 101, 127.
5. *BGBV, App. i, pp. 11, 188; App. ii, pp. 76, 100, 119;*
App. iv, p. 2; USC, i, pp. 249, 259; C. A. Harris and J. A. J. de Villiers, Storm van Gravesande: The Rise of British Guiana 2 vols (London, 1911), ii, p. 624.
6. *BGBV*, App. ii, p. 119; App. iv, pp. 7, 78.
7. *FGB*, App. i, pp. 24-25, 113.
8. *Ibid.*, p. 67.
9. *Ibid.*, p. 70.
10. *Ibid.*, p. 73.
11. *Ibid.*, p. 61.
12. *Ibid.*, pp. 61, 86.
13. *Ibid.* W. Farabee, *The Central Arawaks* (Anthropological Publications, Univ. of Philadelphia), 9 (1918), p. 13; G. W. Bennett, *An Illustrated History of British Guiana* (Georgetown, 1866), p. 87.
14. I. Myers, 'The Makushi of British Guiana', *Timehri*, 27, (1946), p. 18.
15. *FGB*, App. i, p. 139. See also R. M. Schomburgk, *Travels in British Guiana 1848-1844*, 2 vols (originally published 1834, rpt. Georgetown, 1922-23), ii, pp. 318, 343.
16. Schomburgk, *Travels*, i, p. 280, ii, p. 246.
17. *FGB*, App. i, p. 86.
18. *Ibid.*, p. 72.
19. *BGBV*, App. i, p. 91.
20. M. N. Menezes, *British Policy Towards the Indians in British Guiana, 1803-1873* (Oxford, 1977), p. 128
21. *BGBV*, App. i, p. 98.
22. J. Rodway, 'The Indian Policy of the Dutch', *Timehri*, new ser., 15, (1896), p. 28.
23. *BGBV*, App. iii, p. 104; App. iv, pp. 189-90; App. v, p. 73.
24. *Ibid.*, App. iii, p. 112.
25. A van Berkel (trans W. E. Roth), *Adriaan van Berkel's Travels in South America Between the Berbice and Essequibo Rivers and Surinam 1670-1689* (Georgetown, 1941), p. 70.
26. *BGBV*, App. i, p. 90.
27. *Ibid.*, App. iv, p. 188; *FGB*, App. i, p. 134.
28. *BGBV*, App. v, pp. 25-26.
29. Hartsinck, p. 291.
30. *BGBV*, App. iv, pp. 187, 188. *FGB*, App. i, p. 134.
31. *FGB*, App. i, p. 159.
32. V. Roth, 'Hillhouse's "Book of Reconnoissances"', *Timehri*, 25 (1934), pp. 20, 23.
33. Harris & De Villiers, ii, pp. 598-99.
34. *BGBV*, App. i, p. 103.
35. *Ibid.*, p. 105.
36. *Ibid.*, App. v, p. 216.
37. *Ibid.*, App. ii, p. 223.
38. *Ibid.*, App. iv, p. 5.
39. *Ibid.*, p. 124; see also pp. 190, 192.
40. *Ibid.*, p. 11.
41. V. Roth, *op. cit.*, p. 23.
42. J. Rodway, 'Indian Policy', p. 14.
43. *BGBV*, App. ii, p. 9.
44. *Ibid.*, p. 64.
45. *Ibid.*, p. 72-73.
46. *Ibid.*, pp. 182-83.
47. Harris & De Villiers, ii, pp. 661-65.
48. *BGBV*, App. i, p. 86.
49. *Ibid.*, App. ii, pp. 123, 125.
50. Cited by Harris & De Villiers, i, pp. 87-88.
51. *BGBV*, App. ii, pp. 2-3.
52. *Ibid.*, pp. 130-31.
53. Hartsinck, *op cit.*, p. 270. Actually, there were always a few Caribs and Akawois who were willing to give non-military service to the Dutch but their numbers were much smaller than those of the Arawaks and Warraus.
54. *Ibid.*, p. 17; Van Berkel, p. 29.
55. *BGBV*, App. iv, p. 16.

8

First Impressions: Europeans and Island Caribs in the Pre-colonial Era, 1492–1623

PHILIP P. BOUCHER

For more than a century before the English and French colonized the Carib-dominated Lesser Antilles, Europeans possessed significant information - and misinformation - about these "cannibals." In Europe, the literary elite became familiar with Hispanic tales of horror about fierce man-eating opponents of European imperialism. To be sure, French and English readers probably responded somewhat differently to the Spanish accounts, in part due to extensive and generally friendly French contacts with other "cannibal" people, the Tupinambas of Brazil. During the final decades of the pre-colonial era, less learned northern European merchants, sailors, and soldiers of fortune established growing contacts with the Island Caribs. Less familiar with Hispanic stereotypes, these adventurers conducted predominantly civil trade relations with aboriginal populations increasingly dependent on European ironware and spirits. Although these peaceable exchanges in no way altered the negative images of metropolitan intellectuals, they created connections that would later facilitate French, English, and Dutch occupation of the Lesser Antilles.

For most of the sixteenth century, however, Island Caribs had to deal with a most difficult European people, the Spaniards. Until at least the 1530s, Caribs persistently fought Spanish occupation of eastern Puerto Rico while attempting to defend their islands against slave raids, punitive expeditions, and campaigns of conquest. However, over time both sides found it useful to establish fragile periods of entente during which

Spanish fleets could victual in peace at Dominica and Island Caribs could obtain the iron goods - axes, knives, manioc griddles, iron pots - they so ardently desired. Nevertheless, after the Spaniards had occupied parts of Trinidad in the 1570s and supplied the Arawak enemies of all Caribs, war once more became the norm of this relationship. Fortunately for the Caribs, increasing numbers of Spain's enemies - Dutch, French, English - appeared in the Lesser Antilles, and these merchant-pirates provided alternate sources of European technology. In the short run, the abolition of the Spanish monopoly must have benefitted the Island Caribs; in the long run, these northern Europeans came and stayed.

Ironically, before Europeans actually encountered them, Island Caribs already possessed a reputation as blood-thirsty man-eaters. The marvellously fertile imagination of Christopher Columbus created the myth of "Carib cannibalism."[1] On his first voyage, the admiral understood from Taino Arawaks of Hispaniola (or so he thought that's what their sign language and facial grimaces meant) that their feared enemies (the "caniba" or "carib") inhabited islands to the east.[2] His initial description of these "cannibals" as "men with one eye, and others with dogs' noses" obviously reflected inherited classical and medieval notions about anthropophagi inhabiting the far ends of the earth,[3] especially those of the popular late medieval writer John Mandeville. Still, as Peter Hulme points out, Columbus initially was sceptical of Taino claims because he believed it possible that these

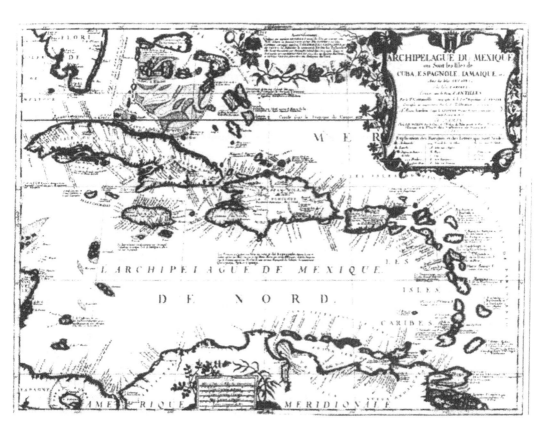

Marco Coronelli's 1688 map of the Lesser Antilles.
Near the island of Dominica is the caption "where live the greatest warriors of America, the anthropophagous Caribs."

"caniba" were soldiers of the Great Khan (*can* in Spanish).[4]

By the conclusion of his wanderings in Caribbean waters, however, Columbus had persuaded himself that Island Caribs were indeed fierce man-eaters and thus subject to enslavement. Although he admitted that he knew few Indian words, he facilely and mistakenly assumed that the first non-Taino to offer resistance to his incursion was a "Carib."[5] Columbus also came to accept the Taino-inspired idea that the "cannibal" islands contained much gold, so it is not surprising to learn that the Lesser Antilles were the initial goal of his second voyage (1493). Columbus intended to investigate reports of gold there and to enslave any "cannibals" he could catch.[6] After cruising about Dominica, he sent a landing party ashore at Guadeloupe, fully expecting a hostile reception. No "Caribs" were found in the village, but their female slaves "confirmed," by sign language presumably, that

their masters were indeed ferocious man-eaters. The landing party retrieved four or five human bones. Not unaware of the Carib - and Taino - practice of burning dead bodies and preserving bones of kin, Columbus nevertheless concluded that Taino accusations were accurate.[7]

In a much publicised letter about this episode, expedition participant and "eyewitness" Dr. Chanca expressed certainty about the anthropophagy of these aborigines and described in sensational detail their culinary practices.[8] All too soon, the very words *Carib* and *cannibal* became synonyms. Despite the absence of first-hand evidence or eye-witness observation, without even much circumstantial evidence, Island Caribs acquired an ironclad reputation that resisted all empirical inquiries and critical examination until recent decades.

As Hulme usefully demonstrates, the term *cannibal* differed significantly from the old established word *anthropophagite*, which ordinarily referred to the ritual consumption of one's relatives after death. In contrast, cannibalism meant from the beginning what anthropologists call *exocannibalism*, the eating of those outside one's community. But it also connoted a ferocious predator-like tearing apart of the limbs.[9] Dr. Chanca, for example, claimed that the bones picked up in the Carib village had been gnawed.[10] As early as 1520 a Spanish writer asserted that the term *cannibal* derived from *canis*, the Latin word for dog.[11] Starting with Peter Martire, European writers often compared Caribs to wolves preying upon the gentle lambs of the Arawak nation.[12]

The emerging concept of Carib cannibalism had almost immediate consequences. Upon his triumphant return to Castile, Columbus urged Isabella and Ferdinand to permit enslavement of "these cannibals, a people very savage and suitable for the purpose, and well-made and of very good intelligence."[13] These qualities made them perfect candidates for the galleys, where, Columbus shrewdly noted for the benefit of the pious queen, they could acquire civilization and Christianity. (Not that the queen refused her royal share of slave-trading proceeds!) These Carib slaves could be payment for the large quantity of cattle needed for the islands. The admiral's view that strong-bodied Caribs would make perfect slaves reflected deep-rooted, Aristotelean conceptions.

In 1503, Isabella authorized the enslavement of those cannibals so inhuman as to resist Spanish arms and evangelism. This decision was reaffirmed by Ferdinand in 1511 and Charles I (Charles V, the Holy Roman Emperor after 1519) in 1525. In 1547, Charles excepted male "Carib" warriors from the New Laws of 1542, which prohibited Indian slavery. Not satisfied, Spanish colonists repeatedly demanded that "Carib" females be subject to enslavement, and the crown so granted in 1569. These edicts in practice allowed open season on all Indians, for anyone resisting Spanish imperialism was now considered "Carib."[14]

King Ferdinand's cedula of 1511, in truth a declaration of war, charged that Island Caribs inspired the Indians of the Greater Antilles, especially those of Puerto Rico, to revolt against their Spanish masters. Records in the Spanish archives indicate intense slave raids and colonization projects in the Lesser Antilles from 1512 to 1517, including the famous armada of Ponce de León in 1515. Not coincidentally, at this time the Arawak population of Hispaniola was in catastrophic decline.[15] How successful these slavers were is uncertain, although later Caribs lamented that Spaniards had killed most of their ancestors.[16] Barbados probably lost its aboriginal population, which may have been Island Carib. Whether this heavy mortality can be attributed to Spanish arms or to the introduction of European diseases is problematical.

The initial European image of Caribs reflected these early decades of hostility. In his widely publicized letter, Columbus created the dichotomy of the gentle, pliable Arawak and the monstrous Carib, warlike and cannibalistic. The immensely influential *Decades* of Columbus's fellow Italian Pietro Martire d'Anghiera (Peter Martire), a courtier of Charles I, propagated this Manichean approach to Amerindians. He felt strong sympathy for those "innocent sheep" the Arawaks, and a vitriolic dislike for those "ravenous wolves," the Caribs. In one of his most cited passages, this humanist scholar asserts that these "brutal men, cruel and terrible, living off human meat" impregnated captured women to assure an ever-fresh supply of human viands. These devils in the new-found Eden evoked from Martire's pen slashing, colourful invective that contrasts greatly with the sweet, bland depictions of his beloved Arawaks. Martire's resonant phrases and striking passages still echoed in geographical accounts two centuries later.[17]

Fierce Carib resistance to Spanish slavers and their subsequent raids on Spanish islands such as Puerto Rico inevitably "confirmed" the validity of the first impressions. Although the aborigines were unable to prevent Spanish ships from taking on water and woodøindeed, Dominica was by the 1530s the official stopping place for Spanish vessels proceeding to the Greater Antilles and the mainlands - they did stop sporadic Spanish colonization efforts, such as that for Guadeloupe in 1525.[18] Carib raids on eastern Puerto Rico apparently started as early as 1511, increased in momentum in the later 1520s, and reached a peak of intensity in the 1570s.[19] The presumed goals of these incursions, beyond revenge for slave raids, were prisoners and iron weapons. Caribs employed the captives as slaves and, if one can assume that European arms and diseases thinned their numbers, as potential recruits. Like other Amerindians, the islanders adopted prisoners into the group, which may explain the numerous episodes in which they tried to prevent captive or shipwrecked Europeans from returning to "civilization."

According to Spanish archives, these Stone Age people scored some remarkable victories against their European tormentors. For example, Caribs killed the survivors of the wreck of a Spanish treasure ship and stowed the mineral riches in a cave near the sea. A decade later a free black woman who escaped from Carib captivity claimed that the looted gold and silver surpassed the height of a man on horseback.[20] Many a European ship anchored off Dominica found its cables cut at night in the hope of a shipwreck. There are even some cases of ships captured at sea by Carib war canoes (periaguas or pirogues).[21] In response to these and other attacks, the Spanish dispatched raiding parties, set traps for Carib bowmen, and endlessly planned the final blow against these "pests of humanity."[22] The government, forever short of funds, sometimes hoped that missionaries might provide a cheaper solution. Many, perhaps most, of these monks were killed (nine alone in 1603-4), although from the 1550s on they no longer purportedly suffered the indignation of being eaten. As a famous legend explained, this reputed change in Carib degustation arose after some cannibals" became ill after feasting on a Spanish Friar.[23]

This account of Spanish-Carib relations is so far primarily one of unremitting and mutual antipathy. Yet, despite the recounted episodes above, there were many years in the sixteenth century without such encounters. Bits of evidence support the view that Spaniards and Island Caribs often exchanged goods with one hand while weapons occupied the other. Spaniards needed, often badly, provisions such as manioc flour, fish, yams, potatoes, and tobacco, whereas Caribs always were short of iron tools.[24] The near silence of the Spanish archives on this issue is no evidence against it; after all, only bad news crossed the Atlantic to the Council of the Indies. There is some linguistic evidence to suggest that the Spanish-Carib relationship was characterized by years of cautious entente as well as periods of war; as late as the 1650s, after many years of intense French contact, the Carib vocabulary contained more Spanish than French

words[25] - despite the contemporary conviction that Caribs loved the French as much as they hated the Spanish.

Given the tensions and outright conflicts between the two peoples, it is not surprising that literary images of Caribs remained abysmally negative. What changed was that Spanish writers, fascinated by the triumphs of Cortés, Pizarro, and other astonishing conquistadors, paid less attention to Island Caribs. Given the retention of the prevailing stereotypes, who could hope to surpass the imaginative Martire in invective? The lush Italian phrases turned to banalities in lesser writers. Gonzalo Fernándes de Oviedo, who twice stopped at Dominica in the 1520s en route to Hispaniola, railed at the abominable sins of these savages.[26] The influential historian Francisco Lopez dé Gomara, who never saw a Carib, merely repeated the horrifying tales of insatiable and epicurean cannibalism he found in earlier sources.[27] These authors expressed a deep abhorrence of what they considered gross inhumanity, but Martire's intense shock at the very existence of such creatures is missing, perhaps because Martire, unlike the Spanish chroniclers, genuinely sympathized with Amerindians like the Arawaks. In the widely translated works of Oviedo and Gomara we see perpetuated the none-more-evil reputation of Island Caribs.

The uniformly negative Spanish image of Caribs meant that two traditions emphasizing either positive or negative cultural traits did not emerge, as was for example the case vis-à-vis the Arawaks, Mexica, and Inca. Further damaging the Carib reputation was the fact that the word *cannibals* elicited a response of horror as well as fascination from European reading audiences. No Amerindian name - probably not even the Mexica and Inca - had greater recognition than Caribs, Tupinambas, and Patagonians.[28] Furthermore, the sensationalism created by man-eating accounts attracted those great popularizers and ethnographic simplifiers, the cosmographers. They pandered to public thirst by endlessly recounting tales lifted from Martire, Oviedo, and, in the case of Brazilian cannibals, accounts attributed to Americus Vespucci. Perhaps Sebastian Münster's *Cosmographia* (1544), which ran through forty-six printings in six languages between 1544 and 1650,[29] most effectively diffused such grotesque stories and illustrations as

A *boucherie* of dog-headed cannibals. From Lorenz Fries, *Uslegung Der Mer Carthen* (Strasbourg, 1525). *This sensationalized representation of American anthropophagy is deeply indebted to late medieval fantasies, especially those of John Mandeville.*

Martire's depiction of the presumed Carib practice of gelding and fattening young prisoners.[30] François Belleforest, who translated Münster into French with much updated material, reiterated the German's description of Caribs as "the nastiest, cruelest, lustful, lying . . . abominable people in the world."[31]

With perhaps competition only from the "Patagonians," Caribs were the ignoble savages par excellence for sixteenth-century reading audiences. To be sure, like other primitives and wild men of medieval lore, Caribs were described as strong, swift, and healthy, thus partaking of the excellencies of the animal world just below men in the chain of being. To readers nurtured on classical concepts, these physical blessings were indicators of their aptitude to serve more delicate, civilized men.[32] Physical and cultural attributes such as nakedness, scarification, long hair and tawny colour, as well as despised customs such as idolatry, crude diet and

filthy "table" manners, sexual "licence" and cannibalism, no doubt scandalized readers.[33]

For traditional Christians, such savages were manifestly the playthings of Satan; indeed, they looked like devils at their infamous drinking feasts (*ouicous*), and they were a stunning example of man's depravity unredeemed by Christ's grace. For those humanists who liked to attribute Golden Age innocence to such Amerindians as "Arawaks," Carib cannibals posed something of a problem. Peter Martire, so well known for his idealization of Arawaks, found not an iota of good to say about Caribs. His fellow Italian Girolamo Benzoni, who on the one hand chastized Spaniards for their unjust treatment of aborigines, nevertheless tagged Caribs with unpleasant epithets.[34] Other humanists, reflecting Aristotle's hostility to uncivilized peoples, found much support for their anti-primitivism in contemporary descriptions of these "bad boys." Of all the sixteenth-century commentators on cannibals, only Bishop Las Casas professed to understand, at least in certain circumstances, the practice of man-eating.[35]

The dominant Spanish view of Caribs received extensive attention in England and France. In France, there were numerous translations of Martire, Oviedo, Gomara, Münster, and other purveyors of the monstrous savage thesis. At the turn of the seventeenth century, the writings of the Spanish Jesuit José de Acosta and the Frenchman Pierre d'Avity firmly placed Caribs and other cannibals at the bottom rung of the human social ladder.[36] French readers also encountered Caribs in Antonio de Herrera's history, which popularized the endlessly quoted anecdote about the Caribs of Dominica who supposedly died after eating a Spanish monk.[37] Theodore DeBry's popular collection of voyages highlighted supposed cannibal feasts.[38] In his travels along northern South America,, Jean Mocquet distinguished in his text and in accompanying graphics friendly "Arawaks" from ferocious, cannibalistic mainland "Caribs."[39] DeBry's and Mocquet's pictorial images probably did as much to foster negative views of these "pests of humanity" as did all previous works.

Despite the extensive sources available to the French reading public, the visible impact of Caribs on intellectuals was relatively slight. That is manifestly not the case for another "cannibal" people, the Tupinambas. Unlike Caribs, these "Brazilians" entranced as often as they horrified readers. The French had an intense acquaintance with these peoples because of strategic and economic ties initiated in the early decades of the sixteenth century. Numerous merchant ships passed annually to Brazil to exchange European merchandise for the famous brazilwood, source of prized red dyes. French boys were left to reside among the "cannibals" in order to learn their language and customs. These interpreters (*truchements*) facilitated the trade and helped the Tupinambas against their Indian and Portuguese adversaries.[40] Their relationship became so close that European captives of the Tupinambas would try to pass as Frenchmen. The well-known narrative of Hans Staden's captivity among the Tupinambas points out dramatically the extent of the French presence on the "cannibal" coast.[41]

This strong economic and cultural relationship engendered distinct French awareness and reasonably precise images of the *Toupinam-*

boux.[42] Whereas the French had only sporadic intercourse with Island Caribs, regular connections with Tupinambas led to their frequent appearance in French ports and in Paris. Fifty Brazilians participated in the *spectacle* of 1550, the *entrée* of Henri II and Catherine de Médicis into Rouen. These Tupinambas, supported by some two hundred French veterans of the Brazil trade, staged a mock battle *à la sauvage* for the enthralled sovereigns.[43] Shortly after this exotic performance, Durand de Villegaignon's colonial expedition to Brazil sparked a bitter polemic between Catholics and Huguenots that further publicized Tupinamba culture.[44]

France's long relationship with these "cannibals" smoothed the path for later colonial encounters with Island Caribs. By the early seventeenth century, one observer of a Parisian extravaganza (in which six Tupinambas were baptised) felt no need to explain to his readers who these *Toupinamboux* were.[45] However the beginning of French - and European - interest in Brazilians really occurred a century earlier with the widespread publication of Americus Vespucci's supposed *Letters*. Although some aboriginal customs, especially cannibalism, were not to his taste, the author presented an imaginative and appealing portrayal of primitive life. He marvelled at the comely bodies of the naked Brazilians, especially those of the maidens. Their seeming lack of private property reminded him of man in the Golden Age.[46] His views spread rapidly, in part thanks to his influence on the cosmographers, although those sensation-mongers tended to place greater emphasis on "cannibal" rites.[47]

Also of European-wide impact were the books of Antonio Pigafetta and Hans Staden. Apparently first published in French in 1525, Pigafetta's account of the Magellan voyage described its encounter with "cannibals." The author insisted that Brazilian man-eating was a tribal ritual rather than a craving for human flesh. These *sauvages* lived long and healthy lives, a point also emphasized by Vespucci, and were of such a temperament that they "would be easy to convert."[48] A quite different impression must have remained with the reader of Staden's famous escapades among the "cannibals." His near stewing in a Tupinamba pot seems to have simultaneously horrified and enthralled European audiences. (His French readers would have been reassured that their countrymen, so greatly loved by these "savages," never served as the entrée.[49])

As part of the polemics aroused by Ville-gaignon's much publicized Brazilian fiasco, which on both sides was attributed to Catholic-Huguenot internecine conflicts, two major works spread knowledge of Tupinamba culture. The *Singularitez* of the Franciscan André Thevet presents lurid descriptions of the "cannibals" accompanied by sensational pictorial images.[50] On the one hand praising such Tupinamba virtues as their charity toward one another, the author on the other hand condemns their nakedness, their barbarism in war, their vindictiveness toward enemies, and, of course, their man-eating. Nevertheless, he trusts that one day Christianity will temper their incivility. Thevet's reader could choose whether to recall the Tupinambas' vices or virtues.[51] One suspects that the general reaction was along the lines of Thevet's English translator, who pointedly praised European arts and sciences, without which man would be "naked, barbarous and brutish."[52] The Genevian Calvinist Jean de Léry, who spent much more time in Brazil than Thevet, presents a more sympathetic portrait of the Brazilians, even placing their "cannibalism" in comparative context by noting that French Catholics had engaged in more ferocious acts of man-eating during the religious wars.[53] Always critical of contemporary European life, Léry praises the superior health, selfless hospitality, and genuine freedom from care (*sans souci*) of these simple people. He refutes Vespucci's claims of sexual libertinism among the Tupinambas, denying that their nakedness induces libidinous acts; just the opposite is true, he points out, as the coquettish half-dress of French courtesans demonstrated. In his most humane moments, Léry liked those charitable children of nature and expressed the exotic wish to be back among them. His readers must have marvelled at the author's peaceable stay with his "cannibal" hosts. In the final analysis, however, Léry the committed Calvinist could not approve intellectually of an idolatrous tribe, descendants of Cham.[54]

These popular works by authors who had firsthand evidence of Tupinamba culture and the numerous visits of Amerindians to France stimulated the interest of metropolitan littérateurs. Disgusted by France's religious wars, the famed poet Pierre Ronsard did not hesitate to depict the Tupinambas as Golden Age men, despite their "cannibalism." Europeans could only corrupt them, he claimed, and as a result should leave them in tranquility.[55] More informed and nuanced were the views of Michel de Montaigne, who shared Ronsard's contempt for contemporary European culture. Consulting the works of Thevet, Benzoni, and Gomara, as well as interviewing unsophisticated, straight-talking interpreters (*truchements*), the sage of Bordeaux praises the "cannibals" for living according to the laws of nature.[56] Tupinamba culture had much to teach corrupt Europeans: "The very words that import lying, falsehood, treason, dissimulations, covetousness were never heard among them."[57] Montaigne explained Tupinamba cannibalism, an obvious perversion of natural law, as a ritualistic rather than dietary trait of aboriginal culture; in any case contemporary Christians engaged in far more contemptible practices. He lauded the Tupinambas for their fidelity toward their wives, perhaps an implicit repudiation of Vespucci's frothy free-sex fantasies. The essayist's use of the word *admirable* in conjunction with the "simplicity and ignorance" of a people "without letters, laws, King or religion" was quite original in sixteenth-century thought.[58] It is crucial, to be sure, to understand the limits of Montaigne's primitivism: "We may then call them barbarous, in regard to reason's rule, but not in respect of us that exceed them in all kinds of barbarism." Montaigne's target was his countrymen, who he felt should have been ashamed that in so many ways *sauvages* lived a superior moral life. While his cannibals are less noble than pedagogical savages, this great thinker's essay "On Cannibals" is nevertheless a remarkable event in the development of modern anthropology.[59]

What accounts for this odd French sympathy toward an idolatrous and "cannibalistic" people who, furthermore, were "disfigured" by facial plugs and scarification? It is possibly germane to point to the strength of humanism in France. Studies of the classics provided examples of primitivism in Greek and Roman letters; however, the tradition of the ignoble savage was at least as prevalent in antiquity. It is tempting to resort to hypotheses about national character and note the anthropological bent of French thought from the sixteenth century forward. But such an observation merely begs the question. Was French sympathy for less-civilized peoples perhaps a result of an intellectual appreciation of the benefits wrought by the romanization of Gaul? Sixteenth-century French historians were well aware of these benefits, but they did not make an explicit analogy with the European occupation of America.

Less speculative approaches to this question of French sympathy for the indigenous people (*indigènes*) might address the following factors. The economic and military imperatives of the French-Tupinamba relationship promoted a policy of *douceur* and the need to understand aboriginal customs. Colonists, *truchements*, ministers, and priests transmitted basic knowledge of Tupinamba culture to metropolitan writers.[60] Is it therefore simply that valued allies would be assessed favourably, as were later the Hurons of New France, but not the Iroquois?[61] Not entirely, because relatively sympathetic views of Hurons, Caribs, and other friendly Amerindians had only a negligible impact on major seventeenth-century writers. Apparently central to the ability of sixteenth-century writers such as Ronsard and Montaigne to overcome the normal Europocentric view of the savage state as the negation of civil society was their disgust at the religiously-inspired barbarisms of their own "Iron Age."

Not all French observers translated discontent with contemporary society into love of savage life, so an image of the Tupinambas as ignoble savages competed with the more positive view. Three participants in the 1555 expedition, Villegaignon himself and the Huguenots Richer and Barre, conveyed very negative impressions of the Brazilians. The commander wondered "whether we had not fallen upon beasts possessed of human form," and the Calvinists held them in such low esteem that their evangelization seemed doubtful.[62] It would be interesting to know their colleague Léry's belief *at the time* of the expedition. Somewhat later, in 1581, a ship captain described Tupinambas as "brutal beasts" who cherished human meat as their "nectar and ambrosia."[63] These and similar views admittedly did not receive as much publicity as those more sympathetic opinions of Vespucci and Léry, but they did have an impact.

From the 1550s on, French "social scientists" were seeking explanations for the increasingly obvious diversity of human customs. Some, like Jean Bodin, used environmental theories to explain these differences. The emerging consensus about people of the "southern" parts of the world as being extremely cruel encompassed Ethiopians, Tupinambas, Patagonians, and Caribs. Bodin deemed New World savages "of all others most devoid of humanity"; he spoke of Brazilians in particular, who are "not content to eat the flesh of their enemies, but will bathe their children in their blood."[64] Louis Le Roy and Voisin de la Popeliniére promoted the emerging hypothesis that primitive cultures constituted the first stage in human social development. Le Roy's view that humans at this stage are "very simple and brutal, hardly different than beasts" was not entirely damning because he made it clear that Europe's first peoples lived as barbarously as do the American savages.[65]

At the turn of the seventeenth century, the influential books of Acosta and d'Avity promoted this idea of cultural, historically based hierarchy. The Jesuit José de Acosta and his intellectual disciple Pierre d'Avity placed Tupinambas in the lowest class of barbarian, the utterly primitive peoples for whom only forced conversion and civilization could exorcise their savagery. These groups, "altogether barbarous without law, without King, and without any certain place of abode, but go in troups like savage beasts," included Floridians, Caribs, and Tupinambas.[66] Father Acosta, much admired for his criticisms of Spanish excesses in the New World and for his contention that "civilized" Amerindians like Incas and Aztecs had the capacity for Christianization, held pessimistic views of "less-developed" peoples of whom he had no direct knowledge.[67] Among others, the works of Bodin, Acosta, and d'Avity suggest that the earlier Golden Age idealization of primitive Amerindians (but never of Caribs) had been swept aside in favour of hierarchical models of cultural evolution, which firmly assigned such peoples as Tupinambas and Caribs to the bottom rung of the human ladder. The intellectual tenor of the late sixteenth and seventeenth centuries was one characterized by increasing pessimism concerning human nature and the concomitant condition of "puritanism" in religion and authoritarianism in politics – singularly unfertile ground for favourable images of *sauvages*.

One final flurry of public interest concerning the Tupinambas occurred in conjunction with the French colony at Maragnan (south of the Amazon river mouth) in 1612-15. The Capuchin missionary Claude d'Abbeville's account envisioned the Tupinambas, upon conversion to Christianity, as the exemplars of a simple, virtuous life far superior to that of corrupt Europe.[68] Here were Léry's and Montaigne's pedagogical savages seen through millenarian Catholic lenses. Returning with Claude on a fund-raiser to Paris in 1613 were six Tupinambas, whose well-publicized and royally attended baptismal ceremony was the social highlight of the season. Paris was ablaze with enthusiasm for these *sauvages*. These events, however, marked the denouement of a century-old French fascination with Brazilians, but that very humanizing experience provided an intellectual and cultural context for the forthcoming colonial encounter with "Carib cannibals."[69]

In the half-century prior to colonization, English impressions of Caribs as established by Columbus, Martire, the Spaniards Oviedo, Gomara, and Acosta, and diffused through the cosmographies, did not perceptibly change. In the 1550s the Hispanophile Richard Eden presented translations of parts of Martire, Oviedo, Gomara, and Münster, especially those passages on the most bizarre Americans, the supposed Patagonian giants and cannibals.[70] With the ascent of Elizabeth I to the throne, growing anti-Hispanic sentiment led to a broader interest in Philip II's rich domains across the Atlantic. Strangely unresponsive to openings to the west previously,[71] Englishmen started dreaming of overseas adventures and soon an accompanying literature appeared. The *Decades* of Martire, especially important for the image of Carib as inhuman monster, was translated by Richard Willes in 1577 and more completely by Michael Lok in 1612.[72]

By the 1580s and 1590s, the heroic exploits of Drake and Hawkins in the Caribbean and the Raleigh-sponsored expeditions to "Roanoke" and Guiana further whetted English interest.[73] Richard Haklyut's collections of voyages both reflected England's new found curiosity and stimulated it. In his *Principal Navigations* (1598), the astute reader *could* have noticed descriptions of amicable English relations with Island Caribs; however, the aborigines in these accounts were usually called "naturals" or, if looked upon hostilely, "savages," but not Caribs. Therefore the reader may not have connected them to the infamous monsters of Martire and Münster.[74] In Raleigh's popular *Discovery of Guiana* and in the account of Charles Leigh, mainland Caribs received negative treatment because of their enmity toward Amerindians friendly to the English.[75]

Other books of these decades undoubtedly reinforced negative impressions of Caribs. The translation of the justly famous work of Acosta reached English readers in the post-Elizabethan era of détente with Spain; as noted previously, his enlightened views of Amerindian "civilizations" did not extend to the "cannibal" vagabonds of the Caribbean basin.[76] An influential

Louis de Jehan, a Tupinamba visitor to Paris, outfitted in courtier garb. From Claude d' Abbeville. *Historie de la mission des péres Capucins . . .* (Paris 1614)

exponent of Acosta's typologies, Pierre d'Avity was available to English readers in 1615 under the name of his translator (Grimstone) and once again Caribs occupied the lowest rank in human societies.[77] Part of Herrera's official history of the Indies, which was deeply indebted to Gomara and which reaffirmed the latter's horror of life among cannibals, was published in Purchase collection.[78] But perhaps George Abbot's unduly popular *Briefe Description,* which had eight printings between 1599 and 1636, best reflects contemporary English views.[79] What good traits Amerindians might possess by the "light of nature" - hospitality, affability, candidness - were snuffed out by Satan-induced vices such as incest, sodomy, adultery, and, among the Tupinambas and Caribs, cannibalism.[80] Abbot's descriptions were indeed "briefe" and sordid.

Any analysis of "American" impact on Elizabethan and Jacobean literature should emphasize the highly impressionistic quality of English images. Although true of French images as well, England had very much less direct contact with Amerindians, especially "cannibals." According to students of Elizabethan literature, mythical Arcadia and the half-mythical Orient held far more enchantment than did America.[81] The New World or the Indies for a Spenser or a Shakespeare were merely other words for fabulous wealth.[82] To be certain, savages depicted in *The Faerie Queene* and in *The Tempest* were more or less influenced by the new-found peoples; however, both of these great authors viewed savagery as the antithesis of civil and especially courtly society. For Spenser, the savage is the negation of his gentlemanly ideal and is placed alongside Irishmen, perhaps - a notch above brute beasts in the chain of being. His cannibals closely resemble, according to one scholar, the monstrous Caribs of Martire's *Decades.*[83] For Spenser, as for most Elizabethan intellectuals, there was no social loss of faith similar to that of Ronsard and Montaigne.

Shakespeare's *Tempest* and especially the character of Caliban, has launched an avalanche of critical studies. It is generally agreed that Shakespeare included and ultimately rejected Montaigne's sympathetic portrayal of cannibal culture.[84] Caliban is probably an anagram of *cannibal,* a term used in *Othello,* although Prospero's slave has no such overt inclinations in the play.[85] If Shakespeare wished to universal-ize the savage state in Caliban, why did he make him so difficult to visualize? Scholars have more or less plausibly linked Caliban to Patagonians, Tupinambas, Caribs, medieval wild men, and others,[86] but they are confounded by Shakespeare, who portrayed him as "half a fish and half a monster." Not only did all contemporary accounts of Amerindians emphatically insist that no natural deformities were found among these "savages," but Shakespeare undoubtedly saw "Virginians" in London.[87] Perhaps this latter assumption helps unravel the mystery about Caliban's monstrous form. Shakespeare accepted the neoplatonic notion that outward bodily form reflects the character and soul of the human being. Because Caliban epitomizes the savage state of man unredeemed by the gentility of civilization, how could he share the comely human form of Amerindian visitors to London? If Caliban is indeed a monster (he is called that thirty-seven times), his origins are perhaps in the fabulous world of Mandeville and Münster, rather than in that of Columbus and Martire.[88]

It is nevertheless plausible to argue that Shakespeare's audience connected Caliban with the new-found peoples.[89] When Caliban is described as speechless, or as babbling "like a thing most brutish," this reflects contemporary attitudes toward Amerindian dialects.[90] It is also notable that the conspiracy against Prospero is hatched only after Stephano plies Caliban with liquor. Caliban's primal sin of unrepenting sexual aggressiveness and his inability to distinguish right from wrong - similar to the beastly kingdom - reflected seemingly popular if not knowledgeable concepts of Amerindians.[91]

To the unknown extent that Caliban reflects the playwright's and his audience's assumptions about Amerindians, some assertions may be hazarded. Shakespeare's primarily unsympathetic depiction of Caliban, "this thing of darkness," probably indicates increasing English pessimism about Amerindians because of the events at Roanoke, the colonial setbacks in Guiana and St. Lucia (1605), and the uncertainty about the contemporary (1612) situation at Jamestown.[92] Caliban and all savages, abroad and at home, are the unrepentant enemies of the processes of civilization. It is no accident that Caliban conspires with the lower-class ruffians Trinculo and Stephano against the authority of Prospero. Secondly, Shakespeare's bizarre sketch of Caliban's physiognomy may have been plausible to an audience nurtured on a concept of a chain of being that barely separated the world of fictitious monsters and factual Amerindians. The popular work of Münster had grouped together these two categories, and English lack of interest in systematic ethnology as typified by Abbot's work did not help clarify the issue.[93] A dozen years before the colonization of the Carib islands, then, England's most popular playwright had produced a monstrous symbol of man's savage state, while across the channel six real "cannibals" in the costume of Renaissance gentlemen charmed the court of Marie de Médicis.[94]

The overwhelmingly negative literary characterizations of "Carib cannibals" had little apparent impact on the increasing numbers of Frenchmen and Englishmen who established sporadic trade contacts with the islands c. 1550-1625. Privateers hunting Iberian shipping, illicit traders, and colonists on their way to Virginia and Guiana often took on provisions at the Carib islands and initiated trade relations.[95] They chose the islands of the Lesser Antilles because the Spanish, who had difficulty protecting even the lifelines of their empire, only occasionally bothered them. Such Euro-Carib encounters were more often than not friendly because of mutual economic advantage and mutual antipathy toward Spaniards. The pithy accounts of some of these interactions suggest between the lines that Caribs were cautiously eager to obtain new sources of ironware, firearms, and spirits.[96] Their actions toward the northern Europeans appear remarkably consistent and civil. (It must be emphasized here that Caribs viewed an exchange of goods as a transfer of gifts between friends; in fact, the Carib word for exchange of goods and exchange of friendship is the same. Also, there is no word for trade, commerce, trader, or merchant, but many for gift and giver.) Only when visitors gave indication of overstaying their welcome, as happened to an English group at St. Lucia in 1605,[97] or when Europeans like those accompanying René de Laudonniére en route to Florida (1564) offended Carib customs were reprisals taken.[98] As for the Europeans, for the most part they appear unfamiliar with the grotesque literary image of the "cannibals." On some occasions when hostilities did erupt, the accounts indicate that the Europeans had received stern warnings by Spaniards or other Indians not to be entrapped by the apparent friendliness of these "sneaky" and "bloodthirsty" savages.[99]

Caribs had strategic as well as economic reasons for encouraging cautious contacts with northern Europeans. From 1569 the Spaniards had renewed efforts to control Trinidad and in so doing aid their Arawak allies in a protracted struggle against Caribs. Trinidad was of great strategic interest to Caribs who visited it frequently when trading and raiding on the continent. Spanish records indicate constant Carib attacks on the island.[100] That contacts with northern Europeans could prove fruitful in this direction was demonstrated in 1613 when a combined foray of Dutch pirates and Carib bowmen seriously threatened Spanish settlers.[101] But the Caribs also had to deal with an increasingly aggressive Spanish threat to their home islands. Perhaps motivated by the killing of Dominican missionaries, the crown granted licences to make war against the Island Caribs and in subsequent years many prisoners were sold at auction.[102]

Carib-Northern European relationships in the "Spanish Caribbean" turned out to be a double-edged sword. Caribs of St. Vincent would see the Dutch - who had from the 1590s established ties with them because of their mutual hostility to the Spaniards and Arawaks at Trinidad - settle at St. Martins and then in 1628 at Tobago. The latter island was as much a threat to Carib communications as Trinidad and thus they expelled the Dutch.[103] Caribs of St. Christopher, Dominica, Martinique, and Guadeloupe, unaware of the tobacco revolution that sent European prices skyrocketing, witnessed increasing settler interest in their islands, especially as colonies in the Amazon valley and Guiana failed to take root. On the other hand, Europeans who supplied Caribs with axes allowed more efficient production of pirogues, and their less frequent furnishing of firearms fostered Carib acquaintance with the Europeans' chief advantage in war.[104]

Thus, in the years prior to colonization of the Lesser Antilles, Englishmen and Frenchmen conducted reasonably civil relations with Island Caribs, whereas in Europe at least some readers must have harboured nightmarish visions of these "assassins of men who drink their blood."[105] The contrast between the realities of cultural contact and the literary images is startling. In 1619 and 1620, a group of stranded

Frenchmen spent some ten peaceable months among anomymous Martiniquan Caribs, an experience that permitted the author of a manuscript to be remarkably free of ingrained prejudices against such strange peoples.[106] At nearly the same time in France, the author of a typical cosmography could dismiss Caribs with one phrase -- "savage, cruel anthropophagites."[107] In England, despite frequent cordial contacts in the islands with these "cannibals," some of which are related in Haklyut, that sensation-monger Samuel Purchas could chuckle to his readers that he had omitted cannibal scenes from one account (Léry) because "we have glutted you already."[108] Whereas Tupinamba visits to France had a humanizing impact, no Island Caribs appeared on the streets of Paris and London or saluted the king at the Louvre or Whitehall. With the advent of the settling in 1623-25 of St. Christopher (modern St. Kitts) and soon other islands, English and French settlers began to deal with Caribs in a much more difficult relationship, that of contestants for limited land. The era of good feelings in the islands rapidly drew to a close: it had never begun in the parlours and studies of the European elite.

Notes

1. Jalil Sued Badillo, *Los Caribes: Realidad o Fabula: Ensayo de Rectificacion Historica*. (Rio Piedras, Puerto Rico: Editorial Antillana, 1978), pp. 36-39 This image would persist for five centuries, especially in Anglo-American literature. See, for example, Samuel Eliot Morison, *The European Discovery of America: The Northern Voyages* (New York: Oxford University Press, 1971), 660, 674; *Admiral of the Ocean Sea* (Boston: Little, Brown, 1942), 407.

2. Richard B. Moore, "Carib 'Cannibalism': A Study in Anthropological Stereotyping," *Caribbean Studies* 13 (1973): 121-22. The Arawak word *carib* signified either "manioc eaters" or "valiant warrior." For the first meaning, see Douglas Taylor, "Carib, Caliban, Cannibal," *International Journal of American Linguistics* 24 (1958): 156-57.

3. Eric Williams, ed., *Documents of West Indian History, 1492-1655* (Port-of-Spain, Trinidad: P.N.M. Publishing, 1963), 48.

4. Peter Hulme, "Columbus and the Cannibals: A Study of Reports of Anthropophagy in the Journal of Christopher Columbus," *Ibero-Amerikanisches Archiv 4* (1978): 121; Christopher Columbus, *The Log of Christopher Columbus*, ed. Robert Fuson (Camden, Maine: International Marine Publishing, 1987),

5. Hulme, "Columbus and the Cannibals," 130-31. See also Williams, ed., *Documents*, 50; Columbus, *The Log*, 172.

6. Patrick Baker, "Ethnogenesis: The Case of the Dominica Caribs," *America Indigena 48*, (1998), p. 380.

7. *Ibid.*; According to Sued Badillo, *Los Caribes*, 42, Columbus had witnessed in Cuba funerary practices that should have provided an explanatory context for these human remains.

8. Letter in Williams, ed., *Documents*, 51. The first Spaniard to die of an Island Carib poison arrow fell at St Croix during Columbus' second expedition; Troy S. Floyd, *The Columbus Dynasty in the Caribbean, 1492-1526* (Albuquerque: University of New Mexico Press, 1973), 20.

9. Hulme, "Columbus and Cannibals," 133-34; see also Hulme, "Hurricanes in the Caribbees: The Constitution of the Discourse of English Colonialsim," in *Literature and Power I the Seventeenth Century: Proceedings of the Essex Conference on the Sociology of Literature*, ed. Francis Baker et al. (Colchester: University of Essex Press, 1981), 64-65.

10. Williams, ed., *Documents*, 51.

11. Hulme, "Hurricanes," 67.

12. Pietro Martire d'Anghiera, *Extrait ou recueil des isles nouvellement trouvées . . .* (Paris: S. de Colines, 1532), 3-9, 23.

13. Williams, ed., *Documents*, 57.

14. Ibid., 62, Sued Badillo, *Los Caribes*, 77-78, 87. For the 1569 decree, see Whitehead, "Carib Cannibalism," 73.

15. C.J.M.R. Gullick, *Myths of a Minority*. (Assen, Netherlands: Van Gorcum, 1985), p. 44. For the tragic Spanish impact on the Taino, see Carl Sauer's admirable *The Early Spanish Main* (Berkeley: University of California Press, 1966).

16. As told to Father Raymond Breton, the first French missionary among the Dominica Caribs. His manuscript relations are printed in Raymond Breton, *Les Caraibes. La Guadeloupe . . . d'apres les Relations du R.P. Breton*, ed. by J. Rennard. (Paris: G. Ficker, 1929), p. 48. The slave raids subsided gradually as the Spanish focus shifted from the Greater Antilles to the mainland; Sued Badillo, *Los Caribes*, 87.

17. Martire, *Extrait*, 4-9, 23, 69, 83, 105. Richard Eden's first English translation of part of the *Decades* may be consulted in Edward Arber, ed., *The First Three Books on America* (Edinburgh: Turnbull and Spears, 1885). An augmentation of Eden's translation appeared as *The History of travayle in the West and East Indies . . .*, trans. Richard Willes (London: Jugge, 1577). Finally, a complete translation reached readers in 1612 as *De novo orbe, or the historie of the West Indies . . .*, trans. Michael Lok (London: Adams, 1612). For further information on the spread of Martire's views throughout Europe, consult Boies Penrose, *Travel and Discovery in the Renaissance, 1420-1620* (Cambridge: Harvard University Press, 1952), 344.

138. It was common for Caribbean basin aborigines to ascribe anthropophagic practices to their neighbors; see Sued Badillo, *Los Caribes*, 74.

18. Joseph Boromé, "Spain and Dominica, 1493-1647," *Caribbean Quarterly* 12 (1966): 33. Although this chapter owes a great debt to Boromé's archival research, his work must be used carefully because he completely accepts his Spanish sources' hostility toward Caribs.

19. *Ibid.*, 33-34. For these conflicts, see also Troy S Floyd, *The Columbus Dynasty in the Caribbean, 1492-1526.* (Albuquerque: University of New Mexico Press, 1973), pp. 102, 105-6, 135. Carl O. Sauer, *The Early Spanish Main.* (Berkeley: University of California, 1966), pp. 180, 192-95. Sued Badillo is skeptical about the official reports of frequent Carib raids, calling them alarmist and self-serving.

20. Boromé, "Spain and Dominica," 3.

21. Gullick, *Myths of a Minority*, 40-41.

22. For this pharse, see Giovanni Magini, *Histoire universelle des Indes* . . . (Douai: Fabri, 1605), 67.

23. Boromé, "Spain and Dominica," 37.

24. See, for example, Thomas Gage, *A new survey of the West India's: or the English American* . . ., 2nd ed. (London: Cotes, 1655), 17. For a more typical example of hostile encounters, see Samuel de Champlain, *Narrative of a Voyage to the West Indies and Mexico in the Years 1599-1602*, trans. Alice Wilmere (London: Haklyut Society, 1859), 6.

25. Douglas M. Taylor, "Diachronic Note on the Carib Contribution to Island Carib." *International Journal of American Linguistics 20.* (1954), p. 29. According to Sued Badillo, Father Breton's famous French-Carib dictionary shows that 10 percent of aboriginal words were European-derived by the mid-seventeenth century; see *Los Caribes*, 93.

26. Gonzalo Fernándes de Oviedo y Valdés, *L'Historie naturelle et générale des Indes* . . ., trans. Jean Poleur (Paris: M. de Vascoson, 1555), 42. Parts of Oviedo were translated into English by Eden; see Arber, ed., *The First Three Books on Ameria*. Samuel Purchas later included parts of Oviedo in *Haklyutus posthumus or Purchas his pilgrimes*, 4 vols. (London: Fetherstone, 1625), 3:970-1000. Consult Sterling Stoudemire's introduction to Oviedo, *Natural History of the West Indies*, trans. Stoudemire (Chapel Hill: University of North Carolina Press, 1959), for biting criticism of Eden's and Purchas' translations.

27. Francisco Lopez dé Gomara, *L'historie générale des Indes occidentales* . . . trans. Martin Fumée, erd ed. (Paris: Sonnius, 1605), 238-39. There were six French editions between 1569 and 1606. Only part of Gomara's writings were translated into English; see Gomara, *The Pleasant historie of the conquest of the West Indies*, trans. Thomas Nicholas (London: T. Creede, 1596). For one example of Gomara's influence, see the negative appraisal of Caribs in Magini's *Histoire universelle des Indies*, 97.

28. For knowledge of the Aztec and Inca, readers could consult in English only Francisco Lopez de Gomara, *The pleasant histoire of the conquest of the West Indies*, trans. by Thomas Nicholas. (London: T. Creede, 1596), one edition of José de Acosta's *The Natural and Moral History of the Indies* . . ., trans.

Edward Grimstone (London, 1604. Reprint [London: Haklyut Society, 1880] and only parts of Garcia Lasso de la Vega in Purchas, *Haklyutus posthumus*, vol. 4. The French had the complete Gomara and Lasso de la Vega (1631) as well as seven printings of the influential Acosta.

29. Margaret Hogden, *Early Anthropology in the Sixteenth and Seventeenth Centuries* (Philadelphia: University of Pennyslvania Press, 1964), 147-49.

30. Münster, in Arber, ed., *The First Three Books on America*, 29, 30. John Mandeville has his anthropophagi fattening children before eating them; Mandeville, *Mandeville's Travels*, ed. Maurice C. Seymour (London: Oxford University Press, 1963), 138-39. Was this the inspiration of European views, perpertrated by Vespucci and Martire, that Brazilians and Caribs gelded and fattenend young captives before eating them? Anthony Pagden asserts that there is a set type of cannibal feast in classical literature that influenced sixteenth-century accounts; Anthony Pagden, *The Fall of Natural Man: The American Indian and the Origins of Comparative Ethnology*. (Cambridge: Cambridge University Press, 1982), pp. 216, 217. He supports Arens' views on cannibalism by saying that he has never encountered a European description of Amerindian anthropophagy not indebted to classical sources.

31. Sebastian Münster, *La cosmographic universelle* . . . *augmentée* . . . par François Belleforest . . . (Paris: Chesneau, 1575), 301, 2071-73. For examples of negative views of other cosmographers, see Ch. Fontaine, *Les nouvelles et Antiques merveilles* (Paris: Le Noir, 1554), 5-6; Petrus Apianus, *Cosmographic, ou description* . . . *du monde* . . . (Antwerp: Bellere, 1581), 153, 157, 171.

32. A concept familiar to Columbus; see Williams, ed., *Documents*, 54.

33. See Olive P. Dickason, *The Myth of the Savage and the Beginnings of French Colonialism in the Americas.* (Edmonton: University of Alberta Press, 1984), p. 144. for the argument that the tawny (Basané) fless of Amerindians was usually considered a negative trait.

34. Girolamo Benzoni, *Histoire nouvelle du Nouveau monde* . . . (Geneva: Eustace Vignon, 1579), pp. 191, 252-259. Benzoni did partially excuse Caribs for barbecuing Spanish captives by noting that revenge, not hunger, motivated their actions; see 252-259.

35. Bartolomé de las Casas, *History of the Indies*, trans. Andrée Collard (New York: Harper and Row, 1971), 127. For translations of las Casas, see Colin Steele, *English Interpreters of the Iberian New World from Purchas to Stevens (1603-1726): A Bibliographical Study* (Oxford: Dolphin, 1975), 70-71. For the ideological context of European translations, see William S. Maltby, *The Black Legend in England* (Durham, N. C: Duke University Press, 1971), 13-20; and Loren S. Pennington, "The Amerindian in English Promotional Literature," in *the Westward Enterprise*, ed. K. N. Andrews, N. P. Canny, and P. E. H. Hair (Detroit: Wayne State University Press, 1979), 183.

36. Acosta, *Histoire naturelle et moralle des Indes . . .*,
trans. Robert Regnault (Paris: Marc Orry, 1616),
209, 224, 275; Jose de Acosta, *The Natural and
Moral History of the West Indies . . .*, trans. and ed.
by Edward Grimstone, (London, 1604. Reprint.
London: Haklyut Society, 1880), 2: 427; Avity, *Les
états, empires . . . du monde*, 18, 281. There were at
least eleven French printings of Avity. In contrast,
the sole English edition is Avity, *The estates,
empires . . . of the world . . .*, trans. Edward
Grimstone (London: Islip, 1615), 236-37, 252.

37. Part of Herrera's history, including this anecdote, is
in Samuel Purchas, *Haklytus posthumus or Purchas
his Pilgrimes*. 4 vols. (London: H. Fetherstone,
1625), 14: 451-53. The anti-Hispanic, anti-Catholic
Purchas could not resis a quip in the margin: "Friar
unwholesome food."

38. William Sturtevant, "First Visual Images of Native
America," In *First Images of America: The Impact
of the New World on the Old*, ed. Fredi Chiapelli, 1:
417-54. 2 vols. (Berkeley: University of California
Press, 1976), 1: 433. For an analysis of Theodore
Debry's powerful pictoral images, see Bernadette
Bucher, *La sauvage aux seins pendants* (Paris:
Hermann, 1977).

39. Jean Mocquet, *Voyages en Afrique, Asie, Indes Ori-
entales et Occidentales . . .* (Rouen: Calloué, 1645),
83, 88-90, 100.

40. For an overview of this question, see Olive P.
Dickason, "The Brazilian Connection: A look at the
Origins of French Technique, for Trading with
Amerindians." *Revue francaise d' histoire d'Outre-
mer 71*, (1984), pp. 129-46; see also Edouard H.
Gosselin, ed., *Documents authentiques . . . à l'his-
toire de la marine normande . . .* (Rouen: Boissel,
1876), 142-45.

41. A French translation of Staden was published in the
same year as the German original (1557). There was
no English translation until Purchas Published extracts in *Purchas his Pilgrimage . . .*, 3rd ed. (London: Fetherstone, 1617). Readers of Latin had access
to Staden in DeBry's *Voyages*. For another example
of a European feigning Frenchness, see Anthony
Knivet's relation in Purchas, *Haklyutus posthumus*,
16:219-33.

42. For the frequent pictorial representations of Brazilian "cannibals," see Sturtevant, "First Visual Images," *in First Images of America*, ed. Fredi
Chiapelli, I:417-54; see also Paul Hulton, "Images
of the New World: Jacques Le Moyne de Morgues
and John White," in *The Westward Enterpise*, ed. K.
R. Andrews, N. P. Canny, and P. E. H. Hair, 197.

43. Ferdinand Denis, *Une Fête Brésilienne celebrée à
Rouen en 1550* (Paris: J. Techener, 1850). He also
describes a similar *spectacle* at Bordeaux in 1556.

44. So much so that Sturtevant, "First Visual Images,"
in *First Images of America*, ed. Fredi Chiapelli,
I:420-21, considers the Tupinambas the best-known
Amerindians in the sixteenth century except for the
half-mythical Patagonians; see also Paul Gaffarel,
Histoire du Brésil français (Paris: Maisonneuve,
1879), 321-23.

45. Michel de Marolles, *Les Mémoires de . . .* (Paris: A.
de Sommaville, 1656-57), 28. François La Mothe Le
Vayer, *Oeuvres . . .* 2 vols. (Paris: Courbé, 1654)
2:808, asserts that "we have so many accounts of the
Tupi."

46. Fracanzano da Montalbodd0, *S'ensuit le Nouveau
Monde . . .*, trans. Mathurin Redouer (Paris, 1515),
109, 113, 14. There wre six French printings. A study
of four libraries in sixteenth-century Paris shows that
two held only Vespucci on America and a third Vespucci and Martire; Roger Coucet, *Les Bibliothèques
parisiennes au xvie siècle* (Paris: Picard, 1956).

47. For examples, see Apianus, *Cosmographie*; Johannes Macer, *Les trois livres de l'histoire des Indes . . .*
(Paris: Guillard, 1555), 77-79; Etienne Pasquier, *Les
lettres . . .* (Lyons: Jean Veyrat, 1597), 83-84.
Pasquier does caution his reader to be prudent about
believing reports that are unverifiable.

48. Antonio Pigafetta, *Le voyage et navigation faict par
les Espagnols* (Paris: S. de Colines, 1525), 3-6.

49. Johann von Staden, *Véritable histoire . . . d'un
pays . . . dans le nouveau monde . . .* (Marbourg:
Koldbe, 1557), 116, 175.

50. André Thevet, *Les Singularitez de la France antarctique . . .* (Paris: :as Porte, 1557). Arens argues
that Thevet, who visited Brazil only briefly, based
his cannibal scenes on Staden's work; William
Arens, *The Man-Eating Myth: Anthropology and
Anthropophagy*. (New York: Oxford University
Press, 1979), pp. 29-30. However, Sturtevant notes
that Thevet used eyewitness accounts as well as
other books; Sturtevant, "First Visual Images of
America." In *First Images of America*, ed. Fredi
Chiapelli, 435-37.

51. Thevet, *Les singularitez*, 86, 123, 143-44, 195-205,
217. He has more detail in *La cosmographie . . .*
(Paris P. L'Huillier, 1575), for which he consulted interpreters. See Ch. André Julien, *Les Français en
Amérique pendant la deuzième moitié du xvie siècle*
(Paris: P. U. F., 1953), vii, viii. See also Frank
Lestringant's introduction to André Thevet, *Les singularitez de la France Antarctique*, ed. Frank Lestringant (Paris: Maspero, 1983).

52. See Hackett's dedication to Thevet, *The New found
World, or Antarctike . . .* (London: Henrie Bynne-
man, 1568). One French poet, praising *Les singularitez*, writes: "More than an inhuman Scythian you
see (here in this book) the Canibale who on human
meat and blood is glutted drunk"; quoted in Ch.
Andre Julien, *Les Francaises en Amerique pendant
la deuxieme moitie du xvie siecle*. (Paris: P.U.F.,
1953), p. 378.

53. Jean de Léry, *Histoire d'un voyage fait en la terre du
Brésil*, ed. Paul Gaffarel, 2 vols. (Paris: A. Lemerre,
1880), 228-30. There were six printings from 1578
to 1611, and fragments appeared in DeBry and Purchas. An anonymous sonnet, dedicated to Léry, reflects the book's puzzlement at who, European or
Tupinamba, is the real savage. "If they [Tupinam-
bas] knew, Léry, how without mercy we eat each
other, they would fear that from here we would quarrel with them over the title savage"; cited in Roger

Le Moine, ed., *L'Améerique et les poètes français de la Renaissance* (Ottawa: University of Ottawa Press, 1972), 124.

54. Jean de Léry, *Histoire d'un voyage fait en la terre du Bresil.*(La Rochelle, 1578), ed. by Paul Gaffarel. 2 vols. (Paris: A Lemerre, 1880), pp. 95, 271, 194, 280. For an example of a sympathetic description of the Tupinambas based on Léry, see Jan Huygen van Linschoten, *Description de l'Amérique . . .* (Amsterdam: I. E. Cloppenburch, 1619), 35-46.

55. Elizabeth Armstrong, *Ronsard and the Age of Gold* (Cambridge: Cambridge University Press, 1968), 27-30. For Ronsard's vagueness about America, see Geoffrey Atkinson, *Les nouveaux horizons de la Renaissance français* (Paris: Froz, 1935), 314-15, 337. In his introduction and notes, Roger Le Moine, ed., *L'Amerique et les poetes francais de la Rennaissance.* (Ottawa: University of Ottawa Preess, 1972). asserts that Ronsard and other French poets had a superficial knowledge of America, emphasizing its spectacular riches and the brutality of the aborigines.

56. Montaigne saw Tupinambas at Rouen during the reign of Charles IX. Hogden claims that he read Léry (1578), but in another place asserts that "Of Cannibals" was probably composed in the first half of the 1570s; Margaret Hogden, *Early Anthropology in the Sixteenth and Seventeenth Centuries.*(Philadelphia: University of Pennsylvania Press, 1964), p. 192. Montaigne proudly possessed a number of Tupi artifacts, including hammock and club.

57. Michel Eyquem de Montaigne, *The Essays of Montaigne*, trans. John Florio, 3 vols. (London, 1892-93. Reprint [New York: AMS Press, 1967]}, I:222.

58. *Ibid.*, I:255-56; I:224; 2:255. The cannibals, who Montaigne says had never heard of Aristotle or philosophy, "enjoy most happily, a long, a quiet, and a peaceful life.

59. For the originality and limits of Montaigne's anthropology, see Hogden, *Early Anthropology*, 191-92. Despite the scores of editions of the essays in seventeenth-century France and England, I have located only rare references to "Of Cannibals" in seventeenth-century literature. Such disciples of Montaigne as Pierre Charron and François La Mothe Le Vayer agreed with his relativistic approach to human culture, but they used references to the ancients; Charron, *De la sagese*, 3 vols. (Paris: Barrois l'ainé, 1789), I:98; La Mothe Le Vayer, *Quatres dialogues . . . d'Orasius Tubero* (Francfort: I. Sarius, 1606), 30-37. One early seventeenth-century French author, *citing* Montaigne, paints a dark picture of the Tupinambas; see Hogden, *Early Anthropology*, 197. See Atkison, *Les nouveaux horizons*, 154, 356, for a few other references; see also Alan Boase, *The Fortunes of Montaigne: A History of the Essays in France, 1580-1689* (London: Methuen, 1935), 10-11, 399-400. Other than Shakespeare's famous lifting of a passage from "On Cannibals (Discussed below), there are few references to Montaingn's relativistic approach to the New World in seventeenth-century English literature.

60. Julien, *Les Français en Amérique*, 571-72, claims that the *truchements* were the catalysts of a more objective French evaluation of the Tupinambas. For a dissent, see Le Moine, ed., *L'Amérique*, 14, 15.

61. As an example of the tendency to evaluate useful Amerindians more positively, see Jacques Auguste de Thou, *Histoire universelle . . .*, 16 vols. (London, 1734), 7:576-78, and 2:652. When de Thou, no admirer of Amerindians, discusses the Brazilian victims of the hated Villegaignon, he elects to substitute the more favorable *naturels for sauvages*, which he uses elsewhere.

62. The Villegaignon and Richer letters are published in Charles Bairds, *History of the Huguenot Emigration to America*, 2 vols. (New York: Dodd, Mead, 1885), I:334-35, 338. Nicholas Barre's views are cited in Gaffarel, *Les Français en Brésil*, 497-98.

63. The letter is published in Gaffarel, *Les Français en Brésil*, 493-501. These examples demonstrate that contact with the Tupinambas did not of itself result in sympathetic appraisals. See also Etienne Pasquier, *Escrits politiques*, ed. D. Thickett (Geneva: Broz, 1956), 83, who espouses negative views of "Brazilians" as a result of conversations with a traveler to that region.

64. Jean Bodin, *The six books of a Commonweale*, ed. Kenneth McRac (Cambridge: Harvard University Press, 1962), 735, 64; *Les six livres de la République* (Geneva:Gamonet, 1629), 680, 682. In his earlier work, *Method for the easy comprehension of history*, trans. Beatrice Rynolds (New York: Octagon Books, 1966), 102, Bodin calls Brazilians "cannnibals" and "bloodsuckers," a view based on Vespucci and Münster. Bodin's only other source for the *Method* was Columbus. For the later *Republic*, he may have read Spanish sources in French translation-for example Oviedo and Gomara-but there are no specific references. For a severe critique of Bodin's anthropological thought, see John H. Rowe, "Ethnography and Ethnology in the sixteenth Century." *Kroeber Anthropological Society Papers* 30 (1964): 4.

65. Cited in Geoffery Atkinson, *Les nouveaux horizons de la Renaissance francaise.*(Paris: Froz, 1935), pp. 154, 356. For Le Roy and La Popelinière as social theorists, see George Huppart, *The Idea of Perfect History: Historical Erudition and Historical Philosophy in Renaissance France* (Urbana: University of Illinois Press, 1970), 110, 150. La Popelinieère so strongly believed that Amerindians held the key to understanding the conditio of early man that he offered to undertake the difficult voyage to American to study them if the Estates of Holland would subsidize him. Nothing came of the offer.

66. Avity, *The estates*, 252; see also Avity, *Les états*, 61, 113-15.

67. Acosta, *The Natural and Moral History*, 2:410, 2:427; see also Acosta, *Histoire naturelle et moralle*, 209, 224, 275.

68. Claude d'Abbeville, *Histoire de la mission des pères Capucins . . .* (Paris, F. Huby, 1614), Preface.

69. Do not these substantial French experiences with the "Brazilians" and "Floridians" help explain their

later commercial and colonial successes in Acadia and New France? This is also the view of Dickason, "The Brazilian Connection."

70. Arber, ed., *The First Three Books on America*. For an analysis of Eden's work, see Richard G. Cole, "Sixteenth Century Travel Books as a Source of European Attitudes toward Non-White and Non-Western Culture," Transactions of the American Philosophical Society 116 (1972): 63.

71. Among others who have discussed this point, see Sydney Lee, *Elizabethans and Other Essays*, ed. F. S. Boas (Oxford: Clarendon Press, 1929), 217; Howard M. Jones, "The Image of the New World," in *Elizabethan Studies and Other Essays in Honor of George F. Reynolds*, ed. J. F. West (Boulder: Colorado University Press, 1945), 62-92; Jarvis Morse, *American Beginnings: Highlights and Sidelights of the Birth of the New World* (Washington, D. C.: Public Affairs Press, 1952); and John Parker, *Books to Build an Empire* (Amsterdam: N. Israel, 1965).

72. See Peter Martire d'Anghiera, *The history of travayle in the West & East Indies . . .* trans. by Richard Willes.(London: Jugge, 1577), pp. 10-13, 137, 144-45, 149. for passages on Caribs. The editor Willes' marginal notes highlight the Italian's sensational discourses on "cannibals."

73. Besides the authors listed in note 71, see E. G. R. Taylor, *Late Tudor and Early Stuart Geography, 1583-1650* (London: Methuen, 1934): Kenneth R. Andrews, *Trade, Plunder and Settlement: Maritime Enterprise and the Genesis of the British Empire, 1480-1630* (Cambridge: Cambridge University Press, 1984); Andrews, *The Spanish Caribbean: Trade and Plunder, 1530-1630* (new Haven: Yale University Press, 1978); and David B. Quinn and A. N. Ryan, *England's Sea Empire, 1550-1642* (London: Allen and Unwin, 1983).

74. Richard Haklyut, *The Principal Navigations . . . of the English Nation*, 12 vols. (London, 1598. Reprint [Glasgow: maclehose and Sons, 1904-5]), 7:88, 7:149, 7:174, 7:165, 7:218; for negative views of Caribs, see 10:29, 10:207, 10:478, 7:383-84.

75. Sir Walter Raleigh, *The Discoverie of Guiana* (London, 1596. Reprint [Amsterdam: Da Capo Press, 1968]), 29, 35, 43;see also 151, where Raleigh remarks that the initially unfriendly Amerindians excused their hostility by asserting that the Spaniards had warned them that the English were man-eaters. Spaniards were old hands at this game. For Leigh's account, see Haklyut, *Principal Navigations*, 10:303-5.

76. Acosta, *The Natural and Moral History*, 2:410. It should be noted tha there was only one edition in English,as compared to seven in French.

77. Avity, *The estates, empires . . .*, 249, 258. Again, one English edition compared to eleven French.

78. Purchas, *Haklyutus posthumus*, 3: book 5, ch. I.

79. George Abbot, *A briefe description of the whole world . . .* (London: Sheares, 1634); on America, see 240-329. For Abbot's popularity, see Hogden, *Early Anthropology*, 200; Parker, *Books to Build an Empire*, 259; and Colin Steele, *English Interpreters of the Iberian New World from Purchas to Stevens, 1603-1726: A Bibliographical Study*.(Oxford: Dolphin, 1975), p. 21. Parker notes that Haklyut's work was not reprinted during all the years of Abbot's popularity.

80. George Abbot, *A briefe description of the whole world . . .* (London: Sheares, 1634), pp. 253, 263, 298-302.

81. Harry Levin, *The Myth of the Golden Age in the Renasisance* (Blookington: Indiana University Press, 1969), 99; Sydney Lee, *Elizabethan and Other Essays*, ed. by F.S. Boas.(Oxford: Clarendon Press, 1929), p. 288.

82. Other than Lee, see Arthur Slavin, "The American Principle from More to Locke," in *First Images of America*, ed. Fredi Chiapelli, I:146.

83. Roy H. Pearce, "Primitivistic Ideas in the *Faerie Queene*, " *Journal of English and German Philology* 64 (1945): 139-42, 150; see also Donald Cheyney, Spenser's *Image of Nature: Wild Man and the Shepherd in the "Faierie Queene"* (New Haven: Yale University Press, 1966), 104-14.

84. Almost alone, Margaret Hogden argues that Gonzalo's famous speech in act 2, scene 1, could have had other sources than Michel Eyquem de Montaigne, "On Cannibals." *The Essays of Montaigne*, trans. by John Florío. 3 vols.(London, 1892-93. Reprint. New York: AMS Press, 1967). Hogden, "Montaigne and Shakespeare Again," *Huntingdon Library Quarterly* 16 (1952): 23-42.

85. "And of the Canibals that eat each other," from *Othello*, act 1, scene 3, *The Complete Works of Shakespeare*, ed. David Bevington, 3rd ed. (Glenview, Ill: Scott, Foresman, 1980).

86. For the Patagonian connection, see Charles Frey, "The Tempest and the New World, " *Shakespeare Quarterly* 30 (1979): 34; J. P. Brockbank links Caliban to *Caraïbe* sorcerers among the Brazilians in "The Tempest: Conventions of Art and Empire," in *Shakespeare's Later commedies*, ed. D. J. Palmer (London: Penquin, 1971), 392-94; Peter Hulme, "Hurricanes in the Caribees: The Constitution of the Discourse of English Colonialism." In *Literature and Power in the Seventeenth Century: Proceedings of the Essex Conference on Sociology of Literature*, ed. by Francis Barker et al, 55-83.(Colchester: University of Essex Press, 1981), pp. 69-70, suggests a composite portrait of mythical monsters joined to contemporary impressions of Carib cannibals. R. R. Cawley insists that Shakespeare did not wish to connect Caliban to any particular group; *Unpathed Waters: Studies in the Influence of the Voyages on Elizabethan Literature* (New York: Octagon Books, 1967), 238-39.

87. According to Lee, in *Elizabethans and other Essays*, 291, organizers of amusements featuring Amerindians emphasized the "farcical" element. If so, tha tcontrasts sharply with the experiences of the Tupinambas in Paris.

88. But contemporary authors, especially cosmographers like Münster, saw close links between primitive men, monstrous beings, baboons, etc. Even the skep-

tical Montaigne repeats stories about monstrous peoples, admittedly with the caution "if any credit may
be given"; *Essays*, ed. Florio, 2:235.

89.   Paul Jorgenson, "Shakespeare's Brave New World, "
in *First Images of America*, ed. Fredi Chiapelli, 1:86.

90.   Steven Greenblatt, "Learning to Curse: Aspects of
Linguistic Colonialism in the Sixteenth Century, " in
First Images of America, ed. Fredi Chiapelli, 2: 568-
76. Greenblatt's article is extremely interesting. In
"An Apologie of Raymond Sebond, " Montaigne
notes that his contemporaries "impute their [Indians]
mutenesse" to "stupiditie of beastliness"; *Essays*,
ed. Florio, 2:163.

91.   Paul Brown, "'This Thing of darkness I acknowledge mine': The Tempest and the Discourse of Colonialism," in *Political Shakespeare*, ed. Johnathan
Dollimore (Ithaca: Cornell University Press, 1985),
59. In *The Life of Henry the Eighth*, Shakespeare
says:" Or have we some strange Indian with the
great tool come to court, the women so besiege us?"
(act 5, scene 4) To Elizabethans, venery characterized savages, Africans, wildmen, baboons, and all
human-like beings beyond the pale of civilisation.

92.   Shakespeare had ties to influential figures in the Virginia Company. Charles M. Gayley, *Shakerspeare
and the Founders of Liberty in America* (New York:
Macmillan, 1917), 225-29. For the possible impact
of the St. Lucia "massacre," see Hulme, "Hurricane
in the Caribbees," 57.

93.   In contrast to Abbot's popularity, there were but single printings of translations of Thevet, Léry, Acost,
and Avity. Nor did Montaigne's "Of Cannibals"
have perceptible influence in England, despite the
popularity of Florio's editions; certainly not on Francis Bacon, who lumps together all "americans" as
"simple and savage peoples"; Bacon, *New Atlantis*,
ed. Robert M. Hutchins (Chicago: Encyclopaedia
Brittanica, 1952), 30:205.

94.   All critiques of *The Tempest* must take into account
Hulme's Chapter 3, Peter Hulme, "Prospero and
Caliban." *Colonial Encounters: Europe and the Native Caribbean*.(London: Methuen, 1986). His is an
intelligent "post-colonial" reading in which Caliban's dignity and Prospero's duplicity are justly highlighted. However, for my purposed, the old
"colonial" readings that see Prospero as toting the
white man's burden and Caliban as the monster he is
described as by is master surely reflect the attitudes
of Shakespeare's audiences and later seventeenth-
century readers.

95.   Kenneth R. Andrews, *Trade, Plunder, and Settlement: Maritime Enterprise and the Genesis of the
British Empire, 1480-1630*. (Cambridge: Cambridge
University Press, 1984), pp. 281-82. He counts
eighty-seven English voyages to the Caribbean from
1570 to 1603. Raleigh said that English ships passed in
the vicinity of the "cannibals" of Dominica; *The Discovery of Guiana*, 22. In *Un Flibustier français*, J. P.

Moreau in Jean-Pierre Moreau, ed. *Un Flibustier
francais dans la mer des Antilles, 1618-1620*. (Paris:
Seghers, 1990), p. 303, n. 7. cites Spanish archives
to show that some French and English ships sold captured Island Caribs as slaves in Puerto Rico; see 303,
n. 7.

96.   For example, George Percy's account in *New American World*, ed. D. B. Quinn, 5:267-68. See also Jac-
ques Petitjean Roget, *La société d'habitation à la
Martinique: Un demi-siècle de formation, 1635-
1685*, 2 vols. (Paris: Champion, 1980), 1:397, 445;
Myers, "Ethnohistorical vs Ecological Considera-
tions," 326-30; Thomas Southey, *Chronological His-
tory of the West Indies*, 3 vols. (London: Longman,
Rees, Orme, Brown, 1827), 1:189-93; and Kenneth
Andrews, ed., *English Privateering Voyages to the
West Indies 1588-1595* . . . (Cambridge: Cambridge
University Press, 1959).

97.   See the account by John Nicholl, *An houre glass of
Indian news* . . . (London: Butter, 1607).

98.   See M. Giraud Mangin, "Une relation inédite d'un
voyage en Floride en 1564," *Revue Renaissance* 13
(192):128-32.

99.   For such examples, see Richard Haklyut, *The Principal Navigations . . . of the English Nation*. 12
vols.(London, 1598. Reprint. Glasgow: Maclehose &
Sons, 1904-5), 7: p. 23, 7: p. 166.

100.   Boromé, "Spain and Dominica," 38.

101.   Joyce Lorimer, "The English Contraband Tobacco
Trade in Trinidad and Guiana, 1590-1617, " in *The
Westward Enterprise*, ed. K. R. Andrews, N. P.
Canny, and P. E. H. Hair, 147.

102.   Neil Whitehead, "Carib Cannibalism: The Historical
Evidence." *Journal de la Societe de Americanistes
70*. (1984), p. 73.

103.   Cornelis Ch. Goslinga, *The Dutch in the Caribbean
and on the Wild Coast, 1580-1680* (Gainesville:
University of Florida Press, 1971), 123-275.

104.   The Spanish archives indicate that in the early seventeenth century, increasingly anxious Spanish officials planned to occupy the Caribbean islands
because European arms made the aborigines so
much more dangerous; see Kenneth R. Andrews,
*The Spanish Caribbean: Trade and Plunder, 1530-
1630*.(New Haven: Yale University Press, 1978), p.
236.

105.   Giovanni Magini, *Histoire universelle des Indes . . .*
(Douai: Fabri, 1605), p. 97.

106.   Moreau, ed., *Un Flibustier français*.

107.   Denis Herion, *Cosmographie . . .* (Paris: D. Henrion,
1627), 897.

108 .   Purchas, *Haklyutus posthumus*, 16:548. In his
one-volume 1617 edition of *Purchas his Pilgrimage*,
Purchas includes Léry on Tupinamba cannibalism,
Martire on Caribs, and Hawkins' misadventure with
"cannibals"; see 1036, 1084, 1085.

9

Kalinago (Carib) Resistance to European Colonization of the Caribbean

HILARY McD. BECKLES

The resistance of native Caribbean people to the colonial dispensation established by Europeans following the Columbus landfall of 1492 has received insufficient attention from scholars. Unlike the case with the experience of enslaved African people few studies have presented systematic accounts of their anti-colonial and anti-slavery struggle. The reasons for this historiographic imbalance are not altogether clear. No one has suggested, for example, that their fight for liberty, life and land was any less endemic or virulent than that of Africans. On the contrary, most accounts of European settlement have indicated in a general sort of way their determination and tenacity in confronting the new order in spite of their relative technological limitations with respect to warfare.[1]

This study seeks to specify some of the political and military responses of the Kalinago people (known in the colonial documentation as Caribs) to the European invasion as they sought to maintain control over lands and lives in the islands of the Lesser Antilles. The examination makes reference to the immediate post-Columbian decades, and touches briefly upon the early eighteenth century to the Treaty of Utrecht in 1713, but is concerned principally with the period 1624 to 1700 when Kalinagos were confronted by considerable military pressures from English and French colonising agents. During this period Kalinagos in the Windward and Leeward Islands launched a protracted war of resistance to colonisation and slavery. They held out against the English and French until the mid-1790's, protecting some territory, maintaining their social freedom, and determining the economic and political history of the region in very important ways.[2]

According to recent archaeological evidence, the Kalinago were the last migrant group to settle in the Caribbean prior to the arrival of the Europeans in 1492. The Columbus mission found three native groups, of different derivation and cultural attainments, but all of whom entered the Caribbean from the region of South America known as the Guianas. These were the Ciboney, the Taino (Arawaks) and the Kalinago. The Ciboney had arrived about 300 B.C., followed by the Taino, their ethnic relatives, about 500 years later and who by 650 A.D. had migrated northwards through the islands establishing large communities in the Greater Antilles. Starting their migration into the islands from about 1000 A.D., Kalinagos were still arriving at the time of the Columbus landfall. They were also in the process of establishing control over territory and communities occupied by Tainos in the Lesser Antilles, and parts of the Greater Antilles. When the Spanish arrived in the northern Caribbean, therefore, they found the Tainos to some extent already on the defensive, but later encountered Kalinagos who they described as more prepared for aggression.[3]

Kalinagos, like their Taino cousins and predecessors, had been inhabiting the islands long enough to perceive them as part of their natural, ancestral, survival environment. As a result, noted G.K. Lewis, they prepared themselves to defend their homeland in a spirit of defiant "patriotism," having wished that the "Europeans had never set foot in their country."[4] From the outset, however, European colonial forces were technologically more prepared for a violent struggle for space since in real terms, the Columbus mission represented in addition to the maritime courage and determination of Europe, the mobilisation of large-scale finance capital, and science and technology for imperialist military ends. This process was also buttressed by the frenzied search for identity and global ranking by Europeans through the conquest and cultural negation of other races.

In the Greater Antilles, Tainos offered a spirited but largely ineffective military resistance to the Spanish even though on occasions they were supported by the Kalinago. This was particularly clear in the early sixteenth century in the case of the struggle for Puerto Rico in which Kalinagos from neighbouring St. Croix came to Taino assistance. In 1494, Columbus led an armed party of 400 men into the interior of Hispaniola in search of food, gold, and slaves to which Taino Caciques mobilised their armies for resistance. Guacanagari, a leading Cacique, who had tried previously to negotiate an accommodating settlement with military commander Alonso de Ojeba, marched unsuccessfully in 1494 with a few thousand men upon the Spanish. In 1503, another forty Caciques were captured at Hispaniola and burnt alive by Governor Ovando's troops; Anacaona, the principal Cacique was hung publicly in Santo Domingo. In Puerto Rico, the Spanish settlement party, led by Ponce de Leon, was attacked frequently by Taino warriors; many Spanish settlers were killed but Tainos and Kalinagos were defeated and crushed in the counter assault. In 1511, resistance in Cuba, led by Cacique Hatuey, was put down; he was captured and burnt alive; another rising in 1529 was also crushed. In these struggles, Taino fatalities were high. Thousands were killed in battle and publicly executed for the purpose of breaking the spirit of collective resistance; some rebels fled to the mountains and forests where they established maroon settlements that continued intermittently the war against the Spanish.[5] By the middle of the sixteenth century, however, Taino and Kalinago resistance had been effectively crushed in the Greater Antilles; their community structures smashed, and members reduced to various forms of enslavement in Spanish agricultural and mining enterprises.

In the Lesser Antilles, however, the Kalinago were more successful in defying first the Spanish, and then later the English and French, thereby preserving their political freedom and maintaining control of their territory. According to Carl Sauer, "As the labor supply on Espanola declined, attention turned to the southern islands" which from St. Croix, neighbouring Puerto Rico, to the Guianas were inhabited by the Kalinagos. Spanish royal edicts dated November 7, 1508 and July 3, 1512, authorised settlers to capture and enslave Kalinagos on "the island of Los Barbados [Barbados], Dominica, Matinino [Martinique], Santa Lucia, San Vincent, la Asuncion [Grenada], and Tavaco [Tobago]," because of their "resistance to Christians."[6] By the end of the sixteenth century, however, the Spanish had decided, having accepted as fact the absence of gold in the Lesser Antilles, and the inevitability of considerable fatalities at the hands of Kalinago warriors, that it was wiser to adopt a "hands off policy" while concentrating their efforts in the Greater Antilles. As a result, the Greater and Lesser Antilles became politically separated at this time by what Troy Floyd described as a "poison arrow curtain."[7] The English and French initiating their colonizing missions during the early seventeenth century, therefore, had a clear choice. They could either confront the Spanish north of the "poison arrow curtain" or Kalinago forces south of it. Either way, they expected to encounter considerable organised armed resistance. They chose the latter, partly because of the perception that Kalinagos were the weaker, but also because of the belief that Kalinagos were the 'common enemy' of all Europeans and that solidarity could be achieved for collective military operations against them.

Having secured some respite from the pressures of Spanish colonisation by the end of the sixteenth century, then, La Kalinagos were immediately confronted by the more economically aggressive and militarily determined English and French colonists. Once again they began to reorganise their communities in preparation for counter strategies. This time, it would be a clear case of resistance on the retreat. By the 1630s, their rapidly diminishing numbers were being consolidated around a smaller group of specially chosen islands – mostly in the Windwards but also in the Leewards. By this time, for instance, Barbados, identified in a Spanish document of 1511 as an island densely populated with Kalinagos, no longer had a native presence. Europeans understood the significance of this reorganisation and resettlement of Kalinago communities, and established their infant colonies in peripheral parts of the Leeward Islands where their presence was less formidable, and in Barbados where it was now absent. The English and French, then, were aware that most of their settlements would have to come to terms with Kalinago resistance. This expectation, however, did not deter them, and they continued to seek out island riches where an effective foothold could be gained until such time as Kalinago forces could be subdued and destroyed by their respective imperial forces.

The English and French sought the pacification of the Kalinago for two distinct, but related reasons, and overtime adopted different strategies and methods but maintained the ideological position that they should be enslaved, driven out, or exterminated. First, lands occupied by the Kalinago were required for large scale commodity production within the expansive, capitalist, North Atlantic agrarian complex. The effective integration of the Caribbean into this mercantile and productive system required the appropriation of land through the agency of the plantation enterprise. Finance capital, then, sought to revolutionize the market value of Kalinago lands by making them available to European commercial interests. By resisting land confiscation Kalinagos were therefore confronting the full ideological and economic force of Atlantic capitalism. Second, European economic activities in the Caribbean were based upon the enslavement of Indigenes and imported Africans. The principal role and relation assigned to these and other non-Europeans within the colonial formation was that of servitude. Europeans in the Lesser Antilles, however, were not successful in reducing an economic number of Kalinago to chattel slavery, or other forms of servitude. Unlike the Taino, their labour could not be effectively commodified, simply because their communities proved impossible to subdue. It was not that the Kalinago were more militant than the Taino. Rather, it was because the nomadic nature of their small communities, and

their emphasis upon territorial acquisition, in part a response to the geographical features of the Lesser Antilles, enabled them to make more effective use of the environment in a "strike and sail" resistance strategy. Kalinago, then, while not prepared to suffer either land or labour to Europeans, were better placed to implement effective counter-aggression.

Primarily because of their irrepressible war of resistance, which intimidated all Europeans in the region, Kalinago were targeted first for an ideological campaign in which they were established within the European mind, not as 'noble savages,' as was the case with the less effective Tainos, but as 'vicious cannibals' worthy of extermination within the context of genocidal military expeditions.[8] Voluminous details were prepared by Spanish and later English and French colonial chroniclers on the political and ideological mentality of the Kalinago, most of whom called for "holy wars" against "*les sauvages*" as a principal way to achieve their subjugation. Literature, dating back to Columbus in 1494, in a contradictory fashion, denied Kalinago humanity while at the same time outlined their general anti-colonial and anti-slavery consciousness and attitudes. In the writings of Jean-Baptiste de Tertre, Sieur de la Borde, and Pere Labat, for example, all late seventeenth century French reporters of Kalinago ontology, they are presented as a people who would "prefer to die of hunger than live as a slave."[9] Labat, who commented most of their psychological profile, found them to be "careless and lazy creatures," not at all suited mentally to arduous, sustained labour. In addition, he considered them a "proud and indomitable" and "exceedingly vindictive" people who "one has to be very careful not to offend," hence the popular French Caribbean proverb, "fight a Caribe and you must kill him or be killed."[10]

The French discovered, like the Spanish before them, noted Labat, that it was always best, if possible, "to have nothing to do with the Kalinago."[11] But this was not possible. Relations had to be established, and here Europeans discovered, Labat noted, that the Kalinago knew "how to look after their own interests very well."[12] "There are no people in the world," he stated, "so jealous of their liberty, or who resent more the smallest check to their freedom."[13] Altogether, Kalinago world view was anathema to Europeans, thus the general view, echoed by Labat, that "no European nation has been able to live in the same island with them without being compelled to destroy them, and drive them out."[14]

The English and French started out simultaneously in 1624 with the establishment of agricultural settlements in St. Kitts. From there, the English moved on to Barbados in 1627, and between 1632 and 1635 to Antigua, Montserrat and Nevis, while the French concentrated their efforts during the 1630s at Martinique and Guadeloupe. The first three years at St. Kitts were difficult for both English and French settlers. They were harassed and attacked by Kalinago soldiers, and in 1635 the French at Guadeloupe were engulfed in a protracted battle. French success in their war with Kalinago at Guadeloupe encouraged them during the remainder of the decade to expand their colonial missions, but failed to gain effective control of the Kalinago inhabited islands of Grenada, Marie Galante, and La Desirada. Meanwhile, a small English expedition from St. Kitts to St. Lucia in the Windwards, the heart of Kalinago territory, was easily repelled in 1639. The following year Kalinagos launched a full-scale attack upon English settlements at Antigua, killing fifty settlers, capturing the Governor's wife and children, and destroying crops and houses.[15]

While English settlements in the Leewards struggled to make progress against Kalinago resistance, Barbados alone of the Windwards, forged ahead uninterrupted. Unlike their Leewards counterparts, early Barbadian planters rapidly expanded their production base, made a living from the exports of tobacco, indigo and cotton, and feared only their indentured servants and few African slaves. By 1650, following the successful cultivation of sugar cane with African slaves, the island was considered by mercantile economic theorists as the richest agricultural colony in the hemisphere. St. Kitts colonists, both English and French, determined to keep up with their Barbadian competitors, were first to adopt a common military front with respect to Kalinago resistance. During the 1630s they entered into agreements, in spite of their rival claims to exclusive ownership of the island, to combine forces against Kalinago communities. On the first occasion, they "pooled their talents," and in a "sneak night attack" killed over eighty Kalinagos and drove many off the island. After celebrating the success of their military alliance, the French and English continued their rivalry over the island until 1713 when the matter was settled in favour of the English by the Treaty of Utrecht.[16]

The success of Kalinagos in holding on to a significant portion of the Windwards, and their weakening of planting settlements in the Leewards, fueled the determination of the English and French to destroy them. By the mid-seventeenth century, European merchants, planters and colonial officials, were in agreement that Kalinagos "were barbarous and cruel set of savages beyond reason or persuasion and must therefore be eliminated."[17] By this time it was also clear that the slave-based plantation system, demanded an "absolute monopoly" of the Caribbean, and tolerated no "alternative system."[18] What Richard Dunn referred to as "Carib independence and self-reliance" constituted a major contradiction to the internal logic of capitalist accumulation within the plantation economy.[19] As a result, therefore, the economic leaders and political representatives of this increasingly powerful production and trade complex were determined to bring the contradiction to a speedy resolution by any means necessary or possible.

By the mid-seventeenth century, the need for a full scale war against the Kalinagos, though clearly established and articulated in Spanish colonial thinking during the sixteenth century, now assumed greater urgency with the English and French. By this time the English were first to successfully establish productive structures based on sugar cultivation and black slavery, and not surprisingly took the lead in attempting the removal of principal obstacles to the smooth and profitable expansion of the system. Also, the English with the largest number of enslaved Africans in the region, were concerned that efficient control on their plantations would be adversely affected by the persistence of Kalinago resistance. It did not take long for the Africans to become aware of Kalinago struggle against Europeans, and to realise that they could possibly secure their freedom by fleeing to their territory. Labat, who studied inter-island slave marronage in the Lesser Antilles, during this period, stated that slaves knew that St. Vincent was easily reached from Barbados, and many escaped there "from their masters in canoes and rafts." During the formative stage of this development, between 1645 and 1660, the Kalinago generally took "the runaway slaves back to their masters, or sold them to the French and Spanish," but as the Kalinago came under more intensive attack during the mid-century, Labat noted, their policy towards African maroons changed. They refused to return the Africans, he stated, and began regarding them "as an addition to their nation." By 1670, Labat estimated that over 500 Barbadian runaways were living in St. Vincent. This community was reinforced in 1675 when a slave ship carrying hundreds of Africans to Jamaica via Barbados ran aground off the coast of Bequia. Survivors came ashore at St. Vincent and were integrated in the maroon communities. By 1700, Labat stated, Africans outnumbered Kalinagos at St. Vincent.[20] In 1675, William Stapleton, governor of the Leewards, noting the significant presence of Africans among the Kalinagos suggested that of the 1,500 native "bowmen" in the Leewards six hundred of them "are negroes, some runaway from Barbados elsewhere."[21]

Throughout the second half of the seventeenth century Europeans tried unsuccessfully to exploit the sometimes strained relations between Kalinagos and Africans by encouraging the former to return runaways to their owners. Miscegenation between the predominantly male African maroon community and Kalinago females was a principal cause of social tension between the two ethnic groups.[22] Both the French and English alleged that Kalinago leaders occasionally sought their assistance in ridding their communities of Africans. The significance of such allegations, however, should be assessed against the background of two important developments in African-Kalinago relations. First, by the mid-seventeenth century, the group mixed bloods, now known as the Garifuna, was increasing rapidly in numbers, and by 1700 had outnumbered both parent groups in St. Vincent.[23] Second, joint African-Kalinago military expeditions against the French and English were common, and represented a principal characteristic feature of anti-European activity - on both land and sea.[24] The full scale attack on the French at Martinique during the mid-1650s, for example, involved both African and Kalinago forces.[25] The warriors who attacked French settlements at Grenada during the same period and kept them in a weak and defensive condition were also described as having an African component, similarly, noted Labat, the English expeditions from Barbados sent to capture St. Vincent during the 1670s were repelled by both Africans and Kalinagos.[26]

The presence of effective anti-colonial Kalinago communities on the outskirts of the slave plantations, therefore, constituted a major problem for slave owners in so far as they fostered and encouraged African anti-slavery. The merging of Kalinago anti-colonial and African anti-slavery struggles, therefore, represented the twin forces that threatened the very survival of the colonising mission in the Windwards. As such, Europeans with the greatest economic stake in the enterprise of the Indies wasted no time in adopting a range of measures to suppress the Kalinago. Both the English and French pursued an initial policy characterised by the projection of anti- Kalinago social images in Europe, while seeking at the same time to promote diplomatic efforts to settle territorial claims.

In 1664 a Barbados document entitled "The State of the Case concerning our Title to St. Lucia," described the island as being "infected" with Kalinagos who were "abetted by the French" in their war against English settlers. In this document, Barbadians sought to reject French claims to the islands by stating that they had purchased it from du Parquet, the Governor of Martinique, who had bought it from the Kalinagos in 1650 for 41,500 livres.[27] Likewise, in 1668, Thomas Modyford, Governor of Jamaica, former Barbados Governor and sugar magnate, described St. Vincent, another Kalinago stronghold in the Windwards, as a place which "the Indians much infect."[28] These statements represent part of the ideological preparation of the English mind for what would be a genocidal offensive against the Kalinago that London merchant houses were eager to finance.

But a full-scale war, the English and French knew, would be costly, both in terms of human life and capital, and hoped it could be averted. The significance of an ultimate military solution was clearly perceived by Kalinago leaders and colonial officials alike. The Kalinago, by participating in tactful diplomatic intrigue designed to exploit differences and conflicts between Europeans, the Kalinago sought to advance their own interests. In 1655, for example, Captain Gregory

Butler informed Oliver Cromwell, the Protector, that the settlement at Antigua was unable to get off to a good start on account of frequent molestations by the Kalinagos, who at that time seemed to be in league with the French.[29] Again, in 1667, Major John Scott, an imperial Commander-in-Chief, reported that the led an expedition against Dutch settlements in Tobago with the "assistance of a party of Caribs."[30] During the second Dutch War, 1665-1667, in which France and Holland allied against the English in the Caribbean, the Kalinago played an important role in shifting the balance of power between Europeans while at the same time seeking to expand the scope and effectiveness of their own war of resistance.[31] In June 1667, Lord Willoughby, stationed in the Leewards informed his father William Lord Willoughby, Governor of Barbados, that when he arrived at St. Kitts he received "intelligence" of further atrocities committed by the Kalinagos against the English which were "instigated" by the French. European rivalry, Michael Craton concluded, was effectively used by the Kalinago nation as evident in the delayed loss of St. Lucia and Grenada, and in the longer retention of full control over St. Vincent and Dominica.[32]

The English and French also targeted the Kalinago for diplomatic offensives. The first systematically pursued diplomatic effort by the English to establish a footing within Kalinago territory in the Windwards was the Willoughby initiative of 1667. William Lord Willoughby, Governor of Barbados, had long recognised the great financial gain that would accrue to himself, Barbados, and England, if the Windwards, the last island frontier, could be converted into slave-based sugar plantations. For over a decade, the sugar kings of Barbados had been signalling their demand for lands on which to expand their operations, and the Windwards were the perfect place given prevailing economic concepts about the conditionalities of slaved-based sugar cultivation. Small scale military expeditions had been repelled by the Kalinago since the 1630s, and so Willoughby, not yet organized for a large scale military assault, opted to send emissaries to open negotiations with Kalinago leaders.

The Kalinagos, in response, showed some degree of flexibility, as is often the case with peoples involved in protracted struggles. Willoughby wanted a peace treaty that would promote English interests by removing obstacles to slave plantation expansionism, but the Kalinago were suspicious and vigilant. In 1666, they were tricked by the English to sign away by treaty their "rights" to inhabit Tortola, and were driven off the island.[33] The Windward islands were their last refuge, and their seige mentality was now more developed than ever.

On March 23, 1667, Kalinago leaders of St. Vincent, Dominica and St. Lucia met with Willoughby's delegation in order to negotiate the peace.[34] At the signing of the Treaty were Anniwatta, the Grand Babba, (or chief of all Kalinagos), Chiefs Wappya, Nay, Le Suroe, Rebura and Aloons. The conditions of the treaty were everything the Barbadian slavers wanted at that particular stage of development:

1. The Caribs of St. Vincent shall ever acknowledge themselves subjects of the King of England, and be friends to all in amity with the English, and enemies to their enemies.
2. The Caribs shall have liberty to come to and depart from, at pleasure, any English islands and receive their protection therein, and the English shall enjoy the same in St. Vincent and St. Lucia.
3. His Majesty's subjects taken by the French and Indians and remaining among the Indians, shall be immediately delivered up, as also any Indian captives among the English when demanded.
4. Negroes formerly run away from Barbados shall be delivered to His Excellency; and such as shall hereafter be fugitives from any English island shall be secured and delivered by as soon as required.[35]

The Willoughby initiative was designed to pave the way for English colonisation of the Windwards, using Barbados as the springboard for settlement. In essence, it was an elaboration of a similar agreement that was made between the defeated Kalinago and victorious French forces at Martinique after the war of 1654-1656. On that occasion, noted Jean-Baptiste du Tertre, who described in detail the nature of the conflict and its resolution, the French were able to obtain settlement rights from the Kalinago as well as guarantees that they would assist in the control of rebel slaves by not encouraging, and more importantly, returning all runaways.36 Within two months of the Kalinago-Willoughby Treaty, a party of fifty-four English colonists from Barbados arrived at St. Vincent in order to pioneer a settlement. The Kalinago, Garifuna, and Africans objected to their presence, drove them off the island, and broke the Treaty with Barbados.

The collapse of the Barbados diplomatic mission angered Governor Willoughby who swiftly moved to the next stage of his plan - full military offensive. His opportunity came in March the following year when English military commander, Sir John Harman, left behind in Barbados a regiment of foot soldiers and five frigates. Willoughby informed the Colonial Office that since he knew not how to "keep the soldiers quiet and without pay" the only course open to him was to "try his fortune among the Caribs in St. Vincent."[37] Once again, the Kalinago proved too much for Willoughby, and the expedition returned to Barbados having suffered heavy losses.

English awareness of Kalinago solidarity and efficient communications throughout the islands of the Lesser Antilles meant that they had reasons to expect reprisals for the Willoughby offensive anywhere and at anytime. Governor Modyford of Jamaica, a most knowledgeable man about Eastern Caribbean affairs, has opposed Willoughby's war plan. He told the Duke of Albemarle that while Willoughby was "making war with the Caribs of St. Vincent" he feared the consequences for settlers at Antigua, and other places. Such an intimely war, he said "may again put those plantations in hazard, or at best into near broils." "It had been far better," he continued, "to have made peace with them," for if they assist the French against us the result would be "the total ruin of all the English Islanders" and a "waste of the revenue of Barbados."[38]

Modyford was perceptive in his assessment of Kalinago responses. A report sent to the Colonial Office in London from officials in Nevis dated April 1669, entitled "An Intelligence of an Indian Design upon the People of Antigua," stated that "The Caribbee Indians have lately broken the peace made with Lord Willoughby, and have killed two and left dead two more of His Majesty's subjects in Antigua." Reference was made to twenty-eight Kalinago warriors who arrived from Montserrat in two canoes and who participated in the raid upon Antigua in response to Willoughby's war in St. Vincent.[39] In addition, Governor Stapleton

of the Leewards, in a separate document, outlined his fear for the lives of Leeward Islanders, including those who had gone to work in a silver mine in Dominica under an agreement with the Kalinago.[40] The Barbadians also offered their criticisms of Willoughby's war effort. In 1676, Governor Atkins described it as a "fruitless design," whose overall result was that there remain "no likelihood of any plantations upon Dominica, St. Vincent, St. Lucia and Tobago."[41] Meanwhile, the Antiguans were forced to keep "fourteen files of men, doubled three days before and after a full moon" as a protective measure against Kalinago warriors.

Governor Stapleton, reflecting on the collapse of the Willoughby initiative, and considering the prospects for English settlements in the Leewards and Windwards, quickly moved to the front stage what had been Willoughby's hidden agenda. Only the destruction of "all the Caribbee Indians" he concluded, could be the "best piece of service for the settlement of these parts."[42] In December 1675, a petition of "Several Merchants of London" addressed to the Lords of Trade and Plantations in support of Governor Stapleton's extermination thesis, called for the granting of a commission to Philip Warner, Stapleton's deputy, to raise soldiers to go into Dominica to "destroy the barbarous savages."[43]

Stapleton, however, had pre-empted the Colonial Office in their response to the London merchants and had already sent Warner "with six small companies of foot," totalling 300 men, into Dominica to "revenge" on the "heathens for their bloody perfidious villanies."[44] One William Hamlyn who participated in the Warner expedition, described the assault upon the Kalinago as a massacre. At least thirty Kalinago, he said, were taken and killed on the first round, not including "three that were drawn by a flag of truce" and shot.[45] After these executions, Hamlyn reported, another "sixty or seventy men, women and children" were invited to Warner's camp to settle matters over entertainment. These were given rum to drink, and when Warner "gave the signal," the English "fell upon them and destroyed them."[46] Included in those killed by the English was Indian Warner, Philip Warner's own half-brother, whose mother was a Kalinago, and who had risen to become a powerful Kalinago leader. Warner was imprisoned in the Tower, tried for the murder of his brother, but was found not guilty. The decision pleased the London merchants who described him as "a man of great loyalty" whose service to the Crown in the destruction of the Kalinagos "who have often attempted to ruin the plantations" should be commended.[47]

In spite of losses sustained in Dominica, Kalinagos there continued to use the island as a military base for expeditions against the English. In July, 1681, 300 Kalinagos from St. Vincent and Dominica in six periagos, led by one who named himself Captain Peter, and who was described as a "good speaker of English having lived for some time in Barbados" attacked the unguarded English settlements in Barbuda.[48] The English were caught by surprise. Eight of them were killed, and their houses destroyed. The action was described as swift and without warning.

Frustrated again by his inability to protect the lives and property of Leeward Islanders, Stapleton reiterated his call for a war of extermination against the Kalinagos. He wrote to the Colonial Office: "I beg your pardon if I am tedious, but I beg you to represent the King the necessity for destroying these Carib Indians." "We are now as much on our guard as if we had a christian enemy, neither can any such surprise us but these cannibals who never come 'marte aperto' . . . If their destruction cannot be "total," insisted Stapleton, at least we must "drive them to the main."[49] He was aware, however, of the inability of Leeward Islanders to finance a major war effort, and had also become respectful for Kalinagos' ability to obtain "intelligence" with respect to their plans. Given these two circumstances, Stapleton instructed London to order the Barbados government to prepare the grand design against the Kalinagos. Barbados, he added, was closer to the Kalinago "infested" islands of St. Vincent and Dominica; also, on account of the colony's wealth, it would be the "best piece of service" they could offer England whilst there was "amity with the French."[50]

Colonial officials in London accepted Stapleton's plan in its entirety. They instructed him to make plans to "utterly suppress" the Kalinagos or "drive them to the main."[51] They also directed Governor Dutton of Barbados to make all possible contributions to the war effort. Dutton, however, would have no part of it, but not wishing to contradict the King's orders, he informed the Colonial Office that though he was in agreement,

Barbadians would support no such design against the Kalinagos for three reasons. First, they consider the affairs of the Leeward Islands none of their business. Second, they do not consider the advancement of the Leewards as a good thing, indeed they consider it in their interest if the Leewards would decline rather than progress. Third, planters considered peace with the Kalinagos in the Windwards a better objective as this would assist them in securing cutwood and other building materials from those islands.[52]

The Leeward Islanders, therefore, had to look to their own resources to finance their military operations. In June 1682, a bill was proposed to the Leewards Assembly requesting funds to outfit an expedition against the Kalinagos in Dominica. The council agreed, but the Assembly of Nevis dissented on the grounds that since they had not been attacked by the Kalinagos in over "twenty years" they did to intend to endanger their peace.[53] Months went by and Stapleton failed to get his planters to agree on a financial plan for the expedition. By 1700, the grand design had not yet materialised.

When on the 11th April, 1713, England and France settled their 'American' difference with the Treaty of Utrecht, Kalinagos were still holding on tenaciously to considerable territory. St. Vincent and Dominica, though inhabited by some Europeans, were still under their control, and they were fighting a rear guard war to retain some space at St. Lucia, Tobago and Grenada. Since the French feared that successful English settlement of Dominica would lead to the cutting of communications between Martinique and Guadeloupe in times of war, they continued to assist the Kalinagos with information and occasionally with weapons in their anti-English resistance. The best the English could do was to continue the attempt to settle private treaties with the French, as they had done during the peace of Ryswick in 1697, which enabled them to go unmolested to Dominica for the sole purpose of purchasing lumber from the Kalinago.

Kalinagos then succeeded in preserving some of their territorial sovereignty and by so doing were able to maintain their freedom from European enslavement. While other native Caribbean peoples suffered large scale slavery at the hands of Europeans, the Kalinagos were never found in large numbers working the mines, *latifundia,* or plantations in the Lesser Antilles. Though Spanish slave raids during the sixteenth century did take many into the Greater Antilles to supplement Taino labour gangs, European controlled productive structures in the Lesser Antilles were not built and maintained on the basis of a Kalinago labour supply.

The involvement of Kalinagos into the colonial economy, then, tended to be small scale, and confined to areas such as fishing, tracking, and hunting, agricultural consulting and a range of petty domestic services. When, for example, a group of Barbadian sugar planters, concerned about the shortage of white indentured servants, and the rising cost of African slaves, encouraged Captain Peter Wroth in 1673 to establish a slave trade in Kalinagos from the Guianas, colonial officials instructed Governor Atkins to make arrangements for the return of all those "captured and enslaved." The reason being, they stated, was that "considering the greater importance of a fair correspondence between the Carib Indians and the English" in establishing settlements on the Amazon coast, it was necessary that "provocation be avoided" and all proper measures be taken to gain their "goodwill and affection."[54] Governor Atkins, in informing his superiors of this compliance indicated his agreement that it was necessary to "keep amity" with Kalinagos, since they have "always been very pernicious, especially to the smaller Leeward Islands."[55]

Between 1492 and 1700 the Kalinago population in the Lesser Antilles may have fallen by as much as 90 per cent, noted Michael Craton, but they had done much to "preserve and extend their independence."[56] By this time the Dominica population, according to Labat, "did not exceed 2000" and warriors were too weak in numbers to do any serious harm" to European colonies.[57] Nonetheless, colonists in the "outlying districts" still had reasons to believe that any night Kalinago warriors could take them by surprise and "cut their throats and burn their houses."[58] By refusing to capitulate under the collective military might of the Europeans, Kalinagos certainly kept the Windward Islands in a marginal relation to the slave plantation complex of the North Atlantic system for two hundred years, and in so doing, made a principal contribution to the Caribbean's anti-colonial and anti-slavery tradition.

Notes

1. See Michael Craton, *Testing the chains: Resistance to Slavery in the British West Indies* (Ithaca, 1982) pp. 21-23; Hilary Beckles, "The 200 Years War: Slave Resistance in the British West Indies: An Overview of the Historiography," *Jamaica Historical Review*, Vol. 13, 1982, 1-10.

2. See J. Paul Thomas, "The Caribs of St. Vincent: A Study in Imperial Maladministration, 1763-73," *Journal of Caribbean History*, Vol. 18, No. 2, 1984, pp. 60-74; *Craton Testing the Chains*, pp. 141-153, 183-194; Richard B. Sheridan, "The Condition of slaves in the Settlement and Economic Development of the British Windward Islands, 1763-1775," *Journal of Caribbean History*, Vol. 24, No. 2, 1991, pp. 128-129; Bernard Marshall, "Slave Resistance and White Reaction in the British Windward Islands, 1763-1833," *Caribbean Quarterly*, Vol. 28, No. 3, 1982, pp. 39-40.

3. David Watts, *The West Indies: Patterns of Development, Culture and Environmental Change since 1492* (Cambridge, 1987) pp. 41, 51-52. W. Borah, "The Historical Demography of Aboriginal and Colonial America: An Attempt at perspective," in W. Denevan, *The Native Population of the Americas in 1492* (Madison, Wisconsin Univ. Press, 1976) pp. 13-34. J.M. Cruxent and I. Rouse, "Early man in the West Indies" *Scientific American*, No. 221, 1969, pp. 42-52. B. Meggers and C. Evans, "Lowland South America and the Antilles," in J.D. Jennings, *Ancient Native Americans* (San Francisco, W.H. Freeman, 1978) pp. 543-92.

4. Gordon Lewis, *Main Currents in Caribbean Thought: The Historical Evolution of Caribbean Society in its Ideological Aspects, 1492-1900* (Heinemann, Kingston, 1983) p. 41.

5. On Kalinago assistance to Tainos in Puerto Rico, see Carl Sauer, *The Early Spanish Main* (Berkeley, Univ. Of California Press, LA, 1966) pp. 58, 192. See Eric Williams, *Documents of West Indian History, 1492-1655* (Port-of-Spain, PNM Publishing Co., 1963) pp. 62-70, 89-94. Robert Greenwood, *A Spetchman History of the Caribbean* (MacMillan, 1991) pp. 18, 23. See also Carl Sauer, *The Early Spanish Main*, p. 32.

6. Sauer, *The Early Spanish Main*, pp. 35, 180, 193; see also Lewis, *Main Currents*, p. 64.

7. Troy S. Floyd, *The Columbian Dynasty in the Caribbean, 1492-1526* (Albuquerque, Univ. Of New Mexico Press, 1973) p. 97. For an account of the Spanish "hands off" policy with respect to the Lesser Antilles, see K.R. Andrews, *Trade, Plunder and Settlement: Maritime Enterprises and the Genesis of the British Empire, 1480-1630* (Cambridge, 1986) p. 282. Craton, *Testing the Chains*, p. 22. See also, Nellie M. Crouse, *The French Struggle for the West Indies 1665-1713* (N.Y. Columbia University Press, 1943) p. 8-10.

8. See Sauer, p. 35; Lewis, p. 64.

9. See Lewis, p. 64; Richard Dunn, *Sugar and Slaves: the rise of the Planter Class in the English West In-*

dies, 1624-1713 (N.Y., 1973) p. 24; Sieur de la Borde, *Relacion de Caraibes* (Paris, Coleccion Billaine, (1694); Jean-Baptiste de Tertre, *Histoire Generale des Antilles Habitees par les Francais* (Paris, 1667-71); John Eaden, ed., *The Memoirs of Pere Labat, 1693-1705* (1970 edition, Frank Cass, London).

10. *Memoirs of Pere Labat,* p. 75.
11. *Ibid.,* p. 83.
12. *Ibid.,* p. 98.
13. *Ibid.,* p. 104.
14. *Ibid.,* p. 109.
15. Watts, pp. 171-172. Richard Sheridan, *Sugar and Slavery: An Economic History of the British West Indies* (Caribbean Universities Press, Bridgetown, 1974) pp. 80, 85, 87, 456.
16. See Dunn, p. 8.
17. Lewis, p. 104.
18. *Ibid.,* p. 105.
19.
20. *Memoirs of Pere Labat,* p. 137.
21. Governor Stapleton of the Leewards to the Lords of Trade and Plantations, Nov. 22, 1676, *Calendar of State Papers,* Colonial Series (C.S.P.C.) 1676, p. 499.
22. See C. Gullick, "Black Caribs Origins and Early Society," in *Transactions of the Seventh International Congress on Pre-Columbian Cultures of the Lesser Antilles* (Quebec, 1978) pp. 283-87.
23. See William Young, *An Account of the Black Caribs in the Island of St. Vincent's* (London, 1795 reprint, London 1971) pp. 5-8; also Vancy Gonzalez, *Sojourners of the Caribbean: Ethnogenesis and Ethnohistory of the Garifunia* (Chicago, 1988).
24. See Vincent Murga, ed., *Historica Document de Puerto Rico,* Vol. 1 (Rio Pedras, n.d.) p. 227.
25. See for an account of the battles at Martinique, Du Tertre, *Histoire General* p. 467-68.
26. See Hilary Beckles, *Black Rebellion in Barbados: the Struggle Adjacent Slavery,* 1627-1838 (Carib Research and Publications, Bridgetown, 1988) p. 36.
27. "The State of the Case Concerning our title to St. Lucia," 1664; C.S.P.C., 1661-68, No. 887. See also, Rev. C. Jessee, "Barbadians buy St. Lucia from Caribs," *Journal of the Barbados Museum and Historical Society,* (J.B.M.H.S.) Vol. 32, Feb. 1968, pp. 180-182.
28. Governor Sir Thomas Modyford to the Duke of Albemarle, March 16, 1668, C.S.P.C. 1661-68, No. 1714.
29. Vere L. Oliver, *The History of the Island of Antigua* (London, 1894-99) Vol. 1, p. xix, xxv; also Sheridan, *Sugar and Slavery,* p. 87.
30. Petition of Major John Scott to the King, 1667, C.S.P.C., 1661-68, No. 1525.
31. Governor Lord William Willoughby to the King, Feb. 11, 1668, C.S.P.C., 1661-68, p. 547; Watts, *the West Indies,* p. 242-43. Henry Willoughby to William Willoughby, June 15, 1667, C.S.P.C., 1661-68, No. 1498.
32. Craton, *Testing the Chains,* pp. 22-23.
33. Governor William Lord Willoughby to the King, July 9, 1668, C.S.P.C., 1661-68; No. 1788.
34. Copy of a Treaty between William Lord Willoughby and several of the Chief Captains of Caribs, March 23, 1668, C.S.P.C., 1661-68, No. 1717.

35. Ibid.
36. Du Tertre, *Histoire Generale,* pp. 467-68.
37. Lord Willoughby to the King, March 13, 1668, *Colonial Papers,* vol. 22, November 5, C.S.P.C., No. 1714.
38. Governor Sir Thomas Modyford to the Duke of Albemarle, March 16, 1668, C.S.P.C. No. 1714.
39. Governor Stapleton to the Lords of Trade and Plantations, May 27, 1672, *Colonial Papers,* Vol. 28, No. 61.
40. *Ibid.* The English claimed that the Dominica silver mine was "lawfully purchased" from the Kalinagos who recognised the contract. Leolin Lloyd to Secretary Arlington, *Colonial Papers,* vol. 29, No. 46; also, *Colonial Papers,* Vol. 28, No. 12.
41. Governor Atkins to Lords of Trade and Plantations, July 4, 1676, *Colonial Papers,* Vol. 37, No. 22.
42. Governor Stapleton to Council of Trade and Plantations, December 1675, *Colonial Papers,* Vol. 35, No. 43. Petition of Several Merchants of London on Adventures to the Caribbean Islands to the Lords of Trade and Plantations, 1676, *Colonial Papers,* Vol. 36, No. 5.
44. Governor Stapleton to the Council for Plantations, February 8, 1675, C.S.P.C. 1675-76, No. 428.
45. Sir Jonathan Atkins to Secretary for Colonies, February 17, 1675, C.S.P.C., 1675-76. No. 439.
46. *Ibid.*
47. Petition of Several Merchants of London Adventurers to the Caribbee Islands to Lords of Trade and Plantations, January 10, 1676, C.S.P.C., 1675-76, No. 774.
48. Governor Stapleton to Lords of Trade and Plantations, August 16, 1681, *Colonial Papers,* Vol. 46, No. 45; see also C.S.P.C., 1681-85 Nos. 410-411.
49. Sir William Stapleton to Lords of Trade and Plantations, August 16, 1681, C.S.P.C., 1681-85 No. 204. See also, *Journal of Lords of Trade and Plantations,* October 18, 1681, No. 259.
50. *Ibid.*
51. The King to Sir William Stapleton, February, 1682, C.S.P.C., 1681-85, No. 411.
52. Sir Richard Dutton to Lords of Trade and Plantations, January 3, 1682, C.S.P.C., 1681-85, p. 181, No. 357; also *Colonial Papers,* Vol. 48, No. 1.
53. Journal of the Assembly of Nevis, June 14, 1682, C.S.P.C. 1681-85.
54. The King to Sir Jonathan Atkins, December 30, 1674, C.S.P.C., 1675-76, No. 401.
55. Sir Jonathan Atkins to Secretary of Plantations, C.S.P.C., February 17, No. 439. See Jerome Handler, "Amerindians and their contribution to Barbados Life in the Seventeenth Century, *J.B.M.H.S.,* 1971, 35, 112-117. "The Amerindian Slave Population of Barbados in the Seventeenth and early Eighteenth Centuries, *J.B.M.H.S.,* Vol. xxxiii, No. 3, May 1970, 111-135. For an account of this attempt to establish a Barbados-Guianas slave trade in Kalinagos, E.G. Breslaw, "Price's - His Desposition: Kidnapping Amerindians in Guyana, 1674," *J.B.M.H.S.,* Vol. 39, 1991, pp. 47-50.
56. Craton, *Testing the Chains,* p. 23.
57. *Memoirs of Pere Labat,* p. 115.
58. *Ibid.,* pp. 110-111.

10

The Caribs of St Vincent: A Study in Imperial Maladministration, 1763-73

J. PAUL THOMAS

In late 1772, at a time when the corruption and cruelty of British rule in India were subjects of massive concern, publicly voiced in Parliament and press, disquieting reports on a military expedition to an obscure West Indian island were taken up by the parliamentary opposition. Reports concerned the sending of two regiments from America to aid local troops in the suppression, and possible deportation or even extermination of a group of free Negroes in St Vincent, whose main crime appeared to be their refusal to sell or exchange their lands to planters, speculators and investors. These, thus thwarted, had appealed to the government for help. There was much material inviting opposition scorn, not only on the grounds of the injustice of the expedition's aims, but also over the foolishness of sending ill-equipped troops in the unpleasant rainy season, when fever, disease and desertion afflicted the force quite as much as the successful tactics of well-armed and resourceful Caribs.[1]

The outcry over the Carib question was not comparable with the great debate in the contemporary press on the American question, or over Indian maladministration. Whereas these latter regularly spawned popular, profitable pamphlet literature, widely reprinted in the periodical press at each successive crisis, the only lengthy piece inspired by the St Vincent question was *Authentic Papers relative to the Expedition against the Caribs and the sale of Lands in the Island of St Vincent*, published by John Almon in February 1773, and this was merely a reprinting of the material laid upon the table of the Commons for consideration in the debates.

This lengthy collection, however, is of immense use to the historian, partly for its ready availability, occupying sixty-five pages of the *Parliamentary History* and finding its way into a number of contemporary periodicals, and partly because its contents, a chronological compendium of official correspondence, reportage and local petitioning, afford a detailed view of the development of a crisis involving a vulnerable native population, an ignorant administration and a number of land-hungry, profiteering colonial adventurers. Irrespective of the rights or wrongs of the Carib question, it was, like Bengal, or indeed the Pennsylvanian frontier, an example of how interested men on the spot could ignore or override the central government's wishes, or even force government intervention in their favour.[2]

The timing of the debates on St Vincent, during the East Indian crisis, was in itself significant. The promoter of the motion of censure on the question, Thomas Townshend Jr, consciously and adroitly remarked on the connection. He asserted, 'such a spirit of gaming is gone forth, that the rapacity of the planters in St Vincent is nearly connected with that rage for making of fortunes, by the most destructive means, which gave such a shock to public credit in the course of last summer.'[3] This was a direct reference to the problems of the banking system and of the East India Company in 1772. Not only was this parallel noted in newspaper correspondence by 'A. Proprietor' in the *Gazetteer*, linking government reluctance to bring to justice 'robbers and murderers of the Moghul' with the 'St Vincent exterminating scheme', but was mischievously compared with the massacre at St George's Fields, in the *Public Advertiser*.[4]

The criticism faced by the government was undoubtedly inconsistent, for Townshend and his parliamentary supporters in these debates, the 'Bostonian', Barlow Trecothick and the Chathamite, Isaac Barré, were as likely to attack administrative land policy and restrictions on

Journal of Caribbean History, Vol. 18, No. 2, 1984, pp. 60-73.

frontier adventurism in America. Sir Richard Sutton indeed pointed out the government's problem when he asserted that the opposition would as happily have attacked the government's failure to protect the allegedly threatened St Vincent planters.[5] This dilemma showed in the court's reluctance to decisively intervene in India's affairs where such intervention would arouse partisan accusations of encroaching on East Indian patronage.

It is difficult to accuse the government of deliberate inhumanity over the St Vincent affair, yet positive morality was by no means conspicuous in the official handling of the Caribs. Certainly, the *Authentic Papers* show official distaste for the planters and no great eagerness to endorse their representations.[6] Official reluctance to countenance the claims and aspirations of frontier and island land speculators and planters, however, did not necessarily derive from humanitarian regard for the rights of native populations already in possession of colonial lands. It stemmed rather from the spirit of the 1763 proclamation, and the Grenvillite policy of limiting expansion, with particular reference to the western American frontier. If this policy of containment involved garrisoning expense, it retained a degree of government control and in revenue projects implied potential in colonial patronage, rather than proliferation of expensive and damaging frontier warfare and the expansion of colonial populations beyond the geographical limits of official control. The Pontiac rebellion had given Whitehall a taste of the dangerous effects of land speculation upon aggrieved natives.[7]

Reluctance to endorse the planters' complaints also stemmed from official distaste for the kind of adventurers and speculators attracted by the opportunities offered by the new lands of the empire. St Vincent offered a quintessential example of the impact of colonial adventurers upon the tentative policy-making of the administrators of 1763. It was to the gaming spirit of these adventurers that Townshend was alluding in his speeches. Such men were making fortunes exploiting the riches of a more sophisticated native civilization in Bengal, and were financing and mortgaging fraudulent stock-jobbing schemes in the ceded islands. Prominent names among such adventurers were those of Lauchlin Macleane, Richard and William Burke and Sir George Colebrooke, all of whom may be implicated in dubious land purchases in Grenada and St Vincent from 1762 onwards, and be shown to have damaged national and company credit in East India stock-boosting schemes during the period.[8] Equally distasteful to traditional-minded administrators and parliamentarians at this time were the West Indian slavers, absentee landlords and planters, and the returning East Indian nabobs whose riches, real and imagined, seemed to be wreaking havoc on the domestic economy, and threatening the traditional grip of 'property' upon Parliament as the newly rich sought to purchase seats in Parliament.[9]

The 'good faith' of such 'avaricious and interested men' was pledged against the Caribs.[10] The latter race was variously described by contemporary commentators, depending on their degree of attachment to the St Vincent land lobby. There were two distinct 'races' of Caribs. The 'yellow' or 'red' Caribs were generally accepted to be a harmless and inoffensive people. They were the original inhabitants of the island and seemed content to co-operate with the European settlers, remaining in proximity with them in the coastal settlements of the island. The 'black' Caribs were, it appears, the descendants of the union of a cargo of shipwrecked slaves marooned about a century previously. They had been accepted by the 'red' Caribs at first but the mixed race, who were universally agreed to be either more aggressive or enterprising, subsequently feuded with their neighbours. Increasingly, neighbouring French colonists came to be involved, and once French settlement of the island proceeded, the black Caribs retreated from the coastal settlements and set up on the rich soil and woodland of the interior and north of the island.

The motives for this separation were sympathetic ones. The black race feared possible French plans to enslave them, and were at all times anxious to emphasize their distinctive status *vis-à-vis* the black slaves brought by the French. Fear of renewed slavery and possibly of the English reclaiming their property (the original shipwrecked slaves were alleged to have been on an English slaver), was evinced in explanation of black reticence and obstruction in the 1760s, with some suspicion being voiced that the French were playing on these fears. The slavery issue was of considerable significance, not only because of Carib sympathy and occasional asylum for British and French 'runaways', but also in determining British racial attitudes to the negroes during the disputes of the 1760s and 1770s.[11]

Attitudes to native races were equivocal at this time. There appears to have been a certain fascination for continental endorsement of the notion of the 'noble' savage. The ideas of Montesquieu and Rousseau were to be found along-side Locke's in popular British and American tracts of the period, while races such as the North American Indians and the Eskimos received a great deal of attention in the popular prints of the era, and a degree of romanticization of their lifestyle and mores. Although the Red Indians were often depicted as scalping, murdering savages, especially by the frontiers-men who had most violent contact with them, British and British American regulars like Major Rogers and Lieutenant Henry Timber-lake wrote idealistic accounts of the bravery and virtue of the Delawares and the Cherokees. En-lightened Americans, notably the Pennsylvan-ians Benjamin Franklin and Anthony Benezet, who were later associated with anti-slavery cam-paigns, were outspokenly sympathetic to Indian rights.[12]

The acquiescent 'red' Caribs were warmly approved by all accounts, but the blacks were tainted with Negro, slave blood. Sympathy for the Negro was at this time a very individual affair, the successes of Granville Sharpe's activi-ties in England being originally guided by per-sonal acquaintance over the case of Jonathan Strong in 1765, and by opportunism in forcing an important test case over the Negro Somerset in 1772.[13] Moreover, just as Red Indians were subject to popular infamy, even anti-slavery campaigners such as Arthur Lee described Negroes as 'a race the most detestable and vile that ever the earth produced'.[14]

Contempt and distrust of the Negroes showed among Carib sympathizers. Thus, 'Sagitta', in the *Gazetteer*, while realistically noting the Caribs' fears for their security and suspicions of the motives of the land speculators, insisted that, 'After all savages are not to be treated upon the same maxims with polished nations', for they were 'a people accustomed to employ treachery for all the purposes of policy'.[15] 'W.W.' in the *Public Advertiser* also threw light upon contemporary attitudes. Evincing 'The sacred legend of our Holy Faith' and 'the fixed law of nature' in support, he argued that 'the weaker shall be subject to the stronger', which advantage he maintained 'we evidently enjoy over the aborigines, as well as the black inhabit-ants of St Vincent'.[16]

The evidence of the planters and their suppor-ters, both in Parliament and press, and most persuasively in their official correspondence with governors Melville, Leybourne and Fitzmaurice, was primarily concerned with emphasizing the Caribs' character defects, their links with the neighbouring French islands, and

their affinity with their slave ancestors and with contemporary slave runaways. Much of the official correspondence which Townshend had called for in the debates of December 1772 dwelt on these themes, their prejudicial effect rein-forced by the testimony of Alexander Campbell, a prominent council member, planter and land speculator, later to pass into history as the plain-tiff in the 1774 *Campbell* v. *Hall* judgement, and that of Messrs Sharpe and Maitland, also planters and council members from the island. Campbell retailed the story of the blacks' approach to M. Denerie, governor of neigh-bouring Martinique, seeking advice and support, while Sharpe 'represented the Caribs to be a set of men void of faith and every senti-ment of morality', who 'loved plurality of women and drinking'.[17] The written evidence of Harry Alexander, president of the Council of St Vincent, and of Richard Maitland, the island's agent, showed that from 1769 onward the local planter community and council, stirred by Carib resistance, were concerned to arrange local self-defence, and to call for extra troops from within the empire.[18]

Why the Caribs had resorted to arms was well documented. They were reluctant to sell or exchange the woodlands they had occupied since the days of French settlement. How these woodlands had come to be a matter of conten-tion lay within the vague arrangements for St Vincent in the 1763 settlement. The island had been occupied by the French, who had, after some friction, tacitly accepted black Carib ownership of and independence within the woodlands. Their terms of surrender did not comprehend the fate of this independent people. Instructions to bear gently on them and not disturb their lands had been handed out in 1764, but the *Authentic Papers* show that with mounting pressure from land-hungry settlers, and with official interest growing in perhaps gaining profit from what could, under asserted sovereignty, be termed Crown lands, moves were made in 1769 to properly survey the black Caribs' territory.

It was the surveying party and its building of a road into the disputed area which led to what can only be termed passive resistance from the blacks who surrounded a body of troops called in to support the alarmed surveyors, and having taken them prisoner returned them unharmed, once assured that the territorial dispute would be referred to the Crown.

Government and private interest in Carib land was not unconnected with the high quality of the property. A memorial from Sir William

Young, first land commissioner for the area, remarked in 1767 that 'the soil was found superlatively excellent — by far more extensive, more level, and a finer country than the part already disposed of; and as the soil is perhaps the best in the world, and it is admirably supplied with rivers, it would probably soon become a more valuable sugar colony than any possessed by the Crown', except Jamaica. Young commented on French acknowledgement of the Caribs' property and suggested the reservation of lands for the blacks, quit rent free and inalienable, in return for making these richer territories available.[19]

Instructions from the lords of the Treasury to the land commissioners followed up Young's suggestions, counselling caution and tolerance in dealing with the blacks, suggesting their separation from the 'red' Caribs and giving guidelines for suitable prices for cleared land sold. The plan was to give the Caribs a price and time to clear or abandon their land.[20] The resulting surveys saw Carib resistance, and, to the credit of the local authorities, a pause for consultation with the government. Sadly, the papers showed that these consultations were coloured by planter emphasis upon Carib unreliability and the physical threat they posed to whites. Official correspondence from the *de facto* Governor of Grenada, Ulysses Fitzmaurice, detailed the negotiations the blacks had had with Martinique, and shrewdly commented on the religious and linguistic links retained with the French, and upon the resentment of dispossessed French and St Lucians who 'consider the present possessors as usurpers of their property and retain an irreconcilable hatred to the English name — these people are exceedingly diligent in working the weak minds of Caribs already prejudiced and suspicious'. Fitzmaurice's testimony was the realistic assessment of a governor actually in trouble for his own acceptance of French Grenadian rights within the council of Grenada. Himself unprejudiced against the local French and enjoying 'a good understanding' with the Governor of Martinique, he recognized that the suspicions of the blacks 'cannot easily be reconciled to the vicinity of white people, whose gradual and successful intrusions upon their Carib neighbours they are sagacious enough to have remarked'.[21]

The government's response to the surveying problems came in a letter from Hillsborough to Fitzmaurice in August 1769 approving the arming of the local settlers and advising a call for reinforcement from the North American establishment if events got out of hand.[22] From then on representations from St Vincent increasingly sought to indicate just such a crisis with depositions in late 1769 alleging further Carib violence. By 1771 an address of the Council and Assembly of St Vincent to the King spoke of 'The dangerous and distressed situation of this colony' and spoke of 'Your Majesty's natural born subjects, who, had purchased lands at very high prices, with an intention of cultivating them, and had met with success — till unexpectedly their properties are rendered very precarious, and their lives endangered by a rebellion of the negroes — without the least provocation from the inhabitants — daily enticing their slaves to join them.' The blacks were accused of violence and genocide against their red counterparts, and the aim of 'totally extirpating the white inhabitants'.[23]

Whether or not these charges were true, it was significant that local representative institutions were totally dominated by the planters and by would-be land speculators whose interests were served by such charges, and by 1772 the government's scepticism seemed to have changed to total acceptance of the planters' viewpoint, as a letter from Hillsborough to Governor Leybourne indicated. He cautioned against 'unnecessary severities that may have the appearance of cruelty and oppression' and looked to secure 'a full submission' from the blacks.[24] The blacks had apparently renounced, or more accurately, denied allegiance to the British Crown during negotiations over land sales in 1770–71, a stance understandable in the light of their history. The dangers inherent in accepting the independence of a free, French-influenced and -speaking Negro race of slave descent in an area of small white and large Negro slave populations were obvious. Fears were bolstered by typical contemporary incredulity that any population within the empire could voluntarily reject the much-vaunted political benefits and freedoms concomitant with submission to the English Crown and constitution. A similar rejection of British values had occurred in Acadia earlier that century; now, prompted by planter suggestions, the government resorted to the policy of forced deportation formerly employed against French, white Acadian habitants, to solve the Carib problem.[25]

The evidence of Messrs Maitland, Otley and Sharpe had suggested that 'any unoccupied tract of 10,000 acres of woodland upon any part of the coast of Africa would afford them [the blacks] all the necessaries of life which they have been accustomed to'. Following this up, Hillsborough advised: 'If necessary demand the removal of the Caribs, do take up such vessels as can be procured, to serve as transports for the conveyance of them to some unfrequented part of the coast of Africa, or to some desert island adjacent thereto'. These instructions, with others to the Governor of the Leeward Islands, were separate and secret 'lest those infatuated savages should become desperate'.[26] 'W.W.' of the *Gazetteer* had expressed similar fears that the Red Indians of America should become desperate if they heard news of this less than enlightened native policy.[27] In the context of often more enlightened policy towards the American Indian at this time, this policy departure is eloquent testimony to the success of the local land lobby and official local representation, and to the awkward position of the mixed, independent Negro race in geographical proximity to French possessions and to a slave economy.

Amid the meagure historiography of this episode, L. J. Ragatz, chronicler of the West Indian planter class, denigrated Townshend and other critics as 'well-meaning but ill-informed individuals' and sternly maintained that the policy was necessary for the proper development of the island as a colony.[28] The well-meaning individuals thus dismissed included a horrified Horace Walpole, and Edmund Burke, as well as a number of distinguished parliamentary critics. If these latter could fairly be accused of having a partisan axe to grind in the debates, this was not necessarily the case with Walpole, already horrified by revelations of the maltreatment of the Bengalese, or of Edmund Burke, whose absence from the debates may well have been due to the possibility of embarrassment over the deep involvement of his younger brother, Richard, in a particularly imprudent land purchase in the Carib territories actually at the centre of the dispute.

Although paradoxically Burke's intense clannishness led him to fervently support the rectitude of Richard's premature and dubiously financed purchases in the area, his private correspondence showed sympathy for the unhappy natives. He attacked 'those who acted in that part' who 'were not possessed of the skill of governing them, or perhaps of the desire of it; and having found or rather made them troublesome neighbours, they could think of no other method to free themselves from that uneasiness, but by removing them by force from their habitations'. He condemned this 'weak and sinister policy' of using troops against 'those unhappy savages'.[29]

Walpole was particularly indignant, like Burke perceiving the malign influence of the governor, council and land commission at work. He sympathized with 'the Caribs' who 'have no representatives in Parliament; they have no agents but God, and he is seldom called to the bar of the House to defend their cause'. Walpole remarked of the note in February on the affair: '206 to 88 gave them up to the mercy of their persecutors'.[30] The Carib cause was defended stoutly within the House and continuing the flavour of military inquiry which had occasioned Townshend's original motion in December, it was the correspondence of serving soldiers on the island and the verbal evidence of senior officers which condemned the military and administrative arrangements for the expedition and called into question the morality behind it all. Lieutenant-Governor Grove cited the peaceable nature of the blacks, and remarked the pressure from white settlers upon their land; Lieutenant-Colonel Fletcher thought them 'well affected to our Government' and 'peaceable until the surveyors had begun to make inroads into their country'. The report of Lieutenant-General Trappaud from the expedition itself confirmed the military attitude. He maintained, 'the poor Caribs have been ill-used — we have only been able to penetrate four miles into the country. God knows how this petty expedition will end; all we hope for is that the promoters and contrivers of it will be brought to a speedy and severe account.'[31] This distaste among the military was voiced in the press, too, with a letter from an officer off the coast of St Vincent who opined at large upon 'the infamy that it will bring upon the national character to butcher a parcel of innocent savages in cold blood'.[32]

The local planters came under some odium. The *Annual Register*, of which Edmund Burke was editor, gave a lengthy and considered account of the expedition and the debates that surrounded it, in which the 'fear and avarice' which 'operated strongly to make them wish removal of the black inhabitants' was remarked. The *Register* made much of the planters' disappointment that they were unable to proceed in 1769 with the reduction of the blacks.[33] In the debates both Isaac Barré and Townshend were severe upon the evidence that planters Sharpe and Alexander had been reluctant to quit the rich inroads made into Carib territory at that time and had regretted 'his Majesty's unfortunate clemency'.

Sharpe in particular was castigated by Townshend as 'a clever, artful, diffuse man — an interested planter' who thought 'sending the Caribs to the coast of Guinea was an eligible plan'.[34] This opinion was backed by at least one newspaper piece, by 'Britannicus' in the *St James's Chronicle*, who likened the planters to the East Indian nabobs, both groups benefiting from a ministry which 'carried on a farce of an enquiry in this as they did in the India Business — the unrighteous Nabobs are to enjoy their millions and *jaghires*, and the St Vincent settlers the estates and plantations seized by force from the natives. Each injured party appeals in vain to English justice.'[35]

Less convincing was the opposition's overzealous depiction of the blacks as defenders of liberty, cast in the mould of English constitutional libertarians. The presumed attractions of allegiance to the British Crown were considered enormous. The offer of the benefits of the British constitution, the settling of provincial assemblies and English laws and customs, had been key clauses in the Proclamation of 1763 relating to the newly acquired territories of the empire. In December Trecothick and Townshend, aided by Whitworth, were right to raise the question of the honour of the British flag, but Barré's heated espousal of the blacks' cause, depicting them as 'in arms for the preservation of their liberty' while calling on 'every English heart' to 'applaud them', strained credulity in its use of conventional Whiggish political jargon.[36] Given such a stance it is unsurprising that opposition oratory received the standard response, voted down in February by a large Northite majority.

The government claimed they were not unduly responsive to settler pressure, and indeed the crux seems to have been reached in 1771 when Carib resistance to further planter negotiations and less attractive offers for their land were met by their references to an independence of ownership and sovereignty, prompting at least one newspaper commentator to remark 'on this occasion, without the least reserve, and in express terms' that the blacks 'denied all allegiance to the King'.[37] This point was reiterated in the local petitions to the Crown. It was notable that, with the military expedition successful but at high cost in sick and wounded, the general approach once the Caribs had submitted, seemed to be lenient, reserving to them rights and privileges as subjects of the British king. When later hostilities with the French saw a further weakening of Carib allegiance, the exasperated authorities finally deported them. Thus, from 1797 the black Caribs were to be located in central America.[38]

If powerful lobbying and a question of sovereignty had stirred the government sufficiently to act against the Caribs, any reluctance was attributable to the low esteem in which the older established West Indian lobbyists were held, and to the suspicion of speculators and *arrivistes* like Macleane and the Burkes. These had made life difficult for the local administrations of Grenada and St Vincent in the early postwar period. Richard Burke was at this time continuing to disrupt local politics through his speculatory activities and his attempts to secure the functions of the local Treasury, and through the procedural wrangling of his 'friends' in the local assembly. His activities centred around purchases of 'red' Carib land in 1770, unsanctioned by local or central government, possibly through the agency of French entrepreneurs known to be operating illegally at that time.[39] Interest in land sales involved not only local officials and planters like Sharpe, Alexander and Campbell, all identifiable as a united and coherent interest group, but outsiders, including the French, and Burke who was identified with the Fitzmaurice interest at Grenada, and whose feud with the officialdom of the ceded islands went back some years. Moreover, the government's insensitivity and ignorance complicated matters such as Richard Burke's land suit in the area by pledging St Vincent property, including Carib land, and indeed land ceded 'inalienably' to the Caribs in the treaty of 1773, to placate the interests of General Monckton, and Dalrymple, the head of the 1772–73 expedition.[40]

The Carib expedition of 1772–73 hinted at problems awaiting imperial administration elsewhere. Although debate on its rights and wrongs never competed with other contemporary outbursts, most notably the East India revelations, the parliamentary proceedings over this episode were covered in detail, including the humanitarian arguments of the opposition, which linked the Carib affair, by inference and coincidence, with the scandal and injustice revealed in Bengal. Moreover, speeches and newspaper correspondence, and detailed and sympathetic coverage by the *Annual Register* provide the imperial historian with useful illustrations of the confused thinking on treatment of indigenous peoples within the empire. There is clear evidence of the fantasy of savage innocence at work, most notably in the ready acceptance by all interested groups of the virtues of the harmless 'red' Caribs, and the doubts over the mixed blood of the blacks. Ambivalence of attitude to the Negro was to be found, for although Trecothick, Barré and various correspondents were eager to equate Carib resistance with more

English, sophisticated concepts of libertarian struggle, just as there had been a certain Whiggish enthusiasm over the case of the slave, Somerset, in the preceding summer, it is clear that the Caribs' association with tainted, slave blood, their own fears of renewed slavery, and geographical proximity to slave populations underlay many of their problems.[41]

Interesting from the racial viewpoint, the Carib episode is most revealing, perhaps, for its evidence of what Edmund Burke termed weak policy. Whitehall knew little of the Caribs or their history. As the *Annual Register* commented, the French surrender terms actually overlooked their existence. There was distaste and distrust, not only from Whitehall of the West India planters, but from the older, established planting class, of the temptations of cheap smallholdings in the new islands which could draw away poorer whites from their employment and control.[42] There was the influence on local and metropolitan politics, both of the older interest and that of maverick investors like the Burkes, and contractors like Sir George Colebrooke who had already made their mark upon East Indian speculations and seemed eager to make a 'quick buck' wherever available. Distrust of irresponsibility and adventurism underlay much of the talk of the good name of the English flag which characterized criticism of the expedition.

The government, based as it was upon response to interest and lobbying, was particularly dependent for advice and information in this affair upon a local hierarchy of planters and politicians who stood to gain by the removal of the Caribs. Whitehall's dependence for information upon local politicians and influence groups, themselves shaped by opportunities for local patronage and aggrandizement, was a feature not only in St Vincent, but in North America. Where in St Vincent the metropolitan authorities were dragged reluctantly into insensitive and ill-judged action, so later in the year, the breakdown of local authority in Boston, and the reports and viewpoint of the Hutchinson-dominated administration led to precipitate clumsy parliamentary reaction. Time and again the history of Whitehall and Parliament's intervention in imperial affairs from 1763 up to the American war was one of reluctance born of ignorance; of foolish and over-enthusiastic implementation of pet theories; or of over-reaction to stimulus from interests and influence on the spot. The Carib affair was an encapsulation in miniature of the problems raised by interaction of central, cautious but ignorant government, and local aims and interests, within a newly expanded empire. As was to happen too often in the future, the interests of indigenous peoples suffered in the resulting confusion.

Notes

1. Commons debate, 9 December 1772: *Parliamentary History of England from the Norman Conquest in 1066 to the year 1803*, ed. W. Cobbett, 36 vols (London, 1886-70), xvii, pp. 568-71.
2. *Ibid.*, pp. 575-639. See also *London Chronicle*, 13-16, 16-18, 23-25 February, 1773; *Critical Review*, xxxv, January 1773, p. 154; *St. James's Chronicle*, 16-18 February 1773.
3. *Parliamentary History*, xvii, pp. 572-73.
4. 'A. Proprietor', *Gazetteer*, 24 February 1773; 'Alfred', *Public Advertiser*, 22 April 1773.
5. *Parliamentary History*, p. 735.
6. See *Authentic Papers relative to the Expedition against the Caribs and the sale of Lands in the Island of St Vincent* (J. Almon, 1773).
7. For newspaper accounts of the effects of frontier expansion and land speculation upon the Indians see *Public Advertiser*, 25 August, 11 November 1763.
8. For the East India speculations of Lord Shelburne, his secretary, Lauchlin Macleane, of the Burkes, Colebrooke *et al.* see L. S. Sutherland, *The East India Company in Eighteenth Century Politics* (Oxford, 1952), pp. 206-12; also L. S. Sutherland and J. Woods, 'The East India Speculations of William Burke', in *Proceedings of the Leeds Philosophical and Literary Society*, xi, 1962.

     For details of Macleane's involvement see particularly J. N. M. Macleane, *Reward is Secondary, the life of a political adventurer and an inquiry into the identity of Junius* (London, 1963), pp. 63, 73-75, 82-85, which discusses his post-war land syndicate in Grenada. See also Dixon Wecter, *Edmund Burke and his Kinsmen* (Boulder, Colorado, 1939), which details the Burkes' speculations in both the East and West Indies.
9. J. M. Holzmann, *The Nabobs in England. A study of the returned Anglo-Indian, 1760-85* (New York, 1926), is also instructive on contemporary hostility in England to the West Indian *nouveaux riches*.
10. *Parliamentary History*, xvii, pp. 730-31, T. Townshend on the evidence of Mr Sharpe, 10 February 1773.
11. See *Annual Register*, 1773, p. 83 on Carib origins. See also C. Shephard, *An Historical Account of St Vincent* (London, 1831), pp. 22-25. For contemporary accounts see 'Sagitta', *Gazetteer*, 7 January 1773; 'Candidus', *London Chronicle*, 1 January 1773; Memorial of Richard Maitland to Lord Hillsborough (not dated), *Parliamentary History*, xvii, pp. 594-95.
12. See, for example, 'G.L.D.', *Gazetteer*, 1 February 1773 on the Esquimaux; Major Rogers' Journal was extensively featured in *London Chronicle*, December 1765, 28-30 January 1766; for Timberlake see *Monthly Review*, January 1776.

     For sympathetic articles see e.g. *London Chronicle*, 21-24 September 1765, 3-6 August 1771, 26-29 October 1771; *Gentleman's Magazine*, August 1765, February 1772. For more savage accounts see *London Chronicle*, 30 July-2 August 1763, 5-8 April 1766. For Franklin and Benezet see G. S. Brookes, *Friend Anthony Benezet* (Philadelphia, 1937), pp. 120-22; L. W. Labaree (ed.), *The Papers of Benjamin Franklin* (New Haven, Conn.,

1957) xi, pp. 69–74, 103–04; *Gentleman's Magazine*, April 1764.

13. See Sir R. Coupland, *The British Anti-Slavery Movement* (London, 1933) pp. 48–56.

14. A. Lee, *Vindication of the Continental Colonies* (London, 1764), p. 25.

15. 'Sagitta', *Gazetteer*, 7 January 1773.

16. 'W.W.', *Public Advertiser*, 15 March 1773.

17. *Parliamentary History*, xvii, pp. 727–28 (Alexander Campbell's testimony); *ibid.*, p. 727 (Mr Sharpe's testimony); *ibid.*, pp. 728–30 T. Townshend on both.

18. *Ibid.*, pp. 580–85, Maitland and Alexander correspondence.

19. *Ibid.*, pp. 575–79.

20. *Ibid.*, pp. 582–87.

21. *Ibid.*, pp. 587–88. For coverage of the scandal of French Grenadian Councillors see Anon, *London Chronicle*, December 1769, pp. 26–29; 'British Indignation', *Ibid.*, January 1770, pp. 25–27.

22. *Parliamentary History*, xvii, p. 597.

23. *Ibid.*, pp. 595–97. Charges of genocide were reiterated by 'Candour', 'Questions from St Vincent', *London Chronicle*, February 1773, pp. 20–23.

24. *Parliamentary History*, xvii, pp. 632–35.

25. For the Acadian affair see Sir R. Coupland, *The Quebec Act: a study in Statesmanship* (Oxford, 1925), pp. 11–14.

26. *Parliamentary History*, xvii, pp. 634–35.

27. See note 15.

28. L. J. Ragatz, *The Fall of the Planter Class in the British Caribbean, 1763–1833* (New York, 1928), p. 116.

29. E. Burke to James de Lancey, 20 August 1772: T. W. Copeland (ed.), *The correspondence of Edmund Burke* (Cambridge, 1860), ii, p. 328 and note.

30. A. F. Steuart (ed.), *The Last Journals of Horace Walpole* (London, 1810), i, pp. 169–71. *Correspondence of H. Walpole* (ed.), Toynbee, viii, pp. 228–41: Walpole to Sir Horace Mann, 21 January, 17 February 1773.

31. Groove, Fletcher and Trappaud's evidence is taken from the account of the Commons proceedings printed in the *Lloyd's Evening Post*, 10–12, 12–15 February 1773.

32. *London Evening Post*, 22 January 1773.

33. *Annual Register*, 1773, pp. 85, 86–87.

34. *Parliamentary History*, xvii, pp. 728–30.

35. *St James's Chronicle*, 16–18 February 1773.

36. *Parliamentary History*, xvii, pp. 569–71; debate of 10 December 1772. A fuller account is available in *Gentleman's Magazine*.

37. 'Candidus', *London Chronicle*, 1 January 1773.

38. The terms of surrender are fully reprinted from the *St Vincent's Gazette* of 27 February in the *London Chronicle*, 10–13 April 1773, and in C. Shephard, *An Historical Account of St Vincent* (London, 1831) pp. 34–36. Sir A. Burns, *History of the British West Indies* (London: 1954) pp. 505–06, details the subsequent treachery and deportation of the black Caribs.

39. See Gov. Melvill to Lord Hillsborough, 16 December 1770, quoted in D. Wecter, *Edmund Burke and his Kinsmen*, p. 57. See also *ibid.*, pp. 60–68.

40. For Burke's and Macleane's political sympathies in the area see, J. N. M. Macleane, *Reward is Secondary*, pp. 171–250. For details of the government land grants see *Burke Correspondence*, ii, pp. 460–64; E. Burke to Rockingham, 21 September 1773.

41. See Franklin's caustic remarks on such 'Whiggish' sympathy over the Somerset affair, *London Chronicle*, 20 June 1772; *Franklin Papers*, xvii, p. 269.

42. L. J. Ragatz, *The Fall of the Planter Class*, pp. 115–17, makes this point.

SECTION THREE

Imperialism and Colonial Slavery

Within a half century of the Columbus enterprise the Caribbean had assumed an importance to European states, Atlantic entrepreneurs and civil society that was unprecedented within the westward imperial drive. The Atlantic islands and West Africa did not excite the imperial imagination in the way the Caribbean did, and its colonization as perceived solutions to countless national ills reached a frenzied intensity. The association of imperialism with colonial settlement therefore became a new formula for migratory activity that reduced the dimensions of the Atlantic ocean, and forged a new identity around the space it occupied.

All European colonizing nations were committed, but with significant variation between them, to slavery as the institution that determined social relations within colonial society. The Spanish tossed and turned with notions of conditionalities, but only in the formative stages. It was considered important to them to set out the principles within which the social actions of colonization could be explained and justified. The northern Europeans, coming to the region at a time when the Spanish had settled the dispute between competing forms of social subjections, made a headlong rush into the chattel enslavement of Africans whenever and wherever it was financially viable and socially necessary.

The economics of colonization were not controversial. Profit from trade, plunder and production were market objectives. Slavery was both a system of trade in itself and a means of generating trade through production. Slave traders and slave owners, merchants and producers, held together the nexus of colonialism and slavery as sanctioned by imperial states and metropolitan civic society.

In this section, a comparative perspective is offered on these experiences, across imperial lines, between places, and through time. Watts' focus is on the methods of effective colonization of the Greater Antilles by the Spaniards who tried to establish viable economic activities in the new settlemens, particularly early agricultural activities. Knight examines the attempt by rival European powers to displace the Iberians and establish their hegemony in the Caribbean, the role of the buccaneers in facilitating the project of North-West Europeans and the formation of resistant maroon enclaves. The Dutch were essential to the creation of the Atlantic systems and played a key role in reducing Spanish influence in the Caribbean. Kopperman look at the role of the Dutch in the creation of the Atlantic systems, in particular their role in settlement, finance and commerce. Zahedieh's focus is the English capture of Jamaica from the Spanish and the creation of an English foothold in the Greater Antilles. More specifically she explores the debate over the capitalization of colonial enterprises. Finally, Butel examines the building up of French commerce and the role of the Caribbean in the expansion of French merchant capital.

11

Early Hispanic New World Agriculture, 1492 to 1509

DAVID WATTS

The first Hispanic agriculture in the New World involved the planting of a selection of Mediterranean crops brought over from Spain on Columbus' second voyage. Although most of these proved to be totally unsuited to the West Indies' environment, a few may have survived, such as the chick peak (*Cicer arietum*), which was always an important, protein-rich part of the diet of Spanish immigrants; and undoubtedly some *Citrus* species.

Prior to his third voyage, the Spanish Crown ordered Columbus to persist in attempts to grow wheat and barley in Española, and in consequence 6,000 fanegas[1] of the former, and 600 of the latter were taken along to the island in 1498; but these presumably suffered the same fate as the original cereal crop (Mercadal, 1959). Following these disasters, it is unlikely that any additional attempts were made to raise European food crop species on any major scale, certainly prior to 1509, the colonists instead turning to indian *conucos* for their food supplies. However, many food products familiar to the Spanish continued to be imported from their homeland: thus a cedula of 9 April 1495 lists cargoes for Española from Sevilla of wheat, barley, pulses, sugar, biscuits, wine, oil, vinegar, dried figs, bacon and salt fish (de Navarette, 1825-9).

Then, towards the middle of this period, the idea of planting commercial crops first began to take root. Members of an unofficial agrarian group, based in Santo Domingo and *villas* nearby, undertook to investigate the possibilities of raising sugar cane, a species with which the Spanish already were well familiar. It is likely that this cultigen had first been brought to Española from Gomera, in the Canary Islands, on Columbus' second voyage, but had not taken (Ratekin, 1954. In the event, its reintroduction was achieved, shortly after the beginning of the sixteenth century, in the neighbourhood of Concepcion de la Vega; and in 1503 a molasses mill was built in this town, the first in the New World. Experiments designed to produce refined sugar were run, at this same locality, from 1506, but all of them appear to have failed. Three major problems seem to have mitigated against the success of this latter venture: first, the type of sugar mill was inefficient, its design dating back to tenth-century Egypt, according to Deerr (1949); secondly, an adequate labour force was unobtainable, since so many settlers directed indians held under *repartimiento* to gold placers rather than elsewhere; and thirdly, the outlet to potential markets was always difficult, bearing in mind the inland position of Concepcion. In effect, the Concepcion experiment in cane production was doomed from the start, and the raising of this crop in the island was not to assume a position of importance to the economy until some ten years subsequent to this date.

Although from the above, it would be correct to conclude that most Spanish settlers at this stage displayed little interest in field cropping, some did indulge in stock-rearing, following open-range Iberian traditions. On Columbus'

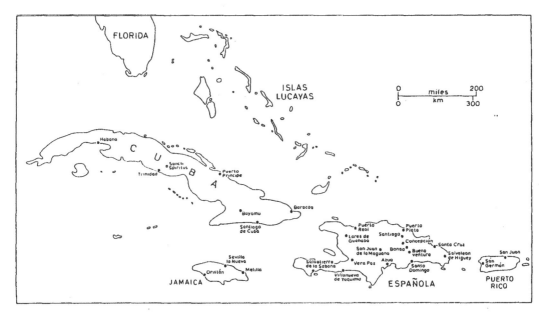

Fig. 11.1 The new *villas* created in Española between 1503 and 1509, and elsewhere in the Hispanic West Indies between 1509 and 1519

second voyage, horses, cattle, swine, sheep and goats all had been introduced, and small numbers of each also arrived regularly thereafter. It should be emphasised that these were the first herbivore domesticates (apart from the indians' guinea pig) to be let loose on the Españolan environment. Most were simply left to run wild; and in the absence of natural predators and competitors, they multiplied rapidly. A rich diet of native grasses, roots and wild fruits, along with cultigens from abandoned *conucos*, supported them. Pigs and cattle thrived especially spectacularly. The fast-running, lean tough hog of the Spanish meseta took well to all but the wettest forest habitats. In Española, at the end of 1498, the rebel Roldan alone owned 120 large and 230 small hogs in Xaragua (Crosby, 1972); and, in some parts of the island, hog population eventually become so large that, by 1508, permission to hunt for 'wild pigs' had been granted to settlers, in attempts to reduce the devastation they caused in the countryside, particularly to the few remaining, productive *conucos*, in which tuberous food plants were uprooted, either to be gnawed or left at the surface to rot. Often, large numbers of cattle complemented the hogs. The contemporary Alonzo de Zuazo suggested that a breeding herd of 30 to 40 cattle might reach a size of 300 to 400 in the space of three or four

years under Españolan conditions; and further to this it should be recalled that Roldan's initial rebellion in the Vega Real was maintained largely by the ready supply of meat obtained from the freely roaming groups of semi-wild cattle which even then were present (De Mendez Natal & Albert, 1947; Sauer, 1966). Horses adapted more slowly, and only 60 or 70 were recorded in the whole of Española by 1503 (Crosby, 1971); but they too grew in numbers, so much so that four years later an edict was issued which prevented any more of them from being imported from Spain. Sheep and goats generally did not prosper during the first years of Spanish settlement (Newson, 1976), although introduced chickens quickly became commonplace.

The peak of Spanish settlement in the West Indies, 1509 to 1519

Expansion from Española: the Greater Antilles and the Lucayas[2]

From 1509, the economic situation in Española became graver. Gold was in increasingly short supply, very little being produced after 1515; and mining had virtually ceased by 1519 (Floyd, 1973). Moreover, the *demora* utilised in its extraction proved to be more and more difficult to maintain, as the decline in indian numbers accelerated. One of the last acts of Ovando, prior to his retirement in 1509, had been to petition King Ferdinand (Isabela had died in 1504) for permission to raid neighbouring 'useless' islands (i.e., those that were known to have no gold placers within them) for the purpose of obtaining additional sources of labour. The King had approved the idea, providing that the indians were not to be made slaves, but rather supplied with wages and necessities, 'just as is being done with the natives of Española' (Simpson, 1966), a sophistry which passed without comment; and indeed, over the subsequent ten years, over two million indians were brought into Española in this way (Las Casas, 1542). At the same time, the search for productive, new gold placers was broadened, to include the adjacent, 'useful' islands of Puerto Rico, Cuba and Jamaica. This two-pronged expansion outwards from Española characterises Spanish policy and settlement between 1509 and 1519.

It was Puerto Rico which first bore the brunt of these activities. Here a small party led by Ponce de Leon, the conqueror of Higuey, arrived late in 1508, to set about determining the location of gold deposits. Some experienced miners went with them. They appear to have been made welcome by the island's Arawak indian population, which then numbered approximately 600,000 (Sauer, 1966). Most of the indians lived close to the southern coast, whereas the known sources of gold were primarily in the north, some distance away. Arising out of this expedition, two major *villas* were founded, one named Puerto Rico San Juan (from which the present city of San Juan derives), and the other San German, this being located at the western end of the island, adjacent to some small-scale placer gravels (Fig. 11.1). For a few months, settlement and gold mining activity were peaceable, both miners and indians being salaried, the latter on a barter basis, according to the King's wishes. But as news of the existence of placers spread back into Española, a miniature gold rush of Spanish incomers developed, and the by now familiar pressures on the indian population and their *conucos* began. Early in 1511, the Arawak in the western end of Puerto Rico rebelled, aided and abetted by a simultaneous, planned attack on the eastern coast by Caribs from Saint Croix: and about 80 Spanish settlers were killed (Oviedo y

Valdes, 1851-5). Thereafter, oppression of the native population was made official policy of this island, through the use of *repartimiento* and *demora*. The gold was worked out, and the island largely depopulated as a result of the repression, in little more than a decade after Ponce de Leon's first contact: and it was then largely abandoned to open-range grazing, the *villas* being deserted, and the main town of San Juan not being reoccupied for several years.

If gold had been the major objective in Puerto Rico, raiding for indians themselves became the primary and profitable activity in the group of islands known as the Lucayas (the Bahamas), in which no precious metals were available. In 1509, when regular incursions into these islands began, they were well peopled with Arawak groups which, as elsewhere in the region, had welcomed the visitors. In Spanish legal terms, Lucayan indians however were classified rather differently to those in Española, being categorised as *naborias perpetuas*, that is as serfs not bound to the land, who therefore could be taken by the colonists to serve their masters in perpetuity; Españolan indians, on the other hand, were known as simple *naborias* with land, who were meant to spend some time cultivating their own *conucos,* and who thus, technically at least (although the principle fell down under *demora*), were not fully tied to those to whom they were assigned in *repartimiento*. This fine distinction effectively made the Lucayan indians extremely vulnerable to Spanish settlers' demands for labour; and moreover they were very handily placed for importation into the placer districts of Española and, for a while, Puerto Rico. The main centres of indian transfer from the Lucayas into the former island were the northern port *villas,* Puerto Real and Puerto Plata, and for a brief time these small towns became exceptionally active in this respect. Peter Martyr (1493-1525) wrote that over 40,000 Lucayans were moved from their homeland in the space of five years, and Las Casas (1542) suggested further that many of these did not survive the short sea crossing, because of overloading and overcrowding on ships' decks: most Spanish ships, he wrote, could 'voyage without compass or chart, merely by following for the distance between the Lucayan Islands and Española, which is sixty or seventy leagues, the trace of those indian corpses floating in the sea, corpses that had been cast overboard by earlier ships'. By 1514, the islands in this group were empty of people, after which they remained depopulated for many years, except for the occasional presence of fugitives from the law and migratory parties of buccaneers.

The occupation of Jamaica, which also commenced in 1509, was one of the first acts ordered by Diego Columbus, Ovando's successor and the explorer's son.[3] Juan de Esquivel, Ponce de Leon's collaborator in the War of Higuey, was assigned to direct events. Jamaica was in the area of high Arawak culture, and native population densities therein seem to have been equal at least to those in Española. A search for gold was undertaken, but none of any consequence was found. On 21 June 1511, King Ferdinand wrote to Diego to express his view that the Jamaican indians might be better treated than those in Española, 'so that they might increase and multiply' (Simpson, 1966); but in point of fact they too were forced to work to excess in the *conucos* in the production of manioc, maize and cotton, produce which initially was sent back to Española, but which later additionally came to be exported to Cuba, and the mainland colonies around Darien. The major *villa* established in Jamaica was Sevilla la Nueva (close to the present St Ann's Bay), first named Santiago. Two other *villas*, of no great subsequent importance, were also founded: Melilla, located at some distance to the east of Sevilla la Nueva on the northern coast; and Oristan, on the southwestern coast, close to the present town of Bluefields (Fig. 11.1). As elsewhere, the decline in Arawak numbers due to their *repartimiento* allocation was rapid: and one may further note in this respect that most appear to have died in their homeland, for there is no record of many having been shipped to Española or other islands. As in Española, livestock (horses, cattle, hogs and, later, goats) were brought in and allowed to run wild on open range and so, inadvertently, hasten *conuco* decline. Overall, Jamaica attracted few Spanish settlers, though the Hispanic population was increased for a while after 1515, as survivors from the ill-fated Panama expedition, organised by Pedrarias d'Avila the year previously, struggled back into the West Indies. But most colonists did not remain for long, preferring to move on to Cuba; and indeed they were encouraged to do so by Panfilo de Narvaez, one of d'Esquivel's lieutenants. By 1519, Jamaica had been mostly forsaken by the Spanish, although a few stayed on to plant subsistence crops, and (with the assistance of negro slaves) periodically round up the open-range livestock which thrived there; the Jamaican Arawak had become extinct, except for the very occasional isolated group which survived for a while in the mountainous interior.

Ultimately, the most important non-mainland expansion out of Española was to Cuba, which the King approved in 1511. Diego Velasquez (p. 000) was appointed to be the main architect of settlement, and he was assisted by the Jamaican party of de Narvaez, the latter directing its attention to the central and western parts of the island. The strategy of Spanish colonisation in Cuba was in certain respects different to that adopted in other islands, an attempt being made to modify the policies of *demora,* which had proved to be so disastrous for indian populations in Española. However, these modifications were, at best, relative, the major point of amelioration being that indians were to be given in service only in those districts in which they already lived (Davis, 1974). Other excesses against them were maintained, so much so that it was in Cuba that Las Casas felt obliged, in 1515, to resign from his commitments to the Crown as an *encomendero,* later (1522) to enter the Dominican order, and devote the remainder of his life to the indian cause; and, in so doing, he commented of de Narvaez' expedition in western Cuba in particular, that he could not remember 'with how much spilling of blood he (de Narvaez) marked that road'. Cuba was put under Spanish control in little less than one year. Gold placers were discovered towards the western end of the Sierra Maestra, in the Trinidad Hills in the centre of the island, and also possibly elsewhere, and they were regarded as being of sufficient importance for a Cuban mint to have been approved in 1512. Indeed, Spanish Cuba prospered from her gold production between that date and 1518. Between 1511 and 1513, seven *villas* were founded in the island in proximity to districts of large aboriginal population, and usually close to gold placers: moreover, and in contrast to Española, all but one were located on or near to the coast. In chronological order of establishment, the first of these was Ascuncion de Baracoa (later, Baracoa), Velasquez' first capital (Fig. 11.1). Trinidad and Sancti Spiritus were the two major mining *villa*s, the first of these being in a district of particularly high Arawak population density, and the second the only inland *villa* in the island. The most populous indian groups in Cuba were controlled by a *villa* at Puerto Principe on the northern coast, which was later relocated to become the town of Camaguey. Two further *villa*s were constructed in the east: Bayamo (or, more correctly, San Salvador de Bayamo), west of the Sierra Maestra; and Santiago, on a sheltered ria harbour. In the west, indian groups (including the remnants of the meso-indian Guanahacabibes,) were subjugated by the *villa* of San Cristobal de la Habana, which was situated not in the north, as is present-day Habana, but on the southern coast opposite.

The severe measures taken against indian populations in Cuba under *repartimiento* and *demora* were such that it was scarcely a decade before the vast majority had been killed off, although small groups of them managed to take refuge in the Sierra Maestra, and in offshore islands. As in Jamaica and Española, they were replaced by open-range grazing animals, notably hogs, cattle and horses; and this trend accelerated after gold production had begun to decline substantially, subsequent to 1518. By the end of the next year, Velasquez had decided to make the (in Cuban terms) remote *villa* of Santiago his new capital, ordering that all gold exports must leave the island from this one town alone; and the rest of Cuba was largely abandoned to be governed very loosely, usually by roving bands of *encomenderos*. The west in particular came to be far from any legal constraints, and it was from here that Hernando Cortez renounced Spanish authority before leaving for Mexico, taking with him some of the open-range hogs that had increased in numbers so rapidly. In 1519, most Cuban gold placers had become exhausted, and those settlers who chose to stay in the island did so solely with a view to developing it further as a stock-rearing centre.

Slave-raiding expeditions to the Lesser Antilles, and the islands north of the Venezuelan coast

Almost from the very beginning of Diego Columbus' tenure of executive office in Española, the permits for slave-raiding granted originally in respect of the Lucayas were quickly extended to include the 'useless' Carib islands of the eastern Caribbean, and the islands north of the Venezuelan coast. For a while, Trinidad was excluded from these attentions, since the King thought that there might be gold placers therein, but this exemption was waived in 1514. Only a few details of the slave-raiding ventures in this broad region have been uncovered thus far, but it is known that by 1512, Barbados, Dominica, Martinique, St Lucia, St Vincent, Grenada and Tobago – in fact, all the islands between Dominica and Tobago – had been approved for incursions. Indians from Barbados appear to have been the most highly prized, being a vigorous Carib-Arawak mix. By 1520, it is likely that all native peoples had been removed from the northern Leeward Islands between the Virgins and Barbuda, except for St Kitts and Nevis; and further to the south, St Lucia, Tobago and Barbados all had been depopulated. Most of the captured indians were transported directly to Española, and at times elsewhere, for work in the gold placers. Native Carib groups in the remaining islands of the Leewards and Windwards retreated as best they could to their mountainous interiors, where they resisted with some skill.

Within the same period, some 100,000 indians had also been taken as slaves from Curaçao; and Bonaire and Aruba had been almost entirely depopulated. Other islands north of the Venezuelan coast suffered the same fate, the main exception being Cubagua and adjacent islands, on which pearls were gathered. Indeed, by order of the King, some Trinidadian and even Lucayan indians were brought into Cubagua in order to assist in the construction of temporary *bohios,* and in the recovery of pearls.[4] Also, some indians were later transferred back to Curaçao from Española, to work on the land (Goslinga, 1979).

On all the islands in the Lesser Antilles, and north of the Venezuelan coast, from which indians had been taken, hogs were left to breed in the wild, and thus serve as an emergency food source, in the event of future shipwreck, or other unforeseen circumstances; and in addition, cattle and horses were brought to the latter group of islands. It was a selection of the open-range cattle and horses derived from Bonaire which eventually were to form the nucleus of the vast, semi-wild herds of these creatures which later ranged the Venezuelan llanos (Crosby, 1972).

Population changes in Española

In Española, the remaining native Arawak declined in numbers exceptionally rapidly from 1509. Between that year and 1512, the price of Lucayan *naborias perpetuas* rose from 5 to 150 gold pesos per head (Sauer, 1966), which gives some indication of the reduction in availability for labour of indians not only in the Lucayas, but also in the Arawak's 'mother island'. By 1518, an official count by the Licenciado Zuazo, who had been sent over from Spain to examine the state of the colonies, indicated that no more than 11,000 Españolan Arawak were then still present, and their continued outrageous treatment under *demora* led many of these shortly afterwards to commit suicide by means of eating the untreated tubers of the bitter manioc, rather than prolong their life-time bondage. A major redistribution of the indian population had also taken place, for at roughly the same time (1514) we know that 25% of it was in Santo Domingo, possibly as house servants; 25% was in Bonao, Buenaventura and Concepcion, the three *villas* nearest to the gold placers; and only 20% remained in the five western *villas*, which formerly had had the highest Arawak population density. The rest were scattered widely throughout the island.

Subsequent to 1518, the position of the Indians belatedly began to change for the better. With the death of Ferdinand in that year, and the accession of Charles V to the Spanish throne, the all-powerful Fonesca was removed from his office as head of the *Casa de Contraccion,* which he had used to negate any previous attempts to restrict indian exploitation; and Diego Columbus was suspended from office. In the place of Diego, three Jeronymite missionaries, who had had no previous links with, or any biases towards former events in the Indies, were appointed to govern Española, with instructions to consider particularly the plight of its indian population. Additional to the representations of Zuazo (see above), they too had reported back to Spain by the end of 1518, advising the abolition of *repartimiento* and *demora,* the resettlement of the remaining indians in agriculturally based *pueblos* of 400 to 500 people each, and the re-establishment of *conucos* in which manioc was once again to be the main crop.

Thirty such *pueblos* had been constructed, and many of the indians resettled, in this tardy attempt to redress the wrongs of the *repartimiento* and *demora* systems within Española when, ironically, an additional final tragedy struck the native population. This was the first recorded appearance in the New World of smallpox, which entered through Santo Domingo in 1518, and then spread quickly to the vicinity of San Juan, Puerto Rico, before dispersing elsewhere (Sauer, 1966). There is still discussion as to whether this complaint was brought in directly by the Spanish or, as Floyd (1973) has suggested, through negro slaves shipped from the Guinea coast of Africa; but whatever the source, the results were devastating for the indians, who, with no previous exposure, had no resistance to it. Few of the Españolan Arawak who were left survived its onslaught, and by 1522 their homeland was almost completely devoid of any remnants of its native peoples. Their final demise may have been accelerated by the further presence, after 1518, of yellow fever and malaria, both of which appear to have been transatlantic imports consequent upon the beginnings of the West African negro slave trade (Wood, 1975). The transmission of these two latter diseases is of course a much more complicated affair than that of smallpox, involving an intermediate vector (usually a mosquito) as a link between the infected individual, originally bitten in Africa, and the recipient of the illness in the New World; but despite this, their effects are likely to have been severe.

As indian populations became increasingly restricted in numbers, negro slaves *(bozales)* came to be introduced more and more into Española, Puerto Rico and, to a lesser extent, Cuba and Jamaica (Floyd, 1973; Lockhart & Otte, 1976). Until 1518, most arrived, under licence from the *Casa,* in Portuguese ships directly from West Africa, or via the Cape Verde islands; but thereafter, the Spanish Crown more often issued its own licences to private traders in order to maintain the flow. At first, like the indians, most were directed to work in the gold placers, but after 1516, as gold became harder to find, a majority at least in Española were sent instead for field labour in the developing sugar plantations of that island's south coast.

In the meantime, the white population of Española stayed essentially footloose and predominantly male. Although exact demographic details for the period are difficult to obtain (see Bowman-Boyd, 1976), it is clear that many rural settlers moved on rapidly elsewhere when the indians assigned to them under *repartimiento* allocations had died. Thus, many of those formerly present in the eastern and western extremities of the island transferred respectively to the new colonies in Puerto Rico, Jamaica and Darien, effectively abandoning to bush the districts which they left. In 1514, one survey suggested that only 718 *vecinos* could be located in Española (Floyd, 1973), and depopulation was such that some of the *villas* established by Ovando had already, by that time, been deserted: Santa Cruz, for example, on Samana Bay, fell into this category, all its inhabitants having gone to Puerto Rico with Ponce de Leon. One year later, Villanueva de Yaquimo was officially disbanded, all the surviving *vecinos* being sent to Vera Paz; and the site of this latter *villa* subsequently was moved to the harbour of Yaguana, the *villa* being renamed Santa Maria del Puerto (Fig. 11.1). Lares de Guahaba was dispersed at about the same time, its vecinos going to Puerto Real. In contrast, Puerto Plata underwent a small increase in population; and Santo Domingo continued to thrive, in consequence of its trading role, and the retention of its position as the controlling town of all the Indies. Towards the end of this period, official attempts were made to try to stabilise the population by encouraging the further emigration from Spain of prospective wives or, alternatively, marriage with indian women; and indeed by 1519 Spanish-born wives had been introduced into every *villa* in Española except Salvatierra, although the great preponderance of them were located in Santo Domingo. Still, however, two-thirds of Spanish residents in the island at this time were unmarried. Most immigrants, both male and female, seem to have come from Andalucia, and to a much lesser extent from Castile (Bowman-Boyd, 1956).

Agricultural development, 1509 to 1519

Probably the most significant, constructive trend of all, in terms of economic development which took place within the Hispanic West Indies, particularly after 1515, was the renewed interest in commercial field crops. Two major influences were responsible for this: economic necessity, as the gold placers began to fail, and then failed

absolutely; and the presence in Española from 1510 of Dominican friars,[5] who saw in commercial crop production a means of stabilisation for the region. From the time of their arrival, the Dominicans had argued the case for agricultural expansion with vigour, but before this could be effected, suitable crops had to be found which were capable of being sold in quantity in European markets, thus recouping the large-scale financial input required for their establishment.

Of those tropical crops which could grow well in the region, and which were immediately available, sugar cane appeared to offer the best possibilities, despite its previous failure in Española, the one island where it had been tried thus far. In 1515, Gonzales de Vellosa, a small-scale landowner with property located a few kilometres to the west of Santo Domingo, took up the Dominicans' challenge, being further encouraged by the then steeply rising sugar prices in Europe (Rodgers, 1866–1902; Ratekin, 1954). He salvaged cane stock from the earlier sugar plantings at Concepcion, and imported a new and better design of sugar mill, and mill technicians, from the Canary Islands. This was patterned on an invention by Pietro Speciale of Palermo, Sicily, who used two upright rollers to squeeze cane and extract cane-juice on the 'clothes-wringer' principle, the rollers being operated by a series of geared wheels. In point of fact, two slightly different types of mill could be utilised, one powered by water and termed an *ingenio*, which was capable of producing an average of 125 t of sugar per year; and the other powered by horses or cattle (*a trapiche*), with a normal output of about one-third that of an *ingenio*. The first mill to be constructed was of *trapiche* design, but by 1517 an *ingenio* was producing sugar on the Nigua river, west of Santo Domingo (Fig. 11.2). The actual technique of sugar production from the cane was well understood, although haphazard production methods often lowered the quality of the product. Once the juice had been removed from the cane stalk, it was channelled into an adjacent boiling house, where it was drained consecutively into a series (5 or 6) of copper cauldrons, each of which had a separate furnace underneath it. The juice was boiled for a while in one cauldron, before being transferred to the next in sequence, where the process was repeated, impurities being skimmed off at each

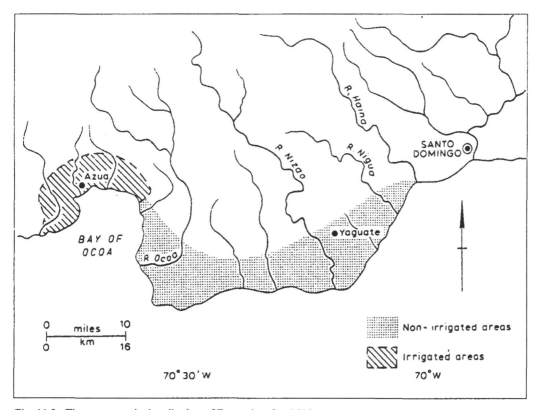

Fig. 11.2 The sugar-producing districts of Española, after 1515

stage. The sticky molasses which resulted increased in density after each transfer; and, following the last boiling, they were scooped into small, clay, sugar-loaf moulds, in which they were left to cool. Any uncrystallised molasses, and any further impurities, then were removed; and the sugar cake (called *mascabado*), which might be coloured anything from a golden yellow to a dark red, was lifted from the moulds to be shipped to Europe for direct sale, or for additional refining into white sugar.

Cane production, then as now, was a costly and complicated business; and in the Hispanic West Indies it always remained to some extent inefficient. In addition to the technical expertise required, the essential components for success were a rapid shipment of cane to the mill once it had been cut (delays of more than 48 hours resulted in a major reduction in the sugar content of the cane juice); an adequate supply of labour, usually provided by negro slaves; sufficient water for the *ingenios*, or animals for the *trapiches;* and ample wood for the furnaces (Morrisey, 1957); and the effective acquisition

and use of these was not always fully mastered or best timed. Yet despite this, once de Vellosa had shown the way, he was followed in his example by many other landowners, especially those along the southern coastlands of Española between Santo Domingo and Azua, and in a few, very restricted districts of Puerto Rico. Most of the costs of development initially were met by the profits gained earlier from the gold placers, or from indian slave factors (Goslinga, 1979). Cane was planted by digging stick on mounds, in a manner which was very similar to indian *conuco* practice, and which was probably derived from it. Labour was most in demand at times of planting, and for weeding and cutting, but for long periods the crop was left to itself; moreover, it could grow back after cutting to be harvested on more than one occasion, secondary and tertiary crops being termed *retonos* (*ratoons*, in English). In the driest parts of Española, and especially in the vicinity of Azua, some irrigation aided cane growth, but by and large this was not necessary.

A few other commercial cultigens were also raised prior to 1519. Some native cotton was produced in small quantities; and the local wild cinnamon (*Canella alba*), which grew especially well in the northwest of Española, was tried and found to be a poor substitute for true cinnamon. The southeast-Asian leguminous tree *Cassia fistula* was introduced from Africa, probably on negro slave ships, and planted for its pods, which were soon to become famous both as a purge, and as a cure for several skin diseases. Another purgative, the castor oil plant (*Ricinus communis*), was also brought in from Africa, and did well.

But perhaps more important than these to the community as a whole were the food crops which were adopted in the region during this period. From 1509, a conspicuous shortage of food had been experienced by Hispanic colonists, especially in Española, as *conuco* abandonment became ever more widespread. We do not know how many *conuco* crops were taken up by the incomers, but certainly enough manioc survived for it to be regarded as the major staple. Attempts were made to supplement the monotonous diet arising from this dominant product by the cultivation of new, non-native plants, from both the Old and New Worlds. Garden vegetables, including cabbages, cauliflowers, carrots, onions, lettuces, radishes, garlic and aubergines, all from southern Europe, began to be grown more widely with varying degrees of success; and new and extended *Citrus* orchards and gardens were authorised, in which were set the sweet orange (*C. sinensis*), sour orange (*C. aurantium*), lime (*C. aurantifolia*), lemon (*C. limon*) and citron (*C. medica*). Small quantities of rice (*Oryza sativa*) were raised from 1512 onwards (Puente y Olea, 1900); and in the same year, the transfer of bananas (*Musa paradisiaca*) from the Canary Islands was effected (Oviedo y Valdes, 1851–5), along with pomegranates (*Punica granatum*) from Spain. The bananas did much better than the pomegranates in their new environment. At the same time, there is little doubt that the Spanish also encouraged the spread of native American cultigens which were not formerly widespread in the Greater Antilles, notably the paw paw (*Carica papaya*) and the cashew (*Anacardium occidentale*). Most of this agricultural activity was, as

in the case of sugar cane, confined to the southern coastal districts of Española, and to Puerto Rico, and was almost entirely absent from Jamaica and Cuba.

In addition to the cultigens brought in by Europeans, the first signs of an intermingling between African and indian garden plants may also be traced to these years (Sauer, 1966). Negro slaves, directed to work in placer mines, and on sugar estates, brought with them from Africa some of their own food crops, such as the yam (*Dioscorea* spp.), which they were allowed to grow on old *conuco* land. Pigeon peas (*Cajanus cajan*) also fell into this category. On the old *conucos*, they in turn came across, and adopted for their own use, several of the cultigens which the indians valued. The precise chronology of these events remains a topic for future research, but they seem to imply at least some overlap between indian and African experience in the raising of foodstuffs, at least in Española. Other African introductions of this period included some of their medicinal plants (the cassia fistula, and the castor oil plant, have already been noted, and the guinea fowl (*Numida meleagris*), which quickly naturalised itself in its new environment.

Further agricultural concerns were largely linked to stock rearing on the open-range basis. As indian raids were undertaken, and/or new colonies founded, grazing animals were left to breed in the wild: the practice of replacing native peoples by beasts was under way. All the evidence indicates that the descendants of these animals thrived and many were still present on most islands over 100 years later. Hogs were conspicuously successful in this respect; thus, in 1514, a note from Velasquez mentioned the existence of 30,000 hogs in Cuba, a number which, though large (bearing in mind that it was only in 1511 that the Spanish arrived), is certainly within the range of possibility. In Jamaica, which by 1515 had become a major open-range hog-rearing island, cattle and horses were numerous as well. All these animals also were widely introduced into Puerto Rico, Curaçao, Bonaire and Aruba while, on the smaller islands of the Lesser Antilles, hogs were the main stock to be left

Summaries of these several introductions of cultivated plants and domesticated animals, and of their source regions, are given in Table 11.1.

Table 11.1: Introduction of Cultivated Plants and Domesticated Animals into Española, 1492–1519*

1493	Wheat	(*Triticum aestivum, L)*	Spain
	Chick pea	(*Cicer arietum, L)*	Spain
	Onion	(*Allium cepa, L)*	Spain
	Radish	(*Raphanus sativus, L)*	Spain
	Melon	(*Cucumis melo, L)*	Spain
	Grapevine	(*Vitis vinifera, L)*	Spain
	Sugar Cane	(*Saccharum officinarum, L)*	Gomera
	(Unspecified salad greens)		Spain
	(Unspecified fruits, including *Citrus*)		Spain
1498	Barley	(*Hordeum vulgare, L)*	Spain
from 1509	Cabbage	(*Brassica sp.)*	Spain
	Cauliflower	(*Brassica sp.)*	Spain
	Carrot	(*Daucus carota, L)*	Spain
	Lettuce	(*Lactuca sativa, L)*	Spain
	Garlic	(*Allium sativum, L)*	Spain
	Aubergine	(*Solanum melongena, L)*	Spain
	Pigeon Pea	(*Cajanus cajan, (L) Millsp.)*	Africa
	Yam	(*Dioscorea spp.)*	Africa
	Cassia fistula	(*Cassia fistula, L)*	Africa
	Castor oil plant	(*Ricinus communis, L)*	Africa
	? Paw Paw	(*Carica papaya, L)*	?S. America
	? Cashew	(*Anacardium occidentale, L)*	?C. America
1512	Rice	(*Oryza sativa, L)*	Spain
	Pomegranate	(*Punica granatum, L)*	Spain
	Banana	(*Musa paradisiaca, L)*	Canary Islands

Animals Cattle, sheep, horses, pigs and goats, all introduced into Española from Spain, from 1493: the guinea fowl (*Numida meleagris*) from Africa, probably about c. 1509.

* Dates of introduction into other islands are uncertain.
? A possibly doubtful date of introduction, or source area.

Environmental changes in 1519

Very little has been elucidated thus far about the patterns of environmental change within the West Indies, which must have accompanied the cultural hiatus between the incoming Spanish and the native indians. Without doubt, though, they must have been far-reaching; and they seem likely to have been at their most visible in those districts which formerly had been characterised by high indian population densities, especially in Española, and also where placer mining and/or European commercial agriculture had begun.

Leaving aside the latter situation for the time being, one of the main agencies of environmental change clearly can be related to the marked decline in extent and quality of indian *conuco* land, which resulted from *repartimiento* and *demora*; and its eventual replacement by forms of secondary vegetation. Most of the evidence for this comes from Española. In the changed economic and cultural circumstances which arose out of the introduction of *repartimiento*, an accelerated reversion to fallow on indian *conucos* came to be the norm. It was set off immediately the time spent by indian populations in *conuco* management was restricted, for this particularly affected the weeding routine, and the scaring off of bird and/or other animal pests. Under aboriginal conditions, both of these tasks had taken up a fair amount of time in the year-on-year cycle, and both were essential for adequate food crop production and the maintenance of *conuco* quality. Additionally, in the enforced absence of indian crop 'guardians', through *demora*, or in consequence of flight as villages were plundered, *conucos* could be expected to deteriorate still further as hogs and cattle unimpededly rampaged through them, uprooting many of the tuberous plants therein and trampling most of the others – a classic case of intercultural land-use conflict. Commenting, in passing, on the predations of the hogs in particular, Las Casas (1875-6) wrote that 'there were great numbers of pigs feeding on sweet roots and delicate fruit . . . the hills were full of them'.

The ecological results of this form of passive-active disturbance (passive, in terms of the absence of the indians; active, in respect of the presence of marauding animals) are fairly easily demarcated. Almost as soon as the weeding process begins to cease, a pioneer vegetation cover of predominantly native weeds at grass and herb level, emerges to reach heights of 1 to 2m, so competing with the cultigens; and these in turn pave the way for an explosive growth of facultative shrubs which, even in the space of a year or two, can overwhelm an old *conuco* almost totally. In practice, this process was at the time facilitated by the tendency of many of the introduced grazing animals to ingest the edible seeds of such grasses, herbs and shrubs, subsequently passing them through their gut, still in viable form, at some considerable distance from the point of ingestion, and so encouraging their rapid dispersal over large areas. Shrub species which are capable of gaining a competitive advantage in this way, and which are certainly present in early secondary growth in Española, include the guava (*Psidium guajava*), a selection of local shrub acacias, possibly the native sage (*Lantana camara*) (one of the world's worst weedy shrubs, according to May, 1981), and several representatives of the *Citrus* group. The spread of the latter appears to have been especially fast. Purchas (1906, quoting Acosta and referring to this period) noted that 'those trees that have most abundantly fructified be orange trees, limon, citrons and other of that sort . . . in some parts there are, at this day, as it were whole woods and forrests of orange trees'. In this way, new but ecologically unstable mixes of both native and introduced shrubs, and no doubt herbs and grasses as well (see below) became conspicuous within the Españolan landscape, in a process which was to be repeated later throughout the West Indies, and in mainland Central and South America.[6] Species which then succeeded these pioneer shrubs in secondary growth woodlands (termed *montes*) often were dominated by representatives of shrub cottons (the *Gossypium*

peruvianum-barbadense complex: Sauer, 1966); and, in time, taller individuals, including many native palms.

Quite how these sequences of change would have affected the faunal communities of former *conucos* and adjacent forest land is not so clear. In the normal course of events, abandoned *conucos* customarily provide good foraging for a wide range of small ground rodents and birds, especially where they are located close to the water and, accordingly, the 'new' plant communities may well have been faunally species-rich. Also as second-growth tree canopies emerged on these sites, many of the birds (e.g., doves, pigeons and parrots) and bats associated with such niche space can be assumed to have moved into them as well, along with the native monkeys. On the other hand, the presence of European grazing animals *en masse* might have scared away some of these creatures from time to time; and others, notably the edible hutias and iguanas but almost certainly many inedible species too, were without doubt expunged from particular localities by Spanish hunting parties. As the secondary vegetation matured, soil structures also were modified, soil organic levels, and probably exchange capacities, being raised to some extent, at least for a while. The microclimate close to the ground became moister and more humid, and soil water levels are likely to have been enhanced too.

On more open land, several other effects arising out of the arrival of the Spanish may be noted. Some native grasses diminished in their areal distribution, through overgrazing by cattle; and at least one, a very palatable Españolan thatch grass, was sought out by them to so great an extent that eventually it became extinct to the island (Las Casas, 1875-6). Often, such grasses were replaced by coarser species, many of them former *conuco* weeds. Further, an interesting question may be posed as to whether savanna vegetation, particularly in Cuba, where it was at its most extensive, was modified both in its distribution and species compositions by the decline in Arawak numbers, and the introduction of large numbers of grazing animals. It may well be that the reduction in frequency of, and ultimately the cessation of indian-set fires, which formerly had kept Cuban savannas largely clear of trees, outweighed the ecological consequences of an increase in grazing activity (which at best must have been species-selective), so allowing some shrub and tree regeneration to have taken place; but the patterns of this change, if indeed it occurred at all, are not clear from the documentary evidence, and they must await the results of pollen analysis from suitable sites before they can be more accurately delineated.

As well as their grazing habits, the likes of which had not been experienced before anywhere in the West Indies, and which in themselves had given rise to the expansion in area of some plant species distributions, and the restriction (and even demise) of others, European field animals also modified the environment more widely, in a more general way, through trampling. In a region in which the heaviest tramplers on land (at least in post-Pleistocene times) previously had been iguanas and hutias, except for Trinidad, the results of this could be profound. Along animal pathways, frequent trampling compacted the soil, so reducing infiltration rates from received precipitation, and eventually encouraging the channelling of rain and soil wash along them, even on slight slopes; and this in turn could lead to minor, and then more major erosion. In Española, there is some documentary evidence that the massive erosional gully forms, termed *barrancas* and *arroyos*, which are now so widespread on mountain land, postdate the advent of European grazing animals; and indeed there is no reason why gullies should have developed, even on steep slopes, under the environmentally conservative indian *conuco* system of pre-Hispanic times . One must say, however, that any gullies which were initiated during the first thirty years of Spanish settlement, seem to have been small in size, for there are no indications at the time of an equivalent, counter-balancing deposition of material downslope, especially in river beds or harbours, which must have been anticipated had major erosion taken place: to be sure, the only descriptions of increased river-bed sedimentation prior to 1519 come from districts located downstream of placer gold workings, such as those of the Rio Haina (Sauer, 1966). The absence of contemporary infill in river valley channels elsewhere in Española also strongly suggests that high forest (tropical rain-forest, seasonal rain-forest and other communities) was left largely undisturbed,

except for the felling of an occasional timber tree, especially since, at other localities in the Caribbean, sedimentation rates are known to have been substantially augmented, once large-scale, and/or clear-cut felling had taken place. In further support of this latter contention, it is known that even close to Santo Domingo, most forest communities, including pine forest, were maintained in the landscape, certainly until the founding of sugar estates; and at Azus, great stands of wood were still reported by settlers in 1515 (Oviedo y Valdes 1851–5).

In addition to *conuco* weeds, both native and introduced, certain other weedy species from the Old World also were present from the earliest days of Spanish settlement, both on open land and in the vicinity of cultivated plots. Thus far, however, we know next to nothing about the speed, or relative success, of the patterns of colonisation of these species in their new environments. According to Coma (Thatcher, 1904), the purslane was the only conspicuous Old World weed in Española in 1494, and if this was the common purslane (*Portulaca oleracea*), it at least must have spread very quickly following its arrival. Source areas for Old World weeds are likely to have been, at first, mainland Spain or the Canary Islands; and later, as the black slave trade commenced, the Guinea Coast of Africa and the Cape Verde Islands.

Except close to the major *villas*, and the main harbour towns, European predation rates on fauna overall appear to have been rather less than in aboriginal times; but near population clusters, the continual shortage of food, and the Spanish predilection for hunting, when put together no doubt meant that some native land animals, notably the hutia and iguana, were removed from selected habitats. In Española, feral dogs too were major agents of ground fauna disturbance, though these were rare in Cuba and Puerto Rico, and never reached Jamaica at this time. Other land fauna was killed off by feral cats and several species of rats, including the black rat (*Rattus rattus*), the brown rat (*R. norvegicus*) and the roof rat (*R. rattus alexandrinus*), all of which were early imports from Europe. In contrast, the culling of marine animals, including inshore and beach animals, always seems to have been slight within this period.

Table 11.2   Patterns of environmental change in selected habitats, to 1519

	(a) Old conucos	(b) Savanna	Mountain slopes
Vegetation	Regrowth of secondary vegetation, of mixed native and introduced species.	Selective grazing from introduced animals alters species balance.	As for (a) and (b)
Fauna	Possible increase in numbers of birds, bats and monkeys in secondary vegetation canopies: mixed effect at surface.	Rapid numerical growth of introduced domesticates.	As for (a) and (b)
Soil	Organic levels, and exchange capacities temporarily raised	Some compaction, lowering of infiltration rate.	Compaction by trampling. Reduction in infiltration rates.
Other effects	Microclimate ameliorated: soil water levels raised.	Cessation of indian fires; possibly some tree and shrub regeneration.	Possibly minor gullying.

A summary of these several environmental changes is given in Table 11.2.

The Hispanic West Indies in decline: the sixteenth century after 1519

Attempts to ameliorate the economic base of the Hispanic West Indies in the second decade of the sixteenth century were interrupted by Cortez' expedition to Mexico in 1519. News of the vast wealth which could be accrued there induced many island settlers to leave in search of their fortune; and the focus of official Court interest in Spain began to shift irrevocably towards the mainland. Shortly afterwards, the position of the West Indies relative to home government was further undermined by the discovery on Magellan's voyage (1519–21) of the real routes to the East Indies which Columbus had sought, around Cape Horn or the Cape of Good Hope, and the development of trading contacts there.

These external events inevitably left their mark on the human geography of the island Caribbean, the Spanish population of which declined again, coming to be concentrated increasingly in the few, relatively large towns, whose

prosperity was ensured through trading interests, and the presence of an administrative sector. Those emigrants from Spain who still sought West Indian destinations, and who after 1519 came predominantly from Andalucia, at first much preferred to settle in Santo Domingo (Table 11.3) than anywhere else, and this city accordingly retained its position as the single largest community in the region for some time; it still had, for example, over 1,000 householders in 1540 (Parry & Sherlock, 1971). Until 1530, most merchants trading in the New World also based themselves in Santo Domingo, but thereafter they tended to move onto the mainland (Bowman-Boyd, 1976). Elsewhere in the region, *villas* struggled to survive, and indeed many were abandoned; and even Santo Domingo itself lost much of its population between 1540 and 1560. In Cuba, in 1550, it was estimated that there were no more than 322 *vecinos* left with 1,000 free indians, and 800 black and indian slaves (Wright, 1916). During the 1560s, the settlement situation worsened further, Lopez de Velasco (1894; see also Andrews, 1978) reporting that only 1,000 Spanish people continued to live in Española, that half of these were in Santo

Table 11.3   New World Destinations of Sixteenth-century Spanish Colonists of known origin

Period	1493-1519	1520-39	1540-59	1560-79	1580-1600	Cumulative	%*
S. Domingo	1,145	1,372	389	1,115	259	4,280	8.5
(Cuba)	(no details)	195	32	191	202	620	1.2
Puerto Rico	109	108	51	152	22	442	0.9

* Percentage figure taken as a measure of the total number of *all* emigrants to the New World, including Hispanic mainland America.

Source: after Bowman-Boyd, 1976

Domingo, and that most of the rest were scattered on agricultural holdings nearby; and at the same time, de Velasco thought that there were only 200 Spanish inhabitants in Puerto Rico, 240 in Cuba and a handful in Jamaica.

Towards the end of the next decade, Habana took over from Santo Domingo as the dominant settlement of the Hispanic Caribbean. This town had been relocated on Cuba's north coast in 1519, when ships on the return journey to Spain from Mexico began to use the newly discovered passage through the Old Bahama Channel and the Florida Straits, instead of the formerly standard exit from the Caribbean through the Windward Passage (Fig 11.3); indeed Santo Domingo came to be avoided entirely on the eastward voyage by the major *flotas*. Habana's new position, on a sheltered ria, was ideal for the construction of a heavily guarded dockside, in which bullion fleets from the American mainland might gather, before they set out on the potentially dangerous Atlantic journey. Just how hazardous this journey might be was realised in full in 1523, when a large part of the treasure booty sent from Mexico City by Cortez to Charles V was captured by the French privateer Jean Fleury; and thereafter, a good deal of Spanish time and money went into the defence of this town (and secondarily, to the rebuilding of fortifications in the three other remaining harbour towns of the region, Santo Domingo; San Juan, Puerto Rico; and Santiago de Cuba), at the expense of more rural districts. By the end of the sixteenth century the Greater Antilles had battened down for siege against corsairs, privateers and buccaneers from several nations, and had begun to adjust to their new military role of providing a defensive shield against such intrud-

ers, for Spanish trade contracts on the American mainland. Little else was attempted in other Caribbean islands during the latter half of the sixteenth century, except for occasional sorties to collect brazilwood and/or pearls from the islands north of the Venezuelan coast (Goslinga, 1979), and spasmodic colonising expeditions sent to Trinidad, which however were not successful until 1592 (Newson, 1976).

As the Spanish population of the region became more and more restricted in size, the way was open for other demographic elements to assume greater importance within it. In particular, increasingly large numbers of negro slaves began to enter from West Africa, so as to satisfy the demand for labour on ranches and sugar estates, particularly those in Española. Frequently the Portuguese, and occasionally northwest-European shipmasters, landed cargoes of slaves illegally, so as to escape the heavy duties imposed on non-Spanish ships by Sevilla; and, as Hispanic control over the remoter parts of her island territories lapsed, the opportunities for this type of smuggling were enhanced. Coastlands in the vicinity of Isabela, Columbus' old town, were a favourite haunt of slave smugglers, for although by mid-century the settlement had been reduced to the status of a hamlet, it retained a small dockside, and it lay a very long way from any representative of government; moreover, new sugar estates were established from time to time in the Vega Real nearby, and thus both sugar, and hides from open range cattle, could be purchased there for the return trip to the Old World, a considerable commercial advantage to the slavers. Many other slaves, of course, also came in 'officially' through Santo Domingo, in Spanish ships, this trade lying largely in the

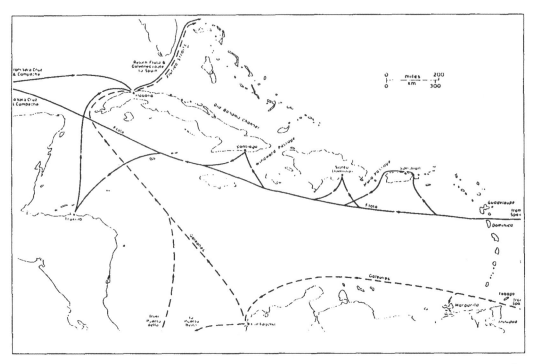

Fig. 11.3 The Florida Straits, and the influence of its location on shipping movements from Habana: revised homeward routes to Spain after 1519

hands of Andalucian Genoese merchants. From 1519 through to the 1560s, Española became the main slave market of the West Indies, handling slaves for other islands as well as on its own behalf. By 1569, between 12,000 and 13,000 African slaves were present on the main island (Sauer, 1966), the colour of whose population accordingly had become overwhelmingly black. The number of slaves on Cuba, Puerto Rico and Jamaica in the sixteenth century is not known. Working conditions for the slaves were poor, causing rebellions as early as 1520 (Parry & Sherlock, 1971); and from these, one may assume that small groups of people of African stock escaped from bondage periodically to live free in remote districts, and thus form the core of an outlaw population, which represented a further potential threat to Spanish authority.

After 1519, the economic base of the Hispanic West Indies lay in two products alone, hides and sugar. From that year, Crown loans for additional development were granted to the sugar industry, enabling the crop to maintain its prece-

dence over cotton, and the purgative cassia fistula. By 1520, three *ingenios* and three *trapiches* were in operation in Española, and several more mills were under construction: sugar exports began in the same year (Davis, 1974). By the late 1530s, 34 sugar mills had been built in this island, on which the crop was largely concentrated (Ratekin, 1954; Crosby, 1972). Most of these continued to be located in the coastal river valleys between Azua and Santo Domingo, although two were in San Juan de la Maguana, and there was a scattering of others elsewhere, in Higuey, and at Bonao, Puerto Plata and La Yaguana. Española's sugar estates at this time tended to be *c* 100 ha in size, of which only one half was cultivated, the rest being left to forest; and of the land which was cropped, normally about one half was put down to vegetables, only 10 to 12 ha being under cane. Such an estate might produce *c* 125 *t* of cane per year, the amount which could be processed by one *ingenio*; and a labour force of about 200 slaves would be required. Most estates also grazed

1,000 to 2,000 cattle on adjacent Crown land, and tried to be as self-sufficient as possible, as regards their food supplies. In 1560, Española's income included 640,000 pesos from her cane crop, as compared to 720,000 received from hides (Crosby, 1972). But for the remainder of the century, the importance of her sugar industry declined sharply as her rural population fell, and as new areas of cheaply produced cane were opened up in both Spanish and Portuguese sectors of the Americas (particularly in Brazil), so flooding Iberian markets. Moreover, problems of shipping costs were beginning to be felt. By the 1560s, the average tonnage per ship sailing to and from the New World had been increased from 100 to 200, in order to handle the augmented flow of bullion. In point of fact, it was most commonly the larger ships which transported the bullion, and only the smaller, older ships which could be persuaded to continue to visit Española to collect her sugar crop; and bearing in mind the higher costs associated with the smaller vessels, transportation charges rose accordingly. However, despite these problems, a few sugar estates remained in work to the end of the century, run by an equally small, aristocratic group of plantation owners, who had by then become the most important political pressure unit in the island.

In many respects, the production of hides was very much easier than that of sugar in that, in its simplest form, it continued to entail merely the periodic round-up of the semi-wild herds of cattle which roamed the countryside. Herds of as many as 8,000 beasts had been noted in Española in the 1520s (Crosby, 1972); and large numbers of cattle were present also in Cuba, Jamaica and Puerto Rico. A steady demand for hides existed in Spain, and was met primarily by exports from Habana and Santo Domingo; some hides also were removed illicitly from Española's northern coast. The period of maximum exploitation seems to have varied from island to island. In Española, very large numbers of cattle were slaughtered for their hides between 1530 and 1540; but the cattle population subsequently was reduced drastically by predations from feral dogs, 100,000 of which were said to have been on the island by 1561 (Las Casas, 1875-6). In Puerto Rico, the trade in hides expanded after 1545, the year in which private farms there were first recognised by the Crown (Mendez Natal &

Albert, 1947). Feral dogs were not present in Jamaica, and may have been scarce in Cuba, and hide exports from both these islands were steady throughout the period. For a while, hogs also were an exportable commodity from the Greater Antilles, being sent to settlements on the Central American mainland, especially from Cuba. Towards the end of the century, some more carefully managed *estancias* were established for raising of livestock, both on Española and in Cuba; and, like the sugar estates, these attempted to be as self-sufficient as possible (Kirkpatrick, 1939). Overall, West Indian ranching activity at this time was seasonal in scale. But large amounts of money could be made from it, and thus it was very well suited to contemporary colonial mores: it was prestigious, and allowed one to live in comfort, off the land and in the towns, for several months each year. But eventually, the same bulk shipping problems which had affected the trade in sugar caused a restriction in the movement of hides, and further aggravated the economic deterioration of the region.

Long before the end of the sixteenth century, large areas of the Greater Antilles, and virtually all of the Lesser Antilles and the islands north of the Venezuelan coast, had been abandoned by the Spanish to the regrowth of secondary forest and scrub, and to the naturalised herds of hogs, cattle and horses that still remained. In ecological terms, most grazing land was severely disturbed, and even by the 1570s, Lopez de Velasco (1894) had noted that pastures in Española were diminishing in size as guava (*Psidium guajava*) bushes and other facultative shrubs encroached along their edges. On mountain land, gullies, induced initially by trampling, continued to grow in size and number. The indian populations had long gone, except in Trinidad and a very few of the Lesser Antilles, which had received minimal attention from the Europeans. In particular, the stable, prosperous, welcoming, agriculturally rich and culturally sophisticated Arawak domains in the Greater Antilles had been destroyed completely, to make way for an ultimately small and predominantly transient Spanish population and many more negro slaves, living in what after 1519 was a fringe, supporting region for Spanish interests on the American mainland. In the West Indies, the attempt to move Iberian land settlement institutions and concepts to the New World had been largely unsuccessful: they had proved to be too rigid, too inflexible, and too incapable of counteracting the greed of individuals which the presence of gold had engendered, or of being adapted without major modification to the totally new cultural and physical environments into which they had been placed. Apart from the immense human tragedy of these events, their end effects were to leave a settlement vacuum in the region, and to create a weak link in the chain of control of Hispanic trade routes to the New World. As the islands became more and more difficult to defend, other European nations began to examine the possibilities of intrusion there, at first tentatively and then more assuredly in the early seventeenth century.

Notes

1. The fanega = 1.68 bushels, or 61.098 dm^3.
2. The Lucayas was the name adopted by the Spanish for the Bahamas group, the English terminology not being taken up until the seventeenth century.
3. Diego Columbus' freedom of action was much less than that accorded to his predecessors. From 1509, the home country increasingly determined the broad outlines of colonial policy, and many of the decisions reached were put into effect by Miguel de Pasamonte, the Royal Treasurer sent to Española in November 1508 to ensure that the monies spent were kept within reasonable bounds. Diego's launch of the Jamaican venture was one of the few decisions taken independently of this new chain of command.
4. Spanish-organised pearl fishing, using indian labour, had commenced in 1499–1502, following expeditions to the Venezuelan coast and adjacent islands by Peralonso Nino, backed by the Guerra brothers of Sevilla; and by Alonso de Hojeda, the man responsible for the first slaughter of indians in Española (p. 92). Both men took advantage of the fact that independent licences (i.e., independent of Columbus and his family) to discover and trade had first been granted in Spain in 1499.
5. Arriving in 1510, the Dominicans took their definitive pro-indian civil rights stance in 1512, following the famous sermon given in Santo Domingo on the last Sunday in Advent in 1511 by Fray Antonio de Montesinos. De Montesinos returned to Spain to present recommendations for the treatment of indians to the Court and, in partial consequence of this, a complete code of laws, the Laws of Burgos, was enacted so that they could be better instructed in the Christian faith. These Laws were, however, largely ignored in Española, and did little to prevent the further destruction of indians at that time.
6. The early naturalisation of the orange, for example, in Paraguay, has recently been discussed by Gade (1976).

References

Mercadal, J.G. 1959. *Lo que Espana llevo a America.* Madrid. Taurus Press.

Navarette, M.F. de. 1825-9. *Colleccion de los viages y descrubimientos que hicieron por mar los Espanoles.* 3 vols. Madrid.

Ratekin, M. 1954. The early sugar industry in Espanola. *Hispanic American Historical Review,* 34: 1-19

Deerr, N. 1949, 1950. *The history of sugar.* 2 vols. London. Chapman & Hall.

Crosby, A.W. Jr. 1972. *The Columbian Exchange: biographical and cultural consequences of 1492.* Westport, Connecticut, Greenwood Press.

Mendez-Natal, D. and Albert, H.W. 1947. "The early history of livestock & Pastures in Puerto Rico. *Agricultural History,* 21: 61-4

Newson, L.A. 1976. *Aboriginal and Spanish colonial Trinidad.* London. Academic Press.

Floyd, T.S. 1973. *The Columbus dynasty in the Caribbean, 1492 to 1526.* Albuquerque, University of New Mexico Press.

Simpson, L.B. 1966. *The encomienda in New Spain.* Berkeley and Los Angeles, University of California Press.

Las Casas, B. de 1542. *Brevissima relacion de la destruccion de las Indias.* Madrid. 1875-6 (reprint). Historia de las Indias, 1520-1561. Madrid.

Sauer, C.O. 1966. *The early Spanish Main.* Berkeley and Los Angeles, University of California Press.

Oviedo y Valdes, G.F. de. 1851-5 (reprint). *Historia general y natural de las Indias.* Madrid.

Martyr, P. 1493-1525. *De orbe nove, the eight decades of Peter Martyr d'Anghira.* (trans. P. MacNutt). Madrid.

Davis, D.D. 1974. The strategy of early Spanish ecosystem management in Cuba. *Journal of Anthropological Research,* 30: 204-314.

Goslinga, C. Ch. 1979. *A short history of the Netherlands Antilles and Surinam.* The Hague, Boston and London, Martinus Nijhoff.

Wood, C.S. 1975. New evidence for a late introduction of malaria into the New World. *Current Anthropology,* 16: 93-104.

Lockhart, J. and Otte, E. 1976. *Letters and people of the Spanish Indies: sixteenth century.* Cambridge, Cambridge University Press.

Bowman-Boyd, P. 1956. Regional origins of the earliest Spanish colonists of America. *Publications of the Modern Language Association,* 71: 1157-72.

Rodgers, J.E.T. 1866-1902. *A history of agriculture and prices in England.* 4 vols. Oxford, Clarendon Press.

Morrisey, R.J. 1957. Colonial agriculture in New Spain. *Agricultural History,* 31: 24-9

Puente y Olea, M. de. 1900. *Los Trabajos geograficos de la Casa de Contracion.* Sevilla.

Purchas, S. 1906, (reprint). *Hakluytus posthumus,* or, *Purchas his pilgrimes.* Glasgow and New York, Hakluyt Society.

Las Casas, B. de. 1875-6 (reprint). *Historia de las Indias, 1520-1561.* Madrid.

Thatcher, J.B. 1904. *Christopher Columbus.* New York.

Parry, J.H. and Sherlock, P.M. 1971. 3 edn. *A Short history of the West Indies.* London, Macmillan Publishing Co.

Wright, I.A. 1916. *The early history of Cuba.* New York.

Velasco, J. Lopez de. 1984. *Geografia descripcion universal de las Indias, recopilada...desde el ano de 1571 al de 1574.* Madrid, Sociedad Geografica de Madrid.

Andrews, K.R. 1978. *The Spanish Caribbean: trade & plunder, 1530-1630.* New Haven and London, Yale University Press.

Kirkpatrick, F.A. 1939. Repartimiento-encomienda. *Hispanic American Historical Review,* 19: 372-9

12

Imperialism and Slavery

FRANKLIN KNIGHT

*It were somewhat difficult, to give you an exact
account, of the number of persons upon the Island;
there being such store of shipping that brings passengers daily to the place, but it has been conjec-
tur'd, by those that are long acquainted, and best
seen in the knowledge of the Island, that there are
not less than 50 thousand souls, besides Negroes;
and some of them who began upon small fortunes,
are now risen to very great and vast estates.*

*The island is divided into three sorts of men, viz:
Masters, Servants and Slaves. The slaves and their
posterity, being subject to their masters for ever,
are kept and preserv'd with greater care than the
servants, who are theirs but for five years, according to the law of the Island. So that for the time, the
servants have the worser lives, for they are put to
very hard labour, ill lodging, and their dyet very
sleight.*

Richard Ligon,
True and Exact History . . . of Barbadoes, 1657

The seventeenth century witnessed some fundamental changes in the political, economic, and
social structure of the Caribbean. This was the
century that marked the transition from settler
communities to exploitation colonies within the
non-Hispanic sphere. The most startling political
change was the balkanization of the imperial
divisions as the Dutch, the French, and the English successfully defied the might of Spain and
established permanent strongholds along the
strategic outer periphery of what had for more
than a century been reluctantly conceded as the
private domain of the monarchs of Castille. After
1700 Caribbean possessions changed hands

among European powers, but the region remained cosmopolitan. Economically those early
outposts of empire began to assume increasing
international importance owing to their conversion into major producers of tropical staples – a
conversion in which the older Spanish colonies
on Cuba, Hispaniola, and Puerto Rico lagged
perceptibly. Socially the Caribbean acquired a
racial-class delineation far more complex than
the simple divisions of Richard Ligon's "three
sorts of men." And the connection between society, economy, and politics was related to the
development and inexorable expansion of the
Caribbean sugar industry.

As late as 1700 – and much later on the larger
islands and mainland possessions – the European
colonies in the Caribbean constituted growing
enclaves with moving frontiers. Until the Peace
of Utrecht in 1713 there were two general types
of society existing in alternating harmony and
discord. The first type comprised the boisterous,
violent society of struggling settlers, prospering
planters, exasperated officials, machinating merchants, suffering slaves, and ambivalent free persons of colour. These were the true colonists who
accepted, albeit under duress, the rules, regulations, and interventions of the metropolis, and
subscribed in varying degrees to the political
integrity of the different imperial systems. The
second social type generated by the considerable
socio-political flux of the times was a variegated
group of individuals, commonly considered
transfrontiersmen. Such transfrontier groups
ranged from the organized communities of Ma-

roons, or escaped slaves, to the defiant, stateless collectivity of buccaneers. These groups – Maroons and buccaneers – were not primarily a threat to settled, organized society, but represented a temporary alternative to the colonial social structure.

The Maroons formed the most successful alternative to organized European colonial society. Born of the resistance to slavery, they were essentially communities of Africans who escaped individually and collectively from the plantations and households of their masters to seek their freedom, thereby continuing a tradition begun by the indigenous indians. The word "maroon" was first used to describe the range cattle that had gone wild after the first attempts at Spanish colonization on the island of Hispaniola. Then the Spanish transferred the term to the escaped indian slaves, and finally to their African successors. In any case, *marronage* – the flight from servitude – became an intrinsic dimension of American slavery, enduring as long as the institution of slavery itself.

American plantation society spawned two forms of resistance to enslavement. The first was the temporary desertion of individual slaves. This form of escape, called frequently *petit marronage*, reflected a strong personal inclination on the part of the slave to resist labour, to procrastinate, to defy a master or a rule, or to visit friends, family, or acquaintances in the neighbourhood without the requisite permission. *Petit marronage* was eventually accepted with due reluctance as one of the inescapable concomitants of the system, and was punished with less severity than other infringements of local regulations, or other patterns of behaviour that jeopardized the social order. At its most serious, *petit marronage* remained a personal conflict between master and slave.

This was not equally true of the second form of resistance, which constituted a fully organized attempt to establish autonomous communities, socially and politically independent of the European colonial enclave. This pattern of conduct was potentially subversive to the entire socioeconomic complex of colonial life. Such communities – variously called *palenques* in the Spanish colonies, *quilombos* or *mocambos* in the Portuguese, and Maroon towns in the English colonies – encompassed varying numbers of individuals. They not only survived for considerable periods of time but also represented the eloquent negative expressions of the Africans and Afro-Americans about the situation in which they found themselves. Organized bands of Maroons prevailed for centuries in Jamaica, outlasting the determined communities of Bahia and Palmares in Brazil, Esmeraldas in Ecuador, and le Maniel in French Saint-Domingue.

Detested and vehemently opposed by the European slave-owning colonists, these misnamed towns taxed the ingenuity and resourcefulness of all the participants both for their sustenance and for their survival. Considering the extreme disadvantages under which the Maroons laboured, it is most surprising that so many communities survived for such long periods of time, often in close proximity to operating plantations. The principal ingredients for success seemed to be the nature of their social organization and the physical location of the communities.

Maroon villages were composed predominantly of able-bodied adults. Bryan Edwards, the Jamaican planter, historian, and later member of parliament in Great Britain, wrote a curiously admiring description of the Maroons, which reveals as much about the writer and his society as his subject:

Savage as they were in manners and disposition, their mode of living and daily pursuits undoubtedly strengthened their frame, and served to exalt them to great bodily perfection. Such fine persons as are seldom beheld among any other class of African or native blacks. Their demeanour is lofty, their walk firm, and their persons erect. Every motion displays a combination of strength and agility. The muscles (neither hidden nor depressed by clothing) are very prominent, and strongly marked. Their sight withal is wonderfully acute, and their hearing remarkably quick. These characteristics, however, are common, I believe, to all savage nations, in warm and temperate climates; and like other savages, the Maroons have only those senses perfect which are kept in constant exercise. Their smell is obtuse, and their taste so depraved, that I have seen them drink new rum fresh from the still, in preference to wine which I offered them; and I remember, at a great festival in one of their towns, which I attended, that their highest luxury, in point of food, was some rotten beef, which had been originally salted in Ireland, and which was probably presented to them, by some person who knew their taste, *because it was putrid.*

Leadership seemed to have been determined by military and political ability, and one of the most successful of the Jamaican Maroon leaders was a formidable lady called Nanny. Like the mature slave society, early Maroon communities revealed a strong masculine sex-dominance. The scarcity of women and the observed polygamy of some leaders forced some unusual practices during the formative years of the community. One such practice was raiding for the express purpose of capturing women. Another was the enforced sharing of females. As the community endured and stabilized, however, the sexual imbalance adjusted itself, especially after the Maroons were able to produce and nurture to adulthood their own offspring. The most successful leaders, such as Cudjoe and Nanny in Jamaica, Macandal or Santiago in Saint-Domingue, combined religious roles with their political positions, thereby reinforcing their authority over their followers. They also showed an unusual understanding of settled colonial society, which facilitated their ability to deal with the white political leaders. Prior to the eighteenth century most leaders tended to be rigidly authoritarian and often needlessly cruel. New recruits to Maroon communities were scrupulously tested, and deserters, wanderers, and suspected spies were brutally killed. Nevertheless, many Maroon villages fell victim to internal feuds or disenchanted defections from the ranks.

Security was the constant preoccupation of the Maroon villages. The physical setting of the village became a prime ingredient in its survival and eventual evolution. All successful villages in the Caribbean depended, at least initially, on their relative inaccessibility. They were strategically located in the densely forested interior of the Sierra Maestra in eastern Cuba, the conical limestone ridges of the Cockpit Country in western Jamaica, the precipitous slopes of the Blue Mountains in eastern Jamaica, the formidable *massifs* of Haiti, the rugged *cordilleras* of Santo Domingo, and the isolated interior of the smaller islands. Where geography was not conducive to hiding, such as in cities, or on very small islands, or less rugged terrain as found in Barbados, Antigua, Martinique, or Guadeloupe, *petit marronage* rather than *gran marronage* seemed to be the order of the day.

Given the inhospitable environment, only the most fit Maroon communities survived. Starvation, malnutrition, dysentery, smallpox, and accidental poisoning from unfamiliar leaves and herbs took a high toll of the original Maroons. Moreover the threat of discovery and attack by the organized colonial society remained constant. Cuban and Jamaican colonists employed specially trained dogs to hunt and recapture Maroons, and throughout the Caribbean the activities of large-scale military search-and-destroy missions were sporadic but important. Notwithstanding the hazards, Maroon communities recruited and trained enough manpower to defy local authorities, wage successful wars, and secure their own peace treaties, as did the Jamaican Maroons in 1739 and 1795. Or they secured a modus vivendi with the local communities and recognition from the political authorities as did the Maroons in le Maniel in southern Saint-Domingue.

Successful *marronage* required the concealed cooperation of slaves and other benefactors within settled society. In this way firearms, tools, utensils, and in some cases food, could be secured to help establish the community and subdue the forest. Not only urban Maroons, but also a large number of rural Maroons, gradually developed a semi-symbiotic relationship with the society from which they had withdrawn their support, and revoked their own servile status.

Unfortunately it was this very semi-symbiosis that proved most lethal to the integrity, cultural distinctiveness, and vitality of Maroon existence. Once the Maroons succeeded in gaining legal or quasi-legal recognition, their structure, internal organization, methods of recruitment, and political attitudes underwent significant changes. In the treaties they signed they accepted severely limited territorial concessions. They also got a legal status. But the price they paid was the surrender of some internal power and control. Runaway slaves could no longer be ascripted to the group, but were handed over to the planter societies – often for a fee. This practice not only restricted the physical size of the community but insidiously undermined the political appeal of the Maroons as a viable alternative to organized slavery. "Following the treaties [between the Jamaican government and the Maroons]," wrote Richard Price in his introduction to *Maroon Societies*, "these same Jamaican Maroons bought, sold, and owned substantial numbers of slaves, hunted new runaways for a price, managed to gain the hatred of much of the slave population, and in many respects may have deserved their common post-treaty nickname, 'The King's Negroes.' " If the Maroons viewed the treaty as a form of collective security, it nevertheless represented a strengthening of the very socio-political structure they formerly had despised. Moreover it strengthened the system of slave control by removing, reducing, or otherwise restricting one option of personal escape from slavery to freedom. Maroon communities, by agreeing to the external legal controls on basic aspects of their life, even regarding the succession of leaders may have done themselves more harm than good. In common with all groups crossing a common frontier, the Maroon societies gradually became virtually indistinct from their neighbouring slave communities. Moreover they lacked adequate facilities for long-term economic and social success. Like other transfrontier groups, the Maroons were like the French Huguenots, ultimately unable to overcome the limitations and internal contradictions of a state within a state.

Like Maroons, the buccaneers were the products of a stage of social evolution in the Caribbean. But buccaneers represented a shorter historical phase, whose period of glory lasted from about the middle of the seventeenth century to the beginning of the eighteenth. This was the period of greatest political and social transition in the Caribbean, of the decline of Spanish influence from the great days of the early sixteenth century and "no peace beyond the line." The boundaries of empires as well as the notions of international law were extremely vague, facilitating fluctuating alliances or associations of European communities within the region. These essentially stateless persons lived comfortably by commerce with the settled communities of European colonists, just as did the Maroons, and with the help of the large numbers of cattle, horses, hogs, and dogs that proliferated on the tropical savannas in the wake of the early Spanish settlement.

It was in this very idyllic existence that legends place the origins of the buccaneers. The word itself derives from the aboriginal Indian custom of slowly drying and curing strips of meat (boucan) over an open fire. This delicious product found a ready market with the increasing number of ships trafficking in Caribbean waters. Small colonies of these hunters and smokers flourished during the middle decades of the sixteenth century on the western parts of Puerto Rico and Hispaniola, vending hides and boucan to the ships passing through the Mona Passage and Windward Passage. Over a period of time the hunters gradually diversified their economic base by adding piracy to their occupation, and extending their operations to the rugged, but easily defensible island of Tortuga – relatively safe from the periodic Spanish search-and-destroy missions, but still very close to the wild herds of northwestern Hispaniola. Eventually the buccaneers forged a community, in which the urge for adventure and plunder overrode the need to settle down. In the Anglophone Caribbean, the term buccaneers adhered to the amorphous group long after they had forsaken the art of hunting and boucaning. The French preferred the term corsairs or "flibustiers," while the Dutch called the group "zee roovers." The more successful buccaneers such as Henry Morgan considered themselves to be "Brethren of the Coasts," with allegiance to no state, and obligation to no laws but their own.

By the middle of the seventeenth century, the buccaneers had achieved international fame and had attracted a motley band throughout the Caribbean probably numbering a few thousand. Their recruits came from shipwrecks, deserters from the regular crews of vessels sailing in the region, fortune seekers, and men and women repelled by the regimentation and coercion of the sugar plantation society then rapidly spreading from island to island. But the international importance of the buccaneers undoubtedly increased because they had the capacity to perform the free-lance attacks on the Spanish possessions in the Caribbean which neither the English nor French, then riddled with civil conflicts or domestic political weakness, could achieve. The buccaneers, by keeping Spain off-balance in the Caribbean, contributed to the permanent success of the non-Spanish attempts at colonization in the tropical Americas. On the other hand Spain, by trying to destroy the communities of buccaneers – especially by hitting at their subsidiary economic activity, boucaning – justified their raison d'être. The myth of Spanish wealth and the reality of Spanish treasure fleets assembling off Havana and sailing to Europe each spring merely sharpened the cupidity of an already rapacious group.

Père Labat, the indefatigable Dominican or Jacobin priest who served in the French West Indies from 1694 to 1705 and whose memories were published posthumously in 1743, left a rare first-hand account of the organization and political importance of the buccaneers, albeit in their waning days. Labat's account compares favourably with that of Exquemelin, and appears to have captured the attitudes and actions of the buccaneers during their predominantly sea-roving phase:

St. Pierre [Martinique], 6th March, 1694. We were busy all this morning confessing a crew of *flibustiers* who had arrived at Les Mouillages with two prizes that they had captured from the English. The Mass of the Virgin was celebrated with all solemnity, and I blessed three large loaves which were presented by the captain and his officers, who arrived at the church accompanied by the drums and trumpets of their corvette. At the beginning of Mass the corvette fired a salute with all her cannons. At the Elevation of the Holy Sacrament, she fired another salvo, at the Benediction a third, and finally a fourth, when we sang the Te Deum after Mass. All the *flibustiers* contributed 30 sols to the sacristy, and did so with much piety and modesty. This may surprise people in Europe where *flibustiers* are not credited with possessing much piety, but as a matter of fact they generally give a portion of their good fortunes to the churches. If church ornament or church linen happen to be in the prizes they capture, the *flibustiers* always present them to their parish church.

The conditions of Roving are set forth in what is called *Chasse Partie*. If the vessel belongs to the *flibustiers* themselves, their booty is shared equally. The captain and the quartermaster (who is always second in command on these ships), the surgeon and the pilot receive no more than anyone else except a gift which is given to them by the rest of the crew. As a rule the captain is given a present which is equivalent to three and sometimes four extra shares. The quartermaster is presented with an additional two shares. The pilot and surgeon each receive an extra share and a half: Boys are given a half-share, and the man who first sights the prize wins an extra share.

Other items in the agreement are: That if a man be wounded he has to receive one *écu* a day as long as he remains in the surgeon's hands up to sixty days, and this has to be paid or allowed for before any man receives his share. A man receives 600 *écus* for the loss of each limb, 300 *écus* for the loss of a thumb or the first finger of the right hand, or an eye, and 100 *écus* for each of the other fingers. If a man has a wooden leg or a hook for his arm and these happen to be destroyed, he receives the same amount as if they were his original limbs.

In the case the ship is chartered by *flibustiers*, the owners have to provision and arm the ship, and receive one-third of the prizes.

In war-time the *flibustiers* are given commissions by the governor of the different islands, who receive a tenth share in the prizes. In peace-time they were given permits to fish. But either with or without commissions, the *flibustiers* pillaged the Spaniards, who hanged them as pirates whenever they caught them.

The description of Labat underlined the principal characteristics of the buccaneers that set them apart from the Maroons as transfrontiersmen. In terms of cultural distinction, the Maroons were patently further removed from settler society than the buccaneers. For the buccaneers won the admiration of their metropolitan public, even though an account such as Exquemelin's history emphasized the savagery, selfishness, excessive avarice, and utter lawlessness of that infamous international horde.

The buccaneers were essentially stateless individuals, but they retained strong links with the general culture and society with which they were familiar. They did not try, as did the American Maroons, to create a culture and a society. They had their culture, and they knew their social origins quite well. What they sought – at least for a time – was freedom from the restraints and obligations of that culture and society. The leaders of the buccaneers had some "national" identity: Alexandre Exquemelin was Dutch; Bartholomé Portuguez – the most famous non-swimmer in the history of the buccaneers – was Portuguese; Rock, the Dutchman, had lived in Brazil; Francis L'Olonnois, the Cruel, was a Frenchman; Henry Morgan of Barbados – later Sir Henry Morgan, lieutenant-governor of Jamaica – was born in Wales; Raveneau de Lassan – in all probability a fictitious character – claimed to be a French buccaneer. To be sure most buccaneers were not from what was then commonly called the "cultivated classes" of Europe. A large number, among them Morgan, Exquemelin, and L'Olonnois, had served as indentured servants or *engagés* in the emergent sugar plantations of the Caribbean. With the demand for labour outstripping the supply, the later accusation that some of these unfortunate indentureds might have been aggressively kidnapped could be true. Moreover the conditions of servitude engendered an enormous antipathy towards the state not unlike that of the African slaves.

The harsh conditions of indenture produced a physically tough and spiritually callous individual, capable of surviving the exacting and hazardous conditions of international piracy. But this occupation did not dissolve their links with settled society, which often found the buccaneers as convenient a bulwark of defence as the Jamaican planters of the eighteenth century found Cudjoe's Maroons. Moreover the ill-gotten plunder of the buccaneers, lavishly dispensed in the local towns, compensated adequately for their otherwise detestable social manners.

The economic importance of the buccaneers contributed in no small way to their general acceptance among the non-Spanish Caribbean authorities. Clarence Haring in his history of the buccaneers describes the English capture of Jamaica and the entire Cromwellian "Grand Design" of 1655 as "a reversion to the Elizabethan gold-hunt . . . the first of the great buccaneering expeditions." John Milton, Oliver Cromwell's Latin secretary, gave the official justification as a response to the cruelties of the Spanish towards the English-American colonists; their cruelty toward the Indians; and the Spanish refusal to sanction English trade with their empire. Sir Charles Lyttleton, the lieutenant-governor of Jamaica in the early 1660's, proposed six practical reasons for official support of the buccaneers, and these seemed to have impressed the English metropolitan government. Privateering, he argued, provided a number of able-bodied men and available ships that served to protect the island in the absence of a navy. Privateers had extremely valuable information on local navigation, and their practical experience would be invaluable in wartime. The international connections of the buccaneers supplied uniquely rich intelligence on the size, preparation, and potential wealth of Spanish towns and Spanish naval activities. The prizes and currency brought to Port Royal attracted merchants, contributed to the economy, and helped to reduce prices. English colonial authorities lacked the requisite naval force to destroy the bands of buccaneers, and English seamen had such great admiration for the brotherhood that it was doubtful they would zealously support such activities. Finally Lyttleton argued that any attempt to destroy the buccaneers might simply serve to attract their aggressive retaliation on English plantations and English commerce.

Lyttleton knew his buccaneers well, and had perhaps personally profited from his short association with them. In any case he was familiar with their modus operandi. For buccaneers did not usually attack the colony from which the leader of the band originated, nor citizens related in nationality or culture to the majority of the members. In practice, therefore, French privateers, led by a Dutchman, would normally attack only Spanish or English towns and ships; and

English buccaneers preferred the spoils of their rivals. Everyone saw the Spanish, however, as fair game. By the beginning of the second half of the seventeenth century, although the lingua franca of the buccaneers remained French, the leadership became English, and, after 1655, the main base of operation shifted from Tortuga to Port Royal. Buccaneer wealth provided a healthy stimulus to the early local economy of the islands. Captain Henry Morgan, admiral-in-chief of the confederacy of Jamaican buccaneers, used his returns from privateering to build a splendid city home in Port Royal, purchase a sugar plantation in the interior, and become the lieutenant-governor of the second most important English Caribbean possession at that time. Apart from the inordinate amounts of bullion and currency which the buccaneers brought and distributed, they dealt in cane, slaves, jewels, silks, spices, wine, and cattle. Buccaneering during the seventeenth century was not only a political weapon; it was also a crude form of imperial revenue-sharing.

Persistent war and conflicts over trade in the Caribbean increased the strategic importance of the buccaneers. Until the late 1670's buccaneers sought formal commissions to engage in privateering raids throughout the region. Ostensibly such commissions made them the legal representatives of the English or French Crown, and their conquests a part of the expansion of empire. But the complicated international situation after the Restoration in England – with Charles II moving toward friendship with Spain, and enmity with France – forced the award of aggressive commissions away from the centre of empire to the local governors, whose authority could then be superseded should diplomatic relations so warrant. The legitimate cover of a commission enabled the buccaneers to equip their ships with powder, shot, cannons, and supplies, as well as recruit men. But from the buccaneer point of view, political support was merely a cover – the interests of empire being of minor importance. In this way, Jérémie Deschamps, Seigneur du Rausset, obtained by duplicity simultaneous commissions from the French and the English and successfully played one power against the other for a short period of time, while the status of his "colony" of Tortuga remained ambiguous. Deschamps finally ended up in the Bastille in Paris, where he was persuaded to cede his interest in Tortuga to Jean-Baptiste Colbert's French West India Company for 15,000 livres and his freedom. On the other hand, Henry Morgan was apparently quite upset by the suggestion of Alexandre Exquemelin that he had sailed without a commission, and sought to have the English edition of Exquemelin's history of the buccaneers suppressed. In 1684, Morgan also brought a charge of libel against the publishers, for the lack of a royal commission erased the legal distinction between piracy, which was illegal, and buccaneering, which was not. At stake also was Morgan's new status as a gentleman, knight, influential planter, and respectable lieutenant-governor of Jamaica. By 1684 the golden age of buccaneering was fading fast.

The conditions that had proved most propitious to buccaneering activity ceased after 1770 – although it was some time before the signals reached the Caribbean. The political significance of a semi-legal, uncontrolled band to further the cause of colonization yielded to the diplomatic adroitness, increased military strength, and self-consciousness of Louis XIV in France and Charles II in England. Moreover Spain was no longer the power it used to be. The possessions of the French West India Company became true colonies after 1674; and Charles II moved to exercise greater control over the English West Indian islands. Greater supervision of the colonies severely undermined the previous reciprocal relationship between settler society and the transfrontier communities. Lyttleton's analysis was no longer valid. The withdrawal of formal commissions during the 1680's and 1690's meant that the same activities formerly hailed in England and France were condemned as piracy, subject to punishment by hanging. The legal end came with the Treaty of Ryswyck in 1697, when France joined the Dutch (the Treaty of The Hague in 1673) and the English (the Treaty of Windsor in 1680) in agreeing to withdraw official support for the buccaneers. These treaties with Spain, signed outside Iberia, underlined her military decline. Individual, uncontrolled marauding became politically counterproductive to the genesis of exploitation societies based on slave-operated plantations and international commerce. Even nature seemed to support the change. In 1692 Port Royal, the most notorious stronghold of bucca-

neers, slipped ominously into the sea after a severe earthquake, taking along the house and tomb of Henry Morgan. The activity which had elevated Morgan and Jean-Baptiste du Casse from transfrontier sea rovers to imperial governors no longer prevailed.

The existence of communities of buccaneers represented a stage in the transition from pioneering colonialism to organized imperialism. And the changes in the Caribbean reflected changes in Europe. England, France, and Holland had become strong enough to dictate aspects of their relations with Spain. But the Spanish had not yet become so weak that her empire could be wrested from her. Trade, not the export of people founding microcosmic European societies, became the major preoccupation; and the exigencies of trade demanded not only a new relationship between metropolis and colony but a new climate of international order. This new climate required the control, coordination, and responsibility that was the anathema of buccaneering. Thus while the buccaneering bands displayed their skills, a series of events and circumstances ushered in a new order. Non-Hispanic European states began to expand their political influence by conquest rather than settlement, exemplified by the capture of Jamaica in 1655 and the French advance on western Hispaniola, conceded at Ryswyck in 1697. The French reorganized their empire under Colbert, and finally brought it under the direct control of the Crown in 1774. Spanish-American mainland silver production declined significantly; domestic Spanish industries virtually disappeared; and Spanish merchant shipping drastically diminished in Caribbean ports. By 1686 more than 90 per cent of the capital and goods handled on the legal Seville-to-the-Indies trade was controlled by French, Genoese, Dutch, English, and German businessmen (often working through Spanish intermediaries), while an estimated two-thirds of the Spanish-American trade was contraband. At this time, too, the Caribbean region had already been experiencing the revolutionary reorganization of its society, its agriculture, and its commerce. With an understandable delay in the Spanish possessions, the exploiters dominated or expelled the subsistence settlers. The age of sugar and slavery had arrived.

The massive introduction of African slaves and the employment of slavery as the main form of labour organization reflected a major socio-political change in the status and role of the Caribbean colonies. The resort to plantation agriculture indicated the failure to re-create viable colonies of Europeans in the tropical islands and lowlands. From about the 1640's, the semi-feudal European settler frontier slowly gave way to the rigidly organized, commercially integrated exploitation society of masters and slaves. The slave society transmitted from east to west across the Caribbean brought greater and quicker profits to the private and public proponents of empire than did the former struggling enclaves of predominantly European farming communities.

The eventual adoption of slavery arose from the severe economic crisis of the seventeenth-century Caribbean, and especially from the overwhelming need to establish a more competitively marketable commodity than tobacco as the basis of a colonial economy. After a short period of trial and error, sugar cane emerged as the most valuable potential agricultural crop. Sugar had become increasingly popular on the European market, and the technique of its production had been known in Mediterranean Europe since the time of the crusades. Moreover sugar provided a balance between bulk and value so crucially important in the days of small sailing ships and distant sea voyages. Sugar production and export, however, demanded a considerable capital outlay and a larger, more reliable, and more consistent supply of labour than was available through contracted servants or irregularly supplied African slaves.

The relationship between a colonial export economy and its metropolis demanded a more structured political organization in the interest of trade. The English circumscribed the political independence of the Barbados Assembly in the late seventeenth century, and the French Crown took over direct control of its overseas colonies. A long series of mercantilist trade and navigation laws were passed during the succeeding century regulating the commerce between the European metropolises and their Caribbean colonies. Metropolitan merchants advancing capital and goods largely on credit desired a stable relationship conducive to long-term planning as well as to the security of their investment. Each European state saw enormous potential gain in the employment of its citizens, the development of its industry, and the expansion of its merchant marine through the twin pursuits of trade within the empire and trade with other Europeans and Africans.

From the colonial perspective, however, the priorities were different. As in the metropolis, colonists viewed the relationship between commerce and wealth as direct. Unlike the metropolitan group, they felt the fewer the restrictions on trade, the more lucrative would be the relationship. Colonial planters enjoyed the partial guarantee of the home market for their tropical commodities, but they wanted a steady supply of slaves from Africa and provisions as well as planting equipment from Europe and America. As they became more successful at their pursuits, they realized that mercantilism did not provide the greatest quantity at the lowest prices. On the other hand, free trade implied a state of commercial insecurity (especially with regard to the unsettled competitive politics of Europe) and the removal of the protection and support derived from being part of an empire. These divergent views, ideals, and practices could never be fully reconciled within the context of empire, and they precipitated within the managerial strata of Caribbean plantation society a resentment that grew more bitter with age. Perhaps no aspect of the commercial relationship bred more mutual irritation than the supply and price of African slaves, the most important single ingredient in the economic success of the plantation society.

As early as the 1630's, the bases of a sugar system were introduced to the Caribbean in an attempt to duplicate the Portuguese and Dutch success along the northeastern coast of Brazil. In 1639 the French *Compagnie des Isles d'Amérique*, acting in response to a number of individual entrepreneurs at home and overseas, signed a contract with a Dutch immigrant from Brazil to build a pioneer sugar estate of approximately 3000 acres on the island of Martinique. It was an ambitious undertaking, but, like other such early experiments, it failed from a combination of uncertain finances and an immature infrastructure unable to coordinate the many features of labour supply, agricultural management, and product marketing. Success necessitated at that period international, especially Dutch, support. The Dutch therefore acted as the organizational middlemen of the Caribbean sugar industry, deploying their capital, expertise, transportation, marketing facilities, and slaves throughout the

English and French Caribbean. In 1647 the first successful cargoes of sugar left Barbados and Guadeloupe in Dutch ships for Europe. By 1650 the Dutch, confident of available supplies, established a number of refineries on their small eastern islands, a development that pleased the sugar planters as much as it irked the metropolises. For the succeeding thirty years the English and French fought a series of anti-Dutch naval wars in an effort to destroy Dutch influence and improve the efficacy of their own mercantile system.

If the English and French sugar industry depended on the benevolence of the Dutch, the same was not true of the early Spanish sugar industry. On his second voyage Christopher Columbus introduced the sugar cane to Hispaniola, and by the middle of the sixteenth century a number of relatively large estates had begun a lucrative export of sugar to Spain. Sugar production from water-powered mills became an attractive economic alternative to the *encomienda*, since both the supply of indians and the quantities of gold had diminished greatly. Many partnerships involving the highest officials of the fledging colony, such as the treasurer Esteban Passamonte, the *fiscal* Pedro Vásquez de Mella, the *contador* Alonso de Avila, and the *oidores* Lebron and Zuazo, imported Africans and participated in the early sugar industry. Diego Columbus had a large estate on the outskirts of the city of Santo Domingo with about forty African slaves producing sugar as early as 1522. Meanwhile Hernando Gorjón of Azua made enough money from the early sugar trade to Spain to endow the *colegio* in Santo Domingo which eventually became the first American university.

Like its Caribbean successors, the early Spanish sugar industry spread throughout the region, island-hopping according to the expansion of settlements and the availability of African slaves. By 1526 Hispaniola had nineteen sugar mills and was importing about four hundred Africans per year. Sugar mills were also established around San German in Puerto Rico and Santiago de la Vega in Jamaica. The gross production of these mills remains uncertain, but their exports totalling several thousand tons went to Spain, Mexico, and Cuba. Most probably as the result of the shortage of available capital, the Cuban sugar industry did not begin until the last decade of the sixteenth century. The first hydrau-

lic mills established in the city of Havana had an export capacity of about three thousand *arrobas* (37.5 short tons) in 1600, sending their product to Spain, Campeche, and Cartagena. Spaniards had produced sugar on estates in southern Iberia, especially around Málaga and Huelva, and transferred the technique to the Americas. But most colonists utilized the sugar cane as a means of making syrup, expressing the juice by a simple manual wooden press or an equally simple, inefficient, rotary animal-powered press called a *trapiche,* and boiling it to the desired state of crystallization. An *ingenio* required both capital and a large quantity of sugar cane which were beyond the individual means of most early colonists. As the numerous petitions to the Spanish Crown frequently repeated, a sugar industry needed African slave labour.

Although the Spanish Crown supported the new industry, even to the extent of lending the early Cuban sugar producers 40,000 ducats in 1595, production faltered. The high volume of Brazilian sugar exports to the European market served to depress further the Spanish-American export trade. But Spanish sugar production for domestic consumption remained high and economically attractive in Peru, Mexico, and the islands. Unfortunately, the technology of Spanish sugar production remained stagnant, and not until the late eighteenth century did the Spanish return to large-scale sugar production for export.

The supply of slaves, on which any large-scale sugar industry depended, did not develop rapidly. African coastal stations had to be found, trade relations with the Africans established, and the exchange of European merchandise for Africans coordinated. So competitive was the international slave trade that, like the earlier experience of colonization, the private entrepreneurs sought and obtained the full support and military resources of their state to assist them in carving and defending their niche in the system. Thus the English and Dutch fought over access rights to the African ports until the Dutch formally recognized the trading rights of the Company of Royal Adventurers of England at the Treaty of Breda in 1667.

The company, succeeded in 1672 by the Royal Africa Company, was the typical private front for a state enterprise. Chartered by Charles II in 1663 and having members of the royal family among its subscribers, it replaced the commerce in dyewoods, gold, and ivory with the slave trade. Enthusiastically promising to deliver 3000 Africans to the English sugar colonies annually at a cost of £17 per head, the company failed miserably in its goal. By March 1664 the company had landed 33 cargoes of 2364 slaves at Barbados, at an average selling price exceeding £20. Despite a cost price of £3 per African, the company proved neither competitive nor profitable and went bankrupt in 1671.

The Royal Africa Company was only marginally more successful. The trans-Atlantic slave trade stubbornly refused to be monopolized by either a chartered company or a trading nation. The records of the Royal Africa Company between 1673 and 1684 illustrate the problems inherent in the slave-delivering component of the south Atlantic system. The average selling price of slaves at Barbados, payable mainly with muscovado sugar, varied between £12 and £20 per slave per cargo, with the highest prices being 29 slaves sold "to a Spaniard at £25 per head" in 1681. This was a profitable price to attract private, non-company traders who did not have the enormous overhead expenses of the company. Given the annual demand in Barbados based on the previous agreement of 1663 to deliver 3000 slaves per year, the performance of the Royal Africa Company fell far short of its promise. Based on the records for twelve years, the company managed to deliver an average yearly supply of only 1356 Africans, and only came close to the required minimum target in 1683 when it brought 2963. Eventually, with its carrying capacity depleted by war, the company resorted to subcontracting its slaves for a fee. Nothing, however, could save the company, and finally in 1698 it lost its legal monopoly of the English trans-Atlantic slave trade.

Despite the constant depredations of war, the importation of slaves expanded rapidly in the Caribbean. The arriving Africans not only completely offset the demographic eradication of the post-conquest and settlement period but also contributed to a greater social and demographic variation. Sugar and slavery provided the catalysts for these changes, and during the eighteenth century the Caribbean distinguished itself in the importation of African slaves and the production of sugar. Every colony sought to produce plantation staples, and every successful plantation maintained its own reservoir of enslaved labour-

ers. During the seventeenth century the Caribbean accepted more than 50 per cent of all arriving Africans in the New World. That figure increased to more than 60 per cent during the plantation heyday of the eighteenth century and declined to a little less than 40 per cent as the system began its rapid disintegration during the nineteenth century.

The Caribbean region received approximately one-half of all Africans brought to the Americas during the nearly 350-year span of the organized trans-Atlantic slave trade.

The islands and coastal perimeter of the Caribbean formed the host society for about 5 million Africans – if we accept the total African arrivals in the Americas to be 10 millions. Given the transportation facilities of the time, this constituted one of the greatest migrations of modern times, although the migrants went unwillingly and with no prospect of ever returning to their homelands. The arrival rate of Africans was more than 14,000 per year, with the concentration varying according to the agricultural development of the particular zone. Prosperity, defined, in terms of quantity of land under cultivation and volume of tropical staple export, was the most powerful magnet for the African slave trade. But a prosperity based on agriculture tended to be transient. As soil fertility and land availability diminished in each territory, so did the prospect of wealth and the number of slaves.

This correlation between new land under cultivation and high volume of slave imports demonstrated a sequential occurrence throughout the Caribbean involving inter-imperial as well as trans-imperial trends. Seen in the conventional terms of the sugar revolution, it is quite clear that the English Caribbean islands tended to experience the first wave of intensification, followed closely by the French, with the Spanish colonies belatedly participating. Barbados was the first English and Caribbean colony to experience the revolution. By 1680 Barbados was perhaps the most valuable tropical colony, and it received the largest supply of Africans. By 1750 Jamaica had superseded Barbados, only to lose its eminence to French Saint-Domingue by 1780. Cuba eclipsed all colonies to become the largest single producer of cane sugar and the "jewel in the Spanish Crown" after 1830. As predominantly monocultural plantation exporters, the Caribbean colonies assumed a commercial importance that transcended the mere buying of slaves and selling of sugar, tobacco, indigo, and cotton. The region demanded such a variety of imports, which not only undermined the structure of imperialist mercantilism but catapulted it into a key element of international trade during the period. The multi-faceted trading system, of which the Caribbean was a part, had connections with North America, Europe, Africa, and South America. From these distant regions came firearms, horses, flour, meat, fish, barrel staves, nails, lumber, tools, slaves, machinery, cloth, and luxury products to supply the economic, dietary, and production needs of the tropical plantation societies.

The so-called "sugar colonies" were never exclusively producers of sugar. But sugar was the mainstay of the export economy. As such the volume of sugar production increased directly proportional to the increase in the slave population. The gross totals tend to disguise the variations in sugar production as well as the fluctuations in the importation of slaves. They do indicate, however, the rapidity with which the colonies moved into high-scale sugar production. This transformation also produced social repercussions.

By the eighteenth century "sugar was king" throughout the Caribbean. Ralph Davis graphically noted this dominance in *The Rise of the Atlantic Economies:*

Sugar production, once it had been introduced, showed a tendency to engulf whole islands in single-crop cultivation, and it created its own form of society whose stamp still lies upon the Caribbean. There were exceptions: the small islands of Grenada and Dominica had single-crop coffee economies for some decades of the eighteenth century, and colonies with great land areas, St. Domingue and especially Brazil, could produce immense sugar crops while still retaining some variety in cultivation. But the value of the Caribbean colonies to Europe came to be in their sugar production. So overwhelming did it dominate island economy and society, so vital was it even to Brazil, that the main features of the life of Europe's tropical colonies are best set out in terms of the movement towards sugar, and the adaptation of society to the needs of its production. After 1660 England's sugar imports always exceeded its combined imports of all other colonial produce; in 1774 sugar made up just half of all French imports from her West Indian colonies; over the colonial period as a whole more than half Brazil's exports of goods were sugar. Sugar made up almost a fifth of the whole English import bill of 1774, far surpassing the share of any other commodity.

Sugar and its associated by-products, rum and molasses, accounted for 81 per cent of the exports from the British Caribbean in 1770. The second-place export commodity was coffee, accounting for 11 per cent. At the same time the French Antilles showed only a slightly higher variation with sugar-related exports amounting to 49 per cent of exports, coffee 24 per cent, indigo 14 per cent, and cotton 8 per cent. In 1855 Cuba had an overwhelming 84 per cent of its export trade in sugar, with second-place tobacco accounting for less than 8 per cent. The situation varied from island to island, but, except for the designedly free-port trading islands, such as St Martin, St Eustatia, and Curaçao, the situation remained the same. Sugar exports dominated the economy.

The export-import economy was only one aspect of the local economic structure, albeit a very important one. The mature plantation complex not only created two societies by the late eighteenth century – one Euro-American, the other Afro-American – it also created two economies. And like the social division, the two economies co-existed in symbiotic relationship. For if the export of plantation products and the import of consumer articles were major activities, they were integrally related to the system of distribution and merchandising done locally by a significant sector of the population.

The import-export trade was more complex than the selling and shipping abroad of the local harvest. Each colony traded not only with its metropolis but also with foreigners. J. Stewart aptly indicated the multilateral dimensions of colonial trade in Jamaica in the 1820s: "The commerce of Jamaica," he wrote, "may be classed under the following heads: The trade with the mother country – which is far more considerable than all the other branches together; the trade with British North America, and the trade with the island of Cuba and other Spanish islands, the Spanish Main or Tierra Firma, and other territories on the American continent formerly belonging to Spain." In the 1850's Cuba traded with Spain, the United States, England, Germany, France, Mexico, Venezuela, and Jamaica. Figures for Puerto Rico in 1843 amply demonstrate how complex external trading had become by that time. The island exported its products in British ships to the West Indian islands, England, and Canada; in Danish, American, Hanseatic, and Dutch ships to England; and in Spanish ships to Spain and Canada. The exported items included sugar, tobacco, dry and salted hides, horses, mules, cattle, coconuts, coffee, beans, tortoise shells, and timber. Imports included olive oil, brandy, beer, gin, wine, salted beef and pork, hams, figs, fish, raisins, rice, cocoa, flour, lard, butter, cheese, potatoes, garlic, onions, barrel staves, lumber, iron hoops, plates and bars, nails, glass, agricultural tools, soap, utensils, medicines, tobacco, candles, perfumes, and domestic supplies. The absence of a coordinated banking system and adequate common currencies restricted much of the trade to the form of a complicated system of barter, in which locally produced goods were accepted and then re-exported along with a variety of coins. This lack of any systematic banking system, plus the eternal shortage of coins for small-scale transactions, were perennial complaints of colonists in the tropics.

Strategically located free ports supplemented the direct importation and export of commodities. Janet Schaw, who visited St Eustatia on January 19, 1775, wrote a very graphic description of one of the most bustling Caribbean free ports:

We landed on St. Eustatia, a free port, which belongs to the Dutch; a place of vast traffic from every quarter of the globe. The ships of various nations which rode before it were very fine, but the Island itself the only ugly one I have seen. Nor do I think I would stay on it for any bribe ... The whole riches of the Island consist in its merchandize, and they are obliged to the neighbouring Islands for subsistence; while they in return furnish them with contraband commodities of all kinds. ... But never did I meet with such variety; here was a merchant vending his goods in Dutch, another in French, a third in Spanish, etc. etc. They all wear the habit of their country and the diversity is really amusing. ... From one end of the town of Eustatia to the other is a continued mart, where goods of the most different uses and qualities are displayed before the shop-doors. Here hang rich embroideries, painted silks, flowered Muslins, with all the Manufactures of the Indies. Just by hang Sailor's Jackets, Trousers, shoes, hats etc. Next stall contains most exquisite silver plate, the most beautiful indeed I ever saw, and close by these iron pots, kettles and shovels. Perhaps the next presents you with French and English Millinary wares. But it were endless to enumerate the variety of merchandize in such a place, for in every store you find everything, be their qualities ever so opposite. I bought a quantity of excellent French gloves for fourteen pence a pair, also English thread-stockings cheaper than I could buy them at home.

The other side of the economic coin was the internal marketing system. The internal economy had two dimensions. The first was the coastal and retail trade, which took the goods of the large-commission merchants in the principal ports and distributed them via small coastal vessels of less than seventy tons to smaller merchants who serviced the planting and free village communities. Again barter and credit were the major operating media, although all items bore a discounted cash price. "A wharfinger's receipt for a puncheon of rum, endorsed by the payer," wrote Stewart, "passes in payment as readily as a bill or draft would do; so that these articles become a sort of circulating medium, and it is not unusual for a puncheon of rum, or other commodity, to pass through twenty or more different hands, without ever being moved from the wharf-store where it was deposited by its original owner, into whose possession it may again ultimately return."

The other dimension of the internal marketing system consisted of the local markets with their higglers, who supplied the plantations and free citizens with ground provisions, livestock, smallstock, poultry, and eggs. Unlike the other facets of trade, however, this sector dealt mainly in cash, further accentuating the scarcity of specie in the colonies. This market was dominated by the free persons of colour. Slaves participated, too, but during the eighteenth century a series of laws gradually proscribed their economic activities. The Jamaica Assembly in 1711 prohibited slaves from owning livestock or from selling meat, fish, sugar, sugar cane, or any manufactured item without the written permission of their masters. St Lucia prevented slaves from dealing in coffee or cotton with laws passed in 1734 and 1735. The French Antilles also passed laws between 1744 and 1765 that removed the opportunities for slaves to trade in cattle or engage in the occupation of butcher, while higglering was prohibited on plantations or in the towns. In 1767 St Vincent forbade slaves to plant or sell any commodity exported from the island. In the 1840's the Cubans restricted the occupations and movements of the free, non-white members of the society.

The planter class which formulated the laws restricting the economic activities of the non-whites were motivated by self-interest. They disliked unnecessary local competition, and economic subordination facilitated the social control of the majority of the population. Nevertheless, the laws could not be enforced, and the gradual collapse of the economic and political worlds of the slaveholders opened more opportunities for the non-whites. By the middle of the nineteenth century non-whites were, individually and collectively, buying bankrupt and abandoned estates throughout the Caribbean and peasant economies were competing with the plantation economies for land and labour.

References

R. Ligon, *A True and Exact History of the Island of Barbadoes*.(London, 1657).

B. Edwards, *The History, Civil and Commercial of the British West Indies*. 5 vols.(Reprint. New York, 1966).

R. Price, (ed.). *Maroon Societies*. (New York, 1973).

J.B. Labat, *The Memoirs of Pere Labat, 1693-1705*, trans. and abridged by J. Eaden. (London, 1931).

A.O. Exquemelin, *The History of Bucaniers*.(London, 1678).

C.H. Haring, *The Bucaneers in the West Indies in the xvii Century*.(Reprint. Hamden, Conn., 1966).

R. Davis, *The Rise of the Atlantic Economies*. (Ithaca, 1973).

13

Ambivalent Allies: Anglo-Dutch Relations and the Struggle against the Spanish Empire in the Caribbean, 1621-1641

PAUL E. KOPPERMAN

In June 1621 the Dutch West India Company was chartered, and it soon began to function as the Netherlands' primary weapon against the New World empire of Spain. For more than a decade the company generally enjoyed success, capped by Piet Heyn's seizure, in 1628, of the entire Mexican silver fleet, and the conquest, beginning in 1624 and accelerating during the 1630s, of most of Brazil.[1]

To many Englishmen, it appeared that the West India Company was doing what their nation should be doing: attacking Spain at the core of its wealth and, hence, its power. They held to the belief that the Spanish empire in the New World was ripe for overthrow, and that a successful sea-war of conquest would more than pay for itself, for it would insure that the bullion that was then fuelling the Spanish war machine would thereafter serve the cause of England. For them, the feats of Drake pointed the way. And the successes of the company showed what boldness might still accomplish.

Those Englishmen who were most impressed by the company's triumphs in many cases also saw the Netherlands and England as potential partners in a crusade against the Spanish empire in the Caribbean. From their perspective, indeed, the English and the Dutch appeared to be natural allies. Protestantism served as a link between the two peoples. Furthermore, they were united by a common hatred and fear of Spain. These factors helped to bring English and Dutch elements together for joint efforts against the Spanish empire, most notably during the years 1637-41. Nevertheless, cooperation was erratic, and on both sides it was effected primarily by small groups. The period 1621-41 was marked as much by rivalry between English and Dutch colonial enterprises as it was by friendly interaction. The nature of Anglo-Dutch cooperation, and the reasons why it was not more extensive, constitute the theme of this article.

Conflict and Cooperation

For its part, the government of the Netherlands, probably with West India Company encouragement, actively promoted cooperative New World expeditions that involved company fleets. In 1621 Dutch ambassadors proposed to the Danes that they organize their own West India Company and that the two companies join in a war of conquest against the Spanish empire, and in the spring of 1624 a second embassy made similar proposals to the French.[2]

A series of negotiations in 1623-25 culminated in the Treaty of Southampton, which bound England and the Netherlands in an offensive and defensive league.[3] At the time the treaty was signed, both nations were at war with Spain, and almost immediately thereafter they joined in an attack on Cadiz. The expedition ended disastrously, however, and although Anglo-Dutch relations remained cordial throughout the later 1620s, they were clearly deteriorating by the time England, in December 1630, concluded peace with Spain.[4]

The crisis that temporarily brought the governments of England and the Netherlands together also prompted major efforts to promote Anglo-Dutch cooperation against the Spanish empire. In early 1624, the Dutch ambassadors who had been sent to England to negotiate an alliance proposed to James I that his government send ships to join in a company expedition to the West Indies, and promised him whatever territories might be conquered by the united fleet. At about the same time, in what may have been a coordinated effort, Sir Edward Conway, the principal secretary, also called on James to join with the Dutch in an attack on the Spanish empire in the New World.[5] It is also possible that the Conway proposal reflected the stance of the most powerful crown favourite, the duke of Buckingham, for Conway was a leading member of Buckingham's retinue, and the duke had recently aligned himself with the anti-Spanish faction at court.[6]

By and large, the English government rejected plans for a joint assault on Spain's New World empire. Nevertheless, the English and Dutch did pursue at least one cooperative enterprise. Had the assault on Cadiz succeeded, the allies would have destroyed the enemy fleet there and then headed to the West Indies, in hopes of plundering Spanish treasure.[7] And the West India Company did gain some temporary advantage. Most notably, its ships were granted free entrance to English ports – useful for refuge, as well as for trade – a principle noted in the Treaty of Southampton and reaffirmed by Charles I in September 1627.[8]

Anglo-Dutch cooperation in the New World was, however, the exception during the 1620s, even while the two nations were allied against Spain. The rule was unilateral action, and England as well as the Netherlands became progressively more involved. Under James, the government had been slow to challenge Spanish hegemony in the Caribbean. Raleigh paid with his life for ignoring crown policy. In April 1620, at the prodding of the Spanish ambassador, Count Gondomar, the Privy Council ordered the imprisonment of Captain Roger North, who had attempted to occupy a tract of land in the Amazon region. One month later, Gondomar persuaded the Council to require that the earl of Warwick surrender his Guiana patent.[9]

With the coming of Charles to the throne, and with the coming of war, there was a dramatic change in direction. In April 1626 North was granted a patent to colonize in the Amazon region. Three years later, the earl of Carlisle received a patent for the Caribbee islands, ending a struggle with several other parties who had sought the proprietary grant. In October 1629 Sir Robert Heath, the attorney-general, was made proprietor of "Carolana," a vast tract that included all North American territory between Virginia and the Floridian peninsula, and encompassed the Bahamas as well. Finally, in December 1630 the Providence Company received a patent that allowed it to take hold of islands in the western Caribbean.[10]

The new attitude of aggressiveness on the part of the government was matched and encouraged by the mercantile classes. During the latter 1620s would-be colonizers fought their private wars against the Spanish empire. In 1660 Captain Henry Powell recalled in a petition that "in the yeare 1626 being warres betweene the kingdome of England and Spaine your petitioner . . . procured a Commission against the estate of the Spaniards and then proceded on a voyage that resulted in the founding of the Caribbee Isles colony." It was also under a letter of marque that Warwick seized Santa Catalina, the island that he renamed "Providence."[11]

Likewise, during the period 1625-30, the court was flooded with petitions and memorials that pressed the government to make war on the Spanish empire. On April 14, 1625, Sir John Coke, a secretary of state, sent Buckingham, his patron, a proposal, "To abate the pride and terror of the Spanish pretended Empire." Coke called for all-out war, suggesting that a fleet be sent to the New World for the purpose of obliterating the Spanish empire in the West Indies and forcing open trade routes to Peru. In July 1629 a Huguenot refugee, M. de Belavene, proposed that the king dispatch a fleet of fifty ships to the Caribbean, there to harass Spanish shipping.[12] Neither he nor Coke suggested that the proposed expeditions be conducted jointly with the Dutch or with any foreign power, and nothing seems to have come from either plan.

The conclusion of peace brought nearly to a halt the wave of proposals for attacking Spain's Caribbean bases. During the first half of the 1630s, only one courtier, Sir Kenelm Digby, is known to have openly counselled aggressive warfare, and his proposal came to nothing.[13]

Furthermore, few new settlement schemes were put forward that related to the West Indies or generally to the region of active Spanish involvement.[14]

In the Caribbean itself, the Dutch remained active, but only the Providence Company was willing to offer assistance. During the early 1630s, Dutch privateers who preyed on Spanish shipping were welcomed at the company property of Tortuga and, albeit less openly, at Providence itself. Company officials back home feared that this hospitality would bring retaliation from Spain, and they ordered the governor of Providence to conceal his dealings with the Dutch. They did not, however, prohibit the use of company territories as a haven for Dutch privateers.[15]

In general, the years 1630-35 saw English passivity or stagnation in the Caribbean. The Heath patent did not result in the planting of any permanent settlements, either on the mainland or in the Bahamas.[16] The Caribbee settlements remained small, as did those of the Providence Company and those belonging to other European nations. Despite this weakness, or perhaps because of it, the Spanish launched a series of attacks in 1633-35, in the process overrunning several English, Dutch, and French colonies. While failing in an attempt to conquer Providence, they did, in March 1635, take Tortuga. There, as elsewhere, they massacred all male settlers. After they departed, the Providence Company established a new settlement, but it languished.[17] The officers of the company now appear to have formulated a new strategy for challenging Spanish hegemony: instead of colonization, privateering.[18]

The mid-1630s, which saw the weakening of England's presence in the Caribbean, was also marked by the collapse of a major effort in Charles' foreign policy. Charles was intent on helping his nephew Charles Louis, the dispossessed Elector Palatine, to regain the Palatinate, and he was hopeful, as James had been before him, that he could persuade the Hapsburgs to effect the transfer. It was essential, he felt, to remain on good terms with the Spanish Court, and to this end he in May 1635 signed a treaty that bound him to support Spain with a naval attack on the Netherlands. Less than a month later, however, the Treaty of Prague was concluded, and it left the Palatinate in the hands of

the duke of Bavaria. In March 1636 Charles sent an envoy to Vienna, trying yet another avenue to regain the electorate for his nephew, but this mission failed to sway the emperor.[19]

Stymied in his diplomacy, and perhaps hoping to pressure the Hapsburgs, Charles began to warm slightly to the Netherlands and to France. He did not, however, confine his new initiative to diplomatic manipulation. Early in 1637 he placed a small fleet at the disposal of Charles Louis.[20] And, as he had done during the period 1625-30, he encouraged those of his subjects who were prepared to challenge Spain in the New World. In January 1636 he granted the Providence Company letters of reprisal.[21] The signs at court once again suggested that an assault on the Spanish empire might be in the offing, and this situation prompted several schemes to drive Spain from the Caribbean.

On September 18, 1637, a lengthy petition, "Propositions for a West Indya Company," was sent to Charles. The petition in some respects hearkened back to others that had been submitted the previous decade, or even as far back as Elizabeth's reign. The petitioners began, "There is no other way, advantagious, and profitable, to make a war upon the King of Spaine, but in the WEST INDYES. A war made in the Indyes, if a good force of shipping be kept there, able to fight with his fleet, and a good port of retrayt be prepared, will separate those Dominions from Spaine: and force those great viceroyes to Cantonize." After the Indies had been "Cantonized," they insisted, trade among the islands would collapse, and the inhabitants would turn to England for supplies. Eventually, the English would be able to incite the "naturalls" to rise against their Spanish masters, by promising them their freedom. The petitioners claimed that their project was altruistic: "The falling off of the Indyes, and cutting the Liver vayne, that supplyes the body of Spayne with such immense sumes of mony, will humble them, and give a generally peace, and securetye, so much Longed for, to all Christendome."

To achieve this dramatic end, the petitioners proposed the establishment of a company whose primary function was to make war on the Spanish Empire. The company was to be empowered "to sease some fitt port, and rendevous in the Indyes"; from this base it would pursue "the oportunitye of the seasons, by invade by Land, and to make prise at Sea."

The proposed project was large-scale and expensive – 10,000 men, £200,000 per annum for the first five years. The necessary cash was to be raised by public subscription, and, in order to win publicity and investment, the king was to announce his support, preferably in print. He was also to grant the patentees the right to establish a joint-stock company, along with the necessary governing machinery, and was to affirm "That they, and their Generalls, and Captaynes, officers, Soldiers, and servants employed by them, [would] have power to surprise, besiege, Conquer, possess, and hold, any part of the West Indyes that they [would] find most conduceable to their deseignes."[22]

Six courtiers signed the petition: Sir Thomas Roe, one of England's leading diplomats; Thomas, Lord Conway, son of the former secretary; Lord Maltravers, who had in 1632 been assigned the Carolana patent by Heath; Sir Dudley Digges, master of the Rolls; Sir John Pennington, rear-admiral of the Fleet; and Sir John Wolstonholme, a wealthy merchant-courtier who, of the six, was perhaps the most experienced in colonial affairs. Roe was probably the prime mover. He was closely associated with Elizabeth of Bohemia – Charles' sister – and with her son Charles Louis, and he appears to have hoped that a two-front war against Spain, in the West Indies and on the Continent, would serve to weaken the Hapsburg cause generally, at least to the point where the Palatinate could be reclaimed.[23]

As the petition was presented to Charles, it spoke only of enemies, not of allies. Yet, it is quite possible that the projectors believed that their company would work with the Dutch, and especially with the West India Company, in carrying on the war in the Caribbean. Not long after the petition was delivered at Court, a second one made direct reference to the possibility that the projected company would, in its assault on the Spanish empire, find an ally in the Netherlands. The petitioner in this case was Heath, a man who was on close terms with most of the projectors and who may, in fact, have been an unnamed partner of theirs. As had the earlier petitioners, Heath attempted to demonstrate the need for prompt action in the Caribbean. Unlike them, he was quite open in proposing a Dutch alliance.

The West Indyes, have been for many years, the support of the house of Austria, & hence hath the Feweel been taken, that hath sett this part of Europe on Fire[.] The hollanders of late have attempted some of thes parts: & by ther interceptions & invasions, have annoyed the kinge of Spayne, & inriched themselves. . . If your Majesty please to interteyne any thoughts of this subject This is humbly offered[:] Eather your Majesty must interpose yourself, openly & avowedly, as your owne, at your pleasure/ or disavowe it, as it may be best for your honor & service/ The first of thes, seemeth to be less safe. . ./ The second way, may happily be attained unto If Some of experience, & quality, & well fitted for such an enterprise, *quasi aliud agentes* will eather interprise somewhat of themselves Or else, shall offer themselves to joyne with the hollanders, to joyn ther Forces & take ther fortunes with them:. . . Such subjects your Majesty hath, who desire nothing else from your majesty for ther incouragement, but that you will take knowledge of ther outward deseigne, which may fairely dessemble ther intentions/ And that if they find that fittest, & shall without your Majestys direction or recommendation, fall in with the hollanders; your Majesty will only take knowledge of, & that such volontiers as for the present or the future shall second them, shall have your free leave, & libertye.[24]

Negotiations directed toward a cooperative venture had in fact been going on for some time. On July 17, 1637, Anzolo Correr, the Venetian ambassador in London, had reported to the Doge and Senate, "They have held long consultations and finally decided to set up a new Company to trade in the West Indies and acquire possessions, after the manner of the Dutch, with whom they are treating, to act in concert."[25] Just who "they" were is not clear, and the exact terms of agreement are unknown. But it is highly probable that before Roe and his partners submitted their petition they had agreed that if the king chartered their company they would join the Dutch in an expedition into the Spanish West Indies.

It is possible that the projectors expected their company fleet to sail with a Dutch naval force, but more likely the plan called for an alliance with the Dutch West India Company. It is likewise probable that the Dutch parties who reached the agreement with them were company officials rather than government representatives. By charter, the company was allowed to negotiate on its own behalf, although the government sometimes interfered.[26]

If the West India Company did negotiate with Roe and his partners, it is likely that one of its leading spokesmen was Johannes de Laet, an influential director. De Laet seems to have had a sincere wish to see England and the Netherlands achieve greater unity. He was an Anglophile, whose brother-in-law was Sir Edward Powell, the master of Requests, and whose English friends included Coke and, on a more intimate basis, Sir William Boswell, a courtier who had been involved in colonizing efforts in Carolana and the West Indies.[27] De Laet was in England throughout the winter of 1637-38.[28] Just when he arrived is unknown, but it may have been in time to join early discussions, and it was probably not so late as to preclude him from attending later meetings with the Roe faction.

Despite the petitions of the Roe faction and of Heath, the English West India Company scheme of 1637 failed to bear fruit. The linkage of their proposed company with the Dutch may have been their undoing. At court, foreign policy was returning to the pro-Spanish, anti-Dutch posture that had obtained 1630-35. The times were no longer favourable to Anglo-Dutch cooperation, particularly when the chief end of that cooperation was an all-out assault on the Spanish West Indies.

Charles' policy toward the Netherlands may have been erratic, but the Providence Company was by now pursuing a clear course, one of cooperation with the Dutch. In early 1637 the West India Company made a formal order to buy Providence Island, and the Providence Company sought the King's permission to sell. Charles, however, refused. He further suggested that the company be reorganized.[29] A committee chaired by John Pym, the treasurer, was appointed to supervise the reorganization. It concluded in part that the company might best serve "by annoying the Spaniard and intercepting his treasure, whereby he hath troubled and endangered most of the States of Christendom and doth foment against the professors of the reformed religion."[30]

The company was already following this plan, and increasingly it was enlisting Dutch aid. In June 1636, company officials ordered Thomas Newman, a captain they had hired, "When you shalbe past the Islands to the Southward, you shall consider the advise by what meanes you may most weaken and disable the Spaniard. . . If you shall in the Indyes meet with Dutch or English ships that will joyne with you Tonne for Tonne . . . we would have you to joyne with them, Takeing Care that the profitts therof to be divided in a due proportion, respect be also had to

us."[31] In July 1638, the company directed another captain, Samuel Axe, to grant "consortship" to Dutch vessels.[32] The following June company officials ordered the governor and council of Providence to allow the Dutch free trade.[33] The most dramatic cooperation came in the spring of 1639, when Captain Nathaniel Butler, governor of the Island, put together a fleet of English and Dutch ships and raided several Spanish colonies. The Dutch ships had a commission, signed by both the Prince of Orange and officials of the West India Company.[34]

Spanish reprisals were quick to come. In the late spring of 1640, Spain tried but failed to capture Providence. However, on May 24, 1641, the island fell to a considerable invading force, and the inhabitants were sent captive to Spain. Only eight months before, Tortuga had been seized by Huguenots from St. Christopher, so mid-1641 found the Providence Company almost entirely stripped of possessions.[35]

The time of the Spanish counterattack was marked also by yet another rapid turnabout in English foreign policy. England was by now almost impotent, and its weakness was generally recognized. In January 1641 the Spanish Council of State wrote of Charles, "we have little cause either to expect anything from him or to fear him." Lacking support in Madrid, the Anglo-Spanish alliance collapsed. The French likewise lost interest in treating with Charles, and in 1640 withdrew their envoy from the English Court. Charles was desperate for allies. With little choice, he turned to the Netherlands and in October 1640 agreed to a marriage alliance involving his daughter and the Prince of Orange.[36]

This agreement virtually coincided with the meeting of the Long Parliament. However much the members resented Charles' policies generally, virtually all of them applauded the apparent end of the Spanish alliance. Some of them went further, openly promoting a war on Spain, or more typically a war on the Spanish empire in the Caribbean. Pym, the dominant force in the Commons 1640-41, showed the way to these hawks. The advocates of war believed that a successful expedition in the Indies would force Spain to effect the return of the Palatinate. So loyal to Charles Louis were the members of the Long Parliament that they refused to approve the marriage alliance unless it was linked to a general league that took his interests into account.[37]

Against the background of diplomatic reorientation and political turmoil that characterized England in 1640-41, English and Dutch elements made one last attempt to establish a league for the purpose of attacking the Spanish empire. De Laet played a leading role in this case, as he probably had in 1637, but neither Roe or any of those who had signed his earlier petition appears to have taken part. The Providence Company was represented, chiefly by Warwick, and Boswell was involved although he remained behind the scenes. Likewise taking part were Charles Louis and Sir Richard Cave, one of his leading English advocates.[38]

The negotiations can best be followed through the medium of de Laet's correspondence with Boswell. On June 18, he wrote Boswell from London:

During these last few days the Prince Elector, the earl of Warwick, Sir Cave, and I as the fourth have met together, and we have had considerable discussion about the American Company, which will be established, under parliamentary authority, in this kingdom, in the name of that illustrious Prince. Many men from the upper nobility, and several more than the commons' delegates, incline even further. . . The aim of our deliberations was that the Prince might impose upon me certain points required to begin the project for the good organization of the society. I have accepted the condition and have completed what I was bidden to do. Next Monday we shall meet together again. Never have I had more hope that I can do something pleasing for the Prince and for the kingdom.[39]

In August, Charles, hoping to find political allies north of the border, departed for Scotland, there to remain for more than three months. Charles Louis went with him. The negotiations appear to have suffered in their absence. Much of de Laet's optimism had faded by August 12, when he again wrote Boswell from London: "Concerning the American Society, which you mention first in your letters, nothing could be done before that king's departure – so much for the negotiations."[40] By October 13 he was back in the Netherlands, fearful that Boswell was holding back information from him: "You will deserve well of me if you will make me a participant, especially concerning what is being considered about the American Society and the restitution of the Palatinate, whose business has disturbed me."[41] On November 11, he wrote in the same vein: "Could you please tell me whether the king has returned from Scotland, or what is the cause of his unexpectedly long delay?

What is the future of the American Society? (I do not doubt in fact that friends have diligently written you honour of this). I beseech you that therefore you open your letters into England."[42]

The projected West India enterprise seemed geared to appeal to most parliamentary leaders. Whatever the precise details of the arrangement – and the evidence is certainly not as complete as one would wish – it is clear from de Laet's remarks that the proposed company was to be led by Parliament's hero, Charles Louis, and that a primary aim of the effort was to win the Palatinate. Almost certainly, the proposed means was to be (as it had been for the Roe faction in 1637) an English West India Company-Dutch West India Company joint assault on the Spanish empire. When the West Indies were conquered, they believed, Spain would be greatly weakened. Then the Palatinate could be reclaimed.

When on September 9, 1641, Parliament began a six-week recess, both houses appointed committees to inquire into certain matters during the break. Included were at least a half-dozen leading members of the Providence Company – notably on the Lord's committee, Warwick; on the Commons' committee, Pym. And among the charges given them was "To consider of framing and constituting a West Indian Company." Other matters were more pressing, however, and colonial affairs were soon left mainly to Warwick and to his secretary, William Jessop.[43]

After the establishment of the Commonwealth, with its strongly Protestant flavour, plans for the establishment of a West India Company were again put forward. One proposal to that end was submitted to Parliament in about 1650. Its author, whose identity is unknown, noted that England was already making headway in the West Indies, thereby "ballancing the greatness and chequing the pride of the SPANIARDS."[44] In 1658 Thomas Povey and a group of English merchants advised the Council of State to establish a West India Company, in order that the company might direct attacks on Spanish colonies and on the treasure fleet, with the ultimate aim of driving the Spanish from the New World. The scheme made some progress, but the chaotic circumstances of the time caused it to drop from view after 1659.[45]

The Civil War-Interregnum period, in many ways unique, mirrored the previous two decades in that the English chose to go it alone in the West

Indies. Even when, in fulfilment of Cromwell's "Western Design," they did attack Spanish holdings in the Caribbean, they worked without allies. There was little talk of making league with the Dutch against Spain's New World empire. Indeed, England and the Netherlands were generally on poor terms, as witness the Anglo-Dutch war of 1652-54. The rule for them, in the New World as in the Old, was non-cooperation. Despite the radical switch in the personnel of government, there was little divergence from the pattern that had obtained 1621-41.

Barriers to Alliance

The period 1621-41 saw England and the Netherlands challenge, more directly than ever before, Spanish hegemony in the West Indies. Yet, had they cooperated they might have greatly weakened Spain's Caribbean empire. These times were propitious. The weakness of Spain was not merely a figment of the imagination of bellicose English protectors. The Spaniards were deeply involved in the Thirty Years' War, and their situation became more desperate after France intervened in that war in 1635. Faced with a revolt in Portugal in 1640, they were incapable even of maintaining their hold there. In that same year, Catalonia also broke away, although this breach was to prove temporary. Spain was weak and beleaguered – in no position to adequately defend a vast New World empire. Indeed, its efforts to quash competitors in the Caribbean were erratic, and they were generally small-scale and half-hearted, successful only when the enemy was few in numbers or poorly armed.

The proponents of an Anglo-Dutch campaign in the Caribbean may at times have been excessively sanguine in estimating Spanish weakness or the strength of the expeditions they envisioned. And they constantly underestimated the cost involved. Nevertheless, their final analysis was substantially correct. If the governments and the monied classes of England and the Netherlands had joined in a single effort – particularly in the period 1635-41, when Spain was at its weakest – it is quite possible that the combined fleets of the Dutch and the English could have conquered a significant part of Spain's empire in the Caribbean. But no cooperative assault took place. Because of this, a golden opportunity was missed, and Spain remained predominant in the Caribbean until the nineteenth century.

The Dutch were not primarily responsible for the failure to cooperate. By and large, they appear to have been willing to join England in a Caribbean war. They were hopeful of making England an ally against the Spanish, and to this end they put forward various schemes to entice the English into a war with Spain, particularly one in the West Indies. As has been noted, by early 1624, the Dutch ambassadors were already proposing a joint West Indian campaign, and 1637 and 1641 saw Dutch and English elements cooperating in attempts to found an English company whose immediate purpose was to make league with the Dutch in attacking Spanish strongholds in the Caribbean.

That at times it was representatives of the Dutch government who encouraged English designs, at other times representatives of the West India Company, does not suggest that there were two groups working independently. Rather, it is probable that in approaching the English company officials were actuated not only by a sense of what would most benefit the company, but by government wishes, even directives. On the other hand, no evidence suggests that the government ever forced them to negotiate to an end that they considered contrary to company interests. De Laet was certainly enthusiastic about the English West India Company project of 1641. By that date, in any case, the company was in great need of allies, for its finances were weak and its hold over Brazil was being endangered by the newly independent Portugal.[46]

While the Dutch promoted cooperative schemes, they viewed with some disdain their prospective English partners. English colonial efforts of the early Stuart period often failed, and even though the record of the Netherlands was far from perfect some Dutch observers considered the English to be rank amateurs in the area of colonization. In the letter that he wrote Boswell on June 18, 1641, de Laet commented rather negatively on certain Englishmen who were interested in the company that was then being projected: "Some of them are talking big, but several men, for me to admit the truth, are not knowledgeable enough of those things that are required for the proper constitution of a society of this kind, nor do they understand how much money may be required for expeditions of this kind and their prosecution." His comment was quite similar to one made by Correr, relative to the negotiations of 1637: "The Dutch . . . doubt whether the English will be prepared to get together the amount of capital required."

It is possible that if the English had openly sided with the Dutch in an attack on the Spanish Empire, they would have found them to be an unreliable ally. In fact, however, they never tested that possibility, and the records do not indicate that during the various negotiations company officials or Dutch emissaries behaved in such a way as to arouse suspicion.

Several factors help to explain why the English were reluctant to ally themselves with the Dutch. Perhaps most obvious is the anti-Dutch attitude of the first two Stuarts. James I and Charles I both considered the Netherlands to be a dangerous competitor, a threat to England's trade and to its colonial schemes. That the Dutch tended to be allied to the French was also a sore point, for the first Stuarts generally considered France to be an enemy.[47] Aside from the mid-1620s, they were seldom willing to accommodate Dutch interests in the New World, even when their subjects were amenable. For his part, Charles was never more open in challenging Dutch colonial interests than he was during the late 1630s, the very time when the Roe clique and the Providence Company were hatching their schemes for Anglo-Dutch cooperation. In April 1637 he sent two letters to similar purpose, one to the governor and council of Virginia, the other to the feoffees of the earl of Carlisle. In both, he noted that the colonists were trading with the Dutch, to the prejudice of crown profits, and he ordered an end to such trade.[48]

Just as they were hostile to the Netherlands, so were the first two Stuarts partial to Spain. In 1631 Charles went so far as to agree to a joint Anglo-Spanish expedition against Holland, a venture ostensibly intended to conquer and partition the Netherlands.[49] It may be that he never intended to follow through on the scheme, but his strong pro-Spanish slant is epitomized in this agreement. Indeed, despite some rocky stretches, particularly 1624-30, Spain was the cornerstone of Charles' foreign policy, as it had been of his father's.

Beyond the fact that James and Charles favoured the cause of Spain over that of the Netherlands, the fear of military consequences also discouraged them from sanctioning an Anglo-Dutch campaign in the Caribbean. Both of them, particularly James, detested war, and consequently pursued a foreign policy that was unlikely to involve England in a major conflict. Both, like many of their subjects, believed that Spain continued to be the greatest power in Europe. They certainly had no desire to trifle with the Spanish, and although they shared an interest in colonization they did not value the West Indies highly enough to go to war over them. There was also the matter of money. The various schemes that projectors of West Indian campaigns put forward between 1621 and 1641 were similar in that they were costly and the projectors generally requested that the government cover the bulk of initial expenses. James and Charles undoubtedly realized also that if the campaigns led to full-scale war with Spain, the cost to England would be great. And this huge expense would have to be borne by a government that was regularly strapped for funds. At no time was the financial crisis greater than it was in 1637-41, the very time when the most ambitious projects were being put forward at Court.

The attitude of James and Charles certainly helps to explain the failure of Anglo-Dutch cooperation, but it was not the sole factor, perhaps not even the primary one. It was not just the kings who were unwilling to see England and the Netherlands join in a Caribbean campaign. Rather, their position appears to have mirrored that of many of their subjects, including those whose support was necessary if any cooperative venture was to succeed.

It is unlikely that any expedition of conquest in the West Indies could have proceeded far without the strong support of the mercantile classes, but the early Stuart period found them unwilling to commit funds to projects that the Court opposed. Like James and Charles, they recognized that there would be great difficulties and expense involved in a major Caribbean offensive, even if the enterprise saw the Dutch as willing and active partners. In the absence of direct governmental support, the risk was heightened. That royal reluctance to support an Anglo-Dutch expedition caused the men of money to hold back may be seen in a letter that the earl of Northumberland wrote to Roe on August 6, 1637, relative to the West India Company scheme of that year.

The West India businesse is doubtlesse the most hopeful and feasable designe we can fall upon if it could be followed as it ought to be, it must constantly be pursued att a greate expence for some yeares without expecting a present profit, and I doubt whether we want not industrie and patience as well as monaie to perfect a worke of that nature, the little incouragement that is given to trade in England makes all men readie to withdraw their stockes, from all parts, out of that consideration I heare men will be very hardly drawne to ingage themselves in any new adventures, and it is to greate an undertaking for a few well affected men to goe through with.[50]

If the crown had been more willing to support the Caribbean schemes, it is quite possible that the mercantile element would have given more financial backing, but even then it might have been unwilling to make a major commitment. Monied men would still have feared, with some cause, that they might lose much or all of their investment. Beyond that, however, was the fact that, for the most part, they preferred to see their country go it alone in colonization, and they saw the Dutch as being competitors on the colonial scene. They fiercely opposed the West India Company, a key to most schemes for Anglo-Dutch cooperation, when it seemed to be competing for New World areas that the English coveted, areas like New Netherlands and Guiana. In April 1625 Jan van Rijn, a company officer who was stationed at Fort Nassau, Wiapoco, reported to the directors of the Zeeland Chamber that the local Indians had become hostile. The main reason for this hostility, he claimed, was that local English traders had told the Indians that the Dutch were planning to kill them.[51] Such tactics, and worse, would likely have won the support of most English merchants who had an interest in colonization. To them, the Dutch, like the Spanish, were a danger, and had to be dealt with accordingly.

A belief that the Netherlands related to England mainly as a competitor was intense. In about 1637 an unidentified projector called on Charles to establish a West India Company. In some respects, his appeal was not unlike that of the Roe clique. But he seemed less concerned with the Spanish threat than with the danger posed by the Dutch. He doubted that Spain would oppose English trade in the West Indies, but if it did, he claimed reassuringly, "shall his Majestie not bee necessitated therby to take up armies against the king of Spayne. For the Masters of this saide English trade shall defind against any nation

whatsoever." Moreover, he went to argue that Spain was in fact too weak to counter any English threat. The real danger lay in the Dutch menace, he claimed: "It is not to bee doubted that if soe bee the Hollanders once become masters of that trade, the same will not soe easily bee taken from them againe without great discontents and disputations." On the other hand, he argued, "by meanes of the trade of such a West India Company his Majestie shall possesse the principall trade in the said quarters which otherwise for Certeyne will fall into the Hollanders hands." He believed that England might advance not only in the West Indies, but in Brazil, "where the Portugals are ready for to yeeld themselves under the protection of his Majestie and of his Subjects trading there.[52]

Even some of the Englishmen who promoted schemes for Anglo-Dutch cooperation in the Caribbean were ambivalent toward the Netherlands. One such was Heath. In the wake of the "Amboina Massacre" of 1623, he joined many of his countrymen in demanding retaliation.[53] Even when he petitioned Charles in 1637, on behalf of the Roe clique, he expressed concern over the fact that the Dutch seemed to be making significant headway in the West Indies, previously Spain's preserve: "That eather of both shold be absolute Lords of the place & the trade therof, is neather profitable nor safe to your Majesty."

Likewise ambivalent was Roe. One basis for his reservations is evident in comments that he made on December 31, 1636, in a letter to Charles Louis – the earliest extant reference to the English West India Company project: "It makes offer of Conniviture with the French and Duch, whick I understand not . . . for to joyne with them in any action, in the Indyes, is to confound, and ruyne it in the beginning, for nothing can be done there, but by surprise, and sudden attempt that must fall like a Clap of thunder." In that same letter, Roe gave vent to suspicions about the Dutch, claiming that they sought only their own advantage, and that they would refuse to ally themselves with England unless Charles withdrew his claims to English control of the Channel. Judging from his letter, Roe appears to have placed more reliance on France than on the Netherlands, as he expressed the hope that Charles Louis would use his fleet, in conjunction with that of the French, to attack first on the Continent, then in the West Indies.[54] For some reason, he and his partners became more willing to work with the Netherlands, and by the summer of 1637 they seem to have been thinking only of Dutch allies, rather than French. Nevertheless, Roe remained suspicious of the Dutch. On October 2, 1637, he wrote to Elizabeth, "I extremely wonder that they who sought less, will not apprehend the greatest and fayrest occasion, that ever was offered to enter into an obliging league with England: which will necessarily accomodate all theyr Sea affayres and all other questions, and engage us with them against the common enemy, upon this treaty many other resolutions depend, as that of the West Indies which must make a breach with Spayne."[55]

If any major element within the mercantile community looked fondly on the prospects of a Dutch alliance against Spain, it was the officials of the Providence Company. To some extent, they were actuated by Protestant zealousness. Still, it appears that the state of company fortunes in the Caribbean played a larger role in deciding policy. It is noteworthy that they did not move decisively toward cooperation until after the Spanish expeditions of 1633-35 had greatly weakened their position and had made them desperate for allies. Prior to this time they had, as has been noted, allowed Dutch privateers to find refuge in the harbours of their New World colonies; yet, they seem to have believed that England should forge its own empire, rather than work in league with states that might prove to be untrustworthy. In these early years they indeed appear to have perceived the Dutch as being rivals first and foremost, and certain incidents encouraged their attitude. For example, in March 1633, they learned that representatives of the West India Company had recently questioned two farmers on Tortuga and had indicated that the company planned to take possession of the island, since the Providence Company was doing so little to effectively occupy and administer it.[56] Distrust remained even in the latter half of the 1630s, the period of cooperation. In May 1636, at a company court, officials discussed the possibility that the Dutch would occupy Tortuga, if the company withdrew.[57]

A major segment of the English mercantile community and many crown officials, therefore, doubted that their nation should align with the Dutch. And even disregarding the issue of alli-

ances, the call for war on the Spanish empire was far from unanimous. Despite the belief of many historians that early-Stuart England seethed with a desire for war with Spain, it is possible that the public, and particularly the influential element, was not truly bellicose. When in November 1621 George Shilleto, a Puritan member, argued that the English should take a hard line against the king of Spain, "To send Ships abroad to take away his West India Treasure," he was laughed down.[58] In a time of crisis, such as existed during the Anglo-Spanish War of 1625-1630, or in an atmosphere highly charged with religious enthusiasm – the atmosphere that prevailed in 1640-41 – there was undoubtedly a warlike spirit, and schemes to destroy the Spanish Empire were probably well received. Normally, however, a sense of caution may have prevailed.

Public apathy is also apparent in the fact that few Englishmen were willing to settle in Caribbean colonies. In 1634, after a plan for West Indian colonization had been scrutinized by the London Court of Aldermen, a critic claimed, "divers are daly Incouraged to transport themselves both to Virginia & New England where specialy In New England they are more secuer from danger of either the spaniard or natives then can bee exported soeveare unto the spaniard as this plantation may bee Intended."[59] For their part, the leaders of the Providence Company campaigned intensively among settlers in New England, hoping to persuade them to move to company properties in the West Indies, but they had little success, despite the fact that the objects of their appeal generally shared their Puritan outlook.[60]

Fear of the Spaniards and concern that the climate was unhealthy dissuaded most Englishmen from settling in Caribbean islands, even in a period when the population of English colonies in North America was burgeoning. There were colonial projectors who sought to ignore this. On April 17, 1641, in the course of promoting his plan for a West Indian campaign, Pym told the Commons, "There are nowe in those parts, in New-England, Virginia, and the Carib Islands, and in the Barmudos, at least sixty thousand persons of this nation, many to them well armed, and their bodies seasoned to the climate, which, with a very small charge, might be set downe in some advantageous parts of these pleasant, rich, and fruitful countries, and easily make his majestie master of all that treasure, which not only foments the warre, but is the great support of peoperie in all parts of Christendome."[61] Pym's scenario was even less practical than were most. As regards the Caribbean, English projectors were many, prospective colonists, few.

When viewed in the general context of English attitudes toward the Dutch, the failure of England and the Netherlands to cooperate against the Spanish empire becomes understandable. Indeed, it would have been surprising if the two nations had mounted any concerted effort. Anti-Dutch feeling in England, spurred by various concerns, was to be found on every level, from king to commonalty. If Spain was hated, the Netherlands was seen in only slightly less negative a light. It had its admirers in England, certainly, and some of them were quite vocal and influential, a fact that may make it appear that they were more numerous and more representative than was actually the case. But the consensus was clearly against alliance. Likewise, the consensus seems to have been against making war on the Spanish empire – at least, the all-out war that the more zealous elements advocated. In view of the national attitude, it is unsurprising that England worked on its own in West Indian colonization, and for the most part proceeded unobtrusively. And the Spanish empire consequently received a respite at a time when Spain itself was wracked by crisis.

Notes

1. The West India Company's monopoly extended to West Africa and to all Pacific islands east of New Guinea, as well as to the New World. On the evolution and chartering of the company, see C.R. Boxer, *The Dutch in Brazil 1624-1654* (Oxford, 1957), pp. 1-15; W.J. Hoboken, "The Dutch West India Company; The Political Background of its Rise and Decline," in J.S. Bromley and E.H. Kossman, eds., *Britain and the Netherlands. Papers delivered at the Oxford-Netherlands Historical Conference, 1959* (London, 1960), pp. 47-51. A good discussion of the organization and purpose of the company is provided by Van Cleaf Bachman, *Peltries or Plantations: The Economic Policies of the Dutch West India Company in New Netherland 1623-1639; The Johns Hopkins University Studies in Historical and Political Science*, 87th ser., no. 2 (Baltimore, 1969), ch. 2. Even in its early years, the company faced significant obstacles: Jonathan I. Israel, *The Dutch Republic and the Hispanic World 1606-1661* (Oxford, 1982), pp. 130-34. After a confused start, the company charter was amplified (June 1622), and the directors met to

plan initial strategy (August 1623): Israel, pp. 124-25, 130.

2. Frances G. Davenport,ed., *European Treaties bearing on the History of the United States and its Dependencies to 1648.*(Washington, 1917), pp. 280-81, 285.

3. George Edmundson, *Anglo-Dutch Rivalry during the First Half of the Seventeenth Century: Being the Ford Lectures delivered at Oxford in 1910* (Oxford, 1911), pp. 86-92. The treaty is printed, in French, in Davenport, pp. 293-99.

4. José Alcalá-Zamora y Quiepo de Llano, *España, Flandes y el Mar del Norte (1618-1639): La última ofensiva europea de los Austrias madrileños* (Barcelona, 1975), p. 224. Although the Dutch had supplied twenty ships for the Cadiz expedition, this was only half of what England had requested (Israel, p. 116). There was significant Anglo-Dutch friction even during the brief period of alliance (Edmundson, pp. 94-96). Fearing the consequences of an end of the Anglo-Spanish War, the Dutch and French interfered in peace talks during the late 1620s (Alcalá-Zamora, p. 265). On the other hand, the Dutch helped to negotiate a peace treaty between England and France, which fought a desultory war, 1626-29 (Edmundson, pp. 102-04).

5. SP 14/147/64; Conway also advised that a company (not necessarily, though probably, one with colonial interests) be established, to the end of drawing off a part of the English poor. Note also Arthur P. Newton, *The Colonising Activities of the English Puritans: The Last Phase of the Elizabethan Struggle with Spain* (New Haven, 1914), p. 28; Davenport, p. 290. In the Parliament of 1624, there seems to have been considerable interest in the establishment of an English West India Company that was intended to make war on Spain's West Indian colonies. Sir Benjamin Rudyerd, a Puritan member, dealt at length with the issue: Leo F. Stock, ed., *Proceedings and Debates of the British Parliaments respecting North America,* (Washington, D.C., 1924), pp. 61-62.

6. The basis for Buckingham's animosity was his humiliating failure in the "Spanish Match" embassy of 1623; note Roger Lockyer, *Buckingham: The Life and Political Career of George Villiers, First Duke of Buckingham, 1592-1628* (London and New York, 1981), ch. 5. During the embassy of 1623, Buckingham is purported to have been approached by a Spanish courtier, "Don Fennyn," with a plan for seizing the Spanish plate fleet. Fennyn's scheme, along with several related documents (all of which may well be bogus), are abstracted in O. Ogle, W.H. Bliss, and W.D. Macray, eds., *Calendar of the Clarendon State Papers,* I (Oxford, 1869), p. 29, No. 237.

7. Israel, p. 116; Alcalá-Zamora, p. 224.

8. W.L. Grant and James Munro, eds., *Acts of the Privy Council of England. Colonial Series,* I (London, 1908), p. 119, No. 194. The pertinent clauses of the Treaty of Southampton are quoted in this entry.

9. *Acts of the Privy Council, Colonial,* I, 31-32 (No. 47); Nos. 35-40, 42-43, 45-46, 54-58, 61-62, 64, 67-69, and 72-73 are also relevant on North. On Warwick, see Newton, pp. 15-16; Wesley F. Craven,

"The Earl of Warwick, A Speculator in Piracy," *The Hispanic American Historical Review*, 10 (1930), pp. 457-79.

10. Public Record Office (London), Colonial Office records (hereafter "*CO*") 1/4/8. State Papers (hereafter "*SP*") 16/24/20, on North. Newton, pp. 52-59, discusses the Providence patent; he also deals (pp. 105-06) with a second which was issued June 17, 1631, for the purpose of bringing Tortuga ("Association") into company purview. The Caribee patent is analyzed by James A. Williamson, *The Caribbee Islands under the Proprietary Patents* (London, 1926), pp. 38-41. On the Heath patent, see Paul E. Kopperman, "Profile of Failure: The Carolana Project, 1629-1640," *The North Carolina Historical Review*, 59 (Winter 1982), pp. 3-7.

11. Newton, pp. 52-53; Bodleian Library (Oxford), Ms. Rawlinson c. 94, f. 33.

12. *CO* 1/5/19. Coke's proposal is *SP* 16/1/59.

13. This document, in English, is appended to Vittorio Gabrieli, *Sir Kenelm Digby: un iglese italianato nell'eta della controriforma* (Rome, 1957), pp. 285-91. It can be tentatively dated as having been written between Digby's temporary conversion to Protestantism (the extreme anti-Catholic tone suggests this), which probably took place in early 1631, and the death of his wife Mary (May 1633), after which he temporarily retired into seclusion.

14. Sir William Boswell and several partners from the Carolana enterprise put forth a proposal in 1632 (British Library [hereafter "BL"], Egerton Ms. 5297, f. 122); *CO* 1/7; *CO* 1/8/19. For a fuller discussion of this project, see Kopperman, "Carolana," p. 13.

15. Newton, pp. 153-55.

16. On the various attempts to settle Carolana, and the reason for their failure, see Kopperman, "Carolana," pp. 12-23. Although little was actually done to settle the proprietary, the Spanish feared that Heath would order that a suitable port-town in Florida be seized, since there was no suitable harbour in Carolana (Donald W. Rowland, trans. and ed., "Spanish Information on Early English Colonization," *Journal of Southern History*, 20 (November, 1954), p. 531). Generally, the Spanish believed the threat to their Caribbean empire to be greater than it was. In 1625 William Semple, a Scot who fought in the service of Spain, bluntly warned Philip IV that he would lose the West Indies if he did not take bold action, particularly against England, which he blamed not only for the West India danger but for arming Spain's enemies on the Continent (Alcalá-Zamora, p. 496).

17. C.C. Goslinga, *The Dutch in the Caribbean and on the Wild Coast, 1580-1680* (Assen, 1971), pp. 205-06; Newton, pp. 189-97.

18. Newton, pp. 199-201.

19. *Ibid.*, pp. 206-07; Edmundson, pp. 106-07.

20. *SP* 16/345/32; *SP* 16/346/34, 35; *SP* 16/349/5.

21. This grant may have been given only in oral form. In any case, the company not only used the letters itself, but issued them to others, finding considerable profit thereby (Newton, pp. 207-08, 266-67). Charles' grant came one month after the earl of Holland, governor of the Providence Company, had petitioned the king in Council to find some means of encouraging new adventurers to join the company, and thereby to "hearten" the company's West Indian colonists, who were demoralized in the wake of the Spanish assault (*CO* 1/8/81).

22. The description of this document, including all quotations, is drawn from *CO* 1/9/62, which is a copy, with some additions, of *CO* 1/9/61.

23. There are articles in the *Dictionary of National Biography* on all of the projectors except for Conway. In addition, note Kopperman, "Carolana," pp. 17-19, on Maltravers' colonial career. Michael J. Brown, *Itinerant Ambassador: The Life of Sir Thomas Roe* (Lexington, Kentucky, 1970), pp. 196-98, notes the project and provides some discussion on Roe's general attitude toward the Spanish Empire. In March 1637 Roe wrote Elizabeth of Bohemia that the West Indies were "the true back door, whereby to entre, undo, or humble Spayne" (*SP* 16/350/16).

24. *CO* 1/3/37.

25. Allen B. Hinds, ed., *Calendar of State Papers and Manuscripts, relating to English Affairs, existing in the Archives and Collections of Venice, and in Other Libraries of Northern Italy*, XXIV (London, 1923), p. 241, No. 261.

26. In theory, the States-General was involved in company affairs only in that it appointed one of the nineteen directors (Boxer, p. 9).

27. A biographical sketch of de Laet is provided in J.A.F. Bekkers, ed., *Correspondence of John Morris with Johannes de Laet* (Assen, 1970), xv-xvii).

28. De Laet was in England by December 25, 1637, for on that date he wrote to Boswell from London (*Add.* 6395, f. 10). He seems to have returned to the Netherlands in early spring, 1638, for in April (precise date uncertain) Boswell wrote to Coke, "I have rd your Honors last by Mr. de Laet (who acknowledgeth himself extreamly obliged to your Honor" (*SP* 84/153/289). De Laet's visit may have also been intended to pave the way for one that his son made, during the summer of 1638; in 1641 de Laet vainly attempted to obtain English naturalization for him (Bekkers, xvi). Interestingly, in this time of need he turned to Roe. On December 28, 1640, he wrote to Roe from Leyden, recommending his son and several other Dutchmen for naturalization (*SP* 84/156/218). The following February 12, Roe responded positively (Bekkers, p. 63).

29. Newton, pp. 238-39.

30. *Ibid.*, pp. 248-49.

31. *CO* 124/1/103.

32. *CO* 124/1/124.

33. *CO* 124/1/139. This order came shortly after the West India Company had established free trade in Brazil (with some exceptions). Boswell was impressed by this move (*SP* 84/153/289, 301).

34. Newton, pp. 256-57. Library of Congress, transcript of Butler's diary (original is in BL), esp. p. 15.

35. Newton, pp. 272-82, 297-302.

36. Gerald M.D. Howat, *Stuart and Cromwellian Foreign Policy* (New York, 1974), pp. 44-46, 65-67;

Alan MacFayden, "Anglo-Spanish Relations 1625-60" (unpub. Ph.D. diss., Liverpool, 1967), p. 47. Plans for the marriage were finalized in early October 1640 (*SP* 84/156/204, 206). At first, the plan was to marry William to Elizabeth, Charles' second daughter, but the Dutch were able to force Charles to agree to the more desirable match. Charles Louis was upset, feeling that Mary should have been reserved for him; note the letters of March 29 and May 16, 1641, from Giovanni Giustinian, Venetian ambassador, to the doge and Senate (*Calendar of State Papers, Venetian*, XXV, pp. 133 (No. 172), 147 (No. 188).

37. Dutch ambassadors in England to Frederick Henry, Prince of Orange, April 19, 1641, G. Groen van Prinsterer, ed., *Archives ou correspondance inedite de la maison d'Orange-Nassau*, 2nd ser., III (Utrecht, 1859), 427.

38. Boswell's involvement with the West India Company is noted in Newton, p. 214. In a speech that he gave in November (apparently) 1641, Roe mentioned that Parliament might "erect a company of the West Indies" (Stock, p. 101). No evidence, however, links him to the project itself. At the same time negotiations were going on between English and Dutch elements regarding the possible establishment of an English West India Company, different parties were discussing terms for resolving various disputes between the English East India Company and its Dutch counterpart. Several letters in the Prinsterer correspondence deal with this effort; note Francois d'Aerssen, Dutch ambassador, to Prince of Orange, September 23, 1641, Prinsterer, 2nd ser., III. 492-93.

39. *BL. Add.* 6395, f. 120. I wish to thank Dr. Gerald Day for assisting me in the translation, from Latin, of this and other letters in *Add.* 6395.

40. *Add.* 6395, f. 126.

41. *Add.* 6395, F. 131. De Laet had returned in mid-September (Bekkers, p. 65).

42. *Add.* 6395, F. 135.

43. Newton, pp. 317-18.

44. *BL. Stowe Ms.* 424, ff. 189-92.

45. Newton, pp. 326-27.

46. Boxer, p. 49; Van Hoboken, pp. 52-56.

47. The French, like the Dutch, represented competition to England in the New World. Note Herbert I. Priestley, *France Overseas through the Old Regime: A Study of European Expansion* (New York, 1939), pp. 77-84.

48. *CO* 1/9/47, 48.

49. Edmundson, p. 106. Although it seems unlikely that England would have made a very determined effort, it is quite possible that Charles would have committed his forces to war against the Netherlands if the Spanish had in fact withdrawn from the Palatinate. He in any case felt that Spain had to make the first move (Martin J. Havran, *Caroline Courtier: The Life of Lord Cottington* (Columbia, South Carolina, 1973), pp. 134-35).

50. *SP* 16/365/28.

51. New York Public Library. Papers of the Dutch West India Company, 1624-1626, relating to New Netherland, trans. J.A.J. Villiers, pp. 15-16; Edmundson, pp. 83-84; Goslinga, pp. 76, 205-06.

52. *CO* 1/9/63.

53. SP 14/120/121. At Amboina, a stronghold of the Dutch East India Company, twelve English merchants were executed by the Dutch governor, who believed that they were part of a conspiracy to take over the island. News of the "massacre" reached England in March 1624.

54. *SP* 16/338/29.

55. *SP* 16/369/4.

56. Newton, p. 214.

57. Noel Sainsbury, ed., *Calendar of State Papers, Colonial Series,* I (London, 1860), 233.

58. Stock, p. 54. Wallace Notestein, F.H. Relf, and Hartley Simpson, eds., *Commons Debates 1621* (New Haven, 1935), V, 406; VI, 201. Stock, like several other historians, mistakenly assigns the speech to Heath; this confusion grows from an error in the *Journals of the House of Commons.*

59. *CO* 1/8/19. iii.

60. Newton, ch. 13.

61. Stock, p. 98.

14

Trade, Plunder, and Economic Development in Early English Jamaica, 1655-89

NUALA ZAHEDIEH

Adam Smith concluded *The Wealth of Nations* with a fierce attack on the value of empire, "not a gold mine, but the project of a gold mine: a project which has cost . . . immense expense without being likely to bring any profit."[1] Smith focused his attention on the West Indian colonies, which contemporaries widely considered to be the most valuable part of the empire. He claimed that from the introduction of the Navigation Acts the stock which had improved and cultivated the sugar colonies had been sent out of England, for "[their] prosperity has been, in a great measure, owing to the great riches of England, of which a part has overflowed, if one may say so, upon those colonies."[2] He added that this investment represented a diversion of resources away from what would have been more profitable employment at home. Furthermore, colonization imposed high costs which offset an additional part of any gains: the costs of preferences on sugar borne by the British consumer and the costs of administration and defence of empire borne by the British taxpayer. Whilst the individual return for many planters and merchants was high, the social rate of return for Britons at large was low or even negative.[3] Smith's assertions have provoked discussion in the last 200 years. However, this has tended to focus on the latter parts of the argument. Little thought has been given to the initial assertion about where the capital for colonization came from and most commentators implicitly assume that it did, as Smith claimed, flow from the mother country.[4] This paper examines his asser-

tion in the light of the funding of what was to be England's richest sugar colony, Jamaica, and concludes by discarding it. It shows how the capital for planting Jamaica was locally generated and, furthermore, that this capital once earned, could not easily have been more profitably employed in the mother country.

Debate about "profit and loss" has focused on the West Indian islands because they most nearly approached the contemporary colonial ideal. The Caribbean colonies stimulated the expansion of long distance trade, "to the benefit of navigation"; they had no manufacturing industries of their own and so imported goods from England; above all, they "cultivated a plentiful soil, productive of commodities not to be had elsewhere".[5] They produced tobacco, cocoa, indigo, ginger, dyeing woods and, most important, sugar. Sugar quickly became England's leading colonial import and, from its first arrival on the market in the 1640s, yielded a far higher and steadier profit than any other American cash crop.[6] Sugar gave rise to levels of wealth and conspicuous consumption which bolstered the image of the Indies as a source of fabulous riches – the land of El Dorado.

There is no one commodity that doth so much encourage navigation advance the King's customs and our land and is at the same time of so great a universal use, virtue and advantage as this king of sweets.[7]

Jamaica was England's leading sugar exporter for most of the eighteenth century and in the 1770s surpassed all the other English islands

Table 14.1. Jamaica's Agricultural Exports According to the Naval Officer, 1671-1678 and 1682-1689

	Sugar (hhds.)	Indigo (hhds.)	Cocoa (hhds.)	Hides	Cotton (bags)	Logwood (tons)
1671 (6 months)	585	32	8	1,616		460
1672	1,169	64	16	3,232		920
1673	1,169	64	16	3,232		920
1674	1,169	64	16	3,232		920
1675	2,512	118	6	4,931		430
1676	2,512	118	6	4,931		430
1677	2,512	118	6	4,931		430
1678	5,165	90	26	11,865		554
1682	10,661	–	–	22,535	1,937	623
1683	9,533	–	–	16,107	1,309	506
1686	12,855	–	–	7,462	1,505	651
1687	11,186	–	–	8,468	1,296	506
1688	12,129	–	–	842	648	1,079
1689	11,574	–	–	576	903	1,132

Sources: 1671-1678, P.R.O. CO 1/43, fo. 59. Given as aggregates, from June 1671-1674, 1675-1677, and 1678; 1682-1689, P.R.O. CO 142/13. These figures are taken from the Naval Officer's returns which were kept to ensure compliance with the Navigation Acts. Thus, they include only legal exports to England or English colonies. It is evident from merchants' papers that illegal exports sent directly ot Europe or via the Dutch entrepôt at Curaçao were very to considerable also. The table excludes indigo and cocoa exports in the 1680s as there is no standard unit of measurement in the records.

combined. Production more than quadrupled between the 1720s and the 1770s and aggregate levels of capital investment must have increased in similar measure.[8] However, as contemporary planters remarked, "a plantation once made may be improved to as much as one will only by its own produce".[9] Once the sugar industry was established the plough-back of profits meant that expansion could be self-financing.[10] This paper looks at the early period when the first English settlers faced the daunting task of amassing the resources to get sugar planting underway – to clear the land; build roads, houses, forts, harbours; support the labour force until the first crops appeared. This was the period when the colonists' need for outside assistance was apparently at its height.

Jamaica was seized by the English in 1655 and was their last Caribbean acquisition in the seventeenth century. The settlers were spared the experimental phase passed through in earlier colonies in which pioneers searched for profitable cash crops and ways to man the fields. Already Barbados had demonstrated the potential profits of tropical agriculture with a firmly established sugar and slave economy. This island, lauded as "one of the richest spots of ground in the wordell"[11] provided a model for Jamaica which her English masters successfully

emulated by the early eighteenth century. This achievement was impressive. The English conquerors had inherited little from the Spaniards, who had scarcely settled or planted the island;[12] Jamaica had only seven sugar works in 1655 producing negligible quantities.[13] In the first decade progress was slow and in 1671 there were still only 57 sugar plantations.[14] Clearly many were as yet in their infancy, as legal exports were only about 1,000 hogsheads (containing 1,000 lbs. each) per annum.[15] Thereafter, progress accelerated. A map of 1685 shows that Jamaica had 246 sugar plantations.[16] By 1689 Jamaican sugar production was over 12,000 hogsheads per year and was approaching the Barbadian level of 15,000 to 20,000 hogsheads (Table 14.1). The French wars caused considerable disruption; progress was temporarily halted. However, it was resumed after the Treaty of Utrecht in 1713, after which Jamaica quickly became England's leading sugar producer.[17]

The Barbadian model for agricultural development was expensive. A sugar plantation, with its combination of industrial and agricultural operations, required a very large-scale capital investment by seventeenth-century standards. The costs of raising a working plantation of 100 acres are laid out in Tables 14.2a and 14.2b which are based on a computation made by

Table 14.2a. Capital Cost of Raising a Plantation of 100 Acres in Jamaica, 1690

	£	s.	d.
50 blacks at average inventoried value of £16 12s.	830	0	0
7 white servants at average inventoried value of £12 for 4 years' service	84	0	0
3 artists which are paid wages	–	–	–
5 horses at average inventoried value of £5	25	0	0
8 bullocks at average inventoried value of £2 4s.	17	12	0
Purchase of uncleared land	–	–	–
Costs of land clearance – 3 years working charges on the plantation as shown in Table 14.2b.	988	19	0
Stills, mills, coppers, etc.; clothes, tools, provisions	1,000	0	0
Interest at 8% p.a. on capital investment for first 3 yers	674	19	10
	3,620	10	10

Table 14.2b. Annual Charges Incurred on the Same Plantation

	£	s.	d.
Wages for 3 artists at 30 shillings per month	54	0	0
Wear and tear on tools, according to Thomas	60	0	0
Clothes and provisions, according to Thomas	120	0	0
Replacement at 10% p.a. of			
Slaves	83	0	0
Servants	8	8	0
Livestock	4	5	0
	329	13	0

Sources: Dalby Thomas, *An Historical Account of the Rise and Growth of the West India Colonies* (1690), pp. 14-15; Jamaica Archives, Spanish Town, Inventories 1B/11/3, III; Lynch to Lord Cornbury, 29 March 1672, B.L. Add. MS 11410 fos. 525-33; Somerset Record Office, Taunton, Helyar MSS, DD/WIIh 1089-90, 1151 Addenda Papers 12.

Dalby Thomas in 1690.[18] However, as Thomas was pleading the case for a reduction in sugar duties he wanted to show that planters' profits were being squeezed and it is assumed he weighted the evidence accordingly. Where possible, his values have been replaced by figures taken from Jamaican inventories and trade papers of the same period. The resulting calculation that it required almost £4,000 to raise a working plantation is borne out by other contemporary comments.[19]

A planter who made an investment of £3,620 could eventually expect a reasonable return even when Jamaican sugar prices were at their lowest as in 1688 (Table 14.3). The annual anticipated output of 80 hogsheads of sugar and 28 hogsheads of molasses on Thomas' plantation[20] would produce a turnover of about £702 per annum in 1688; a net income of £372 7s. (10.28

per cent) if no interest is charged on the capital; a net income of £82 14s. (2.28 per cent) if interest is charged at 8 per cent, a typical level in Jamaica at this time.[21] The rates of return would be substantially greater at 12.46 per cent and 4.46 per cent respectively if allowance is made for a capital appreciation in land values at much the same level as the interest rate of 8 per cent. However the planter could not expect to see any visible return for at least three years after he made the initial investment. A sugar planter needed not only plentiful cash resources to invest, but also had to be in a position to defer gratification for several years. As Governor Thomas Lynch remarked, "planting is a work of time, it requires vast expense . . . wherefore who will plant, must (like the builders in the Gospel) take their measures beforehand, and furnish themselves with money and patience."[22]

Table 14.3. Returns on a Sugar Plantation, 1688

		£	s.	d.	
a)	Capital investment (Table 14.2a)	3,620	10	10	
	Annual charges (Table 14.2b)	329	13	0	
	Average price per hogshead of sugar and molasses in Jamaica	6	10	0	
	Annual turnover	702	0	0	
	Capital appreciation in value of cleared land at 8% p.a.	79	0	0	
	Annual production	80hh. sugar and 28hh. molasses			

		£	s.	d.	Per cent of capital investment
b)	Net income (without interest on capital)	372	7	0	10.28
	Net income + 8% capital appreciation in land value (without interest on capital)	451	7	0	12.46
	Net income (with 8% interest on capital)	82	14	0	2.28
	Net income + 8% capital appreciation in land value (with 8 % interest on capital)	61	14	0	4.46

Clearly it needed a large-scale capital investment to establish Jamaican agriculture in the seventeenth century. Whilst it is not possible to calculate the aggregate sum with precision the preceding calculations do suggest various indicators. They show that it cost £45 5s. to produce one hogshead of sugar per year in good conditions. This indicates that there had been an investment of £540,330 5s. in order to produce the island's annual average recorded exports of 11,941 hogsheads between 1686 and 1689. If allowance is made for illegal exports, which were reported to be considerable,[23] and the many misfortunes which could befall a plantation, the investment must have been far greater.

The main cost of sugar planting was labour. One acre in canes produced one hogshead of sugar per year in good conditions and required one man to cultivate it (Table 14.4). Surviving inventories confirm the literary evidence that, despite concern about security risks, Jamaican planting was largely based on black slave labour from the first. They reveal a servant to slave ratio of 1 to 24 in 1674-1675 and 1 to 54 in 1686-1696 (Table 14.5). This acquisition of a large slave labour force required a substantial outlay and provides yet another indication of the scale of the capital resources required to establish Jamaica's plantation economy. By 1689 the island's 5,000 or so whites owned about 25,000 slaves (Table

14.6). The inventories surviving for the period 1686 to 1689 give an average value of £16 12s. for a slave so that the black labour force was worth at least £415,000. But, the planters needed to spend perhaps twice this sum to acquire their 25,000 slaves as very high mortality rates and desertion caused substantial wastage. Assuming a mortality rate of 10 per cent per annum (as in the estimates in Table 14.6), planters would have had to buy 30,000 slaves between 1680 and 1689 to increase the total from 21,500 to 25,000. This represents an investment of £498,000 in that decade alone, an annual outlay of £49,800.

Table 14.4. Labour Requirements of Sugar Plantation described by Dalby Thomas, 1690

Plantation size	100 acres
Number of slaves	50
Area in cane	80 acres
(area harvested annually)	40 acres
Slaves per acre harvested	1.2
Annual production of muscovado	80 hogsheads (of 1,000 lbs.)
Annual production of muscovado per slave	1,600 lbs.

Source: Dalby Thomas, An Historical Account of the Rise and Growth of the West India Colonies (1690), pp. 14-15.

Table 14.5.   Number of Servants and Slaves on Jamaican Plantations, 1674-5 and 1686-96

	Number of servants											
1674-1675	0	1	2	3	4	5	6	7	8	9	10	Total
Number of plantations with												
0- 10 slaves	25	2	1	–	–	–	–	–	–	–	–	
11- 20	8	1	1	1	–	–	–	–	–	–	–	
21- 50	8	2	3	1	–	–	–	–	1	–	–	
51-100	1	–	–	2	–	1	–	–	–	–	1	
101 +	1	–	–	–	–	–	–	–	–	–	–	
Number of plantations	43	5	5	4	–	1	–	–	1	–	1	60
Number of slaves	718	85	83	165	–	55	–	–	44	–	60	1,210
Number of slaves per plantation	17	17	17	41	–	55	–	–	44	–	60	20
Slave to servant ratio		17	8	14	–	11	–	–	5.5	–	6	24

	Number of servants												
1686-1696	0	1	2	3	4	5	6	7	8	9	10	11	Total
Number of plantations with													
0- 10 slaves	52	5	–	–	–	–	–	–	–	–	–	–	57
11- 20	29	6	1	–	–	–	–	–	–	–	–	–	36
21- 50	26	2	1	2	–	–	–	–	–	–	–	–	31
51-100	12	1	3	1	2	–	2	–	–	–	1	–	22
101+	4	–	–	–	–	–	–	–	–	–	–	1	5
Number of plantations	123	14	5	3	2	–	2	–	–	–	1	1	151
Number of slaves	2,856	266	259	112	184	–	161	–	–	–	64	106	4,008
Number of slaves per plantation	23	19	52	37	92	–	81	–	–	–	64	106	27
Slave to servant ratio		19	26	12	23	–	13	–	–	–	6	11	54

Source: Inventories, Jamaica Archives, Inv. 1B/11/3, I and III

Did this large capital investment made in Jamaican agriculture flow from the mother country as Adam Smith suggested? The manner in which Jamaica was acquired had a considerable bearing on this question. Unlike earlier colonial projects Jamaican settlement was not initiated by a joint stock company or lords proprietors, who might have provided the first capital.[24] The Jamaican project was backed by the state, but more by accident than design. The island was a consolation prize acquired in what was little more than a state-sponsored buccaneering raid on the Spanish Indies;[25] a venture conceived with the intention of making a large, immediate profit in Spanish treasure, not a long-term investment in agriculture.[26] England did retain Jamaica but neither Cromwell, nor his successors, felt disposed to spend money on it. Land was reserved for the state, but it was never developed and was finally abandoned in 1678.[27]

Other outside interests were equally reluctant to make a direct investment in Jamaican agriculture. This is not very surprising. The dramatic profits of the early sugar days in Barbados were over. The returns now looked far less tempting. Production had outstripped demand, and the English price of muscovado fell by 60 per cent from about 40 shillings per hundredweight in 1660 to a low point of 16 shillings per hundredweight in 1686/1687.[28] It was still possible to make a handsome profit from a sugar plantation, even when prices were at bottom, as shown in Table 14.3. However, these profits depended on close, careful supervision of the estate as many an unhappy absentee owner discovered. One such was William Helyar, an English squire who inherited a Jamaican sugar plantation from his brother in 1672. Under the management of irresponsible and corrupt overseers the estate never yielded a penny profit except when the squire's

Table 14.6. The Population of Jamaica, 1662-1689

	1662	1670	1673	1680	1689
White men	2,458	3,000	4,050	c. 4,000	
women	454	1,200	2,006		
children	448		1,712		
Total whites	3,360	4,200	7,768	c. 5,600	c. 4,600
Privateers	1,500	1,500-2,000	1,500	1,200	1,200
Negroes	514	2,500	9,504	21,500	25,000

Sources: 1662: P.R.O. CO 1/15, fo. 192.
1670: Ibid., CO 1/25, fo. 5.
1673: Journals of House of Assembly of Jamaica, 1663-1826 (Jamaica, 1811-29), I, pp. 20, 28.
   There is no head count available for 1680 or 1689. Figures for 1680 based on the Naval Officer's information on arrivals, 1673-1679. The figure for blacks was doubled to allow for illegal deliveries; both figures were adjusted to allow for a mortality rate of 10% p.a. P.R.O. CO 1/43, fo. 59.
   1689: Figure for whites based on annual average arrivals calculated from the Naval Officer's Returns, 1686-1688. The figure for blacks is based on the Royal African Company's deliveries 1680-1689, doubled to allow for illegal deliveries and then reduced by 25% to allow for sales to the Spaniards. Both figures were adjusted to allow for a mortality rate of 10% p.a. P.R.O. CO 142/13; T 70/10, 12, 15, 16; T 70/938-944. The mortality rate is based on planters' expectations in the 1680s. For example, Bodleian Library, Oxford, MS Rawl. A348, fo. 4, "Affairs and instructions for the care of a plantation".
   The figure for slaves is broadly confirmed by the following check. Map of 1685 shows 690 plantations; average number of slaves per plantation in inventories, 1684-1694 is 27. This gives totals of 18,630 slaves. In addition there was an estimated 1,500 slaves in Port Royal and Spanish Town. Total 19,630 slaves.
   The trends are also confirmed by literary evidence. Contemporaries remarked that the white population barely maintained itself in the 1670s and declined in the 1680s. Meanwhile, the black population increased rapidly. P.R.O. CO 138/3, fo. 332, Carlisle to Coventry, 15 Sept. 1679; Institute of Jamaica, Kingston, MS 159, fo. 63. The State of Jamaica under Lord Vaughan; P.R.O. CO 138/7, fo. 129, President and Council to Committee, Sept. 28, 1692; P.R.O. CO 138/9, fo. 14, Some Considerations Relating to the Island of Jamaica, Oct. 1696.

own son took brief control in the 1680s.[29] As Lynch remarked "servants, attorneys, etc. are apt to dye or remove, and this ayre I think disposes people more to covetnousness yn yt of Europe . . . those that are absent can do nothing, but loose all".[30] Absentee investment in sugar planting was a very risky and generally unattractive proposition.

The pattern of land ownership was reflected in a survey of Jamaica of 1670. This shows that a total of almost 210,000 acres had been patented.[31] Contemporaries observed that those aiming to produce cash crops would usually patent over 1,000 acres. There was only one absentee amongst the 13 men with tracts larger than 2,000 acres; Lord Clarendon whose portion was totally uncultivated. The 34 patentees with between 1,000 and 2,000 acres revealed a similar pattern. Of the 26 who could be identified, 25 were residents. There was only one absentee, Josiah Childe, who patented land in partnership with Samuel Bache, a Port Royal merchant. Clearly the group of 47 men who possessed over

1,000 acres (an aggregate of 80,386 acres, or 42.5 per cent of the total patented by 1670) were overwhelmingly Jamaican residents. There was no similar survey at the end of the period, but it is clear that the pattern of land ownership changed little. The file of Land Patents in the Jamaica Archives shows that at least 74 out of the 88 persons who patented over 2,000 acres in the seventeenth century were residents. A sample of conveyances in the Island Record Office in Spanish Town indicates that sales were also overwhelmingly among residents.

Outside interests were almost as wary of making an indirect as a direct investment in early Jamaican planting. The inventories and deeds in the Island Record Office show that it was unusual for planters to owe money outside the island. Meanwhile, there was an active internal credit market. The one important outside creditor was the Royal African Company. The total amount owed to it in Jamaica rose from £56,583 to about £100,000 in 1689.[32] Almost half of this was short-term credit given to planters. Part was interest.[33] However, even the total sum represents the value of only 5,422 slaves at the average inventoried value of £16 12s. or about 10 per cent of the total numbers delivered to the island.

Unwillingness in England to become too heavily involved in the risky business of funding a distant colonial venture is reflected in the dispersed nature of Jamaican trade. The London port books indicate that a large number of individuals were involved in trade with the island, mainly in a small way. Between 29 December 1685 and 30 June 1686, 298 merchants imported goods from Jamaica in 30 ships. Of these, only 62 people had goods on more than one ship, and only 20 had goods on three or more ships.[34] These mainly small-scale adventurers might have felt able to extend short-term trade credit to their Jamaican customers but few wished to make the large, and frequently risky, long-term investment necessary to get Jamaican planting under way.

It is clear that it was largely left to the early Jamaican residents to make what they could of the island's agricultural potential. Outsiders played little part. How did the first colonists accumulate the necessary resources? Very few arrived with sufficient capital to develop a plantation. There was no large-scale transfer of capital (see number of slaves brought from the other colonies, Table 14.7) and expertise from the smaller islands, despite their complaints about land shortage and soil exhaustion.[35] The conquering expedition did recruit 4,000 men (mainly indentured servants) in the Caribbean, but few survived even the first year of settlement. After this, West Indians displayed a marked reluctance to transfer to Jamaica (Table 14.7). Sugar probably did not seem to offer rich enough rewards in this period to offset the stories of disease, death and general gloom which circulated from Jamaica. Some planters of substance made the move – Luke Stokes, Sir Thomas Modyford, who was appointed governor in 1664, the two groups of settlers from Surinam in the 1670s; but they were few and far between. It was often remarked that those who did transfer to Jamaica were usually the "looser sorts" who went "in hopes of plunder" – not to plant.[36]

Settlers who arrived from the mother country also came to the Indies in expectation of making a fortune once there: very few brought one with them. Those whom the diarist, John Taylor,

Table 14. 7. Migration to Jamaica from Other Colonies 1671-8 and 1686-9

	Whites	Blacks
1671-4	793	1,491
1675-7	989	1,585
1678	92	95
Total	1,874	3,171
Annual average	296	396
1686	90	82
1687	49	216
1688	46	109
1689	0	86
Total	185	493
Annual average	46	123

Sources: P.R.O. CO 1/43, fo. 59; CO 142/13.

listed as the island's "chief and principal gentlemen and planters" in 1688 were "for the most part (though now rich) formerly rude and of mean birth, men of their wits, which have here advanct their fortune."[37] They were younger sons like Hender Molesworth or Cary Helyar; junior officers like Thomas Lynch; small traders like Peter Beckford; craftsmen like Robert Bindloss who was said to have been a ship's surgeon. Only one of the 12 residents who had patented over 2,000 acres by 1670 came with sufficient capital to set up a plantation: Thomas Modyford, a successful Barbadian planter. The six army officers and the five merchants who made up the group had first to accumulate funds before they could "fall upon planting".[38]

In fact, the early settlers were not first attracted to Jamaica by its future as a plantation. It was often remarked that "few come particularly or only to plant, but to merchandize."[39] Their interest in Jamaica was aroused by its geographical location, "in the Spaniard's bowels and in the heart of his trade."[40] It was this strategic position which attracted settlers to the island and it was their successful exploitation of the location which enabled them to accumulate the necessary resources to begin planting free of overseas ties.

Men had been attracted to the Indies by visions of El Dorado since the first discoveries. The abundant treasure of the mines of Mexico and Peru aroused the avidity of all Europe. Spain

Table 14.8. Ships Trading at Port Royal, 1686–1688

FROM		England	Ireland	Africa	English West Indies	Spanish Ports	North America including Bermuda	Curaçao	Madeira	Wreck	Other	Total
1686	Ships with recorded arrival and departure	11	14	10	4	–	24	2	15	–	–	80
	Ships with recorded arrival but no recorded departure	2	3	4	20	11	20	6	5	–	–	71
1687	Ships with recorded arrival and departure	12	15	7	2	–	17	1	9	1	–	64
	Ships with recorded arrival but no recorded departure	8	9	5	23	6	23	6	6	22	–	108
1688	Ships with recorded arrival and departure	12	12	1	2	2	18	3	11	1	–	62
	Ships with recorded arrival but no recorded departure	11	7	–	20	33	38	8	9	23	2	151

The returns list all vessels coming into port but only record the departure of those heading for England or English colonies, not Spanish destinations.

Source: P.R.O. CO 142/13, Naval Officer's Returns, Jamaica, 1680-1705.

tried to reserve this wealth for herself by declaring a monopoly of trade and navigation in the area; but what others could not have by agreement, the newcomers took by force or stealth – privateers and smugglers raided and traded.[41] As the Spaniards found it increasingly difficult to defend their empire from depredations it was likened to a "dead carcass upon whom all the rest do prey".[42]

The first half of the seventeenth century was the great age of Dutch commercial expansion; the Hollanders turned the Caribbean almost into a Dutch lake.[43] The acquisition of Curaçao in 1634 gave them an ideal base for expanding their trading operations on the Spanish Main. Meanwhile, the English were hampered in both contraband trading and plunder by their lack of a suitable headquarters in the Caribbean.[44] The English settlements which survived this early period were all situated on the periphery of the region, where they were safely away from Spanish harassment, but equally ill-placed to trade or plunder on the Main.[45] The colonists were confined to agricultural development by necessity rather than choice. Jamaica was different. It was "in the centre of the most valuable part of the West Indies at an easy distance from the Spanish settlements."[46] The island was ideally suited for both trade and plunder.

The English founded a town at Port Royal with its large, sheltered harbour immediately after the seizure of Jamaica. The port quickly became a base for freebooting activities against the Spaniards, attracting disorderly elements from all over the Caribbean. In 1663 Jamaica had a fleet of 15 privateers. By 1670, the island had over 20 such vessels with about 2,000 men.[47] Marauders continued to operate from Port Royal throughout the seventeenth century despite the Anglo-Spanish Treaty of Madrid, promising peace and friendship in 1670. Both opponents and advocates of so-called "forced trade" declared that the town's fortune had the dubious distinction of being founded entirely on the servicing of the privateers' needs and a highly lucrative trade in prize commodities.[48] A report that the 300 men who accompanied Henry Morgan to Portobello in 1668 returned to the town with prize to spend of at least £60 each (two or three times the usual annual plantation wage) leaves little doubt that they were right.[49] Although Jamaican planting had scarcely begun (Table

14.1), the port's trade increased fivefold in the 1660s. It attracted about 20 ships a year in 1660, and 100 by the end of the decade.[50] As Governor Lynch admitted in 1671, scarcely one quarter of what was shipped from the island was of its own growth.[51] The Portobello raid alone produced plunder worth £75,000,[52] more than seven times the annual value of the island's sugar exports, which at Port Royal prices did not exceed £10,000 at this time.

Port Royal was also ideally situated for contraband trade with the Spanish colonists. Foreigners had long obtained a substantial share of the official Spanish colonial trade which was conducted in two, supposedly annual, fleets from Seville or Cadiz. The goods were shipped to Portobello and Vera Cruz where they were exchanged for rich American commodities, mainly bullion. However, the traders' profits were eroded by innumerable difficulties and delays, particularly as the fleets became increasingly irregular and high defence costs pushed up charges.[53] The advantages of direct trade via a base in the Caribbean were apparent to both sellers and customers. Suppliers reduced costs and delays considerably (Peter Beckford, a Port Royal merchant, reckoned that direct trade reduced shipping and freight charges to half what they were with the fleets),[54] which enabled them to increase turnover and profits. The Spanish colonists could buy goods more cheaply and dispose of their own products more regularly which was particularly important if they were *selling perishable agricultural commodities. The economic logic was too strong to be denied and,* despite the Spanish authorities persistent refusal to condone the trade, it grew and flourished, attracting merchants to Port Royal who participated on their own, and their correspondents' behalf.[55] Part of this trade was conducted in the island's own sloop fleet, stimulating its growth from 40 in 1670 to 80 in 1679 and about 100 in 1689.[56] A further considerable part was carried on by English and colonial ships which called at Port Royal before making for the Spanish Indies, but did not return to Jamaica on their way home. Reginald Wilson, the Naval Officer, reported that 40 of the 87 ships which had sailed from Port Royal in 1679, had gone on to trade with the Spaniards in this way.[57] A close examination of Wilson's returns in the 1680s suggests that it continued to be usual for about half the ships

entering Port Royal to be destined for Spanish markets[58] (ships with a recorded arrival but no recorded departure in Table 14.8). Jamaican agents hired skilled supercargoes and strengthened the ships' crews, earning commission for their services.[59] Contemporary comment confirms the importance of the Jamaican entrepôt trade and, as Cary remarked in 1695, its steady growth was also reflected in a decline of English commerce by the old route to the Indies, via Old Spain.[60]

The contraband trade was mainly carried on "underhand" in bays and creeks or the smaller towns. The larger, strongly fortified towns of Portobello, Cartagena and Havana were more difficult and risky to penetrate. The one commodity which could open their doors was slaves, for the Spaniards did not pretend to provide them for themselves, and so had to turn to a middleman who did. The contractors, or *asientistas*, obtained supplies where they could and Jamaica was ideally situated to serve them; transport costs being 20 per cent lower than they were from the rival Dutch base at Curaçao.[61] There is no record of a formal agreement to supply the Spaniards in the early years but there are references to their coming to Jamaica. By the 1680s the trade was substantial. The African Company alone sold about 25 per cent of its annual supplies to the Spaniards (i.e. an average of about 500 slaves, see Table 14.9) and there are also records of large sales by interlopers. However, it was a small group of merchants who benefited

Table 14.9. Royal African Company's Deliveries to Jamaica,1680-1689

	No. of ships	No. of slaves delivered
1680	7	1,602
1681	5	1,561
1682	5	1,577
1683	9	1,892
1684	8	1,905
1685	9	1,908
1686	14	3,574
1687	11	3,075
1688	1	103
1689	7	2,176
Total	76	19,373
Annual Average	7.6	1,937

Sources: P.R.O. T 70/10, 12, 15, 16; T 70/938-944; CO 142/13.

Table 14.10. Population of Port Royal, 1662-1679

	Whites	Blacks	Total	Privateers
1662	630	40	670	1,500
1673	1,669	312	1,981	1,500
1680	2,086	845	2,931	1,200
1689	Approx. 4,000	not available	not available	1,200

Sources: P.R.O. CO 1/15, fo. 192. 'A Brief Account of the Several Inhabitants in the Precincts in the Island', 1662; Journals of Jamaican Assembly, app. 1, p. 40; P.R.O. CO 1/45, fos. 97-109, 'Account of Inhabitants both masters and servants of Port Royal Parish', 26 May 1680. Unfortunately, there is no reliable figure for 1689. The diarist, Taylor, who was prone to exaggerate, claimed that the town had 5,000 white inhabitants and as many slaves in 1688. Institute of Jamaica, Kingston, MS 105, fo. 499. In 1692 the Council asserted that before the earthquake the town could muster 2,000 men which suggests that the total white population was about 4,000. P.R.O. CO 138/7, fo. 129, President and Council to Committee of Trade, Sept. 28, 1692.

most. They bought slaves from the African Company, then sold them to the Spaniards, providing their customers with an armed convoy and accepting payment in the Spanish home port. The Spaniards paid 35 per cent extra for this convenience.[62] It was a highly lucrative and relatively safe business which was, as the planter John Helyar remarked, "a much easier way of making money than making sugar".[63] The *asiento* trade also provided Jamaican merchants with an opportunity to smuggle manufactured goods into the major Spanish towns, which had proved so difficult to penetrate.[64]

Unfortunately the lack of detailed statistical evidence makes it impossible to quantify the value of Port Royal's Spanish trades, either peaceful or forced, with any precision. However, their combined importance is clear. It was most obviously reflected in the unusual abundance of cash in Jamaica, which enabled the islanders to use coins as currency, rather than commodities as in other colonies. In 1683 a visitor remarked that "there was more plenty of running cash proportionately to the number of its inhabitants than is in London."[65] Furthermore, although there were no continuous figures for Jamaica's bullion exports a number of scattered estimates show that they were considerable. Governor Lord Inchiquin claimed that the fleet carried away £100,000 worth of bullion in 1690,[66] whereas sugar exports recorded by the Naval Officer the previous year were worth only £88,000 at the current inland price. In addition a large quantity of bullion was earned in the entrepôt trade with the Spanish colonies and shipped straight back to England.

The value of the Spanish commerce is also indicated by the fact that the growth and prosperity of Port Royal predated the development of the agricultural hinterland. Although the island's sugar trade was in its infancy the port's white population increased from 630 in 1662 to almost 3,000 in 1680 and 3,000 to 4,000 in 1689, making it the largest English town in the Caribbean[67] (Table 14.10). The importance of trading opportunities in attracting people to Port Royal is shown by the very large number of merchants in the town. There are 118 Port Royal inventories surviving from the period 1686-1694, a fairsized sample of a town with about 1,000 households in 1689; 49 of these were merchants.

Port Royal was also the busiest port in the English Caribbean. By the 1680s the Naval Officer's returns show that it was attracting 150 to 200 ships a year. Barbados was still the leading English sugar producer but in 1688, the only complete year for which figures survive in this period, it attracted only 102 ships (although they were of slightly higher average tonnage).[68]

Visitors remarked on Port Royal's easy lifestyle. Taylor, the diarist, described the merchants and gentry living "in the height of splendour", served by negro slaves in livery. The craftsmen also lived better than in England. There was plentiful employment and wages were three times as high as at home. There was abundant food. Three daily markets were well stocked with fruit, fish and meat. Luxuries were easily available too. There was also a wealth of entertainment: a bear-garden, cock-fighting, billiards, music houses, shooting at targets and also "all manner of debauchery" which the prudish

Table 14.11. Values of Port Royal Inventories, 1674-1694

Value in £	Volume I 1674-1675		Volume II 1679-1686		Volume III 1686-1694	
	No.	%	No.	%	No.	%
0–49	8	20.5	7	13	11	9
50–99	8	20.5	7	13	20	17
100–499	10	25	16	30	47	39.5
500–999	7	18	13	24	14	12
1,000–1,999	4	10	6	11	10	8
2,000+	2	5	5	9	17	14
Total	39		54		119	

Source: Jamaica Archives, Inv. 1B/11/3, I-III, Inventories 1674-94.

blamed upon "the privateers and debauched wild blades which come hither". Many raised eyebrows at the large number of alehouses and the "crue of vile strumpets and common prostratures" which crowded the town, undeterred by frequent imprisonment in a cage near the harbour.[69] All this reflected the surplus cash in the place. The Port Royal inventories which survive from the period 1674-1694 also indicate that it was a prosperous town. In the whole period 44 out of a total of 212 left estates worth over £1,000 (Table 14.11). This suggests that the townspeople had succeeded in making themselves at least as rich as their famous New England counterparts.[70] As Taylor remarked "with the help of the Spaniards' purse" inhabitants of the island "have advanced their fortune" and were now rich.[71]

The successful exploitation of Jamaica's strategic geographical location, and the rise of Port Royal as a trading post based on Spanish plunder and contraband, provided the early residents with the capital necessary to embark on plantation agriculture. William Claypole's study of the extensive land records available in Jamaica indicates that Port Royal's merchants provided the largest source of capital investment in agriculture.[72] Many patented and planted land on their own account – at least 275 of 508 merchants identified in Port Royal between 1664 and 1700 purchased agricultural property. Twelve of the 23 Port Royal estates inventoried as over £2,000 indicate an involvement in a plantation. The debts listed in the inventories also show that Port Royal's residents were the major source of credit for the planters. Port Royal grew rich "out of the

Spaniard's purse": the profits of trading and looting were used to build up Jamaica's plantations.

The mechanism is clearly reflected in Taylor's list of the island's "principal gentlemen and planters" in 1688.[73] Almost without exception their debt to the Spaniards is apparent. The most telling example was Henry Morgan, the most celebrated of the privateers, who built up a substantial plantation with 122 negroes, valued at £5,263 on his death.[74] Lynch, Molesworth, Beeston, Bindloss and the others had all participated in Port Royal's rise as a trading post.[75] The most spectacularly successful of these early immigrants was Peter Beckford who arrived in Port Royal in 1661 "bred a seaman and merchant" and at first prospered by doing business in prize commodities.[76] In the 1680s he was *asiento* agent in Jamaica.[77] Meanwhile he also began to patent and plant land.[78] When he died in 1710 he had accumulated 20 estates, 1,200 slaves and had founded, what Noel Deerr described as "perhaps the greatest fortune ever made in planting."[79]

Adam Smith was wrong. The prosperity of Jamaica was not "owing to the great riches of England of which a part had overflowed".[80] Plantation agriculture in Jamaica was largely financed by Spanish silver earned in a lucrative illicit trade based on plunder and contraband. Nor did the investment of these illicit gains in Jamaican agriculture represent a diversion of capital away from what would have been more profitable employment in the mother country. Table 14.3 shows that, even at the end of the period when sugar prices were at their lowest, the net return on a well-managed plantation, unencumbered by debt, was 10.3 per cent (without capital appreciation on the land). This was higher than typical rates of return on rentier-type investment in England.[81] However, there was not, as yet, any mechanism by which a merchant making his living in Port Royal could make a safe, trouble-free investment of his surplus funds in England. There was no government stock and it was risky to make loans or an investment in land without personal supervision. Capital and entrepreneurship are most effective when combined, and rates of return suffer if one or the other is missing. The importance of "enterprise" as a contributory factor of production, with higher returns in Jamaica than in England, made capital far less mobile than might at first seem possible. The failure to recognize this is a prime flaw in the argument that colonies brought "more loss than profit".

Furthermore, the high individual returns to planters and merchants in Jamaican trade were not offset by low or negative social returns in the early period. Defence and administration costs incurred in the mother country were nominal. The island did not have a standing army after the disbandment of Cromwell's troops in 1662. There were never more than two naval frigates stationed at the island in this period. Frequently there were none at all. The governors' expenses and salary were usually paid out of the proceeds of local taxation and prize goods. The Navigation Acts, which compelled the colonial producers to send their sugar to the mother country, rather than to the market of their choice, tended to reinforce the price fall of the 1670s and 1680s in England caused by supply outstripping demand. Thus, in this period, they operated in favour of the home consumer rather than the colonial producer.[82]

The wealth of Jamaica was created out of the profits of Jamaica; far from supporting the liberal theory that empire was a cost and burden on the mother country, the island provides a good example of imperialism as theft,[83] albeit by one colonial power from another, rather than by a developed from a developing country. It was plunder and illegal trade which provided England's largest sugar producer with much of its initial capital. Smith's contemporary, the planter historian William Beckford, was justified in this case in asserting that

the person who acquires a competence in another country does not draw any wealth from his own, at the same time that which he makes or at least the greater part of it flows back again to enrich the parent stream.[84]

England was able to drain some of "the benefit of the Spanish gold and silver mines" without the "labour and expense" of working them.[85] Nothing could have been more attractive in a mercantilist world!

Notes

1.   Adam Smith, *An Inquiry into the Nature and Causes of the Wealth of Nations* (1776), II, p. 587.

2.   "When, by the act of navigation, England assumed to herself the monopoly of the colonial trade, the foreign capitals which had before been employed in it were necessarily withdrawn from it. The English capital which had before carried on but a part of it was now to carry on the whole … [prior to this] the island of Jamaica was an unwholesome desart, little inhabited and less cultivated." Smith contrasted French and English colonial development in the West Indies. "The stock, it is to be observed which has improved the sugar colonies of France … has been raised almost entirely from the gradual improvement and cultivation of those colonies … But the stock which has improved and cultivated the sugar colonies of England has, a great part of it, been sent out from England, and has by no means been altogether the produce of the soil and industry of the colonies." Ibid. pp. 187, 197,199.

3.   Smith expands his views on the financing of the colonies in the sections "Causes of the prosperity of new colonies" and "Of the Advantages which Europe has derived from the discovery of America." Ibid. pp. 157-256.

4.   R.P. Thomas, 'The Sugar Colonies of the Old Empire: Profit or Loss for Great Britain,' *Economic History Review*, 2nd ser. XXI (1968), pp. 30-45; P.R.P. Coelho, 'The Profitability of Imperialism: The British Experience in the West Indies, 1768-1772,' *Explorations in Economic History*, X (1973), pp. 253-80. Sheridan presents the counter argument that the West Indies yielded an economic surplus which contributed to the growth of the metropolitan economy. R. Sheridan, 'The Wealth of Jamaica in the Eighteenth Century,' *Econ. Hist. Rev.* 2nd ser. XVIII (1965), pp. 293-311; idem, 'The Wealth of Jamaica in the Eighteenth Century: A Rejoinder,' ibid. XXI (1968), pp. 46-61. Also see, F.W. Pitman, *The Development of the British West Indies, 1700-63* (New Haven, Conn. 1971), pp. 334-60; Eric Williams, *Capitalism and Slavery* (Chapel Hill, N. Carolina, 1944), pp. 209-12.

5.   The southern colonies were highly valued by contrast with the 'Northward parts' which were seen as very injurious to the mother country. "The Northward parts have drained us most of people and yet

yield commodities of little value": Charles D'Avenant. 'On the Plantation Trade' (1698), in *The Political and Commercial Works of Charles D'Avenant*, ed. C. Whitworth (1771), II, p. 20. See also Josiah Child, *A New Discourse of Trade* (1692), pp. 204-6; John Cary, *An Essay on the State of England in Relation to its Trade* (Bristol, 1695), pp. 68-70, 204-205.

6.   R. Davis, 'English Foreign Trade, 1660-1700,' *Econ. Hist. Rev.* 2nd ser. VII (1954), pp. 150-66; idem, 'English Foreign Trade, 1700-1774,' ibid. XV (1962), pp. 285-303; R. Dunn, *Sugar and Slaves* (Chapel Hill, N. Carolina, 1972), p. 188.

7.   Thomas Tryon, *Tryon's Letters, Domestick and Foreign to Several Persons of Quality Occasionally Distributed in Subjects* (1700), p. 221.

8.   R. Sheridan, *Sugar and Slavery: An Economic History of the British West Indies, 1623-1775* (Barbados, 1974), pp. 487-9.

9.   B.L. Add. MS 11410, fo. 527, Sir Thomas Lynch to Lord Cornbury, 29 March 1671.

10.   Robert Nash claims that the growing indebtedness of the West Indies after the 1730s came from financing conspicuous consumption amongst the planters rather than financing the sugar industry. R. Nash, 'English Transatlantic Trade, 1660-1730: A Quantitative Study' (unpublished Ph.D. thesis, University of Cambridge, 1982), pp. 31-51.

11.   B.L. Sloane MS 3926, fo. 8, 'Henry Whistler's Journal.'

12.   F. Cundall and J. Pietersz, *Jamaica Under the Spaniards* (Kingston, Jamaica, 1919).

13.   'Letters Concerning the English Expedition into the Spanish West Indies in 1655,' in C.H. Firth, ed. *The Narrative of General Venables* (1900), p. 139.

14 .   B.L. Map K123 (44), 'Novissima et Accuratissima Jamaicae Descriptio per Johannum Ogilivium,' 1671.

15.   P.R.O. CO 1/43, fo. 59, 'An Accompt of what Passengers, Servants and Slaves has been brought to this Island with account of what goods hath been exported from 25 January 1671 to 25 March 1679' (hereafter 'Account of what . . . brought to this Island').

16.   B.L. Map 80710 (17), 'A New Map of the Island of Jamaica,' 1685.

17.   Sheridan, *Sugar and Slavery*, pp. 487-9.

18.   Dalby Thomas, *An Historical Account of the Rise and Growth of the West India Colonies* (1690), pp. 14-15.

19.   B.L. Add. MS 11410, fo. 532, Lynch to Cornbury, 29 March 1672.

20.   Thomas expected one acre to yield one hogshead per annum. Thomas, *Historical Account*, pp. 14-15. However the yield of sugar per acre varied widely according to site conditions and levels of management. One writer gave the following information about classes of yields of muscovado: for *plant cane*, 3,200 pounds per acre, "uncommonly great" 2,400 pounds per acre, "10 per cent of all estates"; 1,600 pounds per acre, "may be a saving average"; for *ratoons* 1,600 pounds per acre, "very few"; 1,200 pounds per acre, "good"; 800 pounds per acre,

"above the common medium". Anonymous, *Remarks Upon a Book, Entitled, The Present State of the Sugar Colonies Considered* (1731).

21.   Interest rates usually exceeded English levels in the Caribbean. S.A. Fortune, *Merchants and Jews: The Struggle for British West Indian Commerce, 1650-1750* (Gainesville, Florida, 1984), p. 155. At times they soared. Sir James Modyford's transactions in 1668 reveal "the bare interest of this place" was 16 per cent. By courtesy of the Dean and Chapter of Westminster, Westminster Abbey Muniments (hereafter W.A.M.), 11921, Sir James Modyford to Sir Andrew King, 4 Nov. 1668.

22.   B.L. Add. MS 11410, fo. 532, Lynch to Cornbury, 29 March 1672.

23.   The frequent contemporary assertions that the Navigation laws were widely ignored by the Jamaicans are confirmed by evidence in merchants' papers. P.R.O. C 110/152, Chancery Masters Exhibits, Brailsford v. peers (hereafter Brailsford papers), Halls to Brailsford, 25 Sept. 1688, 20 Sept. 1689.

24.   R. Pares, *Merchants and Planters* (Cambridge, 1960), pp. 1-14.

25.   Cromwell had no provocation for his attack which was launched while Spain was trying to negotiate an alliance with England. A. MacFayden, 'Anglo-Spanish Relations, 1625-1660', (unpublished Ph.D. thesis, University of Liverpool, 1967), pp. 56-65.

26.   B.L. Add. MS 11410, fos. 61-80, 'A Copie of the Original Design upon which Cromwell sett out the fleet for the taking of the island of Hispaniola'.

27.   P.R.O. CO 138/3, fo. 482, Carlisle to Robert Southwell, 11 July 1681.

28.   J.R. Ward, 'The Profitability of Sugar Planting in the British West Indies, 1650-1834', *Econ. Hist. Rev.* 2nd ser. XXXI (1978), pp. 197-213; Dunn, *Sugar and Slaves*, p. 205; Sheridan, *Sugar and Slavery*, pp. 496-7.

29.   Somerset Record Office, Taunton (hereafter S.R.O.), Helyar MSS, DD/WHh 1089-90. 1151 Addenda Papers 12.

30.   B.L. Add. MS 11410, fo. 532, Lynch to Cornbury, 29 March 1672.

31.   P.R.O. CO 138/1, fos. 61-80, 'Survey of Jamaica,' 1670.

32.   P.R.O. T 70/16, fo. 52; P.R.O. CO 138/6, fo. 227, 'Petition of Royal African Company,' 15 July 1689.

33.   Interest charges were high. "The company with their own chapmen . . . taking twenty per cent the first six months and fifteen after." P.R.O. CO 138/3, fo. 479, 'Paper presented by Planters of Jamaica to Lords of Trade', 1680.

34.   P.R.O. E 190/143/1, London Overseas Imports by Denizens, 1686.

35.   E. Hickeringill, *Jamaica Viewed* (1661), p. 59. B.L. Egerton MS 2395, fo. 286B, 'Considerations about the Peopling and Settling the Island Jamaica,' 1660.

36.   B.L. Egerton MS 2395, fos. 640-1, Colonel Lynch 'Concerning the Sugar Plantations'.

37.   Institute of Jamaica, Kingston (hereafter I.J.), MS 105, John Taylor, 'Multum in Parvo', fo. 589.

38.   P.R.O. CO 138/2, fo. 117, 'State of Jamaica', 1675.

39. Ibid.
40. Hickeringill, *Jamaica Viewed*, p. 16.
41. R.D. Hussey, 'Spanish Reaction to Foreign Aggression in the Caribbean to about 1680', *Hispanic American Historical Review*, IX (1929), pp. 286-302; Violet Barbour, 'Privateers and Pirates in the West Indies', *American Historical Review*, XVI (1911), pp. 526-66; K.R. Andrews, *The Spanish Caribbean: Trade and Plunder, 1530-1630* (New Haven, Conn. 1978).
42. I.J. MS 390, Letter to Nottingham, March 1689.
43. Dunn, *Sugar and Slaves*, p. 16; C.H. Goslinga, *The Dutch in the Caribbean, 1580-1680* (Gainesville, Florida, 1971), pp. 52-60.
44. An English Company did settle the islands of Providence (Santa Catalina), Henrietta (San Andreas) and Tortuga in 1630, which provided ideal bases for privateering. The Spanish expelled them from Tortuga in 1635 and Providence in 1641. A.P. Newman, *The Colonising Activities of the English Puritans* (Yale, 1914).
45. All foreign colonies established in the Antilles in the early seventeenth century faced serious danger of a Spanish attack. The Spanish expelled the French and English from Trinidad and Tobago in 1634; they expelled the French and English from St. Christopher and Nevis in 1629; the Dutch from St. Martin in 1633; and the English from St. Catalina in 1641. Hussey, 'Spanish Reaction to Foreign Aggression', p. 299.
46. *H. of L. Journals*, XVII, p. 510. Report of Admiralty Papers Relating to Vice Admiral Greydon, 23 March 1703.
47. B.L. Add. MS 11410, fo. 10, 'An Account of the Private Ships of War belonging to Jamaica and Tortudos in 1663'; P.R.O. CO 1/25, fo. 5. Charles Modyford's Report on Jamaica, 1670; M. Pawson and O. Buisseret, *Port Royal, Jamaica* (Oxford, 1975), pp. 6-19.
48. P.R.O. CO 1/23, fo. 191, Bowne to Williamson, 17 Dec. 1688; W.A.M. 11913, Sir James Modyford to Sir Andrew King, 27 Dec. 1667.
49. W.A.M. 11920, Sir James Modyford to Sir Andrew King, 4 Oct. 1668; P.R.O. CO 1/24, fo. 145, 'Narrative of Sir Thomas Modyford', 23 Aug. 1669; P.R.O. CO 1/24, fo. 1 'Memorial of Spanish Ambassador', 7 Jan. 1669.
50. P.R.O. CO 140/1, fo. 6, Minutes of Council of Jamaica, 18 June 1661; P.R.O. CO 138/1, fo. 107-11, 'List of What Vessels Arrived in Port Royal, 1668-1670'.
51. P.R.O. CO 1/28, fo. 9, Lynch to Williamson, 16 June 1672.
52. W.A.M. 11920, Sir James Modyford to Sir Andrew King, 4 Oct. 1668.
53.

Sailing of Fleets	Galeones	Flota
1670s	3	5
1680s	2	4

H. Kamen, *Spain in the Later Seventeenth Century* (1980), p. 133.
54. *C.S.P. Col. 1675-1676*, No. 735, Peter Beckford to Williamson, 6 Dec. 1675. Cary claimed that direct trade with the Spanish Indies was five times more profitable than the Cadiz route; Cary, *Essay on the State of England*, pp. 115-16.
55. B.L. Add. MS 28140, 'An Essay on the Nature and Method of Carrying on a Trade to the South Seas,' fos. 24-24b; P.R.O. C 110/152, Brailsford Papers.
56. P.R.O. CO 1/43, fo. 59, 'An Account of what . . . brought to this Island; I.J. MS 105, Taylor, 'Multum in Parvo,' fo. 499.
57. P.R.O. CO 1/43, fo. 59, 'An Account of what . . . brought to this island'.
58. P.R.O. CO 142/13, Naval Officer's Returns, Jamaica, 1680-1705.
59. P.R.O. CO 110/152, Halls to Brailsford, 13 and 14 March 1688; Nuala Zahedieh, 'The Merchants of Port Royal, Jamaica and Spanish Contraband Trade, 1655-92', *William and Mary Quarterly*, 3rd ser. XLIII (1986).
60. "The West Indies . . . is very plentifully supply'd by us with manufactures and many other things from Jamaica . . . this I take to be the true reason why our vent for them at Cadiz is lessened because we supply New Spain direct with those things they used to have thence before." Cary, *Essay on the State of England*, pp. 115-16. Kamen claims that the Andalusian trade and English participation declined during the late seventeenth century. There is little statistical evidence but the English in Spain were conscious of a decline. Kamen, *Spain in the Later Seventeenth Century*, p. 118.
61. B.L. Egerton MS 2395, fos. 502-502b, 'Considerations about the Spaniards buying negroes of the English Royal Company'.
62. P.R.O. CO 138/6, fo. 288, 'Address of Council and Assembly of Jamaica', 26 July 1681.
63. S.R.O. Helyar MSS, WIIh/1089, John Helyar to father, 16 Sept. 1686.
64. P.R.O. CO 138/5, fo. 47, Molesworth to Committee of Trade, 24 March 1684; the trade is discussed in C.P. Nettels, 'England and the Spanish American Trade, 1680-1715', *Journal of Modern History*, III (1931), pp. 1-33.
65. F. Hanson, ed. *Laws of Jamaica* (1683), Introduction.
66. P.R.O. CO 138/7, fo. 19, Inchiquin to Lords of Trade, 12 Aug. 1691.
67. The population of Bridgetown, Barbados, was 2,927 in 1680. P.R.O. CO 1/44, fos. 142-397, Census of Barbados, 1680. The population is said to have been stable or falling in the 1680s. The population of Boston, the largest town in mainland North America, was 6,000 in 1690. James A. Henretta, 'Economic Development and Social Structure in Colonial Boston', *William and Mary Quarterly*, 3rd ser. XXII (1965), p. 75.
68. P.R.O. CO 390/6, fo. 26, 'Ships Trading at Barbados'.
69. I.J. MS 105, Taylor, 'Multum in Parvo', fos. 491-507.
70. Bernard Bailyn, *The New England Merchants in the Seventeenth Century* (Harvard, 1979); Henretta, 'Economic Development . . . in Colonial Boston', p. 84.

71. I.J. MS 105, Taylor, 'Multum in Parvo', fo. 589.

72. Island Record Office, Spanish Town (hereafter I.R.O.), Deeds, OS, I-III. Claypole analysed these records with some care in his thesis. W. Claypole, 'The Merchants of Port Royal, 1655-1700' (unpublished Ph.D. thesis, University of the West Indies, 1974), pp. 174-95.

73. I.J. MS 105, Taylor, 'Multum in Parvo', fo. 326.

74. Jamaica Archives, Spanish Town (hereafter J.A.), Inv. 1B/11/3, fos. 259-267, Inventory of Henry Morgan, 1688.

75. Zahedieh, 'The Merchants of Port Royal'.

76. P.R.O. CO 138/4, fo. 25b, 'Names of Persons fit to be Councillors', 16 Feb. 1684; I.R.O. Deeds OS 1 fo. 115b; P.R.O. CO 1/34, fo. 71, Beckford to Williamson, 25 March 1675.

77. P.R.O. CO 138/6, fos. 292-293, Address of Council and Assembly of Jamaica, 26 July 1689; The Royal African company's factors reported Beckford's dealings with interlopers, P.R.O. T 70/10, fo. 296.

78. P.R.O. CO 138/1, fos. 61-80, 'Survey of Jamaica', 1670.

79. N. Deerr, *History of Sugar* (1949), I, pp. 175-6. Beckford's son's inventory of 1739 indicates that his whole fortune may have amounted to £300,000 or so. J.A. Inv. 1B/11/3, XVIII, fo. 108.

80. Smith, *Wealth of Nations*, II, p. 187.

81. R. Grassby, 'The Rate of Profit in Seventeenth-century England', *English Historical Review*, LXXXIV (1969), pp. 721-51.

82. L.A. Harper, The English Navigation Laws (New York, 1939), pp. 241-5; Child, *A New Discourse of Trade*, p. 94; Thomas, *Historical Account*, p. 44.

83. F.C. Lane, 'National Wealth and Protection Costs,' in J.D. Clarkson and T.C. Cochran, eds. *War as a Social Institution: The Historian's Perspective* (New York, 1941), pp. 32-43.

84. William Beckford, *A Descriptive Account of the Island of Jamaica* (1790), II, p. 319.

85. F. Hanson, ed. *Laws of Jamaica* (1683), Introduction.

15

France, the Antilles, and Europe in the Seventeenth and Eighteenth Centuries: Renewals of Foreign Trade

PAUL BUTEL

Thanks to the dynamism of merchant communities along the Atlantic coast and to the exploitation of a young colonial empire, French foreign trade expanded during the eighteenth century. This expansion was based upon the growth in the Antilles trade, which was in turn based upon the mastery of European markets in the re-export of colonial products. The tempo of this growth is estimated to have been greater than that of its rivals – in particular, English commerce. F. Crouzet notes that despite the setback dealt by the collapse of Law's system, French commerce at first grew at a tempo nearing that of English commerce. However, beginning about 1735 it exhibited a more rapid and precocious acceleration that doubled its value in less than seventeen years; from 221 million livres in 1735 to more than 500 million in 1752-4. In Crouzet's words, the years 1735-55 were the golden age of French commerce.[1] Indeed, during the next twenty years, until the American War of Independence, this commerce continued to grow (notwithstanding a clear tapering off caused by the Seven Years' War), although at a slower rate; trade values reached a peak in 1777. On the eve of the American War of Independence, trade remained less than 750 million livres. Not until after the war did an unmistakable recovery occur, which carried trade to its record level on the eve of the

French Revolution.[2] Figure 15.1 shows this growth clearly.

To better understand the factors underlying this growth, one must analyze the heritage of the preceding century. One must not neglect the results of Colbert's policies regarding maritime and colonial trade. Also, the Antilles, colonized since the time of Richelieu, gave French merchants a new position in international commerce. The important naval wars at the end of Louis XIV's reign, between France, Holland, and England, expressed the vigour of international competition created by the early momentum of the Antilles trade in France. Meanwhile, the traditional dynamism of Mediterranean merchants continued, and the first effects of the East Indian trade were also being felt.

This age of the foundation of the French commercial empire cannot be explained unless one tries to discover the situation at the end of the sixteenth century, after the troubles of the Wars of Religion. The financial means for colonial development during the reigns of Louis XIV and Louis XV came from very diverse transactions: those of the Middle Ages, carrying products of the soil (wines, brandies, fruits, and salt), which linked southern France with Nordic Europe; cloth from the north and west of France sold to the Iberian countries; and finally the extension of Atlantic trade, in particular the fisheries of Newfoundland.

Translated by Frederick Suppe, Ball State University.

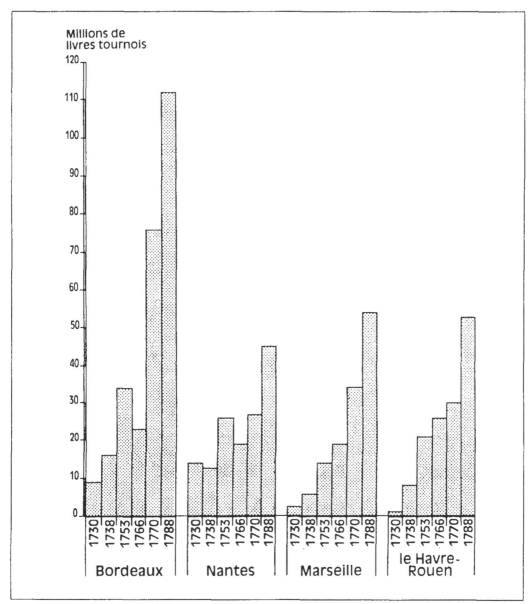

Millions de livres tournois

Figure 15.1. Colonial trade in the eighteenth century *Sources:* J. Meyer, *Histoire du Havre* [Toulouse, 1975], 84; C. Carrière, *Négociantes marseillais au XVIIIe siècle* [Marseille, 1973], 45-65; P. Butel, *Les négociants bordelais, l'Europe et les îles au XVIIIe siècle* [Paris, 1974], 393)

The Legacies of the Fifteenth and Early Seventeenth Centuries

The expansion of the "good" sixteenth century (a period of increasing wealth) allowed merchants to restore traditional trade developed during the preceding centuries. Factors essential for this renewal appeared at the end of the fifteenth century. The long stagnation that had prolonged

the crises of the fourteenth century finally came to an end. As M. Mollat notes, an economy stimulated by new commercial possibilities and the acceleration of monetary circulation succeeded a contracted, regional economy. There was an increase in trade, with new products appearing, such as spices from Lisbon and, more regionally, wood from Languedoc, which, together with wine, composed the cargoes loaded at Bordeaux and Bayonne in Montaigne's day. The French isthmus between the Nordic seas and the Mediterranean assumed its full economic potential.[3]

Growing Mediterranean activity corresponded with the opening of northwestern European markets. The markets of Bruges and then of Antwerp were favoured hereafter with the trade of Rouen, Nantes, and even Bordeaux.[4] At the same time England, Spain, and Portugal constituted the markets for the linens from Brittany, Anjou, and Poitou, which departed from Nantes. This port also shipped Breton grain to the Iberian peninsula; grain remained a major element in the north-south trade between France and the Mediterranean.

At the end of the sixteenth century the impact and stimulus of the early American treasure should not be overestimated. Well before Columbus' discovery, busy centres of production developed in France, working for themselves and for export to England, to the Low Countries, and within France.[5] There was, it has been argued, a fragmentation of the French economy. I. Wallerstein has distinguished continental, northwestern and western, and southern regions. The first, including Paris and the northeast, remained linked with Antwerp; the second was connected to the New World economy, to Baltic and Atlantic commerce; and the third remained an exporter of agricultural products.[6] In fact, trade between north and south still predominated in the greater part of the country and was a source of great unity in the French economy.

But did not the Wars of Religion, together with the long periods of troubles linked with them, call into question the results of the good sixteenth century for more than a generation – from the 1560s to the 1590s? Seemingly, the losses had been great, but in reality the financial means already in place and the maturation of trade would lay the foundation at least half a century in advance for the successes of Colbert's age.

The economic difficulties of this period have been illuminated by work done om Nantes, such as the researches of H. Lapeyre, who analyzed the business of merchants connected with Spain, the Ruiz. Lapeyre has shown that their activities suffered many setbacks in the shipment of linens from Maine and Anjou in Spain from 1568-70 onward.[7] All French textiles were apparently affected; the index of exports of Roman alum, which reflects this activity, shows a decrease during 1566-90 to nearly half of the 1541-66 levels.[8] Normandy was invaded by English cloth produced at low cost, ending the textile-based prosperity of Amiens.[9]

Nonetheless, not all commodities were uniformly affected. J. Tanguy has stressed that for Nantes there was an upsurge after the Treaty of Cateau-Cambrésis (1559) until St. Bartholomew's Day (1572). Trade in wine and salt fed prosperity, as it had earlier.[10] When this trade fell off sharply, certain exports resisted the decline. Such was the case with linens from Brittany, which reached a peak in 1608, attaining nine times the volume exported in 1586. It was not until later that English and Dutch demand replaced that of Iberia as the major outlet for these textiles.[11] One of the essential foundations of France's commercial empire – the, at least partial, mastery of the markets of Spain and Spanish America – was established at the end of the sixteenth century. It was to remain nearly stable until the French Revolution. In the mid-seventeenth century Brittany exported more than 8 million livres worth of linen; if one compares this amount with the total value of exports in 1646, nearly 46 million livres, Breton linens represented nearly 17 per cent of French exports that year.

Close to Nantes and at certain times its opponent, the Protestant republic of La Rochelle flaunted an insolent prosperity at the close of the sixteenth century. Political factors alone are not the only explanation for this. The traditional trade in wine, brandy, and salt, which was the enduring base of La Rochelle's commerce, was more and more controlled by Dutch businessmen. One may note that French salt remained a constant element in the Baltic trade until the mid-eighteenth century. The French share of salt shipped to the Baltic did not fall below 20 per cent during the worst years of the seventeenth century.[12]

In the long term, what is most interesting at La Rochelle is the penetration of foreigners into the re-export trade. The French merchant empire would always be beholden for a great part of its prosperity to the presence of commission agents from Germany and the Low Countries. Dutch merchants, who ascended the Charente as far as Cognac to buy the brandies and wines of the hinterlands, brought industry to this region; they converted windmills in the Charente and Périgord regions into paper factories to produce the "paper of Holland." At La Rochelle the Netherlanders founded sugar refineries. Their close commercial associations with the Protestant merchants proved to be very fruitful in creating the relationships supporting new expansion based on the re-export of colonial products to northern Europe in the eighteenth century.

A similar continuity in the structure of trade is found at Bordeaux, where the traditional ambit of trade with England and the Netherlands expanded at the end of the sixteenth century and even more at the time of Richelieu, thanks to the new growth of the Newfoundland fisheries. For Bordeaux, Newfoundland created the Antilles, by which I mean that it was the fisheries that provided the means of financing trade. Capital for trade came from the Bordeaux region and from a much larger area, including the Paris district, where bankers made sea-venture loans to Bordeaux shipowners during the 1630s. Here, too, as at La Rochelle, the commercial agents of the United Provinces depended upon a network of Protestant merchants that was as dense in the hinterland – in the valleys of the Garonne, the Lot, and the Dordogne – as it was in the Charente. The Netherlanders thereby indirectly stimulated activity in the southwest, developing trade there in brandy and tobacco. Their dominant position was the envy of local merchants.[13]

At Marseille the growth of the silk trade to satisfy the orders of manufacturers in Lyons is clear from the reign of Henry IV to that of Louis XIII, the volume of raw imported silk having doubled between 1613 and 1642. As along the Atlantic coast, what appears to have been a rather modest trade was a preparation for later growth – in this case, trade with the Levant.[14]

The role of the Dutch in stimulating trade is clearly understood in the only comprehensive qualitative source from the mid-seventeenth century, the *Commerce honorable,* written by Jean Eon of Nantes. M. Morineau has studied the mid-seventeenth century Dutch position in France by comparing it with the situation during the following century.[15] In Eon's day Dutch sales rose to 21.4 million livres while purchases increased to 18 million. In the highest rank of sales were the textiles – woollens and serges – with

more than 32 per cent of the total; spices came next with 15 per cent and Brazilian sugar sold by the Dutch middlemen accounted for 9 per cent of the total. The share of goods from the north, which included flax, hemp, lumber, and masts but not grain, was rather small, at 8 per cent. A bit later, during the 1660s, Colbert reckoned the value of northern European goods sold by the Dutch, including grain, at 15 million livres. One must remember that the Dutch seemed masters of French commerce; their total sales greatly exceeded those of the English, estimated at 16 million livres. They controlled the supply to France of spices, commodities from the Antilles, and goods from Nordic Europe. A century later the situation had changed because of the growth of the French Antilles trade and because of the direct relationships between French ports and northern Europe, which led to the decline of Dutch intermediaries.

In 1750 the Dutch no longer furnished sugar to France, contenting themselves with the exotic imported commodities of tea, cocoa, and tobacco. Despite the growth of French shipping, which required more naval stores, Nordic products represented a somewhat reduced share – less than 1.6 million livres, or about 7 per cent of Dutch sales. The restoration of textile prosperity at Amiens, Lille, Beauvais, and Rouen at the end of the seventeenth century reduced textile imports; the Dutch sold no more than 2.3 million livres' worth, though a century earlier they had imported some 7 million livres' worth. The merchants of Amsterdam preserved a sector of the French market for themselves only in spices, because the Vereenigde Oost-Indische Compagnie (VOC) was able to provide much larger quantities than could be supplied by France's Company of the East Indies.

A spectacular reversal in trade had taken place: France was freed from Dutch domination for the supply of sugar and other commodities from the American islands. Moreover, France had become the greatest re-exporter of colonial goods in Europe; this was the basis for its new commercial empire. In the long run Colbert's struggle was successful. France was ultimately the victor of the sugar wars in Martinique and Guadeloupe during the 1650s and then in Santo Domingo around 1700. An Americanization of French commerce then revealed itself, sustained by the growth of shipping to the Antilles under

Colbert. The old commercial networks established by foreigners had ensured the indispensable relationships for re-export to all of northern
Europe; the Netherlands figured here as a powerful intermediary while competing with Hanseatic merchants. In the mid-eighteenth century,
colonial commodities alone represented more
than half of French sales to the United Provinces;
their value reached 12.4 million livres, approximately three times that of traditional goods
(wines and brandies). This compensated for the
decline in Dutch purchases of salt, fruits, and
other products of the soil. Sales of salt declined
as a result of Portuguese shipments from Setúbal,
whose salt replaced that of Brouage and Bour-
gneuf.[16]

The Expansion of Commerce from the 1660s to the 1750s due to Colonial Trade

The rise of the Antilles and the re-export of colonial commodities

French colonial trade commenced at the beginning of Louis XIV's personal rule. In 1664 the
merchant fleet was still of modest size. Statistics
on ships of more than 100 tons, prepared for
Colbert, yield the following comparison of ports.

Le Havre	75	Toulon	9
Saint-Malo	48	Calais	5
Rouen	26	Sables-d'Olonne	5
Marseille	21	Rhuis (Morbihan)	5
Bayonne	19	Dunkirk	4
La Rochelle	18	Granville	4
Honfleur	14	Abbeville	3
Nantes	12	Caudebec	2
Bordeaux	11	Hennebont	2

Ships of less than 100 tons were not counted, and
one must emphasize the imperfection of these
statistics, since many ships of 50 to 80 tons were
used in long-distance trade to the Atlantic archipelagoes and Newfoundland. But the overall
impression is one of a mediocre fleet; colonial
traffic was quite modest, and the European
coastal trade was mainly sustained by foreign
ships.[17] Twenty-two years later ships over 100
tons now numbered:

Saint-Malo	117	Nantes	84
Le Havre	114	Bayonne	61
Dieppe	96	Dunkirk	59
La Rochelle	93	Marseille	47

There is a total increase of 75 per cent. It is
necessary to examine more precisely the Atlantic
traffic at Bordeaux, Nantes, and La Rochelle.
Between 1670 and 1679, 273 ships departed
from La Rochelle for the Antilles, Africa, or
Canada, while 411 departed between 1680 and
1689. From Nantes 64 ships left for the Antilles
between 1674 and 1675, 95 had the same destination in 1684-5, and from 1687 to 1688 the
traffic grew to 128 ships. At Bordeaux trade in
all commodities flourished during the second
half of the seventeenth century (Table 15.1).

In 1674 French ships bound for the Antilles
departed from the following ports.[18]

La Rochelle	35	Marseille	4
Nantes	25	Toulon	2
Dieppe	10	Le Havre	7
Honfleur	10	Rouen	1
Saint-Malo	6	Dunkirk	1

Despite the losses of the Dutch war, a turnaround
in transatlantic commerce occurred during the
decade 1670-1680. As at Bordeaux, growth
henceforth depended upon the vigour of French
transatlantic commerce (exclusively controlled
by local capital in the port) and a major European
north-south coastal commerce (with the exception of Iberian commerce, still a Dutch and Hanseatic quasi monopoly) to handle re-exports.
Nantes, studied by J. Meyer, is a good example
of this growth. The medieval threesome of
wheat, wine, and salt was patently incapable,
even when combined with cod, of ensuring anything more than slow growth in the best of cases,
with small successive advances coupled with
prolonged slumps. On the other hand, the opening of colonies accelerated trade; in less than a
half century, from 1664 to 1704, the high seas
fleet (ships of more than 100 tons) increased
more than tenfold, from 12 to 151 ships.[19]

This acceleration was a result of Colbert's
policies and can be measured in the eighteenth
century, when the rate of expansion for all
French commerce was superior to that for English commerce, this growth being essentially due
to colonial trade.[20] The average annual value of
foreign trade increased from 215 million livres
in 1716-20 to 1,062 million in 1784-8, nearly
quintupling (these figures in current prices).
With a rise in prices of about 60 per cent between
1730 and 1780 (less for agricultural products),
one must deflate the figures from the end of the

Table 15.1 Ship Departures from Bordeaux

	Ships	Tonnage 1651	Ships	Tonnage 1672	Ships	Tonnage 1682
Bordeaux flagged ships	83	(4,972)	107	(5,284)	223	(7,209)
Foreign flagged ships	423	(72,630)	339	(25,613)	935	(94,149)
French flagged ships	1,007	(21,541)	1,699	(45,151)	2,120	(49,164)
Total	1,513	(99,143)	2,145	(76,048)	3,278	(150,552)

Source: Archives de la Gironde, Fonds de l'Amirauté.

century to reduce them to constant values, but this still leaves a very clear progression. In 1716-20 the value of foreign trade barely exceeded half that of English commerce, but on the eve of the revolution it had reached a level close to the latter.

Where did French commerce control local markets?

France was the chief supplier of manufactured goods for Spain and, via Cadiz, for its American empire, whereas the British monopolized the smaller markets of Portugal and Brazil. In 1686 the French consul at Cadiz valued the French linens imported by Spain at 12 million livres; to these should be added the lace, gold, and silver of Tours and Lyons; the hats of Paris; and cloth from Picardy. In return, there were colonial products and especially piastres (12 million livres in 1673).[21] The French also dominated the markets of Italy and the Levant.

Of greatest importance was the spectacular development after 1700 of sugar cane cultivation on new soil on the French portion of Santo Domingo; the French price was very competitive with that of the sugar from the English Antilles, whose exports continued to decrease, in constant livres, from the beginning of colonialization until the middle of the eighteenth century. This growth corresponded to the expansion of European markets, especially those of northern Europe. British exports to the Continent advanced only slowly in absolute terms.[22] The driving force was provided by colonial re-exports, which multiplied eightfold while exports of French products only tripled. For all of France,

the greatest acceleration occurred in the 1730s and 1740s, with the value of foreign trade doubling in less than eight years, between 1736-9 and 1749-55. For re-exports the tempo of growth was higher still for the whole century, at Bordeaux exceeding 6 per cent per year.

Sector by sector, Table 15.2 illustrates the tempo of growth. One is struck by the independent pattern of growth for French trade with the Levant; after having been the most vigorous of all the areas of trade, more than tripling in a decade, its tempo slackened very notably. It is clear nonetheless that this sector participated in the colonial connection, since one stream of re-exportation was directed toward the Levant. The trade with Spain remained one of the most important during this whole period, but its tempo not merely slackened but indeed declined, with a negative balance from 1765 to 1772. The Dutch trade also tended to regress, to the advantage of the trade with the north, the strength of which faithfully echoed that of the colonial trade but which grew even more rapidly during the middle of the century and remained the most vigorous of the European trades after the Seven Years' War.[23]

To be sure, this analysis lacks the final period, that which followed the American War of Independence. If one looks at colonial trade port by port, one finds the volume of trade climbing steeply during the 1780s: compared with mid-century, Bordeaux had tripled its colonial trade by 1787 (110 million livres compared with 34 million), and Le Havre had more than doubled its trade (53 million compared with 21 million).

Table 15.2. The Growth of French Trade (in Millions of Livres)

	1730–1740		1740–1754		1765–1776	
Colonial trade	32.0	70.2	70.2	120.4	108.0	191.0
Increase		119.0%		71.7%		76.7%
Northern trade	10.8	24.4	24.4	51.9	53.5	79.9
Increase		107.6%		109.4%		55.4%
Dutch trade	31.1	44.1	44.1	51.1	52.1	51.01
Increase		29.3%		15.9%		-16.15%
Spanish trade	44.7	64.1	64.1	73.7	76.4	71.7
Increase		43.1%		14.4%		-6.1%
Levant trade	12.3	41.0	41.0	53.2	56.2	65.9
Increase		331.0%		29.7%		17.3%

Source: Bilan du Commerce de la France, Archives Nationales, Paris.

Of all the Atlantic ports, it was Nantes that had the slowest growth (relatively speaking – 45 million livres compared with 26 million). One is also struck by the relative lag in commerce between the Seven Years' War and the American war. The two phases of liveliest expansion were therefore 1730-50 and the few years preceding the French Revolution.

This growth rested upon the redistribution of colonial goods, which were themselves linked to the Dutch-Hanseatic "connection" and by it to the importation into France of grains, textile fibres, and wood from the north. To understand this process we must consider the role of these northern markets in French prosperity.

France, storehouse for northern Europe, and the special position of the Nordic markets

One of the better specialists, P. Jeannin, has shown that one should not be satisfied with measuring the importance of northern markets only in terms of volume of trade. The role of intermediary between France and the countries of northern Europe, filled at first by Amsterdam and then more and more by Hamburg, did not consist solely of importing goods into France for re-export to the north and vice versa. It also included service functions, notably as regards credit, which was so often indispensable to firms since towns in France did not have direct commercial relationships with places beyond the Elbe.[24]

During the 1760s France imported around 10 per cent of the raw materials originating from the Baltic. The country held first rank as a supplier of Hamburg and Bremen, delivering to Hamburg almost half of all it received by sea. As the dynamic colonial economy made its effects felt in the Nordic area, it caused the whole curve of French trade to rise, as well as stimulating further growth in the colonial sphere. One must, however, carefully define the specific characteristics of the flow of colonial goods to the Baltic. For France this commerce drained off its "excess," the goods of its colonies; the productive forces of the kingdom, except for viticulture and the manufacturing sector specializing in luxury and fashion goods, made only a small contribution. In return, the imports from the north were sought more as objects of demand for British commerce than as indispensable raw materials.

In the statistical records meant to show the French balance of trade, the term "north" does not refer to the distant north, the Baltic zone, but rather to the Hanseatic cities and "other countries."[25] Denmark and Sweden were removed from this category in 1734, and Russia was removed in 1744. The area that was left included Prussia and the ports of Germany and Poland, but the Hanseatic cities represented the most important part by far. From 1751 to 1780, the "north" in this narrow sense supplied more than 57 per cent of French imports from the northern sector in the broad sense (pre-1734) and received more than 77 per cent of the exports to the same sector. The "north's" share of the total European trade (not including the Levant) was 7.4 per cent of imports and 8.2 per cent of exports in 1721-40 and increased to 11.8 and 21.3 per cent, respectively, in 1761-80.

The consular reports of Hamburg stress that manufactured articles – items of fashion and silks from Paris and Lyons, all light and valuable – came by road via Strassburg and Frankfurt and did not pass through the ports. The balance-of-trade statistics for France consider only maritime traffic for the north and are therefore incomplete. According to these figures, colonial goods – sugar, coffee, and indigo – greatly predominated, representing 79 per cent of imports coming from France during the 1760s, compared with less than 14 per cent for wines. But colonial goods had attained this rank well before the middle of the century. If one takes account of merchandise arriving by land, worth nearly 5 million livres in 1750, colonial goods represented 60 per cent of French exports to the north and wines 10 per cent.

Aside from the years when France had a very great shortage of cereals (in 1752 grains represented 20 per cent of the exports from Hamburg to France), this trade showed a great deficit for the north.[26] Whereas nearly 100 loaded ships left the Baltic bound for France, 139 loaded ships came from France to the Baltic. The cargoes coming from the west had a greater average value than those from the east. Between 1731 and 1740 nearly 235 ships left French ports for the Baltic, and to these should be added ships bound for Hamburg and Amsterdam, the transfer points where products for the north were reshipped. Between 1749 and 1755 more than 310 ships coming from France passed through The Sound, and Hamburg and Bremen received between 220 and 240 French ships. These two ports allowed access to the German market and were more oriented toward central Europe than northern Europe. One may note the rather traditional role played by Königsberg and neighbouring ports in receiving wine and salt, while Stettin, the port of Frederick II, shipped much wood and received many colonial goods, having overtaken Danzig in this role after 1750.

Of all the French ports, Bordeaux took the greatest share of the northern markets. In 1776-80 Bordeaux shipped more than 78 per cent of its exports to the north.[27] As early as the middle of the century, in 1748-52, this port sold six times as many goods as in 1733-7, whereas exports did not even triple during the same period. Immediately after the American war, in 1783, Hamburg became the principal market for coffee and indigo shipped from Bordeaux – 46 per cent and 25 per cent, respectively, with tonnages of 6,400 and 100 tons – having largely supplanted Amsterdam for these commodities. By the middle of the century Bordeaux had become the greatest French port for the Baltic, assuming, with the help of Dutch and Hanseatic intermediaries, the supply of the wine, brandy, sugar, and coffee markets and a major part in French purchases of merchandise from the north.

This role is explained by the insertion into the Bordeaux merchant milieu of dynamic businessmen, agents from Amsterdam and, particularly during the eighteenth century, from Hamburg, Lübeck, Danzig, and Stettin. Thanks to their arrival in successive stages from the end of Louis XIV's reign to the American war, the agents "doing business with Germany and the Baltic countries" had strengthened their number: the Almanac of 1779 lists sixty-three agents of this type, and one may estimate the number of commercial firms of Germanic origin at some seventy to eighty, representing the largest foreign group in Bordeaux, even more numerous than the important Anglo-Irish colony.[28] New estimates made by W. Henninger put the number of Germans present in Bordeaux during the 1780s higher still, over 130 in 1782-4. This figure represents a very perceptible increase compared with the numbers of Germans present in 1711, 1744, and 1764-5, which the same author sets at 21, 39, and 75, respectively.[29] The inquest by the intendant Aubert de Tourny in 1743 enumerates eighteen traders who were "subjects of the Hanseatic Cities" and gives details of their business.[30] Thus the agent from Hamburg, Jean Christophe Harmensen, carried on northern trade "by the commissions which he has from Hamburg, Danzig, Rotterdam, and Sweden to send wine, sugar, and indigo and to receive in return planks, *merrain*, and *bourdillon*" (these last two products are woods for cooperage).

The recent study by P. Jeannin of the northern trade was based upon the example of one firm in Bordeaux, Schröder and Schyler. This study reveals a clear distribution of Bordeaux's northern clientele into three major levels. One rather large group of merchants regularly imported products from Bordeaux for local or regional distribution. The second level was composed of agents for centres like Danzig who required wine above all and did not indulge in speculation on colonial goods. At the highest level, one finds the traders of Hamburg, some of whom imported considerable quantities of colonial goods and arranged letters of credit for other ports. These Hamburg merchants were, however, far from enjoying a monopoly in this latter sector of credit, since they left an important role to firms from Amsterdam.[31] The dynamism of these commercial networks stands out in Jeannin's analysis of private commercial papers and confirms the conclusions derived from statistical studies of the balance of trade concerning the overriding importance of northern markets for Bordeaux beginning in the mid-eighteenth century.

This leaves an ambivalent picture regarding the strength of France's commercial empire. It was founded, to be sure, on the growth of the shipping firms backed by very diverse investors, in particular, the financiers of Paris and many of its banking houses. But this strength would not have amounted to much without the constant intervention of foreign firms, based in the Atlantic ports (or Marseille) as well as in northern Europe. Thus, French overseas trade was vulnerable in that it was dependent on others, indeed doubly so. First, the transshipping trade that animated France's commercial empire depended on the Antilles trade, and any blows suffered by the latter struck heavily at metropolitan trade. One sees this in dramatic fashion during the "French Wars," the revolution and the Empire, when the colonies were cut off from metropolitan France. Second, French trade could not maintain its growth except by re-exporting to northern Europe. If this trade fell off, as happened during the "French Wars" at the close of the century, the whole trading empire was shaken. It was not until much later, after 1815, that a new equilibrium appeared in French maritime commerce, but by this time the transshipping ports that had been so important in the eighteenth century were banished into the shadow of markets protected by the system of colonial privilege.[32]

Exploitation of Indian Ocean routes and Asian commerce

The most recent research indicates that Colbert's efforts to open Asiatic routes to French trade were crowned with success in the long term. P. Haudrères has analyzed the flood of pamphlets written toward the close of Louis XIV's reign that argued for suppression of the French Company of the East Indies and shows that the company's operations around the middle of the eighteenth century were incontestably a success. Using a comparative approach in presenting the traffic in Asian goods received by Europe by the various companies acting as intermediaries, Haudrères shows that from 1720 onward the sales of the French Company of the East Indies saw a more significant growth than the sales of the rival companies. In 1725 the VOC was well ahead in the surge of sales, the English East India Company was in second position, and the French company was in third place. After 1731 a strong growth in French sales stands out, and in 1735 these sales overtook English sales. There was severe competition between the French and English companies during the twenty years before 1759, the year when the English crushed their rivals. After 1760 the English company obtained the best results, overtaking and surpassing even the Dutch sales at the end of the 1760s.[33]

Some numerical indices may give an idea of the progress of French trade. Sales deriving from Asian trade increased rapidly after 1730, increasing from 7 million livres to 17 million in 1733, approaching 20 million per year in the early 1740s, and reaching more than 25 million annually on the eve of the Seven Years' War (1756-63). But the war was not as disruptive as one might have expected, considering that sales were still at 12.5 million in 1757-58. After the war, there was a perceptible recovery, with sales climbing to a bit less than 24 million livres in 1768. From 1725 until 1769, when the company was suppressed, India provided 72 per cent of the sales, some 7 to 15 million livres per year. China came next with 21 per cent, and 2 to 5 million livres per year, followed by the Mascarene Islands (east of Madagascar) with 7 per cent, some 1 million. The position of India tended to diminish while that of China improved. It is fair to say that the variations in sales were more pronounced than for the other companies because of the effects of the wars.

Converting the value of trade into thousands of pesos, as N. Steansgaard has done, the ten-year averages of sales of the French company can be calculated:

1731-40	1741-50	1751-60
2.823	2.290	2.777

These annual averages are lower than those for the other companies.

Division of sales by products shows that textiles made the strongest advance. White cottons and muslins constituted more than three-quarters of the textile cargoes coming from India, with the remainder composed of dyed linens and silk-stuffs. Sales of these textiles tripled from the 1720s to 1730-45. Orders for the famous "Company of the Indies" porcelains from China, already common during the first half of the century, were increased after the Seven Years' War. Among the bulkier articles, cargoes of cowries (small shells serving as money along the coast of Guinea and therefore indispensable for the slave trade) were always present but were of much lesser value. Of the other commodities, it was tea that had the highest value; cargoes of tea increased rapidly in number, and most of it was destined for Great Britain, as contraband. For most of these articles there was a tendency for prices to sink, which did not prevent the levels of profits from remaining high as volume grew. This Asian commerce was definitely linked with the Antilles trade by way of the slave trade. J. Meyer has shown the importance for Nantes of re-exportation of Indian cotton cloth to Africa,[34] and the importance of cowrie shells for the slave trade was just noted. In all these examples one sees the unity of the French commercial empire in its Asian, African, and American networks. The links between these networks explain why at Lorient, the centre of sales for the Company of the East Indies, purchases by Nantes firms

mainly concentrated upon Indian textiles and cowries; Paris bought spices, silks, and porcelains; Saint-Malo took a great part of the tea (being near England); and Bordeaux was very interested in porcelain. Atlantic coastal France dominated the company's sales just as its businessmen secured the largest part of French maritime commerce.

It is interesting to compare the profits obtained by the French company and by England's East India Company (Table 15.3). The French company's position improved in the middle of the century, before and after the War of the Austrian Succession. This fact is all the more interesting because profits on products from India declined after 1735, and those on Chinese commerce declined after 1745. The increased volume of sales compensated for this tendency.

If one compares the respective positions of the trade with Asia and with America, one sees a difference in scale (sales in millions of livres tournois):

	1750	1772
America	92	157
Asia	20	20.4

It was always America that guided French commercial growth, from mid-century to the eve of the American Revolution. But Asian commerce secured profits that were far from negligible. The Mascarene trade had the closest connections to products traded in the Antilles commerce, and it provided the best profits, especially on coffee. We must add that the disparity between the trade with America and that with Asia grew between 1750 and 1772. By 1772, following the cancel-

Table 15.3. Comparisons in Profits (in Millions of Livres Tournois, Annual Averages)

	French Company	East India Company
1725/6–29/30	4.4	19.7
1735/6–39/40	7.2	19.4
1740/1–44/5	8.3	12.1
1745/6–49/50	2.8	10.8
1751/1–54/5	11.5	7.5
1765/6–69/70	7.8	11.8

Source: Haudrère, Compagnie Fr. des Indes, II, 443.

lation of the company's privileges in 1769, trade with Asia was free, and businessmen from the Atlantic ports and Marseille could undertake voyages to India and China. This does not seem to have increased trade, however. At mid-century, trade with America was almost five times that with Asia, but by 1772 it was more than seven times the value of the Asian trade.

Merchants who had been critical of the commercial privileges of the company met certain difficulties in launching themselves into trade with India and China. Conditions in this trade were much different from those in the American trade: The cycle for turnover of capital was much longer because voyages were longer and wear and tear on ships was heavier. On the route to the American islands a ship could make at least one round-trip voyage per year, sometimes two. A voyage to Asia might last more than twenty months in the 1720s. From 1735 to 1740 the duration of voyages was reduced to nearly eighteen months, but this was still at least twice that of Antilles voyages. In duration the voyages to Asia recall those of the slave trade, but in the latter the shipowners integrated the voyages into the Antilles trade. The Asian voyages remained separate. Their higher costs (the heavier tonnages of ships used for Asia also increased costs) demanded more substantial capital. One notes that the shipowners who devoted themselves to this trade after 1769 had recourse to the procedures of financing, like loans for major ventures, which had disappeared from the Atlantic routes and were relatively costly. Often foreign places had to be called upon to finance these voyages. Thus, at Bordeaux the ship *Maréchal de Mouchy*, equipped in 1783 for India by the firm of Feger and Gramont, combined capital provided by firms from Paris, Basel, Bilbao, and Santo Domingo.[35] Even more than for the Antilles trade, the shipowners had to combine their investments: firms from Bordeaux, Le Havre, and Saint-Malo collaborated during the 1780s for these ventures.

These voyages to Asia via the Ile de France (Mauritius) also represented a far from negligible effort at diversifying trade beyond the too exclusive and dangerous routes to the American islands and the re-export of their products. The spectacular growth of the "Pearl of the Antilles", Santo Domingo, whose progress had eclipsed the trade of its colonial rivals since the beginning of the eighteenth century, had been strongly favoured by the nature of the French commercial empire, which was based upon exploitation of privilege, of colonial exclusivity, and of the re-export trade with northern Europe. During the 1770s and 1780s, however, new relationships began to form between these European markets and the Antilles. Merchants from English North America and then from the United States invaded the Antilles markets. England regained a place among European markets for the re-export of Antilles sugar. The situation became less favourable for French business.

The expansion of the Antilles trade, which had advanced French European commerce thanks to the sustained demand of northern European markets for "excess" colonial products, was the main innovation in French commerce since Colbert. It was able to overshadow traditional trade in wines, brandies, grains, and manufactured goods with both northern and Mediterranean Europe. However, it must be strongly stressed that it was this latter trade that provided the capital necessary to launch trade with the American islands and also to create the market demand. The Dutch-Hanseatic connection and the French commercial networks linked to it had prepared for the later growth. From this trade a commercial empire was born, doubtless favoured by the mercantilist framework desired by Colbert. But changes in trade happening under cover of the wars of the French Revolution and of the Empire and the new importance of Hamburg and especially of London at the beginning of the nineteenth century brought an end to the re-export trade on which the French Atlantic ports had depended for their prosperity during the seventeenth and eighteenth centuries.

Notes

1. "Angleterre et France au XVIIIe siècle: Essai d'analyse comparée de deux croissances économiques," *Annales: Economies, Sociétés, Civilisations* 21 (1966): 264.

2. In current prices, the average annual value for 1784-8 reached 1,062 million livres, nearly five times what it was in 1716-20. Exports led this growth, exceeding 500 million livres in 1787.

3. M. Mollat, *Histoire de Rouen* (Toulouse, 1982), 102.

4. Ibid.

5. M. Morineau, "L'Europe du Nord-Ouest de 1559 à 1642," *Bulletin de la Société d'Histoire Moderne*, 16th ser., 33 (1987).

6. Immanuel Wallerstein, *The Modern World System*, vol. 1, *Capitalist Agriculture and the Origins of the European World-Economy in the Sixteenth Century* (New York, 1974), pp. 263-4.

7. *Une famille de marchands nantais, les Ruiz* (Paris, 1955).

8. J. Delumeau, *L'alun de Rome* (Paris, 1952), 251.

9. P. Deyon, "Variations de la production textile aux XVIe et XVIIe siècles," *Annales: Economies, Sociétés, Civilisations* 18 (1963): 939-55.

10. J. Tanguy, *Le commerce du port de Nantes au milieu de XVIe siècle* (Paris, 1956).

11. J. Tanguy, *La production et le commerce des toiles bretonnes* (Paris, 1978), provides the following statistics for exports: 1585, 440,348 pieces; 1594, 1,585,474; 1608, 3,949,492; 1621, 380,253.

12. J. Delumeau, "Le commerce extérieur de la France au XVIIe siècle," *XVIIe Siècle* 70-71 (1966): 81-105.

13. P. Voss, "Contribution à l'histoire de l'èconomie et de la société marchande à Bordeaux au XVIIe siècle: L'exemple de Jean de Ridder" (Master's diss., University of Bordeaux III, 1986), 152. A certain hostility against immigrant Dutch merchants sometimes developed. This was the case in 1683 after letters of citizenship were granted to Jean de Ridder, when there were complaints against "foreigners who, under the cover of the bourgeoisie, intrude upon all affairs of the country, depriving the king of one part of his rights and hindering the native-born countrymen in their dealings."

14. M. Morineau, "Flottes de commerce et trafics français en Méditerranée au XVIIe siècle (jusqu'en 1669)," *XVIIe Siècle* 86-87 (1970): 135-71.

15. "La balance du commerce frano-néerlandais et le resserrement économique des Provinces-Unies au XVIIIe siècle," *Economische-Historisch Jaarboek* 30 (1963-4): 170-233.

16. M. Delafosse and C. Laveau, *La Commerce du sel de Brouage aux xviie et xviiie siècles* (Paris, 1960), 96-7.

17. Ships of more than 40 tons: Le Havre, 142; Marseille, 91; Bordeaux, 77; Saint-Malo, 77. There were relatively few ships of medium tonnage suited to the European coastal trade.

18. Cf. Jonathan Howes Webster, "The Merchants of Bordeaux in Trade to the French West Indies, 1664-1717" (Ph.D. diss., University of Minnesota, 1972).

19. J. Meyer, *Histoire de Nantes* (Toulouse, 1977), 135.

20. Crouzet, "Angleterre et France au XVIIIe siècle," 261.

21. J. Delumeau, "Le commerce extérieur de la France au XVIIIe siècle," One may contrast the 1669 exports of silk and linen products to England, which had a value of 800,000 livres.

22. Crouzet, "Angleterre et France au XVIIIe siècle," 263.

23. The value of trade with the north increased sixfold from 1730 to 1772, whereas trade with Holland did not even double.

24. "Les marchés du Nord dans le commerce français au XVIIIe siècle," *Actes du Colloque des Historiens Economistes Français* (Paris, 1973), 71.

25 Ibid., 69.

26 Ibid., 62.

27 P. Butel, *Les Négociants Bordelais, L'Europe et les îles au xviiie siècle* (Paris, 1974), 47.

28 P. Butel, "Les Négociants allemands de Bordeaux dans la deuxième moitié du XVIIIe siècle," *Wirtschaftskräfte und Wirtschaftswege*, vol. 2, *Wirtschaftskräfte in der europäischen Expansion* (Klett-Cotta, 1978), 597.

29 *Studien zur Wirtschafts und Sozialgeschichte von Bordeaux im 18. Jahrhundert unter besonderer Berücksichtigung der deutschen Kaufleute*, vol. 1 (Cologne, 1986), 70-1.

30. Archives de la Gironde, C 4439.

31. "La clientèle étrangere de las maison Schröder et Schyler de la guerre de Sept Ans à la guerre d'Indep128. pendance Americaine," *Bulletin du Centre d'Histoire des Espaces Atlantiques* 3 (1986): 21-85. Jeannin calls attention to the dependence of clients in Bremen for their payments, which were always transferred, either through Amsterdam or through Paris (p. 27). Of more than ninety firms in Amsterdam doing business with Schröder and Schyler in 1763-75, seventy-five appear to have had only the right to accept payments for the accounts of clients in other cities, especially Bremen and Danzig (p. 24).

32. P. Butel, "Traditions and Changes in French Atlantic Trade between 1780 and 1830," *Rennaissance and Modern Studies* 30 (1986): 142-3.

33. "La Compagnie Française des Indes (1719-1795)" (thesis, University of Paris IV, 1987), 2:438-40, for the analysis of these sales.

34. *L'armement nantais dans la deuxième moité du xviiie siècle* (Paris, 1969), 161-4, 361. The author stresses very strongly the difference in the value of cargoes bound for the trade with Africa and the value of cargoes bound directly for the American islands. The higher value of the former derived from the place taken in these cargoes by linens from England and Holland before the middle of the century, and then later increasingly from India. Note the importance of these linens in the inventories of shipowners.

35. P. Butel, *Les négociants bordelais*, 41.

SECTION FOUR

Servitude, Slavery and New Economic Orders

European colonial capitalism could see no way to ensure profitable economic activity other than with the mass deployment of servile labour. As the intensity of economic accumulation gripped colonial élites, and the pressures of profits, power and glory fuelled the colonizing enterprise, chattel slavery became the preferred form of servile labour. Other labour institutions were tried for varying periods in most places, but with the development of the productive activities in all colonies, African slavery was centered as critical to economic accumulation and the cultural imperatives of white supremacy. In the Spanish colonies the general model embraced Africans on the periphery of labour systems that extracted greater surplus value from natives. In the English and French colonies, the use of white indentured servitude as a mode of labour exploitation formed part of the strategic economic thinking of wealth accumulators in the seventeenth century. But, as Beckles shows, patterns of social conflict and protest contributed to the instability of seventeenth century Barbados, reinforcing the view that labour protest in the English-colonized Caribbean was not confined to enslaved Africans. White servitude was later to be undermined and replaced by the chattel enslavement of Africans. Everywhere in the Caribbean chattel slavery was established. The extent of its importance in specific places reflected the degree of productive development and depth of integration into the market economy.

The extensive use of servile labour, both Amerindian and African, has origins within the mining and agricultural sectors of Spanish colonies in the Greater Antilles during the sixteenth century.

But the establishment of African slavery as the principal labour institution is related more specifically to the expansion of the sugar industry. As Batie and others show, as large-scale sugar production spread through the entire region, the demand for African slave labour increased at a phenomenal rate. The emergence of the industry gained revolutionizing proportions in the Lesser Antilles during the seventeenth century, and in the Greater Antilles during the eighteenth and nineteenth centuries. Everywhere, the relations between sugar and black slavery were similar. In this section, the peculiar characteristics of sugar and slavery development are explored, mostly for Barbados, Jamaica, Cuba and Puerto Rico. Explanations are given for the transition to large-scale slavery, the uneven pace of development in the use of slave labour throughout the region, and the relations between differential growth and patterns of economic activity accounted for. In this section also, Shepherd reminds us that even though sugar and slavery came to define the economic and social history of the Caribbean after 1640, the large sugar plantation did not absorb all land in all colonies. Jamaica sustained a significant degree of diversification and maintained the livestock industry started by the Spanish colonizers. Of course, the livestock industry hardly had its own independent economic dynamic, being dependent on the dominant sugar industry.

16

Why Sugar?
Economic Cycles and the Changing of Staples
on the English and French Antilles, 1624-54

ROBERT C. BATIE*

One of the enigmas facing scholars investigating the 17th-century West Indies is the phenomenal economic expansion that, from 1624 to 1654, elevated the Caribees into a prominent place among the world's colonies.[1] During most of the 17th and 18th centuries, the English and French Antillean possessions experienced few abrupt changes. Until 1789, no revolutionary waves wracked the islands, intellectual life was negligible, and social and economic patterns remained largely constant. Events of the first thirty turbulent but formative years of settlement, however, stand in sharp contrast to these generalizations. From 1624, when Englishmen founded their first enduring colony on the islands, until 1643, the date when sugar became a significant export, Europeans flocked to the region to raise tobacco, cotton, indigo and ginger. Then in 1643 the Barbadians abruptly turned to sugar, so abruptly in fact that by 1655, when they shipped an estimated 7,787 tons to England,[2] their settlement had achieved very near its full growth. How near will be discussed later, but it is useful to remember that Jamaica, conquered in 1655, required roughly sixty years before its sugar output consistently equalled the level its rival attained in twelve. The differential in their growth rates has hitherto never been adequately explained, but it enabled Barbados to become the most prosperous 17th-century insular colony on the globe. As surprising as the suddenness of that island's transformation is the fact that from 1643 to 1654 other Antillean dominions continued to produce their previous exports. Why

this was the case, why the newly founded colonies enjoyed an unusually high growth rate, why their inhabitants waited until the 1640s before plunging heavily into sugar, and why Barbados enjoyed an advantage over its sisters, constitutes the subject of this article.

The cause of these changes is obscured by the standard and disarmingly simple explanation held by scholars for the popularity of sugar cane during the next two centuries, namely that settlers found it more profitable to raise than alternative products.[3] Having made this assumption, historians have found it reasonable to conclude that, until sugar cane cultivation became widespread, the Caribee enclaves enjoyed only a marginal existence. For a current view of this interpretation, one need but turn to recent works by two eminent historians, Richard S. Dunn and Carl Bridenbaugh. The latter most bluntly stated this thesis: Caribee farmers obtained 'their first truly profitable staple' only with sugar and 'to maintain that the white men made a success of their colonies prior to 1645 is to press the evidence too hard'.[4] Dunn, while also believing that 'no one made much money' from Antillean tobacco and that sugar 'fetched a far higher and steadier profit than any other American commodity', was nevertheless perplexed by the implications of this line of thought. He therefore qualified it by stating 'there are a number of small mysteries about the introduction of sugar culture to Barbados', one presumably being 'that the Barbadians struggled with tobacco and cotton so long

*I am indebted to Dauril Alden, Robert Paul Thomas and Richard Bean for their constructive criticisms of earlier drafts of this paper.

Journal of Caribbean History, Vols 8–9, 1976, pp. 1–41.

before they tried making sugar'.[5] He might also have added that if pre-sugar agriculture was unremunerative, it is almost impossible to explain why thousands of Europeans migrated to the islands during that period.

In contrast to the traditional interpretation, it is a contention of this essay that the pre-sugar era was one of great economic opportunity. The case for this view rests primarily on commodity price data, which serves as a measure of colonial incomes, and on the remnants of both English and French correspondence and travel accounts. That the two groups of colonies experienced the same economic trends is to be expected since their settlers lived under similar free market institutions, raised nearly identical commodities, and bought their slaves from and sold their products to the same Dutch merchants. This placed all planters on as much the same competitive footing as if they were members of a single nationality.

The source of the price data utilized in this paper deserves mentioning. Almost no Caribbean information survives concerning the worth of tropical exports, but scholars have compiled at least two lists of published Chesapeake prices for tobacco,[6] the first staple exported from the Antilles. These figures serve as a reasonable proxy for West Indian values since all planters produced for the same Atlantic seaboard market, raised, with the exception of Barbadians, a quality leaf and paid substantial shipping fees when sending their product to the Old World, fees which dwarfed any transportation advantage the Antillean settlements might have had over Virginia. No accurate substitute exists for New World prices of other Caribbean commodities, but since each was sold in Europe, there remains a record of how much they bought on the Amsterdam exchange,[7] tobacco excepted. This record, which is far fuller, and therefore more reliable, than the spotty series of Virginia tobacco values, largely parallels Caribee price trends, since competition among European merchants forced price changes to be passed back to the original producers. Still the Netherlands market fluctuations are not identical to the New World variations because, as economic theory indicates, the huge transAtlantic carriage costs constituted an unknown but nearly constant burden.[8] As a result, percentage changes in Virginia figures cannot be compared directly with shifts in Dutch values even though the two series convincingly demonstrate that, despite two brief recessions, from 1624 to 1654 settlers enjoyed remarkable prosperity. The evidence for this view is presented in Figures 1 and 2 which show that at no time later

Figure 1

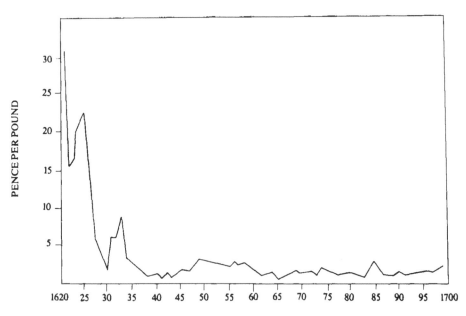

Source: Table 1 and Robert P. Thomas and Terry L. Anderson, 'The Economic Growth of the Chesapeake in the Seventeenth Century', unpublished paper, Department of Economics, University of Washington, n.p.

Figure 2   Netherlands Prices of Sugar and Indigo, 1624–1700

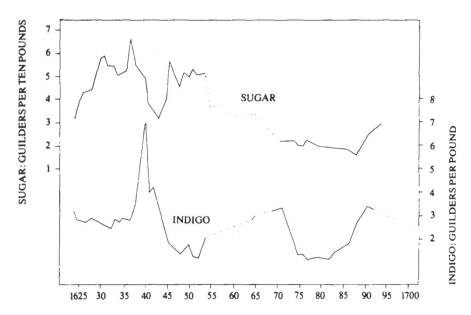

Source: Nicholas W. Posthumaus, 'Inquiry into the History of Prices in Holland' (Leiden, 1946), I, 119-20, 134-5, 415-16.

in the century did the average value of Antillean products attain as high a level as it then achieved. Clearly the first decades of Caribee colonization were boom times. As the next section indicates, the economic basis for that prosperity was laid during an earlier period.

1 The Profitability of Tobacco Cultivation, 1624–34

Historians describing the English colonization of North America have focused much of their attention on either the religious motives contributing to the Puritan migration or on the well-organized and heavily capitalized nature of the Virginia Company and have often lost sight of the economic incentives that led thousands to venture across the Atlantic. Yet for the American habitations to thrive and to be able to import European essentials, they had to export some product of such great value that it could bear the expensive trans-Atlantic shipping costs. Tobacco proved to be the first such staple discovered outside non-Hispanic America, which perhaps explains why over half-a-dozen English colonies,[9] started during the first two decades of the century, but before the leaf became a sure commodity, failed.

Tobacco served as a profitable export because it was in great demand relative to its supply. In the middle of the 16th century, the Spanish introduced it to Europe where it sold as a medicine, until Sir Walter Raleigh popularized pipe smoking.[10] By the early 1600s, the new fashion had become so widespread that Hispanic planters, whose ability to expand commodity output when prices increased was constrained by government regulations and a limited Caribbean labour force, found themselves unable to meet the needs of the new market. As a result, the value of tobacco soared[11] until only the wealthiest gentlemen could afford it. At this time, around 1616, Virginians discovered that they could raise the plant, and in 1619 one New World writer noted that it fetched 3s. 6d. a pound and that a grower could make £200 yearly. Another author stated that a settler could raise 25 bushels of corn and 700 pounds of tobacco a year, which suggests that the latter brought him £122 10s.[12] In either instance the sum was extraordinary, for from 1613 through 1622 unskilled farm labourers in England received an average wage of about 4s. a week or around £10 8s. a year,[13] provided that they were employed throughout each season which was generally not the case. Even after leaf prices had started declining, earnings remained for some time substantial. For instance, from 1624 to 1629, tobacco planters received on an average 19s. 5d. a pound for their product or thirteen times as much as they usually obtained from 1655 to 1700,[14] the half century following the period treated in this article. It is small wonder then that after 1616 the inhabitants of Jamestown rightly believed that they had discovered in tobacco the means by which their faltering village could become a thriving community, and it is also small wonder that thousands of English labourers, unable to afford the passage to America, chose to sell themselves into indentured servitude in the hope of making their fortunes once their terms expired. A great migration wave thus began, and the settlement of the English and French Antilles must be viewed in its context.

The Caribees, which consist of a chain of small islands stretching from Puerto Rico to the Main, provided logical places for Northern Europeans to found tobacco colonies: all but Trinidad were uninhabited by the Spanish; the direction of the prevailing trades placed the islands upwind from Hispanic America, thereby protecting them from attack; and they lay near the famous Spanish tobacco producing areas of Venezuela and Trinidad,[15] a point which led prospective planters to believe that a quality leaf could be raised in the Caribbean. As a consequence, during the 1620s and early 1630s, the English and French founded settlements on seven Caribee islands: St Christopher (1624), Barbados (1627), Nevis (1628), Antigua (1632), Montserrat (1632), Guadeloupe (1635) and Martinique (1635). In addition, Englishmen also settled two isles closer to the mainland, Old Providence (1629) and Tortuga (1630).

The circumstances surrounding the inception of the Lesser Antillean enclaves underscores the early profitability of tobacco farming. Future inhabitants, mainly young males, migrated to the region with the expectation of making a quick killing and then returning to Europe. The promoters who led the procession had similar motives. Thomas Warner, founder of the first successful colony, was typical of such men, nearly all of whom were unwealthy adventurers. A member of Roger North's short-lived settlement on the Amazon, he arrived at St Christopher in 1624 with less than two dozen men. Despite the destruction of one tobacco crop by a hurricane, in 1625 he returned to England with 9,500 pounds of the leaf. This fetched such a high price that in 1626 he was able to sail back to St Christopher with 400 recruits.[16] The French plantations were begun in an equally modest manner. In 1625, a French privateer which had unsuccessfully attacked a Spanish vessel stopped at St Christopher for repairs. After talking with the Englishmen, the officers

decided that farming would be more profitable than buccaneering, and they formed habitations on the unclaimed ends of the island. From there, they later branched out to Martinique and Guadeloupe.[17] Even the Puritan colony of Providence developed because of the efforts of ambitious entrepreneurs seeking to make their fortunes in tobacco. The Puritans had founded a settlement on Bermuda in 1612, but the climate proved inimical to the cultivation of a quality leaf. Aware of Warner's success, Philip Bell, Governor of Bermuda in the late 1620s, decided to plant in the Caribbean, for he believed that a small tropical island could 'in short time be made more rich and bountiful either by tobacco or any other commodities than double or treble any man's estate in all England'.[18] After sending forth settlers from Bermuda, he offered his resignation to the London directors while at the same time asking them for assistance, particularly in obtaining a royal charter for his new venture. The Earl of Warwick, the principal investor in Puritan overseas enterprises, faced with this *fait accompli*, accepted Bell's proposal, formed the Providence Company, made his erstwhile employee its governor, and gave him substantial financial aid.[19] Of course, not all the individuals founding West Indian settlements were of inconsequential stature. The possibility of acquiring wealth appealed to men of all classes and occupations, and two separate groups of powerful London merchants contested for jurisdiction over Barbados, the most windward of the Lesser Antilles. One faction ultimately obtained the assistance of the King's companion, the Earl of Carlisle, who became proprietor of the English Caribees. The Earl then gave his merchant supporters 10,000 acres on Barbados in return for which they voided his considerable debts to them.[20]

Throughout the 1620s, settlers made extraordinary profits from tobacco, even though increased New World production forced its price steadily downward. As late as 1628, when Barbadians apparently sold their leaf, which all agreed was of inferior quality, for 9d. a pound, expected profits were so high that twenty Barbados servants were contracted on a one year lease for £1,000.[21] Given the risk from disease and natural catastrophe, the leasees obviously expected an average net return per person of well above £50. An indirect but more systematic method of determining profits relies on productivity estimates. Assuming that the typical worker raised between 1,000 and 1,500 pounds of tobacco annually,[22] a conservative estimate, yearly incomes would have varied from £37 10s.

to £56 5s., nearly all of which sum would have been net profit since production costs were limited to the purchase of a hoe, an axe and land, each of which cost little. Land, the one item of potential value, was so abundant relative to the population that even by 1640 it fetched only around 10s. an acre on Barbados, making it possible at that late year for an unassisted farmer to more than meet his field needs with an initial investment of only £2. On the French islands settlers experienced even fewer costs, for Martinique and Guadeloupe remained sparsely colonized until near the end of the century, with the result that uncleared property was virtually worthless. This led the Crown to give new planters free tracts 200 paces by 1,000 paces.[23]

With Caribee incomes four to six times as high as those in England, the islands took on the appearance of boom towns, a designation which also aptly fitted contemporary Virginia.[24] Planters put all their efforts into raising the weed: they lived in hastily constructed huts, imported their foodstuffs, which sometimes led to shortages, and avoided expending time on non-essential improvements to their land. As Sir Henry Colt, who visited Barbados in 1631, wrote, 'your grownd & plantations . . . lye like ye ruines of some village lately burned, . . . all ye earth couered black wth cenders nothinge is cleer. What digged or weeded for beautye?' The inhabitants, many of whom were 'younge & hott bloods', did however spice their labour with an 'excess of drinkinge' and engaged in quarrels stemming from their 'fyery spiritts'.[25] The tropical enclaves were indeed boom communities with the violence and rough living conditions associated with early Virginia and the later gold mining towns of the American West.

The adventurers who swarmed over the Caribees usually acquired their substantial incomes with their own hands, a point which gave the islands an egalitarian appearance. Servants could be purchased, but price theory indicates that settlers would bid the price of indentures up to a point nearly equal to their expected earnings, thereby making the shippers who sold the bondsmen the primary beneficiaries of the white slave trade. That this happened is supported by evidence from Edmund Morgan who cites one case where in 1623 a Virginia servant sold for £150 sterling.[26] It is likely that indentures, purchased at inflated values, often failed to repay their original cost. For tobacco prices declined irregularly for nearly two decades, and during that period colonists, uncertain that the trend would continue, probably tended to overestimate future revenues. It is understandable,

then, why most planters chose not to invest heavily in servile labour but rather kept their work force small. One notable exception consisted of setttlers like Warner and the later famous Colonel James Drax, men who returned to England where they obtained indentures cheaply, that country then being in the midst of a depression.[27] Another exception concerns colonists who luckily had merchant relatives able to send them a steady stream of inexpensive servants, generally in return for a partnership in the estate. Such business arrangements proved advantageous to both parties, for planters without cheap, exploitable labour could never hope to enter the small circle of truly successful West Indians. In all likelihood the later well-known connection between leading settlers and merchants began at this point. It was a case where to become an insular magnate, one had to engage in trade, the area where major profits lay, and not a situation where wealthy colonists chose to invest previously acquired fortunes in shipping.

The confidence of this world of men-on-the-make received a rude shock in 1630 when tobacco values temporarily plummeted to around a pence a pound, an unanticipated low level. The price decline, which was naturally accompanied by a profusion of colonial complaints that may have influenced those scholars who have believed that the pre-sugar era was economically disappointing, can be attributed in part to an abrupt increase in the Antillian tobacco output. For, although in 1629 a Spanish expeditionary force destroyed the Nevis and St Christopher crops, by 1630 the inhabitants of those places had renewed their production; Barbados, founded in 1627, was just coming into its own; and planters on Providence were marketing their first harvest.

Despite the glut, the depression of 1630 was short-lived, with prices rebounding in the following year so that from 1631 to 1634 the leaf sold for an average of 5–6d. a pound and planters found it more profitable to cultivate than other commodities. Among the foremost reasons for tobacco's resurgence in 1631 were Governor Harvey's laws designed to restrict Virginia's production, laws which he apparently enforced until dissatisfied colonists removed him from office in 1635. In addition, in 1632 the English Crown reduced imposts on Virginia leaf from 6d. to 2d. a pound and on that from the Antilles from 9d. to 4d.[28] But the new prosperity proved ephemeral, for Englishmen and Frenchmen, attracted by the still substantial profits to be made in agriculture, continued to flock to

America, causing the tobacco supply to increase rapidly. As a result, prices steadily declined, falling from up to 6d. a pound in 1634 to around 2.5d. in 1635.[29] They would not reach the 1624–34 levels again in the century, and the era when unassisted planters could make their own fortunes had ended.

2   A Growing Depression and the Search for a New Staple, 1635–40

During the next five years, 1635 to 1640, tobacco values steadily deteriorated. Colonists complained when prices fell to 2.5d. a pound, even though that figure was still well above the future long-run average of 1.5d., and they were truly distressed when in 1638 and 1639 a bumper Virginia harvest forced leaf values down to 0.75d. a pound. As might be expected, it was during these last years that Antillean planters earnestly began to investigate raising other commodities, one of which was sugar cane, a product whose potential they did not immediately grasp. The breadth of the search for a new staple can be gleaned from the Providence Company correspondence. Concerned about the stability of tobacco prices, the directors wrote Governor Bell as early as 1632, 'Wish silk grass (like hemp) to be planted and sent home, and sugar canes for private use; cotton to be made trial of; mulberry trees to be procured, also bees and fruits from the main'. Pomegranates, peppers and fig trees were also planted that year.[30] Most of these products proved of little commercial value, if only because spoilage during shipping was excessive. But a few appeared highly profitable, for enduring circumstances had combined to reduce the supply of tropical and semi-tropical commodities reaching Europe from elsewhere in the world, a point enhancing their worth. Warfare handicapped the Brazilian economy; high shipping fees restricted the importation of Indian staples; piracy and unfavourable climatic conditions reduced the quantity of cotton and sugar raised in the Southern Mediterranean; and a complex of factors joined to impair Spanish American agriculture, central to them being a merchantile system which impeded the flow of labour to the New World, taxed goods from there at a rate of roughly 27% *ad valorem*, and placed all shipping in the hands of a monopolistic trade guild.[31]

Yet, even with international circumstances favourable for English and French planters to shift to other commodities, colonists hesitated before abandoning tobacco. Unknown products required new and sometimes complex cultivation skills which were difficult to acquire in the 17th century. In addition, European agriculture revenues then fluctuated widely from year to year, and consequently settlers came to realize that leaf values would not rebound only after the 1638 price decline created a crisis in the industry which led to many Antillean producers leaving it. By the end of the decade, the exodus was largely complete, for in 1638–39 English officials on the Antilles and in Virginia formed a cartel designed to drastically reduce the leaf supply. By its terms Caribbean settlers ceased growing the plant almost entirely.[32] That they agreed to do this without serious argument indicates that most colonists believed that other commodities were more profitable to raise.

Fearing that without French participation the cartel would fail to significantly reduce tobacco supplies, Thomas Warner requested that his neighbours also join it. They declined, perhaps because they hoped to capitalize on the expected higher prices. But Warner was not so easily dissuaded, and by threatening to attack Gallic St Christopher, in May 1639 he forced Sieur Lonvilliers de Poincy, the French governor-general, to support the Anglo-Saxon scheme.[33] Yet even with all the non-Hispanic colonies involved, the crop restriction programme clearly failed to achieve its purpose, partly because Chesapeake planters could not be easily policed.[34] The French left the cartel in late 1640 after their eighteen-month agreement with Warner expired, but by then the leaf offered neither them nor anyone else much immediate future.

It may appear that colonists should have begun turning to sugar during the tobacco ban, but they were then still in the process of acquiring information concerning how to make that difficult staple, and so instead planters started raising cotton, a commodity which required little special knowledge to grow and which solitary farmers could easily cultivate without purchasing expensive equipment. A few colonists, whom others could copy, had already produced it commercially, especially on Barbados where the tobacco was so rank that Richard Ligon, an earlier traveller, called it 'the worst I think that grows in the world'[35] and where the southeast littoral, one of the first areas settled, received insufficient rainfall to produce other commodities luxuriantly.[36] Barbadians began exporting cotton around 1630 when leaf values took their first dip, and in 1631 Sir Henry Colt wrote that 'now ye trade of cotton fills them all with hope'.[37] The rebounding of tobacco prices from 1631 to 1634 temporarily slowed the movement to cotton, but the change in the terms of trade after that period again inspired settlers to grow it. In this respect, they, and other West Indians, had the encouragement of proprietary officials. The Company of the Isles of America, for instance, recommended in 1636 that its colonists raise the product.[38] In May of the following year, the proprietary agent on Barbados, Peter Hay, was told to 'incourage every planter to plant Cotton for Barbados Cotton of all other is esteemed best . . . and it is a staple commoditie that will ever be worth money',[39] while in 1637 Providence Island Company officials notified their governor that cotton was more valuable in England than was tobacco.[40]

But despite the shift to a new staple, planters still found themselves plagued by unstable market conditions, for so many settlers turned to cotton in 1638 that in 1639 the extra supply forced the bottom out of the English market. Prices remained depressed for the next four years. Smyrna cotton, for instance, sold at an average of 0.478 guilders a pound in Amsterdam from 1635 through 1638[41] but brought only 65% of that from 1640 to 1644. The reduction in value, however, had desirable side benefits, for it made cotton fabrics less costly to consumers and contributed to the establishment of the English cotton weaving industry. It also meant, however, that Caribee settlers had failed to find a permanent alternative to tobacco.

In searching for a new staple, colonists began experimenting with ginger, long a major export from Santo Domingo and Puerto Rico.[42] Few records remain of this crop, which was soon to be eclipsed by sugar cane, but all indications suggest that it played a large role in West Indian economies. For instance Father Dutertre, author of a respected 17th-century history of the islands, wrote that, when tobacco cultivation was banned, French planters turned primarily to ginger because 'it had a better price'.[43] But ginger faced an inelastic European demand with the result that, as in the case of cotton, the addition to its supply drove its value rapidly downwards.[44]

Thus by 1640, the English and French Antilles were caught in the throes of a depression, one only slightly mitigated by planter attempts to shift from tobacco to cotton and ginger. Islands where only a few years earlier colonists had been tantalized by the dream of affluence now offered their inhabitants a standard of living little, if any, better than that of Europe. As one Barbadian afterwards wrote, 'this island was in a very low condition . . . and small hopes appeared of raising any fortunes there for the future'.[45] Henry Ashton, Governor of Antigua, described planters on St Christopher as reduced 'to this pointe of undoeing',[46] while on Providence the bleak economic outlook influenced many settlers to emigrate, thereby reducing the island's military strength and paving the way for the 1641 Spanish reconquest. The French inhabitants of course fared no better than their rivals, which perhaps explains why Sieur Loinvilliers de Poincy pessimistic about his future capacity to muster enough men to repel Anglo-American assaults, proposed to the Company directors that part of St Christopher be sold or abandoned.[47]

3 The Appearance of Large Plantation Crops: The Coming of Sugar, 1624–43

By 1640, the West Indian economy had deteriorated to the point where a Barbados proprietary agent wrote 'unlesse some New Inventions be founde oute to Make A Commodytie on the Inhabitants are noe wayes able to subsist'.[48] That new invention was fast making its appearance. Starting sometime near 1635 when tobacco prices crumbled, a limited number of colonists began experimenting with indigo, a prominent blue dye, and shortly afterwards a few commenced testing sugar.[49] It is, of course, not at all surprising that settlers waited until those years before raising these products. In fact, any other economic behaviour would have been inexplicable given the earlier profitability of tobacco.

The introduction of indigo and sugar cane must have occurred only gradually, for to produce either commodity required a heavy capital outlay, sizeable labour force and sophisticated knowledge of manufacturing processes, none of which was needed to grow tobacco, cotton or ginger. The distinction was due to the necessity of processing the dye material and cane juice into finished products before marketing them. In the case of indigo, colonists had to erect large stone vats in which the leaves were steeped and their precipitate oxidized,[50] and although some planters employed as few as half-a-dozen workers, upwards of 17–25 men laboured on particularly efficient estates.[51] The cost of these properties served as an obstacle which dissuaded many West Indians from entering the industry, but the barriers to making sugar were even greater. The milling and refining equipment, which on one Jamaican plantation were inventoried at £199 in 1672,[52] and the minimal number of slaves, cost far more than anything used in manufacturing indigo. The smallest competitive sugar plantations, for instance, contained several dozen workers, while noticeably successful properties had between 60 and 200 hands.[53] The latter estates were worth at least £1,000, and during the 1640s one sold for £14,000.[54] In addition to these expenses operators needed a wealth of information that the first sugar planters were forced to acquire through the costly process of trial and error. To provide some idea of the complexity of this lore, in the boiling house alone the refiner had to know how much lye to add to the syrup, how long to heat each type of juice, how hot to maintain the furnaces and when to strike the final cauldron.[55] Clearly, the mastery of the art of making sugar required time, skill and money. It is no wonder, then, that colonists waited until tobacco values reached very near their long-run levels before seriously committing themselves to learning how to produce muscovado, the common brown sugar later exported from the islands. Nor is it any wonder that settlers experimented with indigo first.

By about 1637, West Indians exported enough of the dye for English officials on St Christopher to levy taxes of 'halfe a pound . . . per poll' for 'powder Shott and other Ammunicion'.[56] But the industry began to blossom only as the decade closed when the value of indigo in Amsterdam rose abruptly from 4.43 guilders a pound in 1638 to 8.10 guilders in 1640.[57] This dramatic change was due to the 1639–41 near collapse of the trans-Atlantic Spanish convoy system, a breakdown which was heightened by the secession of Portugal and by the Catalonian revolt, which served to block the shipment of indigo from Guatemala, then Europe's foremost supplier.[58] As a result, from 1640 through 1642 the dye sold for more than at any other time in the century[59] and temporarily became the most profitable commodity raised in the West Indies, a point which induced settlers with capital to prefer it to sugar.

This was true despite abnormal international market conditions in the sugar industry which made the sweetener also unusually high priced. In the last half of the 16th century, Brazil became the major source of the muscovado consumed in Europe; and since she and her mother country, Portugal, had become components of the Spanish empire in 1580, both were drawn into the struggle that began when a twelve-year truce between Madrid and the Netherlands expired in 1621. That war proved unusually disastrous for Brazil in that the directors of the West India Company, a firm created to conduct the Dutch maritime offensive against the New World Luso-Spanish empire, decided to seize prominent Portuguese slave stations in West Africa and to capture Portuguese America, a land particularly vulnerable because it had been settled only along the coast, making the entire area open to seaborne assault. After several years of abortive attacks, in 1630 the Dutch took Recife, the main port of Pernambuco and the capital of one of the two major Brazilian sugar-producing regions and, during the decade of fighting that followed, they gradually expanded the territory under their control until, by 1641, it included the entire area from Maranhão in the far North to the São Francisco River in the South.[60] During this warfare, however, the object of the conquest, the sugar estates, were largely destroyed, and with their output reduced, muscovado prices on the Amsterdam exchange rose from a year average of 0.32 guilders a pound in 1624 to never less than 0.50 guilders a pound during the 1630s. With prices like these, Caribee settlers were likely to find the commodity profitable to grow once they mastered its intricate production processes.

As a prerequisite to accomplishing this feat, planters not only had to find sugar cane relatively more remunerative to cultivate than indigo, but their colonies had to mature to a point where wealthy sugar estates would be secure from confiscation or attack. The threat of invasion particularly worried wealthy investors who stood to loose a fortune in slaves and equipment during even the briefest seaborne raid, for although the Caribees contained few accessible landing places, they straddled the main Hispanic convoy route from Iberia to Peru, which made them a tempting target for passing fleets. The danger became a reality when Spaniards laid ruin to the Nevis and St Christopher colonies (1629) and twice attacked Old Providence (1635 and 1641). In addition, Spain fortified the small island of St Martin from whence supply ships picked off straying Englishmen and Frenchmen. Barbados excepted, Indians also threatened the colonies. Caribs toppled English settlements on Trinidad, St Lucia and Tobago, and in 1640 overran Antigua. At the same time they isolated and harassed the French on Guadeloupe to the extent that until 1640 that community remained on the verge of collapse, and even as late as 1654 they almost conquered Martinique.[61] There remained only one defence against these dangers; namely, for the English and French to increase their insular populations to the point where potential invaders would avoid attacking them; but until the mid-1630s, little advance was made in this direction.

Harried by depression and the ever growing threat of civil war, Englishmen left their homeland in such numbers during the 1630s that their exodus was called the 'Great Migration'. The 1635 collapse of the tobacco market reorientated that human flow, causing many individuals who otherwise would have gone to Virginia to sail to the West Indies where they could cultivate the more profitable cotton, ginger, indigo and later sugar cane. Thus, while the citizenry of Virginia increased from 4,914 in 1635[62] to an estimated 7,738 in 1639,[63] the population of Barbados alone, whose dry climate proved especially appropriate for raising cotton, mushroomed from 1,227 in 1635 to 8,707 in 1639.[64] By that time the island was too heavily settled to succumb easily to foreign invasion. The same was less true of the other Caribee settlements. Under 20,000 Englishmen[65] and perhaps a third as many Frenchmen dwelt on the Antilles by 1640,[66] but only Barbados and St Christopher contained substantial populations, and the joint inhabitants of the latter island lived in mutual fear of each other. The resultant instability so retarded St Christopher's development that its economy fully flourished only after England permanently acquired the French sector in 1713. By 1640, then, Barbados was easily the most heavily populated and securely held West Indian colony, which gave it a substantial advantage over its insular neighbours.

Planter properties were also threatened by the arbitrary actions of Antillean governors, who ruled largely independent of home control until the success of the subsequent sugar boom attracted European attention to the Caribees. Since most of these officials went to the islands expecting to make their fortunes and since they lacked the supportive power sources which both gave and checked authority granted to local leaders in their homelands, they sometimes levied heavy fines on wealthier rivals who committed minor transgressions. Governor Henry Hawley of Barbados exemplifies such a leader. In 1630, he arraigned and executed his predecessor, Sir William Tufton, on flimsy charges following Tufton's protest at the governor's arbitrary rule. Hawley then managed with an iron hand the colony for nearly a decade during which time he once even exiled the Earl of Carlisle's kinsman and proprietary agent, Peter Hay. Upon being given recall orders in 1639, Hawley changed his stand, created an island assembly, and temporarily defied his former patron. Yet the revolt was short-lived, for Hawley lacked widespread popular support and was forced to surrender to Crown officials, leaving behind an established legislature which gave Barbadians a means not found on the other Caribees of countering arbitrary government.[67] For this reason also, the settlers on that island experienced a decrease in investment risks towards the end of the 1630s.

It is no wonder then, that with risk costs and tobacco prices having declined simultaneously on only Barbados, colonists there were more aggressive than those elsewhere in turning to sugar. The precise date when cultivation began remains unclear, but one account stated that the original trials were made in 1637 by a Dutchman, Peeter Brower.[68] At least talk of raising sugar cane was in the air by that time, for in 1638 the Earl of Warwick attempted to purchase the colony's proprietary charter for apparently £12,000 in order to make the commodity.[69] Even so, the year when planting began is unimportant, for the initial experiments were largely unsuccessful. As Richard Ligon noted,

some of the most industrious men, having gotten Plants from Pernambock, a place in *Brazill*, and made tryal of them at the Barbadoes; and finding them to grow, they planted more and more . . . till they had such considerable number, as they were worth the while to set up a very small Ingenio [mill and boiling house] . . . But, the secrets of the work being not well understood, the Sugars they made were very inconsiderable, and little worth, for two or three years. But they finding their errours by their daily practice, began a little to mend; and, by new directions from *Brazil*, sometimes by strangers, and now and then by their own people, who . . . were content sometimes to make a voyage thither, to improve their knowledge in a thing they so much desired . . . And so returning with more Plants, and better knowledge, they went on upon fresh hopes.[70]

Thus, at the earliest, Barbadians became familiar with the intricacies of cultivating sugar only after 1639 when it superseded indigo in profitability.

The French sugar industry was created shortly after that of the English. In 1635, officials of the proprietary firm, the Company of the Isles of America, directed settlers on Guadeloupe 'to work their people principally at cotton and at sugar' and to de-emphasize tobacco.[71] The recommendation concerning muscovado was not followed, but the potential of cane was recognized, and in 1640 one traveller wrote that in time 'it will be far more common to make sugar than tobacco, principally on the islands of Guadeloupe and Martinique, which will be able someday to supply France'.[72] That was on the eve of the founding of the French sugar industry. In 1639, the Company had granted a

Dutchman, Daniel Trezel, a six-year monopoly on all sugar produced on Martinique if he would establish a plantation there. Trezel began clearing land and planting cane, but he also experienced financial difficulties, and in 1642, reportedly when he was ready to produce 25 tons of sugar, Governor Du Parquet, who gained nothing from the arrangement, permitted his milling equipment to be sold for what some said were minor debts.[73]

But despite Trezel's ill fortune, the industry was taking root on the other islands. The first recorded shipment from Barbados reached England in 1643, and according to an enthusiastic proprietary agent, the colony had become 'the most flourishing Island in all those American parts, and I verily believe in all the world, for the producing of sugar Indico Ginger'.[74] According to tradition, the industry began on St Christopher in the same year,[75] and in 1644 the French proprietary company, dissatisfied with what had happened on Martinique, financed the founding of an estate on Guadeloupe, but only after appointing a member of its board of directors, Charles Houel, as governor.

By that time sugar had again replaced indigo as the most remunerative product on the islands. Why this occurred can only be understood in terms of commodity price changes. With the re-establishment of the Spanish convoy system, the value of Amsterdam indigo fell from an average of 8.10 guilders a pound in 1640 to 4.58 guilders in 1643, 3.15 guilders in 1645, 2.78 guilders in 1646, and 2.31 guilders in 1648, with the result that from 1645 to 1649 the dye sold for an average of only 2.70 guilders a pound, well below its long-run value.[76] If the terms of trade during the more competitive and stable second half of the century are any guide, the critical year in this steady decline, when indigo and sugar appeared equally profitable to cultivate, was 1643. For over a decade thereafter, the sweetener easily held the first position.

Much of the credit for the new primacy of muscovado was due to changes in its supply. Following the secession of Portugal and Luso-Brazil from Spain in 1640 and the Dutch consolidation of its conquests during the early 1640s, warfare nearly ceased in Brazil, sugar output expanded, and Dutch prices fell from 0.49 guilders a pound in 1649 to a low of 0.31 guilders in 1643, a point which helps to explain why Trezel failed. But at the same time, the Dutch West India Company, which was experiencing difficulty paying its debts, decreased its Brazilian garrison, ordered its overdue loans collected, and recalled (1644) its popular New

World governor-general Johan Maurits, whose expansive economic policies struck the directors as extravagant. The foreclosure on delinquent loans, a policy implemented by Maurits' successors, threw the colony's financial system into disarray, causing interest rates to rise to as much as 4 per cent a month. With the region in economic upheaval, the Portuguese citizenry revolted in 1645, capturing the hinterland. For the next nine years, the Dutch held the ports and the rebels controlled the agricultural areas.[77] Under such circumstances, sugar cultivation was again thoroughly disrupted, and, with the decrease in supply, prices rose, averaging 0.51 guilders a pound from 1646 through 1654. The new and extraordinary profitability of sugar production was reflected in an abrupt shift in the Amsterdam terms of trade, and consequently it took on an average almost three times as much indigo to purchase a pound of sugar from 1645 to 1649 as it had during the previous five years.

4 The Sugar Boom, 1645–54

With Barbadians secure from foreign invasion or confiscatory decrees, they were in an ideal position to take advantage of the resurgence in sugar prices. As a result, almost overnight the colony was thrust into a boom period much like that of the earlier tobacco era. As a measure of the new prosperity, Ligon wrote that planters sold their muscovado for 50s.–54s. 6d. a cwt, prices far above the 23s.–25s. they received in the late 1650s.[78] The difference between the two levels was nearly all profit for planters and it furthered their buoyant psychology and their get-rich-quick talk. Ligon, for instance, believed that sugar 'will make' Barbados 'one of the richest Spots of earth under the Sun', and he described one man, Colonel James Drax, who had arrived on the island with, at the most, £300 and yet who by 1650 expected to return soon to England with sufficient money to buy an estate large enough to provide a yearly income of £10,000. Colonel Thomas Modyford, who immigrated to Barbados with Ligon in 1647, had similar ambitions, and he also by 1650 was saying that he would not return to the Old Country until he had realized £100,000 on his investment of only £1,000.[79] At the same time William Powrey, who like many other settlers sought financial assistance in England, assured an uncle that £1,000 spent to equip a property with slaves and mill would return £2,000 annually after three years.[80] By any standard, these men expected astronomical profits.

The exceptional value of sugar led to a reduction in the sum needed to enter the industry. James Parker, for instance, wrote in 1646 that 'a man with about 200 off pounds...might quickly gaine an estate by sugar',[81] for even a plantation too small to function efficiently could return a good profit. This made it very easy for colonists who had already developed a work force large enough to raise indigo to switch to sugar cane. Moreover, while £200 was then a substantial figure, amounting to nearly twenty times the yearly wage of unskilled labourers in England, money flowed freely on Barbados. Numerous English gentry, who had shown the bad judgement to side with the King during the Civil War and had fled to the island, were inspired by the price of sugar to invest their funds in the industry. Indicative of the economic and numerical importance of such men is the fact that by 1650 they dominated the Barbados Assembly and helped cause the island to side with the royal family whose prospects were then bleak.

The Dutch also contributed to the availability of capital and, incidentally, of labour. After the Brazilians revolted in 1645, the West India Company directors, believing that the insurrection would soon be squelched, ordered their governor on the Gold Coast, Van der Wel, to continue sending slaves to Brazil. The High Council in Pernambuco, faced with an influx of blacks it could not use, shipped them to the Lesser Antilles where they were sold on lenient credit terms.[82] Of the islands, Barbados lay nearest to Recife, and with conditions on it propitious for cultivating cane, the Dutch found it expedient to sell nearly all their slaves to that colony, a situation aptly described by Sir Robert Harley, who wrote that 'the Dutch being ingaged on the coast of Giney in Affrick for Negros slaves having lost Brasille not knowing where to vent them they trusted them to Barbados, this was the first rise of the Plantacion'.[83] By perhaps 1650 and certainly by 1654, at least 20,000 blacks dwelt on the island,[84] a number equal to over twice what its white population had been only fifteen years earlier.

The influx of slaves and the size requirements for sugar estates altered the nature of Barbados society and led to the creation of a planter elite. The Dutch, forced to dump their blacks in the Caribbees, inundated the market and were unable to obtain a price for their slaves even close to their worth. Ligon wrote that a 'best man *Negroe*' cost £30 sterling and that a woman brought £25–£27.[85] This was 60–100% higher than the Royal African Company had charged

planters during the first twenty years it serviced Barbados,[86] which indicates that the Dutch received a return that more than covered their cost of granting credit. But the income colonists obtained from their slaves was proportionately much higher. One source noted that a black could produce enough sugar to pay for his original cost in only eighteen months,[87] while Ligon's figures show a net profit of £57 10s. yearly per labourer on a plantation containing 130 workers.[88] Consequently, slaves appeared cheap and settlers invested heavily in them. This trend was in sharp contrast to the boom years of the late 1620s, and it resulted in wealth patterns becoming strikingly unequal, with a few planters buying out surrounding small farmers in order to have estates large enough to make sugar.[89]

Adding to this economic growth was an enormous influx of English servants attracted to Barbados by its opulence. These people were sold at rates competitive with slave prices, making it profitable for planters to employ them as field hands. Only too late did indentures discover that on sugar estates men laboured under frightful conditions. As Ligon wrote, 'I have seen an Overseer beat a Servant with a cane about the head, till the blood had followed, for a fault that is not worth the speaking of; and yet he must have patience, or worse will follow. Truly, I have seen such cruelty there done to servants as I did not think one Christian could have done to another.'[90] Additional Englishmen, political prisoners and felons, also found themselves sentenced to the West Indies where they served lengthy indentureships. Cromwell shipped no less than 12,000 captured soldiers to Barbados,[91] while judges sent convicts there in such numbers that Henry Whistler wrote in his journal, 'this Illand is the Dunghill wharone England doth cast forth its rubidg: Rodgs and hors and such like peopel are those which are generally brought heare.'[92]

The impact of this influx of labourers on the insular economy was softened only by their high death rate. In 1647 alone an epidemic, probably of yellow fever, killed an estimated 6,000–10,000 Barbadians.[93] Dysentery, otherwise called the 'bloody flux', also accounted for numerous deaths, perhaps because colonists were unaware of basic sanitary practices. As it was, slaves and evidently servants drank from the same still ponds at which animals were watered. These ponds were further used 'upon all occasions, and to all purposes: to boil their meat, to make their drink, to wash their linen, for it will beare soape'.[94] Despite the ensuing toll, the population continued to increase, and by 1654 perhaps 25,000–30,000 Englishmen inhabited Barbados.[95]

Apart from population changes, the magnitude of the sugar boom can be seen in the extension of the frontier line. When colonists first began to grow cane, Barbados was only partially settled. Ligon indicated that in 1647 at least one-third of it was not cultivated, especially the higher parts where 'passage was stopped by gullies'. Yet the frontiersmen, who probably made their living girding and burning trees, planting provisions and tobacco, and then selling the land, were fast extending the inhabited area, for Ligon also wrote, 'at the time we came first there, we found both *Potatoes, Maies* and *Bonavists*, planted between the boughes, the Trees lying along upon the ground: so far short was the ground then of being clear'd'.[96] In 1652, five years later, the frontier was so far extended that Colonal Modyford wrote, 'this island of Barbados cannot last in an height of trade three year longer especially for sugar, the wood being almost already spent'.[97] He could have added that men already imported lumber from as far away as Surinam.[98] Still, contrary to the impression he gave, the colony was not yet fully settled, for its population stood at only about 70% of the 66,170 who dwelt there in 1684 or 83% of the 54,498 who inhabited the place in 1712.[99] Even so, by 1654 it contained more people per square mile than any agricultural area in Europe.

As the Barbados frontier receded and planters grew affluent, primitive living conditions began to disappear. Ligon had found the dwellings alive with insects and shabbily constructed. Made of roughly cut local wood, the houses were built so low that he could hardly stand upright while wearing his hat. They also lacked window glass. This forced colonists to construct their homes without openings on the side towards the trade winds in order to avoid having rain blown inside during storms. The breezeless rooms were consequently hot and stuffy. In addition, flies, cockroaches, ants and mosquitoes from the undrained swamps so pestered the inhabitants that, to stop insects which crawled, settlers set table legs and bed posts in bowls of water and hung hammocks and shelves containing meat by tarred ropes. Planters also placed sugar at one end of the dinner table to attract flies from food at the other.[100]

Yet the island was fast changing. Father Biet, visiting it in 1654, wrote that the 'plantation master's house is ordinarily handsome and has many rooms'. He also noted that 'one furnishes his house sumptuously. Things that are the finest in England or elsewhere are found in the island',[101] and a year later Henry Whistler wrote, 'the genterey heare doth liue far better than ours doue in England'.[102] The wealth and labour which flowed into Barbados during the sugar boom years had transformed that colony from a raw and primitive frontier region into a mature and affluent settlement.

During those same years, the remaining Caribees failed to turn fully to sugar or to become completely inhabited, partly because most prospective colonists sailed to Barbados but also because an unusual degree of political turmoil swept the other islands. For instance, rebellion intermittently racked the English sector of St Christopher from December 1641 to at least March 1642,[103] after which Governor Warner carefully exiled, or executed, his enemies. Affairs probably remained somewhat unstable for some time following that because Warner was by then an old man according to West Indian standards (he was to die in 1649), and people were perhaps unsure what type of government would replace his autocratic rule. In comparison to this short-lived upheaval, a protracted revolution of major proportions convulsed the French territories. Since their founding, their leading officials had managed with little outside assistance, and when, in 1645, the French proprietary company recalled its governor-general, Sieur de Poincy, he refused to relinquish his command of St Christopher, the only area over which he exercised actual authority. In the struggle which followed, the other governors sided first with the Company of the Isles of America and tried to seize de Poincy; but when this failed and the Crown, which was also involved in a civil war at home and the Thirty Years War abroad, chose not to provide the firm with financial of military support, the governor of Guadeloupe, Charles Houel, also rebelled. There ensued a lengthy and violent rebellion during which major planters who were reluctant to turn against their King found themselves pitted against their governors. These latter, arguing that the Company sought to impose extra duties on settlers, enlisted the assistance of small farmers and confiscated the property of their opponents. The trouble even spread to Martinique, the single island which remained loyal to the firm. The civil war drew to a close in the late 1640s when the Company, which was near bankruptcy, sought to recoup its losses by selling its proprietary claim to the by then clearly victorious governors, thereby legalizing their independent positions. This it did between 1649 and 1651, ending half a decade of strife.[104]

During that period, the French sugar industry remained in an undeveloped state[105] with, primarily, the governors investing heavily in it. A visitor to Guadeloupe wrote around 1647 that Houel had a plantation containing 100 Negroes with 80 more ordered and that he expected to make 75 tons of sugar yearly,[106] but as late as 1656 only about ten mills existed on the island.[107] A traveller staying on St Christopher in 1646 and early 1647 wrote that de Poincy owned over 100 slaves, a sugar mill and an indigo works. Advised by a man called 'Dom Paul Espagnol', the governor supposedly earned annually 30,000 *écus* from sugar, and the commodity was described as 'the first merchandise of our islands', no doubt because of its price. Yet despite this favourable description, the sugar industry appeared relatively undeveloped. De Poincy possessed the largest plantation in the French sector, but his boiling house contained only three cauldrons which made his works of minimal efficient size.[108] Even so, he apparently took advantage of the high sugar prices and rapidly increased his production, for Father Pelleprat, who visited St Christopher in 1654, believed that he owned 600 or 700 slaves.[109] If true, this would have made him very nearly the most wealthy planter on the Antilles, a position in striking contrast to that of his subjects who owned slaves and raised mainly tobacco.

With planters living outside Barbados unable to shift fully to sugar cane, it might be expected that their insular economies would remain depressed. Yet that was not the case, for with the primary flow of English labourers directed towards Barbados and with Spanish America no longer able to compete for European tobacco markets, the tobacco and cotton supplies reaching the Old World ceased expanding at previous rates and may even have decreased. Prices for these commodities consequently rose to profitable levels. The average value of Virginia tobacco, for instance, increased from 0.9d. per pound in 1640–43 to 1.5d. in 1645–49 and 3d. in 1649–50. As a result, all the English Caribbean colonies prospered, and their populations steadily expanded. The citizenry of Anglo-St Christopher, for instance, was estimated at more than 6,000 in 1645 and 12,000–13,000 in 1648.[110] While these figures lack reliability, by 1655 so many people inhabited the colony that one observer wrote, 'this island is almost worne out by reason of the multituds that live upon it'.[111] Even the less defended Leewards participated in the prosperity, and the number of

Englishmen on Antigua rose from about thirty families in 1640 to 350 armed men or 750 'soules' in 1646 and close to 1,200 men in 1655.[112]

Despite the divisive civil war wracking the French colonies, their populations also grew rapidly. In 1642, the Company of the Isles of America, which had every reason to inflate its accomplishments since it sought support from the Crown, declared that over 7,000 Frenchmen lived on the Antilles.[113] Three years later, a priest put the number at 5,000. Of these, 3,000 dwelt on St Christopher and 1,000 each inhabited Guadeloupe and Martinique.[114] Their populations increased substantially during the next decade, and by 1655 the islands contained around 13,000 whites and 10,000 slaves.[115] To put this expansion of perhaps threefold to fivefold over a thirteen-year period into perspective, during the next forty-five years their citizenry increased only one and one-half times.[116] Equally important, during this period the population of Martinique and Guadeloupe surpassed that of French St Christopher: the 1645 estimate of 3,000 living on the latter island is higher than any that followed, while in 1655 Guadeloupe was said to contain 12,000 whites although in 1664 it actually had, according to a census, only 5,009.[117] That was very near the 5,303 persons said to inhabit Martinique in 1658.[118] During the sugar boom era, the French thus became thoroughly entrenched on what later became their two Caribee strongholds.

The end of that period was sealed in January 1654 when the Portuguese expelled the Dutch from Recife, the main port of Pernambuco, thereby enabling Brazilian producers to again market their commodities in Europe. As a result, tropical staple prices dropped to competitive levels, ending the most lucrative age in West Indian agriculture. For Barbadians, however, the period had lost much of its lustre even earlier. In May of 1650, royalists in the island assembly passed a declaration of loyalty to the son of Charles I. Parliament retaliated in August by forbidding Englishmen to trade with the island. Then, in 1651, Cromwell sent a fleet to the Caribees which blockaded the colony; and in January 1652, after James Modyford, then a leading militia officer, defected with his regiment, the insurgents surrendered. Because the warfare interrupted trade, planters doubtless fared poorly.

Since Holland played a major role in the Barbados economy, trade was further disturbed by the Anglo-Dutch War of 1652–54. That engagement however, did benefit the French islands, for the Amsterdam merchants were temporarily forced to orient the bulk of their Caribee shipping to them. Relations became so close between the two nationalities that when Indians attacked Martinique in 1654, Dutch soldiers were used to bear the brunt of the assault and when Protestant refugees fled Brazil, following the Portuguese reconquest, they bypassed the English possessions for Catholic Guadeloupe.

With the 1654 decline in muscovado prices, the Caribee economies experienced a sharp reverse. Numerous sugar-cane planters, hoping to minimize their losses, turned to cotton or ginger, increasing the supply of those commodities so much that their values also fell. Ginger, for instance, declined by 1655-56 from £5 sterling a cwt, to £1.25, a drop in percentage very near that which had occurred in the price of sugar.[119] The ramifications of the recession touched most aspects of Antillean life. Among the noticeable consequences, the number of whites willing to migrate to the region decreased, and as a result the islands experienced a loss in their European populations. The number of Englishmen on Barbados fell from perhaps 25,000 in 1654, apparently the highest figure in its history, to 19,568 by 1684,[120] while the population of sparsely settled Martinique declined by over 1,000.[121] Antiguans expressed the prevailing feeling of the time in a 1656 petition to Cromwell in which they asked for aid because 'many plantations have been deserted'. Their statement further noted that 'no supplies of servants have of late arrived from England' and that the 'number of fighting men is very inconsiderable', so that 'unless some speedy course is taken to remedy these evils, the island will be quite deserted'.[122] Antiguans were not the only ones seeking a political remedy for their economic ills. Barbadians petitioned the home government in 1654 to enforce the law prohibiting the cultivation of tobacco in England,[123] and in 1655-56 they presented the Protector with a carefully prepared request asking that he levy prohibitive duties on Brazilian sugar and reduce tariffs on English colonial commodities. As a result of these and other New World pressures, he revised the customs schedule.[124] In addition, he declared that all earlier loans made by the Dutch to settlers were to be paid to the English government. Colonial officials, who were themselves often planters, failed to collect these accounts, and consequently Englishmen emerged from the boom period largely unencumbered by debts.

The depression of 1654, and the competition characteristic of the following era, hardly proved disastrous for planters. Antigua did not, as the petitioners feared, become deserted, and while Martinique did temporarily lose settlers, it soon became the foremost French colony of the century. These successes, however, occurred in large part because of the firm foundation established during the prosperous years, 1624-54,

Table 1   Anglo-American Tobacco Prices, 1624-50 (pence per lb)

Year	Price	Year	Price
1624	36,[1] 24,[2] 6	1639	4/5
1625	12, 36[3]	1640	1 1/5
1628	3, 9[4]	1641	1/2
1630	2, 1[5]	1642	1 1/2
1631	6	1643	4/5
1632	6	1645	1 1/2
1633	9	1646	1 1/2
1634	1,[6] 6,[7] 4/5, 4-6[8]	1647	1 1/2
1635	2-3, 2-3	1649	3
1636	2	1650	3
1638	4/5		

[1] All uncited prices come from Robert P. Thomas and Terry L. Anderson, 'The Economic Growth of the Chesapeake in the Seventeenth Century'. unpublished paper, Department of Economics, University of Washington, n.p. and Irene W. D. Hecht, 'The Virginia Colony, 1607-40: A study in Frontier Growth' (Ph.D. dissertation, University of Washington, 1969), 356-58.
[2] Edmund S. Morgan, 'The Firth American Boom: Virginia 1618 to 1630', *William and Mary Quarterly*, 3rd ser., 28 (April 1971), 177.
[3] *Ibid.*
[4] *CSP Dom.*, *1628-1629*, ser. 2, III, 411.
[5] George Louis Beer, *The Origins of the British Colonial System 1578-1660* (1908; rpt. Gloucester, Mass., 1959), 93.
[6] Lewis Cecil Gray, *History of Agriculture in the Southern United States to 1860* (1933; rpt. Gloucester, Mass., 1958), I, 260.
[7] Beer, *British Colonial System*, 94.
[8] *Ibid.*

Table 2   Netherlands Prices of Sugar, Cotton and Indigo, 1624-54 (guilders per Dutch lb)

Year	Sugar[1]	Cotton[2]	Indigo[3]	Year	Sugar	Cotton	Indigo
1624	0.32	0.81	4.13	1640	0.49	0.34	8.10
1625	0.38	0.84	3.85	1641	0.38	0.33	4.95
1626	0.42		3.76	1642	0.34	0.29	5.25
1628	0.44	0.60	3.90	1643	0.31	0.29	4.58
1630	0.57	0.53	3.72	1645	0.39	0.56	3.15
1631	0.59	0.48	3.55	1646	0.57	0.61	2.78
1632	0.54	0.50	3.45	1648	0.43	0.28	2.31
1633	0.54	0.48	3.83	1649	0.52	0.29	2.57
1634	0.50	0.48	3.75	1650	0.49	0.28	2.79
1635	0.51	0.56	3.90	1651	0.53	0.34	2.30
1636	0.52	0.50	3.83	1652	0.50	0.34	2.18
1637	0.67	0.47	3.90	1653	0.51	0.43	2.53
1638	0.54	0.38	4.43	1654	0.51	0.46	3.13

[1] Nicholaas Posthumus, *Inquiry into the History of Prices in Holland* (Leiden, 1946), I, 119.
[2] *Ibid.*, 281.
[3] *Ibid.*, 415-16.

successes which elevate those three decades to a prominent place in West Indian history. Yet events during that time are also much misunderstood. Scholars have overlooked the extraordinary incomes planters originally received from producing tobacco and how this influenced the founding of ten English and French colonies in the Caribbean between 1624 and 1635. Also overlooked have been the accompanying increase in tobacco output and consequent decrease in leaf prices, a trend which culminated in a depression around 1640 and which motivated settlers to feverishly search for a new staple. As a result of their investigations, Barbadians and to a lesser extent other colonists began raising sugar and there occurred another intense boom that lasted until 1654. By then the growth in West Indian populations had placed England and France in a position where they felt obliged to assert themselves as major Antillean powers, while Barbados, the most developed of the Caribees, exhibited all the characteristics that prompted men later in the century to call her 'the garden of the world'[125] and Henry Whistler to write in 1655 'This island is one of the riches spotes of ground in the wordell and fully inhabited'.[126] Neither Jamaica nor the larger French colonies of Martinique, Guadeloupe, and later St Dominique would overtake her in population until the 18th century which, as much as anything, indicates the strength and formative influence of the economic forces at work during this early period.

Notes

1. Historians have often stated that, for unspecified reasons, sugar cane cultivation was exceptionally profitable and economic growth unusually rapid during the 1660s. For instance, Richard Sheridan described this period as a 'golden age'. See *The Development of the Plantations to 1750: An Era of West Indian Prosperity 1750–1775, Chapters in Caribbean History*, I (Barbados, 1970), 83, Aside from explaining in detail the causes of that prosperity, this article seeks to move back the chronology of that era to before 1654.

2. Richard S. Dunn, *Sugar and Slaves: The Rise of the Planter Class in the English West Indies, 1624–1713* (Chapel Hill, 1972), 203. This is easily the finest book published on the 17th-century Antilles. Most of the sugar was shipped to London where the customs on the white import amounted to £1,419 12s. and the custom on brown sugar (muscovado) totalled £10,002 10s. See W. Noel Sainsbury (ed.), *Calendar of State Papers, colonial series, American and the West Indies, 1754–1660* (London, 1860), I 434, (hereafter *CSP Col. AWI, 1574–1660*). It should be noted that sugar cane was cultivated on the Caribees quite early, perhaps because the juice from the stalks served as a raw sweetener and as a base for alcoholic beverages. During the 16th century, Indians apparently carried the plant

from Puerto Rico to the larger French islands, for the first settlers found it growing wild, while Captain Powell introduced it to Barbados in 1627. Because of the plant's availability, colonists possibly exported some crude molasses during the 1630s, but until *ca.* 1640 they evidently failed to invest the capital in equipment and knowledge necessary to make a quality product.

3. Accepting this unproven belief makes it difficult to explain why planters turned to sugar cane in the 1640s, for one is then faced with the perplexing question of why Caribee settlers waited nearly twenty years after founding their colonies before raising their most remunerative product. It is the thesis of this paper that sugar was not always their most profitable commodity and that colonists turned to it only when the sweetener increased in value relative to alternative staples. For a different explanation of events, see Matthew Edel, 'The Brazilian Sugar Cycle of the Seventeenth Century and the Rise of West Indian Competition', *Caribbean Studies*, IX (April 1969), 24–44.

4. *No Peace Beyond the Line: The English in the Caribbean 1624–1609* (New York, 1972), 33, 98.

5. *Sugar and Slaves*, 19, 49, 60–1, 188. The appearance of this and the above recent works enables us to delineate the frontiers of Caribbean scholarship. Both authors introduce new archival findings, and both view the early sugar era as a prosperous time, but neither writer systematically utilized price data, the primary basis for the conclusions of his article, to throw light on the course of economic development. For that reason, perhaps, neither noted that the early West Indian economies were subject to violent economic cycles.

6. See Table 1.

7. Nicholaas W. Posthumus, *Inquiry into the History of Prices in Holland* (Leiden, 1946), I, 119, 169–70, 281–86, 413–16.

8. The Amsterdam price of tobacco, or any other New World staple, was the sum of its American price, transportation costs and transaction expenses. Competition rapidly drove the latter down to a point where additional shippers and merchants had little incentive to enter the field, thereby minimizing changes in average profits. Until 1651–52, basic operating costs in these two areas also remained relatively constant for there occurred no major shifts in the balance of sea power, no break in New World Anglo-French hostilities with Spain, and no significant cost reducing shipping innovations. Consequently, European market fluctuations were consistently passed directly to planters, causing colonial incomes to oscillate from one extreme to another. The dynamics of that situation can more fully be understood by examining a hypothetical case. Assume that, as in the 1685 sugar industry, Barbadians sold their produce for 10s. a cwt and that transportation and transaction charges added an additional 10s. burden to the commodity so that it fetched 20s. a cwt wholesale in London. A 4s. or 20% decrease in the London figure, then, would result in a 4s. or 40% decline in its West Indian value.

9. Among these were two on the Amazon, two in Guiana, two on the Caribees and one in New England.

10. F. W. Fairhold, *Tobacco Its History and Associations* (London, 1859), 50. The curative powers of tobacco were widely advertised in natural histories. See John Gerard, *The Herball or General Histoire of Plantes* (London, 1597), 287 and Jacques Gohory, *Instruction sur l'herbe petum ditte en france l'herbe de la Royne ou Medicée* (Paris, 1572), *passim*.

11. Huguette and Pierre Chaunu, *Séville et l'Atlantique* (Paris, 1956), VI, Pt 2, 1033.

12. Lewis Cecil Gray, *History of Agriculture in the Southern United States to 1860* (1933; rpt. Gloucester, Mass., 1958), I, 218-19.

13. In comparison, the lesser gentry lived well. James E. Rogers described one landowner, a man educated at Cambridge, who on £300 or £400 a year kept a stable of horses, lived in some luxury and maintained a considerable number of servants. See *A History of Agriculture and Prices in England* (Oxford, 1887), V, 28-9, 673.

14. See Table 1 and Thomas and Anderson, 'Growth of the Chesapeake'. n.p.

15. Trinidad was actually little more than a contraband centre for Venezuelan tobacco, but many Northern Europeans believed it to be a major producer. John Gerard, for instance, wrote that the best tobacco came from that island but did not mention Venezuela. See *The Herball*, 285, and Eric Eustace Williams, *History of the People of Trinidad and Tobago* (New York, 1964), 14.

16. James A. Williamson, *The Caribee Islands Under the Proprietary Patents* (London, 1926), 22 and John Cordy Jeaffreson, *A Young Squire of the Seventeenth Century* (London, 1878), I, 18.

17. Nellis M. Crouse, *French Pioneers in the West Indies, 1624-44* (New York, 1940), 16-18; and Jean Baptiste Dutertre, *Histoire générale des Antilles habitées par les François* (Paris, 1667), I, 1-113.

18. Arthur Percival Newton, *The Colonising Activities of the English Puritans* (New Haven, 1914), 33.

19. *Ibid.*, 31-34, 44-46.

20. The early history of Barbados is described by Vincent T. Harlow, *A History of Barbados, 1625-85* (1926; rpt. New York, 1969), N. Darnell Davis, *The Cavaliers and Roundheads of Barbados, 1650-1652* (Georgetown, British Guiana, 1887) and Williamson, *The Caribee Islands*. Richard S. Dunn provides the best overview of the colonization of all of the islands in his *Sugar and Slaves*.

21. John Bruce, (ed.), *Calendar of State Papers, domestic series, Charles I, 1628-1629*, ser. 2 (London, 1859), III, 411 and Harlow, *History of Barbados*, 12.

22. Thomas and Anderson have noted seven productivity estimates for Virginia between 1624 and 1645. They are 800 lbs, 800-1,000 lbs, 1,500 lbs, 1,530 lbs, 2,000-2,400 lbs and 2,000-3,000 lbs. To these I added one of 1,000 lbs from the early French Caribbean and took the median which was 1,000-1,500 lbs. This is a conservative figure, for the lower productivity estimates probably applied to planters who spend much of their time raising corn. See 'Growth of the Chesapeake', Appendix Two, and (Anon.), 'La plus ancienne relation de voyage aux colonies françaises des Antilles' (ca. 1640), ed. Louis-Philippe May, *Terre-air-mer, la geographie*, XVIII (July-August 1932), 16. Virginia's productivity estimates clearly provide a reasonable proxy for Caribbean figures. For one thing, cultivation techniques were nearly identical in the two regions, partly because the English and French were unable to improve already existing Spanish husbandry practices. For an understanding of the virtually unchanging state of the art from ca. 1620 to 1779, one need only glance at the works of Vázquez de Espinosa, Father Labat and Jonathan Carver. Second, several West Indian productivity estimates exist for the years following 1645 and these closely resemble those coming from Virginia. John Scott (ca. 1668), for instance, stated that a man who raised his own provisions could grow 2,500 lbs of tobacco yearly while Father Labat (ca. 1700) placed the figure at 1,330 lbs. See Antonio Vázquez de Espinosa, *Description of the Indies* (ca. 1620), trans. Charles Upson Clark (1942; rpt. Washington DC, 1968), 56-57;

Jean Baptiste Labat, *Nouveaux voyage aux isles de l'Amérique* (The Hague, 1725), I, Bk 4, 169-71; Jonathan Carver, *A Treatise on the Cultivation of the Tobacco Plant* (London, 1779), *passim*; and John Scott, 'Description of Barbados', *The Bulletin of the Barbados Museum and Historical Society*, No 11 and 12 (November 1967 and February 1968), n.p.

23. Dunn, *Sugar and Slaves*, 66. Dutertre, *Histoire générale*, II, 452-53. For a more detailed discussion of French land policy, see Mme. G. Desportes, 'Mode d'appropriation des terres', *Annales de Antilles*, No 2 (1955), 71-88. Land began to increase significantly in value only towards the end of the 1630s. Before then it was so cheap that Barbados and St Christopher planters found it advantageous to create patent offices for registration of titles only around 1639. Public surveyors appeared on both the English and French Caribees only in the 1640s, but titles remained vague throughout the century, causing numerous lawsuits when property became valuable. See 'Papers Relating to the Early History of Barbados and St Kitts', ed. N. Barnell Davis, *Timœehri*, new ser., VI (1892), 339-40.

24. Edmund Morgan, 'The First American Boom: Virginia 1618 to 1630', *William and Mary Quarterly*, 3rd ser., 27 (April 1971), 169-98.

25. Henry Colt, 'The Voyage of Sir Henry Colt' (1631), *Colonising Expeditions to the West Indies and Guiana, 1623-1667*, ed. Vincent T. Harlow, Hakluyt Society, 2nd ser., Vol. LVI (1924; rpt. Nendeln/Liechtenstein, 1967), 65-66. Colt considered the planters lazy, in part because they had difficulty controlling their servants. Food shortages were common during the 1620s, but as tobacco prices fell settlers began raising their own eatables, and Barbados apparently even started exporting foodstuffs to the other Caribees.

26. 'The First American Boom', 197.

27. Real wages in England were then very near the lowest levels recorded during the period 1250-1950. One of the foremost causes of this depression was the deterioration of the English woollen industry. See E. H. Phelps Brown and Sheila V. Hopkins, 'Seven Centuries of the Prices of Consumables, Compared with Builders' Wage-rates', *Economica*, new ser., XXIII (November 1956), 302 and B[arry] E. Supple, *Commercial Crisis and Change in England, 1600-1642* (Cambridge, 1959), 5-6, 33-38, 120.

28. George Louis Beer, *The Origins of the British Colonial System 1578-1660* (1908; rpt. Gloucester, Mass., 1959), 204.

29. See Table 1. According to the independent but non-quantitative work by the French historian Louis-Philippe May, tobacco prices broke in 1635. See his *Histoire économique de la Martinique (1635-1763)* (Paris, 1930), 87.

30. *CSP Co AWI, 1574-1660*, I, 146, 148.

31. Clarence H. Haring, *Trade and Navigation Between Spain and the Indies* (1918; rpt. Gloucester, Mass., 1964), 77-78, 84-88.

32. Gray, *History of Agriculture*, I, 261-62, and J. Harry Bennett, 'Peter Hay, Proprietary Agent in Barbados, 1636-1641', *The Jamaican Historical Review*, V (1965), 16. This was not the first time a cartel was attempted. In 1629, 1630, 1631, 1632 and 1633 Virginians attempted to restrict tobacco cultivation, apparently with little success, and in 1634 the Crown succumbed to colonial requests and appointed a commissioner who was to sit on the Council and establish rules for reducing production. See *CSP Col. AWI, 1574-1660*, I, 117, 190. The man, however, died on his way to America. In the Caribbean, there also appears to have been an unsuc-

cessful attempt to reduce the tobacco supply in 1633 or 1634. See Davis (ed.), 'Early History of Barbados and St Kitts', p. 339.

33. M. Moreau de Saint-Méry, *Loix et constitutions des colonies françoises de l'Amérique sous le vent* (Paris, 1784), 1, 43-4; and Dutertre, *Histoire générale*, I, 143-45.

34. The total quantity of tobacco imported at the Port of London amounted to 1,516,050 lbs in 1637, 3,117,600 lbs in 1638, 1338,360 lbs in 1639 and 1,207,100 lbs in 1640. Of this the share from Barbados fell from 124,590 lbs in 1637 and 204,906 lbs in 1638 to 28,010 lbs in 1639 and to 66,900 lbs in 1640, while the share from St Christopher declined from 263,600 lbs in 1637 and 470,730 lbs in 1638 to 107,310 lbs in 1639 and 138,970 lbs in 1640. See 'Imports of Tobacco, 1637-1640', *Caribbeana*, ed. Vere Langford Oliver (London, 1914), III, 197-98. The quantity of Virginia tobacco imported into London greatly exceeded the quantity from the Caribees because the West Indian leaf was more heavily taxed in England. This led Antillean planters to ship their product directly to the Netherlands.

35. Richard Ligon, *A True & Exact History of the Island of Barbados* (1657) (1673; rpt. London, 1970), 113. In the late 1630s, another observer called Barbados tobacco, 'the worst of all tobaccos'. See Bennett, 'Peter Hay', 15.

36. Scott, 'Description of Barbados', n.p.; and David Watts, *Man's Influence on the Vegetation of Barbados, 1627 to 1800*, University of Hull Occasional Papers in Geography, no. 4 (Hull, England, 1966), opposite 16.

37. Colt, 'Voyage of Sir Henry Colt', 69.

38. May, *Histoire économique*, 87-88.

39. Bennett, 'Peter Hay', 16.

40. *CSP Col. AWI, 1574-1660*, I, 277.

41. Posthumus, *Prices in Holland*, I, 119, 284.

42. The detailed Stanto Domingo census of 1606 demonstrates that ginger was the foremost economic product of that island. See Antonio Ossorio, 'Autos y testimonios tocantes a las cossas del estado de la isla Española', in *Relaciónes históricas de Santo Domingo*, ed. E. Rodrigrues Demorizi, (Ciudad Trujillo, 1945), II, 443-44. Ginger also served as a prominent Puerto Rican export and was grown on Jamaica and Cuba. See Irene Wright, 'History of Sugar-IX', *The Louisiana Planter and Sugar Manufacture*, LV (July 17, 1915), 46 and Robert Batie, 'A Comparative Economic History of the Spanish, French, and English on the Caribbean Islands during the Seventeenth Century', (Ph.D dissertation, University of Washington, 1972), 22-27.

43. Dutertre, *Historie générale*, II, 7.

44. Don Diego de Torres Vargas, 'Descripción de la isla y ciudad de Puerto Rico, y de su vecindad y polbaciónes, presidio, gobernadores y obicpos; frutos y minerales' (1647), *Boletín histórico de Puerto Rico*, IV (September-October 1917), 261.

45. Nicholas Foster, *A Briefe Relation of the Late Horrid Rebellion Acted in the Island Barbados, in the West Indies* (1650; rpt. London, 1879), 1-2.

46. J. Harry Bennett, 'The English Caribees in the Period of the Civil War, 1642-1646', *William and Mary Quarterly*, 24 (April 1967), 360.

47. Sieur Lonvilliers de Poincy, 'Mémoires envoyés aux seigneurs de la Compagnie des Iles de l'Amérique' (1640), in *Tricentenaire des Antilles Guadeloupe 1635-1935, documents inédits*, ed. J.[oseph] Rennard, (Basse-Terre, Guadeloupe, 1935), 40.

48. Bennett, 'Peter Hay', 16-17.

49. Scott, 'Description of Barbados', n.p.

50. For background on indigo, see W. A. Vetterli, 'The

History of Indigo', *Ciba Review*, No. 85 (April 1951), 3066-3087, a succinct and balanced study; J. Bridges-Lee, *On Indigo Manufacture: A Practical and Theoretical Guide to the Production of the Dye* (Calcutta, 1892), provides a detailed explanation of the reason for each step in the manufacturing process; James Crokatt (ed.) *Observations Concerning Indigo and Cochineal* (London, 1746), translated selections from authors like Jean Baptiste Labat; George Watt, *Dictionary of the Economic Products of India* (London, 1890), IV, 383-469, or the abridged edition, *Commercial Products of India*, (1908; rpt. New Delhi, 1966), 660-85; Dauril Alden, 'The Growth and Decline of Indigo Production in Colonial Brazil: A Study in Comparative Economic History', *The Journal of Economic History*, XXV (March 1965), 35-60; William F. Leggett, *Ancient and Medieval Dyes* (Brooklyn, 1944), 17-31; and Batie, 'Caribbean Islands during the Seventeenth Century', 68-72.

51. The 18th-century planter-historian Edward Long noted that a twenty-five acre plantation required twenty men, while Patrick Browne wrote that 'seventeen negroes are sufficient to manage twenty acres of indigo'. Neither author stated that estates were commonly that size, but both seemed to assume it. Since techniques for producing indigo appear nearly identical throughout the 17th and 18th centuries, there is no reason to expect the ideal plantation size to have changed. See Edward Long, *The History of Jamaica* (London, 1774), I, 407, and Patrick Browne, *The Civil and Natural History of Jamaica* (London, 1789), 304-05.

52. J. Harry Bennett, 'Cary Helyar, Merchant and Planter of Seventeenth-Century Jamaica', *William and Mary Quarterly*, 21 (January 1964), 74.

53. How many labourers were needed remains difficult to pinpoint, but the number probably varied. Ward Barrett noted that on thirteen 17th- and 18th-century estates the work force ranged from 50 to 500 labourers. But both 50 and 500 were atypical figures, for the second smallest number was 150 and the third largest number was 300. Since estates sufficiently prominent to attract attention might well have been unusually large, it is useful to compare Barrett's findings with those of Richard S. Dunn who, utilizing the Barbados census records of 1679-80, discovered that the 175 settlers who possessed 60 or more slaves owned 53% of the island's acreage and 54% of its Negroes. See Barrett, 'Caribbean Sugar-Production Standards in the Seventeenth and Eighteenth Centuries', in *Merchants and Scholars*, ed. John Parker (Minneapolis, 1965), 166; and Dunn, 'The Barbados Census of 1680: Profile of the Richest Colony in English America', *William and Mary Quarterly*, 26 (October 1969), 12, 17.

54. Ligon, *Islands of Barbadoes*, 22.

55. Accurate accounts of the sugar-making process and of plantation life are rare. See Barrett, 'Caribbean Sugar-Production Standards', 147-70 and his *The Sugar Hacienda of the Marqueses del Valle* (Minneapolis, 1970); Noel Deerr, *The History of Sugar*, 2 vols (London, 1949-50), Labat, *Nouveaux voyage*, II, Bk 3, 224-360, one of the most detailed and useful works available; F. Depons, *A Voyage to the Eastern Part of Terra Firma of the Spanish Main in South America, During the Years 1801, 1802, 1803, and 1804*, trans. (New York, 1806), II, 196-229; Batie, 'Caribbean Islands during the Seventeenth Century', 112-69; Michael Craton and James Walvin, *A Jamaican Plantation* (Toronto and Buffalo, 1970), 95-154; and J. Harry Bennett, *Bondsman and Bishops, Slavery and Apprenticeship on the Codrington Plantations of Barbados,*

1710-1838, University of California Publication in History, LXII (Berkeley and Los Angeles, 1958).

56. N. Darnell Davis (ed.), 'Early History of Barbados and St Kitts', 336.

57. Posthumus, *Prices in Holland*, I, 416.

58. Chaunu, *Séville et l'Atlantique*, VIII, pt. 2, sec. 2, 1797-1848; John Lynch, *Spain Under the Habsburgs* (New York, 1969), II, 94-115.

59. Posthumus, *Prices in Holland*, I, 415-16.

60. C. R. Boxer, *The Dutch in Brazil 1624-1654* (Oxford, 1957), *passim*.

61. Dunn summarizes the well-known English colonizing failures in *Sugar and Slaves*, 17. Thomas G. Mathews, in 'The Spanish Domination of Saint Martin (1633-1648)', *Caribbean Studies*, IX (April 1969), 3-23, insightfully presents the Spanish response to foreign incursions. Details of Indian attempts to obstruct the French colonizing activity are found in C. A. Banbuck, *Histoire politique, économique et sociale de la Martinique sous l'ancien régime (1635-1789)* (Paris, 1935), 30-35; Maurice Satineau, *Histoire de la Guadeloupe sous l'ancien régime (1635-1789)* (Paris 1928), 21-32; and above all Dutertre, *Histoire générale*, 70-2, 81-95, 113-15, 145-53, 496-504. For a discussion of Indian customs by a priest who lived among the natives, see Raymond P. Breton, *Les Caraibes de La Guadeloupe 1635-1656* (1656), ed. Joseph Rennard (Paris, 1929), 45-74.

62. *CSP Col. AWI, 1574-1660*, 1, 201.

63. I am in debt to Kevin P. Kelly of the Institute of Early American History and Culture for providing me with this figure.

64. Bennett, 'Peter Hay', 13.

65. *CSP Col. AWI, 1574-1660*, 1, 295.

66. Early authors gave widely varying accounts as to how many planters they believed lived on the Caribees, but most scholars tend to accept a report by company officials who place the population at 7,000 in 1642. See May, *Histoire économique*, 55. The French were heavily outnumbered because the English depression and Civil War impelled numerous people from that island to sail to America while the more stable economic conditions within France reduced the incentives for individuals from that country to migrate.

67. Harlow, *History of Barbados*, 7-20.

68. Scott, 'Description of Barbados' [7].

69. Bennett, 'Peter Hay', 20.

70. Ligon, *Island of Barbadoes*, 85.

71. Ch[ristian] Schnakenbourg, 'Note sur les origines de l'industrie sucrière en Guadeloupe au XVII siècle (1640-1670)', *Revue française de 'historie d'outremer*, LX No. 200 (1968), 270.

72. [Anon.], 'La plus ancienne relation', 16.

73. Rennard, ed. *Tricentenaire des Antilles*, 49-53.

74. Bennett, 'English Caribbees', 372.

75. Labat, *Nouveaux voyage*, I, Bk 3, 228.

76. Posthumus, *Prices in Holland*, I, 416.

77. This account relies heavily on Boxer, *Dutch in Brazil*, *passim*, and Hermann Watjen, 'The Dutch colonial Empire in Brazil', trans. Peter Guldbrandsen, typescript trans. of a work published at The Hague in 1921 (Bancroft Library, University of California at Berkeley). The sugar supply reaching Europe was also reduced due to a shortage of vessels and to high trans-Atlantic shipping costs, both of which were the result of warfare at sea. From 1623 through 1636, Dutch West-India Company raiders captured 547 Spanish-Portuguese ships valued at 6,710,000 florins, while in 1647 and 1648 they took 259 vesels trading with Bahia alone. See Watjen, 'Empire in Brazil', 125 and Boxer, *Dutch in Brazil*, Appendix III.

78. The 50s.-54s. 6d. estimate was calculated from an anonymous statement that in 1650 slaves cost 1,000-1,100 pounds of sugar apiece and from Ligon's belief that slave prices varied from £25-£30. Ligon wrote in one place that Barbadians received 70s.-124s. per cwt for brown sugar and in another that the lowest price was 25s. The figures are irreconcilable even though it may be surmised that the lower one referred to values after 1654 when he wrote his book. Certainly Posthumus' price data indicate that from 1645 to 1654 sugar was worth a great deal, in fact far more than the 28s. which it fetched in 1658. Other sources support this view. In 1685, a petition to the Crown stated that in earlier times 'our sugar then yielded very high rates in England as from three pounds unto four pounds per cent for our muscovado sugars, and white sugars from 6 lbs to 7 lbs per cent, whereas now our white sugar cleers not the halfe part of what our musco sugar heretofore yielded'. See Ligon, *Island of Barbadoes*, 46-7, 92, 95; [Anon.], ' Breife Discription of the Ilande of Barbados' (1650), in *Colonising Expeditions to the West Indies and Guiana, 1623-1667*, ed. V[incent] T. Harlow, the Hakluyt Society, 2nd. ser., LVI (1925; rpt. Nendeln/Liechtenstein, 1967), 45 and [Anon.], 'Groans of the Plantations' (1685), *The Journal of the Barbados Museum and Historical Society*, XVI (November 1948 and February 1949), 27.

79. Ligon, *Island of Barbadoes*, 86, 96, 22.

80. Dunn, *Sugar and Slaves*, 59.

81. Bridenbaugh, *Beyond the Line*, 79.

82. Watjen, 'Empire in Brazil', 505-06.

83. Elizabeth Donnan (ed.), *Documents Illustrative of the History of the Slave Trade to America* (Washington, DC, 1930), 1, 125. Another author wrote, 'the Hollanders . . . did at the first attempt of makeing sugar give great credit to the most sober inhabitants, and upon the unhappie Civill warr that brake out in England, they managed the whole Trade in or Westerne Collonies, and furnished the Island with Negroes, Coppers, Stills, and all other things Appertaining to the Ingenious for making of sugar'. See Harlow, *History of Barbados*, 42.

84. Harlow, *History of Barbados*, 338.

85. Ligon, *Island of Barbadoes*, 46.

86. K. G. Davies, *The Royal African Company* (New York, 1970), 364.

87. Donnan (ed.), *History of the Slave Trade*, 1, 124.

88. Ligon, *Island of Barbadoes*, 116.

89. Richard Pares who examined Barbadian land records believed that settlers began enlarging their estates around 1646. See *Merchants and Planters, Economic History Supplement*, No. 4 (Cambridge, England, 1960), 57. The long-run economic forces which ultimately resulted in slaves displacing white servants are analyzed by Richard N. Bean in 'The British Trans-Atlantic Slave Trade, 1650-1755' (Ph.D. dissertation, University of Washington, 1971), 103-18.

90. Ligon also noted that both white males and females laboured in the fields alongside blacks (*Island of Barbadoes*, 44, 115). After 1654, Antillean slave prices fell and real wage rates in England rose. As a result fewer people sold themselves into servitude while those men who did fetched comparatively high prices and were generally placed in managerial or skilled labouring positions where they enjoyed improved working conditions. Similar trends occurred, although more slowly, on the French islands. Concerning brutality, for instance, a visitor to Martinique wrote in 1660 that servants were so cruelly handled that they would be better off as slaves among the Turks. See Cosimo Brunetti, 'Three Relations of the West Indies in 1659-60', ed. Susan Heller Anderson, *Transactions of the American*

Philosophical Society, LIX (September 1968), 15.

91. Harlow, *History of Barbados*, 119.

92. Henry Whistler, 'Extracts from Henry Whistler's Journal of the West Indies Expedition' (1655), in *The Narrative of General Venables with an Appendix of Papers Relating to the Expedition to the West Indies III*, ed. C. H. Firth, Royal Historical Society, new ser. (London, 1900), 146.

93. Harlow, *History of Barbados*, 273, and Beauchamp Plantagent, ' Description of the Providence of New Albion', (1648), in *Tracts and Other Papers*, ed. Peter Force, (Washington DC, 1838), II, 5.

94. Ligon, *Island of Barbadoes*, 28-9.

95. Harlow has compiled a list of population estimates. Only three figures exist for the number of whites dwelling on that island at the end of the sugar boom: 30,000 in 1653, 23,000 in 1655, and 'at least' 25,000 in 1655. Considering how many people must have lived there in order to produce the recorded sugar exports, I feel that 25,000 is a conservative figure. See *History of Barbados*, 338.

96. *Illand of Barbadoes*, 24, 94.

97. *CSP Col. AWI, 1574-1660*, 1, 374.

98. Father Antoine Biet, '. . . Visit to Barbados in 1654' (1654), ed. and trans. Jerome S. Handler, *The Journal of Barbados Museum and Historical Society*, XXXII (May, 1967), 56.

99. Dunn, *Sugar and Slaves*, 87.

100. *Illand of Barbadoes*, 40, 59, 63-64, 94.

101. Biet, 'Visit to Barbados', 65, 67-68.

102. Whistler, 'West India Expedition', 146.

103. Bennett, 'English Caribees', 361-65.

104. The fullest account of these struggles was written by Dutertre, *Histoire générale*, I, 146-448, whose interpretation was later closely followed by Crouse, the only modern historian to treat this subject in English. See his *French Pioneers, passim*. The Knights of Malta, of which de Poincy was a member, acquired St Christopher along with St Martin, St Croix and St Bartholomew on 24 May 1651 for 120,000 livres. Du Parquet bought Martinique and the French claims to St Lucia, Grenada and the Grenadines on 27 September 1650 for 60,000 livres, while Houel and his brother-in-law, Boisseret, purchased Guadeloupe, Mariegalante, Desirade and the Saints on 4 September 1649, for 73,000 livres.

105. Planters believed that their principal problem was an inability to acquire sufficient capital for slaves and equipment. As early as 1639, Du Parquet wrote that 'there is not one hero [on Martinique] rich enough' to erect sugar works. At the end of the sugar era, the problem still remained, and Father Breton noted that 'one will make more profit from this merchandize [sugar] than from tobacco, but it takes a great deal of money in order to erect a mill'. In fact, capital may have been scarce because risk costs remained excessive, a point which led investors to place their money elsewhere. See Dutertre, *Histoire générale*, I, 109, and Breton, 'L'isle de la Guadeloupe', 44.

106. Stewart L. Mims, *Colbert's West India Policy* (New Haven, 1912), 34.

107. Schnakenbourg, 'Origines de l'industrie sucrière', 300.

108. F. Maurile de Saint-Michel, *Voyages des isles Camercanes en l'Amérique* (Le Mans, 1652), 44-45, 120.

109. P. Pierre Pelleprat, 'Relation des missions des pères de la Compagnie de Jesus' (1655), in *Mission de Cayenne et de la Guyane Française* (Paris, 1857), 46.

110. Pacifique de Provins, *Breve relation du voyage des îles de l'Amérique* (1645) (Paris, 1939), 16 and Jeaffreson, *Young Squire*, I, 34.

111. Vere, L. Oliver, *The History of Antigua* (London, 1894), I, xxv.

112. *Ibid.*, xxv and Bennett, 'English Caribbees', 37.

113. May, *Histoire économique*, 55. One even higher estimate exists. In about 1640, an anonymous source wrote that 8,000 French bachelors lived on St Christopher, 2,000 on Martinique, and 1,000 on Guadeloupe. While the estimate is obviously excessive, the distribution is informative. [Anon.] 'Plus ancienne relation', 14.

114. de Provins, *Îles de l'Amérique*, 16-17, 20.

115. Only two estimates exist of the total number of people then living on the French Antilles. Father Pelleprat, who visited the Caribbees in 1654, wrote that altogether they contained 15,000-16,000 Frenchmen and 12,000-13,000 slaves, but an examination of the various estimates of specific island populations suggests that these figures are too high. In 1658, Charles Rochfort wrote that there were 9,000-10,000 whites on the French Antilles and nearly as many Indians and Negroes. The present author feels that 13,000 Frenchmen and 10,000 slaves constitutes a reasonable estimate but that either figure could be in error by as much as 2,000. See Pelleprat, 'Missions des pères', 6, 47. May, *Histoire économique*, 54-55.

116. Batie, 'Caribbean Islands during the Seventeenth Century', 174-75.

117. Schnakenbourg, 'Origines de l'industrie sucrière', 300.

118. J. B. Delwarde, *Les défricheurs et les petits colons de la Martinique au XVII siècle* (Paris, 1935), 18.

119. Harlow, *History of Barbados*, 93. The French also complained about the decline in ginger prices. See Dutertre, *Histoire générale*, iI, 95-6.

120. By 1684, the Barbados slave population had risen to 46,602. In 1712, just before Queen Anne's War ended, the island contained 12,528 whites and 41,970 blacks, in 1809, 15,556 whites and 69,119 Negroes, and in 1922, 15,000 whites and 180,000 blacks. See Dunn, *Sugar and Slaves*, 87 and Harlow, *History of Barbados*, 338.

121. Brunetti, 'Relations of the West Indies', 28.

122. Oliver, *History of Antigua*, I, xxvii.

123. *CSP Co. AWI, 1574-1660*, 1, 417.

124. Harlow, *History of Barbados*, 91-3.

125. John Houghton, *A Collection of Letters for the Improvement of Husbandry and Trade* (London, 1681), 1, 2-3. During the second half of the 17th century, English and French colonists expanded sugar production and enjoyed a high standard of living partly at the expense of Brazilian planters. Luso-American sugar output revived briefly following the expulsion of the Dutch but then entered a period of protracted decline, primarily because the Crown levied heavy taxes on its producers, taxes which in 1624 amounted to perhaps 30% of the value of their output and which tended to increase in later years, thereby placing Brazilians at a competitive disadvantage. See Frederic Mauro, *Le Portugal ét l'Atlantique au XVII siècle (1570-1670), Étude économique* (Paris, 1960), 225.

126. Whistler, 'West India Expedition', 145. The rapid economic expansion of the Caribees up to 1654 was a major factor in causing Cromwell to implement the Western Design which led to England conquering Jamaica in 1655. Not realizing that the English Antillean growth rate, and particularly that of Barbados, was artificially high, a view also not grasped by his West Indian advisers such as the optimistic Modyford, Cromwell vastly overestimated the wealth that would accrue to England were she to enlarge her Caribbean dominions. At the same time, he was acutely aware of the fact that by 1654 Barbados had become nearly completely settled and that continued Antillean economic growth depended on seizing one of the larger Spanish islands.

17

A "Riotous and Unruly Lot": Irish Indentured Servants and Freemen in the English West Indies, 1644-1713

HILARY McD. BECKLES

Seventeenth-century English planters in the West Indies, like their mainland counterparts, established plantations with white indentured servants.[1] Like them, they had to control or suppress the unruly behaviour of disgruntled servants and landless ex-servants, or freemen. Historians of seventeenth-century English America have identified and explained patterns of social conflict and protest that contributed to the instability of settler communities. Such research on the mainland colonies has focussed primarily on the anti-servitude activities of disenchanted white indentured servants and wage labourers; primacy of place within the West Indian literature has gone to the anti-slavery actions of blacks and coloureds.[2] Much evidence suggests, however, that this divergence, commonly explained in terms of the regions' differences in demographic structure and race relations, is in need of reassessment. Accordingly, this essay examines the social terms of servitude, the degree of servant protest and resistance to planters' domination of social and economic life, and the extent to which such actions affected labour relations and community development in the West Indies.

Though the behaviour of most servants and freemen was typically restless and insubordinate, sparked by their awareness that West Indian indentureship offered extremely limited opportunities for social or material advancement, it was the Irish who were perceived by English masters as a principal internal enemy – at times more dangerous and feared than blacks.

Planters wrote of their Irish servants as constituting a special problem. Their discussions suggest that long-standing tensions and hostilities in English-Irish relations threatened the stability of white communities and the accomplishments of the English colonizing mission in general.[3]

The presence of large numbers of Irish servants in the West Indies can be accounted for partly in terms of planters' ineffective control over the servant trade. Merchants believed the Irish poor were more willing so seek opportunities in the West Indies than their English, Scottish, or Welsh counterparts, owing to frequent food shortages, high unemployment, and English military disruption in Ireland. Consequently, they looked to Ireland for a ready supply of servants. Emigration facilities became an integral part of the extensive colonial trade with Ireland, and most ships sailing from Irish ports to the West Indies carried servants. Before the Restoration, Ireland was not discriminated against in the West Indian market, and the Navigation Act of 1663 continued the direct trade in servants.[4] Only Barbadians resorted to legislation in an effort to prevent Irish immigration. Their 1664 law failed miserably, and like planters in the other islands, they could not prevent consignments of Irish servants from landing on their shores.

Servant traders presented the West Indies to the Irish poor as an area of great economic opportunity: laborers need only be hard-working and enterprising to become successful colonists. It is unlikely that Irish emigrants believed that

Table 17.1   Population of the English West Indies, 1655-1715

	Barbados			Jamaica			Leeward Island	
Year	White	Black	Year	White	Black	Year	White	Black
1655	23,00	20,00	1660	3,000	500	1660	8,000	2,000
1673	21,309	33,184	1661	2,956	3,479	1670	8,000	3,000
1684	19,568	46,502	1673	7,768	9,504	1678	10,408	8,449
1696	–	42,000	1690	10,000	30,000	1690	10,000	15,000
1715	16,888	–	1713	7,000	55,000	1708	7,311	23,500

Sources: For Barbados for 1655 see Harlow, *History of Barbados*, 338; for 1673, C.S.P.C., 1669-1674, no. 1101; for 1684, Sloan Mss. 2441; for 1696, C.O. 318/2, fol. 115; and for 1715, C. O. 28/16. The founded figures for Jamaica in 1690 and 1713 and the Leewards in 1660, 1670 and 1690 are Dunn's estimates; *Sugar and Slaves*, 312. For Jamaica in 1673 see *Journal of the House of Assembly of Jamaica, 1663-1826*, I, 20. The Leeward figures for 1678 and 1708 are from C.O. 1/42. Fol. 193-243, and C.S.P.C., 1706-1708, nos 1383 and 1396. For other population estimates see David W. Galeson, *Traders, Planters and Slaves: Market Behavior in Early English America* (Cambridge, 1986), 4-5; John J. McCusker, "The Rum Trade and the Balance of Payments of the Thirteen Continental Colonies, 1650-1775" (Ph.D. diss., University of Pittsburgh, 1970), 691-1775; and Robert V. Wells, *The Population of the British Colonies in America before 1776: Survey of Census Data* (Princeton, N. J., 1975), 195-196, 238-239.

working conditions and social relations on English plantations would be as agreeable as merchants suggested, though they must have accepted the general point that the West Indies offered levels of opportunity for betterment that were inconceivable at home. Servants received the cost of their passage and food, clothing, and shelter on the plantations in return for up to seven years of contracted labour. On termination of the indenture masters were legally bound to offer "freedom dues" in the form of a small parcel of land and a sum of money or its commodity equivalent. Labourers who accepted these terms hoped to improve their lives by acquiring some wealth, some status, and greater personal liberty.

The planter elite that emerged in the first decades of West Indian settlement, however, had engrossed all economically viable lands and dominated public institutions. Its members did not identify with egalitarian social ideologies that were conducive to the upward mobility and material advancement of persons arriving in the colonies as indentured servants. In general, planters considered servants and freemen a potentially subversive lot who had to be controlled and kept in a labouring status for the preservation of their own social order and wealth accumulation. This perception was strengthened by the fact that Irish Catholics, who were marked at the outset for the lowest socio-economic status within the West Indies' Anglican-dominated

communities, constituted the largest single ethnic group of white servants on the plantations.

Frequent trade contacts allowed information of varying accuracy to circulate among the Irish poor concerning conditions in the islands. Voluntary servants therefore had some basis for exercising a measure of choice of destination. The records of servant trader Capt. Thomas Anthony show that during the period 1638-1641, for example, Irish labourers held clear preferences for certain islands. Their assessments were based on limited information concerning wage levels, land availability, and general conditions of labour.[5] These records show that labourers were concerned not only with the terms and nature of contracts but also with post-indenture conditions and opportunities.

Not all servants were able to choose their destinations. Many were involuntary emigrants banished by the state. The scarcity of detailed information on the servant trade makes it impossible to ascertain accurately what proportion of servants was involuntary, but the evidence strongly suggests that there was a lively traffic in deportees, especially during the years of the Commonwealth. In 1658, for example, Thomas Povey, an English merchant with extensive West Indian investments stated that the majority of Irish servants in Barbados and St Kitts had been transported by the English state for treasonous engagements against the Protector.[6] Barbados was the favourite West Indian dumping ground for political prisoners during the Commonwealth.[7] On September 15, 1649, after the Battle of Drogheda, Oliver Cromwell informed John Bradshaw, president of the council, that "the Enemy were about 3,000 .... They made a stout resistance .... [but those who] escaped with their lives ... are in safe custody for the Barbados."[8] In October 1655 he ordered that "all English, Scots and Irish" prisoners in Dorchester jail be "forthwith sent to Barbados."[9]

In addition to political prisoners, many hundreds of Irish were legally defined by the state as social undesirables and transported to the West Indies to help meet the insatiable demand of sugar planters for labour.[10] Transporting such people had begun with the English poor under Charles I; Cromwell's regime carried out the practice "on a far larger scale" with the Irish.[11] In 1654, for example, governors of several Irish counties received orders to "arrest ... all wanderers, men and women, and such other Irish within their precincts as should not prove they had such a settled course of industry as yielded them a means of their own to maintain them, all such children as were in hospitals or workhouses, all prisoners, men and women, to be transported to the West Indies."[12] Colonial governors accepted these involuntary servants reluctantly and urged the termination of the traffic from Ireland. Thus Gov. Daniel Searle objected to eighty-seven "Irish rogues" who arrived at Barbados in November 1657 on the grounds that they were not only physically unfit for plantation labour but also unsuited for militia duty since they were opposed to the furtherance of English Protestant interests.[13]

Fragmentary statistical data permit a limited assessment of the size and growth of the Irish servant and freemen population. Richard S. Dunn states that Irish Catholics, "cordially loathed by their English masters," constituted the largest block of servants in Barbados in the middle of the seventeenth century.[14] He offers no estimates, but in 1667 Gov. William Willoughby reported, rather worriedly, that over half of the 4,000 militia men on the island were Irish.[15] He pleaded for additional servants other than Irish, declaring: "I am for the downright Scot who, I am certain, will fight without a crucifix about his neck."[16]

Gov. Sir William Stapleton's 1678 population estimates for the Leeward Islands show a separate listing of Irish inhabitants, who were mostly indentured servants and waged freemen. They composed 9.9, 22.7, 69, and 26.4 per cent of the white population of St Kitts, Nevis, Montserrat, and Antigua respectively (Table 17.2). The census does not provide detailed information on land ownership patterns by nationality, but inventories and deeds show that the planter elite as well as middling sorts on the Leewards were overwhelmingly English. When Irish Catholics were landholders, even in Montserrat, where they outnumbered the English, the picture that emerges is of a disadvantaged group clustered at the lower end of the property-owning scale with very modest holdings. Their economic subordination ensured their "second class" status – as the English took every opportunity to remind them.[17]

Only Jamaica experienced an increase in the Irish population during the last quarter of the seventeenth century. The island, colonized by the English from 1655, some twenty to thirty years after Barbados and the Leewards, had a supply of white labour that officials considered inadequate for agricultural development. Jamaica's increased sugar production during the 1670s resulted from rapid expansion of the slave population, which in turn highlighted the smaller size of the white community. The Lords of Trade and Plantations considered a liberal immigration policy the most effective way to solve the white labour shortage and expand the white population. Successive governors promised immigrants religious tolerance and easy access to landownership, and servants from Ireland as well as Irish freemen from Barbados and the Leewards responded to these incentives during the period 1660-1700. Jamaica became the leading West Indian destination for Irish and English servants departing from Kinsale, Bristol, and London in the last quarter of the century.[18]

Emigration to Jamaica of Irish labourers from St Kitts, Nevis, and Antigua, and to a lesser degree from mainland colonies, was a principal factor in the decline of the Leeward Irish population that began about 1680. The Leewards also found it harder to attract servants from Britain.[19] In 1689 Gov. Christopher Codrington reported that Antigua's Irish population numbered "three hundred in all," a drop of 310 from the 1678 figure. Codrington estimated that the Irish at Montserrat numbered "upwards of eight hundred" in 1689, compared with 1,869 in 1678.[20]

Table 17.2.   Census of the Leeward Islands, 1678

	Men	Women	Children	Total
		St Kitts		
English	370	409	543	1,322
Irish	187	–	–	187
French	130	127	122	379
Dutch	8	3	8	19
Blacks	550	500	386	1,436
Total	1,245	1,039	1,059	3,343
		Nevis		
English	1,050	700	920	2,670
Irish	450	120	230	800
Scots	34	8	9	51
Blacks	1,422	1,322	1,116	3,860
Total	2,956	2,150	2,275	7,381
		Montserrat		
English	346	175	240	761
Irish	769	410	690	1,869
Scots	33	6	13	52
Blacks	400	350	292	1,042
Total	1,548	941	1,235	3,724
		Antigua		
English	800	400	400	1,600
Irish	360	130	120	610
Scots	76	14	8	98
Blacks	805	868	499	2,172
Total	2,041	1,412	1,027	4,480
Grand Total	7,790	5,542	5,596	18,928

Source: Gov. William Stapleton to Lords of Trade , June 29, 1678, C.O. 1/42, fols. 193–243.

Stapleton's figures are estimates compiled by churchwardens on the respective islands. Not all households were enumerated, which accounts for the absence of entries for Irish women and children in St Kitts. Stapleton was resident at Nevis and attempted a more complete census for that island. For most islands the number of blacks was also estimated. See Dunn, *Sugar and Slaves,* 127. The age limit for all children is 16 years.

While Leeward planters continued to complain to London colonial officials about their shortage of white labour and embarked on programmes designed to attract servants – even from the jails of Britain – they were pleased with the diminishing number of Irish inhabitants.

Barbados also experienced a reduction in its white labour force in the last quarter of the century. This was due to migration of freemen to Jamaica, loss of servants in the planters' ill-fated settlement schemes in St Lucia, Tobago, and Suriname, and recruitment of men for military service against the Dutch and French. The Barbadians, like their Leeward counterparts, were happy enough to see the Irish population diminish, though they too continuously petitioned Whitehall for servants. In December 1667 Gov. Willoughby, in a letter to the Privy Council, expressed the typical English opinion on the relationship between the white labour shortage and Irish servants:

There yet remains that I acquainte your Lordships with the great want of servants in this island, which the late war hath occasioned. If labour fayles here, His Majesty's customes will at home; if the supply be not of good and sure men the saifety of this place will always be in question; for though there be noe enemy abroad, the keeping of slaves in subjection must still be provided for. If your Lordship shall offer a trade with Scotland for transporting people of that nation hither and *prevent any excess of Irish in the future,* it will accommodate all the ends propounded.[21]

Willoughby's correspondence reflected anti-Irish attitudes that profoundly affected the conditions of Irish servitude and the quality of servants' lives. English masters considered their Irish servants as belonging to a backward culture, unfit to contribute anything beyond their labour to colonial development. Furthermore, their adherence to the Catholic religion reinforced the planters' perception of them as opposed to the English Protestant colonizing mission that in fact had begun in Ireland. Irish servants, then, were seen by the English planter class as an enemy within and were treated accordingly.

In Barbados, where the planter class achieved the greatest degree of cohesion and political power by mid-century, Irish servants and freemen suffered the most intense day-to-day discrimination and humiliation on the labour market. They were kept in slave-like conditions and rarely given employment that conferred prestige. John Scott, an English adventurer who travelled in the West Indies during the Commonwealth, saw them working in field gangs with slaves, "without stockings" under the "scorching sun." The Irish, he wrote, were "derided by the negroes, and branded with the Epithet of 'white slaves.'"[22] Pere Labat, a French missionary who visited the West Indies toward the end of the century, noted that such descriptions were commonplace.[23] Both Scott and Labat implied that English masters had no objection to reducing Irish servants to a slave-like relationship during their contracts, though the presence of a black slave majority inevitably gave some advantage to white servants.

Irish servants in general experienced servitude as an oppressive labour system in which their condition was nearer slavery than freedom. Like blacks, they resisted this unfamiliar subservience when and how they could. Masters complained about their unwillingness to work according to the terms of their contracts and about their hostile reactions to demands of overseers and managers. They were stereotyped as disobedient, lazy, and aggressive, while Scottish servants in particular were termed loyal and hardworking. In 1673, for example, Christopher Jeaffreson, a leading St. Kitts planter, ranked labourers as follows: "Scotchmen and Welshmen we esteem the best servants, and the Irish the worst, many of them being good for nothing

but mischief."[24] Two years later, in a petition to the Lords of Trade, Barbadian planters supported Jeaffreson's grading and added that they found the Irish "of small value."[25] In 1676 Gov. Atkins of Barbados noted that "the planters are weary of [the Irish] for they prove commonly very idle and [the planters] do find by experience that they can keep three blacks who work better and cheaper."[26]

Atkins' comparison of the economic value of Irish servants and black slaves reflects in part the planters' perception of their interchangeability. With the advent of large-scale black slavery in the 1650s, white women were removed from the sugar fields as part of a general attempt to dissociate whites from ganged labour, for which blacks were imported. By the 1660s, the skilled and supervisory labour elite on most estates was composed of English, Scottish, and Welsh servants and freemen. Irish servants were the exceptions to this clear racial division of labour in planter policy.[27] Since planters experienced no slave labour supply crises after mid-century, Catholic Irish were not needed for the elite labour functions or preferred for militia duties. Under these shifting market conditions the Irish suffered further intensification of English prejudices.

When efforts to restrict the entry of Irish into Barbados and the Leewards proved ineffective, masters resorted to the institutionalization of police and military operations for their surveillance and control. In addition, governors issued directives to parish administrators to monitor Irish community developments. In Barbados such a policy meant, among other things, that Irish Catholic priests would not be given settlement rights. Early in 1655 the arrival of four priests at Speightstown (Barbados' second largest town) caused such consternation among inhabitants that Gov. Daniel Searle instructed Col. Sir John Yeamans of the parish militia to investigate the matter and inform the council. Upon receipt of Yeamans report, the council ordered that the four – Richard Shelton, James Tuite, Robert Eagan, and Richard Moore – "do within three days bring into the secretary's office, the place of their abode, and that they have 15 days liberty to seeke passage for their departure from this island to any place within the Dominion of the Commonwealth of England."[28] On May 21 the council learned that the priests had departed.

Neither were the Barbadians prepared to accept the Irish as unindentured immigrants, free to dispose of themselves as they wished. In 1654, when Garrett Plunkett, Finian Martin, Owen Carthy, and Daniel O'Mehegan arrived at Barbados from Ireland as free persons, without indentures, the governor was forthwith informed by port officials. At its next sitting the council ruled that these four Irishmen should, without delay, "put themselves into some employment with some freeholder of the English Nation; and that they do bring with them before the governor on Monday next their masters with whom they so agree to put in security for their good demeanour for the time they stay on the island."[29] Throughout the century successive councils ruled that Irishmen landing in Barbados without indentures must engage themselves to English masters or leave. English, Scottish, or Welsh immigrants were not subject to this restriction but were allowed to make their own arrangements as long as they did not become a financial charge on the colony.

During the 1650s master-servant relations in Barbados and to a lesser extent in the Leeward Islands deteriorated. This period saw the development of sugar plantation monoculture that excluded ex-servants from participating effectively in the land market. The value of arable land in Barbados more than trebled between 1645 and 1655, and most wage earners found the purchase of even small plots of marginal land beyond their reach. As a result, the cherished ambition of servants to own good land was now removed to the realm of fantasy. It was during the 1650s that the mass influx of Irish political prisoners occurred. This immigration contributed to the hardening of already hostile master-servant relations. For economic as well as ethnic and religious reasons, these two developments, aggravating the crisis of indentured servitude, had their greatest impact upon the Irish. Such social and economic conditions affected servants' attitudes. They soon viewed their existence in the West Indies as similar to the slavery experience of blacks. Masters in turn responded more severely to servants' insubordination and unrest. A 1673 grand jury reported that for many years "the severity of some masters and overseers towards christian servants has been such that some have lately been destroyed."[30] Attorney General Sir Thomas Montgomery, an English merchant resident in Barbados, wrote the Lords of Trade and Plantations in 1688, "I beg also for your care for the poor white servants here who, are used with more barbarous cruelty than if in Algiers."[31]

Court records give some insight into how the crisis of servitude was managed by individual planters and their governments. Magistrates frequently arbitrated in cases of master-servant conflict and referred more serious cases to the governor. The few surviving records of Barbados cases for the 1650s in which Irish servants were involved show the extent to which their anti-English and anti-servitude attitudes hurtled them into social confrontations. They were imprisoned, publicly flogged, deported from the island, and generally victimized for such offenses as Cornelius Bryan, an Irish wage servant, committed; in January 1656 the council sentenced him to "21 lashes on the bare back by the common hangman in Bridgetown" for saying, while refusing a tray of meat, that "if there was so much English blood in the tray as there was meat, he would eat it all." The following month Bryan was arrested and deported for uttering anti-English remarks. In August the same year, Daniel Maligee, an indentured servant, was sentenced to endure the midday sun unclothed in the pillory for talking "scandalously" of Englishmen. The following year, again on the council's order, the provost marshal arrested, whipped, and deported Patrick O'Callaghan, another indentured servant, for speaking "irreverently and profanely of the Holy Bible and uttering bad expressions of Englishmen."[32]

Servants were legally entitled to protection from their masters' excesses. In order to make indentured servitude an attractive institution to voluntary emigrants, it had to be distinguished from slavery. Colonial legislators did this by recognizing servants' liberty to express their rights as free persons under contract. This perception also embraced those shipped out involuntarily by the state. Such persons generally served for ten years. No legal distinction was made between the types of servants on the plantations. Irish servants, then, could petition magistrates in the event of perceived maltreatment and breaches of contract.

In Barbados, servant petitions were few in number, further hardships were likely to follow the exercise of this right. Complaints were investigated by constables and justices of the peace who, like other law officials who made judgments, were also planters. Courts, however, occasionally freed servants in cases of proven ill-usage. Extreme maltreatment was considered to be that which destroyed a servant's normal functions as a producer. Treatment that did not result in such physical injury was accepted. In December 1656, for example, Patrick Cornelius complained in a petition to the local magistrate that his master had punished him so harshly that he could no longer perform his duties. Investigation revealed that he had lost the use of his left leg. The magistrate did consider this a case of maltreatment, removed Cornelius from the estate, and declared him a freeman.[33]

More commonly, servants found that litigation resulted in their exposure to further injustices. In December 1656 an Irish servant, Daniel Duncombe, petitioned a magistrate that his master, Capt. John Symmonds, a prominent planter, had refused to pay his "freedom dues" in accordance with their agreement. The magistrate ruled for Duncombe and ordered Symmonds to make the payment. Symmonds refused. The magistrate then referred the case to the governor, who also ordered Symmonds to make the payments. Symmonds not only still refused but took hold of Duncombe and gave him a "sound beating" for his audacity. The payment was finally made from the public treasury.[34]

The Grimlin case of 1677 best illustrates how planter solidarity in Barbados inevitably helped distort the execution of the laws. In that year, Charles Grimlin, a substantial planter, murdered his Irish maidservant. The case was heard by Gov. Jonathan Atkins, one of the few governors without landed property on the island and one who relied heavily on planters' financial concessions to supplement his small salary from Whitehall. Grimlin was reprieved by Atkins – a decision that angered many propertyless whites. By law Grimlin should have been convicted and either fined severely or imprisoned. Atkins washed his hands of the controversial decision; he had acted, he said, at the request of "most of the Ministers and very many gentlemen of the island."[35] In instances such as this, when a miscarriage of justice was perceived, officials sometimes expressed an interest in the legal protection of servants, while planters invariably emphasized the necessity to suppress servant insubor-

dination. Debates in the legislative assemblies revolved around the assertion that leniency made servants "more refractory than ever."[36]

To control and discipline servants, masters and their managers established a system of authority headed by a chief overseer who delegated responsibilities to sub-overseers and field-gang drivers. If this system failed, a planter could request the services of parish constables, the provost marshal, or, as a last resort, the parish militia. During the 1650s, Barbados officials loosed the full apparatus of law enforcement on their Irish servants, whom some thought a greater threat to peace than their African slaves.

Servant revolts of the 1650s spring from the minutes of the Barbados Council. In 1655, for example, Gov. Searle learned that there were "several Irish servants and negroes out in rebellion in the Thicketts and thereabout," plundering estates in a systematic and arrogant manner, and "making a mockery of the law." The council's response reflected the seriousness with which it viewed this information. It ordered Lt. Col. John Higginbottom of the St Philip parish militia to raise Col. Henry Hawley's regiment, "follow the said servants and runaway negroes," and secure or "destroy" them. On July 15, 1656, the governor once again ordered Higginbottom to examine a case of a "riotous and unruly lot" of Irish servants on the estate of Robert Margott in that parish. The investigation led to several arrests and the imprisonment of five Irishmen who had declared themselves opposed to the "furtherance of the English nation." On September 1, 1657, the council heard the petition of Edward Hollingsheade, who stated that "his Irish servants, Reage Dunnohu and Walter Welch, have rebelliously and mutinously behaved themselves towards him, their said master, and their mistress, whereby they have been in fear of their lives by the said servants." The governor ordered the provost marshal to jail these servants pending a full investigation. It was finally ordered that Dunnohu and Welch should receive thirty-one lashes each, "soundly laid on their bare backs by the common hangman and returned to the common gaol at the pleasure of their master." On this plantation, as on many others, the planters' system of control proved insufficient in the face of Irish aggression, and public law enforcement facilities were called upon.[37]

By the end of September 1657 Gov. Searle became convinced that the English outcry concerning insubordination and rebelliousness among Irish servants required an official public statement. After receiving advice from leading planters, he issued a public proclamation, the preamble of which stated:

It hath been taken notice that several of the Irish nation, freemen and women, who have no certain place of residence, and as vagabonds refusing to labour, or to put themselves into any service, but contriving in a dissolute, leud, and slothful kind of life, put themselves to evil practices, as pilfering, thefts, robberies, and other felonous acts for their subsistency, are endeavouring by their example and persuasion to draw servants unto them of the said nation to the same kind of idle, wicked course; and information having been given that divers of them have of late uttered threatening words and menacing language to several of the inhabitants of this place, and demeaned themselves in a very preemptory and insolent way of carriage and behaviour; and some of them have endeavoured to secure themselves with arms, and other are now forth in rebellion and refuse to come in, by which it appears that could they be in a condition of power, or had opportunity, they would soon put some wicked and malicious design into execution.[38]

Searle adopted a four-point programme of control. First, Irish servants found off their plantation of residence without a "pass," "ticket," or "testimonial" signed by their master or mistress were to be arrested and conveyed by any English person to the nearest constable, who was empowered to whip them and return them to their plantation. Second, Irish freemen or women found about the island who could not give a good account of themselves were to be arrested by constables and, "if they be of no fixed abode," put "to labour for one whole year on some plantation." Third, it became a legal offence for anyone to "sell any kind of arms or ammunition whatsoever to any of the said nation." Fourth, any Irish person found in possession of arms or ammunition, "either on their persons or in their houses, shall be whipped and jailed at the governor's pleasure." Within two weeks of the implementation of this policy, it was reported that the Irish had resorted to more covert forms of resistance. The governor was notified that servants "in rebellion now pass up and down from plantation to plantation with counterfeit and forged testimonials." Furthermore, by using such false documents, many servants were reported to be in transit about the island, "unmolested as freemen."[39] Under these circumstances, Searle urged Englishmen to be circumspect in their enquiries into such tickets or testimonials.

By the end of the 1650s the Barbados government, accepting the failure of these measures to curb servant insubordination and halt the deterioration of plantation labour relations, moved toward adoption of a tough and comprehensive legal framework that took the form of the Master and Servant Code of 1661. The code reflected English perceptions of the Irish as "a profligate race," "turbulent and dangerous spirits," who thought nothing of "joining themselves to runaway slaves." The preamble illustrated the intentions and attitudes of the legislature. Since "much of the interest and substance of the island consists in the servants," who have caused "great damage" to their masters by their "unruliness, obstinacy and refractoriness," the peace of the island could only be maintained by adopting a "continual strict course" to prevent their "bold extravagancy and wandering." The code covered most aspects of servant life; it was especially explicit on the subject of resistance. Clause four, for instance, states that any servant who shall "lay violent hands upon his or her master or mistress, or overseer, or any person put over them in authority to govern them, and being thereof convicted before any of His Majesty's Justices of the Peace shall serve one whole year after his or her time." Clause nine provides a penalty of one extra year of service, and double the time for any term of imprisonment for every two hours' absence from work without permission. Barbados planters were satisfied that this legislation provided a satisfactory framework for the control of servants.[40]

What worried masters in Barbados, above all, was Irish involvement in slave revolts. Fear outran fact in this regard: no certain evidence exists that servants or freemen ever attempted to participate in a large-scale violent uprising of slaves. The reality was that the Irish, as whites, benefited, though marginally, from black slavery, and the slaves knew it. But the English constantly suspected that the Irish might support the slaves' rebellious designs and debated the need for preventive measures.

Following the discovery by the militia of an islandwide slave conspiracy in 1675, suspicions of Irish participation ran deep in Barbados. No Irishmen were arrested on this occasion, but in 1686 Gov. Edwin Stede learned that a party of creole slaves was inviting some of the "Irish Nation" to join in a design to destroy the English. Stede immediately ordered constables in seven of the eleven parishes to "search the negroes' houses within their parishes for arms and ammunition, . . . there being signs of an insurrection of negroes and white servants." Within two weeks of this investigation he informed the council that "some Irish servants have been sent to gaol and others are in recognizance touching the suspicions of their being concerned or privy to the late intended rising of the negroes to destroy all masters and mistresses." Twenty-two Negroes were arrested and executed. Eighteen Irish servants were arrested, then freed owing to insufficient evidence. The arrest of Irish servants was probably no more than a precautionary measure brought about by intense suspicion. Gov. Stede, however, asked his constables to tighten the policing of the Irish.[41]

In January 1692 the Barbadian planters believed they had finally found sufficient evidence to implicate Irishmen in large-scale rebellious organizations of slaves. In that month, creole slaves plotted an islandwide conspiracy to defeat the planters and take control of the island. John Oldmixon, an English historian whose account was based on interviews with absentee planters, described the aborted affair as "the most general the Slaves ever hatched, and brought nearest to Execution."[42] A small party of Irishmen was arrested and imprisoned for participating in the plot. The assembly's commission of enquiry reported that the slaves' strategy for obtaining arms was to send "five or six Irishmen" into Needham Fort to intoxicate the guards with strong drink and then unlock the stores. Of the slaves arrested for involvement in this plot, ninety-two were executed, four died of castration, fourteen of miscellaneous wounds, and four of causes unknown. No record, however, has been found pertaining to the trial or punishment of the Irishmen, and it can be reasonably assumed that, as on the former occasion, there was no evidence and that English suspicion had reached paranoid levels.[43]

Englishmen in the Leewards mainly feared that Irish servants would form an alliance with French Catholics. Their anxiety was heightened by political developments in the Leewards during the war years of the 1660s and the 1680s. While Barbadians suspected that their Irish la-

bourers were providing the French with military intelligence and took measures to prevent their running away to French settlements in the Windward Islands, in the Leewards the Irish determined the pattern of international events in a more fundamental way by contributing to important shifts in the balance of imperial power.

The development of St Kitts in particular was affected considerably by Anglo-French conflict and the role played in it by Irish labourers. Since the late 1620s, English and French colonists had shared the settlement in an uneasy alliance against the Caribs, with the French on the two ends of the island, the English in the fertile central valley, and the Caribs in the mountainous interior. In the summer of 1666, when war was declared between France and England, Irish servants and freemen rose against their English masters, plundered their estates, and burned their buildings before defecting to the French. With this support, the French took full control of the island and forcefully evacuated some 800 English settlers.[44] Francis Sampson, an English colonist who fled to Nevis, stated that at a critical moment of the battle "the Irish in the rear, always a bloody and perfidious people to the English Protestant interest fired volleys into the front and killed more than the enemy of our own forces."[45]

The St Kitts experience was repeated at Montserrat where the Irish population in the Leewards was greatest. Irish servants on English plantations assisted the French in capturing Montserrat in April 1667, threatening England's hold on the Leewards. Montserrat was recaptured in June, but William Willoughby, commander-in-chief of the English forces, noted of the opposition posed by the Irish: "wee, with all other of His Majesty's loyal subjects of this island have so much above any other of our neighbours become devastated, wasted and destroyed in the late unhappye warr, not only by our Ennymes in the tyme of their short staye with us, but have likewise been robbed, plundered, stripped and almost utterly consumed of all that wee had in the world by a party of rebellious and wicked people of the Irish nation."[46] The Peace of Breda in 1667, by which the English regained their portion of St Kitts, put an end to Irish armed hostilities against English masters in the Leewards.

In January 1689, however, as information spread through the islands that William of Orange had been crowned king of England, a new Irish-French military assault was launched in the Leewards. During the first week of February, Irish servants and freemen in St. Kitts plundered English estates in the name of King James II. The revolt weakened English forces, and the French were able to seize the colony. On receiving news of the rising, Leewards Gov. Codrington hastily arrested a large number of Irish servants and freemen. These were subsequently deported to Jamaica, according to Codrington, "lest they should serve us as they did" at St. Kitts. The Antiguan policy was to disarm the Irish, 300 in all, and "confine them to their plantations." The Irish at Montserrat, who were "three to one of the English," openly declared their intention to desert their English masters and give over the island to the French. Sixteen were arrested, charged with treason, and sent for trial to neighbouring Nevis.[47]

The English soon recaptured and pacified their island colonies, but settlers continued to live in fear of Irish-assisted French invasions. In June 1689 Joseph Crispe, a colonial official, reported from St. Kitts that "beside the French we have a still worse enemy in the Irish Catholics, who despite the law to the contrary, remain ... among us and openly exercise their religion." In 1706 Lt. Gov. Anthony Hodges of the Leewards noted that the French still "flatter themselves" that regaining territory in the Leewards would be an easy matter – an impression "derived from some confidence that the Irish here are in their intrest."[48]

Jamaica's receipt of Irish rebels from the Leewards, plus a small but steady flow of freemen from Barbados, intensified Anglo-Irish conflicts there. Hundreds of Barbados freemen arrived at Jamaica under the resettlement schemes of Thomas Modyford and Gov. Thomas Lynch during the 1660s. They were promised up to twenty acres on condition that they reindenture themselves for two or three years. Those who survived their service were allocated lands in the interior of the island, where lived Maroons who were said to oppose any "white inhabitant who attempted to form a settlement in the interior."[49]

By the 1680s many Irish freemen had settled in communities on the internal frontier, outside Maroon country, and represented an important factor in the colony's political turmoil. Christopher Monck, appointed governor in 1687 by James II, welcomed the support of "Irish Catho-

lic small planters and servants" in his plan to weaken the authority of the planter elite. In addition, some English planters suspected that Irish servants were ready to take up arms against them in defence of King James. The suspicions intensified the bitterness of master-servant relations. With Monck's death in 1688 and the appointment of Sir Francis Watson, a wealthy planter, as lieutenant governor, the planter elite implemented a series of actions to crush Irish insubordination generally and the riotous behaviour of servants in particular. One such measure was aimed at improving the efficiency of the militia, which the planters considered "entirely untrustworthy . . . Irish Catholic and pro-French."[50]

As in the Leeward Islands, the fear of an alliance of Irish servants with the French raised much anxiety among English Jamaicans in the last quarter of the century. In 1694 two Irishmen were incorrectly accused of giving military intelligence on the defences of Port Royal that led the French to attack nearby Carlisle Bay on July 19. Such unproven accusations fuelled the widespread belief that the Irish, in league with the French, posed a greater threat to English rule than did the Maroons in the interior.

Against this background of fear, successive governors continuously reported to London that the white population was growing too slowly. Jamaica's deficiency law contributed to the demand for white labour by requiring that a certain number of white men be kept on each estate in proportion to the number of slaves. This law was strictly enforced. Planters accordingly took whatever servants they could find in order to avoid the deficiency fee, and the Irish were most readily available. In 1703 the assembly exempted from port charges all ships carrying thirty or more servants. The prices planters paid for servants reflected discrimination against the Irish, as was also the case in Barbados and the Leewards. English, Welsh, and Scottish servants cost £18 currency, while an Irish servant cost £15.[51] In spite of planters' demand for white servants and lower prices for the Irish, Gov. Robert Hunter informed Whitehall in 1731 that Jamaica's interest would be best served by "deterring at least the native Irish papists, of which our servants and lower rank of people chiefly consist, from pouring in upon us in such sholes as they have done of late years; they are a lazy, useless sort of people . . . and their hearts are not with us."[52]

In Barbados, following widespread suspicion of Irish involvement in the aborted slave revolt of 1692, planters adamantly refused to accept Irish servants. Instead, between 1693 and 1696 they petitioned (in vain) for Scottish servants to strengthen their militia forces. In 1697, when the Colonial Office made an offer of Irish servants, the legislative council made its position explicit: "[W]e desire no Irish rebels may be sent to us; for we want not labourers of that colour to work for us, but men in whom we may confide, to strengthen us." So determined were the Barbadians to refuse the Irish that in 1696 they questioned officials of the Council of Trade and Plantations concerning the possibility of sending a shipment of "malefactors" from Newgate Prison – women, children and the infirm excluded.[53]

Nevis was first among the Leewards to take legislative action to limit the numbers and activities of Irish inhabitants. In 1701 the legislative council passed an act to prevent "papists" and "reputed papists" from settling in the island and to bar those already settled from public office. This act was repealed following disapproval from the Colonial Office. Montserrat also debated similar "Protestant Bills" aimed at excluding Irishmen from public service, including militia duties. The Barbadians, however, who had not passed legislation removing Irish civil liberties, merely imposed oaths of abjuration in order to vote or to hold public office.

Following the Treaty of Utrecht in 1713, by which France ceded its portion of St. Kitts to England and thereby removed "the most irritating source of Anglo-French friction in the eastern Caribbean," Irish rebelliousness virtually ceased in the Leewards.[54] Few plantation labour disturbances occurred in which Irish servants and freemen were involved, and fear of Irish involvement in slave revolts and French invasions greatly diminished. By the 1720s the number of Irish inhabitants in the Leewards had fallen to about half that recorded in 1678. Having lost their strength in numbers, and with the cessation of French hostilities, the Irish sought less confrontation with their English masters. Like their counterparts in Barbados, Irish freemen and women lived quietly and obscurely in the back country, though emigration to Jamaica and the mainland colonies remained an attractive option.

Intense master-servant conflict was therefore not a significant feature of eighteenth-century English West Indian society. For the white community as a whole such conflict gave way to the overriding task of keeping the thousands of slaves in subjection. In all the islands the servant population fell rapidly after 1700, and pressures emanating from the overwhelming presence of the constantly growing slave population removed the problem of servant control from the planters' agenda. If anything, the remaining Irish inhabitants were considered by the English as tolerable social misfits.

Notes

1. In the Leewards, St. Kitts was settled in 1624; Nevis, Antigua and Montserrat were settled between 1632 and 1635. Barbados, the first English colony in the Windward Islands, was settled in 1627. For settlement policies and plans at Barbados see British Library Add. MS, 33845, fols. 6–7; Egerton MS 2395, fol. 662; Sloane MS, 2441, fol. 6; William Duke, *Some Memoirs of the First Settlement of the Island of Barbados and other . . . Carribee Islands . . .* (Barbados, 1741), 1–18; and F.C. Innis, "The Pre-Sugar Era of European Settlement in Barbados," *Journal of Caribbean History* (1970), 1–10. For the Leewards see Egerton MS, 2395, Brit. Lib.; Leeward Islands Manuscript Laws, C.O. 154/1/1–77; and C.S.S. Higham, *The Development of the Leeward Islands Under the Restoration, 1660–1668 . . .* (Cambridge, 1921), 1–4.

2. See Aubrey Gwynn, "Documents Relating to the Irish in the West Indies," *Analecta Hibernica*, Irish Manuscripts Commission, No. 4 (Dublin, 1932), 140–287; [Dalby Thomas], *An Historical Account of the Rise and Growth of the West India Colonies . . .* (London, 1690), 10–18; [Edward Littleton], *The Groans of the Plantations: or A True Account . . . upon Sugar, . . .* (London, 1689), 2–16; Richard B. Sheridan, *Sugar and Slavery: An Economic History of the British West Indies, 1623–1775* (Barbados, 1974), 124–183; and Richard S. Dunn, *Sugar and Slaves: The Rise of the Planter Class in the English West Indies, 1624–1713* (Chapel Hill, N.C., 1972), 46–83, 117–148.

3. On various aspects of white indentured servitude and white wage labourers in the West Indies see Jill Sheppard, *The "Redlegs" of Barbados: Their Origins and History* (Millwood, N.Y., 1977); Gary A. Puckrein, *Little England: Plantation Society and Anglo-Barbadian Politics, 1627-1700* (New York, 1984); David Galenson, "White Servitude and the Growth of Black Slavery in Colonial America", *Journal of Economic History*, XLI (1961), 446-467; Abbot Emerson Smith, *Colonists in Bondage: White Servitude and Convict Labor in America, 1607-1776* (Chapel Hill, 1947: rpt., Gloucester, Mass., 1965). Hilary Beckles, *White Servitude and Black Slavery*

in Barbados, 1627-1715 (Knoxville, Tenn., 1989); and Beckles, "Plantation Production and 'White Proto-Slavery': White Indentured Servants and the Colonization of the English West Indies, 1624-1645", *The Americas*, XLI (1985), 21-45. See also Beckles, "Rebels and Reactionaries: The Political Responses of White Labourers to Planter Class Hegemony in Seventeenth Century Barbados", *Journal of Caribbean History*, XV (1983), 1-19; Beckles, "' Black Men in White Skins': The Formation of a White Proletariat in West Indian Slave Society", *Journal of Imperial and Commonwealth History*, XV (1986), 5-21; and Riva Berleant-Schiller, "Free Labor and the Economy in Seventeenth-Century Montserrat," *William and Mary Quarterly*, 3d Ser., XLVI (1989), 539-564.

4. Sheridan, *Sugar and Slavery*, 313. See also Francis G. James, "Irish Colonial Trade in the Eighteenth Century," *WMQ* 3d Ser., XX (1963), 574-584; R. C. Nash, "Irish Atlantic Trade in the Seventeenth and Eighteenth Centuries," *ibid.*, XLII (1985), 329; L. Cullen, "Merchant Communities Overseas: The Navigation Acts and Irish and Scottish Responses," in L. Cullen and T. Smout, eds., *Comparative Aspects of Scottish and Irish Economic History, 1600-1900* (Edinburgh, 1981); David Beers Quinn, *The Elizabethans and the Irish* (Ithaca, N. Y., 1966); "Ireland and Sixteenth-Century European Expansion" in T. Desmond Williams, ed., *Historical Studies: Papers Read before the Second . . . Irish Conference of Historians* (London, 1958); John J. Silke, "The Irish Abroad, . . . 1534-1691," in T. W. Moody, F. X. Martin and F. J. Byrne, eds., *A New History of Ireland*, vol 3, *Early Modern Ireland, 1534-1691* (Oxford, 1976), 599-604; Audrey Lockhart, *Some Aspects of Emigration from Ireland to the North American Colonies between 1660 and 1775* (New York, 1976); John Tracy Ellis, *Catholics in Colonial America* (Baltimore, Md., 1965); Michael J. O'Brien, "The Irish in the American Colonies," *Journal of the American Historical Society, XXI* (1923); Nicholas P. Canny, *The Elizabethan Conquest of Ireland: A Pattern Established, 1565-1765* (Hassocks, Eng., 1976); and P. J. Drudy, ed., *The Irish in America: Emigration, Assimilation, and Impact*, Irish Studies, no. 4 (Cambridge, 1985)

5. Letters of Thomas Anthony, High Court Admiralty MSS, Misc., bundle 30/636, Public Record Office, London.

6. Thomas Povey's Diary, Brit. Lib. Add. MS 12410, fol. 10.

7. See Thomas Carlyle, *Oliver Cromwell's Letters and Speeches: With Elucidations*, 2d ed., 3 vols. (London, 1844), II, 47. He noted that, so popular was the term "to be Barbadoes," an active verb was made of it during the Commonwealth. See also Hilary Beckles, "English Parliament Debates 'White Slavery' in Barbados, 1659," *Journal of the Barbados Museum and Historical Society*, XXXVI (1982), 344-353; A. Gunkel and J. Handler, eds., "A German Indentured Servant in Barbados in 1656," Ibid., XXXII (1979), 91-100; and *Diary of Thomas Burton, Esq. . . . from 1656 to 1659* (London, 1828), IV, 256-258.

8. Carlyle, *Cromwell's Letters*, II, 56-57.

9. Order of Council of State, 19 Oct. 1655, W. Noel Sainsbury *et al.*, eds., *Calendar of State Papers, Colonial Series*, 45 vols. (London, 1860-), *1574-1660*, 419. See also Marcellus Rivers and Oxenbridge Foyle, *England's Slavery, or Barbados Merchandize, Represented in a Petition to the High Court of Parliament* (London, 1659); David Galenson, "The Social Origins of Some Early Americans: Rejoinder" *WMQ*, 3d Ser., XXXVI (1979), 264-286; and Galenson, " 'Middling People' or 'Common Sort'?: The Social Origins of Some Early Americans Reexamined, With a Rebuttal by Mildred Campbell," *ibid.*, XXXV (1978), 499-524, 526-540.

10. See Vincent T. Harlow, *A History of Barbados, 1625-1685* (Oxford, 1926), 295-296. For the servant trade see David Galenson, *White Servitude in Colonial America: An Economic Analysis* (Cambridge, 1981); Galenson, "Immigration and the Colonial Labour System: An Analysis of the Length of Indenture," *Explorations in Economic History*, XIV (1977), 360-377; Galenson, "White Servitude and the Growth of Black Slavery in Colonial America," *Journal of Economic History*, XLI, (1981), 446-467; and David Souden, " 'Rogues, Whores, and Vagabonds'? Indentured Servants, Emigrants to North America, and the Case of Mid-Seventeenth Century Bristol," *Social History*, III (1978), 23-41.

11. Sheppard, *"Redlegs" of Barbados*, 19.

12. Joseph J. Williams, *Whence the "Black Irish" of Jamaica?* (New York, 1932), 12. See also Robert Dunlop, ed., *Ireland Under the Commonwealth . . .*, II (Manchester, 1913), 477, 549.

13. Minutes of Council, Nov. 27, 1657, Davis transcripts, Box 1.

14. Dunn, *Sugar and Slaves*, 69.

15. Willoughby to Secretary of State for Colonies, 7 May 1667, C.O. 1/21, fol. 108.

16. Willoughby to King, 16 Sept. 1667, Stowe MS 735, fol. 19, Brit. Lib.

17. Stapleton to the Lords of Trade, 29th June, 1678, C.O. 1/42, fols. 193-243. Dunn, *Sugar and Slaves*, 122, 130.

18. The list of indentures recorded at Bristol between 1654 and 1686 reflects the relative attractiveness of Barbados and Jamaica. Between 1660 and 1675, 1,124 servants registered for Barbados but only 64 for Jamaica. Between 1676 and 1686, however, 127 registered for Barbados while 404 registered for Jamaica. The London data for 1720 to 1732 show Jamaica as the most frequent destination for servants. The numbers of indentures recorded are Jamaica 1,146; Maryland 918; Virginia 223; Pennsylvania 432; Antigua 165; Barbados 31; St. Lucia 24; and Nevis 22. For Bristol data see "The Tolzey Book of Indentures," City of Bristol Archives, in N.D. Harding, ed., *Bristol and America: A Record of the First Settlers in the Colonies of North America, 1654-1686* (Bristol, n.d.). For London data see "A register of names and surnames of those persons who have voluntarily contracted and bound themselves to go beyond the seas into His Majesty's Colony's and Plantations in America," City of London Corporation Archives.

19. Account of the militia and inhabitants of Barbados, 1661, *C.S.P.C., 1661–1668*, no. 204; *Journal of the House of Assembly of Jamaica, 1663–1826*, (Jamaica, 1811–1829), I, 20–40; Dunn, *Sugar and Slaves*, 155.

20. Codrington to the Lords of Trade and Plantations, July 31, 1689, *C.S.P.C., 1689–1692*, no. 312; John Netheway to King, July 9, 1689, *ibid.*, no. 237; John Netheway to King, June 27, 1689, *ibid.*, no. 212. Netheway stated that, during the war against the French, "an hundred and thirty armed Irishmen" at St. Kitts joined with the French forces on the island.

21. Willoughby to Privy Council, Dec. 16, 1667, C.O. 1/21, no. 162 (emphasis added).

22. Scott, Some Observations on the Island of Barbados, c. 1667, C.O. 1/21, no. 170. On the white slavery debate and the plight of the poor whites see Sheppard, *"Redlegs" of Barbados;* T. Keagy, "The Poor Whites of Barbados," *Revista de Historia de Americas*, LXXIII–LXXIV (1972), 9–52; E. Price, "The Redlegs of Barbados," *J.B.M.H.S.*, X, (1957); and K. Watson, "The Redlegs of Barbados," (unpub. M.A. thesis, University of Florida, 1970). On the white slave social categorization see also A.B. Ellis, "White Slaves and Bondservants on the Plantations," *The Argosy* (Georgetown, British Guiana, May 6, 1893), and Edward Eggleston, "Social Conditions in the Colonies," *Century Illustrated Monthly Magazine*, XXVIII (Oct. 1884).

23. John Eadon, ed., *Memoirs of Pere Labat, 1693–1705* (London, 1970), 125.

24. Letter of Jeaffreson, Aug. 15, 1673, C.O. 1/22, no. 57.

25. Grievances of the Inhabitants of Barbados, Nov. 25, 1675, C.O. 1/37, no. 22.

26. Atkins to Lords of Trade, Aug. 15, 1676, C.O. 1/38, no. 65.

27. See Beckles, " 'Black Men in White Skins'," *J. Imp. Comm. Hist.*, XV (1986), 5–21.

28. Minutes of the Barbados Council, Jan. 2, 1655, Davis Transcripts, Box 2; *ibid.* May 21, 1655.

29. Minutes of the Barbados Council, Dec. 6, 1654, P.R.O., Microfilm Series.

30. Presentments of the Grand Jury in Barbados, July 8, 1673, *C.S.P.C., 1699–1704*, 507.

31. Montgomery to the Lords of Trade and Plantations, Aug. 3, 1688, *C.S.P.C., 1685–1688*, 577.

32. Minutes of the Barbados Council, Jan. 15, Feb. 6, 1656, Lucas MSS, Microfilm Reel 1, Barbados Public Library; *ibid.*, Aug. 2, 1656, fol. 186; *ibid.*, Dec. 16, 1657, in *ibid.*, Reel 2, fol. 486.

33. Minutes of the Barbados Council, Dec. 1656, Davis MSS, Box 7, no. 21, Royal Commonwealth Society, London.

34. Minutes of the Barbados Council, Dec. 10, 1656, Lucas MSS, Reel 1, fols. 327–338.

35. Atkins to the Lords of Trade and Plantations, Jan. 12, 1677, *C.S.P.C., 1677–1680*, 202.

36. Lt. Gov. Stede to Lords of Trade and Plantations, Aug. 30, 1688, *C.S.P.C., 1685–1688*, 584.

37. Minutes of the Barbados Council, Nov. 6, 1655, Box 12, no. 1, Davis transcripts, also Lucas MSS, Reel 1, fols. 161–162; *ibid.*, July 15, 1656; *ibid.*, Sept. 1, 1657; *ibid.*

38. *Ibid.*, Sept. 22, 1657.

39. *Ibid.*, Dec. 21, 1657, Davis transcripts, Box 1, no. 1, *ibid.*, Jan. 3, 1658, Sept. 30, 1657.

40. Expedition of Admiral Penn and General Venables to the West Indies, Lucas MSS, Misc., vol. V, 342; Minutes of the Barbados Council, Oct. 16, 1660, Lucas MSS; "An Act for the Good Governing of Servants, and Ordaining the Rights between Masters and Servants," in Richard Hall, *Acts Passed in Barbados, 1643–1762* (London, 1764), no. 30, 35–40.

41. Minutes of Council of Barbados, Feb. 16, 1686, *C.S.P.C., 1685–1686*, 155; also C.O. 31/1, fol. 675; Minutes of the Barbados Council, Mar. 1, 1686, Lucas MSS, Reel 2, fol. 160.

42. [John Oldmixon], *The British Empire in America, Containing the History of the . . . Islands of America*, vol. II (London, 1741; rpt. New York, 1969), 53; see also Gov. James Kendal to the Lords of Trade and Plantations, Nov. 15, 1692, C.O. 28/1, fols. 200–206, and C.O. 28/83, fols. 174–176. For an account of the 1692 aborted revolt see Hilary McD. Beckles, *Black Rebellion in Barbados: The Struggle Against Slavery, 1627–1838* (Bridgetown, Barbados, 1984), 42–48.

43. Report of the Commissioners Appointed to Enquire into the Negro Conspiracy at Barbados, Nov. 3, 1692, *C.S.P.C., 1689–1692*, 733–734. See also Hilary Beckles, "Rebels Without Heroes: Slave Politics in Seventeenth Century Barbados," *Journal of Caribbean History*, XVIII (1986), 16–17, and J. Handler, "The Barbados Slave Conspiracies of 1675 and 1692," *J.B.M.H.S.* XIII (1960), 192.

44. Higham, *Leeward Islands*, 40–60; see also Dunn, *Sugar and Slaves*, 123–124, Inhabitants of Montserrat to William Willoughby, Jan. 1668, C.O. 1/22, no. 17, and Report of William Willoughby on the Leeward Islands, June 1668, C.O. 1/24, no. 71.

45. Francis Sampson to John Sampson, June 6, 1668, *C.S.P.C., 1661–1668*, 386.

46. Willoughby to King, Jan. 1668, C.O. 1/22, no. 17; Report of William Willoughby on Montserrat, Feb. 1668, C.O. 1/24, no. 71.

47. Henry Carpenter to Thomas Belchkamber, Aug. 19, 1689, *C.S.P.C., 1689–1692*, 129; Christopher Codrington to Lords of Trade, July 31, 1689, *ibid.*, 111; John Netheway to King, June 27, 1689, *ibid.*, no. 1689; Christopher Codrington to Lords of Trade, July 31, 1689, *ibid.*, no. 312.

48. Crispe to Colonel Bayer, June 10, 1689, *ibid.*, no. 193; Hodges to Lords of Trade, Apr. 6, 1706, *C.S.P.C., 1706–1708*, 103.

49. W.J. Gardner, *A History of Jamaica: From its Discovery by Christopher Columbus to the Year 1872* (London, 1971; orig. pub. 1873), 53.

50. Dunn, *Sugar and Slaves*, 160; *ibid.*, 161.

51. Gardner, *A History of Jamaica*, 170.

52. Hunter to the Board of Trade, Nov. 13, 1731, C.O. 137/19, fols. 108–109.

53. Minutes of the Barbados Council, 1697, *C.S.P.C., 1696–1697*, no. 1108; Journal of the Council of Trade and Plantations, Dec. 28, 1696, *ibid.*, no. 535.

54. Dunn, *Sugar and Slaves*, 146–147.

18

The Economics of Transition to the Black Labour System in Barbados, 1630-1680

HILARY McD. BECKLES AND ANDREW DOWNES

In recent years there has been an expansion of academic interest in the nature of the transition from white indentured servitude to black slavery as the dominant labour base of the English New World colonies during the seventeenth and eighteenth centuries. Studies by Galenson, Menard, Gray and Wood, Gemery and Hogendorn, and Bean and Thomas have explained in detail this change in the labour systems of the Chesapeake area, the Carolinas, Virginia, and Maryland. In this literature, references are made to the West Indian colonies by way of comparison, but no specific studies have yet been presented for these colonies. Only Bean and Thomas attempted to be comprehensive in their comparison and showed the importance of the West Indian experience, but their analysis did not go far enough in correcting the lopsided nature of the historiography.[1]

All of these studies have noted that Englishmen in the West Indian colonies, particularly in Barbados during the late 1640s and 1650s, were the first to employ black slave labour on a large scale in the Americas. This was done by the displacement of white indentured labour. By the end of the seventeenth century these colonies were unable to survive profitably without a large and expanding slave trade. It was not until the eighteenth century that the mainland colonies followed the Barbadian trail. This study applies formal economic theory to the analysis of the transition from white servant labour to black slave labour in the English West Indies. It is specifically a study of the Barbadian case and more generally an essay on the economic history of labour in the English West Indies.[2]

In 1627, William Courteen and Associates, a London merchant company, began the colonization of Barbados. By 1629, the company had invested about £10,000 in preparing the colony for commodity production with an export orientation. Between 1629 and 1634, the cultivation of tobacco dominated the colony's economic activities. As a result of rapidly falling tobacco prices on the London market, plus the inability of the planters to produce a good quality leaf competitive with the Virginians, economic resources were shifted into cotton and indigo production, and by 1637 these two commodities had outstripped tobacco in terms of land use and aggregate export value.

During 1641/42, both cotton and indigo prices fell sharply on the London market, and planters, responding to this crisis, in 1643 began to experiment seriously with the cultivation of sugar cane. The sugar industry, pioneered by a few planters such as James Drax and James Holdip, gained momentum and by 1680 it absorbed some 80 per cent of the island's arable land, 90 per cent of its labour force, and accounted for an estimated 90 per cent of its export earnings. This sugar revolution set the pattern of agricultural development in the English West Indies for 300 years.[3]

The pre-sugar economy was based almost totally upon the employment of white indentured labour recruited from the British isles. Voluntary servants contracted for terms of between two to ten years. In the case of the thousands of political

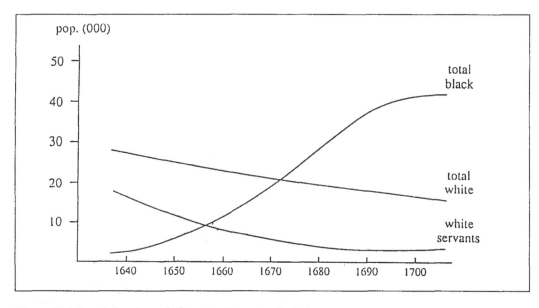

Figure 18.1. Population change in Seventeenth-century Barbados

prisoners adjudged rogues and vagrants, and the defenceless poor who were transported by the State, contracts of ten years were normal. Between 1630 and 1660, the estimated average length of servant contracts on the island was six years.[4]

Empirical evidence suggests that the first phase of sugar production, 1643 to 1648, was also based largely on servant labour. Between 1650 and 1670, planters rapidly replaced servants with black slaves in unskilled field work and other related manual occupations. Subsequently, servants emerged in the second half of the century as a labour elite, monopolizing artisanal and low-level managerial occupations. After the mid-1660s the white servant population began to decrease rapidly, and the black population more than doubled between 1645 and 1665. During the 1670s servants were replaced

by slaves in the skilled plantation roles, and by 1690 servants had a monopoly of only the overseer functions, most carpenters, masons, sugar boilers, and bricklayers being black slaves. Figure 18.1 illustrates the changes in the demographic structure of the colony between 1640 and 1700.[5]

A sample of the few remaining inventories of early Barbados, shown in Table 18.1, illustrates the numerical relationship between servants and slaves. From an insignificant minority in the 1630s, slaves accounted for about 95 per cent of the labour force in the 1680s. Shifts in the slave-servant ratios on the plantations were reflected in the 1679/80 island-wide census. It was about this time that the displacement of white by black labour in the skilled trades was gaining momentum, and these aggregate data reflect this process (see Table 18.2). By 1680, there were seventeen

Table 18. 1. Labour Composition on Thirty-Eight Barbadian Plantations, 1639–1670

Years	No. of Estates	Total Acres	Servants	Slaves
1639–1640	6	1,210	114	0
1641–1643	9	1,568	108	51
1644–1649	6	1,931	112	238
1650–1657	7	1,882	129	168
1658–1662	3	684	6	487
1663–1667	3	380	4	203
1668–1670	4	876	21	421
Totals	38	8,531	494	1,568

Table 18.2. Number and Distribution of Slaves and Servants in Barbados, 1679/80

Parish	Servants	Slaves	Slaves per Servant[a]
St. Michael	303	3,765	12
country	407	1,430	4
town	111	4,316	39
St. George	179	4,789	27
Christ Church	123	4,407	36
St. Phillip	133	2,895	22
St. James	72	2,070	29
St. Joseph	118	1,965	17
St. Lucy	228	3,386	15
St. Thomas	158	3,303	21
St. John	379	2,977	8
St. Peter	47	2,248	48
St. Andrew			
	2,258	37,551	17

[a]To the nearest whole number

slaves to every servant, whereas in 1640 there were about thirty servants to every slave.[6]

The Economics of the Transition

The transition from indentured to slave labour did not represent simply a fundamental adoption of a qualitatively different labour system but primarily a move along a continuum of further labour subjection. The crises of the tobacco and cotton economies had threatened not only investments but also the future of West Indian colonization. The planters, noting that capital investments in servant labour was second only to land in terms of value, developed and implemented an extreme market conception of labour, so that servants became generally known in Barbados as white slaves.[7]

The most effective method by which a wide range of economic functions could be attached to a servant was to establish in custom, if not in law, his use as a form of property. In this categorization the early Barbadian planters succeeded; servants were taxed as property, alienated in wills, used as currency in the financial and monetary system, advanced as security in mortgage agreements, and attached to land to be sold as moveable assets. Some social characteristics of slavery were also present in the development of Barbadian servitude. The master's almost total control over his servant, the common acceptance in custom of his authority over labour outside of civil law, and the general ease with which he was able to obtain social (non-pecuniary) benefits

from his bonds-persons were integral parts of Barbadian servitude. By means of these functions, planters were able to derive most of the critical economic benefits of slave labour from the institution of servitude in early seventeenth-century Barbados.[8]

The dominant traditional interpretation for the transition from white indentureship to black slavery in the West Indies is the climatic theory, which stressed the physical inability of whites, and the ability of blacks to work efficiently on tropical plantations. Partly related to this theory is the argument that West Indian planters, for racist, cultural, and other non-economic reasons, preferred black to white labour. Instead we suggest that during the pre-sugar era and the first phase of the sugar era (1627–1660) indentured labour was more economical than slave labour, hence its general adoption by West Indian planters. In addition, the growing efficiency of the slave trade between 1650 and 1660 allowed slaves to become satisfactory, economic substitutes for servants. It was not until the mid-1660s, when adverse forces affected the servant market, drastically reducing supply and pushing up cost, that slave labour gained a clear cost advantage over servant labour. That the displacement process had accelerated during the 1650s merely suggests that planters had correctly perceived these trends in the two labour markets and were able to absorb, in the short term, the higher marginal cost incurred by black labour because of the extraordinarily large profits generated by early sugar production.[9]

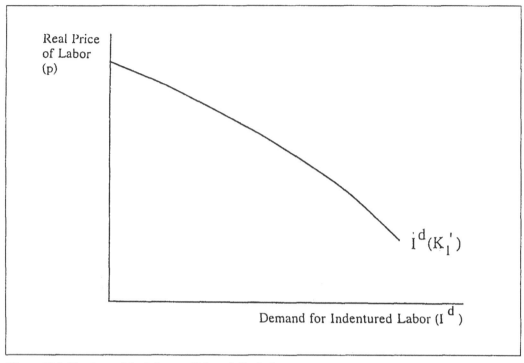

Figure 18.2. The demand for indentured labour in Barbados

Sugar Production and Indentured Labour

The pre-sugar economy and the formative period of expansion in the sugar industry (1627-1650) were not characterized by any labour shortages. The level of demand for servants during the 1640s was estimated at about 2,000 servants per year. In 1652 the estimated annual optimum demand for additional servants was 3,000 per year. The stock of servants on the island in that year was about 13,000. Between 1645 and 1650 at least 8,000 servants arrived in Barbados. These were a mixture of voluntary servants, political refugees, and transported convicts and rogues. The political and economic problems of England and Scotland in this period were analyzed by political economists in demographic terms. Over-population was seen as the central reason for social distress and economic dislocation. The opportunity to emigrate to the West Indies created a labour market which was seen, during the 1640s and 1650s, as quantitatively and qualitatively adequate for sugar production. For servants, the expected real income, including benefits on the expiration of their contracts, exceeded the opportunity cost of staying at home where they would more than likely remain un-

employed. Nonetheless, they characteristically formed part of a pool of surplus labour in Barbados.[10]

Our economic analysis at this stage is fundamentally classical. If we assume that planters were essentially profit maximizers, they would have been willing to hire this migrant labour up to the point where its marginal revenue product equalled the price of an indenture. Alternatively, planters would have hired indentured labour up to the point where the marginal physical productivity of that labour was equal to its real price. (The real price of labour can be taken as the amount of cotton or sugar exchanged for one labour unit.) Given the existing technology in the sugar industry, we assumed that sugar production was subject to diminishing returns; we expected an inverse relationship between the demand for indentured labour and its real price. This inverse relationship is depicted in Figure 18.2, where a demand curve for indentured labour, which is also the marginal product of that factor, is shown for a composite set of factors, for example, plantation capital equipment and land.[11]

Following Lewis, we assumed that planters in Barbados attracted indentured labour at a con-

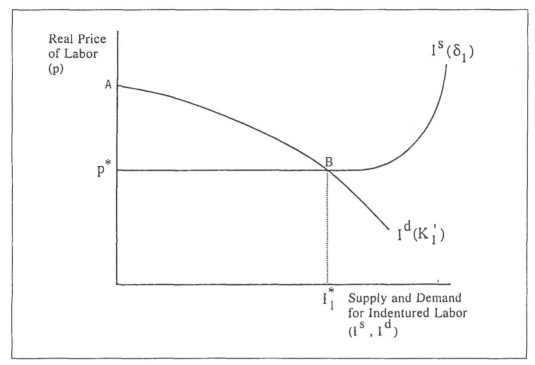

Figure 18.3. Supply and demand for indentured labour in Barbados

stant real price. Equilibrium in the market for indentured labour would require that the real demand and supply prices be equal.[12]

With a given set of exogeneous factors – capital equipment and land – the intersection of the demand and supply labour schedules yields the amount of indentured labourers demanded $(I*p*)$ as illustrated in Figure 18.3. The area under the demand curve for labour, $ABI*_1O$, represents the total output of sugar Q. This output is broadly divided into payment for indentured labour services (i.e., maintenance costs, etc.) – $p*BI_1*O$ – and the surplus going to the planter $(ABp*)$. Broadly defined, we have:

$$Q = C_L + \delta$$

where C_L is the cost of labour and δ is the surplus. We can further assume that part of this surplus is reinvested into the expansion of sugar production and the remainder is used for personal aggrandizement, that is

$$\delta = \delta_1 + \delta_2$$

where δ_1 is reinvested profit and δ_2 is distributed profit.

The development of the sugar economy meant that there was an increased demand for labour,

capital, and land. Since we are dealing with the issue of capital accumulation and labour absorption we can ignore the issue of land. With no changes in the conditions of supply of indentured labour to Barbados, the increased demand for labour to expand the scale of operations can be depicted by pivoting towards the 1^d curve (see Figure 18.4).[13]

The expansion in existing operations, as a result of the consolidation of small estates into large-scale enterprises, and the entry of new planters into large-scale sugar production would have increased the demand for labour. The profit on sugar production would have increased by the area ABC, whereas the costs of indentured labour would have increased by $BCI*I*_1$. With the real supply of indentured labour approximately perfectly elastic up $I*_2$, the increased demand for indentured labour would not have affected the price $(P*)$ which planters paid for their labour.

The process of output expansion, capital accumulation, and labour absorption continues until the real supply price of labour begins to rise about the point D in Figure 18.4. Beyond this stage we move out of our classical world into a

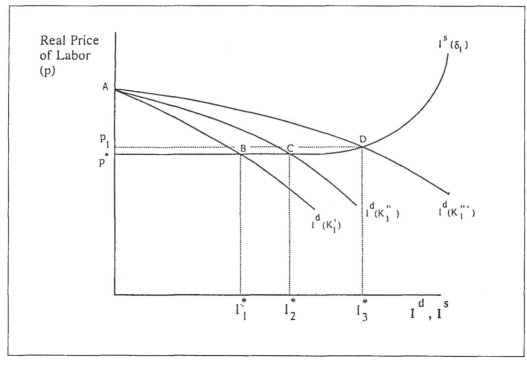

Figure 18.4. Supply and demand for indentured labour over time in Barbados

neoclassical one. The increase in the price of indentured labour and other operating costs, coupled with the competition of capitalists in the production of sugar, gradually reduces the level of profit and hence long-run capital accumulation. In order to maintain profit levels and capital accumulation, Barbadian planters would have had either to substitute capital for indentured labour, assuming the relative price of capital was lower than that for labour, or seek an alternative source of labour. The possibility for rationalization in the sugar industry was limited, since there was little technological progress taking place within the sugar industry. Indeed, Dunn notes that "it was a Sicilian sugar planter, as long ago as 1449, who invented the three-roller vertical mill that the English planters in the Caribbean used throughout the seventeenth and eighteenth centuries to crush their cane and extract their juice."[14]

With the growing demand for sugar in Europe, Barbadian planters were in dire need of labour to expand their operations. They still tapped the European labour market for skilled labour but, by the mid-1660s, the appeal of their incentive package offered on this market rapidly

decreased as newly colonized Jamaica and the expanding mainland colonies, both of which offered greater land ownership possibilities, became more attractive to potential servants. With an increasing demand for sugar and a diminishing supply of indentured labour, the planters were forced to offer servants a better package, such as shorter contracts, better housing and diet, and, most important, the socio-psychological incentive of being excluded from work in the same gangs as blacks. These factors were important in raising the stream of costs associated with indentured labour.

Our analysis points to a number of hypotheses concerning the use of indentured labour in the early phase of sugar production. The majority of servants arriving in Barbados had no ready contracts with specific planters; instead they were recruited and indentures were sold by merchants on the open market. The price of indentures sold was a reflection of several minor costs, such as clothing, food, the surgeon's fee during the middle passage, and the merchant's profit margin. Over the century, the price of supplying servants to the market increased, but at no stage did it exceed £8 sterling per freight, as each servant was referred to by the shippers. A parliamentary debate of 1659 revealed that the normal cost of supplying a servant to Barbados was £4.10.5. In 1664, a committee of the Lords of Trade and Plantations reported that £6 per freight was the norm. By the 1690s, the cost had risen to about £7.10s per freight.[15]

No price series exists for this early period, and analysts therefore have to obtain what they can from fragmented data. The selling price of prime indentures varied minimally according to skills, sex, and nationality. In general, merchants aimed to sell each servant indenture at twice the supply cost. Age and skills were not critical factors on the primary market, as most servants were between the ages of sixteen and thirty, and artisanal skills were not generally applicable to sugar production. Most planters were prepared to pay a marginally higher fee for good Scottish servants, but cared less for Irish Catholics. The fifty-six servants aboard the *Abraham* who were sold at Barbados in January 1637 went for medium and modal prices, male and female, of 500 lbs. of tobacco – about £7 sterling.[16]

During the 1640s and early 1650s, as the demand for servants rapidly increased, so did their price. By the mid 1650s, indentures were being sold in Barbados between £10 and £14 per head. This inflation of servant prices placed considerable financial pressure upon owners of small and mid-sized plantations, most of whom were already heavily indebted to merchants. In 1661, the governor informed the colonial office that the "price of servants," among other commodities, had "doubled what they were," and must inevitably "ruin the planters." He pleaded for an increase in supply in order to reduce price levels, but none was forthcoming. During the 1660s, prices continued to increase, while the length of service was rapidly reduced. By the late 1670s, after many unsuccessful attempts by the planters to increase the supply of servants, the council and assembly enacted legislation to stabilize prices. In 1678, the first of a series of laws was passed entitled "An Act to Encourage the Bringing in of Christian Servants." In 1682, another act was passed which led to direct involvement by local government in the servant market. The act provided that merchants who brought "good servants" to the colony and were unable to dispose of them within ten days would be paid £12.10s per servant by the treasurer.

These servant indentures would then be resold to planters at a rate of £13 per head. The 10 shillings difference was to cover the cost of administering the facility and the fee for allowing the planters to pay by instalments.[17]

In 1688, this price level was changed. The treasurer was now instructed that, since planters consistently complained about the high costs of servant labour, he was to reduce prices by reselling servant indentures at the rate of £10 per male and £10.10s per female. By 1690, the merchants were rejecting the £12.10 price level. They petitioned the assembly stating that the war against the French, which made their business riskier, and raised recruitment costs in England, required a significant price increase. By 1696, the treasurer was paying servant traders the increased price of £18 per freight. For example, in 1699 Nicholas Baker supplied fifty servants to the treasurer and collected £990. Likewise, Roberts and Company supplied 125 servants and collected £2,250.[18]

Meanwhile, the price of slave labour became progressively lower between 1627 and 1680. Between 1630 and 1650, slave prices in Barbados were generally some 200 to 300 per cent higher than servant prices. The limited data available for most of this period suggest an estimated mean price of £35 per slave. These were the years when the Dutch merchants, operating largely from Pernambuco in north-eastern Brazil, had a virtual monopoly of the Barbadian slave market. No price series is presently available for Barbados during the first half of the century. Bean and Thomas presented what Gemery and Hogendorn have considered the most accurate computation available to date. The price series, shown below, is a per capita decimalized sterling list which is based largely upon Watgen's 1921 slave prices.[19]

Fragmentary Barbadian data suggest that the Pernambuco prices were reasonably representative of the colony's market. For example, John Severne, a Dutch slave trader, sold his slaves at Barbados in 1640 for £35 each. In addition, Ligon, who lived in Barbados between 1647 and 1650, noted that £25 to £30 per head was the norm for prime slaves.[20]

In spite of the substantial per unit margin in the initial capital outlay between slave and servant during the pre-1660 period, their respective marginal physical product could be equated.

Table 18.3   Estimated Barbadian Slave Prices, 1638–1645

Year	£ Sterling
1638	40.88
1639	44.15
1640	30.03
1641	36.72
1642	39.75
1643	20.54
1644	13.03
1645	20.98

Both slave and servant worked in gangs doing the same work for the same hours (sunup till sundown), driven by severe overseers. They were fed on the same basic diet and extracted from their masters similar maintenance costs. Although servants might have cost marginally more to clothe than slaves, the difference was not sufficiently significant to influence the overwhelming cost advantage of the servant over the slave.[21]

Planters, however, made more detailed calculations. They were concerned with the estimated longevity of both types of labour in order to make deductions about the relative stream of future net returns on their investment. The sketchy and fragmented mortality data which exist for early Barbadian slave society suggest that planters were generally able to extract no more than seven working years from their average slave. This sum was arrived at after deductions were made for the two or three years of seasoning, when new slaves did little strenuous work, and the estimated aggregate 30 per cent mortality among these slaves for this period. When these data are placed alongside the six years of work extracted from the average servants, and the margin in their purchase price is added, the cost advantage of the servant over the slave prior to 1660 is noticeable.[22]

Planters were usually able to attract prime labourers from the European market. Servants were generally young, largely male, and skilled in some area. An analysis of 836 servants shipped from London to Barbados in 1634 in eight different consignments shows that planters were able to obtain optimal labour. Male servants constituted 94.5 per cent of the total shipment; 72.3 per cent were under twenty-two years of age (see Table18. 4). The skilled component in the servant labour force can be illustrated by the sample of 1,808 servants registered at Bristol between 1654 and 1660 for servitude in Barbados (see Table 18.5).[23]

If we assume a seven-year average working span for slave labour and a six-year working span for servant labour, the former, with an average purchase price of £30 for the period 1635 to 1660, produced a man/year price of £4.2, whereas the latter with an average purchase price of £10, produced a man/year price ratio of £1.6.

Table 18.4   Servants Shipped to Barbados in 1634[a]

| Ship | Age | | | Age Distribution | | | |
	Male	Female	Total	10–19	20–22	23–29	30+
Abraham	99	2	101	20	49	23	9
Hopewell	146	1	147	35	83	16	13
Bonaventure	3	4	7	–	7	–	–
?	86	5	91	25	31	21	14
Falcon	70	10	80	35	28	10	7
Alexander	143	19	162	64	55	22	21
Expedition	202	2	204	56	83	30	35
Falcon	41	3	44	11	23	5	5
Total	790 (94.5)	46 (5.5)	836	246 (29.4)	359 (42.9)	127 (15.2)	104 (12.5)

[a] percentages in parentheses

Source: John Hotten, *The Original List of Persons . . . who went from Great Britain to the American Plantations, 1600–1700* (London, 1874), 38–154.

Table 18.5   Servants Registered for Barbados from Bristol, 1654–1660

Year	No.	No. Skilled	% Skilled
1654	16	14	87.5
1655	115	53	46.0
1656	158	68	43.0
1657	371	225	60.6
1658	415	149	35.9
1659	494	268	54.2
1660	239	142	59.4
Total	1,808	919	50.8

Using such simple economic calculations we can compare the cost advantage of servant labour over slave labour for the pre-Restoration period.

During this early period, the economic policies of sugar planters in Barbados did not encourage inputs into the labour force by internal reproduction, which would have diminished the marginal revenue advantage of servant labour. In fact, the early planters were hostile to the natural reproduction of both slaves and servants, believing that the opportunity cost and the money outlay for rearing juveniles were greater than the expected capital gain.[24]

In the post-Restoration period, however, significant changes took place in both the slave and servant markets. These changes were substantial enough to give slave labour a marginal cost advantage over servant labour, thus reversing the economic pattern of the previous thirty years. By 1665, the ratio of the marginal product of slave labour to the price of a slave was greater than that of an indentured servant. This change in the price/cost ratios of servant and slave labour took place rapidly, and should be accounted for carefully.

During this period, an anti-emigration movement became popular in England, fuelled by the writings of political economists and economic pamphleteers and supported by the government. These writers, still operating within the confines of demographic analysis, argued that England was underpopulated, and the emigration of every servant to the colonies represented a drain upon its resources; hence the trade was seen as contrary to the economic interest of England. Coke and Cary were able to influence the government by the publication of their respective treatises on trade which were strongly anti-emigration. In addition, during the 1660s, for the first time in the seventeenth century, merchants were brought to the courts and charged for kidnapping and inveigling servants away from the realm.[25]

More important, the Navigation Acts of 1660 and 1661 made it illegal for ships to take servants from Scotland to the colonies without first stopping at an English port and registering their cargo. This legislation had the effect of driving Scottish merchants out of the servant trade, thus taking the Scottish labour market out of the orbit of Barbadian planters. In addition, Jamaica emerged after the 1660s as the most attractive destination for British servants going to the West Indies. No land was offered to servants in Barbados, and little opportunity existed for them to acquire land after their servitude expired. The Jamaican planters offered indentured servants contracts of two to four years and up to twenty acres of land at the expiration of their servitude. Barbados became after 1660 the least attractive of the West Indian colonies from the perspective of potential servants, and the larger proportion of servants going to the West Indies after 1670 went to Jamaica.

The data sets for indentured servants departing from Bristol between 1654 and 1684, from London between 1683 and 1686, and from Liverpool in 1702 illustrate the rapidly diminishing attractiveness of Barbados and the increasing preference of servants for Jamaica and the mainland colonies. Of the recorded 10,394 servants leaving Bristol for the plantations, 46.8, 25.7, 11.9, and 4.5 per cent were bound for Virginia, Barbados, the Leeward Islands, and Jamaica respectively. The London data illustrate most clearly the relative ascendancy of Jamaica over Barbados as a favoured destination. Of the 428 servants recorded, only 99 were bound for Barbados, whereas 276 were destined for Jamaica. Furthermore, of the 545 indentured contracts signed at Liverpool for the above dates, 475 stated the destinations of Virginia and Maryland, 34 New England, 20 Barbados and 16 the Leeward Islands.[26]

In spite of the Barbados planters' offer of two-year contracts in 1661, the supply continued to diminish, suggesting that potential servants were probably more responsive to post-servitude conditions, such as land owning possibilities and general socio-economic mobility, than to the actual conditions of servitude. Governor Richard Atkins of Barbados confirmed in 1675 that "there is no encouragement and no land for them, nor anything but hard service for small wages." Furthermore, the governor continued, most servants came from Ireland, and these "prove very idle." As a result, it was well established in Barbados by this time, the governor noted, that "three blacks work better and cheaper than one whiteman." Meanwhile, Carolina was offering 150 acres of land for every able-bodied adult male servant, 100 acres for females, and 100 acres for male youths under the age of sixteen.[27]

The diminishing supply of servants to Barbados, however, should be examined within the general context of falling aggregate supply from England, Wales, and Scotland during the second half of the century. As economic and political conditions in England improved during the second half of the century, the propensity to emigrate lessened. Workers made market evaluations of future earning by comparing their expected income at home with the estimates of income and general accumulation in the colonies. The statistical evidence supplied by Phelps-Brown and Hopkins suggests that the English labour market improved considerably during the second half of the century. As money wages increased steadily, workers in England would have been more reluctant to emigrate to the West Indies, where conditions were worsening for individuals without substantial capital. Small numbers of servants still continued to arrive in Barbados into the eighteenth century, but they had little impact upon the colony's labour market. In addition, increasing socio-political stability in England after the Restoration led to a higher level of inertia among potential emigrants. The numbers fleeing England in order to avoid political persecution diminished toward the end of the century. Those emigrating under indenture in order to avoid religious discrimination, such as Catholics and Quakers, avoided Barbados when they could, as the colony became known as one of the least tolerant of all the English New World possessions.[28]

Meanwhile, the price of slave labour continued to fall. During the late 1650s prices fell to between £24 and £28 for a prime male slave. In 1663, the Company of Royal Adventurers of England Trading to Africa was formed with a charter to supply slaves to Barbados at a price of £17 per head. Between 1663 and 1666 the Company supplied over 5,000 slaves to Barbados at an average price of £18. By the late 1660s, the price of slave labour had fallen some 35 per cent below the level of the 1640s, while the cost of servant labour increased by over 300 per cent. In addition, by the 1670s planters had improved their ability to exploit slave labour effectively, and the encouragement of natural reproduction became a feature of plantation policy – reflecting the maturity and sophistication of management techniques. Planters now valued slave children as an important part of the capital accumulation process, their market value rising from £5 at birth to £6 at the age of one month.[29]

Indentured vs. Slave Labour: Economic Statics and Dynamics

Economic factors were principally at work in the transition from indentured labour to slave labour. With the development of a bottleneck in the indentured labour market, planters were increasingly forced to turn their attention to an alternative labour resource, namely slave labour. This transfer took place on a very limited scale during the initial phase of sugar production since the purchase price of a servant was substantially lower than that of a slave. Figure 18.5 illustrates the relative demands for the two types of labour, given their respective supply conditions.

The real prices of indentured and slave labour are represented by q and p respectively, while I^d, S^d, I^s, and S^s represent their respective demand and supply curves. If we assume, for simplicity, that the conditions in the slave labour market were such that the supply of labour was perfectly inelastic (i.e., a vertical supply curve), then with given demand conditions the equilibrium price of slave labour is given by q_1. As is evident from Figure 18.5, $q_1 > p_1$, where p_1 is the equilibrium price in the indentured labour market. The perfectly elastic supply of indentured servant labour

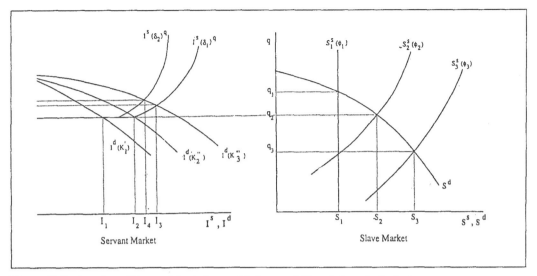

Figure 18.5. Supply and Demand for Indentured Labour and Slave Labour in Barbados

has already been explained in terms of conditions existing in Europe. The high inelasticity of supply of slave labour reflects the early monopoly control of the Dutch in the slave market. Therefore, in the early phase of sugar production, the high price of slave labour relative to servant labour meant that planters would have purchased more of the latter, given that both types of labour yielded similar marginal productivity. With the increase in the demand for indentured labour, its price would have risen once labour supply moved out of the perfectly elastic stage, that is, to p_2. On the other hand, changes in the conditions of the supply of slave labour (ϕ) would have led directly to a decline in the price of slave labour and hence the amount traded in the market.[30]

There were two factors which affected the supply conditions in both the indentured and slave labour markets and hence the movement in labour prices. First, the English attempted to integrate vertically the entire production process by breaking into the slave trade and driving the Dutch out of the Barbadian market. With the breaking of the Dutch monopoly and greater English control over the supply of slaves, Barbadian planters were provided with a steady supply of slave labour with a resultant fall in the price of slaves over time. In Figure 18.5, we represent such a long-run situation with the S^s curve shifting downward and becoming relatively elastic, that is, S^s_2 and S^s_3. Given reason-

ably stable demand conditions, the price of slave labour would gradually have declined and the number of slaves traded would have increased.[31]

The second factor relates to supply conditions in the indentured slave market. The activities of the anti-emigration movement, the regulations in the Navigation Acts of 1660 and 1661 which adversely affected the Scottish servant market, and the emergence of competing markets for servant labour (e.g., Jamaica offered better rewards) all reduced the supply of servant labour to the Barbadian planters. The change in the conditions of supply would therefore have shifted the supply curve for indentured labour from $I^s(\delta_1)$ to $I^s(\delta_2)$ for given demand conditions and hence raised the price of indentured servants.

Underlying the comparatively static analysis of labour market interaction are important dynamic considerations. The market price of the two types of labour was not the only factor affecting the planters' choice of an optimal labour combination. The expected economic life of the labour inputs along with their expected maintenance and supervision costs compared with the gross return from their employment were also decisive factors in the decision-making process. The choice of the optimal combination of slave and indentured labour became an inter-temporal or dynamic optimization problem. If we assume that the planters sought to maximize their long-run profit position, then they would have demanded labour only if the stream of expected (future) net returns, discounted at a given rate of discount, equalled or exceeded the purchase price of labour. We therefore have the decision rule for slave labour as

$$q \leq \sum_{t=o}^{T} \overline{\frac{R_t}{(1+r)^t}}$$

where q is the purchase price of a slave, R_t is the net return at time t, r is the rate of discount, and T is the economic life of the slave.[32]

Given the two types of labour – indentured and slave – provided identical flows of services with roughly the same constant performance during their economic lives, then if one type of labour was expected to survive longer than the other, it would have had a higher present value at a given rate of discount. In effect, if the slave's economic life exceeded the contractual period of an indentured servant, then, with similar marginal productivities, maintenance, and supervisor costs, slave labour would have been in greater demand if slave prices were falling relative to those of indentured servants. The assumption is that the flow of productive services of both types of labour depended on their age structures, quality, health, and general attitude to work.

It was as a result of these changed market conditions that planters came to prefer slaves to servants in the second half of the seventeenth century. After the early 1660s, black labour was not only cheaper but also much easier to procure. West Indian planters had no choice but to obtain slave labour if they wished to remain viable sugar producers. Any other choice would have been irrational from a market point of view.

Notes

1   Richard Bean and Robert Thomas, "The Adoption of Slave Labour in British America" in Henry Gemery and Jan Hogendorn (eds.), *The Uncommon Market: Essays in the Economic History of the Atlantic Slave Trade* (New York, 1979), 377-398. For the Chesapeake area, colonial Georgia and Barbados respectively, see Russell Menard, "From Servants to Slaves: The Transformation of the Chesapeake Labor System," *Southern Studies*, XVI (1977), 391–429; Ralph Gray and Betty Wood, "The Transition from Indentured to Involuntary Servitude in Colonial Georgia," *Explorations in Economic History*, XIII (1976), 353-370; Beckles, "The Economic Origins of Black Slavery in the British West Indies: A Tenta-

tive Analysis of the Barbados Model," *Journal of Caribbean History*, XVI (1982), 36–57. See also the excellent work of David Galenson on the servant trade to early America and the development of colonial servitude: "White Servitude and the Growth of Black Slavery in Colonial America," *Journal of Economic History* XLI (1981), 446–467; idem, "The Market Evaluation of Human Capital: The Case of Indentured Servitude," *Journal of Political Economy*, LXXXIX (1981), 446–457; idem, "Immigrants and the Colonial Labor System: An Analysis of the Length of Indenture," *Explorations in Economic History*, XIV (1977), 360–377.

2.   For the polemic over the pre-sugar era, see Robert C. Batie, "Why Sugar? Economic Cycles and the Changing of Staples in the English and French Antilles, 1624–1654," *Journal of Caribbean History*, VIII and IX (1976), 1–25; Frank C. Innis, "The Pre-Sugar Era of European Settlement in Barbados," *ibid.*, I (1970), 1–20; Beckles, *Black Rebellion in Barbados: The Struggle against Slavery, 1627–1838* (Bridgetown, 1984), 9–20.

3.   For three authoritative accounts of the sugar revolution in Barbados, see Richard Dunn, *Sugar and Slaves: The Rise of the Planter Class in the English West Indies, 1624–1713* (New York, 1973); Richard Sheridan, *Sugar and Slavery: An Economic History of the British West Indies, 1623–1775* (Barbados, 1974), 124–127; idem, *The Development of the Plantation to 1750* (Kingston, 1970), 1–70.

4.   Beckles, "English Parliamentary Debate on 'White Slavery' in Barbados, 1659," *Journal of the Barbados Museum and Historical Society (J.B.M.H.S.)*, XXXVI (1982), 344–352; Thomas Burton, *Parliamentary Diary, 1656–1659* (London, 1838), IV, 252–307; Abbott E. Smith, *Colonists in Bondage: White Servitude and Convict Labor in America, 1607–1776* (Chapel Hill, 1966), 142–168.

5.   Richard Ligon, *A True and Exact History of the Island of Barbados* (London, 1657), 143–146; Frank W. Pitman, *The Development of the British West Indies, 1700–1763* (New York, 1967), 61; Jerome Handler, "The Amerindian Slave Population of Barbados in the Seventeenth and Early Eighteenth Century," *Caribbean Studies*, VIII (1968), 38–64; idem, "Aspects of Amerindian Ethnography in Seventeenth-Century Barbados," *ibid.*, IX (1969), 50–72; Galenson, "White Servitude," 450–460; Beckles, " 'Black Men in White Skins': The Formation of a White Proletariat in West Indian Slave Society," *Journal of Imperial and Commonwealth History*, XV (1986), 10–17. For demographic data on seventeenth-century Barbados, see Governor Atkins to Secretary Blathwayt, Apr. 1, 1680, *Calendar of State Papers, Colonial Series (C.S.P.C.), 1677–1680*, nos. 1336, 1386; Egerton Ms. 2395, British Library; Vincent Harlow, *A History of Barbados, 1625–1685* (Oxford, 1926), 338.

6.   Inventories and Deeds of Barbados, RB 3/1, ff 1–418, RB 3/2, 309, RB 3/3, 27, 58–63. 165–168. 190–199. 273–335, RB 3/8, 6–8, Barbados Archives; Dunn, *Sugar and Slaves*, 68; idem, "Profile of the

Richest Colony: The Barbados Census of 1680," *William and Mary Quarterly,* XXVI (1969), 3–30; Ligon, *A True History,* 22; Census of Barbados, 1679–80, I–II, Barbados Archives.

7. Indentured servants were frequently referred to as white slaves and white niggers by seventeenth-century observers. See, for example, Beckles, "Plantation Production and White 'Proto-Slavery': White Indentured Servants and the Colonization of the English West Indies, 1624–1645," *The Americas,* XLI (1985), 37–45; Eric Williams, *Capitalism and Slavery* (London, 1975), 18; an Anonymous Description of Barbados, circa 1667, CO 1/3, no. 170, Public Record Office (PRO), London.

8. Beckles, "White Labour in Black Slave Plantation Society and Economy: A Case Study of Indentured Labour in Seventeenth-Century Barbados," unpub. Ph.D. diss. (Univ. of Hull, 1980), ch. 5; *idem,* "Economic Origins," 38–39.

9. Eric Thompson, "The Climatic Theory of the Plantations," *Agricultural History,* XV (1941), 49–64; Richard Schomburgk, *The History of Barbados* (London, 1848), 144–145; Harlow, *Barbados,* 292–293. For a critique of the climatic theory see Williams, *Capitalism,* 20–23.

10. "A Description of Barbados," Egerton Ms. 2395, 625. Rough estimates of servants arriving at Barbados during the early years of the sugar revolution can be found in Darnell N. Davis' transcripts of the minutes of Council. See, Davis Mss. Box 4, Royal Commonwealth Society Archives.

11. Because the I^d ($K^1{}_L$) curve in Fig. 18.2 is also the marginal product curve, the surplus is equal to profit.

12. W. Arthur Lewis, "Economic Development with Unlimited Supplies of Labour," *Manchester School of Economics and Social Studies,* XXII (1959), 139–191. We examined the pricing aspects of indentured labour and not other details of their contracts.

13. The issue of land use is discussed by James A. Hansen, "Colonial Economic Development with Unlimited Supply of Land: A Ricardian Case," *Economic Development and Cultural Change,* XXVII (1979), 611–627. Early seventeenth-century Barbados would be considered an economy of surplus land.

14. Dunn, *Sugar and Slaves,* 60.

15. Leo Stock (ed.), *Debates and Proceedings of the British Parliament respecting North America, 1542–1739* (Washington D.C., 1924), I. 256; Report of the Committee of the Council of Foreign Plantations, Aug. 17, 1664, (C.S.P.C.), 1661–68, 229; John C. Jeaffreson (ed.), *A Young Squire of the Seventeenth Century: Papers of Christopher Jeaffreson, 1676–1686* (London, 1876), II, 102.

16. See Tables 18.4 and 18.5. Papers of the Abraham, High Court of Admiralty, Mss. Misc., Bundle 30/635–636, PRO; Galenson, "Market Evaluation of Human Capital," 450.

17. Minutes of Council, June 11, 1654, Davis Mss., Box 7, Royal Commonwealth Society Archives; Petition of the President, Council and Assembly of Barbados to His Majesty's Commissioners for Foreign Planta-

tions, May 11, 1661, C.S.P.C., 1661–68, 29–30; Journal of the Barbados Assembly, Feb. 20, 1678, C.S.P.C., 1677–80, 218; Acts of the Council and Assembly of Barbados, CO 30/5, 44–45.

18. The Agent of Barbados to the Council of Trade and Plantations, Oct. 25, 1696, C.S.P.C., 1696–97, 672; Minutes of Council, Feb. 15, 1700, (C.S.P.C., 1700, 68.

19. Bean and Thomas, "Adoption of Slave Labor," 391; Gemery and Hogendorn, "The Economic Cost of West African Participation in the Atlantic Slave Trade: A Preliminary Sampling for the Eighteenth Century," in *idem, Uncommon Market,* 155–156; H. Watgen, *Das Holländische Kolonialreich in Brasilien* (The Hague, 1921), 30–33. For Barbadian slave prices, 1673–1720, see Galenson, *Traders, Planters, and Slaves: Market Behaviour in Early English America* (Cambridge, 1986), 53–64.

20. Deeds of John Severre, RB 3/1, 27–28; Ligon, *A True History,* 46.

21. Beckles, "Economic Origins of Black Slavery," 50–52.

22. William Dickson concluded his studies of eighteenth-century Barbadian slave society by noting that "the labouring life of bought field slaves . . . exceeds not seven years in gross": *Mitigation of Slavery* (London, 1814), 445. See also, J. Harry Bennett, *Bondsmen and Bishops: Slavery and Apprenticeship on Codrington Plantations of Barbados, 1710–1838* (Los Angeles, 1958), 44, 52–62. For an account of the contracts of political prisoners, see Richard Hall, Manuscripts Laws of Barbados, 1640–1762, CO 21/1, 40.

23. Beckles, "Class Formation," 24–28; John Hotten (ed.), *The Original List of Persons . . . who Went from Great Britain to the American Plantations, 1600–1700* (London, 1874); Tolzey Book of Indentures, B.A.O., 04220, 1654–1686, Bristol Records Office; Smith, *Colonists,* 309; Mildred Campbell, "Social Origins of Some Early Americans," in James M. Smith (ed.), *Seventeenth-Century America* (Chapel Hill, 1959), 1–27; Galenson, "Middling People or Common Sorts?": The Social Origins of Some Early Americans Re-examined," *William and Mary Quarterly,* XXXV (1978), 502.

24. See Alfred Conrad and John Meyer, "The Economics of Slavery in the Ante-Bellum South," *Journal of Political Economy,* LXVI (1958), 95–129.

25. Pitman, *Development of the British West Indies,* 42; Roger Coke, *A Discourse on Trade* (London, 1670), 10–13; John Cary, *Essay on Trade* (London, 1695), 60–66; Memorial of Merchants of England trading to the Plantations to the Lords' Committee of Trade and Plantations, Mar. 14, 1670, C.S.P.C., 1669–74, 58.

26. For the Bristol data, see the Tolzey Book, B.A.O. 04220. The London data are found in seven boxes marked "Indentures to Serve in America," City of London Corporation Record Office. These are also tabulated in Michael Ghirelli, *A List of Emigrants from England to America* (Baltimore, 1968). The Liverpool data are tabulated in Elizabeth French, *A*

List of Emigrants to America, 1697–1707 (Baltimore, 1969).

27.   Petition of the Representatives of Barbados to the King, Sept. 5, 1667, C.S.P.C., 1661–68, 495; Governor Atkins to the Lords of Trade and Plantations, Aug. 15, 1676, C.S.P.C., 1675–76, 445; Instructions from the Lords Proprietor of Carolina to William Sayle, July 27, 1669, C.S.P.C., 1669–74.

28.   E. Henry Phelps-Brown and Sheila V. Hopkins, "Seven Centuries of Building Wages," *Economica,* XXII (1955), 205; Bean and Thomas, "Adoption of Slave Labor," 393.

29.   The initial policy of the Company of Royal Adventurers was to sell slaves at the following prices: Barbados £17 per male, Antigua £18; Jamaica £19. Proposal for the Resettlement of the Royal African Company; Jan. 14, 1662, C.S.P.C., 1661–68, 120. For a discussion of the level of servant prices in mid-seventeenth-century Barbados, see "The President, Council and Assembly of Barbados to the Lords' Committee of Trade and Plantations, May 11, 1661," C.S.P.C., 1661–68, 30; Gentlemen Planters of Barbados to the King, Apr. 20, 1670, CO 31/21, f.27. On the early English slave trade, see Journal of the Company of Adventurers trading into Africa, CO 1/17, no. 2; Harlow, *Barbados,* 311; Sir Thomas Modyford to the Company of Adventurers, Mar. 20, 1664, C.S.P.C., 1661–68, 194. John Oldmixon, *The British Empire in America* (London, 1708), II, 136.

30.   We use the term price of labour to refer to the price of the stock of slaves or servant labour. In formal economic theory, services is the appropriate term. The service flow of labour is equal to the stock of workers' time, the rate of utilization, or average work time per labourer.

31.   For simplicity we assume that demand conditions did not change significantly. In practice, they would have shifted upward and hence the amount traded would have been greater. The equilibrium trading price would have been dependent on the elasticity of demand and supply with respect to the shift parameters.

32.   A similar formula can be applied to indentured labour. We assumed that in spite of the seasoning period the slave began to work as soon as he was purchased. If this was not the case, R_t would be negative for some initial period when he was maintained but not working.

19

Livestock and Sugar: Aspects of Jamaica's Agricultural Development from the Late Seventeenth to the Early Nineteenth Century

VERENE A. SHEPHERD

The study of the agricultural history of Jamaica, particularly after the seventeenth century when England seized the island from Spain, has traditionally been dominated by investigations of the sugar industry. Recently a few scholars have deviated from this path to examine in varying degrees of detail, agrarian activities which did not represent the standard eighteenth-century West Indian route to wealth. Foremost among this growing body of literature are articles and papers on the livestock industry (and livestock farmers), arguably the most lucrative of the non-sugar economic activities in rural Jamaica, perhaps until the advent of coffee later in the eighteenth century.[1] Intended as a contribution to the historiography of non-staple agricultural production in colonial Jamaica, this article traces the early establishment and expansion of the important livestock or 'pen-keeping' industry.[2] But the history of pens must also be located within the context of the dominant sugar economy; for during the period of slavery, pens were largely dependent on the sugar estate to provide markets for their outputs. Indeed, pens expanded as a result of the growth of the sugar industry and, therefore, the importance of the livestock industry in eighteenth- and nineteenth-century Jamaica is best appreciated by examining its economic links with the estates.

The rise of pen-keeping in Jamaica owed much to the Spaniards who occupied the island from 1494 until 1655;[3] for along with soldiers, priests and settlers, the ships of Christopher Co-

lumbus had brought to Hispaniola in 1494 war horses and beasts of burden. In 1495 followed the jennets, mares, cattle and pigs.[4] These animals were later introduced into Jamaica, where they multiplied considerably on the southern savanna lands. Most were reared by open-style ranging; but the Spaniards also seemed to have enclosed cattle in *hatos* or pens in the areas formerly employed by the Arawaks in the cultivation of maize.[5] Both types of stock-rearing had been practised on the lush, warm pastures of Andalucia where this enterprise was a profitable means of earning a living and had been transferred to the Spanish colonies in the Caribbean.[6] By 1515, Jamaica had also become a major open-range hog-rearing island. Such activities took a heavy toll on Arawak *conocu* farming and hastened the decline of the Arawak population by 1519. However, the suitability of these lands for pasture and their accessibility to the ports, and therefore export markets, were important factors determining their conversion into livestock farms and the disregard of indigenous welfare.

The early Spanish settlers also planted subsistence crops, fruits and sugar. Despite this fairly diversified agricultural economy, the livestock industry emerged as the most important economic activity. Two factors accounted for this agrarian pattern. First, the decline of the Arawak population, the shortage of African slaves – increasingly used as an alternative labour force in 'Spanish America'[7] – and the aversion of the soldier-settlers to manual labour, meant that the island suffered an acute labour shortage. As livestock husbandry was less labour intensive than plantation agriculture, cattle and horse-rearing were vigorously pursued. Second, there was a great demand in peninsular Spain for cow hides for the leather industry.[8] Although some lard and smoked meat were exported, primarily to Havana, cattle became increasingly important for their hides, which formed the major item of export from 'Spanish Jamaica'.

This thriving livestock industry was not in evidence at the time of the English capture of the island in 1655. After the first decade of the seventeenth century, the rate of demographic decline on the island accelerated. Not only had the Arawak population been virtually decimated by 1611, but Spanish colonists drifted to areas of the Spanish empire where the presence of mineral wealth offered quicker enrichment possibilities. On the eve of the English conquest, therefore, Sederno, a Spanish resident, noted that 'this island had formerly a large population of Spaniards, so much so that [while] there were [once] seven towns . . . only St. Jago de la Vega now remains'.[9] In 1655, however, there were 'now a little over three hundred colonists, mostly poor people. Nearly four hundred and fifty men bear arms including the hunters and country folks, all of whom are labouring people . . . and lacking in military discipline'.[10] According to contemporary writers, this depopulation of Jamaica not only caused the Spaniards to become too short-handed to pen their 'stock' – which then reverted to a wild state – but facilitated an easy English conquest.[11]

The revival of pen-keeping and the restoration of the lucrative export trade in hides were not immediate concerns of the Cromwellian expeditionary army. Rather, disappointed at the mineral and bullion poverty of Jamaica, the soldiers set about to destroy wantonly evidence of Spanish occupation. Not only did they wreck the buildings of the capital, but, as W.J. Gardner noted, Cromwell's soldiers 'ruthlessly destroyed vast numbers of the herds of cattle which a little before had covered the plains around Spanish Town and that [sic] on the edge of which Kingston now stands'.[12] Gardner, influenced by Edward Long, further records that:

twenty thousand cattle had been killed and the rest driven so wild that it was almost impossible to catch them . . . Horses, once accounted as 'the vermin of the country', had become so scarce by the end of the 17th century that ships had to be sent to fetch some from thence.[13]

This mutinous attitude displayed by the early English soldiers and which was aimed at forcing Cromwell to abandon Jamaica as a possible English colony, did not have the desired effect. By 1657, conditions in the island had reached crisis proportions. Food supplies from England were irregular and according to Long, as 'these early settlers all had a dislike against settling and planting in this part of the world and made no effort to do so',[14] starvation and famine-like conditions resulted.

At this time the English begun to make the first efforts towards reestablishing the pen-keeping industry in the island. Their task was difficult. Lowland tamed animals had been the first to be destroyed, and by 1656 all had been killed. Consequently, hunting parties had to be organized to secure wild cattle from the forested interior. Not surprisingly, the value of horses in this venture was quickly appreciated, giving rise to the development of the 'horse-catchers'.[15] In this pioneer stage of the island's colonial development, livestock were hunted and killed mainly for food. The export of hides was also revived. To facilitate these activities, pens were established in English Jamaica in the late seventeenth century. In this period they had an independent economic dynamic. Their importance grew as, with generous land grants offered as inducements to settle, the population of the island slowly increased and the market for fresh beef expanded. This expansion encouraged more settlers to invest in the pen-keeping industry and the penning and breeding of cattle were protected by law.[16]

In the 1670s and early 1680s, characterized as the extensive diversified production stage of Jamaica's economic development, pen-keeping experienced only moderate expansion. Some future sugar planters in St. John's parish, such as Francis Price, intent on accumulating the capital needed for the establishment of a sugar work, at first engaged in pen-keeping.[17] Indeed, by the time of Sir Hans Sloane's visit to Jamaica in the late seventeenth century, cattle had 'received a proper share of attention from . . . the settlers',[18] the wild cattle had been tamed, and 'the Savanna pens were . . . abundantly stored with neat kine . . .'[19] But plantations of minor staples – tobacco, indigo, cotton, cocoa, ginger – the contraband trade and buccaneering activities engaged the attention of the majority of settlers.[20]

By the end of the seventeenth century, there were still well below 100 pens in the island. As the livestock industry struggled to recover from its earlier destruction, marked expansion was not experienced until well into the eighteenth century.

From a mere seventy-three 'pens' in 1684,[21] located primarily in the southern parishes, the island had over 300 in 1782.[22] By this latter date, the location of pens had been expanded to include parishes in the western and northern sections of the island, most notably St. Ann, St. Elizabeth and Westmoreland. The principal factor in the phenomenal increase in the number of pens in Jamaica was the development of the sugar industry as the principal and dominant economic activity. The change from the cultivation of minor staples and other economic activities to sugar, was not as quick and revolutionary as in Barbados. Indeed, limited capital, and a small labour and settler population for long delayed Jamaica's equivalent of Barbados 'sugar revolution'. By the end of the seventeenth century, however, greater infusions of capital and population, particularly through the forced migration of Africans (the slave trade), and a more generous land policy initiated by Governor Modyford, had combined to set Jamaica on the way to being a 'sugar island'. The island's varied physical environment, though, enabled small-settler entrepreneurs who lacked the capital to invest in sugar, to occupy and farm lands unsuitable for the cultivation of the cane. While some of these non-sugar producers were engaged in production for the export market, others were primarily geared towards the domestic market. The most notable of these internal producers were the livestock farmers, whose growth and expansion by 1740 depended on the sugar sector. The sugar economy had created a new market for a number of products. The estates, for example, provided a large market for food and draught animals – the two types of goods produced on the pens. However, the production of food on independent pens was simply a secondary activity and was not geared towards fulfilling the estates' demand for this commodity. Indeed the sugar estates had a high import co-efficient in foodstuffs, particularly flour, salted beef and fish. Additionally, the establishment of supple-

mentary food-producing units by some sugar planters and the existence of the slave provision ground system combined to limit the part of the estates' food market to which internal producers could have access. Although the estates did purchase fresh beef from the pens – regularly for their white population and periodically for the slaves – pen-keepers sought other outlets among the comparatively small free population not resident on the estates.

Greater opportunities for the growth of interval producers existed in the market for livestock, for the sugar plantation economy created an extraordinary demand for livestock (as well as for pasture and other pen services). This was because before the development of chemical fertilizers and until draught animals were largely displaced by motor transport, sugar estates relied heavily on animals for draught and other purposes.

The types of animals most in demand on sugar estates are clearly indicated by the early Jamaican estate records of accounts called the accounts produce. These were steers (oxen), mules and heifers. Steers and spayed heifers were often referred to in the accounts as 'planters' stock'.[23] Though the pens sold a considerable number of horses, these were used more for the racehorse industry and for riding by the white supervisory class, than as work animals.[24] This was in contrast to the trend in England where by 1850 English farmers, with some regional variations, had virtually dispensed with the working of cattle in favour of the use of horses. After the Napoleonic Wars, more favourable price conditions and the increasing efficiency of horses in farming caused the emphasis in cattle husbandry to shift to beef production.[25] In Jamaica, however, competition from the horse-racing industry and the expense of procuring, feeding and maintaining horses, determined their unattractiveness as a source of draught animals.

Mules were used primarily for draught purposes. They were used to take off the crop from the fields and to transport sugar to the wharf. Up to twelve mules at a time were also frequently used to transport coffee to the wharf.[26] In the early years of the sugar industry, mules were also used along with cattle to turn the rollers which ground the juice out of the canes at the mill. By the nineteenth century, however, they were largely displaced by steers and spayed heifers.

Contemporary sources provide no explanations for this shift, but one can speculate that the dual income yielded by oxen was attractive to both pen-keepers and sugar planters. The former could benefit directly from the sale of young oxen to sugar planters and the sale of beef when oxen had reached the end of their working life. The mule, on the other hand, was not used for meat and realized little of a return upon the completion of its working life. At the same time, the mule was unsurpassed in its hardiness as a draught animal. Sugar planters also perceived the benefits from the use of oxen which could be sold to pen-keepers or butchers as beef cattle at the end of their working life on the estates. In both cases, cattle contributed to the risks involved in farming.

A partial indication of this change is supplied by the data on pens returned in the accounts produce. In 1740, for example, the 'working stock' sold by the twenty pens represented in the accounts included 19 steers, 8 heifers and 7 mules. In 1760, 144 steers, 54 mules and 12 heifers were sold, and in 1780, 278 steers, 181 mules and 19 heifers were disposed of to estates. By 1820, however, 3,162 steers, 1,162 spayed heifers and only 511 mules were sold through the internal trade. By 1840, the number of mules sold by the pens represented in the accounts had fallen to 283, compared to 2,461 steers and 1,006 heifers.[27]

Cattle were important sources of manure for sugar estates. They were also used as draught animals, but predominated as mill animals. This presumably influenced the use of the term 'cattle mills' to refer to all animal mills even those also powered by mules. Up to 1740, cattle mills were almost exclusively used on sugar estates, though other forms of power were being explored. As Charles Leslie records, in that year 'the mills that are most in use here are cattle mills, but lately, some substantial Planters have One or Two Windmills, and some Three'.[28] Windmills were at this time regarded as curiosities, however, and according to Leslie, 'the late President Ascough erected One at his Plantation to Windward, which is a very curious Piece of mechanism'.[29]

As sugar estates proliferated after 1680, the demand for livestock to provide all of the above functions increased. Pens were established to help to meet this demand, and this assured for them a role in Jamaica's colonial economy.

The direct relationship between the expansion of the livestock industry in Jamaica and the evolution and growth of the sugar industry was best established by Edward Long. After discussing what he termed the 'sugar revolution' with its creation of land monopolies by those who bought out the thirty-acre farmers to create larger sugar estates, he explained that 'to sustain these sugar estates, large breeding farms were requisite'.[30] Pens, as a result, did not suffer the fate of coastal provision farms and plantations of 'minor' staples; for whereas the increasing dominance of sugar in Jamaica in the eighteenth century stifled the production of competing staples other than coffee,[31] the growing demand for livestock on sugar estates was met by an increasing number of pens. Far from giving way to sugar, therefore, by 1740 pens along with sugar estates had 'swallowed up by degrees all the little settlements around; which from their contiguity, and being ready cleared for canes or pasturage, the lordly planter has found convenient to be purchased, and added to his territory'.[32]

As further indication that pens were not sacrificed for sugar cultivation, Edward Long explained that:

. . . some have imagined, that the sugar estates have increased at the expense of sacrificing many of the farms or penns; but that this has not been the case is manifest from the great increase in the number of Negroes; which would not have happened if the settlers had done no more than remove their Negroes from penns to sugar estates. . . It is more probable, that the augmentation of sugar estates has been the means of increasing the number of penns, by enlarging the demand for pasturage and stock.[33]

By the outbreak of the American revolution, therefore, Jamaica was being described as an island of 'large sugar plantations and "cattle ranches" '.[34] From beginning as a step towards diversification, therefore, pen-keeping had by the eighteenth century, evolved into a prop for sugar monoculture.

The number of cattle in Jamaica from year to year and the extensive use of cattle mills on sugar estates throughout the island in the period of slavery, help to indicate the extent to which livestock was vital to the plantation economy. In 1734 Jamaica had 74,846 head of cattle.[35] Six years later, Jamaica's colonial agent, James Knight, compiled a table of the number of slaves and cattle in each parish based on the returns of a tax of twelve pence per head on slaves and three pence on cattle. The total was 99,239 slaves and

Table 19.1. Sugar Works and Cattle, by Parish, for 1740 and 1768

	1740		1768	
Parish	Cattle	Sugar works	Cattle	Sugar works
St. Catherine	8,581	3	10,402	?
St. Dorothy	5,468	8	4,661	12
St. John	2,837	28	2,726	21
St. Thomas-in-the-Vale	4,813	48	5,782	41
Clarendon	12,299	?	14,276	70
Vere	8,580	7	7,462	19
St. Mary	2,972	19	7,996	49
St. Ann	2,342	20	6,207	22
St. Andrew	5,244	34	4,626	?
Kingston	607	None	923	None
Port Royal	158	None	170	1
St. Thomas-in-the-East	5,256	44	9,007	66
St. David		No figures available		
Portland	178	3	1,651	29
St. George	1,024	4	3,421	12
St. Elizabeth	9,695	32	16,947	31
Westmoreland	8,921	32	13,750	69
Hanover	2,631	39	8,942	71
St. James	1,204	19	15,137	95
Trelawny	Still part of St James		8,130	4
All Island total	82,810	340	142,216	612

Source: E. Long, *History of Jamaica*, 11, Add. MS 12,405, fos. 39–192.
Note: ? = Not stated. Totals given are thus incomplete.

84,313 cattle.[36] Table 19.1, compiled from Long's *History of Jamaica,* shows that Knight's figure for cattle is somewhat higher than Long's calculations, but the difference might be explained by the absence of figures in the table for St. David, an essentially pen/coffee parish. There is also some discrepancy in the figures for cattle for 1768, by which year, according to calculations from the poll tax roll authorized in that year, cattle had increased to 133,773 head,[37] 6,443 lower than Long's calculations of 142,216 head of cattle in the twenty parishes.[38] However, this confusion could have resulted from the difference between taxable and working stock in the island. Taxes were not levied on working stock and so would not have been represented on the poll tax roll relating to sugar estates.

In 1768 also, there were said to have been 648 sugar estates in the island (three fewer than Long's estimate of 651) of which 369 had cattle mills, 235 had water mills and 44 had wind mills.[39] This means that the number of cattle mills in the island in 1768 was thirteen less than

the number in 1763. (See Table 19.2). On the other hand, the number of water and wind mills had increased since 1763, showing a gradual shift away from cattle mills. Such a shift could have affected pen-keeping by cutting out the need for livestock for mills; but even though rivers, topography and wind currents determined the selection of wind mills, water mills and tide mills in the West Indies, most planters in Jamaica still kept a cattle mill or two in case of emergencies as they were considered more reliable. Drought-prone parishes also realized the necessity of catering for the precariousness of the water supply. The case of St. Jago estate can be cited as an illustration. Throughout 1822, the attorney for the Mitchells' estates in Jamaica complained to the proprietors about the severe drought in the island especially in St. Catherine. This had affected the use of the water mill on St. Jago estate, thus forcing the estate to revert to the cattle mills. According to the attorney, 'St. Jago is now getting on as fast as they can with the Old Cattle Mills – the water having entirely failed

Table 19.2. Distribution of mills in Jamaica by parish, 1763

Parish	Mills		
	Cattle	Water	Wind
St. Thomas-in-the-East	34	17	2
Portland	21	5	–
St. David	2	5	–
Port Royal	1	1	–
St. George	10	4	1
St. Andrew	23	5	–
St. Catherine	3	–	–
St. John	25	2	1
St. Thomas-in-the-Vale	35	7	5
St. Mary	33	15	7
St. Ann	4	12	1
Clarendon	21	38	2
Vere	14	–	3
St. James	38	7	2
St. Elizabeth	18	10	1
Hanover	50	–	8
Westmoreland	42	22	1
St. Dorothy	8	–	–
Total	382	150	34

Source: Simpson and Craskill, Map of Jamaica c. 1763, C.O. 700/16.

and is not likely to return now before the May season'.[40] The rains did come in May, but by December St. Catherine was again in the grip of a drought, forcing the attorney to write that 'St. Jago has lost the use of the . . . water again and will be obliged to go on with the cattle mills'.[41]

An indication that, despite technological changes in power, cattle mills were dominant in Jamaica's sugar economy even in the nineteenth century, is Robertson's map of Jamaica.[42] Table 19.3, compiled from this map, indicates that the island had 656 cattle mills in 1804, compared with 68 wind mills and 333 water mills. Furthermore, as there were 830 estates in Jamaica in 1804, this further strengthens the argument that even where alternative forms of power were utilized, cattle mills were maintained for emergencies, for there were 1,077 mills in all. Again, parishes where the water supply could be unreliable were especially careful to maintain cattle mills in addition to their water mills. Clarendon is a good example. Of 59 estates in Clarendon, only 17 or 29 per cent did not have a water mill; for the proximity of the Rio Minho or its tributaries to most estates made water a natural choice of power. Nevertheless estates such as Danks,

Clarendon Park and St. Toolies also had cattle mills.[43]

This continued dominance of cattle mills indicates the extent to which mill type was dictated not by efficiency but by the state of available technology and by topographical and locational factors. Mills varied in efficiency by up to 50 per cent according to their power source. Water mills (where water was always available) turned fastest, most continuously and reliably and were the cheapest to run once installed;[44] but not every state had access to rivers or ponds or could afford to have aqueducts built for the diversion of water from distant sources. Wind power was cheap but capricious. Wind-powered mills were the most constrained locationally, requiring an exposed hill-top site. Consequently, in contrast to plantations in the Eastern Caribbean which had the advantage of a more favourable location, only a small number of favourably suited plantations in Jamaica utilized them.[45] Estates in the vales of St. John's parish, for example, had no use for wind mills. Animal power, it was true, turned mills slowly and was relatively expensive as there was a constant need to replace the animals and was less efficient than water power. But

Table 19.3. Mill types by Parish and County, 1804

		Mill type		Total no. of	
	Wind	Water	Cattle	Mills	Estates
County of Cornwall					
1 Hanover	13	15	88	116	85
2 St. James	4	29	84	117	89
3 Trelawny	21	14	100	135	95
4 Westmoreland	0	24	59	83	70
5 St. Elizabeth	0	16	12	28	26
Total	38	98	343	479	365
County of Middlesex					
6 St. Catherine	0	1	4	5	4
7 St. Dorothy	0	6	13	19	15
8 St. John	2	8	17	27	19
9 St. Thomas-in-the-Vale	4	13	27	44	34
10 Vere	7	1	35	43	30
11 St. Ann	1	40	25	66	59
12 Clarendon	2	23	27	52	46
13 St. Mary	14	41	54	109	68
Total	30	133	202	365	275
County of Surrey					
14 St. Andrew	0	6	20	26	24
15 Kingston	0	0	0	0	0
16 St. George	1	19	7	27	26
17 St. David	0	12	5	17	15
18 Portland	3	11	21	35	32
19 St. Thomas-in-the-East	16	51	57	124	89
20 Port Royal	0	3	1	4	4
Total	20	102	111	233	190
Grand Total (all counties)	88	333	656	1,077	830

Source: J. Robertson, *Maps of the counties of Cornwall, Middlesex and Surrey* (Jamaica, 1804), N.L.I.
N.B. Manchester and Metcalfe were not yet formed.

animal mills were relatively free of physical constraints and could be placed more easily wherever the planter chose. In addition, the animal supply was fairly reliable. Even in other parts of the Caribbean such as in dry Antigua, unsuitable for water mills, but where nearly every planter had a wind mill, plantations also had at least one cattle mill to use when the north-east trades failed.[46]

Theoretically then, Jamaica's sugar economy afforded a relatively substantial market capable of acting as a dynamic factor in the development of the pen-keeping industry in the island. The average estate in the late eighteenth century, for example, needed a starting livestock supply of 80 steers and 60 mules,[47]

and by the early nineteenth century, at least 100 working steers annually.[48] The total demand for steers alone in 1789 when there were 710 sugar estates, was therefore 71,000. By 1820, the annual demand for steers had dropped to 56,200,[49] matching the decrease in the number of estates and therefore the demand for working animals. At £18 currency each in the late eighteenth century and between £20 and £30 each in 1820, this would still necessitate a considerable annual expenditure on oxen alone.[50] Bryan Edwards records that the annual replacement cost of working animals to each estate was £300 currency in the 1790s,[51] but this would increase with the rising prices of livestock in the nineteenth century.

All Jamaican estates kept some animals, but as the profitability of the sugar business encouraged specialization, some entrepreneurs avoided diverting production factors into secondary activities – at least at times when the prospects of the sugar market seemed favourable. At such times the use of estate lands for livestock rearing was uneconomical for the sugar planters. Thus, from the late seventeenth century when sugar emerged as the dominant crop, most estates were buying livestock from the specialized pens. By 1740 about 23 per cent of the estates owned by absentee proprietors were involved in the purchase of livestock from internal sources.[52] By 1760 they had improved their participation to 36 per cent and this percentage increased each year.[53] The extent of participation of units owned by resident proprietors cannot be substantiated with any degree of accuracy, except to say that there is indication from the accounts produce that they purchased animals from pens owned by absentees.

Cartographic and non-cartographic sources indicate that the main internal sources of supply came from the parishes of Westmoreland, St. Elizabeth, St. Catherine, and St. Ann. Supplies also came from the combined pen/coffee units in Manchester. In these parishes, there were significant acreages unsuited for either cane cultivation or coffee and which were turned over to pasture. By 1820, in fact, a pattern of regional crop specialization had developed in Jamaica with distinct ecological zones supporting particular crops – the result largely of topographical differentiation.[54]

Despite the proliferation of local livestock-producing units across the island from the late seventeenth to the eighteenth centuries, internal supplies of animals were never adequate to meet total demand. In 1768, for example, Edward Long estimated that Jamaica's 651 estates needed 3,900 mules per annum. With 200 pens supplying at most twelve mules each, a shortfall of 1,500 remained.[55] In 1820 when over 56,200 working animals were needed annually, the island's pens supplied only around 39 per cent of this number.[56] The shortfall in this, previous and subsequent years was filled from external sources, chiefly Spanish America. Between 1729 and 1739, for example, an annual average of 826 animals were imported. A total of 14,456 animals were imported in the next decade[57] and

by 1825 the annual average was 11,836. Indeed, 59,182 were imported between 1815 and 1825.[58] In all years, the trade was dominated by South America. In 1832, for example, 97 per cent of the island's expenditure on horses, 98 per cent on asses, 100 per cent on mules and 98.5 per cent on cattle went to Spanish America.[59] Thus, Jamaica was less dependent on Britain and North America as sources for animals. Where the participation of these countries was significant was in the area of supplying thoroughbred horses and at times, high breed cattle to improve the local strain.

Although inadequate numbers, competition for land with sugar estates in some parishes, high cost of production and inability to compete with foreign suppliers whose animals cost considerably less were factors militating against the ability of Jamaican pens to satisfy total internal demand, they nevertheless supplied a far greater proportion of the island's needs than did any other non-staple producers elsewhere in the English-speaking Caribbean.[60]

The accounts produce provide a partial idea of the amount of money that sugar estates spent on the purchase of animals from the pens. In 1782, for example, Golden Grove Estate in St. Thomas-in-the-East spent £3,000 on the purchase of oxen[61] – significantly more than the approximately 16 per cent of total annual estate contingencies estimated by Edwards.[62] Pens benefited greatly from such trade. A small sample of 11 per cent of the pens returned in the accounts produce in 1820 (representing roughly 5 per cent of the island total) reveals total earnings of £20,014 17s. 8½d. currency from livestock sales to estates. These pens earned more from such sales (69 per cent) than from other important income-generating activities such as jobbing, wainage, pasturage, the sale of food (ground provisions and fresh beef) and wood. These other sales and services combined yielded £8,924 13s. 3½d. or 31 per cent of the total earnings of £28,939 10s. 11d. Taken singly, jobbing represented 9 per cent, pasturage 4 per cent, wainage 4 per cent, provisions 9 per cent and miscellaneous items (rent, shingles, wood, staves) 5 per cent. These percentages of course, varied from pen to pen. Forest pen, for example, earned only 2 per cent from non-livestock sources.[63]

In addition to having a ready source of young working animals, sugar estates benefited from the pens in several other ways. Their use of pens for pasturing their 'stock', for providing extra 'hands' especially during crop time and for providing transportation for the crop have already been noted. Pens also supplied estates with food provisions such as plantains and fresh beef, particularly during wartime conditions when external supplies were disrupted. But the pens also provided a ready market for the estates' 'used' animals. Animals at the end of their working life on sugar estates were sold to the pen for fattening. These were then killed in the pens' butcheries or sold to independent butchers. James Stevenson, attorney for the Scarlett's estates noted in 1800 that fat cattle from these properties fetched up to £40 a head – almost as much as for young cattle.[64]

The economic relationship between pens and estates which was unique to Jamaica in the British Caribbean, can best be illustrated by reference to the history of satellite holdings. In Jamaica, sugar planters often established their own pens as an alternative to complete reliance on independent pens or external producers. Such satellite units also not only helped to solve the problem of inadequate pasture-lands on some estates, but were important supplies of working animals, food, grass, fuel and extra labourers. Those located in higher (and cooler) elevations, were vital in the seasoning of African newcomers up to 1807. Thereafter, they assumed increasing importance as a location for sick slaves as planters adopted socially ameliorative measures aimed at preventing the high mortality rates and improving the low rate of fertility among their slave populations.[65]

Golden Grove estate and Batchelor's Hall pen, both located in St. Thomas-in-the-East, typified the relationship between sugar estates and their related pens in Jamaica. Unlike some satellite holdings, Batchelor's Hall was not contiguous to Golden Grove, but as it was located in the same parish, was fairly easily accessible. As was usual in such cases, both properties were run by the same attorney, though they had separate overseers and kept separate records.

Batchelor's Hall served Golden Grove in seven important ways. First and foremost, it provided the livestock needs of the latter. Golden Grove thus did not have to devote much needed cane land to pasture. According to Simon Taylor, the attorney, 'Golden Grove is as good for

Breeding as Batchelor's Hall';[66] but he did not recommend that any part of the estate be developed for this purpose as the land on the estate was more suitable for cane, 'and should be used for such'.[67] In 1765 the pen was still struggling to achieve maximum efficiency, but Taylor assured his employer that as soon as it was well stocked 'that place will ease the contingencies of your estate'.[68]

Second, Batchelor's Hall fattened the estate's old, meagre cattle and pastured its breeding stock after the crop. Later, when a butchery was established at the pen, such fattened stock was killed and the estate provided with fresh beef. This can be considered a third function.

Fourthly, Batchelor's Hall's slaves jobbed on Golden Grove whenever the need arose there, even if this set back the schedule of the pen. Jobbing was especially needed to put in the spring plant 'which never can be done by the Estate people as the mill is then always about'.[69] Jobbers planted guinea grass at the estate and fetched wood from the pen for the mill when coal and trash were in short supply. When Golden Grove's four trash houses were destroyed by fire set by slave pipes in 1793, the pen's slaves had to go to the estate to help to cut brush wood for the mill. Batchelor's Hall's slaves again came to Golden Grove's rescue when floods did extensive damage to the estate in 1793. As the estate's slaves undertook the routine jobs, the pen's slaves did the repairs. Taylor afterwards remarked that 'I do not know what we should have done at Golden Grove after the flood had it not been for the Batchelor's Hall's negroes'.[70]

The pen served three other important functions. It supplied extra provisions for the estate when war conditions or drought disrupted the latter's supply. In 1833 for example, Batchelor's Hall sold 1,359 plantains, 426 cwt. of ground provisions and 80 lbs. of arrowroot to Golden Grove.[71] Batchelor's Hall Pen was used for the recuperation of sick slaves from Golden Grove, especially those afflicted with yaws. The rationale for this is given in the following extract from Taylor's letter:

I desired for the future that when any of them get the yaws, that they might be sent to Batchelor's Hall Penn which is a dryer situation than the estate and to be there kept cleaning the pastures as exercise is reckoned good for that disorder and it is the lightest work negroes can be put to.[72]

Some concern with the high rate of mortality, especially among newly imported slaves, and with the low birth rate caused sugar planters to use their pens for the seasoning of new slaves. Taylor felt that a pen was the best place for seasoning 'new negroes' in the first year as well as to encourage slave women to reproduce. He noted that 'a Penn is certainly better calculated for negroes to breed at than Estates for there is no light work on them [estates] for negro women'.[73] On pens, on the other hand, newly imported slaves could do light tasks such as weeding and cleaning the pastures.

Finally, pens provided an outlet for estates' old, 'weakly' and ineffective slaves. Thus, instead of renewing the labour force for the pen through the purchasing of new slaves, 'weakly' slaves from Golden Grove were drawn off for the pen. These were used to clean pastures already established, 'but by no means to open new land to be put in Grass and make fences, which require able people and such cannot be spared from the estate'.[74] For such tasks, a few new slaves were purchased.

Although the primary role of satellites was to serve the needs of their related estates, in the nineteenth century a significant part of their income was earned from links formed with non-related properties and individuals. In 1833, for example, while Batchelor's Hall Pen earned £1,148 11s. 8d from the sale of beef, provisions and working stock to Golden Grove, it earned £2,380 8s. 11d. from non-related properties and individuals. Restated as a percentage of total earnings for that year, dealings with Golden Grove represented 31 per cent of the total earnings of Batchelor's Hall in 1833.[75]

This article has traced the evolution and expansion of the livestock industry in Jamaica from the occupation of the island by the Spaniards to its capture by the English in the mid-seventeenth century. Before sugar became the dominant export crop, pen-keeping represented an important element of diversification in Jamaica, maintaining its independent economic dynamic. By 1740, pens had become virtual adjuncts of the dominant sugar economy providing in addition to working animals, a variety of services including jobbing, wainage and pasturage. The estates also relied on pens for food and at times utilized them for the seasoning of 'new negroes'. Pen-keeping thus represented an alternative path to wealth for those small-scale entrepreneurs lacking the capital to invest in the more lucrative sugar industry. However, livestock-farming in the period of slavery was a precarious enterprise. In times of buoyancy in the sugar industry, pen-keepers could gain considerable earnings. Conversely, as estates represented their principal markets, any crisis in that industry could cause economic chaos – even ruin – for livestock farmers. The effects of this economic dependence was most marked in the later nineteenth century after the abolition of slavery. A depressed market for livestock and a shortage of labourers forced some pen-keepers out of production. By the 1890s, however, they had broken their link with the sugar estates, assumed an export dimension and were catering for an expanding local consumer market for beef and dairy products.

Notes

1 . Among the most notable of these articles and papers on livestock and livestock farm (farmers) in Jamaica are D.G. Hall, 'Fort George Pen, Jamaica: slaves, tenants and labourers', *Association of Caribbean Historians Conference*, Curaçao, 1979; Hall, 'Runaways in Jamaica in the mid-eighteenth century: one man's record', Department of History, U.W.I., Mona, Seminar Paper 1984; Hall (ed.), 'Thomas Thistlewood in the vineyard 1750-51', *Jamaica Journal*, xxi, 3 (1988), 16-29. (This article is part of Hall's more detailed *In miserable slavery – Thomas Thistlewood in Jamaica, 1750-1786* (London, 1989). Thistlewood became an overseer-pen-keeper in western Jamaica); B.W. Higman, 'The internal economy of Jamaican pens 1760-1890', *Social and Economic Studies*, xxxviii, 1 (1989), 61-86; V.A. Shepherd, 'Problems in the supply of live-stock to sugar estates', Mona, 1986; Shepherd, 'Obstacles to the expansion of the pen-keeping industry in Jamaica', Mona, 1989). (These ideas are more fully developed in Shepherd, 'Pens and pen-keepers in a plantation society: aspects of Jamaica's social and economic history 1740-1845', (unpublished Ph.D. dissertation, University of Cambridge, 1988) and P.D. Morgan, 'Slavery and livestock in eighteenth-century Jamaica', *Conference on Cultivation and Culture, University of Maryland*, April 1989. Higman's *Jamaica surveyed* (Institute of Jamaica, 1988) also devotes a chapter to pens from a cartographic perspective.

2.   Livestock farms were styled 'pens' in Jamaica. The term 'pen-keeping' evolved as a description of the livestock industry and the proprietors of pens were styled 'pen-keepers'. See F.G. Cassidy and R.B. LePage (eds.), *Dictionary of Jamaican English* (Cambridge, 1967), p. 345 and Shepherd, 'Pens and pen-keepers', pp. 4-10.

3. E. Long, *History of Jamaica* (3 vols., London, 1774) in British Library, Add. MS 12,404, fos. 176, 182. See also F. Cundall and J.L. Pieterz, *Jamaica under the Spaniards* (Kingston, 1919), p. 26 and F. Morales Padron, *Jamaica Española* (Seville, 1952), pp. 268-93, 357-72.

4. P. Martyr, *Histoire of the West Indies* (London, 1675), p. 11 and A.P. Whittaker, 'The Spanish contribution to American agriculture', *Agricultural History*, III (1929), 2-3.

5. Long, *History of Jamaica*, 1 in B.L., Add. MS 12,404, fo. 176. Hatos also developed in Cuba for large-sized cattle or steers. See the Cuban economic research project, *A study on Cuba* (Miami, 1965), p. 60.

6. C. Bishko, 'The peninsular background of Latin American cattle-ranching', *Hispanic American Historical Review*, XXXII (1952), 513 and D. Watts, *The West Indies: patterns of development, culture and environmental change since 1402* (Cambridge, 1987), p. 84.

7. For more on this topic see F. Bowser, *The African slave in colonial Peru*, (California, 1974) and L.B. Rout, Jr., *The African experience in Spanish America: 1502 to the present day* (Cambridge, 1976).

8. Bishko attributes the great demand for cowhides in Spain to the late medieval shift of the peninsular tanning and leather traders from goat and sheep skins to the tougher, if less workable cow hide. This item also formed the basis of an important export trade to Italy, France and the Low Countries. As internal production was inadequate to meet the external demands, Spain relied on her colonies to supply hides for re-export. Thus, where mineral wealth was absent, Spanish colonies were developed into important producers of hides. This was equally true of Cuba, Santo Domingo and Puerto Rico. See Bishko, 'The peninsular background', p. 513; F. Knight, *Slave society in Cuba during the nineteenth century* (Madison, 1970), p. 3; M.D. Clausner, *Rural Santo Domingo: settled, unsettled and resettled* (Philadelphia, 1973), p. 71; F.A. Scarano, *Sugar and slavery in Puerto Rico: the plantation economy of Ponce, 1800-1850* (Wisconsin, 1984), pp. 4-40 and J.L. Dietz, *Economic history of Puerto Rico: institutional change and capitalist development* (New Jersey, 1986), pp. 4-8.

9. Cundall and Pieterz, *Jamaica under the Spaniards*, p. 35.

10. Ibid. This figure excludes the black population.

11. Ibid.

12. W.J. Gardner, *History of Jamaica, 1655-1872* (London, 1909 edn), p. 36.

13. Ibid.; Long, *History of Jamaica*, 1 in B.L., Add. MS 12,404, fos. 190, 192.

14. Ibid. fo. 190.

15. See D. Knight, *Gentlemen of fortune: the men who made their fortunes in Britain's slave colonies* (London, 1978), pp. 36-8.

16. Instruction to Governor Modyford from Charles II, 18 Feb. 1664, P.R.O. C.O. 138/1; Proclamation of Charles II, *Laws of Jamaica, 1681-1759*, 1, 9; H.

Barham, *Account of Jamaica*, 1772, London, British Library, Sloane MS 3,918, fo. 56 and Long, *History of Jamaica*, 1, in B.L., Add. MS 12,404, fos. 199-205. The law imposed heavy fines on those found unlawfully killing livestock. It also stipulated that grazing farms be fenced. See C. Leslie, *A new history of Jamaica* (London, 1740), pp. 167-8. See also, *Laws of Jamaica*, 1681, Anno. 33, Caroli, 11, Cap. x, p. 9.

17. M. Craton and J. Walvin, *A Jamaican plantation: the history of Worthy Park, 1670-1970* (London, 1970), pp. 30-42. No precise figures are available to indicate the number of planters who made a start in this manner or established estates on former pen lands.

18. Gardner, *History of Jamaica*, p. 79.

19. J. Roby, *A history of St. James* (Kingston, 1849), p. 100, and Sir Hans Sloane, *A voyage to the islands* (2 vols., London, 1707), 1, pp. xiv-lxxv.

20. See R. Dunn, *Sugar and slaves* (North Carolina, 1972), pp. 149-87; R.B. Sheridan, *Sugar and slavery* (Barbados, 1974), pp. 210-16; N. Zahadieh, 'Trade, plunder and economic development in early English Jamaica, 1655-1689 (unpublished Ph.D. dissertation, University of London, 1984); Zahadieh, 'The merchants of Port Royal, Jamaica and the Spanish contraband trade, 1655-1692', *William and Mary Quarterly*, 3rd Series, XLIII (1986), 570 and Zahadieh, 'Trade, plunder and economic development in early English Jamaica, 1655-1689', *The Economic History Review*, XXXIX (1986), 205-22.

21. Dunn, *Sugar and slaves* p. 169. This calculation was based on Bochart and Knollis, *A new and exact Mapp of the island of Jamaica c. 1684*, C.O. 700/6. This figure probably also included a few hog crawles. Simpson and Craskill's map of 1763 grouped pens with 'non-sugar units', so that this makes it difficult to obtain an accurate idea of the number of livestock farms. See Simpson and Craskill, *Map of Jamaica*, 1763, C.O. 700/16.

22. Gardner, *History of Jamaica*, p. 161.

23. Jamaica Archives, Accounts Produce (J.A., A.P.), 1840, 1B/11/4/84. These Accounts related to the properties of absentees, but provide a window through which the pens can be viewed generally.

24. Phillippo observed in 1843 that 'the stock required for agriculture are . . . oxen, horses, mules'. He acknowledged, however, that horses were used mainly 'for the saddle'. See J.M. Phillippo, *Jamaica: its past and present state* (London, 1843), p. 85.

25. J.A. Perkins, 'The ox, the horse and English farming 1750-1850', Working paper in economic history, 3/1975, University of New South Wales, Dept. of Economic History, School of Economics, pp. 2-15.

26. Radnor Plantation Journal, 1822-6, National Library of Jamaica (N.L.J.), MS 180.

27. J.A., A.P., 1740, 1B/11/4/1; 1760, 1B/11/4/3-4; 1780, 1/B/11/4/9; 1820, 1B/11/4/54-6 and 1840, 1B/11/4/84-5.

28. Leslie, *A new history of Jamaica*, p. 318.

29. Ibid.

30. Long, *History of Jamaica*, 1, in B.L., Add. MS 12,404, fo. 220.

31. Grown on lands unsuitable for either pens or sugar-cane.
32. Add. MS 12,404, fo. 311.
33. Ibid. fo. 308.
34. Sheridan, *Sugar and slavery*, p. 232.
35. Long, *History of Jamaica*, 1, in B.L., Add. MS 12,404, fos. 39-192.
36. F.W. Pitman, *The development of the British West Indies, 1700-1763* (New Haven, 1917), pp. 367-77.
37. Ibid.
38. These figures represented a combination of the production of pens and livestock imported.
39. Pitman, *The development of the British West Indies*, pp. 367-77.
40. Letter from the Attorney to Messrs. W.R. and S. Mitchell, 17 Feb. 1822, Jamaica Archives, Attorneys' Letterbook, 1B/5/83/1.
41. Ibid. Letterbook, 30 Dec. 1822.
42. J. Robertson, 'Maps of the counties of Cornwall, Middlesex and Surrey', 1804, N.L.J.
43. Ibid. 'Map of the county of Middlesex'.
44. M. Craton, *Searching for the invisible man: slaves and plantation life in Jamaica* (Cambridge, 1974), p.2.
45. B.W. Higman, 'The spatial economy of Jamaican sugar plantations; cartographic evidence from the eighteenth and nineteenth centuries', *Journal of Historical Geography*, 13, 1 (1987), 17–39 and Watts, *The West Indies*, p. 193.
46. The estates in Antigua had the advantage of nearby Barbuda – a source of draught animals, slaves, harnesses and leather goods. See D.G. Hall, *Five of the Leewards* (Caribbean Universities Press: Ginn & Co. 1971), p. 59.
47. B. Edwards, *The history of the West Indies* (2 vols., London, 1793), 1, pp. 253–4.
48. Simon Taylor to Chaloner Arcedeckne, 29 Oct. 1782, Cambridge University Library; Vanneck Manuscripts, Jamaican Estate Papers, (J.E.P.), Box 2, Bundle 10.
49. This calculation is based on contemporary accounts indicating that each estate needed 100 oxen annually in addition to mules and heifers. There were 562 sugar estates in 1820.
50. These prices relate to locally bred livestock. Imported animals usually cost less.
51. Edwards, *History of the West Indies*, 1, 259.
52. J.A., A.P., 1B/11/4/1.
53. J.A., A.P., 1B/11/4/3–4.
54. Shepherd, 'Pens and pen-keepers', chap. 3.
55. B.L., Add. MS 12,404, fo. 330.
56. J.A., A.P., 1B/11/4/54–6.
57. B.L., Add. MS 12,404, fo. 330.
58. Naval Officer's Returns, 1815–25, *Jamaica House of Assembly Votes* (J.H.A.V.) 1815–25 and *Blue Books of Jamaica* (*B.B.J.*) 1822–5, C.O. 142/34–8.
59. *B.B.J.* 1832.
60. Shepherd, 'Obstacles to the expansion . . .'.
61. Taylor to Arcedeckne, 29 Oct. 1782.
62. Edwards, *History of the West Indies*, 1, p. 259.
63. J.A., A.P., 1B/11/4/54–6.
64. James Stevenson to Mrs. Scarlett, 8 April 1800, Hull University, Brynmor Jones Library, Scarlett family papers, DDCA/41/17.
65. See J.R. Ward, *British West Indian slavery, 1750–1834: the process of amelioration* (Oxford, 1988).
66. Taylor to Arcedeckne, 27 Sept. 1781, J.E.P., Box 2, Bundle 9.
67. Ibid.
68. Taylor to Arcedeckne, 11 Nov. 1765, J.E.P., Box 2, Bundle 1.
69. Taylor to Arcedeckne, 3 Sept. 1787, J.E.P., Box 2, Bundle 13. A similar relationship between the Blagroves' properties was outlined by Henry Blagrove. He noted in his journal that 'Orange Valley Pen and Orange Valley Estate have a special relationship. At the pen, we breed planters' stock and buy them for Orange Valley Estate, work them for a certain period of time carrying canes to the mill, sugar to the wharf – and other estates' works – and when at Orange Valley they become useless they are draughted or sold to Bell Air Pen and there put in guinea grass pastures, fattened and then sold to the butcher'. See Journal of Henry John Blagrove, Jamaica Archives, Private Deposit 4/4/1–2, 21 March 1842.
70. Taylor to Arcedeckne, 4 Sept. 1794, J.E.P., Box 2, Bundle 19.
71. Crop Accounts, 1833, J.E.P., Box 2, Bundle 60.
72. Taylor to Arcedeckne, 10 April 1768, J.E.P., Box 2, Bundle 3.
73. Taylor to Arcedeckne, 5 July 1789, J.E.P., Box 2, Bundle 11.
74. Ibid. 10 Oct. 1783. See also B.C. Wood and T.R. Clayton, 'Slave birth, death and disease on Golden Grove Estate, Jamaica, 1765–1810', *Slavery and Abolition*, 6 (1985), 99–121. See also Wood, *Slavery in colonial Georgia, 1730–75* (Athens, 1984), pp. 101–2 for a similar pre-occupation of southern planters with morality rates among 'new negroes'.
75. Crop Accounts, 1833, J.E.P., Box 2, Bundle 60.

20

The Transformation of Cuban Agriculture, 1763-1838

FRANKLIN KNIGHT

There is no doubt about it. The era of our happiness has arrived.
Arango Y Parreño, 1793

Over the years from 1763 to 1838, Cuba changed from an underpopulated, underdeveloped settlement of small towns, cattle ranches, and tobacco farms to a community of large sugar and coffee plantations. Any full understanding of the history of slavery in the island after this date must perforce take into account the revolutionary changes in the structure of Cuban society and economy that preceded.

Although Cuban political life had not overcome, by 1838, the uncertainty and corruption which were its bane, the economic condition of the island was extremely promising. The island had 'arrived' among the world's sugar producers. While the other producers of the West Indies complained bitterly about 'rack and ruin', the Cuban sugar cane planters merely complained about the acute shortage of workhands of any color for their estates. The island had become the foremost producer of the world's sugar, but there still remained an abundance of fertile, unworked land of inestimable potential for the growing of sugar cane. The frequent changes of local political leadership in Havana and the incessant alternation of Spanish court parties had hardly affected the steady spread of the plantation throughout the island. From a minor colony in the Spanish imperial domain, Cuba had become the most valuable member of Spain's diminished overseas empire. Indeed, while Isabel II (1833–68) reigned unsteadily in Spain, sugar became 'king' in Cuba. But Cuba was important not merely because it was beginning to make substantial contributions to the Spanish treasury, but also because of the very nature of Cuban production at this time, it had joined the wider world community; metropolitan Spain knew only too well the dire consequences of this development.

The history of the sugar plantation goes as far back as the late sixteenth century in Cuba[1] The early settlers had continually produced small quantities of sugar on the island. And indeed, there were scattered examples of larger plantations, with probably as many as one hundred slaves, both in Cuba and Hispaniola from the late sixteenth century.[2] The technique of production may have been as efficient as that employed anywhere else in the world at that time. Nevertheless, it is important to point out that sugar production was geared exclusively toward internal consumption, and very few producers thought of sugar as a lucrative enterprise.[3] Moreover, the demand for sugar at that time in Europe was adequately supplied from the islands on the other side of the Atlantic and Brazil.

Cuban society at that time was not dominated by the plantation of any sort. It was, instead, an underpopulated island, a settlement colony existing on small ranches, *vegas* (tobacco farms), and in small towns, with a few plantations and a few slaves. Until the second half of the eighteenth century, Cuban agriculture consisted of alternating attempts at monoculture and a mixed economy, neither of which was distinguished in the activities of the overseas Spanish empire taken as a whole. This is not to say that the island was not an important

Slave Society in Cuba During the 19th Century (Madison, 1970), pp. 3–24.

part of the Spanish empire in the New World. It was valuable as a meeting place for ships and men from the diverse parts of the mainland, and it represented a springboard for the colonization attempts on the mainland before it lost its place to the ports and cities of New Spain and New Granada. A few colonists, however, remained in Cuba braving the elements and making a living by raising cattle and planting tobacco. Tobacco was the main export crop; but leather, meat, and dyewoods became important commercial supplements, especially in the immensely valuable inter-island trade.[4] The most important aspect of early Cuban society was the fact that, in accordance with the general pattern of Spanish colonial expansion, the majority of the inhabitants of the island colony lived in towns. Life in Cuba at that time for freedman or slave centered upon the town, the hacienda, or the vega.[5]

As long as the society remained predominantly dependent on the growing of tobacco and the raising of cattle, the labor requirements were low. Since tobacco was not grown as a plantation crop, but as a small-scale cash crop — as indeed it was in the English colonies of the eastern Caribbean before the sugar revolution — and ranching does not require regimented labor, Cuba could remain an island settlement of preponderantly white persons.[6] It is folly to expect that such a society would generate high racial tension, whether or not the whites were racists. The white sector maintained its substantial majority and probably as a result exhibited little or no racial fear of the non-white sector of the population. There was, and could be, little tension of any kind. The society just did not have the kind of divisions which yield strife: no foreigners of note, no Indians, no very rich people, few African slaves. As far as the lack of racial tension went, this resulted less from the benevolence of Spanish legislation or the doctrine and intercession of the single, all-encompassing Roman Catholic Church, than it did from the realities of the situation. In Cuba at this time the African simply represented little economic value and even less economic competition. In terms of services and obligations, therefore, white and non-white complemented each other.[7]

In the pre-plantation era of Cuban slavery, the enslaved persons could live with few rigorous rules. A large number of the slaves were obviously in domestic service, while the others worked in the fields. Often white masters and their slaves worked together in the tobacco vegas, or on the cattle haciendas. In any case, the farms were small and their proprietors poor. Tobacco plantations such as the ones found in Virginia and other areas of the southern United States were the exception in Cuba, where the farmers had few slaves and a lower social position than the cattle rancher. The cattle ranchers tended to be richer than the tobacco growers, but this was not really important since they both used small numbers of slaves and supervised them rather laxly. Regardless of where master and slave found themselves, the relationship tended toward intimacy and patriarchy. In comparison with the other islands of the Caribbean before the late eighteenth century, the relations between masters and slaves were relatively personal. This apparently amiable situation derived less from the differing cultural heritages of the various Caribbean islands than from their varying stages of economic development.

But the placidity and lethargy of Cuban society did not last forever. Between 1762 and 1838 the relatively mixed economy based on cattle-ranching, tobacco-growing, and the small-scale production of sugar gave way to the dominance of plantation agriculture based on the large-scale production of sugar and coffee. There was no single factor which engendered the change in the nature of Cuban society and its agriculture. Instead, a bewildering series of interrelated events and forces over which the Cubans themselves had no control, and which they often did not understand, imposed the radical transformation into a plantation society. Among these powerful agents of change in the history of Cuban society at this time must be included the shifts in international market demands, the English occupation of Havana in 1763–64, the far-reaching economic and administrative reforms of Charles III (1759–88), the sudden destruction of the French colony of St. Domingue, and the disruptive wars of the Latin American independence movement. All these events, occurring in the last decades of the eighteenth century and the early years of the nineteenth, resulted in a truly revolutionary change in the nature of Cuban society.

Once the Cuban agricultural revolution took place, other equally fundamental changes were irrepressible. The entire society began to readjust itself to the new demands of the plantation and the economy. More slaves resulted in a new method of organizing slave labor. More intensive agriculture meant wider markets and greater dissatisfaction with the restrictive measures of Spanish colonial commerce. Greater participation in the international market brought new ideas of economic and political relationship. The Cuban elite which had long complacently accepted Spanish colonial rule began to demand greater intercourse with other countries, particularly France, Great Britain, and the United States. The illegal trade with the British which had always been conducted clandestinely assumed prominent proportions. And the United States became a large market for Cuban sugar as well as the best source of the manufactured goods, skilled laborers, and enlightening ideas so seriously lacking in the island.

The most convenient starting point for this intensification in Cuban agriculture may be taken as the year 1763, when the English captured and occupied Havana for a period of ten months. Of course, seen in isolation that event may not have been crucial to the island's agriculture.[8] The English did nothing that the Cubans were not already doing before they arrived on the scene.[9] Nevertheless, the large number of merchant vessels which visited Havana during the months of the occupation and the importation and sale of more than 10,000 slaves in such a short time constituted a tremendous stimulus to a process already under way. Among other things, the English occupation of Havana emphasized the gigantic gap betwen the prevailing Cuban demand for slaves and its effective supply. It also convinced Charles III and his ministers that the entire colonial situation was ready for the rational reforms which they had already been contemplating.[10]

The real importance of the reforms of Charles III lay in the fact that they were the first major official attempt to integrate the island of Cuba into the mainstream of the wider world. Cuban changes, however, were only a small part of the large scheme of physiocratic ideas to bring Spain up to date by the thorough overhaul of her relations with her overseas colonies. Nor by focusing on the official acts of the Spanish Crown should one lose sight of the important fact that the entire eighteenth century was a period of general European economic progress and enlightenment. To a certain extent, therefore, Charles III was as much the servant of his age as he was the master of his deeds.[11] The island of Cuba was of paramount importance in the imperial plans of Charles III, as a testing ground for the measures that he subsequently applied to the rest of the empire.

Before the late eighteenth century, Cuban property owners had bought their slaves from the English, the French, the Dutch, and the Portuguese.[12] Indeed, before 1792 Spain had never been able to provide her colonies with the required human cargoes, since she lacked the necessary African factories. At first she farmed out the awards for the supply in a series of *asientos*, or contracts. These contracts gave the right to any individual of any country to deliver for sale a stated number of slaves in the Spanish empire. Later the asientos were given to the emerging joint-stock companies of the Portuguese, French, and, after 1713, the British.[13] The companies, like the individuals earlier, promised to transport a specific number of slaves to the Spanish colonies, and to pay a specified tax into the Spanish treasury.

However the awards were made, they were totally inadequate to supply the Spanish colonies. The official asientos were supplemented by a lively, mutually beneficial, inter-island trade throughout the Caribbean. English privateers, often acting on their own initiative, made sporadic trips among the Spanish islands, and by force or judicious bribes sold their cargo of slaves for specie.[14] But there were also well-established markets in Jamaica and Dominica, in which the Cubans regularly made their purchases. Condemned strongly by the Spanish crown, but welcomed openly by the islanders, this inter-island trade fulfilled two acute needs: the Cubans got their slaves, and the English and the French obtained cash, dyewoods, and hides. Spanish silver, dyewoods, and leather products not only enabled the Jamaican and other West Indian merchants to become solvent, but found their way into English domestic industry, and English trade with the Far East.

The Spanish government was always aware of the unsatisfactory conduct of the asiento, and the formation of their own chartered companies in the early eighteenth century was an attempt to rectify the situation. In the case of Cuba, the Real Compañia Mercantil de La Habana was the first attempt to boost the trade in slaves and to stir the waning interest in agriculture[15] The company was formed in 1740 to take over the transportation to and sale of Africans in the island. It disposed of its slaves for cash, credit, or pledged crop returns. In this way the company dominated, though it never monopolized, the island's major exports of sugar, tobacco, and hides before 1763. In the first twenty-six years of its operation the company brought into Cuba and sold officially 9,943 slaves. But of this number, more than 50 per cent were sold in the three years immediately following the British occupation.[16]

The Real Compañía had other counterparts in Spanish America. The Caracas Company, chartered in 1728, monopolized the trade of the Venezuelan coast. A company from Galicia received a charter to trade with the Campeche region in 1734, and the Barcelona Company, chartered in 1755, intended to carry on trade with Puerto Rico and Hispaniola. Most of these new companies had the financial backing of the merchants from the northern provinces of Spain. Only the Caracas Company proved successful over the long run. Nevertheless, the organization of the companies represented Bourbon attempts to liberalize trade in the empire and to break the monopoly of Andalusia.

The organization of the Real Compañía was extremely important, but from the planter's point of view it proved more a liability than an asset. On the one hand it failed to supply an adequate amount of goods or slaves at reasonable or satisfactory rates. On the other hand, it bought the planters' products at the lowest possible prices. Under these conditions, contraband trade became probably the largest outlet for Cuban products and the best method of obtaining necessary imported goods. But the prevalence of the contraband trade made it monumentally difficult to arrive at credible estimates for the island's commerce, or its slave population and annual rate of slave importation. This study takes into account the possibility that the official figures represent the minimum for any particuar time. Nevertheless, I think that the earlier figures may not be too inaccurate since the demands were low; and the later figures at least represent an index of volume.

On the basis of official estimates and intelligent guesswork, Hubert Aimes set the total number of slaves imported into Cuba between 1512 and 1761 at about 60,000 — a figure which seems eminently reasonable for the period.[17] For 1762–1838, the same author put the total at somewhere in the region of 400,000.[18] The mean annual import figure for the first period of nearly 250 years comes to about 250 slaves per year. The mean annual figure for the 76 years prior to 1838 comes to nearly 5,000 slaves per year. These figures dramatically reflect the demographic changes which were brought about in the society as a consequence of the transatlantic slave trade. But the trade, for its part, was merely a local response to the agricultural demand. Cuban planters wanted more adult Africans to provide the labor for the cultivation of their land. And even though they knew that it meant a fundamental change in the composition of their island's population, they were quite prepared for that eventuality. The demand, after all, preceded the fateful events in St. Domingue and France at the end of the century, and so there was less need for worry.

The commercial importance of Havana increased tremendously after the British occupation. During the eighteen years after 1860, the number of ships calling at the port rose from six to more than two hundred per year.[19] As part of the system of modified free trade which had been instituted during the reforms of Charles III, the port became a focal point for the entire gulf area, handling larger and larger quantities of European manufactured goods and slaves. Commodities which were usually scarce became more available, and in the case of slaves a greater supply seemed to be consistently below the local requirements. As far as the Cuban planters were concerned, African laborers were the most valuable commodity which could be imported into the island at that time. The liberalization of the trade afforded by the crown unwittingly paved the way for a succession of unforeseen events towards the end of the eighteenth century which would begin the promotion of the island of Cuba as the foremost producer of sugar in the world.

Once the Creoles in Cuba had begun the agricultural transformation of the island, the supply of slaves became the main concern. For at this time the international competition in the production of tropical staples depended on a sufficient labor force. The continuous agitation by the Cubans led to the complete reexamination of the island's slave supply. Not surprisingly, the consensus was that the means and measures by which the Cubans procured their slaves were totally inconsistent with the agricultural requirements of the island. Over a period of years, therefore, the crown granted permission for an unrestricted number of slaves to be brought to the island.[20] Finally, a royal cedula of February 28, 1789, permitted foreigners and Spaniards to sell as many slaves as they could in a specified number of free ports, including Havana.[21] This was exactly what the Cuban planters had been anxious to achieve for more than a decade. The royal order removed all the previous restrictions on the trade of slaves, suspended all taxes for a period of three years, and allowed the merchants to sell at any price determined by the local market conditions. Indeed, the planters were so delighted by the new situation that they persuaded the royal court in Madrid to extend the free trade beginning in 1792 for a further period of six years.[22] And so great was the interest in Cuban agriculture and the commerce in slaves that a total of eleven royal pronouncements was made between 1789 and 1798 expanding the trade in black workers to the Spanish Indies.[23]

This declaration of a virtual free trade in slaves at the end of the eighteenth century, then, provided the necessary impetus for the development of the plantation society. Nevertheless, the greater trade must also be seen against the general background of events in the Caribbean and elsewhere at that time. For exactly during this period of time international events favored the growth of Cuba's economy and importance. And perhaps the most significant single event was the destruction of the sugar-producing capacity of the French colony of St. Domingue, and the later creation of the independent republic of Haiti.

Until 1789, St. Domingue was the most highly developed plantation society in the world. It was the paragon among sugar islands of the West Indies. Situated on the western part of the island of Hispaniola, and comprising a total area of only 10,700 square miles, the colony's population of 40,000 white persons and 480,000 slaves and free persons of color had long become the ideal of, and comparison for, every other colony in the area that hoped to become rich by growing sugar cane and coffee. The Cubans reasoned that with four times the land area of St. Domingue, and undoubtedly greater soil fertility, they could easily outproduce their neighbors. The only handicap they had was the acute shortage of slaves, which, however, was being rectified at last. And like the sugar producers in St. Domingue a little before, they would have faced the unhappy restrictions of their own exclusive imperial commercial system.[24] But before they could worry about that, there was the immediate concern of raising their sugar production to a competitive level.

The extension of the French revolution to the Caribbean brought two unexpected results beneficial to the Cuban producers. In the first place, the principal producer of the world's sugar and coffee was almost instantly and completely destroyed. The price of sugar on the European market rose sharply as the demand outstripped the available supply, and brought a windfall to producers elsewhere. But in the immediate aftermath of the events in St. Domingue, the Spanish crown was hesitant to sanction the creation of a new slave society in Cuba, even though it would give permission to

the continued increase in the number of Africans imported into the island. Nevertheless, the Cuban planters won a resounding victory over the crown when they got a concession in 1792 for the first Spanish ship ever to sail directly from Africa to Cuba bringing Africans to the slave market in the Antilles. In the second place, from St. Domingue came a number of refugees who brought their skills, their slaves, and an uncertain amount of capital, and initiated the plantation agriculture of coffee in the eastern sections of the island.[25] It seemed, despite the confustion of that era, very clear to Don Francisco de Arango y Parreño, the intelligent, articulate representative of the Cuban planters in Madrid, that the age of their happiness had indeed arrived.

From its very inception, the Cuban plantation agriculture depended upon imported skills, imported capital, and an imported labor force. An uncertain part of the skills and capital came from the early immigrants from St. Domingue. These were joined later by other French emigrés from Louisiana who preferred to go into exile than to endure life under the Anglo-Saxons after Napoleon sold the territory to the United States of America. And even some defeated royalist supporters of the mainlaind Latin American wars settled in Cuba, bringing at least their initiative, if they had no cash.[26]

Cuba derived enormous benefits from the unsettling external situation at the beginning of the nineteenth century. Wars in the area considerably augmented the available supply of capital devoted to agriculture. This led to other necessary changes as well. For since tropical agriculture depended at this time on the availability of land and slaves, intensified agriculture necessitated a fundamental change in the pattern of landholding and land use, and in the demographic composition of the island. In short, to accommodate the newcomers, black and white, the Cubans had to alter the basic structure of landholding in their island.[27]

The old tobacco and cattle holdings rapidly gave way in certain areas to the sugar and coffee plantations. Specific zones developed for each particular form of activity. Tobacco became the principal crop in the region mainly west of Havana. Sugar dominated the central plains and the lowlands around Santiago de Cuba in the eastern end of the island. Coffee, after failing to hold its own on the plains against the inexorable expansion of the sugar plantation, retreated to the mountainous area of the eastern division. But before this pattern attained its final form, it was imperative to abolish the antiquated nature of landholding and land use in Cuba. Only then could valuable land be free for new settlements and new crops.

To understand the revolution in landholding which took place at this time, it is necessary to go back to the early days of Spanish colonization in the new world and to trace the complicated growth of a system of landholding fettered by lethargic, ancestral latifundism. This system, incidentally, was common throughout Latin America before the nationalist wars of liberation in the early eighteenth century. The general pattern was the enormous hacienda with its ill-defined boundaries. Designed to be self-sufficient as much as possible, these estates also produced a few cash crops to meet the royal tax and support the luxurious life of their occupants. This type of hacienda had its roots far back in the frontier conditions of Spanish society, but it underwent some modification when it was transplanted to the New World.

After America was discovered, all land became the personal domain of the Castilian monarch, who had the prerogative to dispose of it either in usufruct or outright grant to any deserving person. Both methods of distribution were used. Originally, each occupied territory was divided into towns which had contiguous boundaries. Within the towns, the land was parceled among the settlers, and enclosed by a common pasture. Beyond this common pasture, the royal lands (*realengos*) were distributed in haphazard, often overlapping grants called *mercedes*, of usufructal tenure.[28] It must, however, be emphasized that the royal grants were modest in size. Latifundism was certainly not the intention of the crown and had its own peculiar historical genesis in the following years.

Each merced was given for the cultivation of a particular crop. Recipients of these mercedes were forbidden to change the designated crop for which they had originally received their parcel of land. The usufructal landlords paid a special annual fee that was determined by the size of the plot or its agricultural purpose. And although the land could be inherited, it could not be sold, sublet, or subdivided. This, then, was the system, which, fraught with abuses and legal complications, prevailed throughout the centuries and was to provide the basis for Creole wealth by the early nineteenth century in Cuba. Over a period of time marriage, as well as other agreements of local interest and dubious legality, converted the modest holdings into larger farms, sometimes of astonishing dimensions.

The absence of a real estate market was only one handicap to the accumulation of wealth by the landholding group. For although a planter may have had the use of his land, he could not cut a large number of the hardwood trees on his hacienda without express royal permission. Until the late eighteenth century, the crown had first lien on all hardwood trees in the island in order that the fleet construction continually taking place at Havana would not be jeopardized.[29] But as the years passed, the rise of the large sugar plantation and the preservation of the hardwood forests became mutually antagonistic. Part of the entire scheme to change the pattern of landholding, therefore, was an alteration of the system of hardwood forest preservation. The sugar revolution — indeed, the entire structure of Cuban society in the nineteenth century — cannot be understood without recognizing the importance of the fundamental change in landholding and land use between the late eighteenth and the early nineteenth century.

The big opportunity for the landholders came with the gradual insolvency of the Spanish crown. As the resources of the treasury decreased the crown ceded for cash the land which its representatives — or local municipal councils — had offered in usufruct. By these means, a small number of wealthy colonists had persevered in the time-consuming legal disentanglements, and finally bought titles in fee simple, to use the Anglo-Saxon term, to the land they used or hoped to own. Nevertheless, by the end of the eighteenth century there had been few concrete achievements in the way of legal security for land. As more immigrants came the demand for land dramatically grew. In order to capitalize on the new source of wealth from land, it became urgent to straighten out the existing confusion or uncertainty over land. That, therefore, became the first obsession of the Sociedad Económica de Amigos del País, or the Havana Economic Society.

The Havana Economic Society, founded by twenty-seven Creole landholders, received its royal sanction in 1791.[30] It was not the only such organization in the island, but another attempt to form a group of the Creoles of Santiago de Cuba ended in failure, leaving the Havana group as the only dynamic social and economic association dominated by the Creoles. Despite the fact that the Havana group later expanded into a body with a membership of nearly two hundred persons, at no time did its influence and activity extend beyond a small enthusiastic core mainly domiciled in Havana. Of the 126 members registered in 1793, 113 resided in the capital city, Havana. The Economic Society was, in every respect an exclusive club, a tightly organized elite group bent on the pursuit of economic power and political influence.

The formation of economic societies was a common response in Latin America to the ideas of the European enlightenment, although this development was interrupted by the wars of separation from Spain in the early nineteenth century. But in Latin America, unlike in Europe, there was a greater emphasis on the pure and applied sciences than on philosophy.[31] In Cuba, the emphasis was on scientific activity and economic interests. The program of the Havana Economic Society encompassed science and arts, commerce and industry, beautification, and agriculture and education. Nevertheless, throughout the long life of the society, agriculture remained its consuming passion.

The Economic Society became the chief advocate for radical changes in the structure of Cuban landholding. Not surprisingly, its members were among the most articulate and influential men on the island. Yet the ultimate success of the society's pleas rested with the nature of political leadership in Havana, and the prevailing state of the Spanish treasury. Interested captains-general and impoverished monarchs were the ingredients of success.

The two most successful periods of the Economic Society coincided with the terms in office of Luis de Las Casas y Arragori (1790-96) and Alejandro Ramírez (1816-19). The supreme political head of the island was also the titular head of the Economic Society (acting in the name of the Spanish monarch) and was able to exert official influence in Madrid, helping or hindering any measure according to his fancy. Regardless of the political ideas held by both Las Casas and Ramírez, they both were themselves landholders in Cuba and probably had a personal interest in reforming the system of land ownership and land use.[32] It was evident that during the periods of office of these two men the landowners would have friends in high places.

On the other hand, the Spanish crown was hardly in a position to resist colonial requests that offered the opportunity of financial rewards. For over a century the royal treasury had barely been solvent, and the long Napoleonic wars further depleted the already slender resources. The Spanish troops and naval forces which at first fought reluctantly with the French emperor in Europe — and then, after experiencing the occupation of their homeland,

turned against him — cost a lot of money to maintain. Neither Charles IV nor Ferdinand VII could be oblivious to the constant need to find new ways of securing money according to the necessities of the state. One such new way, of course, was to accept the advocated changes in the legal nature of land tenure. Unfortunately, the crown derived far fewer returns from that gesture than it had anticipated, and the poverty of the Spanish treasury remained a constant factor throughout the nineteenth century.[33]

Between 1795 and 1820, the landholders won such major concessions from the crown that they altered irrevocably the entire system of land ownership in Cuba. A royal cedula of 1800 broke up the hereditary pattern of the existing *señorios*, or large estates, and permitted the outright ownership of lands previously held in usufruct. Even crown lands became fast-selling real estate. Further royal decrees in 1815 and 1816 gave landowners the right to parcel, sell, sublet, and use their land without legal intervention. But most important of all for the future development of the sugar estate, royal approval was finally given for the destruction of the hardwood forests in the interest of agricultural expansion. After a long dispute, sugar at last took precedence over the royal navy: the Spanish crown had cleared the way for the sugar revolution in Cuba.

The immediate effect of the series of royal decrees was to open the way for real estate speculation. Land values rose rapidly, sometimes as high as five times what they had been in the late 1790s. And as the sugar belt moved out of the area around Havana, it further stimulated the rise in the market price of land. In the Matanzas sugar belt, for example, land that before the turn of the century was priced at 80 pesos per hectare was sold at prices in excess of 500 pesos afterwards. The Economic Society of Havana bought a number of estates and resold them to the new immigrants at moderate profits.[34] Private investors such as Juan Poey, a wealthy Creole planter of Havana, dreamed of making millions of pesos in real estate speculation, though it is unlikely that they made quite that amount. Nevertheless, many new schemes produced new towns, mainly settled by immigrants, such as Guira, Alquizar, Nueva Paz, Palos, Bagäes, and Güines in the outskirts of Havana. The construction of towns was even carried on by private individuals, like Agustín de Cárdenas, marquis of Cárdenas de Monte Hermoso, who founded the town of San Antonio de los Baños on his estate. He also leased small farms to the new immigrants. The exemption from the payment of the alcabala, or sales tax, by the purchasers of new land also served to further encourage a lively real estate market.[35]

The ability to cut and use the timber on private lands did not result in the instant deforestation of the island. Until the middle of the nineteenth century, the landowners zealously protected the forests as their primary source of fuel for their boilers, and timber for general building and the construction of the boxes in which they transported their sugar. Major deforestation only came with the advanced technological era, especially after the use of railroads had become general throughout the sugar-cane-producing area. Rail transport eventually proved so convenient and economical that the cane growers derived more profits by replacing their forests with canefields, and importing their lumber, firewood, and coal. Even the railroads, which had used locally mined coal, found it necessary to import this fuel as local supplies dwindled.[36] By the late 1860s the central section of the island had been almost completely deforested.

The leaders of the Cuban agricultural phenomenon of the nineteenth century were extremely intelligent men, fervently desiring that Cuba should stand second to none in gross agricultural production. Francisco Arango y Parreño and Francisco Frías y Jacott, Count of Pozos Dulces, were amazingly farsighted. They knew that Cuban prosperity had come latest among the West Indian producers of sugar and coffee. Unlike the plantation owners of Jamaica, Barbados, Antigua, and St. Domingue, the Cubans lacked the numbers of slaves to catapult them into competitive production. But this liability, they reasonably assumed, was offset by the vast stretches of deep fertile land in Cuba.[37] Moreover, the Cubans were starting when science and technology offered new scope for profits and production in the sugar industry. With no obsolete machinery on their hands, the Cubans began with the latest equipment and the most proven formula for sugar production.

The Cuban Creoles, in agriculture as in politics, were a restless group. They were always ready to grasp at any innovation which promised to boost the total output, or to cut the costs of production.[38] As the sugar industry got under way, private individuals and public commissions made long trips through the other sugar islands, reporting in detail upon every aspect of the production of sugar and coffee.

In 1795, along with Ignacio Montalvo y Ambulodi, Count of Casa-Montalvo (who died soon afterwards), Arango y Parreño made the first official trip abroad for the Cuban sugar planters. The long voyage took the indefatigable and curious representative of the city of Havana to England, Portugal, Barbados, and Jamaica. Everywhere he went, the extremely inquisitive Arango reported back to his keenly interested audience on a bewildering range of topics, with particular emphasis on agriculture and relevant proposals for adaptation to Cuban conditions.[39]

In his reports from Europe, Arango noted the superior advantage of the English and Portuguese in the slave trade. Both countries, he pointed out, had factories on the African coast. This measure facilitated a steady supply of African slaves to their colonies, and reduced the price of the slaves at the delivery point because the initial cost was lower. English industrial development impressed him most. He sent back models of the newly invented sugar mills, and a detailed description of the refining process. His opinion was that the Cubans stood to gain a far greater advantage from importing 'those marvelous European machines' and thus completing the entire refining process in Cuba, than from selling muscovado (unrefined brown sugar) to the European refiners. This was, perhaps, his most valuable observation. It was partly the result of the British West Indians' failure to mechanize and to refine their sugar which weakened their competitive position in the European market.

In Barbados and Jamaica, Arango visited the foremost sugar producers among the British islands. Nothing in the political, social, and economic position of the islands escaped his careful scrutiny. Long reports relayed information ranging from the total area of land under cane cultivation to the most minute aspect of the production of sugar and rum.

Arango's journey convinced the Cubans that soon Cuba would be the world's leading sugar producer. As a result of his persuasive advocacy new varieties of cane, partiuclarly the Otaheiti, and new types of processing employing steam, water, and wind power were introduced to the island.[40] But along with the imported technique came a new awareness on the part of the Cuban Creole elite. They had joined the stream of ideas of the wider world. A mounting wave of criticism — carefully tendered under the guise of 'suggestions' — of Spanish colonial and economic policies originated in Havana. As the Cubans realized the magnitude of their economic potential, they realized the stifling restrictions of being a part of the Spanish empire. They demanded free international trade to buy the slaves, food, and manufactured goods that Spain could not supply, and to sell in a market larger than that offered by the Iberian peninsula. The Cuban attraction towards Britain and the United States in the early nineteenth century was, therefore, one of practical economic necessity.

Arango's fact-finding tour of Barbados and Jamaica in 1795 became the first of a frequent general practice. To any Cuban sugar producer, the grand tour of the British West Indies became a source of personal prestige, establishing the traveler as an authority on the subject of sugar production. And in some cases, the trip became the prerequisite for the founding of an *ingenio* (sugar estate with factory).[41] The curiosity value aside, the trips did provide much useful knowledge of methods and machines which were brought to Cuba. The 'Jamaican train', the boiling process of sugar manufacture, became standard in the early days of Cuban sugar production. Yet the true value of these trips over the long term came from the restless desire of the Cuban planters to find a process which would combine speed, efficiency, economy, and labor-saving devices. Because they were never able to stock their plantations with slaves the way the Jamaicans or Barbadians did, they had to find some alternative. In the fiercely competitive sugar market, survival depended on the volume of production. To the British West Indies and to Brazil, increased volume resulted from more slaves and more acreage under cane. But in the nineteenth century the British were waging a relentless crusade to abolish the slave trade and, ultimately, slavery. The essential problem for Cuba, therefore, was to devise a method of increasing the total output using the available manpower or, better, less manpower.

By 1828, Cuba had clearly surpassed her British West Indian neighbors in sugar production. A commission of Ramon de Arozarena and Pedro Bauduy made a thorough tour of Jamaica in that year, and reported back to the Cuban government.[42] In a lengthy report filled with interesting and knowledgeable observations, the commissioners described their journeys through the island, and the state of its sugar, coffee, and pimento operations. There were only three aspects in which the Cubans were not as distinguished as their neighbors: in the large-scale manufacture of rum, as a byproduct of sugar; in the extensive use of guinea grass as cattle fodder; and in the possession of pimento, which was native to

Jamaica. They clearly supported the immediate adoption of those three measures. But they thought that Cuba, with her vast areas of virgin land, her large forests, water supply, and mountains would always be in a position to outproduce the sugar and coffee planters of Jamaica. They were amazed, too, that English chemical developments were completely unknown in the Jamaican sugar industry, which produced only muscovado sugar. Jamaica's economic glory lay in her past; Cuba was the land with the future.

The economic and political activities resulting from the progressive reforms of Charles III initiated the complete renovation of Cuban society: a steep rise in population, agricultural production, and profits; a new political awareness as new ideas crept back along the routes of economic and educational contact. The old order slowly dissolved. The new prosperity based on land speculation, slave trading, and sugar and coffee plantations brought to the forefront of Cuban society a new economic elite which accepted the old order on its own terms. This was extremely important, especially for the race relations which were to develop from the demands of plantation management and operation. Men like Muguel Aldama, Juan Poey, Julian Zulueta, Gonzalo José de Herrera y Beltran de Santa Cruz, Count of Fernandina, and Franciso Arango y Parreño were men who had become wealthy during their lifetimes, when the island was undergoing the changes of economy and demography which made it a classic, late-flowering example of the plantation society and the South Atlantic System. But the real importance of this new slave-owning class was that they would not, and could not, be bounded by the patriarchal conventions of the prevous era of Cuban slavery. Their attitude to the Church, the state, and their plantations was one which they themselves worked out — an attitude which reflected the new political power position of the Cuban Creole class.

Between 1775 and 1838 the island underwent profound changes in the composition of its population. In 1775, Cuba had a population of 171,500 persons. Of this total, 96,400 were white persons; 36,300 were free persons of color; and 38,900 were African slaves. But even then, a large proportion of the African slaves were recently imported — a trend which was to continue throughout the period of slavery on the island. By 1841, the official census reported a permanent population of 1,007,624 persons, of whom 418,291 were white, 152,838 were free

Table 1   Cuban Population Growth, 1774–1841

Class	1774	%	1827	%	1841	%
White	06,440	56.9	311,051	44.1	418,291	41.6
Free colored	36,301	20.3	106,494	15.1	152,838	15.1
Slave	38,879	22.8	286,942	40.8	436,495	43.3
Total population	171,620	100.0	704,487	100.0	1,007,624	100.0

Sources: For the census of 1774, Guerra y Sánchez, Historia, 2:78. For 1827 and 1841, Resumen del censo de la población de la isla de Cuba . . . 1841 . . . (Havana, 1842), p. 19.

persons of color, and 436,495 were slaves (see Table 1). In two generations the black element of the population had risen to be a majority in the society. The phenomenal growth of the slave population — from less than 23 per cent of the total population in 1774 to more than 43 per cent in 1841 — may be understood and explained only by looking at the profound concomitant change in the nature of agricultural activity. But the volume of trade to Cuba in the nineteenth century is more surprising, because of Great Britain's hostility to the trade at that time and her attempts to put an end to it.

ᵗ The volume of trade in Africans to Cuba, had, despite fluctuations from year to year, tended to increase generally as the demand grew for workers on the island, and especially since the attempt to import white workers was not succeeding. With the abolition of the English slave trade in 1807, the most efficient suppliers of slaves in the Caribbean were removed. But from the Cuban planters' point of view, the greatest calamity was the agreement of 1817, forced by the English upon a war-weakened Spain, whereby the Spanish agreed to stop the trade to their colonies after 1820.[43] Of course, as an incentive to do so, the English government had paid the Spanish crown £400,000 as 'compensation'. No amount of money, however, especially when it was paid in Spain, could have induced the Cuban planters at that time to cooperate in the cessation of the slave trade. Instead, the Cubans regarded the British offer as a 'monstrous, hypocritical plot' designed to undermine their expanding sugar cane and coffee plantations and eventually stifle their economic progress.[44] The Anglo-Spanish agreement had the effect of increasing the numbers of Africans brought to the island of Cuba. Indeed, with the fear that the trade might be terminated in 1820, the mean annual importation figures between 1816 and 1820 were more than three times the figures for the period between 1812 and 1815.[45] Despite their awareness of the racial tragedy in St. Domingue, and despite the foreboding of the metropolitan power, the Cubans gambled on the risks: the

plantation society had, by then, become the sine qua non in the Caribbean for wealth, stability, civilization, and patriotism.[46]

Yet, after the establishment of the independent republic of Haiti in 1804, slaveowners in the area could never be as complacent as they used to be in the unquestioned days of the eighteenth century. And after about 1817, the official relations between the metropolis and the colony, between Cuba and Spain, changed considerably as a result of the increased inflow of Africans. The white population suddenly became more and more aware of the heightening possibilities of a racial confrontation in the island.[47] Some white persons became fearful. The planters began to see the Spanish government — and especially the Spanish military power on the island — as the best guarantee of their personal safety and the security of their property.[48] Even the native Cubans began to see self-interest and self-preservation as the overriding concerns of the moment. Cuba would remain a faithful colony as long as the planters needed Spain.

Notes

1. José Antonio Saco, Historia de la esclavitud de la raza africana en el nuevo mundo . . . 4 vols (Havana, 1938), 2:96–97.
2. Hubert H. S. Aimes, A History of Slavery in Cuba, 1511–1868 (New York, 1907), p. 13.
3. Actually, sugar cane growing had declined markedly by the end of the seventeenth century. See H. E. Friedlaender, Historia económica de Cuba (Havana, 1944), pp. 18–31.
4. Francisco de Arango y Parreño, Obras 2 vols (Havana, 1952), 1:81; Elizabeth Donnan (ed.), Documents Illustrative of the Slave Trade to America 4 vols (New York, 1965) 2:204–5, 211–12, 254; Allan Christelow, 'Contraband Trade between Jamaica and the Spanish Main, and the Free Port Act of 1766', Hispanic American Historical Review, 22 (1942), 309–43.
5. See Ramiro Guerra y Sánchez et al. (ed.), Historia de la nación cubana 10 vols (Havana, 1952), 1.
6. Aimes, op. cit., p. 8.
7. See Herbert S. Klein, Slavery in the Americas: A Comparative Study of Virginia and Cuba (Chicago, 1967), pp. 131–33.
8. Aimes quite correctly points out that the English

occupation did not 'cause' the awakening and economic development of Cuba (*op. cit.*, p. 33). He does, nevertheless, agree that it marks a period of significant change (*ibid.*, p. 69).

9. Donnan, *op. cit.*, 2: xlv; Aimes, *op. cit.*, pp. 22-25.
10. J. H. Parry, *The Spanish Seaborne Empire* (New York, 1966), pp. 314-25; John E. Fagg, *Latin America: A General History* (New York, 1963), pp. 292-303. My information on the reforms of Charles III is condensed principally from the following: Cayetano Alcázar Molina, *Los virreinatos en el siglo XVIII*, (Madrid, 2nd edn, 1959); R. A. Humphreys and John Lynch, (ed.), *The Origins of Latin American Revolutions, 1808-1826* (New York, 1965); Salvador de Madariaga, *The Fall of the Spanish American Empire.* (New York, rev. edn, 1963); R. J. Shafer, *The Economic Societies in the Spanish World (1763-1821)* (New York, 1958).
11. Richard Herr, *The Eighteenth-Century Revolution in Spain* (Princeton, 1958).
12. J. H. Parry and P. M. Sherlock, *A Short History of the West Indies* (London, 1956), pp. 95-107.
13. Aimes, *op. cit.*, pp. 35-37; Jerónimo Becker y González, *La política española en las Indias* (Madrid, 1920), pp. 412-15.
14. Allan Christelow, *op. cit.*, pp. 309-43; Parry and Sherlock, *op. cit.*, p. 103.
15. Aimes, *op. cit.*, pp.29-30; Donnan, *op. cit.*, 2:xlv.
16. Aimes, *op. cit.*, pp. 23, 36.
17. These figures are taken from Aimes, *op. cit.*, p. 269, who derived them from Alexander von Humboldt, *The Island of Cuba*, trans. J. S. Thrasher (New York, 1856), pp. 216-24. Cuban import figures for this period compare closely with those for Jamaica during its heyday of slavery. See Orlando Patterson, *The Sociology of Slavery* (London, 1967), pp. 290-91.
18. Aimes, *op. cit.*, p. 269.
19. Parry, *op. cit.*, p. 316; Aimes, *op. cit.*, p. 35.
20. Aimes, *op. cit.*, pp. 45-48; Becker y González, *op. cit.*, pp. 412-15.
21. *Real cédula por la que Su Majestad concede libertad para el comercio de negros con las islas de Cuba, Sto. Domingo, Puerto Rico, y provincia de Caracas a los españoles y extranjeros* (Madrid, 1789).
22. Aimes, *op. cit.*, p. 50.
23. Manuel Moreno Fraginals, *El ingenio* (Habana, 1964), p. 8.
24. Arango y Parreño, *op. cit.*, 2:134.
25. Francisco Pérez de la Riva y Pons, *Origen y régimen de la propiedad territorial en Cuba* (Havana, 1946), p. 136; Humboldt, *op. cit.*, p. 46.
26. Antonio Gallenga, *The Pearl of the Antilles* (London: *op. cit.*, 1873), pp. 10-11; Juan Pérez de la Riva, 'Documentos para la historia de las gentes sin historia. El tráfico de culíes chinos', *Revista de la Biblioteca Nacional José Martí*, 6 (1965), 77-90.

27. Moreno Fraginals, *op. cit.*, pp. 18-19; Pérez de la Riva y Pons, *op. cit.*, p. 91; Duvon C. Corbitt, 'Mercedes and Realengos: A Survey of the Public Land System of Cuba', *Hispanic American Historical Review*, 19 (1930), 262-85.
28. Pérez de la Riva, *op. cit.*, pp. 20-21; Corbitt, *op. cit.*, pp. 262-78.
29. Pérez de la Riva, *op. cit.*, pp. 137-48.
30. Shafer, *op. cit.*, pp. 151-54, 183-98; R. Guerra y Sánchez trans. Marjorie M. Urquidi, *Sugar and Society in the Caribbean*, (New Haven, 1964), pp. 56-57.
31. See Arthur P. Whitaker (ed.), *Latin America and the Enlightenment* (Ithaca, N.Y., 2nd edn, 1961).
32. Pérez de la Riva, *op. cit.*, pp. 127-28.
33. See Raymond Carr, *Spain 1808-1939* (Oxford, 1966), pp. 155-319.
34. Moreno Fraginals, *op. cit.*, pp. 14-15; Guerra y Sánchez, *Historia*, pp. 157-63.
35. Pérez de la Riva, *op. cit.*, pp. 132-34; Guerra y Sánchez, *Sugar and Society*, pp. 33-36.
36. Moreno Fraginals, *op. cit.*, pp. 74-78.
37. Arango y Parreño, *op. cit.*, 1:114-74.
38. For a variety of interesting local inventions, especially designed for the sugar cane industry, see the records in Archivo Histórico Nacional, Madrid, Sección de Ultramar (hereafter AHN, Ultramar), Fomento, leg. 49(19, 27, 28).
39. Arango y Parreño, *op. cit.*, 1:234-47.
40. Francisco J. Ponte Dominguez, *Arango Parreño, el estadista colonial* (Havana, 1937), pp. 84-87.
41. Moreno Fraginals, *op. cit.*, p. 24.
42. AHN, Ultramar, Fomento, leg. 37, fol. 91: *Informe sobre . . . Jamayca. Por D. Ramon de Arozarena, y D. Pedro Bauduy* (Havana, 1828).
43. *Ibid.*, Esclavitud, leg. 3547, fol. 1333: governor of Cuba to minister of war and colonies, July 2, 1861 (confidential).
44. Justo Zaragoza, *Las insurrecciones en Cuba*, 2 vols (Madrid, 1872-73), 1:512.
45. Aimes, *op. cit.*, p. 269. gives the imports as follows:

1812:	6,081	*1816:*	17,737
1813:	4,770	*1817:*	25,841
1814:	4,321	*1818:*	19,902
1815:	9,111	*1819:*	15,147
		1820:	17,194

Since these figures are based on official calculations, they probably represent the lowest import statistics.
46. Arango y Parreño, *op. cit.*, 1:148-50.
47. Rafael M. de Labra y Cadrana, *La abolición de la esclavitud en el orden económico* (Madrid, 1873), p. 251; AHN, Ultramar, Esclavitud, leg. 3552(2), ind. 6, fol. 3: confidential despatch of Captain-General O'Donnell, September 30, 1844.
48. *Ibid.*

21

The Origins of Plantation Growth in Puerto Rico

FRANCISCO SCARANO

In attempting to understand the rise of sugar in Puerto Rico, one is impressed by the rather cursory treatment afforded the important societal process of plantation evolution in scholarly literature. In the absence of thorough studies of the nineteenth-century economy, useful guidelines are found only in textbooks and general histories, and in barely a handful of specialized monographs conceived primarily in a legalistic framework.[1] As a result, the standard interpretation suffers serious shortcomings, particularly in regard to two crucial issues: the origins of economic change, and the nature of the plantation labor system, or more precisely, the economic role of slavery in sugar. Because clarification of these issues is essential to an understanding of Puerto Rico's economy and society during the nineteenth century, it is at this point necessary to address several prevailing misconceptions.

The standard interpretation of the resurgence of commercial agriculture in the early 1800s is inadequate primarily because of its excessive emphasis on the administrative measures dictated by Spain and its colonial representatives to promote economic growth. In their sometimes unconscious attempt to explain the historical process as a function of institutional change or political events, historians have offered what amounts to a monocausal explanation of a complex, multifaceted process. With the exception of a few scholars who have stressed the need to view Puerto Rican developments in a broader context, there has been wide agreement on the 'determining' effects of the so-called *Cédula de Gracias*, a royal decree of 1815 which endeavored to promote cash-crop agriculture through increased trade, freer technological exchange, and the attraction of foreign capital. Enacted to 'give renewed impulse to the

prosperity and welfare of the natives of that Island',[2] the Cédula allowed (among other things) the opening of all ports to foreign trade, the abolition of the ecclesiastical tithe and other taxes, the promotion of immigration from friendly Catholic countries, and a reduction of duties on imports of slaves and agricultural implements and machinery. The decree came in the wake of the restoration of Ferdinand VII to the Spanish throne and the conclusion of the first wave of anti-Spanish revolutionary activity in the continental colonies — a rebellion to which segments of the Puerto Rican Creole elite had shown some sympathy, but had not yet resolved to follow. In a way, therefore, the Cédula was designed to appease the island's liberals, whose ideological disposition, though not yet transformed into outright anti-Spanish and pro-independence feelings, alarmed imperial authorities who were conscious of the colony's value as a strategic base for counter-campaigns. In the conception of policymakers in Spain at this difficult junctive insurgency, colonial economic growth was not just an end in itself; it was also a means to obtain the support of influential Creole groups and to thwart the rise of an independence movement.

Regardless of underlying intent, with the Cédula the Spanish crown removed a series of obstacles in the path of plantation development, and partly because of this the production of cash crops took off soon after the decree's promulgation — slowly at first, and more rapidly after about 1825. But the changes in trade regulations, immigration policy, and taxation embodied in the Cédula were hardly sufficient in themselves to spark the plantation boom. Though often overlooked by historians, the facts are that the reform measures actually adopted reduced the scope of the original

Sugar and Slavery in Puerto Rico: The Plantation Economy of Ponce, (Madison, 1984), pp. 16–34.

Table 1   Concentration of Sugar Plantations in Puerto Rico, 1828

Sugar production[a] (tons)	Number of municipalities	Number of plantations[b]	Total production (tons)	% of total output
0	15	2	—	—
1–50	18	17	322.9	2.3
51–200	10	44	1,168.4	8.3
201–1,000	11	125	4,962.4	35.2
More than 1,001	3	88	7,622.4	54.2
Total	57	276	14,076.1	100.0

Source: Córdova, *Memorias geográficas*, Vol. 2, *passim*.
[a] Many districts not reporting sugar output produced molasses in home-made wooden mills.
[b] In one district, Sabana Grande, two plantations were reported but no sugar output was recorded.

decree, and more important, that the ordinance was neither a radical departure from ongoing imperial policy nor a potent catalyst of the larger, pan-Caribbean forces that ultimately sustained Puerto Rico's full incorporation into the international economy. All too frequently in the historical literature these points have been sidelined in favor of a simpler, rigid, causal connection between policy change and economic growth.[3] One would be remiss, however, to accept this conceptualization; reform was an important ingredient in the formula of plantation development, but more as a permissive condition than as an independent agent of change.

The reformist intent of Ferdinand VII's new policy toward Puerto Rico immediately faced several practical challenges. Far from pleasing all of the colonial elites, the Cédula de Gracias aroused the suspicion of Spanish merchants and raised the specter of a total collapse of the island exchequer. It theatened, in other words, two of the most solid foundations of Spanish colonial power. To thwart a dangerous depletion of the treasury and to appease the peninsular merchants, Spanish officials in Puerto Rico did not enforce all of the Cédula's provisions, choosing instead to modify some and postpone others. In the months following the king's declaration, intendant Alejandro Ramírez and governor Salvador Meléndez promulgated a series of regulations governing the Cédula, most of which sought to balance the need for a progressive economic policy with the preservation of merchant interests and the protection of the treasury's solvency. Thus, while the Cédula exempted foreign colonists from all regular taxes for a period of ten years, Ramírez and Meléndez reduced the period to five years; while it authorized forcing trade through all of the island's ports for a period of 15 years, they limited the period to one year, and in the case of the import

trade, to the port of San Juan exclusively; and although the Cédula abolished the ecclesiastical tithe and the *alcabala* (an old sales tax), the two highest ranking officials devised a new tax on gross income, the *subsidio*, to take their place, which amounted to a larger levy than the tithe and alcabala combined.[4] The scope of other minor measures was enlarged, to be sure, and few of the restrictions were later rescinded. But on the whole the limitations imposed on key provisions of the Cédula reduced its potential impact on trade, procurement of outside capital, internal accumulation, and free access to the slave trade — the crucial prerequisites of economic growth.

In the context of long-term Spanish policy toward its Caribbean possessions, moreover, the Cédula did not mark a new departure. Most of the reforms prescribed in 1815 specifically for Puerto Rico had been dictated for the Caribbean in general at various times during the earlier Bourbon reformist period. As Morales Carrión has noted, the Cédula marked 'the formal abandonment of the old Spanish exclusivism in practice as well as in theory ... [as it] brought together principles and measures which at different times had been adopted but never systematized in an official policy'.[5] Restrictions on the immigration of wealthy foreigners and skilled workers had been relaxed in 1778; the slave trade had been declared free of duty and open to foreigners in 1789; and by 1797, when Spain allowed its colonies to conduct trade with 'neutral' nations on a temporary basis — a move which hastened the expansion of trade between Spanish America and the United States — *de facto* commerce with foreign powers had existed for some time.[6]

Institutionally, then, Spain has consistently sought to promote cash-crop agriculture in its Caribbean possessions long before Ferdinand VII handed down his reform packages for Cuba and Puerto Rico. Indeed the consensus among historians is that the revival of Spanish mercantilism in the late colonial period, and its tolerance of colonial trade with the bourgeoning Spaniard periphery (Catalonia and the Basque provinces especially), prescribed a concerted effort to create cash-crop economies oriented towards overseas markets, albeit through the mediation of Spanish merchants and shippers whenever possible.[7] This policy, and the general expansion of markets for tropical staples, enlarged the demand for Puerto Rico's coffee and (to a lesser extent) tobacco, and significant advances in the export of these products were recorded. Yet sugar cane cultivation and sugar exports did not increase correlatively. Why?

In addressing this question it is fruitful to compare the Cuban and Puerto Rican cases, for despite the basic similarity of Spanish policy toward both islands before 1800, Cuba developed the foundations of its industry early, and Puerto Rico did not. In the comparative framework, the critical point turns on differences in economic endowment and possibilities rather than on policy. Given a Spanish policy that was fundamentally the same toward both islands, what accounted for the difference in timing between the two? The answer rests heavily on one factor: the rate of prior capital accumulation and the attendant existence (or lack) of a capital reserve to invest in sugar once the demand arose. There is no doubt that a large gulf separated Puerto Rico and Cuba in this respect during the eighteenth century.

The greater extent to which Creoles participated in the onset of sugar production in Cuba is one clear indication of a difference in prior capital accumulation. Knight has indicated that Creole ownership of the industry predominated in Cuba until the early nineteenth century:

The sugar revolution derived its greatest impetus from the entrepreneurial skills of the oldest families in Cuba. These families, having become rich in land and having access to public offices, found themselves strategically positioned to take every advantage of the early economic development. Until the early nineteenth century — indeed, until the technical and capital transformation of the period beginning around 1838 — this oligarchy maintained control and prominence. Eventually they gave way to new men and newly acquired wealth and the new economies of scale which the industrial age required. Between 1760 and 1810, these old oligarchs had increased per mill production from the vicinity of 165 tons to more than 400 tons [of sugar]. They increased the acreage of sugar cane, and expanded the number of mills. The largest producers remained unchanged: Arango, Montalvo, Duarte, Peñalver, Córdova, Herrera, O'Reilly.[8]

In addition to the sources of accumulation pointed out by Knight, there were in eighteenth-century Cuba other sources from which the Creole elite derived capital that was later invested in sugar. Tobacco was one of them, and the provisioning of Spanish ships at Havana for their return voyage across the Atlantic was another. With the rise of contraband after the peace of Utrecht (1713), the tobacco economy

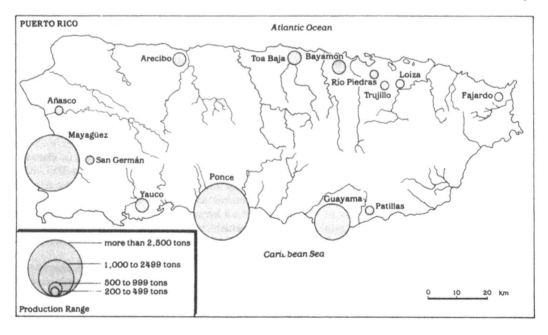

flourished, and although a Crown monopoly established in 1717 curtailed its potential for greater expansion, it became in the first half of the century an important source of commercial wealth.[9] Similarly, the myriad of activities revolving around the use of Havana as a rendezvous for returning Spanish ships received a strong stimulus with the recuperation of intra-imperial trade from its depression of the late seventeenth century. Thus, by the time the English captured Havana during the Seven Years' War — an occupation that lasted several months in 1762–63 — contacts with the European economy, making possible an accumulation of wealth that was soon to be funneled increasingly into the sugar economy.[10]

Puerto Rico, in contrast, remained relatively isolated from European trade during this period, and in its external relations confined mainly to a contraband trade with foreign colonies that was marked by high deficits. Usable to initiate any commercial activity on a scale analogous to Cuba's, Puerto Rican Creoles were generally incapable of harnessing sufficient capital to invest in the machinery and slaves required to begin commercial sugar production. Hubert Aimes, paraphrasing a Crown report of 1781 on ways to develop the colonial economies, summarizes the situation well: 'There are scarcely half a dozen persons in Puerto Rico able to buy twenty negroes each; little advancement can be expected from them.'[11] Nevertheless, the situation had begun to change with the increase in commerce that occurred after 1765, the spread of coffee and tobacco planting, and the Spaniards' investment of enormous sums on military construction in San Juan from the 1760s to the 1780s; by the time of the Crown report the possibility of accumulation had greatly improved. Still, at the turn of the nineteenth century Creoles were not sufficiently wealthy to propel the sugar economy forward, and the export boom owed much of its impetus to foreigners who eagerly seized on the opportunity to settle in Puerto Rico when other plantation colonies began to wane. While Creoles had controlled most of the sugar wealth in Cuba in the early stages of the industry there, foreigners and peninsular Spaniards constituted the bulk of the Puerto Rican planter class at an analogous stage of the Puerto Rican industry's development.

Ultimately, then, the most important objection to the policy-centered conceptualization of structural change is that it does not credit developments taking place outside the island society that both conditioned the demand for sugar and stimulated the migration of foreign planters, merchants, and skilled sugar workers to Puerto Rico. Against a backdrop of sweeping changes throughout the Caribbean, Spanish reforms legitimized and reinforced broad economic trends which sooner or later would have had an impact on Puerto Rican society, regardless of imperial policy. The havoc created in the international sugar market by the destruction of the Saint Domingue industry; the large and growing demand for the product in the United States, as well as that country's enhanced mercantile power in the Caribbean region; the economic decay of neighbouring plantation colonies; the abolition of the British slave trade; and the increasing importance of Saint Thomas as a clearinghouse for all types of plantation commerce — all of these together account for the Puerto Rican ascendence more adequately than enlightened colonial policy. Although the careful implementation of a longstanding Bourbon policy of export promotion undoubtedly facilitated and accelerated it, the shift to cane cultivation in Puerto Rico may be more fruitfully interpreted as part of a complex chain of events that displaced the locus of plantation agriculture in the Caribbean from the exhausted soils of the classic sugar colonies to the virgin lands of the larger Spanish colonies, and to some of the newly opened continental territories (British Guiana, for example).[12] In legitimizing the plantation system in Cuba and Puerto Rico through the liberalizing measures of the 1810s, Spain effectively guaranteed the continuation of its political control of the last of its American colonies. The costs of this transaction were considerable, however, for in so acting the metropolis, which could neither absorb the colonies' exports nor control their productive structures, relinquished many of the economic advantages of the imperial relationship.

Of all the major reorientations that occurred within the Caribbean during the age of revolutions, perhaps none was more instrumental in the development of Puerto Rico's plantation system than the commercial ascent of the Danish free port of Saint Thomas. The Haitian Revolution and the Napoleonic wars precipitated extremely favourable market conditions; the avalanche of the United States–Caribbean commerce created efficient linkages with distant markets; but it was the presence of nearby Saint Thomas that cemented these beneficial conditions for Puerto Rico. 'At the time,' Alejandro Tapia y Rivera reminisced of the 1820s and 1830s, 'St Thomas was ... our Liverpool and

Paris in commercial matters'.[13] This assessment refers basically to the Danish colony's relations with San Juan, but the assessment can easily be extended to the enormous influence Saint Thomas exercised in outports' economies as well. As a centre for commerce, shipping, finance, and the slave trade, and as a source of sugar entrepreneurs, the importance of Saint Thomas to developing sugar districts in Puerto Rico was unsurpassed, in the early period at least.

Unlike its sister colony of Saint Croix in the Danish Virgin Islands, Saint Thomas evolved from earliest times not as a plantation colony, but as a trade depot, one of several commercial links with Europe and North America in the eastern Caribbean. Declared a free port in 1764–67, several years after the abolition of the Danish West India Company, its commercial prosperity benefited from the chaos of Caribbean trade in the 1790s, brought about by war and revolution. In the words of one early chronicler, the Reverend John P. Knox,

an immensely increased impetus was given to the commerce of St Thomas by the breaking out of war in 1792, consequent upon the French revolution. The island then profited by the neutrality maintained by Denmark. It became the only market in the West Indies for the products of all the colonies, and the only channel through which they could be conveyed to the countries in the North of Europe. The resort to it of mercantile speculators from all quarters, brought a large addition to its population; and ... [J.P. Nissen] informs us, that many stores and houses were built, and that in the year 1793 one hundred and four persons took out burgher briefs; that is, paid the tax required to qualify them to begin business in the colony.[14]

The occupation of the island by the British for a brief period in 1801–02 and again between 1807 and 1815 eliminated the advantages of neutrality and curtailed the growth of its commercial wealth. But it is significant that the Puerto Rican branch of the Saint Thomas trade did not suffer correspondingly, particularly during the second British occupation. Relations between the two colonies, which had been close ever since the first half of the eighteenth century (Saint Thomas was considered the nerve centre of the contraband trade at the time) intensified in the early 1810s.[15] Shipping statistics for Saint Thomas in 1811 reveal, for instance, that intercourse with the Spanish islands (mostly Puerto Rico and Santo Domingo) predominated over all other contacts with non-British territories, a situation no doubt reinforced when Great Britain imposed an embargo on United States

merchantmen in 1812 — the second such action in five years.[16] On both geopolitical and economic grounds the trend toward greater interdependence between Puerto Rico and Saint Thomas was inevitable. On the one hand, diplomatic events brought the islands closer together than perhaps at any other time in history, since the provisional Spanish government, recognized by the authorities in Puerto Rico, was allied with Great Britain in a joint struggle against Napoleon, whose armies had invaded Spain the previous year. Thus Saint Thomas became a full ally for most of the duration of the British regime, a status Puerto Rican authorities must have welcomed as a legitimate excuse for a trade which, although deeply rooted in tradition, violated the spirit of Spanish mercantilist policy. On the other hand, the change in the imperial colors of Saint Thomas could not have been more timely from an economic point of view. With peninsular trade disrupted by the war, and the flow of traditional fiscal subsidies (situados) from the viceroyalty of New Spain halted by the rebellion in New Spain, Puerto Rico's external commerce and finances came dangerously close to collapse.[17] This crisis and the outbreak of war between the United States and Great Britain in 1812 created a dilemma for Spanish officials in Puerto Rico: how to balance the conflicting interests of the two powers in order to sustain commerce with both, the sum of which was a significant portion of the Puerto Rican total. The ensuing compromise policy both welcomed the intensified relations with British traders (now including the Saint Thomas merchants) and promoted the arrival of North American vessels, a part of whose merchandise was reportedly sent, oddly enough, to Saint Thomas.[18]

The significance of the British occupation of Saint Thomas for the development of the port's crucial ties with Puerto Rico therefore rests on the unique opportunities it created for reinforcing the islands' commercial and financial interdependence. In Saint Thomas in 1807 the British encountered a rich merchant group made wealthier by war. When they curtailed its activity, they inadvertently strengthened the merchants' disposition to finance commercial and agricultural venture in Puerto Rico. The associations thus established outlived the wartime occupation, and flourished when the island was returned to Danish sovereignty.

When peace was re-established in Europe in 1815, and Saint Thomas regained the advantages of the free port under Danish rule, its merchants recuperated most of the estranged transit trade.

Contacts with the British, French, and Dutch colonies resumed, and the volume of shipping handled by the port steadily increased. 'In the decade 1821–1830,' Waldemar Westergaard notes, 'the tonnage of ships annually visiting St. Thomas harbor was more than double what it had been during the two decades preceding. An average of not less than 2,809 ships of a combined tonnage of 177,444 called there each year.'[19] This frantic pace continued into the 1840s. Through it all, the momentum of the Puerto Rican trade accelerated, partly because of beneficial Spanish legislation and partly because of the collapse of wartime partnerships cultivated by Saint Thomas merchants elsewhere in the Caribbean region. Such was the fate of that island's contacts with the Spanish Main, whose trade had enriched many a Saint Thomas merchant during the independence wars. But as Knox saw it, the penetration of British and other European traders into the new republics of northern South America did not greatly damage the prosperity of the Danish emporium, which only became more dependent on its close ties with Puerto Rico:

When it became evident to the European powers that the South Americans could succeed in throwing off the yoke of the mother country, their enterprising merchants began to mediate the opening of a direct trade with these rich and fertile regions, and as early as 1824 direct importations were made at various of the Colombian ports. This, of course, was so much withdrawn from the commerce of St. Thomas; but, in the meantime, the island of Puerto Rico so increased its population and productions, as in a great degree to make up the loss of South American trade.[20]

Saint Thomas would enjoy its dominance over Puerto Rican plantation commerce for several decades, though it would not be long before traders in the United States and Europe seized on the opportunity to establish direct contacts with the merchants and planters of the booming Puerto Rican outports. In time, Saint Thomas would be edged out — but not before it mediated in the transformation of the Puerto Rican coastal lowlands into sprawling cane fields that thrived on the toil of a subjected population.

Plantation Labor

In the abundant literature on plantation systems of the Americas, Puerto Rico is often singled out as an anomalous case: an economy and society which developed an advanced sugar industry during times of a farily open Atlantic slave trade, yet did not rely to any significant degree on the labor of African slaves. The notion that nineteenth-century Puerto Rico was an exception to the slave-based sugar systems of the time has gained wide historiographical appeal, both in national and international scholary circles. In his authoritative history of sugar, for instance, Noel Deerr asserts that 'a peculiar feature of the Porto Rican industry is that it owes but little to African labor.' And Luis M. Diaz Soler, whose general history of Puerto Rican slavery stands as the only full-length study of the subject, concludes that 'slavery was an accident in the nineteenth century'.[21] The data suggest, however, that as an economic institution slavery flourished co-extensively and in conjunction with the sprouting of sugar haciendas in the first half of the nineteenth century, not by accident, but as a result of the powerful economic rationale of the emerging dominant institutions of the lowland countryside. The haciendas needed a mass of inexpensive disciplined workers, and for nearly three decades after 1815 the African slave trade satisfied that demand. Except on very small farms using a balanced combination of slaves and jornaleros, slaves constituted the majority of sugar workers in the principal producing districts until well beyond the middle of the century.

In reviewing the scholarship on plantation labour, one is impressed by the extent to which the free-labor argument rests on the writings of one observer, George D. Flinter. An Irishman who for 21 years served as an officer of the British Army in the West Indies, Flinter visited Puerto Rico in 1829–32 and wrote two books on his experiences there: *A View of the Present Condition of the Slave Population in the Island of Puerto Rico, Under the Spanish Government*, a short treatise published in 1832; and *An Account of the Present State of the Island of Puerto Rico*, a lengthier work published in London in 1834.[22] Since Flinter, at greater length than any other contemporary observer, addressed the question of the relative importance of free and slave labor, his views have carried particular weight in the writings of modern scholars, just as they shaped the opinions of his contemporaries. Yet in positing his defense of Puerto Rican slavery on the twofold argument that the masters were benevolent with their slaves and that the institution itself was economically unsound, Flinter at best deliberately misled his readers to believe that his generalizations applied to all sectors of the island society and economy; at worst, and probably no less deliberately, he portrayed a false picture of the reality he so fully observed.

Flinter's first work on Puerto Rico — of the two, the only to deal exclusively with slavery — appeared at the height of international agitation over the expectation of British abolition. Published simultaneously in English and Spanish, it was a propaganda piece unquestionably aimed at portraying a benign image of Spanish slavery at a time when Caribbean slavery was coming under severe abolitionist pressures abroad. True to the propaganda genre, the book was an awkward piece. The title was only marginally related to the content, about two-thirds of which was devoted to a philosophical defense of very gradual, long-term abolition. In the section devoted to Puerto Rico, Flinter articulated a defense of the island's slave system which was meant to divorce that system on qualitative grounds, from other slave regimes that were beginning to collapse around it. He skillfully conveyed the impression, so favorably to the interests of the local planter class, that slavery in Puerto Rico was not only of trifling importance to the export economy, but that it was also extremely easy on the slaves themselves because of the 'wise and philanthropic' provisions of the Spanish slave codes. 'The object of this work,' he said in the introduction, 'is to demonstrate the convenience and happiness that black slaves enjoy in this island and in all the Spanish colonies, compared to their previous condition in the colonies of other nations.' To 'substantiate' this, he in effect argued that: (a) Puerto Rican slaves were humanely treated in strict observance of the laws; (b) they generally owned property; (c) all slaves on the plantations cultivated subsistence plots; (d) they lived in family units which promoted stable unions and normal reproduction; (e) the growth of the slave population 'does not in any way owe to importations of African slaves, which have been limited in recent times due to the lack of capital; nor can it be attributed to introductions by new colonists . . .'[23]

I will not attempt a detailed discussion of the issues of slave treatment and the structure of the slave family, for although they are important, they transcend the scope of this work. It is interesting to note, however, that for the most part Flinter's generalizations on these issues rested on the need to explain the 'insignificance' of slave imports in the early 1820s and early 1830s. Because he could not publicize the existence of a full-scale clandestine slave trade — the revelation would have seriously undermined his

defense of the Puerto Rican regime, especially for British readers — Flinter needed an alternative explanation for the enormous recent increase in the slave population, which had grown from 19,000 persons in 1815 to 32,000 in 1828. The only possibility, short of admitting the continuation of the trade, was to portray the slaves' material and family conditions in the most favorable terms possible, on the assumption that under the normally harsh conditions of New World slavery the population would not reproduce itself — indeed, that it would take abnormally high slave incomes and family stability to achieve positive rates of growth. What Flinter perhaps did not realize was that in the period 1815–28 the slave population increased at an annual rate of 4.2 per cent, a phenomenon he would have found almost impossible to explain solely on the basis of stable unions and normal reproduction.

This difficulty underscores the basic problem of Flinter's credibility. Although he lived in Puerto Rico during some of the most intense slave-trading years, he purported to show the outside world that little such activity had occurred. One must suspect, too, his generalizations about slavery which were phrased in such a manner as to conceal differences between plantation and non-plantation phenomena. Undoubtedly familiar with the peculiarities of the emerging hacienda system, he did not endeavor to distinguish between the practice of slavery in the haciendas and its practice in other sectors of the economy. The distinction was a crucial one to make in discussing the economic importance of slavery, for as he knew too well the sugar industry was the raison d'être for the extension of slavery. He must also have known that at least half of the slaves in sugar plantations were of recent importation.

In his second book, which dealt exclusively with Puerto Rico and was based on more extensive observations, Flinter elaborated on his earlier themes but avoided any application of the arguments of free labor and benevolent treatment to the sugar industry. The Puerto Rican experience, he indicated, demonstrated the superiority of free over slave labour 'in security, in economy and in productiveness', as 'free labor on a large scale and attended by the most beneficial consequences, has been for some years in practical operation in Puerto Rico, and . . . the free black and the slave work together in the same field as the white man.'[24] As a general description of labor in a wide range of activities, from subsistence farming to coffee and tobacco production, this statement was probably not incorrect. But Flinter did not clearly specify this range of applications. Instead, he left readers of this voluminous work to discover for themselves how vague and misleading the generalization was in reference to a society in which labor- and capital-intensive agriculture coexisted with several types of small-scale, peasant production.

Furthermore, Flinter's observations concerning sugar labor indicated an exception. In a section of the book dealing with the relative inputs of slave labor in the sugar, coffee, tobacco, and cattle industries, he estimated that fully 80 per cent of the island's sugar was produced by slaves.[25] Accordingly, his detailed description of the principal sugar districts of Mayagüez, Ponce, and Guayama did not once mention the occurrence of free labor (although it existed on a small scale); on the contrary, it abounded in references to the haciendas' reliance on slaves. The remainder of the book offered no further evidence to support his initial implication that free labor 'on a large scale' existed in the plantation context.

David Turnbull's influential book on Cuba and the slave trade, published in 1840, gave notoriety to Flinter's misrepresentation of Puerto Rican slavery and added a new dimension to the incipient argument about free labor: Turnbull applied Flinter's thesis specifically to the sugar industry. Citing Flinter, the British consul in Havana concluded that

the most remarkable fact connected with the history and the present state of Puerto Rico is that the fields are cultivated, *and sugar manufactured*, by the hands of white men under a tropical sun. It is very possible that this might never have occurred had not the island been treated as a penal settlement at an early period of its history. The convicts themselves were condemned to hard labour as a part of their punishment; and when the term of their sentence arrived, they were compelled to continue it in order to obtain the means of subsistence . . . [;] their descendants present at this day a permanent solution to the problem, that white labour can be profitably applied to the cultivation of the sugar-cane, and the manufacture of its products, in one of the warmest regions of the West Indies [emphasis added].[26]

Turnbull also referred in his chapter on Puerto Rico to a population census of 1834 that classified nearly half of the slave population of about 40,000 as African-born, an indication, he thought, that the slave trade had intensified in recent years with the proliferation of sugar estates. This contradiction notwithstanding, his distortion of Flinter's ambiguous conclusions has been accepted literally by many a reputable

scholar, and represents today one of the standard sources of the free-labor argument.[27]

The Flinter-Turnbull thesis contrasts sharply with the testimony of Victor Schoelcher, the renowned French abolitionist, who visited Puerto Rico in 1841 with the purpose of obtaining first-hand knowledge of slavery there — a trip that shocked him deeply and influenced his conversion to radical abolitionism, according to one biographer.[28] In his little-known notes on the Puerto Rican journey, Schoelcher asserted that the primary function of the island's slave system was to sustain the sugar economy and that, consequently, the beneficial aspects of the slave codes were universally violated. He claimed that the 41,000 overworked, mistreated slaves of Puerto Rico, by themselves and without any significant collaboration from the peasantry, produced at least two-thirds as much sugar as the 78,000 slaves of Martinique. His argument was that in the French colony the proportion of elderly slaves and children was higher, and that the planters, unable to purchase new slaves since 1831, had deemed it in their best interst to ameliorate the working and living conditions of the slaves they had.[29] Flinter's 'senseless opinion' on these issues, he thought, was the product of a man who sought to justify slavery in general, and Spanish slavery in particular, on the basis of spurious comparisons between the living conditions of the slaves and those of the laboring classes in Europe.[30] Contrary to Flinter's assertions, Puerto Rican planters were, with few exceptions (Schoelcher cited Cornelius Kortright, owner of a large hacienda on the north coast) exceedingly brutal to their slaves:

One is tempted to praise the charity of our planters when one sees how the unhappy creatures bowed under the great evil of slavery are treated in Puerto Rico. Completely given over to the discretion of the master, their work is only limited by his pleasure. At harvest time one sees the blacks going to the mill by three o'clock in the morning and continuing until eight or nine o'clock in the evening, having as their only compensation, the pleasure of eating cane. They never even get twenty-four hours of respite during the year. On Sundays and feast days they still have to go to work for two hours in the morning and often for two hours in the evening.[31]

Such an inhuman regime, Schoelcher thought, could not be sustained without ample recourse to the African slave trade, which recently had provided as many as 3,000 new slaves in one year.

Schoelcher's remarkable testimony to the Puerto Rican plantations' heavy reliance on

Table 2   Changing Population Balances, Puerto Rican Sugar Municipalities, 1812–28

Sugar production, 1828 (tons)	Municipality	Population in 1812			Population in 1828			Pop. growth 1812–28	
		Free	Slave	% Slave	Free	Slave	% Slave	% Free	% Slave
More than 1,001	Mayagüez	8,640	994	10.3	14,407	3,860	21.1	67	288
	Ponce	8,780	1,060	10.8	11,723	3,204	21.5	61	296
	Guayama	2,191	328	13.0	5,501	2,373	29.8	156	623
	Subtotal	19,611	2,382	10.8	31,631	9,437	23.0	61	296
201–1,000	Bayamón[a]	6,047	1,364	18.4	5,351	899	14.4	− 12	− 34
	Loíza	2,220	696	23.9	3.456	742	17.7	56	7
	Trujillo[b]	2,173	406	15.7	7,576	610	12.9	133	50
	Rió Piedras	1,717	618	26.5	2,063	969	32.0	20	57
	Toa Baja	3,048	337	10.0	3,040	410	11.9	0	22
	Arecibo	6,176	432	6.5	9,048	915	9.2	45	112
	Añasco	7,301	447	5.8	9,257	627	6.3	27	40
	San Germán	15,242	1,281	7.8	30,550	1,673	5.2	105	31
	Yauco	5,447	570	9.5	10,271	834	7.5	89	46
	Patillas	2,531	338	11.8	3,278	407	9.8	47	20
	Fajardo	3,750	444	10.6	3,750	367	8.9	0	− 17
	Subtotal	55,652	6,933	11.1	88,090	8,453	8.8	58	22
	Total	75,263	9,315	8.2	119,721	17,890	13.0	59	92

Sources: AGI, Indiferente General, leg. 1525; Córdova, *Memorias geográficas*, Vol. 2, *passim*.
[a] Loose territory between 1812 and 1828 because of the establisment of new towns.
[b] Segregated into two municipalities between the çensus dates. The data for 1828 represent the sum of both subdivisions (Trujillo Alto and Trujillo Bajo).

slave labor finds corroboration in quantitative data collected by the colonial government, which is summarized in Table 2. The three major sugar-producing districts (Mayagüez, Ponce, and Guayama), where more than half of the added sugar output of the first few decades of the century was recorded, experienced enormous increases in their slave populations between 1812 and 1828. While the expansion of the free population in those districts averaged 62 per cent, the growth of the slave population averaged 296 per cent. In contrast, in the eleven districts that produced only between 201 and 1,000 tons of sugar in 1828, the free population increased by an average of 58 per cent, and the slave population by only 22 per cent. These differences clearly point to a dichotomy in the effects of economic change on the population structures of the various coastal districts of Puerto Rico. In districts that experienced only mild economic change the slave population increased at a fairly rapid pace, but its growth rate fell below that of the non-slave groups. There the connection between sugar and slavery was not overwhelmingly positive, although one cannot overlook the possibility that changes in the nature of the slave regime occurred in those areas in response to the challenge of sugar pro-

duction, and that, as a result, the figures on population growth may conceal potentially significant changes in the organization of labor. On the other hand, in the major sugar areas the data on population change point to a very positive correlation between plantation development and slavery. As the districts most affected by foreign colonization and investment, Puerto Rico's three prime sugar municipios replicated, in their early stages, the previous Caribbean pattern in which a rapid expansion of sugar production entailed a sizeable increase in the African slave population.

The extent to which the islandwide pattern conformed to, or was influenced by, the trend in Mayagüez, Ponce, and Guayama can be statistically ascertained. In order to measure the degree to which a hypothetical prevalence of slave labor in the sugar industry held for all of Puerto Rico, a correlation analysis was performed using Córdova's 1828 data — a large collection of economic and demographic statistics, containing for each of 58 municipios a breakdown of the population into five socioracial categories, as well as figures on land use, production, and (in the case of sugar farms) type of processing machinery. As Table 3 makes plain, the degree of correlation between sugar

Table 3 Correlation of Population Groups, Land Use, and Mill Technology, 1828

Variable	(1)	(2)	(3)	(4)	(5)	(6)	(7)	(8)	(9)	(10)	(11)	(12)
(1) Whites	1.00	.62	.51	.69	.55	.71	.19	.45	.83	.58	.13	.73
(2) Mulattoes		1.00	.64	.46	.51	.62	.37	.51	.58	.31	.14	.70
(3) Free blacks			1.00	.35	.48	.33	.39	.46	.33	.04	.11	.54
(4) Peasant squatters				1.00	.62	.58	.26	.52	.54	.66	.27	.53
(5) Slaves					1.00	.39	.74	.92	.38	.69	.18	.56
(6) Wooden mills						1.00	.10	.35	.66	.48	.07	.64
(7) Iron mills							1.00	.89	.14	.43	.10	.40
(8) Sugar lands								1.00	.31	.60	.14	.52
(9) Subsistence lands									1.00	.64	.15	.72
(10) Coffee lands										1.00	.09	.47
(11) Tobacco lands											1.00	.24
(12) Livestock												1.00

Source: Córdova, *Memorias geográficas*, Vol. 2.
Note: This table makes use of the Pearson Correlation Matrix. Pearson's product-moment coefficient of correlation is a statistical measure of the strength of a bivariate relationship. For two variables suspected of exhibiting a linear relationship (as when, for instance, change in the value of one variable provokes a concomitant change in the value of the other), Pearson's coefficient (r) indicates the direction and strength of the association. When r approaches $+1.0$ or -1.0, a strong linear relationship can be assumed.

cane farming and slavery was very high indeed.

The even greater correlation between the slave population and the capitalized segment of the sugar industry that was represented by the haciendas and associated with the use of iron-roller mills is highly significant. It distinguishes the industry as an economic sphere with a labor organization that differed sharply from the labor systems in other sectors of the economy, in which free labor predominated. This distinction brings up the important issue of the motivation of Puerto Rican hacendados in choosing to stock their estates with imported Africans, rather than resorting to the potentially abundant pool of free labor embodied in the peasantry. The population censuses of this period give evidence of a substantial increase in the free group — from 202,276 persons in 1815 to 267,837 in 1828, and to 317,018 in 1834 (the intercensal annual growth rates were 2.3 and 2.8 per cent, respectively). Yet the slave population grew even faster, from 18,616 persons in 1815 to 31,874 in 1828, and to 41,818 in 1834 (at intercensal average rates of 4.2 and 4.7 per cent).[32]

Why did planters prefer to purchase African slaves if such a large free population existed? Part of the answer may be found in Schoelcher's argument that the foreign planters, many of whom had been engaged in the sugar business in other slaveholding areas, were predisposed to favor slavery as the only profitable method of sugar labor. 'The increment in the slave population,' Salvador Brau wrote of the first decades of the nineteenth century, 'was sustained by the erroneous belief that only the African race could

withstand with impunity the hard labor of the haciendas; the notion that without slaves sugar could not be produced attained the character of an axiom.'[33] Had the incipient planter class encountered objective economic reasons to employ wage workers in the demanding chores of the plantations, these attitudes would probably not have persisted. There is every reason to believe that the planters would have employed free workers instead of slaves if the cost and work discipline of the former matched that of the enslaved blacks.

The problem is, of course, that the existence of a large peasant population — a potential supply of non-slave labor — need not be tantamount to an effective labor supply. For such a correlation to hold, as Witold Kula and others have argued, the peasantry would have had to be in an advanced stage of deterioration, particularly in regard to the means of economic independence — the land.[34] As we have seen, this was not the situation in Puerto Rico during the first half of the nineteenth century, when land to own or to squat on was still available in the interior sections of the country. There are documented cases of peasant migrations from plantation zones to the uplands, where large-scale agriculture had not yet taken hold.[35] Future research on this question may reveal that these were not isolated cases, but part of a widespread movement of freeholders into marginal lands of the interior that were unsuitable for sugar cane and which had not yet been encroached on by coffee haciendas. As long as these lands remained an alternative to the peasantry, the supply of wage labor to the sugar haciendas was bound to remain scarce, and consequently, expensive.

The preceding observations must not be construed as a categorical denial of the occurrence of wage labor on the plantations before 1849. One of the characteristics of the Cuban and Puerto Rican experience with sugar in the nineteenth century, a heritage of three centuries of society-building, was that there was no succession of slave labor to free labor, but a simultaneous juxtaposition of both, as Moreno Fraginals has observed of the Cuban situation.[36] Especially during the harvest, haciendas employed a few jornaleros to complement their permanent slave work force, which normally took care of all the industrial tasks. In the early years there were reports that prospective planters turned to the peasantry for most of the tasks entailed in the founding of new estates. In Guayama, for example, several hundred peasants from all over the region were employed in clearing the land and in hoeing and planting for several years after 1816, but the introduction of large contingents of African slaves terminated the practice, which suggests that the experiment with free labor failed. Most contemporaries believed, moreover, that the trouble with jornaleros was not so much the difficulty in persuading them to work, but their high cost and notorious absenteeism. The cost factor reflected the scarcity of supply, as only the prospect of very high wages could lure peasants away from their subsistence plots, even temporarily, for the demanding work of cane harvesting. Even if population growth may have progressively lowered the cost of free workers, however, there remained the serious problems of irregularity in work attendance and resistance to the intensity of sugar labor. These were critical difficulties in a production process that required uninterrupted labor to avoid grave losses of raw materials and lowered sugar yields; canes must be milled within 48 hours of harvesting lest they begin to rot. This was the crux of the problem: because of their lack of regular work attendance and resistance to prevailing working conditions, jornaleros were ill-suited to the processing phase, which was widely recognized as the bottleneck of sugar production before the advent of the central-mill system. '[The planters] have great difficulty in getting the freemen to work in the manufacture of sugar,' exclaimed John Lindegren, the British consul in San Juan, 'and there are few estates in which they can get them into the boiling houses. . . . '[37] If they succeeded in doing so, one might add, the planters would

have desired to bind the workers to the haciendas in any way possible to preclude costly interruptions. Unable as yet to coerce jornaleros legally, hacendados preferred to employ them in field work, and, as a safeguard against absenteeism, to institute a system of piecework.

The Reglamento of 1849 imposed a series of coercive measures to hold down the price of wage labor and, more important, to force jornaleros into a slavelike productive system on the plantations.[38] Enacted in the wake of a sharp depression in sugar income resulting from low prices, the news of abolition in the French colonies, and the disclosure of at least two serious slave conspiracies (one of them in Ponce), this law attempted to undermine the independence of the peasantry by placing limitations on traditional access to the land and by formulating a legal definition of 'jornaleros' which encompassed peasant smallholders as well as the truly landless.[39] The history of this legislation is the story of a partly successful attempt to maneuvre a Caribbean peasantry into virtual slavery when the possibility of extending black slavery had ended. While I will not attempt to describe this history, it is fitting to observe that for the planters the experiment was not altogether a happy one. Between 1849 and 1873, although armed with legal authority to bind jornaleros to plantation work, hacendados tried desperately to obtain alternative sources of servile labor, whether by contracting with workers in the foreign West Indies, planning to import Chinese coolies, or promising to 'care for' several hundred emancipados (freedmen) from the slaver Majesty shipwrecked off the coast of Humacao in 1859. Planters enthusiastically backed these plans, but the colonial government opposed them.

Such plans were obvious signs of the failure of the coercive laws to satisfy the haciendas' demand for abundant, constant, and disciplined labor; so, too, were the planters' lamentations about the negative impact of abolition in 1873. Slavery continued to be the basis of labor in many coastal estates until the time of emancipation, and the crisis that concerned the Diputación Provincial in 1880, and which echoed throughout the colony's ruling circles, was in part a result of slavery's demise.

Notes

1. Examples of this scholarship are Lidio Cruz Monclova, *Historia de Puerto Rico* (*Siglo XIX*), 6th ed., 6 vols (Rio Piedras, 1970); Tomás Blanco, *Prontuario histórico de*

Puerto Rico, 6th ed. (San Juan, 1970); Isabel Gutiérrez del Arroyo, *El reformismo ilustrado en Puerto Rico* (Mexico, D. F., 1953); and Labour Gomez Acevedo, *Organización y reglamentación del trabajo ent el Puerto Rico del siglo XIX* (San Juan, 1970). Several noteworthy exceptions to the legalistic interpretation of social change may be found in the anthropological literature: Fernández Méndez. *Historia cultural*; Julian Steward *et al.*, *The People of Puerto Rico: A Study in Social Anthropology* (Urbana, 1956); Sidney W. Mintz, 'Labor and Sugar in Puerto Rico and in Jamaica, 1800-1850', *Comparative Studies in Society and History*, Vol. 1, No. 3 (March 1959), pp. 273-83; and Sidney W. Mintz, 'The Role of Forced Labor in Nineteenth Century Puerto Rico', *Caribbean Historical Review* 1, No. 2 (December 1951), pp. 134-51.

2. King Ferdinand VII in the Cédula's preface, cited in Cruz Monclova, *Historia de Puerto Rico*, 1:77. See the text of the decree in Cayetano Coll y Toste, 'La Cédula de Gracias y sus efectos, rectificaciones históricas', Bulltín Histórico de Puerto Rico (*BHPR*) 14:3-24.

3. See, for instance, Coll y Toste, 'La Cédula de Gracias'; and Salvador Brau, 'Las clases jornaleras de Puerto Rico,' *Ensayos (idsquisiciones sociológicas)* (Río Piedras: Editorial Edil, 1972), p. 23. In fairness to Brau, he later embraced a more sophisticated interpretation of the rise of the sugar industry in his essay, 'La caña de azúcar', *Ensayos*, pp. 271-94.

4. Cruz Monclova, *Historia de Puerto Rico*, 1:79-83. The agreements have been transcribed by Coll y Toste, 'La Cédula de Gracias'.

5. Arturo Morales Carrión, *Puerto Rico and the Non-Hispanic Caribbean: A Study in the Decline of Spanish Exclusivism* (Rio Piedras, 1952), p. 141.

6. *Ibid.*, pp. 118-32.

7. Manuel Moreno Fraginals, *El Ingenio: Complejos Económico-Sociales Cubana del Azúcar* 3 vols. (Havana: Editorial de Ciencias Sociales, 1978) vol. 2; J. H. Parry, *The Spanish Seaborne Empire* (London: Hutchinson, 1966), chap. 16.

8. Franklin W. Knight, 'Origins of Wealth and the Sugar Revolution in Cuba, 1750-1850', *The Hispanic American Historical Review*, 57, No. 2 (May 1977), pp. 231-53. Pablo Tornero has recently identified a large number of Cuban hacendados of this period, corroborating Knight's observations on the predominance of the old Creole families. See Pablo Tornero, 'Hacendados y desarrollo azucarero cubano (1763-1818)', *Revista de Indias* 38, Nos. 153-54 (July-December 1978), pp. 715-37.

9. Hubert H. S. Aimes, *A History of Slavery in Cuba, 1511 to 1868* (New York and London, 1907), pp. 20-23.

10. Julio Le Riverend, *Historia económica de Cuba* (Barcelona, 1972), pp. 147-48. A detailed account of the Cuban sugar industry in the early eighteenth century may be found in Leví Marrero, *Cuba: economia y sociedad*, 7 vols to date (Madrid, 1971-78), 7:1-39.

11. Aimes, *op. cit.*, p. 41.

12. Ramiro Guerra y Sánchez, *Sugar and Society in the Caribbean (New Haven, 1964); Joseph L. Ragatz, The Fall of the Planter Class in the British Caribbean, 1753-1833* (New York: The Century Co., 1928); and Sidney W. Mintz, 'Labor and Sugar'.

13. Alejandro Tapia y Rivera, *Mis memorias, o Puerto Rico como lo encontré y como lo dejo* (Barcelona, 1968), p. 17.

14. John P. Knox, *A Historical Account of St. Thomas, W.I.* (New York, 1852), p. 100.

15. For accounts of contraband trade between Saint Thomas and Puerto Rico, see Morales Carrión, *op. cit.*,

pp. 83-86; Manuel Gutiérrez de Arce, *La colonización danesa en las Islas Vírgenes: estudio histórico-jurídico* (Seville, 1945), p. 54; and Birgit Sonesson, 'El papel de Santomás en el hasta 1815', *Anales de Investigación Histórica*, 4, nos. 1-2 (1977), pp. 42-80.

16. The first embargo was imposed in 1807-09. Sonesson, *op. cit.*, pp. 74-75.

17. Luis E. González Vales, *Aljandro Ramírez y su tiempo: ensayos de historia económica e institucional* (Rio Piedras, 1978).

18. Sonesson, *op. cit.*, pp. 74-75.

19. Waldemar Westergaard, *The Danish West Indies Under Company Rule (1671-1754)* (New York, 1917), p. 252. In comparison, the port of Havana — then one of the busiest in the Americas — saw 1,057 arrivals of merchant vessels (excluding a large number of slave ships) in 1828 and 2,524 in 1837. Knight, 'Origins of Wealth', p. 246.

20. Knox, *op. cit.*, p. 104.

21. Noel Deerr, *The History of Sugar*, 2 vols (London, 1948), Vol. 1, p. 126; Luis M. Díaz Soler, *Historia de la Esclavitud Negra en Puerto Rico* (Río Piedras, 3rd edn, 1970), p. 349.

22. The first of his works was published in English in Philadelphia (1832), while a Spanish version appeared the same year in New York. All references in this study are to the Spanish translation: George Flinter, *Examen de estado actual de los esclavos de la Isla de Puerto Rico bajo el dominio español* (1832; rpt, San Juan, 1976). The second work was published in London by Longmans in 1834.

23. Flinter, *Examen*, pp. 16, 46-50.

24. George Flinter, *An Account of the Present State of the Island of Puerto Rico* (London, 1834), p. vii.

25. Significantly, this calculation was flawed by a mathematical error. Having estimated the number of field slaves at 30,000 and the total number of sugar and coffee haciendas at 448, Flinter's average for all slaveholdings should have been 67, not 37 as he indicated in his text. If one accepts his (incorrect) implicit estimate of labor productivity in the sugar sector (obtained by dividing sugar output per estate, of which there were 300, by his incorrect estimate of slaves per unit), scarcely one-third of the 30,000 field slaves would have sufficed to produce the entire crop of 21,000 tons of sugar.

26. David Turnbull, *Travels in the West: Cuba, with Notices of Porto Rico and the Slave Trade* (London, 1840). pp. 559-60.

27. Among the scholars who have referred to Turnbull on these issues are Eric Williams, *From Columbus to Castro: The History of the Caribbean* (New York, 1970); Deerr, *History of Sugar*; Díaz Soler, *Historia de la esclavitud*; and Mintz, 'Labor and Sugar'.

28. Cited by Thomas Mathews. 'The Question of Color in Puerto Rico', in *Slavery and Race Relations in Latin America*, ed. Robert Brent Toplin (Westport, Conn., 1974), pp. 299-323.

29. Victor Schoelcher. *Colonies étrangères et Haiti*, 2 vols (Paris, 1843), 1:320-22.

30. *Ibid.*, 1:332-33.

31. *Ibid.*, 1:330.

32. Censuses of the populations of Puerto Rico, AGI, Indiferente General, leg. 1525; Córdova, *Memorias geográficas*, 2:400; Ormaechea, 'Memoria acerca de la agricultura'.

33. Brau, 'Las clases jornaleras', p. 25.

34. Witold Kula, *Teoría económica del sistema feudal*, trans. Estanislao J. Zembrzuski (Buenos Aires, 1974), pp. 16-17.

35. Félix M. Oritz, in 'Análisis de los registros de matrimonios de la parroquia de Yabucoa, 1813–1850', *Anales de Investigación Histórica* Vol. 1, No. 1 (1974), pp. 73–92, has demonstrated the occurrence of a substantial migration of peasants from Guayama, a plantation district, into Yabucoa. In addition, the 1849–50 jornalero register of the town of Utuado in the interior highlands lists a considerable number of young migrants from coastal areas; see Fernando Picó, comp., *Registro general de jornaleros: Utuado, Puerto Rico, 1849–1850* (Rio Piedras, 1977). For an analysis of this migration, see Picó's excellent study of the dispossession of the highland peasantry, *Libertad y servidumbre*, pp. 69–73.

36. Manuel Moreno Fraginals (trans. Cedric Bellfrage), *The Sugarmill: the socio-economic complex of sugar in Cuba, 1760–1860* (New York, 1976), p. 131. From a broader perspective, Mintz writes: 'Indeed, the history of Caribbean plantations does not show a clear break between a slave mode of production and a capitalist mode of production, but something quite different. The succession of different mixes of forms of labor exaction in specific instances reveals clearly how the plantation systems of different Caribbean societies developed as parts of a worldwide capitalism, each particular case indicating how variant means were employed to provide adequate labor, some successful and some not, all within an international division of labor transformed by capitalism, and to satisfy an international market created by that same capitalist system'. Sidney W. Mintz, 'Was the Plantation Slave a Proletarian?', *Review* 2, No. 1 (Summer 1978), pp. 81–98.

37. Great Britain, *Parliamentary Papers* (PP), Vol. 23 (1847–48), Pt 3 (*Accounts and Papers*, Vol. 17), 'Appendix to the Seventh Report from the Committee on Sugar and Coffee Planting', p. 370.

38. See the text of the Reglamento of 1849 in *BHPR* 6:217–21.

39. The news of French abolition and its consequences touched off a wave of panic among the Puerto Rican planters. In part their fears stemmed from a bloody revolt of the freemen of Martinique which soon spread to the Danish island of Saint Croix, and prompted the Puerto Rican governor, Juan Prim, to dispatch troops to aid the French colonial government in restoring order. Fearful of a general uprising in Puerto Rico in response to the deteriorating material conditions of the plantations and the spread of an insurrectionary spirit in the eastern Caribbean, Governor Prim enacted a repressive ordinance (*Bando contra la raza africana*) imposing severe punishment for even minor offenses committed by blacks, whether free or slave. Shortly thereafter the discovery of conspiracies among the slaves of Ponce and Vega Baja confirmed the worse fears of the ruling class. On these events, see Díaz Soler, *Historia de la esclavitud*, pp. 217–22; Arturo Morales Carrión, *Auge y decadencia de la trata negrera en Puerto Rico (1820–1860)* (San Juan, 1978), pp. 149–75; Guillermo A. Baralt, *Esclavos rebeldes: conspiraciones y sublevaciones de esclavos en Puerto Rico, 1795–1873* (Río Piedras, 1982).

French abolition may have affected some hacendados in another way. Article 8 of the French emancipation decree threatened all French citizens in foreign countries who possessed slaves with abrogation of citizenship unless they disposed of the slaves within three years. Although later it was all but nullified, Article 8 may have intimidated those planters in Puerto Rico who had retained French citizenship. See Lawrence C. Jennings, 'La abolition de l'esclavage par la IIe Republique et ses effets en Louisiane, 1848–1858', *Revue française d'histoire d'outre-mer*, 56, No. 205 (1969), pp. 375–97.

SECTION FIVE
Slavery, Finance and Trade

Financing the trade, production and governance of the colonial system was a major undertaking that required sophisticated instruments and techniques of management. Private entrepreneurs and Governments alike faced these challenges and found creative ways in which to have money available at various points of commercial exchange. Here authors examine several levels of engagement with the financial system of colonialism: how to provide for effective public administration; how to supply the factors of production and plantation inputs; how to secure returns from private investments in trading facilities and productive enterprises; and the importance of maintaining an all-embracing, mushrooming network of commerce and credit.

The European colonization of the Caribbean and the establishment of sugar and slavery as the bases of Caribbean economic development necessitated the maintenance of a complicated trading network. The phenomenal expansion of world trade between 1451 and 1870 which accompanied European colonization depended largely on the employment of African slaves in the exploitation of American resources. This network integrated Africa, the Atlantic islands, Europe and North America. Inikori examines the buying and shipping of slaves to the Americas, two fundamental functions fulfilled by Western Europe in the Atlantic system, as well as the economic, and tragic demographic, consequences of the trade. The United States were integral to Atlantic commerce, as Carrington shows. They were critical suppliers of plantation inputs, and the Caribbean therefore suffered economically from the disruption of trade during the war of independence. The

new economic order after the end of the war also had significant consequences for the profitability of the sugar industry in the Caribbean, though the restrictions on United States commerce gave rise to a circuitous trade that went through non-British colonies.

Stein and Davies focus more on production, the acquisition of input by sugar plantations, and the disposal of output through legal or illicit means. Davies concentrates on the Commission system which was an outstanding characteristic of the elaborate system of marketing, and a means by which credit was transmitted from imperial countries. Unlike Stein and Davies, Shepherd is concerned with the relations between the sugar economy and other producing units in a diversified economy. Her focus is on the internal system of exchange as opposed to the external trade. These essays illustrate some of the major concerns which have gained attention in the past two decades.

The sugar business, and colonial enterprises generally, consumed and produced a greater share of financial resources than any other over the full slavery period. The historiography of the financing and profitability of such enterprises is quite extensive, and is steadily being enlarged. Marichal and Mantecón revisit the vast and complex nature of the fiscal structure of the Spanish monarchy in the metropolis and the overseas possessions. They show that in the financing of Spanish American enterprises, New Spain played a much larger role than the metropolis itself in supporting the American empire. Their conclusions have implications for the debate over whether capital for the colonization project was internally or externally generated.

22

The Slave Trade and the Atlantic Economies, 1451-1870[1]

JOSEPH E. INIKORI

This article deals with all the regions of Africa directly affected by the external slave trade from that continent across the Sahara, the Atlantic Ocean, the Red Sea and the Indian Ocean. Other territories included are South and North America, the West Indies and all Europe bordering on the Atlantic, including those European countries affected by the activities of the Atlantic countries. In some ways this definition of the scope of this paper is arbitrary. It excludes some of the slave receiving economies of the period, in particular, those of the Middle East.[2] On the other hand, the economies included were not all affected to the same degree by the slave trade; indeed, some were only indirectly affected. However, the coverage of the territories mentioned makes it possible to analyse in one broad sweep the effects of the slave trade on all the economies most significantly affected.

The slave trade and slavery is a subject on which a great deal has already been said and written, starting from the eighteenth century and continuing to the present day.[3]

But the existing studies have failed to fit the slave trade as a causal factor, positive or negative, into a process analysis of economic development in the major countries or territories that participated in it. This is what this article tries to do. For that purpose the external slave trade from Africa is viewed as a form of international trade whose effects on the countries or regions involved in it, directly or indirectly, are analysed in economic terms. The paper is based essentially on development as opposed to growth

analysis. The distinction between these two concepts is not always observed by writers. Modern economic growth is usually defined in terms of a sustained annual increase in income per head of the entire population in a given economy, over a long period of time, while economic development relates to the transformation of an economy from a customary, subsistence, rural and regional stage, to a rational, commercial, urban and national stage, with appropriate institutions for the efficient mobility of factors. Often the transformation includes a major structural shift in the economy, from primarily agricultural to primarily industrial. In the context of Rostovian analysis, development belongs to the 'pre-condition' and 'take-off' stages, while growth belongs to the post-take-off stages. The main question which this article tries to tackle, therefore, is the extent to which the movements of the various economies under review were accelerated or retarded by the slave trade in those crucial stages of development. The analysis draws on the concept of dynamic gains from international trade as opposed to the static gains of classical analysis.[4]

Magnitude of the external slave trade

One problem which is central to our question is the magnitude of the external slave trade from Africa during the period 1451-1870. This means a computation of the total number of slaves actually carried away from sub-Saharan Africa by way of the Sahara, the Atlantic, the Red Sea and the Indian Ocean, during that period. From the point of view of the European sector of the Atlantic, this is necessary because the development of resources required by the trade forms an important part of the analysis and this will have to be weighted by the estimated magnitude of the European portion of the trade. For the African part of the analysis the computed magnitude will form a useful starting point for an estimate of the demographic impact of the trade and the consequences of that for economic development in the regions affected.

Most writers dealing with the slave trade across the Sahara and the Atlantic have always found it necessary to estimate the total number of slaves involved. For the Atlantic portion, the most recent of these estimates is that of Professor Curtin,[5] which was based on published data. However, his global estimates have now been shown to be generally on the low side of the mark.[6] At present much work is going on relating to the number of slaves exported from Africa by way of the Atlantic trade. It may take another decade or more before the outcome can be stated in terms of global figures. For the purposes of the analysis in this article, the figure of 11 million slaves provided by Professor Curtin has been taken as representing the barest minimum for the Atlantic trade. This, together with the European share of the unknown magnitude of the Indian Ocean trade, makes up the European portion of the external slave trade from Africa.

For the trans-Saharan trade, a recent attempt to summarize the implications of some of the existing estimates put the total number of slaves taken away from sub-Saharan Africa to meet the demands of the desert trade, for the whole period 850-1910, at 10 million. The distribution of this total over time shows that for our period, 1451-1870, a little under 6 million people were taken away.[7] These data are extremely weak, and some think the present estimate may be on the high side.[8] If the trans-Saharan figure should be proved to be an overestimate, this may compensate to some extent the underestimate for the trans-Atlantic trade.

As for the slave trade from East Africa to the Red Sea, Arabia, the Persian Gulf, India and the islands on the Indian Ocean, no aggregate estimates of the total numbers involved have been made. From the information available,[9] we may not be exaggerating if we put the total figures for the whole of our period at some 2 million.

Thus, the external slave trade from Africa south of the Sahara between the fifteenth and nineteenth centuries, involved the export of not less than 19 million people.

The slave trade and the expansion of international trade

The buying, shipping and employment of over 11 million slaves in capitalistic production for an international market on the one hand, and the shipping and marketing of the commodities produced by those slaves on the other, constituted a very large part, in volume, of all international economic transactions in the period 1451-1870. In order to relate this international transaction of immense proportions to Western development, we shall try to answer the following questions which in some ways are related:

1. To what extent did the requirements for buying and transporting over 11 million slaves contribute towards development in Western economies?
2. Was the process of economic development in Atlantic Europe and the Americas critically influenced by the growth of world trade between 1500 and 1870?
3. To what extent did the expansion of international trade between 1500 and 1870 depend on the slave trade?

Before answering these questions, something must be said about the division of functions in the Atlantic system within which the slave trade and slavery operated. The main functional categories in that system were: trade and finance; transportation; manufacturing; mining; export staple agriculture in plantations; commercial foodstuff agriculture in medium-sized freehold farms; and the sale of labour. Western Europe overwhelmingly dominated trade, finance, transportation and manufacturing. Portuguese and Spanish America also did some trading and transportation, including some manufacturing for internal consumption. But their main function in the Atlantic system was the mining of precious metals and export staple agriculture in plantations. The middle and north-eastern states of North America, right from the colonial days, concentrated on commercial foodstuff production for export to the slave plantations of the West Indian islands, import and export trade, shipping, finance, shipbuilding, lumber production, fishing and, later, manufacturing. The southern states specialized in plantation agriculture, first, mainly tobacco, but later, mainly cotton. The special function of all the West Indian islands was plantation agriculture – coffee, cotton, indigo, but in particular, sugar cane. Africa did not perform any real production function in the Atlantic system. Its function was limited to the acquisition and sale of slave labour. On the whole, of all the territories under review, only the north-eastern States of North America per-formed economic functions closely resembling those performed by Western Europe in the Atlantic system.

The character of functions performed by a given territory in the Atlantic system was a crucial factor explaining the type of developmental effect which the system produced in that territory. Trade, finance, shipping, manufacturing, and commercial foodstuff production in medium-sized freehold farms tended to produce much greater positive developmental effects than plantation agriculture. However, the character of the functions does not fully explain the differing developmental effects. It is significant that the territories which were engaged mostly in plantation agriculture were also those in which 'foreign factors of production' were most largely employed, using this concept in Jonathan Levin's sense.[10] As a consequence, a very large proportion of the total income produced in the Atlantic sectors of these economies was remitted abroad. This was particularly so for the West Indian islands. This, together with the character of the functions performed, left little or no room for a self-sustained internal development to accompany the growth of activities in production for an international market. In the Latin American territories the operation of some internal factors, partly connected with the character of the European colonists and the institutions they brought with them, further reduced the overall positive effects of the Atlantic system for the internal development of those economies. For these various reasons, the positive developmental effects of the Atlantic system were largely concentrated in Western Europe and North America.

The buying and shipping of slaves to the Americas formed one of the most important functions fulfilled by Western Europe in the Atlantic system. This proved to be a very de-manding task, requiring considerable mercantile skills, highly sophisticated financial arrangements, refinements in shipbuilding technology, and production of new types of goods demanded by the slave-producing regions of tropical Africa. The creative response of the economies of Atlantic Europe to the requirements of this function formed an important part of the development process in those economies. Unfortunately, a detailed study of the character of this response and an assessment of its place in the process of economic development in Western Europe is only just receiving the attention of scholars employing the analytical tools of development economics. The first of such studies, which has been made on the British economy for the period 1750-1807,[11] shows that during this period of about sixty years when Great Britain dominated the buying and shipping of slaves to the Americas, the peculiar requirements of this function stimulated important developments in key sectors and regions of the British economy. The slave merchants were constantly exposed to considerable risks and so their regular and growing demand for insurance cover was important in the development of marine insurance in Great Britain. The trade required the extension of credit[12] at various stages – credit to slave-dealers on the African coast, and more important, credit to the employers of slave labour in the Americas. In addition, a long space of time, usually over a year, elapsed between the time a merchant in Great Britain invested in goods and shipping and the time the slaves were finally sold in the Americas. In consequence, the financial resources of the slave merchants were more than ordinarily stretched. In fact, the commercial capital required by the slave trade – in shipping, in stock of goods, and in trade credits – was far in excess of the annual volume of the trade. Rather than sink the whole of their fortunes in the trade, the slave-merchants always preferred to obtain credit in various forms. They obtained export credit from the producers of goods for the trade, a requirement which in turn compelled the latter to look for sources of credit for their operation. More important, the slave-merchants obtained credit through the discounting of the voluminous bills of exchange they obtained from the sale of slaves in the Americas.

The favourable demand conditions created in this way were important for the development of banking and the discount market in Great Britain. In fact, some of the provincial banks that sprang up at this time, especially in Lancashire, were motivated primarily by the desire to profit from the discounting of slave bills and other bills resulting from the credit relationship between the slave-merchants and producers of goods for the slave trade.[13]

The special shipping requirements of the trade stimulated considerable activities in British shipyards for the building of a special class of vessel and for the repair and costly outfit of slave vessels. From a calculation based on 137 slave-ships, measuring 24,180 tons, it is found that about 60 per cent of British slave vessels were built in British shipyards, the remaining 40 per cent being made up of prizes taken in wartime, and foreign-built ships purchased abroad, mostly in the colonies. After deducting this proportion, an elaborate calculation based on a large amount of shipping data, shows that between 1791 and 1807 about 15 per cent of all tonnage built in Great Britain was destined for the Guinea trade, about 95 per cent of which went into the shipping of slaves.[14] Between 1750 and 1807, an average of £2,625,959 per decade was invested by British slave-merchants in the building, repairing and outfit of their vessels in British shipyards, ranging from an average of about £1 1/2 million per decade for the period 1750-80, to an average of almost £4 million per decade in the period, 1781-1807. The input requirements of these activities had important linkage effects on other industries, particularly the metal and metal-using trades, and hence the mining of metal ore and coal, and their transportation. They also made an important contribution to the process of urbanization.

The manufacturing sectors significantly influenced were the metal and metal-using industries, copper, brass and iron. The manufacture of guns for the purchase of slaves was an important Birmingham industry. The production of special copper and brass goods for the slave trade, and the employment of copper in sheathing the bottoms of slave vessels were important activities in the London, Bristol and Liverpool regions. But the British industry whose development was most critically influenced by the slave trade was the cotton textile industry.

Between 1750 and 1776, the proportion of total annual British cotton exports, by value, which went to the west coast of Africa varied from 30 to 50 per cent.[15] This proportion fell drastically during the American War of Independence, but recovered after the war, and between 1783 and 1792, varied from 11 to 32 per cent. After 1792, the faster growth of exports to Europe and the Americas meant that exports to the African coast formed a diminishing percentage of total British cotton exports, by value. Thus, in terms of volume, exports to the African coast were important for the development of the export sector of the British cotton textile industry. The cotton goods exported to the African coast were the cheap type for common consumers and this made them adaptable to mass production by mechanical methods. But, by far the most important contribution which exports to the African coast made towards the development of the British cotton textile industry was in terms of exposure to competition.

In the early years of the industry, its home market was protected, the sale of East Indian cotton textiles for domestic consumption having been prohibited in Great Britain early in the eighteenth century. Sales in Europe remained insignificant until after 1776. In those early years, it was mainly on the west coast of Africa that the British cotton textile industry faced very serious competition from similar goods from all parts of the world, in particular, East Indian cotton textiles. The industry's response to this competition was very important for its competitiveness from the last years of the eighteenth century onwards.[16]

Thus, as far as the British economy in the eighteenth century is concerned, the requirements for buying and transporting slaves to the Americas made an important contribution to development. No similar studies have been made for the other European countries that performed this same function in the Atlantic system. But the limited studies of Simone Berbain, Gaston Martin and Pierre Boulle, show that, at least, for Nantes, Rouen and Montpellier, the slave-merchants' demand for cheaply produced goods stimulated the growth of large-scale industry in the eighteenth century.[17] And the export of German linens to the African coast through British and other European slave-merchants was an important outlet for the textile industries of Westphalia, Saxony and Silesia.

The buying and shipping of slaves to the Americas represented just a part of the greatly expanded world trade in which the Atlantic economies participated in the period 1451-1870. It will be shown later that thus phenomenal expansion of world trade was due largely to the availability of African slave labour in the Americas. But for the moment we have to establish the relationship between this growth of world trade and the economic development of Western Europe and North America.

Between the late Middle Ages and the first half of the seventeenth century some very important internal developments occurred in West European economies, which were due to changes in some internal factors, such as population, leading to the growth of intra-European trade, particularly in raw wool, woollen products, metal products and silver, as well as interregional trade within the individual West European countries. These early developments stimulated in the different West European countries differing institutional changes, political, social and economic. Particularly in Great Britain and Holland, the changes which occurred at this time created

a hospitable environment for the evolution of a body of property rights which promoted institutional arrangements, leading to fee-simple absolute ownership in land, free labour, the protection of privately owned goods, patent laws and other encouragements to ownership of intellectual property, and a host of institutional arrangements to reduce market imperfection in product and capital markets.[18]

The main contribution of the Atlantic system to these early developments was in the supply of bullion which greatly promoted the growth of exchange in all Western Europe, thereby giving a fillip to the expansion of the market sector of West European economies. Besides this contribution, much of West European development at this early stage depended on European resources. The 'hospitable environment' created by these early developments are very important in explaining the responsiveness of West European economies to the external stimuli emanating from the growth of world trade from the second half of the seventeenth century onwards.

But, it is one thing to say that these early internal developments made West European economies responsive to external stimuli arising from the growth of the Atlantic system. It is quite another thing to say that from these early developments the institutional arrangements that evolved in Western Europe between the seventeenth and eighteenth centuries, and that great structural transformation called the Industrial Revolution which occurred in Great Britain during this period, were inevitable. The explanation for those developments is to be found in the new problems and possibilities created by the growth of world trade in the seventeenth and eighteenth centuries: the new problems of regularly carrying large quantities of goods over very long distances across turbulent seas; of processing and distributing large quantities of products imported from distant places; of accommodation in a trade system stretching to every part of the globe; the opportunities offered for developing new industries based on raw materials previously scarce and expensive, or wholly unavailable, such as sugar, tobacco, cotton, etc., and for developing new products in response to new demands and tastes; the economies of scale associated with production for a greatly extended world market – these and many other factors stimulated the institutional developments and the radical structural shifts which occurred in Western Europe at that time. They were all produced by the growth of world trade in this period. The technical developments and the technological innovations of the period were all called forth and made economic by the practical problems of production for an extended world market. It is the verdict of a British economic historian that

Colonial trade introduced to English industry the quite new possibility of exporting in great quantities manufactures other than woollen goods, to markets where there was no question of the exchange of manufactures for other manufactures. . . . The process of industrialization in England from the second quarter of the eighteenth century was to an important extent a response to colonial demands for nails, axes, firearms, buckets, coaches, clocks, saddles, handkerchiefs, buttons, cordage and a thousand other things.[19]

It was this which made possible the concentration of large-scale industrial production at all levels in the small country that England was in the seventeenth and eighteenth centuries, being peopled by less than 7 million inhabitants by the mid-eighteenth century, and by just over 8 million by 1790,[20] and with no unusual endowment of natural resources. The opportunities offered for large exports of ironwares and later of cottons 'played a vital part in the building of those industries to the point where technical change transformed their momentum of growth'.[21] For

Europe generally, and for France in particular, a French economic historian wrote:

The eighteenth century can be truly called the Atlantic stage of European economic development. Foreign trade, and especially trade with the Americas, was the most dynamic sector of the whole economy (for instance, French colonial trade increased tenfold between 1716 and 1787), and furthermore the demand from overseas was stimulating the growth of a wide range of industries as well as increased specialization and division of labour. Owing to the superiority of sea transport over land transport, the eighteenth-century European economy was organized around a number of big seaports, the most prosperous being those with the largest share in the growing colonial trade, such as Bordeaux or Nantes; each of these had, not only its own industries, but also its industrial hinterland in the river base of which it was the outlet.[22]

He further points out that if

'Americanization' of trade and industry was the most pronounced for countries which owned a colonial empire (such as Great Britain, France, Holland and Spain), its influence extended also farther to the east, to countries which had no colonies but were able to send goods to America as re-exports from the colonial powers, especially through Cadiz; so German linens, cutlery, and hardware reached the West Indian and Spanish American markets.[23]

For North America in the colonial period, it has been shown that the proportion of total economic activity devoted to production for overseas markets was relatively large at the beginning of the eighteenth century, being about one-fifth of total output, and that though that proportion declined over the century, it still remained about one-sixth in 1768-72 .[24] This was made up of shipping and other commercial services sold by the north-eastern colonies to the West Indian islands and southern Europe, export of foodstuffs, horses and lumber from the middle and north-eastern colonies to the West Indies and southern Europe, and the export of tobacco, rice and other minor crops from the southern colonies to Great Britain and other European countries. From this analysis of the colonial economy of North America, it is concluded:

While overseas trade and market activity may not have comprised the major portion of all colonial economic activity, the importance of the market was that of improving resource allocation . . . We argue that while subsistence agriculture provided an important base to colonial incomes and was a substantial part of average per capita income, changes in incomes and improvements in welfare came largely through overseas trade and other market activities. Not only did improvements in productivity occur primarily through market activity, but the pattern of settlement and production was determined by market forces. This pattern changed slowly and unevenly, spreading from the waterways and distribution centres along the Atlantic seaboard into the interior.[25]

For the period, 1790-1860, Professor D. C. North has shown that the export of raw cotton from the southern states was the most crucial factor in the growth and development of the United States economy. As the southern states concentrated all their resources on the production of raw cotton for export, they had to buy their foodstuffs from the producers in the west, and this stimulated the settlement of the west and its specialization in foodstuff production. Also, the south had to depend on the north-east for its transportation, financial and other commercial services. Incomes earned from the production of cotton for export and spent on western food and north-eastern services, provided the base for the growth of import substitution industries in the north-east. And so the north-east graduated from exporting southern cotton and supplying the south and west with imported foreign manufactures, to the domestic production of those goods for consumers in the south and west, as well as in the north-east itself, using southern cotton as part of the inputs for the new industries. It was this regional specialization based originally on the production of cotton in the south for export that made economic the establishment of large-scale industries in the United States between 1790 and 1860.[26]

It can, therefore, be concluded that economic development in Atlantic Europe and North America was critically influenced by the growth of world trade between 1500 and 1870. The next question is the extent to which the growth of world trade in this period depended on the slave trade. Since this growth depended almost entirely on the exploitation of the resources in the Americas, the question boils down to whether the exploitation of those resources would have been possible at all, or whether the scale of their exploitation would have come anywhere near to what it was, without the availability of slave labour. This is looking at the problem from the point of view of supply. Another way is to look at it from the point of view of demand and ask whether the employment of non-slave labour would not have considerably advanced the cost of production and therefore have raised the prices of the products in Europe to a level that would have considerably reduced their consumption and therefore the quantity imported into Europe. If this had happened, the level of incomes in the Americas would have been reduced, thereby reducing the volume of goods imported from Europe. The overall effect would have been a drastic reduction in the volume of world trade. All this would have depended on the price elasticity of demand in Europe for the products of the Americas.

Recent publications on the subject of slave labour show that in some cases it was either slave labour or nothing. It has been pointed out that Spain and Portugal, the possessors of the majority of the American tropical colonies, were not in a position to provide workers 'who were prepared to emigrate at any price'.[27] For the capitalistic production of sugar in the West Indies generally, it is stated that 'free labour was simply not available in sufficient quantity and what there was would not (*would* not rather than *could* not) put up with the conditions of work on a plantation so long as cheap farmland was to be had in other colonies. It was slavery or nothing.'[28] As a general statement for all the Americas outside Spanish and Portuguese America, it is argued that

Wage or indentured labour would have been forthcoming in some additional numbers at some high wage. Such wage levels would have been high owing to certain factors impeding labour movement into plantation agriculture, [so that] any attempt at sizeable increases in the production of agricultural staples under the inelastic supply patterns characterizing free and indentured labour would have advanced those labour prices substantially.[29]

Apart from the foregoing arguments, it has been shown that in the decade before the civil war southern slave farms produced 28 per cent more output per unit of input than southern free farms, and 40 per cent more than family based northern farms.[30] When this superior efficiency of slave labour over free labour is added to the very much higher labour costs that would have prevailed in the absence of slave labour, it can be easily seen why production costs, even in the areas where it was possible to obtain some additional wage or indentured labour at a high price, would have been terribly high in the absence of slave labour. As Ralph Davis has shown, the phenomenal expansion of European consumption of products imported from the Americas depended largely on the very low levels to which

their prices dropped in the course of the seventeenth and eighteenth centuries.[31] European demand for products from the Americas was therefore highly price elastic, so that a manifold increase in the prices of those products in the absence of slave labour would have greatly reduced their consumption in Europe and therefore the volume of trade based on them. Hence, taking into account the large areas in the Americas where no production at all would have taken place without slave labour, and the greatly reduced level of production and sale in areas where some wage or indentured labour would have been forthcoming at a high price, the conclusion can be drawn that the growth of world trade between 1500 and 1870 was due very largely to the availability of African slave labour supplied through the slave trade. It is important to stress that even the growth of trade between West European countries at this time depended greatly on the re-export of American products from one European country to another, and the export of European goods from one European country to another for onward trans-shipment to the Americas. Before these developments, autarchic practices by various West European nations in their efforts to encourage home industries militated against the growth of intra-European trade.[32] Even the greatly enlarged trade with the East Indies during this period still depended largely on the Atlantic system, for a large proportion of the oriental goods was re-exported to Africa and the Americas.

Economic consequences of the external slave trade from Africa

This question has just begun to receive the attention of scholars.[33] One recent attempt in this field is based on a static model derived from the classical theory of international trade. The costs and benefits of the slave trade for Africa were computed on the basis of the difference between an estimated total amount of goods that would have been produced (at the subsistence level of production) in Africa by the estimated number of all slaves that were exported and the total value of import goods received in exchange for the slaves. If the former exceeds the latter then the material welfare of Africans deteriorated as a result of the slave trade; but if the latter exceeds the former, then the material welfare of Africans improved as a result of the slave trade.[34] Apart from the conceptual weaknesses of this model, it has no power to determine the dynamic gains or losses that may be associated with the slave trade. As John H. Williams points out:

the relation of international trade to the development of new resources and productive forces is a more significant part of the explanation of the present status of nations, of incomes, prices, well-being, than is the cross-section value analysis of the classical economists, with its assumption of given quanta of productive factors, already existent and employed [with fixed technology and fixed market and productive organization].[35]

It is sometimes said that the slave trade brought from the Americas to Africa new food crops, such as manioc, sweet potato, maize, groundnuts and some others.[36] If we leave aside the controversy over the American origin of these crops, and accept that as a fact, the argument that those crops came to Africa *because* of the slave trade cannot be sustained on any ground, since these crops are said to have been introduced into West Africa 'by Portuguese traders early in the sixteenth century',[37] a period during which Portuguese slave trade in West Africa was far less important, in volume and value, than Portuguese trade in West African products, such as gold, pepper and so on.[38]

Another way of relating the slave trade positively to African economic development may be through the investment of profits made in the trade by African dealers. It is possible that after the effective abolition of the external slave trade late in the nineteenth century, profits earlier accumulated from it by some African dealers may have flowed into the development of trade in African products, such as palm oil, then in demand. This could be regarded as a positive contribution by the slave trade to African economic development. But during the 400 years or so of the slave trade before its abolition, profits from that trade added nothing in terms of capital formation to the production capacity of African economies.[39] Duke Ephraim, one of the greatest Efik traders of pre-colonial times, 'peopled the vast agricultural area of Akpabuyo to the east of Calabar with slaves purchased from the profits of his trade, not so much to produce oil or even food, but to strengthen the power of his house or ward.'[40] In general, this was how slave-trade profits were employed in the Cross River region of present-day Nigeria. It would seem, therefore,

that the economic conditions associated with the slave trade provided no demand incentives for capital formation to take place. Hence economic development in Africa was not stimulated by the slave trade. Indeed, it can be argued that institutions and habits inimical to economic development, which developed and became hardened during over 400 years of slave trade, became, in later years, great obstacles to economic transformation in Africa.

If it is so difficult to isolate any positive contribution by the slave trade to African economic development, two other propositions remain to be examined. First, we propose to show that the slave trade had an ascertainable direct negative impact on the economic development processes in Africa; secondly, that, while it lasted, it prevented the growth and development of 'normal' international trade between Africa and the rest of the world.

The first direct negative impact was its retardative or contractionary effects on African population during a period of over 400 years. This is an issue on which historians hold differing views.[41] With regard to Africa south of the Equator, there seems to be a general consensus of opinion among them that external slave trade led to an outright depopulation in the Congo-Angola region, broadly defined. As for West Africa, there is disagreement as to whether it led to an outright depopulation, but what no one seems to contend is that, at best, the population there was stationary during the period of the external slave trade – that is, the rate of population growth was equal to the rate of population loss due to that trade.

One general weakness of the existing studies of the subject is that population movements in Africa have been related only to the Atlantic slave trade. A proper understanding of African demographic processes in the period 1451-1870 requires an assessment of population losses due to the external slave trade in all its branches. Also, even in the Atlantic trade, only the numbers of slaves actually exported are considered, when it is known that the processes leading to the export of those numbers – the wars, raids and other methods of slave gathering; the long march to the coast; the 'warehousing' of slaves on the coast awaiting shipment; the long keeping of slaves in ship holds before the vessels actually departed the African coast with their full cargoes

– involved population losses that probably have been far in excess of the numbers actually exported. The most serious weakness, however, is that no effort has been made to assess, albeit roughly, the additional population the slaves exported would have produced in Africa had they been left there.

It is difficult to make such an estimate. In the first place, no data exist on birth rates and survival rates in Africa at this time. Even if they existed the data would not have reflected the effects of the slave trade on birth and survival rates through its retardative effects on economic growth and the high incidence of war. On the other hand, the Africans exported were all people in their prime of life so that the rate of reproduction among them should have been higher than that of the rest of society left behind.

One way of getting round the problem would have been to employ the reproduction rates among the Africans received in the slave-importing territories of the Americas. But this, again, poses problems. Of all the slave-receiving territories in the Americas it was only in the United States that the imported Africans achieved some rate of net natural increase during much of our period. In the other territories, the effect of a lengthy journey from Africa by sea, strange disease environment, the harsh conditions of plantation slavery, particularly on the sugar-cane plantations, etc., actually led to rates of net natural decrease among the slave populations. Since rates of net natural decrease did not operate in the African territories from which people were exported,[42] the only usable rate is that among the Africans in North America. For this territory, Professor Curtin's calculations show that about 430,000 Africans imported, largely between 1700 and 1810, produced a black population of about 4.5 million by 1863.[43]

Before this rate of reproduction can be refined to provide a rough approximation of the numbers that would have been reproduced in Africa by the people exported, some qualifications are necessary. The North American imports were concentrated in the second half of the eighteenth century so that it actually took the 430,000 imported Africans very much less than a century to produce a population of 4.5 million by 1863. By the time a large number of Africans began to arrive in North America in the second half of the eighteenth century, the first million people to leave Africa as a result of the external slave trade in all its sectors had done so for more than 100 years. On the other hand, the harsh conditions of slavery, its psychological effects on the fecundity of female slaves and the strange disease environment still reduced to some extent the rate of reproduction among the imported Africans in the United States.

On the other side of the coin, it may be argued that the mortality rate in tropical Africa during our period was higher than that of North America during the same period. If this was the case, then the survival rate among the children of Africans in North America, from about the second generation onward, would be higher than that in Africa. In addition the slaves in North America did receive some modern medical attention, however minimal the effect may have been on their health. Another consideration is the fact that the population of Afro-Americans in 1863 was produced with the input of some white fathers. It has been shown that the proportion of mulattos in the total slave population of the United States of America in 1860 was 10.4 per cent.[44]

When these two sets of opposing factors are matched it is not easy to decide the direction of the net result. To be conservative let us assume that, notwithstanding all the points made above, the reproduction rates which prevailed among the Africans imported into North America were higher than the rates that would have prevailed among the 19 million Africans exported had they been left in Africa. Let us even assume that, when all the facts stated earlier have been considered, only 50 per cent of the North American rates would have prevailed in Africa. Applying this rate to the 19 million earlier estimated, the result is that had those Africans not been exported they would have produced an additional population of at least about 99,420,000 in Africa by about 1870. This calculation does not take into account the fact that the large number of Africans who were exported several years before North American imports started would have produced proportionately far more descendants in Africa than those imported into North America produced in that territory by 1863.

It must be understood that this estimate is a very rough one. It is likely that Professor Curtin underestimated United States slave imports to a greater extent than he did for imports into other territories. If so, reproduction rates based on

Curtin's United States figures will be an exaggeration which will make our estimates somewhat too high. On the other hand, in our estimate we have not included the numbers lost in the various stages of producing the 19 million actually exported. Besides, an assessment of the demographic consequences of the external slave trade for Africa has to take into account the indirect effects as well. The unsettled conditions produced by the slave trade and its retardative effects on economic growth had adverse effects on population growth in Africa during a period of over 400 years. It is significant that, from 1500 to 1870, the growth of the African population lagged far behind that of any other continent during the same period. When the external demand for Africans as slaves was cut off in the late nineteenth century, peaceful conditions prevailed, international trade in the products of the African soil developed, the flow of goods within Africa expanded and became more regular, and general economic improvement took place. Under these conditions, population growth rates in Africa came to be among some of the highest in the world between 1900 and 1950. No one should be misled into thinking that this population growth in Africa was due to the availability of modern medicine, whose contribution was minimal, because only a tiny proportion of the total population benefited from the limited modern medical facilities that existed. 'Traditional' African medicine remained the only means of treatment for most people, and 'traditional' African midwives remained the only physicians known to most expectant mothers, as was the case during the slave-trade period. The only new elements that were significant as far as population growth was concerned, were peace and economic improvement.

Thus, however rough it may be there is no doubt that the figure we have produced is a very conservative estimate of the additional population that would have existed in Africa by 1870 in the absence of the external slave trade. It should be pointed out that the operation of the Malthusian checks could not have made it impossible to maintain this additional population since the amount of land in Africa suitable for food production completely eliminates the possibility of their operation. The inescapable conclusion to be drawn from the foregoing, therefore, is that the extremely low ratio of population to cultivable land which prevailed in Africa south of the Sahara up to the present century was the direct repercussion of the external slave trade from Africa.

This underpopulation prevented for several centuries the growth of a virile market sector in the African economies by eliminating population pressures that would have led to internal colonization, taming the forests, and greater population concentration. Internal colonization would have led to interregional differentiation of economic functions arising from climatic differences, differential natural-resource endowments, and differing population densities. The taming of the forests and greater population concentration would have led to a reduction in distribution costs by lowering costs of transportation. All this would have stimulated interregional trade and therefore the growth of production for the market and all the institutional developments associated with that growth. But because the ratio of population to land remained extremely low, population remained largely dispersed, the forests remained untamed, extensive, rather than intensive, cultivation was encouraged, and subsistence production and local self-sufficiency remained the rule. Because land was never a scarce resource no market for land developed and agriculture generally remained uncommercialized. The land-tenure system which became hardened under the conditions produced by the slave trade is one of those institutions inimical to the growth of capitalism which took root in Africa as a result of the external slave trade. In most of Africa, this system is often talked about as if it were something inherently African, without it being realized that the persistence of the system has its history in the slave trade, which prevented the growth of demand for land that would have made it a scarce and, therefore, marketable resource. The present development of a market for urban land in many African countries, following the pressure of population in the urban centres, shows clearly why a land market (urban and agricultural) failed to develop in much of Africa many years ago. In the absence of a large population, the existence of a very great and growing external demand for African products that were land-intensive in production would gradually have reduced land to a scarce and marketable resource and hence led to the commercialization of agriculture and the whole rural economy. This was what the export of raw wool and woollen cloths did for British land tenure and agriculture in the sixteenth century and after; what the export of foodstuffs to the West Indies did for the agriculture of the middle and northern colonies of North America in the seventeenth and eighteenth centuries; and what the export of cocoa is doing for the western State of Nigeria .[45] But, as we shall show later, the opportunity cost of the slave trade made impossible the growth of such an external demand during the period of that trade. Dr Hopkins suggests that, in the absence of population growth, technical innovation would have encouraged the growth of market activities by reducing production costs.[46] This is rather a case of putting the cart before the horse since, historically, the growth of market activities preceded technical innovation. This is to say that, historically, technical innovation was not an autonomous variable, having always been stimulated by demand pressures, although in its turn, it later stimulated the growth of market activities.

The other direct negative effect of the external slave trade on African economic development is associated with the general socio-economic and socio-political conditions created by the trade. Every economic activity has a way of creating such conditions which not only help to sustain its earlier levels but provide it with further momentum. This is the major idea behind Professor Rostow's 'take-off' analysis. That self-reinforcing process was crucial in sustaining the slave trade. The socio-economic and socio-political forces created by the slave trade in Africa which sustained it for several centuries, operated in the form of increased warfare based on the use of firearms and horses supplied by the European and Arab slave-merchants, the emergence of professional slave-raiders or man-hunters, the gearing of political, social and economic institutions to the needs of slave acquisition and marketing and so on. The incentives behind all these innovative activities were the increased variety of European and Oriental products available to those with slaves to sell.

The mechanism of this self-sustaining process is well elaborated by many writers on the slave trade. The account by Leo Africanus shows that the king of Bornu (Borno) at the beginning of the sixteenth century sold slaves to Barbary merchants and received horses for use in his cavalry in return. With these horses the king carried out his annual slave-raiding expeditions.[47] The horses may also have been used to acquire territorial fiefs through which tribute slaves were obtained. In fact, the important slave market of Kuka is said to have been supplied with slaves captured in government raids in the surrounding non-Muslim territories south, west and south-west of Bornu (Borno), and with tribute slaves paid by vassal princes who, in order to discharge this obligation, carried on continuous warfare against their non-Muslim neighbours.[48]

In the Atlantic sector, firearms took the place of horses, and the proliferation of firearms in the coastal and forest states was an important part of the self-reinforcing mechanism. The firearms gave steam to imperial ventures aimed at controlling the sources of slave supply. The conflict between these nascent empires over the control of slave supply on the one hand, and the need for self-defence against their activities by their victims or potential victims on the other hand, created a slave-gun circle. This is why it does not make much sense to talk of these wars as being politically motivated, for beneath what one may describe as a political motive lay what was primarily economic. This is not to say that all the wars of the slave-trade period were caused by the conditions created by the trade, nor that some non-economic motives were not also present in wars that were largely due to the slave trade. But it does mean that the self-reinforcing conditions created by the trade were responsible for much of the wars of the period. As one writer puts it:

The two-way pressures of the ocean trade – European demand for captives and African demand for European goods – worked powerfully toward the institutionalization of the system. Whether making wars in order to capture prisoners for sale or defending themselves against neighbours with similar ambitions, coastal and near-coastal rulers found firearms indispensable to their security. The firearms did much to fasten powerful rulers, as well as weak ones, into a trading system which required the sale of captives.[49]

Of central and eastern Africa it is said:

The opportunity for gaining durable material wealth from the slave trade obviously encouraged rulers to expand their possessions and increase the number of people over whom they ruled. Such expansion often took place by warfare which initially provided prisoners of war, a ready source of slaves, and subsequently provided new subjects on whom taxes could be levied in the form of men. By expanding his fief the ruler also acquired a position of being the final arbiter in judicial matters. This position brought the ruler export slaves through a manipulation of the judicial processes. Thus, for various reasons, the gains to be derived from the slave trade provided one of the sharpest incentives to imperial expansion in Central Africa.[50]

On the other hand, while the European and Arab slave merchants may not have openly encouraged inter-State wars in Africa, apart from Portuguese military activities in Angola, their willingness to loan firearms to warring groups in return for war captives may have played an important role among the African States in reaching decisions to make war or peace. For example, a European slave merchant, resident on the Guinea coast, wrote to his co-partner in Great Britain in August 1740:

We have been greatly disappointed in our trade. Ever since the Fanteens went to engage Elmena no thinking man that knew the coast could have expected otherwise; all the trading paths were stopped; nothing going forward but thieving and panyarring; had the said Fanteens become conquerors it's certain we should for our own parts have got eight hundred or one thousand slaves at pretty easy terms; but as they came back repulsed and were even forced to run away, we have suffered to be sure considerably, for I credited the headmen pretty largely to secure their interest on their return that I might have the preference of what slaves they took in the war.[51]

Earlier on this same merchant had written:

General Shampoo is encamped at the head of the River Vutta [Volta] with 20 thousand men ready to engage Dahomee King of Whydah; the said king has an army equal to the other's, encamped within two miles of each other. On the success of the former we have a large interest depending and until that battle is decided in some shape or another there are no trade to be expected. Young in the *Africa* I am loading him with a proper assortment of goods and to dispatch him with all expedition for Little Popo to attend the result of the Battle.[52]

These are not isolated cases, for similar references can be found in the works of other writers on the subject.[53]

Historians have always tried to relate the socio-political and socio-economic conditions created in Africa by the slave trade to political processes, particularly those connected with the rise and decline of States, kingdoms and empires. What has been neglected is an analysis that will explicitly relate those conditions to the process of economic development in Africa. In the matter of state formation, for instance, if the slave trade gave rise to some larger and more powerful states, one would like to know whether such states directed or took part in economic activities likely to bring about economic devel-

opment; whether they made conscious efforts to provide peaceful conditions under which private enterprise could have helped to bring about economic development; or, finally, whether they consciously made any efforts to evolve or encourage the evolution of institutional arrangements essential for economic development. If the answers to all these questions are negative, one would like to know why.

It is well known that during the period of the slave trade not only did the states whose rise may be associated with that trade fail to do any of the things specified above, but even others, like the kingdom of Benin failed to do so. The explanation is simple. The former remained largely slave-trading states and so had no political or economic incentives to develop other resources, or to encourage private enterprise to do so by providing peaceful conditions, while the other states also became largely involved in the slave trade, or in defending themselves against the activities of slave-trading states. On the other hand, the requirements of the slave trade were such that they could not stimulate any infrastructural developments in the slave-trading states. For instance, the fact that the slaves transported themselves along bush paths eliminated any possible pressure to build good roads and to encourage artisans to build 'the wheel' to facilitate the flow of trade.

From the point of view of the private sector, the chaotic conditions which the slave trade created and which helped to sustain its momentum for several centuries raised transaction costs enormously and so retarded the growth of market activities. Any reading of the European company records bears this out. In a letter to the Royal African Company in Great Britain, an official of the company resident on the African Coast wrote:

at best the Waterside Kings, and Great Cabbasheers (so called) are but poor great rogues, for when they do not disturb the traders, and are not at war with one another for a livelihood combine and lay their heads together to contrive how to abuse and cheat your honours and the Dutch West India Company.[54]

Obviously, the slave trade was not a gentleman's trade, and what the Europeans say about the African dealers, the former also say about each other, for the same writer quoted above had cause to say:

Were I to characterize the Dutch as I by experience have found them to be, I should give the same character of them, as I have herein given of the Natives of this country, for I have often seriously considered with myself whether they or the Natives here were of the most villanous, falsest temper and could never come to a resolution thereon.[55]

No doubt the Dutch and the Africans had much the same thing to say about the British.

What is more, the wars and raids of the slave trade encouraged the location of settlements

in good defensive positions and their location in relation to natural obstacles makes settlements inaccessible at the cost of ease of communications or even good building sites [and good agricultural land].[56]

This encouraged subsistence and discouraged market activities. But what is more serious, by hiding away from slave gatherers these settlements were also hiding away from the flow of modernizing ideas.

Thus, it is hard to exaggerate the consequences of the chaotic conditions created by the slave trade for African economic development. For Central and Eastern Africa, in particular, it has been shown that 'the pre-colonial economic tragedy' consists of the 'dissipation and disruption' of industrial and specialized skills developed in pre-slave-trade days, 'under the impact of violence and the slave trade'.[57]

Not only did the external slave trade retard the development of African economies through its demographic and disruptive effects, but it also prevented the growth of a 'normal' international trade between Africa and the rest of the world at a time when such trade was acting as a powerful engine of economic development in a number of territories. The loss to Africa of the developmental effects of this type of international trade represents one of the most important opportunity costs of the slave trade for African economies.

There is evidence to show that opportunities for the development of international trade in commodities capable of being produced in Africa did exist and that the foreign merchants who came to Africa in the period 1451-1870, were aware of those opportunities, and there is proof that the operation of the slave trade prevented in various ways the development of such a trade.

In the trans-Saharan sector of African international trade, transport costs prevented the development of trade in commodities with low value-to weight ratio. In fact, it is possible that the problem of finding suitable commodities with which to pay for goods coming across the

Sahara may have compelled people in the western Sudan to look for slaves as the preferred commodity. It was in the Atlantic that the first opportunity appeared to develop international trade with Africa in bulky goods.

It is important to note that all the Europeans who came to Africa following the Portuguese discovery of an ocean route to that continent were attracted in the first instance by the desire to develop trade with Africa in the products of her soil – gold, pepper, ivory, etc. – and for a time these remained the most valuable commodities in the Atlantic trade between Africa and Europe. In addition, the European merchants even acted in those early years as distributors of African products from one African region to another. Between 1633 and 1634 the Dutch alone imported about 12,641 pieces of Benin cloth into the Gold Coast, present-day Ghana .[58] Again, in 1645, a Dutch vessel brought to the Gold Coast from Ardra and Benin, 588 pieces of Ardra cloth and 1,755 pieces of Benin cloth, respectively.[59] Between 1486 and 1506 the Portuguese developed an important trade with Benin in Benin pepper.[60] The latter example clearly shows that the rulers of the coastal states took keen interest in this early trading in African products. For instance, when large-scale importation of European and oriental cotton cloths reduced demand for Benin cloth on the Gold Coast, and the Dutch, therefore, failed to buy Benin cloth as they did previously, the king of Benin protested and forced them to take at least 1,700 pieces a year.[61]

Apart from gold, pepper, ivory and some other minor products, the European merchants, quite early in their contact with Africa, were aware of the possibilities of producing in Africa a wide range of products for which there was a demand in Europe. The records of the European companies that traded with Africa are full of correspondence from their officials on the African coast relating to such possibilities. For example, in July 1708, the governor of the Royal African Company resident on the coast, wrote to the Company:

The ground of this country is as fertile as any ground in the West Indies, taking places according as they lye nearer or farther from the sea, but the natives are such scothful sordid wretches, and so given to stealing from one another rather than labour that little or nothing is made of it . . .[62]

The governor recommended that the company should establish a settlement at Fetue on the Gold Coast, which 'will be an inlet to all manner of Plantations'. The success of such company-owned plantations would encourage people to apply to the company 'to come and settle here upon such terms as you may think convenient to permit to settle on'. The company's plantations were to contain corn, sugar cane, indigo, cotton and cattle. The governor refers to the Dutch 'laying out ground on the River Butteroe near their fort there' for the development of a sugar-cane plantation, 'for to make sugar and rum here they have lately sent to Whydah for two hundred slaves, and they expect by their next shipping all sorts of materials for their making sugar and rum . . .'[63]

Later in the eighteenth century, when the Royal African Company's slave trade became increasingly unprofitable due to long credits and bad debts in the West Indies, the company made some frantic efforts to develop trade in African products, not only with the coastal States but also with States in the far interior. In March 1722 the company wrote to its officials on the coast:

We have already in divers letters acquainted you with our thoughts concerning the carrying on of our trade, and as the negroe branch of it grows every day less and less profitable it is from the article of the home returns we see our chief advantage must arise .[64]

From then on, the company endeavoured to make its officials on the coast open up trade with Africa along these lines. It suggested a number of ways of doing so, from the development of company plantations and encouraging Africans on the coast to cultivate sugar cane, cotton, indigo, tobacco and other crops, to the questioning of slaves brought from the interior about the opportunities for opening up trade with them in the products of the soil. It was even suggested by the company's officials on the coast that 'from the notion we have of the Whydah natives industry', the cotton grown on the company's plantations and by the Africans could be sent to Whydah and

be worked up there into assortments proper for the West Indies and as you have encouragement or profit by that branch of trade your honours slaving vessels will be capable of taking on board such quantities as you shall please to direct from hence to be wrought up at Whydah.[65]

Thus, from the available records, it is clear that not only were the European merchants

aware of the possibilities of developing trade with Africa in the products of the African soil, but also they made some efforts to develop such trade. However, they all tended to see the trade in African products as subordinate to the slave trade, which they were unwilling to give up in favour of devoting full attention to the development of trade in the products of the soil. Hence, the zeal and enthusiasm with which late nineteenth- and twentieth-century European merchants encouraged the development of trade in the products of the African soil through trial and error were completely lacking in the slave-trade period.

The explanation for the European merchants' attitude is that the development of trade in products of the African soil would have been a slow process compared with the development of trade in commodities produced in the Americas with African slave labour, and such development would have required a mass withdrawal of factors from the exploitation of the American resources and the shipping and marketing of the output. In other words, the exploitation of the American resources was making a very heavy demand on the same production factors that were needed for the development of African resources. But as long as African slave labour was available, production factors from Europe could be more profitably employed in the exploitation of American resources than in the development of trade in the products of the African soil.

This was so because the employment of African slaves by European planters to produce tropical products in Africa on the scale that prevailed in the Americas would have been very costly in terms of resistance by African governments, the ease with which the slaves employed in Africa could escape from their white masters (possibly with the connivance of African governments), and, most seriously, in terms of mortality among whites in Africa at a time when tropical medicine was unknown to Europeans. The most likely method would have been through co-operation between the European merchants and African rulers to encourage African peoples to cultivate the crops in demand, as was done in the late nineteenth and twentieth centuries. But this method would definitely have been slow in producing a trade on the scale then prevailing in commodities being produced in the Americas with African slave labour.

In this circumstance, so long as African slave labour was available, the Americas remained far more attractive to European production factors. The buying and shipping of the slaves to the Americas, the exploitation of the American resources, and the shipping and marketing of the American commodities internationally, absorbed so many production factors from Europe and Africa that little or nothing was left for the development of trade in the products of the African soil. That development was further hampered by the unsettled conditions which attended the acquisition of captives for sale as slaves.

But the important point is that the advantages of the Americas depended very largely on African slave labour. If there had been no slave trade from Africa to the Americas, the advantage would have been on the side of encouraging Africans to produce a wide range of commodities in Africa for an international market. From the evidence before us, it is clear that this is what would have happened. But the conditions which prevailed under the slave trade made that trade more profitable both to a majority of the European merchants and to the African rulers and entrepreneurs whose talents would have been required for the production and marketing of these commodities in Africa. Consequently, African products imported into Europe during the slave-trade period remained those which required very little entrepreneurship and little or no capital investment to produce – ivory, gum, palm oil, redwood, etc. – being all commodities that were either hunted or gathered from wild trees.

Some European governments fully realized that the development of international trade in the products of the African soil would mean a mass withdrawal of production factors from the exploitation of the American resources. Since they saw this as conflicting directly with what they thought to be their own true interests [66] they did all they could to discourage such development. Thus following the recommendation in 1708 to the Royal African Company by the company's governor in Africa to encourage the cultivation of sugar cane, tobacco, cotton and indigo in Africa, a bill was introduced into the British Parliament to prohibit the cultivation of those crops on the Gold Coast.[67]

Again, in the 1750s, when the officials of the Company of Merchants Trading to Africa tried to encourage the cultivation of some of the American crops in Africa, the British Board of Trade quickly summoned the members of the company's ruling committee and told them,

That the introducing of culture and Industry amongst the Negroes was contrary to the known established policy of this trade. That there was no saying where this might stop and that it might extend to tobacco, sugar & every other commodity which we now take from our colonies, and thereby the Africans who now support themselves by war would become planters & their slaves be employed in the culture of these articles in Africa which they are now employed in America. That our possessions in America were firmly secured to us, whereas those in Africa were more open to the invasions of an enemy, and besides that in Africa we were only tenants in the soil which we held at the good will of the natives.[68]

The members of the company's committee were therefore ordered to ask their officials on the coast to put an end to this type of activity. Thus, in order to ensure that Africa provided a regular supply of slaves required for the exploitation of American resources, the British Government through the Board of Trade had to discourage the development of African economies. In a letter to the British Treasury in April 1812, about five years after the slave trade had been abolished in Great Britain, the Committee of the Company of Merchants Trading to Africa summed up the whole matter thus:

It is a lamentable but certain fact, that Africa has hitherto been sacrificed to our West India colonies. Her commerce has been confined to a trade which seemed to preclude all advancement in civilization. Her cultivators have been sold to labour on lands not their own, while all endeavours to promote cultivation and improvement in agriculture have been discouraged by the Government of this country, lest her products should interfere with those of our more favoured colonies.[69]

Conclusion

In conclusion, it is clear that the phenomenal expansion of world trade between 1451 and 1870, depended largely on the employment of African slaves in the exploitation of American resources, and that the development and growth of West European and North American economies during this period were greatly influenced by the expanded world trade. This leads to the inference that the slave trade was a critical factor in the development of West European and North American economies in the period of this study. The benefits of the Atlantic system to Latin America and the West Indies generally were minimal, due to the type of economic functions performed, the large amount of 'foreign factors of production' employed and some other reasons. But, the clear losers in the growth of the Atlantic system, and woefully so, were the African economies. The demographic and disruptive effects of a trade which required the forceful capture and sale of human beings retarded the development of market activities and the evolution of institutional arrangements essential for the growth of capitalism. What is more, the operation of the slave trade prevented in various ways the growth of a 'normal' international trade between Africa and the rest of the world. From the evidence presented above, it is clear that, without the supply of African slave labour to the Americas, European merchants and governments would have been compelled by purely economic considerations to encourage the production of a wide range of commodities, including some of the American commodities, in Africa. This would have meant that the growth of world trade in the period under review would have been very much slower, and hence the rate of development in Western Europe and North America. But the History of Africa would have been entirely different. The level of economic and social development would not have been the same in all the regions of Africa, south of the Sahara. But all of them would have been far richer, the regions poorly endowed with resources benefiting from the development of the better endowed ones through trade and other contacts. In the final analysis, it can be said that the Atlantic economies that developed between 1451 and 1870, did so at the expense of the African economies.

Notes

1. I am grateful to Professor Michael Crowder of the Centre for Cultural Studies, University of Lagos, Professor R. J. Gavin of the Department of History, Ahmadu Bello University, Zaria, and Dr E. J. Usoro of the Department of Economics, University of Ibadan, for reading through the first draft of this paper and making helpful criticisms and suggestions. They are, however, not responsible for any errors there may be in the paper.
2. It is not easy to assess the contribution of slavery to the Middle East economies.
3. A great deal of the literature centres round Eric Williams' *Capitalism and Slavery*. A Seminar held at the Centre of African Studies, University of Edinburgh, on 4-5 June 1965, dealt with the issues of abolition raised by Eric Williams. The proceedings of the seminar have appeared under the title *The Trans-Atlantic Slave Trade from West Africa*, University of Edinburgh, Centre of African Studies, 1965. Some of the papers are of particular interest: Roger Anstey, 'Capitalism and Slavery-A Critique'; John Hargreaves, 'Synopsis of a Critique of Eric Williams' *Capitalism and Slavery'*; C. Duncan Rise, 'Critique of the Eric Williams Thesis: "The Anti- Slavery Interest and the Sugar Duties, 1841-1853" '; Christopher Fyfe, 'A Historiographical Survey of the Transatlantic Slave Trade from West Africa'. The latter is a useful survey of the literature and the type of study available on the slave trade. Also to be noted are, Roger T. Anstey, 'Capitalism and Slavery: A Critique', *Econ. Hist. Rev.*, Vol. XXI, 1968, p. 307-20; Roger T. Anstey, *The Atlantic Slave Trade and British Abolition, 1760-1810*, London, Macmillan, 1975.

Some of the literature on the private profitability of the slave trade antedated Eric Williams' book: James Wallace, *A General and Descriptive History of the Ancient and Present State of the Town of Liverpool*, Liverpool, R. Phillips, 1795; Gomer Williams, *History of the Liverpool Privateers and Letters of Marque with an Account of the Liverpool Slave Trade*, London, W. Heinemann, 1897; S. Dumbell, 'The Profits of the Guinea Trade', *Economic History* (Supplement to *Economic Journal*), Vol. 11, January 1931. But since the publication of Eric Williams' book the literature on this aspect of the slave trade has grown enormously. Some of the more important works include: F. E. Hyde, B. B. Parkinson and S. Marriner, 'The Nature and Profitability of the Liverpool Slave Trade', *Econ. Hist. Rev.*, Vol. V, No. 3, 1953; K. G. Davies, 'Essays in Bibliography and Criticism XLIV. Empire and Capital, *Econ. Hist. Rey.*, 2nd Ser., Vol. XII 1960-61, p. 105-10; R. B. Sheridan, 'The Wealth of Jamaica in the Eighteenth Century', *Econ. Hist. Rev.*, 2nd Ser., Vol. XVIII, August 1965; Robert Paul Thomas, 'The Sugar Colonies of the Old Empire: Profit or loss for Great Britain?', *Econ. Hist. Rev.*, 2nd Ser., Vol. XXI, April 1968; R. B. Sheridan, 'The Wealth of Jamaica in the Eighteenth Century: A Rejoinder', *Econ. Hist. Rev.*, 2nd Ser., Vol. XXI, April 1968; Stanley L. Engerman, 'The Slave Trade and British Capital Formation in the Eighteenth Century: Comment on the Williams Thesis', *The Business History Review, Vol. XLVI*, No. 4, Winter 1972, p. 430-3; Roger T. Anstey, 'The Volume and Profitability of the British Slave Trade, 1761-1807', in Stanley L. Engerman and Eugene D. Genovese (eds.), *Race and Slavery in the Western Hemisphere: Quantitative Studies*, Princeton University Press, 1975; David Richardson, 'Profitability in the Bristol-Liverpool Slave Trade' (paper read at the VIth International Congress of Economic History, Copenhagen, 19-23 August 1974).

See Stanley L. Engerman, 'The Effects of Slavery upon the Southern Economy: A Review of the Recent Debate', *Explorations in Entrepreneurial History*, Vol. 4, 1967; R. W. Fogel and S. L. Engerman, *Time on the Cross : The Economics of American Negro Slavery*, London, Wildwood House, 1974; Stanley L. Engerman, 'Comments on the Study of Race and Slavery', in Engerman and Genovese (eds.), *Race and Slavery*, p. 495-526.

K. Onwuka Dike, *Trade and Politics in the Niger Delta, 1830-1885: An Introduction to the Economic and Political History of Nigeria*, Oxford University Press, 1956; A. Akinjogbin, *Dahomey and its Neighbours, 1708-1818*, Cambridge University Press, 1967; K. Y. Daaku, *Trade and Politics on the Gold Coast 1600-1720*, Oxford University Press, 1970; Walter Rodney, A *History of the Upper Guinea Coast 1545-1800*, Oxford University Press, 1970; A. J. H. Latham, *Old Calabar 1600-1891: The Impact of the International Economy upon a Traditional Society*, Oxford, Clarendon Press, 1973; M. D. Kilson,'West African Society and the Atlantic Slave Trade, 1441-1865', in N. I. Huggins, M. Kilson and D. M. Fox (eds.), *Key Issues in the Afro-American Experience*, Vol. 1, New York, 1971 ; David Birmingham, *Trade and Conflict in Angola: The Mbundu and their Neighbours under the Influence of the Portuguese, 1483-1790*, Oxford University Press, 1966; Phyllis Martin, *The External Trade of the Loango Coast 1576-1860*, Oxford Clarendon Press 1972; Edward A. Alpers, *Ivory and Slaves in East Central Africa: Changing Patterns of International Trade to the Later Nineteenth Century*, London, Heinemann, 1975.

4. See John H. Williams, 'The Theory of International Trade Reconsidered', in Lord Keynes, Joan Robinson, *et al.* (eds.), *Readings in the Theory of International Trade*, p. 253-71, London, 1950, where this distinction is clearly made.

5. P. D. Curtin, *The Atlantic Slave Trade: A Census*, Madison, Wis., University of Wisconsin Press, 1969.

6. J. E. Inikori, 'Measuring the Atlantic Slave Trade: An Assessment of Curtin and Anstey', *Journal of African History*, Vol. XVII, No. 2 (1976); D. Eltis,'The Direction and Fluctuation of the Trans-Atlantic Slave Trade 1821-43: A Revision of the 1845 Parliamentary Paper' (paper presented at the Mathematical Social Science Board Seminar on the Economics of the Slave Trade, Colby College, Waterville, Maine, 20-22 August 1975); Roger Anstey, *The Atlantic Slave Trade and British Abolition 1760-1810*, London, Macmillan, 1975.

7. Ralph A. Austen, 'A Census of the Trans-Saharan Slave Trade, or approximating the uncountable' (paper presented at the Mathematical Social Science Board Seminar on the Economics of the Slave Trade, Colby College, Waterville, Maine, 20-22 August 1975).

8. This view was expressed by some of the participants at the Colby College Seminar.

9. C. S. Nicholls, *The Swahili Coast: Politics, Diplomacy and Trade on the East African Littoral 1798-1856*, London, Allen & Unwin 1971.

10. Jonathan Levin emphasized the proportion of total income from export production, which is remitted abroad by'migrated factors' of production, as one of the important determinants of the magnitude of the contribution of export production to internal development processes in export economies. Consequently, he applied the term, 'foreign factors of production', only to those factors which remit their income abroad. Conversely, he applied the term, 'domestic factors of production', to 'those factors which spend their income within the economy in which it is earned, for consumation, investment, imports, or any other purpose'. See Jonathan V. Levin, 'The Export Economies', in James D. Theberge (ed.), *The Economics of Trade and Development*, p. 17-18. New York, London, Wiley, 1968. In the case of Latin America, remittances (especially bullion remittances) to imperial governments in Europe form parts of factors' remittance abroad.

11. J. E. Inikori, 'English Trade to Guinea: A Study in the Impact of Foreign Trade on the English Economy, 1750-1807'. (Ph.D. thesis, University of Ibadan, 1973.)

12. In some aspects, the credit requirements of the British slave trade are similar to those required today by the trading of capital goods internationally.

13. Inikori, 'English Trade to Guinea', op. cit., Chap. VII.

14. Inikori, 'English Trade to Guinea, op. cit., p. 234-41 ; J. E. Inikori, ' Measuring the Atlantic Slave Trade'.

15. Inikori, 'English Trade to Guinea', op. cit., Chap. IV.

16. See Inikori, 'English Trade to Guinea', op. cit., Chap. IV, for more details.

17. Simone Berbain, 'Études sur la Traite des Noirs au Golfe du Guinée: Le Comptoir Français de Juda (Ouidah) au XVIIIe Siècle', *Memoires de l'Institut Français d'Afrique Noire*, No. 3, 1942, p. 85-6; Gaston Martin, *Nantes au XVIII^l, Siècle: l'Ere des Negriers, 1714-1774*, Paris, 1931; Pierre M. Boulle, 'Slave Trade, Commercial Organisation and Industrial Growth in Eighteenth Century Nantes', *Revue Française d'Histoire d'Outre-Mer, Vol. LIX*, No. 214, 1st quarter, 1972.

18. Douglas C. North and Robert Paul Thomas, *The Rise of the Western World: A New Economic History*, p. 18. Cambridge University Press, 1973.

19. Ralph Davis,'English Foreign Trade, 1700-1774', *Economic History Review*, 2nd ser., Vol. XV, 1962, p. 290.

20. Phyllis Deane and W. A. Cole, *British Economic Growth, 1688-1959*, 2nd ed. Table 2, p. 6, Cambridge University Press, 1967.

21. Ralph Davis, *The Rise of the English Shipping Industry in the Seventeenth and Eighteenth Centuries*, p. 393, London, Macmillan, 1962.

22. François Crouzet, 'Wars, Blockade, and Economic Change in Europe, 1792-1815', *Journal of Economic History*, Vol. XXIV, No. 4, December 1964, p. 568.

23. Crouzet, op. cit., p. 569.

24. James F. Shepherd and Gray M. Walton, *Shipping, Maritime Trade, and the Economic Development of Colonial North America*, p. 44, Cambridge, Cambridge University Press, 1972.

25. Shepherd and Walton, op. cit., p. 25.
26. D. C. North, *The Economic Growth of the United States, 1700-1860*, Englewood Cliffs, N.J., Prentice-Hall, *1961*.
27. Henry A. Gemery and Jan S. Hogendorn, 'The Atlantic Slave Trade: A Tentative Economic Model', *Journal of African History*, Vol. XV, No. 2, 1974, p. 229, quoting C. Padro, Jr, *The Colonial Background of Modern Brazil*, p. 19, Berkeley, Calif., University of California Press, 1967.
28. K. G. Davies,'Empire and Capital', p. 107.
29. Gemery and Hogendorn, op. cit., p. 229-3 1. For some other aspects of the slave-labour issue, see Robert P. Thomas and Richard N. Bean,'The Adoption of Slave Labour in British America' (paper presented to the Mathematical Social Science Board Seminar at Colby College, Waterville, Maine, 20-22 August 1975.
30. Robert W. Fogel and Stanley L. Engerman, *Time on the Cross: The Economics of American Negro Slavery*, p. 192, London, Wildwood House, 1974.
31. Ralph Davis, *A Commercial Revolution, English Overseas Trade in the Seventeenth and Eighteenth Centuries*, p. 10, London, Historical Association, 1967. Professor Davis shows that the large reduction in the prices of the products brought them within the reach of more consumers and made them 'near-necessities rather than luxuries'.
32. For the points made here, See W. E. Minchinton (ed.), *The Growth of English Overseas Trade in the 17th and 18th centuries*, London, Methuen, 1969, Chapters 2 and 3 by Ralph Davis on English foreign trade, 1660-1774, and Chapter 5, by H. E. S. Fisher, on Anglo-Portuguese Trade, 1700-70. See also Allan Christelow, 'Great Britain and the Trades from Cadiz and Lisbon to Spanish America and Brazil, 1759 1783', *Hispanic American History Review*, Vol. XXVIII, No. 1, February, 1948, Part *2;* and Jean O. McLachlan, *Trade and Peace with Old Spain 1667-1750*, Cambridge, Cambridge University Press, 1940.
33. Walter Rodney, *How Europe Underdeveloped Africa*, p. 103-12, London and Dar es Salaam, Bogle-L'Ouverture Publications, 1972; Henry A. Gemery and Jan S. Hogendorn, 'The Economic Costs of West African Participation in the Atlantic Slave Trade: A Preliminary Sampling for the Eighteenth Century' (paper presented to the Mathematical Social Science Board Seminar at Colby College, Waterville, Maine, 20-22 August 1975); H. A. Gemery and J. S. Hogendorn, 'Technological Change, Slavery, and the Slave Trade', forthcoming in C. J. Dewey and A. G. Hopkins (eds.), *Studies in the Economic History of India and Africa*, London, Athlone Press, in press; A. G. Hopkins, *An Economic History of West Africa*, London, Longman, 1973.
34. Gemery and Hogendorn, 'The Economic Costs of West African Participation in the Atlantic Slave Trade'.
35. Williams, op. cit., p. 255.
36. Gemery and Hogendorn, 'Technological Change, Slavery, and the Slave Trade'.
37. Ibid.
38. John W. Blake, *European Beginnings in West Africa, 1454-1578*, p. 23, London, Longman, 1937.
39. It is said that the plantation economy of Zanzibar and Pemba developed in the 1820s following restrictions imposed by the British on the slave trade of the Swahili coast. Thereafter profits from the slave trade contributed to the expansion of those plantations: Nicholls, *The Swahili Coast*, p. 203.
40. A. J. H. Latham, 'Currency, Credit and Capitalism on the Cross River in the Pre-Colonial Era', *Journal of African History*, Vol. X11, No. 4, 1971, p. 604.
41. J. D. Fage, 'Slavery and the Slave Trade in the Context of West African History', *Journal of African History*, Vol. X, No. 3, 1969; Peter Morton-Williams, 'The Oyo Yoruba and the Atlantic Trade, 1670-1830', *Journal of the Historical Society of Nigeria*, Vol. III, No. 1, December 1964; Michael Mason, 'Population Density and "Slave Raiding" – the Case of the Middle Belt of Nigeria', *Journal of African History*, Vol. X, No. 4, 1969; M. B. Gleave and R. M. Prothero, 'Population Density and "Slave Raiding"-A Comment', *Journal* of *African History*, Vol. XII, No. 2, 1971; Roger T. Anstey, *The Atlantic Slave Trade*, p. 58-88.
42. If that had been the case those territories could not have sustained the slave trade for over 400 years.
43. P. D. Curtin, 'The Slave Trade and the Atlantic Basin: Intercontinental Perspectives', in N. 1. Huggins, M. Kilson and D. M. Fox (eds.), *Key Issues in the Afro-American Experience*, p. 39-53, Vol. 1, New York, 1971.
44. Fogel and Engerman, *Time on the Cross*, p. 132. The factor of slave breeding is dismissed by the authors as an erroneous idea disseminated by the anti-slavery movement. In fact, they argue that if slave-breeding methods were adopted by the slave holders the effects on reproduction rates would have been negative due to the psychological effects they would have had on the female slaves. See Fogel and Engerman, op. cit., p. 78-86.
45. Sara S. Berry, *Cocoa, Custom, and Socio-Economic Change in Rural Western Nigeria*, Oxford, Clarendon Press, 1975.
46. Hopkins, op. cit., p. 77.
47. Allan G. B. Fisher and Humphrey J. Fisher, *Slavery and Muslim Society in Africa: The Institution in Saharan and Sudanic Africa and the Trans-Saharan Trade*, p. 59, London, C. Hurst, 1970.
48. Fisher and Fisher, op. cit., p. 160.
49. Basil Davidson, 'Slaves or Captives? Some Notes on Fantasy and Fact', in Huggins, Kilson and Fox (eds.), op. cit., p. 69.
50. J. R. Gray and D. Birmingham, 'Some Economic and Political Consequences of Trade in Central and Eastern Africa in the Pre-Colonial Period', in J. R. Gray and D. Birmingham (eds.), *Pre-Colonial African Trade: Essays on Trade in Central and Eastern Africa before 1900*, p. 18-19, London, 1970.
51. C.103/130: 'Captain George Hamilton to Thomas Hall', Annamaboe, 3 August 1740.

52. Ibid., 24 December 1738.
53. K. Y. Daaku cites two cases among British slave-merchants in 1689 and 1706, respectively: K. Y. Daaku, *Trade and Politics*, op. cit., p. 30.
54. C. 113/274 Part 4, folios 275-6. The letter is un-dated, but it should be early eighteenth century.
55. Ibid., folios 277-8.
56. Peter Morton-Williams, 'The Oyo Yoruba', p. 27; See Mason, op. cit., and Gleave and Prothero, op. cit., for a discussion of this subject in connection with the Middle Belt of Nigeria.
57. Gray and Birmingham, 'Some Economic and Political Consequences of Trade in Central and Eastern Africa', p. 12.
58. Daaku, *Trade and Politics*, op. cit., p. 24.
59. J. K. Fynn, *Asante and Its Neighbours 1700-1807*, p. 11, London, Longman, 1971.
60. Blake, *European Beginnings*, op. cit., p. 84.
61. Fynn, *Asante and Its Neighbours*, op. cit., p. 12.
62. C.113/273: Part 1, Sir Dalby Thomas to the Royal African Company, Cape Coast Castle, 30 July 1708, folios 17-18. What this statement shows clearly is the absence of opportunities for the gainful employ-ment of available resources.
63. Ibid., folios, 27-9.
64. C. 113/272 Part 2, folio 235: 'Court of Assistants to James Phipps and Others', African House, London 13 March 1721-22.
65. C. 113/274 Part 3, folios 216-17: 'Cape Coast Castle to Royal African Company', 2 July 1722.
66. The thinking of these governments was that the Americas belonged to them as colonies while Africa did not. Therefore, while they could control the ex-ploitation of resources in the Americas they were not in a position to do the same in Africa.
67. T.70/5 folio 64: Abstract of Sir Dalby Thomas' letter to the Royal African Company, 29 November 1709.
68. C.O.391/60, p. 66-71: 'Minutes of the Board of Trade Meeting of Friday, 14 February 1752.'
69. T.70/73, p. 139-40: 'The Committee of the Company of Merchants Trading to Africa to the Treasury, 9 April 1812.'

23

Silver and Situados: New Spain and the Financing of the Spanish Empire in the Caribbean in the Eighteenth Century

CARLOS MARICHAL and MATILDE SOUTO MANTECÓN

The transfer of royal silver and gold from the American viceroyalties to the Spanish metropolis has long been judged by historians to constitute one of the key measures of the costs of empire for the Spanish American territories. It may be argued, however, that such a focus underestimates the total costs of empire and does not allow for a full understanding of the importance of the intra-American transfers of funds from royal treasuries (*reales cajas*) with financial surpluses to those with perennial deficits. It is the principal purpose of this essay to demonstrate that the maintenance of the Spanish civil and military administration in the Caribbean depended, during the eighteenth century, on large and rising transfers of silver from the royal treasuries of New Spain. These transfers bespeak the highly complex nature of the financial integration of the empire and reflect the fiscal interdependence of its different parts.

Over the last decade, major progress has been made in the historical reconstruction of the finances of the Spanish Empire in the eighteenth century. The laborus of a diverse cohort of scholars from Spain, the United States, Canada, and Latin America have illuminated the vast and complex nature of the fiscal structure of the Spanish monarchy both in the metropolis and in its overseas possessions, particularly in the Americas.[1] Such research has laid the groundwork for a deeper understanding of the common dynamics of financial administration over the extremely extensive and multiethnic mosaic of territories under Spanish rule. It has also provided the quantitative data for the detailed study of income and expenditure in most parts of the American empire.

The statistical series of the *real hacienda* of New Spain (and especially that of the *real caja* of Veracruz) published by Herbert Klein and John Jay TePaske make possible a year-by-year reconstruction and analysis of the financial transfers from the viceroyalty to the metropolis and to different parts of the American empire.[2] We have complemented this data with additional archival information on the situados from New Spain, among the most important of which were financial remittances initiated at the end of the sixteenth century for the support of military and administrative bastions in the Caribbean.[3]

The study of these situados reveals the existence of a dense network of intra-imperial financial transfers. It also demonstrates that the remittances sent by the royal treasury of New Spain during the eighteenth century to the Caribbean military posts tended to **surpass** the value of the royal silver transferred annually to the metropolis. The Viceroyalty of New Spain thus not only provided important sums of precious metals for the Spanish metropolitan state but also financed the bulk of the empire's defenses in the greater Caribbean.

This essay offers an estimate of the total overseas remittances by the royal treasury of New

Spain, followed by a comparison of remittances to the Iberian peninsula between 1720 and 1800 with those sent on account for the *situados ultramarinos*.[4] Then it presents an analysis of the specific problems associated with the financial transfers by the royal treasury at Veracruz to the greater Caribbean for the sustenance of the civil and military administrations in Cuba, Santo Domingo, Puerto Rico, Florida, Louisiana, and several secondary military outposts.[5] Finally, it demonstrates the importance of the financial transfers in times of international war, and particularly the huge contribution of the royal treasury of New Spain to cover the costs of the military operations conducted by the Spanish crown against Great Britain in the greater Caribbean, including Louisiana and Florida, during the years 1779 to 1783, at the time of the American war of independence.

Fiscal Surplus and Overseas Remittances from New Spain in the Eighteenth Century

New Spain traditionally distinguished itself as a viceroyalty that enjoyed regular annual surpluses in what we could call the consolidated accounts of the royal treasury.[6] Such a situation contrasted to that of other territories in the Spanish Empire, such as Cuba, Puerto Rico, Santo Domingo, or the Philippines, which – over centuries – were unable to produce sufficient internal fiscal resources to meet the total civil and military costs of their own administration. To cover their considerable and regular deficits, those territories were obliged to rely on remittances of silver from other parts of the empire, most particularly from New Spain.[7]

During the eight decades from 1720 to 1800, the remittances by the royal treasury of New Spain both to Castile and to the greater Caribbean showed a sustained increase (in current values). Before 1740 these surplus funds – which were concentrated at Veracruz, whence they were sent abroad – did not usually exceed a combined total of two million pesos per annum. Subsequently, however, they rose systematically, especially as a result of the outbreak of wars, which impelled a surge of financial demands for the defense of the Spanish Empire.

Figures 23.1, 23.2, and 23.3 indicate certain peaks in the royal remittances from New Spain that correspond clearly to the war periods: the Seven Years War (1756-1763), the war against Great Britain (1779-1783), and the war against the French Convention (1793-1795). It was, logically enough, during these periods that the military, and therefore also the financial, demands of the metropolis and the empire as a whole intensified, although they became especially marked in the last two decades of the eighteenth century. By that time, the remittances abroad by the royal treasury from Veracruz were equivalent to approximately 40 per cent of the viceroyalty's total annual silver production – a

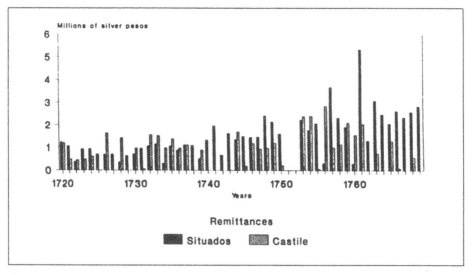

Figure 23.1: Royal Remittances from New Spain to Caribbean Situados and Castile, 1720-1769
Source: Klein and TePaske, *Ingresos y egresos.*

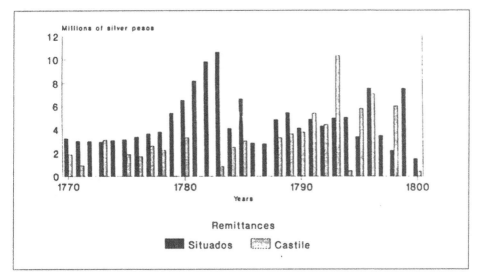

Figure 23.2: Royal Remittances from New Spain to Caribbean Situados and Castile, 1770-1800
Source: Klein and TePaske, *Ingresos y egresos.*

clear indication of the state's enormous weight on the economy.

The decennial totals of silver exported are impressive from any point of view. In the decade 1770-79, the royal treasury exported 4.8 million pesos; in 1780-89 the figure rose to 7.8 million; and in 1790-99 it reached the extraordinary level of 9.0 million. Never in the history of New Spain (or, for that matter, Spanish America) had so great a volume of monetary resources been extracted to assist in the defense and survival of the empire as a whole.

Insofar as the overseas remittances of precious metals and coin on account of the royal treasury represented a "unilateral" contribution of New Spain to the empire, it can be argued that the analysis of these series provides one particularly good indicator of the costs of the colonial relationship for Bourbon Mexico – a factor that has been suggested previously by John Coatsworth, among other historians.[8] During each successive decade a huge volume of royal silver left the viceroyalty with a remarkably low degree of recompense.[9] Furthermore, the export

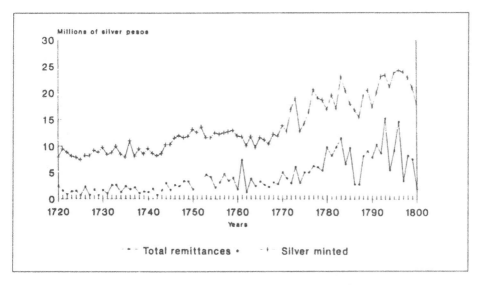

Figure 23.3: Royal Remittances and Silver Minted, New Spain, 1720-1800

Table 23.1   Growth of various Cajas of New Spain

	Caja of Mexico	Caja of Veracruz	Caja of Guanajuato	Remittances to Castile	Remittances to situados	Total remittances
1720–29	14	4	20	17	16	15
1730–39	18	4	29	20	19	20
1740–49	24	12	41	19	33	24
1750–59	30	5	33	28	42	39
1760–69	31	10	34	15	52	34
1770–79	41	11	60	33	73	54
1780–89	63	53	72	44	130	86
1790–99	100	100	100	100	100	100

Sources: Klein, "La economía de la Nueva España, 1680–1809"; Klein and TePaske, *Ingresos y egresos*; Humboldt, *Ensayo político sobre el reino de la Nueva España.*

of such a large volume of coin implied a major drain not only on New Spain's monetary system but also on its working capital.[10]

It is indeed remarkable that throughout most of the eighteenth century the rising volume of overseas remittances did not provoke substantial deficits for the royal treasury of New Spain. Evidently, the growth of fiscal income raised in the viceroyalty was sufficient to meet both the increase in internal expenses and the overseas financial demands. Thus, although the rise in overseas remittances by the royal treasury proved fairly constant throughout the eighteenth century (see figure 23.3), it was matched by a parallel increase in ordinary tax income until the 1780s, and later by a combination of taxes and a large volume of loans and forced contributions. These became necessary supplements to fulfil the extraordinary financial requirements of the crown as it became involved in ever more costly international wars.[11]

In an innovative and suggestive study on the fiscal boom experienced by New Spain in the eighteenth century, Herbert Klein has constructed a series of indexes that measure the growth of the income of the various regional *cajas reales* of the viceroyalty.[12] We have compared those with indexes of the expansion of the remittances to the Caribbean situados and Castile (see table 23.1). Such a comparison indicates that the growth rates of the overseas transfers followed quite closely those of fiscal income. This pattern is particularly evident in the data on income of the caja de México (which concentrated the bulk of total revenues of the

viceroyalty) and the data on total overseas remittances.[13]

While the figures on global income of the main cajas certainly help discern the general trends of the fiscal revenues, they do not sufficiently explain the economic resources that permitted the large remittances to the Caribbean and to Spain. For this purpose we have carried out a simple exercise: comparing remittances with silver mint production in New Spain (see appendix, table A).[14] The analysis of both series clearly indicates the increasing proportion of overseas remittances as a per centage of total silver minted: in the period 1720-1750, the average was slightly under 20 per cent; in the two decades 1750-1770, approximately 27 per cent; in the 1770s, 30 per cent; and in the last two decades of the century, the extraordinary figure of 40 per cent of total silver minted was exported by the royal treasury of New Spain alone (see table 23.2).[15]

In sum, the close correlation between silver production and overseas remittances by the royal treasury of New Spain suggests that future research must delve even deeper into the crucial silver-mining sector, so as to evaluate in detail the dynamics of an economic sector that – despite signs of crisis – continued to be a veritable fountain of monetary riches. These riches, however, apparently did not contribute to the viceregal economy as much as would be expected, because of the royal treasury's increasing extraction of silver from circulation for export.

Table 23.2   Annual Average by Decade of Remittances from the *Real Caja* of Veracruz
and Silver Production in New Spain, in pesos

	Remittances to Castile	Remittances to situados	Total remittances	Silver minted
1720–29	899,181	758,412	1,387,839	8,392,218
1730–39	1,053,294	85,363	1,833,328	9,052,963
1740–49	1,037,145	1,587,247	2,209,534	10,257,122
1750–59	1,521,875	1,767,234	3,510,012	12,574,809
1760–69	792,261	2,490,556	3,124,365	11,288,730
1770–79	1,793,828	3,453,880	4,888,942	16,457,011
1780–89	2,365,150	6,170,565	7,826,170	18,742,871
1790–99	5,396,817	4,748,523	9,065,976	22,118,065

Sources: Klein and TePaske, *Ingresos y egresos*; Humboldt, *Ensayo político sobre el reino de la Nueva España.*

Remittances to Spain: The Surges of the 1750s, 1770s, and 1790s

The comparison of the viceroyalty's remittances to Spain with those sent to the various colonial administrations in the Caribbean yields several observations. First, while remittances to the Caribbean situados tended to grow more steadily and rapidly through most of the century than remittances to Spain, shipments of royal silver to the metropolis were especially voluminous in the decades of the 1750s, 1770s, and 1790s. In the early decades of the century (1720s to 1750s), Mexican royal silver's contribution to the metropolitan fiscal regime was probably important but relatively limited in scope; during this 30-year period, transfers to Castile did not ordinarily surpass one million pesos per year. In the 1750s, by contrast, average remittances rose to nearly two million pesos a year, a trend that roughly coincides with data published by Jacques A. Barbier in an important article on the income received by the Depositaría de Indias in Cádiz during the last decade of the reign of Ferdinand VI.[16]

After the Seven Years' War, royal remittances from New Spain to Spain declined markedly, a short-term trend that may be attributed essentially to the huge expansion of expenditures to reinforce the defensive infrastructure in the greater Caribbean. But by the 1770s, shipments of royal silver to Cádiz returned to the levels of the 1750s (almost two million pesos per year). This new tendency contradicts the general argument advanced by Barbier, who suggests that the

regime of Carlos III was less efficient than that of Ferdinand VI in extracting revenue from the American empire.[17]

Another significant observation derived from the specific analysis of the royal remittances is that in the 1780s and 1790s the bulk of American revenues received by the metropolitan treasury came from New Spain. According to various authors, in the last 15 years of the eighteenth century approximately 20 per cent of total income registered by the Tesoreria General in Madrid can be attributed to American silver shipments.[18] However, if the analysis is limited to the remittances from New Spain in the years 1784-1793 (the last, long phase of fiscal prosperity for the empire), it can be estimated that Mexican silver **alone** accounted for 18 per cent of the total revenues of the Tesorería General.[19] These figures tend to reinforce the observations of Klein and Barbier on the importance of American remittances for the metropolitan fiscal system in the last years of the eighteenth century, but they magnify the role of New Spain within the structure of imperial finance.[20]

From 1793 on, the relative importance of American silver apparently fell in relation to total metropolitan income. But the story has an interesting twist. While ordinary income became less important, extraordinary revenues (that is, debt income) skyrocketed. Both the external and internal debt of the Spanish crown became the principal base of support to cover rapidly growing military expenditures and deficits. And once again, silver from New Spain was the linchpin of much of the new financial policy. All contracts for foreign loans taken by the Spanish government in Amsterdam, for example, specified payment in Mexican silver. Thus, as soon as news spread of ships arriving at Cadiz from Veracruz, Dutch bankers would demand shipment of the precious metal to Holland for debt service.[21]

Mexican silver was equally significant for Spain's internal debt. As most authors who have dealt with this topic have indicated, the fundamental instrument of this debt was the issue of *vales reales* (begun in 1781), and the receipt of American silver was the determining factor in the *vales*' fluctuating market value. News of the arrival of important shipments of silver at Cádiz repeatedly spurred a recovery of the *vales,* which became the favourite instrument of extraordinary finance in the latter years of the reign of Carlos III and that of Carlos IV.[22]

Remittances to the Caribbean: Sustained Growth

While historians generally recognize the importance of New Spain to metropolitan finance in the final decades of the eighteenth century, they have paid less attention to the crucial significance of the viceroyalty's financial contribution to the maintenance of the American empire itself, particularly in the greater Caribbean. Our analysis of these remittances (situados) in figures 23.1 and 23.2 shows that from 1720 to 1790, such shipments of royal silver grew more rapidly and systematically than those to the Iberian peninsula. The data also, however, reveal certain observable swings in the remittances of both categories, alternating in strength and time span.

During a period of almost two decades, 1720 to 1739, the contribution of royal silver from New Spain to the situados in the Caribbean remained fairly stable at somewhat under one million pesos a year, similar to the level of remittances to Spain proper (see table 23.2). But after the outbreak of the conflict with Great Britain known as the War of Jenkins' Ear, military expenditures tended to expand; this can be observed in the increase in situado payments, whose annual average surpassed 1.5 million pesos in the 1740s while transfers to the metropolis remained stable.

The situado remittances remained at the same levels during the 1750s, but that was when ship-

ments to Spain tended to increase more rapidly. Once again, after the intensification of hostilities with Great Britain (which climaxed in the occupation of Havana in 1762), military requirements in the Caribbean intensified and spurred a new and much stronger trend of silver shipments from Veracruz to the region's key Spanish military garrisons. Average annual remittances from Veracruz rose from approximately 2.5 million pesos in the 1760s to 3.5 million in the 1770s and an extraordinary 8 million in the early 1780s. Subsequently, Caribbean shipments declined somewhat (to approximately 4 million pesos a year), while remittances to the metropolis rose enormously, particularly from 1788 to 1796.

The phase of most rapid increase in the situado payments (1760-1782) clearly corresponds to the period when the Bourbon regime made its most formidable effort to strengthen its defenses throughout the greater Caribbean – not only in terms of fortifications and naval squadrons but also with local infantry. In addition, Mexican silver helped pay for a great number of powerful battleships built in the Havana shipyards – and supported the royal tobacco monopolies in Cuba and Louisiana. While it is still too early to evaluate the particular importance of the situado payments to the overall defense of the Caribbean or to the income of the region's territories – Cuba, Puerto Rico, Santo Domingo, Trinidad, Louisiana, and Florida – the large volume of silver sent suggests that New Spain became, in effect, the area's financial bulwark of imperial defense. But to grasp the nature and complexity of the transactions between the royal treasury of New Spain and the Caribbean colonial administrations, it would seem useful to continue our exploration by commenting on the specific destination of the silver sent for the situados.[23]

Origins and Strategic Objectives of the Situados in the Greater Caribbean

The remittance of royal silver from New Spain to support military defenses in the Caribbean was an old mechanism of imperial finance, although its significance increased enormously in the eighteenth century. During the reign of Philip II, precisely when the basic legislation governing commerce and navigation in the empire was ratified, the practice of situado finance became institutionalized and came to constitute a regular part of the *real hacienda* throughout the Americas. It is not surprising that the bulk of the situados were financial transfers to key ports on the major naval routes or, alternatively, to the most important frontier posts of the empire.

The principal providers of situados were the royal treasuries of New Spain and of Peru, although they were not the only ones. A lesser but still significant role in this regard was exercised by the treasuries of Tierra Firme and Caracas. In 1584 the crown ordered New Spain to send financial support to Cuba, Santo Domingo, Puerto Rico, and Florida, and from this time on the port of Havana was the key redistributing point for the situados in the greater Caribbean.[24]

The tendency for the greater part of the situados to go to the Caribbean possessions of the crown is not strange, for it was there that – because of ocean currents and winds – virtually all European-American trade converged, making the Spanish-controlled Caribbean ports the critical nodes of the famous *flotas* on their annual transatlantic journeys. Because foreign shipping (particularly British, French, Dutch, and Danish) also used the same sea routes, the Spanish authorities found it necessary to create a defense system based on the protection of the most vulnerable and strategic ports and channels of passage, and it was there that the major fortifications and garrisons were established.[25]

The costs that such a defense system entailed could not be covered by the Caribbean provinces, and as a result, the crown made recourse to remittances from the more prosperous American possessions – a tendency that was progressively accentuated as military expenses rose during the seventeenth and eighteenth centuries. Thus it became established practice that the Viceroyalty of New Spain would send large annual sums of royal funds to help pay for garrisons and fortifications throughout the greater Caribbean as well as in the Gulf of Mexico. Furthermore, New Spain was charged with the financial support of the Armada de Barlovento, whose task was to protect the main Caribbean sea lanes used by Spanish shipping.[26]

The main predators along these routes were pirates and privateers of different European nationalities, and their numbers increased throughout the seventeenth century. The eighteenth century, by contrast, witnessed an increase in regular naval squadrons, particularly those of Great Britain and France, which eliminated most of the pirates but at the same time represented a new and more serious threat to the Spanish colonies. The occupation of Havana in 1762 by British forces threw Spanish imperial administrators into a state of shock; it also forced the adoption of a much more systematic policy to strengthen fortifications and military garrisons throughout the Americas and especially in the Caribbean. As military expenditures in the region rose steeply, the demand for financial subsidies intensified and, logically enough, situado payments from New Spain increased substantially, as noted in the trends visible in figures 23.1 and 23.2.

Specific Expenses Covered by the Situados

The growing military expenditures included the salaries of troops and officers (infantry and artillery) stationed in the different garrisons and the costs of maintaining the fortifications in the principal ports. The strategic importance of the situados in sustaining the naval lifeline of the empire in the Caribbean and the Gulf of Mexico can be judged by their contribution to the extremely costly reinforcement of the great fortifications of Havana, San Juan, and Veracruz, particularly during the second half of the eighteenth century.[27] It is worth emphasizing that the 70 battleships and frigates built in Havana between 1723 and the end of the century were among the key contributions to the resurgence of the Spanish armada by midcentury – although in total force the armada remained somewhat less powerful than those of France and Great Britain.[28] Most of these ships were financed with the royal remittances from New Spain, but the armada also received some private contributions. In the 1780s, two of the largest battleships, the *Regla* and the *Mexicano* (each with 114 cannon) were built in Havana shipyards with million-peso contributions from New Spain's wealthiest silver miners.

During the reign of Carlos III, a considerable portion of the situados were also used to reinforce fixed garrisons, composed mostly of infantry, in the principal Caribbean ports. New regulations were ratified at the same time that the size and number of local units (both regular troops and militia) increased, provoking a parallel rise in expenditures for salaries, provisions, and equipment. In addition, throughout the century various military expeditions were sent from Spain to the Caribbean to strengthen local forces, and this required the dispatch of extraordinary situados from New Spain on various occasions.[29]

Although the situados were employed principally to cover costs of the defensive apparatus of the empire, this was not their only function. From an early date the funds remitted were also used to support religious missions involved in subduing and indoctrinating Indian tribes, both in northern New Spain and in different parts of the greater Caribbean.[30] The situados not infrequently were utilized to provide salaries of civil functionaries and clergy.[31] Occasionally they also helped finance certain specific colonization projects, such as in Santo Domingo, where a considerable number of families from the Canary Islands were transferred with support from the royal treasury; and in Trinidad, when the Spanish government decided to promote agricultural development there.[32]

The importance of those situados not directly related to imperial defense increased during the eighteenth century especially as a result of the Bourbon policy of promoting the expansion of the royal tobacco monopoly. With the increasing control established by the crown over the production and sale of tobacco throughout the empire, orders were dispatched to New Spain for the allocation of a fixed annual sum of the situados to be sent to the royal treasury in Cuba to assist in the large volume of annual payments due to local tobacco farmers. In 1723 the sum allocated for Havana was two hundred thousand pesos; but by 1744 the figure had risen to five hundred thousand pesos per year, at a time when the amount destined for the military garrison of that city was but four hundred thousand pesos.[33] Both the tobacco and the military remittances were ratified in 1768 and continued to be sent annually from New Spain until the beginning of the nineteenth century. (Additional military remittances made the total situados much higher, as will be discussed below.)

The significance of the tobacco situado is emphasized in the classic study by Ramón de la Sagra, who points out the strategic importance of the Mexican silver transfers in greasing the wheels of the royal tobacco monopoly, probably the largest state enterprise in the eighteenth-century world.[34] According to de la Sagra, approximately 200 million pesos' worth of tobacco leaf was shipped from Cuba to the metropolitan tobacco factories between 1750 and 1800. This enormous quantity certainly suggests the crucial importance of the situados of New Spain not only for tobacco production in Cuba but also for the fiscal prosperity of the metropolitan treasury.[35]

Geographic Distribution of the Situados

The increase in volume of the situados during the eighteenth century was of such considerable significance that the distinguished Cuban historian Julio Le Riverend Brusone has called this period the "golden age of the situados."[36] Nevertheless, an analysis of the growth in the overall volume of silver shipments from New Spain to the Caribbean does not provide an adequate idea of the geographical distribution of the funds and their varying impact once they reached their different destinations. As previously indicated, the bulk of the situados were normally sent in ships of the armada from Veracruz to Havana and from there distributed to other points in the greater Caribbean, although some royal silver transfers were sent via other routes.

The sum of situados assigned to each different territory or port was, generally speaking, a function of its strategic importance, and was calculated on the basis of military needs on both land and sea.[37] Although the remittance of fixed annual sums to each destination was ratified by particular royal orders, the actual sums sent varied considerably from year to year, depending on a variety of factors (see table 23.3). Among the strictly military factors involved was total troop strength. Besides normal fluctuations in the garrisons because of death or desertion, important changes occurred in the number of soldiers and officers with the outbreak or conclusion of military conflicts in the region. Likewise, the numbers in naval squadrons could change dramatically as a result of battles or storms; the loss of a large number of ships inevitably led to extraordinary expenditures.

Fiscal factors also help explain the variation in remittances. Liquidity problems in the royal treasury of New Spain and adjustments in the accounting methods could result in substantial decreases in the sums sent, while accumulation of surplus income could increase the situados.[38]

Table 23.3   Estimated average annual amounts of Situados to the Caribbean, in pesos

	1750–59	1760–69	1770–79	1780–89	1790–99
Havana	1,400,000	1,900,000	1,900,000	5,219,000	2,674,000
Santo Domingo	170,993	—	274,892	—	347,813
Puerto Rico	82,819	253,465	—	376,896	376,896
Cumaná	41,360	41,360	41,360	(a)	(a)
Trinidad	—	—	—	186,519	—
Louisiana	(b)	150,000	150,000	315,000	577,695
Pensacola	28,461	(c)	(c)	(c)	47,126
San Agustín, Florida	57,399	(c)	(c)	66,666	151,031

ᵃ Under Caracas jurisdiction
ᵇ Under French rule
ᶜ Under British rule

Sources: For Havana, see text, notes 38–40. For remaining situados, estimates based on the following primary sources: AGN, Archivo Histórico de Hacienda, leg. 395, e. 7; leg. 537, e. 5; leg. 573, e. 5; leg. 1210, e. 1 and 2. For 1758 and 1791: Libros manuales; Correspondencia de Virreyes, 1a. serie, v. 183, e. 616, f. 89–90; Historia, v. 569, 570, 571; Reales Cédulas Originales, v. 83, e. 126, v. 87, e. 45, v. 86, e. 155, f. 331, v. 90, e. 133, f. 227. Secondary sources: Arcila Forías, *Comercio entre México y Venezuela*; Fonseca y Urrutia, *Historia general de la real hacienda*; Glascock, "New Spain and the War"; Humboldt, *Ensayo político sobre la isla de Cuba*; Klein and TePaske, *Ingresos y egresos*; Lewis, "New Spain During the American Revolution"; Maniau, *Compendio*; Marchena, "Financiación militar y situados"; De la Sagra, *Historia económico-política*; Velázquez, "El siglo XVIII."

The way the situados were sent could make a difference in the sums registered. Frequently, the total amount of the specific situado was sent not in one shipment but in smaller quantities in various ships, so as to reduce the risk of loss from storms or pirates. Yet despite the variations this traditionally would imply, during the eighteenth century the transfers became more regular, as the royal functionaries complied quite strictly with the transmittal of the annual sums designated.

Although it is difficult to find detailed and complete information on the exact amounts of the situados sent to each point in the Caribbean in each year of the eighteenth century, it is possible to make estimates by using a variety of sources that allow observation of the major variations, decade by decade, from the 1750s on. The data from these sources, which do not include remittances to Havana, are presented in table 23.3. The sums sent to Havana, however, were by far the most important – and they are also the most difficult to estimate. Because the royal treasury in Havana was only the first depository of most of the situados sent to the greater Caribbean from Veracruz, the available information on the total remittances to Cuba is much greater than information on the final distribution. This makes it difficult to determine how much was actually disbursed on the island or, alternatively, how much went to other points.

Throughout the eighteenth century, the Havana situado comprised three principal categories: *tierra*, *marina*, and *tabaco*. The first two were essentially defense expenditures. The first royal order we have found that refers to the ordinary annual situado to Havana is that of August 2, 1744, establishing that five hundred thousand pesos should be sent from New Spain to cover the annual expenses of Cuba's royal treasury officers in the acquisition of the tobacco harvest.[39] During the 1750s, additional archival sources indicate, the situado for infantry in Havana was four hundred thousand pesos a year and for naval affairs five hundred thousand pesos.[40]

After the British invasion and occupation of Havana in 1762, during which local shipyards and forts were seriously damaged, royal officers stationed in Cuba called for increased financial assistance. Thus, in 1765, orders were made on the treasuries of New Spain to send three hundred thousand pesos for the fortifications in Havana and one hundred thousand pesos for those in Santiago de Cuba. Three years later, the situado to Havana was increased substantially, reaching 1.9 million pesos, of which seven hundred thousand was intended for naval purposes, four hundred thousand for troops, three hundred thousand for fortifications, and five hundred thousand for the tobacco harvest.[41] Nevertheless, the annual sums remitted frequently varied, especially in cases of extraordinary expenditures .[42]

In the mid-1780s, the funds sent from New Spain for Cuban defense expenditures remained at the same levels as in previous decades, while those involving fortifications decreased substantially. But the analysis of the total ordinary Havana situado for this period is complicated because the estimates offered by the various available sources differ considerably. The classic eighteenth-century administrative experts, Fonseca and Urrutia, calculated the average annual value of this situado at 1,285,000 pesos between 1785 and 1789 (without including the tobacco subsidy); whereas their equally expert colleague, Joaquín Maniau y Torquemada, proposed a figure of 2,674,213 pesos as the average between 1788 and 1792. On the other hand, the accounting book of the royal treasury of Veracruz for the year 1791 gives a total of 1,050,000 pesos, but omits the category of naval expenses .[43] Finally, a comparison of the annual series offered by Alexander von Humboldt (1812), de la Sagra (1831), and, more recently, Klein and TePaske (1989) reveals somewhat diverse (although relatively close) estimates of the total .[44] More considerable differences are found in comparing the extraordinary sums registered at times of war in the Caribbean, particularly the 1760s, early 1780s, and 1790s. Evidently, more extensive research is required to provide a detailed breakdown of the geographical and functional distribution of the total situados as depicted in figures 23.1 and 23.2.

To provide an idea of the complexities involved in analyzing the remittances in times of military conflicts, it would seem useful to comment briefly on the remittances from New Spain during the war of 1779-1783, when the situados reached their highest peak.

The War Against Great Britain, 1779-1783

Both the French and the Spanish monarchies took advantage of the war of independence of Great Britain's 13 North American colonies to launch their own offensive simultaneously in Europe and the Caribbean. The central objectives of Spain's military campaigns in the latter region were the reconquest of Florida; the reinforcement of Spanish positions in Louisiana, mainly along the southern Mississippi River;

and the capture of British positions in the Bahamas, Jamaica, and Honduras.[45] The costs of the war required enormously increased expenditures by all the Spanish military forces in the Caribbean, but particularly those in Havana, where the bulk of the troops and ships were concentrated. As a result, the crown made large demands on the treasuries of New Spain to provide huge sums that far surpassed the standard levels of the situados. So great were these expenditures that by the early 1780s they exceeded the capacity of New Spain's tax structure to provide funds, and thus obliged the viceroy to call for a series of forced and voluntary loans from all sectors of the Mexican population.[46]

Space does not permit a detailed account here of all the remittances sent by order of Viceroy Martín de Mayorga from New Spain to Havana, but the volume of financial support and other types of assistance sent from Veracruz – including provisions and manpower – was extraordinary.[47] As Melvin Glascock suggests, during the war years of 1779 to 1783 New Spain " was virtually the sole support of Spanish arms in the Americas . . . and made for the mother country and her allies a contribution unmatched in the history of colonial Spanish America."[48]

The estimates by Glascock and by James A. Lewis of such huge shipments of silver from Veracruz to Havana during the war are similar, although they use different sources. Lewis indicates that some 34 million silver pesos were sent as situados to the Caribbean during the military conflict, while Glascock asserts that these remittances reached 37 million pesos in the same five years.[49] Remarkably, these figures agree almost exactly with those in the treasury summaries of Veracruz published by Klein and TePaske: the total amount registered as leaving Veracruz for Havana between 1779 and 1783 is 37.8 million pesos.

The contribution that these remittances represented for the overall war effort of the Spanish crown can be judged only indirectly, but their critical importance is clear. At 20 reales vellón to each silver peso, it can be estimated that New Spain sustained the crown's military effort in the Caribbean with a financial subsidy of more than 750 million reales vellón, an extraordinary sum for the period, considering that it was equivalent to almost twice the total ordinary annual defense expenditures of the metropolitan treasury at Madrid.[50]

A difficult problem is finding out exactly how these monies were spent, since only one portion remained in Cuba while the rest was distributed throughout the greater Caribbean. It is known that most of the funds went to support three major defense expenditures: the expeditionary army, commanded by Bernardo Gálvez, which was headquartered in Havana but which operated in Florida and Louisiana; the armada, under Admiral José Solano, which carried out various naval operations against the British throughout the greater Caribbean; and the military garrisons in Cuba itself, headed by Captain General Juan Manuel Cacigal and including Spanish, Cuban, and Mexican troops. While quite a number of historical studies have analyzed aspects of the military campaigns undertaken by these forces, few refer to the precise disbursement of funds.[51]

The financial documentation generated by the war is abundant, but relatively dispersed and sometimes contradictory. The information found, for example, in the Correspondencia de Virreyes in the Mexican archives includes the confidential reports of Viceroy Mayorga of New Spain to the crown's minister of the Indies, José de Gálvez, on the silver remittances sent to Havana on Spanish warships. Significantly, however, the viceroy complained that the functionaries rarely acknowledged receipt of the shipments, and that therefore he had insufficient information on disbursements in Cuba; he even went so far as to suggest to Gálvez that he believed important sums were used for illicit purposes. The intendant of Havana, José Iguano de Gaviria, had written to Gálvez arguing that insufficient funds had been sent from Veracruz to cover large military expenditures in Cuba. But in October 1781, Viceroy Mayorga informed Gálvez that he had sent large sums to Havana that year, and that therefore the intendant's complaints were unjustified. The funds included 12 million silver pesos, 1.5 million pesos in provisions (flour and biscuits, ham, bacon, salted meat, powder, and other commodities), and a force of 1,913 Mexicans who were to be employed by the Spanish naval squadrons operating out of Cuba.[52]

That New Spain was expected not only to send funds and supplies but also to evaluate the scale of the financial effort required to sustain the war in the Caribbean is confirmed by the viceroy's correspondence with a variety of func-tionaries. In October 1782, the chief treasury officer (*fiscal de la real hacienda*) of New Spain informed Mayorga that he had constructed a provisional estimate of war expenditures in the previous year and was using it to calculate future disbursements. On the basis of the correspondence between Admiral Solano, General Bernardo Gálvez, and Intendant Pedro Antonio de Cosío of New Spain, it is possible to calculate that the armada operating out of Havana had absorbed 5.6 million pesos, whereas the expeditionary army and the Cuban garrisons required an additional 7 million pesos.[53] Moreover, Cosío noted that all these funds had been sent punctually to Havana on various warships, adding that this surpassed all previous expectations of the financial resources that could be obtained in New Spain for this costly war.

Despite the assurances from Mexico, Minister José de Gálvez remained profoundly concerned that the military expenses might not be covered when the war reached its climax. He therefore dispatched a high-ranking commissioner, Francisco de Saavedra (later minister of finance under Charles IV), to supervise and expedite the remittances from Veracruz to Havana and to coordinate the provision of additional funds and supplies to the allied French fleet in the Caribbean. Perhaps to vindicate his reputation, in a letter to Gálvez in September 1782, Viceroy Mayorga made a point of recalling that when Saavedra had arrived with royal orders to remit ten million pesos for the war, everyone had thought this impossible; nevertheless, the order had been fulfilled, as one warship after another left Veracruz carrying silver for Havana. The first to depart was the battleship *San Francisco de Assis*, which carried Saavedra himself plus one million pesos. A few days later another ship followed, bearing two million pesos. Subsequently, the *San Agustín* took more than four million pesos to Cuba, and the *San Francisco de Assis*, on a second journey, boarded another two million pesos. Mayorga argued that this effort constituted "an increase never before seen in shipments of silver on account of the royal treasury" and added that this had been possible in part because of his success in raising a combination of forced and voluntary loans from all sectors of the population of the viceroyalty.[54]

Although the transfer of silver was New Spain's most valuable contribution to the war waged against Great Britain in the Caribbean, the viceroyalty also sent food provisions for the troops and other war supplies. The latter included large amounts of gunpowder from the royal powder factory in Mexico City, which supplied not only Havana but also troops at New Orleans, Campeche, El Carmen, Tabasco, and El Guarico. Copper sheets for ship repairs and cargoes of lead also were sent from Veracruz. Among the food provisions (for which yearly lists exist), flour, dried vegetables, and ham were the most important. The amount of flour (almost all from the region of Atlixco-Puebla) was considerable, totaling 39,834 *tercios* to Havana between 1779 and 1783.[55]

The provisions and supplies sent out from Veracruz also supported the several thousand troops operating out of Mobile and Pensacola, who successfully carried out the reconquest of Florida. In addition, a considerable portion of the soldiers and sailors who participated in the diverse battles were Mexican: as of 1780, a total of almost two thousand seamen had been sent from Veracruz to reinforce the naval squadrons at Havana; in 1782, three thousand men of the crown regiment from Mexico City and one thousand troops of the Puebla regiment were incorporated into the infantry in Cuba, Louisiana, and Florida. Furthermore, between one and two thousand Mexican convicts were sent out to fulfil their sentences of forced labour in Cuban shipyards and fortresses.[56]

Finally, apart from covering strictly military expenditures, the remittances of Mexican silver to Cuba also were used to cover an important part of the Spanish government's international debt. A total of three million pesos was paid at Havana between 1781 and 1783 to the agents of the Franco-Spanish syndicate of bankers headed by Francisco de Cabarrús. This official was instrumental in the establishment of the Banco de San Carlos (1782), the bank charged with handling the new Spanish internal debt (*vales reales*) and with the service of the external debt, held mostly in Amsterdam. The Mexican silver constituted repayment for loans advanced to the Madrid administration to guarantee the successful issue of the *vales reales* and to launch this first great Spanish bank.

In summary, it is clear that during the war years of 1779 to 1783, the great economic contributions of New Spain were of strategic impor-

tance to imperial policy for not only military but also financial reasons. In this respect, our data tend to suggest a need to broaden the argument offered by Pedro Tedde with respect to the success of the administration of Carlos III in meeting rising expenditures in the 1780s without risking bankruptcy, as was the case in those years in neighbouring France. Tedde suggests that this financial success obtained from the crown's ability to cover steeply rising public expenditures by intelligent handling of its debt policy.[57]

Our analysis indicates, however, that this argument tends to leave New Spain largely out of the picture – and without the viceroyalty it is impossible to understand the course of imperial finance during the military confrontation with Great Britain. In reality, the bulk of the American war expenses were covered not with Spanish funds but by Mexican silver. Furthermore, both during the war and, even more so, after the conclusion of hostilities, the remittances of silver to the metropolis proved to be essential pillars of the relatively successful debt policies of the administration of Carlos III.

Conclusions

Our historical review of the situados sent from New Spain during the eighteenth century provokes a series of general observations. First, our study indicates that while the situados to the greater Caribbean were a traditional element of imperial Spanish-American finance, it was in the eighteenth century that they acquired a central importance. By the end of that period it was clear that New Spain was playing a much larger role than the metropolis itself in supporting the American empire.

This initial conclusion suggests the need for future studies on the role of intra-American financial transactions as one of the fundamental factors in the comprehension of imperial economics. In other words, it is plainly insufficient to deal with remittances from America to Spain without simultaneously analyzing the volume and trajectories of capital flows from one American colony to another. Thus to comprehend the multilayered, multitiered structure of imperial finance requires a study of the complex web of fiscal transfers that bound the different royal treasuries together in America as well as in Spain.

A second observation has to do with evaluating the dramatic increase in absolute values of the situados during the eighteenth century. The spectacle of New Spain's phenomenal effort in covering both the expenditures in the greater Caribbean and the rising demand for funds by the metropolis signifies the colonial government's ability to extract a growing volume of ordinary tax income as well as extraordinary revenues from the population of the viceroyalty. Indeed, by the end of the century, it is possible to argue, the treasury of Mexico City rivaled the General Treasury of Madrid in tax revenues, making New Spain the unquestioned financial jewel of Spain's American empire. If this is truly the case, however, it provides all the more reason for further research into the much-debated question of the nature of the Bourbon fiscal reforms in the viceroyalty and, in particular, their long-term impact on the local economy and society.

Finally, our study suggests that the financial and commercial relations between New Spain and different parts of the Spanish greater Caribbean should be the subject of deeper analysis – breaking with the traditional historiography that tends to look at the Mexican experience in an overly ingrown way, and instead placing that experience in the context of a financial, commercial, political, and military dynamic that had much broader geographic frontiers. Certainly, during the eighteenth century, New Spain became the financial bulwark of the greater part of the military and administrative structure of the Spanish Empire in the Caribbean.

We have emphasized the key role of Havana as receptor of the royal funds sent from Veracruz and as redistributor of Mexican silver throughout the region. In this regard, three "subzones" of the Caribbean need more analysis: the subzone known as Barlovento, which included Cuba, Puerto Rico, Santo Domingo, and the lesser Antilles; the Venezuelan coast and part of the coast of Nueva Granada, which received occasional silver transfers; and Louisiana and Florida, both of which acquired extraordinary importance in the 1780s relative to imperial financial transactions originating in New Spain. In sum, to reconstruct the multiple trajectories of royal silver shipments from Veracruz is to learn that a new and much wider outlook is needed to understand the structure and dynamics of the Spanish Empire in the Americas in its final century.

Notes

1. See Herbert Klein and John Jay TePaske, *Ingresos y egresos de la real hacienda de, Nueva España*, 2 vols. (Mexico City-: Instituto Nacional de Antropologia e Historia, 1987-1989). See also Klein and Jacques A. Barbier, 'Revolutionary Wars and Public Finances: The Madrid Treasury, 1784-1807," *Journal of Economic History* 41:2- (1981), 315-39. Additional works by TePaske: "The Financial Disintegration of the Royal Government of Mexico During the Epoch of Independence, 1791-1821," in *The Independence of Mexico and the Creation of the New Nation*, ed. Jaime E. Rodriguez O. (Los Angeles: Univ. of California Press, 1989), 63-84: TePaske, José Hernández Palomo, and Mari Luz Hernández Palomo, *La real hacienda de Nueva España: la real caja de Mexico, 1576-1816* (Mexico City: Colección Científica INAH, 1976). See also Barbier, "Peninsular Finance and Colonial Trade: The Dilemma of Charles IV's Spain," *Journal of Latin American Studies* 12:1 (1980), 21-37; Barbier and Klein, "Las prioridades de un virrey ilustrado: el gasto público bajo el reinado de Carlos III," *Revista de Historia Economica* 3:3 (1986), 473-96; Alvaro Jara and John Jay TePaske, *The Royal Treasuries of the Spanish Empire in America* (Durham: Duke Univ. Press, 1982); José P. Merino Navarro, "La hacienda de Carlos IV," *Hacienda Pública Española* 69 (1981), 131-81; Javier Cuenca, "Ingresos netos del estado español, 1788-1820," *Hacienda Pública Española* 49 (1981), 183-208; Miguel Artola, *La hacienda del antiguo régimen* (Madrid, Alianza, 1982); Eduardo Arcila Farías, *Libros de la real hacienda en la ultima década del siglo, XVI* (Caracas: Banco Central de Venezuela, 1983); idem, *El primer libro de la hacienda pública colonial de Venezuela, 1529-1538* (Caracas: Instituto de Investigaciones Históricas, Univ. Central de Venezuela, 1979).

2. To determine the levels of remittances on account of the royal treasury from New Spain to Spain and to the American situados, we used the series from the *real caja* of Vera cruz, which we consider the most complete sources of information. We used the data of the *cartas cuenta* in the Archivo General de Indias for Veracruz, published in Klein and TePaske, *Ingresos y egresos*. But first we compared these data with those registered in various volumes of the *Libro manual de cargo y data de la Real Caja de Veracruz* (hereafter *Libro manual*), which we located in the Caja Matriz, Archivo General de la Nación, Mexico City (hereafter AGN). Those data almost perfectly match the preceding source.

3. Although the term *situado* means salary or rent paid or remitted, in the Spanish Empire it was used specifically to refer to the remittance or transfer of royal funds from one caja of the royal treasury to another

to cover expenses of strategic importance. For the early eighteenth-century definition, see *Diccionario de la lengua castellana* in its first edition of *1739*, known as "Autoridades." A later definition: "Llevaban este nombre [situados] las cantidades que anualmente se remitían desde las cajas reales de América a otras provincias, para suplir con su importe la falta de los productos de sus rentas y atender al pago de las obligaciones del erario en ellas." José Canga Argüelles, *Diccionario de hacienda* (Madrid: imprenta de Marcelino Calero, 1833 [reprint, Madrid: Instituto de Estudios Fiscales, 1968]), 2:509.

4. The few discrepancies between our data and those summarized in John Jay TePaske's pioneering essay on situados are explained mainly by the difference that under situados, TePaske has not included "Armada de Barlovento" and " 1 percent de Armada de Barlovento." Moreover, we have not included the data on supposed remittances *(remisibles)* to Castile for the years 1786 and 1799 that TePaske does, because we have not found sufficient evidence to confirm that these were the exact sums sent in either year. See TePaske, "La política española en el Caribe durante los siglos XVII y XVIII," in *La influencia de España en el Caribe, la Florida, y la Luisiana (1500-1800)*, ed. Antonio Acosta and Juan Marchena Fernández (Madrid: Instituto de Cooperación Iberoamericana, 1983), 61-87.

5. Among the few, important studies that deal with the problems related to the financing of the situados are John Jay TePaske, "New World Silver, Castile, and the Philippines, 1590-1800," in *Precious Metals in the Later Medieval and Early Modern Worlds*, ed. J. F. Richards (Durham: Carolina Academic Press, 1983), 425-45; Juan Marchena Fernández, "La financiación militar en Indias: introducción a su estudio," *Anuario de Estudios Americanos* 36 (1979), 93-110; and idem, "Financiación militar y situados," in *Temas de historia militar*, Ponencias del 2. Congreso de Historia Militar (celebrado en Zaragoza, 1988) (Madrid: Servicio de Publicaciones del EME, Colección Adalid, 1988) 1:263-307.

6. The Klein and TePaske series in *Ingresos y egresos* does not provide consolidated accounts of all *23 reales cajas* of the Viceroyalty of New Spain in the eighteenth century, but the accounts of the two most important cajas, Mexico City and Veracruz, permit analysis of the respective surpluses.

7. The data we analyze are only from remittances to Spain and to the situados in the greater Caribbean. We do not include estimates of remittances to the Philippine situados, which were also considerable. For comparative data, see Leslie Bauzon, "Deficit Government: Mexico and the Philippine Situado (1606-1804)" (Ph.D. diss., Duke Univ., 1970).

8. John Coatsworth, *Los orígenes del atraso: nueve ensayos de historia económica de México en los siglos XVIII y XIX* (Mexico City: Alianza Editorial Mexicana, 1990), 108-9.

9. It may be argued that a small compensation for the remittances can be observed in the merchandise sent by the *real hacienda* from Castile to New Spain; this included mercury and paper sent from Cádiz, paid for with a small percentage of the Mexican silver received. It may also be noted that a small portion of the silver sent to Cuba and other Caribbean situados benefited producers in New Spain, who received orders for hard biscuits, ham, and other merchandise.

10. Coatsworth provides some estimates of this drainage and of possible effects on the colonial economy. *Los orígenes del atraso*, 108-9. Richard L. Garner says loans to the crown between 1790 and 1810 diminished the sources of capital available to the private sector. Garner, "Price Trends inEighteenth-Century Mexico," *HAHR*, 65:2 (May 1985), 305

11. The first large deficits appeared in the year 1782-83, when the royal treasury in New Spain was obliged to make recourse to forced loans *(donativos)*, interest-bearing loans, and fund transfers from a variety of *ramos particulares y ajenos* to the central treasury in Mexico City for remittance overseas. See Carlos Marichal, "Las guerras imperiales y los préstamos novohispanos, 1781-1804, "- Historia Mexicana 39:4 [156] (Apr.-Jun. 1990), 881-907.

12. Herbert Klein, "La economía de la Nueva España, 1680-1809: un analisis a partir de las cajas reales," Historia Mexicana 34:4 [36] (1985), 561-60.

13. As various researchers have suggested, interpreting the fiscal series in current values may lead to certain errors, which suggests the need for an adequate deflator to account for the inflation that gained strength in the economy of New Spain at the end of the eighteenth century. At present, however, the number of complete price series for the colonial economy is insufficient to construct a completely satisfactory general price index. In this sense, we agree with Pedro Pérez Herrero, who emphasizes the need to deflate the series but also cautious against using premature estimates (as Coatsworth would apparently justify) in order to avoid costly subsequent errors. See essays by Pedro Pérez Herrero: "El creciluiento económico novohispano durante el sigio XVIII: una revisión," *Reuista de Historia Económica* 7:1 (1989), 111-32; and "Los beneficiarios (del reformisnio borbónico: metrópoli versus élites novohispanos," *Historia Mexicana* 41:2 [162] (1991), 207-64.

14. For the annual series of silver minted we have used the data provided by Alejandro de Humboldt [Alexander von Humboldt], *Ensayo politico sobre el reino de la Nueva España*, edición y revisión de texto por Juan Ortega y Medina (Mexico City: Ediciones Porrúa, 1991), 386.

15. Another statistical exercise indicates that the annual growth rates of remittances tended to surpass those of silver production. From 1720 to 1800 the annual average increase of remittances in regard to silver production was 0.3 per cent. This would suggest quite clearly that increases in overseas remittances exerted a constant, growing pressure on the mining sector. If Z denotes the ratio of the annual remittances divided by silver production, the statistical results of the regression are the following:
$Z = 0.173 + 0\text{-}003t$ $(6.561) + (5\text{-}804)$ $R_2 = 0.3595$
$DW = 2.13$ where the numbers in parentheses corre-

spond to the t-value statistics, and t takes the value of o for the year 1720, 1 for 1721, and so on.

16. The income series presented by Barbier require careful analysis, as the various sources are not specified in sufficient detail to determine how much revenue was derived from transfer of royal income from America. In some years, furthermore, there would appear to be significant discrepancies with the Veracruz data. See Jacques Barbier, "Towards a New Chronology for Bourbon Colonialism: The "Depositaria de Indias" of Cádiz, 1722-1789," *Ibero-Anerikanisches Archiv*, n. f, jg. 6, h 4 (1980), *335-53-*

17. For instance, Barbier affirms: "One certainly would not have supposed from the existing secondary literature that Ferdinand drew more Indias money than his half-brother [Carlos III] . . ." Barbier, "Towards a New Chronology," 342. Renate Pieper, however, on the basis of a major quantitative study, argues: "De esta evolución de los ingresos americanos en España no se puede deducir una mayor eficacia administrativa o presión en ultramar durante el reinado de Fernando VI. . . ." Pieper, "La aportación americana a la real hacienda española en la segunda mitad del siglo XVIII,- *Estudios de Historia Social y Económica de América* (Alcalá) 6 *(1990),* 72. See also idem, *Die spanischen Kronfinanzen in der zweiten Halfte des M. Jahrhunderts* (1753-1788) (Stuttgart: Franz Steiner Verlag, 1988).

18. Cuenca, "Ingresos netos"; Jose P. Merino Navarro, *Las cuentas de la administración central espaiiola, 175O-1820* (Madrid: *Instituto de Estudios Fiscales, 1988),* and "La hacienda de Carlos IV"; Leandro Prados de la Escosura, *De imperio a nación: crecimiento y atraso económico en España, i78o*-1936 (Madrid: Alianza, 1988*),* chap. *2.*

19. It should be underscored that the series of "Indias" income registered as going to the Madrid Treasury by Barbier and Klein, "Revolutionary Wars," 323 and 338, does not check with the figures collected by Cuenca, "Ingresos netos," and Merino, "La hacienda de Carlos IV."

20. As they affirm: "When the related receipts from the Cádiz royal treasury are added in, American-related funds may have accounted for one-fifth of total Madrid treasury revenues in this period, making the Indies the largest ultimate source of Madrid income." Barbier and Klein, "Revolutionary Wars," 328.

21. On this question see the excellent study by Marten G. Buist, At Spes Non Fracta, Hope and Company, 1770-1815: Merchant Bankers and Diplomats at Work (The Hague: Nijhoff, 1975).

22. The most detailed analysis of these operations is found in Pedro Tedde's monumental *Historia del Banco de San Carlos* (Madrid: Banco de España/Alianza, 1987*)* and in his essay "Política financiera y política comercial en el reinado de Carlos III, "- *Actas del Congreso internacional sobre Carlos III y la Illustracion,* vol. *2, Economía y sociedad* (Madrid: Ministerio de Cultura,1989*),* 139-217.

23. It should be recalled that the situados of New Spain also included funds that went to other points apart from the greater Caribbean, such as the northern

presidios of New Spain itself and occasional transfers to Guatemala, Nueva Granada, and - via Acapulco the Philippines, which received some 250,000 pesos annually from the mid-eighteenth century on. On internal military expenses in the viceroyalty of New Spain, see Christon I. Archer, "Bourbon Finances and Military Policy in New Spain, *1759—1812, " The Americas* 37:3 (1981), 315-50.

24. Julio Le Riverend Brusone, "Relaciones entre Nueva España v Cuba (1518-1520)," *Revista de Historia de America* (Mexico City) 37-38 (1954), *90.* The exact date of the establishment of situados in the Caribbean islands has not yet been determined. According to the references cited by Le Riverend, more or less regular remittances were made to Havana from the 1570s on. But the only exact date for a royal order in this respect – Sept. 18, 1584 – is provided by Manuel Villanova, "Economía y civismo," *Revista Cubana* (1892), 157-90 (reprinted, Havana: Ministerio de Educación, 1945), 43. Ramón de la Sagra refers to the same royal cédula but gives the date of November 18, 1584. De la Sagra, *Historia económico política y estadistica de la isla de Cuba, a sea de sus progresos en la población, la agricultura, el comercio, y las rentas* (Havana: Imprenta de las viudas de Arazoza y Soler, 1831), 276.

25. Paul E. Hoffman, *The Spanish Crown and the Defense of the Caribbean, 1535– 1585: Precedent, Patrimonialism, and Royal Parsimony* (Baton Rouge: Louisiana State Univ. Press, 1980); Pedro Vives, "Tres siglos de fortificación e infraestructura portuaria en la América Española," in *Puertos y fortificaciones en América y Filipinas* (Madrid: Comisión de Estudios Históricos de Obras Públicas y Urbanismo, 1985), 49-50; Ricardo Cerezo Martínez, "Las rutas marítimas espafiolas en el siglo XVI,"- in *España y el ultramar hispanico hasta la Ilustración* (Madrid: Instituto de Historia y Cultura Naval, 1989), 72.

26. Bibiano Torres Ramírez, *La Armada de Barlovento* (Seville: Escuela de Estudios Americanos, 1981), chap. 8, pp. 221ff.; Manuel Alvarado Morales, "El cabildo de la ciudad de México ante la fundación de la Armada de Barlovento, 1635-1643" (Ph.D. diss., El Colegio de México, 1979), 11-17.

27. A description of the fortifications constructed during the colonial period can be found in José Antonio Calderón Quijano, *Historia de las fortificaciones en Nueva España* (Seville: Escuela de Estudios Hispanoamericanos, 1955), which focuses on the fortifications in New Spain.

28. For a general overview of the resurgence of the Spanish armada in this period, see John D. Harbron, *Trafalgar and the Spanish Navy* (Annapolis: Naval Institute Press, 1988), 59-60, 91-92, which includes a complete list of all warships built in Havana in the eighteenth century. See also the seminal article by Jacques A. Barbier, "Indies Revenues and Naval Spending: The Cost of Colonialism for the Spanish Bourbons, 1763-1805," *Jahrbuch für Geschichte von Staat, Wirtschaft, und Gesellschaft Lateinamerikas* 21 (1984), 171-84.

29. For the increase in military expenditures and the expansion of military forces in Spanish America in the eighteenth century, see Marchena Fernández, "Financiación militar y situados." On Cuba, see Allan J. Kuethe and C. Douglas Inglis, "Absolutism and Enlightened Reform: Charles III, the Establishment of the Alcabala, and Commercial Reorganization in Cuba," *Past and Present* 109 (1985), 118-43

30. Engel Sluiter, *The Florida Situado: Quantifying the First Eighty Years, 1571-1651* (Gainesville: Univ. of Florida Libraries, 1985), 5-6. As late as the eighteenth century the situados were used to cover these expenses, as can be seen in the *reales cédulas* of Nov. 20, 1741, (Oct- 13, 1756, and Apr. 6, 1763, AGN, Reales Cédulas Originales, v. 61, e. 91, f. 334; v. 76, e. 123, f 290 and v. 86, e. 66.;

31. See, for example, AGN, Reales Cédulas Originales, v. 62, e. 60, f 185; v. 76, e. 144, 331; and v. 63, e. 60, f. 159; Historia, v. 570, f. 57; and Archivo Histórico de Hacienda, leg. 1210, e. i.

32. See AGN, Reales Cédulas Originales, v. 64, e. 33, f. 103, and Historia, v. 570, f 25; and Eduardo Arcila Farias, Comercio entre Mexico y Venezuela en los siglos XVI y XVII (Mexico City: Instituto Mexicano de Comercio Exterior, 1975), 218.

33. The 1723 figure comes from De la Sagra, Historia económico-política, 272.

34. Beginning in 1770, the production sphere of the Spanish royal tobacco monopoly included factories both in Spain (Seville employed more than five thousand workers) and in Mexico City (more than four thousand workers), as well as in other parts of the empire. The official tobacco sales outlets employed additional thousands. And several thousand tobacco farmers in Cuba and Mexico, plus a lesser number in Louisiana, Puerto Rico, and Santo Domingo, depended for their living on the royal monopoly.

35. De la Sagra, *Historia económico-política*, 264-65.

36. Le Riverend was one of the first Latin American historians to underscore the significance of the situados. See "Relaciones entre Nueva España y Cuba," 92 and 143-44. His estimates of remittances to Cuba from New Spain appear to be based on De la Sagra, *Historia económico-politica.*

37. Each American province was obliged to send documents that justified the level of de fense expenditures; this explains why the AGN contains numerous reports on the regiments in each garrison and the number of deaths and deserters. See, e.g., reports on garrisons in Puerto Rico, AGN, Archivo Histórico de Hacienda, leg. 1210.

38. In 1697 the crown ordered that when the Caribbean treasuries receiving the situados accumulated fiscal surpluses, these sums should be deducted from the remittances sent from New Spain. AGN, Historia, v. 570, f. 9. This occurred with surpluses generated in the fiscal branch of the Cruzada in Cumaná, the Santa Bula in Florida, and the Media Anata in Santo Domingo. AGN, Historia, v. 570, f. 14, 45, 109.

39. Arcila Farias confirms the figure of five hundred thousand silver pesos *(Cornercio entre Afixico, y Venezuela,* 203), but Marchena Fernindez registers

only four hundred thousand pesos ("Financiación military situados," 271-73).

40. Libro manual, 1758; Marchena Fernández, "Financiación militar y situados," 271-73. It should be noted that the category of marina is one of the most difficult to specify; some of the funds went for the salaries of sailors and officers and others for provisions and ship repair or construction. E.g., a report of Oct. 19, 1758, indicates that of 1,016,094 pesos sent to Havana for "marina," 407,123 pesos were designated for expenses of the naval squadron, 100,924 pesos for ship construction, and 508,047 pesos for especially urgent naval disbursements. AGN, Historia, v. 570, f. 204.

41. AGN, Reales Cédulas Originales, v. 92, e. 48, 188.

42. E.g., in 1774, a sum f. 1,990,122 pesos was sent from Veracruz to Havana, of which 216,714 pesos were registered as *extraordinarios.* In 1778, relevant documents indicate that the figures designated for remittance to Havana were 986,866 for tierra; 1,015,204 for marina; and 600,000 for tabaco, although the actual amounts sent were only 290,400, 680,607, and 200,000 pesos, respectively. María del Carmen Velazquez, "El siglo XVIII, in *Historia documental de México,* Miguel León-Portilla et al. (Mexico City: Instituto de Investigaciones Históricas, UNAM, 1964), 1:321-419.

43. Fabian Fonseca and Carlos de Urrutia. *Historia general de la real hacienda* (Mexico City: Imprenta de Vicente G. Torres, 1845-1853), vols. 13-27; Joaquin Maniau y Torquemada, *Compendio de la historia de la real hacienda de Nueva España, escrito en el año de 1794* (Mexico City: Sociedad Mexicana de Geografia y Estadistica, 1914), 43-46; Libro manual, 1791.

44. Humboldt, *Ensayo político sobre la isla de Cuba,* edición e introducción de Fernando Ortiz (Havana: Archivo Nacional de Cuba, 1960), 273-74; De la Sagra, *Historia económico-política,* 282; Klein and TePaske, *Ingresos y egresos.*

45. The first three objectives were achieved, but the raids on Honduras were a failure, and the naval campaign off Jamaica proved a major defeat because of the British Navy's sea victories under the command of Admiral Rodney. On the Bahama campaign, see James A. Lewis' recent monograph, The Final Campaign of the American Revolution: Rise and Fall of the Spanish Bahamas (Columbia: Univ. of South Carolina Press, 1991).

46. A previous study of these loans can be found in Marichal, "Las guerras imperiales."

47. Information on shipments to Spanish military garrisons throughout the greater Caribbean is found in a variety of sources in the Archivo General de la Nación, as well as in two excellent and infrequently cited doctoral theses that provide an abundance of data on New Spain's crucial role in the war. See Melvin Bruce Glascock, "New Spain and the War for America, 1779-1783" (Ph.D. diss., Louisiana State Univ., 1969); and James A. Lewis, "New Spain During the American Revolution, 1779-1783: A Viceroyalty at War" (Ph.D. diss., Duke Univ.,

1975). Both texts are under consideration for publication in Spanish translation by the Instituto Mora, Mexico City.

48. Glascock, "New Spain and the War," 285.

49. The source Glascock used is a very detailed document titled "Decretos, planos, certificaciones sobre el costo de la guerra," Archivo Histórico Nacional, Madrid, Consejo de Indias, leg. 20721, cuad. V, f 77-109, cited in Glascock, "New Spain and the War," 265-74. Lewis' estimates come from documents in the AGN, Mexico City. See "New Spain During the American Revolution," 157.

50. For comparative data on metropolitan finance, see Tedde, " Politica financiera," 143.

51. A detailed study of the financial transactions would considerably help to elucidate the methods used to finance imperial wars. Apart from the financial documents noted in this essay, an important source is the documentary section titled Marina in the AGN.

52. AGN, Correspondencia. de Virreyes, v. 129, e. 1317, f. 281-83.

53. AGN, Marina, v. 12, f. 144-49.

54. AGN, Correspondencia de Virreyes, v. 129, e. 1317, f. 281-83.

55. Glascock provides detailed lists of provisions sent year by year. "New Spain and the War," 265-73.

56. For details on the soldiers of the Mexican crown regiment, see Christon I. Archer, *El ejército en el México borbónico, 1760-1810* (Mexico City: Fondo de Cultura Económica, 1983). Glascock provides annual information on the transfer of seamen from Veracruz. "New Spain and the War," 265-73.

57. Tedde, "Política financiera."

24

The Origins of the Commission System in the West India Trade

The Alexander Prize Essay

K.G. DAVIES, M.A.

Read 16 June 1951

The half-century which followed the capture of Jamaica in 1655 was characterized by the consolidation rather than by the expansion of the English interest in the West Indies.[1] In the political sphere this consolidation took several forms. The acquisition of Jamaica, by far the largest English West Indian colony, and the termination of proprietary rule in the Caribee Islands in 1663 brought the greater part of the English West Indian empire under the direct adminstration of the Crown.[2] As a corollary to this extension of Crown rule, the creation of effective institutions for the government of these and other colonies became a matter of urgent necessity. After a series of experiments in the decade following the Restoration, the constitution in 1672 of the Council of Trade and Plantations inaugurated 'a more thorough system of colonial control than had been established by any of its predecessors'.[3] The sum effect of these developments was that London became, in a way that it had never been before, the place where all the major decisions affecting the destinies of the West Indies were taken. From London there issued not only Crown-appointed governors and a stream of Orders-in-Council, but also declarations of the King's pleasure on such minor questions as appointments to colonial judgeships and seats in colonial councils.[4] To London there flowed, besides acts of colonial legislatures for approval or rejection, a torrent of complaints and petitions for redress.

To such a process of centralization the West Indians could not be expected to remain indifferent. Their immediate reaction was to seek for some representation at the centre of business whereby they could obtain reliable, up-to-date information, and through which they could bring pressure to bear on those in whose power they found themselves. These objects were achieved by the formation of associations of West Indian planters resident in England together with London merchants with West Indian connections, and by the appointment of political agents nominated and paid by the several colonial legislatures. The first of these associations, the Committee for the Concern of Barbados, was established in 1671, and shortly afterwards the Jamaica Coffee-House in St. Michael's Alley became a recognized meeting-place for persons interested in that colony.[5] Such associations, whether formal record-keeping bodies like the Barbados Committee or informal like the Coffee-House, provided not only a medium for the exchange of views and co-ordination of private interests but also a repository of expert knowledge and opinion on which the government could and did draw. The political agents, on the other hand, were more directly representative of the interests of the colonies; their duties included the presentation and management of petitions, lobbying of all kinds and the transmission of information.[6]

The growth of absenteeism, especially amongst the planters of substance, helped to divert the interests of many away from the colonies to the wider stage which England afforded. The first generation of English settlers in the West Indies may have been genuine exiles

Transactions of the Royal Historical Society (London), Fifth Series, 001-2, (1952), pp. 89-107.

seeking a fresh start and a clean break from home. But by the later seventeenth century a different type was in the ascendant, and in Barbados at least had already established itself. To some of the second and third generation of planters the West Indies were no more than a point of departure; to others they offered a tolerable fortune followed by retirement to quiet estates in Kent; to others their West Indian estates were mere appendages to more valuable property in England.[7] Some West Indians, like John Blake of Barbados, were already in the seventies of the seventeenth century sending their children to be educated in England.[8] Many, like the Littletons, the Merricks and the Freres, retained family ties with England. Almost, it seems, as soon as the 'frontier phase' in a West Indian colony's history was ended and the estate put on a working footing, the planter and his family began to aspire to the pleasures of civilized life 'at home'.

This focusing of the political interests and social aspirations of the West Indies upon England has its economic counterpart in the post-Restoration period. It is with the concentration of the economic interests of the sugar colonies upon the London market and the machinery by which this concentration was effected that this paper is concerned.[9] Just as the last 40 years of the seventeenth century witnessed the development of political agencies, so they saw also the foundations laid of the commission or 'factorage' system which in the eighteenth century was to become an outstanding characteristic of the West India trade.[10] In its heyday this commission system grew to be something more than a widely adopted method of marketing the most important commodity produced by the Old Empire: it became the means whereby credit, the very life-blood of the West Indies in the eighteenth century, was transmitted from the mother country. For this reason its origins and early development deserve a brief inquiry.

During the seventeenth century trade between England and the West Indies was carried on in at least four different ways. The first settlers had to rely on the fortuitous arrival of a ship bringing reinforcements, stores and provisions, for which they could barter their tobacco, indigo, cotton and other products. But as soon as a settlement had demonstrated its will to survive and its ability to pay, a more regular form of trade sprang up. In 1628, for example, Thomas Littleton, a London merchant, sent three ships to Nevis with provisions, munitions and clothing to the value of £5,000. These goods were consigned to Littleton's factor or agent, whose duty it was to sell them and make suitable returns.[11] This mode of trading was particularly apt for the early years of a new colony's existence. The merchant in London (or in many instances the Dutch merchant) supplied the capital which enabled the necessities of life and labour to be brought to the colonist.[12] In these early days the planter's main concern was to plant, to produce larger crops, to buy more food, more land and more labour. Individual holdings of land in Barbados and the Leeward Islands before the elevation of sugar to the status of main crop tended to be small; and planters to be men of little fortune. In such a trade, the merchant, English or Dutch, made the running, and could and no doubt did exploit the initiative which he held. But the small planter drew certain benefits from his subordinate position. By selling in the island, he could without any delay translate his crops into the commodities he needed; no calls were made on his small capital for customs, freight or insurance, though all three would be reflected in the value set upon his crop; and if the ship which carried the produce of his land was lost on the homeward voyage, not he but the merchant was the sufferer.

This method of trading begat in the islands a class of merchants or 'shop-keepers' who handled the goods of their principals, collected debts and made up return cargoes. Richard Ligon described how during his residence in Barbados from 1647 to 1650 an English merchant might accumulate the money to buy a plantation by trading in this way.[13] Ten years later Thomas Povey's letter-book shows us Edward Bradbourn acting as factor in Barbados for Povey and Martin Noell in London.[14] Although this method of trading began to be superseded soon after the Restoration it did not die out altogether; during the remainder of the seventeenth century and in the eighteenth, middlemen factors continued to ply their trade in the islands. Azariah Pinney, on his arrival in Nevis in 1686, set up as factor for his family and soon began to gather other commissions from England.[15] The yearly cargoes which William Stout, the Lancaster Quaker, sent to Barbados between 1699 and 1702 were consigned to factors resident in the island.[16] Alternatively, the roles might be reversed, the island merchant setting up in business on his own account and himself employing an agent in England to make consignments to him.[17] Unpopular as they were and the target of spiteful legislation which doubled the difficulties of their business, these island merchants and factors served a useful purpose in reducing the demands put upon the capital of the smaller planter.

But the future belonged neither to the speculative ship, nor to the London merchant with his island factor, nor to the island merchant with his English factor. The future belonged to a trade in which the planter himself assumed responsibility for the marketing of his products, consigning them on his own account to an agent, at first in London and later in other towns, who for a consideration saw to their ultimate disposal. This system reached its full flowering in the eighteenth century, when it can be studied in the records of such firms as Pinney and Tobin, and Lascelles and Maxwell. But it was in full working order, though on a smaller scale, by the end of the third quarter of the seventeenth century. The great commission houses which later dominate the scene have their seventeenth-century counterparts in firms such as Bawden & Gardiner and John Eyles & Company, and in individuals such as Thomas Tryon, Anthony Wallinger and Nathaniel Bridges.

The duties performed by the London agent of a West Indian planter in the later seventeenth century were much the same as those under-taken in the eighteenth century. He received the goods off the ship, having previously made whatever insurance on them might be necessary; he obtained the certificate of discharge and paid the customs; he warehoused the goods; and either personally or through a broker he conducted the sale. From the gross proceeds he first deducted his own commission of $2\frac{1}{2}$ per cent, plus an additional $\frac{1}{2}$ of 1 per cent for brokerage if he had himself negotiated the sale. Further deductions were made in respect of charges which the agent had defrayed on behalf of his correspondent for freight, customs, and so on. The net proceeds were then placed to the credit of the planter and could be used either for the purchase of goods which he might order out from England (on which the agent collected a further $2\frac{1}{2}$ per cent) or as a fund on which bills could be drawn for the payment of debts due in England or in the West Indies.[18] To the planter therefore his English factor stood at once as selling and buying agent and as banker.

The bill of exchange, by means of which the planter was enabled to draw upon the funds he had accumulated in the hands of his agent, represented a credit transaction involving at least three parties, the drawer (in this case the planter), the drawee (his agent in London) and the payee (the planter's creditor). The principal

evidence for the operation of commission agents in the West India trade in the later seventeenth century derives from the records neither of a planter nor of an agent, but of a payee, the largest single business engaged in that trade, the Royal African Company.[19] The nature of the trade pursued by this company is well known. Goods of English, European or East Indian manufacture sent out from London were bartered on the coast of West Africa for negro slaves; these were shipped to the West Indies where they were sold sometimes to contractors but more often directly to the planters. Payment for the Company's slaves could be made in one of three ways. First, the Company's accepted coin, for the most part the Spanish pieces-of-eight which circulated in Barbados and Jamaica. Secondly, payment might be in kind, usually sugar but sometimes indigo, cotton or other products. This method was almost universally practised in the Leeward Islands where sugar was current, and it was by no means rare in the other colonies. The third mode of payment was by the planter's bill of exchange drawn on his London agent or on some other person in England and made payable to the Company in London. It is these bills, entered in the Company's books, which with scattered references from other sources provide the material for studying the commission system in the early stages of its development. For the years 1672-94 record is preserved of about 1,500 bills, of a gross value of nearly £350,000. The yearly average for the whole period is £16,000, and for the years of the Company's greatest activity, 1676-87, it is over £21,000.[20]

Not all these 1,500 hundred bills are evidence of the operation of a commission system. Nearly a half of the two hundred persons on whom they were drawn were concerned in only one bill. The acceptance and payment of a single bill does not make the acceptor a commission agent; nor need it imply the existence of any well-founded commercial relationship between the parties concerned. It may denote merely the discharge of an obligation of a non-commercial nature; and in many instances in which a single bill was drawn the parties appear to have had some family connection.[21] If we may take the five bills spread over a period of at least two years as evidence of a regular correspondence between planter and agent, nearly 60 such attachments can be discerned in these years. The degree of permanence which they enjoyed varied widely. Generally the practice seems to have been for the planter to employ only one agent at a time and to continue with him over a number of years. The

Bulkeleys, the Farmers, the Silvesters and the Hothersalls, all planters of Barbados, retained their agents for thirteen years or longer, while John Gibbes was associated with the firm of Eyles & Co. for nineteen years. But that the planter retained some freedom of action is clear. John Davies, for example, who had a 200-acre estate in Barbados, employed Robert Chaplin as his factor from 1672 to 1682. But while continuing to drawn on Chaplin, he began in 1676 to draw also on Eyles & Co. In 1682 he gave up both agents and began to draw on a third, John Eston. Similarly Humphrey Waterman, after two years with Edward Thornburgh, transferred his commission to Christopher Fowler, while John Pierce, whose 1,000-acre estate was one of the largest in Barbados, employed simultaneously Robert Chaplin and the firm of Bawden & Co. as his factors. At the end of the seventeenth century, therefore, it was still possible for a planter to change his correspondent. Thus the agents of the African Company in Barbados reported in 1693 that several of the planters who employed John Gardiner 'have such regrett at his unkind useage that they Change theire factors'.[22] In the eighteenth century a planter might have no alternative but to confine his business to the agent to whom he owed money.[23] But in the seventeenth century these bonds of debt had not been firmly or finally riveted. Chronic indebtedness was already a West Indian characteristic,[24] but the principal creditors do not as yet seem to have been the London agents. The largest single creditor in the West Indian colonies in the last quarter of the seventeenth century was the Royal African Company itself. The standing debt owing to it never fell below £100,000 and frequently rose above £150,000.[25] Credit for the purchase of labour, the commodity of most vital importance to the planter, was thus being supplied from outside the commission mechanism. The replacement in the early eighteenth century of the African Company by private slave-traders, less able and less disposed to sell on trust, deprived the planters of a source of credit which they could ill afford to lose, and probably threw a heavier burden upon the commission agents.[26]

Without the records of a seventeenth-century commission agent, it is difficult to reconstruct the precise relationship which existed between his kind and the West Indian planters. It is possible that even at this date such agents as John Bawden, John Eyles and John Gardiner were making advances to their correspondents on the security of their West Indian estates. But no evidence has so far come to light to confirm such an hypothesis. What is fairly certain is that agents were not disposed to make advances on the bills drawn upon them. Ideally the planter should have kept a sufficient reserve in the hands of his agent to meet all contingencies. But it was general practice to draw on the bill of lading, that is to say, to send off the bills of exchange at the same time as the goods which were intended to meet them.[27] In other words, planters were writing cheques and then hastening to the bank to pay in sufficient to cover them. If the goods and the bill came to hand together, well and good. But if the ship which carried the planter's sugars was lost, his bill could expect no mercy; it was promptly protested and returned to drawer.[28] To some extent this contingency could be provided for by long-dated bills, but in fact these were uncommon. Thirty or forty days after sight were the periods at which the majority of West India bills became payable in the seventies of the seventeenth century, though somewhat longer-dated bills became more common in later years.[29] Attempts by the planters to anticipate the proceeds of their consignments were met by firm protests from the agents. In the early years of the war which began in 1689, the West India trade was severely dislocated by embargoes, shipping losses and a scarcity of freight. Two bills drawn at this time by Thomas Walrond of Barbados were entered in the Company's books with a note: 'Mr. Walrond does not doubt but thro' the blessing of God to have Sugars timely for the full discharge of these bills of Exchange If Fraight may then be had.'[30] Freight was apparently not to be had, and the bills were protested. In normal times very few bills had to be returned to drawer. Between 1672 and 1687 Bawden & Co. protested only six, Eyles & Co. seven, Hinchman two and Tryon three. But with the outbreak of war the number rose steeply. Of eighteen bills drawn on John Gardiner between 1689 and 1694, all but four were protested;[31] Eyles & Co. protested nine of the bills drawn on them in the early years of the war, and Henry Hale ten. Of twenty-eight bills which the African Company received on 7 November 1692, only seven were paid. This manifestation of the factors' unwillingness to make advances on bills came at a time when the planters were in particular need of credit; for sugar prices were booming and maximum output was called for.[32] It is therefore reasonable to suppose that agents were not yet convinced either of the necessity or of the profit to themselves of making advances to planters on their bills. Only further inquiry can show if they were supplying extensive credit in any other form.

The intimate social relationship which was later to subsist between planter and factor[33] does not appear to have fully developed in the seventeenth century. John Blake, for example, employed a distant kinsman to oversee the education of his children in England, whereas a century later he would probably have commended them to Nathaniel Bridges, his factor.[34] On the other hand, there are signs that already the relationship was growing into something more than a business convenience. When John Hothersall of Barbados made his will in 1694, he appointed his good friends Sir John and Francis Eyles guardians of his children and besought them to advise his widow in her investments.[35] Eyles & Co. had been factors for the Hothersalls for at least fourteen years, and by the will were made receivers of the products of the plantation during the minority of the children.

The task of inquiring into the origins of this commission system is somewhat simplified by the knowledge that as yet it did not extend to the trade of every West Indian colony. We have already noticed the persistence into the eighteenth century of the earlier forms of trading controlled either by London or by island merchants. Of the 1,500 bills which the African Company received between 1672 and 1694, only 58 originated in Jamaica and 25 in the Leeward Islands; the remainder were drawn in Barbados. This is not to suggest that the commission system was unknown outside the trade of Barbados; Christopher Jeaffreson has left evidence of its existence in the trade of the island of St. Christopher's.[36] But the extensive use of the bill of exchange in Barbados and its rarity elsewhere imply that it was to the conditions which prevailed in Barbados that the system was thought to be particularly apt.

Barbados at the Restoration was unique amongst the English colonies, and not only on account of her riches. As the first island to cultivate sugar as a commercial crop she had a start of several years over her rivals, and throughout the seventeenth century she continued one or more jumps ahead of them. The concomitants of sugar planting, a large slave population, intensive cultivation of the soil, and the large estate, all manifested themselves first in Barbados. While Jamaica continued a 'frontier colony' until well into the eighteenth century,[37] Barbados was already in the fifties of the seventeenth century so fully settled that she could afford, indeed was

constrained, to get rid of her surplus population to the newer colonies.[38] By 1676 it could be said that 'there is not a foot of land in Barbados that is not employed even to the seaside', and, despite the falling price of sugar, land values were high.[39] The rapid growth of the slave population in the fifties and sixties is itself evidence of the heavy capitalization and intensive cultivation of the soil.[40] With the possible exception of the little island of Nevis, Barbados alone in the last quarter of the seventeenth century had reached a point beyond which further economic progress could take place only at a much reduced rate.

Although the average size of a plantation was certainly under 100 acres,[41] Barbados in the second half of the seventeenth century was already a land of comparatively large estates.[42] In 1673 she could boast of no less than 74 'eminent planters' with estates of 200–1,000 acres,[43] many of whom were aristocrats by birth as well as by inclination. 'Whoever will look over the Map of Barbadoes,' wrote John Oldmixon, 'will find the Country is not possessed by such a set of Men as inhabit the other Plantations', but by 'families of the most ancient and honourable in England'.[44] Such were the Draxes, the Stedes, the Codringtons, the Littletons, the Willoughbys and the Fortescues. Though they might be debtors, they were still men of substance, men whose promissory bills might be expected to command acceptance, men whose estates were such that they did not feel the same urgency as their lesser brethren to turn their crops immediately to account, men, in short, who could forbear returns long enough to send their products to the best accessible market, however distant it might be. The commission system was in origin the method of disposal for the sugar produced by the large, intensively cultivated, highly capitalized estate; and since it was in Barbados that such estates were mainly to be found in the seventeenth century, it was in the trade of that colony that the system made its first appearance. In the eighteenth century, as Jamaica began to be more intensively cultivated and families like the Pinneys built up large estates in other islands, the system spread into the entire West Indian trade.

The evidence for this statement lies in the bills of exchange already mentioned. Of the 74 'eminent planters' of Barbados, all but fourteen appear in the records as drawing bills in favour of the Company, and the majority of them did so regularly and may therefore be assumed to have employed London agents. Of the 122 bills drawn between 1672 and 1680 on the three leading agents of the time, John Bawden, John Eyles and Edward Thornburgh, 82 were drawn by 'eminent planters',[45] and ten others by men who, though not appearing in this list of 'eminent planters', are found a few years later holding offices in the island which tended to be the preserves of the greater landowners.[46] From the point of view of the London agent it is understandable that this should have been so. Only the larger fish could have been really worth the catching. The labour of correspondence and accounting could scarcely be recompensed if consignments of sugar were not to be large enough for the commission thereon to amount to a worthwhile sum.

The growth of the large estate and the emergence of a class of substantial planters were the prerequisites of the commission system. But other factors help to explain its rise, in particular the concentration of the economic interests of the West Indies upon England to which reference has already been made. In the main this concentration was arbitrary; the planters did not want it and never ceased in the seventeenth century to campaign against it. The imperial economic programme which took shape between 1650 and 1665 was not intended to benefit them. By the Navigation Act of 1660 and the Staple Act of 1663 their interests were completely subordinated to those of the mother country. They lost above all the right to buy from and sell to the Dutch traders whose ready acceptance of 'moderate gains by Trade' had done so much to set the English colonies on their feet. The planters were left at the mercy of the English and island merchants, and as early as 1655 they were resenting the position in which they found themselves.[47] 'The Merchants,' they complained in 1661, 'having us in their power that wee can send our sugars noe where else, they give us what they please and soe having the markett in themselves to send it for other countryes, they sell it for what they list, and make us simple planters only the propertie of their gaine, and sell the poor for bread and the rich for shoes.'[48] In such straits any planter who could afford to do so must have been encouraged to reach out to a wider and freer market than that provided by his own island. Since Europe was closed to him, he could look only to England. In London he would find at least a measure of competition for his sugars amongst English grocers, refiners, distillers and re-exporters. Thus the invasion of the London market by the West Indian planters may be seen partly as a reply to the prohibition of free trade and the alleged excesses of the local merchants and factors.[49]

Fundamentally there could be only one motive for a planter to switch his products from the island market to London. Richard Ligon told the Barbados planter of the early fifties that he could expect 3d. a lb for muscovado sugar sold in the island. 'But if,' he continued, 'you run the Hazards of the Sea, as all Marchants doe and bring it for England, it will sell in London for 12d. a lb.'[50] Already, therefore, an incentive existed for the planter to forbear his returns in the expectation of a greater profit. Later in the century it is less easy to assess the relative margins of profit to be gained from the two alternative methods of trade. They certainly may not be regarded as constant; a heavy sugar crop could mean high freight charges as shippers competed for cargo space, but low wholesale prices in London. On such occasions the planter's profit might disappear altogether.[51] But the fact that in the later seventeenth century planters were making consignments to England on their own accounts of itself suggests that generally this method of disposal through London agents was thought to be the more profitable.

At the time when Ligon wrote, sugar was a crop of such golden possibilities that the risks and trouble of making consignments to London may not have been compensated by the extra gain accruing. But the sellers' market which Barbados enjoyed in the forties and early fifties disappeared under the impact of an increase in world production of sugar with which consumption did not keep pace. From the mid-fifties almost until the outbreak of war in 1689 prices were falling; in June 1686 good Barbados sugar was selling for no more than 15s. 9d. a 100 lbs in the London wholesale market, a price such as would obtain only two or three times in the next 200 years.[52] These falling prices magnified the difference in the margin of profit accruing to the planter by the alternative methods of marketing his sugar. When profits were being cut to the bone and possibly in some years annihilated, the chance of an extra shilling or even of a few pence on 100 lbs of sugar could not be ignored by those planters who could afford the delay involved in dispatching their goods to London. Like the navigation laws, falling prices bore equally on all the sugar islands; yet only in the trade of Barbados did the commission system play an important part in the seventeenth century. As yet it was only in Barbados that there was to be found a sufficiency of planters of substance wedded to a one-crop method of agriculture.[53] For the most part the products of Jamaica continued to be sold in the old way and the planters of that island remained in subjection to local merchants and factors long after those of Barbados had emancipated themselves.[54] The navigation laws and the falling price of sugar, which promoted the commission system in Barbados, produced different effects in the other English islands because those colonies were at different levels of economic development and specialization. As Jamaica and Antigua came more into line with Barbados in the eighteenth century, the commission system became practically universal.

It remains to consider briefly the London agents themselves, the first generation of new-style West Indian merchants, who operated the system. It has already been pointed out that the 1,500 bills of exchange which are the principal evidence for this paper were drawn on more than 200 people and that only a small number of these men were acting as commission agents. In fact, a group of about twenty engrossed nearly two-thirds of the business.[55] The connection between these leading commission agents and the West Indian political agencies is notable; Edward Thornburgh, the first agent appointed by Barbados, Thomas Hinchman, chosen for the same office in 1671, John Gardiner, nominated for the position in 1694, Bartholomew Gracedieu, agent for Jamaica from 1693 to 1704, Robert Chaplin, personal agent to the governors of Barbados, all these in their private capacities were commission agents to West Indian planters.[56]

These new West Indian merchants were of diverse origins. Some like John Bawden were absentee planters whose commission business may have grown out of the practice of receiving the products of their own and their friends' estates for sale in London.[57] Some like Thomas Tryon knew the colonies from experience but had no territorial interest in the island whose planters they served.[58] Others like John and Francis Eyles had no apparent hereditary or personal connections with the plantations or their trade.[59] Few as yet were specialists. Bawden for instance had trading interests in Holland and the Canaries, dabbled in the slave trade and was part-owner of a number of ships plying for hire.[60] His West Indian affairs, however, were his main concern, and his usual designation was that of West Indian merchant. His commission business certainly prospered. In 1682 he was able to take John Gardiner into partnership, and these two, according to

Oldmixon, 'had then the largest Commissions from Barbadoes of any Merchants in England, and perhaps the largest that ever were lodg'd in one House in the West-India Trade', a verdict which coincides exactly with the evidence of the bills of exchange.[61]

Bawden's greatest competitors were Eyles & Co. With the two partners in this firm is associated one of the great mercantile dynasties of eighteenth-century London. The eldest daughter of John Eyles, the senior partner, married a nephew of Robert Stiles, the 'millionaire' merchant of Amsterdam, while two other daughters married into the gentry. The two sons of Francis Eyles, the junior partner, John and Joseph, are too well known in eighteenth-century political and business history to need any comment. The founder of the firm, John Eyles, son of a Devizes mercer, applied himself to the West Indian commission business at least as early as 1674. From the African Company's records we can see that at different times more than 30 people drew bills on him from Barbados. Like Bawden's, his agency was large enough to warrant a partner, and the volume of business which the firm handled was only a little less than that of Bawden & Gardiner. That his career was successful and that he died a wealthy man there can be no doubt. Member for Devizes in the Exclusion Parliament, under James II he became successively knight, alderman of the City of London and Lord Mayor. How much of the property which he left at his death, and how much of the £29,000 which he lent to the government in 1689, represented the profits of his commission business it is impossible to say.[62] One fact, however, does emerge clearly: the leading commission agents of the seventeenth century were men of substance and influence who can stand comparison with the great houses of 50 or 100 years later.

One final piece of evidence of the growth of the commission system remains, the curious project sponsored by Dalby Thomas in 1687 for a West India Company. The objects of this scheme were two-fold, first to make loans to the colonies, and second, in the words which the projector addressed to the planters:

to have had all your Goods that came to England brought to one Body of Men, which we call'd a Common Factory, and they constantly to be chosen by you in your Assemblies, and they to have been Accountable to every Consignor for the Nett proceed of every parcel of Goods Sold.[63]

The project failed, killed (so it was said and so it might be expected) by those who stood to lose most by it, the commission agents led by Bawden and Gardiner.[64] The significance of this storm-in-a-teacup could easily be exaggerated; it was never anything more than a project. But it does show that the commission business had made such progress that a projector could contemplate erecting it into an organized system; and the failure of the scheme itself testifies to the strength of the established agents. The foundations of the system which, it is hardly too much to say, was to keep the English West Indies in being during the eighteenth century had been well and truly laid.

Notes

1. Barbados 'expanded' in the sense that she helped to people other colonies; many left in the sixties and seventies of the seventeenth century to settle Surinam, Jamaica and St. Lucia. But taking the West Indies as a whole, the movement was an increase and redistribution of population rather than a territorial expansion. See A. D. Chandler, 'The Expansion of Barbados', *Journal of the Barbados Museum and Historical Society*, xiii 1945–46, 106–36.

2. J. A. Williamson, *The Caribee Islands under the Proprietary Patents*, Chapter X.

3. C. M. Andrews, *British Committees, Commissions and Councils of Trade and Plantations, 1622–1675*, p. 111.

4. For example, *Calendar of State Papers, Colonial (Cal. S. P. Col.), 1677–80*, Nos. 387 and 889; Public Record Office (P.R.O), Treasury (Expired Commissions), 70, 169, fo. 45r.

5. L. M. Penson, *The Colonial Agents of the British West Indies*, pp. 181–83.

6. *Ibid.*, Chapters II, III, IX.

7. Sir Peter Colleton, Sir Edwin Stede and Christopher Jeaffreson are examples of these three types of West Indian.

8. Blake family records, described in *Caribbeans*, ed. V. L. Oliver, i. 51–57.

9. The principal authorities are the works of G. L. Beer; C. M. Andrews, *The Colonial Period in American History*, especially Vols II and IV; V. T. Harlow, *A History of Barbados, 1625–1685*; C. S. S. Higham, *The Development of the Leeward Islands under the Restoration*; F. W. Pitman, *The Development of the British West Indies*; Richard Pares, *A West-India Fortune*; O. P. Starkey, *The Economic Geography of Barbados*; Noel Deerr, *A History of Sugar*; *Caribbeana*, ed. V. L. Oliver; *A Young Squire of the Seventeenth Century*, ed. J. C. Jeaffreson; *Autobiography of William Stout*, ed. J. Harland; Richard Ligon, *A True and Exact History of the Island of Barbadoes*, (1673); Dalby Thomas, *An Historical Account of the Rise and Growth of the West-India Collonies*, (1690); John Oldmixon, *The British Empire in America*, (1708); Edward Littleton, *The Groans of the Plantations*; Thomas Tryon, *Letters Domestick and Foreign to Several Persons of Quality*, (1700). The manuscript sources used in this paper are the Entry Books of Bills of Exchange of the Royal African Company, P.R.O., Treasury 70, 269–77 and 282, and the Letter Books of the same Company, principally T.70/1, 10, 12, 15–17, 20.

10. A brilliant picture of the working of a commission house in the later eighteenth century has been given by Professor Pares in *A West-India Fortune*. Unfortunately the Pinneys did not go into the business until 1783. The subject of the rise of the commission system was touched upon by Professor Penson, *The Colonial Agents of the British West Indies*, pp. 10 ff. Material for comparison is to be found in J. S. Bassett, 'The Relations between the Virginia Planter and the London Merchant', *Annual Report of the American Historical Association for 1901*, i, 553–75, and in Elizabeth Donnan, 'Eighteenth-Century English Merchants: Micajah Perry', *Journal of Economic and Business History*, iv, 1931–32, 70.

11. *Caribbeana*, ii, 2–7, for a description of a Chancery suit, Littleton *v.* Bullock.

12. For the extent of Dutch trade, see G. L. Beer, *The Origins of the British Colonial System*, pp. 357–59; British Museum add. ms. 11411, fos. 3v–5v; Dalby Thomas, *An Historical Account of the Rise and Growth of the West-India Collonies*, pp. 36–37.

13. *A True and Exact History of the Island of Barbadoes*, pp. 109–12.

14. British Museum add. ms. 11411, fos. 78v–79v, Thomas Povey to Edward Bradbourn.

15. *A West-India Fortune*, pp. 32–35.

16. *Autobiography*, pp. 54 ff.

17. *A West-India Fortune*, p. 35.

18. J. Oldmixon, *The British Empire in America*, ii, 155. An account rendered by Edward Thornburgh to the Assembly of Barbados of the sale of 30 butts of sugar illustrates the type and scale of charges which an agent defrayed, P.R.O., Colonial Office, 31, 2, pp. 112–13. Three per cent was the regular charge for commission and brokerage combined; see a report by John Eyles, Benjamin Skutt and John Bawden (all commission agents) on the accounts of the Barbados Four-and-a-half Per Cent Duty in *Calendar of Treasury Books, 1679–80*, p. 513.

19. P.R.O., T.70/269–77 and 282. The entry books for the years 1700–27 are of little value.

20. These are gross figures, including bills drawn not by planters but by syndicates of contractors who bought negroes from the Company. They include also the very small (until 1690) number of bills which were protested.

21. Thus Justus Birkin drew on James Birkin, Katherine Bentley on Sir Martin Bentley, Emanuel Hulson on Thomas Hulson, etc.

22. P.R.O., T.70/14, fo. 61r.

23. *A West-India Fortune*, pp. 172, 254–58.

24. For example, *A Young Squire of the Seventeenth Century*, ed. J. C. Jeaffreson, ii, 50.

25. In 1681 the debt stood at £120,000; in 1685 at £136,000; in 1690 at £170,000; in 1694 at £128,000; in 1696 at £140,000; details from annual statements of the assets of the Company in P.R.O., T.70/101. The floating debt must at times had made the total outstanding very much larger.

26. In 1700 the Governor of Jamaica (a former agent of the Company and possibly a prejudiced witness) wrote to the Council of Trade and Plantations: 'Another fatal thing to the settling and increasing these Plantations is the merchants of London have never left soliciting against the Royal Company under pretence they would supply negroes more plentiful and cheap, till they have gotten them out and themselves in, and whereas the Royal Company usually supplied negroes at £22 and £24 per head and gave 6, 8 and 12 months' credit, now the

Merchants sell for £34 per head and give no credit at all' (*Cal. S. P. Col.*, 1700, p. 19).

27. J. Oldmixon, *op. cit.*, ii, 167.

28. J. Oldmixon, *op. cit.*, ii, 167. Three copies of a bill were normally sent by different ships, so that if one miscarried the others would arrive.

29. Of the first 112 bills received by the Company between 1672 and 1675, 61 were payable at 30 or 40 days' sight, and 40 at 50 or 60 days' sight. Of 55 bills drawn in 1688, 26 were payable not at so many days' sight but on a certain date written into the bill, generally from six to twelve months after the bill was drawn. An interesting and (amongst these bills) rare form is a bill in which the date of payment was made contingent upon some event, for example, 'Three months after the safe arrival of the *George*, Samuel Jones, Commander, in the Port of London.'

30. P.R.O., T.70/276, under date 7 November 1692.

31. This action made Gardiner unpopular in Barbados and may have prejudiced his candidature for the political agency of the island. His conduct, the African Company's agents reported, 'extreamly disobligeth his freinds by exposeing Theire reputation and for Bringing it into contempt here to there Great Damage (P.R.O., T.70/17, fo.61r.).

32. The average London wholesale price of Barbados sugar in December 1688 was 23s. 6d. a 100 lbs; in December 1689 it was 33s. 6d.; in November 1690, 34s.; in December 1693, 38s.; in December 1695, 55s.; details from an index of sugar prices compiled from the records of the African Company's sales.

33. *A West-India Fortune*, pp. 186–87.

34. *Caribbeana*, ed. V. L. Oliver, i, 51–57.

35. P.R.O., Chancery Proceedings, C. 5, 238/47.

36. *A Young Squire of the Seventeenth Century*, ii, 213–14.

37. F. W. Pitman, 'The Settlement and Financing of British West India Plantations in the Eighteenth Century', *Essays in Colonial History presented to C. M. Andrews*.

38. V. T. Harlow, *A History of Barbados*, p. 203; A. D. Chandler, 'The Expansion of Barbados', *Journal of the Barbados Museum and Historical Society*, xiii, 1946, 106.

39. *Cal. S. P. Col., 1675–76*, p. 421.

40. In 1680 Barbados had 37,000 slaves; *Cal. S. P. Col., 1677–80*, No. 1336, xxiv. In 1748 she had 47,000, an increase of only 27 per cent; F. W. Pitman, *The Development of the British West Indies*, Appendix I. Jamaica, on the other hand, had 9,000 in 1673 and 112,000 in 1746, an increase of 1,150 per cent (*ibid.*).

41. 80 acres in 1712 (Pitman in *Essays in Colonial History presented to C. M. Andrews*, p. 260).

42. Harlow, *op. cit.*, pp. 306–07.

43. *Cal. S. P. Col., 1669–74*, No. 1101, ii.

44. J. Oldmixon, *op. cit.*, ii, 111.

45. If owners employed managers or attorneys with power to draw bills, the number emanating from the large estates might well be greater than appears.

46. British Museum, Sloane MS., 2441, fos. 21r–22r.

47. Butler to Cromwell, 'The islanders heer much desire commerce with strangers, our English merchants trafficquing to those parts being generally great extortioners', quoted in Harlow, *op. cit.*, p. 88.

48. P.R.O., C.O. 1/15, No. 70. Further evidence of the notorious animosity between planters and merchants is to be found in C.O. 1/23, No. 20, and in Oldmixon, *op. cit.*, ii, 155.

49. Compare L. M. Penson, *The Colonial Agents of the British West Indies*, pp. 10–11.

50. *A True and Exact History of the Island of Barbadoes*, pp. 95–96.

51. Limitation of production was preached by Thomas Tryon, *Letters, Domestick and Foreign to Several Persons of Quality*, Nos. xxxii and xxxiii.

52. This quotation and the evidence for falling prices derive from an index of wholesale sugar prices for the years 1674 to 1695 compiled from the records of sales of sugar by the African Company. Cf. N. Deerr, *A History of Sugar*, ii, 530–31.

53. Jamaica, presumably because sugar slumped before she was too deeply committed to it, remained an island of 'mixed planting' in the eighteenth century (F. W. Pitman, *Essays in Colonial History presented to C. M. Andrews*, pp. 263–64).

54. An instance of what this subjection could mean is to be found in the records of the African Company. In 1682 the Company's agents entered into an agreement with other factors in Jamaica to depress the price of sugar by holding up their purchases. So strong was the combination that the agents believed nothing could mar its success but the insistence of principals in England upon early returns (P.R.O., T.70/10, fo. 28r, T.70/15, fos. 30r, 31r).

55. The names of the most active agents with the number of bills drawn on them in favour of the African Company are: Paul Allestree (53 bills), Sir John Bawden, trading in his own name and as Bawden & Co. (136), Robert Chaplin (26), Thomas Clarke (47), Sir John Eyles, in his own name and as Eyles & Co. (126), Christopher Fowler (39), Henry Hale (24), Thomas Hart (24), John Harwood (46), Thomas Hinchman (39), John Hill (20), Thomas Robson (23), John Sadler (30), Benjamin Skutt (22), Edward Thornburgh (37), Richard Tilden (37), Thomas Tryon (40), Anthony Wallinger (39) and Richard Worsam (21).

56. L. M. Penson, *The Colonial Agents of the British West Indies*, pp. 250–51; *Cal. S. P. Col., 1677–80*, Nos. 197 and 413; *Cal. S. P. Col., 1681–85*, No. 274.

57. Compare Christopher Jeaffreson, who marketed his own sugars but refused the commissions of his friends (*op. cit.*, ii, 213–14).

58. *Some Memoirs of the Life of Mr. Thomas Tryon* (1705), pp. 40–41. Tryon spent five years in Barbados making hats.

59. The Eyles were a Wiltshire family; see below.

60. P.R.O., Chancery Proceedings, C.5/455/40 and C.5/97/4; T.70/79–82 for hiring of ships belonging to Bawden; *Cal. S. P. Col., 1681–85*, No. 1106.

61. J. Oldmixon, *op. cit.*, ii, 47–48. Bawden was knighted in 1687 and in the same year became an alderman of the City of London.

62. For the Eyles family, see *Wiltshire Notes and Queries*, i, 213, 265, 301, 366–67. 390–1; v 431; vi 371; vii 444; viii 145–51; P.R.O., Chancery Proceedings, C.8/242/138, C.7/405/40, C.7/530/76; Will of John Eyles, P.C.C. 109 Degg; *Calendar of Treasury Books, 1689–92*, Part V, 1972, 1974, 1983, 1984.

63. Dalby Thomas, *op. cit.*, Dedication and pp. 48–49.

64. Oldmixon, *op. cit.*, ii, 47–48.

25

The French West Indian Sugar Business

ROBERT STEIN

Political reason insists the the colonies always be dependent upon the mother country.
— 'Sur les retours des colonies' (anonymous memoir)

Once the cane was grown and processed, it remained for the plantation director to sell the sugar, preferably at a profit. In selling his sugar, the planter entered into a complex relationship with French or colonical merchants that was often characterized by bitterness on both sides. The planters believed that the merchants were abusing their monopoly privileges over trade with islands, while the merchants accused the planters of subverting the entire colonial system by illegally trading with foreigners. The debate became particularly acrimonious late in the eighteenth century, when colonial debts to French merchants reached unprecedented heights. It is against the background of increasing colonial indebtedness and growing French frustration that the West Indian aspects of the sugar business must be considered.

Any examination of the sugar trade in the colonies must begin with the quantities involved, both per plantation and per colony. In spite of limited and occasionally conflicting evidence, it appears that the average sugar plantation in the French West Indies produced anywhere from 100,000 to 250,000 pounds of sugar. The most reliable figures come from Christian Schnakenbourg's study of Guadeloupe: he estimated that in the late eighteenth century the average Guadeloupe sugar plantation of 181 carrés, of which 57.5 were planted in cane, produced some 900 quintaux (about 90,000 pounds) of sugar. This was clayed sugar, however, and must be converted into its equivalent in muscovado. Using Seymour Drescher's conversion factor of

1.42, the average Guadeloupe plantation produced 1,250–1,300 quintaux of muscovado. This was considerably lower than contemporary estimates of good or even modest yields. Tascher de la Pagerie, for example, claimed in 1787 that an average 100-carré plantation should yield 3,500 quintaux of sugar, and a good one 4,000 quintaux. Even if Tascher was talking about muscovado and even if he meant 100 planted carrés, his figures would still be almost double Schnakenbourg's. D'Auberteuil was even more extravagant in 1776, believing that a 150-carré plantation should yield 12,000 quintaux of muscovado. Similar discrepancies existed in productivity-per-slave figures. Schnakenbourg has calculated that on Guadeloupe it took 112 slaves (of whom 85 were adult) to produce 900 quintaux of clayed sugar, each adult slave yielding some 1,500 pounds of muscovado. But contemporary estimates were again much higher. Tascher believed that 100 (adult?) slaves could produce 3,500–4,000 pounds of muscovado, a figure unequalled even by d'Auberteuil, who claimed 2,400 pounds each on a good plantation. D'Auberteuil admitted elsewhere that his figures were somewhat optimistic and that planters could hope to get 2,000 pounds per slave only on exceptionally fertile land.[1]

The contemporary estimates for Saint Domingue seem more reliable, although the data are incomplete. In 1791 Saint Domingue planters exported some 163 million pounds of sugar to France, a figure that rises to 192 million pounds when the 70 million pounds of clayed sugar it includes are converted to their equivalent in muscovado.[2] This was produced on 800 sugar plantations for an average yield of nearly 240,000 pounds (2,400 quintaux) each; the 350 muscovado plantations produced 93

The French Sugar Business in the 18th Century (Baton Rouge, 1988), pp. 74–89.

million pounds, or 270,000 pounds (2,700 quintaux) each, while the 450 clayed-sugar plantations produced a bit more than 200,000 pounds (2,000 quintaux) each (muscovado equivalent). These figures are much higher than their Guadeloupe counterparts, reflecting the larger plantation sizes on Saint Domingue and, perhaps, their greater fertility. Some Saint Dominque plantations were immense, like Grande Place, owned by the Marquis de Gallifet.[3] With nearly 400 slaves, it produced up to 650,000 pounds of sugar (muscovado equivalent) in one year. This was nearly ten times the output of a small plantation on Martinique, such as the one at Anse à l'Ane owned by the Comtesse de la Rochefoucault and the Marquise de Cheylarfont. There some 150 slaves produced about 70,000 pounds of sugar per year (muscovado equivalent) in the 1770s.[4]

Colonial production figures would be even higher if they were complete. Unfortunately, reliable statistics exist only for exports to France, and there is no sure way of ascertaining gross production figures. There are a few eighteenth-century estimates of colonial sugar production, but these are of limited value and usually ignore the problem of smuggling.[5] In spite of numerous laws to the contrary, smuggling was a major business in the French West Indies, and it undoubtedly consumed a significant portion of the French colonial sugar crop. The most notorious smugglers were the Guadeloupeans, although they may well have been rivalled by residents of the south of Saint Domingue. Schnakenbourg has estimated that between 1667 and 1789, anywhere from 17 to 60 per cent of the annual Guadeloupe sugar crop went to smugglers, with the overall average approaching 40 per cent.[6] This is probably higher than the rest of the French colonies, but there is no way of knowing for sure. It is dangerous enough to assume a constant rate of smuggling, let alone attempt to identify that rate.[7] All that can be said for certain is that Saint Domingue produced from two-thirds to three-quarters of all French West Indian sugar late in the Old Regime.

In selling his quarter of a million pounds, or 250 barrels, of sugar each year, the typical planter wanted both high prices and the security of a guaranteed market, a combination not always feasible. In practice, therefore, planters had to decide whether to use the services of a middleman based either in the colonies or in France. Although most planters opted for these services, many did not and instead tried to market their own sugar. Basically, there were two ways of disposing of sugar without having recourse to merchant intermediaries.[8] Planters could sell directly to ship captains or to foreigners. Selling directly to captains was the time-honored means that had been so useful in the colonies' early days. It was essentially a barter system: the passing ship captain traded flour, wine, or manufactured goods from Europe to the planter for sugar either on hand or to be produced after harvest. Although such a system was apparently declining by the eighteenth century, it was still used until the Revolution, particularly by small shippers and out-of-the-way planters. Now, however, the shippers exchanged slaves for sugar, with both sides saving the commissions charged by merchants.

The second direct-sale system was illegal because it involved selling sugar to foreigners. Throughout most of the Old Regime, it was illegal for French West Indian planters either to sell sugar to foreigners or to purchase most commodities from them. However, in areas that proved to be unpopular with French merchants, such as the Lesser Antilles and the south of Saint Domingue, many planters came to depend upon the services of British, American, or even Dutch smugglers. Although present from the earliest days of colonial settlement, smuggling first became a major factor in the colonial economy during the War of the Austrian Succession (1744–48). As the Conseil Supérieur of Martinique notes in 1759: 'That war, so glorious for the nation through its victories, became harmful for our colonies through the weakness of our navy . . . . The need to turn abroad forced the creation of a trading system.'[9] This new system relied upon the sale of French colonial commodities to foreigners in return for flour, cod, manufactured goods, and especially slaves.

Illegal deals with foreigners took place in several ways.[10] One was quite traditional, with transfers of merchandise made in secluded inlets at night. Variations of this method were numerous and sophisticated, but all involved some nocturnal sleight of hand, such as this sugar-for-slaves trade described in 1730:

To go to this island [the Dutch Colony of Saint Eustatius] in total security to buy Negroes with the intent of reselling them, the French on Martinique make simulated declarations to the Bureau des Domaines claiming that they are shipping to Saint Domingue a certain number of local Negroes that [in reality] they have borrowed from their neighbors. The declaration made for form's sake, the Negroes return to their masters, and during the night the false claimants load their boats with sugar or other commodities and sail to Saint Eustatius, where they trade their cargo for the number of Negroes claimed on their declaration and proceed to sell them on Saint Domingue.[11]

Another means of smuggling was more innovative; it involved filling barrels labelled SYRUP with sugar and selling them openly to foreigners. After the Seven Years' War, the government allowed the colonists to sell the largely unwanted beverages to foreigners under the well-defined — but scarcely obeyed — conditions. The planters viewed this as an open invitation to fraud and were encouraged to do so by the generally benign neglect of the colonial administration. As one observer put it: 'Whole lots are sold in molds to be shipped to Havana and new England. How many other Americans are there who, while declaring "syrups" and "tafias", are actually exporting [clayed sugar] ... ?' So common were these and similar practices that the French consul in Boston wrote to his superior that 'the illegal commerce is conducted openly between our islands and my department'.[12]

Illicit transactions affected the colonial economy and aroused the ire of French merchants. According to the merchants, massive foreign purchases raised sugar prices in the islands, but low foreign shipping costs plus government subsidies prevented similar price increases in Europe.[13] Unaided by subsidies and faced with high shipping costs, the French merchants were hurt by high purchase prices and low sale prices. The French merchants also lost when foreigners illegally sold goods to the French West Indian planters. Although the French merchants had a theoretical monopoly over most kinds of sales to the islands, foreigners subverted that monopoly, particularly from 1744 to 1783, and introduced vast quantities of slaves, flour, cod, and manufactured goods. In 1765 one person observed, 'The English are selling Negroes all over Saint Domingue.' And the previous year he noted that 'English flour continues to be introduced freely and with all kinds of abuses.' The Dutch also participated in the illicit trade, although they specialized in selling manufactured goods to the planters. As Frances Armytage remarked: 'The Dutch at St. Eustatius were rich and prosperous solely because they were the distributors of European manufacturers to all the French islands in the vicinity .... The French had not been able to supply their own colonies with enough provisions and manufactures for some time,

and St. Eustatius had become their chief source of supply.' These purchases claimed a significant quantity of French West Indian commodities: 'A paper ... stated that the French West Indian produce loaded at St. Eustatius was enough to fill forty or fifty large ships in a year.'[14]

Even so, most exports of sugar were legal and were facilitated by the services of one or two merchants. Basically, the planter had his sugar shipped to a French merchant, either with or without the intermediary of a local merchant, and then the sugar was usually sold to a Dutchman or a German. The contractual relationships, first, between the planter and the local and/or French merchant and, then, between the colonial and the metropolitan merchants varied according to the size and financial health of all concerned. Depending on the relative strength of the parties involved, the planter was either in control of the entire affair or very much at the mercy of the merchant(s).

Owners of small plantations had to limit their dealing to local merchants or, in the special case of Guadeloupe before the Seven Years' War, to merchants on Martinique.[15] The production of these small plantations was too small to necessitate direct dealings with the French ports, and local intermediaries were capable of handling it all. The colonial merchant, usually located in the larger towns, such as Cap Français, Port-au-Prince, or Saint Marc on Saint Domingue, Fort Royal on Martinique, and Pointe-à-Pitre or Basse Terre on Guadeloupe, could purchase the sugar from the planter for resale to French captains. More often, he could act as a commissioned agent, finding a buyer for the sugar and taking a substantial (usually 5 per cent) commission on the transaction. In either case the merchant profited from the deal, and the small planter made a quick sale.

Larger planters required more sophisticated arrangements involving the active participation of merchants in France. The planter's sugar was shipped to France, where it was sold by a merchant who kept a commission on the sale and remitted the rest to the planter. Financially healthy planters had great freedom in choosing which French merchants to patronize and were under no obligation to be faithful to any one agent. Of course, sugar tended to follow family lines, with planters preferring to use the trustworthy services of relatives, but in the absence of convenient family connections good service was the only criterion to adopt. Not having a long-term contract with a French merchant house, the planter was free to ship his goods on the first available ship going to the preferred destination, and solvent planters could deal with merchants in several French ports.

Once planters were in financial difficulties, their range of options was limited, at least on paper. They had to accept long-term arrangements with French merchant firms even though such arrangements were often draconian.[16] In extreme cases, hard-pressed planters had to abandon real control over their plantations to the French merchants, who in turn took over the often substantial debts of the plantation. Some French merchant houses specialized in this type of transaction, and the Bordeaux firm of Henry Romberg, Bapst and Company had contracts with nearly sixty planters on Saint Domingue in the 1780s.[17] Romberg, Bapst and Company agreed to pay off plantation debts, guarantee the delivery of European merchandise and African slaves to the plantations, and run the estates efficiently; in return the company had exclusive rights to sell the products of one plantation and priority in shipping the commodities in its ships. Such arrangements had certain advantages for the planters. Relieved of his debts and usually guaranteed a reasonable pension by the merchant, the planter was put back on his feet while retaining ownership of, albeit not control over, his plantation. The merchant, on the other hand, was drawn into the quagmire of colonial debt and could be extricated only in the unlikely case of the plantation turning a profit. But to transform virtually bankrupt plantations into profitable enterprises took more time and more money than most companies could afford, and the new plantation owners — the French merchants — quickly became overextended.

As Françoise Thésée noted, indebted planters used the French merchants more as bankers than as commissioned agents. Planters in effect used their merchant associates to finance inefficient operations, and by the end of the Old Regime the colonies were in considerable debt to the port merchants. Most of this money represented slave purchases that the planters had made but could not afford. This was not necessarily a new phenomenon; even in 1765 Stanislas Foache of Le Havre remarked, 'The old cargo debts are almost all for Negroes; there are very few for merchandise.'[18] Since it was difficult to force colonial debtors to pay, especially with foreclosure almost unknown on the islands, the only way the merchants could get their money back was to lend or invest even

more money, take over running the plantations, and once again hope to make a profit. The planter was well protected by local custom and had little reason to fear the loss of his estate. Local authorities were reluctant to force planters to pay their debts and all but refused to consider seizing real property. The problem originated in the early days of colonial settlement, when it appeared that a period of planter indebtedness was inevitable before profits could accrue. In order to protect the pioneering planters, laws were passed prohibiting the seizure of parts of the estate; in other words, slaves could not be seized by creditors. With the colonies developed, planters used their legal immunity to force loans from metropolitan merchants; they did this simply by contracting debts that they had no intention of repaying.[19]

Needless to say, merchant creditors did not acquiesce in this matter, but they had little chance of winning the battle. The legal administration on Saint Domingue sided with the planters, and exasperated merchants could only lament 'the sad job of recovering debts on Saint Domingue'. Actually, persistent efforts could reap come rewards, but only at the expense of alienating the debtor and losing future business. Most merchants simply considered it impossible to get anywhere with the authorities. 'Real seizures,' wrote one merchant in 1749, 'although permitted in America as in France, have not yet been concluded [successfully] on Saint Domingue. Some have tried this route more than once, but the infinite number of formalities, the lengths of time, and the dearth of legal procedures have disgusted all who have been involved with it.'[20] Ship's captains seemed to have somewhat better luck in dealing with colonists, but even they had to give up when faced with the expenses involved. After a while it simply became too expensive to wait for all payments to be made.

The impossibility of foreclosing left the merchant with little leverage over the planter once the initial commitment was made. The merchant could refuse to make a commitment; he could simply serve as a commissioned agent with no banking role. This, however, was to run the risk of accepting a secondary position permanently. By not offering any exceptional services to the planter, the merchant could not hope to attract as much business. Of course, not all planters were in desperate straits, but it seems that enough were to affect the health of the entire system by the 1780s. On the eve of the French Revolution, economic difficulties put into sharper relief both the similarities and the differences between merchant and planter. On one hand the colonists had to rely heavily on the frequently willing merchant for money; on the other hand the colonists viewed this money as a long-term capital investment, while the merchant thought it was a short-term loan. The result was considerable misunderstanding and bitterness.

In the middle of the dispute were the major colonial merchants. Whereas the smaller colonial merchants were independent retailers purchasing European goods from arriving ships and speculating in small quantities of colonial commodities, larger merchants were usually associated with French commercial houses and acted primarily as representatives of French interests.[21] The major colonial merchants served almost as frontline soldiers in the battle waged against the planters. As such, they had somehow to balance the unrelenting demands of the home office with the realities of colonial life. This was not always an easy task, a fact to which numerous impatient letters bear witness. As one colonial merchant complained to the head office, 'We are between the hammer and the anvil, between your interests and those of our landowners.'[22] The French merchant wanted all of his money immediately, the planter wanted to postpone repayment indefinitely, and the colonial merchant wanted to receive as much as possible from the former without forever losing the latter as a customer.

Most of the major colonial merchant houses were subsidiaries of French companies, although they did not necessarily begin that way. It was not at all unusual for small merchants in the French ports to go to Saint Domingue and make modest fortunes as commissioned agents; they then returned to France to establish major commercial houses using the services of the colonial companies they had created. But whether formed originally by a French merchant temporarily residing in the colonies or by one who had never left France, most significant colonial companies were accountable to parent companies in France. The French company always retained a controlling interest in the colonial one. For example, Stanislas Foache of Le Havre organized a company in Saint Domingue in 1777; Foache held a 50 per cent interest, and two colonial merchants split the remaining 50 per cent. Five years later, Foache reorganized the company as Stanislas Foache, Morange and Company, but again kept a 50 per cent interest personally, in addition to advancing money to two of his three

partners. This was quite typical, and similar arrangements existed for other colonial companies.[23] The French supplied the capital and the colonial agent the labor; profits were split accordingly.

Large colonial merchant houses handled all the French merchant's affairs in the area. Among other things, this included running plantations either owned or managed by the merchant; acting as commissioned agents on purchases and sales of slaves, colonial commodities, and European goods; and collecting debts. One overworked colonial merchant complained of his burden in a letter to the main office: 'I beg you to pay a moment's attention to our affairs and to their nature: five plantations in sugar that require constant surveillance: trials, credits . . . and all the costs of exploitation. Three coffee plantations that have the same needs to fill as the sugar plantations. In the office; books, letters, accounts, purchases, barreling, goods to sell, and finally recovering debts, this terrible thing in town and country.'[24]

The colonial merchant also had to be a shrewd observer of the colonial scene: he frequently speculated in sugar or other commodities and had to know what, when, and at what price to buy and sell. Such a wide range of activities required a large staff, and the major colonial merchant houses employed several skilled workers. Preparing to return to France from Cap Français in 1777, Stanislas Foache described his staff in a lengthy letter to his brother in Le Havre.[25] Foache was particularly pleased with the abilities of his workers, whom he preferred above almost all others in the town. The chef de maison described no fewer than eight office workers, at least two of whom later became partners in the company. These two were Hellot, pictured as an honest, intelligent young man of twenty-two who already handled many of the legal affairs of the company and who was to assume responsibility for the company after Foache's departure, and Morange, the meticulous cashier from Saint Domingue who had never been outside Cap Français or seen a plantation. The other employees included the hard-working Pellier; Gerard, the book-keeper from Martinique; Corneille, a local Creole who kept the books rather unsatisfactorily; La Croix, the director of the store or warehouse; and two travelling clerks.

Colonial agents were probably the only people in the colonies certain to make the profits from colonial commerce. Taking a commission on all transactions, they were able to avoid the problems besetting the planters. Although it was commonly believed that sugar planters made vast sums of money, such as was not the case. In spite of hypothetical calculations showing that a well-run estate should net profits of 25 per cent per year, few planters ever realized such profits in practice, and plantation records show losses almost as frequently as gains.[26] Even large, well-organized, and presumably well-run plantations did not necessarily make money. This was the case with the five plantations owned by the Marquis de Gallifet.[27] Worth some 5,500,000 livres in 1784, Gallifet's three sugar plantations (worth 5 million livres) and two coffee plantations (worth 500,000 livres) produced up to 300,000 livres' worth of goods per year. Unfortunately, expenses could be just as high, and in the thirty-two quarters from July 1, 1783, through June, 1791, the estate showed a profit in only sixteen. After eight years the five plantations actually had a net loss of 2,507 livres, even though revenues were nearly 3 million livres. The more modest Bongars sugar plantation did little better in the 1770s.[28] With about 200 slaves it produced 200,000 pounds of sugar per year, and from 1769 to 1779, total income was 1,114,000 livres. Expenses over the same period were 1,108,000 livres, leaving the plantation with a trivial surplus of 6,000 livres on what probably amounted to a capital investment of nearly 1 million livres. Individual plantations were clearly not always prosperous.

The overall picture was similar, especially later in the Old Regime. Very rough estimates indicate that the French colonists sold a maximum of 300 million livres' worth of goods annually before the Revolution. Jean Tarrade estimated that from 1784 to 1790 'imports from the colonies and from the Newfoundland fisheries' were worth some 200 million livres per year, a figure that should be augmented by a maximum of 50 per cent to account for smuggling and losses in transit. Colonial imports during the same period probably amounted to some 175 million to 200 million livres per year: close to 90 million livres for goods shipped directly from France, some 80 million livres for slaves, and the rest for goods purchased illegally from foreigners.[29]. Thus, the colonies had an annual profit of from 100 million to 125 million livres. This, however, was based on a total capital investment of over 2,000, million livres, for a profit of some 5–6 per cent.[30] This figure must be lowered somewhat to ascertain the planters' net profit; commissions charged by middlemen, taxes, and the like

prevented the planters from actually receiving all of their money. Indeed, the comité intermédaire of Martinique estimated in 1787 that net profits for all plantations on the island were in the neighborhood of only 2 per cent.[31]

It is commonly assumed that profit rates were higher earlier in the eighteenth century, but the data are not entirely convincing. Indeed, many historians seem to accept the notion of diminishing profits in order to explain the apparently unprecedented rancor that characterized merchant-planter relations following the American Revolution. Christian Schnakenbourg, for example, wrote of an economic crisis afflicting Guadeloupe, the other French West Indies, and perhaps even the entire Caribbean area from 1785 to 1790, an argument also advanced by Jean Tarrade for the French islands. Similar crises have been discerned in the French ports: Jean Meyer spoke of Nantes's declining profits, and François Crouzet implied much the same for Bordeaux.[32] The evidence for such statements, however, is often slight and usually rests on an unproven belief in an earlier golden age of high profits. Unfortunately, such a golden age, if it ever existed, was probably brief and of little significance. It is possible, as Schnakenbourg believes, that the first planters on Guadeloupe made annual profits of 25 per cent or, as Meyer implies, that early slave traders made profits of over 100 per cent, but such examples testify more to the high-risk nature of the early colonial and slave trades than to a subsequent crisis of declining profits. Once transatlantic commerce ceased being the preserve of a few adventurous souls and became another business run by calculating businessmen, it followed the normal laws of the marketplace, reflecting competition and supply and demand. In such conditions, astronomical profits were most unlikely and were due to some exceptional stroke of fortune, such as a sudden and unexpected dearth of ships in port. These quirks notwithstanding, colonial commerce normally provided a 5 per cent annual profit, about the same as good investments in France. Colonial trade did involve greater risks, but it also held out the possibility of greater profits and perhaps the prospect of greater or at least more rapid growth based on loans. In other words, credit was much looser in the colonies than in France.

What was unique about the last decade of the Old Regime was the very size of the entire operation, the increasing needs for captial to keep it functioning smoothly, and the sources of that capital. After the American war, the volume of trade between France and the colonies doubled, and debts increased accordingly. Instead of a recession, as in France, there was a tremendous boom in the 1780s for colonial commerce, and this boom was ultimately financed by credits provided — often voluntarily — by French port merchants on the verge of overextention. The central problem was with the slave trade, and for French slavers the American war was a critical turning point. Before the war, English slavers provided the French West Indies with a large proportion of its slaves, perhaps up to 50 per cent.[33] These slaves were notoriously cheap and provided the French planters with an economical source of labor. After the war the English were effectively excluded from the French West Indian slave market just when that market was expanding appreciably. Now the French merchants were supplying the colonies with virtually all the required slaves, and the French slave trade nearly doubled relative to prewar levels, going from an average of less than 60 expeditions per year to 110 per year. This meant that more than twice as much of the merchants' capital was being tied up for lengthy periods of time in slaving, and colonists' delays in repaying debts provoked an exceptionally strident response from the merchants.[34] Also, it should be noted that during the last decade of the Old Regime more medium-sized merchants were involved in slaving than ever before; these men had far smaller reserves than the large merchants who had dominated slaving in earlier periods, and they were affected more directly by the delays in payment.

Things looked no better from the planters' point of view. Expansion forced them to purchase more slaves than ever before, and the slave population of Saint Domingue alone went from an estimated 260,000 in 1775 to 465,000 in 1789.[35] The new slaves were supplied almost exclusively by French traders and were much more expensive than prewar English (or even French) slaves. In short, planters' expenses were rising rapidly, but revenues were temporarily lagging behind. It would be two or three years before the large labor force affected harvest sizes and plantation income, and it was the question of who was to finance the waiting period that sharply divided merchants from the planters during the 1780s. Thus, the impressive growth of colonial trade created short-term problems of considerable proportion. Had there been sufficient time available, these problems probably would have been resolved to the satisfaction of both planter and merchant, but

the French and Haitian revolutions brought the postwar period to an early end and made any such readjustments impossible.

The problems of the 1780s were 'growing pains', aggravated by the intense dislike of the merchants by the planters and the deep suspicions of the planters by the merchants. Tied together in a colonial economy and dependent upon that economy for their prosperity, the merchant and planter nonetheless pursued conflicting short-term policies and had opposing views of their respective roles in the system. The planter believed that the health of the colonial economy was the first priority; as one planter said in 1791 or 1792: 'There are two classes of men on Saint Domingue: the planter and the merchant. The first is the true colonist; he belongs to the land, either through possession or his work. Behold the citizen. The merchant . . . sacrifices all to his cupidity. He lives in Saint Domingue as a gambler lives by a gaming table. Behold the troublemaker.'[36] The French merchant, on the other hand, believed in the subordination of colonial interests to French commercial ones. The colonies should consume French goods and produce exotic commodities that French merchants could sell throughout Europe. Typical were the sentiments of the deputies of commerce: The colonies, they declared, 'consume the excess of the production of our soil and our manufactures . . . . They deliver in return luxury commodities that we lack and that habit has made necessary . . . . It is through sales of colonial commodities — after our own consumption — that we obtain a tribute of 70 million livres from foreign lands.'[37]

Thus, on the eve of the Revolution, there was a split between merchant and planter, but this must not overshadow the close ties between the two throughout the Old Regime. Although neither was completely satisfied with the colonial system and although both tried to gain advantages during the early days of the French Revolution, they realized that their fates were closely linked and that they both relied on the continuation of the slave trade and the slave system for their livelihood. The eighteenth-century French colonial economy depended on the use of slave labor, and slaves bore the burden of the entire operation. In determining just who profited and who lost from the system, it appeared that all were winners save the slaves, Planters, colonial merchants, French merchants, and African merchants made profits from the sales of either slaves or sugar or both, while the use of slave labor helped keep sugar prices relatively low in eighteenth-century Europe.[38] By keeping prices down, merchants helped to create a demand for sugar and coffee, which alone seemed to justify the entire operation.

Notes

1. C. Schnakenbourg, *Les sucreries de la Guadeloupe* (Paris, 1972), 88–89; Seymour Drescher, *Econocide* (Pittsburgh, 1977), 192; Tascher de la Pageine, 'Mes délassements', III, 110–11; Hilliard d'Auberteuil, *Considérations*, I, 236.
2. *Archives de la Chambre de Commerce, masseiles* (hereafter ACCM), H19 (printed in M. Avalle, *Tableau comparatif des pronitions des colonies françaises aux Antilles avec celles des colonies complanises, espagoles et hollandaises de l'anneé 1787 à 1788* (Paris, 1799), Table 11). The manuscript says 1794, but this is clearly impossible; internal evidence suggests 1791.
3. *Archives Nationeles* (hereafter AN), 107AP127, May 22, 1775; AN, 107AP128, dossier 4, May 12, 1784. For production figures see AN, 197AP130, dossier 1 (1790–91).
4. AN, T256/2.
5. See, for example, AN, F12 1639A, 'Mémoire sur les sucres', by an anonymous author. This claims that the French West Indies produced 160,000,000 lbs of sugar annually, but it does not break this figure down by colony or by type of sugar. It also ignores smuggling.
6. Schnakenbourg, *op. cit.*, 118, See also Jean Tarrade, *Le commerce colonial de la France à la fin de l'annien régime* (Paris, 1972), 111.
7. Drescher, *Econocide*, 46–47, 195–96, assumes a 'steady rate of smuggling from 1770 to 1787' and sets his rate at 11.1 per cent of total production. Unfortunately, evidence for these statements appears to be lacking. For a contemporary estimate of illegal sales to foreigners, see M. Weuves, *Réflexions historiques et politiques sur le commerce de France avec des colonies de l'Amérique* (Geneva, 1780), 54, Weuves believed that one-quarter of the production of the Lesser Antilles and one-eight of that of Saint Domingue went to smugglers. Avalle, *op. cit.*, Table 8, put the value of smuggled goods from the French islands at 5 per cent of total production in 1787.
8. On sales see Schnakenbourg, *op. cit.*, 100–26.
9. *Archives Départementales, Bouches du Rhône* (hereafter ADBR), C2561, March 7, 1759.
10. Schnakenbourg, *Les sucreries de la Guadeloupe*, 120–21. See also C. Frostin, *Histoire de l'autonomisme colon de la partie française de Saint Domingue anx* XVII² et XVIII² siècles (Paris, 1975), Chaps. 9–11; Tarrade, *op. cit.*, 101–12; Frances Armytage, *The Free Port System in the British West Indies, 1766–1822* (London, 1953), Chap. 3.
11. *Archive Départementales, Loire Attantigne* (hereafter ADLA), C735, mémoire by the Chamber of Commerce of Guienne (Bordeaux), September 2, 1730.
12. ADSM, BDM, 1.48, January 28, 1784; AN, Col F2B 8, July 21, 1784.
13. This was a common complaint. See for example, *Archives commerce Bordeuax* (hereafter ACB), HH49, April 22, 1786, and ADSM, BDM, 1.48, January 28, 1784. On the problems caused by the smugglers, see P. Butel, *La croissance commerciale bordelaise dans la seconde moitié du XVIII² siècle* (Paris, 1976), 216–21.
14. *Archive Départementales, Seine Maritime* (herafter ADSM), Funds Begoven Demeaux, 1.47, January 14, 1764 [sic; it should read 1765], and September 19, 1764; Armytage, *op. cit.*, 35–36.
15. Schnakenbourg, *op. cit.*, III.
16. Pierre Léon, *Marchands et speculateurs dauphinois dans le monde antillais au XVIII siècle* (Paris, 1963), 81.
17. This company is the subject of F. Thésée, *Les négociants bordelais et les wlons de Saint Domingue* (Paris 1972), upon which this section is largely based.
18. ADSM, BDM 1.47, June 13, 1765.
19. Thésée, *op. cit.*, 261. See also ADSM, BDM, 1.47, May 22, 1765, ADSM, BDM 1.48, February 7, 1784; and Article 48 of the Code Noir.
20. ADSM, BDM, 1.48, February 7 and August 25, 1784; ACCM, BDM, 1.48, June 4, 1749. According to Schnakenbourg, *op. cit.*, 235, there were but six foreclosures on Guadeloupe from 1778 to 1788, and this was a time of economic crisis.
21. For a description of the purchases made by merchants, see Weuves, *op. cit.*, 29.
22. ADSM, BDM, 1.48, May 18, 1784.
23. ADSM, BDM, 1.53, December 28, 1777, and May 15, 1782. For other companies, see Thésée, *op. cit.*, 29–30.
24. ADSM, BDM, 1.47, May 18, 1784.
25. ADSM, BDM, 1.47, January 3, 1777.
26. For example, see Tascher, 'Mes délassements', III, 110–11.
27. AN, 107AP128, dossier, 4, May 12, 1784, and dossier 1, July 1, 1783, to June 30, 1784 (brouillard).
28. AN, T520/2.
29. Tarrade, *op. cit.*, 740 says that 70,000,000 livres' worth were exported, but the colonists paid far more than that once commissions, taxes, and profits — all paid by the colonists — were added.
30. On total investment, see ACCM, H19, which evaluates Saint Domingue plantations at 1,488,000,000 livres. Schnakenbourg, *op. cit.*, 88–89, estimates Guadeloupe's sugar plantations to have been worth 155,000,000 livres; other Guadeloupe plantations plus all of Martinique's plantations would easily amount to more than 357,000,000 livres. For a comparison of profits, see Richard B. Sheridan, *The Development of the Plantations* (Barbados, 1970), 102, which estimates a similar profit on investments in Jamaica at this time. J. R. Ward, 'The Profitability of Sugar Planting in the British West Indies, 1650–1835', *Economic History Review*, XXXI (1978), 208, says that profits averaged about 10 per cent in the eighteenth century.
31. AN, Col F3 84, 'Examen des observations du commerce de la Martinique sur le procès verbal colonial par le comité intermédaire de cette assemblée', 1787.
32. Schnakenbourg, *op. cit.*, 127–239; Tarrade, *op. cit.*, 776, 783; Jo Meyer, *L'armement nantais dans la deuxième moitié du XVII² siècle* (Paris, 1969), 248, 250; François Crouzet in François Pariset (ed.) *Histoire de Bordeaux* (Bordeaux, 1968), V, 316–17.
33. P. Curtin, *The Atlantic Slave Trade* (Madison, 1969), 211, 216, as corrected by Stein, 'Measuring the French Slave Trade', *Journal of African History*, XIX (1978), 519–20.
34. Stein, 'Profitability of the Nantes Slave Trade, 1753–92', *Journal of Economic History, xxxv (1975)*, 791.
35. C. Frostin, *Les révoltes blanchesà St Domingue aux XVII² et XVIII² siècles* (Paris, 1975), 28.
36. *Discours historique sur la cause des désastres de la partie française de Saint Dominque* (Paris, [1792?]), 56–57.
37. AN, Col F2B 8, 'Avis de deputés du commerce', 1785.
38. Robert Paul Thomas and Richard Nelson Bean, 'The Fishers of Men: The Profit of the Slave Trade', *Journal of Economic History*, XXXIV (1974), 885–914.

26

The United States and the British West Indian Trade, 1783-1807[1]

SELWYN H.H. CARRINGTON

The War of American Independence (1775-83) had brought significant hardships to British West Indian planters. The islands suffered in different ways and experienced varying levels of deprivation during the war. All emerged with weakened economies, however, and the planters must have had doubts as to their ability to continue sugar planting in a changed commercial environment.

The return of peace certainly did not satisfy the hopes and expectations which the planters had for the sugar industry. While they wished for better crops, they were not sanguine about the direction in which their businesses were heading. Many wanted the relations between the newly-independent United States and the West Indian colonies to be re-established on their pre-war commercial basis in order to promote and maintain the economic viability of the sugar islands, whose war-time experiences clearly demonstrated their dependence on United States trade. But planter preferences ran counter to the aims and goals of the British policymakers and pro-imperialist groups, such as the Canadian loyalists and the British shipping industry. Even the Committee of West India Merchants and Planters found a spokesman in Lord Sheffield who fervently supported the exclusion of North American ships, and some of their foodstuffs and lumber, from the West Indian trade. Hence, by Order-in-Council of 2 July 1783, the United States was excluded from colonial markets on the principles of the Navigation Acts. Some articles such as salted beef, pork, fish and dairy products were prohibited, while the monopoly for supplying the islands went to the Irish and Canadians. After their war-time problems, the sugar islands encountered further insecurity, and the destabilization of the sugar industry continued.

The response to the post-war restrictions was critical. Most West Indian colonial governments supported the overall British policy, but were unhappy with its expected long-term impact on the islands. The only consolation discerned by David Parry, Governor of Barbados, was "that the advantages which may accrue to the Empire at large will highly compensate for the inconveniences His Majesty's West Indian Islands must for a long time sustain."[2] All West Indian Governors rejected the argument that Canada could supply the islands, and preferred to see the implementation of a strict, yet positive, trade arrangement between the United States and the West Indies.[3] Some recommended the admission of United States vessels under one hundred tons for about three years, or until Canadian production could meet the demands of the islands. Planters were equally critical of British policy. Simon Taylor, who had looked forward to peace, now dreaded it and accused the British Government of entering "into a combination to Ruin" the islands "with their high duties and Prohibition of the American Trade. Indeed they seem to be tired of the islands and look on the inhabitants as their Gibionites," he wrote.[4] Those who had expected relief from the large debts accumulated during the Revolutionary War, saw British policy as maintaining indebtedness by forcing them:

to pay a double price for their supplies which means their Debts to the Mother Country, which were considerable, before the capture of the island, instead of being diminished are greatly increased, to which is to be added a load of public debt for the payment of which such heavy taxes are about to be imposed on the People, as will almost be unsuperable in the present state of the reduced value of their produce, loaded with late additional duties imposed on it in the Mother Country, by which means the sugar yields but little to the Planter, and the high duty on Rum operates as a Prohibition to its Importation. While at the same time, from the present state of their commerce with America, they are in great measure deprived of the Benefits of the Market and likewise obliged to pay much higher than formerly for various Articles, indispensably necessary, which they chiefly depended on being supplied with, from that Quarter.[5]

British Policy was formulated on the belief that the United States was unable or unwilling to take effective retaliatory action. Under-Secretary of State, John Knox, based his opinion on the fact that the United States was importing more and more manufactured goods from Britain in spite of the Proclamation of 2 July 1783. He testified:

the orders from thence for our Manufactures are at this Time greater than at any period of the former Peace – And if they were inclined to enforce it . . . they could not find the means. They were not able to do it in the height of the War – the United States have not . . . but little Trade with any other Nation of Europe.[6]

Despite the optimism of British officials, the retaliatory measures adopted by many states in the new United States against British shipping and West Indian products had some effect. For example, Massachusetts, New Hampshire, and Rhode Island, prohibited British ships from loading any United States products, under penalty of seizure and condemnation. Maryland, North Carolina, and Pennsylvania, imposed an extra tax on British shipping, while the New England states placed an added charge on goods imported in British vessels.[7] New Hampshire, Massachusetts, Rhode Island, Virginia, North and South Carolina, and Georgia, charged higher duties on British than on French West Indian sugar and rum, thus discouraging importation.[8] These protective regulations, although without cohesion and probably not very strictly enforced, nevertheless adversely affected British shipping and the importation of West Indian staples into the United States.[9]

Imperial policy towards the United States trade created conditions which forced West Indians to adopt surreptitious practices for obtaining North American provisions and lumber. Some islands provided United States ships with British register,[10] while most colonies allowed illegal entrances of United States ships, expediting their handling to avoid detection, while ships from Canada remained idle.[11] British attempts to stop this trade by capturing the vessels involved resulted in the harassment of her naval officers by the colonists.[12]

As efforts to trade with their United States counterparts in their own ports failed, British West Indian merchants resorted to free ports in the neighbouring French islands to buy North American supplies.[13] This caused a massive depletion of the money supply from all the British islands, with an estimated 200,000 pounds annually leaving Barbados alone.[14] In his efforts to prevent this trade, Parry issued a proclamation restating British policy, and encouraging British ships to go to the United States for supplies.

Yet, on the whole, the operation of British policy did not achieve its goals. The prohibition of shipping did not lead to an increase of British seamen; rather, the number of slaves employed as sailors grew, especially on Bermudan vessels.[15] Canada was unable to supply the necessary foodstuffs, or even lumber. For example, none of the vessels arriving in Dominica after the Order-in-Council of 2 July 1783 came from Canada. Governor John Orde told Lord Sydney "as yet sorry am I to add, not a single vessel with any article of their produce had arrived."[16] Instead, St. Eustatius, St. Pierre in Martinique, and several ports in St. Domingue, became entrepôts for United States products destined for the British Islands.

The restrictions on United States commerce gave rise to a circuitous trade that went through the foreign islands. Consequently, the largest quantities of most United States supplies of lumber and provisions prohibited by law reached the British West Indian sugar plantations this way. Canada could not supply the demands of the islands; more plantation supplies were reaching the British sugar colonies through the foreign West Indies than from Canada.

Moreover, the systematic smuggling which developed as a result of British policy meant that the British sugar colonies were relying on foreign islands for most of their supplies: Montserrat, St. Kitts, Nevis and St. Vincent, for example, imported most of their United States supplies from St. Eustatius.[17] Table 26.1 gives the statistics illustrating trade between the United States, Canada, the foreign islands and the British West Indies, and shows that the quantities of most items imported from Canada were smaller than from the foreign islands, except for fish, and to a lesser extent, beef and pork. Although the quantities of some United States exports declined after 1785, combining the United States and the foreign figures, shows minimal, if any, decrease.

While goods from the United States were always in demand, the sugar planters suffered. The United States trade was simply "thrown into a new Channel, not destroyed by their separation from the Mother Country."[18] The trade with the foreign islands was, however, subverting British monopoly of the commerce of the British West Indies, so in April 1787, Parliament passed an Act prohibiting the entry of flour, bread, wheat, rice and lumber from the foreign West Indies into the British colonies, except when governors, on advice from their Councils, were empowered to permit the importation of a list of enumerated goods for a limited time only,[19] in cases of "real and very great necessity."[20]

After the issuance of the Prohibitory Act in 1776, and the Order-in-Council of 1783, the commanders-in-chief of every West Indian island were repeatedly requested to use the discretionary powers those measures allowed. In 1784, for example, when a severe gale did irreparable damage to property in St. Thomas in the East, residents there petitioned the Jamaican Assembly to request that the governor open the ports to United States provisions and lumber for six months. Initially, he refused, arguing that British shipowners should despatch their vessels to the United States for supplies. After being informed that there were no ships, and that he was bound to take the advice of the Council before refusing the petition, the governor conceded, and opened Jamaica's ports. His refusal may not have mattered, because some planters and merchants were in such a defiant mood over British policy that they were prepared to resort to unusual methods to secure supplies. Simon Taylor indicated:

if the importation is not allowed we must inevitably perish or bring in provisions without permission and indeed if some intercourse is not opened with America we must throw up the sugar estates into Provision Grounds and Penns or Migrate with our Negroes to the French Islands. Was Lyssons my sole property I would immediately throw it up for we are only labouring there to throw a Revenue into Britain without the least Benefit of ourselves. Indeed if the same rigorous Laws and high Dutys are continued I am determined to throw up my Properties. If I cannot sell them and move to some Government where the Laws will allow me to buy bread from Foreigners when I am starving. If we can get Provisions we may save the greatest part of our Negroes, if not they must be carried off with fluxes and Famine.[21]

British policy was not consistent with the continued development of a healthy sugar economy. The April 1787 Act (27 Geo. 111 C.7) was passed to diminish the commercial importance of the foreign West Indies, and to reduce migration there from the Leeward and Windward Islands and Barbados. It also sought to restrain the commerce of the United States with the West Indies because, some British officials conjectured, commercial jealousy between the several states might limit united action against Britain.[22] But the Act had hardly been proclaimed in the West Indies when its enforcement was suspended and the discretionary clause implemented. As Governor Shirley reported:

Soon after the receipt of the Act . . . I found the immediate operation of it would have been attended with such ruinous and fatal consequences to the British islands that I ventured to permit the intercourse with the foreign islands to continue for a short time...until the first day of October next, and I have also signified publicly that then the provisions of the Act will be strictly adhered to and carried into execution according to their full force.[23]

Governors used their discretionary powers to open West Indian ports to United States trade throughout the period from 1782-1807. The general practice was for petitions to be made to the Assembly and/or Council to permit the importation of provisions and lumber from the foreign West Indian islands in British vessels. If governors rejected the Council Boards' advice, their members were usually supported by planters and merchants in the ensuing conflict. But a governor's refusal could at times signal division between groups on the island, being used, as the Council of St. Kitts noted, by "some designing Persons to serve their own particular Purposes regardless of the general good."[24] The interpretation of the role of the Councils was also subjected to query on occasions when their recommendations were rejected. Since governors were obliged to take the advice of their

Table 26.1   Account of North American Provisions and Lumber imported into the British West Indies

Year	Ships	Tonnage	Flour (Bbls.)	Bread (Bbls.)	Rice (Bbls.)	Fish (Hhds.)	Beef & Pork (Bbls.)	Lumber (1,000 ft.)	Staves (No.)	Disassembled ("Shaken") Hogshead	Hoops (No.)	Corn (Bushels)	Horses (No.)	Oxen (No.)
THE UNITED STATES														
1785	635	49,021	82,887	14,834	6,415	449	-	12,497	27,201	3,572	258	132,451	1,667	176
1786	502	38,421	100,033	21,106	7,239	-	18	6,851	17,368	1,284	206	192,163	573	76
1787	417	89,641	95.406	15,789	7,366	33	-	4,409	16,708	466	157	154,550	224	20
BRITISH NORTH AMERICA (CANADA)														
1785	161	11,508	1,666	10	121	5,016	103	2,585	2,862	677	28	3,600	47	8
1786	192	13,974	3,623	582	51	4,988	290	3,666	3,999	188	6	6,624	131	9
1787	192	14,344	7,554	1,451	287	7,618	497	1,450	3,618	393	70	6,252	149	33
FOREIGN ISLANDS														
1785	-	-	-	-	-	-	-	-	-	-	-	-	-	-
1786	479	-	27,260	27,260	330	25	84	3,413	5,437	991	262	59,171	258	97
1787	479	41,491	15,933	15,933	776	-	166	3,975	14,783	563	300	37,631	390	203

Sources: A Comparative State of Trade between the West Indian Islands, the United States of America, the British Colonies in 1785-1786, Add. MSS. 38, 347, fos. 336-37, British Library, London; A Comparative State of Trade between the West Indies and North America from 1 October 1785 to 1 October 1787, showing No. of Vessels, Tonnages, and their Cargoes, C.O. 318/1, fo. 135, Public Record Office, London.

Council Boards when considering requests for allowing United States trade, Council members believed that Parliament had placed its confidence in the Boards to judge such emergencies. Consequently, when their recommendations were disregarded, the members contended that this confidential trust had been violated.[25]

Claims of shortages and the clamour for opening the ports throughout the British West Indies were tied to interest groups. Early in the practice of suspending the Act and opening the ports, many merchants benefitted from the trade, contrary to the interest of the planters, by re-exporting the goods to neighbouring islands, and reaping exorbitant profits. These merchants who had no commitment to the sugar industry, saw their businesses prosper from restrictions on the United States trade. In order to curb this practice, proclamations suspending the Act began to include a clause "obliging the importer to bond at entry" all goods and lumber, "and not to export without previous permission from the Governor."[26] Different interest groups within the merchant class also adopted metropolitan alliances throughout the years, and became associated with efforts to control opening or closing of West Indian ports. In Barbados, for example, when Governor Seaforth closed the ports to United States trade on the petition of some merchants, public meetings were held at which Customs House Officers and other officials reportedly appeared in support of groups opposing his action. Several pro-United States sentiments were loudly voiced. One colonial official exclaimed: "Mother Country! America is the Natural Mother of these Colonies." Governors, on the other hand, by enforcing British policies, were usually linked with the imperialist faction. Governor Seaforth highlighted this conflicting situation:

in this manner I left the council not very easy in my mind for I knew that parties would not rest till they either drove me to some harsh measure or compelled me to give up the point. They imagined or effected to imagine that I was acting in contradiction to my orders from home and the Americans who were on the spot were not idle in assisting to increase the clamour against me by insinuating that if they were not allowed to sell their salt meat and fish they would sell nothing – they had even the impertinence to insinuate this to me.[27]

At times the governors must have felt that, irrespective of their decisions, they would face severe criticism. On occasion, some tried to steer a middle course by making exemptions in order to satisfy those groups not linked to the United States trade. This was particularly the case of Governor Nugent in Jamaica who, faced with general demands throughout the island for opening the ports to United States trade, acceded to the requests. He was equally conscious, however, of the need to pay "due attention to the interests of the British and Irish provision merchants and 'Graziers' as well as the fisheries by excluding the articles they supplied to Jamaica."[28] The enforcement of the Act posed continued problems for all governors. British policy was from its inception seen as retrogressive commercial action. Governor Parry of Barbados was the first to point out this limitation:

The Dismemberment of the American Colonies from the British Empire, leaving them at perfect freedom to exercise their Talents and to improve the materials with which nature had supplied them for the purpose of Commerce, had in effect estranged the objects and circumscribed the Power of the Navigation Act. The Act being no longer capable of enforcing obedience to its restraints over so large a territory as it formerly controlled, the purpose for which it was passed are in a great measure defeated.[29]

The reinforcement of the Navigation Act by the April 1787 Act (28 Geo. 111C. 7) caused ongoing tension and conflict in societies whose declining economic systems were linked to the exclusionist policy established by the 1783 Order-in-Council. The policy was occasionally evaded, and was unable to function smoothly, since it tried to suppress the interests of the very men who advised the governors. Thus, it created conflict between the merchant and the planter classes.

By the 1790s, the operation of British policy became even more difficult to enforce. Governor Shirley of the Leeward Islands observed:

The Council Board appears to consider itself entitled to compliance whenever it represents the necessity of opening the ports, notwithstanding any other information which the Governor may have received. So that the Governor must either desert his duty to the Nation at large by constantly complying with the requisitions made by the Council to open the Ports or keep himself in disagreement with the Colony, by refusing to comply with requisitions when he had received information that there is not any necessity for opening the Ports . . . If the requisition for opening the Ports is always to be complied with when made by the Council the restrictions contained in the Act will be totally nugatory.[30]

Throughout the period of the French Wars (1789-1815), severe shortages, and depressed economic times resulted in repeated appeals from legislative bodies, merchants and planters for the reinstatement of all levels of United States trade with the West Indies, including the use of United States ships. Many members of the colonial interest groups viewed the continued policy of carrying on the trade in British ships as "fatal to the islands'" economic development.[31]

The justification for the continued practice of using the discretionary clause to open the ports to North American trade in United States ships was because of the trifling quantity of supplies, compounded by unreliable shipping, from Ireland, Britain, and Canada.[32] The shortages which planters experienced during the American War of Independence were exacerbated by British exclusionist policy in the 1780s and by the French Wars during the 1790s and afterwards. Generally, the planters experienced grave hardships after 1776, and these continued beyond the first decade of the nineteenth century, with most of the British West Indies remaining almost totally dependent on regular supplies of foodstuffs and lumber from the United States. In addition there was a severe diminution of rum sales to the North American market.

Hence, in order to meet the quantities of provisions and lumber adequate to the local West Indian demand, proclamations were issued periodically permitting United States vessels to the trade, although these were directly contrary to the law. Consequently, Parliament passed Acts of Indemnity to protect the governors from being penalized for their actions. The permission for United States ships to enter West Indian ports by proclamations was for stipulated periods of time. In a few cases, such as Barbados, these were continued indefinitely, with succeeding commanders-in-chief simply reissuing the original document.

Consequently, the policy which was to be the exception became the rule. From 1794 on, Customs House Officers throughout the British West Indies annually admitted the entry of those articles which were listed in the original proclamation. Governors, however, were not allowed to include the importation of salted beef and pork, but since the quantity of these products imported from Britain, Ireland and Canada was very small, they were illegally brought with legitimate cargoes and landed either surreptitiously, or with the governors' permission, along with those articles allowed by proclamation. Not

all colonial officials adhered assiduously to the tenets of British policy. Some governors refused to open the ports even when conditions of famine were apparent. Others simply turned a blind eye to the operation of the North American trade. Yet others adopted the recommendations of their Councils without question. This was especially the case when the governor was replaced by the President of the Council who acted as commander-in-chief.[33]

Opening the ports did not always achieve the intended results. In some instances as, for example, in 1794, there was only minimal response from United States traders because their government had imposed an embargo on trade with the West Indies because of the Royal Navy's impressment of United States seamen and its capture of United States ships.[34] Furthermore, in some instances, the wrong goal was achieved, since opening the ports not only gave rise to significant illegal trade, but also led to the exportation of sugar in United States vessels. The Colonial Office was incensed by this latter action, with West Indian officials offering as an excuse the refusal of the North Americans to take rum, or the lack of sufficient specie with which to pay them. The export of sugar in United States vessels defeated the British government's policy of forcing down sugar prices since imports to Britain would be reduced, thus maintaining or even forcing up prices on the London market. In spite of the British government's efforts, the United States became the chief neutral carrier of tropical products to Europe. This angered the Duke of Portland, Secretary of State for the Colonies, who wrote to Governor George Poyntz Ricketts of Barbados:

it is with concern . . . that I feel myself under the necessity of representing to you how, materially, the interests of the island, and his Majesty's Property in general have been injured by the exercise of the liberty you have assumed, even exclusive of the National Evil arising from it – For it ought not to have escaped you that it is through this very channel and by these very means that Neutral Markets are supplied by American and other countries, and you should have recollected that exactly, in proportion as that supply is furnished them, the price of the Markets here must fall – it is impossible in this respect to separate the Public interest from that of the individuals – and I therefore cannot too strongly state to you my expectation that you will forthwith proceed to diminish the proportion of sugar now allowed to be exported, in return for American Produce, and that you would disallow it altogether as soon as possible.[35]

Table 26.2   Rates of Exchange at War Prices (1776-1782) for North American and Jamaican products

North American Produce					Jamaican Produce				
Item	Quantity	Price			Item	Quantity	Price		
		£	s.	d.			£	s.	d.
Staves	(1,000 ft.)	40							
Saltbeef	(bbl.)	5			Sugar	(cwt.)	3		
Salt pork	(bbl.)	7	10		Coffee	(cwt.)	5		
Fish	(bbl.)	3	10		Rum	(gal.)	4		6
Salt Fish	(cwt.)	25			Pimento	(lb.)			7½
Superfine flour	(bbl.)	7	10						
Inferior flour	(bbl.)	6	10						
Cornmeal	(bbl.)	3	10						
Corn	(bushel)	13							

Source: Tariff at war prices of American produce imported into Jamaica and of the produce of that island to be allowed to be taken away in return (no date). C.O. 137/106, Public Record Office, London.

The practice of permitting North Americans to take sugar as barter for lumber and provisions became general throughout the British West Indies, and the objections of the Colonial Office did not seem to terminate it. Indeed, some commanders-in-chief objected to the Duke of Portland's criticism. Robert Thompson of the Leeward Islands was obviously upset and displeased with Portland's language, and his response got to the heart of the problem with British policy on trade between the United States and the West Indies. He replied:

If his Majesty's Ministers would be pleased to take the Commercial Intercourse between the United States of America and the Islands into their consideration and to settle it upon some permanent basis, the Governors would then be exempted from all Solicitations for indulgences on the one hand, and from Censure on the other for that compliance with them.[36]

In order to expedite their trade with the North Americans, Jamaica established a system of tariffs formalising exchanges to guide the Customs House officers. Whereas most of the islands were giving a part of their local produce to pay for North American supplies (for example, Barbados reduced its payment in local produce from ⅓ to ¼ of the value of American goods[37]), the Jamaica Council Board recommended that the full value of the imports from the United States was to be paid in Jamaican products. Table 26.2

shows the rate of exchanges between American and Jamaican goods.

Numerous complaints from colonial officials and merchants involved in Irish, British and Canadian commerce with the islands, resulted in the termination of trade between the British West Indies and the United States. Lord Camden's directive of 5 September 1804 prohibited British West Indian governors from opening their ports to goods from the United States which were not permitted by law, "except in cases of real and very great necessity."[38] All commanders-in-chief also had to inform the Secretary of State when such cases arose, and provide justification. In essence, applications for relief now had to be made directly to the King through his ministers, and it was widely circulated "that the prohibitory order . . . would remain in force except his Majesty's pleasure should signify that it ought to be revoked."[39]

The reaction to British policy was swift and vociferous. The Assembly of Jamaica voiced serious opposition to Governor Nugent's order of 21 November 1804 terminating the trade between Jamaica and the United States as of 1 May 1805, and the controversy spread throughout the sugar islands.[40] West Indian interest groups in England also took up the matter. Lord Camden drafted an immediate response to West Indian governors:

I am now to acquaint you that the alarm which you state to have been excited in Jamaica has been extended to America, and to the Jamaica Merchants here; in consequence whereby a Meeting has been held at Mr. Pitt's upon the subject which was attended by the Duke of Montrose, Mr. Rose and myself.[41]

Camden now assured the Jamaicans that the governors still had the power to open the ports to neutral shipping "in cases of urgent and real necessity," while in the United States, Congress threatened to retaliate to British exclusion by forcing all exports of provisions and lumber to be carried in United States vessels.[42]

The British government was sensitive to the problems that its exclusionist policy caused in the United States, and sought to assure the North Americans that the policy was not discriminatory. The Colonial Office thus published a notice in the United States press that West Indian governors still retained the discretionary powers to relax, when necessary, "the rigid Provisions of the Navigation Laws," to allow the importation of provisions and lumber in North American or neutral bottoms,[43] and Lord Musgrave, the Foreign Secretary, was directed to instruct the British representative in Washington that Lord Camden's letter was not intended to discriminate against the United States. On the contrary,

the British Administration had nothing in view but restoring the Trade with our Colonies as far as can conveniently be done, to the Provisions of the Laws which had been in force for a century and a half, a due attention to which had been interrupted only by the late [French Revolutionary] War, and that instead of having been made more strict they had of late years been very much relaxed.[44]

In its diplomatic communique, the imperial government recognised the dependence of the West Indian colonies on supplies of provisions and lumber from the United States. Consequently, the Board of Trade took up the question of North America trade with the West Indies, and ruled that it was necessary to continue the practice of allowing the importation of provisions and lumber into the islands in exchange for molasses and rum during the Napoleonic War, since there was not a sufficient number of British ships to go to the United States for supplies.

The Board recommended that the governors' discretionary powers be retained and that they be allowed to suspend the Navigation Laws for limited periods according to the necessity of each colony. West Indians who had long been frustrated by the attitudes of the British government, and who knew that United States lumber and provisions were needed for a profitable sugar industry, now pushed for a clearly defined policy. The Assembly of Jamaica stressed:

the indispensable necessity which exists of the permanent establishment of an intercourse between the United States of America and the Island of Jamaica upon a liberal footing, and not to be rendered liable to the recurrence of an interruption, similar to that which has been recently experienced is established by referring to authentic documents.[45]

The dependency of the sugar colonies on the United States is nowhere more clearly highlighted than in the statistics giving the trade in provisions and lumber between each island and the United States between 1772 and 1806. The other revelation which the statistics show conclusively is that the imperial policy of restricting the transport of North American foodstuffs and lumber in British vessels did not work. It is also clear that overall, smaller quantities of all categories of goods were imported into the islands in the period after 1794 than in 1772.

The reduced supplies of North American provisions and lumber reaching the West Indies after the issuance of the Prohibitory Act in 1776, led to a marked increase in the prices of all articles. Hence, operating their estates became a severe burden to most planters after 1776. The price of lumber, for example rose significantly during the War of American Independence and continued at a high level thereafter, and although the price declined in the 1780s and for some periods in the 1790s, it never again fell to pre-1775 levels.

The resumption of war with the outbreak of the French Revolution forced up prices of all supplies to new heights, especially since British policy prohibited the direct flow of goods between the United States and the West Indies. Herrings, the principal protein source for slaves, rose from 45s. per barrel in 1791 to 65s. in 1793; shads were only a couple of shillings cheaper. Flour, which before 1775 was relatively cheap (thereby allowing managers to sell plantation-grown plantains at high prices and buy good quality flour for the slaves with the proceeds) rose by 220 per cent, from 37s 6d. to 6 pounds per barrel. The price of corn, the staple of the slaves' diet, increased dramatically on all the islands, rising from 7s. 6d.-8s. Per bushel in 1790 to 10s.-14s. in 1792-93.[46] The impressment of United States citizens by British captains deepened the crisis in Anglo-United States relations, and made life difficult for the West Indian planters, because the United States government retaliated by imposing an embargo on trade with the British West Indies. This further reduced supplies to the islands and corn prices soared to as much as 24s. 9d. per bushel early in 1797.[47]

In Barbados, prices of plantation supplies and lumber were 225 and 440 per cent above pre-American Revolution prices, and while the Windward Islands were generally more self-sufficient in food supplies than the older sugar colonies, they too suffered from exceptionally high prices. In Dominica and St. Vincent, commodities such as salted pork and lumber cost 325-1220 per cent more than they had before 1775, although in Grenada the level of increase was much lower.[48]

All the sugar colonies needed vast quantities of North American lumber for making hogsheads and barrels to ship their sugar and rum. On the older islands, most of the woodlands had been cut down, but more importantly, tropical rain forests did not contain large quantities of lumber well-suited to shipping edible commodities. Hence the reliance on North America for supplying staves and hoops and even the lumber, shingles and frames for building houses. Lumber prices soared. Indeed, some colonies had no price quotations for lumber, because none was available. In other cases, lumber prices were from 600 to 1,200 per cent higher than the 1775 figures.[49]

Such massive price increases, of course, significantly increased the costs of running a sugar estate and diminished its profitability. Moreover, there was no reciprocal trend in the price of rum. While sugar was central to the West Indian economy, the islands' profitability also depended on the production and sale of other crops, and of rum, whose value to eighteenth-century West Indian commerce cannot be overstated. The sugar planters used rum to procure supplies for their estates, bartering it with the North Americans for lumber and provisions, or selling it locally to meet the contingencies of the estates. Rum normally paid for all the local expenses of West Indian plantations, including the purchase of slaves, and the main consumers of West Indian rum were the North American colonies. But beginning with the American Revolution, and for the most part because of British policy, rum sales to this market were restricted. The British government's failure to allow the West Indies to establish reciprocal commerce with the United States weakened the islands' bargaining position in the rum trade, and the problems continued through the 1780s, worsening in the 1790s with the outbreak of the French Wars. Canada and Ireland, which were expected to replace the United States market, did not contribute in any meaningful way to relieving the islands' inability to dispose of their rum, although the destruction of the sugar industry in St. Domingue provided temporary relief.

The Haitian revolution rejuvenated the British markets on which the West Indians depended. The planters hoped the high prices that resulted from the revolution would persist, allowing them to meet their high food and lumber bills and repay their longstanding debts. Between 1795 and 1796, the average prices for rum in Jamaica increased from 5s. 6d. to 8s.8d. Similar trends existed in St. Vincent, where the price of rum skyrocketed from 3s.5d. per gallon in 1794 to 8s.3d, in 1796, although it fell to 7s.7d. per gallon in 1797. The market was limited, however, and West Indian planters found themselves unable to dispose of their rum readily, and prices began to fall again. In Dominica, rum sold for 4s. 3d. To 4s. 6d. per gallon between 1804 and 1807, while the lowest prices were for Grenadian rum – 2s. 9d. to 3s. 7d. per gallon in the years 1805-07. Jamaican rum did only marginally better, selling at 3s. 2d. to 3s. 8d. between 1805 and 1807.[50]

In the British West Indies, rum could not command satisfactory markets and sales. Moreover, changes in production were occurring throughout the world: the United States, for example, was now distilling its own products. Nor did Canada and Ireland, which were given the West Indian market for their lumber, fish, dairy products, beef and pork, reciprocate by purchasing West Indian rum, which now became a drug on local markets. By the abolition of the slave trade in 1807, conditions on the islands were precarious, and rum's traditional role in the economy of the British West Indies could no longer be maintained. In spite of warnings to the contrary, estate managers were forced to defy their absentee landlords and draw bills on them to make up the deficiency in rum sales and thus meet the contingency costs. This was a significant departure from the system that financed the operation of West Indian estates during the eighteenth century.

The dependence of the West Indian islands on external supplies was clearly evident in the years between 1783 and 1807, as the planters struggled to maintain the plantation system with only limited access to United States markets. Hence, the Council Boards seized every opportunity to open West Indies ports to North American trade. While not always in conformity with the Act of April 1787, and often at variance with the policies and expectations of the Colonial Office and even some local officials, the Boards' actions were imperative to the survival of the West Indian plantations. Consequently, attempts in 1804 to terminate the discretionary powers of the governors met with opposition from the legislatures of all the islands, and the British government was forced to continue the opening of West Indian ports, even though this was more closely monitored.

It was clear that the profitability of the sugar economy and its continued economic benefits to Britain could not be maintained without unlimited trade with the United States. The results of the restrictions on British West Indian – United States commerce were frequent and sometimes led to terrible sufferings in the sugar colonies. The conditions which had existed on the islands during the American War of Independence changed very little between 1783 and 1807. The planters were forced to continue to grow provisions, and the colonies were repeatedly faced with periods of severe scarcity. The aspirations of the British merchants to establish their shipping as the major carrier did not succeed: their supplies to the West Indies were infrequent and unreliable. The North Americans continued to trade with the West Indies as British shipping made no major gains between 1783 and 1807. On the whole, the West Indian economy could not adjust to the new Atlantic commercial system and hence declined markedly, while the discriminatory duties imposed on West Indian products by some states in the United States reduced their consumption.[51]

The advantages to be derived by Britain from a healthy West Indian economy were potentially great, but were lost because of the restrictions contained in the order-in-council of July 1783 and the regulations embodied in the Act of 1787. The aim of the British government to bring the Canadian and Caribbean colonies closer together during this period failed, as the British sugar colonies remained dependent on the United States for their economic survival.[52]

Notes

1. The research for the paper was funded in part from grants received in 1989 and 1993 from Dame Professor Lillian Penson Memorial Fund and from several grants made by the Research and Publication Fund of the St. Augustine Campus, University of the West Indies. Some of the information used in this chapter is incorporated in Selwyn H. H. Carrington, "The American Revolution, British Policy and the West Indian Economy, 1775-1808," *Revista Interamericana* 22 (1992): 72-108.

2. David Parry to Lord Sydney, 23 June 1784 and 7 September 1785, C.O. 28/60, fos. 104d and 158-160m Public Record Office, (PRO), London.

3. Thomas Shirley to Lord Sydney, January 1785, C.O. 152/64, No. 95. PRO.

4. Simon Taylor to Sir John Taylor, 2 November 1783, Simon Taylor Letter Books, Vol. 1A, Institute of Commonwealth Studies (ICS), University of London. Taylor appears to be referring to Gibeonites, the citizens of Gibeon in ancient Palestine who were condemned to being hewers of wood and fetchers of water.

5. Alexander Winnett to Governor Mathews, 4 May 1874, C.O. 101/25, PRO.

6. "Minutes of the Privy Council for Trade," 18 March 1784, B.T. 5/1, fol. 43, PRO

7. See Samuel Flagg Bemis, *Jay's Treaty: A Study in Commerce and Diplomacy* (New Haven and London: Yale University Press, 1962), pp. 32-33; and "Report of the Committee of the Privy Council for Trade and Foreign Plantations," 28 January 1791, PC 1/19/A24, pp. 14-15,PRO.

8. See The Committee of Merchants in the Trade between the Dominions of Great Britain and the United States (hereafter referred to as the Committee of Merchants), "Memorial to the Rt. Hon. William Pitt and the Rt. Hon. the Marquis of Camathan," 21 January 1786. B.T. 6/20, fos. 412-416, PRO; and The Committee of Merchants Trading to North America, "Memorial to the Committee at the Privy Council for Trade, 30 March 1787. B.T. 6/20, fos. 18-20d, PRO.

9. See "Answers to Questions to the Merchants of London, Bristol, Liverpool and Glasgow relative to the American Import and Tonnage Bill," 1789, B.T. 6/20, fos. 373, 381, 383, PRO; and "Case of Messirs Spiers, Bownan and Company, Merchants in Glasgow, 1756. B.T. 6/51, fos. 6/81, fos. 248-249, PRO; Vernon G. Sester, *The Commercial Reciprocity Policy of the United States 1774-1829* (Philadelphia:

9. University of Pennsylvania Press, 1937), pp. 62-65; and Memo respecting American Duties, no date, B.T. 6/20, fol. 373, PRO.

10. Colonial Secretary to David Parry, 8 July 1785, C.O. 28/60, PRO; and Lord Sydney to Shirley, 2 June 1785, C.O. 152/64, PRO.

11. Lord Sydney to David Parry, 5 August 1785, C.O. 52/64, PRO.

12. See Parry to Lord Sydney, 5 April 1786, C.O. 28/60, PRO; and David Parry to Lord Sydney, 14th October 1784, CO. 28/60, fol.172,PRO.

13. Parry to Lord Sydney, 15 November 1786, C.O, 28/61, fol.4, PRO.

14. Parry to Lord Sydney, 21 October 1787, C.O. 28/61, PRO.

15. Gov. Orde to Lord Sydney, 11 January 1785, C.O.71/9, fol.57, PRO.

16. See "An Account of Ships and their cargoes entered inwards in the British Islands, from the United States, British North America and the Foreign West Indies," (no date), C.O.318/1, fos. 142-148, PRO; and for Dominica see C.O. 318/1, fol.264, PRO, and John Phillip Wise, "British Commercial Policy, 1794: The Aftermath of American Independence" (PhD dissertation, University of London, (1972), pp.74-75,79.

17. Edward Lincoln to Lord Sydney, 1 December 1785, B.T. 6/85, fos. 185-186, PRO.

18. See Geo. 111. C. 7; and Lord Sydney to David Parry, 6 January 1787, C.O. 28/61, fos. 1-1d, PRO.

19. Shirley to Lord Sydney, 7 June 1787, C.O. 152/65, No. 169,PRO.

20. Simon Taylor to Jack (Sir John Taylor), 4 August 1787, Simon Taylor Letter Books, Vol. 1A.

21. Shirley to Lord Sydney, 7 June 1787, C.O. 152/65, No. 169, PRO.

22. Shirley to Lord Sydney, 24 July 1787, C.O. 152/65, No. 172, PRO.

23. "Minutes of A Meeting of the Council of St. Christopher," 31 December 1789, C.O. 152/69, fos. 5-5d, PRO.

24. "Minutes of A Meeting of the Council of St. Christopher," 31 December 1789, C.O. 152/69, fos. 5-5d, PRO.

25. John Nugent to Lord Sydney, 9 October 1788, C.O. 152/67, No. 12, PRO.

26. Lord Seaforth to the Earl of Camden, 12 December 1804, C.O. 28/71, fos. 198d-200, PRO.

27. John Nugent to the Earl of Camden, 19 May 1805, C.O. 137/114, PRO.

28. Parry to Lord Sydney, 16 June 1785, C.O. 28/42, fos. 88d-90, PRO.

29. Shirley to Lord Sydney, 13 January 1790, C.O. 152/69, fos. 3.3d,PRO

30. Stephen Fuller to John King, 23 August 1793, C.O. 137/93, fol. 275, PRO.

31. Major General Adam Williamson to Henry Dundas, 18 January 1794, C.O. 137/92, PRO.

32. See President Esdaile to the Duke of Portland, 20 September 1776, C.O. 152/78, 12-12d, PRO; and the Earl of Balcarres to the Duke of Portland, 11 May 1795, C.O. 137/95, PRO.

33. Lieutenant-Governor Williamson to Dundas, 23 June 1794, C.O. 101/33, PRO.

34. The Duke of Portland to George Ricketts, November 1799, C.O. 28/65, PRO.

35. Robert Thompson to the Duke of Portland, 3 September 1789, C.O. 152/79, PRO.

36. Ricketts to the Duke of Portland, 4 January 1800, C.O. 28/66, fol. 3. PRO.

37. See Barbados Mercury and Bridgetown Gazette, 8 April 1805, C.O. 28/72, fol. 9, PRO; and Lowell J. Ragatz, The Fall of the Planter Class in the British West Indies (New York: The Century Company, 1928), p.299.

38. See Edward P. Lyon to the Earl of Camden, 7 March 1805, C.O. 137/115,PRO;and Edward Cooke to Edward P. Lyon, 13 March 1805, C.O. 137/115, PRO.

39. The Assembly of Jamaica to George Nugent, 7 December 1804, C.O.137/113,PRO.

40. Lord Camden to George Nugent, 7 March 1805, C.O. 137/113, PRO.

41. Anthony Merry to Lord Harrowby, 25 January 1805, C.O. 137/115, PRO.

42. Extract of Despatch from Mr. Bond to Lord Musgrave, 3 June 1805, C.O. 137/115, PRO.

43. William Fawkner to Edward Cooke, 21 October 1805, C.O. 137/115, PRO.

44. William Fawkner to Edward Cooke, 21 October 1805, C.O. 137/115, PRO.

45. James Cragg to Henry Goulburn, 13 December 1793, Goulburn Papers, Acc 319, Box 53, Surrey Record Office, Kingston, England.

46. Samuel Eliot to Clement Tudway, 2 March 1797, Tudway Papers, DD/TD, Box 11/71, Somerset County Record Office, Somerset; see David Evans to Lord Penrhyn (do date), Penrhyn Mss. 1475, University of North Wales Library, Bangor.

47. For Barbados prices, see Comparative Prices for Provisions & other Articles in Barbados, 26 December 1784, C.O. 28/60, fos. 183, 206, 243, 312, PRO; Average Prices at Barbados Market in January, February, March & April 1787, 25 May 1787, C.O. 28/71, fo. 47, PRO; see also, Average Prices at Barbados Market for October 1804, fos. 22-23, C.O. 28/71, fo. 205, PRO; C.O. 28/73, 7 May 1805, fos. 4, 15, 34, 80, 81, 96, 197, 198, PRO; C.O. 28/74, February & August 1806, fos. 42, 43, 81, 110, PRO; C.O. 28/75, fos. 18, 31, 49, PRO.

48. For Dominica, see Prices Current in Dominica, December 1786 - December 1808. C.O. 71/12, 13, 14, 38, 39, 40, 42, 43, PRO. For St. Vincent, see Extract of a Letter from a Planter in St. Vincent (no date), B.T. 6/77, PRO; The Prices of Lumber, Horned Cattle, Livestock and Indian Corn compared with the Average Prices Before and During the War [of the American Revolution], in Edward Lincoln to Lord Sydney, 8 January 1785, C.O. 260/7, No. 14, PRO; also see Prices Current, in C.O. 260/8, 9, 11, 13, 14, 15, 23, PRO. For Grenada, Answers to Queries 1st, 5th and 6th of Heads of Inquiry, 1 January 1785, C.O. 101/26, PRO; Weekly Prices Current of the Produce, Provisions and Lumber exported and imported from and to Grenada, August 1785-March 1790,

C.O. 101/26, 27, 28, 29, 30, PRO; Prices Current, August 1805, C.O. 101/42, PRO; Prices Current 1806, C.O. 101/45, PRO, January 1808, C.O. 101/47, PRO.

49. Ibid.; for increase in prices in Jamaica, see Prices Current in Kingston (1792 - 1810). C.O. 137/91, 95, 97, 114, 116, 117, 118, 121, 122, 124, 128, PRO; Prices in 1775 in Jamaica, Long Papers, Add.MS. 12, 404, British Library, London; Prices of Lumber at Kingston, 1772-1791, *Journal of the Assembly of Jamaica* 11 (no date), pp. 149-150, 436, University of the West Indies Library, Mona, Kingston, Jamaica.

50. Current Prices of the Market at Barbados, August, November 1785 & March 1786. C.O. 28/60, PRO; C.O. 28/61, PRO; Prices in the Leeward Islands, C.O. 101/42, 43, PRO; Average Prices Current in St.. Vincent, 1 October 1786-3 January 1787, C.O. 260/8, PRO; 5 April-5 July 1789, C.O. 260/9, PRO; see also the following C.O. 260/12-15, 23, PRO; Prices Current in Dominica for the years 1786-87, 1805-1808, (no dates), C.O. 71/12-14, 38-39, PRO; Wholesale Prices at Kingston, Jamaica, 5 January - 5 July 1801; 5 December 1801, C.O. 137/105, vols. 114-118, 121-122, PRO. See also Van Keelen to Sir Joseph Barham, 24 July 1786, 24 July 1787, Barham Papers, Bodl. Mss. Clarendon, Dep. c. 357, Bun. 1, Bodelian Library, Oxford.

51. Statements made to the contrary by two historians are not, in my opinion, supported by their research. My manuscript, *The Sugar Industry and the Abolition of the Slave Trade, 1775-1810*, develops this theme fully, and provides ample statistical information to show that the greatest part of the West Indian trade remained under the control of U.S. merchants. I also demonstrate the decline of the West Indian economy during the French Revolutionary and Napoleonic Wars. The contradictory conclusions are discussed in Seymour Drescher, *Econocide: British Slavery in The Era of Abolition* (Pittsburgh: University of Pittsburgh Press, 1977), and subsequent publications by him, and J.R. Ward, "The Profitability of Sugar Planting in the British West Indies, 1650-1834," *Economic History Review*, 2nd series, 31 (1978): 197-213.

52. Trade figures found throughout Colonial Office papers and plantation records testify to the dependence of the islands on supplies from the United States.

27

Trade and Exchange in Jamaica in the Period of Slavery

VERENE A. SHEPHERD

I

Traditional accounts of commercial transactions in British Caribbean sugar plantation societies have been located within the context of external trading relations. Where domestic trade and exchange have been addressed, the focus has been on the marketing system of the slaves. Scholars have been less concerned with the other dimension of local trade — that which developed among the different rural agrarian units. Such inter-property relations were most evident in Jamaica among Britain's mercantilist empire in the Caribbean; for unlike in the classical plantation economies of the Eastern Caribbean, sugar monoculture was never a persistent feature of the island's colonial economy. Jamaica produced and exported, in addition to sugar, significant quantities of coffee, cotton, ginger, pimento, dyewoods and hardwood. The island also produced food and livestock. Most of these commodities were produced on properties geared towards the export market although some output was exchanged locally from the estates and 'minor' staple plantations. Indeed, Barry Higman indicated that towards the time of emancipation, the flow of goods and labour from one unit to another resulted in about 17% of the total production on sugar estates and coffee plantations remaining in Jamaica.[1] Unlike sugar estates, coffee plantations and other monocultural 'minor staple' units, however, the island's livestock farmers catered primarily to the domestic market. Livestock farmers were able to sustain a vibrant trade with other properties, but especially with the sugar estates which needed large numbers of working animals (as well as grass and pasturage facilities) for the production of sugar. Animals were especially vital where planters did not utilize wind, steam or water power. Even where

alternative forms of power existed, 'standby' 'cattle' mills were often maintained.

This essay, using examples from the Accounts Produce,[2] illustrates another dimension of the domestic system of trade and exchange which developed during the period of slavery — the economic relations which developed between the locally based 'pens' (livestock farms) and the dominant sugar estates, arguably the best example of inter-property trade in the island. It examines the pens' transition from primarily export-based production in the 17th century to the dominant form of domestic trade and exchange by the 19th century. The essay, while intended as a contribution to the empirical base of knowledge on commercial relations in Caribbean plantation societies, has the potential to contribute to theoretical discussions on the nature and socio-economic implications of diversification of commodity production in colonial economies within a region characterized by sugar monoculture.

II The Transition from Export to a Dominant Local Trade

The Accounts Produce show quite clearly that by the mid-19th century Jamaica's livestock farms participated only minimally in the direct export trade. This was in contrast to their participation in the export trade in the preceding century. Indeed, the early history of the livestock industry in the 16th and 17th centuries indicates that the export dimension of trade was highly developed. In that period, these farms had an independent economic dynamic, exporting hides, lard and dried meat to the Spanish Indies and Spain. By 1740, the majority of the livestock farms disposed of their output on the domestic market, principally the sugar estates. Quantitative data on the disposal of pen output are not abundant, especially for those units owned by resident proprietors. The available trade statistics provided by the Accounts Produce from 1740 relate primarily to the properties of absentees; nevertheless, they can be used effectively to demonstrate some broad trends in the extent of pen participation in the export trade.

From the data available, it would seem that from the mid-18th century, where pens produced goods for export, the value of such goods did not, in general, exceed the proceeds from local transaction. Before 1800, the commodities exported were ginger, pimento, cotton, dyewoods and hardwood (logwood, fustic, mahogany). These products could be related clearly to specific parishes. Ginger was sold from the pens in St. Andrew; pimento from St. Ann and Trelawny, but mostly from the former; dyewoods, fustic and cotton from St. Elizabeth with some cotton also from the pens in St. Catherine.

Two distinct patterns of trade seemed to have existed. One method was to ship the commodity to Britain, presumably to an agent who handled the sale there. The most frequently observed practice, however, and one which was in direct contract to the usual method of disposing of sugar, was to sell the product to merchants in Kingston, who then arranged the sale.

Evidence of the participation of pens in the export trade was most available from the 1770s. Accounts for the earlier period were scanty, perhaps because of the greater residency of the penkeepers then. In 1740, for example, whereas it was evident that estates were exporting minor staples in addition to sugar (such crops also being exported from plantations of minor staples), only two of the eighteen pens for which returns were seen exported any commodity, in this case, cotton. In this period, most of the pens were located on the southside, particularly St. Catherine, and supplied primarily grass and provisions to the urban markets.[3] Forty years later, of the 21 returns relating to livestock farms, only five participated in the export trade. From Dornoch, Riverhead and Gordon Valley pens in St. Ann were shipped 118 bags of pimento valued at £256 17s. Several other bags valued at £161 0s.4d. were sold in Kingston, presumably for later export. In all then, pimento sales totalled £417 17s. 4d., but this represented only 11 per cent of the total earnings of the pen which amounted to £38,587 7s. 7d.[4]

Taking the period 1776–85 together, it is evident that the pens continued to export ginger, pimento, fustic, mahogany, logwood and

cotton. A similar commodity-parish relationship existed as in 1740.[5] The just over 40 returns seen (representing 25 pens), showed a mere seven pens active in the export market. In all cases, the value of exports fell far below the receipts from internal transactions. The best example in this period is from Luana Pen in St. Elizabeth which had eight separate returns in the period under review. Between 1776 and 1785, Luana exported 58 tons of fustic (£340 16s. 9d.), 65 tons of logwood (£325) and 995 lbs of cotton (£87 1s. 3d.), totalling £1,083 10s. 6d; but over the same period, receipts from livestock sales and pen services totalled £3,156 12s. 0d. Exports thus represented 34% of total earnings of just over £4,240.[6] In the other accounts, the percentage represented by exports was lower. The receipts of Dornoch, Riverhead and Gordon Valley pens from exports together represented 11 per cent of all goods and services sold.

Accounts for 1800 and 1820, the other years sampled, also replicated these earlier trends with respect to commodities produced, parishes in which produced, patterns of trade and comparative receipts from sales — with one important exception, the addition of coffee to the list of exports. In 1800, coffee was shipped from pens in St. Ann, Clarendon and St. James. Cotton, logwood and fustic continued to be produced in St. Elizabeth and Westmoreland, by this time an important exporter of logwood. One pen in St. Dorothy shipped a quantity of lignum vitae wood, and pimento continued to be associated with the St. Ann pens.[7]

Unlike in the preceding period, the value of exports from the pens in 1800 and 1820 at times exceeded earnings from internal transactions. Two notable examples were firstly Bellemont Pen which in 1800 exported coffee valued at £1,117 6s. 8d., 67% of total receipts for that year. The second case was Patherton Pen whose coffee exports formed 82 per cent of total earnings. As not all the accounts contained the volume and value of the commodities and as it is not at all times safe to assign current prices to the crops (if sold in Jamaica, for example, commodities fetched a different price from those exported directly to Great Britain), it is impossible to ascertain the extent to which Patherton and Bellemont typified the situation with the pens in 1800 with respect to value of exports *vs* internal trade. A further complication limiting generalization about the trend is that it would seem that it is those pen/coffee combined units, mostly in Manchester, which showed an increase of exports over internal sales. Pens like Luana, which were primarily devoted to livestock rearing, continued to show an excess of internal transactions over exports. In 1800, Luana earned 32% from export sales, for example. Indeed, of the eight complete accounts seen for this year, six recorded that sales from internal transactions exceeded those from exports. It should also be added that of 73 returns of pens in 1800, 21 (29%) participated in the external trade — a significant enough improvement over previous years in numbers, though not necessarily in percentage. This improvement seemed attributable to the increase of pens producing and exporting coffee.

In 1820, 153 returns of pens were seen. Of this number 43 or 28% participated in the direct export trade. The products exported were coffee, pimento, fustic, lignum vitae, logwood and hides. One pen, Castille Fort, provided ballast for outgoing ships. Most pens exported only one commodity. Only a minority[8] exported two. The usual combination was pimento and coffee (four pens) or logwood and fustic (two pens). One pen exported both pimento and fustic. St. Ann's pens continued to be overrepresented in the export of pimento. The combined pen/coffee units in Manchester most likely dominated the export of coffee, but because of the high residency among the coffee farmers, were underrepresented in the Accounts Produce. In the 1820 returns, it is the St. Ann pens which seemed to be exporting most of the coffee.

Most of the products were recorded as having been 'sent to Kingston'. Again, as not all commodity prices were included, only tentative statements can be made about the value of the products sold abroad. What seems clear is that of the 18 pens which had detailed information on prices and volume of goods, only three seemed to have earned more from exports than from internal transactions, the percentage from exports ranging from 59% to 71%. The others earned between 0.2% and 39% from external trade. The limited quantitative data, therefore, serve to reinforce the impression from qualitative sources that unlike the sugar estates, by the 19th century, pens catered essentially to the domestic market in the island.

III The Domestic Trade

In contrast to their relatively minimal involvement in the direct export trade, Jamaican pens participated actively in the domestic system of exchange. The pens conducted two levels of exchange locally. One was the domestic trade in provisions and livestock in which money was used as a medium of exchange. The other was a form of barter, an informal, non-monetary exchange of commodities among properties. A variety of goods were involved in the internal system of exchange among Jamaican properties. The primary product was livestock, comprising working steers, spayed heifers, breeding cows, mules, horses, bulls, calves, asses, fat cattle, old, wornout estate cattle and small stock. Other goods included food provisions (mainly corn and plantains), grass, milk, bricks, white lime, shingles, fresh beef, fish, timber, staves, sugar, rum, coffee and miscellaneous items. Most of these goods were sold by the pens. Those sold or exchanged by estates were sugar, rum and old working cattle. Where pen/coffee units or monocultural coffee units were involved in the trade, they sold coffee and livestock in the case of the former.

Various services (including labour) were also provided. The principal services provided by pens were jobbing, pasturage and wainage (cartage). Sugar estates rented excess land, at times in exchange for more pastureland from nearby properties. They also jobbed their tradesmen. Jobbing was, however, probably dominated by pens and specialized, independent jobbing gangs.

Of the goods listed above, the trade in livestock was the most lucrative for pens. According to Bryan Edwards, an eighteenth-century estate spent a minimum of £300 per annum to replace 'stock'.[9] The majority, indeed, spent far more. In 1783, Simon Taylor, the attorney for Golden Grove estate in St. Thomas-in-the-East, reported that that estate needed 100 working steers annually.[10] At around £30 each in 1820, this would cost this estate £3,000 per annum. As estates also bought mules and spayed heifers annually, pens stood to gain considerably from the trade in working stock, especially around 1820 when the price of a mule was £40 and for a young, spayed heifer, £22 10s.–26 each. J. B. Moreton recorded that an estate with even 100 acres of cane needed to buy 40 mules annually and maintain 100 always on the estate in the late eighteenth century.[11] Horses, proof asses and fat stock sold to the butchers also fetched considerable sums.

Of the services provided by pens, jobbing was the most financially rewarding. Jobbing consisted chiefly of digging cane holes and planting the spring canes on estates. In 1834, the have . . . '.[17] Third, pen-keepers or pen overseers themselves visited estates to enquire about the availability of livestock for sale. Over time, estates developed a relationship with particular pens, getting to know their routine and approximate selling time for young steers, heifers and mules.

In the majority of cases, pen slaves supplied the orders sent in by estates for livestock. The driving of cattle and horsekind to and from estates provided the slaves involved with a great deal of mobility. On 27 July 1750, for example, Charles Guy and Julius left Vineyard Pen with 15 steers, two young horses, ten heifers and two mules for a property in Westmoreland. They did not all return until August 2. Their explanation was that they had been delayed unduly because several people asked them to collect and deliver letters.[18] Pen slaves often covered longer distances than were involved in the case of Vineyard Pen's labourers. Slaves from Agualta Vale Pen in St Mary, for example, drove animals to Spring Estate in St Andrew, approximately 34 miles away.[19] Slaves from other properties, or those belonging to individual butchers, also went to the pens to collect goods for their masters. Mr. Markham, for example, 'sent his negroes for one dozen crabs caught by Titus and a he-lamb'.[20] Markham similarly sent his slaves to purchase fat cattle from Vineyard Pen. According to Thistlewood, however, his 'hands' were inadequate to manage the nine cows and calves; so that Charles and Cuffie had to help with them as far as Black River.[21] In some cases, the butchers, or estate overseers, visited the pen personally to make arrangements for purchase.[22]

In addition to driving livestock to 'markets', pen slaves fetched animals bought for the pen or to be pastured on its lands. In 1807, for example, the overseer of Thetford Hall Pen in St John sent slaves from that property to Mile Gully in Clarendon for a bull purchased from that pen.[23] Similarly, Thistlewood sent the slaves Dick, Guy, Charles, Julius and Simon to Mr. Allen's pen to fetch the mares for pasturage.[24] When pen slaves themselves delivered livestock to markets, or fetched and returned animals for fattening or pasturage, an extra cost was added.

The method by which other pen products were disposed of seemed less systematic. On Vineyard and Breadnut Island pens, for example, no letters were exchanged respecting the sale of vegetables and food crops. Also, no advertisements appeared in the newspapers relating to the sale of products other than large stock and its by-products. Products such as

cost of digging cane holes was £8 per acre. In this and previous years, some pens profited considerably from this service provided by their hired slaves. Stoneyfield Pen in St. Ann, for example, earned £660 1s. 6d. in 1820 for jobbing done on Fellowship Hall estate. This represented 52.54% of its total earnings from internal transactions.[12]

Pasturage, particularly for St. Catherine's pens, was also quite lucrative. In the eighteenth century, the typical rates charged for this service were 15s. per month for each horse or mule, and 10s. per month for each head of cattle. If pastured in batches of 20, rates were slightly lower. For example, 7s. 6d. for each animal was charged where cattle were pastured in batches of 20 or more. Rates increased in the nineteenth century to a maximum of 20s. for each horse.[13]

For sugar estates, the sale of their old, meagre or fat cattle after the crop to pens or butchers gave them handsome returns on their initial investment in young working stock. James Stevenson, the attorney for the Scarlett's estates in Jamaica, noted in 1800 that fat cattle from the estates sold at around £40 each. He stressed that formerly, old, fat cattle sold at between £18 and £25 each, but now fetched almost as much as for young cattle. Even though estates then had to buy fresh beef from such stock, at 1s.-1s. 8d. a pound, he felt they still made a profit in the sale of fat stock.[14] The army used a substantial proportion of the fresh beef sold by pens, at times up to 425 head per annum.[15]

The internal sale of rum also provided estates with money to help with local contingencies. As most of this product would have eventually been re-exported by Kingston merchants, however, this was, perhaps, not a true part of the domestic trade. However, sugar estates still participated in local transactions by providing the sugar and rum needs of non-sugar producing units.

The availability of goods and services provided by Jamaican pens was made known to potential customers in one of three ways. First, the sale of livestock was advertised in various newspapers. One hundred and twenty pens advertised the sale of animals in various newspapers sampled between 1780 and the end of slavery.[16] Second, pen-keepers or overseers, utilizing the services of slave couriers, sent letters to sugar planters or their representatives and butchers indicating the availability of planters' stock and fat cattle respectively. Thomas Thistlewood, owner of Vineyard Pen, noted in 1751, for example, that he 'sent Julius to Mr. Markham [a butcher in Black River] with a letter to let him know what fat cattle we capons, crabs, poultry,[25] eggs, fruits, sheep, goats and vegetables were sent to market in Westmoreland or Black River each week.[26] These were clearly not marketed by slaves on their own account as such sales were not usually made on Saturdays or Sundays. On some Saturdays, however, products were prepared for sale the following week.[27] In addition to these producta, Phibbah, Thistlewood's 'house-keeper', frequently sold cloth (usually check) in Westmoreland.

Few pens returned in the Accounts Produce established butcheries in the period under review. Those that did also developed significant links with properties and individuals within and outside of the area of their location. The best example of the scale of transactions in fresh beef from a pen is provided by Batchelor's Hall Pen's accounts. In 1833, this pen earned £2,120 2s. 11d. from its sale of fresh beef to estates, individuals, the troops and ships. This represented 57.63% of its total earnings for that year.[28]

The participation of the various units in the internal commodity trade varied in extent, volume and value from year to year. In 1740, when the Accounts Produce returns begin, 175 accounts were sent in by overseers. These represented 85 sugar estates, 20 pens, five plantations of minor staples, 19 jobbing gangs, 19 multiple crop combinations and 27 returns relating to merchants' earnings or house rents collected. Eighteen of the 20 pens, 20 of the 85 estates and the plantations of minor staples participated in the internal trade. Unfortunately, there is no detailed accounts of the buyers involved, so that the extent of economic links for 1740 cannot be measured.

The returns for 1760 indicate that interproperty transactions remained essentially the same as for 1740 in terms of the total number of properties involved. Sugar estates had, however, improved their participation, moving from 23.52% in 1740 to 35.68% in 1760. Pens basically remained at the same level, but the participation by plantations had declined. By 1780, 120 properties of the 266 returned were involved in local transactions. The number of properties involved continued to increase along with the increase in the number of returns. These indications are for units owned by absentees, but resident proprietors also participated in the trade, though the extent of their involvement cannot be ascertained. In the post-slavery period, however, the nature of transactions underwent slight changes. While the sale of livestock continued between pens and

estates, there was a drastic reduction in the jobbing of pen labourers on the estates. Indeed, only five such cases were noted in the 152 returns of pens in 1840, compared with 64 of the 145 such units in the 1820 return.

The extent of trade is clearer in the nineteenth-century returns. The majority of estates relied either on pens or local butchers to buy their old stock. Pens dominated this trade, however, as they were better placed than the butchers to fatten such animals prior to their being killed for fresh beef. Only five of the pens returned in 1820 had their own butcheries, and the supply of beef — a form of final demand linkage — was probably in the hands of urban butchers and independent pens not returned.

The volume of livestock being sold in the island can be partially ascertained from the Accounts Produce. In the first return when pens were not as numerous as later on, these units supplied only 34 head of working stock to estates. In that year, few pens were monocultural livestock units, and St. Catherine's units, in particular, sold more sheep and small stock than cattle and mules. By 1780, 21 of the 266 returns were pens. The latter were involved in the sale of livestock to the number of 942. This represented 50.7 per cent of the 1,881 sold by the 120 units involved in local trading. Table 1, showing the specific breakdown of the numbers traded, indicates the relative importance of each type of livestock in the eighteenth century. It is clear that in the late eighteenth century, heifers and mules were overrepresented in terms of working animals. The mule, indeed, was recognizedly unsurpassed in its hardiness as a work animal. The horses, on the other hand, and the 'steers' were underrepresented as work animals, the

Table 1 Breakdown of Livestock Sales by Type and Volume, 1780

All properties		Pens only	%
Working steers	278	137	49.28
Heifers	19	15	78.94
Cows	30	24	80.00
Calves	56	38	67.85
Horses	123*	91	73.98
Old/fat/cattle	1,039	407	39.17
Bulls	3	—	—
Sheep	140	95	67.85
Mules	181	131	72.37
Asses	12	4	33.33
	1,881	942	50.70

*Including six mill horses.
Source: J.A., A.P., 1780, 18/11/4/9.

former being more important for transportation and the horse-racing industry. This was in contrast to the trend in England where by 1850, English farmers, with some regional variations, had virtually dispersed with the working of cattle in favour of the use of horses. This was because after the Napoleonic Wars, more favourable price conditions and the increasing efficiency of horses in farming caused the emphasis in cattle husbandry to shift to beef production.[29] In Jamaica, however, competition from horse-racing and the expensiveness of procuring and maintaining horses determined their unattractiveness as draught animals.

By the mid-nineteenth century, however, mules had largely been displaced by steers and spayed heifers. A partial indication of this shift is that by 1820, and in contrast to 1780, an estimated 3,162 steers, 1,162 spayed heifers and only 511 mules were sold or exchanged internally. By the post-slavery period, the number of mules sold by the pens represented in the Accounts Produce had fallen significantly. In 1840, for example, the 283 mules compared with 2,461 steers and 1,006 heifers were sold from the pens.[30]

Contemporary sources provide no explanations for this shift, but one can speculate that the dual income yielded by oxen was attractive to both planters and pen-keepers.

Unlike the oxen, mules realized little of a return on initial investment at the end of their working life. Indeed, the table also reinforces qualitative statements about the lucrative nature of the sale of old stock from the estates and the dominance of pens in the trade in working stock.

By 1820, when the total number of livestock traded internally was 14,134 head, pens were responsible for 8,267 or 54.49%, an improvement over their 1780 level. In the former year, the returns included 145 pens and 470 sugar estates. As in previous years, sugar estates dominated the sale of old, meagre stock, while pens controlled the sale of working animals. Pens acted as 'middlemen' in the trade in old stock which could not be sold straight to the butcher. These were fattened on the pens' pastures prior to sale to urban butchers. This enabled them to make a profit on their purchases from the estates.

As a result of the trade in livestock, therefore, a significant degree of economic links developed among the island's main economic units. These links typified the relations between estates and pens throughout the island.

The Accounts Produce give some indication of the relative value of each type of good and service to properties involved in the internal trade, as is demonstrated by Table 2, based on examples drawn from the 1820 Accounts (which are far more detailed than previous samples

Table 2　Sample of Interproperty Trade, 1820

Property	Type	Parish	Total earnings from the internal trade			Proportion earned from dealings with estates/pens			
			£	s.	d.	£	s.	d	%
1　Golden Grove	Sugar estate	Hanover	2,405	2	0	84	2	0	3.5
2　Silver Grove	Sugar estate	Hanover	1,923	14	0	157	2	0	8.2
3　Steelfield	Sugar estate	Trelawny	1,318	10	6	135	0	0	10.2
4　Unity Hall	Sugar estate	St. James	2,300	16	6	179	0	0	7.8
5　Seven Rivers	Sugar estate	St. James	267	3	0	267	3	0	100
6　Old Montpelier	Sugar estate	St. James	3,896	18	0	219	0	0	5.6
7　Grange	Sugar estate	Hanover	1,540	15	8	115	0	0	7.5
8　Fontabelle	Sugar estate	Westmoreland	695	9	4	622	0	0	89.4
9　Frome	Sugar estate	Westmoreland	178	15	7	82	4	7	46.0
10　Spring Garden	Sugar estate	Westmoreland	186	0	0	128	0	0	56.06
11　Silver Grove	Sugar estate	Trelawny	169	10	0	136	0	0	80.2
12　Golden Grove	Sugar estate	Trelawny	134	10	0	119	10	0	88.8
13　Harding Hall	Sugar estate	Hanover	1,348	5	8	108	0	0	8.0
14　Old Shafston	Pen	Westmoreland	1,321	0	6	204	0	0	15.4
15　Carysfort	Pen	Westmoreland	3,998	19	3½	3,396	19	3½	84.9
16　Midgham	Pen	Westmoreland	1,451	12	11	1,251	15	0	86.2
17　Paradise	Pen	Westmoreland	790	6	8	218	18	0	27.6
18　Mount Edgecombe	Pen	Westmoreland	2,120	13	0½	1,350	8	10½	63.6
19　Hamstead	Pen	St. Mary	428	8	0	428	8	0	100

Source: J.A., A.P., 1B/11/4/54–6.

Table 3   The Internal Trade: Relative Value of Goods and Services from Selected Properties, 1820

Property	Livestock £	s.	d.	Jobbing £	s.	d.	Pasturage £	s.	d.	Wainage £	s.	d.	Provisions £	s.	d.	Wood, staves shingles £	s.	d.	Misc. rents, etc £	s.	d.
1 Forest Pen	4,027	16	8	75	0	0	—			—			—			—			134	4	11
2 Maverly Estate	137	0	0	—			—			—			—			363	7	6	—		
3 Lyndhurst Plan.	620	0	0	—			—			—			—			554	7	7	—		
4 Pindar's River Estate	124	0	0	—			—			20	0	0	—			—			150	0	0
5 Phantilland's Pen	356	13	4	746	16	8	45	6	8	—			—			—			122	4	5
6 Chudleigh Plan	1,326	10	0	—			—			—			—			—			—		
7 Brazellita Est.	174	0	0	294	0	9½	—			40	0	0	—			—			37	3	4
8 Crescent Park Pen	787	0	0	20	0	0	—			—			—			—			—		
9 Batchelor's Hall Pen	1,304	0	0	—			—			84	0	0	2,272	3	9	—			—		
10 Petersville Est.	1,655	10	0	—			—			—			—			—			—		
11 Monymusk Estate	—			60	0	0	—			—			—			—			45	0	0
12 Spring Gdn. Pen	1,740	13	0	—			18	10	0	—			—			—			16	5	0
13 Worthy Part Est.	225	0	0	—			—			—			—			—			—		
14 Aboukir Plan.	72	10	0	—			—			97	0	0	38	1	3	70	16	0	—		
15 Paynestown Pen	640	0	0	1	5	0	—			3	0	0	39	0	0	—			—		
16 New Forest Pen	219	16	0	47	10	0	207	2	6	263	13	4	—			—			—		
17 Chesterfield Est.	220	0	0	—			—			10	0	0	32	8	4	—			25	0	0
18 Crawle Pen	2,379	0	8	211	7	9	446	5	10	393	3	8½	—			—			—		
19 Lower Works Pen	1049	0	0¼	—			375	0	0¼	50	18	9	—			—			—		
20 Palmyra Pen	167	6	8	662	0	0	—			5	6	8	—			—			—		
21 Rosehall Estate	148	0	0	50	10	0	—			—			—			—			—		
22 Cherry Gdns. Est	52	0	0	—			—			—			—			—			—		
23 Holland Estate	400	0	0	—			—			—			—			—			—		
24 Sevens Plan	300	0	0	—			—			—			88	5	0	—			—		
25 Santa Cruz Park Pen	924	0	0	72	0	0	—			—			—			10	0	0	—		
26 Ramble Pen	1,450	0	0	—			—			105	5	0	78	0	0	427	15	0	155	0	0
27 St. Faith's Pen	1,386	7	0	99	14	10¼	6	18	4	—			—			403	1	6	—		
28 Ardoch Pen	574	0	0	190	9	7¼	20	8	0	—			—			16	0	0	—		
29 Bryan's Pen	980	7	8	476	0	0	—			368	0	0	115	0	0	—			78	17	6
30 New Ground Est.	108	0	0	—			—			38	0	0	—			—			—		
31 Dunbarton Est.	—			80	0	0	—			—			522	0	2	—			—		
32 Phoenix Park Pen	2,028	6	8	—			—			—			—			202	0	0	—		
33 Prospect Est.	368	8	0	—			—			—			88	8	0	—			—		
35 Roaring River Est.	32	0	0	—			—			—			58	4	6	—			47	0	0
35 Williamsfield Est.	12	10	0	85	0	0	—			—			—			—			—		

Source: J.A., A.P., 1B/11/4/54–6.

returned). In 1740, for example, though 35 units indicated earnings from the domestic trade, the purchases of these goods and services were rarely given. Values were equally generally absent, making calculations based on known price rates virtually impossible. Table 2 indicates that 11 of the 16 pens involved earned most from the sale of livestock and its by-product, beef. It should be stressed that not all transactions involved money, but all could be reduced to monetary value. Where goods were exchanged for other goods or services, however, a money value was not given. Flamstead Estate in St. James, for example, bartered 110 gallons of rum for stock in 1780.[31] Unlike in other West Indian islands, however, the products of the island were not made legal tender after 1751, despite an attempt to get the Assembly to sanction this. Where it occurred, it was more custom than law. Indeed, Edward Long confirmed that 'money is the chief agent for carrying on any trade'.[32] Increased draining of money from the island by American and Spanish merchants, however, not only made bartering common, but according to Long, 'credit became a part of Commerce'.[33] Although pens diversified their activities to a greater extent after the abolition of slavery, up to 1840, earnings from the livestock trade still accounted for the largest share of their income. A sample of 24% of the pens returned in 1820 (representing 9–10% of the estimated island total) reveals earnings of £25,990 5s. 8½d. from livestock sales to estates. These pens earned more from such sales (69%) than from other important income-generating activities such as jobbing, wainage, pasturage, the sale of food (ground provisions and fresh beef) and wood. These other sales and services combined yielded £11,974 19s. 0d. or 31 per cent of the total earnings of £37,965. Taken singly, jobbing represented 8%, pasturage 3%, wainage 4%, provisions 9% and miscellaneous items (rents, shingles, wood, staves) 7%. These percentages varied, of course, from pen to pen. Forest pen, for example, earned only 2% from non-livestock sources.

It should be pointed out that on the whole, estates and pens were unequal partners in the internal trade. In the majority of cases, as Table 3 illustrates, estates accumulated less from their internal transactions with pens than they did from other sources such as the sale of rum to Kingston merchants and fat cattle to butchers. On the other hand, pens relied on the estates for the greater portion of their earnings. Additionally, the estates' gains from the internal trade represented an insignificant part of their total earnings from the domestic export trade. For example, Prospect Estate in Hanover earned £12,650 18s. 0d. from the sale of sugar and rum and only £183 10s. 0d. from internal transactions. Of the money accumulated locally, £128 10s. 0d. resulted from trade with pens. Similarly, Mint Estate in Westmoreland earned £7,818 17s. 0d. from the export of sugar and rum and £420 14s. 0d. from the domestic trade.[34]

Conclusion

It should be clear from the foregoing analysis that commercial relations in 18th- and 19th-century Jamaica did not conform to the trade patterns in monocultural or classic plantation economies. The island's colonial economy was diversified and led not only to the availability of a wider range of export crops, but to the emergence of non-staple producers who traded their goods on the domestic market.

Despite the importance of this domestic trade in livestock, however, local producers were never able to supply the total livestock requirements of the island. The competition between estates and pens for land made the pens unable to maintain the required livestock density which would cater to the island's needs. Furthermore, the high cost of production of local livestock made pen-keepers unable to compete with external producers, notably Hispanic America. This lack of self-sufficiency in working animals encouraged the development and maintenance of a vibrant import trade with Spanish America. Between 1815 and 1825, for example, the Spanish Main and Islands supplied 57,704 of the total 59,182 mules, horses, asses and cattle imported into the island.[35] Nevertheless, the domestic trade in livestock reduced the island's dependence on foreign sources and supplied locally a larger share of Jamaica's total demand for plantation animals than did any other island in the British Caribbean.

Notes

1. B. W. Higman, 'Slave Population and Economy in Jamaica at the time of Emancipation' (Ph.D. diss., UWI, Mona, 1970), p. 313.
2. Accounts Produce contain returns of commodities produced, method of disposal and value of goods and services in some cases. These accounts related to the properties of absentees, but information pertaining to pens owned by residents is available where the latter traded with the former.

3. Jamaica Archives (J.A.), Accounts Produce (A.P.), 1B/11/4/1.
4. *Ibid.*, 1B/11/4/9.
5. *Ibid.*
6. *Ibid.*
7. *Ibid.*, 1B/11/4/27–28.
8. *Ibid.*, 1B/11/4/54–56.
9. B. Edwards, *The History of the West Indies*, 2 vols (London, 1793), I, p. 259.
10. Simon Taylor to Chaloner Arcedeckne, 29 October 1782, Jamaica Estate Paper, Vanneck Manuscripts, Box 2, Bundle 10.
11. J. B. Moreton, *Manners and Customs in the West Indian Islands* (London, 1790), p. 57.
12. A.P. 1B/11/4/56.
13. *St. Jago de la Vega Gazette*, 4–11 April 1801, p. 93.
14. James Stevenson to Mrs Scarlett, 8 April 1800. Scarlett Family Collection, DDCA/41/17, Hull University Library (Brynmor Jones).
15. *Jamaica House of Assembly Votes (J.H.A.V.)* 1795–6, p. 282.
16. *Royal Gazette*, 1780–1834; *St. Jago de la Vega Gazette*, 1791–1831; *Falmouth Post*, 1791–1836.
17. Thomas Thistlewood's Journal, Vineyard Pen, 15 January 1751, Monson 31/2 fol. 8, Lincolnshire Archives Office.
18. *Ibid.*, Monson 31/1, fols. 342, 348.
19. V. Shepherd, 'Problems in the Supply of Livestock to Sugar Estates in the Period of Slavery', UWI, Mona, 1987.
20. Thistlewood's Journal, 26 January 1751, Monson 31/2, fol. 14.
21. *Ibid.*, 10 April 1751, fol. 58.
22. *Ibid.*, 23 April 1751, fol. 59.
23. Thetford Hall Pen Accounts, 1807. D.M. 444, Special Collections, Bristol University Library.
24. Thistlewood's Journal, 11 April 1751, Monson 31/2, fol. 25.
25. *Ibid.*, 5 September 1750, Monson 31/1, fol. 374.
26. *Ibid.*, 1750–51, Monson 31/1–2.
27. *Ibid.*, 11 July 1750, Monson 31/1, fol. 355.
28. Accounts Produce, Batchelor's Hall Pen, January–December 1833, Vanneck MSS; Jamaica Estate Papers, Box 2, Bundle 60.
29. J. A. Perkins, 'The Ox, the Horse, and English Farming, 1750–1850', Working Papers in Economic History, 3/1975, University of New South Wales, Dept, of Economic History, School of Economics, pp. 2–15. (I am grateful to Prof. Barry Higman for this source).
30. A.P. 1B/11/4/84–5, 1840.
31. *Ibid.*, 1B/11/4/9, 1780.
32. Add. MS 12,404, fols. 450–2, E. Long, *History of Jamaica*, 3 vols. (London, 1774), I, fols. 450–52.
33. *Ibid.*, fol. 450.
34. A.P. 1B/11/4/54–56.
35. V. Shepherd, 'Pens and Penkeepers in a Plantation Society', Ph.D., Cambridge, 1988, p. 163.

SECTION SIX

The Work Culture of the Enslaved

As Higman, Knight and Hall demonstrate, economic diversification was the principal feature of the Caribbean slave complex. From the post-Columbian mining economy in the sixteenth century to the sugar and coffee revolutions in the Spanish colonies during the mid-nineteenth century, economic systems responded to both domestic, imperial, and transimperial demands. While it is true that agriculture ultimately dominated the productive endeavours of colonists, and that imperial interests tended over time to focus upon the exportation of primary goods, no colony was ever in reality a pure export economy. At best we should describe them as mixed economies, though the sugar industry of Barbados and the Leeward Islands in the seventeenth century came rather close to being monocultural systems.

Higman's account of the occupational distribution of the British Caribbean slave population, while emphasizing that work was central to the experience of the enslaved in all colonial settings, demonstrates that there was no homogeneous slave experience. The enslaved worked in a variety of physical environments and were engaged in a wide range of economic activities. While most were probably confined to the agricultural sector, many worked at industrial crafts, in the mercantile and social services sectors, fishing and domestic economies. In the sugar plantation industry, enslaved peoples ultimately came to dominate skilled, technological occupations. The boilerman, distillers, and mechanic were considered special crafts that conferred prestige. In addition, slaves were employed in lower-level management roles, performing the tasks of driver, overseer, and ranger. They worked with sugar, coffee, tobacco, indigo and cotton, and tended to cattle in the well established husbandry culture of the Greater Antilles.

Tomich's analysis allows us to view the everyday routine of the "hands and feet of the planters". Even the elderly and children worked; and as Mair shows, women worked just as hard as men. Women by the end of the eighteenth century were the majority workers in the gangs of the English sugar economy. Full employment was the objective of slave economies. Enslaved people worked in the towns in a wide range of occupations. They worked as domestics, vendors, prostitutes, musicians and street cleaners among other jobs; some men were also slave catchers and militiamen. The nature of work determined to a considerable degree the general nature of their life experiences as slaves. It influenced their mortality, fertility, and domestic life. It might very well have shaped their consciousness in ways that determined political responses. Essays in this section explore these themes and provide a range of theoretical insights for detailed research.

28

Physical and Economic Environments

B.W. HIGMAN

Variations in the character of slavery and in the demographic experience of slave populations may be traced, in part to the contrasting physical and economic environments in which slaves were forced to live. In order to determine the nature of these parameters for the British Caribbean in the early nineteenth century, it is necessary to describe briefly the physical geographies and settlement histories of the colonies, the spatial distribution of the slave populations within these contrasting physical contexts, and distribution between the different types of economic activity. On the basis of these patterns, a typology of the colonies is advanced.

Physical Environments

Differences in the physical geographies of the British Caribbean colonies related chiefly to the elements of size, slope, size, and rainfall.[1]

Variations in size were great (Table 28.1). The mainland colonies, British Honduras and British Guiana, exceeded the islands by far, but their slave populations were confined to narrow coastal and riverine belts. The Bahamas, the largest of the island colonies, was made up of some 700 islands and 2,000 cays and rocks spread through 90,000 square miles of sea; the largest of these islands were Andros (2,300 square miles), Inagua (599), Grand Bahama (530), and Abaco (395). Jamaica was easily the largest of the colonies occupying a single island, and its slave population was almost as numerous as that of the other colonies combined. The smallest of the island colonies, each with its own legislature, were Montserrat, Nevis, and Anguilla, in the Leewards. Thus, while some slaves lived on the fringes of massive hinterlands, most found themselves on small islands, only occa-

sionally being able to see neighbouring islands across the sea. But this had little significance for the mobility of the slaves, since the majority were tied to particular plantations or locations.

A systematic analysis of slope is not available, and maximum altitudes tend to be misleading at the colony level (Table 28.1). The populated coastal strip of British Guiana was in fact largely below sea level and was protected by a sea wall; its waterlogged agricultural lands were criss-crossed by canals. The mountains were far distant in the interior, known only to the Amerindians and a few explorers.[2] The slaves could not look unto the hills for strength. Along the coastline of British Guiana was a narrow clay lowland, rarely more than 30 miles wide, backed by a sandy lowland that took up about one-quarter of the territory. Further inland, to the west and south, were uplands under heavy forest cover.

The topography and settlement pattern of British Honduras were similar to those of British Guiana. The populated northern third of the territory was lowland, less than 500 feet above sea level. Along the entire length of the 200 miles of coast were many swamps, lagoons, and cays, covered by mangrove. Only in the southwestern third of the territory were there uplands rising above 3,000 feet.

Some of the island colonies were low-lying: the Cayman Islands, the Bahamas, Anguilla, and Barbuda. None of these rose above 200 feet. Made up of shallow limestone banks and coral reefs, many of them were covered by low scrub and surrounded by mangrove swamps. The islands and cays of the Bahamas stood on a shallow bank of limestone through which it was difficult for shipping to find a passage. The soil

Table 28.1   The British Colonies in the Caribbean c. 1834

Colony	Area (sq mi)	Maximum Altitude (ft)	Slave Population	Slaves per sq mi	Year of British Colonization
Barbados	166	1,100	83,150	500.9	1627
St. Kitts	65	3,792	17,525	269.6	1625
Nevis	36	3,232	8,840	245.6	1628
Antigua	108	1,319	28,130	260.5	1632
Montserrat	39	3,002	6,400	164.1	1632
Virgin Islands	59	1,760	5,135	87.0	1672
Jamaica	4,411	7,402	311,070	70.5	1655
Dominica	305	4,672	14,165	46.4	1763
St. Lucia	233	3,145	13,275	57.0	1803
St. Vincent	150	4,048	22,250	148.3	1763
Grenada	133	2,756	23,645	177.8	1763
Tobago	114	1,860	11,545	101.3	1763
Trinidad	1,864	3,085	20,655	11.1	1797
British Guiana	83,000	9,000	83,545	1.0	1803
British Honduras	8,867	3,000	1,895	0.2	1670
Cayman Islands	100	165	985	9.9	1734
Bahamas	5,548	200	9,995	1.8	1648
Anguilla	35	200	2,260	64.6	1650
Barbuda	62	100	505	8.1	1685

Sources: B.W. Higman, *The Caribbean Today* (1975).

tended to be sandy and infertile, while the uplands weathered to create karstic landscapes. Anegada, one of the Virgin Islands, was simply a flat limestone block. Anguilla and Barbuda were coral islands with only occasional ridges interrupting their flatness. The soil was thin, and bare rock and sand common.

The remaining islands, in which local variations in relief were generally considerable, belonged to three partially submerged mountain systems. The most important of these stretched from the Virgin Islands in the east through Jamaica and southern Cuba to Central America: the Greater Antilles. The second extended southward from the Leeward Islands to Grenada: the Lesser Antilles. Here the volcanic peaks were separated by deep sea passages, creating a succession of small, mountainous islands. In the Leeward Islands the volcanoes were inactive and eroded to form relatively low-lying islands, as in the case of Antigua. In the Windward Islands volcanic activity continued, and the land was much more mountainous. The third mountain system was that extending from the South American mainland through Trinidad and Tobago. Tobago had a very limited fringe of level land, whereas the northern and southern ranges

of Trinidad were separated by an extensive plain. Barbados rested on the same submarine ridge and was composed of coral terraces surrounded by barrier reefs. But, excepting the northeastern area where the terraces had been raised to create steep cliffs, the whole of Barbados was arable.

Temperatures in the Caribbean were uniformly high, in spite of the wide latitudinal spread of the colonies. Seasonal variations were also limited. Diurnal contrasts tended to be greater, occasionally exceeding those between summer and winter. Local variations were important, with altitudinal differences in the more mountainous islands having an effect on their patterns of settlement and land use.

Rainfall patterns were much less uniform. Great variations occurred both within and between colonies. Differences in altitude were basic, with the small low-lying islands receiving less than 60 inches per year. These islands also tended to suffer the longest droughts and to lose most by percolation. In Barbados rainfall exceeded 75 inches only in the most hilly area of the island. By contrast, the Windward Islands received less than 70 inches only in their coastal fringes, with rainfall being above 100 inches for the greater part of their area and exceeding 250 inches in Dominica. In Tobago the range was greater (40–150 inches), but in Trinidad less (50–100 inches). Coastal Guyana received an average 90 inches per year. But the greatest local variations occurred in Jamaica, with the southern plains receiving an average less than 70 inches while the eastern mountains received over 200 inches. It must be noted that all of these rainfall data derive from twentieth century averages and take no account of secular change. There is evidence of change in rainfall levels since 1870, but no studies of the early nineteenth century are available, so it must be assumed that the pattern of variation found in modern times is similar to that in the last years of slavery.

The colonies of the British Caribbean, then, contained a variety of physical environments and contrasting landscapes. The colonies can be sorted roughly into types using these criteria, but the extremes of size mean that some colonies contained more than one of these types within their borders. Local, small-scale variation was common.

Settlement Histories

Variations in the economic and demographic patterns of the British Caribbean colonies between 1807 and 1834 were also affected by their contrasting settlement histories. Some had been a part of the British Empire for the entire length of their colonial history; some had begun as Spanish, French, or Dutch colonies; and others were constantly passed back and forth between the European imperial powers. Some had been densely settled sugar colonies since the middle of the seventeenth century, some still possessed active frontiers in 1807, and others had never really moved beyond the pre-sugar settlement pattern.

The British invasion of the Caribbean fell into three major phases: the second and third quarters of the seventeenth century, the 1760s, and the turn of the nineteenth century.[3]

In the first phase of British colonial expansion, settlements were established between 1625 and 1632 in St. Kitts, Barbados, Nevis, Antigua, and Montserrat; in Jamaica in 1655; and, rather more tenuously, in the Virgin Islands, Anguilla, Barbuda, the Bahamas, the Cayman Islands, and British Honduras (table 28.1). All of these settlements were largely the product of private enter-

prise rather than of government action. Jamaica was captured from the Spanish, the Virgin Islands from the Dutch, and St. Kitts was shared with the French until 1702. With the exception of British Honduras, all of these settlements were to remain in British possession, and they were firmly stamped with British influence. Barbados and the Leeward Islands, with high proportions of level land and moderate rainfall, were quickly transformed into full-blown sugar colonies. Jamaica, however, was never as strictly mono-cultural, and the expansion of settlement continued throughout the eighteenth century.

Jamaica's slave population continued to grow rapidly until the abolition of the Atlantic slave trade, whereas the populations of Barbados and the Leeward Islands leveled off after about 1710.[4] In the Virgin Islands the sugar revolution was retarded, gaining momentum only after 1750. The other colonies established in this first phase never endured the sugar revolution. The Bahamas experienced a short-lived plantation revolution based on cotton, following the influx of Loyalists after the American Revolution, but by 1800 the poor soil had been exhausted and salt raking and "wrecking" again became dominant activities. Anguilla depended on salt, British Honduras on logwood and mahogany, the Cayman Islands on turtles, and Barbuda on livestock. But none of these colonies produced major agricultural export staples, and they always remained marginal to the imperial plantation economy.

The sugar colonies established in the first phase all had their own planter-controlled legislatures by the end of the seventeenth century. The British attempted to establish a joint legislature in the Leeward Islands (including the Virgin Islands) in 1798, but it was dissolved in 1800, the island assemblies resuming their legislative autonomy.[5] The marginal, non-plantation colonies were much less successful in gaining control over their political affairs. Only the Bahamas established and maintained a legislative assembly, incorporating the Turks and Caicos Islands from 1804. Anguilla's assembly was annexed to St. Kitts in 1825 and the island placed under a Deputy-Governor. Barbuda was effectively the private property of the Codrington family, and the Cayman Islands were administered from Jamaica. British Honduras, generally referred to in the early nineteenth century as "the British settlement in the Bay of Honduras," was aberrant since it existed within territory that remained legally Spanish until 1862. It was placed under a Superintendent rather than a Governor, and its legislation proceeded from a rough-and-ready "public meeting," not an elected assembly.[6] All of the non-plantation colonies lacking assemblies had small white populations and few slaves.

The second phase of British settlement in the Caribbean lacked the private enterprise characteristics of the first. All of the islands added to the empire in the 1760s were "conquered" colonies, acquired through European treaties rather than taken directly from Amerindians. The Peace of Paris, concluded in 1763, ceded to Britain the islands of Dominica, St. Vincent, Tobago, Grenada, and the Grenadines. Dominica and St. Vincent were "neutral" islands, still effectively occupied by the Caribs. Grenada, a French colony since 1645, had a partially developed plantation economy. Tobago was the scene of attempted settlement by the French and Dutch in the seventeenth century, but became "neutral" territory after 1690 and fell again into the hands of the French between 1780 and 1803. There was also a brief French occupation of Dominica in 1778-84. The total land area added to the British Empire through the cession of these islands was 702 square miles, much less than the area acquired in the seventeenth century.

This second phase of settlement took place during what Richard Pares called the "silver age" of sugar (the golden age being the 1640s).[7] Sugar prices were consistently high between 1750 and 1775, and British colonization transformed the ceded islands from diversified agricultural economies, producing cocoa, coffee, and cotton, into sugar colonies. But this transformation was nowhere as complete as it had been in Barbados and the Leeward Islands, the environments of the ceded islands being too mountainous and wet to permit the development of an encompassing sugar monoculture. The colonies of the second phase were, however, were all granted elected legislatures, like the first-phase sugar colonies. The Grenadines were divided between the colonies of Grenada and St. Vincent.

In the third and final phase of British colonization, Trinidad was taken from the Spanish in 1797, St. Lucia from the French in 1803, and Demerara, Essequibo, and Berbice from the

Dutch in the same year. Trinidad had remained a backwater until the *cédula* for population of 1783 opened the island to foreign Catholics, offering land in proportion to the number of slaves brought with them.[8] The result was a considerable influx of planters, slaves, and freedmen, most coming from the troubled French Antillean colonies. From a mere 1,500 (including only 200 slaves) in 1780, the population of Trinidad grew to 17,500 (10,000 of them slaves) by 1797. But the buoyancy of the 1760s sugar market had passed, and the British placed a restraining hand on the expansion of the sugar plantation and the slave trade. In order to effect this control, Trinidad was refused an elective legislature. It became the first crown colony, with its government originating in the imperial metropolis.[9] It was this direct control that made Trinidad the ideal colony for the first trial of the slave registration system.

St. Lucia had been the site of several abortive British settlements in the seventeenth century, but from 1748 was regarded as neutral. Britain occupied the island during the Seven Years' War, but it was ceded to the French in 1763. Between 1763 and 1803 St. Lucia was repeatedly lost and retaken by the French and British, until the final capture by the British in 1803. Sugar planting began only after 1763 and was interrupted by the uncertainty of control and supplies. As in the other Windward Islands, the firm establishment of the British led to the development of sugar at the expense of cotton, coffee, and cocoa, but the monocultural tendency was limited by the wet and mountainous character of the island. St. Lucia was not granted an assembly, and government was left largely in the hands of the Governor.[10]

Abortive British colonization of the Guianas in the seventeenth century had been followed by Dutch occupation between 1667 and 1803. At first settlement centred on the up-river regions, but by 1750 the locus shifted to the coastal clay soils protected by the sea wall. The British conquest of Demerara, Essequibo, and Berbice resulted in a large immigration of planters from colonies established in the first phase. The mainland colonies became the British Empire's leading producer of cotton and coffee for a brief period, but these crops were soon to fall off as sugar production was promoted and competition from United States cotton increased. Like Trinidad, the colonies possessed an open frontier in 1807. Similar forces operated to prevent the granting of an assembly, but pure crown colony government was not imposed. The Dutch legislative institutions, the Court of Policy and the Combined Court, were retained, together with their elective element. The colonies of Demerara and Essequibo were united in 1813 and combined with Berbice in 1831 to create British Guiana.[11]

By 1807, when the Atlantic slave trade was abolished, the territorial expansion of the British Empire in the Caribbean was complete. The phasing of this expansion over almost 200 years meant that the colonies were inevitably at different stages of economic and demographic development. They were also subject to differing political and cultural forces. But the plantocracy was generally strongest in the longest-settled, most monocultural, most British of the colonies, and weakest in the recently settled colonies of diversified agriculture and cosmopolitan population. Thus, the political power of the plantocracy was strongest where the ratio of slaves to free people was greatest. In general, the first-phase colonies tended to have the slighter slopes, the thinner soil, and the lighter rainfall, whereas the later-settled tended to be rugged and wet. The nature of the economic activities in which the slaves were employed was determined by the interaction of these contrasting physical environments with phases of settlement. Thus, any classification of the colonies based simply on stage of settlement is likely to prove inadequate as a basis for understanding variations in the character of slavery and economic-demographic relationships in the West Indian colonies.

Types of Economic Activity

The primary object in this section is to determine the number of slaves employed in particular types of economic enterprise. The discussion begins with an overview of the structure of the slave labour force at about 1834, then treats the pattern of land and labour use in individual colonies for the period 1807-34. Finally, the colonies are classified into types according to their economic structure.

For an overall view of the occupational distribution of the British Caribbean slave population, the most comprehensive data available are those generated as a by-product of the compensation of the masters at emancipation. This compensation was calculated according to the money value of the slaves. The valuers' returns produced by this system provided a source of data for the detailed geographical location of the population, but their main purpose was to classify the slaves belonging to the individual masters. This classification (table 28.2) was used to value the slaves on the basis of the average prices paid for slaves sold between 1823 and 1830 (a total of 74,000 transfers). The £20 million compensation money was then divided between the masters at a rate ranging from 42 to 55 per cent of the valuation.[12] The slaves were classified after actual inspection by the Assistant Commissioners for Compensation, except that in the Bahamas the occupations listed in the registration returns of 31 July 1834 were used to avoid the cost of visiting the scattered islands. The Cayman Islands were excluded entirely. The system required that slaves be classified according to their usual occupations before August 1834, but the masters had a monetary incentive to try to have slaves placed in a higher class.[13] There also seems to have been some inconsistency between colonies in the allocation of occupational groups. But in spite of these deficiencies, the compensation data do provide a very valuable picture of the total slave labour force.

In the British Caribbean as a whole, 81.7 per cent of the slaves were classified as active in the labour force (table 28.3). Indeed, the only slaves excluded were children under 6 years of age (13.6 per cent of the population) and those classed as "aged [70 years and over], diseased, or otherwise non-effective" (4.7 per cent). There were some significant differences between the colonies, but only in Anguilla and Barbuda did the active labour force fall below 75 per cent of the total population, and only in Trinidad, British Guiana, and the Virgin Islands did it exceed 84 per cent. These variations were a product of differing age structures.

Praedial slaves, who made up 85 per cent of the total labour force, were those employed in agriculture or the extraction of other produce from the land (table 28.2). Many of the "non-praedial" slaves lived on agricultural units, of course, but most of these served in the masters' households. The largest proportions of praedials were found in the sugar colonies of Tobago and

Table 28.2   British Caribbean Slave Population as Classified for Compensation, 1834

Compensation Classification	Number of Slaves	Percentage of Slaves	Percentage of Employed Slaves
Praedial attached			
Head people	25,658	3.8	4.7
Tradesmen	18,735	2.8	3.4
Inferior tradesmen	5,999	0.9	1.1
Field labourers	241,177	36.2	44.3
Inferior field labourers	132,008	19.8	24.2
Praedial unattached			
Head people	1,772	0.3	0.3
Tradesmen	1,639	0.3	0.3
Inferior tradesmen	643	0.1	0.1
Field labourers	22,218	3.3	4.1
Inferior field labourers	10,730	1.6	2.0
Non-praedial			
Head tradesmen	4,151	0.6	0.8
Inferior tradesmen	2,439	0.4	0.5
Head people on wharves, shipping, etc.	3,335	0.5	0.6
Inferior people on wharves, shipping	3,928	0.6	0.7
Head domestic servants	29,387	4.4	5.4
Inferior domestic servants	40,718	6.1	7.5
Children under 6 years of age	91,037	13.6	–
Aged, diseased, or otherwise non-effective	30,088	4.5	–
Runaways	1,075	0.2	–
Total	666,737	100	100

Source: T.71/851 and 1522.

British Guiana (exceeding 90 per cent of the active labour force), and the smallest in the marginal colonies of Anguilla and the Bahamas (less than 60 per cent). Slaves working on lands owned by their masters were classified as "praedial attached" and those employed elsewhere as "praedial unattached." The latter were hired out by their masters under a variety of arrangements. Some led relatively settled lives, working for years on a single plantation. Others belonged to jobbers who moved them about frequently, while some, especially tradesmen, were employed on a daily basis. In British Honduras, at one extreme, no slaves were defined as praedial attached, since plantation agriculture was proscribed and the woodcutters divided their year between town and interior. High ratios of unattached praedials also occurred in the Virgin Islands and Anguilla, together with high percentages of non-praedials. But elsewhere this relationship did not hold, and in many more of

the mature sugar colonies a settled agricultural labour force went together with a large non-praedial class.

Below these broad divisions, comparisons of the occupational composition of the colonies are affected more strongly by inconsistencies in classification. In particular, the principles used to separate "inferior" from other slaves in a class varied form colony to colony.[14] It is more useful to ignore this distinction and consider the five main occupational categories into which the slaves were grouped (table 28.3) Overall, "field labourers" accounted for almost 75 per cent of the active labour force. Only in British Honduras and the Bahamas did this proportion fall below 60 per cent. Low proportions were also found in Trinidad, Anguilla, and surprisingly, Nevis.

After field labourers, the most numerous category comprised "domestics." In the marginal colonies of British Honduras, the Bahamas, and Anguilla, domestics made up more than 25 per

Table 28.3 Distribution of Slaves between Compensation Categories by Colony, 1834

| | Percentage of Employed Slaves | | | | | | Percentage of Total Slaves | | |
Colony	Field Labourers	Domestics	Tradesmen	Head People	On Wharves	Employed	Children under 6	Aged, diseased
Barbados	70.8	18.8	5.7	3.0	1.7	80.2	17.7	2.1
St. Kitts	72.4	16.4	5.0	4.4	1.7	79.2	16.2	4.6
Nevis	64.1	16.8	6.8	3.9	8.4	82.0	14.3	3.7
Antigua	78.9	9.6	7.7	2.6	1.2	80.3	14.7	5.0
Montserrat	81.2	8.1	4.7	5.0	1.0	79.0	17.6	3.4
Virgin Islands	71.5	17.1	4.7	3.8	2.9	84.1	14.5	1.4
Jamaica	73.5	12.5	7.0	6.0	0.9	82.1	12.5	5.4
Dominica	81.3	9.2	3.6	5.4	0.5	82.3	14.9	2.8
St. Lucia	78.6	14.0	3.3	3.3	0.8	77.7	14.7	7.6
St. Vincent	75.5	12.2	5.0	5.2	2.1	81.4	13.3	5.3
Grenada	77.4	6.9	6.7	6.2	2.8	80.4	14.0	5.6
Tobago	82.1	6.9	7.3	2.4	1.3	78.3	12.8	8.9
Trinidad	67.4	18.6	6.1	6.8	1.1	84.9	10.9	4.2
British Guiana	82.8	7.0	4.9	4.9	0.4	84.2	11.8	4.0
British Honduras	48.1	46.4	2.8	1.5	1.2	83.7	11.5	4.7
Bahamas	54.5	31.8	2.7	0.9	10.1	77.2	19.9	2.9
Anguilla	67.9	28.4	1.4	0.7	1.5	74.9	20.3	4.8
Barbuda	80.4	5.3	8.4	2.0	3.9	72.5	23.0	4.5
Total	74.6	12.9	6.2	5.0	1.3	81.7	13.6	4.7

Source: T.71/851 and 1522.

cent of the slave labour force. They were less numerous in the sugar colonies, where the proportion varied with the urban concentration of the slaves. More than half of the domestics lived in capital towns.[15]

Slave "tradesmen," employed in manufacturing processes or the production of intermediate goods on plantations, accounted for 6.2 per cent of the labour force. The largest proportions occurred in the first-phase sugar colonies, whereas the marginal colonies with large numbers of domestics had the smallest. Although the compensation records rarely summarized the data by sex, it is clear that the trades were the occupations most strictly reserved for male slaves.

Slaves classified as "head people," the supervisors, overlapped the tradesman and field labourer categories. If they were distributed thus, there would be a significant inflation of the tradesman category (probably raising it to 10 per cent of the labour force) and a slighter inflation of the field labourer class. Greater changes might result from this adjustment at the colony level, but there seem to have been inconsistencies in classification. It is obvious that head people would be most numerous in those colonies where the slaveholdings were large. In the Bahamas,

for example, no headman was assigned to a master unless he owned at least 10 slaves.[16] In the sugar colonies the proportion of head people was inevitably larger, a reflection of the structure of slave ownership and of the internal hierarchy of the slave system.

The fifth major occupational category, accounting for only 1.3 per cent of the labour force, comprised slaves "employed on wharves, shipping, etc." Such occupations were most important in colonies made up of small islands, the Bahamas having the largest proportion.

In broad terms, the occupational distribution of the slave labour force was determined by the extent to which a colony was dominated by sugar or other plantation crops. Of the nineteen British Caribbean colonies, only five were not significant producers of sugar in the period 1807-34: British Honduras, the Cayman Islands, the Bahamas, Anguilla, and Barbuda, with a total slave population of only 16,000 in 1834. The sugar colonies may be divided into three groups, according to their phase of settlement. The first-phase sugar colonies (Barbados, the Leeward Islands, and Jamaica) accounted for 463,000 slaves, the second-phase group 71,000, and the third-phase, frontier colonies 117,000.

Table 28.4   Tons of Sugar Produced per Slave by Colony, 1815–34

Colony	1815–19	1820–24	1825–29	1830–34
Barbados	0.16	0.17	0.19	0.21
St. Kitts	0.34	0.27	0.27	0.24
Nevis	0.34	0.24	0.27	0.27
Antigua	0.29	0.26	0.26	0.30
Montserrat	0.24	0.23	0.19	0.14
Virgin Islands	0.36	0.16	0.17	0.16
Jamaica	0.23	0.23	0.21	0.22
Dominica	0.12	0.13	0.15	0.19
St. Lucia	0.20	0.26	0.24	0.24
St. Vincent	0.50	0.49	0.56	0.47
Grenada	0.40	0.50	0.46	0.42
Tobago	0.41	0.41	0.39	0.40
Trinidad	0.29	0.35	0.53	0.71
British Guiana	0.20	0.32	0.63	0.65

Source: Calculated from data in Noel Deerr, *The History of Sugar* (1949), and T.71.

Within these three groups of sugar colonies, however, there were significant differences in the dominance of the crop. A rough measure of its relative importance is the average production of sugar per slave. This ratio has been calculated for the years 1815 to 1834 (table 28.4). But the results are of limited value because the ratio contains three separate elements: the proportion of the slave labour force employed in sugar production, the proportion of the slave population comprising the active labour force, and the productivity of labour. The presence of the last two components weakens the ratio's ability to measure the first. In 1830-34 slaves in the first group of colonies produced only 0.14 to 0.30 tons of sugar per annum, those in the second 0.19 to 0.40, and those in the third 0.65 to 0.71. Obviously the long-settled monocultural colonies suffer in this comparison because of low labour productivity. Changes in the ratio over the period are more revealing but to tend to mirror changes in total output. Barbados, the only colony in the first-phase group to show an increase in ratio, also experienced a substantial increase in output (figure 28.1).

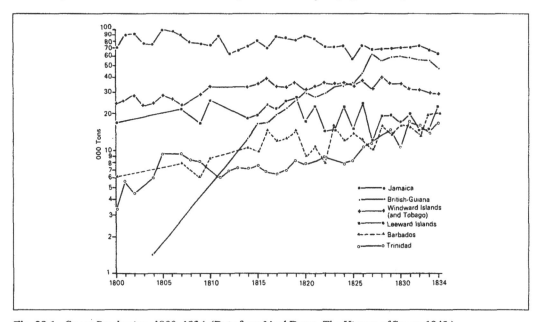

Fig. 28.1   *Sugar Production, 1800–1834.* (Data from Noel Deerr, *The History of Sugar*, 1949.)

Although these gross data provide some insights into the employment and productivity of the slave labour force, they cannot elicit a precise picture of the distribution of the slave population between the different types of economic activity. In order to build up such a picture, it will be necessary to discuss the data for individual colonies seriatim, within the framework of the phases of settlement outlined above.

First-Phase Sugar Colonies

Barbados. Between 1807 and 1834 Barbados more than doubled its sugar production, but this gain in output was not won at the expense of other crops. A summary of the registration returns for 1834 defined 49.5 per cent of the island's 82,807 slaves as "labourers in sugar cultivation," 5.8 per cent as "labourers in cotton and other agriculture," 11.6 per cent as "labourers not in agriculture," 13.0 per cent as "domestics," and 20.1 per cent as having no occupation.[17] Comparison with the 1834 compensation returns shows, however, that these registration data understated the number of domestics (by about 2,000) and agricultural labourers (by 7,000). It appears that the group "labourers not in agriculture" included tradesmen living on rural holdings, and these should be redistributed to the agricultural and urban categories.[18] It is also necessary to distribute the domestics and those with no occupation according to the proportions found in the compensation records. The derivation of the estimated size of the urban population will be discussed fully in the next chapter. On the basis of these manipulations, it seems that no more than 78 per cent of the Barbados slave population lived on sugar estates in 1834, while 11 per cent lived on plantations or "places" producing cotton, provisions, ginger and other crops, and 11 per cent lived in towns.[19]

Sugar estates were spread almost uniformly throughout Barbados, thinning out only around Bridgetown, and in the rugged country of Mt. Hillaby, the Scotland District, and Hackleton's Cliff. There were no significant changes in distribution between 1807 and 1834, the number of mills remaining steady at around 340.[20] But, whereas the windward (eastern) parishes were rather less densely covered by sugar mills, there the concentration of slaves into the sugar sector was at a maximum. Cotton and other agriculture were relatively concentrated in the leeward parishes, especially around Bridgetown. Barbados was effectively a vast sugar plantation, with sugar and its by-products, molasses and rum, accounting for almost 98 per cent of the value of exports.[21] Molasses was more important than rum as an export item, the rum being largely consumed within the island, lubricating the internal market.[22] The only export other than sugar and molasses to exceed 1 per cent of the total value was cotton. Ginger, arrowroot, and aloes were also exported on some scale, but were insignificant relative to sugar. The minor staples were produced by small settlers and slaves as well as planters.[23] In spite of the many acts passed to encourage the cultivation of these crops, the planters maintained a strictly monocultural orientation.[24] But the sugar planters of Barbados did use a significant proportion of their land space and the labour time of their slaves for the production of food crops to be consumed on the plantation. Even in such a monocultural economy, almost one-quarter of the slaves did not actually live on the sugar estates.

St. Kitts. Detailed data are not available for St. Kitts, but the distribution of slaves between economic activities must have been similar to that found in Barbados. Sugar, molasses, and rum accounted for 97 per cent of the value of exports.[25] Between 1760 and 1810 St. Kitts had consistently produced more sugar than Barbados. It then entered a period of decline, but the ratio of sugar to slaves remained higher than in Barbados until 1834 (table 28.4). Few slaves in St. Kitts were employed in agriculture other than sugar, and only a small number were engaged in salt raking. Thus, the concentration of the slave population on the sugar estates was even greater than in Barbados.

The sugar estates of St. Kitts formed a fringe around the island's coast, interrupted only in the dry eastern peninsula where the salt ponds were located. According to William McMahon's map of 1828, 44 per cent of the island was cane land, the remainder being taken up in "works, negro huts, pasture, mountain, and uncultivated land." Some of the cane land was planted in food crops, but the planters became increasingly dependent on imported food and increasingly monocultural in orientation.[26] Few slaves on St. Kitts knew any life other than that of sugar cultivation.

Nevis. The land use pattern of Nevis was a simplified version of that of St. Kitts. Its conical form meant that there was almost no break in the succession of wedge-shaped estates, and the island lacked even the salt ponds of St. Kitts. The proportion of cane land (40 per cent) matched that in St. Kitts, as did the ratio of sugar production to slaves. In 1765 some 75 per cent of the slave population of Nevis was said to be located on sugar estates, and it is clear that this proportion had increased considerably by 1834.[27] In the early nineteenth century, Nevis was a sugar monoculture pure and simple.

Antigua. With its gentler slopes, Antigua approximated more closely the land use pattern of Barbados. Although it had been an important producer of cotton until the end of the eighteenth century, sugar gained complete mastery between 1800 and 1834, covering the greater part of the island.[28] Food crops were grown as a part of estate cultivation, as in Barbados, but Antigua imported most of its corn. An important contrast with Barbados, however, lay in the fact that some Antiguan properties were devoted to raising livestock for use on the estates. Sheep were also grazed, there being some demand for their wool.[29] Only in the more rugged southern parishes of Antigua were cattle and provisions properties numerous. Elsewhere sugar dominated. Antigua was the largest producer of sugar in the Leeward Islands for most of the period 1807-34, though the ratio of sugar to slaves did not exceed that in St. Kitts and Nevis until about 1830. Detailed data on the distribution of the Antiguan slave population are not available, but it can be estimated on the basis of these comparisons that almost 80 per cent worked on sugar estates, while 10 per cent were on holdings producing other crops and livestock, and 10 per cent lived in towns.

Montserrat. Sugar, molasses, and rum were the only significant exports of Montserrat. Output remained fairly steady until 1820, then declined rapidly, so that by 1834 the sugar to slaves ratio was the lowest of all the British Caribbean sugar colonies (table 28.4). As in Antigua, cotton had declined rapidly in the late eighteenth century

and reappeared only after 1838. The rugged topography of Montserrat confined sugar estates to the eastern and western coastal strips and the valley crossing the island. Food crops were rarely planted on the estates' limited potential cane land, and the slaves were expected to produce most of their own food on provision grounds allotted to them in the marginal hills.[30] The distribution of the slaves between enterprises was similar to that in Nevis.

Virgin Islands. In the Virgin Islands the sugar industry did not become dominant until 1800, and even then it was concentrated on one island, Tortola. Sugar exports increased rapidly between 1800 and 1819, but the extent to which this resulted from local production is uncertain. Tortola was declared a free port in 1801, permitted to import foreign sugar and coffee and re-export these goods to Britain. But since Tortola had to compete with free-trading St. Thomas, it is doubtful that it captured much non-British production.[31] In any case, by 1820 the Virgin Islands had become the smallest sugar producer in the Leeward Islands, rarely making more than 1,000 tons.

The most detailed source materials for the Virgin Islands are the tables prepared in 1823 by John Stobo for the Colonial Office.[32] Stobo provided data for 1815 and 1823, his intention being to show the great decline in the fortunes of the islands over the period. He named 47 islands, 15 being less than 10 acres in extent. In 1815 some 24 were under cultivation, but 2 (Ginger Island and Great Tobago) were abandoned by 1823. Four of the exploited islands had no people living on them, and others were occupied solely by slaves. Only a small proportion of the land was cultivated.

In 1823 only Tortola produced sugar, and even on that island scarcely more than 20 per cent of the area was cultivated. The acreage under cane, according to Stobo, fell from 3,125 in 1815 to 2,400 in 1823. By contrast, King's map of 1798 showed 58 sugar estates on Tortola, covering the western two-thirds of the island.[33] Cotton, too, showed a minor decline in Tortola between 1815 and 1823, but in the Virgin Islands as a whole there was a slight increase, and cotton remained the major export staple of most of the smaller islands. Exports of cotton fluctuated but maintained a fair level until the end of the

Table 28.5 Employment of Slaves in the Virgin Islands, 1815 and 1823

	1815		1823	
Employment	Number	Percentage	Number	Percentage
In trade in town	178	2.4	159	2.5
Domestics in town	554	7.6	469	7.3
In fishing	136	1.9	124	1.9
Domestics in country	80	1.1	122	1.9
On sugar estates	4,569	62.6	4,131	64.1
On cotton plantations	1,725	23.7	1,343	20.8
Cultivating provisions	53	0.7	96	1.5
Total	7,295	100.0	6,444	100.0

Source: Stobo, "Statistical Table," C.O. 239/9.

1820s.[34] Land under cotton, according to Stobo, was valued at only half the amount for that under cane (£15 and £32 currency per acre, in 1815). Stobo also listed coffee produced in the larger islands, but most of this must have been imported from foreign colonies under the Free Port Act, the amount falling steeply after 1815. Salt was most important for Anegada, with 655 acres in salt ponds in 1815. Salt Island, Tortola, and Beef Island were also significant producers.

Stobo also provided estimates of the distribution of the slave population between these types of economic enterprise (table 28.5). The source of his information is not known, but the total populations conform closely to those found in the registration returns. In 1823 sugar estates accounted for almost 65 per cent of the slaves, and cotton plantations for 21 per cent. But, whereas the area under cane declined between 1815 and 1823, the estates increased their proportion of the slave labour force; hence the great fall in productivity. The dominance of sugar no doubt continued to increase, but even in 1834 the slaves of the Virgin islands were employed in a much wider range of enterprises than those in other sugar colonies of the Leeward Islands.

Jamaica. The use of land and labour in Jamaica has been discussed in detail elsewhere.[35] The available data are excellent, compared to those for the Leeward Islands and Barbados. Jamaica's economy was much more diverse than that of any of the other first-phase sugar colonies. This diversity resulted from the island's varied physical environments and the relatively slow movement of the frontier of settlement. Around 1832

slightly less than 50 per cent of the slaves lived on sugar estates, 14 per cent on coffee plantations, 13 per cent on livestock pens, and 7 per cent belonged to mobile jobbing gangs, and 8 per cent lived in towns.

Second-Phase Sugar Colonies

Dominica. Dominica was the least important sugar producer of all the colonies settled by Britain after 1763. But its level of output did remain fairly constant between 1807 and 1834, with a definite growth after 1825, and there was a steady increase in sugar production per slave. To a certain extent, the British did convert Dominica into a sugar colony from the coffee-cotton-cocoa-provisions economy it had been in 1763. Immediately following the cession of the island, sugar estates were established on a large scale by British planters, to the neglect of all other crops. By 1800 indigo, cotton, and ginger had all disappeared as significant crops.[36] Yet sugar failed to attain an absolute dominance, and coffee continued to employ a larger proportion of the slave population until 1834.

The most detailed data available for Dominica are found in the poll tax returns for 1827. By that year, 80.6 per cent of the slaves lived on sugar estates or coffee plantations. There were 42 sugar estates, 219 coffee plantations and 11 properties that combined sugar and coffee in varying proportions. A few properties combined the production of coffee and molasses, but these may be placed with the coffee plantations since the quantity of molasses made was always small. If the slaves located on sugar-coffee units are divided equally between sugar and coffee plantations, it follows that 46.3 per cent of the total slave population worked on coffee plantations and 34.3 per cent on sugar plantations. If anything, this estimate overstates the proportion in sugar. It assumes 7,131 slaves in coffee and 5,271 in sugar, whereas a planters' petition of the late 1820s or early 1830s claimed 7,700 were in coffee and 4,500 in sugar.[37] The remaining praedial slaves were employed on smaller holdings, producing minor staples such as cocoa and arrowroot,[38] and ground provisions. Thus, although there was a significant shift in land use patterns between 1763 and 1834, sugar never dominated the slave population of Dominica. Coffee cultivation in Dominica was heavily concentrated in the windward parishes, the estates clinging to the limited level lands around river mouths. The sugar-coffee units were well scattered. They were relatively large, suggesting that they took advantage of diverse land types within their boundaries.

St. Vincent. For the greater part of the period 1807-34, St. Vincent was the leading sugar producer in the Windward Islands, with the highest ratio of sugar to slaves. Sugar had overtaken coffee and cocoa as the leading crop before 1800. Production increased until about 1828, after which there was a definite decline.

Detailed data on land and labour use in St. Vincent are available in the official annual returns made by the landowners to special commissioners.[39] These data show that sugar dominated in the windward parishes but was cultivated in coastal niches throughout the island. The windward parishes became increasingly monocultural, and by the 1830s coffee and cocoa production was largely confined to the leeward parishes of St. Patrick and St. David. Coffee output reached a peak about 1809 and then fell off steadily, while cocoa production increased until 1826. Arrowroot emerged as a significant crop during the 1820s, and by 1834 it accounted for as much as 50 per cent of St. Vincent's minor exports (that is, excluding sugar, rum and molasses). It was grown by slaves in their garden plots, as well as by small holders and planters, but the greater part of the crop came from St. Patrick parish.[40]

The data in the annual returns show that around 1830 some 70 per cent of the slaves living on the island of St. Vincent worked on sugar plantations, and 20 per cent worked on plantations and small holdings producing combinations of coffee, cocoa, arrowroot, and food crops. To this estimate must be added those slaves living on the islands of the Grenadines, divided between the colonies of St. Vincent and Grenada.

The Grenadines were miniature plantation economies dominated by sugar and cotton. Unlike St. Vincent and Grenada, they produced no coffee or cocoa. But the Grenadines experienced the same monocultural tendency as the larger islands in the early nineteenth century, sugar-replacing cotton. The most dramatic decline in cotton production occurred in Carriacou, especially after 1820. In the St. Vincent Genadines, cotton production fell from 225,000 lb in 1810 to 55,000 in 1831, though Union Island maintained a high level of output into the 1820s. Sugar production increased steadily after 1800, with particularly rapid growth in Carriacou. By 1830 sugar was produced only on Carriacou, Bequia and Mustique. Using comparative labour output ratios, it can be estimated that by 1830 approximately 50 per cent of the slaves in the Grenadines worked on sugar plantations and 35 per cent on cotton plantations. The remaining 15 per cent worked on small agricultural holdings or in fishing, shipping, or town occupations. The plantation system dominated only in Bequia, Mustique, Canouan, Union Island, and Carriacou. The other islands were all very small, supporting only rudimentary economies and tiny slave populations.[41] Even in the larger islands the pattern of landholding was simple: Mustique, for example, was divided up between only seven plantations (figure 28.2).

Grenada. The agricultural economy of Grenada was relatively diversified, though the nineteenth century saw the ascendancy of sugar. Sugar production rose rapidly after 1763, then more gradually after 1807, reaching a peak in 1828. Coffee went into decline from 1800, cotton from 1820, and by 1834 both crops dropped into insignificance. Cocoa production doubled during the 1820s, and Grenada also exported small quantities of arrowroot, ginger, and coconuts. The rugged topography meant that little estate land was planted in food crops, but the total area allocated to slave provision grounds was considerable, equalling the area under cane.[42]

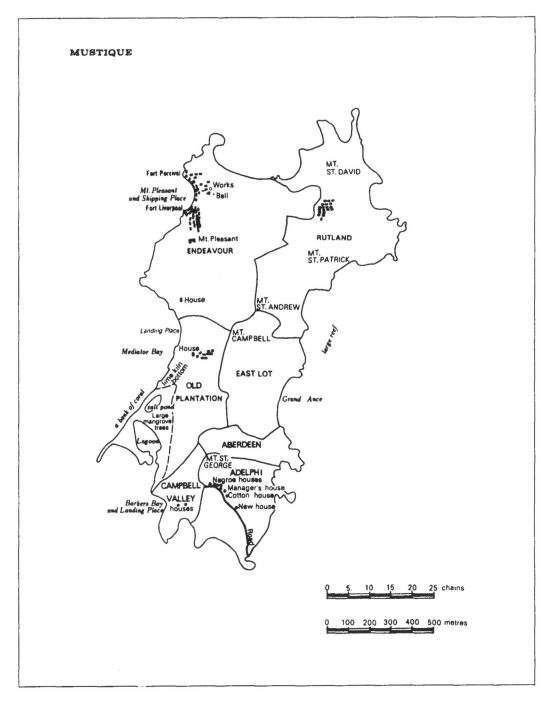

Fig. 28.2 Mustique, 1804 (*Source:* MS plan [Survey Department, Kingstown, St. Vincent].)

Sugar occupied the coastal fringe of Grenada, penetrating more than two miles into the interior only in the northeastern corner of the island. The relative concentration of estates on the windward side of the island was matched by a relative decline in output in the leeward parishes of St. John and St. Mark during the 1820s. Most of the cotton plantations were located in the southwestern peninsula. Coffee and cocoa plantations were heavily concentrated in the leeward parishes on the steeper slopes behind the sugar estates, though there were also a few in the interior of the windward parishes. Coffee and cocoa were generally produced in combination, but it was very rare for sugar to be grown together with either of these crops or with cotton. An occasional holding combined coffee and cotton production.[43] Thus, the windward parishes were dominated by monocultural sugar estates, whereas the leeward parishes combined a variety of crops, monocultural estates being intermixed with diversified minor staples plantations.

The distribution of the slave population of Grenada between these types of enterprise can be calculated directly for 1819.[44] In that year, 83 per cent of the slaves worked on sugar estates, 4 per cent on cotton plantations, and 4 per cent on holdings combining the cultivation of coffee, cocoa, and provisions. The remainder lived in the towns. As elsewhere, a small number of slaves were employed in fishing, charcoal burning, lime burning, and quarrying. The inclusion of the Granada Grenadines, discussed in the section dealing with St. Vincent, changes these proportions somewhat. The proportion in cotton rises to 14.5 per cent in 1819, while sugar drops to 72 per cent. By 1834, however, Carriacou had come to resemble Grenada much more closely as sugar expanded at the expense of cotton.

Tobago. Sugar production increased steadily throughout the period 1800–34 in all of the second-phase sugar colonies with the exception of Tobago, which experienced a steady decline. In spite of this decline Tobago was the most monocultural of the group. The island had developed very rapidly as a sugar plantation economy in the late eighteenth century, leading to the abandonment of indigo and the almost total collapse of cotton cultivation.[45] No detailed records on slave employment are available for Tobago,

but it can be estimated, on the basis of the export data, that by 1834 probably 90 per cent of the slaves worked on sugar plantations. This proportion was similar to that in Nevis and Montserrat. To a greater extent than in any other colony of the British Caribbean, the life of the typical slave in Tobago was one dominated by sugar.

Third-Phase Sugar Colonies

St. Lucia. The slave registration returns for the third-phase sugar colonies identified the crops cultivated by the slaves on each holding. Estimates of the distribution of the slaves between types of economic activity may thus be regarded as more reliable than those achieved by indirect methods for the first- and second-phase colonies. But problems remain because some masters failed to identify the crops produced on their holdings. In St. Lucia, the registration returns for 1815 omitted the crop cultivated on holdings accounting for 17.4 per cent of the total slave population. All of these were defined as "plantation" slaves, so it is clear that they were all involved in agriculture. The owners of these slaves were not atypical in terms of their sex, colour, or nationality, and the distribution of slaveholding size was very similar to that in the total population. Some 20.2 per cent were defined as "personal" slaves, but only half of these lived in towns.

Thus, it is necessary to distribute these two unknown categories between the identified crop types pro rata, assuming that they were typical of the general pattern.

Table 28.6 Distribution of Slaves by Crop-type: St. Lucia, 1815

Crop	Number of Slaves	percentage
Sugar	9,713	59.7
Coffee	3,256	20.0
Cocoa	586	3.6
Cotton	321	2.0
Other agriculture	640	3.9
Livestock	25	0.2
Lime	94	0.6
Personal: urban	1,647	10.1
Total	16,282	100.0

Source: T.71/378û79.

In St. Lucia in 1815, sugar accounted for barely 60 per cent of the slave population, while 20 per cent worked on coffee plantations (table 28.6). Cocoa and cotton were also significant, cultivated either as monocultures or in combination with coffee, sugar, cassava, and other provision crops. This land-use pattern was similar to that of Dominica, but sugar achieved a greater domination in St. Lucia. By 1831, cane covered 4,752 acres and coffee only 696 acres. Cotton was gradually abandoned, with only 18 acres planted by 1831. Cocoa production stagnated. A further 4,049 acres were under provisions in 1831, but it is uncertain how far this incorporated ground cultivated by slaves living on sugar estates.[46] Coffee cultivation was concentrated in the leeward parishes. Sugar also found its center here, especially in castries and Soufriere parishes, but spread into the windward parishes.

Trinidad. Although it came to be dominated by sugar after 1800, Trinidad retained a relatively diversified agricultural economy. Sugar production grew very rapidly at first, but the peak of 1805 was not reached again until 1826, after which it once more expanded rapidly (figure 28.1). The cocoa industry expanded even more rapidly than sugar. But cocoa was a small holder's crop, largely cultivated by the considerable free coloured and free black population of Trinidad and not dependent on slave labour in the same way as sugar. Unlike sugar and cocoa, the output of cotton fell drastically between 1800 and 1834, and coffee suffered a significant, though more gradual, decline (figure 28.3). By 1832 sugar and its by-products accounted for more than 90 per cent of the total value of exports from Trinidad.[47] The island exported 90 per cent of the sugar it produced, 99 per cent of the

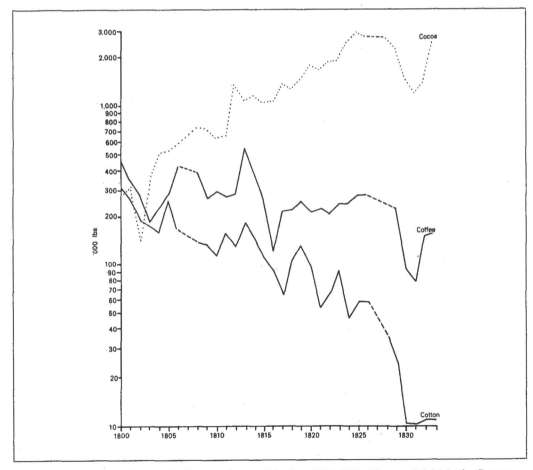

Fig. 28.3 *Production of Cocoa, Coffee, and Cotton: Trinidad, 1800–1833. (Source: R.M. Martin, Statistics of the Colonies of the British Empire, 1839, p. 34)*

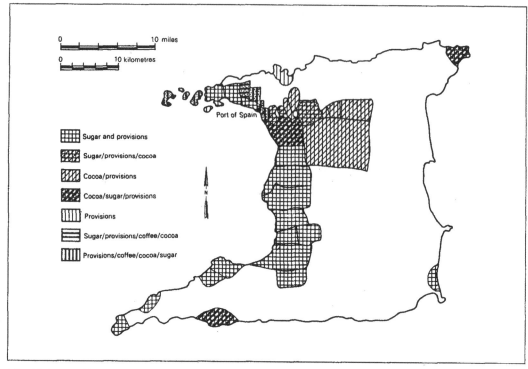

Fig. 28.4   *Land Use: Trinidad, 1832. (Source:* C.O. 295/46, p. 158. Crops are included only if they covered more than 10 per cent of the total cultivated area of a quarter, and they are ordered in terms of area.)

molasses, and only 3 per cent of the rum. Cocoa, in spite of its meteoric rise, contributed only 6.2 per cent of total exports, and coffee a mere 2 per cent.

The area planted in sugar cane doubled between 1808 and 1832, as did the area in food crops. But for the greater part the cultivation of food crops was contained within the plantation economy, since almost two-thirds of the provisions seem to have been produced on "Negro grounds," and at least a proportion of the remaining third must have been cultivated by planters rather than free small holders. Land under food crops was valued as highly as land under cane.[48] A considerable area of Trinidad was under pasture, but this too was contained within the plantation sector and it did not give rise to independent livestock pens.[49] Tobacco, annatto, nutmeg, cloves, and coconuts were all produced on a small scale, in combination with the more important minor staples.[50]

Agricultural settlement in Trinidad was restricted to the western edge of the island, fringing the Gulf of Paria, throughout the period 1807-34. But within this zone there was a major southward

shift in the location of the sugar industry.[51] Old estates were abandoned and new ones established on fertile virgin soils. In many of the northern quarters, in a belt stretching from Bocas to the Maracas Valley, there was an absolute decrease in the area under cane. The regions of greatest growth, exceeding the general doubling, were Chaguanas, Point à Pierre, and South Naparima. By 1832 South Naparima alone was cultivating more than 20 per cent of the island's cane. In 1807 it had been a leading coffee producer, but by 1832 the crop had all but disappeared from the quarter. The expansion of cocoa took place mainly in the northern upland interior quarters, while coffee survived best in the northern upland region around Port of Spain. Thus, by 1832 a distinct pattern of agricultural regionalization had emerged in Trinidad (figure 28.4), with a sharp line drawn between north and south at about Chaguanas. The southern region was strictly a sugar monoculture, cultivating only provision crops as a subsidiary. Only in the quarter of Erin, on the southern coastal uplands, was cocoa significant. In the north, only Tragarete, Mucurapo, and Carenage remained sugar

Table 28.7   Distribution of Slaves by Crop-type: Trinidad, 1810 and 1813

	1810		1813	
Crop	Number of Slaves	Percentage	Number of Slaves	Percentage
Sugar	13,219	60.1	14,498	56.4
Coffee	1,732	7.9	1,742	6.8
Cocoa	859	3.9	1,421	5.5
Cotton ⎫			765	3.0
Other agriculture ⎬	2,492	11.3	971	3.8
Fishing, shipping	–	–	128	0.5
Personal: urban	3,680	16.8	6,171	24.0
Total	21,982	100.0	25,696	100.0

Sources: 1810: C.O. 295/23, f.57: Hislop to Liverpool, 16 Apr. 1810. 1813: T.71/501–3.

monocultures, with cocoa, coffee, and provisions dominating elsewhere.

A small number of slaves were employed in manufacturing and extractive industries. They worked in lime, brick, and tile kilns, and in quarrying and charcoal burning.[52] More than 100 fishing boats operated out of Port of Spain, but there were only 63 slave fishermen in the town in 1813. A whale fishery was established at Gasper Grande Island in 1826, but it was said to be difficult to find men accustomed to whaling in Trinidad, and schemes were proposed to bring forty slaves from Bermuda; so it is doubtful that the station employed many slaves.[53]

The distribution of the slave population of Trinidad between types of economic activity can be established directly from the slave registration returns for 1813. In table 28.7, slaves belonging to units combining more than one crop have been allocated to the leading, first-named crop, but these account for a small proportion of the total since most plantations were described as monocultural. Only 3.4 per cent of the slaves attributed to sugar lived on sugar-cocoa, sugar-coffee-cocoa, or sugar-coffee units. Diversification was greater outside sugar. Some 22.7 per cent of the slaves in coffee were on units that also produced cocoa and provisions, and 14.6 per cent on diversified cocoa plantations. Provision crops dominated the units attributed to "other agriculture." Trinidad possessed a very large urban slave population in 1813, but the towns did not account for all the "personal" slaves on the island, and the remainder (9.6 per cent of the total population) have been distributed pro rata. A check on the pattern derived from the 1813 reg-

istration returns is found in an official estimate of 1810, based on the annual returns made to the Commissary of Population (table 28.7). The latter underestimated the urban slave population, but otherwise the pattern was very similar to that found in the more comprehensive registration returns.

In 1813 about 56 per cent of the Trinidad slave population worked on sugar estates, and another 19 per cent on plantations producing combinations of coffee, cocoa, cotton, and provisions. The pattern in 1830 cannot be determined directly, but the data on output and cultivated area (figure 28.4) can be compared with the geographical distribution of the slaves to derive an estimate. It is certain that sugar increased its share significantly, to about 70 per cent, at the expense of the towns and cotton and coffee. But the growth of cocoa meant that the minor plantation staples still accounted for 14.5 per cent of the slaves and created a clear regional distinction between sugar monoculture and small-scale diversified agriculture.

Demerara-Essequibo and Berbice. At the end of the eighteenth century Demerara, Essequibo, and Berbice (combined to form British Guiana in 1831) were the leading British colonial producers of coffee and cotton. These two crops reached their peaks about 1810 and thereafter were increasingly eclipsed by sugar. Between 1810 and 1834 sugar output increased more rapidly than in any other colony, levelling off only after 1827 (figure 28.1), and production per slave more than tripled. But coffee production dropped from 19.2 to 1.4 million lb in Demerara between 1810 and 1831, and from 2.3 million to a mere 27,000 lb in Essequibo. Cotton production showed a similar pattern: between 1810 and 1831 it fell from 5.8 million to 400,000 lb in Demerara, and from 1.3 million to 41,000 lb in Essequibo. A similar decline in cotton and coffee occurred in Berbice, though sugar proved far less dominant than in Essequibo, where the shift was most marked. Some of the old cotton and coffee plantations were converted to sugar estates or cattle farms but, particularly in Berbice, great tracts of land were simply abandoned and left in waste.

The distribution of the slave population between the major agricultural activities can be established for Demerara-Essequibo in considerable detail, using data provided in the registration returns. But Berbice is less well served, the returns giving no real clues as to the crops cultivated. In Essequibo 97.2 per cent of the slaves lived on sugar estates, very few of which grew coffee as a subsidiary crop, and on the islands in the mouth of the Essequibo River sugar monoculture was almost total in its dominance. Coastal Demerara was much less completely dominated by sugar, with cotton and coffee plantations remaining significant until the time of emancipation, and some large estates produced coffee as well as sugar. But overall 78.5 per cent of the slaves in Demerara-Essequibo lived on sugar estates by 1832, a proportion very similar to that found in Barbados. This pattern may be compared with that in 1813, when only 32.6 per cent of the slaves in Demerara-Essequibo lived on sugar estates, 31.3 per cent were on cotton plantations, and 22.3 per cent on coffee plantations.[55] The contrast with 1832 is great.

For Berbice, only total numbers of holdings are known, by simplified land uses, and the slave populations attached to them must be estimated by applying the mean holding sizes found in Demerara-Essequibo. These calculations show that less than 50 per cent of the slaves lived on sugar estates in 1832, while at least 35 per cent were on plantations producing coffee, cotton, and provisions. The contrast with Demerara-Essequibo is confirmed by production data: in Berbice sugar production per slave was less than half that in Essequibo, but in coffee and cotton the ratio was double that for Demerara. Berbice also had a larger livestock industry, selling twice as many cattle as Demerara-Essequibo.[56]

By 1832 sugar cultivation was spread throughout the settled coastland of British Guiana, but it was everywhere mixed with other crops except on the islands in the mouth of the Essequibo. Cotton, however, was chiefly concentrated in the coastal belt between the Berbice and Demerara rivers. Up-river settlements tended to combine sugar and coffee cultivation, the majority of coffee plantations favouring this location over the coast. Food crops, particularly plantains, were produced extensively, with Demerara the leading area.[57] Woodcutting, which employed only a small number of slaves, was most important in areas accessible to the Georgetown market.

First-Phase Marginal Colonies

British Honduras. Plantation agriculture and manufacturing enterprises were prohibited in the British settlement in the Bay of Honduras under the terms of the 1786 Convention of London. Thus, no slaves were classified as "praedial attached" in the compensation returns of 1834. The occupational distribution of the slaves was quite simple, most males working as woodcutters and females as domestics.[58] But most of the boys, to about the age of 15 years, lived in town with their mothers, who were employed as domestics. Thus, almost exactly 50 per cent of the slaves lived in town, working as domestics or tradesmen, the other 50 per cent being employed as woodcutters. The latter did not live permanently in the interior and spent several months of each year in Belize Town.

The export of mahogany, the leading timber cut in British Honduras in the early nineteenth century, fluctuated from year to year but maintained a consistent level of about 5 million feet during the 1820s. The profitability of mahogany cutting led to the large scale cutting out of reserves by about 1830, especially on the Belize and Sibun rivers, and to the extraction of timber from outside the limits of settlement (north of the Rio Hondo) in spite of a heavy tax levied on it after 1818.[59] Logwood was relatively unimportant between 1807 and 1834, and the output of cedar was slight. Indigo production declined, but cochineal emerged as a minor export after 1828.[60] Some boats were built in Belize, using local timber, but the industry was hampered because such boats could not be registered as

British shipping before 1820, and thereafter only under rigid restrictions, due to the ambiguous legal position of the settlement.[61]

Cayman Islands. The Cayman Islands were known in the early nineteenth century for their turtle meat and shell, otherwise producing only a little cotton, logwood, and livestock for export.[62] But the occupational data in the 1834 registration returns, the only material available on the distribution of the slaves between activities, suggest that few slaves were fully employed in fishing. Only 29 of the 490 male slaves were listed as fishermen or mariners. Another 25 were carpenters, sawyers, caulkers, mechanics, and coopers, who may have been employed in boat building. The great majority of the slaves were field labourers or domestics, and it seems that most were engaged in an agriculture primarily directed toward food crops for domestic consumption. Some cane was grown for home sugar processing, but the more important products were yams, plantains, and cassava, and pigs, poultry, and goats. All of the holdings were small, with fewer than 50 slaves.

It may be estimated, rather crudely, that in 1834 some 80 per cent of the slaves in the Cayman Islands lived on diversified food-producing holdings, 15 per cent in town (Georgetown),[63] and 5 per cent in units directed towards the sea (fishing turtling, sailing, and boat building).

Bahamas. In the Bahamas, the collapse of the cotton plantation economy had occurred by about 1800, the crop surviving in the following decades only as part of a diversified agriculture similar to that of the Cayman Islands. In 1816 the assembly complained that "our almost worn out islands" were reduced to the export of a few tons of cotton, dyewoods, salt, and turtle, and the scavenging of stranded cargoes.[64] By 1829 salt was declared the only real staple, the exhausted soil yielding but meagre crops of cotton and provisions.[65]

The occupational data for 1834 compensation returns show that, in the working age groups, about 55 per cent of the slaves were field labourers, 32 per cent domestics, and 10 per cent employed in fishing and shipping.[66] It can be estimated, then, that 15 per cent lived in the towns, 10 per cent belonged to sea-oriented units, and 75 per cent worked on agricultural and salt-raking holdings. It is difficult to separate the slaves involved in salt-raking, since the activity was seasonal, but they may have comprised 10 per cent of the total. Thus, the pattern in the Bahamas was similar to that in the Cayman Islands, except that there was a greater emphasis on fishing and shipping. The scattered nature of the islands of the Bahamas and the concentration of trade in Nassau were the major causes of this contrast.

Salt ponds were found on six of the islands, the largest being on Rum Key, Long Island, and Exuma, but the leading producers were Turks and Caicos. By 1832, cotton production was concentrated on Exuma and Long Island, and the nearby Rum Key and Crooked Island. Elsewhere cotton was never more than a marginal part of the land use pattern. Most islands cultivated a diversity of crops, but some were able to specialize to some degree by supplying the town and port markets of Nassau. Eleuthera was the leading producer of provision crops, harvesting one-third of the corn, half of the yams and potatoes, half the cassava and arrowroot, one third of the pumpkins and lemons, and one-quarter of the peas, beans, garlic, onions, and eschalots. Eleuthera also supplied almost all of the pineapples produced for the emerging export trade (40,000) dozen in 1832).[67] Fishing, turtling, and sponge gathering were carried out on the Bahama Bank, off the coast of Cuba. The banks also provided favourable conditions for that other prop to the Bahamas economy in the nineteenth century, "wrecking," gathering up stranded goods from unfortunate vessels.[68]

Anguilla. Less than one-tenth of Anguilla's land area was cultivated, only a fringe around the central pond, which in the eighteenth century had been a leading supplier of salt to the American trade. In the early nineteenth century the annual yield of salt was 3 million bushels. Sugar was cultivated, but even in favourable seasons the crop amounted to little more than 100 tons of inferior quality, and most of it was consumed locally. A trifling amount of cotton was produced, but the major crops were corn, yams, potatoes, and other ground provisions. Cultivation was diffused over many small parcels of land.[69] Anguilla struck contemporary travellers in the West Indies by its lack of typicality, the landscape forming "the exact antipode of large plantations of sugar."[70]

The American Revolution destroyed the market for Anguilla's basic resource salt, and even when restrictions on British West Indian-United States trade were relaxed in 1822 Anguilla was overlooked, so that American vessels went elsewhere. In the same year the island was affected by drought, and the ports were opened to foreign vessels to prevent famine. In 1823 no salt was made, heavy rains dissolving it in the pond just when it was ready for gathering, but in 1824 the ports were opened to dispose of an abundant salt crop.[71] In 1832 it was said that the salt crop, "the staple commodity of the island," had failed for the past six years, and that the provision crops had been destroyed by an intense year-long drought, resulting in actual starvation. Subscription lists were opened in the British colonies of the eastern Caribbean for the relief of the ill-fated Anguillans.[72]

The occupational distribution of the 2,260 slaves living on Anguilla in 1834 is uncertain. But the failure of salt, the apparent small scale of sugar production, and the absence of any urban settlement or even a store on the island, suggest that at least 90 per cent of the slaves must have lived on small diversified agricultural holdings.

Barbuda. Sir Bethel Codrington's lease on Barbuda meant that the island comprised a single economic unit, an adjunct to his Antiguan sugar estates. It supplied the estates with livestock, harness and leather goods, timber, meat, fish, and provisions. But it produced no export staples, and the island developed a life of its own. The economy was essentially self-sufficient.[73] The livestock – cattle, horses, sheep and deer – roamed wild and were run down by mounted slave "huntsmen." The provision grounds were fenced to protect them from the animals. Some slaves were fishermen, drawing the seine in the lagoon; others were sailors; and a small group of domestics tended the few supervisory whites who occupied the "castle." Thus, it is difficult to categorize Barbuda.

A Classification of The Colonial Economies

An attempt can now be made to classify the colonies in terms of the types of economic environments in which the slaves were employed. Table 28.8 summarizes the estimates made for each colony at about 1810, 1820, and 1830.

These estimates relate to the number of slaves living on particular types of units, not their actual occupations. Slaves attributed to "sugar," for instance, all lived on sugar plantations, but some worked as domestics or cattle keepers rather than in the cane field or mill. Slaves attached to diversified agricultural holdings have been distributed according to the leading crop, where this was sugar, coffee, or cotton; but those in which cocoa, provisions, or other minor staples predominated have been allocated to "other agriculture." The problem of definition is least in the case of sugar, which was usually cultivated as a mono-culture, and greatest in those small holdings in which slaves were variously employed in fishing, agriculture, and salt raking. It must also be emphasized that for only 11 of the 20 colonies are the estimates calculated directly from employment or labour use data. But these 11 colonies accounted for as many as 552,000 slaves around 1830, and the estimates for the largest colonies (Jamaica, Barbados, and Demerara-Essequibo) all rest on strong data. For the remaining 9 colonies, with 133,000 slaves, the estimates are derived from output/export data, applied to the labour-output ratios found in comparable colonies. Again, the data are generally stronger for 1830 than for the earlier years, except in Trinidad, St. Lucia, Grenada, and the Virgin Islands. In most cases, the data permit an exact estimate for only one of the reference years, and the estimates for the others are based on extrapolations within the general trends established in the discussion of individual colonies. The slave populations for 1820 and 1830 are derived from the registration returns, but those for 1810 are extrapolations.

In spite of these reservations about the data, the general patterns that emerge are quite clear. The phase-of-settlement classification employed in this chapter thus far is shown to be inadequate, in terms of economic environments. Of the first-phase colonies, it is patent that the "marginal" colonies had a very different pattern from that in the sugar colonies, but it is also apparent that Jamaica must be separated form the other sugar colonies because of its diversification. The second- and third-phase sugar colonies can be combined to form a single class, the "new sugar colonies." The pattern in the latter class was, however, distinct from that in Jamaica and that in the old sugar colonies. Within the four classes

Table 28.8   Estimated Distribution of Slaves by Crop-type and Colony, 1810, 1820 and 1830

Colony	Sugar	Coffee	Cotton	Other Agriculture	Livestock	Salt, Timber	Fishing, Shipping	Urban	Number of Slaves
1810									
Old sugar colonies									
Barbados	76.5	–	4.0	7.0	–	–	0.5	12.0	75,000
St. Kitts	87.0	–	1.0	2.0	–	0.5	0.5	9.0	20,800
Nevis	90.0	–	–	1.5	–	–	0.5	8.0	10,400
Antigua	73.5	–	5.0	5.0	5.0	–	0.5	11.0	35,650
Montserrat	80.5	–	8.0	2.0	–	–	0.5	9.0	6,800
Virgin Islands	60.0	–	27.0	0.5	–	0.5	2.0	10.0	7,500
Jamaica	51.5	17.0	–	8.0	14.0	–	0.5	9.0	347,00
New sugar colonies									
Dominica	30.0	50.0	0.5	10.0	–	–	0.5	9.0	19,000
St. Lucia	55.0	22.0	3.0	9.3	0.2	–	0.5	10.0	18,500
St. Vincent	60.0	5.0	8.0	16.0	–	–	2.0	9.0	27,400
Grenada	70.0	1.0	15.0	3.5	–	–	1.5	9.0	30,000
Tobago	88.0	–	2.0	2.5	–	–	0.5	7.0	18,000
Trinidad	55.0	8.0	4.0	7.5	–	–	0.5	25.0	26,200
Demerara-Essequibo	58.0	10.0	20.0	3.0	0.5	0.2	0.3	8.0	80,000
Berbice	18.0	35.0	30.0	1.5	5.0	0.2	0.3	10.0	27,300
Marginal colonies									
British Honduras	–	–	–		–	50.0	–	50.0	2,900
Cayman Islands	–	–	–	80.0	–	–	5.0	15.0	850
Bahamas	–	–	5.0	60.0	–	10.0	10.0	15.0	10,000
Anguilla	–	–	–	90.0	–	8.0	2.0	–	1,700
Barbuda	–	–	–	90.0	5.0	–	5.0	–	350
1820									
Old sugar colonies									
Barbados	77.0	–	3.5	7.5	–	–	0.5	11.5	78,350
St. Kitts	87.0	–	0.5	3.0	–	0.5	0.5	8.5	20,000
Nevis	90.0	–	–	1.5	–	–	0.5	8.0	9,350
Antigua	77.0	–	2.0	5.0	5.0	–	0.5	10.5	30,850
Montserrat	85.0	–	4.0	2.0	–	–	0.5	8.5	6,550
Virgin Islands	64.0	–	22.0	1.5	–	0.5	2.0	10.0	6,600
Jamaica	52.0	16.0	–	9.0	14.0	–	0.5	8.5	342,380
New sugar colonies									
Dominica	33.0	48.0	–	10.0	–	–	0.5	8.5	16,505
St. Lucia	64.0	17.0	1.0	7.4	0.1	–	0.5	10.0	14,750
St. Vincent	66.0	1.0	6.0	16.0	–	–	2.0	9.0	24,750
Grenada	72.0	–	14.0	4.0	–	–	1.5	8.5	26,900

Table continues

Table 28.8　(Continued)

Colony	Sugar	Coffee	Cotton	Other Agriculture	Livestock	Salt, Timber	Fishing, Shipping	Urban	Number of Slaves
				Percentage of Slaves					
Tobago	90.0	–	–	2.5	–	–	0.5	7.0	15,050
Trinidad	65.0	4.0	0.5	10.0	–	–	0.5	20.0	23,400
Demerara-Essequibo	72.0	6.0	10.0	2.0	0.5	0.2	0.3	9.0	77,400
Berbice	32.0	30.0	20.0	3.0	4.5	0.2	0.3	10.0	23,400
Marginal colonies									
British Honduras	–	–	–	–	–	50.0	–	50.0	2,560
Cayman Islands	–	–	–	80.0	–	–	5.0	15.0	900
Bahamas	–	–	–	65.0	–	10.0	10.0	15.0	11,000
Anguilla	–	–	–	90.0	–	8.0	2.0	–	2,100
Barbuda	–	–	–	90.0	5.0	–	5.0	–	400
1830									
Old sugar colonies									
Barbados	77.5	–	3.0	8.0	–	–	0.5	11.0	82,000
St. Kitts	87.0	–	–	4.0	–	0.5	0.5	8.0	19,100
Nevis	90.0	–	–	1.5	–	–	0.5	8.0	9,200
Antigua	79.5	–	–	5.0	5.0	–	0.5	10.0	29,120
Montserrat	89.5	–	–	2.0	–	–	0.5	8.0	6,300
Virgin Islands	65.0	–	17.5	5.0	–	0.5	2.0	10.0	5,150
Jamaica	52.7	15.2	–	9.9	13.7	–	0.5	8.0	319,000
New sugar colonies									
Dominica	35.0	45.0	–	12.5	–	–	0.5	7.0	14,700
St. Lucia	72.0	10.0	–	7.5	–	–	0.5	10.0	13,400
St. Vincent	68.5	0.5	4.0	16.0	–	–	2.0	9.0	23,100
Grenada	80.0	–	4.5	6.0	–	–	1.5	8.0	23,880
Tobago	90.0	–	–	2.5	–	–	0.5	7.0	12,550
Trinidad	70.0	2.0	–	12.5	–	–	0.5	15.0	22,750
Demerara-Essequibo	78.5	4.4	5.9	0.0	0.7	0.2	0.3	10.0	68,160
Berbice	48.3	21.7	9.7	5.5	4.3	0.2	0.3	10.0	20,700
Marginal colonies									
British Honduras	–	–	–	–	–	50.0	–	50.0	1,900
Cayman Islands	–	–	–	80.0	–	–	5.0	15.0	1,000
Bahamas	–	–	–	65.0	–	10.0	10.0	15.0	9,500
Anguilla	–	–	–	90.0	–	8.0	2.0	–	2,600
Barbuda	–	–	–	90.0	5.0	–	5.0	–	480

Sources: See text.

Table 28.9   Estimated Distribution of Slaves by Crop-type: Classes of Colonies, 1810, 1820, and 1830

	Percentage of Slaves								
Colony	Sugar	Coffee	Cotton	Other Agriculture	Livestock	Salt, Timber	Fishing, Shipping	Urban	Number of Slaves
1810									
Old sugar colonies	77.5	–	4.8	5.0	1.1	0.1	0.6	10.9	156,150
Jamaica	51.5	17.0	–	8.0	14.0	–	0.5	9.0	347,000
New sugar colonies	·54.7	14.2	13.4	5.8	0.7	0.1	0.7	10.4	246,400
Marginal colonies	–	–	3.2	54.0	0.1	16.4	6.9	19.4	15,800
Total	56.8	12.3	5.4	7.6	6.8	·0.4	0.7	10.0	765,350
1820									
Old sugar colonies	78.9	–	3.4	5.5	1.0·	0.1	0.6	10.5	151,700
Jamaica	52.0	16.0	–	9.0	14.0	–	0.5	8.5	342,380
New sugar colonies	64.2	10.5	8.1	5.7	0.6	0.1	0.7	10.1	222,200
Marginal colonies	–	–	–	59.9	0.1	14.9	7.1	18.0	16,960
Total	60.1	10.6	3.2	8.5	6.9	0.4	0.7	9.6	733,240
1830									
Old sugar colonies	79.9	–	2.2	6.2	1.0	0.1	0.5	10.1	150,870
Jamaica	52.7	15.2	–	9.9	3.71	–	0.5	8.0	319,000
New sugar colonies	70.5	8.0	4.0	6.2	0.7	0.1	0.7	9.8	199,250
Marginal colonies	–	–	–	63.0	0.2	13.6	6.9	16.3	15,480
Total	62.7	9.4	1.7	9.2	6.8	0.3	0.7	9.2	684,600

Source: Calculated from data in table 28.8.

of colonies, the Virgin Islands approached the pattern of the new sugar colonies, and Tobago that of the old sugar colonies, but it seems more useful to retain the settlement history element of the classification rather than moving these two colonies. Thus, the colonies can be classified efficiently as follows: old sugar colonies, new sugar colonies, Jamaica, and marginal colonies.

It is obvious that the principal factor underlying this typology is the relative dominance of sugar (table 28.9). In 1830 roughly 80 per cent of the slaves in the old sugar colonies worked on sugar estates, compared to 71 per cent in the new sugar colonies, 53 per cent in Jamaica, and none in the marginal colonies. The proportion changed little between 1810 and 1830, except in the new sugar colonies where the crop significantly increased its share of the population. There was also a clear pattern of agricultural

diversification outside of sugar, with cotton predominating in the old sugar colonies; coffee, pimento, and livestock in Jamaica; and coffee, cotton, and cocoa in the new sugar colonies. But it is probable that this pattern especially in the years immediately before emancipation, was the most monocultural in the history of the British Caribbean, since the peasantry that emerged after 1838 was quick to restore minor staples to a more important place in colonial agriculture. Thus the dominant role of the sugar estate in determining the character of slavery was at its most intense in this period. Even in 1830, however, more than one-third of the slaves were not employed in sugar, but lived and worked in a variety of economic, social, and physical environments, each with a differing potential for shaping their demographic experience.

Notes

1. Barry Higman, *The Caribbean Today*.(Kingston. Social Development Commission, 1975).
2. M.C.P.B.G., 24 May 1833; Petition of William Hilhouse.
3. Franklin W. Knight, *The Caribbean: The Genesis of a Fragmented Nationalism*. (New York: Oxford University Press, 1978). Eric Williams, *From Columbus to Castro: The History of the Caribbean, 1492-1969*.(London: Andre Deutsch, 1970). Richard S. Dunn, *Sugar and Slaves: The Rise of the Planter Class in the English West Indies, 1624-1713*.(Chapel Hill: University of North Carolina Press, 1972). Richard B. Sheridan, *Sugar and Slavery: An Economic History of the British West Indies, 1623-1775*.(Barbados: Caribbean University Press, 1974).
4. Phillip D. Curtin, *The Atlantic Slave Trade*.(Madison: University of Wisconsin Press, 1969), p. 56.
5. Elsa V. Goveia, *Slave Society in the British Leeward Islands at the End of the Eighteenth Century*.(New Haven: Yale University Press, 1965), pp. 52-58.
6. Narda Dobson, *A History of Belize*.(London. Longmans, 1973). R.A. Humphreys, *The Diplomatic History of British Honduras, 1638-1901*.(Oxford: Oxford University Press, 1961). Neville Williams, *A History of the Cayman Islands*.(Grand Cayman: Government of the Cayman Islands, 1970). Michael Craton, *A History of the Bahamas* (London: 1963); *Royal Gazette* (Nassau), 3 October 1804.
7. Richard Pares, *Merchants and Planters. Economic History Review*, suppl. no. 4, (1960), p. 40.
8. Linda A. Newson, *Aboriginal and Spanish Colonial Trinidad: A Study in Culture Contact*.(London: Academic Press, 1976), p. 180.
9. D.J. Murray, *The West Indies and the Development of Colonial Government, 1801-1834*.(Oxford: Oxford University Press, 1965), pp. 67-68. James Millette, *The Genesis of Crown Colony Government: Trinidad, 1783-1810*.(Curepe, Trinidad: Moko Enterprises, 1970).
10. Murray, *Development of Colonial Government*, pp. 56, 161; Joseph Lowell Ragatz, *The Fall of the Planter Class in the British Caribbean, 1763-1833*.(Reprint. New York: Octagon Press, 1963), pp. 218, 332, 351.
11. Ragatz, *Fall of the Planter Class*, p. 332; Alan H. Adamson, *Sugar without Slaves: The Political Economy of British Guiana, 1838-1904*.(New Haven: Yale University Press, 1972), p. 24.
12. R.E.P. Wastell, *The History of the Slave Compensation, 1833 to 1845* (Master's thesis, University of London, 1932), pp. 29-47; T.71/685-851; Lt. Governor's Correspondence, Tobago, 1835: 6 April 1835, "Report of the committee appointed to inspect the books of the Compensation Commissioners"(T.A.).
13. Wastell, *History of Slave Compensation*, p. 80; Woodville K. Marshall, ed. *The Colthurst Journal: Journal of a Special Magistrate in the Islands of Barbados and St. Vincent, July 1835-September 1838*.(Millwood, N.Y.: KTO Press, 1977), pp. 68-69.
14. Wastell, *History of Slave Compensation*, p. 77. In Barbados, "field labourers" were aged 16-60 or 60-69 years, whereas in the Bahamas these ages were 15-49 and 6-14 or 50-70.
15. T.71/851.
16. Wastell, *History of Slave Compensation*, p. 77.
17. Index 10493, following Y; the index to T.71/553-64 (P.R.O.).
18. The original of the 1 August 1834 return for Drax Hall classified the plantation's slaves as follows:

	M	F	Total
Domestics	3	4	7
Labourers in sugar	61	77	138
Labourers in cotton	–	–	–
Labourers in agriculture	9	3	12
None	17	13	30

See Drax Hall Estate Papers (D.A.B.).
19. Cf. Keith R. Aufhauser, "Profitability of Slavery in the British Caribbean." *Journal of Interdisciplinary History* 5.(1974): p. 51. and Barbados, Agents' Letterbooks, 1829-33: J.P. Mayers to miscount Goderich, 2 March 1833 (D.A.B.)
20. For lists of mills by parish, see *Minute Book*, Barbados Agricultural Society, p. 31 (1811), p. 167 (1812), p. 245 (1813) (University of Keele); *Barbados Almanack*,1818.
21. *The Barbadian*, 16 March 1833; *Barbados Almanack*, 1835, p. 65.
22. Robert Haynes to Thomas Lane, 12 and 24 February, and 23 June 1814 (Newton Estate Papers, University of London), MS 523/715, 716, 730.
23. J.S. Handler. "The History of Arrowroot and the Origin of Peasantries in the British West Indies." *Journal of Caribbean History*, 2 (1971); 46-93.
24. Barbados Acts of 4 November 1806 and 18 January 1822 (cotton), 28 May 1811 and 23 March 1813 (aloes), and 30 June and 27 August 1824 (ginger). See also *The Barbadian* (Bridgetown), 18 January 1825.
25. St. Kitts *Bluebook*, 1832, p. 148 (S.K.G.A.).
26. St. Kitts. *Record Book of the Court of Special Sessions, 1815-25*: 22 September 1820 (S.K.G.A.): Goveia, *Slave Society in the British Leeward Islands*, pp. 136-37; Douglas Hall, *Five of the Leewards* (1971), p. 29.
27. Richard Pares, *A West-India Fortune*.(London: Longmans, Green, 1950), p. 354. Gordon C. Merrill, *The Historical Geography of St Kitts and Nevis, the West Indies*.(Mexico: Instituto Panamericano de Geografía e Historia, 1958).
28. Douglas Hall, *Five of the Leewards, 1834-1870: The Major Problems of the Post-Emancipation Period in Antigua, Barbuda, Monserrat, Nevis and St Kitts*.(Barbados: Caribbean Universities Press, 1971), p. 4.
29. P.P., Lords, 1832, 13 May 1819; *Antigua Gazette*, 18 March 1819.
30. Hall, *Five of the Leewards*, p. 29.
31. Frances Armytage, *The Free Port System in the British West Indies: A Study in Commercial Policy, 1766-1822*.(London: Longmans, Green, 1953), pp. 104, 141.
32. John Stobo, "Statistical Table of the British Virgin Islands at two periods, 1815 and 1823," April 1823, C.O. 239/9. Stobo put the total area of the Virgin Islands at 58,649 acres, rather than the actual 38,000. He put Tortola at 13,300 acres (instead of 15,360), Anegada at 21,200 (8,320), Virgin Gorda at 9,500 (5,760), and Jos Van Dykes at 3,200 (2,560). But if his remnant categories, "forest and brush wood" and "barren," are ignored, it is probable that the acres said to be under crop were close to the reality.
33. *Plan of Tortola, from Actual Survey* by George King 1798).
34. Armytage, *Free Port System*, p. 154; Robert Montgomery Martin, *Statistics of the Colonies of the British Empire*.(London: William H. Allen, 1839), p. 101.

35. B.W. Higman, *Slave Population and Economy in Jamaica, 1807-1834*.(Cambridge: Cambridge University Press, 1976), chaps. 2-4.

36. *Census of Dominica* in 1763, printed in *Dominica Chronicle*, 16 March 1825; Thomas Atwood, *The History of the Island of Dominica*.(London: J. Johnson, 1971), pp. 82-83.

37. Planters' Petition to Council and Assembly [Dominica], n.d. (Archive Room, Old Ministerial Building, Roseau).

38. Martin, *Statistics of the Colonies*, p. 78.

39. See *Royal St. Vincent Gazette*. 1 January 1825, and 7 April and 22 December 1827. The returns were published in *An Account of the Number of Slaves Employed, and Quantity of Produce Grown, on the Several Estates in the Island of Saint Vincent and Its Dependencies, 1801–24* (1825).

40. Jerome S. Handler, "The History of Arrowroot and the Origin of Peasantries in the British West Indies." *Journal of Caribbean History 2*, (1971), p. 70.

41. Charles Shephard, *An Historical Account of the Island of St Vincent*.(London: W. Nichol, 1831), p. 215.

42. C.O. 106/22, p. 154. For examples, see Grenada, Deeds, vols. M/5, pp. 280, 282; L/5, p. 271 (Supreme Court Registry, St. Georges).

43. *Proceedings of the Grenada Agricultural Society, 1820 and 1821* (1821); [Robert Wilkinson], *A Topographical Description of the Island of Grenada* (1805) (microfilm of typescript at U.W.I. Library, Mona)

44. *Proceedings of the Grenada Agricultural Society*, pp. 29-41.

45. Custom House, Tobago, Letterbook, 1814–26, p. 66 (T.A.); Martin, *Statistics of the Colonies*, p. 40; Jean-Claude Nardin, *La Mise en valeur de l'ile de Tabago, (1763-1783)*.(Paris: Mouton, 1969), pp. 227-37. Jean-Claude Nardin, "Tabago, Antille Francaise, 1781-1793." *Annales de Antilles 14*, (1966); *Tobago Bluebook*, 1838, p. 162 (T.A.).

46. Martin, *Statistics of the Colonies*, pp. 72-73; Ragatz, *Fall of the Planter Class*, p. 351.

47. C.O. 300/46.

48. *Port of Spain Gazette*, 17 May 1833; C.O. 295/14, f. 49.

49. C.O. 295/53, f.341; 295/75, f. 138; 295/78, f. 55; 295/89, f. 152.

50. C.O. 300/40 (Report); 300/47, p. 162

51. C.O. 295/21, f. 107; 295/33, f. 437; 295/66 f. 299; 295/46, p. 158; C.O. 300/40; *Port of Spain Gazette*, 17 May 1833.

52. C.O. 295/44, f. 15, 3 August 1817: Woodford to Goulburn; Protocols of Wills, Trinidad, 1826, f. 96, and 1829, p. 107 (Registrar General's Department, Port of Spain); T.71/501-3

53. C.O. 300/40, f. 18; 300/46, p. 163; 300/47, p. 163; C.O. 295/78, f. 105; 295/85, f. 14; C.O. 298/6, 2 May 1826: Memorial of C.A. Whyte; T.71/501–3.

54. Adamson, *Sugar Without Slaves*, p. 25; Martin, *Statistics of the Colonies*, p. 135; M.C.P.D.E., 1833, vol. 1, p. 502: 19 March 1833.

55. *Demerary and Essequebo, The Annual Miscellany, or Local Guide for 1817*.(Georgetown: William Baker), p. 96.

56. M.C.P.D.E., 1833, vol. 1, p. 502; 19 March 1833.

57. Ibid.

58. T.71/251.

59. British Honduras, Mr. Miller's Mission to England, 1834-35; Journal, 6 March 1835 (N.A.B.); Legislative Meetings, 1830-36, p. 166: 2 July 1833, and pp. 188-93: 4 November 1833 (Supreme Court Registry, Belize); George Henderson, *An Account of the British Settlement of Honduras*.(London: C. and R. Baldwin, 1809), pp. 39-43.

60. Martin. *Statistics of the Colonies*, p. 141; Alan K. Craig, "Logwood as a factor in the Settlement of British Honduras." *Caribbean Studies 9*.(1969), pp. 53-62. Nardo Dobson, *A History of Belize*.(London: Longman, 1814), p. 129.

61. Dobson, *History of Belize*, p 130; Mr. Miller's Mission to England: Memoranda, 24 November 1834 4; British Honduras," Miscellaneous, Inwards and Outwards, 1830-39; Magistrates to Arthur, 16 January 1820 (N.A.B.).

62. Williams, *History of the Cayman Islands*, pp. 32-45: George S.S. Hirst, *Notes on the History of the Cayman Islands*.(Kingston: P.A. Benjamin Manufacturing Co., 1910), pp. 119-21.

63. T.71/851. Another 425 slaves lived in the parish of Bodden Town.

64. Minutes of Meetings of the Commissioners of Correspondence, 1796–1833: 2 May 1816 (House of Assembly, Nassau).

65. Ibid., 31 January 1829.

66. T.71/851.

67. Martin. *Statistics of the Colonies*, p. 110; *Royal Gazette and Bahama Advertiser* 26 May 1832.

68. *Royal Gazette* and *Bahama Advertiser*, 18 February 1832.

69. C.O. 239/12, No. 157, Maxwell to Bathurst, 10 January 1825 (Report of Pickwood and Rawlins, 1 December 1824).

70. Henry Nelson Coleridge, *Six Months in the West Indies in 1825*.(London: John Murray, 1832), p. 212.

71. Ragatz, *Fall of the Planter Class*, p. 357; C.O. 239/9, Maxwell to Bathurst, 11 March 1823 and 28 August 1823; C.O. 239/10, Maxwell to Bathurst, 8 August 1824; Customs 34/721 and 726, James Hay, Waiter and Searcher, Anguilla, to Commissioners of Customs 10 October 1822 and 20 October 1823 (H.M. Customs and Excise Archives London).

72. C.O. 239/29, No. 39 Nicolay to Goderich, 2 May 1832; *Grenada Free Press*, 19 September, 10 and 31 October 1832; *The Barbadian*, 6 February 1833.

73. David Lowenthal and Colin G. Clarke, "Slave-Breeding in Barbuda: The Past of a Negro Myth," *Annals of the New York Academy of Sciences*, 292 (1977) 510-35; Hall. *Five of the Leewards*, pp. 59-60; Coleridge, *Six Months in the West Indies*, pp. 256–59.

29

Women Field Workers in Jamaica During Slavery

LUCILLE MATHURIN MAIR

Any attempt to reconstruct the past of Jamaican female agricultural labour is bedevilled by the colonial/metropolitan orientation of much of Caribbean historiography. This is perhaps inevitable, given the primacy of European strategic and commercial interests in the establishment of New World plantations. So that the enslaved African men and women who laboured in those plantations have been for centuries submerged in the archives, barely making it to the footnotes. Women have suffered as well from the invisibility which has been the nearly universal fate of women's work, whether slave or free, in or out of the field, in the past or the present. When noticed, it is usually seen as marginal to the national, not to mention the international economy. This applies to that wide range of essential goods and services which women produce in the home: they are seldom if ever quantified, seldom if ever regarded as significant enough to be reflected in calculations of national income. It is equally true of women's enterprises in that sector of the economy, which in Jamaica and the rest of the Caribbean is dominated by women, and is variously labelled the informal or parallel or underground sector, all of which imply activities that are imprecise, irregular and out-of-sight.

This syndrome of virtual non-existence constricts research. Economists who, for example, wish to compute female rural labour in regions of Africa, Latin America or Asia, find their attempts to get hard sex-aggregated data frustrated by a widespread insistence on the part of men, but of women too, that women do not work. And this, despite the clear evidence of the vital agricultural tasks in which women are engaged in so many areas of these continents, and have been

engaged for centuries. For the Caribbean region, the new history of slavery, in which Elsa Goveia's work is a major landmark, now allows us to adjust that distortion of female reality.[1] In contrast to a generation ago, the greater body of knowledge at our disposal today about that formative period of Caribbean societies gives us the ammunition to reject the stereotype of a female labour force which is peripheral to the dominant sectors of the economy. Recent and current scholarship, such as Orlando Patterson's work on the sociology of Jamaican slavery, Michael Craton's and James Walvin's study of Worthy Park estate, my own research findings, and Barry Higman's meticulous demographic analysis of the Jamaica slave population on the eve of Emancipation, all testify to the extensive involvement of slave women in Jamaica's agricultural enterprises, and notably the prime productive processes of the sugar industry.[2]

It was sugar which placed Jamaica at a strategic point in the emerging international capitalist system of the eighteenth century, establishing it as Britain's most prized transatlantic colony. In 1805 it was the world's largest individual exporter of sugar. Sugar commanded the island's major resources of land, capital and labour. In 1832, sugar employed 49.5 per cent of the slave work force. The majority of those workers were women, the ratio being 920 males to 1,000 females.[3] It was the requirements of sugar that set the occupational norms for the bulk of the population, even for those workers not directly involved in sugar production: and it was those requirements as identified by the captains of the sugar industry that dictated a conscious policy of job allocation which concentrated black enslaved women in the fields in the most menial and least versatile areas of cultivation in excess of men, and in excess of all persons, male and female, who were not black.

Patterson examined the distribution of the slave labour force on Orange River and Green Park estates in the parish of Trelawny, in 1832, as well as on Rose Hall estate in St. James in the 1830's. He was struck by the large numbers of women who were engaged in field tasks as contrasted with men who were spread over a wider range of skilled, non-praedial jobs. He concluded that the most distinctive occupational feature of Rose Hall estate was the preponderance of field women – 1 to every 2 – as compared with 1 man in every 8. He attributed this partly to the fact that men had more job options available to them, and partly to the fact that women outnumbered men in the Rose Hall work force. This indeed was typical of the demographic situation throughout the island after the abolition of the slave trade in 1807, when the population structure was no longer manipulated by human importation, and moved by natural increase from a male to a female excess. However, there is considerable evidence to indicate that women were tilling Jamaica's valleys for nearly a century before that period, and had been performing the most arduous tasks of agricultural cultivation, in greater numbers than men, even at an earlier time in the island's development when men outnumbered women in the slave population.

The pattern of sex-differentiated labour deployment evolved out of colonial socio-economic imperatives as well as out of traditional concepts about the sexual division of labour. In the seventeenth century, Jamaica was largely an island of small proprietors engaged in hunting, and in subsistence planting, with some cash crops such as tobacco. During this stage of relative under-development, estate work was structured roughly along the following lines: a class of white indentured servants did some field work, but for the most part, supervised the slaves and carried out the skilled and technical functions of the estate: this servile white group numbered approximately 20 per cent to 30 per cent of the labour force. One of the rare censuses of the period, for example, in the parish of St. John in 1680, listed 95 white servants and 527 slaves.[4] Male slaves bore the brunt of the more physically

demanding field labour. Female slaves, who at that period were present in approximately equal numbers to male slaves, supplemented male labour in the lighter tasks of the field, and worked as domestics in the planters' houses.

White indentured servants had the advantage of race and of short-term bondage: and these enabled many to climb the creole socio-economic ladder, eventually to become property owners, or to migrate. As they moved up or out, taking with them their skills, male slaves were recruited into those areas of greater expertise which whites were vacating. The colonial establishment only grudgingly conceded this process, and the local assembly, by a series of legislative measures up to the early eighteenth century attempted to bar male slaves from supervisory positions, from trades, and from the more expert technologies of the plantation.[5] But the turn of the eighteenth century saw Jamaica's transition to a highly capitalised monocultural export economy operating in large plantations. This process accelerated the flight of small proprietors as well as of the white indentured class. Male slaves continued to fill those work slots originally conceived for lesser whites. The occupational vacuum which they, in turn, left in the fields, was filled by women.

Estate inventories, of the 1720s and 1760s which have been examined make clear the wide range of specialisations available to male slaves: they indicate also the limited choices which women had.[6] Particularly rich archival material exists in the estate papers of the absentee planter, William Beckford who was also the Lord Mayor of London in the 1780s. He owned a complex of 12 properties, spread throughout the parishes of Clarendon, Westmoreland and St. Ann: the majority produced sugar, the others were livestock and cattle pens. Together, they provide revealing evidence of the conscious deployment of a labour force of 2,204 slaves containing a slight excess of men – 802 males and 778 females.[7] A minority of the men, viz., 291 or 36 per cent of the male total were field workers, compared with a majority of the women, 444 or 57 per cent of the female total. The men who were not field labourers, were among other things, stonemasons, blacksmiths, fishermen, farriers, wheelwrights, wharfmen, coopers, sawyers, doctor's assistants, tailors, distillers, bricklayers. Many of these jobs involved the kind of special expertise which placed such men among the elite of the slave hierarchy. They sometimes combined praedial jobs with skilled occupations, so that a field man might also be a boiler. In contrast, women were confined within a much more restricted area, and field women were exclusively field women. Where they were listed in other categories of work apart from that of the field, a close look shows that they were often engaged in ancillary field tasks such as cutting grass.

Domestic work was the most significant work category next to agriculture and accounted for 59 or 13 per cent of the sample: within this group were washerwomen, housewomen and cooks. A significant number of house slaves, 9 out of 18, were mulattoes, consistent with the creole view of coloureds as being incapable of physically demanding labour, such as that of the field. Elsa Goveia's observation on the occupational rating of domestics is here relevant: the female house slave on the plantation, she noted, was not so much a "skilled" as a "favoured" worker.

Women with acknowledged "skills" numbered 34 or 8 per cent of the Beckford slaves, and included midwives, doctresses, field nurses and seamstresses. But even this group of non-praedial female workers overrates the black woman's access to special expertise. For mulattoes dominated as seamstresses – 11 out of a total of 14; and the labels of doctress, midwife and nurse were often euphemisms for superannuated field workers, regarded as physically unable to continue in arduous agricultural work, but just about capable of providing services for younger workers.

The period of the 1780's to which these data relate, was a period when the traffic in African slaves was at its peak, and planters had a clear policy of sex-selective importation of labour with a preference for men: as a consequence, African men constituted the majority of the workers on the plantation, outnumbering women right until the time when the slave trade ended. It was in the context of this sex ratio of male excess in the work force that a pattern of job allocation evolved in which not only were the majority of the African women field labourers, but the majority of field labourers were African women. And this had profound implications for their working lives.

The routine of plantation agriculture with its para-military regimentation is widely docu-mented. Youth and physical fitness were the main criteria by which manual tasks were distributed. The first or great gang of the work force, "the flower of all the field battalions" was comprised both sexes, from ages 15 to about 50 years, and was "employed in the most laborious work": on a sugar estate, that involved digging cane holes, planting, trashing, cutting, tying, loading and carting.

Female labourers used the same implements as male, the bill and the hoe. The most strenuous operation in the agro-industrial cycle of sugar production was the crop-time when continuous supplies of freshly cut stalks of ripe cane had to be processed without delay. Workers were then occupied from sunrise to sunset, averaging six days and three nights each week. In the words of one contemporary, "In the extraction of this labour, no distinction is made between men and women."[8]

A witness to the British Parliamentary Commission of Inquiry into the state of West Indian Slavery in 1832 testified as follows:

Q. Are the women employed for the same number of hours as the men?
   Yes, except the women who have children at the breast.
Q. And at the same description of labour as the man?
   Almost entirely, there are of course different branches of labour which they cannot undertake; they cannot undertake the management of cattle; they are excused from night work out of crop, in watching.
Q. Are they employed in digging cane holes?
   Yes
Q. In gangs with men?
   Yes.
Q. And exposed to the same degree of labour?
   Yes.[9]

And it is here worth noting that as Higman's data reveal, women spent more of their working years in the field than did men.

It is interesting to consider what became of two prevalent gender assumptions regarding women's physical and intellectual capacities, assumptions which can be bluntly stated as follows: women are not strong enough to do tough manual work, nor are they clever enough to master things technical – both assumptions well proven to be without foundation, but both frequently invoked as strategies of female subordination. The Jamaican colonial establishment was, however, distinguished among other things for its pragmatism, which was unfailingly inspired by economic self-interest: and this enabled planters, without reservation, to discard the image of woman as frail creature and convert her into the mainstay of estate manual labour. At the core of that mental flip-flop was the racist ideology which supported African enslavement and which denied Africans normal criteria for judging human potential. Racism eased the process by which black women, and black women only, were massively drafted into the assembly line of the field.

The other gender assumption concerning women's technical capabilities proved to be of hardier stock. It was bad enough that planters had to overcome their aversion to the idea of a male slave with expertise, but to be female and skilled, was unthinkable. And this had wider consequences for the political economy of the plantation system, functioning as it did in a vicious circle of labour exploitation and retarded technology.

The Jamaican economist, Norman Girvan has analysed this phenomenon with great insight, and in so doing, has placed today's Caribbean technology policies in a relevant historical continuum. He writes, viz.:

If the artisan workshops of Europe were the basis of technological innovation, the mines and plantations of America were a prescription for technological stagnation ... The slave plantation system systematically underdeveloped the technical capacities of the population.[10]

A gender dimension to that analysis even further sharpens its relevance. Little scope existed in Jamaica's mono-crop economy for the mixed farming enterprises, dairy production, and cottage craft industries which rural people in other economies developed: and of all labourers on the plantation, it was the black female who was the least able to diversify or upgrade her economic potential. She could not, for instance, perpetuate the considerable range of skills and crafts characteristic of the African rural economy in which she had been a central productive figure before she crossed the Middle Passage.

Furthermore, female labour on the estate account book was expensive labour because of the inevitably high rates of absenteeism associated with child bearing and child rearing. So unless she was producing children and providing additional work units in numbers sufficient to compensate for her absences from the field gangs, the female slave offered relatively minimal returns on capital outlay. To offset the cost of her maintenance, she had to be heavily utilized, and this need to extract maximum manual output from female labour was a factor in the plantation's reluctance to rationalize its operations. The planter/novelist Matthew "Monk" Lewis tried to promote "the labour of oxen for that of negroes, whenever it can possibly be done".[11] The creole historian/proprietor Edward Long estimated that "one plough could do the work of a hundred slaves and should be encouraged ... for no other work on a plantation is so severe and so detrimental as that of holing or turning up the ground in trenches with hoes".[12] But both the economics and the politics of slavery mitigated against the introduction of oxen and ploughs. Estate managers and overseers, for example, had vested interests in their own slave property, whom they hired profitably to the estates for miscellaneous jobs such as holing, hoeing and planting. They were a significant pressure group in the creole resistance to technological progress. Moreover, the power-relationship inherent in a coercive labour system obscured considerations of managerial efficiency. The plantation establishment saw the slave as a special kind of multi-purpose work equipment, a flexible capital asset which, unlike animals or machinery, could be deployed for almost any use at any time. Women were even more multi-functional, for, of course, they could also replenish the labour supply. So as long as the most technically backward, but versatile section of the labour force, viz., slave women, serviced the plantation in large and growing numbers, little incentive to technological progress existed: and as long as Jamaican agriculture remained technologically retarded, women continued to be used in the field in overwhelming numbers as substitutes for animals and for machines.

And what did this mean for women's status? Elsa Goveia wrote of the "ordinary field slave" that "no other group of slaves was so completely subject to the harsh necessities of slavery as an industrial system . . . they lived and worked under the discipline of the whip . . . they had fewer opportunities for earning a cash income than most other slaves . . . they were maintained on the bare margin of subsistence . . . although they did the most laborious work, their standard of living was severely lower than that of any other group of slaves." An important index of status was the monetary value of the slave. The highest figure attached to a female slave was normally that of "a strong, able field worker". For the man, that tended to be his lowest price, for his market value rose as he acquired a skill. An official valuation of 1789 showed the most expensive women, field women, averaging between £75 and £85, with the exception of one mid-wife who was worth between £150 and £200. Male praedial workers were slightly more costly than their female equivalents, being priced at between £80 and £100. Eleven different categories of skilled male workers were also listed: their prices started at £120 and rose to £300.[13] The market's low assessment of field labour was also reflected in its regular use as punishment. No greater disgrace could fall to the lot of an artisan or a house slave than to be demoted to the field for some misdemeanour. And this, more often than not implied not only an instant decline in status, but physical indignities imposed "under the discipline of the whip".

Not surprisingly, field women's health was generally poor: 188 or 13 per cent of the 604 women and girls found on the Beckford estates were in various stages of physical disability: of 199 who were over the age of 40, 68 per cent suffered from impaired health. The condition of the young female adults was particularly revealing, because they, presumably were in the fittest condition to perform the demanding field tasks allocated to them. In fact, 22 per cent of that prime group were listed as in poor shape. Few diseases or illnesses as such were diagnosed, but these young women were variously described as "weakly", "infirm", "distempered", etc., suggesting a general debility associated with inadequate diet, inadequate care, excessive exertion and physical abuse. And this had grave consequences for, among other things, women's childbearing functions. Beckford's Clarendon estate with a population of 274 women of childbearing age produced 19 live infants in 1780, a year in which slave deaths numbered 34.

The decrease of the slave population was in fact an island-wide phenomenon estimated to be approximately 2 per cent per annum in the 1770's and 1780's. It was within this depressing

demographic context that the abolitionist/humanitarian movement gained momentum, and generated pro-natalist measures, starting with the Consolidated Slave Acts of 1792 which gave official cognizance for the first time to the role of the female in population growth: clause XXXVI of such legislation, for example, provided that every woman with six children living should be "exempted from hard labour in the field or otherwise".[14] The abolition of the slave trade in 1807 saw such policies intensified. The legislation of the period, while containing some elements of concern for the well-being of slaves, was primarily motivated by the need to sustain labour supplies: various rewards were devised for mothers, adopted mothers and midwives who produced healthy children. An example of the favoured status which prolific women received during the last decades of slavery is found on Matthew Lewis' estate at Canaan in the parish of Westmoreland. He instituted an order of honour for mothers, which gave them the privilege of wearing a "scarlet girdle with a silver medal in the centre" and entitled them to "marks of peculiar respect and attention". He even declared a "play day" for the whole estate, at which the mothers were special guests. He made sure that all the slaves knew they owed their good fortune of a holiday to the "piccaninny mothers; that is, for the women who had children living". At about the same time, however, between 1816 and 1817, that Lewis was celebrating motherhood on Canaan estate, the slave population had reached its numerical peak of 346,150 and moved steadily into a decline which only ended with emancipation.[15]

One is perhaps here observing an example of that well known propensity of colonial designs to self-destruct. The Jamaican establishment, while ostensibly assuming social responsibility for reproducing the labour force, was simultaneously pursuing economic policies virtually guaranteed to diminish that labour force. For official urgings and incentives to women to be fruitful and to multiply went hand in hand with the oppressive work loads of the field and punitive practices which had profound impact on women's ability and desire to bear and rear children. The highest mortality and the lowest fertility rates were found on the sugar estates, establishing a strong correlation between the labour requirements of the island's main industry and the decrease of the slave population. Slave women also themselves exercised effective control over their reproduction. They practised abortion, they prolonged lactation, they drew extensively on the midwives' knowledge of birth processes in order deliberately to depress their fertility. Both voluntarily and involuntarily, they frustrated the establishment's hopes for a self-reproducing labour force. They could not escape the backlash of that frustration.

Creole attitudes towards women noticeably hardened in the latter years of slavery, almost in direct proportion to the plantocracy's dependence on women as a key source of their labour power. The most highly publicized cases of planter brutality are recorded in the 1830's; in most instances the victims were female slaves.[16] A telling example of the heightened antagonism towards women is the Jamaican Assembly's refusal to regulate or to abolish the flogging of women, despite repeated recommendations for reform from the colonial administration in Westminister. Not even for aged or pregnant women would the plantocracy consider exemption from corporal punishment. Jamaica exactly reflected the view of the Barbadian Council which debated the issue at the time, and which declared that to abolish the flogging of female slaves . . . "would mean adieu to all peace and comfort on plantations".[17]

Women became even more conspicuous targets of planter hostility during the Apprenticeship period which was mandated under the Abolition Bill of 1834 to phase out slavery in gradual stages. Ex-slaves, now apprentices, were required to give 40 ½ hours of work weekly on the estates to which they were attached. The rest of their time was theirs to place and barter on the wage market, if they chose. This stage of quasi-bondage was originally conceived as a 6 year transition from a forced to a free labour system: it proved to be "an impossible compromise" and was terminated after 4 years. For the period that it lasted, planters used apprenticeship as a last stand to retain maximum control over what they saw as a dwindling labour force.[18] The increasing withdrawal of the female apprentice from the cane field was a critical factor in that perception. One contemporary analysed it aptly as women's rejection of that type of labour "which is inseparably associated in their minds with the idea of torture, oppression and degradation."[19]

Thomas McNeil, attorney for the estate of Lord Holland in western Jamaica, expressed the plantocracy's obsessive fear of a labour shortage and the need for an adequate supply of female workers to avert such a disaster. He calculated that even if the men gave sustained labour it would still be "quite impossible to continue sugar cultivation to give any remuneration to the proprietors unless the females also be induced to labour regularly".[20] "Inducement" of women took many forms, and was facilitated by the Abolition Act itself, which entrusted to the planter-dominated local legislature the detailed subordinate arrangements necessary for the implementation of the law: important aspects of the apprentice's welfare fell to its discretion; and, despite the appointment of special stipendiary magistrates to mediate between masters and apprentices, abuses and injustices were rampant and bore heavily on women. The Select Committee of the House of Commons appointed to inquire into the workings of the Apprenticeship system reported in 1837 that women were "the principal sufferers" from various measures devised to manipulate and coerce the labour force.[21]

The maternal allowances and privileges which had been customary before 1834 fell into a grey area of the law and were frequently either curtailed or abolished. Women were being called on to work in the field in advanced stages of pregnancy, whereas they had previously been entitled to exemption. One stipendiary magistrate maintained that on several occasions when he attempted to protect such women from excessive labour he was threatened with action for damages by the estate owners involved. Mothers with over six children found their pre-emancipation right of work exemption reversed and they were frequently sent back to the field. The services for field workers which were provided by cooks, water carriers, midwives and nurses were often withdrawn and the women providing such services were re-deployed to the field gangs.

Planters feared that apprentices, given an opportunity, would seek and find other occupational options, outside of their obligatory 40 1/2 hours estate time. And they had good reason to fear. For during slavery, women, despite overwhelming odds, had been engaging in semi-independent economic activities which offered prospects for a viable peasantry in a free society.

It was the plantation system itself which inadvertently gave them the main resource for such initiatives; for the priority which the macro-economic system placed on cash crops for export, to the exclusion of food crops for local consumption, resulted in slaves having to assume responsibility for feeding themselves. Female slaves, as a consequence, like male slaves, enjoyed customary, and after the 1792 slave legislation, legal entitlement to their provision grounds. And there they put to their own and their family's use the chief expertise which the economy allowed them: women laboured hard and profitably in their own fields. They thereby generated a historical process which was to give Jamaican women, as food producers and distributors, a pivotal role in the domestic economy.

The diary of a St. Ann doctor/planter, James Archer, reveals how threatening such slave entrepreneurship appeared to estate owners. Archer imposed strict taboos on the type of crops which apprentices could plant on their ground allotments. He also ordered that no additional help should be used for cultivating these plots: "The person, male or female, who has any sanction to work such land must work the same himself, or herself; no brother, sister or any other person to assist."[22] This created special hardships for women accustomed, as they frequently were, to pooling land and labour in a family enterprise. Women provoked such spiteful measures from the establishment, not only because they could divert their time and energy to their own purposes and could so undermine the estate's labour power; in addition, they could withhold their children's labour. For according to the Abolition Act, children under six years of age were to be free: as they became of age to be apprenticed, they could be employed with their mother's consent. Planters never lost sight of young blacks as potential estate workers.

But women stood in the way of their designs. As a contemporary observer expressed it in 1835, "A greater insult could not be offered to a mother than by asking her free child to work." At Silver Hill in St. Andrew, an overseer asked a woman to let her 8 year old son do light work on the estate in return for his clothing and an allowance. She flatly refused.[23] The Select Committee of the House of Commons on the workings of the Apprenticeship system reported the evidence of one witness, viz., "Negro mothers have been known to say, pressing their child to their bosoms, 'we would rather see them die, than become apprentices'." Jamaica's fractious females became the subject of extensive official dispatches. They were singled out for their "lack of co-operation, their ingratitude, and their insulting conduct. They were on all occasions, the most clamorous, the most troublesome and insubordinate, and least respectful to all authority. None of their freed children have they in any instance apprenticed to their former masters."[24] Women unequivocally stood firm on this issue; and of the 39,013 slave children who were less than 6 years of age on August 1, 1834, only 9 were released by their mothers for estate work during the 4 years of apprenticeship.[25]

Motherhood with its biological and customary social implications is frequently perceived as a conservative force which imposes constraints on female activism. It became, however, in this instance, a catalyst for much of women's subversive and aggressive strategies directed against the might of the plantation. When they could, they withheld their labour and that of their children from the dominant socio-economic system. By their actions during slavery and apprenticeship, they placed themselves in the very eye of the storm of Jamaica's post-emancipation crisis. It was the crisis of land and labour, which reached a flashpoint in the Morant Bay Rebellion of 1865, and which ultimately created the jobless, landless proletariat of today – a proletariat which is largely urban and largely female, and whose significance in the evolution of Jamaica's modern labour movement is only now beginning to be illuminated by feminist scholarship.[26]

Some measure of the agony of free labour in nineteenth century Jamaica was manifested in the exodus of the black population in large numbers from estate labour, a partly voluntary and partly involuntary process. In 1844, the year of the first official census, 80 per cent of the island's work force were engaged in agriculture. A hundred years later, the proportion was 47 per cent, and it continues to fall. Female participation in agriculture fell from 57 per cent in 1921 to 28 per cent in 1943. In the eighties, it averages 15 per cent.[27]. As women attempted to escape the assembly line of the field, they moved into the peasant domestic food economy, and increasingly into the urban service economy, in search of new options for economic viability and dignity. They encountered forces in the free society which would deny them these options: and so their search continues.

Notes

1. Goveia, Elsa. *Slave society in the British Leeward Islands at the end of the eighteenth century*. New Haven and London: Yale University Press, 1965.
2. Patterson, Orlando. *The sociology of slavery*. London: McGibbon & Kee, 1967.
    Craton, Michael and Walvin, James. *A Jamaican plantation: the history of Worthy Park, 1670-1970*. London and New York: W.H. Allen, 1970.
    Mathurin, Lucille. *A historical study of women in Jamaica, 1655-1844*. Unpublished Ph.D. Thesis, U.W.I., 1974.
    Higman, Barry. *Slave population and economy in Jamaica, 1807-1834*. Cambridge: Cambridge University Press, 1976.
3. Higman, Barry. Ibid.
4. Bennett, J.H. "Cary Helyar, merchant and planter of seventeenth century Jamaica." *William and Mary Quarterly*, January, 1964. Colonial Office 1/45.
5. *The Laws of Jamaica*, passed by the Assembly in 1683. CSP Col., 1716-1717.
6. Inventories, Libers 14, 44, 46 (Jamaica Archives).
7. C. 107/43, *Plantation papers of William Beckford, 1773-1784*.
8. Cooper, Thomas. *Facts illustrative of the condition of the negro slaves in Jamaica*. London: 1824.
9. Parliamentary Papers 1832. I (127)
10. Girvan, Norman. "White magic: the Caribbean and modern technology." Papers presented at a seminar on Caribbean issues related to UNCTAD IV, University of the West Indies, Mona, February 5-7, 1976.
11. Lewis, Matthew G. *Journal of a West India proprietor, kept during a residence in the island of Jamaica*. London: John Murray, 1834.
12. Long, Edward. *The history of Jamaica*. 3 vols. London: T. Lowndes, 1774.
13. Parliamentary Papers 1789. XXVI (84), 646(a).
14. Edwards, Bryan. *The history, civil and commercial of the British colonies in the West Indies*. 3 vols. London: 1801.
15. Roberts, George W. *The population of Jamaica*. Cambridge, England: Cambridge University Press, 1957.
16. Parliamentary Papers 1832. II (127).
17. Williams, Eric. *Documents on British West Indian history 1807-1833*. Port of Spain, Trinidad: Historical Society of Trinidad and Tobago, 1952.
18. Hall, Douglas. "The apprenticeship period in Jamaica, 1834-1838." *Caribbean Quarterly*, 3:3, December, 1953.
19. Add. Mss. 51818, 1839 (British Museum).
20. Add. Mss. 51819, 1838 (British Musuem).
21. *Negro apprenticeship in the colonies: a review of the report of the Select Committee of the House of Commons . . .* London: J. Hatchard [etc.] 1837.
22. Add. Mss. 27970 (British Museum).
23. Sturge, J. and Harvey, T. *The West Indies in 1837*. London: Hamilton, Adams and Co., 1838.
24. Colonial Office 137/2.
25. Hall, Douglas. *Ibid.*
26. French, Joan and Ford-Smith, H. "Women's work and organisation in Jamaica, 1900-1944." 1986. Unpublished ms.
27. *Statistical Yearbook of Jamaica*, 1980. Kingston: Dept. of Statistics, 1981.

30

Slavery in a Plantation Society

FRANKLIN KNIGHT

With twenty hours of unremitting toil,
Twelve in the field, and eight indoors to boil,
Or grind the cane – believe me few grow old,
But life is cheap, and Sugar, Sir! – is gold.

R. R. Madden, *Poems by a Slave*, p. 45.

Cuban slave society, like any other slave society, was subdivided into castes and classes. The castes corresponded very roughly to the racial divisions in which membership was hereditary and defined by laws: the white population first, and then, in descending order of social rank, the free persons of color and the slaves. A class stratification characterized each caste. The term class is appropriate in this context, referring as it does to those who had a certain degree of social mobility, and whose status and position were not necessarily either heritable or legally prescribed. This combination of caste and class provided a certain stability to the society by allowing a dynamism within the separate classes of each racial group, while retaining and constraining the various elements within the castes.

The two classes within the slave caste were the urban and domestic, and the field slaves. Arriving Africans joined either of these two classes. But the number of domestic and urban slaves in the nineteenth century was relatively small, and the chance of a recent arrival finding his way into this group was extremely slim. A small minority of the slaves lived in the towns, where they were employed mainly as domestic servants, or in minor skills and simple professions (though these Services formed an important economic function in the society as a whole). The vast majority of the Africans imported dur-ing the nineteenth century-more than 80 per cent of those brought in between 1840 and 1860- ended up working on the plantations of the interior. It was precisely this preponderance of rural slaves which made Cuban slave society in the nineteenth century a plantation society, and hence distinct from Cuban slavery in the earlier period. Urban slaves were the exceptions; urban slavery could not be considered the norm for the society. Yet many visitors to Cuba, and a great many historians of Cuban slavery from 1800 to the present have probably honestly, though nonetheless erroneously, based their opinions on Cuban slavery from a limited exposure to, or inference from, this type of urban slave conditions. Any attempt to generalize about Cuban slavery must bear in mind some important distinctions, and not the least of these is the separate environment of the two slave groups. The two classes were a world apart. Urban slaves had some unique opportunities and resources which their rural counterparts lacked or were denied. Moreover, the entire organization of urban and domestic slavery in Cuba, as in other parts of the world, lent itself to moderation and liberality. Some observers did compare and comment on the vast differences evident between the two types. Fernando Ortiz, with some degree of exaggeration, insisted that the conditions surrounding urban slaves were more closely comparable to the conditions of the master group than to the conditions of rural slaves.[1] The urban slave enjoyed advantages denied his rural counterpart in three crucial -areas: in the method of labor and participation in the cash economy; in social and sexual conduct; and in the available legal resources.[2]

Urban slaves fell into three large groups. Many were domestic helpers, with some women being wet nurses for the infants of the white people, and females in general dominating the domestic occupations. Many others conducted some specific occupation – coachmen, carpenters, dressmakers, gardeners, musicians-or small trade. A third group hired out their labor either for their own gain, or for their master's.[3] No group, however, was entirely exclusive, and sometimes circumstances superseded preferences. Ortiz remarked that within the urban slave community during a certain period in the nineteenth century it was considered somewhat ignominious to be rented, as such a gesture indicated the poverty and low social position of the owners.[4] Writers on slavery generally conceded that the urban slaves, regardless of their occupations, established an understanding and a relationship with their masters which was completely absent elsewhere. Not only was the life of slaves in the towns far less regimented, but also the opportunities to get cash enabled them to buy their freedom with relatively greater facility than rural slaves. Urban slaves also mixed with the free colored people, and escaped from their masters with greater ease.

With far more cash and far more freedom, the urban slave both fed and dressed himself better, and enjoyed himself more. Instead of the striped, coarse clothes and simple dress of the plantation slave, the urban slave was sometimes smartly-if uncomfortably-uniformed if he were a coachman or she a preferred domestic helper. Otherwise, the slaves in the city generally dressed in the style of the whites. In the towns, too, the slaves participated in a wide variety of common attractions, ranging from membership in an Afro-Cuban *cabildo*, or lodge, to dances and drinking in their *bodegas*, or taverns.[5] Such forms of entertainment took place with their friends of the same accepted "tribe," or their *carabelas* – their shipmates from Africa. Sexual union was facilitated by the consistently larger proportion of black women in the towns. Apart from this, sexual relations with the whites were common, and often rewarding for the black parties involved. For not only did the whites offer handsome material rewards in cash or other valuables which assisted in coartación, the method by which the slave gained his freedom, but also,

albeit quite rarely, they gave their slaves freedom in their wills.[6]

Legal stipulations had some meaning and effect in the towns. Urban slaves were aware of their legal rights and resources, and often resorted to them. If the relationship between a particular master and his slave broke down, then either party could effect the sale of the slave. In that case, the *síndico*, or protector of slaves, intervened to see that the slave's .right to permission to seek a new master was observed. The physical punishment possible in the rural areas was not necessary in the towns. Masters with troublesome slaves either sent them to the country or sold them. Besides, slaves were more expendable in the cities than they were in the fields.

Unfortunately the mitigating influences, of the cities did not extend to the vast majority of Cuban slaves, who found themselves circumscribed by the regimented requirements of plantation agriculture. Planters usually bought slaves when they wanted them, and sold them when they thought that they were redundant. In the countryside-in sharp distinction from the towns – the practice of renting slaves was frowned upon as being uneconomical and *déclassé*.[7] As a result the avenues of mobility for the rural slaves were, naturally, far more limited, and depended upon special skills. Sometimes, however, a slave possessing a light skin color and a sympathetic character might win the affection or the goodwill of a kind master, with enormous benefits occurring as a consequence of this coincidence. Such slaves – the skilled and the loved – might then be transferred to the city from the farm, and in the course of time could gain their freedom through the accustomed urban avenues.[8]

Not surprisingly, the general tendency of the slave population before the end of the slave trade was for the number of urban slaves to decline steadily, while the rural slaves, constantly augmented from Africa, increased. Since the urban slaves had a higher birthrate than those in the fields, and since there is no evidence of massive transfer of slaves from the cities to the plantations, the decrease of urban slaves could perhaps be due to manumissions. On the other hand, the steady increase in rural slaves reflected the healthy state of the illegal slave trade. Nevertheless, the cessation of the trade after the mid-1860's brought a sharp increase in the proportion of urban slaves (see Table 30.1).

Table 30.1:   Cuban Slave Population, 1855–57 and 1871

Year*	Urban	% of all slaves	Rural	% of all slaves	Total slaves
1855	70,691	19.0	304,115	81.0	374,806
1856	66,123	17.8	305,243	82.2	371,366
1857	65,610	17.5	307,375	82.5	372,985
1871	55,830	20.9	231,790	79.1	287,620

*All figures are for January

Source: Figures for 1855 to 1857 are taken from the capitation censuses found in AHN, Ultramar, Esclavitud, leg. 3551; for 1871, from *Cuba desde 1850 á 1873* (Madrid: Impr. Nacional, 1873), pp. 152-53.

The official declaration of an end to the slave trade agreed upon by Britain and Spain for a second time in 1835 made it impossible to continue the former system of large barracones or slave markets in the principal cities of the island. After the last barracón was destroyed in 1836, the arrival of slaves and their distribution took place clandestinely, often at night.[9] Traders called their slaves *piezas* (pieces), and divided them into three outstanding categories: "bozales," "ladinos," and "criollos."[10]

Bozales were raw Africans who could not speak Spanish. These were also called "negro de nación," a reference to their foreign origin. Traders referred to such Negroes between the ages of six and fourteen as *muleques*; and those between the ages of fourteen and eighteen as *mulecones*. Most traders, however, had no way of ascertaining the age of the slave, and resorted to physical appearance as the best index of age. Ladinos were slaves who, although foreign born, were baptized into the Roman Catholic faith, and could speak Spanish or Portuguese, or in some cases French. Criollos were slaves born in Cuba. On the markets, criollos fetched the highest prices, especially if they possessed certain skills, and were destined for city or domestic use. Until the end of the trade in the mid-1860's, bozales fetched an ever-increasing price owing to the high demand for them on the plantations.

Most rural slaves found themselves working on tobacco farms, coffee plantations, or sugar plantations. Rural life and conditions for the slaves were so far removed from city or great house conditions that banishment to the plantation was a frequent threat against recalcitrant slaves. David Turnbull reported that the most

dreadful threat which the wealthy inhabitants of Havana used to terrify their delinquent domestic servants was the hint of sending them back to the plantation under the special charge of the *mayoral*, the supervisor of slaves.[11]

There was a general consensus that conditions of labor varied according to the nature of the agricultural enterprise. The tobacco farms were thought to offer the easiest life, followed by the coffee plantations, where the work was not very arduous. Life on the sugar plantations, however, was seen in Hobbesian terms as "nasty, brutish, and short." The life and conditions of any particular group of slaves depended, of course, on the personality of the master. Notwithstanding, two factors corresponded to make the labor and living conditions on the coffee and tobacco farms more favorable than on the sugar plantations. In the first place, the nature of the tasks differed and the need for regimentation was less: only sugar demanded a great number of workers who had to accomplish their tasks in a very important and specific period of time. In the second place, many white planters lived on their farms, and often worked with their slaves in tending and reaping the harvests of tobacco or coffee.

Traditionally, tobacco-growing in Cuba was a small, cash crop undertaking on small farms, just as it had been in the Eastern Caribbean islands in the early seventeenth century, before the sugar revolution there. In the areas where the tobacco thrived best, it was a meticulous culture, as lyrically described by Fernando Ortiz. Far from being an enormous, impersonal, capitalistic enterprise, it was essentially an activity dominated by the fastidious individualist:

The best smoker looks for the best cigar, the best cigar for the best wrapper, the best wrapper for the best leaf, the best leaf for the best cultivation, the best cultivation for the best seed, the best seed for the best field. This is why tobacco-raising is such a meticulous affair, in contrast to cane, which demands little attention. The tobacco-grower has to tend his tobacco not by fields, not even by plants, but leaf by leaf. The good cultivation of good tobacco does not consist in having the plant give more leaves, but the best possible. In tobacco quality is the goal; in sugar, quantity. The ideal of the tobacco man, grower or manufacturer, is distinction, for his product to be in a class by itself, the best. For both sugar-grower and refiner, the aim is the most.[12]

By the middle of the nineteenth century, tobacco-farming was an activity of free white and free colored people, with very little use of slave labor.[13] In reality, therefore, relatively few slaves participated in the delights of the vegas, compared to those on the sugar estates. In 1846, García de Arboleya claimed that only about 4,000 slaves, or 40 per cent of the total tobacco labor force, worked in urban tobacco concerns.[14] Although the author did not give the number of rural slaves engaged in cultivating tobacco, he pointed out that the tobacco haciendas were generally found along the banks of rivers, and that the total area of the farms seldom exceeded thirty-three acres, only one-half of which was in tobacco. Tobacco farms had, in addition to the dwelling house, a drying house for curing the tobacco leaves after they had been collected. The labor force varied between four and twenty workers, who were not always blacks, since that branch of agriculture was, above all others, "the chief concern of the whites."[15]

The principal tobacco-growing areas of Cuba were in Pinar del Río, San Cristóbal, Villa Clara, Manzanillo, Bayamo, Jiguaní, Santiago de Cuba, and Guantánamo. (See Map 30.1.) Confined to specific zones, the tobacco farms increased in number from 9,102 in 1846 to 9,482 in 1861, while the total value of tobacco products remained constant.[16] Quite probably, the number of vegas did not suffer marked fluctuations after 1846, because tobacco no longer competed with sugar cane either for land or manpower.

Coffee, unlike tobacco or sugar cane, grew best on shaded slopes. But coffee was successfully grown on the plains of central Cuba before it was displaced by the sugar cane, in the middle of the nineteenth century. After that, the coffee areas remained in the more hilly regions of Guanajay, San Antonio de los Baños, Cienfue-

gos, and Mantanzas in the western department, and the mountains of Santiago de Cuba and Guantánamo in the eastern department.

Large-scale coffee cultivation in Cuba began with the arrival of the French refugees from St. Domingue. The plantations were modest in size, and carefully tended by a resident proprietor, who adorned the farms with exotic shade trees and valuable timber. The coffee plants grew to a height of six feet, and yielded their berries twice a year. So that the trees could be cleaned and the fruit gathered at harvest, wide wagontrails intersected the plantation at regular distances, presenting the visual aspect of a charming garden – an idea continually in the mind of the coffee planter, who spent a very long time perfecting the picture of resplendent beauty.[17]

When the coffee berries turned purple, they were collected, dried in the sun, and thrashed to separate the grain from the useless dried cuticle. It was not a very arduous job, and one in which females could be as adept as males. Slaves on coffee plantations did not suffer the sexual imbalance characteristic of the sugar plantations. Coffee cultivation, therefore, required no extraordinary capital outlay, no elaborate mechanical power, no large factories, and no specialized scientific knowledge beyond a simple familiarity with soils, plants, and cultivation.

In 1846, García de Arboleya stated that coffee plantations varied in size from four to twenty caballerías (133 to 666 acres), with a maximum labor force of one hundred slaves.[18] But a recent scholar of the Cuban coffee plantation, Francisco Pérez de la Riva, has pointed out that tile average size of the cafetal by the later 1850's – the twilight of coffee cultivation in the island – was only eight caballerías (267 acres), employing forty slaves.[19] In short, the cafetal was the closest approximation to the cotton plantation of the United States southern belt.

Unlike the great sugar estates, coffee plantations, in common with all the other forms of small, rural, agricultural enterprises, also embodied large areas devoted to the growing of their own food crops, or the rearing of cattle and small stock used mainly for their domestic food supply. Almost all the land of the ingenio went into sugar cane or cattle, and the enormous size of its slave labor force made food importation both more desirable and more economical than domestic production.

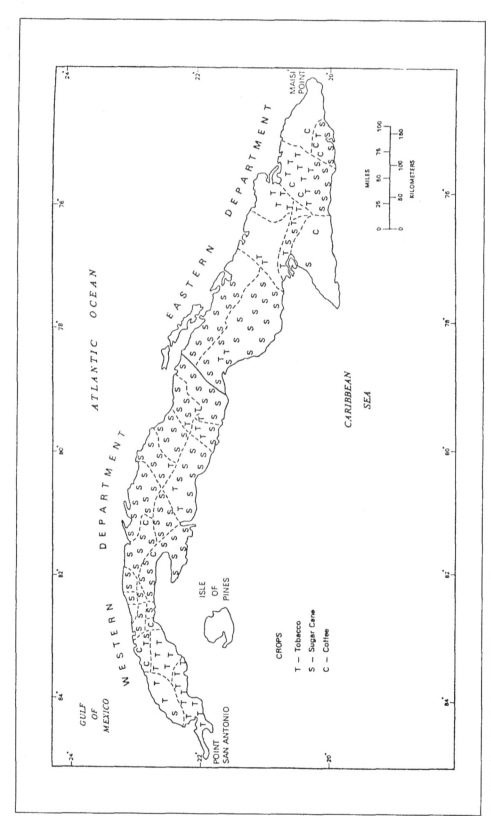

Map 30.1: Crop Distribution, 1861. Map courtesy of UW Cartographic Lab.

By the late 1860's, nearly 50 per cent of all slaves in Cuba worked directly on the sugar estates, while a substantial proportion of the remainder were in some way involved in the sugar industry. And on some sugar estates, the slave was considered as "little else than an item of labor raised or bought."[20] However different were the conditions outside the sugar industry, its economic influence was so great that the entire course of slavery was affected by the decisions of the sugar manufacturers.

The successful operation of the sugar plantation demanded a change in the treatment and operation of slave labor. As the size of slave gangs became larger, the slaves were more alienated from the traditional semiextended family relationship. Apart from the change in treatment, the slaves saw and felt other physical alterations of their status. Large infirmaries became necessary to treat the real and pretended illnesses. The collection of individual huts gave way to long, connected barracks which the owners thought were more secure, since the two main doors could be locked at night.[21] The *conucos*, the small, slave-worked plots of land which had so long provided food for the hacienda and a source of private gain for the slaves themselves, gradually succumbed to economic necessity as the planters put more area under sugar cane and relied on imported flour, salt pork, and codfish to feed the laborers.[22] Naturally, therefore, the number of slave uprisings increased in the nineteenth century. And with the constant example of Haiti before them, the white planters responded with even more severe regimentation, as evidenced by the slave laws of 1842.

The entire operation of a sugar estate was set out in a handbook written by a planter in Havana, and published in Spain in 1862. Called *Cartilla práctica del manejo de ingenios* – "practical handbook for the management of sugar estates" – it covered every aspect of sugar production: selection and required -area of land, choice of cane, labor needs, and the advisability of renting laborers rather than contracting out the work in times of insufficient labor supply.

We have already seen that in Cuba, as elsewhere, the sugar industry was highly capitalized, with an inordinate need for land, slaves, and oxen. By the middle of the nineteenth century the most important planters aimed at an annual production of between 5,000 and 6,000 boxes of sugar, or a little more than 1,000 tons.[23] Cristóbal Madan, however, thought the average size was a little less: "one of 4,000 boxes, which, while not one of the recent colossal factories, cannot be classified as small."[24] Production in this range demanded an acreage in excess of 3,000 acres, of which more than 1,300 acres were in sugar cane. Furthermore, the handbook stated that such an estate needed "a minimum of 317 slaves and 326 head of oxen."[25] To establish an estate of this sort would cost far more than $300,000, with annual maintenance costs being around $40,000, and net profits nearly $20,000 per year.[26]

The crucial role of labor in sugar production led to the wretched conditions of the slaves on the plantation. The Planter had to supervise his workers in such a way that he would have them at exactly the right time, as well as ensure maximum output,[27] Richard Dana reflected planter opinion when he wrote:

The sugar estate is not valuable, like the coffee estate, for what the land will produce, aided by quiet manual labor only. Its value is in the skill, and the character of the labor. The land is there, and the Negroes are there, but the result is loss or gain, according to the amount of labor that can be obtained, and the skill with which the manual labor and the mechanical powers are applied.[28]

After the 1850's most large sugar estates employed a mixed group of laborers; free, wage-paid whites, indentured Asians, and slaves. The labor organization was hierarchical, corresponding, to the racial divisions. Occupying the topmost administrative and skilled positions were the whites. Asians did the intermediate, semi-skilled tasks. Slaves did unskilled, manual jobs.

Since most sugar estates had absentee proprietors – a characteristic common to all the Caribbean sugar islands – the operation and management of the estate devolved upon the *administrador* or overseer, who often lived in the palatial great house. Below the administrador was the mayoral, or supervisor of Negroes, and a boyero, a supervisor of animals. Other important white jobs regularly held were the *maestro de azúcar*, or boiling-house chief, noted more for his cooking ability and guesswork than for any knowledge of chemistry; the machinist, usually from Europe or the United States, and employed only for the crop-time season; and the *mayordomo*, or bookkeeper – a term applied in its most literal sense. Some estates had a part-time nurse or doctor, who paid periodical visits for an agreed sum of money.

Cristóbal Madan gave the following salaries for the white employees on a medium-sized estate at the middle of the nineteenth century:

Overseer	$1,500
Supervisor of Negroes	600
Supervisor of animals	300
Book-keeper	408
Nurse (part-time)	240
Doctor (part-time)	300
Maestro de azúcar and his assistant	1,600
Machinist for five months	698.50[29]

Apart from his basic salary the overseer enjoyed many additional perquisites, including an annual bonus, and unusually great opportunities for fraud and other means of private accumulation of wealth. With the exception of the machinist, and sometimes the maestro de azúcar, the other white people on the estates were locally recruited. In nineteenth-century Cuba, as two centuries before in Barbados and the other West Indian islands, the sugar revolution uprooted many small farmers, ranchers, and gardeners. In Cuba, these were absorbed into the labor force of the ingenios, and even dockyard workers, foundry workers, and other small artisans of the urban areas like Bejucal and Santiago followed suit – sometimes under pressure, sometimes attracted by the higher wages. The slaves suffered indirectly from the displacement of these small poor farmers: many of the guajiros (landless whites) developed a strong racial prejudice which they), vented in severe punishments for simple misdemeanors, or brutal hunting excursions after runaways.[30]

The Asians, who bridged the gap between black and white, assisted the slaves in the field and in the factories. Unlike the slaves, however, they did simple semiskilled jobs, and handled some machines.[31] Although the Asians were classified as whites, their conditions of labor tended to be identical to those of slaves. Antonio Gallenga asserted that on the few estates with an all-Asian labor force the organization and working conditions were identical to the slave-worked estates.[32]

An American visitor to Cuba in 1853 expressed the opinion that Chinese would eventually "occupy the place of the Negroes in all agricultural districts."[33] The Cubans did not seem to share that opinion. Some planters thought the Chinese a poor substitute for Negro slave labor, but admitted that they were an indispensable link in the transition from slavery to free labor if sugar production was not to be seriously disrupted. Other planters thought that the importation of the Chinese should be discontinued as they only further complicated the racial problem on the island.[34]

Both indentured laborers and slaves fell into the subordinate group of "purchased" labor, a cardinal point of calculation in the value of any estate.[35] Slaves did any kind of job in the process of sugar manufacture leading up to the machine-performed tasks, and then on afterwards.[36] Some black men became contramayorales or assistants to the whites, an extremely prestigious position for any slave, and one which carried some authority with it.[37]

The regimentation of the slavery system and of the system of indenture in Cuba was a logical outgrowth of the process of sugar production. It was, in fact, the most simple form of labor organization for a process which had extremely unbalanced labor requirements, especially in a situation of great labor scarcity. To ensure sufficient manpower for harvest, the planter had to buy and keep his slaves throughout the year. Once he had bought them and had to maintain them, it was judicious to keep them fully occupied. That was easy during the hectic months of harvest between late December and early May, when the slaves had to work for extremely long periods. After the harvest, the estate required fewer laborers, but still had its full complement of men. Every serious sugar planter, therefore, had a carefully planned annual cycle of work calculated to use his force as fully as possible throughout the entire year.

For the Cuban slave the year had two significant divisions: zafra, or crop-time and tiempo muerto, or dead season. These two divisions not only composed his yearly cycle but also decided his daily activities.

The beginning of the calendar year often coincided with the beginning of the harvest. All the slaves were given the first of two changes of clothes (the other being given at the end of the harvest).[38] Each man received one loosely-fitting cotton shirt, and one pair of pants, which reached just below the knees, a woolen cap, a short, thick flannel jacket, and a blanket. Each woman received one striped cotton dress and a cotton scarf (pañuelo). At the end of the harvest, the rations were almost identical, except that the men were given straw hats instead of woolen caps. A holiday usually followed this first distribution of clothing, the signal that the harvest was about to begin.

Before the actual work began, however, it was important that all the slaves knew precisely where they worked, and the order of their rotation. At the first session on a new estate, this was done by an assembly of the entire working force, and their division.[39] First the men for the boiler house were called forward. They were the strongest men in the force, and were handed over to the maestro de azúcar. The number of boilers determined the number of men. Each boiler needed about 7 attendants, with an additional 4 or 5 for odd jobs. A factory of 5 boilers had about 39 men.

The cartmen who hauled the canes were next selected. If the estate lacked its own domestic railroad, the number of cartmen was equal to the number of men in the boiling house, since they took over the first night shift from these men, after their own day's work in the fields. For that reason they had to be the second strongest team of men.

Following in descending order of strength came the cutters. Numbering about fifty for a medium-sized estate, they had to be taught the way of cutting in order to achieve maximum safety and maximum output. The cutter held the cane in his left hand, then first cut off the leaves with one swift stroke of his machete. He then cut the cane as near as possible to the ground with a second stroke of the machete, and threw the stalk behind him. At night the canecutters relieved the men in the purging house, and those carrying the bagasse on the compound.

Lesser duties followed in this order of selection: 25 men for the purging house; 50 women and boys to collect the cane, stack it, and help to load the carts; 4 boys to change the teams of oxen; 2 older men and women to collect the cane which fell from the carts or railway wagons along the way; 8 men to take away the green bagasse (crushed canes) from the mills; 10 men to carry the dry bagasse and tend to the fires; and 60 additional women and a few boys to attend to the cooking, and to serve water to the men in the fields.

Harvest was the time of work for everyone on an estate. It presented a scene of concentrated and determined labor.[40] During these months, the slaves averaged a workday of nearly twenty hours, even on the best-run estates.[41] The slaves worked almost to the maximum of their physical ability:

The hour for ringing the morning bell should be so arranged that nothing from a full day's work is lost. On the other hand, the Negroes should not be unnecessarily disturbed, depriving them of that part of their rest which they may enjoy without jeopardizing their labor.[42]

In order to keep the slaves awake, and as a stimulus to work, the whip became the chief instrument of the mayorales and contramayorales, Sometimes, the slaves were flogged owing to the sadism of the supervisory personnel, but during crop-time, whipping was, by some reports, almost incessantly employed to keep the slaves on the job and to prevent their malingering or falling asleep.[43]

Indeed, the need for continuous labor was so great at this time that the handbook recommended that the men in the boiler house be given their night meals on the job.[44] Nevertheless, despite the rigorous regime of crop-time, many reporters remarked that the slaves not only survived, but even displayed a robust physical appearance.

The second distribution of clothing signaled the end of harvest. The slaves cleared the land and planted new fields of sugar cane, weeded the old fields of "ratoon" cane, and cut wood to prepare for the next harvest. These occupations were time-consuming and made reasonably heavy demands on the labor force.

Planting the canes involved a system of digging holes or trenches in the cleared land. The land was divided into small squares, and in each square two slaves, working together, opened a furrow with a hoe. The strongest men did this work, which could be very difficult in soils laced with stones or roots or lowland soils of plastic mud. The rest of the slaves were divided into sowers and carriers. The sowers placed the canes longitudinally in the holes and covered them with loose soil hauled from the banks. The carriers supplied the canes from the stockpiles. Later, as the canes began to grow, the male slaves moved in to weed the fields and loosen the soil around the young plants.[45] The planting season usually lasted from September to December.

More often, however, the scarcity of labor forced the planters to continue the operation long after the close of the conventional season. At such time the planters might be forced to hire additional slaves to cut wood or tend the cattle.[46]

The great fertility of Cuban soils allowed a lengthy ratooning of canes. Nevertheless, the soils became exhausted eventually, and the farmers had to move on to new plots. Many attempts were made to popularize the use of manures, but those met with little success while land was available at reasonable cost. Some of the richer producers such as Miguel Aldama, Pedro Diago, and Joaquín de Ayesterán, however, made serious efforts to get fertilizers from abroad, either in the form of crushed bones from New York, or guano from Peru.[47] Not until the end of the century and the arrival of the large corporation did fertilizers play an important part in Cuban agricultural practices.

Many attempts were made to use steam-driven plows to replace the hand plows used by the slaves. But although the machines were far more efficient, their high cost, coupled with the fact that they could not be easily operated by slaves, tended to make them prohibitive for all but the richest planters. The first steam-driven plow was demonstrated on Friday, April 24, 1863, on the ingenio Concepción, owned by Miguel Aldama.[48] Many farmers traveled very far to view the plow which promised a new breakthrough in the labor-land dilemma. They were impressed by the speed and efficiency of the machine. Its cost and the additional requirement of an imported, salaried operator and mechanic considerably dampened their enthusiasm. Following the path of least resistance, many planters preferred to take fullest advantage of the wretched system of slavery while it still existed, or sought simply to replace their slave labor by equally wretched indentured Asians.

One of the innovations of plantation agriculture in Cuba, at least in the history of slavery there, was the provision of facilities for medical care for the sick, and a nursery for the small children. The sick room, or miniature hospital, catered to the small eventualities of the estate. It possessed all the medicines required for the frequent injuries, small infections, or the colds and influenza epidemics which accompanied the rainy summer months.

Many slaves used the facilities of the infirmary as an excuse for procrastination. The result of this was that some planters were particularly skeptical about admitting the illnesses of their slaves.[49] In the earlier days of slavery, some plantation owners had held the assumption that it was more economical to work a slave to death as quickly as possible and then replace him with a new purchase than to care for the slave properly and encourage reproduction.[50] Cristóbal Madan openly confessed that the care given to a slave was generally related to the costs of production: the lower the price of slaves, the less was their general welfare considered, and vice versa. ''The reduction in the trade with Africa and the consequent reduction in the facility to replace the workforce at a low cost, has forced some proprietors to take better care of their slaves, and to promote their well-being and comfort,'' he wrote in the 1850's.[51]

According to the handbook for slave-run sugar estates, pregnancy and birth were not classified as illnesses.[52] Forty-five days after giving birth, a mother went back to work, often in the fields, while the offspring was given to the *criollera*, an old slave woman who supervised the nursery.

Under the arduous conditions of labor, the rural slave population found it impossible to maintain its own equilibrium of births and deaths. One important factor, of course, was the tremendous imbalance of the sexes on the plantations, where productive males outnumbered productive females by over 2:1, as very few planters made any attempt to supply an adequate number of females to satisfy the males on their estates.[53] Women were considered to be less productive than men. Apart from the sexual imbalance, women could not produce healthy babies under conditions of labor entirely devoid of hygiene, and where they often had to do field work for the entire time of their pregnancy. The practice of having women in their ninth month of pregnancy working alongside men and cutting canes in the field perhaps contributed to a number of deformed or stillborn babies.[54] Many women lost their babies during the terrible punishments they underwent for individual misdemeanors.[55]

Corporal punishment was at once a measure of discipline and of intimidation for the slaves. The slave code of 1842 sanctioned the more

Table 30.2:   Slaves: Sex and Age Groups, 1855–57

Year	Males			Females			Total
	Under 12	Useful 12–60	All males*	Under 12	Useful 12–60	All females*	
1855							
Urban	6,991	21,438	33,140	7,911	26,111	37,551	70,691
Rural	32,566	143,767	192,919	30,128	78,456	111,196	304,115
1856							
Urban	7,083	22,616	30,303	7,975	26,561	36,820	66,123
Rural	35,476	143,183	190,327	32,719	77,749	114,916	305,243
1857							
Urban	7,673	21,478	30,848	7,743	25,649	34,762	65,610
Rural	35,147	144,310	193,187	33,160	75,416	114,188	307,375

*Includes slaves over the age of 60, and invalids between 12 and 60.

Source: AHN, Ultramar, Esclavitud, leg. 3553.

popular forms – flogging, stocks, shackles, chains, and imprisonment – which were administered on the estates.

Flogging was the most common and the most convenient form of punishment. It was legally limited to twenty-five lashes, but was often given on a brutal installment plan called the *novenario* which consisted of nine strokes daily over a period of nine days. Not only was the legal limit exceeded, but the slave did not run the risk of an immediate loss of life during the procedure. Some estates had a special flogging section called a *tumbadero*. Flogging, however, was dealt to the slaves anywhere and everywhere, either as a consequence of the anger of a white person, or as an incentive to work harder.

Next in popular use on the plantations came the stocks and shackles (*cepo* and *grillete*). Both forms had many styles. The most common form of stocks consisted of an enormous, fixed board with holes through which fitted the head, hands, and feet of the delinquent slaves, either separately, or in any combination. Left in the open in a number of uncomfortable positions, the slaves suffered from the weather as well as from the many varieties of insects found in the tropics without being able to protect themselves.

Shackles varied from simple chains and padlocks attached to the ankles or wrists and fastened around the neck to the types that were attached to a large log, which the slave had to lift whenever he desired to move from one place to another. The heavy iron of the shackles sometimes chafed the skin, resulting in serious infection of the wounds. That such forms of punishment should have led directly or indirectly to miscarriages among pregnant females was not surprising.

The degree to which these measures operated depended on the individual slave master and the supervisory personnel on the estate, who had the authority to inflict punishment in the absence of the proprietors. All the above forms of physical abuse remained on the law books until 1882.[56]

The slaves never remained indifferent or acquiescent to their conditions. Not many were literate and therefore able to leave a written account of their impressions and experiences, although at least one probably did.[57] Instead, the reactions of the slaves must be deduced from their actions.

As long as the Cuban economy had remained relatively underdeveloped, and the increase of Africans small, the social problems of a multiracial society were neither obvious nor frightening. Both elite and subordinate groups had the kind of close, personal relationship characteristic of patriarchal societies. On the one hand, the number of slaves held by any one master was unlikely to be very large. On the other hand, the absence of any great economic incentive on the part of the master permitted him to be fairly liberal in his regimentation of the lives of the slaves. Besides, as Herbert Klein has revealed, the diversification of the economic system in the rural areas and the growth of urban zones lent themselves to quite a relaxed form of slavery.[58] Nevertheless, the slaves, despite the often vaunted "Spanish Catholic kindness," consistently and in a variety of ways expressed their opposition to their servitude. And with the harsher conditions of a plantation type of slavery, such resistance became more widespread. The slaves resisted slavery in many ways. Some simply poisoned their masters, destroyed machines, or set canefields on fire.[59] Such manifestations of resistance, however, neither alleviated their suffering nor affected their status, and represented individual responses of anger, jealousy, or revenge in particular situations.

Far more serious reflections on the general state of slavery came from the evidence of voluntary abortions, suicides, and runaways. Many women practiced abortion by drinking a brew concocted from wild herbs, in order to save their offspring from undergoing the life that they themselves were leading.[60] Suicide was so frequent that the problem was taken up by the highest authorities in Madrid in 1847, and continued under active consideration until 1855.[61] Initially, the Cuban captain-general proposed that more religious instruction offered the most efficacious method of fighting a practice inimical to the "propagation and conservation of that caste not only necessary to the country, but also difficult to replace by any other."[62] Eventually the officials realized that something, else had to be tried. A royal order in 1855, noting that males outnumbered females on some estates by a ratio of 4: 1, insisted that all proprietors be forced to balance the sex ratio on their farms. It also suggested that tax rebates could be used as incentives for the successful procreation of the slaves on the estates.[63] The figures given in the royal order, however, are not borne out by an examination of the census returns for slaves. The incidence of such one-sided masculinity among the slave populations on estates was extremely rare. Among all the rural slave population, the ratio of males to females was far nearer the proportion of 2:1 which even then represented an exaggeration of the male sector.

Wherever the plantation society existed-as indeed, wherever slavery existed-slaveowners faced the recurrent problem of escapees. Herbert S. Klein noted in his study of slavery in both Cuba and the state of Virginia that the occurrence of runaways in the island was "far out of proportion to anything experienced in Virginia," and was so serious a problem that the Cuban proprietors found it more expedient to be lenient with the malady, equating it to no worse an offense than simple malingering.[64] But it was not merely that the masters feared losing forever the slave who might have intended to desert only temporarily in the initial stages. Rather it was more significant that the master could not afford to lose a slave who might be required for the harvest time. Part of the idea of leniency, therefore, stemmed from the acute shortage of laborers on the island. Masters could have been motivated by kindness and economic considerations with equal validity. But lenience did not seem to reduce the desire for freedom. This desire could be frustrated; it could never be extinguished.

Desertion, temporary or permanent, was as common among urban slaves as it was among plantation slaves. Slaves with ideas of permanent escape created their abodes in the most inaccessible parts of the mountains. Called *cimarrones*, or maroons, these runaways in their villages or *palenques* often defied the concerted attacks of the whites for extremely long periods. Not only did they carry on their own regular social and political organization independent of the white society, but they practiced cultivation to supplement foraging and stealing from the plantations. Their weapons for defense included machetes stolen from the plantations – still one of the most useful devices in Latin America and the Caribbean – poisoned arrows and wooden spears with improvised iron heads.[65] In addition, the maroons also defended their villages with sharpened bamboo poles, fixed firmly in the ground, and covered with dried leaves.

The main Negro palenques were in the mountains of the east, especially the Sierra del Cristal, "where white men hardly dare to go."[66] One famous palenque there was called Moa, or El Frijol. Other outstanding palenques existed in the Cuzco hills of the Vuelta Abajo region, the marshes of Zapata, and the Organos mountains of Pinar del Río.[67] Some runaways, however, did not live in the palenques, but rather led a wandering life in the country, or drifted to the larger towns where they tried to blend in with the free colored population. White response to the *apalencado,* or Negro slave living in the palenque, was considerably less lenient than to the temporary absconder, who, by the intervention of a third party, called a *padriño,* could be pardoned and restored to the farm.[68] Many whites were semiprofessional slavehunters. These *ranchadores,* accompanied by bloodhounds, led expeditions into the mountains, often to eliminate a troublesome palenque, or its diminutive, the ranchería, but more often to get the four dollars per head reward each captive brought from the *capitanes de partido* (the district military or judicial commanders). Sometimes large military expeditions went out to destroy the more formidable maroon villages in the mountains.

The most emphatic form of resistance to slavery consisted of open rebellion.[69] In a number of cases, most notably in 1825 and 1843 in Matanzas, the slave revolts revealed widespread planning, and even included whites and free persons of color. Far more frequently, however, all the slaves on a single estate would erupt in violence, destroying property and killing those whites they could get their hands on. Spontaneous uprisings, confined to the slaves of the same owner, were very common throughout the Caribbean region. Proslavery writers tended to explain them as symptomatic of lax supervision and absenteeism.[70] More objective observers realized that servility bred revolt, and that men subordinate to hostile overseers reacted with hostility themselves.[71]

Of the numerous slave disturbances after 1840, two deserve special attention. One occurred in 1844, and the other in 1866. The supposed slave "revolt" of 1844 had absolutely no foundation in fact.[72] Basing its actions upon the testimony of a female slave that the blacks on a Matanzas plantation were conspiring with many outsiders to foment a rebellion, the government of Leopoldo O'Donnell precipitately moved in and arrested nearly two thousand whites, free colored persons, and slaves. No one knew the exact number of executions, which included the well-known free colored men Andrés Dodge and Gabriel de la Concepción Valdés, otherwise known as "El Plácido". Many innocent free persons suffered imprisonment and exile to

Melilla and Ceuta, while the slaves who escaped death were brutally flogged.

In March, 1866, the slaves on the estates of Zulueta, Aldama and some other prominent proprietors of Matanzas simultaneously withheld their labor, claiming that they had been declared free by the Cortes in Spain. The Negroes demanded that they be paid for their services. Although there was no report of any violence by the slaves, a large number of troops was deployed to force the men to go back to work.[73] The slaves were in all probability misled by the general excitement among the whites on the island about the election of representatives to the Cortes in Madrid, scheduled for 1866.

The opinions expressed about slave mortality as about everything else in the island differed considerably. The only general consensus seemed to be that mortality rates were higher in the rural areas than in the towns, and highest of all on the sugar plantations. Both in town and country, infant mortality was extremely high. One infant sickness alone, a convulsive complaint locally called *espasmo,* or *mal de los siete días,* was purported to have been responsible for over fifty per cent of infant slave deaths.[74] Adult mortality however was far less uniformly presented.

Antonio Gallenga thought that the mean life of a slave on the plantation was about five years, which would give an overall mortality rate of 20 per cent.[75] Gallenga, of course, wrote in the 1870's, when the trade had ceased and replacements had become impossible. In the 1850's, Cristóbal Madan put the annual plantation loss at 7 per cent, Urbano Feijóo Sotomayor at 10 per cent.[76] J. S. Thrasher thought the loss to be nearer to 8 per cent on sugar estates.[77] Vicente Vásquez Queipo, writing in 1845, thought that the average life span of a plantation slave was twenty years and the mortality rate 5 per cent per annum.[78] The most reasonable figure seems to be about 4 per cent – a mortality rate comparable with that of other West Indian islands during their plantation era.

The prevalence of diseases certainly played a part in the high mortality figures. Nevertheless, conditions of labor for the Cuban slaves in the nineteenth century were also responsible. Moreno Fraginals asserts that between the last years of the eighteenth century and the decade beginning in 1840, the slave numbers on the sugar estates were maintained exclusively by new purchases.[79] Nor could the slaves be expected to reproduce or resist diseases when they suffered from sexual imbalance, dietary deficiencies, and consistent overwork. The most telling indictment of the severity of Cuban slavery came from the dramatic decline of the black population after the abolition of the slave trade.

The number of slaves fell from 363,288 in 1869 to 227,902 in 1878, a decline of 135,386, of which at least 50 per cent were freed by the Moret Law of 1870.[80] The entire Negroid population decreased from 596,396, or 43.7 per cent of the total population of the island in 1860, to 528,798, or 32.5 per cent of the same total in 1887.[81] The decline was relative as well as absolute, and it is further accentuated if one accepts the general view that the slave census of 1860 underestimated the numbers (some think by the unlikely proportion of 30 per cent) and that the free colored population increased by 70 per cent between 1840 and 1860. Such startling decline in this sector of the population in the island sharply exposes the myth that the Cubans were humane to their slaves, or that the society was less racist than slave societies which lacked an Iberian heritage and Roman Catholic religious tradition. Writing in 1902, Rafael María de Labra laconically remarked on the earlier proslavery propagandists whom he had fought for nearly a generation in the Spanish Cortes:

One has to admire, Señores, the nerve by which they propagated the belief that the slaves in the Antilles lived happily and contentedly . . . without even mentioning the dungeons, the stocks and the irons, or the awful mortality rates among the slaves.[82]

Unfortunately, the perspicacity of the heroic Spanish liberal has not been shared by many writers of slavery. For what is abundantly clear from any study of Cuban slavery during the nineteenth century is not merely that it was significantly different from slavery in the southern United States. That was almost self-evident. Instead, what emerges, somewhat surprisingly, is that slavery on the sugar plantations of Cuba and slavery on the sugar plantations of the other West Indian islands bore a strong resemblance and were comparable. Plantation slavery – and particularly of the sugar plantation type – was a distinctive system which lent itself to systadial comparisons throughout history. Sugar and slavery had a markedly similar development and course from Barbados in the seventeenth century, through Jamaica and St. Domingue in the eighteenth century, and ended up being not very different in Cuba and Brazil in the nineteenth century. Everywhere, slavery was extremely wasteful in human terms. Everywhere its differences were in degrees of wretchedness, not in variations of humanity. One does not have to catalogue the evils of the system to support that assertion – at least not any more. In Cuba the plantation society challenged the traditions of humanitarianism and protectiveness of the Catholic Church and the royal bureaucracy. To find out how well they withstood the challenge we must look more closely at the social structure of the island during the nineteenth century.

Notes

1.   Fernando Ortiz Fernández, *Hampa afro-cubana, los negros esclavos* (Havana: Revista Bimestre Cubana, 1916), p. 320.

2.   Two historical novels which clearly exemplify the gulf between rural and urban slaves are Cirilo Villaverde, *Cecilia Valdés or Angel's Hill*, trans. Sydney G. Gest (New York: Vintage, 1962), first published in 1882; and Anselmo Suárez y Romero, Francisco. *El ingenio o las delicias del campo* (Havana: Ministro de Educación, 1947), written in the late 1840s, and originally published in 1880. The latter was the basis of accounts by Medden and Fernando Ortiz, and is often compared with *Uncle Tom's Cabin.*

3.   Ortiz, *Negros esclavos*, pp. 307-13; Herbert S. Klein, *Slavery in the Americas: A Comparative Study of Virginia and Cuba* (Chicago: University of Chicago Press, *1967*), pp. *145-51.*

4.   Ortiz, *Negros esclavos, p. 313.*

5.   See Fernando Ortiz Fernández, "La fiesta afro-cubana del dia de reyes," *Revista Bimestre Cubana*, 15 (1920), 5-26; and "Los cabildos afro-cubanos," ibid., *16 (1921), 5-39.* See also Villaverde, *Cecilia Valdés.*

6.   Ortiz, *Negros esclavos, p. 312.*

7.   *Cartilla práctica del manejo de ingenios* . . .(Irun: Impr. de la Elegancia, 1862), p. 94.

8.   See Anselmo Suarez y Romero, *Francisco. El ingenio o las delicias del campo.* New ed., (Havana: Ministro de Educacion, 1947).

9.   Ortiz, Negros esclavos, p. 168, fn.

10.   Ibid., pp. 171-73.

11.   David Turnbull, *Travels in the West. Cuba . . . (London:* Longman, Orme, Brown, Green, and Longmans, *1840),* p. 51. *Also* Suárez y Romero, *Francisco,*

12.   Fernando Ortiz Fernández, *Cuban Counterpoint: Tobacco and Sugar,* trans. Harriet de Onís (New York: Knopf, *1947),* p. 24.

13. See Jacobo de la Pezuela, *Diccionario geográfico, estadístico, histórico de la isla de Cuba (4 vols.;* Madrid: Mellado, 1863-66), 1:38-39.

14. José García de Arboleya, *Manual de la isla de Cuba . . .* (Havana: Impr. del Tiempo, 1859), p. 180.

15. Ibid., p. 142.

16. For 1846, ibid., p. 144; For 1861, *Pezuela, Diccionario,* pp. 38-39.

17. Richard H. Dana, *To Cuba and Back: A Vacation Voyage,* new ed. (Carbondale: Southern Illinois University Press, 1966), p. 53. This book was first published in 1859.

18. *Arboleya, Manual, pp. 140-41.*

19. Francisco Pérez de la Riva, *El caé: Historia de su cultivo y explotación en Cuba* (Havana: Montero, 1944), pp. 170-71.

20. Richard H. Dana, Jr., *To Cuba and back: A Vacation Voyage.*(Boston: Ticknor and Fields, 1859). New ed.,(Carbondale: Southern Illinois University Press, 1966), p. 56.

21. *Cartilla práctica,* pp. 75-80.

22. Manuel Moreno Fraginals, *El ingenio: El complejo economico social cubano del azucar. Tomo 1, 1760-1860.*(Havana: UNESCO, 1964), pp. 15-16. Of course, the conucos were never entirely abolished.

23. Cartilla práctica, p. 15.

24. [Cristóbal Madan], *Llamamiento de la isla de Cuba a la nación española* (New York: Hallet, 1854), p. 11.

25. *Cartilla práctica, pp.* 15-18, 46. I have converted the caballerías to acres, and rounded the figures. Madan gives a requirement of 300 slaves.

26. [Madan], *Llamamiento, pp.* 15-17. prices are in U.S. dollars, 1854 value.

27. *Cartilla práctica,* pp. 31, 53-58.

28. Dana, *To Cuba,* pp. 54-55.

29. [Madan], *Llamamiento,* p. 12.

30. Roland T. Ely, *Cuando reinaba su, majestad el azúcar* (Buenos Aires : Ed Sudamericana, *1963),* pp. 464-72; Moreno Fraginals *El ingenio p 8;* Samuel . Hazard, *Cuba with Pen and Pencil (Hartford,* Conn.: Hartford Pub. *'Co., 1871 pp. 3S2-71.* For comparisons with the West Indies see *J. H.* Parry and P. M. Sherlock, *A Short History of the West Indies* (London: Macmillan, *1957),* chapter 5. Most travel books on Cuba at this time included extensive references to the white workers on the sugar estates-Dana, *To Cuba ' pp. 60-64, is* the best, but See also Demoticus Philalethes [pseud.], *Yankee Travels through the Island of Cuba* (New York: Appleton, *1856), pp. 33-36.* For evidence *of* increased racial prejudice, see *José J. Ribó, Historia de los voluntarios cubanos* (2 vols.; Madrid: González, 1872), 1:21-23.

31. Moreno Fraginals, *El ingenio,* p. 118.

32. Antonio C. Gallenga, *The Pearl of the Antilles* (London: Chapman & Hall, *1873), pp. 127-28.*

33. Philalethes, *Yankee Travels,* p. 75.

34. AHN, Ultramar, Esclavitud, leg. 3550: El Correo de España, Sept. 13-27, 1863.

35. Justo German Cantero, *Los ingenios . . .*(Havana: Marquier, 1857).

36. Moreno Fraginals, *El ingenio, p.* 118. Richard H. Dana visited an estate, however, on which one free

person of color was trained to operate the machines so that he could relieve the white machinist at night. This was the highest position to which a free colored person could rise on any plantation.

37. *Cartilla práctica,* pp. 43-46.

38. Ibid., pp. 75-76.

39. This pattern is taken from ibid., pp. 43-46: "Fuerzas que se necesitan para. la zafra y distribución de ellas."

40. Dana, *To Cuba,* pp. 48, 56-59.

41. *The slave laws of 1842* stipulated that the crop-time work should be *"16* hours daily with *2* for rest in the days, and *6* at night's to sleep." These became the minimal requirements observed only on the very best estates. Many travellers remarked that during crop-time the slaves got no more than 3 hours of sleep per day. Edwin F. Atkins, *Sixty Years in Cuba* (Cambridge: Riverside Press, 1926), p. 98, states that the Negroes on his estates worked regularly for 18 hours during the harvest, and that some became crippled by their work.

42. *Cartilla práctica,* p. 58.

43. Hazard, *Cuba,* p. 360; for other contemporary reports, see Noel Deerr, *The History of Sugar* (2 vols.; London: Chapman & Hall, 1949-50), 2:359.

44. *Cartilla práctica,* p. 58.

45. Ibid., p. 31.

46. Moreno Fraginals, *El ingenio, pp.* 90-94; *Cartilla práctica,* p. 94.

47. Ely, *Cuando reinaba,* pp. 569-75.

48. Moreno Fraginals, *El ingenio,* p. 91.

49. *Cartilla práctica,* pp. 82-83.

50. Alexander Humboldt, *The Island of Cuba,* trans. J. S. Thrasher (New York: Derby & Jackson, 1856), pp. 227-28.

51. [Cristóbal Madan], *El trabajo libre y el libre cambio en Cuba* (Paris: n.p., 1864), p. 3. See also AHN, Ultramar, Esclavitud, leg. 3552: Serrano al M. de la Guerra y Ultramar, April 15, 1862 (confidential).

52. *Cartilla práctica,* pp. 82-83.

53. See census returns in AHN, Ultramar, Esclavitud, legs. 3553-54.

54. Moreno Fraginals, *El ingenio,* pp. 157-58.

55. Ortiz describes, with illustrations, the wide variety of corporal punishments used by the masters to ensure discipline, in *Negros esclavos, pp.* 245-69.

56. AHN, Ultramar, Gobierno, leg. 4815, 1880-82: "Exposiciones abolicionistas alas Cortes, 1881-1882"; and leg. 4814, fols. 279-80, 1883.

57. See, Robert R. Madden, *Poems by a Slave on the Island of Cuba recently liberated . . . (London:* Ward, 1840), which contains the poems supposedly written by the ex-slave Juan Francisco Manzano, along with his autobiography.

58. Herbert S. Klein, *Slavery in the Americas: A Comparative Study of Virginia and Cuba.*(Chicago: University of Chicago Press, 1967), pp. 142-50. In a personal communication, Sidney W. Mintz of Yale University has suggested the term "lagging capitalistic" to describe this earlier period of Cuban history.

59. Philalethes, *Yankee Travels, pp.* 14-15, and Dana, *Cuba,* p. 61.

60. Moreno Fraginals, *El ingenio*, p. 157.

61. AHN, Ultramar, Esclavitud, leg. 3550: "Expediente sobre los medios de evitar los frecuentes suicidios de los esclavos." Also Ortiz, *Negros esclavos, pp.* 391-423.

62. AHN, Ultramar, Esclavitud, leg. 3550(l), ind. 17.

63. Ibid ind 18: "Proyecto de importación de mugeres esclavas en la Isla de Cuba."

64. Klein, *Slavery in, the Americas*, p. 155.

65. For the life of a runaway slave, see Esteban Montejo, "The Day I Stopped being a Slave," *Observer Review*, April 14, 1968 (an extract from his book, *The Autobiography* of *a Runaway Slave*, ed. Miguel Barnet [London: Bodley Head, 1968]). Also Ortiz, *Negros esclavos*, p. 413.

66. Dana, *To Cuba*, p. 127.

67. Ortiz, *Negros esclavos*, p. 412.

68. [J. G. F. Wurdemann], *Notes on Cuba* (Boston: Munroe, 1844), pp.260-61; Philalethes, *Yankee Travels*, pp. 38-43

69. See Ely, *Cuando reinaba, pp.* 492-501; Ortiz, *Negros esclavos*, pp. 429- 35.

70. For example, [Wurdemann], Notes, p. 273.

71. Suárez y Romero, *Francisco*, pp. 22-23.

72. For the complete report of the commission of inquiry, see AHN, Estado, Esclavitud, leg. 8057. The abolition of slavery in the British West Indies, the large number of slave uprisings in 1843, and the general rumors of a race war on the island all contributed to the government's testiness. There can be no doubt that the government used the opportunity to remove some of the Creoles from the island.

73. Ely, *Cuando reinaba*, p. 495.

74. Ortiz, *Negros esclavos*, pp. 284-85.

75. Gallenga, *Pearl of the Antilles, p. 80.*

76. [Madan], Llamamiento, p. 14; Urbano Feijo de Sotomayor, *Isla de Cuba* . . . (Madrid: J. Peña, 1855), pp. 44-45.

77. Humboldt, *Cuba*, pp. 206-7.

78. [Vincente Vásquez Quiepo], *Informe fiscal* . . . *(Madrid:* Alegria, *1845),* p. 18-19.

79 Moreno Fraginals, *El ingenio*, p. 155.

80. Arthur F. Corwin, *Spain and the Abolition of Slavery in Cuba, 1817-1886* (Austin: University of Texas Press, *1967),* p. 294.

81. Spain, Instituto Geográfico y Estadístico, *Censo* . . . *1860* (Madrid: Impr. Nacional, 1863), and ibid., *Censo. . . 1887* (Madrid: Inst. Geog. y Estadistico, 1891).

82. Rafael M. de Labra y Cadrana, *La reforma política de Ultramar 1868-1900* (Madrid: Alonso, 1902), p . 22.

31

Slavery in Martinique in the French Caribbean

DALE TOMICH

Through the social relations of slavery, the demand for surplus labor was imposed upon the labor process. The technical-material conditions of sugar production were developed and extended as commodity production, and pressure was exerted for the optimal utilization of available laborers and labor time. Thus, neither "technical necessity" nor the master's domination over the slave alone determined the actual work relations – the mode of cooperation, division of labor, division of laborers. Within the technical framework established by the *habitation sucrière,* the slave relation permitted the increase of the mass of workers, the prolongation of labor time, and the intensification of effort. Concern for regularity, efficiency, quantification, and standardization increasingly came to dominate the organization of the labor process in order to secure its integration and expand the surplus product. Capital here does not appear as the so-called external reality of the market but enters into the inner constitution of the slave labor process itself.

However, the very processes that increased surplus production revealed the ever greater inadequacy of the slave relation as the means of both securing the necessary combination of workers and disciplining their activity to the technical and social requirements of the large-scale commercial production of sugar. While the adoption of new techniques and efforts to maximize output integrated the division of labor on each plantation ever more closely and filled in the "empty spaces" in the potentially available labor time, the slave form limited the kind and amount of labor at the disposition of the planter, and hence the potential surplus product. Within the limits and conditions of the slave relation, the planter could increase the surplus product only by adapting the activity of a given body of workers to the technically determined conditions of production for a period of fixed duration that was itself subject to natural, technical, and social constraints. As the result of these structural limitations, planters attempted to intensify the exploitation of labor and to discipline more effectively the productive activity of the slaves within the prevailing social and technical conditions. The integration of the slave laborers into the productive mechanism of the plantation was both the condition and the limit of the expansion of surplus production. In this context, labor discipline consisted of the attempt to bind the slaves to the social and technical conditions of production more effectively and to secure the maximum effort possible in conformity with the technical requirements of production.

Thus, the social relations of slave production were not only categories of political economy and value production. They were at the same time processes of social action through which work was imposed on the subject population. For the African bondman, slave labor in the New World required a radical restructuring of the social relations of work under the most brutal conditions. In the plantation societies of the Americas, the goals and organization of work, as well as the role of work in daily life, were very different from what they had been in Africa. A complex system of political and legal sanctions established the domination of the master over the person of the slave and allowed him to control the labor of the latter. The master regarded the slave as a mere instrument of production, and the pattern of labor he imposed upon the slave population formed the matrix of plantation life. Work was separated from ritual and community. Its organization and purposes were no longer defined by mutual obligation, kinship ties, or social duty. It was carried out independently of the subsistence needs of the laborers, and they had no personal interest in it. Instead, work was separated from all other human activities and subordinated to the alien claims of production embodied in the master, while all other aspects of life on the plantation were subordinated to work.[1]

Work assumed new forms and took on new social meanings for the African slave. Systematic production for the abstract market, not direct or indirect consumption, required that the enslaved adapt to a new organization and new purposes of production, appropriation, and distribution imposed and structured through the slave relation. The slaves were forced to adopt new work habits, adjust to new work discipline, and learn new values and incentives to work. They had to become accustomed to different motor habits and physiological rhythms, as well as a new range of social conduct. They had to learn to accept the authority of the master and his supervisors, to become proficient at new skills, and to work together in large gangs continuously and regularly at repetitive tasks within a developed division of labor for a period of fixed duration, day after day. The burden of this transition lay heavily on the minds and bodies of the enslaved, and it required a painful cultural adaptation on a vast scale – if not as the personal experience of each individual bondman, then as the historical experience of the slave population as a whole.[2]

The socialization of African slaves and their descendants into the labor regime of the sugar plantation entailed subtle and complex historical processes of cultural change, accommodation, and resistance that were central both to their adaptation to the New World environment and to the formation of Afro-Caribbean identity and culture. Indeed, the adaptability and creativity of the enslaved made the plantation system possible. But more than this, the irreducible autonomy of the slaves' responses to the conditions that confronted them not only presented a barrier to surplus production but transformed the character of slave relations and the organization of production itself.[3]

With the assimilation of the slave population into the regime of plantation labor, the social relationships of work became increasingly important in shaping their lives. Yet, neither were the slaves simply reducible to factors of production nor was work a sphere of activity completely dominated by the master. Instead, the slave labor process was an arena where the cultural definitions of work and its relation to the larger matrix of plantation life were formed and contested. Europeans and Africans encountered one another through the unequal relations of slavery and engaged in a day-to-day struggle, sometimes implicit, sometimes overt, over the organization of work and the norms and values it entailed. The master sought to discipline the slaves to the technical and social conditions of plantation production and to inculcate in them appropriate skills, attitudes, and values. But if the enslaved successfully adapted to the exigencies of the new labor regime, their behavior and values did not imitate those of their masters nor were their motives, meanings, and goals identical with those of the latter. For their part, the slaves, in a complex mixture of accommodation and resistance, struggled both within and against the framework dictated to them and, in the course of their struggle, developed other values, ideas, and cultural forms that enabled them to assert their own purposes, needs, and rhythms in work and social life and to resist the definitions imposed by the masters.

The ability of the slaves to adapt to the routine of the plantation, to organize their own capacity for collective activity, and to physically carry out the tasks assigned to them, even under the most adverse circumstances, discloses the contradictory process at the heart of New World slave systems. The labor process is not the one-dimensional creation of the master. Rather, on the one side, the master sought continually to appropriate this slave initiative and turn it to his purpose, while, on the other side, this slave self-organization thrust itself against his domination. Within the context formed by antagonistic needs and purposes and by the asymmetrical relations of power, norms of behavior as well as work loads and routines to which both master and slave must acquiesce were established as "customary" and "normal" through this confrontation. The slave relation was simultaneously strengthened and weakened, while the ground of confrontation between master and slave shifted.

However, while the social relationships of work more and more became the focal point of slave resistance, their actions are not simply reducible to economic struggle in its narrow meaning. Rather, they also entailed more generalized and complex cultural resistance to the imposition of a whole way of life on a subject population. At issue in this conflict were not only the specific conditions of labor but the broader question of the place of work in social life. For the slaves, the plantation was the locus of a network of solidarities and institutions, beliefs, and values that formed a distinctive and autonomous community and culture. Historically these were created and sustained by the slaves themselves, and slave resistance sought to protect and maintain them and to enforce their claims against the economic rationality of the plantation. In this context, specific struggles over work could shape and reinforce broader patterns of community solidarity and cultural resistance and vice versa, while the result of both was to establish and maintain a community and way of life not completely subordinated to the relations of work, property, and social hierarchy of the plantation system. While the integration of the slave population into the relations and processes of the plantation enterprise was one pole of development, the other was the creation of the slave community and the formation and transformation of new solidarities among the slave group. The slave plantations embodied both enterprise and community and evolved through their mutual dependence and antagonism.[4]

Thus, the relation between master and slave was not static but underwent a continual process of evolution. The very ability of the masters to compel the slaves' participation in the new conditions of life and labor and the complexity and originality of the slaves' responses altered the masterslave relation itself. New forms, meanings, and goals of social action emerged alongside older ones and became the focal points of a new constellation of conditions, needs, and capacities on both sides, which moved the struggle between them onto a new terrain. This process of "creolization" expressed the historical limits of the master-slave relation and of slave production.

The Hands and Feet of the Planter

Under slavery, as Max Weber pointed out, workers could not be selected according to technical abilities and needs. In the face of this structural constraint, planters were compelled to adapt the particular workers at hand to the specific requirements of the production process. The goal of the master was to use the slave labor force optimally within the given technical master w division of labor by making the best use of individual capacities over the course of the slaves' working lives. "It is your business . . . " Dr. Collins enjoined the planters in his important *Practical Rules for the Management and Medical Treatment of Negro Slaves in the Sugar Colonies,* published anonymously in 1811, "to adapt their stations to their qualities and talents." The division of labor on the plantation was organized as a social process on the basis of the personal attributes of individual slaves. Factors such as age, gender, size, strength, dexterity, aptitude, and reliability entered into determining the distribution of slaves among the various occupations and activities of the sugar estate.[5]

However, even these efforts to rationalize the labor force were mitigated by incorporating the master's residence and the slave community into the plantation. A variety of tasks essential to operating the estate but not directly concerned with sugar production – ranging from domestic service to child care – emerged "naturally" in the course of plantation life and were performed by slaves. The division of labor thus became more complex, and a large number of slaves were absorbed in activities whose contribution to the plantation as a productive enterprise were minimal. The difficulties these activities presented for the rationalization of the labor force were exacerbated by the decline of the slave trade to the French Lesser Antilles during the second half of the eighteenth century and its abolition in the 1830s. Without the opportunity to appropriate new slaves, providing for the daily and generational reproduction of the labor force assumed greater importance in the social and economic organization of the plantation, while the demographic composition of the slave population raised on the estate did not coincide with the demand for labor.[6]

Only a portion of the slaves attached to the estate were actually engaged in agricultural production. According to Sainte Croix, 210 slaves were required to produce 450 hogsheads of sugar. But, of these, less than half were actually engaged in sugar manufacture. The remainder consisted of the aged and infirm, caretakers, wet nurses, children unable to work, and so forth. Though not complete in detail, the report by the planter De Lavigne showed a larger proportion of active workers among his 200 slaves. He recorded that 63 were younger than fourteen years of age; 102 were workers between 14 and 60 years old employed in agriculture; 14 were artisans, drivers, or domestics; and 21 were over 6o years of age and too old to work. Jabrun, in the neighboring colony of Guadeloupe, had 154 slaves more or less evenly divided between men and women. Of these, 104 were between the ages of 14 and 6o and formed the active working population of the plantation. Counted among these were 65 slaves engaged in agriculture, 2 drivers, 3 masons, 2 carpenters, 2 coopers, 2 cart drivers, 2 refiners, 3 herdsmen, 6 domestics, 2 nurses *(gardes-malades)*, 4 sick in the hospital, and *8* women pregnant or lying in. The remaining slaves included 35 children under 14 years of age and 15 slaves over 60 years old. In another another account, de la Cornillère describes a plantation in Martinique which cultivated 120 carrés of land and produced *521* boucauts of sugar annually (1 boucaut = 489.5 kilograms). There were *255* slaves living on this plantation, but only *54* men and *56* women worked in the fields. There were also *9* skilled workers. The remainder included 18 boys, 18 girls, *6* domestics, 1 midwife, 2 nurses *(hospitalières)*, 7 herdsmen, 18 infirm and aged, and 28 small boys and 28 small girls too young to leave the quarters.

The smaller plantations were similarly handicapped by the high proportion of unproductive labor. Cassius Linval owned 56 slaves, but only 25 of them were adult workers between the ages of 14 and 60 years, and it is not known how many of these were suited for heavy labor.[7]

The productive force of the slaves resident on the estate was organized and coordinated by the gang system, and the gangs, or *ateliers,* provided the means through which work was imposed on the slaves from childhood to old age. The number, size, and composition of the gangs varied from plantation to plantation depending particularly on the size of the estate. On the majority of plantations, the field slaves were typically di-

vided into two gangs. The adults formed the great gang *(grand atelier)*, while adolescents and older children formed the second gang *(petit atelier)*. However, many planters felt that this arrangement was insufficient. Strength and ability could not be inferred from age. Collins wrote that the consequence of this division is that "either the weaker negroes must retard the progress of the stronger ones, or your drivers, insensible of the cause of their backwardness, or not weighing it properly, will incessantly urge them, either with stripes or threats, to keep up with the others; by which means they are overwrought, and compelled to resort to the sick-house." He concluded that the solution to this problem was to divide the slaves into a greater number of gangs according to their physical capacity. "In order that the weak may not work too much nor the strong too little, it is advisable to divide your force into a greater number of sections or gangs." Such an arrangement created more homogeneity within each gang and allowed for more effective supervision, though it also complicated the task of management. There were thus a variety of arrangements and combinations in use as each planter sought to maximize the force of the laborers at his disposal and make the most effective use of his supervisory staff, and, of course, gangs could be combined or divided or individuals shifted from one gang to another according to particular circumstances.[8]

The *grand atelier* was the pride of the plantation, and its physical strength was the motive force of the production process. Ideally, this gang was made up of adult slaves of both sexes and was selected on the basis of strength and ability. The *grand atelier* ordinarily comprised a bit more than one-third of the total number of slaves on the plantation. On very large estates, these slaves could be divided into two separate gangs in order to permit separate tasks to be performed simultaneously and for administrative and supervisory purposes Women generally outnumbered men in the *grand atelier*. This reflected, in part the greater proportion of females than males in the slave population in Martinique; and, in part, the demand for other types of labor for slaves of each gender on the plantation. The need for refiners, coopers, carpenters, masons, blacksmiths, and other skilled workers as well as slave drivers reduced the number of men available for work in the fields, whereas domestic service provided female slaves with their sole major alternative to the field gang. When a slave became too old or too weak to continue to work in the fields, he or she was given less demanding work such as watching over buildings, cornfields, and provision grounds, or else was retired completely from labor, though that individual was often still regarded as part of the *grand atelier* from an administrative point of view.[9]

The most difficult jobs on the plantation, those requiring strength and skill, were assigned to the *grand atelier*. These included digging the cane holes, planting cane and provisions, trashing heavy canes, woodcutting, feeding the mill, and carrying green bagasse from the mill to the drying shed. Beyond this, road construction and repair as well as building stone walls were counted among their duties. Sainte Croix also included stoking the furnace of the boiling house and skimming the evaporating pans among the jobs assigned to the great gang. These were two of the most physically exhausting jobs on the plantation, and females were exempt from them. The great gang always performed the agricultural tasks on the plantation collectively under the supervision of the overseers and drivers. On large plantations, a gang of between 30 and 50 slaves, each equipped with a hoe or a cane knife, formed a single line across the field with a driver at each end and the overseer in the middle. The line advanced step by step as each slave completed the required task and then moved ahead to repeat it. The overseer and the drivers followed behind, inspecting the work, shouting and threatening, exhorting the slaves on, and, if necessary, reprimanding or whipping the lazy and insubordinate in order to prevent delays in completing the day's assignment or to punish some serious mistake.[10]

The *petit atelier* was composed of slaves who were not physically capable of working in the great gang. These included the aged and other adults who were not strong enough for strenuous field work, nursing mothers, those convalescing from childbirth or illness, and most importantly, older children and adolescents between the ages of 10 and 16. If not working in conjunction with the great gang as happened during planting, the second gang worked under the supervision of a driver, often a woman, and was charged with the lighter tasks on the plantation, including planting "seed," cleaning and banking young cane,

weeding, bundling the cut cane stalks, helping to transport the cane to the mill, and carrying dried bagasse to the furnace in the boiling house. On larger plantations, this gang may have been subdivided into two groups on the basis of strength and assigned to lighter or heavier tasks respectively. Children too big for the grass gang, but not strong enough for the second gang, and convalescents were often employed in jobs such as light weeding and spreading manure over the cane pieces under the supervision of an older woman slave. After two or three years in the *petit atelier,* the young slave was sent to the *grand atelier,* usually between the ages of 14 and 16 when he or she was capable of working with the adults.[11]

Finally, the grass, or weeding, gang included the children of the estate from the time they left the nursery at the age of 5 or 6 years until they graduated to one of the adult gangs. They were gathered under the supervision of an old woman and assigned a number of light tasks to perform, chief among which were cutting grass to feed the livestock and weeding the cane pieces. Beyond these jobs, the grass gang was expected to assist the great gang during planting by throwing manure into the cane holes. The children were supervised, instructed, and encouraged in their efforts by a negro woman experienced in all manner of field work and "armed with a pliant twig, more to create dread, than inflict chastisement." Aside from the practical advantages to be drawn from the employment of the "supple hand of the negro child" in the grass gang, its other purpose was to initiate these children into the discipline of collective labor and to acquaint them with the skills and practices of the plantation routine. Planters feared that if the slave children were neglected and left to their own devices even at a young age, they might acquire habits prejudicial to their future reliability as laborers. Instead, industry, order, and discipline must be carefully cultivated among them. Collins was explicit about the evils inherent in an idle childhood and their remedy. Such small slaves, he cautioned, "for want of other employment, would escape from their nurses, and employ themselves in mischief, such as in breaking canes, or pilfering from absent negroes, or in setting fire to their houses, and in many such amusements, by the practice of which, they are initiated into early roguery and become adepts in the science in time. To prevent this, let them be employed; for employment is the parent of honesty as idleness is of vice." The idiom of this Jamaica planter may have differed from that of his French compatriots, but the sentiment grew from the soil of slavery itself and was common to those who had appropriated their labor force from birth to old age and death. After the children were indoctrinated into collective labor, obedience to authority, and the routines of the plantation, they were graduated into the adolescent and adult gangs according to their age, gender, strength, and dexterity. Thus, the grass gang provided a continual supply of creole slaves formed from infancy to the regimen of plantation labor. In it were shaped the field hands, drivers, cattlemen, mulemen, carpenters, Coopers, masons. and refiners upon whose toil the planter would depend in years to come.[12]

Not all of the work on the plantation was done by gang labor. Slaves also performed a variety of more specialized and skilled jobs that were required by the processes of sugar manufacture. The integration of manufacturing operations into the sugar plantation created complexity and diversity in its division of labor and established a hierarchy among the laborers. The skilled slaves and those with specialized jobs had greater personal responsibility in their work and enjoyed greater autonomy in its execution than did field slaves. Many were exempt from direct supervision and had only minimal contact with those in authority. While it was necessary that such slaves function within-and, to some degree, accept-the norms and routines of the plantation, the master was in large measure dependent upon their knowledge, initiative, and judgment for the successful operation of the estate. The acquisition of skills allowed these slaves to appropriate aspects of the work routine. Instead of being simply the instruments of the planter's will, their command of essential techniques and the master's dependence on their abilities provided them with a voice in determining their conditions of work as well as the means to contest what they considered to be the excessive demands of the planter. In addition, slave artisans received greater material rewards and had more opportunity to engage in what Sidney Mintz terms "economic self- defense" than did the slaves in the *ateliers*. The acquisition of skills enhanced individuals' chances of acquiring cash and property within slavery and gave them an advantage on the market for their services or their product should they become free. No less importantly, the acquisition of such skills also opened an avenue for the exercise of individual capabilities and an assertion of individual worth and self-respect in a system that attempted to deny them.[13]

The mill and the refinery together employed between 10 and 20 slaves at a time, depending upon the size of the estate. The mill was supervised by the *maître du moulin*, a post to which great prestige was attached. The slave was responsible for the arrival and unloading of the carts, preventing the mules and oxen from being overworked, maintaining the mill and the other equipment, and caring for the stables. The other slaves in the mill were under his supervision. These were generally females aided by slaves who "lacked intelligence and strength." One woman fed the cane into the mill, while another took out the bagasse. One or two young boys were charged with keeping the table of the mill and the gutter carrying the juice to the boiling house free from debris. Two or three women carried the bagasse from the mill to the drying shed and the dried bagasse to the boiling house to be used as fuel.[14]

Work in the boiling house was difficult and hazardous. It demanded long hours of constant attention without rest and involved prolonged exposure to heat, humidity, and the stench of boiling cane juice, yet it had its rewards and was prized by the slaves. According to one author, "The business of a boiler, during the crop, I consider as the most unhealthy of any to which a negro can be applied, and yet so fond they are of heat, and of the privileges of the boiling-house, which comprise unlimited use of hot liquor and sugar, that it is pretty generally coveted." The number of slaves employed in the boiling house depended, of course, upon the size of the operation and the organization of the shifts. Ordinarily, two stokers were necessary to keep the fires under the boilers going. This was an extremely fatiguing job. Only the strongest slaves were assigned to it, and it had to be rotated every few hours. Inside the boiling house, four male slaves, including the refiner, worked at the kettles. Skimming the cane juice was also physically demanding work, and only the most robust slaves were given this job. In addition there were perhaps two or three slaves charged with taking care of the sugar after it was struck.[15]

The head refiner, or "boiler," as he was called in the English colonies, was the most important slave on the plantation. The fate of the entire crop, thus profit or loss for the estate, was in his hands. The entire operation of manufacturing the sugar took place under his guidance and demanded his constant attention around the clock during the harvest season. He supervised his assistants in the refinery, and the furnace, mill, *cases à bagasses,* and *purgerie* were under his overall command. The job required intimate knowledge of the processes of sugar making and the particularities of the cane juice, furnace, and kettles. The head refiner had to judge the quality of the cane juice and, therefore, had to be familiar with "the way the cane has been raised and treated; the kind of soil it grows upon; if that soil has been high or low manured; the age of the cane; the species it is of; whether it has been topped short or long in the cutting; if it has been arrowed, bored, or rat-eaten . . ." He had to prepare and apply the temper according to the quality of the cane juice. He determined how long the juice boiled in each of the kettles, supervised its transfer from one to another, and, most importantly, decided when the sugar was ready to strike. He also had to see to the proper crystallization, packing, and draining of the sugar. In the absence of scientific instruments and methods of sugar refining, control over these processes depended upon individual skill, judgment, and a wide range of empirical knowledge. The refiner's job was difficult and entailed great responsibility. If he failed to demonstrate the requisite skill or trustworthiness, the consequences for the estate could be severe. "The fairest fruits of a cane field have been destroyed, perverted, and rendered a mass of thick, slimy, dark, sour, cloddy, unprofitable, unmarketable substance (disappointing the expectations of the overseer,) by an improper choice of such a member, or having a villain for conducting such a business. The labor of the negroes and stock have often been lost by this means; the trash-house consumed or emptied, shipments disappointed, and adulterated juices sent to the distilling-house, where it will scarcely pay for its boiling," lamented Roughley.[16]

Despite growing scientific interest and inquiry, for all practical purposes knowledge of the techniques of sugar refining remained a craft secret and could be acquired only by long practice and experience. This knowledge was the property of the slaves whose permanence on the estate was assured, and, in a society organized by the most extreme social and racial hierarchy, the exercise of the refiner's art came to be seen as their special province. Wrote one observer, "The negro boilers must be more perfect in their business than any white can pretend to be." Although the white sugar master nominally oversaw the boiling house, the slave refiner was in practical control of its activities.

It often occurs, that this man has a very general knowledge of the method of making good sugar, from almost every cane-piece on the estate, is conversant with the soils, the management the canes have received, and when the overseer may be in a dilemma, knows how to correct some perverseness in the cane liquor. The useful slave may by his ready experience, explain the cause, and apply a remedy to prevent its bad consequences. The head boiler and the boatswain of the mill are the leading, ostensible, and confidential persons about the works in crop time, while sugar is manufacturing.

His technical qualifications made the slave refiner indispensable to the operation of the estate, and the master was obliged to concede control over the most strategic aspect of the labor process to this craftsman.[17]

The highly subjective judgment and skills of his craft were the source of the slave refiner's power and prestige. The slave's domination of his craft placed the master in a dependent position. The refiner was thereby able to compel an exceptional degree of autonomy and control over his work and, despite his servile status, delimit if not challenge the master's authority. As Roughley expressed the generally held opinion, "it will be well for overseers not to chide or check the head boiler much, except a glaring fault occurs in him; he may become despirited, diffident, and careless by so doing." To prevent such friction, an elaborate etiquette marked the interaction between the slave refiner and the white sugar master that expressed the several inequalities in their relationship and the ways in which each was constrained to defer to the other, as Reed illustrates with an example from a Cuban refinery.

The diplomacy that takes place between Sambo and the master is edifying. Some old negro, who may have worked on the estate for twenty years, and who knows all about this particular battery, goes to the teache, when –

taking a little of the syrup between his finger and thumb – he draws it out in a thread, and infers from the appearance of the latter that the juice has been boiled enough. Meantime the sugar master is away though accessible; smoking his cigarette. Sambo tells him the skip is ready; but it would never do for the sugar master to seem to be taught by Sambo. He knows that a few moments will make no practical difference, so he pulls out his watch, and affects to look with much edifying mystery at the dial. At length he lets Pancho, or Pedro, adjust the gutters leading from the teache to the cooler ten feet away, and the skip of emptying the teache is effected.

This ritualized behavior delineates the spheres of authority of the slave refiner and the white sugar master. 'The sugar master defers to the superior practical knowledge of the slave and does not interfere with his activity. The abstract homogeneous time of the watch cannot be abstracted from and imposed back upon a material production process regulated by "natural" time. On the other hand, the illusion of scientific measurement in a totally empirical process upholds the pretense that the slave's expertise is secondary, if not inessential. It masks the social domination that the slave in turn acknowledges by going through the ceremony of the sugar master's making the final decision.[18]

The slaves were not powerless in this game. They carefully prevented the whites from learning the secrets of their trade and protected their position in the production process. If the conventions and usages of the boiling house were violated, the slave refiner had the ultimate sanction at his disposal. "Even in the old times of slavery," recollected Reed, "the master or estate proprietor was obliged to humour his slaves whilst the boiling season lasted . . . should [the boiler] have been spited in any way, he had the means at command for taking revenge out of his owner's sugar. A few tablespoonsful of lemon-juice squeezed into the clarifier, or the grand copper, or the striking teache, and the ruin was accomplished. By this simple process the crystallization of the sugar would be almost completely destroyed. "[19]

The strategic position of the slave refiner calls for a reexamination of the prejudice in favor of the brute character of slave labor that has become almost axiomatic in much historical writing. Moreno Fraginals, for example, suggests that the clarifier was too complicated for slaves to use. However, opening a spigot does not seem to be an overly difficult operation, and deciding when

to turn it off also seems rather straightforward, given the more difficult and subtle judgments regularly made by the slaves in the boiling house. Yet, when it is recognized that with the perfect clarification of the juice, the rest of the refining process would be reduced to the extremely simple operation of evaporation, the argument that the ignorance and awkwardness of the slave made him an obstacle to technological innovation must be seriously questioned. Rather, it becomes at least plausible that the slave's desire to protect established customs and norms in production provided the motive for him to resist such change. To claim that individuals were incapable of performing certain tasks because they were slaves both misreads the historical evidence and misunderstands the nature of social relations, that they really are *relations* and not attributes of individuals. (Still less convincing are attempts to continue this line of argument by ascribing the systemic features of slavery to the characteristics of the slaves: slavery was backward and inefficient because the slaves were backward and inefficient. If one persists in this methodological approach, it is but a short step to the alternative theoretical formulation: the problem was not that the subject population was enslaved but that it was African. While the substantive character of this latter formulation may be disquieting, from a logical point of view it at least has the virtue of avoiding the tautological character of the first proposition.)[20]

In addition to the specialized workers in the mill and the refinery, the sugar estate required the services of carpenters, coopers, smiths, masons, and wheelwrights. The large estates tended to become self-sufficient productive units. It was cheaper for the master to train slaves whose labor was always at his disposal than to hire outsiders to do it. While this practice may have degraded manual labor in society generally, the acquisition of special skills was an important economic and social resource for the slaves. As a consequence of the skilled nature of their work, artisans tended to form a more stable and closed group than the domestics or the field slaves. Apprenticeships were often long and represented a great expenditure that would be lost if the slave were sent back to the fields. Craftsmen whose work was seasonal, such as refiners or coopers, ordinarily assisted the other artisans during periods when their particular skills were not needed. However, they could also find themselves working in the fields, either temporarily, for some special task, or permanently, if they failed to perform their duties to their master's satisfaction. The permanence and stability of the group of artisans depended, among other things, upon the size of the estate, the planting and manufacturing routine, and the patterns of recruitment and formation of the labor force.[21]

The livestock of the estate represented a large portion of the proprietor's capital and were crucial to the operation of the plantation. Tending them was a full-time job. Roughley stressed that the herdsmen should specialize in caring for the cattle and mules in and out of the crop season and not be drafted into other labor. The head cattle and mule men were charged not only with the care of the animals but with their integration into the work process as well. It was their duty to organize the transport of a constant supply of cane from the fields to the mill and to carry the barrels of sugar to the wharf. They had to select the animals most suited to the fields, mill, or roadwork; see to it that proper harnesses and other equipment were ready for them; spell tired animals and have others ready to replace them; keep them fed and rested; and treat their injuries. They were assisted in these duties by cattle and mule boys. These were preferably creole youth who knew how to lead and yoke cattle and ride and tackle mules. Each boy was charged with the care, harnessing, and working of a number of individual animals assigned to him. The head cattle and mule men had to keep close check not only on the animals but also on the men in their charge. Carters were noted for pilfering the sugar and rum they carried down to the wharf or the supplies, especially salt, they carried back up to the estate. Similarly, mule drivers were notorious for taking mules off the property or using them for private purposes. It was the responsibility of the head mule and cattle men to exercise vigilance and prevent these practices.[22]

Finally, the planters' love of luxury and desire for prestige could swell the ranks of domestic servants. The duties of the house slaves included cleaning, cooking, sewing, laundering, and other domestic chores such as making clothes for slaves without wives. On a large plantation, the master and each member of his family ordinarily had their own personal servant. The rest of the household staff typically included a cook, two washerwomen, two or three seamstresses, and two or three women to run errands. The domestics were generally creoles born on the property, and mulatto girls were favored for household chores. These slaves had opportunities for better quality food, clothing, and shelter for themselves and their families as well as having less arduous work to do than did the field slaves. Household slaves had closer personal contact with the master and his family and were thereby both in a position to win rewards by gaining their favor and more exposed to their caprice. For many, household service was a road to freedom. Perhaps because of closer personal relations with the master and a greater opportunity to amass savings, domestics were often given their freedom or were able to save enough to purchase it. However, Gabriel Debien, in his study of the plantation "l'Anse-à-l'Ane" in the eighteenth century, suggests that more typical were household slaves who served faithfully without attempting to gain their freedom, knowing that they would be treated as freed upon reaching their sixtieth birthdays.[23]

The craftsmen, mechanics, and domestic servants formed what were in many respects privileged groups among the slaves, and their presence increased the internal differentiation within the slave population. They commonly lived apart from the other slaves and enjoyed better food, housing, and clothing. There were considerable avenues for mobility between' groups of slaves on the plantation. Slaves could pass from the fields into domestic service, a path particularly open to females, or if one were particularly talented or intelligent, to apprenticeship in a trade. Jamaican planter Monk Lewis suggests that mulatto children were always employed as craftsmen if male or as domestics if female, but never as field hands. On the other hand, Orlando Patterson, basing his conclusions on several Jamaican sources, cautions that field hands preferred the independence and stability of their position to the constant daily contact with the master and the insecurity of domestic service. Craft labor, however, appears to have been universally aspired to. The advantages that these groups of slaves enjoyed may have created an ambivalent but not necessarily conservative response to the slave system on their part. For if they had privileges to protect, intimate contact with the master and his family gave them insights into the nature and limits of power while it exposed them to the arbitrariness and eccentricity of those in authority. Indeed, the contradiction between individual dignity and self-worth, on the one hand, and slave status, on the other, may have been experienced more palpably by these slaves than others as numerous and varied acts of poisoning, arson, and revolt committed by them throughout the Americas attest.[24]

Rhythms of Work: Economy of Time

The sugar plantation engaged the slaves in a year-round cycle of work that followed the rhythm of the crop. Planting and harvesting dominated the agricultural year and defined its division. However, the agrarian rhythm formed by this alternation was not simply natural but rather was manipulated to make full use of the productive capacity of the slave gang over the entire course of the planting and harvest seasons. As has been discussed previously, the slaves had to be supported by the estate whether they were working or not, but they contributed to its revenue only while they were engaged in commodity production. In addition, idle hands were the enemy of every slaveowner, and maintaining discipline and regular work habits among the slaves was their constant concern. Consequently, an agricultural routine was adopted that minimized the effects of the natural seasonal break while the crop matured and kept the slaves continuously engaged in sugar production throughout the year. The rotation of the fields was carefully planned so that over the 15-18 month maturation period of the sugar cane the planting of one crop could be constantly alternated with the harvesting of a previous crop. Planting and harvesting the crop each took place over the course of a period of several months, and one followed upon the other as quickly as possible. In this way, the planter was able to make greater use of the productive potential of the slave labor force and to obtain an annual crop while increasing the yield within the natural limits of the planting and harvest seasons.[25]

The demand for labor was most intensive during the harvest season, but even in the so-called dead season between harvests the slaves were kept continually busy with a variety of tasks essential to the operation of the plantation.

These included not only planting and caring for the cane but also auxiliary tasks (*petits travaux*) such as clearing new fields; planting provisions; carrying manure to the fields; ditching; building and maintaining roads, buildings, and animal pens; cleaning canals; building and repairing carts; and other types of repairs and maintenance. If these jobs were not enough to keep the slaves occupied, new work was created for them. Such a routine encouraged the generalization rather than the specialization of slave labor. Individual slaves were constantly shifted from one task to another and thus acquired a broad range of general skills, but at the same time the development of the division of labor on the plantation and therefore the collective level of skill and the productive capacity of the slave gang as a group was retarded. Furthermore, although the dead season was in principle less demanding than the harvest season, this regime harnessed the slaves to a pattern of year-round drudgery that dulled their incentive and efficiency and exposed them to the burdens of prolonged fatigue and overwork. This situation was aggravated when heavy rains or extended periods of drought impeded work during the off-season. There then followed a push to make up for lost time and to complete these tasks before the harvest season renewed its claims on the full energy of the labor force.[26]

The unit of labor time in the Caribbean sugar colonies was the day. This was a variable, natural unit of measurement lasting from sunrise to sunset. Marking the length of the parts of the working day depended upon the overseer's judgment. Beyond the technical problem of measurement, this could lead to conflict between the overseer, who was under pressure to produce as much sugar as possible, and the master, who, particularly after the abolition of the slave trade, wished to protect the well-being of his slaves. The divisions of the day were signaled by the crack of the overseer's whip, the blowing of a whistle or conch shell, or, more rarely on large plantations, the ringing of a bell. Mechanical timekeeping was conspicuous by its absence in the French Antilles. Indeed, even bells were scarce, and the elaborate system utilizing the clerical hours of the church bells to mark the working day. described by Moreno Fraqinals for Cuba, appears to have been unknown in Martinique. According to Schoelcher's description: "The whip is the bell of the plantations. It announces the moment of awakening and that of retirement. The whip marks the hour of work, and also it marks the hour of rest. It is to the sound of the whip that punishes the guilty that the people of the plantation are assembled morning and evening for prayer. The day of death is the only one where the slave enjoys respite without being awakened by the whip." Domination and time, symbol and act, are joined and woven into the texture of everyday life. Through the whip, emblem of the planter's authority and the physical subjugation of the slave, the temporal organization of the plantation is imposed upon the lives of the enslaved as an external and alien demand.[27]

In the French colonies, work in the fields before sunrise and after sunset as well as from noon until two in the afternoon for whatever reason was forbidden by law. Although it was sometimes attempted during the harvest season, fieldwork done in the dark was both dangerous and difficult to supervise, and this legislation more or less coincided with common practice in the colonies, according to Baron Mackau, a former governor of Martinique. In order to take maximum advantage of the daylight hours, the slaves were awakened before dawn. After assembly for communal prayers, roll call, and the assignment of the day's tasks, they went off to the fields, accompanied by the overseer (économe) and the drivers (commandeurs). The slaves' workday began between 5:00 and 6:00 a.m. with the rising of the sun. At eight or nine o'clock, they stopped work for between 3 0 and 4 5 minutes while breakfast was brought to them in the fields. Work was then resumed and lasted until midday. Work in the fields was avoided during the hottest part of the day, and the slaves had the time from noon until two o'clock to themselves in order to eat and rest. The slaves were free to return to their cabins, and many of them devoted this time to cultivating their private garden plots or provision grounds if these were located near enough to the fields. At two o'clock, they were summoned back for the afternoon work session, which lasted until five o'clock in the summer and sunset in the winter. At the end of the workday, and sometimes during the midday break as well, each slave was required to pick up a bundle of guinea grass for fodder for the animals and carry it back to the animal pens. There was a final assembly and an evening prayer, though this was not as regular or

as formal as the morning assembly. The remaining time belonged to the slaves. Each household prepared its own evening meal. The slaves were then relatively free, and all that was required for the remainder of the evening was that general order and tranquillity be maintained.[28]

Thus, the effective working day spent in the fields normally lasted between nine and ten hours, depending upon the amount of daylight. Further, the technical division of labor left gaps in the working day, and Schoelcher reported that there was much more give and take in the time discipline of the sugar plantations in Martinique than in a European factory. Not infrequently he witnessed the afternoon work session begin at 2:15 or 2:20 rather than at 2:00 p.m. In addition, many planters, especially after the end of the slave trade, were very attentive to rest periods and meals and thought them to be essential for the efficiency and well-being of their *ateliers*. However, to the time spent in fieldwork must be added the time spent going to and from the work site and carrying fodder. At the time of the passage of the Law of July 18, 1845, Mackau argued that, contrary to common usage, this time should not be taken out of the slaves' rest periods, while a growing number of planters thought that carrying fodder merely added to the fatigue of the slaves after a long day's work and ought to be given over to a special gang. Nevertheless, both pro- and antislavery commentators agreed that this regime did not make excessive demands on the strength and health of the slaves even in the tropical climate. In Schoelcher's words, "The slaves do what they must, and today the masters demand no more of them than they can do."[29]

The "natural" agrarian rhythm of the daily plantation routine was interrupted during the harvest season when the industrial character of sugar manufacture emerged and revealed its dominion over the organization of the entire crop cycle. The harvest season (*roulaison*) was the busiest time of the year and mobilized the entire labor force of the plantation. "The work of making sugar from cane juice is most anxious," warns Reed. "It admits of no irregularity, no laziness. The crop being ripe will not wait long without deterioration, and the juice once expressed will not keep twenty minutes without fermenting if proper treatment not be followed." During this period, the legal restrictions on the working day were suspended, and the slaves were harnessed to the continuous mechanical movement of the mill and the flow of the boiling house, where work went on ceaselessly around the clock.[30]

Both the Royal Ordinance of October 15, 1786, which regulated the length of the working day, and the Law of July 18, 1845, which supplemented it, explicitly distinguished between ordinary work and the extraordinary circumstances of the sugar harvest, which absolutely demanded continuity of work, and specifically excluded the latter from the normal prohibitions. The Law of July 18, 1845, or the Mackau Law, as it was known, attempted to limit the working day to the period between six in the morning and six in the evening under ordinary circumstances and required rest periods totaling two- and-one-half hours during this time. During the harvest season, when continuous labor was necessary, the maximum amount of labor time could be prolonged by two hours and the hours of work could be transferred from the day to the night, so long as the legal maximum was not exceeded during each 24-hour period and the obligatory rest periods were observed. If work was required during days or hours when it was not obligatory, this legislation prescribed a minimum salary of 10 centimes per hour or 5 francs per month for both male and female slaves.[31]

In some parts of Martinique, attention had to be devoted entirely to sugar production to the exclusion of other activities during the harvest season. Sainte Croix has left an account of the division of labor and number of slaves involved in the harvest on a plantation producing 450 hogsheads of sugar annually. Twenty slaves, supervised by the économe and the commandeurs, cut the cane. In half a day, 20 cutters could cut about 10 grandes of cane. (A grande was the quantity of cane necessary to provide enough juice to fill the grande, the largest kettle in the boiling train. Thus, the grande served as the measure of both the amount of cane and the volume of juice. One grande yielded enough syrup for seven or eight formes of raw sugar weighing between 52, and 54 livres.) The 20 cane-cutters required 10 other slaves to handle the cut stalks and load them on the mules or oxcarts to be transported to the mill. Eight or 10 mule drivers or two or three men driving oxcarts were necessary to keep the cane flowing quickly

and steadily to the mill. During this period, the maximum effort was demanded of the slave gang, and work in the fields was often prolonged until total darkness made it impossible to continue.[32]

While the available daylight limited work in the fields, this was not the case in the mill and the refinery. During the harvest, night work and work on Sundays was a necessity, and an enormous strain was placed on the work force, especially on large plantations. Although night work seems to have been exceptional on small and medium plantations, on large estates work in the refinery continued around the clock without interruption. In order to maintain this effort, the atelier was divided into three groups called quarts. According to Sainte Croix, on successive days each of these was rotated from the fields to the mill and the refinery, where work went on around the clock in 7½-hour shifts. Ideally, the slaves worked one night every five to eight days depending upon the size of the gang. Sainte Croix suggests that 150 slaves were necessary to organize a complete system of shifts and to make sure that no slave worked more than 7½ hours a day in the mill. Planters with fewer slaves had to restrict themselves to manufacturing sugar only during the day. However, this was an exceptionally large number of active workers for Martinique, and other sources indicate that around-the-clock shifts were carried on with smaller complements of slaves.[33]

This schedule placed an enormous physical burden on the slaves. Depending upon the size of the gang and the schedule of rotation, a full day's work in the fields during the most demanding period of the year could be followed by a shift in the mill or the refinery at night as well. During the harvest season, 18-20 hours of intensive effort without a break was not uncommon. The refiners in particular were subjected to long and exhausting hours in order to guarantee the continuity of the manufacturing process. The need to supervise the preparation and application of the temper, the continual skimming of the kettles, and striking the sugar required their constant attention day and night. This unrelenting pace could continue for weeks on end. The exhausting veilliés, as the night shifts were known, led to fatigue, and negligence and mistakes that threatened both sugar and men were inevitable. The result was often horrible accidents, as tired and overworked slaves got a hand or arm caught in the cylinders of the mill or fell into the cauldrons of boiling cane juice.[34]

Despite the enormous and prolonged effort demanded of the slaves, crop time also had its rewards and was the high point of the agricultural year. "Even in the days of slavery," writes Reed, it "has been described as a period of mingled hard work and hilarity, during which man and beast – animals even to swine – grow fat." This was particularly true on small and medium plantations where there was no night work. As compensation for their extra efforts during this season, the slaves were given a ration of sugar and syrup, and the harvest afforded ample opportunity for the slaves to supplement this ration on their own initiative as well. The end of the harvest was an occasion for feasting and dancing. Money was given to the slaves according to their ability to work. Sheep were slaughtered and divided among the slaves, as were vegetables, syrup, and other rewards. The celebration culminated with two days of dancing.[35]

Superimposed on the agricultural calendar was the religious calendar. The Edict of 1685 (the *Codenoir*) and the Royal Ordinance of 1786 exempted the slaves from labor on Sundays and holidays, and, according to all available accounts, these provisions were generally observed. There were, however, fewer religious holidays in the colonies than in France. In prerevolutionary Saint-Domingue, Dutrône calculated that 52 Sundays and 16 feast days, in addition to about *17* rainy days, left the planter with 280 work days a year. (This compares with Kuczynski's figure of 250 days for an ancient régime France and 300 days for Protestant Britain.) After the French Revolution, divine virtues gave way to secular ones, and the number of religious holidays was reduced to four: Christmas, Ascension Day, Assumption, and All Saints' Day. In addition, the slaves were customarily given all or part of Saturday off in order to work in their own gardens and grow their own food. These regulations were suspended during the harvest season, when the demands of production were continuous. The days remaining after these exemptions were deducted were available for the work of the plantation.[36]

The temporal requirements of sugar production coincided imperfectly with the social relations of slavery. The intensive overwork of the

harvest combined with other periods when there was little to do and the work routines were much more flexible. There was careful time discipline, but time was not an abstract and homogeneous standard external to the processes of material production. Instead, time was determined by the physical requirements of sugar making. Indeed, the measurement of tasks by the *grande* – a necessarily imprecise measure depending upon the relationship between the amount of cane cut, ground, and boiled-suggests the domination of physical processes over the temporal organization of the labor process. Under these conditions, economy of time could mean only that the "natural" temporal limits of these processes were extended and more juice was processed more quickly. However, the rationalization of labor time was not possible. There was no economy of labor time. Instead, the laborers had to be regimented to perform the given tasks at hand.

Because the labor force was appropriated as slaves, the number of workers and the quantity of labor time available over the crop cycle were fixed, and the potential output was limited. Under these circumstances, and particularly as changing market conditions put a greater premium on efficiency, there was pressure on planters to manage the time at their disposal effectively. According to Dutrône: "This sum of the working days and the force of the Negroes being determined, their product is also necessarily determined. From this it is easy to see that the time which is lost by not seizing what could be done in the day is lost forever. The Master who governs must handle [*ménager*] time and the force of his Negroes with the greatest care and make the best use of them." Already in the second half of the eighteenth century, the planters in the French Caribbean demonstrated a concern with the systematic measurement and regulation of the activities of the slaves and the rationalization of sugar production. Dutrône pioneered the attempt to establish precise technical control over the labor process. In monthly and annual tables, he kept a careful daily inventory of the number of slaves and their age, sex, occupation, and condition. He then followed each step in the process of sugar production and recorded the number of slaves employed in each department of the plantation, the amount of work done each day in each sector, and information on temperature and rainfall as well as on the final product and its price. The master could then follow in detail the particular and the general movement of the labor force and compare one year with another, while absentee owners could have an exact account of their operations. Dutrône's method of organization was influential not only in the French sugar colonies but also in Cuba, Brazil, and elsewhere, and it served as a model for the elaboration of more refined and precise systems of management that were developed during the nineteenth century.[37]

Various authors have interpreted this concern for the rationalization of the slave labor process, particularly on the sugar plantation, as anticipating the purposes and techniques of modern management, especially Taylorism. Aufhauser, for example, stresses that contrary to conventional belief, both the slave plantation and the modern factory offer similar conditions for the application of management techniques, and he enthusiastically identifies task-work on the slave plantation, which establishes daily quotas for each worker, with time-motion studies in the modern factory.

The efforts to keep up the accustomed routine were facilitated by the existence of work that could be divided into distinct tasks. Instructions to overseers read like Taylor's directions in the Midvale Steel Company. First, reduce everything to system; second, introduce daily accountability in every department. Work teams were designed and made responsible for the completion of specific tasks; if the job was not satisfactory, the team would be punished the next day with more arduous labors. ... The slave plantation shared with modern industry the technological prerequisites for systematic task work: a large number of very simple operations amenable to time-motion studies. This circumstance both explains why the routine of the plantation seemed anomalous to contemporary observers and why it so closely resembles modern management techniques.

According to Aufhauser, the slaveowners, like Taylor, had to rely on a "strict system of rules, laws, and formulae" to guarantee strict labor control. For both, constant supervision was necessary because individual initiative could not be relied upon to increase productivity. The common denominator of both systems is that the workers, whether slave or free, are lazy and inefficient.[38]

However, while these two types of labor management share many apparent similarities, and there is arguably an important historical connection between them, their resemblance is superficial and can be misleading. They are constituted within extremely different processes and relations, and they lead to opposite results. Leaving aside its general applicability on the slave plantation, which will be discussed in more detail below, task work, far from establishing the similarity between slave and wage labor, illustrates their difference.

The techniques of modern management have radically restructured the organization of the labor process and transformed the nature of work. They have seized upon the individual actions of workers and reduced them to abstract activity. The labor process has been fragmented, and the activity of the worker engaged in production has been broken down into its constituent elements. The division of labor has been altered, and the activities of work recomposed under the control of the manager in order to increase the productivity of the socialized laborer. In this context, time-motion studies have attempted to subordinate the activity of the wage worker to an objective standard of productivity. With the development of the detail division of labor, the knowledge, skill, and subjective capacities of each worker have come to count for less and less. Space for individual initiative in production is sharply delimited, and every laborer must adapt his action to the objective organization of the production process. Abstract social labor appears to each worker as an external standard, and the individual characteristics of each laborer are subordinated to it, while the wage secures the continuity of effort for the duration of the entire working day.

Slaveowners, on the contrary, regimented a preestablished number of individual workers to perform within a technically predetermined structure of production. The technical organization appeared as something given, immutable, and external, and labor was adapted to it. Thus, an examination of eighteenth- and nineteenth-century sugar manuals reveals that characteristically the planters were considerably more preoccupied with the technical problems of sugar production than with questions of slave management. The purpose of task-work on the slave plantation was to to create some interest for the slave in executing the labor of the estate and subjectively to bind him to the performance of his work. Task-work quotas were assigned to each individual in the *atelier* on the basis of the amount of work customarily performed by the average adult slave in a day. The slaves could do the job when they pleased and were free to enjoy the time remaining after its completion for their own use. The organization of the division of labor on the estate thus remained intact, and the planter surrendered control over the actual execution of the work in order to obtain the regular application of a fixed amount of labor during a given period of time. But, without the wage relation, both to bind the worker to his job for the entire duration of the working day and to offer him the promise of a higher monetary reward for his efforts, the only inducement slavery could offer was a reduction in the hours of compulsory labor. With the task system, an industrious slave could get some free time each day to work in his garden or at some other job for his own benefit, while for his part, the planter guaranteed the performance of a minimal amount of work during this period. But the productive force of labor was not modified at all.[39]

Domination, Hierarchy, and Labor Discipline

Slavery remained a crude and coercive form of extracting labor. The property relation was the necessary condition for the slave labor process, but it by no means guaranteed that the slaves would work. The actual expenditure of slave labor was dependent upon and organized through the explicit domination of the slaveowner. Although the slaveowner could appropriate the capacity of the slave gang to work collectively, the slave relation provided no systemic incentive for the individual workers to prolong the duration or increase the intensity of their activity. For the slaves, labor was perpetual drudgery without reward. Their needs were reduced to a minimum, and meeting them was independent of their labor in the canefields. As Schoelcher observed,

If he [the slave] puts one or two more arpents of land under cultivation, I clearly see the increase of his effort, but I search in vain for the increase in his well-being. Let us admit it, to bend down each day to a job without pay, to remain a stranger to a greater abundance that one has created, is a situation that must lead to indifference ... In compensation for the five full days of labor given by him to his master, the slave, on the whole ... really only has the right to work the sixth in order to gain his nourishment for the entire week!

The activity of work could only be an alien imposition under slavery. The slave could be compensated for production, but he could not be made self-interested in production itself. There could be trade-offs in exchange for work (consistent with the maintenance of domination and the property relation), but there is nothing in work itself that could ever reward the slave.[40]

Slavery created indifference to work among the slaves, and they gave their labor reluctantly. "The Negro in the Antilles," wrote Schoelcher,

shows no ardor for work. It is repugnant to him precisely because he is forced to do it. He does not hurry because he gains nothing by hurrying. Forced to give all of his time, he gives the least effort possible. It is completely straightforward. . . . It necessarily sets up a struggle between the master and the slave. The latter seeks to give little because as much as he withholds effort is he spared from fatigue. The former seeks to get a great deal because as much extra as the other does is gained for his benefit. Is it surprising that the Negro does not at all like steady, perpetual work for the profit and at the will of others? How could this work have the least attraction in his eyes since the whole harvest is for another? The feeling of no personal advantage being attached to the results of the task that is imposed upon him, it is completely natural that this task is odious to him or at least indifferent.

There were, of course, a variety of individual adaptations to slave labor, but, if the Afro-Caribbean slave was integrated into the productive mechanism of the sugar plantation and adjusted his behavior to its routines, this by no means implied the internalization of the norms and values of a European "work ethic" nor the mere imitation of planter desires, beliefs, or behavior. The slave was too often an apathetic and untrustworthy worker. Even "good" slaves could not be trusted by their masters, and practices such as malingering and feigning illness were common among them. However, the slave was not simply a lazy, inept, or unproductive worker. Rather, such behavior, where it existed, was engendered by the social relations of slavery. The productive force of slave labor (and thus the relative efficiency of the plantation system) rested upon its collective and cooperative character, while the motivation of individual slaves was retarded. The same process that created the image of paternalism and conspicuous consumption on the side of the master created the image of the lazy Negro on the side of the slave.[41]

Under these conditions, constant surveillance and at least the threat of punishment were required to secure the minimal performance of the slaves' duties. Collins stresses this necessity:

To one point you ought particularly to attend, and never let it escape from your memory, that a negro is an instrument, which requires to be incessantly acted upon to the performance of its duty. Whenever work is to be done, your white servants ought to see that it is done, and not to satisfy themselves with giving orders to the negroes, and trusting to their memories for the execution; for it is ten to one but that they forget it, and by that means incur your displeasure; and it is certainly, in all cases, more pleasant to prevent an offence than to punish the commission of it. The neglect of this rule is the occasion of many severities, which, with a little attention, might easily be avoided.

A hierarchical staff of supervisors was required to organize the work process on the sugar plantation and discipline the workers. Through them the master's antagonistic demand for surplus production was imposed on the slave labor force. Their job was to coordinate the activity of the slave gang and to see to it that the energies of the slaves were put to the master's best advantage. The presupposition and the goal of their activity was not a responsible and self-acting worker, but an automaton integrated into a collective mechanism. "You cannot resign him to the guidance of his own discretion," continued Collins, "but like a soldier in the ranks, he must be a mere machine, without will or motion, other than you impress upon him."[42]

The planter, of course, was at the top of the plantation hierarchy. He personified power on the estate. All of its activities were subordinated to his control, and he was the source of all authority. But he in turn had to conform to the requirements of the market and the technical conditions of sugar production. The sugar plantation as a commercial enterprise formed an impersonal productive apparatus that translated the planter's personal dominion over the slaves into a concern with extracting the necessary quantity, type, and intensity of labor as he sought to obtain the optimal effort of the collectivity within the prevailing technical conditions. The result was the objectification and instrumentalization of the laborers, which was secured by direct domination and force. "That the population in his power adopts regular habits is the last concern of a planter," lamented Schoelcher. "He only sees, he is only able to see instruments of labor in the negroes, and provided that they make a lot of sugar, he is happy. The rest does not concern

him. On the contrary, the less the slaves pass from the crude state of nature, the less they are to be feared and the less they appear worthy of liberty. Everything that the slaves have acquired in servitude, they owe only to themselves. The masters have never done anything in this respect. What use would it have had for them?"[43]

If the planter was an absentee, the *géreur*, or administrator, was responsible for the overall operation of the estate. If there was an administrator, he lived on the plantation, either in the big house or in a separate house with his family, if they were in the colony. Unlike the subordinate whites who came and went, he often remained in his position for a long period of time. He maintained a regular correspondence with the owner to whom he was responsible. "His task," according to Debien, "is to squeeze the agricultural and industrial machine by every means possible in order to increase the yield. His activity is translated abroad by numbers. He thus can be pitiless if he decides that the principal goal of his position is to ship the most hogsheads of sugar that he can."[44]

Next in rank were the *économes*, or overseers, who were in charge of the practical day-to-day work of the plantation. The head overseer was responsible for keeping a record of births, deaths, accidents, and the condition of the animals, equipment, and provisions, as well as of the work performed each day. He had to keep an eye on the animals, the fields, the provision grounds, the slave cabins, and the condition of the mill, the refinery, and the storehouses. But above all he was entrusted with supervising the slaves. With the exception of the domestics, the overseers were in charge of all the slaves of the estate, including the artisans and the sick as well as the agricultural workers. Beyond directing their work, the overseers administered rations and were generally responsible for the good order of the slaves.[45]

This was an extremely important position. The overseer could make or break the estate. The master or the *géreur* was often far removed from the direct management of slaves, and the overseer was the one directly responsible for them. He had to be familiar with the individual characteristics and condition of every slave in the gang. He had to know their character, the state of their health, and their physical capacity in order to coordinate their efforts and utilize their labor most effectively. The job was demanding and required constant activity day and night, especially during the harvest season. Early each morning, he had to tour the plantation to survey the progress of the work and plan the disposition of his forces with the care and precision of a military commander, while his nights were often spent watching over the sugar making and the activities of the slaves in the refinery. The life was hard, and the pay low. According to Hilliard d'Auberteuil of Saint Domingue, talent and good conduct were not enough. The job required physical and mental toughness and preferably a sufficiently imposing physique to command the respect of the slaves.[46]

The overseers were at the point of confrontation between the master's drive for surplus production and his demand for the maintenance of social control, on the one side, and the recalcitrance of the slaves, on the other. The difficulty of their situation could affect the way that they handled the slaves. They were callous and unrelenting toward the slaves. They often believed themselves capable of accomplishing any task, and, if the master or administrator did not watch over them, they were capable of pushing the slaves without regard for fatigue. A few weeks of this treatment could disrupt the slave gang, upsetting their habitual routine and harassing them without any effect. The slave gang then responded with bad will, working slowly and under the force of the whip, when that had not been necessary before. The overseer was recalled and a new one brought in. The process then began all over again.[47]

Beneath the *économes* in authority were the slave *commandeurs,* or drivers. Laborie, a planter from Saint Domingue, described the driver as the "soul of the plantation." Slaves themselves, the drivers were responsible for the immediate control of the field hands, but not for the workers in the mill or the refinery or for the carters, who had their own supervisors. The drivers directed the execution of the tasks performed by the slave gang and regulated the pace of the work. Each morning it was the responsibility of the head driver to assemble the slaves, report the missing and sick to the overseer, and then accompany the gang to the fields. The drivers carried to the fields the two great emblems of their rank, the whip and an iron-tipped staff on which to lean while supervising the day's tasks.

These symbolized both their authority and their exemption from physical labor and clearly delineated them from the body of the slaves. On large estates, it was frequently the head driver who calculated the amount of work to be done during each morning and afternoon session and designated which slaves were to be assigned to which jobs. If inclement weather retarded the work, the driver had the power to decide whether to try to wait out the storm or simply suspend work for the day. However, if, under certain circumstances, the driver could reduce the assigned task, he could not increase it or substitute one job for another once the overseer had made his decision. Each evening the drivers reported the progress of the day's work to the *économe* to be recorded in the plantation log. The information included such details as the weather, the number of slaves present for the various tasks in the morning and the afternoon, those slaves who were sick, those assigned to extraordinary work outside of the fields, and the number or the name of the cane pieces where the *atelier* had worked, as well as runaways, serious quarrels, punishments, accidents, and unmanageable slaves. In the evening and on Sundays when there was no work to be done, they were charged with maintaining order and tranquillity in the slave quarters and with keeping an eye on the comings and goings and general behavior of the slaves. The driver was of crucial importance for the smooth operation of the *atelier* and the economic success of the estate, and the planters had to exercise great care in their selection and training. "Good order in the *atelier,*" wrote one planter, "depends absolutely on the intelligence, good conduct, activity and firmness of the *commandeurs.* A good *commandeur* is a rare man and of inestimable value."[48]

Physical coercion remained an integral part of the organization of the slave labor process. Ultimately, the exploitation of slave labor rested upon the threat of compulsion, and the slave was exposed to the daily possibility of violence. Force created and sustained the slave as property and as the instrument of labor and was in turn shaped and sustained by the slave relation. But the use of this force was not arbitrary or capricious. On the one hand, it was the means of organizing and animating labor and establishing industrial discipline; on the other hand, it was embedded within and constrained by the purposes, organization, and requirements of production itself. Thus, as many authors have indicated, the treatment of the slaves was restrained by the economic self-interest of the master. But the apparent and carefully constructed rationality of the slaveholder as selfinterested economic man could quickly show its other face, irrational violence. If the economic self-interest of the master provided the motive to care for the material well-being of the slave, it by no means guaranteed it. This self-interest was inscribed within and operated through an explicit system of domination that had its own logic. The planter had to maintain control over a broad range of activities of social life in order to guarantee production, and at any point the fabric that held together domination and material production could rupture. If domination failed to function as an effective means of labor discipline, it could easily become an end in itself and disrupt both production and property.[49]

Slave discipline in the French Antilles underwent considerable amelioration during the July Monarchy, and some of the more brutal aspects of the slave regime were removed. Reports from magistrates sent to inspect the plantations commented almost universally on the moderation of discipline and the mildness of punishments, at least in comparison with earlier conditions. Yet, it remained a harsh system, and the whip played a central and perhaps expanding role in the organization of colonial production and the maintenance of order throughout the last decades of the slave period. While a handful of planters experimented with various other means of securing the cooperation of their laborers and enforcing discipline without corporal punishment, the great majority of the planter class defended the whip as the only means of compelling labor from the slaves. It was the most common means of punishing laziness, insubordination, or any serious breach of discipline. The whip was particularly suited to the conditions prevailing after the abolition of the slave trade, as it could be used to inflict punishment without necessarily causing permanent injury. According to one source: "Previously, during the period when the health and the life of the slaves had less pecuniary value, anything went to punish those miserable creatures. Since the abolition (of the slave trade] the creoles have been given this problem to solve: How to make a guilty Negro suffer with-

out making him seriously ill or killing him. They believe that they have found the answer to it in the whip. Today it is the punishment inflicted on the slaves for every type of fault." The whip was regarded as an essential element of labor discipline, and the threat of its use and abuse was always present. In Schoelcher's words: "The whip is an integral part of the colonial regime. It is its principal agent. It is its soul . . . The whip, in a word, is the expression of work in the Antilles. If one wanted to symbolize the colonies such as they still are, it would be necessary to stack a sugar cane stalk together with the driver's whip."[50]

The *Code noir* gave masters the power to beat their slaves with a rod or cord if they thought that a slave deserved it. But from 1783 onward in Martinique, the number of lashes a master could give a slave was fixed at 29, except for a brief period when 50 were allowed. While some planters protested this legal restriction as an infringement on their absolute authority and right to property as well as a threat to public safety, this number allowed the infliction of an ample amount of pain. As Schoelcher testified: "The force of the executioner depends upon the humanity of the master. If he so wishes, twenty-nine blows of the whip will not produce any effect, but, if it is desired, the most robust man can be disabled for six months with only fifteen." Indeed, the case of Braffin, a planter who severely injured four of his slaves without exceeding the legal maximum number of lashes, is evidence of the potential for violence and physical harm that might be inflicted on the enslaved within the limit of the law. Further, even if punishments were normally "mild," the slaves had little formal protection and few recourses from abuses by the master or his staff. Yet, while the colonial court records more than enough examples of excessive brutality (and paltry success in prosecuting them), such cases were the exception.[51]

The magistrates who inspected the plantations in Martinique during the 1840s reported that the use of the whip was "moderate" and becoming increasingly mild throughout the colony. In general, the slaves were whipped only enough to maintain good discipline. Punishments did not ordinarily go beyond 10 or 15 lashes, and only in the most serious offenses did they reach the legal maximum of 29. Excessive punishment might create more problems among the *atelier* than it solved, and the master ran the risk of injuring his property. Further, as Gutman has argued, the significance of whipping as an instrument of labor discipline is not only its effect on the recipient of the blows but also its social visibility among the other slaves. According to Schoelcher, half of the slaves in the rural gangs in the French Antilles had never felt the lash. Intimidation was sufficient to ensure adequate behavior.[52]

Discipline was generally milder on small plantations than on large ones. The master usually lived in close proximity with the slaves, and frequently there was no driver. According to contemporary sources, corporal punishment was unknown on a great many small estates. Prisons, irons, and even the whip were not used. Instead, the master carried a sort of heavy riding crop (*rigoise*) and used it to administer punishment. Self-interest, proximity to the slaves and familiarity with them, and relatively mild demands on labor served to check brutality and excessive punishment. It was frequently reported that often reprimands alone sufficed to discipline the slaves, and the number of lashes only rarely attained the legal maximum. However, routines and duties were less clearly defined on small estates, and the slaves were more directly exposed to the personal eccentricities of the master. One official warned that the very informality prevailing on many small plantations could cause discipline to become capricious and irregular. The master might tolerate misbehavior for a long time without reproach, and suddenly explode in anger for a frivolous cause. Punishments could then become severe without any motive, and give way to unrestrained brutality on the part of the master.[53]

In contrast, discipline on large plantations was both more severe and more regular. Whipping could be authorized by the master, the administrator, or the overseer, and the number of blows varied with the offense. Serious offenses were always punished some time after they were committed. These cases were decided by the master or the administrator. On well-run estates, great effort was made to ensure that duties were clearly delineated and that punishments were regular, calculable, impersonal, and in proportion to the offense. According to one report: "On a large plantation, an offense almost never goes unpun-

ished. But before inflicting the punishment, the master reflects. He thinks. It is a guarantee that the punishment be just and measured. Furthermore, on each large plantation there is a code based on custom which sanctions certain penalties for habitual offenses." Another report elaborates this point. The slave "knows his duties. He is subject to an invariable rule and knows in advance the punishment that will result from his error. The contact not being immediate, the punishment is administered without passion or anger." Indeed, on some estates punishment was sufficiently rationalized that there was a formal set of written rules and punishments.[54]

The drivers on large estates were also given a considerable amount of discretionary power in administering punishment. In the fields, the *commandeurs* were normally authorized to give between four and seven lashes without the master's permission in cases that demanded immediate attention. The planters and overseers realized that these slaves bore direct responsibility for the regular performance of the most difficult tasks and needed this authority in order to maintain the continuity of the production process. Thus, it was the drivers who most frequently used the whip to enforce labor discipline. However, the planters' ability to regulate the actions of these subordinates who were subject to pressures to produce and a relation to property and production very different from those of the planter was an important problem. Their power to punish could easily escape the planter's control. Necessary autonomy could become misuse and at worst degenerate into private vendettas with the slaves.[55]

Yet, physical coercion alone provided insufficient motivation for the slaves. It produced sullen and recalcitrant slaves who worked only because of the threat of punishment and did only enough work to avoid punishment. According to Schoelcher: "The whip, or rather the threat of the whip is almost the sole stimulus of a slave. It is very conceivable that he only does exactly what is necessary to escape the whip." Some sign of encouragement or favor or small rewards of food or clothing from the plantation's stores for obedience or good work were necessary to temper fear of the lash and obtain some degree of goodwill and cooperation from the slaves. By themselves, such "positive incentives" were at best of limited effectiveness and needed to be backed up by the threat of coercion. If individuals or groups of slaves responded favorably to such rewards, the degree of voluntary cooperation thus obtained was circumscribed and uncertain. Nevertheless, by the 1830s a growing number of planters were attempting to move beyond overt physical coercion and develop more effective means of labor discipline and social control. On many estates, the use of the whip was reduced or abolished. Instead, for ordinary offenses, slaves were confined in the plantation hospital or a special detention cell during the night, assigned extra work during their free time, or not allowed to go to town on the weekend. Similarly, one planter testified that fines were a more effective means of discipline than the whip, the chain, or detention, and the latter were to be used sparingly. "When . . . one of my Negroes [acquires] some savings, he is in my control from then on. Pride and self-love dominate him, and the desire to protect what is his makes him more careful and rarely at fault. If one of my slaves steals a day or more of work from me or commits some injury to one of his comrades, he owes a reparation and [must] repay the damage. His savings diminish, and that is the most severe punishment of all for him." The slaves feared such penalties more than corporal punishment. One magistrate expressed the general opinion: "These means of correction which are less shocking to humanity are also more effective. There are few Negroes who would not prefer to receive a considerable number of strokes of the whip than pass the night confined."[56]

Measures such as these suggest the limits of pure coercion as a means of enforcing labor discipline. Their success was dependent upon the integration of the enslaved population into the productive and social system. For them to work, both master and slave had to recognize the existence of certain privileges and at least a limited degree of independence for the slave. Their manipulation became a means of modifying work habits and disciplining slave labor. Paradoxically, however, both master and slave became more closely tied to the maintenance of these privileges. The possible range of action of each was restricted, and the character if not the content of industrial relations was altered decisively. However, while such measures may have been more effective punishments for breaches of

labor discipline, they still failed to provide a positive incentive to work.

The lack of incentive for slave labor constrained the productive capacity of the *atelier* and made it resistant to the modification or intensification of work routines. "The Negro, addicted to routine by nature," commented Lavollée,

becomes by position the enemy of all amelioration. As no personal interest attaches him to the land, as an increase in its products must result in no benefit for him, the change displeases him, and he resists it from the first without another thought. Often, the planter seeks in vain to demonstrate to him that by the adoption of a new process his task will become less long and less difficult. Whether his intelligence cannot grasp the import of such an explanation or rather whether a change that could eventually prove to be of advantage to him does not appear to him to be worth the present disruption of his habits, it is only after a long time and with the greatest difficulties that the planters have introduced some changes among them.

Confronted with the inertia of the slaves, the planters could only resign themselves to utilizing productive forces already at hand as effectively as possible and maintaining the discipline and morale of the slave gang.[57]

The system of task work was implemented to remedy this lack of incentive and to animate the slave gang. Its purpose was to create an inducement for the slave to work and thus guarantee the performance of a given amount of labor during the day. According to Soleau, "Currently the black in the Antilles, having no interest in working quickly since he must remain in the master's field the entire day whether he works a lot or a little, does not hurry." However, Soleau continued, "if the quantity of work were fixed he would go more quickly in order to have time to himself." Task work, according to Collins, was the best way of rewarding the slaves: "Wherever there is the least prospect of its being done, it should certainly be attempted; for nothing is so encouraging to your negroes, as the idea of a holiday at the end of their work; nor can anything depress them more, than a tiresome routine of duty, which presents no prospect of end, relief or recompence. In such cases, they labor with incessant regret; rather seeming to work than to work, and anxious only to consume the time, not to dispatch the business."[58]

Through experience, the planter was able to calculate for each of the different types of work to be done how much the average slave could do in a day without being overworked. Every morning, each slave in the gang was assigned his daily task based on this customary amount of labor. The slaves could do their daily quota of work as they liked, and were free to dispose of the time remaining after its completion as they wished. "This will encourage every negro to make his utmost exertion, in consequence of which, the work of twelve hours will be dispatched in ten, and with much more satisfaction to themselves," declared Collins.[59]

Under the task system, an industrious slave could gain several hours each day that could be employed in the cultivation of his own garden or some other employment. The slave thus had the opportunity to improve his condition, while the master obtained the required amount of labor. Soleau commented, undoubtedly with some exaggeration, "In the Antilles the organization of work by tasks, with all the opportunity that the blacks have to take advantage of the hours at their disposal, would make the great majority of them rich in a few years without diminishing the revenue of the master." On the other hand, a slave who did not use the time well had to spend the whole day working in the master's fields in order to complete the required task. The punishment was proportional to the lack of effort, and if the failure to meet the assignment was too great, the free day given to the slaves could be jeopardized.[60]

Despite the advantages presented by the task system, it was not universally applicable to all types of work on the sugar plantation. Both Soleau and Collins record that this method could be employed only with the *grand atelier*. Only the slaves in this gang commanded sufficient force to perform a definite and quantifiable amount of labor on a regular basis. In the case of illness or other absence, its numbers could be maintained by occasional or temporary drafts from the second gang, which always contained some slaves sufficiently strong to provide such a substitution. Such manipulation, however, was not possible in the case of the second gang. The weaker slaves of the *petite atelier* performed tasks that were not susceptible to such evaluation. They always worked under the supervision of a driver, and, in Soleau's description, performed indifferently the entire day. In addition, certain jobs on the plantation, such as cane

cutting, weeding, and carrying manure, were subject to great variation, depending respectively on the type and quality of the cane, the quantity of weeds, and the distance the dung had to be carried, that they were not, as a rule, amenable to a standard evaluation.[61]

Task work could function only when the slave population had sufficiently assimilated the routine of plantation labor to respond to its incentives. For self-regulation to replace external domination, it was necessary for the slaves to understand and accept the rhythm of work, organization of time, and system of rewards and punishments that characterized the plantation regime. Only then could the notion of free time appear as a reward to the slave. Only if the slave formed a concept of his self-interest and appropriated time for himself within this framework could the task system operate and the larger appropriation of the slave's activity by the master take place. This change itself contributed to the mutation of the relations of work. Soleau, writing from the point of view of a defender of slavery, described the task system as a form of contractual agreement: "It is easy to see all the advantages of this system of labor which represents a type of contract between master and slave. The former pledges to feed, dress, lodge, and care for the slave in sickness, in childhood, in old age. The slave, who, for his part, must give a certain determined quantity of labor each day of good health, is thus sheltered from the caprice and arbitrariness of the driver or overseer who directs the work." In Soleau's view, if master and slave fulfilled their obligations to each other, the mutual self-interest expressed by this contract could guarantee social peace in the colonies. The contractual character of task work was a mystification, since the slave could not bargain among employers and enter freely into the agreement. Yet, Soleau did catch something of the changing character of the relation between master and slave. Once the slave had a recognized interest, the system could no longer rest upon absolute domination and authority, but instead had to give way to bargaining and negotiation between interested parties, however unequal and antagonistic their relationship might have been. Thus, task work marked a further transformation of the master-slave relation and the adaptation of the African slave to the American environment which was both cause and effect of this change.[62]

However, the integration of the slave into the system of task work was itself an expression of the social limit of the slave relation and an element in its crisis. While planters might influence individual behavior and set the parameters of the action of the group through the systematic manipulation of rewards and punishments, such measures merely adapted the slaves to the existing organization of production with a greater or lesser degree of enthusiasm. While the task system guaranteed the completion of a minimum amount of work, and perhaps somewhat reduced the costs of supervision, it did not alter the composition of the working day or increase surplus production. The self-interest created by this system was not a reward earned through commodity-producing activity; instead, it was formed outside of this work and through a release from it. After the slaves completed their predetermined task, they were free to look after their own affairs literally, they were free to tend their own gardens. Such a system might provide the slaves with an incentive to give a bit more of themselves, but it demonstrates slavery's incapacity to create individual self-interest in production itself. Rather, individual self-interest and identification with the job and the plantation were created, not in commodity production, but in social reproduction. Garden plot cultivation did not lower the value of labor, but rather represented a deduction from the total potential surplus without changing the conditions of surplus production.

Notes

1. J.F. Dutrone, *Precis sur la canne et les moyens d'en extraire le sel essentiel, suivi de plusieurs memoires sur le sucre, sur le vin de canne, sur l'indigo, sur les habitations & sur l'etat actuel de Saint-Domingue.* (Paris, 1791), pp. 334-40. M. Moreno Fraginal, *EL ingenio: Complexo economico social cubano del azucar.* 3 vols. (Havana: Editorial de ciencias sociales, 1978), 2: 15-29.

2. George P. Rawick, *From Sundown to Sunup: The Making of the Black Community.* (Westport, Conn.: Greenwood Press, 1972), pp. 27-28. Sidney Mintz, "Toward an Afro-American History." *Cahiers de' histoire mondiale 13, no. 2.* (1971). Eric Wolf, "Specific Aspects of Plantation Systems in the New World: Community Sub-Cultures and Social Classes." *Pan- American Union Science Monographs 7.* (Washington D.C., 1959), pp. 136-137. Norman Klein, "West African Unfree Labour before and after the Rise of the Atlantic Slave Trade." In *Slavery in the New World: A Reader in Comparative History*, ed. by Laura Foner and Eugene D. Genovese. pp. 87-95 (Englewood Cliffs, N.J.: Prentice Hall, 1969). Moses I. Finley, "Slavery." *International Encyclopedia of the Social Sciences, vol. 14* (1968). Roger Bastide, *African Civilizations in the New World.* trans. by Peter Green. (New York: Harper & Row, 1971), pp. 89-90.

3. Gerald W. Mullin, *Flight and rebellion: Slave Resistance in Eighteenth Century Virginia.* (New York: Oxford University Press, 1974), pp. 37-38. Herbert G. Gutman, *Slavery and the Numbers Game: A Critique of "Time on the Cross."* (Urbana: University of Illinois Press, 1975), p. 171. Rawick, *From Sundown to Sunup*, pp. 27, 30-31; Mintz, "Toward an Afro-American History."

4. Sidney W. Mintz and Richard Price, *An Anthropological Approach to the Afro-American Past: A Caribbean Perspective.* (Philadelphia Institute for the Study of Human Issues, 1976), esp. pp. 7, 9-10, 20-21. Rawick, *From Sundown to Sunup*, pp. 31-32; Bastide, *African Civilizations in the New World*, pp. 154-56; Roger Bastide, *The African Religions of Brazil: Toward a Sociology of the Interpretation of Civilizations*, trans. by Helen Sabba. (Baltimore: John Hopkins University Press, 1978), p. 96. Yvan Debbasch, "Le Maroonage: Essai sur la desertion de l'esclave antillais." *Annec sociologique.* (1961), p. 85.

5. Max Weber, *Economy and Society.* 2 vols. (Berkeley: University of California Press, 1978), 1:129, 162-164. Anon. [Collins], *Practical Rules for the Management & Medical Treatment of Negro Slaves in the Sugar Colonies.* (London, 1811), pp. 168-69.

6. Fernando Ortiz, *Los negros esclavos.* (Havana: Editorial de ciencias sociales, 1975), p. 182. Mintz and Price, *An Anthropological Approach to the Afro-American Past*, p.14.

7. Marquis de Felix Renouard Sainte Croix, *Statistique de la Martinique.* 2 vols. (Paris, 1822), 2: 156. Ministere de Commerce et des Manufactures, *Commission formee avec l'approbation du Roi...pour l'examen de certaines questiones de legislation commerciale: Enquete sur les sucres.* (Paris, 1829), pp. 48-49, 72. M. Le Comte E. de la Cornillere., *La Martinique en 1842: Interets coloniaux, souvenirs du voyage.* (Paris, 1843), p. 98.Ministere de la Marine et des Colonies, *Compte rendu au Roi de l'emploi des fonds allouees depuis 1839, pour l'enseignement religieux et elementaire des noirs, et de l'execution des lois des 18 et 19 juillet 1845 relatives au regime des esclaves, a l'introduction de travailleurs libres aux colonies, etc.* (Paris, 1846). Gaston Martin, *Histoire de l'esclavage dans les colonies francaises.* (Paris: Presses universitaires de France, 1948), pp. 122-23. W.A. Green, "The Planter Class and British West Indian Sugar Production, before & after Emancipation." *Economic History Review 26.* (1973), p. 449.

8. Anon. [Collins], *Practical Rules*, pp. 150-51, 157-58; Sainte Croix, *Statistique*, 2:125; Orlando Patterson, *The Sociology of Slavery: An Analysis of the Origins, Development and Structure of Negro Slavery in Jamaica.* (Cranbury, N.J.: Associateed University Presses, 1969), pp. 59-61.

9. Anon. [Collins], *Practical Rules*, pp. 151-52; homas Roughley, *The Jamaican Planter's Guide; or A System for Planting and Managing a Sugar Estate or other Plantations in the Island and Throughout the British West Indies in General.* (London, 1823), pp. 99-100, 113-18. Victor Schoelcher, *Des colonies francaises: Abolition immediate de l'esclavage.* (Paris, 1842), pp. 59-61. Patterson, *Sociology of Slavery*, pp. 59-61.

10. Roughley, *Jamaica Planter's Guide*, pp. 99-102; Anon [Collins], *Practical Rules*, pp. 151-52; Sainte Croix, *Statistique*, 2:125; Charles Derosne, *Memoire sur la fabrication du sucre dans les colonies par de nouveaux procedes*.(Paris, 1824), pp. 23, 44-45. P. Lavollee, *Notes sur les cultures et la production de la Martinique et de la Guadeloupe*. (Paris, 1841), p. 123. Ministere de la Marine et des Colonies, *Expose general de resultats du patronage des esclaves dans les colonies francaises*. (Paris, 1844), pp. 380-97. Gabriel Debien, *Les esclaves aux Antilles francaises (xviie-xviiie siecles)*. (Basse-Terre: Societe d'histoire de la Guadeloupe; Fort-de-France: Societe d'histoire de la Martinique, 1974), p. 125. Richard Thurnwald, *Economics in Primitive Societies*.(London: Oxford University Press, 1932), pp. 213-214. Karl Marx, *Capital*. Vol. 1. (Harmondsworth: Penguin Books, 1976), 1: 443.

11. Sainte Croix, *Statistique*, 2:125-26; Roughley, *Jamaica Planter's Guide*, pp. 102-3; Anon. [Collins], *Practical Rules*, pp. 154-55; *Enquête sur le sucres*, pp. 48-49.

12. Roughley, *Jamaica Planter's Guide*, pp. 103-9, 121-22; Anon. [Collins], *Practical Rules*, pp. 155-57.

13. Mintz and Price, *Anthropological Approach to the Afro-American Past*, p.13.; Mintz, "Toward an Afro-American History," esp. pp. 327-30; Marx, *Capital*, 1:468-70.

14. Dutrône, *Précis sur la canne*, p. 109; Derosne, *Mémoire sur la fabrication du sucre*, pp. 23, 44-45; Anselme Payen, *Traite de la fabrication et du raffinage des sucres*.(Paris: Thomine Libraire, 1832), p. 70. Lavollée, *Notes sur les cultures*, pp. 122-23; Moreau de Saint-Mery, cited in Martin, *Histoire de l'esclavage*, p. 123.

15. Dutrône, *Précis sur la canne*, p. 109; Derosne, *Mémoire sur la fabrication du sucre*, pp. 23, 44-45; Payen, *Traité*, p. 70; Lavollée, *Notes sur les cultures*, pp. 122-23; Anon. [Collins], *Practical Rules*, p. 159; Moreau de Saint-Mery, cited in Martin, *Histoire de l'esclavage*, p. 123.

16. Dutrône, *Précis sur la canne*, p. 111-12, 140-41, 225; Lavollée, *Notes sue les cultures*, p. 74; Roughley, *Jamaica Planter's Guide*, pp. 85-87; Richard Sheridan, *Sugar and Slavery*.(Eagle Hall, Barbados: Caribbean Universities Press, 1974), pp. 115-17.

17. E.O. von Lippman, *Historia do acucar desde a epoca mais remota ate o comeco da fabricacao do acucar de beterraba*. (trans by Rodolfo Coutinho). 2 vols. (Rio de Janeiro: Instituto do acucar e do alcool, 1942), 2: 241. A. De Lachàrière, "Une lettre de M. A. De Lachàrière," p. 91; Dutrône, *Précis sur la canne*, p. 175; Roughley, *Jamaica Planter's Guide*, pp. 339-41; Clement Caines, *Letters on the cultivation of Otaiti Cane. . .* (London, 1801), p. 98, cited in Elsa V. Goveia, *Slave Society in the British Leeward Islands at the End of the Eighteenth Century*. (New Haven: Yale University Press, 1965), p. 133.

18. William Reed, *A History of Sugar and Sugar Yielding Plants Together with an Epitome of Every Notable Process of Sugar Extraction and Manufacture from the Earliest Times to the Present*. London: Longmans, Green, 1866), pp. 32-33. Roughley, *Jamaica Planter's Guide*, pp. 339-41.

19. William Reed, *History of Sugar*, p. 54; Roughley, *Jamaica Planter's Guide*, p. 364; Goveia, *Leeward Islands*, p. 133; Noel Deerr, *The History of Sugar*. 2 vols. (London; Chapman and Hall, 1945), 2: 582.

20. M. Moreno Fraginals, *The Sugarmill: The Socioeconomic Complex of Sugar in Cuba*, trans. by Cedric Belfrage. (New York: Monthly Review Press, 1976), p. 39.

21. Lavollée, *Notes sur les cultures*, pp. 97-98; Sainte Croix, *Statistique*, 2:114-15; Schoelcher, *Abolition immédiate*, pp. 23-24; M.G. Lewis, *Journal of a West Indian Proprietor, 1815-1817*. (Boston, 1929), p. 70. Roughley, *Jamaica Planter's Guide*, p. 87; Martin, *Histoire de l'esclavage*, pp. 126-27; Gabriel Debien, "Destinées d'esclaves à la Martinique (1776-1778)," pp. 32-35; Patterson, *Sociology of Slavery*, pp. 57-64.

22. Roughley, *Jamaica Planter's Guide*, pp. 83-85, 110-13.

23. Schoelcher, *Abolition immédiate*, pp. 2, 23-24; Adolphe Granier de Cassagnac, *Voyage aux Antilles*. (Paris, 1842), pp. 116-19. Roughley, *Jamaica Planter's Guide*, pp. 97-98; Debien, "Destinées d'esclaves." pp. 22-31; A.N.S.O.M., Généralitiés 167 (1348).

24. Lewis, *Journal of a West India Proprietor*, p. 70; Patterson, *Sociology of Slavery*, pp. 57-64; Roughley, *Jamaica Planter's Guide*, p. 87; Schoelcher, *Abolition immédiate*, pp. 23-24; Martin, *Histoire de l'esclavage*, pp. 126-27; Debien, "Destinées d'esclaves." pp. 32-35; Ministère de la marine et des Colonies, Exposé général des résultats du patronage, pp. 345-46.

25. Goveia, *Leeward Islands*, pp. 127-29.

26. Goveia, *Leeward Islands*, pp. 127-29; Gwendolyn M. Hall., Social Control in Slave Plantation Societies: A Comparison of St Dominque and Cuba. (Baltimore: John Hopkins University Press, 1971), pp. 15-19. M. Moreno Fraginals, "Aportes culturales y deculturacion." In *Africa en America Latina*, ed. by M. Moreno Fraginals. (Mexico: Siglo 21 & UNESCO, 1977), pp. 28-29.

27. Anon. [Collins], *Practical Rules*, pp. 162-63; Moreno Fraginals, *El ingenio*, 2:32; Lavollée, *Notes sur les cultures*, pp. 122-23; Schoelcher, *Abolition immédiate*, pp. 22, 84; Jacques Le Goff, *Time, Work and Culture in the Middle Ages*. (trans. by Arthur Goldhammer). (Chicago: University of Chicago Press, 1980), pp. 44-49.

28. Ministère de la Marine et des Colonies, Exposi général des resultats du Patronage, PP- 301-5; Lavoll6e, Notes Sur les cultures, pp. 12.2-Z3; De la Cornillere, *La Martinique en 1842*, pp. 124-26; Sainte Croix, *Statistique*, 2:I25-26; Schoelcher, Abolition immédiate, p. 22; A.N.S.O.M., Martinique 9 (99), De Moges, "Mémoire" (1840); Debien, Les esclaves aux Antilles françaises, pp. 147-49; Christian Schnakenberg, *Histoire de l'industrie sucriere en Gaudeloupe (xixe-xxe siecles)*. Vol. 1, *La crise du systeme esclavagiste, 1835-1847*. (Paris: L' Harmattan, 1980), pp. 53-54. Goveia, Leeward Islands, p. 130; Ortiz, Los negros esclavos, pp. 182-91; Patterson, Sociology of Slavery, pp. 67-69.

29. Schoelcher, *Abolition immédiate*, p. 22; A.N.S.O.M., Martinique 9 (99), De Moges, "Mémoire" (840); Ministère de la Marine et des Colonies, *Exposé général des résultats du patronage*, p. 107; Lavollée, *Notes Sur les cultures*, pp. 122-23.

30. Reed, *History of Sugar*, pp. 53-54

31 Ministère de la Marine et des Colonies, *Exposé général des résultats du patronage*, pp. 213, 223, 301-3; Ministère de la Marine et des Colonies, *Compte rendu au Roi de l'emploi des fonds alloues depuis 1839*, pp. 99-105.

32. Sainte Croix, *Statistique*, 2:110-11, 128-29, 131-35; Lavollée, *Notes Sur les cultures*, pp. 73-74, 122; Adolphe

Gueroult, *De la question coloniale en 1842: Les colonies francaises et le sucre de betterave.* (Paris, 1842), pp. 64-67. Richard Pares, *A West-India Fortune.*(London: Longmans, Green, 1950), p. 1516.

33.   Ministère de la Marine et des Colonies, *Exposé général des résultats du patronage,* p. 108; Sainte Croix, *Statistique,* 2: 13 9; Lavollée, *Notes Sur les cultures,* pp. 73, 122-73, 132.; A.N.S.O.M., Martinique 9 (99), Dc Moges, "Mémoire" (1840); Dutrône, *Pricis sur la canne,* pp. 140-41; Debien, Les esclaves aux Antilles françaises, pp. 149-52; Schnakenbourg, *Crise,* pp. 53-54; Ortiz, *Los negros esclavos,* p. 18 6; Goveia, *Leeward Islands,* pp. 12.9-31; Moreno Fraginals, *El ingenio,* 2:32-34.

34.   Lavollée, *Notes sures cultures,* pp. 73, 122-23, 132; Sainte Croix, *Statistique,* 2:139; Dutrône, *Pricis sur la canne,* pp 140-41; A.N.S.O.M., Martinique 9 (99), De Moges, "Mémoire" (1840); Dcbien, *Les esclaves aux Antilles françaises,* pp. 149-5 2; Schnakcnbourg, *Crise,* pp. 53-54; Ortiz, *Los negros esclavos,* p. 186; Goveia, *Leeward Islands,* pp. 129-31; Moreno Fraginals, *El ingenio,* 2:3 2-34.

35.   Reed, *History of Sugar,* pp. 53-54; A.N.S.O.M., Martinique 9 (99), Dc Moges, "Mémoire" (1840); Ministère de la Marine et des Colonies, Exposé général des résultats du patronage, pp. 108, 303-5, 392; Ministère de la Marine et des Colonies, Compte rendu au Roi de l exe-cution des lois des 18 et 19 juillet, pp. 657-59.

36.   Debien, *Les esclaves aux Antilles francaines,* p. 154; Dutrône, *Précis sur la canne,* pp. 335-36; Jurgen Kuczynski, *A Short History of Labour Conditions under Industrial Capitalism.* 4 vols.(London: F. Muller, 1945), pp. 44-45. A.N.S.O.M., Martinique 9 (99), De Moges, "Mémoire" (1840); Ministère de la Marine et des Colonies, *Exposé général des réultats du patronage,* pp- 301-1; Sainte Croix, *Statistique,* 2:128-29; Moreno Fraginals, *The Sugarmill,* p. 56.

37.   Dutrône, *Précis sur la canne,* pp. 334-40; Moreno Fraginals, *El ingenio,* 2:15-29.

38.   Keith R. Aufhauser, "Slavery and Scientific Management." *Journal of Economic History 33, no. 4.* (1977), esp. pp. 812-18. R.W. Fogel, and S.L. Engerman, *Time on the Cross: The Economics of American Slavery.* 2 vols. (Boston: Little, Brown, 1974), 1: 208. Herbert Gutman, *Slavery and the Numbers Game,* pp. 82-83.

39.   A. Soleau, *Notes sur les Guyanes francaise, hollandaise, anglaise, et sur les Antilles françaises (Cayenne, Surinam, Demèrary, la Martinique, la Guadeloupe).* (Paris, 1835), pp. 8-10. Anon. [Collins], *Practical Rules,* pp. 152-54.

40.   Anon. [Collins], *Practical Rules,* pp. 169-70; Schoelcher, *Abolition immédiate,* P. 274

41.   Schoelcher, *Abolition immédiate,* pp. 273-74; Roughley, *Jamaica Planter's Guide,* p. 94; Anon. (Collins), *Practical Rules,* pp. 165, 170-71. Cf. Gutman, *Slavery and the*

Numbers Game, esp- pp. 14, 171; Fogel and Engerman, *Time on the Cross,* 1:146- 53.

42.   Anon. (Collins], *Practical Rules,* pp. r65, 171-72.

43.   Schoelcher, *Abolition immédiate,* pp. 5-6; Sainte Croix, *Statistique,* 2:101-5, 126- 28, 157-58; Lavollée, *Notes sur les cultures,* pp. 66, r13; A. de Chazelles, *Etude sur le systeme colonial.* (Paris,1860), pp. 131, 156.

44.   Debien, *Les esclaves aux Antilles françaises,* p. 108.

45   Ibid., pp. 114-15

46   Ibid.,pp. 2-15; Hilliard d'Auberteuil, 1:165, in ibid., p. 115; Roughley, *Jamaica Planter's Guide,* pp. 40-41.

47.   Debien, *Les esclaves aux Antilles françaises,* pp. 116-17.

48.   Ibid.,pp. 119, 124-25, 128; Marquis de Casaux, *Essai sur l'art de cultiver la canne et den extraire le sucre,* p. 267, in ibid., p. 124; Roughley, *Jamaica Planter's Guide,* pp. 79-80.

49.   Anon. (Collins), *Practical Rules,* pp. 169-70.

50.   Schoelcher, *Abolition immédiate,* pp. 84, 90-93; Ministère de la Marine et des Colonies, *Exposé général des résultats du patronage,* p. 130- See also David Brion Davis, *The Problem of Slavery in an Age of Revolution, 1770-1823.* (Ithaca: Cornell University Press, 1975), p. 464.

51.   Schoelcher, *Abolition immédiate,* pp. 89-90; Ministère de la Marine et des Colonies, *Exposé général des résultats du patronage,* p. 359.

52.   Ministère de la Marine et des Colonies, *Exposé général des résultats du patronage,* pp. 380-82, 384-85; Schoelcher, *Abolition immédiate,* pp. 89-90; Gutman, *Slavery and the Numbers Game,* pp. 19, 32.

53.   Ministère de la Marine et des Colonies, *Exposé général des résultats du patronage,* pp.380, 382-85, 392, 394-95

54.   Ibid., pp- 380-85, 394-95; Debien, *Les esclaves aux Antilles franqaises,* pp. 125-26; Schoelcher, *RAbolition immédiate,* p. 85.

55.   Schoelcher, *Abolition immédiate,* p. 8 5; Ministère de la Marine et des Colonies, *Exposé général des résultats du patronage,* pp. 380-85- See also Debien, *Les esclaves aux Antilles françaises,* p. 126.

56.   Anon. [Collins], *Practical Rules,* pp. 170-71; Schoelcher, *Abolition immédiate* pp. 90-94, 273-74; Ministère de la Marine edes Colonies, *Exposé général des résultats du patronage,* pp. 384-95

57.   Lavollée, *Notes sur les cultures,* pp. 45-46.

58.   Soleau, *Notes sur les Guyanes,* pp. 8-9; Anon. [Collins,] *Practical Rules,* pp. 152-54.

59.   Soleau, *Notes sur les Guyanes,* pp. 8-10; Anon. [Collins,] *Practical Rules,* pp. 152-54.

60.   Soleau, *Notes sur les Guyanes,* pp. 8-10.

61.   Anon. [Collins,] *Practical Rules,* pp. 152-54.; Soleau, *Notes sur les Guyanes,* pp. 8-9.

62.   Soleau, *Notes sur les Guyanes,* pp. 8-9; Edward Brathwaite, *The Development of Creole Society in Jamaica, 1770-1820.* (Oxford: Oxford University Press, 1971), pp. 298-99.

32

Slavery in Three West Indian Towns: Christiansted, Fredericksted and Charlotte Amalie in the late Eighteenth and early Nineteenth Century

N.A.T. HALL

Urban slavery as a phenomenon was well established in Denmark's West Indian colonies by the middle of the eighteenth century. In St. Croix, for which the data are more plentiful at this time, slaves by 1758 already dominated the populations of the island's two towns, Christiansted and Fredericksted, comprising in each case more than 60 per cent (Tables 32.1 and 32.2). In the ensuing years of the eighteenth century and until the turn of the nineteenth, slaves at no time comprised less than half of the population of either town. By 1803, as the tables show, the island's urban slave population had grown absolutely from 1,454 in 1758 to 3,879. This represented a relative decline from 65.2 to 56.0 per cent of the total urban population. But that decline has to be seen in the context of a rapidly growing urban freedman population that increased, almost five-fold in the case of Christiansted and more than three-fold in the case of Fredericksted, between 1775 and the turn of the nineteenth century. This largely explains the relative decline of some 10 per cent in Christiansted's slave population in that period. Fredericksted, on the other hand, with a less significant exponential growth of its freedman population,

Table 32.1   Growth of the Urban Slave Population: Christiansted, St. Croix, 1759–1803

Year	Slaves	Freedmen	Whites	Total Urban	Island Total Free & Slave	Urban as % of Island Total	Slaves as % of Urban Total
1758	1,422	–	753	2,175	13,497	16.1	65.3
1766	1,342	–	861	2,203	19,043	11.5	60.9
1775	2,364	290	944	3,598	15,873	13.9	65.7
1786	2,850	730	1,207	4,787	25,102	19.0	59.5
1789	2,977	797	1,055	4,829	25,377	19.0	61.6
1792	2,488	797	961	4,246	24,663	17.2	58.5
1797	2,998	973	1,085	5,056	28,803	17.5	59.2
1803	3,038	1,407	1,065	5,510	30,155	18.2	55.1

Sources: P.L. Oxholm, De Danske Øers Tilstand (Copenhagen: 1797); Jens Vibaek, Vore Gamle Tropekolonier (Copenhagen: Fremad, 1966); Hans West, Beretning om det dansk Eilande St. Croix (Copenhagen: 1791).

Table 32.2   Growth of the Urban Slave Population: Fredericksted, St. Croix, 1758–1803

Year	Slaves	Freedmen	Whites	Total Urban	Island Total Free & Slave	Urban as % of Island Total	Slaves as % of Urban Total
1758	32	–	20	52	13,497	0.3	61.5
1766	209	–	132	341	19,043	1.7	61.2
1775	405	71	236	712	25,873	2.7	56.8
1786	487	133	302	922	25,102	3.6	52.8
1789	597	156	298	1,061	25,377	4.1	56.2
1792	649	174	270	1,093*	24,663	4.4	59.3
1797	712	191	267	1,170	28,803	4.0	60.8
1803	841	249	237	1,327	30,155	4.4	63.3

*Vibaek, through an error in aggregating, gives this figure as 1,087.
Sources: As for Table 32.1

and an absolute decline of its white population from 1786, shows a slight relative increase of almost 2 per cent.

Data available for Charlotte Amalie, St. Thomas, in the late eighteenth and early nineteenth century indicate that there too the urban slave presence was substantial. Table 32.3 indicates that in 1797 two-thirds of the town's population were slaves; yet despite absolute growth since 1789 there had been a relative decrease of some 6 per cent. This absolute growth had been offset by the near doubling of the white population and an increase by half as much again of the freedman population. Nevertheless, in Charlotte Amalie as in Christiansted and Fredericksted, the urban slave population outnumbered whites and freedmen combined at the end of the eighteenth century.

By the 1830s however, the situation of the 1780s and 1790s no longer obtained. The progressive urbanization of St. Thomas was reflected by Charlotte Amalie accounting for more than three-quarters of the island's population in 1838. The relative size of the urban slave popu-

Table 32.3   Growth of the Urban Slave Population: Charlotte Amalie, St. Thomas, 1789-1838

Year	Slaves	Freedmen	Whites	Total Urban	Island Total Free & Slave	Urban as % of Island Total	Slaves as % of Urban Total
1789	1,527	260	398	2,085	5,266	39.5	73.2
1791	1,527	160	400	2,087	7,353	28.3	73.1
1797*	1,943	239	726	2,908	5,734	50.7	66.8
1831	2,894	8,177+	–	11,071	13,492	82.0	26.1
1838	2,093	5,024	1,770	8,887	11,433	77.7	23.5

*I have taken Oxholm's figures for 'house negroes' to refer to those in Charlotte Amalie, on the assumption that since he does not give any separate figures for house slaves among his figures for plantation slaves in St. Thomas or St. Croix, but confines the term 'house negro' to Christiansted and Fredericksted, his 'house negro' was an urban slave.
+ This figure includes the total for whites as well.

Sources: P.L. Oxholm, *De Danske Vestindiske Øers Tilstand; Hans West, Beretning om det dansk Eilande St. Croix; Hans West, Bidrag til Beskrivelse over St. Croix* (Copenhagen: 1793); J.P. Nissen, *Reminiscences of a 46-year residence in the Island of St. Thomas in the West Indies* (Nazareth, Pa.: 1838).

lation had declined *pari passu*. A corresponding development can be observed for St. Croix in the 1830s (Table 32.5), and in both islands the development is largely to be explained by the introduction of the free port system in 1782, the importance of Charlotte Amalie in that system, and the opportunities offered by it to whites and freedmen.

The preponderance of slaves in these towns in the late eighteenth century was the direct result of their expansion as service ports for the prospering plantations; of their role as free ports and centres of distribution and exchange in the overseas trade. As the white community responded to the commercial opportunities, it generated a demand for labour; in service areas related to commerce, such as porters, stevedores and wainmen; in the production and distribution of goods to meet the everyday needs of the white community; in the provision of personal service. In all of these areas slave labour in the three towns occupied a position of cardinal importance.

The provision of personal service heavily skewed the sex ratio in favour of female slaves. In 1797, as Table 32.4 shows, there were only 83 males per 100 females in Christiansted and Fredericksted, and 68 in Charlotte Amalie. This pattern was in marked contrast to that on the plantations. The balance in favour of female slaves did not alter over time in St. Croix (Table 32.5), and there is good reason to assume that the same was true of St. Thomas.

Table 32.4: Sex Composition of Urban and Rural Slaves, St. Croix & St. Thomas, 1797

	Males	Females	Males per 100 females
St. Croix – Rural	11,670	10,036	116.2
Christiansted	1,361	1,637	83.1
Fredericksted	323	389	83.0
St. Thomas – Rural	1,472	1,354	108.7
Charlotte Amalie	791	1,152	68.6

Source: Oxholm, *De Danske Vestindiske Øers Tilstand*

The domestic staff of the Lutheran priest Ohm was not a typical. In 1792 it consisted of a cook, a washer and her two female children, and a seamstress.[1] It is these females slaves who cooked, baked, laundered, made and repaired clothes, fetched water from Christiansted's well in the case of poorer whites, or from private wells in the case of the more well-to-do, waited at table, attended their masters and mistresses in public, carried messages etc.

If Ohm's slave retinue was more or less average size, there were others whose staffs were even larger. Carl Holten, adjutant to the governor general, who arrived in 1799, records in his memoirs that he had a staff of fourteen including five children: 'A mulatto servant; 2 black boys;

Table 32.5 Sex Composition and Growth of Urban Slavery in St. Croix, 1831–1839

Year	Female Urban	Male Urban	Total Urban Slaves	Urban Total Free & Slaves	Island Total Free & Slaves	Urban as % of Island Total	Slaves as % of Urban Total	Females % of Urban Slaves
1831	1,613	1,103	2,677	7,905+	25,208	31.3	34.3	59.3
1835	1,463	911	2,374	8,154	25,087	32.7	29.1	61.6
1839	1,196	713	1,909	7,322	23,826	30.7	26.0	62.6

*These totals are probaly inflated as Alexander does not separate country whites from town whites. The urban free total is thus probably inflated by 300.
+ Alexander gives a figure of 1,589 for the freedman and white population in 1832. This was without a doubt a transposition of the two initial digits. His figure would be less than the known total of the free urban population of 2,472 in 1803. The figure of 5,189 used in this calculation accords with what is known of the growth of the freedman and white populations in St. Croix at the end of the 1820's. See N.A.T. Hall, 'The 1816 Freedman Petition in the Danish West Indies: Its' Background and Consequences', paper presented at the 11th Conference of Caribbean Historians, 1979.

Source: G.W. Alexander, *Om den moralsk Forpligtelse til og det hensigtemaessige af strax og fuldstaendigt at ophaeve Slaveriet i de danske vestindiske Kolonier* (Copenhagen: 1843).)

a cook; an assistant cook; a washer; two chamber maids and an old biddy who supervised the women and looked after the children.'[2] Hans West, Rector of Christiansted's school for white children, and, like Ohm and Holten, part of the town's Danish official classes, nevertheless disapproved heartily of the numbers and efficiency of these establishments. Compared to their European counterparts, he observed, what such slaves did was more pastime than work.[3] This comment, however, must be seen in the context of West's negrophobic views.

West complained further that so far as the size of the establishments went, the white women, particularly the creoles, were largely to blame. They were so possessed by vanity that they could not see an attractive female slave without wanting her in their entourage as a servant.[4] Many years later, Governor General Bentzon similarly criticized what he described as a form of idleness supporting a creole tendency to luxury, and called for a reduction in the number of household slaves.[5]

In 1792, Governor General Walterstorff, in attempting to explain the inflated numbers of household servants, pointed out that for one thing townsfolk tended to have less spartan lifestyle than planters; that for another, the open doors and windows of West Indian houses invited more dust and more cleaning and polishing than houses in Europe. Thirdly, West Indian children were not confined to a nursery, as in Europe, where a single child could oversee them. In explaining the practice, Walterstorff was not attempting its justification. Like West and Bentzon, he identified vanity as an operative factor among several families in Christiansted, but added that it had also become hallowed practice to have a particularly large retinue of servants, whose numbers were increased over time by reproduction. In one decade, he claimed, the household slave staff could double its number by natural increase; and no master, in Walterstorff's view, would sell the children of slaves who had been in his service for some time. There was also the factor of over-specialization of functions, whereby a cook could be used to do nothing else but cooking. The end result was that one became surrounded by 'a large army of useless persons who cost more than a little to feed and clothe'.[6]

Domestics represented but a fraction of the wide range of occupational skills through which slaves made an important contribution to urban life and economic activity. Their production of goods and services, and their distribution, and the generation of income for white townsfolk, were critical inputs into the urban economy, particularly of St. Croix. Nowhere was this more applicable than in the itinerant retail trade, an important generator of income and cash. White townsfolk, poor and better-off alike, had their slaves take to the streets hawking a variety of goods and food. These slaves, mostly women, armed with their passes, and trays on their heads, pictures of grace if West is to be believed,[7] were a constant feature of the landscape in town and country. The stock in trade consisted of such items as bread, butter, coffee, beans, fruit, meat, vegetables, candles, cushions and haberdashery notions. Plying their trade on behalf of their masters and mistresses, they were the lifeline of an internal marketing system, complementing the Sunday market of the country slaves. Huckstering was an ideal outlet for stolen goods, but neither the concern of the Burgher Council at Christiansted nor the police as late as 1812, seemed to have made any appreciable difference to the use of higglers as "fences".[8]

Higglers were particularly important as sources of income for poor whites. The same would also be true for freedmen, who by 1802 were estimated to own 30 per cent of the slaves in Charlotte Amalie.[9] The frequency distribution of slave-ownership in Christiansted in 1792 (Table 32.6) shows that most households owned a maximum of four slaves. The same held true for Fredericksted. If it is assumed that the ownership of a large number of slaves was a measure of substance in eighteenth century Christiansted and Fredericksted, it would be reasonable to conclude from the data in Table 32.6, that by far the great majority of households in those two towns were peopled by the less well to do. This has important implications for the quality of shelter and food provided by such households, and raises doubts of the authenticity of West's claim that each slave in Christiansted was comfortably housed and adequately fed.[10]

In relation to what Table 32.6 indicates, the comment of the Burgher Council of St. Croix in 1792 is very instructive. Many persons, it informed the Danish West Indian government, had no other property than a few slaves and nothing else to live from apart from what these slaves

Table 32.6   Frequency Distribution of Slaves in Christiansted and Fredericksted, 1792

	Slaves per Household	No. of Households	Estimated No. of Slaves*	% of Households	% of Slaves
Christiansted	1-4	238	476	59.5	19.6
	5-9	93	651	23.2	26.8
	10-14	30	360	7.5	14.8
	15-19	18	306	4.5	12.6
	20+	21	630	5.2	26.0
Total		400	2,423	99.9	99.8
Fredericksted	1-4	53	106	49.0	15.7
	5-9	33	231	30.5	34.2
	10-14	15	180	13.8	26.6
	15-19	4	68	3.7	10.0
	20+	3	90	2.7	13.3
Total		108	675	99.7	99.9

*Estimated number of slaves derived from the assumed mean of each size-group: 2,7,12,17, and 30.

Source: R/A, VJ 1793, # 911.

brought in. Such persons were reduced to the necessity of sending out their slaves to earn whatever they could to ensure their support.[11] That observation was confirmed in its turn by the Danish West Indian government in its comment on the raw data from which Table 32.6 derives:

It should be noted that the apparent superfluity of house slaves can in many instances be justified having regard to the fact that such slaves are their owners sole means of support, either as craftsmen or hired help.[12]

Skilled craftsmen, particularly carpenters, and other skilled slaves like seamen, were as important as itinerant vendors as "sole means of support' for some of the towns' whites and freedmen. Hired out, such slaves could bring in the not inconsiderable sums of $2-3 per week at the start of the nineteenth century.[13] In the dry docks carpenters were always in demand, and in the boats which put into port, slaves on hire as crew were always indispensable.[14] In Charlotte Amalie in particular, this was an important consideration as more and more after 1782 it became the free port crossroads of the Caribbean.

The range of artisan skills commanded by slaves in the towns covers an impressive spectrum. A random sample will suffice. J.B. Moreton, a Christiansted butcher, claimed in 1808 to have one slave 'the most active butcher in the West Indies' and another a 'nimble segar-maker' capable of rolling up to 100 per day.[15] To such well promoted individuals and skills, one can add others: silversmiths like Creole Jimmy; saddlers like Jasper; Major de Nully's Osmond, who was a tailor; masons such as Nathaniel; jockeys like John Jones, alias Anguilla Johnny; slaves who combined more than one skill like Benjamin who 'tripled' as barber, hairdresser and fiddler; Lewis, who was both tailor and barber; Mulatto, carpenters as well as wheelwright; and Commodore Morgenstern's Cuffy who was a tailor and also played the violin.[16] Even Hans West, who was nothing if not negrophobe, was forced to the grudging admission that there were no artisan skills which slaves found difficulty in acquiring, and the range of skills seems to have been matched by excellence in execution. West had nothing but the highest praise for the women's needlework, and his comments on the men bordered on the rapturous:

Some of them acquire artisan skills which they bring to such a point of refinement, that I would be prepared to wager that no fully accomplished journeyman in any of Copenhagen's many famous guilds could stitch a pair of shoes, a garment or a buttonhole with the fit and finesse of a creole black.[17]

The cash incomes generated by these slaves on their masters' behalf was estimated in 1784 at about 100,000 Rigsdaler,[18] a not inconsiderable sum.

The importance of these skills and services to the towns was paralleled in significant ways by an input from slaves who, although sometimes forming part of the towns' populations, belonged in fact to contiguous estates. The proximity of La Princess to Christiansted and of La Grange to Fredericksted made them peculiarly suitable to supply such skills and services. The opportunities in Fredericksted were of lesser magnitude than those in Christiansted and related largely to the presence of the Fort there. In 1759, only three of La Grange's work force of 104 were hired out in the town, all at the Fort: a water carrier, a barber and a baker.[19] For La Princess the attractions of Christiansted were more compelling . The estate's inventory for 1759 shows the importance qualitatively and quantitatively of the support services it provided for the town. Seven men of a total male workforce of 193 were engaged in the towns: two permanently in Christiansted; four on a daily basis and one permanently in Fredericksted. In addition there were fourteen boys who went on a daily basis to provide fodder for the governor general's stables. Apart from supplying fodder, the other services included that of a stable boy, an apprentice mason and a drummer with the garrison in Fredericksted.

This 1759 inventory also illustrates the bias in favour of females for service in the town, and the high degree to which white officialdom made use of their services. In 1759 La Princess had a total of 103 women and girls, nineteen of whom were employed in some capacity in Christiansted: seven on a daily basis and twelve permanently. Their occupations ranged from fodder-carrier, to baker, to cook and washer, and they were employed variously at the governor general's, the Fort, the priest's the police prefecture, the Regimental Quarter master's. Of the estate's overall workforce of 194 in 1759, a total of 42 or some 22.8 per cent were employed in activities related to the urban milieu. The inventory list, if nothing else, conveys the important symbiotic relationship which bound the estate to Christiansted.[20]

In addition there were the country slaves who lived and worked permanently on the plantations, but who maintained continuous contact with the towns. It was common practice for these country slaves, especially those from the nearby estates, to come to town every evening, selling fodder in the form of grass, corn stalks and leaves for the town's horses, and firewood. Without this service, Von Roepstorff, a former governor general, expressed the view in the 1780s that the towns would have been severely embarrassed.[21] The towns' provisioning through the slave Sunday market is discussed elsewhere;[22] suffice it to say here that the Sunday market merely illustrated on a larger scale the towns' daily dependence on slaves goods and services.

It would also appear that the supply of grass and firewood was responsible for a significant cash flow among those country slaves who supplied those articles. This was cash which remained as disposable income to these slaves and quantitatively was about one-half of the income generated by urban artisans for their owners in St. Croix in the late eighteenth century. West attempted to measure this cash flow in the early 1790s. On the basis of an estimate of 250 horses for Christiansted and 50 for Fredericksted, each of which cost 24 skillings per day for fodder, West calculated that the gross annual intake was 22,812.5 Rigsdaler from Christiansted and 4,562.5 Rigsdaler from Fredericksted, or a total of 27,375 Rigsdaler from both towns.[23] The income from the sale of firewood was of almost a similar order of magnitude. West calculated that providing the 664 houses in Christiansted with firewood at 8 skillings per day represented a yearly expenditure of 20,141.3 Rigsdaler. In the case of Fredericksted with 190 houses, the yearly cost was calculated at 5,971.6 Rigsdaler, making a total for both towns of 26,112.9 Rigsdaler.[24] The sale of fodder and firewood therefore grossed 53,487.9 Rigsdaler annually. Slaves in this kind of contact with the urban milieu, were collectively earning incomes that were probably the near equivalent of the cost of maintaining the Danish West Indian garrison, estimated in 1826 to cost some 68,000 Rigsdaler.[25]

The income derived from the sources outlined above, and those, which are to be assumed, from urban artisans working on their own account, gave such slaves independent purchasing power. This in turn enabled them to establish one of many bases of interaction with urban whites patronage of the punch and beer houses and grog shops. Mutual interest ensured a degree of collusion between slaves and spirit retailers in the towns, to defeat the laws or ordinances governing the sale of alcohol. No spirits were permitted to be sold on the plantations, but in the towns no such prohibition applied. Access to the *vaertshus* or tavern was one of the smalls areas of freedom which the urban slave and his country counterpart could enjoy. Despite the fact that drunkenness was not a widespread phenomenon in these islands, at least not in the nineteenth century,[26] the conditions of spirit sales to slaves were rigidly prescribed for obvious reasons of public order: none on Sundays or feast and fast days of the Church, or after the sundown drum. By and large, however, publicans seem to have treated the stipulations none too seriously at least in the later eighteenth century.[27] Further infractions are suggested by Governor General Clausen's proclamation in 1766 which emphasized that slaves were to be sent on their way after buying one drink, and in any event were to be served outside the tavern.[28]

The publican for their part, had every interest in encouraging loiterers and in offering service to their slave clientele inside their establishments. The considerations involved were not merely pecuniary, i.e. cashing in on the liquidity of the urban artisans or the grass and firewood vendors from the country estates. The *vaertshus* was identified by white officialdom in the later eighteenth century as the centre of a traffic by slaves in stolen goods. The law deemed the reception and handling of stolen goods as criminal as the theft itself.[29] The goods stolen were usually of moderate value[30] and readily vendable in the comparative privacy of the taverns. Sometimes they were of greater value, such as gold and silver coins and watches.[31] Sometimes, too, they were of greater bulk than the latter but of no less value: items such as fence posts and lumber for carriage wheels,[32] or even the traditional staples, run, sugar and cotton.[33]

Bulk does not appear to have been any obstacle to the disposal of stolen goods, however. The Burgher Council of St. Croix, expressing great alarm at the traffic in 1787, pointed to the channel of procurement of the staples and a method of disposal that implicated the towns' free population, white as well as non-white:

Particularly during crop time, itinerant slaves hucksters betake themselves to the estates, encouraging the slave there to theft. By barter they obtain what rum, sugar and cotton they can and finally consign the goods to good-for-nothing whites and freedmen in the towns. Greater quantities can be disposed of in this way and in complete security.[34]

This urban demi-monde of slaves, 'good-for-nothing whites and freedmen' shared, as marginal groups, a community of interest expressed in a variety of ways, all of which were in violation of the law. In St. Croix, it appears that whilst the 1766 ordinance to serve slaves outside the grog shops was being observed in the 1780s, an earlier ordinance prohibiting sale on Sundays etc. was being flagrantly ignored. The Burgher Council noted that sales in the back of premises on Sundays and holidays gave rise to gambling with cards and dice, which the owners of such premises found it advantageous to encourage and permit.[35] Colbjornsen, a judge in the colonial service, also expressed unease about the operation of the grog shops: the rum puncheons were located inside the shops and could easily be set alight by an overturned candle, if they remained open after sunset. Such indeed had been the origin of one Christiansted fire. More importantly, however, Colbjornsen independently confirmed the Burgher Council's observation about gambling, and the comparative security of the backyards for this purpose. He also reinforced the view that they constituted ideal locations for the disposal of illegal merchandise.[36] The two activities were not of course unconnected, or as Governor General Clausen remarked in 1774, gambling was the father of 'theft, swindles and roguery'.[37] Whites in this urban demi-monde were not mere spectators at these sessions of gambling and drinking. As early as 1741, an ordinance forbade whites to sit and drink and or gamble with slaves. The severity of the punishment, which was eight days imprisonment on bread and water, is indicative of the seriousness with which the offence was viewed.[38]

The other important basis of communal interaction was undoubtedly the dance. Elsewhere, the author has discussed the compelling attractions of the dance for urban slaves.[39] Here it only needs to be re-emphasized that a Clausen ordinance of 1774 prohibited whites from attending any dances at which slaves were present, or to drink and dance with them – on pain of a fine of 100 Rigsdaler or imprisonment on bread and water for fourteen days.[40] Such dances to which whites ventured for enjoyment, rather than as monitors of law and order, were not, however, exclusively slave dances. They were as likely to be revels put on by freedmen at which were consistent but illegal participants. Persistent attempts were made to prevent this form of social intercourse between freedmen and urban slaves.[41] Such attempts were aimed at disrupting important links in the stolen goods trade, and at preventing, as was tried in the cities of the United States South, the forging of common links between slaves and freedmen. On neither of these counts did official policy enjoy noteworthy success. It was difficult to legislate against the natural affinities of kin, and, where these did not exist, of ethnic affiliations and marginality. This helps to explain also the enthusiasm with which the freedmen of the towns patronized the tea and coffee party treats that town slaves were regularly holding in the later eighteenth century.[42]

The communal interaction of urban slave and freedmen can be perceived not merely as pleasurable forms of inter-ethnic social commerce. In an important sense it existed also as a defense mechanism against the whites' hold on hegemonic power; in another sense, as an offensive instrument aimed at containing that power's effectiveness, or, under proper auspices, of defeating it. It is of interest that both contemporary literary and archival sources carry the conviction that the traffic in stolen goods was an important point of contact between slave and urban freedman. Hans West, for example, excoriated Christiansted's Free Gut, the freedman quarter, not only as a den of carnal iniquity, but also as a storehouse of every conceivable stolen good.[43]

The Burgher Council of St. Croix, as mentioned earlier, was convinced of such collusion in illegal trafficking. On another, occasion it described with grave disquiet 'the Free Negroes' connection and too great familiarity' with slaves, hinting darkly that no good would come of it.[44] Governor de Maleville, writing from St. Thomas in the 1780s, was prepared to be far more explicit. He deplored equally the stolen goods trade and the games of chance in which slaves became involved with freedmen.[45] His concerns were coloured by the austere morality of the good Moravian convert that he was. However, he was as determined to undermine the forging of any sense of community through 'too great familiarity'. Such a determination shared by many of his contemporaries, was a form of insurance against the re-occurrence of the St. Jan uprising of 1733 and after 1791, prophylaxis against infection from St. Domingue.

In St. Thomas, de Maleville had recorded instances where the 'close connections' between slaves and freedmen in Charlotte Amalie had resulted in the slave receiving assistance by gift or loan to obtain his freedom.[46] For him this was not matter for celebration, praying as he fervently did for a reduction in the numbers of freedmen whom he perceived more as 'a burden and a plague than an advantage'.[47] What was worse, he asserted, was that the freedmen in the town were a source of encouragement for marronage, as they were known to provide refuge for slaves on the run.[48]

Some contemporary whites, then, were convinced that they urban slave found among the freedmen of the towns companions in crime and spiritual succour. This is not to say, however, that the relationship between urban non-whites, free and un-free, was void of tension, contradiction and conflict. Certainly slaves were no less prone to run away from freedmen owners.[49] Contemporary whites would no doubt have explained such slaves' escape by attributing to freedmen as slave owners, a capacity for cruelty which was a form of over-compensation for their lowliness in the societal scale. Writing about the situation in Jamaica, Bryan Edwards commented quite unfavourably on the treatment freedmen meted out to the slaves they owned.[50] An anonymous memorialist in the Danish West Indies at the beginning of the nineteenth century, believed that the worst tyrants over their slaves were not only vain creole white women – when not in their overindulgent mood – and Jews, but also the 'emancipated coloured'. This memorialist claimed that such owners seldom handed over their slaves to the public authorities for punishment, preferring the limitless correction which domestic privacy permitted. It was not uncommon, he observed, to have several hundred lashes administered with a riding crop. Examples were supposed to abound of such owners taking it upon themselves to punish the weak and pregnant when the police had refused.[51] And yet, there are indications of charity and humanity to belie the lurid tales of sadism portrayed above. In St. Thomas in 1822, for example, two freedwomen Nancy Westphall and Petronella Moller secreted their slaves to avoid public punishment for offences unspecified.[52]

In the final analysis, however, the relationship between urban slaves and freedmen appears to have been one of some ambivalence. On the one hand, there are indications of co-operation: in the traffic in stolen goods, the use of the Guts as havens for runaways, in assistance to achieve manumission, in protection from the law. On the other hand, there is evidence of marronage from freedmen, and suggestions of extreme cruelty on their part. The ambiguities were further reinforced by the developments of the early nineteenth century which stratified freedmen on the basis of wealth, social standing and freeborn or manumitted status.[53] Urban slaves were not unaffected by these developments, for they provided the basis of conflict between the two groups. Adrian Bentzon, governor general, submitted in 1818 a detailed memorandum to the Danish government in which he gave a plausible explanation of the grounds for conflict, or its absence, between slaves and freedmen in the towns. It was his view that the 'lower classes' or freedmen, i.e. those manumitted, not freeborn, or as Bentzon described them, the 'transitional class', regarded slaves with a suspicion and deep hatred which was reciprocated. Many a worthy and intelligent bondsman, he observed, worked for the most contemptible freedman, and the slave themselves had taken notice that the fact of being in their ownership and employ was a guarantee of the worst treatment. The slaves' negative perception of such owners had been expressed in several uncomplimentary proverbs of which he was aware.[54]

Urban slaves and the poorer freedmen were in daily contact, and given the undercurrent of tension, it was little wonder that they were in perpetual collision and conflict. Bentzon noted that whilst the slaves' relationship with the poorer freedmen was marked by uneasiness, the same could not be said of their relationship with freeborn and better off freedmen.[55] He does suggest that the urban bondsman regarded light complexioned freedmen with favour because the latter approached the whites in phenotype. But in as much as he also admits that even noticeably black freedmen who were freeborn were also held in high regard by town slaves, it would appear that the respect was not exclusively a function of colour, nor necessarily mediated by it.

What the evidence might suggest is that as the freedman population in the towns expanded, the less privileged among them were in direct competition with urban slaves for economic opportunity. That was the circumstance which kept the town slave and the more privileged freedman apart, and explains Bentzon's remark that the 'opportunities for confrontation which arise from too close association do not exist with this class [of freedmen], who keep a marked degree of distance between themselves and slaves'. There is no direct literary or archival evidence of economic competition in the towns between slaves and freedmen, but it must be assumed, from the range of occupation skills which the former possessed, that those skills coincided at many points with those listed for the latter by contemporary authors such as Hans West.[56] There is evidence of competition between slave artisans and whites of similar skills.[57] Poorer freedmen, for their part, might have had neither enough means nor sufficient self-confidence and literacy skills to air grievances of this kind for public consumption and posterity.

As in the American South,[58] urban slavery in the Danish West Indies posed the problem of enforcing white authority in circumstances where the institution of servitude was at its most flexible. That being the case, the presumption of the slave's potential criminality was even greater in the towns than in the plantation country-side. The continuing concern with the maintenance of public order in the towns is well illustrated in the case of Charlotte Amalie in the later decades of the eighteenth century. As the town grew in economic importance as a result of the free port system, there was an increasing demand for labour associated with the port and warehouses. This was an area of occupation for those slaves whose owners depended on their hireage for a livelihood. But it was clear from contemporary comment that the supply was sometimes in excess of demand. De Maleville and Lillienschiold, the administrators of St. Thomas, commented in 1792 that it was as difficult in the West Indies to keep slaves with no fixed employment out of the towns, as it was to keep *Strand Cadetter* or 'Shore Cadets' out of Copenhagen.[59] Work in the West Indian customs houses where porters were mostly engaged, was seasonal; in between times, therefore, they tended to congregate on the streets. This was a source of annoyance and alarm to officialdom. De Maleville and Lillienschiold, for example, thought that their numbers should be controlled, that they should be made to carry passes and assemble for hire only in the customs house.[60]

The governor general at the time, Walterstorff, was similarly concerned about the porters as a potential public nuisance. Their threat to public order was made all the worse in his mind by an indolent and inefficient constabulary.[61] The Burgher Council of St. Croix, with whom he consulted, was as apprehensive, although they hesitated to prescribe a remedy that was worse than the disease. They recognized that many white townsfolk had no other property, no other source of income than the few slaves and the cash which these brought in. They recognized further that it was a convenience, as in any commercial centre, to have porters on hand for hire. That convenience, however, came at a price: runaway slaves from the country districts often passed themselves off in town as porters. The only solution the Burgher Council envisaged was that slave porters should have a readily distinguishable badge – like the hucksters' ticket – with their owner's name on it; that, as a general principle, all slaves hiring themselves out in town should have a ticket of authorization and that stricter police measures should be taken against urban vagrancy.[62] The problem of accommodating slavery to the environment of the towns, and the effect of urban slavery on the laws affecting servitude, were graphically illustrated in the case of Jochum and Sam, indicted for beating a white ship's captain, John Hart, in January 1784, at the request of their owner, ship's agent Lorentz Ebbesen. The petty sessions court or *Byting* handed down a judgement of a public beating and transportation for both. According to three witnesses to the event, Hart was vigorously set about in a public street and from the cudgel blows to his head and elsewhere, especially from Jochum the more violent of the two, lost a great deal of blood. Hart required a fortnight to recover, and there seems to be no doubt of the violence of the assault.

When the case came before the Landsting or Magistrate's Court, however, the presiding judge Colbjørnsen took cognisance of the slaves' circumscribed choice in obeying their master's orders. Their first duty, he said, was an unquestioning obedience to their master's commands, and in any event they had been assured by Ebbesen that he would take responsibility for the consequences of the assault.[63] In confirming the sentence of the lower court, Colbjørnsen was influenced like it by a notion of the slaves' diminished responsibility. Paradoxically, however, the sentence was also influenced by a notion of the slave as primarily property, no different in fact from a well trained guard dog that was ever responsive to its immediate source of authority, its master, and not responsible to the law. The judgement conveniently or otherwise failed to address itself to the fact of the slave as a person, and it was precisely in this capacity that the slave posed a threat to public order in the towns.

It is therefore of interest that the following year, the Governor General, Schimmelmann, drew up a proclamation which attempted to speak to those issues which Colbjørnsen's judgement had not. In cases such as Jochum's and Sam's there would be an investigation to establish whether the assault was justifiable, using as a criterion the necessity to save a master's life or property. If proven otherwise, the slave would be suitably punished.[64] The proclamation, however, failed to differentiate between town and country. It prescribed the same law for both, on the assumption presumably that the town's problem of public order was of a higher order of magnitude than the countryside's, and that the lesser would be comprehended by the greater. But writing from St. Thomas two years after Schimmelmann's ordinance, de Maleville was strongly in favour of differentiating the contexts. In the country parts the slave's help was virtually an unavoidable necessity. The situation in Charlotte Amalie, he argued, was entirely different. It was very seldom the case that in an emergency in that town, one could not do without the assistance of slaves since there were always whites about.[65]

In recognizing that the different circumstances of town and country called for different prescriptions, de Maleville was responding, in a way that Schimmelmann was not, to the legal tradition of half a century. As early as 1733 the use of iron-tipped sticks or knives as sidearms in Charlotte Amalie had been forbidden, and the presence of plantation slaves in town after the sundown drum prohibited.[66] The importance of the curfew generally and its specific application to dances was emphasized in ordinances in 1741, 1765 and 1774.[67] In a series of ordinances proclaimed between 1756 and 1759 Governor General von Prock required patterns of public behaviour that were to be at once deferential and free from suspicion: no galloping in the streets; no gambling on pavements; no throwing of firecrackers during the celebrations of Christmas or the New Year.[68] In St. Thomas in the 1760s, Governor de Gunthelberg made it an offence for slaves to ride horses through the town when they were to be watered. Nor was he overjoyed at the scant respect which slaves showed for police patrols, nor at the loud noises and derisive laughter which sometimes characterized their behaviour on the streets.[69] Indeed, any occasion on which slaves assembled in numbers in the towns was a source of misgiving whether it involved casual loitering or organized activities like dances, funerals or tea and coffee party treats.[70]

These laws specific to the urban bondsman merely delineate prescribed areas of unacceptable conduct without any helpful indication of frequency. In the case of marronage, however, there is an abundance of evidence of its frequency and persistence over time, and the way in which the flexible milieu of the towns facilitated running away from or to them. The contemporary newspapers are a rich source of information by way of their advertisements. They do pose a problem, however, in distinguishing which slaves were urban where the address of the owner was not given. One admittedly crude method employed for this study has been to regard as urban any of the slaves advertised as runaways who belonged to the following categories of persons: government and public officials, merchants, professionals. Sephardic and other Jews where identifiable by name, and freedmen.

The difficulty of identifying runaways to the towns is less unmanageable. As mentioned earlier, the greater anonymity of the town setting and the laxity of the police, made it possible for country slaves to pass themselves off as porters on the docks and in the warehouses. Governor General Clausen had taken note as early as the 1770s of Christiansted's attraction for runaways, who took day's work to support themselves while getting to know stores and warehouses.

For this reason he passed an ordinance requiring daily and weekly hired slaves to have passes.[71] But some twenty years later the concern over the unregulated wharf and warehouse porters suggests that Clausen's ordinance was a dead letter, and that Christiansted, at least, offered opportunities for an inventive runaway to find semi-regular employment. In the Basin or Bass End as the town was variously known, there were possibilities for the gifted or the skilled; like Matthias in 1808 whose mother was already there. Known by his aliases Dunlop and Tom Quinn, he was 'very active, smart and artful in conversation; a great frequenter of negro dances and frolics, where he is useful in beating the tambourin and creating sport'.[72] Clearly neither the plantation nor slavery could contain his zest for life nor accommodate his love of freedom; for him Christiansted was likely to cater to both.

The pull effect of the towns for runaways is best illustrated by Charlotte Amalie in the early nineteenth century. As the town grew as a commercial centre and Caribbean entrepot, so too did its population and the demand for labour services; with increasing complexity came increasing anonymity and the possibility of escaping detection. The expanding size of the freedman population provided an additional mask behind which runaways could conceal their identity. Charlotte Amalie had a particular attraction for runaways from nearby islands like Tortola or St. Croix.[73] The same was true for St. Jan. Jefferson, a cooper, who ran away from that island in 1827, was probably typical in his demonstration of ingenuity and capacity for survival. An African with country marks, he was described by his owner William Ruan as about 40 and *inter alia* 'plausible and cunning'. Jefferson was bilingual in creole and English, lived from fishing on St. Thomas' north side and came ashore only very infrequently. When he did, he was known to wear women's clothing, and although "well known in town' did not seem to be deterred by this fact.[74]

Other islands in the not so immediate environs of the northern Leewards are well represented in the catalogue of deserters to Charlotte Amalie. From St. Bartholomew in 1825 there was Gabriel, also known as Benjamin Powell. His upbringing as a seafarer conceivably assisted in his getaway. His trilingual skills in English, French and Spanish would also have been important pieces of equipment in his survival kit.[75] Jim, who came in on the inter-island schooner Isabella from Nevis in 1832, represents a category of runaways whose points of origin were even further afield.[76] There are several other examples from Antigua, Curacao and Barbados.[77] All of these slaves uniformly seized the opportunity of sea traffic into St. Thomas to develop in the early decades of the nineteenth century a species of underground railroad which, however, came by sea and at whose terminal point there was not unequivocal freedom.

Nor was movement unidirectional. Charlotte Amalie as port provided the hope of a life on the margins of freedom, but it was also a porthole on the world of freedom and escape hatch to it. In 1819 James Hazel's schooner, the Waterloo, which had made a trip from St. Thomas to St. Vincent, lost at one go a complement of eight slaves, seven men and one woman.[78] For those who did not seek escape to distant destinations, there were always the opportunities created by itinerant vending to seek a freedom, however parlous, in the countryside. This was perhaps more the case in St. Croix where relatively greater land mass, easier terrain and more numerous rural estates enhanced the prospects for slaves running away from the towns. It was this possibility to which the Burgher Council of St. Croix was very much alive when it noted in 1778 that many urban runaways were hawking bread, meat, fish and other items around the countryside.[79]

"Mulatto Nancy" was a typical case in point in the 1770s. She was owned by John Peter O'Donnel who carried on a tailoring establishment in Christiansted's Company Street, and had diversified into mosquito nets and bed curtains. Nancy was seen trafficking goods in Fredericksted and on country plantations. Like Jefferson, mentioned above, and so many others later and before, Nancy was 'well known in town and country' but avoided arrest with the plausible story that she was working for her owner. Neither the beatings which left 'sundry scars' on her face, nor the shackles on one foot and sores from them on the other, were able to deter her from her continuous attempts at a precarious freedom. One such attempt was with her eleven week old child.[80] Running away from the towns with a tray was a phenomenon that persisted well into the nineteenth century.[81]

Women vendors from the towns formed part of the aristocracy of servitude, enjoying latitude, mobility, flexibility in their working arrangements, and opportunities to handle on trust sums of cash that were sometimes substantial. The nature of their work permitted them to develop an intimate knowledge of the countryside and a network of connections that could be useful for future escape. Where huckstering was not a manifestation of this aristocracy of servitude, it helped to create and reinforce it. As an occupation, huckstering called for levels of articulation and savoir faire that were arguably of a higher order than those of other slaves, urban or rural. Dry goods had to be measured, salt beef, pork or fish weighed and priced, and competition with other higglers necessitated a competitive sales pitch. J.C. Leinburner's Nanette who ran away in 1808 with the goods she was selling was in all probability not atypically described as having 'a very smooth and insinuating tongue'.[82] James Aylmer's Fanny was no less gifted or enterprising. Seller as well as house servant, Fanny took off from Christiansted with a tray of goods of considerable value, having forged her own pass, and kept a brisk step ahead of the law by changing her name frequently.[83]

The male elites, the skilled and the artisans, figure continuously among runaways from the towns.[84] But men were not normally among the towns' itinerant slave vendors, an occupation dominated by women. For that reason, therefore, they were not usually to be found among bondsmen running away from the towns *qua* higglers. The records have yielded a single such: teenage Hector who ran away from his owner Kirksteen in Christiansted in July 1818.[85] This is not to say, however, that there were not male slaves in the towns who, deciding to run away, proceeded to use a tray and its contents as cover to escape. For example, in May 1810, John broke and entered his master's store in Christiansted, took dry goods and provisions valued at $200, informed another slave he was going to sell for his master, and was last seen heading for the West End, i.e. Fredericksted.[86]

Marronage from the town was also prompted by past or prospective punishment. Fred Rohde's whipmarked Hazard who ran away from Fredericksted in 1771 had perhaps had enough of the whip.[87] Freedwoman Bobkitta's Samuel was sought by Christiansted's chief of police

Mouritzen in 1807, suspected of having been 'of that Plot who (sic) breaks open the sugar hogsheads on the wharf.[88] Detention in the forts of any of the three towns was also a factor motivating marronage from the towns. It is not always possible to establish whether the provenance of fort detainees was urban or rural. But the forts existed as the ultimate symbols of the white's power of coercion and control. Rural slaves who had escaped to the towns in the hope of acquiring anonymity and freedom, had every motivation to escape from them once their apprehension and detention had returned them to that power. Whether rural or urban, however, there is every indication that slaves incarcerated in the forts escaped regularly, although the incidence appears to have been higher in St. Croix than St. Thomas.[89]

Urban slaves also responded to the same basic human motivation to reunite with kin and sexual partners that often inspired plantation slaves to petit and grand marronage. Rachel ran away in 1771 from Christiansted and the employment of Col. Kraus to the West End, 'being a favourite of Sergeant Deneyer' at the fort there. The records do not indicate whether this sergeant had a hand in the enterprise, but a sexual liaison must be assumed, the discretion of the phraseology notwithstanding.[90] Susannah who was a house servant to C.C. Henninges, the Christiansted printer, ran away thrice between 1804 and 1807 to join either her family on Dr, Stevens' plantation or her husband on Moses Titcombe's estate. Henninges was convinced that she was being harboured by a 'planter' he did not name, but duly threatened with the 'consequences of the Law.'[91] Planters and estate personnel may or may not have been guilty of such collusion. What is clear, however, is that a strong sense of kinship was an important catalyst of such attempted reunions.

The importance with which they could be regarded and the extreme steps taken to preserve those reunions, were illustrated in spectacular measure in the case of Sophina, house servant to Christiansted's vendue master Eylitz in 1802. Sophina ran away to rejoin her mother on a north-side estate. When a hunter went after her for the first time, he was prevented from apprehending her; on the second occasion he came back with his arm in a sling, 'being beaten up by one of the Negroes on the said Estate'.[92] There is no record of whether and or how the offending

slave was punished, nor whether Sophina was ever taken back to Christiansted. The incident does provide, however, an important index not only of the strength of kinship ties but also of a sense of loyalty that transcended the urban-rural dichotomy.

That dichotomy was at its most pronounced in the material conditions which tended to favour the existence of urban slaves in some important areas. In this regard housing was a key factor. In the slave cantonments on the plantations, the quality of the housing provided was notoriously indifferent throughout the eighteenth and early nineteenth century until it became the subject of ameliorative reform by Governor General von Scholten.[93] There is little or no data on housing for urban slaves except for West's tendentious claim of its adequacy, mentioned earlier. Bearing in mind, however, the extent of ownership by freedmen and poor whites, a substantial proportion of the towns' slaves could not have enjoyed housing considerably superior to the plantation quarters. Nothwithstanding, one would hazard the guess that most urban slaves were assured of rain-proof and draught-free accommodation. In relation to food, the data are equally sketchy. West's claim of universal plenty in Christiansted is not to be treated with seriousness. But the urban setting would have provided the possibility, at least, of more frequent access to a wider variety of nourishing food than was possibile on the plantation. There was a daily market in the towns on weekdays, conducted by the town slaves themselves,[94] and slaves with purchasing power to take advantage of this facility.

What probably holds true for housing and food, can be demonstrated with more certainty for clothing, for slaves resident in the towns, contact with white society was more sustained, intimate, frequent and broadly based than was the case on the estates. Indeed, Oxholm's use of the term, 'house negro' to apply exclusively to urban slaves, was perhaps influenced by that consideration. In the circumstances, there was an almost automatic assumption on the part of white society that slaves in their households should wear clothes of better quality than field slaves; an assumption for which the reported vanity of white creole women would have served as reinforcement. It was this assumption which informed Schimmelmann's sumptuary ordinance which dealt with household slaves and artisans. Plantation field slaves were allowed coarse cotton or linen for daily use, and, as a concession for Sundays and public holidays, old castoffs of little value. On the other hand, household slaves and artisans were permitted shoes, coarse stockings and items of cheap jewellery in addition to coarse cotton for daily use, and on Sundays clothes of better quality cotton or linen. Schimmelmann added that in any case, slaves in personal service could use whatever livery their owners provided, as well as cast-offs of whatever description. He pointedly concluded with the hope that no owner, in clothing his household slaves, would overstep those boundaries defined by the slaves' station and status, nor encourage them in extravagance, even if the latter of their own resources could buy clothing more costly than the ordinance permitted.[95]

There were other respects in which the constraining regimen of the plantation by its absence in the towns, favoured the urban slave. As West cryptically observed, no household slave could be made to do anything he or she had set his or her face against. How far this was true is difficult to determine. However, both West and Holten independently remark that urban house slaves were not normally sold by public auction except when the owner's estate came under the jurisdiction of the probate court. According to Holten:

The usual practice when a house slave is to be sold is to give him a ticket which says he is to be sold and at what price. He then goes about looking for another owner and if he is known to be a good-natured sort, he can count on finding a good master or mistress.[96]

What this therefore implies, is that until von Scholten's reforms of the 1830s which abolished the sale of slaves by public auction as inhuman and degrading, it was the exception for urban slaves to be publicly sold. The convention of allowing urban slaves to seek new masters can be substantiated by two examples. When 14 year old Jane, described as the mustee and 'somewhat freckled' child of Rachel Malcolm, ran away from 15 Company Street, Christiansted, in August 1817, her owner indicated that should she come home voluntarily, 'she shall have the choice of an owner.'[97] There was also Anthony Houseman who belonged to the Charlotte Amalie baker Delov. At the time Houseman ran away in May 1821, he had a permit to seek a new owner.[98]

Such comparatively favourable conditions relating to food, shelter, clothing and relationships with authority would suggest a lower mortality rate for urban than for plantation slaves. Oxholm, in the debate on Abolition in 1792, made the explicit claim that slaves in or close to the urban ambience were materially better off than their rural based counterparts. In support of that position, he produced a rare but important statistic: the death rate among slaves in Christiansted during the influenza epidemic of 1789 was 1:77, while the mean for the rest of the island exclusive of Fredericksted was 1:16. Fredericksted registered a death rate of 1:45, but this poor showing by the West End was explained, in Oxholm's view, by the presence of "an evil smelling lagoon behind Fredericksted town'.[99] However tendentious these data are, they are supportive of an inference which it would be reasonable to draw on the basis of the other evidence.

What this paper has attempted to demonstrate, is that in the later eighteenth and early nineteenth century, the three Danish West Indian towns of Christiansted, Fredericksted and Charlotte Amalie had a slave presence that was significant in the extreme. That presence had a very important bearing on the quantitative composition of the towns' populations, as well as an important qualitative effect by way of the provision of goods, crucial services and skills. There is evidence to suggest that their role in the urban economy was one of some importance. The shape of life in these towns was affected not only by the slaves who lived in them, but also by estate slaves who were attracted to them as market vendors of food, firewood and grass suppliers, servants or artisans contracted out. The towns also acted as powerful magnets for runaway slaves from the plantations, and other islands nearby and not so nearby. With poorer whites and free people of colour, urban slaves established and sustained a fraternity of the marginalised. The authorities complained of common interests embracing dances, games of chance, traffic in stolen goods and the illegal sale of alcohol. But in addition to this there would have been among urban blacks as a group, whatever their legal status, ties of kinship, residence, language and many shared values.

The polyglot white population,[100] concentrated in the towns was only slightly less vulnerable to the slaves' numerical strength than the plantation whites. But the very flexibility of the urban milieu created special problems of social control to which the law was obliged to address itself. The cultural fragmentation of this white population because of the diversity of its national provenance and confessional allegiances created a situation of startling paradox. It can be claimed without exaggeration that the slaves were the major source of whatever culturally unifying tendencies there were: in language, by way of the lingua franca, creolsk, and the celebration of Christmas and the New Year in which the towns played a dominant role.[101]

But whatever else the towns were, they enshrined and symbolised the dominant power of the whites over the slaves. It was here that the gallows and the public whipping posts were situated; it was here that the auctions were held into the 1830s, even though few if any urban slaves were so sold after the 1780s. It was here too that the forts were located, serving not only as prisons for delinquent bondsmen but also as the embodiment of that ultimate sanction which kept all slaves, urban and rural alike, in subjection. It is therefore of more than passing significance that the ultimate confrontation with white authority which ended in emancipation in July 1848, took place in one of the three towns of the Danish West Indies, Frederiksted, and that the greater part of that drama was played out in front of its fort.

Notes

1. *RDAG* 30 June and 15 Sept. 1792.
2. C.H. Holten, 'Af en Gammel Hofmands Mindeblade. Konferensraad Carl Henrik Holtens Optegnelser' *Memoirer og Breve* 11 (1909) 51. In contrast Holten observed that in Europe he had two chambermaids and a man servant. Cf, also R/A, VJ 1793 #911, where it was claimed that in the West Indies a married man needed a household staff of 5, an additional servant for each member of the family, one for each child, plus a coachman.
3. Hans West, *Bidrag til Beskrivelse over St. Croix*, (Copenhagen: 1793)p.61.
4. Hans West, 'Beretning om det dansk Eilande St. Croix i Vestindien', *Iris*, 3(1791)64.
5. R/A, *AVS/FC*, Betaenkning no.3, 10 Fe.1818.Cf.VJ1793#911.
6. R/A, *Dokumenter Vedkommende kommissionen Vedrørende negerhandelen Samt Efterretninger om Negerhandelen og Slaveriet i Vestindien*, Gen. Walterstorff's 'Foreløbige Anmaerkninger', 21 Sept. 1792.
7. West, "Beretning", p.42.
8. R/A, *Udkast og Betaenkning ang. Negerloven m.Bilag 1783-1789*, no. 27, Placat #43,2 Dec. 1778. See also Frederiksted Police Chief Behagen's call for an inventory of trays' contents as a means of preventing the sale of stolen goods: St.C.G. 13 Feb. 1812.
9. R/A, *Om Negerhandelens Afskaffelse (korrespondence m. kommissioner etc.)* 1789-1847, Anonymous Pro Memoria c. 1802f. 11.
10. West, "beretning".p. 47.
11. R/A, *Dokumenter Vedkommende Kommissionen*, Burgher Council of St. Croix to Danish West Indian Government, 5 Sept. 1792.
12. R/A, VJ 1793 #911:
    den tilsyneladende Overflødighed af Huusneger i Mange Tilfaeld kan fortjene Forsvar, naar man laegge Maerke til, at ofte ere de deres Ejers eneste Opholds-Middel, der enten gjør sig Fordeel ved dennes Haandarbejde eller ved atudleje den.
    * All translations in this paper are the author's and he accepts sole responsibility for their accuracy.
13. R/A, *Om Negerhandelens Afskaffelse*, Anonymous Pro Memoria c. 1802.
14. R/A, VJ 1793 #911.
15. St. C.G. 25 July 1808.
16. See respectively *RDAG* 1 Feb. 1770; *RDAG* 25 June 1777; *RDAG* 17 Oct. 1770; St. C.G. 14 Jan. 1815; *RDAG* 4 Aug. 1770; St. C.G. 24 Mar. 1817; *RDAG* 30 Oct. 1776; *RDAG* 25 Aug. 1770. These bits of bio-data all derive from advertisements for runaways.
17. West, "Beretning", p. 42:
    Nogle laere haandevaerke, og bringe det saavidt i deres kunst, at jeg nedlaegge min Aere paa, at ingen fuld udlaest Mesterssvend immelem Kiøbenhavns høiberømte Laug, der indskraenke al muelig Industrie, skal kunne sye et Par Sko eller en Klaedning, end ikke et Knaphul saa net og skønt, some en creolsk Neger.
18. R/A, *Udkast og Betaenkning*, no. 17, von Roepstorffs Nota, 7 Feb 1784.
19. Jens Vibaek, *Vore Gamle Tropekolonier*, (Copenhagen, Fremad: 1966) vol. 2 p. 13.
20. R/A, *Vestindisk Kommissionsforretning vedr. Salg af Plantager og Ulovlig Handel paa St. Croix, 1759.*
21. R/A, *Udkast og Betaenkning*, no. 17, von Roepstorff's Nota, 7 Feb. 1784.
22. N.A.T. Hall, 'Slaves' Use of their 'Free Time' in the danish Virgin Islands in the late Eighteenth and early Nineteenth Century', *Journal of Caribbean History*, 13 (1979) 28-29.
23. West, *Bidrag*, p.75.
24. Ibid, p. 76.
25. N.A.T. Hall, *Forslag til Ordning af Vestindisk Forfatnings Forhold Angaaende Negerne m.m. Translated with an Introduction and Notes*, Occasional Paper No. 5 (St. Thomas, Bureau of Libraries Museums & Archaelogical Services, Dept. Of Conservation & Cultural Affairs: 1979), p.18.
26. Holten, "Af en Gammel Hofmands Mindeblade. . .", p. 52.
27. R/A, *Udkast og Betaenkning . . . 27 #22*, von Prock's Placat, 23 Dec. 1759 para. 7 See also *Udkast og*

Betaenkning . . ., no. 1,Moth's "Articuler for Negerne' 11 Dec. 1741 para 2. Cf. *Udkast og Betaenkning . . .* no. 27, #35, Schimmelmann's Placat, 20 Aug. 1773. Para. 4;#38, Clausen's Placat, 5 Oct. 1774, para. 2. For the situation regarding St. Thomas see #27, 12 Nov. 1762.

28. Ibid, #30, 18 Oct. 1766.
29. Ibid, #39, 27 Sept. 1775.
30. For some early nineteenth century examples see St. C.G. 29 Feb. 1808;DVRA 21 Mar. 1808;26 Feb.1816.
31. West, "Beretning", pp. 48-49.
32. R/A, *Udkast og Betaenkning . . .* no. 27, #34, Clausen's Placat, 27 Sept. 1775.
33. R/A, *Kommissionsforslag og Anmaerkning ang. Negerloven med Genpartner af Anordninger og Publikationer 1785*, Bind 2, Borger Raads Betaenkning, 1 Aug. 1787, f. 76.
34. Ibid, f. 76:
     Saelge Neger infinde sig isaer i Crop Tiden paa Plantagerne, op muntre Slaverne til Tyverie, selv tilbytte for Skamkjøbe hvad Run, Sukker eller Bomuld de kunde have i Besiddelse, og emdligen anvisse dem nederdraegtige Blank og Frie Negere i Byerne, hos hvem de frit og i Sikkerheden kan afsaettes større QVANTITER.
35. Ibid.
36. Ibid, Colbjørsen's Anmaerkninger, 20 Sept. 1788, f. 114.
37. R/A, *Udkast og Betaenkning...*no. 27 #38, 5 Oct. 1774.
38. Ibid, no. 1, Moth's "Articuler', 11 Dec. 1741.
39. Hall, 'Slaves' Use of their 'Free' Time', pp. 30-33.
40. R/A, *Udkast og Betaenkning . . .* no. 27 #38, 5 Oct. 1774.
41. See for example R/A, *Udkast og Betaenkning...*no. 27 #38, Clausen's Placat 5 Oct. 1774 para. 6. Cf. Ibid, no. 1 #24, "Forslag til en Neger Lov for de Kongelige Danske Vestindiske Eylande", Part 1 para.83,1773; and *Kommissionsforslag og Anmaerkning. . .* Bind 2, Neger Lov for de Danske Vestindiske Eylande", Part 2 par. 38.
42. Hall, 'Slaves' Use of their 'Free' Time', pp. 31-33.
43. West, 'Beretning', p.49.
44. R/A, *Udkast og Betaenkning . . .* no. 27#43, 2 Dec, 1773.
45. R/A, *Kommissionsforslag og Anmaerkning. . .* Bind 2, de Maleville's Betaenkninger 19 Oct. 1787, f.94.
46. Ibid, de Maleville's Anmaerkninger, 7 April 1784, f.33.
47. Ibid, de Maleville's Betaenkninger, 19 Oct. 1787, f.84.
48. Ibid.
49. For examples see *RDAG* 14 June 1775; *DVRA* 23 April 1807; Ibid, 25 May 1807.
50. Bryan Edwards, *The History Civil and Commercial, of the British Colonies in the West Indies* (London: 1793) vol.2, p. 25.
51. R/A, *Om Negerhandelens Afskaffelse 1738-1847*, Anonymous Pro Memoria c. 1802, f.8.
52. St. T.T., 29 Jan. 1822.
53   N.A.T. Hall, 'The 1816 Freedman Petition in the Danish West Indies: Its Background and Conse-

quences'. *Boletin de Estudios Latinoamericanos y del Caribe*, No. 29 (December 1980).
54. R/A, *AVS/FC*, Bentzon's Betaenkning no.3, 10 Feb. 1818.
55. Ibid.
56. West, "Beretning", p. 42 and footnote, 17 above. For coincident freedmen's skills see West, *Bidrag*, pp. 57-58.
57. See for examples RDAG, 19 Sept. 1772 reporting the case of the runaway tailor Wanico who 'tis well known . . . would not absent himself so often from his master, if there was (sic) not bad people to employ him in hopes of getting their work cheaper done than by a white person'.
58. C.D. Goldin, *Urban Slavery in the American South* (Chicago: University of Chicago Press, 1976) pp. 47 et seq.
59. R/A, *Dokumenter Vedkommende Kommissionen . . .*, St. Thomas Raad to Danish West Indian Government, 9 Nov. 1792.
60. Ibid.
61. Ibid, Walterstorff's 'Forelobige Anmaerkninger,' 21 Sept. 1792.
62. Ibid, St. Croix Burgher Council to Danish West Indian Government, 5 Sept. 1792.
63. R/A, *Udkast og Betaenkning. . .* Miscellaneous Papers, Bilag 5a.
64. R/A, *Kommissionsforslag og anmaerkning. . .* Bind 1, 'Gienpart af Adskillige. Placater Negerne Betraeffende 1672-1787', no. 60, Schimmelmann's Placat, 14 Oct. 1785, para. 1.
65. Ibid, de Maleville's 'Uforgribelige Taenker over Heer General Gouverneurens Placat', 10 Dec. 1787.
66. R/A, *Udkast og Betaenkning . . .* no. 4, 5 Sept. 1733, paras. 12, 17, 18.
67. Ibid, no. 1, Moth's Articular for Negerne', 11 Dec. 1741, para. 1; Ibid, no. 27 #29, de Gunthelberg's St. Thomas Placat, 9 Feb. 1765, paras. 2 & 3; Ibid, no. 27 #38, para. 6.
68. Ibid, no. 27 #18, 17 May 1756 para 8; #22, 23 Dec. 1759 para. 12;#22, 23 Dec. 1759 para 9 (cf. #38 Clausen's Placat, 5 Oct, 1774 para. 3); no. 1, 30 Dec. 1758 para. 2 (Cf. No. 27 #33, Clausen's Placat, 21 Oct. 1770) and #41 Clausen's Placat, 21 Oct. 1771.
69. Ibid, no. 27 #29, 9 Feb. 1765, paras. 6, 8, 10, 14. Cf. #38, 5 Oct. 1774 para. 4.
70. Ibid, no. 27 #43, St. Croix Burgher Council's Forestilling, 2 Dec. 1778, paras. 4 and 5.
71. Ibid. No. 27 #30, 27 Sept. 1775.
72. St. C.G., 11 Feb. 1808.
73. St. T.T. 23 June 1818 & 9 July 1819.
74. Ibid, 28 Mar. 1827.
75. Ibid, 13 Apr. 1825.
76. Ibid, 15 Aug. 1832.
77. Ibid, 30 June 1817; 17 Mar. 1821; 6 Sept. 1821; 11 Jan. 1822; 23 Nov. 1825; 15 Aug. 1832 constitute some good examples.
78. Ibid, 10 Apr. 1819.
79. R/A, *Udkast og Betaenkning . . .* no. 27 #43, St. Croix Burgher Council's Forestilling, 2 Dec. 1778.

80. Her various attempts are catalogued in RDAG 17 Feb. 1773; 27 Mar. 1773; 11 Aug. 1773; 27 Mar. 1774; 13 Apr. 1774; 7 June 1775.

81. For examples see RDAG 31 Mar. 1802,; 5 May 1802; 26 June 1802; 4 Oct. 1803; 21 Mar. 1805 and St. C.G. 3 Mar. 1809; 9 June 1809; 19 July 1811.

82. *DVRA*, 21 Mar. 1808.

83. St. C.G. 16 Oct. 1810.

84. See above, footnote 16.

85. St. C.G. 30 July 1816.

86. Ibid, 4 May 1810.

87. *RDAG* 21 Nov. 1771.

88. *DVRA* 23 Apr. 1807.

89. Examples of slaves escaping from town forts can be found in *DVRA* 12 July 1802; 27 May 1805; 4 April. 1807; 22 June 1807; 29 Oct. 1807; *St. C.G.* 26 Mar. 1811; 21 July 1812; *St. T.T.* 1 Jan 1816; *DVRA* 7 Jan. 1819; 5 Jan. 1824.

90. *RDAG* 12 Jan. 1771.

91. *DVRA* 10 Sept. 1804; 3 Oct. 1805; 26 Jan. 1807.

92. *RDAG* 24 Mar. 1802.

93. Victor Schoelcher, *Colonies Estrangeres et Haiti. Resultats de l'Emancipation Anglais* (Paris: 1843) vol. 2,pp. 20-21.

94. West, 'Beretning', p. 47.

95. R/A, *Kommissionsforslag og Anmaerkning . . .* Bind 1, no. 63, Schimmelmann's Placat, 26 May 1786, para. 2(b), ff. 72-73.

96. Holten, 'Af en Gammel hofmands Mindeblade . . .', pp. 51-52. West makes a comparable observation in Bidrag, p. 60.

97. *RDAG* 14 Aug. 1817.

98. St. T.T. 24 May 1821.

99. R/A, *Dokumenter Vedkommende kommissionen...* Oxholm's Anmaerkninger ved kongl. Kommissionen', 1 Aug. 1792, para 8(b).

100. Hall, 'Slaves' Use of their 'Free' Time . . .', p. 22.

101. Ibid., pp. 26, 33-36.

SECTION SEVEN

Slavery and Capitalist Globalization: The First Phase

Marxist historians have been in the vanguard of the discourse that locates slavery within the first phase of Atlantic capitalist development. Colonial exploitation, using slavery as the mode of extracting surplus value from workers, provided the wider market economy required by merchant capital during the seventeenth century. The emergence of Western Europe as the political centre of an Atlantic economy signalled the importance of imperial exploitation to its development. Indeed, development discourse, centering around the new discipline of political economy, privileged colonialism as the transformative engine of capitalist growth. Colonies meant trade, finance and plunder. These essays explore the details of these discussions, and illustrate the intensity of their political significance.

The conclusions of Eric Williams and CLR James were clearly stated before 1945. First, they stated that both the slave and sugar trades were lucrative, and that the plantation system provided a significant amount of the critical surplus capital which propelled England and France into self-sustained economic growth in the eighteenth and nineteenth centuries. Second, that with the ability of European capitalism to reproduce internally its own surplus capital, largely associated with the ascendancy of industrial capital over merchant finance in the late eighteenth century and early nineteenth century, came the economic context for the reduced economic significance of the West Indian plantation system. Declining importance and adverse market forces led to long-term crisis in the West Indian plantation economy and hence the movement towards the abolition. Over these theses, rigorous polemics, with transatlantic dimensions, have developed. The intention of these essays by Williams, James, Knight, and Darity is simply to provide a brief summary of the intellectual loci of the various arguments.

33

Capitalism and Slavery

ERIC WILLIAMS

'There is nothing which contributes more to the development of the colonies and the cultivation of their soil than the laborious toil of the Negroes.' So reads a decree of King Louis XIV of France, on August 26, 1670. It was the consensus of seventeenth-century European opinion. Negroes became the 'life' of the Caribbean, as George Downing said of Barbados in 1645. Without Negroes, said the Spanish Council of the Indies in 1685, the food needed for the support of the whole kingdom would cease to be produced, and America would face absolute ruin. Europe has seldom been as unanimous on any issue as it has been on the value of Negro slave labour.

In 1645, before the introduction of the sugar economy, Barbados had 5,680 Negro slaves, or more than three able-bodied white men to every slave. In 1667, after the introduction of the sugar industry, the island, by one account, contained 82,023 slaves, or nearly ten slaves to every white man fit to bear arms. By 1698, a more accurate estimate of the population gave the figures as 2,330 white males and 42,000 slaves, or a ratio of more than eighteen slaves to every white male.

In Jamaica the ratio of slaves to whites was one to three in 1658, nearly six to one in 1698. There were 1,400 slaves in the former year, 40,000 in the latter. The ratio of slaves and mulattoes to whites increased from more than two to one in Martinique in 1664 to more than three to one in 1701. The coloured population amounted to 2,434 in 1664 and 23,362 in 1701. In Guadeloupe, by 1697, the coloured population outnumbered the whites by more than three to two. In Grenada in 1700 the Negro slaves and mulattoes were more than double the number of whites. In the Leeward Islands and in St Thomas the whites steadily lost ground.

By 1688 it was estimated that Jamaica required annually 10,000 slaves, the Leeward Islands 6,000 and Barbados 4,000. A contract of October, 1675, with one Jean Oudiette, called for the supply of 800 slaves a year for four years in the French West Indies. Four years later, in 1679, the Senegal Company undertook to supply 2,000 slaves a year for eight years to the French Islands. Between 1680 and 1688 the Royal African Company supplied 46,396 slaves to the British West Indies, an annual average of 5,155.

The Negro slave trade became one of the most important business enterprises of the seventeenth century. In accordance with sixteenth-century precedents its organization was entrusted to a company which was given the sole right by a particular nation to trade in slaves on the coast of West Africa, erect and maintain the forts necessary for the protection of the trade, and transport and sell the slaves in the West Indies. Individuals, free traders or 'interlopers', as they were called, were excluded. Thus the British incorporated the Company of Royal Adventurers trading to Africa, in 1663, and later replaced this company by the Royal African Company, in 1672, the royal patronage and participation reflecting the importance of the trade and continuing the fashion set by the Spanish monarchy of increasing its revenues thereby. The monopoly of the French slave trade was at first assigned to the French West India Company in 1664, and then transferred, in 1673, to the Senegal Company. The monopoly of the Dutch slave trade was given to the Dutch West India Company, incorporated in 1621. Sweden organized a Guinea Company in 1647. The Danish West India Company, chartered in 1671, with the royal family among its shareholders, was allowed in 1674 to extend its activities to Guinea. Brandenburg established a Brandenburg African Company, and established its first trading post on the coast of West Africa in 1682. The Negro slave trade, begun about 1450 as a Portuguese monopoly, had, by the end of the seventeenth century, become an international free-for-all.

The organization of the slave trade gave rise to one of the most heated and far-reaching economic polemics of the period. Typical of the argument in favour of the monopoly was a paper in 1680 regarding the Royal African Company of England. The argument, summarised, was as follows: firstly, experience demonstrated that the slave trade could not be carried on without forts on the West African coast costing £20,000 a year, too heavy a charge for private traders, and it was not practicable to apportion it among them; secondly, the trade was exposed to attack by other nations, and it was the losses from such attacks prior to 1663 which had resulted in the formation of the chartered company; thirdly, the maintenance of forts and warships could not be undertaken by the Company unless it had an exclusive control; fourthly, private traders enslaved all and sundry, even Negroes of high rank, and this led to reprisals on the coast; finally, England's great rival, Holland, was only waiting for the dissolution of the English company to engross the entire trade.

The monopolistic company had to face two opponents: the planter in the colonies and the merchant at home, both of whom combined to advocate free trade. The planters complained of the insufficient quantity, the poor quality, and the high prices of the slaves supplied by the Company; the latter countered by pointing out that the planters were heavily in debt to it, estimated in 1671 at £70,000, and four years later at £60,000 for Jamaica alone. The British merchants claimed that free trade would mean the purchase of a larger number of Negroes, which would mean the production of a larger quantity of British goods for the purchase and upkeep of the slaves.

The controversy ended in a victory for free trade. On July 5, 1698, Parliament passed an act abrogating the monopoly of the Royal African Company, and throwing open the trade to all British subjects on payment of a duty of 10 per cent *ad valorem* on all goods exported to Africa for the purchase of slaves.

The acrimonious controversy retained no trace of the pseudo-humanitarianism of the Spaniards in the sixteenth century, that Negro slavery was essential to the preservation of the Indians. In its place was a solid economic fact, that Negro slavery was essential to the preservation of the sugar plantations. The considerations were purely economic. The slaves were denominated 'black ivory'. The best slave was, in Spanish parlance, a 'piece of the Indies', a slave 30-35 years old, about five feet eleven inches in height, without any physical defect. Adults who were not so tall and children were measured, and the total reduced to 'pieces of the Indies'. A contract in 1676 between the Spaniards and the Portuguese called for the supply of 10,000 'tons' of slaves; to avoid fraud and argument, it was stipulated that three Negroes should be considered the equivalent of one ton. In 1651 the English Guinea Company instructed its agent to load one of its ships with as many Negroes as it could carry, and, in default, to fill the ship with cattle.

The mortality in the Middle Passage was regarded merely as an unfortunate trading loss, except for the fact that Negroes were more costly than cattle. Losses in fact ran quite high, but such concern as was evinced had to deal merely with profits. In 1659, a Dutch slaver, the *St. Jan*, lost 110 slaves out of a cargo of 219 – for every two slaves purchased, one died in transit to the West Indies. In 1678, the *Arthur*, one of the ships of the Royal African Company, suffered a mortality of 88 out of 417 slaves – that is, more than 20 per cent. The *Martha*, another ship, landed 385 in Barbados out of 447 taken on the coast – the mortality amounted to 62, or a little less than 15 per cent. The *Coaster* lost 37 out of 150, a mortality of approximately 25 per cent. The *Hannibal*, in 1694, with a cargo of 700 slaves, buried 320 on the voyage, a mortality of 43 per cent; the Royal African Company lost £10 and the owner of the vessel 10 guineas on each slave, the total loss amounting to £6,650. The losses sustained by these five vessels amounted to 617 out of a total cargo of 1,933, that is, 32 per cent. Three out of every ten slaves perished in the

Middle Passage. Hence the note of exasperation in the account of his voyage by the captain of the *Hannibal*:

No gold-finders can endure so much noisome slavery as they do who carry Negroes; for those have some respite and satisfaction, but we endure twice the misery; and yet by their mortality our voyages are ruin'd, and we pine and fret our selves to death to think we should undergo so much misery, and take so much pains to so little purpose.

The lamentations of an individual slave trader or sugar planter were drowned out by the seventeenth-century chorus of approbation. Negro slavery and the Negro slave trade fitted beautifully into the economic theory of the age. This theory, known as mercantilism, stated that the wealth of a nation depended upon its possession of bullion, the precious metals. If, however, bullion was not available through possession of the mines, the new doctrine went further than its Spanish predecessor in emphasising that a country could increase its stock by a favourable balance of trade, exporting more than it imported. One of the best and clearest statements of the theory was made by Edward Misselden, in his *Circle of Commerce*, in 1623:

For as a pair of scales is an invention to show us the weight of things, whereby we may discern the heavy from the light . . . so is also the balance of trade an excellent and politique invention to show us the difference of weight in the commerce of one kingdom with another: that is, whether the native commodities exported, and all the foreign commodities imported do balance or over-balance one another in the scale of commerce. . . If the native commodities exported do weight down and exceed in value the foreign commodities imported, it is a rule that never fails that then the kingdom grows rich and prospers in estate and stock: because the overplus thereof must needs come in in treasure . . . But if the foreign commodities imported do exceed in value the native commodities exported, it is a manifest sign that the trade decayeth, and the stock of the kingdom wasteth apace; because the overplus must needs go out in treasure.

National policy of the leading European nations concentrated on achieving a favourable balance of trade. Colonial possessions were highly prized as a means to this end; they increased the exports of the metropolitan country, prevented the drain of treasure by the purchase of necessary tropical produce, and provided freights for the ships of the metropolis and employment for its sailors.

The combination of the Negro slave trade, Negro slavery and Caribbean sugar production is known as the triangular trade. A ship left the metropolitan country with a cargo of metropolitan goods, which it exchanged on the coast of West Africa for slaves. This constituted the first side of the triangle. The second consisted of the Middle Passage, the voyage from West Africa to the West Indies with the slaves. The triangle was completed by the voyage from the West Indies to the metropolitan country with sugar and other Caribbean products received in exchange for the slaves. As the slave ships were not always adequate for the transportation of the West Indian produce, the triangular trade was supplemented by a direct trade between the metropolitan country and the West Indian islands.

The triangular trade provided a market in West Africa and the West Indies for metropolitan products, thereby increasing metropolitan exports and contributing to full employment at home. The purchase of the slaves on the coast of West Africa and their maintenance in the West Indies gave an enormous stimulus to metropolitan industry and agriculture. For example, the British woollen industry was heavily dependent on the triangular trade. A parliamentary committee of 1695 emphasised that the slave trade was an encouragement to Britain's woollen industry. In addition, wool was required in the West Indies for blankets and clothing for the slaves on the plantations.

Iron, guns and brass also figured prominently in the triangular trade and the ancillary West Indian trade. Iron bars were the trading medium on a large part of the West African coast, and by 1682 Britain was exporting about 10,000 bars of iron a year to Africa. Sugar stoves, iron rollers, nails found a ready market on the West Indian plantations. Brass pans and kettles were customarily included in the slave trader's cargo.

The triangular trade presented an impressive statistical picture. Britain's trade in 1697 may be taken as an illustration.

	Imports £	Exports £
British West Indies	326,536	142,795
North America	279,582	140,129
Africa	6,615	13,435
Antigua	28,209	8,029
Barbados	196,532	77,465
Jamaica	70,00	40,726

	Imports £	Exports £
Montserrat	14,699	3,532
Nevis	17,096	13,043
Carolina	12,374	5,289
New England	26,282	64,468
New York	10,093	4,579
Pennsylvania	3,347	2,997
Virgina and Maryland	227,756	58,796
Total	1,220,121	575,283

Barbados was the most important single colony in the British Empire, worth almost as much, in its total trade, as the two tobacco colonies of Virginia and Maryland combined, and nearly three times as valuable as Jamaica. The tiny sugar island was more valuable to Britain than Carolina, New England, New York and Pennsylvania together. 'Go ahead, England, Barbados is behind you,' is today a stock joke in the British West Indies of the Barbadian's view of his own importance. Two and a half centuries ago, it was no joke. It was sound politics, based on sound economics. Jamaica's external trade was larger than New England's as far as Britain was concerned; Nevis was more important in the commercial firmament than New York; Antigua surpassed Carolina; Montserrat rated higher than Pennsylvania. Total British trade with Africa was larger than total trade with Pennsylvania, New York and Carolina. In 1697 the triangular trade accounted for nearly 10 per cent of total British imports and over 4 per cent of total British exports. Barbados alone accounted for nearly 4 per cent of Britain's external trade.

Mercantilists were jubilant. The West Indian colonies were ideal colonies, providing a market, directly as well as indirectly, through the slave trade, for British manufactures and foodstuffs, whilst they supplied sugar and other tropical commodities that would otherwise have had to be imported from foreigners or dispensed with entirely. The West Indies thus contributed to Britain's balance of trade in two ways, by buying Britain's exports and by rendering the expenditure of bullion on foreign tropical imports unnecessary. On the other hand, the mainland colonies, Virginia and Maryland, and, to a lesser extent, Carolina excepted, where the conditions of labour and production duplicated those of the West Indies, were nuisances; they produced the same agricultural commodities as England, gave early

evidence of competing with the metropolitan countries in manufactured goods as well, and were rivals in fishing and shipbuilding.

The British economists enthused. Sir Josiah Child in his *New Discourse of Trade* in 1668, wrote:

The people that evacuate from us to Barbados, and the other West India Plantations . . . do commonly work one Englishman to ten or eight Blacks; and if we keep the trade of our said plantations entirely to England, England would have no less inhabitants, but rather an increase of people by such evacuation, because that one Englishman, with the Blacks that work with him, accounting what they eat, use and wear, would make employment for four men in England . . . whereas peradventure of ten men that issue from us to New England and Ireland, what we send to or receive from them, doth not employ one man in England.

In 1690, Sir Dalby Thomas stated that every white man in the West Indies was one hundred and thirty times more valuable to Britain than those who stayed at home:

Each white man, woman and child, residing in the sugar plantations, occasions the consumption of more of our native commodities, and manufactures, than ten at home do – beef, pork, salt, fish, butter, cheese, corn, flour, beer, cyder, bridles, coaches, beds, chairs, stools, pictures, clocks, watches; pewter, brass, copper, iron vessels and instruments; sail-cloth and cordage; of which, in their building, shipping, mills, boiling, and distilling-houses, field-labour and domestic uses, they consume infinite quantities.

Charles Davenant, perhaps the ablest of the seventeenth-century economists, estimated at the end of the century that Britain's total profit from trade amounted to £2,000,000. Of this figure the plantation trade accounted for £600,000, and the re-export of plantation produce for £120,000. Trade with Africa, Europe and the Levant brought in another £600,000. The triangular trade thus represented a minimum of 36 per cent of Britain's commercial profits. Davenant added that every individual in the West Indies, white or Negro, was as profitable as seven in England.

What the West Indies had done for Seville in Spain in the sixteenth century, they did for Bristol in England and Bordeaux in France in the seventeenth. Each town became the metropolis of its country's trade with the Caribbean, though neither Bristol nor Bordeaux enjoyed the monopoly that had been granted to Seville. In 1661 only one ship, and that ship a Dutch one, came to Bordeaux from the West Indies. Ten years later twelve ships sailed from that port to the

West Indies, and six returned from there. In 1683 the number of sailings to the sugar islands had risen to twenty-six. La Rochelle for a time eclipsed Bordeaux. In 1685 forty-nine ships sailed from that port to the West Indies. Nantes also was intimately connected with West Indian trade; in 1684 twenty-four ships belonging to the port were engaged in West Indian trade.

As a result of the triangular trade Bristol became a city of shopkeepers. It was said in 1685 that there was scarcely a shopkeeper in the city who had not a venture on board some ship bound for Virginia or the West Indies. The port took the lead in the struggle for the abrogation of the Royal African Company's monopoly, and in the first nine years of free trade shipped slaves to the West Indies at the rate of 17,883 a year. In 1700 Bristol had forty-six ships in the West Indian trade.

The basis of this astounding commercial efflorescence was the Negro slaves, 'the strength and sinews of this western world'. In 1662 the Company of Royal Adventurers trading to Africa pointed to the 'profit and honour' that had accrued to British subjects from the slave trade, which King Charles II himself described as that 'beneficial trade . . . so much importing our service, and the enriching of this Our Kingdom'. According to Colbert in France, no commerce in the world produced as many advantages as the slave trade. Benjamin Raule exhorted the Elector of Prussia, on October 26, 1685, not to be left behind in the race: 'Everyone knows that the slave trade is the source of the wealth which the Spaniards wring out of the West Indies, and that whoever knows how to furnish them slaves, will share their wealth. Who can say by how many millions of hard cash the Dutch West India Company has enriched itself in this slave trade!' At the end of the seventeenth century all Europe, and not England only, was impressed with the words of Sir Dalby Thomas: 'The pleasure, glory and grandeur of England has been advanced more by sugar than by any other commodity, wool not excepted.'

The Negro slave trade in the eighteenth century constituted one of the greatest migrations in recorded history. Its volume is indicated in the following table, prepared from various statistics that are available. (See table 33.1)

Average annual importations do not provide a complete picture. In 1774 the importation into Jamaica was 18,448. In fourteen of the years 1702-75, the annual importation exceeded 10,000. Imports into Saint-Domingue averaged 12,559 in the years 1764-68; in 1768 they were 15,279. In 1718 Barbados imported 7,126 slaves. During the nine months in which Cuba was under British occupation in 1762, 10,700 slaves were introduced. The British introduced 41,000 slaves in three years into Guadeloupe whilst they were in occupation of the island during the Seven Years' War.

These large importations represented one of the greatest advantages which the slave trade had over other trades. The frightful mortality of the slaves on the plantations made annual increments essential. Consider the case of Saint-

Table 33.1 The Nego Slave Trade in the Eighteenth Century

Years	Colony	Importation	Average importation per year
1700-86	Jamaica	610,000	7,000
1708-35 & 1747-66	Barbados	148,821	3,100
1680-1776	Saint Domingue	800,000	8,247
1720-29	Antigua	12,278	1,362
1721-30	St. Kitts	10,358	1,035
1721-29	Montserrat	3,210	357
1721-26	Nevis	1,267	253
1767-73	Dominica	19,194	2,742
1763-89	Cuba	30,875	1,143
1700-54	Danish Islands	11,750	214

Domingue. In 1763 the slave population amounted to 206,539. Imports from 1764 to 1774 numbered 102,474. The slave population in 1776 was 290,000. Thus, despite an importation of over 1,000,000, without taking into account the annual births, the increase of the slave population in thirteen years was less than 85,000. Taking only importations into consideration, the slave population in 1776 was 19,000 less than the figure of 1763 with the importations added, and the imports for one year are not available.

A much clearer illustration of the mortality is available for Barbados. In 1764 there were 70,706 slaves in the island. Importations to 1783, with no figures available for the years 1779 and 1780, totalled 41,840. The total population allowing for neither deaths nor births, should, therefore, have been 112,546 in 1783. Actually, it was 62,258. Thus despite an annual importation for the eighteen years for which statistics are available of 2,324, the population in 1783 was 8,448 less than it was in 1764, or an annual decline of 469. The appalling mortality is brought out in table 33.2.

Thus, after eight years of importations, averaging 4,424 a year, the population of Barbados was only 3,411 larger. 35,397 slaves had been imported; 31,897 had disappeared. In 1770 and 1771 the mortality was so high that the importation in those years, heavy though it was, was not adequate to supply the deficit. Half the population had had to be renewed in eight years.

In 1703 Jamaica had 45,000 Negroes; in 1778, 205,261, an average annual increase from all causes of 2,109. Between 1703 and 1775, 469,893 slaves had been imported, an average annual importation of 6,807. For every additional slave in its population, Jamaica had had to import three. The total population in 1778, excluding births and based only on imports, should have been 541,893, and that figure excludes imports for 1776, 1777 and 1778. Allowing 11,000 a year for those three years, the total population in 1778 should have been 547,893. The actual population in that year was less than 40 per cent of the potential total.

Economic development has never been purchased at so high a price. According to one of the leading planters of Saint-Domingue, one in every three imported Negroes died in the first three years. To the mortality on the plantations must be added the mortality on the slave ships. On the slave ships belonging to the port of Nantes in France, that mortality varied from 5 per cent in 1746 and 1774 to as high as 34 per cent in 1732. For all the slave cargoes transported by them between 1715 and 1775, the mortality amounted to 16 per cent. Of 100 Negroes who left the coast of Africa, therefore, only 84 reached the West Indies; one-third of these died in three years. For every 56 Negroes, therefore, on the plantations at the end of three years, 44 had perished.

The slave trade thus represented a wear and tear, a depreciation which no other trade

Table 33.2   Slave Population in Barbados, 1764-71

Year	Slaves	Imports	Potential pop. of next year	Actual pop. of next year	Decrease	Decrease as % of imports
1764	70,706	3,936	74,642	72,255	2,387	60
1765	72,255	3,228	75,483	73,651	1,832	57
1766	73,651	4,061	77,712	74,656	3,056	75
1767	74,656	4,154	78,810	76,275	2,535	61
1768	76,275	4,628	80,903	75,658	4,345	90
1769	75,658	6,837	82,495	76,334	6,161	90
1770	76,334	5,825	82,159	75,998	6,171	106
1771	75,998	2,728	78,716	74,485	4,231	155
1764-71	—	35,397	106,103	74,206	31,897	90

equalled. The loss of an individual planter or trader was insignificant compared with the basic fact that every cargo of slaves, including the quick and the dead, represented so much industrial development and employment, so much employment of ships and sailors, in the metropolitan country. No other commercial undertaking required so large a capital as the slave trade. In addition to the ship, there was its equipment, armament, cargo, its unusually large supply of water and foodstuffs, its abnormally large crew. In 1765 it was estimated that in France the cost of fitting out and arming a vessel for 300 slaves was 242,500 livres. The cargo of a vessel from Nantes in 1757 was valued at 141,500 livres; it purchased 500 slaves. The cargo of the *Prince de Conty*, of 300 tons, was valued at 221,224 livres, with which 800 slaves were purchased.

Large profits were realised from the slave trade. The *King Solomon*, belonging to the Royal African Company, carried a cargo worth £4,252 in 1720. It took on 296 Negroes who were sold in St Kitts for £9,228. The profit was thus 117 per cent. From 1698 to 1707 the Royal African Company exported from England to Africa goods to the value of £293,740. The Company sold 5,982 Negroes in Barbados for £156,425, an average of £26 per head. It sold 2,178 slaves in Antigua for £80,522, an average of £37 per head. The total number of Negroes imported into the British islands by the Company in these years was 17,760. The sale of 8,160 Negroes in Barbados and Antigua, less than half the total imports into all the islands, thus realised 80 per cent of the total exports from England. Allowing an average price of £26 per head for the remaining 9,600 Negroes, the total amount realised from the sale of the Company's Negroes was £488,107. The profit on the Company's exports was thus 66 per cent. For every £3 worth of merchandise exported from England, the Company obtained an additional £2 by way of profit.

The Negroes taken on by the *Prince de Conty* on the coast of Africa averaged 275 livres each; the survivors of the Middle Passage fetched 1,300 livres each in Saint-Domingue. In 1700 a cargo of 238 slaves was purchased by the Danish West Indies at prices ranging from 90 to 100 rixdollars. In 1753 the wholesale price on the coast of Africa was 100 rixdollars; the retail price in the Danish West Indies was 150-300 rixdollars. In 1724 the Danish West India Company made a profit of 28 per cent on its slave imports; in 1725, 30 per cent; 70 per cent on the survivors of a cargo of 1733 despite a mortality in transit of 45 per cent; 50 per cent on a cargo of 1754. It need occasion no surprise, therefore, that one of the eighteenth-century slave dealers admitted that, of all the places he had lived in, England, Ireland, America, Portugal, the West Indies, the Cape Verde Islands, the Azores and Africa, it was in Africa that he could most quickly make his fortune.

The slave trade was central to the triangular trade. It was, in the words of one British mercantilist, 'the spring and parent whence the others flow'; 'the first principle and foundation of all the rest', echoed another, ' the mainspring of the machine which sets every wheel in motion'. The slave trade kept the wheels of metropolitan industry turning; it stimulated navigation and shipbuilding and employed seamen; it raised fishing villages into flourishing cities; it gave sustenance to new industries based on the processing of colonial raw materials; it yielded large profits which were ploughed back into metropolitan industry; and, finally, it gave rise to an unprecedented commerce in the West Indies and made the Caribbean territories among the most valuable colonies the world has ever known.

Examples must suffice. In 1729 the British West Indies absorbed one-quarter of Britain's iron exports, and Africa, where the price of a Negro was commonly reckoned at one Birmingham gun, was one of the most important markets for the British armaments industry. In 1753 there were 120 sugar refineries in England – eighty in London, twenty in Bristol. In 1780 the British West Indies supplied two-thirds of the 6,500,000 pounds of raw cotton imported by Britain. Up to 1770 one-third of Manchester's textile exports went to Africa, one-half to the West Indian and American colonies. In 1709 the British West Indies employed one-tenth of all British shipping engaged in foreign trade. Between 1710 and 1714, 122,000 tons of British shipping sailed to the West Indies, 112,000 tons to the mainland colonies. Between 1709 and 1787, British shipping engaged in foreign trade quadrupled; ships clearing for Africa multiplied twelve times and the tonnage eleven times.

The triangular trade marked the ascendancy of two additional European ports in the eighteenth century, Liverpool in England and Nantes in France, and further contributed to the development of Bristol and Bordeaux, begun in the seventeenth century. Liverpool's first slave ship, of 30 tons, sailed for Africa in 1709. In 1783 the port had 85 ships, of 12,294 tons, in the trade. Between 1709 and 1783, a total of 2,249 ships, of 240,657 tons, sailed from Liverpool to Africa – an annual average of 30 ships and 3,200 tons. The proportion of slave ships to the total shipping of the port was one in a hundred in 1709, one in nine in 1730, one in four in 1763, one in three in 1771. In 1752, 88 Liverpool vessels carried upwards of 24,730 slaves from Africa. Seven firms, owning 26 vessels, carried 7,030 slaves.

Liverpool's exports to Africa in 1770 read like a census of British manufactures: beans, brass, beer, textiles, copper, candles, chairs, cider, cordage, earthenware, gunpowder, glass, haberdashery, iron, lead, looking glasses, pewter, pipes, paper, stockings, silver, sugar, salt, kettles.

In 1774 there were eight sugar refineries in Liverpool. Two distilleries were established in the town for the express purpose of supplying slave ships. There were many chain and anchor foundries, and manufacturers of and dealers in iron, copper, brass and lead in the town. In 1774 there were fifteen roperies. Half of Liverpool's sailors were engaged in the slave trade, which, by 1783, was estimated to bring the town a clear annual profit of £300,000. The slave trade transformed Liverpool from a fishing village into a great centre of international commerce. The population rose from 5,000 in 1700 to 34,000 in 1773. It was a common saying in the town that its principal streets had been marked out by the chains, and the walls of its houses cemented by the blood of the African slaves. The red brick Customs House, blazoned with Negro heads, bore mute but eloquent testimony to the origins of Liverpool's rise by 1783 to the position of one of the most famous – or infamous, depending on the point of view – towns in the world of commerce.

What Liverpool was to England, Nantes was to France. Between 1715 and 1775, vessels belonging to the port exported 229,525 slaves from Africa, an annual average of 3,763. In 1751 Nantes ships transported 10,003 Negroes. Slave ships constituted about one-fifth of the total shipping of the port. But the slave trade conditioned all others. The slavers brought back sugar and other tropical produce. The number of sugar refineries declined from fifteen in 1700 to four in 1750. But five textile factories were established in 1769, together with manufactures of jams and sweetmeats dependent on sugar. As in Liverpool, a slave trading aristocracy developed, of big capitalists each owning four or six ships.

The West Indian trade was worth twice as much to eighteenth-century Bristol as the remainder of her other overseas commerce. In the 1780s the town had 30 vessels engaged in the slave trade, and 72 in the West Indian trade. Some of its most prominent citizens were engaged in sugar refining. The Baptist Mills of Bristol produced brass manufactures for the slave trade.

As Nantes was the slave trading port *par excellence* of France, Bordeaux was the sugar port. In 1720, Bordeaux had 74 ships, of 6,882 tons, in the West Indian trade; in 1782, 310 ships, of 108,000 tons. In 1749 the town's trade with the West Indies exceeded 27 million livres; in 1771, at its peak, it approximated 171 million. An enormous stimulus was given to shipbuilding: 14 ships, of 3,640 tons, in 1754; 245 totalling 74,485 tons, between 1763 and 1778. Sugar imports into Bordeaux, less than 10 million livres in 1749, attained the huge figure of 101 million in 1780. A mere 22 livres of coffee were imported in 1724; in 1771 the figure was 112 million. Indigo, less than 5 million livres up to 1770, amounted to 22 million in 1772. Bordeaux, in return, exported codfish from Newfoundland, salted fish from Holland, salted beef from Ireland, flour and wine to the West Indies. There were 26 sugar refineries in the town in 1789. Population rose from 43,000 in 1698 to 110,000 in 1790.

The West Indian basis of Bordeaux' prosperity was symbolised by the aggrandisement of a naturalised Portuguese Jew, Gradis. The founder of the dynasty was David, who became a citizen in 1731. Devoting himself exclusively to West Indian trade, he established a branch in Saint-Domingue, which he entrusted to a brother-in-law, Jacob, and another in Martinique, which was supervised by a nephew. His son, Abraham, became the greatest merchant in eighteenth-century Bordeaux. At the government's order, he supplied Canada in the Seven Years' War, six ships in 1756, fourteen in 1758. He loaned large sums to the state and to the greatest in the land. He died in 1780 leaving a fortune of 8 million livres having lived to hear himself denominated by contemporaries, 'the famous Jew Gradis, King of Bordeaux'.

The remarkable value of the triangular trade can best be presented statistically. As for the seventeenth century, we shall take as an illustration the British West Indies. The table that follows gives British imports from, and British exports to, the several colonies for the year 1773 and the period 1714 to 1773.

Thus Jamaica in the eighteenth century was what Barbados had been in the seventeenth century, the most important colony in the British Empire. Its exports to Britain from 1714 to 1773 were three times those of Barbados; its imports from Britain more than double. In these years one-twelfth of total British imports came from Jamaica, nearly one-fortieth of total British exports went to Jamaica. In 1773 one-ninth of total British imports came from the island, one-twenty-second of British exports went to it. Jamaica's exports to Britain were ten times those of New England; the exports to the two colonies were about the same. Jamaica's exports to Britain from 1714 to 1773 were one-fifth larger than those of Virginia and Maryland combined; its imports from Britain about one-tenth less.

From 1714 to 1773 Barbados' exports to Britain were more than one quarter larger than those of Carolina, imports from Britain about one-tenth less. Antigua's exports to Britain were 15 per cent larger than those of Pennsylvania; imports from Britain about two-fifths the figure for that mainland colony. St Kitts' exports to Britain were seven times the figure for New York; its imports more than one quarter those of New York. Grenada's exports to Britain in twelve years, 1762-73, were more than five times as large as Georgia's in forty-two, 1732-73; Grenada's imports were half as large as those of Georgia.

In 1773 total British imports from the British West Indies amounted to one quarter of total British imports, British exports to the West Indies to about one-eleventh of the total export trade. Imports from the mainland colonies were one half the West Indian figure; exports less than double. For the years 1714-73, British imports from the West Indies were one-fifth of the total import trade; from the mainland colonies they were slightly more than half the West Indian figure; from Africa they were 0.5 per cent. British exports to the West Indies during the period were one-sixteenth of the total export trade; to the mainland, they were one-tenth; to Africa, one-fiftieth. For these sixty years the triangular trade accounted for 21 per cent of British im-

Colony	Imports (1773)	Exports (1773)	Imports (1714-73)	Exports (1714-73)
Total British	11,406,841	14,763,252	492,146,670	730,962,105
Antigua	112,779	93,323	12,785,262	3,821,726
Barbados	168,682	148,817	14,506,497	7,442,652
Jamaica	1,286,888	683,451	42,259,749	16,844,990
Montserrat	47,911	14,947	3,387,237	537,831
Nevis	39,299	9,181	3,636,504	549,564
St. Kitts	150,512	62,607	13,305,659*	3,181,901*
Tobago	20,453	30,049	49,587†	122,093†
Grenada	445,041	102,761	3,620,504‡	1,179,279‡
St. Vincent	145,619	38,444	672,991	235,665
Dominica	248,868	43,679	1,469,704§	322,294§
Tortola	48,000	26,927	863,931‖	220,038‖
Carolina	456,513	344,859	11,410,480	8,423,588
New England	124,624	527,055	4,134,392	16,934,316
New York	76,246	289,214	1,910,796	11,377,696
Pennsylvania	36,652	426,448	1,115,112	9,627,409
Virginia & Maryland	589,803	328,904	35,158,481	18,391,097
British West Indies	2,830,583	1,270,846	101,264,818	45,389,988
Mainland Colonies	1,420,471	2,375,797	55,552,675	69,903,613
Africa	68,424	662,112	2,407,447	15,235,829

*1732-73   †1764-73   ‡1762-73   §1763-73   ‖1748-73

ports; 8 per cent of British exports; and nearly 14 per cent of Britain's total external trade.

The population of the British West Indies in 1787 was 58,353 whites; 7,706 free Negroes; 461,864 slaves – a total of 527,923. The annual British export of slaves from Africa by 1783 was approximately 34,000. This was the human and social basis of one in every five pounds of British imports, one in every twelve British exports, and one in every seven of Britain's total trade.

The situation in the French West Indies was essentially similar. In 1715 France's external trade amounted to 175 million livres – imports, 75; exports, 100. West Indian trade accounted for one-sixth of the whole, 30 million; their imports, of 20 million, amounted to one-fifth of France's export trade; their exports, 10 million, constituted one-eighth of France's import trade. In 1776, though France had lost some of the smaller West Indian islands, exports from the French West Indies amounted to 200 million livres, imports to 70 million, the total external trade of the islands representing more than one-third of total French commerce, which oscillated between 600 and 700 million livres; West Indian trade employed 1,000 ships, outward and inward cargoes in the proportion of 5 to 4. The population of the French West Indies about 1780 amounted to 63,682 whites, 13,429 free Negroes, and 437,738 slaves – a total of 514,849. France's annual export of slaves from Africa was estimated at 20,000.

Magnum est saccharum et prevalebit! Great is sugar, and it will prevail! Mercantilists were jubilant. The colonies, wrote Horace Walpole, were 'the source of all our riches, and preserve the balance of trade in our favour, for I don't know where we have it but by the means of our colonies'. The statistics given above identify the colonies which Walpole had in mind. An annual profit of 7s per head was sufficient to enrich a country, said William Wood; each white man in the colonies brought a profit of over £7, twenty times as much. The Negro slaves, said Postleth-wayt, were 'the fundamental prop and support' of the colonies, 'valuable people', and the British Empire was 'a magnificent superstructure of American commerce and naval power on an African foundation'. Rule Britannia! Britannia rules the waves. For Britons never shall be slaves.

But the sons of France arose to glory. France joined in the homage to the triangular trade. 'What commerce' asked the Chamber of Commerce of Nantes, 'can be compared to that which obtains men in exchange for commodities?' Profound question! The abandonment of the slave trade, continued the Chamber, would be inevitably followed by the ruin of colonial commerce; 'whence follows the fact that we have no branch of trade so precious to the State and so worthy of protection as the Guinea trade'. The triangular trade was incomparable, the slave trade precious, and the West Indies perfect colonies. 'The more colonies differ from the metropolis,' said Nantes, 'the more perfect they are . . . Such are the Caribbean colonies; they have none of our objects of trade; they have others which we lack and cannot produce.'

But there were discordant notes in the mercantilist harmony. The first was opposition to the slave trade. In 1774, in Jamaica, the very centre of Negro slavery, a debating society voted that the slave trade was not consistent with sound policy, or with the laws of nature and of morality. In 1776 Thomas Jefferson wrote into the Declaration of Independence three paragraphs attacking the King of England for his 'piratical warfare' on the coast of Africa against people who never offended him, and for his veto of colonial legislation attempting to prohibit or restrain the slave trade. The paragraphs were only deleted on the representations of the states of South Carolina, Georgia and New England. Two petitions were presented to Parliament, in 1774 and 1776, for abolition of the slave trade. A third, more important, was presented in 1783 by the Quakers. The Prime Minister, Lord North, complimented them on their humanity, but regretted that abolition was an impossibility, as the slave trade had become necessary to every nation in Europe. European public opinion accepted the position stated by Postlethwayt: 'We shall take things as they are, and reason from them in their present state, and not from that wherein we could hope them to be. . . . We cannot think of giving up the slave trade, notwithstanding my good wishes that it could be done.'

The second discordant note was more disturbing. Between 1772 and 1778, Liverpool slave traders were estimated to have lost £700,000 in the slave trade. By 1788 twelve of the thirty leading houses which had dominated the trade from 1773 had gone bankrupt. Slave trading, like sugar production, had its casualties. A slave trader in 1754, as his supreme defence of the slave trade, had adumbrated that 'from this trade proceed benefits, far outweighing all, either real or pretended mischiefs and inconveniencies'. If and when the slave trade ceased to be profitable, it would not be so easy to defend it.

The third discordant note came also from the British colonies. The British government's ambition was to become the slave carriers and sugar suppliers of the whole world. Britain had fought for and obtained the *asiento*. The supply of slaves to foreign nations became an integral part of the British slave trade. Of 497,736 slaves imported in Jamaica between 1702 and 1775, 137,114 had been re-exported, one out of every four. In 1731, imports were 10,079; re-exports 5,708. From 1775 to 1783, Antigua imported 5,673 slaves and re-exported 1,972, one out of every three. Jamaica resorted to its seventeenth-century policy, an export tax on all Negroes re-exported. In 1774, the Board of Trade, on the representation of the slave traders of London, Liverpool and Bristol, disallowed the law as unjustifiable, improper and prejudicial to British commerce, pointed out that legislative autonomy in the colonies did not extend to the imposition of duties upon British ships and goods or to the prejudice and obstruction of British commerce, and reprimanded the Governor of the island for dereliction of duty in not stopping efforts to 'check and discourage a traffic . . . beneficial to the nation'.

34

French Capitalism and Caribbean Slavery

C.L.R. JAMES

The slave trade and slavery were the economic basis of the French Revolution. 'Sad irony of human history,' comments Jaurès. 'The fortunes created at Bordeaux, at Nantes, by the slave trade, gave to the bourgeoisie that pride which needed liberty and contributed to human emancipation.' Nantes was the centre of the slave trade. As early as 1666, 108 ships went to the coast of Guinea and took on board 37,430[1] slaves, to a total value of more than 37 million, giving the Nantes bourgeoisie 15-20 per cent on their money. In 1700 Nantes was sending 50 ships a year to the West Indies with Irish salt beef, linen for the household and for clothing the slaves, and machinery for sugar-mills. *Nearly all the industries which developed in France during the eighteenth century had their origin in goods or commodities destined for the coast of Guinea or for America.* The capital from the slave-trade fertilized them; though the bourgeoisie traded in other things than slaves, upon the success or failure of the traffic everything else depended.[2]

Some ships took on the way wine from Maderia for the colonists and dried turtle from Cape Verde for the slaves. In return they brought back colonial produce to Nantes whence Dutch vessels took it to Northern Europe. Some made the return journey by the way of Spain and Portugal, exchanging their colonial cargo for the products of those countries. Sixty ships from Rochelle and Oberon brought their salted cod to Nantes, to go to the inland market or out to the colonies to feed the slaves. The year 1758 saw the first manufactory of Indian cloth, to weave the raw cotton of India and the West Indian islands.

The planters and small manufacturers of San Domingo were able to establish themselves only by means of the capital advanced by the maritime bourgeoisie. By 1789 the Nantes merchants alone had 50 million invested in the West Indies.

Bordeaux had begun with the wine industry which gave its ship-builders and navigators an opportunity to trade all over the world; then came brandy, also to all ports, but above all to the colonies. By the middle of the eighteenth century, 16 factories refined 10,000 tons of raw sugar from San Domingo every year, using nearly 4,000 tons of charcoal. Local factories supplied the town with jars, dishes and bottles. The trade was cosmopolitan — Flemings, Germans, Dutchmen, Irishmen and Englishmen came to live in Bordeaux, contributing to the general expansion and amassing riches for themselves. Bordeaux traded with Holland, Germany, Portugal, Venice and Ireland, but slavery and the colonial trade were the fount and origin and sustenance of this thriving industry and farflung commerce.

Marseilles was the great centre for the Mediterranean and Eastern trade, and a royal decree at the beginning of the century had attempted to exclude it from the trade with the colonies. The attempt failed. San Domingo was the special centre of the Marseilles trade. Marseilles sent there not only the wines of Provence: in 1789 there were in Marseilles 12 sugar refineries, nearly as many as in Bordeaux.

In the early years most of this trade had been carried in foreign-built or foreign-owned ships. But by 1730 the maritime bourgeois began to build themselves. In 1778 Bordeaux ship-owners constructed seven vessels, in 1784 they constructed 32, with a total of 115 for the six years. A Marseilles ship-owner, Georges Roux, could fit out a fleet on his own account in order

The Black Jacobins: Toussaint L'Ouverture and the San Domingo Revolution (Vintage Books, 1963), pp. 47–61.

to take vengeance on the English fleet for the prizes it had taken.

Nantes, Bordeaux and Marseilles were the chief centres of the maritime bourgeoisie, bur Orlenas, Dieppe, Bercy-Paris, a dozen great towns, refined raw sugar and shared in the subsidiary industries.[3] A large part of the hides worked in France came from San Domingo. The flourishing cotton industry of Normandy drew its raw cotton in part from the West Indies, and in all its ramifications the cotton trade occupied the population of more than a hundred French towns. In 1789 exchanges with the American colonies were 296 million. France exported to the islands 78 million of flour, salted meats, wines and stuffs. The colonies sent to France 218 million of sugar, coffee, cocoa, wood, indigo and hides. Of the 218 million imported only 71 million were consumed in France. The rest was exported after preparation. The total value of the colonies represented 3,000 million, and on them depended the livelihood of a number of Frenchmen variously estimated at between two and six million. By 1759 San Domingo was the market of the new world. It received in its ports 1,587 ships, a greater number than Marseilles, and France used for the San Domingo trade alone 750 great vessels employing 24,000 sailors. In 1789 Britain's export trade would be £27 million, that of France £17 million, of which the trade of San Domingo would account for nearly £11 million. The whole of Britain's colonial trade in that year amounted to only £5 million.[4]

The maritime bourgeoisie would not hear of any change in the Exclusive. They had the ear of the Minister and the Government, and not only were the colonists refused permission to trade with foreign countries, but the circulation of all French currency, except the very lowest, was forbidden in the islands, lest the colonists use it to purchase foreign goods. In such a method of trade they were at the mercy of the bourgeoisie. In 1774 their indebtedness was 200 million, and by 1789 it was estimated at between 300 and 500 million.[5] If the colonists complained of the Exclusive, the bourgeoisie complained that the colonists would not pay their debts, and agitated for stricter measures against the contraband.

Rich as was the French bourgeoisie, the colonial trade was too big for it. The British bourgeois, most successful of slave-traders, sold thousands of smuggled slaves every year to the French colonists and particularly to San Domingo. But even while they sold the slaves to San Domingo, the British were watching the progress of this colony with alarm and with envy. After the independence of America in 1783, this amazing French colony suddenly made such a leap as almost to double its production between 1783 and 1789. In those years Bordeaux alone invested 100 million in San Domingo. The British bourgeois were the great rivals of the French. All through the eighteenth century they fought in every part of the world. The French had jumped gleefully in to help drive them out of America. San Domingo was now incomparably the finest colony in the world and its possibilities seemed limitless. The British bourgeoisie investigated the new situation in the West Indies, and on the basis of what it saw, prepared a bombshell for its rivals. Without slaves San Domingo was doomed. The British colonies had enough slaves for all the trade they were ever likely to do. With the tears rolling down their cheeks for the poor suffering blacks, those British bourgeois who had no West Indian interests set up a great howl for the abolition of the slave trade.

A venal race of scholars, profiteering panders to national vanity, have conspired to obscure the truth about abolition. Up to 1783 the British bourgeoisie had taken the slave trade for granted. In 1773 and again in 1774, the Jamaica Assembly, afraid of insurrection and seeking to raise revenue, taxed the importation of slaves. In great wrath the British Board of Trade disallowed the measures and told the Governor that he would be sacked if he gave his sanction to any similar bill.[6] Well-meaning persons talked of the iniquity of slavery and the slave trade, as well-meaning persons in 1938 talked about the native question in Africa or the misery of the Indian peasant. Dr. Johnson toasted the next slave insurrection in the West Indies. Stray members of parliament introduced Bills for the abolition of the slave trade which the House rejected without much bother. In 1783 Lord North turned down a petition against the trade:[7] the petition did credit to the Christian feelings, and to the humane breast, etc, etc, but the trade was necessary. With the loss of America, however, a new situation arose.

The British found that by the abolition of the mercantile system with America, they gained instead of losing. It was the first great lesson in the advantages of free trade. But if Britain gained the British West Indies suffered. The rising industrial bourgeoisie, feeling its way to free trade and a greater exploitation of India, began to abuse the West Indies, called them 'sterile rocks',[8] and asked if the interest and independence of the nation should be sacrificed to 72,000 masters and 400,000 slaves.[9]

The industrial bourgeois were beginning their victorious attack upon the agricultural monopoly which was to culminate in the Repeal of the Corn Laws in 1846. The West Indian sugar-producers were monopolists whose methods of production afforded an easy target, and Adam Smith[10] and Arthur Young,[11] the fore-runners of the new era, condemned the whole principle of slave labour as the most expensive in the world. Besides, why not get sugar from India? India, after the loss of America, assumed a new importance. The British experimented with sugar in Bengal, received glowing reports and in 1791 the first shipments arrived.[12] In 1793 Mr. Randle Jackson would preach to the company's shareholders a little sermon on the new orientation. 'It seemed as if Providence, when it took from us America, would not leave its favourite people without an ample substitute; or who should say that Providence had not taken from us one member, more seriously to impress us with the value of another.'[13] It might not be good theology, but it was very good economics. Pitt and Dundas saw a chance of capturing the continental market from France by East India sugar. There was cotton and indigo. The production of cotton in India doubled in a few years. Indian free labour cost a penny a day.

But the West Indian vested interests were strong, statesmen do not act merely on speculation, and these possibilities by themselves would not have accounted for any sudden change in British policy. It was the miraculous growth of San Domingo that was decisive. Pitt found that some 50 per cent of the slaves imported into the British islands were sold to the French colonies.[14] It was the British slave trade, therefore, which was increasing French colonial produce and putting the European market into French hands. Britain was cutting its own throat. And even the profits from this export were not likely to last. Already a few years before the slave merchants had failed for £700,000 in a year.[15] The French, seeking to provide their own slaves, were encroaching in Africa and increasing their share of the trade every year. Why should they continue to buy from Britain? Holland and Spain were doing the same. By 1786 Pitt, a disciple of Adam Smith, had seen the light clearly. He asked Wilberforce to undertake the campaign.[16] Wilberforce represented the important division of Yorkshire, he had a great reputation, all the humanity, justice, stain on national character, etc, etc, would sound well coming from him. Pitt was in a hurry — it was important to bring the trade to a complete stop quickly and suddenly. The French had neither the capital nor the organisation to make good the deficiency at once and he would ruin San Domingo at a stroke. In 1787 he warned Wilberforce that if he did not bring the motion in, somebody else would,[17] and in 1788 he informed the Cabinet that he would not stay in it with those who opposed.[18] Pitt was fairly certain of success in England. With truly British nerve he tried to persuade the European governments to abolish the trade on the score of inhumanity. The French government discussed the proposal amicably, but by May, 1789, the British Ambassador wrote sadly that it seemed as if all the French government's negotiations had been to 'compliment us and to keep us quiet and in good humour'.[19] The Dutch, less polite, gave a more abrupt negative. But here a great stroke of luck befell Pitt. France was then stirring with pre-revolutionary attacks on all obvious abuses, and one year after the Abolitionist Society had been formed in Britain, a group of Liberals in France, Brissot, Mirabeau, Pétion, Condorcet, Abbé Grégoire, all the great names of the first years of the revolution, followed the British example and formed a society, the Friends of the Negro. The leading spirit was Brissot, a journalist who had seen slavery in the United States. The society aimed at the abolition of slavery, published a journal, agitated. This suited the British down to the ground. Clarkson went to Paris, to stimulate 'the slumbering energies'[20] of the society, gave it money, supplied France with British anti-slavery propaganda.[21] Despite the names that were to become so famous and a large membership, we must beware of thinking that the Friends of the Negro represented a force. The colonists took them seriously, the maritime bourgeoisie did not. It was the French Revolution which, with unexpected swiftness, would drag these eloquent Frenchmen out of the stimulating excitement of philanthropic propaganda and put them face to face with economic reality.

These then were the forces which in the decade preceding the French Revolution linked San Domingo to the economic destiny of three continents and the social and political conflicts of that pregnant age. A trade and method of production so cruel and so immoral that it would wilt before the publicity which a great revolution throws upon the sources of wealth; the powerful British Government determined to wreck French commerce in the Antilles, agitating at home and intriguing in France among men who, unbeknown to themselves, would soon have power in their hands; the colonial world (itself divided) and the French bourgeoisie, each intent on its own purposes and, unaware of the approaching danger, drawing apart instead of closer together. Not one courageous leader, many courageous leaders were needed, but the science of history was not what it is today and no man living then could foresee, as we can foresee today, the coming upheavals.[22] Mirabeau indeed said that the colonists slept on the edge of Vesuvius, but for centuries the same thing had been said and the slaves had never done anything.

How could anyone seriously fear for such a wonderful colony? Slavery seemed eternal and the profits mounted. Never before, and perhaps never since, has the world seen anything proportionately so dazzling as the last years of pre-revolutionary San Domingo. Between 1783 and 1789 production nearly doubled. Between 1764 and 1771 the average importation of slaves varied between 10,000 and 15,000. In 1786 it was 27,000, and from 1787 onwards the colony was taking more than 40,000 slaves a year. But economic prosperity is no guarantee of social stability. That rests on the constantly shifting equilibrium between the classes. It was the prosperity of the bourgeoisie that started the English revolution of the seventeenth century. With every stride in production the colony was marching to its doom.

The enormous increase of slaves was filling the colony with native Africans, more resentful, more intractable, more ready for rebellion than the Creole Negro. Of the 500,000 slaves in the colony in 1789, more than two-thirds had been born in Africa.

These slaves were being used for the opening up of new lands. There was no time to allow for the period of acclimatisation, known as the seasoning, and they died like flies. From the earliest days of the colony towards the middle of the eighteenth century, there had been some improvement in the treatment of the slaves, but this enormous number of newcomers who had to be broken and terrorised into labour and submission caused an increase in fear and severity. In 1784 the administrators, who visited one of the slave shops which sometimes served as a market-place instead of the deck of the slaver, reported a revolting picture of dead and dying thrown pell-mell into the filth. The Le Jeune case took place in 1788. In 1790 de Wimpffen states that not one article of the Negro Code was obeyed. He himself had sat at table with a woman, beautiful, rich and very much admired, who had had a careless cook thrown into the oven.

The problem of feeding this enormous increase in the slave population was making the struggle between the planters and the maritime bourgeoisie over the Exclusive more bitter than ever, and the planters after 1783 had forced a slight breach in the straitjacket which clasped them. Having tasted blood, they wanted more.

Mulattoes educated in Paris during the Seven Years' War had come home, and their education and accomplishments filled the colonists with hatred and envy and fear. It was these last years that saw the fiercest legislation against them. Forbidden to go to France, where they learnt things that were not good for them, they stayed at home to increase the strength of the dissatisfied.

With the growth of trade and of profits, the number of planters who could afford to leave their estates in charge of managers grew, and by 1789, in addition to the maritime bourgeoisie, there was a large group of absentee proprietors in France linked to the aristocracy by marriage, for whom San Domingo was nothing else but a source of revenue to be spent in the luxurious living of aristocratic Paris. So far had these parasites penetrated into the French aristocracy that a memoir from San Domingo to the King could say: 'Sire, your court is Creole', without too much stretching of the truth.

The prosperity affected even the slaves. More of them could save money, buy their freedom, and enter the promised land.

This was the San Domingo of 1789, the most profitable colony the world had ever known; to the casual eye the most flourishing and prosperous possession on the face of the globe; to the analyst a society torn by inner and outer contradictions which in four years would split that structure into so many pieces that they could never be put together again.

It was the French bourgeoisie which pressed the button. This strange San Domingo society was but a garish exaggeration, a crazy caricature, of the *ancien régime* in France. The royalist bureaucracy, incompetent and wasteful, could not manage the finances of France; the aristocracy and the clergy had bled the peasantry dry, impeded the economic development of the country, gobbled up all the best places, and considered themselves almost as superior to the able and vigorous bourgeois as the white planters considered themselves superior to the mulattoes.

But the French bourgeoisie too was proud

and no members of it were prouder than the maritime bourgeois. We have seen their wealth. They knew that they were the foundation of the country's prosperity. They were buying up the land of the aristocracy. They built great schools and universities, they read Voltaire and Rousseau, they sent their linen to the colonies to be washed and to get the right colour and scent, they sent their wine for two or three voyages to the colonies and back to give it the right flavour. They, along with the other bourgeois, chafed at their social disadvantages; the chaotic state of French administration and finance handicapped them in their business. A hard winter in 1788 brought matters to a head. The monarchy was already bankrupt, the aristocracy made a bid to recover its former power, the peasants began to revolt, and the bourgeoisie saw that the time had come for it to govern the country on the English model in collaboration with its allies, the radical aristocracy. In the agitation which began the French Revolution, the maritime bourgeoisie took the lead. The bourgeoisie of Dauphiné and Brittany, with their ports of Marseilles and Nantes, attacked the monarchy even before the official opening of the States-General, and Mirabeau, the first leader of the revolution, was the deputy for Marseilles.

From all over the country the *cahiers*, or lists of grievances, poured in. But the French people, like the vast majority of Europeans today, had too many grievances of their own to be concerned about the sufferings of Africans, and only a few *cahiers*, chiefly from clergymen, demanded the abolition of slavery. The States-General met. Mirabeau, Pétion, Mayor of Paris, Abbé Grégoire, Condorcet, all members of the Friends of the Negro, were deputies, all pledged to abolition. But abolition for the maritime bourgeois was ruin. For the moment, however, the States-General grappled with the King.

While the French bourgeoisie led the assault on the absolute monarchy at home, the planters followed suit in the colonies. And, as in France, the geographical divisions of San Domingo and their historical development shaped the revolutionary movement and the coming insurrection of the slaves.

The pride of the colony was the great North Plain of which Le Cap was the chief port. Bounded on the north by the ocean, and on the south by a ridge of mountains running almost the length of the island, it was about 50 miles in length and between 10 and 20 miles in breadth. Cultivated since 1670, it was covered with plantations within easy reach of each other. Le Cap was the centre of the island's economic, social and political life. In any revolutionary upheaval, the planters of the North Plain and the merchants and lawyers of Le Cap would take the lead. (But the slave-gangs of the North Plain, in close proximity to each other and the sooner aware of the various changes in the political situation, would be correspondingly ready for political action.)

Very different was the West Province, with its isolated plantations scattered over wide areas. In districts like the Artibonite, Verrettes, Mirabelais, and St Marc, there were many mulatto proprietors, some of great wealth.

The South Province was a sort of pariah, somewhat sparsely populated, with a majority of mulattoes. The eastern end, Cape Tiburon, was only some 50 miles from Jamaica and here the contraband trade was particularly strong.

Early in 1788 the North Province took the lead. It formed a secret committee to secure representation in the States-General. In Paris the group of wealthy absentee noblemen formed a committee for the same purpose, the two groups collaborated and the Paris noblemen refused to accept the veto of the King. At the end of 1788 the colonists summoned electoral assemblies and elected a delegation, some of whom consisted of their allies in Paris. In their *cahier* they claimed abolition of military justice and the institution of a civil judiciary; all legislation and taxes to be voted by provincial assemblies subject only to the approval of the King and a Colonial Committee sitting at Paris but elected by themselves. By restricting political rights to owners of land the planters effectively excluded the small whites who took little interest in all this agitation. Of the slaves and mulattoes, they said not a word. Slaves did not count, and the mulattoes secured permission from the frightened bureaucracy to send a deputation to Paris on their own account. But a number of the planters at home, and quite a few in Paris, the Club Massiac, viewed this desire to be represented in the States-General with distrust. The agitation for abolition of the slave trade in England, the propaganda of the Friends of the Negro, the revolutionary temper of France, filled them with foreboding. Representation in the States-General by a few deputies could effect nothing, and it would bring the full glare of publicity and awakening political interest on the state of society in San Domingo, which was exactly what they did not want. But while the pro-representation group were in a minority, having a positive aim they were bold and confident. Their opponents, with bad consciences and aiming only at avoiding trouble, could oppose no effective resistance. Colonial representation in a metropolitan assembly was an innovation unheard of at that time, but the San Domingo representatives, profiting by the revolutionary ferment in Paris, circumvented the objections of the King and Minister. They petitioned the nobility who cold-shouldered them. But when Louis tried to intimidate the Third Estate, and the deputies went to the tennis-court and swore that being the representatives of the people they would never adjourn, Gouy d'Arsy, leader of the colonists, boldly led his group of colonial noblemen into this historic meeting. Out of gratitude for this unexpected support, the bourgeoisie welcomed them, and thus France admitted the principle of colonial representation. Full of confidence these slave owners claimed 18 seats, but Mirabeau turned fiercely on them: 'You claim representation proportionate to the number of the inhabitants. The free blacks are proprietors and tax-payers, and yet they have not been allowed to vote. And as for the slaves, either they are men or they are not; if the colonists consider them to be men, let them free them and make them electors and eligible for seats; if the contrary is the case, have we, in apportioning deputies according to the population of France, taken into consideration the number of our horses and our mules?'

San Domingo was allowed only six deputies. In less than five minutes the great Liberal orator had placed the case of the Friends of the Negro squarely before the whole of France in unforgettable words. The San Domingo representatives realised at last what they had done; they had tied the fortunes of San Domingo to the assembly of a people in revolution and thenceforth the history of liberty in France and of slave emancipation in San Domingo was one and indivisible.

Unaware of these portentous developments, the colonists in San Domingo were going from victory to victory. As in France, the last months of 1788 in San Domingo had been hard. France had had to prohibit the export of grain, and under these circumstances the Exclusive was a tyrannical imposition threatening the island with famine. The Governor opened certain ports to foreign ships; the Intendant, Barbé de Marbois, agreed to the first small breaches but

refused to sanction their extension. The matter went to the King's Council which repudiated the Governor, recalled him, and appointed a new Governor, with the colonists calling for the blood of the Intendant. This was the situation when on a day in September a boat sailed into the harbour, and the captain, hurrying ashore, ran down the streets of Le Cap, shouting the news of July 14th. The King had been preparing to disperse the Constituent Assembly by force, and the Paris masses, arming themselves, had stormed the Bastille as the symbol of feudal reaction. The great French Revolution had begun.

Notes

1. This section is based on the work of Jaurès, *Histoire Socialiste de la Révolution Francaise*, (Paris, 1922), pp. 62–84.
2. Gaston-Martin, *L'Ere des Négriers, 1714–1774*. Paris, 1931, p. 424.
3. L. Deschamps, *Les Colonies pendant la Revolution* (Paris, 1898), pp. 3–8.
4. H. Brougham, *The Colonial Policy of the European Powers*, 2 vols (Edinburgh, 1803), Vol. II, pp. 538–40.
5. Deschamps, *op. cit.*, p. 25.
6. Great Britain, *House of Commons: Accounts and Papers, 1795–1796*, Vol. 100.
7. *Parliamentary History*, XXIII, pp. 1026–27.
8. *The Right in the West India Merchants to a Double Monopoly of the Sugar Market of Great Britain, and the Expedience of all monopolies examined*. (n.d.).
9. J. Chalmers, *Opinions on Interesting Subjects of Law and Commercial Policy arising from American Independence* (London, 1784), p. 60.
10. A. Smith, *The wealth of Nations*, Vol. I, p. 123.
11. A. Young, *Annals of Agriculture* (1788), Vol. IX, pp. 88–96.
12. *East India Sugar*, 1822, Appendix I, p. 3.
13. *Debate on the Expediency of Cultivating Sugar in the Territories of the East India Company*, East India House (1793).
14. *Report of the Committee of Privy Council for Trade and Plantations* (1798), Pt IV, Tables for Dominica and Jamaica.
15. T. Clarkson, *Essay on the Impolicy of the African Slave Trade* (London, 1784), p. 29.
16. R. Coupland, *The British Antislavery Movement* (London, 1933), p. 73.
17. R. Coupland, *Wilberforce* (Oxford, 1923), p. 93.
18. *Fortescue MSS.* (Historical Manuscripts Commission, British Museum). Pitt to Grenville, June 29, 1788. Vol. I, p. 342.
19. *Liverpool Papers.* (Add. MSS. British Museum), Lord Dorset to Lord Hawkesbury, Vol. 38224, p. 118.
20. R. I. and S. Wilberforce, *Life of Wilberforce* (London, 1838), Vol. I, p. 228.
21. *Cahiers de la Révolution Francaise* (Paris, 1935), No. III, p. 25.
22. Written in 1938.

35

Slavery and Lagging Capitalism in the Spanish and Portuguese American Empires, 1492-1713

FRANKLIN KNIGHT

The long and complicated historical relationship between slavery and capitalism is both elusive and unclear. This is true both in its initial phase and in its later development. As elsewhere in Europe, the Iberians had employed slaves in various social and economic situations long before the manifestation of what may be properly termed the advent of capitalism. Indeed, slavery formed an integral part of the social and organizational structure of society from distant antiquity. Capitalism, on the other hand, represented a relatively modern innovation in European societies, dating probably no earlier than the seventeenth century – with some understandable lag time for the Spanish and Portuguese states.[1] Both slavery and capitalism, however, were essential characteristics of the new, dynamic imperialism that fuelled the expansion of Europe after the fifteenth century. Although the connection between slavery and imperialistic capitalism may not have been either linear or direct, it is difficult to deny the catalytic function of the former for the latter. Expansion of slavery and the slave trade became an important instrument in the expansion of empire.

Portugal and Spain did not initiate their overseas empires merely to derive economic benefits from slavery and the slave trade. Slave trading was not foremost in their plans. Nevertheless, economic pursuits constituted an integral component of the early restless expansion of these two Iberian states across the Atlantic and into the Indian and Pacific oceans. The Portuguese explained their relentless overseas quest in terms of "Christians and Spices", meaning that their goal was as much the conversion of souls as the acquisition of wealth, and their first formal trading post – the first constructed by any European state overseas – was a slave trading factory on Arguim island established by Prince Henry of Portugal in 1448.[2] Overt missionary activity was notoriously inconspicuous until the Portuguese reached India.[3] It was more than half a century after they established their slave trading activity, and well after their arrival in India, that spices would temporarily supersede slaves among the commercial commodities of the Portuguese.[4] The early Spanish empire also combined equally the religious and economic motives of overseas expansion. In the words of the inimitable Bernal Diaz del Castillo, the intrepid soldier of Hernán Cortés, the Spanish went to the Americas "for the service of God and His Majesty, to give light to those who were in darkness, and to procure wealth, as all men desire."[5] This combination of acquisitive materialism and spiritual idealism was characteristic of the age.[6] The compatibility between the business of saving souls and the notion of acquiring material wealth formed a tradition extending back to the time of the crusades.[7]

In the earliest stages of the modern evolution of this international and intercontinental trade involving Europeans, slaves did not feature as one of the more important items. This should hardly be surprising. Slavery had virtually ceased to be a mode of production or an important commercial commodity in Europe (although forms of serfdom prevailed). By contrast, slaves remained important trade items, and an important mode of production in most areas of Africa.[8] In the Mediterranean world's border disputes, certain social transgressions and religious rivalry produced victims who were sentenced to lifetime service in the galleys. Apart from the galleys, slaves comprised one segment of the category of unfree labour. This changed when the Europeans tried to break into the African and Muslim markets and found that slaves were valuable items of trade.

From the European perspective, colonial expansion involved the transportation of groups of settlers from the home country with the overt idea of re-creating a microcosm of the domestic model overseas. This certainly was the Portuguese model on the eastern Atlantic islands from the Cape Verdes to São Tomé, despite their relatively, small domestic population.[9] In the elaborate agreement between Christopher Columbus, a professional explorer, and the monarchs of Castille there is no direct mention of slaves. The crucial part of the text relating to commerce, in characteristic legal language, states,

that of all merchandise, whether pearls, precious stones, gold, silver, spices, or other things of whatever kind, name or description they may be, which may be bought, bartered, found, acquired, or obtained within the bounds of the said Admiralty, Your Highnesses will, and decree that the said Don Cristobal Colon shall take and keep for himself one tenth part of the whole, after all expenses have been deducted so that of all that remains he may take the tenth part for himself and dispose of it as he pleases, the other nine parts to belong to Your Highnesses.[10]

It is tempting to think that the order of listing reflected the priority placed on such trade items by the Spanish court. But the available evidence does not warrant an assumption. On the other hand, it seems certain that the lack of a general appreciation for the economic importance of slaves complicated the ability of the Spanish court to promote this branch of commerce aggressively in the early centuries of the transatlantic slave trade.[11]

As they evolved during the fifteenth, sixteenth, seventeenth, and early eighteenth centuries, the Portuguese and Spanish empires depended greatly on an extensive legal and administrative system and a coherent set of economic relations between the centre and the constantly changing periphery. Neither an empire – the unit of administrative authority – nor an economy – the basis of interdependent acquisition and management of wealth – could be established or maintained as complementary, watertight entities within any one community. The logic of total self-sufficiency simply did not work in practice. And the inadequacy was not confined to the Iberian powers. Mercantilism, constructed as a theory for imperial economic hegemony, floundered due to the changing and expanding needs of both centre and periphery. The "economy world" (to employ the phrase of Fernand Braudel) of both the Portuguese and Spanish empires eventually evolved into an integral component of a much larger Atlantic economy world involving non-Iberians such as the English, French, Dutch, Danes, Swedes, and Italians, with the network of trade, commerce, and contacts spreading well beyond the geographical boundaries of the Atlantic Ocean or the American continent.[12]

What was the catalyst for this dynamic, ever-expanding commercial system? How did an international marketing system manage to operate smoothly and relatively efficiently in the absence of established and recognized institutions of capital such as banks and other clearing houses, accepted currencies, or standardized rates of exchange?

These questions are not easily answered, but any satisfactory answers depend on an examination of the role of a number of commodities including precious metals, luxury items such as spices, tobacco and sugar, and slaves, as well as the expansion within participating societies of the mentality of capitalism. The quest for profit was a driving force in the creation and continuation of markets. For states such as the Portuguese and Spanish, which were relatively resource poor for market engagement in the early modern age, the trade in slaves offered an unusual and novel opportunity to expand their commerce as well as to create new wealth.

Slavery offered two important advantages among the competitive preconditions of capitalism. In the first place, slaves were commodities of exchange as well as units of potential labour. As goods, they could be moved from market to market and sold or exchanged readily, thereby producing wealth. Excess slaves could, and were, incorporated into the society as additional labour and eventually, in some cases, as productive citizens.[13] In the second place, slavery provided the multifaceted linkages that promoted the rise of capitalism. The trade in slaves worked in concert with other trades and demanded a variety of exchange products on both sides of the market. In both the supplying African societies and the receiving American communities, the increasing commercial use of slaves accelerated the mechanisms of production and exchange, altering significantly the participating groups.[14]

Like any other market involving commodities of exchange, the slave market generally responded to the normal supply and demand characteristics of the marketplace. Nevertheless, social and political conditions within Africa, as well as political and economic conditions across the Atlantic, greatly influenced the operation and volume of the trade. When supply exceeded demand, prices tended to be depressed; conversely, excessive demand tended to increase prices. The Portuguese empire, with ready access to African supply points during the years of the transatlantic slave trade, invariably had a supply of cheaper slaves than the Spanish empire, which - apart from the period between 1580 and 1640, when both empires were united - lacked such facilities. But until well into the eighteenth century, prices were more nominal than real, since price was a function of barter rather than a straight exchange between commodity and cash. Moreover, many factors other than the market conditions at the point of exchange affected prices.[15] Since slavery represented one form of coerced labour organization, its viability depended on the degree to which its competitive systems remained feasible. Where alternate forms of labour were available and adequate for local needs, slavery involving Africans did not assume great significance. In the Americas, an active slave market indicated a high level of productive enterprises, usually in agriculture or mining, and significant changes in the local economy and society. The presence and availability of substantial numbers of indigenous Americans as alternate forms of servile labour weakened the demand for imported African slaves or bonded workers from Europe. This was an advantage that the Spanish had in some parts of the Americas – for example, in Mexico and Peru – but that the Portuguese lacked in their fledgling donatary colonies in Brazil.

In the early era of the slave trade, neither Portugal nor Spain possessed a domestic economy that by itself could provide adequate exchange commodities for the successful pursuit of African trade. Although market demands varied considerably across the continent, the principal foreign items required for profitable trade in Africa were salt, rice, cattle, glazed pottery (especially of the type brought by the Arabs from Persia and China), porcelain, glass beads, shells, iron bars, copper basins, brass ornaments, dried fish, cloth (especially Indian cloths), horses, tobacco, rum and other forms of alcohol, and sugar. Of these items, the Portuguese and Spanish could supply from domestic production only cattle, horses, pottery (especially from Talavera), and beads. In return, the Africans offered incense, ivory, tortoiseshell, rhinoceros horns, coconut oil, timber, grain, pig iron, gold, pepper, copper, indigo, amber, wax, hides, and beads. Most of these items reflected the long-established trade pattern with India and China, conducted through the overland caravan routes dominated by Jews and Arabs. Almost all could be sold in Europe, although not all could be sold profitably. For the Portuguese, the initial problem along the African coast involved the collection of information on the correspondence between items and markets, as well as the acquisition of local commodities that would reward the freight for the long sea voyage back to Europe. Successful trade was eventually a matter of trial and error. At the end of the fifteenth century, experience had already demonstrated that spices and precious metals were definitely profitable in Europe, adequately repaying the cost of the freight. In order to get these spices and precious metals, the Europeans had to supply transport services or locally desirable goods.

The initial Spanish experience in the New World was similar. Columbus, no doubt with some idea of the nature of Portuguese trade along the West African coast and with the firm conviction that he would reach China, had loaded drums, tambourines, glass beads, small bells, knitted caps (probably woollen), and samples of gold, silver, spices, pearls, and other jewels.[16] This collection of trade items represented the notion of what the Spanish conceived as important international trade items, as well as the relative scarcity of commodities of exchange that met their criteria for long-distance trade.

Throughout the Caribbean there was no ready market for the Spanish products. As Columbus confided to his journal a few days after his encounter with the original people of the Bahamas and Cuba, trade prospects were slim:

They afterwards swam out to the ship's boats in which we were sitting, bringing us parrots and balls of cotton thread and spears and many other things, which they exchanged with us for such objects as glass beads, hawks and bells. In fact, they very willingly traded everything they had. But they seemed to me a people very short of everything.[17]

For those who followed Columbus and went farther afield, things were not much different on the mainland.[18] Normal trade was difficult but plunder for the small amounts of ornamental precious metals was rewarding enough to lead to the final conquest of the Aztec and Incan empires. Among the "many other things" that the indigenous Indians offered Columbus and his crew were tobacco, maize, cocoa, and manioc (cassava), which would become important international trade commodities much later. But the mechanics of the Atlantic market were not fully developed by the early sixteenth century – and, what is more, to develop this market fully would require a massive infusion of labour and basic reorganization of the local societies. Labour constituted a form of capital investment.

As mentioned before, neither Spain nor Portugal produced a variety of trade items that fit easily into the marketing system that they first encountered in the world beyond Europe. As basically agricultural societies, they were not especially geared to international trade (or to the type of trade that seemed most profitable in the Americas and Africa), though they both included elements of a flourishing, sometimes foreign, bourgeois class.[19] One example of this commercial incompatibility can be seen in the textile trade in Africa. The African market for textiles usually required woven cottons, not the woollen and silken fabrics that were common in the European markets. The Portuguese (and later the Dutch and English) brought these cotton fabrics from India for resale along the African coast. Only much later were the Europeans capable of producing comparable textiles. The indigenous Americans wove their own cloths and hammocks from locally grown cotton and, in some places, henequen.

The Portuguese, nevertheless, did manage to penetrate the African trade system slowly, beginning as transporters of commodities from one regional market to another and only gradually converting the nature of the market to their advantage.[20] To facilitate this conversion of the indigenous African market, the Portuguese had to do two things. In the first place, they had to create a plantation system on the tropical Atlantic islands of São Tomé and Fernando Po. This system allowed them to convert excess slaves derived from their coastal trade into servile labourers on the islands, producing principally sugar and alcohol. Most of the sugar was exported to Portugal, but some of the sugar and most of the alcohol became valuable items exchanged for slaves and gold with the mainland Africans. After 1500 these slaves were also shipped to Brazil and elsewhere in the Americas. In the second place, the Portuguese had to establish their hegemony (later lost to the Dutch) over the Arabs in the Indian Ocean trade, gaining access to Indian sources of spices and cotton textiles – commodities of high value in the European and African markets. The spices were shipped to Europe and the cotton textiles were incorporated into the African trade. In the Americas the Spanish were either unable or unwilling to enter and convert the local trading system. The commerce of the Americas in 1492 involved cotton cloths, cacao (which was also used as money in some places), quetzal feathers, onyx and jade, as well as wooden and stone knives.[21] Instead the Spanish created an entirely new system of trade, linking the Americas irrevocably to Spain (especially Seville and Cadiz) and the wider Atlantic pattern of commerce and emphasizing goods of value to Europeans.

Slavery formed the basis of this new commercial construct, and the American labour needs in large measure determined the volume of the trade in Africans and others to Iberia and the Iberian empires beyond Europe.[22] Indeed, the first forays of the English into the Iberian-American world of the sixteenth century involved selling slaves as well as plundering Spanish treasure ships. The tradition of slavery had survived longer in Iberia than north of the Pyrenees. As early as the tenth century, slaves were employed – along with other types of coerced labourers – throughout the Mediterranean world.

By the beginning of the sixteenth century, African slaves (recently purchased from the Portuguese) frequently worked in agriculture throughout southern Iberia, and in the Spanish port cities of Huelva, Cadiz, Sevilla, Málaga and Valencia, as porters, domestic servants, and labourers in the olive oil and soap factories. Though their use was extensive, slaves (within the category of bondsmen) did not constitute the major form of labour in Iberia, and their economic importance was somewhat obscured.[23] The Spanish monarchs, Ferdinand and Isabella, were reluctant to sanction the unmitigated sale of American Indian slaves in their mainland territories or in the Canary Islands, and as early as 1500 had prohibited the practice, although with some loopholes to allow a supply nearly adequate to the demand in their American possessions. They flatly rejected the offer of Columbus that the Indians of the Americas could be sold as slaves in Iberia.[24] But the demographic disaster among the indigenous populations during the first two centuries after the conquest forced the Castillian monarchs and the Council of the Indies to adopt measures to increase the importation and sale of African labourers in their overseas possessions.[25] Several thousand African slaves were shipped from Spain to the Indies between 1500 and 1518, but that measure was inadequate. Finally, in 1518, Charles I began to issue formal *asientos* (commercial licenses) to various individuals, who could then ship slaves directly from Africa to the Spanish Indies, free of customs duties paid in Spain. After 1713 these *asientos* became an English monopoly, and English slave traders dominated the transatlantic slave trade.

The adoption of the large-scale use of African slaves was a reluctant concession on the part of the Spanish authorities. Some of the reluctance to exploit fully the commercial advantages of slavery stemmed from the hallowed tradition of Hispanic law, especially the *Siete Partidas* of Alfonso X, King of Castile and Leon (1252-84). This was reinforced by a papal declaration in 1462 by Pope Pius II.[26] Iberian domestic slavery, however, was quite distinct from the later American practice. Both the *Siete Partidas* and the papal pronouncements referred to a type of slavery that was less capitalist, less phenotypically African than its development after the sixteenth century.[27] The steadfast refusal to permit the open enslavement of non-belligerent Indians in the Americas meant that non-Indian slaves had to be imported to supply needed labour and the *encomienda* – that ancient feudal Castillian system of *señorio* – had to be transformed in the Americas to serve as an instrument of local coercion.[28] The expansion of the Spanish slave trade to the Americas, therefore, served not only to provide ready labour where and when it was needed, but also to expand the capital base of both the metropolis and the colonies.

Wealth in the early modern world was closely identified with the possession of gold and silver.[29] If one purpose of the establishment of empire was the creation of wealth not only for individuals but also for the emergent nation-states, then the Iberians thought of only two ways to acquire it: by trade and by mining for precious metals. The Portuguese began with an emphasis on trade. That worked successfully along the West African coast and in India. But trading simply did not work well along the Brazilian coast, with its seminomadic, poorly organized, and relatively sparsely settled population of Tupi and Guarani Indians. When a central administration arrived with the Tomé de Sousa expedition of 1549, sounding the death knell to the modified feudal system of *sesmarias* (land grants), the general expectation was that Brazil would eventually become another slave-importing, sugar-producing colony like Sao Tomé. It quickly did, surpassing production elsewhere and creating a glut on the European sugar market. For their part, the Spanish, disappointed with the prospects of trade in the Americas, and lucky enough to find substantial deposits of gold and silver in Mexico and Peru, began to exploit the mines. Bullion was more profitable than spices. Both mining and sugar producing required enormous amounts of labour and a far more complex, interdependent economic system than the Spanish and Portuguese first realized.[30]

Once formalized, the European slave trade expanded rapidly. The volume of the trade at the various import points in the Atlantic islands and the Americas increased from less than 300,000 between 1451 and 1600 to nearly 1.5 million between 1601 and 1700.[31] The Spanish American colonies received about 27% of the total transatlantic trade before 1600, with Brazil getting 18%. For the entire seventeenth century, Spanish America received nearly 22% of the volume, with Brazil getting nearly 42%, reflecting the growing importance of the sugar revolution there. But the volume of the trade had expanded so much that the 22% that the Spanish Americas received during the seventeenth century almost equalled the number of the previous half century.

Without African slaves and the transatlantic slave trade, the potential economic value of the Americas could never have been realized, since neither Portugal nor Spain had the reserves of labour needed to explore and develop their new possessions. Access to supplies of slaves made possible the "taming of the wilderness," construction of cities, pacification of the hostile frontiers, exploitation of the mines, and the establishment of haciendas, *fazendas,* and plantations. By enabling the development of a viable economy on the American frontier, slavery stimulated the accumulation of wealth and power in Spain and Portugal, as well as among the upper segments of American colonial society. The ownership of slaves even became one index of wealth and status.

Several sectors of the economy reflected the enormously increased trade. Shipping expanded, with thousands of slave ships crossing the Atlantic and specializing in the slave trade. To supply these ships, a wide range of goods had to be provided. According to Ray Kea, "one Dutch factor, referring to the late seventeenth century market demands, remarked that more than 150 different commodities were needed to conduct a proper trade at the Gold Coast ports" and that "textiles and metalware were in greatest demand."[32] No other type of trade could equal the broad-based economic stimulus of the slave trade. The requirements of successful intercontinental trade were often beyond the scope of a single European state. Countries that could not produce the necessary commodities and wanted to engage in the African trade simply had no other recourse than to purchase them. Portugal, with its access to India, Africa, and the Americas, had access to a variety of complementary markets. Spain, with its access to American-derived precious metals, was able to purchase commodities from any source – legally if it could and illegally if it had to. At the same time, American buyers of African slaves used their tropical sta-

ple products to finance their needs. Most of these tropical staples were sold in markets in Europe, giving rise to the misleading description that the slave trade was part of a "triangular trade" linking Europe, Africa, and the Americas. In reality, most trade was bilateral, although the trading system itself was enormously complex, involving Asian and Indian states as well as those of the Atlantic littoral. The slave trade was a lucrative enterprise that had extensive repercussions throughout the wider world of commerce in the period, affecting sectors of the economy and groups such as artisans and metalworkers that might seem peripheral to the trade itself.[33] For the local administrations of the precious metals-scarce Caribbean and circum-Caribbean regions, the slave trade provided a source of substantial public income, often ranking second only to the *situado,* or subsidy, sent from New Spain.[34]

By the beginning of the eighteenth century, the Atlantic marketing systems – in Africa, Europe, and the Americas – were already established. The mechanisms for obtaining and selling slaves were perfected, including the construction of ships specially designed for efficiently transporting slaves. During this century, the Europeans would transport and sell far more slaves than ever throughout the Americas.[35] But toward the end of the century, and especially after the French Revolution, the volume of the transatlantic slave trade began to decline and its proportional relationship to world trade progressively fell. Slavery as a mode of production, and the slave trade as a mechanism for capital accumulation, yielded priority to other forms of commerce. Industrial capitalism took precedence over commercial capitalism. Ironically, this change coincided with the Spanish realization of the full economic potential of the slave trade and their attempts to exploit it more thoroughly.[36] Those dramatic changes of the eighteenth century lie outside the scope of this chapter. Industrial capitalism required new networks, new international measures of exchange, and a new order of commercial relations. Slavery created a commercial revolution that evolved until the arrival of the Industrial Revolution. Industrial capitalism, therefore, has part of its foundations in the existence of American slavery and the transatlantic slave trade.

Notes

1. Without becoming too involved in the endless dispute concerning the origins of capitalism in Europe, it may be important to indicate what I understand by capitalism and how it is employed in this chapter. I understand capitalism to be the coherent system of economic relations based on individual private property and private control of the means of production. Fundamental to this system is the pervasive *mentality* that the accumulation of profit for private purposes represents a worthwhile end in itself. See David Harvey, *Tire Urbanization of Capital: Studies in the History and Theory of Capitalist Urbanization* (Baltimore, 1985); and *Consciousness and the Urban Experience* (Baltimore, 1985)

2. See J. H. Parry, *Europe and a Wider World, 1415-1715* (London, 1949), pp. 29-43

3. This is not to deny the missionaries' efforts beyond the Muslim region north of the Sahara, but by their own admission, the activities were not zealously prosecuted. See C. R. Boxer, *Race Relations in the Portuguese Colonial Empire 1415-1825* (Oxford, 1963), pp. 6-9.

4. Slaves are not frequently mentioned in the commercial activities noted by Martin Fernandez de Figueroa during the early years in India. See James B. McKenna, *A Spaniard in the Portuguese Indies: The Narrative of Martín Fernández de Figueroa* (Cambridge, (Mass.), 1967).

5. Bernal Díaz del Castillo, *The True History of the Conquest of Mexico*, translated from the Spanish by Maufice Keatinge, esq. London, 1800 (facsimile edition, La Jolla, Calif.: 1979), p. 502. Varying translations of this quotation appear elsewhere – for example, in John Parry, *The Age of Reconnaissance: Discovery, Exploration and Settlement, 1450-1650* (New York, 1963), p. 19.

6. Gianni Granzotto, *Christopher Columbus: The Dream and the Obsession*, trans. Stephen Sartarelli (Garden City, N.Y., 1985).

7. Steven Runciman, *A History (of the Crusades,* 3 vols (Cambridge, 1951, rev. ed. 1987).

8. Paul Lovejoy, *Transformations in Slavery: A History of Slavery In Africa* (Cambridge, 1983), pp. 23-35.

9. T. Bentley Duncan, *Atlantic Islands: Madeira, The Azores and the Cape Verdes in, Seventeenth Century Commerce and Navigation* (Chicago, 1972); Felipe Fernández-Armesto, *The Canary Islands After Conquest: The Making of a Colonial Society in the Early Sixteenth Century* (Oxford, 1982); Demietrio Castro Alfin, *Historia de las Islas Canarias: De la prehistoria al descubrimiento* (Madrid, 1983).

10. Quoted in Bjorn Landström, *Columbus* (New York, 1966), p. 44.

11. This might indicate a relative underdevelopment of the slave mode of production in Iberia. It seems that the Spanish monarchs had difficulty distinguishing between slaves and vassals. Of course, the conquest of Mexico and Peru in the early sixteenth century, and the resulting discovery of vast quantities of precious metals made the official consideration of in-creased wealth from agriculture and slave trading less important before the eighteenth century.

12. Peggy K. Liss, *Atlantic empires: The Network of Trade and Revolution, 1713-1826* (Baltimore, 1983).

13. See *Slavery in Africa. Historical and Anthropological Perspectives*, ed. by Suzanne Miers and Igor Kopytoff (Madison, Wisc., 1977), pp. 3-75.

14. See, for example, Philip D. Curtin, *Economic Change in Precolonial Africa: Senegambia in the Era of the Slave Trade* (Madison, Wisc., 1975), pp. 6-58; Ray Kea, *Settlements, Trade, and Politics in the Seventeenth Century Gold Coast* (Baltimore, 1982), pp. 206-47; Paul Lovejoy, *Transformations in Slavery* (Cambridge, 1983), pp. 88-107.

15. Philip D. Curtin, *The Atlantic Slave Trade: A Census* (Madison, Wisc., 1969); Herbert S. Klein, *African Slavery in Latin America and the Caribbean* (New York, 1986); Paul Lovejoy, "The Volume of the Atlantic Slave Trade: A Synthesis," *Journal of African History*, Vol. 23, No. 4 (1982), pp. 473-501.

16. Landström, pp. 49-50.

17. *The Four Voyages of Columbus*, ed. and trans. J. M. Cohen (Baltimore, 1969), p. 55. See also *The Log of Christopher Columbus*, trans. Robert H. Fuson (Camden, Me., 1987), p. 76.

18. Carl Orwin Sauer, *The Early Spanish Main* (Berkeley, 1966).

19. It should be remembered that during the reign of Ferdinand and Isabella, latifundism was rife in Spain. In Castille, according to John Elliott, some "2 per cent or 3 per cent of the population owned 97 per cent of the soil of Castille, and that over half of this 97 per cent belonged to a handful of great families." See J. H. Elliott, *Imperial Spain 1469-1716* (New York, 1966), p. 111. On the foreign elements in Spanish trade, see, for cxample, Ruth Pike, *Enterprise and Adventure: The Genoese in Seville and the Opening of the New World* (Ithaca, N.Y., 1966).

20. C. R. Boxer, *Four Centuries of Portuguese Expansion, 1415-1825* (Berkeley, 1969), pp. 32-3; Philip D. Curtin, *Cross-Cultural Trade in World History* (Cambridge, 1984), pp. 57-9.

21. Sauer, pp. 128-9.

22. Pike, p. 40; Leslie B. Rout, *The African Experience in Spanish America, 1502 to the Present* Day (New York, 1976), pp. 15-18; Vicenta Cortes, *La esclavitud en Valencia durante el reinado de los Reyes Catolicos* (Valencia, 1964); Antonio Dominguez Ortiz, "La esclavitud en Castilla durante la edad moderna", *Estudios de Historia social de España*, 2 vols. (Madrid, 1952), Vol. 2, p. 380.

23. Elliot, pp. 68-9.

24. Landström, p. 121; Elliott, p. 68. Presumably the suggestion referred to the more warlike Carib Indians. Columbus also sent back Arawaks to be trained as translators. The majority of the Indians died before they arrived in Cadiz, and this might also have affected court opinion on their suitability as slaves in Iberia.

25. See, Enriqueta Vila Vilar, *Hispanoamérica y el comercio de esclavos: Los asientos portugueses* (Seville, 1977); Colin A. Palmer, *Human Car-*

goes: *The British Slave Trade to Spanish America, 1700-1739* (Urbana, Ill., 1981). The entire profile of the transatlantic slave trade may be reviewed in Curtin, *The Atlantic Slave Trade,* and an excellent summary of the various post-1969 revisions is offered by Lovejoy.

26. E. N. Van Kleffens, *Hispanic Law Until the End of the Middle Ages* (Edinburgh, 1968), pp. 199-200; John Esten Keller, *Alfonso X, El Sabio* (New York, 1967), pp. 111-33.

27. Even the category of slaves was somewhat imprecise, and among the bondsmen in Iberia at the time were Spaniards, Jews, Moors, Canary Islanders, Arabs, Turks, and Russians, many of whom were condemned to the galleys. See Orlando Patterson, *Slavery and Social Death: A Comparative Study* (Cambridge, Mass., 1982), p. 44; Rout, p. 17; Herbert S. Klein, *African Slavery in Latin America and the Caribbean* (New York, 1986), pp. 21-43.

28. Lesley Bird Simpson, *The Encomienda in New Spain* (Berkeley, 1950), S. Padilla, M. L. López Arellano,

and A. Gonzalez, *La Encomienda en Popayan: Tres Estudios* (Seville, 1977); Antonio Muro Orejon, *Las leyes nuevas* (Seville, 1961).

29. See J. F. Richards, ed., *Precious Metals in the Later Medieval and Early Modern World* (Durham, N.C., 1982).

30. James Lockhart and Stuart B Schwartz, *Early Latin America: A History of Colonial Spanish America and Brazil* (Cambridge, 1983), pp. 181-252.

31. Lovejoy, pp. 480-1.

32 Kea, p. 207.

33. Pere Molas Ribalta, *La burguesia mercantil en la España del antiquo regimen* (Madrid, 1985).

34. Levi Marrero, *Cuba: Economia y sociedad,* 14 vols. (Madrid, 1974-86), Vol. V11 47-8.

35. Lovejoy.

36. See *Reglamento y Aranceles reales para el comercio libre de España a Indias de 12 de Octubre de 1778* (Madrid. 1778; reprinted, Seville, 1979).

36

Mercantilism, Slavery and the Industrial Revolution

WILLIAM A. DARITY, JR.

"To discuss trade between Africans and Europeans in the four centuries before colonial rule is virtually to discuss slave trade."

Walter Rodney

How Europe Underdeveloped Africa p.103

A Methodological Prelude

This is primarily an essay in clarification, making no special claims at originality. It represents an attempt to present a consistently Marxist view of the relationship between the Atlantic slave trade and the Industrial Revolution. Moreover, the exploration undertaken here should reveal why the origin of the Industrial Revolution is not a mystery for Marxist scholars and, moreover, how the Marxist method of inquiry facilities a clean break with the circularities that beset other "theories" of early European industrialization.

In addition, this essay is intended to demonstrate how the insights of the Caribbean School of historians – C.L. R. James (1963), Eric Williams (1966), and Walter Rodney (1972) – constitute a coherent whole. Elsewhere this author has sought to offer a "canonical" neoclassical model of the triangle trade to examine the ideas of James, Williams, and Rodney (see Darity, 1981). Unfortunately, the neoclassical approach, due to its general equilibrium method, leads to the possibility of demonstrating the logical validity of virtually any result.[1] For example, the author (Darity 1981) showed in the earlier paper, depending upon the parameter values chosen,

one could demonstrate that the slave trade either aided or hindered growth prospects for Africa. The very same model can be used to "prove" the logic of either conventional Smithian free trade optimism or less conventional neo-Smithian free trade pessimism.[2]

The most extreme variant of the application of the general equilibrium method to the analysis of the Industrial Revolution can be found in the argument of Nicholas Crafts (1977). Crafts argues that the possible "systematic" determinants of the cluster of technical innovations in the late 18th century were swamped by random effects. This position amounts to treating the Industrial Revolution as the outcome of a stochastic process – a sheer accident. It is still a conclusion that can be drawn from an application of the general equilibrium method to the analysis of this even as long as the effects of all the variables typically identified as systematic influences were small, relative to the effects of random disturbances. It reveals plainly how sophisticated intellectual surrender can become when the analyst works within a problematic that breathes, as its life's blood, causal agnosticism.

Aside from the intermediateness of the conclusions that can be drawn from the general equilibrium method, it suffers from a fundamental problem of abstraction. "General equilibrium" models in economics stay confined to an analysis of the sphere of circulation or commodity exchange. Causation is as circular as the actual movement of commodities. Causal primacy vanishes. The general equilibrium method

– the essence of modern economics – completely lacks what Althusser (1979) refers to as "determination in the last instance," Marxism, in contrast, genuinely "sees" the sphere of production that lies behind circulation phenomena and, furthermore, assigns causal primacy to the social relations men and women enter into while engaging in material production.[3]

A mode of production is defined by those social relations that govern the appropriation of surplus labour time. A social formation is an articulated combination of modes of production. From a Marxist perspective, the social relations of production define the mode of production – the historically specific form that material production takes in a given community subject to investigation. It is only by grasping the core importance assigned to the social relations in Marxism that one can grasp the full flavour of the research of the Caribbean School's historians. The deep significance of class or social relations in the politics of slavery in England and France – especially the roles of their respective West Indian planter classes – are central aspects of the work of Williams (1966) and James (1963) respectively. Rodney (1972), pp. 9-82) even undertakes a broad discussion of the comparative character of the dominant modes of production in 16th and 17th century Africa and Europe at the start of his book, *How Europe Underdeveloped Africa.*

In fact, Rodney's discussion openly gives primacy to the social relations of production, although he fails to extend the analysis systematically throughout later parts of his work. His work also is plagued somewhat by an emphasis on prospects for "human development" or an ideological "humanism."[4] Moreover, at various points Rodney (1972, p. 47) conflates his correct and rigorous usage of the concept of a mode of production with more anthropological categorizations of society, for example, his comments on "pastoralists and cultivators, fishing societies and trading societies, raiders and nomads."

However, Rodney does manage to unlock the central issue from a Marxist perspective: what will happen when two societies having different histories of development – development of the social relations – come into contact? Why did the interaction of the African and European modes of productions lead to the triangle trade and Caribbean and North American slavery? What consequences did this interaction have for European industrialization?

Rodney even asks, is it possible in the 16th century to conceive of an "African mode of production" applicable to all regions and peoples of the continent? His conclusion is that it is unreasonable to treat all of Africa as sharing a single mode of production, but that the modes he identifies – ranging from forms resembling communalism and feudalism – were all noncapitalist (or "precapitalist") in character (Rodney, pp. 46-7).

One just as reasonably can question whether or not a single mode of production was applicable to all regions and peoples of 16th century Europe. It seems legitimate to characterize Eastern and Southern Europe as predominantly feudal while northwestern Europe, especially England and France, was in transition from feudal to capitalist social relations.[5] The central claim common to Rodney's discussion and to the approach of this paper is that substantial evidence of capitalist penetration of the sphere of production was present in post-medieval Europe but not in Africa. England stood at the centre of capitalism as the site of the first development of the capital-labour relation, while Africa was on the periphery with the rest of the world.

It was this difference in prevailing social relationships that constitutes the Marxist entry point for a scientific inquiry into the place in history of slavery in the Americas. The object of inquiry here is the specific social formation that existed during the 16th through 18th centuries that interfaced non-capitalist Africa and nascent capitalist Europe.

Rodney (1972-9) hypothesized that there are two major conclusions about the effects of interaction between two societies characterized by different modes of production:

The fact that capitalism today is still around alongside of socialism should warn us that the modes of production cannot simply be viewed as a question of successive stages. Uneven development has always ensured that societies have come into contact when they were at different levels – for example, one that was communal and one that was capitalist.

When two societies of different sorts come into prolonged and effective contact, the rate and character of change taking place in both is seriously affected to the extent that entirely new patterns are created. Two general rules can be observed to apply in such cases. Firstly, the weaker of the two societies (i.e. the one with less economic capacity) is bound to be adversely affected – and the bigger the gap between the two societies concerned the more detrimental are the consequences. For example, when European capitalism came into contact with the indigenous hunting societies of America and the Caribbean, the latter were virtually exterminated. Secondly, assuming that the weaker society does survive, then ultimately it can resume its own independent development only if it proceeds to a level higher than that of the economy which had previously dominated it. The concrete instances of the operation of this second rule are found in the experience of the Soviet Union, China and Korea.

One of the purposes in this paper is to evaluate Rodney's "two general rules," which will require examining whether or not there is a rigorous meaning to the notion of a "weaker" mode of production. The conclusion is that Rodney's concept is inadequate but can point in theoretically interesting directions.

Foundations of Racism and Mecantilism

Before going further, it is important to clarify the conception of ideology to be used in this paper. The definition is borrowed from Althusser (see Althusser and Balibar, 1979, p. 314):

[Ideology is] the lived relation between men and the world, or a reflected form of this unconscious relation, for instance a "philosophy" (q.v.) Etc. It is distinguished from a science not by its falsity, for it can be coherent and logical (for instance, theology), but by the fact that the practico-social predominates in it over the theoretical, over knowledge.

Put differently, an "ideology" is the set of ideas guiding day-to-day practice – or daily activities. There is nothing pejorative or judgmental in this definition of ideology. Ideologies are not necessarily "wrong." It is clear that people cannot live without ideologies for that would be to live without beliefs. Ideology, in this sense, places the emphasis on ideas having a direct bearing on activity and practice.

Furthermore, ideologies are produced. They are products of the social relations. For example, the idea of the inferiority of the Africans – the idea of white supremacy – has a specificity to the period of slavery in the Americas. The fact, the notion of racial superiority was first directed by the Spanish toward the native population of the Caribbean, the peoples whom the Spanish enslaved first. The translation of the idea of racial superiority into white over black only comes with the expansion of the use of Africans as slaves in the New World Eric Williams (1966, p. 7) concludes ". . . racism was a consequence of slavery."

The slavery of the Americas arose out of the particular social formation that existed during the era of the rise of capitalism in Europe.

Caribbean and North American slavery was specific in character and purpose to the development of capitalism. It might be reasonable to conceive of the slavery of antiquity as constituting a separate slave mode of production.[7] One would be hard-pressed to do the same for slavery in the New World from the 15th century onward.[8] Although slavery in ancient Greece and Rome was a mechanism for appropriation of surplus labour time by the citizens, the appropriation was not conducted with a lust for profit. As Orlando Patterson has argued, Caribbean and North American slavery, in contrast, was conducted on a capitalistic basis with the slaves mobilized for the production of surplus value, the form of surplus labour time specific to capitalism (p. 38) then identifies differences in the notion of property associated with particular episodes of slavery – even differences between the concept of property between ancient Greece and ancient Rome. The key point is that wherever slavery has appeared it has not had the same meaning, although many of its institutional characteristics may look much the same.

Because of the geographical origin and racial characteristics of the vast majority of the slaves, slavery in the Americas produced an ideology of white supremacy that was absent from the slavery of ancient Greece and Rome. For instance, Oliver Cox (1970, p. 324) observes:

The next great organization of peoples about the Mediterranean Sea – and insofar as European civilization is concerned this may be thought of as constituting the whole world – was the Roman Empire. In this civilization also we do not find racial antagonism, for the norm of superiority in the Roman system remained a cultural-class attribute. The basic distinction was Roman citizenship, and gradually this was extended to all freeborn persons in the municipalities of the empire. Slaves came from every province, and there was no racial distinction among them. Sometimes the slaves, especially the Greeks, were the teachers of the masters; indeed very much of the cultural enlightenment of the Romans came through slaves from the East. Because slavery was not a racial stigma, educated freedmen, who were granted citizenship upon emancipation, might rise to high positions in government or industry. There were no inter-racial laws governing the relationship of the great mass of obscure common people of different origin.

The idea of white supremacy was a product of the trade in Africans and the building of the plantation system in the "New World." But what was the basis for the introduction of the slave-plantation system itself into the Americas? It arose from a programme of social policy that evolved in the recently consolidated European nations in the 16th and 17th centuries, setting as a goal national power and expansion of output, the programme of social policy that can be labeled "mercantilism" (see Eli Heckscher, 1935). Mercantilism covers the web of principles that guided statecraft in the European nations throughout the period in question.

Marx identified capitalism's beginnings with the rise of a class that achieved self-valourization through the sphere of circulation. Capital originated in the far past with the activities of long distance trade and money lending, accessing surplus labour time generated in precapitalist modes of production in the forms it took in commodity – money exchange. Marx (1977. p. 247) described the initial confrontation of the emerging capitalist class with the feudal landlords in the following way:

The circulation of commodities is the starting-point of capital. The production of commodities and their circulation in its developed form, namely trade, form the historic presuppositions under which capital arises. World trade and the world market date from the sixteenth century, and from then on, the modern history of capital starts to unfold.

If we disregard the material content of the circulation of commodities, i.e. the exchange of the various use-values, and consider only the economic forms brought into being by their process, we find that its ultimate product is money. This ultimate product of commodity circulation is the first form of appearance of capital. Historically speaking, capital invariably first confronts landed property in the form of money; in the form of monetary wealth, merchants' capital and usurers' capital. However, we do not need to look back at the history of capital's origins in order to recognize that money is its first form of appearance. Every day the same story is played out before our eyes. Even up to the present day, all new capital, in the first instance, steps onto

the stage – i.e. the market, whether it is the commodity-market, the labour-market, or the money-market – in the shape of money, money which has to be transformed into capital by definite processes.

Merchant and interest-bearing capital's agenda for its own development and for its eventual penetration into the sphere of production was embodied in the doctrines of mercantilism. Mercantilism was the programme for the 16th century transformation of money into capital. Mercantilism was also the ideology produced by the advance of merchant capital that sought to mobilize the absolutist state on its own behalf. The array of mercantilist restraints on imports – the "monopolies" – were recognized by their most severe critic, Adam Smith (1937, pp. 420-39), to be instrumental in advancing specific sectors of home manufacturing important in the export trade.

Although the absolutist state was a product of advanced feudalism, as long as merchant capital did not disturb the sphere of production, there was in Perry Anderson's (1974 a, p. 41) words a "field of compatability" between the nascent bourgeoisie and the feudal lords. Utilization of this arena of accord permitted merchant capital to employ the state power as a means for its own class development to the point that its class strength was sufficient to transform the sphere of production in its own image. The long series of serf revolts or "The Peasant Wars" weakened the feudal lords to such an extent that the way was paved through their own state apparatus for the ascendancy of capital.

Mercantilism and "Primitive Accumulation"

Central to the mercantilist agenda was the creation of the conditions of labour market, the conditions that permit "the owner of money (to) find labour-power on the market as a commodity . . ." (Marx, 1977, p. 270). Capital only could consolidate its penetration of the sphere of production when labour-power appeared on the commodity market. Mercantilism promoted the legal arrangements that contributed to the making of a market for labour: the process of expropriation of the land from the peasantry, the subsequent "bloody legislation" directed against the expropriated, the process that Marx (1977, po. 873-904) called "primitive accumulation."

Primitive accumulation and the associated Poor Laws were so thoroughly developed by the close of the 18th century that Adam Smith's disciple, Frederic Morton Eden (1929, p. 1), could claim that the true source of wealth was control over human labour:

It is not the possession of land or money, but the command of labour that distinguishes the opulent from the labouring part of the community.

Eden (1929, pp. 3-4) plainly linked evidence of widespread poverty to the "releasing" of the peasantry from the land:

The answer to Rousseau's enquiry: 'Why is it that in a thriving city the Poor are miserable, while such extreme distress is hardly ever experienced in those countries where there are no instances of extreme wealth?' is that in cities people are poor because they are more independent than in the country. It is one of the natural consequences of freedom that those who are left to shift for themselves must sometimes be reduced to want. Dr. Johnson's remarks on marriage and celibacy may perhaps be applied with propriety to freedom and servitude: the one has many pains, the other no pleasures.

The decrease of villeinage seems necessarily to have been the era of the origin of the Poor. Without, therefore, disparaging the benefits of commerce the result of this investigation seems to lead to the inevitable conclusion that manufactures and commerce are the true parents of our nation's Poor.

From the outset the ideology of merchant capital was deeply conscious of the importance of the problem of "the command of labour." Moreover, 17th century mercantilist writers with rare exception – the exceptions were Cary, North and Defoe – believed in a principle of large numbers of labourers and low wages (Coleman, 1956, pop. 280-1). There was little "humanitarian" sentiment in their thinking and an acceptance of the view that many were to live in poverty while the few would live well. When it was decided that a workforce was needed for the West Indies, there was nothing in mercantilist thought to restrain the hunger for labour. The limitation on capitalist development always came not from the thinking of capital itself but from accommodations forced upon it by its working class.

The Tendency of The Rate of Profit To Fall And The Tade In Africans

In the mercantile scheme the Americas were valuable sites for access to mineral wealth, cheaper foodstuffs, and raw materials; and, like West Africa, any outlet for export of new manufactures (Spengler, 1960). Adam Smith saw the importance of the extension of the market to promote the division of labour. His inability to grasp the critical abstraction between the spheres of circulation and production precluded Smith's recognition that foreign trade retarded the fall of the rate of profit, Marx's "pure form" of the rate of profit specific to the sphere of production and not to be confused with the Ricardian rate of profit:

Since foreign trade partly cheapens the elements of constant capital, and partly the necessities of life for which the variable capital is exchanged, it tends to raise the rate of profit by increasing the rate of surplus – value and lowering the value of constant capital. It generally acts in this direction by permitting an expansion of the scale of production. It thereby hastens the process of accumulation, on the one hand, but causes the variable capital to shrink in relation to the constant capital, on the other, and thus hastens a fall in the rate of profit. In the same way, the expansion of foreign trade, although the basis of the capitalist mode of production in its infancy, has become its own product, however, with the further progress of the capitalist mode of production, through the innate necessity of this mode of production, its need for an ever-expanding market... (Marx, 1967, p. 237, emphasis added).

The "extension of the market" was a means of overcoming the contradictory character of productivity growth with increasing capitalist production. Rather than promoting the division of labour, foreign trade expansion could validate capital's efforts to slow the fall in the rate of profit precipitated by the introduction of new machinery. More extensive use of machinery raised relative surplus value but more than proportionately raised the ratio of constant to variable capital.

In volume 3 of *Capital*, Marx (1967, pp. 232-7) enumerated several steps capital might pursue to brake the fall in the rate of profit, steps that could be taken in addition to expansion of foreign trade:

1. Increase the intensity of exploitation of labour power.
2. Depress wages below the value of labour power.
3. Cheapen or devalue the elements of constant capital, that is, raise the ratio of constant to vari-

able capital in the manufacture of means of production.

4. Use the relative overpopulation associated with the advance of the capitalist mode of production – the population cast off as older sectors mechanize – to open up new industries where the proportions of constant to variable capital are low, thus having a higher rate of profit and pulling up the general rate of profit. This counter-effect on the decline of the profit rate is temporary for "These new lines start out predominantly with living labour, and by degrees pass through the same evolution as the other lines of production."

Marx concluded (1967, p. 239) that these counteracting influences would confine the tendency of the rate of profit to fall but would not eliminate it:

We have thus seen in a general way that the same influences which produce a tendency in the general rate of profit to fall also call forth counter effects, which hamper, retard and partly paralyze this fall. The latter do not do away with the law, but impair its effect.

The rising productivity of labour was the source of the tendency. What is of interest here are the various ways the mercantilist programmes for the colonies could serve as a counter-effect to the fall of profit rate.

The falling profit rate was associated with the transition from raising the rate of absolute surplus value to raising relative surplus value in the history of capital. This transition did not occur uniformly across all industries. As Domenico Sella (1974, p. 397) observed, "Before the eighteenth century, examples of labour-saving techniques and devices are notoriously rare . . ." Since the capacity to raise absolute surplus value was still great, there had been no need to introduce machinery, even when capitalist production was in heated competition with precapitalist producers throughout the globe. If the working day still could be lengthened, the rates of surplus value and profit could be raised in concert. But the working class ultimately set the limit to the extent of extraction of absolute value. The working day was not to be lengthened beyond the astonishing 14 – 16 hour days characteristic of early to mid-18th century factory labour. In fact the working day was to be reduced.

After the working class placed its block on the extraction of absolute surplus value, development of large-scale manufacturing to a degree that would extinguish small-scale handicrafts

necessitated productivity increases that could be accomplished via introduction of machinery. Since precapitalist/handicraft producers were, for the most part, makers of wage-goods, it is no surprise, as Perez Sainz (1977, p. 6) has argued, that those industries were the first to experience substantial mechanization. Perez Sainz (p. 6) has noted further that it is not until later in capital's history – the phase of intercapitalist rivalry - that devaluation occurs for the means of production themselves.

Consistent with the preliminary mechanization of wage goods industries was the preeminence of the textile industry in foreshadowing the growing embrace of machinery in the capitalist labour process. Attempts to mechanize textile production appeared at least as early as the 17th century in experiments with braking flax in England. Mechanical looms in weaving achieved significant use in the same century (Kellenbenz, 1974, pp. 214-17).

The relatively early introduction of machinery into textile production meant that this industry would be among the first to reveal the contradictory character of capitalist production (Perez Sainz, 1977, p. 6). In addition, it is no surprise that textiles were a leading arm of foreign trade expansion even in the 17th century - exchanged abroad for cheaper primary goods and cheaper wage-goods. Sella (1974, p. 363) identifies linens as a large aspect of the American-bound trade in the late 1600s, "a not negligible if much smaller outlet in West Africa where it was used alongside silks, firearms and trinkets to secure slaves" for Brazil and the West Indian sugar plantations. Linen was also shipped from Normandy to Africa in the late 16th century! In the late 17th century the Royal African Company traded Dutch linens in Guinea.

A comparable expansion in production was internally evident in England in the construction sector, particularly in meeting growing housing requirements and in supporting the shipping industry. The expansion was so pronounced that when the American War of Independence deprived England of access to North American timber, the first centre of capitalism experienced a late 18th century "energy crisis." Binley Thomas (1980, pp. 1-13) has argued that England's Industrial Revolution was a consequence of a response to adversity associated with this crisis of the 1770s and 1780s. But Thomas has it backward: the increased hunger for energy was the result of the most extensive adoption of machine production up to that time rather than the cause.

The rapid advance of the wage-good sectors, especially the textile industry, could contribute in Western Europe to the emergence of the relative surplus-population, ready to be absorbed into new industries. The new industries would begin with a low organic composition of capital and have, due in part to the downward pressure on wages exercised by the "over-population", a higher rate of profit than the previously existing general rate.

Colonial production also could retard the fall in the rate of profit for much the same reasons. Marx (1967, p. 238) himself observed:

As concerns capitals invested in colonies . . . they may yield higher rates of profit for the simple reason that the rate of profit is higher there due to backward development, and likewise the exploitation of labour, because of the use of slaves, coolies, etc.

In the colonies surplus value could be raised in the absolute form for a far long period of time, under a regimen of slavery, than it could be in West Europe. The lengthening of the working day was being extended in the sugar islands while it was being contracted in England and France.

The mercantile agenda mandated building the American colonies, and building the American colonies required access to labour, an initial accumulation that would permit the Caribbean and North America to fit into the mercantile system. Even free trader Adam Smith, whose *Wealth of Nations* defined the developed bourgeois class' ideology that was to supplant mercantilism, still believed that the colonies were invaluable for ongoing capitalist development. Smith objected to restraint in trade with the colonies, not the procurement and maintenance of the colonies. Even with the objectionable mercantile restrictions the colonies were a net benefit for Smith (1937, p. 573):

We must carefully distinguish between the effects of the colony trade and those of the monopoly of that trade. The former are always and necessarily beneficial; the latter always and necessarily hurtful. But the former are so beneficial, that the colony trade though subject to a monopoly, and notwithstanding the hurtful effects of that monopoly, is still upon the whole beneficial; though a good deal less so than it otherwise would be.

To reap the "net benefits" the indigenous population of the Americas was turned to first as a source of labour. The consequences were devastating for the natives. The combination of European diseases from which the natives lacked immunity and the uncustomary toil in mines run by the Spanish and Portuguese led to decimation of their numbers. Perhaps of greater importance in explaining the failure of the indigenous population to provide an "effective" workforce for European efforts to economically develop the Americas was the ability of the natives to flee further inland – to run away from merchant capital's agenda for development of their land.

Next to be turned to were indentured servants, kidnapped European youths, and European prisoners.

The mercantile system in operation was well equipped to conduct a large-scale migration to the New World. Williams (1966, p. 15) provides the following example from the City of Bristol in the mid-17th century:

The merchants and justices were in the habit of straining the law to increase the number of felons who could be transported to the sugar plantations they owned in the West Indies.

By the close of the 17th century, mercantile thinkers were fully cognizant of the mixed effects of their efforts to send large numbers of the working class to the Americas. Although it aided in the building of the colonies, it also was a strategy that ran counter to their efforts to maintain a large population at home to sustain low wages for industry. Clearly emigration contradicted their populationist instincts (William, 1966, p. 16). Mercantilist fears of external competition in manufacturing from Europeans transplanted to the Americas also was a concern (Williams, 1966, p. 18). Williams (p. 19) also argues that the indentured servant was harder to keep in a proletarian condition once the term of servitude was over than a black slave:

On the plantations, escape was easy for the white servant; less easy for the Negro who if freed, tended in self-defence to stay in his locality where he was well known and least likely to be apprehended as a vagrant or runaway slave. The servant expected land at the end of his contract; the Negro, in a strange environment, conspicuous by his colour and features, and ignorant of the white man's language and ways, could be kept permanently divorced from the land. But Williams (1966, p. 19) concluded that "the decisive factor" leading to the virtually complete turn to Africa as the source of labour for the West Indies by the 1700s was the relative cost of the black slave:

The money which procured a white man's service for ten years could buy a Negro for life.

The claim that blacks were better suited to be slaves due to a greater African familiarity with slavery is not a persuasive explanation for the turn toward Africa. Such a claim presumes an unlikely homogeneity in the character of African and American slavery. It also overlooks the long European experience with slavery, as well, that did not end even with the breakdown of the social relations of antiquity and the rise of feudalism (Anderson, 1974, passim.). Africa was turned to because a detribalized and enslaved people proved to be the only workforce from which surplus value could be extracted effectively in the Americas.

Thus the initial accumulation (of labour) that enabled merchant capital to economically develop the Caribbean and North America meant the proletarianization of large numbers of Africans. For **proletarianization** should not be confused merely with the appearance of wage-labour. It must be understood as a condition where workers truly have nothing to sell but their skins. Although the African's labour-power was not his own to dispose of as he pleased, if "freed" from slavery, dispose of it he must, by hiring it out, or starve. Moreover, as was argued above, the use to which labour-power is put by the dominant class is a crucial determinant of its character, regardless of the form that labour-power takes.

Merchant capital at its height of development reached "backward" to the slave form of production because it could not get sufficient number of workers to build the Caribbean as "free" labourers. The problems with free European labourers have been documented above. **Even** with Europeans, "backward" labour forms akin to those of feudalism were utilized, for example indentured servitude.

Africans were not likely to come as "voluntary migrants" with a lure of high salaries, since the customary incentives associated with the market for labour were alien to the social relations within which Africans were living. Labor-

power had not become a commodity to be sold by the labourer himself in Africa like it had in Europe. Africa had not experienced a "primitive accumulation" of the sort that occurred in the post-medieval Europe. Besides capital is never anxious to pay high wages for labour-power when it can be had more cheaply.

On the eve of contact, Africa's communities largely stood outside even the nascent forms of the capitalist mode of production. Therefore, to obtain labour from Africa would require a process quite different from "voluntary" migration. Instead of purchasing African labour-power from African labourers' individually, merchant capital purchased African labour-power by buying blacks from other blacks. The African labourer did not enter into "equality" in the market with the buyer of his labour-power. Thus, while the divorce of the peasants from the land in Europe turned them into "free labourers, the divorce of Africans from the continent turned them into slaves. In either case, the process was designed to satisfy that incredible hunger for labour that early capitalism expressed so plainly. Cox (1970, p. 332) notes succinctly the case of the African Trade:

Sometimes, probably because of its very obviousness, it is not realized that the slave trade was simply a way of recruiting labour for the purpose of exploiting the great natural resource of America.

Williams (1966, p. 9) is more blunt:

The Indian reservoir, too, was limited, the African inexhaustible. Negroes therefore were stolen in Africa to work the lands stolen from the Indians in America.

The hunger for labour in the Americas was aggravated by the resistance of the proletariat in Western Europe to further expropriation of surplus value in the absolute form. To the extent that the development of the colonies served to retard the fall in the general rate of profit for capital as a whole, the capacity of the working class in Western Europe to achieve "victories," intensified capital's need for African labour in the Caribbean and North America.

The Nature of African "Underdevelopment"

In fact, however, it is unlikely that a large proportion of the millions of Africans transported to the New World were "stolen" literally. A complex and elaborate system of "production" of slaves developed on the continent, in conjunction with the expanding trade, inclusive of vast networks to transport slaves from deep within the interior to the western coastal entrepôts. Merchant activity had a long history in Africa prior to the Atlantic trade in slaves, but the genuinely rapid development of the merchant class in Africa must be associated with the era after contact and trade with Europe.

The African merchants also flourished in collabouration with a strong ruler, for the major source of slaves was successful warfare waged against other tribes. Replication of the European style of capitalist development was out of the question, for African mercantilism was based on the export of labour, not its accumulation! As Rodney (1972, p. 108) observes, "Captives were shipped outside instead of being utilized within any given African community for creating wealth from nature." "Elsewhere he (p. 115) writes, ". . . even the busiest African in West, Central or East Africa was concerned more with trade than with production . . ."

The character of the advance of African merchant capital contradicted the possibility of capitalist penetration of the African sphere of production, a penetration which would require large pools of available labour-power. Therefore, African capital was to linger far longer than European capital in the sphere of circulation. In fact, when European capital set about "developing" West Africa in the mid-19th century – through plantation agriculture and extraction of mineral wealth – the "shortage" of labour led to a variety of schemes (Shuler, 1980) to encourage freed blacks to repatriate to the continent.

African rulers whose strength increased via participation in the slave trade, consolidated their power in ways that were inimical to the European style of capitalist development. Reconstitution of their dominance did not require the use of wealth for valorization purposes. Robin Law (1978, pp. 48-50) concludes that West African rulers' wealth acquired either directly from the trade of slave or indirectly through taxation was "used for prestigious conspicuous consumption, to attract support or buy off the opposition, or to exchange against military supplies such as horses and firearms." The rulers who were effective producers of slaves also could use the trade with the Europeans as an additional vehicle for preserving their power and order in their communities. They could sell their own malcontents, dissidents, and criminals into slavery.

This is not to say that there was not a substantial and sometimes organized opposition within Africa to the slave trade. Classic cases of sustained resistance were those of the legendary Queen Nzinga, who helped found "the Angolan state of Matamba around 1630 as a direct reaction to the Portuguese," and the Agaja Trudo king of Dahomey, in 1724 and 1726.[9] But the combined weight of the European commercial interests, eager to buy slave labour, and African commercial interests, eager to sell slave labour, was too great. European merchant capital's divide-and-rule tactics, coupled with its access to military power and active collabouration from African merchant capital, gave sustenance to the trade in Africans. It is doubtful that European military superiority would have been decisive without such collabouration.

What were the consequences of the slave trade for Africa? Rodney in Chapter 4 of *How Europe Underdeveloped Africa* cites four major reasons why the Atlantic slave trade had an adverse effect on prospects for African economic development.

First, Rodney (1972, pp. 103-112) contends that depopulation led to technological arrest, suggesting a population pressure theory of technical change. Perhaps such a theory is appropriate to a specific precapitalist mode of production, but Rodney does not develop the argument in such a fashion. The Marxist law of population specific to the capitalist mode of production – the law of relative surplus population – severs *any direct relationship between population growth and the technical characteristics of production* . As Perez Sainz (1977, p. 4) observes, "[Capitalism] is the first mode of production which frees itself from the natural constraint of population growth and other possible social constraints." Rodney's argument would have been improved if he had elabourated a theory of population specific to the mode's of production characterizing Africa in the 16th and 17th centuries. There is substantial anthropological evidence to suggest that in so-called "primitive agrarian" societies there is a relationship between population pressure and technological change (Boserup, 1965).

Second, Rodney (1972, p. 115) argues the Atlantic slave trade meant the loss of bright young minds for Africa, youths who might have been great inventors. Again, Rodney seems to be giving preeminence to a factor – technology – that must be, in a Marxist analysis, tied to a specific mode of production. Do bright young minds always manifest "inventiveness," regardless of the societal context?

Third, Rodney (1972, p. 115) suggests that the warfare that wracked the continent of Africa to produce slaves for the trade led to severe social disruption that stymied technological advance. But Europe during the same period underwent a long string of wars. Yet by the end of the 18th century there is strong evidence of an Industrial Revolution in England.

Finally, Rodney argues that the quality of the compensation Africans received for their brothers and sisters sold into slavery was inadequate. In fact, he (p. 111) claims the Europeans dumped their worst quality manufactures in Africa – "cheap gin, cheap gunpowder, pots and kettles full of holes, beads, and other assorted rubbish." This ignores the substantial evidence of the sophistication of the African traders and the hard bargains they typically struck (A. G. Hopkins, 1973). But, moreover, from a Marxist perspective an "unequal exchange" at the level of circulation has no meaning. A more interesting argument would be the obvious impossibility in having capitalist economic development in Africa when the source of value – labour-power – was being sold abroad rather than being put to work at home.

The key point in explaining African "economic backwardness" is not simply that African precapitalist social relations, when confronted with European nascent capitalist social relations, were "weaker" and hence Africa was pushed into underdevelopment. The *dominant classes* in precapitalist Africa had no strong reason to conduct, and did not conduct, a European-styled programme of economic development after entering into trade relations with the centre of capitalist development. Prevailing African class relations within the social formation some call "the Atlantic economy" were not to produce the same sort of economic growth witnessed in northwestern Europe during the same period.

If the slave trade was arguably a block on African development, in the precise Marxist sense of development of the social relations, then it must be treated as aiding the backward or older classes in maintaining their power. As noted above, African merchant capital was tied so deeply to the trade in slaves, it was sending abroad what it needed most to penetrate the sphere of production – labour. Thus Rodney's first general rule is at best an oversimplification.

In addition, communal societies disintegrated under the impact of slave raidings. Surviving modes of production may have been closer to what Marxist anthropologists Dupré and Rey (1973) describe as "lineage" societies in modern Africa, where the dominant class is comprised of the older, male members of the community. The survival of such societies may have been the consequence of the importance of younger males as objects of the slave trade.

Consolidation of The Capitalist Mode of Production

In contrast, the trade in Africans and the enslavement of Africans in the New World thoroughly aided the rise of the newer class in Europe, the capitalist class, both in its merchant form and later in its industrial form. Access to African labour for the colonies aided the maintenance of an adequate reservoir of labour required for European industry. After all, the mercantilist writers were well aware that "the command of labour" was their central problem.

It is at this stage that the singular importance of the title of Eric Williams' book, *Capitalism and Slavery*, can be understood most clearly. For capitalism needed the enslavement of Africans to proceed – to break through the barriers to its development. The manifestations of this intimate relationship – merchant capital producing African slavery in the Americas, and African slavery in the Americas facilitating the rise of industrial capital – are especially evident in Chapter Three, "British Commerce and the Triangular Trade" and Chapter Five, "British Industry and the Triangular Trade" of Williams' classic (Williams, 1966, pp. 51-84 and 98-107). Rodney (1972, pp. 84-102) repeats much the same argument in the third chapter of his book. But perhaps Marx's (1977, p. 918) own incandescent rhetoric captures the nature of relationship most forcefully:

The colonial system ripened trade and navigation as in a hothouse. The 'companies called Monopolia'. . . were powerful levers for the concentration of capital. The colonies provided a market for the budding manufactures, and a vast increase in accumulation which was guaranteed by the mother country's monopoly of the market. The treasures captured outside Europe by undisguised looting, enslavement and murder flowed back to the mother-country and were turned into capital there . . .

Capitalism needed colonies; to have colonies, capitalism needed slaves.

Consider also Williams' (1966, pp. 106-7) profound summary statement of the effects of the Atlantic slave trade in Britain:

Thus it was that Abbé Raynal, one of the most progressive spirits of his day, a man of wide learning in close touch with the French bourgeoisie, was able to see that the labours of the people in the West Indies "may be considered as the principal cause of the rapid motion which now agitates the universe.' The triangular trade made an enormous contribution to Britain's industrial development. The profits from this trade fertilized the entire productive system of the country. Three instances must suffice. The slate industry in Wales, which provided material for roofing, was revolutionized by the new methods adopted on his Caravonshire estate by Lord Penrhyn, who . . . owned sugar plantations in Jamaica and was chairman of the West India Committee at the end of the eighteenth century. The leading figure in the first great railway project in England, which linked Liverpool and Manchester was Joseph Sandars, of whom little is known. But his withdrawal in 1824 from the Liverpool Anti-Slavery Society is of great importance, as at least showing a reluctance to press the sugar planters. Three other men prominently identified with the undertaking had close connections with the triangular trade – General Gascoyne of Liverpool, a stalwart champion of the West India interest, John Gladstone and John Moss. The British West India interest also played a prominent part in the construction of the Great Western Railway.

But it must not be inferred that the triangular trade was solely and entirely responsible for the economic development. The growth of the internal market in England, the ploughing-in of the profits from industry to generate still further capital and achieve still greater expansion, played a large part. But this industrial development, stimulated by mercantilism, later outgrew mercantilism and destroyed it.

The destruction of mercantilism was signaled by Adam Smith's (1937) *Wealth of Nations* as a statement of the new liberal ideology of the industrial bourgeoisie, but by then mercantilism and slavery had accomplished their purpose. Immediately after the quotation just above, Williams (1966, p. 107) says, "In 1783 the shape of things to come was clearly visible." He (p. 107) then catalogues a wide range of industrial innovations with a direct or indirect link to the slave plantation system: the steam engine, improved methods of coal mining and the growth of the iron industry, and innovations in cotton/textile production, the latter "the queen of the Industrial Revolution."

Williams has drawn us carefully toward a theory of the Industrial Revolution in such a way that the British factory the West Indian plantation, and the West African trading port must be seen in their essential unity. *The ideologies of white supremacy and mercantilism also then must be seen as supportive of the development of capitalism.* Both ideologies shared roots in Judaeo-Protestant religious beliefs that placed many outside of "salvation," whether African slaves or European peasants. Jewell Mazique (1959) has written the following about the North American colonies:

The identification of the industrial and commercial classes with a religious radicalism which rejected restrains on usury and avarice established a bond of interest between psuedo-Christian Christians and Marranos which has lasted to this day. The precepts of Calvinism, implemented and expounded most completely by the Puritans, supplied the dynamism for the slave movement in America and gave rise to the Yankee spirit. The marriage of the Puritan 'elect' gospel with the Jewish 'chosen' theology in a free climate beyond the restraining influence of Catholic authoritarianism and the limitations of Lutheran ethics, gave birth to a 'capitalico-religion' morality guaranteeing the sanctity of 'buying cheap and selling dear'. Thus with God's approval Yankee merchants entered freely in the selling of Negroes and Indians with impunity and barbaric cruelty and were encouraged just as long as they kept the Sabbath, steered clear of obscenity and avoided profanity and alcohol.

The Catholic Church once had managed to temper the maltreatment of the natives in the early period of colonization in the West Indies. No such restrain was effectively forthcoming on behalf of the blacks. For by then, merchant capital was attaining its greatest hour of glory. In fostering and eventually yielding to industrial capital, merchant capital paved a bloody way for the Industrial Revolution – from enclosure of the common land to the enslavement of Africans.[10] It is no grievous misstatement to say that the Industrial Revolution was in major part borne on the backs of Africans toiling in West Indian sugar cane and cotton fields.

Finally, in return to Rodney's second general rule, his claim that if the "weaker" society survives, "it can resume its own independent development only if it proceeds to a level higher than that of the economy which had previously dominated it." Obviously, this is Rodney's ideological admonition to Africa that it must turn toward socialism rather than capitalism. Disregarding Rodney's still unsatisfactory notion of a "weaker" society, resumption of "independent development" is probably an impossibility. For it raises the thorny question of whether a society can consciously "withdraw" from a social formation, once a part of it. The real issue is transformation from within and the ability of the masses to liberate themselves from domination by any of the backward classes, whether capitalist or noncapitalist.

Notes

1. Roy Weintraub (1979, pp. 71-5) has claimed the method of modern economics, "general equilibrium," is a case of "general systems" theory. The "general equilibrium method" - the application of systems of circular-cum-cumulative causation-spans the sweep of modern social science. Even the institutionalist tradition in economics embraces the same methodology; see, for example, Gunnar Myrdal's (1974) discussion in his essay *What is Development?* The mainstream epitome of the general equilibrium method applied to historical phenomena crystallizes in Peter Temin's (1971) *General Equilibrium Models in Economic History*. The intricate confusions that arise in the use of the general equilibrium method in analyzing the process of technical change are uncovered with painstaking care in Paul David's (1975) *Technical Choice, Innovation and Economic Growth: Essays on American and British Experience in the Nineteenth Century*.
2. Neo-Smithian pessimism about the consequences of international trade is reflected fully in the work of Immanuel Wallerstein (1979), e.g. *The Capitalist World-Economy*, Wallerstein's work, the "dark side" of Adam Smith's (1937) *Wealth of Nations*, parades improperly as Marxist since Wallerstein never can get past circulation of commodities. For substantive critiques see Robert Brenner (1977) and C.H. George (1980).
3. In *Capital Volume One*, Marx (1977) was quite explicit in ascribing causal primacy to the social relations governing the appropriation of surplus labour-time. Marx (p. 325) wrote, "What distinguishes the various economic formations of society . . . is the form in which this surplus labour is in each case extorted from the immediate producer, the worker."
An alternative view of causal primacy in Marxism is offered by G.A. Cohen (1978), Cohen contends that modes of production are distinguished by the forces of production – by technology – rather than by the social relations, and he contends that the social relations are produced by the forces of production rather than vice versa. The inanities to which this leads are apparent in Chapter 6 of Cohen's book, *The Primacy of the Productive Forces*, especially his disastrous discussion of slavery and technology (p. 158). To find textual support from Marx for determination in the last instance in the productive forces, Cohen relies heavily on the more ambiguous position Marx took in works **prior** to *Capital*. In *Capital*, however, Marx's position (1977, p. 286) is quite clear: the instruments of production are an indicator or an index of the underlying social relations. Marx speaks continuously of the social relations of the capitalist mode of production as being responsible for the most rapid development of the means of production in history. The agnostic position is presented by E.K. Hunt (1979) in *History of Economic Thought: A Critical Perspective* where a mode of production is defined by both the forces and social relations of production placed on an equivalent plane. This escape from a commitment to fundamental causation, unfortunately, presses the analysis back onto the terrain of circular causation, general equilibrium, and theoretical intedeminateness.
4. Rodney (1972, especially p. 17). As my colleague, Michael Pyne, repeatedly asks of "humanists": "How do you make people *more* 'human' than they already are?"
5. On the persistence of feudal relations in eastern and southern Europe, see Perry Anderson (1974a). Adam Smith (1937, 238-9) was aware of "backwardness" of Poland, Spain, and Portugal relative to other parts of Europe in the late 18th century – attributing Poland's backwardness to the persistence of feudalism and the failure of Spain and Portugal to achieve capitalism with the decline of feudalism. Smith (p. 239) wrote, 'Though the feudal system has been abolished in Spain and Portugal, it has not been succeeded by a much better."
6. See Oliver Cox (1970, pp. 334-5) and Winthrop Jordan (1968). Western images of blacks in art were quite positive until the advent of the African slave trade (Olmsted, 1980, p. 2069).
7. See Perry Anderson (1974b) and Barry Hindess and Paul Q. Hirst (1975, pp. 109-77). The latter work precedes Hindess and Hirst's (1977) remarkable hasty retreat from Marxism with their own self-criticism.
8. Nevertheless, such attempts have been made especially in the case of the plantation South in North American, e.g. Eugene Genovese (1974).
9. Rodney (1972, pp. 90-1). Also see the fascinating description of Queen Nzinga's resistance in an otherwise mediocre work by Chancellor Williams (1968), pp. 273-89).
10. The position taken here is largely consistent with the discussion in Chapter 5 of Geoffrey Kay's (1975, pp. 96-112). See especially his comments on merchant capital on p. 97 of his book: "Rising out of the pores of feudal society, [merchant capital] broke down the coherence of the old economic order subjecting production to the rationality of the market and acted as the medium consummating the process that it set in motion. It could never overcome its specific nature of merchant capital and realise its general nature as capital; it could never break out of the sphere of circulation and impose the law of value directly on the sphere of production. It corroded the feudal order but in the last analysis was always dependent upon it. It was revolutionary and conservative at the same time. It opened the way for industrial capitalism but also blocked its progress. In eighteenth-century Britain it frustrated the rising class of industrial capitalists by

denying them free access to markets and forcing them to operate within its own monopolistic market structures; it prevented free competition between the new and the old orders. It created the pre-conditions for a thorough-going revolution in the means of production, but its fractional interests, its desire to protect narrow monopolistic privileges, blocked their realisation. As a result the first struggle of industrial capitalism was against its own progenitor: the industrial revolution was a historic defeat for merchant capital. Its monopolistic privileges were attached and destroyed by the new order whose call to battle was *laisser-faire*, free trade and competition.''

References

Althusser, L. (1979), ''Contradiction and Overdetermination,'' in *For Marx*, London: Verso Editions.

Althusser, L. and Balibar, E. (1979) *Reading Capital*. London: Verso Editions.

Anderson, P. (1947a), *Passages From Antiquity to Feudalism*. London: New Left Books.

Anderson, P. (1947b) *Lineages of the Absolutist State*. London: New Left Books.

Boserup, E. (1965), *The Conditions of Agricultural Growth: The Economics of Agrarian Change Under Population Pressure*. Chicago: Aldine.

Brenner, R. (1977), ''The Origins of Capitalist development: A Critique of Neo-Smithian Marxism,'' *New Left Review*. #104.

Cohen, G. A. (1978), *Karl Marx's Theory of History: A Defense*. Princeton: Princeton University Press.

Coleman, D. C., (1956), ''Labour in the English Economy of the Seventeenth Century,'' *Economic History Review*, Vol. 8, pp. 280-95.

Cox, O. (1970) *Caste, Class and Race*. London: Modern Reader.

Crafts, N. (1977), ''Industrial Revolution in England and France: Some Thoughts on the Question, 'Why Was England First?''' *Economic History Review*, Vol. 30, pp. 429-42.

Darity, W. A. Jr. (1981), ''A General Equilibrium Model fo the Atlantic Slave Trade: A Least-Likely Test for the Caribbean School,'' in Paul Uselding (ed.) *Research in Economic History*, Vol.7

David, P. (1975), *Technical Choice, Innovation and Economic Growth: Essays on American and British Experience in the Nineteenth Century*. Cambridge: Cambridge University Press.

Dupre, G. and Ray, P. (1973), ''Reflections on the Pertinence of A Theory of the History of Exchange,'' *Economy and Society*, Vol 2, pp. 131-63.

Eden, F. M. (1929), *The State of the Poor: A History of the Labouring Classes in England with Parochial Reports*. New York: E. P. Dutton & Company.

Genovese, E. (1974), *Roll Jordan Roll: The World the Slaves Made*. New York: Pantheon Books.

George, C. H. (1980), ''The Origins of Capitalism: A Marxist Epitome and A Critique of Immanuel Wallerstein's Modern World-systems,'' *Marxist Perspectives*, Vol. 3, pp. 70-100.

Heckscher, E. (1935), *Mercantilism Volumes 1 and 2*. London: George Allen & Unwin.

Hindess, B. and Hirst, P. (1975) *Precapitalist Modes of Production* London: Routledge and Kegan Paul.

Hindess, B. and Hirst, P. (1977) *Mode of Production and Social Formation: An Auto-Critique of Pre-Capitalist Modes of Production*. London: The Macmillan Press.

Hopkins, A. G. (1973), *An Economic History of West Africa*. New York: Columbia University Press.

Hunt, E. K. (1979), *History of Economic Thought: A Critical Perspective*. Belmont: Wadsworth Publishing Company.

James, C.L.R. (1963) *The Black Jacobins: Toussaint L'Ouverture and the San Domingo Revolution*. New York: Random House.

Jordan, W. (1968), *White Over Black: American Attitudes Toward the Negro, 1550-1812* Baltimore: Penguin Books.

Kay,. G (1975) *Development and Underdevelopment: A Marxist Analysis*. New York: St Martin's Press.

Kellenbenz, H. (1974) ''Technology in the Age of the Scientific Revolution, 1500-1700,''in Carlo M. Cipolla (ed.) *The Fontana Economic History of Europe: The Sixteenth Centuries*. Glasgow, Colins.

Law, R. (1978), ''Slaves, Trade and Taxes in Precolonial Africa,'' in George Dalton (ed.) *Research in Economic Anthropology*, Vol. 1.

Marx, K. (1977) , *Capital: A Critique of Political Economy Volume One* New York: Vintage Books.

Marx, K. (1967) , *Capital: A Critique of Political Economy Volume Three* New York: International Publishers

Mazique, J. R. (1959), ''The Role of the Church in the Establishment of Slavery and Segregation in the United States.'' Unpublished manuscript. Wesley Theological Seminary.

Myrday, G. (1974) ''What is Development?'' *Journal of Economic Issues*, Vol 8, pp. 729-36.

Olmsted, N. (1980), '' Images of Blacks in Western Art,'' *West Africa*, October 20. p. 2069.

Patterson, O. (1979), ''On Slavery and Slave Formations,'' *New Left Review* #117.

Perez Sainz, J. P. (1977), ''Basic Remarks on Peripheral Accumulation,'' Working Paper #65. The Hague: Institute of Social Studies.

Rodney, W. (1972) *How Europe Underdeveloped Africa*. London Bogle L'Overture.

Sella, D. (1974), ''European Industries, 1500-1700,'' in Carlo M. Cipolla (ed.) *The Fontana Economic History of Eurpoe the Sixteenth and Seventeenth Centuries*. Glasgow: Collins.

Shuler, M. (1980), ''*Alas, Alas, Kongo*'': A Social History of Identured African Immigration into Jamaica, 1841-1865. Baltimore: The Johns Hopkins Press.

Smith, A. (1937), *The Wealth of Nations*, New York: Modern Library.

Speagler,J. (1960), ''Mercantilist and Physiocratic Growth Theory.'' in B.F. Hoselitz (ed.) *Theories of Economic Growth*. Glencoe: Free Press

Temin, P. (1971), ''General Equilibrium Models in Economic History,'' *Journal of Economic History*, Vol. 31 pp.58-75.

Thomas, B. (1980).''Towards an Energy Interpretation of the Industrial Revolution,'' *Atlantic Economic Journal*, Vol 8, pp.1-13.

Wallerstein, 1. (1979), *The Capitalist World Economy*. Cambridge: Cambridge University Press.

Weintraub, E.R. (1979), *Microfoundations: The Compatibility of Microeconomics and Macroeconomics*. Cambridge: Cambridge Univeristy Press.

Williams, C. (1968) *The Destruction of Black Civilization: Great Issues of a Race From 4500 B.C. to 2000 A.D.* Chicago World Press.

Williams, E. (1966) *Capitalism and Slavery*. New York: Capricorn Books.

SECTION EIGHT

Slavery and Capitalist Globalization: The Second Phase

If the first phase of slavery and capitalist globalization was initiated by Spanish colonialism in the Greater Antilles during the sixteenth century and revolutionized by the English, Dutch and French in the Lesser Antilles in the following century, it was the resurgence of the Spanish in the nineteenth century, with economies based on sugar and coffee, that redefined the parameters of industrial capitalism and slavery. The first phase found the Dutch, French and English committed to an alliance against Spanish monopoly colonialism which they found restrictive and suppressive of the economic potential of Atlantic capitalism. Indeed, critics and opponents of Spanish colonialism even suggested that it sought to confront the advance of modernity. The Spanish clearly had their problems, and their opponents found their weaknesses and exploited them.

The second phase of capitalist globalization, as Bergad, Fraginals and others show, found the Spanish, still in colonial possession of some of the largest Caribbean territories, coming to terms, though reluctantly, with their inability to defeat the forces of Protestant aggression. The Industrial Revolution in England, particularly, had empowered its colonial interests in ways that threatened the viability of Spanish colonialism. Spain either had to remove barriers to its colonial markets or be swept from the region as an impe-

rial power. The end of the eighteenth century, and the first half of the nineteenth century, saw the penetration of the Spanish-colonized Caribbean by English, French and to some extent, American capital. The traditional process of sugar and slavery gained revolutionary momentum in Cuba after 1763, and the colony emerged as the Atlantic's largest sugar producer by the 1840s.

European capitalists, however, had a greater interest in Cuba other than sugar and slavery. They were looking for markets to dispose of a range of industrial goods and finance capital. The industrial modernization of the sugar industry attracted entrepreneurial interests. Industrial capitalism and slavery proved to be a contradictory relationship, particularly in the area of labour productivity. As Satchell shows, the application of scientific technology to production was seen as a way to resolve this contradiction. In Jamaica, Puerto Rico and Cuba, investments in steam power in the sugar industry, as well as the railroads, had a considerable impact upon the dominant sugar industry. The essays in this section trace the varying contexts of the relationship between industrial capitalism and Caribbean slavery, and explore the concept of contradiction from the perspective of productivity and efficiency in the agricultural sector.

37

Plantations in the Caribbean: Cuba, Puerto Rico and the Dominican Republic in the Late Nineteenth Century

MANUEL MORENO FRAGINALS

Historical phenomena, obviously, have never been static; but there are certain periods in which transformations occur slowly, and others in which the rate of change is such that in a few short years everything seems different. An example of this may be found in the industrial history of the Caribbean.

During the eighteenth century and the first half of the nineteenth century, the patterns of sugar production and commerce changed very little, and what changes occurred were either geographical (shifts in production from one island to another) or determined by the partial adoption of certain technologies. On the other hand, starting about 1860 and within not more than thirty years, the centuries-old structure of the sugar industry was shattered, to be replaced by completely new forms of production and commerce and even by a new form of the final product itself, a sugar produced to different standards and shipped in different packaging. It is no exaggeration to say that as regards sugar in the Caribbean, in the nineties everything was completely different from what existed in the sixties.

It is almost impossible to list the successive developments in the sugar world from the 1860s on, and even more so to establish causal relationships among these developments in order to follow them like a chain reaction. These changes equally affected sugar producers, merchants, and consumers; they modified human and labour relations and altered age-old habits of consumption. This great transformation was at once the cause and the consequence of other economic, social, and political factors and was at the same time connected by innumerable links to other world events such as the crisis of the Spanish colonialism, the emergence of the United States as a world power, the rapid developments in science and technology, the universal increase in population, and the new systems of communications.

Changes in the Sugar Industry

Technical Changes

An overview of the process allows us to point out that, in the first place, from a technical point of view, Caribbean sugar-producing methods changed completely in the last thirty years of the nineteenth century. A series of radical innovations sprung up at every stage of the sugar-making process, causing the old manual machines (run by untrained workers) to be junked and replaced by highly sophisticated machinery that required skilled operators and efficient technical supervision.

The installing of this new machinery required an extremely large economic investment and the scrapping of the existing production lines and even of most of the buildings constructed under the previous system. Consequently, the new enterprise cannot be considered an old mill that had been modernised (as was the case with the introduction of the first steam engines into the sugar mills); rather, the old sugar mill was demolished, and in its place – or elsewhere – new buildings were erected to house new machinery run by new types of workers. The only holdovers of the old sugar mill complex were, in general, certain structures for social use, the communications infrastructure, and the cane fields, which in any case supplied only a small part of the new production centre's needs: obviously, to be profitable, the new industrial plant had to process much greater quantities of cane than the old sugar mill.

This was the case when the new industrial plantation (the central or centralized factory, as it came to be known at the end of the nineteenth century) was set up in the zone previously occupied by one or more *ingenios*, the old sugar mills. One other solution, also quite typical, was for the organizers of the new central to seek out fertile new low-priced lands.

This change is both quantitative and qualitative. From the point of view of quantity, the old central differed from the old *ingenio* both in grinding capacity and a higher rate of extraction of sugar from the cane that it ground. For example, the so-called modern mechanized sugar mills of 1860 ground, on an average, the cane from 30 to 35 *caballerías* of land (roughly 400 to 500 hectares or about 1,000 to 1,250 acres); the central of 1890 could handle the production of 100 to 120 *caballerías* and those that could grind the cane from up to 150 to 200 *caballerías* were not uncommon. But production increased at an even greater rate than milling capacity because the new factories could extract almost twice the amount of sugar from the same amount of cane as the old mill.

This increase in production capacity accelerated the process of consolidation. In 1860 there were 1,318 sugar mills in Cuba producing some 515,000 metric tons of sugar; by 1895 the number had decreased to 250 while production was up to almost 1 million tons. In Puerto Rico, where a similar process began somewhat later, there were 550 mills in 1870 producing about 100,000 tons, the highest figure achieved there in the nineteenth century; by 1910, fifteen centrales were producing 233,000 tons.

This consolidation affected land owning practices from a legal standpoint and brought about the emergence of the sugar latifundia in Cuba and Puerto Rico; socially, the consolidation process undermined the old class of slave-owning planters, who were replaced to a great extent

by a new type of industrial entrepreneur. In Cuba, by 1895 only 17 per cent of the owners of centrales came from the old plantation-owning families.

This industrial revolution in the sugar industry also made it necessary to transform labour relations over the next thirty years, having finally triggered the crisis of the slave system on which the old *ingenio* had been based. But the industrial revolution of the Caribbean was not accompanied by a complementary agricultural revolution. On the contrary, the agricultural side of the sugar industry (planting, cultivation, and harvesting) retained its traditional backwardness, which had originated in slave-owning cultural patterns, though under a new political climate, for by 1873 (in Puerto Rico) and 1881 (in Cuba) slavery had been abolished.

Thus a technological gap arose between the industrial sector and its agricultural base. In contrast to the modernity of the central, the agricultural sector retained its obsolete ways: within a few years the law of diminishing returns (which applies where, as in this case, no efforts were made to improve crop yields by modern methods of cultivation) made its appearance, marked by the trend toward smaller cane yields.

The first response to this situation, aggravated by other social and legal factors, was to create an administrative separation between the manufacture of sugar (the industrial sector) and the supply of raw material, cane (the agricultural sector). The relationship between these two sectors was to be a permanent source of conflict from the end of the nineteenth century. The old Creole sugar oligarchy, sugarocracy of Cuba and Puerto Rico, was for the most part forced out of the manufacturing side of the industry, but in many cases stayed on as owners of cane plantations.

As a result of the industrialization process, the productivity of the industrial worker in the central rose steeply; but the productivity of the agricultural worker, especially that of the cane cutter, remained the same, for, as mentioned, the methods of cultivation and harvesting had not evolved. In order to take advantage of the enormous capacities of the new industrial installations, the *zafras*, or cane harvests, became bigger and bigger but were carried on in shorter periods, generally starting in January and ending in April.

This, in turn, created two problems of far-reaching magnitude: one with labour, the other with the amortization and the optimal utilization of the expensive industrial equipment. With respect to labour, the amount of cane required by the modern industry made it necessary to employ hundreds of thousands of agricultural workers (cane cutters) simultaneously in Cuba, Puerto Rico, and Santo Domingo for a period of three or four months of the year. Thus there arose, in all its tragic dimensions, the problem of seasonal employment during four months of the year, which for the majority of the labourers meant seasonal unemployment for eight months of the year. This situation had not occurred previously because with unskilled slave labour (which in any case had to be supported all year round), rudimentary manufacturing equipment, small daily millings, and long harvest seasons, there was always work for all hands. But the modern plantation required, for its optimal running, the existence of an army of unemployed workers, ideally located off the *ingenio* grounds but subjected to economic pressure that forced them to sell their services cheaply and with a minimum of social benefits, as cane cutters. These workers made up a migratory mass, and their migration could be either internal (from one part of the country to another) or external (from one country to another). A mixture of both kinds became the normal pattern.

The other problem created by the installation of modern industrial equipment was the need to find additional sources of income, not necessarily connected with the sugar industry, that would help to amortize the enormous economic investment. Certain double-purpose equipment (railways, power plants, foundries, etc.), as well as some specific services, became "independent" enterprises, with autonomous economic existence. Thus in typical centrales the cane-hauling railway also offered passenger services; the power plant provided electricity for the centrales' facilities as well as for the nearby settlements that would pay for it; the foundry made items ranging from park benches to manhole covers for the municipality – and all at high prices because the central enjoyed a monopoly of these services in its region, besides decisive economic and political influence. The typical Cuban central of the nineties controlled the general store where labourers bought, the hotels, houses, and barracks, either permanent or temporary, the barbershop, the butcher, the drug-store, and sometimes even the gaming house and the brothel.

Partly for its own financial benefit and partly for increased control on all the surrounding region, the centrales issued their own coinage, in the form of tokens, as legal tender. By this system of private coinage, Cuba, Puerto Rico, and the Dominican Republic reproduced, under conditions of colonialism and underdevelopment, one of the most typical aspects of the English Industrial Revolution. There were two ways in which the sugar token was employed. One was for the central to pay its workers in tokens. These tokens were legal tender in all the shops and facilities around the mill and could be redeemed there, though at a discount (often this was the result of a "secret" agreement between the management of the mill and the owner or manager of the store), which was the equivalent of a wage reduction. The other system was for the central to pay wages monthly in official currency; but since workers had to pay for their daily needs from their first day on the job, the storeowner would advance them small loans in tokens that could be spent only in his store or in the establishment of other members of the group. The storeowner would notify the management of the central of the advances made to each worker, and the totals would be automatically docked from his wages at the end of the month. In cases of illness or layoff, the mill would immediately notify the shopowners to withhold credit. Payrolls for Cuban and Puerto Rican mills show that at the end of the month many workers received only 10 per cent of their wages in cash, the balance having been advanced.

In 1892, the Santa Lucía sugar mill in Gibara, Cuba, ran as subsidiaries five general stores, seven grocery stores, one shoe shop, one distillery, three barbershops, one drugstore, nine bars, one school, one confectioner's, two eating houses, three blacksmiths, three bakers, three clothing stores, two tailor shops, and one leather goods or saddlery. All of these accepted payments in the nickel tokens issued by the central. And what made this case even more unusual was that the official paper currency issued by the Bank of Spain was not accepted by these establishments; it had to be exchanged for Santa Lucía company tokens – at more than 10 per cent off face value.

Within this group of transformations, there was one further and extremely important change that has been little noticed: the end product, the sugar produced by the new-style industry, was as different from the previous product as the central was different from the old slave-run *ingenio*. Indeed, it is enough to glance at any market report of the 1860s, in any market of colonial products to see that they do not give the prices of **sugar** (in the singular) but for **sugars** (in the plural). The Colleges of Brokers of Havana and Puerto Rico (up to the sixties, the Havana market played a key role in fixing world sugar prices) daily quoted prices for fourteen different types of sugar. And the Dutch Standard (Tipo Holandes in Spanish-speaking countries), which was accepted worldwide as the most suitable set of standards for trading in sugar, listed twenty-one different grades, based on colour, where grade 1 was practically muscovado and 21 was powdered white sugar.

This plethora of kinds of sugar was the logical consequence of sugars being manufactured with primitive equipment, set up in different ways in hundreds of small factories throughout the Caribbean: mills in which the quality of sugar depended on natural factors (the degree of ripeness of the cane), on the purity of the cane juice obtained by manual operations, on the intensity of the fire that heated the boilers (a fire fed by slaves who might throw more wood or less wood on), and, in the final event, on the skill of a maestro (generally illiterate) who was guided only by his senses (smell, taste, touch, hearing), by his long experience, and by orally transmitted tradition.

On the other hand, the industrial processes of the sugar mills of the nineties were standard, supervised by technically trained professionals, who were aided by internationally recognized analytical methods carried out on modern laboratory equipment. Thanks to these controls, by the end of the century all the Caribbean mills were producing centrifugal sugar Pol 95 degrees. In the first few years of this century a sugar purity of Pol 95 degrees became the standard.

The different types of sugar produced in the pre-industrial stage required at least three types of packing: the box, the hogshead, and the bag. This last was little-used in the sixties (only 4 per cent of total New York market sales), but by 1890 the situation had changed completely, with more than 95 per cent of U.S. sugar imports in bags. By the beginning of the twentieth century the box and the *bocoy* (the hogshead) were virtually museum pieces.

One type of sugar, one type of packing: these factors influenced the transformation of the sugar trade. The Pol 95 degrees sugar of the new industrial period, as we have seen, was a standardized product, whose source (cane or beet) or region of origin (Cuba, Puerto Rico, Java, Australia, Mauritius, Brazil, or whatever place in the sugar-producing world) was impossible to determine. It was also a long-lasting product, that packed in bags could be stacked and stored cheaply. In contrast, the muscovadoes of the sixties differed widely in quality and spoiled easily; the hogsheads in which they were shipped could be stacked only three high without those on the bottom bursting. There were other essential differences; the hogshead was expensive, the bag was cheap; the hogshead was heavy (10 to 14 per cent of the weight of the sugar it contained), the bag was light (less than 1 per cent); the hogshead was hard to handle and raised shipping costs enormously, the bag was easy to handle.

Commercial Changes

All these factors brought about a new commercial practice that had hitherto been little observed: the storing of large surpluses from successive sugar crops. As the new-type centrifugal sugar came more and more to be packed in bags, it became feasible to store it indefinitely. This was the beginning of a new dimension of the problem of initial stocks as a factor affecting sugar prices. Sugar traders had always taken initial stocks into account in fixing their prices, so it was not a new phenomenon: what changed was its magnitude. Before 1860, stocks on hand rarely were as much as 10 per cent of the estimated annual consumption; by the nineties it was common for them to run over 50 per cent of estimated consumption, and the trend was constantly upward. The bigger the stocks sugar importers had in their warehouses, the more pressure they could bring to bear on the producers to lower their prices.

All these new conditions (uniform product, packing in bags, worldwide standards, large on-hand stocks) inevitably led to what can be called the revolution of the sugar trade. This commercial revolution was in part the result of the factors already detailed, but it was also caused by other features of the world's economy in the last third of the century. There were several significant dates in the sixties and the seventies. For example, historians point to 1871 as the year in which the tonnage carried by sailing ships, subject to the whims of the winds, was first surpassed by that shipped in steamers – fast, punctual, and with low freight rates. A steamer could carry five times the cargo that a sailing ship of the same displacement could. In addition, the opening of the Suez Canal had eliminated sailing ships from the regular Europe–Far East runs. In general, freight rates between America and Europe fell, on the average, 25 per cent between 1860 and 1880, while those between Europe and the eastern sugar colonies (India, Java, Mauritius, Philippines) fell 63 per cent. As a result, sugar could finally breach the wall that high freight rates had built around the colonies, thereby limiting their development. At the same time, sugar from Hawaii began to reach California.

So far, these new factors affected those countries that produced cane sugar. But simultaneously the last decades of the century saw a tremendous boom in beet sugar. In 1860 the 352,000 tons of beet sugar produced made up 20 per cent of total world sugar production. By 1890, however, beet sugar production was up to 3.7 million tons, for a total of 59 per cent of the world's production. From being a net importer of sugar, Europe became an exporter. And logically what had resulted was not by any means "fair competition": an immensely intricate protectionist system, complemented by every sort of subsidy and direct aid, brought beet sugar prices below any possible competition and drove Cuban, Puerto Rican, and Dominican sugar off the European markets.

The three Spanish-speaking countries (of which two were still Spanish colonies) had only one customer left for their sugar, the United States. Java increased its sugar production thanks to the protected Dutch market: India and Mauritius benefitted, to a certain degree, from English protectionism, as did Reunion (formerly Bourbon Island) from French policy. Cuba and Puerto Rico (and the Philippines), on the other hand, had never had a protected market: of all the colonial countries of Europe, Spain had the lowest sugar consumption per capita, and, besides, its poor commercial and maritime development did not allow it to become a re-exporter of its colonies' raw materials. Santo Domingo's sugar was also in the hands of its almost exclusive customer, the United States.

By 1890 the commercial sugar world had required the same characteristics it was to keep until 1960. On one hand were the beet sugar-producing countries, highly developed and defended by protectionist barriers. On the other were the colonial countries that produced cane sugar (except Cuba, Puerto Rico and the Philippines) with the protected markets offered by their respective mother countries (Hawaii, at this time a colony, must be included in this group). The difference between total European sugar consumption and the supply of local beet sugar plus the cane sugar from protected colonies made up the prize that Cuba, Puerto Rico, Santo Domingo, and Brazil, principally, competed for. This minimal breach in the protectionist barrier – irregular, unstable, and residual – was to receive, in the twentieth century, the imposing name of *free market*.

As may be seen, then, at the end of the nineteenth century the European market for sugar imports was characterized by its lack of elasticity: only to a very limited degree (the "free" or residual market) can we speak of free competition or of the interplay of supply and demand. The foregoing, obviously, refers to the European market. At that time the other great importer was the United States, which possessed characteristics of a free market in that its local producers, benefitting from protectionism, supplied a minimal per centage of the country's needs. Cuba was its principal supplier: in the 1860s Cuban sugar exports to the United States covered more than 60 per cent of that country's consumption and the share was a rising one. The balance was supplied mainly by Puerto Rico and Brazil and to a lesser degree by Santo Domingo.

This overall picture shows a key fact: the European beet sugar producers were industrial powers (independently of sugar), countries with solid economies, a high degree of culture, and extraordinary political development. They thus met all the conditions necessary for being able to establish effective protectionist policies and, further, to set up a system of subsidies, the Sugar Bounties, that permitted beet sugar to compete all the more advantageously with cane sugar. For example, French and German raws drove sugar from Cuba, Puerto Rico, Santo Domingo, and Brazil off the British domestic market. In the eighties French refined sugar was selling in London at 15 per cent under its cost of production.

Cuba, Puerto Rico, and Santo Domingo were colonial countries (even though Santo Domingo had become an independent country in the second half of the century, from an economic point of view it must be considered a colony), poor, tied to a single major crop and a single major export to a single major market, and completely lacked the means of economic self-defence. Nor did they have the remotest chance of forming a producers' pool to safeguard the prices of their raw materials. It was not until far into the twentieth century that the developing sugar-producing countries were able to bring about the holding of the first international sugar conference, which would set forth their points of view.

Since the cane sugar-producing countries were virtually defenceless, the sugar trade was rapidly dominated by the great international trade interests that drove out even the local traders: these became simple intermediaries of the great international firms. There was a corresponding shift in the location of the price-setting markets: in 1884 the FOB Hamburg price played a more decisive part in commercial decisions than the FOB Havana quotations. Another important development, moreover, marked the coming of a new age to the sugar trade.

Until the sixties sugar prices were fixed in the market. But until that time the concept of the *market* was a strictly physical one: it referred to the geographical, urban region where warehouses were located and where the traders carried out their operations. In London it was Mincing Lane; in New York, lower Wall Street; in Le Havre, the great square where the Exchange Building stands today; in Havana, the dock area near the College of Brokers, where the principal trading firms – Drake and Brothers, Sama and Company, Ajuria and Brothers, and others – were located. What was meant by market prices were the highs and lows of the day's most important sales, that is, the maximum and minimum spot prices paid for sugar for immediate (fast or prompt) delivery. Payment for purchases was generally made on delivery (although it was also customary to ship sugar on consignment to European or U.S. markets to be sold through agents there, again for immediate delivery).

In this world of commerce, physical and tangible, the parameters to be fixed were equally objective and concrete, requiring the trader's personal attention in the solution of specific problems rather than the theoretical analysis of market conditions and trends. The trader's calculations were done with elementary arithmetic – thus the figure of the rich but illiterate sugar merchant. Just as the old slave-operated sugar factories were swept away by the modern industry, this type of trading (and consequently this type of trader) would be replaced by new firms, using new methods, in the last thirty years of the nineteenth century. There was a simple physical reality: the old trading organizations could no longer cope with the multiple factors that went into the making of a sugar sales agreement, or dealing with futures, on the exchanges of New York, Paris, London, or Hamburg.

In brief, then, the modern sugar industry of the late nineteenth century – an intricate economic complex with an enormous volume of production that had to meet international standards of quality – came into being in a world that since the sixties was being constantly shaken by new developments: the rise of monopolistic world capitalism, the ever-increasing speed of transport, and the radical techniques of handling information.

The application of mathematics to business (especially sampling surveys, the concept of indexes, the improvement of economic statistics); modern data processing (the decimal classification system, other coding and retrieval systems, punched cards); new methods of transmitting information (the telegraph, telegraphic codes, the telephone, the Atlantic cable, the stock ticker); the concept of marketing; new methods for evaluating the efficacy of management and for manipulating public opinion; the use of sociological, and anthropological studies to help the incipient international trusts achieve economic domination – all of this can be found in the large-scale sugar speculation of the last years of the nineteenth century. In that sense, the sugar trade led the field in international trade.

For example, the German firm of F.O. Licht, founded in 1861, was the first firm of sugar brokers to use successfully, and on a large scale, sampling to predict world sugar production. Licht's figures, published in the famous "Monthly Report of Sugar" from 1868 on, were a fundamental tool of the big sugar speculators. C. Czarnikow Ltd., of London, did similar work to Licht but concentrated on the Caribbean. In 1897 this firm opened in New York a branch office that was to play a decisive role in the sugar trade of Cuba, Puerto Rico, and Santo Domingo: merging with the New York-based Cuban broker Manuel Rionda in 1909 as the Czarnikow-Rionda Company, within a few years it had so dominated the market that it could act as sole broker for the Cuban crops of the war years (1914–18) and for some 80 per cent of both Puerto Rican and Dominican crops of the same period.

These and similar firms functioned simultaneously as market researchers, trade publishers, and brokers and acted as agents for certain powerful sugar interests, although this last was done more or less discretely: for example, Willet and Hallem (later Willet and Gray Inc.) acted for the American Sugar Refining Company, at one time one of the world's largest trusts.

In the last thirty years of the nineteenth century, the world sugar market fell into the hands of a small group of refiners and bankers, who used the most up-to-date big business methods to control the producers of raw sugar and eliminate the old traders. In this struggle the key strategy was to create a price-fixing mechanism that while appearing to observe the rules of supply and demand, would allow them to take over the market. The commodity exchanges played a fundamental role, opening a new era in the trade of colonial products. For the West Indies, especially Cuba, Puerto Rico, and Santo Domingo, the London Sugar Exchange and the New York Produce Exchange (which later became the famous New York Coffee and Sugar Exchange) were especially significant.

These exchanges, in theory at least, were of ancient origin: some scholars claimed that they were the direct descendants of the medieval bourses. But whatever the kinship, the similarity was only skin-deep. Commodity exchanges, before this commercial revolution, had been organizations made up jointly of buyers and sellers, a kind of organized market where the forces of supply and demand would meet to carry out commercial transaction. But the new exchanges were marked by an essential difference: here the products were not sold directly; the transactions carried out were exclusively speculative. Briefly stated, the commodity operations consisted of signing sales contracts in which one party undertook to supply a certain amount of sugar on a certain date: that is, a sale was made at the prices of the day for future delivery. When the date of delivery arrived, no sugar was delivered. The price of the sugar involved was calculated on the basis of the prices in effect on the delivery date, and the difference between the two prices was paid by one party to the other, in cash, less a commission paid to the exchange for its services. As there were many such operations daily, the exchange provided the means for setting the transaction: that is, it acted as a clearing-house. Only in less than 1 per cent of the deals did any sugar actually change hands. Thus the exchange did not replace the real market in which the actual sugar was bought and sold: it simply dominated it, imposing prices and terms. It is clear why in the nineties London's authoritative *Economist* described the London Sugar Exchange as "Monte Carlo in Mincing Lane."

As stated, however, the exchanges were not only places where one could gamble in commodity prices but also the brain children of economically dominant groups, whose purpose was to consolidate and broaden their control of the market. Appearing before a U.S. Senate hearing that was investigating a great sugar antitrust scandal, Theodore Havemeyer, president of the American Sugar Refining Company, stated that he used the stock exchange to bribe government officials and the commodities exchange to impose the prices that he wanted on the raw sugars of Cuba, Santo Domingo, and Puerto Rico.

As may be expected, in the last decade of the nineteenth century there was little regulation of the activities of the commodity exchanges. This allowed the carrying out, daily, of operations that could not even be attempted on today's exchanges. It must be remembered that data gathering and handling were new phenomena at the time and that there were no regulations affecting relations between different exchanges; it was possible to take advantage of the five-hour time difference between England and the East Coast to learn London's closing prices before the New York Exchange opened (thanks to the international telegraph, which was also poorly regulated and, furthermore, controlled by a group of speculators) and use this information advantageously. In general, in the United States (practically the only market for Cuban, Puerto Rican, and Dominican sugar at the time) sales of sugar futures lacked any regulatory legislation until the incredible speculating of 1920–21 led to the controversial Futures Trading Act of August 24, 1921, which was declared unconstitutional shortly afterward, though passed again, with minor changes, on September 21, 1922.

An interesting commentary on the changes at this time may be found in the following, first published in 1888: "In the good old days merchandise seldom arrived to a loss, except in time of severe panic: dealers, when they speculated at all, had visible evidence of the goods in warehouses and docks, and prudence, foresight and intelligence reaped their reward. The introduction of steamships changed all this, and the telegraph completed the revolution . . ."[1]

Cuba and Puerto Rico: Growth of Production

Throughout the nineteenth century Cuba's sugar production increased steadily, year by year, until 1875, when the slave plantations, which for some time had been showing clear signs of crisis, started on the path to their definite disintegration. Plotted on a graph, the fortunes of the sugar industry would show marked fluctuations, especially for the 1876–89 period, reflecting the transition from the old *ingenio* to the modern *central*. By the nineties, however, Cuba had regained its sceptre as the world's largest sugar producer, with five successive crops of over or just under a million tons, only to fall into the great slump brought about by the War of Independence and the subsequent U.S. occupation of the island.

Puerto Rico, on the contrary, maintained its upward economic trend only until the fifties, when the series of ups and downs started that bore witness to the instability of its slave-based production. In 1873 (before Cuba, notwithstanding the fact that both islands were Spanish colonies) slavery was abolished in Puerto Rico. This occurred during a period marked by large harvests; but abolition in Puerto Rico was not accompanied by a general process of modernization, and production fell sharply in the nineties.

Diverse factors contributed to the dissimilar development of these two colonies of the same mother country and therefore with the same form of government, countries with similar climate and in the same geographical region. In the first place, historically they had different pasts. From the sixteenth to the eighteenth centuries and into the first two decades of the nineteenth, Cuba was a centre of defence of the Spanish Empire, a main maritime base (for both the navy and the merchant fleets), and an important productive region. Due to these factors, there developed on the island an oligarchy that came to wield almost unique political power and from the start accumulated large sums of capital derived from the service sector (trade, shipbuilding for the Spanish state, building of forts, etc.). This capital was subsequently invested in agro-industrial resources: tobacco, coffee, and sugar. The Cubans took advantage of the favourable conditions of foreign trade, which had been upset by the 1791 revolution in Haiti (until then the largest sugar producer in the world), emerging in the first third of the nineteenth century as the possessor of an important sugar complex that by 1829 was outproducing all the British West Indies together.

During the long process of formation of the Cuban oligarchy, its accumulated wealth and political experience also led to a cultural development of the highest order. In addition, it was able to impose, uniquely, its own terms on the home government: for example, the right to trade freely and directly with any foreign port and in ships of any nationality was a privilege won by the native oligarchy in 1792 (though officially recognized only from 1818 on).

Unlike the French or English West Indian colonies, in Cuba the sugar mills were the result of native investments, and with very few exceptions they were never the property of absentee owners. These owners, on the contrary, lived in Cuba and as a general rule at the beginning of the sugar harvest would move into their *ingenios* to watch over and manage their interests directly. Like modern entrepreneurs, they kept up to date regarding world technological developments and quite rapidly incorporated into the Cuban sugar complex those items of equipment and technical advances that could improve the capacity or the profitability of the industry.

As early as 1796 these native businessmen carried out the first experiments in adapting the steam engine to the cane mill; in 1837 they inaugurated the world's first railway devoted to hauling sugar and molasses from the mills to the ports (and the first railway of any kind in Latin America); in 1842 they started using vacuum evaporation for obtaining sugar; in 1844 (the same year as in the United States) they put up the first telegraph wires; in 1849 they installed sugar centrifuges. Cuba, a colonial possession, outpaced all the other Latin American countries in technological developments during the nineteenth century. Under the influence of legislative privileges and a dynamic class of entrepreneurs, and helped by extraordinarily favourable natural conditions (highly fertile lands, ideal weather conditions, large forestry resources, etc.), Cuba understandably was the world's largest sugar producer from 1829 to 1883. (Puerto Rico, which did not share these characteristics, was a much smaller producer.)

With the arrival of the sixties, however, both Cuban and Puerto Rican plantations began to show the first symptoms of a crisis. Put briefly, the crisis was a structural one, provoked by the steadily decreasing profitability of slave-based labour and by the difficulties resulting from the adoption of the new technologies.

Thus there came into being a state of permanent instability in which the principal problem faced by the producers—and therefore by officialdom—was to find a viable solution to the transition from slavery to wage-earning labour. The objective of the producers was to obtain from Spain a law of abolition that would include indemnification to allow them to recoup the capital that they had invested in slaves for reinvesting in modern equipment. They also hoped for related legislation that would provide a cheap and constant supply of free labourers (by *free* meaning semi-enslaved, obliged to work 12 hours a day for starvation wages and then laid off at the end of the harvest). In Cuban in 1863 over 95 per cent of all sugar properties were mortgaged. Economic studies of the period showed that the 300 million pesos invested in the sugar industry bore 200 million pesos in mortgages. That is to say, two-thirds of the sugar industry was in the hands of merchants who in Cuba and Puerto Rico carried out the functions of bankers.

In the sixties this critical situation on the two islands abruptly entered a stage wherein a series of external events acted favourably, not by solving the inherent structural difficulties (for the slave plantation had exhausted all possibilities of internal reform) but by extending the system's lease on life. The U.S. Civil War and the Franco-Prussian War for years created their classical effect of upsetting market conditions, bringing about increased demand and very high prices. In Cuba, the Ten Years' War (1868–78), the first gigantic struggle for independence, also heightened the panic in the sugar trade and extended favourable market conditions. There were almost ten years of good harvests and high prices (even though most of these, in Cuba, occurred during the Ten Years' War), which allowed the Cuban sugar producers to pay off a great part of their mortgages, and their Puerto Rican counterparts to begin the mechanization of their sugar mills, which in general lagged behind Cuba in this respect. But this period was an exception to the trend, and once it had passed, the crisis made itself felt stronger than ever.

In Puerto Rico the process of disintegration of the old-style sugar plantations was extremely rapid. In 1870 there were 550 mills with a total production of 96,000 tons; by 1880 there were 325, producing 50,000 tons. Due to the existing backwardness, the crisis in production was matched by a crisis in quality, and many U.S. importers refused to buy the Puerto Rican raw sugars that were rejected by refiners. But there was a more significant reason for the island's crisis: the basic problem was that Puerto Rico lacked the necessary physical and economic infrastructure on which to base its industrialization. Without investment capital or an adequate railway system, without concerted action by the producers, without what might be called the vision of sugar, the few efforts made were individual and for the most part limited to the purchase of machines (which were not always logically installed) and to the building of a few centrales that until the end of the century alternated between good and bad years, and generally with heavy debts. To cite but one example, Central San Vicente, in Vega Baja, founded by Leonardo Igaravidez, Marquis of Cabo Caribe, by 1873 had taken over the larger surrounding plantations to ensure a supply of cane for his mill and was using the services of as many as several hundred cane cutters. But by 1879 his debts were over a million pesos (one peso = one dollar), an incredible amount for the time. In

1880, besides the San Vicente, there were four other centrales: the Luisa, San Francisco, Coloso, and Canovanas. All through the nineteenth century, from the economic point of view, their histories were the same.

Another key point that limited the development of Puerto Rico's sugar industry was the failure to find a successful means of transition from slavery to free labour. It is generally said that slavery was abolished in Puerto Rico in 1873, but this is true only in the legal sense. In fact, the institution of slavery had for a long time been in a state of collapse, and by the seventies the island lacked a labour force that could be subjected to the conditions that the plantation owners considered necessary. Unlike Cuba, in Puerto Rico there was no significant influx of migrant labour: only small numbers of coolies came in from China; efforts to set up a system of migrant workers from Spain (colourfully known at the time as *golondrinos* – swallows) met with no success; and the experiment of importing labourers from the British West Indies ended with a handful of groups that settled on offshore Vieques and on the sugar mills of Ponce, Humacao, Loiza, and Carolina.

The Cuban case was different. The great sugar boom took place in regions that had easy access to ports that by mid-century were already served by an excellent rail network. In general, this railway system, originally designed to carry hogsheads and boxes of sugar, turned out to be exceptionally useful for carrying cane from the fields to the mills. As far as the labour force was concerned, 1847 saw the beginning of an impressive immigration of coolies that probably reached as high as 150,000 by the end of the century. Another source of labour for Cuba's sugar mills had an unusual origin. The Spanish regular army being needed at home for the Carlist Wars, garrisons in Cuba were manned chiefly by *quintos*, or conscripts from Spain. A series of Cuban regulations – which were considered thoroughly illegal in Spain – gave the draftee the choice of serving out his full term as a soldier or of signing on as a hand in a sugar mill. The Ten Years' War being fought in Cuba at the time, many *quintos* not unnaturally became cane cutters. And in the eighties the owners of the new centrales were able to set up an efficient flow of migrant workers, who would arrive in Cuba at the beginning of January and leave at the end of April, from the Canary Islands and from the Spanish provinces of Galicia and Asturias, where there were extremely low standards of living, overpopulation, and high rates of unemployment.

Large sums of capital being available, many Spanish merchants and some families belonging to the old *criollo* (Cuban-born) oligarchy invested in centrales, especially from the eighties. From an economic point of view, Cuba's bloody Ten Years' War for independence turned out to be profitable for the modernized sugar industry. The war, which was fought mainly at the eastern end of the island, destroyed over a hundred old sugar mills, all of which were technologically backward and unproductive. The western part of the country where the new "giant" mills were located, and which produced 80 per cent of Cuban sugar, did not suffer the ravages of the war.

Moreover, the *Banco Colonial* and the *Banco Español de la Isla de Cuba*, both controlled by the big Spanish merchants and some members of the Cuban oligarchy, had been charged with the financing of the war by the Spanish government, and this turned out to be an enormously profitable deal. Cuban-Spanish shipping and railway companies handled the transportation of military supplies. With a military colonial administration and under the psychological state-of-war pressures, legitimate business and shady deals of all types were made, and illicit enrichment became the norm. It is evident that at the end of the war these groups would have the necessary liquid capital to invest in the great "new" (i.e. radically modernized) sugar industry.

There were still other factors. With a sugar-oriented background and political experience, united by long-time common interests, the Cuban producers were well aware of the needs of the times and began to create a group of institutions to steer the new industry. In this way came into being the *Asociación de Hacendados de la Isla de Cuba* (Association of Mill Owners of the Island of Cuba) in 1879 for the purpose of coordinating the action of the principal brains (and capital) in the sugar world. From its beginnings, the association guided the activities of the producers, promoted projects for bringing in migrant workers, set up agricultural and industrial training schools, sponsored research, set up direct communications with the sugar exchanges in New York and London, published a widely read magazine, and formed a powerful lobby to defend the industry's interests. During this period arose many similar but local associations of *colonos* or cane planters.

Slavery was abolished in Cuba in 1881 (eight years later than in Puerto Rico). The concept of the abolition of slavery may suggest to many the picture of a mass of people, chattels subjected to their masters' every whim who suddenly, at a given point in time, find themselves free and in full possession of civil rights and responsibilities. Had this really been so, the abolition of slavery would have brought the total collapse of the sugar industry, for as late as 1877 (the last year for which reliable statistics on Cuban slavery are available) more than 70 per cent of sugar production was based on slave labour. That this did not occur was due to the simple fact that the Law of Abolition was merely the de jure recognition of a situation characterized by the de facto disintegration of the slave system.

As a matter of fact, as early as the 1860s, and more so in the seventies, the term *slavery* covered a wide range of means of exploiting labour. To begin with, there was the "pure" slave, physically forced to work on the sugar mill. Next to him was the hired slave. These slaves were subject to totally different conditions from the first type: physical punishments were banned, and they received part of the money paid for their hire. There was the *jornalero* or wage earner, a variant of the preceding, the slave who personally signed on at a sugar mill for a certain figure and who periodically handed part of his wages to his nominal owner as payment for the status of a semi-freedman with the right to sell his services freely. There was the salaried slave (a very common feature of the time), whose wages were generally 50 to 70 per cent of those of a freedman. Many slaves of all types enjoyed usufruct of small plots of land where they grew produce and raised animals, selling part to the *ingenio*. With them worked free blacks and whites, Chinese and contract labourers from the Yucatán (virtual slaves themselves), and, at times, convicts whom the state provided to the mills and who were paid a small wage. This anomalous situation in the labour supply acted as a break on capitalistic industrial development: the Law of Abolition was a means to the end of rationalizing the confused labour system efficiently.

Thus, the essence of the changes brought about in Cuban sugar production from the eighties were much more economic and social than technical. This does not mean that there were no significant improvements in equipment and processes – there were. But the complete renovation of the process of production was not a mere question of installing modern industrial equipment (which had begun in numerous Cuban sugar mills since the middle of the century); it also implied a renovation on the social, institutional level that could simply not be carried out by slaveowners. The more reactionary among these retained and exploited their slaves as long as they could: clinging to a past that was doomed to disappear, they held on to their slaves because they considered them part of their investment. Perhaps, for them, there was no alternative.

One other key point refers to the process of consolidation in Cuba. Industrialization, as we have seen, led to the early disappearance of the less efficient units. In Matanzas, Cuba's most important sugar region, there were 517 mills in 1877, producing some 350,000 tons; in 1895 the number of mills was down to 99, but production was almost doubled, at 600,000 tons.

During these last years of the nineteenth century, however, the concentration of production in fewer but larger mills did not find a counterpart in land ownership. Possibly the liens and other obligations of land ownership (especially the unredeemable and indivisible type of *censo* or living pledge) conspired against all efforts to bring about a consolidation of lands that would complement industrial concentration. This led to a broad discrepancy between agriculture and industry and in part explains the backwardness of cane planting in a period of industrial and technological advance.

From the point of view of direct ownership, either of land or of mills, there are a few signs of the presence of U.S. capital in the Cuban sugar industry of the nineteenth century. There were, of course, individual American millowners, just as there were French, Canadians, and Germans. The figures of the U.S. forces, which occupied the island in 1898, show that at the time 93.5 per cent of the sugar mills belonged to Cuban and Spanish capital, and only the remaining 6.5 per cent belonged to foreigners, including U.S. citizens. Moreover, many of the mills then listed as American really belonged to native Cubans and

Spaniards who had only recently acquired U.S. citizenship.

The preceding, in the main, has referred to the behaviour of those internal factors that shaped the development of the Cuban sugar industry during the last decades of the nineteenth century. But external factors also played a decisive role in the process. Thus, the statement about the lack of a U.S. presence in the sugar period refers exclusively to an internal situation. But from the point of view of international trade, the United States had long exercised hegemony. By the 1870s the Golden Age of Competition had disappeared from that country, at least where sugar was concerned: there existed an oligopolistic structure that, though legally established in 1887, had in fact come into being a decade before. The Sugar Act of 1871 was the first legislative tool of neocolonial domination forged in the United States, under pressure of the East Coast refiners, for the specific purpose of economically dominating Cuba, Puerto Rico and Santo Domingo. By the eighties all three islands were selling virtually all their sugar to the United States, dealing with one sole firm in the market; their sugar was shipped in U.S. vessels; the sugar prices were fixed by the New York Produce Exchange; island planters and millowners got their market prices and production estimates from Willet and Gray, in news items reported by Associated Press and carried by Western Union. Without direct investment in lands or mills, the economic annexation of the three islands was underway: physical annexation by forcible means would come a few years later.

Cuban sugar development suffered an abrupt interruption. On February 24, 1895, in the middle of the harvest season, a new war of independence broke out, one that unlike the Ten Years' War was fought over the entire island. The magnitude of the war may be gathered from a few figures: Spain moved 400,000 soldiers, the largest army ever to cross the Atlantic until the days of World War II. This signified one Spanish soldier for each three inhabitants of the island. During the War of Independence, (1895–98) thousands of hectares of cane fields were repeatedly set afire (cane is an easy crop to burn). An indeterminate number of sugar mills were also destroyed. Unfortunately, quantitative documentation is lacking that would allow an exact appreciation of war damages inflicted on the sugar industry. From the point of

view of production, the last five years of the century are presented in table 37.1. Using these figures as their basis, traditional Cuban historiography, influenced by the interests of the sugar magnates, created the myth of the total destruction of the sugar industry during the war. As no censuses of sugar plantations were taken during the period, the theory of total ruin still prevails among modern historians.

Table 37.1 Cuban Sugar Production, 1895–99
(unit: metric tons)

1895	983,265
1896	286,229
1897	271,505
1898	259,331
1899[a]	322,337

Source: Manuel Moreno Fraginals, *El ingenio* (Havana: Editorial de Ciencias Sociales, 1978), 3:38.

[a]First year of peace

But painstaking qualitative studies, which analyzed thousands of dispersed sources, would seem to prove that although an enormous drop in production was evident in cane production (the result of repeated burnings), the industrial sector, on the contrary, received much less damage. Of the fifty largest centrales to grind in 1895, only seven were destroyed during the war, four received some damage, and thirty-nine remained standing, ready to start a new grinding season. It is probable that the effective overall loss suffered by the industry was 20 to 25 per cent of installed producing capacity, as a maximum. To start up the industry anew required an extensive programme of cane planting at a time when the traditional farm labourers had been widely dispersed (the war had completely changed the pattern of settlements in many areas). This explains the drop in production in the war and immediate post-war years and why, within three years after the war, sugar production reached almost a million tons, which was about the total installed capacity in 1895.

Notes

This paper draws on the work that will be published in more detail and with full documentation elsewhere. The translation was done by Arturo Ross.

1.   "The London Produce Clearing House," *Financial News* (London), as reprinted in *The Sugar Cane* (Manchester), July 2, 1888, pp. 350ff.

38

The Sweet and the Bitter: Cuban and Puerto Rican Responses to the Mid-Nineteenth-Century Sugar Challenge

LUIS MARTÍNEZ-FERNÁNDEZ

Despite the enormous potential for regional and comparative approaches to the history of Cuba, Puerto Rico and the Dominican Republic, few students of the Hispanic Caribbean have produced works that transcend the traditional and island-by-island approach. Studies put forth in the 1980s by Laird W. Bergad, Andrés Ramos Mattei, Roberto Marte, and the editors of *Between Slavery and Free Labour*, however, have begun to point in the direction of comparative possibilities and a less fractionalized vew of the region.[1] This article attempts to contribute to the still very modest body of historiography that seeks to integrate more than one of the components of the Hispanic Caribbean. It focuses on one particular aspect of the region's history: the mid-nineteenth-century world market sugar pressures, and how Cuba and Puerto Rico responded to them

The 1840s and 1850s were a period in which international market exigencies put enormous pressures on the economies of Cuba and Puerto Rico, in fact, on those of all sugar-exporting regions. Sugar consumption increased tremendously in countries like Great Britain and the United States as new, lower tariffs for the sweetener were put in place. As Sidney W. Mintz (1985:148) aptly put it: "A rarity in 1650, a luxury in 1750, sugar had been transformed into a virtual necessity by 1850." Increased demand for sugar – an apparently favourable development for sugar producers – was, however, only

half the story. The supply of cane sugar from a variety of regions and beet sugar from Western and Central Europe also increased exponentially during this period with world beet sugar production jumping from 60,857 metric tons in 1845 to 351,602 metric tons in 1860 (Moreno Fraginals 1978, III:36).[2] Sugar prices, thus, fell or at best remained stagnant during the 1840-1856 period, shrinking the profit margins of sugar producers around the world.[3] Under such pressing circumstances, sugar planters in the Caribbean had to adjust to the new exigencies of the world market; planters in Cuba and Puerto Rico responded differently to these pressures, a reflection of divergent levels of capital resources and adaptability.

The Cuban Response

Cuban planters as a whole responded to the new realities of the world market by accepting the sugar challenge: in light of diminishing profit rates they sought to expand sugar production. During this critical time, Cuba's economy continued to steer away from diversification and relative self-sufficiency toward sugar monoculture and dependency. By 1855, sugar and its by-products represented 84 per cent of Cuba's exports, and by 1862 this category represented 58 per cent of the island's entire agricultural production (García de Arboleya 1859:238, Marrero 1984 X:101). Other traditional staples like coffee, tobacco, and cotton suffered serious setbacks as land, labour and capital previously linked to these crops were siphoned off to the insatiable world of sugar. The number of coffee farms in Cuba, for example, fell from 2,067 in 1827 to 1,670 in 1846, and to 782 in 1862, a 62 per cent drop in thirty-five years (Schroeder 1982:239).[4] By the late 1870s, there remained less than 200 coffee estates in the entire island. In contrast, the number of sugar estates grew considerably during the same period from 1,000 in 1827 to 1,422 in 1846, to 1,650 in 1850. During the 1850s, the number of sugar estates actually declined somewhat to 1,365, a reduction, however, that indicated concentration rather than contraction.[5] Not only did the Cuban economy accept foreign dictates to produce more sugar, but also specific kinds of sugar. The core nations with refining sectors to protect, the United Sates and Britain, shut off their markets for Cuban semi-refined sugar and called upon Cuba to produce more, of a lesser quality and for a smaller number of markets.

By the end of the 1850s, Cuba was a full-fledged sugar island. Seventy per cent of the island's agricultural production consisted of sugar, close to 50 per cent of all its slaves worked in sugar plantations, and more than 25 per cent of its cultivated land was destined to sugar cane (Knight 1970:40-41). These transformations were apparent to contemporary observers. "There are no manufactures of any consequence" wrote Richard H. Dana (1859:129), "the mineral exports are not great; and, in fact, sugar is the one staple. All Cuba has but one neck – the worst wish of the tyrant." A year later, Ramón de la Sagra (1963) warned against the island's dependence on a single export crop and coined the phrase "*agricultura de rapiña*" (preying agriculture). The problem of monoculture was aggravated by the fact that sugar went primarily to one market: the United States.

To stay competitive and to meet the quantitative and qualitative international demands, Cuba's planter class embarked on expansion resting on two simultaneous, although seemingly contradictory, strategies: the mechanization of the sugar industry and the expansion of the servile labour force. New machines had always been a symbol of status among Cuban planters. Their mouthpiece of the late eighteenth and early nineteenth centuries, Francisco de

Arango y Parreño, had emphasized the necessity of integrating Europe's latest technology into the island's *ingenios*. Steam-powered engines made their debut in Cuba as early as 1796 and the island's first railroad system was in place by 1837, more than a decade before it would appear in Cuba's *de jure* metropolis.

The mechanization of Cuba's sugar industry in the 1840s and 1850s did not, however, touch upon all aspects of sugar production and transportation. Despite some efforts to introduce steam-powered plows, planting and harvesting remained in their primitive forms as labour-intensive, manual tasks. New technology, however, transformed dramatically most of the manufacturing stages of sugar production. Steam engines to power larger and more sophisticated cane grinders became common in the 1840s and 1850s. Whereas in 1827 only 2.5 per cent of the island's sugar mills were run by steam engines, in 1860 close to 70 per cent of the island's sugar mills used this type of energy. Some estimates put this proportion near 91 per cent by the end of the 1850s.[6] This transition from muscular and hydraulic power to steam increased the grinding capacity and speed of the average *ingenio* enormously.

The next major step in sugar production, the crystallization of the *guarapo* (cane juice), also required improved mechanization in order to keep pace with the greater and faster outputs of the grinding phase. In this area the major technological innovation was the vacuum pan, known in the region as *tacho al vacío* or *tren Derosne*. In 1844, Wenceslao de Villaurrutia introduced one such device in his *ingenio*, replacing the open pans system (*trenes jamaiquinos*) in which boiling cane juice had to be manually transported through a succession of pans of different sizes (Marrero 1984:250). Because of their exorbitant price tags, however, Derosne and similar crystallizing devices were much slower in their penetration of Cuban sugar-making. Only the largest and most financially sound – or the most daring – of the *ingenios* managed to acquire vacuum pans in this period. By 1863, only 4 per cent of Cuba's *ingenios* had them. Four years later, a total of seventy-five *tachos al vacío* were operating at a staggering average cost of $120,000 (Ely 1963:539).[7] The rest of the planters had no option but to multiply the number of open *trenes* in order to keep up with the increased grinding capacity achieved with steam.

The following step, the *purga* or separation of sugar crystals and molasses, was the next phase in the mechanization orgy of the mid-century. Bottlenecks now occurred in this slow and simple procedure. Traditionally, the *purga* was achieved through a long process of filtration (lasting thirty to fifty days), which consisted of pouring the saturated molasses into conical containers with a cloth-covered hole on the bottom. By force of gravity most of the molasses covering the crystals dripped out into special containers, leaving behind sugar crystals of various degrees of purity. This stage was revolutionized by yet another innovation of the industrial age: the centrifuge – a spinning device with a metallic screen which pushed the excess molasses out of its inner drum, leaving dried sugar crystals in the inner chamber. Cuba's pioneer in the use of the centrifuge was Joaquín de Ayestarán in his *ingenio* La Amistad in 1850 (Marrero 1984:194-5). These devices were popularized to such an extent that 116 of them were purchased in 1862 alone (Marte 1988:296).

Students of Cuban agrarian and social history have underscored the importance of yet another aspect of the industry's mechanization: railroads. According to Manuel Moreno Fraginals (1987, 1:272) the establishment of the Güines railroad in 1837 marked "a fundamental milestone" in the rapid expansion of sugar in the 1840s and 1850s. In the same vein, Franklin Knight (1970:38) concludes that railroads were instrumental in freeing sugar production from earlier constraints that limited the extension of single *ingenios*. Knight stresses that the introduction of locomotives reduced transportation expenses and liberated a considerable segment of the plantation labour force, which could now be transferred to the production stages. Indicative of the railroad's importance is the use of 1837 as a periodization watershed by Laird W. Bergad (1990:109-14) in his recent book on Matanzas. Twenty-two years after the Güines locomotive puffed its first clouds of smoke, the Cuban railroad network consisted of 378 completed miles and 184 more miles under construction (García de Arboleya 1859:200-1). By 1865 the railroad network stretched along 754 operating miles.[8]

The mechanization of the Cuban sugar industry was not as simple as choosing models from the catalogues of the West Point Foundry or Derosne and Cail. It required enormous amounts of money which planters often did not have. Since the addition of new machines had to be coordinated with the acreage, the number of slaves, and the rest of the machines in the complex, one addition in any particular phase usually translated into the necessity of further investments in more machines, land, and slaves. To set up a mid-size sugar plantation in the 1850s required an original investment of between $300,000 and $350,000 with yearly injections of $40,000 for upkeep and renovation of the slave force (Ely 1963:446-47; Knight 1970:69). Because of the costs involved only a small segment of the old Cuban planter class managed to reorganize and expand their sugar operations to meet the challenges of the mid-century. Between 1838 and 1851, Francisco Pedroso y Herrera, Nicolás Peñalvar y Cárdenas, Ignacio Peñalvar y Angulo, Gonzalo de Herrera, Nicolás Martínez de Campos, and José Luis Alfonso and his brother José Eusebio Alfonso either set up new mechanized *ingenios* or reorganized the ones they had (García de Arboleya 1859:137-38; Knight 1970:39). Many others could not produce the cash or credit required to buy the expensive machinery and continued to struggle along with what they had for as long as they could. Between 1850 and 1860, 385 *ingenios* ceased operations, a 23 per cent decrease.[9] According to Moreno Fraginals (1987, 1:222), the incapacity to purchase vacuum pans ruined the old planter class. One could also argue that it was precisely the disorderly, yet seemingly unavoidable, purchase of sugar-producing equipment that paved the road to their eventual ruin. Meanwhile, new capital from licit and illicit commercial enterprises moved in to accept the sugar challenge and establish fully mechanized sugar operations. The Aldamas, the Diagos, and Julián Zulueta were salient members of the new planter class composed mostly of first and second-generation immigrants.

Another goal of most planters wishing to mechanize was to reduce the industry's dependence on imported slave labour. The growing number of slaves and their majority status, first revealed by the census of 1841, were a constant source of anxiety among the propertied classes, which feared a St Domingue-style racial war. Moreover, international pressures for the cessation of the slave trade sent clear signals to the Cuban plantocracy that they better start looking for alternative sources of labour. In 1854, Cristóbal Madan estimated that the application of the latest technology could reduce labour demands by seventy-nine men in a medium-sized, 4,000 hogshead *ingenio* (Hacendado 1854:32). He continued to state that it was not possible,

to enumerate the changes fostered by the exclusion of ignorant and barbaric hands, substituting them by a higher intelligence, one manifested in machines and inventions as well as direction and rational structuring of the work process.

Since the mechanization of the sugar industry failed to touch the planting and harvesting of sugar cane, the process did not alleviate labour needs; on the contrary, it increased them. The voracious appetite of the new mills had to be satisfied, thus requiring the expansion of the cultivated area and the addition of new planting and cutting hands to allow the costly new machines to operate at full capacity. Alternative sources to bonded labour, however, were not easily forthcoming. Immigrants from the Peninsula and the Canary Islands tended to avoid plantation labour, and by the 1850s the island's planter class gave up hopes of promoting white colonization after innumerable failures and frustrations during the previous decade. Attempts were also made to reduce the dependence on black slavery by introducing coolie labourers from the Orient. During the second half of the 1850s, some 37,000 Chinese coolies arrived in Cuba as contract labourers.[10] An anonymous member of the Creole elite dramatized the labour crisis when he stated in *La Gaceta de la Habana* that he would welcome not only Asian labourers, but even "orangutans if these were susceptible to domestication."[11] Thus, a paradox arose whereby, on the one hand, the planter class was stepping into the future, embracing the latest technology in sugar manufacturing, while on the other, it remained deeply attached to slavery and other forms of servile labour.

The relationship between mechanization and slave labour has long been a central issue of Cuban historiography. In the late 1940s, Raúl Cepero Bonilla (1948) put forth the thesis that the continuation of slavery was incompatible with the modernization of Cuba's sugar industry. He argued, rather dogmatically, that the enormous cost of slavery hindered the accumulation of capital necessary for successful mechanization and that slaves were not capable of operating the new complex machinery. Other Cuban historians have built upon Cepero Bonilla's interpretation, most notably Moreno Fraginals (1978, I: 27, 49) and Fe Iglesias García (1985:59). Iglesias García recently asserted that slavery was a barrier to industrialization, and estimated that slaves represented between 38 and 40 per cent of a mill's investments. Herbert S. Klein (1973:307-15) challenged the "incompatibility" thesis in the early 1970s. He pointed out that sugar producers in Louisiana had successfully modernized their industry before the abolition of slavery. More recently, Rebecca J. Scott (1985:89) concluded that "during the 1860s and 1870s, when the 'contradictions' within Cuban slavery were in theory becoming most apparent, the major sugar areas were nonetheless holding on to most of their slaves ..." According to Scott, it was precisely in the most advanced and mechanized sugar regions where slavery persisted. More recent studies by Bergad (1989, 1990) emphasize both the viability and profitability of slavery well into the late 1860s. Actually, the Cuban planter class had no alternative but to mechanize and expand if it was to stay in business; this demanded more labour, and since alternative sources failed to provide it, the only reasonable response was to remain attached to slavery. Neither theoretical incompatibilities, which do not affect the course of history, nor slave resistance, which is sometimes romanticized, brought about the institution's eventual demise.

During the 1850s, following four years of sharply reduced slave importation after the conspiracy of La Escalera, slave trading boomed once again (Eltis 1987: 109-38). Increased demand and the slave population's inability to reproduce itself spurred the growth of the slave trade. According to estimates reported by the British judges of the Havana Mixed Commission, a total of 67,422 slaves were imported between 1849 and 1858. On October 6, 1855, British Consul Joseph Crawford reported: "This Island seems to be beset with slavers; they are swarming and what is worse, they appear to succeed in landing their Slaves eluding the vigilance of the Spanish authorities always." The high watermark of slave importation was reached in 1859-1861, when the Mixed Commission registered 58,705 importations and ninety-four enslaving expeditions (Murray 1980:244, 259).

Growing demand for labour during this period and the increasing legal difficulty faced by slave traders translated into higher slave prices. The average price for a *bozal* (African-born) jumped from between $300 and $350 in 1845 to between $1000 and $1,500 in 1860.[12] Another indicator of Cuba's desperate demand for labour were recurrent attempts to siphon slaves from Puerto Rico and Brazil.[13] According to the late Arturo Morales Carrión (1978: 200-3), a student of Puerto Rico's slave trade, the 1850 epidemic in Cuba with a toll of 30,000 slaves, spurred the flow of slaves from Puerto Rico to Cuba. Speculators were accused of buying up entire estates in Puerto Rico just to gain control over their bonded labour force for export to Cuba. This practice continued even after authorities in Puerto Rico established a $75 export tax (per slave) in 1853. Harsher labour conditions in Cuba made the threat of being sold there, one of the most effective disciplinary measures that a planter in Puerto Rico could use against his slaves. In fact, Cuba was to the Puerto Rican slave what Mississippi and Alabama were to slaves in the Middle Atlantic region of the United States: hell.[14] In March 1854, Captain-General Fernando de Norzagaray effectively put a stop to this flow of slaves out of Puerto Rico. In his decree's preamble he alluded to constant complaints by Puerto Rico's planter class. Cuba also imported slaves from Brazil, most probably from that country's depressed sugar regions of the Northeast (Díaz Soler 1967:407-8).

If planters' labour needs were the main stimulus behind slave trading, bribes and traders' profits insured the continuation of the trade. Captain-General Leopoldo O'Donnell was said to have left Cuba in 1848 with a fortune of over half a million dollars derived from slave importation bribes (*La Verdad* 1851:4). His successor, Federico Roncali, true to O'Donnell's precedent, charged a bribe of fifty-one pesos per imported slave (Ely 1963:585). In an 1853 dispatch British Consul Joseph Crawford reported on the extent of official corruption regarding the slave trade.

[T]he Spanish Officers are bribed; the Slave Traders interested commit their offences and repeat them with the most complete impunity; Commissions sent by the Chief Authority of the Island to investigate such offences are baffled, or corrupted, the Masters and Crews are not punished, the Vessels are allowed to escape ...[15]

In one instance the smugglers of 468 *bozales* to the Southern coast of Cuba had to pay bribes amounting to 468 gold ounces to the port's commanding officer, 234 gold ounces to the captain of the port, and 200 gold ounces, each, to the port's collector and tide-surveyor, a total of 1,102 gold ounces. Rumours circulated that Captain-General José de la Concha received one gold ounce ($17) for each slave landing on Cuban shores and that in 1859 alone these fees earned him $680,000.[16] Despite this high rate of 'taxation', slave trading brought enormous profits for traders bringing slaves into Cuba. According to an 1860 report by the British consul, slavers could afford to lose four vessels to every successful expedition and still make a profit (Murray 1980:266). In an 1861 report to Judge Truman Smith of the New York Mixed Commission, Robert W. Schufeldt estimated that a five-hundred-slave expedition could net $236,500. He calculated costs to be $37,500 for the slaves, $7,000 for the ship, $19,000 for wages and $100,000 (the largest single category) for bribes. Later estimates stated that slaves costing only $40 worth of cheap liquor and rusty rifles in Africa could be sold in Cuba for $600 and more. According to Hiram Fuller of the *New York Mirror,* an individual investor could buy $500 worth of stock in a slave trading company and expect to return $10,000 in a year or two.[17]

The mechanization and slave trading orgy of the 1840s and 1850s provided a means for social mobility that eventually led to the subordination of one elite by another. New machines and fresh slaves came at no small cost to Cuban planters. As a class, they soon found themselves indebted to the Spanish-born merchants who grew wealthy from speculation in slaves, capital, dry goods, and machines deemed necessary for the expansion of the sugar industry.

The Cuban sugar boom of the late 1700s and early 1800s stands as the deviant case of the Caribbean; it was the only such experience fuelled by domestic capital and *native* skill. On this matter Knight (1977:249) has written:

The sugar revolution derived its greatest impetus from the entrepreneurial skills of the oldest families in Cuba. These families, having become rich in land and having access to public offices, found themselves strategically positioned to take every advantage of the early economic development.

Among the most salient names of these old families stood those of Arango, Montalvo, Duarte, Peñalvar, Cárdenas, Herrera, Chacón, O'Reilly, Calvo de la Puerta, O'Farrill, Pedroso, and Nuñez del Castillo.[18] The sugar operations of these and other planters consisted of patriarchal, self-sufficient units, requiring little financing and only a primitive technology. According to Moreno Fraginals (1978, I:63) the magical numbers of these units were one hundred slaves, producing 115 tons of sugar. Growth beyond that was achieved simply by establishing additional *ingenios*.

Evidence suggests that by the late 1830s, the majority of Cuba's sugar planters lacked the capital needed to expand and reorganize their enterprises. "[T]here are many known cases," wrote one observer, "who while having estates worth 200 or 300,000 pesos, can not dispose of 2,000 without needing them" (Zaragoza 1837:24). Thus, for many Cuban planters willing to accept the expansion challenge, mechanization meant recourse to outside sources of credit. In a society where, with few exceptions, there were no real banks until the 1850s, merchants played the role of money-lenders by advancing cash and imported goods in exchange for the guarantee of the planters' next harvest. The recourse to this mechanism, known as *refacción*, represented the subordination of the planters' interests to those of the mercantile class and eventually the takeover of landed wealth by the latter. Interests stipulated in *refacción* contracts ranged between 18 and 20 per cent, a virtually confiscatory rate if compared to the going rate for credit in Europe, 4 to 5 per cent (Ely 1963: 324-25). Aside from profits derived from interests, merchants were able to extract profits by forcing planters to buy overpriced hogsheads, by charging excessive sales commissions and storage fees, and by speculating with the sugar that they bought at an agreed price before the harvest (Bergad 1990: 174).

Many contemporary observers and more recent students of the region's history have blamed these high rates of interest on a specific piece of sixteenth-century Spanish colonial legislation: *el privilegio de ingenios* (privilege of the sugar estates). This law protected sugar producers from having their land, slaves and equipment seized for debt. Francisco de Arango y Parreño was among the first Cubans to blame the ills of the island's sugar culture on the maligned *privilegio*. In a May 24, 1797 deposition to the Development Board, Arango y Parreño called for its abolition. He argued that the *privilegio* kept good land in bad hands and that it favoured not only those suffering misfortune but also the "treacherous swindlers" (Marrero 1984:210). Another critic implied that such laws favored the debtors as he recounted the anecdote of a merchant who was sentenced to forty years in prison for attempting to collect from a delinquent marquis (Se Roches 1869:15-17). In the middle of the nineteenth century, colonial administrators in Cuba and Puerto Rico stepped in to remedy some of the problems of the sugar industry by attacking the centuries old *privilegio*. On November 10, 1848, Captain-General Juan de la Pezuela promulgated a decree granting sugar planters in Puerto Rico the dubious right to renounce the *privilegio*. Four years later, a royal decree provided that *ingenios* established hence would no longer enjoy the *privilegio,* and that all others would lose it by 1865.[19] Although no actual documentation supports this contention, it is likely that in light of their pressing needs for credit, planters were willing to forfeit their *privilegio* as a precondition for credit.[20]

In summation, by accepting the expansion challenge, Cuban planters prepared the scenario for their downfall. Having little capital to finance their industry's modernization, the most daring resorted to expensive sources of credit. Others simply backed away from expansion. By the end of the 1850s the planter class had lost financial control over the sugar industry. With the *privilegio* gone or about to expire, the actual loss of its property became a matter of time. The economic and financial crisis of 1857 further aided this process. In that year alone 250 bankruptcies were registered in Havana (Pérez 1988: 113). Francisco López Segrera (1979: 114) has concluded in his study of the Cuban economy that by 1860 Spanish commercial capital had gained almost complete control of the sugar business. According to Moreno Fraginals (1985: 16), two-thirds of the Cuban sugar industry were mortgaged, and consequently in the hands of the mostly foreign merchant class by 1863. At that point 95 per cent of the *ingenios* were mortgaged to some degree.

The mechanization of the Cuban sugar industry and the consequent rise of slave importations, the two processes that sealed the fatal destiny of Cuban planters, were precisely the circumstances favouring the ascendancy of Spanish commercial capital. During the 1840s and 1850s, the Peninsular element gradually moved into territory heretofore monopolized by the Creole elite. Spaniards seeking a fortune in Cuba usually found it in one or more of three ways: first, government service through high salaries and access to even higher bribes[21]; second, usury and speculative trading-lending; and finally, contraband, particularly in slaves.

Spaniards migrating to Cuba usually carved niches in either the colonial bureaucracy, Church, military, or commercial sector. Only on rare occasions would Spanish immigrants engage directly in agricultural ventures of their own; Julián Zulueta being a notable exception to this. Zulueta, a poor and illiterate Basque immigrant, started out as a *dependiente* (shop clerk) gradually moving up to become an independent merchant, and later (1844) a plantation owner as well. By 1857, Zulueta, who was active in slave trading, was Havana's largest slave-owner, with 1,475 slaves. [22] "I have not seen during the time I have been in this island," wrote a visiting traveller, "a single Spaniard cultivating the soil."[23] Most Spaniards started out as *dependientes* in commercial establishments, perhaps working for a so-called tio (distant relative, called uncle) or a paisano (fellow-countryman). Through thrift, cunning, or deceit, or a combination of all three, some *dependientes* managed to amass small fortunes which eventually allowed them to set up their own commercial enterprises.

Comprised mostly of Peninsulars, the commercial sector exploited and subordinated the planter class through a multitude of mechanisms. First, it advanced overpriced goods and cash at the exorbitant rate of 18 to 20 per cent. Second, it set the price at which sugar was received as payment. Third, it collected fees, commissions and other charges for transporting, storing and selling the sugar. As if this was not enough, some merchants refused to accept sugar not packed in the containers that they sold. Their hogsheads and barrels were, thus, forced upon indebted planters at prices far above their market value. An extreme practice by some merchants consisted of collecting the molasses that dripped

from the sugar hogsheads during their storage. These dripping molasses were not credited to the planters at the time of shipping, rather they were retained by greedy merchants as an additional source of profit. For them, it was obvious, every drop counted (Ely 1963:306-7; 1964:470-72).

Rather than wait for the drops of molasses to accumulate slowly, some merchants opted for quicker ways to make their fortunes. None was quicker than trading in slaves. Roland T. Ely (1963:330-31), a student of Cuba's commercial sector in the nineteenth century, concluded that a great many of the island's commercial fortunes were made by importing and selling slaves. Another student of Cuban society in the nineteenth century, Robert L. Paquette (1988:46-47), asserts that slave trading was one of two ways in which newcomers became members of the elite – marrying into it being the other. The previously mentioned Julían Zulueta was one of the nouveaux riches and to cite just another example, José Suárez Argudín arrived penniless from Asturias and within a few years became one of the island's wealthiest men, elected deputy to Madrid in 1867.[24] Interestingly, contrary to the trend during the eighteenth and early nineteenth centuries whereby the new Spanish immigrants soon became "Cubanized" through absorption into older Cuban clans, the newer waves now tended to retain their Spanish identity and acted and saw themselves as superior non-permanent residents of the island. Spanish cultural clubs, such as *el Casino Español*, and participation in the infamous Volunteer Corps increasingly served to reinforce this sense of separateness during the later decades of the nineteenth century. The origins of this divide can, perhaps, be found in the anti-Creole policies of Captain-General Miguel Tacón and in the mid-century ideological split over the issue of the slave trade. This issue clearly drew the line separating the mostly Creole planter segment, opposed to the continuation of the slave trade, and mostly foreign commercial sector, intimately linked to slave trading activities.

Finally, simultaneously with the process of economic subordination outlined above, the colonial state through banishment and confiscation aided in the displacement of the Cuban elite; the *coup de grace* would come with the Ten Years' War (1868-78).[25]

Puerto Rico's Response

Puerto Rico responded quite differently to mid-nineteenth-century world market demands for tropical staples. Whereas Cuban planters attempted to remain competitive by increasing output through expansion and mechanization, in Puerto Rico planters fell victim to a sustained crisis marked by stagnation and decline. Between 1850 and 1859, Puerto Rico's sugar exports declined at an average yearly change rate of 26,317 *quintales*; the decade started with exports of 1,121,294 quintals and ended with exports of 884,443 *quintales*.[26] In the light of the crisis some of the capital backing sugar production was diverted to other agricultural ventures or commerce or simply faded away in the face of a prolonged crisis that reached its nadir in the 1870s.

A series of basic differences separated Cuba and Puerto Rico in terms of their economic history and their capacity to meet the challenges of the mid-century. Above all, Puerto Rico's sugar boom, which started some fifty years later than Cuba's was fuelled, financed and managed by foreign capital and immigrant entrepreneurs. Interestingly, while the origins of the Cuban sugar revolution are usually traced back to the British occupation of Havana 1762-63 (an eleven-month period during which the port city received an influx of ten thousand slaves), the boom in Puerto Rico is attributed to the measures of the 1815 *Cédula de Gracias*, which, among other things, promoted the immigration of foreign capitalists. In short, while Cuba imported its labour force, Puerto Rico began by importing its bourgeoisie.

A prosopographic analysis of Ponce's planter class by Francisco A. Scarano (1981) has demonstrated that only 28 to 30 per cent of the municipality's sugar planters were Puerto Rican (1827-45). As he points out, even these percentages do not give a full picture because the estates owned by Creoles were among the smallest of the holdings.

By the middle of the century, the privileged strata of Ponce's society were primarily composed of first or second generation immigrant families, while only a minority of the sugar estate owners could trace their origins to the old elite of hateros and estancieros, the patriarchical rural elite of the eighteenth century. (Scarano 1981:23)

One of the drawbacks of having a foreign-born bourgeoisie leading Puerto Rico's transition to an export economy was that the capital behind the process was uncommitted and highly mobile. French, Spanish, or German planters in Puerto Rico could easily sell their land, slaves, and equipment and retire back to Europe if pressed too hard, or they could shift their capital resources into commerce, where most of the plantation capital had originated. In contrast, the Cuban planter class had an additional incentive to face the sugar challenge. For them, holding on to their land meant keeping an ancestral symbol of status and prestige; their lands, many times linked to titles of nobility, had passed from generation to generation, deemed the most important legacy they could hand on to their heirs. Besides, Cuban sugar estates were larger and could resist times of crisis better than their smaller counterparts in Puerto Rico.[27]

If Cuba's sugar boom was a revolution, Puerto Rico's was a revolt. Puerto Rican expansion was shorter (through the 1820s and 1830s), localized and not as far reaching. As pointed out earlier, during the 1840s the island's sugar industry began to show signs of debilitation. The number of sugar estates dropped by two-thirds from 1,552 in 1830 to 550 in 1860, while sugar output remained stagnant (Ramos Mattei 1981:126; Bergad 1983:68). Puerto Rico's newer planters did not exhibit the same staying power as their Cuban colleagues. Moreover, mechanization in Puerto Rico lagged decades behind, which meant that modernization to competitive levels required larger sums of money. For example, as late as 1867 vacuum pans had not been adopted in Puerto Rico; that year there were seventy-five such units operating in Cuba. Three years later, only 120, or 20 per cent of the island's sugar estates used steam to run their mills.[28] Significantly, while Cuban planters were downgrading their sugar production to meet the quality standards of the United States market, Puerto Rico's sugar, with a high content of molasses was not deemed appropriate for the needs of the United States and other North Atlantic markets. Moreover, Puerto Rico was geographically farther than Cuba from the United States, which made Puerto Rico's sugar less competitive when transportation expenses were added to the costs. Finally, chronic droughts and declining soil fertility affected the southern coast of Puerto Rico beginning in the 1840s.

Another significant contrast between Puerto Rico and Cuba was that large proportions of the arable land and labour force in the smaller island remained on the fringes of the plantation economy. Sugar plantations had sprung up only in select pockets of Puerto Rico like Ponce, Guayama, and Mayagüez, while most of the work force and tillable land remained allocated to minor crops and subsistence agriculture. In fact, it could be argued that Puerto Rico was not a plantation society. In the same sense, Cuba's Eastern Department was not a plantation society although it harboured pockets of plantations in Santiago and Guantánamo. According to 1862 estimates, the amount of land for minor crops (i.e. plantains, tubers, and corn) in Puerto Rico was about equivalent to that destined to the island's chief staples: sugar and coffee (Scarano 1984:5). Moreover, Puerto Rico had a massive population of independent or subordinate peasants who remained on the fringes of the plantation economy. In 1844, the British Consul at San Juan described this element of the island's population as follows:

[T]he natives who are free surpass by far the slaves, many of them possess small plots in which they live, and since their needs are minimal, they only cultivate that which they find necessary to sustain themselves, they care little about improving their crops or their condition. . . .(quoted in Morales Carrión 1978:134-35)

The availability of land had made this kind of life-style possible for centuries. According to the historian Laird W. Bergad (1983), unoccupied lands were still plentiful in the first half of the nineteenth century, a circumstance that made labour-control difficult. The dual expansion of the state and staple agriculture, however, soon pushed this autonomous population into the frontier interior of the island.

During the late 1830s and the 1840s, efforts were made to regiment the island's independent workforce through antivagrancy laws and other coercive means. In June 1838, Captain-General Miguel López de Baños passed his notorious "Bando contra la Vagancia" (vagrancy law). Antivagrancy tribunals called "Juntas de Vagos y Amancebados," were set up to punish those who preferred to subsist off officially vacant plots rather than become servile peons in export-oriented units. The crown jewel of Puerto Rico's coercive labour legislation was Juan de la Pezuela's "Ley de la Libreta" of 1849. It stipu-lated that those without land or a profession either had to become tenants or had to search for employment under a landholder and carry with them their *libreta de jornalero* (journeyman's passbook) at all times. The *libretas* were used to make annotations about each *jornalero's* work, wages, debts, and conduct. *Jornaleros* were also forced to remain in one particular municipality and to continue working for the same estate until their debts were cleared. To further control the mobility of the labour force, land owners commonly advanced overpriced goods to their workers from their own estate shops. British Consul Augustus Cowper praised the results of *libreta*. "It has been in practice for fifteen years," he wrote in 1866, "and the results have been that every man, without distinction of color, has been forced to work; the productions of the soil have annually increased; and vagrancy, and the higher crimes are almost unknown."[29] The dual expansion of the state and the export economy eventually caught up with the people and the land of Puerto Rico's interior. As Fernando Picó (1979) has demonstrated in his studies of the Utuado municipality, the rolls of the *jornalero* class became filled with the names of descendants of the town's founding families and its former local elite.

Perhaps the sharpest contrasts to be drawn between Cuba and Puerto Rico in this period are those relating to slavery and racial patterns. In Puerto Rico slavery never played the crucial role it did in Cuba. According to Philip D. Curtin's estimates, a total of about 702,000 slaves arrived in Cuba, but only 77,000, close to a mere tenth of that, were imported into the smaller island. Moreover, in Cuba the slave population reached its peak in 1841, with 436,500 or 43 per cent of the population; in Puerto Rico it peaked around 1846, with 51,300 or less than 12 per cent of the population. Patterns of change in the importation of slaves into Cuba and Puerto Rico further reveal divergent developments since the crisis of the sugar industry in Puerto Rico had a considerable impact on the demand for slave labour. While an estimated 1,410 slaves entered Puerto Rico yearly between 1830 and 1845, during the following fifteen years only an average of 700 slaves arrived each year, a decrease upwards of 50 per cent. In contrast, in Cuba, where the sugar industry continued to expand, yearly average imports of slaves increased from 10,014 during

1827-1847 to 10,546 during 1848-1860, a modest 5 per cent increase (Curtin 1969:31-44, 88).

A series of factors explain the crisis of slavery in Puerto Rico. First, as suggested before, the island's economic reorientation away from sugar and toward coffee reduced the demand for slave labour. Second, those who continued to produce sugar were not always in the best position to invest in new slaves. Third, as demonstrated by the studies of José A. Curet (1982:84-85), the low technological level of most sugar estates meant that the addition of more slaves in estates with fifty or more slaves produced only marginal returns. These factors also help explain the loose attachment of planters in Puerto Rico to the continuation of the slave trade. In 1860, when slave imports were breaking records in Cuba, Consul Charles De Ronceray described the prevailing attitude in Puerto Rico in the following terms:

[T]he sentiments of the natives, including the planters are opposed to the transportation of slaves from Africa and very little encouragement is therefore given to the slave trade either by the people or Government of the island notwithstanding the want of labour.[30]

The lesser importance of slavery was also reflected in Puerto Rico's racial patterns. The existence of large sectors of society outside the grip of the state and the export economy during three centuries favoured the population's miscegenation. Enlightened European visitors to Puerto Rico noted a high degree of race mixture among the population, a characteristic attributed to activities lying outside the sphere of the state and the official economy: piracy, smuggling, illegal immigrations, desertion, and marronage (Morales Carrión 1978: 11-14). Census data for San Juan's districts between 1823 and 1833 show that the proportion of free people of colour in the different barrios ranged between 38 to 59 per cent of the entire population (Kinsbruner 1990: 445). By 1860, according to census figures, Puerto Rico's non-white free population was 241,015 out of a total of 583,308 inhabitants, that is 41 per cent. According to one abolitionist active in Puerto Rican politics, "there is no radical separation of the races in this country, and mulattoes constitute more than 50 per cent of the population" (De Labra 1871:25). Contrastingly, in Cuba, particularly in the western districts where plantations played such a central role, there was a far more defined separation of

the races and a much stronger correlation between colour and status. The Cuban census of 1841 for example, reflected a population consisting of 418,291 whites (41.5 per cent), 490,305 blacks (48.7 per cent), and 99,028 mulattoes (9.8 per cent) (Knight 1970:86, 93). Regarding Matanzas, specifically, the 1862 census reflected that 40 per cent of the population was white, 46 per cent was black slave, and only 6 per cent was either free or emancipado of colour, while the remaining 896 was Asian (Bergad 1990:99). Racism, the ideology which sought to preserve this kind of stratification and a close association between colour and status was also considerably stronger in Cuba than in Puerto Rico.

In summation, the world market demands put enormous pressures on the economies of the Spanish colonies of the Caribbean during the middle decades of the nineteenth century. Sugar planters were forced either to accept the sugar challenge, by modernizing the industry and expanding slavery or to withdraw from the industry altogether. Despite belonging to the same geographical region, sharing similar climatic and geological conditions, and being subjected under the same empire, Cuba and Puerto Rico took different economic paths during the mid-nineteenth century. Conditions in Cuba were favourable to the acceptance of the sugar challenge. Planters there resorted to expensive credit in order to modernize and expand sugar production. The result of this was that by 1863 two-thirds of the industry were in the hands of Spanish merchant-bankers, who held mortgages to the amount of $200,000,000. Meanwhile, in Puerto Rico the mostly foreign planter class had no choice but to continue operating at a reduced level or to back away and diversify into other crops, coffee in particular. Both societies faced similar challenges from the outside world; both responded to them as best they could, but in the end both floundered, each in its own particular way.

Notes

1. See, for example, Manuel Moreno Fraginals, Frank Moya Pons and Stanley Engerman (eds.), *Between Slavery and Free Labor. The Spanish Speaking Caribbean in the Nineteenth* (Johns Hopkins Univ. Press, 1985), Laird Bergad, 'Dos alas del mismo pajaro?: notas sobre la historia socioeconomica compa-

rativa de Cuba y Puerto Rico', *Historia y Sociedad*, 1, (1988). See also Luis Martinez-Frenandez, *The Hispanic Caribbean between Empires, 1840-1868*, (Ph.D. diss, Duke University, 1990). Research for the broader project from which this article stems was made possible by the generous support of the following institutions: Duke University; the Tinker Foundation; the Program in Atlantic History, Culture, and Society of the Johns Hopkins University; Bowdoin College; the National Hispanic Scholarship Fund; the American Historical Association; and the National Endowment for the Humanities.

2. The percentage of beet sugar among British sugar imports increased consistently during the second half of the nineteenth century, from 14% in 1853 to 23% in 1863, and further to 38% in 1873, in Eric Williams, *From Columbus to Castro: The History of the Caribbean 1492-1969* (Vintage Books, 1984), p. 383.

3. According to Sidney Mintz, in *Sweetness and Power: The Place of Sugar in Modern History* (New York: Viking, 1985), p.144, sugar prices fell by 30 per cent between 1840 and 1850, and by a further 25 per cent between 1851 and 1870. Laird Bergad's *Cuban Rural Society in the Nineteenth Century: The Social and Economic History of Monoculture in Matanzas* (Princeton Univ. Press, 1990), p. 162, figures show that in Matanzas sugar prices remained fairly stable during 1840-56 and then shot up in 1857-58.

4. A series of ravishing hurricanes hit the Cuban coffee regions in the mid 1840s, causing enormous destruction.

5. A variety of sources provide data on the number of estates, among them: Thomas Wilson, *The Island of Cuba in 1850* (New Orleans: La Patria, 1850), p. 7, Arthur Corwin, *Spain and the Abolition of Slavery in Cuba, 1817-1886* (Univ. of Texas Press, 1967), p. 295, Franklin Knight, *Slave Society in Cuba in the Nineteenth Century*, (Univ. of Wisconsin Press, 1970), p. 39, and Levi Marrero, Cuba economia y sociedad (Madrid: Editorial Playor, 1984), p. 176.

6. For information on numbers and proportion of steam-run mills see Thomas Wilson, Franklin Knight, Levi Marrero, Ibid. and David Denslow, *Sugar Production in Northeastern Brazil and Cuba, 1858-1908*, (Ph.D. diss., Yale Univ. 1974), p. 74.

7. See also the testimony of Jose Julian Acosta in the Junta de Informacion, February 6, 1867 (Espania, Ministerio de Ultramar, 1873), p. 72.

8. For an assessment on the origins, development, and impact of the Cuban railroads, see Gert Oostindie, 'La burguesia cubana y sus caminos de hierro, 1830-1868', *Boletin de Estudios Latinoamericanos y del Caribe*, 37, (1984), and 'Cuban Railroads, 1803-1868: Origins and Effects of Progressive Entrepreneurialism', *Caribbean Studies*, 20, 3\4, (1988).

9. See Thomas Wilson, *Island of Cuba in 1850* (New Orleans: La Patria, 1850), p. 7, Arthur Corwin, *Spain and the Abolition of Slavery in Cuba, 1817-1886* (Univ. of Texas Press, 1967), p. 295, Franklin Knight, *Slave Society in Cuba during the Nineteenth Century* (Univ. of Wisconsin Press, 1970), p.39, and

Levi Marrero, Cuba: economia y sociedad. Vol. 10. (Madrid: Editorial Playor, 1984), p.176.

10. For data on coolie and Yucatecan labor imports, see Crawford to Lord Clarendon, August 7 and 16, 1855, Great Britain, Parliament, British Parliamentary Papers (hereafter cited as BPP), vol. 42, Class B: 397-401; see also Laird Bergad, *Cuban Rural Society in the Nineteenth Century: The Social and Economic History of Monoculture in Matanzas* (Princeton Univ. Press, 1990), 250-1.

11. Roland Ely, *Cuando reinaba su majestad el azucar* (Buenos Aires: Editorial Sud americana, 1963), p. 616; "Report of Coolie Importations to Cuba, June 14, 1858," National Archives, Washington, D.C. (hereafter cited as NAWDC), Records of the Department of State, Record Group 59, Despatches from U.S. Consuls in Havana, roll 39; La Gaceta de La Habana, January 30, 1856.

12. Commenting on the scarcity and expense of labor and referring to Chinese contract workers, Richard Dana, *To Cuba and Back: A Vacation Voyage* (Southern Illinois Univ. Press, 1859), wrote "such is the value of labor in Cuba, that a citizen will give $400, in cash, for the chance of enforcing eight years' labor, at $4 per month, from a man speaking a strange language, worshipping strange gods or none, thinking suicide a virtue..." See also Susan Schroeder, *Cuba: A Handbook of Historical Statistics* (G.K. Hall, 1982), p. 107; Franklin Knight, *Slave Society in Cuba During the Nineteenth Century* (Univ. of Wisconsin Press, 1970), p. 181; Richard Dana, *To Cuba and Back: A Vacation Voyage* (Southern Illinois Univ. Press, Reprint 1966), p. 45.

13. According to an 1850 report by the British judge of the Havana Mixed Commission, three or four cargoes of Brazilian slaves arrived yearly to the island, BPP, vol. 7, pp. 173-177.

14. Arturo Morales Carrion, *Auge y decadencia de la trata negrera en Puerto Rico, 1820-1860* (San Juan: Instituto de Cultura, 1978), p. 203, recounts dramatic instances of slaves jumping off ships to avoid being sent to Cuba.

15. Crawford to Lord Clarendon, August 29, 1853, quoted in David Murray, *Odious Commerce: Britain, Spain, and the Abolition of the Cuban Slave Trade* (Cambridge Univ. Press, 1980), pp. 247-48.

16. U.S. Congress, 'Stephen R. Mallory on the Acquisition of Cuba,' 35th Congress, 2nd session, Congressional Globe (February 25, 1859) vol. 28, pt. 2, 13, 28; Robert Gibbes, *Cuba for Invalids* (New York: W.A Townsend, 1860), p. 39.

17. Robert Shufeldt, 'Secret History of the Slave Trade in Cuba', *Journal of Negro History*, 55, (1970); quotation of Hiram Fuller of the New York Mirror, in Levi Marrero, *Cuba: economia y sociedad. Vol. 10* (Madrid: Editorial Playor, 1984), p. 269; Arthur Corwin, *Spain and the Abolition of Slavery in Cuba, 1817-1886* (Univ. of Texas Press, 1967), p. 118. Similar estimates were produced by the British consul at Havana, who calculated that a 450-slave expedition could net a $389, 850 profit, and that twice as much was spent in bribes ("blood money") and in

purchasing the slaves; Crawford to Lord Russell, February 5, 1861, Great Britain, Foreign Office, General Correspondence before 1906, Slave Trade (microfilm), vol. 5, Class B, 16-19.

18. Franklin Knight, *Slave Society in Cuba During the Nineteenth Century* (Univ. of Wisconsin Press, 1970), pp. 231-253; Robert Paquette, Sugar is Made with Blood: The Conspiracy of La Escalera and the Conflict between Empires over Slavery in Cuba (Wesleyan Univ. Press, 1988), p. 45. For a discussion of native wealth expanding to Matanzas, see Laird Bergad, *Cuban Rural Society in the Nineteenth Century; The Social and Economic History of Monoculture in Matanzas* (Princeton Univ. Press, 1990) pp. 14-15, 22-23.

19. *La Gaceta de Puerto Rico,* vol. 17, no. 137, quoted in Lidio Cruz Monclova, *Historia de Puerto Rico* (siglo XIX). Vol. 1 (Rio Piedras: Editorial Universitaria, 1952), p. 292.

20. Between 1850 and 1853 planter Fernando Diago paid a total of $333,815 in interest for his debt to refaccionistas while his colleague Joaquin de Ayestaran paid $284,691, Louis Perez, *Cuba: Between Reform and Revolution* (Oxford Univ. Press, 1988), p. 94.

21. Mariano Cancio Villa-Amil, *Situacion Economica de la isla de Cuba* (Madrid: M. Ginesta, 1875), p. 44, list a variety of popular sayings describing the extent of official corruption in Cuba: "To leave one's shame in Cadiz," "Nobody comes to Cuba for the fresh air," "To kill leaves" (To destroy incriminating government documents).

22. See Arthur Corwin, *Spain and the Abolition of Slavery in Cuba, 1817-1886* (Univ. of Texas Press, 1967), pp. 136-137 and Levi Marrero, *Cuba: economia y sociedad.* Vol. 10 (Madrid: Editorial Playor, 1984), pp. 269-71. Laird Bergad, *Cuban World Society in the Nineteenth Century: The Social and Economic History of Monoculture in Matanzas* (Princeton Univ. Press, 1990), pp. 51-52, contends that Zulueta's humble origins were fictional. He, however, fails to present supporting evidence for this contention.

23. See Demoticus Philalethes, *Yankee Travels Through the Island of Cuba* (New York: D.A. Appleton, 1856), pp. 64-65. Similar information is provided in Richard Dana, *To Cuba and Back: A Vacation Voyage* (Southern Illinois Univ. Press, 1966), pp. 111-

12, John Thrasher, *A Preliminary Essay on the Purchase of Cuba* (New York: Derby & Jackson, 1859), p. 77, and James Rawson, *Cuba* (New York: Lane & Tippet, 1847), p. 12.

24. Roberto Matre, *Cuba y la Republica Dominicana* (Santo Domingo: Universidad APEC, 1988), pp. 178-79, mentions other examples such as Antonio Telleria, Ramon Herrera and Rafael Toca.

25. By 1895 only 17% of the island's planter class could trace its origins to the "old plantation owning families", Manuel Moreno Fraginals, 'Plantations in the Caribbean: Cuba, Puerto Rico, and the Dominican Republic in the Late Nineteenth Century', in Manuel Moreno Fraginals, Frank Moya Pons and Stanley Engermans (eds.), *Between Slavery and Free Labor: The Spanish-Speaking Caribbean in the Nineteenth Century* (Johns Hopkins Univ. Press, 1985), p. 5.

26. Data from Balanzas mercantiles, housed in the Centro de Investigaciones Historicas de la Universidad de Puerto Rico. The average yearly change rate is calculated by determining all the yearly fluctuations between 1850 and 1859, and then calculating the average.

27. Francisco Scarano, *Sugar and Slavery in Puerto Rico: The Plantation Economy of Ponce, 1800-1850* (Univ. of Wisconsin Press, 1984), pp. 66-67, writes that Cuban ingenios produce a mean of 391 tons (1860) while the Puerto Rican average remain at around 87 tons (1845).

28. Indicative of the stagnation of Puerto Rico's sugar industry is the fact that in 1899 one half of the sugar mills were still driven by oxen. The railroad too arrived in Puerto Rico some forty years later than in Cuba; Andres Ramos Mattei, 'La importacion de trabajadores contratados para la industria azucarera puertorriquena: 1860-1880', in Francisco Scarano (ed.) *Inmigracion y clases sociales en el Puerto Rico del Siglo XIX* (Rio Piedras: Ediciones Huracan, 1981), pp. 22-23 and Laird Bergad, 'Agrarian History of Puerto Rico, 1870-1930', *Latin American Research Revue*, 13, 3 (1978), pp. 65-66.

29. H. Agustus Cowper to Lord Clarendon, February 11, 1866 (Centro de Investigaciones Historicas, 1974, p. 53).

30. De Ronceray to Cass, August 22, 1860; NAWDC, Records of Foreign Service Post, San Juan, Capital Record Group 84, vol. 7228.

39

The Early Use of Steam Power in the Jamaican Sugar Industry, 1768-1810

VERONT M. SATCHELL

Introduction

Galloway in his discussion of the sugar industry argues that, since its inception nearly 1000 years ago, the Jamaican sugar industry has been extremely conservative in its adoption of innovations in the milling and manufacturing of sugar.[1] Tomich accounts for this supposedly technical backwardness in the industry in the '. . . contradiction between slave labour and technological innovations'.[2] Galloway however, concedes that after 1800, ' . . . innovations becomes a major theme in the history of the industry'.[3] Steam, he notes, was the first innovation of the nineteenth century and inquiries were made by West Indian sugar planters from the very early days of its invention, about its application to power mills on their estates.[4] Watts, contends, however, that despite these early inquiries, steam in cane estate mill was . . . never common in the West Indies prior to 1833. Most planters regarded the idea with disfavour.[5]

This paper assesses Watts' claim by presenting an analysis of the extent of the diffusion of steam power in Jamaica between 1768, when James Watt made his first visit to Boulton's Soho Works near Birmingham and 1810, when the first Boulton and Watt engine arrived in the island's plantation economy. Through an examination of the early experimentation and uses of steam as a motive force in Jamaica, it is argued that the diffusion of steam power was well under way in the island before the advent of the Watt engine.

The evolution of steam power began in 1698, when Thomas Savery was granted the historic patent for 'Raising water by the impellent force of fire', for a period of 21 years.[6] The solution for growing power needs in England was, however, not achieved in Savery's machine but rather with the invention of the steam engine in 1712, by Thomas Newcomen, an ironmonger of Dartmouth, in Devon, England.[7] The Newcomen engine was a low pressure engine which provided power in reciprocating motion which was ideal for operating pumps.[8] Notwithstanding the benefits of the Newcomen engine it had many problems.[9] James Watt remedied the defects of his predecessors and made the steam engine an instrument of wide application.[10] Like the Newcomen engine, the early Watt engine was a reciprocating low pressure engine.

During the 1760s there was demand for rotative engines to drive mills and engine builders started to adapt motion to the Newcomen engine.[11] Watt also followed suit and in 1781 he received a patent for fourteen years for his new invention of a rotative steam engine. Watt's first double acting steam engine was erected in 1786 at the Albion mills in England,[12] and it set the firm of Boulton and Watt on the road to fame and fortune. The engine became the standard design for producing rotative power everywhere. Although Watt held his patent, the company of Boulton and Watt did not have a monopoly of steam engine manufacturing. Neither did the company monopolise the steam engine market. Watt's patent did not preclude the manufacturing of Savery and Newcomen type engines.[13] The firms of Bateman and Sherratt of Manchester and Francis Thompson of Ashover, Derbyshire, for example, continued to build these engines in large numbers for both the British and overseas markets.[14]

There were also the pirating of Watt engine designs. Many companies constructed engines on Watt's principles, a noted example being Bateman and Sherratt.[15] In a court battle over infringements, it was revealed that 29 pirated Watt engines were made by this company between 1791 and 1796, one of which was built and shipped from Liverpool to Jamaica, for Lord Penrhyn's sugar estate.[16] Although the court ruled in favour of Boulton and Watt, Bateman and Sherratt continued to have a great deal of engine business and they were still copying Boulton and Watt's engines exactly leaving everything in readiness only to put on the condenser as soon as Watt's patent had expired in 1800.[17] With the expiry of Watt's patent, the use of the double acting engine was rapidly extended and competition from rival manufacturers intensified with these manufacturers selling to both the domestic and foreign markets. By the beginning of the 1800s the diffusion of the Newcomen, Watt and other steam engines was rapid. Steam power was widely adopted not only throughout Britain but also in Europe and America.[18]

Steam Power in Jamaica 1768-1810

During the period between 1760 and 1810 sugar mills in Jamaica were powered either by natural forces wind or water, animals or steam engines. Craskell and Simpson's map of 1763 shows that there were 566 estates in the island in 1763. Of this total, 382 or 67.5 per cent, used animals to turn sugar mills, 150 or 26.5 per cent depended on water powered mills and 36 or 6.3% utilised wind power. Ragatz estimated that there were 648 sugar estates in the island in 1768, of which 369 or 56.9 per cent were cattle mills, 235 or 36.3 per cent were water powered and 44 or 6.8 per cent were wind operated.[19] He made only passing mention of the use of steam to power mills, arguing that there were experiments in the use of steam power from as early as 1768 but nothing came of these. Robertson's map of Jamaica which indicates clearly the geographical distri-

bution of sugar mills in Jamaica and the power sources each utilised around 1804, recorded 830 sugar estates. Of this total 48.1 per cent depended on animal power, 31.6 per cent depended solely on water power, 9.8 per cent depended on wind mills. Estates utilising a combination of water and cattle accounted for 5.8 per cent; cattle and wind 4.2 per cent and wind, water and cattle 0.5 per cent. The map does not record the existence of steam engines in the island during this period, which would suggest that none was in operation locally at that time.

The empirical evidence, however, indicates that as soon as the Newcomen engine had acquired rotative motion, experiments were made in Jamaica to adapt it to power sugar cane mills. Contacts were also made by some planters residing in England with steam engine manufacturers in an effort to have engines erected on their Jamaican plantations, most importantly engines were being erected on estates locally. According to Deerr, the first attempt to apply steam to power sugar cane mills was made in Jamaica.[20] In 1768 John Stewart, otherwise known as Robert Rainey, a millwright, presented a petition to the Jamaican House of Assembly for a patent for his newly invented fire engine to power sugar mills. The petition read thus:

The petitioner had by great study and application invented a mill of a new construction for grinding sugar canes and the petitioner had great reason to believe will be of infinite service to the island. That the petitioner went to London and had made a compleat mill of a proper size and dimension and arrived in the island a few days ago and brought with him the same praying for the House to take the same into consideration and give him such encouragement as to them seem fit.[21]

A sub-committee of the House which was appointed to investigate the claim, reported that the complete mill was in the hands of Messrs Read and Chambers to whom it 'stands mortgated for £343 sterling'.[22] A resolution was passed, recommending that, the House direct the Receiver General to pay the said Read and Chambers the sum of £343 sterling and that the said John Stewart be at liberty to erect the same where 'he thinks proper ...'[23] In 1770 a Committee of the House reporting on Stewart's engine stated that:

... John Stewart ... has put up the same [a fire engine for grinding sugar canes] at Greenwich plantation in the parish of St. Andrew and that there is the greatest prospect of it answering for the purpose for which it was intended, as the power of the said fire engine is found to be sufficient for the grinding of canes . . . [24]

It was recommended that, a bill be brought to give Stewart the sole right of erecting mills on his design for grinding sugar canes for a certain time. The enabling Act was passed in that same year.[25] Deerr states that Stewart was granted an English patent prior to this Jamaican patent.[26]

In promoting his engine Stewart enumerated the advantages, which in many cases he either overstated or exaggerated, that steam engines had over other sources of power for sugar cane mills, namely, locational flexibility, reliability and dependability, lower initial, operational and maintenance costs, labour saving, fuel efficiency and simplicity of operation hence its compatibility with slave labour. In emphasising the locational flexibility of the steam engine he noted that:

. . . it may be set in the most convenient spot of the plantation, for water and easy carriage of canes, which must be considerable saving in every plantation, and in some very great.[27]

It was more dependable and could be relied upon during the crucial period of crop time. According to Stewart, it was always ready to work, day and night, right through the crop time without stopping, except for every five or six weeks when the piston was being reclothed and this took about half an hour or when the boiler was being cleaned, which operation took about twelve hours including the time the boiler was cooling.[28] It could be easily stopped and therefore, not subjected to accidents.[29] This aspect of reliability and dependability was of extreme importance to the island's sugar planters. They indeed could ill afford a mill that was constantly breaking down. The expeditious processing of the cane once it was cut, was crucial for a successful crop. Steam engines indeed may be reliable but they, like all machines, are subjected to malfunctioning especially in the early period of their installation. In fact, mill engineers had to accompany early engines to see to their maintenance. There was also the problem of spare parts, which in many cases were not manufactured locally and therefore, had to be imported from the engine manufacturers overseas. There is no doubt that whether parts were available locally or imported there were lengthy waiting periods for these parts. Which in turn could adversely affect the production process. In fact Watt, recognising the problems of breakdowns and the continued need for parts, insisted that spare parts accompany his engines destined for overseas.

The estimated price quoted by Stewart for his engine was £700, a great contrast to the £2000 he estimated for a wind- and cattle-mill and mules.

. . . The first cost of a Wind mill, with a Cattle mill, and thirty Mules, that is Twenty-Four constant in work, and Six in reserve . . . at a moderate Computation may be estimated at £2000 sterling or upwards . . . [the steam engine] may not exceed Seven Hundred Pounds . . . [30]

This estimated cost for his engine was comparable to the £640 for Watt's 6 horsepower engines which were sent to Jamaica during the 1800s. But it seems hardly likely, however, that at this early stage of the development of the steam engine that the price could be so low. His estimate for the wind mill and cattle mill together was double the £1000 sterling estimated by Bryan Edwards for these two mills in 1793.[31] He was, however, promoting his engine from which he had hoped to make some monetary gains through sales. Hence it is to be expected that he would be emphasising all the advantages, real or imagined, that his engine had over all other competing sources of power. His showing comparative prices of competing power sources was one measure he was using in advertising his invention.

He was of the view that since the engine would require very few repairs and replacement parts, maintenance cost would be low.

. . . Repairs . . . for the first four or five Years, may not amount to five pounds Yearly and Boylers made from Iron Plates, generally lasts twelve or fifteen Years . . . But some are made of Copper, which lasts for 20 to 30 years.[32]

This low maintenance cost, according to Stewart, was in contrast to his estimated annual costs of £632.16s for a wind and cattle mill.[33] To emphasise further the economy of his engine, he argued that, with the exception of the brick work for the boiler, the engine did not require any expensive buildings, a shed to shelter the mill, machinery and boilers and people were all that were needed.

Stewart asserted that his engine was fuel efficient. According to him, the manner in which he had arranged the boiler in relation to the sugar cane boiling house made the need for additional fuel unnecessary.

. . . by setting the boiler of the engine close by, or partly on the Gavel of the boiling house; and one of the clarifiers, (that is the largest Coppers)... next to the Gavel so as the flame from the clarifier may come to the boiler to boil it . . . [34]

This heat he claimed was sufficient for the boiler, since it did not require any excessive heat to maintain the boiler pressure. If the heat was excessive, it impaired steam generation, causing the engine to slow down or even stop. Thus the fuel in the boiling house was all that would be required. He strongly recommended wood and cane trash, rather than imported coal as fuel. Thus there were sufficient materials locally that could be used as fuel.[35] This was indeed a practical expedient since it saved the added expenditure of purchasing imported coal. Indeed bagasse and local wood became the chief sources of fuel for engines operating in the island.

In contradiction to the popularly held view that the slaves would not be able to operate the steam engine, Stewart argued that the machinery of the engine was simple and easily understood. Hence there would be no difficulty in training local personnel to man it. He further contended that in England young boys and women were left in charge of steam engines. He, therefore, saw no difficulty in implementing steam engines on plantations worked by slave labour. According to him:

It may be objected that . . . it may not be practicable to make Negroes understand them . . . But although Fire Engines are very curious and appear misterious to those to whom the principles of them have not been explained, yet there are few Machines more simple and easier understood, or managed . . . Any man of tolerable capacity (especially if he is a carpenter) may be instructed to manage them, and to set them up to work, by attending ten to fourteen days. They are frequently attended by boys not more than twelve years old and women of the collieries for several days together.[36]

It should be noted that, given the paucity of whites and most especially those in the artisan groups, in the Jamaican population during the period of slavery, the chief technicians and artisans in the island and other slave societies of the Caribbean were slaves.[37]

Stewart contended that in its ability to save labour, it was superior to other power sources. Whereas wind and cattle mills demanded 18 attendants, the steam powered mill required only five, three to work the rollers, one to take out the trash and one to carry the canes.[38] This feature of saving labour, however, was secondary to the other economic gains to be had by using his engine.

An added feature of this engine according to Stewart was that it could supply water for the boiler house and distillery as well as irrigating the cane pieces in times of drought in addition to its normal task of powering mills.[39] There is, however, nothing novel about this feature since waterwheels had a similar advantage and were being so utilised on several estates. The island indeed suffered from periods of drought and, depending on their severity, they could have serious effects on the estates' output. Any power source that facilitated irrigation schemes would certainly have been attractive to the local planters.

Stewart argued that he could have, erected on any plantation, an engine set in good working order within ten to fifteen days of its arrival in the island from England.[40] This was unrealistic and impractical. To erect the boiler and engine houses plus digging the well for the water to supply the boiler and finally to assemble the engine and boiler, were operations that took weeks if not months. Nowhere has it been shown, in the case of the Watt engines erected in the island, that this operation took less than several months. The difficulties encountered in the establishment of the first Watt engine in the island has been documented fully elsewhere.[41] Stewart had, however, invented a very versatile engine. It could grind sugar canes, grind corn, and raise water for irrigation purposes, for plantation use and for itself, simultaneously. His method of setting the boiler made it energy efficient since it used the same fire in the boiling house.

There is no doubt that this steam engine successfully powered a sugar cane mill on a sugar estate in Jamaica for at least a short time and other sugar producing areas in the Caribbean had full knowledge of its existence and apparent success. In a paper read before the Royal Society in 1780, by the Marquis de Cazaud, a planter from Grenada, reference was made to a steam engine having worked eleven years previously in Jamaica.[42] The engine, however, did not pass rapidly into general use. But nonetheless this was a most remarkable and significant achievement in the sugar industry.

Stewart, however, has been credited by Deerr, with being the first to apply steam power to the operation of machinery in the sugar manufacturing process.[43] The Jamaican plantocracy made a commendable gesture in encouraging Stewart's attempts locally. In so far as Jamaica was the first place where such an attempt was made, it may be concluded that Jamaica pioneered experimentation in the use of steam power as a motive force in the sugar industry. Deerr, however, contends that Cuba rather than Jamaica was the first country in which steam was successfully applied to power the operation of cane crushing mills.[44] This claim was based on a report made by Alexander von Humboldt, who had visited Cuba in 1797. In this account it was claimed that the first plant was erected in that year on an estate owned by Count Jaruco y Mopex. The report further stated that by 1808 there were 25 steam engines powering mills in that country.[45] This suggested rapid diffusion of steam power in Cuba. However, pieces of correspondence between the firm of Boulton and Watt and Cuban sugar interests during the early 1800s, cast some doubts on this account. Several letters addressed to Boulton and Watt from Cuban planters were simply requests for information on the efficiency and efficacy of steam power in cane mills in these planters bid to introduce this new technology to the sugar industry.[46] In the light of von Humboldt's account, it seems odd for such requests to be coming from these planters. Cuba is a relatively small island, the sugar industry was confined to even smaller geographical areas and the planters formed a small closely knit group, certainly with the existence of so many steam engines planters should have had full knowledge of their efficiency and efficacy. Apparently, however, this does not seem to be the case, thus casting doubt on the report. Watt's response to these queries are also very instructive. In each case the firm referred the Cuban planters to Jamaica, not that there were several engines operating in that country, so that either a visit to the island or corresponding with Jamaican planters should supply the desired information.[47] It may be necessary to note that the chief suppliers of steam engines to Cuba, during the nineteenth century, was the firm of Fawcett and Preston of Liverpool and not Boulton and Watt. The point however, is that it is hardly likely that Cuba would have had mills operating prior to or as early as, 1768. The empirical evidence indicate that engines were successfully operating mills in Jamaica as early as 1768. In so far as there are doubts about the accuracy of von Humboldt's

account, it would appear that Jamaica and not Cuba should be considered as being the first country in which steam was successfully used to operate cane mills.

The introduction, erection and actual operation of Stewart's engine in Jamaica corresponds to the first stage of diffusion or the dispersal stage in the Tann and Breckin model of Diffusion.[48] Stewart, however, was not alone in these early attempts at applying steam to power sugar cane mills in the island. Dugald Clarke obtained a patent from the Legislature of Jamaica in 1770, for his 'New Method of Constructing and Hanging the Boiler and of Applying the power of the Machine (commonly called a Fire or Steam engine) to the working of my new constructed sugar mill and of all kinds of mills and engines whatsoever'.[49] Deerr states that Clarke had obtained an English patent (no. 949), for this invention in 1769/70.[50]

Deerr described the patent drawings of Clarke's engine as novel,

... in that it shows two steam cylinders working alternatively, continuous circular motion of the shaft being obtained by the system of open and crossed ropes working on the drums in combination with pawls. The boiler was fitted with a internal tubular heating element ... [51]

No record has been found indicating that this engine was ever built. Wickes Skurray, gentleman, presented a petition to the House in 1773 stating that:

In the year 1772 [he] did contrive and with great trouble executed a very small model of a new method of applying the steam engine to a mill for the grinding of sugar canes, which [he] apprehends to be more compact than any hitherto exhibited in public, and that by a more immediate application of the lever and the small numbers of wheels the friction being lessened, the canes will be ground with more facility, and from the simpleness of the work will be less liable to be out of order, and sooner repaired when such case happens than any machines that are more complex.[52]

A full size version of this engine was erected for the examination of a Committee of the House. It seemed satisfactory to the members and as a result in 1773 he obtained a Private Act enabling him to carry into execution his, '. . . newly invented method of applying the steam or fire engine to the work of mills for grinding sugar canes'.[53] No evidence has been found to indicate that the engine was ever used commercially.

Josias Robins, a millwright of St. Mary and Thomas Bunker Parker of Great Britain, represented by Rob___ Jackson of St. James, received patents in 1793 for their inventions of methods of applying the power of steam to drive sugar cane mills.[54] Robins stated in his petition that he had introduced in the island a steam pump or machine for the purpose of grinding sugar canes. That he had erected one according to his plan on Markham Hall Estate in St. Mary, the property of John Cozens Esq. and that he, . . . can advance the most satisfactory proof to the House of the utility and advance thereof . . . [55] Nothing more has so far been found on this engine. What is important, however, is that this engine worked successfully. Parker claimed in his petition that he had invented an instrument, engine or machine to be wrought by means of air and water or by fire, air and water by which any work may be performed by mills, engines or by any of the known mechanical powers.[56] Again nothing further is known of this machine.

John Ashley, planter of Vere, in an effort to employ the more efficient waterwheel to power his mill, invented a steam pump in 1787, to raise water to throw on a waterwheel to power a sugar mill. Although his invention did not deal with the direct application of steam to power mills, it gives an indication of the keen interest in steam and the tremendous efforts that were being made by the locals to utilise the power of steam to the benefit of the sugar industry. Vere was one of the driest parishes of the island, and there was a scarcity of running streams suitable to power waterwheels. The use of steam engines to pump water to power waterwheels was indeed the first use made of steam engines and hence now new. Ashley, being aware of this principle, was applying it to local situations in order to overcome the constraints imposed by geographical conditions. Ashley's method, however, did not pass into general use. This is understandable since by that time steam engines were producing rotative motion, thus enabling them to power mills directly.

The discussion has so far indicated the level of experimentation that took place in the island in applying steam as a motive force and the relative success these achieved. Planters themselves were actively investigating, seeking further information and actually adapting steam engines on their estates before 1800. On 28 May, 1790 a memorandum was sent to Watt, by a Mr. Whitehead informing him that Mr. Dawkins, a Jamaican planter would be meeting him at 10 o'clock the following Thursday morning to see the engine subsequent to a previous discussion between them concerning steam engines for his West Indian plantations.[57] But even before this date Lord Penrhyn (Richard Pennant), owner of several estates in the island corresponded with the firm of Boulton and Watt on the subject of employing steam engines on his Jamaican estates. In 1786 he wrote to Watt proposing a dinner meeting with him during one of his [Penrhyn's] visits to Birmingham to discuss the matter further. In this letter he wrote:

I wish much to have the pleasure of conversing with you on the subject of steam engine for Jamaica. I propose coming to Lichfield to a late dinner . . . Saturday the 10th February and I shall be very glad of your company to dine with me . . . But should it not be agreeable to you to come to Lichfield I will alter my plans and I will be at the Hotel at Birmingham Saturday morning the 10th when I hope I shall have the pleasure of seeing you .[58]

Nothing further has been found concerning these early extracts. However, a Boulton and Watt engine was erected on his Denbeigh estate in Jamaica in 1815. But this was certainly not the first steam engine erected on one of his estates in Jamaica. Reference was made earlier to a pirated Boulton and Watt engine manufactured by Bateman and Sherratt and shipped from Liverpool to Jamaica before or during 1796 for one of Lord Penrhyn's Jamaican estates. The name of the estate to which this engine was sent by the company was not given. Information on the number of engines this company shipped to the island during this early stage would be of tremendous benefit to this study. Despite enquiries, however, this information has proven difficult to come by, thus suggesting either, that this company kept no record of its business transactions or, if it did, these records have not survived. It is hardly likely that this was the only engine shipped to Jamaica by this company, especially after 1800.

Jean Lindsay in her work on the Pennants in Jamaica 1665-1808, argues that in the late eighteenth century Jamaican planters and their attorneys were beginning to show an interest in steam engines. She refers to a letter from a J. Davis, a London merchant responsible for sending provisions for estates, to Lord Penrhyn concerning a suggestion made by Alexander Falconer, Penrhyn's attorney in 1797, regarding the application of steam engines on Penrhyn's estates. In supporting Falconer's suggestion, Davis stated that,

... If Mr. Falconer can get water for the engine have no doubt it will repay the expence of two or three Steam Engines, Clarendon being a very uncertain part of the island, so subject to dry weather ...[59]

No other reference is made to steam engines on Penrhyn's estates in Lindsay's work, until that of an 1804 report from Rowland William Fearon, the new attorney, to Lord Penrhyn. In this report Fearon stated that he had ordered a steam engine, which was then on trial at Denbeigh. It was, however, used for pumping water for estate use rather than for turning sugar cane mills. In that same report he stated that a rotative mill was to be used to take off the crop, and that he had ordered '... the young men on the estate to be instructed in the use of the machinery ...'[60]

There was some initial opposition to the introduction of steam to power the mill on Denbeigh during this early period. Fearon stated that this opposition came from the overseers, who had tried to sabotage it. The reason for their attitude was the extra time which was necessary to look after the machinery. Fearon went on to assure Lord Penrhyn that he would do everything to thwart their schemes.[61] Fearon himself, had some apprehension about the steam powered mill, he proposed to re-establish the disused windmill on Denbeigh.[62] No evidence has been found to indicate that this mill was ever re-activated. What is certain is that by 1806 the rotative steam engine on Denbeigh was in full operation. It was used solely for grinding canes and was producing '25 hogsheads of sugar per week'. The pump engine on the other hand made very little progress. In September of that year the well digger and mechanic died. Apparently he had taken to drinking, which seemed to be the cause of his death.[63] It would appear that excessive drinking was a hallmark of the millwrights and engine keepers. This was clearly indicated in a reply by Watt to a West Indian customer who had requested that sobriety be a key qualification in the man who was being sent to erect his engine.[64] To this request Watt replied:

One qualification you required that of sobriety is very rarely met with in engine keepers and formed an objection to the otherwise good characters and ability ... they may be supposed like the blacksmith to have an unquenchable spark in their throats.[65]

On the subject of replacing the mechanic, Fearon advised Lord Penrhyn that he need not send out a replacement mechanic, because 'the people have sufficient knowledge ... to proceed ...'[66] This is clear indication that the local population was becoming conversant with steam engines and steam engineering, which leads to the conclusion that there were several steam engines in operation in the island by this time. There were two engines on this estate alone, one to which rotative motion was adapted to turn the cane mill, and which was fully operational, the other a pump engine.

James Mitchell, proprietor of Moreland estate in Vere also owned a steam engine by 1800. His was larger than that of Lord Penrhyn's but unlike Penrhyn's which was used for irrigation his was used to power the sugar cane mill.[67] Mitchell was described by Rennie in 1811 as a great enthusiast for steam mills in Jamaica.[68]

There was competition, during this early period among plantation owners and attorneys, for local personnel to man these engines. Fearon reported to Lord Penrhyn in 1806, that James Mitchell had attempted to entice the carpenter away to attend to his engine by offering him a salary of £500 per annum. To avert what Fearon referred to as a disaster, he offered the carpenter a salary of £300 and put him in charge of carpenters on Thomas River and Denbeigh Estates.[69]

This is clear indication that the island was on the threshold of the diffusion stage in the Tann-Breckin model by this time. This stage was to be developed with the wide scale importation of the Watt engine beginning in 1810.

Conclusions

The evidence is clear. Jamaica not only pioneered experiments in the utilisation of steam power in the sugar cane mills but was also the first Caribbean country in which this technology was successfully used to grind sugar canes commercially. Beginning with Stewart's steam engine in 1768, engines were invented locally and were erected on estates. As the technology of steam engines improved in England, however, local inventions ceased and engines were imported from England. As a consequence of these local experiments and importations, by 1810 the diffusion of steam power in Jamaica was well under way.

Notes

Note: *JAJ* as used in the reference notes is the abbreviation for *Journal of the Honourable House of Assembly of Jamaica.*

1. J. H. Galloway, *The Sugar Cane Industry An Historical Geography From its Origins to 1914* (Cambridge, Cambridge University Press, 1989) p. 134.
2. Dale Tomich, *Slavery in the Circuit of Sugar Martinique and the World Economy 1830-1848* (Johns Hopkins, Baltimore, 1990), p. 201. There is much controversy among economic historians as to the extent of technological change that developed in the slave societies of the New World during the era of slavery. The popularly held view is that slavery impeded progress for the simple reason that innovations are incompatible with slavery/slave labour. See for example Tomich; Eugene Genovese, *The Political Economy of Slavery: Studies in the Economy and Society of the Slave South* (New York, 1976). The contradictory view of this 'Incompatibility thesis is that in slave societies innovations were widely implemented and these were integral to economic development recorded in these societies. See Rebecca Scott, *Slave Emancipation in Cuba* (Princeton, 1987); J. R. Ward, *British West Indian Slavery, 1750-1834: The Process of Amelioration* (Oxford: Clarendon Press 1988).
3. Galloway, op. cit., p. 134; See also Noel Deerr, *The History of Sugar* (Chapman & Hall, London: 1949).
4. Galloway, op. cit., p. 135.
5. David Watts, *The West Indies Patterns of Development, Culture and Environmental Change Since 1492* (Cambridge: 1987), p. 421. Ragatz similarly argues that there was very little or no advance in technology of sugar production during this period of slavery in the British Caribbean. He claims that the introduction of steam power in the British Caribbean, during this period when its employment in the 'mother country' had become common [did not] make much headway . . .' This he argues was a result of West Indian planter conservatism. According to him 'the change from animal to steam as a motive force was too great for West Indian conservatism' Lowell Ragatz, *The Fall of the Planter Class in the British Caribbean 1763-1833* [1928] Reprint (Octagon, New York, 1963).
6. L. T C. Rolt, *Thomas Newcomen. The Prehistory of the Steam Engine*, (Augustus Kelley, New York, 1964) 35; 2nd ed (Moorland, Harlington, 1977).
7. *Ibid.*, p. 35.
8. Richard Hills, *Power From Steam: A History of the Steam Engine* (Cambridge University Press, Cambridge, 1989), p. 31.
9. Its construction was crude and its machinery cumbrous. It had an insatiable appetite for fuel; hence it was costly to operate. It also had low thermal capacity. Because of these imperfections steam engineers looked to see how they could improve the performance of existing engines. See Von Tunzelmann, *Steam Power and British Industrialization to 1860*, (Clarendon Press, Oxford, 1978) pp. 16-17.
10. James Renwick, *Treatise on the Steam Engine*, (New York: 1836) p. 197.
11. Hills, op. cit., p. 40.
12. Carroll Pursell, *Early Stationary Steam Engines in America: A Study in the Migration of a Technology* (Smithsonian Press, Washington, 1969), p. 14.
13. Hills, op. cit., p. 70.
14. A. E. Musson and E. Robinson, 'Science and Industry in the Late Eighteenth Century' *Economic History Review*, Vol. 13:1 (1960) p. 424.
15. *Ibid.*, pp. 428-429.
16. *Ibid.*, p. 433.
17. *Ibid.*, p. 437.
18. Eric Robinson, 'The Early Diffusion of Steam Power,' *Journal of Economic History*, Vol. 34:1 (1974), p. 95.
19. Ragatz, op. cit., p. 61.
20. Noel Deerr and A. Brooks, 'The Early Use of Steam Power in the Cane Sugar Industry' *Transactions of the Newcomen Society*, Vol. 21 (1940/41), p. 12.
21. See, Petition of John Stewart, Millwright, *JAJ*, (December 9, 1768).
22. See, *JAJ* (December 16, 1768).
23. See, 'A Bill for vesting in John Stewart the sole right for erecting Mills for grinding Canes upon his new invented plan.' *JAJ* (December 23, 1768). See also, Deerr and Brooks, 'Steam Power,' p. 550. 24. See, *JAJ* (December 16, 1770).
25. See Private Act entitled 'An Act enabling Robert Rainey, otherwise known as John Stewart, to carry into execution his newly invented mill for grinding sugar canes with the power of a fire engine'. *JAJ* (December 29, 1770).
26. Deerr and Brooks, 'Steam Power,' p. 11.
27. John Stewart, *A Description of a Machine or Invention to Grind Sugar Canes By the Power of a Fire Engine: Such as are used in Raising Water Out of Mines &c.* (1768), p. 9.
28. *Ibid.*, p. 9.
29. *Ibid.*, p. 6.
30. *Ibid.*, pp. 5, 17.
31. 'Bryan Edwards . . . Jamaican Plantation,' In Michael Craton, James Walvin et al. Eds. *Slavery, Abolition and Emancipation: Black Slaves and the British Empire. A Thematic Documentary* (Longmans, London, 1976), pp. 70-71.
32. Stewart, op. cit., p. 10.
33. Stewart's estimated operating costs of the wind- and cattle-mills:

The labour of ten Negroes	£120	0	0
A white Overseer . . .	£ 60	0	0
A carpenter and a Smith Extraordinary, to keep the mills in repairs, and their maintenance £60 each . . .	£120	0	0
Corn to feed 24 Mules while working, 2 quarts each twice a day, is 3 bushels per day, suppose for 8 months each year, or 34 weeks, is 612 bushels at 3s. per bushel	£ 91	16	0
Purchasing mules to keep up the Number, five yearly, at £20 each	£100	0	0

Sail cloth, Ropes and Twine
for the Wind mill, computed at   £ 30   0   0
Iron, nails, planks, timber &c.   £ 15   0   0
Negroes time in bringing cane
tops to the pens and watching
cattle in the pasture, and other
attendance, computed at
4 constant, at £12   £ 48   0   0

And every Negroes on the Plantation except the
boylers and house servants, go out every morning
before the sun is up, and pull and bring in grass by
the roots, which they carry to feed the cattle in the
pens, which prevents their so regular to other work,
and going out in the dew so early bare footed, brings
fevers on some; and on the whole it may be
computed that the labour of four more constant
may be lost by this, at £12 each

$$£ 48 \quad 0 \quad 0$$
$$£632 \quad 16 \quad 0$$

Source: *Ibid.*, pp. 14-15.

34.   *Ibid.*, pp. 17-23.
35.   *Ibid.*, pp. 18, 21, 22.
36.   *Ibid.*, p. 25.
37.   For a discussion on this topic, see Barry Higman, *Slave Population and Economy in Jamaica 1807 - 1834* (Cambridge, Cambridge, 1976).
38.   Stewart, op. cit., p. 13.
39.   *Ibid.*, p. 25.
40.   *Ibid.*, p. 17.
41.   See Veront Satchell, 'Technology and Productivity Change in the Jamaican Sugar Economy, 1760-1830'. Unpublished PhD Dissertation (UWI, Mona) 1993.
42.   Deerr and Brooks, 'Steam Power' p. 13.
43.   *Ibid.*, p. 14.
44.   *Ibid.*, p. 15.
45.   *Ibid.*, pp. 15-16.
46.   Boulton and Watt *Letter Book*, vol. 36 (1814).
47.   See for example the following response: 26, Sept. 1814

> . . . We have your favour 'of the 23rd. relative to the introduction of steam engines in Cuba for the use of the sugar works there. We are sorry and may we say surprised that you should have been unable when in Jamaica to procure the information you wanted . . . that they answer the satisfaction of the planters we may fairly say so far from the increase of the demand for. . .' Boulton and Watt to

Messrs Mitchell (Cuban Agent), #2 New Bank Building, *Letter Book*, vol. 36, Dec. 1813-Feby. 1815. See also Letter Boulton and Watt to Joseph Malagamba [?] 26, Aug. 1815. *Letter Book* vol. 39 Feby. 1815-Feby. 1816.

48.   Tann and Breckin proposed a simple three stage model in their discussion of the diffusion of the Watt engine. Viz. DISPERSAL (purchases are made but there is no band wagon appeal) → DIFFUSION (spread of information, interests are shown, wide scale purchases are made) → ASSIMILATION (new technology is absorbed in the host country to the point where knowledge and manufacture of the product have been assimilated by the nationals). Jennifer Tann and M. J. Breckin, 'The International Diffusion of the Watt Engine 1775-1825', *Economic History Review*, Vol. 31:4 (1978), p. 545.
49.   See, Petition of Dugald Clarke, *JAJ* (December 17, 1770).
50.   Deerr and Brooks, 'Steam Power' pp. 11-12.
51.   *Ibid.*, p. 15.
52.   See, Petition of Wickes Skurray to the Hon. House, *JAJ* (November 27, 1773).
53.   See, 'An Act to enable Wickes Skurray . . .' Private Acts Passed by the Hon. House of Assembly, *JAJ* (December 30, 1773).
54.   See Petition of Josias Robins to the House and Petition of Thomas Bunker Parker of Great Britain presented by his attorney Robert Jackson of St. James *JAJ* (November 21, 22, 1793).
55.   See *JAJ* (November 23, 1793).
56.   *JAJ*, (November 21, 1793).
57.   In Letter to Watt re Mr. Dawkins visit, Letter Book, *B & W Coll.*
58.   'Letter Lord Penrhyn to Watt re Steam for Jamaica,' Letter Book 34/13 1786/87 No. 56-57 (January 30,1786), *B & W Coll.*
59.   Jean Lindsay, 'The Pennants and Jamaica 1665-1808' *Transaction of the Caernarvonshire Historical Society*, Vol. 43:7 (1982), p. 79.
60.   *Ibid.*, p. 79.
61.   *Ibid.*, p. 79.
62.   *Ibid.*, p. 80.
63.   *Ibid.*, p. 8 1.
64.   John Rennie to Watt, Letter book, *B & W Coll.*
65.   Watt to Simon McKinns, January 3, 1820, Letter Book vol. 42, *B & W Coll.*
66.   Lindsay, op. cit., p. 80.
67.   *Ibid.*, p. 80.
68.   John Rennie to Watt, Letter Book *B & W Coll.*
69.   Lindsay, op. cit., p. 81.

40

Slave Prices in Cuba, 1840–1875

LAIRD W. BERGAD*

The transition from slavery to free labour in the Hispanic Caribbean has recently become a topic of considerable scholarly interest.[1] Although the close linkages between slavery and Caribbean sugar production have long been recognized, after 1850 slave labour and sugar remained inexorably bound only in Cuba.[2] The Cuban sugar economy's persistent dependency on slaves through the eve of emancipation has generated two multifaceted questions concerning slave labour, abolition, and the economics of sugar production.

The first centres on the relationship of slavery to the sweeping technological transformations the sugar economy experienced from the 1830s on. The installation of steam engines, Rillieux double vacuum pan evaporators, centrifuges, and British or U.S.-built railway systems to transport cane from fields to mills and sugar from mills to ports were among the most widespread and costly innovations gradually employed by sugar planters from the mid-1830s through the late 1870s.[3] Did the increased refining capacity resulting from these transformations, and the rising capital investments their adoption mandated, make slavery an antiquated labour system incompatible with changing technological forms? Did new productive methods lead to emancipation because slavery was no longer economically viable? While refining was becoming more and more capital intensive, was the sugar economy's continuing dependence on slave labour responsible for decreasing profitability?[4]

The second question concerns the adaptations of Cuban sugar planters in the aftermath of abolition. The end of slavery was followed by an unprecedented increase in sugar production between 1880 and 1894.[5] Did abolition indeed release productive forces that were stifled because of the economic limitations of slavery, thus confirming the sugar economy's pre-abolition "internal contradictions" alluded to above? Or was this increase in production due to a combination of other factors?

Although a number of suggestive, and sometimes emphatic, answers to these questions have appeared in the works cited above, it should be stressed that systematic economic data on the functional mechanisms of Cuba's slave/sugar complex are conspicuous for their scarcity. Whether slavery had reached its maximum productive potential in Cuba by the 1860s is closely tied to the crucial question of profitability. To date, however, there have been few studies attempting to examine rates of return on investments in slaves and their variations through time.[6] This is hardly surprising, since time-series data on the most fundamental economic variables needed to calculate the profitability of Cuban slave labour are currently unavailable. These include local sugar prices, land values, land/cane and cane/sugar yields, costs of technological innovations and their depreciation, maintenance costs of slave populations, productive life expectancies of slaves, and slave prices.[7]

The movement of slave prices can be used as an analytical tool to provide insights into the economic dynamics of Cuba's nineteenth-century sugar economy. An a priori assumption is that planter willingness to support rising slave prices indicates the economic viability of slave-labour-based sugar production. Trends in slave prices during the late 1860s and early 1870s are particularly important indicators for the slave/sugar economy since by then the abolition process was initiated and the final end of slavery was no longer in doubt. It is assumed that if slavery were no longer profitable at this point in the history of Cuba's sugar economy, demand for slaves would soften and prices would decline. The exact opposite occurred, suggesting the continuing economic compatibility of slavery and sugar production.

Despite increasing utilization of expensive imported technology, slaves continued to account for a substantial share of capital assets on most Cuban sugar *ingenios* through the mid-1870s.[8] Clearly, therefore, it is impossible to analyze the economics of sugar production or the viability of slave labour without a precise understanding of trends in slave prices.[9] This article does not pretend to definitively answer the broader questions outlined above; its purpose is to provide an accurate account of tendencies in Cuban slave prices between 1840 and 1875, which can be used to understand the economic dynamics of Cuba's slave-based sugar economy on the eve of abolition.

Sources and Data

This study is based on slave transactions recorded in the city of Matanzas between 1840 and 1875 and in the town of Colón between 1863 and 1875. On the eve of the nineteenth century, the Matanzas region was largely an unexploited frontier. Sugar and coffee production expanded gradually around the Matanzas Bay area in the first two decades of the century. During the 1830s and 1840s, railroads opened the interior and large, capital-intensive mills were constructed in the Colón region which became one of the most important centres of the Cuban slave/sugar economy.

Slave sales were recorded by local notaries in bound protocol volumes preserved in various Cuban archival collections. The complete records from 1863 through 1900 of one Colón notary, Manuel Vega Lavarría, were discovered in the Archivo Histórico Provincial de Matanzas, located in the centre of the port city of Matanzas. The volumes for 1863, 1864, 1867, 1870, 1872, and 1875 were read and 522 slave transactions

were analyzed for this study. A number of notaries recorded slave sales in the city of Matanzas, and their protocol records have been maintained in the Archivo Nacional de Cuba, Havana. The notaries studied for this article were chosen randomly, and a total of 1,006 slave sales were examined for the years 1840, 1843, 1846, 1850, 1854, 1857, 1860, 1865, 1870, and 1875.[10]

By and large the data are consistent but not ideal. Notaries routinely recorded the sex, age, national origin, and the price of each slave sold, but did not uniformly report on occupations, skills, or physical impairments. Nor was there any indication of whether slaves were destined for urban or rural areas, sugar plantations or other types of farms. Thus, the latter factors have not been used to calculate average prices of the different categories discussed below. It is also lamentable that between 1837 and 1843 few transactions noted ages and that no age data were recorded by Matanzas notaries from 1846 through 1857.

Prices for slaves have been analyzed by sex, origin, and age, when this information was available. Three age groups have been defined: 1 through 14 years of age; 15 through 40; and slaves 41 years of age and older. This was not done idiosyncratically, but because an initial perusal of price frequency distributions by age indicated a notable increase in slave prices at age 15, and a sharp decline at age 41 for African and creole slaves, whether males or females.[11]

General Trends and Sex Differentials in Slave Prices

Slave prices for both males and females exhibited marked downward trends in the first half of the 1840s. Average prices for males dropped 19.5 per cent between 1840 and 1846 (from 328 to 264 pesos); while average prices for females fell 29.4 per cent (from 316 to 223 pesos).[12] Although Cuban sugar production expanded significantly in the Matanzas region during this period and demand for slave labour was considerable, slaves were available in abundant quantities because of a surge in African imports from the mid-1830s through 1841.[13] The slave market's apparent oversupply meant downward pressure on prices.

Price differentials between males and females indicate no discernible trend before 1846. Females sold for 96 per cent of male prices in 1840 and 84 per cent in 1846. Yet, in 1843 females were priced at 111 per cent the value of males.

From 1846 to 1854, average prices for male slaves recovered (+30.3 per cent) and slightly surpassed 1840 levels (328 pesos in 1840; 344 pesos in 1854). However, differentials in prices between males and females widened considerably. Females were sold at 65 per cent of average male prices in 1850 and 81 per cent in 1854. In addition, by 1854 average female prices (278 pesos) remained lower than in 1840 (316 pesos), although there was a 24.7 per cent increase from 1846.

Between 1846 and 1854, two factors exerted upward pressure on male slave prices. The first was the strong demand for labour accompanying the constant construction of new *ingenios* and the resulting increase in sugar production.[14] The second factor was a decrease in slave supplies due to a downturn in African imports which began in 1841 and continued to the early 1850s. Between 1834 and 1841, an average of 13,469 African slaves landed in Cuba annually. But between 1842 and 1852 annual imports averaged 4,639 slaves.[15]

Average prices for all slaves increased sharply after 1855, soaring in Matanzas to 581 pesos in 1857; softening to 558 pesos in 1860; and peaking to 600 pesos in 1865. These prices were more than double slave prices before 1850.

In Colón prices reached their highest levels somewhat later, in 1870, when the average price per slave was 673 pesos, after which there was a gradual decline as the onset of the legal abolition process heralded the end of slavery.[16] The willingness of Colón planters to pay the highest prices of the century for slaves, at the precise historical moment when the end of slavery was no longer in doubt, suggests the continuing economic viability of slave-labour-based sugar production. In 1872, Colón planters continued to actively purchase slaves and paid average prices (630 pesos) only slightly lower than the 1870 peak.

In Matanzas after 1855, sex differences in slave prices were insignificant and no discernable trend can be noted until 1870. In some years females sold at slightly lower average prices, 98.2 per cent of males in 1860 and 93.0 per cent in 1870. But in 1857 and 1865, female slaves sold for higher average prices (104 per cent) than males.

A significant divergence in slave prices by sex took place in Matanzas after the promulgation of the 1870 Moret Law. In 1875, males sold at average prices of 518 pesos, females at 247 pesos (47.7 per cent of male values). Under pressure to maximize productivity and extract optimum labour from slave populations in the short term due to the imminent end of slavery, planters placed a greater premium on males, more so than at any other time during the nineteenth century. Although not as extreme, the same phenomenon was found in Colón where males prices averaged 391 pesos and females 344 pesos in 1875 (88 per cent of male values).

Declining female slave values were related to the fact that newborns had no future economic value since they were theoretically free under the terms of the 1870 Moret Law. Slave owners may also have viewed females as less viable economically because those bearing children would become a liability through lost labour time, and because the children themselves would have to be supported by masters under the terms of the 1870 law. (See Figures 1 and 2 for a graphic presentation of price differences by sex in Matanzas and Colón.)

What factors supported significantly higher slave price levels after 1855, and what does the willingness of plantation owners to actively purchase slaves at relatively high prices through the early 1870s indicate about the economic viability of slave labour?

On the supply side, a resurgence of the slave trade from the mid-1850s to the early 1860s meant an abundance of *bozales* landing in Cuba. According to British consular estimates, imports between 1853 and 1857 averaged 9,640 slaves per year, while from 1858 to 1864 over 120,000 Africans were brought to Cuba, 17,413 annually.[17] It was only after 1863 that a variety of factors effectively curbed, then eliminated, the Cuban slave trade.

Not only were slave supplies abundant, but slave prices on the African coast seem to have remained remarkably stable from the 1840s through the mid-1860s, although shipping and operating costs for slave traders seem to have risen considerably. In addition, increased bribes to Spanish colonial officials effectively raised operating costs for slavers.[18] These factors did not restrict the number of Africans embarking for Cuba, nor can they be used alone to explain

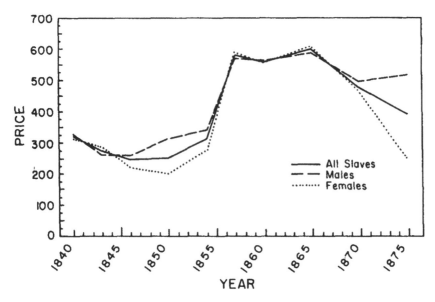

Figure 1: Matanzas Slave Sales 1840-1875; Average prices by Sex

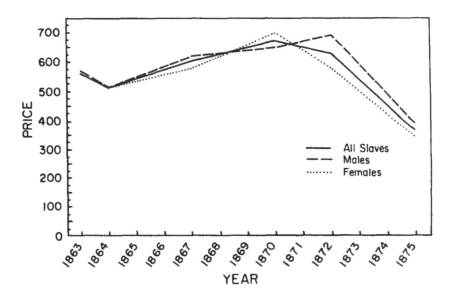

Figure 2: Colón Slave Sales 1863-1875; Average prices by Sex

Cuban slave price rises in the late 1850s and early 1860s.

Three interacting factors produced the overwhelming demand for slaves responsible for pushing prices to the high levels noted above. The first was the uncertainty surrounding the future of the slave trade itself. The long and persistent British campaign to force an end to the Cuban slave trade had traditionally been circum-

vented by collusion between Spanish colonial officials and Cuban slave traders. An additional obstacle to British efforts was the unwillingness of the United States to permit the search of U.S.-flag vessels suspected of involvement in the slave trade.

However, policy toward the Cuban slave trade shifted as the U.S. Civil War deepened. The United States began to support British efforts to

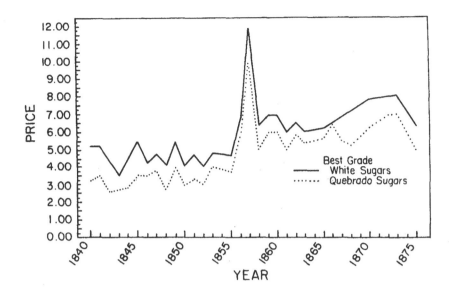

Figure 3: Sugar Prices in Matanzas, 1840-1875 (in cents per pound) *Source:* Aurora de Matanzas

curb slaving in the Caribbean, and Spain was increasing pressured to effectively patrol the Cuban coast. The result was the reduction of slave landings in 1865, and the trade's virtual elimination by 1867.[19] Thus, from the beginning of the U.S. Civil War, Cuban planters experienced increasing uncertainty on the critical question of future labour supplies. Planter response was to stock *ingenios* with large numbers of slaves, thus exerting upward pressure on prices.

After 1855, the Cuban slave market was also transformed by a second factor, the sharp upward trend in sugar prices on international markets and the maintenance of higher prices through the early 1870s (Figure 3). In May 1855, the price for top grade Cuban white sugar in the port of Matanzas was 4.63 cents per pound. By March 1856, prices were quoted at 6.88 cents per pound (+48.6 per cent); by August, 1857, Matanzas planters were receiving 12 cents per pound for top grade (*florete*) white sugar. Prices retreated to an average of 6.47 cents per pound in 1858, but remained at 6 cents or more per pound through 1870. Thus, even though there was a sharp rise and subsequent decline in sugar prices between 1855 and 1857, the overall trend after 1855 was an upward movement in sugar prices to 1873. Prices in the 1860s and 1870s were considerably higher than prices in the 1840s.[20]

Supported by the highest prices of the nineteenth century, Cuban sugar production increased by 51.8 per cent between 1855 and 1870, from 462,960 to 702,974 metric tons.[21] The growth in income resulting from price rises and productive expansion meant that Cuban sugar planters could well afford higher slave prices.[22]

The third factor was related to the mechanics of Cuban sugar expansion during the nineteenth century. Despite innovative, capital-intensive refining methods, the growth of sugar output was heavily dependent on the constant integration of newly planted cane fields into the productive process. In part this was linked to the need for ever increasing quantities of cane to efficiently utilize installed refining capacity at the mill. Railroads facilitated the industry's mobility, and the centre of Cuban sugar production shifted incessantly from Havana toward the high-yielding virgin soils of an eastward-moving frontier throughout the nineteenth century. However, unlike its industrial counterpart, the agricultural phase of sugar production experienced few technological transformations, remaining both land extensive and labour intensive through the 1870s.

Despite constant efforts to find alternative sources of labour, including the importation of over 120,000 Chinese between 1848 and 1874, Cuban sugar production remained as dependent

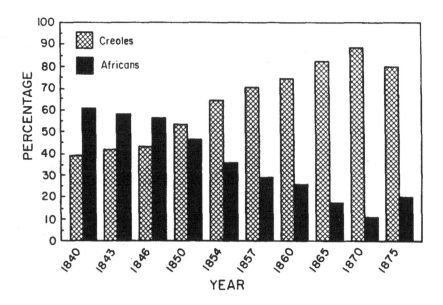

Figure 4: Matanzas Slave Sales by Origin 1840-1875 (in percentages)

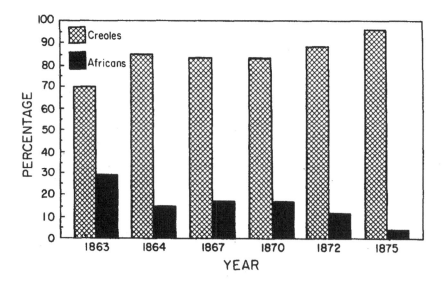

Figure 5: Colón Slave Sales by Origin 1863-1875 (in percentages)

on slave labour in the late 1860s as a century before.[23] To increase sugar production new cane fields had to be planted, and this meant that slave labour forces had to be maintained or expanded. With the relatively high sugar prices of the post-1855 period, new mills were also constructed, and *ingenio* owners continued actively purchasing slaves despite their higher prices.[24] The cost of slave labour was supported by the evident profitability of a dynamically expanding labour-intensive industry, exhibiting few signs of contraction on the eve of abolition.

Slave Prices by Origin and Age Groupings

Before 1850, African-born slaves accounted for a majority of slave sales in Matanzas. After mid-century, however, sales of creoles outnum-

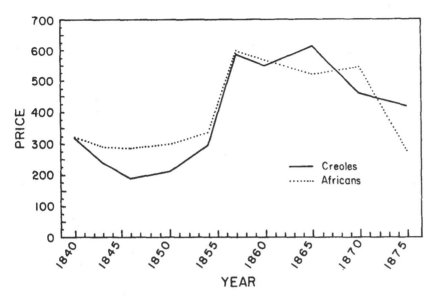

Figure 6: Matanzas Slave Sales 1840-1875 Average prices by Origin

bered Africans by ever increasing margins despite the vigour of the transatlantic trade in the 1850s and early 1860s. Creoles were more actively sold in Colón in the 1860s as well (see Figures 4 and 5).

Explanations are hardly complex. The natural reproduction of the Cuban slave population resulted in a large creole to African ratio by the 1860s despite the continuing imports, especially in the prime working age group of 15 to 40 years old.[25] In addition, it is likely that the high price structure of the slave market after 1855 induced some slaveholders to take profits on prior investments, especially those who had purchased young creoles at low prices in the 1840s, or who benefitted from the natural reproduction of their slave populations. These factors, which revolved around slave demographics and higher slave prices, resulted in the abundance of Cuban-born slaves placed on the market after 1855.[26]

Until the price increases of the post-1855 period, the data seem to indicate that creole slaves sold at lower prices than Africans in Matanzas (see Figure 6). However, this impression is distorted. Although age information is fragmentary in Matanzas between 1840 and 1860, on the basis of data from the 1830s it is likely that a high percentage of marketed African slaves were between 15 and 40 years old, the highest-priced age category. (See Figures 7

and 8 for slave prices by age group in Matanzas and Colón.) In addition, a greater percentage of creole slaves was in the lowest-valued age group, under 15 years of age. Combined, these factors effectively lowered the relative average price of creoles compared to Africans.[27]

As the price structure of the slave market moved upward after 1855, and more creole slaves between 15 and 40 years of age were marketed, the overall differential in prices by origin narrowed. In 1857 and 1860 there was very little difference in average prices between creoles and Africans, and by 1865 Cuban-born slaves not only overwhelmed the Matanzas slave market (83 per cent of all sales), they also sold at higher average prices than Africans, 611 to 523 pesos.

The marked increase in the sale of higher priced creoles was linked to the changing age structure of the slave population. The offspring of the voluminous African imports of the 1830s and the early 1840s were just entering the prime working age group in the 1850s and early 1860s. Despite continuing imports, the African-born slave population was generally much older, which meant declining market values. For example, in Guanajayabo, the Cárdenas *partido* referred to above, the 1871 slave census revealed the mean age of Cuban-born slaves to be 19.3 years, while the African-born slave population had a mean age of 32.2 years.[28]

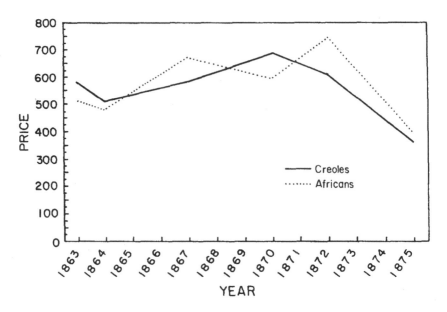

Figure 7: Colón Slave Sales 1863-1875; Average Prices by Origin

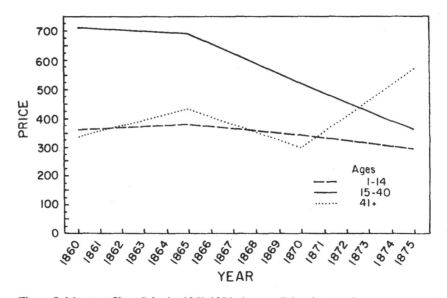

Figure 8: Matanzas Slave Sales by 1860-1875; Average Prices by Age Group

The data for Colón on slave prices by origin indicate no discernible trend (see Figure 9). The higher price structure of the overall slave market in the 1860s and early 1870s is confirmed, but the comparative market values of Africans and creoles is inconsistent through time. In 1863, 1864, and 1870 creoles sold at average higher prices. But in 1867, 1872, and 1875 Africans were more costly, even though most transactions

involving creoles consisted of prime working age slaves.

By the mid-1860s, with the waning and then collapse of the slave trade, sales of nonprime age slaves declined notably. Although the slave market remained surprisingly active in the early 1870s, buyers were interested primarily in working age slaves of either sex. In Matanzas, 1860 data reveal that 39.6 per cent of all sales con-

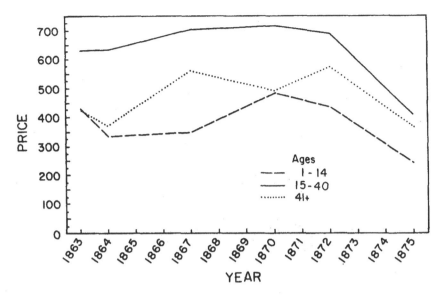

Figure 9: Colón Slave Sales 1863-1875; Average Prices by Age Group

sisted of prime age slaves, but in 1865 this figure stood at 66.7 per cent; in 1870, 74.3 per cent; and in 1875 at 80.8 per cent. In Colón, a similar pattern can be noted; over two-thirds of all slave sales after 1863 involved prime working age slaves (Figures 10 and 11).[29]

Prices for prime working age slaves in the 1860s and 1870s peaked at different times in Matanzas and Colón. In Colón, where almost all slaves worked on sugar plantations, average prices for this group reached their apex in 1870 at 717 pesos. In more urbanized Matanzas, where it is likely that a significant portion of marketed slaves were destined for non-sugar sector occupations, general prices for prime age slaves peaked a decade earlier, in 1860 when they reached 714 pesos. It is also conspicuous that in 1870 average prices for prime age slaves in Matanzas had fallen to 521 pesos, a decline of 27.0 per cent from 1860, and that these prices were 72.7 per cent the value of Colón's average-priced prime age slaves.

The importance of these comparative data is worth stressing. They indicate the persistence of strong demand for working age slaves in a major Cuban plantation zone (Colón) to the very beginning of the legal abolition process. Although the ongoing revolutionary war in eastern Cuba certainly caused a great deal of political uncertainty among planters, the rebellion had little impact on

sugar production in the major cane-growing areas of western Cuba. In Matanzas province, sugar cultivation expanded and new *ingenios* were constantly established throughout the Ten Years' War.

When prime age slave sales in Colón are broken down by sex and national origin, the strong demand for slaves is apparent, even in 1872 when the end of slavery was no longer in doubt. Prime age creole males sold for average prices of 737 pesos in 1870 and for exactly the same price in 1872. The average price for prime age African males increased from 638 pesos in 1870 to a peak of 837 pesos in 1872. It should be underlined that in Colón the price peak for all male slaves was 1872, at average prices of 694 pesos. Demand for males was so strong in this major sugar-producing zone that prices thus continued to rise after legal abolition began. It is also interesting to note that labour demands pushed prices higher for slaves 41 years of age and older in both Matanzas and Colón between 1870 and 1872. (See Figures 8 and 9.)

Creole females sold for average prices of 738 pesos in 1870, almost precisely the price for males, but declined to 634 pesos in 1872, 86 per cent of male values. African females, like African males, increased in value between those two dates, from 550 to 700 pesos.

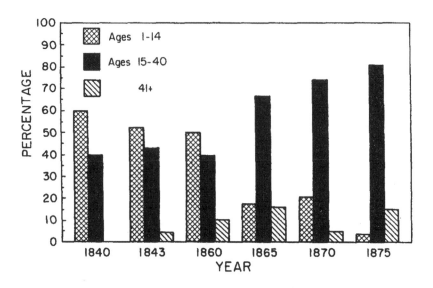

Figure 10: Matanzas Slave Sales by Age Groups, 1840-1875 (in percentages)

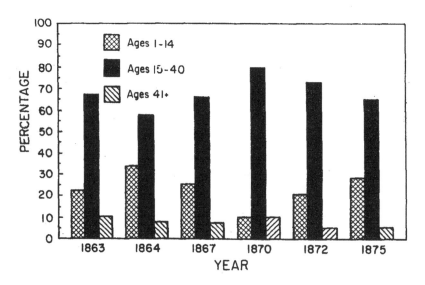

Figure 11: Colón Slave Sales by Age Groups, 1863-1875 (in percentages)

If slave labour was no longer economically viable by the 1860s and 1870s, it is puzzling that Colón's sugar planters would underwrite the highest prices in the history of Cuban slavery for prime working age slaves, particularly with final abolition no longer a theoretical debate. In fact, the continuing rise in sugar prices to 1873 evidently meant that slave-labour-based sugar production continued to remain completely viable

despite the highest labour replacement costs of the nineteenth century.

It was only after 1873, when sugar prices declined sharply, that demand for slaves softened and prices plummeted. Inflation, the political uncertainty caused by the continuation of the Ten Years' War, and the imminence of final abolition were other critical factors. In 1875, the average price of prime age slaves of both sexes

Table 40.I: Average Prime Age Slave Prices in Coln, 1863–1875 (Ages 15–40)

	1863	1864	1867	1870	1872	1875
Creole males	698	628	714	737	737	440
Creole females	653	662	692	738	634	380
African males	557	533	653	638	837	400
African females	520	na	850	550	700	na

Table 40.2: Average Prime Age Slave Prices in Matanzas, 1860–1875 (Ages 15–40)

	1860	1865	1870	1875
Creole males	775	706	517	547
Creole females	759	708	499	200
African males	500	641	677	263
African females	725	475	500	308

and nationalities was 366 pesos in Matanzas (–29.8 per cent from 1870) and 408 pesos in Colón (–43.1 per cent from 1870).[30] (see Tables 40.1 and 40.2, and Figures 12 and 13). The data presented here can accordingly be used to challenge the notion that Cuban slavery collapsed because it was no longer economically viable, nor compatible with the industrial modernization of sugar refining.

Conclusion

The movement of slave prices in Cuba between 1840 and 1875 can be broken down into two broad periods. The first was between 1840 and 1855 when prices seemed to have responded exclusively to fluctuations in supplies of newly arrived Africans. The Cuban slave trade's high level of activity in the late 1830s drove down prices in the 1840s. The contraction of African imports through the early 1850s was followed by a recovery of slave prices. There seems to have been a lag time in the response of the slave market to changes in supplies, prices shifting after supply levels were clearly defined over several years. Since slaves represented the principle source of labour on almost all sugar plantations, and Cuban sugar production increased steadily in this period, strong demand for slaves was constant or increasing.

The second period was between 1855 and 1875 when a number of other variables exerted more influence on slave prices than supplies of

newly arrived *bozales*. The most important factor was the rise of sugar prices on world markets. Sugar prices fluctuated wildly between 1855 and 1857 but settled at substantially higher levels in the early 1860s, and moved gradually upward between 1865 and 1872. Even though the slave trade reached its highest nineteenth-century level in the late 1850s and early 1860s, slave prices soared on the strength of intense labour demand linked to rising sugar prices. A new plateau was reached in the early 1860s and prices for males even increased in the sugar-producing region of Colón in the early 1870s. Other factors acting to sustain high slave prices included: a reduction of African imports after 1862; the effective end of the Cuban slave trade after 1867; and planter uncertainty over future labour supplies. Sugar price levels played a critical role in maintaining high slave prices even after the onset of the legal abolition process. Between 1870 and 1872, when sugar prices continued to gradually rise, prices for male slaves increased in Colón, prices for creole males rose in Matanzas, and prices for males over 40 years of age moved upward in both regions. It was only after 1872, when sugar prices dropped, that slave prices declined precipitously.

The strong demand for slave labour indicated by the high price structure of the Cuban slave market in the 1860s and early 1870s seems to indicate the continuing viability of slave-labour-based sugar production.[31] Cuban sugar planters

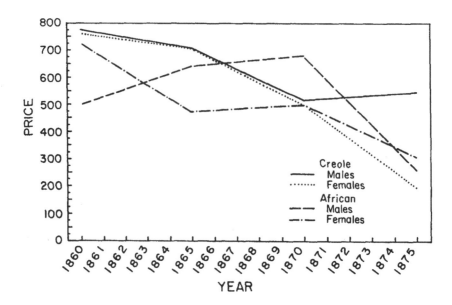

Figure 12: Matanzas Slave Sales 1860-1875; Average Prices by Sex and Origin, Ages 15-40

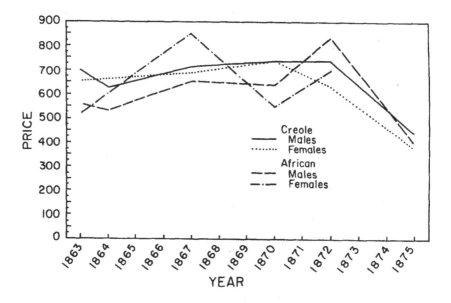

Figure 13: Colón Slave Sales 1863-1875; Average Prices by Sex and Origin, Ages 15-40

were hardly naïve, nor were they under any illusions about the long-term future of slavery by the late 1860s, and certainly not after 1870. Yet, they continued to support high slave prices. Planters apparently acted on the basis of short-term economic considerations, which revolved around maximizing income by producing as much sugar as possible to take advantage of high world market sugar prices. Construction of new mills, clearing and planting of virgin land, and maintenance of slave labour forces were all part of their activities. Although plantation owners attempted to diversify their work forces, dependence on slave labour continued through the mid-1870s.[32]

Notes

* I would like to thank the Professional Staff Congress, City University of New York, the John Simon Guggenheim Memorial Foundation, and the Social Science Research Council for providing funds to support the research and writing of this article. I want to thank Luis M. Rodríguez for his much appreciated research assistance in Cuban archives, and Stanley Engerman, David Eltis, and Rebecca Scott for comments on an earlier draft.

1. In June 1981, a "Conference on Problems of Transitions from Slavery to Free Labour in the Caribbean" was held in Santo Domingo, Dominican Republic. The papers were published in Manuel Moreno Fraginals, Frank Moya Pons, and Stanley L. Engerman, eds., *Between Slavery and Free Labor: The Spanish-Speaking Caribbean in the Nineteenth Century* (Baltimore, 1985).

    In Nov. 1986, an international colloquium "L'Abolition de L'Esclavage dans les Antilles Hispaniques (Cuba, Puerto Rico, Santo Domingo)" convened in Paris sponsored by the research group "Histoire des Antilles Hispaniques" of the University of Paris.

2. The British Foreign Office estimated that 178,852 slaves landed in Cuba between 1850 and 1867. David R. Murray, *Odious Commerce. Britain, Spain and the Abolition of the Cuban Slave Trade* (Cambridge, 1980), 244.

    These data have recently been revised in David Eltis, "The Nineteenth-Century Transatlantic Slave Trade: An Annual Time Series of Imports into the Americas Broken Down by Region," *HAHR*, 67: 1 (Feb. 1987), 109–138.

    In the central sugar producing regions, most slaves resided on sugar *ingenios*. For example, in the *jurisdicciones* of Matanzas, Colón, and Cárdenas the percentage of total slaves residing on ingenios in 1862 was 64.2, 82.2, and 74.3 respectively. See "Distribución de la población en los pueblos y fincas de la isla" in Cuba, Centro de Estadística, *Noticias estadísticas de la isla de Cuba en 1862* (Havana, 1864).

    The slave trade to Puerto Rico fell dramatically after 1850 along with a general decline in the importance of sugar. For a discussion of the Puerto Rican sugar economy in the first half of the nineteenth century, see Francisco A. Scarano, *Sugar and Slavery in Puerto Rico: The Plantation Economy of Ponce, 1800–1850* (Madison, 1984). For the second half, see Andrés Ramos Mattei, *La hacienda azucarera: Su crecimiento y crisis en Puerto Rico* (siglo XIX) (San Juan, 1981) and the essays in Ramos Mattei, ed., *Azúcar y esclavitud* (San Juan, 1982).

3. For a description of the technological transformations of the sugar mill to 1860, see Moreno Fraginals, El ingenio. *Complejo económico social cubano del azúcar*, 3 vols. (Havana, 1978), I, 203–237.

4. Since the publication of Raúl Cepero Bonilla's *Azúcar y abolición* (Havana, 1948), which argued that abolition was due to the incompatibility of slave labour with a modernizing sugar industry, every Cuban historian writing about sugar and slavery has adopted this same view. The most influential proponent has been Moreno Fraginals who emphasizes this in *El ingenio* and in a series of articles, the most important of which are "El esclavo y la mecanización de los ingenios," *Bohemia*, 61:4 (June 13, 1969); "Abolición o disintegración" and "Plantaciones en el Caribe: El caso Cuba – Puerto Rico – Santo Domingo (1860–1940)" in Moreno Fraginals, *La historia como arma y otros estudios sobre esclavos, ingenios y plantaciones* (Barcelona, 1983), 50–117. Fe Iglesias García, who has conducted extensive research on the Cuban sugar economy from 1860 to 1900, also emphasizes the above. See "The Development of Capitalism in Cuban Sugar Production, 1860–1900" in Moreno Fraginals et al., eds., *Between Slavery and Free Labour*, 54–76. Also see her unpublished manuscript "Formación del capitalismo en la producción de azúcar en Cuba (1860–1900)" and "Changes in Cane Cultivation in Cuba, 1860–1900," paper presented to the Symposium on Caribbean Economic History, University of the West Indies, Jamaica, Nov. 7–8, 1986.

    Franklin Knight, *Slave Society in Cuba during the Nineteenth Century* (Madison, 1970) asserts that slavery was not economical in nineteenth-century Cuba. See p. 183. However, Rebecca J. Scott's *Slave Emancipation in Cuba: The Transition to Free Labor, 1860–1899* (Princeton, 1985) dissents from that view. She has studied the abolition process from a regional perspective within Cuba, and found that in the areas of the great sugar estates, planters strove to keep producing sugar with slaves well after emancipation began. She questions, convincingly, the validity of the "internal contradiction" theory of Cuban abolition.

5. Cuban production increased from 618,654 to 1,110,991 metric tons between 1880 and 1894. See Moreno Fraginals, *El ingenio*, III, 37–38.

6. On a very narrow data base, José Curet has made a pioneering calculation of slave profitability on plantations in Ponce, Puerto Rico between 1845 and 1861. See Curet, "From Slave to *Liberto*: A Study on Slavery and Its Abolition in Puerto Rico, 1840–1880" (Ph.D. diss., Columbia University, 1980), especially ch. 4, "Slave Labor versus Free Labor: A Question of Profitability?" Also see Curet, "About Slavery and the Order of Things: Puerto Rico, 1845–1873" in Moreno Fraginals, et. al., eds., *Between Slavery and Free Labor*, 117–140.

7. Curet, "From Slave to *Liberto*," using a small sample of transactions, calculated Puerto Rican slave prices between 1845 and 1872.

    Cuban slave prices between 1856 and 1863, based on plantation assessments, have been calculated in Engerman, Moreno Fraginals, and Herbert S. Klein, "The Level and Structure of Slave Prices on Cuban Plantations in the Midnineteenth Century: Some Comparative Perspectives," *American Historical Review*, 88:5 (Dec. 1983), 1201–1218. This article, based on market transactions, has arrived at substantially lower calculations.

8. Eltis offers systematic data on prices for newly arrived prime age male *bozales* in Cuba between 1815 and 1864, gleaned largely from British archival sources. See Eltis, *Economic Growth and the Ending of the Transatlantic Slave Trade* (New York, 1987). I should like to thank him for sending me the manuscript of app. 3, "Prices of Slaves in the Atlantic Slave Trade After 1810."

8. Complete ingenio inventories are exceedingly rare in Cuban documentary collections. However, an example is provided by the case of the ingenio Nuestra Señora de la Paz, located in the Cárdenas partido of Guamacaro. In 1867 this property extended for 52 *caballerías* (1 *caballería* = 33.6 acres) and was worked by 198 African slaves assessed at 140,250 pesos ($708/slave), which accounted for 39.4 per cent of the estate's total value. The mill was powered by a 14-horsepower, English-manufactured steam engine, and utilized two Jamaican trains. See "Testamentaria de María Eugenia Álvarez de Marril," Archivo Histórico Provincial de Matanzas (hereafter AHPM), Gobierno Provincial, *Ingenios*, leg. 3, no. 40. While other mills utilized more costly machinery, they also used much larger slave populations.

9. Engerman, Moreno Fraginals, and Klein have pointed out that slave price trends also indicate other aspects of slave-based societies such as planter expectations on the future of slavery. See "The Level and Structure of Slave Prices," 1201, 1218.

10. Only sales from one individual to another were used to calculate prices for this article. *Coartaciones*, or down payments on self-purchase by slaves themselves, were not used, nor were sales of slaves who had been previously *coartados*. These slaves, by law, had their prices fixed at the date of *coartación* and thus cannot be considered as part of current market values.

11. All values were listed in pesos. The 1875 data, however, were listed in "billetes" (paper money) or "oro" (gold). To finance the Spanish military during the Ten Years' War (1868–78), the Banco Español de la Habana began printing paper money in the early 1870s which resulted in rampant inflation by the middle of the decade. For 1875 I have determined that the value of "billetes" was half that of gold, two pesos in "billetes" worth one peso in gold. This was done by separately analyzing transactions in each type of currency. The mean prices for different categories of slaves (males, females, Africans, creoles, age groupings) were compared by type of currency utilized. In almost every grouping, the value rate was two pesos in paper for every one peso in gold. Thus, for the 1875 mean prices, "billetes" have been converted to gold at the 2:1 rate.

12. Unless otherwise noted, data for all slave prices included in the text, tables, and figures have been based on slave sales recorded in the following sources: Archivo Nacional de Cuba (hereafter ANC), Protocolos Notariales (hereafter PN), Matanzas, Joaquín de la Fuente, 1840; ANC, PN, Matanzas, Manuel Morales, 1843; ANC, PN, Matanzas,

Manuel Morales, 1846; ANC, PN, Matanzas, Manuel Morales, 1850; ANC, PN, Matanzas, Manuel Morales, 1854; ANC, PN, Matanzas, Clemente Mihoura, 1857; ANC, PN, Matanzas, Clemente Mihoura, 1860; ANC, PN, Matanzas, Manuel Padrón, 1865; ANC, PN, Matanzas, Manuel del Portillo, 1870; ANC, PN, Matanzas, Manuel del Portillo, 1875; AHPM, PN, Colón, Manuel Vega Lavarría, 1863, 1864, 1867, 1870, 1872, 1875. It should be noted that since specific age data are unavailable for the 1840s, trends can only be indicated by the average price of all slaves by sex and origin.

13. From 1840 to 1846 Cuban sugar production increased 27.5 per cent from 161,248 to 205,608 metric tons. See Moreno *Fraginals, El ingenio*, III, 36. For data on total Cuban slave imports, see Murray, *Odious Commerce*, 111–112, 244. Murray used British Consul David Tolmé's reports of slave landings in Cuba and estimated 70,038 slaves imported between 1834 and 1838 (approximately 14,008 per year). Tolmé estimated that 20 per cent would have to be added to this figure for unknown landings (see p. 111).

The total Cuban slave population was 286,900 in 1827. No reliable subsequent data are available until 1841, when the number of slaves was estimated at 436,500. According to the British consular reports cited by Murray, between 1830 and 1841, 189,497 slaves were imported (66 per cent of the slave population of 1827). Based on these statistics, 43.4 per cent of Cuba's slave population in 1841 was imported between 1830 and 1841. See Murray, *Odious Commerce*, 111–112. Klein, *The Middle Passage: Comparative Studies in the Atlantic Slave Trade* (Princeton, 1978), table 9.8, p. 226, examines imports by known region of origin.

14. Sugar production increased from 205,608 to 397,713 metric tons between 1846 and 1854 (+ 93.4 per cent). See Moreno Fraginals, *El ingenio* III, 36. This expansion was largely due to the founding of new mills and planting of sugar cane in virgin land, which assured high yields. For example, in the province of Matanzas (not officially constituted until 1878) there were 9,150 *caballerías* of land cultivated in 1846, but 15,877 in 1862 (+ 73.5 per cent). See Cuba, Gobernador y Capitán General, *Cuadro estadístico de la siempre fiel isla de Cuba, correspondiente al año de 1846* (Havana, 1847), 41–42; and "Estadística territorial caballerías de tierra" in Cuba, Centro de Estadística, *Noticías estadísticas de la isla de Cuba en 1862*.

15. See Murray, Odious Commerce, 244. These estimates include the British consul's addition of one-third the number of slaves known to have landed, which account for the widespread activities of smugglers. This decline in imports reflects the total saturation of the Cuban slave market because of high imports during the 1830s.

16. Prices peaked later in Colón because almost all slaves in that *jurisdicción* were employed on *ingenios* where demand for slaves continued even after the Moret Law was decreed in 1870. This law initi-

ated the legal abolition process by freeing all slaves reaching 60 years of age and those born after Sept. 1868. In Matanzas, a large portion of the slave population lived in the city or on other types of farms where demand for labour was not as strong. In 1876, for example, 94 per cent of Colón's slaves lived on sugar estates. See "Padrón general de fincas rústicas de este distrito, año de 1875 a 1876," ANC, Gobierno General, leg. 270, no. 13563. In 1862, when similar data are available for Matanzas, 64.1 per cent of all slaves lived on *ingenios*. See "Distribución de la población en los pueblos y fincas de la isla" in Cuba, Centro de Estadística, *Noticias estadísticas de la isla de Cuba en 1862.*

It should be noted that Engerman, Moreno Fraginals, and Klein, "The Level and Structure of Slave Prices," 1207, found that prices for prime age slaves peaked in 1859. My findings for prime age slaves (to be discussed below) confirm this for Matanzas, but in Colón prices for this category peaked in 1870.

17. Murray, *Odious Commerce*, 244. The slave trade peaked in 1859 when British consuls estimated 30,473 African imports. There were 24,895 in 1860 and 23,964 in 1861. These three years constitute the highest levels of Cuban slave imports in the nineteenth century.

18. Eltis found the absence of slave price rises on the African coast. See *Economic Growth and the Ending of the Transatlantic Slave Trade*, app. 3, fig. 1. This is supported by E. Phillip Leveen, "A Quantitative Analysis of the Impact of British Suppression Policies on the Volume of the Nineteenth Century Atlantic Slave Trade" in *Race and Slavery in the Western Hemisphere: Quantitative Studies*, Engerman and Eugene D. Genovese, eds. (Princeton, 1975), 51–81, who found that slave prices in Africa declined between 1820 and 1860. However, Leveen found a considerable rise in shipping and distribution costs involved in the Cuban trade in the 1850s and 1860s (see p. 56). I want to thank Eltis for pointing out the role of increased bribes in raising slaves costs.

19. Murray, *Odious Commerce*, 304–305. Also see Arthur F. Corwin, *Spain and the Abolition of Slavery in Cuba, 1817–1886* (Austin, 1967), 129–151.

20. For sugar prices, see the respective years of *La Aurora de Matanzas*, which was also published under the name *La Aurora or Aurora de Yumurí*. The Biblioteca Gener y Del Monte, in the town of Matanzas, has a complete collection of this valuable provincial newspaper from 1828 through 1895. I would like to thank Mirta Martínez of the library's Fondos Raros y Valiosos for helping me locate and examine these newspapers.

For monthly sugar prices in Havana from 1857 through 1866, see Great Britain, Public Record Office (hereafter PRO), Foreign Office (hereafter FO) 72/1153.

21. Moreno Fraginals, *El ingenio*, III, 36–37.

22. For example, Colón sugar planters experienced a 55.7 per cent increase in income between 1865 and 1876, from 5,396,337 to 8,402,088 pesos. See "Padrón de fincas rústicas de la jurisdicción de Colón,

1865," ANC, Gobierno General, leg. 405, no. 19209 and "Padrón general de fincas rústicas de este distrito, año de 1875 a 1876," ANC, Gobierno General, leg. 270, no. 13563. Data on income for Colón and Cárdenas are summarized in Laird W. Bergad, "Land Tenure, Slave Ownership, and Income Distribution in Nineteenth-Century Cuba: Colón and Cárdenas, 1859–1876" (*Social and Economic Studies*, University of the West Indies).

23. For a statistical summary of Chinese landing in Cuba, see J. Pérez de la Riva, *El barracón y otros ensayos* (Havana, 1975), 469–507. For general treatment of the Chinese in Cuba see Duvon C. Corbitt, *A Study of the Chinese in Cuba, 1847–1947* (Wilmore, KY, 1971) and Denise Helly, *Idéologie et ethnicité: Les chinois Macao à Cuba: 1847-1886* (Montreal, 1979).

My research on the social and economic history of Matanzas province indicates that even in the mid-1870s almost every major sugar plantation depended almost entirely on slave labour. See Bergad, "Land Tenure, Slave Ownership, and Income Distribution in Nineteenth-Century Cuba."

24. The construction of new sugar mills, and accompanying demand for slave labour, continued through the Ten Years War in Matanzas province. For example, in Colón, the largest sugar-producing *jurisdicción* in Cuba, 33 new *ingenios* were constructed between 1865 and 1876, a 45.2 per cent increase in the number of mills. All were based on slave labour in this late period in the history of Cuban slavery. "Padrón de fincas rústicas de la jurisdicción de Colón, 1865" and "Padrón general de fincas rústicas . . . 1875 a 1876,: ANC, Gobierno General, leg. 405, no. 19209 and leg. 270, no. 13563.

25. For data on Cuban slave population increase, see Jack Ericson Eblen, "On the Natural Increase of Slave Populations: The Example of the Cuban Black Population, 1775–1900" in Engerman and Genovese, eds., *Race and Slavery in the Western Hemisphere*, 211–247.

Even on plantations with large African-born slave populations, age-structure differentiations between Africans and creoles were sometimes extreme. For example, in 1854 in the Matanzas *partido* of Sabanilla, the Ingenio San Juan owned 197 creoles and 503 Africans. The mean age of the Africans was 44.0 years while the creoles had a mean age of 15.9 years. See AHPM, Gobierno Provincial, Esclavos, leg. 6, no exp. number.

Although global nineteenth-century Cuban census data do not provide national origins of the slave population, surviving manuscript slave census data include this information. For example in Guanajayabo, a major sugar-producing *partido* of Cárdenas, in 1871 75.5 per cent of the 2,107 slaves registered were creoles. See "Provincia Matanzas, Término mpal. de Guanajayabo. Cuandeno para tomar razón de las certificaciones espedidas por la central sobre derechos de patronato," AHPM, Gobierno Provincial, Provisional, leg. 60, exp. 1731 (this leg. is provisionally catalogued).

26. Another factor was the increased demand for slaves by the sugar sector. There is evidence that high prices and plantation demand induced the transfer of slaves in the late 1860s and early 1870s from non-sugar sector slaveholders to *ingenios*. For example, in Colón 83 per cent of all slaves lived on *ingenios* in 1859, but 94 per cent in 1876. See "Repartos municipales de la jurisdicción de Colón, 1859," ANC, Miscelánca de Expedientes, leg. 4120, no. M. and "Padrón general de fincas rústicas1875 a 1876," ANC, Gobierno General, leg. 270, no. 13563.

27. For example, in 1834, when age data are available in the Matanzas protocol records, of 54 Africans sold 43 (79.6 per cent) were between the ages of 15 and 40; of 28 creoles sold 53.9 per cent fell into this category; and 42.9 per cent were under 15 years of age. See slave sales, ANC, PN, Matanzas, 1834, Joaquín de la Fuente.

28. See "Provincia Matanzas. Término mpal. de Guanajayabo," AHPM, Gobierno Provincial, Provisional, leg. 60, exp. 1731.

29. The only exception to this was in 1864 when 58 per cent of slave sales were in this category. In 1870, 79.7 per cent of marketed slaves were between the ages of 15 and 40.

30. It should be noted that the prices listed for African males and females in Matanzas are based on very few transactions. (see app.). They are presented here, not as authoritative data, but because they are the only data available. Data on the other groups are more reliable since they are based on a larger number of transactions.

The average slave prices presented here are significantly lower than the data presented by Engerman, Moreno Fraginals, and Klein in "The Level and Structure of Slave Prices," 1207. Data in the two articles are comparable for 1863 (for Colón in this article). The average prices for 1863 presented here are 23.6 per cent lower for creole males; 21.3 per cent lower for creole females; 31.1 per cent lower for African males; and 28.3 per cent lower for African females.

Several explanations may account for these discrepancies. The first and most probable is that values presented for slaves in plantation assessments, the source material utilized by Engerman, Moreno Fraginals, and Klein were inflated and did not reflect real market values. Motives for inflating prices were many, including fear of abolition and the quest for possible indemnification. Most slaves were also insured by various slave life insurance companies such as José María Morales's *La Protectora. Compañía general de los seguros mutuos sobre la vida de los esclavos,* founded in 1855. It was in the planters' interest to present high slave values in case of slave death. That slaves were assessed by "independent" assessors is of little importance, since they, as all other Spanish officials, could be handsomely rewarded for presenting "correct" figures. There is also the possibility that what planters considered to be the "value" of slaves was more subjective for many reasons, including self-serving calculations of their own worth. In sum, I feel that the data presented here reflect the real prices of slaves on the Cuban slave market and are more reliable as a measure of slave value than plantation assessments.

It is conceivable that plantation slaves were generally more "seasoned" and thus worth more in the marketplace. Unfortunately, the data used to calculate average prices in this article do not indicate occupation or place of residence. Thus, it is impossible to determine how many were plantation slaves. However since over 90 per cent of all slaves lived on *ingenios* in Colón in the 1860s, it is very likely that Colón's slaves were destined for plantations. In addition, I doubt that the value of "seasoning" in an epoch of strong slave demand could account for over 20 per cent higher values in each category.

31. I have recently completed an article-length manuscript which explores the economics of slave labour, "The Economic Viability of Slave-Labour Based Sugar Production in Cuba, 1859–1876."

32. See, Scott, *Slave Emancipation in Cuba,* 84–110 for a discussion of planter attempts to diversify labour forces. For data on planters' continuing dependence on slave labour, see Bergad, "Land Tenure, Slave Ownership, and Income Distribution."

SECTION NINE

Race, Class, Colour and the Power Order

The dynamics of colour, race and class within Caribbean societies from the earliest years of colonization, have been popular foci of historical research. Racism dictated the emergence of a pro-slavery ideology as Lewis shows, and planters developed a legal framework, enshrined in laws, to control the slave population. Some colonialists inveighed against miscegenation; but wherever blacks laboured as slaves and whites mastered in the Caribbean, and indeed the Americas, a prominent feature of society was the existence of people of mixed racial ancestry, their numbers and rate of growth varying according to situational demographic, ideological and economic factors. Since legal codes for governing the enslaved blacks provided that all juveniles should at birth take the socio-legal status of their mothers, most peoples of mixed racial origins, particularly those born of slave mothers, were at birth designated slaves.

However, partly because some empowered white males could not comfortably enslave for life their own progenitor, and partly because the application of white supremacist ideology required some socio-economic adjustment, a general tendency was for the manumission of some mixed-race people, as well as Blacks. Consequently, as Campbell shows, a group of 'free-coloured' people emerged, and was to be found in most Caribbean societies. In general, they cherished their legal freedom, the most highly valued commodity in slave society, but were rejected by white society on the basis of their colour – the common mark of servitude and inferiority. Living within these two psychological worlds, the free-coloureds developed a unique perspective on society which has been identified as being worthy of special study.

Marginality, however, as Shepherd demonstrates, embraced other social groups. The power order was complex and dynamic. Intense competition for scarce resources and institutional privilege determined that a white male élite, composed mainly of the sugar planters, came to dominate all colonial societies. Small farmers, women, free non-sugar producers and landless whites felt in varying ways the effects of economic alienation and social oppression. In this section, authors examine these processes in a number of specific circumstances. The slave laws as Goveia shows, were designed to assure social stability and the protection of private property, but in effect represented much more. Gender, cultural and racial denomination also underpinned the white supremacy ideology of élite slave holders.

41

Pro-Slavery Ideology

GORDON LEWIS

The Discussion on Indian and Negro

The planter ideology starts, in effect, with the early movement to replace Indian labour with imported African labour. The continuous campaign of the Dominicans and Franciscans in defence of the Indians; the increasing requests from the settlers for Negro slaves; the profit to the Crown to be reaped from the slave trade: all of these factors facilitated the change. Even Oviedo, anti-Indian as he was, could argue that the rapid decimation of the Indians was due to their maltreatment at the hands of Spanish factors and overseers, acting on behalf of powerful court favourites who never visited the islands.[1] The enslavement of the African thus, through a cruel paradox, was justified in terms of the salvation of the Indian; the argument can be seen as the first expression of the general pro-slavery apologetic that African slavery, as an institution, worked for beneficent results. Even Las Casas petitioned the Crown in support of the trade.[2] But it would be historically inaccurate to accept the thesis, advanced by his enemies, that Las Casas was responsible for the change of policy. The thesis rested for a long time on the assumed veracity of Herrera's original accusation, on the basis of which eighteenth century writers as different as Robertson, Raynal, and Corneille de Pau repeated the charge. But the extracts of documents on the Negro trade put together in the great collection of Juan Bautista Muñoz, during the late eighteenth century, and on which Quintana in part based his corrective monograph on Las Casas of 1833, prove conclusively that the trade was already flourishing even before Las Casas suggestion of 1518.[3] Las Casas Sevillian background may have been responsible for his initial acceptance of Negro slavery. But the institution had its roots in collective interests and vague ideas present in the mental climate of the sixteenth century that could have had little to do with the outlook of one man, even although that man was as influential as Las Casas.

The theme of Indian emancipation thus became recruited into the slavery apologetic. The arguments were varied. The new African trade would bring profit to the Crown. Negroes were better than Indians since, as Judge Zuazo of Hispaniola told the regent of Spain in 1518, it was very rarely that a Negro died in the islands.[4] Negro slaves, as the bishop of San Juan advised in 1579, would revive the former prosperity of the Puerto Rican colony, since they could be made to work in the gold mines.[5] Or there was the argument that if the Spanish did not enter the slave trade, it would remain in the hands of the Portuguese, to the detriment of Spanish wealth and security. There was even the curious argument that slaves brought from overseas were much less likely to attempt escape than Indians enslaved locally; yet the argument had little ground in fact, for as early as 1574 the Havana *audiencia* was obliged to reprimand in stern tones those persons who helped runaway slaves – already by that time, obviously, a serious problem.[6] Underpinning all of these arguments there rested the general European ethnocentric tendency to place all non-European peoples in a sort of colour continuum, with those more closely approximating white appearance being regarded as the more pleasing. Not even Las Casas himself was exempt from that prejudice; and in those chapters of the *Historia* in which he denounced the Portuguese slave raids in Africa, he innocently described the various gradations of the captives, "those who were reasonably white, handsome and elegant, others less white, who seemed to be *pardos* (gray or dusky), and others as black as Ethiopians, so malformed in their faces and bodies that they appeared to those who looked at them to be the image of another and lower hemisphere."[7] The prejudice helps to explain why African slavery failed to generate in the Spanish theologians and jurists of the time anything comparable to the great controversy on the Indian question.

The anti-African feeling finally matured, of course, into the pro-slavery ideology. Yet it is worth emphasizing the truth that it was neither an easy nor a rapid victory. The European mind was still dominated by the virtually universal assumption, dictated by both church and scripture, that all mankind stemmed from a single source and therefore enjoyed a common brotherhood. Notwithstanding their religious hatred of each other, the sentiment was voiced by both Spanish Catholic and English Protestant. As early as 1573 Bartolome de Albornoz, in his *Arte de los Contratos*, answered the specious argument that slavery was justified because it saved men from an African paganism with the assertion that it would be better for an African to be king in his own country than a slave in Spanish America; in any case, the argument about the welfare of the slave did not justify, but rather aggravated, the reason for holding him in servitude. "I do not believe," added Albornoz finally, "those persons who will tell me that there is anything in Christ's law to the effect that freedom of the soul must be paid for by slavery of the body."[8] Fray Tomás Mercado described in grim detail the horrors of the Middle Passage in his *Suma de Tratos y Contratos* of 1587; his account makes it clear how the theory of the just war – half-plausible enough when used against Arab, Moor, and Mohammedan – had become dishonestly twisted into an excuse for the forcible capture of innocent African women and children.[9] Finally, Fray Alonso de Sandoval, in

his treatise of 1627, invoked the authority of Plato, Philo Judaeus, and Euripides to deliver an impassioned condemnation of the slavery institution. "For if," he exclaimed, "the civil laws classify exile as a form of civil death, with how much more reason may we call abject slavery death? For it involves not only exile but also subjugation, and hunger, gloom, nakedness, outrage, imprisonment, perpetual persecution, and is, finally, a combination of all evils."[10] English writers echoed similar sentiments. The Reverend Samuel Purchas, who completed Hakluyt's work of compilation, expressed it in his elegantly worded declaration that "the tawney Moore, black Negro, duskie Libyan, ash-coloured Indian, olive-coloured American, should with the whiter European become one sheep-fold, under one great sheep-heard, till this mortalitie being swallowed up of Life, we may all be one ... without any more distinction of Colour, Nation, Language, Sexe, Condition."[11]

Attitudes such as these, undoubtedly, were important. They came, especially in the Spanish case, from priests and officials who were often colonial residents, so that it could not be said of them that they were armchair critics who had never set foot in the islands (a frequent charge of the pro-slavery writers against their opponents). At the same time, they were clearly not much more than ideological survivals of the older medieval teachings. They lasted longer in Spain, where the influence of the priest maintained itself more effectively than in England and Holland. But outside of Spain the new forces of the age – mercantilism, capitalist acquisitiveness, the victory of the commercial bourgeoisie over the landed aristocracy, and the general secularizing tendency – combined to discredit the moralistic viewpoint. Slavery, when discussed at all, was seen in economic and not in religious terms, as is evident enough, in the English case, in the economic writings of men like Locke and Sir Josiah Child. By 1700, possibly even before, slavery had not only become an integral part of the new Atlantic industrial system but had also been accepted by the European mind, at all social levels, as a part of the natural order of things.

There is yet another sense in which the European-Indian confrontation constituted, as it were, a dress rehearsal for the later chattel-slavery regime. It gave a new impetus, in a new environment, to the values of the European master class. Those values, essentially, were two: that Europe possessed a natural right to arbitrary rule over non-European peoples, and that it was the obligation of the new subject-peoples, again by natural law, to work for their new masters. They are evident, from the very beginning, in the literature of the Conquest. After the first enraptured impressions, it is the common complaint of Columbus and his successors that the Indians do not like to work. Even Las Casas was not prepared to give the Indians complete liberty; his reform schemes envisaged that they would be organized in new communities along more rational lines in a regime of humanely controlled communal work. The Indians, it is charged against them, show no real appreciation of the value of gold and silver, which they use only for ornamental purposes (in a similar fashion, it was held against the Aztec and Inca Indians that they hoarded their wealth in palace treasure rooms instead of putting it to productive use). This is clearly the genesis of the later argument of the pro-slavery apologetic that if the slave is not forced to work, he will lie under a tree and live on mangoes and bananas. There is present here, first, the old Christian-medieval conviction that man must work by the sweat of his brow and, second, the new capitalist belief that natural resources must not be allowed to lie idle, but must be rationally exploited for the purpose of accumulating wealth.

The Settler Historians

The general sense of Europe as a superior civilization with a manifest destiny to develop the New World was shared by all the colonizing powers. In the English case, it makes its appearance in the eighteenth century with the writings of the settler-historians and their like such as Atwood in Dominica, Poyer in Barbados, Dallas in Jamaica, and Sir William Young in St Vincent. As early "local" historians, they wrote openly as apologists, mainly addressing British public opinion in defence of the West Indian social order. Their essentially paternalistic and favourable view of the planter society was complemented by their tendency to regard the stability of the slave system as a vital element in the continued viability of the political and social structure of the British colonial empire in the region as a whole. For Atwood, Dominica is an

island healthier than St Lucia and more capable of planned economic improvement than Trinidad. A combination of English immigration and free grants of the unappropriated Crown lands would soon put it ahead, in terms of commercial prosperity, of the old and exhausted sugar islands. In addition, the island's strategic position, situated between the two main French colonies, was inestimable. Atwood, again, writes almost as a tourist agent as he describes, in classic Arcadian style, the beauties of the island, not to mention its importance as a watering spa for invalids; he even manages to claim that lovers of astronomy would find in the island new opportunity to advance their science. The only urgent problem that threatens the island's development is the existence of the runaway-slave settlements. They must be crushed, if only because the cost involved in pacification – which Atwood describes in detail – places a tax burden so onerous on the planters that it threatens to put them out of business. The note of jealous island particularism, so much a part of the planter creed, is clearly struck in Atwood's book: Dominica is healthy virgin territory awaiting the energetic settler, while St Lucia is only the burying place of thousands of brave Englishmen.[12] The insularism was only overcome when planters needed help from other islands to repress a slave revolt, for rebellion in one island encouraged rebellion in another. A sense of regional identity was fragile at best, essentially narrow and selfish in its motives.

The Young book on St Vincent was even more expansionist in its tone. It is the voice of the white settler on the frontier, righteously indignant at the continued existence of an aboriginal group – in this case, the Black Caribs of St Vincent – which by its endemic hostility to the settler presence places the whole white European "civilizing" process in jeopardy. Young obviously felt it necessary to construct some plausible thesis to justify the group's deportation since, unlike the Negro slaves, its members were keepers of an original aboriginal heritage that rested on prior occupancy. He found the thesis in the doctrine of the right by conquest .The English had conquered them, and therefore, they possessed no rights beyond those granted by the Crown; correspondingly, those rights were forfeited by their rebellion and by their partiality for the French. The thesis was completed by the typical method of defamation of character: the Caribs were a barbarous and cruel set of savages beyond reason or persuasion and must therefore be eliminated.[13] It is worth noting, comparing Atwood and Young, how the planter ideology singled out for that defamatory process the group or groups that posed the greatest danger to the planter interest. In Dominica, the real danger came from the runaway slaves, not from the Caribs, who formed no more than twenty or thirty families; in St Vincent, by contrast, the Carib himself was the danger, constituting as he did a strong and militant tribal enclave. So, Atwood saw the Carib, in benign terms, as a "native Indian," while Young saw him as a predominantly Negro person, with all of the Negro's negative traits. So again, Atwood wanted to organize a political union with the Caribs, so that they could become hunters of escaped slaves, following the Jamaica policy; Young saw deportation as the only solution. Both apologists, with an unerring instinct based on the sentiment of English moral paramountcy, identified their main enemy and then proceeded to vilify him, which in turn justified his extinction.

This theme of the white settler battling against a hostile internal enemy reached its fullest expression, however, in the Dallas account of the Jamaican Maroon wars. As an ex-liberal, Dallas felt compelled to embellish his defense of slavery as a civilizing force with pseudo-learned observations. Like a lesser Burke, he saw the root cause of the Maroon revolt in the "mischievous effect" of the Enlightenment philosophy, although he provides no evidence that any Maroon leader had ever even heard about it. He also saw that philosophy as influencing planters to more humane treatment of their slave charges, again without supporting evidence. He even managed to defend the Maroons against the shrill invective of Bryan Edward's portrait of them as a lawless banditti of cruel animals; their marriage customs, he acutely argues, ought not to be judged by alien European standards, and far from being animals they possessed most, if not all, of the senses in a superior degree.[14] He even gives the benefit of the doubt to the Maroons concerning the original cause of the war in his admission of the Maroon argument that they had been forced into hostilities out of self-preservation, being persuaded that the whites planned

their destruction. He goes yet further, and admits that the technical violation of the treaty on the part of the whites – against which only General Walpole, to his credit, earnestly protested – and which was made the pretext by the local Assembly for their deportation, was probably due to the Maroons' suspicions of bad faith on the part of the colonial authorities.[15] Despite making all these concessions, Dallas arrived at substantially the same conclusions as the more reactionary Edwards. The Maroons had committed "horrid atrocities." They had rebelled against the legitimate authority of the Jamaica Assembly. Enslavement, after all, was not only God's will but also necessary in the light of the fact that the Negro "character" could never itself operate the sugar economy without the guidance of the whites.[16]

Three leading themes, characteristic of the planter outlook, infuse these writings of the settler-historians. First, there is the theme of the absolute monopoly of the slave-worked plantation system. It cannot tolerate any alternative system, nor indeed coexist with any alternative system. It must, therefore, crush any attempt at creating such an alternative, such as the elementary Maroon food-crop economy or the Carib self-sufficient economy; or such alternatives as with the Carib regime, must at least be safely isolated by a policy of controlled reservations. Nor, of course, could any such alternative be allowed to become the economic basis for organized resistance to the plantation regime. "A cordial reconciliation between them [the Maroons] and the white people," Dallas concluded, "was hardly to be expected."[17] The white settler has taken that intransigent view of native peoples who stand in his way everywhere, and the treatment of the Maroons and Caribs in the West Indies anticipated the later treatment of the Maori tribes in Australasia and of the Plains Indians in the American West – with the same perfidious record of military repression, governmental treachery, broken treaties, and forced evacuation from lands coveted by the whites.

Second, there is the theme of the "divide and rule" strategy, devised to prevent the emergence of a united front against the whites, pitting one set of native interests against another. Dallas saw that clearly. "Had the Maroons," he wrote, "shown that their rebellion was not a temporary struggle but a permanent and successful opposition to the government, it is highly probable that the example might in time have united all the turbulent spirits among the slaves in a similar experiment; if not in the same interest; or indeed such a decided triumph might have tempted numbers of the plantation negroes, unwilling before to change a state of peace for warfare, to join the Maroons. At all events, they would have been a rallying point for every discontented slave, and for all who dreading punishment were incited by their fears to escape." Such an event, he adds, would have meant total economic ruin for the island.[18] The danger was avoided by the policy of tolerating the Maroons so long as they faithfully served as hunters of runaway slaves and, indeed, of making that role a condition of their final surrender. Had there been such a body at Santo Domingo, General Walpole wrote to Lord Balcarres at the end of the war, the brigands would never have risen. The remark sums up a whole policy.

Third, there is the theme of Negro incapacity for freedom. For Atwood, there was, he wrote, "something so very unaccountable in the genius of all negroes, so very different from that of white people in general, that there is not to be produced an instance in the West Indies, of any of them ever arriving to any degree of perfection in the liberal arts or sciences, notwithstanding the greatest pains taken with them"; although, illogically, he conceded, as against that theme of natural inferiority, that second-generation Negroes, under the proper social influence, were capable of losing some of their "stupidity," thus allowing, inferentially, that their state was related to environment and not to inherent deficiency. For Dallas, as he put it in turn, "the notion of a free, active, negro republic, does not seem to have any reasonable foundation."[19] Such a republic, if it came to pass, would simply reveal a people without direction, union, or energy; he seems not to have realized that his own description of the Maroon social organization and fighting strategy belied the accusation. It was left to Edwards, in that section of his book that was originally written as an introduction to the published proceedings of the Jamaica Assembly on the Maroon affair, to develop the theme into an argument against slavery abolition. The "calm and unprejudiced reader," he wrote hopefully, will agree with him that the "wild and lawless freedom" of the Maroons proves that abolition would be nothing more than a state of things without control or restraint, neither benefiting society at large nor promoting the happiness of the slaves themselves.[20] The particular circumstance of a beleaguered racial minority engaged in a death struggle with a more complex and ruthless exploiting civilization was thus arbitrarily identified with the general circumstance of Negro freedom understood in its larger context.

These settler-historians, notably Atwood, Young, and Dallas, may properly be seen, as it were, as the Robinson Crusoe apologists of the slave regime; that is to say, they were all concerned with a crucial period when the colonial society was threatened, in Robinson Crusoe fashion, by a hostile force – runaway slaves in Dominica, Caribs in St. Vincent, the Maroons in Jamaica. The analogy is an apt one. For far from being the epic of primitive life, an idyll of tropical island life away from it all, that it has been popularly supposed to be. Defoe's famous book is better seen as a celebration of the heroic exploits of the *homo faber europeanus* in the New World, utilizing his European technology, in the form of goods and tools salvaged from his wrecked ship, to cultivate his island, once he had at hand a subordinate labour supply in the person of Man Friday; undertaking, that is to say, an economy of primitive capital accumulation. Along with that there went a sort of neo-revolutionary view in which the bands of *mauvais sauvages* (evil savages), the rescued native Friday, and Crusoe himself embodied perceived different stages, from lower to higher, in the growth of "civilization." Only the tropical setting of the story, facilely invoking the European dream of the idyllic island paradise, made it seem to the European reader to be something else, so that it was ironic that the book should have been seen by Rousseau's Emile as a picture of the ideal state of nature. It is closer to the truth to say that in its portraiture of Crusoe, incessantly working each day to build up his little empire against the threat of dark and unknown enemies, the book describes the European settler struggling to maintain his supremacy in the colonial world, just like the white groups of settler-historians. Nor was it incidental that Defoe should have made the foundation of Crusoe's success his earlier venture as a slave owner in Brazil, for it was from Brazil that many of the early Caribbean planters emigrated in order to establish the slave-based sugar economy in the islands.

The pro-slavery ideology reached its zenith in the period between the mid-eighteenth century and the latter part of the nineteenth century, when the slave economy entered into its golden age. It was centred primarily in the English Jamaica, French Saint Domingue, and Spanish Cuba, with a distinct and recognizable literature of books and pamphlets written by various schools of historians and publicists that developed in those three leading societies: the Jamaican planter historians; the publicists, both white colonist and "free coloureds," of Saint Domingue; the Cuban Creole writers and political leaders. To these sources must be added others, of course: colonial assembly debates, metropolitan state papers, the correspondence of governors, the vast literature of travellers' reports, not least of all the growing local press – all of which enable the student to catch glimpses of the self-image of the plantocracy and the images that class entertained of the other actors in the dramatis personae of the colonial scene. For the essence of ideology is perceived self-image, how any societal group sees its function within the general matrix of the social structure, how it sees other groups, and what particular arguments it produces as a means of self-justification.

Particular Considerations

Concerning the pro-slavery ideology, certain particular considerations present themselves to the reader of the vast literature. In the first place, it is a defensive literature. Historically, every ruling class had been mainly concerned with power and the uses of power and has only attempted some sort of philosophic rationalization of its position when challenged by hostile forces. The Caribbean plantocracy was no exception. Its English echelon was responding to the abolitionist campaign mounted after the 1770s its French echelon was reacting to the attack of the philosophies of the Enlightenment, given practical impetus by the assault of its position unleashed by the revolution of 1789; while its Cuban echelon, after the abolition of the slave trade in 1807, had to meet the hostile public opinion of nineteenth-century liberal Europe. It is enough to glance through the exhaustive compilation of the literature spawned by the English abolitionist campaign put together by the historian Lowell Joseph Ragatz – *A Guide for the Study of British Caribbean History, 1763-1834, Including the Abolition and Emancipation Movements* – to realize how the majority of pro-West Indian titles were improvised answers to the abolitionist writers.[21]

Second, it is noteworthy that, almost in the nature of things, the defensive literature was usually written not by planters themselves but by publicists who, sympathetic to the planter cause, were marginally placed in relationship to the slave institution. Although they were planters themselves, both of the Jamaican planter-historians, Long and Edwards, were educated Englishmen who had become creolized; men like Moreau de Saint-Méry in Saint Domingue were moderates distrusted by the *colon;* and the most ardent defender of Cuban slavery, for a while, was José Antonio Saco, not so much a planter as a leading member of the Cuban Creole intelligentsia. It is not surprising then that the pro-slavery movement in the Caribbean did not produce a Calhoun – who, in the North American case, fashioned a formidable and persuasive case for the Southern cause that was at once a brilliant defence of the plantation economy, an astute critique of the economic principle of the rival Northern industrial capitalist organization, and a presentation of the slave South as a civilization nobler and of finer texture than the coarse materialism of the North. Those particular arguments were also present in the Caribbean literature, of course, but they were never presented with the learning of a Calhoun. And that, probably, is due to the fact that the Caribbean plantocracy constituted the most crudely philistine of all dominant classes in the history of Western slavery. Even Labat, worldly realist that he was, lamented that everything had been imported into the Indies except books. One whole minor theme of Caribbean literature – Luffman's account of the Antigua planter class; Schomburgk's description of Guianese planter society with its ceremonial stiffness and affection; or the description of a decadent Cuban creole society penned by nineteenth century visitors such as Atkins, Turnbull, Hazard, and others[22] – is almost unanimous in its general portrait of a planter way of life that is at once crassly materialist and spiritually empty. Anything even remotely approaching the intellectual was unlikely to make its own appearance in such a milieu. Mental excitement, indeed, was provided by the outsider; reading Labat's diary or Lady Nugent's journal, for example, one is struck by the fact that in both cases intelligent conversation was provided by the resident and visiting-officer class present in the islands as a consequence of a wartime situation – the War of the Spanish Succession in Labat's case, the Napoleonic Wars in Lady Nugent's case. *Le luxe est grand dans les Isles* (Luxury is rampant in the islands), wrote Du Tertre early on. As much as anything else, the remark explains the intellectual paucity of the planter mind. It explains, equally, why the planter ideology cannot be seen in any way as constituting a serious philosophical system. It was, rather, little more than a series of rationalized prejudices and unexamined assumptions, trying to justify the vested interest of the dominant Caribbean groups.

Edward Long and Bryan Edwards

The Jamaican contribution to the ideology is essentially that of Edward Long and Bryan Edwards in their respective histories, although there were lesser histories like those of Renny and Leslie and Browne. Long – to begin with – is concerned to argue the legitimacy of slavery against its critics. He argues the case within the framework of two general principles. In the first place, he posits an eternal struggle for power between warring factions in society. He declares:

History evinces that, in all ages, there has been one set of persons uniting its efforts to enslave mankind; and another set, to oppose such attempts, and vindicate the cause of freedom. The accidental circumstances of men may, perhaps, occasion this difference: the rich are the natural enemies of the poor; and the poor, of the rich; like the ingredients of a boiling cauldron, they seem to be in perpetual warfare, and struggle which shall be uppermost; yet, if both parties compose themselves, the *faeces* would remain peaceably at the bottom; and all the other particles range themselves in different strata, according to their quality, the most refined floating always at top.[23]

Second, writing as a colonial Whig on the eve of the revolt of the North American colonies, Long advances the Whig concept of liberty. Much of his book, indeed, is an impassioned denunciation of the Crown for its abrogations of "British freedom" in its treatment of the colonies. There is, he argues, in the best Lockean

manner, a contractual obligation that links government and citizen: "All societies of men, wherever constituted, can subsist together only by certain obligations and restrictions, to which all the individual members must necessarily yield obedience for the general good; or they can have no just claim to those rights, and that protection, which are held by all, under this common sanction."[24]

Long, hardheaded realist that he is, perceives, and admits readily, that slavery, on the face of it, cannot easily be reconciled with those principles. The first principle must meet the fact that, in colonial societies based on slavery, the war of rich and poor is made worse by the fact that the rich are white and the poor are black. The second principle is likewise embarrassing, for it is used by the enemies of the West Indian planters to point out the hypocrisy of claming liberty for themselves while denying it to their slaves; indeed, Long himself admits at one point that slavery is repugnant to the spirit of the English laws. To make the difficulty even more pressing, Long also notes, (with typical candour) how the spirit of liberty infects the slave population itself. The contagion of faction spreads; even our very Negroes, he laments, turn politicians.[25] That Long, indeed, was fully aware of the basic contradiction between the general principles that he espoused and the social order he sought to defend is evident from his citation of Montesquieu's argument that a large slave population is always dangerous in a moderate state, since the political liberty of the rulers only serves to accumulate in the slaves the keener awareness of their own lack of civil liberty, and the slaves, much more than in despotic states, consequently become the natural enemies of the society.

Faced with this fundamental problem – the tension between his English liberalism and his attachment to the moral validity of slavery – Long retreats into a farrago of inherited prejudices. He begins with a highly selective and prejudiced account of the African background of "Negro-land," drawn from the more negative sections of travellers' reports like those of Bosman, Snelgrove, Goguet, Le Maire, and others. It is a picture of unrelieved barbarity: all of these peoples – following, Long claims, a similar portrait painted by the ancient Greek and Roman authors – possess, "in abstract, every species of inherent turpitude that is to be found dispersed

at large among the rest of the human creation."
It follows, logically, that the slave trade must be
seen, not through the perspective of British concepts of freedom, but though the perspective of
African realities: the slave is transported from a
condition of pure slavery in Africa into a condition of relative slavery in the Americas, where
his servitude is tempered with lenity. Even the
objection of the critics that many die in transportation to the colonies cannot be accepted, since
the objection "does not bear against the trade
itself, but against some defect or impropriety in
the mode of conducting it."[26] Once settled in his
new home, the slave enters into a "limited freedom" supervised by the white master who is his
friend and father. "His authority," writes Long
of the typical gentleman-proprietor it is his ultimate purpose to vindicate, "over them is like that
of an ancient patriarch: conciliating affection by
the mildness of its exertion, and claiming respect
by the justice and propriety of its decisions and
discipline, it attracts the love of the honest and
good; while it awes the worthless into reformation."[27] That authority receives further legitimacy from the general character of the slave
population. the creole slaves are in general, iras-
cible, conceited, proud, indolent, lascivious,
credulous, and artful; although the author is willing to admit that as far as the habit of drunkenness is concerned they are superior to the order
of the lower-class white servants.[28] The "Guiney
slaves," or newly imported Africans, are, if possible, even worse, which leads Long to conclude
that any missionary effort among them is
doomed to failure, since their "barbarous stupidity" and ignorance of the English language make
them hopelessly intractable. Of these, the Coro-
mantins, being warlike, are the worst, and the
source of all slave conspiracies – so much so that
the Jamaica planters should follow the example
of the French islands and prohibit their further
importation.[29]

If there is any scientific foundation for all this,
Long claims to find it in a pre-Darwinite fixity-
of-species theory, thus applying the popular "design of nature" argument to the problem, as he
saw it, of the species of mankind. Within that
scheme there are "gradations of the intellectual
faculty," from the monkey at the bottom through
the ape and the Negro man, on to pure white
homo sapiens at the top: "Let us then not doubt,
but that every member of the creation is wisely

fitted and adapted to the certain uses, and confined within the certain bounds, to which it was
ordained by the Divine Fabricator. The measure
of the several orders and varieties of these Blacks
may be as complete as that of any other race of
mortals; filling up that space, or degree, beyond
which they are not destined to pass; and discriminating them from the rest of men, not in kind, but
in species."[30]

That position leads the author into some fairly
severe strictures on the general plantation system, which, all in all, he has supported as the
necessary order of things. Obsessed with racial
purity, he inveighs bitterly against white miscegenative habits. White and black, he avers, are
two tinctures that nature has dissociated, like oil
and vinegar. Their unnatural mixture has produced in Spanish America, a "vicious, brutal,
and degenerate breed of mongrels." The solution, Long insists, is to strengthen the institution
of marriage, in order to counteract illicit connections. That, in turn, requires incentives, among
which should be the better education of the Creole white woman so as to render her a more
agreeable wife. Even more than that, the law
governing transmission of property should be
revised, going back to the old feudal doctrine of
non-alienation, in order to discourage the prevalent habit of white fathers willing their property
to their coloured children. The right to make
wills and dispose of property is the creature of
the civil law, and in slave societies it should be
even more rigorously limited than in societies,
like England, where "rational freedom" prevails. Nothing could illustrate better than this
particular argument, in its proposal to circum-
scribe the right of private property, how far the
racial apprehensions of the West Indian plantocracy could persuade them to subordinate economic to non-economic considerations. The
same consideration leads Long to advocate a
policy of enfranchisement for all mulatto children, even at public cost; such a policy, he argues, will create a new class of trained
lower-class artisans, who will become "orderly
subjects, and faithful defenders of the country."[31]

All in all, Long is trapped in the inconsistencies between his eighteenth-century secular moralism and his pro-slavery stance. He claims that
in charity, philanthropy, and clemency the Jamaican Creole gentlemen match at any time their

English peers; yet he is appalled, as much as any missionary, by their reckless fornication. In that sense, he is the Puritan in Babylon. "To cast general reflections on any body of men," he writes in the best Burkean tradition, "is certainly illiberal"; he properly adheres to that principle in his discussion of the Jews and the Moravians in Jamaican society but throws it overboard in his discussion of the blacks. In his discussion, again, of the French *Code Noir* of 1685 – which he reprints as an appendix – he can fully see the difference between the literary theory of slave-protective legislation and the actual reality of slave life: "It is not enough to make laws," he wisely observes, "it is also necessary to provide for their execution." Yet he seems incapable of applying the same pragmatic test to the slave laws of his own English islands. There is, finally, the glaring discrepancy between Long's view of the colonial-metropolitan relationship and his view, quite different, of the master-slave relationship. He perceives clearly the absence of any mutually beneficial contractual principle in the former, and unequivocally denounces it; yet he cannot see the absence of the same principle in the internal master-slave relationship. What, at best he does is to attempt an unconvincing argument promulgating the curious thesis that, from the original point of purchase in Africa, there exists, so to speak, a "sort of compact" that buyer, seller, and bought slave all implicitly accept; and, once in the final point of destination in the islands, the compact is renewed between slave and master, in which a "reciprocal obligation" connects them, producing "protection and maintenance on the one hand, fidelity and service on the other." This, Long admits, is not a "voluntary banishment" on the part of the African. It is, however, he insists, an unwritten agreement, based on custom, to which all parties are tied.[32] The argument, ingenious enough, omits to note that the fulfillment of the compact depends exclusively on the will of the master. Long is capable of appreciating the weakness of such an arrangement when he discusses the British-West Indian system of colonial government. "We are not to expect," he opines, "that men, invested with power at discretion, will forbear, from an innate principle of goodness, to make an ill use of it, while they can abuse it with impunity and profit."[33] Yet the Jamaican social order that he describes, more or less approvingly, is made to rest upon the accidental possession of that very same "principle of goodness" on the part of the master class.

The final problem with which Long felt obliged to deal was that of the theme, so central to the discussion of slavery, of black capability. It was a problem that also preoccupied Jefferson at the same time. It is easy to see why. For once admit that the black, given access to education, could match the white, it would have been necessary to make a damaging exception to the racist assumption of a natural inequality of mental powers. So, Long felt it necessary to write a separate chapter, full of amused contempt, on the figure of Francis Williams, the Jamaican who was put through a course of English education by the Duke of Montagu in order to prove the intellectual capacities of the coloured person. The best that Long can bring himself to say is that the Latinate compositions of Williams are no better than what might have been expected from a middling scholar at the seminaries of Eton or Winchester; the worst is to quote Hume's comment that a black scholar, thus educated, could become nothing more than a parrot who speaks a few words plainly. Long can even manage, unfairly, to laugh at Williams because of his habit of composing laudatory odes to successive Jamaican governors, despite the fact that the fulsome dedicatory preface to the aristocratic patron was the common practice of the eighteenth-century world of letters. He thus failed to see – as did Dr. Johnson in the case of the woman preacher – that the surprising thing about the black writer like Williams was not that the thing was well done but that it was done at all. The failure, no doubt, had its own psychological roots. For Long, no more than Jefferson, could not have endured, even temporarily, the continued existence of slavery had he thought that he was thereby maintaining in subjugation hundreds of mute, inglorious Miltons. In order to avoid that intolerable thought, it was necessary for him to rationalize the conviction that the Negro was by nature incapable of reasoning or of higher imagination.[34]

Edwards, by contrast with Long– whose help and friendship he acknowledged – is generally regarded as the "moderate" voice of the West Indian plantocracy. Humane and intelligent, he never lost his capacity to look at the slavery institution with some objectivity, despite the fact that he wrote at the time of the French Revolution and the Saint Domingue upheaval. He was that rare species, the educated planter – more at home, perhaps, in the study than on the plantation. Despite the fact, then, that his work was, in the final analysis, a reasoned defence of slavery, he was himself infected with the humanitarian temper of the age. He sought to reconcile the two outlooks and inevitably involved himself in irreconcilable contradictions. It was, of course, an impossible task. It was made even more impossible by the pressure of events; so that whereas in his earlier work on the British West Indies he managed to maintain the "moderate" pose, in his later work on Saint Domingue he reflected the mood of panic that engulfed the propertied class and delayed abolition for a whole generation.

Edwards begins by establishing his humanitarian credentials. He is, he claims, no friend of slavery, for so degrading is its nature that "fortitude of mind is lost as free agency is restricted"; "cowardice and dissimulation," he adds, "have been the properties of slavery in all ages and will continue to be so, to the end of the world." He can even perceive that behaviour patterns within the slavery institution may be shaped by culturally conditioning factors rather than being the expression of an assumed human nature, so, while he dismisses the popular theory about the impact of climate, he can observe that "it is no easy matter. . . to discriminate those circumstances which are the result of proximate causes, from those which are the effects of national customs and early habits in savage life."[35] He can even perceive, further, the interconnection of economic factors and group behaviour; the notorious profligacy of the planter class, he notes perceptively, is traceable to the fact that (as he puts it) the West Indian property is a species of lottery, arising out of the fact that the island planter, unlike an English landed proprietor, cannot sublet to tenants and is obliged to become a practical farmer in an occupation full of uncertainty.

Yet, once having made these concessions, so damaging to the unconditional racism of Long, he proceeds to rob them of meaning by reverting, in the last resort, to moral absolutes unrelated to empirical reasoning. There is either the Hobbist argument that power makes right: "In countries where slavery is established, the leading principle on which the government is supported is fear;

or a sense of that absolute coercive necessity, which leaving no choice of action, supersedes all questions of right." Or there is the Burkean argument of relapse into religious obscurantism: "Yet that the slavery of some part of the human species, in a very abject degree, has existed in all ages of the world, among the most civilized, as well as the most barbarous nations, no man who has consulted the records of history disputes. Perhaps like pain, poverty, sickness, and sorrow and all the various other calamities of our condition, it may have been originally interwoven into the constitution of the world for purposes inscrutable to man."[36]

Having thus bypassed the dilemma posed by the simultaneous entertainment of the argument of nature and the argument of environment, Edwards passes on to a defence, point by point, of the slave-based social order. Admitting the many abuses connected with the slave trade, he invokes the popular argument that the slave is rescued from a barbarous Africa, although the evidence that he invokes – his own cross-examination of slaves concerning their original status in their homelands – is hardly credible when his earlier statements concerning the habitual mendacity of slaves are recalled. His account, in turn, of the slavers is hardly more convincing than the highly coloured account of African society:[37] he makes the Middle Passage sound almost like a pleasant sea cruise. In any case, he adds, recent parliamentary legislation regulates the trade and makes it more humane; he neglects to note that that piece of legislation, like all ameliorative legislation, was vigorously opposed by the planter lobby. Even admitting, he goes on, that some slaves are originally free men, and not just war captives or domestic slaves, he insists that the West Indian planter, as the buyer, is completely innocent of the manner in which the trade is conducted, although we know from Labat's account that a century earlier the full details were already common knowledge in the islands. The trade, he concludes, should not be abolished but, at best, ameliorated.[38] Its sudden unilateral abolition by the British would merely benefit the other European powers involved in the traffic, and in any case an effective maritime blockade of the traffic, once it had been declared illegal, would be practically impossible. Any such attempt would be like chaining the winds or giving laws to the ocean.

Edwards' subsequent discussion of the life on the West Indian plantation betrays a similar effort, almost desperate at times, to see things in terms of rosy optimism, playing down the dark side and exaggerating the bright aspects. The much-aligned West Indian planter, he insists, is a generous, proud, frank, hospitable person, possessed of a high degree of compassion and kindness towards his inferiors and dependents. He rules, it is true, a "miserable people. . . condemned to perpetual exile and servitude." But he rules them with paternal kindness. His interest concurs with his humanity, and a well-regulated plantation, as Edwards describes it, is a model of mild labour, decent housing, and adequate medical care. If there are abuses of this "plenitude of power" – and Edwards is sufficiently honest not to deny the charge – they are, he argues, the exception and not the rule. The difference between my view and that of the abolitionist critics, he writes, is that they claim that cruelty is the general rule, while I insist that it is only occasional; and he quotes Ramsay's remark that adventurers from Europe are universally more cruel towards the slave than are the Creoles or the native West Indians. The humane spirit of the age, he argues, notwithstanding the critics, is also present in the islands, and is felt where the law is a dead letter. Yet he admits at the same time that, granted the absolute discretion of the slave owner, the sense of decorum alone "affords but a feeble restraint against the corrupt passions and infirmities of our nature, the hardness of avarice, the pride of power, the sallies of anger, and the thirst of revenge."[39] Thus, in the last resort, he falls back on the argument, so typical of the eighteenth century, that however unjust a social order may be, the leading ills of mankind are traceable to a human nature that law cannot alter. His is, altogether, a generous moral nature unable to see the full evil of a way of life of which – so typical of West Indian estate ownership – he had become a member only by an accident of family relationship.

The histories of Long and Edwards were, of course, only two items in the voluminous war of words – one of the first of the modern wars of literary propaganda – that took place between the friends and the opponents of the West Indian slavocracy cause in the fifty years before Emancipation in the 1830s. It addressed itself, both in England and France, to the rise to power of the bourgeois public opinion of the age. The verdict of history has decided in favour of the abolitionist argument, sustaining Wilberforce's remark – which anticipated Lincoln's more famous dictum – that to unite slavery and freedom in one condition is impracticable. The English abolitionist groups tended to emphasize the principle of Christian liberty; the French groups, the principle of the rights of man. There was, of course, wild exaggeration on the part of both general protagonists in this great debate for and against slavery; for if the one side was tempted to portray the West Indian scene as a heaven of happy feudal relationships, the other was tempted to expose it as a veritable hell in which every plantation owner was a Simon Legree. The lines of division of course, were much more complicated than that, for there were pro-slavery advocates, like Edwards himself, who could admit to the defects of the slavery regime, just as the abolitionist leaders could decide, illogically, to make a distinction between the slave trade and slavery itself for the purposes of parliamentary strategy. Even so, the long debate provides valuable material for understanding the basic principles on which both arguments were based.

The West Indian Planter Response

The essentials of the planter outlook can be garnered from the colonial responses, reluctant and indeed recalcitrant, to the various stages of the increasingly critical metropolitan debate – the parliamentary debates on Wilberforce's various motions leading to the 1807 abolition of the trade. Wilberforce's Slave Registry Bill of 1815, Canning's Resolutions of 1823, and the final emancipatiory act of 1833. Eric Williams has extracted the leading contributions of the parliamentary debates for his volume *The British West Indies at Westminster*.[40] But what more particularly concerns our enquiry is the character of the planter outlook as it appears in the titles published during the period of those of its advocates who – sometimes as planters themselves, sometimes as clergymen, sometimes as visitors – had resided in the islands and had absorbed, through the famous West Indian hospitality, the planter ideology. Very little of that literature was written by Creole planters themselves, for as one of their partisans – John Stewart in his 1823 volume *A View of the Past and Present State of the Island of Jamaica* – himself confessed, the arbitrary character of slavery was inimical to the improvement of mind and manners: "Intellectual pleasures," he wrote, "are not so much suited to the taste of the inhabitants as something that will create a bustle, and bring a crowd of well-dressed persons in pursuit of amusements of a more tangible nature – such, for instance, as the parish races, where, in one week, there is as much money spent as would establish a superb public library."[41] It was a very rare West Indian-born planter who could write anything at all. It was even more rare for him to write an intelligent autobiography such as the anonymous *Memoirs of a West Indian Planter* edited by the Reverend John Riland in 1827; and even then the many improbable scenes described in that book, including the conversation of a planter to Christian retribution, cast some doubt on its authenticity.[42]

The pro-West Indian literature runs the entire gamut of planter pride and prejudice. There is the hackneyed theme of "barbarous" Africa, although it became an increasingly implausible argument as early nineteenth century African exploration revealed a more realistic picture of the African state systems. The slave trade, it is claimed, was a nursery of English seamanship – had not Nelson learned his apprenticeship in the West Indies? – so that if the battle of Waterloo was won on the playing fields of Eton it was equally true that the battle of Trafalgar had been won in the naval stations of the West Indies. There are the usual citations from Scripture – the laws of Leviticus or Saint Peter's letter to the slave owner Philemon – to justify slavery, although they became less frequent as the spirit of the age became more secular. There is the argument that the critics, in their detailed accounts of cruelty, are speaking of the island society as it was, say, twenty years ago; things are now much improved. It is instructive, with respect to that argument, to read the apologetic report of 1824 of a committee of the Barbados Council that proves, to its own satisfaction, that the slaves are "cheerful, happy, and contented," and cites as its "impartial" witnesses plantation owners and high-ranking officers of the local military establishment. There is the argument, again, that West Indian planters have to face problems unknown to English landlords; the garrulous Beckford, in his 1790 *Descriptive Account of the Island of Jamaica*, even managed to recruit his graphic

description of the hurricane of 1780 into the service of the argument.[43] The planter, it is added, must deal with a labour force that is lazy, mendacious, contumacious, unreliable, and full of thievery; yet almost in the same breath, the author who makes those charges will regale his reader with sentimental stories of the slaves' childlike loyalty to their masters in times of distress, in order to disprove the abolitionist charge that they are unhappy and discontented wretches. That contradiction is even more pronounced in a more fundamental sense. For if, on the one hand, the pro-planter literature portrays the West Indian society as almost idyllic – aptly illustrated in the hand-coloured engravings of the artist James Hakewill in his 1825 book *A Picturesque Tour of the Island of Jamaica*, where classically composed tropical landscapes present, Watteau-like, pleasing prospects of plantation life[44] – on the other hand, it warns the would-be reformer that he is playing with fire, since slave discontent at any moment can explode into another Haitian *servile bellum* (servile war). The contradiction is even more painfully clear in the contrast between the optimistic account of amelioration by Edwards and the awful *Jamaican Slave Code*, which he printed as illustrative proof of his case.[45] To the modern reader there is an almost unbearable, indeed a tragic, tension between the need of the literature to show the slave as almost an animal in human form – for to admit his humanity would be to strike a mortal blow at the very basic principle of the system – and its need to defend the slave against the embrace of what the planters called the English "pseudo-philanthropists."

The leading argument in all this, however, was that based on the doctrine of legislative amelioration. The argument was persuasive, and was enthusiastically advanced by all of the writers who, although sometimes with serious reservations, could be regarded as defenders of the slave system, with knowledge based on their own experience in the islands: Edwards himself, Stewart, Collins, Williamson, Jordon, Barham, Barclay, and others. A gradual amelioration, it is argued, would be better than a precipitate abolition. In proportion, wrote Barclay, as moral improvement, religion, and habits of industry civilize the slave, "the arbitrary power of the master will become unnecessary, and slavery will gradually assimilate to the servitude of

Europe." To the degree that we extract all its ingredients from the condition of slavery, added Barham, the "whole mass of slaves shall at once glide, as it were, into freedom."[46] The means to that end was to be colonial legislative enactment, for the doctrine of amelioration went hand in hand with the doctrine of local colonial jurisdiction – might be viewed, indeed, as a particular tactic under cover of which the larger doctrine could be advanced. It received a definite expression in Jordan's 1816 *Examination of the Principles of the Slave Registry Bill,* composed in his capacity as Colonial Agent for Barbados. Barbados, he reminds his readers, flew the royal flag in the seventeenth century, when democracy and puritanism triumphed over the monarchy in England itself. But that does not give the Westminster Parliament the right to unilaterally legislate for the colonies. Extension of parliamentary power can only be effected by extension of parliamentary representation. Of such, there are two kinds: extended representation united and inclusive, as in the cases of Ireland and Wales, and representation separate and exclusive, which is the case of the West Indian colonies. The concept of sovereignty, as stated in Blackstone, belongs to metaphysical jurisprudence; what we appeal to is English statutory law, which, since Henry I, has always recognized the exclusive power of localities where, as in the West Indies, there exist duly established local parliaments based on the common rights of all English subjects. British commercial regulation excepted, then, London cannot legislate for Barbados in matters that concern the liberty and property of Barbadians.[47]

The argument notwithstanding, however, the amelioration doctrine, was an empty one. Never seriously implemented by the colonial assemblies, as Goveia and Williams have shown, it was merely a desperate effort to save time; emancipation was accepted, but always at some safe, distant future date, never at the present moment.[48] It emphasized the need to improve the slave, through education and religion, in order to fit him for freedom; but at the same time it was openly hostile to the only force, that of the island sectarian missionaries, who took that task seriously, and the author of the 1824 Barbados committee report frankly conceded Wilberforce's charges on that matter.[49] Humane observers like Edwards could learn from events, and it is impossible to read the final paragraphs of his account of Santo Domingo, with its anguished appeal to the resident plantocracy to rise above "the foggy atmosphere of local prejudices" and accept the cessation of the trade before its intransigence leads it to the terrible fate of the French colony (which is the handwriting on the wall)[50] and then to compare it with the adamant refusal of the same plantocracy to listen to the warning without a realization of the completely Bourbonese, purblind, and reactionary character of the planter establishment. Even its friends recognized that aspect of it: "It would have reflected more honour upon those who live so much in the community of slaves," lamented Beckford, "if those alterations had been the spontaneous effects of their humanity, and had not originated in, and been enforced by the persevering compassion of England."[51] Every piece of circumstantial evidence (the Parliamentary returns, the reports of island correspondents, the dispatches of island governors, the reports of the Berbice Fiscal, or adjudicator) shows conclusively that every suggested reform of the ameliorative literature – the right of the slave to testify in court proceedings, the right to a free Sabbath, the elimination of the use of the cart whip – was frustrated by the fact that the administrative machinery of slave society was monopolized by the very class that stood to lose by their implementation. To use Burke's phrase in his letter of 1792 to Dundas, all of the ameliorative measures passed by the various colonial assemblies were good for nothing because, as Burke put it, they were totally destitute of an executory principle. It was, in sum, a losing battle. The moral climate of slavery itself made it so. "Doubtless, too," wrote Stewart, himself no friend to serious reform, "there is in the very nature of slavery, in its mildest form, something unfavourable to the cultivation of moral feeling. Men may be restrained. . . by very good and well-intentioned laws, from exercising acts of cruelty and oppression on the slaves, but still harsh ideas and arbitrary habits, which may find innumerable petty occasions for venting themselves, grow up, wherever slavery exists, in minds where principle has not taken a deep hold."[52]

That climate of opinion helps explain the other ingredients of the planter ideology. The planter mind lived in a world of self-sustaining myth. The mythology constituted the energizing principle of all colonial attitudes: the myth of

African degeneracy, the myth of Negro happiness, the myth of King Sugar. When those myths were challenged, the plantocracy responded with yet another final exculpatory myth: that the challenge came from demonic, subversive forces ready to risk even slave rebellion for the purpose of destroying a social order they hated too much to understand. Those forces, of course, were seen as, first, the Baptist and Methodist missionaries and, second, the English and French philanthropists. The Nonconformist chapels were seen, in Bleby's words, as "dens of sedition, infamy, and blasphemy" deserving to be destroyed; and the account of white vigilante burnings, aided and abetted by conniving magistrates, perjured juries, and a venal press, in the Jamaica of the 1830s, which is described in Henry Bleby's first-hand account, *Death Struggles of Slavery*, testifies to the spirit of virulent hatred felt by the Creole white community for men who were no more socially radical than Wesley or Wilberforce. It is especially instructive to read the excerpts from the colonial press cited in that volume, for they tell us much more about the planter mentality than the books and pamphlets that, written for an English public, had to accommodate themselves to a quite different opinion. They show, indeed, a contemptuous disdain for English public opinion – as well as an open defiance of the British Parliament – that could more properly itself be described as seditious.[53] The hatred became even more splenetic in its attitude to metropolitan humanitarians. Even Edwards, confronted with the horrors of the Saint Domingue civil war, came to write more with the zeal of a fanatic waging a holy war than in his usually moderate temper, exhorting Britain not to encourage "the pestilent doctrines of those hot-brained fanatics, and detestable incendiaries, who, under the vile pretence of philanthropy and zeal for the interests of suffering humanity, preach up rebellion and murder to the contented and orderly negroes in our own territories."[54]

The myth of the agitator thus provided the planter defendants with what was for them a half-plausible answer to the crucial question raised by the humanitarian criticism: if the Negroes were so contented, why then did they revolt – as they did so frequently? Like all conservative thought, the planter ideology thus failed to see that the "agitator" is not so much the cause as the consequence of discontent; he simply articulates the protest of general social forces against oppression too intolerable to be borne any longer. Equally, it failed to see that metaphysical systems do not subvert established orders but simply provide the intellectual justification for revolutions that would have taken place anyway. Therefore, in the wake of the 1831 rebellion, there were few members of the Jamaican colonial legislature like Beaumont – who could tell his fellow members that the sectarian ministers were no more guilty of that insurrection than were the advocates of reform in the British Parliament guilty of the conflagration of Bristol.[55] Nor were many legislators disposed to heed the observation, made indeed by one of their friends, that there are "those who can distinguish black from white in the colour of the human skin, but who cannot discriminate what is black from white in the integral conduct of man to man." They talked endlessly of the need for the moral reformation of the slave as a necessary prerequisite of freedom; they could not see, as the same friend insisted, that any meaningful reformation must begin with the white people themselves.[56] Their own gross irreligiosity, indeed, was a byword in the islands, as testified to by Lady Nugent in her Jane Austen-like journal, written in the early 1800s, and by "Monk" Lewis somewhat later in his own journal. They saw their adversaries as nothing more than self-seeking publicists looking for advancement; the Popish plot, wrote a group of their defenders, was never a better stalking horse than Negro slavery is at the present day.[57] They were, altogether, the champions of a dying social order. They were even wrong in their apocalyptic prophecies about the dire consequences that would follow its demise.

Yet it would be misleading to conclude that the West Indian planters always had the worse of the argument. They were, of course, doomed to lose the larger argument, for ever since Adam Smith's monumental demolition of protectionist mercantilism, they were on the defensive against the new vested interests of British industrial capitalism as a world economic system that demanded free trade as its instrument of expansion. But they were quick to point out the hypocrisy of that policy. The West Indian connection, their literature argued, was cherished by Britain so long as it was profitable in the regime of commercial capitalism, and was ruthlessly abandoned once it became unprofitable in the regime of industrial capitalism. Their exclusive possession of the home market, the argument continued, was their just reward for the restrictions imposed on them by the colonial system.[58] If Britain claimed the right to secure its supplies in the cheapest market, as in the case of East Indian sugar, then the West Indies ought to be granted the same right by means, for example, of an uninhibited trade with North America; that principle of reciprocal right was made as early as 1784 in Edwards' first published work.[59] The whole system, in brief, was "an implicit compact. . . for a mutual monopoly."[60] For one side to abrogate it unilaterally was a violation of trust.

The argument was carried even further. If, the West Indians claimed, slavery was in fact original sin, then who invented it in the first place? The English themselves. "Many persons," wrote Barham in his 1823 *Considerations on the Abolition of Negro Slavery*, "have been so used to charge all the odium of that system on those, who by accident happen to be the present owners of slaves, that they will be surprised to learn how much larger a share Great Britain has had, than the Colonies, in the formation, maintenance, and present extent of Slavery"; and he proceeds to prove his point by referring to the Elizabethan slave traders, the support of the trade by the Stuart and Hanoverian monarchies, the Asiento treaty with Spain of 1713, and the vast profits that the city of Liverpool gained from the enormities of the Middle Passage.[61] Barclay drove the point home four years later, in *A Practical View of the Present State of Slavery in the West Indies*, his answer to James Stephen's book. "Without stopping to enquire whether or not the condition of savages has been improved by the change," he wrote, "one thing is certain, that the merit or odium of it is due, not to the inhabitants of the colonies, but to the people of England. They reaped the advantages of establishing slavery in the West Indies; it was *their* ships and *their* capital that conveyed the negroes from their native land to these fertile islands, from the cultivation of which, the British people have derived much of the wealth they now possess; and if any of the existing interests are now to be broken up, these surely ought, in common justice, to be indemnified at the public expense."[62] The note of "perfidious Albion" is clear. The

West Indians, true, were the most visible agents of the system. But they were not prepared to be made the scapegoats of its unpopularity. The argument is an embryonic form of colonial nationalism.

But the adroitness of the West Indian counterattack was best exhibited in its use of the vexed question, so prominent in the lengthy debate: which was the happier person, the West Indian slave or the English peasant and factory worker? It was the Achilles heel of the abolitionist-emancipationist assault, and the West Indians assailed it shrewdly. Edwards noted that the slave housing in the islands, allowing for the difference of climate, was superior to the cabins of the Scotch and Irish peasants described by Young and other travellers of the time. Beckford argued that the lot of the Negroes compared favourably with that of European peasants, soldiers and sailors, and imprisoned debtors – an argument not entirely of an abstract character since he wrote his *Remarks* of 1788, when he was himself a debt-ridden slave-owner incarcerated in the Fleet Prison. Others echoed the argument, as good an example as any being an anonymous pamphlet of 1833, *The Condition of the West Indian Slave Contrasted with that of the Infant Slave in our English Factories,* embellished with pictures drawn by the celebrated cartoonist Cruikshank.[63] This, altogether, was the one argument that the humanitarians were never able satisfactorily to answer, for too many of them exemplified in their attitudes toward the struggle for factory legislation at home the hypocrisy that Dickens castigated in the figure of Mrs. Jellyby, the religious philanthropist speechifying in defence of the sufferings of the poor African yet oblivious to that of the new factory proletariat at home. The West Indians, indeed, might have carried their argument even further, for in one of their remarkable chapters the English historians, the Hammonds, have shown how the apologies for child labour in the new factory system were precisely the same as the earlier apologies for the slave trade – as the London workhouses of early Victorian England came to serve the purpose of the Lancashire cotton mills as surely as the Guinea coast had served that of the West Indian plantations.[64] The West Indians could not have been expected, naturally, to have appreciated the grim lesson of that fact: that, as in all imperialisms, the moral atmosphere of the colony becomes a breeding ground from whence retrogressive social ideas are imported into the metropolis.

Looked at in the larger perspective of course, the truth of the matter was that both West Indian slave and English factory operative were the exploited labour force of the modern industrial capitalism, the one in its earlier Atlantic phase, the other in its later world phase. The master class of the one was the West Indian plantocracy, of the other the rising English factory capitalist After the period of the Napoleonic Wars, their interests began to diverge, and they used the suffering of their respective slave populations as a stick with which to beat each other. Men like Edwards could clearly see the oppression of the English factory hand but seemed to develop a moral blind spot when it came to the question of oppression of the West Indian slave; similarly, men like Wilberforce could indignantly admonish the planters about their treatment of the slave yet be silent on the issue of protective factory legislation in England itself. It was a struggle between two self-interested segments of a common ruling class similar to that between the territorial aristocracy and the capitalist industrialists in England itself: Lord Shaftesbury, the noble leader of the factory-legislation movement, could view the efforts of Joseph Arch to organize the labourers of the agricultural districts with hostility; John Bright, whose economic liberalism made him the enemy of all colonial enterprises, saw trade unions as a menace to industrial peace. Class interest, in each case, made it impossible for the protagonists to see that all of the exploited classes involved, English village labourer and factory hand as well as West Indian slave, were common victims of a system that had become truly global in its character. It was left to the socialist thinkers to perceive the real truth. In the eighteenth century it was the French philosopher like Mably; in the nineteenth century, the English Christian Socialist like Ludlow of the 1848 movement. Rather than simply reproach the American colonists for holding slaves, in the indignant manner of Raynal, Mably saw slavery as a variant of the wage-labour system of the bourgeois order, "I beg to remark," he wrote in his 1788 volume, *Recherches historiques et politiques sur les Etats-Unis de l'Amérique septentrionale*, "that the liberty which every European believes himself to enjoy is nothing but the possibility of breaking his chain in order to give himself up to a new master. Want here makes the slaves; and they are the more miserable, since no law provides for their subsistence." Ludlow, in his turn, saw the worldwide character of the new oppression. "You cannot do justice to India," he wrote, "without striking a blow at the fetters of the American slave; you cannot free the latter without giving an enormous impetus to the development of India." Everything was tied together, so that "the over-taxation of India and the exactions of London slop-sellers, the massacres of Ceylon or Cephalonia and the beating to death of parish-apprentices at home, are but pustules of the same plague."[65]

The French Antilles

The historical evolution of French Saint Domingue was, of course, intrinsically different from that of the English colonies. It grew during the eighteenth century into the richest of all the sugar colonies; in 1776 it produced for France more wealth than did the whole of Spanish America for Spain. But the tremendous events of 1789–1804, which passed over the colony with all the destructive force of a tropical hurricane, transformed it, within a brief generation, into a new society that, politically, was the first independent black republic in the hemisphere and, economically, was a neo-feudal system with the new Haitian peasant as its backbone. The change was swift and violent. There did not take place, then, the protracted controversy on the morality of slavery that took place between the West Indians and the English humanitarians. The philosophes, it is true, attacked slavery. But they did not constitute, as did the English humanitarians, a powerful political force with friends in government; the court at Versailles was not the House of Commons. The very nature of the cataclysmic changes after 1789, which were at once, in Saint Domingue, a generalized slave rebellion and a war for national liberation, necessarily precluded the growth of any sort of debate comparable to what took place in London.

Yet the Saint Domingue colonial society produced, in its manners, values, and attitudes, its own unique expression of the slavery theme. The older historical scholarship of Peytraud, Frossard, and Boissonade, as well as the later modern scholarship of Lepkowski, Pierre-Charles, Debien, Franco, and Hector and Moise, have together painted a graphic picture of its character. Historically, it had its origins in the early Tortuga island-stronghold of the filibusters and buccaneers, and although they soon disappeared, the colony retained much of their spirit of unbridled individualism and rapacity. Economically, it was a typically Caribbean hybrid economy, composed of the most advanced European elements of capital and technology mixed with the archaic (from the European viewpoint) element of slave labour, producing a tremendously complicated unit of organization in the form of the huge sugar plantations described by the contemporary observer Barré de Saint Venant. Politically, it was ruled with a strong hand by the centralized bureaucracy of the *ancien régime*, thus allowing little of the limited democracy of the assertive colonial assemblies of the English islands. Socially, all of those factors combined to shape a society of almost caste-like distinctions, composed of *grands blancs, petits blancs*, mulattoes, blacks, governmental and military personnel, and impoverished French nobility; a pyramidal social structure in which the leading criterion of wealth and status was the ownership of slaves, *têtes de negres* in the telling parlance of the colony – bought and sold, and sometimes rented out, like so many head of cattle.

It was not without reason that the colony, in its brief heyday between the Treaty of Paris of 1763 and the French Revolution, was regarded as the Babylon of the Antilles. Its corruption, venality, brutality, and rascality would have taken the genius of a Molière or a Balzac fully to describe. The testimony of contemporaries, both Creole writers and European visitors, is overwhelming. Its descriptive detail helps to illuminate the principles on which the colonial life was conducted and how each group in the general concatenation of forces saw itself and saw the others. The general tone was one of ferocious cupidity and greed. The tone was set at the very top by the repressive administrative machine, led by the Governor and the Intendant – representing the monarchy and its ally, the rich maritime bourgeoisie of the French slave ports. "The Governor," wrote Pons, "exercises a monstrous power, the source of infinite vexations. At once head of justice and military chief, he holds in his hand the life and the fortune of everybody." "This office," added Baron de Wimpffen in his

letter written on the eve of the French Revolution, "has ceased to be granted for merit, to become the prey of ignorance, irresponsibility, of the ability of some great person impoverished when he arrives, to reappear later in France, after three years, and at the risk of seeming to be a bad citizen or even a fool, with a fortune equal to what it would have been difficult for three generations of wastrels to consume."[66] It was a rare governor, such as Bellecombe, who could spend his brief tenure translating the *Anabasis* of Xenophon, or a rare Intendant, such as Barbé-Marbois, who could use his retirement to publish his two definite works on Saint Domingue finances. The consequent nepotism, peculation, and bribery seeped down into every level of the system: the administration of justice, the regulation of trade and commerce, the licensing regime, the organization of public works, the award of land titles. And what was bad enough in France itself became doubly worse in the colony by reason of the vast geographical separation between metropolis and American dependency. A Choiseul or a Necker was possible in Paris but unthinkable in Saint Domingue. Even the parasitic sinecurism was worse, since every new governor added to the administrative chaos with his own mass of edicts, letters patent, and ordinances; the massive volumes of laws and administrative regulations that Moreau de Saint-Méry put together in his monumental *Loix et Constitutions des colonies françaises de l'Amerique sous le vent de 1550 à 1785* would have been sufficient to discourage any functionary with a taste for reforming codification.

In sum, the leading normative value of the society – and certainly of its warring and turbulent white groups – was that of the old pirate dream of easy plunder. Pons, Gel Chast, Girod-Chantrans, Moreau de Saint-Méry, Baron de Wimpffen, d'Auberteuil, all testify in one way or another to the chronic pervasiveness of the disease. To become rich and therefore socially respected; to rise into the local plutocracy; then to return to France with sufficient money to buy a title of nobility: it was the common aspiration of all. The means were legion: to connive at contraband trade; to exact exorbitant fees from clients; to swindle an absentee planter by mismanaging his property; to form a *mésalliance* with a rich and aged Negress. Even more than in the English colonies, it led to the even worse disease of absenteeism. In place of citizens, observed Wimpffen, in Saint Domingue there are only birds of passage. It is wrong to believe, added d'Auberteuil, that it is the climate that drives away the richest inhabitants, for here there are health and wealth, it is only a sense of security that is lacking. Everybody, concluded Moreau de Saint-Méry, says that he is leaving next year and considers himself merely a *voyageur* (transient) in a land where only too often he finds his final resting place.[67] Nor was this the aspiration of only the improvident and the rapacious. It infected all who came to the colony; and Victor Advielle's memoir of the architect Pierre Lefranc de Saint-Haulde shows how a prudent bourgeois, by means of speculating in the colonial stock-market of slaves, could amass a sufficiently tidy fortune to return to his native Normandy for a comfortable retirement.[68]

What shocked most of the observers, most of whom shared the new bourgeois philosophy of the age, was the sheer waste of the system. The wealth of the colony, they argue, is drained, by means of the infamous colonial pact, to France, to be spent by absentee planters and merchant princes. If it remains in the colony, it is drained from the countryside to the cities. The *corvée* system robs the plantations of their slave labour. The industrious planter, and especially the absentee owner, is swindled by the resident attorney-agent in charge of the estate. Agriculture, the most important resource of the colonial wealth, is the least protected. Its cultivators, writes Wimpffen, who owe in debt more than they possess, languish in misery and inertia; in the words of one resident planter quoted by Pons, agriculture is the slowest means of gaining a fortune, and often the quickest road to ruin.[69] The fabulous wealth of the country, in fact, is more apparent than real. Rather than being genuinely productive, it is wasted in habits of profligate consumption; and the French visitor Laujon described in tones of disgust the typical *soir de fête* held at the governor's palace – where fashionable society, richly dressed and bejewelled, danced to the steps of Vestris, listened to the latest *chanson* of Garat or of Blondel: the men splendidly arrogant, the women pursuing the only art known to them, that of Creole coquetry. Saint Domingue, exclaimed the comte d'Ennery, is a second Sodom, which the fire of heaven will destroy.[70] The habits of industry are thus sacri-

ficed to a *luxe asiatique*; the whole society, in the phrase of the later historian Ardouin, confident in its delusive security, slept on the crater of a volcano ready at any moment to erupt and devour it.

Social morality and civic spirit alike withered in such a society. Wimpffen, noting the municipal squalor of Port-au-Prince, termed it a Tartar camp, and Moreau de Saint-Méry, while deprecating the sharpness of the expression, admitted that it was not entirely inapplicable.[71] The very paucity of architecture, both private and public, testified to a general disinterest in civic improvement; certainly, neither Port-au-Prince nor Cap Français produced anything to rival the cathedrals of Mexico or the churches of Havana, while no resident planter managed to build a "great house" in any way comparable, say, to Worthy Park in Jamaica or Sam Lord's Castle in Barbados. Moreau de Saint-Méry described at length the scandal of the sewage and drainage systems. Nor was the intellectual aspect of colonial life any more prepossessing. True, the local Philadelphian Circle discussed the latest books from Paris. But the generality of the society regarded such publications as little more than fancies indulged by a politically powerless elite of *beaux esprits* rather than warnings of the gathering storm. True, too, there was a handful of thoughtful and intelligent Creoles. Men like the merchant Delaire and the president of the colonial assembly, De Cadusch, provided Bryan Edwards with written narratives that he incorporated into his *Historical Survey of Santo Domingo*. The interest of the age in science, technology, and industry was also reflected in the colony in, variously, the work of Thierry de Menonville in tropical botany, of Trembley and de Saint-Ouen in hydraulic engineering, of Chastenet de Puysegur in maritime cartography, and of de Neufchateau in the general field of economic science.[72] But, even so, that had little impact upon a slave mode of production where the availability of plentiful servile labour, notwithstanding its high morality rate, gave little incentive to the planter class to develop a practical interest in technological innovation along purely capitalist lines. The very hedonism of the society, the prevailing urge to make a rapid profit and decamp, precluded the growth of such an interest. The English observers of the society during the same period noted its anti-community spirit, notwithstanding the fact that they themselves were friends to the principle of slavery. Bryan Edwards, in his visit to Santo Domingo in 1791, was unimpressed by the majority of whites who were left after the first exodus, seeing them as a lower order of *noblesse* preoccupied solely with the restoration of their properties; and Lady Nugent, somewhat later, could find nothing charitable to say of the exiles she met in Jamaica.

Saint Domingue, in sum, was a bizarre exaggeration, a tropical caricature, of the *ancien régime* in France. The sole difference was that created by slavery: The only cement that held the society together, in, that is, its white groups, was unanimity on the issue of white supremacy. It all rested on a simple catechism: The black was inferior both in cultural and biological terms; the white, however low on the social ladder, was a superior being; nothing must ever be countenanced that would seem – even in subtle ways that the eye of a European could not appreciate – to compromise the moral authority of the white master class.

The social history of Saint Domingue provided plentiful illustration of those imperatives. Adam Smith, in a frequently noted passage of his famous work, had argued that the condition of the slave was better under an arbitrary government, as in the case of the French West Indian islands, than it was under a free government, as in the British islands, since in the latter case the power of the colonial state was in large part coincidental with the interests of the class of slave owners who were also the controlling force in the colonial legislative assemblies.[73] But the record of slave treatment in Saint Domingue does not bear out the accuracy of that assertion. The Lejeune case of 1788 proved that white Santo Domingo would not tolerate any interference with white masters, even when they were proved guilty of the most barbarous methods of slave treatment.[74] The case of the Sieur Chapuzet in the 1770s, in its turn, proved that the privileges of white status would not be accorded to anyone possessing even the faintest traces of black ancestry, even if, as in that celebrated case, the plaintiff could prove that his forebears were not African imports but the free and noble Caribs that the old seventeenth-century French writers had celebrated.[75] To read, even today, the savage and punitive legislation passed by the local councils against the rising mulatto group is to realize,

albeit faintly, how the paranoic obsession with racial purity was so intense that it even superseded consideration of class interest: the propertied mulatto group, in the white view, was dangerous not because it was bourgeois but because it was tainted with blackness.[76]

There is, indeed, almost a note of sexual guilt in the contemporary accounts of the attitude, as if the white mentality recognized in the figures of the *affranchis* (freedmen) and *gens de couleur* (people of colour) the biological consequence of its own miscegenative habits. Originally, perhaps, an instinct of social preservation, the attitude became congealed into an institutionalized form of prejudice, so built into the very structure of social relations that, as events proved, only the destruction of society itself could end it. The Swiss Girod-Chantrans noted that whiteness was a *titre of commandemente* (sign of authority), blackness the *livrée du mépris* (badge of disdain). The prejudice of colour, added Moreau de Saint-Méry, was the *ressort caché* (hidden spring) of the social machine.[77] Wimpffen noted, in his turn, that the prejudice took the place of *distinctions de rang, mérite de la naissance, honneurs et même de la fortune*. In such a way, he added graphically, that even if a black could prove his descent from the Negro king who came to adore Jesus Christ in the manger, even if he combined in his person the genius of a celestial intelligence with all the gold from the bowels of the earth, he would still be regarded as a vile slave, a *noir*, by the most cretinous, the most foolish, the poorest of whites.[78]

It is in this sense that colonial society differed, in its fundamentals, from metropolitan society. The French *ancien régime* was divided, horizontally, into the three estates of nobility, bourgeois, and peasantry. The Saint Domingue society was divided, vertically, into the three estates of whites, people of colour, and blacks. There developed, in the colonial sense, neither a discernible nobility based on title nor a distinctively clerical group. The rivalries that did exist – between the large planter and small planter, between the civilian and the military arms of government, between town and country populations, between planters and merchants, and between the local petite bourgeoisie and the *petits blancs* – were real enough, as the insurrection of the 1760s on the part of the *petits blancs* shows. But they were overshadowed by the overriding sentiment of race solidarity, reinforced by the terrifying imbalance of sheer numbers between whites and non-whites. That, as much as anything else, explains why the colonial historians, including Moreau de Saint-Méry, divided their material into sections and chapters subtitled in racial terms – the whites, the mulattoes, the blacks – to the practical exclusion of other differentiating criteria. It left behind a legacy of implacable race hatred that made impossible the continuance of a white presence in the new black republic after 1804; nicely summed up in the nineteenth-century anecdote of the encounter between the editor of the journal *Le Sauveteur,* Turpin de Sanzay, and President Salomon, in which the Frenchman's insulting remark, "Retirez-vous, vous occupez la propriété de mes ancêtres, et je ne peux souffrir ici votre présence" (Go away, you occupy the property of my ancestors, and I cannot tolerate your presence here), was countered with the dignified retort that de Sanzay's own ancestor was a filibuster and that he, the President of the Republic, had no need to make an excuse for himself.[79]

Moreau de Saint-Méry and Hilliard d'Auberteuil

Just as Jamaica gave birth to its own school of local historians and writers, so did Saint Domingue. They were, most notably, Moreau de Saint-Méry himself and Hilliard d'Auberteuil, the first a Creole (his grandfather had been *sénéschal* of Martinique), the second a creolized *métropolitain*, and both of them eminent lawyers who held high office in the colony. In addition to the volumes of *Loix de Constitutions des colonies françaises de l'Amérique* (1784–90) already mentioned, Moreau de Saint-Méry also wrote *La Description de la partie française de Saint-Domingue* (1792). He was twice exiled by the Revolution – the first time from the colony and the second time from France itself – and the journal of his Philadelphia stay is a charming record of how his bookshop became the centre of exile life; his friends included Volney, de Noailles, Talon, the duc d'Orléans (the future Louis Phillipe) and the redoubtable Talleyrand himself, not to mention the English Radical Cobbett, who translated Moreau de Saint-Méry's other book on the Spanish part of Saint Domingue.[80] A historian and born researcher (he com-

plained bitterly of the Spanish neglect of the riches of the Seville archives), he provides in his books a valuable commentary on all aspects of colonial life. In his turn, d'Auberteuil, of Rennes origin and domiciled in the colony, provided an equally valuable commentary in his volume of 1776–77, *Considérations sur l'état prèsent de la colonie française de Saint-Domingue.* Much more than Raynal, who used only secondary sources for his famous work, Moreau de Saint-Méry and d'Auberteuil constitute together an intimate and detailed description of colonial manners and values based on direct experience.

In the history of the Caribbean political thought – as Charles Frostin has shown in his exhaustive study, *Les Révoltes blanches à Saint-Domingue aux XVII*–*XVIII*_siècles* – these two colonial writers are important because they gave eloquent expression to the ideology of *autonisme colon,* (local self-government), using what has aptly been termed "the American spirit" to attack the French colonial regime of oppressive royal administration and restrictive economic mercantilism. Just as in the case of the British West Indies Long and Edwards fashioned a theory of colonial Whiggery against the English Crown and Parliament, so in the French West Indies Moreau de Saint-Méry and d'Auberteuil shaped arguments of an advanced politico-constitutional radicalism against a monarchy and a bureaucracy that they saw as the instruments of the vested interests of absentee planters, metropolitan merchants, and royal appointees. But because that movement of thought, in both cases, belongs more properly to the study of Caribbean colonial nationalism – despite the fact that it never flowered, as it did in the British North American colonies, into open rebellion. What is more pertinent, at this point, is the manner in which these writers throw light on the planter collective mentality and how they came, despite their exposure to the ideas of the Enlightenment, to justify and rationalize its psychological assumptions.

Reading the three tomes of Moreau de Saint-Méry's *Description* compels admiration. A Freemason, vaguely deistical in his religious beliefs, an avowed disciple of Diderot and Rousseau, he evinces all the characteristics of the Enlightenment: its romantic sensibility, its intellectual curiosity, its belief in the goodness of man. If he is sufficiently a colonial snob to record with pride the brief visit to Saint Domingue in 1783 of the English royal heir-apparent Prince William Henry, he is also the *savant* who catalogues with equal pride the list of residents who adorned the colony with their learning: the Jesuit Père Boutin with his study of African languages, the medical doctor Desportes who almost single-handedly created the science of colonial pharmacology, the M. Dubourg who wrote on colonial botany, and the younger Weuves who sought, in his book of 1780, to refute the accusation that the colonies constituted an onerous burden for the metropolis.[81] His account makes it clear, too, that notwithstanding colonial philistinism, the exciting ferment of ideas taking place in France had its repercussions in the West Indies. For if there was an ideology of trade, institutionalized in the notorious *Exclusif* system, there was also a trade of ideology.

The influence of the French ideas comes through, loud and clear, in Moreau de Saint-Méry's incisive analysis of colonial habits and manners. He writes as an ethnologist would write. Seeing the colonial life as an eternal triangle, as it were, between whites, mulattoes, and blacks, he subjects each group to a rigorous examination. His bourgeois sense of business prudence is offended by the extravagance of colonial luxury, the passion for gambling (cock-fighting for the slaves, card games for the white gentry), the obsession with expensive finery that penetrates every social level, including the slaves, the pervasive spirit of tropical hedonism. His spirit of *bon civisme* leads him to lament the general absence of public and private morality. Every group is indictable. Luxury, he observes, flourishes in the colony, and no profession is safe from its assault. Everywhere, he asserts, the military, who are the defenders of the country, are rarely the guardians of its morals; and Saint Domingue is no exception. The European residents imagine that a single day in the colony entitles them to ennoblement so much so that they break off their family connections at home lest their low social origins be discovered.[82] The *creol blanc*, even although in his youth he may have received a French education, rapidly learns that his station in life predisposes him to cultivate his physical pleasures rather than his moral inclinations. The *creole blanche*, in her turn, is destined for a life of forced early marriage, obsession with sexual intrigue, and the torture of

jealousy caused by the general practice of white male liaisons with mulatto mistresses.[83] The *affranchis*, likewise, are so devoted to the pursuit of pleasure that it becomes their despotic master; their three passions are dancing, horse riding, and *la volupté*.[84] As for the slaves, the transplanted African system of polygamy makes a happy family life even more impossible. Whether it is the languorous creole or the lascivious *mulâtre* or the lazy black, Moreau de Saint-Méry sees in all of them the dehumanizing influence of a laxity of sexual morals that, as he observes, takes the form, not of the scandalous public prostitution of the European cities, but of a total absence of any sense of morality. Nor is this the expression of an outraged puritan conscience in the English fashion. There are passages in both the Philadelphia journal and the Saint Domingue volumes that reveal the author as a sort of French-colonial Boswell, with a keen scientific curiosity, for example, about sexual aberrations. So, for him, colonial sexual licence and marital infidelity are obnoxious not because they are sinful but because they are antisocial. It is the clear inference of the argument that in such an environment there can be neither moral happiness nor social utility.

In all of this Moreau de Saint-Méry speaks as a social critic after the manner of a Diderot or a Rousseau. Yet, interestingly enough, he refuses to draw the necessary radical conclusions from his critique. He recognizes the symptoms of the colonial social disease. But he stops short of indicting the system itself. He clearly perceives that the symptoms are related to the system. So, in his telling description of the upbringing of the white Creole child, he sees that its character of imperious arrogance is a consequence of being surrounded, from birth, by a fawning court of slaves – never was there a despot, he writes, that had adulation so assiduous; he is corrupted by being at once the object of parental indulgence and of slave idolatry.[85] Similarly, his portrait of the *mulâtresse*, half-admiring, half-censorious, condemns her indolence and her obsession with the sexual art, yet fails to insist upon its real cause in the sexual depredations of the white class; all the author will admit is that the general promiscuity is a necessary evil of the system, so much so that no legislation can touch it: the law remains silent, he comments, where nature speaks so imperiously.[86] He prints an exhaustive list of the 128 grades of colour, officially enforced, of the resultant mélange, but he fails to recognize its comic absurdity. He even manages to imply that the slave trade, the origin of it all, was more the fault of the French than of the colonials.[87] But the most astonishing omission of the account is in its treatment of the slaves. It discusses, variously and with intense curiosity, the different tribal origins of the slave population, their distinctive characteristics, their intramural prejudices one against the other, their remarkable command of music, their passion for the dance, their bodily cleanliness, their religion of *vaudoux* or vodun, their sexual preferences, and much else. But it says hardly anything about their daily work, almost as if it did not exist[88]

For all of his sensibility, Moreau de Saint-Méry was, in sum, an apologist for the planter cause. So part of the natural order of things did the system seem to him that he did not even attempt its defence in any serious fashion. The slave mind, he observed, was incapable of understanding religious ideas; he could not see that the real reason for the deficiency lay in the bitter resistance of the planters to any kind of religious instruction at all for their charges, although the evidence is overwhelming as much in Père Charlevoix's early account of 1730–31 as in the planter Malenfant's oddly sympathetic account published later, in 1814.[89] Many of the slaves, he wrote, were lazy, quarrelsome, liars, and thieves. Yet his own further account of their concern with cleanliness, their avoidance of drunkenness, the habit of breast-feeding their children on the part of slave mothers (which especially enthused him as a disciple of Rousseau), indicates an at least partial realization that nurture, as much as nature, shaped slave behaviour patterns.[90] His reference to the Negroes as forming part of *les peuples non-civilisés,* suggests that, as with his English colonial counterpart, Edwards, his prejudice against them was cultural rather than racial. But prejudice of either kind could help buttress the same general conclusion that the slave order was sacrosanct. It is possible that he was even vaguely aware of the profound contradiction in which his argument placed him, for there is a curious passage in his book, omitted after the 1797 edition, that sought to excuse his failure to discuss the moral problem involved. "It is not pertinent," he wrote, ". . . to examine the question of slavery and to determine if such

a state of things, over which humanity and philosophy can only heave a sigh, is to be made a matter of accusation against the colonies. . . . A great nation has opened up a discussion on the subject which has attracted everybody. . .I very well know the interest it can inspire in the man of sensibility. . . .But it is not by wishes alone that moral ills can be ended; for the deeper they are the more their cure requires genius, care, and time. Experience has unhappily shown that it would have been better for the man of sensibility that this cause, undoubtedly so appealing, had not been broached at all, that it would have been far better for him to have realized the impossibility of putting an end to slavery and to have considered only its amelioration, alleviating its rigours by means which would have gained, through self-interest, even the support of the slave owners."[91] The sentiment was in keeping with the main purpose of the book itself, which, as the author stated, was to remind Paris of the spendours of a colony created by the French genius and which, even after the events of the Revolution, could still be restored to its pristine prosperity. It was only logical, then, that in his role in those events after 1789 he should have acted as the spokesman of the planters and merchants as against the Parisian reformers; and his pamphlet of 1791, *Considérations présentées aux vrais amis du repos et du bonheur de la France,* was a characteristic attack on the Sociéte des Amis des Noirs, the pro-Negro club of the French Revolution, assailing their effort (as Moreau de Saint-Méry saw it) to overthrow a social structure so nobly tested by history and experience in favour of fantastic theories presupposing an ideal human nature that had never really existed. The disciple of the philosophes thus ended as the supporter of the Napoleonic reaction.

Contemporary accounts testify to the sensation occasioned by the publication of Hilliard d'Auberteuil's book. It is easy to see why. It is a highly censorious account of French colonial administration written from the viewpoint of a bourgeois reformer (notwithstanding some sharp strictures passed on the philosophes). It has the spirit, in that respect, of Raynal; and it is suggestive that the author's plan to compose a more extensive work was dropped because the publication of Raynal's book forestalled it. Yet it was one thing to be a critic of Versailles, quite another to be a critic of the slave regime; and d'Auberteuil's section on that subject graphically reveals how, just as with Moreau de Saint-Méry, the prejudice of the colon effectively stifled the spirit of the reformer. It is almost as if a split intellectual personality is at work. Nothing could better illustrate how slavery suborned the critical instinct.

D'Auberteuil begins with the ritualistic obeisance to the spirit of liberty. The love of country, he says, is the first of the civic virtues. The best government is that in which no one shall find his interest in the misfortune of others. Law and administration should be accommodated to the peculiarities of the people, so that, in the case of Saint Domingue, many metropolitan laws are inapplicable because of the differences of climate and manners.[92] These truths, the argument continues, even apply to slavery. "The country where slavery rules," opines the author with candour, "is the anchorage of the man who possesses only the appearance of virtue. The habit of being obeyed makes the master proud, precipitate, harsh, angry, unjust, and cruel, and insensibly encourages an absence of all the moral virtues...he is alone in the midst of his enemies." He concedes even more when he argues that the vices usually attributed to the slave are not intrinsic to him but the direct consequence of his condition: "It is not surprising that the negroes, on becoming our slaves, contract an infinity of vices they do not possess in their natural state. They lose the sentiment of pity towards us, we, in our turn, because we are estranged from nature, have no sentimental feeling towards them."[93] The concession is all the more significant when it is remembered that even those French writers and travellers of the time who were critics of slavery – Lambert, Chanvalon, Pierre Poivre, Delacroix, Sonnerat – tended to accept the negative and unflattering portrait of the slave presented in the pro-slavery literature.

Yet, for all this, d'Auberteuil is no champion of emancipation. At best, he repeats the old amelioration recipe. Let the slaves have adequate medical care, rest periods, time to cultivate their own provision grounds. Let them be granted the right to lodge complaints against their masters. Above all, let them be governed by a revised civil law, in place of the present law of the master, which in reality confers the right of life and death upon the individual slave proprietor. If, he observes, we want to get the best from them, we must treat them humanely. We must accustom them gradually to an exact, but unchanging discipline. It is urgent to make them happy; which, he adds, is not at all difficult, for they are content with little. If this is done, all will have a happy ending. Lighten the burden of your slaves, he admonishes the *créoles volupteaux* (indolent colonists), and you will find at home the happiness you vainly seek in France.[94] Having said all this, he assumes that the argument is closed. "I will not pause," he concludes disarmingly, "to examine the point as to whether this property of slaves is legitimate, it is at least profitable. If we treat the slaves with humanity, their condition will hardly seem to them to be unfortunate."[95]

The gross naiveté of the argument illustrates the fatal weakness of the pro-slavery thesis. With its tone of Panglossian optimism and sweet reasonableness, it refuses to face up to the two crucial contradictions of the situation. First, if the slave – as d'Auberteuil admits – is innately intelligent and capable of comprehending the nature of liberty, how could he be expected to accept the state of slavery? Second, if (as, again, d'Auberteuil honestly admits) the existing legislation of the 1685 *Code Noir* has turned out to be ineffective in its effort to protect the slave – so much so that, in his own phrase, any white in Saint Domingue can ill-treat blacks with impunity – then of what use is it to advocate even more legislative amelioration? Neither d'Auberteuil nor Moreau de Saint-Méry proffered a satisfactory answer to those questions. The truth is that both of them were men of colonial bourgeois prudence. Even when they seem to sympathise with the lot of the slave, it is more an exercise in elegance of diction than the expression of deeply felt compassion. It is suggestive that d'Auberteuil's criticism of the slave trade rests on utilitarian rather than moral argumentation; the trade must end, he argues, because of its economics of high mortality, so that it would be more advisable to adopt a public policy of encouraging the natural increase of the resident slave population, for the costs of natural reproduction are bound to be less than those of continued importation. Likewise, he is against the religious instruction of the slaves on the ground, again utilitarian, that the contemplation of a future life will make them inattentive to their work.

A final example of this general temper of prudent pragmatism is the manner in which both writers treat the question of colonial luxury. They write on this topic, not as old-fashioned clerical moralists but as hardheaded colonial gentleman-politicians. Luxury, they argue, bleeds the colony and benefits France, since it requires an unending stream of useless imported items. It leads to dissipation and downgrades the honour of work. Reading all this, it is instructive to compare it with the temper of the book written earlier, in the 1730s, by the Jesuit missionary Père Charlevoix, *Histoire de l'isle Espagnole ou de St Domingue.* For the spirit that breathes through the pages of Charlevoix is that of a genuine Christianity, a note altogether absent in the two later writers. The grim picture that he painted of the slave population at that earlier date, in all of their misery, "despised of men and rejected by nature," is full of a compassionate pity his successors failed to repeat.[96] In this sense, the difference of tone between Charlevoix and d'Auberteuil is the same as the difference in the previous century, between Du Tertre and Labat. As the slave regime solidified itself, its unconditional defence became more urgent.

Yet perhaps neither Moreau de Saint-Méry nor Hilliard d'Auberteuil may be viewed as the most representative voice of the French West Indian colonial ideology. They were both too much touched by the metropolitan currents of thought. A much more representative presentation of the planter outlook is that of the French resident Dubuisson who, in his *Nouvelles considérations sur Saint-Domingue* of 1780 attempted a rebuttal, point by point and page by page, of d'Auberteuil's work. All three writers are defenders of the slave regime. But if the first two are liberals, the third is unrepentingly conservative, even reactionary. At every point, he is incensed by each concession that his rival makes to the Enlightenment outlook. Where d'Auberteuil castigates colonial governors, Dubuisson eulogizes them. The idea that the colonists are alienated from the mother country, he insists, is as impossible as it is imaginary. The advocacy of free trade with foreign countries is misconceived. Even the criticism of absentee plantation owners is misguided, since the more they spend of their net income in France, the more they require that their colonial agents make the plantation operation more efficient and more profitable.[97] As for the matter of slavery, Dubuisson becomes almost apoplectic. We whites, he answers d'Auberteuil, with our arts and science, do not need the pity of the slave: in fact, the pity a slave might feel for a white is something *si peu natural* (so very unnatural) that the idea could only have entered the head of somebody like d'Auberteuil who has not been long enough in the colony to understand things. The qualities attributed to the Negro, such as intelligence, pity, and tenderness, are nonexistent. All they possess, in reality, is a sort of mechanical attitude for music. Far from being obedient and affectionate, they are rebellious people, and d'Auberteuil's assertions about the state of security in the colony are belied by the prevalence of marauding Maroon Negro bands.[98] And how can we expect the sentiment of tenderness, he asks in a long harangue, from black women or even the *sangmêlees* (those of mixed blood), who are so much the carriers of a *debauche effrenée* (frightening debauchery) that they may inspire love but never the delicious emotions of a tender heart?[99] These people, he concludes, should in fact be grateful for slavery, for, *vainqueurs inhumains* (vengeful conquerors) or *captifs malheureux* (unhappy captives) in Africa, they have been brought to America to become beneficiaries of a new life. He finally admonishes those philanthropists who mourn over their condition to remember that the well-being of the slave lies safely in the care of masters whose self-interest alone guarantees the prevention of cruelty.[100]

Whereas Moreau de Saint-Méry and Hilliard d'Auberteuil are partial racists, Dubuisson is the complete racist. In an interesting passage Moreau de Saint-Méry described how so many whites, coming to the colony, failed to recognize one Negro from another, seeing only a faceless black crowd, and how he himself had suffered from the embarrassment, but had managed to overcome it. For Dubuisson, however, the blacks remain forever a generic object of undistinguishable anatomic and physiological features. The slave, for him, is not a person. He is not even a nonperson. He becomes almost an anti-person. The term *l'homme sauvage,* he declares, applies only to the aboriginal Indians and not to the African slaves; he thus shows once again how the European mind could only idealize an American group that was no longer a threat to its hegemony. He is scandalized by the idea that blacks and whites could share human sentiments; the very thought is unthinkable. Merely to entertain it is to endanger the very existence of the colony.[101] There is, all in all, in all of these three writers, composing their work almost on the eve of the upheaval of 1789, a total absence of any awareness of the forces that, once that event took place, would put an end to their world.

The Contribution of the French Revolution

These accounts, of course, were only one part of the rearguard action conducted by the French Antillean slavery vested interests against their enemies. They had to wage a war on three fronts: first, against the growing metropolitan antislavery opinion; second, against the free mulatto group on their own home ground; and, third, against the slave proletariat itself. The struggle was finally resolved with the abolition of slavery by the Paris Revolutionary Convention in 1794, consolidated ten years later by the victory of the black war of liberation and the establishment of the new black republic. The war was accompanied by an extensive pamphlet literature, as well as the debates in the three successive revolutionary assemblies between 1789 and 1794 on the various issues that arose: the colonial grievances contained in the 1789 cahiers, the problem of colonial representation, the status of the free blacks, and the meaning of the Declaration of the Rights of Man for slavery and the slave trade. Both the literature and the debates throw additional light on the planter ideology as it was forced to come to grips with those issues.

The nature of the problem that confronted the colonial representatives – early on accepted by the States General as a legitimate delegation and organized in the form of the Massiac Club – is easily stated. They accepted the revolution because it promised the overthrow of Bourbon despotism in the islands and consideration of the grievances catalogued in their *cahiers de doléances*; that is, the official reports of complaints: discontent with the trade laws, the discriminatory tax system, and the repressive colonial administration, in which they wanted a share. They even took the Tennis Court Oath. But they saw, correctly, that the universalistic principles of the Declaration of the Rights of Man logically threatened their slaveholding propertied interests, and so claimed that it did not

apply to the colonies. They had to answer the argument of the Paris radicals and of the Société des Amis des Noirs that natural law and justice required the termination of slavery, or at least of the slave trade. They saw clearly that it was a fundamental conflict between the interests of property and the claim of principle, summed up in Moreau de Saint-Méry's defence of the May 1791 colonial constitution law: "You must renounce your wealth and your commerce," he told the National Assembly, "or declare frankly that the Declaration of Rights does not apply to the colonies."[102] That conflict, of course, had been fully publicized for some fifty years in the form of the French antislavery intellectual movement. But with 1789 it became, as the colonists clearly perceived, a clear and present danger with the radical parties in control of Paris. As Boissonade has put it, what had hitherto been dismissed as the paradoxes of an elite set of *beaux esprits* had become for the first time a practical threat both to metropolitan slave-based commerce and to the Saint Domingue colonists.[103] As Moreau de Saint-Méry put it in his apologetic pamphlet of 1791, the arrival at Cap-Français in 1788 of the issues of the *Mercure de France* that contained details of the discussion among the negrophiles of the problem created *une grande sensation*.[104] Faced with that challenge, the slave-owning interest – a combination of *grands planteurs*, metropolitan merchants, and high-ranking aristocrats possessed of lucrative properties in the colony, usually through marriage – was compelled to spell out some sort of reasoned defence.

The defence took the form of a virulent propaganda campaign effectively conducted by the colonial deputation and its friends, representing, as did the delegation, the colonial aristocracy *de fortune et de nom*; that is to say, the nobility both of wealth and title. It is worth noting that only two of its members, Jean-Baptiste Gérard and Bodkin Fitzgerald, dared to inscribe themselves as members of the Jacobin Club.[105] First and foremost, of course, there is the scurrilous libelling of the anti-trade forces. They are seen as unrealistic philosophes, impractical dreamers, *enthousiastes* and *frondeurs*. The fact that the highly respectable membership of the Amis des Noirs included the King of Poland and the Duc de Charost, and did not include either Mirabeau or Robespierre, does not prevent the charge that the Society seeks to destroy all religions, all empires, and all forms of government.[106] The admirable Abbé Gregoire was admired by all; but that does not deter the colon pamphleteers from spreading the calumny that he defends the *gens de couleur* because his brother is married to one of them; in a spirited reply, the Abbé remarked that he would prefer such a sister-in-law to all the vaunted amiability of the white colonial womenfolk.[107] Despite the moderate character of his views, based on his American travels, Brissot is denounced by his colonial detractor Louis-Marthe Gouy d'Aray as an irresponsible demagogue who would be hanged a hundred feet in the air by the very Negroes he cherishes should he ever set foot in Saint Domingue.[108] The double charge, even more serious, is then made that the Society is responsible for the Saint Domingue civil war, since its writings incite the slaves to revolt, and that some of its members are even paid agents of the English cause: a charge formally presented to the National Assembly by the Martiniquan deputy Dillon.[109] The particular charge of treason takes on piquant irony when it is remembered that the colonists themselves were at this time in secret negotiations with the English and even anticipated calling in North American aid, as the colonials' secret correspondence, published in Paris by the Society, makes clear; and Guy-Kersaint noted correctly in his 1792 address to the National Assembly that the ultimate aim of the colonists was independence. The Abbé Gregoire warned his countrymen in his *Lettre aux Citoyens de Couleur* of 1791 of the same secessionist temper, present in both white and mulatto elements of the colonial opposition.[110] To all of this there is added the occasionally quixotic note, such as the charge that the abolitionists employ women publicists as a means of provoking the colonists; one of them, Olympe de Gouge, replied to the charge in a vigorous polemic: without knowing anything of the history of America, she writes, this odious traffic of Negroes has always excited my indignation.[111] Our enemies, all in all, the colonists urge, are drunk with the language of liberty and must be stopped at all costs.

To this assault on abolitionist motives there were appended other theses. There is the argument that the peculiar social structure of the colony absolves it from the application of the social reforms mooted in Paris. "There is hardly any Third Estate in Saint Domingue," writes the colonial committee to the naval ministry in 1788, "since there are no free people, the slaves taking the place of a working class; there are no clergy; there is only one order of citizens, that of the planter proprietors, who from this viewpoint are all equals, all soldiers, and all officers, and all entitled as a result to enjoy the privileges of nobility."[112] It was a shrewd point: the Revolution in France is geared to the interests of the Third Estate; there is no Third Estate in the sugar colonies; therefore the colonies do not need the Revolution. The leading characteristic of the colonial society that from the liberal viewpoint demanded its transformation – its racial polarization – was thus perversely invoked by its defenders to nullify the demand. Or again, there is the argument that emphasizes the theme of the legendary colonial loyalty. If, as the colonists charged, Mirabeau was in the pay of Pitt and Clarkson was a British spy, we, they claimed are the true defenders of French honour and interests. We are loyal Frenchmen, the planters tell the king in their address of May 1788, and the ocean cannot prevent us from being the first to approach the throne.[113] Saint Domingue, reiterate the commissioners of the colonial deputation in the same year, is the most precious province of France, and should indeed be considered a second kingdom.[114] That argument is logically tied to the further compelling argument of the economic importance of the colony. Interfere with either slavery or the trade, and the commerce of France, along with its prosperity, will be annihilated. Commerce, in turn, is the necessary agent of navigation, agriculture, and the arts; destroy commerce, and you destroy everything.[115]

Like overseas colonists everywhere, the Saint Domingue plantocracy thus grossly exaggerated their importance for the mother country. The argument of loyalty, in any case, was patently insincere, for its lyrical effusions were accompanied by a tone of haughty arrogance that at times bordered on sedition. Your Majesty, they told the king, cannot pass over us any more than we can pass over you. Yesterday, we were weak; today, we are strong and vigorous, and we have the strength of adolescence. You cannot regard us , they told the National Assembly, as you did before the American war of independence, as if we were destined merely to serve the interests of France. You should consider the example of the schism provoked by the English. England still permits the Jamaican planters only to approach it as suppliants; but we ourselves are not asking favours but rights founded on our wealth, industry, and loyalty.[116] The argument received its practical expression in the organization of the colonial provincial councils based on an openly racial suffrage, in clear defiance of the sovereignty of the National Assembly, effectively constituting an assertion of the constitutional principle, so fatal to that sovereignty, that the colonies alone should exercise the right to initiate legislation concerning slavery and the coloured population.[117]

The final argument of the planter ideology, it goes without saying, was the racist one. Both the Abbé Sibire, in his *L'Aristocracie negrière*, and Lecointe-Marsillac in his *Le More-Lack* noted the unexamined dogmas of the planter creed with respect to the slave: slavery is justified by customary law or by the right of captivity in war or by ecclesiastical and civil law; the Church condones it, as is evident in St Paul's epistles, church council edicts, and even the Decalogue itself; the slave enters the system as an integral part of the necessary miseries of mankind; the slave is happier in America, where he gains physical safety and spiritual salvation through the ministrations of the Christian religion; the blacks are a race of men devoid of talent, reason, and intelligence; without slave labour it would be impossible to work the American plantations; the natural indolence of the African can only be overcome by harsh treatment; and the ever-present danger of servile revolt makes the harsh treatment even more obligatory.[118] The racist disdain extended even to the mulattoes, for to the "aristocrats of the skin" the people of mixed colour were at once an affront to their racial pride and a reproach to their own miscegenative behaviour. Malicious-minded genealogists, observed the abbé de Cournand scathingly, spend their time in odious investigations for the purpose of injuring innocent citizens.[119] The prejudice accounts for the fierce campaigns of the whites to deny the bastard-people of the mulattoes any sort of colonial representation in the prolonged struggle over the issue of the colonial suffrage after 1788, a campaign fought to the bitter end, even when the colony went up in flames after 1791.

All of the scholarly studies on the colonial question in the Revolution of 1789, albeit from different viewpoints – Dalmas, Boissonade, James, Deschamps, Garrett, Hardy – substantiate the general opinion of contemporary liberal observers like Brissot, Destuut de Tracy, Pétion de Villeneuve, and Condorcet that the Saint Domingue whites constituted a dominant, reactionary colonial ruling group of truly Bourbonese proportions. Their cast of mind was more authoritarian than that of the governors and intendants they so much hated. They saw the slave population simply as *une canaille abominable* (an abominable scum of the earth). Both the chevalier de Laborie and the Abbé Gregoire noted how the colonists' mode of argumentation, such as it was, was based not so much on reason as on blind prejudice and hatred.[120] They had no sense of compromise, because the habit of compromise was unknown to their experience. They sought to sabotage the conciliatory mission of the Commissioners sent out to the colony by the French government as surely as they refused to forge an alliance with the mulatto class with which, from the standpoint of economic interest, they had so much in common, and when they did finally bring themselves to countenance such an alliance, it was too late. For them, everything – in both racial and moral terms – was either black or white. The Amis des Noirs were evil-minded, misguided fools; the slave-generals of the revolution, who later became the black republic's slave-kings, were black monsters; and men of their own caste who showed even the slightest touch of the liberal disease were mercilessly destroyed: the Abbé Gregoire recounted in one of his works how Hilliard d'Auberteuil, who was certainly no Jacobin, was arrested and imprisoned in Port-au-Prince on suspicion of preparing to write an advising brief in favour of the *sangmêlés* and was then released after two months to die.[121] Even Père Labat, uncritical loyalist to the slave regime that he was, had been able to write in bitter terms of the rapacity of the French Company in Senegal in its slave-raiding missions; and Lanthenas, who noted Labat's accusation in his rebuttal of the apologist Lamiral, added that you could expect not even that much from the present-day defenders of slavery who, as a class, knew only the routine of amassing wealth and lacked both taste and philosophy.[122] They knew only two slogans, Lanthenas went on to say, the "balance of commerce" and the "interest of the nation."[123]

The Cuban Apologetic

After the English Antilles and French Hispaniola (Saint Domingue), the third case study of the planter mind is, of course, that of Spanish Cuba. With the disappearance of Saint Domingue as a rival sugar producer (which the Cuban sugarocracy welcomed, even at the terrible price of a successful slave uprising, thus demonstrating once again the absence of any genuine regional loyalty in the planter mentality), and with the English colonies hampered by the abolition of the trade and the subsequent efforts of the British navy to suppress the continuing illegal trade (those efforts being seen by the non-English Caribbean planter interests, perhaps justifiably, not as an exercise in British disinterested philanthropy, but as a sinister attempt to ruin their own Atlantic trade), Cuba moved into first place as the sugar bowl of the Caribbean and the last bastion of the slavery regime. A whole school of Cuban historians – Rivero Muñiz, Benito Celorio, Cepero Bonilla, Ramiro Guerra y Sànchez, Julio Le Riverend – has documented the century-long process whereby the island progressed from the status of a backward rural community in the eighteenth century, retarded by a restrictive Spanish colonial exclusivism, to that in the nineteenth century of a n opulent slave-based capitalism dominated by sugar tycoons, cigar magnates, and wealthy landowners. Notwithstanding the fact that the island economy was far more diversified than the earlier English and French slave regimes – coffee and cattle raising held their own up until the very end – it was sugar, founded on eternally escalating illegal slave imports, that laid the foundations of the new fabulous wealth; so much so that all the leading works of the Cuban socioeconomic literature – Saco's *Historia de la Esclavitud*, Guerra's *Azúcar y poblacion en las Antillas,* Ortiz's *Contrapunteo cubano*, Fraginals' *El Ingenio* – have been concerned in one way or another with the creoledom of sugar and its massive distorting effects upon Cuban society.[124]

What strikes the reader of the Cuban pro-slavery apologetic, as it developed throughout the nineteenth century, is that fact that despite uniquely different conditions that theoretically should have encouraged more civilized attitudes than those of the earlier eighteenth-century English and French defenders of the cause, that apologetic, in its substantive elements, remained as fixed and obdurate as ever. The different conditions are well known. The white-black population ratio was far more in favour of the whites than it had been in English Jamaica or French Saint Domingue. Heavy miscegenation patterns, in turn, spawned a free mulatto class much larger, statistically speaking, than its counterpart elsewhere, thus taking the edge off the endemic hatred between white master and black slave, and facilitating the rise of at once a free mulatto professional class and a negro-mulatto intelligentsia. The slave regime, in its turn, was not necessarily exclusively identified with the sugar-plantation regime, for there were sizable elements of slaves both on the coffee plantations and in the urban centres; and contemporary accounts strongly suggest that they led a more tolerable life than the English factory operatives of the period. Added to all that was the fact that nineteenth-century Cuba existed within the framework of the era of victorious liberalism; internationally, in the form of a hostile world opinion spearheaded by the British naval power, and internally, in the form of a cosmopolitan, articulate, and well-educated Creole elite oriented toward the outside world. Internally, it was apparent by the 1860s that slavery was an inefficient mechanism for a continuing profitable sugar industry; externally, the defeat of the South in the American Civil War made it clear that slavery could not survive within the modernizing Atlantic slave system.

It is chilling testimony to the habit of ideological persistency – the capacity, that is to say, of ideological systems to survive even when their social and economic infrastructures have been seriously weakened or have even disappeared – that all of these factors did not prevent a continuing defence of the slave system on the part of the Cuban plantocracy and its allies throughout the better part of the century. Despite the fact that Cuba never became, like Barbados or Jamaica, one vast, undifferentiated sugar plantation and that the investment, both economic and psychological, in the slave system was unequal in different strata of the Cuban top groups – making possible, for example, the well-known distinction between the Creole sugar oligarchs of the Occidente region and the more diversified Cuban agriculturists of the Oriente region, which generated as it did a fundamental rift in political ideology as the irrepressible conflict with Spain sharpened – it was the psychopathology engendered by slavery that shaped the dominant values and attitudes of the society. Wealth replaced birth as the badge of social status, and the most fabulous wealth in the perennial "dance of the millions" came from sugar. The continuing vague stigma that attached to men who – like the Tomás Terry who became the Cuban Croesus of his time – dealt directly in the clandestine trade did not prevent either social recognition or political advancement. Every generation witnessed the same spectacle of yet another new group of sugar barons, often self-made men without a genuine claim to any aristocratic title, being received into the Havana *haut monde*: the O'Farrills and Arangos came to be accepted by the Montalvos and Calvos, just as, later, the Zuluetas were accepted by the O'Farrills. The sole, impregnable barrier to that social mobility was the inability to parade the *limpieza de sangre* (purification of blood). Whereas inbreeding was rampant, interracial marriage was the one unforgivable offence. The testimony of practically all of the travellers who reported on the society agrees in noting these twin characteristics, feeding on each other: its insensate profligacy and its paranoid racism.[125]

It was in those terms that white Cuba, including much of its educated intelligence, saw itself and perceived others. That self-image, and that image of others, expressed itself in a variety of ways. The Havana commercial and agricultural societies, reflecting the influence of Benthamite utilitarianism, undertook, early on, extensive statistical studies of trade, commerce, and industry; but the official indifference to and general distaste for the class of free Negroes carried over into census investigations, so much so that no real effort was made to ascertain their true numbers. It was left to visitors like Humboldt in the early part of the century and De la Sagra in his *Historia económico-politica y estadística* of 1831 to attempt any sort of reliable statistics in that field, while it was not until the 1860s, with the publication of Pezuela's extraordinary geographical dictionary, that another Spanish scholar completed the task.[126] Visitors were constantly startled to hear praise heaped on the bozal, the newly arrived, raw African, while little but contempt was expressed for the Creole-born black, whose claim to be Cuban was clearly regarded as an intolerable affront.[127] A veritable hierarchy of colour prejudice offset the democracy of wealth; so, just as the resident Spanish *peninsulares* despised all Creoles as *mestizos* and defended their own often brown skin colour evasively as proof of a manly "Moorish blood," and just as publicists like Cristóbal Madán in his *El trabajo libre* of 1864 dismissed the mulattoes as a lazy and vicious crowd,[128] so the mulattoes in turn took out their own frustrated feelings of racial identity in a brutal contempt for the blacks, so much so that there is evidence galore to show that in Cuba, as much as in Saint Domingue earlier, the worst planter-masters were often the mulatto rich and that the slaves feared them even more than they feared the whites. The ingrained obsession with heredity, so typically Spanish, was reinforced by an acute anxiety over racial purity, again so typically Spanish; and it is no accident that the most famous of all nineteenth-century Cuban novels, Villaverde's *Cecilia Valdés*, treated the theme of the *parda,* the coloured woman, cruelly frustrated in her love for a scion of a Havana white family who, unbeknownst to her, is in fact her half brother, thus constituting in her figure at once a victim of white sexual exploitation and a casualty of a fiercely hierarchical system.

The key element in this set of attitudes was, of course, that of sex. Every ruling class has sought to use that element, through its marriage customs, as a means of collective self-defence. But in a racially divided society, the psychopathology of sexual anxiety is immeasurably intensified, for the fear of sexual pollution becomes not simply a matter of class integrity but one of racial purity. A racism of sex emerges. Martínez-Alier's study of racial attitudes and sexual values in nineteenth-century Cuba shows how that racism was perfected in the last of the Caribbean slave societies. Interracial marriage legislation, going back to the older edicts of the Council of the Indies, though often honoured in the breach rather than in the observance, accurately reflected the ideological stance of upper-class white Cuba on the matter; inequality in colour constituted a civil impediment to marriage that it was the business of both church and state to uphold. The civil legislation that controlled the marriage system was, in turn, accompanied by an obligatory ritual controlling seduction and elopement.

Two leading institutive principles lay at the heart of this discriminatory regime. There was, first, the Spanish concept of family honour, traditionally enforced by patterns of social class and endogamy and, second, the metaphysical notion of pure blood. The Martínez-Alier study demonstrates clearly how the Cuban slave regime gave both principles a new lease on life. Family, honour, originally concerned with the dangers of lower-class penetration of aristocratic homes, became transmuted into a defence-mechanism against racial pollution on the part of socially aspiring coloured adventurers. Similarly, the concept of purity of blood, originally used to distinguish old Christians from the new Christians in Spain itself, and largely discredited in the mother country by the end of the eighteenth century, gradually acquired the new meaning of distinction between people of African-slave origin and people of European-free origin. In the Cuban context, both of those principles became subtly transmuted to mean, more than anything else, protective shields against the ominous stain of slavery origin. It is true that the realities of the society– progressive miscegenation, the rise of a large free-coloured group, the widespread practice of the policy of *adelantar la familia* (keeping intact the family whiteness), and the consequent ambiguity surrounding racial identity – all made nonsense of any effort to determine social stratification along strictly racial lines. The point to note is that the ideologues of the system persisted to the end in portraying a dream world in which only coloured people should be slaves, and only free people white. The system contained its own seeds of destruction. But its dominant ideology, conceiving the system as it ought to have been rather than as it was, remained intact.[129]

Yet, however intact, the Cuban pro-slavery ideology was on the defensive throughout the century. If, in world opinion, Spain itself was regarded contemptuously as being nothing more than a geographical expression, its leading American colony was regarded as the immoral protagonist of the dying slave system. Internally, liberal movements of thought, from Varela's

constitutionalist liberalism at the beginning of the period, through the autonomist ideas of the liberal reformers, on to the radical populism of Martí at the end of the period, compelled a critical reevaluation of slavery, although the reevaluation was by no means always in favour of abolition. Attitudes to slavery, indeed, were inextricably mixed with attitudes, variously, to the independence movement against Spain and the pro-American stance of the annexationist ideologues. The social question, the race question, and the national question were necessarily interwoven, making it difficult to impose any neat classification upon the competing intellectual positions.

Arango y Parreño and José Antonio Saco

The two leading figures in the prolonged discussion of slavery were, it is generally agreed, Francisco de Arango y Parreño and José Antonio Saco. Both sons of the Cuban social respectability, they have long been enshrined by orthodox Cuban scholarship in the national pantheon of patriots, statesmen, and shapers of the Cuban national destiny. Both of them, intellectually, were self-confessed disciples of the European liberal movement, from Adam Smith to the Utilitarians, and employed their genius in a prolonged campaign to rid Cuba of an outmoded Spanish colonial mercantilism. They wanted to remake Cuba in the image of the England of triumphant technology, political liberty, and constitutional government that (as for so much of the Latin American intelligentsia of the period) was their model of the ideal society. But just as in Victorian England, liberalism, in practice, turned out to be an ideology working mainly for the interests of the rising industrial bourgeoisie, so in colonial Cuba it catered to the interests of the new wealth of sugar as against the interests of the masses; and since, furthermore, those masses were overwhelmingly black, it meant the perpetuation of Negrophobia. The writings of both Arango and Saco graphically illustrate the philosophical contradictions that arose, then, out of their effort, ultimately unsuccessful, to reconcile their liberalism with the slavery question.

Arango has been called "the colonial statesman" by the most uncritically admiring of his biographers.[130] The encomium is undoubtedly deserved. Appointed at a youthful age as *Apod-*

erado General of the Havana *ayuntamiento*, he devoted his intellectual gifts to a lifelong campaign in defence of the expansionist interests of the new, rising sugar wealth in the colony. One the one hand, it was a sort of Creole nationalist revolt against the old Spanish mercantilist closed system, a system rooted in the contemptuous observation by the Viceroy of Peru that "the American ought to know nothing more than how to read, write and pray"; on the other hand, it was a frank and completely unsentimental defence of the interests of the new Cuban bourgeois wealth, incarnated in the dictum of the Spanish minister of the time, Floridablanca, that "greed and interest are the main incentive for all human toil and they should only be checked in public matters when they are prejudicial to other persons or to the State."[131] Arango's work, it follows, was essentially that of the well-placed lobbyist who wrote important state papers seeking to influence the policymakers of Havana and Madrid. Despite his mastery of the problems of the Cuban economy, despite even his wide reading in, for example, the French encyclopaedists, his vision was limited to the single purpose of transforming Cuba into an opulent sugar palace; so, although he could have written the first monumental history of Cuba had he so wished, it was left to the young Spanish scholar Pezuela to lament, on his arrival in Havana in the 1840s, that such a history did not exist and to prepare to undertake the task of composing it himself.

Accordingly, it is in Arango's state documents that we meet the first reasoned apologetic for the slave system in Cuban historiography. His very first memorial of 1789, significantly enough, was an extensive examination and defence of the Havana claim for a thoroughgoing liberalization of the restrictive Spanish legislation that inhibited the free entry of slaves into the colonial market. The old laws of the Indies – based on the traditional Spanish reluctance to allow an unrestricted import of Africans into the colonies – the argument went, have been rendered anachronistic by the vast contraband trade, which benefits foreign nations and defrauds both Spain and Cuba. The crying need of Cuba was for a rapid and cheap supply of Negro labour; and if it was impossible to give the trade entirely to Spanish ships, it should at least be made free to all nationalities as the only way to avoid the evils of monopoly.[132] Arango's famous *Discurso*

of 1792 on the state of the Cuban agriculture pressed the argument further. It is the central theme of the *Discurso* to emphasize the irony of the fact that with the most fertile soil of the Antilles, Cuba remains the most backward of the New World colonies. The reasons are clear: the lower costs of slave importation in the rival islands; the equally lower costs of slave maintenance, including the fact that the French and the English slave owners permit fewer holidays to their slaves than do the Cubans; the technological backwardness of the Cuban agriculturist, due in part, as Arango sees it, to the *indolencia criolla* (Creole indolence) of Latin Americans in general; and the subjection of the Cuban planter to the merchant houses of Spain and the usury-mongers of the Havana financial class, also mainly Spanish. Only a free-trade system, ultimately giving the Cuban planter the direct access to the African slave market hitherto denied him, can in the long run override most of those disabilities.[133]

In all of this, Arango is the shrewd, hard-headed business ideologue ready to employ any argument, however jesuitical, to foment a Cuban slave-based capitalism. In that effort he had to meet the older conservative humanism of the Council of the Indies, where the spirit of Las Casas was still very much alive, and the new humanitarianism of the English and French abolitionists. Both were met with the argument that theirs was a grossly misplaced concern, since the Negro was a piece of chattel property only, not a person with rights; and in any case, he and his kind "were all becoming much happier than they used to be." The Haitian revolt was due to the insidious propaganda of the abolitionists, which the Saint Domingue planters had mistakenly imbibed, thus teaching their slaves the fatal lesson that they were deserving of rights. In any case, the revolt is to be welcomed, since it annihilates a dangerous sugar rival: it was necessary to look at the French colony, "not only with compassion but with the eyes of hard political sense."[134] If slavery is unchristian (as even Arango cannot deny), it is nonetheless necessary, for the tropical climate makes work by whites impossible (a myth later on vigorously denied by Saco). In any case, continues Arango, the original sin is not Cuban, but European (thus avoiding the question, surely pertinent, as to whether it was not an equal sin to continue an offence launched by others). "The inconsequential piety of Las Casas," Arango tells the Crown, "introduced negroes among us: a stupid policy has paralysed the process of the world and the vigour and number of the whites. We are just awakening with all the lethargy of three centuries of exhaustion and neglect. . .we see that without remedying our internal situation, without having any regard for it or providing new aids for us, it is made a question of depriving us suddenly of the means given us by the old laws and customs for our subsistence, or for keeping up the culture which maintains our existence."[135] A policy originally misconceived thus becomes a policy absolutely necessary to a Cuban "culture" identified exclusively with the interests of its white men of property. Even as late as the prolonged controversy over the Spanish 1812 Constitution, the Council of the Indies still managed to see the issue in moral terms, summed up in its statement that "We ought, therefore, never to forget that the question is not one between Men and Brutes, but between Men and Men, lest our judgment should overlook the cause of humanity and lean towards that of Interests."[136] Arango's answer in the strongly worded *Memorial* of 1811 was to reassert the paramountcy of the rights of Interests. Arango admonished the Crown:

Think, Señor, about the political slavery of these regions before civil slavery, about the Spaniards before the Africans, about the rights and privileges of citizens here before determining the size and numbers of doors that should be opened or closed to people of colour, about ways to breathe life into our inert police force, and all branches of our dead and decayed public administration, before increasing their risks and their burdens, define the role and powers of the Spanish and of the colonial government before undertaking to cure ills which are neither urgent nor paramount, fortify the old government's corrupted organs and adjust its defective spectacles before exposing the wounds and infections of remote sectors of our social body.[137]

The significance of all this, in the history of Cuban racism, is that it reveals Arango as the exponent of the slavery apologetic in its purest form. His arguments are those of a matured bourgeois consciousness. He sees the slave as the objectively necessary labour force of a new Cuba. If that end had been possible without slavery, he would have welcomed it. But Cuban conditions, including the aversion of white labourers to plantation work, made recourse to the African market inescapable. So while, on the one hand, his work is completely bereft of any of the romantic humanitarianism of the time, it is equally bereft of the Negrophobic racism of other Cuban ideologues like that of Lorenzo Allo in his *La esclavitud doméstica* and that of Betancourt Cisneros in his letters to Saco.[138] Or, to put it in another way, if on the one hand there is nothing in Arango's work of the doubts that assailed other slavery defenders like Edwards and Moreau de Saint-Méry, on the other hand there is very little of the Negrophobic hatred of writers like Delmonte and Echeverría – so little, in fact, that later on in his life he was capable of championing the idea of race admixture, whereby the black Cuban would eventually, by a process of genetic evolution, be obliterated by the white Cuban, thereby (in his own phrase) wiping out the memory of slavery.[139] For Arango, then, it is not a matter of slavery for slavery's sake. Rather, it is that since slavery will always exist where human nature exists, the statesman has no other choice than to put it to use for his own purposes. Brought up and educated in the age of Bonaparte and Metternich, Arango is the worldly-wise cynic for whom the only rationale is that of *raison d'état*. It is for that reason that his work constitutes, in Moreno Fraginals' phrase, the first great expression of the Cuban sugarcrat ideology, the most sincere, and hence, perhaps, the most significant, the most cynical, and the most pathetic.[140]

The importance of Arango's work, then, is that it confers intellectual letters of credit upon the rising native bourgeoisie and its incipient capitalism. Its gross and pathetic contradiction, of course, was that it sought, unsuccessfully, to marry the bourgeois ethic with the pre-bourgeois material base of slavery. For the essence of the bourgeois ethic was the concept of contract between capitalist and worker, a concept fatally compromised by the denial of contractual relationships in the master-slave system. That contradiction was reflected in the new ideology; Arango, as its chief intellectual protagonist, had (again in Moreno Fraginals' terms) one foot in the bourgeois future and the other in the remote slave past. That basic contradiction helps to explain all of the argumentative contradictions of Arango's work. The examples are numerous. There is the perpetuation of the legend (which Arango helped to create and which survives even into modern scholarship) that Cuban history starts with the English occupation of Havana in 1763 – that is, with the first step in the realization of the paranoid dream of the Havana slavery group of a free and unrestricted importation of slaves, almost as if the previous two centuries of Cuban social development could be arbitrarily forgotten. For if that legend, as one American scholar has sharply put it, is yet another instance of Anglo-Saxon self-glorification,[141] it can also be seen as an instance of self-congratulatory Cuban bourgeois historiography that only sees Cuban history as a real thing once its slave base becomes assured. Without slaves, Arango seems to be saying, we are nothing; with slaves, we are everything. Arango, in turn, defended the stability of the Cuban social order, founded as it was – unlike the English and French colonies – on a resident Creole proprietary class. Yet he was ready to weaken that stability with a heavy black influx, cavalierly ignoring the warnings – prolific in the official Spanish literature and reiterated for example, in the objections of the directors of the Real Compañía in 1760 – to the effect that an immoderate introduction of Negroes would jeopardize the security of the whole island.[142] The contrast, here, with the argument of an earlier Cuban economist like Arrate is instructive. For it was one of the theses of Arrate's work *Llave del Nuevo Mundo*, composed in the 1750s, that Cuban society would have been far better served if, instead of importing alien Africans who rapidly became an economic burden to their masters, it had nurtured its aboriginal Indians, who had shown themselves willing to work industriously for food and a modest wage return – by comparison with which slavery was wasteful and expensive.[143]

There emerged finally, then, the ultimate contradiction between Arango's real sense of Cuban nationalism and his obsession with the accumulation of riches. He shared with Arrate a real pride in Cuban identity. But whereas for Arrate that meant a *familia cubana* in which all shared full citizenship – as his appreciative observations on the positive role of Negroes and *pardos* in the eighteenth century civic militia clearly show[144] – for Arango it meant a socially exclusive club for the white respectability only. The club would only bend its rules to make way for the growth of the mulatto class, as a part of Arangos' racial hygiene plan – which class, following the Haitian example (as Arango read it) would ally itself

to the whites in a combined effort to keep the repressed black class in order.[145] Arangos' concern with racial harmony, this is to say, was wholly that of the realpolitiker who thinks in terms of power-group alliances rather than in terms of social justice. If, then, the attempt throughout the century by the liberal party in Spain to instill its institutions into Cuba failed, the failure must be attributed in main part to the prevalence of Arango's ideology, which could see no way of saving the wealth of the island colony without slaves, nor of admitting democratic institutions without setting free a hazardously large number of Negroes. As a young colonial student of the work of the great Spanish agrarian reformer Jovellanos, Arango dreamed of a modernized Cuba. But the very institution of slavery that he had himself helped to create made its realization impossible. Its fulfilment was only made possible, later, by the growth of the *ideología mambisa* (ideology of the revolting slaves) and its acknowledgment of the truth that only the abolition of slavery could create the indispensable condition for a liberal Cuba. The social base of Arango's thought made that failure inevitable, for if Arrate was the expression of the old Havana town oligarchy, Arango was the expression of the new sugar aristocracy.

Notes

1. Fernando de Oviedo y Valdés, *Historia general y natural de las Indias* (Madrid, 1535–1556), cited ibid., pp. 111–13.
2. Bartolomé de Las Casas, *Historia de las Indias* (Mexico City: Fondo de Cultura Económico, 1951), cited ibid., p. 141.
3. Henry Raup Wagner, *The Life and Writings of Bartolome de Las Casas*.(Albuquerque: University of New Mexico Press, 1967), p. 11.
4. Alonzo Zuazo, Judge of Hispaniola, to Cardinal Ximenes, Regent of Spain, January 22, 1518, cited in Eric Williams, ed., *Documents of West Indian History, 1492-1655*.(Port-of-Spain, Trinidad: People's National Movement Publishing Co., 1963), pp. 144-45.
5. Diego de Salamanca, Bishop of San Juan, to Philip II, King of Spain, April 6, 1579, cited ibid., p. 144.
6. *Ordenanzas para el cabildo y regimiento de la villa de la Habana y las demás villas y lugares de esta isla que hizo y ordeno el ilustre Sr. Dr. Alonso de Caceres, oidor de la dicha Audiencia real de la cuidad*, January 14, 1574, cited ibid., pp. 153–54.
7. Quoted in Wagner, *The Life and Writings of Las Casas*, p. 247.

8.   Bartolomé de Albornoz, *Arte de los Contratos* (Valencia, 1573), quoted in Williams, *Documents of West Indian History*, p. 161.

9.   Fray Tomás Mercado, *Suma de Tratos y Contratos* (Seville, 1587), cited ibid., pp. 158–60.

10. Fray Alonso de Sandoval, *De Instauranda Aethiopum Salute* (Seville, 1627), quoted ibid., p. 163.

11. Samuel Purchas, *Purchas his Pilgrimage. Or Relations of the World and the Religions Observed in all Ages and Places Discovered, from the Creation unto This present* (London, 1614), cited in Jordan, *White over Black*, pp. 12–13.

12. Thomas Atwood, *The History of the Island of Dominica* (London, 1791, reprint ed., London: Frank Cass and Co., 1971).

13. Sir William Young, *An Account of the Black Charaibs in the Island of St Vincent's* (London, 1795).

14. R.C. Dallas, *History of the Maroons*, 2 vols. (London, 1803). 1:viii, 87–95.

15. Ibid., 1:148.

16. Ibid., 1:45.

17. Ibid., 1:180–81.

18. Ibid., 2:2-3.

19. Atwood, *History of the Island*, p. 257; Dallas, *History of the Maroons*, 2:453–54.

20. Bryan Edwards, *The History, Civil and Commercial, of the British West Indies*, 5 vols. (London, 1819), 1:522–79.

21. Lowell Joseph Ragatz, *A Guide for the Study of British Caribbean History, 1763–1834, Including the Abolition and Emancipation Movements* (Washington, D.C.: U.S. Government Printing Office, 1932).

22. John Luffman, *A Brief Account of the Island of Antigua, 1786–1788* (London, 1789), reprinted in Vere Langford Oliver, *History of the Island of Antigua*, 3 vols. (London: Mitchell and Hughes, 1894), pp. cxxxviii–cxxxviii; Richard Schomburgk, *Travels in British Guiana, 1840–1844*, ed. Vincent Roth (Georgetown, British Guiana: Guiana edition, *Daily Chronicle*, 1953), 1:47; noted in Roland T. Ely, *Cuando reinaba su majestad el azúcar* (Buenos Aires: Editorial Sudamericana, 1963), ch. 28.

23. Edward Long, *History of Jamaica*, 3 vols. (London, 1774, reprint ed., London: Frank Cass and Co., 1970), 1:25.

24. Ibid., 2:324.

25. Ibid., 1:25.

26. Ibid., 2:354, 398.

27. Ibid., 2:271.

28. Ibid., 2:407.

29. Ibid., 2:429–30.

30. Ibid., 2:375.

31. Ibid., 2:326–27, 332–33.

32. Ibid., 2:393–94, 400–404.

33. Ibid., 1:4.

34. Ibid., vol. 2, ch. 4.

35. Edwards, *History of the British West Indies*, 2:93–94.

36. Ibid., 3:13, 2:179.

37. Ibid., 2:124–28, 140–44.

38. Ibid., 2:148–49.

39. Ibid., 2:169–70.

40. Eric Williams, ed., *The British West Indies at Westminster*, Part 1:*1789–1823* (Port-of-Spain, Trinidad: Historical Society of Trinidad and Tobago, Government Printing Office, 1954).

41. John Stewart, *A View of the Past and Present State of the Island of Jamaica* (1823; reprint ed., Westport, Conn.: Negro Universities Press, 1969), p. 205.

42. Rev. John Riland, ed., *Memoirs of a West Indian Planter* (London, 1827); and note in Ragatz, *Guide for the Study of British Caribbean History*, pp. 232–33.

43. *A report of a committee of the Council of Barbados, appointed to inquire into the actual conditions of the slaves in this island* (1824), in *West Indian Slavery: Selected Pamphlets* (Westport, Conn.: Negro Universities Press, 1970), pp. 6–9; Wm. Beckford, *A Descriptive Account of the Island of Jamaica*, 2 vols. (London, 1790).

44. James Hakewell, *A picturesque tour of the Island of Jamaica* (London, 1825).

45. Edwards, *History of the British West Indies*, vol. 2, app. 1, bk. 4, pp. 187–225.

46. Alexander Barclay, *A Practical View of the Present State of Slavery in the West Indies*, 2d ed. (London, 1827), p. 42; J.F. Barham, *Considerations on the Abolition of Negro Slavery and the Means of Practically Effecting It* (1823), on *West Indian Slavery: Selected Pamphlets*, p. 9.

47. G.W. Jordan, *An Examination of the Principles of the Slave Registry Bill and of the Means of Emancipation* (1816), on *West Indian Slavery: Selected Pamphlets*, pp. 43–46, 61–66, 68–70, 75–84.

48. Elsa Goveia, *Slave Society in the British Leeward Islands at the End of the Eighteenth Century* (New Haven: Yale University Press, 1965; reprint ed., Río Piedras: Institute of Caribbean Studies, University of Puerto Rico, 1969), p. 330; Eric Williams, *Capitalism and Slavery* (Chapel Hill: University of North Carolina Press, 1944), pp. 184–85.

49. *A report of a Committee* (1824), pp. 30–31.

50. Edwards, *An Historical Survey of the French Colony of St Domingo*, vol. 3 in *History of the British West Indies*, pp. 208–10.

51. Beckford, *Descriptive Account of Jamaica*, p. 6.

52. John Stewart, *A View of the Past and Present State of the Island of Jamaica*.(1823; reprint ed., Westport, Conn.: Negro Universities Press, 1969), pp. 181-82.

53. Henry Bleby, *Death Struggles of Slavery*, 3 ed.(London, 1868), ch.11, "Pernicious Influence of a Licentious Press."

54. Edwards, *History of the British West Indies*, 3:208–9.

55. Beaumont, cited in Bleby, *Death Struggles*, p. 27.

56. Beckford, *Descriptive Account of Jamaica*, pp. 117, 48.

57. *A report of a committee* (1824), p. 40.

58. Williams, *Documents of West Indian History*, p. 244.

59. G.W. Jordan, *The Claims of the West Indian Colonists to the Right of Obtaining Necessary Supplies from America* (1804), noted in Ragatz, *A Guide*, pp. 301-2; and Bryan Edwards, *Thoughts on the Late Proceedings of Government, Respecting the Trade of the West India Islands with the United States of America* (1784), noted ibid., p. 292.

60. Edwards, *History of the British West Indies*, 2:281.

61. Barham, *Considérations*, p. 27.
62. Barclay, *A Practical View*, p. 15.
63. Edwards, *History of the British West Indies*, 2:163–64; Wm. Beckford, *Remarks upon the Situation of the Negroes in Jamaica*, noted in Ragatz, *A Guide*, p. 479; *The Condition of the West Indian Slave Contrasted with That of the Infant Slave in Our English Factories* (London, c. 1833), noted ibid., p. 420.
64. J.L. Hammond and Barbara Hammond, *The Rise of Modern Industry* (London: Methuen and Co., 1944), ch. 12.
65. Abbé de Mably, *Recherches historiques et politiques sur les Etats-Unis de l'Amerique septentrionale* (1788), cited in W. Stark, *America: Ideal and Reality* (London: Kegan Paul, Trench, Trubner and Co., 1947), p. 48; John Ludlow, *Progress of the Working Class* (London, 1867), cited in Gordon K. Lewis, *Slavery, Imperialism, and Freedom: Essays in English Radical Thought* (New York and London: Monthly Review Press, 1978), p. 184.
66. A. Pons, *Observations sur la situation politique de St-Domingue*, cited in Placide David, *L'Héritage colonial en Haité* (Madrid, 1959), p. 279; Baron Alexandre de Wimpffen, *A Voyage to Santo Domingo in the Years 1788, 1789, and 1790*, English edition, cited ibid., p. 279.
67. Baron Alexandre de Wimpffen, *Voyage à St-Domingue: Souvenirs du Baron de Wimpffen* (Paris: Allbert Savine, 1911), letter 22, p. 277; Hilliard d'Auberteuil, *Considérations sur l'état présent de la colonie française de Saint-Domingue*, 2 vols. (Paris, 1776–77), vol. 1, Discours preliminaire: Médéric-Louis-Elie Moreau de Saint-Méry, *Description topographique, physique, civil, politique, et historique de la partie française de l'île Saint-Domingue*, 3 vols. (Philadelphia, 1797), 1:2.
68. Victor Adveille, *L'Odyssée d'un Normand à St-Domingue au dix-huitième siècle* (Paris: Librarie Chaltenel, 1901).
69. Wimpffen, *Voyage à St-Domingue*, letter 10, p. 103; Pons, *Observations*, p. 3.
70. A. De Lauzon, *Souvenirs de trente années de voyage à Saint-Domingue*, cited in David, *L'Héritage colonial*, pp. 48–50; Comte d'Ennery, cited in D'Auberteuil, *Considérations*, vol. 2, Discours preliminaire.
71. Wimpffen, *Voyage à St-Domingue*, letter 22; Moreau de Saint-Méry, *Description*, 3: 227–31.
72. Moreau de Saint-Méry, *Description*, pp. 227–31.
73. Adam Smith, *The Wealth of Nations* (London: Everyman's Library, 1917); bk. 4, pt. 2, pp. 84–85.
74. Cited in Antoine Gisler, *L'esclavage aux Antilles Françaises, XVII–XVIII siècle* (Fribourg: Editions Universitaires, 1965), pp. 117–21.
75. Noted in C.L.R. James, *The Black Jacobins* (London: Secker and Warburg, 1938), p. 30.
76. Noted in P. Boissonade, *Saint Domingue à la veille de la Révolution* (Paris and New York: Librarie G.E. Stechert and Co., 1906), pp. 33–34. See also James G. Leyburn, *The Haitian People* (New Haven: Yale University Press, 1942), pp. 17–20.
77. Girod-Chantrans, *Voyage d'un Suisse dans differentes colonies d'Amérique* (Neufchatel, 1785), cited in David, *L'Héritage colonial*, p. 87; Moreau de Saint-Méry, *Description*, cited ibid., p. 87.
78. Wimpffen, *Voyage à St-Domingue*, pp. 54–55.
79. Cited in Adveille, *L'odyssée*, p. 142.
80. *Moreau de Saint-Méry: American Journey, 1793–1798*, trans. and ed. Kenneth Roberts and Anna M. Roberts (Garden City, N.Y.: Doubleday and Co., 1947).
81. Moreau de Saint-Méry, *Description*, 3 vols. (Paris: Theodore Morgand, Librarie-Dépositaire, 1875), 3:216–18.
82. Ibid., 1:7–8, 11–12.
83. Ibid., 1:17–18, 20–27.
84. Ibid., 1:79–82.
85. Ibid., 1:15–16.
86. Ibid., 1:82.
87. Ibid., 1:83–89, 82.
88. Ibid., 1:27–46.
89. Píerre de Charlevoix, *Histoire de l'île Espagnoleou de St-Domingue* (Paris, 1730–31); Malenfant, *Des Colonies et particuliérement de cette de Saint-Domingue* (Paris, 1814).
90. Moreau de Saint-Méry, *Description*, 1:51.
91. Ibid., vol. 1, Discours preliminaire.
92. D'Auberteuil, *Considérations*, 1:4–5.
93. Ibid., 1:136–37, 130–33.
94. Ibid., 1:143, 133, 135.
95. Ibid., 1:132.
96. Charlevoix, *Histoire de l'île espagnole*, 1:496–97.
97. Paul Ulric Dubuisson, *Nouvelles considérations sur Saint-Domingue* (Paris, 1790), 1:6, 146–47, 154–56.
98. Ibid., 1:69, 72–73, 77–78.
99. Ibid., 1:80–81.
100. Ibid., 1:83–84.
101. Ibid., 1:67–68, 69.
102. Moreau de Saint-Méry, debate of May 7, 1791, *Moniteur Universel* (Paris), edition of 1853–63, pp. viii, 333–36, cited in Charles Oscar Hardy, *The Negro Question in the French Revolution* (Menasha, Wis.: George Banta Publishing Company, 1919), p. 45.
103. Pierre Boissonade, *Saint-Domingue à la vielle de la Révolution et la question de la représentation coloniale aux Etats Generaux* (Paris: Paul Geuthner, 1906), p. 36.
104. Moreau de Saint-Méry, *Considérations présentées aux vrais amis du repos et du bonheur de la France* (1791) cited in Boissonade, *Saint-Domingue*, p. 42.
105. Boissonade, *Saint-Domingue*, pp. 166–67.
106. *Il est encore des Aristocrates, ou Réponse a l'infame auteur d'un Ecrit institué: Decouverte d'un conspiration contre les intérêts de la France* (Paris, 1790), pp. 3–4; reprinted in Ediciones d'Histoire Sociales (EDHIS), *La Révolution française et l'abolition de l'esclavage*, 12 vols. (Paris: EDHIS, 1968), vol. 4.
107. M. Gregoire, *Lettre aux citoyens de couleur et Nègres libres de Saint-Domingue* (Paris, 1791), p. 19; reprinted in EDHIS, *La Révolution Française*, vol. 4.

108. Louis-Marte Gouy d'Aray, *Premiére et dernière lettre à Jean Pierre Brissot* (Paris, 1791), p. 11.

109. Armand Guy-Kersaint, *Moyens proposés à l'Assemblée Nationale pour rétablir la paix et l'ordre dans les colonies* (Paris, 1792); reprinted in EDHIS, *La Révolution française*, vol. 5; Gregoire, *Lettre*, pp. 14–15.

110. Cited in Hardy, *The Negro Question*, pp. 38–40.

111. Olympe de Gouge, *Réponse au champion américain ou colon très-aisé à connaître* (Paris, 1790), p. 5; reprinted in EDHIS, *La Révolution française*, vol. 4.

112. *Mémoire instructif à consulter et consultation* (1788), cited in Boissonade, *Saint-Domingue*, pp. 115–16.

113. "Lettre des colons à Saint-Domingue au Roi" (May, 1788), Bibliothèque Nationale, Paris, bk. 12, vol. 23).

114. *Lettre des commissaires de la colonie de Saint-Domingue aux présidents des Bureaux de l'Association des Notables* (November 1788), cited in Boissonade, *Saint-Domingue*, pp. 123–24.

115. Boissonade, *Saint-Domingue*, pp. 95–97.

116. Ibid., pp. 95–96, 118–19.

117. Hardy, *The Negro Question*, pp. 34–35; Boissonade, *Saint-Domingue*, pp. 74–76.

118. Abbé Sibire, *L'Aristocracie négriere* (Paris, 1789), reprinted in EDHIS, *La Révolution française*, vol. 2; and Lecointe-Marsillac, *Le More-Lack* (Paris, 1789), reprinted (ibid.,) vol. 3.

119. Abbé Antoine de Cournand, *Requête présentée à Nos Seigneurs de l'Assemblée Nationale, en faveur des gens de couleur de l'île de Saint-Domingue* (Paris, 1790), p. 5, reprinted in EDHIS, *La Révolution Française*, vol. 4.

120. Chevalier de Laborie, *Propositions soumises à l'éxamen du Comité de Marine de l'Assemblée Nationale* (Paris, 1790), pp. 11–12, reprinted in EDHIS, *La Révolution Française*, vol. 4; Gregoire, *Lettre*, p. 20.

121. Gregoire, *Lettre*, p. 9–10.

122. François-Xavier Lanthenas, *M. Lamiral Réfuté par lui-même* (Paris, 1790), pp. 58–59, reprinted in EDHIS, *La Révolution Française*, vol. 7.

123. Ibid., p. 69

124. José Antonio Saco, *Historia de la esclavitud de la raza africana en el Nuevo Mundo y en especial en los paises américohispanos*, 6 vols. (Barcelona, 1879); Ramiro Guerra, *Azúcar y población en las Antillas* (Havana: Instituto del Libro, Ciencias Sociales, 1970); Fernando Ortiz, *Contrapunteo cubano del tobaco y el azúcar* (Havana: Casa Montero, 1940)—translated into English by Cedric Belfrage as *Cuban Counterpoint, Tobacco and Sugar* (New York: Knopf, 1947); Manuel Moreno Fraginals, *El Ingenio: El complejo económico—social cubano del azúcar* (Havana: Casa Montero, 1964)—translated into English by Cedric Belfrage as *The Sugar Mill: The Socioeconomic Complex of Sugar in Cuba, 1760–1860* (New York: Monthly Review Press, 1976).

125. Ramon Guerra et. al., eds., *Historia de la Nación Cubana*, 10 vols. (Havana: Editorial Nacional, 1952);

Willis Fletcher Johnson, *The History of Cuba*, 5 vols. (New York, 1920).

126. Friedrich H.A. von Humboldt, *The Island of Cuba* (New York, 1856); Ramón de la Sagra, *Historia económica-política y estadistica de la Isla de Cuba* (Havana, 1831); Jacobo de la Pezuela, *Diccionario geográfico, estadístico, histórico, de la isla de Cuba*, 4 vols. (Madrid, 1859).

127. Kenneth F. Kiple, *Blacks in Colonial Cuba, 1174–1899* (Gainesville: Center for Latin American Studies, University of Florida, 1976), pp. 42–43.

128. Cristóbal F. Madán, *El trabajo libre* (1864), cited in Franklin W. Knight, *Slave Society in Cuba during the Nineteenth Century* (Madison: University of Wisconsin Press, 1970), p. 97.

129. Verena Martínez-Alier, *Marriage, Class, and Colour in Nineteenth-Century Cuba: A Study of Racial Attitudes an Sexual Values in a Slave Society*, Cambridge Latin American Studies (Cambridge: At the University Press, 1974).

130. Francisco J. Ponte Domínguez, *Arango Parreño: El estadista colonial* (Havana: Editorial Trópico, 1937).

131. Viceroy of Peru and Floridablanca, cited in Manuel Colmeiro, *Historia de la economía política en España*, 2 vols. (Madrid, 1863) 2:243.

132. Ibid., pp. 28–30.

133. Francisco de Arango y Parreño, *Discurso sobre la agricultura de la Habana y medios de formentarlo*, in *De la factoria á la colonia* (Havana: Cuadernos de Cultura, 1936), pp. 1–113, and especially "Proyecto," pp. 94–112.

134. Arango y Parreño, *Memorial* (1791), in *Obras del Excmo. Señor D. Francisco de Arango y Parreño* (Havana, 1888), 1:49–52, 93.

135. Arango y Parreño, *Memorial* (1811), cited in Hubert H.S. Aimes, *A History of Slavery in Cuba, 1511 to 1868* (New York and London: G.P. Putman's Sons, 1907), p. 66.

136. Aimes, *History of Slavery*, p. 77.

137. Arango y Parreño, *Memorial* (1811), in *Obras*, 2:208.

138. Lorenzo Allo, *La esclavitud doméstica en sus relaciones con la riqueza*, cited in Raul Cepero Bonilla, *Azúcar y abolición: Apuntes para una historia crítica del abolicionismo* (Havana, 1948), p. 24; Ibid., p. 43.

139. Ibid., pp. 94–96.

140. Moreno Fraginals, *The Sugar Mill*, p. 60.

141. Aimes, *History of Slavery*, p. 33.

142. Ibid., pp. 30–31.

143. José Martin Félix de Arrate, *Llave del Mundo Nuevo, antemural de las Indias Occidentales* (Mexico City: Biblioteca Americana. 1949), ch. 6. See also José Manuel Pérez Cabrera *Historiografía de Cuba* (Mexico City: Instituto Panamericano de Geografía e Historia, 1962), pp. 93–102.

144. Arrate, *Llave del Mundo Nuevo*, ch. 19.

145. 145.Cepero Bonilla, *Azucar y abolicion: Apuntes para una historia critica del abolicionismo.*(Havana, 1948), p. 96.

42

The West Indian Slave Laws of the Eighteenth Century

ELSA V. GOVEIA*

The West Indian slave laws of the eighteenth century mirror the society that created them. They reflect the political traditions of the European colonizers and the political necessities of a way of life based upon plantation slavery.

The foundation of these laws was laid in the earliest days of colonization; and the body of slave laws existing in the eighteenth century included a substantial proportion of laws made at an earlier time. The thirteenth-century code of laws, known as the *Siete Partidas*, was from the beginning incorporated in the common law of the Spanish colonies and provided a series of principles for the government of slaves.[1] The great slave code of the French West Indies, which came to be called the *Code Noir*, was promulgated during the seventeenth century. The early slave laws of the British colonies, though they were not codified in this way, were generally retained as part of the slave law of the islands during the eighteenth century; and even when these laws were repealed in detail, a continuity of principle can be traced. The early laws were elaborated. Their emphasis changed with changes in the life of the islands. But the structure of the eighteenth-century slave laws rested upon older laws and was moulded by forces, early at work in the islands, which had shaped not only the law but also the society of these slave colonies.

Both in the creation and in the maintenance of the slave laws, opinion was a factor of great significance. Law is not the original basis of slavery in the West India colonies, though slave laws were essential for the continued existence of slavery as an institution. Before the slave laws could be made, it was necessary for the opinion to be accepted that persons could be made slaves and held as slaves. To keep the slave laws in being, it was necessary for this opinion to persist. Without this, the legal structure would have been impossible. Spain's role in establishing slavery as part of the pattern of European colonization in the West Indies is thus of primary importance. Of equal importance, is the influence exerted by developments within the West Indies in sustaining the legal structure, first introduced by the Spaniards, and, to a greater or lesser extent, transforming its content.

Slavery was an accepted part of Spanish law at the time of the discovery. It was legal to hold slaves, and it was accepted in law that slavery was transmitted by birth, through the mother to her children. This was the core of the system of enslavement transferred from Spain to the West Indies.[2] But in Spain, at this time, slavery was a relatively insignificant and declining institution, and by no means the dominant force that it was to become in the West Indies. The early and vigorous growth of plantations and slavery in the Spanish West Indies, though it was sharply checked, revealed the dynamic, expansive force of slavery in the new environment. With the growth of the French and English plantation colonies, slavery came to provide the economic

*Elsa V. Goveia is Professor of West Indian History at the University of the West Indies, Jamaica. She is the author of *Slave Society in the British Leeward Islands at the End of the 18th Century* (1965) and a recognized authority on West Indian history.

Reprinted from Elsa V. Goveia, 'The West Indian Slave Laws of the Eighteenth Century,' *Revista de Ciencias Sociales*, IV, No. 1 (March, 1960), 75–105, by permission of the *Revista de Ciencias Sociales*.

Revista de Ciencias Sociales, IV, No. 1 (1960), pp. 75–105. Also in Laura Foner and Eugene Genovese (eds), Slavery in the New World: A Reader in Comparative History (New Jersey, 1969).

and social framework of a whole society Both the institution and the society were radically transformed.

In the Spanish colonies, the decline of the plantation system, after its first phase of rapid growth, created a situation still different from that of Spain, but different also from the classic pattern of plantation slavery to be found elsewhere in the West Indies. The Spanish slave laws were less completely adapted to the will of the slave-owning 'planter' than was the case elsewhere, during the eighteenth century. In addition, the strong conservatism of the Spanish crown and government made possible the retention of some of the fundamental concepts borrowed originally from the slave laws of Spain.

These concepts are very clearly expressed in the *Siete Partidas*, in which may be found what is chronologically the earliest legal view of the slave and slavery in the history of the West Indian slave laws. In the *Siete Partidas*, the slave is considered as part of the 'familia', and the distinction between slaves and serfs is not clear-cut. The term 'servitude', which may cover the unfree condition of both, is defined, as is the concept of liberty, which is its opposite. According to the *Siete Partidas*: 'Servitude is an agreement and regulation which people established in ancient times, by means of which men who were originally free became slaves and were subjected to the authority of others contrary to natural reason.' (Partida IV, Tit. XXI, Ley i). Slavery is defined as 'something which men naturally abhor and . . . not only does a slave live in servitude, but also anyone who has not free power to leave the place where he resides.' (Partida VII, Tit. XXXIV, Reg. ii) Logically then, liberty is 'the power which every man has by nature to do what he wishes, except where the force of law or *fuero* (privilege) prevent him'. The preamble to the section on liberty states: 'All creatures in the world naturally love and desire liberty, and much more do men, who have intelligence superior to that of others.' (Part. IV, Tit. XXII).

Deriving from these premises, the principle of the Spanish slave law was, on the whole, a principle friendly to the protection of the slave and to his claims of freedom. For the *Partidas* envisaged the slave as a 'persona' and not as 'mere property'. The master was regarded as having duties toward his slaves, as well as rights over them: 'A master has complete authority over his slave to dispose of him as he pleases. Nevertheless, he should not kill or wound him, although he may give cause for it, except by order of the judge of the district, nor should he strike him in a way contrary to natural reason, or put him to death by starvation.' (Part. IV, Tit. XXI). In the *Partidas*, slavery is undoubtedly accepted as legal. It is not accepted as good. Liberty is the good which the law strives to serve: 'it is a rule of law that all judges should aid liberty, for the reason that it is a friend of nature, because not only men, but all animals love it.' (Partida IV, Tit. XXXIV, Reg. i).

The liberty of these principles relating to slaves cannot be denied, though it may be doubted whether they were ever fully enforced in Spain. In the *Partidas*, it is clear that slavery is looked upon as a misfortune, from the consequences of which slaves should be protected as far as possible, because they are men, and because man is a noble animal not meant for servitude. The growth of enslavement in the West Indies undermined and even reversed this view; and many later apologists of slavery attempted to prove that enslavement is not an evil but a good. The myth of 'inevitable progress' has prevented for long an appreciation of the fact that humaneness predates humanitarianism. The truth is that this 'medieval' slave code was probably the most humane in its principles ever to be introduced in the West Indies. It appears to have been the one section of the West India slave law in which was made the unequivocal assertion that liberty is the natural and proper condition of man.

The case of the *Siete Partidas* illustrates that, within the general agreement that slavery could legally exist, a considerable latitude of opinion about the institution itself was possible. The slave laws of the Spanish West Indies tended positively to favor the good treatment of slaves and their individual emancipation. From the beginning, under the provisons of the *Sieta Partidas*, the slave was legally protected in life and limb. As the celebrated jurist Solórzano pointed out, the slave was, in law, entitled to the protection and intervention of the law on his behalf, and the master could actually lose his property in the slave as a result of proved maltreatment of him.[3] Failure to subsist the slave adequately was, from the standpoint of the law, a serious abuse. So was the infliction upon the slave of inordinate work. In addition, slaves might be compulsorily manumitted for specific kinds of abuse — for example, in the case of women slaves, for violation or prostitution of the slave by her owner.[4] Under the Spanish slave laws codified in 1680, *audiencias* were instructed to hear cases of slaves who claimed to be free, and to see that justice was done to them.[5] When slaves of mixed blood were to be sold, it was provided that their Spanish fathers, if willing, should be allowed to buy them so that they might become free.[6] Orders were also given that peaceful settlements of free Negroes were not to be molested, and, throughout the eighteenth century, Puerto Rico followed the practice of giving asylum to fugitive slaves from non-Spanish islands, with very little variation from the principle that, once they had embraced the Roman Catholic religion, they were not to be returned.[7]

Custom, as well as law, appears to have favored the growth of the free colored group. By the custom of *coartación*, slaves by degrees bought themselves free from the ownership of their masters.[8] When the customary institution was incorporated in the slave laws, it had to be made clear that the master retained his property in the slave undiminished until the last payment was made. The law, which was more severe than custom had been, acknowledged a right in the master to claim all the *coartado*'s time if he wished.[9]

Customary *coartación* was widespread in the Spanish islands in the eighteenth century, and it was probably of great importance in increasing the numbers of freed men in these territories at the time. One estimate of Cuban population in 1774, which Friedlander apparently considers not too wide of the mark, gives a total of 171,620, of whom 96,440 were whites, 30,847 were free colored, and only 44,333 were slaves.[10] Figures for Puerto Rico, which was even slower than Cuba in turning to sugar and the great plantation, are equally interesting. As late as 1827, Puerto Rico was still a country with a predominantly free and even predominantly white population, though here the margin of difference between whites and non-whites was less than in Cuba of 1774.

The spirit of the Spanish slave laws, which was relatively liberal, undoubtedly influenced the form of these societies, in particular by aiding the growth of the free colored group. In turn, the less rigid and less slave-centered societies of these islands enabled the liberality of the Spanish law to survive and to exercise its influence upon them. When the changeover to sugar and the great plantation came in real earnest, the processes consequent on this changeover had to be worked out in a social environment different from that of other islands which had suffered transformation during the seventeenth and early eighteenth centuries. Despite the brutalities of the nineteenth century,

slavery in the Spanish islands was, on the whole, milder than was the case elsewhere in the West Indies.

Nevertheless, this is a contrast which can be overemphasized. As Ortiz points out in his illuminating study *Los negros esclavos*, the attitude of the Cuban upper class throughout its history has not been so far different from that of the slave-owners of other islands as the difference in their slave laws might suggest. The relative despotism of the Spanish government acted as a check on the local oligarchies, which did not necessarily share the view of slavery expressed in the *Siete Partidas*. In fact Ortiz suggests that, if the task of making slave laws had been placed as firmly in the hands of these men as it was in the hands of a slave-owning ruling class in the British islands, there might not be so much to choose between Spanish and English slave laws.[11] Certainly, when this class became strong enough in Cuba to resist official policy successfully, one of its earliest successes was the defeat of the humane Slave Code of 1789, in which the Spanish government had attempted to provide for the amelioration of conditions among a growing slave population. Certainly also, it is generally agreed that the increase in the numbers of slaves in Cuba, which accompanied the expansion of the sugar industry there, brought a marked and general deterioration in their treatment. As Cuba became a sugar colony, its slave conditions more approximately resembled those of the other sugar colonies.[12]

What is more, even in the period of relatively mild treatment of slaves in the Spanish colonies, enacted law and practice were not one and the same thing.[13] The custom of *coartación*, which existed before it was recognized in law, serves to illustrate a case where custom was in advance of the law from the point of view of the slaves. In other cases, the law was decidedly more humane than was custom. The existence of the slave laws of the *Siete Partidas*, and of later enactments, did not prevent the existence of numbers of slaves who were underfed, overworked, and badly treated.

Lastly, though this is by no means of least importance, the humane regulations do not tell the whole story of the enacted slave law in the Spanish colonies. In addition to the structure of protective regulations already described, there existed other and different laws governing slaves and free colored, and these show the direct influence of the necessities of the slave system which depended in part upon force for its maintenance. In his discussion of the Cuban slave laws, Ortiz has pointed out how much the Spanish and local governments were concerned with the problem of slavery as a problem of public order. He shows that in the evolution of the slave laws, as in the restictions on the slave trade in the Spanish colonies, political consider- ations were often of great weight. The slave laws very clearly reflect this concern.[14]

In the Code of 1680,[15] for example, the police regulations governing slaves already outnumber all others, and there were also several restrictions on the free colored. (Vol. II, Lib. 7, Tít. 5). All of these were based upon the determination to preserve public order. It was provided, for instance, that Negroes were subject to a curfew in cities; and the magistrates were enjoined to try them for any disturbances which they might commit. (Leyes 12, 13.) No Negro, whether slave or free, and no person of Negro descent, except in special cases, was to be permitted to carry arms. (Leyes 14-18.) There were several regulations for the policing of runaway slaves. (Leyes 20-25.) One provided for their protection by forbidding that they should be mutilated in punishment. (Ley 24.) But it is fair to say that this was exceptional. Most of the provisions were made with an eye to the control and suppression of the runaways as a threat to public order. Finally, there were regulations for preventing, defeating, and punishing the risings of slaves, and for the summary arrest of any Negro found wandering or engaged in similar suspicious activities. (Ley 26.)

As for the free colored, they were supposed to live under the supervision of a patron, even though free; and, by a special law, they were forbidden to wear gold, silk, cloaks, or other kinds of clothing considered unsuitable to their station in society. (Leyes 3, 28). From the first too, the Spanish government tried to prevent race mixture in its colonies between Spaniards, Indians, and Negroes, whether slave or free. (Ley 5). In this, it was, of course, generally unsuccessful.

Among the provisions made to secure public order in Cuba during the seventeenth century, Ortiz lists laws prohibiting the sale of wine to slaves, regulations governing the work of hired slaves, the perennial restrictions against the bearing of arms by slaves, and provisions for the pursuit of runaways and their punishment. These, rather than purely protective measures, continued most to occupy the active attention of the authorities until the ameliorative codific- ation of 1789.

This code included provisions regulating the work and recreation of slaves, their housing and medical care, their maintenance in old age, their marriages and similar subjects, their punish- ments, and their formal protection in law. Besides providing for the protection of slaves, the code of 1789 made provision for the detection and punishment of abuses by the colonists in the management of slaves. Unlike the police regulations, this code ran into strong opposition from the colonists, especially in Cuba, where the resistance was so determined that the government was forced virtually to withdraw the new code in 1791.[16]

There was in Puerto Rico a comparative neglect of those regulations which affected the activities of the master, while the laws penal- izing the criminal actions of slaves were far more effectively enforced.[17] The intention behind protective regulations could thus be defeated, and the law was given an emphasis in practice which does not emerge to the same extent in its enactment. Even in these relatively liberal slave islands, therefore, it can be seen that slavery presented a minimum requirement of rigor, which pressed upon the slave because of his status, and because of the necessity to maintain it.

In the British islands, during the eighteenth century, the marks left by the slave system upon the law are less ambiguous. This is not only because the plantation system had here taken a very firm hold, but also because of the nature of the British political tradition. England, which was earlier freed of slavery and even of serfdom than was Spain, had no *Siete Partidas* to transfer to her West India colonies when they were acquired, even though these colonies quickly adopted the slave system brought to the West Indies by the Spaniards. The English government never, until the nineteenth century, showed so careful and sustained an interest in the subject of slave regulations as did the government of Spain from earliest times. Most important of all, perhaps, tradition of representative government determined that the slave laws of the British colonies were made directly by a slave-owning ruling class. These laws were, therefore, an immediate reflection of what the slave-owner conceived to be the necessities of the slave system.

It has often been said that the greater freedom incorporated in the British constitutional system helped to breed respect for the property of the subject, as well as for his liberty. This may be part of the explanation of the legal convention which, in the British slave colonies, left the power of the master over his property, the slave, virtually unlimited, even in some cases as to life and limb. For this convention to apply, however, it had to be made clear that the slave was property and subject to police regulations. In fact, the experience of the British colonies makes it particularly clear that police regulations lay at the very heart of the slave system and that, without them, the system became impossible to maintain.

This was the moral of Somersett's case decided by the Chief Justice, Lord Mansfield, in 1771–72, and also of the case of the slave Grace decided by Lord Stowell in 1827.[18] Given police regulations, the English law in the West Indies worked against the slave, because he was there mere property or something very near it. In the absence of such regulations, the slave had to be regarded as an ordinary man; and, in this context, the respect for liberty of the subject, which was also a part of the English legal tradition, worked in his favor. Somersett's case illustrates the operation of the principle of liberty of the subject. There was no law against slavery in England. But the absence of a law providing sanctions for slavery enabled Somersett to win his freedom by refusing any longer to be held as a slave. The case of the slave Grace shows the potency of police provisions in maintaining the slave system. For on returning voluntarily to Antigua, she lost the temporary freedom gained by a visit to England.

English respect for the liberty of the subject was thus restricted by the erection of a slave system, and had to be so restricted to keep the slave system in being. Under the English slave system in the West Indies, the slave was not regarded as a subject, but as a property; and when the English humanitarians attempted to take the view that he was a subject, they were advocating an innovation which only slowly gained acceptance in the controversies over amelioration and emancipation.

The basic conception of the English law in relation to the slave was not, as with the Spaniards, that he was an inferior kind of subject. It was rather that he was a special kind of property. First of all, he was merchandise when bought and sold in the course of the slave trade. Once acquired by a planter, the slave became private property — regarded in part as a chattel, in part as real property. As a chattel, for instance, he could be sold up for debts if other moveable assets were exhausted. But in other cases, he was subject to the laws of inheritance of real estate. He could be entailed, was subject to the widow's right of dower, and could be mortgaged.[19]

These aspects of the law appeared both in the law of the West Indies and in the law of England. Under both, trading in slaves was a recognized and legal activity. Under both, there were provisions for regulating the mortgage of slaves and obliging their sale as chattels in cases of debt.[20] This point is worth stressing. The idea of slaves as property was as firmly accepted in the law of England as it was in that of the colonies; and it was not for lack of this provision that Somersett had to be freed. It was the lack of the superstructure raised on this basis — in the form of police law governing slaves — which made it impossible for Somersett to be held in slavery by force in England. Before and after the Somersett case, slaves were taken to and from England, as the case of the slave Grace shows; and, so long as they did not refuse to serve, as Somersett did, it may be said that they remained property and did not become subjects in fact, though in theory this change was supposed to take place on their arrival in England.

In the West Indies, they were slaves because the superstructure, lacking in England, was there available. By the eighteenth century, it was elaborate and, generally speaking, comprehensive. On the basic idea of the slave as property, a whole system of laws was built up. Some concerned the disposal of the slaves as property, others governed the actions of slaves as an aspect of public order. Some gave slaves a species of legal protection. But, up to the time when organized humanitarian agitation began in the 1780s, the protective enactments were relatively few and sometimes rather ambiguous. Police regulations occupied the most ample proportion of the attention of the British West India legislators.

Some of the regulations made are clearly related to the conception that the slave was property, but even those border on the idea of police. Thus, owners whose slaves suffered the judicial penalty of death were usually compensated for the loss. Obviously, this was because their property in the slave was recognized. But the intention was also to reduce the temptation of owners to conceal criminal slaves from justice. Again, persons who employed or hired the slaves of others without proper consent were guilty of a form of trespass, which was subject to both civil and criminal proceedings. Taking the slaves of another by violence was robbery. To carry off a slave from the provisions safe-guarded the slave as private property. They also penalized those aiding runaways, either by enabling them to support themselves away from the master or by aiding their flight directly. They are part of a whole series of laws which penalized all persons, whether slave or free, who sheltered or otherwise assisted the runaway slave.[21]

Every island passed laws for the pursuit, capture, suppression, and punishment of runaway slaves; and these laws were usually severe. Similar police regulations were made in islands other than those of the British. Slaves were not to wander abroad without written passes, they were not to have any firearms or to assemble together in numbers. Usually they were forbidden to beat drums and blow horns, since these were means of communication which might be used to help runaways.[22] All such activities were dangerous, too, as means of concerting uprisings — another reason for the existence of these laws. Not all of them were enforced at all times with equal rigor. Slave dances, feasts, and drumming were often allowed; and even the pass laws were not strictly observed. The laws remained in force, however, and they were used when necessary to prevent or to control emergencies.

The function served by the laws may be illustrated by a comparison. In Barbados, under an early law of the seventeenth century, it was provided that if a Negro slave died under punishment by his master and no malice was proved, the master killing his own slave was to pay a fine of £15. If the slave belonged to another master, the fine to be paid was £25, and an additional payment of double the slave's value was to be made to compensate his owner.[23] This law was made notorious by abolitionist criticism. It is one of the worst of its type, but its singularity lay rather in the lowness of its fines than in its principle. It was a brutal law, but its brutality flowed in well defined, socially accepted channels. This is why a struggle was necessary to achieve a change of principle. Few islands in the British West Indies, until the later eighteenth century, showed any willingness to recognize that the willful killing of a slave was an act of homicide or murder. It was usually regarded in theory, though not always in practice, as a criminal offence. But generally it was a criminal offence of a lesser order, to which it was not felt necessary to attach so heavy a penalty as that of death.

By contrast, heavy penalties were attached to the commission of a crime, the gravity of which depended entirely on its social context. For striking or insulting a white, slaves were subject to the penalties of whipping, mutilation, or death; and usually the law provided that if the white was in any way hurt or if the blow drew blood, then the more severe punishments should be inflicted.[24] Even free persons of color were often made liable to similar punishments for similar offences against whites — and this meant all whites, from the great planter to the poor white, and white indenture servant.[25] The contrast in treatment of the crime of striking or abusing a white is due in each case to the social significance attached to the crime.

Yet the slave was a special kind of property, as these laws attest. For to kill even one's own slave maliciously was penalized, though not usually as much as the killing either of the slave of another or of a free man. The law with regard to the striking or wounding of whites also had to envisage the slave as something more than a 'thing'. The dilemma was that he was not 'mere property', as the law wished to suppose him, but a creature possessing volition, and the capacity for resistance which must be checked, indeed crushed, if the society were to survive. Obviously, the slaves were also regarded as a special kind of property in the laws governing them as runaways, and punishing them as conspirators or rebels. If the slave had been truly a thing in fact, as well as in the fiction of the law, such legislation would not have been necessary. Because he was a person, he posed a problem of public order, which the police regulation tended to cover. The law was forced to allow the slave some kind of 'persona' for the purpose of dealing with him under this aspect of his activity as a special kind of property.

In the earlier British slave laws, and even up to the beginning of the humanitarian controversy, the dominant tendency was to recognize the slave as a 'persona' in a sphere far more limited than that allowed him in either Spanish or French slave law. Early English slave law almost totally neglects the slave as a subject for religious instruction, as a member of a family, or as a member of society possessing some rights, however inferior. Insofar as the slave is allowed personality before the law, he is regarded chiefly, almost solely, as a potential criminal.

This is true of the police regulations governing the movements of slaves. It is true of the regulations to restrain and punish thefts by slaves, which were numerous. It is true even of the regulations governing the economic activities of slaves, in which may be traced a constant preoccupation with the problems of running away and theft, as well as a desire to limit the economic competition of slaves with whites.

The humanitarians, in their criticism of the

West India slave laws, attacked this limited legal concept of the slave, and, in the course of their long struggle with the West Indians, substantial changes were made in the laws by the island legislatures. In particular, attempts were made, during the controversies over amelioration, to define the duties of masters towards their slaves, and the degree of protection to which slaves were entitled in law. During this phase, the status of the slave as a 'persona', in the eyes of the law, was significantly broadened. But this development came relatively late, and was, to a considerable extent, due to the pressure built up by the humanitarian critics of the West Indies.

Before the beginning of the humanitarian assault, the British West India slave laws included relatively few protective clauses, and even these often seem to rest on an ambiguous view of the slave. Indeed, it is misleading to regard many of these regulations as providing anything comparable to the 'positive protection' sought for in later laws. There was, for instance, a Montserrat regulation of 1693, which provided that one acre of provisions should be cultivated for every eight slaves belonging to a plantation. But this is only one clause of an extremely severe act intended to punish thefts by slaves, and especially thefts of provisions. The act was concerned with a problem of public order, rather than with any idea of the rights of slaves to sufficient food in return for their services.[26]

Provisions for holidays to be given to slaves at particular times reflect similar police problems. In these laws, fines were often imposed on those who gave more, as well as those who gave less, than the prescribed holidays, and this practice only gradually came to be modified later in the eighteenth century.[27]

Laws to prevent old and disabled slaves from being abandoned by their masters have a similar ambiguity. For wandering and destitute slaves always constituted a serious problem of public order; and local authorities usually refused to have them become a burden on poor relief. The most obvious expedient was, therefore, to insist upon the master's obligation to keep even useless slaves, rather than have this burden thrown on the public.[28] Here, for once, the idea that the slave was private property operated against, rather than in favor of, the master's will. The result of this insistence upon the private responsibility of the master was not always favorable to the slave, however. For it led to severe laws providing life sentences of hard labor for destitute slaves whose masters could not be found, and to an unwillingness on the part of the legislators to permit even the manumission of able-bodied slaves unless the public was indemnified beforehand against the possibility that the new freedman might become destitute. During the second half of the eighteenth century, in particular, several laws were passed, imposing a tax for this purpose upon manumissions.[29] Even where the object was not directly to check the growth in numbers of the free population, the effect was certainly to make the achievement of manumission more difficult, because more costly.

In the British West India slave laws in force during the eighteenth century, there were, of course, some unambiguous protective clauses. But some of these carry little weight in comparison with the other kinds of regulation. For example, Barbados in 1668 had provided that slaves should be given clothing once a year, specifying drawers and caps for men, and petticoats and caps for women. The penalty for failure to comply with this law was 5 shillings per slave.[30] In the newer colonies of the eighteenth century, for instance, St. Vincent and Dominica, heavier fines were imposed, but the amount of clothing provided as a compulsory allowance was still either small or inadequately defined in the law.[31] Even under the consolidated slave law passed at Jamaica in 1781, where the penalty of £50 was inflicted for neglect, the allowances to be made to slaves were stated without proper definition.[32] It can hardly be doubted that such weaknesses must have lessened the effectiveness of these protective laws.

Other more considerable regulations for the protection of slaves were also instituted. But their comparatively small number indicates that they were exceptional. It has already been noticed that the willful killing of slaves was not generally considered to be murder, but was nevertheless judged to be a criminal offense of some gravity. Jamaica, from relatively early days, went a step further than the other islands by providing under an act of 1696 that anyone found guilty of a second offense of willingly, wantonly, or 'bloodymindedly' killing a Negro or slave, should be convicted of murder. The first offence was declared a felony, and, as this was found to be an insufficient deterrent, an additional punishment of imprisonment was provided in 1751.[33]

There were also laws penalizing the dismemberment or mutilation of slaves, by fine or imprisonment or both. The range of fines ran from a minimum fine of £20, provided at Antigua in 1723, to the much heavier fine of

£500, provided by the St. Kitts legislature 60 years later.[34] But such provisions were by no means ubiquitous, and in many of the islands it remained true that, as one report of 1788 states: 'Very little Measure appears to have been assigned by any general laws, to the Authority of the Master in punishing Slaves.'[35] In particular, the regulation of lesser punishments by laws was very generally neglected, and the partial nature of such legislation is illustrated by the fact that a St. Vincent law which provided against mutilation of slaves also contained a clause inflicting a £10 fine on persons taking off iron collars and similar instruments of punishment from slaves, without the consent of the master.

When the controversy over abolition of the slave trade drew attention to the inadequacy of statutory protection offered slaves in the matter of punishment and maltreatment, defenders of the West India interest had recourse to the argument that common law protection was available, where statutory protection was lacking.[36] Insofar as this was clearly true, however, it affected the slave as a piece of property rather than as a person. The master had the right to bring suit for damages against anyone harming his slave, even where there was no statutory provision for this. Indeed, acts which added a criminal penalty for such offenses generally made specific reference to this civil right. The more dubious part of the case concerns not this right, but the right of slaves to personal protection, without the intervention of the owner, or against the owner or his representatives.[37] A thorough search of judicial records throughout the Britsh islands at this time would be necessary to determine whether, before the matter became a contentious one, cases against owners and their representatives were normally, or even occasionally, brought to the common law courts in any of the islands.

The evidence already available does not suggest that the personal protection of slaves under the common law was very effective. As late as 1823, when Fortunatus Dwarris, as a member of the legal commission of the West Indies, investigated this matter, he was forced to report a 'want of remedy' for slaves at common law in Barbados, and a conflict of opinion on the subject there and throughout the British islands.[38] Dwarris wished to have the situation clarified and recommended that

it might be advantageous, that in the Windward as well as in the Leeward Islands, the common law of England should be declared to be the 'certain rule for all descriptions of persons being subjects of His Majesty, and to obviate all doubts real or pretended upon this head, it might be recited and set forth explicitly in such declaratory law, that all African, or Creole slaves admitted within the King's allegiance, are, and shall at all times be taken and held to be, entitled to the protection, and subject to the penalties, of the common law; and to this, the slave code carefully compiled would properly be supplemental.'[39]

Yet he doubted that even when this had been done, the common law would protect the slave from other than scandalous abuse.[40]

Dwarris' report, and his doubts, reflect an uncertainty as to the degree of protection offered under the common law. At St. Kitts, in 1786, a jury trying a case of maltreatment involving a slave also questioned whether 'immoderate correction of a slave by the Master be a Crime indictable'.[41] On this occasion, the judge decided that it was. But, what the attorney-general of Dominica said in 1823 of the whole question of common law protection is true here too: 'the rule upon this subject is so vague, and so little understood in the colonies, that decisions founded upon it will be often contradictory.'[42]

Even graver doubts about the application of the common law to slaves were current in the West Indies, and these may have sprung from an unwillingness to recognize the slave as having personal status in law. In 1823, Dwarris reported many assertions made by the judge and crown law officer of St. Kitts to the effect that 'the justices have no jurisdiction over slaves except what is expressly given them by Colonial Acts'. It was not their duty, or even their right, to hear and deal with the complaints of slaves.[43]

The existence of this belief in the West Indies underlines the contrast, already noted in the discussion of Somersett's case and of the case of the slave Grace, between the situation of the slave in England and in the West Indies. Somersett's freedom was due to the common law, the slavery of Grace was secured by enacted law. In the West Indies, the slave was a 'thing' rather than a person, a 'property' rather than a subject. The same conception, which led to inadequate protection of slaves under enacted law, explains the uncertainty regarding their protection under the common law. The legal nullity of the slave's personality, except when he was to be controlled or punished, was the greatest obstacle to his adequate personal protection.

The law of evidence with regard to slaves reveals both the nullity and the anomaly of the conception of the slave as property. Any free man could give evidence against or for a slave. But during the eighteenth century, the evidence of slaves was not admitted for or against free persons in the British islands. Nevertheless, at the discretion of the courts, the evidence of slaves was admitted for or against other slaves. Thus the legal disability of the slave reinforced his inferior position. Still exposed to detection for his own crimes, he was deprived of protection against the crimes of all but his fellow slaves. He had no real redress against those very abuses of power to which his inferior position already exposed him.

The existence of special forms of trial for slaves in the British islands, as well as the limited validity of their evidence, served to mark them off from the rest of the body politic. In many cases, they were placed under the summary jurisdiction of judges, acting without a jury, for the trial even of capital crimes.[44] When a solemn form of trial was provided, as for instance in Montserrat, where capital cases were tried by the Governor in Council, the form of trial still differed from that given to free men.[45] The Barbados legislature put the matter succinctly in 1688, when it provided a solemn court for capital cases but omitted the usual jury of twelve men, on the ground that the accused 'being British Slaves, deserve, not from the Baseness of their condition, to be tried by the legal trial of twelve men of their Peers, or Neighbourhood, which truly neither can be rightly done, as the Subjects of England are.'[46]

Every aspect of the slave law of the British islands reveals the fundamental political concern with the subordination and control of slaves. This emphasis was characteristic right up to the beginning of the abolitionist struggle and beyond. In 1784, when their first cautious ameliorated slave code, the Act of 1781, expired, the members of the Jamaican legislature were apparently too busy to bring in a new improved slave law. But this did not prevent them from passing an act providing for parties to hunt runaway slaves, nor from reviving the very severe laws under which thefts and destruction of horses and cattle by slaves were visited with the punishment of death.[47] It seems fair to conclude not only that these were less controversial than improvements in the slave laws, but also that they were regarded as being more urgently necessary than, for instance, the new provisions against mutilation and dismemberment of slaves which lapsed when the Act of 1781 did.

It was not that the West Indians were always disinclined to serve the cause of humanity, but simply that they considered the cause of self-preservation infinitely more important. The primary function of the British West India slave laws was either directly or indirectly repressive. For, as Bryan Edwards, who was himself a planter and a slave-owner, put it: 'In countries where slavery is established, the leading principle on which the government is supported is fear: or a sense of that absolute coercive necessity which, leaving no choice of action, supercedes all questions of right. It is vain to deny that such actually is, and necessarily must be, the case in all countries where slavery is allowed.'[48]

The French West Indies, unlike the British islands, had, after 1685, a slave code drawn up by the metropolitan government as the basis of their slave laws.[49] However, the contrast between these groups of islands, with regard to their slave laws, was not as great as that between the Spanish and British islands. The *Siete Partidas* was a code of Spanish laws, containing provisions relating to slaves. The *Partidas* came into existence long before the creation of a West Indian empire. They were not framed to deal with the circumstances of the West Indies, though they were incorporated into the law of the Spanish colonies there. But the *Code Noir*, though drawn up in France, was never intended to be a code of French laws. Like the laws of the British islands, the *Code Noir* of the French West Indies was made with West Indian conditions firmly in mind, and for the purpose of dealing with problems already posed by the existence and acceptance of slavery in the West Indian colonies. The *Code Noir* bears some resemblance to the *Siete Partidas* because both were influenced to some extent, by the concepts of Roman and canon law. Nevertheless, it more fundamentally resembles the slave laws of the British West Indies by reason of its intention and function.

The fact that the *Code Noir* was a metropolitan code is, nevertheless, important. Even in the early 1680s, the French monarchical government was less limited than that of England, a difference reflected in the government of the French and English colonies. In the English colonies, the crown's legislative power was incorporated in the structure of a representative legislature, including council and assembly. In the French colonies, the crown retained more autonomous powers of legislation. The laws of the French colonies were made by the royal government in France, by the royal officials in the West Indies, and by the local councils. The *Code Noir* is described as a metropolitan code, because it was made by the exercise of the legislative power of the royal government in France.

However, the *Code*, although made in France, was based upon earlier local laws and was prepared in consultation with the local authorities in the West Indies. Even after promulgation, it was revised to meet strong local criticisms on some points. Long before the *Code Noir* was prepared, local authorities had concerned themselves with the problems of religious conformity, with the regulation of the status and conduct of slaves, with the necessity for public security, and with the protection to be given to slaves as property and as persons. These were the matters which also occupied the framers of the *Code Noir*; and a few examples will show the similarities between the earlier laws and the later *Code*.

As early as 1638, it was provided that Protestants should not be allowed to own slaves in the islands; and, by later laws, made by representatives of the crown in the West Indies, provisions were added for the punishment of blasphemers, and the regulation of Jews and non-Catholics, and also to encourage the Christianization of slaves.[50] Undoubtedly, the crown may be regarded as having special interests in religious conformity; and it is hardly surprising that the *Code Noir*, which was promulgated in the same year that saw the Revocation of the Edict of Nantes, should have given great prominence and emphasis to the provisions enforcing religious conformity. But the regulations of the crown in this matter already had precedents in the accepted local law, and did not arouse much local opposition. On the one subject — the abolition of Negro markets on Sundays and holidays — where local opinion showed itself immediately hostile to the provisions of the crown for enforcing religious observance, the crown quickly gave way.[51] In the matter of religious conformity, the predilections of the crown enjoyed the general support of a large body of local opinion.

As for regulations concerned more directly with slaves, a good many may be cited which occur in the earlier laws and recur in some form in the *Code Noir*. They illustrate that, before the *Code Noir* was instituted, the French colonies already possessed a fairly comprehensive series of slave laws, and that the *Code Noir* really may be regarded as an extended codification of these laws.

Some of these laws were made by officials and some by the Council; and perhaps it is significant that the Council appears to have concerned itself mainly with police laws. It is notable, however, that the Council, as a court, heard cases arising from the cruelty of masters to their slaves, and already, before 1685, had made judgments punishing cruelty.[52] This point is probably significant of a contrast in attitudes in the British and French islands arising from a contrast in their political traditions.

In British law, the tendency was to limit the sphere of interference of the crown, and to foster, in particular, a respect for the rights of private property. In France and its colonies, because the power of the crown was less limited, its sphere of interference, even with private property, was commonly accepted to be much wider. The slave, by being private property, did not cease to be in his person a matter of public concern; and public interference in the management of slaves was more taken for granted at this stage of development in the French West Indies than it was in the British islands at the same time. With the continued growth of slavery in the French West Indies, and with the related development of a feeling of white solidarity in those colonies, two very important changes of sentiment with regard to slaves made themselves felt. Public concern for their welfare declined rapidly, and public acceptance of interference between the master and his property became less and less certain.

An analysis of the content of the *Code Noir* reveals the same concern for public order which marks the slave laws of the British West Indies. But the *Code Noir* was, nevertheless, based on a wider conception of the slave as a 'person' and on a different conception of the elements of public order. The contents of the code may be placed under a number of heads. Provisions regarding religious conformity are laid down in the earlier clauses; provisions governing the status of slaves and their political control follow. The protection of slaves is then provided for, after which their civil disabilities are carefully listed. These disabilities arose, of course, from the legal view that the slave was property, though as in the British law, he had to be admitted to be a peculiar kind of property. The element of political control over slaves, which was inseparable from their regulation as property, appears clearly in the section of the code which deals with the slave as property, as it does in the slave laws elsewhere. In this section however, the police regulations are accompanied by protective regulations; and, in fact, these two categories make up a large part of the code. Lastly, there are clauses providing for the manumission of slaves and for the regulation of the status of freedom. Underlying these provisions is the assumption that all groups in the community are subject to the will and direction of the state.

A short summary of the more important clauses of the code shows this assumption in operation. Under the provisions of the code, Jews were to be expelled from the colonies, and Protestants were subjected to religious and civil disabilities — such as incapacity for legal marriage by their own rites. The object was to secure public conformity of all, and not even the slaves were excluded. They were to be baptized and instructed as Catholics; and their overseers could be of no other religious persuasion. They were to observe Sundays, and the holidays of the church, to be married, and if baptized, buried on holy ground. The concubinage of free men with slaves was penalized, except in those cases where the irregular union was converted into marriage. (Cls. 1–11) Under this section, conformity to the state religion is the duty enforced on all.

The regulations concerning slavery provided that children should take the status of the mother in all cases. (Cls. 12, 13) The slave mother being property, the slave child was property. This property was to be kept in a state of subordination by the usual means. Slaves were forbidden to carry arms or other weapons, to assemble together, to engage in certain kinds of trade, to strike the master or mistress or to use violence against free persons. Penalties were provided for those slaves who were guilty of thefts, and for those slaves who were guilty of running away. Finally, it was expressly provided that slaves could be criminally prosecuted, without involving the master if he was not responsible for the crime. (Cls. 15–21, 33–38) As in the British law, therefore, the slave was subject to coercion; and was treated as being personally responsible to the state before the law.

He was also viewed as, to some extent, a person in a state of dependence. As such, the master who owned him was obliged to give him fixed allowances of food and clothing, to care for old and disabled slaves, to avoid concubinage with his slaves, and to leave them free to observe the rules of the church. His property in the slaves was regarded as conferring on him the right to punish them by whipping, or by putting them in irons. But he was expressly prohibited from torturing or mutilating them; and a master killing a slave was to be prosecuted as a criminal, and penalized 'according to the atrocity of the

circumstances'. The clergy were enjoined not to marry slaves without the master's consent, but also not to constrain slaves to marry if they were unwilling to do so. Under the law, families were not to be broken up when slaves were sold; and those slaves between the ages of 14 and 60 who were employed in sugar — or indigo — works and plantations were attached to the soil and could not be sold except with the estate. Slaves not falling within these categories were, however, regarded as chattels. (Cls. 9–11, 22–25, 27, 42, 43, 47–54)

As a piece of property, rather than a person, the slave was incapable of legally possessing property or of legally making contracts, and he was, of course, incapable of holding any public office or acting legally as a responsible agent. The code declared that slaves could not legally be parties to a trial, though they themselves were subject to criminal prosecution. Masters received compensation for their loss when criminal slaves were executed. But they were also liable to make good losses caused by their slaves. (Cls. 28, 30–32, 37, 40)

All these clauses with regard to the protection and disabilities of the slave assumed that the master, in return for public recognition of the dependency of the slave, accepted certain conditions of obligation laid down by the state. His property in the slave was held subject to these obligations, and could be forfeited as a result of failure to observe the limitations on his authority, imposed by the state as a condition of its support. Under the British slave laws, where the disabilities arising from the slave's dependency were the same, the conditions of this dependency, as they affected the master, were less carefully defined. In both British and French slave law, the inferior position of the slave was accepted. But in the British slave law, the state showed far greater unwillingness to interpose in the relations between masters and slaves.

The inferior position of the slave, though it was recognized in the French slave laws, was not directly reflected in the forms of trial provided for slaves under the *Code Noir*. The slave was to be tried before the ordinary judges, and he had the right of appealing his case to the Council — 'the process to be carried on with the same formalities as in the case of free persons'. (Cl. 32) In 1711, however, the slave's right of appealing against his sentence was restricted to capital cases and sentences of hamstringing.[53] This was one of the symptoms of the change which gradually transformed the French West Indian slave code. But, at the time of the promulgation of the *Code Noir*, concern for the protection of the slave in law was still strong. Clause 30 of that code, which provided that slave evidence was inadmissible except against slaves, was immediately protested by the Martinique Council, on the grounds that this would result in an impunity for many crimes committed against slaves. As a result of this protest, the crown, in 1686, amended the code so as to allow the admission of evidence by slaves, in the absence of evidence by whites, in all cases except against their own masters.[65]

Even here, at one of the most touchy points in the whole slave system, the *Code Noir* provided for the protection of the slave in law, by enabling him, under clause 26, to make complaints to the crown's *procureur-général* against his master in cases where the master failed to give him subsistence, or treated him cruelly. The attorney-general was thus given a status as protector of slaves which compensated, to some extent, for the unwillingness to admit slave evidence against masters. In keeping with this relative liberality, manumissions were made easy for all masters who had attained their legal majority; and, once freed, the former slave was to be treated as a freeborn subject of the king, entitled to the same rights as other subjects, so long as he lived in obedience to the law and performed the duties of the subject — with this difference only that he was expected to give due respect to his former master, the source of his freedom. (Cls. 26, 55–59)

In one respect, the provisions of the *Code Noir* regarding manumissions were restrictive. Until the promulgation of the code, it was customary for children of mixed blood to be freed during their teens.[55] But the crown, in its desire to secure religious conformity, was most anxious to discourage concubinage; and therefore, it provided that the illegitimate offspring and their mothers could never be free, except by the marriage of the parents. (Cl. 9) But in this matter, the will of the crown was at variance with the will of the local society, and was defeated. Masters continued to engage in irregular sexual unions with their slaves and continued to free their offspring. In the end, the crown itself expressly withdrew from its former position, in the belief that the mulattoes, being sworn enemies of the Negroes, might safely be freed.[56]

While the special provisions against manumission of mulattoes fell into disuse, the general provisions for manumission became more difficult. Early in the eighteenth century, the royal representatives in the colonies made it a rule that their written permission was necessary to validate all manumissions of slaves.[57] In 1713, this rule was confirmed by the crown, and it continued to be enforced during the century.[58] Instead of encouraging manumissions, the crown and its officers in the colonies showed a constant determination to control the accession of slaves to freedom. Even in France, where it was an accepted axiom of law that slaves became free on entering the realm, the crown proved willing to protect West Indian property by altering the law so as to nullify this usage.[59] The crown and its officers also allowed the wide privileges, originally granted to freedmen under the *Code Noir*, to be gradually contracted, and joined with the councils in multiplying laws against them and in subjecting them to increasing disabilities.[60]

This series of changes in the laws reflects the process by which the law was adapted to fit in with the development of society in the French colonies. In framing the *Code Noir*, the metropolitan government had shown itself generally disposed to follow local practice and to respect local opinion, even though, as in the case of the mulattoes, it occasionally rejected local customs. Unlike the Spanish government which, for long, showed a tendency to limit the increase of slaves in its colonies, the government in France was early committed to a policy of increasing slave numbers and even, though somewhat more reluctantly, to encouraging the growth of large plantations. In line with mercantile thought, it regarded these as the means of acquiring wealth and power from its West India possessions. Slavery must be maintained if these benefits were to be secured and enjoyed.

In his monumental study of French West Indian slavery, Peytraud supports the view that Colbert, who was largely responsible for preparing the *Code Noir*, was moved to protect the slaves by commercial, rather than humane, considerations.[61] Material considerations, a concern for public security, and a strengthening of race prejudice later produced a much greater hardening in the attitude of the crown and its officials towards the Negroes. The crown's desire for order, which had led the regulation of masters as well as of slaves under the *Code Noir*, led on to a certain tolerance of the abuses committed by masters against their slaves.

In 1713, the crown expressed great indignation on learning that masters were torturing their slaves barbarously.[62] In 1742, disapproval was also expressed, this time concerning a case in which a slave had been killed.[63] But the crown was now rather more concerned with the need for maintaining subordination among the Negroes. In the following year, the crown declared that 'while the Slaves should be maintained and favorably treated by their Masters, the necessary precautions should also be taken to contain them within the bounds of their duty, and to prevent all that might be feared from them.'[64]

The humaneness of the *Code Noir* itself can be overstated. The allowances of food and clothing fixed in the code were small. In the matter of punishments, the code prohibited the private infliction of torture and mutilation, but did not prevent their use by judicial authorities. Slaves could still be tortured in official investigations, and judges were left free to sentence slaves to be burnt alive, to be broken on the wheel (a favorite punishment), to be dismembered, to be branded, or to be crippled by hamstringing — a penalty expressly provided for runaways under the code.[65] Masters maltreating or killing slaves were liable to prosecution, and there are records of cases having been brought against them, although no master appears to have suffered the death penalty for killing a slave. By contrast, atrocious sentences were usually passed on slaves guilty of killing whites; and even for the crime of raising a hand against one of the children of his mistress, a slave was sentenced to have his hand cut off and to be hanged.[66] The attorney-general, who was appointed as guardian of slaves under the *Code Noir*, was far oftener engaged in prosecuting slaves, or in complaining of abuses by them, than in presenting the abuses committed against them. Like his employer, the crown, he was preoccupied with the task of securing public order.

A glance through the very numerous police regulations, passed with the object of enforcing or of supplementing the police clauses in the *Code Noir*, shows that many of these were initiated by a complaint on the part of the *procureur-général*, citing incipient or actual disorders. Thus, at the beginning of the eighteenth century, the Council of Léogane passed laws forbidding slaves to carry arms, or to assemble together, and providing for a hunt of runaways. At Le Cap, a pass-system was enforced; and the attention of masters was again called to the prohibitions against slaves carrying arms. Later, the council at Port-au-Prince penalized those selling arms and ammunitions to slaves without the master's written authority.[67]

The attorney-general also occupied himself with the suppression of thefts by slaves and with the restrictions on their trading. In 1710, complaint was made that the clauses of the *Code Noir* regulating trade by slaves were not being properly enforced. In the same year, the council at Petit-Goâve, on advice from the crown attorney, forbade gold- and silver-smiths to buy anything from slaves without express permission. Neglect of the rules against trading with slaves in the staple crops at Guadeloupe was similarly brought to the attention of the council there during the eighteenth century.[68]

Even in performing those duties which might be regarded as protective, the *procureur-général* showed a tendency to consider the public interest rather than the slave. Thus, one source of unfailing annoyance was the practice adopted by masters in giving their slaves Saturday or some other day of the week to work for themselves, instead of giving an allowance. This was presented as an abuse, not only because it might lead to thefts of provisions by slaves, or to want among those who paid no attention to their cultivations, but also because the gain made by industrious slaves as a result of this practice 'has made them so proud that they can scarcely be recognized for what they are.'[69] The laws for the planting of provisions by estates, constantly reiterated and constantly neglected, were not motivated only by the desire to protect the slaves.[70] Similarly, though the attorney-general complained when colonists had their slaves beaten in the streets, the disorder caused in the towns by this practice was obviously important in calling forth an objection to it.[71]

The crown, the royal officials, and the councils did not need much urging to concern themselves with police regulations in any case. These made up the large majority of the laws passed after the *Code Noir* was instituted. The subjects of these laws are, generally speaking, those to which attention has already been drawn in discussing the complaints made by the crown's attorney — the control of runaways, the general subordination of slaves and the need to prevent them from concerting risings, the prevention and detection of thefts, and the limiting of their economic opportunities, as well as of their physical mobility. The laws emphasized their dependence, because it was an element of social stability, directly related to their subordination. The regulations occasionally made, enforcing the allowances fixed under the *Code Noir*, have to be seen in this context.

In 1712, the crown returned to its insistence that slaves should not be privately tortured, and the cases brought against masters from time to time for cruelty to slaves were a reminder that the principle of governmental supervision was not forgotten.[72] But the crown would have needed to maintain a much closer watch than it did, if it had meant to enforce those protective clauses which were included in the *Code Noir*. Religious instruction, at first so much insisted on, was neglected or prevented by the colonists, and their attitudes were in turn defeated by government officials like Fénelon, who had come to believe that: 'The safety of the Whites, less numerous than the slaves, surrounded by them on their estates, and almost completely at their mercy, demands that the slaves be kept in the most profound ignorance.'[73] Pierre Regis Desalles, himself a colonist, writing in the second half of the eighteenth century, admitted that regulations favoring the marriage of slaves, and providing fixed allowances of food and clothing for them, were generally neglected. The laws against concubinage were notoriously ineffective. Abuse against slaves went undetected because 'No one cares to inform on his neighbor; and it is so dangerous to let Negroes make complaints against their masters.'[74]

All evidence points to one conclusion. As they were actually administered during the eighteenth century, the French slave laws differed far less from their English counterparts than might be imagined. The enforcement of the *Code Noir* during this period, in fact, shows a well-defined emphasis markedly similar to that already noticed in the British slave laws before the period of amelioration. Thus the provisions safeguarding the slave as 'persona' were either laxly enforced or neglected. His religious instruction, his protection against ill-treatment, his right to food, clothing, and care, provided for in the law, depended in practice far more on the will of the master than on enacted regulations. The law tended to become more and more a dead letter in these matters. Changes in the law made his manumission less easy, and deprived him, when free, of equality with other free men. Thus, the benefits which the law had originally conferred upon the slave and the freedman were either lost or reduced in their value by practice or by legislative change. Meanwhile, the part of the law which was provided for his control and submission continued in vigor — as the activities of the crowns' attorney serve to make abundantly clear. As in the British islands, so in practice in the French, police laws were the heart of the slave code. They were not neglected because the continuance of slavery depended upon them, and was understood to depend upon them. The law actually and continuously enforced was here, as

in the Spanish colonies, different from the law as enacted. As Peytraud says: 'Reality is sometimes far from corresponding to legal prescriptions.'[75]

The will to bring about a correspondence was also much weaker than it had been. In 1771, the crown issued official instructions which show this change at work:

It is only by leaving to the masters a power that is nearly absolute, that it will be possible to keep so large a number of men in that state of submission which is made necessarry to their numerical superiority over the whites. If some masters abuse their power, they must be reproved in secret, so that the slaves may always be kept in the belief that the master can do no wrong in his dealing with them.[76]

That the feeling of white solidarity had grown even stronger in the colonies is indicated by the well-known case involving the coffee-planter, Le Jeune, who was alleged to have killed four slaves and to have severely burnt two others, in the course of torturing them. Heavy pressure was brought to bear upon the governor; and the judges, afraid to go against local opinion, dismissed the case. The Council also refused to see Le Jeune punished, and he suffered no legal penalty whatever for his crimes.[77]

The Le Jeune case occurred in 1788, about four years after the crown had made several new provisions for the protection of slaves in its act 'concerning Attorneys and Managers of Estates situated in the Leeward Islands'. This order which was intended to correct abuses at St. Domingue, where the Le Jeune case occurred, contained clauses limiting the working hours of slaves and fixing their holidays, and allowing them to cultivate small plots of land for their own profit, besides compelling proprietors to plant provisions and to make allowances of food and clothing to their slaves. Provision was also made for the care of pregnant women and the sick, and for encouraging child-bearing. The protection against physical maltreatment given the slaves under the *Code Noir* was renewed, and a limitation was placed on the number of lashes which a master might give his slave.[78] These last clauses did not prevent Le Jeune's escape, and it is difficult to believe that the rest of the code can have been much more effective. Peytraud appears to be justified in his conclusion that 'the material condition of the Negroes did not cease to be miserable. As for their legal condition, so for their moral education, the advances achieved were very small. The facts cry aloud the condemnation of slavery, which reduced so many human beings to being scarcely more than beasts of burden.'[79]

The rule of force inherent in slavery produced comparable results in the Spanish, British, and French colonies in the West Indies, though variations were introduced by the degree of their dependence on slavery and by differences in their political traditions. The experience of the Dutch and Danish colonies supports this conclusion. Westergaard, in his study of the Danish islands, has said that the slave laws, which were made by the local government, 'became more severe as the ratio of negro to white population increased.' He cites repressive measures against runaways, who were specially aided by the nearness of the islands to Puerto Rico, and against thefts and the trading carried on by slaves without the permission of their owners.[80] In particular, he refers to the very severe ordinance of 1733, which, in his opinion, precipitated the serious slave rebellion of that year at St. John's. This ordinance provided such punishments for the crimes of slaves as pinching and branding with hot irons, dismemberment, hanging, and flogging. It was a police law, entirely concerned with the prevention of revolts and conspiracies, the control of runaways, thefts, and slave assemblies. It forbade the carrying of weapons by slaves, and punished severely any Negro found guilty of raising his hand against a white. These were the elements which attracted most attention in the government of slaves. Other laws protected the master's property in the slaves, and masters were indemnified for their losses when their slaves were judicially punished.[81] There was also supposed to be official supervision of the punishment of slaves, but, generally speaking, their protection was left to custom rather than law. The Company, which governed the islands, was more interested in the slaves as objects of trade and sources of manual labor for the production of wealth, than as persons. Here as elsewhere, they were subject to public repression and private tyranny.

The Danish West Indies under Company rule were at once entrepôts and plantation colonies. The Dutch also held both plantation colonies and trading colonies in the region; but these were geographically separate. In the main trading centres, Curaçao and St. Eustatius, and in the other small islands held by the Dutch, planting was of almost negligible importance. They lived by trade. The Guiana colonies, by contrast, developed a planting economy.

Throughout these Dutch colonies, the slaves were considered in law as things rather than as persons.[82] But the difference in the economic functions of the two types of colonies was reflected in a difference of slave conditions within them, despite their common basic law. The slaves in the Guiana colonies were subject to very harsh conditions of enslavement. The resident slave populations of the trading colonies — as distinct from the slave cargoes merely brought to be sold through these ports — generally enjoyed more humane treatment. In the Guianas, also, the slave laws, especially those for the control of runaways, were extremely severe in comparison with the laws of the islands. The influence of the plantation economy on slavery is thus again demonstrated.

In many of its aspects, the Dutch slave law resembled the slave law of the French West Indies — a resemblance due no doubt to their common origins in Roman law. Under the Dutch law, slaves could be bought and sold as chattels, and slave status was transmitted by birth through the mother. Plantation slaves were attached to the soil, and could only be sold with the estate. The dependency of the slave on his master was held to imply an obligation on the master to feed, clothe, and otherwise care for his slave; and a degree of protection was, in principle, made available to the slave through the fiscal of each colony. For a time, also, the Dutch West India Company showed some interest in the religious instruction of slaves, and made provisions to prevent their masters from forcing them to work on Sundays.

But the divorce of law and practice was as characteristic of the Dutch as of other colonies in the West Indies. In general, the Dutch Company, like the Danish, regarded the slaves primarily as objects of profit; and the settlers in the Dutch colonies took a similar view. The police regulations, which were numerous and often severe, were constantly invoked. Extralegal and illegal punishments were privately inflicted on slaves, especially in the Guiana colonies, where the existence of bands of runaway slaves in the hinterland encouraged a brutal stringency in estate discipline. Fear of the Bush Negro threat increased also the repressive tendencies of public policy. Inhuman punishments were inflicted on slaves, not merely by masters privately and illegally, but also by the judicial authorities acting under the law.

As in the French colonies, a conflict arose between the principle of repression and that of protection; and, on the whole, it was repression that triumphed.

Scandalous mistreatment of slaves by plantation-managers and others, acting on their own authority, was more than once punished by banishment or otherwise; but the persons responsible for the punishment were themselves slave-holders and this was reflected in the kind of punishment inflicted. The slave laws, which were revised from time to time, also failed to achieve the end in view. Those who administered them were all slave-holders. At the beginning of the nineteenth century, there was humane treatment of the slaves because of the abolition of the slave trade, but long after that time very crude punishments were apparently still in existence and the slaves were looked upon as a sort of cattle.83

Both in their content and in their enforcement, the West India slave laws follow a remarkably consistent pattern, imposed by the function of the law in maintaining the stability of those forms of social organization on which rested the whole of the West India colonies during the eighteenth century.

Notes

1. Samuel P. Scott, C. S. Lobingier, and John Vance (Eds), *Las Siete Partidas* (New York, 1931) is an English translation of the code, based upon the 1834-44 edition of the text of the original printed editions by Gregorio López (Salamanca: 1st edn, 1555; 2nd edn, 1565-98).
2. See C. Verlinden, *L'Esclavage dans l'Europe médievale* Vol. I, *Péninsule Ibérique-France*, (Bruges, 1955).
3. Juan de Solórzano, *Política indiana*, 5 vols (Madrid and Buenos Aires, 1930), Vol. I, Lib. 2, c. 4, n. 34 and c. 7, n. 77.
4. *Ibid.*, Vol. I, Lib. 2, c. 7, n. 13 and Vol. II, Lib. 3, c. 17, n. 23.
5. *Recopilación de leyes de las Indias* 3 vols. (Madrid, 1943), Vol. II, Lib. 7, tit. 5, ley 8.
6. *Ibid.*, ley 6.
7. *Ibid.*, ley 19. See also Luis M. Díaz Soler, *Historia de la esclavitud negra en Puerto Rico* (Madrid, 1953), p. 235; Fernando Ortiz, *Los negros esclavos, estudio sociológico y de derecho público* (Havana, 1916), p. 351; Arturo Morales Carrión, *Puerto Rico and the Non-Hispanic Caribbean* (Río Piedras, 1952).
8. On *coartación* see H. H. S. Aimes, 'Coartación', *Yale Review* (February, 1909), 412-31; Díaz Soler, *op. cit.*, especially Chap. X; Ortiz, *op. cit.*, especially Chap. XVII.
9. Aimes, *op. cit.*, pp. 424-25.
10. H. E. Friedlaender, *Historia economica de Cuba* (Havana, 1944), p. 84.
11. Ortiz, *op. cit.*, pp. 335-44.
12. *Ibid.*, *passim*. See also H. H. S. Aimes, *A History in Cuba, 1511-1865* (New York, 1907).
13. For an illustration see Javier Malagón, *Un documento del siglo XVIII para la historia de la esclavitud en las Antillas* (Havana, 1956).
14. Ortiz, *op. cit.*, pp. 342 ff.
15. *Recopilación*.
16. Ortiz, *op. cit.*, Chap. XX.
17. Díaz Soler, *op. cit.*, pp. 192-93.
18. H. T. Catterall, *Judicial Cases Concerning American Slavery and the Negro*, 5 Vols. (Washington, 1926-36), vol. I, pp. 1-8, 14-18, 34-37.
19. A good summary of the basic provisions of the British West Indian slave law during the eighteenth century is given in Reeves' 'General View of the Principles on which this System of Laws Appears to have been Originally Founded' in House of Commons Accounts and Papers, Vol. XXVI (1789), No. 646a, Part III. See the section dealing with 'Slaves Considered as Property'.
20. Statute 5 Geo. II, c. 7, and Statute 13 Geo. III, c. 14. For a West Indian example see *Laws of Jamaica*, 2 vols. (St. Jago de la Vega, 1792), Vol. II, 23 Geo. III, c. 14.
21. See for example *Laws of the Island of Antigua*, 4 vols., London, 1805), Vol. I, No. 130 (1702), No. 176 (1723).
22. Reeves, 'General Views', *loc. cit.*
23. *Ibid.*, section on 'Punishment by Masters'. See Act No. 82 (1688) in *Acts Passed in the Island of Barbados (1643-1762)* (London, 1764); a ms. copy is in C. O. 30/5, P.R.O. London.
24. For examples, see the Virgin Islands slave act (1783) in C. O. 152/67, the St. Kitts Act No. 2 (1711) 'for the better government of Negroes and other slaves' in C. O. 240/4, and the St. Vincent Act (July 11, 1767) in C. O. 262/1, P.R.O. London.
25. See the Antigua Act No. 130 (1702) and the Virgin Islands Slave Act (1783).
26. Montserrat Act No. 36 (1693)
27. Compare Antigua Act No. 176 (1723) and Antigua Act No. 390 (1778) in *Laws . . . of Antigua, op. cit.*, Vol. I.
28. Virgin Islands Slave Act (1783).
29. See Reeves, 'General View', *loc. cit.*, section 'of Manumissions.'
30. Barbados Act No. 82 (1688).
31. St. Vincent Act (July 11, 1767), in C. O. 262/1, P.R.O. London
32. 22 Geo. III, in *Laws* (Spanish Town, Jamaica), Lib. 8, I. R. O.
33. Jamaica Acts 8 Wm. III, c. 2, and 24 Geo. II, c. 17, in *Laws* (Spanish Town, Jamaica), Lib. 4, R. O.
34. Antigua Act No. 176 (1723); St. Kitts Act (1783) in C. O. 152/66, P. R. O. London.
35. Reeves. 'General View', *loc. cit.*
36. For instance, evidence given by James Tobin before a Select Committee of the House of Commons (1790), printed in House of Commons Accounts and Papers, Vol. XXIX (1790), No. 695/5, esp. pp. 272-73.
37. This view of the case is put by Drewry Ottley, Chief Justice of St. Vincent, in his evidence, reported in House of Commons Accounts and Papers, Vol. XXIV (1790-91), No. 476, pp. 158 ff.
38. F. Dwarris, 'Substance of the Three Reports of the Commissioners of Enquiry into the Administration of Civil and Criminal Justice in the West Indies', extracted from the *Parliamentary Papers* (London, 1827), pp. 113ff., 431ff.
39. *Ibid.*, p. 433.
40. *Ibid.*, pp. 114-16.
41. House of Commons Accounts and Papers, Vol. XXVI (1789), No. 646a. Pt 3 (St. Kitts), Appendix A.
42. Dwarris, *op. cit.*, p. 543.
43. *Ibid.*, pp. 431ff., 113ff.
44. Antigua Act No. 130 (1702).
45. Reeves, 'General View', *loc. cit.*
46. Barbados Act No. 82 (1688).
47. 25 Geo. III, c. 23 and 22, in *Laws of Jamaica, op. cit.*, Vol. II.
48. Bryan Edwards, *History of the British Colonies in the West Indies*, 3 vols (London, 1801), Vol. III, p. 36.
49. See the definitive text of the *Code Noir* of 1685 in L. Peytraud, *L'Esclavage aux Antilles Françaises avant 1789* (Paris, 1897), pp. 158-66.
50. France, Archives Nationales. Colonies F3 247, p. 63

(Martinique), règlement of September 1, 1638; F3 221, pp. 477–80 (Guadeloupe), ordonnance of September 14, 1672. Louis Elie Moreau de St.-Méry, *Loix et constitutions des colonies français de l'Amérique sous le vent*, 6 vols (Paris, 1784–90), Vol. I, pp. 117–22 (règlement of June 19, 1664).

51. *Ibid.*, Vol. I, pp. 447–48 (arrêt of October. 13, 1686).

52. *Ibid.*, Vol. I, p. 203 (arrêt of October 20, 1670). Arch. Nat. Cols. F3 247, pp. 825–26 (Martinique), arrêt of May 10, 1671.

53. Moreau de St.-Méry, *op. cit.*, Vol. II, pp. 241, 242–43 (letter and ordonnance of April 20, 1711).

54. *Ibid.*, Vol. I, pp. 447–48 (arrêt of October 13, 1686).

55. See R. P. DuTertre, *Histoire général des Antilles habitées par les français*, 3 vols (Paris, 1667–71), Vol. II, pp. 511–13; H. A. Wyndham, *The Atlantic and Slavery* (Oxford, 1935), pp. 256–57.

56. Moreau de St.-Méry, *op. cit.*, Vol. III, pp. 453–54 (letter of March 29, 1735).

57. *Ibid.*, Vol. II, pp. 272–73 (ordonnance of August 15, 1711). Arch. Nat. Cols. F³ 222, pp. 189–90.

58. Moreau de St.-Méry, *op. cit.*, Vol. II, pp. 398–99 (ordonnance of Oct. 24, 1713). Wyndham, *op. cit.*, pp. 256–57. An instance of a later law regulating manumissions is found in Arch. Nat. Cols. F³ 233 (Guadeloupe), ordonnance of March 3, 178.

59. Arch. Nat. Cols. F³ 249, p. 818 (Martinique). Moreau de St.-Méry, *op. cit.*, Vol. II, pp. 535–28.

60. Wyndham, *op. cit.*, pp. 367ff.

61. Peytraud, *op. cit.*, pp. 150–57.

62. *Ibid.*, p. 326.

63. Arch. Nat. Cols. F³ 225, p. 777 (Guadeloupe), letter of May 17, 1742.

64. Moreau de St.-Méry, *op. cit.*, Vol. III, pp. 727–29 (déclaration of February 1, 1743); pp. 500–502, (jugement of November 11, 1691); Vol. II, p. 103 (arrêt of August 1, 1707).

65. For examples see *ibid.*, Vol. I, p. 805 (arrêt of December 11, 1777); Vol. I, Arch. Nat. Cols. F³ 221, pp. 925–28

(Guadeloupe), arrêt of March 4, 1698. Also, *Code Noir*, Cl. 38.

66. Moreau de St.-Méry, *op. cit.*, Vol. V, p. 744 (arrêt of November 20, 1776); Vol. IV, p. 136 (arrêt of November 5, 1753).

67. *Ibid.*, Vol. II, pp. 25–27 (arrêt of March 16, 1705), p. 117 (arrêt of May 9, 1708), pp. 568–69 (ordonnance of July 1, 1717); Vol. III, pp. 177–78 (arrêts of July 2 and 8, 1726); Vol. V, pp. 97–98 (arrêt of March 9, 1767).

68. *Ibid.*, Vol. II, pp. 208, 213 (arrêts of September 1 and October 6, 1710). Arch. Nat. Cols. F³ 223, pp. 717–23 (Guadeloupe), arrêt of September 6, 1725; F³ 225, pp. 139–45, arrêt of Nov. 8, 1735.

69. Arch. Nat. Cols. F³ 226, pp. 269–82 (Guadeloupe), arrêt of July 9, 1746.

70. Moreau de St.-Méry, *op. cit.*, Vol. IV, pp. 401–03 (ordonnance of August 19, 1761).

71. *Ibid.*, Vol. IV, p. 566 (ordonnance of March 24, 1763).

72. Arch. Nat. Cols. B.34, ordonnance of December 30, 1712.

73. Peytraud, *op. cit.*, pp. 193–94.

74. Adrien Desalles, *Histoire générale des Antilles* (Paris, 1847), III, pp. 21ff.

75. Peytraud, *op. cit.*, p. 150.

76. Pierre de Vaissière, *St. Domingue (1629–1789)* (Paris, 1909), p. 181.

77. *Ibid.*, pp. 186–89.

78. Arch. Nat. Cols. F³ 233, pp. 231–35 (Guadeloupe), ordonnance of December 17, 1784.

79. Peytraud, *op. cit.*, p. 241.

80. W. Westergaard, *The Danish West Indies under Company Rule (1671–1754)* (New York, 1917), pp. 158ff.

81. *Ibid.*, pp. 162ff.

82. The discussion of the Dutch West Indian slave law is based upon the article 'Slavernij' in *Encyclopaedie van Nederlandsch West Indie* (The Hague, 1914–17), pp. 637ff.

83. *Ibid.*, p. 640.

43

Trinidad's Free Coloureds in Comparative Caribbean Perspectives

CARL CAMPBELL

The free coloured population of Trinidad have always possessed grounds for pretension, to which no other coloured colonists could aspire. During the whole period of Spanish administration, they were as impartially treated as the whites.

J. B. Philip: *Free Mulatto*, p. 16

The Two Charters

A very convenient point at which to begin the discussion of the position of the free coloureds in Trinidad is the Cedula of 1783. This Cedula represents Spain's deliberate attempt in the late 18th century to develop a plantation economy in Trinidad by relaxing restrictions on access to land, by freeing trade and investment, and by creating a safer climate for capital. For the moment our attention must be confined to the two clauses which most directly related to the question of the status of the free coloureds. Since the Cedula of 1783 was not abrogated by the English when they captured the island in 1797, its terms were at the centre of the debate in the 1820s on the status of free coloureds. The famous 5th clause reads as follows:

After the first five years' establishment of foreign settlers on the said island, they shall, by obliging themselves to continue therein perpetually, have all the rights and privileges of naturalization granted to them, and to the children they may have brought with them, as well as those that may be born in the island, in order to be admitted in consequence to the honorary employments of the public, and of the militia, agreeable to the quality and talents of each.[1]

This clause was the bedrock of the case of the free coloureds that the Spanish government had given them civil equality with the whites. As settlers they were convinced that they were entitled to the benefits of this clause. The final clause of the Cedula of 1783, though less often quoted, also provided the free coloureds a welcomed shelter. They claimed that it abolished any and all pre-1783 Spanish laws hostile to them. It reads in part:

And in order that all the articles contained in this regulation should have their full force, we dispense with all the laws and customs which may be contradictory to them; and we command our councils of the Indies, the chancellors and courts of justice thereof, vice-kings, captains and commanders-in-chief, governors and intendants, common justice, the officers of our royal revenues, and our consuls in the ports of France, to keep, comply with, and execute, and cause to be kept, complied with, and execute the regulation inserted in this our royal shedule.[2]

Another document which was vital to the free coloureds' case, and indeed to all the Roman Catholics of the island, was the Capitulation of 1797. This treaty between a defeated Spanish governor and a victorious British general was often regarded as an irrevocable part of the constitution of the island, and even as late as the early 20th century a few persons sought to protect their rights by appealing to it. The clause which was of most importance for the free coloureds was no. XII which reads:

The free coloured people, who have been acknowledged as such by the laws of Spain, shall be protected in their liberty, persons and property, like other inhabitants, they taking the oath of allegiance and demeaning themselves as becomes good and peaceable subjects of His Britannic Majesty.[3]

What could be clearer than this, asked the free coloured leaders? By clutching to the 12th clause the free coloureds turned the Capitulation into a sort of victory for themselves, and the term 'capitulant' used to describe those who were present when the English took over the island, instead of a badge of shame, became a mark of pride and privilege. The Cedula of 1783 gave them equal civil rights, and the Capitulation of 1797 confirmed it. Yet the English authorities, as we shall see, placed a wholly different interpretation on these clauses.

Immigration into the Spanish Antilles

There is to date no full-scale study of the free coloureds in Trinidad.[4] This present study is the first in the field. The island falls firmly within the three-tier socio-racial pattern prevailing in the Caribbean. As a Spanish colony for nearly three hundred years, Trinidad shared the fate of Cuba, Santo Domigo, Jamaica and Puerto Rico: neglected and under-populated, perhaps even more so that the larger Spanish islands in the Greater Antilles, Trinidad at the southern end of the Antillean chain of islands possessed some of the pre-conditions for the early birth of a free coloured population. White men were few, white women very rare, and a small number of African women were available. The persistence of Aboriginal Indian communities for longer periods in Trinidad than in other Spanish islands ensured that Indian blood was mixed with those of Europeans and Africans.[5] The small number of white colonists limited the growth of the free coloured population with white fathers.

It cannot be argued that the need to defend the island gave the early free coloureds any advantages in status. Trinidad was more or less defenceless for at least two-and-a-half centuries. It was not avidly sought by rival European nations, nor was it on the route of Spanish fleets to the centres of the Spanish American empire. The level of colonization in Cuba, Santo Domingo and Puerto Rico was higher than in Trinidad in the first two-and-a-half centuries of Spanish rule. Those colonies already had the beginnings of a Spanish creole identity by the middle of the 18th century. There were at this time too few colonists for anything similar to have happened in Trinidad.

Towards the end of the 18th century Trinidad, like Cuba and Santo Domingo and Puerto Rico,

was stimulated economically by new types of policies from the Spanish Crown acting in its own interest and those of the creole landowning and slave-owning class.[6] Basic to this economic stimulation was an increase in the population through immigration. Some of the immigrants were refugees, white and coloured, sometimes with their slaves, from the rebellious French Antilles. The ports of all the Spanish islands were opened to a freer flow of the African slave trade. However, the three-tier socio-racial structure was filled out by these immigrants in a somewhat different matter. The white population of Cuba and Puerto Rico, especially Cuba, was heavily reinforced; comparatively speaking, white immigration into Trinidad in the 1780s and 1790s was feeble.[7] The capture of the island in 1797 by the British and its distance from Saint Domingue and Santo Domingo limited its role as a destination for frightened Spaniards and dispossessed Frenchmen. Because the white population was small, and because Trinidad never went into an era of sugar development in the 1780s and 1790s with the surge and power of Cuba, there were far fewer slaves imported, although Trinidad like Cuba had new privileges of free trade in slaves.[8] Trinidad very likely imported more slaves than Puerto Rico in the 1780s and 1790s, although Puerto Rico had a larger white population than Trinidad.[9] The apparent results of these varying patterns of immigration was that a larger proportion of free coloured immigrants entered Trinidad than either Cuba or Puerto Rico. Hence the three-tier structure of Trinidad was mostly reinforced in the middle, the intermediate level, by coloureds. While Cuba and Puerto Rico entered into the early 19th century with white majorities, Trinidad continued with a white minority, adding by the 1780s a slave majority, and a strongly represented free coloured section.[10] Superficially at least the pattern in Trinidad was a hybrid of the traditional Spanish Caribbean and British Caribbean patterns. Like the British Caribbean Trinidad in 1797 had a white minority, and a slave majority; like the Spanish Caribbean, especially Puerto Rico, it had a large free coloured sector. This pattern persisted down to the abolition of slavery (1838), with the free coloureds making significant gains over the white population. Compared to most other Caribbean islands the demographic strength of the free coloured popu-

Table 43.1   Population of Trinidad 1813, 1819, 1825

Groups	1813		1819		1825	
White						
Male	1,695		2,047		)	
Female	1,201		1,669		)	
Total	2,896		3,716		3,310	
% of total population		7.6%		9.3%		7.8%
Free Coloureds						
Male	3,774		5,956		)	
Female	4,328		6,529		)	
Total	8,102		12,485		14,983	
% of total population		21.3%		31.2%		35.4%
Slave						
Male	)		)		)	
Female	)		)		)	
Total	25,717		22,854		23,230	
% of total population		67.7%		57.2%		54.9%
Indians						
Male	)		)		)	
Female	)		)		)	
Total	1,265		850		727	
% of total population		3.3%		2.1%		1.7%
Total population	37,980		39,905		42,250	

Sources: C.O. 295/55, p.366, Return of E. Hodkinson, Commissary of Population
Cecil Goodridge: Land, Labour and Immigration into Trinidad 1783–1833 (unpublished Ph.D. thesis, Cambridge University, 1970), p.219

lation in Trinidad was outstanding. Table II demonstrates the comparative demographic strengths at a high period of the struggle in the British islands. Only Grenada which also had a large free coloured population, and Puerto Rico which was characterised by a notoriously small slave population, could compare favourably with Trinidad.

The Colour Scale

Of the older British West Indian islands Jamaica is the only one which had a well-established, sophisticated colour scale measuring the distance of persons of mixed ancestry from white persons. It is recognised that these internal gradations were first created in the New World by Spaniards and distilled into a fine art by the French. No researcher has explained how Jamaica came to adopt such a sophisticated colour scale so uncharacteristic of the English in the other British islands. Trinidad which was Spanish for nearly three hundred years received a substantial influx of Frenchmen and free coloureds of French extraction in the last two decades of the 18th century. It is not therefore surprising (and one must not forget its vital links with neighbouring Venezuela) that Trinidad had a definite colour scale. In this respect the island

Table 43.2   Comparative Demographic Strength of Freedman Populations

Year	Colony	Freedmen as % of free population	Freedmen as % of non-white population
1825	Barbados	23.6	6.0
1817	Cuba	30.1	33.2
1827	Puerto Rico	38.2	74.5
1817	Curacao	44.6	24.8
1820	Jamaica	48.5	8.8
1826	Martinique	52.0	11.7
1826	St. Kitts	57.3	11.3
1830	Surinam	66.0	9.3
1829	Guyana	67.7	8.4
1824	St. Lucia	75.4	21.2
1823	Dominica)	)	)
	St. Vincent)	75.4	16.0
	Grenadines)	)	)
1825	Trinidad	81.9	39.2
1826	Grenada	82.4	13.7

Sources: E. Williams: *From Columbus to Castro*, pp. 290-1; D. Cohen and J. Greene: *Neither Slave nor Free*, p.62, 71, 151; B. Marshall: *Social Stratification in the Slave Society of the British Windward Islands*, op. cit., p. 35; E. Cox: *The Shadow of Freedom*, op. cit., p.59, 61; B. Gaspar: *The Emancipation of the Free Coloureds of St. Lucia 1824-31*, op. cit., p.3; R. Schomburgk: *A Description of British Guiana*, p.42; E. Brathwaite: *The Development of Creole Society 1770-1820*, op. cit., p. 152, 168.

Notes: The figures include free blacks except in Surinam and Curacao. Guyana means Demerara and Essequibo.

was more like Jamaica and unlike the rest of the British islands.

The main evidence for a detailed colour scale in Trinidad comes from the classification of slaves in the Slave Registry.[11] Our assumption is that the colour scale used for slaves was not peculiar to them, but applied to the free non-white population generally. The colour rating in descending order was something like this:

whites
quadroon
mestee
costee
mulatto
cabre
mongrel
sambo
blacks

As usual the sexual union of a white man and a black woman, African or creole, produced the best known type of coloured person, the mulatto. The majority of coloured slaves were mulat-

toes,[12] and the term, as elsewhere in the Caribbean, came to be synonymous with the entire group of coloureds. It seems that a cabre woman and a white man could have a mulatto child. A mulatto woman and a white man produced a mestee offspring; and a mestee and a mulatto produced a costee. A mulatto and a black person would usually have a cabre child, occasionally a black child, rarely a mongrel or a sambo child.[13] A cabre and a black person would usually produce a black child, occasionally a cabre child. A black person and an Amerindian would produce a sambo child or a black child. But a mulatto and a black person could also produce a sambo offspring. A quadroon could result from mating between a mestee and a white person.[14]

Unlike Jamaica where a law specifically named the cut-off grade above which coloured persons could legally be white,[15] no law has been found in Trinidad regulating the colour scale or assimilating grades to the white population. But there were persons who were so nearly white in appearance as to pass for white.[16] And there were others white enough to be confused sometimes with whites.[17] As elsewhere, the detailed colour scale does not seem to have been employed in everyday life, but chiefly when it was necessary to describe someone with particular accuracy. Thus wills, for instance, might specifically name a cabre or mestee inheritor.[18] As might be expected it was Frenchmen and blacks and free coloureds of French extraction who seemed most adept at distinguishing the different shades of colour. Apparently the term most often used in the street was mulatto, with the adjective 'dark' added when appropriate.[19] The English authorities, especially from the time of Governor Woodford, preferred to speak of coloured persons.

Comparative Disabilities

A review of the literature in English indicates that for the élite free coloureds the most fundamental disabilities were related to inability to exercise the electoral franchise, incapacity to get civil service posts, or to serve in the courts as witnesses, jurors or magistrates. Trinidad did not quite fall into this pattern. It did not have an elected Assembly; not did it have a jury system; hence free coloureds and whites had a kind of "negative equality" to use the term of Chief Justice George Smith. The magistrates of the colony in descending order of importance were the governor, three senior judges (often sitting together), the Alcaldes of the Cabildo of Port of Spain, and the Commandants of Quarters. Free coloureds never occupied any of these positions, but they could be witnesses in any civil court against anybody in all kinds of action. Since the whites also could not be elected to an Assembly (there being none), the supreme disability of the free coloureds came to be their failure to get jobs in the civil service, and in particular their failure to achieve officer rank in the militia. It was their conviction that they were entitled to these rights from the Cedula of 1783.

The free coloureds of Trinidad had no limit set on the amount of land or slaves they could own; they were not subjected to any special taxes;[20] marriages between whites and coloureds were not legally prohibited, though they were socially disapproved. No sumptuary laws were in force in Trinidad. It is important however to mention the confused legal position in the island. It was a point of frequent dispute which or how many Spanish laws were still in force in the island. The British adopted the strategy of leaving Spanish law in place except where they conflicted with obligatory English law or were specifically abrogated. Additionally some Spanish laws conflicted confusingly with others, and there was from 1797 a most important disagreement about the interpretation of two documents which were fundamental to the people of the island. Suffice it to say at present that it would have been perfectly possible for some lawyer to produce an ancient Spanish American law, for example on dress, which appeared to apply to a Spanish American province of which Trinidad was a part. When we say there was no Spanish law in Trinidad to cover a case we usually mean that the debate (if there was one) was not conducted as if there was such a law.

In the category of disabilities which we have regarded as humiliating, but not fundamental, Trinidad shared the same sort of grievances with many other colonies in the Caribbean. There were the usual grievances of having to carry lighted lanterns, obey curfews, endure segregation in public places, and refusals to call free coloureds 'Mr.' or 'Madam'. A somewhat unusual disability in Trinidad was the device of asking free coloureds to pay less for the same type of medical treatment as whites.[21] The élite free coloureds not appreciating the economy, saw the indignity, and feared a lower standard of treatment.

On the whole the free coloureds of Trinidad seemed among the least disadvantaged in the Caribbean. They were discouraged from being professionals, but they were not prohibited lucrative trades and occupations. They could buy, sell or own anything. While other islands to a great or lesser extent allowed free coloureds to have some or all of these privileges, Trinidad combined them with a scheme of free land grants which lasted from 1783 to 1812. If the Trinidad free coloureds had economic rights equal to the whites, they had in a political sense a negative equality of a sort, since neither they nor the whites had the vote. But of course in practice Crown Colony government was conducted by the governor with the aid of an all-white Council, and in this sense the free coloureds were in fact disadvantaged. But the incessant arguments in the colonies with Assemblies about the franchise did not arise in Trinidad except where the more fundamental question of achieving an elected Assembly arose in the first instance. The need for an Assembly was discussed more often than a franchise.

Another advantage which the free coloureds of Trinidad had, or thought they had, was the strategic position of being able to argue that they had lost under the English rights which they possessed under the Spanish. The free coloureds of the French Antilles, especially those of Saint Domingue, were the counterparts in the Caribbean most clearly in a similar position. They could and did argue that they had rights under the Code Noir which they subsequently lost, though without a change of flag. There was a sense though in which most of the free coloureds of the other British islands knew that their position had been eroded by legislation in the 18th century. The difference in their position was that they could not point to any Magna Carta like the Code Noir, or the Cedula of 1783. Some accepted this erosion as understandable at the time it was done.[22] The free coloureds in Trinidad, when the British government came to adjudge the question of their rights, did benefit from their restorationist posture.

The response of the Trinidad free coloureds to their disabilities cannot be said to have taken long to mature, because on their own account they were protesting against disabilities introduced by the English; the English administration began in 1797, and by the second decade of the 19th century the free coloureds had commenced to organize themselves for resistance. This did not mean that the free coloured population was exempt from internal weakness or devoid of disunity; for one thing there were those who were oriented to the culture of Spain, others to that of France and still others to that of England,[23] some were Roman Catholics and others Methodists or Anglicans. Then there were divisions between urban free coloureds and élite free coloured planters. It was not really that the free coloureds acted earlier than in other British islands, but that the discrimination came late. In some other Caribbean islands the disabilities were piled on by legislation from the early and mid-18th century. In Trinidad free coloureds claimed that the English immigrants and governors, especially Governor Woodford who arrived in 1813, were the evil ones who overturned the policy of tolerance and equality which characterised the Spanish regime, especially the governorship of Chacon.

Very likely there were important élite free coloureds who stayed outside the incipient movement of protest, but their were no reports of splits arising from special concessions to individual élite free coloureds. Because there was no elected Assembly there was no local authority capable of dividing the élite free coloureds by concessions to individuals such as happened in Jamaica through the means of private privilege bills. The whites in Trinidad did feel insecure, especially from revolution from the Spanish mainland, and from the local free coloureds. The insecurity did not arise from the proximity of black generals in Haiti, or from slave rebellions or maroon attacks.[24] There was no slave rebellion in the colony, nor clusters of hostile maroons. Free coloureds were probably feared more than the slaves. It was not plausible therefore to meet the insecurity by concession to the local free coloureds. An alternative strategy was available to the soldier governors of the island, which was to frighten the free coloureds and troublesome whites by the use of their extensive powers.

The Debate over Status

Between 1800 and 1823 the slaves in the colony apparently were governed by Picton's Slave Code of 1800; in the decade before this, it was Chacon's Code of 1789 which applied.[25] Neither of these codes had clauses applicable to free coloureds as well as to slaves. The famous English ameliorative slave code of 1823 did not confuse slaves with free coloureds. Nor did generally the regulations issued by Woodford in his long governorship (1813-1828). It cannot therefore be said that the legal status of the free coloureds in Trinidad, as in some other islands, was complex because slave laws applied to them. The legal ambiguity of the status of the free coloureds in Trinidad arose from differences in the interpretation of the Cedula of 1783 and the Capitulation of 1797. Behind these documents was the potential ambiguity of little-known Spanish laws.[26] For instance if the Cedula of 1783 had not abrogated all the old disabling laws of the Spanish empire, as the opponents of the free coloureds claimed, then their status was open to great uncertainties.

The main difference therefore between the status of the free coloureds in Trinidad and their counterparts in other British islands was that in Trinidad the first problem was to decide the legal status of the free coloureds and then to redress it; in the other British islands it was more a problem of improving on a legal status which was complex but undisputed. There was therefore in Trinidad a dimension of protest not present in the other Caribbean islands: the interpretation of fundamental laws defining the legal status of free coloureds was itself in question.

Free coloureds in Trinidad were not required to have a white patron, but were still thought of as subordinate children. John Sanderson, an ambitious English lawyer, wrote a polemical book rejecting the claims to civil equality in which he argued that coloureds, as a race derived from European, should be strictly subordinated to them as children to adults or as women to men.[27] To Woodford the free coloureds were out of control; they were too numerous, too wealthy and too independent of white society. An essential part of his programme was to create a society of settled ranks in which no free coloured was in a situation of command over a white person. This was one reason why a free coloured could not be given officer status in the militia.

In Trinidad the status of free coloureds in the militia was not just another grievance. The free coloureds claimed to have enjoyed officer status under Chacon. Officer status was the most important position which they actually claimed that they once had. Their role in the militia therefore became a test case for civil equality. It was as if the entire civil service could be penetrated by free coloureds if indeed it was true that coloured militia officers not only existed but did so on terms of equality with white officers. The élite free coloured leaders as owners of landed property in the country were exactly the sort of persons who would qualify for officer status if coloureds had a right to be officers. The deprivation was therefore most personal: the leaders were talking about posts which they themselves should have. And their white upper class opponents were equally determined on the point of officer status because they might have to serve under these very coloured militia officers. The

power of a militia officer could be used to great effect to wound social enemies.

The supreme leader of the free coloureds, Dr John Baptiste Philip, a medical practitioner whose family were wealthy landowners and slave owners, was humiliated by having to serve in the militia as a private and by being sent into the forested interior to hunt runaway slaves.[28] He had expected to enlist as an officer. It mattered to Philip to have officer status for élite free coloureds even if in the short run coloureds and whites were not integrated in the militia. For the situation was rather like other places in the Caribbean: there were separate militia companies of whites and free coloureds, and the coloured militia units were officered by whites.

The Stronghold in the Naparimas

The free coloureds of Trinidad had a strong position on the land because of the vital head start in land ownership provided by the free distribution of land to immigrants under the Cedula of 1783. Contemporaries did not portray the free coloureds as a poor community, but as in other Caribbean islands the majority had little or no property. It is not possible to quantify the extent of free coloureds' land ownership in the entire island, but of the free land distribution between 1783 and 1812 free coloureds received at least five per cent. Subdivision of these lands spread free coloured land ownership over many families. There was in Trinidad, as in the south of Saint Domingue, a territorial area in which free coloured land ownership was particularly pronounced. This was the Naparimas, the hinterland of San Fernando. In the Naparimas in 1813 there was a total of thirty-eight coloured proprietors with seventeen sugar estates, three coffee estates, one coffee/provision estate and ten provision estates. In this particular area of the island free coloureds had 35% of the estates and 30.1% of the slaves.[29] In other parts of the island there were scores of free coloured landowners cultivating their own land. A general impression is that land owning among the free coloureds was more widespread in Trinidad after 1783 than in any other British Caribbean island. The situation was somewhat more like that in Puerto Rico where free coloureds' access to the land was widespread. A difference though was that in

Trinidad legal ownership, not squatter rights, distinguished the position of the coloured land-holders. Because of their strength on the land the free coloureds in Trinidad were not particularly an urban community, a pattern which distinguished them from many other Caribbean slave societies. In 1811 aout 52.9% lived in the countryside; in 1825 the figure was 65.2%.[30]

Free coloureds in Trinidad did not confine themselves to urban occupations. In the towns they did the usual range of jobs from domestics to skilled artisans, shopkeepers and hucksters. But a class of free coloured small farmers and peasants existed in the countryside; Trinidad, like Puerto Rico, had a coloured peasantry before the abolition of slavery. Since these small farmers could not afford slave labour it must be assumed that they employed members of their families or occasionally coloured or black wage labour. Trinidad had settlements of disbanded soldiers and some of them from the USA, the so-called American refugees, might have been coloureds. On land given by the government these settlers grew their own food.[31] It has often been said that free coloureds generally spurned field labour on the estates. Regular field work on sugar estates did not have prestige in Trinidad or anywhere else, and this was avoided if possible. There was however in Trinidad a category of coloureds who specialised in clearing estate land. These were the peons some of whom moved between Trinidad and Venezuela.

As in the other Caribbean islands the free coloureds of Trinidad were less prominent as slaveowners than as owners of land or houses. They were also represented as cruel slave masters. It is wise however to apply the same skeptical attitude to this stereotype in Trinidad as Handler did in Barbados. The stereotype of the cruel free coloured slave master had less to do with the statistical reality of cruelty and more with the sense of moral outrage which whites, and the slaves themselves, felt in observing punishment being meted out by non-white owners to slaves racially akin to them. It was a privilege to beat slaves and in the literature created by the whites there was more talk of the disabilities of free coloureds as coloureds than of their privileges as free persons.

In Trinidad land was in plentiful supply and there was no substantial body of poor whites. Poor whites from Venezuela were the objects of the feeble charity of the Cabildo of Port of Spain and not recipients of land. Thus competition for resources and markets between free coloureds and poor whites was minimal. There was no attempt to exclude coloureds from growing export crops. For the most part what they grew were provisions. There was no pressure to turn the free coloured farmer into an estate worker. Not even Woodford had such a daring objective. Woodford tried to get all social groups to cultivate their land more intensively, and by implication he did not think free coloureds produced as much as they should. The free coloureds were blamed for slovenly agricultural methods and they were never publicly praised as an energetic enterprising sector of the society. Woodford badgered free coloured landowners. But on the whole the theme of the useless free coloured was not heavily stressed by the authorities.

Trinidad did not experience any massive white immigration which depressed the conditions of the free coloureds. The whites who came in the period of free land distribution came into a society of expanding economic opportunities, not only for themselves but for free coloureds as well. Labour and capital, not land, were the missing elements in commercial agriculture. Because of the supervisory power of the British government the colony's labour problems could not be solved either by the clandestine importation of slaves (after 1807) or by the reduction of the landless or unemployed population as in Puerto Rico in the early 19th century, to forced labour.[32]

Resistance without Violence

The free coloureds of Trinidad never resorted to violence to achieve the goal of civil equality. In the 1780s and 1790s when refugees and immigrants, some free coloureds, were entering the island, there was considerable apprehension especially in 1796 by the Spanish authorities that free coloureds of French extraction might carry the revolutionary ideas of their brothers from the French Antilles into the colony.[33] The British inherited these apprehensions even after the immigration had ceased. There were coloured republicans, but as in many other areas in the world revolutionary refuges did not carry revolution to the country of exile. Indeed the refugees and immigrants found new economic opportunities to become landowners in Trinidad, and to settle down to become peaceful fathers of families. In Venezuela there was a war of liberation in which coloureds participated as rebels and conservatives. Some of the coloured rebels camped occasionally on the shores of Trinidad, whose neighbouring coastline was strategically part of their battlefield. But Venezuela, not Trinidad, was the object of their subversive attention.

Trinidad did appear to be a colony where free coloured violence could erupt. Of the British islands the political experience of Grenada between 1763 and 1795 seems most closely to resemble the situation in Trinidad. Grenada had once been French; then the English took it over, and a war of nationalities and cultures began. The free coloureds were also well represented in Grenada.[34] Then came 1795. The abortive Julien Fedon revolt in neighbouring Grenada was not only a bad memory, but an experience of some who were now ex-Grenadians resident in Trinidad, which had a mixed population of Spaniards, Frenchmen and Englishmen, and the different groups of coloureds and slaves oriented to the culture of each of these major European groups. It had absorbed refugees whose antecedents were not always clear. It was near to revolutionary Venezuela. But on the other hand it had tough English military governors, and behind them a powerful British military capability. Free coloured violence for civil equality would have been foolhardy in a colony where free coloureds had more privileges than in many other colonies.

Yet the image of the revolutionary free coloureds existed also in Trinidad as in other parts of the Caribbean. Trinidad was not too far from Haiti for the authorities to escape the powerful reverberations of events in that country. As elsewhere in the Caribbean it was remembered that it was the free coloureds of Haiti (Saint Domingue) who by opposing the whites opened the door to slave rebellion and the loss of the colony.[35] No amount of peaceful behaviour could shake the stereotype of the subversive free coloured.

If Trinidad had remained a Spanish colony it might possibly not have had any collective resistance by free coloureds to the civil and political dominance of the whites. With the coming of the English in 1797, anti-free coloured policies were stepped up at the same time that the new controlling metropolitan power began to develop anti-slavery attitudes and policies. Thus Trinidad's free coloureds felt that need for collective resistance, and also perceived the possibility of success. Not having any local elected assembly to appeal to, the free coloured leaders down to 1825 requested relief directly from the British government. This was unlike the British colonies with Assemblies where many years of early appeals to the Assemblies preceded the change of strategy in the 1820s.

In Trinidad the main organs of government were a governor and a Council. The governor, with or without the Council, could make regulations for the government of the colony, including orders affecting the status of the free coloureds. All the governors, with the exceptions of Col. Fullerton and later acting Governor Col. Young, were hostile to free coloureds, and there were no friendly voices among the all-white members of the Council. There was therefore no political basis for an appeal for relief to the governor or the Council, for it was these very bodies which had passed the regulations of which the free coloureds complained. In most of the British colonies with Assemblies the free coloureds of the 1820s were complaining against laws made in an earlier period; sometimes as far back as a previous generation. In Trinidad, free coloureds in the 1820s were protesting against regulations made or executive action taken in their own times, certainly since 1797, and especially since 1813. It was constitutionally normal to expect an Assembly to reverse decisions made by a previous Assembly; the balance of forces and views were subject to change in an elected body, and each new Assembly was not bound by the views of its predecessors. But matters were somewhat different with an appointed Council completely dependent on the will of the governor. The views of the governors were that the subordination of the free coloureds was socially necessary for the continuation of the slave society. Consistency of policy was easier in an appointed Council than in an elected Assembly; and consistency in this case worked against the free coloureds.

Because the first appeal was to the British government and not to the local authorities, there was no need to ask for redress in a piecemeal fashion. With the British government there was no need to bargain, to ask for little and expect less or to accept a new privilege while agreeing to some new disability. The 1823 petition of the free coloureds to the British government was a full exposition of their grievances and a direct request for full civil equality.[36] It was followed closely by an even fuller revelation of their agonies in the form of a book, *Free Mulatto*, written by the free coloured leader, Dr John Baptiste Philip.

The absence of an elected Assembly also helped to shape the nature of the collective resistance. There was no need to lobby members of the Council; no opportunity to attempt to shape opinions in the Council by public agitation. All that was necessary was the collection of sufficient names on a petition to impress the metropolitan government, and ability to win a sympathetic hearing at the Colonial Office or in Parliament by the use of contact men in England or the despatch of special delegates from the colony. It is not that signatures could be obtained without raising the level of consciousness of grievances, but the emphasis was on the appeal to the external authority, not on internal agitation to influence the local authorities. It was not until after 1825 when the British government was half way to a favourable decision, and when the collective resistance moved into a new phase and to the capital, Port of Spain, that the new leaders, chief of whom was the rebel coloured Roman Catholic priest, Francis DeRidder, sought to appeal politically to a local audience of coloureds. This phase of the movement, though the peak of it came ironically after the free coloureds had won the first giant step towards legal equality, gave the authorities more problems than the 1810-1825 phase which was dominated by the respectable élite planters. Port-of-Spain was a more volatile community than the Naparima sugar district, more middle and lower class people were involved in the post-1825 period of the movement; and new camouflaged political organizations with a following had sprung up. This was nearer to 'grass roots' political agitation among the free population than the activities of a rural planter committee in the pre-1825 period.

Because the free coloureds asked for full civil equality all at once, the British government responded in like manner with full civil equality. In the drafting of the 1826 Order-in-Council though, certain problems arose which meant that in the eyes of the free coloureds full civil equality had not been granted to all of them. The adjust-

ments came by 1829 through an unequivocal Order-in-Council. Thus there was a sense in which we can say that it took two attempts to reach the goal of civil equality; the first big step occurring in January 1826, and the final step in 1829; yet the process of getting there was not as fragmented as in the British colonies which had Assemblies. Of course we should remember that one question which occasioned the toughest struggle in British colonies with Assemblies, namely the franchise, was not an issue in Trinidad where the British government resolutely maintained Crown Colony government. The free coloured leaders supported the status of Crown Colony, but not the policies of the Crown Colony government.[37]

In Trinidad the 'split' in the movement for civil equality was not a confrontation between conservative free coloureds who would be satisfied with less than full civil equality and radical free coloureds who would stop at nothing short of it. There were two discreet phases of the same movement: a pre-1825 phase and a post-1825 phase, each of which had a distinct leader, each of which was located in a different area of the colony, and each of which attracted a somewhat different audience. However some of the junior leaders overlapped both phases of the movement. In the second phase a schism occurred in the Roman Catholic congregation of Port of Spain as DeRidder set up his own chapel and attracted a following. In 1811 a serious disagreement had flared up between Church of England free coloureds and Methodist free coloureds, but this did not reflect directly a split on the question of civil rights.[38]

If there were any white liberals among the white élite in Trinidad supportive of the free coloureds' thrust to civil equality we do not know of them.[39] Col. Fullerton, one of the triumvirate of governors in 1803, was opposed to needless oppression of free coloureds. Chief Justice George Smith was so unfriendly to the social pretensions of creole whites in the colony that he looked like a potentially ally of the coloureds. But neither Fullerton nor Smith argued that free coloureds should have civil equality with whites. John Lewis, a white English lawyer, was an opponent of Woodford; Lewis once argued the case of the free coloureds as a paid advocate.[40] He did a poor job. Chief Justice George Scotland was the first genuine white liberal in high office, but his administration started after the struggle for civil equality had come to an end. The free coloureds' petitions for equality did not have the support of any whites; nor do we know of any white groups which petitioned on behalf of the free coloureds as was done in Jamaica and St.Kitts. In the post-1825 phase of the movement DeRidder was joined by Abbe Power, a rebel Irish Roman Catholic priest from Grenada. Power was expelled from the island, but later returned and was reconciled to the Church.

Though Fullerton and Young failed the test as white liberals the free coloureds did recognise that during their administrations a less hostile attitude emanated from the governors themselves. Fullerton tried to act legally and this alone won him the reputation as a friend of coloureds.[41] Col. Young, commander of the troops who once acted for Woodford during the latter's absence, had a tolerant attitude to coloureds, but not wishing to anger Woodford, did not reverse any of his policies. In the end Fullerton's and Young's reputed friendliness to coloureds was a matter of personal attitude and not favourable legislation. But personal attitude was important to oppressed free coloureds looking for relief. On the whole Trinidad had no friendly governor who took the lead on behalf of free coloureds.

The Free Blacks

It is not known how many free blacks were in the colony since they were lumped with free coloureds in the official statistics. There is however a strong impression that people of mixed racial ancestry were in a sizeable majority.[42] This arises from the large influx of free coloured immigrants in the late 18th century at a time when the pre-existing slave population was small. This headstart of the true free coloureds, plus the likelihood of coloured slaves being favoured in manumissions, left them with a solid position in the island. Some free blacks owned houses and lots in Port of Spain and small plots of land in the countryside.[43] They too were entitled to land under the Cedula of 1873. Among the free blacks there is evidence of Mandingos who organized themselves to purchase the freedom of fellow tribesmen, and to continue their religious life. But the free Mandingo community was thinking of re-

turning to Africa rather than of winning civil rights in the colony.[44]

There is no indication that free blacks participated in the struggle of the free coloureds to gain civil equality. In neither of the two phases of the movement were they mentioned as participants. No free black petition was presented as in Jamaica and Guyana. In the first phase of the movement élite free coloureds' leaders charged Governor Woodford and his chief agent in the Naparimas, Robert Mitchell, with oppression of the American refugees settled in the Naparimas. Some of these were blacks. They were however a special group living near the centre of free coloureds' protest. The other free blacks of the colony, as individuals or as groups, were not mentioned.

In neither of the two phases of the free coloured movement did the leaders refer to the contemporary struggles in other parts of the Caribbean. But this does not mean that they were ignorant of it. The year of the major petition (1823) fell within the period 1822 to 1823 in which most of the other British islands sent in their major petitions to the British government. The free coloureds' leaders in Trinidad did not collaborate with any other colony in choosing a spokesman to represent their case. They chose their own delegates and sent them to London. The passage of refugees from Martinique to Trinidad in 1824, subsequent to serious reprisals on free coloureds there (the Bissette affair) must have provided the opportunity for many persons in Trinidad to become well informed of the situation there.[45] But the conduct of the campaign in Trinidad was in accordance with the general picture in the Caribbean: the free coloureds of each island chose to fight their own battles separately.

The British Government

The British government did not have the opportunity actively to protect the free coloureds of Trinidad against unfriendly regulations between 1797 and 1824. This was because these regulations were not usually sent up to the British government, but were simply implemented by the solider governors on security grounds. The normal correspondence between governors and the Colonial Office did not contain any discussion of these regulations, nor the regulations themselves, which became known to the Colonial Office only when the free coloureds denounced them. It was therefore in an atmosphere of profound ignorance that the Colonial Office, under the influence of James Stephen Jr., set about in the 1820s to discover what the grievances of the free coloureds were.

When the British government became interested in the free coloureds, it did not railroad the local authorities into immediate action. The Judicial commissioners who visited so many of the British islands had their terms of reference extended specifically to include an investigation of the grievances of the free coloureds in Trinidad.[46] Governor Woodford was given a chance to explain himself. James Stephen Jr. was asked to review the recommendations of the Judicial commissioners. All of this happened because of the complexity of the free coloureds' claims in Trinidad. Their claims to civil equality were based on a Spanish Cedula which seemed to couple land grants, and a period of residence, with the rights of full citizenship. One question which the metropolitan government had to sort out was whether free coloureds who had not received land grants were entitled under the Cedula to civil equality.[47] These difficulties delayed a decision by the British government. Hence the irony that in a Crown Colony where the British government had power to act directly, a five-year lag occurred between the presentation of the main petition and the decisive Order-in-Council in 1829.

In view of the reports of the Judicial commissioners and James Stephen Jr. it seems correct to say that in imposing civil equality in 1829 the British government was restoring an old right rather than establishing a new privilege. That is the British government seemed to have agreed that the Cedula of 1783 did establish civil equality. Of course in selling the idea of civil equality using Trinidad as a model, the British government sought to get the other islands to legislate free coloureds' equality as a new principle; and in Trinidad itself in subsequent years, the Order-in-Council of 1829 was apparently celebrated as the beginning of a new principle rather than the restoration of an old right.

Slavery

The slave system of Trinidad after 1783 has unfortunately not yet been fully investigated.[48]

In defense of slavery the planters of the colony in the 1820s asserted that slavery was mild and paternal.[49] On the surface some of the conditions of pre-plantation Spanish colonies which had, together with Spanish traditions and institutions, disposed the authorities of Spanish colonies to mild treatment of non-whites, free and enslaved, in the sense of relatively easy access to manumissions and to partial rights of citizenship for those so manumitted, existed in Trinidad. The sugar plantation system was not well developed although it experienced growth in the early 19th century. It is known that in 1813 most slave holdings were small, the economy still not monocultural, and that a significant proportion of the slaves were domestics. This pattern still existed basically on the eve of slave emancipation.[50] But the capitalistic drive of the English sugar planter class, restrained by the scarcity of slaves, was a force in the countryside; and at any rate in assessing the relative harshness of slave systems, it is well to point out as Genovese has done, that day-to-day living and working conditions of slaves varied independently from opportunities for religious instruction or access to manumission, or partial recognition of some rights after manumission.[51] The predominance of African-born slaves in a frontier colony where new estates had to be established by arduous land clearing contributed to a high rate of mortality. There is also ambivalent evidence that the material conditions of life, such as work, diet and disease, affected unfavourably the physical growth of the slaves.[52] The general shortage of labour tended in the direction of pressure of work on the declining slave population. All this suggests that the slave system was generally positioned towards the harsh end of the scale. While therefore the French creole legend of paternal treatment by Frenchmen or French creole masters might apply to some small cocoa estates, it should be realised that sugar production for export demanded hard labour for long hours.[53] There is no evidence of mild day-to-day living and working conditions on sugar plantations.

It is clear from what has been said so far that race relations between whites and free coloureds in Trinidad slave society between 1797 and 1829 was characterised by legal discrimination, but that on the whole this discrimination was not as severe as in some other islands. Nor was there a violent conflict between the two parties such as happened in the French Antilles. By contemporary early 19th century Caribbean standards race relations between whites and free coloureds in Trinidad were less harsh than in many other islands. A tentative conclusion then would be that Trinidad experienced a somewhat harsh slavery coupled with relatively less harsh race relations outside slavery between whites and free coloureds.[54] Trinidad was a good place to be manumitted. It is hardly safe therefore to attempt to use the status of the free coloureds in Trinidad as an index of the condition of the slave population. In explaining the condition of the free coloureds one could call attention to the relative availability of land and the existence of a moving frontier which interposed distance between competing races; and then there was the supervisory power of the British government, which offered, however limited at first, some protection against the legislation of the local white authorities.

In the first phase of the movement in Trinidad, Dr John Baptiste Philip, the first coloured leader, wrote a book in which he called attention to the anomaly of having a slave-holding public officer as the Protector of Slaves. The élite free coloured leaders, like free coloureds generally, were owners of slaves, and the Philip family held a large number. The free coloured leaders did not call for the abolition of slavery. Dr Philip himself though was in a slightly different position from the rest of his élite supporters. As a medical practitioner his personal income was not dependent on slave labour. His book leaves the impression that he himself would not have been averse to abolition if done in an orderly manner and with compensation.

In the second phase of the movement free coloureds in Port of Spain were dominant; and many of the rank and file did not depend on slave labour. When called upon to assist the whites in defending slavery many urban free coloureds, by and large, supported the slave emancipation policy of the British government, and began to use the term 'People of African Descent' which might be seen as a sign that they understood that emancipation was on the horizon, and were willing to acknowledge publicly their blood relationship with the blacks.[55] The élite free coloured planters however who were dependent on slave labour on their estates were generally not supportive of these urban free coloureds though they did not as a group openly join with the white

slaveowners. There is thus some evidence that in Trinidad, as in Jamaica, St Kitts and Antigua, some free coloureds, at the eleventh hour, were willing to see the end of slavery. But the threatening, though belated, anti-slavery posture of Edward Jordan in Jamaica in 1832 did not have a parallel in Trinidad. The people of colour in Trinidad did not have their own newspaper.

In 1842 there was a brief exchange of letters in a newspaper which revealed that the theme of betrayal was not absent from the free coloured movement for equality. One writer, possibly a person of the same generation as the free coloured élite of the first phase of the movement, wrote appealing to the youths of the colony to acknowledge Dr John Baptiste Philip and John Welsh Hobson (one of the leaders) as heroes and patriots,[56] a monument should be erected to their honour. A reply came from another correspondent who charged that these élite leaders selfishly campaigned for their own freedom while neglecting that of the slaves.[57] In the politics of the post-emancipation period it seems that the non-holders of slave property, or those who had possessed only a few slaves, had a moral advantage over those who had owned substantial slave property. It is possibly significant that it was not until the late 19th century when a generation which had not experienced slavery had come to manhood that Dr John Baptiste Philip began to get recognition from blacks and coloureds as a fighter for freedom which implicitly was broader than that of free coloureds alone.[58]

Summary

The free coloureds of Trinidad were among the most privileged in the Caribbean, and were better off in land ownership than their counterparts in the other British West Indies, with the possible exception of Jamaica.[59] Their leaders were acutely aware of this superior position in the British West Indies. A distribution of free land between 1783 and 1812 had given them a vital headstart in land ownership, which does not have any parallel in the other British islands. Their demographic strength in the mid-1820s vis-à-vis other sections of the population was also unmatched in the British West Indies except for Grenada. In the struggle for civil equality they had the advantage, unlike their counterparts in other British islands, of being able to argue that they were seeking a restoration of lost rights rather than a bestowal of new privileges. But the struggle for civil equality was complicated by the investigation into the Cedula of 1783, and the lateness of the legal discrimination against free coloureds by the English authorities meant that the protest against it was almost contemporaneous with the imposition of the disabilities themselves. The Crown Colony form of government placed the governor, not a group of planter legislators, (as in the colonies with Assemblies) in the limelight as the enemy. This helped to personalise the struggle.

The absence of an elected Assembly encouraged the free coloureds of Trinidad to appeal directly and immediately to the British government for full civil equality. There was no hope of relief from the local authorities from which white liberals were notably absent. It was only the intervention of the British government which gave the free coloureds victory which came earlier than in any other island except St Lucia, itself a Crown Colony. But there was a sense in which the free coloureds of Trinidad had received less than their counterparts in most other British islands. Crown Colony government still remained and the subsequent political history of Trinidad in the 19th century was to show that the whites were able to use it to protect their political supremacy against the coloureds better than the whites in the colonies with elected Assemblies. Finally, it is prudent to add - since in comparative analysis the temptation is to underplay similarities - that despite important contrasts the free coloureds of Trinidad were not in a totally different position from those of other British islands. They too were an intermediate, subordinated group, the victim of racial prejudice and discrimination; neither free nor slave.

Notes

1. PP. House of Commons, 1826-1827 (428) XXII, Report of the Commissioners of Inquiry into the subject of Land Titles in Trinidad, pp. 191-194.
2. Ibid.
3. G. Carmichael: *The History of the West Indian Islands of Trinidad and Tobago 1498-1900* (Alvin Redman, 1961), pp. 374-375.
4. The most extensive treatment of the free coloureds between 1783 and 1810 can be found in Millette's excellent study of politics of that period. See J. Millette: *The Genesis of Crown Colony Government.*

Trinidad 1783-1810. (Moko Enterprises Ltd., Trinidad 1970). For other works with references to free coloureds in Trinidad, see Eric Williams (ed.) *Documents on British West Indian History* (Port of Spain, 1952); and D. Horowitz: "Colour Differentiation in American Systems of Slavery", *Journal of Interdisciplinary History*, vol. 3, Winter 1973.
5. The best treatment of the Aboriginal population under Spanish rule is that of Newson. See. L. Newson: *Aboriginal and Spanish Colonial Trinidad. A Study in Culture Contact* (Academic Press, London, 1976).
6. Carl Campbell: Credulants and Capitulants (Paria Publishing Co., Port of Spain 1992)
7. Millette: *The Genesis of Crown Colony Government,* Table X, Abstract of Population. The white population in 1782 was 126 and in 1797 it was 2,151. The figure given by Newson for 'freemen' (white plus free coloureds) in 1784 is 2,550 which is much higher than Millette's for 1782 (viz. 421). Even if Newson's higher figure is nearer to the truth, and assuming that not more than 30% were whites, the white population would not be more than 850 persons. See Newson, op. cit., p. 186.
8. Millette: *The Genesis of Crown Colony Government,* Table X. The slave population in 1782 was about 310 with an increase to 10,009 by 1797. There is also a huge discrepancy between Millette's figures for the slave population in 1782 and Newson's figure for 1784 (viz. 2,462). The problem arises from the use of different sources: the figures in the Archivo General de Indias being considerably higher than those provided by English investigators such as Capt. Mallet. Newson's figures indicate that there was a higher level of colonisation in Trinidad before the Cedula of 1783 came into effect. See Newson: *Aboriginal and Spanish Colonial Trinidad,* op. cit., p. 186.
9. There are no reliable figures for the slave trade into Puerto Rico at this time. See Francisco Serrano: *Sugar and Slavery in Puerto Rico. The Plantation Economy of Ponce 1800-1850* (University of Wisconsin Press, 1984), pp. 120-124.
10. In 1810 the population pattern was as follows: whites 2,495 (7.9%); coloureds 6,264 (20.0%); slaves 20,821 (66.6%), Indians 1,683 (5.3%). See Millette: *The Genesis of Crown Colony Government,* Table IX
11. The entire analysis of the colour scale is based on information in the Slave Registry, T 71/501 and 502. In 1813 coloured slaves (field and domestic) formed 5.9% of the total slave population.
12. About 56.4% of slaves of colour on the estates in 1813 were mulattoes, and about 56.9% of coloured domestic slaves were mulattoes. Together mulattoes and cabres made up 91 % of the coloured slave population. Higman is of the opinion that in Jamaica the Slave Registry overestimated the size of the mulatto section of the slave population, See B. Higman: *Slave Population and Economy of Jamaica 1807-1834,* (Cambridge University Press, 1976), p. 140.
13. In Spanish times the offspring of a black and an Amerindian was called a "grifo." See Newson. op.

cit., p. 311. In Jamaica the coloured slave might be called a "mongrel" when his classification was uncertain, See Higman: *Slave Population and Economy*, op. cit., p. 140.

14. In Jamaica the child of a white and "mustee" would be a mustifino, See .Edward Brathwaite, *The Development of Creole Society in Jamaica 1770-1820.* (Clarendon Press, Oxford, 1971), op. cit., p. 167. In Trinidad only 1 quadroon was recorded, a child of 3 years. The classification "copper" does not seem to describe the blending of racial types, but rather skin tone of certain persons, including some Mandingos and Ibos. The term "yellow" also refers to skin tone, See T 71/501, p. 89. Seville Estates: Alex Sommerville; Betway Morgan.

15. Arnold Sio, "Race and Colour in the Status of the Free Coloureds in the West Indies: Jamaica & Barbados." *Journal of Belizean Affairs.* There is however some confusion about the exact cut-off point, See Barry Higman, *Slave Population and Economy in Jamaica, 1807-1834.* (Cambridge University Press, 1976), op. cit.ff. 4, p. 298.

16. C.O. 295/63, Woodford to Horton, 4 Aug., 1824, Enclosure; Report of Le Goffe. These coloureds who were nearly white were called "cafe-au-lait".

17. In 1803 two white magistrates refused to allow Jose Alvarez, the Deputy Keeper of the Records (of Port of Spain) to act as Keeper on the grounds that he "might have a portion of mulatto blood in his veins", although he looked like a white man. C.O. 295/10, Fullerton to Hobert, 27 March, 1804.

18. PW., 1822 Will 47/1822, James Innis; also PW., 1827 Will 41 /1827. Jean Baptiste Geoffroy.

19. For the effrontry of a certain "dark mulatto" who dared to allow himself to be seated in the same dining room with white people (1803), see W. Fullerton: A Statement, Letters and Documents respecting the affairs of Trinidad, including a reply to Col. Picton's Address to the Council of that Island (London, 1804), p. 164.

20. A Tax of $16 was placed on free coloureds' balls apparently by Hislop, but was allegedly never collected. C.O. 295/63, Woodford to Bathurst, 3 Sept., 1824, no.571.

21. J.B. Philip, *Free Mulatto.* (London, 1824), op. cit., pp. 112-115

22. C.O. 318/76, Humble Petition and Memorial of the coloured inhabitants of Dominica.

23. Millette: The Genesis of Crown Colony Government, op. cit., Table III. This shows inter-alia that the number of coloureds in 1803 who were of English, Spanish or French extraction were: English, 282 (18.8% of coloureds); Spanish, 290 (19.4% of coloureds); French, 922 (61.6% of coloureds).

24. In 1819 there was a report of maroon camps in the forest behind the Naparimas, see J. Philip: *Free Mulatto*, op. cit., p. 149. The absence of studies on slavery in Trinidad makes it difficult to assess the security problem of the planters. Horowitz has faced the same problem, see Horowitz: "Colour Differentiation in American Slavery", op. cit, p. 520. note 48.

25. For the provisions of the Codes, see E. Williams: *History of the People of Trinidad and Tobago* (Andre Deutsch, 1964), pp. 45-46; Carmichael: *The History of the West Indian Islands*, op. cit., pp. 379-383.

26. C.O. 318/76, pp. 333-346, Answer of Henry Fuller.

27. J. Sanderson: An Appeal to the Imperial Parliament of the United Kingdom of Great Britain and Ireland (London, 1812), pp. 135-186.

28. J. Philip: *Free Mulatto*, op. cit., pp. 101-102.

29. Calculated from T 71/501, 502, and numerous supporting documents.

30. Compiled from C.O. 295/28, p. 9. A General Return of Population, 1811; Also from C.O. 295/62, p. 263. Return of Population, 1824, The towns counted were Port of Spain and St. Joseph. San Fernando, destroyed by fire in 1818 and described in 1824 as a "wretched borough" was not entered separately as a town in the above censuses. The inclusion of San Fernando would not have greatly altered the balance of residential location. Newson noted that in 1797 the free coloured population was evenly distributed over the island. See Newson: op. cit., pp. 188-190.

31. K.O. Laurence: "The Settlement of Free Negroes in Trinidad before Emancipation", *Caribbean Quarterly* vol. XIX, no. 1 and 2,1963, pp. 26-52.

32. For a discussion of the Puerto Rican situation. See S. Mintz: "The Role of Forced Labour in Nineteenth Century Puerto Rico", *Caribbean Historical Review* no. 2, Dec., 1951, pp. 134-141.

33. B. Brereton: *A History of Modern Trinidad 1783-1962,* (Heinemann, Port of Spain, 1982), pp. 27-31.

34. For the socio-political configuration of Grenada 1763 1795, see Edward Cox, *The Shadow of Freedom: Freedmen in the Slave Societies of Grenada & St Kitts 1763-1838.* (PhD Thesis, The Johns Hopkins University, 1977), op. cit., chaps., iv,v.

35. C.O. 295/9, Kingston to Sullivan 17 Jan, 1804.

36. C.O. 295/61, pp. 173-189, Memorial of Philip and Congnet, 19 Nov., 1823.

37. For the free coloureds' attitude to Crown Colony government before emancipation, see C. Campbell: The Opposition to Crown Colony Government in Trinidad before and after Emancipation 1813-1846, in B. Higman (ed.): T*rade, Government and Society in Caribbean History.* Essays presented to Douglas Hall (Heinemann Educational Books, Caribbean Ltd., 1983), pp. 53-68.

38. C.O. 295/27, p. 227, Petition of 27 free coloureds; also p. 224, Petition of 23 free coloureds.

39. Millette: The Genesis of Crown Colony Government, op. cit., pp. 234-235. An investigation of white colonists' attitude to free blacks also led Brereton to notice the absence of white liberals, see B. Brereton: Changing Racial Attitudes in Trinidad. Slavery and after, in Some Papers on Social, Political and Economic Adjustment to the Ending of Slavery in the Caribbean (A.C.H., Jamaica, 1975), pp. 1-24.

40. C.O. 318/76, pp. 347-362, Reply of John Lewis.

41. C.O. 295/4, pp. 273-275, Letter of E. Noel to Commissioners, 21 Feb., 1803; also Millette: The Genesis of Crown Colony Government, op. cit., pp. 143-144.

42. A "guestimate" by W. Green of the percentage of free blacks in free coloured populations of the British islands was "at least" 15.0% (with the exception of Barbados), See. W. Green: *British Slave Emancipation* (Clarendon Press, 1976), p. 13.

43. An outstanding black was Jonas Mohammed Bath, a free Mandingo priest. See C. Campbell: "Jonas Mohammed Bath and the Free Mandingos in Trinidad. The Question of their repatriation to Africa 1831-1838" *Journal of African Studies* vol. 2 no. 4,1975/76, pp. 467 495. On the question of economic assets of some free blacks, see C. Campbell: "Black Testators. Fragments of the lives of free Africans and free creole blacks in Trinidad 1813-1877".

44. C. Campbell: "Jonas Mohammed Bath", op. cit.; also C. Campbell: "Mohammed Sesei of Gambia and Trinidad c. 1788-1833", *African Studies Association of the West Indies*, Bulletin no. 7, Dec., 1974, pp. 29-38.

45. C.O. 295/62, Woodford to Bathurst, 31 July 1824, no. 562.

46. C.O. 295/63, Woodford to Bathurst, 3 Sept., 1824, no. 571.

47. C.O. 295/83, p. 88, Colonial Office notes. Stephen to Hay (undated).

48. Recent Quantitative studies of the slave population include G. Friedman: "The Heights of Slaves in Trinidad", *Social Science History* vol. 6.1982, no. 4, pp. 482-515; B. Higman: "Growth in Afro-Caribbean Slave Population", *American Journal of Physical Anthropology* vol. 50., March 1979, pp. 373-385. A considerable amount of new information about the slave population of Trinidad has appeared since 1983. See for example Ann John: 'The Slave Population of 19th Century Trinidad' (unpublished Ph.D. thesis, Princeton University 1983); and B. Higman: *Slave Populations of the British Caribbean 1807-1834* (Johns Hopkins Press, 1985). A specific study of slavery in Trinidad remains to be written.

49. Brereton: *Changing Racial Attitudes*, op. cit., pp. 2-11.

50. Eric Williams: *History of the People of Trinidad and Tobago* (Andre Deutsch, London, 1964), p. 84.

51. E. Genovese: 'The Treatment of Slaves in Different Countries. Problems in the application of the Comparative Method', in L. Foner and E. Genovese (eds): *Slavery in the New World*, op. cit., pp. 202-210.

52. In 1813 the African born slaves were 56.1% of the field slaves, See Carl Campbell, *The Rise of a Free Coloured Plantocracy in Trinidad 1783-1813.* Boletin de Estudios Latinoamericanos y del Caribe. No. 29, Dec., (1980), pp. 33-54., Table IV. Also M. Craton: *Sinews of Empire. A Short History of British Slavery* (Anchor Books 1974), Campbell: "The Rise of a Free Coloured Plantocracy", op. cit,p. 268, note 50. Also Barry Higman, " Growth in Afro-Caribbean Slave Populations." *American Journal of Physical Anthropology 50.* (1979).Gerald Friedman, The heights of slaves in Trinidad, *Social Science History.* Vol. 6. (1982), No. 4, pp. 482-515. Higman: *Slave Populations of the British Caribbean* op. cit., pp. 280-292.

53. The non-professional historians of Trinidad have tended to follow the interpretation that slavery was mild, while the professionals have been more skeptical. See J. Millete: The Genesis of Crown Colony Government, op. cit., pp. 63-65; B. Brereton: *A History of Modern Trinidad 1783-1962* (Heinemann, 1981), pp. 25- 27.

54. For arguments about the absence of any necessary connection between the nature of slavery and the nature of race relations outside it, see H. Hoetink: *Slavery and Race Relations in the Americas. Comparative Notes on their Nature and Nexus* (Harper & Row, New York, 1973), Chap. 1.

55. C.O. 295/92 Grant to Woodford, 26 March, 1832 no. 24, Enclosure, A Petition.

56. Standard 8 Oct., 1842, Letter from "Dominican".

57. Standard 24 Oct., 1842, Letter from "Franciscan".

58. New Era, 18 Nov., 1872, Report of a Torch Light Procession to the Grave of Dr. Philip.

59. One does not get the impression that the value of the property of the élite free coloured planters in Trinidad was as great as the top 40 free coloureds of Jamaica. The spread of land ownership among the comparatively smaller free coloured population of Trinidad might have been in favour of Trinidad. See William Green, *British Slave Emancipation. The Sugar Colonies and the Great Experiment 1830-1865.* (Clarendon Press, 1976), op. cit., Table 2, p. 15.

44

Livestock Farmers and Marginality in Jamaica's Sugar-Plantation Society: A Tentative Analysis*

VERENE A. SHEPHERD

The sugar plantation as a socio-economic institution dominated Jamaican history from the beginning of the 18th century. Both contemporary and modern writers stress the superordinate position occupied within this plantation structure by the sugar plantocracy – that class which owned and controlled most of the means and markets of production, and dominated the social and political life of the island.[1] The resultant socio-economic order, defined by George Beckford as the plantation system, constituted the empirical basis for the formulation of the classic 'plantation economy model'. [Beckford, 2] Among the stated characteristics of plantation societies are the limited possibilities for internal capital accumulation, the absence of a significant home market, monoculture, the importation of inputs, usually from the 'mother country', and the exportation of all outputs. [Ibid.][2]. But some colonial economies conformed more rigidly than others to this model. Studies have shown that in contrast to Eastern Caribbean islands like Barbados and St. Kitts, Jamaica's more varied physical environment resulted in significant entrepreneurial and economic diversification and the evolution of an important group of non-sugar producers. [Higman, 15 and 14, Shepherd 25]. While some of these, notably the 'minor staple' cultivators like the coffee farmers, catered primarily to the export market, others geared their activities essentially to the domestic market. Among those producing primarily for the local market were the penkeepers or livestock farmers who participated only minimally in the direct export trade, accumulating their capital locally. They dominated the internal trade in livestock and by catering primarily to the sugar estate market determined that plantations did not conform to the traditional 'enclave theory'. [Dupuy, 8, pp. 169-226].

However, despite their importance to the domestic economy, Jamaican livestock farmers were never successful in challenging the institutional arrangement of the sugar plantation society. They, like other non-staple producers, were relegated to secondary roles and remained ancillary to the sugar sector. The dominant sugar sector, indeed, exploited those dependent on it, thereby reinforcing its superordinate position and the marginality of other sectors.

It should be pointed out from the outset that the article is essentially exploratory. It examines the marginality construct, considers its applicability to the penkeepers, and gives an overview of the evolution and demographic composition of the penkeepers. The paper is also concerned with the interrelationships between the sugar and the penkeeping sectors and will use the example of the interaction between these economic sectors to examine the notion of the dominance of the sugar plantocracy and the subordinate position of other producers.

The Marginality Construct

Marginality and the marginalization process have been operative throughout Caribbean history and have been recognized and acknowledged in several works. Influenced, perhaps, by the functionalist or integrationist model of society, these studies present marginalization as the antithesis of integration. The overwhelming majority of historical works on marginality deals with slaves and freed people of colour. Very few deal with the poor whites[3]. More modern works focus on the gender issue, specifically the legacies of partriarchal domination [Miller, 20] or on the rural and urban poor. [Perlman, 22; Giddens and Held, 10; Price, 23]. Thus a review of the many schools of thought leading into the marginality construct, reveals a common focus either on the underclass who remain unintegrated into the mainstream economy or on those disadvantaged because of race, legal status, or gender. Furthermore, in most cases, the marginals studied in the Caribbean context are non-white, or whites socio-economically closer to the lowest echelons of society. The Barbadian 'redlegs' for example, hardly voted prior to 1840 because of the property qualifications attached to the franchise and the fact that few of them owned over 10 acres of land. [Sheppard, 28, pp. 5-6]. In addition, existing studies tend to deal with homogeneous groups in terms of gender, race, colour or class.

This article, by focusing on the interaction and interrelationships between economic sectors, attempts to broaden the debate on marginality as it is applied to colonial plantation societies. Admittedly, it departs from the traditional and classic interpretations of marginality because it suggests that members of the lower strata of white society who engaged in penkeeping were marginalized partly because of the economic activity in which they were engaged. A further problematic aspect of the article is that it also includes in the discussion traditionally marginalized people – the freed people of colour and women. These were already marginalized because of race, colour and gender – factors which had nothing to do with their occupation. But it would seem that if those who were agriculturalists depended solely on penkeeping for the means of upward social mobility (and not, for example, on export commodities like sugar and coffee) within their group and within a planter-dominated society, then their prospects were not very great.

The other analytical problem, of course, is that because of the great heterogeneity existing among the penkeepers, it is arguable whether they can be accorded a 'group' status in the strict sociological sense of the word. However, it seems clear from the contempo-

rary records that the larger society regarded the penkeepers as a type of group. Planters and urban consumers often blamed 'the penkeepers' for the high price of beef and 'the penkeepers' often called their members to meetings to discuss matters affecting their industry. There is no evidence to indicate that at such meetings race, colour or gender barriers prevented united action in the interest of 'the penkeepers'.

Despite these obvious problematic issues an attempt will still be made to highlight, from the available empirical data, certain characteristics of the penkeepers which could be deemed marginal. Chief among these were their occupation of marginal lands, their economic dependence on the dominant sugar sector, internal disorganization, external isolation, exclusion from the mainstream political process and their resorting to unconventional politics such as petitions. Livestock farmers were also ascribed a social position inferior to the sugar planters, particularly if they were free coloureds. Above all, as they lacked political power, they were unable to influence legislation favourable to the livestock industry and were often passed over in favour of foreign suppliers.

The Livestock Farmers: Definitions, Historical Development and Demographic Composition

Many people kept livestock in Jamaica in the 18th and 19th centuries – slaves, free people of colour, free blacks, the large sugar planters, coffee farmers and other small-scale white entrepreneurs. The article is, however, primarily concerned with those specialized livestock farmers commonly styled 'penkeepers' in the contemporary literature. [M'Mahon, 19, p. 172]. They are to be distinguished from the slave 'penkeepers' in charge of animals on sugar estates and other units and from the overseers of livestock farms, who were also frequently styled 'penkeepers'. Large sugar planters, resident or absentee, who established satellite pens must also be excluded from this analysis.

The livestock industry pre-dated the establishment of sugar as the dominant crop and the rise of the plantation system. The earliest livestock farmers were, in fact, the Spaniards whose *hatos* dotted the southern savannah lands of early

17th century-Jamaica. At that time, the industry was more export-oriented, supplying dried, cured meat to passing ships and to Cuba, and lard, hides, and tallow to the metropolitan Spanish market. With the English invasion, subsequent settlement and the rise of the sugar economy, livestock farmers increasingly catered to the estates' demand for animals for draught purposes and millwork. Edward Long, for example, stressed the positive correlation between the expansion of the livestock industry and the extension of the sugar culture. [Long, 18, fol. 308]. By 1782, there were an estimated 300 livestock farms in the island. [Gardner, 9, p. 161].

The earliest penkeepers in English Jamaica were among the soldier- settlers of the Cromwellian expeditionary force. At first they established pens on the south coast, but with the competition for land resulting from the development and expansion of the more lucrative sugar industry, some were pushed onto marginal interior lands. In this regard, they were among the pioneers of the frontier society and were early numbered among the settlers in the Pedro's Cockpit area of St. Ann. The social position of the livestock farmers was early distinguished from the sugar planter class. In his seminal work on the development of creole society in Jamaica, Kamau Brathwaite outlined the main social divisions within the society and differentiated between the several categories of settlers. [Brathwaite, 6, pp. 105-150]. White penkeepers along with 'minor staple' producers were grouped among those he categorized as 'other whites' and 'small settlers', not numbered among the 'upperclass whites'. [Ibid., pp. 135-148].

Jamaica's varied topography and physical environment then, clearly provided possibilities for small-scale entrepreneurs and together with the ready market for livestock on the sugar estates, contributed to the growth of the small-settler population. By 1820, penkeepers also included attorneys and overseers in charge of estates. Attorneys and overseers, according to M'Mahon's somewhat exaggerated description, made their 'fortunes' while in charge of properties belonging to their absentee proprietors. They invested these 'fortunes' in pens, which provided not only a ready source of animals for the estates they managed but also markets for the estates' old animals which were fattened and sold to the butchers. [M'Mahon, 19 pp. 171- 173]

In addition to whites from the lower strata of the segmented white group, the penkeepers also comprised free coloureds already marginalized because of their colour and legal disabilities. Before the enactment of a law in 1761 curtailing the value of inheritance, free coloureds had managed to acquire substantial property[4]. Some inherited pens. Benjamin Scott-Moncrieffe, for example, inherited Soho Pen from his father and later also acquired Thatch Hill Pen in St. Ann. [Shepherd, 25, p. 182]. Livestock farmers also included women, though Brathwaite was essentially correct in his impression that it was a male-dominated occupation. [Brathwaite 6, pp. 146-147]. Female penkeepers comprised whites, free coloureds, and freed blacks. White female farmers seemed to have been essentially widows and were less numerous among the penkeepers than freed women. [Boa, 5, pp. 64-69]. Catherine Buckeridge from Sonning, County Berks in England, for example, was a widow and owner of a rather substantial pen – Salt Pond Hut -in St. Catherine. [Shepherd, 25, p. 183].

Free coloured and freed black women were more numerous among the female penkeepers and only a few were numbered among the sugar planting class. Anna Woodart was, arguably, the wealthiest free coloured woman in 1762, owning Dirty Pit and Hoghole pens; in St. Catherine. Freed women were also noted among the penkeepers in Westmoreland, St. Elizabeth, St. Thomas-in-the East, and St. David The pens owned by freed women were among the smallest and were also confined to marginal lands. [Boa, 5. p. 66]. For these freed women, marginality was derived from race, colour and gender. Penkeeping offered a chance for upward social mobility within the free coloured society but certain obstacles unique to this industry frustrated their efforts.

Other distinguishing characteristics of penkeepers were that they were primarily creole born and resident.

Economic Dependence

An examination of the economic relations between penkeepers and the dominant sugar sector, reveals a heavy dependence on the sugar industry. In this regard, it must be stressed that sugar estates provided the largest outlet for the products of the pens. A small sample of 11 per cent of the pens returned in the Accounts Produce for

1820 revealed that these units earned more from the sale of working animals to the estates than from other income-generating activities such as jobbing, wainage, pasturage and the sale of food and miscellaneous items. While livestock sales represented 69 per cent of total earnings, other resources combined accounted for 31 per cent. Taken as single categories, jobbing represented 9 per cent, pasturage 4 per cent, wainage 4 per cent, provisions 9 per cent and miscellaneous items 5 per cent. On individual pens, however, livestock sales often accounted for as high as 98 per cent.[5]

The size of the sugar estate market for livestock was considerable. Large estates like Golden Grove in St. Thomas-in-the-East needed an estimated 100 'steers' (oxen) annually in addition to mules and spayed heifers.[6] Indeed, between the late 18th century and the early 19th century, the estimated annual total island demand for working animals was put at somewhere between 56,000 and 71,000[7]. At £18 (currency) each in the late 18th century and between £20 and £30 in the early 19th century, estates would need to spend a considerable sum on oxen alone.[8]

Theoretically then, Jamaica's sugar economy afforded a relatively substantial market capable of acting as a dynamic factor in the development of the pen sector. In reality, this dynamism was not directed towards the local livestock industry. In the first place, Jamaican sugar planters continued to import working animals, primarily from Spanish America, even after the local penkeeping industry had been well-established. Sugar planters also established their own pens or rented existing ones in an attempt to exclude the middleman supplier. The In-givings of 1815 reveal that 84 sugar planters owned 96 satellite pens serving 122 estates.[9] As their sugar states could not always use all the animals reared on such related units, planter-penkeepers competed on the local market with the specialized penkeepers. Even the section of the sugar market to which livestock farmers had access was not always stable.

During and after the period of slavery, fluctuations in the demand for livestock on the sugar estates resulting from depression in the sugar market, often resulted in bankruptcy for some penkeepers. Between 1810 and 1817, for example, George Forbes of Thatchfield Pen in St. Elizabeth was confident of making profits of between £2,000 and £2,500 from his property.[10]

The decline in profitability of some estates in the mid-19th century which resulted in a decrease in the demand for livestock on the estates soon wiped out his savings.[11] In the immediate post-slavery period too, the depressed state of the sugar sector affected by labour and capital shortage, caused an oversupply of animals on the market and a drop in their prices. Livestock farmers then complained of the 'death of pen-keeping'.[12] Competition from foreign suppliers and the precariousness of depending solely on the sugar estates caused penkeepers to diversify their activities and restrict their output of animals. This further contributed to the reinforcement of their marginal and dependent position.

Social and Political Marginality

In her analysis of white society in the British Leeward Islands in the 18th century, Elsa Goveia suggested that despite existing stratification among whites an unconscious sense of solidarity existed and that, further, they were all because of their colour, members of the elite. [Goveia, 11 pp. 314-315]. In referring to this statement in his analysis of white society in Jamaica, Brathwaite stressed that in the island, phenotype affinity did not seem to have been a sufficient guarantee of elite status. This is supported by aspects of the history of the livestock farmers because white penkeepers, particularly those who were overseers and managers, were clearly socially differentiated from the top echelons of white society, and typically represented a contradictory location within the classs configuration of 18th and 19th century Jamaican slave society. Neither Brathwaite's nor M. G. Smith's account of white society listed such whites among the elite or 'principal' whites. According to Smith, 'principal whites' formed a closed social class from which 'secondary' whites, coloureds and blacks were vigorously excluded – with the possible exception of mistresses. [Brathwaite, 6, pp. 105-150; Smith, 31 pp. 55-59]. The bases of social marginality for lower class whites were linked to economic factors and social class differences. From the early 18th century, pens were considered to be less prestigious properties and their differential rate of remuneration made them unable to attract white workers. J.B. Moreton emphasized that 'grass pens were considered as despicable objects for enterprising individuals to hunt after, nor would any man accept the management of one who had hopes of preferment on sugar plantations'. [Moreton, 21 p. 58]. He stressed that managers and overseers of sugar estates, would not even associate with people in similar occupations on the pens. Furthermore, because pens were considered to be simply 'moderate sized farms' their owners were more likely to be residents and less likely to join the elite group of absentees. Resident proprietors – and particularly Creoles – were viewed as socially inferior. [Bigelow, 4, 104; Shepherd, 25, pp. 100, 180]. Relationships of superordination and subordination were also clearly discernible between 'principal' and 'secondary' whites according to Smith's categorization. [Smith, 31, pp. 55- 59]. This was because a significant number of Jamaican penkeepers comprised attorneys and overseers. Dominant – subordinate relations were thus partly the result of the delegation of authority in the administration of estates.

The free coloured penkeepers; were already regarded as socially inferior by white society. Even those like Robert Anguin and Benjamin Scott-Moncrieffe whose economic position ranked them at the top of the free coloured social ladder were socially marginal to white elite society along with other members of the 'unappropriated people'.[13]

Despite the fact that social differences separated sugar planters and penkeepers, the necessity for the forging of economic links between economic sectors in the island, determined that a certain level of interaction occurred. [Shepherd, 25, pp. 135-150].[14]

Sugar planters or their representatives at times visited pens to select the stock for their estates. Penkeepers similarly visited the sugar plantations to seek business and to see about the welfare of their jobbers. The crucial question is: did such interaction extend beyond that dictated by economic necessity? There is no definitive answer. Caribbean social history highlights the social divisions between broad social groups but sheds very little light on the more complex subject of intra- and inter-class interaction within racial and colour groupings. Nevertheless, it can be safely assumed that interaction dictated by economic necessity did not necessarily imply egalitarianism.

Jamaican society of the 18th and 19th centuries was politically dominated by the sugar plantocracy. In this society, many groups were politically marginalized. Race, colour, or gender factors had already marginalized women and free coloureds of all categories (except for those free coloureds who had successfully applied for privileges). But even among the whites – traditionally viewed as the ruling class in plantation societies – there was differential access to political power. 'Secondary whites', among whom rural penkeepers were numerous, were clearly politically subordinate to the 'principal whites'. Thus, white penkeepers were among those who existed on the margins of the political process. Admittedly, most possessed the franchise. In 1757, for example, white penkeepers formed a significant proportion of agriculturalists in St. Catherine applying for the franchise. [Shepherd, 25, p. 216]. But, in general, specialized penkeepers never occupied high political positions. Up to 1845, none was noted in the Assembly or Legislative Council. Even where – such as in prominent penkeeping parishes – penkeepers managed to occupy public positions, these were usually low-status parochial positions (such as waywardens and jurors). [Ibid., pp. 218-220]. To gain access to positions of political power meant that rural penkeepers had to diversify into export-oriented economic activities – particularly the sugar industry. Only those penkeepers who joined the sugar planter class eventually gained seats in the Assembly. A notable example was Hamilton Brown.

Responses to Marginality

The majority of Jamaican penkeepers could do very little about their dependent economic position. Until the late 19th century, they lacked a viable alternative market for their outputs, were restricted in the scale of their operations as sugar planters engrossed most of the suitable pasturelands, and could not compete effectively with foreign suppliers of livestock. For the majority of penkeepers, therefore, economic constraints affected the extent to which they could improve their socio-political position. This situation, in fact, caused some to sell out and emigrate. Others were frustrated in their attempts to achieve an economic position which would enable them to join the ranks of the absentee class; for, as J. Bigelow pointed out, very often residency was forced by low economic status. He noted that nothing less than the profits of a very large estate could compensate ... for the trouble and expenses of keeping up a force of attornies [sic] agents and book-keepers, and for the absence of that personal devotion to its management which none but a proprietor ever feels. [Bigelow, 4, p. 104].

Thus, the St. Elizabeth penkeeper, George Forbes, had informed his brother that he would return to live in the United Kingdom as soon as his financial circumstances allowed him to do so.[15]

Others invested in alternative economic activities such as sugar, coffee, pimento, and logwood, often in combination with penkeeping, or sought jobs as overseers on sugar estates.[16]

Free coloured penkeepers, notably Anguin and Scott-Moncrieffe, were among those freed people who successfully petitioned the Assembly for privileges in order to improve their social position. But these strategies were largely individualistic. Internal diversities, and disorganization, notably the absence of group cohesion and consciousness, and the acceptance of the dominant social ideology by lower-class white and free coloured penkeepers, meant that responses to marginality were not all designed to achieve the upliftment of the penkeepers as a 'group'.

Collective group action was not totally absent, however. Despite the existence of internal divisions, when their economic welfare was threatened, penkeepers collectively agitated for favourable legislation in their economic interests. The primary form of political action was petitioning the Assembly. This action was taken by white and free coloured male penkeepers and white female penkeepers. It would seem that free coloured women were directly affected by the sexist attitudes prevalent during this period. Boa records that as it was considered 'unseemly' for women to be involved in political activities, free coloured women were excluded by their male counterparts from the civil rights movement. Free coloured men did not even seek free coloured women's signatures on petitions. [Boa, 5, p. 202]. By contrast, petitions at times originated with white female penkeepers. For example, in 1843, Catherine Buckeridge spearheaded the protest over the planned diversion of the Rio Cobre to facilitate the laying of railway lines. The construction of the railway from Spanish Town to Kingston would have encroached on the lands of some of the St. Catherine penkeepers including Mrs. Buckeridge. She petitioned the Assembly to reconsider its plans as the diversion

of the river would create hardships for penkeepers who relied on it as 'in its present course [the river] had afforded a constant supply of water to the grass pieces of petitioner's pen and had thereby fertilized them, and given the occupier the means of conveying grass to market'.[17] Her petition was unsuccessful. Most of the other petitions related to the import trade in livestock from Spanish America, the low level of import duties imposed and general matters of taxation.

The planters' continued support for imported animals caused the penkeepers to restrict production to a low level to avoid having a surplus that they could not dispose of, and the consequent price fall. As early as 1790 the penkeepers in the St. Ann Vestry petitioned the governor about the 'distressing Prospect arising [in] the Community in general . . . and this Parish in Particular of the trade carried on between the Spaniards of Cuba and a few of the trading or commercial Persons of this country . . . '.[18] They stressed that the trade posed an obstacle to the further expansion of the industry 'which is being partly discontinued by the introduction of Spanish horses, mules, mares and meat cattle, subject to no Impost or Duty whatsoever, and at a time when we are paying Taxes towards the support of Government from the time of sale . . .'[19] The penkeepers of Manchester and St. Elizabeth echoed these sentiments in the early 19th century. In 1816 they implored the House of Assembly to impose a tax on imported 'stock'. The St. Elizabeth graziers complained that 'from the late large importation of horned or meat cattle, mules and horses, the stock of the native breeder and grazier has become unsaleable.'[20] The petitioners of Manchester complained similarly that

the petitioner are sorely aggrieved by the constant importations into this island of horses, mules, asses and meat cattle from the Spanish Main and other ports, to the great loss and injury of the petitioners; and that such importations enable the importers very considerably to undersell the breeders of the island.[21]

In their defense, the sugar planters maintained that the trade with Spanish America was vital as animals from that source sold at cheaper rates and this served to regulate better the price of beef and planters' stock. Long, however, accused them of being prejudiced in favour of foreign articles 'despising their own though far superior in value'.[22] In addition to differences in cost, however, planters maintained that the form of payment demanded by the local penkeepers was at variance with the customary method employed by the importers of foreign cattle. That is, while local producers wanted immediate cash payment, importers supplied animals on a one-year credit at interest of 6 per cent. Although by the mid-nineteenth century some penkeepers had adopted the credit system, this did not significantly reduce the level of importations; for though the few penkeepers in the Assembly were able to press for the importation of a tax on animals imported, this was too low to stem importation. Hamilton Brown, for example, had proposed a tax of 80s. but instead the low level of 20s. (£1) per head of livestock was implemented in 1817.[23] Though changes occurred afterwards, the duty never exceeded £2 per head of livestock in the period of slavery.

In the post-slavery period, livestock farmers collectively protested the Assembly's attempt to tax them unfairly. Where the parish vestry was planter-dominated, the fight for fair taxation was even more protracted. In 1840, for example, the penkeepers of St. Mary consistently petitioned the Assembly to get the Vestry to remove the five shillings tax imposed on all breeding stock. The Vestry had levied this charge with the explanation that it was to offset the cost of road repair incurred in the parish in the previous year. The penkeepers objected on the grounds that in the past, when money was raised for this purpose, little of it was actually correctly applied. Rather, it was 'appropriated towards the disbursement of the general accumulated debts of the parish'.[24] They accused the Vestry of using this devious means of achieving its real purpose which was 'to evade a recent law prohibiting Vestries from assessing any tax on stock for parochial purposes, to an amount exceeding treble the amount per head, levied as a public tax on stock'.[25] The penkeepers claimed that 'the nominal road tax . . . is most unequal and oppressive in its operation and amount, falling on a description of property which makes no use of the roads for the repairs of which it is alleged to be imposed'.[26] They claimed that estates had been assessed only one-third of the sum levied on pens.

In 1843, other penkeepers from various pen parishes added their voices to those of the St. Mary protestors. They claimed that the 'petitioners are heavier taxed than any other proprietors in the island'.[27] Without adequate representation in the Assembly, however, the penkeepers could not hope to win favourable legislation to protect their industry.

In conclusion, the history of livestock farmers in Jamaica from the 18th to the mid-nineteenth century reveals certain aspects of socio-economic and political marginalization. While it is undeniable that for some penkeepers marginalization derived from race, colour, gender and class considerations, the nature of their primary economic activity seemed to have been a crucial **contributory** factor. Non-staple producers were relegated to secondary roles and social positions in a plantation society dominated by the sugar sector. A retrospective examination of the ideas presented in this paper reveals certain other essential conclusions. First, the Jamaican plantation society, though characterized in a generalized sense by a dichotomy of classes – the white exploiting class and an exploited non-white class – showed significant intra-class diversities. In the case of the whites, internal socio-economic and political differentiation and antagonistic class relationships derived from competitive economic activity, lend support to the notion that Caribbean plantation societies were not characterized by a homogeneous white race, forming the ruling class. Second, political power was not exclusively held by the sugar planters as a few non-sugar producers managed to gain access to the Assembly – the traditional bastion of 'sugar power'. Admittedly, the success of a few individuals did not significantly change the position of the marginal groups. Finally, the effectiveness of the penkeepers' attempts to change this position of marginality was diminished by external factors relating to the state of the sugar market, economic dependence on the sugar sector, their own internal disorganization and the absence of a true coalition which cut across colour, race, class and gender lines, and their acceptance of the dominant ideology. In the case of the free coloured penkeepers, responses to marginalization represented individualistic and pragmatic strategies for upward social mobility in a society where social position was determined not only by class considerations but also by colour and race. They used their education and wealth accumulated from the livestock industry to seek acceptance within white elite society, not to challenge the dominant ideology.

Notes

*This article was first presented as a paper to the 22nd Conference of Caribbean Historians, Trinidad, 1990. I should like to express my thanks to all those who participated in the discussion of the paper.

1. See the works of E. Long [18], J.B. Moreton [21], M.G.Smith [31], E.K. Brathwaite [6], R. Sheridan [29], and B.W. Higman [14].
2. See also L. Best [3, pp. 283-326], F.L. Pryor [24, pp. 288-317] and A. Dupuy [8, p. 239].
3. See, for example, S. Boa [5], A. Sio. [30, pp. 166-182]. R.B. Allen [1, pp. 26-150]. In Allen's article, comparisons are made with the Caribbean and he suggests that perhaps free coloured marginality had to do with factors other than local, internal circumstances. For a discussion of the poor whites see J. Sheppard [28].
4. See G. Heuman [13].
5. Jamaica Archives, Accounts Produce, IB/1 1/4154-56
6. Simon Taylor to Chaloner Arcedeckne, 29 October 1792, Vanneck MSS, Jamaican Estate Papers [hereafter J.E.P.] box 2, bundle 10
7. Calculated on the basis of the number of estates each year and their .estimated demand for workng animals.
8. Accounts Produce, I B/ 11/4/3, 4, 9, 54.
9. Jamaica Almanack, 1815, pp. 221-83. Satellite pens represented about one-third of the total number of pens.
10. George Forbes to Peter Forbes, 12 Jany. 1811 and 11 June 1817, Jamaica Archives, Private Deposit (Gunnis Papers), 4/110/17, 30, 40-46.
11. Ibid.
12. For further information on the experiences of livestock farmers during the Apprenticeship and post Apprenticeship periods-, see Shepherd [26] and Shepherd [27].
13. See Heuman [13], D. Cohen and J. Green [7], J. Handier [12] and Boa [5].
14 See also Higman [16] and Higman [17].
15. George Forbes to Peter Forbes, 12 Jany. 1811.
16. The Crop Accounts and the Returns of the Registration of Slaves were usually made up by the overseers. Many of these overseers were pen owners.
17. Jamaica House of Assembly Votes (J.H.A.V.) 1843, pp. 113-114.
18. Jamaica Archives, St. Ann Vestry Minutes, 2/911
19. Ibid.
20. Petition of the Stockbreeders and Graziers of St. Elizabeth', 27 Nov. 1816, J.H.A.V., 1816 p. 114.
21. H.A. V., 1816, p. 115.
22. Add. Ms 12,404, fol. 329.
23. Blue Book of Jamaica (B.B.J.), 1832, C.O. 142/45
24. Petition of Certain Proprietors of St. Mary', J.A.H.V., 1840.
25. Ibid.
26 Ibid.
27. J.H.A.V., 16 Nov. 1843.

References

Allen, R. B., 'Economic Marginality and the Rise of the Free Population of Colour in Mauritius, 1767-1830', Slavery and Abolition, 10, 2 (1981), 126-150.

Beckford, G., Persistent Poverty: Underdevelopment in Plantation Economies of the Third World (New York, 1972).

Best, L., 'Outlines of the Model of a Pure Plantation Economy', Social and Economic Studies, 17 (1968).

Bigelow, J., Jamaica in 1850 (London, 1851).

Boa, S., 'Free Black and Coloured Women in a White Man's Slave Society', M. Phil thesis, UWI, Mona, 1985.

Brathwaite, E. K., The Development of Creole Society in Jamaica 1770-1820 (Oxford, 1971).

Cohen, D. & Green, J. eds., Neither Slave nor Free (Baltimore, 1972).

Dupuy, A., 'Slavery and Underdevelopment in the Caribbean: A Critique of the Plantation Economy "Perspective"', Dialectical Anthropology, 7 (1983).

Gardner, W. J., History of Jamaica (London, 1909 end).

Giddens, A. & Held, D., eds., Class, Power and Conflict: Classical and Contemporary Debates (Berkeley, 1972)

Goveia, E., Slave Society in the British Leeward Islands at the end of the 18th Century (New Haven, 1965).

Handler, J., The Unappropriated People (Baltimore, 1973).

Heuman, G., Between Black and White: Race, Politics and the Free Coloureds in Jamaica, 1792-1865 (Connecticut, 1981).

Higman, B. W., Slave Populations and Economy in Jamaica, 1807-1834 (Cambridge, 1976)

_____, Slave Populations of the British Caribbean, 1807-1834 (Baltimore, 1984)

_____, 'Slave Population and Economy in Jamaica at the time of Emancipation', Ph.D. Diss., UWI, Mona, 1970.

_____, 'The Internal economy of the Jamaican Pens, 1760-1890', Social and Economic Studies, 1 (1989), 61-86

Long, E., History of Jamaica (Add. Ms 12, 4-4-6, British Library), 3. Vols., (London, 1774)

M'Mahon, B., Jamaican Plantership, (London, 1935)

Miller, E., ' Marginalization of the Black Male: Insights from the Development of the Teaching Profession', Inaugural Aubrey Phillips Memorial Lecture, UWI, Mona, 30 April 1986 (Institute of Social and Economic Research, 1986).

Moreton, J. B., Manners and Customs of our West India Islands (London, 1790).

Perlman, J. E., The Myth of Marginality: Urban Poverty and Politics in Rio de Janeiro (Los Angeles, 1976).

Price, N., Behind the Planter's Back: Lower Class responses to Marginality in Bequia Island, St. Vincent (London, 1988)

Pryor, F. L., 'The Plantation Economy as an Economic System, Journal of Comparative Economics, 6 (1982)

Shepherd, V. A., 'Pens and Penkeepers in a Plantation Society: Aspects of Jamaican Social and Economic History, 1740-1845', Ph.D. Diss., University of Cambridge, 1988 .

_____. 'The Apprenticeship Experience of Jamaican Livestock Pens', Jamaica Journal, 22:1 (1989) 48-55.

_____, 'The Effects of the Abolition of Slavery on Jamaican Livestock Farms (Pens), Slavery and Abolition, 10,2 (1989), 187-211.

Sheppard, J. The 'Red Legs' of Barbados: Their Origin and History (New York, 1977).

Sheridan, R. B., Sugar and Slavery: An Economic History of the British West Indies, 1623-1775 (Barbados, 1974).

Sio, A., Marginality and Free Coloured Identity in Caribbean Slave Society', Slavery and Abolition, 8,2 (1987), 166-183.

Smith, M. G., 'Social Structure in the British Caribbean about 1820'. Social and Economic Studies, 1, 4, (1955), 55-78.

45

The Cuban Sugar Planters 1790–1820
"The Most Solid and Brilliant Bourgeois Class in all of Latin America"[1]

ANTÓN L. ALLAHAR

One of the dominant themes stressed in the literature on development and underdevelopment in Latin America, is that the landowners in this region have historically played a negative role. They are portrayed as having been politically reactionary, economically passive, lacking in entrepreneurial drive, and generally unconcerned with promoting the development of the productive forces in their respective countries. Further, their attitudes have been branded as "traditional," and the policies which they pursued are seen to have been "defective." As a consequence, the general economic underdevelopment of the area has to be understood as a product of this class' inaction and its "conscious willingness"[2] to be subordinated to foreign capital.

Such an image of the Latin American landowner is associated with the traditional understanding of the *latifundio,* which was the common form of property ownership during the early colonial period.[3] In later years, however, as the so-called feudal structure of the Latin American countryside underwent changes,. and capitalist relations of production increasingly penetrated the rural sectors, the *latifundio* rapidly began to give way to the *hacienda.* With the establishment of agro-export oriented economies in the region, the *hacendados* who controlled the large landed estates came to be seen as more "modern" types of landowners, whose activities were largely geared to the pursuit of profit and the expanded reproduction of commodities for the world capitalist market.

The role played by these *hacendados* in either promoting or retarding the development of the productive forces in agriculture is not very clearly spelled out in the literature. Writers such as Suchlicki, for example, continue to promote the view that they were traditional, inward-looking, and anti-progressive.[4] Further, the actual labels used to characterise this class have neither been very specific nor of much analytical value. We are thus presented with such terms as "land-owning oligarchy,"[5] "agro-commercial export" or "lumpen" bourgeoisie,[6] "native" bourgeoisie,[7] and "national" bourgeoisie,[8] among many others. What do these terms tell us about the Latin American landowners? About their attitudes to development? Or about the economic conditions confronting them?

To arrive at some answers to these questions we will use Gunder Frank[9] as a point of departure. This author, though making a distinction between the anti-national (understood in the patriotic sense) bourgeoisie dedicated to raw material exports, and the national bourgeoisie concerned with the development of local manufacturing and industrial operations, focuses on the former and criticises it for having promoted the so-called "development of underdevelopment." The main thrust of his argument is that the lumpen-bourgeoisie, by seeking to export raw materials and unfinished products, serves to (a) export jobs abroad, (b) commit the country to being a net importer of finished goods, (c) impede the growth of an internal market, and (d) guarantee the dominance of foreign capital. The policy of free trade, therefore, which Gunder Frank labels a defective policy, favoured the economic interests of this class and simultaneously weakened the small manufacturers who produced mainly for the local market and who demanded protective tariffs and restrictions on imports.

On this basis, therefore, Gunder Frank sees the lumpen-bourgeoisie as "no more than the passive, though I would prefer to call it active, tool of foreign industry and commerce." [10] He then goes on to state that, given their strong links with foreign capital, the policies of the lumpen-bourgeoisie

further strengthen the very same bonds of economic dependence which produced the policy, and thus aggravate still further the development of underdevelopment in Latin America. [11]

For Gunder Frank, then, who seeks to discuss the concrete economic limitations to development in the context of Latin America, it is clear that the problem was one of strategy. Instead of attempting to forge an alliance with local industrial forces, the lumpen-bourgeoisie, which had grown strong under the regime of free trade in the early nineteenth century, chose to reinforce the *status quo* of foreign (colonial) domination, by continuing to produce raw materials primarily for export. They thus served to strengthen industrial development in other countries, while at the same time tending to neglect local industrial development:

in order to increase still further its capacity to export raw materials, the Latin American bourgeoisie chose an economic policy which increased economic dependence and, with it, the development of underdevelopment. [12]

The argument that the landowners in the underdeveloped countries are, or have been responsible for promoting underdevelopment, has another dimension which is related to, but also goes beyond the mere fact that they pursued free trade and neglected the development of local manufacturing operations. This "further" dimension is more psychological in nature, and seeks to portray the landowners in these countries as lacking initiative and drive. They were thus capable of offering only passive responses to the challenges facing them. The general absence of a "progressive," adventurous and enterprising spirit is seen as a major explanation of economic backwardness.

In the psychological literature on the question of what factors are responsible for promoting development (especially in the underdeveloped countries), the works of David McClelland, [13] among many others, are most instructive. McClelland stresses such "internal" factors as values, attitudes and motives, as being central in explaining development and underdevelopment. Of special significance to McClelland is the level of achievement motivation within a given population or society. The higher the level of "need for achievement" (n'Ach), the greater the likelihood that development would occur. Thus, in a study to determine the level of achievement motivation among potential entrepreneurs, McClelland said of those who scored low that

They thus manifested behaviour like that of many people in underdeveloped countries who, while they act very traditionally economically, at the same time love to indulge in lotteries – risking a little to make a great deal on a very long shot. [14]

That tendency to shy away from taking risks, he argues, is symptomatic of low entrepreneurial drive, since "one defining characteristic of an entrepreneur is *taking risks* and/or innovating." [15] Further,

if people with high need for achievement are to behave in an entrepreneurial way, they must seek out and perform in situations, in which there is some moderate risk of failure – a risk which can, presumably, be reduced by increased effort or skill. [16]

Such a view seems, therefore, to support the contention that "it is values, motives or psychological forces that determine ultimately the rate of economic and social development." [17] According to McClelland, the problem faced by the Third World underdeveloped countries is that such positions of responsibility are usually filled by members of the "upper class" or "elite," who are not always the most competent or highly motivated to achieve. [18] Such a system of recruitment, therefore, tends to promote and perpetuate an upper-class bias, while excluding members of the lower and middle classes.

The relevance of this discussion lies in the fact that it is the dominant groups or classes within the underdeveloped countries that are seen to be responsible for the backward conditions which prevailed in the past and even continue into the present. This is a salient point which is stressed in the literature, whether written from a psychological, historical or economic point of view.

In sum, therefore, though coming from clearly distinct intellectual traditions, both McClelland and Gunder Frank tend to see the main causes of economic backwardness as residing in the specific orientations and policies of the ruling groups in the underdeveloped countries. These groups were presumably incapable of pursuing policies which would have resulted in development. In the case of McClelland this was due to the general lack of entrepreneurial skills among the dominant elites in underdeveloped countries, while for Gunder Frank it stemmed from the terms of subordination of those elites (landowners) to foreign capital. [19]

While there is some merit in the points of view expressed by these authors, it appears to me that their treatment of the topics they address was conducted at far too general a level. In other words, I do not dispute the fact that the export-oriented landowners in Latin America were to some extent responsible for the backward conditions which came to prevail in some areas. Nor do I reject the position that certain values and attitudes lend themselves more readily to the promotion of development strategies. My immediate concerns, however, are with (a) those countries in which there *was* evidence of "entrepreneurial spirit" among the dominant groups, and yet development did not result; and (b) the fact that in those countries, the failure to develop did not result from a lack of effort in that direction, or from pursuing policies of "lumpen-development." Rather it was closely tied in with a series of objective conditions, which were often accompanied by a number of subjective and ideological considerations.

In this context, the classic work of Paul Baran,[20] is most instructive. Speaking about the specific case of India, Baran shows, as do so man others, that this country was very advanced in its methods of production, industrial and commercial organization, etc., before its colonial conquest. India had a well developed handicraft industry and exported "the finest muslins and other luxurious fabrics and articles, at a time when the ancestors of the British were living an extremely primitive life . . . ."[21]

Today, however, India is an underdeveloped country – one which has failed to take part in the economic revolution initiated by the descendants of those same wild barbarians" (the ancestors of the British).[22] But what was the reason for

this "failure"? Was it due to some historical accident or a peculiar inaptitude of the Indian "race"? No, says Baran,

It was caused by the elaborate, ruthless and systematic despoliation of India by British capital from the very onset of British rule."[23]

To support his point, Baran also quotes from Marx's "The Future Results British Rule in India":

the great mass of the Indian people possess a great industrial energy, is well fitted to accumulate capital, and remarkable for a mathematical clearness of head and talent for figures and exact sciences. Their intellects are excellent. [24]

The key point to be examined, therefore, is not whether or not entrepreneurial talent, as a "factor of production" exists, but what are the conditions under which it is permitted to be actualised? In developing his argument that the underdeveloped countries possess a superabundance of entrepreneurial ability, Baran states that

in all countries of the world, and at all times in history, there have been ambitious, ruthless, and enterprising men, who had an opportunity and were willing to innovate, to move to the fore, to seize power and to exercise authority.[25]

Following from Baran's discussion, therefore, and in the specific case of nineteenth-century Cuba, I plan to show that the types of backward conditions which came to prevail, did so in spite of the fact that the planters possessed entrepreneurial drive. In other words, by using their own initiative, the planters were able to amass considerable amounts of wealth by the third decade of the nineteenth century. And on this basis, they attempted, within certain limits, to overcome the obstacles to the development of the productive forces within the sugar sector, and actively sought ways of dealing with the practical political and economic situations they faced. When the conditions changed, however, opportunities for accumulation became more limited and the planters had to devise new strategies.

Thus, though a relevant consideration, I do not accept the argument that one could identify a set of responses which are "modern" or "progressive" by definition, and which will not tend to vary when changes in the material conditions of existence occur. Surely the planters often met with only limited success, but this was not due simply to their "lack of enterprising spirit" or to their pursuit of "defective" policies. The point, therefore, is to examine the nature of the challenges which they faced and the types of strategies devised to combat them.

In my analysis of the responses offered by the Cuban landowners to the challenges faced during the nineteenth century, attention will be focused on the sugar planters, who represented the most wealthy and powerful set of economic interests on the island at the turn of the century. The tobacco growers – *vegueros* – and cattle ranchers – *ganaderos* – who had formerly occupied key positions in Cuba's national economy, fell victim to the growing strength of the sugar barons – *hacendados azucareros* – owing largely to three interrelated international developments which took place in the second half of the eighteenth century.

Chronologically speaking, the first of these occurred in 1761-1762, when, during the Seven Years War, Britain captured and occupied Havana for a period of eleven months and introduced major changes which served as the foundation for the building of the future sugar empire. As Knight tells us, the four major factors of production required for establishing an *ingenio* (a steam-powered mill) in those days were: land, oxen, forests and labour. The first three were no problem in Cuba where there were abundant lands and fine forests, along with

an adequate supply of oxen for agricultural purposes, thanks to the long standing tradition of ranching on the island. Most plantations had their own ranches or *potreros*, in order to eliminate the expense of renting draught animals.[26]

The only score on which the planters found themselves wanting, therefore, was with regard to a labour force. The reasons for this had little to do with Cuba *per se*, for as Merivale[27] shows, it was a situation common to all colonies in the New World at the time. Where land was cheap, abundant and easily available, as it was in the colonies, those Europeans who migrated did so with the hope of owning land and bettering their conditions of existence, and understandably avoided becoming agricultural wage labourers. And this general absence of a body of wage workers acted as serious fetter on the development of the sugar industry up until the early 1960s.

As Robin Blackburn[28] tells us, "between 1720 and 1762 the economy of the country was so undeveloped that its entire European trade was carried by an average of only five or six merchant ships each year." During the short period of the English occupation, however, over one hundred trading ships called at the port of Havana, and some 10,000 African slaves were introduced into the country: "The take-off point of the plantation economy can be dated from this brief but overpowering intervention. Sugar production began to expand rapidly, assisted by the international conjuncture."[29] During this period, also, the monopolistic powers of control wielded by certain interests residing in Cadiz and Seville were broken, and the first steps were taken in the direction of the liberalisation of trade. The creole *hacendados* then availed themselves of the opportunity to purchase large numbers of slaves, along with machinery and various other bits of technology to be used in the grinding mills.

This represented only the beginning of the sugar revolution, for with the increased installed capacity of the mills, and the phenomenal growth of the slave labour forces,[30] the sugar *hacendados* were very well placed to engage in a greatly expanded scale of operations. But one problem remained. For whom were they going to produce? Up until this point, the expansion of sugar production was not only limited by the general unavailability of a labour force, but there was also the question of the market. The small free population in Cuba did not constitute a sufficiently large market capable of absorbing increased production. And, with the Spanish home market being amply supplied by producers in Granada and Santo Domingo, it did not appear as though the Cuban planters woud be able to take advantage of their increased capacity for production.

The solution to this problem came with the second major development of the period – the American War of Independence (1776) – which saw the curtailment of exports of sugar from the British West Indian islands to the former Anglo-American colonies. Suddenly huge market possibilities were opened up and the Cuban producers were able to respond immediately to fill the vacuum which was created.[31] More slaves were imported, production soared, forests were destroyed, and a general "sugar-fever", seized the island.

Then there came the third international development which contributed to the take-off of the Cuban sugar industry. This one took the form of the slave uprisings in Haiti, which culminated in 1792 with the utter destruction of that country's sugar empire. The almost immediate ruin of the Haitian planters, who produced fifty per cent of the world's sugar in 1792 and none in 1793[32] added to the frenzy in Cuba, spelling instant riches for the cane growers, both big and small. And from exports totalling 4,969 tons in 1760, Moreno Fraginals shows that in 1799 Cuba exported over 32,500 tons of sugar.[33]

The Economic Response

Given the wider developments taking place in the second half of the eighteenth century, the years 1790-1820 came to represent a boom period for the Cuban sugar industry and those who controlled its fortunes. It was a period which effectively began with the elimination of Haiti as a major sugar producer, and ended with the signing of a treaty in 1818 to legally abolish the slave trade by 1820. Between these years the Cuban planters did in fact establish themselves as the most dynamic and aggressive of local contending classes.

They founded several important economic organizations, and at the same time played a leading role in the development of school and university curricula. The latter was mainly centred around the teaching of physics, chemistry, agronomy, etc., and directly related to the needs of the sugar industry. As a class they were also responsible for the introduction of steam-driven machinery, the appearance of the railroad, and the development of a highly lucrative export trade. In the area of more sociocultural activities, the planters were again instrumental in pioneering the first newspapers, in drafting and sponsoring all the economic, political and social reforms instituted during the early part of the century, and were constantly embroiled in disputes with the colonial authorities, seeking a "fair" deal for Cuba.[34] "They were," as Moreno Fraginals commented, "men of bourgeois consciousness and thus a revolutionary element within their world."[35]

The Cuban creoles, in agriculture as in politics, were a restless group. They were always ready to grasp at any innovation which promised to boost the total output, or to cut the costs of production. As the sugar industry got under way, private individuals and public commissions made long trips through the other sugar islands. reporting in detail upon every aspect of the production of sugar ...

back to their keenly interested audience a bewildering range of topics, with particular emphasis on agriculture and relevant proposals for adaption to Cuban conditions.[36]

Oscar Pino Santos also writes:

The Cuban *hacendados* – whose sharp entrepreneurial talent can scarcely be denied – understood very well the brilliant opportunities which the business of sugar offered. Their alertness, for example, can be shown by the great attention which they paid to technical developments which were taking place in the outside world.[37]

Thus, as opposed to the image of Havana as being "apparently feudal" and reminiscent of "Eastern bazaars,"[38] there are those who paint a picture of a vibrant and expanding society during the early decades of the nineteenth century.[39] And far from living in a parasitic relationship off of this society, there is evidence to show that the planters actively pursued the enactment of different types of legislation, which served to enhance the development of the sugar industry and the rest of the economy.

Up until the decade of the 1820s, the planters were able to participate in an international market where the laws of capitalist production and exchange dominated every facet of existence, and they were also made to be fully aware of the fact that the socioeconomic complex of sugar production entailed a great deal more than just obtaining the highest possible price for their product. Their economic reality encompassed the slave trade and the massive problem of policing, feeding and caring for a huge, totally dependent work force; the securing of credit; the importation of machinery; the establishment of transportation and communication networks; the manufacture of rum, molasses and other by-products of cane; the constant acquisition of new lands for planting and forests for woodfuel, etc.

In this context, three examples can be cited. The first concerns the formal passage of free trade laws on February 10, 1818, which served to ratify certain informal practices which had come into existence ever since the British capture and occupation of Havana in 1762. As Foner[40] noted, especially in the context of trade with the United States, the colonial authorities were powerless to prevent the growing numbers of American ships calling at Cuban ports in the years preceding the free trade legislation. And even if the legal trade could have been stopped, there was no official remedy to counter the highly developed channels of contraband activities. Thus, in an effort to compromise, and also to enhance the flow of tax revenues into the royal coffers, the Crown capitulated and granted free trade privileges to the *hacendados*, but not before the latter had made it clear that there was no alternative open to the Crown.

The second example relates to the slave trade and its growing importance for the Cuban economy. The *hacendados*, though already involved in an unofficial sense in the direct transportation of slaves from Africa to Cuba, had been making repeated representations to the Cortes for the right to import their own slaves. They argued that such a move would be in the best interests of the country, since it would eliminate the rapacious middleman (the Spanish *negrero),* who waxed rich on the basis of the high prices he commanded, and would in turn permit greater direct investments in sugar production. This permission was finally granted in 1789, thus giving legal recognition to a process which was begun ten years earlier, when Spanish ships became actively and directly involved in the traffic of human cargo. The colonial authorities were again embarrassed into a situation of having to give legal sanction to a practice which had existed for several years prior, in a *de facto* manner. As Moreno Fraginals[41] indicated, even before the royal cédula of February 6, 1789, official representatives of various slaving companies were already resident in Havana. In effect, as was noted in the Decreto de la Libertad de Comercio de Esclavos,

that decision of the Crown was the first great victory for the creole landowning class, which saw the expansion of the sugar industry blocked by the general scarcity of available wage workers.[42]

Finally, a third example of the manner in which the *hacendados* were able to influence or effect superstructural changes, is that of the royal cédula of August 15, 1815, which authorised the clearing of forests for sugar expansion. Severely weakened and impoverished by the effects of the Napoleonic wars, the general state of turbulence in Europe, and the rebellions in the continental Latin American colonies, the Spanish crown was in no position to refuse requests from the *hacendados* with respect to the further consolidation of the interests of this group. Thus came the concession of 1815, which merely sped up the process of deforestation, but did not initiate it,

since before the release of the royal cédula, over ten thousand caballerias (330,000 acres) of forest lands had been cleared for the planting of sugar cane.

On the basis of the foregoing, therefore, it is clear that the Cuban planters made great attempts to modify the terms of their subordination, while at the same time actively seeking means by which to expand their sugar operations. The fact, therefore, that they may have been given to conspicuous consumption and lavish spending, etc., does not appear as the most salient feature of this group, as Thomas[43] would have us believe, and as Enrique Gay-Calbó attests, when he says that the planters wasted

millions on luxury goods, trips abroad, the high life in grand cities and on fashionable beaches, in European castles, on ostentatious displays of wealth, buying titles of nobility . . ..[44]

A very different picture is the one painted by Philip Foner which shows that the planters' interests were tied in with the promotion of the development of the productive forces and "eliminating the backwardness of the island's economy" He writes that:

The planters were ambitious to advance their own interests, but understood that the progress of the island and the advancement of their own interests were interrelated . . . They were interested in raising the yield from the soil, developing the island industrially, and expanding trade and commerce with other countries besides Spain.[45]

The impact of these actions, when translated into economic terms, provides us with a profile of the Cuban sugar planter which is radically different from the one we are led to expect, if we were to rely on the general discussion of the Latin American landowners in the literature. Moreno Fraginals[46] for example, notes that overall sugar output increased from 4,300 tons in 1761 to 32,500 tons in 1799, and 56,150 tons by 1825. In addition, the price of sugar rose from 2 and 4 *reales per arroba* (1 arroba = 25 lbs), for brown and white sugar respectively in 1790,[47] to 3 and 7 *reales* in 1807, and peaked at 24 and 28 *reales* in 1818.[48] Nor was this all, for the number of sugar mills and *trapiches* had increased from 473 in 1792,[49] to 870 in 1803 and over one thousand by 1827.[50]

Thus we can appreciate the extent to which the sugar planters were able to seize the initiative and take advantage of the opportunities presented by the favourable market conditions which prevailed. These were not the actions or characteristics of a "passive" and "unenterprising" class. By the 1820s, therefore, after having secured certain free trade agreements, the planters finally became a force to be reckoned with by the colonial authorities. As Foner tells us

A powerful class of rich sugar planters emerged as a consequence, living sumptuously on the wealth created by a swelling number of slaves. More and more capital went into sugar production and more and more land was devoted to it.[51]

The vast new opportunities which were opened up for sugar as a result of the Haitian "disaster" and the exposure to American trade, had great repercussions for the economic and social structure of the island. The *haciendas comuneras,* which had remained largely intact until the first two decades of the nineteenth century, increasingly began to come under attack. Individual landholders, eager to cash in on the windfall profits of sugar, started to demand legal title to the lands which they occupied, in order that they may be exploited in accordance with their own interests. It was a period during which many of these landholders (big and small) who were not previously involved in the cultivation of cane, swiftly began to convert their fields to the growing of this crop, undertaking the simultaneous construction of numerous *trapiches* (small, inefficient, animal-driven, grinding operations), and abandoning the production of minor food crops which were so vital to the growth of the internal market. On this basis, therefore, the Cuban sugar planters sought to put the entire social organization of the countryside in the service of sugar.

Occupying what could be termed a dominant position in the circuit of capital, the sugar planters attempted to give greater coherence to their interests and began to demand economic concessions from Spain. The tremendous opportunities for the amassing of wealth which had been created by the initial flowering of the sugar industry, had offered the planters a fair measure of economic independence, and given the still generally backward state of technology within this sector, it was not difficult for them to undertake the new (non-technical) improvements which had been necessitated. These improvements centered mainly around two considerations: (a) the expansion of the labour force (slaves), and (b) the acquisition of new lands. Up until this point

(the second decade of the nineteenth century) the planters were able to maintain control over the organization of production, since slaves were cheap, land was plentiful, and foreign competition was minimal.

This last consideration is important since it meant that pressures to revolutionise the technology and techniques of production were not very great and the general question of the development of the forces of production would not be addressed in any serious manner for some years to come. Though **increases in production** resulted from the addition of new slaves and the incorporation of new lands, there was not an **increase in productivity**, which could only have come from the scientific application of technology and the use of more skilled labour in the production process. Thus, given the state of the world market for sugar, the low level of competition and the high prices which obtained, the Cuban planters could feel secure within their world of sugar. And on the basis of this security they began calling for free trade.

As a policy which was consciously pursued, however, free trade had potentially positive and negative consequences. On the one hand, it could increase the possibilities of amassing even more wealth by increasing the number of buyers: on the other hand, it could render the internal market for local manufacturers highly vulnerable in the face of low cost imports. To realise the positive benefits, three conditions had to be met: (a) a low level of foreign competition, (b) high demand, and (c) high prices for the product. During the period in question, when the economic ideology of free trade was embraced by the planters, these conditions were in fact present.

If any or all of these conditions (variables) changed (as they often do), problems were bound to ensue. And in the case of Cuba, when foreign competition increased, and demand and prices fell, major difficulties were encountered by the planters. For example, the phenomenal rise in the price of sugar which followed the Haitian disaster led to a vastly enlarged scale of production and for a time served to strengthen the economic base of the planters even further. However, higher prices stimulated increased production not only in Cuba, but also in the islands of the British West Indies; before long an over-supply on the world market resulted, leading in turn to a decline in prices. In Cuba this was directly translated into the almost immediate ruin of many small farmers, the destruction of over thirty sugar mills, and the weakening of many more.[52] The uncertainties and fluctuations in the market price for sugar thus meant that in good years everyone tended to do well; but when prices fell significantly, the smaller, weaker and less efficient producers were the first to be ruined.

This, then, was the situation facing the Cuban planters during the second decade of the nineteenth century. Since the local market was very small, and since demand in Spain was insufficient for absorbing any major increases in output from Cuban mills (it must be noted that within the Spanish empire Cuba was not the only sugar producer), protectionism did not constitute a viable economic strategy. For the more wealthy planters who could compete and survive on the open market, therefore, free trade was a rational demand. But, when once the planters began to lose the ability to compete effectively, and when neither free trade nor protectionism served their best interests, how did they respond?

The answer to this question, though very relevant to an assessment of the planters' actions over time, will have to be sought in concrete developments which occurred during the middle and later decades of the century, and will more properly constitute the subject matter for another follow-up study. For the moment, therefore, we will focus on the early decades of the 1900s, during which time the planters had amply demonstrated both the willingness and capability to promote the development of the sugar industry (and consequently of the entire national economy). Their economic actions appeared to have been rationally calculated and, where the economic ideology and practice of free trade were concerned, they sought to pursue a course of action which was consistent with the interests of their class. They transported sugar cane to Cuba, planted it, manufactured sugar, and sold it on the world market. In doing so, they secured along the way the necessary economic and political reforms which served to transform Cuba from being just another Spanish colonial military outpost with a stagnant economy, into the "Pearl of the Antilles" – Spain's richest and most treasured colonial possession. There is no more fitting testimony to the achievements of this class than the words uttered by Moses Yale Beach,

Latin American advisor to President Polk in 1847: "Give us Cuba and our possessions are complete."[53]

The Political Response

Apart from the purely economic changes taking place within the sugar industry during the period 1790 to 1820, we must also consider the political conditions attending the rise of the planters. In this context, special attention will be paid to questions relating to the abolition of (a) the slave trade and (b) the institution of slavery itself, and what these meant for the structure of colonial relations. Having achieved a secure place for themselves within the sphere of economic activities, the political projects of the wealthiest sugar planters were aimed at the consolidation of that position. Since slavery had come to assume such a central role in the continued functioning of the sugar industry, their path to security lay in the preservation of that institution. What, then, were the prices they paid for such a stand? What were the implications for their future development and the development of the forces of production in sugar?

To answer these questions, the writing of the "Representación de la Ciudad de la Habana a las Cortes Españolas" (1811) may serve as a point of departure.[54] This document, though actually written by Arango y Parreno, does not necessarily reflect the personal views of the author alone, for, as probably the most perceptive, astute and articulate representative of his class, he was commissioned to write it by the Court of Agriculture and Commerce (Consulado de Agricultura y Comercio), the City Council of Havana (Ayuntamiento de la Habana), and the very powerful Society of Friends of the Country (Sociedad Patriótica de Amigos del País), bodies that contained several representatives of the growing sugar interests.

The writing of the "Representación" was provoked by the actions of two Mexican representatives to the Cortes of Cadiz, José Miguel Guridi y Alcocer and Agustín de Argüelles, when they entered a plea for the abolition of slavery in the Americas. Realising that an end to slavery would spell ruin for sugar and themselves, the *hacendados* were stirred to action and through the pen of Arango launched an attack on Spain, the crown, the church, and all else who stood in their way. They reminded the king that "sovereignty resides essentially in the Nation, and the Spanish Nation (of which Cuba is a part), is not, and cannot be the patrimony of any individual family or person." [55] This could be interpreted as a veiled threat to the king, who, still having the memory of France 1789 in his head, would think twice before acting against the immediate interests of the most powerful group in the colony. Added to this, was the fact that by 1811 the continental Latin American colonies were rising up in arms and demanding their independence, and Spain needed to keep Cuba as a faithful ally. Fully cognisant of the heavy financial losses suffered by the crown as a result of the long Napoleonic wars, the Cuban planters capitalised on this weakness, speaking openly and defiantly to the king, and even criticising the practice of democracy as it applied to the Cortes where they were not permitted a voice, and where the decision to abolish slavery was debated:

Pardon us your Majesty for pointing out, with profound respectfulness, that the absolute majority of votes, even within one congress, however informed they are, however numerous, has rarely yielded good laws. [56]

Slavery, they argued, was a necessary evil introduced into Cuba by the crown and the church and, now that their (the *hacendados*) very lives had come to depend on it, sudden abolition would represent a harsh punishment for a crime they were forced to commit. In other words, their maintenance and use of the institution of slavery amounted to nothing more than "obeying certain laws, which did not only authorise us, but also obliged and even pressured us into the ownership of slaves." [57] Even the Church, for its part, they continued, "participated in and sanctioned the violence of bringing human beings in chains and shackles from such remote countries":

We must never become tired of repeating that the Blacks came and are here ... not due to our own fault, but rather to those who opened the way with guns and the full support of the law, and even the Church, which was so interested in liberating their souls from eternal damnation. [58]

Thus the pro-slavery political stance, of the *hacendados*, epitomised in their 'Representación,' was to have a decisive influence on the unfolding of events related to their own class and the overall politico-economic growth and development of Cuba. Although essentially a conservative position, nevertheless, this attitude has to be understood contextually. Surely it meant that the planters would not and did not participate in the revolutionary conspiracies of 1809-1812, which were aimed at the independence or political separation of Cuba from Spain. [59] But this was a calculated and rational response to the conditions they faced. They understood how easy it would be for the slaves to free themselves during a general state of war, and even set up a black republic (as was done in Haiti). And, since Cuba did not have any army of its own, attempting to seize independence by violent means was far too risky a proposition.

The pro-slavery stand of the planters was thus Spain's main guarantee of continued domination of Cuba. And though unhappy about the oppressive system of taxation, bribery, tributes, duties, etc., they chose, albeit reluctantly, to submit to Spanish domination as the surest means of security against the ever-present threat of a massive slave rebellion. Thus Pino Santos writes:

The Cuban oligarchy of sugar planters, coffee growers, and cattlemen lived on the basis of their exploitation of slaves, and to maintain that regime, they needed the support of a powerful state. To maintain slavery it was necessary to ensure the existence of the state's coercive and repressive power. And on this score the creole slave-owners were weak; they felt incapable of sustaining, on their own, a state apparatus which could guarantee their system of exploitation. [60]

And arguing along similar lines, the Spanish Minister Calatrava noted that

the fear which the Cubans have of the Blacks is the surest means which Spain has for guaranteeing her continued domination in that country. [61]

Thus, although economic prosperity produced a *liberal economic ideology* (mainly free trade and other questions related to it), politically the outcome was the reverse: to maintain their favourable economic position, the pillar of which was slavery, the planters had to seek protection or security against a slave uprising and this implied a *conservative political ideology*, which resulted in their continued political subordination to the Crown and the colonial state. Their demands of Spain were always limited to very clearly defined economic and political concessions, taking special care not to hint at rebellion lest the black population should perceive this rift as a sign of weakness or division among the colonisers, and use it as the signal for sparking off their own war of liberation. The Cuban planters, therefore, as Pino Santos affirmed,

saw themselves forced to remain within the bounds of the Spanish colonial system, and their projections were thus limited to obtaining minor concessions and reforms within this system, without attempting to break away from it.[62]

Given their objective situation of colonial dependence, the planters knew just how far they could go without jeopardizing their relatively privileged economic position. They thus opted for political subordination to Spain: but this stand has to be understood as one that was rationally calculated. To push for political independence would have amounted to class suicide, since this would have inevitably involved a war against Spain and possibly against their own slaves. They thus chose to use tact and persuasion, securing minor reforms, and gradually entrenching their class interests even further. Far from being either submissive or impulsive, therefore, the sugar planters evinced a great deal of political cunning, economic initiative, and a sober rationality in their dealings with Spain.

By way of conclusion, then, the conservative politics of the Cuban hacendados during this period has to be understood as having been directly related to the manner in which they perceived a threat to their own interests. Further, their conciliatory stance seemed to be yielding positive benefits, for between the years 1816-1819, Ferdinand decided to reward them generously for their continued fidelity to the Spanish cause. This reward came in the form of the granting of various reforms which they had long been seeking. Along with earlier concessions related to the freedom of importation of slaves, the granting of equal political rights, etc., to the Spaniards resident in the colonies, the crown in 1817 agreed to lift the one hundred year old government monopoly on tobacco and also approved legislation for the promotion of free, white Catholic immigrant workers. In 1818, the long awaited granting of unrestricted free trade became a reality, opening up Cuban ports to foreign vessels and permitting free trade with foreign nations. Finally, in 1819 there came a decree giving the hacendados full legal title to the lands they had been occupying. In a sense this signalled the birth of private property for the creoles, since for the first time they were permitted to cut-up, sub-divide, sell and rent out their lands.

The bulk of these reforms, it must be noted, were of an economic nature, since Ferdinand, still very much an absolute monarch, was most wary of any political aspirations on the part of the hacendados. Nevertheless, the latter appeared to be contented with their new economic gains, which afforded a great measure of social mobility and tended to blur any early signs of significant discontent or antagonism, as may have emerged between the peninsula and creole interests. Politically, too, through their various organizations, cabildos, etc., the hacendados were given some say in the management of Cuba's internal affairs:

Around this time, the wealthy class of creole planters had access to, and participated in the direction of the state apparatus, which governed the so called "ever faithful pearl of the Antilles."[63]

And, as Moreno Fraginals added, during this period:

The Cuban sacarocracia [sugarocracy] shared with the merchants and the Spanish authorities the effective government of the island. They dominated the city councils of all the municipalities, the Sociedad Patriótica of Havana, the Real Consulado, the Junta de Tabacos; and they counted on the support of the governor and captain general, whom they were able to control through bribes (Luís de las Casas) or bribery and political blackmail (Marqués de Someruelos).[64]

On the basis of the foregoing case study of the landowning Cuban azucareros, therefore, it is clear that they do not fit the traditional passive roles which are usually ascribed to the Latin American landowners in the literature. On the contrary, during the period studied, they demonstrated a great dynamism and participated successfully in the tremendously competitive international sugar market. At both the economic and political levels, their ideological and practical responses to the challenges faced in the early nineteenth century were carefully calculated and reflected the type of maturity that was required if they were to survive as a class. Of course, they met with setbacks along the way, and surely their survival was not without social, economic and political costs; but what is important is the fact that they *actively* sought ways out of their dilemmas, and managed to promote an important measure of economic development in Cuba.

Notes

1. This appreciation of the Cuban sugar planters is offered by Manuel Moreno Fraginals in "Azucar, Escalvos y Revolución," *Casa de las Americas* 50 (1968): 36.
2. André Gunder Frank, *Lumpenbourgeoise: Lumpendevelopment: Dependence, Class and Politics in Latin America* (New York: Monthly Review Press, 1972), p. 3.
3. For a detailed and comprehensive treatment of the period see Jacques Lambert, *Latin America: Social Structures and Political Institutions* (Berkeley: University of California Press, 1967), especially pp. 59-64.
4. Jaime Suchlicki. *Cuba: From Columbus to Castro* (New York: Charles Scribners and Sons, 1974), p. 67.
5. Carlos Romeo, "Revolutionary Practice and Theory in Latin America," in *Latin American Radicalism*, ed. Irving Louis Horowitz et al., (New York, Vintage Books, 1969), pp. 595-606.
6. Gunder Frank, *Lumpenbourgeoisie*, p. 5 and passim.
7. Ramón de Armas, "La Evolución de la Burguesia Latinoamericana," in *Feudalismo, Capitalismo y Subdesarrollo*, ed., Luis Vitale (Madrid, 1977), pp. 123-138.
8. Ronald Chilcote and Joel Edelstein, *Latin America: The Struggle with Dependency and Beyond,* (New York: John Wiley and Sons, 1974), pp. 32-34.
9. Gunder Frank, *Lumpenbourgeoisie*, pp. 4-8.
10. Ibid., p. 5.
11. Ibid., p. 13.
12. Ibid., p. 14.
13. David G. McClelland, "The Achievement Motive in Economic Growth," in *Development and Society: The Dynamics of Economic Change,* ed. David Novack and Robert Lekachman (New York: St. Martins Press, 1964). See also David McClelland "Motivational Patterns in Southeast Asia with Special Reference to the Chinese Case," in *Journal of Social Issues,* Vol. 29 (1963).
14. McClelland, "The Achievement Motive," p. 183.
15. Ibid., p. 182.
16. Ibid., p. 183.
17. Ibid., p. 188.
18. Ibid., pp. 185-86..
19. It is interesting to note that the conclusions of both these authors are stated in the form of tautologies. For McClelland, development is impossible without entrepreneurs; thus, where there is no development, this is due to the lack or absence of entrepreneurial skill. And Gunder Frank, on the other hand, after investigating the concrete limitations to developmental strategies faced by the landowners, concludes that underdeveloped results in those situations where development fails to take place:

    underdevelopment is the result of exploitation of the colonial and class structure based on ultra exploitation: development was achieved where the structure of underdevelopment was not established because it was impossible to establish. (p. 19)

20. Paul Baran, *The Political Economy of Growth* (New York: Monthly Review Press, 1957).
21. Vera Anstey quoted in ibid., p. 144.
22. Ibid., pp. 144-45.
23. Ibid., p. 145.
24. Ibid.
25. Ibid., p. 235..
26. Franklin W. Knight, *Slave Society in Cuba during the 19th Century* (Madison: University of Wisconsin Press, 1970). p. 28.
27. Herman Merivale, *Lectures on Colonisation and Colonies,* 2 vols. (London: Longman, Orme, Green, Brown and Longman, 1841); see especially chaps. 9, 10, 11, 20.
28. "Prologue to the Cuban Revolution," in *New Left Review* 21 (1963): 54.
29. Ibid.
30. See the authoritative study done by Hubert H. S. Aimes, *The History of Slavery in Cuba, 1511-1868* (New York: Octagon Books, 1967), Aimes shows that in the two hundred and fifty years from 1512-1762, a total of roughly 60,000 slaves were imported into the island, thus averaging about 240 slaves per year. This was the period of relatively slow overall economic growth, during which time the sugar sector showed very little expansionary tendencies. In the thirty-year period beginning with the British occupation of 1762, however 50, 435 slaves, an average of over 1600 per year, were introduced and came to represent that all-important work force which was so sorely lacking, and which was a vital requirement for the flourishing of the sugar industry.
31. Eric Williams, *Capitalism and Slavery.* (New York: G. P. Putman's Sons, 1966). pp. 149-153.
32. Manuel Moreno Fraginals, *El Ingenio: Complejo Económico-Social Cubano del Azúcar* (La Habana: Editorial de Ciencias Sociales, 1978) 1:43.
33. Ibid.
34. Ramiro Guerra y Sánchez, *Sugar and Society in the Caribbean* (London: Yale University Press, 1964), p. 56.
35. Manuel Moreno Fraginals, *The Sugarmill: The Socioeconomic Complex of Cuban Sugar - 1760 to 1860* (New York: Monthly Review Pess, 1976), p. 133.
36. Knight, *Slave Society*, p. 19
37. *Historia de Cuba, Aspectos Fundamentales* (La Habana: Editorial Nacional de Cuba, 1964), p. 161.
38. Hugh Thomas, *Cuba, or the Pursuit of Freedom* (London: Eyre and Spottiswoode, 1971), p. 143.
39. See, for example, Julio LeRiverend's *Economic History of Cuba* (La Habana: Book Institute, 1967), pp. 162-63; and Robert B. Hoernel's "Sugar and Social Change in Oriente, Cuba: 1898-1946." in *Journal of Latin American Studies,* 8 (1976): 217-219.
40. Philip S. Foner. *A History of Cuba and its Relations with the United States* (New York: International Publishers, 1962), I: 68-69.
41. "Azúcar, Escalvos." p. 37.
42. Hortensia Pichardo, *Documentos para la historia de Cuba* (La Habana: Editorial de Ciencias Sociales, 1971) I: 158.
43. *Cuba, or the Pursuit,* p. 143.

44. "Colonialismo." In *Cuadernos de Historia Habanera* 23 (1943): 24-25.
45. *A History of Cuba,* I. 54.
46. *El Ingenio,* I: 35.
47. Foner, *A History of Cuba,* I:70.
48. Alexander Von Humboldt, *Ensayo politico sobre la isla de Cuba* (La Habana: Cultural S. A, 1930).p. 187.
49. Leland Hamilton Jenks. *Our Cuban Colony: A Study in Sugar (*New York: Vanguard Press, 1928), p. 25.
50. Julio LeRiverend, *Historia Económica de Cuba* (La Habana: Instituto Cubano del Libro, 1974), pp. 195-96.
51. *A History of Cuba.* I: 70.
52. Guerra y Sánchez, *Sugar and Society,* p. 52.
53. Quoted in Basil Rauch, *American Interest in Cuba, 1848-1855* (New York: Columbia University Press, 1948), p. 59.
54. Contained in Pichardo's *Documentos para la historia.* I: 217-252.

55. Ibid., p. 217.
56. Ibid., p. 225.
57. Ibid., p. 229.
58. Ibid., pp. 236-37.
59. A brief outline of the movements which came to the fore during this period is given by Fernando Portuondo del Prado, *Historia de Cuba* (La Habana: Editorial Nacional de Cuba, 1965) I: 266-68.
60. *Historia de Cuba,* pp. 128: 176.
61. This speech is reported in José Luciano Franco's *Antonio Maceo: Apuntes para una historia de su vida (*La Habana: Editorial de Ciencias Sociales, 1975) I:32.
62. *Historia de Cuba.* p. 176.
63. Ibid., p. 171.
64. "Azúcar, Esclavos" p. 37.

SECTION TEN

Sex, Race and the Gender Order

Recent scholarship, attempting to compensate for past discursive shortsightedness, has emphasized that there was no homogeneous slave experience and that analyses of slave conditions, and, indeed, of slave society, must take gender differentiation into consideration. As part of this project of differentiation, historians have been engaged in research on the slave family and reproduction (more intimately linked with women than with men), as well as on the gender differences in work régimes, access to 'privileges', enslaver-enslaved relations and representation. They have sought to uncover details on women in Caribbean slave society which can inform comparative debates on gender and slavery.

The conclusions from researchers have been instructive. They emphasize that women did not live the way men did, and that slavery as a social system of oppression, had a different impact on them. The experiences of women sharply varied between particular colonies, but less so across imperial lines. There was also a sharp differentiation in the lives of women of different ethnic, class and colour groups and little solidarity existed across these lines. As Beckles shows, white women, active contributors to the development of a proslavery ideology in the Caribbean, were assigned special roles within the slave system which in turn determined their experiences as free persons within the gender order. Black women, both free and enslaved, field-hand and domestics, also experienced society in fundamentally different ways, though categories were not always clear, and edges invariably blurred.

The essays in this section look at women in the gender order by reexamining notions of difference and seeking points of commonality. They reinforce the multifaceted importance of slave women in the Americas, the contradictory productive, reproductive and sexual roles they were called upon to play, and their objectification and mostly negative treatment in the narratives of Europeans who observed Caribbean slave society.

46

Women Without History: Slavery and the International Politics of Partus Sequitur Ventrem in the Spanish Caribbean

JOSEPH C. DORSEY

We felt betrayed by historians whose liberal views allowed them to envision the reality of male slaves (to a degree) but not that of female slaves . . . Since Black women held it in their power to reproduce the labor force, does this not make them central to an understanding of slave history?

> *Gloria Hull et al, eds, **But Some Of Us Are Brave***

Introduction

This essay explores the political and juridical significance of female slaves in Anglo-Spanish diplomatic relations. It argues: 1. That the slow and often fractured results of Great Britain's antislave trade diplomacy are traceable to a certain brand of discursive shortsightedness in the composition and implementation of its bilateral antislave trade accords. 2. That the problem centres on Great Britain's failure to grasp and act upon the subsumptive subtlety of matrifocal determinants within the discourse of antislave trade diplomacy. 3. That this point is best illustrated in Great Britain's twenty-year effort to liberate its own black subjects from illegal bondage in the Spanish Caribbean islands of Cuba and Puerto Rico. 4. That while it was necessary for proslavery Spanish agents to author and carry out complex stratagems to circumvent Anglo-Spanish antislave trade agreements vis-à-vis the traffic from Africa to the Caribbean, inter-Caribbean slave trading required no such ploys because Spanish international, national, and colonial legislation sufficed to protect it. 5. That in Spain's archival arsenal of counter-abolition-

ist subterfuge, the womb-oriented dictum of *partus sequitur ventrem* was at once its most formidable and its most understated source of motivation and resistance.

Section I summarizes the multifaceted importance of slave women in the Americas. In doing so, it also suggests the various ways that *partus sequitur ventrem* defined and shaped the contours of historical otherness, a dialectical construction of master-slave relations predicated on the conscious objectification of an unconscious subject. Section II considers Latin American legal systems (Spanish and Portuguese) as they relate to the amelioration of the slave condition. With emphasis on slave-initiated litigation, by parallel and differentiation, male slaves are included specifically to highlight the political and juridical encumbrances foreign-born slave women faced. Despite the international implications of some of these examples, juridical decisions discussed in this section were limited strictly to internal concerns. Section III examines full case histories of Afro-Britons enslaved in Cuba. With discussions and illustrations of the inter-Caribbean slave trade as its preface, Section IV focuses on the international dimensions of womb-oriented politics in Puerto Rico.

Rooted firmly in the legal traditions of imperial Rome, *partus sequitur ventrem* was a simple measure that extended immediate slave status to any child born of a slave mother, irrespective of the status of the father. Under favourable conditions in the Americas, it guaranteed that black slave populations would reproduce themselves naturally, thus freeing slaveholding polities from continued dependence on external acquisitions. When avenues of external acquisition were threatened, especially in the absence of acceptable birth rates among Creole slaves, its importance increased dramatically. In identifying *partus sequitur ventrem* as a force to be reckoned with in the arena of international abolitionist politics, this essay maintains not only that British agents underestimated its might, it will be argued further that Spanish officialdom exploited it for the explicit retention of black British subjects – male and female – enslaved illegally in Spanish Caribbean dominions. The overriding paradox of this ancient matrifocal safeguard is that it was seldom referred to. Among the primary source materials used for this essay, it is mentioned but once, and by a British rather than Spanish functionary whose textualization reduced it to a rather bland afterthought.

It seems, therefore, that *partus sequitur ventrem* was a quiet oppressor, a mute autocrat whose tyranny was spread so effectively that it was taken for granted. In Latin America, such slave-related issues as food, clothing, and shelter, labour conditions, punishments, and spiritual affairs were continuously, and often uselessly, legislated and amended. *Partus sequitur ventrem,* however, was a legal device designed to expand slavery – or at least conserve it – not compromise it with ameliorative risks. In Peru and Venezuela, for example, where black slavery did not dominate relationships between capital and labour, as well as in Cuba, Puerto Rico, and Brazil, where it did, *partus sequitur ventrem* was an uncontested given that did not warrant serious attention until free-womb laws were promulgated as steps towards aggregate emancipation.

Cuba and Puerto Rico rose to slaveholding pre-eminence comparatively late, between the 1760s and 1820s. Inasmuch as this period corresponded with the rise of Britain's national and international antislave campaign, British diplomatic pressures on Spain were relentless. Thus it is to the credit of desperate and ruthlessly creative slaveholder interest groups that both Spanish islands became bona fide slave-based economies. The success of nineteenth-century Spanish Antillean slave-based sugar production was contingent upon liberal access to African captives. Slave increase by natural reproduction was not reliable. African kings, paramount chiefs, and prime merchants habitually undersupplied European and American buyers with female captives because of their higher value in local markets. Furthermore, for reasons related to the trauma of captivity, the rigours of the Atlantic crossing, and the emotional impact of permanent dislocation and marginalization, African-born slave women in the Americas were consistently less fertile than their Creole sisters and progeny. Few experts today would generally label one slave occupation as more desirable than another – be it coffee or rice production, the mining of gold and diamonds, railroad construction, masonry, smithing, lumberjacking, cattle ranching, dock porterage, or domestic assignments, including concubinage. Sugar cultivation, however, was exceptionally hazardous. Of all slave occupations readily associated with premature death – pearl diving in Panama (shark attack and lung collapse), prostitution in Brazil (sadistic brutality and sexually-transmitted diseases), and the supervision of Native American conscripts for the mining of mercury in Mexico, Peru, Bolivia, and Brazil (blood poisoning and lung collapse) – labour-intensive sugar production resulted in the highest rates of mortality. Small wonder that Spanish life insurance companies limited the coverage of slaves assigned to sugar plantations. All these factors militated against dependable demographic increase among Creole slaves in the Spanish Caribbean, where sugar was king.[1] Hence Cuba and Puerto Rico looked to their non-Hispanic Caribbean neighbours for supplements, no matter how small their numbers or channels compared to the larger but equally illicit influx of African captives. Though women did not dominate numerically in the inter-Antillean traffic of Anglophone slaves, once Britain began strident efforts to free its black subjects, the Spanish bureaucracy proved to be fairly liberal toward certain male slaves, but utterly inflexible toward female slaves and their offspring, regardless of age or sex.

Many sources testify to the various roles women played in the history of modern black slavery, often as victims of oppression but at times as oppressors themselves. But it is only in recent decades that scholars of various disciplines have begun to address the importance of women in slavery studies. In the area of women's studies, in particular for students of radical feminist theory in search of historically classless sources of women's solidarity, research thus far addressing the sex-specificity of slavery studies must be disappointing. Universal sisterhood is not found in the history of institutionalized bondage. With keen feminist and abolitionist sensitivities, Sarah and Angelina Grimké observed that slavery in the United States demeaned black and white women alike. The controversial novelist, Gertrudis Gómez de Avellaneda, equated the oppression of women with the bondage of black people she witnessed in her native Cuba. Nonetheless, using different methods and documents, for different periods, cultures, and hemispheres, Gerda Lerner and Elizabeth Fox-Genovese show that slavery and universal sisterhood are thematically irreconcilable.[2]

The Victorian illusion of female constitutional delicacy was an elitist construction intended for the consumption of elitist classes of whites. It excluded all other classes, especially the working class poor. It is therefore obvious – but worth repeating *ad infinitum* – that neither sex nor gender afforded slave women in the Americas any semblance of long-term privilege, influence, comfort, or sympathy. Wherever slavery represented pervasive capital-labour relationships, women in bondage were usually charged with the same or similar duties as men. It follows that they were exposed to parallel occupational hazards, drudgery, and tedium.[3] Along similar lines, it should be noted that the expression, "White women for marriage, black women for work, and mulatto women for sex play," is fictive. The equivocal intimations directed towards the women of colour targeted in this pejorative adage are easily corrected with queries into black maternity. More importantly, the variant exigencies of a system whose success depended on social insecurity could offer few ameliorative guarantees for the subalterns whose forced labour supported it.[4]

Regardless of background or phenotype, all slave women occupied a special position in the white male-dominated world of American slavery. In the absence of rigorous cross-disciplinary research, the extent to which slaveholders appreciated the equal or near-equal labour potential of slave women remains open to question. On the one hand, for example, it is clear that both sexes performed similar tasks. On the other hand, throughout history of slavery in this hemisphere, males brought higher prices than females. There are also the matters of concubinage – or at least sexual gratification on demand – and *partus sequitur ventrem*, slave children are born of slave mothers. Issues of comparative vulnerability are prickly, for any attempt to differentiate physical and psychological adversity invites circulatory dispute. The master who flogged his male slaves and engaged in forced sex with his female slaves demonstrated the equality of symbolic dominance. The flogging of female slaves was hardly novel, of course, regardless of such critical factors as pregnancy and age. Furthermore, only the most unenlightened of scholars would dismiss the probability of sexual activity between male slaveholders so inclined and the male slave partners they selected – though documentation for this type of liaison in American slave societies appears scant. Sex, gender, and genderization processes, however, remain viable factors when we consider that women, not men, were the main targets of rape and such added horrors as involuntary prostitution – both of which exposed slave women to then-fatal syphilis and gonorrhea. That black people saw black women as more susceptible to the intrinsic vulgarities and fatalities of slavery is borne out by the tendency of newly manumitted slaves of both sexes to purchase the freedom of their nearest female relatives first.[5]

Sex and gender are not interchangeable codes. If it cannot be said that slave women were never genderized – with the exception of cooks, housekeepers, and nannies – it is feasible to postulate that slave women were never genderized the way free women were. With respect to sex, it was the happenstance of birth, rather than any socialization process (here, genderization), that determined the comparative value of slave women and slave men. Historical hindsight remedies historical uncertainty. In all American slave societies, buyers purchased slave women at lower prices; more often than not, slave women worked under the same rigours as slave men; by tradition all slave women were the potential sex partners of their masters; and by law, the children of the slave women were also slaves. If male slavocrats bore these four points in mind, then the purchase of any young, healthy female of child-bearing age represented a bargain and a sound investment. However, the first three points of this winning, master-class combination were wholly dependent on the strength of the final point. Auction-block cost-effectiveness, together with relative job-performance parity, and the traditional promise of free sexual access, stood for nothing or little without *partus sequitur ventrem.*

Slave women experienced multiple conditions of subaltern status. Women, black people, and slaves were separate representations of historical otherness, each capable of standing alone as objectified paradigms of white Western male domination. For slave women, these hallmarks of individual subaltern consciousness and subconsciousness – female identity, black identity, and slave identity – were the components of an externally imposed whole.The entirety of their objectified existence constituted a series of subjectified oscillations between the imposition of their complete selves, and the imposition of the separate yet consubstantive components that completed the whole of their objectified reality. In other words, as the subjects and the objects of socially constructed identity, slave women in the Americas were compelled to broker numerous and often simultaneous sets of internal and external consciousness.

From ancient to modern times, all slaveholders believed that slave women were more easily managed than slave men. Their convictions were based on comparative strength and objectified temperament, both reflecting the genderization of behaviour. With control ranking as a primary concern, it made more sense – especially but not exclusively in the Armericas – to foist the onerous dictum of *partus sequitur ventrem* on women. From the beginning of modern times, such issues as Euro-American legal mechanisms and genderization processes compromised slavemaster control over the reproductive activities of slave men. Laws alone denied slavemaster control over the reproductive activities of free women, regardless of birth, class, or colour. Thus black slave women experienced a special brand of historical otherness. It was an otherness, a phenomenological impasse of consciousness, that limited their access to self-accountability. *Partus sequitur ventrem* commandeered their reproductive independence, the very essence of a woman's ability to determine the course and content of her historical continuity.

II

Constant slave resistance was a major attribute in modern American slave regimes.[6] It took two distinct but sometimes overlapping paths: channels beyond the legal system and channels within it. Discussions here focus on the politics of the latter. At one time or another all American slave-based economies had institutions, or branches of institutions, that were responsible for the well-being of slaves.[7] Yet the importance of slave rights, irrespective of the polity that feigned such concerns, lay less in their existence than in their purpose and their applicability. For many years, Western scholars were fascinated by the fine corpus Iberian law and canonical theory that recognized the enslaved as homo sapiens with baptizable bodies and redeemable souls – that is, human beings who, under certain conditions, had a limited number of civil rights. The academic admiration for Latin American slave systems stemmed from the apparent contrast with slavery in Anglophone America, especially in the northern colonies that became the United States, where the humanity of Africans and their descendants was denied legally on the basis of fractional computations. Greater access to manumission, mandatory holy sacraments, and ethnic hybridization all seemed to corroborate the gentility of Spanish and Portuguese American slavery. Evidence was convincing. One would be hard pressed to imagine a Virginian governor personally investigating slave complaints of poor nutrition, as did Governor Rafael Arístegüi of Puerto Rico in 1847. Yet the historical literature antithetical to this "friendly master" thesis is immense. Suffice it to say, in the words of one revisionist, "One race cannot systemically enslave members of another, on a large scale, over three centuries, without acquiring a conscious or unconscious feeling of racial superiority."[8]

In response to higher imports of African captives, which related to variegated political shifts that radically modified the contours of Spanish imperialism between the 1760s and the 1820s, the Spanish Bourbons passed new legislation to improve the material and the emotional conditions of slaves. Salient among them was the creation of the *Sindico Protector de Esclavos* or the Magistracy for Slave Defense, a conduit that allowed slaves to file formal grievances against their masters.[9] In his *Slavery and Social Death,* Orlando Patterson alludes to the ameliorative futility of this agency and any other conduit of legal redress when he says:

The master's authority was derived from his control over symbolic instruments which effectively persuaded both slaves and others that the master was the only mediator between the living community to which he belonged, and the living death that his slave encountered.[10]

In Vega Baja, Puerto Rico, in 1845, Joaquin protested excessive workloads and physical abuse. The arbiter was himself a slaveholder. When a plantation administrator informed him that the plaintiff was incorrigible, he dismissed the case. Obliged to return to the offending master, Joaquín was placed in shackles for three months. Once unfettered, he fled.[11] In San Juan in 1859, María Balbina complained:

On the promise of freeing me, when I was barely a teenager, my master made me the mother of his three children, born one after another. But now, unmindful of his given word and the lamentations of his conscience, he intends to sell me.[12]

Medieval Castillian laws discouraged slave sales of this type, but in modern seaborne imperial situations such cases probably elicited more tribunal laughter than anything else. Anxious over the slow process of the suit, two years thus far, María Balbina's statement was a direct appeal to the governor for hands-on intervention. Though he seemed cooperative, she had no faith in his efforts. Like Joaquín, she finally resorted to flight.[13]

Perhaps because of greater experience in the business of African slave acquisition, in conjunction with a less fastidious bureaucracy, Portuguese America was not subject to a body of laws developed expressly to protect slaves. Slave codes were plentiful enough, but statutes to buffer abusive treatment were not requisite.[14] Honorata was a pre-adolescent mulatto who was raped by her master. He was not only a known child molester, four physicians concurred that the plaintiff exhibited no anatomical indications of forthcoming puberty. Nonetheless, the Brazilian high court, on the eve of aggregate emancipation, ruled in favour of the defendant, on the grounds of insufficient evidence to prove that Honorata was a minor.[15]

Oppositional forces against María Balbina clearly included the strength of *partus sequitur ventrem.* It did not factor, however, in Hono-

rata's defeat. She was not only a child yet capable of producing slave children for the system – an issue that would not have helped her case in any event – the trial took place after Brazil had passed its free womb law. Thus, while still a slave, any children she had would be free-born. In both suits, however, plaintiff victory would have resulted in freedom. Where there were no grounds for liberty, slaves such as Joaquín sued to improve tangible conditions alone. When freedom did not hang in the balance of slave-initiated law suits, plaintiffs in Spanish America were required to seek new masters – a risky endeavour that many masters were known to block by treating their slave litigants as runaways. When law suits included bids for emancipation, slave plaintiffs were removed from their masters under escort and placed in the protective custody of the Real Casa de Beneficencia (Royal House of Public Charity), in jail, or in private homes, at times in the homes of defending lawyers themselves. Slave advocates were lower court barristers called *hombres buenos.* Regardless of any lower court decision (with the exception of the Síndico de Juicios de Paz y de Conciliación, a pre-trial civil court), all final verdicts rested with the High Court of Appeals: the Audiencia Pretorial for Cuba, and the Audiencia Territorial for Puerto Rico.[16]

After ratification of the Moret law of 1870, which freed slave children up to two years and older slaves, among others, it seems that more slaves sued their masters for misrepresenting their ages.[17] Before 1870, however, slave suits were wide and varied. Though there are few studies on slave advocacy in the Spanish Caribbean, and no systematic examination of legal slave defence according to sex, primary sources for Cuba and Puerto Rico show that many slaves of both sexes sought to take advantage of laws designed ostensibly for their protection.[18] Frequent protests in both colonies focused on severe punishments, malnutrition, and excessive work hours, on the one hand, and the defence of loved ones, on the other. Without the benefit of scientific scrutiny, two trends are in evidence here. Men sued more often on the basis of harsh treatment, while women sued more frequently for the unlawful enslavement of close kin, especially children. These tentative observations are not meant to suggest spousal indifference among slave women or spousal indifference and parenting flaws among slave men. Outside the law, some slave men found the added dangers of family marronage to be the best protective expedient. Within the law, black men – slave and free – operated at severe disadvantages vis-à-vis the protection of their wives and children. Juan José Aliende, a free black Puerto Rican, fought a losing battle to secure the freedom of Juana Negrón, his wife and the mother of his children. As if to intimate some sinister delusion of comparative power, the Spanish legal system deemed slave women, especially slave mothers, more acceptable plaintiffs in struggles of this type. In cases reminiscent of Dred Scott and James Somerset, María Cándida Mejía of Puerto Rico and Gabriela Arencibia of Cuba sued for the liberty of their daughters, Paula and Tomasa, whose masters took them on visits to Spain, where slavery was abolished in 1836. Manuela Celiz launched an energetic campaign to obtain the return of her daughter, Estefanía, who was taken as property in cabotage commerce from San Juan to Havana. She filed suit on the grounds of deceit, violent kidnapping, illegal sale, and wrongful export. If any of these girls had black fathers, slave or free (an issue the records do not reveal, as was often the custom), who might have initiated these claims on their behalf, their cases might never have reached the *sumaria* or hearing stage. Slaveholders had the right to deny black male assertions of paternity, for any reason, including no reason at all. Mejía and Arencibia won their suits; Celiz did not. Therefore deception ranked in the silent salience of *partus sequitur ventrem,* for in Celiz's case, separation from the parent, rather than freedom, hung in the balance.[19]

International abolitionist politics and diplomacy rendered law suits for wrongful enslavement a special threat to the tenuous stability of slavery in the Spanish Caribbean. Spain exercised particular caution to protect rights, given that slaves were chattels. The avoidance of precedent was paramount. It has been shown that the legal concept of slave property was a judiciously fabricated myth that dated back to pre-principate Rome.[20] Yet fictive or not, among other determinants, slave ownership was a legislated and practised reality, secure in the protective shroud of property rights.

Whether for the manumission or the amelioration of locally-born slaves or African-born slaves, district arbiters, municipal magistrates, and high court judges were more than ideological sentinels who helped monitor slavery as a superstructural field of production. They were skilled vanguards who knew the contours of their fronts. For these colonial officials, law suits filed to liberate slaves of non-Hispanic Antillean origin in Cuba and Puerto Rico presented few challenges. As long as they were taken to Spanish dominion as slaves from neighbouring islands where slavery still existed, Spain refused to proscribe the inter-Caribbean influx. This meant that slaves from the French and Danish islands were welcomed until 1848, as were slaves from the Dutch islands until 1863.[21] Many non-Hispanic Antillean-born slaves were introduced by this route, a path Britain insisted was in violation of the Anglo-Spanish anti-slave trade conventions of 1817 and 1835. It provided Puerto Rico especially with a safety-valve for the continued importation of African captives as re-exports from its neighbours. This influx slowed to a halt between 1828 and 1830, revived, apparently, in 1845, and climaxed between 1847 and 1848.[22]

In the next decade, several non-Hispanic Antilleans claimed fraudulent enslavement in Puerto Rico on grounds directly and indirectly related to the abolition of slavery, or the abolition of the international slave trade in their native islands. Proslavist resolution was easy. In the complex case of Richard Lawrence of Danish St. Croix, pivotal papers turned up missing. For Anna Maria Salomons, a Jewish mulatto from Dutch Curacao, Spanish judges spent greater energy identifying pitfalls in diplomatic protocol.[23] With dauntless, discursive elegance, slave plaintiff Frédéric Othon, of French Guadeloupe, stated to the governor of Puerto Rico in final appeal:

My problem and its remedy, Most Excellent Sir, are quite simple. Let he who claims the right to me present legitimate papers verifying that I am a slave, and I will resign myself to my fate. But if they are not brought forth ... I should be declared legally free immediately and without the introduction of measures prejudicial to my right to claim compensation for damages occasioned by my lengthy bondage.[24]

Othon's appeal was denied.

III

The introduction of British slaves, and the claims to liberty that followed, were separate matters altogether. Britain abolished the slave trade to its colonies in 1807, and ended slavery itself in 1834. Spain's illegal slave trade diplomacy with the subjects and governments of France, Denmark, and the Netherlands ranged from hot to chilly, but it was never cold and was often warm. Hence, non-Hispanic Antilleans enslaved in the Spanish islands found little reason to seek the solace of their consulates in San Juan, Havana, and Santiago de Cuba.[25] With Britain having abolished slavery and the trade in its dominions, and with its unpopular resolve to influence the abolition of slavery worldwide, black British subjects held in bondage in Spanish territories would seem to have stood a better chance at gaining their freedom. But they did not. The Spanish government first realized that such claims could threaten Puerto Rico's supply of slave labourers in 1838, when Britain unsuccessfully demanded the return of its black subjects.[26] This rather strange and poorly organized effort led Spanish metropolitan authorities to re-examine their position on the international trafficking of slaves. With Cuba enjoying far greater success than Puerto Rico in the clandestine introduction of African captives directly from the coast, Spanish reassessments, and the measures resulting from them, would have different meanings for the two islands. For both, however, until mid-century, the fortification of proslave trade policy would include special – albeit understated – considerations for slave women.[27]

Britain's anxiety over the new or prolonged enslavement of its technically free black subjects had just begun to surface at the time their efforts failed in Puerto Rico in 1838. Blacks from the British Caribbean, and from as far afield as British outposts and settlements along the Gambia, the Gold Coast, and Freetown, Sierra Leone, were discovered in bondage in Dutch Suriname and St. Eustatius, Portuguese Guinea Bissau, and the United States South.[28] They were more thickly concentrated, however, in the municipalities of eastern Cuba. Estimated to number some 5,000 in Holguín alone, and, consisting mainly of Bahamians, Jamaicans, and Sierra Leonian Creoles, their bondage was especially problematic from the standpoint of international law. With the conspicuous exception of Lord Aberdeen, most British politicians, and their seaborne agents, viewed all enslaved black British subjects as victims of kidnapping. But such a

conviction was questionable, considering that most of them were Antillean-born slaves whom British subjects took to neighbouring slaveholding polities before Parliament abolished slavery in 1834.[29]

In 1805-1806, Britain banned the export of slaves from its territories under the parliamentary act 46 Geo. III c. 52. The following year, it prohibited its subjects from participation in the international slave trade. In 1825, 5 Geo. IV c. 113 specifically outlawed the transport of English slaves to foreign dominions.[30] These statutes nonetheless were flaccid, as consuls would note in reporting their diplomatic confrontations with Spain to their superiors in London. They were British national and colonial rulings that were never re-worked for incorporation into international accords with Spain. Britain had no legal international leverage to combat the inter-Caribbean slave trade. Indeed Spain never failed to remind the British that its few concessions were gifts strictly limited to representational good will. Such gestures, as we shall see, excluded the return of any child-bearing black woman born in a British colony.

Britain's growing parliamentary antislavist activity met with fierce opposition in its colonies. In the wake of threats to himself and his family, British envoy Richard Madden had to leave Jamaica very quickly.[31] Some Britons sold their slaves to Spanish and French Caribbean planters for fear of insufficient indemnification. Others, in more militant protest, relocated, taking their slaves with them. By the early 1840s, some British communities in the Cuban province of Oriente were so large that many, including slaves, saw no need to learn Spanish. Whenever Viscount Palmerston held office (twice as foreign minister, later as prime minister), he pressed his consuls to ferret out slaveholding nationals in foreign dominions. But for all the efforts of antislave trade functionaries at home and abroad, colonial and consular correspondence show that few overseas Britons were ever prosecuted for slaveholding.[32] Some shed their British nationality for others – mainly Spanish, Danish, and Dutch – and so doing, they escaped the spheres of British domestic and colonial policy. Others, retaining their nationality, could be quite brazen in their resistance to antislavism. David Turnbull, the most vigorous abolitionist agent ever assigned overseas, incurred the wrath of proslavists everywhere, including that of his country-men.[33] Samuel Driggs was a British national residing in Candelaria, Holquín. He owned twenty-four British Caribbean-born slaves, in addition to slaves born in Cuba and Africa. Driggs threatened to decapitate Turnbull if he tried to deprive him of his human chattels. Others less openly hostile preferred to own slaves in the names of Spanish friends and in-laws.[34]

Some black British subjects, most of them men, and apparently few by comparison, were victims of outright kidnapping. From separate regions of the Upper Guinea Coast, two West African Creoles, Daniel Speck and John Fontanales, were sold at Gúines, near Havana. James Thompson, a free-born Bahamian mulatto, was enslaved in Santiago de Cuba by his Anglo-American brother-in-law. Antoine Ledamaux shanghaied Henry Shirley and others at Montego Bay and carried them off to Puerto Principe (Camagüey), and Pedro García, a debt-ridden sailor, entrapped George Wellington Crawford in Kingston, to sell him in Santiago.[35] To secure the freedom of over 100 black British men, women, and children, together with their Cuban-born descendants, Britain wrangled with Spain in 22 court cases between 1838 and 1856. But with respect to the thousands of other victims reported, their cases were never heard.

In law suits for liberty, the litigation process for all slaves was usually the same: protective custody, the pre-trial hearing (juicio de paz y de conciliación), the appointing of hombres buenos, lower court decisions from district and municipal tribunals – both of which were linked to Síndicos Protectores de Esclavos – with the final verdict resting in the hands of the pretorial high court. Naturally the major difference with plaintiffs who were British subjects was that British diplomatic officers and Spanish colonial government officers monitored every step of procedure, and both sides exerted as much pressure as possible. Sentiment, however, along national lines was not always uniform. Juan de la Pezuela, governor of Puerto Rico and later Cuba, was usually cooperative. Fernando de Norzagaray of Puerto Rico, and later the Philippines, simply followed directives from metropolitan-based superiors – unless the problem involved Puerto Rican-born slaves. And Leopoldo O'Donnell, governor of Cuba, mastermind of the great black Cuban purge of 1844, captain general of Tetuan,

Morocco, and caudillo of Spain was, in a word, ruthless. On the other hand, Aberdeen's soft-pedal, anti-Palmerstonian abolitionism thwarted the emancipation of more than one British subject in the Spanish Caribbean and elsewhere.[36]

Many such subjects, whose cases reached the courts, were eventually freed but problems persisted. Some men with Spanish mates remaining in slavery decided to stay, while other cases of couples enslaved together were tried separately and with different outcomes. Still others elected to remain because they had grown accustomed to life in a Spanish dominion. The question was never British identity versus Spanish identity. It was a matter of freedom versus slavery.[37]

Though fewer British females than males were known to be held in slavery in Cuba, precisely due to partus sequitur ventrem, their cases endured longer and they were the objects of more complex legal and diplomatic attention. Moreover, freedom came only to women whose circumstances separated them from matrilineal concerns, as the following cases indicate. In 1822, Elizabeth Kelsall left the Bahamian island of Exuma to settle in Holquín with a retinue of black servants, slave and free. Among them were two sets of brothers, sharing the same surname but not related by blood. The larger group consisted of six brothers, the smaller, of two. Some arrived with spouses, others as bachelors. Of the eight men, Kelsall freed half before leaving the Bahamas. The status of the other men and their accompanying wives is not clear. Henrietta Kelsall Eysing inherited her mother's Cuban estate and she considered the Bahamian-born servitors to be a part of it.[38]

For two of the Kelsalls, Newton and John, manumission came easily by lower courts. In matters related to slavery, the Audiencia rarely overturned lower court decisions. Newton died in the protective custody of prison. John remained to earn money to free his wife, Polly Gaythorne, who was the slave of a Jamaican planter-class family of immigrants. Of the other Kelsalls, Jacob died years before the suit, and Henry was never found. The governor of Cuba upheld the high court's decision to free the remaining brothers. Of these freedmen, Daniel was single; Bill had two children with Petronilla, a mulatto slave and the daughter of an unnamed member of the Samuel Driggs clan; Nat had five children with his wife Teresa, a Spanish Dominican-born slave now deceased; and Cuffee had ten children with his Bahamian wife Eve, also a slave, in addition to a Cuban-born mulatto grandchild. Given Teresa's status as a Spanish-born slave, *partus sequitur ventrem* could be relied on with customary silence and confidence, but as a token of good faith, the Audiencia Pretorial permitted Nat to attempt to raise money to purchase one of the five children, the couple's only son. Eve's case was litigated apart from her husband's. Predicting her defeat, he also left to earn money for her freedom, choosing Jamaica over his native Exuma because it was the closest British colony to Oriente Province. Eve's outcry at his departure prompted the police to fetter and jail her for disturbing the peace.[39] Ultimately, Polly, of child-bearing age but childless, Eve with her ten children and grandchild, Petronilla and her two children, and Nat's five children, were never freed.

Other cases testify to Spanish concerns for older female slaves. In Jamaica in 1799, George MacKenzie gave Betsy her freedom. She then worked as a domestic for Christain Clabor until a Madame Lefevre convinced her to immigrate with her to Cuba. Clabor died in Kingston in 1826, as did Lefevre in Santiago de Cuba shortly after. In the same city, Marie Geneviève Bastienne Clabor (whose relationship to the defunct Clabor was not spelled out) retained the services of Miguel Linares, a black Cuban barrister, to establish legally that she was the executrix of the Jamaican gentlemen's will, and that she inherited Betsy and her three sons from him. At the time Betsy approached the British consul of Santiago for help, her son Juan, Jamaican-born, was free. José also born in Jamaica, was the property of Cipriano Casamadrid. Luis, born in Cuba, was owned by Francisco Griñón.[40]

Betsy's *hombre bueno* argued that because she was taken away after Britain ended its participation in the international slave trade, she and her sons were entitled to emancipation. British agents elaborated, invoking first 46 Geo. III c. 52, then 5 Geo. IV c. 113. Though British consuls cited these acts in Cuba, and to a lesser extent in Puerto Rico, between 1838 and 1856, the Spanish response was always the same: "The parliamentary acts of foreign states have no bearing on the affairs of Her Catholic Majesty's Government." Repeated references to the statutes were nothing more than matters of form.

True to traditional resistance, the pretorial judges in Betsy's case scoffed at British national legislation, but they were impressed with other evidence: Betsy's manumission papers and ample proof that Clabor's will was a forgery. But before reaching a final verdict, both the Audiencia Pretorial in Havana and the Audiencia Territorial de Oriente in Santiago prevailed on the British to produce her baptismal record.[41] Meanwhile, more pressing matters needed attention. Casamadrid had José kidnapped from protective custody, carried him back to his plantation, administered him fifty lashes (twenty-five more than the law allowed in one installment), and forced him to work in shackles. Only strong political pressure induced him to release the slave-litigant.[42]

On the condition that Betsy return for her final decision of her cause, the governor of Santiago permitted her to go to Jamaica to testify against Bastienne Clabor, extradited to face multiple charges of fraud. When Betsy arrived in November 1849, the governor of Jamaica recorded that he had no authority to force her to return to Cuba. When the British consul of Santiago reported to London that further evidence of Betsy's free status emerged during Clabor's trial in Kingston, Palmerston reacted with typical verbosity:

With respect to sending the negress Betsy to Jamaica as a witness in the trial of Bastienne Clabor, I am apprehensive that you have taken an engagement in regard to the reappearance of Betsy in Santiago at a time when she may be wanted for pending judicial inquiry in her own case, which you have no certain means of making good.[43]

He stipulated that Betsy was not to return to Spanish soil, but, as we shall see later, the directive meant little.

Before his death, John Clarke of Jamaica bequeathed his slave Nancy to his Haitian mistress, Louise Defournet. The beneficiary immigrated to Santiago, accompanied by her mother, Bonne Castain, her compatriot and paramour, Joseph Toucon, and Nancy, the slave. The lovers married but Toucon soon died, and in 1838, the widow relocated to France, leaving the estate to her mother. Before departing, she sold two of Nancy's three Cuban-born sons. Juan went to Salvador Benítez and José, to Francisco Prado. Castain kept Lucien, and freed him before she died in 1848. The Tribunal de Bienes de Difuntos (The Tribunal of Intestate Affairs) froze Castain's assets. Evidently her death motivated

Nancy to enlist the aid of the British consul general, who helped place her in protective custody. On learning of his mother's actions, Juan attempted to follow the same course. Benítez, his master, intercepted him, charged him with marronage, and orchestrated his assignment to chain-gang labour. José disappeared, Nancy died in 1852, and the case fizzled out unresolved.[44]

Mary Gallagher was a free black British subject from Nassau. She had a curious relationship with British diplomats in Cuba. She sought David Turnbull's aid because her sixteen-year-old Congolese slave, Enrique, was framed, arrested, and severely beaten by a district chief of police. Writing to his superiors, Turnbull assessed that British support, based on her natal identity, would provide his government with the opportunity to aid in curbing Spanish colonial extortion, which he perceived as rampant enough to stir the Cuban population to revolution.[45] During Enrique's two-month detention, district authorities demanded and received cash and gold from Gallagher, said to be requisite for the slave's release. Though they released him, they threatened re-arrest unless Gallagher continued to pay. Captain General Gerónimo Valdés denied Turnbull's request for intervention. Nonetheless, the matter must have been resolved, for when Gallagher died in 1843, her estate included the teenager, as well as another slave, a Bahamian-born laundress named Charolette, who would soon sue for her freedom.

Gallagher named Tomás de Almeida executor of her will. As such, he took temporary possession of the two slaves. Charlotte's case was simple enough. The Bahamian Slave Register of 1822 revealed that she was never owned by the deceased, but by her daughter, Susan Buchanan Brathwaite, then a minor but now residing in Europe with her English husband. Valdés expelled Turnbull for radical abolitionist activity. With reduced diplomatic responsibilities, James Crawford succeeded him. On Charlotte's behalf, he invoked 46 Geo. III c. 52. Because her case had no bearing on Anglo-Spanish antislave trade accords, Intestate Affairs, rather than other lower courts, was responsible for initial adjudications, and it ruled that Gallagher's estate had no claim on the plaintiff. Charlotte returned to her laundry business and awaited pretorial ratification from the governor. Shortly after, a policeman appeared with a warrant to escort her to the Casa de Beneficencia. Crawford filed another claim to indemnify her loss of time and money while in the custody of Almeida and the Casa. Compensation was denied but she was freed. As with many others, she requested to remain in Cuba.[46]

Mary Ann was born a slave in Eleuthera, in the Bahamas. Her owner, Elizabeth Bethel, married a German resident of Mexico named Stoltz. Bethel moved to Veracruz to join her husband, taking the slave woman with her. When Mexico abolished slavery, Stoltz sold Mary Ann to a Madame Fellet, a French mulatto residing in Santiago. In turn, she sold her to Aurora Rossi of Havana.[47] The British consul argued for Mary Ann's freedom and compensation for thirty years of illegal servitude. By royal order she was manumitted in late 1851, receiving her freedom papers early the next year. The Spanish treasury awarded compensation to Doñla Aurora rather than Mary Ann. Her petition to remain in Cuba was denied. Vision-impaired, elderly, childless, and thoroughly dysfunctional in her native English, she was forced to leave the island in 1853.[48]

In this sampling of older, individual women, the case of Plassy Laurence is the shortest. She belonged to the Laurence family, one of the ten largest plantation dynasties on the British island of Nevis, in the Eastern Caribbean. Freed in 1834, she went to the sister island of St. Kitts to serve out the required apprenticeship. While she may have had some choice in the decision to change her venue of apprenticeship, it is fairly certain that she was kidnapped from St. Kitts, and taken to Cuba. There is also the possibility of an interim tenure in Puerto Rico.[49] Whatever the course of Plassy's re-enslavement, she exhibited neither patience with nor confidence in the Spanish bureaucracy to correct her status in Cuba. Exasperated with the slow process of litigation, she took advantage of the mother superior's absence from the Casa de Beneficencia and fled. When the governor inquired as to her whereabouts, the consul general deadpanned, "She has returned to her native island by British steamer."[50]

IV

Compared to the influx of African captives from across the Atlantic, the influx of bona fide Creole (or Creolized) slaves from the non-Hispanic Caribbean to Cuba and Puerto Rico was no deeper than a dimple. But no matter how shallow, the indentations varied in basic structure and content. Obviously national and international politics minimized British input compared to other non-Hispanic slaveholding powers. The majority of Cuba's comparatively small population of slaves of British origin came from the Bahamas, usually a result of British planter-class relocation in the early 1820s, and from Jamaica, a result of planter-class relocation and kidnapping, both during the 1830s. Cuba's French Caribbean slave population was older, pre-dating the 1815 starting point of international abolitionist politics and diplomacy, and probably larger, especially in Santiago, the island's main sanctuary of French refugees from the Haitian Revolution. Puerto Rico's British Caribbean slave population was even smaller than Cuba's, or at least less-publicized as a group, with the glaring exception of the diplomatic fiasco of 1838. In addition, most of them came from the Eastern Caribbean rather than Jamaica or the Bahamas. As with eastern Cuba, for reasons directly related to events in Haiti and Spanish imperial responses to them between 1791 and 1830, most free immigrants in Puerto Rico were Francophone. But their numerical predominance did not extend to the slaves they brought with them between 1815 and 1830, the peak years of their arrival. More non-Hispanic Creole slaves in Puerto Rico came from Dutch and Danish sources, with one important qualification. The re-export traffic of newly arrived African captives from the French, Dutch, and Danish Caribbean climaxed between 1828 and 1830. In theory, all subsequent introductions of non-Hispanic Caribbean slaves consisted of Creoles. The risks involved in landing Creole slaves from the British islands were greater for Puerto Rico than Cuba. Puerto Rico's proximity to the Eastern Caribbean invited such efforts, but Barbados was the Caribbean base of operations for the British Admiralty's antislave trade maneuvers. The tables below illustrate how and why Puerto Rico attempted to exercise greater caution than Cuba. Table 46.1 is a small sample of petitions for slaves between 1835 and 1846.

Table 46.1 Slave Introductions by Puerto Rican Residents, 1835–1846

Year	Petitioner	National Origin	Male Slaves	Female Slaves	Immediate Slave Origin
1835	Pedro Basbe	Spanish	1	0	Vieques
	Mary Wallace Henry	United States	1	1	St. Thomas
	Mary Wallace Henry	United States	3	3	Martinique
	Fortunato Benallo	Brazilian	1	1	Brazil
1842	Juan and José García	Spanish	10	8	St. Thomas (2 African-born women included)
	Julia Flavanger	United States	0	1	New York
	Pedro Martínez Novato	Spanish	1	0	Venezuela
	Jeanne Marie Sourffront	French	0	1	St. Thomas
	Antonio Aubaredes	Spanish	0	1	St. Thomas
	Nicolás Larraz	Spanish	1	1	St. Thomas
	Pierre Danois	French	0	1	St. Thomas
1845	Ana María Espinosa	Spanish	0	1	Venezuela
	Joseph Dizac	French	0	1	St. Thomas
	Francesco Margotti	French (Corsican)	0	2	St. Thomas
	Laureano de Castro	Spanish	1	0	Cuba (African birth specified)

Source: Archivo General de Puerto Rico, Gobernadores Españoles: Asuntos Fiscales, cajas 66 and 222.

The absence of Anglophone Caribbean input reflects apprehension of the Anglo-Spanish treaty of 1835, even though its force lay in a clause, which targeted the African rather than the inter-Caribbean influx of slaves. The case of the García family highlights this point. For unspecified reasons, the Garcia brothers, Juan and José, took their family for an extended stay in Danish St. Thomas. With them went a large retinue of domestic slaves, said to be requisite for, " . . . nuestros servicios y comodidades en el viaje."

The García family returned, with slaves, in segments between 1842 and 1843. As in three other cases cited in this table, and three cases in Table 46.3, the García slaves were already based in Puerto Rico with their masters; they only accompanied them abroad as domestic retainers. Perhaps annoyed or encouraged by the family's display of conspicuous consumption, customs officials encumbered the re-entry of several slaves in the entourage. Alejandro, Simona and María Rufina were detained six weeks awaiting certified copies of their baptismal records. The García brothers had to retain a lawyer to secure the return of African-born Manuela, to establish that she had arrived initially in Puerto Rico before the Anglo-Spanish conventions of 1835. It did not seem to matter that her captivity violated the first conventions of 1817. Clotilde, also African-born, and the mother of a son, gave birth to two more children while in St. Thomas. For reasons probably more related to bribery than anything else, customs and municipal authorities allowed their re-entry. The detentions suggest that *partus sequitur ventrem* functioned not only in favour of slaveholders, it worked in favour of government hustlers as well. It seems that customs officers focused on women of child-bearing age, whom they suspected were foreign-born. Alejandro and Simona were minors and certified criollos del país. They were probably included to ward off suspicion. María Rufina was also Puerto Rican-born, but she was of child bearing age. Manuela and Clotilde were not only African-born women of child-bearing age, the latter had established her fecundity and therefore her importance to the Garcia estate, an importance well worth the outrage of bribery.

Table 46.2 identifies slaves targeted in Puerto Rico in 1838 for repatriation to the British Caribbean as free people. Their presence, in the main, reflected British slaveholder fears of in-adequate compensation on the eve of abolition in the Eastern Caribbean in 1834. The failure of this genuine but isolated bilateral initiative resulted from diplomatic bungling on both sides. Their numbers, for example, are not reliable. In the confusion to speed up the emancipation and repatriation of Anglophone slaves, Francophone slaves were also included. The following tables demonstrate significant inter-Caribbean slave traffic on the eve of abolition in the French and Danish islands.

While Tables 46.3 and 46.4 reflect the proslave trade policies of Governor Rafael de Arístegüi in 1847, the former illustrates small requests, mainly for personal reasons not associated with concerns to fortify the island's slave-based economy. Four of the eleven petitioners owned a total of twenty slaves they inherited from estates on other islands. Six of them owned their slaves previously on other islands. And seven of the applicants lived in the capital, far from the slave-dependent sugar-producing centres in the south and southwest. But there was nothing to prevent the applicants in Table 46.3 from selling to large-scale slaveholders at considerable profit.

Antonio Salvador de Vizcarrondo and Marcelino Classe, for example, did not cite motives in their petitions. More suspect should be those who cited "any island" as a source, for it intimates profiteering activity, no matter how small-scale. Yet desperate planters, such as Nicasio Viña, had no intention of selling their slaves, at this point. And figures ranging from intermediate to high in this small-scale category would be suspect were it not for the fact that most of the petitioners gave detailed explanations for their requests. Claude Abraham, for example, requested the four Thomian slaves in the name of his daughter, Antoinette, a minor and the sole beneficiary of her late mother's estate. And Federico Menar Hagenbergh, a Puerto Rican-born postmaster, inherited six slaves from his mother's property in Maracaibo. The preponderance of slave women named in most of these requests raises a curious rather than suspicious connection to *partus sequitur ventrem*. Antoinette Abraham's Thomian inheritance consisted of Daphne and Celestine and their children Joseph and Thomas. Menar Hagenbergh's Venezuelan estate included Platina and her small children, Pierter and Andrés Corsino, Kato and her

Table 46.2   British Subjects Enslaved in Puerto Rico, 1834–1838

Municipality	Slave	Slaveholder
Juana Díaz	Pedro	Teresa Lara
	Andrés	Gregoria Dávila
	Agustina	Petrona Ortiz
Lugillo	John	Manuel Román
Naguabo	Tom Bom	William Bedlow
	Fanny	
	María	Buitrío Brothers
	Luis (son of María)	
	Opio	Beneficiaries of Cristóbal Ramírez
Juncos	Francisco	Mayor of Juncos (not named)
Trujillo Alto	Jorge	Louis Couvertier
Las Piedras	Belén	Josefa Ortiz
Humacao	John	López and Margueti
	Juan	José María Ríos
	Francisco Carlos	Ramón Berrios
	Johnny	Juan Antonio Miranda
Aguadilla	Pedro	Louis Duprey
	Silvestre	
	Florencia	Bruno Moreu
	Rosa	José (surname illegible)
	Jacob	Mayor of Aguadilla (not named)
Toa Baja	Enrique	Francisca Dávila
Añasco	Enrique	Gabriel Rodríguez
	Santiago	
	Vicente	Victoriano Calderón
	Manuel Eduardo	Andrés Basilis
	Carlos	Manuel Pagani
Patillas	James	Pedro Bodini
Fajardo	Carlos	Thomas O'Neill
	Flora	
	Moriah	
	Tom White	Juan Campos
	John	
	Francisco	María de Jesús Delgado
	Santiago	
	Dick	
	Andrés	
	Lupeni (?)	
Río Piedras	Luis	Jacobo de Castro
	Sofía	
	Norberta (daughter of Sofía)	
	Pedro	
	Domingo	

Table 46.2 British Subjects Enslaved in Puerto Rico, 1834–1838 (cont'd)

Municipality	Slave	Slaveholder
Hatillo	Pedro	Patricio Gandía
San Juan	Pedro	Aranzamendi
	Pedro	Juan Guillén
	Abelina	Joseph Giraud
	Nancy	
Ponce	José	Mora (given name illegible)
	Isidora	
	Luis	
	Juan Luis	
	Federico	
	Rita	
	Janet	
	María Agustina	Ana Bire
	Louis Creole	Jules DuBocq
	Juan de Velis	
	Guillermo	Martorell Brothers
	Isabel	Francisco Salas
	Susana	N. Viqnuit
	María	
	Tomás	Thomas Souffront
	Juliana	Manuel Rosario
	Gweny	
	Julian	
	Johnny	James Fraser
	María	Felicita Ferrer
	Julián	Rev. Father Joaquín Ollería
	Adelaida	Juan Salomas

Source: Archivo Histórico Nacional, Madrid, Spain. Gobierno: Puerto Rico, 5070/29. no. 23. Orthographic modifications from original: John/Yan, Johnny/Yani, and Souffront/Soufron.

toddler son, Castile Alcée, and an adolescent, María Herminia.

Table 46.4 clearly indicates planter concern in Puerto Rico, for more than half of these petitioners came from the sugar-producing municipalities of the south and the southwest. Furthermore, all of them owned one or more sugar plantations. In 1845, Spain promulgated its own law for the abolition of the African slave trade. Though slaveholder panic in Cuba and Puerto Rico was brief, resolution came from different directions of support. Both islands relied on old friends. For most of the 1850s, the United States provided Cuba with even greater assistance, in direct Africa-to-Cuba transport, than it did between the late 1830s and the early 1840s. Puerto Rico, however, could not maintain direct access to this corridor. Thus in 1847, and possibly sooner, it successfully returned to the French, Danish, and

Dutch Caribbean channels. Such channels serviced the island well throughout the 1820s, particularly – and in many instances, exclusively– in the area of re-export operations. This point leads to the matter of true versus immediate slave provenance with respect to the large-scale petitions of 1847. Dutch St. Maarten abolished slavery along with the French and Danish Caribbean in 1848. The remainder of the Dutch Caribbean territories did not abolish it until 1863. Why then did Puerto Rican petitioners for large-scale introductions target the non-slave-dependent, free port Dutch colony of Curacao as their principal source? It seems certain that the introductions of 1847 revived, however briefly, the inter-Caribbean re-export of newly landed African captives, probably, if not exclusively, from Dutch Accra. Indeed several of the petitioners were veterans of international slave commerce. Tito

Table 46.3   Sample of Petitioners for Small-Scale Introductions, 1847 (Puerto Rico)

Petition Date	Petitioner	Municipality	No. of Slaves	Source
January 9	Juan Montaña	San Juan	1	St. Thomas
January 25	Ramón Cestero	Mayagüez	4	Any island
January 25	José Ramón Fernández	San Juan	2	St. Eustatius
February 27	Antonio Moncerrate	Guayama	3	St. Thomas
March 5	Claude Abraham	Guayama	4	St. Thomas
March 6	F. Menar Hagenbergh	Guayama	6	Venezuela via Curaçao
March 12	Juan Liaño	San Juan	2	St. Thomas
March 13	Marcelino Classe	Guayama	2	St. Barthélemy
March 25	José Antonio Sánchez	Guayama	7	Curaçao via St. Thomas
March 30	Domingo Pelati	San Juan	8	any island
August 4	José María Sánchez	San Juan	1	St. Thomas
August 16	Nicasio Viña	San Juan	9	Any island
September 1	A. Salvador de Vizcarro	San Juan	2	St. Thomas

Source: Same as Table 46.1.

Patxot Gurnach, Casimiro Capetillo, and Antonio Casbasa were known slave merchants. And Antonio Canales was not only named as ship's captain for a number of the inter-Caribbean requests in Table 46.1, British antislave trade correspondence also cited him occasionally as ship's captain for African expeditions between 1834 and 1842.

Table 46.5, therefore, holds few surprises. Figures for African-born slaves reaffirm the acquisitional problem of sex disparity, though the gap is not as broad as it was a few decades earlier. Dutch sources provided the greatest input for the inter-Caribbean influx of 1847 specifically, for few slaves, Creole or African, from Dutch sources in the 1820s would have been alive by the census of 1872. Finally, it also shows that by 1872, Puerto Rico's largest slaveholding municipalities were nearly empty of British Caribbean-born slaves; only three out of 1,332 slaves are identified as British. Island officials certainly appeared reluctant to antagonize British diplomatic relations. Their reluctance, however, was specialized. From 1838 onward, Anglo-Spanish correspondence reveals no further trends in British provenance. On the other hand, the same officials barred no holds to retain black British subjects already held in slavery.

The welfare of these subjects was one of the several motives the British Foreign Office cited for establishing a consulate in San Juan in 1844. But with one exception – a Briton taken from Jamaica to Puerto Rico and then to Cuba – Consul John Lindegren found no cases related to the wrongful enslavement of British subjects in the 1840s.[51] Much of the new consul's time was spent trying to prevent the illegal landing of African captives from present-day Guinea-Conakry, in Upper Guinea (Accra, in Lower Guinea, was not mentioned), and to encourage Governor Arístegüi to discourage the brief revival of inter-Caribbean slave commerce, which, according to the consul, consisted mainly of women. By his reckoning he succeeded on both fronts. In reality, he failed on both fronts, and miserably so, by not considering that the two flows of traffic might come from the same source. Regardless of this display of naivete, inspired no doubt by his blind faith in the slippery governor, by the 1850s, he was well prepared to face the greatest challenge of his diplomatic career.[52]

Though Puerto Rico did not compare to Cuba with respect to the quantity of cases filed for wrongful enslavement at the international level, it could boast of endurance. Lasting from 1851

Table 46.4   Sample of Petitioners for Large-Scale Introductions, 1847

Municipality (Puerto Rico)	Petitioner	Maximum No. of Slaves Requested	Source	Motive Given
Guayama	Isabel Batable de Romano	21	St. Thomas	Sugar production
	Juan Bentejead	20	Curaçao	Sugar production
	Antonio Canales	50	Curaçao	Turned from sea transport to agriculture
	Juan Luis Ramís	12	Any island	Factory work
	Francisco Luis Ramírez	12	Any island	Sugar production
	Constantino Souteyran	10	St. Thomas	Sugar production
	Jean Toubert	26	Curaçao	Sugar production
San Germán	Luisa Belvis	30	Curaçao	Last year's petitions not acted on
	José Manchaní & F. de Silva	20	Curaçao	Sugar production
	Narcisco Pujois	30	Curaçao	Sugar production
	José Romagnera	50	Curaçao	Sugar production
	José Saldaña	30	Curaçao	Slave decreases due to illness
Cabo Rojo/ Mayaqüez	Beltrán Sant Laurent	15	Curaçao	Coffee and sugar
	Nicholás Más	50	Curaçao	Sugar production
	Mariano Antonio Ponce de León	40	Curaçao	No response to earlier petition
	James Byron	30	Curaçao	Coffee and sugar
Vega Baja	Casimiro Capetillo	15	Curaçao or St. Thomas	Sugar production
Naguabo	Tito Patxot Gurnach	25	Curaçao	Debt collection: slaves in lieu of cash
	Marino Joaquín Polo	50	Any Dutch island	Sugar production
Humacao	José María Ríos	50	St. Thomas	Sugar production
	Achilles Stuart	20	St. Thomas	Debt collection: slaves in lieu of cash
	Juan López de Alicea	20	any island	Sugar: slaves for new hydraulics complex

Source: Same as Table 46.1.

to 1856, Mary Gordon's case broke the longevity record for claims of this sort. Born free in British St. Kitts of a free-born father and a legally manumitted mother, Gordon was kidnapped in 1811 at age ten while bathing with playmates at Pump Bay, in the district of Sandy Point, St. Anne's Parish. She was carried off by Francisco Monge, the Venezuelan captain of a vessel that had

Table 46.5   Foreign-born Slaves in Three Municipalities, 1872 (Puerto Rico)

Origin	Guayama	Mayagüez	Ponce
African	502 (31.5%)	385 (41.4%)	262 (26.6%)
Danish:			
St. Thomas	5	14	2
St. Croix	0	1	0
Unknown	2	1	0
Total:	7 (71.4%)	16 (87.5%)	2 (50.0%)
Dutch:			
Curaçao	19	94	10
St. Maarten	3	0	0
Unknown	1	6	0
Total:	23 (82.6%)	100 (86.0%)	10 (80.0%)
French:			
Guadaloupe	3	2	0
Martinique	0	2	1
St. Barthélemy	2	3	1
Unknown	3	2	1
Total:	8 (100%)	9 (57.5%)	3 (66.6%)
British:			
Anguilla	1	0	0
Unknown	0	2	0
Total:	1 (100%)	2 (100%)	0 (00.0%)
Totals:	541	514	277

(%) = Percentage of Women

Omitted : Cuba–1, Portuguese Macao–1, and Venezuela–12

Source: Registro Central de Esclavos de Puerto Rico, 1872 National Archives, Washington, D.C. (microfilm)

docked at Pump Bay's bleak and desolate shore to sell citrus fruits. He took her to St. Thomas, where Danish merchant Samuel Hokeb sold her to Antonio Guadalupe Colón of Caguas, a municipality in central eastern Puerto Rico.[53]

There were undeniable cases of the kidnapping of free black British subjects for enslavement in Cuba, mainly from Jamaica, but also from the Bahamas, and the intermittent Anglophone littoral of Upper Guinea. Mary Gordon's case differed not only because it was isolated in both time and place; patterns in Cuba point to the abduction of young men explicitly for enslavement on sugar plantations. Her plight also differed from that of black British subjects enslaved in Puerto Rico in the 1830s. They like the majority of Anglophone slaves found in Cuba throughout the 1840s and 1850s, were the slaves of British subjects who moved to a Spanish dominion, or slaves sold from a British to a Spanish

dominion prior to abolition in 1834. Three factors form the basis of singularity in this case. First, shelving the viable possibility of pedophilia as one of several motives for kidnapping, Gordon's market value was more potential than real at the age of captivity. Second, her haphazard capture and reduction to slavery formed no part of a larger organized design, though Consul Lindegren, without an ounce of proof, said it did. Third. She was unequivocally freeborn.[54]

Early in 1851, Governor Juan de la Pezuela visited Caguas as part of routine island-wide tour. Mary took advantage of his visit by appealing directly to him for help. She based her grievance on excessive physical abuse and wrongful enslavement. Finding multiple lacerations on her limbs, and discovering irregularities in the ownership papers, Pezuela had Antonio Colón investigated, and authorized Mary's placement in the

Casa de Beneficencia. The governor and his wife provided her with pocket money.[55]

Under the auspices of the Síndico Protector de Esclavos a suit was initiated. Like many before her, and many to follow, Mary found the proceedings lengthy and ineffective. Moreover, she discovered that her master had begun selling her children and grandchildren. This time her efforts to seek Pezuela's intervention were futile; he had accepted the Queen's commission to govern Cuba.[56] However, when Gordon learned that Britain had a consul in San Juan, she solicited his aid. Of their first meeting, Lindegren wrote:

From the very particular account she gave of herself and speaking English so well after so long an absence, I find myself bound to render her all the assistance I could, and stating her case to the governor, I claimed the freedom of herself as well as her children . . . and grandchildren, all of whom are equally entitled to their freedom.[57]

Bypassing public defenders, the consul retained the private services of Estéban Calderón who, by authority of the interim governor, placed a lien on Colón's estate to stop him from selling more of the children. Margarita and her daughter, María Ignacia, were already sold to Miguel Saron of Caguas; and Juana María was sold to Juan Plá in Río Piedras. With the injunction, Juan de la Cruz and Gertrudis with her children, Genaro and Clemencia, joined Mary at the Casa.[58] Lindegren handled most of the international particulars. He requested Mary's baptismal record from St. Kitts, and depositions from people who knew her as a child. Networking in St. Thomas, he secured modest evidence that the Danish bill of sale was either forged or filled out incorrectly and therefore, void. Calderón obtained permission for Mary to go to St. Thomas to find anyone who might remember her, Monge, or Hokeb. In San Juan, he also discovered an ageing British subject who recalled her childhood in Sandy Point.[59]

Proofs to verify Gordon's free-born identity were overwhelming, but the Puerto Rican Audiencia Territorial ruled against her repeatedly, as did the lower courts before it. Many factors worked against the plaintiff. Estéban Calderón, Mary's primary lawyer, died mid-trial, and possibly because of nervousness, the defendant's lawyer was able to lead her into verbal traps. Colón bribed witnesses to testify that she agreed to go with Monge on the promise of money and jewelry. When the judges learned of the perjuries, they were indifferent. Lindegren's urgent, pushy style probably annoyed colonial bureaucrats in St. Kitts, who proved to be less cooperative than they could have been. Moreover, parochial record-keeping in early nineteenth century St. Kitts was disorganized and sometimes non-existent. Lindegren erred in his description of the St. Thomas-based lawyer he retained as "Danish America's cleverest advocate." The barrister's understanding of key aspects of Danish slave laws and Danish slave classifications according to sex, age, and occupation were not only inadequate, his interpretation of these laws and his translations of descriptive slave labels made no sense. The high court must have recognised the severity of his shortcomings. It is also noteworthy that Pezuela was the island's first abolitionist governor. As both governor and captain general of Puerto Rico, he was also president of the territorial appellate court; the final decision for almost all juridical processes rested in his hands alone. Had he remained in Puerto Rico, Mary would have won the case, and easily so. But his replacement followed a different brand of abolitionism: Norzagaray loathed the African slave trade, but he was in less of a hurry than his predecessor to end slavery itself. Furthermore, most of his administrative energy was spent in failed efforts to stop the interstate slave trade from Puerto Rico to Cuba. Nothing short of a royal directive from Madrid would have convinced him to free Mary Gordon.

In most respects, Lindegren went beyond the call of duty in the Gordon case, but a David Turnbull he was not. To liberate British subjects enslaved in foreign countries, Turnbull and others sometimes stretched their diplomatic responsibilities to the point of illegal maneuvering, especially when they found themselves restricted under the direction of Lord Aberdeen. Lindegren, however, would not allow his passionate outrage to exceed the limits of the law. Exhausted from litigation Antonio Colon expressed his willingness to sell Mary to him. Instead of seizing the moment, as other British consuls had done in identical situations elsewhere, he took umbrage.[60] He also considered Norzagaray's unusual suggestion that the case be moved to Spain, to be heard by the ancient High Court of Grace and Justice (Audiencia de Gracia y Justicia).[61] The governor's advice was rather disingenuous, for he must have known that Gordon's case lay outside metropolitan jurisprudence. Nearly two decades earlier, Spain had abolished slavery within its contiguous borders.

We will never know if any force might have compelled Lindegren to break Spanish law by helping Mary escape, or to break British law by purchasing her. What is certain is that she lost a true champion when he died in early 1855. In Madrid, throughout the summer of that year, there were blistering diplomatic exchanges between Ambassador Otway and Minister Zavala over the plight of the Gordon family. After Otway summarized the case, he declared it to be analogous to the case of Mary Ann in Cuba. After comparing both cases, and criticizing the actions of the late consul, Zavala observed that the governor of Cuba freed Mary Ann as

.. an act of friendship and mere favour . . . not founded on legal reasons or considerations of any kind . . . It could not be referred to, in the future, as a precedent for reclamations of the same kind. Because Doña Aurora Rossi was the possessor in legitimate right of the slave Mary Ann, 438 hard dollars [pesos fuertes] were paid to her by the treasury as indemnification for compelling her to grant the letter of freedom.[62]

Ardour and eloquence are standard styles of dissent in the antislave trade correspondence of Governor Norzagaray. But in support of a slave system he purported to despise, he curtly dismissed Mary Gordon as, ". . . una mujer sin historia." The case closed in early 1856, when Charles Lindegren requested reimbursement for money his father spent in defence of . . . a woman without history.[63] Gordon was not alone. *Partus sequitur ventrem* denied historical accountability to all slave mothers. Their bodies sealed their bondage. By law, slave women who reproduced confirmed the perpetuity of their enslavement.

Conclusion

It would seem that the Kelsall wives stood less chance of gaining their freedom than the middle-aged litigants who followed them, for in addition to bearing many children – of whom females slightly outnumbered males – they were still of childbearing age at the time of their proceedings. The other plaintiffs were post-menopausal and were the mothers of sons, Furthermore, their emancipation represented minimal loss because none served in the plantation sector. Nancy, for

example was partially blind, yet until her death, her case was as inconclusive as those of the Kelsall wives. Betsy's individual freedom was a hollow victory because it was unresolved, and as such, her sons remained in bondage. While the Spanish government usually cited its support for slaveholding defendants on the grounds of proprietor sovereignty, Mary Ann's case is the only instance where property status proved to be the real issue. By comparison, local Cuban courts recognized Charlotte's case as hardly worth the effort. The status of a slave as chattel was no small argument, for wherever bondage was contested on legal grounds in the Americas, the defendant's proof of ownership almost always resulted in judgement against the plaintiff.[64] British officials in London, Madrid, Havana, and Santiago concurred that the cases of Mary Ann and Charlotte were one and the same. Cuban and metropolitan authorities were quick to point out that they were not, for lack of evidence to verify that Charlotte was owned legally by a Spanish subject or a legal Spanish resident. Yet both women were manumitted. Plassy Laurence's escape marked a turning point. It demonstrated that by the early 1850s British diplomats were willing to bypass dilatory Spanish jurisprudence by aiding and abetting flight. Though the Laurence case was one of the last of its kind in Cuba, Spanish bureaucrats feared that its resolution could set a disastrous precedent vis-à-vis the Gordon case in Puerto Rico. Other factors, however, contributed equally in the decision against Mary and her family.

With the spectacular exception of the African slave ship *Majesty* in 1859, and a few minor reports before, by 1848 Puerto Rico had ceased to import slaves from any source.[65] In that year, slavery was abolished in French and Danish islands, thereby officially cutting off Puerto Rico's access to a small number of non-Hispanic Caribbean-born slaves and, until 1835, a larger number of African-born slaves. From 1830 to 1848, as active conspirators in slave acquisitions for Puerto Rico, Danish merchants and independent renegade Frenchmen played roles that ranged from minor to inconsequential. Dutch complicity lasted longer, and the forces that motivated its cessation were more complex. If it is certain that African rather that Caribbean provenance dominated Dutch brokerage in the large scale slave introductions of 1847, then Dutch succour was destined to end by 1848, along with that of the French and Danish. Indeed Africa helps explain the suspicious gaps between the end of Dutch-assisted slave acquisitions for Puerto Rico in late 1847 and the abolition of Dutch Caribbean slavery in 1863. Though the Netherlands was the last non-Hispanic imperial power to end slavery in the Caribbean, for some time it had given serious attention to the prospects of selling its property leases on the Gold Coast to Britain. The two nations reached an agreement in 1850.[66] This transaction practically invalidated any pretext for the presence of Dutch ships anywhere along the West African littoral, even for legitimate commerce, in view of Dutch colonialism in Southeast Asia. Therefore, by mid-century, Dutch links to slave acquisitions for Puerto Rico were cut off.[67]

Spanish cabotage commerce was an additional factor in Mary Gordon's defeat. Beginning in 1841, but more specifically between 1848 and 1873, there were recurrent outflows of slave traffic from Puerto Rico to Cuba. Figures for this trade have never been tabulated, and in all likelihood, they never will be. What is known is that by 1852, Cuba had received at least a thousand slaves – mainly Creoles – from its sister island, and that such relocations continued in mercurial spurts until slavery was abolished in Puerto Rico. Unsuccessfully attempting to counter the efforts of local and transient slave merchants now catering to the higher prices of Cuban markets, a small number of Puerto Rican antislavists (mainly in exile) united briefly with larger numbers of local proslavists (mainly sugar producers) in an emotion-charged *cause celebre* led by the Governor Norzagaray himself.[68]

In view of the fact that Cuba continued to import slaves directly from West Africa and Mozambique up to some unknown date in the 1870s, or possibly beyond, the diplomatic inertia for the liberation of several thousand black British subjects – along with new ideals of multiracial British patriotism – had diminished a great deal by the 1850s. By this time, Puerto Rico had greater reason than Cuba to resist the legal claims of British slaves. It had a much smaller slave population, never exceeding 52,000; the influx of slaves was nearly terminated; and, to be sure, more slave traffic flowed outward (against the wishes of the slaveholding class) than inward. Of all the slave women discussed, Mary Gordon was the only bona fide free-born litigant. But with a teen-age son close to the age of field labour, and three daughters of child-bearing age – two of whom were already the mothers of two daughters and a son – Mary's continued bondage was crucial for the fiscal and political stability of slavery. Had circumstances permitted her to file for wrongful enslavement some years earlier, chances for a verdict in her favour would have been slim. But by the early 1850s, it was impossible. Her victory would have encouraged other Anglophone slaves in Puerto Rico – and, at that time, there were still many from the 1830s – to sue for their freedom. Ever-sensitive to precedent, Spanish officialdom in San Juan and Madrid could not afford to let her go.

For slave men, the link to maternity remains important. For all the arguments of market value and owner nationality, elderly Mary Ann and Charlotte were freed precisely because they had no children. While the motives that stimulated the carefully orchestrated defeat of Mary Gordon and the Kelsall wives are obvious, ultimately the cases of Betsy and Nancy followed the same line of reasoning. Even in the absence of female off-spring, they bore the symbols of *partus sequitur ventrem*. The liberation of these two women would have contributed not only to the loss of four very expensive young adult male slaves, but the loss of potential slave children as well. Following the geographic requisite for profitable, labour intensive production, most sugar plantations were isolated and relatively self-sufficient entities. Slave men labouring under such conditions had little opportunity to form social relations with free women. In other words, slave men usually fathered children with slave women in nineteenth century Cuba and Puerto Rico.

The British abolitionist movement politicized and internationalized the matricentric concerns of Spanish colonial law. It did so, however, inadvertently. In fact it was so inadvertent that it rendered itself useless. The internationalization of womb-oriented politics was connected at once to the silence of Spanish victory and the silence of British default. In essence, *partus sequitur ventrem* became a diplomatic weapon that Spain deployed frequently and namelessly by stealth. In this international war of nerves, Britain not only misread Spain's silence as an underestimation of womb-oriented politics, it imitated it. The imitation was facilitated by a new era of Victorian patriarchy. Western genderization processes operated from traditional assumptions of female inferiority. Race – and class, to lesser degrees in this regard – determined what kinds of women merited social and legal protection because of their natural weakness, and what kinds of women did not. Prior to the Victorian Age, white women could not bear slave children. The old order protected them from the endemic brutality of slavery with social concepts that quickly produced the promulgated support of legal disassociation. The new order stipulated that the natural inferiority of women remain bifurcated along the lines of race. Decreasing the theoretical distance between the rising conceptual uniformity of European colonialism in Africa (despite future proclamations of British "association" and French "assimilation," along with the latter's extension, or inspiration, Portuguese "tropicalism"), and the ever-fragmented politics of Euro-American antislavism (radicalism, gradualism, repatriatism, bourgeois feminism, Catholic papal "pecadism," and Protestant fundamentalism), the mediation of Victorian thought deemed black women yet unworthy of protection. Therefore, Great Britain's silence vis-à-vis *partus sequitur ventrem* represented a sociopolitical lien of continuity between the old order and the new. In other words, the authors of British foreign policy and diplomacy failed to recognize the strength of *partus sequitur ventrem* as an abolitionist tool because of the on-going interference from their own cultural convictions of patriarchy. Nothing better illustrates this point than a perusal of documents that illustrate the treatment of ex-slave women in the British Caribbean, particularly in the context of interracial sexual abuse during and after the apprenticeship period. The juridical outcomes of these women's efforts to reconstruct their identity as free subjects is most telling.[69]

In theory, the slave's right to legal protest arose from the slaveholder's need to buffer the stress of rigid social control. This was achieved by relaxing the definition of slave property as absolute property. However, when slave suits included claims for liberty, the plaintiffs, as units of labour-power, were perceived exclusively as marketable commodities, with specific characteristics that increased or decreased their value.[70] Legislation in American slave-based economies was never designed to compromise the established order of master-slave relations. Under the strain of abolitionism, juridical institutions reaffirmed the doctrine of absolute ownership. During the most tumultuous decades of the abolitionist era, black British subjects in the Spanish Caribbean exposed the futility of slave rights in Latin America. In addition, their quest for freedom further demonstrated the difficult role of foreign diplomacy as a referee between sovereignty and international law. In the thick of these contretemps, the Spanish imperial bureaucracy expanded the matrifocal function of *partus sequitur ventrem* from its juridical centre, as a slaveocratic safety device, to its international frontier, as a counter-abolitionist offensive. As a diplomatic device, nuanced perhaps by the confidence of its internal longevity, it compounded the exploitability of slave women, less by denying their humanity than by subverting their natural hegemony in the physiological realm of historical accountability. Such was the power and frequency of its whispered voice that it ultimately tempered the destruction of slavery with its continuity.

Notes

The author wishes to thank Janet Evelyn-Dorsey, Franklin Knight, Robert Paquette and the anonymous reader of the **Journal of Caribbean History** *for their suggestions and comments on earlier drafts of this article. All translations from the original Spanish in archival sources are by the author.*

1. On *partus sequitur ventrem* in different slave societies over time, see Orlando Patterson, *Slavery and Social Death* (Cambridge: Harvard, 1982), 132-147. For the British Caribbean, see B. W. Higman, *Slave Populations in the British Caribbean, 1807-1834* (Baltimore: Johns Hopkins, 1984), 147-148, and his *Slave Population and Economy in Jamaica, 1807-1834* (Cambridge: University Press, 1976), 139-140. For political comparisons of slavery in Cuba and Puerto Rico see Arthur Corwin, *Spain and the Abolition of Slavery in Cuba, 1817-1886* (Austin: University of Texas, 1967) and Franklin Knight, *Slave Society in Cuba during the Nineteenth Century* (Madison: University of Wisconsin, 1970). For the political economy of slavery in the context of municipal divisions, see Laird Bergad, *Cuban Rural Society in the Nineteenth Century* (Princeton: University Press, 1990) and Francisco Scarano, *Sugar and Slavery in Puerto Rico: The Plantation Economy of Ponce, 1800-1850* (Madison: University of Wisconsin, 1984). For general studies, see Luis M. Díaz

Soler, *Historia de la esclavitud negra en Puerto Rico* (Río Piedras: Editorial Universitaria. 1970) and Levi Marrero, *Cuba: economía y sociedad* (Madrid: Editorial Playor, 1972), v.11. For discussions and illustrations of slave occupations in the Caribbean, see Higman (1984); Benjamnín Nistal Moret, "Problems in the Social Structure of Slavery in Puerto Rico during the Process of Abolition," in Manuel Moreno Fraginals, et al., eds. *Between Slavery and Free Labor: The Spanish-Speaking Caribbean in the Nineteenth Century* (Baltimore: Johns Hopkins, 1985) 141-157; and Rebecca Scott, *Slave Emancipation in Cuba: The Transition to Free Labor, 1860-1899* (Princeton: University Press, 1985).

2. On impossible sisterhood between female slaves and female members of slaveholding classes, see Elizabeth Fox-Genovese, *Within the Plantation Household: Black Women and White Women in the Old South* (Chapel Hill: University of North Carolina, 1988) and Gerda Lerner, *The Creation of Patriarchy* (New York: Oxford, 1986). For the most recent assessment of Gómez de Avellaneda as an abolitionist novelist, see Lorna Williams, *The Representation of Slavery in Cuban Fiction* (Columbia: University of Missouri 1994).

3. See Higman (1976 and 1984), Nistal Moret, and Scarano for occupational differentiation according to sex. Also see David Barry Gaspar, *Bondmen and Rebels: A Study of Master-Slave Relations in Antigua* (Baltimore: Johns Hopkins, 1985), 97-107. For a comprehensive examination of slave labour differentiations in the United States, see Robert Fogel, *Without Consent or Contract: The Rise and Fall of American Slavery* (New York: Knopf, 1975),45-52.

4. Sociologist-historian Gilberto Freyre first shared this popular Brazilian proverb with Anglophone audiences in the translation of his *The Masters and the Slaves: A Study of the Development of Brazilian Civilization* (New York: Knopf, 1946). Reflecting Freyre's defunct theory of Luso-Brazilian tropicalism, this nonsensical refrain has roots as much in the antislavery novels of the United States as in their Latin American counterparts.

5. For discussions of rape and concubinage, see Hilary Beckles, *Natural Rebels: A Social History of Enslaved Black Women in Barbados* (New Brunswick, NJ: Rutgers University,1989); Angela Davis, *Women, Race, and Class* (New York: Vintage, 1983); Gloria Hull, et al., eds., *But Some of Us Are Brave* (Old Westbury, NY: Feminist Press, 1982); Mary Karasch, *Slave Life in Rio de Janeiro, 1808-1850* (Princeton: University Press, 1987); and Marietta Morrissey, *Slave Women in the New World: Gender Stratification in the Caribbean* (Lawrence, Kansas: University of Kansas, 1989). On interpersonal relations among slave women in the United States, see Debra Grey White's *Arn't I a Woman? Female Slaves in the Old South* (New York: Norton, 1985). On acquiescence as a form of resistance, see the case of María Balbina, discussed briefly in this paper. Also see Jean Fagan Yellin, "The Text and Contexts of Harriet Jacobs' *Incidents in the Life of a Slave Girl,"* in Henry Gates, Jr. and Charles Davis. eds., *The Slave's Narrative* (New York: Oxford, 1985), and Valerie Smith, "Loopholes of Retreat: Architecture and Ideology in Harriet Jacobs' *Incidents in the Life of a Slave Girl,"* in Henry Gates, Jr., *Reading Black, Reading Feminist: A Critical Anthology* (New York: Meridan, 1990). For modest references to slavery and male homosexuality, see Miguel Barnet, ed., *Biografía de un cimarrón* (Havana: Academia de Ciencias de Cuba, 1966); Manuel Moreno Fraginals, "Africa in Cuba: A Quantitative Analysis of the African Population of the Island of Cuba" in Vera Rubin and Arthur Tuden, eds., *Comparative Perspectives on Slavery in the New World Plantation Societies* (New York: Academy of Sciences, 1977), and Antonio Zambrana, *El negro Francisco* (Havana: P. Fernáindez. (1951). For slavery, prostitution, and STD, see Robert Conrad, ed., *Children of God's Fire: A Documentary History of Black Slavery in Brazil* (Princeton: University Press, 1983). Without negating the possibility of prostitution in the history of slavery in the United States, Herbert Gutman and Richard Sutch disqualify the evidence thus far presented in "Victorians All?" in Paul David, et al., eds. *Reckoning with Slavery* (New York: Oxford,1976). For manumission patterns, see David Cohen and Jack Greene, eds., *Neither Slave nor Free: Freedmen of African Descent in the Slave Societies of the New World* (Baltimore: Johns Hopkins, 1972), 7-8, 31-32, and 58.

6. The historical literature on militant slave resistance is copious. For hemispheric perspectives, see Richard Price, ed., *Maroon Societies* (Garden City NJ: Anchor, 1973). Also see Eugene Genovese, *From Rebellion to Revolution* (New York: Vintage, 1979). For radical antislavist activity among free black people, see Robert Paquette, *Sugar is Made with Blood* (Middletown CN: Wesleyan University Press, 1988).

7. For summaries of Spanish Caribbean slave codes, see Knight, 131-132 and Guillermo Baralt, *Esclavos rebeldes: en Puerto Rico* (Río Piedras, Ediciones Huracán), 67-72. For slave codes promulgated elsewhere in the Americas, see Cohen and Greene.

8. This oft-repeated and paraphrased quote comes from a review of Charles Boxer's *Race Relations in the Portuguese Colonial Empire, 1415-1825* (New York: Oxford, 1963). On visits to Puerto Rican slave plantations, see Archivo Histórico Nacional, Madrid, Gobierno: Puerto Rico, legajo 5065/12. Hereafter, AHN, GPR, and leg.

9. Díaz Soler, 190-195.

10. Patterson, 8.

11. Baralt, 140,

12. Benjamín Nistal Moret, ed., *Esclavos prófugos y cimarrones de Puerto Rico, 1770-1870* (Río Piedras: Editorial Universitaria, 1984), 201-203. Considering that María Balbina was entrusted to the care of the intrepid abolitionist, Julio Vizcarrondo y Coronado, her marronage was probably encouraged, if not assisted. For Vizcarrondo, founder of the first Hispanophone abolitionist society, and the influence of his Quaker spouse, Harriet Brewster, see, Corwin 151-

159. For the most recent study of slave women and the ambiguities of sexual negotiation and consent, see Melton McLaurin, *Celia, a Slave Girl* (New York: Avon, 1991).

13. Nistal Moret, *Esclavos*, 201.

14. A.I.R. Russell-Wood, *The Black Man in Slavery and in Freedom in Colonial Brazil* (New York: St. Martin, 1982), 151 and 172-173.

15. Conrad, 274-281.

16. Jesús Lalinde Abadía, *La administración española en el siglo XIX puertorriqueño* (Seville: Escuela de Estudios Hispanoamericanos de Sevilla, 1980), 35-38.

17. Discussions of the Moret Law are found in Díaz Soler, 306-315, Knight, 171-174, Corwin, chapters 13-16, passim, Scott, chapters 34, and Nistal Moret in Moreno Fraginals, et al.

18. A welcomed exception to the dearth is Nistal Moret's compilation, "Catorce querellas de esclavos de Manatí 1869-1873," in *Sin Nombre* (VI:2, 1973), 78-100. It includes four lawsuits initiated by slave women.

19. On slavermaster negation of slave paternity, see Nistal] Moret, "Catorce querellas." On slave suits resulting from slaveholder violations of the Moret Law, see Arturo Morales Carrión, ed., *El processe abolicionista en Puerto Rico; Documentos para su estudio* v. 11., 235-240. On Manuela Celiz, Archivo General de Puerto Rico, Gobeadores Espaloles: Comercio, caja 222, 1859. Hereafter, AGPR, GE: C. On Gabriela Arencibla, AHN Ultrarmar, leg. 4763/288, 1880. Hereafter, AHN, U. Also see Don Fehrenbacher, *The Dred Scott Case* (New York: Oxford, 1978) and James Walvin, "The Somerset Case," in *Black and White: The History of the Negro in England, 1555-1954* (London: Longmans, 1972).

20. Patterson, 17-22 and 28-32.

21. For French, Dutch, and Danish slavery and slave trading in the nineteenth century, see David Eltis and James Walvin, eds., *The Abolition of the Atlantic Slave Trade* (Madison: University of Wisconsin, 1981). Dutch St. Maarten abolished slavery in 1848 for fear of slave responses to the abolition of slavery on the French side of the island.

22. From 1848 onward, no governor of Puerto Rico issued "legal" permits for the introduction of slaves for the purpose of sale. The cessation would make future illegal introductions impossible.

23. AGPR, GE: C, caja 444,1847, and AHN, GPR, leg. 5076/24,1858.

24. AGPR. GE: C, caja 69, 1856-1859.

25. Neither the Danes nor the Dutch had consulates in Spanish colonial Puerto Rico.

26. English-speaking slaves first began to appear in Puerto Rico in groups in 1834. See Table 46.2.

27. Great Britain, *Parliamentary Papers, Slave Trade Series*, Lindegren to Palmerston, May 25, 1847. On the consolidation of Spanish Caribbean slave trading policy, see the author's forthcoming "Puerto Rico and the Cabotage Slave Trade to Cuba, 1848-1873," in *Slavery and Abolition*. It is common knowledge that the voluminous *Parliamentary Papers* on the slave trade constitute no more than a fraction of the origi-

nal correspondence for the same theme, in the Foreign Office series 84 (hereafter, PP and FO 94), in the Public Record Office of London (Kew). While both sources are used in this essay, the author relies on FO references only in instances where their greater volume enhances the scope of the cases discussed.

28. See, for example, PP, Palmerston to Wynn, December 12,1835; Rendall to Aberdeen, December 24, 1841; and Schenley to Aberdeen, July 15, 1842.

29. For Holguín, see Cuffee Kelsall's petition, Ibid, in Palmerston to Bulwer, August 14, 1847, second enclosure.

30. The act of 1825, which nullified the act of 1805-1806, applied only to British subjects attempting to remove British slaves from British possessions. It did not protect slaves removed by resident or transient foreigners. See FO 84-965, Lindegren to Ward, April 4, 1854. Furthermore, consular authorities initially underestimated the enormity of the influx. "I do not think it likely, however, that such kidnapped negroes, unless introduced long ago, will be found in Cuba; for the authorities [in Cuba], though tolerant enough in receiving bozales [newly arrived, non-westernized Africans], they are dreadfully apprehensive of the effects in the island of the coloured people [free blacks), who have imbibed notions of freedom. . . ." PP, Tolme to Palmerston, September 11, 1838.

31. Richard R. Madden, *Memoirs* (London: Ward and Downey, 1891); David R. Murray, "Richard R. Madden. . Abolitionist", *Studies* 61 (Spring 1972), 41-53; and Philip Curtin, ed., *Africa Remembered: Narratives by West Africans from the Era of the Slave Trade* (Madison: University of Wisconsin, 1967).

32. On this issue, Palmerston sent frequent reminders to British diplomats worldwide. For Cuba, see PP. Crawford to Palmerston, December 31. 1948. For Puerto Rico, Lindegren to Palmerston, January 22, 1849.

33. There is no biography of Turnbull. For his abolitionist activity prior to succeeding Madden as Superintendent of Liberated Africans, see his *Travels to the West: Cuba, with Notices of Puerto Rico and the Slave Trade* (London: Longman, 1840) For his controversial tenure in Cuba, see Paquette, *Sugar is Made with Blood*, and David R. Murray, *Odious Commerce: Great Britain, Spain, and the Abolition of the Cuban Slave Trade* (Cambridge: University Press, 1980).

34. To a lesser extent, the same chicanery was practised in Puerto Rico. See AGPR, GE, Esclavos, caja 66, "La consignación de los negros del *Majesty,*" 1859.

35. PP, Tolme to Palmerston, December 17, 1839; Turnbull to Palmerston, December 27, 1840; Turnbull to Aberdeen, January 31, 1842; Turnbull to Palmerston, May 17, 1841; and Aberdeen to Crawford, February 1, 1843. In Cuba, Ledamaux was called Antonio Ledesma, a Spanish subject. García, however. turned out to be Pierre Garcie, a Frenchmen.

36. In the Spanish Caribbean for most of the nineteenth century, with the exception of Santiago de Cuba, the offices of governor, captain general, and president of the high court of appeals were one and the same, that is, one man held all three positions simultaneously. Knight and Corwin provide extensive discussions on the relationship between the continuity of the external slave trade and the captaincy general of Cuba. For Puerto Rico, see Arturo Morales Carrión, *Auge y decadencia de la trata negrera a Puerto Rico, 1820-1860* (San Juan: Centro de Estudios Avanzados de Puerto Rico y el Caribe and Instituto de Cultura Puertorriqueña, 1978). On Aberdeen's abolitionism vis-à-vis African and British slaves, see PP, Aberdeen to Turnbull, February 9, 1842, along with the critical analysis by Johnson Asiegbu, *Slavery and the Politics of Liberation 1787-1861: A Study of Liberated African Emigration and British Antislavery Policy* (London: Longman and Green, 1969).

37. Anglophone West African Creoles, who found themselves enslaved in Cuba, were especially concerned about having to return once they were freed. They ran the risk of reenslavement and transshipment back to the Americas. See PP, Tolme to Palmerston, July 16, 1840.

38. PP, v. 26, 41 and 43-46; v. 28, 98-105; v. 32, Class B. 233-235 and Class A, 233-236; and v. 33, 37-60, especially 47-48 and 50-53.

39. Eve was probably detained to prevent riotous responses from sympathetic on-lookers. Crowds witnessing the separation of slave families or cabotage slave sales were known to exhibit violent collective behaviour in favour of the slaves. See the case of Gregoria and her children in Morales Carrión, ed., *Proceso abolicionista*, v. 1.

40. PP, v. 36, 308-322 and v. 39, 368-378.

41. Ibid. Forbes to Palmerston, February 2, 1849.

42. Ibid, Forbes to MacCrohon, May 28, 1848.

43. Ibid. Palmerston to Forbes, February 6, 1850.

44. Ibid. v. 38, 363-369 and 378-382.

45. Ibid. v. 23, 49-52 and v. 30, 121-122 and 126-130.

46. The failure of the British Consulate to act on behalf of Enrique's Emancipation – for the presence of all African slaves landed in Cuba after 1821 was illegal – is probably linked to Turnbull's double expulsion from the island, and the subsequent wholesale slaughter of Cuban blacks that followed.

47. PP, v. 39, 249-326, 336-340, and 361-362.

48. Ibid. Alcoy to Kennedy, November 26, 1849 and Palmerston to Kennedy, December 30,1849.

49. Courthouse of Nevis, Charlestown, Books of Common Record: v. 2, 1819-1825; v.4, 1830-1834; and v. 5, 1835-1842. For patterns of apprenticeship in St. Kitts as well as Nevis, see Higman (1984). On protests among women apprentices in St. Kitts, see Barbara Bush, *Slave Women in Caribbean Society, 1650-1838* (Bloomington: University of Indiana. 1990).

50. PP, Crawford to Clarendon, April 26, 1853.

51. Ibid. Crawford to Palmerston, September 3. 1847.

52. For Arístegui's true feelings about Lindegren, see AHN, GPR 5065/19.

53. For Colón's planter-class pedigree, see Oscar Bunker, *Historia de Caguas* (Caguas, Puerto Rico: Bunker, 1975) For examples of his activities as a member of town council of Caguas, see AHN, GPR 5064/10 and 5107/18.

54. Unless Lindegren referred to the presence of St. Kitts-born slaves in Puerto Rico in the 1830s, before his arrival as consul, he erred in his assertion of slave acquisition through kidnapping from the British islands after 1838. After that year, the problem persisted between Montego Bay and Santiago de Cuba. Puerto Rico, however, was not involved.

55. PP, Lindegren to Clarendon, October 18, 1854. Pezuela's concern for Mary seemed genuine. He ordered Colón to his palace and subjected him to a rather scathing tirade which began, "How dare you treat a free women in this manner!" Elsewhere the present writer has questioned the effectiveness of Pezuela's abolitionism in Puerto Rico: See note 27. Regarding the Gordon case specifically, one wonders why he left Puerto Rico without mentioning the problem in his instructions to his successor. See Archivo del Ministerio de Asuntos Exteriores, Madrid, Ultramar y Colonias, leg. 2966. Hereafter, AMAE, UC.

56. PP, Lindegren to Clarendon, October 18, 1854.

57. Ibid.

58. Ibid.

59. Ibid. Kittitian responses included depositions from Mary's playmates, who managed to escape abduction. Their statements suggest deep feelings of guilt. Out of fear, they remained hidden for hours after the vessel departed. The abduction occurred in the morning; authorities were not notified until late in the afternoon.

60. Ibid., Lindegren to Clarendon, December 13, 1854; FO 84-935, Lindegren to an unnamed informant, February 13, 1854; and FO 84- 935, Lindegren to Ward, April 24, 1854. For Kittitian record-keeping problems, see Richard Frucht, "From Slavery to Unfreedom," in Rubin and Tuden, eds., 379-389. When Aberdeen (Clarendon) expressed his unwillingness to authorize Consul Schenley to demand the liberation of John Claver, a Kittitian mulatto enslaved in Dutch Suriname, he purchased him, via an intermediary, for 505 guilders. PP, Aberdeen to Schenley, April 28, 1845.

61. In one of his last letters to the Foreign Office, the consul described the judges of the Puerto Rican High Court as unscrupulous. FO 84-964, Lindegren to Clarendon, February 10, 1855. In Spain all final decisions respecting colonial affairs rested in the hands of the Consejo Real and the Junta de Ultramar, not the Audiencia de Gracia y Justicia.

62. For the complete correspondence between Zavala and Otway, including directives from their superiors, as well summaries of Mary Gordon's testimony, see PP, v. 42, 343-351; AHN, Gracia y Justicia, Puerto Rico, 2044/19 and AMAE, UC, leg. 2966 and 2967.

63. FO 84-0988, Lindegren (fils) to the Lord Commissioners of Her Majesty's Treasury, March 15, 1856. The term "A woman without history" is cognatively exaggerated here. The more appropriate translation

for "una mujer sin historia," is "a woman without a proper account of herself," as Consul Lindegren stated correctly in his last letter to the Foreign Office. By explicated semantics, the two translations are identical.

64. For critical discussions of slaves as legal property in American slave-based economics, see Elizabeth Fox-Genovese and Eugene Genovese, *The Fruits of Merchant Capitalism: Slavery and Bourgeois Property* (New York: Oxford, 1983), 338-387.

65. The documentation for this memorable landing of 1,600 Bantu-speaking children is immense but largely unexploited. For summaries, see Díaz. Soler, 237-239 and Morales Carrión, 217-222. For detailed assessments, see Luis de la Rosa Martínez, "Los negros del brig-barca 'Majesty,'" (An unpublished manuscript submitted to the Centro de Estudios Avanzados de Puerto Rico y el Caribe, May 1982) and the present writer's "Puerto Rico and the Atlantic Slave Trade, 1815-1873" (Ph.D. dissertation, University of California Santa Barbara, 1989), 232-257.

66. PP, Colonies: West Africa, 1812-1874, v. 50, "Report on the Conditions of the Gold Coast," 458-463.

67. While British and Spanish archival sources support the position maintained here, that the large-scale (not small scale) influx of Dutch Caribbean slaves to Puerto Rico in 1847 was a revival of re-export methods popular in the 1820s, without source materials from The Hague and the municipal archives of Ponce, Guyama, and Mayaguez – where most of the slaves were landed-the author's posture remains theoretical.

68. Pezuela's odd support for the outflux was as formidable as Norzagaray's opposition to it. See all enclosures for AHN, GPR 5072/38.

69. See, for example, the case of "Patty, Negress versus William Paddar, Planter," Parish of St. John Figtree. Courthouse of Nevis, Books of Common Record, v. 1, March 10, 1836. Such adverse features of emancipation adaptation were not limited to Victorian cultures. It is likely they were as much in evidence in "Comptian cultures" (i.e., Francophone, Hispanophone, and Lusophone cultures) as well. See, "Isabel Carvalho Miranda, Serviçal, queixa-se do Dom António Simas, Patrão," Roça da Conceição, Provincia de São Tomé e Príncipe, Curadoria Geral de Serviçais, April 25, 1913. Arquivo Histórico Ultramarino, Lisbon Portugal. Unlike Michel Foucault and many others, nonetheless, the present author does not support the notion of Victorian thought as pervasive in the West. It would seem, for example, that in Latin America, southern Europe, and even France, its influence was limited haute-couture.

70. Fox-Genovese and Genovese, 338-340. For similar concerns, but in the context of master-slave interdependence and the law, see Patricia J. Williams, "On Being the Object of Property" in Micheline R. Malson, et al., *Black Women in America: Social Science Perspectives* (Chicago: University Press, 1988), 19-38.

47

White Women and Slavery in the Caribbean

HILARY McD. BECKLES

Caribbean historiography before the mid 1980s, unlike that of the United States, offers but whispers in response to the challenging call for major revisions to the traditional concepts and methodologies that have negated and marginalized the writing of women's history.[1] On the surface, it would appear that most Caribbean historians have displayed a surprising (or suspicious!) reluctance in adopting gender as an instrument of investigation and analysis. Interpretative inertia has resulted in the study of women's history being defined, or claimed, as a sort of 'minority' area – the special responsibility and reserve of feminist scholars. This condition, in turn, is used as part of an on-going effort to devalue feminist scholarship, and promote dissonance in relation to the dominant male-centred historiography.[2]

Fortunately, however, historians of slavery, feminist and otherwise, have succeeded in avoiding the conceptual pitfall inevitable in the perception of women as socially homogeneous. Rather, most have subjected women's experiences to investigation with respect to caste, class, race, colour and occupation. To date the primary focus of research (and this is reflected in the structure of the historiography) is the black woman, with the coloured woman running a competitive second, and the white woman trailing behind at a distance. Recently, for example, three major monographs on the subject of black women's enslavement were published, all of which addressed directly, and in detail, the experiences of the 'coloured' women, but paid little attention to the lives of white creole or European women. Scholarly articles and essays reflect a similar research bias.[3] By way of contrast, how-

ever, a major subject of post-war Caribbean historians has been the study of white males within the colonial enterprise. This work focuses primarily upon the politics and entrepreneurship of white males in shaping the Caribbean world, and suggests the insignificance of ideological, social and economic inputs from white women.

These research patterns and trends can be accounted for in three ways. First, they are endemic to an earlier imperialist scholarship that conceptually subsumed white women to their male counterparts in assessments of agricultural and mercantile activities and their corresponding colonial cultures. Studies of the rise and fall of the planter class in Caribbean societies, for instance, have not paid systematic attention to the planter's wife as a socio-economic agent. Ignored to an even greater extent is the white woman as owner of slaves, agricultural lands, and other forms of property. Second, historians and social anthropologists, inspired by considerations of cultural decolonization and nation building, targeted black women's history in search of general explanations for problems identified as resulting from the legacy of slavery; this included matters such as the perceived instability and matrifocality of the black family, and the role it played in shaping social life and community development. Third, emerging from both these types of scholarship is the notion of white women's relative unimportance to ideological formation within the history of the colonial complex.

The argument that Caribbean white women were of marginal historical importance in fashioning the colonial complex is striking when placed alongside interpretations found within the historiography of slavery in the southern United States.[4] Here, historians suggested that white women, particularly planters' wives, represented a kinder, gentler authority within the totalitarian power structure of the plantation. Some historians have gone further and argued that the plantation mistress was the unifying element within southern patriarchy. It is through her, according to this argument, that slaves were emotionally and socially integrated into the white household, rather than rejected and used primarily as natally alienated, disposable chattel. Against the ideological background of patriarchy, the southern plantation mistress, Morrissey states, came to consider herself 'the conscience' of society, while her Caribbean counterpart is conceived within the literature as a person who 'contributed little' and 'benefitted shamelessly from slave labour'.

Recently, this perception of the Caribbean white women received an important boost from the work of Barbara Bush. In discussing the socio-sexual manipulation and exploitations of all women by empowered white males, she produces a typology in which women's societal roles were defined by race and colour, and prescribed by the ideological weight of racism within the colonizing tradition. While Bush recognizes the privileges afforded white women within the slave system, many of which were predicated upon the subjection and brutalisation of non-white women, she seeks, nonetheless, to highlight the common ground where womanhood in general was the target and prey of white male patriarchal authority.[5]

Lucille Mair, pioneer in Caribbean feminist historiography, moreover, in outlining a framework for detailed historical research, reinforced the parasitic view of the white woman by stating that in Caribbean plantation society 'the black woman produced, the brown woman served, and the white woman consumed'.[6] Again, the diverse productive roles played by white women in the development and maintenance of the slave mode of production are peripheralized by the projection of an hegemonic, culturally moronic consumerism in which they were apparently imprisoned. Caribbean historiography, then, lacks a clearly articulated and empirically sound conceptualization of white women in their roles as pro-slavery agencies within the world made by the slave holders.

None of these approaches addresses adequately questions concerning, white women as economic actors, managers of slave-based households, and conduits in the process of socio-ideological transmission. As a result, the traditional conception of the slave owner as male remains unchallenged, and the socio-economic limit of patriarchy not identified. Nowhere is there to be found within the historiography, for instance, a systematic assessment of white women's autonomous roles as economic agents and positive participators in the formulation of pro-slavery values and institutions. Yet there is no shortage of documentary evidence to show white women as accumulators of property and profits through involvement on their own account in commercial and service activities, and as ideological enforcers within the social organization of slave society. The complex pattern of women's roles, in addition, should be understood in terms of the internal evolution of colonial society, particularly in relation to its patriarchal foundations.

In 1797, Moreau de Saint Méry noted, with respect to the eighteenth century developments in the French colony of St Domingue, that white women were initially the ideological victims of the male-centred colonization mission. He argued that they acquiesced under intense social pressure to support the institution of black slavery by managing the plantation household and projecting it to slaves as the centre of all legitimate power and justice .[7] In committing themselves to this socio-economic role, however, they emerged over time as critical parts of its internal logic, and became inseparable from its cultural legacy. At the centre of Saint Méry's argument is a conception of white women's removal from the process of production and integration into the plantation system at the level of reproduction as mothers and wives. This analysis runs along the same course as that by Pollack Petchesky, who suggests that women with a large investment in reproductive relations tend to exert a conservative influence on gender-role attitudes and in so doing become critical to the consolidation of patriarchal structures and ideologies.[8]

It would be consistent, therefore, following Saint Méry, to state that once white women's socio-economic interest had become linked to the reproduction of slavery, their consciousness and social behaviour would be fashioned by its social laws, customs, and culture. As a result, the sight of creole white women examining the genitals of male slaves in the markets before making purchases, which offended the sensibilities of some European travellers, should not be considered necessarily as evidence of social degeneration, but rather as a product of the dialectical relations between social and economic forces within the slave mode of production. Neither should such action be considered contrary to their roles as good mothers and wives within the plantation household. Rather, it suggests that white women were acting fully within the epistemological framework of slavery by ensuring that rational market choices were made. The slave plantation enterprise, it must be emphasized, was considered a principal expression of Renaissance rationality within the colonial realm.

It is important to recognize the contradictions inherent within the attempt of plantation patriarchs to import and impose elements of aristocratic and bourgeois domestic values upon the metamorphic creole culture of frontier civilization. These can be seen in their effort to insulate white women, as much as possible, from the aesthetically crudest aspects of slavery. They went about this by passing legislation and using specific aspects of social custom as moral strictures. For example, in order to protect white women from the hallmark of enslavement - field labour - Caribbean planters by the early eighteenth century refused to employ white working-class women as fieldhands. By the end of the century most fieldhands in the English colonies were black women.[9] Also, from the beginning of the plantation system laws were framed and implemented in order to disassociate white womanhood from the reproduction of the slave status by linking it solely to black women. When white women produced children with enslaved black men, which was not as uncommon as generally suggested, infants were born legally free. In this way the offspring of white women would not experience social relations as human property, nor suffer legal alienation from social freedom. White women, then, were constitutionally placed to participate in the slave-based world as privileged persons, and to adopt ideological positions consistent with this condition.

The linking of white womanhood to the reproduction of freedom meant that the entire ideological fabric of the slave-based civilization was conceived in terms of sex, gender and race. This was the only way that black slavery and white patriarchy could coexist without encountering major legal contradictions. As a result, it became necessary for white males to limit the sexual freedom of white women and at the same time to enforce the sexual exploitation of black women as a 'normal benefit' of masterhood. In so doing white males valued black women's fertility solely in terms of the reproduction of labour for the plantation enterprise, and placed a premium on white women's maternity for its role in the reproduction of patriarchy.

The 'victim' approach to the study of white women in the slave formation, however, has severe conceptual limitations. These can be identified immediately by an empirical assessment of the white women's autonomous participation in the shaping of economic and social relations. The demographic data, for instance, show the extent to which slave ownership correlated to differences of class, race and sex. While white males were the predominant owners of slaves in the plantation sector, the same cannot be said for the urban sector. White women were generally the owners of small properties, rather than large estates, but their small properties were more proportionately stocked with slaves than the large, male owned properties. In 1815, they owned about 24 per cent of the slaves in St. Lucia; 12 per cent of the slaves on properties of more than 50 slaves, and 48 per cent of the properties with less than ten slaves. In Barbados in 1817, less than five of the holdings of 50 slaves or more were owned by white women, but they owned 40 per cent of the properties with less than ten slaves. White women were 50 per cent of the owners of slaves in Bridgetown, the capital, on properties stocked with less than 10 slaves. In general, 58 per cent of slave owners in the capital were female, mostly white, though some were also 'coloured' and black. Overall, women owned 54 per cent of the slaves in the town. The typology of slave owning in the West Indies as a whole shows a male predominance in the rural areas, and a female predominance in the urban areas where property sizes were relatively smaller.[10]

White women also owned more female slaves than male slaves. The extensive female ownership of slaves in the towns was matched by the unusually high proportion of females in the slave population; female slave owners owned more female slaves than male slave owners. The evidence shows, furthermore, that in Bridgetown in 1817, the sex ratio (males per 100 females) of slaves belonging to males was more than double that for female slave owners. The majority of slaves in the town were owned by male slave owners. The sex ratio of slaves belonging to males was 111 and that for slaves belonging to females 49. The sex ratio of slaves belonging to white females, when separated from other non-white females, was even higher at 53. For Berbice in 1819, slaves owned by males had a sex ratio of 132, while those owned by females had a ratio of only 81.[11]

From these data the image that emerges of the white female slave owner is that she was generally urban, in possession of less than ten slaves, the majority of whom were female. That female slave owners generally owned female slaves, indicates the nature of enterprises, and hence labour regimes, managed and owned by white women. It is reasonable, then, to argue that any conceptualization of urban slavery, especially with reference to the experiences of enslaved black women, should proceed with an explicit articulation of white women as principal slave owners. Such a departure is an analytically necessary precondition for the correct identification of white women within the slave owning ethos, and for a more rigorous assessment of urban-rural differentiations within the slave mode of production. Furthermore, it would enhance a real situational understanding which is necessary for the theoretical interpretation of black women's slavery experience, by linking it also to the power and authority of white matriarchs.

An empirical understanding of this reality should be presented against the background of the sexual composition of white communities. Demographic structures and patterns indicate and determine the nature of white women's functions as economic and social agents. Reports for the eighteenth century, for example, illustrate significant differences in the sex structure of Caribbean white communities. Statements ranging from the chronic shortage of white women in Jamaica to an over-abundance in Barbados have been used by contemporaries to account for important socio-political variations between these two colonies. In Jamaica, white women consti-

tuted no more than 40 per cent of the white community up to 1780, while as early as 1715 white women outnumbered white men in Barbados by one per cent, and by seven per cent in 1748 – levelling off at about two per cent for the remainder of the slavery period.

Eighteenth-century observers, such as William Dickson, argued persuasively that the white female majority in Barbados tempered the brutish frontier mentality of white men and promoted at an early stage a mature hegemonic paternalism. By 'civilizing' the white community in many respects, he suggests, the overwhelming presence of white women tended towards the gradual amelioration of slave relations. Conversely, it has been suggested that the shortage of white women in eighteenth-century Jamaica explains in part the rapid rise of the mulatto population, and accounts for the undeveloped state of the planter households, as well as the violence endemic to relations between white and black males, much of which resulted from competition for black females.[12] More importantly, however, the larger numbers of white women in Barbados meant that many remained unmarried, untied to plantation households, and financially independent of males. As a result, there was a greater tendency for white women in Barbados to participate in the market economy as autonomous agents, and to establish independent accumulationist strategies based upon the ownership and possession of slaves.

Explaining the structure and distribution of white women's slave holdings requires, however, a precise grasp of the socio-economic forces operating within the white community. For example, it requires an understanding of the extent to which white women were subordinate to white men within the domestic economy, constitutional provisions, and social culture. Indeed, white women were not 'free', in the sense that white men were, to participate in the polity and market economy as unrestricted colonizing agents. On marriage, unless complicated trust arrangements were made, their properties were legally transferred to their husbands, an alienation of resources which ensured their subordination to men and promoted their second class status within the 'free' society.

Many unmarried white women were forced to find whatever niche was available within the market economy in order to make an independent living. Generally, most of what they found was in areas that propertied white males considered inadequate, in terms of low rate of returns, or socially dishonourable. Many operated within the periphery of the urban economy, dominating the ownership and management of enterprises in the service sector such as taverns, sex-houses, slave rental services, petty shop-keeping and huckstering. Small scale urban slave rental businesses were typically controlled by single white women, who leased domestic servants for miscellaneous household tasks. These businesses operated with a greater female than male labour force which accounts for the relatively larger number of female slaves owned by white women in the towns.

Invariably, then, white women's businesses were concentrated in the informal sector, especially in those areas that bordered on the illicit and illegal as defined by white male officials. In most Caribbean societies, prostitution was illegal, but white women made a thriving business from the rental of black and coloured women for sexual services in the port towns. The testimony of Captain Cook, a British military officer, before the 1791 Parliamentary Committee on the Slave System, gives insights into the way that white women in Barbados rented black women as prostitutes. He noted that the use of black women, both free and slave, as prostitutes in all the colony's towns, 'was a very common practice'. White mistresses in the towns, he stressed, frequently 'rented out' female slaves as prostitutes to sailors. These slaves, he added, would 'go on board ships of war for the purpose' of selling sex for money. Cook had no objection to this activity on board his ship, but on one occasion became rather indignant when a 'negro girl' he knew was 'severely punished on her return home to her owner without the full wages of her prostitution'.[13]

The hiring of slave women for various purposes was an integral part of the urban and rural labour markets. Many white and free-coloured families, and quite often single white women, made their living from the wage earnings of hired female slaves who worked not only as prostitutes but as nannies, nurses, cooks, washerwomen, hucksters, seamstresses, and general labourers. The hiring out of women for sex ran parallel to these markets. In 1806, for example, a British naval officer reported knowledge of a 'respectable Creole white lady' who, for a living, 'Lets out her negro girls to anyone who will pay her for their persons, under the denomination of washerwoman, and becomes very angry if they don't come home in the family way'.[14] John Waller, who toured Barbados in 1808, made a similar report on the relations between prostitution and the 'hiring out' labour system. He stated in his 'travel' book:

In the family where I lodged, a respectable lady . . . was regretting to the company at dinner, that a young female slave, whom she had let out for several months, was about to return, as she would lose twelve dollars a month, the price of her hire, and besides, be at the expense of maintaining her . . . I made inquiry respecting the subject of hiring slaves, and learned that the one in question has been let out to an officer in the garrison, with whom she had been living as a mistress . . . I felt extremely shocked at the idea of so strange a traffic; but . . . a few days later, this very slave [was] publicly advertised, in the 'Bridge-town Gazette,' in the following curious terms: 'To let, a Sempstress, a well-looking mulatto girl, seventeen years of age, an excellent hand at the needle, etc. To prevent needless application – terms twelve dollars per month. Apply, etc.' I had previously noticed advertisements of this description, and . . . few weeks pass without them; they are, however, frequently intended only for the purposes literally expressed.[15]

Infants of slave prostitutes were owned by their mothers' owners and often sold when weaned as an additional product. At the end of the eighteenth century weaned slave infants fetched up to ten dollars local currency on English Caribbean markets. The accumulation of such lump sums of capital also accounted in part for white women's preference for female slaves. The economics of slave reproduction suggests the rationality of a market preference for female slaves, since several streams of return could be derived from such an investment. The marketing of black women's sexuality, and the sale of their progeny, were therefore associated directly with the economic accumulation strategies of white women, and ought to be considered an integral part of the overall capitalist exploitation of slave labour. In 1811, Elizabeth Fenwick, an English resident in Barbados explained this double process as follows:

The female slaves are really encouraged to prostitution because their children are the property of the owners of the mothers. These children are reared by the ladies as pets, are frequently brought from negro houses to their chambers to feed and to sleep, and reared with every care and indulgence till grown up, when they are at once dismissed to labour and slave-like treatment.[16]

This evidence can be interpreted to suggest that many black women probably suffered their greatest degree of social exploitation at the hands of white women, since the direct sale of women's sexuality for accumulation purposes represents a crucial distinction between the general experience of plantation and urban slaves. It is precisely in this area that the inhumane forces of slavery entered the inner world of women with its greatest devastation. For this reason, it becomes problematic to root an empirical argument which suggests that white women might have been more humane owners of slaves.

The pro-slavery ideology of white women was seen by some contemporaries as emerging from their realisation that non-white women competed effectively for the attention, favours and resources owned and controlled by white men. White women were said to react with jealousy to patterns of white male sexuality, and invariably directed their anger against non-white women.[17] Many contemporaries suggest that white males in the Caribbean possessed a sexual preference for mulatto or brown-skinned black women over white women. One individual ironically, explained this preference in terms of white males cohabiting with coloured women 'at a very early age' under the guidance and encouragement of their mothers.[18] White women, according to this observation, played a critical role in shaping the ideological content of white male's sexual attitude towards black women.

Bayley's observations in the 1820s perhaps betrayed the white male's norm when he spoke of the attractiveness of 'coloured' women. He described them as having 'captivated' with ease the 'hearts of English, Irish, and Scotch' men on the island.[19] He added:

If I accord the palm of female beauty to the ladies of colour, I do not at the same time deteriorate the attractions of the fairer [white] Creoles; the stately and graceful demeanor which calls upon us to admire the one, does not forbid us to be fascinated by the modest loveliness of the other; yet I will acknowledge that I prefer the complexion that is tinged, if not too darkly, with the richness of the olive, to the face which, however fair in its paleness, can never look as lovely as when it wore the rose-blush of beauty which has faded away. I know no prettier scene than a group of young and handsome coloured girls taking their evening walk . .[20]

Bayley and Waller, who visited the West Indies between the 1790s and the 1820s, suggest that white males possessed a sexual typology in which white women were valued for domestic formality and respectability, 'coloured' women for exciting socio-sexual companionship, and black women for irresponsible, covert sexual adventurism .[21] Enslaved black women, then, produced thousands of socially fatherless mulatto daughters, many of whom on becoming adults, 'enjoyed' levels of recognition and attention unknown to their mothers. Waller explained the critical role played by white women in the reproduction of white male sexual ideology:

A very respectable matron, who had shewn a kind and motherly affection for a young friend of mine who came over to settle here as a merchant, advised him in the most serious manner to look out for a young mulatto or Mustee girl for his housekeeper, urging that it would greatly increase his domestic comforts and diminish his expenses; and, in addition to this, she hinted very delicately, that, by being confined to one object, his health and reputation would be better secured, than by the promiscuous libertinism to which she seemed to consider every young man as habitually addicted.[22]

Elizabeth Fenwick's letters from Barbados illustrate the extent to which white women, even unwittingly, shared and contributed to the racist ideologies and values of the plantation world. Fenwick arrived at Barbados from England at the turn of the nineteenth century, and established a school for white children in Bridgetown. Her correspondence with her friend Mary Hays in England spans the period 1814 to 1822, and gives detailed and critical insights into the colony's slave-based social culture. Her primary problem related to the management of domestic slaves, most of whom were females. Undoubtedly, Fenwick's judgement is that of an Anglo-centric foreigner, but her keen eye renders her evidence most valuable. First, she assessed the worth of domestic slaves in both economic and moral terms:

Our domestics are Negroes, hired from their owners, and paid at what seems to me an exorbitant rate. . . . They are a sluggish, inert, self-willed race of people, apparently inaccessible to gentle and kindly impulses. Nothing, but the dread of the whip seems capable of rousing them to exertion, and not even that, as I understand, can make them honest. Pilfering seems habitual and instinctive among domestic slaves. It is said they are worse slaves and servants in this island than in many others because they are less severely made use of.[23]

As a single woman and a stranger to the island, Fenwick fell victim to the cunning of hired domestics who considered her ignorant of local social life and, in the process, incurred her moral wrath; but she was no defender of slavery. For her, the slave system was 'horrid', and 'the vices and mischiefs found among the slaves' were to be 'traced back' to it.[24] This judgement mitigated her responses to the horrors she experienced as a mistress of domestic slaves whom she accused of preventing her speedy social adjustment to the colony, and of continuously threatening to drive her away. After several complaints of being systematically robbed by them, Fenwick finally admitted that her female slaves were responsible for her adverse judgement of the society:

I recollect perfectly that in struggles and pecuniary difficulties I used to think any place would be paradise where I could secure a living. The means are now abundant, but Barbados is not my paradise . . . the endless trouble and vexation that black servants involve you in, renders domestic comfort unattainable.[25]

Finally, in May 1817, unable to endure her domestics any more, Fenwick discharged most of them - including the chief housekeeper.[26]

Unable to do without a housekeeper to supervise the maids, she hired one from a friend. She complained, however, that this decision merely added to, rather than diminished, the amount of work she was required to do; the management of domestics, she intimates, is 'a labour so great, so constant, so oppressive in this country, where every order must be executed under the eye of the mistress'. Disturbed by the 'heavy sums paid for wages of hired servants', Fenwick decided to purchase a male slave cook who was given the responsibility of supervising female domestics. Concerned about her friend's reaction to this development, she wrote: 'it will no doubt be repugnant to your feelings to hear me talk of buying men', but it was the only way to reduce the costly dependence upon the female domestics. By August 1821, she had eight slaves – three hired and five (two men, two boys and one woman) owned. With this reduced female labour force, Fenwick seemed to have found the domestic peace which had eluded her since her arrival in the colony.

But she was also concerned with the wider social 'problems' associated with white males' socio-sexual use of domestic slaves. For her, white males were locked into a perverse sexual culture which corrupted their personal values

and public morality. Worried about Orlando, her young son, she stated how easy it was for young men to 'acquire those vices of manhood' by intimate relations with domestic slaves.[27] In her overall view, however, slave women, because of their constant and casual contact with masters and their sons, were the victims of sexual domination. For this and related reasons she rejected slavery as a 'disgraceful system' not consistent with the cultivation of 'excellence of character' in white men. [28] On a more personal note, she informed Mrs Hays:

I strongly suspect that a very fine mulatto boy about 14 who comes here to help wait on the breakfast and luncheon of two young ladies, our pupils, is their own brother, from the likeness he bears to their father. It is a common case and not thought of as an enormity. It gives me disgusted antipathy and I am ready to hail the slave and reject the master.[29]

In December 1821, Mrs Fenwick departed from Barbados for New Haven in the United States, 'disposing' of her five slaves for half their value.

Fenwick's recognition that slavery was a 'disgraceful system' but one, nonetheless, within which one had to struggle to make a living, explains in part her emphasis upon discipline, honesty and orderliness. The enforcement of a productive ethic among slaves meant in social terms the use of authoritarian power – the very core of any definition of slavery. She therefore encountered women slaves with a profound moral dilemma, as well as the major contradiction that results from women's need for solidarity within a capitalist economy. The need to engage in productive activity, then, meant compliance with the logic of slavery – its modes of ideological rationalisation and social culture.

Acts of extreme cruelty to black women by white women are documented in much of the eighteenth- and nineteenth-century literature. European travellers seemed rather surprised and disturbed that white women should display attitudes to human suffering and impose punishments that held them indistinguishable from their male counterparts. Bayley, for instance, deplored the standard forms of torture used on slaves, but concluded from his four years' residence in the West Indies: 'I will state, however, my conviction that female owners are more cruel than male; their revenge is more durable and their methods of punishment more refined, particularly towards slaves of their own sex'.[30] If Bayley's conclusion erred on the side of popular stereotype, David Turnbull correctly located the expression of white female authority within the specific context of the overriding need for effective slave control. Reporting from his experiences of Cuban slave society, he stated in 1840:

The mistress of many a great family in Havana will not scruple to tell you that such is the proneness of her people (slaves) to vice and idleness, she finds it necessary to send one or more of them once a month to the whipping post, not so much on account of any positive delinquency, as because without these periodic advertisements the whole family would become unmanageable, and the master and mistress would lose their authority.[31]

Such policies were consistent with the material and social interest of the white community in general, and should not be considered surprising, given that white women participated fully in the accumulationist and elitist colonial culture that depended upon the successful control of slave labour.

Mary Prince, the only West Indian female slave who, to the best of our knowledge, produced an autobiography, gave an account of her mistress that confirms impressions presented by Turnbull. She wrote of her mistress:

She taught me to do all sorts of household work; to wash and bake, pick cotton and wool, and wash floors, and cook. And she taught me (how can I ever forget it!) more things than these; she caused me to know the exact differences between the smart [inflicted pain] of the rope, the cart-whip, and the cow-skin, when applied to my naked body by her own cruel hand. And there was scarcely any punishment more dreadful than the blows I received on my face and head from her hard heavy fist. She was a fearful woman, and a savage mistress to her slaves.[32]

The value of Mary Prince's account has to do with the nature of relations between female slaves and mistresses. 'Both my master and mistress,' she stated, 'seemed to think that they had a right to ill-use [the slaves] at their pleasure.' This is clearly illustrated in the case of the punishment of her friend Hetty:

One of the cows had dragged the rope away from the stake to which Hetty had fastened it, and got loose. My master flew into a terrible passion, and ordered the poor creature to be stripped quite naked, notwithstanding her pregnancy, and to be tied up to a tree in the yard. He then flogged her as hard as he could lick, both with the whip and the cow-skin, till she was all over streaming in blood. He rested, and then beat her again and again. Her shrieks were terrible. The consequence was that poor Hetty was brought to bed before her time, and was delivered after severe labour of a dead child. She appeared to recover after her confinement, so far that she was repeatedly flogged by both master and mistress afterwards . . . till the water burst out of her body and she died.[33]

Throughout her narrative, Mary Prince argues that the execution of owners' authority was not affected by their sex, and gave no indication of being surprised by the pro-slavery role of white women.

Since the plantation economy was capitalist by nature, and market forces generally took precedence over the ideological need for racial solidarity at the frontier, many white women found themselves in a labouring relationship to the planter dominated economic system. For those in the rural sector, the custom was to attempt subsistence farming on uncultivated, 'rab' lands not used for sugar but denied the blacks. Many of these 'poor-white' women, noted Dickson at the end of the eighteenth century, could be found tilling small patches of land without the assistance of slaves, and walking 'many miles loaded with the produce of their little spots, which they exchange in the towns for such European goods as they can afford to purchase'.[34]

The relationship between black and white female hucksters was complex, and was never far removed from legislative considerations. Dickson commented that their marketing patterns and associated customs were similar in many ways. White women typically carried baskets on their heads and children strapped on their hips in the traditional African manner, which was perhaps due to some degree of cross-cultural fertilization between the two groups. For him, this illustrated the extent to which slave women defined the behavioural patterns and customs of huckstering. He also believed that white female hucksters depended to a large extent upon their trading association with slaves, especially those who owned retail outlets in the towns.

The intimacy of relations between working-class white women and slaves inevitably found expression in socio-sexual activity and family formation. In the formative decades of slave society, when social ideologies were not yet fully rooted, the evidence of sexual relations between black men and white women was recorded. In the St Michael parish register for 4 December 1685, for example, a marriage is entered between 'Peter Perkins, a negro, and Jane

Table 47.1   The Inter-racial family ties of white women in the parish of St. Phillip, Barbados, in 1715

Name	Age	Description given in Census
John Goddard	40	A mulatto, born of a white woman
Jane Goddard	32	White, husband a mulatto
Elizabeth Shepherd	52	White, husband a mulatto
Thomas Goddard	30	Mulatto, born of a white woman
Ann Goddard	30	White woman, husband a mulatto
Mary Shepherd	13	Mother a white woman, father a negro
John Wake	5 ⎱	Father negro, mother white
Elizabeth Wake	8 ⎰	
Simon Kitteridge	18	Son of a white woman and coloured man
Sarah Avery	15	Mulatto, born of a white woman
Charles Sergent	36	Mother white, father a mulatto
Mary Sergent	31	White woman, husband a negro
Elizabeth Sinckler	48	Born of a white woman and negro man

Source: Census of Barbados, 1715: Barbados Archives

Long, a white woman'. The 1715 census shows that they had a son; three other children of such relations were recorded as: Elizabeth X, a mulatto born of a white woman; Mary K, the daughter of a white woman and begotten by the extract of a negro; John L, a mulatto born of a white woman.[35] (See Table 47.1). During the mid-century, however, as the slave society matured, the role of racial and gender ideologies became increasingly important to the white male élite as tools of social control, and reports of such relations more or less vanished from official documents. Black men faced punishments such as castration, dismemberment, and execution for having sexual relations with white women, who in turn were socially disgraced and ostracized. In this way, the sexual freedom of white women was curtailed, and white males reported no problems with their authority system in this area for the remainder of the slavery period.

Commonplace within the historiography is the assertion that the white male sought to prevent the social access of black males to the white female in order to project her as a symbol of moral purity and ideal domesticity.[37] Indeed, such an interpretation has contributed to the spawning of stereo types about the lives of white women and the views of white men within the development of patriarchal ideology. Though it is unnecessary to deny the validity of such claims, emphasis should be placed upon the white male's principal concern which was to limit the size of the free non-white group within society. Since the most natural way in which this could be done was to greatly reduce the incidence of white women's cohabitation with slave men, it was logical for white men to see the white woman as an avenue to freedom for blacks that had to be blocked. By restricting the sexual lives of white women, then, white males moved to ensure that the progeny of black males were not lost to the slave gangs, while at the same time maintaining the status of freedom as the most prized commodity within their society. Evidence of this reasoning can be found in the nature of race relations during the formative years of slavery, and in white men's indifference to black men's sexual access to white prostitutes who were considered outside of the fertility considerations of the slave régime.

The obvious influence of African social culture upon European and creole white women did not meet with the approval of visitors to the 'Indies'. Edward Long, the eighteenth-century Jamaica historian, was saddened by the cultural deterioration he thought white women experienced from 'constant intercourse' with black household servants. He suggests that these women 'insensibly adopted' the dress, speech, and manners of blacks, which rendered them further removed from European culture than the colour of their skin suggests. According to Long:

We may see in some of these places, a very fine young woman awkwardly dangling her arms, with the air of a negro servant lolling almost the whole day upon beds or settees, her head muffed up with two or three handker-chiefs, her dress loose, and without stays. At noon, we find her employed in gobbling pepper-pot, seated on the floor, with her sable hand-maids around her. [36]

Maria Nugent, the famous wife of a Jamaican Governor, reported that creole white women were 'not untainted' by their close relations to blacks, and implied, like Long, their cultural inferiority to their European counterpart.[37]

The white female voice was rarely heard on issues of this nature. They certainly did not organize an anti-slavery core within the islands, nor did they exert any special influence upon the reconstruction of social life after emancipation. Since they were excluded from holding public office and participating in political administration, their views are absent from official annals. Even when disturbing crises, such as slave revolts, surrounded and impacted upon their lives, their voices were silenced by officialdom and subordinated even to those of free non-white males. After revolts, for example, when evidence was submitted to official commissions, their views were not sought; neither was it assumed that they were in possession of a gender-specific interpretation of events that was valuable.

Since white women in the Caribbean did not emerge as part of an anti-slavery front, unlike their counterparts in the United States, it would be folly to expect manumission records to indicate that they were more active participants in the promotion of black freedom. Available data suggest that white women were less inclined to manumit their slaves than white men. These records show that the typical manumitter was a white male, while the typical manumitted slave was a female domestic. Since white women owned a significant proportion of domestic slaves, it can be inferred that white women were less inclined than white men to free slaves. Most white males who freed their female slaves did so as a result of repayment for socio-sexual services rendered. Since white women might not have benefitted from slave owning in these ways (to

the same degree) part of the explanation for the divergence might also be found in the fact that white males were better able to pay the large fees involved in manumission procedures.

The images that emerged of white women as slave owners in the Caribbean context, then, suggest that they were generally pro-slavery, socially illiberal, and economically exploitative of black women. They were assigned the primary role of symbolic matrons of the slavery culture, but were also active participants in their own right in the socio-economic accumulations that slavery made possible. They made valuable contributions to the development of the colonial economy and society, not only as the domestic partners of planters, merchants, overseers, and managers, but also as large and small-scale owners of slaves and other forms of property. Their participation in the consolidation and defence of the slave system, then, cannot be explained solely in terms of their dependent status – social and economic victim of patriarchy. Rather, emphasis should also be placed in their autonomous survival strategies within the unstable and socially hostile colonial culture fashioned by competitive market forces.

Finally, the theoretical discourse on the relations between race, sex, gender and class forces in slave society requires an empirically sound grasp of the process of socio-economic construction and transformation. The search for such an understanding should involve a careful assessment of the diverse and complex manifestations of patriarchal ideologies, the precise location of women within productive structures, as well as their reproductive relations within households and communities. This research should then be informed by the culturally embracing process of social creolization in which European immigrants were transformed at the frontier into natives who possessed an increasingly distinct value system and sensibility.

Notes

1.   See for example, Barbara Bush, *Slave Women in Caribbean Society, 1650-1838*, Bloomington, 1990; Hilary Beckles, *Natural Rebels: A Social History of Enslaved Black Women in Barbados*, New Brunswick, 1989; Marietta Morrissey, *Slave Women in the New World: Gender Stratification in the Caribbean*, Lawrence, Kansas, 1989; Lucille Mair, *Women Field Workers in Jamaica During Slavery*, Department of

History, University of the West Indies, Mona, 1986; Blanca Silvestrini, *Women and Resistance: Herstory in Contemporary Caribbean History*, Department of History, University of the West Indies, Mona, 1989.

2. Rhoda Reddock,'Women and Slavery in the Caribbean: A Feminist Perspective', *Latin American Perspectives* Issue 40, 12: 1, 1985, pp. 63-80. Arlette Gautier, 'Les Esclaves femmes aux Antilles Francaises, 1635-1848', *Reflexions Historiques* 10: 3, Fall, 1983, pp. 409-35. Lucille Mair, *The Rebel Woman in the British West Indies During Slavery*, Kingston, 1975.

3. Beckles, *Natural Rebels;* Bush, *Slave Women in the Caribbean;* and Morrissey, *Slave Women in the New World.*

4. See for example, Catherine Clinton, *The Plantation Mistress: Women's World in the Old South*, New York, 1982; C. L. R. James, *The Black Jacobins: Toussaint L'Ouverture and the San Domingo Revolution*, New York, 1963 pp. 30-31; Morrissey, *Slave Women in the New World*, p. 150. Barbara Bush, 'White "Ladies", Coloured "Favourites" and Black "Wenches". Some Considerations on Sex, Race and Class Factors in Social Relations in White Creole Society in the British Caribbean', *Slavery and Abolition*, 2, December 1981, pp. 245-62; Joan Gunderson, 'The Double Bonds of Race and Sex: Black and White Women in a Colonial Virginia Parish', *Journal of Southern History*, 52, 1986, pp, 351-72.

5. Bush, *Slave Women*, pp. 8, 134.

6. Ibid. p. xii; See Lucille Mair, 'An Historical Study of Women in Jamaica from 1655 to 1844' (PhD, University of the West Indies, Mona, Jamaica, 1974); *The Rebel Woman in the British West Indies During Slavery*, Kingston, 1975; 'The Arrival of Black Women', *Jamaica Journal*, 9: 2 and 3, Feb 1975; see also Jacqueline Jones, '"My Mother was Much of a Woman". Black Women, Work, and the Family under Slavery', *Feminist Studies*, 8, 1982, pp. 235-69. Marietta Morrissey, 'Women's Work, Family Formation and Reproduction among Caribbean Slaves', *Review*, 9, 1986, pp. 339-67.

7. Moreau de Saint Méry, [1797], *Description topographique physique, civile politique et historique de la partie française de Visle Saint Domingue*, Paris, 1958, p. 10. Morrissey, *Slave Women in the New World*, p. 150.

8. See R. Pollack Petchesky, 'Reproduction and Class Divisions among Women', in A. Swerdlow and H. Lessinger (eds), *Class, Race and Sex: The Dynamics of Control*, Boston. 1983, pp. 221-31; Alwin Thornton and D. Camburn,'Causes and Consequences of Sex-Roles, Attitudes and Attitude Change'. *American Sociological Review*, 48, 1983, pp. 211-27; Alwin Thornton and D. Freedman, 'Sex-Role Socialisation: A Focus on Women' in J. Freeman (ed) *Women: A Feminist Perspective*, California 1984, pp. 157-62.

9. See Hilary Beckles, *White Servitude and Black Slavery in Barbados 1627-1715*, Knoxville, 1989, pp. 115-68;'Black Men in White Skins: The Formation of a White Proletariat in West Indian Slave Society', *Journal of Imperial and Commonwealth History*, 15: 1, 1986, pp. 5-22; *Natural Rebels*, pp. 24-54.

10. Barry W. Higman, *Slave Populations of the British Caribbean, 1807-1834*, Baltimore, 1984, p. 107; also, *The Slave Population and Economy of Jamaica 1807-34*, Cambridge, 1978.

11. *Slave Populations.*

12. See for the Structure of the Barbados and Jamaica white population, Hilary Beckles, *Natural Rebels*, p. 15. Also Hilary Beckles, *Black Rebellion in Barbados: The Struggle Against Slavery, 1727-1838*, Bridgetown, 1985, pp. 58-9; William Dickson, *Mitigation of Slavery* [1841] Westport, 1970, pp. 439-41.

13. Parliamentary Papers, 1791, vol. 34, Testimony of Evidence of Captain Cook, p. 202; also, evidence of Mr. Husbands, p. 13.

14. Major Wyvill, 'Memoirs of an Old Officer', 1815, p. 386, MSS. Division, Library of Congress.

15. John Waller, *A Voyage to the West Indies*, 1820, pp. 20-21.

16. A. F. Fenwick (ed) *The Fate of the Fenwicks: Letters to Mary Hays, 1798-1828*, 1927, p. 169.

17. See Bush, *Slave Women*, pp. 44, 114.

18. Waller, *A Voyage*, p. 19.

19. F. W. Bayley, *Four Years' Residence in the West Indies*, 1833, p. 493; Bush. *Slave Women*, p. 115.

20. Bayley, pp. 493-4.

21. See Bush 'White "Ladies"'.

22. Waller, p. 20.

23. Fenwick, pp. 163-4.

24. Ibid., p. 164.

25. Ibid.

26. Ibid., p, 175.

27. Ibid., p. 170.

28. Ibid., p. 169.

29. Ibid.

30. Bayley, pp. 417-8.

31. David Turnbull, *Travels in the West*, 1840, p. 53.

32. Moira Ferguson (ed), *The History of Mary Prince: A West Indian Slave, Related by herself* t[1831], 1987, p. 56.

33. Ibid.

34. William Dickson, *Letters on Slavery*, 1789, Westport, 1970, p. 41.

35. St Michael Parish Register, vol. IA, RL 1/1, Barbados Archives; see also, Richard Dunn, *Sugar and Slaves: The Role of the Planter Class in the English West Indies, 1624-1713*, New York, 1973, pp. 255-6. Census of Barbados, 1715. Barbados Archives.

36. Edward Long, *The History of Jamaica* (5 vols), 1774, vol. 2, pp. 412-13; see also 278-80. Bush, *Slave Women*, p. 25.

37. Bush, Ibid.

48

Women's Work, Family Formation, and Reproduction Among Caribbean Slaves

MARIETTA MORRISSEY

Introduction

The organization of slave families in the American South has received new, sustained attention from Genovese (1976), Fogel and Engerman (1974), Gutman (1977), and others. It is argued, first, that slave families were more likely to be nuclear — a male, a female, and their children — than matrifocal as previously proposed, and, secondly, that families maintained intergenerational ties. Hence, family stability is now said to be prevailed among American slaves. This proposition contradicts the findings of Stampp (1956) and others who argued that slavery broke up families, that with 'these conditions — the absence of legal marriage, the family's minor social and economic significance, and the father's limited role — it is hardly surprising to find that slave families were highly unstable' (Stampp, 1956: 344). And it challenges Patterson's (1979) more recent hypothesis that slaves were 'natally alienated', or symbolically estranged from natal ties by the slave condition.

For the West Indies, it is more difficult to establish the existence of 'stable' family patterns. Slaves were rarely able to reproduce their numbers, certainly not at the level found among slaves in the United States (Fogel and Engerman, 1974). Still, statistical evidence of high levels of nuclear family formation has been found for Jamaica (Higman, 1976a), Trinidad (Higman, 1978; 1979), and the Bahamas (Craton, 1979; 1978). Indeed, Craton concludes that patterned family life, 'even in patterns recognizable to Europeans', was sometimes the norm for West Indian slaves, in particular, 'nuclear, two-headed households' (1979: 2).

The evidence of conjugal domestic units among British West Indian slaves is an important empirical breakthrough in the study of the family, although there is still little quantifiable evidence of intergenerational kinship. But a body of critique has developed, focusing on the failure of contemporary quantitative research to identify fully the meaning and origins of nuclear families among Caribbean slaves and thus to account for the considerable variation in Caribbean slave family organization (Patterson, 1976; 1982). That is, why did nuclear families form, instead of other arrangements? And why are nuclear families found in some settings, while the mother–child unit predominates elsewhere?

Major findings on Caribbean slave families and critical reaction will be reviewed. It is suggested that both propositions of stable nuclear family formation among Caribbean slaves and critical commentary have failed to consider women as a complementary unit of analysis to the family and thus have missed a crucial source of explanation of changing patterns of Caribbean slave families.

Research on Nuclear Families Among British West Indian Slaves

The recent examination of slave registration figures presented to British colonial authorities shortly before emancipation extends aggregate and plantation-specific research on nuclear family formation. The methodological approach and findings differ dramatically from those of earlier research on slave families based on occasional and incomplete plantation records, diaries of slave owners and travelers, and other documents of the period.

Higman studied three plantations in Jamaica and aggregate figures for Trinidad. He

Review, IX, 3 (Winter 1986), pp. 339–67.

concludes that the nuclear family was the modal type on three estates in Jamaica on the eve of emancipation (1976a). His findings for Trinidad in 1813 are similar (1978; 1979). Craton's (1979) study of the Bahamas echoes Higman's work in methods and substance. According to the 1821–22 census, most Bahamian slaves lived in nuclear families.

Three competing but tentative hypotheses have been offered by historians and demographers about the origins of West Indian nuclear families.

First, it has been argued that nuclear families were sometimes a demographic possibility: for example, where sex ratios were even or populations stable and isolated (Craton, 1979). Thus, it is suggested that in the absence of material and ideological constraints, and given the demographic opportunity, nuclear families developed. This explanation is so broad as to be nearly tautological: nuclear families can exist, therefore they do exist. It does not offer in sufficiently specific terms the conditions that unite a variety of New World national and plantation settings that produced nuclear families.

Secondly, it has been hypothesized that African traditions predisposed slaves to stable, co-residential conjugal patterns. Indeed, Africans appear to have been more likely than Creoles to establish stable, two-headed households in urban Trinidad (Higman, 1978: 170), although contradictory evidence has been found in other settings, for example, Martinique (Debien, 1960). Still, no evidence is offered of what particular African family forms were represented in nuclear units, so no hypotheses can be developed about the meaning of slave families based on links to the slaves' African past. Higman suggests, however, that African-born slaves may have perceived the nuclear family as a 'building-block of extended or polygynous family types rooted in lineage or locality' (1978: 171).

Finally, for high-status males or males with productive garden plots and well-developed marketing skills and opportunities, nuclear families served an economic function not unlike that of early Western nuclear families (Patterson, 1969; Higman, 1976a). This is an important explanation of Caribbean nuclear family formation, supported by the statistical evidence of nuclear and polygamous families among slaves with prestigious occupations and/or lighter skin color in Trinidad and Jamaica. However, this explanation applies only to some Caribbean slaves. Field hands were

found in equal proportions among all family types in Higman's Jamaican sample, suggesting that the family economic function may have reinforced other tendencies toward nuclear family formation.

Women as a Unit of Analysis

The new scholarship on women has made clear that their roles as producers and reproducers of the future labor force have profound effects on family organization (Goody, 1976; Quick, 1977). A materialist analysis suggests that women's roles are established through the system of production (in particular, the labor market) and reinforced by ideological agents such as the state and church (Boserup, 1970; Blumberg, 1977). An important factor emerges from these assumptions for analysis of West Indian slave families. That is, the time at which New World slave societies reached their peak need for labor relative to the availability of slaves on the world market may have influenced women's work, family membership and fertility. Craton, Higman, and others have distinguished between the demographic profiles (in particular, the sex ratios of older and newer slave societies) in accounting for differential patterns of family formation and reproduction in the study of Caribbean slaves; I suggest refining that distinction to the more fundamental one of societies with labor shortage and those with labor surpluses.

At times of labor shortage, particularly towards the end of the slave trade, when young male slaves were not easily purchased, women were used in increasing proportions as field laborers rather than as household workers. At the same time, slave holders tried to breed new slaves by encouraging nuclear family formation and the reproduction of children. Given the nearly constant historical tendency towards the natural decrease of slaves in the West Indies, stimulation of reproduction was generally ineffective, particularly, it seems, when women's production roles in agriculture were also emphasized. It is hypothesized, then, that women's increased contributions to agricultural production mitigated the effects of planter incentives and reduced women's tendencies to live in nuclear families and to produce children. In formal terms:

1. At time of severe labor shortage, West Indian slave women
   (a) were employed more often than males in field labor;

(b) lived, in the main, by themselves or with their children;

(c) produced relatively few children (fewer than 30 per 1,000 population annually)[1]

2. At times of adequate labor supply, West Indian slave women

(a) were employed in equal numbers to males, or less often, in field labor;

(b) lived, in the main, in nuclear families;

(c) produced a relatively large number of children (more than 30 per 1,000).

These propositions will be examined in light of six cases; the Bahamas, the Leeward Islands, Martinique, Jamaica, Barbados, and Cuba. These societies represent three stages in the evolution of New World plantation agriculture. The Bahamas and the Leewards, although different in agricultural and social structure, both had sizable labor surpluses by the late eighteenth and early nineteenth centuries, the time of our inquiry. We can expect women to work in the fields as often or less so than males in the Leewards and the Bahamas, nuclear families to predominate, and slave reproduction rates to be high. Barbados and Martinique, our second set of cases, present a second stage in the evolution of Caribbean plantation agriculture. Both areas suffered a labor shortage at the turn of the nineteenth century. Therefore, we can expect a predominance of single female or mother–child units, low levels of reproduction (below 30 per 1,000 population), and the disproportionate presence of women in field work. However, the competitive position of these islands had diminished in the world sugar market by the era under investigation. Labor shortage was a serious problem, but the high levels of productivity demanded of an earlier slave population in Barbados and Martinique were not required of workers during this era. By introducing a third paired comparison, that of Jamaica and Cuba, we can explore in greater depth the independent variable — labor shortage — and its impact on women's lives. These societies reached peak levels of labor productivity and agricultural capacity as the slave trade ended. We can expect women to predominate heavily in agricultural work, natural production to be extremely low (approaching natural decrease), and mother–child units or women alone to be most common familial patterns.

The Bahamas and the Leeward Islands

British settlers occupied the Bahamas in the 1650s and contributed to the mercantile character that distinguished the area from the agricultural West Indies to the south. Cotton cultivation by slaves was established, but 'in such colonies the conditions did not exist which led, in the West Indies proper, to the development of a fully fashioned slave society of the plantation type' (Lewis, 1968: 309). The area never experienced severe labor shortages, as its agricultural development preceded the intensification and competition of later sugar planting.

As predicted, most of the 10,000 Bahamian slaves (54 per cent) registered from 1821 to 1822 lived in 'simple nuclear families' (Craton, 1979: 7, 11). Craton argues that three factors contributed to the slaves' likely preference for conjugal domestic units: (1) 'Eurocentric, pronatalist, or publicity-conscious masters'; (2) the widespread existence of provision gardens, apparently in male slaves' control, that required the labor of women and children; and (3) the tendency for nuclear families to be on larger, more isolated estates in a fairly stable cohort.[2]

These factors lead Craton to suggest a continuum of family types among Caribbean slaves. At one pole were the 'virtual peasants of the Bahamas, Barbuda, and, perhaps, the Grenadines with locational stability, a small proportion of African slaves, natural increase and a relatively high incidence of nuclear and stable families. At the opposite pole were the over-worked slaves of new plantations such as those of Trinidad, Guyana, and St. Vincent, with a high rate of natural decrease, a majority of slaves living alone or in 'barrack' conditions, and a high proportion of 'denuded', female-headed families' (1979: 25). Indeed, Craton reports the reluctance of one group of Bahamian slaves to be moved to Trinidad's more productive plantations, where slaves reputedly worked much harder.

The missing factor in Craton's discussion is an account of how relative productivity affected women's work roles. We have little information about what kinds of work women did on Bahamian plantations. The overall sex ratio was nearly even in contrast to more intensely cultivated areas of the Caribbean, where males predominated. This is a probable indication that high productivity was not demanded, as the apparently more productive male slave labor force was still available through trade. Craton (1978: 350–52) offers ample evidence of declining productivity, production, and profitability on the large cotton estate of Lord John

Rolle, said to be typical of Bahamian plantations after the 1790s. Craton suggests that slave masters took advantage of the nearly even sex ratio to pursue pronatalism, but with only moderate success. Higman (1976: 67) finds a natural increase among Bahamian slaves of about 16 per 1,000 population from 1825 to 1828, up from an earlier period and the highest in the British West Indies at the time (see Appendix). But the birth rate climbed to barely more than 30 per 1,000 from 1825 to 1828, well after labor productivity reached its peak in the Bahamas.

The Leeward Islands (St. Christopher, Nevis Montserrat, and Antigua) were settled from 1623 to 1632. These small islands were the sight of wars among the French, English, and Amerindians until the early 1700s, when plantation sugar production became a consistent, lucrative enterprise. Among them there has been considerable variation in productivity, sugar exports levels, and slave populations. Antigua, with 37,808 (mostly slaves) and more than 25,000 acres in cane, surpassed Barbados in sugar exports in the mid-eighteenth century, as indicated in Table 1. The other islands had less agricultural land than Antigua, and fewer slaves (in 1775, St. Kitts recorded 23,462 Blacks; Nevis, 11,000; Monserrat, 9,834 [Sheridan, 1973: 150]).

By the end of the eighteenth century, sugar planting had peaked in the British Leewards, and planters enjoyed a relative surplus of labor. 'Originally the slave system had been intended to relieve the shortage of field labour for the plantations. But by the end of the eighteenth century its influence had created a pattern of profuse consumption of relatively unproductive forced labour, as well as of wealth, which was proving ruinously expensive to maintain' (Goveia, 1965: 150). Goveia offers several indicators of labour surplus. a smaller proportion of slaves was used in the field work, leading to a decline in productivity from a mid-century peak. More slaves were employed in domestic service: 27 per cent of the slave population on Montserrat engaged in domestic service or worked as tradesmen or fisherman (Goveia, 1965: 146). The custom of hiring out slaves was well developed, manumissions were relatively numerous, and a cash economy among slaves were extensive. Slaves customerily supplemented food and clothing allotments through earnings from provision sales and hiring out (Goveia, 1965: 135-39).

The population of the Leewards was highly Creolized by the late eighteenth century.

Women outnumbered men on Nevis and probably on Montserrat, and children and old people made up more than a third of the population on both islands (Goveia, 1956: 124). Women's work is not treated directly by Goveia, but we can infer that women were not especially valued as field workers. Most of the numerous domestics were women; some slaves were hired out for domestic service. Other groups commonly able to evade field work along with women workers were able to do so in the Leewards. People of mixed ethnicity, in particular, were not attractive to Leewards' planters for field work.

We expect the Leewards to exhibit a relatively high proportion of nuclear families and a high birth rate. Higman's population estimates are for the 1800s, well after the peak in sugar production. All of the Leewards had an increase in births from 1817 to 1831, with all except Nevis showing a small natural increase, but never more than Montserrat's 6 births per 1,000 population in the period from 1824 to 1827. More relevant to our hypotheses, only Montserrat exhibited a crude birth rate over 30 per 1,000.[3]

Slave families are said by Goveia to have consisted of a mother and her children, all belonging to the mother's owner, regardless of the parentage of the children. Goveia does report on the success of Methodist and Moravian churches in the Leewards, both of which advocated 'Christian monogamy' for their slave converts (1965: 271-99). Goveia is of an earlier school of thought that rejects on logical grounds the possibility of stable conjugal unions among slaves. One set of nineteenth-century observers may partially confirm Goveia's findings. Sturge and Harvey, travelling through Antigua after emancipation, claimed this about the earlier slave condition: 'Husbands and wives are not helpmeets to one another; they rarely reside in the same hut, or even on the same estate' (1838: 76).

What, so far, does our exploration of women's roles reveal about their contribution to nuclear family formation in early Caribbean plantation societies? The Bahamas and the Leewards enjoyed an adequate labor supply in the eighteenth century. A majority of Bahamian slaves lived in nuclear families, although we know little about women's work. In contrast, slave women of the Leewards appear to have worked in domestic service and less demanding areas of field work. Yet nuclear families appear not to have formed in the Leewards, and the crude birth rate was high by early nineteenth-century   Caribbean   standards   only   in Montserrat.

Barbados and Martinique

Barbados reached its peak productive capacity in the late 1600s, 'the first [English colony] to transform its society from a smallholder, semi-subsistence base to a slave-plantation, near-monoculture regime which was dominated by a class of wealthy sugar planters' (Sheridan, 1973: 124). An expanding African slave population made possible this dramatic transition. From a reported 6,000 slaves in 1643, the slave population grew to more than 68,000 in 1783 (Sheridan, 1973: 133; Watson, 1975: 48), primarily through the massive purchase of young male Africans. But by the late 1700s, the abolition of the slave trade was certain, and Barbados had entered a stage of productive decline.

Our best source of information on the daily lives of slaves during the transition from highly successful to less lucrative planting in Barbados comes from two Codrington estates, left to the Society for the Propagation of the Gospel in Foreign Parts in 1710 (Bennett, 1958). In the early 1700s, Codrington shared the remarkable good fortune of the Barbados plantocracy, depending on the heavy purchase of highly productive slaves, and thus maximizing their gain from the sugar boom. And, by the end of the century, the Codrington estates suffered labor shortage and financial loss.

The slave trade lost its relevance for the Codrington plantations in 1761. After fifty years of trial, the policy of restocking with new African Negroes was discarded forever. From 1712 to 1761 the Society had purchased about 450 Negroes at a cost of about £15,000. It had spent two and one-half times the value of the Negroes left by Christopher Codrington, and had added one-half times the number of slaves that had come from him. The outcome of this investment after five decades was a population smaller by more than one-third (Bennett, 1958: 52).

New categories of workers were now brought to the fields. 'Young Negroes who would formerly have been apprenticed to artisans were now kept at work in the secondary great gangs' (Bennett, 1958: 19). Other schemes were tried, including 'recruiting Africans, hiring slaves on an occasional basis, reducing crops and production, concentrating available strength in the field gangs, purchasing parcels of seasoned slaves' (1958: 19). None of these efforts succeeded.

Women became an increased portion of the slave population through purchase and creolization. In 1732, there had been 123 males to 58 females on the Society's estates. Females slightly outnumbered male slaves byu the end of the century. At that time 'one-half of the men worked in the fields, but only one-third of the women were spared the heavy duty on the land' (Bennett, 1958: 13). Table 2 presents the occupational distribution of males and females at Codrington in 1781. Women did some domestic work (personnel workers), but men had more opportunities to evade field work by serving as skilled workers. Moreover, a 1775 price listing indicates that women were engaged in heavy field work, with most in the first gang, and were valued at the same price as first-gang male field hands.

At the same time, estate officials arrived at what they saw as the last resort in solving labor supply problems: 'amelioration' of the slaves' conditions. One goal of amelioration was to 'encourage the Negroes to breed' (Bennett, 1958: 100). Women were now sometimes given a small reward for delivering a child. The resulting birth rate of 2 per cent was an improvement, but was lower than before, and still less than the death rate (2.5 per cent) (1958: 98). Better houses and garden plots were offered, and field work decreased at Codrington with the use of plows in 1812.

Amelioration eventually brought a small natural increase in Codrington's slaves, with a net gain of three slaves in 1795, eleven in 1800, five in 1804, and seven in 1805. By this time, Codrington had moved beyond other estates in Barbados in amelioration and would shortly adopt ways to ease the emancipation of its slaves. The Codrington records are puzzling on marital patterns, as passing sexual unions were often mistaken for polygamous ones (Bennett, 1958: 35). Polygamy was believed to dominate conjugal forms throughout the island. For example, in 1787, Barbados's governor claimed that male slaves generally had several wives (Watson, 1975: 176). It is likely that women and children were often housed separately from men; there are examples in the Codrington records of slaves helping a 'new mother' to build a house (Bennett, 1958: 33). But a mix of single women,   mother–child,   and   polygamous residential patterns probably prevailed, with only some 'enduring monogamous unions' (Bennett, 1958: 35).

The evidence for a natural increase of slaves on the Codrington estates would seem to contradict our hypothesis that labor shortages inhibited reproduction. By 1834, women substantially outnumbered men (173 females to 135 males, counting boys and girls), and worked almost exclusively in field labor, along with girls and boys. Yet 'the breeding program had brought spectacular results in Barbados generally after the abolition of the slave trade in 1807, [with] the Codrington gain thought to be unequaled by any other sugar estate' (Bennett, 1958: 131). Still, the number of new slaves born yearly was small, particularly in comparison with the number purchased earlier. The net gain in slaves was also influenced by the absences of new adult Africans; about 43 per cent of African slaves died soon after reaching Codrington.

Our information on Barbados as a whole, pertaining to a later period, points to the relative success of amelioration. Higman (1976b) calculates Barbados's rate of natural increase at about 10 per 1,000 population by 1823, more than the Leewards' at the same time, but less than the Bahamas'. But as many as 40.7 births per 1,000 population were registered in 1823 (1976b: 68), and 30.6 deaths per 1,000 population. Indeed, the number of slaves increased from 69,400 in 1809 to 82,000 in 1834 (Curtin, 1969: 59). On Codrington, manumissions increased along with task labor as the estate prepared for emancipation. Slaves were also permitted to buy free days (Bennett, 1958: 125). Eventually, slaves were granted plots on which to grow provisions. They paid rent to estate owners in exchange for labor (Bennett, 1958: 129). Women continued to predominate in field work, but it is likely that overall productivity fell as slaves became 'apprentices', and those with lots devoted time to cash crops (1958: 132–33).

It appears, then, that our hypothesis is only partially supported for Barbados. Women experienced an increased role in agricultural production, although reproduction also increased. It is likely, however, that by the 1800s increases in crude birth rate accompanied reductions in labor productivity for both men and women. Although nuclear families seem to have been largely absent, it is unclear whether mother–child units and single females or polygamous family forms prevailed.

Martinique was settled by the French in 1635. Plantation agriculture was quickly established, with more than 21,000 slaves by 1700. Martinique reached its zenith in sugar production from 1763 to 1789 by trading with the United States. On the eve of the French Revolution, Martinique exported more than 8,000 tons of sugar annually, surpassing

Table 1 Sugar Exports of the Ten Leading Caribbean Islands, 1766–70 (annual averages in tons)

	Exports	Areas in square miles
Saint-Domingue	61,247 (1767–68)	10,200
Jamaica	36,021	4,411
Antigua	10,690	108
Cuba	10,000 (1770–78)	44,206
St. Christopher	9,701	68
Martinique	8,778	380
St. Croix	8,230 (1770)	84
Guadeloupe	7,898 (1767)	619
Barbados	7,819	166
Grenada	6,552	120
	166,936	60,362

Source: Sheridan (1973:101).

Barbados (see Table 1).[4] With the start of the nineteenth century, the French West Indies suffered the abolition of the slave trade, changes in colonial administration, and the effects of European wars. By 1815, the sugar industry had recovered, but not to its earlier level of prosperity. French planters purchased some slaves illegally until emancipation in 1848, but maintained a small work force and relatively little agricultural land in cane.

Debien's research on Martinique may offer the most complete assessment of women's work roles and family formation for Caribbean slave societies of the mid- to late eighteenth century. Debien studied records from a single plantation, L'Anse-à-l'Ane, from 1743 to 1778. As early as 1746, adult males and females were about equal in number, with 56 men and 52 women (Debien, 1960: 5). No purchases of slaves were made after 1753, resulting in a small natural population increment after 1763 and continuing near parity in sex ratio. This gender distribution was typical of Martinique's estates in the 1800s (Tomich, 1976: 106).

There was never a labor surplus on L'Anse-à-l'Ane, so both men and women were used as field laborers, mostly in the first gang, with teenagers and children in second and third gangs. This distribution of personnel became

Table 2 Occupations of Slaves at Codrington, 1781

Occupation	Men	Women	Boys	Girls	Total
Field workers	37	52	34	39	162
Artisans and watchmen	17	0	1	0	18
Stockkeepers	10	5	7	1	23
Personnel workers	3	15	0	1	19
Non-workers	4	4	19	27	54

Source: Bennett (1958:12).

common on Martinique's estates (Tomich, 1976: 185–88). Indeed, in 1772, the first gang of 60 field slaves was composed of 20 males and 40 females (Debien, 1960: 18). As in Barbados, male slaves worked in skilled tasks and sugar refining. Debien argues further that women's reproduction was not highly valued, as price data indicate that female slaves were considerably less costly than males aged 18–40. 'Their relatively low price underscores that their reproductive function was secondary; and the constant decline shows that masters were not concerned with an increase in women in order to increase the number of children. Children were always numerous at L'Anse-à-l'Ane, but not as a result of a demographic policy. Simply it is a general custom of the island' (Debien, 1960: 44–45).[5] Women had few paths out of field work, as in other areas of labor shortage. This can be attributed, however, to the rate of planter absenteeism and resulting low need for domestic service. Other evidence of labor shortage is manifest in eighteenth-century Martinique: for example, children increasingly performed field labor in the first gang after 1763 (1960: 23).

Still other indicators suggest that labor shortage was not acute, or at least was mitigated by declining production. For example, although women and children were increasingly drawn into field work, the overall number of field workers fell. Proportionately more slaves were old, sick, freed, or in skilled jobs after 1763. The first gang had 98 workers in 1746, and only 66 by 1773 (Debien, 1960: 5). Moreover, women did hire themselves out for domestic work, a phenomenon not generally associated with an intense need for female labor on New World plantations.

There is evidence of low fertility accompanying high levels of nuclear family formation at L'Anse. There were 58 children born of about 50 slave women at L'Anse from 1762 to 1777, a period for which records were fairly well kept (Debien, 1960: 77). The number of children per 100 women from 1753 to 1773 is recorded in Table 3, and ranges from 69.38 in 1753 to 98.14 in 1763, and then falls to 81.48 in 1767 and 60.41 in 1773. This suggests a decline in fertility, perhaps associated with women's expanding agricultural role. Extending data from L'Anse to the society level, the annual crude birth rate would not be high from 1762 to 1777, only about 21 births per 1,000 population. Debien speculates that infant mortality rates were artifically low in plantation computations. Listings by slaves' names suggest high infant mortality with the death of 29 of 58 babies born from 1762 to the end of 1777 (1960: 77).

Successes in reproduction at L'Anse were largely limited to conjugal families, about 52 of which are recorded for the period from 1761 to 1776. These families produced 215 children, slightly more than four per couple (1960: 58). Conjugal families predominated among Creoles, who made up nine-tenths of the L'Anse population from 1746. 'Maternal families' were less numerous than conjugal units, but more frequent than 'passing units'. The relationships 'approached' conjugal units, with a male maintaining a provision garden for the women and her children. Still, women in such families were less fertile than those in conjugal families.

There was a labor shortage in Martinique from 1763 to 1789, and, like Barbados, it confirms some dimensions of our hypotheses. Women participated in field work disproportionately to their numbers at L'Anse, predominating in the first gang. As expected, the birth rate was well below 30 per 1,000 population. Nevertheless, many couples lived in nuclear families, particularly creoles.[6] Their birth rate was probably higher than 30 per 1,000.

Jamaica and Cuba

Jamaica reached its peak in number of slaves, gross output of sugar, and labor productivity from 1805 to 1809. In 1808, 324,000 slaves were owned by Jamaican planters. Owners found it

Table 3 Demographic Indices, L'Anse-à-L'Ane, 1753–73

	Total slaves	Women older than 17	Number of children younger than 11	Number of children per 100 women
1753	152	49	34	69.38
1763	—	54	53	98.14
1767	163	54	44	81.48
1773	154	48	29	60.41

Source: Debien (1960:73).

cheaper to purchase slaves than to breed them, and tried to purchase males from about 15 to 30 years of age. With the rise of sugar production in the French islands and erosion of Jamaican soil, sugar production became more intense. At the same time, labor was in short supply with the abolition of the slave trade in 1807. This labor shortage greatly influenced the demographic profile of the slave population, as it had in Barbados and Martinique.

Like slave populations in our earlier cases, Jamaica's became proportionately more female, older, and lighter through the early 1800s. The sex ratio favored women on Jamaican estates by 1820. For example, at Worthy Park, records from which have been studied extensively by Craton, 65 per cent of the field labor force was female by 1832 (Craton, 1977: 142). At Rosehall, half of the women were in the field, but only one-eighth of the men. Women also remained in the fields longer than did men (Higman, 1976a: 194). At the Irwin estate in St. James, females constituted the majority in the first and second gangs (1976a: 199). At Maryland, a coffee plantation in St. Andrew, women worked in the fields longer than did men; of those in the 20–59 year age group, only nine women were not in the fields, whereas 20 men were not (1976a: 196). There was also an increase in whiteness among Jamaican slaves, and light skin ceased to be an easy path to manumission or to more highly skilled occupations. Slave owners complained also that too many slaves were over 40 or under 20. Higman comments:

After 1807 the structure of the slave population of Jamaica changed in a manner contrary to the planters' ideal. It became less 'effective' and less 'flexible'. Not only was the number of slaves in the most productive age groups decreasing absolutely and relatively, but the slaves in these groups were also increasingly female and coloured (1976a: 211).

What was the effect on fertility and family form of intensification of women's role in production? Higman (1976a: 156–73) found these relationships on three properties: Old Montpelier, New Montpelier, and Shettlewood Pen. (1) More than half of the 864 slaves on the three properties lived in units with a man, a woman, and her children, or, in a related family type, a woman, her children, and others, while 'probably 100 of the [slave] households... contained mates' (1976a: 164). (2) Other significant household types includes the slave living alone or with friends (about 30 per cent), polygamous units (in which about 11 per cent of slaves resided), mother–child households (about 11 per cent), and male–female households (including about 11 per cent of the slave population). (3) Africans were more likely to live alone or in simple nuclear families (man, woman, his and/or her children) than were Creoles. (4) Slaves of color 'with their privileged occupations and blood allying them to the great house and the whites, formed households in which slave men had no part and which were tightly organized around the maternal connection' (1976a: 162).

At the plantation level there is little relationship between a tendency for a female to work in the fields and to live in a nuclear family. There was a strong tendency for domestics, mostly colored, to live in female-dominated units, for mulatto and quadroon slaves (with white fathers) to live in female-dominated units. Male slaves with authority in the field constituted the male groups most likely to be in the household with women and children. Athough 'co-residence of a mate was conducive, though not essential, to relatively high fertility', colored females were significantly more fertile than black women. The Colored population of Jamaica was only about 10 per cent in 1832, yet colored births constituted 18 per cent of registered slave births from 1829–32. Among 15–19 year olds, the fertility of colored women was five times that of blacks (Higman, 1976a: 154). Higman concludes that the Colored woman, with a higher status occupation and economic security through her likely links to a white man, was more willing to bear children than was the black woman.

Thus, because of the essential economic impotence of the slave, the normal relationship between social status and fertility was reversed. The slave woman of colour and status was therefore more prepared to expose herself to the risk of pregnancy than was the black woman (1976a: 155).

There is no direct evidence that colored women were more fertile because they did not work in the fields. On the other hand, that domestic workers produced more children than field workers on the three plantations studied by Higman is consistent with our hypothesis of a tension between female agricultural work and reproduction. Moreover, Jamaican planters did make some efforts to encourage breeding. By the 1820s, planters exempted women from field work as soon as pregnancy was suspected. After birth, women were permitted to remain in the second gang for as long as they nursed their children, which could be two years (Higman, 1976a: 206–07).[7]

Higman presents some evidence that production did intensify on Jamaican plantations during the 1830s. Although supposedly less productive slaves (i.e., women and teenagers) were now used in the fields, productivity remained fairly consistent from 1800 to 1834. 'Productivity declined less rapidly than the slave population and even more slowly than gross output' (1976a: 213). On the other hand, where slave women were fertile, productivity fell — a relationship supporting our hypothesis. 'The more the slaves were able to maintain and augment their numbers the lower their productivity' (1976a: 221). Higman hypothesizes further that manumissions fell and slave rights were eroded as masters faced labor shortages. Jamaican slaves were tied increasingly to plantation sugar production. Probably 90 per cent were on agricultural units in the 1830s; even in 1834, more than 70 per cent of the active slave labor force was field labor (1976a: 36–42).

Craton's (1977) findings for Worthy Park echo Higman's. Worthy Park was one of the largest and best managed of Jamaica's sugar estates, one of twelve with more than 500 slaves in 1820. With the abolition of the slave trade in 1808, the number of slaves at Worthy Park fell, and with it the profits from sugar production declined. The demographic profile of the field gangs also changed. Women were relied upon increasingly for field labor, with males making up 92.4 per cent of the work force for skilled occupations. In the 1790s women made up 58 per cent of the field labor force; and 65 per cent in the 1830s. Craton comments, 'It was indeed a curious society, as well as an inefficient agricultural economy, in which women for the most part were the laborers and men the specialist workers' (1977: 146).

Efforts to ameliorate slaves' lives eased the natural decrease of slaves at Worthy Park, but the birth rate remained less than the death rate. Planters tried to intensify production in response to falling sugar prices. Productivity actually fell with the 'increasing frailty of the slave labor force', but so did the number of slaves at Worthy Park (Craton, 1977: 172).

The effect of amelioration on overall fertility in Jamaica cannot be assessed accurately. Roberts (1957) speculates that Jamaica's rate of natural decrease fell from a higher, although unspecified, rate in the 1700s to about 5 per 1,000 slaves annually in 1829. Given a close ratio of sexes and a fairly young population, it is likely that a rise in fertility accounts for much of the fall in natural decrease (1957: 245). Roberts

notes, however, that planters reported disappointment in the results of their amelioration programs. M.G. Lewis, for example, complained that after his various efforts in the early 1800s to improve the birth rate on his estates, there was little change. No more than 12 or 13 new babies were born of 330 slaves annually (Lewis, 1834: 320). Registration figures (Appendix) indicate little change in the birth rate, despite the improved sex ratio, but an increase in slave deaths.

The last great sugar island, Cuba, reached its peak well after the abolition of the slave trade and, thus, with Jamaica, suffered dramatic consequences of labor shortage. Seventeenth- and early eighteenth-century Cuba had been only a modest sugar producer; tobacco was the main Cuban export crop. From 1762 to 1838, a transition to large-scale sugar production was completed (Knight, 1970: 6). During that period, 400,000 slaves were imported to Cuba; the slave population increased from nearly 39,000 in 1774 to well over 400,000 in 1841 (1970: 21).

As Cuban sugar production intensified, male slaves were favored; many estates had exclusively male labor force. Half the population was aged from 16 to 25, the rest from 26 to 40 (Moreno Fraginals, 1978: 39). This highly productive demographic profile changed when the slave trade was abolished and as the Spanish metropolitan government urged the importation of African women to curtail the perceived violence and homosexuality of the heavy male slave population. With the new techniques of sugar production adopted in Cuba, women and children could be employed more productively than ever before in sugar agriculture. From 1850, about 45 per cent of African slaves imported to Cuba were women, and nearly all worked in some phase of sugar production, with virtually no mobility to more skilled positions. Moreno Fraginals contends that productivity per capita dropped as the sex ratio equalized, but indicates also that productivity levels demanded of Cuban women slaves surpassed those of other Caribbean slave societies.

As slaves became more difficult to procure, planters attempted to encourage the reproduction of slaves. Nuclear families were rare, Moreno Fraginals tells us, because couples were so often broken up for slaves; mothers and children constituted the basic kinship unit. Some planters encouraged monogamy to increase the birth rate. Several slave breeding farms were established. But the housing of slaves in barracks on many plantations, the related eradication of garden plots to supplement plantation rations, and the supervision of children in plantation nurseries all inhibited nuclear family formation. Nor were many births effected through planters' coercion. Pregnant women received few rewards for giving birth until the 1860s and 1870s, when they were permitted to work only ten house a day and received prizes for children who survived to two years (Moreno Fraginals, 1978: 43-57).

Amelioration efforts of the mid-nineteenth century did reduce slave mortality, especially among infants, and reproduction rates increased. The overall mortality of Cuban slaves from 1835 to 1841 was 63 per 1,000 population, falling to 61 per 1,000 from 1856 to 1860; infant mortality fell from 575 per 1,000 annually to 283 per 1,000 for the same periods. The natural decrease of population improved only slightly from a loss of 44 per 1,000 population annually from 1835 to 1841 to a loss of 33 per 1,000 from 1856 to 1860 (Moreno Fraginals, 1978: 88). From 1860 to 1880, and the emancipation of Cuban slaves, amelioraton measures increased. Still numbers continued to decline through natural decrease and manumissions. In 1883, there were somewhat fewer than 100,000 slaves registered in Cuba.

The Cuban and Jamaican cases offer the same mixed results as those of Barbados and Martinique. Cuban and Jamaican planters used more women than men in agricultural production, with few alternatives or avenues for mobility; these tendencies are not significantly greater for Jamaica and Cuba than for Barbados and Martinique. It appears, however, that women were under more pressure to maintain high labor productivity in Cuba and Jamaica than in Barbados and Martinique. In neither Jamaica nor Cuba were even low levels of natural increase achieved. As for Martinique and Barbados, family patterns are not related to reproduction in the expected way for either Jamaica or Cuba. Nuclear families were common, if not prevalent, in Jamaica, but nearly non-existent in Cuba. The Cuban case,

perhaps along with Barbados, confirms the hypothesized relationships between labor supply and family formation, whereas neither Jamaica nor Martinique does so.[8]

Summary and Conclusions

The two major hypotheses examined are these:

Hypothesis 1: At times of labour shortage, West Indian slave women
(a) were employed in larger numbers than male slaves in field labor;
(b) lived mainly by themselves or with children;
(c) produced relatively few children, resulting in a crude birth rate of less than 30 per 1,000.

Hypothesis 2: At times of adequate labor supply, West Indian slave women
(a) were employed in field labor in the same numbers as males, or less frequently;
(b) lived mainly in nuclear families;
(c) produced relatively large number of children, resulting in a crude birth rate of 30 or more children per 1,000 population.

The cases of labor shortage were late eighteenth-century/early nineteenth-century Barbados, Martinique, Jamaica, and Cuba. The results of my analysis of these cases are presented schematically in Table 4.

All four societies utilized women increasingly in field work as male slaves became scarce. It appears that only slightly larger proportions of the female work force worked in agriculture in Jamaica and Cuba than in Martinique and Barbados. But high levels of labor productivity were probably achieved by women in Jamaica and Cuba. Only Cuba and perhaps Barbados conform to our hypothesis about family patterns. Jamaica and Martinique exhibited higher levels of nuclear family formation than mother–child and single female units. Extensive provision grounds in Jamaica and Martinique

Table 4 Results for Hypothesis 1

	(a) Women outnumber men in fields	(b) Mother–child unit predominates	(c) Crude birth rate is low
Barbados	yes	?	no
Martinique	yes	no	yes
Jamaica	yes	no	yes
Cuba	yes	yes	yes

Table 5   Results for Hypothesis 2

	(a) Women employed equally or less frequently than men in fields	(b) Nuclear families predominate	(c) Crude birth rate is high
Bahamas	yes	yes	yes
Leewards			
Antigua	yes	no	no
Montserrat	yes	no	yes
St. Kitts	yes	no	no
Nevis	yes	no	no

may thus have mitigated the effects of labor shortage on family organization.[9] Reproduction patterns conform more closely to our hypothesis for all societies, although emphasis on amelioration caused dramatic increases in slaves' crude birth rate in Barbados. Nuclear family formation did little to increase reproduction at the aggregate level; amelioration contributed to increased birth rates more powerfully than did nuclear family formation.

The findings related to Hypothesis 2 are presented in Table 5. For the Bahamas and the Leewards, women performed agricultural work as much as or less often than men. In the Bahamas, an adequate labor supply is related to nuclear family formation and increasing birth rate, as predicted. The relationship is not especially strong, however, given that the crude birth rate reached little more than 30 per 1,000 only after 1825. For the Leewards, adequate supplies of labor did not lead to the creation of nuclear families. Only in Montserrat is a crude birth rate over 30 per 1,000 recorded for the early nineteenth century. These cases suggest that labor supply per se does not explain the birth rate of West Indian slaves, and neither does family organization.

This investigation of several West Indian cases suggests that labor shortages did draw women into the most rigorous forms of field labor as the abolition of the slave trade approached. Women's presence in agricultural work seems not to have precluded nuclear family formation in Jamaica and Martinique. Women's agricultural work does seem to have discouraged reproduction in the absence of strenuous amelioration efforts such as those of Barbados in the early 1800s. However, labor supply did not strongly encourage reproduction, as the cases of the Bahamas and Leewards demonstrate.

Theories that unite production and reproduction assume individual or familial incentives for both (Goody, 1976; Boserup, 1970; Blumberg, 1970). In slavery, owners obtained maximum benefits by slaves' reproduction, but had little direct interest in family formation. It may be that in Caribbean slavery family formation related directly to slaves' self-interest, particularly where provision gardening was possible. On the other hand, children may have brought little joy or comfort to Caribbean slaves,[10] given the conditions of life — more difficult than those of more fertile U.S. slaves — and thus reproduction depended on strenuous planter efforts at amelioration.

References

Bennett, J. Harry, Jr. *Bondsmen and Bishops: Slavery and Apprenticeship on the Codrington Plantations of Barbados, 1710–1838* (Berkeley, 1958).

Blumberg, Rae Lesser. *Stratification: Socioeconomic and Sexual Inequality* (Dubuque, IA, 1977).

Boserup, Ester. *The Role of Women in Economic Development* (New York, 1970).

Craton, Michael. *Searching for the Invisible Man: Slaves and Plantation Life in Jamaica*. Cambridge (MA, 1977).

Craton, Michael. 'Hobbesian or Panglossian? The Two Extremes of Slave Conditions in the British Caribbean, 1783–1834', *William and Mary Quarterly*, XXXV, 2 (April 1978), 324–56.

Craton, Michael. 'Changing Patterns of Slave Families in the British West Indies', *Journal of Interdisciplinary History*, X, 1, (Summer 1979), 1–35.

Curtin, Philip. *The Atlantic Slave Trade* (Madison, 1969).

Debien, Gabriel. *Destinées d'esclaves à la Martinique, 1746–1778* (Dakar, 1960).

Dirks, Robert. 'Resource Fluctuations and Competitive Transformation in West Indian Slave Societies,' in C. D. Laughlin, Jr. & Ivan A. Brady (Eds), *Extinction and Survival in Human Populations* (New York, 1978), 122–180.

Fogel, R. W. & Engerman, S. L. *Time on the Cross* (Boston, 1974).

Fraginals, Manuel Moreno. *El Ingenio: Complejo Econmico Social Cubano del Azúcar* (Havana, 1978).

Genovese, Eugene, D. *Roll, Jordan, Roll* (New York, 1976).

Goody, Jack. *Production and Reproduction* (Cambridge, 1976).

Goveia, Elsa V. *Slave Society in the British Leeward Islands at the End of the Eighteenth Century* (New Haven, CT, 1965).

Gutman, Herbert. *The Black Family in Slavery and Freedom, 1750–1925* (New York, 1977).

Higman, Barry W. *Slave Population and Economy in Jamaica, 1807–1834* (Cambridge, 1976a).

Higman, Barry W. 'The Slave Population of the British Caribbean: Some Nineteenth Century Variations', in Samuel Proctor (ed.), *Eighteenth Century Florida and the Caribbean* (Gainesville, 1976b), 60-70.

Higman, Barry W. 'African and Creole Slave Family Patterns in Trinidad', *Journal of Family History*, III, 2 (Summmer, 1978), 163-80.

Higman, Barry W. 'African and Creole Family Patterns in Trinidad', in Margaret E. Crahan & Franklin W. Knight (Eds), *Africa and the Caribbean: The Legacy of a Link* (Baltimore, 1979), 41-64.

Klein, Herbert S. & Engerman, Stanley, L. 'Fertility Differentials Between Slaves in the United States and the British West Indies: A Note on Lactation Practices', *William and Mary Quarterly*, XXXV, 2 (April, 1978), 257-74.

Knight, Franklin W. *Slave Society in Cuba During the Nineteenth Century* (Madison, 1970).

Lewis, Gordon K. *The Growth of the Modern West Indies* (New York, 1968).

Lewis, Matthew Gregory. *Journal of a West Indian Proprietor* (London, 1834).

Mathieson, William Law. *British Slavery and Its Abolition* (London, 1926).

Patterson, Orlando. *The Sociology of Slavery* (Rutherford, NJ, 1969).

Patterson, Orlando. 'From Endo-Deme to Matri-Deme: An Interpretation of the Development of Kinship and Social Organization Among the Slaves of Jamaica, 1655-1830,' in Samuel Proctor (Ed.), *Eighteenth Century Florida and the Caribbean* (Gainesville, 1976), 50-59.

Patterson, Orlando. 'On Slavery and Slave Formations', *New Left Review*, No. 117 (September, 1979), 31-67.

Patterson, Orlando. 'Persistance, Continuity and Change in the Jamaican Working-Class Family', *Journal of Family History*, VII, 2 (Summer, 1982), 135-61.

Quick, Paddy. 'The Class Nature of Women's Oppression', *Review of Radical Political Economics*, IX, 3 (Fall, 1977), 42-53.

Roberts, G. W. *The Population of Jamaica* (Cambridge, 1957).

Sheridan, Richard B. *Sugar and Slavery* (Baltimore, 1973).

Stampp, Kenneth M. *The Peculiar Institution* (New York, 1956).

Sturge, Joseph & Harvey, Thomas. *The West Indies in 1837* (London, 1938).

Tomich, Dale. 'Prelude to Emancipation: Sugar and Slavery in Martinique, 1830-1848', unpubl. Ph.D. diss., Univ. of Wisconsin (1976).

Watson, Karl Steward. 'The Civilised Island, Barbados', unpubl. Ph.D. diss., Gainesville, Univ. of Florida (1975).

Notes

1. The criterion based on crude birth rates during the early nineteenth century. Klein and Eagerman (1978) report that the birth rate among U.S. slaves was 55 per cent 1,000, considered high for mid-nineteenth-century populations in general. Jamaica's low crude birth rate of 23 per 1,000 from 1817 to 1829 is comparable to European birth rates during the same period.

2. Craton (1978) compares the Rolle estate in Grand Exuma in the Bahamas with Jamaica's Worthy Park, and considers many factors important in the higher rates of fertility and nuclear family formation found in the Bahamas. Included among them are the closer sex ratio, the small number of Africans, and a favorable age distribution. He concludes, however, 'The essential differences between the two populations clearly lay in the nature of the economic system in which each was employed. Worthy Park's system was the "factory-in-a-field" of sugar production, while Exuma's was an almost decayed open plantation system with a negligible "industrial" component' (1978: 349).

3. Higman (1976: 65–66) contends that Caribbean slave populations increased their birth rates as the Creole population increased and the sex ratio became more even. 'Thus in the sugar colonies it appears that natural increases did not occur until the populations were disproportionately female' (1976: 66–67). Eventually, feminization, 'aging and wasting' of the population occurred (Craton, 1978), causing a decline in fertility. Sex ratios were similar in St. Kitts, Nevis, Montserrat, and Antigua, and related to an increasing birth rate, but in a strong way only in Montserrat.

4. Martinique was long attractive to France's rival metropoles. English and Dutch attacks had been repulsed in the seventeenth century. The English again tried but failed to capture Martinique in 1759; a British seige succeeded in 1762, but the island was returned to the French by the Treaty of Paris in 1763. The French Revolution threatened Martinique's sugar planters, with talk of rights for black slaves and the free colored population. The French Revolutionary government abolished slavery in 1790, and Martinique's and Guadeloupe's elites surrendered themselves to Britian in 1794. With access to British markets, Martinique once again prospered, until 1802, when Martinique was returned again to France by the terms of the Treaty of Amiens. The British seized Martinique again in 1809, permanently restoring the island to France in 1814. In the meantime, Napoleon had made slavery legal once again.

5. All translations are mine.

6. Debien comments that on the more intensely cultivated Saint-Domingue, there were fewer than two or three families per plantation at any time. The birth rate was also very low.

7. To permit women to nurse their children for two years ran counter to the planters' desire to increase labor productivity. Nursing took women from the fields altogether or removed them to lighter tasks they could complete while breastfeeding a child. Still, planters perceived nursing as a necessary incentive to increase women's fertility, and some associated it with infant health and development — major issues in societies with high infant and child death rates.

8. There is considerable evidence that nuclear families did have more children than other family forms, at the plantation level. At Montpelier, analyzed by Higman (1976a), and L'Anse-à-L'Ane, studied by Debien, nuclear families had more children than did other families. Craton (1978) made the same discovery about slaves at the Rolle estate in the Bahamas.

9. Food allocations and distribution may hold the key to the small population increments and possible propensity for mother–child units in the Leewards. These islands had little non-estate land, although slaves received a small provision garden near their huts to supplement estate-grown and imported provisions. Frequent drought affected ground provisions more than

it did sugar (Mathieson, 1926; 72; Sturge & Harvey, 1838). Rations allotted to slaves were small, 'much less, indeed, than was given in the prisons in Jamaica' (Mathieson, 1926: 72). Slaves in the Leewards may have lacked both the material basis in extensive and productive provision-gardening for the formation of residential conjugal units and the health and welfare conducive to rapid population growth (see also Dirks, 1978).

10. We have no way of knowing how many children were conceived by Caribbean slaves, but were miscarried or stillborn. Craton (1978: 343) reports that 21.8% of 'births' among females at Worthy Park in 1795 were said to be miscarriages in plantation records.

Appendix   Basic Demographic Indices, Early Nineteenth-Century Bahamas, Montserrat, Antigua, Nevis, St. Christopher, Barbados, and Jamaica

	Date	Total slave populations	Males per 100 females	Births per 1,000	Deaths per 1,000	Natural increases per 1,000
Bahamas	1819–22	10,908	104.6	—	—	—
	1822–25	10,036	103.3	26.9	14.2	12.7
	1825–28	9,266	100.2	31.0	14.9	16.1
Leewards						
Montserrat						
	1817–21	6,558	86.4	31.0	30.4	0.6
	1821–24	6,392	86.0	31.4	32.0	− 0.6
	1824–27	6,270	84.6	34.1	28.1	6.0
St. Christopher						
(St. Kitts)						
	1817–21	19,993	92.3	25.2	28.4	− 3.2
	1821–25	19,667	91.9	28.2	29.3	− 0.8
	1825–28	19,413	91.2	29.3	27.5	1.8
	1828–31	19,198	91.5	28.3	26.3	2.0
Antigua						
	1817–21	31,627	87.4	18.5	22.8	− 4.3
	1821–24	30,650	87.9	27.1	27.6	− 0.5
	1824–27	30,077	88.8	25.5	25.2	0.3
Nevis						
	1817–22	9,432	96.6	22.5	25.9	− 3.4
	1822–25	9,274	97.9	23.9	24.9	− 1.0
	1825–28	9,273	97.7	22.9	22.6	0.3
	1828–31	9,201	97.8	23.3	24.6	− 1.3
Barbados						
	1817–20	77,919	86.1	31.7	28.3	3.4
	1820–23	78,581	86.5	34.9	28.5	6.4
	1823–26	79,684	84.9	40.2	28.1	12.1
	1826–29	81,227	85.1	38.0	28.0	10.0
	1829–32	81,701	85.8	40.7	30.6	10.1
Jamaica						
	1817–20	334,266	99.7	23.6	24.3	− 0.7
	1820–23	339,318	98.7	22.8	25.9	− 3.1
	1823–26	333,686	97.4	23.0	25.1	− 2.1
	1826–29	326,770	96.5	22.2	25.6	− 3.4
	1829–32	317,649	95.5	23.2	28.0	− 4.8

Source: Higman (1976b:67–69).

49

The Female Slave in Cuba During the First Half of the Nineteenth Century

DIGNA CASTAÑEDA

African slavery, a historical phenomenon of the New World, is seen with the greatest clarity and depth in Cuban colonial society, in the role and place of the slave woman. The African slave women, despite the great suffering they endured, managed to keep in their minds their native land and part of their culture. As a consequence, they not only fed and protected their offspring, but also taught them about Africa, life, freedom and survival. In this way, they ensured that the slaves would not become mere biological fuel[1] for the economic and cultural development of Europe but helped to establish the slaves' biological and cultural footprints. In brief, they guaranteed the survival of their race, and even more, they played an outstanding part in the wars for national independence in Cuba.

In the Caribbean, and therefore in Cuba, it is impossible to evaluate properly the black woman's present position if her slave predecessors are not taken into account. The study of slavery points towards the future; there is no alternative for those who study this form of oppression but to denounce continuously its evils as well as to find in it the inspiration that can identify ideas for any type of social change.

In this article, the first section of a major work about the black slave woman in Cuba, the examples discussed are drawn mainly from the western regions of the island during the first half of the nineteenth century. It is argued that the coincidence of social class, race and gender came about and manifested itself within African slavery at the same time that these three elements became a means of exploitation. In this context, the black female slave is triply discriminated against: for being black, for being a slave, and for being a woman.

Historical Framework: First Half of The Nineteenth Century

During the first quarter of the nineteenth century in Cuba, there were traces of the initial symptoms of a revolutionary consciousness expressed by, among others, Captain General Marqués de Someruelos, who led a local autonomist movement in which the representatives of the Cuban oligarchy demanded judicial and political equality for all Americans, Antilleans and *peninsulares*; the sending of deputies to the Spanish Cortés, and the autonomy of the colony, a task in which the Cuban priest Félix Varela stood out. Also, the political atmosphere prevailing was clearly seen in the publication of the first constitutional draft document of the island of Cuba, written in Venezuela in 1812 by the Cuban Joaquín Infante.

Consequently, when Captain General Dionisio Vives assumed command of the island in 1823, the conspiratorial activity which was the normal and permanent state of a large number of young Cubans was no longer confined to them.[2] The unrest also affected almost all social classes, and this is the time when the Masonic lodges and secret societies achieved their golden age. A good example was the 'Suns and Rays of Bolivar' conspiracy, founded in 1821, which sought to create the Republic of Cubanacán. To this atmosphere of political unrest can be added the threat of liberating expeditions initiated by Cubans from Colombia and Mexico, such as the one organized by the conspirators of the secret society named 'Great Legion of the Black Eagle', which collapsed in 1829.

Other symptoms that foretold the end of the colonial era in Cuba were the subversive writings of José Antonio Saco in *The Weekly Messenger*, published from 1828 to 1830, the writings of Félix Varela, published in *El Habanero* between 1824 and 1826, and the patriotic verses written by José María Heredia.

Nevertheless, from the 1830s, there was a period – that did not end until the second half of the nineteenth century – characterised by the weakening of the independence movement, as a result, among other reasons, of the effective work of Captain General Francisco Dionisio Vives.[3] Vives managed to guarantee the failure of Cuban separatism and to silence the opposition, to the extent that on 17 May 1824 Fernando VII described the island of Cuba as 'ever faithful' in a *Real Ordenanza*. There were also other events that influenced the new situation: the end of the independence movements against Spain on the continent, and the attitude of England and the United States who lessened their anti-Spain activities because they preferred Cuba to remain Spanish for the time being. Coincidentally, for the rising creole bourgeois aristocracy, independence was not a necessity because they had already achieved the right to free trade. At the same time, their position was strengthened by that of the landowners who tried to preserve their wealth, of which slave ownership formed a part.

In this part of the century, classic marronage and slave revolts suddenly became the 'black peril', so that slavery constituted a source of social and ideological contradiction, giving a new shade of meaning to the political trends prevailing in that epoch.[4] The frequent revolts had the new characteristics of insubordination, premeditation and coordination.[5] Among the most noted conspiracies was the Aponte Conspiracy of 1812, the first conspiracy of free blacks, and 'La Escalera' in 1843.

In short, blacks were feared, whether free[6] or slave. This alarmist notion will be understood if the happenings around Cuba between 1789 and 1850 are examined in time and space. First, the Haitian Revolution[7] became known in Cuba and was seen as a concrete threat.[8] Second, fear increased when the ruling sector became aware of the numerical increase of the black population,

whether free or slave, which in 1817 represented 57 per cent of the population. This increased to 59 per cent in 1847 and 61 per cent in 1855.[9] In addition to this, during the years 1842 and 1843, the English, under the pretext of fighting against the slave trade, stimulated several slave revolts through their consul in Havana, David Turnbull.

Also during this period, the activities of abolitionists like William Wilberforce, Victor Schoelcher and Abraham Lincoln, inspired by the abolitionist ideas of the philosophers Charles-Louis de Secondat Montesquieu, François-Marie Arouet, who called himself Voltaire and Abbe Raynal, contributed to the abolition of slavery in the English-speaking Caribbean colonies (1834), the French-speaking colonies (1848) and in the United States of America (1865). Thus, in the 1840s the internal situation of the colony, in addition to the factors stated above, led to the breakdown of the slave system in Cuba.[10]

The Cuban abolitionist movement found its followers among individuals of liberal thinking and, in general, among writers. The first Cuban novels, like *Autobiography* by Juan Francisco Manzano, *Francisco* by Anselmo Suárez Romero, *Sab* by Gertrude Gómez de Avellaneda and especially *Cecilia Valdés,* by Cirilo Villaverde, had a pronounced anti-slavery character. These works became primary sources of information on slavery in Cuba.

These were the main socio-political features of the period. The Spanish governors, pressed by the international situation mentioned above as well as by the slave rebelliousness, had been forced almost since the beginning of slavery to pass laws aimed at ameliorating slavery. But although most of these laws remained dead letters in some way, they allowed the slaves to defend themselves against their owners. The female slaves played critical roles in these activities.

During the first centuries of the slave trade, few female slaves were imported. Although on 5 May 1523, the solicitors of the already founded cities expressed their interest in introducing black females, the landowners refused to do so, basically because they could get male slaves on the African coasts relatively easily, and they never thought that the trade would end. Only in Baracoa did the Belemnite monks admit black females in their sugar mill, and married them to their male slaves.[11]

Nevertheless, at the beginning of the nineteenth century, after the slave trade was restricted, landowners began to acknowledge the need to bring female slaves from Africa in order to increase their slave stock through natural reproduction. This line of action was strongly supported by the creole economist Francisco de Arango y Parreño, who proposed at a meeting of the *Consulado* of Havana, of which he was a *síndico*,[12] an increase in the number of slaves by encouraging *hacendados* to ensure that one-third of the slaves introduced on to the estates should be female. To facilitate the process, their importation to the island would be exempt from all import duties.

At another meeting of the same institution, the deputies proposed, among other things,

that the master of a male slave married to a female slave of another master will be obliged to sell the male slave after valuation, if the owner of the female slave would like to buy, also taking into consideration the male slave's wishes and with the understanding that the owner of the male slave did not have one-third female slaves on his estate and the owner of the male slave did not allow him to marry.[13]

Within this framework the Royal Decree of 27 April 1804 was promulgated, and it stated: 'The sugar mills and estates where there were only male slaves, should also include female slaves, restricting the license for the introduction of slaves to those properties to that sex (female) only until all the male slaves who wanted to, got married.'[14]

Although this was not totally fulfilled, in the mid-nineteenth century, there were black female slaves on all the estates sharing the harsh tasks of the plantation with their male partners. The fulfillment of the assignments given to black female slaves was done with such effectiveness that some foremen could say, 'black females slaves are hardier and more consistent than males . . .'[15]

This assertion was based on the fact that the duties of female slaves were not limited to agricultural tasks, but consisted also of others both in the city and in the countryside. They served their owners directly or were hired as wet nurses or dressmakers, and performed other domestic chores, such as ironing and cooking. They also became midwives.[16] Most of these tasks, especially being midwives, helped enslaved women to acquire their freedom, which could also be obtained through ordinary sexual life with a white man.

Apart from the rigours of the regime of work to which female slaves were subjected in city and countryside, they were also victims of the most cruel and outrageous punishments like lashing, being sent to the stocks, or being whipped with their face downward even during pregnancy.[17] At the same time they were the targets of some sadist masters who manifested their sexual aberrations through activities that were inconceivable for the mentally sound. Don Ramón Saíz, from Havana, for example, promised his 14-year-old female slave, the mulatto Florencia Rodriquez or Hernandez,[18] to grant her freedom if she had sexual relations with him. Once his goal was achieved, he withheld her freedom and more than that, he punished her very often and forced her to work in the blacksmith's shop and even, according to the slave's own words, 'he tried to place silver rings in the most secret parts of her nature'.

In the face of this situation in October 1834, she complained to the mayor who asked if she was wearing the rings, to which the accuser answered no, but that her master had tried to put the rings on her, as he had previously with her friend, the *mulata Inés*, after he had had her as his woman for some time.

Despite these facts, the mayor did not do a thing except to offer to talk to the master and to send her home. In the circumstances, she continued urging her claims by other petitions as nobody paid attention to her in the village because, as she declared, the master had money and, she added, she sought help because if they were to send her back to him, she would die.[19]

The female slaves were also victims of such abuses as their owners stealing their belongings. Thus, for example, in Guanabacoa village on 1 March 1828, María del Carmen Gangá made an accusation against her master to the first mayor of the village, because her master had stolen 21 ounces of gold from her as well as some jewellery that was the product of her husband's savings. Although the master was summoned to appear in court many times, the records indicate that he never showed up.[20] Meanwhile the fact that the female slave remained in the hands of the *síndico* testified to the partiality of the colonial authorities.

In August 1860, the female slave Rosa Novantes presented to the síndico a document that credited her right to the money obtained for a lottery bill that she had bought with her mistress Doña Rosa Fuentes, priced at 50,000 pesos in 1855. According to the plaintiff, Don José Fuentes had not given the corresponding share either to her or to her mistress. Having lost the case at the Nueva Bermeja Court, she went to see the Regent of the Royal Audience where owing to the delay, she insisted on having a defence attorney, or the necessary means for her defence and on the taking of testimony from witnesses.[21]

Of all these abuses, the most outrageous was the separation of the slave family. During the first half of the nineteen century in Cuba, the slave family had unique characteristics, and although the family was recognised[22] and theoretically protected by the Hispanic legislation that ruled the colony, its capacity to survive under such inhumane conditions was truly dramatic.

Within this slave colonial context, the role of the black female, whether enslaved or free, was outstanding. In accordance with her possibilities, she fought boldly with all the means at her disposal, including legal ones, to protect her relatives; she helped them to obtain their freedom or get it back, and to keep them united. This was a hard and complex struggle, because generally the family nucleus was dispersed, subject to the will of different slaveholders who violated the laws with impunity, almost always with the connivance of the colonial authorities who were supposedly responsible for defending the slaves.

One of the methods used by the owners of slaves to violate the laws established to protect the slaves and the integrity of their families was to send the urban slaves to the countryside and hide them there. Thus, for instance, a document of the Superior Government Secretariat of the island of Cuba (12 September 1837) revealed, based on the story of the plaintiff, María Dolores Fría, that her daughter Ana María, slave of Marcos Podrón, came to her 15 days before and complained that her master habitually ill-treated her. She therefore asked the *síndico* for a licence to find a new master. But when a potential purchaser turned up, the master discouraged him by accusing her of being a runaway and of having several shortcomings. After achieving his objective, he sent the slave to Alquízar where she continued to be equally ill-treated and although she had been assessed[23] at 350 pesos, the master managed to prevent her from being sold. As a consequence, when in 1838 the master, Podrón, was commanded to allow the slave to go to the capital to find a new master because there was a potential buyer, he said she had already been sold to the administrator of Dolores sugar mill a few days before.[24]

The same method was used against the town slave, María de la Cruz Pedroso, age 25, slave of Don Joaquín García, who was sent to the countryside to prevent her from being bought by the purchaser, whom Rosalía Pedroso, an African native who was her mother and a free brown, had found for her. This was the reason for her decision to approach the authorities.[25]

Slave mothers had also to face other arbitrary acts. For example, their children who had been born free were sold as slaves. They were separated from their small offspring, or their owners failed to protect them according to the stipulation of the colonial laws. There are many such examples: among them is the situation faced by the female slave María Dolores Español, property of Don Juan Peraza. She presented a claim to the síndico in 1851 because her daughter, María Francisca, a free brown, was unfairly enslaved. This young woman was born in Madrid in 1832, the year in which her mother travelled to the Peninsula, and in which the girl was baptised in the San Sebastian parish church. On coming back to Cuba they stole her daughter and sold her as a slave for 6 ounces of gold, which her mother discovered after some time; and although she did all she could to obtain the baptismal certificate from the Spanish capital, she never succeeded.

Likewise, although the *síndico* from Bejucal filed a suit against Don Isidro Fernández who had bought the said freed slave, he could only get her sent in deposit to the Royal House of Welfare, where she was hired like the other slaves. This decision did not resolve the problems because it did not restore her freedom.[26]

Something similar happened to María Francisco Cañedo, free brown, whose daughter was in Doña Loreta García's possession for 22 years, out of which the slave spent more than 12 as a *coortada*, leaving only 5 ounces of gold to pay for her freedom. But the young slave got sick and she was given to her mother, for two years, to cure her. In this span of time, the free brown woman not only assisted her sick daughter at her own expense, and without receiving any help from the mistress, but also raised the mistress' son, which led her to believe that out of gratitude for her services plus the small amount of money left to pay for the young slave's freedom, her daughter would be granted her letter of freedom. Instead, she was cheated and as soon as her daughter recovered, she was taken away to the Malverde coffee plantation in Quivicán, where she was in 1849 when her mother took the case to the colonial authorities to claim payment for her services and for her daughter to be placed in deposit. To conclude, the young female slave was valued at 85 pesos, but the process could not continue because the slave did not appear in court, naturally, because she was in captivity.[27]

The violation of the colonial laws was constant, therefore the *coartación* process was violated constantly. This happened to María Justina, slave of Don José Came, who received 50 pesos from the slave's mother, the free brown Josefa Ramírez, as a payment for her freedom. Later on, the master sold her to Doña Maria Ana Betancourt without the requirements of a valuation. The new mistress, in turn, also tried to sell her to someone who was going to taker her abroad. That was the reason why the slave's mother took the case to the *síndico* to request that her daughter be assessed at 50 pesos to allow her to find a new master of her choice.[28]

The constant increase in the slave's estimated price was another method used to hinder the sale of slaves already assessed. This is the reason why generally the female relatives, mothers, wives and daughters went to the court room to seek justice. This was the case of María Encarnación, a free brown from Cárdenas who in 1835 complained to the authorities in Havana because Doña Rosalía del Corral, owner of her mother Joaquina Gonga, did not want to accept the amount of money she offered to free her mother. She explained that the owner wanted 200 pesos for someone whose value was barely 100 pesos, because her mother was so gravely ill that she was unable to stand up straight, but still the mistress insisted on the same price.[29]

The marriage of the brown slaves, Hilario and Inés, who belonged to the slave crew of the Nazareno sugar mill, property of Juan de Larrinaga, in Guanajay, furnishes another example of the abuses suffered by the slave family. This couple, in 1852, asked that their four-year-old son, Juan Criollo, be given back to them. They explained that Don Juan Benítez, declaring himself the owner of the little black boy, had taken him away to another place, they said that they did not want to live without their son who constituted all their happiness. The *síndico,* arguing on the basis of the Slave Regulations of 1842, said that this set of rules tended, in all its articles, to develop the principles of morality and family among slaves and that Article 31 said: 'When the master of the male slave husband buys the woman, he should also buy along with her, the children who are under three years old, based on the right that up to this age the children should be breast-fed and nurtured.'[30]

For this reason, Don Juan Benítez was asked to come to the captain's office with the little boy, Juan, to sign the bill of sale with Jan de Larrinaga, in accordance with the previous valuation by the *síndico,* and because the parents wanted Larrinaga to buy their little son. Juan Benítez refused, arguing that he had raised the little boy as his own son and would not therefore, under any circumstances, sell him; that with him, the boy was better fed and cared for and that, besides, he wanted to give him his letter of freedom so that by the time he became an adult, he would inherit it. Moreover, he proposed to buy for 2,000 pesos the boy's parents, his sister Eulogía, and by valuation, another slave, to collect from Jan de Larrinaga who owed him and thereby unite the whole family. To conclude, it appears that there was an agreement between the masters, because the authorities gave Juan Benítez the opportunity to buy the little boy who was given his freedom letter and it was decided that the boy should remain under the care of Juan Benítez, who was obliged to feed him. To sum up all these facts, the family remained separated.[31]

The kidnapping or sale of slaves was also another type of abuse suffered by blacks, including black women. Testimony presented by the United States' consul in Santiago de Cuba on behalf of the black woman Carolina, born in Savannah City, Georgia, gives further evidence. Carolina declared in her testimony that she was the daughter of free parents , and that she had been sold, together with her children and a sister, by Mr. Francisco Fabars, businessman of the city, who also kept her brother as a slave. In the face of this situation, the consul demanded that the law be respected, because although he was not authorised to explain the measures the United States government would take if he got no response to his claim, he was sure that this crime would be mercilessly punished. Moreover, the female slave stated that her mother had her letter of freedom, given to her in payment for having raised Fabars himself in Baracoa, and that she went to the United States to accompany Fabars' mother; once there, she decided, being free, to go to Charleston. After some time she wrote back to her mistress because she wanted to return. The mistress immediately sent a cousin for her, but on their way back, they experienced shipwreck and in the accident the female slave lost her letter of freedom., the original copy of which must have been in Baracoa City. She also made it clear that the father of her children was Don Francisco de Mesa Garibaldo, who had bought their freedom. Therefore all three of them were free. Since she was short of money, she had claimed for the money that belonged to her, but Fabars had not given it to her, so she took the matter to court.

Fabars' defence was that Carolina's mother was the property of his mother; that they came from Santo Domingo and that on arriving in Cuba she decided to send some of her slaves to the United States, where Carolina was born. He also declared that the plaintiff's mother got pregnant in Cuba and died as a slave. Based on the circumstances, the authorities agreed to send Carolina to the slave depot. In the mistresss' will she and her children were registered as slaves, and no letter of freedom was found. However, the Military-Political Government of Santiago de Cuba, taking into consideration the fact that her freedom had been paid for, acknowledged Carolina Fabars' free status and gave her letter of freedom.[32]

Maybe the most famous case of deception in the nineteenth century, and one which became an international lawsuit, was that of Plassy Laurence. This brown woman, also known in Havana as María del Carmen, was the slave of Don Pedro Pino when the claim was first presented to the English Consul on 15 February 1851. The female slave stated that she had been unfairly submitted to slavery for over 30 years, although she was a native of the British island of Nevis.

According to her statement, in 1819 or 1820, counselled by Juan Scabraugh, she ran away from her mother who was a slave at the Farm. This man took her to the island of St. Thomas, at that time a Danish island, where they were caught and handed over by the governor to be sent back to Nevis. But as she did not want to go back, she ran away from the detaining officers, and hid in the house of a native of that island named Jane Huggins, who took her to another black female from whose house she was placed in a boat captained by a white man, heading for Fagard Port in the island of Puerto Rico. From there, she travelled on horseback to another point called Cadgoa, and was taken to the house of Captain Florencio. She ran away from this place and went to the judges of the village, but found no mercy and was put in jail under the custody of the mayor, Don Victoriano Sancalo, who sold her for 200 pesos to Don Joaquín Delgado. She defied this master because he wanted to send her to the field; so he exchanged her for a French cook from don Leopoldo Román, who enslaved her for two years. She refused to work or to be sold, insisting that she was free, so this master sent her to Havana on a ship with a group of African blacks and a shipment of wood that was unloaded in Talla Piedra, where she was warned not to say where she was coming from. From there, she was taken to the house of Don Antonio Vida o Vilá on Cuba Street. Upon the latter's death, his butler Don Pablo Soler, in the light of her refusal to work on the grounds that she was free, sent her to the consulate where she stayed for approximately six months. She was then sold to Don Francisco Muñoz, who lived in front of the consulate on the road to Cerro. He, in his turn, sold her to Ramón Hernandez in Jesús del Monte, who gave her to Don José Buciano, who was murdered shortly afterwards, but his papers went to Pedro Rizo who made her his slave. Plassy commented that his intentions were not clear.

María del Carmen or Plácida Lawrence or Plassy Lawrence – as her name appears interchangeably – wanted to go back to her family in Nevis; which is why she went to the consul of England in Cuba, who took up her case and presented a claim to the government of the island. While the investigations were going on as usual the slave was kept in the Paula hospital where she was forced to assist all patients and was exposed to infections. The consul pointed out this situation in a letter to the captain general and requested that she be removed from that place and freed because she had committed no crime.

Six months after all this began, the English consul again wrote to the captain general asking him to wrap up the case since, in his opinion, sufficient time had passed for the proper searches abroad. He added that at that moment, moreover, (2 February 1852) Plassy was in the Royal House of Welfare, but they wanted to send her back to the Hospital of San Lázaro to work as a hired slave there. In addition, the diplomat insisted on speeding up the investigation and freeing her from slave work, because she should be considered a British subject. In May 1852 the black male Fippo Laurence, an adult and relative of the slave, arrived from Nevis to identify her officially, which he did before the authorities, adding that he knew Plassy's mother, Elsie.

Meanwhile, the English consul made investigations in Nevis and received documents that gave credibility to Plassy's statements. They even checked the lists of slaves on the Farm estate as of 14 July 1817. This estate, which belonged to William Lawrence, listed Plassy as number 70, and 14 years old, and in the Nevis slave register of 1 January 1825, Plácida was mentioned as missing. The British diplomat sent the evidence to the Spanish governor of the island, and also insisted that she had been taken out of the island as a slave and sold with impunity, and that Plácida was a subject of Her Majesty Queen Victoria by birth. It was also proved by the scars on her leg, arm and body, that Plácida and María del Carmen were one and the same person. The consul demanded monetary compensation for his client for more than 30 years of enslavement in Cuba and Puerto Rico. The compensation would take the form of a salary of 10 pesos per month, although she had earned more for her master, which amounted to 3,600 pesos. The consul was, however, willing to accept 2,000 pesos.

In the investigations carried out in Cuba, some masters denied Plassy was their slave. Other masters had died. The governor of the Danish island, St. Thomas, also sent a report stating that there was no trace of Plassy's stay there. In these circumstances, the British consul declared in a letter to the captain general, dated 15 June 1852, that once she was properly identified as Plassy Lawrence, belonging to the Nevis island, she should be freed and allowed to go back in the ship that would leave Havana harbour on the 22nd of that month. As he received no answer, he sent another letter on July 1, in which he asked the captain general to send back the witness together with Plassy in the ship that was to leave on 10 July 1852. Finally, the diplomat sent another letter on 4 December 1852, indicating that the process had been too prolonged, therefore he considered the captain general had had time enough to consult his government.

Plassy then ran away onboard an English Frigate, *La Vestal*. The event became an international scandal that was reported in the English press, mainly by the *Morning Post,* whose article was reproduced by *La Gaceta de la Habana* on Wednesday, 23 February 1853. In one of its paragraphs, it stated:

(On) the 10th of December there was great excitement in Havana owing to the kidnapping from Nevis island, belonging to Great Britain, of a subject of her Majesty the Queen, the female black Plassy Lawrence, who was sold as a slave in Havana. The British Government had demanded the return of this poor woman who found refuge on Her majesty's frigate La Vesta Vestal, whose gallant Captain kept her safe under the British Flag and ignored all proposals to restore Plassy to her masters, despite being under the cannons of the Spanish batteries and surrounded by the Spanish squadron.

The reporter from *La Gaceta de la Habana*, the official newspaper of the Spanish government, said the delay of the Spanish authorities was:

not only just but also indispensable in a country where the sacred right of property is guaranteed by the law and under the custody of zealous authorities, who before presenting the desires of the Government of Her Majesty the Queen of Great Britain, in relation to the handing over of the mentioned Plácida Lorenza, should firstly find out the facts on which such a claim was based, and that it was also necessary even when her place of birth was positively identified, to answer a matter of international law of such importance for the interests of this Antillean island.

Furthermore, the article stated, 'We consider no less worthy of praise the correct decision of our government to submit such behaviour to the resolution of His Majesty, because as we had said before, it was a matter of international law and in such matters only the Supreme Power can decide.'

In another paragraph, the article accused the people from the ship of performing a despicable act which favoured the escape of a person whose case was before the courts, pending a sovereign's resolution. In addition, the reporter asked what could be expected of a person who ran away from home at the age of 17.

The piece of news was also published by the French and American newspapers, for instance, the *Journal des Debats Politiques et Literaire* of 18 January 1853, *The Morning Courier* and T*he New York Enquirer.* The last two under the title, 'Importante de la Havana', reported Plassy's escape and featured *La Vestal,* commanded by Captain Cospabrick Baillie Hamilton, as a ship that served in the naval station of North America and the West Indies. The press defended Plassy and even referred to the fact that she was forced to become a prostitute and that her children were sold as slaves.

Further investigations proved that Plassy had run away, after she had conversed (in English) with the British consul, who had gone to the House of Welfare to talk to her. After Plassy's escape, the captain general replied to the British consul on 15 December, telling him he had not yet received a decision from Her Majesty the Queen.

As a consequence of the international scandal provoked by Plassy's escape, the captain general of the island of Cuba suggested in a letter to the President of the Council of Ministers Overseas, the convenience of 'declaring the freedom of the forementioned black slave, so they could show a clear sample of disinterest and respect for the most severe and strict justice'. He also criticised the behaviour of the English consul, who, as the captain general said, offended the dignity and good faith of the Spanish government and abused the immunities and privileges that went with his position.

Finally, the search of the Spanish government to find the fugitive proved fruitless, as the letter sent on 29 August 1853 from the Spanish consulate in Nassau to Havana demonstrated, stating that they could not find Plassy either in Nevis or in the surrounding islands.[33]

To conclude, this unhappy woman was in the hands of nine persons, had eight masters, was sold four times, bartered once and inherited once, all within the context of fraud and deceit in four Caribbean countries. The case became notorious not only because of the human significance, but mainly because by that date slavery had already been abolished in the British and French Caribbean colonies. Therefore, England and France did not give away this opportunity to harass publicly, the slaveholding Spain.

Conclusions

In conclusion, the black African and creole female slaves during the first half of the nineteenth century played an important role in the entire society of Cuba. They not only helped the masters' families with their work on the plantations and in the cities, but were also the foundation of their households, because they breast-fed the children, fed the adults, sewed their clothes, took good care of them when they were ill, and were even – as had been related – frequently forced to satisfy the sexual needs of their masters.

In the slave community, the role of women was all the more outstanding because apart from procreating, they were the centre of their homes. They were responsible for all the domestic chores and they were also the ones who fought all the legal battles, based on slave legislation, to defend their rights and those of their relatives and even to keep united the battered family, which is well known to have been the target of multiple disruptive attacks.

The tremendous battle that the slave women must have fought forced them to encounter complex judicial processes, the violation of the law and other arbitrary acts that reduced the possibilities of victory. However, their demands were far from being in vain, because not only did they serve to secure their rights, but they also allowed them to reveal, for posterity, the horrors of slavery and the true situation of the black female slave.

Notes

1. The term is used by Rene Depestre in 'Buenos Dias y Adiós a la Negritud', *Cuaderno Casa de las Americas*, Havana, No. 29, p. 9.
2. See Cirilo Villaverde, *Cecilia Valdés*, p. 266, quoted by Alain Yacou in *Esclavage et Conscience Revolutionnaire à Cuba (Dans la Prémière Moitie du XIXe Siécle)*, (Pointe-a-Pitre: April 1969), p.3.
3. Ibid., p. 5.
4. That is, integrism, autonomism, annexionism and independentism.
5. See Alain Yacou, *Esclavage et Conscience*, p. 16.
6. Ibid., p. 18.
7. See Digna Casteñada Fuertes, *La Revolución Haitiana, 1791–1804*, (Havana City: Social Sciences Publishing House, 1992).
8. See Alain Yacou, *Esclavage et Conscience*, p. 9.
9. Ibid., p. 13.
10. See Fernando Portuondo, *Historia de Cuba*, (Havana: National Publishing House, 1975), p. 196.

11.   Fernando Ortíz, *Los Negros Esclavos*, (Havana: Social Sciences Publishing House, 1975), p. 196.

12.   He was the official appointed in the cities to protect the rights of the slaves and to administer justice.

13.   Ortíz, *Los Negros*, p. 197.

14.   Ibid., p. 198

15.   Aselmo, Suárez Romero, quoted by Ortíz, *Los Negros*, pp. 193-99.

16.   See Pedro y Deschamps Chapeaux, *El Negro en la Economía Habanera del Siglo XIX*, pp. 169-84.

17.   Ortíz, *Los Negros*, p. 285.

18.   In the documents, these surnames are used interchangeably.

19.   Fondo Gobierno Superior Civil, Sheaf 936, no. 33109, Cuban National Archives (ANC).

20.   Ibid., Sheaf 938, no. 33655.

21.   Ibid., Sheaf 953, no. 33655.

22.   Supporting the family were the Royal Provision of Emperor Charles V and Cardinal Cisneros, dated 11 May 1527, confirmed repeatedly. See Fernando Ortíz, *Los Negros*, p. 401.

23.   According to Fernando Ortíz 'The *coartación* consisted of the right granted by the slave by giving his/her master a given amount of money if he/she was not sold at an agreed price, from which such an amount was discounted; and so the slave could become free by giving to his/her master the difference in money between the one already handed to his master as estimated and the fixed price.' For more information, see, Ortíz, *Los Negros*, pp . 285-90.

24.   Fondo Gobierno Civil Superior, Sheaf 938, no. 33087.

25.   Ibid., Sheaf 946, no. 33353.

26.   Ibid., Sheaf 946, no. 33376.

27.   Ibid., Sheaf 946, no. 33365.

28.   Ibid., Sheaf 948, no. 33497.

29.   Ibid., Sheaf 937, no. 33060.

30.   Ibid., Sheaf 948, no. 33487.

31.   Ibid., Sheaf 947, no. 33312.

32.   Ibid., Sheaf 944, no. 33312.

33.   Ibid., Sheaf 947, no. 33381.

50

Property Rights in Pleasure:
The Marketing of Enslaved Women's Sexuality

HILARY McD. BECKLES

Visitors to Britain's West Indian plantations during the last decades of slavery frequently commented on what they considered the culturally endemic and morally regressive socio-sexual practices of white creoles. Comments reflecting aspects of the moral outrage that characterized popular anti-slavery literature, tended to focus on the values of domesticity within which racial groups were forging a new social sensibility. In general, they contained informed judgements on how the ethical character and aesthetic standards of creoles were shaped within the ideological sphere of the colonial mission, and highlighted the principal interest of slaveowners in maintaining and defending comprehensive property rights in persons.

Some proslavery practitioners, in addition, also seemed concerned by the extreme power held by slaveowners with respect to their right to intervene and manipulate the social world of the enslaved, especially its bio-social reproductive capacity. Ideologically, slaveowners understood well that they were entitled to commodify fully all the capabilities of slaves, as part of the search for maximum economic and social returns on their investment. Properly understood, this meant, among other things, the slaveowners' right to extract a wide range of non-pecuniary socio-sexual benefits from slaves as a legitimate stream of returns on capital, and an important part of the meaning of colonial mastery.

In real terms, then, slavery in the islands led to the legal and customary institutionalization of the slaveowners' right to unrestricted sexual access to slaves as an intrinsic and discrete prod-

uct.[1] The circuitous route of capital accumulation within the slave system, furthermore, recognized no clear distinction between the slave-based production of material goods, and the delivery of sexual services. Production and reproduction oftentimes were indistinguishable within the market economy of slavery. With respect to slave women, then, household work, which ordinarily meant manual labour, also included the supply of socio-sexual services and the (re)production of children as a measurable marginal product that enhanced the domestic capitalization process.

An exploration into the dynamic, multidimensional system of slaveowning which focuses on slaveowners' property rights in slave sexuality is essential to a psycho-social and economic grasp of the accumulating mechanisms that emerged from slavery as a mode of (re)production. The contours of such an excavation and display, furthermore, are particularly relevant to any discursive journey into the 'inner' worlds of enslaved women whose deeper integration into the market economy remains largely uncharted on account of the undeveloped discourse on the gender implication of slaveowning.

The outer sphere of this investigation touches upon the violent access to slave women's bodies by their owners, and the sale of their persons for money upon the sex market. Laws did not allow slaves to refuse social demands made by owner, but did provide for the punishment of recalcitrant, disobedient, rebellious and unruly slaves. Rape as a form, or degree, of sexual violation perpetrated against enslaved women by males -

black, white, free or enslaved – was not considered a legal offense, and evidence of it does not appear in the litigation records.

Neither colonial statutes nor slave codes, then, invested slaves with any rights over their own bodies, but rather transferred and consolidated such rights within the legal person of slaveowners. This direct translation of legal entitlement into social power and authority meant that white men especially were located at the convergence where the racial, sexual, and class domination of slave women provided a totality of terror and tyranny. This judicial patriarchy supported and buttressed the ideological representation of white mastery, and illuminated the hegemonic maleness of the colonial enterprise.

The rape of the enslaved woman was first and foremost an attack upon her as a woman. Her powerlessness enters the scene of the offense only insofar as it serves as a confirmation of the totality of enslavement. It is for this reason that Orlando Patterson, attempting to compare violent rape with the coercive mechanisms of sexual manipulation, laid bare the social reality of plantation life when he stated that rape was often 'unnecessary since the slave negress soon gave into the overwhelming pressures and made the best of its rewards.'[2] This argument rises directly from the many assertions found in the tortured texts of slaveowners' narratives in which rape is rarely admitted but where clear prominence is given to slave women accepting offers they could not easily reject.[3]

The inner sphere of the investigation concerns the theme of the commercialization of slave women's sexuality as cash-receiving prostitutes. This subject also has several important implications for the way in which gender, race, and class relations are viewed within the market worlds of the slave mode of production. The roles of slaves as mistresses and concubines, and their use as prostitutes, is analyzed in connection with the formal institutional presence of 'leisure houses'; these two processes in turn are considered against the general background of the passage and reform of slave laws and the complex ideological world of miscegenation.

Unlike the Antiguan colonial elite of the seventeenth century, Barbadian colonists did not legislate against miscegenation. In 1644, Antiguans passed a law which prohibited the 'carnall coppullation between Christian and Heathen.'[4] Barbadians, however, hoped that the bio-social aspects of their white supremacy ideology, enshrined in the slave laws, would function as an adequate deterrent. The dominant ideological charge of the slave laws was that blacks were heathens and should not share the same psycho-social space as Christians. The use of dehumanizing animal analogies and demonisation references to blacks were common. Blacks, therefore, were not to be integrated into the emotional and sexual spheres of whites, either as domestic equals or as leisure-seeking partners.[5]

Representations of racial inequality in this social idealism, however, could not find real-life roots in the colonial setting; here societal standards were being fashioned in a rather hurried and ad hoc manner. The social and demographic realities of plantation life oftentimes required pragmatic social approaches to race relations, which included, among other things, submission to the tendencies of human sexuality to transcend ideological boundaries no matter how firmly established. Consequently, the earliest Barbadian slaveowners came to consider it their legitimate right and privilege to engage in sexual liaisons with blacks. According to Richard Dunn, seventeenth-century plantation records indicate that 'the master enjoyed commandeering his prettiest slave girl and exacting his presumed rights from her.'[6] This tradition is further illuminated by John Oldmixon in 1708. Reporting on the domestic lives of slaveowners in Barbados, he noted that the 'handsomest, cleanliest (black) maidens are bred to menial services' in order to satisfy their masters in 'divers' ways.'[7]

As the anti-slavery movement gained momentum towards the end of the eighteenth century, promoting its ideas by focussing upon the exploitation of black women and the destruction of slaves' family life, the moral authority of slaveowners came under intense scrutiny. Indicative of popular European opinion was the reaction of an English military officer, Colonel Hilton. He reported in 1816 his horror and outrage at the sight of a white woman in the slave market preparing to make a purchase by examining the genitals of male slaves 'with all possible indelicacy.'[8] Likewise, F. W. Bayley, an English traveller in the 1820s, found organized slave prostitution in Bridgetown rather distasteful, but reported that white males considered the houses of 'ill repute' socially indispensable.[9] Mrs. E. Fenwick, an English schoolteacher living in Bridgetown during the 1810s, tried desperately but failed ultimately to accept a social culture in which young white males commonly underwent their sexual apprenticeship with domestic slaves and prostitutes 'brought into the household solely and explicitly for the purpose of sex.' Fearing for the moral character of her young nephew, she prepared to remove him to Philadelphia, but was defeated in the effort by a 'raging fever' that took his life.[10]

Creole slaveowners seemed undisturbed by such searching critical comments on their social lives and personal struggles. In general, they considered it no evidence of degenerate taste to retain black or coloured female slaves as sexual partners. The evidence suggests, furthermore, that such social relations were popular in Bridgetown, while probably less so on the plantations, although estate owners and managers had social access to a larger number of slave women. In Bridgetown, organized prostitution, and the formal integration of slave mistresses into white households, were common enough, while on the sugar estates sexual access to slave women took more covert forms and was less visible to outsiders.

Urban society was influenced considerably by the maritime activity on which its economy depended. Here, prostitution was as much in demand as any social institution. The large, transient, maritime personnel expected to be able to purchase sex and the liberal values and ideological openness of urban society allowed for the proliferation of facilities that promoted slave prostitution. Claude Levy informs us that from the seventeenth century, Barbados was one of the region's busiest entrepots, and that slave prostitution was 'an occupation which was more common at Bridgetown than in any other city in the British West Indies.'[11] With reference to Jamaica, Higman states: 'Prostitution was common in the towns but rare on the plantations. No slaves were listed in the registration returns as prostitutes. But the inns and taverns of the towns were very often brothels as well, and the slaves attached to them were used as prostitutes as well as domestics.'[12] Prostitution was illegal in Barbados and Jamaica, but there is no evidence to show that the laws were enforced vigorously, a circumstance which suggests that this criminal activity was condoned if not encouraged by imperial and colonial officials.

Elizabeth Fenwick could find no significant reason to differentiate morally between urban slaveowners who engaged slave women as prostitutes and resident mistresses, and plantation owners who used them as 'breeding wenches' in search of a greater labor supply. For her, these roles overlapped, because many prostitutes were often the kept mistresses of white males, who also encouraged them, from time to time, to have children so as to benefit financially from the sale of the child. In Fenwick's value system, slavery, in this specific context, was 'a horrid and disgraceful' institution, and while she expressed a marked sympathy for 'victimized' slave women, she was particularly disturbed by the manner in which slave prostitutes and resident mistresses (invariably housekeepers) constituted a subgroup within many white households – a kind of informal socio-sexual domestic service sector. According to her:

The female slaves are really encouraged to prostitution because their children are the property of the owners of the mothers. These children are reared by the ladies as pets, are frequently brought from negro houses to their chambers to feed and to sleep, and reared with every care and indulgence till grown up, when they are at once dismissed to labour and slave-like treatment.

Domestic arrangements that sought to conceal the practice of prostitution, she added, were 'common' to both urban and rural white households, and not considered 'an enormity.'[13]

Plantation owners, however, consistently denied that female slaves were sexually abused or used for sex-related 'immoral gain.' They maintained that slave women were generally promiscuous, and pursued sexual relations with white males for their own material and social betterment. With respect to Newton Plantation in Barbados, the data for the late-eighteenth century show that female slaves feared, and sought to escape sexual violence at the hands of white personnel. Slaveowners reports also indicate that domestic slaves sought sexual relations with white men, both on and off the estate. In 1796, Manager Sampson Wood informed the estate owner that one woman had fled the estate, charging sexual abuse by the overseer, but that most domestics 'either have or have had white husbands, that is, men who keep them.'

Dolly, the thirty-year-old daughter of Old Doll, the retired housekeeper, was the resident mistress of Wood's predecessor at Newton. Jenny, her twenty-eight-year-old sister, also had an intimate relation with the overseer, while Mary, her cousin, whom Wood described as 'extremely heavy, lazy and ignorant,' had a long-standing sexual relation wth the white book-keeper by whom she had a son.[14] Yet, for this plantation the evidence of sexual coercion and rape is implicit in the same records, which show that all four field women listed in 1796 as having 'mulatto' children, Membah Jubah, Fanny Ann, Jemenema and Little Dolly, were impregnated between the ages of thirteen and sixteen.[15]

The few cases in which slaveowners conceded the occurrence of rape and sexual violence they attributed such behaviour specifically to whites whom they described as persons without 'social breeding', such as dishonoured indentured servants, overseers, and other waged labourers. In 1822, for example, William Sharpe, a prominent Barbadian planter, informed a committee of the Legislative Council:

illicit intercourse with the whites does sometimes take place, but it is principally confined to the inferior servants on the estates, who are young men whose circumstances in life will not admit of their marrying and supporting a family:- when a connexion of this kind takes place between them and the young black women, it is done by persuasion, and because they have it more in their power to gratify the vanity of the females in their fondness for dress; punishment however awaits the offender when his improper conduct is discovered, for he seldom escapes being turned out of the estates. A manager's moral conduct is a great recommendation of him: glaring instances of immoral conduct would not be tolerated.[16]

In Bridgetown, however, such rationalizations and apologies were considered unnecessary and irrelevant. White males, including planters who sometimes resided in town, made a gainful business by prostituting female slaves. William Dickson found that men would often 'lease out' their slave mistresses for the purpose of prostitution as a convenient way of obtaining cash. These women, he added, were 'rented out' especially to visiting merchants, naval officers, and other such clients, for specified periods.[17] The money paid to owners of slave women for sexual services frequently exceeded the slaves' market value.

During the period immediately after the sugar harvest the number of slave women placed on the urban market as prostitutes by rural slaveowners increased, as did the number of male artisans put out to sell their technical skills on a contractual basis. In both instances, slaveowners expected all, or a proportion of the money earned; the slaves, on the other hand, considered themselves fortunate to have a greater degree of 'control' over the disposal of their time.

The question of slave prostitution was raised before the 1790-91 House of Commons inquiry into the slave trade. Evidence submitted showed that in spite of its illegality, it was 'a very common thing' for 'female slaves to be let out by their owners for purposes of prostitution.'[18] The Commissioners heard, furthermore, that rural slaves were sent to town, and town slaves were sent to the barracks at the Garrison, in order to raise money from prostitution. The evidence suggests that prostitution posed no major problems for colonial administrators, and may have been less widespread than in the cities of Europe.[19]

Early nineteenth-century references to slave prostitution emphasized the distinction between the urban and rural contexts. In 1824, Thomas Cooper, looking at the wider Caribbean situation, stated that elite slaves on the estate, notably midwives, were frequently the suppliers of young girls to urban clients.[20] J. B. Moreton, however, noted in 1790, that urban slave prostitutes were controlled by their mothers who arranged clients and received monies. He argued, furthermore, that coloured slaves 'from their youth are taught to be whores' and to expect their living to be derived from immoral earnings.[21]

In support of his abolitionist position, Cooper attributed part of the failure of slave populations on the sugar colonies to reproduce themselves naturally to the prevalence of prostitution among young females – on the estates as well as in towns. Slaveowners, however, did not accept that prostitution had adverse effects upon slaves' domestic arrangements or their fertility.[22] Edward Long's proslavery ideologue of late-eighteenth-century Jamaica echoed the Barbadian planters' sentiments when he stated that black women were predisposed towards prostitution, and performed this function with efficiency and without moral reflection.[23]

The evidence is not always clear on the distinction in occupational terms between slave mistresses, prostitutes, and housekeepers. Certainly, housekeepers were typically selected by white male householders via the sexual relation route, which suggests the inevitability of interchangeable functions. Captain Cook, a British military officer, giving testimony before the 1790-91 parliamentary committee, illustrated the many ways that Barbados' slaveowners prostituted female slaves. His knowledge of colonial society was derived from several visits to the colony in 1780 and 1782; he knew first hand the domestic culture of whites, and was attentive to the sexual practices of creole males. He described how enslaved domestics, black and coloured, were used as prostitutes in the colony's towns, and concluded that the purchase of sex by maritime crews 'was a very common practice.'[24] Slave prostitutes, he stated, would go on board ships under special arrangements with port officials for the purpose of selling sex for money. He confessed to accepting this activity on board the ship under his command, since it was part of colonial maritime life, but seemed rather indignant when he discovered that a 'negro girl' he knew well was 'severely punished on her return home to her owner without the full wages of her prostitution.'[25]

White creoles in Barbados never accepted that organized prostitution was of any economic importance. Slave women, they argued, were frequently given time to 'work out', which meant that they were free to pursue whatever gainful employment they wished, and though many would enter the business of prostitution for quick and large sums of money, it was their own 'voluntary' choice. Hiring slave women for multifarious social purposes, then, was considered part of the urban labour market in which slaves had some autonomy. Many free black and free coloured slaveowners, following the pattern set by white slaveowners, earned their living from the wages of hired-out female slaves; these worked formally as nannies, nurses, cooks, washerwomen, hucksters, seamstresses, and general labourers. The hiring-out of women specifically for sex ran parallel to this market, and the general expectation of white males who hired female slaves, under whatever pretence, was that sexual benefits, if needed, were included. Prices for hired women invariably reflected this dual function, even when it was not made explicit at the outset.

The covert organization of slave prostitution was also a popular business activity of 'well-to-do' white women, especially widows or those without influential or financially-sound husbands. White elite colonial society insisted on the projection of images of social respectability, and as such, distanced itself from formal association with prostitution as an enterprise. For financially-insecure white women, however, it was the best they could do, and they were described as displaying their involvement without shame or remorse. In 1806, for example, a British naval officer reported that he knew a respectable creole lady who, for a living 'lets out her negro girls to anyone who will pay her for their persons, under the denomination of washer woman, and becomes very angry if they don't come home in the family way.'[26]

John Waller, an Englishman who visited Barbados in 1808, made a similar report on the relations between high 'society' white women, slave prostitution, and the 'hiring-out' labour system. He stated in his travel book:

In the family where I lodged, a respectable lady was regretting to the company at dinner, that a young female slave whom she had let out for several months was about to return as she would lose twelve dollars a month, the price of her hire, and besides, be at the expense of maintaining her. After dinner, I made inquiry respecting the subject of hiring slaves and learned that the one in question had been let out to an officer in the garrison, with whom she had been living as a mistress. I felt extremely shocked at the idea of so strange a traffic; but I found, a few days later, this very slave advertised in the "Bridgetown Gazette," in the following curious terms: "To let, a Sempstress, a well-looking mulatto girl, seventeen years of age, an excellent hand at the needle, etc. To prevent needless application – terms twelve dollars per month. Apply, etc." I had previously noticed advertisements of this description, and I believe that few weeks pass without them; they are, however, frequently intended only for the purpose literally expressed.[27]

The institutional framework of prostitution, however, centred on the taverns, bars, and inns of Bridgetown. By the late-eighteenth century many of these leisure houses were owned, or managed, by free black or free coloured women, who were more restricted occupationally than their white counterparts in the search for economic niches. Dr. George Pinckard who frequented Barbados during the 1790s as a medical officer aboard a war vessel, provides us with insights into the practice of prostitution in Bridgetown's taverns:

The hostess of the tavern, usually, a black or mulatto woman, who has been the favoured enamorata of some backra [white man] from whom she has obtained her freedom, and perhaps two or three slaves to assist her in carrying on the business of the house, where she now indulges in indolence, and the good things of life, grows fat, and feels herself of importance in society. It is to her advantage that the female attendants of her family should be as handsome as she can procure them. Being slaves, the only recompense of their services, is the food they eat, the hard bed they sleep on, and the few loose clothes which are hung upon them. One privilege, indeed, is allowed them, which is that of tenderly disposing of their persons; and this offers the only hope they have of procuring a sum of money, where with to purchase their freedom. [28]

Such taverns, according to Pinckard, were 'commonly known by the names of the persons who keep them.'[29] The most frequented at Bridgetown were 'those of Nancy Clarke, and Mary Bella Green; the former a black, the latter a mulatto woman.' The white public, he intimates, would scarcely accept the terms 'Mrs. Clarke,' or 'Mrs. Green,' and so a 'party is said to dine at Mary Bella Green's, or at Nancy Clarke's,' the title Mrs. is reserved 'solely for the ladies from Europe.'[30]

In any of these taverns, Pinckard informs, a 'bed may be had for half a dollar per night, or three dollars per week; and, for an additional sum well understood, the choice of an attendant to draw the curtains.'[31] 'Prostitute girls,' he suggested, 'were treated in the most cruel manner by their mistresses, whose objectives were to earn as much money from their duties as possible. My considered response to such treatment,' Pinckard says, 'was much tempered by the realization that these women 'showed' neither shame nor disgrace' in their prostitution. Rather, he added, the one 'who is most sought becomes an object of envy and is proud of the distinction shewn her.'[32]

It was generally recognized that in these taverns, slave women were offered the boon of freedom as an incentive for maintaining their enthusiasm. For any category of slave, freedom was a legal status not easily rejected.[33] There were prominent freedwomen such as Sabina Brade who was described in 1807 as 'an old, fat black woman' Betsy Lemon, a well-known mulatto figure in Bridgetown; Betsy Austin, whose hotel was said to offer the best in 'mental and corporeal' entertainment, though at exorbitant rates; Caroline Lee, Betsy Austin's diminutive

mulatto sister, after whom the well-known Barbadian yellow sweet potato is named; and Hannah Lewis, arch-rival of Betsy Austin, also a 'brown-skin lady.'[34] Dr. Walker, an Englishman who resided in Barbados during 1802-03, stated that these women possessed 'considerable property, both in houses and slaves.' He stated, furthermore:

Nor can they fail to amass large fortunes, as their houses are generally filled with strangers, who must submit to the most exorbitant charges for every article of eating, drinking, as well as for the accommodation of lodging and washing. These taverns are besides houses of debauchery, a number of young women of colour being always procurable in them for the purpose of prostitution.[35]

In 1837, when English abolitionists, Joseph Sturge and Thomas Harvey, conducted their 'emancipation' tour of the British West Indies, most hotels and taverns in Bridgetown were still considered 'houses of debauchery where a number of slave women were kept for the purpose of prostitution.'[36] Most observers of slave prostitution in Barbados noted, like Sturge and Harvey, that coloured women, both slave and free, were more in demand than black women, and fetched higher prices for their services. Coloured women, however, were less available for this role than their black counterparts in Bridgetown, because they were more likely to be mistresses of white men or married to coloured men. The records attest to the favoured status of 'yellow-skinned' women, most of whom operated from the more exclusive taverns and hotels. In 1804, for example, an English naval officer made reference to a white woman he knew who made 'a round sum' by trafficking her prostitute 'coloured' girls to Europeans as 'housekeepers' in disguise, or as she preferred to call it, 'marrying them off for a certain time.'[37]

White men publicly displayed a preference for coloured women, though black women were more likely to bear the fruit of their secretive sexual exploits. The 'mulatto' girl was paraded as the kept mistress, but the black housekeeper was more likely to be the 'invisible lover.' One contemporary explained that white men's mulatto preference resulted from their cohabiting with them 'at a very early age,' and few denied that the 'brown' or 'yellow' skin 'coloured' women, outside of respectable family relations, were socially and sexually desired – more so than were white or black women.[38]

Bayley's observations in the 1820s were perhaps representative of the white male's norm when he spoke of the sexual attractiveness of coloured women. He described them as having 'captivated' with ease the 'hearts of English, Irish, and Scotch' men on the island.[39] He added the following statement by way of personal judgement:

If I accord the palm of female beauty to the ladies of colour, I do not at the same time deteriorate the attractions of the fairer [white] creoles; the stately and graceful demeanour which calls upon us to admire the one, does not forbid us to be fascinated by the modest loveliness of the other; yet I will acknowledge that I prefer the complexion that is tinged, if not too darkly, with the richness of the olive, to the face which, however fair in its paleness, can never look as lovely as when it wore the rose-blush of beauty which has faded away. I know no prettier scene than a group of young and handsome colored girls taking their evening walk.[40]

From the comments of Bayley, Waller and Pinkcard it seems that white elite males possessed a sexual typology in which white women were valued for domestic formality and respectability, coloured women for exciting socio-sexual companionship, and black women for less-structured covert sexual adventurism. Generations of black women, then, produced mulatto daughters who were priced higher on the market than themselves. Waller explained the forces which led to this differentiation:

A very respectable matron, who had shewn a kind of motherly affection for a young friend of mine who came over [from England] to settle here as a merchant, advised him in the most serious manner to look out for a young mulatto or Mustee girl for his housekeeper, urging that it would greatly increase his domestic comforts and diminish his expenses; and, in addition to this, she hinted very delicately, that, by being confined to one object, his health and reputation would be better secured, than by the promiscuous libertinism to which she seemed to consider every young man as habitually addicted.[41]

North American abolitionists, J. A. Thome and J. H. Kimball, suggested that, during the 1830s, Europeans generally took this advice on 'first going to the island.' It was in vogue, they added, for new arrivants to engage 'colored females to live with them as housekeepers and mistresses.' Furthermore, 'it was not unusual for a man to have more than one.'[42] Bayley believed that this sexual culture arose principally from slavery, which corrupted the moral character of those who depended upon it, but he was not prepared to deny the sexual attractiveness of 'the

proud and haughty spirits of the coloured ladies themselves.'[43]

Black women, whether slave or free, were generally not as successful in extracting socio-economic benefits from propertied white males as were coloured women. Data for Bridgetown suggest that whereas black women remained in the 'small-time' fringe of this illicit social culture, larger numbers of coloured women successfully fashioned their socio-ideological vision around the need to entertain white males, in return for social and material betterment. As free persons, coloured women's opportunities were severely limited, so this realization encouraged them to adopt a professional attitude towards the sex industry that brought them into intimate contact with propertied white males.

Social custom dictated that prominent white men should neither marry coloured women, nor allow them in any way to transcend white women in social respectability. In this way, coloured women's social ambitions could be kept in check without alienating their sexual usefulness. In spite of their intimacy and loyalty to eminent white males, coloured women could not be accepted as equal members of official elite society. When, for example, the newly-appointed Governor George Ricketts, arrived at Barbados from Tobago in 1794 accompanied by his mulatto mistress, it caused a tremendous uproar among his councilors and assemblymen, although many had similar social relations.[44]

Illicit social relations with white men were considered the most rewarding options for coloured women, the recognition of which, some observers noted, frequently drove them to reject respectable domestic life with coloured men, and to consider black men socially unacceptable. A United States citizen resident in Barbados noted in 1814 that 'colored parents educated their female children for this special purpose.'[45] Likewise, Thome and Kimball, observing the social culture of urban whites and free coloreds, took the view that coloured women were 'taught to believe that it was more honourable, and quite as virtuous, to be kept mistresses of white gentlemen, than the lawfully-wedded wives of coloured men.'[46] For Bayley, only the removal of civil disabilities that adversely affected the status of free coloured men would enable society to affect 'the weakening of those motives which induce the colored women to live in immorality with a white protector.'[47] General emancipation, he argued, could bring about a slow 'change in this system.'[48] Even then, he insisted, moral society would have to 'contend with strong and established prejudices, and the mighty influence of long custom and habit.'[49]

While the evidence points to whites and coloured women as the primary owners of slave prostitutes, occasional references to free black women and men suggest their marginal involvement. Free blacks were sometimes wholly dependent upon 'immoral gains' to maintain their status. It was not uncommon to find runaway female slaves being harboured by such persons, who in turn arranged their prostitution in return for protection. It was at this end of the business that black owners of prostitutes were to be found in large numbers, often catering for black clients, both slave and free.

Some slave women gained legal freedom through the route of the overlapping roles of prostitution and concubinage.[50] In these ways, they earned the necessary money to effect their manumission, or came in contact with clients who were prepared to assist them in doing so. Legal freedom, however, did not always result in a distancing from these roles. It was, therefore, very common to find freed women continuing as prostitutes and mistresses. In 1811, the Rector of the St. Michael Parish Church, commenting on the 'very rapid' increase in the number of slaves freed by whites since 1802, suggested that 'out of every four at least three were females who obtained that privilege by

becoming favourites of white men.'[51] He was supported by Joseph Husbands who claimed that in 1831:

By far the greater number of free colored persons in Barbados have either obtained their freedom by their own prostitution, or claimed it under some of their female ancestors who in like manner obtained it and have transmitted it to the descendants.[52]

From the mid-eighteenth century, legislators seemed determined to restrain white males from manumitting their black and coloured sex favourites. In 1739, the manumission fee had been legally set at £50 plus an annuity of £4 local currency; the annuity was insisted upon by poor law officials as one way to prevent slaveowners from freeing old and infirmed persons who could not reasonably be expected to earn their subsistence. In 1774, a bill was introduced into the Assembly aimed at curtailing the number of females being manumitted. It was designed to raise the manumission fee to £100, but was rejected on the grounds that slaveowners should not be deprived of the right to assist the 'most deserving part' of their slaves – 'the females who have generally recommended themselves to our "kindest notice."' It was defeated by a vote of eleven to five; opposition was led by Sir John Gay Alleyne who argued that female slaves who gave their loyalty, love and service to masters should not be denied the opportunity to gain freedom.[53]

Barbadian whites debated the subject once again in 1801, following Governor Seaforth's proposed bill to limit female slave manumission,

Table 50:1: Slave Manumissions in Barbados, 1809–32

Years	No. Males	No. Females	Total	% Male	% Female
1809–11	168	263	431	39.0	61.0
1812–14	88	148	236	37.3	62.7
1815–17	191	279	470	40.6	59.4
1818–20	167	245	412	41.0	59.0
1821–23	131	166	297	44.1	55.9
1824–26	126	196	322	39.1	60.9
1827–29	212	458	670	31.6	68.4
1830–32	–	–	1,089	–	–

Source: Jerome Handler, *The Unappropriated People: Freedmen in the Slave Society of Barbados* (Baltimore, Johns Hopkins University Press, 1974) p. 49.

and to ensure that proper provisions were made by slaveowners for their manumitted slaves. The bill became law, and raised the manumission fee to £300 for females and £200 for males. Slave women continued to be freed in significantly larger numbers than men for the rest of the slavery period (see Table 50:1), though the 1801 Act was repealed in 1816 following the Bussa Rebellion (14-17 April), and the £50 plus £4 annuity fee for both sexes was re-established.

Against this background, the Assembly continued to be notified that too many freed black women survived on income derived from prostitution. Since the 1780s Joshua Steele had expressed concerned for free black women who were forced to subsist by 'gallantry.'[54] He was supported by Governor Parry who was earlier informed by his Council that many freed women sustained 'themselves by the prostitution of their persons.'[55] The Assembly, however, was aware that the urban economy provided few outlets for free black women, most of whom were unable to compete with slave labourers in the huckster trade, or as general labourers, housekeepers, seamstresses, and the like. It was difficult, then, for free black women to break out of the prostitute/mistress cycle, unless they were able to marry those few free black men who earned a steady income.

The socio-economic integration of slavewomen into the plantation system, therefore allowed for their use at various points along the circuit of capital accumulation. Their contribution to the overall wealth creation process of slaveowners involved not only their roles as labourers, and reproducers of labour, but also as suppliers of socio-sexual services. The sex industry was an important part of the urban economy, and the relations of slavery, protected by slave codes, created societal conditions under which the maximum benefits offered by property ownership in humans accrued to slaveowners. The use of slave women as prostitutes, therefore, was another way in which slaveowners extracted surplus value and emphasized their status as colonial masters.

For the slave women, whether black or coloured, life as a concubine or prostitute was characterized by more than the omnipresent forces of relentless sexual exploitation at the hands of slaveowners. Their life chances were shaped by socially-complex and dialetically-changing circumstances. Some of them gained materially from the relations of sex in diverse ways. Many obtained legal freedom, which for slaves was the most important social commodity. Few became slaveowners and tavern proprietors, but most gained greater social mobility than plantation field gang women, who, according to the economic and pathological indicators, were the more dispensable and shortlived 'beast of burden' in the productive sector.[56]

Notes

1. See for example, George Pinckard, *Notes on the West Indies*, 3 vols. (London: Longman, 1806), I; 245-46; John Waller, *A Voyage to the West Indies* (London; Richard Phillips, 1820), pp 9-10,20-21; J. Thome and J. Kimball, *Emancipation in the West Indies* (New York: Anti-Slavery Society, 1838), p. 79; J. Sturge and T. Harvey, *The West Indies in 1837* (London: Hamilton and Adams, 1837), p. I; William Dickson, *Letters on Slavery* (1789; reprint, Westport: Negro University Press, 1970), p. 39; F. W. Bayley, *Four Years' Residence in the West Indies* (London: William Kidd, 1833), pp. 496-97.

2. Orlando Patterson, *The Sociology of Slavery* (London: University Press, 1967), p. 160. See also Hilary Beckles, *Afro-Caribbean Women and Resistance to Slavery in Barbados* (London: Karnak House, 1988), pp. 77-78. Most accounts of slavery in the West Indies comment upon the use of slave women as prostitutes but do not theorize the significance of this form of exploitation for an understanding of female slavery. For example, see Elsa Goveia, *Slave Society in the British Leeward Islands at the end of the 18th Century* (London: Yale University Press, 1965), pp. 216-17; Edward Brathwaite, *The Development of Creole Society in Jamaica, 1770-1820* (Oxford: Clarendon Press, 1971), p. 160; B. W. Higman, *Population and Economy of Jamaica, 1807-1834* (Cambridge: Cambridge University Press, 1976), p. 42

3. See, for example, the Diary of Thomas Thistlewood, Jamaican slaveowner, Lincolnshire Records Office, England; for extensive references to this point, see Douglas Hall, *In Miserable Slavery: Thomas Thistlewood in Jamaica, 1750-86* (London: MacMillan, 1989); also Hilary Beckles, *Natural Rebels: A Social History of Enslaved Black Women in Barbados* (New Brunswick: Rutgers University Press, 1989), pp. 131-38.

4. See Leeward Islands MSS Laws, 1644-1673.CO 154/1, CO 154/1/49-50, Public Record Office (PRO), London.

5. The preamble to the 1661 Slave Laws of Barbados described blacks as 'heathenish,' 'brutish,' and a 'dangerous kind of people.' The 1688 Code de-

scribed blacks as 'of a barbarous, wild and savage nature, and as such render them wholly unqualified to
be governed by the laws, customs and practices of
[the white] nation.' Acts of Barbados, 1645-1682,
CO 30/2, CO 30/5, PRO. Richard Hall, *Acts Passed
in the Island of Barbados, 1643-1762* (London: Richard Hall, Jnr., 1764), no. 42; also ff. 112-13. See also
Richard Dunn, *Sugar and Slaves: The Rise of the
Planter Class in the English West Indies, 1624-1713*
(Chapel Hill: University of North Carolina Press,
1972), pp. 240, 246.

6.   Dunn, *Sugar and Slaves*, p. 253.

7.   John Oldmixon, *The British Empire in America*, 2
vols. (London: Mapp, 1708), 2: 129.

8.   Colonel Hilton to Reverend John Snow, 16 August
1816, Codrington MSS, Barbados Accounts , 1721
to 1838, Lambeth Palace Library, London.

9.   Bayley, *Four Years' Residence*, op. cit., p. 497.

10.   The Barbados Letters of Elizabeth Fenwick are to be
found in A. F. Fenwick, ed., *The Fate of the Fenwicks: Letters to Mary Hays, 1798-1828* (London:
Methuen, 1927), pp. 163-207.

11.   Claude Levy, *Emancipation, Sugar and Federalism:
Barbados and the West Indies, 1833-1876* (Gainesville: University of Florida Press, 1980), p.30.

12.   B. W. Higman, *Slave Populations of the British Caribbean, 1807-1834* (Baltimore: Johns Hopkins University Press, 1984), p. 231.

13.   Fenwick, *Letters*, p. 169.

14.   Report on the Negroes at Newton Plantation, 1796,
Newton Papers, M523/288, ff 1-20, Senate House
Library, University of London, London.

15.   Ibid.

16.   Evidence of William Sharpe, in *A Report of a Committee of the Council of Barbados, appointed to Inquire into the Actual Condition of the slaves of this
Island* (Bridgetown: W. Walker,1822), pp. 5-6.

17.   Dickson, *Letters*, p. 39.

18.   Evidence of Nicholas Brathwaite, *British Sessional
Papers: House of Commons,* 1791 (34), Vol. 42, 9.
183.

19.   See Bryan Edwards, *The History, Civil and Commercial, of the British Colonies in the West Indies,* 3
vols. (1793; reprint, London: G. and W. D. Whittaker, 1801), 2: 23.

20.   Thomas Cooper, *Facts Illustrative of the Condition
of the Negro Slaves in Jamaica* (London: Hatchard,
1824), p. 42.

21.   J. B. Moreton, *Manners and Customs of the West
India Islands* (London: Richardson, 1790), p. 132.

22.   See *A Report of a Committee of the Council of Barbados*, pp. 4-10.

23.   Edward Long, *The History of Jamaica*, 3 vols.
(London: T. Lowndes, 1774), 2: 436.

24.   Testimony of Captain Cook, *British Sessional Papers: House of Commons*, 1791 (34), Vol. 42, p. 202.

25.   Ibid.

26.   Major Wyvill, "Memoirs of an Old Officer, 1776-
1807." p. 386, MSS Division, Library of Congress,
Washington, D.C.

27.   Waller, *A Voyage to the West Indies*, pp. 20-21.

28.   Pinckard, *Notes*, 1: 245-46

29.   Ibid., p. 249.

30.   Ibid.

31.   Ibid., p. 245.

32.   Ibid., p. 137.

33.   Neville Connell, "Hotel Keepers and Hotels," in
Chapters in Barbados History, ed. P. F. Campbell
(Bridgetown: Barbados Museum, 1986), p. 107.

34.   Ibid., pp. 111-16.

35.   Ibid., p. 108.

36.   Sturge and Harvey, *The West Indies in 1837*, p. l.

37.   Major Wyvill, "Memoirs," p. 383.

38.   Waller, *A Voyage to the West Indies*, p. 19.

39.   Bayley, *Four Years' Residence*, op. cit., p. 493.

40.   Ibid., pp. 493-94.

41.   Waller, *A Voyage to the West Indies*, p. 20.

42.   Thome and Kimball, *Emancipation, op. cit.*, p. 79.

43.   Bayley, *Four Years' Residence*, op. cit., p. 195.

44.   John Poyer, *The History of Barbados from the First
Discovery of the Island in the Year 1605 till the Accession of Lord Seaforth 1801* (London: J. Mauman,
1808), p.639.

45.   Jerome Handler, *The Unappropriated People: Freedmen in the Slave Society of Barbados* (Baltimore:
Johns Hopkins University Press, 1974), p. 199.

46.   Thome and Kimball, *Emancipation, op. cit.*, p.

47.   Bayley, *Four Years' Residence*, op. cit., p. 497.

48.   Ibid., p. 496.

49.   Ibid.

50.   Handler, *The Unappropriated People*, p. 137.

51.   Evidence of Garnette Beckwith, December 5, 1811,
Parliamentary Papers (PP), 1814-1815, Vol. 7,
p. 478.

52.   Joseph Husbands, *An Answer to the Charge of Inhabitants of Barbados* (New York; Richardson,
1831), p. 19.

53.   Minutes of the Barbados Assembly, 15 March 1744,
Barbados Archives, Bridgetown, Barbados.

54.   Joshua Steele's reply to Governor Parry, *Parliamentary Papers (PP)*, 1789, Vol. 26, p.33.

55.   See Handler, *The Unappropriated People*, p. 137.

56.   Both terms – 'worn out' and 'beast of burden' –
were used by William Dickson to describe the condition of slave women in the late-eighteenth century.
See Dickson, *Letters*, op. cit.,

51

Gender and Representation in European Accounts of Pre-emancipation Jamaica

VERENE A. SHEPHERD

During the colonial era large parts of the non-European world were produced for Europe through the narratives of the early colonizers, missionaries, planters, short-term visitors and others who observed Caribbean society and recorded their observations. Indeed, each new arrivant went through what Peter Hulme refers to as a 'gesture of discovery'. This 'gesture of discovery' was repeated over a period of three centuries and gave rise to a series of narratives, the first being the encounter between European and 'native', which provided a window through which to analyse the attitudes and views toward the inhabitants of the region.[1]

This preliminary paper, part of a larger project, uses a small sample of the narratives to illustrate some aspects of this 'colonialist discourse', specifically as it related to the representation of women and gender relations in Jamaica by explorers, adventurers, and other visitors, and resident and absentee planters in the island from the 15th to the 19th century. The majority of the sources are male-authored, reflecting the pattern in Caribbean historiography in the period up to 1834.[2]

While the narratives of the pre-emancipation era were preoccupied with such issues as colonization, climate, the flora and fauna, slavery, the sugar industry, trade, politics, race, colour and class, gender was also a crucial site of struggle. Indeed, these works give an insight into the historiography of the textual invention of the Jamaican and Caribbean woman, in particular, the African-Caribbean woman. Admittedly, contemporary writers were often 'gender blind' in their narratives; but some did single out women and exposed their biases towards the social relations between the sexes, the gender division of labour and the place of women in society. In her seminal work on gender and history, Joan Wallach-Scott argues that relations of power are organised along at least three axes – race, class and gender –; and that gender is a primary way of signifying relationships of power. If one supports her view, then one must view these narratives as important for what they reveal about power relations in colonial society.[3] The narratives also reveal a configuration of ethnocentrism towards the issues of ethnicity/race, identity and empire; and when these attitudes are combined with views on male dominance and the inferiority of women, what results is a portrayal of the enslaved African and African-Caribbean woman in a particularly negative light. For example, while clearly recognising their importance as producers and reproducers of the labour force, enslaved women were nevertheless represented by some of these male writers in the historical literature as ugly, lacking in intelligence and promiscuous. The view of the sensual and promiscuous, 'easy-going', exotic island black woman still persists and is manifested in overseas popular culture, particularly in posters and brochures which push tourist destinations. The indigenous women were painted as 'innocent' and 'simple' and in need of 'civilisation'. European women, especially creoles, did not escape the notice of the contemporary writers; and were usually represented as 'uncultured'. The elite white woman was accorded the title of 'lady', a designation not applied to other classes of women.

Many of these narratives were written without reference to the historical Caribbean and its inhabitants; and fall into the realm of historical [even fictional] literature. The narratives and accounts sampled for this paper fall into three categories: the first hand accounts of colonists and travellers from the Columbus mission onwards; planters' letters and journals, and the histories of Jamaica by planters and others. The latter sometimes draw on these 'first hand accounts' but also rely on the official documents and reports lodged in European archives. Whatever the type, these narratives were all engaged in the ideological production of Jamaica and the Caribbean for Europe, and provide a glimpse into the heterogeneity of the historical experience of women in the colonised, non-European world in the period of slavery.

The Discourse of Discovery

Predictably, one must begin with the Columbus mission which landed on Jamaica's north coast – now quintessentially the island's premier tourist area in 1494. The Columbian discourse is important for it initiated the age of modernity and created the context for the evolution of the plantation system, a multi-ethnic Caribbean society, the devaluation of what was indigenous and provided a background for the colonialist discourse of Long and others. The Columbian discourse is also important for its representation of indigenous women, its insights into the evolution of indigenous slavery and the justification for the transition to the enslavement of African captives.

Columbus kept a detailed journal of his voyages in which he recorded the geography of the region [sometimes inaccurately] as well as the habits of the people. He does not seem to have left a written account of the second voyage and his time in Jamaica on the fourth voyage; but there are surviving accounts and histories of those who were on the voyage with him or to whom he related his experiences. The articulating principles of the Columbian discourse after the encounter with Jamaica are those of conflict and accommodation with the indigenous people as well as of mild censure for the simplicity/'primitiveness' of their lives. The impression

of innocent transgressors of the rules of civilisation is also evident.

The principal historians of this period of the second voyage were Ferdinand Columbus, Peter Martyr and the priest Andres Bernaldez. Diego Mendez, Columbus' interpreter on his fourth voyage, also gave an account of parts of the fourth voyage. Peter Martyr, an Italian by origin but who was domiciled in Spain, and who claimed to have been a personal friend of Columbus, never set foot in Jamaica; but that did not prevent him from giving his views, based on documents from Columbus to which he claimed access. He was a member of the Royal Council of the Indies and one of the early abbots of Jamaica. Columbus' son, Ferdinand wrote a biography of his father which is an important record, second only to Columbus' own journals.

These 15th, 16th and 17th-century narratives are important for not only do they represent a kind of 'first hand' account of the region's history; but they influenced later historical accounts.

Bernaldez' history is relevant to Jamaica and of all the 15th and 16th century narratives, gives the most colourful and detailed account. But Bernaldez never went to the so-called 'New World'; he may never even have ever gone to sea. He was parish priest of Los Palacios near Seville from 1488 up to about 1513 when he died. He claimed to have been a friend of Columbus and Columbus allegedly stayed with him after his return from his second voyage.[4] Columbus apparently also gave or lent Bernaldez written and verbal descriptions of the voyage. His account provides only a glimpse of the island women. He described the cacique's 18 year old daughter for example as a 'very lovely girl . . . entirely nude, as they are wont to be there, and very modest . . .'[5] The cacique's wife, he recorded,

'. . . was likewise adorned, naked and exposed, except that she had one single part of her person covered with a little piece of cotton, no bigger than an orange leaf. On her arms, about the armpits she wore a roll of cotton, made like the upper part of the sleeve of old-fashioned French doublets. She also wore two others, also made of cotton, like these and larger, on each leg below the knees, as ajorcas. The elder and more lovely daughter was completely nude. She only wore round her waist a single string of stones, very black and small, from which hung something shaped like an ivy leaf, made of green and red stones fastened on woven cotton.[6]

This account by Bernaldez is typical of other early accounts of the Spanish period in its focus on the physical characteristics of the island women. More is said about their beauty and other physical traits than about their productive roles. The accounts of the men also focus on physical traits but are fuller in the description of their prowess in war, hunting and other supposedly 'manly' tasks.

During the 17th century, rival European powers continued to invade the Spanish Indies and generated their own historiography. Many books written outside of the period also focussed on the 17th century history. The principal concern of most of these was the socio-economic and political conditions of Spanish Jamaica, the English capture of the island from the Spaniards and the problems of establishing a viable English colony, particularly the problems associated with securing a labour force and establishing a sugar industry.[7]

The Discourse of the Slavery Era

There was a greater demand for knowledge on the empire in the 18th century. The controversy over the slave trade and the social upheavals of the last years of the 18th century and the early years of the 19th century focussed attention on the affairs of the Caribbean and produced a new spate of works. It is clear that the consciousness of fear and crisis underpins pre-emancipation writings; for they were written in a period of international rivalry, wars, the revolts of the enslaved and the emancipation and independence struggles in Haiti. Predictably, most are pro-plantocracy and pro-slavery and give an insight into the repressive slave regimes imposed on the Caribbean. Those written by individual planters towards the end of slavery often exaggerated the 'good' treatment of their enslaved peoples to stem the tide of abolitionism. Jamaica formed a significant part of the British Empire, so that, predictably, there were many works focussed on this island. The histories of Jamaica written during the 18th and early 19th century include the works of Charles Leslie, Edward Long, William Beckford, Robert Renny, M.G. Lewis [whose text was composed after the Napoleonic wars] and Cynric Williams [who wrote just at the start of the organized antislavery campaigns in Britain]. There were, in addition, accounts of travellers, planters' letters and journals and diaries [such as those of Thomas Thistlewood and Lady Maria Nugent].

Charles Leslie's *A New and Exact Account of Jamaica* was the earliest of the published historical books. The work was first published in 1739 and was re-issued in two expanded editions in 1740. It was written under the form of a series of letters from the author to the young Earl of Eglington and it was designed to be informative not only on historical events but also on the laws, geography, religion, government, trade and manners of Jamaica. As a stranger or visitor to the island, Leslie stood a little outside of the society which he described in the book – a fact which he indicates indirectly by what he wrote concerning his arrival in Jamaica:

"I was now to settle in a Place not half inhabited, cursed with intestine Broils, where slavery was established, and the poor toiling wretches worked in the sultry Heat, and never knew the sweets of Liberty, or reap'd the Advantages of their painful Industry, in a Place, which except the Verdure of its Fields has nothing to recommend it".[8]

Like most visitors, Leslie made hasty remarks in the first few days of his arrival. He noted:

I . . . scarce see a Face that resembles the gay Bloom of a Briton. The people seem all sickly, their complexion is muddy, their colour wan, and their Bodies meagre; they look like so many corpses and their Dress resembles a Shroud; however, they are frank and good humoured, and make the best of life they can.[9]

But he also promised that: "I'll take another Opportunity to draw their character when Time shall increase my knowledge and my acquaintance with them becomes more general."[10] And true to his word, by the time he wrote his second letter, he had changed his impressions somewhat as is indicated by the following:

Sir, whatever dismal Apprehensions I might have formed on my first arrival, I now find this place has too many Beauties not to engage my attention. It produces a thousand surprising curiosities; kind nature in return for a sultry sun has blessed it with varieties few countries can boast of.[11]

In addition to his comments on the natural beauty of the island, Leslie also remarked on the abundance of fish and fruit; the lovely flora and fauna; the absence of seasons and the 'scorching heat of the sun.'

Leslie came to take on the attitudes of the society towards, for example, the Africans. He wrote concerning the Africans: "When they first arrive, 'tis observed they are simple and very innocent creatures; but they soon turn to be roguish enough".[12]

Leslie made comparatively few references to women in Jamaica and about gender relations in general. His aim seemed to have been rather to provide future immigrants with a view of the island and made comments about the opportunities for wealth, opportunities for work for whites, the hospitality of other whites, the climate and its effects on the inhabitants; the hazards of earthquakes and hurricanes.

From the little he writes about women, it is clear that he differentiates between the different classes and ethnicities of women and refers to white women as 'ladies', and well dressed ones too:

the ladies are as gay as anywhere in Europe, dress as richly and appear with as good a Grace. Their morning habit is a loose nightgown carelessly wrapped around them. Before dinner they get out of their Dishabille and shew themselves in all the Advantages of a becoming, rich, neat dress.[13]

The white female indentured house servants are clearly regarded as inferior and he refers to them as 'the servant maids' who dress in 'a Linen or striped Holland Gown and plain headcloths'.[14]

Like later writers, he discusses the 'Negro women' separately;[15] and also like other contemporary observers he gives the impression that black women were shameless in their exposure of their bodies:

the negro women go many of them quite naked; they do not know what shame is and are surprised at an European's bashfulness who perhaps turns his head aside at the sight. Their masters give them a kind of Petticoat but they do not care to wear it. In the towns they are obliged to do it; but these are the favourites of young squires who keep them for a certain use.[16]

These writers, while also commenting on the nudity of the indigenous women, portray such state of nakedness as 'innocence' rather than shamelessness.

As Leslie was in Jamaica at a time when white indentured servitude was still being utilised as a form of labour exploitation, we learn some interesting things about gender and white servitude - at least from the perspective of the laws of the island. For example, it is evident that sexual relations between male and female servants was prohibited and that if this happened and the female servant became pregnant, the male servant was blamed and either had to find a replacement for the woman he impregnated [if she was still under indentureship] or himself be liable to serve double the time left unexpired in her contract. Male servants also needed the permission of their employers if they wished to get married. Failure to get such a permission would result in a penalty; and a free man who married a female indentured servant had to pay a fine to the woman's employer and be freed subsequently.[17]

As Trevor Burnard observes, most of Leslie's comments about the island are probably typical of most other descriptions made about mid-18th century Jamaica.[18]

The accounts of the later 18th and 19th centuries took on a different character. This was the heyday of the slave-based sugar plantation economy. In fact by the 18th century the Caribbean plantation economy had become wholly and exclusively identified with the African slave. The enslaved population comprised imported African captives, 'an outsider' group of a different racial category from that of their owners. Predictably racial prejudice became mixed up with class prejudice and had important consequences for the general character of the Caribbean settler planter ideology. There developed a systematic racist ideology that identified the slave with non-human and anti-natural attributes.[19]

This ideology, evident in the island, was also reflected in planter histories and travellers accounts of the 18th and 19th centuries. These were decidedly pro-slavery and justificatory in their orientation, particularly if they were written after the late 1770s in response to the emergence of the abolitionist campaign. Those written after the Haitian revolution reflected the fear of the whites of 'another Haiti'.

Among the genre of pro-slavery accounts are those of Thomas Thistlewood, a visitor turned native. Thistlewood came to Jamaica in 1751 from Tupholme, Lincolnshire, England. Throughout his life he kept a detailed journal which reveals his activities in the island. It is clear that he accepted the social stratification and the system of white dominance in a slave society. He also accepted that the use of force was the way to control the slave societies; and was not at all averse to perpetrating the use of brutal force on male and female slaves alike. He was very quick to understand the customs in Jamaica with respect to sexual behaviour of whites with enslaved black women. Unlike Edward Long, Thistlewood does not make many negative statements about the physical character and attributes of women. He did on occasion comment on the fact that some slave women were liars and he did observe that slave women were sensual.[20] Nevertheless, his physical and sexual abuse of enslaved women leaves us in no doubt about his attitude towards them. He learnt from very early after his arrival that living openly with slave or free mulatto women brought no social condemnation from white society and indeed was 'accepted behaviou'r. Thistlewood, like other white men, seemed to have believed that one advantage of coming to the island was the chance of sexually exploiting many black and coloured women. While working for Mr Vassell on Vineyard Pen in Westmoreland and Mr Cope on Egypt plantation, he sexually abused practically every female slave. From 5 slave women [Marina, Juba, Betty, Hago, Sylvia] in 1750, his sexual contact expanded to 11 enslaved women by 1751. When he established his own property, Breadnut Island Pen in 1768, he continued with this habit.

Like most overseers, Thistlewood kept in 'faithful' concubinage a black woman, Phibbah, but showed no loyalty at all to her in terms of his sexual behaviour, having had sexual relations with 9 of the 16 female slaves on his property. He also evinced no interest in marriage. In fact, single white men saw no need to marry in the Caribbean, preferring to sexually exploit enslaved women. In response to his brother's query about his marital status, Stephen Harmer, overseer on Old Hope pen, said in his reply: "Now the candid truth is that I have got no wife and have never been married. It is not the fashion for overseers to be married in this country except over the broomstick".[21] Harmer, however, had four children by a slave woman. These black slave partners were euphemistically called 'house-keepers' in the Caribbean, and several 18th and 19th writers remark on their existence. Alfred Caldecott remarked, perhaps exaggeratedly, that it "nine-tenths of the coloured women were 'housekeepers' to white men".[22] As M'Mahon explained in *Jamaica Plantership,* the overseers in Jamaica usually kept one particular mistress called by themselves housekeepers but by the labourers their wives".[23] He further added that these "housekeepers were expected to yield to the sexual demands of these overseers."[24]

The behaviour of Thomas Thilstlewood and Stephen Harmer was consistent with the belief in white superiority and black inferiority, demonstrated in the physical abuse of the black male and the physical and sexual abuse of enslaved women.

The Jamaican contribution to the ideology of racism and sexism is essentially that of Edward Long in his multi-volumed history of Jamaica. He wrote when the pro-slavery ideology had reached its zenith – that is in the period between the mid-18th century and the latter part of the 19th century – when the slave economy had entered its 'golden age'. This period saw the emergence of the settler planter historians. Along with other sources such as the correspondence of governors and the vast literature of travellers, these planter histories allow for a glimpse of the self-image of the plantocracy and the images that class entertained of the people in the colonies.[25]

Edward Long was born on August 23, 1734 in Cornwall, England. He was a member of a wealthy family and his writings often reflect his elitist attitudes to those outside of his class. He came to Jamaica at age 23 in 1757 and joined the plantocracy. He returned to England in 1769 after a period of 12 years in the island.[26] His book reveals that he was creole and colonial in his sympathies but his remarks on women and Africa – two objects of his analysis reveal his elitist, racist views. Long clearly had an attachment to the moral validity of slavery and was concerned with arguing the legitimacy of slavery against its critics.

His anti-African stance eventually matured into a pro-slavery ideology. He also displays a clear antipathy towards miscegenation. Obsessed with racial purity, he inveighs against white male miscegenative habits and decries the black woman in the most negative and racist of terms.[27] He constructed a hierarchy among women in Jamaica based on his racist and classist notions. Predictably, he placed white women at the top of this social ladder and black women at the base; and the faults he finds with white women are almost always attributable to a) lack of education, b) lack of sufficient association with Europeans and c) their too close association with black women.

He saw some good characteristics in white creole women: their humane and charitable disposition, their faithfulness as partners, their attentiveness to domestic things and therefore their observance of their 'proper gender role'.[28] But Long was not always complimentary in his remarks; for he criticised the creole women as a little 'uncouth for the taste of any gentleman'.[29] He was especially harsh on rural white women who he claimed were less cultured than their urban counterparts. He wrote:

those who have been bred up entirely in the sequestered country parts, and had no opportunity of forming themselves either by example or tuition, are truly to be pitied. We may see in some of these places, a very fine young woman awkwardly dangling her arms with the air of a negro servant.[30]

Long opposed the custom in Jamaica of black slaves nannies suckling the babies of white women on the basis that these nannies had 'diseased milk' which they would then pass on to 'the poor victims of this pernicious custom'.[31] He accused slave domestics of having a bad influence on the language of the white children.[32] The last of the 18th century narratives to be considered is that of William Beckford whose two-volumed account of Jamaica was published in 1790. William Beckford's description of Jamaica is similar in tone and focus to the later account by Robert Renny. Like Renny, he was pre-occupied with the consequences of the possible abolition of the slave trade and was equally sparse in his observations on women. His only reference was to enslaved black women involved in the production process who sang plaintive songs as they fed the canes into the mills. He observed that the men were less likely to engage in this type of singing.[33] He was one of the few contemporary writers to oppose the representation of black women as vulgar and rude, arguing instead that some of them possessed 'a decency, a propriety of behaviour . . . that would shame many of the lower classes of the white women'.[34] He emphasised that black women took great pride in their festive, holiday clothes.[35]

Among the most influential 19th century narratives on Jamaica are those of Lady Maria Nugent, Robert Renny, M.G. Lewis and Cynric Williams. Maria Nugent was born in New Jersey in 1771 of parents whose ancestry was Scottish, Irish and Dutch. She later went to live in England and married George, also of Irish decent. George Nugent was appointed Lieutenant Governor and Commander-in-Chief of Jamaica after the Governor designate, Major General Knot, was drowned at sea on his way to Jamaica to take up his appointment. The Nugents landed in Jamaica at the end of July 1801; and Maria Nugent kept a detailed Journal of her life in Jamaica from 1801-1805. Her Journal, recognised as one of the most interesting of the contemporary accounts of colonial Jamaica, was first published in 1839 for private circulation only. An edited version by Frank Cundall, which also included her years in India and England, was published in 1907. Two subsequent editions appeared in 1934 and 1939. Yet another edited version which limited itself largely to the Jamaica period was done by Phillip Wright and published in 1966.[36] Maria Nugent was concerned primarily with life in the household of the Governor and with the activities of her husband.

She had first hand experience with household domestic staff, mostly enslaved but also white; and because she accompanied her husband on a tour of the island, also recorded valuable snippets of information about issues outside of her immediate social world. She commented on various aspects of life in Jamaica: the prevalence of diseases, the suddenness of death, the fear of slave revolt and the shadow of Haiti; the maroons, the social activities of whites and blacks; the economic activities in the island, issues of fertility, slave reproduction and the emancipation movement; the tendency of whites to overindulge in food and drink; gender relations and race relations and her own family life.

Maria Nugent was decidedly pro-slavery, though she displayed a certain benevolence towards the enslaved, forever "teaching the blackies their catechisms"[37]; and on one occasion at a slave fete, she opened the dance floor with one of the enslaved men, to the chagrin of all. In her defence, she claimed that "I did exactly the same as I would have done at a servants' hall birthday".[38] Despite her seeming benevolence, Maria Nugent shared the white stereotype of the enslaved, on two occasions describing Africans as savages and cannibal-like, yet somehow contented with slavery. Of the new black recruits in the West India Regiment she wrote: "They made a most savage appearance, having just arrived from Africa"[39]; and on another occasion:

In returning home from our drive this morning, we met a gang of Eboe negroes, just landed and marching up the country. I ordered the postilions to stop, that I might observe their countenances. . . and see if they looked unhappy; but they appeared perfectly the reverse. . . The women in particular seemed pleased. . . One man attempted to shew more pleasure than the rest by opening his mouth as wide as possible to laugh, which was rather a horrible grin. He showed such truly cannibal teeth, all filed as they had them, that I could not help shuddering.[40]

On first coming to King's House in Spanish Town, she remarked upon the way in which the house was untidy and tried to get the enslaved domestics to improve on their care of the house. She noted that she " reflect[ed] all night on slavery, and made up my mind that the want of exertion in the blackies must proceed from that cause".[41] So she assembled them after breakfast one morning and talked to them, "promising every kindness and indulgence".[42] She denied that the enslaved were as ill-treated as the abolitionists claimed, noting that "I believe the slaves are extremely well-used."[43]

On Hope Estate in St Andrew, she commented on the habit of working class whites like overseers to keep enslaved women as mistresses. On that particular estate, the overseer was "a civil, vulgar Scotch Officer on half-pay. . .; vulgar, ugly, dirty and with a dingy, sallow-brown complexion and only two yellow, discoloured tusks by way of teeth."[44] His *chere amie*, and no man was without one according to Mrs Nugent, was a tall black woman "well-made, with a very flat nose, thick lips, a skin of ebony, highly polished and shining."[45] On her visit to Golden Grove Estate in St Thomas-in-the-East, the mulatto women told her that Simon Taylor, the Attorney, had children on almost all the estates he owned or operated. In St Mary she herself encountered many mulatto ladies who were the daughters of Assembly men and officers. She also bemoaned the habit of white men to leave money and property to their black mistresses and coloured offspring, at times leaving nothing to their white wives; and detailed the case of a white man murdering his servant in a fit of jealousy over a mulatto woman.

Maria Nugent, in fact, blamed the failure of the enslaved population to increase by natural means on the failure of white men to set good and moral examples for the enslaved population. She noted:

...it appears to me, there would be certainly no necessity for the slave trade, if religion, decency and good order were established among negroes; if they could be pre-

vailed upon to marry; and if our white men would but set them a better example."

She claimed that when slaves lived together in families they had lots of children;

"but white men of all descriptions, married or single, live in a state of licentiousness with their female slaves and until a great reformation takes place on their part, neither religion, decency nor morality, can be established among the negroes".[46]

Planters did not often allow their slaves to marry; yet writers like Nugent and others accused slaves of being promiscuous and disinclined to marry. Alfred Caldecott, in his 1898 work on the Church in the West Indies, noted that marriage was confined to the elite whites, while the working class whites consorted with black women "without restraint either from their own corrupted consciences or from public opinion"; that " the slaves were not allowed to marry, not indeed did their own stage of moral development lead them to desire the institution".[47] In a 1937 work, Richardson Wright noted, "Marriage between slaves was unknown. Doubtless plenty of romance waxed and waned between sable Venuses and sooty Adonises, but it never entered their head s. . . Polygamy was common among the slaves. Most men managed to have half-a-dozen wives scattered through the neighbourhood, their huts being convenient ports of call."[48] He also described the maroon men as 'gay Lotharios'.[49]

Mrs Nugent says something about the conditions of enslaved women who had to work up to the last six weeks of their pregnancy and return to work within two to three weeks of delivery. She was influenced by the local women to believe that "it was astonishing how fast black women bred, what healthy children they had and how soon they recovered after lying-in" in contrast to mulatto women who were "constantly liable to miscarry and subject to a thousand little complaints."[50]

Jamaica was clearly marked by an excess of white males over white females, despite her observations that women tended to outlive men and her constant references to white widows like Mrs Simpson who ran Monymusk Estate. "Women rarely lose their health, but men as rarely keep theirs."[51] Some of the single white women were nursemaids to white children and housekeepers in charge of the enslaved domestics. Lady Nugent had several of these women in her employ as nurses after she had her two children, George and Louisa; and these women were expected to serve faithfully, even suppressing their own feelings in the interest of their charges. When George's nurses husband died, she "made great efforts to conquer her own feelings on account of my precious boy".[52] By 1804, Mrs Nugent had become "most heartily sick of dissipation and politics and long[ed] for a little rest of body and mind."[53] She left Jamaica in 1805.

Robert Renny's history of Jamaica, dedicated to the Earl of Balcarres and published in 1807, was more concerned with observations on the climate, scenery, trade, agriculture, diseases of Europeans in the tropics and the implications of the abolition of the slave trade than he was with the women of the island. His intention was to produce a more concise historical account of the island which would be cheaper and of use to "those who may be led by inclination or necessity to visit that country."[54] Prior accounts by Long and Bryan Edwards he described as "voluminous, ill-digested and unconnected".[55] However he gave a passing mention of them. His description of the simple, naked, innocent indigenous women is based on the narratives of the members of the Columbus mission. But his remarks on black, coloured and white women are made from first-hand observations as a visitor.

Renny was clearly convinced that Africans were 'untutored savages' destined to be enslaved on biological and climatic reasons; for they could not have the same ancestors as white Europeans and "slavery is peculiarly congenial and seems to be natural, to the inhabitants of warm climates".[56] He did not inveigh against miscegenation as Long did, but clearly pitied the mixed race women. He remarked: "The females of this class are still more objects of compassion than the males".[57] Why? Because, as Long also observed, they lacked education and therefore "they have no ideas of a dignified propriety of thought or of conduct; and their notions of virtue are confused and depraved".[58]

Renny also pitied coloured women on the basis that they had no marriage prospects. The free-coloured men were:

much too degraded to think of marriage; and for a white man to marry a mulatto would be a degradation which would forever exclude him from the respectable company of his own colour and sink him to a level with those who are excluded from all consideration in society.[59]

The choice open to the free woman of colour was to become the mistress of a white man "in which station she behaves with a fidelity, modesty and tenderness and prudence which are highly exemplary and which might furnish an important lesson to many a married European lady".[60] Renny was favourable in his remarks about the attitude of free coloured women towards the care of the sick and unlike the usual representation of black women, he commended the free women of colour for their "unbounded attachment to their children".[61]

Renny said very little about enslaved black women, only implying that they were crucial, as first gang workers in the field, to the production process. He gave more space to a discussion of white women. First, he emphasised that they were few in number, a situation he interpreted as an unfortunate one for white men who had to put up with the women of colour as partners. The 'white creole ladies' he described as 'handsome, elegant and engaging', kind to the sick and 'in their mode of living, they are in the highest degree abstemious'. He also described them as 'faithful wives and mothers' who seemed content to play their proper gender role in the domestic sphere'. Predictably, in the tradition of the dichotomous representation of black women as promiscuous and non-black women as virtuous, Renny comments that the white women, though few in number, "are seldom seen gadding abroad".[62]

Finally, the accounts of M. G. Lewis and Cynric Williams must be mentioned. M. G. Lewis owned estates in Jamaica but was an absentee owner. He made periodic visits to Jamaica and wrote accounts of these visits. He died in 1818 on his way back to England from the Caribbean. On his 1815-1817 visit he had several observations to make about the women on his properties. Lewis is regarded by many as a liberal, but his rather complex and contradictory narrative which typifies the struggle between ameliorative/liberal humanism and the abolitionist regime of the plantation, reproduces most of the pro-slavery arguments of the period; at the same time he tries to introduce reforms on his own estates, thus incurring the hostility of the Jamaican plantocracy. He gives insight into the enslaved as individuals, as human beings, unlike others who reduce the enslaved to undifferentiated masses with a constancy of character. But one must remember that Lewis was writing after the abolition of the transatlantic trade in enslaved Africans and would have been more conscious of the need to appease the anti-slavery elements who were marshalling evidence of the ill-treatment of the enslaved. It is quite clear, for example, that he was more favourable in his views of the female 'brownings' [the current term in Jamaica for 'mulatto' women]. His mulatto slave, Mary Wiggins, was described as beautiful – a description not applied to black women. He observed, in one sense unflatteringly [?] that "Mary Wiggins and an old cotton tree are the most picturesque objects that I have seen for these 20 years".[63]

He, like others, commended the coloured housekeepers for their kindness to the sick and their faithful attachment to their white male 'protectors'. On the other hand, black women, such as Psyche, were represented as unfaithful and ever ready to leave black or coloured men for white men. He related a conversation he had with the slave Cubina as an illustration of the deep social divisions created by the colour hierarchy, even among the enslaved. When Cubina told Lewis that he had gotten married, Lewis remarked that he hoped Cubina had married a pretty woman, for example, Mary Wiggins. Cubina reportedly ". . . seemed quite shocked at the very idea. Oh Massa, me black, Mary Wiggins sambo; that not allowed",[64] he remarked.

Unlike some of his fellow writers, Lewis did not paint a generalised picture of uncaring black slave mothers, though he identified a few of those. The general impression he gave was that once born, infants were cared for by enslaved women who were anxious for them to live. But he suggests that black women deliberately chose at times not to reproduce. According to him, "I really believe that the negresses can produce children at pleasure; and where they are barren, it is just as hens will frequently not lay eggs on ship-board, because they do not like their situation."[65]

Finally, Cynric Williams had a similar bias towards coloured women. He visited and toured Jamaica in 1823 and wrote an account of his visit. He learnt from very early to make the distinctions of colour among the racially mixed groups. He stated that: "an Englishman considers all people of colour as mulattoes until he has occasion to remark the different shades by which they are distinguished".[66] One of the first women he wrote about was the 'mahogany tone' Polly Vidal, a lodging-house keeper in Falmouth whom he characterised as rather a chatterbox whose questions "crowded me faster than I could reply to them",[67] but who nevertheless he found courteous and hospitable. He admired the 'tawny' damsels who worked for Polly Vidal and who occasionally peeped out at him from behind jalousies. He described them as having elegantly formed, graceful and elastic bodies, though like other European visitors he felt compelled to comment on their colour and manner of speech. He observed that: "I was not as yet reconciled to their dingy hue, and there was something I thought rather too languid in the drawling tone of their speech."[68]

The other woman of colour he admired was the 16 year old quadroon girl, Diana whose complexion he described as "very little darker than the European"[69] Diana was the daughter of a wealthy white planter and a slave woman [whose freedom he offered to buy from her owner, Mr 'S' but who refused to accept his offer] but he studiously avoided too much reference to her African origin, extolling those aspects of her physique which reminded him of European, classical Greek and Roman women. In fact, though he regarded Diana as a beautiful coloured woman, her features were only 'near' perfect; for "the features [of the Quadroon]retain too often the inclination to the African lips, or cast of countenance that reminds one of their origin."[70] In his view, as in the view of other visitors, "the European cast of countenance is vastly superior to the African."[71] When he fell ill he was nursed by the beautiful Diana. He remarked that Diana had "youth, beauty and all the etceteras". He on the other hand, 20 years her senior, had "neither youth, nor beauty nor any of the etceteras that can engage the attention of the young damsel."[72] While lauding her beauty though, Williams typically represented Diana as stupid – the stereotypical beauty without brains. He concluded that she was a 'pretty, simple creature',[73] unable to learn European customs and beliefs no matter how hard she tried. This 'revelation' came to him after he had asked her if she were a Christian, and she said 'no'. In response to his request for a reason for her failure to convert to christianity, she replied [rather sensibly, I think], "because me can't believe what me can't understand. Massa preaches to the ears but not to the heart".[74]

Williams commented on the habit of sexual relations between coloured women and white men but had no scathing comments to make about this, as Edward Long had done. On the contrary he was at pains to point out that "there is no misery here among the class of females who had become the companions of European gentlemen"; and certainly coloured women were not prostitutes.[75]

His comments about creole white women replicated those of previous observers. That is, that they excelled at domestic duties and skills such as embroidery and needlework.[76] On the other hand, "European beauty cuts but a mean figure in this climate contrasted with the healthy countenances and elastic figures of the Mulatto and Quadroon women".[77] He stated quite bluntly that single white women, particularly those who were educated in England, had little prospects of finding a mate because only a sorry crop of white single men were in Jamaica.

His comments on the black women are sparse. He commented on the unrepentant stance of a slave woman who was beaten by the driver for having, in a fit of jealous rage, herself beaten a young girl. She told the driver to "go to hell and walked off".[78] We also learn from his narrative that the people of colour stayed aloof from black Christmas festivities.[79]

In conclusion, most of the narratives are marked throughout by a disdain and contempt for the indigenous Caribbean people, inspired by racial animosity, religious intolerance and cultural ethnocentrism. These narratives were clearly linked to an imperialist project in which 'natives' [or subjugated 'aliens'] are perceived as 'savage' and 'barbaric', to be subject to the 'civilizing' influence of the colonizers. This involved taking over land, imposing an empire and colonial rule, and making all of this acceptable to intellectuals, humanitarians and financial backers in Europe. One would have to look to the post-slavery writers like Mary Seacole, Nancy Prince and J. J. Thomas[80] for engagements with counter-discourse. The post-slavery period did usher in writings in a more revisionist genre; but despite emancipation, the negative representations of Caribbean people did not cease. People like Thomas Carlyle in his *Ocassional Discourse on the Nigger Question*, and J.

J. Froude in *Froudacity*, insisted on painting a picture of the lazy island men and women, contented with colonialism.

Notes

1. Peter Hulme, *Colonial Encounters: Europe and the Native Caribbean, 1492-1797* [Methuen & Co. Ltd., London & New York, 1986]. p. 1.
2. For a perspective on the representations in female-authored texts, see Bridget Brereton, 'Text, testimony and gender: an examination of some texts by women in the English-speaking Caribbean, 1770s-1920s', Paper presented at the symposium on women and gender, UWI, Mona, November 1993.
3. Joan Wallach Scott, *Gender and the Politics of History* (New York: Columbia University Press, 1988, p. 42).
4. D. J.R. Walker *Columbus and the Golden World of the Island Arawaks*, Ian Randle Publishers: Kingston, 1992, p.233.
5. Andres Bernaldez, *Historia de los Reyes Catolicos*, quoted in Walker, *Columbus and the Golden World*, p. 269.
6. Walker, p. 270.
7. Some of these issues are taken up in P. Martyr, *Historie of the West Indies* (London, 1675) & W.J. Gardner, *History of Jamaica, 1655-1872* (London, 1909 edn.).
8. Goveia, pp. 51; Leslie. Letter 1, p. 14.
9. Leslie, Letter 1, p. 1.
10. Ibid, p.2.
11. Ibid., Letter 2, p. 17.
12. Goveia, p. 53; Leslie, Letter XI, pp 305-6.
13. Ibid., p.34
14. Ibid., p. 35.
15. Ibid.
16. Ibid.
17. Ibid., Letter 7, pp. 206-7.
18. T. Burnard, 'Thomas Thistlewood Becomes a Creole', unpublished 1994 paper, p.8.
19. Gordon Lewis, *Main Currents in Caribbean Thought: The Historical Evolution of Caribbean Society in its Ideological Aspects, 1492-1900*, Heinemann Educational Books, [Caribbean] Ltd., Kingston : Port of Spain, The Johns Hopkins University Press, Baltimore, 1983, pp. 97-8.
20. Monson 31/1. 26 June; 17 July, 1750.
21. MS. 675, National Library of Jamaica. Stephen Harmer to Saul Harmer, 21 June 1842.
22. Alfred Caldecott, *The Church in the West Indies* (London: Frank Cass, 1970 edition), p. 37.
23. Benjamin M'Mahon, *Jamaica plantership* [London, 1839], p. 186.
24. Ibid., p. 181.
25. Lewis, *Main Currents*, pp. 107-8.
26. Carol Francis, 'Edward Long: The Man, the Historian', M. A. Research Paper, University of the West Indies, 1992.

27. Edward Long, *History of Jamaica* (London, 1774).
28. Ibid., p. 280.
29. Vol. 11, ch. xiii, sec. 1, p. 260.
30. Ibid.
31. Ibid., pp. 276-77.
32. Ibid., p. 279. For an excellent recent analysis of Long's textual invention of the Caribbean woman, see Veronica Gregg, 'The Caribbean (as a certain kind of) woman', paper presented at the symposium 'Engendering History', UWI, Mona, November 1993.
33. William Beckford, *A descriptive account of the island of Jamaica* (London: T & J. Egerton, MDCCXC), Vol 2, pp. 120-21.
34. Ibid., p. 385.
35. Ibid., p. 386.
36. Philip Wright (ed.), *Lady Nugent's Journal of her residence in Jamaica from 1801-1805* (Kingston: Institute of Jamaica Publications, 1966).
37. Ibid., p. 53, January 1802.
38. Ibid., p. 156, April 1803.
39. Ibid., Jany. 1804, p. 199.
40. Ibid., 22 Feby. 1805, p. 220.
41. Ibid., 6th August 1801, p. 14.
42. Ibid.
43. Ibid., April 1802, p. 86.
44. Ibid., p. 29: August 1801.
45. Ibid.
46. Ibid., p. 87. This seems to be a corollary of the planters' view that promiscuity among enslaved women was the chief cause of their infertility.
47. Caldecott, p. 37.
48. Richardson Wright, *Revels in Jamaica, 1682-1838* (Kingston: Bolivar Press, 1986 reprint), pp. 230-31.
49. Ibid., p. 232.
50. Wright (ed) *Lady Nugent's Journal*, Feby. 1802, p. 59.
51. Ibid., p. 59.
52. Ibid., p. 155, April 1803.
53. Ibid., Nov. 1804, p. 217
54. Robert Renny, *An history of Jamaica* (London: J. Cawthorn, 1807), p. ix.
55. Ibid.
56. Ibid., p. 161.
57. Ibid., p. 189.
58. Ibid.
59. Ibid., pp. 189-90.
60. Ibid., p. 190.
61. Ibid.
62. Ibid., pp. 209, 211-12, 315, 325.
63. M. G. Lewis, *Journal of a residence among the negroes* (London, 1861), p. 35.
64. Ibid., p. 39.
65. Ibid., pp. 41-55.
66. Cynric Williams, p. 53.
67. Cynric Williams, *A tour through the island of Jamaica* (2nd ed., London, 1827), p. 2.
68. Ibid.
69. Ibid., p. 54.
70. Ibid., p. 254.
71. Ibid., p. 255.
72. Cynric Williams, *A tour through the island of Jamaica* [1823], p. 128.
73. Ibid., p. 57.
74. Ibid.
75. Ibid., p. 310-11.
76. Ibid., p. 129.
77. Ibid., p. 254.
78. Ibid., p. 13.
79. Ibid., p. 27.
80. *A Black Woman's Odyssey through Russia and Jamaica: the Narrative of Nancy Prince* (1850. Marcus Wiener Pub, 1990) with an introduction by R. G. Walters; Mary Seacole, *Wonderful Adventures of Mrs Seacole in Many Lands*, eds. Z. Alexander & A. Dewjee (Bristol: Falling Wall Press, 1984; originally pub. 1857); J. J. Thomas' *Froudacity: West Indian Fables Explained* (London, 1889) was a response to J. J. Froude's racist and ethnocentric *The English in the West Indies* (London, 1888). Alfred Caldecott said of Froude: "He must go down to posterity as a man who could speak irresponsibly from a position of responsibility in which he was placed by his talents, and could write carelessly when his evidence was important, and with bias when justice was imperative.' See his *The Church in the West Indies*, p. 255.

SECTION ELEVEN

Subaltern Autonomy: Social & Economic Culture

The subalterns, or enslaved Africans and other racially marginalized groups, demanded room for themselves. Demands generated tension. The relations between African cultural and ideological world views and those of their European overlords within the Caribbean environment, furthermore, have produced a vibrant and fascinating literature. Issues surrounding the degree and depth of cultural retention and adaptation to slavery, especially from the perspective of the historian centred within a nativist consciousness, are seen as critical to social development and institutional formation. Lamur, for example, addresses the important issue of the dynamics of cultural interaction within the social theatre of religious formation and evolution.

The ways in which the enslaved pursued the right to be autonomous economic agents, as part of the legitimate use of their 'leisure' times, are also major concerns. As Mintz and Hall, among others, show, the culture of marketing emerged among Blacks as a common expression, and material and social conditions on the plantations as well as in the towns made it particularly attractive. Marketing allowed enslaved peoples to improve the quality and quantity of their diets in a context of general malnutrition, to own and possess property in a system that also defined them as property, and offered them time to travel, and to attempt to 'normalize' their social lives as much as possible under generally restrictive circumstances. These benefits, however, had to be militantly pursued, as Turner demonstrates and it is here that women in particular displayed great tenacity. Marketing symbolized a spirit of independence and was central to the process of non-violent protest and resistance which characterized day-to-day anti-slavery behaviour.

The essays in this section are divided into categories. It is understood that for the sake of analysis social and economic activities can be separated and treated distinctly. Africans sought to promote and protect social cosmologies that enabled them to make sense and create order from their environments. Leisure and entertainment were as important as religion in this regard, and as a result the pursuit of cultural autonomy and a sense of spiritual happiness pervaded the nature of daily decision-making. Likewise, the right to property possession, and open engagement in the market as autonomous buyers and sellers, was aggressively demanded. These essays place the discourse in clear perspective and illustrate the extent to which Africans were not members of 'total' plantation societies.

52

Slave Religion on the Vossenburg Plantation (Suriname) and Missionaries' Reaction

HUMPHREY E. LAMUR

In the course of years much has been published on both the religion of slave populations and the proselytizing of the descendants of slaves in the Caribbean and in the United States. There also exist numerous publications dealing with Afro-Caribbean religions in the Danish and Spanish Caribbean and Brazil.

However, very little is known about the religion of slaves in the Western hemisphere and their proselytizing. In particular, in the seventeenth and eighteenth centuries, the planters were opposed to the conversion of slaves to Christianity for fear that religious instruction would automatically lead to manumission. Only after the mid-eighteenth century had the proselytizing of slaves started, but not even in all slave societies. In most Caribbean slave societies missionary activities began around 1850 (Genovese 1976, 185; Jackson 1931, 168-239; Lamur 1984; Oldendorp 1770; Olwig 1985; Rooke 1979). Most of the available information on this subject concerns primarily the slave population in the American state Virginia. Thus, most of the comparison which follows will be with this slave society. In the remainder of this paper I shall present a brief overview of the achievements of missionary activities among the slave population in Virginia. In doing so I shall rely on Genovese (1976, 183-209) and Jackson (1931, 168-239). Subsequently, some remarks will be made on the religious beliefs of the slave population on the sugar estate Vossenburg. This is followed by a discussion of the Protestant missionaries' efforts to convert the slaves of this plantation to Christianity.

Black Conversion in Virginia

The history of Christianity of the slave population in Virginia can be divided into three periods, namely 1750-90, 1790-1830, and 1830-60 (Genovese 1976; Jackson 1931). One of the criteria used by the authors to distinguish these periods is the missionaries' attitude toward slavery. In the period 1750-90, the Baptists and Methodists 'expressed hostility towards slavery and a hope that it would vanish'. They argued that the slaves were brothers in Christ. During the period 1790-1830, antislavery attitudes in the churches began to decline under pressure by the slaveowners. The Nat Turner uprising in 1822 meant a turning point in the history of black Christianity in Virginia and ushered in the third phase. 'Whereas previously many slaveholders had feared slaves with religion – and the example of Turner confirmed their fears – now they feared slaves without religion even more.' Hence they began to accept Christianity as a means of social control. In response (Genovese 1976, 186-87), 'several churches embraced the pro-slavery argument. They won the trust of the masters and freed themselves to preach the gospel to the slaves.' However, the slaveowners remained reluctant to the missionaries' wish to teach the slaves to read and write. How did the slave population in Virginia respond to the new efforts of the preachers after 1822 to convert them? It seems that the missionaries failed in eliminating the remnants of African religion of the slaves. Genovese (1976, 184) claims that 'the conditions of their new social life forced them to combine their African inheritance with the dominant power they confronted and to shape a religion of their own'. He examines a number of sources which support this statement. One is Jones, a Presbyterian missionary who preached the gospel to the slaves in Georgia around 1840. Genovese quotes him as saying that the slaves still believed in 'second-sight, apparitions, charms, witchcraft, and in a kind of irresistible Satanic influence' (see also Jones 1847, 127-28). A second source, Hundley (1860, 328-29, cited in Genovese) was a slaveowner. Around 1860 he claimed that the slaves still believed in 'witchcraft, sorcery, conjuring and other forms of paganism'. About the same time, another slaveowner, Eliza Andrews, described the attitudes of the slaves to Christianity as indifferent but not hostile. Several times she attended religious services for the slaves and noticed that they fell asleep through the sermons. Similar remarks on the retention of African religious elements by the slaves were also made by medical doctors who worked in the Southern States around the mid-nineteenth century. Among them were Carpenter (1844, 165), Cartwright (1857,11) and Wilson (1860, 319). Thus, it may be concluded that the missionaries failed to fully eliminate the African beliefs of the slave population in Virginia. This finding of Genovese is consistent with the conclusion reached by Jernegan in the early twentieth century that the efforts to convert the slaves to Christianity were not successful.

Slaves Religion on Vossenburg

Does the conclusion concerning black Christianity in Virginia in the period prior to 1860 hold also for the slave population at Vossenburg, a sugar estate in Suriname? I have chosen this plantation for the following reason. To date, it is the only plantation in Suriname for which the material on missionaries' activities has ben analyzed in relation to other aspects of plantation life.

In the late seventeenth and early eighteenth centuries Vossenburg was owned by Adriaan de Graff. It covered 3,000 acres and was situated on the Commewijne river in the coastal area of Suriname. In 1705, the number of slaves amounted to 92, and increased to 196 in 1747. A few years before the abolition of slavery in 1863 the slave force had increased to 240.

As said before, I shall first present some information on the religious beliefs of the slave population at Vossenburg, and then discuss both the missionaries' efforts to convert the slaves to Christianity and the slaves' response to these endeavours. Both the missionaries' account and the oral histories of the informants that I collected in the period 1980-82 and thereafter were used to gain an insight into the religion of the slave population at Vossenburg. The information, though fragmentary, shows that the system of belief of the slaves at Vossenburg consisted of the following elements:

– A Supreme being and lower Gods
– Priests and mediums of lower Gods
– Religious objects
– Rituals

Adangra was the name by which the slaves denoted their God. The available information does not reveal in what respect the Gods affected the life of the slaves. The main religious objects were a wooden image of a God used for group worship and some small icons kept in each house for private use. Among the functionaries who played an important role in religious ceremonies were the priest the obeahman (*lukuman*). In addition there was also the witchdoctor (*wissiman*) who affected the life of the slaves, although he cannot be considered as a religious functionary. The priests were in charge of leading the services intended to worship the God. The primary task of the obeahman was to divine the cause of sickness or death of fellow slaves. In particular they tried to deduce whether sickness/death was of a supernatural origin for which a human being was to blame, or whether a natural cause was involved. Obeahmen also prescribed medicines for illness. These tasks were performed at the request of the interested party. The obeahman rarely acted on his own initiative. While the obeahman was seen by the slaves as a benefactor, the witchdoctor was perceived as antisocial. The latter was thought to cause illness and death, and acted both at the request of others and on his own initiative. This is a summary of the system of belief of the slave population at Vossenburg which the Moravian Mission confronted when it started its activities on 27 December 1847.

The aim of the Moravian Brotherhood Mission was to convert the slaves to Christianity, and at the same time to eliminate the religion of the slave population since it was considered inconsistent with Christianity. Did the Moravian preachers succeed in this? To answer this question I shall discuss a number of cases of conflicts between the slaves and the missionaries which took place in the period of 1847-77, i.e. the last year for which archival material is available on missionary accounts at Vossenburg.

Conversion of Slaves on Vossenburg

The missionaries visited Vossenburg every six weeks. They arrived on Saturdays and stayed with the director of Vossenburg. The next day, on Sunday, they held two religious services, one in the morning, the other in the evening. The sermons took place in the engineer's or the carpenter's shed. In addition, the missionaries gave religious instructions (catechism) and they baptized both children and adults. In addition, they visited the sick, the needy, and the older people.

One of the problems in analyzing the missionary accounts on the conversion of the slaves at Vossenburg was the question what different missionaries meant by conversion and what religious tactics they applied. Further, it was of importance to know whether the notions held by the missionaries on conversion had changed in the course of years between 1847 and 1877. Unfortunately, it was not possible to find a satisfactory answer to these questions. Yet, to give an impression of the notions of conversion held by the missionaries, I will report two events. In 1861 an epidemic broke out which claimed many victims among the slave population. The missionary saw it as a punishment by God and assumed that the slaves shared his view: 'For the first time . . . the Negroes were quiet and attentive, . . . The Lord had addressed them seriously, ...' The next event: a slave who had been excommunicated by the missionary, was later, on his death, 'buried as a pagan'. The missionary claimed that this made a strong impression on another slave, a sick one who had also been excommunicated. The slave showed repentance and asked the missionary to report that 'God's Spirit has touched his heart'. This case is also

interesting because it reveals what religious tactics the missionary used to convert this penitent. He told him that the slave who had been buried earlier as a 'pagan' was 'now standing before God's judgement seat' to be punished for his 'idolatry'. Having told the penitent all this, he was proposed to be readmitted as a member of the church, but only on the condition that he would 'publicly in the church in front of the whole idolatrous slave force express his repentance for his wrongdoing.' The slave did so, as the missionary informed us in his monthly report. Let me repeat that this case only shows how that particular missionary went about converting the slaves. Thus, I am not suggesting that this event was representative of the religious tactics applied by other missionaries who worked at Vossenburg between 1847 and 1877, because of the lack of more information on this subject.

J. G. F. Jansa, the first Moravian missionary to preach the gospel to the slaves at Vossenburg, started his work on 28 December 1847. Before doing so he asked the slaves who were gathered if they were in favour of his work. A driver backed by a small group of slaves answered, 'No, we do not want it.' However, the majority reacted favourably. Thus Jansa soon realized that he would face a difficult task among a group which he described as the most superstitious of all slave populations in Suriname. Their God which is the biggest of its kind in this country was called *Andranga* or the 'most secret'. This remark is correct. The cult of the slaves at Vossenburg was apparently so important that the place of worship in the bush where the icon of the Supreme God was located was also attended by slaves from the nearby plantations, namely Breukelerwaard, Fairfield, Fortuin and Schoonoord. These were plantations where the Moravian Mission has started their activities some years earlier. In 1847 a new wooden image of the God, five feet in height, was built to replace an older one which had rotted. The new one was placed standing in a hut with a roof of leaves, while the old one was placed to the side near the new image. This altar where the God was worshipped was located at a distance of one hour walking from the centre of the plantation.

It was at the place of worship, on 16 July 1849, that the first serious confrontation between the missionary Jansa and the slaves took place. That morning, following the religious service in the converted prayer house, Jansa was invited by a mulatto slave to destroy their God in the bush. The missionary accepted the invitation and in the afternoon went to the slaves' place of worship accompanied by a few slaves, among whom was one of the drivers. Jansa, proceeded to destroy the hut and seized the religious images. Subsequently, they returned to the centre of the plantation where the missionary asked the slaves if they had any more religious objects in their huts. The head driver, a slave priest, responded in slave creole that the icons would be delivered to the missionary the next day: 'they will be available tomorrow' (*Tamara sa de*'). But the missionary insisted and the slaves handed over the objects to the nmissionary on the spot. Then the missionary went into the huts to see for himself if the slaves had hidden more of the icons.

The news that the missionary had dared to destroy the altar astonished director Uhlenkamp of Vossenburg. He noticed that of old the slaves of this sugar estate were known as 'idolatrous'. Why had the slaves invited the missionary to the centre of their religious activities? Is this event a sign that the slaves had deserted their own African beliefs? I do not think so, because the slaves still defended their own religion against criticism by the missionary, as the following event shows. During a service in the prayer house on 26 October 1849 the missionary depicted the slaves as stupid because they worshipped their own God. This remark annoyed the slaves. A driver, who probably acted as spokesman of the group, responded that the missionary should control himself. He did so by using the following rhetorical question, in creole: 'If you are living among the negroes, you have to speak their language.' A more reasonable explanation for the slaves' willingness to destroy their own religious objects is to perceive this behaviour as an act of iconoclasm. The replacement of old relics by a new one had probably occurred in the past. Thus, the incident in 1849 was not intended by the slaves as a rejection of their religion as such, but rather as a destruction of the religious objects they had in use at that time. In my view the missionary's demand was only a cause for the slaves to do what they had done periodically in the past.

Similar events have recently occurred in West Africa. This is clear from an analysis of the anti-witchcraft movement among the Bashilele (le Mupele); here too relics were destroyed (Ngokwey 1978).

There is another possible explanation for the slaves' willingness to hand over their religious objects to the missionary. Their behaviour can also be judged as a gesture of goodwill in return for the missionaries' readiness to accept them as equals. Whatever explanation is correct, the destruction of the religious objects did not mean that the slaves had lapsed from their own African beliefs. This is clear from the following case. On Sunday morning 22 May 1850 a conflict broke out between the director of the plantation, Uhlenkamp, and the slaves. They declined an order by the director to work on that day because Sundays were usually a day off. Some time later, during the sermon in the prayer house, the missionary tried to persuade the slaves to obey the director and to carry out his orders after the service. The slaves rejected the missionary's plea and made clear that they had already made numerous sacrifices for the church. They reminded him that his predecessor, the missionary Jansa, had taken away their beloved religious objects a year ago. They also threatened to reclaim all this if they did not get the whole Sunday off to attend the church meeting. From this incident it is also clear that the slaves began to see the missionary as an appendage of the director and they resented it.

The following event also shows that the introduction of Christianity in 1847 had not resulted in a full surrender to Christian ideas. On 20 November 1853, the slave woman Dina went to the missionary to inform him that she no longer wanted to live together with the slave October. The latter did not let it pass and a few hours later, after the sermon, he also made his way to the missionary to give his version of their matrimonial problems. Dina was ill which led her sister Paulina to consult an obeahman. The latter consulted the gods and then concluded that Dina's sickness was of a supernatural origin, for which October was to be blamed. This, October claimed, was the real motive for Dina to leave him, despite his humble appeal not to do so.

Another indication that the slaves still defended their own belief, concerns the so called '*kwa kwa banji*', small benches, which the missionary considered one of the slaves' religious objects. When the issue was first raised on 11 August 1857, the slaves responded with reserve. They were reluctant to discuss the subject and they only admitted that a certain man named Staars was 'the father of the seats'. Staars, at that time living as a free black at the nearby plantation of Fairfield, was a slave at Vossenburg before his manumission. One month later, on 25 September 1857, the 'religious' seats were a cause of a dispute again, when the missionary discovered three of them in the prayer house during the service. Moreover he learned that many converted slaves owned these seats and used them as drums at their religious dances. At that sermon, another driver was one of the slaves who had brought his seat to the prayer house. In a discussion with the missionary that followed he denied that the seats were used as objects of worship and thus he refused to put away his bench. Following the dispute the missionary explained that it was sinful to possess the seats. However, the slaves did not share that view and were determined not to give in. The missionary went to the director and the white overseer to discuss the conflict. On his return to the prayer house he told the slaves that he had decided to postpone the ceremony of baptism to his next visit on 9 November 1857. Probably, he expected that the slaves would change their minds after some time. At this next visit he made a third effort to persuade them to dispose of the seats. However, he failed again.

Two years later another incident occurred which reveals that even baptized slaves had not fully accepted Christian ideas. In 1859 the slave Hiob Hermanses complained that his sickness was of a supernatural origin, for which he blamed Abraham Hermanus. The missionary was astonished to learn that Hermanses, who had only recently been baptized a Christian, still believed in what he described as witchcraft. As he saw it Hermanses had slid back into 'paganism'.

A major blow to the work of the Moravian Mission was the discovery by the missionary on 25 July 1860 that 22 converted male slaves had continued to hold religious meetings at their altar in the place of worship in the bush. He also learned that these slaves had built a new wooden image of their god. In addition he was informed that the slaves were performing *Pakasaka*, a

religious ritual, in their huts. Apparently, on the same day that the missionary received the information on the new wooden image, it was agreed that the slaves would take the idol from the bush to the slave quarters to show it to the missionary at his next visit to Vossenburg. However, six weeks later, on 14 September 1860 on his arrival at the plantation, the missionary found that the icon was removed but not destroyed and probably installed in another place. He demanded that the image be delivered to him immediately, as missionary Jansa had done some 13 years ago. But this time the slaves refused to grant his request, despite his threat that a curse would rest on them as long as their god was among them. The missionary also decided not to baptize new candidates at that time. It seems that this incident had depressed the missionary. He considered it as a sign of the influence of Satan but continued to believe that Jesus Christ would finally gain the victory.

Not long after this incident the missionary had to admit that he had not yet succeeded in converting the slaves to Christianity. On 22 October 1860 it came to his attention that a few slaves had taken part in a dance ritual near the sluice gate. When questioned, the slaves – all the 15 participants and 6 spectators – gave their names. Three of the fifteen participants, all of them converted males, promised to refrain from further participation. The remaining 12, none of them converted, refused to make such a promise. All of these, except one, were female slaves.

The small number of slaves who attended the services in the prayer house was also a disappointing experience for the Moravian Mission. In 1861 this led the missionary to conclude that the devil had got the upper hand:

When I arrived at the prayer house for the afternoon service only 50 people were present. The others did not consider it worth attending the sermon, but preferred to pursue their pleasures instead . . . (Lamur 1984,94)

Whether the small number of slaves that attended the services points to indifference rather than hostility towards Christianity is not clear.

On 1 July 1863, slavery was abolished in Suriname. The ex-slaves remained on Vossenburg as (semi-) free labourers and the Moravian Mission continued to preach the gospel to them. Did this change in the legal status of the slaves affect their relationship to the missionaries? To answer this question let us consider a few more cases. On Christmas Eve of the year 1863 a child died. According to former slave Leptonis, it was caused by a witchdoctor who had used supernatural means. hence Leptonis decided to find out which of his fellows was to blame for it. To do so, he took the corpse and, while carrying it on his head, walked along the huts in the old slave quarters in order to divine the cause of death. This case is interesting since it shows that witchdoctors were considered as antisocial individuals who should be punished. But more important is to note that the slaves' African-based religion still affected their behaviour.

The slaves often spoke out openly in defending their religion against criticism from the missionaries. On 8 February 1869 a conflict arose between a few freedmen and the missionary. He had learned from Heering, who had succeeded Uhlenkamp as director, on 21 June 1864, that the ex-slaves were still holding the bench dance-rituals. When they were gathered the missionary demanded them to stop these activities. Samson Winston, a 29-year-old field hand who had been baptized on 1 September 1866, stepped forward in the direction of the missionary. Furiously he looked at the missionary and gave him to understand that he did not intend to grant this request and that the 'bench' had cost him a lot of money. 'I shall not stop playing, preacher. You can take against me whatever measure you like, the bench has cost me money,' he said in the Creole language. Consider also the following incident. On 22 April 1869, the missionary told the blacks during a service that he believed most of them were still worshipping their 'idols'. One of those present confirmed this on behalf of the audience by saying: 'Yes Sir, that is correct.'

A few months later on 19 August 1869, the missionary suffered another setback in his work. On that day he learned that the blacks were again 'worshipping the *Mamasneki*' (a serpent deity). A member of the church council, and ex-slave who was questioned by the missionary, said that he was unaware of it. 'If the snake finds himself in one of the houses, he certainly has got there on his own efforts', the member of the council added soberly. Then all began search for the snake and it was found in the garret of the prayer house. At the request of the missionary the reptile was killed and the Christian services could be started.

Even the blacks who were converted to Christianity did not accept all regulations imposed on them by the missionaries. On 14 July 1872 Markus Vreede Cornelius told the missionary that he was not prepared to pay more than 32 cents ('*drisren*') as financial contribution for the church. When the missionary told him that it was not enough, he became angry and threatened to pay nothing. The missionary in turn took a strong position and threatened to expel Cornelius as a member of the church if he did not reverse his decision.

The cases presented above reveal that the Moravian Mission made little progress in converting the slaves to Christianity at the sugar estate Vossenburg. Nor did the missionaries succeed in eliminating the African-based religion of the slave-population. Quite the opposite. The slaves retained their own system of beliefs and practised their religion along with attending the religious services of the Mission.

While it is difficult to give a sufficient explanation of the retention of slave religion at Vossenburg, it may be concluded that the role played by the slave priests was an important factor. When the missionary Jansa introduced Christianity at Vossenburg in 1847, it was a black slave driver who opposed this effort. Two years later the missionary visited the place where the slaves worshipped their god. That time the head driver, who also was a slave priest, played a crucial role in the discussion with the missionary. Three months later the missionary criticized the slaves for what he described as their idolatrous way of life, and again it was a driver who admonished the missionary to control himself. On 2 July 1850, the missionary expelled a slave from the prayer house during a service, just because he did not like the remarks he made. It concerned the slaves' admiration for a driver. In one of the clashes in the prayer house over the benches ('*kwa kwa banji*') on 25 December 1857 the slave who declined the demand of the preacher to put away his bench was the second-driver. In 1864 Leptonis tried to uncover the witchdoctor who he thought to be responsible for the death of a child. While it was not possible to know the social position of Leptonis in the slave community, apparently he was one of the obeahmen, since it was they who were responsible for finding out the causes of sickness and death of fellow members in the community. Finally, the case of Samson Winst can be mentioned. He said that he did not care a bit about the missionary's demand to stop holding ritual dancings, Samson was a 29-year-old driver. In sum, in most of the recorded clashes or cases of deliberation with the missionary concerning the religion of the slaves, it was the drivers (acting at the same time as religious functionaries, priests or obeahmen) who were involved. They did so as spokesmen of the slave community or of a group of slaves.

The missionaries were aware of the fact that the drivers/priests had a great influence on the success or failure of the Moravian Mission. Consider the following case. On 24 February 1851 a driver expressed his wish to become a member of the Moravian church. When the missionary responded in astonishment to the slave's intentions, the latter assured him that he was serious. This incident led the missionary to write the following in his monthly report to the headquarters: 'If he becomes so faithful to the Saviour as he now is to the Devil, then he can be of great help to the Saviour's affair.'

Why was it in particular the drivers/priests who opposed the Moravian Mission and tried to retain their own religion? To answer this question it should be kept in mind that the religion of the slaves at Vossenburg emerged as a response to oppressive slavery conditions and, psychologically, it offered some protection against exploitation by the planters. However, the Moravian Mission considered the religion of the slaves as pagan and attempted to destroy it. In doing so the mission threatened the emotional support, the feelings of security, and group solidarity rendered to the slaves by their beliefs. No wonder the missionaries clashed with the drivers/priests who were looked upon by the fellow slaves as functionaries responsible for maintaining the slaves' religious system. There is another factor which helps to explain why the missionaries interfered in the conflict between the slaves and the director of Vossenburg. Often they called on the slaves to obey the members of the dominant white group, the director, the overseers, the book-keeper, the artisans, and to carry out their orders. In some cases the missionaries made their appeal because they were fearful that the conflicts between the blacks and the whites would get out of control. But whatever the motives of the missionaries to interfere, by trying to inculcate in the slaves such virtues as patience, submission and obedience, they hoped to contribute to maintaining the social order. The mere fact that they acted this way provoked resentment among the slaves and thus led them to depict the Moravian preachers as an appendage of the dominant white planter class. Thus, the slaves also saw the missionaries as preservers of the interests of the planter class.

How to explain the missionaries' attitudes in this respect? To answer this question we have to go back to the year 1734 when the Moravian Mission negotiated an agreement with the Society of Suriname. This governing board of Suriname represented the interest of the planter class. In this agreement the conditions were spelled out under which the society allowed the Moravian Mission to preach the gospel to the slaves in Suriname. To indicate what conditions were involved, let me quote a paragraph from the letter of agreement dated 7 December 1734:

On 4 December I met again with the directors in the West Indian House, to have talks. They only asked me how I felt about the slaves. I replied that one should try to convert them, but at the same time to admonish them to be loyal and industrious and therefore not to long for freedom. However, to accept it with thanks when it is granted to them. They were satisfied with my answer (Lamur 1984,112).

To fully understand this paragraph it should be kept in mind that cooperation between Christian churches and private Western organizations in the colonies was quite normal, in particular in the eighteenth and nineteenth centuries. In Suriname, for example, the Dutch Reformed Church held a similar view. One of its preachers, J. W. Kals, who lived in Suriname between 1731 and 1756, linked the need to preach the gospel and the importance of the mission to the planter class (Van der Linde 1987, 141-56).

The missionaries admitted that slavery conditions were harsh, but they considered slavery as a system that was imposed by God and that it should only be abolished by Him (on the slant of the Moravian Mission, see Van Raalte 1973, 113-25; Zeefuik 1973, 138-52). This point of view held by the Moravian Mission led to inconsistency, contradiction, and lack of clarity in the behaviour of the missionaries who preached the gospel at Vossenburg and elsewhere in Suriname. One of the few missionaries who openly criticized his colleagues for interfering in conflicts in favour of the dominant white group is N.O. Tank, who lived in Suriname between 1846 and 1848. His view was that the missionaries were used 'to keep the negroes in subordination and under control, as if one had a presentiment that the whip would once prove insufficient' (Tank 1848, 24, 25).

Whether the missionaries who preached the gospel at Vossenburg thought that way is not clear to me. Ironically, they despised the morals of the dominant white group and saw them as godless and lapsed Christians.

Conclusion

In both slave societies, namely Virginia and Vossenburg, the missionaries failed to fully eliminate the African-based religion of the slave populations. In the case of Vossenburg the slave population apparently retained more elements of their religion than did the slaves in Virginia. At Vossenburg the missionaries started their activities much later compared with Virginia, as at Vossenburg the history of Christianity began in 1847, when major changes in the occupational structure of the slave population has already taken place. These changes include the emergence of a group of relatively privileged slaves. It was they who contributed most to the retention of the African-based religion of the slave group. As spokesmen of the slave community, these drivers/priests spoke out openly and defended the slaves' religion. Thus, I found no indication that Christianity rendered the slaves docile. However, neither did it lead them to rebel.

References

Bilby, K. M., ''The Kromanti dance of the Windward Maroons of Jamaica', *Nieuw West Indische Gids* (1981) 55.1.-2:52-101.

Carpenter, W. M., 'Observations on the Cachexia Africana. New Orleans'. *Medical and Surgical Journal* (1844), 1:146-65.

Cartwright, S. A., *Ethnology of the Negro or Prognathous Race* (New Orleans, 1857).

Earnest, J. B., *The Religious Development of the Negro in Virginia* (Charlottesville, Va, 1914).

Genovese, E. D., *Roll, Jordan Roll* (New York, 1976).

Hundley, D. R., *Social Relations in our Southern States* (New York, 1860).

Jackson, L. P., 'Religious development in the Negro in Virginia from 1760 to 1860', *Journal of Negro History* (1931), 16: 168-239.

Jernegan, M. W., 'Slavery and Conversion in the American Colonies', *American Historical Review* (1916), 21:504-27.

Jones, C. C., *Suggestions on the Religious Instruction of the Negroes in the Southern States* (Philadelphia, 1847).

Lamur, H. E., *Dekerstening van de Slaven van de Surinaamse plantage Vossenburg, 1847-1877* (Amsterdam, 1984).

Linde, J. M. van der, *Jan Willem Kals, 1700-1781* (Kampen, 1987).

Ngokwey, Ndolamb, 'Le désenchantement enchanteur ou d'un mouvement religieuse à l'outre', *Les Cahiers du Cedaf* (1978), No. 8

Oldendorp, C. G. A., *Geschichte der Mission der evangelischen Brueder auf den Caraibischen Inslen St. Thomas, S. Croix und S. Jan. Johann Jakob Bossard* (Barby, 1770).

Olwig, K. F., 'Slaves and Masters on Eighteenth-Century St. John', *Ethnos* (1985), 50.3/4:2124-30.

Van Raalte, J., *Secularisatie en zending in Suriname* (Wageningen, 1973).

Rooke, P. T., 'The World they Made: the Politics of Missionary Education to British West Indian Slaves, 1800-1833', *Caribbean Studies* (1979), 18.3/4:47-68.

Simpson, G. E., *Religious cults of the Caribbean: Trinidad, Jamaica and Haiti* (Puerto Rico, 1982).

Tank. N.O., 'Circulaire aan de Heeren Eigenaars en administrateurs van plantaadjes in de kolonie Suriname', in E. van Emden *et al., Onderzoek ten gevolge der circulaire van de heer Otto Tank* (Paramirbo, 1848).

Thoden van Velzen, H. U. and van Wetering, W., 'Voorspoed, angsten en demonen', *Antropologische Verkenningen* (1982), 1.2: 85-118.

Thoden van Velzen, H. U. and van Wetering, W., 'Affluence and the Flowering of Bush Negro Religious Movements', *Bijdragen tot de Taal-, Land en Volkenkunde* (1983), 139: 99-139.

Wilson, J. S., 'The Pecularities and Diseases of Negroes', *American Cotton Planter and Soil of the South New Series*: 4 (1860).

Wooding, J. C., *Winti: een afroamerikaanse godsdienst in Suriname* (Meppel, 1972).

Zeefuik, K.A., Herrnhutter Zending en Haagsche Maatschappij, 1828-1867 (Utrecht, 1973)

53

Slaves' Use of Their 'Free' Time in the Danish Virgin Island in the Later Eighteenth and Early Nineteenth Century

N.A.T. HALL

Europe's expansion into the New World and the African diaspora that, by forced march, accompanied the former's progress had as one of their unforeseen consequences, a process of cultural change. That process has from time to time been described as 'acculturation', but the use of that conceals a value judgement, a presumption of a *terminus ad quem*, and the accommodation by the enslaved majority to the normative values of the white minority. Conceptualized in this way, the interaction of Europe and Africa in the New World locates the African exclusively as object, never as subject; and by a kind of hubristic Eurocentrism, ignores the double process of 'transculturation', in which each cultural legacy is stimulated by and responds to the other.

Bronislaw Malinowski observed in this regard that, 'the two races exist[ed] upon elements taken from Europe as well as from Africa... from both stores of culture. In so doing both races transform[ed] the borrowed elements and incorporate[d] them into a completely new and independent cultural reality.'[1] Recently, Edward Brathwaite, in examining this cultural process, which he describes as creolization, not only concurs implicitly with Malinowski's basic propositions, but also goes further to identify this process as 'the single most important factor in the development of Jamaica',[2] affecting whites no less than slaves. Further, in situations of cross-cultural contact, as Serghei Arutuniev has concluded, 'the dissimilarities, the morphological heterogeneities and the polymorphism existing even within the same population will... serve man as a means to cultural adaptation. The fact is that the plurality of cultures and of cultural variants... constitutes the adaptation mechanism which enables man to develop by selection of the best elements and renewal of his cultural heritage.'[3]

The cultural cross-currents of the Danish Virgin Islands in the period under review flowed from a variety of sources, and involved the intermingling of several cultural influences of the Danish official classes, Dutch and German missionaries, Jewish and French traders and craftsmen, English and Irish plantation owners and Scots-Irish overseers with an African cultural input that was itself by no means monolithic. Following Arutuniev's analysis, the foundations for the adaptation mechanism would have been well established by the middle of the eighteenth century, when the maximal exploitation of the Danish Virgin Islands began under Crown Rule.

What this paper sets out to do, as closely as the sources will permit, is to investigate one region of 'the world the slaves made', to shed some light on the process of cultural change, on the interplay of adaptation and adoption, or in Arutuniev's words, 'the independent creation of a new element (invention), and... the borrowing of an existing element from another culture... the first resembl[ing] mutation, the second, cross breeding'.[4] It would be idle to pretend that what is being attempted is in any way exhaustive. Nevertheless, it is the basic premise of this paper that the heterogeneous aggregate of Danish Virgin Islands slaves — more than 20,000 by the beginning of the nineteenth century — originating in an area that extended from Upper Guinea to Angola, came to comprise a community, achieve coherence, and evolve a discrete slave culture, involving, to precis Handler and Lange, behavioural patterns that were shared by the slaves as a group, and socially learned and transmitted.[5] The slaves' use of leisure, or if the phrase is not a contradiction in terms, 'free' time, will provide, it is hoped, important indicators of transculturation and a deeper understanding of this particular slave society.

Journal of Caribbean History, Vol. 13 (1980), pp. 21–43.

Despite the all-encompassing nature of slavery in these islands, as elsewhere in the Caribbean, it is nevertheless true to say that the slaves' occupational spread and the nature of the work routine allowed many slaves to have discretionary time. Those slaves, for example, who were involved in roles and specialities independent of plantation production and associated activities, viz. — urban jobbers and artisans, wharf and warehouse porters and seamen, were in no way bound by the sunrise to sunset regimen of the plantations. Even on the plantations themselves, custom not to mention self-interest had come to dictate that one day in the week, namely Sunday, was to be allowed to the slaves to rest from their labours. There were moreover individual planters who, in addition to Sunday, were in the habit of giving slaves an extra day for purposes of cultivating their provision grounds in lieu of plantation rations.[6] Long before 1843, therefore, when Saturday was legally created into a 'free' day and Sunday, the feast of the Lutheran Church and royal birthdays, likewise, there was ample opportunity for slaves in the towns and on the plantations to have discretionary leisure.

Both before and after 1843, a significant proportion of the work-free Sunday was spent in religious observance. The slaves of ten responded with fair enthusiasm to the stimulus of missionary proselytizing. Although the state Lutheran church was not itself a vigorous campaigner for slaves' souls, there were other denominations that entered the field with official concurrence and with varying degrees of success. The Moravians who were earliest in the field by 1732 had by far the largest number of slave adherents, followed by the Roman Catholics, the Anglicans, the Dutch Reformed Church and the Methodists in that order. Among slaves who became Moravians it was not uncommon to spend part of a week-day evening receiving instruction from a Moravian brother on the plantation, or walking to the nearest mission station.[7] Attendance at church on Sunday had also assumed significance before the end of the eighteenth century. One observer noted in 1788 as many as 200 slaves from a single estate on their way to church on Sunday. His description of the phenomenon, moreover, suggests strongly that those occasions had also been seized as opportunities for group activity and social interaction, for the display by some of 'chintz and other finery, such that a stranger would not think they were slaves'.[8]

At the beginning of the nineteenth century, church affiliation among slaves had achieved significant levels. The first complete figures indicate, as Table 1 illustrates, that in all three islands church affiliation exceeded 50 per cent of the total slave population. As the century grew older, despite the fact that the slave population was declining in all the islands except St. Thomas, as Table 2 shows, the numbers of church affiliated slaves had grown not only relatively but also absolutely. In the island of St. Croix, those numbers had reached an astonishing 99 per cent.

It is therefore surprising, given this significant response to the religion of the Europeans, that the slaves of the Danish Virgin islands showed no inclination whatever to graft their African religious beliefs and practices onto Christianity, to produce a syncretic religion of their own or to indigenize Christianity. There were no Moses Bakers or George Leisles, nor the emergence of any sect like the 'native' Baptists, as in Jamaica. The explanation probably inheres in the fact, firstly, that the missionary penetration was thorough, particularly on the part of the Moravians. Secondly, that penetration was a function of two variables: the islands' relatively small size, and their topography. None of these islands exceeded 85 sq. miles in area, and it was

Table 1 Christian Slaves in the Danish Virgin Islands, 1805

Island	Baptised slaves	Total slave population	Baptised slaves as % of total
St. John	1,294	2,417	53.5
St. Thomas	2,103	3,344	62.8
St. Croix	14,603	22,076	66.1
Total	18,000	27,837	64.6

Source: Dokumenter Vedkommende Kommissionen for Negerhandelens bedre Indrething og Ophaevelse, samt Efterrethinger om Negerhandelen og Slaveriet i Vestindien, 1783–1806, Rigsarkiv, Copenhagen.

Table 2 Christian Slaves in the Danish Virgin Islands, 1835

Island	Baptised slaves	Total slave population	Baptised slaves as % of total
St. John	1,636	1,943	84.1
St. Thomas	5,064	5,315	85.2
St. Croix	19,692	19,876	99.0
Total	26,392	27,134	87.2

Source: Originale Forestillinger fra Kommission Angaaende Negernes Stilling i Vestindien 1834–43, (5), Governor General von Scholten's Report, 2 January 1839, Bilag 16 B. Rigsarkiv, Copenhagen.

possible for a denomination as indefatigable as the Moravians, or as zealous as the Roman Catholics, to saturate an island like St. Croix, with its relatively easy topography, with Christian teaching. It is worthy of note that the missionaries' efforts were relatively less rewarding in St. John; not, one suspects, because the slaves on that island were any more resistant. Its breathtaking vistas notwithstanding — indeed precisely because of them — St. John is an island of notoriously difficult terrain. The lower percentages of converts from that island indicated in Tables 1 and 2 have a direct correlation with this geophysical fact.

Thirdly, there are grounds for believing that as the slave population became more and more creole or native-born after the slave trade's abolition in 1802, it was distanced with each passing year from aspects of its African roots. Missionary endeavour, it would seem, had pre-empted the population's leadership cadres, lessening the possibility thereby of cultural continuities, at least so far as religion went. Such a co-opted leadership could also help to explain why, between the aborted conspiracy of 1759 in St. Croix[9] and the uprising of 1848 which brought emancipation, there was neither conspiracy nor uprising. As the process of pre-emption and co-option took place, African magico-religious practices *pari-passu* fell into abeyance. Whereas in the eighteenth century, proscriptions against obeah figure very prominently in the slave codes and the proposed drafts for codes,[10] in the nineteenth century neither regulatory ordinances nor the accounts of contemporary travellers have anything to say on the subject of obeah.

It is not to be assumed, however, that the culture contact between European and African religions, was unidirectional. The flow in the other direction was equally noteworthy. The slaves' adoption of Christianity compelled the acquisition and more widespread use by the Europeans of the slaves' *lingua franca*, 'creolsk'. Dutch based, creole originated in St. Thomas from the need for a common medium of communication between the original Dutch colonizers and the multiple language slave community. Creole became a compound of African idiomatic expressions and sentence construction, with a vocabulary drawn from German and Dutch, Danish, French, Spanish and the Portuguese of the Sephardic Jewish community. It was a linguistic situation from which the English in the islands remained aloof, although their children, like other white children, learned creole from their slave nurses.[11] At a time when the 'art of writing a book was so seldom practised in Denmark',[12] two ABC creole books, a creole grammar, a hymnal and a catechism had been produced by 1770; a creole translation of the New Testament in 1779; a translation of the Old Testament, unpublished, in 1781; and in the remaining years before emancipation an impressive run of readers (1798, 1827); hymnals (1799, 1823); children's Bibles (1822); and catechisms (1827). By invention and cross-breeding a new element was created in creole and the *de facto* domination of Malinowski's 'new and independent cultural reality' remained basically unchanged, until the introduction by Governor General von Scholten of a Lancastrian school system for slaves in 1838, with English as the official medium of instruction.[13]

At its introduction von Scholten's school system catered for younger children aged four to eight on Monday to Friday mornings, and older children, up to age fourteen, on Saturday mornings and Sunday afternoons. When the school system was finally formalized in 1846, instruction to the older children was confined to three morning hours of the 'free' day, Saturday, established in 1843.[14] In St. Croix, where eight of the eleven schools were located, all the contemporary accounts bear witness to the children's enthusiasm. According to one account, they were attentive and responsive and showed a quicker grasp than white children in general. Their parents were no less enthusiastic about what they had missed, and obviously made special efforts to send their children to school clean and well dressed.[15]

I have argued elsewhere that this positive response on the part of the slaves to increased leisure and its opportunities, bears a direct causal relationship with the uprising of 1848. The availability of education at state expense, the adjustments to plantation routines which it necessitated, between them heightened the slaves' perception of their own worth. The Law of Free Birth of 28 July 1847 simply reinforced that perception and acted as a catalyst on the impatience which had slowly emerged in the previous decade with the introduction of education and the 'free' day associated with it.[16]

The declaration of that 'free' day in 1843 also introduced Saturday as market day, rescheduling it from Sunday on which it was traditionally held. By the middle of the eighteenth century the markets were well established in the islands' towns. They represent an important contribution on the slaves' part to the internal distribution system, no less important than what Hall and Mintz have identified for Jamaica in the eighteenth century.[17] The markets moreover provided an important opportunity for social interaction among the slaves from different plantations, an opportunity further to supplement their rations by barter or purchase, and to earn cash.

The market in Christianstead was usually open until 8 p.m., but as it got dark by 7 p.m., the slaves lit their stalls with candles. A variety of products was offered for sale: vegetables such as cabbages, green pulses and tomatoes; peas; poultry, pigeons, eggs; yams, potatoes, maize, guinea corn and cassava, known collectively as Indian provisions; pumpkins; melons, oranges, wild plums and berries from the hills on St. Croix's north side; rope tobacco; cassava bread, which many whites, particularly creoles, were especially fond of; fish, firewood and fodder.[18]

Market regulations were first codified as part of the Slave *Reglement* of 1775, and they called for two white market supervisors and the permission of slaves' owners, as a deterrent to the sale of stolen goods.[19] The convention was also established in the course of the eighteenth century that slaves could not offer for sale any of the export staples such as cotton and sugar or rum.[20] The *Reglement* was never enforced and in practice supervision appears to have been lax. Nevertheless there is little evidence to suggest that goods sold in the markets were stolen, or that the markets provided an outlet for illegal trafficking in the way that itinerant vending did. The available market produce was, overwhelmingly, the result of the slaves' creative initiative in the use of their 'free' time, particularly in the cultivation of their provision grounds. The literary evidence in the eighteenth century certainly identifies the same kind of goods for sale in the market as were grown on the provision grounds.[21] This creative initiative was particularly in evidence in identifying and satisfying the market demands for grass and firewood. Hans West who lived in St. Croix in the 1780s reckoned that the sale of these two items in Christianstead and Frederickstead amounted to the not inconsiderable sum of 61,488 *Rigsdaler* per annum,[22] and Thurlow Weed who wrote in the 1840s supplies evidence for the continuing vigour of this traffic.[23] What the evidence also helps to identify was that there was a rationalization of this activity, and a sex-specific distribution of the work involved at least by the 1840s. Like itinerant huckstering, market vending was largely a female monopoly; work on the provision grounds was largely the

province of the males.[24] For West Indian purposes, the slaves had adopted the prevalent practice of the Gold Coast, from which many of them had originated.

The cultivation of provision grounds and the Sunday, subsequently Saturday, market apart, a major portion of slaves' discretionay time was spent in dancing. As early as the first codified slave laws of 1733, there were indications that 'fetes, balls, dances and divertissements with Negro instruments' were sufficiently established to warrant the imposition of conditions under which they could be held.[25] In the 1740s Governor Moth's *Articuler for Negerne* stipulated that such revelries should end at sundown or at 8 p.m. on moonlight nights.[26] In St. Thomas in the 1760s a proclamation of Governor de Gunthelberg extended the time limit to 10 p.m.; thereafter police permission was required but in no circumstances was the use of Goombay drums permitted.[27]

Understandably, dancing or the opportunity and energy to engage in it, was a greater likelihood for urban slaves. In St. Croix in the 1770s Governor General Clausen permitted dances in town but not beyond the 8 p.m. curfew. The same proclamation allowed free people of colour to hold dances until 10 p.m. but both slaves and whites were prohibited, on pain of severe punishment in the one case, and fines and imprisonment in the other, from either attending or participating.[28] The prohibition would suggest that in the towns at least the inflexible lines of slavery were being both bent and breached by the compelling attractions such as that contained in Lindemann's draft slave code for 1783.[29] There are, therefore, strong presumptive grounds for believing that some slaves and some whites by deliberate choice shared, in the eighteenth century at least, one common social activity, albeit illegally and under the cover of darkness.

Such violence to the society's implicit premises was not the only remarkable feature of the slaves' preoccupation with the dance. In 1791 Hans West reported that dances were held several times per week, with an entrance fee as much as three *Rigsdaler* per couple. It was this frequency he concluded, that was a prime consideration in the limitation of the activity.[30] Carl Holten, brother of Christian, the commandant of St. Thomas in 1815, was another contemporary observer who shed some light on the subject of slave dances. With a good eye for detail, Holten noted that formal styles of address were often in use at these occasions: Mister, Mrs., Councillor, Captain, etc. Holten put this down to mere mimicry. But that hardly exhausts the possibilities. It might just as probably have been ridicule, and there is the third alternative that the slaves could have been investing the occasion with special significance by the adaptation of European styles of address and the usages in contemporary 'society'. At any rate the adaptations were subject to the slaves' own sobering sense of the appropriate, an eye for the absurd, and a capacity to poke fun at each other. The point is well borne out by one of Holten's numerous anecdotes:

Jeg mindes iblandt andet en Haarskjaerer, som anskaffede sig et Par Briller til at valse med, fordi han havde seet Waltersdorffs Secretair Captain Manthey at gjore dette, og at han, da de andre Couleurte dog fandte dette vel latterligt, svarede den ganske muggent: 'I ere nogle Tosser, some vide at dette er Mode ved Hoffet'.[31]

Non-dancing parties, at which tea and coffee were served, was another favourite diversion of slaves. The evidence, however, points to this being a particularly urban activity. They had become popular enough by the 1770s to attract the notice of officialdom, and the Burgher Council of St. Croix gave it their attention in 1778, declaring that those entertainments had got completely out of hand. Some slave owners not only turned a blind eye to these occurrences, but also used permission to attend them as a means of granting favours to some slaves. An entrance fee was charged, as with the dances on which West reported. The payments involved were more than likely one use to which the proceeds of marketeering or own-account jobbing were put. Like the dances too, these tea and coffee parties were opportunities for social intercourse among legally segregated strata of the society. The parties were attended by free people of colour, whose 'connections and too great familiarity' with slaves were, in the Burgher Council's opinion, a cause for concern. They thought these revelries should be either limited or forbidden altogether.[32]

Above all, the parties gave the slaves a chance to bring out their finery, finery of the sort that was the subject of a detailed sumptuary ordinance in 1786. The ordinance mentions accessories of gold and silver and precious stones, silk, lace and other expensive fabrics as items all prohibited to field and house slaves alike, although the latter were allowed a silver clasp of simple design.[33] The implication was that the silks and jewellery were, if not cast offs, stolen. The Danish West Indian, like the British West Indian, slave law tended to view the slave as above all a potential criminal. However,

Governor General Schimmelmann, who drew up the ordinance, did not calculate for the slaves' insistence on carving out of the wilderness of servitude the oasis of his own humanity by individual idiosyncracies of dress or dressing up when he had unencumbered time. How effective the 1786 ordinance was is difficult to judge, but in 1814 the police chief of St. Croix, Gjellerup, issued a notice referring to 'wearing apparel, jewellery and beads too numerous to specify found at a slave ball', and inviting their 'owners' to claim them.[34] Despite Schimmelmann, the slaves had clearly not ceased to wear their best to balls, whether that best was the end product of their own sweat or borrowed surreptitiously from their masters' or mistresses' wardrobes, as the police chief broadly implied.

By convention and latterly by royal instructions of 1 May 1840, slaves were allowed all the recognized feast days and high holy days of the state Lutheran church, as well as the monarch's birthday. No special significance appears to have been attached to these by the slave population, although it can be assumed that where appropriate they would have gone to church. Of the public holidays, the two days of Christmas and the New Year stand in a category by themselves. According to Thurlow Weed who visited in 1844-45, in the week that intervened 'they contrive...to do very little work....And on these occasions the slaves' cup of enjoyment fills to the brim.'[35] These days produced their own kinds of diversion and dynamics. The European practice of throwing firecrackers and letting off fireworks was a particularly pervasive practice among slaves in this holiday period; indeed, before — during the 'several weeks preceding' in which they were 'busied with preparations for their festivities' — and after.[36] Proclamations over several decades, particularly in St. Thomas, had failed to arrest the practice.[37]

A colonial law officer commenting in 1783 blamed it on the indolence of the police. But in part the explanation also lay in the fact that 'the throwing of fire-crackers was reckoned to be one of those innocent pleasures wherewith one distinguished special from ordinary days, and even whites themselves participated'.[38] Annual ordinances, issued by the police prefects just before Christmas, continued into the nineteenth century.[39] Their very issuance, however, are grounds for believing that this was one 'innocent pleasure' in which whites and slaves found common enjoyment.

Itinerant minstrelsy at Christmas and New

Year was well enough established by 1759 for Governor General von Prøck to issue a proclamation against it. It involved the use of violins, 'other instruments' which von Prøck did not specify, and begging for money as minstrels everywhere did and still do. It was also the practice among some slave owners to have these slaves playing for them, and it can also be reasonably inferred from the proclamation that they were sent to, or were hired by, other owners to perform.[40] Lindemann's draft slave laws of 1783 and van der Østen's of 1785 repeat the prohibitory paragraph of 1759, and indicate that the practice could not be legislated away.[41] It seems hardly likely that these slave musicians were performing African music on the violin for an audience of Europeans. It can safely be assumed therefore, that the music was, if not European, at the very least a creolized variant of it.

In connection with the New Year festivities, Johann Nissen who lived in St. Thomas for 46 years from 1792, noted in 1832:

It is the custom here, especially among the coloured persons to celebrate old year's night with music, dancing, singing and in short, making a great noise. They commenced this uproar as early as 4 o'clock in the afternoon, passing in great crowds through all the streets, crying out in their creole tongue, 'Old Year's night'.[42]

These street processions to which Nissen calls attention were probably not new in 1832. Some 80 years before, von Prøck in condemning the minstrels with their violins, makes mention of '*de andre Negere som ombløber*': the other negroes who go around.[43] This is hardly conclusive, although tantalizingly suggestive.

Nissen further remarked:

At 9 o'clock they pass through all the streets with music and continue to do so through the whole night. Some of them have a certain place, where they have put up a tent of coconut leaves, and dance there during the night. Many of them again dance in their own rooms, which are certainly very small, and are so full that the dancers have scarcely room to move.[44]

In St. Thomas then, the dance took over at the New Year's festivities, and the Goombay did duty here as with other dances. Nissen did not think a great deal of the slaves' dancing. Their free-form improvisatory style contrasted sharply in his mind with the then prescribed European measures of his day. Dancing was something which 'well-educated' people learnt and performed. On the other hand, 'the dances of the negroes are of one sort; turning and moving about — they have no regular dances'.[45]

In St. Croix, nominally more Christian by far, the situation described by Weed at the beginning of 1845 is not very different. Indeed, he describes dancing as the slaves' 'only festive resource' and notes that for the New Year frolic, there was 'turban, calico, ribbon, gewgaw and trinket' in abundance. Estate slaves elected Kings and Queens, Princes and Princesses, Maids of Honour and Pages; a somewhat more formalized structure than anything reported for St. Thomas. The dance was opened with 'much gravity' by the King and Queen, to the accompaniment of ballads led by a 'Prima Donna' supported by a chorus, and the ubiquitous Goombay 'discours[ing] most eloquent music'. As the dance progressed, the enthusiasm rose, as did the Prima Donna's voice, the chorus swelled, the drummer was carried away and the Queen eventually swooned, to be revived by her attendants sprinkling bay rum and plying their fans. But once recovered she joined the dance with renewed energy, having called upon the Princess to replace her as leader; she in her turn, and the King and Princess in theirs, calling on those of 'inferior rank' when exhausted. The chorus accompaniment did not actually join in the dance; indeed they constituted, according to Weed, the greater proportion of those present. 'Towards the close of the festivities, however, all join in the dance, all, at the same time, singing most vociferously.'[46]

Weed enables us to see not only the all-consuming nature of the event for the slave population. His information enables us equally to see the event's all-encompassing character for the entire population:

The first privilege (or duty as they esteem it) of the slaves on Christmas day New Year's day, is to pay their respects, in a body, to their master, before whom they dance for an hour or more, paying tribute, in their songs to his liberality, generosity &c., after which they are regaled with cakes, cordial &c., and generally receive presents from their mistress.[47]

While plantation whites were touched in this way, the free coloureds confined to the towns residentially, were in their turn touched by the celebrations of the urban slave population. Both groups, we are told, 'form their parties, elect their Kings, Queens &c., and dance in like manner'.[48]

The renditions of the Prima Donna and chorus were not mere accompaniments to the dance. They were sometimes complimentary — to greet, impromptu, some passer-by; or congratulatory — to the King, Queen Victoria or the Americans. In this regard the slaves were displaying in song a good grasp of current events. But nowhere was this grasp put to better use than in the songs of incisive social comment, indeed of social protest;

All we girls must keep heads together; King Christian have sent to free us all; Governor SHOLTON had a vote for us; King Christian have sent to grant us all; we have signed for liberty; our Crown Prince had a vote in it; our Gracious Queen had the highest vote; King Christian have sent to say he will crown us all.
Oh yes! oh, yes! hurra! hurra!
All we girls must keep head together.[49]

Some 60 years before Schmidt had warned that slaves sang songs for the courage to rebel; that if Europeans paid more attention to them than they did the possibilities of uprising would be considerably lessened.[50] Weed, an outsider visiting from North America, may very well have recorded without realising it, the first audible rumble of the eruption which took place three years later.

There are no explicit references in the literature to end of year mummery of the John Canoe type, which Brathwaite has argued was an African retention in Jamaica.[51] However, the Jamaican procession of 'Set Girls' had an inexact equivalent in the organised processions from some estates that went into town on New Year's morning. The rivalries between the women of different estates was certainly as intense as that between the 'Set Girls'. They abused each other roundly for the poverty of parsimoniousness of their masters, cast slurs on the colour of mistresses, and did not cavil to use that most approbrious of epithets, 'Guinea Bird'.[52]

At least one slave diversion could be classified under the heading of the martial arts. Particularly among plantation or country slaves who had long distances to travel, it was not unusual for them to walk with a stick for support. Indeed, the surviving newspapers of the eighteenth century bear this out. On the longest journey the slave could contemplate, namely when he ran away, the advertisements almost invariably represented him with a stick. The sticks were obviously large enough to be considered cudgels, and could be gnarled, pointed, metal-tipped or banded with metal. The slave's staff had the potential for becoming a murderous weapon, and was so regarded by white authority, which proceeded to ban it.[53] But the ban of the Bangelar, as it was known, was never very successful. It was difficult to suppress like Goombay drumming, and perhaps for the same reason: probable ritual

significance, definite entertainment value and a high degree of skill required, in the case of the Bangelar, for its effective use. At the same time, white encouragement is also to be accounted a causal factor in its survival. According to Clausen, whites not only found pleasure in the spectacle of these stick-fighting contests but attended to egg on the contestants.[54] Stick-fighting, like cock-fighting which survived into the nineteenth century and was favoured among whites no less than slaves,[55] was a blood sport; a brutal business for a brutal time. Whites and slaves could both find pleasure in the structured violence the contest involved, for co-existing in a society based upon an identical premise, neither could escape its logic.

One other pastime which served a second function as defence in situations of conflict, was the use of stones with and without slingshots. In 1873, a colonial law officer deemed stone-throwing a habit dangerous enough to merit 20 lashes. The habit, he said, was acquired in childhood: the slave child's first amusement as soon as it began to creep being stone throwing. It persisted into adult life, and stones were used not only for chasing dogs, pigs, goats and other animals but were also employed against each other in moments of irritation or during disputes:

Sielden seer man en Neger paa Gaden uden en Steen i Haanden. Det gaar endog saavidt, at man ei kan vaere sikker i huusene og paa Gallerierne for saadan letsindig Steenkasten hen i Veiret. Man hitter allerede paa at bruge Slynger. En saadan Øvelser, naar de blev almindelig, vist blive en farlig Tidsfordriv og Fornøielse.[56]

These remarks which apply to St. Croix, could equally have applied to St. Thomas. That island's commandant in the 1780s, de Maleville, reported with concern the growing proportions that stone-throwing had assumed. In the years 1774, 1775, 1776, for several nights at a particular time of the year which de Maleville did not specify, stones rained down upon the houses and galleries of Charlotte Amalie from the sea and from the hill above. Those stones were large enough to kill and made it unsafe to sit outside after dark.[57] If one rules out a poltergeist theory, the only likely explanations with which one is left, are gestures of defiance towards whites — a not uncommon phenomenon in the urban setting of Charlotte Amalie[58] — or a stone 'war' between individual slaves or groups of slaves under the cover of darkness.

If the facility with stones for diversion and

defence was African in origin, there is evidence of cultural cross-breeding in the West Indies. Lindemann suggested in his draft slave code that slaves should not be allowed to play·'Kag'.[59] But that game was almost certainly metropolitan Danish, for it is described in Verner Dahlerup's *Ordbog over det Danske Sprog* (Dictionary of the Danish Language) not as a game of African origin, but simply as: 'Name of a children's game, the object of which is to hit down with a stonethrow, the uppermost stone in a pyramid-formed stone-heap; or to knock over a ninepin or a forked stick'. Borrowing from a European children's game, the slaves had made it theirs, transformed it into an adult's game and used it as target practice to sharpen their stone-throwing skills.

Gaming was an important social activity among whites in Virgin Island slave society. Card games such as *L'Hombre*, whist and boston with 300 *piastre* stakes were an important part of official entertaining, at least under Governor General von Scholten; among the *haute monde* in the elegant public salons of Charlotte Amalie in the 1840s or among the less respectable and in secret in St. Croix.[60] Slaves no less than their masters were given to games of chance, especially to cards and dice. However, none of the official proclamations · from Gardelin's time in the 1730s takes any notice of the practice before the 1770s. Since it is unlikely that slaves could have played without attracting attention to themselves, one possible conclusion is that gambling as 'leisure' time activity became popular after mid-century, and is probably one index of the creolization process. Calusen, in prohibiting all forms of gambling among slaves in 1774, claimed that 'daily experience had taught that slaves had an insatiable lust for gambling' which had gone completely out of control. It was taking place, it would appear, not only in houses and on galleries, but also on the streets.[61] This suggested a largely urban manifestation. Lindemann's draft code of 1783 on the other hand is not specific as to place in recommending prohibition of 'dice, cards . . . or any such games',[62] but Van der Østen's does speak of gambling in the towns.[63] However, the St. Croix Burgher Council did indicate in 1787 that there was gambling on the plantation as well; during the religious feast days and fast days, on Sundays and the two days of Christmas and the New Year.[64] De Maleville, writing in the same year from St. Thomas, also expressed concern about the extent of card playing and all forms of gambling among the slave population, and the participation of free coloureds in these games of chance.[65]

Gambling was associated in the minds of some whites with other 'vices' such as rum drinking, which officialdom did its best to discourage if it could not stop.[66] Some publicans apparently allowed slaves to sit in their rum shops when they were open on weekdays, Sundays and holidays. Some officials thought slaves should only be sold from the back yards of the shops and not permitted to loiter; others that such loitering and the gambling to which it gave rise was allowed and encouraged by the publicans for pecuniary advantage or for trafficking in stolen goods.[67] Rum, traditionally, was never sold on the plantations, so that a slave 'on his own time' wanting to acquire his own liquor without stealing or to buy himself a drink had to wait until there was an opportunity to be in town and have cash: an opportunity which the market provided. The market's attraction as an opportunity for release from the boredom and brutality of plantation life, was enormously enhanced, therefore, by the prospect of a few drams of· 'kill-devil'.

A similar kind of release appears to have been found in horseback riding. The imperatives of the society, however, with its high premiums on discipline and deference, made such use of slaves' time in an essentially individualistic activity, problematic in the extreme — particularly if slaves were given to hard riding. For both whites and slaves, it was as if the physical act of mounting a horse had a corresponding metaphysical significance, lessening the status gap between both groups. Lindemann in drafting his slave code in 1783, emphasised white concern in this regard. Any mounted slave should either dismount or ride slowly out of the way for approaching whites, but in no circumstances was he to gallop past, nor ride side by side with, whites.[68] This was in the spirit of Gardelin's earlier code of 1733, which had insisted on similar shows of public submissiveness, even when the situations were reversed and the slave on foot.[69] In Van der Østen's draft code of 1785, we again meet with this continuing concern with the slaves on horseback. In his view, slaves' use of horses without permission was to be regarded as theft and punished accordingly.[70]

The abandon with which slaves apparently rode, as they savoured these brief moments of glory, was the occasion of adverse white comment from time to time, for as a group whites were as much concerned about 'public order' as they were about deference. Indeed, in their minds the two were closely related, if not synonymous. Governor General von Prøck noted in 1756 that hard riding in the streets of Christianstead had become a daily and dangerous practice on the part of slaves, and proceeded to prohibit it.[71] Lindemann too would have prohibited slaves riding in streets of towns or their immediate environs, unless there were evidence of some urgent errand. He remarked further that more often than not, the offenders were small boys,[72] who obviously rode with no less enthusiasm than their elders.

If there were constraints on this method of release in the towns and their vicinity, the country roads offered better opportunity. Estate slaves who were not professional jockeys like John Jones who ran away in 1815,[75] nevertheless continued to organize their own equestrian diversion. The following public notice in 1815 signed by the Chief of Police, Mouritzen, in St. Croix, suggests a well established practice, involving as dancing and stick-fighting did, whites no less than slaves, and conducted in such a way as to avoid official attention:

It has been reported to this office that it has been customary even among slaves to run Horse Races on the high-roads in the Country: This being contrary to the Laws and good order, each and every one is admonished to desist from such bad practice; and, it is requested, that any one who might know of such races give information to this office, where the offended will be treated as the Law directs.[74]

Horse racing as a sport did not have any currency before the first two decades of the nineteenth century. This was the period, at any rate, during which it was considered important enough to be advertised in the public prints.[75] The slaves had not only co-opted the sport among themselves for pleasure and, where possible, profit; they had also played a clear part in their role as jockeys in establishing the sport for whites.

In the last hundred years or so of slavery in the Danish Virgin Islands, the slaves by the use of the discretionary time, legally and illegally at their disposal, had created certain modes of being and behaviour that were distinctly theirs. The use of 'free' time was far more conducive to this purpose, having regard to the demanding nature of the routines and discipline associated with plantation production. By emancipation they had created a culture, neither wholly African nor yet European, retaining, adapting, borrowing and adopting. The transition from disaggregation to community was only possible by a process of cultural change. As Mintz and Price have observed, 'in order for slave communities to take shape, normative patterns

of behaviour had to be established, and these patterns could be created only on the basis of particular forms of social interaction'.[76]

The creation was taking place not in a vacuum but in a dynamic context: of interaction among themselves and contact, sometimes intimate, with the other dominant cultural elements which were European. Masters as well as slaves were caught up in the process of cultural interchange. They enjoyed, or learnt to enjoy, foods like cassava bread, and some at any rate, slaves' sports like stick-fighting. Donors of their religions, they became recipients of the slaves' language, and in several respects provide empirical justification for the conclusion that 'the role of the powerless in affecting, and even controlling important parts of the lives of the masters was also typical of slave colonies'.[77]

Notes

1. B. Malinowski, 'Methods of Study of Culture Contract in Africa', *Institute of African Languages and Cultures*, Memorandum XV (1938), p. xvii.
2. Edward Brathwaite, *The Development of Creole Society in Jamaica 1770–1820* (Oxford, 1971), p. 296.
3. S. Arutuniev, 'Cultural Paradigms: The Process of Change Through Cultural Borrowings', *Cultures*, Vol. 5, No. 1 (1978):p. 95.
4. *Ibid.*, p. 95.
5. J. S. Handler and F. W. Lange, *Plantation Slavery in Barbados. An Archaeological and Historical Investigation*, (Cambridge, Mass, 1978), p. 289 n.1.
6. Rigsarkiv, Copenhagen (cited hereafter as R/A), *Originale Forestillinger fra en Commission angaaende Negernes Stilling i Vestindien m.m. og dertil hørende Kongelige Resolutioner 1834–1843*, von Scholten to Christian VIII, 15 January 1841, Encl. 3, d/d 29 October 1840; Encl. 5, d/d 26 May 1840. For an earlier instance see I. Schmidt, 'Blandede Anmaearkninger', *Samleren*, Vol. 2, No. 42, (1788): p. 244.
7. Schmidt, *op. cit.*, p. 239. See also R/A, *Kommissions Forslag og Anmaerkning ang. negerhandelen med genparter af anordninger og publikationer* (1785), Bind 2. Commandant de Malevilles Bataenkninger, 19 October 1787, f. 92.
8. Schmidt, *op. cit.*, p. 245
9. R/A, *Udkast og Betaenkning ang, negerloven m. bilag*, No. 4, Philip Gardelin's Placat (cited hereafter as Gardelin), 5 September 1733, para. 13 Cf. *ibid.*, No. 24, Forslag til en Neger Lov for de Kongelife Danske Vestindicke Eylande, 1783 (cited hereafter as Lindemann), Pt 1, para. 10. Cf. also *Kommissions Forslag og Anmaerkning* .... Bind 1, Negerlov for de Danske Vestindiske Eylande (cited hereafter as *Van der østen*), Pt 3, para. 18.
10. Monica Schuler, 'Akan Slave Rebellions in the British Caribbean', *Savacou*, Vol. 1., No. 1 (June 1970): pp. 21–23.
11. Jens Larsen, *Virgin Islands Story* (Philadelphia, 1950), Chaps. 10 and 11 give an extremely useful survey of these developments.
12. H. B. Dahlerup, *Mit Livs Begivenheder* (Copenhagen, 1909), Vol. 2, p. 277.

M

13. This subject is dealt with by N. A. T. Hall, 'Establishing a Public Elementary School System for Slaves in the Danish Virgin Islands 1732-1846', *Caribbean Journal of Education* (January 1979).

14. *Ibid.*

15. Dahlerup, *Mit Livs*, Vol. 2, pp. 296-97. See also Dahlerup, 'Skizzer fra et kort Besog paa vore vestindiske Øer i Sommeren 1841', *Nyt Archiv for Søvaesnet, 1* (1842): p. 28.

16. N. A. T. Hall, 'Establishing a Public Elementary School System'.

17. Sidney Mintz and D. G. Hall, 'The origins of the Jamaican internal marketing system'. In Mintz S. (ed.), *Papers in Caribbean Anthropology*, (New Haven, 1960).

18. On the market see H. West, *Bidrag til Beskrivelse over Eylandet St. Croix i America in Vestindien* (Copenhagen, 1793), pp. 75-76; West, *Beretning om det dansk Eilande St. Croix i Vestindien* (Copenhagen, 1791), pp. 72-74; Schmidt, *op. cit.*, pp. 242-44; J. P. Nissen, *Reminiscences of a 46 years' residence in the Island of St. Thomas in the West Indies* (Nazareth, Pa, 1838), p. 34 and Thurlow Weed, *Letters from West Indies* (Albany, 1866), pp. 353-55.

19. R/A, *Udkast og Betaenkning*, No. 2, paras 14 and 15.

20. R/A, *Udkast og Betaenkning*, No. 27, Governor Clausen's Placat, 11 August 1767, paras 1-5.

21. West, *Beretning*, p. 72. Cf. Schmidt, *op. cit.*, pp. 241-43.

22. West, *Bidrag*, pp. 75-76.

23. Weed, *op. cit.*, p. 354.

24. Weeds, *op. cit.*, p. 353.

25. Gardelin, para. 16.

26. R/A, *Udkast og Betaenkning*, No. 1, 11 December 1941, para. 6. Cf. *ibid.*, No. 27, #18, Governor von Prøck's Placat, 17 May 1756, para. 7.

27. *Ibid.*, No. 27 #29, 9 February 1765, para. 9.

28. *Ibid.*, No. 27, #38, 5 October 1774, para. 6.

29. Lindemann, Pt 3, paras 33-36.

30. West, *Beretning*, p. 77. Although he does not specifically say so, it is likely that his remarks were based on his own observations of, or reports on, the situation in Christiansted, not on the plantations.

31. Carl Holtens Dagbog. In Clausen, J., & Rist, F. P. (Eds), *Memoirer og Breve*, ix (1909): 53. I recall among the other things a barber who got himself a pair of spectacles to waltz in, because he had seen Walterstoff's secretary Capt. Manthey doing so and when the other coloureds found this entirely ridiculous, replied surlily: 'You are a bunch of fools if you don't know that is the style at court.'

32. R/A, *Udkast og Betaenkning*, no. 27, #43, 2 December 1778, para. 5.

33. R/A, *Kommissions Forslag og Anmaerkning* . . . . Bind 1, Schimmelmann's Placat, 26 May 1786, paras 1 and 2.

34. *St. Croix Gazette*, 27 July 1814.

35. Weed, *op. cit.*, p. 346.

36. *Ibid.* See also R/A, *Udkast og Betaenkning*, No. 33, Clausen's Placat, 21 October 1770.

37. For representative samples of proclamations see R/A, *Udkast og Betaenkning*, No. 1, 30 December 1758, *ibid*, No. 27, 12 December 1761; *ibid*, No. 33, 21 October 1170; *ibid;* No. 41, 21 October 1777.

38. Lindemann, Pt. 1, para. 93. My emphasis.

39. See for example *St. Croix Gazette*, 25 December. 1813.

40. R/A, *Udkast og Betaenkning*, No. 27, #22, 23 December 1758, Para. 3.

41. Lindemann, Pt 1, para. 98, Van der Østen, Pt 3, para. 104.

42. Nissen, *Reminiscences*, p. 164.

43. R/A, *Udkast og Betaenkning*, No. 27, #22, 23 December 1759, para. 3.

44. Nissen, *Reminiscences*, p. 164.

45. *Ibid.*, pp. 164-65. My emphasis.

46. Weed, *op. cit.*, pp. 346-47.

47. *Ibid.*, p. 347.

48. *Ibid.*

49. *Ibid.*, p. 348.

50. Schmidt, *op. cit.*, pp. 232-33.

51. Brathwaite, *The Development of Creole Society*, p. 230.

52. Weed, *op. cit.*, pp. 349-350. On 'Set Girls', see Brathwaite, *The Development of Creole Society*, p. 231.

53. R/A, *Udkast og Betaenkning*, No. 27, #38, Governor General Clausen's Proclamation, 5 Oct. 1774, paras 1 and 5. Cf. *Lindemann*, Pt 1, para. 87; Van der Østen, Pt 3, para. 74.

54. R/A, *Udkast og Betaenkning*, No. 27, #38, 5 October 1774, para. 5.

55. Dahlerup, *Mit Livs*, p. 48. See also *Dansk Vestindisk Regerings Avis*, 25 August 1836.

56. Lindemann, Pt. 1, para. 94. One does not often see a Negro on the street without a stone in his hand. It has gone so far that one can no longer be secure in one's house or gallery from such careless stone-throwing Already they have hit upon using sling shots. If such a practice became common, it would be a dangerous pastime.

57. R/A, *Kommissions Forslag og Anmaerkning* . . . Bind 2, Commandant de Maleville's Bataenkninger, 19 October 1787.

58. See for example R/A, *Udkast og Betaenkning*, No. 27, #29, Commandant de Gunthelberg's Proclamation, 9 February 1765.

59. Lindemann, Pt 1, para. 76.

60. Dahlerup, *Mit Livs*, pp. 47-48, 274.

61. R/A, *Udkast og Betaenkning*, No. 27, #38, 5 October 1774, para. 3.

62. Lindemann, Pt 1, para. 77.

63. Van der Østen, Pt 3, para. 73.

64. R/A, *Kommissions Forslag og Anmaerkning* . . . . Bind 2, 1 August 1787, f. 68.

65. *Ibid.*, de Maleville's Betaenkninger, 19 October 1787, f. 91.

66. Lindemann, Pt 1, para. 84.

67. Van der Østen, Pt 3, para. 98. Cf. R/A, *Kommissions Forslag og Anmaerkning*, Bind 2, 1 August 1787, f. 76, and *ibid.*, Etatz Raad Colbiornsens Anmaerkninger, 24 September 1788.

68. Lindemann, Pt 1, para. 2.

69. Gardelin, para. 11.

70. Van der Østen, Pt 3, para. 59.

71. R/A, *Udkast og Betaenkning*, No. 27, #18, 17 May 1756, paras, 8, 22. Cf. *ibid.*, #22, 23 December 1759, para. 12 and *St. Croix Gazette*, 7 July 1812, Police Chief Gjellerup's Ordinance.

72. Lindemann, Pt 1, para. 97.

73. *St. Croix Gazette*, 14 January 1815. Cf. *St. Croix Gazette*, 5 October 1814 wich announces the running away of 'mulatto Michael', another slave jockey.

74. *Dansk Vestindisk Regerings Avis*, 13.May 1815.

75. See for example *St. Croix Gazette*, 9 February 1807; 5 October 1814.

76. Mintz, S. W. and Price Richard, *An Anthropological Approach to the Afro-American Past: A Caribbean Perspective* (Philadelphia, 1976), p. 10.

77. *Ibid.*, p. 16.

54

An Economic Life of Their Own: Slaves as Commodity Producers and Distributors in Barbados

HILARY McD. BECKLES

Studies of patterns of property ownership and resource use in Caribbean slave societies have generally focused on the economic conditions within the free, mostly white, communities. Particular attention has been given, for example, to the manner in which economic relations developed between the dominant mercantile and planting communities. Examinations of the economic experiences of free people of colour have reinforced opinions held about the tendencies of the white elite to monopolize the market. The slaves' independent economic behaviour, especially for the English colonies, has received less attention. The neglect of this subject is surprising since slave hucksters had great influence over the informal commercial sector of most island economies. Comprehending the economic role of slave marketing practices will provide both a more accurate understanding of slave life and a firmer basis for interpreting the nature of owner-slave relations in the economic sphere of plantation culture.

Much evidence exists to illustrate that slaves, like free persons, sought to increase their share of colonial wealth by participating in the market economy as commodity producers and distributors, with and without their owners' permission. Although they were undoubtedly the primary victims of colonial economies, in which they were defined and used as property, generations of slaves managed, nonetheless, to identify and pursue their own material interests.[1] By combining their work as fieldhands, artisans, domestics, or whatever with their own productive and commercial activities, slaves made economic decisions as 'free' persons. At least such was the case on the island of Barbados.

In nearly all instances, property owning whites, who dominated colonial governments in the Caribbean, objected to market competition from slaves and enacted legislation that gradually proscribed their economic activities.[2] Since slave owners considered the slaves' subordination critical to systems of control, they sought to assert their dominance in all economic relations, no matter how petty. On Barbados, slaves tenaciously resisted such legislative assaults upon this aspect of their independent economic activities and made from the outset a determined effort to maintain their market participation. At times, Barbadian slave owners adopted concessionary policies, prompted generally by their desire to secure the wider goals of social stability and high levels of labour productivity. Slaves, in turn converted the most limited concessions into customary rights and defended them adamantly.

Huckstering, the distributive dimension of small-scale productive domestic activity, was an important part of the socio-economic culture of African women. It was certainly as much part of their gender culture as other more well-known aspects of social life, such as religion and the arts. Its continued attractiveness to women in the Caribbean, however, had much to do with the social and material conditions of their enslavement. Huckstering afforded women the opportunity to improve the quantity and quality of their nutrition in environments where malnutrition was the norm.[3] It allowed them to possess and later own property, which in itself represented an important symbolic offensive mission against the established order. It enabled them to make profitable use of their leisure time. And it afforded them the chance to travel and normalize their social lives as much as possible under highly restrictive circumstances.

The relations between slaves' independent production and huckstering provides the context in which the development of the internal marketing systems can be understood. In what accounts to a typology of food production, Sidney Mintz and Douglas Hall[4] have shown how the autonomous economic life of slaves in Barbados, and other smaller sugar monoculture plantation colonies, differed from that of their Jamaican counterparts. Within this analysis, they divided plantation systems into two basic categories: first, those in which slaves were fed by their owners, such as Barbados; and, second, those in which slaves were largely responsible for producing their own subsistence, such as Jamaica.

In Barbados especially, planters allotted 'land to food cultivation only by impinging on areas which, generally, could be more profitably planted in cane'. The planters' policy was to 'restrict the land at the disposal of the slaves to small house plots', import food for the slaves, and include 'some food production in the general estate program'.[5] In Jamaica, owners allotted their slaves large tracts of land unsuited to cane production in the foothills of the mountain ranges and there encouraged slaves to produce their own food. These provision grounds or polinks represented the primary form of food cultivation, and slaves were given managerial authority in this activity. In addition to these provision grounds, which were generally located miles from their homes, Jamaican slaves also cultivated little 'house spots'.

The provision grounds on which Jamaican female slaves became experienced proto-peasants constituted the basis of their entry into, and subsequent domination of, the internal marketing system. White society came to depend heavily upon the slaves' produce. There was, as a result, no persistent legislative attempt to arrest and eradicate the slaves commercial activities and, by the mid-eighteenth century, the slaves'

domination of the provisions market was institutionalized.[6]

The experience of slaves in Barbados was somewhat different in scale and character than that of those in Jamaica. Barbadian slaves had no provision grounds. They were fed from the masters' stocks, which were both imported and locally produced. Imported salted meat and plantation grown grain were allocated to slaves by their overseers, sometimes on Friday night, but mostly on Sunday morning. Slaves possessed only little house spots, generally no more than 25 yards square, on which to root their independent production and marketing activity. They could not therefore be defined as anything more than 'petty proto-peasants', and yet the vibrancy of their huckstering activities was no less developed than that in Jamaica where slaves cultivated acres of land.

Several visitors to Barbados paid attention to the relationship between slaves' receipt of food allowances and their huckstering. Dr George Pinckard who toured the island during the mid-1790s, was especially perceptive. He noted that slaves received their subsistence on a weekly basis, 'mostly guinea corn, with a small bit of salt meat or salt fish', which served for 'breakfast, dinner and supper'. This diet, he added, was 'for the most part the same throughout the year', though 'rice, maize, yams, eddoes, and sweet potatoes form an occasional change'. But the slaves, 'in order to obtain some variety of food', were often seen 'offering guinea corn for sale' and using the proceeds obtained to 'buy salt meat or vegetables'. When slaves were asked why they preferred to sell or barter their food allocations, Pinckard declared, they would commonly

express themselves: "Me no like for have guinea corn always! Massa gib me guinea corn too much – guinea corn today – guinea corn tomorrow – guinea corn cb'ry day – Me no like him guinea corn – him guinea corn no good for guhyaam".[7]

In his 1808 *History of Barbados,* John Poyer, a white creole social commentator, agreed with Pinckard that slaves would generally 'barter the crude, unsavory, substantial allowance of the plantations for more palatable and nutritious food'.[8]

Pinckard, however, recognized that slaves did not rely fully on food rations in creating supplies of marketable goods. Rather, he observed, 'those who are industrious have little additions of their own, either from vegetables grown on the spot of ground allotted to them, or purchased with money obtained for the pig, the goat, or other stock raised about their huts in the negro yard'.[9] He regarded it as 'common for the slaves to plant fruit and vegetables, and to raise stocks'. At one hut on the Spendlove estate Pinckard 'saw a pig, a goat, a young kid, some pigeons, and some chickens, all the property of an individual slave'. He observed the advantages of these activities for both slave and owner, for he thought garden plots and livestock afforded slaves 'occupation and amusement for their leisure moments', and created ' a degree of interest in the spot'.[10]

Thirty years later F.W. Bayley's account of the slaves' domestic economy, like that of Pinckard's, emphasized the raising of poultry and animals, as well as the cultivation of roots, vegetables, and fruits. He described as 'pretty well cultivated' the 'small gardens' attatched to slave huts. For him, 'slaves have always time' to cultivate their 'yams, tannias, plantains, bananas, sweet potatoes, okras, pineapples, and Indian corn'. To shade their homes from the 'burning rays and scorching heat of the tropic sun', noted Bayley, slaves planted a 'luxuriant foliage' of trees that bear 'sweet and pleasant fruits', such as the 'mango, the Java plum, the breadfruit, the soursop, the sabadilla and the pomegranate'. In 'every garden' could be found 'a hen coop' for some 'half dozen of fowls' and, in many, ' a pigsty', and 'goats tied under the shade of some tree'. Bayley also observed that while the animals were 'grazing or taking a nap' a watchful 'old negro woman was stationed near' to ensure that 'they were not kidnapped'.[11]

Retailing was slaves principal means of raising the cash necessary for their purchases, and many produced commodities specifically for sale. Sunday was their main market day (until 1826, when it became Saturday), although it was customary for 'respectable overseers and managers' to grant slaves time off during the week when 'work was not pressing' in order to market 'valuable articles of property'[12]. The established Anglican Church was never happy with Sunday marketing. In 1725 the catechist at Codrington Plantation informed the Bishop of London, under whose See Barbados fell: 'In this Island the Negroes work all week for their masters, and on the Lord's Day they work and merchandize for

themselves; in the latter of which they are assisted, not only by the Jews, but many of those who call themselves Christians'.[13] Efforts made by the estate's managers to prevent Sunday trading were unsuccessful, and many insurbordinate slaves went to their beds 'with very sore backsides unmercifully laid on'. The catechist suggested that the 'force of custom' among slaves in this regard would inevitably break through 'managerial resolve'.[14]

Descriptions of slave huckstering illustrate the extent to which these fettered entrepreneurs made inroads into the colony's internal economy. William Dickson reported in the late eighteenth century that slaves were seen all over the island on Sundays walking 'several miles to market with a few roots, or fruits, or canes, sometimes a fowl or a kid, or a pig from their little spots of ground which have been dignified with the illusive name of gardens'.[15] J. A. Thome and J. H. Kimball, who witnessed the disintegration of Barbados slavery, in the nineteenth century had much to say about the role of black women – slave and free – in the internal marketing system. They were impressed by the spectacle of these 'busy marketeers', both men and women, 'pouring into the highways' at the 'crosspaths leading through the estates'. These plantation hucksters were seen 'strung' all along the road 'moving peaceably forward'. Thome and Kimball described as 'amusing' the 'almost infinite diversity of products' being transported, such as 'sweet potatoes, yams, eddoes, Guinea and Indian corn, various fruits and berries, vegetables, nuts, cakes, bundles of fire wood and bundles of sugar canes'. The women, as elsewhere in the Caribbean, were in the majority. They described one woman with 'a small black pig doubled up under her arm'; two girls, one with 'a brood of chickens, with a nest coop and all, on her head', and another with 'an immense turkey' also elevated on her head. Thome and Kimball were not only impressed with the 'spectacle' of this march to the Bridgetown market, but also with their commercial organization, especially the manner in which their information network conveyed 'news concerning the state of the market'.[16]

Huckster slaves dominated the sale of food provisions in the Bridgetown market. Numerous urban slaves, however, retailed their cakes, drinks, and a range of imported goods. According to Bayley, many Bridgetown inhabitants gained a livelihood by sending slaves about the town and suburbs with articles of various kinds for sale. These hucksters, mostly women, carried 'on their heads in wooden trays' all sorts of 'eatables, wearables, jewelry and dry goods'. Bayley also commented on the social origins of free persons who directed huckster slaves. Most, he stated, were less fortunate whites, but it was common for members of the 'higher classes of society' to 'endeavour to turn a penny by sending their slaves on such money-making excursions'.[17] Such slaves retailed exotic items such as 'pickles and preserves, oil, noyau, anisette, eau-de-cologne, toys, ribbons, handkerchiefs, and other little nick-knacks', most of which were imported from the neighbouring French island of Martinque.

Town slaves, who sold on their own account, marketed items such as 'sweets and sugar cakes'. Bayley described these items as 'about the most unwholesome eatables that the West Indies produce'. Hucksters could be found 'at the corner of almost every street' in Bridgetown, 'sitting on little stools' with their goods neatly displayed on trays. Plantation hucksters, then, posed no competition for their urban counterparts. There was a mutually beneficial relationship in which each provided a market for the other's goods.[18]

From the early eighteenth century, government policies respecting slave hucksters were informed by the planters' beliefs that a significant proportion of the goods sold at the Sunday markets were stolen from their estates. The assumptions that the tiny garden plots cultivated by slaves could not support the quantity of produce marketed and that hucksters were not sufficiently diligent and organized to sustain an honest trade throughout the year underpinned the debates in the Assemblies and Legislative Councils. It was more in the slaves' nature, planters argued, to seek the easier option of appropriating plantation stocks. The charge of theft, therefore, featured prominently in the planters' opinions and policies towards slave hucksters.

The acquisition of plantation stocks by slaves was one likely way to obtain items for the Sunday markets, though such acts of appropriation were difficult to separate from scavenging by malnourished slaves looking to improve their diet. There was little planters could do to eradi-

cated the leakage of stocks into slave villages. In spite of the employment of numerous watchmen and guards to protect their property, they complained constantly about the cunning and deviousness of slaves in this regard.

Contrary to the planters, Pinckard found evidence of a sort of moral economy in which slaves asserted a legitimate right over a satisfactory share of the produce of their labour. Many slaves, he stated, were firm in the opinion that it was not immoral to appropriate plantation stock, but rather it was the master's inhumanity that denied them what was rightfully theirs, an adequate proportion of estate production. Slaves, he said, 'have no remorse in stealing whensoever and wheresoever' and do not accept the notion of 'robbing their masters'. They would commonly respond to the charge of theft, Pinckard added, with the expression: 'me no tief him; me take him from Massa'.[19] The slaves' perception of the planter as the guilty party may have fuelled the highly organized system through which they sought redress by the clandestine appropriation of estate goods.

A case illustrative of slaves' determination to increase their share of estate produce can be extracted from events on the Newton plantation between 1795 and 1797. During this time the manager, Mr Wood, made several references to the confiscation of stocks by slaves and considered it a major problem. Wood's account of the slaves' organized appropriation under the management of his predecessor, Mr Yard, provides a detailed view of extensive contact between plantation theft and huckstering. Dolly, the daughter of Old Doll, the estate's retired housekeeper, was brought into the house by Yard and kept as his mistress. On account of their intimate relations, Dolly obtained access to all stores, and it was believed that she 'pilfered' for the enrichment of her family.

Sir John Alleyne, the estate's attorney, discovered the sexual relation between Yard and Dolly on a surprise visit to the property, and Yard's services were terminated. Dolly was removed from the household, but the flow of goods continued. When Wood conducted his investigation he realized that Billy Thomas, Dolly's cousin, who worked for Yard and was held 'in great confidence' and 'trusted with everything', was the culprit. Billy, noted Wood, 'had an opportunity of stealing the key of the box which held the key of the building'. This gave him and his family access to 'the rum, sugar, corn, and everything else which lay at their mercy'. Billy's aunt, Betsy, also a plantation slave, was married to a free black huckster who, 'through these connections', was 'supplied plentifully with everything'. Old Doll also did some huckstering and her home was described by Wood as a 'perfect out-shop for dry goods, rum, sugar, and other commodities'.[20]

A greater problem was posed for planters, however, when their slaves plundered the property of other persons, which was also another way of obtaining articles – especially fresh meat – for sale. Such cases involved more than estate discipline, and at times required criminal litigation. The records of Codrington Estate, for example, show that neighbouring planters commonly sought compensation outside of court when Codrington slaves were presumed guilty of theft. In some instances, however, courts settled such matters. In 1746, for example, Richard Coombs was paid £1 by the estate 'for a hog of his kill'd by the plantation negroes'. The following year James Toppin was paid 3s 9d 'for a turkey stolen from him by the negro John', and in 1779 the manager paid William Gall £8 when he agreed not to sue at law 'for a bull stolen' from him by a group of field slaves.[21] It was suspected that these stocks found their way onto the market through white intermediaries who worked in league with slaves.

Most contemporaries believed that the typical huckster's income, outside of what was earned from the occasional sale of high priced fresh meats, was meagre.[22] Bayley offered an account of their annual earnings by estimating the values of produce she sold. In normal times, he noted, 'a tray of vegetables, fruits, calabashes, etc.' brought in gross annual receipts of six or seven shillings. The sale of poultry and animals, in addition to 'cane, cloth, and sugar', would increase receipts to about 'ten shillings'.[23] Such an income level, Bayley suggested, could not sustain a slave's life without plantation allowances. Free blacks or poor whites with such an income would have had to resort to the parish for relief.

Bayley, however, considered such modest incomes the result of the slave huckster's lack of the accumulationist spirit. Slavery, he believed, was responsible for the suppression of their acquisitive impulse. He made reference to slaves who had 'the power of earning' but 'frequently neglected it'. He attributed this to 'the cursed spirit of slavery' which 'leaves too many contented with what they deem sufficient for nature, without spurring them to exert themselves to gain an overplus'. Such persons, he added, would 'only cultivate sufficient ground to yield them as much fruit, as many vegetables as they require for their own consumption'. As a result, according to Bayley 'they have none to sell'.[24]

Bayley believed a minority of 'more enterprising' hucksters, who 'strive to make as much as they can', generally do very well. Some even accumulated enough cash to purchase their freedom. Most financially successful slaves in Bayley's opinion, however, lacked the appetite for freedom. 'I have known several negroes', he averred, who had

'accumulated large sums of money, more than enough to purchase their emancipation, but that as they saw no necessity for changing their condition, and were very well contented with a state of slavery, they preferred remaining in that state and allowing their money to increase'.[25]

His belief, however, was tempered by the recognition that many slaves realized that free black's material and social life was frequently not an improvement over their own. Consequently, for some slaves it made more sense to seek the amelioration of their condition by the purchase of a 'host of comforts'. The use of cash to facilitate the education of their children was as important as the purchase of a 'few luxuries for their huts', Bayley concluded.[26] Plantation hucksters, who were mostly field slaves, did not live as well as the mechanics, artisans, domestics and drivers or other members of the slave elite. One was more likely to find a driver in a position to offer a visitor 'a glass of wine and a bit of plumcake' than a huckster.[27]

The poor white, living on the margins of plantation society, developed the most noticeable contacts with slave hucksters. From the seventeenth century, many white women labourers, mostly former indentured servants and their descendants, made a living by selling homegrown vegetables and poultry in the urban market. Largely Irish catholics, they were discriminated against in the predominantly English protestant community. They formed their own communities in back country areas of the St. Lucy, St. John, St. Andrew, St. Joseph, and St. Philip parishes, where they cultivated crops as subsistence peasants on a variety of rocky, wet and sandy, non-sugar lands. Descriptions of their huckstering activity differ little from those of the slaves.

William Dickson, who studied the poor whites closely, offered a detailed account of their huckstering culture. Labouring Europeans, mostly women, he stated, 'till the ground without any assistance from negroes', and the 'women often walk many miles loaded with the produce of their little spots, which they exchange in the towns for such European goods as they can afford to purchase'.[28] Their gardens were generally larger than those utilized by slaves, as was the volume of commodities they traded. But in spite of their disadvantage, slaves offered their white counterparts stiff competition especially at the Sunday markets.

The relationship between slave and white hucksters was complex. Both Dickson and Pinckard commented that the marketing patterns and customs of the two showed similarities. White women hucksters were typically seen carrying baskets on their heads and children strapped to the hip in a typical African manner, which suggests some degree of cultural transfer. Dickson stated that some white hucksters owned small stores in the towns and most of these depended upon the exchange of goods with slaves. These hucksters, he said, 'make a practice of buying stolen goods from the negroes, whom they encourage to plunder their owners of everything that is portable'.[29]

Dickson made a strong moral plea for the protection of slave hucksters in their unequal relationship with their white counterparts. Until 1826 slaves had no legal right to own property, and they suffered frequent injustices in their transactions with whites. Many white hucksters, Dickson stated, 'depend for a subsistence on robbing the slaves' by taking their goods 'at their own price' or simply 'by seizing and illegally converting to their own use, articles of greater value', which the 'poor things may be carrying to market'. 'For such usage', he added, 'the injured party has no redress' and so 'a poor field negro, after having travelled eight or ten miles, on Sunday, is frequently robbed by some town plunderer, within a short distance of his or her market, and returns home fatigued by the journey, and chagrined from having lost a precious day's labour'.[30] Slave owners were not prepared

to offer huckster slaves – even those who sold on their account – protection from these white 'plunderers'. Many saw the matter as nothing more than thieves stealing from thieves, from which honest folk should distance themselves.

The detailed descriptions and accounts of slave huckstering offered by visitors to Barbados present a static image which underestimates the social and political tension and conflict that surrounded it. Concealed in these reports was an important social crisis. However common, huckstering was never fully accepted, and slaves struggled to maintain their marketing rights against hostile legislation. From the mid-seventeenth century Barbadian lawmakers designed legislation to prevent slave huckstering by linking it directly to a range of illicit activities. In addition, authorities formulated policies to mobilize the entire white community against the slaves' involvement in marketing by stereotyping slaves as thieves and receivers of stolen goods. Against this background of persistent efforts to criminalize huckstering, slaves attempted to maintain an economic life of their own.

Initially, legislators considered it possible to prevent slaves going from 'house to house' with their 'goods and wares'. But a difficulty was recognized in that so many whites declared a willingness to accept slave hucksters. Legislators, therefore, had to differentiate this 'deviant' element within the white community and target it for legal consideration. The 1688 Slave Code provided, for instance, that Justices of the Peace were required to identify such whites and warn them against transacting business with slave hucksters.[31] The law also empowered Justices to take legal action against persistent offenders.

In 1694 an assemblyman who considered the 1688 provisions insufficient, introduced two bills designed to remove slaves from the internal market economy. The first bill prohibited 'the sale of goods to negroes' and the second barred 'the employment of negroes in selling'.[32] The debate over this legislation focused on the need to prevent the employment of slaves in activities other than those related to plantations. Some planters, however, expressed concern that a curtailment of slaves' 'leisure' would impair already fragile labour relations on the estates. Slaves had grown accustomed to considerable freedom of movement during non-labouring hours and marketing was a direct consequence of this independent use of leisure time. The implementation of the proposed restrictions would entail closer surveillance of slaves – undoubtedly a major administrative task for local officials and slave owners alike.

The legislation never became law, but persistent complaints from small-scale white cash-crop producers, urban shopkeepers, and other of the slaves' competitors kept the subject at the forefront of discussion concerning the 'governing' of slaves. In 1708 the first of many eighteenth-century laws was finally passed attempting to undermine the huckstering culture of slaves. This 1708 law tackled every aspect of slave huckstering, both as a planter-controlled enterprise and as an independent slave activity. The preamble to the act linked huckstering to slave insubordination and criminality, stating that 'sundry persons do daily send their negroes and other slaves to the several towns in this island to sell and dispose of all sorts of quick stock, corn, fruit, and pulse, and other things', with the result that slaves 'traffick among themselves, and buy, receive and dispose of all sorts of stolen goods'. The 1708 law, therefore, flatly disallowed any white person from sending or employing a slave to sell, barter, or dispose 'of any goods, wares, merchandize, stocks, poultry, corn, fruit, roots, or other effects, or things whatsoever'.[33]

While provisions were made for the punishment of whites – who either transacted with or employed slave hucksters, as well as for the hucksters themselves, the law of 1708 also implicitly recognized the hucksters' existence by stating conditions and terms under which they could legally function. Offending white persons found guilty could be fined £5, while slaves convicted for selling or bartering could receive 'one and 20 stripes on his or her bare back upon proof thereof made by any white person'. Exempted hucksters were allowed to sell 'stocks' to their masters, overseers and managers, and 'milk, horse meat or firewood' to any person. But this concession was also granted on terms that dehumanized the huckster and symbolized criminality, for the huckster had to wear 'a metaled collar' locked about his or her neck or legs. The collar had to display the master's and maker's name and place of residence.[34]

Legislators were concerned specifically with plantation slaves huckstering in Bridgetown, as they had suspected collusion between these slaves, white hucksters and shopkeepers. The 1708 law thus required 'the clerk of the market' to hire annually two able men to apprehend slaves that 'come into the said town to sell' without 'a metal collar' or accompanied by a white person. Magistrates were also empowered to remove all slaves from 'tippling houses, huckstering shops, markets, and all other suspected place' where they might trade with whites.[35]

During the eighteenth century, elements in the white community and their elected representatives remained dissatisfied with the ineffectual nature of the 1708 law. Bridgetown continued to attract large numbers of hucksters from the countryside, who, like the residents in the town, appeared determined to ignore the law. During the 20 years after 1708 reports reaching the government confirmed the continued expansion of huckstering in Bridgetown. In 1733 the island's assembly passed a new law to strengthen and expand the provisions of the 1708 Act. This time the law enumerated the foodstuffs and other items that hucksters were allowed to sell. It also enlarged the range of commodities which slaves could not trade, either on their own or their masters' account.[36]

The 1733 law was undoubtedly a response to the growing number of slave hucksters in the years after 1708. It suggests that the planter-controlled government saw hucksters as a threat to efficient slave control and its own economic dominance. The list of commodities that constables and market clerks were empowered to confiscate from slave hucksters now included sugar cane, 'whole or in pieces, syrup, molasses, cotton, ginger, copper, pewter, brass, tin, corn, and grain'. Particular concern was expressed for the welfare of *petit white* and small planters, whose profits were adversely affected by intense slave competition. In order to protect these persons, the act made it unlawful for slaves to plant crops for the use of anyone but their masters.

Cotton and ginger were singled out; any slave found selling these two crops could be charged for selling 'stolen goods'.[37] In addition, white persons who purchased such items from slave hucksters could be prosecuted for receiving stolen goods. The 1733 Act was amended in 1749, making it illegal for slaves to assemble 'together at Huckster shops' for any reason.[38] Still slaves refused to comply, rendering these provisions ineffective. For example, in 1741 the manager of Codrington plantation, reporting on his slaves' attitudes towards these laws, stated that nothing short of 'locking them up' could keep slaves away from the markets, and such an action would probably result in a riot.[39]

In spite of these laws, then, slaves continued to participate actively in the internal marketing system. In 1773 the legislature came under pressure from Bridgetown merchants who claimed that slave and white hucksters posed unfair competition for their businesses and a public nuisance on account of the noise and litter the slaves created. The Legislative Assembly responded by appointing a committee to 'settle and bring in a bill for putting a stop to the Traffick of Huckster Negroes'.[40] The committee's bill became law in 1774, proscribing 'free mulattoes and negroes', who hitherto were not singled out for legal discrimination, from the marketplace.[41]

The 1774 Act sought to diffuse three decades of accumulated grievances among the island's merchants. This time, however, the Legislature's emphasis was not to attempt the impossible – that is, eradicate huckstering – but to seek its containment. Provisions were made for the punishment of slaves and free people of colour who sold meat to butchers and who operated on 'Sunday, on Christmas Day and Good Friday'. The 1774 law also outlawed slave huckstering 'in or about any of the streets, alleys, passages, or wharfs of any of the towns' and on 'any of the highways, broad-paths and bays'.[42] Slaves found guilty of these offences were to be imprisoned and have their goods confiscated.

The small measure of legitimacy given 'country' hucksters by the 1733 Act was retained in 1774. Such slave hucksters could 'sell firewood and horse meat', items which posed no competition to small white merchants and planters. No mention was made of milk, the sale of which had been allowed under the 1708 Act. To those enterprising hucksters, however, who were accused of creating commodity shortages and inflating prices, legislators were particulary hostile. They singled out slave hucksters 'who go on board vessels' and who 'go a considerable way out of the respective towns to meet' country hucksters, in order to 'buy and engross' produce with the result that 'the price of stock and provi-

sions are greatly advanced'. Such attempts by slaves to manipulate even corner, the market were outlawed. Offending slave hucksters were liable to receive 21 lashes. Since some offenders were likely to be women, law makers, sensitive to the ameliorative spirit of the time, included a provision that 'the punishment of slaves with child may, in all cases, be respited'.[43]

Established Bridgetown merchants remained dissatisfied with these legal provisions and they lobbied for still tougher measures. In 1779 the 1774 Act, like its predecessors, was amended.[44] The new law aimed to end the 'traffick carried on by slaves' and limit the number of free hucksters – white, coloured, and black. For the first time white hucksters were subject to official regulation, and categorized with free coloureds and free blacks. All free hucksters were now required to obtain a trade licence from the Treasurer at an annual cost of £10, in addition to a processing fee of 25 shillings. This levy, which also served as a revenue measure, sought to eliminate marginal hucksters.

In 1784 an amendment to the 1779 Act provided for a penalty of up to three months imprisonment for white persons convicted of buying 'cotton or ginger' from slaves.[45] In November 1784, shortly after the 1779 Act was amended, the *Barbados Mercury* reported that the number of hucksters on the streets of Bridgetown continued to increase.[46] The Court of Quarter Session subsequently urged the government to adopt a policy towards huckstering which emphasized formal organization and legitimization rather than opposition. The government agreed, and hucksters in Bridgetown were instructed to confine themselves to the 'public market place called the Shambles adjoining the Old Church Yard'.[47]

John Poyer, the local historian, opposed the reasoning behind the legislative provisions of 1774, 1779 and 1784, and welcomed, the institutionalization of the huckster market.[48] Attempts to eradicate slave hucksters and penalize free hucksters, he argued, reflected the monopolistic thinking and tendencies of the commercial elite, which ultimately burdened the majority of the island's inhabitants. Both free and slave hucksters, he insisted, displayed survival skills and energy under adverse circumstances which should be encouraged. White hucksters, he stated, were in great part 'aged and infirm' and women whose capital 'in very few instances' was equal to the 'sum required for a licence'. These persons, he added, could not afford to pay such a levy, and would be forced out of business, resulting in their families becoming 'burdensome to their parish'.[49] As for the slaves, the huckster trade allowed them an income with which they could vary their nutrition. 'Let not the hapless slave', he argued, 'be denied these needful comforts by absurd and unnatural policies.'[50] Poyer led the lobby which in 1794 succeeded in repealing the 1774 and 1779 laws. As a result, huckster markets, such as the Shambles, became accepted in law, and a victory against discriminatory legislation partly won.

During the June 1811 sittings of the Assembly, members were informed that "Roebuck (a central Bridgetown street) was as much crowded as ever by country negroes selling their goods'.[51] Reportedly, hucksters refused to be confined to the Shambles, which they considered out of the way of pedestrians. From their perspective, Roebuck Street was ideally situated, and it attracted hucksters in spite of stiff penalties attached to street vending. The Assembly also learned that slave hucksters 'do not like to go there [Shambles] because the persons about the market set whatever price upon their commodities and the poor negroes are compelled to take that price'. Hucksters associated the old market with consumer domination, something they were determined to destroy. Freedom of movement, they believed, was the most effective way of gaining some measure of control over prices.

The Shambles became a place of open hostility between hucksters and constables. Disagreements among hucksters and between hucksters and customers sometimes resulted in affrays. In these instances the clerk of the market would instruct constables to arrest offending hucksters and confine them to the stocks. Stocks were eventually fixed adjoining the market where 'disorderly' hucksters were imprisoned and flogged. In 1811 the Grand Session was notified that the Shambles had become a public flogging place to the great disgust and annoyance of all who go there and to buy and sell.

By the beginning of the nineteenth century the huckster market had become an entrenched institution within the colony, commonly described by visitors as colourful, exciting and attractive. Alongside this formal arrangement, street vend-

ing proliferated, and each was an important part of the internal marketing system. In 1826 the 'Sunday and Marriage Act', designed to accelerated the pace of slave Christianization, finally outlawed Sunday markets and Saturday became the major market day until the present time. After emancipation hucksters continued to dominate in the marketing of food provisions, although plantations sometimes sold food directly to the public. As in other Caribbean colonies, former slaves took to other types of work, but huckstering remained an attractive occupation. It was an economic niche which they had identified and protected during slavery, and which, in freedom, became a cornerstone in the survival strategies for many households.[52]

During slavery the Barbadian internal marketing system revealed the slaves' struggle to achieve an economic life of their own. Unlike their Jamaican counterparts, Barbadian slaves pursued this objective within the context of persistently hostile legislative interventions from their owners. Evidence confirms the aspect of the Mintz and Hall account which shows that in the sugar monoculture colonies of the English Caribbean slave owners did not or could not make provisions that would enable slaves to produce their own subsistence. A close look at slave huckstering in Barbados, however, requires an important revision of the Mintz and Hall analysis by demonstrating that, in spite of the land handicap suffered by 'small island' slaves, they too were able to establish their own vibrant economic culture based upon the exchange of food allocations, the raising of poultry and stocks, and the intensive cultivation of lands that surrounded their huts.

Notes

1.   Hilary Beckles, *Natural Rebels: A Social History of Enslaved Black Women in Barbados* (New Brunswick, NJ, 1989) pp. 72-7; Robert Dirks, *The Black Saturnalia: Conflict and Its Ritual Expression on British West Indian Slave Plantations* (Gainesville, 1987), 69-80; Handler, *The Unappropriated People*, op. cit., pp.125-33; Hilary Beckles and Karl Watson, 'Social Protest and Labor Bargaining: The Changing Nature of Slaves' Responses to Plantation Life in 18th Century Barbados', *Slavery and Abolition*, 8 (1987), pp. 272-93; Edward Brathwaite, *Contradictory Omens: Cultural Diversity and Integration in the Caribbean* (Kingston, 1974), 41-3; Sid-

ney W. Mintz and Douglas Hall, *The Origins of the Jamaican Internal Marketing System*, Yale University Publications in Anthropology No. 57 (New Haven, 1960); Sidney W. Mintz, 'Caribbean Market Places and Caribbean History', *Nova Americana*, 1, (1980-81), 333-44; John H. Parry, 'Plantation and Provision Ground: An Historical Sketch of the Introduction of Food Crops in Jamaica', *Revista de Historia de America*, 39 (1955), 15-18.

2.   In 1711, the Jamaican Assembly prohibited slaves from owning livestock, or from selling meat, fish, sugar cane, or any manufactured items without their masters' permission. In 1734 and 1735, the St. Lucian Assembly prevented slaves from selling coffee or cotton. Between 1744 and 1765, the French Antillean slave owners passed laws prohibiting slaves from huckstering in towns or trading in coffee. In 1767, the St Vincent Assembly forbade slaves to plant or sell any commodities that whites export from the colony. See Franklin Knight, *The Caribbean: the Genesis of a Fragmented Nationalism* (New York, 1978), p. 92; Beckles, *Black Rebellion in Barbados: The Struggle against Slavery, 1727-1838* (Bridgetown, 1984) pp. 71-72; Edward Long, *The History of Jamaica . . .* 3 vols (London, 1974 [1774]) 2: 486-87.

3.   For an account of slave nutrition, see Kiple, *The Caribbean Slave: A Biological History (Cambridge, 1984)*. On the impact of malnutrition upon mortality levels, see Richard B. Sheridan, *Doctors and Slaves: A Medical and Demographic History of Slavery in the British West Indies, 1680-1834* (Cambridge, 1985): 'The Crisis of Slave Subsistence in the British West Indies during and after the American Revolution', *William and Mary Quarterly*, 3rd series, 23 (1976), 615-43.

4.   Mintz and Hall, *Origins*, op. cit., p. 23.

5.   Ibid., 10.

6.   Mintz and Hall note that laws in force during the seventeenth century 'make plain that a number of markets were established, formalized, and maintained under government provision. . .', and that 'formal legal acknowledgment of the slaves' right to market had been in negative form at least, as early as 1711'. Restrictions were applied to the slaves' sale of beef, veal and mutton, but they were allowed to market provisions, fruits, fish, milk, poultry and small stocks. Ibid., 15.

7.   George Pinckard, *Notes on the West Indies...*, 3 vols. (London, 1806), 2: 116.

8.   John Poyer, *The History of Barbados* , (London, 1971 [1808]), 400.

9.   Pinckard, *Notes*, op. cit., 2: 116-17.

10.   Ibid., 1: 368.

11.   F. W. Bayley, *Four Years Residence in the West Indies* (London, 1830), 92.

12.   *Report of a Debate in Council on a Dispatch from Lord Bathurst* (Bridgetown, 1822), p. 8.

13.   J. Harry Bennett Jr. *Bondsmen and Bishops: Slavery and Apprenticeship on the Codrington Plantations of Barbados, 1710-1838*, University of California Publications in History, 62 (Berkeley, 1958), 26.

14.   Ibid., 24-5.

15.   William Dickson, *Letters on Slavery* (London, 1814), 11.

16.   J. A. Thorne and J. H. Kimball, *Emancipation in the West Indies: A Six Month's Tour in Antigua, Barbados, and Jamaica in the Year 1837* (New York, 1838), 66.

17.   Bayley, *Four Years Residence*, op. cit., pp. 60-61.

18.   Ibid.

19.   Pinckard, *Notes*, op. cit., vol. 2: p. 118.

20.   Sampson Wood to Thomas Lane, 1796, M523/288, Newton Papers, Senate House Library, University of London.

21.   Bennett, *Bondsmen and Bishops*, op. cit., p. 25.

22.   In 1822, Mr Hamden, a member of the Legislative Council, reported, 'The goods which they have to take to market are comparatively insignificant; nor are the supplies which they procure from thence less so. The poultry which they raise with the superfluity of their allowance, or the surplus of allowance in kind, which can never be considerable, are the only objects of honest traffic which they have', *Report of a Debate in Council*, 8.

23.   Bayley, *Four Years Residence*, op. cit., p. 422.

24.   Ibid., p. 423.

25.   Ibid., p. 425.

26.   See also Hilary Beckles, 'The Literate Few; An Historical Sketch of the Slavery Origins of Black Elites in the English West Indies', *Caribbean Journal of Education*, 11 (1984), 19-35; Claude Levy, *Emancipation, Sugar, and Federalism: Barbados and the West Indies, 1838-1876* (Gainesville, 1980), 19.

27.   Bayley, *Four Years Residence*, op. cit., p. 425

28.   Dickson, *Letters*, op. cit., p. 41.

29.   Ibid., 41-2. In 1741, Abel Alleyne, manager of Codrington Plantation informed the estate owner that the white hucksters are 'often worse than the negroes, by receiving all stolen goods'. Alleyne to the Society for the Propagation of the Gospel in Foreign Parts, 9 Dec. 1741, Letter Book, Vol B8, 51, SPGFP Archives, London. Whites were protected by law from slaves' evidence; also, white hucksters could not be prosecuted if their slave suppliers informed legal authorities. In 1788, Joshua Steele informed Governor Parry that 'under the disqualification of Negro evidence the crime of *receiver of stolen goods* cannot be proven against' white hucksters, and that this acts as an encouragement to them. Reply of Joshua Steele to Governor Parry, 1788, *Parliamentary Papers*, 1789, Vol. 26, 33 (italics in original).

30.   Dickson, *Letters*, op. cit., pp. 41-2.

31.   An Act for the Governing of Negroes, 1688, in Richard Hall, *Acts Passed in the Island of Barbados from 1643-1762 inclusive* (London, 1764), 70-71.

32.   Journal of the Assembly of Barbados, 17 Oct. 1694, Colonial Entry Book, Vol. 12, 484-6, Public Record Office, London. Also, *Calendar of State Papers, Colonial Series*, 1693-6, 381.

33.   An Act to Prohibit the Inhabitants of this island from employing their Negroes and other slaves in selling

and Bartering; passed 6 Jan. 1708. See Hall, *Laws*, op. cit., pp. 185-7.

34. Ibid., 185-6.
35. Ibid., 187.
36. An Act for the Better Governing of Negroes, and the more Effectual Preventing the Inhabitants of this Island from Employing their Negroes or Other Slaves in Selling and Bartering, Passed 22 May 1733, Hall, *Laws*, op. cit., pp. 295-9.
37. Ibid., 298.
38. An Act for Governing Negroes, 1749, in Hall, *Laws*, op. cit., pp. 355-6.
39. Bennett, *Bondsmen and Bishops*, op. cit., pp. 24-5.
40. Minutes of the House of Assembly, 6 July 1773, HA 3/15, 1772-4, Barbados Archives.
41. 'An Act for the better to Prohibit Goods, Wares, and Merchandize, and other things from being carried from House to House, or about the roads or streets in this Island, to be sold, bartered, or dispose of . . . and to remedy the mischief and inconveniences arising to the Inhabitants of this Island from the Traffic of Huckster Slaves, Free Mulattos, and Negroes', passed 15 March 1774, in Samuel Moore, *The Public Acts in Force, Passed by the Legislature of Barbados, from May 11th, 1762 to April 8th, 1800, inclusive* (London, 1801), 154-71.
42. Ibid., 164.
43. Ibid., 167.
44. Ibid., 212-7.
45. Ibid., 251-5.
46. *Barbados Mercury*, 20 Nov. 1784.
47. Ibid.
48. Poyer, *History of Barbados*, op. cit., pp. 398-419.
49. Ibid., 400-401.
50. Ibid., 400.
51. Minutes of the House of Assembly, 14 June 1811, CO 31/45, PRO.
52. See Handler, *The Unappropriated People*, op. cit., pp. 125.

55

The Other Face of Slave Labour: Provision Grounds and Internal Marketing in Martinique

DALE W. TOMICH

The slaves' working activity was not confined to the production of export commodities. The planters of Martinique were under constant pressure to reduce the costs of their operations. The easiest and most readily available means to do this was simply to squeeze more out of the slaves. The latter were obliged to produce for their own subsistence in their 'free' time, that is outside the time devoted to producing the plantation's commercial crop. Instead of receiving the legally required amounts of food and clothing, the slaves were commonly given plots of marginal land and a free day on Saturday in order to provide for at least a portion of their own consumption needs on their own accounts. (Some planters gave only half a day on Saturday and continued to supply a part of the slaves' rations themselves.) By encouraging the slave to work for himself, the master could avoid the effort and expense of the large-scale cultivation of provisions. Instead, he had to furnish only some clothing, a fixed weekly ration of salt meat or fish and perhaps rum, and occasional medical care.[1]

This arrangement directly benefited the master, because the expense of maintaining the slave population placed a heavy economic burden on him. Goods imported for consumption were always expensive and their supply was often irregular, while both land and time for provision cultivation emerged almost naturally from the conditions of sugar production itself. The planters perceived it in their interest to spend as little money, time, or energy as possible on slave maintenance. This perception did not change appreciably, at least as long as the slave trade lasted, and for many it went beyond the end of the slave trade and even of slavery itself. Allowing the slaves to produce for their own subsistence from resources already at hand instead of purchasing the necessary items on the market represented a saving to the master and a reduction of the cash expenses of the estate. The burden of reproduction costs was shifted directly to the slaves themselves, and they were kept usefully employed even during periods when there was no work to be done on the sugar crop. Althouth it meant that after long hours of toil in the canefields the slaves had to work still more just to secure the basic necessities of life, many planters hoped that it would give them a stake in the plantation and instill regular habits and the virtues of work and property.[2]

The possibility of self-organized subsistence production emerged from the contradictory nature of the slave relation itself. The same social relation that shaped labor as a mass, disciplined, cooperative force also created the possibility for autonomous individual subsistence production and marketing by the slaves. The commodification of the person of the laborer compressed these two kinds of labor — commodity production and the reproduction of the labor force — into the same social space and defined the relation between them. Slavery thus made possible, and in some respects even required, the development of provision crop cultivation by the slaves as a means of reducing or avoiding market expenditures for their maintenance. But this labor of reproduction developed within the antagonistic relation between master and slave. For the master, the provision ground was the means of guaranteeing cheap labor. For slaves, it was the means of elaborating an autonomous style of life. From these conflicting perspectives evolved a struggle over the conditions of material and social reproduction in which the slaves were able to appropriate aspects of these activities and

Slavery in the Circuit of Sugar: Martinique and The World Economy, 1830–1848 (Baltimore, 1990), pp. 259-80.

develop them around their own interests and needs.

These simultaneously complementary and antagonistic processes crystallized in the practices and embryonic property relations that Sidney Mintz has described as the formation of a 'proto-peasantry'. He uses this term to characterize those activities that allowed the subsequent adaptation to a peasant way of life by people while they were still enslaved. As Mintz emphasizes, the formation of this proto-peasantry was both a mode of response and a mode of resistance by the enslaved to the conditions imposed upon them by the plantation system. Thus, it was not a traditional peasantry attacked from the outside by commodity production, the market economy, and the colonial state; rather, it was formed from within the processes of the historical development of slavery and the plantation system. The cultivation and marketing of provision crops and the acquisition of the necessary agricultural and craft skills emerged seemingly as a matter of course from the interstices of the slave plantation. They were interstitial, not just in the sense that final authority over the use of the land and the disposition of labor resided with the master, but also because the time and space for such activities arose out of the rhythm of plantation life and labor. These were not activities and relations separate from the plantation system but were intertwined with its logic; they developed within, and were dependent upon, its temporal and spatial constraints. Slave provision-ground cultivation was thus intimately linked to the organization of export commodity production and developed in close association with it.[3]

Mintz has been primarily concerned to demonstrate the originality of the proto-peasant and subsequent peasant adaptations that were precipitated out of Caribbean slavery. I would like to extend and qualify this concept by examining the historical interrelation between the various types of laboring activities performed by the slave population. Rather than looking toward the formation of an independent peasantry, as some readers of Mintz have done (though not Mintz himself), I would suggest that the focal point of the development of these autonomous cultivation and marketing activities was the struggle between master and slave over the conditions of labor and of social and material life within slavery. Beyond the formal juridical distinction between free and unfree labor, these activities indicate the sub-

stantive complexity of slave labor, which combined both 'proletarian' labor in the canefields, mill, and boiling house, and the 'peasant labor' of the provision ground. This 'peasant' dimension of slave labor emerged within its 'proletarian' dimension and formed a counterpoint to it. While provision-ground cultivation arose from the planter's attempts to reduce costs and create an interest for the slave in the well-being of the estate, its further elaboration depended upon the slaves' assertion of their own individual and collective needs within and against the predominant slave relation. The condition of the development of autonomous provision-ground cultivation and marketing was the slaves' appropriation of a portion of the estate's labor time. This struggle for 'free' time entailed, and was reinforced and conditioned by, struggles to appropriate physical space and to establish the right to property and disposition over their own activity. In turn, the consolidation of slave autonomy in provision-ground cultivation provided leverage for more struggles over the conditions of staple crop production. These interrelated practices transformed and subverted the organization of labor within slavery as they reinforced it.[4]

This process reveals both the contradictoriness and the historically developing character of the master-slave relation. As the assertion of slave autonomy had a continual tendency to push 'beyond' the limits of the slave relation, the master was compelled to try to recapture and rationalize labor under these changing conditions. Thus, for example, task work may be seen as an attempt to create a new, more effective form of labor discipline whose premise was autonomous slave self-interest. Industrial discipline depended on the existence of provision grounds and adequate material incentives recognized by both parties, though meaning something different to each. Slave struggles for autonomy and planter efforts to contain them within the bounds of the prevailing relations of production developed the slave relation to its fullest extent and created both the embryo of post-emancipation class structure within slavery and the conditions for the transition to 'free labor'. Seen from this perspective, the reconstruction of the post-emancipation plantation system was not simply a unilateral and functional shift to a more adequate and rational 'capitalist' form of organization. Rather, it was a process whose outcome was problematic, requiring violence and compulsion to recapture labor in the face of material and social resources acquired by the laboring population while still enslaved. The struggle over conditions of labor and of social and material life was continued in a new historical context.

Slavery and Subsistence

While the slaves had been given small gardens to supplement their rations since the beginning of slavery in the French colonies, the practice of giving the slaves gardens and a free day each week to grow their own food was brought by Dutch refugees from Pernambuco who introduced sugar cane into the French Antilles during the first half of the seventeenth century. The origins of this practice can be traced back to São Tomé in the sixteenth century. Thus, the diffusion of sugar cane entailed not merely the movement of a commodity but the spread of a whole way of life. With the appearance of sugar cultivation in the French Caribbean, subsistence crops for the slaves were neglected in favor of planting cane, and the 'Brazilian custom' was rapidly adapted by planters eager to reduce their expenses. Masters no longer distributed rations to their slaves. Instead, the latter were expected to provide their own food, shelter, clothing, and other material needs from the labor of their 'free' day.[5]

But this practice had negative consequences. Food production was chaotic, and the slaves were often poorly nourished. Indeed, frequent food shortages prevented the masters from dispensing altogether with the distribution of rations. Critics of the custom of free Saturdays claimed that it gave the slaves too much freedom and encouraged theft and disorder. The metropolitan authorities were in agreement with the critics and sought both to stop what they perceived to be the excesses resulting from the free Saturday and to ensure adequate treatment for the slave population. The proclamation of the Royal Edict of 1685 (the *Code noir*) by the metropolitan govenment was the first attempt to establish a uniform dietary standard for slaves in all the French colonies and to put an end to the prevailing disorder. It sought to make the master totally responsible for the maintenance of his slaves and to prescribe standards for food, shelter, and clothing to be provided to the slaves. The practice of individual slave gardens and free Saturdays in lieu of rations was to be suppressed, and regular weekly food allowances of determined composition and quanity (the *ordinaire*) were mandated.[6]

This edict remained the fundamental legislation governing slavery in the French colonies throughout the *ancien régime*. The distribution of slave rations seems to have been more widely practiced in Martinique than elsewhere in the French Antilles, and the slaves there had the reputation of being better fed than elsewhere in the French colonies during the *ancien régime*. Even so, the writings of administrators in Martinique throughout the course of the eighteenth century complain continuously that the slaveowners were concerned only with sugar, and if they provided a part of the slaves' nourishment, they obliged them to secure the rest on their own account. The persistent failure to regulate slave diet and treatment and especially to prohibit the practice of slave provision grounds is evidenced by the succession of declarations, edicts, ordinances, regulations, and decrees, too numerous to recount, promulgated on these matters by both metropolitan and colonial authorities during the seventeenth and eighteenth centuries. The colonial authorities lacked the means to enforce the regulations in a society dominated by slaveholders, who were usually hostile to any tinkering with their 'property rights', particularly if it cost them time or money. Planters expressed their preference for slave self-subsistence, and the reluctance to spend money on slave maintenance, especially food, persisted throughout the *ancien régime* and into the nineteenth century. Far from dying out, the practice of free Saturdays and private provision grounds expanded and increasingly became an established part of colonial life during those years.[7]

Ordinances enacted in 1784 and 1786 revised the *Code noir* and represent an important attempt to ameliorate the lot of slaves and reconcile the law with the growing importance of provision grounds in the colonies. The practice of the free Saturday was still forbidden, but, instead of prohibiting slave provision grounds, this legislation recognized their existence and attempted to regulate their use. It decreed that each adult slave was to receive a small plot of land to cultivate on his or her own account. However, the produce of these plots was to supplement the *ordinaire*, not to replace it. The distribution of rations was still required by the law. This prohibition against substituting the free Saturday for the legal ration was restated by the Royal Ordinance of October 29, 1828, which reformed the Colonial Penal Code. However, the custom was stronger than the law, and ministerial instructions advised colonial authorities to tolerate this arrangement when it was voluntary on the part of the slave.[8]

This legislation was a step toward recognizing the realities of colonial life, but provision-ground cultivation was still regarded as only a supplemental activity, and the slave codes continued to insist on the distribution of *ordinaire* as the primary means of providing for slave maintenance. However, postwar economic conditions made complete dependence on the ration impractical, and scarcities caused planters to increase their reliance on provision-ground cultivation. According to evidence presented before the commission of inquiry into the sugar industry, before 1823 the majority of plantations could only rarely provide their slaves with the *ordinaire* and had to abandon them to the necessity of providing for their own subsistence, thus depriving themselves of the labor of their slaves. In his testimony before the commission, Jabrun stated that the slaves were better fed, better dressed, and better housed than they had been some years previously. However, he added that the lack of affluence and shortage of credit — and, consequently, the difficulty in obtaining provisions opportunely — still caused some planters to substitute the free Saturday for the ration. De Lavigne testified that in general this practice had ceased in Martinique. Almost all the Negroes now received the quantity of codfish and other food prescribed by the regulations, and provision grounds supplemented the ration. While this claim seems exaggerated, De Lavigne also suggests a cyclical aspect of provision-ground cultivation. In contrast to periods of low sugar prices, when land and labor could be given over to provision grounds, with the high prices of the sugar boom of the 1820s many planters may have preferred to devote their attention entirely to sugar cultivation and purchase necessary provisions. Undoubtedly, a variety of individual strategies were possible, and while the historical continuity of provision-ground cultivation may be demonstrated for the colony as a whole, it may not necessarily have been the case for individual estates.[9]

Despite the shortcomings and abuses of the practice of free Saturdays and slave provision grounds and the repeated attempts to suppress or regulate them, the scale of these activities increased steadily, and by the nineteenth century they had become more and more central to the functioning of the colonial economy. By the 1830s, the masters, with few exceptions, were encouraging their slaves to grow their own foodstuffs, and the substitution of free

Saturdays for rations had become widespread. The slaves were given as much land as they could cultivate. They not only produced but also marketed their crops without supervision, and the colony became dependent upon their produce for a substantial portion of its food. As one observer stated, 'The plantations which produce foodstuffs (*habitations vivrières*) and the slaves who cultivate gardens more than guarantee that the colony is supplied with local produce.' Measures prohibiting these activities were disregarded with the common consent of both masters and slaves. Enforcement not only would have inhibited the efforts of the independent slave cultivators but also would have reduced the island's food supply.[10]

By the 1840s, colonial authorities no longer regarded these practices as threats to order but, rather, felt that they contributed to social harmony. The reports of local officials particularly stressed the social benefits of independent cultivation by slaves. One of them expressed the opinion that the free Saturday was an 'effective means of giving [the slave] the taste for property and well-being, and consequently, to make them useful craftsmen and agriculturalists desirous of family ties.' For another, writing in 1842, it means nothing less than bringing the slaves up to the standards of the civilized world: 'But the slaves, for whom the custom of free Saturdays is established, prefer it to the ration because they work on their own account and find some profit from that state of affairs. It is clear evidence that man, even though a slave, has an interest in money and likes to enjoy the fruits of his labors while freely disposing of that which belongs to him. The black is forced to enter into types of social transaction that can only serve as a means of civilizing him.' This latter aspect was seen to be especially important because of the imminent prospect of emancipation. The report continued: 'In this regard, the custom of the free Saturday must be preferred to the legally sanctioned ration because, beyond everything else, it is a road toward free labor.'[11]

Thus, slavery, instead of separating the direct producers from the means of subsistence, provided them with the means of producing a livelihood. While the slaves acquired access to the use of property and the possibility of improving the material conditions of life, for them the price of subsistence was work beyond that required for sugar production. With these developments, the time devoted to the slaves' reproduction became separate from commodity production, and a de facto distinction between time belonging to the master and time belonging to the slave was created. However, instead of permitting the rationalization of the labor process, this distinction blocked it. The relation between time devoted to commodity production and time devoted to the reproduction of the labor force became fixed and rigid. The prevailing conditions of production were thereby reinforced. The economy of time and labor was dissolved into the maintenance and reproduction of a given body of laborers and the regular performance of a predetermined quantity of labor: it thus resolved itself into a social-political question as the master-slave relation was challenged from within.

The Self-Appropriation of the Appropriated

The successful development of autonomous provision-ground cultivation and marketing in Martinique depended upon the response of the enslaved. It was the result of the slaves' adapting to New World conditions and acquiring the skills and habits necessary to produce and market these crops. One contemporary document stresses the importance of cultural adaptation on the part of the slaves in developing subsistence agriculture and also suggests that slave provision grounds became more prevalent after the slave trade was abolished.

Thus, previously, the progress of the population did not take place in accordance with the laws of nature. Each year, the irregular introduction of considerable numbers of blacks increased the possibility of a scarce food supply in the country. These new arrivals in the colonies, knowing neither the soil, the climate, nor the special agriculture of the Antilles, could not count on themselves for their support. It was necessary to provide sufficient and regular nourishment for them, but they had no skills to contribute. Thus, the proprietors were quite properly compelled to plant a certain amount of provisions since their slaves did not know how or were unable to plant enough..... The slaves required more prompt and rigorous discipline (than today) because of the savage stage in which almost all of them had been taken, their ignorance of the work of a sugar plantation, the tiring labor to which they had perhaps not been accustomed, and their sorrow for their country which could lead some of them to commit crimes .... The slaves of today have less need of constant tutelage than previously. They are able to supply themselves without depending upon the generosity of their masters. The latter hardly plant provisions at all any more because the slaves plant well beyond the amount that is necessary for consumption.

Indeed, nineteenth-century accounts indicate that the slaves by and large preferred to have an extra day to themselves and to raise their own provisions rather than to receive an allowance of food from the master. 'This practice,' observed one government official, 'is completely to the advantage of the slave who wants to work. A day spent by him cultivating his garden or in some other manner, will bring him more than the value of the nourishment the law prescribes for him. I will add that there is no *atelier* which does not prefer this arrangement to the execution of the edict [*Code noir*]. Once it has been set, it would be dangerous for the master to renounce it.'[12]

The provision grounds and 'proto-peasant' activities were not merely functional for the reproduction of the social and material relations of the slave plantation. They also offered a space for slave initiative and self-assertion that cannot simply be deduced from their economic form. Through them the slaves themselves organized and controlled a secondary economic network that originated within the social and spatial boundaries of the plantation, but that allowed them to begin to construct an alternative way of life that went beyond it. In this process, the bonds of dependence of the slave upon the master slowly began to dissolve, and the activities of the slaves gradually transformed the foundations of slave society itself. The changing role and meaning of these activities was both cause and response to the increased pressure on the plantation system during the first half of the nineteenth century. While these practices had existed virtually since the beginning of slavery in the colony, they assumed new importance with the changing economic and political conditions of those decades and the imminent prospect of emancipation.

The reforms of the July Monarchy were a decisive step in the recognition of existing practices in the colonies and prepared the way for emancipation. The law of July 18 and 19, 1845, known as the Mackau Law, allowed the substitution of provision grounds for the *ordinaire*. While the land itself remained the property of the master, its produce belonged to the slave, and the law recognized the latter's legal personality and right to chattel property. The slaves could not represent themselves in civil action, but they had the right to administer their personal property and dispose of it as they saw fit in accordance with the civil code. This legislation confirmed and regularized what was already a customary practice and gave it the sanction of law. It thus extended the scope of previous legislation and further legitimized the existing custom. In the words of its authors, 'The law only recognizes a state that has long existed in practice and makes it a right to the great advantage of the black and without detriment to the master.' These legally enforceable rights were less precarious and dependent upon the proprietor's whim than was the previous custom. The slaves could now assert their purposes with the backing of the colonial state. The authorities saw in these practices not the source of disorder but the means to regulate slavery and provide a transition to free labor. The purpose of the legislation was to ease the transition to freedom by giving slaves skills, property, and therefore a stake in society. 'On the eve of complete emancipation, it is in the interest of the masters to see the taste for labor and the spirit of economy develop in the slaves. Now, without property there is no industrious activity. It is only for oneself that one has the heart to work. Without property there is no economy. One does not economize for another.'[13]

The Royal Ordinance of June 5, 1846, allowed the slaves to choose between the Saturday and the *ordinaire*. Upon request, each adult slave over 14 years of age could have the disposition of one free day per week to provide his or her own nourishment in place of the weekly ration. The minimum size of the plot to be allotted to each individual slave was set at six ares for slaves on a sugar estate, four ares for a coffee plantation, and three ares for other types of estates, and the master was not to make deductions for plots claimed by other members of the same family. The plot was to be located no more than one kilometer from the center of the plantation unless approved by the authorities. In addition, the master was also to supply the seeds and tools necessary to begin cultivation for the first year, but he was not obliged to renew the supply of these items. The extent of these plots could be reduced by half if the master could justify to colonial authorities that the total arable land at his disposal compared to the number of slaves made it necessary. The slave could be made to leave the assigned plot only when (1) it had been at his disposition for at least a full year; (2) his harvest was completed, and he had been advised not to plant again; and (3) a plot equivalent in size and as far as possible in quality was put at his disposal. Further, on the day reserved to him, the slave had the right to rent himself out, either to his master or to another proprietor in the commune on the condition that he demonstrate

that his provision grounds were well maintained.[14]

The slave who claimed a free day had to provide only for his or her own personal nourishment from the provision ground. The husband, wife, children, or other family members to whom the disposition of a free day did not apply were to continue receiving the *ordinaire*, which this new legislation set at 6 liters of manioc flour, 6 kilograms of rice or 7 kilograms of corn, and 1½ kilograms of cod or salt beef for an adult slave over 14 years. (Although there were some complaints about the lack of meat, all observers, including abolitionists like Schoelcher, reported that the diet of the slaves who received the *ordinaire* was adequate, if plain, and that planters supplemented the legal requirements with salt and rice.) However, an arrangement could be made between the master and the slave mother or father to replace the ration due to the children with additional free time. In this case, the size of the plot allotted was to be increased by one-sixth for each child over six years of age. But the right to this supplemental land ended when the child for whom it was claimed reached 14 years of age. Such arrangements also had to be submitted to the local authorities for approval.[15]

In order to prevent abuses of this system and to ensure adequate maintenance of the slaves, the request for the free day was to be made verbally in the presence of four adult slaves of the *atelier*, and each planter was to present a list of the slaves on his estate to the justice of the peace with an indication of those who requested the free day. The judge, on his own office or at the planter's request, could void the arrangement when the slave was recognized as incapable of providing his nourishment by his own labor, when he neglected the cultivation of his plot, or when he abused the time at his disposal. This arrangement could also be suspended or annulled at the slave's request, but in this case he could not claim the right to a provision ground again for at least six months without showing sufficient motive to the justice of the peace.[16]

Table 1 indicates the extent of provision-ground cultivation and the practice of free Saturdays in Martinique in the 1840s. However, it must be noted that these figures refer to the number of visits made by the inspecting magistrates, not to the number of plantations or slaves in the colony. Many estates were visited several times. Between May 1841 and May 1843, the colonial magistrates charged under the law with inspecting slave conditions made 968 visits

Table 1 Summary of Magistrates' Inspection Reports on Slave
Conditions 1841–43

	Arrondissement		
	St. Piere	Fort Royal	Total
Number of plantations visited			
Sugar	205	309	514
Coffee	38	176	214
Provision & minor crops	112	100	212
Mixed crops	16	12	28
Total	371	597	968
Number of slaves			
Below 14 years old	6,556	9,670	16,226
14–60 years old	14,491	21,548	36,039
Over 60 years old	1,520	2,173	3,693
Total	22,567	33,391	55,958
Food distribution (by plantation)			
Legally prescribed ration	67	129	196
Free Saturday	252	400	652
Mixed regime	33	60	93
No information	19	8	27
Clothing distribution (by plantation)			
Legally prescribed ration	244	256	500
Partial ration	54	52	106
No distribution	60	287	347
No information	13	2	15
Gardens (by plantation)			
Well or adequately cultivated	304	384	688
Poorly cultivated	49	159	208[a]
No gardens	14	48	62
No information	12	6	18

Source: Ministère de la Marine et des Colonies, *Exposé générale des résultats
de patronage*, pp. 89–90.
[a]Table gives figure as 200. Presumed addition error.

to plantations (of these, 514 were to sugar plantations, 214 to coffee plantations, and 240 to other types of plantation).[17]

With few exceptions, masters encouraged their slaves to grow their own foodstuffs wherever possible. Among the estates included in this sample, the practice of giving free Saturdays to the slaves appears to have been far more common than the distribution of the legally prescribed *ordinaire* as the means of providing for slave subsistence. The substitution of free Saturdays for the legal ration was almost general throughout the colony, while garden plots were almost universal and appear to have existed even where the *ordinaire* was distributed. For example, according to one report, in Lamentin, where free Saturdays were denied on almost all the plantations and the slaves received the legal allotments, the slaves nevertheless kept well-tended gardens and drew considerable revenues from selling to the local markets. Alternatively, many planters, especially if they were well-to-do, like the owners of the large plantations in Sainte Marie, preferrred to give rations to their slaves rather than to allow them to cultivate gardens independently. Not surprisingly, the distribution of clothing allowances was more widely practiced than food rations, although the plantation inspection reports reveal that many planters expected their slaves to provide their own clothing as well as their food from the income of their gardens. This practice was especially widespread among the less prosperous planters, particularly in the poorer southern *arrondissement* of Fort Royal. Only planters who were well-off could afford to buy clothing to give to their slaves. Others could do so only when the harvest was good, if at all. Several public prosecutors objected to making the slaves provide their own clothing and admonished the planters to stop the practice. Thus, while there were diverse combinations and possibilities of conditions of subsistence, the slaves appear to have provided a substantial amount of their maintenance through their independent labors beyond their toil in the canefields, and the gardens and free Saturdays were a widespread experience of the majority of the slaves.[18]

However, not all parts of the island nor all planters were amenable to the cultivation of provision grounds. The instances where there were no gardens or where they were reported as poorly cultivated appear to be overrepresented in the arid and poorer southern part of the island (the *arrondissement* of Fort Royal). In Vauclin, Marin, Sainte Anne, Diamant, Anses d'Arlets, Trois Ilets, and parts of Carbet, dry weather and poor soil prevented the slaves from producing enough to feed themselves and contributed to the malaise of the plantations as well. In 1843, a public prosecutor inspecting plantations in Vauclin wrote: 'In the *quartier*, the masters could not substitute the free Saturday for allowances of food without compromising the existence of their *ateliers*. The drought and the quality of the soil would prevent the slaves from satisfying their needs by their own labor. For several years, the products of some very important plantations have not covered their expenses.'[19]

For even the most industrious slave, the paternalism of the planter was inescapable. As Schoelcher remarked, 'The greater or lesser wealth of the slaves depends a great deal on the benevolence of the master.' Whichever mode of providing for the slaves was adopted, one inspection report noted, 'their nourishment is assured everywhere, and the master is always ready . . . to come to the aid of the slave when the latter has need of him.' Indeed, seasonal fluctuations could require the master to come to the assistance of his slaves. 'In years of great drought,' de Cassagnac writes, 'subsistence crops do not grow. Then planters who previously gave the free Saturday once again give the *ordinaire*. Those are disastrous years.'[20]

Although the actual cultivation of the crops was not subject to the direct discipline of the planter, this labor could be compulsory. According to the inspection report of one public prosecutor: 'the good or bad state of his provision is the doing of the slave. However, the master can be accused of negligence if he does not use all the means of encouragement or of correction in his power to compel the slave to

work for himself and thus improve his lot. Also, I have given my approval to those planters who have told me that they are just as severe or even more so with the slave who will not cultivate his garden than with the one who will not work with them.' But compulsion was not usually necessary, and often individual planters went to great lengths to support the efforts of their slaves. Sieur Telliam-Maillet, who managed the Ceron plantation in Diamant, had the land that his slaves were going to use for their provision grounds plowed. Even though he supplied his slaves with the *ordinaire*, M. Delite-Loture, who owned nearly 300 slaves in the *quartier* of Sainte Anne, bought or rented land in the highlands of Rivière Pilote which he cleared so his slaves could work it for themselves. Each week, he had them taken nearly two leagues from the plantation to these gardens, and he paid for the transport of their produce as well. Schoelcher reports that in some *quartiers*, the masters provided the slaves who worked such gardens with tools, carts, mules, and a *corvée* of workers, and the masters and the slave cultivators divided the harvest in half. Other masters considered such an arrangement beneath their dignity and simply abandoned the land to the slaves.[21]

According to Schoelcher, the garden was the principal source of well-being available to the slaves in Martinique. Customarily, slaves who were given half a free day a week were given only half a ration, while those who received a full day were to provide their food by themselves. In addition, Sundays belonged to the slaves and could also be devoted to subsistence activities, as could rest periods and evenings during the week. Schoelcher records that on a great number of plantations in Martinique, this arrangement had become a sort of exchange between the master and his slaves. 'This transaction', he writes, 'is very favorable for the master who no longer has capital to lay out to ensure the supply of provisions. And it is accepted with good will by the black who in working Saturday and Sunday in his garden derives great benefits.'[22]

The slaves who wanted to plant gardens were given as much land as they could cultivate. The provision grounds were usually on the uncultivated lands on the margins of the estate, often scattered in the hills above the canefields. However, both de Cassagnac and Schoelcher write that some planters in the 1840s used the gardens to practice crop rotation. When the sugar cane had exhausted the soil in a field, the slaves were permitted to plant provisions there until the land was again fit for cane. The gardens were then shifted to other fields. (According to historian Gabriel Debien, larger gardens located away from the slave quarters appeared only after 1770, but these were still intended to supplement the rations provided by the master rather than to furnish the main items of the slave diet. The staples of the slave diet, manioc, potatoes, and yams, were grown by the master in the gardens belonging to the plantation.) The plots were frequently quite extensive, as much as one or two *arpents*, according to Schoelcher (1 *arpent* = 0.85 acre). All the available sources agree that the slave provision grounds were very well kept. The produce of the gardens was abundant, and the land was not allowed to stand idle. Manioc, the principal source of nourishment of the slave population, was harvested as often as four times a year. Besides manioc, the slaves raised bananas, potatoes, yams, and other vegetables on these provision grounds.[23]

In addition to the provision grounds, there were also small gardens in the yards surrounding the slave cabins. They were intended to supplement the weekly ration, not replace it, and all the slaves, including those who received the *ordinaire*, had them. There the slaves grew sorrel (*oiselle de Guinée*), a type of squash (*giraumon*), cucumbers from France and Guinea (*concombres de France et de Guinée*), green peppers (*poivrons*), hot peppers (*piment z'oiseau*), calabash vines (*liane à calebasse*), okra (*petites racines gombo*), and perhaps some tobacco. They also planted fruit trees and, if the master permitted, kept a few chickens there as well.[24]

The 'little Guineas', as the provision ground have been called, allowed collective self-expression by the slaves and form what Roger Bastide describes as a 'niche' within slavery where Afro-Caribbean culture could develop. The slaves had complete responsibility for the provision grounds and were able to organize their own activity there without supervision. The use of these parcels and their product was not simply a narrow economic activity but was integrated into broader cultural patterns. The work of preparing the soil, planting, cultivating, harvesting, and the disposition of the product were organized through ritual, kinship, and community and were important aspects of slave life as diverse as kinship, cuisine, and healing practices. These activities provided an avenue for the slaves to exercise decision making and to demonstrate self-worth otherwise closed off by slavery. But, except for Schoelcher's vague

comment that the slaves cultivated them 'communally', there is little detailed information on how the slaves organized their activities. This lack of documentation is perhaps mute testimony to the genuine autonomy that the slaves enjoyed in the conduct of these activities.[25]

Even at best, the slaves who produced their own provisions were exposed to risk and uncertainty. They were generally given land of inferior quality that was incapable of supporting sugar or coffee. At times, the planters deprived them of their free day under various pretexts. If for some reason they fell ill and could not work, their food supply was jeopardized. Drought or bad weather might make cultivation impossible. The prospect of theft and disorder was then increased, and at the extreme the physical well-being of the labor force was threatened.[26]

Nevertheless, this arrangement could be advantageous for an industrious slave. Access to this property meant that the slaves' consumption was no longer entirely dependent on the economic condition of the master. Rather, they could use their free time and the produce of their gardens to improve their standard of living. They demonstrated exceptional initiative and skill and used the opportunities presented to them to secure at least relative control over their subsistence and a degree of independence from the master. According to one contemporary estimate, the incentive provided by the gardens doubled slave output, while Higman's data suggest an inverse relation between provision-ground cultivation and mortality on Jamaican sugar estates. With the free day and the other free time that could be husbanded during the week during rest periods and after tasks were finished, the slave could produce beyond his or her immediate sub-sistence needs. The slaves sold this produce in the towns and cities and developed a network of markets that was an important feature of the economic and social life of the colony. The sale of this surplus in the town market allowed the slaves to improve both the quantity and the quality of goods available to them and to satisfy tastes and desires that the master could not. Thus, improvement in the slaves' well-being was due to their own effort, not to any amelioration of the regime.[27]

Of course, not all slaves were willing or able to endure the burden of extra work which the provision grounds represented. Infants, the aged, the infirm, expectant mothers or those nursing children — all those who could not provide for themselves received a food allowance from the master, even on the plantations where the slaves grew their own foodstuffs. Also included among this number were those slaves who refused to raise a garden. In Fort Royal, a public prosecutor wrote, 'Only the lazy receive a ration and they are almost ashamed of it.' Of these 'lazy' slaves, Schoelcher commented. 'We do not want to deny, however, that there are many Negroes who show a great indifference to the benefit of free Saturdays. It is necessary to force them to work for themselves on that day. It does not surprise us that beings, saturated with disgust and struck by malediction, are litte concerned to improve their lot during the moments of respite that are given to them. Instead, they prefer to surrender to idleness or become intoxicated to the point of delirium from the melancholy agitation of their African dances.' The free Saturday, while generally received enthusiastically by the slaves, was not universally accepted. For many slaves, it simply meant more work, and they refused. They withdrew their voluntary cooperation and threw the burden of maintenance back on the master. De Cassagnac expressed surprise that on many plantations, if the slaves were given the free Saturday, they would not work. They had, in his view, to be treated like children and be forced to work for themselves. It was necessary to have a driver lead them to the gardens and watch them as carefully as when they were working for the estate.[28]

Long before the promulgation of the Mackau Law, the slaves established rights and prerogatives with regard not only to the produce of the land but to the provision grounds and gardens themselves that the masters were compelled to recognize. 'The masters no longer acknowledge any rights over the gardens of the *atelier*. The slave is the sovereign master over the terrain that is conceded to him,' admitted the Colonial Council of Martinique. 'This practice has become a custom for the slaves who regard it as a right which cannot be taken from them without the possibility of disrupting the discipline and good order of the *ateliers*,' reported one official. The slaves regarded the provision grounds as their own. When they died, the garden and its produce was passed on to their relatives. 'They pass them on from father to son, from mother to daughter, and, if they do not have any children, they bequeath them to their nearest kin or even their friends,' wrote Schoelcher. Often, if no relatives remained on the estate, it was reported that

kinsmen came from other plantations to receive their inheritance with the consent of the master. Here as elsewhere the autonomous kinship organization of the slave community served as a counterpoint to the economic rationality of the plantation, and the master was obliged to respect its claims.[29]

The slaves defended their rights even at the expense of the master, and there was often a subtle game of give-and-take between the two parties. While traveling through the *quartier* of Robert, Schoelcher was surprised to find two small patches of manioc in the midst of a large, well-tended canefield. M. Tiberge, the proprietor, explained that the slaves had planted the manioc when the field had been abandoned. When he wanted to cultivate the field he offered to buy the crop, but they demanded an exorbitant price. The master then called upon the other slaves to set what they considered to be a fair price, but this too was rejected by the slaves who had planted the manioc. 'I'll have to wait six or seven months until that damned manioc is ripe,' Tiberge continued. Another planter, M. Latuillerie of Lamentin, upon returning from a long trip, found that his slaves had abandoned the plots allotted to them in favor of his canefields. He could not simply reclaim his land, but instead he first had to agree to give the occupants another field. Schoelcher also observed large mango trees in the middle of canefields which stunted the cane plants in their shadow. The masters would have cut them down, but they remained standing because they were bequeathed to some yet-unborn slave. He continued, 'There are some planters who do not have fruit trees on their plantations because tradition establishes that such and such a tree belongs to such and such a Negro, and they (the planters) have litte hope of ever enjoying them because the slave bequeaths his tree just like the rest of his property.'[30]

The Fruits of Their Labour

Beyond filling the personal consumption needs of the slaves, the provision grounds produced a marketable surplus of food that was sold to the plantations and in the towns and cities. The main source of revenue for the slaves was the sale of manioc flour and other agricultural products, and among the main customers were the plantations themselves. Almost all of the manioc consumed on the majority of medium and large estates was purchased from the slaves. The planters bought these provisions to replace or supplement provisions cultivated as an estate crop and to distribute as rations to those slaves who were unable to provide their own food. The abundance of slave produce, especially in the years when agricultural conditions were favorable, caused the price of provisions on the local markets to fall sharply. When this happened, the more prosperous planters bought manioc flour from their slaves at a constant price above that of the market and, according to De Moges, gave it right back to them as a ration. One official observed that 'every time that manioc flour is cheap, the master buys it from them, usually at a price above the market price. Sometimes he pays double the market price.' The report of a deputy public prosecutor in 1843 describes the difficulties caused by low provision prices:

The worthless price to which provisions, especially manioc flour, . . . sometimes falls causes even the most industrious slave to become disgusted with labor. In these circumstances, many masters, I believe one could say the majority of them, come to the aid of their slaves, buying from them the quantity of flour which is necessary for the needs of their plantations at a price well above the market price. But sometimes the discouragement of men whose hopes for a better price for their labor have been betrayed is such that they do not plant at all in the following year. Thus dearth often follows abundance.

By subsidizing their slaves' production in hard times, the planters hoped to encourage them to continue growing provisions and thereby avoid a scarcity that would drive prices up, increase the colony's reliance on food imports, and disrupt general economic activity. Instead, they could keep prices low and guarantee a stable supply of essential provisions by supporting the market.[31]

The slaves also developed a network of markets beyond the plantation that was an important feature of the economic and social life of Martinique, and the colony came to rely on the produce of the slave gardens for a substantial portion of its food. Important market towns such as the ones at Lamentin, François, Trinité, and Robert attracted slaves from all parts of the island and brought them into contact with the world beyond the plantation. Soleau describes the Lamentin market: 'This town is one of the most frequently visited by the slaves of the colony. It has a fairly large market where they come to sell their produce on Sunday. I have been told that the number of slaves that gather there is often as high as five or six thousand. I passed through

there that day while going to the *quartier* of Robert, and encountered many blacks on the road who were going to the town. All were carrying something that they were doubtlessly going to sell — manioc flour, potatoes, yams, poultry, etc.' Sunday was the major market day in the towns; however, smaller markets were held on other days. These markets allowed the masters to have their slaves acquire goods that were not available on the plantation and would otherwise have to be purchased. An astonishing variety of goods were exchanged at the town markets. These, of course, included manioc, fruits, vegetables, yams, fresh or salted fish, animals, and slave handicrafts, but also manufactured goods such as shoes, dry goods, porcelain, crystal, perfume, jewelry, and furniture. Undoubtedly, barter played a large part in these exchanges, especially in local markets, but the money economy was significant, and prices were set in major towns for the main articles of trade. The scale of exchanges at these town markets was so great that they caused the urban merchants to complain, but, in the words of Sainte Croix, they were nevertheless a great resource for the interior of the island.[32]

The Sunday market was as much a social event as an occasion for exchanging goods. Slaves went to town to attend mass, meet friends from other parts of the island, drink tafia, smoke, eat roast corn, exchange news and gossip, and perhaps dance, sing, or gamble. It was an opportunity for display, and the slaves wore their best. One observer paints a striking picture of the appearance made by the slaves at the Lamentin market: 'These slaves are almost always very well dressed and present the exterior signs of material well-being. The men have trousers, shirts, vests, and hats of oilskin or straw. The women have skirts of Indian cotton, white blouses, and scarves, some of which are luxurious, as well as earrings, pins and even some chains of gold.' According to Soleau, the signs of prosperity presented by the slaves of Martinique on market day were unusual in the Caribbean and even in rural France: 'One thing struck me that I have never seen in Cayenne, Surinam, or Demerara. It is the cleanliness and the luxury of the clothing of the slaves that I encountered. The lazy, having nothing to sell, remained on the plantations, but in France, generally, the peasants, except for their shoes, were not better dressed on Sunday and did not wear such fine material.'[33]

The colorful and bustling markets punctuated the drudgery and isolation of plantation life. Slaves from town and country, young and old, male and female, as well as freedmen, sailors, merchants, planters — anyone who wanted to buy or sell — mingled in the crowds. Such gatherings were potentially dangerous and posed a threat to order and security in a slave society, as Governor Mathieu recognized: 'I have posted thirty men and an officer at St. Esprit. This measure was welcomed by the entire commune. St. Esprit is a center of commerce. A great number of people, including many strangers, gather there for the markets that are held each week, especially on Sundays. Thus, police measures are necessary and are linked to those that have been established to prevent bad subjects from stirring up the *ateliers* and inciting unrest.'[34]

These markets offered incentives to the slaves and enabled them to improve the material conditions of life as well as to acquire skills, knowledge, and social contacts that increased their independence and allowed them to assert their individuality and vary the texture of their lives. Their initiative led to the development of new economic and social patterns and the mobilization of productive forces that otherwise would have remained dormant.

They were able to obtain money and to purchase a range of goods that would otherwise be unavailable to them. Particularly important were items of clothing, and the more industrious slaves were able to forgo the ration and provide for themselves. According to one inspection report: 'In general, the slaves are well-dressed. The most industrious of them renounce the distribution of clothing and are well enough off to consider it a disgrace to ask the master for a shirt or a pair of trousers. On the other hand, the laziest of them sometimes oblige the masters to give them more than the regulations prescribe.' With the ability to acquire their own clothing, dress became an important expression of independence and status during their free time. While they were working, the slaves dressed poorly. Schoelcher marveled at the tatters they wore. But on 'their' time the slaves' appearance could undergo a drastic transformation. On Sundays or special occasions, the slaves wore frock coats and well-made outfits with satin vests, ruffled shirts, boots, and the ever-present umbrella. A public prosecutor described the appearance of slaves at a New Year's celebration on one plantation: 'The costumes of some dancers were luxurious so to speak. For the women, there were skirts of fine material, cambric shirts, coral or jet necklaces, and gold earrings. For the men, costumes of linen or broadcloth. Shoes had been abandoned as unnecessary encumbrances.' Another attorney reported a runaway slave who wore a black frock coat, boots, and a new silk hat, and who passed for a freedman for several days. 'Meeting them like this,' wrote Schoelcher, 'one does not suspect that they are the same men that were seen the day before working in rags.' Boots or shoes were an especially important status symbol among the slaves. In the early days of the colony, they were forbidden to wear shoes. Although these ordinances were no longer enforced, most slaves went barefoot. Schoelcher wrote that it was not uncommon to meet a well-dressed slave on the road to town carrying his shoes and putting them on only after his arrival.[35]

Household goods also figured prominently among the items bought by the slaves. The more prosperous of them often furnished their cabins elaborately. Commentators on slave conditions, both official and unofficial, in favor of slavery and opposed to it, noted such articles as chairs, tables, chests of drawers, mirror wardrobes, and even four-poster beds with pillows, sheets, and mattresses. However, as Schoelcher emphasized, such relative luxury could be found only among a privileged few such as artisans and *commandeurs*. The less prosperous had only a broken-down bedstead, a chair or bench, some crockery, a cooking pot, a storage box or two, and an earthen floor, while the poorest possessed only a cooking pot, a board or mat to sleep on, a bamboo stalk to store water, and a few pieces of tattered clothing hanging from a string stretched across the room.[36]

The slaves often made great efforts to increase their property during their free time, and in the process they developed a variety of skills. Many slaves raised chickens, rabbits, pigs, sheep, cows, and even horses. Slave-owned herds could be surprisingly large. In addition to their provision grounds, the slaves on the Lacouet plantation had 25 hectares on which to graze their animals. The slaves on the Fabrique plantation in Rivière Salée owned 15 head of cattle. The head carpenter on the plantation of Peter Maillet in Saint Esprit personally owned seven cows in addition to pigs, chickens, and rabbits, while the *commandeur* on the same plantation had two horses. Schoelcher reports a herd of 100 sheep belonging to the slaves of M. Douville on the neighboring island of Guadeloupe. Slaves also found other means of augmenting their income or acquiring property if circumstances did not permit them to have provision grounds. Where the soil was poor and little garden produce could be grown, slaves cut wood and made charcoal for sale. Fishing was an important resource for slaves near the coast, although their activities were curtailed after 1837 by an ordinance, designed to prevent slaves from escaping to freedom in the neighboring British islands, which forbade slaves to use boats. Slaves on plantations near towns cut guinea grass during their midday break and carried bundles of it into the town to sell as fodder after work in the evening. A young lawyer from Martinique remarked to Schoelcher that the slaves sometimes walked as far as a league with bundles of fodder weighing up to 75 livres merely in order to earn 20 francs a month. Other slaves earned money by hiring themselves out during their free time, either on or off the plantation. In the context of such opportunities to earn money, any skills a slave could acquire were an extremely important resource. A notable example of this was a cook in Vauclin who acquired considerable wealth by preparing most of the banquets in the *quartier*. He was given his freedom when his master died, and he bought his wife's freedom for 1,500 francs.[37]

The provision grounds could be very profitable for industrious slaves. Lavollée estimated that the revenue from $1\frac{1}{2}$ hectares near the Pitons du Carbet, which was worked by three male and three female slaves, was no less than 10 francs per day. Schoelcher wrote that a slave could earn between 200 and 400 francs yearly with free Saturdays — men a little more and women a little less. An official source puts the figure at 700–800 francs per year. One public prosecutor reported that many slaves on one exemplary plantation had savings amounting to more than three times their purchase price but had not thought of buying their freedom. According to another public prosecutor, the slaves at the Grand-Ceron plantation had 18,000 francs in doubloons and quadruples, while a third attorney claimed that the slaves of another plantation had more than 5,000 doubloons worth 432,000 francs. Such estimates must be judged with caution, since we do not know the basis upon which they were made nor the number of slaves involved. Neither is it very likely that the slaves made a habit of showing their money to visiting public officials. Nevertheless, it is certain that slaves in Martinique were able to accumulate substantial sums of cash as well as other property.[38]

Perhaps the most surprising and extraordinary aspect of the independent economic life of the slaves in Martinique is that some slaves used their earnings to hire other slaves or freedmen to work in their gardens, and a few even owned slaves themselves. One public prosecutor commented on the practice of slaves hiring other slaves and on the source of their labor force: 'The Negroes have as much land as they can cultivate. It has reached the point that several of them hire Negroes from outside or belonging to the plantation to work in their gardens. This supposes that the latter do not cultivate the land on their own account. In fact, on almost all the plantations there are lazy slaves who do not have gardens. But these men, who cannot be motivated to work by the hope of a harvest for which one must wait several months, can be drawn by the lure of an immediate gain, at least to satisfy the needs of their moment.' Not only did slaves hire other laborers, including free men to work for them, but there are also recorded instances of slaves owning other slaves. On the Perpigna plantation in Vauclin, the *commandeur* owned a slave, but this *commandeur*, like so many other slaveowners, found that his slave was 'never as industrious as he could be'. There were several slaves on the plantation of Sieur Telliam-Maillet who owned slaves. 'It is a reward from a master who is very happy with his slave,' wrote a public prosecutor. 'He permits him to buy slaves to replace him when he does not want to work, even in the master's fields.' This is probably the ultimate expression of the slave's access to property in a slave society. With it the gap between slave and master, bondman and free man, was narrowed considerably. But, at the same time, such conditions cannot be exaggerated. The slave's access to property and the opportunity for independent activity are extremely important for understanding the contradictions of the slave system as well as the role of the slaves in shaping their New World environment. However, only a small minority ever acquired even moderate property, and independence was always limited and conditional upon the benevolence of the master. The social distance between the most prosperous and industrious slave and the most impoverished and recalcitrant slave was always much less than between the former and the most destitute master.[39]

This process of the slaves' appropriating the free Saturday and elaborating these 'proto-peasant' activities had far-reaching consequences for the development of slavery in the French West Indies and was itself an aspect of the crisis of the slave system. It was an initiative by a population that, over the course of its historical experience, had learned to adapt to the labor routine, discipline, and organization of time of the slave plantation and confronted slavery within its own relations and processes. The result was simultaneously to strengthen and to weaken the slave system. On the one hand, the slaves became more effectively integrated into slavery and responsive to its rewards and punishments. The operating expenses of the plantation were reduced, and a greater surplus was available to the planter. On the other hand, the slaves were able to appropriate aspects of these processes and to establish a degree of control over their own subsistence and reproduction. They claimed rights to property and disposition over time and labor that the masters were forced to recognize, and they were able to resist infringements upon them. While it meant more work for the slaves, they were able to improve their material well-being substantially and to increase their independence from the master. They restricted his capacity to exploit labor and presented a fixed obstacle to surplus production. The amount of labor time at the disposition of the planter was frozen, and the slaves acquired a means of resisting the intensification of work at the very moment that the transformation of the world sugar market demanded higher levels of productivity and greater exploitation of labor from French West Indian planters.

In this process, the character of the slave relation itself was altered. The assertion of these rights and the exercise of autonomy by the slaves reduced their dependence on the master and undermined his authority. Custom, consent, and accommodation assumed greater weight in the conduct of daily life where coercion had prevailed. The acquisition of skills and property and the establishment of economic and social networks enabled the enslaved to realize important material and psychological gains. The slaves thus began to fashion an alternative way of life that played an important role not only in eroding the slave regime but also in forming a transition to a new society. In it can be seen nuclei of the post-emancipation social structure. Significantly, after emancipation the system of petty production and marketing organized by the slaves was to play an important part in helping them to resist the new encroachments of plantation agriculture and shape a new relation between labor and capital.[40]

The ability to elaborate autunomous provision-ground cultivation and marketing within slavery provided the slaves with an alternative to plantation labor after emancipation and allowed them to resist its reimposition. The very activities that the planters had encouraged during slavery now incurred their wrath. Carlyle scorned Quashee and his pumpkin; but far from representing the 'lazy Negro', it is a testimony to the capacity of the Afro-Caribbean population to learn, adapt, create, and articulate an alternative conception of their needs despite the harshness of slavery. Probably few could escape the plantation entirely after emancipation, but for the great majority of the freed slaves the existence of provision-ground cultivation and marketing networks enabled them to struggle effectively over the conditions of their labor. Jamaican historian Douglas Hall suggests that upon emancipation the freed slaves sought to separate their place of residence from their place of work. Where planters tried to compel a resident labor force, the workers left to establish free villages on lands off the plantations. In either case, the skills, resources, and associations formed through 'proto-peasant' activities during slavery were of decisive importance in enabling the free population to secure control over their own conditions of reproduction and to establish an independent bargaining position vis-à-vis the planters.[41]

The immediate consequence of emancipation throughout the French and British Caribbean was the withdrawal of labor, particularly the labor of women and children, from the plantation sector, and struggles with the planters over time, wages, and conditions of work in which the laboring population was able to assert a great deal of independence and initiative. It represented, in Walter Rodney's expression, an attempt to impose the rhythm of the village on the plantation. The successful separation of work and residence forced a new relation of production and reproduction on the plantation system itself as the planters attempted to recapture the labor of the emancipated population or find a substitute for it under conditions that guaranteed profitability. This resulted in the formation of new coercive control over subsistence activities and petty commodity production to one degree or another. This transformation of the plantation system and the transition from one form of coerced labor to another was not the inevitable result of unfolding capitalist rationality but rather is best understood as the product of the contradictory relation between production and social reproduction within the relations of slavery and of the struggle between masters and slaves over alternative purposes, conceptions of needs, and modes of organization of social and material life.[42]

Notes

1. A. Soleau, *Notes sur les Guyanes francaise, hollandaise, anglaise, et sur les Antilles francaises*, (Cayenne, Surinam, Demerary, La Martinique, La Guadeloupe) (Paris, 1835), pp. 9–10; Ministère de la Marine et des Colonies, Commission, 26 (1840), p. 205.
2. Félix Sainte Croix, *Statistique de la Martinique*, Vol. 2 (Paris, 1822), p. 105.
3. Sidney W. Mintz, *Caribbean Transformations* (Baltimore, 1974), pp. 132–33; Ministère de la Marine et des Colonies, *Exposé général des résultats du patronage* (Paris, 1844), pp. 303–05.
4. Walter Rodney, 'Plantation Society in Guyana', *Review*, 4, No. 4 (1981), pp. 643–66; Sidney W. Mintz, 'Descrying the Peasantry', *Review*, 6, No. 2 (1982), pp. 209–25.
5. Gabriel Debien, *Les esclaves aux Antilles françaises, XVIIe–XVIIIe siècles*, (Basse-Terre: Société d'histoire de la Guadeloupe; Fort-de-France, 1974), pp. 178–86; Lucien Peytraud, *L'esclavage aux Antilles françaises avant 1789 d'après des documents inédits des Archives Coloniales*, (Guadeloupe, 1973), p. 217.
6. Debien, *op. cit.*, pp. 176–86; Peytraud, *op. cit.*, pp. 216–24.
7. Debien, *op. cit.*, pp. 176–77, 181, 183–86, 215; Antoine Gisler, *L'esclavage aux Antilles françaises, XVIIe–XIXe siècles: Contribution au problème de l'esclavage* (Fribourg, 1965), pp. 23–25, 35–38.
8. Victor Schoelcher, *Des colonies françaises: Abolition immédiate de l'esclavage* (Paris, 1842), pp. 8–9.
9. Ministère du Commerce et des Manufactures, *Enquête sur les sucres* (Paris, 1829), pp. 23, 52, 67, 156, 248.
10. Sainte Croix, *Statistique*, 2:p. 105. P. Lavollée, *Notes sur les cultures et la production de la Martinique et de la Guadeloupe* (Paris, 1841), p. 10.
11. Ministère de la Marine et des Colonies, *Exposé général des résultats du patronage* (Paris, 1844), pp. 183–84, 290.
12. *Ibid.*, pp. 104–05, 180–88, 290.
13. Ministère de la Marine et des Colonies, *Exposé général*, pp. 177–88, 288–91, 332–33.
14. Archives Nationales — Section Outre — Mer (A.N.S.O.M.), Généralités 167 (1350).
15. *Ibid.*
16. *Ibid.*
17. Ministère de la Marine et des Colonies, *Exposé général*, pp. 89–90.
18. *Ibid.*, pp. 89–90, 182–85, 177, 219–25, 288–91, 332–33.
19. Ministère de la Marine et des Colonies, *Exposé général*, pp. 183–85; Gisler, *op. cit.*, p. 48; Schoelcher, *op. cit.*, p. 7.
20. Ministère de la Marine et des Colonies, *op. cit.*, Schoelcher, *op. cit.*, pp. 12–13; A.N.S.O.M., Martinique 7 (83), Dupotêt à Ministre de la Marine et des colonies, Fort Royal, 5 April 1832.
21. *Ibid.*; Adolphe Granier de Cassagnac, *Voyage aux Antilles*, (Paris, 1842), pp.174–75.
22. Schoelcher, *op. cit.*, p. 11; Lavollée, *Notes sur les cultures*, p. 123.
23. Debien, *op. cit.*, pp. 178–91, 205–07; Sainte Croix, *Statistique*, 2, p. 105.
24. Ministère de la Marine et des Colonies, *Exposé général*, pp. 180–88; Schoelcher, *op. cit.*, pp. 9–13; A.N.S.O.M., Généralités 144 (1221); Debien, *op. cit.*, pp. 178–91; Mintz, *op. cit.*, pp. 225–50.
25. Melville Herskovits, *Life in a Haitian Valley* (New York, 1937), pp. 67–68, 76–81; M. G. Lewis, *Journal of a West India Proprietor, 1815–1817* (Boston, 1929), p. 88; Roger Bastide, *The African Religions of Brazil* (Baltmiore, 1978), p. 58.
26. Soleau, *op. cit.*, pp. 9–10; Lavollée, *Notes sur les culvures*, p. 123.
27. Ministère de la des Colonies, *Exposé général*, pp. 110–188, 305; Barry Higman, *Slave Population and Economy of Jamaica, 1807* (Cambridge, 1976), p. 129; A.N.S.O.M., Martinique, 7 (83).
28. De Cassagnac, *op. cit.*, p. 176; Schoelcher, *op. cit.*, p. 12.
29. Schoelcher, *op. cit.*, pp. 9–13; A.N.S.O.M., Généralités, 144 (1221), Ministère de la Marine et des Colonies, *Exposé général*, pp. 180–88, 290.
30. *Ibid.*
31. A.N.S.O.M., Martinique 9 (99); Schoelcher, *op. cit.*, p. 11; Ministère de la Marine et des colonies, Commission 26, May 1840, p. 206.
32. Soleau, *op. cit.*, p. 59; Herskovits, *op. cit.*, pp. 81–85; A.N.S.O.M., Généralités, 144 (1221); A.N.S.O.M., Martinique 7 (83); Sainte Croix, *Statistique*, Vol. 2, pp. 13–15; M. Le Comte E. De la Cornillère, *La Martinique en 1842: Intérêts coloniaux, souvenirs du voyage* (Paris, 1843), pp. 123–24.
33. Cornillère, *op. cit.*, pp.123–24; Soleau, *op. cit.*, p. 59; Ministère de la Marine et des Colonies, *Exposé général*, p. 102.
34. A.N.S.O.M., Martinique 7 (83), Mathieu à Ministre de la Marine et des Colonies, 10 March 1847, No. 1508.
35. *Ibid.*; Benoît Duschene-Devernay, *Mémoire sur la Martinique avec des notes explicatives* (Paris, 1832), p. 22–27; Schoelcher, *op. cit.*, pp. 4–7, 14–15.
36. Schoelcher, *op. cit.*, pp. 1–3; Ministère de la Marine et des Colonies, *Exposé général*, pp. 111, 268–77, 288–91, 332–33.
37. *Ibid.*; A.N.S.O.M., Martinique 7 (83), Duschene-Duvernay, *op. cit.*, pp. 17–19.
38. Ministère de la marine et des Colonies, *Exposé général*, p. 100, 111, 332–33; Schoelcher, *op. cit.*, p. 11; Lavollée, *Notes sur les cultures*, p. 10.
39. *Ibid.*; Sidney W. Mintz, 'Was the Plantation Slave a Proletarian?', *Review*, Vol. 2. No. 1 (1978), 81–98.
40. Mintz, *op. cit.*
41. *Ibid.*; Douglas Hall, 'The Flight from the Plantations Reconsidered: The British West Indies, 1838–1842', *Journal of Caribbean History*, Vol 10–11 (1978), pp. 7–23.
42. Rodney, 'Plantation Society in Guyana'.

56

The Origins of the Jamaican Internal Marketing System

SIDNEY MINTZ AND DOUGLAS HALL*

This paper deals with the origins and growth of the Jamaican internal market system and the local small-scale agriculture whose products are served by that system. The Jamaica Census of 1943 indicates that out of an agricultural labor force of 221,376, there were 49,200 peasants operating holdings of ten acres or less, while 16,972 operators had larger holdings. Moreover, a significant proportion of the agricultural labor force listed as wage earners was simultaneously engaged in cultivating owned land in plots of less than one acre, or in cultivating rented land (Cumper, n.d.).

The Jamaican peasantry of today originated within the physical boundaries of the slave-worked sugar estates and within the normal pattern of slave-estate administration of two centuries ago. Since the slave plantation elsewhere in much of the Caribbean region, as in Puerto Rico, served to destroy the peasantry rather than to create it (Mintz, 1951, 1959), the forces at work in the Jamaican case are of interest, and what is known of the history of Jamaican internal marketing is closely intermeshed with the rise of that country's peasant class (Mintz, 1955).

In the British Caribbean under slavery, the owners and managers of estates faced the problem of feeding their slaves. The alternative extremes were either to use the slaves to produce as much as possible of their own diet, by compulsion or by incentive, or else to import all of what they ate. Of these two courses the first, though not always practicable, was ideally the more desirable. If the slaves could feed themselves the estates would be saved expenditure of money on imported foods and avoid the risks contingent upon importation. When warfare disturbed merchant shipping, as occurred so often in the eighteenth century, and shortages of imported food resulted, food prices rose (Ragatz, 1927). Moreover, when shortages of imports prevailed, the slaves could not be adequately fed even if the planter could afford to purchase at high prices. Prolonged interference with the importation of food introduced a vicious circle of high prices, malnutrition, and reduced production and profits.

Yet there were often difficulties in the way of local food production, and it is no accident that today in the British Caribbean the peasantry and food production are found chiefly in mountain areas or in areas otherwise, by reason of location, or of soil or weather conditions, unsuitable for sugar production. Until the 1830s land and slave labor were the essential factors of sugar production. Capital equipment and technical know-how became important only after the emancipation and the opening of the British sugar market to foreign competition in the second half of the nineteenth century (Goveia, 1959).

On this emphasis on land and labor rested the expedient decisions of the sugar planter who wanted to plant sugar wherever it could profitably be planted, but at the same time had either to provide land for food growing for his labor force or risk the uncertainties of the food-import trade. Generally speaking, where land was flat and fertile the cane was planted; where it was not, food was grown for the slaves and the dependence on food imports was considerably reduced. Thus, throughout the archipelago as a whole, the flat or gently sloping islands (e.g.

The authors are grateful to Mr H. P. Jacobs of Kingston, Jamaica, and to Mr Peter Newman of the University College of the West Indies, Mona, Jamaica, for reading this paper and offering helpful criticism.

Papers in Caribbean Anthropology, No. 57 (New Haven, 1970), pp. 3–26.

Barbados, Antigua, St. Kitts) were almost entirely planted in sugar, whereas in the mountainous islands (e.g. Grenada, St. Vincent, Jamaica) planters, limited by topography in their sugar cultivation, had at their disposal relatively extensive areas which might be allotted to the growing of food crops.

Jamaica, largest of the British islands, contains distinctive coastal plains and interior valleys as well as mountain areas. In this island, therefore, both patterns developed (Beckford, 1790, 1: 154-70). On the few estates which lay quite apart from steep mountain slopes the food-import plan tended to prevail; but on those estates (the majority by far) which included rough hills or slopes or other poor-quality sugar land within their boundaries, the tendency was to food production. Clearly, whatever might be the individual planter's preference in the choice between food importing and food producing for his slaves, his actual practice was much influenced by sugar prices, the lay of his land, and the condition of the soil.

Where food production was undertaken the planter had to decide whether to include the work in the regular supervised agricultural program of the estate, or whether to offer inducements to the slaves to undertake the work voluntarily. It will be demonstrated that a thoroughgoing dependence on the regulated production of food was never achieved; in large measure, food production by the slaves grew in the absence of compulsion, and under conditions which implicitly acknowledged their responsiveness to the same incentives which operated for the free Jamaican.

In short, there was no generally accepted policy for supplying the slaves with food. Where an estate had land not wanted for cane, the slaves were usually allowed to cultivate provisions on it in their spare time. When war threatened or when for other reasons the importations of food were insufficient to meet the demand for them, laws were usually passed requiring estate owners to undertake the cultivation of a stipulated quantity of land in foodstuffs as an estate operation (Leslie, 1739: 233; Edwards, 1793, 2: 132). It is relevant that in years of warfare the prices offered for sugar tended to rise, thus encouraging the expansion of cane fields. In Jamaica the laws requiring local food production were customarily honored only in the breach. In all the islands, and especially in those in which the food-import system prevailed, the provident planter attempted to time his purchases of imported foods judiciously in order to keep his costs down

and his stocks ready in case of shortage (Pares, 1950: 126-7, 136). At the same time, unsupervised cultivation of food stocks by the slaves themselves grew steadily more important, whenever the estate contained land to support their activity.

The slaves used such lands to produce a variety of foods, such as tree crops, vegetables, edible herbs and roots, as well as craft materials. This produce was primarily intended for their own domestic use. But eventually — and the details of the process are regrettably dim — surpluses came to be taken to local markets and exchanged for other commodities, or sold for cash. The proceeds of these transactions accrued entirely to the slaves, apparently from the very first. Market day, customarily held on Sunday so as not to interfere with estate cultivation, became an important social and economic institution.

Consideration of the system of agricultural production and marketing by slaves briefly noted above raises questions which are a prime concern of this paper. It is not at first apparent, for instance, why this food production should have been left to the slaves' initiative and not have been more commonly regulated as a part of the estate's program of cultivation. It is even less apparent why the slaves were permitted to go to market, sell or exchange surplus produce, and retain the goods or money received. Further, there is the question of the origins of the markets themselves. Also, we may ask precisely what crops the slaves chose to cultivate, why these were chosen, and with what skill and proficiency the enterprises of production and marketing were executed.

Exact and wholly satisfactory answers to these questions are not yet possible. For most of them we have been able to formulate reasonable explanations based on the available data, and it is convenient to begin with the subjects of crops and agricultural skills.

There had been a background for cultivation and for its associated processes before the English conquest of Jamaica and the rise of plantation agriculture, and even before the Spanish discovery and conquest of the island. To some extent at least, later patterns of subsistence were derivative from these older adjustments. Jamaica was occupied by Arawak Indian cultivators at the time of its discovery and early colonization by Spain.

Parry writes that the native Arawak cultivated cassava and perhaps a soft variety of maize, and gathered shellfish, roots, and berries (Parry, n.d.:30). Further information suggests that the Jamaican aboriginal crop repertory included 'tannier' (*Xanthosoma* sp.), arrowroot, sweet potatoes, coconuts, plantain, and a variety of uncultivated fruits. The diet was apparently sufficient and well-balanced (Sauer, 1950: 487–543; 1954: 20–1).

The Spanish settlement of Jamaica substantially eliminated the Arawak, but not their crops. Las Casas and others note the continued cultivation of the foods mentioned above, and the only important innovations mentioned are the raising of livestock and the curing of pork and bacon (Cundall and Pietersz, 1919: 15). Nonetheless, some of the earliest references to cultivated plants after the English occupation in 1655 make it clear that new crops had been added during the Spanish period, or introduced very early after the English landed. The Spaniards certainly were responsible for the introduction of the banana, nearly all the then known varieties of citrus, and the sugar cane. The English may, perhaps, be accredited with the introduction of the potato (Blome, 1672: 25; Hickeringill, 1661: 20; Parry, n.d.: 31).

The root crops which emerged as so important in later peasant agriculture and diet are of great interest, some of them spanning the three periods. Cassava and sweet potatoes, as we have noted, were cultivated aboriginally. Arrowroot and tannier were probably present, possibly cultivated. The 'yampee' or 'cushcush', a true New World cultivated yam (*Dioscorea trifida*), is popular to this day in Jamaica. Sloane did not mention it in his exhaustive botanical work (1707), and Parry thinks it fair to assume it was introduced from the American mainland after that time. Sloane does mention *Dioscorea cayenensis*, the 'yellow Guinea yam', which came to Jamaica from Oceania, probably via West Africa in the eighteenth century, Parry believes. By the start of the nineteenth century, there were at least six cultivated yam varieties in Jamaica, and there were the taros, the so-called 'eddoes, dasheens, and cocoes or cocoyams', which are of Oceanian origin and probably became established in Jamaican peasant cultivation and cuisine in the eighteenth century. Finally, there are several important plants whose dates of entry can be precisely fixed. Parry (1955) refers to the ackee (from West Africa, 1778), the mango (from Oceania, 1782), and the breadfruit (from Oceania, 1793, carried by Bligh on his second voyage).

From these enumerations, it will be seen that the crop possibilities open for Jamaican cultivators were considerable indeed. But very

little, unfortunately, is ever afforded in the early reports concerning the agricultural methods themselves. Beckford, writing in 1790, probably provides the fullest description, and that all too sketchy and vague:

When a tract of negro-provisions is regularly planted, is well cultivated, and kept clean, it makes a very husbandlike and a beautiful appearance; and it is astonishing of the common necessaries of life it will produce. A quarter of an acre of this description will be fully sufficient for the supply of a moderate family, and may enable the proprietor [read 'cultivator'] to carry some to market besides; but then the land must be of a productive quality, be in a situation that cannot fail of seasons, be sheltered from the wind, and protected from the trespass of cattle, and the theft of negroes.

If a small portion of land of this description will give such returns, a very considerable number of acres, if not attended to, will on the contrary, yield but little; and those negroes will hardly ever have good grounds, and of consequence plenty of provisions, who are not allowed to make for themselves a choice of situation, and who are not well assured that it will be well guarded and protected (Beckford, 1790, 1: 256–7).

At a later point, Beckford states:

All kinds of ground provisions and corn are, as well as the plantain, successfully cultivated in the mountains; but as this is done by the negroes in their own grounds [i.e., provided individually by the owner or overseer] and on those days which are given to them for this particular purpose, it does not enter into the mass of plantation-labor.... (Beckford, 1790, 2: 129–30).

And further:

The manner in which the negroes occupy themselves in their grounds is rather an employment than a toil, particularly if the wood be felled, and the land be cleared: but if they have heavy timber to cut down, the labour will be much, and the danger will be great; for they often get maimed or killed in this precarious operation, in which are required not only strength but likewise foresight.

They generally make choice of such sorts of land for their grounds as are encompassed by lofty mountains; and I think that they commonly prefer the sides of hills, which are covered with loose stones, to the bottoms upon which they are not so abundant. Some will have a mixture of both, and will cultivate the plantain-tree upon the flat, and their provisions upon the rising ground; and some will pursue a contrary method; for in the choice as well as change of situation, they seem to be directed more by novelty and caprice, than by convenience or expediency.

They prepare their land, and put in their crops on the Saturdays that are given to them, and they bring home their provisions at night; and if their grounds be at a considerable distance from the plantation, as they often are to the amount of five or seven miles, or more, the journey backwards and forwards makes this rather a day of labour and fatigue, than of enjoyment and rest; but .if, on the contrary, they be within any tolerable reach, it may be said to partake of both.

The negroes, when working in their grounds, *exhibit a picture of which it will be difficult to give a minute description.* They scatter themselves over the face, and form themselves into distinct parties at the bottom of the mountains; and being consequently much divided, their general exertions can only be observed from a distance.

If the land be hilly, it is generally broken by rocks, or encumbered by stones; the first they cannot displace, but the last they gently remove as they proceed in their work, and thus make a bed for the deposit of the plantain-sucker and the coco, or of the corn and yam.

Upon these occasions they move, with all their family, into the place of cultivation; the children of different ages are loaded with baskets, which are burdened in proportion to their strength and age; and it is pleasing to observe under what considerable weights they will bear themselves up, without either murmur or fatigue. The infants are flung at the backs of the mothers, and very little incommode them in their walks or labour.

The provision-grounds in the mountains, or polinks as they are called in the Island, admit of not much picturesque variety. Upon these are cultivated, and particularly upon those in Liguanea (a fertile tract of ground in the neighbourhood of Kingston), all kinds of fruit and garden stuff, or coffee, coco, ginger and other minor productions of the country (Beckford, 1790, 2: 151–87, *passim*).

It is known that the slave cultivators burned off the land they were preparing to plant. This technique, contemptuously referred to as 'fire-stick cultivation' in Jamaica, is of doubtful origin. It may have been continuous with aboriginal practice, but this cannot easily be proved.

The provision grounds, which normally lay at some distance from the huts of the slaves grouped near the center of the estate, were set apart agriculturally from the tiny house plots or 'yards'. On the patches of land around their huts, the slaves cultivated fruit trees, garden herbs, and crops which were very easily stolen, or very delicate. The distinction between house plot and provision ground persists to the present and is characteristic of Jamaican peasant agriculture. Stewart, writing in the first quarter of the nineteenth century, makes clear reference to the distinction between house plot and 'polink':[1]

Adjoining to the house is usually a small spot of ground, laid out into a sort of garden, and shaded by various fruit-trees. Here the family deposit their dead, to whose memory they invariably, if they can afford it, erect a rude tomb. Each slave has, besides this spot, a piece of ground (about half an acre) allotted to him as a provision ground. This is the principal means of his support; and so productive is the soil, where it is good and the seasons regular, that this spot will not only furnish him with sufficient food for his own consumption, but an overplus to carry to market. By means of this ground, and of the hogs and poultry which he may raise (most of which he sells), an industrious negro may not only support himself comfortably, but save something. If he has a family, an additional proportion of ground is allowed him, and all his children from five years upward assist him in his labours in some way or other (Stewart, 1823: 267).

The major local source of food appears to have been the provision grounds, or polinks. That these normally lay upon the slopes where cane was not grown suggests that the particular techniques of cultivation were adjusted to the terrain, a pattern which persisted long after emancipation and still largely characterizes peasant agriculture in Jamaica. This is of more than passing importance. Peasant agriculture in Jamaica has been repeatedly criticized for its erosive effects. It is true that failure to make long-range investment of labor and materials on such land is destructive. But it ought to be borne in mind that it is not necessarily the cultivation methods as such, or even the crops, which are destructive.

The 'choice' of hilly land for such cultivation followed from the monopolization of coastal plains and interior valleys by the plantations. It has never been conclusively proved, in fact, that the small-scale production of the Jamaican peasantry is in itself inherently less productive or more destructive than other systems of production *on the same land*. (This does not contradict the justifiable claim that productivity would be increased and erosion slowed by proper terracing, crop rotation, manuring, and the building of retainer structures, and so on.)

Sauer has written very explicitly of the *conuco*, or garden plot of the Antilles:

When Indians gave way to Negro slaves, the latter took over for themselves, rather than for their masters, the cultivation of the Indian crops, and added thereto such African things as the greater yam, the pigeon pea or *guandul* [sic], okra, and the keeping of fowls.

The food potential of the traditional *conuco* planting, or provision ground, is hardly appreciated by ourselves, be we agricultural scientists, economists, or planners, because its tradition as well as content are so different from what we know and practice. Yields are much higher than from grains, production is continuous the year round, storage is hardly needed, individual kinds are not grown separately in fields but are assembled together in one planted ground, to which our habits of order would apply neither the name of field or garden. And so we are likely to miss the merits of the system.

The proper *conuco* is, in fact an imitation by man of tropical nature, a many-storied cultural vegetation, producing at all levels, from tubers underground through the understory of pigeon peas and coffee, a second story of cacao and bananas, to a canopy of fruit trees and palms. Such an assemblage makes full use of light, moisture, and soil — its messy appearance to our eyes meaning really that all of the niches are filled. A proper planting of this sort is about as protective of the soil as is the wild vegetation. The *conuco* system can make intensive use of steep slopes and thereby may encounter erosion hazards that should not be blamed on the system itself, as commonly they have been (Sauer, 1954: 21-2).

Sauer's contentions, while unproved, certainly demand reflection. In fact, the whole nature of the adjustment of Caribbean peasantries to the aftermath of slavery, to the circumstances of a ruined economy, and to freedom, deserves more study than it has yet received. Such study can profitably examine the view that the patterns of human and horticultural occupance, the system of cultivation, the paths of distribution of products, and the economic relationships of the peasantry to other classes, form one interwoven system. We contend that this system had begun to evolve long before the emancipation.

Information on the agricultural implements used by the slaves is discouragingly scanty. The most important were the bush knife, or cutlass, and the short-handled hoe. We have been unable to ascribe an origin to these tools; a case might be made for either England or Africa. It is likely that at first they were provided by the plantation, and this might argue against an African origin (Public Record Office, 1836).

Both with regard to the crops generally preferred for cultivation and to cuisine, our information is again less than satisfactory. Several early authors suggest that the slaves preferred to cultivate plantains (and bananas?), corn, and vegetables rather than root crops, attributing this preference either to imprudence or to laziness. The planters themselves preferred to see root crops planted since these would better survive hurricanes (Edwards, 1793, 2: 132). Renny (1807: 87) believed it was the slaves' taste preference for plantains and corn that led them to neglect the root crops. And yet yams,

sweet potatoes, dasheen, tanniers, cassava, etc, could hardly have become embedded in peasant taste choices only after the start of the nineteenth century. It seems fair to suppose, therefore, that any favoritism the slave cultivators may have shown for plantain, corn, and vegetables over root crops could have arisen as much from the market situation as from anything else, and it is possible that these items were supplied in significant quantities to naval and merchant vessels. That the planters never actively interfered with the slave cultivators' crop choices in any case is of great interest, and seems to underline the mutual respect of customary arrangements which held between the estate owners or managers and the slaves. It also explains the vagueness of the accounts given by Beckford and others of the cultivation of the provision grounds. The only points which these commentators make with clarity are the distinction between house plots and polinks, the 'high' productivity of the latter if conscientiously cultivated, and the fact that the slaves were allowed to take surpluses to market, dispose of them, and keep the proceeds.

The first of these points is of interest because it indicates that even where estates were limited in size and did not contain slave provision grounds, the slaves were not absolutely dependent on imports. Even in Barbados and St. Kitts, for example, there were house plots (Coleridge 1826: 132). But it is upon the polinks that the foundations of the free peasantry were established, and here we turn to the local trading of the slaves, and the origins and early growth of the market places.

Extracts from the writings of two West Indian proprietors of the late eighteenth century will serve to give the planter's view of the relative advantages of food production as against food importation and to suggest one very powerful motive for the reluctance of masters to supervise production on the polinks.

FRIDAY, FEB. 10TH, 1792. My voyage to Antigua has put me in full possession of the question concerning the best mode of feeding the negroes. I am speaking of the difference in this situation in regard to plenty and comfort, when fed by allowance from the master, as in Antigua; or when by provision grounds of their own, as in St. Vincent. In the first case, oppression may, and certainly in some instances, and in different degrees doth actually exist, either as to quantity or quality of food; besides the circumstances of food for himself, the negro too suffers in his poultry and little stock, which are his wealth. The maintenance of his pigs, turkeys, or chickens must often subtract from his own dinner, and that perhaps a scanty one, or he cannot keep stock at all; and a negro without stock, and means to purchase tobacco, and other little conveniences, and some finery too for his wife, is miserable.

In the second case, of the negro feeding himself with his own provisions, assisted only with salt provisions from his master (three pounds of salt-fish, or an adequate quantity of herrings, per week as in St. Vincent's) the situation of the negro is in proportion to his industry; but generally speaking, it affords him a plenty that amounts to comparative wealth, viewing any peasantry in Europe (Young, 1801: 287-8).

Bryan Edwards, a contemporary observer whose main experience was of Jamaica, wrote on the same subject:

The practice which prevails in Jamaica of giving the Negroes lands to cultivate, from the produce of which they are expected to maintain themselves (except in times of scarcity, arising from hurricanes and droughts, when assistance is never denied them) is universally allowed to be judicious and beneficial; producing a happy coalition of interests between the master and the slave. The negro who has acquired by his own labour a property in his master's land, has much to lose, and is therefore less inclined to desert his work. He earns a little money, by which he is enabled to indulge himself in fine clothes on holidays, and gratify his palate with salted meats and other provisions that otherwise he could not obtain; and the proprietor is eased, in a great measure, of the expense of feeding him (Edwards, 1793, 2: 131).

Both these observers mention the advantages of having the slaves produce their own food, but it is interesting that Edwards, the Jamaican planter, is more explicit about the consequent savings enjoyed by the master. In the small, relatively flat, arable islands such as Barbados or Antigua, the planter could allot land to food cultivation only by impinging on areas which, generally, could be more profitably planted in cane. He tended therefore to restrict the land at the disposal of the slaves to small house plots, to depend heavily on imports of food, and, when the food trade was disturbed, to include, however reluctantly, some food production in the general estate program.

In St. Vincent and the other mountainous islands of the Windwards, the planter's decision was affected by the relative unsuitability of his land for sugar production. The 'sacrifice' of allotting land to food cultivation was not so strong a deterrent, and the advantages of having a comparatively well-fed slave force and of reduced dependence on food imports were clear.

In Jamaica, the largest of the British islands, with the largest estates and the greatest variety of soil, topography, and climate, the planter usually had land on his estate which, except in periods of unusually high sugar prices, he would never consider using for cane. There is much evidence that in Jamaica the area in sugar cultivation expanded and contracted under the influence of rising and falling sugar prices (Hall, 1959: 13). As prices fell, marginal sugar areas became submarginal and were, at least temporarily, thrown out of cane cultivation. But even when the process worked the other way and cane fields were extended in response to the promise of higher prices, there was generally a significant area which, because of its high unsuitability, would remain beyond the sugar line.

It is worth noting that in Barbados and the Leewards (except Montserrat which is mountainous) there is still a heavy reliance on food imports; that in the Windward Islands and in Montserrat the sugar industry declined under the competitive conditions of nineteenth-century free trade in sugar, and these islands now export foodstuffs to Barbados and the Leewards; and that only in Jamaica have food production and sugar production managed to survive together.

But, from the two extracts quoted above, the decision whether or not to allow the slaves to cultivate foodstuffs was apparently affected by more than 'classical' considerations of diminishing returns to land. We have shown that even where polinks were not usually allowed house plots were, and in many of the contemporary explanations of the system there is a sort of medievalism modified by the realities of colonial slave-plantation life in the eighteenth-century. There is the implied concept of the estate community, of the advantages to be gained from 'a happy coalition of interests between the master and the slave'; and indeed, the eighteenth century sugar estate with its great house and surrounding fields, its 'village' of workshops and slave quarters, its unfree agricultural population, and its complement of skilled craftsmen, was, superficially, not unlike the medieval manor. Even further, although sugar cultivation was the basic occupation, the workers had access to estate 'waste' land (the polinks), where they labored on their own behalf, not only growing food but also grazing small livestock and collecting the raw materials for their handicraft products. But superficialities apart, there was a second very important reason why masters should be concerned with securing this happy coalition of interest. It was simply that, since there was neither ethical nor economic basis for any such coalition (and here we begin to diverge from the medieval pattern), they must try to introduce and stimulate it. At any rate, the wiser masters would because, as our two writers argued, the slave with a better diet, a small source of income, and a feeling of proprietorship in land was less discontented, less likely to run away, and less dangerous as a potential rebel.[2]

For this reason, too, the slave was not supervised in his food cultivation, and this activity was never included, except in brief periods of shortage or threatening shortage of food, in 'the mass of plantation-labor.' Supervised field labor was repugnant to the slaves, and in the social hierarchy of the slave population the field slaves sat on the lowest rung (Smith, 1953). Supervised cultivation of food would have necessitated either a reduction of the time spent in cane cultivation, which the masters would not have willingly conceded, or an increase of the daily hours of compulsory estate labor, which would have encouraged disaffection and rebellious sentiments among the slaves.

But the accounts quoted above were written more than a century after the practice of allowing slaves to cultivate estate backlands, or polinks, had been established. The writers, therefore, might simply have been trying to explain, in the light of their own experience, the reasons for a custom of which the beginning and original intention were unknown to them. They tell us not how the practice began but only why it was still favored in the late eighteenth century.

Blome, writing in 1672 from the notes of Governor Sir Thomas Lynch, in Jamaica, gives detailed instructions for the setting up of a 'Cocao [sic] Walk' or plantation, and his advice includes careful explanations of the need for provision grounds for servants and slaves (Blome, 1672: 15–21). Sloane's introductory notes to his great work on the flora of Jamaica, published 1707–25, say of the slaves:

They have *Saturdays* in the Afternoon, and *Sundays*, with *Christmas* Holidays, *Easter* call'd little or *Piganinny*, Christmas, and some other great Feasts allow'd them for the Culture of their own Plantations to feed themselves from Potatoes, Yams and Plantains, etc., which they plant in Ground allow'd them by their Masters, beside a small Plantain-Walk they have by themselves (Sloane, 1707, 1: 52).

Leslie, writing in 1739, states:

Their owners set aside for each a small Ground, and allow them the Sundays to manure it: In it they generally plant Maiz, Guiney Corn, Plantanes, Yams, Cocoes, Potatoes, Etc. This is the food which supports them . . . (Leslie, 1739: 322).

Though we have not been able to establish a precise date for the beginning of this practice, Blome's statements, coming but 17 years after the English occupation, make it clear that it was generally adopted even on the earliest estates.

We do not know if it became the practice to provide slaves with provision grounds immediately upon the establishment of a new plantation, however. Conceivably, the managers of a new estate might attempt to supervise food production as a matter of course at the time it was set up. But this would not be likely. Precisely at the time that a new estate was brought into being, when slaves were being bought, land cleared, buildings erected, and factory machinery installed, managerial attention would be almost exclusively directed toward the main objective of getting the first sugar away to market. Probably imported foods would bulk large in the first years. If food production by the estate slaves were undertaken, it would doubtless be in their free time. When such production became stabilized, the need for imports would presumably decline. Much of this is surmise, but we have so far found no contrary evidence. Estate-supervised production of provisions never seems to have been undertaken without pressure from the island legislature and, as we have stressed, unsupervised cultivation by the slaves goes back to the early years of the occupation and may have been conjoined with the start of the estates. By the late eighteenth century what might have begun as a conveniently casual system of industrial feeding had become a tradition with which it would have been profitless and dangerous to interfere.

In these circumstances the emergence of local marketing arrangements is not surprising. The unsupervised production of food crops by the slaves provided the very basis of an open market system. Each slave cultivated as, and what, he wanted to cultivate. His primary concern, originally, might well have been his own household needs. But because his neighbors also had free choice of whether to plant, what to plant, and how much of it, the range of small transactions which might take place even among the slaves of a single estate was considerable. For instance, the volume of exchange would have been increased by the fact that some slaves would prefer to produce minor handicrafts, some to raise small livestock, some to grow food, and some to find profit by acting as intermediaries among these diverse interests. The Jamaican higgler, or middleman, also finds his prototype in the slave society (Lewis, 1861: 41). Under a straight system of estate-organized food production this variety of interests could never have emerged. It would have been choked off by the routine and the compulsory conformity of estate agriculture.

Exactly how the first slave producers came to market their surplus stock is not known; nor can we pin down with assurance the date of founding of the first market in Jamaica. The first legally established market place, however, was created in Spanish Town (Santiago de la Vega) in the year 1662, seven years after the English occupation, at the request of English settlers.

Whereas the settlement of our Island of Jamaica is much hindered or obstructed for want of a Faire or Markett for the sale and buying of Horses, Mares, Mules, Assinegoes, Cowes, Bulls and other Cattle and many other necessaries for the use of our subjects there and whereas our Towne of Snt. Jago de la Vega in our said Island is commodiously situated for the keeping of wuch a Faire or Markett therein . . . [we] by this our present Charter doe grant and confirm that . . . [the] inhabitants of our said Towne of Snt. Jago de la Vega for ever have a Faire or Markett in our said Towne . . . four times in every year . . . for the sale of horses, mares, mules, assinegoes, cows, bulls, and all or any other cattle and all or any other goods and commodities whatsoever of the groweth or produce of our said Island and all or any goods, wares and merchandizes whatsoever with all liberties . . . according to the usage and customs of our kingdome of England (Institute of Jamaica, 1895: 146).

The emphasis in this statement is upon the establishment of a market for livestock. Furthermore, this is a quarterly market only, and one may judge that its original intent was to serve the free population of Jamaica. Yet we learn that the need for a market place had been recognized and acted upon less than a decade after the occupation; it is also worth noting that the market here described was set up quite matter-of-factly according to English law. Though the slaves came to play a central role in Jamaican internal marketing, it is clear that this first legal market was English, not African, in conception and form.

Edward Long, describing events in the 1660s, tells of large numbers of small cultivators who produced food for the markets of Spanish Town (the capital) and of Port Royal, then a headquarters of the buccaneers where the great consumption of provisions of all sorts in that town, and for the outfit of so many privateers, created a very large demand for cattle, sheep, hogs, poultry, corn, and every other similar supply furnished by planters and settlers. . . . And it is owing to this cause that we find such a prodigious number of these little settlements grouped together in all the environs of St. Jago de la Vega [Spanish Town], and in the maritime parts not far from Port Royal harbour, which were then full of people, all subsisting well by their traffic with that town . . .

But, he continues, the suppression of the buccaneers and the founding of the sugar industry led to 'the declension of Port Royal, and the dissipation of the petty settlers, who from that period began to spread themselves more into the inland parts', while the establishment of large estates led to the buying out of many of these small settlers 'by the more opulent planters or merchants' (Long, 1774, 1: 282–3).

But as settlement and the sugar industry and trade increased, activity in the capital town and in the ports of the island would also have grown. New demands for food supplies would have arisen to be met, not by those early European small-scale farmers whom Long described, and mainly in whose interest this first market had been officially established, but by their successors in the business of food production. The great majority of these successors, we believe, were slaves working in their spare time on estate lands, and selling their produce in officially designated and other market places.

Since it was the individual slaves or slave households who produced provisions on the estate backlands, then clearly it would be they who would sell any surplus produce. Either individual slaves would go marketing, or else they would make voluntary agreements among themselves for marketing each other's produce. Certainly no sane estate manager would ever have conceived the idea of collecting and selling produce from separate slave provision grounds. The effort would have been pointless. If the estate kept all or even a share of the proceeds, voluntary food production by the slaves would be discouraged. In any case, the prevention of competitive transactions between slaves of the same estate, or even of adjacent estates would have been physically impossible for the limited and generally inefficient subordinate managerial staff.

Undoubtedly, the earliest transactions between slave producers were not conducted in markets. What seems probable is that the establishment of markets on the English model afforded a setting in which the slave producer could most readily buy and sell what he wished. The slave's part in market activity probably grew swiftly more important, but the details are nearly all obscure. Hickeringill (1661) and Blome (1672), two of the earliest observers, do not refer directly to markets, though Blome does state that *'provisions are very dear'* in Kingston at the time of his writing, and the reference seems to be to locally produced foodstuffs (Blome, 1672: 32). Cundall mentions a passing reference to a market for the year 1685, less than a quarter of a century after the first legally recognized market was established, in revealing terms: 'In May, the negroes at a usual Saturday market at Passage Fort having made some little disturbance, the market was suppressed by the Council' (Cundall, 1936: 99). That this market was 'usual', and that Negroes were in it, bears noting.

Leslie (1739) provides an abstract of laws in force, compiled mostly under the second government of Sir Thomas Lynch (1671–74), and these laws make plain that a number of markets were established, formalized, and maintained under government provision even in this early period. Laws regarding the weighing of meats, occasions of sale, market days, etc, were put into force in the seventeenth century (Leslie, 1739: 170–8).

Formal legal acknowledgment of the slaves' rights to market had been given, in negative form at least, as early as 1711: 'Hawking about and selling goods (except provisions, fruits, and other enumerated articles) to be punished, on conviction before a magistrate, by whipping, not exceeding *thirty-one lashes*' (Long, 1774, 2: 486–7). The exception is more important than the law, since it read: 'This restraint is construed to extend only to beef, veal, mutton and saltfish; and to manufactures, except baskets, ropes of bark, earthen pots and such like' (Long, 1774, 2: 486). In 1735, the law is stated in positive terms: 'Slaves may carry about, and sell, all manner of provisions, fruits, fresh fish, milk, poultry, and other small stock of all kinds, having a ticket from their owner or employer' (Long, 1774, 2: 492). It is interesting to compare the lists of goods which slaves were allowed to trade. The purpose of restriction was, of course, to prevent them from dealing in stolen goods. A slave with a carcass of beef was, prima facie, guilty of having slaughtered his owner's cattle. A slave offering metalware or saltfish, neither of which was produced in the island, was clearly suspect of having raided the estate stores. But clearly, between 1711 and 1735 there was some change.

In the first year, slaves are forbidden to sell 'beef, veal, mutton and saltfish', in 1735 they are permitted to trade 'fresh fish, milk, poultry, and other small stock of all kinds'. This suggests either a belated legal acknowledgment of the range of slave production or, more likely because the laws were generally permissive and not restrictive in this matter, a fairly rapid extension of productive activities by the slaves in response to a growing market for their produce. Accounts of the later eighteenth century and after almost invariably list pigs, goats, fish, poultry, eggs, and milk,[3] as sold by the slaves. It will be a matter for further discussion that later laws restricting the free movement of slaves always excepted their marketing operations.

The importance, in the third quarter of the eighteenth century, of slaves to the Jamaican domestic economy is revealed at length in the intelligent and thorough discussions provided by Long, one of the most careful and thoughtful writers of the eighteenth century. In 1774, by Long's estimate, of the £50,000 in currency circulating in the island at least £10,000, or 20 per cent, was in the hands of the slaves, most of it in the form of small coins. Money was scarce, and this scarcity adversely affected daily commerce and interfered with transactions. The island had serious need of small silver to

enable the housekeepers and Negroes to carry on their marketing for butchers meat, poultry, hogs, fish, corn, eggs, plantains and the like (Long, 1774, 2: 562).

. . . a small copper coin might be found extremely convenient here, as enabling the lower class of inhabitants not only to exchange their silver without a drawback, but likewise to keep down the prices of the small necessaries of life: which is a matter that has been thought of great importance to every trading community; and is especially of moment to this island, where the Negroes, who supply the market with small stock, and other necessaries, as well as the white families supplied from those markets, must be very much distressed, if they should ever be wholly deprived of a minor currency accommodated to their dealings with each other (Long, 1774, 2: 570).

Long describes a number of markets, but his description of Kingston market is particularly revealing:

At the bottom of the town, near the water side, is the market place, which is plentifully supplied with butchers meat, poultry, fish, fruits, and vegetables of all sorts. Here are found not only a great variety of American, but also of European, vegetables: such as pease, beans, cabbage, lettuce, cucumbers, French beans, artichokes, potatoes, carrots, turnips, radishes, celery, onions, etc. These are brought from the Liguanea mountains, and are all excellent in their kind. Here are likewise strawberries, not inferior to the production of our English gardens; grapes and melons in the utmost perfection; mulberries, figs, and apples, exceedingly good, but in general gathered before they are thoroughly ripe. In short, the most luxurious epicure cannot fail of meeting here with sufficient in quantity, variety, and excellence, for the gratification of his appetite the whole year round. The prices are but little different from those of Spanish Town: but, where they disagree, they are more reasonable at Kingston, the supplies being more regular, and the market superintended by the magistracy. The beef is chiefly from the pastures of Pedro's, in St. Ann; the mutton, from the salt-pan lands, in St. Catherine's: what they draw from the penns in St. Andrew's parish being very indifferent meat (Long, 1774, 2: 105).

Long did not criticize the virtual monopoly which the slaves had come to exercise in internal marketing; rather, he repeatedly suggested means to broaden and extend it. He objected to the pay system in country barracks of the Army, where the officers disbursed the pay. It would have been better, he argued, had the common soldiers received their pay directly:

with the money in their hands, the men might purchase much better in quality, and more in quantity, of fresh meat and wholesome victuals... every country-barrack would attract a market for the sale of hogs, poultry, fresh fish, fruits, and roots, which are articles produced and vended by almost all the Negroes (Long, 1774, 2: 303-4).

Indeed, by the time Long was writing, the slaves were not only central to the economy as the producers of the cash export commodities, principally sugar, but had also become the most important suppliers of foodstuffs and utilitarian craft items to all Jamaicans.

The customs of slave-based subsistence farming and marketing clearly provided the slaves with their best opportunities to accumulate liquid capital, as Hall (1954: 161-3) and others have demonstrated. Long, too, writes:

even among these slaves, as they are called, the black grandfather, or father, directs in what manner his money, his hogs, poultry, furniture, cloaths, and other effects and acquisitions, shall descend, or be disposed of, after his decease. He nominates a sort of trustees, or executors, from the nearest of kin, who distribute them among the legatees, according to the will of the testator, without any molestation or interruption, most often without the enquiry, of their master; though some of these Negroes have been known to possess from £50 to £200 at their death; and few among them, that are at all industrious and

frugal, lay up less than £20 or £30. For in this island they have the greatest part of the small silver circulating among them, which they gain by sale of their hogs, poultry, fish, corn, fruits, and other commodities, at the markets in town and country (Long, 1774, 2: 410-1).

Thus, one century after the first legal Jamaican market was created, the slaves had made a place for themselves in the free economic activity of the country which would never thereafter be challenged.

Our continuing emphasis upon the slaves' role in supplying and maintaining the internal markets, however, should not obscure another aspect of the economy as it was constituted under slavery. At the end of the eighteenth century, Jamaica's major exports, measured either in bulk or in value, were typical plantation products: cotton, coffee, ginger, and pimento to a lesser extent, and most important, sugar and rum. But other items also reached foreign markets, and quantities of these were derived from slave holdings; that is, they were produced on estate backlands by the slaves. Here may be mentioned gums, arrowroot, castor oil, turmeric, hides, supplejacks, oil nuts, cows' horns, goatskins, and wood products. These items were exported through a growing class of small merchants resident in towns and doing their business in conjunction with local markets. There is scarcely any descriptive information on these traders and their commercial relationships with slave producers; yet such relationships, well reported in the years after emancipation (Sewell, 1861: 219-20, 248-51), must have taken on their characteristic form under slavery. Large quantities of imported goods consumed by the slaves passed through the hands of local importers, the largest traffic being in clothes, household wares, and other items of comfort and convenience not provided by the estate owners.

By the start of the nineteenth century, reports by observers on slave production of provisions and acquisition of buying power had become quite matter of fact in character. Dallas, writing in 1803, reports:

Every proprietor is compelled by law, to cultivate in ground provisions (of course indestructible by hurricanes) one acre for every ten negroes; besides the allotment of negro territory. To cultivate this allotment, one day in every fortnight, belongs to the slaves, exclusive of Sundays and holidays. Thus they raise vegetables, poultry, pigs, or goats, which they consume, bestow, or sell. While some raise provisions, others fabricate coarse chairs, baskets, or common tables. These are bartered for salted meat, or pickled fish, utensils, or gaudy dresses; of which they are very fond. Their right of property in what they thus acquire, is never questioned; but seems completely established by custom (Dallas, 1803, 1: cviii).

It will be seen that certain customary arrangements had been secured, and these appear to have been observed by master and slave alike. The marketing arrangements, the increasing dependence of townsmen and free people on slave production, the customary system of slave inheritance, and the slave's attitudes concerning his property rights in the fruits of his labors, all must have grown up gradually and to some extent at least outside the law. They were maintained and accepted by the small group which wielded overwhelming power in the society because they were economically and socially convenient, even necessary, once they had taken shape.

By the time the nineteenth-century observers had begun to write of the markets and the slaves' role in them, the pattern had well over a century of traditional practice behind it. No really important new crops would be introduced after 1800, to enter into the slaves' cultivation, diet, or marketing; the slave code which guaranteed rights to market was long in force. After emancipation, many new markets would appear, and the scope of economic activity open to the freedmen would be much increased. But emancipation, insofar as marketing and cultivation practices were concerned, widened opportunities and increased alternatives; apparently it did not change their nature substantially.

Matthew Gregory ('Monk') Lewis, an estate owner, reported on his 1815-17 visit to his Jamaica estates:

In my evening's drive I met the negroes returning from the mountains, with baskets of provisions sufficient to last them for the week. By law they are only allowed every other Saturday for the purpose of cultivating their own grounds, which, indeed, is sufficient; but by giving them every alternate Saturday into the bargain, it enables them to perform their task with so much ease as almost converts it into an amusement; and the frequent visiting their grounds makes them grow habitually as much attached to them as they are to their houses and gardens. It is also advisable for them to bring home only a week's provisions at a time, rather than a fortnight's; for they are so thoughtless and improvident that, when they find themselves in possession of a larger supply than is requisite for their immediate occasions, they will sell half to the wandering higglers, or at Savannah la Mar, in exchange for spirits; and then, at the end of the

week, they find themselves entirely unprovided with food, and come to beg a supply from the master's storehouse (Lewis, 1861: 41).

Lewis's comments indicate that the slaves were inclined to make much of their provision grounds. Certainly they must have found it a relief to escape from the regimen of labor in the cane fields and to work on 'their own' cultivations. His observations of their attachments to these far-off fields are even shrewder than he knew. The assumption some observers had made that the slave, once free, would be unable to give up his residence at the center of the estate, because of his emotional attachment to his house and garden there, turned out to be very mistaken. The slaves must also have responded well to the feeling of autonomy which work on their provision grounds afforded. As the day of emancipation approached, other observers, particularly missionaries intent on establishing the slaves' capacity for freedom, tried to confirm this:

If the vices of the slave belong then to his condition, that condition should be changed before the nature of the negro is deemed incapable of elevation, or susceptible of improvement. That his defects are redeemed by no good qualities would be a bold assertion; that they are mingled with so many good ones as they are, is to me a matter of the greatest wonder.

To say that he is not industrious without reference to the object for which his exertions are employed would be an absurd remark; to say he is indolent, where his labour is exacted without reward, is to prove nothing.

But where the negro labours on his own ground, for his own advantage, — where his wife and children have the price of his own commodities to fetch him from the market-town, no matter how many miles they have to trudge, or how heavy the load they have to bear, — where the wages he received for his services are at his own disposal, — where his own time is duly paid for, not in shads and herrings, but in money a little more than equivalent to the advantages he deprives his own ground of, by transferring his extra time to the estate he is employed on — the negro is not the indolent slothful being he is everywhere considered, both at home and in the colonies (Madden, 1835, 1: 136-7).

In fact, the marketing system in which the slave had been long involved not only prepared him for freedom but, in the way in which he rose to make the fullest use of it, established his capacity to live as a freedman.

At the same time that the missionaries used all their means to work courageously for emancipation, they deplored the Sunday markets. Their pronouncements provide some useful (though rather mournful) information on the markets themselves. Bickell describes a market in Kingston on the day of his arrival in August, 1819:

It was on a Sunday, and I had to pass by the Negro Market, where several thousands of human beings, of various nations and colours, but principally Negroes, instead of worshipping their Maker on His Holy Day, were busily employed in all kinds of traffick in the open streets. Here were Jews with shops and standings as at a fair, selling old and new clothes, trinkets and small wares at cent. per cent. to adorn the Negro person; there were some low Frenchmen and Spaniards, and people of colour, in petty shops and with stalls; some selling their bad rum, gin, tobacco, etc.; others, salt provisions, and small articles of dress; and many of them bartering with the Slave or purchasing his surplus provisions to retail again; poor free people and servants also, from all parts of the city to purchase vegetables, etc., for the following week (Bickell, 1835: 66).

Concern that the slave did his marketing on Sunday was not restricted to the missionaries, however. The shopkeepers who kept the Sabbath were effectively cut off from sharing in the consumer market the slave represented. Long, in 1774, had sought to demonstrate that there was more to the profaning of the Sabbath than met the eye. He noted the comment of a contemporary:

It is certain that the sabbath-day, as at present it is passed, is by no means a respite from labour: on the contrary, the Negroes, either employing it on their grounds, or in travelling a great distance to some market, fatigue themselves much more on that day, than on any other in the week. The forenoon of that day, at least, might be given to religious duties; but I think it rather desirable than otherwise, that the after-part of it should be spent on their grounds, instead of being uselessly dissipated in idleness and lounging, or (what is worse) in riot, drunkenness, and wickedness. If such an alteration should take place, Thursday might be assigned for the market day, instead of the sabbath, and prove of great advantage to all Christian shop-keepers and retailers; the Jews now grossing the whole business of trafficking with the Negroes every Sunday, at which time there is a prodigious resort of them to the towns, and a vast sum expended for drams, necessaries, and manufactures. This alteration would therefor place the Christian dealers upon an equal footing, which they do not at present enjoy (Long, 1774, 2: 492).

'No Sunday markets' was probably the only issue in Jamaican history on which missionaries and proslavery writers were able to agree, though their reasons were wholly different.

The significance of this concern is the proof it offers that the marketing activities of the slaves were in fact very important to the Jamaican economy. The economy itself rested on the plantation system and slave labor; but the circumstances were such that the slaves could make a second valuable capital-building contribution through their individual efforts. And the same observers who debated whether the slaves were capable of learning even the fundamentals of Christian teaching were surely aware of their very human capacity for creating and employing wealth by cultivation and commerce. Had it not been for the slaves' skills as producers and distributors and their needs as consumers, there could scarcely have appeared in the Jamaican economy a numerous class of middlemen, import and export dealers, retailers, etc. The importance of slave marketing was legally recognized in the laws which regulated the behavior of the slave population. Renny cites a law in 1807 which is revelatory of this:

And whereas it is absolutely necessary, that the slaves in this island should be kept in due obedience to their owners, and in due subordination to the white people in general, and, as much as in the power of the legislature, all means and opportunities of slaves committing rebellious conspiracies, and other crimes, to the ruin and destruction of the white people, and others in this island, prevented, and that proper punishments should be appointed for all crimes to be by them committed; be it further enacted by the authority aforesaid, that no slave, *such only excepted as are going with firewood, grass, fruit, provisions, or small stock and other goods, which they may lawfully sell, to market, and returning therefrom,* shall here after be suffered or permitted to go out of his or her master or owner's plantation or settlement, or to travel from one town or place to another, unless such slave shall have a ticket from his master, owner, employer, or overseer.... (Renny, 1807: 255 [italics ours])

For the marketing practices of the slaves, even the sharpest vigilance was relaxed, and the exceptions cry for explanation. It would be hard to explain this wholly and with certainty. But it may be fair to contend that the growth of town populations and the demand for the products of the slaves' spare time labor encouraged the participation of slaves as sellers and suppliers; that the growth of the market and the emergence of new demands enlarged the quantity and the variety of items which reached the markets; that the activity of the markets increased the slaves' buying power, and led in turn to increases in the numbers of local merchants, retailers, moneylenders, etc, who became dependent on the slaves' surpluses and buying needs for their share of profits from the economy; that the free people in the towns gradually grew reliant upon the slaves' marketing activities for their daily needs; and that long before emancipation came, the markets and all of the related institutions which maintained them had become core features of Jamaican society and economy. Such seems to have been the situation in Jamaica in 1834, when slavery ended and the 'apprenticeship system' began.

In most of the British West Indian colonies an attempt was made to bridge the gap between slavery and freedom by the intervention of a number of years of 'apprenticeship' during which masters and slaves were to condition themselves for the new order of a free society. But the 'apprenticeship system' asked too much of mere mortals. It allowed the masters the labor of their slaves for a stated number of hours per week. Beyond this limit the slaves (or 'apprentices') had the right either to refuse to work for their masters or to demand wages for what they did. The apprenticeship system failed to serve its purposes, however, and was curtailed. It was too much to ask that a man should be a slave on weekdays and a wage earner over the weekend. The Monday morning master found the Friday evening transition to wage-labor employer beyond his power. The apprenticeship system ended at midnight, July 31, 1838, exactly four years after it had begun, and the expected disagreements between ex-masters and ex-slaves set in.

The great variety of those disagreements need not detain us. They have been fully described elsewhere (Burn, 1937; Hall, 1953) and our present concern is with only one of the sources of discontent. Estate slaves had been housed in huts or tenements provided by their owners, and they had been allowed to cultivate estate backlands. Now, as free wage workers, they were asked to pay rents for huts and land, and ex-masters and ex-slaves faced each other as landlord employers and tenant employees.

This situation was full of potential misunderstanding and reprisal. Under slavery the Jamaican planters had made much of the freedom which they allowed the slaves in their cultivation of the backlands.

I do not believe that an instance can be produced of a master's indifference with his Negroes in their *peculium* thus acquired. They are permitted also to dispose at their deaths of what little property they possess; and even to bequeath their grounds or gardens to such of their fellow-slaves as they think proper. These principles are so well established, that whenever it is found convenient for the owner to exchange the negro-grounds for other lands, the Negroes must be satisfied, in money or otherwise, before the exchange takes place. It is universally the practice (Edwards, 1793, 2: 133).

There, precisely stated, are three points of immediate and important relevance to the post-emancipation squabbles over rents and wages. The first is that slaves were allowed to acquire and bequeath property of various kinds; the second, that they were even allowed to bequeath their provision grounds, or gardens; and the third, that planters so fully recognized the slaves' rights to these grounds that they offered compensation wherever it became necessary to convert an area of slave cultivation to estate purposes.

There is no need to discuss further the reasons why the slaves were allowed to keep the money and goods they received in their marketing transactions, and as they were allowed to keep them it was thus logical to allow bequests. The alternative would have been an unworkable estate tax system of 100 per cent death duties on the 'property' of deceased slaves. It would have been impossible without the full cooperation of the slaves themselves to assess the property of any individual slave in the crowded living conditions of the slave quarters and in the circumstances of a lifetime of unaccounted small purchases and transactions.

The fact that planters usually compensated slaves who were made to give up provision grounds to estate uses is reasonable enough. If the slaves were to provide most of their own food they would clearly have to have the necessary resources at their disposal. If they were to be deprived of certain plots of provision grounds they would have to be given other grounds with yielding crops, or a supply of food, or else money with which to fulfill their needs until other land was allowed them and they could collect their first harvest. From the planter's point of view this would be an obvious need unless he were disposed to see his slaves starve.

It is the fact that slaves were allowed to bequeath provision grounds which is least clearly explicable. At first glance this would seem to imply that for each estate a time would come when, all of the backlands having been appropriated, there would be no marginal areas left free for cultivation by newly arrived slaves. Yet this could never happen, in part because of the high rate of slave mortality, more so because of the way in which newly imported slaves were absorbed into the estate organization.

The practice is that of distributing the newly-imported Africans among the old Negroes, as pensioners (with some little assistance occasionally given), on their little *peculium*, and provision-grounds (Edwards, 1793, 2: 126).

Thus, new arrivals were simply taken into the existing pattern of provision ground production, and slave importation did not necessitate the setting aside of more land for spare-time cultivation.

The system appears to have been favored by all concerned. From our point of view, it is of interest because it was the course of action least likely to encourage continued introduction of West African methods into Jamaican slave estate agriculture. Admittedly, the newly arrived slaves would, by their language and behavior, revive memories of Africa among a few of the longer enslaved, but in their new households they were the newcomers, the trainees, and the minority voice. As Edwards points out, the new slaves were in fact pleased with the arrangement,

and afterwards considered themselves as the adopted children of those by whom they were thus protected, calling them parents, and venerating them as such; and I never knew an instance of the violation of a trust thus solicited and bestowed. In the course of eight or ten months, provided they are mildly used and kept free of disease, new people, under these circumstances, begin to get well established in their families, their houses and provision-grounds; and prove in all respects as valuable as the native or Creole negroes (Edwards, 1793, 2: 127).

The new slaves thus became operators on the household's provision grounds, and later, perhaps, as heads of the households in a succeeding generation, inherited the right of use of the land. And this is where the emphasis must be placed, for as Edwards himself showed, no slaves held provision grounds by legal right of property in land (1793, 2: 147). The land belonged to the estate owner. The use of it was allowed to the slaves. What slaves were permitted to bequeath was certainly not a plot of land, but rather the right to continue to cultivate a certain piece of land for as long as the owner or estate manager permitted that land to be cultivated in provisions. The slaves, never disillusioned in the matter, may well have considered a certain piece of land as their

'property'; the master, under no illusions, recognized the arrangement for what it was, namely, a free letting of land in return for which he hoped to have a well-fed and contented slave labor force. After emancipation, of course, employers were no longer directly concerned with the condition of their workers' minds and stomachs, the *peculium* was quickly forgotten, and money rents were imposed.

The emancipation was the most important event in Jamaican history after the English conquest of the island. The Jamaican freedman of 1838 had to work out his style of life anew. The material needs of daily living would be met by personal effort and because of personal motivation; the hated compulsion of the planter was no longer a spur to effort and the freedman easily learned to live without it.

The freedman's most important means for establishing his independence was by repudiating his previous status as an estate laborer and becoming a peasant, that is, an agriculturist who produced the bulk of his own food needs and a surplus for sale, wholly or mainly on his own land. The inspiring transformation of the Jamaican people into a free and independent peasantry has been written about many times in the large; but the immediate concern is with the freedman's preparation for this transformation. Aside from the basic question of funds for the acquisition of land and housing, the freedman needed to have skills and knowledge which would enable him to live independently. In this he had been prepared for independence by certain conditions of slavery, notably the initial insistence or concession that he provide his own food (Mintz, 1955, 1958). At the same time it must be made clear that the newly enslaved Africans carried to Jamaica and absorbed into the estate system and the slave household did not have to learn everything anew. Some of native America's most important foods, such as maize and cassava, were carried to West Africa as early as the sixteenth century and were adopted there with incredible rapidity and success. Later, food-bearing plants had been brought from West Africa to the West Indies. In certain major crops, therefore, and perhaps in the technology and equipment of cultivation, there was much that was already familiar.

Nevertheless, we have largely avoided dealing with the important question of Africanisms, either in agriculture or in marketing. In the case of Jamaican agriculture, the available historical data have not yet been totally and thoroughly analyzed, while sufficient data simply are not available to assess the degree to which Jamaican marketing could have been derived directly from West African practices. Such common West African features as separate royal and commoner markets, royal monopolies in certain products, and price fixing by the court (Herskovits, 1938) were of course absent and could not have been expected to occur. The first formal Jamaican market was a wholly English innovation, and there is no need to look to Africa in this connection. It is true that women carry on most marketing activity in Jamaica today, as they do, and did, in large part in much of West Africa. But even this likeness may be a parallel rather than a historical derivation. Until specific historical documentation for such a derivation can be amassed, to claim this division of labor to be an Africanism is no more than an unproved assertion.

Slavery meant forced removal from familiar landscapes, institutions, and, often, kinsfolk. It meant sudden introduction into an estate system with a social order and an economic objective quite foreign to the newly arrived slave (Hall, 1954: 153–4). And because among each shipload of new arrivals the men usually far outnumbered the women, slavery demanded a total reconsideration of the place and functions of men and women in society, beginning with fundamental questions about new mating patterns.

In Jamaica, life was as the master ordered it; the master was European, or oriented toward Europe (Curtin, 1955: 42 ff.), with his eyes on overseas markets, prices, laws, and fashions. What we have seen already of the rise of slave-based food production and activity in the markets should make it abundantly clear that what may have survived from Africa was what the master ignored, or permitted to survive. Yet admittedly, the African content of this aspect of slave culture remains unassessed. Its weighing will not depend on a search for likenesses, but on precise and detailed historical research.

We do not attempt here to carry the description of Jamaican markets and marketing further forward in time than those first years following the emancipation. Nor can our findings be claimed to do more than state some of the fundamental features of the market system in the early period of Jamaica's history as a British possession. We think it established that both the peasant economy and its marketing pattern originated within the slave population. We feel the role of European culture and culture history may have been slighted in the past tendency to attribute so many features of Jamaican peasant culture to the African culture stream. Adequate study, both historical and ethnographic, of the Jamaican peasantry, is only now beginning. As Ansell Hart has said:

Plantation economy, absentee proprietorship and the overlordship of Britain combined to produce Jamaican traits of delegation, dependence, and 'tek a chance', above which however, tower the Jamaican's humor, sentiment, physique, capacity for hard work and generosity. There are of course many strands to the story of the undesirable traits which emerges from the plantation economy: neglect, economic insufficiency, malnutrition, disease, etc. Subsistence economy on the other hand developed into the main source of supply of staple food; and besides giving the slave a 'bellyful', produced directly by himself for himself, also gave him access to the Sunday market, a money economy, important social contacts in field and market and some degree of self-reliance and independence. The cultural and economic effect of what began as subsistence production was immense (Hart, 1955: 1).

Bibliography

Beckford, William, *A Descriptive Account of the ISLAND OF JAMAICA*, 2 vols. (London, 1790).

Bickell, Reverend R., *The West Indies as They Are* (London, 1835).

Blome, Richard, *Description of Jamaica* (London, 1672).

Burn, W. L., *Emancipation and Apprenticeship in the British West Indies* (London, 1937).

Coleridge, H. N., *Six Months in the West Indies in 1825* (London, 1826).

Cumper, George, *The Social Structure of Jamaica* (Mona, Jamaica, n.d.).

Cundall, Frank, *The Governors of Jamaica in the Seventeenth Century* (London, 1936).

Cundall, Frank, and Pietersz, J., *Jamaica under the Spaniards* (Kingston, Jamaica, 1919).

Curtin, Philip, *Two Jamaicas* (Cambridge, Mass., 1955).

Dallas, R. C., *The History of the Maroons*, 2 vols. (London, 1803).

Edwards, Bryan, *The History, Civil and Commercial, of the British Colonies in the West Indies*, 2 vols. (London, 1793).

Goveia, Elsa, 1959, Comment in 'Labour and Sugar in Puerto Rico and Jamaica', *Comparative Studies in Society and History*, Vol. 1, No. 3 (1959), pp. 281–83.

Hall, Douglas, The Apprenticeship Period in Jamaica, 1834–1838, *Caribbean Quarterly*, Vol. 3, No. 3 (1953), pp. 142–66.

Hall, Douglas, 'The Social and Economic Background to Sugar in Slave Days', *Caribbean Historical Review*, Nos. 3–4 (1954), pp. 149–69.

Hall, Douglas, *Free Jamaica* (New Haven, 1959).

Hart, Ansell, 'Causeries', *Monthly Comments*, Vol. 1, No. 15 (1955), p. 1.

Herskovits, M. J., *Dahomey*, 2 vols. (New York, 1938).

Hickeringill, Edmund, *Jamaica Viewed* (London, 1661).

Institute of Jamaica, 'Notes and Queries: Early Fairs in Jamaica', *Journal of the Institute of Jamaica*, Vol. 2, No. 2 (1895), p. 146.

Leslie, Charles, *A New and Exact Account of Jamaica* (Edinburgh, 1739).

Lewis, M. G., *Journal of a Residence Among the Negroes in the West Indies* (London, 1861).

Long, Edward, *The History of Jamaica*, 3 vols. (London, 1774).

Madden, R. R., *A Twelvemonth's Residence in the West Indies*, 2 vols. (London, 1835).

Mintz, Sidney W., 'The Role of Forced Labour in Nineteenth Century Puerto Rico', *Caribbean Historical Review*, No. 2 (1951), pp. 134–41.

Mintz, Sidney W., 'The Jamaican Internal Marketing Pattern', *Social and Economic Studies*, Vol. 4, No. 1 (1955), pp. 95–103.

Mintz, Sidney W., 'Historical Sociology of the Jamaican Church-Founded Free Village System', *De West-Indische Gids*, Vol. 38, Nos. 1–2 (1958), pp. 46–70.

Mintz, Sidney W., 'Labor and Sugar in Puerto Rico and Jamaica, 1800–1850', *Comparative Studies in Society and History*, Vol. 1, No. 3 (1959), pp. 273–83.

Pares, Richard, *A West India Fortune* (London, 1950).

Parry, John H., 'Salt Fish and Ackee', *Caribbean Quarterly*, Vol. 2, No. 4 (n.d.), pp. 29–35.

Parry, John H., 'Plantation and Provision Ground', *Revista de Historia*, No. 39 (1955), pp. 1–20.

Public Record Office, Letter from Magistrate Harris to the Governor, 27 July, 1856, *Colonial Office Documents*, No. 137/216, 'Jamaica Apprentices', Pt 3 (London, 1836).

Ragatz, L. J., *Statistics for the Study of British Caribbean Economic History, 1763–1833* (London, 1927).

Renny, Robert, *An History of Jamaica* (London, 1807).

Sauer, Carl O., Cultivated Plants of South and Central America, in *Handbook of South American Indians*, edited by Julian Steward, *Bulletin*, Bureau of American Ethnology, Vol. 6, No. 143 (1950), pp. 487–543.

Sauer, Carl O., 'Economic Prospects of the Caribbean', in *The Caribbean: Its Economy*, edited by A. C. Wilgus (Gainesville, Florida, 1954), pp. 15–27.

Sewell, William G., *The Ordeal of Free Labour in the British West Indies* (New York, 1861).

Sloane, Sir Hans, *A Description of a Voyage to the Islands of Madera, Barbados, Etc. . . .*, Vol. 1 (London, 1707).

Smith, M. G., 'Some Aspects of Social Structure in the British Caribbean About 1820', *Social and Economic Studies*, Vol. 1, No. 4 (1953), pp. 55–80.

Stewart, J., *A View of the Past and Present State of the Island of Jamaica* (Edinburgh, 1823).

Young, Sir William, *A Tour Through the Several Islands of Barbados, St. Vincent, Antigua, Tobago and Grenada, in the Years 1791 and 1792* (London, 1801).

Notes

1. Mr H. P. Jacobs has suggested a connection between the words 'polink' and 'palenque', the latter being a place where the Negro hunters of Spanish times lived and cultivated foodstuffs. In Cuba, the term 'palenque' was used to refer to a palisaded village established by runaway slaves.

2. It would be of interest to test this opinion by comparing data on slave desertions, riots, and other indices of disaffection in, for example, Antigua and St. Vincent. But such a comparison would have to take into account the disincentives to desertion, etc, in flat, fully occupied, and small islands, and the greater chances for success in the larger, mountainous, and less fully occupied islands.

3. It may have been goats' milk or perhaps cows' milk bought by the slaves from the estate owners for retail trading. Yet the cattle may have been owned by the slaves themselves. In his journal entry for March 2, 1816, Lewis (1861: 102–3) writes that he purchased from his slaves at 15 pounds per head, cattle which they owned and used to graze on the estate's pastures.

57

Chattel Slaves into Wage Slaves:
A Jamaican Case Study

MARY TURNER

Slaves were distinguished from other categories of labour by being persons whose labour was denied exchange value. They faced as workers, however, fundamentally the same problems as serfs, or wage workers; they were forced to spend their lives expending labour over and above what was necessary for their own subsistence. Improvement in work conditions for all categories of workers meant improving rewards for labour extracted and cutting down on the coercive power(s) of the owners of the means of production. The question arises, therefore, whether these fundamental similarities in the nature of exploitation and in the goals of the exploited indicate some similarities in their methods of struggle?[1]

The structure of slave based sugar production in the British Caribbean suggests this possibility. The plantations were set up as specialized, export oriented, agro-manufacturing units of 200-600 workers, supervised by a skeleton staff of owners and their waged employees as an integral part of an economy characterized by wage labour. These specialized export crop production units developed as part and parcel of a commercial economy with internal and external market connections in which the slaves themselves were gradually integrated through the development of their provision grounds. These plots, allocated for subsistence to cut production costs, generated surpluses necessary to the development of the colonial economy and provided the body of slaves, as petty producers, with cash rewards.

Skilled slaves, hired out for payment as the towns grew, became proxy wage earners. Supplying labour in response to direct physical coercion in societies characterized by wage labour and from workers involved in the cash economy, dictated struggles over the degree of coercion and the quantities of reward.

This chapter investigates, in relation to Jamaican sugar estate workers, the dynamics generated by this contradiction. It is based on estate papers for the parish of St Thomas in the East, one of the most important sugar producing parishes in Jamaica with a slave population, in 1832, of 23, 000.[2] It shows that the forms of class struggle which characterized contract and wage sugar estate workers, such as group and collective verbal protests as well as appeals for mediation backed up by strike action, were adopted by slaves and contributed to undermining the slave labour based economy.

Early Labour Protest and Strikes

The fundamental impetus which generated collective organization among the slaves, these records suggest, was the struggle for survival. The provision ground system, usually regarded as in itself a mitigation of the slaves' work conditions, represented simply an alternative use of the slaves' labour by the owner who dictated that the slaves subsist the labour power they used. In the early stages of estate development this system subjected the slaves to additional problems. Blue

Mountain estate, for example, was developed for sugar in the latter half of the eighteenth century in a fertile interior valley by an influx of predominantly male Africans who increased the estate labour force from 170 to 350.[3] The demands for estate work were such that only some of the more privileged and longest settled slaves were able to establish provision grounds.

This situation surfaced in 1787 after Jamaica had been pounded by successive hurricanes and was suffering the effects of new trade restrictions with the United States. Consequent food shortages dictated that, in the Jamaica Assembly's own estimate, 15,000 slaves died.[4] Conditions at Blue Mountain contributed to this death toll. The 1786 hurricane destroyed the slaves' plantain walks; emergency supplies of potatoes and black-eye peas brought in from Kingston proved inadequate. As a result, the great gang could not carry out its routine. Cane holing, which was particularly strenuous work on the heavy soil of a valley bottom, was curtailed because the workers were beginning to 'drop off fast'.[5]

In these circumstances the planting attorney, William Sutherland, in charge of the estate between 1780-1804, discovered that the 'better sort' of slaves had established grounds and were using the 'poorer sort' to work them in return for a share of the produce. The system broke down when provisions were scarce and the 'poorer sort' required subsistence from the estate.[6] Sutherland's terminology clearly suggests that the 'better sort' were skilled and confidential slaves and the policy he pursued confirms this. He did not challenge the system directly. The fight for subsistence had created a slave village interest bloc which could not be simply disciplined out of existence. He proposed, rather, to provide the 'poorer sort' with the means to develop their grounds by supplying all their food for a year.[7]

No such arrangement was made. Substantial losses to the work force threatened if the provision ground problem was not resolved, but despite Sutherland's pleas that the 'odd slice' of salt pork saved lives, the owner refused to undertake the expense involved. When the same subsistence problem surfaced a decade later during a prolonged drought, Sutherland strongly recommended more drastic action, recruiting 'a small gang of about 15 or 16 Negroes . . . for the sole purpose of raising provisions'; in other words, workers should be withdrawn from sugar pro-

duction to specialize in food production. Again, nothing was done; the workers were left to subsist themselves as best they could.[8]

The slave village interest bloc underpinned efforts to exert some control over work conditions and, in particular, to protest unjust and excessive use of coercion by overseers. Blue Mountain attorneys tried to minimize this problem by stocking the estate with new Africans; Jamaican born workers with 'bad habits' and 'connections outside the state', that is those familiar with local labour conditions and protest patterns, as well as experienced American slaves on sale after the revolution, were excluded.[9] Their method calls into question the rebellious qualities commonly attributed to 'wild Africans', but is, of course, consistent with industrial employers' preference for unorganized immigrant labour.

Despite these precautions Blue Mountain slaves effected the removal of two overseers between 1795 and 1800. In one case the action they took is not specified; in the paternalist language attorneys used, the overseer, William Grant, was described as having lost their (the slaves') affections. He had a 'peevish temper' and 'teasing methods' and his successor was recommended as a man of 'mild disposition'[10] In this instance the slaves timed their protest well. The planters' fight against the Maroons, itself partly inspired by revolutionary infection spreading from Haiti at the instigation of French agents, was in progress. Martial law, which drew overseers and bookkeepers away from the plantations was still in force and, when Grant was dismissed, had been extended for another month.[11] It was a moment which put a premium on management maintaining the 'affections' of the work-force.

In the second instance, the attorney masked the slaves' success by delaying the overseer's departure until the crop was over so that his removal appeared to be part of the turnover customary for white estate personnel.[12] The overseer, his reputation as a good planter (i.e. maximum sugar producer) at risk in an excessively rainy crop season, extracted labour 'by harsh . . . bordering on cruel treatment of the Negroes, particularly the Pregnant Women'.[13] The pregnant women, despite the fact that they had most to lose by physical punishment, resisted work demands beyond their capabilities and won enough support among their fellows to make the overseer's position untenable.

The earliest and most developed form of labour protest in these records, however, took place at Grange Hill estate in 1770 during the attorneyship of Malcolm Laing (1759-78) who first developed Blue Mountain estate for sugar. The Grange Hill slaves' struggle was facilitated by two circum stances: the land was only marginally suitable for sugar so its anticipated profit margins were lower than at Blue Mountain and, more significantly, the estate slaves were intertwined with the wage work economy of Manchioneal, a port and market town where the demand for skilled workers and the ready sale of ground provisions demonstrated the cash value of labour.[14]

By 1770 the slaves, some 200 strong, had secured terms of service distinctly in advance of existing slave code provisions: they had Thursdays as well as Sundays to work their provision grounds[15] and estate artisans enjoyed material benefits which reflected their value as wage earners: benefits intended, presumably, to curb any ambition for free status. Carpenter Joe, for example, lived in Kingston at Laing's house for three months every year, perhaps at his own insistence,[16] either to be hired out or to earn something for himself. His services on the estate earned the same rations of meat, salt fish and rum as the white managers had.

An artisan, once valued at a rate comparable to white wage earners, naturally appealed in the event of dispute with them, to the land owner's representative and, since an artisan was less replaceable than an overseer or a bookkeeper, such an appeal was likely to succeed. The Grange Hill records exemplify this process. Joe, in a dispute with the overseer, instantly appealed to the attorney who 'gave credit to the Carpenter' and sacked the overseer. The success of this grievance procedure naturally afforded 'a great triumph' and set a useful precedent to the whole work-force.[17]

In February 1770 a new overseer, David Munro, an ex-soldier with a military man's view of slave labour, took charge. He considered 'the same Discipline and Subordination . . . proper to slaves, as is practised in the Army and Navy, and without which they can't be kept to their Duty . . . It is a well known Maxim that a relaxation of Discipline, has the same effect on Slaves which it has on Soldiers: inclining them to Dissolute Indulgence and Loose passions'.[18]

The slaves' response to Munro's methods was to strike; early in September they took to the woods and sent four delegates 60 miles to Laing in Kingston to state their case. What ill-usage sparked the strike does not emerge; Laing had a clearly articulated policy of listening to both sides of 'Negro Stories' and his reaction to the crisis suggests that it was not, in his experience, altogether unusual. He told the slaves to return to work, told the overseer to withhold any punishments and promised to investigate affairs in two weeks' time when he had attended to business in Clarendon parish. In the upshot Munro, the military style disciplinarian, was sacked.[19]

The Struggle for Informal Contract Terms

In all these cases management, by judiciously responding to an immediate grievance, conceded very little and won a great deal. Laing, for example, by placating the work-force before crop commenced in December, secured his income and reputation, and prevented another flight to the woods which risked the permanent loss of some slaves, the disruption of neighbouring estates and the threat of small-scale rebellion. At the same time, the attorney impressed on propertyless whites respect for property in slaves. This class conflict was reflected also in the island courts; Laing himself took a white mason who shot one of the slaves in his charge to court 'as if the Man had perpetrated Murder'. Laing lost the case and the accused was awarded; £5 for shooting a rebellious negro. As Grange Hill attorney, however, Laing had no intention of allowing Munro liberties with live investments and was perfectly prepared to give what the overseer termed 'glaring encouragement' to the slaves' 'contempt of Authority and of the White Colour'.[20]

Slave protests against the overseer's use of his coercive powers neatly exploited this class division and contributed to the turnover rate of white estate personnel. More significantly, this bargaining process secured the slaves material advantages which constituted informal contract terms, always disputed, but always likely to be reconfirmed and possibly improved upon. The bargaining process contributed, as Munro observed, to developing their political consciousness.

Island-wide developments fed and watered this consciousness in the early decades of the nineteenth century. The abolition of the slave trade in 1807 did not effect the transformation of the slave labour system the abolitionists hoped for, but it cut off the plantation owners' capacity to increase their effective labour force (i.e. workers aged 18-49) at will. The fixed labour force, with its own internally determined age structure, dwindled in numbers with the highest rates of loss on the sugar estates where the proportion of effective workers was reduced to some 40 per cent of the population by 1832.[21]

These circumstances generated new areas of struggle for the slave work-force and contributed to important new gains. In the first place, efforts to rationalize the available labour power removed workers wholesale from marginal to more profitable properties.[22] This robbed the workers of property (houses and grounds) and of the burial plots which contained their history. Removals prompted widespread resistance and induced some careful managers to offer compensation - houses and grounds already prepared at the new location - but conflict and coercion were always anticipated.[23] Thousands of slaves were removed; some however, as one of the cases discussed below indicates, secured *de facto* occupation of their estate.

The overall labour shortage, however, in some ways improved the slaves' bargaining position. Coloured slaves claimed by custom a right to differentiated functions as skilled and domestic as opposed to field workers; estates short of blacks for field work advertised coloured slaves for exchange.[24] More significantly, a substantial proportion of slaves secured, like the Grange Hill workers, more time for the provision grounds. Their success was reflected in the 1816 Slave Code in which planters officially designated 26 days a year in addition to Sundays for provision ground cultivation. The slaves made it clear that they regarded the grounds and the time to work on them as a form of wages for their work on the estate. 'The slave thinks he has a right to those grounds on account of his labour on the property to which he belongs', one observer commented; at the same time, work on the grounds secured the slaves' foothold in the island's commercial economy and strengthened their bargaining position on the estate.[25]

The slaves' capacity to connect themselves to the island's commercial economy and to contribute to the export trade exacerbated the tension between coerced labour and 'waged' labour. Consciousness was raised, struggles with management intensified and, as a result, slave workers were able to establish customary norms for estate work and respect for their expertise. As Robert Scott, proprietor and attorney (1802-26) for 4,000 slaves in the important sugar producing parish of Trelawny commented:

They are excessively impatient of control, if you exact more from them than you ought to do, *they will not submit to it*, but they know very well what duty [i.e. informal contract obligation] they have to do on a plantation and if no more is exacted, they are very easily managed and require no harsh treatment whatever.[26] (emphasis and brackets added)

Labour bargaining and re-negotiation of informal contract terms consequently took place whenever new overseers took charge. Overseers expected to 'encounter opposition' rather than, as in the cases reviewed, stir it up, and claimed that the whip was an essential weapon in their initial struggle to determine terms of work, including work loads.[27]

The establishment of work norms opened the way to demands for task work, sharpening the division between masters' time and slaves' time and led to forms of outright wage bargaining. The slaves pressed for time, food or cash payments for work over and above the production routine, such as the repair or extension of the existing infrastructure, roads, buildings, fences, bridges and ditches.

Task work characterized coffee and pimento production in Jamaica just as it characterized lowland rice cultivation in central South Carolina because, as Philip Morgan argues, this was the most efficient form of labour organization.[28] Investigation may prove, however, that the task work system reflected worker demands as much as staple crop 'requirements'. Certainly, no later than the 1820s slaves were pressing for task work in sugar production, traditionally characterized by gang labour and team work. The method seems to have been limited to cane holing, but it was suitable for both planting and cutting as continental experience in low country rice production demonstrated.[29] From management's point of view, task work, while recognizing work norms, also promoted productivity and reduced jobbing costs; the danger for the slaves, as some slave foremen realized, was that established work norms would be undercut.[30] Task work opened the way, however, to the demand for wages.

The slaves were always ready, as one observer put it, to work for pay. The slaves paid each other wages; Sunday work on the provision grounds, for example, could earn 1s. 8d per day plus breakfast. Sunday work on an attorney's garden might earn 2s. 11d plus breakfast; and cash payments were incorporated into task work deals. The planters faced the uncomfortable realization, articulated to the 1832 Commons Committee on Slavery, that they simply could not afford to pay both wages and maintenance.[31] From their foothold in the island's commercial economy, the slaves attacked directly the form of exploitation to which they were subjected.

The political implications of the struggle to secure free time and cash rewards for estate work were clearly spelt out for the slaves by the free coloured and black population which more than quadrupled (10,000-46,000) between 1800 and 1834. Freedmen, traditionally urban based, jostling with the slaves at market, now appeared in little colonies adjacent to some plantations, on land rented from ruinate estates. They worked as small producers and traders, and, in some cases, established family connections with estate slaves.[32] They translated into material terms the slaves' vision of the future implicit in the provision grounds, and their campaign for full civil rights which succeeded in 1830, extended that vision to embrace citizen status, a hope also fostered by the Protestant missionaries and the abolition campaigners.

The planter class rallied to hold back the creeping tide of economic and political pressure undermining their economy by improving management techniques. *The Jamaica Planter's Guide* (1823), for example, explicitly advocated security of tenure for occupations usually dominated by coloured slaves (artisans and domestics) and dismissal of overseers who wantonly interfered with the authority of drivers and head men; it celebrated the expertise of sugar boilers and their crucial role in production and specified, as great gang requirements, good tools, rum rations in wet weather and shelter from persistent rain.[33]

The Challenge to White Authority

The impact of these general circumstances and the limitations of management techniques are well illustrated by developments at Grange Hill and Blue Mountain which were in the hands (1825-9) of a reforming attorney, Charles Lewsey, imported by the absentee owner from Barbados to make his Jamaican properties pay. Lewsey's correspondence, suffused with awareness of labour problems, contrasts sharply with that of Laing and Sutherland and suggests one measure, though refracted through Barbadian experience, of the shift in the balance of power between workers and owners since the end of the slave trade. The estate workers indicate the new spectrum of these relations: one work-force bargaining within the parameters set by demands for sugar production while the other challenged those parameters.

The slave population at Blue Mountain in 1825 was just 176 – about the size it was before sugar production developed, a reduction Lewsey unhesitatingly attributed to malnutrition and mismanagement after studying the estate records.[34] Cultivation was carried on with the assistance of jobbing gangs. The use of jobbers could mean that estate slaves had successfully transferred part of the work load to hired gangs; at Blue Mountain it was symptomatic, rather, of estate slaves working, in industrial terms 'at stretch', in planter terminology, being subjected to 'the pushing system'. The 'pushing system' served merchant rather than planter interests by pushing for maximum profit crop by crop, at the expense of the owners' reputedly long-term profit interest.[35]

The slaves, nevertheless, had consolidated their village life and had their own social centre, a religious meeting-house with a regular priest, an elderly African, in charge. The priest is not characterized as an obeah man, perhaps because Lewsey did not wish to risk the effects of taking legal action against him, but may have been one of the syncretic sect leaders engendered by the Black Baptists (active since the 1780s) and the missions established in St Thomas in 1802. Whatever the case, the slaves made it clear to Lewsey that their religion was their own affair by resisting his efforts to make them good Anglicans; very few consented to be baptised even at the ceremony held for Lewsey's own infant daughter.[36]

On the estate, apparently under the leadership of Becky, the head driver, the slaves used a variety of methods to limit white authority and to assert their own expertise. They threatened strike action in response to manifestly unjust as well as cruel punishment. Conscious that the take-over period was a testing time for managers and workers Lewsey, in good Barbadian fashion, set out to establish that he ran a tight ship; in pursuit of economy and efficiency he systematically attacked infringements of estate property rights and consequently curtailed traditional slave property rights. One such move sparked instant collective protest: he ordered the slaughter, without warning, of hogs found straying in the cane. Outraged property owners surrounded Lewsey, long discussions ensued, and though the slaves finally (in Lewsey's account) admitted they were wrong to let the hogs stray, the attorney was left in no doubt as to the injustice of his action. [37]

The slaves had their revenge; the head driver, Becky, made a mockery of Lewsey's efficiency campaign by demonstrating the incompetence of his assistant, overseer Parkinson, a trainee planter also from Barbados. Ordered to close up a drain trench that needed to be open, Becky defied the order. Parkinson compounded his error and called the second driver to take Becky to the stocks. Lewsey, who met the punishment detail on the way, instantly recognized 'all is done here with Mr Parkinson ... The negroes find out he knows nothing'. Slave expertise had discredited white management; Lewsey raged privately that 'it was the overseer that ought to be put in the stocks'. Publicly, he tried to save face, told Becky he would 'beg Mr Parkinson for him' and put the trainee back on probation.[38]

Becky's exposure of Parkinson, nevertheless, undermined his authority. When he tried to solace himself by commanding new sexual favours and sent male slaves to solicit for him, they did not meet with instant success. Customarily, slave women sought alliances with white managers for there were immediate material benefits and the children were whitened. Parkinson, however, already had a resident 'housekeeper' and some male relatives of the girls solicited, concerned perhaps to assert their family's autonomy or to comment obliquely on Parkinson's career pros-

pects with Lewsey, refused on their behalf. The three girls who were recruited were made a common laughing stock by field women next day. Parkinson, desperate to assert his authority, took advantage of Lewsey's absence in Vere and had the women flogged, 18 lashes on their naked shoulders.

The women, an important component in the first gang, sent a delegation to Mrs Lewsey and threatened to walk off the job to go to Vere and complain to Lewsey. Mrs Lewsey played mediator; she sent for Lewsey and promised Parkinson would cease all punishments if the women returned to work. Lewsey in contrast to Laing who, confronted by an actual strike could order the slaves back to work on the promise of an investigation two weeks later, was on the spot in 48 hours, heard all parties and immediately sent Parkinson off the estate.[39]

The intensity of the contract bargaining process at Blue Mountain permeates the correspondence and it is clear that agreement was reached chiefly because labour shortages forced Lewsey to rationalize production; this meant reduced work loads and improved work routines. The land laid out in sugar was 'beyond the strength' of the estate workers and jobbers were expensive: great gang work cost 2s. 1d, cane holing 2s. 6d per day per worker, or £7.10s. an acre and their use tended to be cumulative, from clearing land, to cane holing, weeding and cutting.[40] Lewsey reduced the acreage in cane and organized sugar production to cut down on night work during crop. The Blue Mountain slaves became part of an experimental routine which attracted comment throughout the parish and was brought to the attention of the House of Commons Select Committee on Slavery in 1832. The mill was shut down for 6-8 hours every week night and from Saturday evening until Monday morning. This gave a 16-18 hour production day, worked in spells, but allowed for 6-8 hours sleep every night.[41]

The slaves at first regarded these innovations with suspicion and skepticism, suspecting that some new loss of privilege or property would make them pay for apparent improvement. As the new work routine continued, however, the reduced acreage to hole and weed and a reduced working day at the mill achieved cooperation. The benefits to management were measured when the 1826 crop was taken off. Like the crop of 1800, it was done in the face of heavy rains which fell from January through to July; 'not two days together have we had in those months fair'. The weather made extra work: the cattle pens became swamps and had to be moved seven or eight times. But, in marked contrast to 1800, the workers' health and spirits stayed good. They let Lewsey know they were trying their best; 'Let us put our shoulder to the wheel and break out a good crop for Massa'. Lewsey took the hint and put up an old steer (value £8cy) to fatten for the harvest home. Almost lyrical with success, he wrote, 'It is truly gratifying to see we can make such an improvement [in the quality of sugar] in the same copper and with the same people'. All this was achieved without a single case of insubordination or a single complaint 'presenting itself for some months'.[42]

The benefits to the slaves were described by the head driver. Lewsey, characteristically, asked him if the cane cutters did more work after they had a night's rest.

He said that the Negroes did not require to be *Drove* that frequently *before time* when the officer had to look for the people in the morning they would find 5 or 6 absent, or Gone to some cane piece to sleep, that those that had *Heart* to take the Flogging would come up and receive it and go to work and those that had none would *Run*.

The results had been bad sugar, bad returns and 'disgraceful depopulation on this estate'.[43]

The slaves at Blue Mountain, as sugar workers, had something to gain from improved contract terms; at Grange Hill they had everything to lose. Grange Hill slaves had successfully cut down on estate work and devoted themselves to provision ground production and marketing. On their grounds they employed, for payment in cash or kind, slaves from other estates and runaways and took the produce to market on the estate mules. Manchioneal was no longer their main outlet; they travelled 30 miles to Morant Bay and shipped from there to the Kingston market.[44]

It is not clear how all the slaves fitted into this system; certainly some enjoyed a higher than average standard of living. Slaves usually owned a few chickens, a hog and sometimes a goat, but only headmen had mules to ride. At Grange Hill slaves commonly owned donkeys with a market value of £8cy.[45] Sugar production was marginalized; the 'Engine ground the Cane juice and the Coppers Stewed the same into what they call

Sugar'. Local jobbing gangs did most of the work, not because the estate slaves were subjected to the 'pushing system', but because they had minimized their work loads and 'enjoyed a Life of Idleness'.[46]

Lewsey initially held his predecessor ('a sinecurist') responsible for this state of affairs but experience taught that his real enemy was John Reay, the head driver. Reay had a reputation in the parish as a man of good character – a court case was settled in his favour on that account – and his support among the Grange Hill workforce made him, virtually, ruler of the estate. Lewsey's efforts to tighten discipline and improve production met with collective non-cooperation. His threat to sell the slaves if runaways were found on the provision grounds was met by silence, possibly of disbelief, since slave prices were low. The promise of cash rewards ($1 a head) and the threat of the work house for Reay if he was not the first to inform on culprits, produced no results.[47] The threat to rent out their provision lands and supply them with corn instead (the practice in Vere parish) provoked, however, a strong verbal response; drivers and people in a grand chorus, nicely calculated for the ear of a man himself devoted to their owners' service, begged for forgiveness, and promised to work their lands. Led by the drivers they pleaded with special fervour that Lewsey not 'write and inform *Master* of their bad conduct'.[48]

The chorus of assurance expressed primarily, as Lewsey rapidly discovered, the collective determination to defend the status quo. Lewsey resorted to physical punishment of individuals; slaves identified as 'trouble makers' were weeded out periodically and sent to 'cool' in the work house. The punishment of individuals did not provoke any overt retaliation from the slaves and no work stoppages or grievance meetings ensued. Management hopes of 'redeeming this property from ruin' were sustained.[49] But such punishments did not alter the power structure on the estate; Lewsey's threats against Reay intensified – he promised to destroy him by sending him from one work house to another through the island, 'unless an immediate emendation takes place in the conduct of the people' – but he never judged it appropriate to do so. The only slave to lose office, in fact, was the woman driver of the productively least important third gang. Mary Tait was 'broke from her Office' for 'winking at the Idleness of those under her charge and for not paying attention to the children and reporting the dirt eaters to the Overseer and the Head Man'.[50] Lewsey made no attempt, either, to move the slaves collectively to Blue Mountain. Although desirable in economic terms, this threatened resistance at Grange Hill and disruption at Blue Mountain. Transfers were individual and voluntary and on this basis ten young men, prime workers, moved to Blue Mountain.[51]

The processes which undermined productivity and with it white authority, are illustrated by the case of Mr Fry the bookkeeper. Sent with a driver and the head watchman to clear a yam piece, he left at least half the yams in the ground 'and those the pick Yams of the whole piece', the overseer reported that 'they took good care not to dig one good one for me'. This 'neglect of duty' by the bookkeeper, together with similar instances, and an old grievance against his 'shameful conduct in attempting mauling a female in the Hot House' secured his dismissal.

The bookkeeper's 'neglect of duty' may have been just that; the circumstances suggest, however, that the level of disaffection among the slaves made it more politic to leave a job half done than coerce them to complete it, Mr Fry did not make an issue of the yam digging and neither, in fact, did the overseer; he sacked Mr Fry, but makes no mention of punishing the slaves.[52] The bookkeeper and the overseer seem to have agreed that, given the state of labour relations on the estate, disciplinary action was not appropriate.

The slaves won this round in the struggle; Lewsey reluctantly concluded he could never promote at Grange Hill 'the Great Work of Reform' achieved at Blue Mountain. Surrounded by 'A set of subjects which meet me on every Quarter with Low Cunning and Vile Cant' efficient sugar production was out of the question; he could only 'extinguish it' as a sugar estate.[53] The property was turned to pasture and livestock, which complemented the slaves' provision ground production and rationalized the economic transformation they had effected.

Conclusion

The slaves at Blue Mountain and Grange Hill demonstrate that the methods of struggle customarily identified with wage workers were first developed by slave workers cognisant of the crucial value of labour power. Collective withdrawal of labour, the presentation of grievances and the use by owners and managers of mediation were methods developed by 1770. Group action by slaves with particular grievances was also used, notably by women, and secured positive results. Skilled and confidential slaves pioneered these processes and the head men on both estates emerge as instigators and, by inference, organizers of group and collective action.

The immediate cause of action was physical coercion: the whip used to extract more intensive, or longer hours of labour and to exert arbitrary authority. The protests recorded were directed against the slaves' immediate oppressors, a realistic objective given the sharp class difference between owners and their representatives and their hirelings. It is clear, however, that the slaves also fought to command their own labour and their own produce, including a 50 per cent share in the estate yam piece. The records reflect primarily the *results* of these struggles which were facilitated by long term trends - the diminution in the labour force and the expansion of the internal market. The *methods* used can also be inferred – 1770 style strike action together with informal 'deals' and 'understandings' between head men and overseers. The problems presented by 'managing' slaves practically dictated that overseers were either strict disciplinarians (like Munro), or time servers. In either case, their transience assisted the modification of work loads and increased rewards. The attorneys themselves were no more than occasional visitors whose self-interest, like Laing's, was often best served by acceding to the slaves' demands – a pattern sufficiently common by the 1820s for attorneys to attempt to conceal from the slaves their key role in overseer dismissals.[54]

· The Blue Mountain and Grange Hill experience suggests more than one parallel with nineteenth-century Russian serf bargaining procedures. Many serfs were also owned by absentees, supervised by stewards (attorneys) and managed by bailiffs (overseers). Deterioration of work conditions, excessive work demands, excessive punishments, removal of livestock, and seduction of women, also prompted grievance procedures. In this case, written petitions to a higher authority – the owners, a local official (magistrate) or even the Tsar – were carried by delegates who risked flogging.

Complaints often focused on the bailiff and, if nothing was done, the serfs went on strike until a special land court composed of local officials (a form of Council of Protection) reviewed the complaint. The end result, which affected the fortunes of several hundreds of thousands of workers on vast estates, was frequently armed resistance and military confrontation.[55]

The slaves' use of strike action and their long tradition of bargaining for informal contract terms places in a new perspective the role played by strike action in slave rebellions (e.g. the 1831 Jamaica rebellion) and invites revision and re-assessment of small-scale events currently labelled 'rebellion'. Small-scale outbreaks may represent spontaneous reactions to the failure of mediation processes.

The struggle of the Jamaican slaves also places in context their astonishing performance as apprentices. The Apprenticeship scheme, implemented in August 1834, incited the workers to bring to bear on a published contract all the skills they had acquired in making, maintaining and developing informal contract terms. The new contract, which established the working week at 40 1/2 hours a week and also rolled back customary allowances to the levels sanctioned by the slave code, resulted in island-wide confrontations. For several months Jamaica teetered on the verge of some form of general strike. The crisis was only resolved when, with crop season looming, 'all the prominent attorneys' and all the big sugar producers conceded the old allowances for the shorter working week.[56] The part-time wage slaves' first task, under the new contract, was to consolidate the gains they had made as chattel slaves.

The records also demonstrate the crucial role in these developments of the slaves' connection with the world of wage labour outside the plantation. The differences between Grange Hill and Blue Mountain derive to a large extent from the fact that Grange Hill slaves were closely intertwined with that economy no later than 1770. Their access to cash returns for labour on their provision grounds exacerbated the tension between coerced labour on the estate and exchange-valued labour on the grounds. In the last decade of slavery these workers were able to carry this struggle a significant step further and take the estate out of sugar production. Grange Hill represents, perhaps, one extreme of a spec-

trum with Blue Mountain, a profitable sugar property where workers still bargained for terms as sugar producers, at the other.

By 1832 Jamaica's gross domestic product was worth £5.5 million sterling of which exports from the plantation sector represented just under 50 per cent (£2.2 million). The slaves' contribution to the economic pie 'outside the canefields' has been calculated at £1.5 million and included almost complete dominance of food production for local consumption (£847,000 of £900,000) as well as contributing arrowroot and ginger, for example, to the export trade. No less than 27 per cent of Jamaica's total agricultural output came from the slaves' provision grounds and was the product of waged labour. The slaves in Jamaica were bursting the bonds of the coerced labour economy by the same processes which undermined the serf economy in western Europe.[57]

The slave labour system, instituted by capitalists to foment rapid capital accumulation, was undermined by the slaves' participation in the capitalist economy they were intended simply to serve. This development reached its apogee in the 1831 rebel slaves' demand, reinforced by the destruction of a million pounds' worth of their owners' crops and property, for wages. In the context created by the re-formation in 1832 of Britain's own ruling class, the Jamaican slaves' militancy destroyed slave labour as a separate category throughout the British Empire and forced acknowledgement of their right to wages for their work.

Notes

1.   Slave labour is more usually considered a 'peculiar institution': E. Foner for example, in *Nothing But Freedom*, (Baton Rouge, University of Louisiana Press 1983) writes of the slave plantation as generating 'a distinct system of social relations as well as ts own characteristic class system and political economy' (p.9) This analysis was presented in April 1986 at the Association of Caribbean Historians' Conference, Nassau, Bahamas and published in *Labour in the Caribbean*, M. Cross and G. Heuman (eds), (London, 1988). While any shortcomings remain my own I am indebted to friends and colleagues for encouragement and advice, including Nigel Bolland, Paul Burgwin, Stanley Engerman, Gad Heuman, Barry Higman, Woodville Marshall, Sidney Mintz and Robert Shenton.

2.   Fitzherbert Papers 239M/E, Derbyshire County Record Office, Matlock, Derbyshire; Barry Higman, *Slave Population and Economy in Jamaica 1807-1834*, (Cambridge 1976), 53, Table 6:123, Table 24.

3. Fitzherbert Papers 239M/E 17766, William Sutherland (planting attorney) to Jacques and Fisher (mercantile attorneys) 24 Nov. 1783; hereafter referred to as 239M/E.

4. Hurricanes stuck Feb., Oct., 1780: Aug. 1781: Oct. 1786. Richard S. Sheridan, 'The Crisis of Subsistence in the British West Indies during and after the American Revolution,' *William and Mary Quarterly*, 33: Oct. 1976, 625, 632.

5. 239M/E 17787, 17803, Sutherland to Jacques and Fisher, 29 Aug. 1785; 9 April 1787.

6. 239M/E 17803, ibid., 9 April 1787.

7. Ibid., Great Britain, Parliamentary papers, (Commons) *Report from the Select Committee on the Extinction of Slavery Throughout the British Dominions*, (no. 721) 1831-2, 20: Q: 6398, William Shand (hereafter cited as P. P. (Commons) (no. 721), 1831-2, 20):Q: 6398, William Shand (hereafter cited as P.P. (Commons) (no. 721), 1831-2, 20) corn took 4, yams 8, and plantains 11 months to mature.

8. 239M/E 17834 Sutherland to Sir William Philip Perrin (absentee owner), 14 Jan. 1798. Some sugar estates (e.g. Worthy Park) resolved the subsistence problem by importing Jamaican food (yams, cocos, plantains) from specialized provision grounds. It is not clear, however, that the slaves' conditions there were significantly better than at Blue Mountain. Michael Craton and James Walvin, *A Jamaican Plantation: The History of Worthy Park, 1670-1970*, (London, 1970), 135.

9. 239M/E 16972-3, Jacques and Fisher to Perrin, 24 April 1783; 17766, Sutherland to Jacques and Fisher, 24 Nov. 1783; 17143, Jacques to Perrin, 28 Feb. 1794.

10. 239M/E 17177, Jacques to Perrin, 7 Sept. 1795.

11. 239M/E 17177, 17179, Jacques to Perrin, 7 Sept., 6 Oct., 1795.

12. 239M/E 17322, Jacques, Laing and Ewing to Perrin, 26 July 1800; Craton and Walvin, *A Jamaican Plantation*, 145.

13. 239M/E 17323, Jacques, Laing and Ewing to Perrin, 26 July 1800.

14. 239M/E 17084, Jacques and Fisher to Perrin, 12 April 1785, 17733, James Blaw (overseer) to Mrs Frances Perrin, 7 Feb. 1775.

15. 239M/E 17717, David Munro (overseer) to Mrs Frances Perrin, narrative account.

16. Charles B. Drew, 'David Ross and the Oxford Iron Works: a study in Industrial Slavery in the early nineteenth century', *William and Mary Quarterly*, 31: April 1974, 205. c.f. case of Billy Bacon, skilled slave who insisted on being hired out in Richmond; his owner had to employ a white miller to replace him.

17. 239M/E 17717, Munro, narrative account.

18. Ibid.

19. 239M/E 17711, Malcolm Laing (planting attorney) to Munro, 11 Sept. 1770. US planters recognized that disciplinarian overseers had the greatest difficulties in managing slaves. Wm. K. Scarborough. *The Overseer*, Baton Rouge, Louisiana State University Press, 1966, 79-80.

20. 239M/E 17717, Munro, narrative account

21. Higman, op. cit., 206

22. Ibid. 224-5.

23. P. P. (Commons) (no. 721), 1831-2, 20: Q. 25, W. Taylor; Q. 513, J.B. Wildman.

24. Higman, op. cit., 208-9.

25. P. P. (Commons) (no. 721), 1831-2, 20: Q. 1406, 1495, Rev. P. Duncan.

26. Ibid. Q. 5283, Robert Scott.

27. Ibid. Q. 510-11, William Taylor.

28. Higman, op. cit., 23, 29, 220; Philip S. Morgan, 'Work and Culture: the task system and the World of Low Country Blacks 1700-1880', *William and Mary Quarterly*, 39, Oct. 1982, 563-99.

29. Ibid. p. 538.

30. P. P. (Commons) (no. 721), 1831-2, 20: Q. 63, 90, William Taylor.

31. Ibid. Q. 89, 90, 111, 570, William Taylor.

32. Ibid Q. 129, William Taylor

33. T. Roughley, *The Jamaican Planter's Guide*, (London, 1823), 82, 97, 101-2, 340-1.

34. 239M/E 21021, Lewsey to Fitzherbert, 9 May 1826.

35. 239M/E 21032, Lewsey to Fitzherbert, 2 July 1826.

36. 239M/E 20992, Lewsey to Fitzherbert, 9 Aug 1825.

37. 239M/E 20985, Lewsey to Fitzherbert, 12 June, 18 July 1825.

38. 239M/E 20985, Lewsey to Fitzherbert, 12 June 1825.

39. 239M/E 20993, Lewsey to Fitzherbert, 25 July 1825.

40. Higman, op. cit., 238, Table A1, 1.

41. 239M/E 21021, Lewsey to Fitzherbert, 9 May 1826; P. P. (Commons) (no. 721), 1831-2, 20: Q. 563, William Taylor.

42. 239M/E 21032, 21021, Lewsey to Fitzherbert, 9 May, 2 July 1826; Higman op. Cit., 237.

43. 239M/E 21021, Lewsey to Fitzherbert, 9 May 1826.

44. 239M/E 20986, Lewsey to Fitzherbert, 18 July 1825.

45. Higman, op. Cit., 238.

46. 239M/E 21039, Lewsey to Fitzherbert, 22 Aug 1826.

47. 239M/E 20985, 20986, 20987, Lewsey to Fitzherbert, 12 June, 8, 18 July 1825.

48. 239M/E 20986, Lewsey to Fitzherbert, 8 July 1825.

49. 239M/E 21004, Lewsey to Fitzherbert, 28 Feb. 1826.

50. 239M/E 21039, Lewsey to Fitzherbert, 22 Aug 1826.

51. 239M/E 21021, Lewsey to Fitzherbert, 9 May 1826.

52. 239M/E 21004,, William Duncan (overseer) to Lewsey, 28 Feb 1826.

53. 239M/E 21039, Lewsey to Fitzherbert, 22 Aug 1826

54. P. P. (Commons) (no. 721), 1831-2, 20: Q. 6510, William Shand.

55. Peter Kolchin, 'The Process of Confrontation; Patterns of resistance to Bondage in 19th Century Russia and the United States', *Journal of Social History*, vol. 11, 1977-8, 459-63.

56. W. L. Burn, *Emancipation and Apprenticeship*, London 1970, 176-7.

57. M. Craton, ed., *Roots and Branches*, Toronto 1979, S. W. Mintz. 'Slavery and the Rise of Peasantries', 231 quoting A.J.G. Knox, 'Opportunities and Opposition, The Rise of Jamaica's Black Peasantry and the Nature of Planter Resistance', *Canadian Review of Sociology and Anthropology*, 14, 1977, 386. C. f. Robert Brenner, 'Agrarian Class Structure and Economic Development in Preindustrial Europe', *Past and Present*, no. 70, Feb. 1976, 30-75.

SECTION TWELVE

A Deadly Business: Mortality, Health, Nutrition and the Crisis of Social Reproduction

Enslavers were caught in the web of a major dilemma. As rational entrepreneurs they sought to maximize profits by reducing the cost of productive inputs. Expenditures on slaves were suppressed to subsistence levels. At the same time, however, the protection of property rights in those they enslaved was a top priority that required careful policy formulation and implementation. The effective social maintenance of the enslaved then, meant that the daily management of subsistence and health care could not be left to chance. Enslaved peoples had to be properly nourished and medically assisted if they were to be productive workers. At the same time the impact of class and race prejudice upon economic thinking oftentimes led to subsistence levels being located below what was required to maintain general health.

Research on slavery has confirmed that enslaved peoples were generally malnourished and preyed upon by a range of diseases related to malnutrition. Not only did food availability fluctuate seasonally, but the enslaved experienced long periods of hunger after hurricanes, during droughts and major war. Crop cycles in Europe and North America also affected food availability. Kiple and Kiple, and Craton have suggested that enslaved peoples suffered from severe deficiencies in important vitamins and minerals, and that the root cause of their vulnerability to fatal and damaging diseases was malnutrition. These authors, however, recognize the problems inherent in any research that attempts to diagnose symptoms known to be the result of nutritional deficiency that were widespread among those enslaved. By discussing labour in relation to food supplies within a hostile disease environment, they have provided pioneer accounts of the biological history of enslaved peoples.

Poor health and nutrition, as well as demographic and other socio-economic factors, contributed to the general inability of Caribbean slave populations to reproduce themselves naturally until the closing years of the slave system. Demographic historians have emphasized the need to analyze the composition of all societies and to identify the variables that determine performance over time. These essays by Craton, Kiple and Kiple and Lamur address the major structural and methodological issues involved in the discourse on slave demography.

58

Deficiency Diseases in the Caribbean

KENNETH F. KIPLE AND VIRGINA H. KIPLE*

The history of slavery in the Americas has recently taken on a new biological dimension as historians have begun to appreciate the importance of pathogenic agents in any holistic understanding of their subject. Of special interest is the impact of these agents on slave mortality and, more specifically, the extent of the role that they played in preventing most Caribbean slave populations from sustaining a natural rate of growth.

Historians are also looking beyond pathogens to the nutritional factor, which may have figured prominently in the etiologies of slave diseases. Seldom does a new work appear which does not allege that malnutrition was a serious problem of Caribbean slave health. However, no attempt has been made to single out specific nutritional deficiencies in the Caribbean slave diet and in the process prove that Caribbean bondsmen were malnourished. Nor for that matter has any effort been made to link suspected nutritional deficiencies with some of the more important West Indian slave diseases.

This study makes such an attempt by investigating the West African nutritional heritage of Caribbean slaves, by analyzing the Caribbean slave diet, and by matching nutritional deficiencies revealed by this analysis with the symptoms of the diseases which plagued slaves exclusively.

The African Nutritional Heritage

Although there were some exceptions, West African diets were poor. Prior to the sixteenth century, they consisted of bananas, taro, the small African yam, millet, and rice crops, which researchers believe did little more than sustain life. In the sixteenth century, American cassava and maize were imported, and are credited with stimulating the growth of West Africa's population — a growth that kept pace, or even exceeded, the drain of the slave trade.[1]

Although the introduction of these two starchy plants may have resolved problems of quantity, the quality of West African diets remained deficient. Animal protein has never played a major role in West African nutrition, with much of the blame belonging to the tsetse fly — a bloodsucking insect which imparts African sleeping sickness to animals as well as to man. In much of West Africa the tsetse fly was so prevalent that it made the raising of cattle and other large animals, if not in all cases impossible, at least unprofitable. Thus many West Africans were limited to keeping a few goats, chickens, and dogs and sometimes a pig — animals so scarce and highly prized that they were slaughtered only on special occasions.[2]

Bovine milk was thus excluded fron West African diets, which may be a reason for the

Kenneth F. Kiple is Associate Professor of History at Bowling Green State University. He is the co-author with Virginia H. Kiple of a book-length study on the biological history of blacks in the United States.

This study is an elaboration of the Caribbean portion of the paper 'Slave Nutrition and Disease during the Nineteenth Century: The United States and the Caribbean', which was delivered at the annual meeting of the organization of American Historians (1979). The authors wish to thank the Joint Committee on Latin American Studies of the Social Science Research Council and the American Council of Learned Societies for an award to support the project out of which this research was generated. They are grateful also to the Bowling Green Faculty Research Committee for assistance with supplementary travel funds.

Journal of Interdisciplinary History, Vol. 11, No. 2 (1980), pp. 197-215.

high frequency of lactose intolerance today among blacks of West African origin. Such intolerance occurs among people with a history of low milk consumption. Also excluded in many places were eggs, for some because of taboos against their consumption, and for others because it seemed wasteful to eat the egg rather than wait for the chicken. Finally, because of cultural beliefs, fruit consumption was frequently frowned upon as was the use of most vegetables, except the yam, taro, cassava, and maize.[3]

One consequence of this background was that many West Africans must have reached the New World with a history of malnutrition. Empirical data suggest that this was the case. Research conducted by Fogel, Engerman, and Higman concerning the height of some 25,000 Trinidadian slaves indicates that newly imported Africans were significantly shorter on average than Creole-born slaves. Fraginals has found the same to be true for Cuba. First-generation Creole slaves were significantly taller than freshly imported Africans.[4]

Research has demonstrated that a radical change in dietary habits produces a dramatic increase in height. The rapid growth of New World slaves over the course of a generation or so implies that West Indian diets were at least more protein laden than those of West Africa and were probably also of better overall quality. We discuss West Africa in order to emphasize the poor nutritional status of a sizeable portion of slaves in the Caribbean.[5]

West Indian slave populations were seldom self-sustaining so long as the slave trade endured. Rather, they received massive injections of fresh imports from that traffic until the beginning of the nineteenth century and, in the case of Cuba, through the middle of that century. Hence Caribbean slave populations always had many badly nourished newcomers crowding their ranks — a condition which the circumstances of the Middle Passage could only have aggravated. The standard menu for slaves making the passage was a boiled cereal (usually rice) with a 'sauce' made by boiling salted fish — a diet lacking in many important nutrients. Moreover, the dysentery and diarrhea, always rife aboard a slaver, would have leached away many of those nutrients which such a diet could have provided.[6]

Thus many West Africans, badly nourished to begin with and then subjected to the disastrous nutritional circumstances of the Middle Passage, reached the New World in a malnourished condition. Doubtless some never recovered, which must count as an important reason for the high incidence of 'seasoning' mortality.

Malnutrition, in addition to its own inherent destructiveness, also renders the body susceptible to pathogenic invasion and, in the case of slaves moving into a new disease environment, to pathogens and strains of pathogens against which they had inefficient defenses. Assuming, however, that the newly imported slaves did survive, they did so on a diet which, although in many ways superior to their accustomed diets in West Africa, may nonetheless have been seriously deficient in some nutrients.

Diet

Our technique for constructing the Caribbean slave diet reflected in Table 1 has been to assign to slaves the amount of meat and cereal that planters claimed that they issued — the kind of standardized *ideal* allotment which is mentioned over and over again in everything from instructions to overseers, to travel accounts, to tracts on slave care — and then to 'build up' that basic allotment with the most commonly mentioned and readily available or easy to store supplements to reach a caloric intake of about 3,000 calories daily. Three thousand calories would be too low for a young male laboring during a sugar harvest; 3,200–4,000 calories would be closer to his requirement for this fraction of the year. However, not all islands employed a majority of their slaves in sugar cultivation, and female requirements run in the average about 1,200 calories fewer than males. Thus 3,000 calories seems a reasonable intake for the average adult slave for at least most of the year.[7]

By employing this technique, we may assume that, ideally, Caribbean slaves received an allotment of a little less than a half pound of animal protein daily, either as dried beef or salted fish, and about a pint of cereal in the form of either cornmeal or rice. This core allotment would have provided in the neighborhood of a third of the daily calorie requirements but about twice as much protein as today's recommendations suggest.[8]

Because of a lack of calories provided by the core, Caribbean slaves were dependent upon

Table 1   Analysis of Caribbean Slave Diets Computed on a Daily Basis[a]

	Calories	Protein	Fat[b]	Calcium	Phosphorus	Iron	Vitamin A	Thiamine	Riboflavin	Niacin	Vitamin C
.42 lb beef	387	65	12	38	791	9.7	0	.13	.60	7.2	0
1 pint cornmeal	884	22	8	42	544	4.4	1180	.74	.20	4.6[c]	0
Core plus vegetable supplements (see below)	2630	104	20	374	1941	26.1	4540	1.80	1.40	20.5	142
% RDA	88[d]	189[e]		47	243		91	123	81	108	316
.42 lb fish[f]	440	67	1	311	790	2.5	0	.15	.80	5.2	0
1 pint rice	1416	26	2	94	366	3.2	0	.28	.12	6.2	0
Core plus supplements	3215	110	3	473	1763	17.7	3360	1.35	1.49	20.1	142
% of RDA	107	200		87	220		67	93	88	106	316
Vegetable supplements											
¼ lb. yams	197	4		39	135	1.1	0	.20	.08	1.0	17
½ lb. taro[g]	236	3		187	218	4.5	0	.22	.04	1.8	16
1 lb. bananas	386	5		36	118	3.2	860	.23	.27	3.2	45
1 lb. plantains[g]	540.	5		32	136	3.2	2500	.27	.18	2.7	64

a Unless otherwise specified, all food values have been calculated from C. F. Adams, *Nutritive Value of American Foods* (Washington D.C., 1975).

b The fat content of vegetable supplements has not been included because that contribution is negligible.

c The niacin figure for corn is particularly misleading, because the niacin contained in corn is chemically bound. Thus without special treatment, most of the vitamin B_3 in cornmeal is unavailable to the consumer.

d All RDAS established by the Food and Nutrition Board, National Academy of Sciences, National Research Council (*Recommended Dietary Allowances* [Washington D.C., 1974; 8th revised ed]) are for a male aged 18–35 years, although — except for protein and iron — female allowances are virtually the same. Pregnant and lactating women have increased requirements for all nutrients.

e The RDA in the past few years has been lowered from 70 to 55 grams in keeping with an increasingly sedentary life style. However, this seems too low for the nineteenth-century slave, and indeed some experts believe that even 70 grams is too low an RDA to maintain long-term health. See N. S. Scrimshaw, 'Shattuck Lecture — Strengths and Weaknesses of the Committee Approach: An Analysis of Past and Present Recommended Allowances for Protein in Health and Disease'. *New England Journal of Medicine*, CCXCIV (1976), 136–42, 198–203. In agreement are C. Frank Consolazio et al., 'Protein Metabolism during Intensive Physical Training in the Young Adult', *American Journal of Clinical Nutrition*, XXVIII (1975), 29–33, who believe that those engaged in sufficient physical activity to cause perspiration need at least 100 grams of protein every day.

f The 3 lbs of fish allotted to Caribbean slaves every week was either dried or pickled cod or herring. Thus we have averaged the nutrients for which information is available yielded by fish submitted to both processes. The difficulty is that no recent reliable data exist to specify the quantity of most minerals and all vitamins provided by dried, salted, or pickled fish. Therefore, we have relied on older data for dried but unsalted cod and herring. (Found in the 1950 edition of the *Agriculture Handbook*.) This means that nutritive values are probably high at least for the B vitamins.

g Computed from A. von Muralt (ed.), *Protein-Calorie Malnutrition* (Heidelberg, 1969), Tables, 147–77.

supplements to that core, which explains the importance of their provision grounds and vegetable gardens often mentioned in the literature on Caribbean plantations: Although West Indian plants and dietary preferences varied from place to place, yams, taro, plantains, and bananas are the most frequently cited supplements. The usual practice was to boil all of these foods (save the bananas) with the ration of animal protein and cereal; and, assuming that out of the cooking pot the average slave plucked a half pound of yam, another of taro root, and perhaps a pound of plantains, he would have satisfied his caloric needs for the day.[9]

Surprisingly, despite the usual description of these basic diets as 'starchy' and 'protein poor', they seem to have supplied most of the basic nutrients. The diets were poor in calcium, and with milk — the one food which might have remedied the problem — in short supply and most slaves lactose intolerant, a widespread calcium deficiency must have been a nutritional fact of life. Caribbean slaves seem also to have been slightly deficient in vitamin A, but, superficially at least, the slave diets of the Caribbean might be characterized as not that poor by eighteenth- and nineteenth-century standards.[10]

A closer look, however, reveals some serious problems, in part because of the chemical composition of some of the foods in question and in part because of the peculiar relationships among some of the nutrients. For example, an enormously complicating factor is the absence of sufficient fats. In both the beef and fish slave diets the animal protein and cereal were the only items to supply any amount of fat. However, because of the low fat content of dried fish and jerked beef, this meant only 20 grams of fat daily for West Indian slaves on a beef-corn core, and a measly 3 grams for those on a fish-rice core. Yet the established world standard for fat intake suggests 80–125 grams as a safe minimum.[11]

Although the low fat intake of slaves may have been good for cholesterol levels, such a diet means that the amount of vitamin A that Table 1 shows West Indian bondsmen as receiving is considerably overstated. Vitamin A is fat-soluble; hence a low fat diet impairs the ability of the body to absorb that vitamin. Moreover, the fish or meat allotment to slaves was usually reported as rancid; indeed, slaves allegedly preferred it that way. Unfortunately rancidity has a destructive effect on fat-soluble vitamins. Thus, instead of being only mildly vitamin A deficient, many West Indian slaves, because of an absence of dietary fat and the rancidity of much of the fat that they did ingest, must have been severely vitamin A deficient.[12]

Less well known is the relationship between fat and thiamine or vitamin B_1. Because thiamine is part of the water soluble vitamin B complex, fat has little to do with its absorption. But in the case of low-fat diets, such as those of Caribbean slaves, carbohydrates replace fat as the major energy source, and carbohydrates require thiamine for metabolism. Thus the low fat/high carbohydrate content of the Caribbean slave diets would have greatly accelerated thiamine requirements. For West Indian slaves thiamine requirements would have been higher than for the whites on the islands whose diets were heavily fat-laden. But even more to the point, it is highly doubtful that Caribbean bondsmen actually received as much thiamine as is suggested by Table 1.[13]

The process of pickling, salting, and drying beef or fish treats thiamine poorly. Both alkaline solutions and prolonged dehydration have a destructive effect on thiamine, the least stable of the B complex vitamins. This lack of stability also means that heat is more destructive to thiamine than to riboflavin or niacin. Thus data on the thiamine content of foods are usually given, as they are in Table 1, before cooking because of the losses which occur in the process. The loss from cornmeal, for example, runs between 15 and 25 per cent. In the case of meat, however, that loss can be as high as 85 per cent.[14]

Moreover, because thiamine is so highly soluble in water, it is readily leached out of the food during boiling, the standard method of cooking on most West Indian plantations. Fish or beef was tossed into the family or communal pot where it simmered all day along with yams, plantains, taro root, and, quite possibly, the cereal ration as well. Because of such factors as dehydration and cooking losses, the thiamine delivered by the West Indian slave diet is probably overstated by at least 50 per cent. Those slaves especially whose cereal allotment was rice were bound to be seriously B_1 deficient because, when rice is subjected to a polishing process to retard spoilage, the process also strips away the thiamine-rich husk of the grain.[15]

Finally, it bears repeating that the low-fat diet of Caribbean slaves would have severely exacerbated a condition of thiamine deficiency by elevating thiamine requirements. To this factor should be added two more exacerbating difficulties: a diet high in carbohydrates also accelerates thiamine requirements; and thiamine is the most poorly stored of all of the B vitamins.[16]

Not all Caribbean bondsmen suffered from the deficiencies of calcium, vitamin A, and thiamine. Red peppers provided much in the way of vitamin A, as did mangoes and ackee, both of which came into widespread West Indian use at about the turn of the nineteenth century. Milk was not totally unavailable to Caribbean slaves and, although most blacks were lactose intolerant, a few ounces in cornbread or coffee would have made a nutritional contribution — especially in the areas of sorely needed tryptophan and calcium — without necessarily producing symptoms of lactose intolerance.[17]

Disease

Not all slaves had access to a variety of supplementary comestibles, and many had access to very few. Even assuming that slave diets were marginally, rather than severely, deficient in one or another vitamin, economic, political, and climatic circumstances could quickly have changed those diets for the worse. The English-French global struggle frequently deprived West Indian slaves of their meat and cereal core diet, as did the end of North American imports to the British West Indies after the American Revolution. Hurricanes were always destructive to slave provision grounds, particularly to the fragile plantain and banana trees, and high prices for meat and cereal or low prices for sugar reduced supplies for slave rations.[18]

Even during good times Caribbean slave diets were badly out of balance, and times were often far from good. Yet all that a nutritional analysis of the basic foodstuffs in the slave regimen has done is to create the suspicion of widespread deficiencies of vitamins A and B₁. That suspicion can only be transformed into something more concrete if the diseases triggered by these deficiencies can be found to have afflicted slaves in large numbers. A correlation could then be established be-een a nutritional deficiency and a deficiency disease.

In any search for a deficiency disease one is quickly confronted with the phenomenon of so-called 'Negro diseases', given much prominence by West Indian physicians of the period. These were diseases from which blacks were far more likely to suffer than whites. Yaws, for example, was reportedly an affliction with an enormous color prejudice. The prejudice, however, is easily explicable in terms of a slave trade which constantly introduced persons infected in West Africa. Because of skin-to-skin transmission, the disease flourished among a people who lived in close contact and wore few clothes. Another such disease — a major killer of infants — was the 'jawful', or neonatal tetanus. The affliction singled out black infants for special grim attention because of the frequency of umbilical stump infections. The unsanitary condition of many slave quarters, on the one hand, and West African practices such as packing the stump with mud, on the other, guaranteed a high black as opposed to white death rate from the disease. There are, however, other Negro diseases the etiologies of which are not so easily understood in terms of pathogenic discrimination, but the symptoms of which do suggest problems of nutrition.[19]

Nutritional analysis has suggested that many Caribbean slaves would have been vitamin A and thiamine deficient, both because the diet itself was low in these vitamins and because a low-fat diet meant that much vitamin A was not absorbed and that thiamine requirements were elevated. Considering vitamin A first, one discovers among those peculiarly 'Negro afflictions' which occupied the attention of Caribbean slave physicians the malady 'sore eyes'. Eye afflictions were so widespread among the slaves that whole chapters in books on slave medicine were devoted to the problem, which is characteristic of several nutrient deficiencies. Night blindness, described as a 'disease which is so frequently seen among Negroes', is prominently mentioned in those chapters, and is a classic sign of vitamin A deficiency. Its prevalence among the slaves, along with the high incidence of sore eyes, does much to strengthen the suspicion born of nutritional analysis that many Caribbean bondsmen were vitamin A deficient.[20]

Another sizeable body of literature amassed by Caribbean physicians concerns one of the worst curses to befall a West Indian slave — the *mal d'estomach*. Also called *mal de estomágo*, *hati-weri*, *cachexia africana*, and just plain dirt-eating, the disease afflicted the black population of the West Indies exclusively. In Puerto Rico it was reportedly one of the two worst diseases of the slaves. In Jamaica it was portrayed as 'common upon almost every plantation' and on some estates the cause of about half the deaths. At first, doctors were powerless against it, and iron masks were used to break the pica habit. However, by the last decades of the eighteenth century, physicians were nearly unanimous in their prescibed cure — a better, more balanced diet.[21]

This mysterious malady, as described by eighteenth-century physicians, made its victims 'languid and listless', 'short breathed', and 'giddy', and afflicted them with 'palpitations of the heart' and 'loss of appetite.' With the progression of the sickness, legs swelled, the countenance became bloated and 'dropsy ensue(d)'. These symptoms are a classic portrayal of beriberi advancing from the dry to wet stage — and beriberi is caused by thiamine deficiency.[22]

In addition to these outstanding symptoms of thiamine deficiency, many other reasons exist for suspecting that *mal d'estomach* was in fact beriberi. Pregnant and lactating females were reported as the most susceptible to the disease, and pregnant and lactating females have historically proven the most vulnerable to beriberi because of accelerated requirements for most nutrients, including the B complex. Also vulnerable were young girls who suffered a disproportionately heavy incidence of the disease 'at a certain time in their life...(just) before their periodical evacuations appear'. The females in question, who probably consumed less food than their brothers of the same age, would have been experiencing the period of growth when requirements for all the B vitamins accelerate. The children susceptible to *mal d'estomach* were depicted as nutritionally deprived and often rickety in appearance. Whether the disease struck at the young or old, male or female, the remedy that physicians prescribed was 'wholesome food'; that the cure worked does nothing to weaken the hypothesis that the disease was indeed beriberi.[23]

There are other explanations for the symptoms. Slaves who manifested dirt-eating symptoms were sometimes thought to be attempting suicide, and slaves who developed *mal d'estomach* often personally diagnosed their problem as the result of having been poisoned or cursed by an 'obeah man'. More recently *mal d'estomach* has been pronounced to be the result of ankylostomiasis or hookworm infection, and indeed dirt-eating among slaves in the United States has also been attributed to hookworm. Yet this explanation ignores the relative immunity that blacks have to hookworm 'expressed as a resistance both to invasion by the parasite and to the injurious effects after invasion'. Another problem with hookworm infection as the culprit is that the disease was not unknown to colonial physicians; rather it was commonly diagnosed in British

troops and thus presumably would have been recognized in blacks had they manifested similar symptoms.[24]

Others have confused the *mal d'estomach* with the dry belly ache, which was also frequently fatal. This affliction, however, was accompanied by enormous intestinal pains that often had individuals begging to be shot or otherwise put out of their misery and which terminated in convulsions or epileptic seizures. Benjamin Franklin became interested in the problem and speculated in a letter to a West Indian physician that the dry belly ache was the result of drinking rum distilled in apparatuses using lead fastenings and pipes. Franklin's speculation may have been correct, for other physicians observed that the dry belly ache often caused lead poisoning. *Mal d'estomach* and dry belly ache were clearly two separate afflictions, with only the former, according to contemporary doctors, having a nutritional etiology.[25]

Evidence of a general B vitamin deficiency in the West Indies is contained in a seasonal phenomenon which occurred at crop time on sugar plantations; despite the long hours of extraordinary hard labor, blacks paradoxically enjoyed better health throughout the harvest. Physicians commented on the 'peculiar glossiness of the skin, so indicative of health (which) is never seen to the same extent at any other season'. Moreover, it was accepted wisdom that slaves purchased during crop time would do better in terms of health than slaves purchased at any other time of the year. Physicians and planters attributed this condition to the drinking of sugar cane juice. Custom allowed slaves to drink as much as they wished of the 'hot liquor' from the 'last copper', which contained a mixture of brown sugar and molasses. Thus slaves who drank from the 'last copper' were imbibing a liquid rich in iron and the B vitamins. If island physicians were not certain why, they nonetheless knew that this annual infusion of minerals and vitamins was beneficial for slaves.[26]

Physicians also (significantly in terms of thiamine deficiency) periodically suspected rice of producing bad health. A Jamaican physician reported early in the nineteenth century that rice had lately 'fallen into disuse' because it caused 'dropsical swellings'. Edema can be symptomatic of many disorders but, because they were linked to rice consumption, the 'dropsical swellings' do suggest beriberi, and dropsy had the reputation of being a major killer of adult Caribbean slaves.[27]

Mortality records bear out dropsy's deadliness; in those consulted for Barbados, dropsy dominated as a cause of plantation deaths. In Jamaica, on the Worthy Park estate between 1811 and 1834, dropsy accounted for fully 10 per cent of the 222 deaths, ranking only behind deaths from old age (53) and fever (23); of 357 slave deaths in St. James Parish, Jamaica, between 1817 and 1820, dropsy accounted for 11 per cent of the deaths, second only to old age. If dirt-eating and *mal d'estomach* deaths are added to those from dropsy, the three accounted for 16 per cent of the deaths. Dropsy alone claimed 11 per cent of the 288 deaths on three other Jamaican estates from 1817 to 1829. If other diseases with symptoms suggestive of beriberi, such as 'fits', 'convulsions', and 'bloated', are included with dropsy, the diseases in question accounted for 22 per cent of the deaths registered.[28]

On the Newton plantation in Barbados from 1796 to 1801 and from 1811 to 1825, dropsy accounted for 9 per cent of the 153 deaths (14), tying with consumption for third place behind old age (22) and 'no cause given' (19). By race the death records for the dioceses of Havana for 1843 recorded a black death rate from *anasarea* (general dropsy) of about three times that for whites. Finally, slave death statistics compiled by a West Indian physician during the 1820s for a Jamaican parish credits dropsy, plus other beriberi-like afflictions, with fully 20 per cent of the victims aged over one year of age in the district in question.[29]

As with *mal d'estomach* and 'cachexias', there was a cure for dropsy. In the words of Long, 'Sometimes they [the slaves] fall into dropsies, which generally prove mortal; for this disorder requires a very nutritious diet'. In the minds of white planters good nutrition was equated with fresh meat, and fresh meat contains that thiamine which could have cured the 'dropsies'.[30]

Fertility and Infant Mortality

Beriberi is one of those nutritional diseases, like pellagra, which escaped identification as a disease *sui generis* for many years, largely because its protean symptoms misled physicians into thinking that they were confronting a number of diseases. Because it was in the Far East that beriberi was finally identified, it subsequently was associated with rice-eating cultures; hence, beriberi is not usually thought of in a Caribbean context. Yet in 1865, early in the

effort to conquer beriberi, Hava reported that the disease was epidemic among blacks on Cuban plantations and described all of the symptoms of wet beriberi. In 1871 a French physician observed the disease on Cuban *ingenios* (plantations) and attempted, not very successfully, to treat it with arsenic. Finally in 1873 the disease was reported as raging with virulence on some Cuban plantations, causing a mortality rate of between 60 and 75 per cent. Because the slave diet in Cuba could and did produce beriberi, there are grounds for the suspicion that the disease was fairly widespread among West Indian slaves and that many of those who died from *mal d'estomach*, dropsy, or convulsions were actually dying of beriberi.[31]

If these deaths were caused by beriberi, then the dietary deficiency which produced this disease may have significantly altered the demographic history of West Indian slave populations — not so much because of the adult deaths, but because of infant mortality. For all the major nutritional diseases, only beriberi is a killer of otherwise normal infants receiving an adequate supply of breast milk. Adult slaves in the United States, for example, suffered from pellagra caused by niacin deficiency. Yet it is almost impossible for infants to be niacin deficient, because human milk supplies an adequate amount of both niacin and tryptophan (naicin's precursor), even if the mother is niacin deficient. However, a mother deficient in thiamine will invariably have milk deficient in that vitamin. To complicate matters for medical personnel, she may show few or even no signs of thiamine deficiency herself; in other words, a mother whose child develops infantile beriberi may not display overt signs of the malady.[32]

Infantile beriberi symptoms are very different from adult symptoms, and edema is only occasionally seen. The disease begins with vomiting, pallor, restlessness, loss of appetite, and insomnia and terminates life with convulsions and/or cardiac failure. Clearly the variety of symptoms makes it difficult to pin down the disease on West Indian plantations of yesterday. But if beriberi were fairly widespread, then infantile beriberi had unquestionably to be a major destroyer of West Indian slave infants. How major a destroyer may be gauged by looking at the Philippines, where beriberi has been and still is a chronic problem; in the late 1950s between 75 and 85 per cent of the 25,000 beriberi deaths reported there annually were infants. By the turn of the century, nearly half of all infants born alive in Manila failed to reach one year of age; infantile beriberi bears much of the blame for this mortality.[33]

How major a killer beriberi was in the West Indies can only be speculated upon. The disease usually strikes infants between the first and sixth months of life, before supplements have been added to their diets. If the attack is acute, the infant has difficulty in breathing, becomes cyanosed, and dies of cardiac failure with 'unnerving rapidity'. If it is chronic, the infant grows thin and wasted, edema occasionally occurs, and convulsions are frequently seen in the terminal stages.[34]

To be sure, the infant slave had to live long enough to contract infantile beriberi by first escaping that primary destroyer of the newborn in the Caribbean — neonatal tetanus. The fearsome reputation of this affliction was well deserved; indeed, the ailment has been credited with carrying off about one quarter of all slave infants within their first two weeks of life. However, as pointed out by students of Caribbean slave mortality, 'it is evident that the majority of fatalities among slave children born at Worthy Park occurred not at birth but in the children's early years.'[35]

A consultation of the literature produced by West Indian physicians and of the mortality data suggests that the latter statement applies not only to Worthy Park but to the Caribbean slave population as a whole. Rivaling neonatal tetanus as major causes of infant deaths were marasmus, convulsions, and tetanic convulsions. Researchers today looking for evidence of beriberi's presence in a region scrutinize any death that is classified under the rubric of convulsions or marasmus. Convulsions were also associated with teething difficulties, yet infants do not convulse simply because of teething. However, the months of teething are also those months during which infants would be most likely to succumb to beriberi.[36]

Another signal to researchers is the phenomenon of mothers with a history of losing one baby after another within the first few months of life. The West Indian literature offers many examples of mothers who had produced fifteen children and lost all but two, or who 'had borne ten children, and yet has now but one alive', or 'the instances of those who have had four, five, six children, without succeeding in bringing up one in spite of the utmost attention and indulgence . . .'[37]

Further analysis of mortality data and plantation records is needed. But this study does show that there is a correlation between a thiamine deficiency in the West Indian slave diet and diseases with beriberi-like symptoms, which ranked among the most important causes of slave mortality. If beriberi were as widespread as the evidence gathered thus far suggests, then thiamine deficiency must join with other factors produced by the slave trade and sugar monoculture to explain why Caribbean slave populations did not sustain themselves by natural means as did the slave population of the United States. It has often been urged that low fertility was at fault. Yet none of the islands have adequate birth records either to confirm or refute this suggestion. A possible measure of fertility relates the number of children under one year to the number of women able to bear those children. But if something is killing those infants at a brisk rate, then this kind of fertility ratio is a very misleading statistic.

Finally, it has been suggested that low fertility may have been partially the result of the practice of West African mothers to nurse their children for periods as long as three years. West Indian planters tried to discourage prolonged nursing but were not so successful in combating West African cultural practices as were United States planters, who were dealing with a people much further removed in time from their homeland. United States' slaves tended to nurse their babies for a year or less. Although the ability of lactation to prevent pregnancy after a few months of nursing is in doubt, there seems no question that prolonged lactation substantially increased the risk of death by thiamine deficiency for many West Indian slave infants.[38]

Although the slave diets of both the United States and the West Indies contained the potential for precipitating a B vitamin deficiency disease, pellagra, the deficiency disease of United States slaves, would not have killed the very young. But beriberi, the disease of Caribbean slaves, most certainly would have. The result may well help to account for the 'astounding fact, that while the blacks in the United States have increased *tenfold*, those of the British West Indies [and the West Indies] generally have decreased in the proportion of five to two'.[39]

Notes

1. Oliver Davis, *West Africa Before the Europeans: Archeology and Prehistory* (New York, 1967), 8, 149; Alfred W. Crosby, *The Columbian Exchange: Biological and Cultural Consequences of 1492* (Westport, Conn., 1972), 186–88; Bruce F. Johnston, *The Staple Food Economics of Western Tropical Africa* (Stanford, 1958), 174–81.

2. J. P. Glasgow, *The Distribution and Abundance of Tsetse* (London, 1963), 1-3; John Ford, *The Role of the Trypanosomiases in African Ecology: A Study of the Tsetse Fly Problem* (Oxford, 1971), 88-89; Frederick J. Simoons, *Eat Not This Flesh: Food Avoidances in the Old World* (Madison, 1961), 56.

3. Although West Indian figures are not available, about three-quarters of the Afro-Americans living in the United States are lactose intolerant, meaning that, because they have low levels of the lactase enzyme which breaks down milk sugars, they cannot drink milk. For a discussion, see K. and V. Kiple, 'Slave Child Mortality: Some Nutritional Answers to a Perennial Puzzle', *Journal of Social History*, X, (1977), 284-309. For West African dietary habits, consult Simoons, *op. cit.*, 73-78; Tadeuz Lewicki. *West African Food in the Middle Ages* (London, 1974), 79, 116-27; Michael Gelfand, *Diet and Tradition in African Culture* (Edinburgh, 1971), 206.

4. Robert W. Fogel and Stanley L. Engerman, 'Recent Findings in the Study of Slave Demography and Family Structure', *Sociology and Social Research*, LXIII, (1979), 566-89; Barry W. Higman, 'Growth in Afro-Caribbean Slave Populations.' *American Journal of Physical Anthropology*, L (1979), 373-85; Manuel Moreno Fraginals, 'Africa in Cuba: A Quantitative Analysis of the African Populations in the island of Cuba', in Vera Rubin and Arthur Tuden (eds), 'Comparative Perspectives on Slavery in New World Plantation Societies,' *Journal of the New York Academy of Science*, CCXCII (1979), 197-98.

5. J. M. Tanner, 'Earlier Maturation in Man,' *Scientific American*, CCXVIII (1968), 26-27; Albert Damon, 'Secular Trend in Height and Weight within Old American Families at Harvard, 1870-1965: Within Twelve Four-generation Families', *American Journal of Physical Anthropology*, XXIX (1968), 45-50; Phyllis Eveleth and Tanner, *Worldwide Variation in Human Growth* (Oxford, 1976), 274.

6. Philip D. Curtin, *The Atlantic Slave Trade: A Census* (Madison, 1969), remains the authority for measuring the magnitude of the various slave trades to the Americas. See also Herbert S. Klein, *The Middle Passage: Comparative Studies in the Atlantic Slave Trade* (Princeton, 1978). For the diets of blacks in the middle passage consult *ibid*, 200-01; John Riland, *Memoirs of a West-India Planter* (London, 1827), 56.

7. Food and Agriculture Organization, *Calorie Requirements* (Washington, D.C., 1950), 23-24.

8. The fish or meat ration in particular varied erratically from the ideal. For example, slave laws in the Leeward Islands required planters to issue a slave 1½ lbs. of salt fish weekly. Elsa V. Goveia, *Slave Society in the British Leeward Islands at the End of the Eighteenth Century* (New Haven, 1965), 193. Barbadian planters, however, claimed that they issued a pound of fish daily: *A Report on a Committee of the Council of Barbados, Appointed to Inquire into the Actual Condition of the Slaves* (London, 1824), 106, 113. Yet Jerome S. Handler and Frederick W. Lange in *Plantation Slavery in Barbados* (Cambridge, 1977), 87, an investigation on the Newton plantation, found that its slaves received only ½ lb of salt fish every two weeks, although for the island as a whole the norm was about 1 lb weekly. Richard N. Bean, 'Food Imports into the British West Indies: 1680-1845', *Journal of the New Academy of Sciences*, CCXCII (1977), 581-90, also found the average to be 'just a bit over one pound of preserved fish per slave per week' (587). For Cuba, Fraginals, 'Africa in Cuba', 198, states that 'the daily norm was some 200 grams (about one-

half pound) of jerked beef'. The point is that by accepting planters' claims of about ¼ lb of fish or meat daily, we are doubtless erring on the high side.

9. For two contemporaries who stressed importance of slave provision grounds see Robert Collins, *Practical Rules for the Management and Medical Treatment of Negro Slaves in the Sugar Colonies* (London, 1811; rpt. edn, 1971), 87, 99; Bryan Edwards, *The History, Civil and Commercial, of the British Colonies in the West Indies* (London, 1807; 4th edn), II, 160-63.

10. Ignio Abbad y Lasierra, *Historia Geografica de Puerto Rico* (San Juan, 1886; rpt. edn 1970), 183; Humphrey E. Lamur, 'Demography of Surinam Plantation Slaves in the Last Decade before Emancipation: The Case of Catherine Sophia', *Journal of the New York Academy of Sciences*, CCXCII (1977), 161-73; Michael Craton, 'Hobbesian or Panglossian? The Two Extremes of State Conditions in the British Caribbean, 1783-1834', *William and Mary Quarterly*, XXXV (1978), 345.

11. League of Nations Technical Commission on Nutrition, *The Problems of Nutrition* (New York, 1936).

12. Edward Long, *The History of Jamaica* (London, 1774), II, 413; Michael Craton and James Walvin, *A Jamaican Plantation, The History of Worthy Park* (Toronto, 1970), 135. Leonard W. Autrand and A. E. Woods, *Food Chemistry* (Westport, Conn., 1973), 122.

13. L. E. Lloyd, B. E. McDonald, and E. Crampton, *Fundamentals of Nutrition* (San Francisco, 1978; 2nd edn), 166. Roger J. Williams *et. al. The Biochemistry of B Vitamins* (Austin Texas, 1950), 276, 282; Aurand and Woods, *op. cit.*, 210. The relationship between fat and thiamine requirements may help to explain a puzzle that nutritionists recently encountered in Puerto Rico. The diet of their subjects clearly supplied a sufficiency of thiamine, yet measurements revealed them to be slightly deficient. Throughout the article, frequent mention is made of the extremely *low fat* yield of the diet. Nelson A. Fernandez *et. al.,* 'Nutrition Survey of Two Rural Puerto Rican Areas Before and After a Community Improvement Program', *American Journal of Clinical Nutrition*, XXII (1969), 1639-51.

14. Aurand and Woods, *op. cit.*, 211; E. E. Rice, 'The Nutritional Content and Value of Meat and Meat Products', in J. F. Price and B. S. Schweigert (eds), *The Science of Meat and Meat Products* (San Francisco, 1971; 2nd ed), 307; Lloyd, McDonald, and Crampton, *op. cit.*, 163.

15. A. Barclay, *A Practical View of the Present State of Slavery in the West Indies* (London, 1827; 2nd edn), 307. Analysis of Caribbean diets today consisting principally of rice, beans, bananas, and codfish indicates that they would be seriously thiamine deficient were it not for 'enriched' rice. See for example Diva Sanjur, *Puerto Rican Food Habits: A Socio-Cultural Approach* (Ithaca, 1970), 23.

16. Lloyd, McDonald, and Crampton, *op. cit.*, 163.

17. John H. Parry, 'Plantation and Provision Ground: An Historical Sketch of the Introduction of Food Crops into Jamaica', *Revista de Historia de America*, XXXIX (155), 16-17.

18. David Lowenthal, 'The Population of Barbados', *Social Economic Studies*, VI (157), 445-501; Richard B. Sheridan, 'The Crisis of Slave Subsistence in the British West Indies during and after the American Revolution', *William and Mary Quarterly*, XXXIII (1976), 615-41; Berta Cabanillas, *Origenes de los Habitos Alimenticios del Pueblo de Puerto Rico* (Madrid, 1955), 274-75, 290.

19. For works that deal exclusively with West Indian black-related diseases see Jean Barthelemy, *Observations sur les Maladies des Negres, leurs causes, leurs traitemens,*

et les moyens de les prevenir (Paris, 1892; 2nd edn), 2; James Thompson, *A Treatise on the Diseases of Negroes as They Occur in the Island of Jamaica* (Kingston, Jamaica, 1820).

20. See William Hilary, *Observations on the Changes of the Air and the Concomitant Epidemical Diseases, in the Island of Barbados* (London, 1811; 2nd edn), 297–304, for a discussion of nyctalopia. See also Collins, *Practical Rules*, 287; James Grainger, *Essay on the More Common West Indian Diseases* (London, 1807; 2nd edn), 60.

21. Bengt Ansell and State Lagercrantz, *Geophagical Customs* (Uppsala, 1958), 60; John Stewart, *An Account of Jamaica* (London, 1808), 273; Abbad y Lasierra, *op. cit.*, 207; John Imray, 'Observations on the Mal d'estomach or Cachexia Africana, as it Takes place among the Negroes of Dominica', *Edinburgh Medical and Surgical Journal*, CIX (1843), 314; John Williamso, *Medical and Miscellaneous Observations Relative to the West India Islands* (Edinburgh, 1817), I, 177–82; II, 267; Edwards, *History of British in West Indies*, II, 167; Collins, *Practical Rules*, 274.

22. *Ibid.*, 293, 295; Williamson, *Medical and Miscellaneous Observations*, I, 110, Abbad y Lasierra, *op. cit.*, 207; John Hunter, *Observations on the Diseases of the Army in Jamaica* (London, 1808; 3rd ed.), 249.

23. David Mason, 'On Atrophia a Ventriculo (Mal D'Estomach) or Dirt-Eating', *Edinburgh Medical and Surgical Journal*, XXXIX (1833), 292; Orlando Patterson, *The Sociology of Slavery* (London, 167), 102; Williamson, *Medical and Miscellaneous Observations*, I, 182; II, 267; Collins, *Practical Rules*, 294; Imray, *op. cit.*, 314; Edwards, *History of British in West Indies*, II, 167.

24. This 'very pronounced' black resistance to hookworm infection was discovered by investigators in the American South during the early decades of this century. See for example, A. E. Keller, W. S. Leathers, and H. C. Ricks, 'An Investigation of the Incidence and Intensity of Infestation of Hookworm in Mississippi', *American Journal of Hygiene*, XIX (1934), 629–56.

25. Hillary, *op. cit.*, 182; Hunter, *Diseases of the Army in Jamaica*, 195, 211–216; Grainger, *West Indian Diseases*, 32.

26. Claude Levy, 'Slavery and the Emancipation Movement in Barbados, 1650–1833', *Journal of Negro History*, LV (1970), 6; Williamson, *Medical and Miscellaneous Observations*, I, 73; Long, *History of Jamaica*, II, 548, 551; Frank Wesley Pitman, 'Slavery on the British West Indian Plantations in the Eighteenth Century', *Journal of Negro History*, II (1926), 632; Richard Henry Dana, *To Cuba and Back: a Vacation Voyage* (Carbondale, Ill., 1966; rpt. edn).

27. Collins, *Practical Rules*, 85; Patterson, *op. cit.*, 99: J. Harry Bennett, *Bondsmen and Bishops: Slavery and Apprenticeship on the Codrington Plantations of Barbados, 1710–1838* (Berkeley, 1958), 56–58; George W. Roberts. *The Population of Jamaica* (Cambridge, England, 1957), 175; Richard S. Dunn, *Sugar and Slaves: The Rise of the Planter Class in the English West Indies, 1624–1713* (Chapel Hill, 1972), 302, 305–06; Higman, *Slave Population and Economy in Jamaica* (Oxford, 1976), 112–13.

28. Craton and Walvin, *A Jamaica Plantation*, 113, 197–98; Higman, *Slave Population*, 112. Deaths were substantially understated because of a failure to report infant deaths.

29. Handler and Lange, *Plantation Slavery in Barbados*, 99; D. Angel Jose Crowley (ed.), *Un Ensayo Estadistico-Medico de la Mortalidad de la Diocesis de la Habana durante el Ano de 1843* (Havana, 1845); William Sells, *Remarks on the Condition of the Slaves in the Island of Jamaica* (London, 1823; rpt. edn 1972), 19–20.

30. Long, *History of Jamaica*, II, 433; Pittman, *The Development of the British West Indies, 1760–1763* (New Haven, 1917), 13, 386.

31. Juan G. Hava, 'Communicacion Dirigida a la Academia sobre una Epidemia de Beriberi', *Academia de Ciencias Medical de la Habana: Anales*, II (165), 160–61: J. Minteguiaga, 'Lettre sur le Beriberi', *Gazette Medicale de Paris*, XLV (1874), 35; August Hirsch, *Handbook of Geographical and Historical Pathology* (London, 1883), II, 576.

32. C. C. de Silva and N. G. Baptist, *Tropical Nutritional Disorders of Infants and Children* (London, 1969), 114–15; Robert R. Williams, *Toward the Conquest of Beriberi* (Cambridge, 1961), 153, 156–57.

33. Michael Latham *et. al.*, *Scopes Manual on Nutrition* (New York, 1972), 39; Stanley Davidson *et. al.*, *Human Nutrition and Dietetics* (Edinburgh, 1975; 6th ed.), 415; Williams, *Toward the Conquest of Beriberi*, 81.

34. Davidson *et al.*, *Human Nutrition*, 415; Latham *et al.*, *Scope on Nutrition*, 39.

35. Craton and Walvin, *op. cit.*, 134. See also the parochial records for Barbados: the Parish of St. Thomas, for example, buried 168 slave children aged ten and under for the period 1816–34. Only 36 of the deaths were one year of age or less. In St. Phillips Parish, 33 of their 106 burials were infants. The records for other parishes are incomplete, yet what data are available continue to suggest that only about one third of those aged ten and under of those slave children who died were infants aged one or less.

36. Collins, *Practical Rules*, 393–94; Roberts, *Population of Jamaica*, 175; Williams, *Toward the Conquest of Beriberi*, 85.

37. M. G. Lewis, *Journal of a West Indian Proprietor, 1815–1817* (London, 1929), 97, 111.

38. Engerman, 'Some Economic and Demographic Comparisons of Slavery in the United States and the British Indies', *Economic History Review*, XXIX (1976), 264–66; Anrudh K. Jain, 'Demographic Aspects of Lactation and Postpartum Amenorrhea,' *Demography*, VII (1970), 250–71; Lamur, 'Demography of Surinam Plantation Slaves in the Last Decade before Emancipation', 168; Klein and Engerman, 'Fertility Differentials between Slaves in the United States and the British West Indies: A Note on Lactation Practices and their Possible Implications', *William and Mary Quarterly*, XXXV (1978), 357–74; Collins, *Practical Rules*, 146.

39. Josiah Clark Nott and George R. Gliddon (eds), *Indigenous Places of the Earth: or New Chapters of Ethnological Inquiry* (Philadelphia, 1857), 387.

59

Death, Disease and Medicine on the Jamaican Slave Plantations: the Example of Worthy Park 1767–1838

MICHAEL CRATON*

Even while condemning the institution of slavery, many modern writers on the subject have echoed the early apologists of slavery in assuming that the health of plantation slaves can be positively correlated with the number of doctors and the amount of medicine used.[1] The motives of the slaveowners are usually acknowledged to have been economic calculation rather than disinterested philanthropy, but the facts that there were more 'doctors' in Jamaica in 1800 than in 1900, that nearly all plantations had their own practitioners, and that medicines featured largely in any list of imported plantation supplies, are taken as evidence that slaves were relatively well cared for. Without such care, it is assumed, slave health conditions would have been far worse; perhaps even as bad as those in the notorious 'graveyard' of the West African coast.[2]

More careful research, however, revises — even reverses — these views. Ignorance of the etiology of tropical diseases placed them largely beyond human control, and this situation was compounded by treatments based upon a purblind ignorance of human physiology, and an irrelevant pharmacopeia. Even at Worthy Park plantation in central Jamaica, which was serviced for 55 years by a doctor famous for his efficiency, slave medicine was a mixed blessing indeed.[3]

Under the Jamaican Consolidated Slave Law of 1792, not only were overseers to hand in to the vestries annual lists of births and deaths on their plantations on a penalty of £50 for non-compliance, but every plantation doctor was also 'on oath, to give-in an account of slaves dying, with, to the best of his judgement, the causes thereof, under penalty of £100 for each neglect'.[4]

Thus, for at least those estates for which records have survived, there exist cause-of-death diagnoses up to the standard attained by eighteenth-century plantation doctors. In addition, at Worthy Park, and some other estates the slave ledgers included, rather less systematically, comments on the health of slaves whose efficiency was impaired, and lists of medicines used. Besides this, Worthy Park's chief slave doctor, John Quier (1739–1822), published an account of seven years of his practice in the district.[5]

What follows is a table (Table 1) showing all the causes of death ascribed in the Worthy Park records between 1792 and 1838, applying to 401 slaves. Wherever possible, the slave doctor's diagnoses have been translated into modern terms, and grouped together into classes along the lines of the World Health Organisation[6] categories. Further on, the significance of the diagnoses given in the 'Condition' columns of the Worthy Park slave ledgers is also discussed, but the Condition listings are so much less systematic and conclusive — so much less final — than Causes of Death, that they cannot easily be tabulated.

The 401 specific causes of death from Worthy Park represent perhaps the largest sample it is now possible to recover from a single Jamaican estate. However, any such single source needs careful preliminary evaluation before its general value is established. The two chief deficiencies of the data are that they are not complete, and that they are derived from a population which

*Department of History, University of Waterloo.

Histoire Sociale — Social History, Vol. 9, No. 18 November (1976), pp. 237–55.

G

Table 1   Worthy Park: Incidence of Causes of Death Noted, 1783–1838 (Assigned by World Health Organisation Categories)

Worthy Park diagnoses	Incidences	Modern diagnoses (where different)	W.H.O.	Categories
Dysentery	10	Bacillary Dysentery	I	004
Flux	25	Diarrhoeal Disease		009
Phthisis Consumption	15	Tuberculosis		011
Coco Bays	2	Leprosy (Arabian)		030
Whooping Cough. Croup	4			033
Locked Jaw	2	Tetanus		037
Measles	5			055
Smallpox	2			056
Diseased Brain. Water on the Brain	2	Encephalitis		062
Yaws	24			102
Dirt Eating	9	Helminthiasis		127
Worms, Worm Fever	14	Internal parasites		129
Fever	26			
Palsy	3	Cerebral palsy	VI	343
Fits, Convulsions, Epilepsy	7	Epilepsy		345
Complaint in Spine	1	Spinal chord disease		349
Apoplexy, Stroke	2		VII	436
Elephantiasis	1			457
Violent Cold, Cough, Catarrh	11	Acute Common Cold	VIII	460
Influenza	2			470
Pneumonia	1			480
Asthma	4			493
Pleurisy	10			511
Abcess in Lungs	2			513
Rupture	3	Hernia	IX	551
Suppression of Menses	2	Menstrual disorder	X	626
Childbed	7			644
Puny from Birth, At Birth, Still Born	18		XI	677
Ulcers, Ulceration	14	Chronic skin ulcers	XIII	707
Spasms	1	Nervous system	XVI	780
Dropsy, 'Cold, Bloated & Dropsical'	38	Cardiovascular. lympathic		782
Lung Trouble, Sore Throat	3	Respiratory system		783
Stomach Complaint	1	Upper gastro-intestinal		784
Bloated, Swelled & Bloated, Inflammation of Bowels	4	Lower gastro-intestinal		785
Swelled Leg, Sore Foot	4	Limbs & joints		787
Old Age, Decline, Weakness, Informity, Invalid (where old)	89	Senility		794
Suddenly, In the Night, Sudden, Act of God, Vindication of God	7	Sudden Death (Unknown Cause)		795
Diseased Many Years, Infirmity, Invalid (not aged), Sick Some Time, Worthless, At Hospital in Kingston	7	Other sicknesses, unspecified		796
Accident	14		XVII	880
Ate Poison, Suicide by Poison	3	Suicide		950
Shot while Stealing	1	Legal Intervention		970
Suffocation	1			994
	401			

changed considerably during the 46 years covered, particularly in the gradual increase in the proportion of Creole (island-born), and thus fully 'seasoned' (acclimatised) slaves. It is likely that between 1792 and 1838 some 1,000 slaves actually died at Worthy Park, so that causes of death are specifically unknown for almost two-thirds. However, the nature of the records determines that these causes of death can be regarded as virtually a random sample, scattered evenly over the entire period and over the whole range of the population.

Causes of death data are deficient for two periods of exceptional mortality, following a large influx of new Africans in the 1790s, and the arrival of more than 100 new Creoles in 1830. This may have led to a slight understatement of the deaths by 'fever' and 'flux'. Yet these periods of exceptional mortality occurred in only about four of the 46 years covered. Were all causes of death in those years specifically known and recorded, this would surely have led to a severe distortion of the overall situation. Moreover, only a minority of Jamaican estates had comparable influxes of population in slavery's last years.

Another area of slight doubt was the degree to which causes of infant death were underrepresented. It is well known that infant mortality itself was commonly understated by plantation records, though not quite to the degree that some writers believe.[7] At Worthy Park, the number of those who were born and died during the intercensal periods and thus went unrecorded was probably no more than one in five overall. Over the period 1792–1838 just over 30 per cent of those born on the estate died in their first five years. Only about 20 per cent of the known causes of death related to deaths in this age range. But since about a third of Worthy Park's slaves were African-born and never were infants at Worthy Park it seems likely that causes of death were not underrepresented at all.

It is a commonplace of plantation studies that new African slaves suffered far higher mortality rates and died from different diseases than seasoned Creoles. Yet it should be rememberd that by the beginning of the period covered an established plantation of 500 slaves would, on the average, receive only two or three new Africans a year, and that from the ending of the British slave trade in 1808 the flow dried up altogether. Accordingly, for Jamaica as a whole, and for most long-established estates, the proportion of Africans in the slave plantation declined from only about 50 per cent

in 1792, to no more than 10 per cent in 1838. The Worthy Park figures were 42.1 per cent in 1784, soaring to 63.4 per cent in 1794, and then declining gradually to 37.9 per cent in 1813 and 9.6 per cent in 1838.[8]

If it is accepted then that the causes of death from Worthy Park for the last half century of slavery were more or less random and representative, it is worth stating here what were the average demographic characteristics of that plantation during that period, in respect of the sex ratio, age cohorts, mortality and fertility levels, and life expectancies.

Worthy Park was a typical Jamaican sugar plantation in most respects, though somewhat larger, further inland, and consequently even more self-contained than the average. How then did its pattern of death and disease compare with other types of settlement and other areas? Although comparable vital statistics were not obtainable, it has at least proved possible to compare the Worthy Park causes of death figures for 1792–1838 with the only previously published cause-of-death analysis for a West Indian slave population, derived from British Guiana, 1829–32, and with figures for the total population of heavily urbanised St. Catherine's Parish, Jamaica, between 1774 and 1778, including free whites, coloureds and black as well as slaves.[10]

In fact, when looking for comparisons with the Worthy Park causes of death, it was the data from St. Catherine's — a lowland area with some sugar plantations but heavily dominated by Spanish Town, the Jamaican capital — which were first employed. The contrasts between a tightly-knit but closed and rural population of slaves, and largely urbanised and geographically mobile population, including all races and classes, were immediately apparent. This was particularly so in the far greater incidence of death by 'fever' and the far smaller number of deaths by old age in Spanish Town and its environs. A tragically high proportion of those who died from fever in Spanish Town were members of the white army garrison who, during their period of acclimatisation, suffered from one of the highest mortality rates in the world.[11] The evidence for mortality among urban slaves is ambivalent,[12] but it is almost certain that the beneficial effects stemming from the fact that they were largely Creoles, and from rather better food and working conditions than on plantations, were offset by a vulnerability induced by slum crowding, poor sanitation, nearby swamps, and the chances of reinfection by transients, particularly in respect of

Table 2 Worthy Park: Average Population Pyramid, 1784–1813

Cohort	Ages	Numbers in each cohort	% of total in each cohort	Recorded deaths in each cohort	% dead in each cohort	Dead each year per 1,000 (av. mortality 39.37)	Annual death rate (per 1,000)	Probability of dying in cohort period	Dead in each cohort period of 10,000 at year 0	Survivors at end of each cohort period	Expectation of life at beginning of each cohort period
1	0– 4	488*	10.76	63**	14.26	5.61	52.14	.2607	2607	7393	27.4
2	5– 9	447	9.86	24	5.43	2.14	21.70	.1085	802	6591	31.2
3	10–14	393	8.64	17	3.85	1.52	17.59	.0879	579	6012	29.7
4	15–19	350	7.72	13	2.94	1.16	15.03	.0752	452	5560	27.3
5	20–24	459	10.12	55	12.44	4.90	48.42	.2421	1346	4214	24.3
6	25–29	451	9.95	28	6.33	2.49	25.03	.1252	528	3686	26.3
7	30–34	417	9.20	28	6.33	2.49	27.07	.1354	499	3187	24.7
8	35–39	335	7.39	26	5.88	2.31	31.26	.1563	498	2689	22.8
9	40–44	325	7.17	33	7.47	2.94	41.00	.2050	551	2138	20.6
10	45–49	205	4.52	27	6.11	2.41	53.32	.2666	570	1568	19.0
11	50–54	220	4.85	21	4.75	1.87	38.56	.1928	302	1266	18.2
12	55–59	181	3.99	17	3.85	1.52	38.10	.1905	241	1025	15.3
13	60–64	126	2.77	19	4.30	1.69	61.01	.3050	386	639	12.0
14	65–69	69	1.52	26	5.88	2.31	151.97	.7594	485	154	4.9
15	70+	70	1.54	45	10.18	4.01	—	1.0000	154	0	2.5
Totals		4535	100.00	442	100.00	39.37					

* 21 added for under-recording
** Increased by 50 per cent from 42 for under-recording

epidemics. All in all, the mortality rates in tropical towns were probably twice the average for whole colonies, and higher than for any plantations.[13]

Though largely explicable, the very great differences between the causes of death from Worthy Park and from St. Catherine's left the question of the typicality of Worthy Park as a sugar plantation up in the air. The discovery of the remarkable correlation between Worthy Park's figures and those for a far larger sample drawn from sugar plantations in a colony a thousand miles distant in a rather later period, was therefore very exciting. Many contemporary writers spoke of sugar plantations as if they were standard in every respect, and of the contrasts between different types of settlement and locations within the Caribbean. Some analysis has recently been made of differences in overall mortality figures.[14] But here for the first time was statistical evidence by specific causes of death. Moreover, from this it was clear that there were health characteristics common and peculiar to sugar plantations wherever they were found within the Caribbean region. These contrasted to a marked degree with West Indian towns, and probably differed to a lesser but significant degree from smaller, less intensively cultivated plantations growing staples other than sugar, in hillier areas, for which similar work remains to be undertaken.

In drawing up both cause-of-death tables there were many difficulties of classification. Too many of the alleged explanations of death from Worthy Park were non-specific or downright evasive. What, for example, is learned from 'Accident'? And what can be made of 'At Hospital in Kingston', 'Suddenly', 'In the Night', or 'A Vindication of God'? In a dismaying number of cases the doctor was describing — and presumably had been treating — symptoms rather than actual diseases. 'Convulsions' and gastro-intestinal complications were particularly difficult to identify, but even the common diagnoses of 'flux', 'fever', 'ulcers', and "dropsy' proved troublesome. At first sight there also seemed to be a remarkably high number of different causes of death. However, discriminating reclassification — first along World Health Organisation lines and then, less scientifically, into the categories used for the British Guiana slaves — elicited a much clearer picture.

Despite the depredations of epidemics (not all of which were killers) and the decimation of the 'seasoning' process among new slaves, the chief single cause of death on sugar plantations was still old age — or at least debility among elderly adults. That over a fifth of the slaves lived long enough to die of what were regarded as natural causes surely runs counter to the impression given by *average* survival rates, which suggest a life expectancy at birth of less than 30 years for Creoles, and for newly-arrived Africans an average expectation of no more than a dozen more years.

Epidemics of measles, smallpox and yellow fever carried off numbers of plantation slaves in some years, but the dreaded 'fluxes' struck more regularly and killed even more overall. Known

Table 3   Comparative Causes of Death: Worthy Park, 1792–1838: British Guiana, 1829–32; St. Catherine's (Spanish town), 1774–78[15]

	Worthy Park slaves 1795–1838	British Guiana slaves 1829–32	St. Catherine's (Spanish Town) 1774–78
Old Age, Debility	22.2	19.1	3.6
Dysentery, Flux	8.7	12.0	9.3
Dropsy	9.5	9.2	3.4
Pulmonary Diseases	11.4	9.2	5.7
Fevers (inc. Measles, Smallpox)	9.2	8.1	39.9
Yaws, Ulcers	9.5	6.1	6.1
Inflammations, etc.	2.0	4.4	3.8
Gastro-Intestinal	6.0	4.3	3.8
Accidents	4.3	4.2	1.6
Leprosy	0.5	3.8	—
Convulsions	3.8	3.7	6.3
Lockjaw	0.5	2.6	0.8
Syphilis	—	1.0	1.1
Others & Unknown	12.4	12.3	14.6
Totals	100.0	100.0	100.0

by their symptoms either as the 'white' or 'bloody' flux, these were nearly all varieties of bacillary dysentery, particularly infection by the protozoa *shigella shigae*. Bacillary dysentery could kill quickly by dehydration and poisoning by bacterial toxins. Amoebic dysentery was probably less common, and where fatal was not always identified as a flux, killing more slowly by chronic infection and secondary ulcerations in intestines, liver or lungs.

Plantation deaths from 'inflammation' and 'mortification' were rather less common than might be expected. On the other hand, intestinal and subcutaneous parasites were extremely common, and it was not the most evident types — such as the nauseating tape and guinea worms — which were necessarily the most dangerous. The tiny hookworm in particular was a far more serious and widespread cause of ill health, debility and death than was recognised by contemporary doctors. The larvae of these creatures were picked up by bare feet, causing what was known as 'ground itch' between the toes. Shedding their skin and burrowing, the larvae travelled through the bloodstream to the lymph glands or lungs, where they caused a cough. Migrating to the mouth, they were ingested, finding a home in the intestines, where they came to maturity. Still only about a centimetre long, hookworms, if undisturbed, could live in their host for seven or even ten years. Females in season laid thousands of eggs a day which, deposited in faeces, restarted the cycle.

Where colonies of over 500 hookworms developed, ancyclostomiasis, or hookworm disease, resulted. This was characterised by symptoms often regarded as separate diseases: flux-like emissions, fluid retention ('dropsy'), convulsions, and the mysterious craving to eat strange substances, particularly clay ('dirt eating').[16] Besides this, non-fatal ancyclostomiasis could stunt growth and delay puberty, and caused chronic anaemia, which brought on the fatigue, dullness and apathy which were often regarded as natural African traits.

Dysentery and intestinal parasites were promoted by unhygienic overcrowding, especially where drinking water, earth closets and cooking facilities were in close proximity, and lack of washing water made personal cleanliness difficult. In these respects, Worthy Park, with good running water from an aqueduct, was rather more fortunate than some estates and most of the crowded 'yards' of the Jamaican towns. This may have been the reason why the recorded cases of tetanus, or lockjaw, in infants — normally contracted through umbilical infection in unhygienic conditions, and invariably fatal — were fewer at Worthy Park than elsewhere. Another reason, though, might have been that the doctor was less ready than other plantation doctors to diagnose lockjaw as a cause of death.[17]

At least two fevers which were later recognised as tropical scourges, the food and water-borne typhoid, and the louse, flea and mite-borne typhus, were also encouraged by unhygienic conditions such as were found in West Indian plantations and towns. Unfortunately, certain identification of these fevers in the West Indies during slavery days is now impossible. However, if they did occur, typhoid was probably more common in the towns than on rural plantations, and of the three main types of typhus, scrub typhus, carried by ticks and chiggers and characterised by dropsy-causing myocarditis, was that most likely to have occurred on plantations. Cholera was apparently not known in the West Indies until after British slavery ended, though there were disastrous outbreaks later. Diphtheria, if it existed, was not recognised during slavery days.

Of the endemic fevers, detectable in the records, malaria ('ague') and dengue were widespread, but the chief killer was probably yellow fever. This disease, so-called for the jaundicing that followed from liver infection, was technically endemic, but went through epidemic phases as different strains of virus went the rounds. Doctors correctly associated fevers with marshes, but erroneously attributed infection to 'miasmas' rising from them at night, rather than to the *anopheles and aedes aegypti* mosquitoes that bred in them and carried the viruses. Slaves did what they could to repel mosquitoes by sleeping with permanently smoking fires nearby, but this was to reduce the nuisance rather than through a perception of danger. It was the immunisation process of the passage of time rather than such preventative measures which brought about the gradual decline in deaths from fevers. Many slaves indeed were already less likely to suffer from certain types of disease notoriously fatal to Europeans in the tropics. Most types of malaria and yellow fever were African in origin, and African slaves at least had inbuilt immunities. Sleeping sickness (trypanosomiasis), however, was only known among the African-born, since the infection was carried by the tsetse fly, which never migrated from Central Africa to the West Indies.

Rather more common killers than fever on plantations, even among acclimatised slaves, were the many varieties of pulmonary infection

Worthy Park: Average Population Pyramid, 1784–1813

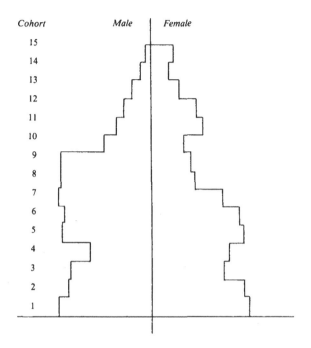

Cohort	Ages	Totals in cohorts	Males	Females	% in cohort of total	% males in cohort of total	% females in cohort of total
1	0– 4	488	242	247	10.76	5.32	5.45
2	5– 9	447	215	232	9.86	4.74	5.12
3	10–14	392	208	184	8.64	4.59	4.05
4	15–19	350	158	192	7.71	3.48	4.24
5	20–24	459	230	229	10.12	5.07	5.05
6	25–29	451	225	226	9.95	4.96	4.99
7	30–34	417	236	181	9.20	5.20	4.00
8	35–39	335	230	105	7.39	5.07	2.32
9	40–44	325	227	98	7.17	5.01	2.16
10	45–49	205	123	82	4.52	2.71	1.81
11	50–54	220	89	131	4.85	1.96	2.89
12	55–59	181	68	113	3.99	1.50	2.49
13	60–64	126	50	76	2.77	1.10	1.67
14	65–69	69	27	42	1.52	0.60	0.92
15	70 +	70	11	59	1.54	0.24	1.30
Totals		4535	2338	2197	100.00	51.55	48.45

imported from Europe. In these cases, resistance was low through lack of immunisation, but also was sapped by overcrowding, overwork and deficient diet. Influenza could kill directly, but even the common cold could accelerate into fatal pneumonia, or a cough or 'catarrh' degenerate into 'galloping consumption'. Whooping cough, though not common, could be fatal to slave children. Diet and vitamin deficiencies also contributed to the high incidence of dropsy, a diagnosis applied to any swelling thought to be caused by an excess of one of the bodily fluids.

Yet dropsies were at least as common among the whites as among blacks in Jamaica, with liver, heart and urinary conditions often exacerbated by excessive drinking. Though some writers deplored the intemperance of town slaves, few slaves in fact had opportunities for such 'over-indulgence. This probably also explains why they so rarely suffered from the gout, or the myterious 'dry belly-ache' so common among Jamaican whites, now known to have been lead poisoning due to drinking rum distilled in vessels made of lead, and drink from pewter pots.

Some 'dropsies' and 'ulcers' among slaves were symptoms of horrifying diseases originally imported from Africa which remained endemic among blacks, though whites were seemingly immune; elephantiasis, 'coco bays' (alias 'Arabian leprosy'), scrofula, true leprosy, and yaws. Of these, yaws, a highly contagious but non-venereal variant of syphilis, was especially virulent. Often contracted in childhood, it was characterised first by raspberry-like eruptions, then by scarring and ulceration, and, with the prolonged tertiary stages, often by excruciating 'bone-ache' and damage to cartilages, spleen and brain. Many sufferers died of old age or general debility rather than of yaws itself, but the disease progressively sapped energy and will, as well as making the victims pathetically unsightly. On some Jamaican estates about a sixth of the slaves, at any one time, suffered seriously from yaws, and there was a separate 'yaws hothouse', or isolation hospital, where the worst cases withered away.[18] At Worthy Park, however, the disease was rather less serious and a second hothouse was not considered necessary.

From the death diagnoses, true venereal disease seems to have been relatively uncommon at Worthy Park and elsewhere, though the effects of yaws were often indistinguishable from those of syphilis, and gonorrhea may have been so common as to be considered unworthy

of notice.[19] Certain other diseases which afflict modern society, such as heart disease, stomach ulcers and cancers, were noticeably rare on slave plantations, either because the slaves did not have the opportunities to contract them, or did not live long enough to develop the symptoms. With the possible exception of the single slave 'shot while stealing', no deaths recorded at Worthy Park were directly attributable to the slave condition. Deaths by accident were no more common than one would expect in any industrial situation with minimal safeguards; and suicides (of whom only three were certainly recorded) were probably no more common than in the British army during National Service, or among undergraduates at a modern university.

The data derived from the Condition listings at Worthy Park are not only more fragmentary and capricious than those for Causes of Death; for several reasons they also seriously understate the low level of general health on the plantation. Even for the years for which full records survive, the health of individual slaves was only noted if their condition incapacitated them. For example, there is no reference at all in the Worthy Park records to eye diseases, though it is unlikely that the plantation was entirely free from all forms of opthalmia common among slaves elsewhere. Short-term or non-fatal illnesses such as colds and malaria were rarely recorded either. Cases of measles and smallpox which did not kill, however, sometimes were; for though immunisation theory was not yet developed, it was already recognised that these diseases rarely recurred.

Many other diseases were too common for diagnosis, not diagnosed in their early stages, or not recognised at all. From the incidence of death from yaws, 'coco bays', scrofula and 'dropsy', it seems likely that at least a third of the slaves suffered from diseases of the skin and tissues at some time during their lives, and perhaps half from serious internal disorders. In most cases these diseases were incurable and progressive, though not invariably fatal in themselves. If the debilitating effects of deficient diet and parasites less crippling than hookworm are included, nearly all slaves were subject to tropical ailments which lowered their efficiency, their fertility and enjoyment of life.

In sum, though seasoned slaves on established sugar plantations were not more subject to fatality than most persons in the tropics — and much less so than those living in towns in the lowlands — the general level of their health was dismally low.

Masters and doctors alike were disposed by

their 'interest' and ignorance to minimise slave ailments. Owners and overseers were determined to keep all but the dying at work, and to trim the costs of medical treatment. To their eyes, a successsful doctor was one who satisfied these requirements. Paid a *per capita* fee, plantation doctors were rewarded positively for cursory treatment, and encouraged to ignore failure and simulate success. Faced with a level of general health that condemned the plantation system by which they lived, or was beyond their care or ken, doctors tended to disguise the inadequacy of the treatments and the ignorance of their diagnoses with accusations of malingering, self-inflicted injury and 'natural' unhealthiness stemming from the slaves' racial origins. In this they perpetuated the malign ignorance of Dr John Trapham, who in 1679 attributed the high incidence of yaws among blacks to the alleged fact that they were an 'animal people', subject to an 'unhappy jumble of the rational with the brutal Nature',[20] or even the distasteful fatalism of a slave trader in 1694:

[. . .] What the small-pox spar'd, the flux swept off to our great regret, after all our pains and care to give their messes in due order and season, keeping their lodgings as clean and sweet as possible, and enduring so much misery and stench so long among a parcel of creatures nastier than swine: and after all our expectations to be defeated by their mortality.[21]

The medical profession, like all self-legislating and self-perpetuating 'misteries', has always been a conservatising force. What particularly bedevilled eighteenth- and even nineteenth-century medicine were the persistence of the fallacy of the four 'humours' in the teeth of the clinical evidence, and the tradition that devalued surgery in favour of 'physic'. When Dr Trapham wrote his *Discourse on the State of Health in Jamaica* in 1679, belief in humoral theory was still absolute. Every human ailment, from hookworm to cancer, was said to be due to an excess of one of the four vital fluids which flowed from liver to heart: melancholy, phlegm, blood, choler — the counterparts of earth, water, air and fire. The sole purpose of medicine, it was held, was to keep the elements in balance, the chief methods being bloodletting, 'salivation', blistering and purging. Physicians were neither willing nor able to use the surgeon's knife, save in emergencies such as amputations.

Besides this, doctors made undiscriminate use of at least two dangerous specifics: mercury and opium. The first, beloved of alchemists as 'quicksilver', had some success with 'the pox', but produced crippling side-effects which until recent times were thought to be symptoms of the disease it purported to cure.[22] The second quelled pain but was demoralisingly addictive, including withdrawal symptoms after very little use. That both mercurials and opiates were relatively expensive may have been positively beneficial to such dependent patients as slaves. The herbal remedies preferred for cheapness's sake were, where ineffectual, generally harmless. It might be argued that in the absence of antiseptics and anaesthetics the reluctance of doctors to operate was also to the slaves' advantage.[23]

What medical progress was made during the slavery period was not due to any revolution in theory or dramatic new methods (save inoculation for smallpox), but a slightly more empirical attitude, a greater attention to the individual patient, and the first glimmerings of a belief in cleanliness, rest and restorative diet. In these respects, the pioneers were the English Thomas Sydenham (1624–89) and the Dutch clinicians such as Hermann Boerhaave of Leyden (1688–1738).[24] Hans Sloane, a disciple of Sydenham, displayed a comparatively open mind and a willingness to experiment (honestly recording failures as well as successes) in the descriptions he published of the many cases he treated during his brief stay in Jamaica (1688–89).[25] But neither Sloane nor his eighteenth-century successors made any systematic discoveries concerning causes or cures. At best they simply learned, through bitter experience, that a West Indian doctor was more likely to succeed the less he applied the 'scientific' humoral theory and the pharmacy he had learned in the European schools.

This gradual awareness can be well illustrated by the career of Dr John Quier, graduate of Leyden and London, who was Worthy Park's doctor from 1767 to 1822, from six published letters written to a former colleague during Quier's first years in Jamaica,[26] and from his later practice. From the letters it seems that Quier was not obsessed by humoral theory, but still placed too great an emphasis upon bodily fluids and the efficacy of 'cleansing the blood'. From the descriptions of some of his early treatments it seems that his patients might well have stood a better chance with no treatment at all. For the eye disease he called 'the dry opthalmies', for example, he specified a copious bleeding, 'antiphlogistic' purges, a 'cooling regimen' with nitre, and blisters behind the ears and on the side of the neck, as well as the 'emollient poultices' which alone might have brought any relief.

What caused Dr Quier most concern were smallpox and measles, serious outbreaks of which occurred in Lluidas Vale during his first few years there. Indeed, he has been given credit, almost certainly exaggerated, for advances in the prevention and diagnosis of these diseases.[27] Although distinguishing clearly between smallpox and measles, he attributed quite distinct afflictions such as dysentery, dry bellyache and even tetanus as 'secondary manifestations' of them. In these respects, only in being able to diagnose whooping cough was Dr Quier farther advanced than the Persian medical authority Rhazes (AD 860–932) who, while being the earliest correctly to identify smallpox and measles, was apparently not aware of any other endemic diseases.[28]

At least John Quier differed from the majority of his fellow slave doctors in learning somewhat from his failures. At first he believed that excessive heat made the blood 'putrescent', and he tended to let blood by venesection at the onset of any fever. He also administered savage purgatives such as the mercuric calomel, nitre, or jalap, in almost all cases of serious illness. When in some measles cases these led not to a 'salutary salivation' and gentle evacuation, but to bloody vomiting and diarrhoea, he bled the patients more, applying blisters to the thighs. If the internal spasm and pains became too severe, he administered — literally almost as a last resort — heroic doses, up to four grains a day, of opium.

Although he never admitted that it was the medicine rather than the disease which was killing his patients, John Quier soon realised that excessive purging and bleeding weakened them, and gradually relented. Ironically, strong 'medicine' became reserved for those unfortunates whom the well-intentioned doctor regarded as strong enough to stand them. In the cases of the very old or young, the seriously undernourished and 'naturally' debilitated, nature was 'allowed to take its course', and some patients' clearly gained a fortuitous reprieve. In the eighteenth century it was medicine as often as death itself which acted as a great leveller.

As to inoculation for smallpox, John Quier was certainly no innovator. The technique of inoculation had been introduced into England from Turkey by Lady Mary Wortley Montagu as early as 1717, and there is some evidence that some form of 'variolation', or intentional inoculative infection with the disease, was known in West Africa.[29] Quier himself acknowledged that he used the method developed by Thomas, Baron Dimsdale, consultant to Catherine the Great — infecting those who had not yet had the disease through a scratch on the arm, with matter drawn from smallpox pustules. Although effective in most individual cases — inducing only a mild form of the disease — it did not avert or check the general spread of smallpox, and could lead to serious cases and death. There is no evidence that John Quier or any slave doctor in Jamaica adopted the much more satisfactory system of vaccination by cowpox matter introduced by Edward Jenner, even when it gained widespread acceptance in England after 1800.

John Quier's method was to wait until a smallpox outbreak threatened, and then to inoculate large numbers of slaves together. In 1768 he treated over 700 slaves, receiving a flat fee of 6s. 8d. a head. As with his treatments, at first Quier's methods were almost indiscriminate. Yet experience and empirical observation taught him that it was pointless to 'inoculate' those who already had the disease, and dangerous to infect the young, the old, weakly, those far gone in pregnancy, and anyone he classified as having 'putrid blood'. By exercising such discrimination Quier diminished his income at first; but as his reputation for success grew, the call upon his services increased.

Success for all West Indian doctors indeed came with moderation and common sense. A wise and humane doctor, such as John Quier clearly became, was one who realised that since his medication could rarely cure, and no doctor could — or ought to — persuade planters to improve slave conditions in general, he should concentrate on ameliorating symptoms and, by providing care, cleanliness, fresh air and decent food, encourage any natural tendency towards a cure, as well as the will to survive. Harsh medicine was simply for the peace of mind of those who paid, and those patients strong enough to take it who believed in it.

Thus, while he continued to pay lip service to the crude, irrelevant, and harmful mysteries of his craft such as bleeding, blistering and purging, John Quier more often came to prescribe strengthening diets, emollients, cooling lotions and analgesics such as the opiate laudanum. It was also during his regime that the slave 'hothouse' still standing at Worthy Park was built, as on many Jamaican properties one of the most substantial buildings erected. For women in childbirth, John Quier recommended that they be allowed to 'lie in' at least two weeks. Observing that the blacks who worked in the stillhouse (distillery) were the fattest on the estate, he recommended that infants be drafted there to fatten up. Although Dr Quier disapproved of the African customs of swaddling newborn infants and suckling children into their second year, there is at least one scrap of evidence that he came to place as much credence in 'African' medicine as in his own received pharmacy. Noticing that his black slave 'doctoress' assistant was in the habit of bathing the swollen feet of yaws sufferers in urine he did not tell her to desist, and honesty compelled him to admit that the patients came to no further harm.

To modern eyes, the wisest section of Dr John Quier's letters from Jamaica concerns a regimen for maintaining general health in a tropical climate. It could serve as a model in most respects even today: choose a dry, healthy location; practise temperance, drinking a little wine but selecting a diet more vegetable than animal, including fresh fruit; rise early, take a moderate amount of exercise, and avoid the night-time damp; bathe frequently, and change clothing according to the time of day and season; maintain a cheerful disposition. Unfortunately, however, these excellent suggestions (which John Quier perhaps followed himself, for he lived to 83) were absolutely irrelevant to the lives of slaves. As Hans Sloane had found long before, they were also almost reversed by the habits of most of the Jamaican whites.

From the Worthy Park evidence for 1792–1838 it is clear that the level of health on slave plantations was low. Yet the situation should not be exaggerated. Disease alone did not account for the continuing natural decrease in the population, which was also influenced by purely demographic characteristics.[30] If sugar plantations, with their large cramped populations and intensive agriculture, were less healthy than mountain pens and coffee plantations, estates like Worthy Park in spacious highland areas were healthier than those in the swampy lowlands of St. Catherine, St. Thomas-in-the-East, St. Mary, or St. James; and all were far less disease-ridden than the kennels and yards of Spanish Town, Kingston and the other ports, the ships on the Middle Passage, and the barracoons of the African coast.[31] Besides this, the health situation which the Worthy Park records for 1792–1838 disclosed was almost certainly better than that which obtained in the plantation's earlier days — though the improvement, like that in the population's demographic balance, was largely beyond the understanding or control of planters, doctors and 'amelioration' laws.

The 'triangle trade' of trade goods, slaves and sugar made the West Indies a crossroads for the diseases of Europe, Africa and tropical America. Until immunities built up over the years, newcomers were infected by unfamiliar strains of virus, germ and parasite. This well-documented but unexplained phenomenon accounted for perhaps half of all African slaves between the time of their original seizure and the conclusion of the seasoning process on a West Indian plantation four years later. It likewise killed almost as high a ratio of all whites newly arriving in the sugar islands, and an even higher proportion of white crewmen on the slave ships, or white soldiers cramped and ill-fed in barracks in the West Indies and West Africa.[32]

Owing to the fallacies of humoral theory, medical treatment for diseases was totally inadequate: never curative, at best palliative or innocuous, at worst positively baneful. The greatest improvement came fortuitously, with the process of creolisation. The increasingly closed nature of the plantation population made it a closed disease environment, rather less subject to attack from passing epidemics than towns or villages.

What remained, however, was serious enough; the general debility from ailments associated with unhygienic conditions, poor diet and overwork. Here, it might be argued, 'amelioration' legislation, such as was passed in all British West Indian colonies from about 1787, and particularly after 1823, should have improved health conditions, by regulating the workload, and establishing standards of food, clothing and medical care.[33] Yet these regulations were minimal, reflecting standards rather than improving them, often a form of 'window-dressing'. Medical treatment was effectively beyond the control of legislation. Besides this, towards the very end of slavery the effects of any improvements were offset by the decline in plantation profits, which made masters inclined to work their slaves harder and spend less on their upkeep and care. If slaves towards the end of formal slavery were able to grow more food, to expand their homes, and to improve their clothing, this was mainly through their own efforts. It might also be argued that there was an ironic virtue in necessity, since the decline in expenditure on slave medicine may have been actually beneficial to health.

Notes

1. Not excluding Michael Craton, *Sinews of Empire: A Short History of British Slavery* (New York and London, 1974), 192–94. The ideas in this paper largely stemmed from remarks concerning the dubious benefits of European medicine practised in West Africa, made by Philip D. Curtin while commenting on a paper on West Indian slave-doctors by Richard B. Sheridan at the M.S.S.B. comparative slavery conference at Rochester, New York, in March 1972. Curtin's own article, 'Epidemiology and the Slave Trade'. *Political Science Quarterly*, LXXXIII (June 1968), 2: 190–216, was the pioneer work on this subject. See also Richard H. Shyrock, 'Medical Practice in the Old South', *South Atlantic Quarterly*, XXIX (April 1930) 2, reprinted in *Medicine in America: Historical Essays* (Baltimore, 1966), 49–70. Much of the material here is to be included in a chapter in a forthcoming study of slaves, slave society and ex-slaves, *Searching for the Invisible Man* (Harvard, 1976).

2. For an analysis of the mortality in West Africa, mainly white, which shaped European views, see K. G. Davies, 'The Living and the Dead: White Mortality in West Africa, 1684–1732', in S. Engerman and E. Genovese (eds), *Race and Slavery in the Western Hemisphere; Quantitative Studies* (Princeton, 1975).

3. Hans Sloane's strictures against black doctors (1707) could indeed be turned by modern commentators against such white practitioners as Sloane himself: '[. . .] There are many such *Indian* and Black Doctors, who pretend, and are supposed to understand, and cure several Distempers, but what I could see of their practice [. . .] they do not perform what they pretend, unless in the vertues of some few Simples. Their ignorance of Anatomy, Diseases, Method, &c. renders even that knowledge of the vertues of Herbs, not only useless, but even sometimes hurtful to those who employ them [. . .].' *A Voyage to Madera . . . and Jamaica*, 2 vols (London, 1707, 1725), I, cxli.

4. Jamaican Act of 32 George III, c. xxiii, 33–5.

5. J. Quier, J. Hume *et. atl.*, *Letters and Essays on the Smallpox* (London, 1778).

6. *Manual of the International Statistical Classification of Diseases, Injuries, and Causes of Death, Based on the Recommendations of the Eighth Revision of Conference, 1965, and Adopted by the Nineteenth World Health Assembly*, 2 vols (Geneva: World Health Organisation, 1967).

7. For example, George W. Roberts, *The Population of Jamaica* (Cambridge, England, 1957), 165–75. Roberts, however, does not prove his contention; he asserts it, substituting figures for a later period of the worst known infant mortality (the 1890s), on the assumption that slavery must have been as bad, or worse.

8. Michael Craton, 'Jamaican Slave Mortality: Fresh Light from Worthy Park. Longville and the Tharp Estates', *Journal of Caribbean History* (November 1971): 1–27. The percentage of Africans at Worthy Park actually rose steeply in 1792 itself because of the influx of over 200 new Africans. It was 45.7 per cent in 1791 and 60.3 per cent in 1793.

9. These tables are all taken from *Searching for the Invisible Man* (*op. cit.*), Chapter III.

10. The British Guiana data are cited in Roberts, *op. cit.*, 175. The St. Catherine's data are derived from Jamaica, Island Record Office, *St. Catherine's Copy Register, Causes of Death*. Vol. I. There is a list of death causes in Edward Braithwaite, *The Development of Creole Society in Jamaica* (Oxford, 1971), but since these refer

to the deaths of soldiers in the military hospital, it is not comparable. Barry Higman, 'Slave Population and Economy in Jamaica at the Time of Emancipation' (unpublished Ph.D. thesis, UWI, 1971) also has a cause of death table for parts of Jamaica in the Registration period (1817–29). This suggests close parallels, but cannot be correlated with those given here because of the smallness of the sample (125) and the differing categories. Between 1817 and 1836 the average annual mortality for white troops stationed in Jamaica was 121.3 per 1,000, of whom 101.9 died from fevers. This compared with total figures for black troops of 30 per 1,000 (fevers 8.7). The comparable figures for the Windwards and Leewards station were 78.5 per 1,000 for white troops (fevers, 36.9), and 40 (fevers, 7.1) for black troops. Roberts, 165–72, quoting Tulloch and Marshall.

12. Barry Higman believes that 'race/geographic' origin was more important than rural/urban dichotomy, and that 'urban' slaves were healthier than plantation slaves. However, his definition of 'urban' includes concentrations no larger than a hamlet, as well as the few true Jamaican towns; Kingston, Port Royal, Spanish Town, Montego Bay.

13. As late as 1851, the annual mortality rate in New Orleans was 81 per 1,000, three times as high as contemporary rates in London, New York and Philadelphia. The rate for Jamaica as a whole in the last decades of slavery was about 35 per 1,000, compared with the 1792–1838 average for Worthy Park of 40 per cent.

14. For example, Higman, *op. cit.*

15. Basic categories from British Guiana slave data; Roberts, *Population of Jamaica*, 175. Data for St. Catherine's from Jamaica, Island Record Office, *St. Catherine's Copy Register, Causes of Death*, Vol. I. Total sample of 472 made up and allocated as follows: Old Age, Debility — 'Old Age', 17; Dysentery, Flux — 'Putrid Fever', 40; 'Flux', 4; Dropsy — 'Dropsy', 16; Pulmonary Diseases — 'Consumption', 25; 'Pleurisy', 2; Fevers (inc. Measles, Smallpox) — 'Fever', 159, 'Fever and Worms', 4, 'Nervous Fever', 2, 'Smallpox', 21, 'Spotted Fever', 1, 'Putrid Sore Throat', 1; Yaws, Ulcers — 'Decayed', 28, 'Sore Leg', 1; Inflammations, etc. — 'Swelling', 1; 'Gout', 9, 'Schirrous Liver', 1, 'Gout in Stomach', 2, 'Bilious Fever', 5, 'Bellyache', 2, 'Swollen Liver', 1, 'Gravel', 1, 'Obstruction', 1; Accidents — 'Accident', 2, 'Murdered', 2, 'A Fall', 3; Convulsions — 'Fits', 26, 'Convulsions', 3, 'Palsy', 1; Lockjaw — 'Lockjaw', 4; Syphilis — 'Sores & Ill Habits', 5; Others and Unknown — 'Unknown', 28, 'Not stated' 7, 'Infancy', 1, 'Childbirth', 6, 'Rheumatism', 1, 'Surfeit', 1, 'Mortification', 1, 'Apoplexy', 3, 'Teething', 1, 'Suspicious', 2, 'Suddenly', 7, 'Hystericks & Broken Hearted', 2, 'Hanged' (for forgery), 1, 'Insobriety', 4, 'Cancer', 1, 'Want', 1. In these St. Catherine's diagnoses 'Decay' might well be a synonym for the 'Debility' used in British Guiana. 'Putrid Fever' may well be a synonym for the 'Flux'. The incidence of fever was disastrously high among the garrison. The two victims of Bellyache were both planters. Some of those listed with convulsions may well have suffered from worms. Leprosy (like Venereal Disease) was probably not specifically diagnosed for social reasons. A high proportion of the population of St. Catherine's was white, coloured and free, though persons were not invariably identified by race or status in the Register.

16. For contemporary views on 'dirt-eating' see Thomas Dancer, *The Medical Assistant: or Jamaican Practice of Physic* [. . .] (Kingston, Jamaica, 1801); James

Thompson, *A Treatise on the Diseases of Negroes as they occur in the Island of Jamaica* (Kingston, Jamaica, 1820), 24, 32: James Stewart, *A View of the Past and Present State of the Island of Jamaica* (Edinburgh, 1823), 307. Some modern commentators have suggested a connection between dirt-eating and the deficiency disease beriberi; Shyrock, 'Old South', 50.

17. In his report to a committee of the Jamaican House of Assembly in 1788, Dr. Quier was reported as saying: 'That he has not in general observed any very great Mortality amongst the Negro Infants, soon after their Birth, in that part of the Country where he practises, nor any peculiar Disease to which they are more subject, than any other Children would be under the same Circumstances [. . .]. That in his Opinion, difficult Labours happen as frequently amongst Negro Women here as amongst the Females of the Labouring Poor in England; but that he has not observed a greater proportion of the Infants of the former perish in the Delivery than of the latter; that he does not conceive the Tetanus or Locked Jaw to be a disease common to Infants in the part where he practices; that he apprehends there may be a reason to suppose that a Symptom which generally attends approaching Death, from whatever Cause it may proceed, in Children vizt. a Paralysis of the Muscle of the Lower Jaw, has been frequently mistaken by People unacquainted with Medicine, for the Tetanus, as he has often observed the same name to be given in common discourse to both those Afflictions though of so very different a Nature [. . .].' *Report of the Assembly on the Slave Issues*, enclosed in Lt. Gov. Clark's No. 92, 20 November 1788, London Public Record Office, *C.O. 137/88*.

   Relative to the common belief that many slave infants died of tetanus before they reached the age of nine days it is worth pointing out both that tetanus is rarely fatal in less than two weeks, and also that slave mothers probably regarded the killing of an ailing infant less than nine days old as abortion, not infanticide, since the humanising spirit was believed to be acquired after the ninth day. For tetanus, see also, Edward Long, *The History of Jamaica*, 3 vols (London, 1774), III, 713: Dancer, *op. cit.*, 269.

18 At Braco Estate, Trelawny, for example, there were an average of 68 slaves 'In the Hothouse, in Yaws house with sores. Pregnant, lying in & attendants' in June 1796, out of a population of 402; *Braco Slave Book, April 1795–December 1797* (Braco: Trelawny).

19. Modern Worthy Park offers an illuminating parallel. When the Sugar Industry Labour Welfare Board clinic was set up on the estate in 1951, the doctor was called upon to treat no less than 331 cases of yaws and 250 of syphilis, but only 28 gonorrhea. In a comparatively short time yaws and syphilis were contained, but the cases of gonorrhea treated multiplied to hundreds. Such is progress. Michael Craton and James Walvin, *A Jamaican Plantation: The History of Jamaica, 1670–1970* (London: W. H. Allen, and Toronto, 1970), 308. That gonorrhea was in fact common among the Worthy Park slaves, at least around 1824, is suggested by the purchase by the estate of six penis syringes included in the list of medicines and equipment appended.

20. Thomas Trapham, *A Discourse on the State of Health in the Island of Jamaica* (London: Boulter, 1679), *passim*. The equating of black slaves with animals by a plantation doctor immediately brings to mind a parallel between slave and veterinary medicine. If planters and their doctors regarded slaves as little more than valuable animals, it is not surprising that slave medicine was little

better than 'horse doctor cures'. Veterinary science — probably because the treatment of animals has been required to remain cheap, and animal doctors are even less regarded as colleagues by MBs and MDs than once they were — has made comparatively far less progress than medicine for humans. For example, horses are still poulticed, blistered and cauterised, much like eighteenth-century slaves.

21. Elizabeth Donnan, *Documents Illustrative of the History of the Slave Trade to America*, 4 vols (Washington, 1930–31), I, 410.

22. The miners of quicksilver at Almadén in Spain, the Japanese of Minimata who ate mercury-poisoned fish, and the thousands of Iraquis who ate mercury-dusted seed grain, were alike found to be suffering from *locomotor ataxia* and other manifestations thought to be classic symptoms of tertiary syphilis. It would be instructive to discover how often *locomotor ataxia* and the other symptoms occurred in persons with syphilis before they were treated with mercurials.

23. It was not long since surgery had been entirely in the hands of barbers. Readers of Samuel Pepys' diaries will recall with what trepidation Pepys submitted to surgery for the stone, and his gratitude to the Almighty for allowing him to survive what was technically a very simple operation. In Pepys' case the 'miracle' was almost certainly that the surgeon used a brand new knife. Until the days of Lister, deaths from appendicitis were far more common among those operated on than those with whom nature was allowed to take its course.

24. Douglas Guthrie, *A History of Medicine* (London, revised edn, 1958), 216–31.

25. Hans Sloane, *A Voyage to . . . Jamaica*, I, *passim*. This work was not published until 1707, 18 years after Sloane's sojourn in Jamaica as physician to his kinsman. Governor Albermarle.

26. Quier *et. al.*, *Letters and Essays on the Smallpox*. The letters, dating from 1769 to 1776, were addressed to Dr. Donald Munro of London, a member of the famous Edinburgh medical clan of that name.

27. Heinz Goerke, 'The Life and Scientific Works of Dr. John Quier, Practitioner of Physic and Surgery, Jamaica, 1738–1822', *West Indian Medical Journal*, V, xviii, 22–27.

28. Guthrie, *op. cit.*, 89.

29. Cotton Mather, who promoted inoculation in Boston in 1721, wrote to a fellow member of the Royal Society in London in 1716 that he had heard of variolation from one of his own slaves, a 'Guaramantee' fittingly named Onesimus; Frederick C. Kalgan, 'The Rise of Scientific Activity in Colonial New England', *Yale Journal of Biology and Medicine*, XXII (December 1949), 130.

30. This argument is developed in Craton, 'Jamaican Slave Mortality' (1971); *Sinews of Empire*, 194–99; 'Jamaican Slavery' (1974).

31. The mortality of the slaves on the Middle Passage was probably about 20 per cent per voyage on the average at the beginning of the eighteenth century, and just about 15 per cent by the end of the century. This represented an annual rate of nearly double these figures, since voyages averaged only about six months. These rates of 300–400 per 1,000 per year were probably equalled among the slaves from the time of their capture until the time of shipment: Craton, *Sinews of Empire*, 96–98.

32. The annual rate among white troops stationed in Jamaica of 121.3 deaths per 1,000, though the second highest in the world, was made to seem quite moderate by the West African figures. As late as 1823–6, the death rate for British troops stationed in Sierra Leone was 483 per 1,000, and for the Gold Coast, 668 per 1,000. In the

slave trade, 20–25 per cent of all white crewmen died on each round trip, which averaged about a year, in the 1780s, compared with less than 3 per cent on ships sailing simply between England and the West Indies. Roberts, *Population of Jamaica*, 167; Davies, 'The Living and the Dead': Craton, *Sinews of Empire*, 97.

33. See, for example, Elsa Goveia, *Slave Society in the British Leeward Islands at the End of the Eighteenth Century* (New Haven, 1965), 183–88.

60

Demographic Performance of Two Slave Populations of the Dutch-speaking Caribbean

HUMPHREY E. LAMUR*

1. Introduction

One of the most challenging issues of slave demography in the Western hemisphere is the great difference in the natural increase of the U.S. slave population compared with the slave societies in the Caribbean and Latin America. This differential persisted during the entire period of slavery. The U.S. slave population increased at a rate of 2.4 per cent annually during the 1810–60 period, while in Cuba the slave population declined by 7 per cent between 1816 and 1860. For Jamaica and Brazil the corresponding figures are around 0.5 per cent (1817–32) and 3.5 per cent (between 1798 and 1825) (Fogel and Engerman 1979: 567; Klein and Engerman 1978: 360). One of the few exceptions to this Caribbean pattern of declining slave population growth is the demographic performance of the slaves of the Dutch Antilles. Since their population growth has been so different from that of Suriname, the other Dutch speaking Caribbean country, it will be interesting to draw comparisons between them in order to explain the differentials (Section 3). Before doing so, a brief overview of the demographic evolution of the two slave populations during the second half of the nineteenth century is presented in Section 2. Section 4 summarises the findings of this paper.

2. Natural increase of slaves in Curaçao and Suriname

Two sources regarding the Dutch Antilles slave population are of importance. First, the official population are of importance. First, the official vital statistics that are provided by the planters and published annually by the *Distrikt-en Wijkmeesters (Curaçaose verslagen van 1840–1862)*. The second source is an 1854 report of *Gouverneurs en Gezaghebbers* of the Dutch Antilles compiled on request of the Dutch government, in connection with the abolition of slavery (*Rapport der Staatscommissie II 1856*). As far as Curaçao, the largest of the six islands constituting the Dutch Antilles, is concerned, the population figures derived from the two sources differ significantly. The higher rates provided by the Governor are justified by the fact that the planners failed to register the slaves aged 60 years or older since these had not been taken into account in computing the tax (*hoofdenbelasting*). The smaller deviation from the census total of January 5, 1857 is another test of the reliability of the material provided by the Governor. Nevertheless, I have decided to use the official vital statistics since they cover a number of consecutive years and provide us with a breakdown of the data according to demographic components. Regarding the nature and reliability of the Suriname data, I refer to an earlier publication (Lamur 1977).

Because of the great availability of information, most of the comparisons will be between Suriname and Curaçao, excluding the other five islands of the Dutch Antilles. For the same reason the article will focus on the second half of the nineteenth century. Moreover, this confinement to the period when the slave imports ceased precludes the effect of factors which can distort the comparison. These variables include the uneven sex ratios, the age

*I am grateful to Bob Scholte for his contribution in preparing the English version of this paper. For their comments and suggestions, I wish to record my debt to S. Engerman, H. Hoetink and Richard Steckel. Richard Steckel was also extremely helpful in providing me with material from his Ph.D. dissertation. I am also grateful to Hanneke Kossen for typing several drafts of the paper.

Boletin de Estudios Latino Americanos y del Caribe, No. 30 (June, 1981), pp. 87–102.

structure of slave women entering Curaçao and Suriname after their child-bearing period had begun.

During the last decades before emancipation both slave societies showed a decline in population size with a 4.3 per cent rate of decrease from 1840 to 1863 and an 11.6 per cent in the case of Suriname for the years 1849–63 (Table 1). The decline in the total slave population of Curaçao resulted from manumissions. As far as the natural increase is concerned, however, Curaçao showed a positive rate during the entire 1840–61 period, while the Suriname rate was negative for nearly all the years between 1849 and 1861. The 0.3 per cent rate of decrease of the Suriname slave population has resulted from a birth rate of 3.1 per cent and a mortality rate of 3.4 per cent. For Curaçao the average annual rate of increase is composed of a birth rate of 4.2 per cent and a death rate of 2.4 per cent (Table 2).

The other islands of the Dutch Antilles have also displayed rates of natural increase between 1850 and 1861, as Table 3 indicates. The trend of the natural increase is another aspect of slave

Table 1 Population growth

January of the year	Curaçao *	Curaçao **	Suriname
1840	5750	n.a.	n.a.
1841	6023	n.a.	n.a.
1842	5979	n.a.	n.a.
1843	5772	n.a.	n.a.
1844	5793	6869	n.a.
1845	5569	6555	n.a.
1846	5619	6931	n.a.
1847	5436	6923	n.a.
1848	5479	6809	n.a.
1849	5585	6703	41310
1850	5638	6854	40311
1851	5573	6893	39697
1852	5542	6891	39157
1853	5503	6981	38690
1854	5418	n.a.	38545
1855	5615	n.a.	38051
1856	5585	n.a.	38592
1857	6986	n.a.	38404
1858	6309	n.a.	37961
1859	5855	n.a.	38142
1860	5962	n.a.	37796
1861	5398	n.a.	37001
1862	5524	n.a.	36732
1863	5498	n.a.	36484

Source: * Annual reports of the *Distrikt-en Wijkmeesters* and *Koloniale Verslagen*
** *Gouverneu en Gezaghebbers Rapport der Staatscommissie II* 1856 pp.136–37
n.a.: not available

demography which differentiates the two societies. While the Suriname rate has changed from negative to positive after emancipation, in the case of Curaçao Hartog (1961: 446) dates this change as early as 1778. However, he presents no evidence to support his statement and currently available data do not as yet permit an analysis of this issue.

The differences in fertility level between Curaçao and Suriname are also discernible when a more exact guide to the reproductive performance, namely the cohort fertility, is used. For Curaçao, the calculation of this rate is based on the accounts of emancipation (*Archief van de Algemene Rekenkamer* 1863). These plantation records list the ages of female slaves and their children, if there were children living with them (for problems relating to the estimation of demographic variables used in this article, see appendix). Of a total of 148 plantations in 1863, 123 have been omitted from the analysis, since the number of slaves per estate, 25–30, is too small to warrant reliable statistical calculation. Eight of the remaining 25 plantations included mothers aged 45 and have been selected for further analysis. For each of these mothers the average number of children living with her and registered in the archives has been calculated; subsequently the same has been done for the group of women as a whole, yielding a value of 5.5. Table 4 demonstrates that the rate has been highest (7.5) and the average birth interval quite small (3.6) on the smaller units, whilst child-bearing has begun at earlier ages. This seems to be consistent with the findings for the U.S. slave population around 1830 (Fogel and Engerman 1979: 574). Taking into account both the children who were born alive but died before the 1863 census and those unlisted for other reasons (sales, manumissions, runaways), it is safe to conclude that the true value of the cohort fertility rate exceeds the number of 5.5 children computed on the basis of the records. To make an assessment of the correct figure, adjusting only for infant deaths, the following steps have been taken:

1. For the 1840–61 period the birth rate of 4.2 per cent and the death rate of 2.4 per cent which have been computed earlier, are considered as minimum values, taking into account the under-registration of births and deaths.

2. It has been assumed that the Curaçao slave population satisfies the four criteria characterising a stable population, namely, a constant rate of natural increase and age-

Table 2 Rates of natural increase of slave population, Curaçao and Suriname

Year	Curaçao			Suriname		
			Natural increase per 100 slaves			
	Birth	Death	Nat. increase	Birth	Death	Nat. increase
1840	3.7	1.6	2.1			
1841	4.5	2.8	1.7			
1842	3.3	2.3	1.0			
1843	4.1	2.5	1.6			
1844	4.2	2.7	1.5			
1845	2.5	1.7	0.8			
1846	4.1	2.5	1.6			
1847	3.9	2.1	1.8			
1848	4.5	1.6	2.9			
1849	4.4	1.9	2.5	2.7	3.4	−0.7
1850	5.0	2.4	2.6	3.3	3.0	+0.3
1851	4.7	2.4	2.3	3.1	3.9	−0.8
1852	3.7	3.2	0.5	3.1	3.2	−0.1
1853	4.6	2.7	1.9	3.1	2.7	+0.4
1854	5.2	2.7	2.5	3.0	3.2	−0.2
1855	5.1	2.7	2.4	2.8	3.8	−1.0
1856	4.0	2.7	1.3	3.2	3.1	+0.1
1857	3.9	2.0	1.9	3.1	4.1	−0.1
1858	5.0	2.0	3.0	3.3	3.1	+0.2
1859	3.9	2.8	1.1	3.2	4.6	−1.4
1860	4.7	4.1	0.6	3.1	3.4	−0.3
1861	5.2	2.6	2.6	3.1	3.8	−0.7
1840–49	3.9	2.1	1.8	—	—	—
1850–61	4.5	2.6	1.9	3.1	3.4	−0.3
1840–61	4.2	2.4	1.8	—	—	—

Source: (Curaçao): Annual reports of the *Distriki-en Wijkmeesters* and *Koloniale Verslagen*

specific fertility, unchanged age structure and negligible migration rate.

3. Given a 1.8 per cent rate of natural increase computed on the basis of vital statistics and a gross reduction rate of 2.70 (m = 27) which has been calculated as 5.5/2.05, the Coale/Demeny stable population table (United Nations 1967: 85, 89) points to the West model (female) level 9. This choice implies that the birth rate has been somewhere between 3.8 and 4.3 per cent, while the death rate has amounted to 2.3 per cent.

4. But since the cohort fertility rate has exceeded the value of 5.5, as pointed out earlier, the true figure for the gross reproduction rate has also been higher than 2.7, corresponding to 5.5 (= 2.7 × 2.05). This means that the birth rate has also exceeded 4.3, while the death rate has been over 2.3 per cent, which implies a 2.0 per cent rate of natural increase.

This preliminary conclusion is supported by an analysis of the age structure of Savonet, the largest estate of Curaçao during slavery (274 slaves). The 'proportions at age x', one of the criteria for comparing the age structure of Savonet with the stable population model, has not yielded satisfactory results since it does not conform to any of the age structures of the model. The other criteria, 'proportions up to age x', however, points more or less to an age structure of the model corresponding to a value of R equal to 0.025 (Table 5). This rate of natural increase has resulted from a birth rate of 4.86 per cent and a death rate of 2.36 per cent. If this is correct, the estimated cohort fertility rate of the Savonet female slaves in 1863 was 6.4 while their expectation of life at birth amounted to 40.0 years. This finding is more or less consistent with the results for the Curaçao slave population as a whole, which point to vital rates exceeding 4.3 per cent and 2.3 per cent. So it is likely that the values computed for Savonet have

Table 3 Population and vital rates, 1850–61, Dutch Antilles

Year	Aruba B	Aruba D	Aruba N	Bonaire B	Bonaire D	Bonaire N	Curaçao B	Curaçao D	Curaçao N	Saba B	Saba D	Saba N	St. Eustatius B	St. Eustatius D	St. Eustatius N	St. Maarten B	St. Maarten D	St. Maarten N
1850	3.6	0.8	2.8	4.7	2.5	2.2	5.0	2.4	2.6	1.5	0.9	0.6	1.9	1.8	0.1	4.2	1.5	2.7
1851	3.9	1.0	2.9	4.2	2.3	1.9	4.7	2.4	2.3	1.9	0.7	1.2	2.1	1.3	0.8	3.3	0.8	2.5
1852	2.4	1.0	1.4	3.5	1.4	2.1	3.7	3.2	0.5	1.2	0.4	0.8	3.5	2.7	0.8	3.6	1.5	2.1
1853	3.8	1.5	2.3	3.9	1.8	2.1	4.6	2.7	1.9	1.0	0.6	0.4	3.1	1.6	1.5	3.3	1.0	2.3
1854	6.2	1.5	4.7	5.6	2.0	3.6	5.2	2.7	2.5	2.4	0.3	2.1	2.7	2.1	0.6	3.5	1.2	2.3
1855	3.0	1.5	1.5	5.7	2.0	3.7	5.1	2.7	2.4	3.5	0.3	3.2	3.3	2.1	1.2	3.1	1.1	2.0
1856	4.3	1.4	2.9	5.1	5.2	0.1	4.0	2.7	1.3	3.7	1.3	2.4	4.1	2.8	1.3	2.7	1.4	1.3
1857	4.2	1.5	2.7	4.1	1.2	2.9	3.9	2.0	1.9	4.3	0.5	3.8	3.2	1.7	1.5	2.0	1.4	0.6
1858	4.5	2.4	2.1	5.7	2.2	3.5	5.0	2.0	3.0	4.0	1.9	2.1	4.1	2.2	1.9	2.9	1.3	1.6
1859	3.6	2.1	1.5	4.0	2.0	2.0	3.9	2.8	1.1	4.3	1.0	3.3	3.7	3.1	0.6	2.4	0.8	1.6
1860	4.8	2.4	2.4	5.7	1.6	4.1	4.7	4.1	0.6	3.5	1.4	2.1	5.2	4.6	0.6	1.4	1.0	0.4
1861	7.0	1.5	5.5	4.6	1.1	3.5	5.2	2.6	2.6	3.9	1.9	2.0	3.5	2.6	0.9	3.0	9.8	2.2
1850–61	4.2	1.5	2.7	2.1	2.6	4.5	2.6	1.9	2.9	2.3	2.0	3.3.	2.3	1.0	2.9	1.1	1.8	

Source: Koloniale Verslagen

B = Birth per 100
D = Death per 100
N = Natural increase per 100

Table 4   Cohort fertility rate and its determinants for Curaçao slave population in 1863, before adjusting for unregistered infant mortality

Plant. size	Cohort fert. rate	Age at first birth	Age at last birth	Average child-bearing period	Average birth interval	Proportion ever bearing children
	R	F	L	(L – F)	S	
1–50	7.5 (2)	19.5	43.0	23.5	3.6	n.a.
51–100	4.3 (3)	22.0	32.0	10.0	3.5	n.a.
101–150	5.3 (3)	24.0	40.3	16.3	4.2	n.a.
Total	5.5 (8)	22.1	38.0	15.9	3.8	0.80

Source: Archief van de Algemene Rekenkamer 1863
( )   Absolute number of women aged 45 years
n.a.:   not available

prevailed for the slaves of Curaçao as a whole.

The fertility level of the slaves of the Richardson plantation on St. Maarten is another case which underscores the unusually high rate of reproduction of the Dutch Antilles. Of a total of 69 slaves belonging to Ann Louisa Richardson, 26 have been recorded as living in units consisting of five mothers who were living with their surviving children (*Archief van de Algemene Rekenkamer* 1863). Based on data for the two mothers aged 42 and 51, while excluding the others for reasons indicated in Table 6, a

family size of 8.5 has been computed. This figure is even higher than the 6.4 rate calculated for Curaçao, in spite of the fact that no adjustments have been made both for children who have died before registration and those unlisted for other reasons. However, the very small number of women upon which the calcuation has been based does not permit reliable statistical analysis.

An adjustment for the other demographic variables, namely the birth interval and the child-bearing period, can now be made using the

Table 5   Age distribution of the West model, level 9 (females) for R equals 0.025 and 0.030, and the female slave population of Savonet, 1863

Age	R (0.025)	Proportions up to age (x) Sav.	R (0.030)	Age group	R (0.025)	Proportions at age (x) Sav.	R (0.030)
1	4.2	4.2	4.7	0–1	4.2	4.2	4.7
5	17.9	22.8	19.6	1–4	13.6	18.5	14.9
10	32.2	37.8	35.0	5–9	14.3	15.0	15.3
15	44.5	46.4	47.9	10–14	12.2	8.5	12.8
20	55.0	53.5	58.6	15–19	10.5	7.1	10.7
25	63.9	62.8	67.4	20–24	8.9	9.2	8.8
30	71.4	74.2	74.7	25–29	7.5	11.4	7.2
35	77.7	80.0	80.6	30–34	6.2	5.7	5.9
40	82.9	85.0	85.4	35–39	5.2	5.0	4.8
45	87.2	88.5	89.3	40–44	4.3	3.5	3.8
50	90.7	92.1	92.4	45–49	3.5	3.5	3.0
55	93.6	94.2	94.8	50–54	2.8	2.1	2.4
60	95.8	94.2	96.7	55–59	2.2	0.0	1.8
65	97.5	95.0	98.0	60–64	1.6	0.7	1.3
				65–69	1.1	0.7	0.9
				70–74	0.7	2.1	0.5
				75–79	0.3	0.7	0.2
				80 +	0.1	1.4	0.1

Source: Archief van de Algemene Rekenkamer 1863

Table 6 Richardson plantations, St. Maarten, November 17, 1862

Name of the mother	Age of the mother			Birth interval										Average	No. of live births
	on Nov. 17 1862	at birth of first child	at birth of last child	1–2	2–3	3–4	4–5	5–6	6–7	7–8	8–9	9–10			
Phillis Richardson*	73	28	37	3	6									4.5	3**
Minverva Richardson***	36	17		2	8	5									
Maria Richardson	42	17	40	3	1	2	2	5	1	2	6	3		2.7	10
Polyninal Richardson****	19	16		3											
Hetty Daniels	51	25	46	3	4	2	3	4	4					3.3	7

Source: *Archief van de Rekenkamer* 1863
*   Mother of Minverva, Maria and Polyninal
**   Some of the children may have died already since the time when the mother reached age 45
***   Incomplete (age under 45)
****   Incomplete (age under 45)

following equation developed by Steckel (1977: 96–103).

$$R = \frac{(\bar{L} - \bar{F})}{\bar{S}} + 1$$

where:
R	=	cohort fertility rate
(L − F)	=	child-bearing period
L	=	age of mother at the birth of her first child
F	=	age of mother at the birth of her last child
S	=	birth interval

Based on the data of the plantation records, the average number of live births per mother has proven to be 5.5, while the ages at first and last surviving children have been 22.1 and 38.0 years respectively. Adjustment for the unregistered live births has raised the cohort fertility rate to 6.4. In order to estimate the average birth interval, information on the birth order of the additional child who died before the 1863 registration is required. The following alternatives are of importance:

1. Assuming that the unlisted child was born between the birth dates of the first and the last registered children, the correction for the additional birth lowers the average birth interval to 2.8 years.
2. If the child was born before the birth date of the oldest of the registered children or after that of the youngest, it is not possible to compute the average birth interval since the exact date of birth of the missing child is unknown. However, there is no reason to doubt that the interval is different from the one computed for the surviving children, namely 3.8 (Table 4). This implies a child-bearing period of 19.7 years. Comparison with the Richardson estate of St. Maarten, however, points to birth intervals of 2.7 and

3.3 years for the mothers aged 42 and 51. This tends to suggest that the first assumption is more likely to be correct, which implies an average birth interval of 2.8 years and a child-bearing period of 15.9. This extremely short birth interval, relative to that of the American slave population (Table 7), is surprising and raises a number of questions, which will be dealt with in Section 3.

The unusual high fertility level of the Curaçao slave population is demonstrated if compared with the two other slave populations indicated in Table 7. Curaçao holds a middle position between the U.S. and Suriname. It should be emphasized that in the case of Suriname the fertility has been measured in terms of the total fertility rate instead of the cohort fertility figure based on material of three plantations, namely Andressa (timber), Catharina Sophia (sugar) and Mijn Vermaak (coffee). None of these estates has shown a higher rate than Curaçao.

In trying to explain the differences in fertility level between Curaçao and Suriname, both demographic and socio-economic factors are of importance. The demographic variables include: the age of the mother at the birth of her first and last children, the average birth interval and the proportion of women ever bearing children (Fogel and Engerman 1979: 574). Since the differences in child-bearing period between the two slave societies have been small, as Table 7 demonstrates, it is unlikely that this demographic component can account for the Curaçao-Suriname differential in fertility. Data on the rate of childlessness point to an estimated 29 per cent for Suriname and 20 per cent for Curaçao. While the rate for Curaçao exceeds that of Suriname, the difference is too small to explain a large proportion of the fertility differential between Curaçao and Suriname. As Klein and Engerman (1979: 366) have pointed

Table 7   Fertility rate for three slave populations

Country	Cohort fertility rate R	Average child-bearing period in years (L − F)	Average birth interval in years S	Proportion ever bearing children
US 1830–60	7.2	18.0	2.9	0.76
Curaçao 1840–60	6.4	15.9 / 19.7	2.8 / 3.8	0.80 / 0.80
Suriname 1850–60	3.0	12.1	3.1	0.71

Source: (U.S.)—Fogel 1976; Klein and Engerman 1978: 360–368.

H

out in the case of Jamaica, these relatively low rates of childlessness for Suriname tend to contradict the notion that infertility (possibly caused by venereal disease) has been widespread in Suriname, and has accounted for the low fertility of slave women of this Dutch speaking Caribbean country. It is more likely that the differential average birth interval has caused the observed differences in fertility between Curaçao and Suriname. But what accounts for the smaller birth interval of the Curaçao slave women? Since no other demographic factor is of importance in this connection, I shall now turn to social variables to investigate their possible contribution to the substantial differences in average birth interval between the two slave populations.

3. Fertility and labour conditions

In dealing with slavery in the Dutch speaking Caribbean it has often been pointed out that the treatment of slaves in Curaçao has been less cruel than in Suriname (among others, Hoetink 1958; 1969; Van Lier 1971: 117–176; Paula 1969; *Rapport der Staatscommissie* 1856; Römer 1977). Hence, it may be useful to discuss whether this factor has contributed to the differences in fertility level. However, the conclusions have to be tentative since the relevant archive material both on this factor and the other social variables has not yet been fully explored.

Because of its favourable geographical location on the coast, Willemstad, the capital of Curaçao, functioned as a commercial centre during the eighteenth and early nineteenth centuries. Slaves brought from Africa to Curaçao were sold to Spanish planters in Colombia, Venezuela and other Latin American countries (Goslinga 1977). Since the slaves were used as merchandise, a less harsh treatment served the interest of their owners (*Brief der Kamer van Amsterdam van 24 december 1694*; Hamelberg 1901. I: *documenten blz.* 107). The decision taken in 1642 to build two hospitals in Curaçao for the treatment of the slaves, long before such facilities existed for civilians and soldiers, was aimed at enhancing the exchange value of the slaves. The appointment of a medical doctor around 1682 charged with the slaves' treatment points in the same direction (Hamelberg 1901. I: 77–78; Hartog 1961: 446–51; Römer 1977: 31–35).

Another factor indicating the less cruel treatment of the slaves in Curaçao in

comparison with Suriname is the nature of the work. To the extent that plantation labour existed in Curaçao, it primarily concerned cattle raising, planting of corn and growing of sorghum. Only six months a year were spent on these activities, while during the second half of the year the slaves were kept busy on the pens with turning the cattle out to grass repairing or building fences on the pasture land, cleaning the pastures of weeds, cleaning the wells, timber cutting and so on (*Rapport der Staatscommissie* 1856. II: 134–54, 226). Sugar estates producing for the world market, where heavy physically demanding labour and long working hours usually prevent slave fertility from rising as in Suriname, were non-existent in Curaçao. The importance of this factor in explaining the Curaçao-Suriname fertility differential is supported by a comparison of the slave fertility by crop in Suriname. Preliminary data show that around 1860 the child/woman ratio of the slaves of sugar plantations was 25–30 per cent lower than the rate on plantations growing other crops such as cotton or coffee (Lamur, *Slave Fertility and Plantation Labour in Suriname*).

The findings for Suriname are consistent with Higman's analysis of the Jamaican slave fertility: 'it appears that the only units to approach the extremely high rate of natural decrease on the sugar estates were the jobbing gangs' (1967: 122–123). The fertility-reducing effect of the nature of the work was reinforced by the influence of the size of the plantations. In the case of Suriname, the fertility rate of the slaves of smaller units was higher than the rate for those on the large plantations (Lamur, *Slave Fertility*.). In this respect the Suriname data are also comparable with those for Jamaica (Higman, *op. cit.* 127–28). In addtion, at the end of the eighteenth century the ratio of whites to slaves was about 60 per cent for Curaçao, while in the case of Suriname the rate amounted to 5 per cent in 1834. Since the Curaçao plantations were on the average smaller than those in Suriname (Table 8), it is likely that this factor contributed to the higher fertility rate of the Curaçao slave population.

The smaller size of the Curaçao plantations, the nature of the work as well as the greater share of whites, relative to Suriname, all these factors combined, imply that the Curaçao slaves had more contact with the white society in their daily lives. 'In general the relation of the master to his slaves in Curaçao was one of individual contact, there was no fear on the part of the owners, and therefore no insecurity or sadism' (Hoetink 1969: 182–83; compare also Paula

Table 8   Plantations and plantation slaves by size of slave population, Curaçao and Suriname, 1862

| Size of slave pop. | Plantations | | Slaves | | | |
| | Number | | Number | | Percentage | |
	Curaçao	Suriname	Curaçao	Suriname	Curaçao	Suriname
1–50	128	64	1523	1075	41.9	3.9
51–100	13	57	961	4320	26.4	15.7
101–150	8	51	876	6139	24.1	22.4
151–200	0	15	0	2579	0	9.4
201–250	0	19	0	4291	0	15.7
251–300	1	7	274	1903	7.5	6.9
301–350	0	7	0	2282	0	8.3
351–400	0	5	0	1932	0	7.1
401–450	0	1	0	410	0	1.5
451–500	0	1	0	450	0	1.6
500 +	0	3	0	2012	0	7.3
TOTAL	150	230	3634	27393	100.0	100.0

Source: *Archief van de Algemene Rekenkamer*

1967; Römer 1977: 24–64; for Suriname, see Van Lier 1971: 51–84, 117–76). Hence it is conceivable that the Curaçao slaves partly adopted some of the white masters' customs, among them the European childnursing practices which imply shorter birth intervals associated with shorter lactation periods. The Suriname data on the other hand point to the retention of African patterns of a lactation period of two to three years, as well as to the practice of abstention from sexual intercourse during lactation (Lamur, *Slave Fertility*). However, no information is as yet available on the lactational practices of the Curaçao slave women. The only source which provides data which is probably related to this subject is a publication by Brenneker (1973: 1314–15; 1975: 2518) on the folklore of the Dutch Antilles. One of his informants who was interviewed in the 1970s claimed that in older times the lactation period was two years, while only a three months' period of abstention from sexual intercourse during lactation was observed. This information is consistent with the small birth interval for the Curaçao slave population (2.9 years) calculated earlier on the basis of cohort analysis. However, Brenneker provides no indication that the expression 'in older time' refers to the Curaçao slave period (for a discussion of variations in cultural adaptation in analysing the Jamaican-U.S. fertility differential, see Engerman 1976: 265–66; 1977: 607–08).

While important, the medical treatment, the plantation size and the nature of the work are not the only factors which are related to the high

fertility level of the Curaçao slave population. It has frequently been argued that a poor diet has a negative effect on human fertility. A deficiency of protein (in meat and fish for example) tends to lower the age of menopause and to raise the age of menarche, while the frequency of irregular and anovulatory cycli is increased. In addition, the probability of a miscarriage and a still-birth is higher than for an inadequately nourished female. And in the adult male, loss of sperm mobility and cessation of sperm production may be the result of undernutrition (Frisch 1978: 22). Fragmentary information shows that regarding nutrition the slaves of Curaçao were also better off than their partners in distress in Suriname. In 1662 provision grounds were established to make the provision of the slaves less dependent on imported food supplies (Hartog 1961: 448). Though some authors claim that the diet of the Curaçao slaves was poor (Goslinga 1961: 381), most contemporaries characterise their diet as adequate and certainly superior to that of the slaves in Suriname. J. J. Putman, a Roman Catholic priest who lived in Curaçao between 1835 and 1853, claims that the food provided by some owners was below legal standards. He adds, however, the even in those cases the slaves did not suffer because of the possibility for stealing food (*Rapport der Staatscommissie* 1856. II: 284, 285; Teenstra 1836 I: 171, 172). In addition, the Curaçao diet consisting of corn, fruit, meat and fish was rich in protein, while the nutritional content of the diet in Suriname was very low, consisting of mainly plantains, yams and some dried fish (Emmer and Van den

Boogaart 1977: 210–13; Van der Kuyp 1958). Putman's observation that low birth rates had been observed in Curaçao in the years of bad harvest, points to a coherence between fertility and the quality of nutrition. In spite of the plausibility of this relationship the evidence for it provided in this paper is quite weak. More information on this factor is required before firm conclusions can be drawn.

The same applies to other factors which may also have contributed to the Curaçao-Suriname fertility differentials. One is the unhealthy, swampy climate of Suriname in comparision with Curaçao (Teenstra 1836. I: 177). Another variable is the presumed breeding of slaves on the Dutch Antillian island Bonaire. The offsprings of this stud farm, situated in a valley called Rincón, are said to have been reared for sale to planters in Curaçao and slave importing countries (Teenstra 1836. I: 188, 189). It may be mentioned in this connection that the Bonaire birth rate was higher than that of the other islands between 1850 and 1861, as Table 3 indicates. An even higher rate, namely 3 per cent, has been observed for Bonaire during the 1817–36 period (*Rapport der Staatscommissie* 1856. II: 10–11). However, since Teenstra presents no evidence to support his statement on the *aanfokkerij van slaven* or its demographic effects, his claim is misleading. Lowenthal and Clark (1977: 512, 527–30) may be correct in stating that the rapid natural increase of the slave population in Barbuda has probably misled modern commentators to conclude that slave breeding occurred. Nevertheless, Lowenthal and Clark's rejection of stud farms in Barbuda, or my remarks in the case of Bonaire, are not sufficient arguments against the plausibility of slave breeding in the Western hemisphere.

The family and household structure of the slaves is a third factor worth mentioning in a study on the fertility differential between slave societies. But here too no information is available for Suriname, while in the case of the Dutch Antilles only the Richardson plantation provides some data on this factor. As indicated earlier, of a total of 69 slaves 26 are listed in the plantation records as living in units, namely five mothers each registered with their surviving children. For the remaining slaves, consisting of seven women of child-bearing age and eleven children below the age of 15, no kinship relation is indicated. So it is not possible to trace whether or not they were residing outside the woman-and-children household type.

Hence, it is too soon to state that only 37 per cent of the slaves of the Richardson plantation were living in units, consisting of a woman and her children. Nor is it correct to assume that these five households were mother-headed. An important aspect of this issue concerns the relative occurrence of two-parent households. As pointed out by Fogel and Engerman (1979: 578), 'recent work has led to a substantial revision of earlier views on the slave family. Earlier writings presumed a relative absence of stable mating patterns among slaves . . . , thus linking the slave experience to issues relating to the twentieth century black family'. This view has recently been questioned for the United States. Data published by Higman (1973; 1975: 266–70) suggest a higher frequency of living in two-parent households among West Indian slaves than was previously believed (see also Fogel and Engerman 1979: 575). For the Dutch speaking Caribbean, data are now being processed to test the plausibility of the view that stable mating patterns were virtually non-existent among the slaves in those areas.

4. Summary

The American slave population grew much faster than the slave societies of the Caribbean and Latin America, even after the closing of the slave trade. Brazil, Cuba, Guyana, Jamaica, as well as Martinique and Suriname, showed a substantial natural decrease. One of the few exceptions to this Caribbean pattern of declining slave population is the demographic performance of the slaves of the Dutch Antilles. A comparison beween Curaçao and Suriname suggests that the fertility rate of the former is twice as high as that of the latter. It is likely that this differential is caused by differences in the average birth interval between the two populations. This demographic variable, in turn, is probably related to differences in both the nature of slavery and the labour conditions on the plantations. Nutrition is another factor which may have contributed to the differences in fertility. No information is as yet available on the role that other variables may have played in causing the differential.

Appendix:
Calculation of the age of the mother at the birth of her first child, the number of children ever born, the rate of childlessness

It must be emphasized that some of the demographic variables used in this article have been estimated. Here I only list both the steps involved and the limitations imposed by the nature of the material or the method employed.

Children ever born

In calculating the cohort fertility rate, data on the number of children ever born to a woman are required. However, the exact number is not known since only data on the number of children who survived to be recorded in the plantation archive of 1863 are available. In addition, the records also omit the children no longer living at home; for example, older children who were sold or left the maternal household for any other reason. Besides, it is likely that older women aged 60 or over have been misclassified as non-mothers because their children no longer lived at home (Trussel and Steckel 1978: 488–89). All these biases combined may have produced a cohort fertility rate which is lower than the number of surviving children ever born to a woman. In Section 2 of this paper an attempt has been made to adjust for these biases. The names of the eight Curaçao plantations used in this context are Valentijn, Rondeklip, Zevenhuizen, Suikertuintje, St. Jacob, St. Barber en Fuik, Koraal and Rustenburg. As mentioned earlier, in the case of Suriname, fertility has been measured in terms of the general fertility rate, based on material from the following estates: Andressa, Catharina Sophia and Mijn Vermasak.

Ages at first birth

The plantation records used for this article list the ages of female slaves and their children for the year 1863, if there were children living with them. I have simply subtracted the age of the mother at the birth of her first child. However, there is no guarantee that the children listed with the woman were her own, and in case the eldest is an adopted child the computed age at first birth is biased downwards. No information is available on the occurrence of adoption during slavery in the Dutch Antilles and Suriname. For the U.S., Sutch (cited in Trussel and Steckel

1978: 478) claims that adoption was rare among slaves and 'estimated that only 1 per cent of slave children under age thirteen were orphans'. The nature of the data in the Dutch Antilles and Suriname archives may have caused another bias, though working in the opposite direction, since no information is available on children who were born and died before the registration of the data in 1863. Since it is likely that some first-born children had died before being recorded and since the probability of this occurrence rises with the time elapsed since the first birth, the computed age of the mother at first birth tends to be overstated. This issue has been raised earlier by, among others, Trussel and Steckel regarding the U.S. slave population (1978: 482–83).

Rate of childlessness

Of a total of ten women of the Curaçao plantation Savonet belonging to the 40–49 age category, eight are recorded in the 1863 plantation archive as having borne one or more children. As indicated earlier, the average number of children per mother aged 45 amounts to 6.5, after adjusting for the unlisted child who died before registration. This means that the chance for a child to die before recording is 0.15 (1/6.5). When applied to the two women classified as childless, this chance yields a 0.3 child which is quite small and may be neglected. The rate of childlessness estimated in this way is 20 per cent, two to a total of ten women, but has to be used with caution, taking into account that the calculation is based on only one plantation. This limitation holds also for Suriname since only three plantations are involved in computing the 29 per cent rate of childlessness.

References

Archief van de Algemene Rekenkamer, *Afrekeningen van de Emancipatie in het Archief van de Algemene Rekenkamer* (Schaarsbergen: Algemeen Rijksarchief, 1863).

Brenneker, P., *Sambumbu, Volkskinde van Curaçao, Aruba en Bonaire* (Curaçao, 1973–75).

Engerman, S. L., 'Some economic and demographic comparisions of slavery in the United States and the British West Indies'. *Economic History Review*, 29 (April, 1976), 258–75.

Engerman, S. L., 'Quantitative and economic analysis of West Indian slave societies: research problems', in V. Rubin and A. Tuden (Eds), *Comparative perspectives on slavery in New World-plantation societies* (New York, 1977).

Fogel, R. W., (Lecture given in Amsterdam, 1976).

Fogel, R. W. and Engerman, S. L., 'Recent findings in the

study of the slave demography and family structure', *Sociology and Social Research*, 63, No. 3 (1979) 566-89.

Frisch, R. E., 'Population, food intake and fertility', *Science*, 199, (1978), 22—30.

Goslinga, C. Ch., 'Curaçao as a slave-trading center during the War of the Spanish Succession (1702-1714)', *Nieuwe West Indische Gids*, 1-2 (1977), 1-50.

Hamelberg, J. H. J. 1901 *De Nederlanders op de West Indische Eilanden*, I, (Amsterdam, 1901).

Hartog, J., *Curaçao van kolonie tot autonomie* (2 delen), (Aruba, 1961).

Higman, B. W., 'Household structure and fertility on Jamaican slave plantations', *Population Studies*, 27 (1973), 527-50.

Higman, B. W., 'The slave family and household in the British West Indies', *Journal of Interdisciplinary History*, 6 (1975), 261-287.

Higman, B. W. 1976 *Slave population and economy in Jamaica, 1807-1834*', (New York, 1976).

Hoetink, H., *Het patroon van de oudse Curaçaose samenleving*, (Assen, 1958).

Hoetink, H., 'Race relations in Curaçao and Surinam', in F. Foner and E. D. Genovese (Eds), *Slavery in the New World* (New York, 1969).

Klein, H. S. and Engerman, S. L., 'Fertility differentials between slaves in the United States and the British West Indies, *William and Mary Quarterly*, 35 (1978), 357-74.

Koloniale Verslagen, 1849-63.

Lamur, H. E., 'Demography of Surinam plantation slaves in the last decade before Emancipation: the case of Catharina Sophia', in V. Rubin and A. Tuden *op. cit.*, *Slave fertility and plantation labour in Surinam*.

Lowenthal, D., and Clarke, C. G., 'Slave-breeding in Barbuda: the past of a negro myth', in V. Rubin and A. Tuden.

Paula, A. F., *From objective to subjective social barriers* (Curaçao, 1967).

Rapport der Staatscommissie, *Erste rapport der Staatscommissie benoemd bij K. B. van 29 november 1853 no. 66, tot het voorstellen van maatregelen t.a.v. de slaven in de Nederlandse Koloniën* (The Hague, 1855).

Rapport der Staatscommissie, *Tweede rapport der Staatscommissie benoemd bij K. B. van 29 november 1853 no. 66, tot het voorstellen van maatregelen t.a.v. de slaven in de Nederlandse Koloniën* (The Hague, 1856).

Römer, R. A., *Un pueblo na kaminda*, (1977).

Steckel, R. H., *The economics of U.S. slave and southern white fertility*, Ph.D. dissertation, University of Chicago, (1977).

Teenstra, M. D., *De Nederlandsch West Indische Eilanden* (2 delen) (Amsterdam, 1836).

Trussel, J. and Steckel, R., 'The age of slaves at menarche and their first birth', *Journal of Interdisciplinary History*, 8, No. 3, (1978) 477-505.

United Nations, *Methods of estimating basic demographic measures from incomplete data* (New York, 1967).

Van den Boogaart, E., and Emmer, P. C., 'Plantation slavery in the last decade before emancipation: the case of Catharina Sophia', in V. Rubin and A. Tuden *op. cit.*

Van der Kuyp, E. E., 'De voeding van de slaaf en de betekenis daarvan voor zijn nakomelingen', in *Emancipatieblad* (1958).

Van Lier, R. A. J., *Frontier Society* (The Hague, 1971).

Wijkregisters van de Nederlandse Antillen.

SECTION THIRTEEN

Rejecting Slavery: Blacks Speak Back

It is recognized that texts written by oppressed people occupy special places within literary traditions. Texts written by enslaved peoples as the most suppressed of the oppressed, represent something altogether revolutionary in that their very existence constitutes a fundamental contradiction to the assumptions and presumptions of slave owners' world.

The enslaved were defined and categorized under the laws in all Caribbean jurisdictions as chattel – property with real estate values. In effect, they were categorized under these provisions as "things", and appear in the accounting culture of the colonial order alongside cattle, horses, furniture, barns, sugar and so on. But the problem for slave owners was that enslaved peoples had developed cosmologies, and would commit their thoughts to paper thereby creating a special literature more enduring perhaps than those of free people.

The enslaved, then, not only spoke back; they wrote back as part of an ontological positioning with colonialism that placed slavery under their literary gaze. The written and spoken word oftentimes converged to produce texts that leave little doubt about enslaved peoples' intention to do away with slavery, or reform it.

Many slaves wrote letters, petitions, gave oral testimony to commissions of inquiry, and made arrangements for the recording and publication of memoirs. Collectively, they produced a literary tradition that situates their struggle at the core of the Atlantic liberationist culture. The memoirs of Olaudah Equiano, the Ibo man who survived kidnapping as a child and decades of slavery in Barbados and elsewhere in the hemisphere to emerge as a major anti-slavery voice has no equal in the literature of 19th century anti-slavery and pan-Africanism. The autobiographies of Esteban Montejo and Mary Prince, together with the speeches of Toussaint L'Overture, represent the anti-slavery voices of Blacks in their many tones and textures. As searchers for social freedom, for social justice, and for political power, enslaved peoples were not homogeneous. Their ideological visions were mediated through the actions of individuals whose situations required complex readings and strategic replies. It is not possible to write of slavery without reference to these texts. Historians are now sufficiently sensitized to the importance of the subjective knowledge of those who lived the experience of colonial slavery. Also, they are aware that their own subjectivity as writers requires firm rooting within the expressions of those who are the targets of study. The entry of the slaves' texts into the historiographical canon is in itself a major achievement of conceptual liberation.

61

The Life of Olaudah Equiano

OLAUDAH EQUIANO

I hope that the reader will not think I have trespassed on his patience in introducing myself to him with some account of the manners and customs of my country. They had been implanted in me with great care, and made an impression on my mind, which time could not erase, and which all the adversity and variety of fortune I have since experienced served only to rivet and record; for, whether the love of one's country be real or imaginary, or a lesson of reason, or an instinct of nature, I still look back with pleasure on the first scenes of my life, though that pleasure has been for the most part mingled with sorrow.

My father, besides many slaves, had a numerous family, of which seven lived to grow up, including myself and a sister, who was the only daughter. As I was the youngest of the sons, I became, of course, the greatest favourite with my mother, and was always with her; and she used to take particular pains to form my mind. I was trained up from my earliest years in the art of war; my daily exercise was shooting and throwing javelins; and my mother adorned me with emblems, after the manner of our greatest warriors. In this way I grew up till I was turned the age of eleven, when an end was put to my happiness in the following manner:– Generally when the grown people in the neighbourhood were gone far in the fields to labour, the children assembled together in some of the neighbours' premises to play; and commonly some of us used to get up a tree to look out for any assailant, or kidnapper, that might come upon us; for they sometimes took those opportunities of our parents' absence to attack and carry off as many as they could

seize. One day, as I was watching at the top of a tree in our yard, I saw one of those people come into the yard of our next neighbour but one, to kidnap, there being many stout young people in it. Immediately on this I gave the alarm of the rogue, and he was surrounded by the stoutest of them, who entangled him with cords so that he could not escape till some of the grown people came and secured him. But alas! ere long it was my fate to be thus attacked, and to be carried off, when none of the grown people were nigh. One day, when all our people were gone out to their works as usual, and only I and my dear sister were left to mind the house, two men and a woman got over our walls, and in a moment seized us both, and, without giving us time to cry out, or make resistance, they stopped our mouths, and ran off with us into the nearest wood. Here they tied our hands, and continued to carry us as far as they could, till night came on, when we reached a small house, where the robbers halted for refreshment, and spent the night.

We were then unbound, but were unable to take any food; and, being quite overpowered by fatigue and grief, our only relief was some sleep, which allayed our misfortune for a short time. The next morning we left the house, and continued travelling all the day. For a long time we had kept the woods, but at last we came into a road which I believed I knew. I had now some hopes of being delivered; for we had advanced but a little way before I discovered some people at a distance, on which I began to cry out for their assistance; but my cries had no other effect than to make them tie me faster and stop my mouth, and then they put me in a large sack. They also stopped my sister's mouth, and tied her hands; and in this manner we proceeded till we were out of the sight of these people. When we went to rest the following night they offered us some victuals; but we refused it; and the only comfort we had was in one another's arms all that night, and bathing each other with our tears. But alas! we were soon deprived of even the small comfort of weeping together. The next day proved a day of greater sorrow than I had yet experienced; for my sister and I were then separated, while we lay clasped in each other's arms. It was in vain that we besought them not to part us; she was torn from me, and immediately carried away, while I was left in a state of distraction not to be described. I cried and grieved continually; and for several days I did not eat any thing but what they forced into my mouth.

At length, after many days travelling, during which I had often changed masters, I got into the hands of a chieftain, in a very pleasant country. This man had two wives and some children, and they all used me extremely well, and did all they could to comfort me; particularly the first wife, who was something like my mother. Although I was a great many days journey from my father's house, yet these people spoke exactly the same language with us. This first master of mine, as I may call him, was a smith, and my principal employment was working his bellows, which were the same kind as I had seen in my vicinity. They were in some respects not unlike the stoves here in gentlemen's kitchens; and were covered over with leather and in the middle of that leather a stick was fixed, and a person stood up, and worked it, in the same manner as is done to pump water out of a cask with a hand pump. I believe it was gold he worked, for it was of a lovely bright yellow colour, and was worn by the women on their wrists and ankles. I was there I suppose about a month, and they at last used to trust me some little distance from the house. This liberty I used in embracing every opportunity to inquire the way to my own home: and I also sometimes, for the same purpose, went with the maidens, in the cool of the evenings, to bring pitchers of water from the springs for the use of the house. I had also remarked where the sun rose in the morning, and set in the evening, as I had travelled along; and I had observed that my father's house was towards the rising of the sun.

I therefore determined to seize the first opportunity of making my escape, and to shape my course for that quarter; for I was quite oppressed and weighed down by grief after my mother and friends; and my love of liberty, ever great, was strengthened by the mortifying circumstances of not daring to eat with the free-born children, although I was mostly their companion.

Here follows an anecdote about Equiano's fears after he has accidentally killed a chicken and run off in terror. He is found however, and his African master, 'having slightly reprimanded me, ordered me to be taken care of, and not to be ill-treated'.

Soon after this my master's only daughter, and child by his first wife, sickened and died, which affected him so much that for some time he was almost frantic, and really would have killed himself, had he not been watched and prevented. However, in a small time afterwards he recovered, and I was again sold. I was now carried to the left of the sun's rising, through many different countries, and a number of large woods. The people I was sold to used to carry me very often, when I was tired, either on their shoulders or on their backs. I saw many convenient well-built sheds along the roads, at proper distances, to accommodate the merchants and travellers, who lay in those buildings along with their wives, who often accompany them; and they always go well armed.

From the time I left my own nation I always found somebody that understood me till I came to the sea coast. The languages of different nations did not totally differ, nor were they so copious as those of the Europeans, particularly the English. They were therefore easily learned; and, while I was journeying thus through Africa, I acquired two or three different tongues. In this manner I had been travelling for a considerable time, when one evening, to my great surprise, whom should I see brought to the house where I was but my dear sister! As soon as she saw me she gave a loud shriek, and ran into my arms – I was quite overpowered: neither of us could speak; but, for a considerable time, clung to each other in mutual embraces, unable to do any thing but weep. Our meeting affected all who saw us; and indeed I must acknowledge, in honour of those sable destroyers of human rights, that I never met with any ill treatment, or saw any offered to their slaves, except tying them, when necessary, to keep them from running away. When these people knew we were brother and sister they indulged us together; and the man, to whom I supposed we belonged, lay with us, he in the middle, while she and I held one another by the hands across his breast all night; and thus for a while we forgot our misfortunes in the joy of being together: but even this small comfort was soon to have an end; for scarcely had the fatal morning appeared, when she was again torn from me for ever! I was now more miserable, if possible, than before. The small relief which her presence gave me from pain was gone, and the wretchedness of my situation was redoubled by my anxiety after her fate, and my apprehensions lest her sufferings should be greater than mine, when I could not be with her to alleviate them. Yes, thou dear partner of all my childish sports! thou sharer of my joys and sorrows! happy should I have ever esteemed myself to encounter every misery for you, and to procure your freedom by the sacrifice of my own. Though you were early forced from my arms, your image has been always riveted in my heart, from which neither *time nor fortune* have been able to remove it; so that, while the thoughts of your sufferings have damped my prosperity, they have mingled with adversity and increased its bitterness. To that Heaven which protects the weak from the strong, I commit the care of your innocence and virtues, if they have not already received their full reward, and if your youth and delicacy have not long fallen victims to the violence of the African trader, the pestilential stench of a Guinea ship, the lash and lust of a brutal and unrelenting overseer.

I did not long remain after my sister. I was again sold, and carried through a number of places, till, after travelling a considerable time, I came to a town called Tinmah, in the most beautiful country I had yet seen in Africa. It was extremely rich, and there were many rivulets which flowed through it, and supplied a large pond in the centre of the town, where the people washed. Here I first saw and tasted coco-nuts, which I thought superior to any nuts I had ever tasted before; and the trees which were loaded, were also interspersed amongst the houses, which had commodious shades adjoining, and were in the same manner as ours, the insides being neatly plastered and whitewashed. Here I also saw and tasted for the first time sugar-cane.

Their money consisted of little white shells, the size of the finger nail. I was sold here for one hundred and seventy-two of them by a merchant who lived and brought me there. I had been about two or three days at his house, when a wealthy widow, a neighbour of his, came there one evening, and brought with her an only son, a young gentleman about my own age and size. Here they saw me; and, having taken a fancy to me, I was bought of the merchant, and went home with them. Her house and premises were situated close to one of those rivulets I have mentioned, and were the finest I ever saw in Africa: they were very extensive, and she had a number of slaves to attend her. The next day I was washed and perfumed, and when meal-time came I was led into the presence of my mistress, and ate and drank before her with her son. This filled me with astonishment; and I could scarce help expressing my surprise that the young gentleman should suffer me, who was bound, to eat with him who was free; and not only so, but that he would not at any time either eat or drink till I had taken first, because I was the eldest, which was agreeable to our custom. Indeed everything here, and all their treatment of me, made me forget that I was a slave. The language of these people resembled ours so nearly, that we understood each other perfectly. They had also the very same customs as we. There were likewise slaves daily to attend us, while my young master and I with other boys sported with our darts and bows and arrows, as I had been used to do at home. In this resemblance to my former happy state I passed about two months; and I now began to think I was to be adopted into the family, and was beginning to be reconciled to my situation, and to forget by degrees my misfortunes, when all at once the delusion vanished; for, without the least previous knowledge, one morning early, while my dear master and companion was still asleep, I was wakened out of my reverie to fresh sorrow, and hurried away even amongst the uncircumcised.

Thus, at the very moment I dreamed of the greatest happiness, I found myself most miserable; and it seemed as if fortune wished to give me this taste of joy, only to render the reverse more poignant. The change I now experienced was as painful as it was sudden and unexpected. It was a change indeed from a state of bliss to a scene which is inexpressible by me, as it discovered to me an element I had never before beheld, and till then had no idea of, and wherein such instances of hardship and cruelty continually occurred as I can never reflect on but with horror.

All the nations and people I had hitherto passed through resembled our own in their manners, customs, and language: but I came at length to a country, the inhabitants of which differred from us in all those particulars. I was very much struck with this difference, especially when I came among a people who did not circumcise, and ate without washing their hands. They cooked also in iron pots, and had European cutlasses and cross bows, which were unknown to us, and fought with their fists amongst themselves. Their women were not so modest as ours, for they ate, and drank, and slept with their men. But, above all, I was amazed to see no sacrifices or offerings among them. In some of those places the people ornamented themselves with scars, and likewise filed their teeth very sharp. They wanted sometimes to ornament me in the same manner, but I would not suffer them; hoping that I might some time be among a people who did not thus disfigure themselves, as I thought they did. At last I came to the banks of a large river, which was covered with canoes, in which the people appeared to live with their household utensils and provisions of all kinds. I was beyond measure astonished at this, as I had never before seen any water larger than a pond or a rivulet: and my surprise was mingled with no small fear when I was put into one of these canoes, and we began to paddle and move along the river. We continued going on thus till night; and when we came to land, and made fires on the banks, each family by themselves, some dragged their canoes on shore, others stayed and cooked in theirs, and laid in them all night. Those on the land had mats, of which they made tents, some in the shape of little houses: in these we slept; and after the morning meal we embarked again and proceeded as before. I was often very much astonished to see some of the women, as well as the men, jump into the water, dive to the bottom, come up again, and swim about. Thus I continued to travel, sometimes by land, sometimes by water, through different countries and various nations, till, at the end of six or seven months after I had been kidnapped, I arrived at the sea coast. It would be tedious and uninteresting to relate all the incidents which befell me during

this journey, and which I have not yet forgotten; of the various hands I passed through, and the manners and customs of all the different people among whom I lived: I shall therefore only observe, that in all the places where I was the soil was exceedingly rich; the pomkins, eddoes, plantains, yams, &c.&c. were in great abundance, and of incredible size. There was also vast quantities of different gums, though not used for any purpose; and every where a great deal of tobacco. The cotton even grew quite wild; and there was plenty of red-wood, I saw no mechanics whatever in all the way, except such as I have mentioned. The chief employment in all these countries was agriculture, and both the males and females, as with us, were brought up to it, and trained in the arts of war.

The first object which saluted my eyes when I arrived on the coast was the sea, and a slave ship, which was then riding at anchor, and waiting for its cargo. These filled me with astonishment, which was soon converted into terror when I was carried on board. I was immediately handled and tossed up to see if I were sound by some of the crew; and I was now persuaded that I had gotten into a world of bad spirits, and that they were going to kill me. Their complexions too differing so much from ours, their long hair, and the language they spoke, (which was very different from any I had ever heard) united to confirm me in this belief. Indeed such were the horrors of my views and fears at the moment, that, if ten thousand worlds had been my own, I would have freely parted with them all to have exchanged my condition with that of the meanest slave in my own country. When I looked round the ship too and saw a large furnace or copper boiling, and a multitude of black people of every description chained together, every one of their countenances expressing dejection and sorrow, I no longer doubted of my fate; and, quite overpowered with horror and anguish, I fell motionless on the deck and fainted. When I recovered a little I found some black people about me, who I believe were some of those who brought me on board; and had been receiving their pay; they talked to me in order to cheer me, but all in vain. I asked them if we were not to be eaten by those white men with horrible looks, red faces, and loose hair. They told me I was not; and one of the crew brought me a small portion of spirituous liquor in a wine glass; but being afraid of him, I would not take it out of his hand. One of the blacks therefore took it from him and gave it to me, and I took a little down my palate, which, instead of reviving me, as they thought it would, threw me into the greatest consternation at the strange feeling it produced, having never tasted any such liquor before. Soon after this the blacks who brought me on board went off, and left me abandoned to despair. I now saw myself deprived of all chance of returning to my native country, or even the least glimpse of hope of gaining the shore, which I now considered as friendly; and I even wished for my former slavery in preference to my present situation, which was filled with horrors of every kind, still heightened by my ignorance of what I was to undergo. I was not long suffered to indulge my grief; I was soon put down under the decks, and there I received such a salutation in my nostrils as I had never experienced in my life: so that, with the loathsomeness of the stench, and crying together, I became so sick and low that I was not able to eat, nor had I the least desire to taste any thing. I now wished for the last friend, death, to relieve me; but soon, to my grief, two of the white men offered me eatables; and, on my refusing to eat, one of them held me fast by the hands, laid me across I think the windlass, and tied my feet, while the other flogged me severely. I had never experienced any thing of this kind before; and although, not being used to the water, I naturally feared that element the first time I saw it, yet nevertheless, could I have got over the nettings, I would have jumped over the side, but I could not; and besides the crew used to watch us very closely who were not chained down to the decks, lest we should leap into the water: and I have seen some of these poor African prisoners most severely cut for attempting to do so, and hourly whipped for not eating. This indeed was often the case with myself. In a little time after, amongst the poor chained men, I found some of my own nation, which in a small degree gave ease t my mind. I inquired of these what was to be done with us; they gave me to understand we were to be carried to these white people's country to work for them. I then was a little revived, and thought, if it were no worse than working, my situation was not so desperate: but still I feared I should be put to death, the white people looked and acted, as I thought, in so savage a manner; for I had never seen among

any people such instances of brutal cruelty; and this not only shown towards us blacks, but also to some of the whites themselves.

One white man in particular I saw, when we were permitted to be on deck, flogged so unmercifully with a large rope near the foremast, that he died in consequence of it; and they tossed him over the side as they would have done a brute. This made me fear these people the more; and I expected nothing less than to be treated in the same manner. I could not help expressing my fears and apprehensions to some of my countrymen: I asked them if these people had no country, but lived in this hollow place (the ship): they told me they did not, but came from a distant one. 'Then,' said I, 'how comes it in all our country we never heard of them?' They told me because they lived so very far off. I then asked where were their women? had they any like themselves? I was told they had: 'and why,' said I, 'do we not see them?' they answered because they were left behind. I asked how the vessel could go? they told me they could not tell; but that there were cloths put upon the masts by the help of the ropes I saw, and then the vessel went on; and the white men had some spell or magic they put in the water when they liked in order to stop the vessel. I was exceedingly amazed at this account, and really thought they were spirits. I therefore wished much to be from amongst them, for I expected they would sacrifice me: but my wishes were vain; for we were so quartered that it was impossible for any of us to make our escape.

While we stayed on the coast I was mostly on deck; and one day, to my great astonishment, I saw one of these vessels coming in with the sails up. As soon as the whites saw it, they gave a great shout, at which we were amazed; and the more so as the vessel appeared larger by approaching nearer. At last she came to an anchor in my sight, and when the anchor was let go I and my countrymen who saw it were lost in astonishment to observe the vessel stop; and were now convinced it was done by magic. Soon after this the other ship got her boats out and they came on board of us, and the people of both ships seemed very glad to see each other. Several of the strangers also shook hands with us black people and made motions with their hands, signifying I suppose we were to go to their country; but we did not understand them. At last, when the ship we were in had got in all her cargo, they made ready with many fearful noises, and we were all put under deck, so that we could not see how they managed the vessel. But this disappointment was the least of my sorrow. The stench of the hold while we were on the coast was so intolerably loathsome, that it was dangerous to remain there for any time, and some of us had been permitted to stay on the deck for the fresh air; but now that the whole ship's cargo were confined together, it became absolutely pestilential. The closeness of the place, and the heat of the climate, added to the number in the ship, which was so crowded that each had scarcely room to turn himself, almost suffocated us. This produced copious perspirations, so that the air soon became unfit for respiration, from a variety of loathsome smells, and brought on a sickness among the slaves, of which many died, thus falling victims to the improvident avarice, as I may call it, of their purchasers.

This wretched situation was again aggravated by the galling of the chains, now become insupportable; and the filth of the necessary tubs, into which the children often fell, and were almost suffocated. The shrieks of the women, and the groans of the dying, rendered the whole a scene of horror almost inconceivable. Happily perhaps for myself I was soon reduced so low here that it was thought necessary to keep me almost always on deck; and from my extreme youth I was not put in fetters. In this situation I expected every hour to share the fate of my companions, some of whom were almost daily brought upon deck at the point of death, which I began to hope would soon put an end to my miseries. Often did I think many of the inhabitants of the deep much more happy than myself. I envied them the freedom they enjoyed, and as often wished I could change my condition for theirs. Every circumstance I met with served only to render my state more painful, and heighten my apprehensions, and my opinion of the cruelty of the whites. One day they had taken a number of fishes; and when they had killed them and satisfied themselves with as many they thought fit, to our astonishment who were on the deck, rather than give any of them to us to eat as we expected they tossed the remaining fish into the sea again, although we begged and prayed for some as well as we could, but in vain; and some of my countrymen, being pressed by hunger, took an opportunity, when they thought no one saw them, of trying to get a little privately; but they were discovered, and the attempt procured them some very severe floggings.

One day, when we had a smooth sea and moderate wind, two of my wearied countrymen who were chained together (I was near them at the time), preferring death to such a life of misery, somehow made through the nettings and jumped into the sea: immediately another quite dejected fellow, who, on account of his illness, was suffered to be out of irons, also followed their example; and I believe many more would very soon have done the same if they had not been prevented by the ship's crew, who were instantly alarmed. Those of us that were the most active were in a moment put down under the deck, and there was such a noise and confusion amongst the people of the ship as I never heard before, to stop her, and get the boat out to go after the slaves. However two of the wretches were drowned, but they got the other, and afterwards flogged him unmercifully for thus attempting to prefer death to slavery. In this manner we continued to undergo more hardships than I can now relate, hardships which are inseparable from this accursed trade. Many a time we were near suffocation from the want of fresh air, which we were often without for whole days together. This, and the stench of the necessary tubs, carried off many. During our passage I first saw flying fishes, which surprised me very much: they used frequently to fly across the ship, and many of them fell on the deck. I also now first saw the use of the quadrant; I had often with astonishment seen the mariners make observations with it, and I could not think what it meant. They at last took notice of my surprise; and one of them, willing to increase it, as well as to gratify my curiosity, made me one day look through it. The clouds appeared to me to be land, which disappeared as they passed along. This heightened my wonder; and I was now more persuaded than ever that I was in another world, and that every thing about me was magic. At last we came in sight of the island of Barbados, at which the whites on board gave a great shout, and made many signs of joy to us. We did not know what to think of this; but as the vessel drew nearer we plainly saw the harbour, and other ships of different kinds and sizes; and we soon anchored amongst them off Bridge Town.

Many merchants and planters now came on board, though it was in the evening. They put us in separate parcels, and examined us attentively. They also made us jump, and pointed to the land, signifying we were to go there. We thought by this we should be eaten by these ugly men, as they appeared to us; and, when soon after we were all put down under the deck again, there was much dread and trembling among us, and nothing but bitter cries to be heard all the night from these apprehensions, insomuch that at last the white people got some old slaves from the land to pacify us. They told us we were not to be eaten, but to work, and were soon to go on land, where we should see many of our country people. This report eased us much; and sure enough, soon after we were landed, they came to us Africans of all languages. We were conducted immediately to the merchant's yard, where we were pent up altogether like so many sheep in a fold, without regard to sex or age. As every object was new to me every thing I saw filled me with surprise. What struck me first was that the houses were built with stories, and in every other respect different from those in Africa: but I was still more astonished on seeing people on horseback. I did not know what this could mean; and indeed I thought these people were full of nothing but magical arts.

While I was in this astonishment one of my fellow prisoners spoke to a countryman of his about the horses, who said they were the same kind they had in their country. I understood them, though they were from a distant part of Africa, and I thought it odd I had not seen any horses there; but afterwards, when I came to converse with different Africans, I found they had many horses amongst them, and much larger than those I then saw. We were not many days in the merchant's custody before we were sold after their usual manner, which is this:– On a signal given, (as the beat of a drum) the buyers rush at once into the yard where the slaves are confined, and make a choice of that parcel they like best. The noise and clamour with which this is attended, and the eagerness visible in the countenances of the buyers, serve not a little to increase the apprehensions of the terrified Africans, who may well be supposed to consider them as the ministers of that destruction to which they think themselves devoted. In this manner, without scruple, are relations and friends separated, most of them never to see each other again. I remember in the vessel in which I was brought over, in the men's apartment, there were several brothers, who, in the sale, were sold in different lots; and it was very moving on this occasion to see and hear their cries at parting. O, ye nominal Christians! might not an African ask you, learned you this from your God, who says unto you, Do unto all men as you would men should do unto you? Is it not enough that we are torn from our country and friends to toil for your luxury and lust of gain? Must every tender feeling be likewise sacrificed to your avarice? Are the dearest friends and relations, now rendered more dear by their separation from their kindred, still to be parted from each other, and thus prevented from cheering the gloom of slavery with the small comfort of being together and mingling their sufferings and sorrows? Why are parents to lose their children, brothers their sisters, or husbands their wives? Surely this is a new refinement in cruelty, which, while it has no advantage to atone for it, thus aggravates distress, and adds fresh horrors even to the wretchedness of slavery.

62

The Autobiography of a Runaway Slave

ESTEBAN MONTEJO

All the slaves lived in barracoons. These dwelling places no longer exist, so one cannot see them. But I saw them and I never thought well of them. The masters, of course, said they were as clean as new pins. The slaves disliked living under those conditions: being locked up stifled them. The barracoons were large, though some plantations had smaller ones; it depended on the number of slaves in the settlement. Around two hundred slaves of all colours lived in the Flor de Sagua barracoon. This was laid out in rows: two rows facing each other with a door in the middle and a massive padlock to shut the slaves in at night. There were barracoons of wood and barracoons of masonry with tiled roofs. Both types had mud floors and were as dirty as hell. And there was no modern ventilation there! Just a hole in the wall or a small barred window. The result was that the place swarmed with fleas and ticks, which made the inmates ill with infections and evil spells, for those ticks were witches. The only way to get rid of them was with hot wax, and sometimes even that did not work. The masters wanted the barracoons to look clean outside, so they were whitewashed. The job was given to the Negroes themselves. The master would say, 'Get some whitewash and spread it on evenly.' They prepared the whitewash in large pots inside the barracoons, in the central courtyard.

Horses and goats did not go inside the barracoons, but there was always some mongrel sniffing about the place for food. People stayed inside the rooms, which were small and hot. One says rooms, but they were really ovens. They had doors with latchkeys to prevent stealing. You had to be particularly wary of the *criollitos*, who were born thieving little rascals. They learned to steal like monkeys.

In the central patio the women washed their own, their husbands' and their children's clothes in tubs. Those tubs were not like the ones people use now, they were much cruder. And they had to be taken first to the river to swell the wood, because they were made out of fishcrates, the big ones.

There were no trees either outside or inside the barracoons, just empty solitary spaces. The Negroes could never get used to this. The Negro likes trees, forests. But the Chinese! Africa was full of trees, god-trees, banyans, cedars. But not China – there they have weeds, purslaine, morning-glory, the sort of thing that creeps along. As the rooms were so small the slaves relieved themselves in a so-called toilet standing in one corner of the barracoon. Everyone used it. And to wipe your arse afterwards you had to pick leaves and maize husks.

The bell was at the entrance to the mill. The deputy overseer used to ring it. At four-thirty in the morning they rang the Ave Maria – I think there were nine strokes of the bell – and one had to get up immediately. At six they rang another bell called the line-up bell, and everyone had to form up in a place just outside the barracoon, men one side, women the other. Then off to the canefields till eleven, when we ate jerked beef, vegetables and bread. Then, at sunset, came the prayer bell. At half-past eight they rang the last bell for everyone to go to sleep, the silence bell.

The deputy overseer slept inside the barracoon and kept watch. In the mill town there was a white watchman, a Spaniard, to keep an eye on things. Everything was based on watchfulness and the whip. When time passed and the *esquifación,* the slaves' issue of clothing, began to wear out, they would be given a new one. The men's clothes were made of Russian cloth, a coarse linen, sturdy and good for work in the fields – trousers which had large pockets and stood up stiff, a shirt, and a wool cap for the cold. The shoes were generally of rawhide, low-cut with little straps to keep them on. The old men wore sandals, flat-soled with a thong around the big toe. This has always been an African fashion, though white women wear them now and call them mules or slippers. The women were given blouses, skirts and petticoats, and if they owned plots of land they bought their own petticoats, white ones, which were prettier and smarter. They also wore gold rings and earrings. They bought these trophies from the Turks and Moors who sometimes came to the barracoons, carrying boxes slung from their shoulders by a wide leather strap. Lottery-ticket-sellers also came round, who cheated the Negroes and sold them all their most expensive tickets. If any of the tickets came up on the lottery you wouldn't see them for dust. The *guajiros*, or white country-men, also came to barter milk for jerked beef, or sell it at four cents a bottle. The Negroes used to buy it because the owners did not provide milk, and it is necessary because it cures infections and cleans the system.

These plots of land were the salvation of many slaves, where they got their real nourishment from. Almost all of them had their little strips of land to be sown close to the barracoons, almost behind them. Everything grew there: sweet potatoes, gourds, okra, kidney beans, which were like lima beans, yucca and peanuts. They also raised pigs. And they sold all these products to the whites who came out from the villages. The Negroes were honest, it was natural for them to be honest, not knowing much about things. They sold their goods very cheap. Whole pigs fetched a doubloon, or a doubloon and a half, in gold coin, as the money was then, but the blacks didn't like selling their vegetables. I learned to eat vegetables from the elders, because they said they were very healthy food, but during slavery pigs were the mainstay. Pigs gave more lard then than now, and I think it's because they led a more natural life. A pig was left to wallow about in the piggeries. The lard cost ten pennies a pound, and

the white countrymen came all week long to get their portion. They always paid in silver half-dollars. Later it became quarter-dollars.

Cents were still unknown because they had not crowned Alfonso XIII king as yet, and cents came after his coronation. King Alfonso wanted everything changed, right down to the coinage. Copper money came to Cuba then, worth two cents, if I remember right, and other novelties in the way of money, all due to the King.

Strange as it may seem, the Negroes were able to keep themselves amused in the barracoons. They had their games and pastimes. They played games in the taverns too, but these were different. The favourite game in the barracoons was *tejo.* A split corn-cob was placed on the ground with a coin balanced on top, a line was drawn not far off, and you had to throw a stone from there to hit the cob. If the stone hit the cob so that the coin fell on top of it, the player won the coin, but if it fell nearby, he didn't. This game gave rise to great disputes, and then you had to take a straw to measure whether the coin was nearer the player or the cob.

Tejo was played in the courtyard like skittles, though skittles was not played often, only two or three times altogether that I can remember. Negro coopers used to make the bottle-shaped skittles and wooden balls to play with. This game was open to all comers, and everyone had a go, except the Chinese, who didn't join in much. The balls were rolled along the ground so as to knock down the four or five skittles. It was played just like the modern game they have in the city except that they used to fight over the betting money in those days. The masters didn't like that at all. They forbade certain games, and you had to play those when the overseer was not looking. The overseer was the one who passed on the news and gossip.

The game of *mayombe*[1] was connected with religion. The overseers themselves used to get involved, hoping to benefit. They believed in the witches too, so no one today need be surprised that whites believe in such things. Drumming was part of the *mayombe.* A *nganga,* or large pot, was placed in the centre of the patio. The powers were inside the pot: the saints. People started drumming and singing. They took offerings to the pot and asked for health for themselves and their brothers and peace among themselves. They also made *enkangues,* which are charms of earth from the cemetery; the earth was made into little heaps in four corners, representing the points of the universe. Inside the pot they put a plant called star-shake, together with corn straw to protect the men. When a master punished a slave, the others would collect a little earth and put it in the pot. With the help of this earth they could make the master fall sick or bring some harm upon his family, for so long as the earth was inside the pot the master was imprisoned there and the Devil himself couldn't get him out. This was how the Congolese revenged themselves upon their master. The taverns were near the plantations. There were more taverns than ticks in the forest. They were a sort of store where one could buy everything. The slaves themselves used to trade in the taverns selling the jerked beef which they accumulated in the barracoons. They were usually allowed to visit the taverns during the daylight hours and sometimes even in the evenings, but this was not the rule in all the plantations. There was always some master who forbade the slaves to go. The Negroes went to the taverns for brandy. They drank a lot of it to keep their strength up. A glass of good brandy costs half a peso. The owners drank a lot of brandy too, and the quarrels which brewed were no joke. Some of the tavern-keepers were old Spaniards, retired from the army on very little money, five or six pesos' pension.

The taverns were made of wood and palm-bark; no masonry like the modern stores. You had to sit on piled jute sacks or stand. They sold rice, jerked beef, lard and every variety of bean. I knew cases of unscrupulous owners cheating slaves by quoting the wrong prices, and I saw brawls in which a Negro came off worse and was forbidden to return. They noted down anything you bought in a book; when you spent half a peso they made one stroke in the book, and two for a peso. This was the system for buying everything else: round sweet biscuits, salt biscuits, sweets the size of a pea made of different coloured flours, water-bread and lard. Water-bread cost five cents a stick. It was quite different from the sort you get now. I preferred it. I also remember that they sold sweet cakes, called 'caprices', made of peanut flour and sesame seed. The sesame seed was a Chinese thing; there were Chinese pedlars who went round the plantations

selling it, old indentured labourers whose arms were too weak to cut cane and who had taken up peddling.

The taverns were stinking places. A strong smell came from all the goods hanging from the ceiling, sausages, smoked hams, red mortadellas. In spite of this, people used to hold their games there. They spent half their lives at this foolishness. The Negroes were eager to shine at these games. I remember one game they called 'the biscuit', which was played by putting four or five hard salt biscuits on a wooden counter and striking them hard with your prick to see who could break them. Money and drinks were wagered on this game. Whites and blacks played it alike.

Another competition was the jug game. You took a large earthenware jug with a hole in the top and stuck your prick into it. The bottom of the jug was covered with a fine layer of ash, so you could see whether a man had reached the bottom or not when he took it out again.

Then there were other things they played, like cards. It was preferable to play with oil-painted cards which are the correct ones to play with. There were many types of card games. Some people liked playing with the cards face up, others with them face down, which was a game where you could win a lot of money, but I preferred *monte*, which began in the private houses and then spread to the countryside. *Monte* was played during slavery, in the tavern and in the masters' homes, but I took it up after Abolition. It is very complicated. You have to put two cards on the table and guess which of the two is the highest of the three you still have in your hand. It was always played for money, which is what made it attractive. The banker dealt the cards and the players put on the money. You could win a lot of money, and I won every day. The fact is, *monte* was my weakness; *monte* and women. And with some reason, for you would have had to look hard to find a better player than me. Each card had its name, like now, except that the cards today are not so colourful. In my day they had queens, kings, aces and knaves, and then came all the numbers from two to seven. The cards had pictures on them of men on horseback or wearing crowns, obviously Spaniards, because they never had fellows like that in Cuba, with those lace collars and long hair. They had Indians here in the old days.

Sunday was the liveliest day in the plantations. I don't know where the slaves found the energy for it. Their biggest fiestas were held on that day. On some plantations the drumming started at midday or one o'clock. At Flor de Sagua it began very early. The excitement, the games, and children rushing about started at sunrise. The barracoon came to life in a flash; it was like the end of the world. And in spite of work and everything the people woke up cheerful. The overseer and deputy overseer came into the barracoon and started chatting up the black women. I noticed that the Chinese kept apart; those buggers had no ear for drums and they stayed in their little corners. But they thought a lot; to my mind they spent more time thinking than the blacks. No one took any notice of them, and people went on with their dances.

The one I remember best is the *yuka*. Three drums were played for the *yuka*: the *caja*, the *mula*, and the *cachimbo*, which was the smallest one. In the background they drummed with two sticks on hollowed-out cedar trunks. The slaves made those themselves, and I think they were called *cata'*. The *yuka* was danced in couples, with wild movements. Sometimes they swooped about like birds, and it almost looked as if they were going to fly, they moved so fast. They gave little hops with their hands on their waists. Everyone sang to excite the dancers.

There was another more complicated dance. I don't know whether it was really a dance or a game, because they punched each other really hard. This dance they called the *maní* or peanut dance. The dancers formed a circle of forty or fifty men, and they started hitting each other. Whoever got hit went in to dance. They wore ordinary work clothes, with coloured print scarves round their heads and at their waists. (These scarves were used to bundle up the slaves' clothing and take it to the wash: they were called *vayajá* scarves.) The men used to weight their fists with magic charms to make the *maní* blows more effective. The women didn't dance but stood round in a chorus, clapping, and they used to scream with fright, for often a Negro fell and failed to get up again. Maní was a cruel game. The dancers did not make bets on the outcome. On some plantations the masters themselves made bets, but I don't remember this happening at Flor de Sagua. What they did was to forbid slaves to hit each other so hard, because

sometimes they were too bruised to work. The boys could not take part, but they watched and took it all in. I haven't forgotten a thing myself.

As soon as the drums started on Sunday the Negroes went down to the stream to bathe – there was always a little stream near every plantation. It sometimes happened that a woman lingered behind and met a man just as he was about to go into the water. Then they would go off together and get down to business. If not, they would go to the reservoirs, which were the pools they dug to store water. They also used to play hide-and-seek there, chasing the women and trying to catch them.

The women who were not involved in this little game stayed in the barracoons and washed themselves in a tub. These tubs were very big and there were one or two for the whole settlement.

Shaving and cutting hair was done by the slaves themselves. They took a long knife and, like someone grooming a horse, they sliced off the woolly hair. There was always someone who liked to clip, and he became the expert. They cut hair the way they do now. And it never hurt, because hair is the most peculiar stuff; although you can see it growing and everything, it's dead. The women arranged their hair with curls and little partings. Their heads used to look like melon skins. They liked the excitement of fixing their hair one way one day and another way the next. One day it would have little partings, the next day ringlets, another day it would be combed flat. They cleaned their teeth with strips of soap-tree bark, and this made them very white. All this excitement was reserved for Sundays.

Everyone had a special outfit that day. The Negroes bought themselves rawhide boots, in a style I haven't seen since, from nearby shops where they went with the master's permission. They wore red and green *vayajá* scarves around their necks, and round their heads and waists too, like in the maní dance. And they decked themselves with rings in their ears and rings on all their fingers, real gold. Some of them wore not gold but fine silver bracelets which came as high as their elbows, and patent leather shoes.

The slaves of French descent danced in pairs, not touching, circling slowly around. If one of them danced outstandingly well they tied silk scarves of all colours to his knees as a prize. They sang in patois and played two big drums with their hands. This was called the French dance.

I remember one instrument called a *marímbula*, which was very small. It was made of wickerwork and sounded as loud as a drum and had a little hole for the voice to come out of. They used this to accompany the Congo drums, and possibly the French too, but I can't be sure. The *marímbulas* made a very strange noise, and lots of people, particularly the *guajiros*[2] didn't like them because they said they sounded like voices from another world.

As I recall, their own music at that time was made with the guitar only. Later, in the Nineties, they played *danzónes*[3] on pianolas, with accordions and gourds. But the white man has always had a very different music from the black man. White man's music is without the drumming and is more insipid.

More or less the same goes for religion. The African gods are different, though they resemble the others, the priests' gods. They are more powerful and less adorned. Right now if you were to go to a Catholic church you would not see apples, stones or cock's feathers. But this is the first thing you see in an African house. The African is cruder.

I knew of two African religions in the barracoons: the Lucumí and the Congolese. The Congolese was the more important. It was well known at the Flor de Sagua because their magicmen used to put spells on people and get possession of them, and their practice of soothsaying won them the confidence of all the slaves. I got to know the elders of both religions after Abolition.

I remember the *Chicherekú*[4] at Flor de Sagua. The *Chicherekú* was a Congolese by birth who did not speak Spanish. He was a little man with a big head who used to run about the barracoons and jump upon you from behind. I often saw him and heard him squealing like a rat. This is true. Until recently in Porfuerza there was a man who ran about in the same way. People used to run away from him because they said he was the Devil himself and he was bound up with *mayombe* and death. You dared not play with the *Chicherekú* because it could be dangerous. Personally I don't much like talking of him, because I have never laid eyes on him again, and if by some chance . . . Well, these things are the Devil's own!

The Congolese used the dead and snakes for their religious rites. They called the dead *nkise*

and the snakes *emiboba*. They prepared big pots called *ngangas* which would walk about and all, and that was where the secret of their spells lay. All the Congolese had these pots for *mayombe*. The *ngangas* had to work with the sun, because the sun has always been the strength and wisdom of men, as the moon is of women. But the sun is more important because it is he who gives life to the moon. The Congolese worked magic with the sun almost every day. When they had trouble with a particular person they would follow him along a path, collect up some of the dust he walked upon and put it in the *nganga* or in some little secret place. As the sun went down that person's life would begin to ebb away, and at sunset he would be dying. I mention this because it is something I often saw under slavery.

If you think about it, the Congolese were murderers, although they only killed people who were harming them. No one ever tried to put a spell on me because I have always kept apart and not meddled in other people's affairs.

The Congolese were more involved with witchcraft than the Lucumí, who had more to do with the saints and with God. The Lucumí liked rising early with the strength of the morning and looking up into the sky and saying prayers and sprinkling water on the ground. The Lucumí were at it when you least expected it. I have seen old Negroes kneel on the ground for more than three hours at a time, speaking in their own tongue and prophesying. The difference between the Congolese and the Lucumí was that the former solved problems while the latter told the future. This they did with *diloggunes,* which are round, white shells from Africa with mystery inside. The god Eleggua's[5] eyes are made from this shell.

The old Lucumís would shut themselves up in rooms in the barracoon and they could rid you of even the wickedness you were doing. If a Negro lusted after a woman, the Lucumís would calm him. I think they did this with coconut shells, *obi,* which were sacred. They were the same as the coconuts today, which are still sacred and may not be touched. If a man defiled a coconut, a great punishment befell him. I knew when things went well, because the coconut said so. He would command *Alafia*[6] to be said so that people would know that all was well. The saints spoke through the coconuts and the chief of these was Obatalá, who was an old man, they said, and only wore white. They also said it was Obatalá who made you and I don't know what else, but it is from Nature one comes, and this is true of Obatalá too.

The old Lucumis liked to have their wooden figures of the gods with them in the barracoon. All these figures had big heads and were called *oché*. Elegguá was made of cement, but Changó and Yemaya were of wood, made by the carpenters themselves.

They made the saints' marks on the walls of their rooms with charcoal and white chalk, long lines and circles, each one standing for a saint, but they said that they were secrets. These blacks made a secret of everything. They have changed a lot now, but in those days the hardest thing you could do was to try to win the confidence of one of them.

The other religion was the Catholic one. This was introduced by the priests, but nothing in the world would induce them to enter the slaves' quarters. They were fastidious people, with a solemn air which did not fit the barracoons – so solemn that there were Negroes who took everything they said literally. This had a bad effect on them. They read the catechism and read it to the others with all the words and prayers. Those Negroes who were household slaves came as messengers of the priests and got together with the others, the field slaves, in the sugar mill towns. The fact is I never learned that doctrine because I did not understand a thing about it. I don't think the household slaves did either, although, being so refined and well-treated, they all made out they were Christian. The household slaves were given rewards by the masters, and I never saw one of them badly punished. When they were ordered to go to the fields to cut cane or tend the pigs, they would pretend to be ill so they needn't work. For this reason the field slaves could not stand the sight of them. The household slaves sometimes came to the barracoons to visit relations and used to take back fruit and vegetables for the master's house; I don't know whether the slaves made them presents from their plots of land or whether they just took them. They caused a lot of trouble in the barracoons. The men came and tried to take liberties with the women. That was the source of the worst tensions. I was about twelve then, and I saw the whole rumpus.

There were other tensions. For instance, there was no love lost between the Congolese magic-men and the Congolese Christians, each of whom thought they were good and the others wicked. This still goes on in Cuba. The Lucumi and Congolese did not get on either; it went back to the difference between saints and witchcraft. The only ones who had no problems were the old men born in Africa. They were special people and had to be treated differently because they knew all religious matters. Many brawls were avoided because the masters changed the slaves around. They kept them divided among themselves to prevent a rash of escapes. That was why the slaves of different plantations never got together with each other.

The Lucumis didn't like cutting cane, and many of them ran away. They were the most rebellious and courageous slaves. Not so the Congolese; they were cowardly as a rule, but strong workers who worked hard without complaining. There is a common rat called Congolese, and very cowardly it is too.

In the plantations there were Negroes from different countries, all different physically. The Congolese were black-skinned, though there were many of mixed blood with yellowish skins and light hair. They were usually small. The Mandingas were reddish-skinned, tall and very strong. I swear by my mother they were a bunch of crooks, too! They kept apart from the rest. The Gangas were nice people, rather short and freckled. Many of them became runaways. The Carabalis were like the Musungo Congolese, uncivilised brutes. They only killed pigs on Sundays and at Easter and, being good businessmen, they killed them to sell, not to eat themselves. From this comes a saying, 'Clever Carabalí, kills pig on Sunday,' I got to know all these people better after slavery was abolished.

All the plantations had an infirmary near the barracoon, a big wooden hut where they took the pregnant women. You were born there and stayed there till you were six or seven, when you went to live in the barracoons and began work, like the rest. There were Negro wet nurses and cooks there to look after the *criollitos* and feed them. If anyone was injured in the fields or fell ill, these women would doctor him with herbs and brews. They could cure anything. Sometimes a *criollito* never saw his parents again because the boss moved them to another plantation, and so the wet-nurses would be in sole charge of the child. But who wants to bother with another person's child ? They used to bath the children, and cut their hair in the infirmaries too. A child of good stock cost five hundred pesos, that is the child of strong, tall parents. Tall Negroes were privileged. The masters picked them out to mate them with tall, healthy women and shut them up together in the barracoon and forced them to sleep together. The women had to produce healthy babies every year. I tell you, it was like breeding animals. Well if the Negress did't produce as expected, the couple were separated and she was sent to work in the fields again. Women who were barren were unlucky because they had to go back to being beasts of burden again, but they were allowed to chose their own husbands. It often happened that a woman would be chasing one man with twenty more after her. The magic-men would settle these problems with their potions.

If you went to a magic-man to ask his help in getting a woman, he would tell you to get hold of a shred of her tobacco, if she smoked. This was ground together with a Cantharis fly, one of the green harmful ones, into a powder which you gave to the woman in water. That was the way to seduce them. Another spell consisted of grinding up a hummingbird's heart to powder and giving this to a woman in her tobacco. If you merely wanted to make fun of a woman, you only had to send for some snuff from the apothecary's. This was enough to make any woman die of shame. You put it in a place where they used to sit down, and if only a little touched their bums they started farting. It was something to see those women with cosmetics all over their faces farting about the place!

The old Negroes were entertained by these carryings on. When they were over sixty they stopped working in the fields. Not that any of them ever knew their ages exactly. What happened was that when a man grew weak and stayed huddled in a corner, the overseers would make him a doorkeeper or watchman stationed at the gate of the barracoon or outside the pigsties, or he would be sent to help the women in the kitchen. Some of the old men had their little plots of ground and passed their time working in them. Doing this sort of job gave them time for witchcraft. They were not punished or taken much notice of, but they had to be quiet and obedient. That much was expected.

I saw many horrors in the way of punishment under slavery. That was why I didn't like the life. The stocks, which were in the boiler-house, were the cruellest. Some were for standing and others for lying down. They were made of thick planks with holes for the head, hands and feet. They would keep slaves fastened up like this for two or three months for some trivial offence. They whipped the pregnant women too, but lying face down with a hollow in the ground for their bellies. They whipped them hard, but they took good care not to damage the babies because they wanted as many of those as possible. The most common punishment was flogging; this was given by the overseer with a rawhide lash which made weals on the skin. They also had whips made of the fibres of some jungle plant which stung like the devil and flayed the skin off in strips. I saw many handsome big Negroes with raw backs. Afterwards the cuts were covered with compresses of tobacco leaves, urine and salt.

Life was hard and bodies wore out. Anyone who did not take to the hills as a runaway when he was young had to become a slave. It was preferable to be on your own on the loose than locked up in all that dirt and rottenness. In any event, life tended to be solitary because there were none too many women around. To have one of your own you had either to be over twenty-five or catch yourself one in the fields. The old men did not want the youths to have women. They said a man should wait until he was twenty-five to have experiences. Some men did not suffer much, being used to this life. Others had sex between themselves and did not want to know anything of women. This was their life – sodomy. The effeminate men washed the clothes and did the cooking too, if they had a 'husband'. They were good workers and occupied themselves with their plots of land, giving the produce to their 'husbands' to sell to the white farmers. It was after Abolition that the term 'effeminate' came into use, for the practice persisted. I don't think it can have come from Africa, because the old men hated it. They would have nothing to do with queers. To tell the truth, it never bothered me. I am of the opinion that a man can stick his arse where he wants.

Everyone wearied of the life, and the ones who got used to it were broken in spirit. Life in the forest was healthier. You caught lots of illnesses in the barracoons, in fact men got sicker there than anywhere else. It was not unusual to find a Negro with as many as three sicknesses at once. If it wasn't colic it was whooping cough. Colic gave you a pain in the gut which lasted a few hours and left you shagged. Whooping cough and measles were catching. But the worst sicknesses, which made a skeleton of everyone, were smallpox and the black sickness. Smallpox left men all swollen, and the black sickness took them by surprise; it struck suddenly and between one bout of vomiting and the next you ended up a corpse. There was one type of sickness the whites picked up, a sickness of the veins and male organs. It could only be got rid of with black women; if the man who had it slept with a Negress he was cured immediately. There were no powerful medicines in those days and no doctors to be found anywhere. It was the nurses who were half witches who cured people with their home-made remedies. They often cured illnesses the doctors couldn't understand. The solution doesn't lie in feeling you and pinching your tongue; the secret is to trust the plants and herbs, which are the mother of medicine. Africans from the other side, across the sea, are never sick because they have the necessary plants at hand. If a slave caught an infectious disease, they would take him from his room and move him to the infirmary and try to cure him. If he died they put him in a big box and carried him off to the cemetery. The overseer usually came and gave instructions to the settlement to bury him. He would say, 'We are going to bury this Negro who has done his time.' And the slaves hurried along there, for when someone died everyone mourned.

The cemetery was in the plantation itself, about a hundred yards from the barracoon. To bury slaves, they dug a hole in the ground, filled it in and stuck a cross on top to keep away enemies and the Devil. Now they call it a crucifix. If anyone wears a cross around his neck it is because someone has tried to harm him.

Once they buried a Congolese and he raised his head. He was still alive. I was told this story in Santo Domingo, after Abolition. The whole district of Jicotea knows of it. It happened on a small plantation called El Diamante which belonged to Marinello's father, the one who talks a lot about Martí.[7] Everyone took fright and ran away. A few days later the Congolese appeared in the barracoon; they say he entered very slowly so as not to scare everyone, but when people saw him they took fright again. When the overseer asked what had happened, he said, 'They put me in a hole because of my cholera and when I was cured I came out.' After that, whenever anyone caught cholera or another disease, they left him for days and days in the coffin until he grew as cold as ice.

These stories are true, but one I am convinced is a fabrication because I never saw such a thing, and that is that some Negroes committed suicide. Before, when the Indians were in Cuba, suicide did happen. They did not want to become Christians, and they hanged themselves from trees. But the Negroes did not do that, they escaped by flying. They flew through the sky and returned to their own lands. The Musundi Congolese were the ones that flew the most; they disappeared by means of witchcraft. They did the same as the Canary Island witches, but without making a sound. There are those who say the Negroes threw themselves into rivers. This is untrue. The truth is they fastened a chain to their waists which was full of magic. That was where their power came from. I know all this intimately, and it is true beyond a doubt.

The Chinese did not fly, nor did they want to go back to their own country, but they did commit suicide. They did it silently. After several days they would turn up hanging from a tree or dead on the ground. They did everything in silence. They used to kill the very overseers themselves with sticks or knives. The Chinese respected no one. They were born rebels. Often the master would appoint an overseer of their own race so that he might win their trust. Then they did not kill him. When slavery ended I met other Chinese in Sagua la Grande, but they were different and very civilised.

I have never forgotten the first time I tried to escape. That time I failed, and I stayed a slave for several years longer from fear of having the shackles put on me again. But I had the spirit of a runaway watching over me, which never left me. And I kept my plans to myself so that no one could give me away. I thought of nothing else; the idea went round and round my head and would not leave me in peace; nothing could get rid of it, at times it almost tormented me. The old Negroes did not care for escaping, the women still less. There were few runaways. People were afraid of the forest. They said anyone who ran away was bound to be recaptured. But I gave more thought to this idea than the others did. I always had the feeling that I would like the forest and I knew that it was hell working in the fields, for you couldn't do anything for yourself. Everything went by what the master said.

One day I began to keep my eye on the overseer. I had already been sizing him up for some time. That son-of-a bitch obsessed me, and nothing could make me forget him. I think he was Spanish. I remember that he was tall and never took his hat off. All the blacks respected him because he would take the skin off your back with a single stroke of his whip. The fact is I was hot-headed that day. I don't know what came over me, but I was filled with a rage which burned me up just to look at the man.

I whistled at him from a distance, and he looked round and then turned his back; that was when I picked up a stone and threw it at his head. I know it must have hit him because he shouted to the others to seize me. But that was the last he saw of me, because I took to the forest there and then.

I spent several days walking about in no particular direction. I had never left the plantation before. I walked uphill, downhill, in every direction. I know I got to a farm near the Siguanea, where I was forced to rest. My feet were blistered and my hands were swollen and festering. I camped under a tree. I made myself a shelter of banana-leaves in a few hours and I stayed there four or five days. I only had to hear the sound of a human voice to be off like a bullet. It was a terrible thing to be captured again after you had run away.

Then I had the idea of hiding in a cave. I lived there for something like a year and a half. The reason I chose it was that I thought it might save me wandering about so much and also that all the pigs in the district, from the farms and smallholdings and allotments, used to come to a sort of marsh near the mouth of the cave to bathe and wallow in the water. I caught them very easily because they came up one behind the other. I used to cook myself up a pig every week. This cave of mine was very big and as black as a wolf's mouth. Its name was Guajabán, near the village of Remedios. It was very dangerous because there was no other way out; you had to enter and leave by the mouth. I was very curious to find another exit, but I preferred to stay in the mouth of the cave with the *majases* which are very dangerous snakes.[8] They knock a person down with their breath, a snake breath you cannot feel, and then they put you to sleep to suck your blood. That was why I was always on guard and lit a fire to frighten them off. Anyone who dozes off in a cave is in a bad way. I did not want to see a snake even from a distance. The Congolese, and this is a fact, told me that the *majases* lived for over a thousand years, and when they got to a thousand they turned into marine creatures and went off to live in the sea like any other fish.

The cave was like a house inside, only a little darker, as you would expect. Ah, and the stink! Yes, it stank of bat droppings! I used to walk about on them because they were as soft as a feather bed. The bats lead a free life in caves. They were and are the masters of caves. It is the same everywhere in the world. As no one kills them they live for scores of years, though not as long as the *majases*. Their droppings turn to dust and are thrown on the ground to make pasture for animals and to fertilise crops.

Once I almost set fire to the place. I struck a spark and flames leapt through the cave. It was because of the bat droppings. After Abolition I told a Congolese the story of how I lived with the bats, and the liar – the Congolese were even worse than you could imagine – said, 'A Creole like you doesn't know a thing. In my country what you call a bat is as big as a pigeon.' I knew this was untrue. They fooled half the world with their tales. But I just listened and was inwardly amused.

The cave was silent. The only sound was the bats going 'Chui, chui, chui'. They didn't know how to sing, but they spoke to each other, they understood each other. I noticed that one of them would go 'Chui, chui, chui and the whole band would follow him wherever he went. They were very united in everything. Bats don't have wings. They are nothing but a scrap of black rag with a little black head, very dark and ugly, and if you look closely at them they are like mice. In that cave I was, as it were, just summering. What I really liked was the forest, and after a year and a half I left that dark place and took to the forest tracks. I went into the Siguanea forests again and spent a long time there. I cared for myself as if I were a pampered child. I didn't want to be taken into slavery again. It was repugnant to me, it was shameful. I have always felt like that about slavery. It was like a plague – it still seems like that today.

I was careful about making sounds or showing lights. If I left a trail they would follow me and catch me. I walked up and down so many hills that my arms and legs became as hard as wood. I came to know the forest gradually, and I began to like it. Sometimes I forgot I was a runaway and started whistling. I used to whistle to dispel the fear of the first days. They say whistling drives away evil spirits. But in the forest a runaway had to be on his guard, and I stopped in case the *ranchadores* came after me. To track down runaway slaves, the masters used to send for a posse of *ranchadores,* brutal white countrymen with hunting dogs which would drag you out of the forest with their teeth. I never ran into any of them or even saw one close up. They were trained to catch Negroes; if one of them saw a Negro he would give chase. If I happened to hear barking nearby I would take off my clothes immediately, because once you are naked the dogs can't smell anything. Now I see a dog and it doesn't mean a thing, but if I had seen one then you wouldn't have seen my heels for miles around. I have never felt drawn to dogs. To my mind they have wicked instincts.

When a *ranchador* caught a slave, the master would give him money, a gold onza or more. In those days an onza was worth seventeen pesos. There's no knowing how many white countrymen were involved in that business!

To tell the truth, I lived very well as a runaway, hidden but comfortable. I did not let the other runaways catch sight of me: 'Runaway meets runaway, sells runaway.' There were many things I didn't do. For a long time I didn't speak to a soul. I liked this solitude. The other runaways always stayed in groups of twos and threes, but this was dangerous because when it rained their footprints showed up in the mud, and lots of idiots were caught that way.

There were some freed slaves around. I saw them going into the forest to look for herbs and jutías, edible rats. I never spoke to them or went near them, in fact I took good care to hide from them. Some of them worked on the land, and as soon as they left the coast clear, I took advantage of their absence to steal their vegetables and pigs. Most of them raised pigs on their plots of land.

But I preferred to steal from the smallholdings because there was more of everything and it was easier. The smallholdings were bigger than the plots, far bigger, almost like big farms. The Negroes didn't have such luxuries. Those *guajíros* really lived very well in their palm-bark houses. I used to watch them at their music making from a safe distance. Sometimes I could even hear them. They played small accordions, kettledrums, gourds, maraccas and calabashes. Those were their favourite instruments. I didn't learn their names till after I left the forest because, as a runaway, I was ignorant of everything.

They enjoyed dancing. But they didn't dance to the black man's music. They liked the *zapateo* and the *caringa.*[9] They all used to get together to dance the *zapateo* in the evenings, around five o'clock. The men wore coloured scarves around their necks and the women wore them around their heads. If one man excelled in the dance, his woman would come up and put a hat on top of the one he was wearing. This was the prize. I watched it all from a safe distance, taking it all in. I even saw them playing their pianolas. They played every sort of instrument there. They made a lot of noise, but it was as pretty as could be. From time to time one of the men would grab a gourd to accompany the pianola. The pianolas played the music that was popular at the time, the *danzón.*

On Sundays the *guajíros* wore white and their women put flowers on their heads and wore their hair loose, then they joined the rest of the festive company and got together in the taverns to celebrate. The men liked linen and drill. They made themselves long shirts like jackets, with big pockets. The *guajíros* in those days lived better than people realise. They got tips from the masters almost every day. Naturally the two got along very well and did their dirty work together. But in my view the runaway lived better than the *guajíro*; he had greater freedom.

I had to forage for food for a long time, but there was always enough. 'The careful tortoise carries his house on his back.' I liked vegetables and beans and pork best. I think it is because of the pork that I have lived so long. I used to eat it every day, and it never disagreed with me. I would creep up to the smallholdings at night to catch piglets, taking care that no one heard me. I gabbed the first one I saw by the neck, clapped a halter round it, slung it over my shoulder and started to run, keeping my hand over its snout to stop it squealing. When I reached my camp I set it down and looked it over. If it was well fed and weighed twenty pounds or so, I had meals for a fortnight.

I led a half-wild existence as a runaway. I hunted animals like *jutías*. The *jutía* runs like the devil, and you need wings on your feet to catch it. I was very fond of smoked *jutía*. I don't know what people think of it today, but they never eat it. I used to catch one and smoke it without salt, and it lasted me months. The *jutía* is the healthiest food there is, though vegetables are better for the bones. The man who eats vegetables daily, particularly malanga roots, has no trouble from his bones. There are plenty of these wild vegetables in the forest. The malanga, has a big leaf which shines at night. You can recognise it at once.

All the forest leaves have their uses. The leaves of tobacco plants and mulberry-trees cure stings. If I saw some insect bite was festering, I picked a tobacco leaf and chewed it thoroughly, then I laid it on the sting and the swelling went. Often, when it was cold, my bones would ache, a dry pain which would not go away. Then I made myself an infusion of rosemary leaves to soothe it, and it was cured at once. The cold also gave me bad coughs. When I got catarrh and a cough, I would pick this big leaf and lay it on my chest. I never knew its name, but it gave out a whitish liquid which was very warming; that soothed my cough. When I caught a cold, my eyes used to itch maddeningly, and the same used to happen as a result of the sun; in that case I laid a few leaves of the *Itamo* plant out to catch the dew overnight, and the next day I washed my eyes carefully with them. *Itamo* is the best thing for this. The stuff they sell in pharmacies today is *Itamo*, but what happens is that they put it into little bottles and it looks like something else. As one grows older this eye trouble disappears. I have not had any itching bouts for years now.

The macaw-tree leaf provided me with smokes. I made tight-rolled neat little cigarettes with it. Tobacco was one of my relaxations. After I left the forest I stopped smoking tobacco, but while I was a runaway I smoked all the time.

And I drank coffee which I made with roast *guanina* leaves. I had to grind the leaves with the bottom of a bottle. When the mixture was ground right down, I filtered it and there was my coffee. I could always add a little wild honey to give it flavour. Coffee with honey strengthens the organism. You were always fit and strong in the forest.

Townsfolk are feeble because they are mad about lard. I have never liked lard because it weakens the body. The person who eats a lot of it grows fat and sluggish. Lard is bad for the circulation and it strangles people. Bees' honey is one of the best things there is for health. It was easy to get in the forest. I used to find it in the hollows of hardwood trees. I used it to make *chanchanchara*, a delicious drink made of stream-water and honey, and best drunk cold. It was better for you than any modern medicine; it was natural. When there was no stream nearby I hunted around till I found a spring. In the forest there are springs of sweet water – the coldest and clearest I have seen in my life – which run downhill.

The truth is I lacked for nothing in the forest. The only thing I could not manage was sex. Since there were no women around I had to keep the appetite in check. It wasn't even possible to fuck a mare because they whinnied like demons, and if the white countrymen had heard the din they would have come rushing out immediately. I was not going to have anyone clap me in irons for a mare.

I was never short of fire. During my first few days in the forest I had matches. Then they ran out, and I had to use my *yesca*, a black ash that I kept in one of the tinderboxes the Spaniards sold in taverns. It was easy to get a fire going. All you had to do was rub a stone on the tinderbox till it sparked. I learned this from the Canary Islanders while I was a slave. I never liked them as they were domineering and petty. The Galicians were nicer and got on better with the Negroes.

As I have always liked being my own man, I kept well away from everyone. I even kept away from the insects. To frighten off snakes I fired a big log and left it burning all night. They did not come near because they thought the log was a devil or an enemy of theirs. That's why I say I enjoyed my life as a runaway. I looked after myself, and I protected myself too. I used knives and half-sized machetes made by the firm of Collins, which were the ones used by the rural police, to clear the undergrowth and hunt animals, and I kept them ready in case a *ranchador* tried to take me by surprise – though that would have been difficult, as I kept on the move. I walked so much in the sun that at times my head began to burn and become, I imagined, quite red. Then I would be seized with a strong fever which I got rid of by wrapping myself up a bit or putting fresh leaves on my forehead, plantain as a rule. The problem was that I had no hat. I used to imagine the heat must be getting into my head and softening my brain.

When the fever passed, and it sometimes lasted several days, I dipped myself in the first river I came across and came out like new. The river water did me no harm. I think river water is the best thing for health, because it's so cold. This is good, because it hardens you. The bones feel firm. The rain used to give me a touch of catarrh which I cured with a brew of *cuajaní* berries and bees' honey. So as not to get wet I sheltered myself with palm leaves, piling them on top of a frame made of four forked sticks to make a hut. These huts were often seen after slavery and during the war. They looked like Indian shacks.

I spent most of the time walking or sleeping. At midday and at five in the afternoon I could hear the *fotuto*,[10] which the women blew to call their husbands home. It sounded like this: 'Fuuuu, fu, fu, fu, fu.' At night I slept at my ease. That was why I got so fat. I never thought about anything. My life was all eating, sleeping and keeping watch. I liked going to the hills at night, they were quieter and safer. *Ranchadores* and wild animals found difficulty in getting there. I went as far as Trinidad. From the top of those hills you could see the town and the sea.

The nearer I got to the coast the bigger the sea got. I always imagined the sea like an immense river. Sometimes I stared hard at it and it went the strangest white colour and was swallowed up in my eyes. The sea is another great mystery of Nature, and it is very important, because it can take men and close over them and never give them up. Those are what they call shipwrecked men.

One thing I remember really clearly is the forest birds. They are something I cannot forget. I remember them all. Some were pretty and some were hellishly ugly. They frightened me a lot at first, but then I got used to hearing them. I even got so I felt they were taking care of me. The *cotunto* was a real bastard. It was a black, *black*

bird, which said, 'You, you, you, you, you, you, you ate the cheese up.' And it kept on saying this till I answered, 'Get away!' and it went. I heard it crystal clear. There was another bird which used to answer it as well; it went, 'Cu, cu, cu, cu, cu, cu' and sounded like a ghost.

The *sijú* was one of the birds which tormented me most. It always came at night. That creature was the ugliest thing in the forest! It had white feet and yellow eyes. It shrieked out something like this: 'Cus, cus, cuuuus'.

The barn-owl had a sad song, but then it was a witch. It looked for dead mice. It cried, 'Chua, chua, chua, kui, kui,' and flew off like a ray of light. When I saw a barn-owl in my path, especially when it was flying to and fro, I used to take a different way because I knew it was warning me of an enemy nearby, or death itself. The barn-owl is wise and strange. I recollect that the witches had a great respect for her and worked magic with her, the *sunsumdamba,* as she is called in Africa. The barn owl may well have left Cuba. I have never seen one again. Those birds go from country to country.

The sparrow came here from Spain and has founded an immense tribe here. Also the *tocororo*, which is half a greenish colour. It wears a scarlet sash across its breast, just like one the King of Spain has. The overseers used to say that it was a messenger from the King. I know it was forbidden even to look at a *tocororo*. The Negro who killed one was killing the King. I saw lots of men get the lash for killing sparrows and *tocororo*. I liked the *tocororo* because it sang as if it was hopping about, like this: 'Có, co, có, co, có, co'.

A bird which was a real son-of-a-bitch was the *ciguapa.* It whistled just like a man and it froze the soul to hear it. I don't like to think how often those creatures upset me.

I got used to living with trees in the forest. They have their noises too, because the leaves hiss in the air. There is one tree with a big white leaf which looks like a bird at night. I could swear that tree spoke. It went, 'Uch, uch, uch, ui, ui, ui, uch, uch.' Trees also cast shadows which do no harm, although one should not walk on them at night. I think trees' shadows must be like men's spirits. The spirit is the reflection of the soul, this is clear.

One thing it is not given to us men to see is the soul. We cannot say whether it is of such or such a colour. The soul is one of the greatest things in the world. Dreams are there to put us in touch with it. The Congolese elders used to say that the soul was like a witchcraft inside you and that there were good spirits and bad spirits, or rather, good souls and bad souls, and that everybody had them. As far as I can see, some people only have the magic sort of souls, while others have ordinary ones. But the ordinary ones are better, I think, because the others are in league with the Devil. It can happen that the soul leaves the body – when a person dies or sleeps – and joins the other souls wandering in space. It does this to rest itself, because so much strife at all times would be unbearable. There are people who don't like being called while they are asleep, because they are easily frightened and could die suddenly. This is because the soul travels far away during sleep and leaves the body empty. I sometimes get the shivers at night, and the same used to happen in the forest. Then I cover myself well because this is God's warning to one to take care of oneself. People who get the shivers need to pray a lot.

The heart is very different. It never leaves its post. If you put your hand on your left side you can make sure that it is beating. But the day it stops no one can help but go stiff. That is why you should not trust it.

Now the most important thing of all is the guardian angel. It is he who makes you go forwards or back. To my mind, the angel ranks higher than the soul or heart. He is always at your feet, watching over you and seeing everything. Nothing will ever make him go. I have thought a lot about these things, and I still find them a bit obscure. These are the thoughts which come when one is alone. Man is thinking at all times. Even when he dreams, it is as though he were thinking. It is not good to speak of these thoughts. There is danger of decadence setting in. You cannot put much trust in people. How many people ask you questions so as to be able to use the information against you afterwards! Besides, this business of the spirits is infinite, like debts which keep piling up. No one knows the end. The truth is I don't even trust the Holy Ghost. That was why I stayed on my own as a runaway. I did nothing except listen to the birds and trees, and eat, but I never spoke to a soul. I remember I was so hairy my whiskers hung in ringlets. It was a sight to inspire fear. When I

came out of the forest and went into the villages an old man called Ta Migue cropped me with a big pair of scissors. He gave me such a close crop I looked like a thoroughbred. I felt strange with all that wool gone, tremendously cold. The hair started growing again in a few days. Negroes have this tendency – I have never seen a bald Negro, not one. It was the Galicians who brought baldness to Cuba.

All my life I have liked the forest, but when slavery ended I stopped being a runaway. I realised from the way the people were cheering and shouting that slavery had ended, and so I came out of the forest. They were shouting, 'We're free now.' But I didn't join in, I thought it might be a lie. I don't know . . . anyway, I went up to a plantation and let my head appear little by little till I was out in the open. That was while Martinez Campos was Governor, the slaves said it was he who had freed them. All the same, years passed and there were still slaves in Cuba. It lasted longer than people think. When I left the forest and began walking, I met an old woman carrying two children in her arms. I called to her, and when she came up I asked her, 'Tell me, is it true we are no longer slaves?' She replied No, son we are free now.' I went on walking the way I was going and began to look for work. Lots of Negroes wanted to be friends with me, and they used to ask me what I had done as a runaway. I told them, 'Nothing.' I have always been one for my independence. Idle gossip never helped anyone. I went for years and years without talking to anyone at all.

Notes

1. African word meaning evil spirit; hence name given to the branch of the Stick Cult which concentrates on black magic.
2. Peasants, originally white settlers, but by this time black and Mulatto also.
3. *Danzón*: a slow, stately Cuban dance popular in the last century.
4. African word for bogey-man.
5. Elegguá, Obatalá, Changó, Yemaya: gods of the Yoruba, a Nigerian tribe, worshipped in Cuba by the followers of *santeria*.
6. Lucumi expression meaning 'all goes well', used particularly in the system of divination with sacred coconuts.
7. Martí, often known as the 'Apostle' or 'the Father of Cuba', was the leader of Cuba's national War of Independence and also a poet and essayist of great influence in the Spanish-speaking world. Juan

Marinello, one of Cuba's leading Communists, is an important critic of Martí's literary work.

8.   In fact they are harmless.

9.   Folk dances popular in the nineteenth century, especially among white country people. The *caringa* was of African origin and usually took the form of a scurrilous song accompanied by a dance.

10.   A large conch used as a trumpet in the country districts.

63

The History of Mary Prince: A West Indian Slave Related by Herself

MARY PRINCE

I was born at Brackish-Pond, in Bermuda, on a farm belonging to Mr. Charles Myners. My mother was a household slave; and my father, whose name was Prince, was a sawyer belonging to Mr. Trimmingham, a shipbuilder at Crow-Lane. When I was an infant, old Mr. Myners died, and there was a division of the slaves and other property among the family. I was bought along with my mother by old Captain Darrel, and given to his grandchild, little Miss Betsey Williams. Captain Williams, Mr. Darrel's son-in-law, was master of a vessel which traded to several places in America and the West Indies, and he was seldom at home long together.

Mrs. Williams was a kind-hearted good woman and she treated all her slaves well. She had only one daughter, Miss Betsey, for whom I was purchased, and who was about my own age. I was made quite a pet of by Miss Betsey, and loved her very much. She used to lead me about by the hand, and call me her little nigger. This was the happiest period of my life; for I was too young to understand rightly my condition as a slave, and too thoughtless and full of spirits to look forward to the days of toil and sorrow.

My mother was a household slave in the same family. I was under her own care, and my little brothers and sisters were my play-fellows and companions. My mother had several fine children after she came to Mrs. Williams, three girls and two boys. The tasks given out to us children were light, and we used to play together with Miss Betsey, with as much freedom almost as if she had been our sister.

My master, however, was a very harsh, selfish man; and we always dreaded his return from sea. His wife was herself much afraid of him; and, during his stay at home, seldom dared to shew her usual kindness to the slaves. He often left her, in the most distressed circumstances, to reside in other female society, at some place in the West Indies of which I have forgot the name. My poor mistress bore his ill-treatment with great patience, and all her slaves loved and pitied her. I was truly attached to her, and, next to my own mother, loved her better than any creature in the world. My obedience to her commands was cheerfully given: it sprung solely from the affection I felt for her, and not from fear of the power which the white people's law had given her over me.

I had scarcely reached my twelfth year when my mistress became too poor to keep so many of us at home; and she hired me out to Mrs. Pruden, a lady who lived about five miles off, in the adjoining parish, in a large house near the sea. I cried bitterly at parting with my dear mistress and Miss Betsey, and when I kissed my mother and brothers and sisters, I thought my young heart would break, it pained me so. But there was no help; I was forced to go. Good Mrs. Williams comforted me by saying that I should still be near the home I was about to quit, and might come over and see her and my kindred whenever I could obtain leave of absence from Mrs. Pruden. A few hours after this I was taken to a strange house, and found myself among strange people. This separation seemed a sore trial to me then;

but oh! 'twas light, light to the trials I have since endured! – 'twas nothing – nothing to be mentioned with them; but I was a child then, and it was according to my strength.

I knew that Mrs. Williams could no longer maintain me, that she was fain to part with me for my food and clothing; and I tried to submit myself to the change. My new mistress was a passionate woman but yet she did not treat me very unkindly. I do not remember her striking me but once, and that was for going to see Mrs. Williams when I heard she was sick, and staying longer than she had given me leave to do. All my employment at this time was nursing a sweet baby, little Master Daniel; and I grew so fond of my nursling that it was my greatest delight to walk out with him by the sea-shore, accompanied by his brother and sister, Miss Fanny and Master James. – Dear Miss Fanny! She was a sweet, kind young lady, and so fond of me that she wished me to learn all that she knew herself; and her method of teaching me was as follows: Directly she had said her lessons to her grandmamma, she used to come running to me, and make me repeat them one by one after her; and in a few months I was able not only to say my letters but to spell many small words. But this happy state was not to last long. Those days were too pleasant to last. My heart always softens when I think of them.

At this time Mrs. Williams died. I was told suddenly of her death, and my grief was so great that, forgetting I had the baby in my arms, I ran away directly to my poor mistress's house; but reached it only in time to see the corpse carried Out. Oh, that was a day of sorrow – a heavy day! All the slaves cried. My mother cried and lamented her sore; and I (foolish creature!) vainly entreated them to bring my dear mistress back to life. I knew nothing rightly about death then, and it seemed a hard thing to bear. When I thought about my mistress I felt as if the world was all gone wrong; and for many days and weeks I could think of nothing else. I returned to Mrs. Pruden's; but my sorrow was too great to be comforted, for my own dear mistress was always in my mind. Whether in the house or abroad, my thoughts were always talking to me about her.

I staid at Mrs. Pruden's about three months after this; I was then sent back to Mr. Williams to be sold. Oh, that was a sad sad time! I recollect the day well. Mrs. Pruden came to me and said, 'Mary, you will have to go home directly; your master is going to be married, and he means to sell you and two of your sisters to raise money for the wedding.' Hearing this I burst out a crying, though I was then far from being sensible of the full weight of my misfortune, or of the misery that waited for me. Besides, I did not like to leave Mrs. Pruden, and the dear baby, who had grown very fond of me. For some time I could scarcely believe that Mrs. Pruden was in earnest, till I received orders for my immediate return. Dear Miss Fanny! how she cried at parting with me, whilst I kissed and hugged the baby, thinking I should never see him again. I left Mrs. Pruden's, and walked home with a heart full of sorrow. The idea of being sold away from my mother and Miss Betsey was so frightful, that I dared not trust myself to think about it. We had been bought of Mrs. Myners, as I have mentioned, by Miss Betsey's grandfather, and given to her, so that we were by right **her** property, and I never thought we should be separated or sold away from her.

When I reached the house, I went in directly to Miss Betsey. I found her in great distress; and she cried out as soon as she saw me, 'Oh, Mary! my father is going to sell you all to raise money to marry that wicked woman. You are **my** slaves, and he has no right to sell you; but it is all to please her.' She then told me that my mother was living with her father's sister at a house close by, and I went there to see her. It was a sorrowful meeting; and we lamented with a great and sore crying our unfortunate situation. 'Here comes one of my poor piccaninnies!' she said, the moment I came in, 'one of the poor slave-brood who are to be sold tomorrow.'

Oh dear! I cannot bear to think of that day, – it is too much. It recalls the great grief that filled my heart, and the woeful thoughts that passed to and fro through my mind, whilst listening to the pitiful words of my poor mother, weeping for the loss of her children. I wish I could find words to tell you all I then felt and suffered. The great God above alone knows the thoughts of the poor slave's heart, and the bitter pains which follow such separations as these. All that we love taken away from us – oh, it is sad, sad! and sore to be borne! – I got no sleep that night for thinking of the morrow; and dear Miss Betsey was scarcely less distressed. She could not bear to part with her old playmates and she cried sore and would not be pacified.

The black morning at length came; it came too soon for my poor mother and us. Whilst she was putting on us the new osnaburgs in which we were to be sold, she said, in a sorrowful voice, (I shall never forget it!) 'See, I am *shrouding* my poor children; what a task for a mother!' She then called Miss Betsey to take leave of us. 'I am going to carry my little chickens to market,' (these were her very words) 'take your last look of them; may be you will see them no more.' 'Oh, my poor slaves! my own slaves!' said dear Miss Betsey, 'you belong to me; and it grieves my heart to part with you.' – Miss Betsey kissed us all, and, when she left us, my mother called the rest of the slaves to bid us good bye. One of them, a woman named Moll, came with her infant in her arms. 'Ay!' said my mother, seeing her turn away and look at her child with the tears in her eyes, 'your turn will come next.' The slaves could say nothing to comfort us; they could only weep and lament with us. When I left my dear little brothers and the house in which I had been brought up, I thought my heart would burst.

Our mother, weeping as she went, called me away with the children Hannah and Dinah, and we took the road that led to Hamble Town, which we reached about four o'clock in the afternoon. We followed my mother to the market-place, where she placed us in a row against a large house, with our backs to the wall and our arms folded across our breasts. I, as the eldest, stood first, Hannah next to the, then Dinah; and our mother stood beside, crying over us. My heart throbbed with grief and terror so violently, that I pressed my hands quite tightly across my breast, but I could not keep it still, and it continued to leap as though it would burst out of my body. But who cared for that? Did one of the many bystanders, who were looking at us so carelessly, think of the pain that wrung the hearts of the negro woman and her young ones? No, no! They were not all bad, I dare say, but slavery hardens white people's hearts towards the blacks; and many of them were not slow to make their remarks upon us aloud, without regard to our grief – though their light words fell like cayenne on the fresh wounds of our hearts. Oh those white people have small hearts who call only feel for themselves.

At length the vendue master, who was to offer us for sale like sheep or cattle, arrived, and asked my mother which was the eldest. She said nothing, but pointed to me. He took me by the hand, and led me out into the middle of the street, and, turning me slowly round, exposed me to the view of those who attended the vendue. I was soon surrounded by strange men, who examined and handled me in the same manner that a butcher would a calf or a lamb he was about to purchase, and who talked about my shape and size in like words – as if I could no more understand their meaning than the dumb beasts. I was then put up for sale. The bidding commenced at a few pounds, and gradually rose to fifty-seven,[1] when I was knocked down to the highest bidder; and the people who stood by said that I had fetched a great sum for so young a slave.

I then saw my sisters led forth, and sold to different owners; so that we had not the sad satisfaction of being partners in bondage. When the sale was over, my mother hugged and kissed us, and mourned over us, begging of us to keep up a good heart, and do our duty to our new masters. It was a sad parting; one went one way, one another, and our poor mammy went home with nothing.

My new master was a Captain I-, who lived at Spanish Point. After parting with my mother and sisters, I followed him to his store, and he gave me into the charge of his son, a lad about my own age, Master Benjy, who took me to my new home. I did not know where I was going, or what my new master would do with me. My heart was quite broken with grief, and my thoughts went back continually to those from whom I had been so suddenly parted. 'Oh, my mother! my mother!' I kept saying to myself, 'Oh, my mammy and my sisters and my brothers, shall I never see you again!'

Oh, the trials! the trials! they make the salt water come into my eyes when I think of the days in which I was afflicted – the times that are gone; when I mourned and grieved with a young heart for those whom I loved. It was night when I reached my new home. The house was large, and built at the bottom of a very high hill; but I could not see much of it that night. I saw too much of it afterwards. The stones and the timber were the best things in it; they were not so hard as the hearts of the owners.

Before I entered the house, two slave women, hired from another owner, who were at work in the yard, spoke to me, and asked who I belonged to? I replied, 'I am come to live here.' 'Poor child, poor child!' they both said; 'You must keep a good heart, if you are to live here.' – When I went in, I stood up crying in a corner. Mrs. I came and took off my hat, a little black silk hat Miss Pruden made for me, and said in a rough voice, 'You are not come here to stand up in corners and cry, you are come here to work.' She then put a child into my arms, and, tired as I was, I was forced instantly to take up my old occupation of a nurse. – I could not bear to look at my mistress, her countenance was so stern. She was a stout tall woman with a very dark complexion, and her brows were always drawn together into a frown. I thought of the words of the two slave women when I saw Mrs. I-, and heard the harsh sound of her voice.

The person I took the most notice of that night was a French Black called Hetty, whom my master took in privateering from another vessel, and made his slave. She was the most active woman I ever saw, and she was tasked to her utmost. A few minutes after my arrival she came in from milking the cows, and put the sweet potatoes on for supper. She then fetched home the sheep, and penned them in the fold; drove home the cattle, and staked them about the pond side; fed and rubbed down my master's horse, and gave the hog and the fed cow[2] their suppers; prepared the beds, and undressed the children, and laid them to sleep. I liked to look at her and watch all her doings, for her's was the only friendly face I had as yet seen, and I felt glad that she was there. She gave me my supper of potatoes and milk, and a blanket to sleep upon, which she spread for me in the passage before the door of Mrs. I-'s chamber.

I got a sad fright, that night. I was just going to sleep, when I heard a noise in my mistress's room; and she presently called out to inquire if some work was finished that she had ordered Hetty to do. 'No, Ma'am, not yet,' was Hetty's answer from below. On hearing this, my master started up from his bed, and just as he was, in his shirt, ran down stairs with a long cow-skin[3] in his hand. I heard immediately after, the cracking of the thong, and the house rang to the shrieks of poor Hetty, who kept crying out, 'Oh, Massa! Massa! me dead. Massa! have mercy upon me –

don't kill me outright.' – This was a sad beginning for me. I sat up upon my blanket, trembling with terror, like a frightened hound, and thinking that my turn would come next. At length the house became still, and I forgot for a little while all my sorrows by falling fast asleep.

The next morning my mistress set about instructing me in my tasks. She taught me to do all sorts of household work; to wash and bake, pick cotton and wool, and wash floors, and cook. And she taught me (how can I ever forget it!) more things than these; she caused me to know the exact difference between the smart of the rope, the cart-whip, and the cow-skin, when applied to my naked body by her own cruel hand. And there was scarcely any punishment more dreadful than the blows I received on my face and head from her hard heavy fist. She was a fearful woman, and a savage mistress to her slaves.

There were two little slave boys in the house, on whom she vented her bad temper in a special manner. One of these children was a mulatto, called Cyrus, who had been bought while an infant in his mother's arms; the other, Jack, was an African from the coast of Guinea, whom a sailor had given or sold to my master. Seldom a day passed without these boys receiving the most severe treatment, and often for no fault at all. Both my master and mistress seemed to think that they had a right to ill-use them at their pleasure; and very often accompanied their commands with blows, whether the children were behaving well or ill. I have seen their flesh ragged and raw with licks. – Lick – lick – they were never secure one moment from a blow, and their lives were passed in continual fear. My mistress was not contented with using the whip, but often pinched their cheeks and arms in the most cruel manner. My pity for these poor boys was soon transferred to myself; for I was licked, and flogged, and pinched by her pitiless fingers in the neck and arms, exactly as they were. To strip me naked – to hang me up by the wrists and lay my flesh open with the cow-skin, was an ordinary punishment for even a slight offence. My mistress often robbed me too of the hours that belong to sleep. She used to sit up very late, frequently even until morning; and I had then to stand at a bench and wash during the greater part of the night, or pick wool and cotton and often I have dropped down overcome by sleep and fatigue, till roused from a state of stupor by the whip, and forced to start up to my tasks.

Poor Hetty, my fellow slave, was very kind to me, and I used to call her my Aunt; but she led a most miserable life, and her death was hastened (at least the slaves all believed and said so) by the dreadful chastisement she received from my master during her pregnancy. It happened as follows. One of the cows had dragged the rope away from the stake to which Hetty had fastened it, and got loose. My master flew into a terrible passion, and ordered the poor creature to be stripped quite naked, notwithstanding her pregnancy, and to be tied up to a tree in the yard. He then flogged her as hard as he could lick, both with the whip and cow-skin, till she was all over streaming with blood. He rested, and then beat her again and again. Her shrieks were terrible. The consequence was that poor Hetty was brought to bed before her time, and was delivered after severe labour of a dead child. She appeared to recover after her confinement, so far that she was repeatedly flogged by both master and mistress afterwards; but her former strength never returned to her. Ere long her body and limbs swelled to a great size; and she lay on a mat in the kitchen, till the water burst out of her body and she died. All the slaves said that death was a good thing for poor Hetty; but I cried very much for her death. The manner of it filled me with horror. I could not hear to think about it; yet it was always present to my mind for many a day.

After Hetty died all her labours fell upon me. In addition to my own. I had now to milk eleven cows every morning before sunrise, sitting among the damp weeds; to take care of the cattle as well as the children; and to do the work of the house. There was no end to my toils – no end to my blows. I lay down at night and rose up in the morning in fear and sorrow; and often wished that like poor Hetty I could escape from this cruel bondage and be at rest in the grave. But the hand of that God whom then I knew not, was stretched over me; and I was mercifully preserved for better things. It was then, however, my heavy lot to weep, weep, weep, and that for years; to pass from one misery to another, and from one cruel master to a worse. But I must go on with the thread of my story.

One day a heavy squall of wind and rain came on suddenly, and my mistress sent me round the corner of the house to empty a large earthen jar. The jar was already cracked with an old deep crack that divided it in the middle, and in turning it upside down to empty it, it parted in my hand. I could not help the accident, but I was dreadfully frightened, looking forward to a severe punishment. I ran crying to my mistress, 'O mistress, the jar has come in two.' 'You have broken it, have you?' she replied; 'come directly here to me.' I came trembling: she stripped and flogged me long and severely with the cow-skin; as long as she had strength to use the lash, for she did not give over till she was quite tired. – When my master came home at night, she told him of my fault; and oh, frightful! how he fell a swearing. After abusing me with every ill name he could think of, (too, too bad to speak in England,) and giving me several heavy blows with his hand, he said, 'I shall come home tomorrow morning at twelve, on purpose to give you a round hundred.' He kept his word - Oh sad for me! I cannot easily forget it. He tied me up upon a ladder, and gave me a hundred lashes with his own hand, and master Benjy stood by to count them for him. When he had licked me for some time he sat down to take breath; then after resting, he beat me again and again, until he was quite wearied, and so hot (for the weather was very sultry), that he sank back in his chair, almost like to faint. While my mistress went to bring him drink, there was a dreadful earthquake. Part of the roof fell down, and every thing in the house went – clatter, clatter, clatter. Oh I thought the end of all things near at hand; and I was so sore with the flogging, that I scarcely cared whether I lived or died. The earth was groaning and shaking; every thing tumbling about; and my mistress and the slaves were shrieking and crying out, 'The earthquake! the earthquake!' It was an awful day for us all.

During the confusion I crawled away on my hands and knees, and laid myself down under the steps of the piazza, in front of the house. I was in a dreadful state – my body all blood and bruises, and I could not help moaning piteously. The other slaves, when they saw me, shook their heads and said, 'Poor child! poor child' – I lay there till the morning, careless of what might happen, for life was very weak in me, and I wished more than ever to die. But when we are very young, death always seems a great way off, and it would not come that night to me. The next morning I was forced by my master to rise and go about my usual work, though my body and limbs were so stiff and sore, that I could not move without the greatest pain. Nevertheless, even after all this severe punishment, I never heard the last of that jar; my mistress was always throwing it in my face.

Some little time after this, one of the cows got loose from the stake, and ate one of the sweet-potatoe slips. I was milking when my master found it out. He came to me, and without any more ado, stooped down, and taking off his heavy boot, he struck me such a severe blow in the small of my back, that I shrieked with agony, and thought I was killed; and I feel a weakness in that part to this day. The cow was frightened by his violence, and kicked down the pail and spilt the milk all about. My master knew that this accident was his own fault, but he was so enraged that he seemed glad of an excuse to go on with his ill usage. I cannot remember how many licks he gave me then, but he beat me till I was unable to stand, and till he himself was weary.

After this I ran away and went to my mother, who was living with Mr. Richard Darrel. My poor mother was both grieved and glad to see me; grieved because I had been so ill used, and glad because she had not seen me for a long, long while. She dared not receive me into the house, but she hid me up in a hole in the rocks near, and brought me food at night, after every body was asleep. My father, who lived at Crow-Lane, over the salt-water channel, at last heard of my being hid up in the cavern, and he came and took me back to my master. Oh I was loth, loth to go back; but as there was no remedy, I was obliged to submit.

When we got home, my poor father said to Capt. I – 'Sir, I am sorry that my child should be forced to run away from her owner; but the treatment she has received is enough to break her heart. The sight of her wounds has nearly broke mine. – I entreat you, for the love of God, to forgive her for running away, and that you will be a kind Master to her in future.' Capt. I – said I was used as well as I deserved, and that I ought to be punished for running away. I then took courage and said that I could stand the floggings no longer; that I was weary of my life, and therefore I had run away to my mother; but mothers could only weep and mourn over their children, they could not save them from cruel

masters – from the whip, the rope, and the cow-skin. He told me to hold my tongue and go about my work, or he would find a way to settle me. He did not, however, flog me that day.

For five years after this I remained in his house, and almost daily received the same harsh treatment. At length he put me on board a sloop, and to my great joy sent me away to Turk's Island. I was not permitted to see my mother or father, or poor sisters and brothers, to say good bye, though going away to a strange land, and might never see them again. Oh the Buckra people who keep slaves think that black people are like cattle, without natural affection. But my heart tells me it is far otherwise.

We were nearly four weeks on the voyage, which was unusually long. Sometimes we had a light breeze, sometimes a great calm, and the ship made no way; so that our provisions and water ran very low, and we were put upon short allowance. I should almost have been starved had it not been for the kindness of a black man called Anthony, and his wife, who had brought their own victuals, and shared them with me.

When we went ashore at the Grand Quay, the Captain sent me to the house of my new master, Mr. D-, to whom Captain I– had sold me. Grand Quay is a small town upon a sandbank; the houses low and built of wood. Such was my new master's. The first person I saw, on my arrival, was Mr. D-, a stout sulky looking man who carried me through the hall to show me to his wife and children. Next day I was put up by the vendue master to know how much I was worth, and I was valued at one hundred pounds currency.

My new master was one of the owners or holders of the salt ponds, and he received a certain sum for every slave that worked upon his premises, whether they were young or old. This sum was allowed him out of the profits arising from the salt works. I was immediately sent to work in the salt water with the rest of the slaves. This work was perfectly new to me. I was given a half barrel and a shovel, and had to stand up to my knees in the water, from four o'clock in the morning till nine, when we were given some Indian corn boiled in water, which we were obliged to swallow as fast as we could for fear the rain should come on and melt the salt. We were then called again to our tasks, and worked through the heat of the day; the sun flaming upon our heads like fire, and raising salt blisters in those parts which were not completely covered. Our feet and legs, from standing in the salt water for so many hours, soon became full of dreadful boils, which ate down in some cases to the very bone, afflicting the sufferers with great torment. We came home at twelve; ate our corn soup, called *blawly,* as fast as we could, and went back to our employment till dark at night. We then shovelled up the salt in large heaps, and went down to the sea, where we washed the pickle from our limbs, and cleaned the barrows and shovels from the salt. When we returned to the house, our master gave us each our allowance of raw Indian corn, which we pounded in a mortar and boiled in water for our suppers. We slept in a long shed, divided into narrow slips, like the stalls used for cattle. Boards fixed upon stakes driven into the ground, without mat or covering, were our only beds. On Sundays, after we had washed the salt bags, and done other work required of us, we went into the bush and cut the long soft grass, of which we made trusses for our legs and feet to rest upon, for they were so full of the salt boils that we could get no rest lying upon the bare boards.

Though we worked from morning till night, there was no satisfying Mr. D-. I hoped, when I left Capt. I-, that I should have been better off, but I found it was but going from one butcher to another. There was this difference between them: my former master used to beat me while raging and foaming with passion; Mr. D- was usually quite calm. He would stand by and give orders for a slave to be cruelly whipped, and assist in the punishment, without moving a muscle of his face; walking about and taking snuff with the greatest composure. Nothing could touch his hard heart - neither sighs, nor tears, nor prayers, nor streaming blood; he was deaf to our cries, and careless of our sufferings. – Mr. D- has often stripped me naked, hung me up by the wrists, and beat me with the cow-skin, with his own hand, till my body was raw with gashes. Yet there was nothing very remarkable in this; for it might serve as a sample of the common usage of the slaves on that horrible island.

Owing to the boils in my feet, I was unable to wheel the barrow fast through the sand, which got into the sores, and made me stumble at every step; and my master, having no pity for my sufferings from this cause, rendered them far more intolerable, by chastising me for not being able to move so fast as he wished me. Another of our employments was to row a little way off from the shore in a boat, and dive for large stones to build a wall round our master's house. This was very hard work; and the great waves breaking over us continually, made us often so giddy that we lost our footing, and were in danger of being drowned.

Ah, poor me! – my tasks were never ended. Sick or well, it was work – work – work! – After the diving season was over, we were sent to the South Creek, with large bills, to cut up mangoes to burn lime with. Whilst one party of slaves were thus employed, another were sent to the other side of the island to break up coral out of the sea.

When we were ill, let our complaint be what it might, the only medicine given to us was a great bowl of hot salt water, with salt mixed with it, which made us very sick. If we could not keep up with the rest of the gang of slaves, we were put in the stocks, and severely flogged the next morning. Yet, not the less, our master expected, after we had thus been kept from our rest, and our limbs rendered stiff and sore with ill usage, that we should still go through the ordinary tasks of the day all the same. Sometimes we had to work all night, measuring salt to load a vessel; or turning a machine to draw water out of the sea for the salt-making. Then we had no sleep – no rest – but were forced to work as fast as we could, and go on again all next day the same as usual. Work - work - work - Oh that Turk's Island was a horrible place! The people in England, I am sure, have never found out what is carried on there. Cruel, horrible place!

Mr. D- had a slave called old Daniel, whom he used to treat in the most cruel manner. Poor Daniel was lame in the hip, and could not keep up with the rest of the slaves; and our master would order him to be stripped and laid down on the ground, and have him beaten with a rod of rough briar till his skin was quite red and raw. He would then call for a bucket of salt, and fling upon the raw flesh till the man writhed on the ground like a worm, and screamed aloud with agony. This poor man's wounds were never healed, and I have often seen them full of maggots, which increased his torments to an intolerable degree. He was an object of pity and terror to the whole gang of slaves, and in his wretched case we saw, each of us, our own lot, if we should live to be as old.

Oh the horrors of slavery! – How the thought of it pains my heart! But the truth ought to be told of it; and what my eyes have seen I think it is my duty to relate; for few people in England know what slavery is. I have been a slave – I have felt what a slave feels, and I know what a slave knows; and I would have all the good people in England to know it too, that they may break our chains, and set us free.

Mr. D- had another slave called Ben. He being very hungry, stole a little rice one night after he came in from work, and cooked it for his supper. But his master soon discovered the theft; locked him up all night; and kept him without food till one o'clock the next day. He then hung Ben up by his hands, and beat him from time to time till the slaves came in at night. We found the poor creature hung up when we came home; with a pool of blood beneath him, and our master still licking him, but this was not the worst. My master's son was in the habit of stealing the rice and rum. Ben had seen him do this, and thought he might do the same, and when master found out that Ben had stolen the rice and swore to punish him, he tried to excuse himself by saying that Master Dickey did the same thing every night. The lad denied it to his father, and was so angry with Ben for informing against him, that out of revenge he ran and got a bayonet, and whilst the poor wretch was suspended by his hands and writhing under his wounds, he run it quite through his foot. I was not by when he did it, but I saw the wound when I came home, and heard Ben tell the manner in which it was done.

I must say something more about this cruel son of a cruel father. He had no heart – no fear of God; he had been brought up by a bad father in a bad path, and he delighted to follow in the same steps. There was a little old woman among the slaves called Sarah, who was nearly past work; and, Master Dickey being the overseer of the slaves just then, this poor creature, who was subject to several bodily infirmities, and was not quite right in her head, did not wheel the barrow fast enough to please him. He threw her down on the ground, and after beating her severely, he took her up in his arms and flung her among the prickly-pear bushes, which are all covered over with sharp venomous prickles. By this her naked flesh was so grievously wounded, that her body swelled and festered all over, and she died in a few days after. In telling my own sorrows, I cannot pass by those of my fellow-slaves - for when I think of my own griefs, I remember theirs.

I think it was about ten years I had worked in the salt ponds at Turk's Island, when my master left off business, and retired to a house he had in Bermuda, leaving his son to succeed him in the island. He took me with him to wait upon his daughters; and I was joyful, for I was sick, sick of Turk's Island, and my heart yearned to see my native place again, my mother, and my kindred.

I had seen my poor mother during the time I was a slave in Turk's Island. One Sunday morning I was on the beach with some of the slaves, and we saw a sloop come in loaded with slaves to work in the salt water. We got a boat and went aboard. When I came upon the deck I asked the black people, 'Is there any one here for me?' 'Yes,' they said, 'your mother.' I thought they said this in jest – I could scarcely believe them for joy; but when I saw my poor mammy my joy was turned to sorrow, for she had gone from her senses. 'Mammy,' I said, 'is this you!' She did not know me. 'Mammy,' I said, 'what's the matter?' She began to talk foolishly and said that she had been under the vessel's bottom. They had been overtaken by a violent storm at sea. My poor mother had never been on the sea before, and she was so ill, that she lost her senses, and it was long before she came quite to herself again. She had a sweet child with her - a little sister I had never seen, about four years of age, called Rebecca. I took her on shore with me, for I felt I should love her directly; and I kept her with me a week. Poor little thing! her's has been a sad life, and continues so to this day. My mother worked for some years on the island, but was taken back to Bermuda some time before my master carried me again thither.

After I left Turk's Island, I was told by some negroes that came over from it, that the poor slaves had built up a place with boughs and leaves, where they might meet for prayers, but the white people pulled it down twice, and would not allow them even a shed for prayers. A flood came down soon after and washed away many houses, filled the place with sand, and overflowed the ponds: and I do think that this was for their wickedness; for the Buckra men there were very wicked. I saw and heard much that was very very bad at that place.

I was several years the slave of Mr. D- after I returned to my native place. Here I worked in the grounds. My work was planting and hoeing sweet-potatoes, Indian corn, plantains, bananas, cabbages, pumpkins, onions, &c. I did all the household work, and attended upon a horse and cow besides, – going also upon all errands. I had to curry the horse – to clean and feed him – and sometimes to ride him a little. I had more than enough to do – but still it was not so very bad as Turk's Island. My old master often got drunk, and then he would get in a fury with his daughter, and beat her till she was not fit to be seen. I remember on one occasion, I had gone to fetch water, and when I was coming up the hill I heard a great screaming; I ran as fast as I could to the house, put down the water, and went into the chamber, where I found my master beating Miss D- dreadfully. I strove with all my strength to get her away from him; for she was all black and blue with bruises. He had beat her with his fist, and almost killed her. The people gave me credit for getting her away. He turned round and began to lick me. Then I said, 'Sir, this is not Turk's Island.' I can't repeat his answer, the words were too wicked – too bad to say. He wanted to treat me the same in Bermuda as he had done in Turk's Island.

He had an ugly fashion of stripping himself quite naked and ordering me then to wash him in a tub of water. This was worse to me than all the licks. Sometimes when he called me to wash him I would not come, my eyes were so full of shame. He would then come to beat me. One time I had plates and knives in my hand, and I dropped both plates and knives, and some of the plates were broken. He struck me so severely for this, that at last I defended myself, for I thought it was high time to do so. I then told him I would not live longer with him, for he was a very indecent man – very spiteful, and too indecent; with no shame for his servants, no shame for his own flesh. So I went away to a neighbouring house and sat down and cried till the next morning, when I went home again, not knowing what else to do.

After that I was hired to work at Cedar Hills, and every Saturday night I paid the money to my master. I had plenty of work to do there – plenty of washing; but yet I made myself pretty comfortable. I earned two dollars and a quarter a week, which is twenty pence a day. During the time I worked there, I heard that Mr. John Wood was going to Antigua. I felt a great wish to go there, and I went to Mr. D-, and asked him to let me go in Mr. Wood's service. Mr. Wood did not then want to purchase me; it was my own fault that I came under him, I was so anxious to go. It was ordained to be, I suppose; God led me there. The truth is, I did not wish to be any longer the slave of my indecent master.

Mr. Wood took me with him to Antigua, to the town of St. John's, where he lived. This was about fifteen years ago. He did not then know whether I was to be sold; but Mrs. Wood found that I could work, and she wanted to buy me. Her husband then wrote to my master to inquire whether I was to be sold? Mr. D- wrote in reply, 'that I should not be sold to any one that would treat me ill.' It was strange he should say this, when he had treated me so ill himself. So I was purchased by Mr. Wood for 300 dollars (or £100 Bermuda currency)[4]

My work there was to attend the chambers and nurse the child, and to go down to the pond and wash clothes. But I soon fell ill of the rheumatism, and grew so very lame that I was forced to walk with a stick. I got the Saint Anthony's fire, also, in my left leg, and became quite a cripple. No one cared much to come near me, and I was ill a long long time; for several months I could not lift the limb. I had to lie in a little old out-house, that was swarming with bugs and other vermin, which tormented me greatly; but I had no other place to lie in. I got the rheumatism by catching cold at the pond side, from washing in the fresh water; in the salt water I never got cold. The person who lived in next yard, (a Mrs. Greene,) could not bear to hear my cries and groans. She was kind, and used to send an old slave woman to help me, who sometimes brought me a little soup. When the doctor found I was so ill, he said I must be put into a bath of hot water. The old slave got the bark of some bush that was good for pains, which she boiled in the hot water, and every night she came and put me into the bath, and did what she could for me; I don't know what I should have done, or what would have become of me, had it not been for her. My mistress, it is true, did send me a little food; but no one fronm our family came near me but the cook, who used to shove my food in at the door, and say, 'Molly, Molly, there's your dinner.' My mistress did not care to take any trouble about me; and if the Lord had not put it into the hearts of the neighbours to be kind to me, I must, I really think, have lain and died.

It was a long time before I got well enough to work in the house. Mrs. Wood, in the meanwhile, hired a mulatto woman to nurse the child; but she was such a fine lady she wanted to be mistress over me. I thought it very hard for a coloured woman to have rule over me because I was a slave and she was free. Her name was Martha Wilcox; she was a saucy woman, very saucy; and she went and complained of me, without cause, to my mistress, and made her angry with me. Mrs. Wood told me that if I did not mind what I was about, she would get my master to strip me and give me fifty lashes: 'You have been used to the whip,' she said, 'and you shall have it here.' This was the first time she threatened to have me flogged; and she gave me the threatening so strong of what she would have done to me, that I thought I should have fallen down at her feet, I was so vexed and hurt by her words. The mulatto woman was rejoiced to have power to keep me down. She was constantly making mischief; there was no living for the slaves – no peace after she came.

I was also sent by Mrs. Wood to be put in the Cage one night, and was next morning flogged, by the magistrate's order, at her desire; and this all for a quarrel I had about a pig with another slave woman. I was flogged on my naked back on this occasion; although I was in no fault after all; for old Justice Dyett, when we came before him, said that I was in the right, and ordered the pig to be given to me. This was about two or three years after I came to Antigua.

When we moved from the middle of the town to the Point, I used to be in the house and do all the work and mind the children, though still very ill with the rheumatism. Every week I had to wash two large bundles of clothes, as much as a boy could help me to lift; but I could give no satisfaction. My mistress was always abusing and fretting after me. It is not possible to tell all her ill language. One day she followed me foot after foot scolding and rating me. I bore in silence a great deal of ill words: at last my heart was quite full, and I told her that she ought not to use me so; – that when I was ill I might have lain and died for what she cared; and no one would then come near me to nurse me, because

they were afraid of my mistress. This was a great affront. She called her husband and told him what I had said. He flew into a passion: but did not beat me then; he only abused and swore at me; and then gave me a note and bade me go and look for an owner. Not that he meant to sell me; but he did this to please his wife and to frighten me. I went to Adam White, a cooper, a free black who had money, and asked him to buy me. He went directly to Mr. Wood, but was informed that I was not to be sold. The next day my master whipped me.

Another time (about five years ago) my mistress got vexed with me because I fell sick and I could not keep on with my work. She complained to her husband, and he sent me off again to look for an owner. I went to a Mr. Burchell, showed him the note, and asked him to buy me for my own benefit; for I had saved about 100 dollars, and hoped with a little help, to purchase my freedom. He accordingly went to my master: 'Mr. Wood,' he said, 'Molly has brought me a note that she wants an owner. If you intend to sell her, I may as well buy her as another.' My master put him off and said that he did not mean to sell me. I was very sorry at this, for I had no comfort with Mrs. Wood, and I wished greatly to get my freedom.

The way in which I made my money was this. When my master and mistress went from home, as they sometimes did, and left me to take care of the house and premises, I had a good deal of time to myself and made the most of it. I took in washing, and sold coffee and yams and other provisions to the captains of ships. I did not sit still idling during the absence of my owners; for I wanted, by all honest means, to earn money to buy my freedom. Sometimes I bought a hog cheap on board ship, and sold it for double the money on shore; and I also earned a good deal by selling coffee. By this means I by degrees acquired a little cash. A gentleman also lent me some to help to buy my freedom – but when I could not get free he got it back again. His name was Captain Abbot.

My master and mistress went on one occasion into the country, to Date Hill, for a change of air, and carried me with them to take charge of the children, and to do the work of the house. While I was in the country, I saw how the field negroes are worked in Antigua. They are worked very hard and fed but scantily. They are called out to work before daybreak, and come home after dark; and then each has to heave his bundle of grass for the cattle in the pen. Then, on Sunday morning, each slave has to go out and gather a large bundle of grass; and, when they bring it home, they have all to sit at the manager's door and wait till he comes out: often have they to wait there till past eleven o'clock without any breakfast. After that, those that have yams or potatoes, or fire-wood to sell, hasten to market to buy a dog's worth[5] of salt fish, or pork, which is a great treat for them. Some of them buy a little pickle out of the shad barrels, which they call sauce, to season their yarms and Indian corn. It is very wrong, I know, to work on Sunday or go to market; but will not God call the Buckra men to answer for this on the great day of judgment – since they will give the slaves no other day?

While we were at Date Hill Christmas came; and the slave woman who had the care of the place (which then belonged to Mr. Roberts the marshal), asked me to go with her to her husband's house, to a Methodist meeting for prayer, at a plantation called Winthorps. I went; and they were the first prayers I ever understood. One woman prayed; and then they all sung a hymn; then there was another prayer and another hymn; and then they all spoke by turns of their own griefs as sinners. The husband of the woman I went with was a black driver. His name was Henry. He confessed that he had treated the slaves very cruelly; but said that he was compelled to obey the orders of his master. He prayed them all to forgive him, and he prayed that God would forgive him. He said it was a horrid thing for a ranger to have sometimes to beat his own wife or sister; but he must do so if ordered by his master.

I felt sorry for my sins also. I cried the whole night, but I was too much ashamed to speak. I prayed God to forgive me. This meeting had a great impression on my mind, and led my spirit to the Moravian church; so that when I got back to town, I went and prayed to have my name put down in the Missionaries' book; and I followed the church earnestly every opportunity. I did not then tell my mistress about it; for I knew that she would not give me leave to go. But I felt *I must* go. Whenever I carried the children their lunch at school, I ran round and went to hear the teachers.

The Moravian ladies (Mrs. Richter, Mrs. Olufsen, and Mrs. Sauter) taught me to read in the class; and I got on very fast. In this class there were all sorts of people, old and young, grey headed folks and children; but most of them were free people. After we had done spelling, we tried to read in the Bible. After the reading was over, the missionary gave out a hymn for us to sing. I dearly loved to go to the church, it was so solemn. I never knew rightly that I had much sin till I went there. When I found out that I was a great sinner, I was very sorely grieved, and very much frightened. I used to pray God to pardon my sins for Christ's sake, and forgive me for every thing I had done amiss; and when I went home to my work, I always thought about what I had heard from the missionaries, and wished to be good that I might go to heaven. After a while I was admitted a candidate for the holy Communion. I had been baptized long before this, in August 1817, by the Rev. Mr. Curtin, of the English Church, after I had been taught to repeat the Creed and the Lord's Prayer. I wished at that time to attend a Sunday School taught by Mr. Curtin, but he would not receive me without a written note from my master, granting his permission. I did not ask my owner's permission, from the belief that it would be refused; so that I got no farther instruction at that time from the English Church.

Some time after I began to attend the Moravian church, I met with Daniel James, afterwards my dear husband. He was a carpenter and cooper to his trade; an honest, hard-working, decent black man, and a widower. He had purchased his freedom of his mistress, old Mrs. Baker, with money he had earned whilst a slave. When he asked me to marry him, I took time to consider the matter over with myself, and would not say yes till he went to church with me and joined the Moravians. He was very industrious after he bought his freedom; and he had hired a comfortable house, and had convenient things about him. We were joined in marriage, about Christmas 1826, in the Moravian Chapel at Spring Gardens, by the Rev. Mr. Olufsen. We could not be married in the English Church. English marriage is not allowed to slaves; and no free man can marry a slave woman.

When Mr. Wood heard of my marriage, he flew into a great rage, and sent for Daniel, who was helping to build a house for his old mistress.

Mr. Wood asked him who gave him a right to marry a slave of his? My husband said, 'Sir, I am a free man, and thought I had a right to choose a wife; but if I had known Molly was not allowed to have a husband, I should not have asked her to marry me.' Mrs. Wood was more vexed about my marriage than her husband. She could not forgive me for getting married, but stirred up Mr. Wood to flog me dreadfully with his horsewhip. I thought it very hard to be whipped at my time of life for getting a husband – I told her so. She said that she would not have nigger men about the yards and premises, or allow a nigger man's clothes to be washed in the same tub where hers were washed. She was fearful, I think, that I should lose her time, in order to wash and do things for my husband: but I had then no time to wash for myself; I was obliged to put out my own clothes, though I was always at the wash-tub.

I had not much happiness in my marriage, owing to my being a slave. It made my husband sad to see me so ill-treated. Mrs. Wood was always abusing me about him. She did not lick me herself, but she got her husband to do it for her, whilst she fretted the flesh off my bones. Yet for all this she would not sell me. She sold five slaves whilst I was with her; but though she was always finding fault with me, she would not part with me. However, Mr. Wood afterwards allowed Daniel to have a place to live in our yard, which we were very thankful for.

After this, I fell ill again with the rheumatism, and was sick a long time; but whether sick or well, I had my work to do. About this time I asked my master and mistress to let me buy my own freedom. With the help of Mr. Burchell, I could have found the means to pay Mr. Wood; for it was agreed that I should afterwards serve Mr. Burchell a while, for the cash he was to advance for me. I was earnest in the request to my owners; but their hearts were hard – too hard to consent. Mrs. Wood was very angry – she grew quite outrageous – she called me a black devil, and asked me who had put freedom into my head. 'To be free is very sweet,' I said: but she took good care to keep me a slave. I saw her change colour, and I left the room.

About this time my master and mistress were going to England to put their son in school, and bring their daughters home; and they took me with them to take care of the child. I was willing to come to England: I thought that by going there I should probably get cured of my rheumatism, and should return with my master and mistress, quite well, to my husband. My husband was willing for me to come away, for he had heard that my master would free me, – and I also hoped this might prove true; but it was all a false report.

The steward of the ship was very kind to me. He and my husband were in the same class in the Moravian Church. I was thankful that he was so friendly, for my mistress was not kind to me on the passage; and she told me, when she was angry, that she did not intend to treat me any better in England than in the West Indies - that I need not expect it. And she was as good as her word.

When we drew near to England, the rheumatism seized all my limbs worse than ever, and my body was dreadfully swelled. When we landed at the Tower, I shewed my flesh to my mistress, but she took no great notice of it. We were obliged to stop at the tavern till my master got a house; and a day or two after, my mistress sent me down into the wash-house to learn to wash in the English way. In the West Indies we wash with cold water – in England with hot. I told my mistress I was afraid that putting my hands first into the hot water and then into the cold, would increase the pain in my limbs. The doctor had told my mistress long before I came from the West Indies, that I was a sickly body and the washing did not agree with me. But Mrs. Wood would not release me from the tub, so I was forced to do as I could. I grew worse, and could not stand to wash. I was then forced to sit down with the tub before me, and often through pain and weakness was reduced to kneel or to sit down on the floor, to finish my task. When I complained to my mistress of this, she only got into a passion as usual, and said washing in hot water could not hurt any one; – that I was lazy and insolent, and wanted to be free of my work; but that she would make me do it. I thought her very hard on me, and my heart rose up within me. However I kept still at that time, and went down again to wash the child's things; but the English washerwomen who were at work there, when they saw that I was so ill, had pity upon me and washed them for me.

After that, when we came up to live in Leigh Street, Mrs. Wood sorted out five bags of clothes which we had used at sea, and also such as had been worn since we came on shore, for me and the cook to wash. Elizabeth the cook told her, that she did not think that I was able to stand to the tub, and that she had better hire a woman. I also said myself, that I had come over to nurse the child, and that I was sorry I had come from Antigua, since mistress would work me so hard, without compassion for my rheumatism. Mr. and Mrs. Wood, when they heard this, rose up in a passion against me. They opened the door and made me get out. But I was a stranger, and did not know one door in the street from another, and was unwilling to go away. They made a dreadful uproar, and from that day they constantly kept cursing and abusing me. I was obliged to wash, though I was very ill. Mrs. Wood, indeed once hired a washerwoman, but she was not well treated, and would come no more.

My master quarrelled with me another time, about one of our great washings, his wife having stirred him up to do so. He said he would compel me to do the whole of the washing given out to me, or if I again refused, he would take a short course with me: he would either send me down to the brig in the river, to carry me back to Antigua, or he would turn me at once out of doors, and let me provide for myself. I said I would willingly go back, if he would let me purchase my own freedom. But this enraged him more than all the rest: he cursed and swore at me dreadfully, and said he would never sell my freedom – if I wished to be free, I was free in England, and I might go and try what freedom would do for me, and be d——d. My heart was very sore with this treatment, but I had to go on. I continued to do my work, and did all I could to give satisfaction, but all would not do.

Shortly after, the cook left them, and then matters went on ten times worse. I always washed the child's clothes without being commanded to do it, and any thing else that was wanted in the family; though still I was very sick – very sick indeed. When the great washing came round, which was every two months, my mistress got together again a great many heavy things, such as bed-ticks, bed coverlets, &c. for me to wash. I told her I was too ill to wash such heavy things that day. She said, she supposed I thought myself a free woman, but I was not; and if I did not do it directly I should be instantly turned out of doors. I stood a long time before I could answer, for I did not know well what to do.

I knew that I was free in England, but I did not know where to go, or how to get my living; and therefore, I did not like to leave the house. But Mr. Wood said he would send for a constable to thrust me out; and at last I took courage and resolved that I would not be longer thus treated, but would go and trust to Providence. This was the fourth time they had threatened to turn me out, and, go where I might, I was determined now to take them at their word; though I thought it very hard, after I had lived with them for thirteen years, and worked for them like a horse, to be driven out in this way, like a beggar. My only fault was being sick, and therefore unable to please my mistress, who thought she never could get work enough out of her slaves; and I told them so: but they only abused me and drove me out. This took place from two to three months, I think, after we came to England.

When I came away, I went to the man (one Mash) who used to black the shoes of the family, and asked his wife to get somebody to go with me to Hatton Garden to the Moravian Missionaries: these were the only persons I knew in England. The woman sent a young girl with me to the mission house, and I saw there a gentleman called Mr. Moore. I told him my whole story, and how my owners had treated me, and asked him to take in my trunk with what few clothes I had. The missionaries were very kind to me – they were sorry for my destitute situation, and gave me leave to bring my things to be placed under their care. They were very good people, and they told me to come to the church.

When I went back to Mr. Wood's to get my trunk, I saw a lady, Mrs. Pell, who was on a visit to my mistress. When Mr. and Mrs. Wood heard me come in, they set this lady to stop me, finding that they had gone too far with me. Mrs. Pell came out to me, and said, 'Are you really going to leave, Molly? Don't leave, but come into the country with me.' I believe she said this because she thought Mrs. Wood would easily get me back again. I replied to her, 'Ma'am, this is the fourth time my master and mistress have driven me out, or threatened to drive me – and I will give them no more occasion to bid me go. I was not willing to leave them, for I am a stranger in this country, but now I must go – I can stay no longer to be used.' Mrs. Pell then went upstairs to my mistress, and told that I would go, and that she could not stop me. Mrs. Wood was very much hurt and frightened when she found I was determined to go out that day. She said, 'If she goes the people will rob her, and then turn her adrift.' She did not say this to me, but she spoke it loud enough for me to hear; that it might induce me not to go, I suppose. Mr. Wood also asked me where I was going to. I told him where I had been, and that I should never have gone away had I not been driven out by my owners. He had given me a written paper some time before, which said that I had come with them to England by my own desire; and that was true. It said also that I left them of my own free will, because I was a free woman in England; and that I was idle and would not do my work – which was not true. I gave this paper afterwards to a gentleman who inquired into my case.

I went into the kitchen and got my clothes out. The nurse and the servant girl were there, and I said to the man who was going to take out my trunk, 'Stop, before you take up this trunk, and hear what I have to say before these people. I am going out of this house, as I was ordered; but I have done no wrong at all to my owners, neither here nor in the West Indies. I always worked very hard to please them, both by night and day; but there was no giving satisfaction, for my mistress could never be satisfied with reasonable service. I told my mistress I was sick, and yet she has ordered me out of doors. This is the fourth time; and now I am going out.'

And so I came out, and went and carried my trunk to the Moravians. I then returned back to Mash the shoeblack's house, and begged his wife to take me in. I had a little West Indian money in my trunk; and they got it changed for me. This helped to support me for a little while. The man's wife was very kind to me. I was very sick, and she boiled nourishing things up for me. She also sent for a doctor to see me, and sent me medicine, which did me good, though I was ill for a long time with the rheumatic pains. I lived a good many months with these poor people, and they nursed me, and did all that lay in their power to serve me. The man was well acquainted with my situation, as he used to go to and fro to Mr. Wood's house to clean shoes and knives; and he and his wife were sorry for me.

About this time, a woman of the name of Hill told me of the Anti-Slavery Society, and went with me to their office, to inquire if they could do any thing to get me my freedom, and send me back to the West Indies. The gentlemen of the Society took me to a lawyer, who examined very strictly into my case; but told me that the laws of England could do nothing to make me free in Antigua. However they did all they could for me: they gave me a little money from time to time to keep me from want; and some of them went to Mr. Wood to try to persuade him to let me return a free woman to my husband; but though they offered him, as I have heard, a large sum for my freedom, he was sulky and obstinate, and would not consent to let me go free.

This was the first winter I spent in England, and I suffered much from the severe cold, and from the rheumatic pains, which still at times torment me. However, Providence was very good to me; and I got many friends – especially some Quaker ladies, who hearing of my case, came and sought me out, and gave me good warm clothing and money. Thus I had great cause to bless God in my affliction.

When I got better I was anxious to get some work to do, as I was unwilling to eat the bread of idleness. Mrs. Mash, who was a laundress, recommended me to a lady for a charwoman. She paid me very handsomely for what work I did, and I divided the money with Mrs. Mash; for though very poor, they gave me food when my own money was done, and never suffered me to want.

In the spring, I got into service with a lady, who saw me at the house where I sometimes worked as a charwoman. This lady's name was Mrs. Forsyth. She had been in the West Indies, and was accustomed to Blacks, and liked them. I was with her six months, and went with her to Margate. She treated me well, and gave me a good character when she left London.

After Mrs. Forsyth went away, I was again out of place, and went to lodgings, for which I paid two shillings a week, and found coals and candle. After eleven weeks, the money I had saved in service was all gone, and I was forced to go back to the Anti-Slavery office to ask a supply, till I could get another situation. I did not like to go back – I did not like to be idle. I would rather work for my living than get it for nothing. They were very good to give me a supply, but I felt shame at being obliged to apply for relief whilst I had strength to work.

At last I went into the service of Mr. and Mrs. Pringle, where I have been ever since, and am as comfortable as I can be while separated from my dear husband, and away from my own country and all old friends and connections. My dear mistress teaches me daily to read the word of God, and takes great pains to make me understand it. I enjoy the great privilege of being enabled to attend Church three times on the Sunday; and I have met with many kind friends since I have been here, both clergymen and others. The Rev. Mr. Young, who lives in the next house, has shown me much kindness, and taken much pains to instruct me, particularly while my master and mistress were absent in Scotland. Nor must I forget, among my friends, the Rev. Mr. Mortimer, the good clergyman of the parish, under whose ministry I have now sat for upwards of twelve months. I trust in God I have profited by what I have heard from him. He never keeps back the truth, and I think he has been the means of opening my eyes and ears much better to understand the word of God. Mr. Mortimer tells me that he cannot open the eyes of my heart, but that I must pray to God to change my heart, and make me to know the truth, and the truth will make me free.

I still live in the hope that God will find a way to give me my liberty, and give me back to my husband. I endeavour to keep down my fretting, and to leave all to Him, for he knows what is good for me better than I know myself. Yet, I must confess, I find it a hard and heavy task to do so.

I am often much vexed, and I feel great sorrow when I hear some people in this country say, that the slaves do not need better usage, and do not want to be free. They believe the foreign people, who deceive them, and say slaves are happy. I say, not so. How can slaves be happy when they have the halter round their neck and the whip upon their back? and are disgraced and thought no more of than beasts? – and are separated from their mothers, and husbands, and children, and sisters, just as cattle are sold and separated? Is it happiness for a driver in the field to take down his wife or sister or child, and strip them, and whip them in such a disgraceful manner? – women that have had children exposed in the open field to shame! There is no modesty or decency shown by the owner to his slaves; men, women, and children are exposed alike. Since I have been here I have often wondered how English people can go out into the West Indies and act in such a beastly manner. But when they go to the West Indies, they forget God and all feel-ing of shame, I think, since they can see and do such things. They tie up slaves like hogs – moor[6] them up like cattle, and they lick them, so as hogs, or cattle, or horses never were flogged; - and yet they come home and say, and make some good people believe, that slaves don't want to get out of slavery. But they put a cloak about the truth. It is not so. All slaves want to be free – to be free is very sweet. I will say the truth to English people who may read this history that my good friend, Miss S-, is now writing down for me. I have been a slave myself – I know what slaves feel – I can tell by myself what other slaves feel, and by what they have told me. The man that says slaves be quite happy in slavery – that they don't want to be free – that man is either ignorant or a lying person. I never heard a slave say so. I never heard a Bucka man say so, till I heard tell of it in England. Such people ought to be ashamed of themselves. They can't do without slaves, they say. What's the reason they can't do without slaves as well as in England? No slaves here – no whips – no stocks – no punishment, except for wicked people. They hire servants in England; and if they don't like them, they send them away: they can't lick them. Let them work ever so hard in England, they are far better off than slaves. If they get a bad master, they give warning and go hire to another. They have their liberty. That's just what we want. We don't mind hard work, if we had proper treatment, and proper wages like English servants, and proper time given in the week to keep us from breaking the Sabbath. But they won't give it; they will have work - work - work, night and day, sick or well, till we are quite done up; and we must not speak up nor look amiss, however much we be abused. And then when we are quite done up, who cares for us, more than for a lame horse? This is slavery. I tell it to let English people know the truth; and I hope they will never leave off to pray God, and call loud to the great King of England, till all the poor blacks be given free, and slavery done up for evermore.

Notes

1. Bermuda currency. About £38 sterling.
2. A cow fed for slaughter
3. A thong of hard twisted hide, known by the name in the West Indies.
4. About £67.10s sterling.
5. A dog is the 72nd part of a dollar.
6. A West Indian phrase: to fasten or tie up.

64

Speeches and Letters of Toussaint L'Overture

TOUSSAINT L'OVERTURE

The following two proclamations are among the first issued by Toussaint. Intended to offset Sonthonax's unofficial emancipation of the slaves on August 29, 1793, they reflect Toussaint's conviction that the blacks should gain their liberty by their own struggle rather than as a gift from the whites. In the first proclamation, the messianic element of Toussaint's leadership is obvious. Throughout his political career, Toussaint endeavoured to capitalize on the religious ecstaticism that had characterized the slave rebellion from the outset. There can be no doubt that this was not merely political expediency but that he shared the general 'delirium' — as he liked to call it — of his brothers. However, he did attempt, with varying degrees of success, to shift the locus of this prophetic movement from the beliefs and practices of African voodoo to Western Christianity. The second proclamation makes it clear that during the period he was fighting in the service of the Spanish his commitment was not to the cause of royalism but to the liberty and equality of the blacks.[1]

Proclamation of 25 August 1793

Having been the first to champion your cause, it is my duty to continue to labour for it. I cannot permit another to rob me of the initiative. Since I have begun, I will know how to conclude. Join me and you will enjoy the rights of freemen sooner than any other way. Neither whites nor mulattoes have formulated my plans; it is to the Supreme Being alone that I owe my inspiration. We have begun, we have carried on, we will know how to reach the goal.

Proclamation of 29 August 1793

Brothers and Friends:

I am Toussaint L'Ouverture. My name is perhaps known to you. I have undertaken to avenge you. I want liberty and equality to reign throughout St. Domingue. I am working towards that end. Come and join me, brothers, and combat by our side for the same cause.

Toussaint Joins the French Republic

In the next two selections, Toussaint presents his reasons for joining the French in May, 1794. In the first he stresses the ideological factor. The Spanish and French royalists were only using the slaves with the ultimate intention of returning them to slavery. Freedom could be achieved solely through a French victory. In the second excerpt — from an official report to the Ministry of the Marine in 1799, which Gerard Laurent refers to as Toussaint's "political testament"- Toussaint offers his interpretation of the early stages of the St. Domingue revolution and suggests that he deliberately chose to join the French at a critical moment when he could wring the maximum number of concessions from Laveaux. Notable in his analysis of events is Toussaint's opinion that the slaves joined the Spanish only after the whites had bought off the persons of color who had initially been their allies.

Some writers have suggested two other motives for Toussaint's decision to join the French: He had fallen out of favour with the Spanish and

English, and his ambitions to further advancement were blocked by Jean François.

Letter To General Laveaux, 18 May 1794[2]

It is true, General, that I had been deceived by the enemies of the Republic; but what man can pride himself on avoiding all the traps of wickedness? In truth, I fell into their snares, but not without knowing the reason. You must recall the advances I had made to you before the disasters at Le Cap, in which I stated that my only goal was to unite us in the struggle against the enemies of France.

Unhappily for everyone, the means of reconciliation that I proposed -*the recognition of the liberty of the blacks and a general amnesty – were rejected. My heart bled, and I shed tears over the unfortunate fate of my country, perceiving the misfortunes that must follow. I wasn't mistaken: fatal experience proved the reality of my predictions. Meanwhile, the Spanish offered their protection to me and to all* those who would fight for the cause of the kings, and having always fought in order to have liberty I accepted their offers, seeing myself abandoned by my brothers the French. But a later experience opened my eyes to these perfidious protectors, and having understood their villainous deceit, I saw clearly that they intended to make us slaughter one another in order to diminish our numbers so as to overwhelm the survivors and re-enslave them. No, they will never attain their infamous objective, and we will avenge ourselves in our turn upon these contemptible beings. Therefore, let us unite forever and, forgetting the past, occupy ourselves hereafter only with exterminating our enemies and avenging ourselves, in particular, upon our perfidious neighbours.

Letter to the Minister of Marine, 13 April 1799[3]

The first successes obtained in Europe by the partisans of liberty over the agents of despotism were not slow to ignite the sacred fire of patriotism in the souls of all Frenchmen in St. Domingue. At that time, men's hopes turned to France, whose first steps toward her regeneration promised them a happier future; . . . they wanted to escape from their arbitrary government, but they did not intend the revolution to destroy either the prejudice that debased the men of colour or the slavery of the blacks, whom they held in dependency by the strongest law. In their opinion, the benefits of the French regeneration were only for them. They proved it by their obstinate refusal to allow the people of colour to enjoy their political rights and the slaves to enjoy the liberty that they claimed. Thus, while the whites were erecting another form of government upon the rubble of despotism, the men of colour and the blacks united themselves in order to claim their political existence; the resistance of the former having become stronger, it was necessary for the latter to rise up in order to obtain [political recognition] by force of arms. The whites, fearing that this legitimate resistance would bring general liberty to St. Domingue, sought to separate the men of colour from the cause of the blacks in accordance with Machiavelli's principle of divide and rule. Renouncing their claims over the men of colour, they accepted the April Decree [1792]. As they had anticipated, the men of colour, many of whom were slaveholders, had only been using the blacks to gain their own political demands. Fearing the enfranchisement of the blacks, the men of colour deserted their comrades in arms, their companions in misfortune, and aligned themselves with the whites to subdue them.

Treacherously abandoned, the blacks fought for some time against the reunited whites and the men of colour; but, pressed on all sides, losing hope, they accepted the offers of the Spanish king, who, having at that time declared war on France, offered freedom to those blacks of St. Domingue who would join his armies. Indeed, the silence of pre-Republican France on the long-standing claims for their natural rights made by the most interested, the noblest, the most useful portion of the population of St. Domingue . . . extinguished all glimmer of hope in the hearts of the black slaves and forced them, in spite of themselves, to throw themselves into the arms of a protective power that offered the only benefit for which they would fight. More unfortunate than guilty, they turned their arms against their fatherland . . . .

Such were the crimes of these blacks, which have earned them to this day the insulting titles of brigands, insurgents, rebels under the orders of Jean François. At that time I was one of the leaders of these auxiliary troops, and I can say without fear of contradiction that I owed my elevation in these circumstances only to the confidence that I had inspired in my brothers by the virtues for which I am still honoured today. Meanwhile, the Spanish, benefiting from the internal divisions to which the French part of St. Domingue had fallen prey and aided by the courage that gave to these same blacks the hope of imminent freedom, seized almost all of the North and a large part of the West. Le Cap, surrounded by them on all sides and beseiged by land and sea, was experiencing all the horrors of the cruelest famine. . . . The Republic that had just been proclaimed in St. Domingue was recognized only in the territory from Le Cap to Port-de-Paix, and the guilty excesses of its agents were not calculated to gain it adherents. But, following their departure for France, they [the Civil Commissioners] left the reins of power in the hands of General Laveaux, who lost no time endearing himself by a wise and paternal administration. It was sometime after this period that, having received the order to attack Le Cap and convinced by my information about the distressing state to which this city was reduced, of its powerlessness to resist the torrent that must engulf it, I went over to the Republic with the blacks under my command.

Proclamation on the Villate Affair, March 1795[4]

In the following proclamation Toussaint explains his actions during the Villate affair. He denies any prejudice against the people of colour, but affirms his determination to destroy any disruptive elements, whatever their colour. Religion and nothing else he insists, has served as his guide.

My heart and my feelings are rent upon learning every day of the new plots of the evil-doers, of these corrupt men, of these guilty men and greatly culpable toward the mother country. It is for you to prepare against their false declamations about which I am going to talk to you as a brother, friend and father; too happy I would be if I could get them to come back to themselves, oblige them to recognize and to renounce their errors, inspire them with wholesome remorse and finally put them back on the right path.

Ah my friends, my brothers, my children!- these men are guilty who try by a few quotations

from my letters, to persuade you that I have sworn the Destruction of all men of colour; they judge my heart by their own hateful and vindictive heart. It is not colour that I am fighting; it is crime that I am pursuing and shall always pursue in whatever place it is hidden; this is the reason that:

Considering that it is my duty to enlighten you, I am going to do it, as briefly and as clearly as I possibly can; I am going to speak to you in the Language of reason, truth and religion.

I have written to certain chiefs to be on guard against men of colour, because I knew, before the criminal arrest of the General in Chief, that some men of colour were at the head of this infernal conspiracy; because I knew that in several quarters of the Colony, the emissaries of these bold chiefs were preaching disobedience, revolt against the lawfully constituted authorities; you have the proof of it today. Who arrested General Laveux? Who dared bring a heinous and sacrilegious hand upon the representatives of the Nation? Men of colour; it was quite necessary then that I warn my subordinates to suspect these men. God forbid, however, that I confuse the Innocent ones with the guilty! No, my brothers, I am not prejudiced against any particular class; I know that there are men of colour who are estimable and virtuous, irreproachable and I have the great satisfaction of having some of them near me, to whom I accord my Esteem, my Friendship and my Confidence; I love them, because, faithful to their duties, they have not participated in perfidious manoeuvres; I have several of them among my Officers, who have never strayed from the right path; and those as well as all faithful soldiers, can count on me; I cherish all virtuous men; I owe them protection, and they shall always obtain it, when they make themselves worthy of it.

When murders were being committed in the Mountain Port of Paix, in the name Etienne, did I not say that Black men were committing these crimes? Let us be just, when we want to accuse; but does calumny know any Limits?

Religion, I remind you, my brothers, is my Guide, it is the rule of my conduct, whatever others might say; Religion tells us, commands us to give back to Caesar that which belongs to Caesar, and to God that which belongs to God; it commands us to give the most complete subordination to our chiefs, to our superiors. A Colonel wishes his body officers to obey him, a

Captain wishes his Lieutenants and second-lieutenants to obey him, the Lieutenant wishes his non-commissioned officers to obey him, and the Officers exact the same obedience from their Companies. Why? because they know that subordination is essential to armed Force; there can be no army without subordination.

Supposing that in the presence of a Captain, a Lieutenant, a second-lieutenant, some rebels were to insult, maltreat and arrest the Colonel; what shall they do? Shall they remain peaceful spectators of that criminal conspiracy? They would become guilty themselves, if they did not put forth their efforts to defend him, to snatch him from the hands of those wicked chiefs and they take it ill that I have hurried to the assistance of my chief, of my superior, of the representative of the Republic: they take it ill that I have arrested those who have participated in this Heinous plot. The French nation is going to judge us. I place into its hands those whom I believe guilty.

Officers, the least insubordination arouses you, you mete out severe punishment, sometimes you even stray from the Law in the severity of your punishments; remember that to command well, you must know how to obey.

And you Colonists, you the beloved Children of the Republic; you, whom this tender mother carries in her bosom, you whom she had overwhelmed with kindness, would allow yourselves to be drawn into the artificial suggestions of the wicked! Ah! my brothers, France has decreed, has sanctioned general Liberty; twenty-five million men have ratified this glorious and consoling Decree for humanity, and you fear that she may return you to your former state of Bondage, while she has so long been fighting for her own Liberty and for the Liberty of all Nations. How mistaken you are!

No, my Friends, you are being deceived, they are jealous of your happiness, they want to rob you of it, and you know the ones who are deceiving you; they are those who slander the intentions, the operations of the Governor general and myself, for we act together. Believe me then, my brothers, you know me, you know my Religion, you have regarded me up to this day as your Father, I believe I merit this title, I hope to always merit it, it is so near to my heart. I implore you for your happiness, shun the rebels, the wicked; busy yourselves with work, France, your good Mother, will reward you.

The mask is going to fall, the evil-doers feel that the Day of vengeance is approaching; they would like to have a great many accomplices so as to be assured of Impunity; but let them fall alone into the abyss they have dug under their Feet; the hand of God, the Avenger, is going to weigh down upon them, for one does not always defy the Supreme Being with impunity; they have scorned Religion; they have defied the terrible thunder bolts of a God in His Anger; they feel the earth falling in beneath their feet, and they would like to drag you along with them in the depths of their anguish.

Denounce then the wrong doers, those who slander my intentions and actions. I take God as my witness, who must judge us all, that they are pure; I long only for your happiness; one moment more and you will be convinced of it. Close your ears to the voice of the wicked and the Agitator; God lets him act a short while, but often in the midst of his course, He stops him. Look at the proud Haman, the favourite of Ahasuerus, he would like to have had the humble Mordecai perish unjustly. The Gallows, which he had had prepared for this faithful Israelite, served for himself.

Everywhere the Holy Bible (I am pleased to mention it because it consoles me) everywhere the Holy Bible, tells us of the proud being humbled and of the humble being elevated; everywhere it shows us terrible Examples of Divine Justice against great Criminals; now it is an Antiochus, who satiated with crimes, at the approach of death asks for mercy and does not obtain it: now it is a heinous son, an Absalom, urged to insurrection against the most tender of all Fathers and who died miserably; finally, everywhere it proves to us that great scoundrels are punished sooner or later.

Alas! we ask, in the Example of our Divine Master, only the conversion of the Sinner, that he may come back to himself, that he may recognize his mistakes, his errors, his crimes, that he may renounce them, that he may come back to us, and we are ready to give him the "kiss of peace and of reconciliation."

The present letter will be printed, read, published and posted everywhere where there will be need, in order that the wicked persuaded by my peaceable sentiments, may profit by the pardon that I offer them, and that the Good may be cautioned against the snares of Error and seduction.

Toussaint Defends the Revolution and His Race

Following the fall of the Jacobins in 1794, the revolution in France moved steadily to the right. From November 1795, the reactionaries who formed a large bloc in the French assemblies began clamouring for a "restoration of order" in the colonies. The elections of March 1797 brought even more of them into the assemblies. Led by Vienot Vaublanc, they deplored the situation in St. Domingue and condemned the policies of the Civil Commissioners. Their speeches were violently antinegro and openly questioned the capacity of the blacks for freedom. Toussaint himself was the victim of a scurrilous attack by Vaublanc. In September 1797, however, Vaublanc and his followers were arrested and deported from France because of their involvement in a royalist plot, and the rightward drift of the revolution was momentarily checked. Toussaint had been watching these events with mounting alarm. Fearful that Vaublanc's faction was having too much influence on public and official opinion in France and unaware that its members had been deported, Toussaint sent several letters to the Directory. Two of these eloquent statements on behalf of the freedom of the blacks are reproduced below.

In the first, Toussaint presents a stirring defence of the revolution and his race, cleverly attacking Vaublanc and his partisans as the real antirepublicans. Admitting the shortcomings of the blacks, which he attributes to slavery and the influence of evil-minded whites, Toussaint insists that the cause of republicanism in St. Domingue can only be identified with that of the blacks. In defense of his brothers, he exposes the double standards by which colonial nations have always condemned the colonized people while justifying their own crimes and hypocrisy.

In the second reading, Toussaint reiterates more forcibly his dedication to the cause of freedom and the determination of his brothers to resist any attempt to deprive them of their natural rights.

Taken together, these selections constitute the most concise and compelling statement of Toussaint's commitment to the ideals of liberty and equality and to Republican France as long as she shared that commitment.

Letter to the Directory, 28 October 1797[5]

Citizen Directors,

At the moment when I thought I had just rendered eminent service to the Republic and to my fellow citizens, when I had just proven my recognition of the justice of the French people toward us, when I believed myself worthy of the confidence that the Government had placed in me and which I will never cease to merit, a speech was made in the *Corps Legislatif* during the meeting of 22 May 1797 by Vienot Vaublanc ... and, while going through it, I had the sorrow of seeing my intentions slandered on every page and the political existence of my brothers threatened.

A similar speech from the mouth of a man whose fortune had been momentarily wiped out by the revolution in St. Domingue would not surprise me, the loser has the right to complain up to a certain point, but what must profoundly affect me is that the *Corps Legislatif* could have approved and sanctioned such declamations, which are so unsuitable to the restoration of our tranquility; which, instead of spurring the field-negroes to work, can only arouse them by allowing them to believe that the representatives of the French people were their enemies.

In order to justify myself in your eyes and in the eyes of my fellow citizens, whose esteem I so eagerly desire, I am going to apply myself to refuting the assertions of citizen Vaublanc ... and ... prove that the enemies of our liberty have only been motivated in this event by a spirit of personal vengeance and that the public interest and respect for the Constitution have been continually trampled under foot by them. ...

Second Assertion: "Everyone is agreed in portraying the Colony in the most shocking state of disorder and groaning under the military government. And what a military government! In whose hands is it confined? In that of ignorant and gross negroes, incapable of distinguishing between unrestrained license and austere liberty." ...

This shocking disorder in which the Commission found St. Domingue was not the consequence of the liberty given to the blacks but the result of the uprising of thirty Ventôse [the Villate affair], for, prior to this period, order and harmony reigned in all Republican territory as far as the absence of laws would allow. All citizens blindly obeyed the orders of General Laveaux; his will was the national will for them, and they submitted to him as a man invested with the authority emanating from the generous nation that had shattered their chains.

If, upon the arrival of the Commission, St. Domingue groaned under a military government, this power was not in the hands of the blacks; they were subordinate to it, and they only executed the orders of General Laveaux. These were the blacks who, when France was threatened with the loss of this Colony, employed their arms and their weapons to conserve it, to reconquer the greatest part of its territory that treason had handed over to the Spanish and English. . . . These were the blacks who, with the good citizens of the other two colours, flew to the rescue of General Laveaux in the Villate Affair and who, by repressing the audacious rebels who wished to destroy the national representation, restored it to its rightful depository.

Such was the conduct of those blacks in whose hands citizen Vienot Vaublanc said the military government of St. Domingue found itself, such are those negroes he accuses of being ignorant and gross; undoubtedly they are, because without education there can only be ignorance and grossness. But must one impute to them the crime of this educational deficiency or, more correctly, accuse those who prevented them by the most atrocious punishments from obtaining it? And are only civilized people capable of distinguishing between good and evil, of having notions of charity and justice? The men of St. Domingue have been deprived of an education; but even so, they no longer remain in a state of nature, and because they haven't arrived at the degree of perfection that education bestows, they do not merit being classed apart from the rest of mankind, being confused with animals. . . .

Undoubtedly, one can reproach the inhabitants of St. Domingue, including the blacks, for many faults, even terrible crimes. But even in France, where the limits of sociability are clearly drawn, doesn't one see its inhabitants, in the struggle between despotism and liberty, going to all the excesses for which the blacks are reproached by their enemies? The fury of the two parties has been equal in St. Domingue; and if the excesses of the blacks in these critical moments haven't exceeded those committed in Europe, must not an impartial judge pronounce in favour of the former? Since it is our enemies themselves who present us as ignorant and gross,

aren't we more excusable than those who, unlike us, were not deprived of the advantages of education and civilization? Surrounded by fierce enemies, oft cruel masters; without any other support than the charitable intentions of the friends of freedom in France, of whose existence we were hardly aware; driven to excessive errors by opposing parties who were rapidly destroying each other; knowing, at first, only the laws of the Mother-Country that favoured the pretensions of our enemies and, since our liberty, receiving only the semiyearly or yearly instructions of our government, and no assistance, but almost always slanders or diatribes from our old oppressors – how can we not be pardoned some moments of ill-conduct, some gross faults, of which we were the first victims? Why, above all, reflect upon unreproachable men, upon the vast majority of the blacks, the faults of the lesser part, who, in time, had been reclaimed by the attentions of the majority to order and respect for the superior authorities? . . .

Fourth Assertion: 'I believed upon my arrival here [in St. Domingue]," continues General Rochambeau, "that I was going to find the laws of liberty and equality established in a positive manner; but I was grievously mistaken; there is liberty in this land only for the commanders of Africans and men of colour, who treat the rest of their fellows like beasts of burden. The whites are everywhere vexed and humiliated."

If General Rochambeau had reflected philosophically on the course of events, especially those of the human spirit, he would not find it so astonishing that the laws of liberty and equality were not precisely established in an American country whose connection with the Mother Country had been neglected for so long; he would have felt that at a time when Europeans daily perjured themselves by handing over their quarters to the enemies of their country, prudence dictated that Government entrust its defence to the men of colour and blacks whose interests were intimately linked to the triumph of the Republic; he would have felt that the military government then ruling the colony, by giving great power to the district commanders, could have led them astray in the labyrinths of uncertainty resulting from the absence of laws; he would have recalled that Martinique, defended by Europeans, fell prey to the English, whereas, St. Domingue, defended by the blacks and men of colour whom Rochambeau accuses, remained constantly faithful to France. More accurately, if he had made the slightest effort to familiarize himself impartially with the law before his pronouncement, he wouldn't have generalized on the intentions of the blacks in respect to some antirepublican whites; he wouldn't have been so certain that they were all vexed and humiliated. I shall not call upon those among the whites who remained faithful to the principles of the Constitution by respecting them regardless of men's colour . . . : it was natural for the blacks to pay them the tribute of their gratitude; but it is to those who, openly declaring themselves the enemies of the principles of the Constitution, fought against them and whom a change of mind, more or less sincere, has brought back amongst us and reconciled with the country; it is these people whom I call upon to report the truth, to tell whether they weren't welcomed and protected and if, when they professed republican sentiments, they experienced the least vexation. When the proprietors of St. Domingue, when the Europeans who go there, instead of becoming the echoes of citizen Vaublanc by seeking to spread doubt about the liberty of the black people, show the intention of respecting this liberty, they will see growing in the hearts of these men the love and attachment that they have never ceased to hold for the whites in general and their former masters in particular, despite all of those who have tried to re-establish slavery and restore the rule of tyranny in St. Domingue.

Fifth Assertion: "I believe," continues General Rochambeau, "it will be difficult to reestablish order amongst the squanderers because by proscribing the Africans they will push them to revolt when they want to reduce their influence and credit; I am not even afraid to predict that after having armed them it will one day be necessary to fight to make them return to work."

The prediction of General Rochambeau, will undoubtedly be fulfilled should he reappear at the head of an army in order to return the blacks to slavery, because they will be forced to defend the liberty that the Constitution guarantees; but that this army may be necessary to force them to return to their rustic work is already flatly contradicted by what they have done in agriculture for the past year. . . I will not be contradicted when I assert that agriculture prospers in St. Domingue beyond even the hopes of this colony's truest friends, that the zeal of the field-negroes is also as satisfactory as can be desired, and

that the results of their rustic work are surprising when one reflects that in the middle of a war they were frequently obliged to take up arms in our own defence and that of our freedom, which we hold dearer than life; and, if he finds among them some men who are so stupid as not to feel the need for work, their chiefs have enough control to make them understand that without work there is no freedom. France must be just toward her colonial children, and soon her commerce and inhabitants will no longer miss the riches they will extract from their greatest prosperity; but, should the projects of citizen Vaublanc have some influence upon the French government, it is reminded that in the heart of Jamaica – the Blue Mountains – there exists a small number of men [the Maroons] so jealous of their liberty as to have forced the pride and power of the English to respect, to this very day, their natural rights, which the French Constitution guaranteed to us. . . .

Eighth Assertion: "A little after their arrival, the Agents had the impudence to welcome the negroes who had fought under the rebel chief Jean François, who had burned the plain and destroyed the greatest part of the colony. . . . These negroes had everywhere abandoned agriculture; their current cry is that this country belongs to them, that they don't want to see a single white man there. At the same time that they are swearing a fierce hatred of the whites, that is to say, the only true Frenchmen, they are fighting a civil war among themselves."

I swear to God, that in order to better the cause of the blacks, I disavow the excesses to which some of them were carried; subterfuge is far from me, I will speak the truth, even against myself. I confess that the reproaches made here against the rebel band of Jean François are justly merited. I haven't waited until today to deplore his blindness; but it was the delirium of some individuals and not of all the blacks, and must one confuse, under the same appellation of brigands, those who persisted in a guilty conduct with those who fought them and made them return to their duty? If, because some blacks have committed some cruelties, it can be deduced that all blacks are cruel, then it would be right to accuse of barbarity the European French and all the nations of the world. But the French Senate will not participate in such an injustice; it knows how to repulse the passions agitated by the enemies of liberty; it will not confuse one unbridled, undisciplined rebel band with men who since the rule of liberty in St. Domingue have given unquestionable proofs of loyalty to the Republic, have shed their blood for it, have assured its triumph, and who, by acts of goodness and humanity, by their return to order and to work, by their attachment to France, have redeemed a part of the errors to which their enemies had driven them and their ignorance had led them.

If it were true that the blacks were so wrong to think that the properties on St. Domingue belonged to them, why wouldn't they make themselves masters by driving off men of other colours, whom they could easily master by their numerical superiority? If they had sworn a fierce hatred against the whites, how is it that at this moment the white population of Le Cap equals that of the blacks and men of colour? How is it that more than half of the sugar planters of the Le Cap plain are white? If union and fraternity didn't reign among men of all classes, would whites, reds, and blacks be seen living in perfect equality? Without the union of all classes would European soldiers, along with blacks, be seen pursuing the same careers as their fellow citizens in Europe? Would one see them so lively in combat and often only to obtain the same triumphs as their noble rivals?

And then citizen Vaublanc proceeded to apply himself to inflaming the passions of the men of St. Domingue, to reviving barbarous prejudices, by proclaiming that the whites in St. Domingue are the only true Frenchmen! Does he include under this appellation the traitors paid by the English, those who following odious treachery introduced this perfidious nation into the territory of freedom? In this case, we retain the honour of not meriting this honourable name; but if the friends of freedom classify under this respectable denomination men submitting heart and soul to the French Constitution, to its beneficial laws, men who cherish the French friends of our country, we swear that we have, and will always have, the right to be called French citizens.

Ninth Assertion: "Alternately tyrants and victims, they outrage the sweetest natural sentiments, they renounce the kindest affections and sell their own children to the English, an infamous traffic which dishonors both buyer and seller in the eyes of humanity."

I acknowledge with a shudder that the charge made against the black rebels in the mountains of Grand-Rivière, who are fighting under the English flag and are led by French *émigrés*, of having sold some blacks is unfortunately too well founded; but has this charge ever been made against the blacks loyal to the Republic? And haven't these miserable rebels been driven to these infamous acts by the whites, . . . partisans of the system citizen Vaublanc seems to want to restore to the colony? Against these misguided men, simultaneously guilty and victims, citizen Vaublanc pours all the odium merited by actions so criminal as to be equally reproved by the laws of nature and the social order; but why, at the same time, doesn't he apply himself to tarnishing the monsters who have taught these crimes to the blacks and who have all been, by a barbarous guild on the coast of Africa, wrenching the son from his mother, the brother from his sister, the father from his son? Why does he only accuse those who, kept in ignorance by unjust laws that he undoubtedly wishes to see revived, were at first unable to recognize their rights and duties to the point of becoming the instruments of their own misfortune, while glossing over the outrages committed in cold blood by civilized men like himself who were therefore even more atrocious since they committed evil knowingly, allowing the lure of gold to suppress the cry of their conscience? Will the crimes of powerful men always be glorified? And will the error of weak men always be a source of oppression for them and their posterity? No! . . . I appeal to the justice of the French Nation. . . .

Thirteenth Assertion: "It is impossible to ignore that the existence of the Europeans in the colony is extremely precarious. In the South, in the mountains of the East, when the blacks are in revolt it is always against their European managers. Since our arrival, a great number have perished in this manner, and we have the misfortune to see that we are without means to suppress them."

An unanswerable proof that these partial revolts were only the effect of the perfidious machinations of the enemies of St. Domingue's prosperity is that they were always suppressed by the authority of the law, is that by executing those who were its leaders, the sword of justice stopped their propagation . . . But even supposing that the evils brought about by these movements should be the work of some villainous blacks, must those who did not participate in them and trembled with horror at the news of these disasters also be accused? This, however, is the injustice repeatedly done to black people; for the crime committed by some individuals, people feel free to condemn us all. Instantly forgotten are our past services, our future services, our fidelity and gratitude to France. And what would citizen Vaublanc say if, because the French Revolution produced some Marats, Robespierres, Carriers, Sonthonaxs, etc. etc. etc., the traitors who handed over Toulon to the English; because it produced the bloody scenes of the Vendée, the September massacres, the slaughter of a great part of the most virtuous members of the National Convention, the most sincere friends of the Republic and Liberty in France and the colonies; if, because some *émigré* troops took up arms against their country, which they had previously sold to the foreign powers, a voice arose from St. Domingue and cried to the French people:

You have committed inexcusable crimes because you shunned those more informed and civilized than you. The discussions of the legislative bodies, their laws which were rapidly transmitted to you, the enlightened magistrates charged with executing them, were before your eyes, at your side; you have ignored their voice, you have trampled upon your most sacred duties, you have reviled the Fatherland. Men unworthy of liberty, you were only made for slavery; restore the kings and their iron scepture; only those who opposed revolution were right, only they had good intentions; and the ancien regime that you had the barbarity to destroy was a government much too kind and just for you.

Far be it from me to want to excuse the crimes of the revolution in St. Domingue by comparing them to even greater crimes, but citizen Vaublanc, while threatening us in the *Corps Legislatif,* didn't bother to justify the crimes that have afflicted uts and which could only be attributed to a small number. . . . However, this former proprietor of slaves couldn't ignore what slavery was like; perhaps he had witnessed the cruelties exercised upon the miserable blacks, victims of their capricious masters, some of whom were kind but the greatest number of whom were true tyrants. And what would Vaublanc say . . . if, having only the same natural rights as us, he was in his turn reduced to slavery? Would he endure without complaint the insults, the miseries, the tortures, the whippings? And if he had tile good fortune to recover his liberty, would he listen without shuddering to the howls of those who wished to tear it from him? . . . Certainly not; in the same way he so indecently accuses the black people of the excesses of a few of their members, we would unjustly accuse the entirety of France

of the excesses of a small number of partisans of the old system. Less enlightened than citizen Vaublanc, we know, nevertheless, that whatever their colour, only one distinction must exist between men, that of good and evil. When blacks, men of colour, and whites are under the same laws, they must be equally protected and they must be equally repressed when they deviate from them. Such is my opinion; such are my desires.

Letter to the Directory, 5 November 1797[6]

The impolitic and incendiary discourse of Vaublanc has not affected the blacks nearly so much as their certainty of the projects which the proprietors of San Domingo are planning: insidious declarations should not have any effect in the eyes of wise legislators who have decreed liberty for the nations. But the attempts on that liberty which the colonists propose are all the more to be feared because it is with the veil of patriotism that they cover their detestable plans. We know that they seek to impose some of them on you by illusory and specious promises, in order to see renewed in this colony its former scenes of horror. Already perfidious emissaries have stepped in among us to ferment the destructive leaven prepared by the hands of liberticides. But they will not succeed. I swear it by all that liberty holds most sacred. My attachment to France, my knowledge of the blacks, make it my duty not to leave you ignorant either of the crimes which they meditate or the oath that we renew, to bury ourselves under the ruins of a country revived by liberty rather than stuffer the return of slavery.

It is for you, Citizens Directors, to turn from over our heads the storm which the eternal enemies of our liberty are preparing in the shades of silence. It is for you to enlighten the legislature, it is for you to prevent the enemies of the present system from spreading themselves on our unfortunate shores to sully it with new crimes. Do not allow our brothers, our friends, to be sacrificed to men who wish to reign over the ruins of the human species. But no, your wisdom will enable you to avoid the dangerous snares which our common enemies hold out for you. . . .

I send you with this letter a declaration which will acquaint you with the unity that exists between the proprietors of San Domingo who are in France, those in the United States, and those who serve under the English banner. You will see there a resolution, unequivocal and carefully constructed, for the restoration of slavery; you will see there that their determination to succeed has led them to envelop themselves in the mantle of liberty in order to strike it more deadly blows. You will see that they are counting heavily on my complacency in lending myself to their perfidious views by my fear for my children. It is not astonishing that these men who sacrifice their country to their interests are unable to conceive how many sacrifices a true love of country can support in a better father than they, since I unhesitatingly base the happiness of my children on that of my country, which they and they alone wish to destroy.

I shall never hesitate between the safety of San Domingo and my personal happiness; but I have nothing to fear. It is to the solicitude of the French Government that I have confided my children. . . . I would tremble with horror if it was into the hands of the colonists that I had sent them as hostages; but even if it were so, let them know that in punishing them for the fidelity of their father, they would only add one degree more to their barbarism, without any hope of ever making me fail in my duty. . . . Blind as they are! They cannot see how this odious conduct on their part can become the signal of new disasters and irreparable misfortunes, and that far from making them regain what in their eyes liberty for all has made them lose, they expose themselves to a total ruin and the colony to its inevitable destruction. Do they think that men who have been able to enjoy the blessing of liberty will calmly see it snatched away? They supported their chains only so long as they did not know any condition of life more happy than that of slavery. But today when they have left it, if they had a thousand lives they would sacrifice them all rather than be forced into slavery again. But no, the same hand which has broken our chains will not enslave us anew. France will not revoke her principles, she will not withdraw from us the greatest of her benefits. She will protect us

against all our enemies; she will not permit her sublime morality to be perverted, those principles which do her most honour to be destroyed, her most beautiful achievement to be degraded, and her Decree of 16 Pluviôse which so honours humanity to be revoked. *But if, to re-establish slavery in San Domingo, this was done, then I declare to you it would be to attempt the impossible: we have known how to face dangers to obtain our liberty, we shall know how to brave death to maintain it.*

This, Citizens Directors, is the morale of the people of San Domingo, those are the principles that they transmit to you by me.

My own you know. It is sufficient to renew, my hand in yours, the oath that I have made, to cease to live before gratitude dies in my heart, before I cease to be faithful to France and to my duty, before the god of liberty is profaned and sullied by the liberticides, before they can snatch from my hands that sword, those arms, which France confided to me for the defence of its rights and those of humanity, for the triumph of liberty and equality.

Notes

1. From Ralph Korngold, *Citizen Toussaint* (London, 1945), p. 85.
2. From Victor Schoelcher, *Vie de Toussaint-Louverture* (Paris, 1889), pp. 98-99; trans. George F. Tyson, Jr.
3. Trans. George F. Tyson, Jr.
4. From *Proclamations of Toussaint Louverture* (New York: New York Public Library, The Schomburg Collection); trans. Eleanor Johnson.
5. From *La Révolution française et l'abolition de l'esclavage*, 14 vols. (Paris, n.d.) 11:1-32; trans. George F. Tyson, Jr.
6. From, C. L. R. James, *The Black Jacobins: Toussaint L'Ouverture and the San Domingo Revolution*, 2nd rev. ed. (New York: Vintage Books, Random House, Inc., (1963), pp. 195-97. Reprinted by permission of the author.

SECTION FOURTEEN

Caribbean Wars: Marronage and Rebellion

Blacks pursued their freedom by all means possible. They declared war on the system and fought bloody battles in the process. But slave societies were able to persist partly because of the complex and pervasive structures of control and regulation. Imperial control agencies were primarily concerned with those enslaved as the lowest social levels of colonial society, though they did not ignore the colonial elites. Spanish and French governments asserted greatest external control over their colonies, an issue which cannot be ignored and is a major argument in explaining the occurrence of the first successful slave revolt in a French colony, and why Creole nationalism reached the most revolutionary level in Spanish territories.

These essays suggest that differences in the stage of material and ideological development in imperial countries determined to a large extent the nature of colonial control systems, though their effectiveness resulted significantly from the peculiarity of problems encountered in the colony. Slaves, (Africans and creoles), free coloured, poor whites, and Amerindians constantly opposed internal socio-political arrangements. Indeed, historians are now in agreement that in the Caribbean anti-slavery revolt was endemic; it has also been suggested that the period of slavery was characterized primarily by one protracted war launched by the enslaved against enslavers.

Detailed studies of the patterns and forms of resistance are now available. It is possible, therefore, to identify the major events and ideas that have shaped the development of Caribbean anti-slavery. Though highly structured revolts and long-term marronage have been considered the most advanced rebellious acts, the relations between such levels of political organizations and the more spontaneous day-to-day slavery responses have not been adequately assessed. This record of resistance illustrates, nonetheless, that there was hardly a generation of male or female slaves in the Caribbean who did not take their anti-slavery actions to the level of violent armed encounters in the pursuit of freedom. Persistent slave rebellions were punctuated by daily rumour and suspicion of conspiracy. It was the general belief among free people that slaves were always in the process of plotting to gain their freedom. Some rumours were investigated and punitive actions taken against slaves. Oftentimes it was not possible for slave owners to verify the existence of planned rebellion. Savage methods were used to extort information from slaves.

The rebellions, however, would come and were expected in very much the same way that hurricanes were. There was dread of revolt, but it was considered part of the climate of the times, and slave owners' prime objective was to weather the storm and live to press on with business. These essays look at the relationships between marronage, rebellion and the struggle for freedom. They are pan-Caribbean in their coverage and deal with varying contexts of slave existence: from rural sugar estates and livestock farms to urban centres; from the large Spanish colony of Cuba to smaller Danish Caribbean outposts: from the highly Africanized to the increasing creolized phases of Caribbean slave society.

65

Caribbean Anti-Slavery: The Self-Liberation Ethos of Enslaved Blacks

HILARY McD. BECKLES

It is now commonly accepted by historians that in the British West Indies anti-slavery conflict was frequently of a revolutionary nature. In earlier articles, I have suggested that the many slave revolts and plots in these territories between 1638 and 1838 could be conceived of as the '200 Years' War' — one protracted struggle launched by Africans and their Afro-West Indian progeny against slave owners. Such endemic anti-slavery activity represented, furthermore, the most immediately striking characteristic of the West Indian world. Current anglophone historiography outlines in detail the empirical contours of this struggle — what amounts to an indigenous anti-slavery movement — though its philosophical and ideological aspects remain less researched.[1]

Anglophone literature on anti-slavery, however, has emphasised above other features, its trans-atlantic dimension. This perspective has enriched significantly our general understanding of the diverse forces that succeeded ultimately in toppling the region's heterogeneous slave regimes. To some extent, this panoramic vision of the anti-slavery movement results from a more theoretical reading of slave resistance which suggests the need for closer investigation of slaves' political culture. Such an examination is necessary not only for an empirical understanding of resistance, but also for a fuller evaluation of slaves' consciousness and depth of political awareness. Such insights would make it possible for the historian to illustrate more precisely those linkages, real or imaginary, that existed between plantation-based politics and the international anti-slavery ethos.[2]

Many historians have responded to this challenge, and the theme of slave resistance or, more appropriately, the blacks' anti-slavery movement, has now become a leading growth area in Caribbean historiography. From the works of leading scholars, particularly Orlando Patterson, Michael Craton, Edward Brathwaite, Barry Gaspar, Mary Turner, Barbara Kopytoff and Monica Schuler, it is possible to demarcate some structural features in the development of Caribbean anti-slavery. Three basic stages have so far been identified. The first stage relates to early plantation construction, and corresponds approximately with the period 1500–1750. The second basic stage is characterised by mature plantation society and declining dependency on slave importation — 1750–1800. The third stage relates to the 'general crisis' in plantation slavery; it is linked with the impact of Haitian politics and serious anti-slavery discussions in the metropole — 1804–1838.

Within these three general phases, three types/levels of anti-slavery struggle have been described — though no systematic effort has been made to articulate them within the historical continuum. Firstly, a proliferation of acts of 'day-to-day' resistance are identified; these were generally designed not to overthrow the slave system, but to undermine its efficiency in order to hasten its eventual abandonment. Secondly, evidence is adduced of the large number of unsuccessful plots and revolts which were characterised by collective organisation with reformist and revolutionary objectives. Thirdly, there is the incidence, 'successful' rebellion, from long-term marronage to the St. Domingue revolution.[3]

Highly structured revolts, considered generally as the most advanced rebellious acts, have been given more research attention within the wide range of anti-slavery politics. Unfortunately, no attempt has been made to illustrate how, and under what conditions, non-violent day-to-day anti-slavery protest evolved into violent revolutionary designs.[4] According to Robert Dirks there are references within the literature to some 70 slave uprisings between 1649 and 1833, including large-scale insurrections that engulfed entire colonies and small-scale violence limited to single estates. Of this total, Dirks states that some 32 revolts did not materialise due to discovery, and some were undoubtedly the invented product of planters' paranoia. Craton's chronology of resistance between 1638 and 1837, however, lists some 75 aborted revolts and actual rebellions; in this computation some of these actions have been grouped together and appear as one event.[5] This record of resistance illustrates that there was hardly a generation of slaves in the English West Indies that did not confront their masters collectively with arms in pursuit of freedom. In this sense, therefore, the relations between slaves and masters in the West Indies can be shown as characterised by ongoing psychological warfare and intermittent bloody battles.

It is now a major concern of scholars interpreting this extensive record of resistance to assess the extent to which slaves' rebellious actions were informed by ideological choices in the context of maturing political consciousness. It has taken scholars many years of revising interpretations to arrive at this position in regard to slave politics, though it remains an influential argument that slaves wanted much less than what some recent historians now suggest. This interpretive inertia reflects, in part, a compulsive assumption within western historical science that the working classes rarely perceived effectively their group interest, an argument supported by what some refer to as irrationality and inhibiting conservatism in their collective responses to oppression.

Not surprisingly, recent revisionist literature produced by most Caribbean, European and American scholars, has centred upon the need to distinguish as clearly as possible the Caribbean and metropolitan anti-slavery movements, and to assess their relative potency. Technically, this is an important development because slave resistance had long been conceived of as a lower species of political behaviour, lacking in ideological cohesion, intellectual qualities and a philosophical direction. Generally considered as marginally more advanced than basic primitive responses to a crude and oppressive material and social world, it was not seen to be possessing anything

resembling theoretical significance. These perceptions have survived in spite of C. L. R. James' 1938 classic work, *The Black Jacobins*, which sought, perhaps with too much theoretical enthusiasm, to link rebel slaves in colonial St. Domingue with the philosophically progressive Jacobin equalitarianism of France that ultimately weakened the ideological hegemony of slave holders in that colony. The 'Black Jacobins' seized the colonial state and established an independent republic in 1804 — an achievement that cannot be divorced, according to James, from its European theoretical roots.[6]

At first glance the immediate goals of the Caribbean and European anti-slavery movements seem ideologically polarised and at variance. The metropolitan movement was essentially philosophical and respectably radical in character. It relied initially upon a strong moral perspective, though with an increasing reliance upon economic arguments in latter years. The Caribbean movement, on the other hand, spearheaded by enslaved blacks, with some Amerindian and free coloured support, was also generally non-violent, but occasionally erupted into revolutionary warfare. The metropolitan movement depended upon popular mobilisation and parliamentary lobbying in a legislative approach to emancipation. The slaves' approach, it may be implied, was more complex; they wanted freedom by all means necessary or possible, and engaged in activities which ranged from self-purchase to violent armed struggle for territory and political sovereignty.

There is some evidence, fragmented though it is, to suggest that more informed slaves saw their anti-slavery actions as articulated to those of metropolitan lobbyists, though they were not prepared to lose the initiative in terms of striking for freedom when circumstances, local or foreign, dictated autonomous actions. Some slaves, whether in revolutionary St. Domingue or rebellious Barbados and Jamaica in 1816 and 1831 respectively, had knowledge, considered crude and inaccurate by most historians, of developments in metropolitan anti-slavery ideas and strategies. This information base, it has been argued, assisted in shaping their costly movement for liberation (measured in human life) and thus illustrating, even if in a tamed manner, the internationalism of their political consciousness.[7]

Evaluating the relative potency of the two segments of the transatlantic anti-slavery movement cannot be an easy task for the historian. Contemporaneous writers on the English Caribbean did not attempt such analyses. Indeed, they generally saw the slaves' movement, most of the time, as having little more than nuisance value, and on those infrequent occasions when they recognised within it revolutionary proportions, their analyses degenerated into negrophobic descriptions and commentaries.[8] Such outpourings were based, in varying degrees, upon the racist notion of angry and savage blacks in a vengeful and mindless lust for blood and white women.[9]

The most sophisticated pro-slavery writer, Jamaica's Edward Long, does not best illustrate this particular point, but he does demonstrate in the clearest manner slave owners' reluctant recognition of slaves' maturing anti-slavery consciousness. Furthermore, he understood fully what it meant for the Caribbean world in particular and the politics of abolitionism in general.

Long was aware of the contradiction inherent in white colonists' claims for 'liberty' within the late eighteenth-century Whig ideological framework, while at the same time denying black colonists any legitimate right to their own liberty. He admitted, moreover, that the 'spirit of liberty' was also a deep-rooted feature of the slave community, though for him this consciousness had its origins in the white community — the blacks being ideological victims of its 'contagious fever'.[10] The resolution of this contradiction within Long's thought was found in a headlong plunge into racial arguments, the structure of which had long been a feature of colonial elite social consciousness. He argued, for example, that the condition of colonial slavery for blacks was in itself an advancement in their claim to liberty. That is, blacks in general enjoyed more social and material rights on the West Indian plantations than they did in West Africa where their lot was generally one of abject poverty and submission to monarchical tyranny. Gordon Lewis suggests that social relations within eighteenth-century planter ideology were based on the tenet that the slave required patronage in return for his labour. Long articulates this point by stating that the slave, once settled in his new home, enters into a limited freedom supervised by the master who is his 'friend and father'. This authority, Long adds,

is like that of an ancient patriarch: conciliating affection by the mildness of its exertion, and claiming respect by the justice and propriety of its decisions

and discipline, it attracts the love of the honest and good; while it awes the worthless into reformation.[11]

This unrealistic view of stability in master–slave relations fell apart precisely at the stage where slaves rejected those reforms which meant the abandonment of their claim to liberty. The extensive record of rebellion and protest provides the empirical and theoretical evidence to support their stance on this question. It points, furthermore, to a refusal within the slave community to accept as legitimate any kind of slave-relation whatsoever, and the search for avenues to freedom was persistent.

Ideally, it could be said that rebel slaves and metropolitan anti-slavery lobbyists shared the same goals, and hence their respective movements ought to be considered as different levels of a general process. The attractiveness of this position is partly betrayed by its simplicity, and is easily abandoned when tested under the weight of empirical evidence. It may very well be suggested that slaves wanted more than legal freedom on many occasions; that they also wanted political power and economic autonomy. These were certainly objectives that most 'humanitarians' preferred blacks not to have. The records of slave rebellion also show, it is true, that in some instances slaves might well have wanted only the right to reasonable wages and conditions of work under their old masters. The 1831 Sam Sharpe rebellion of Jamaica has recently been so interpreted.[12] But rebellions in St. Domingue, 1791–1804, and Barbados in 1816 also suggest that blacks understood that meaningful freedom could be guaranteed only by means of seizing the organs of law and government and by imposing a revolutionary constitutionalism thereafter in order to enforce the reality of freedom.

Wilberforce, for instance, had no time for slaves' revolutionary approach to emancipation in the English colonies, and considered such actions, in spite of his friendship with King Henry of Haiti, as detrimental to the survival of English authority in America — not only in terms of economic and political leverage, but also in terms of the hegemony of western civilisation. The scenario of black revolution and the formation of Afro-Caribbean republics or monarchies, in addition to the subsequent freezing of 'things European', did not excite English anti-slavery lobbyists.[13] From this point of view, then, it may be suggested that the two segments of the transatlantic anti-slavery movement were heading in different directions most of the time. It was not simply a matter of the divergence of strategies and radically different levels of procedure, but also a matter of the kind of worlds that were to be created in the aftermath.

A simple statistical analysis might show that given some 400,000 blacks who gained revolutionary freedom in St. Domingue, together with the large numbers who freed themselves by means of marronage and otherwise, no concrete basis exists for the claim that European legislative emancipation should be given an obvious right to first consideration. Though the numbers analysis is not necessarily the best way to proceed on this question, it would perhaps impose some demographic constraints upon the ideological charge involved in the argument that, by and large, freedom was brought to the blacks, and that self-attained freedom was of marginal significance. In addition, it would illustrate more clearly the impressive record of achievement of slave communities as sponsors of the libertarian ideology.

Such an analysis is particularly relevant at this stage partly because one of the most striking features of the recent historiography has been the establishment of a dichotomous core/periphery structure within the transatlantic anti-slavery movement. Eric Williams was perhaps first to pose this dichotomous paradigm when he argued that, while metropolitan anti-slavery lobbyists intensified their campaign, during the early nineteenth century, the slaves had done likewise. By 1833, he said, 'the alternatives were clear', 'emancipation from above or emancipation from below, but Emancipation'.[14] Not surprisingly, only radical scholars seem perturbed by the assignment of the peripheral status to the slaves' movement and the core status to the metropolitan lobbyists. This has been the case in spite of a revisionist attempt to give greater value within the emancipation process to the autonomous anti-slavery actions of blacks. That is, whereas the traditional interpretations crudely negated the slaves' role, the modernist view sought the subordination of slaves' struggle within international abolitionism. The hands-on political movement of slaves, then, is yet to free itself conceptually of the hegemonic constraints imposed by a revised anti-slavery interpretation. Symbolically, the images of Wilberforce, Schoelcher, *et al.* still stalk the literature, transcending those of slave leaders such as Bussa, Kofi and Sam Sharpe.

It is not clear, however, why the slaves' struggle for freedom should be considered secondary or peripheral to the activities of European emancipationists. No coherent arguments have been given for this outside of the general statement that ultimately it was imperial law rather than colonial war which terminated the 'not very peculiar' institution of slavery. Michael Craton, for example, after evaluating the record of slave resistance in the English colonies, though in a rather technical and 'eventist' manner, considered it necessary to add, by way of not distancing himself from what he perceived to be substantial empirical evidence, that white abolitionists won the day, though black abolitionists helped in no small way. He has also treated us to other variations on this theme. There is the view, for example, that slaves created in part the ideological context for parliamentary legislation by rendering their societies irretrievably unstable. In this way they assisted in forcing the imperial legislature into action in order to protect colonial life (white) and property (black and non-human). In addition, there is the argument that slave rebels had illustrated by 1832 that the colonial elite could rule in the long term only by means of extreme repression, and that Parliament was not prepared to pay the economic nor political cost implied, and acted to defuse an increasingly explosive situation.[15]

Whatever the perspectives, the perception that rebel slaves were featured in abolitionist debates by the imperial governments cannot be ignored. If these arguments have any weight, then it becomes less clear what precisely was the overwhelming and more critical role of the 'humanitarians'. Unfortunately, analyses of these and related matters are hampered by insufficient data on specific ways in which the imperial government perceived the political action of slaves in relation to that of its own anti-slavery members.

The assignment of a peripheral status within anti-slavery thought to slaves is also to be found in the 'intellectual' work of David Brion Davis and more so in Roger Anstey's several accounts of British abolitionism. Following Davis, it could be argued that while the conceptual separation of Caribbean and European processes are perhaps inevitable, owing to different historiographic and philosophical traditions, the projection of an hierarchical order in the emergence of democratic ideology, and in the partial and full attainment of freedom, constitutes a major problem of anti-slavery in western culture.[16]

Two recent works on anti-slavery, the first by

a long-standing anti-Marxist American scholar of British abolitionism, and the other by an English Marxist political historian, best illustrate this historiographical condition. First, in Seymour Drescher's 1986 work, *Capitalism and Anti-Slavery*, which represents a mild revision of Anstey's thesis, there are no references to Caribbean anti-slavery activities in the opening chapter entitled the 'Foundations of anti-slavery'. Drescher, however, offered what can be interpreted as a dismissive aside in his summary where it is stated that 'the expansion of freedom was the central problem of abolitionists (including the slaves)'.[17] Second, Robin Blackburn in his recent impressively comprehensive study, *The Overthrow of Colonial Slavery*, argues in the opening chapter on the 'origins of anti-slavery' that since the publication of Thomas Clarkson's seminal work on British slave trade abolition (1808), 'it has been common to identify the origins of anti-slavery within the works of the learned men who first published critiques of slavery or the slave trade.'[18]

Recognising the persistence of this perspective in the study of anti-slavery, Marxist historians such as C. L. R. James, Richard Hart and Gordon Lewis, among others, have been suggesting for some time that slave politics be conceived of as the 'on the ground' (core) dimension of a general struggle to remove slavery from Caribbean and European political culture. James has long been concerned with illustrating how revolutionary ideology transcended the political barriers implicit in colonial slavery and racism. He insists that there should be no surprise in the fact that Caribbean slaves hammered out a political reality of anti-slavery with the assistance of European thought.

The equally vintage work of Hart on Jamaican slave resistance and rebellion now represents an historiographic core that illustrates as well as any other source the evolution of a hardened anti-slavery consciousness among blacks in that country. For him, the core of the anti-slavery movement resided undoubtedly within the Caribbean, and his personal political feel for contemporary consciousness gives a strong sense of continuity in his analysis.[19] Lewis, in addition, in his well-known style, attempted to flesh out the theoretical and conceptual dimensions of international anti-slavery ideology, and gave full credit to the intellectual contribution of Caribbean slaves. He is not the kind of scholar who is limited by what has been said already.

Furthermore, he had the courage to travel along uncharted areas in search of the 'hidden' ideological elements of the past world. What he found were the outer limits of a grand Caribbean anti-slavery tradition, whose actors were not only black and coloured, but also Amerindian and creole white. Conceptually, he does not detract from the achievements of Wilberforce, Clarkson, Buxton and Schoelcher, but he does suggest that the world created, even if temporarily, by the anti-slavery energies of Toussaint and Dessalines, Sam Sharpe, Tackey and other slave leaders, seemed comparatively more 'hell-bent' on destroying Caribbean slavery.[20]

English abolitionist leaders, of course, perceived themselves as constituting the vanguard of anti-slavery thought and practice, a vision which historians have continued to perpetuate. This perception, not surprisingly, has managed to survive long after the 1790s when blacks in St. Domingue overthrew the slave regime and established in 1804 the state of Haiti which boasted an aggressive anti-slavery constitution and foreign policy.[21] Haiti had emerged regionally and internationally as the real symbol and manifestation of anti-slavery, Toussaint having beforehand eclipsed Wilberforce in the watchful eyes of the western world as the prime anti-slavery leader. For the hard-working and determined English abolitionists, however, the presence of Haiti was, in general, more of a hindrance to their crusade than an asset, and they continued to see anti-slavery as being endangered by Caribbean slaves' impatient tendency to resort to arms. Eltis suggests that this is why abolitionists, in general, were in favour of the establishment of a strong police force, an independent magistracy, draconian vagrancy laws and increased missionary activity.[22]

Historians have had little difficulty in endorsing the humanitarians' claim to possession of the philosophic 'mind' — and hence the core — of anti-slavery, and by extension in suggesting that slaves lived out at best the cruder socio-material aspects of the movement. According to David Geggus, no major figure appears to have openly approved of violent self-liberation by blacks. Wilberforce thought them still unready for freedom, however obtained, and he deplored the 'cruel' and 'dreadful' revolt in St. Domingue. Even Charles James Fox, the well-known radical and abolitionist, uttered negrophobic statements which culminated in his call for an assurance by his government that the spirit of revolt would not find roots within English colonies. Thomas Clarkson, however, respected for his unemotional consistency on the question of anti-slavery, rejected the popular sentiments of abolitionists, and spoke of Haiti as representing, not the upsurge of brutish savagery, but the affirmation of the 'unalterable Rights of Men' to freedom. Clarkson had only few supporters within the abolitionists' camp, the most famous being the long-standing abolitionist, Percival Stockdale, who saw in the St. Domingue experience a movement against tyranny, led by Africans 'acting like men', fulfilling the most honourable destiny of mankind as directed by 'Nature and by God'.[23]

It was the treacherous removal of Toussaint from St. Domingue, the scene of the greatest single anti-slavery triumph, that allowed the best in England's journalism and the finest in its philosophic and artistic tradition to address the real meaning of Caribbean anti-slavery. In 1802, for example, the *Annual Register* voted him the man of the year, while Samuel Coleridge rated him in terms of 'true dignity of character' the better of Napoleon, his captor.[24] William Wordsworth, perhaps, more so than any other thinker, concretised in 1802 the value of Toussaint to mankind's search for liberty in general and the anti-slavery cause specifically with his sonnet, 'To Toussaint L'Ouverture':[25]

Though fallen thyself, never to rise again,
Live and take comfort. Thou has left behind
Powers that will work for thee; air, earth, and skies;
There's not a breathing of the common wind
That will forget thee; thou hast great allies;
Thy friends are exultations, agonies,
And love, and man's unconquerable mind.

But Wordsworth, like Toussaint, did not breathe 'the common wind', as Geggus assures us in his treatment of British opinion on black self-liberation in the Caribbean. On the St. Domingue question, Geggus asserts: 'Among the abolitionists, with the exception of a few fringe figures, the black rebels found apologists rather than supporters; most avoided the question of the legitimacy of the use of violence, and none seem to have spoken out against Britain's brief, but traumatic attempt to restore slavery in the colony'. Geggus is not surprised that 'the response of the British Romantics' to this struggle for personal freedom and national self-liberation was 'surprisingly slight', since the evidence suggests that although 'the blacks' resistance won them respect, prejudice persisted'.[26]

Persistent anti-black prejudice within western

thought, Eric Williams affirmed, has influenced considerably the development of British and European colonial historiography, which forces us to examine the extent to which it remains a feature of the theoretical claims of anti-slavery literature.[27] It can be argued, within the limits of reasonable deductions from the data available, that English abolitionists' rejection of the slaves' revolutionary approach to freedom suggests that they had conceived liberation strictly in legal and sociological terms. That is, they did not support slave politics which sought to undermine the hegemony of the planter elite and the supportive Christian missions. They wished slaves legally free and to some extent recognised as social and biological equals to whites. But they did argue, however, that the economic dependency and political subordination of blacks to whites were necessary and desirable for their own advancement as well as for the continued growth of the Caribbean. Blacks, they generally believed, had nothing of superior merit to offer the new world in advancing its civilisation, and therefore they were to play a submissive role in the expansion of Eurocentric culture via the white-controlled plantation economic regime.[28]

The racism implied within this perception of black liberation was an entrenched feature of abolitionists' thought. Emancipation was not conceived in terms of liberation from Europeans' power, values and domination. From this point of view, then, it was only when Toussaint showed himself, like King Christophe did at a later date, to be receptive of the European educational and religious mission and its cultural-language baggage, that he received some measure of ideological acceptance by English statesmen and humanitarians. Furthermore, the abolitionists' tendency to conceive of slaves as unfortunate children to be liberated from tyrannical parents, with the moral outrage which that implied for the reasonable mind, served to deepen the racist perception of their audience and enhance a fear among them that blacks seeking independence, economic autonomy and political power, were irresponsible, rash, ungrateful, in addition to being naive.

With these ideological tenets so deeply embedded in abolitionist perceptions of blacks in struggle, it would have been a formidable, but necessary task for historians to transcend or penetrate them in order to observe as objectively as possible the intellectual features of the political culture of blacks. This remains a most necessary precondition for a proper evaluation of the Caribbean anti-slavery tradition as well as for an understanding of how it is related to the European movement.

Logically, then, a feature of anti-slavery that should have been addressed at the outset is the history of blacks' political consciousness in the general evolution of their conceptual understanding of their wants, needs and means. To do this, it would have been necessary to say something meaningful about the 'slave mind' — hence ideology. Gordon Lewis quite perceptively punctuated his fascinating treatment of Caribbean anti-slavery with this reference to the state of the 'slave mind' within the historiography:

If, then, there was a planter mind, there was also a slave mind. This has not always been fully appreciated, even by authors sympathetic to the slave cause.[29]

Refusal to recognise black rebels at this level of consciousness, more than any other factor, has held back the advance of the kind of conceptual analysis which is necessary for an incisive understanding of slave resistance, and the subject remains today a soft spot within the modern anti-slavery literature.

To conceive rebel slaves as intelligent political activists (in spite of their material and socio-legal oppression), who were capable of evaluating pro-slavery strengths and weaknesses, has not been an easy task for most historians. Occasionally, references are made to this inhibition in terms of it being rooted within a racist perception of blacks which, in part, relates to the abolitionist view of slaves as primitive, anti-intellectual beings in need simply of paternalistic and moral care. Take Michael Craton's conceptual development, for example. For many years he worked diligently on slave resistance in the English Caribbean. In 1974 he presented what he described as a typology, morphology and etiology of resistance — neatly packaged in what he also termed 'a sequential model'. Since then he has published several works on slave resistance, illustrating a praiseworthy need to revise and fine-tune his analysis. Indeed, he is generally considered to be a leading authority within this aspect of Caribbean historiography. It is interesting to note, however, what happened when he encountered the need to comment on the 'slave mind' — an encounter which resulted from a general recognition that structuralist models based squarely on demographic, topographic and economic forces were insufficient in

explaining why the slaves rebelled and what their motivating ideas were. He ran into the minefield of his own [unconscious] race attitude and attempted to deal with it as follows:

Because of my seduction by the neat model and simple causes, I went so far as to dismiss the influence upon the British West Indies slaves of all the ideology of the Age of Revolution (1775-1815), even of the slave rebellion in Haiti between 1791 and 1804 . . . , finally, it seems to me now that to deprive the slaves of an ideology such as that normally ascribed to the rebellious Americans, the French Revolutionaries . . . is to be guilty once more of a racist denigration.[30]

Having cleared this hurdle, a major achievement within Euro-American historiography of black struggle, Craton goes on to assert what for him was the ideology of the rebel slaves throughout Caribbean history; it 'was that of all unfree men — that is the vast majority throughout history — freedom to make, or create, life of their own'.[31]

Craton's admission and subsequent assertion came some 30 years after C. L. R. James had illustrated quite remarkably in *The Black Jacobins* that a proliferation of conflicting ideas and socio-political visions existed within the Haitian revolutionary ranks on the issues of foreign policy, economic strategy, race relations, education and government. Indeed one could argue that, like Lenin, Stalin, and Trotsky, the Haitian leaders, Toussaint, Dessalines and Christophe, differed fundamentally from each other on ideology, and thus the revolution was characterised by deep-rooted conceptual heterogeneity.[32] The real tribute to slaves in Craton's point, then, is perhaps to be found more succinctly stated in Gordon Lewis' political theorem — 'without intelligence there can be no ideology'.[33]

Leading on from these conceptual developments, though not in a logical manner, is the belief, now generally associated with the work of Sidney Mintz and Douglas Hall, that rebel slaves wanted a limited measure of economic and social autonomy as represented by a peasant culture rather than formal political power.[34] It is not clearly stated whether this objective was that of rebel leaders or the generally non-violent majority of slaves. Neither is it clearly stated whether this 'peasanthood' was considered the end product of their politics — that is, after they had defeated their masters — or merely a base for a future revolutionary onslaught upon planter power. For Craton, 'the black majority' wanted to be 'free to work for planters or themselves as and when they wished', ambitions he considered to be 'comparatively moderate', but in 'consonance with what seems to have been the wishes of the mass following'.[35]

It is not difficult to recognise that these projections of rebel slaves' objectives represent the most conservative and restricted interpretation of their ascribed ideology — 'freedom to make a life of their own'. Is it not a little odd to state that rebel slaves would have used whatever means possible to win their freedom and then to suggest that this end could be realised by a 'moderate' peasanthood cocooned within a plantation/planter dominated world? Would slaves not have realised that this idea as an end itself was unattainable under plantation hegemony? If we look solely at the British West Indies where slaves failed, after 200 years, to wrest political power from masters by means of arms, we also see that, in the period 1838–1870, landownership was used as a political tool with far-reaching constitutional implications, especially for Jamaica where the peasantry was numerically most advanced.

Where slaves succeeded in freeing themselves, whether in Haiti, in long-lasting maroon communities, and in temporary slave regimes, the value of political power to their sense of freedom was considered critical. The labourers' and peasants' riots and voting practices in the mid-nineteenth-century British West Indies clearly illustrate that blacks were aware that without political power their 'reconstituted' peasant culture could not deliver the quality of freedom envisaged. Historians, then, seemed to have taken one step forward in the recognition of a slave ideology of struggle, but have taken two backwards in implying that it was a depoliticised peasant world, dialectically opposed to plantation hegemony, which rebel slaves pursued.

More recently, this regressive trend within the historiography has received a significant boost from Dirks in what he describes as an analysis of 'conflict and its ritual expression' on British West Indian slave plantations. Dirks' thesis is that slaves possessed a 'proclivity to turn the holidays [especially Christmas] into a bloodbath and to try to topple their masters' regime'.[36] He computes that of the 70 slave revolts reported, aborted, imagined and actual, some 37 occurred in the month of December, producing what he terms the 'darkside of Christmas'.[37] Dirks' analysis of this time-based phenomenon falls within the category identified by Craton as racist

denigration — dark for whom! For him, the slaves were not driven by a political and military understanding, sophisticated or otherwise, of the impact of the Christmas festivities within the white community, but by forces of the belly rather than the brain. The month of December, he claims, without the presentation of adequate supportive data, was associated with a rather sudden increase in slave nutrition — preceding months being characterised by extensive hunger:

The onset of dry weather in December brought immediate and dramatic relief. The energy-rich fields of cane started to ripen. At the same time yams, sweet potatoes, maize, plantains, and bananas, as well as a great number of other fruits and vegetables, began to mature. Field-work slackened off for a brief interlude before the cane harvest. And the end of the hurricane season brought hundreds of vessels laden with provisions, much of it for holiday distribution. Together these events broke the pattern of hunger and lethargy and disease of the previous months and gave way to vigor and better health all around.

'This upsurge in available food energy,' Dirks argues, 'is also related to tumultous celebrations' and aggressiveness among slaves in general. He asserts that 'the effect of this nutritional boost and the availability of other fresh sources of nourishment was nothing short of explosive'. Typically, some of this excessive energy went into 'jolly sport', but most went into 'extraordinary aggressiveness'.[38]

One of Dirks' achievements is that he has managed to turn upside down the traditional analysis without attempting to remove it from nutritional or biological levels of conception. In 1974, for example, Richard Sheridan had argued that slaves 'tended to revolt when they were underfed, overworked, and maltreated'.[39] We are now told by Dirks that, on the contrary, they tended to revolt when overfed, underworked and well-treated. The assumption underlying both arguments is that it was possible to produce in a general way an anti-rebellious consciousness by a sensitive, well-planned manipulation of labour and nutritional factors. This suggests an objection to the notion that slaves practised 'politics' on a sophisticated and intellectually conscious level. Yet, the evidence illustrates fully that slaves made definite political analyses of the power structures they encountered, and used almost every force — natural and human — in their struggle. They rebelled when they could, and accommodated when they had to. The ebb and flow of rebellion and accommodation suggest that they understood 'time', including Christmas time, as a political factor in struggle. As a result, some planters were forced to appreciate the political skills and conscious determination of rebel slaves, in spite of the negrophobic nature of their social commentaries.

It can no longer be generally accepted, then, that slaves existed in an atheoretical world which was devoid of ideas, political concepts and an alternative socio-political vision. Their tradition of anti-slavery activity impacted upon the social culture and polity of the Caribbean world in more fundamental ways than anti-slavery lobbyists ever did in metropolitan societies. Indeed, the entire Caribbean reality was shaped and informed by the persistent forces of slavery and anti-slavery as long as the slave regimes lasted. From a Caribbean perspective, slaves' struggle for freedom should not be diminished when placed alongside the legislative interventions of European parliaments. These metropolitan actions were part of the final episode in an epic struggle — initiated and propelled by its greatest sufferers — the slave population. Only in Haiti were blacks able to overthrow the slave regime and achieve their freedom. Yet, slaves throughout the region consistently rebelled in order to gain freedom, employing over time a wide range of political tools and methods in their struggle.

In terms of the Caribbean anti-slavery movement, no iron laws of slave resistance exist, and consequently most scholars have tended to emphasise the uniqueness of each colony's case. While recognising, at least philosophically, the temporal and spatial uniqueness of each historical moment, one can still illustrate that the fundamental ideological core of anti-slavery was almost identical: the slaves were saying to their masters, 'we want to be free, and we will pursue that freedom by all means necessary.' This was the essential stream of thought that ran through the region, from colony to colony, from plantation to plantation. Indeed, it was anti-slavery rather than sugar production which stamped the most prominent unifying marks upon the region. In this sense, then, black-led anti-slavery resided at the root of the Caribbean experience, and represented a critical element of the core of what was perhaps the first international political movement of the modern era — transatlantic abolitionism.

Notes

1. Hilary Beckles, 'The 200 Years War: Slave Resistance in the British West Indies: An Overview of the Historiography', *Jamaican Historical Review*, 13 (1982), 1-10; also 'Slave Ideology and Self-Emancipation in the British West Indies', *Bulletin of Eastern Caribbean Affairs*, 10:4 (1984), 1-8. See also Michael Craton, 'The Passion to Exist: Slave Rebellion in the British West Indies, 1650-1832', *Journal of Caribbean History*, 13, 1 (1980); Edward Long, *The History of Jamaica*, (London, 1774, rpt 1970), 348-55, 465-69; Bryan Edwards, *The History, Civil and Commercial of the British Colonies in the West Indies* (London, 1794), 1, 60-65.
2. See, for example, the following revisionist analyses of slave resistance: Barry Gaspar, *Bondsmen and Rebels: A Study of Master-Slave Relations in Antigua (with Implications for colonial British America)* (Baltimore, 1985), xiv-20. Michael Craton, *Testing the Chains: Resistance to Slavery in the British West Indies* (London, 1982), 19-51. Hilary Beckles, *Black Rebellion in Barbados: The Struggle Against Slavery, 1627-1838* (Bridgetown, 1984), 1-8.
3. See Orlando Patterson, 'Slavery and Slave Revolts: A Socio-historical Analysis of the First Maroon War, Jamaica 1655-1740', *Social and Economic Studies*, 19:3 (1970), 289-325. Michael Craton, *Sinews of Empire: A Short History of British Slavery* (New York, 1974), 225-40. Edward Braithwaite, *Wars of Respect: Nanny, Sam Sharpe and the Struggle* (Kingston, 1977); also 'Caliban, Ariel and Unprospero in the Conflict of Creolisation: A Study of the Slave Revolt of Jamaica, 1831-32', in V. Rubin and A. Tuden (eds), *Comparative Perspectives on Slavery in New World Plantation Societies* (New York, 1977), 41-62. Barbara Kopytoff, 'The Early Political Development of Jamaican Maroon Societies', *William and Mary Quarterly*, 35:2 (1978), 287-307; 'The Development of Jamaican Maroon Ethnicity', *Caribbean Quarterly*, 22 (1976), 35-50. Monica Schuler, 'Akan Slave Rebellion in the British Caribbean', *Savacou*, 1:1 (1970); also 'Ethnic Slave Rebellions in the Caribbean and the Guianas', *Journal of Social History*, 3 (1970), 374-85. Barry Gaspar, 'The Antigua Slave Conspiracy of 1736: A Case Study of the Origins of Collective Resistance', *William and Mary Quarterly*, 35:2 (1978), 308-24. Mary Reckord-Turner, 'The Jamaican Slave Rebellion of 1831', *Past and Present*, No. 40 (July 1968), 108-25.
4. See Monica Schuler, 'Day-to-Day Resistance to Slavery in the Caribbean during the Eighteenth Century', *African Studies Association of the West Indies*, Bulletin 6 (December 1973), 57-77. Also, Richard Sheridan, 'The Jamaican Slave Insurrection Scare of 1776 and the American Revolution', *Journal of Negro History*, 61:3 (1976), 290-308.
5. Robert Dirks, *The Black Saturnalia: Conflict and its ritual expression on British West Indian Slave Plantations* (Gainesville, 1987). M. Craton, *Testing the Chains*, 335-39.
6. C. L. R. James, *The Black Jacobins: Toussaint L'Ouverture and the San Domingo Revolution* (rpt. 1963). See also Gordon K. Lewis, *Main Currents in Caribbean Thought: The Historical Evolution of Caribbean Society in its Ideological Aspects, 1492-1900* (Baltimore, 1983), 171-239.
7. For example, the Report of the House of Assembly's Select Committee which investigated the causes of the 1816 rebellion in Barbados concluded that the rebellion originated 'solely and entirely in consequence of the

intelligence imparted to the slaves, which intelligence was obtained from the English newspapers, that their freedom had been granted them in England'; and that their hopes for emancipation were 'kept alive' by the information that 'party in England and particularly in Wilberforce . . . were exerting themselves to ameliorate their condition, and ultimately effect their emancipation'. (*Report from a Select Committee Appointed to Inquire into the Origins, Causes, and Progress of the Late Insurrection — April 1816*, Barbados, 1818).

8. For example, J. Oldmixon (*The British Empire in America*, London, 1708) wrote of the rebels involved in the 1692 slave conspiracy in Barbados: 'Did they imagine that Christians would have suffered them to set up a Negro Monarchy, or Republick, in the midst of their Governments? . . . The English, Dutch and French . . . would rather have leagued than suffer this unnatural and dangerous independence. . . . They would have been looked upon as common enemies by all nations . . .' (p. 53). See Beckles, *Black Rebellion*, 48.

9. See Craton, *Testing the Chains*, 109; Beckles, *Black Rebellion*, 110.

10. Edward Long, *The History of Jamaica* (London, 1774); (rpt. 1970), 1, 25.

11. Lewis, *Main Currents*, 111; Long, 11, 270–271.

12. See Mary Turner, *Slaves and Missionaries: The Disintegration of Jamaican Slave Society, 1787–1834* (Chicago, 1982), 153–54, 158; Craton, *Testing the Chains*, 301.

13. See David Geggus, 'British Opinion and the Emergence of Haiti, 1791–1805', in James Walvin (ed.), *Slavery and British Society, 1776–1846* (London, 1982), 123–50; Michael Craton, 'Slave Culture, Resistance and the Achievement of Emancipation in the British West Indies, 1783–1838', in J. Walvin (ed.) *Slavery and British Society, 1776–1846* (Macmillan, 1982), 100–123. See also Hilary Beckles, 'Emancipation by War or Law? Wilberforce and the 1816 Barbados Slave Rebellion', in David Richardson (ed.), *Abolition and its Aftermath: The Historical Context, 1790–1916* (London, 1985), 80–105.

14. Eric Williams, *Capitalism and Slavery* (London, 1944), (rpt. 1964), 208.

15. Craton, 'Slave Culture', 122; also 'Proto-Peasant Revolts? The Late Slave Rebellions in the British West Indies, 1816–1832', *Past and Present*, No. 85 (1979), 99–126; 'What and Who to Whom and What: The Significance of Slave Resistance', in Barbara Solow and Stanley Engerman (eds), *British Capitalism and Caribbean Slavery: The Legacy of Eric Williams* (New York, 1987), 259–82.

16. Davis, in *The Problem of Slavery in the Age of Revolution, 1770–1823* (Ithaca, 1975), marginalised the philosophical impact which persistent slave rebellions in the Caribbean had upon English (European) anti-slavery thought, though conceptually this matter would have been critical to the thought of Locke and Hegel, both of whom he dealt with extensively. He attempted to address the matter in a rather peripheral manner by means of an epilogue entitled 'Toussaint L'Ouverture and the Phenomenology of Mind', which does no

justice to the historical and philosophical vision of either Toussaint or Hegel. See Roger Anstey's two most impressive works: *The Atlantic Slave Trade and British Abolition, 1769–1810* (London, 1975); 'Parliamentary Reform, Methodism, and Anti-Slavery Politics, 1829–1833', *Slavery and Abolition*, 2:3 (1981), 209–26.

17. Seymour Drescher, *Capitalism and Anti-Slavery: British Mobilisation in Comparative Perspective* (London, 1986), 162.

18. Robin Blackburn, *The Overthrow of Colonial Slavery, 1776–1848* (London, 1988), 35.

19. Richard Hart, 'The Formation of a Caribbean Working Class', *The Black Liberator*, 2:2 (1973/74), 131–48; *Slaves who Abolished Slavery: Vol. 1 Blacks in Bondage* (Kingston, 1980); *Blacks in Rebellion* (Kingston, 1985); *Black Jamaicans' Struggle Against Slavery* (London, 1977); 'Cudjoe and the First Maroon War in Jamaica', *Caribbean Historical Review*, 1 (1950), 46–79.

20. See G. Lewis, *Main Currents*, Chap. 4, for an exciting analysis of Caribbean anti-slavery thought and actions.

21. For an interesting case of Haiti's anti-slavery foreign policy in action, see Richard Sheridan, 'From Jamaican Slavery to Haitian Freedom: The Case of the Black Crew of the Pilot Boat, Deep Nine', *Journal of Negro History*, 67:4 (1982), 328–39. See also David Geggus, 'The Enigma of Jamaica in the 1790s: New Light on the Causes of Slave Rebellions', *William and Mary Quarterly*, 44:2 (1987), 274–79.

22. D. Eltis, 'Abolitionist Perceptions of Society after Slavery', in James Walvin (ed.), *Slavery and British Society*, 202–03.

23. Geggus, 'British Opinion', 127.

24. *Annual Register*, 1802, 210–20.

25. Published in the *Morning Post*, 9 November 1802.

26. Geggus, 'British Opinion', 149.

27. Eric Williams, *British Historians and the West Indies* (Trinidad, 1964), 1–13.

28. For an excellent analysis of this theme, see David Eltis, 'Abolitionist Perceptions of Society after Slavery', 195–214. See also W. A. Green, 'Was British Emancipation a Success? The Abolitionist Perspective', in David Richardson (ed.) *Abolition*, 183–203.

29. Lewis, *Main Currents*, 182.

30. Craton, 'The Passion to Exist', 2.

31. *Ibid.*, p. 18.

32. See Beckles, *Black Rebellion*, 4.

33. Lewis, *Main Currents*, 180.

34. See Sidney Mintz and Douglas Hall, 'The Origins of the Jamaican Internal Marketing System', in this volume.

35. Craton, 'Slave Culture', 118. He further states: 'The chief of these aspirations was, naturally, to be free. Yet the form of that freedom seems to have become visualised as that of an independent peasantry, about which the slaves had quite clear notions and of which, in most cases, they already had considerable experience.'

36. Dirks, *Black Saturnalia*, xvi–xvii.

37. *Ibid.*, 167.

38. *Ibid.*, 171.

39. Richard Sheridan, *Sugar and Slavery: An Economic History of the British West Indies, 1625–1775* (Bridgetown, 1974), 254.

66

Caliban, Ariel, and Unprospero in the Conflict of Creolization: A Study of the Slave Revolt in Jamaica in 1831-32

KAMAU BRATHWAITE

> I think he will carry this island home in his pocket, and give it to his son for an apple.
>
> William Shakespeare, *The Tempest*

Introduction

Since setting out the ideas and outlines of creolization in *The Development of Creole Society in Jamaica, 1770-1820,*[1] I have attempted to continue my exploration of the subject/concept in several ways. In *Contradictory Omens*[2] I did what I said ought to be done: I tested and extended the concept to the post-emancipation period, when creolization became "complicated" by the introduction of Asian immigrants from China and India, and by significant changes in the role of blacks and coloureds in the local society. There was also a significant change in the role of the metropole increasingly with "modernization," and the "cultural influence" of Americanization (films, TV, tourists, etc.) has carried this a stage further and has set up new pressures and challenges within the post-emancipation/contemporary context. In *Kumina*[3] and in this study I have attempted to examine, in some detail, the creolizing influence on Afro-Caribbeans (specifically of Jamaicans) of African culture, as handed down and present in the society as (1) *lore* (direct and conscious teaching), (2) *behaviour* (energy patterns of expression, speech, movement and socio-intellectual praxis) and (3) *ideological myth* (all three of these being subsumed into the term *nam,* used in the text), which have somehow kept Afro-Carib-

bean cultural expression "African" and/or "black," especially at moments of crisis or in the so-called margins of the society despite the obvious material and social advantages of Afro-Saxonism, for instance. *Kumina* is a socio-cultural and linguistic study of Afro-creolization; while this article is a historical account of the 1831 slave revolt in Jamaica, seen as a crucial moment of competing orientations within the developing creole matrix. My model of creolization has therefore in many senses been considerably extended; it has become, for one thing, less linear and "progressive," more prismatic, and includes more comprehensively than formerly a sense of cultural interaction not only among all elements of the "tropical plantation," but also between these elements at certain metropolitan aspects (look at popular music for instance) of the continent.

The Process

Our sense of the process must begin with a firm sense of the nature and qualities of the ancestral/originating cultures of our complex. Since nearly all these ancestral cultures originated outside the New World, their characteristics with regard to transferability – and the shape and nature of their transport – must be understood and discussed; as must their shape and nature after impact, as it were: debasements, renewals, survivals, alliances, growth/decline, influence. The *missile* European transport, for example, was quite different in nature and impact and influence, from that, say, of the African *capsule* We have, too, to be aware of and consider the attitude of the new-impacted ancestors to their old homelands (the Spaniards, for instance, proudly brought their flags and crosses; the indentured Indians who elected to become "creole" tried to pretend that they were no longer Indian); and this, in many ways, also influenced their attitude to the new environment: discover explore, exploit, destroy (the missile); learn, conserve, nourish (the capsule); and this in turn affected attitudes to the other cultures of the environment. And it was that same ancestral past the shape of the transport from that past, the fragmentations of impact and its consequences in death and resurrection, which slowly influenced what the various creole elements would define, essentially, as their *future*: their vision of continuation/fragment (the plural society) or wholeness (prismatic possibility).

Product(s)

This is above all a question/problem of perception. One view – the monolithic, paradoxically plural-conceives of society as being a single sacred construct, with a single socio-cultural product: political nationality. But practice has never made much sense of this theory; and for a long time we have had to bear the burden of perceiving of ourselves as "nations" ("West Indians") without norms (somatic, intellectual, aesthetic); and to counter this breakdown in expectation, we developed the pessimistic notion of a plural society of one "official" nation/caste, ruling by force and alliance with the metropole, and a number of inferior and deprived subcultures, with their peculiar mores: linguistic, kin-sense, cook-style, etc; but having no viability or visibility as long as they remained eccentric or marginal. The prismatic concept, on the other hand, conceives of all resident cultures as equal and contiguous, despite the accidents of political history, each developing its own lifestyle from the spirit of its ancestors, but modified – and increasingly so – through interaction with the environment and the other cultures of the environment, until residence within the environment – *nativization* – becomes the process (creolization) through which all begin to share a style, even though that style will retain vestiges (with

occasional national/cultural revivals back towards particular ancestors) of their original/ancestral heritage.

Other Aspects of the Subject

These, it will be readily seen, are general comments and refer largely to the theoretical aspects of the subject. My paper, however, raises the historical problem of the effect of *colonialism* on creolization: in a situation where inter-culturation was being made to take place (or rather, where a very conscious attempt was made to force the process into certain forms and channels, cut by whip and legislation) in a predetermined manner, with the inferior/superior ranking of the inherited system maintained and extended. In such a situation, the persons and communities involved in this colonial/creolization had certain choices, each with its consequences. There could be an *acceptance* of the colonial system: as was done of course by nearly all, if not all, the whites of the culture, and by those nonwhites who felt that acceptance was worth their while, or who had been bribed or coerced into it, or who had come into it through some accident or design of birth. There was also, arising from this acceptance situation, the *ambiguous product*: the freedom faced with the possibility of privileges and "perks," the coloured or cultural mulatto, somatically defined as one thing; often socially promoted as something else; but never "pure," since he was without ancestors. The *Ariel personality type*, discussed in this paper, comes out of this; as do all the other personality types of creole culture: Prospero and Unprospero; Quashie/Sambo, Caliban (the would-be rebel or house slave), Tacky, (the rebel), Ananse (the conscious trickster), Kwesi (the anancy-man who has come to believe his own deceptions); the maroon; Sycorax, the obeahman or native preacher, suggesting an alternative to the system; Ariel (already mentioned);Alonso (the metropolitical presence), and Gonzalo, the metropolitan philosopher in the tropics: liberal, well-meaning, utopian and single-mindedly devoted to his own monolith and – logue.

Finally, as the developments from 1820 to 1831 suggest we must also constantly consider *creolization* and *time*, *creolization* and *change;* the effect of education on the process; the effect of changing vision and self-image; the effect of ideology on the system (the Revolutions of France, Haiti, Industry, the cosmos; word into print, etc.); and, connected with this, the effect of outside influences as a form not only of colonization but also of *modernization.*

Perception and Description of the Process

All that I have said above implies a certain kind of (prismatic) perception and the ability – at least the attempt – to describe that perception: the development of a *quadrilateral* rather than a linear approach: collage, metaphor, nonarchival sources, which have their own shape, their own pressure of outline. "Classical" historiography assumes a more or less ordered development of society, based on ancient residential contact between the elements of its culture. On the other hand, New World history and society, based upon the enigma of the Amerindians and involving immigrant cultures of essentially different paradigms, connected through violence and the self-concepts we call racism, and the ordinations of colonialism, which yet produced something creative and new, needs its surrealism (or sourealism) to express what it can of the extraordinary complicity of what we call creolization. In *The Development of Creole Society in Jamaica*,[1] I was more or less concerned with the foundations (if not the origins) of the process, during the "high" period of slavery (1770-1820) in a particular territory. I was concerned, in that first essay, with this process as it affected social institutions, private and public cultural expression, habit, custom and attitude of the various groups involved to their inherited sense of norm/ideal:

the ancestor; and to the new development: the creole. In *Caribbean Man in Space and Time* and more especially in *Contradictory Omens*,[2] I tried to move the concept closer to my growing sense of reality by trying to recognize and deal with the extension of the process in *time*; from slavery then, through to the shadow of independence; and in *prismatic, space*: not simply as white: black: brown; but as aboriginal, maroon and multivariate: the various orientations of the fixed and mixed . . .

But all this was based upon the assumption that it was taking place within a context of (involuntary) consensus, which meant, to give one example, that marronage and slave revolts could be viewed only as eccentric to creolization: though it was/is obvious that the reality of the situation encompassed both crisis and consensus, bread and bomb-blast.

In this paper, therefore, I am taking a look at the 1831-32 slave rebellion in Jamaica, examining, as it were, its trigger(s) and explosion, trying to determine what effect it had on the existing structure, the existing, developing product; how far, indeed, the revolt with its nomen of break and fracture was in fact inscrutable paradox: cement of process, re-encreolization.

At the basis of this discussion will be certain (well known) symbols from Shakespeare's *The Tempest* already used by several Third World writers and representative here of certain throats or throttles (forces) within slave society:

Alonso: Political metropole;
Prospero, or rather *Unprospero*: slave-owning planter;
Ariel, the go-between, sometimes mistaken for *Aerial* (the press, mass media), usually an

Table 66.1: Vital Statistics: All-Parish

	Tried	Executed	Killed	Transported	Whipped	Wounded
Slaves	406	96	209	–	–	23
Freemen	14	6	–	5	3	–
White	1	–	14	–	–	12
pfc	7	–	3	–	–	2
Free blacks	–	–	–	–	–	–
Women (black/slave)	38	2	–	–	–	–
Women (col/slave)	1	–	–	–	–	–

Source: CO 137/185:52-59, 61, 63, 94-97, 220-221, 237-241.

Table 66.2:   Vital Statistics: St James

	Tried	Executed	Killed	Wounded
Slaves	109	82/77	124/82	14
Freemen	–	–	–	–
White	–	–	8	–
pfc	–	–	–	–
Free blacks	–	–	–	–
African	21	18/19	25	–
Creole	88	64/58	57	–
Women (black)	3	1	–	–
Women (col)	–	–	–	–
Women (african)	–	–	1	–
Women (creole)	–	1	5	–
Women (slave)	–	–	6	–

Sources :CO 137/185:53-59, 61, 94-97, 220-221, 237-241; Higman's Thesis:[8] 432, Table 54.

educated slave or freedman open to "white" creolization and technology;

Caliban, the black/slave rebel, trying, from cultural impulse, to return to or align himself with his submerged/maroon ancestral heritage as represented by *Sycorax*, his mother, in whom resides the quality of soul grit or kernel, known as *nam*.

But by 1831-32, despite their differences, Prospero, Ariel and Caliban were all creoles: that is, they had a lifestyle that was tropical, slave/colonial and dependent on/independent of the metropole. But to be "creole" didn't completely mean or imply satisfaction, stabilization or completion of a process quite the opposite, in fact. To be creole in the changing world of the early nineteenth century was to be in a state of constant bias (from/towards) the ancestral cultures. Prospero wanted to be more white again. Caliban wished to assert, more comprehensively than his equipment allowed, his negritude. (Ariel produced/picked up/transmitted the various vibrations). But because of metropolitan actions and precautions – and the history of their own local development – neither Prospero nor Caliban could return to the imagined idyll. Nor could they, since their sense of identity was, in a sense, in crisis, cease from striving towards it. We shall soon see how the local white establishment expressed itself on this. Caliban's action is what they were reacting to: the most widespread and significant revolt in Jamaica's history: the Christmas Rebellion of 1831/1832: an insurrec-

tion involving 20,000[4]/50,000[5] slaves, nine parishes, [6,7] hundreds of deaths (See Tables 66.1 and 66.2) and over a £1 million worth of damage to the planter [16] and which led to the almost immediate emancipation of Caliban by Alonso. My contention is that the revolt was itself an aspect of creolization.

Causes of the Rebellion

The "causes" of the rebellion varied, depending on the viewpoint of the following:

1. *Local white establishment.*
2. *Metropolitan establishment*
3. *Metropolitan nonestablishment*. This included missionaries, colonial reformers, etc.
4. *The nam/ariel crisis among the slaves.*

Only the viewpoint of the local white Establishment will be documented here, since it is the one that raises issues and images pertinent to the subject.

The primary and most powerful cause arose from a civil excitement created in the minds of our Slaves generally, by the unceasing and unconstitutional interference of His Majesty's Ministers with our local legislature, in regard to the passing of laws for their government, with the intemperate expression of the sentiments of the present Ministers, as well as other individuals in the Commons House of Parliament in Great Britain, on the subject of slavery; such discussions, coupled with the false and wicked reports of the Anti-Slavery Society, having been industriously circulated, by the aid of the press, throughout the Island as well as the British Empire.

Secondly, from a delusive expectation produced among the whole of the Slave Population of the machinations of crafty and evil-disposed persons, who, taking advantage of the prevailing excitement, imposed upon their disturbed imaginations a belief that they were to be free after Christmas; and in the event of freedom being withheld from them, they must be prepared to fight for it.

Thirdly, from a mischievous abuse existing in the system adopted by different religious sects in this Island, termed Baptists, Wesleyan Methodists and Moravians, by their recognizing gradations of rank among such of our Slaves as had become converts to their doctrines, whereby the less ambitious and more peaceable among them were made the dupes of the artful and intelligent, who had been selected by the preachers of those particular sects to fill the higher offices in their chapels under the denomination of rulers, elders, leaders and helpers.

And lastly, the public discussions of the free inhabitants here, consequent upon the continued suggestions made by the King's Ministers regarding further measures of amelioration to be introduced into the Slave Code of this Island, and the preaching and teaching of the religious sects called Baptists, Wesleyan Methodists and Moravians (but more particularly the sect termed Baptists), which had the effect of producing in the minds of the Slaves a belief that they could not serve both a Spiritual and a Temporal Master; thereby occasioning them to resist the lawful authority of their Temporal, under the delusion of rendering themselves more acceptable to a Spiritual Master.[9]

Commentary

Three basic image/concepts will be observed above:

1. Fear/dislike of external/metropolitan intrusion from Alonso (the British Parliament), from Gonzalo (the anti-slavery/humanitarian movement) and from Aerial (the liberal press).
2. Mythologies of servitude: that there was a link, among the slaves, between Christmas and freedom, and that the missionaries (Gonzalo) and certain intelligent (!) slave leaders (Caliban) were connected with this.
3. That there were worlds alternative to the plantation: a temporal world of amelioration, if not freedom; a spiritual world of Christianity and "heavenly" freedom; and a new cultural world of literate, informed subordinates, with sources of imagination (negritude) of their own.

Had Prospero (UnProspero) been able to cope with these life/metaphors, there would obviously have been no rebellion, since the culture – forces of the *status quo* would have been successfully

in operation. But ever since the abolition of the slave trade, the alliance between Prospero and Alonso had been breaking down; and ever since the Haitian revolution, Caliban was beginning to discount the omnipotence of Prospero's magic and was at last learning how to circumvent the influence of his servant, Ariel. But it was not until the 1820s, with the loss of metaphorical initiative by Prospero, that the two nodes of the mercantilist/ plantation system began to overload under the pressure of what had become a crisis.

The Prospero/Alonso Crisis

Prospero, despite his books, was a product of the *alter-Renaissance*: the movement towards anti-spiritual and anti-intellectual materialism fostered by the slave plantation. Despite his books, Prospero's tropical polity regressed from nation-state to barbarian estate, from developing to reactionary world, from science to magical unreality. Attempts by Metropolitan Alonso, therefore, to maintain control, to keep in touch, even, were resented as (liberal) *Intrusion*, interference in the internal affairs, etc. *Reform* was resisted because it would remove planter influence at Court and introduce Amelioration at home. Renaissance scientific and technological developments were ignored because of the fear that they would adversely affect the local feudal-manpowered labour force. New ideas – romanticism, humanitarianism, laissez-faire, evangelical Christianity – and the spread of literacy through the printing press/newspaper were also to be resisted. And not of course in the name of local illiberalism, but with the contention that such intrusions from the inner metropole would (could) only upset the (delicate) balance, as already displayed in the extract above, between citizen and slave, white and black, in the society. Had the creolization process turned the way Prospero had (naturally) wanted it to: ac/culturation: the imitation of his fractured image by Caliban, it might not have been so bad. But Caliban was already (had in fact been all along) creating for himself a language of resistance/revolt based upon his own mythology of survival (what Prospero would have called the mythology of servitude). And this creation was real in that it was a force that could (would) affect the Other. Flexible (organically growing) Prospero could open himself to it and absorb it and its consequences; and he could be organically altered in the process, even though he continued to "control" (something his American cousins seem to have understood or at least are beginning to understand); or inflexible Unprospero, he could ignore, shut out, resist the Caliban alternative so that change would appear only as crack in the armour: riot, revolt, rebellion.

The Slave Ariel/Caliban Crisis

Unprospero, in other words, had created a fortress for Caliban to attack. But within the slave/plantation culture, there was also a growing crisis of identity and orientation,[17] the unresolution of which was causing tension and conflict – as it still does today – within the "less fortunate" (?) culture; and the two main groups involved were those (Ariels) increasingly concerned with (what their masters called) Liberal Metropolitan Intrusions (receivers of messages) and those (*nams*) increasingly concerned with a return to the Ancestral Heritage.

. . . they were in the habit of reading the newspapers themselves, or paying a gratuity of five pence to persons who would when they happened to hear it contained good news for them.

These circumstances together perhaps with the progress of civilization brought about by the provisions of the legislature here, and by the facility afforded for instruction by the proprietors themselves, by which the slaves begin to form some imperfect idea of the moral distinction between freedom and slavery, have, in my opinion, been the cause of the rebellion; for it is a very remarkable fact, that the head and confidential slaves, and consequently the most intelligent, have been the most active rebels.[18]

When we had sat down, Baily looked for an old newspaper and said, "This is not the right one; this is four months old, and this tells us that eight years back, women were not to get any flogging . . .

Richard Baily said that he had found the other paper under his bed . . . he knew it by the ship on the top . . . he said that the paper said, that the English people will not submit under the *brutish custom any longer.*[19]

What is interesting here is that slave Ariel Baily is not only receiving messages from the Liberal Intrusive Metropole, but that he recognizes its role and function in the creolizing process: that the Englishman at home, as part of the mercantilist empire, was himself being affected by the corruption at the extremities. It was a view also held, of course, by the missionaries (at least it was an argument employed by them), and since a missionary is here reporting on Baily, he might of course have put the notion into Baily's mouth. But it doesn't deny the awareness, among Ariels (since the missionaries were themselves white Ariels) of the structural/functional relationship between colony and metropole and its culturative significance on both colony *and* metropole. Hence Ariel's alliance – and here we differ significantly and not unnaturally with Shakespeare's interpretation – not only with Unprospero, but with Alonso. Ariel, in fact, because of his liberal and metropolitan allegiances, was as much a rebel as Caliban would be (the difference would lie in the aesthetic paradigms of the new regime) and indeed was more ready (fatal trap) than Caliban to take over and assume Unprospero's symbolic hat and hauteur.

I was sitting on the steps of the Great House the day it was burnt . . . I took up my Master's hat, and Alick took it out of my hand and went into the Stables and took Masters big mare – saddled it, and rode round the canes . . . [20]

This leads in the end to nothing – or nothing but recapture and disaster – and comes about because, as I shall try to demonstrate later, Ariel, moving towards the metropole from too shallow a base, becomes acculturated (assimilated saxonized, or what have you) so that he becomes a new *thing*, a product, rather than a new and continuing force. Compare Ariel's action above, for instance, with Caliban's:

On Friday [after Christmas] Busha came and said we must go to work, if they did not . . . he would bring a Guard. John Baillie then got vexed because Busha told him . . . to work, and run down the Hill, and when the Busha rode down the hill to the road they meet and John Baillie, Thomas Baillie, John Brown, John Gordon and John Haughton stopped the Busha at the well – heard Thomas Baillie say he carried his hoe and gave it to the Busha . . . [21]

Which is interpreted: that symbol of the hoe or plough: from *item* to *loa*: by George Lamming, meditating upon the Haitian Revolution, as follows:

It must have been clear to the owner that the mournful silence of this property contained a danger which would last as long as their hands were alive. One day some change akin to mystery would reveal itself through these man-shaped ploughs. The mystery would assume the behavior of a plough which refused contact with a free hand. Imagine a plough in the field. Ordinary as ever, prongs and spine unchanged, it is simply there, stuck to its post beside the cane shoot. Then some hand, identical with the routine of its work, reaches to lift this familiar instrument. But the plough escapes contact. It refuses to surrender its present position. There is a change in the relation between this plough and one free hand. The crops wait and wonder what will happen next. More hands arrive to confirm the extraordinary conduct of this plough; but no one can explain the terror of those hands as they withdraw from the plough. Some new sight as well as some new sense of language is required to bear witness to the miracle of the plough which now talks. For as those hands in unison move forward, the plough achieves a somersault which reverses its traditional posture. Its head goes into the ground, and the prongs, throat-near, stand erect in the air, ten points of steel announcing danger.[22]

The Missionaries

But the most important, most intimate (as intimate, that is, as the structural racism and apartheid system would allow) ally of slave Ariel was the Christian missionary, especially the Baptist evangelical, product of the metropolitan plantation: the great, crowded, spreading wastelands of the burgeoning industrial ghettoes of midland and northern England.[23] Themselves Aerials of this situation, the missionaries came from a hard tradition of reading – the Bible, schoolbook, Bunyan – and it was this need to read the word, literacy, that they passed on to their Ariel slaves. And it was the symbolic power of this new *nommo*, plus the obvious *rite de passage* that baptism involved, that attracted the bondsmen to the Baptists.

Literacy

The number of children attending the mission schools is . . . little guide to the number of slaves affected by missionary education. In the vicinity of the mission stations any ambitious adult could find means of instruction; school children in Kingston, for example, earned 3d to 10d a week teaching adults to read.[24]

The first mission school – the East Queen Street Baptist School in Kingston – was established in 1822. There followed the Spanish Town Baptist School in 1825, the Anglican Day School, Kingston, in 1826, the Spanish Town Anglican in 1828 and the Wesleyan Day School, Kingston, in 1829. By 1830, according to Mary Reckord,[25] the Mission day schools served in all some 1300 children, of whom about 900 were slaves.

Baptism

Baptist candidates were admitted to their church at an impressive ceremony. During the night before Baptism

they came in with their friends from the surrounding country to spend the night in the chapel. In the very early hours of the morning the missionary joined them for prayer; then, before sunrise, the company moved to the nearest river or sea-shore. The candidates, all robed in white, were assembled by the class leaders while the missionary waded waist-deep into the water and the ceremony began. Each candidate was led by his class leader to the missionary who, emphasising once more that Baptism must mark a change of heart, immersed him ... The orderly crowds, the white robed candidates, the sacrificial [?] fires and the holy music under the luminous dome of the sky before sunrise, created a memorable occasion.[26]

But above all the Ariel slave, and especially the radical Ariel slave, gained two important advantages (in addition, that is, to literacy) from the missionary contact: a public ("permitted") organization: the church/congregation: and the smaller, even more vital, because less visible, classes; and an ideology: salvation: (emancipation): and its sociopolitical spinoffs and consequences: liberty, equality, fraternity. It was on this front, and from this alliance, that Prospero most acutely perceived the assault on his fortress to have been launched.

There was a chapel at Montego Bay capable of holding from 2000 to 3000 persons. At that chapel a Baptist missionary regularly preached and taught. He had another chapel at some distance in the country where he also occasionally attended. At these places of worship the congregation was frequently altogether slaves. It is no wonder if, among so large a body, there were persons of violent passions and criminal intentions; the meeting, under a religious pretext, afforded such persons opportunities of disseminating their mischievous principles. The division of the Baptists into leaders and inferior grades prepared the slaves to act under command. The doctrines of the Baptist minister himself may have been free from intentional guilt, but nevertheless many have *been peverted by ill-disposed slaves* to forward their malpractices . . . I am of opinion, that whenever societies are permitted to be formed in this island, under whatever denomination they may pass, if they are composed entirely of slaves, are permitted to congregate in large masses without the admixture of those superiors whom they are in the habit of being controlled by; if they act under leaders and have passports under the name of tickets, which will carry them all over the island, that under such circumstances we may expect periodical rebellions.[27]

Coloured Ariel

The question of possession: true ownership/belonging: is one that will always exercise creole societies: non-native natives: and especially slave Caliban, most dispossessed of all:

This island's mine, by Sycorax my mother,
Which 'thou tak'st from me. When thou cam'st first
Thou strok'st me and made much of me, wouldst give me
Water with berries in't, and teach me how
To name the bigger light, and how the less,
That burn by day and night; and then I lov'd thee,
And show'd thee all the qualities o' th' isle,
The fresh springs, brine-pits, barren place and fertile.
Curs'd be I that did so: All the charms
Of Sycorax, toads, beetles, bats, light on you!
For I am all the subjects that you have,
Which first was mine own king . . . [28]

To which, of course, Prospero replies with the stereotypes: liar, sale negro and sexual violator of Miss Ann's pale purity: which forces Caliban to articulate the barb and crux of the issue: "The red plague rid you/For learning me your language."[29] But for Ariel/Aerial, already in love with that language and committed to its technology of transmission, there could be no such freedom of repudiation. There would always be a sense of obligation. The life of Edward Jordon provides an example.

Edward Jordon

Edward Jordon, mulatto, born slave, perhaps born free,[30] son of a (white) planter from Barbados, and a black (?) submerged mother,[31] was 31-32 years old when Caliban's last great rebellion took place. If not born free, he was probably manumitted quite early on, because by the age of 23, we find him an active member of the Kingston Committee of Coloureds, agitating for civil rights. In July 1829, with Robert Osborne, another free coloured, he launched *The Watchman*, the first coloured-owned and run newspaper in the British colonies, which immediately identified itself with the Liberal Metropolitan Intrusion: the humanitarian movement in Britain and the rights of dissenting ministers in Jamaica.[32] Jordon's position as a free coloured journalist-politician and his alliance with the inner metropole were both strengthened by the victory of the metropolitan liberals in the Lescence-Escoffery case against the plantocracy in 1829, which led to the final surge of free coloured agitation, which in turn led to the Disabilities Act of 1830, which granted "freedmen" the same civil rights as born Englishmen.

It is at this juncture that the real problems started: the old abiding/lurking problem of iden-

tity, identification, allegiance. The Disabilities Act meant that from henceforward Jordon had a choice. He could continue his alliance with the metropole (though since the "victory," as so often happens, there was a cooling off of the connection), or he could (try to) become a Jamaican, which in turn involved other choices: what kind of Jamaican? There was Prospero's isle and Caliban's island. George William Gordon, another political free coloured, also probably born a slave, was in 1865 to make one kind of choice: Caliban and the gallows. Jordon went the other way. Even during the period of agitation for civil rights he could not bring himself to include free blacks in his programme,[33] and in fact it was Alonso, the British Government, not Ariel Jordon, who insisted on an equality of freedom if there was to be such for freedmen: blacks and coloured. So that, like Prospero, Jordon's sense of possession of the island, *excluded* certain people/forces; and partial possessions, to defend themselves, have to become conservative, which is what happened to Jordon, although this was obscured for some time because of the lingering influence upon him of the metropolitan liberal alliance. But, as usual, the test and rubicon came with the crisis of the black majority rebellion. Jordon could not but deplore the violent planter reaction to the revolt of Christmas 1831; and when in *The Watchman* (7 April 1832) there appeared to be a gloat over the apparent triumph of Jordon's interests (another white alliance), the local elite decided it was time to break him for seditious libel.

We have been consistent throughout [Jordon said], and now that the Member for Westmoreland [planter Beaumont] has come over to our side, we shall be happy with him, and the other friends of humanity, to give a long pull, a strong pull together until we bring the system down by the run – knock off the fetters, and let the oppressed go free.[34]

Jordon, in the Lescence-Escoffery tradition, was rescued by the metropolitan liberals, but it was the end of his "faceteyness". Coloured Ariel had learnt his lesson: one had to make a choice of one's cultural (and political) orientation if one were to live (and succeed) in the barbarian planter environment. That same year (1832) there was a post-Disabilities Act election at which the free coloureds and the free blacks both put up candidates for the Kingston Common Council. With black support, the coloured candidate, Watkis, was elected. But instead of supporting, in their turn, the black candidate, Rugless, as agreed, the coloureds engineered the election of Jordon instead.[35] It was the beginning of Ariel's apprenticeship to UnProspero: vestryman, assemblyman, lieutenant of militia, invitations to King's House, Asst. Judge of the Court of Common Pleas ... By 1838, Ariel had become editor of the planters' *Morning Journal*; by 1839 he was a manager of a planter's bank, a Companion of the Order of Bath (1860), Speaker of the House of Assembly (1861-64) and Island Secretary (almost Governor!), 1864.

In the end, under pressure of the second great black crisis, the Rebellion of 1865 and its aftermath, Jordon had to make (for him) an even bitterer choice: between Alonso and Unprospero. On his deathbed, in 1869, he had his C.B. returned to Alonso "out of bitterness and disappointment with what his obituary called the galling and oppressive restriction [the abrogation of the (white) Jamaica constitution by the British Government] which at present excludes a Jamaican, however well qualified otherwise, from filling permanently [he had been so close!] the higher offices of trust in Jamaica".[36] But even here there was a twist, because it was UnProspero, for whom Jordon had betrayed so much, who had moved to stop him from assuming permanent high office.

The Slave/Ariel Crisis

The case of slave Ariel is of course different. Sam Sharpe, leader of the 1831 slave rebellion, could read, and to this extent he was involved in the Liberal Metropolitan Intrusion. He was also a deacon in the Baptist Church; which gave him an even more intimate relationship with metropolitan values. But the quality of the alliance differed radically from that of the other Ariels because, for one thing, he had no sense of obligation to the inner metropole – or to any metropole for that matter. He was one of the "ingrates." Nor could he, like Jordon, *invest* in aerials. There was no chance of his ever owning a printing press or becoming a newspaper editor or proprietor, and so the great entanglements of renaissance technology were denied to him. And when he used the press or print, he used it not to browse or graze but to *confirm*: "Sharpe said I know we are *free*, I have read it in the English papers." [37] Besides, the oral context of knowledge in which Sharpe was rooted meant that unlike Jordon, who (had to) believe the written word as Word, Sharpe absorbed and converted into the communal literacy of his time, what the books call *rumour*. So that the *ship*, which was used by Richard Baily (mentioned above) to identify a particular newspaper, was also the *freedom ship* on which Missionary Burchell was supposed to be bringing the Freedom Paper from Alonso and is the same ship that the present day Rastafari know will come to take them back to Ityopia. Here, in other words, was subversive material that couldn't be charged with seditious libel; which couldn't even be controlled by Gonzalo, the well-meaning missionaries. Hence William Knibb's sermon at Crooked Spring on the verge of the volcano: 27 December 1831. I shall attempt, during this quotation, to indicate the various syndromes or signals employed by Knibb in his effort to retain control over a force of slave Ariels who were in fact Lamming's converted ploughs – cannon: cannibal: calibans:

Gonzalo

My dear hearers, and especially those of you who constantly attend at the chapel, and are members of Crooked Spring, or other Baptist churches, pay great attention to what I am about to say. It is now seven years since I left England to preach the gospel to you, and when I came, I made up my mind to live and die to promote your spiritual welfare. Never did I enter the pulpit with such painful feelings as at present. Till yesterday I had hoped that God had blessed my poor labours and the labours of your dear minister [Burchell] now in England for his health, who loves you and prays for you, and who tells me that he hopes soon to return to you. But I am pained to the soul to hear that many of you have agreed not to go to your work after Christmas; and I fear it is too true. I learn that some wicked persons have persuaded you that the king

Alonso Syndrome

has made you free. Hear me, I love your souls ... I would not tell you a lie for the world. What you have been told is false – false as hell can make it. I entreat you not to believe it, but go to your work as usual. If you have any love for Jesus Christ, to religion, to your ministers:

Metro/Lib Syndrome

to those kind friends in England who have given money to help you build this chapel, be not led away by wicked men. You are too ready to listen to and believe what they tell you, instead of

Patronage

coming to your minister who you know will tell you the truth. God commands you to be obedient to your master;

God/Master

if you do as he commands, you may expect his blessing; but if you do not, he will call you to account for it at the Judgement day. If you refuse to work and are punished, you will suffer justly;

Communal Rejection Syndrome

and every friend you have must and will turn his back upon you.[38]

It was a perfectly judged and executed appeal from Gonzalo to Ariel, and it would no doubt have worked if the transformation from Ariel to Caliban hadn't taken place in that congregation/community. As the missionary recorder reports it:

Much dissatisfaction was manifested by some of the slaves . . ., and many murmurs were heard. This plain contradiction of their error – this sudden dashing of their fond hopes of freedom – overcame their patience, and called forth the bad [black?] passions of their nature. They said that 'Parson Knibb had no business to meddle with the free paper – *that the white people had bribed Mr. Blyth to tell lie, and that Mr. Blyth had given Mr. Knibb half the money to keep free-paper from them'*

So angry were they with Mr. Knibb, for this interference to frustrate their intentions, that they declared they would have maltreated him, had he not had so many [black] ministers, with him.[39]

Of course, for political reasons, the missionaries had to claim that their congregations remained loyal during the disturbances; that is, it was claimed that Christianized (pacified) communities did not take part in the insurrection. This was shifted, as the evidence to the contrary shifted, to the claim that they (the missionaries) were ignorant (had been kept ignorant) of slave Ariel's secret activities, and finally, twenty years after the revolt and its liberation outcome, we find the Baptists acknowledging, indeed claiming Sharpe's role as leader of the revolt; but of course as martyr; crusader in the cause of (Christian) freedom. In a letter to *The Freeman*, dated 21 November 1855, we find the Rev. P.H. Cornford, Burchell's successor at Montego Bay, speaking of Sharpe's "piety and patriotism." Indeed, as the missionaries warmed to their new acculturation of Caliban, the martyred Sharpe begins to take on a Christ-like suffering hagiography. Cornford, the chief architect of the new conceptual monument, in his account of victim/victor's death and burial, introduces the sacred ikon of Joseph of Arimathaea, a Mobay Jew referred to in the texts as "L" (probably Levien), who approached Pilate and asked if he could take

the body from the cross or gallows; while Sharpe himself, condemned by all for administering dreaded African and obeah oaths and sealing them with gunpowder and blood, the murderer, was now transfigured:

But where [asked Cornford] [in the midst of all that bloodshed and violence]was the holy man? What part now would the Christian play? Does he still hold fast to his integrity? Can his garments be always white?[40]

And for that purity of raiment there could be no bloodshed; Sharpe, even in the midst of daggers, had determined to remain nonviolent and holy holy holy now in nomine:

But mark, he can take no part with them: He will take no arms of any kind. He simply dwells in their [the rebels] midst to counsel, to restrain . . . to *bless*.[41]

And finally there is the long walk to Montego Bay, giving himself up for the sake of the missionaries and the Church's one foundation; the "long lonely cavalry" [sic] to Calvary and apotheosis:

I saw him come [Cornford reporting Levien] with his face as bright, and his form as sweet, as if he had achieved some glorious victory.[42]

Which indeed he had, except that it was inverted: a *post facto* Ariel deliberately created by Gonzalo, again using the technology of communication (the press) in order to give the impression that his relationship and control of slave Ariel had been closer than it was. A deliberate, in fact, rewriting of history in order to retain the sense that it was the liberal European whose cultural initiative (influence upon the pagan mass) was essentially responsible for the revolutionary changes wrought within Jamaica (and the plantation generally) by the emancipation of the slaves. According to Aerial, therefore, the slave revolt of 1831 and the victory of emancipation that followed was a result of an alliance between the Inner Metropole, the missionary Gonzalos and local loyal Ariels. But there is an alternative reading: that the revolt and victory were achieved, with ambiguous and tangential "alliance" with the inner metropole it is true; but with leadership and spiritual fuel supplied by Caliban.

Caliban and the Slave/Ariel Crisis

The concept of slave Ariel contains a contradiction, as William Styron recognized in his fictional account of Nat Turner's rebellion, which was taking place at almost the same time as Sam Sharpe's in Jamaica. The contradiction has to do with the concepts/reality of *free* and *unfree*. Ariel is a "free" spirit, even if under the control of some mundane magic or busha. But *slave* doesn't have this quality, but its opposite. Here is an earthbound, earth nourished creature, legally and temporally mastered, but answering to no metaphysical owner (since none existed under the unspiritual terms of his servitude). Any act or action not prescribed by the routine of the plantation could therefore be an act of rebellion and every act of rebellion could be a step of (self-) discovery, an illumination of the existential cosmos as Fanon and before him Garvey declared:

Where is the black man's Government? where is his King and his kingdom? Where is his President, his country and his ambassador, his army, his navy, his men of big affairs? I could not find them, and then I declared, "I will help to make them."[43]

Without nation the slave could have no notion of patriotism; without God, he could have no religion; without philosophers and priests, he could develop no ethical system; without a sense of self, he could have no conscience; with chains, in other words, he could not be an Ariel. But he could learn, he could receive information, he could become an Aerial. And this, throughout the period of slavery, is what he was doing; and thanks to the missionary teachers, the process was significantly accelerated after 1815. But any tendency or desire or urge to go further and convert the Aerial to Ariel, to enter fully into the Euro-creolizing or ac/culturative process, was resisted by all the living forces that defined him: the "negative," invisible, "forbidden," submerged culture of Sycorax, his mother. There were of course individual slaves who desired to make the break; some who could be bribed into making the break. But these were exceptions; and even for them there had to be a symbolic, even a psychological *rite de passage*.[44] But the average and majority of slaves were bound by instinct and their custom to their custom: to their mother's milk and buried navel string. So that Sam Sharpe could never have been the Christian hero made him by the missionaries because although he was a deacon in the Baptist church he was also, unknown and invisible to the missionaries who thought they patronized his soul, a

"ruler" in his own right in his own people's church.

Maroon/Ancestral "Cults"

This is an important aspect of this study, subject to some reiteration, because we should observe, as we undertake an examination of its origins and development, that the idea of creolization as an ac/culturative, even an inter-culturative process between "black" and "white," with the (subordinate) black absorbing "progressive" ideas and technology from the white, has to be modified into a more complex vision in which appears the notion of *negative* or *regressive creolization:* a self-conscious refusal to borrow or be influenced by the Other, and a coincident desire to fall back upon, unearth, recognize elements in the maroon or ancestral culture that will preserve or apparently preserve the unique identity of the group. This quality of consciousness is recognized in all modern societies as one of the roots of nationalism. But it should be noted that the history of the American plantation begins with this: Palmares, Black Caribs, the Jamaican maroons. The formation of these root communities was no whim or overnight affair, result of no neglect from Prospero-Alonso forces. The Jamaican community, for instance, established itself in 1655, using the opportunity of the British takeover of the island, and they were engaged in almost constant combat with the army, pioneers and militia volunteers until 1739, when a truce established maroon independence within the colony. And this victory was won and nourished not on "syncretisms" (imitations of the enemy), but on creative improvisations based upon the sure and shored-up fragments of a living "native" culture. Indeed, it is only because the local white establishment was, at that time still flexible and growing enough to learn from/ absorb some of the techniques/culture of the maroons (making that truce, for example, and on those terms) that Euro-Culture survived that test at all. After this, of course, the plantation system, taking root, recovered and thrived. But the alternative tradition also survived and thrived: Haiti, 1802; Jamaica 1831-32; Morant Bay, 1865; the all-West Indian riots, 1937-38. In every case the insubordinates appeared and flared against the odds; surprising, unexpected; fed from deep resonating sources of black energy; *mabrak*, which Unprospero found his magic knew too little of. And this source of energy, rooted in the maroon hills and gullies, dry river courses, was not, however, there only: only there, it would have been too easily cut off, truly marooned. But it had spread; indeed it had been always part of the whole plantation experience and reality; *vodun, santeria, shango, condomble*. What, for Jamaica, I shall be calling *kumina*.

Kumina

Kumina, creative adaptation of slaves from a wide arc of continental Africa, is in itself a remarkable example of creolization; although not in the old black/white terms. Here was a "creole" adjustment to a new psychophysical landscape and to new circumstances of a formidable and extraordinary character; an adaptation, too, of a variety of African cultures to each other and to the white colonists. As a transfer from one nexus to another, *kumina*, the religious core of African culture, was not by any means perfect (but then neither was the better circumstanced Euro-Christian culture); but it was certainly effective and more effective than might be imagined.

Missile and Capsule Cultures

Assessment of this cannot be measured in index or quantitative terms; but an understanding of the shape of parent cultures will provide a way of seeing. Euroculture I would characterize as *missile*:[45] projectile nation states, stratified into national classes specialized into "warhead" of government/monarchy, aristocracy (warrior/military), bourgeois and proletarian/peasant fuel chambers: labour and taxable wealth. From this, certain symbolic ikons emerge: crossbow, fusil, long-range cannon, gothic spire, skyscraper, Eiffel tower, even Quixote, pylon, moonshot rocket – all highly adapted to transport, transmission, exploration. Hence colonization (the ship and printing press are other forms of missile), seeking out the target capsule culture. But because of the very nature of the missile: streamline efficiency: malfunctions were disastrous: low survival value: break-up, burn-up, break-down. The cultural transfers then were either almost perfect – the Pilgrim Fathers; or deformed – as on the Caribbean plantations,

characterized by Patterson in *The Sociology of Slavery*.

The African capsule or circle culture, on the other hand, was concerned with equilibrium, and was inward-looking and conservative: drum, round mud hut, village, sense of time. It was not designed for conquest, but survival; and it was the capsule powered by that rocket of the slave trade, middle passage transplantation, that brought miraculously intact – more intact than missile-culture writers would instinctively perceive – what we now call the culture of the slaves; with *kumina* the core, atomic nucleus and colonel. In other words, the slave continued aware of an active relationship with the life force/cosmos through priests, ritual observance, charms ("fetish"), sacrifice/propitiation ("obeah"); and this continued to influence all other aspects of his life/expression, though many of the more public forms of this (e.g., *jonkonnu*) were limited and eventually eroded; while other life-forms (politics, economics and several aspects of the arts, for example) were truncated and submerged; and all were legislated against. What was "permitted" is what (parts of wholes; "creolized," watered down versions) pleased the local establishment.[46] So the masks had to become less "ugly," drum-beat less complex, dances more "formal" less "frenzied." But obeah and the obeahman persisted despite the legislation increasingly secularized; true; increasingly commercialized; increasingly malfunctioning and malevolent in many cases; but still the religious *nam* remained; nourishing the "cults," distracting attention from the priests:

. . . on several estates in the parish of Manchester, the people worshipped a cotton tree and had an idol in every house.[47]

. . . he took me to his own house first. There I found bottles, horns and other things . . . some of them buried . . .[48]

The things which you find here, you will find the like in every house, for this is the way we all live. [slave informant].[49]

And this persisted, despite "conversion" to Christianity:

There was certainly much superstition mingled with their religious exercises [the reference is to black Baptist converts]; many had wonderful dreams to tell, which they considered as prophetic visions; some excited themselves by fanatical notions, and fell into wild extravagances, which they called "the convince" in which they had full faith, as much as in Divine Revelation.[50]

Alongside these mutations; often, out of them: after 1780, were an increasing number of Afro-Christian churches, started in Jamaica not by missionaries at all, but by black converts and preachers, the first of whom was probably George Liele, a freed slave from Virginia/Georgia.[51] With Moses Baker, George Lewis, George Gibb, Parson Kellick and others, these churches multiplied, Baker's, for instance, claiming a fellowship of thousands[52] before the "white" Baptists arrived in 1814 [53] whereupon, of course, none of the black Baptist preachers was found theologically acceptable, all being accused or spoken of as being "superstitious."[54] After 1825, with the white missionaries firmly settled in and in control of their own Aerials, we hear less and less of the black Church though it would be absurd to think that it had disappeared. Today's po/kumina is a direct and distinctly flourishing descendant. But what we do note – since this recorded by Gonzalo's Ariels – is the steady rise of black/slave deacons, with increasingly independent powers and authority as the chapel lengthened in distance from the mission station. Four[55] such deacons, not to mention Sharpe, from St James alone, appeared in the Montego Bay Slave Courts charged with fomenting rebellion . . .

The Black Church

Black churches were set up during the period of slavery (as they still are) as self-supporting, autonomous bodies under a leader/shepherd who "owned" (owns) it. The more formal of them probably had, or based their organization upon, the kind of document that guided the formation of Liele's church: *The Covenant of the Anabaptist Church begun in America in 1777and in Jamaica in 1788*. Here is set out the main principles of (local) Anabaptist faith: reliance on the Word (Lord of Scripture); baptism; moral conduct and deportment; fellowship. So far, so general. But there was, within this, a sense of definition/boundary that is significant; and it is revealed in the provision (it surfaces again in 1865 [56] and was no doubt present also during the 1831-32 revolt) for church or people's courts:

We hold to appoint Judges and such other officers among us to settle any matter according to the Word of God. (Acts vi: 1-3)[57]

We are forbidden to go to law one with another before the unjust, but to settle any matter" we have before the Saints[58] . . .

The "Daddy" who "ruled" these congregations, therefore, had more than an administrative/counseling role. He was the ancient, classical and pre-Renaissance *ecclesia: unam sanctam* of sacred and secular, controlled by the priest-politician; *utraqu e potestas scilicet apostolica et imperialis, est a Deo, et neutra pendet ex altera;* though again, with these African churches, we are dealing with a capsule, self-contained concept, rather than the missile imperialism implicit in Huguccio's words. And when the Daddy's judicial authority was reinforced by the dreaded obeah oath-swearing, it will be appreciated how much (potential) power and influence the black preachers had within their communities: *communities, it must be remembered, who shared, despite increasing creolization, an African religious core and custom.*[59]

These churches ran the whole gamut of black slave/plantation experience from Baptist, through black Baptist and varieties of Afro-Christian, to the Afro and Afro-creole *convince* (above) and *kumina,* where the entire worldview shifted from *mono* to *poly,* and the plural gods of Africa were polyrhythmically recognized: *possessed:* within the worship/dancer. And the spectrum of identification, even within the continuum of increasing creolization, shifted from Christo to Afro according to crisis: 1720, 1760, 1795, 1830, 1865, 1938, and 1970 bringing up the "darker" manifestations of *nam.* So that creolization cannot be seen as a "progress," as assumed by scholars from missile cultures, from black to white, from pagan to civilized, dark to light;[60] but a tidal thing, in addition to the already discussed rest, to the moon/maroon. Creolization "progresses" in fact, as much from linear osmosis (inter-culturation through time), as through hold-up, breakdown, crisis; appearance of Caliban: the participants halting or separating themselves from the process for re-evaluation of themselves; hence re-definition; hence greater clarity of expression; hence greater understanding of both self and other; and so, after the crisis: since after all it, too, took place within the shared continuum: a vivid, new continuation.

The Rebellion

Sharpe

Now he was oft in reverie by day, and oft in dreams by night. Secret converse began. Now there were low whispers – then eager gesticulation – then all was still.

But the stone which dropped so noiselessly from on high into the quiet lake threw upon its bosom those concentric rings which were destined to increase at once in multitude and power. A secret society was formed, with both "the power" and the passion "to add to its number". . . . Multitudes had taken the secret oath.[61]

Cornford here, as ever, romanticises or rather, converts what he doesn't understand into romance. The low whispers and eager gesticulation were not disciple-like conversation and behaviour, but hard-headed para-military plotting: the guns, companies and campaign plans that were soon to reveal themselves, support this contention. The "church" was being used as cover: disguise or *mask:*

... when they came out of the Baptist church, at Montego Bay, on Christmas day . . . Guthrie gave a large dinner, at which he, Gardner, Dove, Sharp of Hazelymph, Samuel Sharp of Croydon, and several other head men, attended. Samuel Sharp swore every man. The oath was that every man should fight to his utmost to drive the white men and free people out of the country and to take it; if they succeeded ... a governor was to be appointed to each parish. This same Sharp of Croydon was the only ruler; he used to go occasionally to Montego Bay and elsewhere for information; he read the newspapers to them from England, as well as pamphlets, and some got letters; that they were led to believe the King's troops in this island and the men-of-war would not fight against them . . .[62]

The Forces

On Thursday the 29th I saw a great many strange negroes who, as I understood, belonged to Chesterfield, Retrieve, Richmond-hill and Belvidere; some of them with fire-arms and others with lances, cutlasses, etc. They had scouts posted on all the hills around, from Y.S. Estate, extending towards St James's, to give them notice of the approach of the militia.[62a]

Ruler

The active person in this scene, and who seemed to have the command of them was a slave named SAMUEL SHARP, belonging, I was told, to T.G. GREY, Esquire of CROYDON in St James's and who, I understood, is a ruler (so called) of the sect of the Baptists. He said he did not wish to take away the life of any person who did not stand between him and his rights; that it was but lately he had begun to know much of religion. . .[62a]

The contradictory image of Sam Sharpe will always remain in the records[63] because of the invisible transformation voltage that was converting Ariel Sharpe to Caliban: deacon into ruler, man of god to "murderer". How else, for instance, could a reliable (?) officer of the Church be admitted to be "new" to religion? That there appeared to be *two* Samuel Sharpes in the disaster area (Knibb symbolically chose one and denied the other: though it is my view that the two represented merely his own schizophrenia of selection: white church/black church) didn't help matters either. But there is no doubt that by Christmas 1831, Ariel had become Caliban: exploiting the mythology of servitude (that lurking image of the *ship:* "letters sent": to justify and claim his freedom/bomb):

Metropolitan Intrusion

but that now he knew, and I knew as well, that freedom was their right, and freedom they would have; that letters had long ago been sent out from England to that effect

Unprospero

but that the people of Jamaica

Aerial

kept them as slaves without any authority for doing so. He said a great deal more, all tending to show that from the religious notions he had imbibed

Caliban

he conceived that the slaves had a right to be free.[64]

The Indictment

This was no "Christian Hero" as conceived by Gonzalo, but

the said Negro man slave [who] . . . with divers Negro and other slaves . . . was present at divers meetings of Slaves formed for the purpose of administering unlawful Oaths in order to Alienate and withdraw the affection fidelity and obedience of divers Negro and other slaves from their Owners and Exciting and Moving them to hatred and dislike of their state and condition as by law. Established and for the unlawful and dangerous purposes of Exciting and stirring up the said Negro and other slaves . . .[65]

CONCLUSION

In this paper I have attempted to indicate (if not demonstrate) that our present notions of creolization – the inter-culturative process between Europe and Africa which started during and as a result of the period of slavery – have to be revised: modified: extended in several important areas and ways:

1. Our ideas of slavery and creolization have so far been too confined to the "classical" period of slavery (I'm referring here to the anglophone Caribbean): 1750-1820. We need now to know more about the foreday morning of the affair and the long twilight: crepuscule: subtle grey areas; especially those last years when Unprospero had been fatally affected by the rise of the free coloureds, by Gonzalo's missionary and libertarian activity, by growing literacy (appearance of Ariel); and by social and ideological changes among the slaves stemming from these things. These changes, plus the important *nam* or "negative" creolization impulses arising from the meaning and achievement of Haiti and the resurgence of black cultural pride which resulted: more *kumina*, more revolt: from this it would have made a significant difference not only in how Unprospero saw himself: pushed onto the defensive; but how the slaves began to see themselves and him. And the quality of all this affected also the quality of increasing familiarity, especially in the growing urban areas,[66] between what was soon to be former master and former slave .[67]

2. Therefore we need to study creolization not only as it affected the slave vis-à-vis Unprospero; i.e., in the towns or through the eyes of literary reporters often recording from hearsay or what was seen *driving through;* but on the inner plantations, where the main tension and competition for influence: models of procedure: was probably not so much between "white" and "black" but between Ariel blacks and Calibans.

3. We need, too, to understand much more of what happened to the course of the process during periods of high visibility: crisis (earthquake, epidemic, and drought, as well as insurrection).

4. We need to know more, also, as I've been implying throughout this piece, about how the increasing Metropolitan Intrusion affected all creoles: black and white: in the period after 1820 and how the image of Alonso: IKON OF THE KING: affected all the orientations.

5. Finally, our picture of the process must include, as best we can, the attitudes, opinions, and observations not only of the elite – leaders, heroes, martyrs: those trapped in print – but also of the little fellas, the folk . . .

There were one or two parties of the Bogue negroes, who had assembled there (at the Bogue Great House, on Christmas Day] with their *John Canoes*. They had been there about one or two hours when prisoner came over from the church, they were dancing, and I saw Mr. Pfeiffer [a missionary] lay hold of one or two of them, who I suppose belong to the church [68]

On Monday morning the 1901 December last, I was sitting at the window when I observed a great stillness in the [Montego Bay] market; there were several groups of Negro men in the market. I then observed this woman, she was dressed in white, and another girl dressed in black; the one in white addressed a group of the men; she said, My Brothers, what is this you are about; you no see them backra and mulatto they keep guard at Court House because M. Grignon woman [slave] take three piece of Cane – him beat the woman, most kill him, then no satisfy with that, but them call out militia so say they go fight for me Colour.[69]

ELIZABETH BALL, FREE COLOURED WOMAN OF MONTEGO BAY. GUILTY. TWO DOZEN LASHES AT FOOT OF GALLOWS: LUCKY:AND SIX MONTHS SOLITARY. ARIEL BECOMING CALIBAN. OKAY?

No mind that, that is nothing [her colour];what them da do, them just da do so to frighten us; you no know say *callalo set down too long.* [my italics] *send another man long road make ochro pye.* Me been married to one Mulatto man, they got him da stick up at Court-house with Gun – *me no care if you can kill him, do something. Buckra and mulatto na do too much for me; you can say you no hear it da the Newspaper say you are all free* . . .

Notes

1. Brathwaite, E. 1971. *The Development of Creole Society in Jamaica, 1770-1820.* The Clarendon Press. Oxford, England

2. Brathwaite, E. 1974. *Contradictory Omens: Cultural Diversity and Integration in the Caribbean.* Savacou Publications. Mona, Kingston, Jamaica.

3. Brathwaite, E. 1976. *Kumina.* Afro-American Studies Department. Boston University. Boston, Mass.

4. Patterson, O. 1967. *The Sociology of Slavery*:273 (citing CO 137/184 and CO 137/ 185). MacGibbon & Kee, London, England.

5. Burns, A. 1954. *History of the British West Indies.* Allen & Unwin. London, England.

6. House of Commons Sessional Papers. Vol. xlvii (561) of 1831-32: Jamaica Slave Insurrection. Report:4. [BM 184].

7. A plan of the parish of St. James, together with a part of the parishes of Hanover, Westmoreland and St. Elizabeth situated in the County of Cornwall & Island of Jamaica, shewing the District and properties Therein Deystroyed during the late Rebellion . . .

Morris, Cunninghame 8 Woodbridge. 1832. J. Gardiner London, England.

8. Higman, B. 1970. Slave Population and Economy in Jamaica at the Time of Emancipation. Ph.D. thesis, University of the West Indies, Mona, Kingston, Jamaica. (A revised version of this thesis will appear in 1976 as *Slave Population and Economy in Jamaica, 1807-1834* to be published by the Cambridge University Press.)

9. House of Commons Sessional Papers. *Ibid.* Copies of the Report of a Committee of the H. of A. of Jamaica, appointed to inquire into the Cause of, and Injury sustained by, the recent REBELLION in that Colony . . . :3-4 [BM 183-84].

10 Brathwaite, E. 1974. *Caribbean Man in Space and Time: A Bibliographical and Conceptual Approach.* Savacou Publications. Mona, Kingston, Jamaica. Revised September 1975.

11. Rodo, J.E. 1900. *Ariel.* Madrid, Spain.

12. Mannoni, O. 1956. *Prospero and Caliban: The Psychology of Colonization.* New York, N.Y. Translated from *Psychologie de la Colonisation.* 1950. Paris, France.

13. Lamming, G. 1960. *The Pleasures of Exile.* London, England.

14. Cesaire, A. 1969. *Une Tempête, Adaptation de la Tempête de Shakespeare pour Une Theatre Negre.* Paris. France.

15. Retamar, R.F. Caliban: Notes toward a discussion of culture in Our America. The Massachusetts Review, Winter-Spring, 1974:7-72.Translated from *Casa de las Americas* 68 (Sept.-Oct. 1971).

16. House of Commons Sessional Papers. Op. Cit. :3945 [BM 219-225].

17. For a rundown of some of the various orientations found (possible) within Creole society see Reference 2 (pp. 24-30 and *passim).*

18. Rev. Thos. Stewart, Rector of Westmoreland: before the Cttce apptd. to inquire into the causes of . . . the recent Rebellion among the Slaves of this Island. BPP Accounts & Papers, vol. xlvii (561), 18 31-32 :203-204.

19. Edward Hilton to Knibb. *In* Facts and Documents Connected with the Late Insurrection in Jamaica: 12-13. 1832. London, England, italics in text. The literature is full of such references to Aerial/Ariel, e.g. "I have understood that Gardiner and Dove could read, and that several of the rebel chiefs could write well." Thomas M'Neel BPP :193.

20. CO 137/185: 108.

21. CO 137/185 :246 v. St James Slave Court, February 1832; my italics.

22. Lamming, G. 1960. Op. cit. :121.

23. Reckord, Mary. 1956. Missionary Activity in Jamaica before Emancipation. Ph.D. thesis. University of London, England.

24. Hinton, John. 1847. *Memoir of William Knibb, Missionary in Jamaica.* :52.

25. Reckord, M. Op. cit.: 192.

26. Reckord, M. Op. cit.:174-175. From *Miss. Herald,* Feb. 1832:853, Nov. 1830:494 and BMS Archives,

Box X1, Letter from Thos. Knibb, Kingston 11 Feb. 1823.

27. The Hon. Richard Barrett before the Cttee appt'd to inquire into the cause of... the recent Rebellion. House of Commons Sessional Papers, *op. cit.* :7-8 [BM 187-188]; my italics.

28. Shakespeare, W. *The Tempest,* Act 1, Scene 2.

29. Ibid.

30. W. Adolph Roberts (1951). *Six Great Jamaicans.* 4. Pioneer Press. Kingston, Jamaica) claims that Jordon (sometimes the name is written Jordan) was "a light-coloured freeman." Mavis Campbell (1968. *Edward Jordan and the Free Coloureds: Jamaica 1800-1865:* 227. Ph.D. Thesis, University of London) says "it's not clear whether he was born a slave."

31. The West Indies and West Indian Literature are full of these. As in Mittelholzer's novel, *The Life and Death of Sylvia* (1953) where the mother of a "mixed" household: white father, black mother, coloured child: lurks in the background/backrooms of the story, little regarded by the novel. She gives the impression that she accepts it as her place to be so low profiled. In Jordon's case we know nothing about his mother. The idea of submerged mother as "type" is introduced in *Contradictory Omens* (:17-18) and applied in two reviews "The unappropriated people: freedmen in the slave society of Barbados" (Handler) HAHR, May 1975; reprinted *Caribbean Quarterly,* Vol. 20(3 & 4) :85-88; and "Submerged mothers," *Jamaica Journal* 9 (2 & 3): 48-49, a comment on Lucille Mathurin's *The Rebel Woman in the British West Indies during Slavery* (1975).

32. Campbell, M, op. cit. :228, 229.

33. See *The Watchman,* the newspaper edited by Jordon (1823-38); although he remained more complex and contradictory than more "simple" Ariels like Alexander Scholar, (appropriate name): see for instance CO 137/175; and Michael Hanby, the Ariel agent in Britain; see CO 137/161.

34. *The Watchman,* 7 April 1832.

35. Campbell, M. op. cit. : 249-250.

36. Ibid.:641-42.

37. Knibb, W. 1832. *Facts and Documents Connected with the Late Insurrection in Jamaica* : 10. London, England.

38. Clarke, John. 1869. *Memorials of Baptist Missionaries in Jamaica.* :28-29. London, England.

39. Ibid.: 29.

40. Cornford, P.H., Rev. Missionary reminiscences. *The Freeman,* 21 November 1855.

41. Ibid.

42. Ibid. 10 October 1855.

43. Garvey, Marcus. 1969. *Philosophy and Opinions.* Amy Jacques Garvey, Ed.:126.Atheneum. New York, N.Y.

44. See Ellison's *Invisible Man* (1952) and for the opposite—return—see Lamming's *Season of Adventure* (1960).

45. For treatment of this idea in detail see my unpublished *The Love Axe/1:A Short History of the Development of a West Indian Aesthetic,* published in a shorter version by Cornell University Press.

46. See Sylvia Wynter's "Jonkonnu in Jamaica" (in *Jamaica Journal* 4(2): 3448 [June 1970]) for an account of the change in Afro-Jamaican art forms and world-view.

47. Clarke, John. op. cit. :13.

48. Ibid. :25.

49. Ibid. :26.

50. Ibid. :15.

51. The best detailed account of Liele's life and work is by Beverly Brown ("George Liele: Black Baptist and Pan-Africanist, 1750-1826." *Savacou* 11/12: 58-67 [Sept 1975]).

52. See *The Baptist Annual Register, 1801-1802* and Brathwaite, *Creole Society* op. cit.: 163.

53. Brathwaite, E. *Creole Society,* op. cit. :253-54; and *Periodical Accounts Relative to the Baptist Missionary Society,* Vol. 5. :502.1800-17. Clipstone.

54. Clarke, John. Op. cit. 11-15, 18, 24 32.

55. See Montego Bay Militia Trials in CO 137/135.

56. Chutkan, Noelle. The administration of justice in Jamaica as contributing factor in the Morant Bay Rebellion of 1865. *Savacou* 11/12: 85. Sept. 1975.

57. *Covenant,* Art. 9, quoted in Brown, op. cit. :62.

58. Ibid., Art. 11, :62.

59. For background, see my four *nam* pieces: "Africa in the Caribbean" (unpublished, "Creative literature of the British West Indies during the period of slavery." *Savacou* 1:46-73; "The African presence in Caribbean literature [and culture]." *Daedalus,* Spring 1974:73-109, and *Kumina* op. cit.).

60. See for instance my "Race and the divided self." *Black World,* July 1972 :54-68; and *Caribbean Studies* 14 (3): 119-131.

61. Cornford,, op. cit.

62. The Examination of Thomas M'Neel, of the parish of Westmoreland, Esquire, Proprietor . . . in House of Commons Sessional Papers, 1831-32 (185),Vol. 13: 623-24.

62a. Deposition on oath of William Annand, Overseer of Ginger Hill Plantation in the Parish of St. Elizabeth. House of Lords Sessional Papers, 18 31- 32 (92), Vol. 13, no. 18 [BM 576-77].

63. Brathwaite, E.K. 1975. Nanny and Samuel Sharp as National Heroes of Jamaica: a Justification. Government of Jamaica, Kingston (unpublished).

64. Deposition on oath of Wm. Annand, Overseer of Ginger Hill Plantation in the Parish of St. Elizabeth. House of Lords Sessional Papers 1831-32 (92), Vol. 13, No. 18 :5 76-77.

65. CO 137/185 :304-305; Trial of Sam Sharpe.

66. Williams-Bailey, Wilma. 1974. Kingston, 1692-1843: A Colonial City. Ph.D. thesis. University of the West Indies. Mona, Kingston, Jamaica.

67. The insights tendered by "Copies of Communications from Jamaica relating to the trial of Samuel Swiney, a Negro Slave . . ." (in the House of Lords Sessional Papers, Vol. 13, No. 254) are particularly helpful here.

68. House of Lords Sessional Papers, op. cit.:291. Was it an accident that the revolt of 1831 took place at Christmas, the *time of Jonkonnu*?

69. Abigail Pacifico in evidence against Elizabeth Ball. Montego Bay Trials, 1831; CO 137/185:116.

67

Liberation Struggles on Livestock Farms in Jamaica during Slavery

VERENE A. SHEPHERD

In a recent article, David Blight, using the autobiography of Frederick Douglass, emphasized the complex nature of the world inhabited by the enslaved, showing how diverse slavery and the enslaveds' response to it could vary even within the same geographical location.[1] Sidney Mintz has also recently prolemtatized the issue of slave resistance, stressing the multidimentionality of slaves' resistant behaviour despite the difficulty of unambiguously distinguishing resistance from individual acts of 'non-violent resistance' and other acts he terms 'non-violent non-resistance'.[2] These observations hold true for Jamaica, a British-held colony in the Caribbean in the period of slavery, where the island's diversified nature facilitated the existence of slavery in different contexts – under the rigid régime of the sugar estates, as well as under alternative régimes on non-sugar properties. But the history of Jamaica demonstrates that from the inception of the slave mode of production, whether on sugar estates or on non-sugar properties, resistance to enslavement and the development of anti-slavery politics were endemic. Slavery is, of course, the antithesis of freedom; therefore, it is not surprising that the enslaved in Jamaica, as in the antebellum South and elsewhere in the Caribbean, launched an opposing struggle for liberation, regardless of their location. Both enslaved men and women struggled to reclaim their natural right to liberty and to create the intellectual basis of the culture of resistance.

The historiography of slave resistance in Jamaica has traditionally been located within the context of maroon struggles, and revolts and day-to-day resistance among the enslaved people on the dominant sugar estates. This article departs from the traditional pattern to probe an alternative context: enslaved peoples on the island's livestock farms (styled 'pens' in Jamaica). This alternative focus is informed by i) the significant crop diversification which existed in Jamaica during slavery and ii) the need to broaden the study of slave resistance and resist the totalizing tendencies in the traditional historiography.

The Context of Resistance: The Livestock Industry & Slavery

The English captured the island of Jamaica from the Spanish colonizers in 1655 and by 1740 had established a plantation economy dominated by the production and export of sugar. From the inception of the plantation system a slave mode of production was instituted and Jamaica imported around 747,500 African captives to service her numerous agricultural and non-agricultural enterprises. An additional 15% is estimated to have died on the journey from Africa.[3] Although sugar dominated the economy, Jamaica's varied physical environment facilitated the emergence of a significant number of properties devoted to alternative economic activities. Among these was the livestock or "pen-keeping" industry. The livestock industry in Jamaica actually pre-dated the establishment of sugar as the dominant export commodity in the island and continued to occupy an important role in the economy even after the island switched to sugar. By 1782, the island had 300 pens[4] which helped to meet the heavy demand for animals generated by the sugar plantations. By 1832, this number had increased to 400.[5]

The existence of the Jamaican livestock industry provided an alternative occupation and social lifestyle to sugar estate labour and sugar plantation residence for a significant proportion of Africans imported to the island. Statistics are sketchy for the 17th and 18th centuries, but by 1832, according to one estimate, the island's pens employed 13% of the enslaved population - the third largest concentration on rural units in the island, surpassed only by sugar estates and coffee plantations.[6] The percentage of the enslaved employed primarily in livestock-rearing in Jamaica was also greater than in any other British Caribbean colony. In 1810, for example, the percentage of bondspeople engaged mainly in livestock-rearing was 5% in Antigua, 5% in Barbuda, 5% in Berbice, 0.2% in St. Lucia and 0.5% in Demerara-Essequibo.[7]

The principal role of enslaved people on Jamaican pens was to produce goods - most importantly, large and small stock, meat, grass, and food provisions – for the domestic market; they participated only marginally in the direct export trade. Enslaved pen labourers were involved in a variety of daily and annual routines not all directly related to livestock husbandry. The work of enslaved people on the pens was extremely varied and less intensive than on the sugar estates. The daily work régime included tending animals, cleaning and preparing pastures, planting guinea grass and provisions, and shelling corn. Some had more specialized responsibilities as domestics, field cooks, nurses, washerwomen, seamstresses, drivers, wagoners, marketers and watchmen. Some did odd jobs. Others laboured at crafts. Pen labourers also periodically jobbed on sugar estates. On economically diversified units, workers chipped logwood, reaped pimento and pruned and picked coffee. Enslaved men also performed the services of grooms, saddlers, jockeys ('raceboys') and butchers.

Field labourers on large pens were divided into gangs, as on sugar estates. But on the pens, these gangs tended to be smaller and their workload bore no relationship to the extraordinarily arduous tasks of sugar-cane cultivation. Most pens had three gangs although a few had four. On the smaller pens, the organization of labourers into gangs was not always practical, and workers were shifted from one task to the next as the need arose. Many of the enslaved worked on their own without constant supervision. Among the most individualistic jobs were those of watchmen, grooms, saddlers, drivers, domestics, traders of stock, and butchers.

The work régime of pens was even and regular. Their labour routines involved no intense periods of work comparable to harvest-time on the sugar estates, no peaks and troughs, no long night hours like those which estate slaves had to endure during the manufacturing of sugar. It was these diverse, at times 'lighter' occupations, the less regimented work organization and less rigid supervision which influenced contemporary writers to characterize the work of those enslaved on pens as less arduous than on sugar estates and pen slaves as having an 'easier' life. The planter-historian, Edward Long, was among the earliest to observe that the work on non-sugar units such as pens was easiest on slaves. Similarly, Cynric Williams remarked, perhaps somewhat exaggeratedly, after a visit to a St. Ann pen that, 'if I had observed on [sugar] estates the bustle of sugar-making, I was no less struck with the tranquility that prevailed here . . .'[8] He also wrote that the negroes [on the pen] have a comparatively idle life, being engaged in cleaning the guinea grass or repairing the stone walls which divide the pastures. David Barclay, owner of Unity Valley Pen in St.Ann, also noted that:

the labour on a pen is much lighter than on a sugar plantation, the employment of the former being only to look after cattle, horses and mules, etc. and to attend to them in the same manner as is practiced by graziers in England.[9]

Demographic historians have indicated that the small 'advantages' pen labourers enjoyed over sugar estate bondsmen and women seem to have caused them to enjoy better life chances. Indeed, the work of Barry Higman demonstrates that in 1834, the principal pen parishes had a higher percentage of children – an indicator of a higher birth rate – than sugar parishes. He also noted that between 1817 and 1832 deaths exceeded births for the whole island, but that natural increase occurred in the pen parishes.[10] The contrasting demographic profiles of pens and sugar estates account for these differences. In addition to the work régime and internal demographic factors, the physical environment of the pens and the material conditions of their enslaved populations also played significant roles in helping to explain the differences in mortality and fertility on pens and estates. Many Jamaican livestock farms were located in physical environments which some proprietors and medical practitioners considered healthier than those of sugar estates. The monopolization of eminently suitable coastal pasturelands by the sugar plantocracy – the result of competition for land between the planters and the penkeepers – had pushed pens onto marginal interior lands. In some parishes, notably St. Ann, such lands were located at higher elevations and were regarded as having healthier physical environments, conducive to the natural increase of the slave population [though some in St Elizabeth could be extremely hot). The intention here is not to construct some simplistic environmental reductionist deterministic model designed to explain population growth, because the effect of environment cannot be absolutely proven. But it is quite evident from the actions of doctors, planters and penkeepers that the location of pens had certain perceived benefits – if only because they were located in drier spots. Chippenham Park Pen in St. Ann, one of the many properties of John Tharp, was used by both whites and slaves for the purpose of recuperation because of its alleged 'healthier environment'.[11] Similarly, the wealthy planter-Attorney, Simon Taylor, claimed that Batchelor's Hall Pen – a satellite of Golden Grove Estate – was ideally located for the recuperation of sick slaves, particularly those suffering from yaws. In a letter to his employer in 1768, he wrote that he 'desired for the future that when any of them get the yaws, that they might be sent to Batchelor's Hall Penn which is a dryer [sic] situation than the estate.[12] When the book-keeper on Retirement Estate contracted a fever, he was advised by his doctor to go to Bromley Pen in St. Ann which had a healthier physical environment than the estate.[13] John Cooper, reporting on the condition of the apprentices on Montrose and Burrowfield pens indicated that all the labourers were healthy and attributed this partly to the location of these properties.[14]

Both planters and penkeepers also seemed to have deliberately chosen to place newly imported African captives on the pens for seasoning before sending them to the more arduous work of the sugar estates. The mortality rate was customarily high in the first years of the slaves' lives in the Caribbean, and after the abolition of the slave trade 'amelioration fervour' caused proprietors to take more positive steps to reduce the death rate.[15] Simon Taylor believed that a pen was the best place for seasoning new slaves in their first year as well as to encourage female slaves to reproduce, noting that ' a Penn is certainly better calculated for Negroes to breed at than Estates for there is no [right?] light work on them [estates] for negro women'.[16] On pens, on the other hand, recently-arrived Africans were put to 'light' tasks such as weeding and cleaning pastures.

The health of the enslaved was also buttressed by their access to beef, pork, and fish, some of which they sold, but some of which they used to supplement their diet. Pen slaves were more likely than estate slaves to keep small stock, pigs and a few head of cattle. On a visit to 'Mr. Matthews' pen' in St. Ann, Cynric Williams wrote that 'the Negroes here are allowed to have as many hogs as they please, a privilege they cannot enjoy on sugar estates where the canes would tempt them into destruction'.[17] Slaves commonly sold surplus pork to the white population on both pens and sugar estates.[18] On some pens, fresh beef broth was given to those in the sick house and extra allowances of fresh beef made to mothers and children. William Dickinson, for example, instructed his attorney in 1792 to issue one pound of fresh beef per week to all children under ten years of age.[19] At Matthews' pen, Williams also observed that the labourers fished in the morning and that after the penkeeper had selected the supply for his family, 'the Negroes came in a body and took away as much fish as they pleased, not less than a bushel a piece, and left many on the shore.' The slaves reportedly salted some of this fish and traded salted fish for 'jerked hog' with slaves in the interior.[20]

Pens cultivated significant quantities of corn, some of which was used for animals, but some of which was given to the slaves. As on sugar estates, pen slaves also had provision grounds which were intended to supply them with most of their food needs.

Control and supervision

The supervision of the enslaved on pens appeared to have been less rigid than on sugar estates. On sugar estates, the attorney and overseer system made for close oversight of all tasks. On modest-sized pens, with their resident owners, smaller white populations, and closer relationships between the resident owner and the enslaved, supervision tended to be less rigid and close.[21] Pens were legally required to maintain a white presence in the ratio of one white to every 30 enslaved persons and 150 head of livestock.[22] Given the average size of the labouring and livestock populations on the pens, at least three whites ought to have resided on each pen. This was rarely the case. On Vineyard Pen in St Elizabeth in 1750, for example, there were 40 enslaved Africans and one white overseer who, on occasions, left the slaves under the supervision of a coloured male driver while he overnighted elsewhere.[23] Despite the legal requirement, most pens experienced difficulties, especially in the 18th century, in attracting white men, and they often had to pay the deficiency tax levied on non-compliance. In addition, though there was some supervision of field gangs whether by the white overseer or the driver, there was little supervision of the more varied, individualistic tasks.

While most owners of pens encountered difficulties in hiring white overseers, those owned by women (white or coloured) and by free-coloureds (men or women) had the greatest difficulties in attracting whites. The reports of Stipendiary Magistrates in the postslavery period indicate that such pens were characterized by 'indiscipline and lax control'.[24] Apparently, sugar planters recognized the potentially disruptive effects on their enslaved labourers, which labourers from the 'freer life style' of the island's pens could have, and sought to restrict mixture. White-owned pens had problems in hiring whites too, chiefly because of the low salaries they offered and the low social status ascribed to pens and penkeepers in this sugar-dominated society. One contemporary noted that up to the late 18th century, pens were considered to be 'despicable objects for enterprising adventurers to hunt after . . . Nor would any man accept the management of one who had hopes of preferment on sugar plantations'.[25]

In the end though, the material conditions and varied demographic profiles of the enslaved and the rigid or lax control to which they were subjected had very little impact on their passion to resist. Indeed, resistance was just as likely to result from indulgence and rising expectations as from brutalizing treatment. Comparative data from properties in the Southern United States where the enslaved lived in small communities in close contact with owners reveal that most revolts occurred in areas of diversified agriculture where the slave régime was more undulgent than in the plantations of the 'Cotton Kingdom'.[26]

Rather than viewing pens as oases of social stability, sugar planters and legislators regarded them as 'storm centres of radical ideas, racial mixing and rapid change' and tried to isolate their slaves from them.[27] They could not, of course, prevent the mixing of slaves from different units. In the first place, pens and estates often shared boundaries. Second, as adjuncts of the sugar economy, pens were essential for the supply of goods and services vital to the sugar estates. This necessitated frequent contacts between pen and estate and their slaves often formed close social ties. Pen slaves who were involved in jobbing and in the marketing of the produce of the farms had a greater degree of mobility than the estate slaves. They could, indeed, have used the legitimate movements allowed them by marketing tasks to plan or spearhead revolts.

The main focus of slave resistance studies now, however, is not on whether slaves were contented or discontented with their lot, but on how they resisted. The specific evidence relating to the response of the enslaved on pens to their servile conditions is fragmentary. They left no record of their intentions and traditional works have generalized about slave resistance, showing little or no property differentiation. From the few surviving accounts, though, [mainly slave court records, newspaper reports and the journals of Thomas Thistlewood], it is clear that the enslaved on pens employed a variety of means to subvert the system of slavery, overthrow it, facilitate their own escape from it through marronage or manumission, sabotage it or regularize their conditions within it. They used these resistant strategies independently or in collusion with others [at times with those from sugar estates].

The majority of the enslaved did not resort to armed revolt but negotiated their daily lives under slavery in various ways, including pressing for greater economic autonomy and day-to-day strategies of non-violent resistance.

Negotiation for Economic Autonomy

One response to slavery by pen slaves was by participating in the informal economy and seeking to maintain customary rights and privileges under slavery. To reduce their cost of production and their expenditure on imported food, slave owners in the Americas shifted part of the burden of slave provisioning onto the shoulders of the enslaved. Neither estates nor pens relied on the ration system exclusively. The 1792 Consolidated Slave Act provided that each proprietor was to provide provision grounds for slaves in the ratio of one acre for every ten slaves. It appears that the act was more nearly put into practice on pens than on sugar estates. The comparatively smaller size of the pens meant that pen slaves travelled less distance to reach their grounds. Furthermore, the work day on pens was probably shorter than on the estates – at least for men. Finally, as much of the labour on pens was not done in gangs, pens slaves no doubt had more time to attend to their grounds, and consequently more opportunity to grow their own food. The enslaved rigorously guarded their access to provision grounds and resisted all attempts to reduce time for their informal economic activities and marketing.[28] Wise slaveowners allowed the enslaved to engage in their own economic activities to improve their conditions under slavery and stem the tide of violent revolts.

Pen slaves seemed to have had a wider range of possibilities to earn money in exchange for their labour. They participated in the internal marketing system by selling goods grown in their grounds and gardens. They also sold cattle, pigs, poultry, dried salted fish, crabs, fresh beef and pork to other slaves as well as to the whites. Pen slaves had more opportunity to rear small stock on their own account than those on the sugar estates. On Vineyard Pen, the slaves Titus and Scipio regularly sold crabs to Thomas Thistlewood. Other Vineyard slaves were also remunerated for several services they performed. When Dick built a house for Marina, he earned ten bits; and Phibbah earned six bits for each shirt and two bitts for each pair of trousers she sewed. She received one bitt for each garment mended.[29] On Breadnut Island Pen, Phibbah earned enough cash to be able to lend Thistlewood £9.15.0 in May 1768 and £2.7.6 in June of the same year.[30]

Enslaved pen labourers had other means of earning extra cash. 'Raceboys' and other slave men who accompanied their owners to the races were given money with which to bet on the horses, although their degree of success is unknown. Enslaved men who drove animals to and from estate markets were also given small financial rewards or incentives as planters and penkeepers tried to ensure the good treatment of livestock.

The enslaved used their earnings for a variety of purposes. While some no doubt contributed to their churches, others purchased their freedom, improved their diet, bought property and fineries that served to improve their status among fellow slaves. Phibbah, a seemingly "independent" enslaved woman on Vineyard Pen who was also Thistlewood's concubine [euphemistically called 'housekeeper'], and who had opportunity to acquire property and earn cash, used some of her money to acquire livestock. In 1834, Whitehall Ellis, the headman on Farm Pen in St. Catherine, owned nine slaves. Three years later, he had acquired 20 head of cattle and 70 sheep. He also lived in 'a large and comfortable and furnished cottage with **jalousies** in the casements' and served madeira wine in 'real wine glasses' to his important visitors.[31]

Day-to-day resistance: evidence from the Thistlewood Journals

Surviving evidence [mostly from the daily journals of Thomas Thistlewood] indicate the wide range of day-to-day strategies adopted by the enslaved peoples on pens to undermine the system of slavery. When he was overseer on Vineyard Pen from 1750-51, Thistlewood recorded that the enslaved stole animals, ran away, malingered, lied, stole, feigned illness, deliberately opened old sores and destroyed or abused property [particularly animals]. He seemed particularly disturbed about the extent to which the enslaved on Vineyard Pen stole goods, at times as part of the activities of runaways, and described them as "a nest of thieves and villains".[32]

Thistlewood also recorded the ways in which the enslaved were punished for acts of resistance, some of which whites deemed 'crime'. On Vineyard and Breadnut Island pens, the enslaved were punished severely by whipping, having faeces rubbed over their faces or put in their mouths, denied privileges, were put 'in the bilboes' and in chains and collars. Rape was also used as punishment.[33]

The abuse and stealing of animals was a common means of sabotage used by slaves who worked closely with animals. In the Old South, Eugene Genovese claims that:

slaves seem to have taken the greatest delight in abusing the horses, oxen and mules that were so essential to the day-to-day work of the plantations. If the hogs were not attended to, pork could be purchased but there was no substitute for work animals.[34]

As pen slaves worked more closely with animals than estate slaves, this act of resistance was predictably quite marked. Thomas Thistlewood constantly punished slave men for abusing horses and cattle and enslaved women for losing small stock. He punished Old Sambo when he brought him 'the bones of a missing goat, pretending that he found them in a hole'.[35]

Thistlewood did not believe Old Sambo's story, but 'as there was no certain proof to me what was become of the flesh, had him given 100 lashes to make him more careful for the pasture'.[36] Cuffee and Joe were whipped for ' catching the old horse and keeping him tied up all day'.[37] Mimba and her children on Vineyard Pen, whose job was to watch small stock, were punished for neglecting the animals and for losing an ewe. Mimba received 50 lashes.

At a slave trial held in St. Elizabeth in 1815, Prosper from Hounslow Pen was sentenced to two months in gaol for 'stealing and killing a bull ... and for having upwards of 20 lbs. of beef in his possession'.[38] He received 39 lashes on first going to prison and was to get another 39 on his release.[39] Three men from Haughton Pen were tried for stealing goats but were acquitted.[40] Despite the severe punishment attached to it, horse stealing was common among the enslaved men on pens.

Stealing, lying and malingering were also strategies of day-to-day resistance. Thomas Thistlewood tied up Mimba and gave her 50 lashes for stealing corns; he beat Titus for allowing the runaway, Robin, to raid the storehouse

on Vineyard Pen. Mimba, Juba, Cynthia, Jenny and Deborah were all punished for theft of pen supplies. Juba was whipped for both these 'crimes' and was described by Thistlewood as an 'incorrigible liar ... there is no taking any notice of what she says'.[41] Malingering was a common strategy of resistance and the enslaved were punished accordingly. Old Titus received 50 lashes for malingering on another occasion.[42] On April 8th 1751, he gave Scipio 50 lashes for "delaying his time coming home from Westmoreland".[43]

Thistlewood also punished slaves whom he accused of laziness and negligence. For example, he recorded that Dick, a mulatto boy was tied to an orange tree in the garden and 'whipped to some purpose' [300 lashes!] for 'his many crimes and naughtiness'. He was so severely beaten that he could not report for work until nine days later.[44]

Marronage was a constant plague for Thistlewood and involved several slaves. The slaves seemed to have engaged more in small scale and temporary marronage rather than permanent flight. This may have been explained by the existence of the British Treaty with the maroons made in 1739. One of the provisions of the treaty was that maroons should return runaway slaves. Incorrigible runaways included Robin, Bank, Charles, Chelsea, George, Joan, Juba, Simon, Sussex and Old Titus. The punishment for marronage [depending on the length of absence] ranged from whipping and confinement, to being sent away from the estate [sale or transportation]. Whipping of from 50-300 lashes was usual for absences of a few days or months; where slaves stayed away for 6 months or over, necessitating advertisements in the press, punishment was more severe. Such marronage was interpreted as political resistance, an attempt to undermine the productivity of the property. George, whom he gave 100 lashes for some misdemeanour and who he sent back to work almost immediately, ran away shortly after. He was said to have returned and raided the pen. Charles also ran away; and after he had accused Juba of lying and had severely whipped her, she also ran away. Other slaves on the pen obviously collaborated with the runaways.[45]

George and Gubby of Cornwall Pen were transported out of the island for life for marronage in 1809 and 1810 respectively. A similar fate befell Oxford of Friendship Pen in St. Elizabeth in 1815. Female runaways seemed not to have been transported to the same degree. They were whipped and imprisoned for three months or more, depending on the time away.[46]

When Thistlewood established his own property of 144 acres in 1767, his 27 slaves behaved in much the same way as those he had supervised on Vineyard Pen. As on other properties, he recorded that they stole, deliberately walked through his corn piece, illtreated the animals, malingered, loitered, lied, stole, engaged in marronage, and were generally lazy and negligent. He used various forms of punishment to keep the Breadnut Island Pen slaves in line, including flogging, branding, putting slaves in chains, collars and in the 'bilboes'. In early January 1768, he flogged the fisherman Chub for "neglect and roguery".[47] In the same month, he recorded that he "flogged ... field negroes for laziness".[48] Cudjoe, Nanny and Coobah were flogged for 'misdemeanors'.[49] Sally, who seemed to have put up great resistance to his constant rape, ran away frequently. He punished her severely each time she returned. On 22 August 1768 he "put a collar and chain about Sally's neck; also branded her TT on her right cheek".[50] Resistance continued into the 1770s. In 1770, several slaves were punished for marronage and day-to-day acts of resistance. Coobah ran away frequently and each time she was caught and returned, she was severely punished. She was also accused of malingering and [like another field woman, Franke], feigning illness to escape field labour. Between 1770 and 1774 [when she was sold], she ran away 4 times.[51] She was flogged, branded in her face, chained and collared, and even had faeces rubbed over her face. In September 1774, he "flogged Solon for neglect in bringing fish".[52] He also flogged Solon for leaving the canoe so that other slaves could steal it; and for running away, I guess to escape the punishment meted out to him for his various offenses. Thistlewood also recorded that female slaves deliberately tried to abort their pregnancies by drinking various herbs.

Even if some of these actions on the part of the enslaved fall into the category of non-violent non-resistance in Mintz's model, their frequency and the punishment they attracted are indications that they had the result of inconveniencing the penkeeper and undermining the order and efficiency of production on the pen. Some of these acts were deliberate acts on the part of the enslaved and must be deemed resistance.

Armed Revolt

The enslaved on pens also participated in armed revolt though the evidence of their participation is more abundant for the 19th century than for earlier centuries. They were involved, for example in the 1824 slave conspiracy discovered in the parish of Hanover in the western end of the island. In June 1824 the planters in that parish reported that they had discovered rebellious conspiracy of 'a very alarming nature' involving the enslaved on the parish's sugar estates as well as on Argyle, Ramble, Burnt Ground, Silver Grove and Knockalva pens.[53] The plan had been for the slaves to set fire to the properties in the parish and to kill any whites who attempted to put out the blaze. A slave on Argyle Pen, William Roach, allegedly revealed the plot and prevented the revolt. Those implicated as leaders were hanged.[54]

Pen slaves also played an active role in the 1831 'Christmas Rebellion' which has come to be intimately associated with one of its outstanding leaders, Sam Sharpe. The 1831 revolt erupted in the western parish of St James. The main cause of the revolt was the slaves' belief that they were to be freed at Christmas,.'. . . and that their freedom order had actually come out from England but was being withheld and that they only had to strike en masse, and they should gain their object'.[55] Slaves from Trelawny and St James parish had apparently agreed that any attempt to force them back to work after the Christmas holidays was to be met by setting fire to the properties, [though not their huts or provision grounds].[56] This revolt is important for the history of pens for two reasons: it was pen slaves who gave the signal for the start of the revolt and pens proved to be important revictualing centres for the roving bands of rebels. Kensington Pen [referred to as an estate in earlier accounts of this rebellion] was the first to be set on fire as a beacon to other properties to activate the plans for the revolt. Its strategic location on an elevation made it ideal for this important function as a beacon to other properties to activate the plans for the revolt. After reports were heard that whites were attempting to break the strike on Salt Spring Estate, the male slave John Dunbar set fire to the proprietor's house on Kensington. He ordered the other slaves to plunder the house of all its furniture and shared it among them. Once the fires on Kensington were seen, the enslaved on Leogan and other properties started similar fires. In the days that followed, pen after pen, estate after estate joined the rebellion. Richard Trail from Shettlewood Pen, with rebels gathered from Ramble, Alexandria and 'nearly the whole of Silver Grove negro men',[57] went to Haughton Pen with a gun and forced the slaves working in the pastures to take the oath of revolt. This oath, 'to fight against the white people as long as there was one of them left in the country' was executed on a bible which Trail's assistant, Thomas Haughton, headman at Shettlewood Pen, reportedly passed along the lines of slaves he had mustered. A slave, Daniel Malcolm of Ramble Pen, testified that Trail accompanied Haughton along the line 'with his musket cocked, and swore that if any man refused to take the oath, he would blow his brains out'.[58]

The male slave, Bob Peterkin, was said to have led the other slaves on Springvale Pen in revolt. Along with Richard Grey, he broke into the Great House, declared themselves the penkeepers and demanded freedom and a share of the cattle on the pen. Similarly James Bernard of Bandon Pen set fire to the house of the white residents, armed himself and joined the revolt.[59]

The activities of some of the enslaved on pens during the course of this revolt demonstrate how essential these units were for the bands of rebels. The latter often stopped at pens and used them as revictualing centres. With their large livestock populations, large quantities of provisions and small supervisory white populations, pens were, in fact, ideal targets for the slave 'captains' and their 'armies'. Some pen slaves had to be forced to provide these food supplies; others willingly slaughtered animals to feed the rebels and still others carried provisions to the rebel camps.[60]

In his evidence against James Bernard of Brandon Pen who was said to have been 'captain' of the 'fort' at the pen, a slave eyewitness stated that it was Bernard who helped to organize dinner for Captain McLennan's party when the latter invaded Bandon. When the slaves had brought the yam '. . . he said he had nothing fresh and ordered two men to shoot two cows'.[61] The white troops also took over pens as their revictualling centres.

When it was over, more than 200 slaves [about 13 from 6 pens in Hanover and St James] had been killed by the militia. A total of 287 non-pen properties and 42 pens in the parishes of St James, Hanover, Westmoreland and St Elizabeth suffered losses due to arson and the commandeering of provisions and cattle for the troops and rebels.[62] In Hanover alone, 10 pens, 31 settlements and 21 sugar estates suffered damage estimated at £429,922.1 5.0d. The total losses to the pens [Burnt Ground, Prosper, Shettlewood, Coventry, Cacoon Castle, Ramble, Friendship Grove, Knockalva, Brae and Haughton] was estimated at £38,231.

Records of the slave trials held after the revolt reveal that 406 slaves were tried before civil slave courts in 1832; 46 of these were pen slaves. The majority of the participants from the pens were from among the male slave elite: the coloured, creole artisans; about 13 were field slaves.

Eugene Genovese is thus basically correct when he asserts that: enslavement in any form has figured as the antithesis of that individual autonomy considered the essence of freedom.[63] The revolt against slavery emerged as the basic assertion of human dignity, and, clearly, resistance was just as likely to result from rising expectations and indulgence as from brutal treatment and poor material conditions.

Notes

*Extracted from V. Shepherd, "Liberation struggles on livestock farms in Jamaica during and after slavery, in K. Agorsah, ed., 'Struggles in Black Freedom' [forthcoming.

1. David Blight, "Analyze the Sounds": Frederick Douglass's Invitation to Modern Historians of Slavery", in Stephan Palmié, Pd., Slave Cultures and the Cultures of Slavery (Tennessee, 1995), pp.1-22.
2. Sidney Mintz, " Slave Life on Caribbean Sugar Plantations: Some Unanswered Questions", in Palmié, pp. 14, 15.
3. Philip D. Curtin, The Atlantic Slave Trade: A Census (Wisconsin, 1969), p. 268.
4. W.J. Gardner, History of Jamaica 1655-1872 (London, 1909 edn.), p. 161.
5. B.W. Higman, Slave Population and Economy in Jamaica 1807-1834 (Cambridge Univ. Press, 1976).
6. B.W. Higman, Slave Population and Economy in Jamaica 1807-1834 (Cambridge Univ. Press, 1976), p. 16.
7. B.W. Higman, Slave Populations of the British Caribbean, 1807-1834 (Baltimore, 1984), pp. 67-71.

8. British Library, Department of Manuscripts, Add. Ms 12,404, fol.308 & C. Williams, *A Tour Through The Island of Jamaica* (London, 1826), p. 59.

9. D. Barclay, *An Account of the Emancipation of Slaves on Unity Valley Pen* (London, 1801), p. 19.

10. Higman, *Slave Population and Economy*, p. 26.

11. Tharp Family Papers, Cambridgeshire County Archives, R:81/41.

12. Simon Taylor to Arcedeckne, 10 April 1768, Jamaica Estate Papers, [hereafter J.E.P.] box 2, bundle 3. See also B.C. Wood and T.R. Clayton, 'Slave Birth, Death and Disease on Golden Grove Estate, Jamaica, 1765-1810', *Slavery and Abolition*, 6 (1985), pp. 99-121.

13. Philo Scotus, *Reminiscences of a Scottish Gentleman*, (London, 1861), p. 217.

14. Jamaica Archives, Gifts and Deposits, 7/177/1-2, 1835.

15. J.R. Ward, *British West Indian Slavery, 1750-1834: The Process of Amelioration* (Oxford, 1988), pp. 121-44, 179-88.

16. Taylor to Arcedeckne, 5 July 1789, J. E. P. box 2, bundle 15.

17. Williams, p. 61.

18. V. Shepherd, 'Pens and Penkeepers in a Plantation Society', Ph. D Diss., University of Cambridge, 1988, p. 238, and Jamaica Archives, 1B/1 1/5/19, Accounts Current, Mt. Plenty Pen, 1820.

19. Dickinson Papers, DD/DN/468, Somerset Record Office.

20. Williams, pp. 79-80.

21. Higman, *Slave Population and Economy*, pp. 101-138.

22. Add. Ms. 12,404, fol. 308.

23. Some of Thistlewood's trips were undertaken in order to 'give in' returns of slaves and livestock for tax purposes. Journal Mon. 31/1-2, 1750-51.

24. Enclosure in C.O. 137/210 (11), Sligo to Glenelg, 2 April 1836.

25. J.B. Moreton, *Manners and Customs of The West India Islands* (London, 1790), p. 58.

26. M.D. de B. Kilson, "Towards Freedom: an Analysis of Slave Revolts in the United States", *Phylon* xxv (1964), 179-83, cited in George Frederickson & Christopher Lasch, "Resistance to Slavery", *Civil War History*, 13 (1967), p. 316.

27. Michael Craton, *Sinews of Empire: A Short History of British Slavery*, (London, 1974), p. 188 47.

28. For a good discussion of this topic see Mary Turner, ed., *From Chattel Slaves to Wage Slaves: The Dy-namics of Labour Bargaining in the Americas* (Kingston, London, Indiana, 1995), pp. 1-47.

29. Mon. 31/2, fols. 73; 31 /1 fols. 372, 518.

30. Mon. 31/20.

31. J. Sturge and T. Harvey, *Jamaica in 1837* (London, 1838), pp. 18, 186.

32. Mon. 31/1, fol. 333.

33. Mon. 31/1-3; Mon. 31/18-19.

34. E. Genovese, *The Political Economy of Slavery* (New York, 1967), p. 112.

35. Mon. 31/1, fol. 331

36. Ibid.

37. Mon. 31/1, fol. 338, 386.

38. Return of Slave Trials, in Shepherd, "Pens and Penkeepers", p. 264.

39. Ibid.

40. Ibid.

41. Mon. 31 /1, fol. 420.

42. Mon. 31/2, fol. 382.

43. Ibid. fol. 55.

44. Mon. 31/1, fol. 340.

45. Ibid., fol. 381.

46. Shepherd, "Pens and Penkeepers", p. 268.

47. Mon. 31/19.

48. Ibid, fol. 123.

49. Ibid., 9 February 1768.

50. Mon. 31/19

51. D. G. Hall, "Runaways in Jamaica in the Mid-19th Century", UWI, Mona, Staff/Graduate Seminar Paper, p. 191.

52. Mon. 31/19, 1774 .

53. Shepherd, "Pens and Penkeepers", p. 270.

54. Ibid.

55. Viscount Goderich to the Governors of the West India Colonies, 16 March 1832, Enclosure in Despatch No. 137, C.O. 137/181.

56. Ibid.

57. Slave Trials, 1832. Jamaica House of Assembly Votes, 1832.

58. Ibid.

59. Shepherd, "Pens and Penkeepers", pp. 272-73

60. Ibid., p. 275.

61. Ibid.

62. Ibid. See also Philip D. Curtin, *Two Jamaicas: The Role of Ideas in a Tropical Colony* (New York, 1970, pp. 83-89) & Mary Turner, *Slaves and Missionaries: The Disintegration of Jamaican Slave Society, 1787-1834* [Illinois, 1982].

63. E. Genovese, *From Rebellion to Revolution*, (London, 1979), p. xiii .

68

Maritime Maroons: Grand Marronage from the Danish West Indies

N.A.T. HALL

The islands of St. Croix, St. Thomas, and St. Jan — now the Virgin Islands of the United States — were Denmark's outposts of empire in the Caribbean. Denmark was a late entrant in the seventeenth-century scramble for West Indian colonies. Its colonization of St. Thomas, beginning in 1671, and of St. Jan in 1718, occurred at a time when England, France, and Holland had long since broken, de facto and de jure, Spain's monopoly in the hemisphere and were consolidating their New World gains. Denmark's choice was limited in the extreme; its acquisition of St. Thomas and St. Jan was determined not by choice but by lack of feasible alternatives. St. Croix, bought from France in 1733, was the last of the Lesser Antilles to come under European rule, and the purchase has the dubious distinction of bringing to a close the first century of non-Hispanic colonization in the Caribbean. The acquisition completed Denmark's territorial empire in the New World. Apart from two British occupations during the Napoleonic Wars, in 1801 and again from 1807 to 1815, the islands remained in Denmark's possession until 1917, when they were sold to the United States.[1]

The geological origins of the Lesser Antilles fall between the Eocene and Pliocene intervals of the tertiary period, when tectonic activity produced the collision of the floors of the Atlantic Ocean and Caribbean Sea that created an inner arc of volcanic islands to which the Danish West Indies belonged. These islands, unlike those of the outer arc such as Antigua or Barbuda, are characterized by serrated ridges and rugged peaks. St. Thomas and St. Jan rise respectively to 517 meters (1,700 feet) and 396 meters (1,300 feet). St. Croix has a range of hills along its northern coast rising to 367 meters (1,200 feet) in its northwestern corner but contains in its center and south an area of flat and fairly well-watered land totaling about 100 square kilometers (39 square miles) that is particularly well adapted to agriculture. This fact, combined with its greater area of 217 square kilometers (84 square miles), determined that neither St. Thomas, with an area of 72 square kilometers (28 square miles), nor St. Jan, 52 square kilometers (20 square miles), ever rivaled St. Croix in sugar production.[2]

Sugar integrated these tropical islands into the economy of their metropolitan center, and it was notoriously labor-intensive. Although the use of white indentured workers was attempted,[3] African slave labor soon became the exclusive basis of the monocrop culture of each island. As Table 1 demonstrates, the eighteenth century was a period of almost unvaryingly upward growth in the number of slaves, which peaked at the turn of the nineteenth century, coincident with Denmark's decision in 1792 to abolish the transatlantic slave trade in 1802 and with consequent feverish importations during that ten-year grace period.[4] Relatively and absolutely, the increments of growth were largest for St. Croix. As the

A version of this article was presented at the XVIth annual conference of the Association of Caribbean Historians, Bridgetown, Barbados, April 1984. Acknowledgments: the author would like to thank Teresita Martínez Vergne and Richard Price for their helpful suggestions of additional material relating to Puerto Rico, Julius Scott and Lorna Simmonds for material relating respectively to St. Domingue and Jamaica, Poul Olsen for identifying the William Gilbert letter, Dahlia Riedel for translations from the German, and the Department of Geography, University of the West Indies, for assistance with the map. Their generosity in no way implicates them in any shortcomings the article may have.

William and Mary Quarterly, 3rd Sents, Vol. XLII, October 1985, pp. 476–97.

Table 1   Slave, White and Freedman Populations of the Danish West Indies, 1688–1846

	St. Croix			St. Thomas			St. Jan		
Year	Slaves	Whites	Freedmen	Slaves	Whites	Freedmen	Slaves	Whites	Freedmen
1688				422	317				
1691				547	389				
1715				3,042	555				
1733				**	**	**	1,087	208	**
1755	8,897	1,303*		3,949	325	138	2,031	213*	
1770	18,884	1,515	**	4,338	428	67	2,302	118	**
1789	22,488	1,952	953	4,614	492	160	2,200	167	16
1797	25,452	2,223	1,164	4,769	726	239	1,992	113	15
1815	24,330	1,840	2,840	4,393	2,122	2,284	2,306	157	271
1835	19,876	6,805*		5,315	8,707*		1,943	532*	
1846	16,706	7,359*		3,494	9,579*		1,790	660*	

*These figures include freedmen as well as whites.
**No data.
Note: Between 1688 and 1715, neither St. Jan nor St. Croix had been acquired by the Danes. St. Jan was acquired in 1718 and was Danish at the time of the slave uprising there in 1733.
Sources: Forskellige Oplysninger, VI, General Toldkammer, Rigsarkiv, Copenhagen; Oxholm's 'Statistik Tabelle over de danske Amerikanske Eilande St. Croix, St. Thomas og St. Jan, 1797', *Dokumenter vedkommende Kommissionen for Negerhandelen, ibid.*; 'Viisdomsbog', *Diverse Dokumenter, Vestindiske Sager, ibid.*; *Originale Forestillinger fra Kommissionen angaaende Negernes Stilling, ibid.*; Westergaard, *op. cit.*; J. O. Bro-Jørgensen, *Vore Gamle Tropekolonier* (Copenhagen, 1966); Hans West, *Beretning om det dansk eilande St. Croix i Vestindien* (Copenhagen, 1791).

nineteenth century progressed, however, all the Danish islands experienced a gradual decline of slave populations as rates of mortality exceeded those of birth.[5]

But even as their numbers dwindled, slaves remained in the majority, a position held almost from the outset of each island's exploitation. Even after 1835, when freedmen, having obtained their civil liberties, were enumerated with whites in the category 'free', slaves never lost numerical superiority vis-à-vis non-slaves. St. Thomas, however, had become an exception in this regard by 1835, and the explanation inheres in that island's large number of freedmen, who then composed well above 70 per cent of the entire population.[6]

The increase of freedmen was closely related to the expansion of mercantile activity in St. Croix's port towns of Christiansted and Frederiksted and, most dramatically, in St. Thomas's port of Charlotte Amalie. That growth also greatly enlarged the number of slaves in those towns. By 1838, slaves composed some 26 per cent of Charlotte Amalie's population. Many were women, engaged mostly as domestics and constituting, in St. Croix, some 62 per cent of the urban slave population in 1839.[7] The data for male slaves do not permit quantification of their employment, although it is a fair assumption that most were occupied in maritime work — loading and unloading vessels, driving the wains that delivered or removed cargo, and laboring in warehouses or

as crew in inter-island or other seagoing traffic. As market centers the towns drew slaves from the countryside to sell fruit, vegetables, poultry, grass, and firewood.[8] At least in St. Thomas and St. Croix, almost the entire slave population was thus in constant contact with the port towns.

The sex distribution of slaves reflected, for the eighteenth century, a general preference for males in plantation America, since planters assumed that females were less able to withstand the rigors of labor. Indeed, the Danish Slave Trade Abolition Commission, in order to redress the imbalance and promote self-sustaining growth, exempted female slaves imported after 1792 from the usual taxes.[9] For St. Croix, for example, the bias against females and its reversal over time is indicated by a comparison of the sex composition of that island's slave population of 1792 (when abolition was announced), 1804 (when the trade had just ended), 1815, 1835, and 1840, eight years before emancipation. Table 2 shows a dramatic half-century shift from a ratio of 85.8 female slaves to 100 males in 1792 to a ratio of 109 to 100 in 1840.

This change does not appear to have resulted in larger numbers of females than males among the slaves who escaped from the islands. Maroons from the Danish West Indies, as from Jamaica, Surinam, and Brazil, were preponderantly male.[10] The reason was not that women were physically less resilient or robust than men, but, more probably, that men were

Table 2 Sex Distribution of the Slave Population of St. Croix, 1792–1840.

Year	Female	Male	Total	Ratio of females per 100 males
1792*	7,364	8,579	15,943	85.8
1804	10,475	11,601	22,076	90.2
1815	12,250	12,080	24,330	101
1835	10,423	9,453	19,876	110
1840	9,714	8,891	18,605	109

*Figures do not include disabled and runaway slaves, numbering 96 and 2,082 respectively.
Sources: Oxholm's 'General Tabelle for St. Croix, 1792', *Dokumenter vedkommende Kommissionen for Negerhandelen*, General Toldkammer, Rigsarkiv; *Forskellige Oplysninger*, VI, *ibid.*; 'Extract af General Tabellerne over Folkmængden paa de danske vestindiske Øer, den 1ste Oktober 1835', *Originale Forestillinger fra Kommissionen angaaende Negernes Stilling*, *ibid.*; G. W. Alexander, *Om den moralske Forpligtelse til og den hensigstmæssige af strax og fuldstændigt at ophæve Slaveriet i de dansk-vestindiske Kolonier* (Copenhagen, 1843).

more likely to have acquired skills needed to survive in forests, swamps, or at sea, while, in addition, women were rendered less mobile by pregnancy or the responsibilities of maternity. In the Danish West Indies, moreover, women began to predominate in the slave population at a time when the creolization of that population was well advanced. (See Table 3.) By the nineteenth century, creole slave women were arguably further deterred from deserting by attachments of family, sentiment, or a sense of place.

Table 3 Creoles and Africans in the Slave Population of the Danish West Indies, 1804–05.

	Creoles	Africans	Total	% Creoles
St. Croix	11,530	10,546	22,076	52.2
St. Thomas	2,096	1,248	3,344	62.7
St. Jan	1,521	896	2,417	62.9
Total	15,147	12,690	27,837	54.4

Source: Raw data from *Forskellige Oplysninger*, V, General Toldkammer, Rigsarkiv.

The three islands lie within sight of each other just east of Puerto Rico and at the northern end of the eastern Antillean chain as it curves gently westward in the vicinity of 18 degrees north latitude. Under Danish administration, they constituted a wedge, as it were, between Spanish Puerto Rico with its dependencies to the west and Britain's Virgin Islands to the east. This factor of insular proximity in a patchwork of national properties had an important bearing on how *grand marronage* from the Danish West Indies developed. There were significant differences from the pattern in the rest of the hemisphere, where aggregates of single fugitives created discrete communities that threatened

the plantation system militarily and economically. Irrespective of their location, the viability of such communities, as Richard Price has noted, was a function of topography.[11] Natural barriers such as jungle, swamp, and hardly penetrable mountain fastnesses enabled maroon communities to develop in isolation and successfully defend themselves against attack. Slaves on the Danish islands enjoyed none of these advantages. The extensive cutting of forests to make way for sugar plantations removed nature's only benefaction from which maroons could profit. The experience of the Danish West Indies therefore provides empirical foundation for a theorem: that in small islands where geographical factors were hostile to the formation of permanent maroon communities, *grand marronage* tended to mean maritime marronage.

Grand marronage was the most viable of alternatives to servitude short of the supreme act of rebellion. From the beginning of Danish colonization to the time of emancipation in 1848, this form of resistance was continuous, indicating that its incidence was not significantly affected by the degree of acculturation or creolization of the slave population or by the changing proportions of male and female slaves. The numbers involved, however, were never very great. Hans West, a Danish pedagogue in St. Croix, reported 1,340 slaves at large in 1789, when the slave population stood at 22,448 — a mere 5.9 per cent.[12] P. L. Oxholm, a military engineer who later became governor-general, identified 96 deserters in 1792, only 0.5 per cent[13] of Croix's 18,121 slaves. In St. Thomas the 86 known deserters in 1802 constituted 2.7 per cent of the slave population of 3,150.[14]

The evidence indicates that *grand marronage* commenced shortly after the settlement of St.

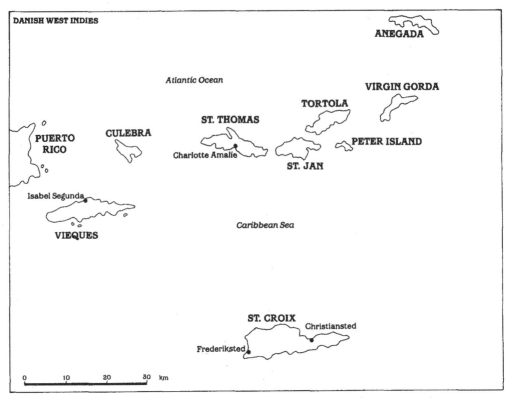

Thomas and the beginnings of that island's development as a plantation colony, which Waldemar Westergaard dates at 1688.[15] During the governorship of Johan Lorentz in the 1690s, proclamations were issued on the subject of runaways,[16] and the Privy Council of St. Thomas resolved early in 1706 to take action against *grand marronage*. Accordingly, it was ordered on October 2 that all trees on the island from which slaves could make canoes were to be cut down; a proclamation of December 30 offered a reward of fifty Rigsdaler for the return of any slave dead or alive who had escaped to Puerto Rico.[17]

The proclamations of 1706 demonstrate two factors that had an important bearing on the phenomenon of *marronage* immediately and over time: environment and geography. In the early years of settlement, before the apotheosis of sugar, the primeval forest provided superb cover and supplied wood for canoes in which slaves could seek freedom in nearby islands. The 'marine underground' to Puerto Rico and Vieques (Crab Island), and farther afield to islands in the northern Leewards and elsewhere, ultimately became a major route of escape.

When the expansion of the plantations removed the forest cover, in St. Thomas and St. Jan by the 1730s and a generation or so later in St. Croix,[18] the best chances for permanent escape lay overseas, although, as we shall see, the islands' towns, as their populations grew, also provided havens. J. L. Carstens, who was born in St. Thomas in 1705 and died there in 1747, noted in his memoirs that in those early years runaways occupied the island's coastal cliffs, where they sheltered in almost inaccessible caves. Those first maroons chose well, with a keen strategic eye, for the cliffs could not be scaled from the seaward side and vegetation obstructed the landward approaches. Such refugees went naked and subsisted on fish, fruit, small game such as land turtles, or stolen provender. Slave hunts, organized three times a year, could neither loosen their grip on freedom nor dislodge them from the cliffs.[19]

Regrettably, Carstens recorded nothing of the size and social organization of this early community or its relationship with plantation slaves. It was the only such community that St. Thomas ever had, and it did not last long. The Danish authorities could ill afford to stand idly by, especially when St. Thomas was not yet self-sustaining.[20] During the War of the Spanish Succession they began to organize the *klappe jagt* or slave hunt more effectively, using planters, soldiers, and trusty slaves.[21] The forests then became less safe, while at the same time the agricultural exploitation of St. Thomas, peaking in the 1720,[22] reduced the vegetational cover. As a result, slaves turned to the sea. Their line of escape led west, with favorable northeast trade winds and currents, toward Puerto Rico and other islands, none of which lay more than 60 kilometers from St. Thomas. Slaves had opportunities to become familiar with the surrounding waters on fishing expeditions for sea turtles around Vieques, and the same boats they manned on their masters' behalf could be used to make a break for Puerto Rico.[23] In 1747, 19 slaves deserted from St. Croix, and the following year 42 seized a sloop there and sailed to comparative freedom among the Spaniards.[24]

Puerto Rico, which became their preferred destination, was sparsely populated before the *Cédula de Gracias* of 1815, and its authorities, perhaps for this very reason, looked leniently if not encouragingly on runaways from the Danish islands. As early as 1714, Gov. Don Juan de Rivera organized 80 deserters from Danish and other islands into a community at San Mateo de Cangrejos east of San Juan, gave them public land, and required them to function as an auxiliary militia.[25] The Spanish government ratified these arrangements in *cédulas* of 1738 and 1750, and in the latter decreed freedom for runaways who embraced Catholicism.[26] Eugenio Fernández Méndez has argued that the Spanish acted largely from religious motives.[27] But there was also an element of calculating realpolitik: in addition to providing manpower, maroons were potential sources of useful intelligence in the event of hostilities. It is instructive to note that slaves from South Carolina found an equally agreeable haven in Spanish Florida in the early eighteenth century and were used by the Spaniards in border incursions that kept the British colony in a state of apprehension.[28]

Early legislative prescriptions against *grand marronage* authorized such physical deterrents as leg amputations, hamstring attenuation, and leg irons or neck collars.[29] Such measures hampered but did not prevent escape by water. Later laws elaborated rules for access to and use of boats. Even before 1750, legislation limited the size of canoes and barges that whites could keep and specified conditions of ownership.[30] Although mutilations and hardware such as neck irons fell out of use pari passu with the disappearance of the forests,[31] regulation of boats persisted until the very end of the era of slavery. The ordinance of October 2, 1706, was the forerunner of many, the necessity for which

was proof of the problem they sought to eradicate. But despite a flurry of laws in the 1740s and 1750s, probably inspired by the beginning of the agricultural exploitation of St. Croix, *grand marronage* could not be suppressed.

Reimert Haagensen, who lived in St. Croix in the 1750s, noted in an account of that island that planter families were being ruined by the running away of slaves in groups of as many as 20–25 in a single night. He instanced occasions when slaves seized boats by surprise attack and forced their crews to sail to Puerto Rico. Many plantation owners, Haagensen complained, had '*capital staaende iblandt de Spanske, hvoraf dog ingen Interesse svares.*'[32] It was commonly supposed in the Danish islands that a year in the service of the Spanish crown brought freedom. This Haagensen said he could neither confirm nor deny; but he had personal knowledge of slaves who had escaped to Spanish territory, lived well and in freedom, and sent back messages of greeting to their former masters and slave companions.[33] Similarly, C. G. A. Oldendorp, a Moravian missionary inspector, writing in the 1760s, noted that Maronbjerg — Maroon Mountain, in the northwestern corner of St. Croix — was no longer a secure retreat, and that as a result the proximity of Puerto Rico and the promise of freedom there acted as powerful stimulants. The still largely African-born slave population demonstrated the same levels of inventiveness and daring that Haagensen observed in the previous decade. Slaves secretly built canoes large enough to accommodate whole families, commandeered when they could not build, forced sailors to take them to Puerto Rico, and, when all else failed, bravely swam out to sea in hope of accomplishing the same objective.[34]

Legislation dealing with *marronage* at the end of the eighteenth century and in the early years of the nineteenth shows a continuing preoccupation with the problem. Gov.-Gen. Ernst von Walterstorff attempted to introduce a boat registry in St. Croix in 1791 and insisted that all canoes must have bungs that were to be put away, along with oars and sails, when the canoes were not in use. All craft were to be stamped with the royal arms and bear a registration number as well as the owner's name; none was to be sold or rented outside the towns' harbors.[35] In 1811 the police chief of Christiansted announced a fine of ten *pistoles* for employing slaves on the wharves or on boats in the harbor without a police permit.[36] The Danish West Indian government in 1816 expressed concern at the persistence of escapes by boat and contemplated introducing regulatory measures such as prohibition of boat ownership except in towns.[37] Finally, as late as 1845, three years before emancipation, Adam Søbøtker, the acting governor-general, promulgated a decree permitting plantations to keep only flat-bottomed boats, as slaves were unlikely to try to escape in such craft.[38] By then, however, the marine underground had other destinations than Puerto Rico, as will be shown below.

Over time, legislation to cauterize the hemorrhage proved only minimally effective. The failure of preventative measures prompted a search for other solutions. The absence of a formal extradition convention had enabled runaways to Puerto Rico to cock their snooks at former owners, a form of salutation that Haagensen for one found less than amusing.[39] The establishment of such a convention, it was thought, would resolve the difficulty. Accordingly, a series of cartels between Spain and Denmark in 1742, 1765, 1767, and 1776 established that deserters would have to be claimed within one year by their owners; that the latter would pay the expenses of their slaves' maintenance for that period; that reclaimed fugitives would not be punished; that those who embraced Catholicism would be allowed to remain in Puerto Rico; and, finally, that a Catholic church and residence for its priest would be built in St. Thomas at Denmark's expense.[40]

These diplomatic initiatives, however, proved disappointing. The cartels applied to future deserters but not to slaves already in Puerto Rico. The Spanish authorities, moreover, were less than expeditious in dealing with claims. The Danish West India Company filed a claim in 1745 for the return of some 300 deserters known to be in San Mateo de Cangrejos, but 21 years passed before it was adjusted.[41] Less than a decade after the 1767 convention, Gov.-Gen Clausen was engaged in a brisk correspondence with Don Miguel de Muesos, captain general of Puerto Rico. Several slaves had decamped from St. Thomas early in 1775, but the envoy sent to claim them was met by Spanish professions of ignorance of their whereabouts.[42] Grosso modo, the Spaniards showed little inclination to cooperate in the matter of runaways. Occupation of the Danish West Indies in the early years of the nineteenth century by Spain's wartime ally England appears to have made little difference. The British lieutenant governor of St. Croix in 1811, Brig. G. W. Harcourt,

issued a proclamation asserting that slaves had been carried off in Puerto Rican boats and declared that such boats found illegally four weeks thereafter in any harbor except Christiansted and Frederiksted would be seized and confiscated.[43] Two months later, the British authorities invited persons who had recently lost slaves and believed them to be in Puerto Rico to submit information on the slaves' age, sex, appearance, and time of desertion.[44]

As late as 1841, the 'long-standing difficulties' with Puerto Rico were the subject of exchanges between the Danish West Indian governor-general and King Christian VIII, each hoping that the new Puerto Rican captain general, Mendez Vigo, would be more disposed to 'friendly conclusions' than some of his predecessors had been.[45] An incident reported by Van Dockum in the early 1840s reveals the nature of the difficulties. Acting on information that two slaves had been spirited away to Vieques in boats from that island, the authorities in St. Croix sent the frigate on patrol duty in the West Indies to reclaim them. When the frigate arrived at Isabel Segunda, the main town of Vieques, that island's governor, though full of conviviality and consideration, would admit only that a boat had in fact taken slaves from St. Croix to Vieques.[46] It appears that the shortage of labor in the Spanish islands after the legal suspension of the slave trade in the 1820s bred illegal trafficking, often with the collusion of Spanish authorities.[47] The episode to which Van Dockum referred seems to have been an instance of labor piracy willingly embraced by the slaves of St. Croix as an avenue of *grand marronage*.

Taking refuge in forested hills and fleeing to Puerto Rico or Vieques were the most dramatic early acts of *grand marronage*. While slaves continued to escape by water, the disappearance of primeval vegetation prompted others to find ways of deserting without leaving the islands. Sugar served their needs and turn. Harvesting began in late December or early January when the canes approached maturity and had grown high enough to conceal even the tallest person. Until the end of the 'crop' or reaping season in July, therefore, each unreaped field provided an artificial forest in which slaves could continue to conceal themselves over a six-month period. The work of these months of harvest made the most strenuous and exacting demands on slaves' endurance. This was also the dry season, before high summer brought the heavy showers associated with the movement of the intertropical convergence zone. A slave thus had multiple inducements: he could find cover, escape the period of hardest labor, and keep dry. A Danish official in the late eighteenth century noted that the expansion of plantations on St. Croix made it difficult for runaway slaves to find shelter in forests that were disappearing or in fields that no longer contained scrub. The alternative, he observed, rendered them secure but posed a constant fire hazard: 'Fleeing to the cane fields in which the cane and leaves can exceed a man's height, they put down poles of about a meter and a half and make a bower over these with the leaves of the nearest canes plaited together. In this way they form a little hut about four and a half feet by six to seven feet around. Having cleared the ground in the hut of dry leaves and left an opening, they then use the place to lie up, to store whatever ground provisions they can, and as a fireplace.'[48] The existence of maroon hideouts in the cane fields was authenticated by discoveries of corner posts, ashes, and coal. A causal link between such hideouts and cane fires was also established by remnants of pork and other meat abandoned to and partially consumed by fires out of control.[49]

Another variant of *grand marronage* was desertion to the coastal towns. Christiansted and Frederiksted in St. Croix, and Charlotte Amalie in St. Thomas, grew in population and commercial importance in the prosperous years of the late eighteenth century: plantations flourished, trade expanded, and Charlotte Amalie was established as a free port.[50] For slaves on islands as small as the Danish West Indies, towns offered advantages of comparative anonymity; a prospect of work on the wharves, in warehouses, and aboard coastal or other vessels; the likelihood of finding a sympathetic reception and succor in the areas of these towns designated by law for free persons of color; concealment, incongruously enough, by whites; and the chance of using the town as a staging post in what might become a step-migration to freedom.

Anonymity was enormously enhanced when a slave on the run shipped from one Danish island to another. One cannot quantify this type of *marronage*, but it was known to have taken place, and as the bustle of free-port commerce in Charlotte Amalie arguably rendered that town a more impersonal place than either Christiansted or Frederiksted, it must be presumed that the tendency would have been toward St. Thomas. Newspaper advertisements appear to support such a hypothesis, although there is also evidence of *marronage* from Charlotte Amalie

to St. Jan and St. Croix. Most notorious was the case of Jane George, who in an advanced state of pregnancy escaped from St. Thomas in a canoe with a white man early in September 1815 paddling for St. Jan or St. Croix.[51] Another runaway, James Dougharty, an artisan apprentice, headed for St. Jan in 1822. A reward of $20 was offered for information, 'as it [was] not likely [he] had walked all the way.'[52] By and large, however, advertisements for maroons in St. Thomas over the first 15 years of the publication of the *Sankt Thomœ Tidende* (1815-30) show approximately twice as many desertions to St. Thomas as to St. Croix or St. Jan from St. Thomas.

The variety of employment in the growing towns facilitated *grand marronage* into them, and the anonymity they offered was compounded by the notorious laxity of the Danish West Indian police,[53] so that it was possible for runaways to sustain a livelihood in wharf-related work or itinerant vending without too great a risk of discovery.[54] Fugitives enjoyed the normally supportive presence of freedmen in their legally prescribed areas of residence, the Free Guts. With freedmen, urban slaves, and poor whites, deserters composed a demi-monde of the marginalized. Governor-General Clausen in St. Croix in the 1770s and Lt. Gov. Thomas de Maleville in St. Thomas in the 1780s expressed only more explicitly than most the sense of community that prevailed among runaways and freedmen in the Guts.[55] Poor whites involved in petty retail trading or artisan trades were known to consort with and provide shelter for runaways. The latter were potential sources of stolen goods and, if they had an artisanal skill, could be hired out to earn an income for their protectors. Throughout the late eighteenth and early nineteenth centuries, therefore, one finds legislation aimed at curtailing the mutually reinforcing liaison of fugitives and their patrons, especially in the towns. The preamble to an ordinance issued by Gov.-Gen. Adrian Bentzon in 1817 spoke of the long history of this liaison; the ordinance prescribed severe penalties for whites and free persons of color who either hired or hid slaves on the run.[56] As late as 1831, Adam Søbøtker, acting as governor-general, was still vainly attempting to curb that sort of collusion.[57]

For runaways, the coastal towns were above all a porthole of opportunity to a wider world. *Marronage* overseas to foreign destinations, before the significant growth of the towns, had been limited to Vieques and Puerto Rico. However, as towns grew, they attracted an increasing number of vessels from distant ports, widening the escape hatch for slaves. The schooners, brigs, sloops, yawls, and snows that called at these towns, especially. Charlotte Amalie as it became ·a Caribbean entrepôt, brought St. Domingue/Haiti and Jamaica in the Greater Antilles, the islands of the Leewards and Windwards, the North American continent, and even Europe within reach, though after 1802 Denmark ruled itself out as a haven for escapees. A Supreme Court decision that year in the case of the slave Hans Jonathan decreed that the free soil of the mother country did not confer freedom on the enslaved.[58]

Access to avenues of flight depended in some measure on the collusion of masters of vessels. Service at sea in the eighteenth and early nineteenth centuries was such as to suggest a parallel between masters of vessels and slave masters, between ships and regimented slave plantations, between crews and enslaved estate labor. Ship masters, not surprisingly, had their own problems of *marronage* in the form of desertion. It was not unusual for crewmen, singly or in numbers, to jump ship in West Indian waters. One Swedish sloop, the *William*, Capt. Joseph Almeida, lost five hands in St. Thomas harbor on February 5, 1827.[59] Such incidents meant that additional or substitute crews were often needed, and since the white population of Caribbean coastal towns was too small to meet the need, it was unlikely that runaway slaves who offered themselves would be interrogated closely, if at all, about their status. Black crewmen were therefore commonplace. Many of Almeida's men were Africans of unspecified status, and slave shiphands were by no means extraordinary. One such, Jan Maloney, deserted from a vessel of British registry in St. Thomas in 1819.[60]

In 1778 regulations were adopted to obstruct this avenue of *grand marronage* by forbidding shipboard employment of any slave without a sailor's pass and written permission from his owner. Significantly, it was considered necessary to reissue these regulations in 1806.[61] The 1833 royal proclamation of Frederik VII, by offering the extravagant reward of 1,500 *pistoles* for information on masters of vessels secretly exporting slaves, suggests that the problem still persisted even at that late date.[62] The size of the reward indicated the seriousness with which the problem was viewed, particularly at a time when the slave population of the Danish islands was steadily declining.[63]

Some ship captains, even before the end of the eighteenth century, were free persons of color. One such was Nicholas Manuel, whose ship, the *Trimmer*, plied between St. Thomas and Jeremie, St. Domingue, in 1796.[64] In such a vessel, arguably, a slave could find the maritime equivalent of a house of safety in a Free Gut. The legislation directed at captains thus took into account a potential collaborator, the colored shipmaster, while it also expressed the paranoia prevailing after the revolution in St. Domingue and accompanying disturbances in the French West Indies. Vulnerability to revolutionary contamination from these trouble spots was a recurring concern of Danish West Indian authorities, who lived in constant fear that their slaves would emulate the St. Domingue example. The years from 1791 to about 1807 were therefore· punctuated by measures to establish a *cordon sanitaire* against St. Domingue. These involved, *inter alia*, the confiscation of any boats arriving from St. Domingue/Haiti and the imposition of a fine of 1,000 Rigsdaler. Yet there is evidence to suggest that such prophylaxis achieved only indifferent results. The traffic to St. Domingue/Haiti, especially from St. Thomas, continued, and in the early 1840s Governor-General von Scholten felt moved to remark on the 'significant' number of 'unavoidable' desertions to that island.[66]

Legislation could not prevent desertions, for the movement of inter-island maritime traffic depended to a degree on slave crews, and the law permitted slaves with seamen's passes to be so engaged, making a pragmatic virtue. out of necessity, considering the shallowness of the white labor pool.[67] Engaged as crews in their island of origin, slaves embraced the opportunity to escape on reaching a foreign port. Jamaica was one such destination in the western Caribbean at which goods from the emporium that was St. Thomas were arriving well before the end of the eighteenth century. Both the *Royal Gazette* and the *Jamaica Courant* carried information that confirms that slaves considered any port a station in the maritime underground. The St. Thomas sloop *Martha*, Capt. John Simmons Blyden, arrived in Kingston in August 1788 and promptly lost Jack, a sailor aged 25, and Tony, 23, described as a 'waiting man and occasional fiddler'. Another St. Thomas sloop, the *Hope*, Capt. John Winfield, lost George, aged 19, at about the same time.[68] Joe, 25, jumped ship in Kingston from the schooner *Eagle*, registered in St. Croix, in May 1806.[69] Not all the deserting slave seamen from the Danish West Indies appear to have made it to freedom. Some like

Sam, a St. Thomas creole who arrived in Kingston on a sloop commanded by Captain Capp in 1797, were apprehended.[70] No doubt a reasonable competence in an English creole tongue must have helped a slave negotiate the narrows of early freedom in a strange English-speaking island, and in this regard slaves from St. Croix may have enjoyed an advantage. In that island, step by step with the creolization of the slave population, there developed an English-based creole lingua franca, whereas in St. Thomas it was Dutch-based.[71] Having an employable skill in addition to seafaring would also have helped. Another Sam, for example, who deserted from a Danish island schooner in Kingston late in 1793, was a hairdresser by trade. Since he was American-born and spoke good English,[72] he stood a doubly good chance of gettng past the exit turnstiles of this station in the maritime underground.

In the Caribbean, the same flows of trade that took vessels to St. Domingue/Haiti or farther away to Jamaica also took Danish West Indian vessels to the Lesser Antilles in the opposite direction. These flows presented like opportunities to slave for employment as crew, and such employment, legitimate or illegitimate, created chances for desertion to the Leewards, Windwards, and elsewhere. That traffic, moreover, complemented the trade originating to leeward of St. Thomas and St. Croix, thereby widening the possibilities for maritime *marronage*. This branch of eastern Carribean intercourse in the early nineteenth century was part of the expanding seaborne commerce into St. Thomas[73] and opened a major escape route for runaways to St. Thomas from islands in the northern Leewards and from as far away as Curaçao and Barbados.[74] Danish slaves were not slow to exploit the situation. One reported example from St. Thomas in 1819 indicates that eight slaves — seven men and one woman — probably crew on the 17-ton inter-island schooner *Waterloo*, stole the ship when it arrived in St. Vincent in the British Windwards.[75]

This episode is remarkable for its daring and also for the fact that it is the only incident of running away to the non-Danish islands of the eastern Caribbean, excluding Tortola, that the newspapers report. Though one of the best sources for the study of all forms of *marronage*, the Danish West Indian newspapers are in fact less helpful than one would like on maritime *marronage* to the foreign islands of the eastern Caribbean — perhaps understandably so, for the logical place in which to advertise for

deserters was the *terminus a quo* or point of escape. The Danish West Indian papers therefore report desertions from other islands more fully than desertions from the Danish islands. The local advertisement placed in the *Sankt Thomœ Tidende* by James Hazel, owner of the above-mentioned *Waterloo*, was thus unusual. Recovery of this lost schooner and slaves would have been better served by insertions in the foreign press. But perhaps the size of his loss — schooner, cargo, and eight slaves — obliged him to issue, in modern police parlance, an all points bulletin.[76]

From the inception of Danish colonization, slaves showed their capacity for creating possibilities for *grand marronage* overseas from each new set of circumstances. They responded ingeniously to the openings presented by the islands' ecology, the proximity of the Spanish islands, and the growing volume of traffic to and from the Danish ports. But of all the circumstances affecting *grand marronage*, none appears to have had a more quickening effect than emancipation in the neighboring British Leeward Islands, particularly Tortola. Desertions to Tortola began to increase from 1839, the year after the post-emancipation period of apprenticeship ended in the British West Indies.[77] Especially in St. Jan, no more than a cannon shot's distance from Tortola, the urge to run away then appears to have become irresistible.

Slaves were well aware that once they set foot on Tortola their freedom was secure, for the effect of the British Emancipation Act of 1833 was to confer on them on arrival the free status that the West Indian slave James Somerset had acquired in England in 1772 only after litigation at the highest level. For example, in reporting the incident of the early 1840s involving the two slaves from St. Croix, Van Dockum noted that before proceeding to Vieques they had requested to be taken to Tortola, where they went ashore. The authorities in Vieques used this fact to explain why they could not return persons who were in law free men.[78] The difficulties that British West Indian emancipation posed for the Danish authorities were practically insurmountable. Louis Rothe, an observant judge of probate who came to St. Croix in the 1840s, noted that desertions from St. Jan were almost impossible to control — and not only because of the proximity of Tortola. Overlooked by precipitous cliffs, St. Jan's innumerable bays made coastal patrols for the most part ineffective. Moreover, the patrols were too few to police bays that, even when

914 Caribbean Slavery in the Atlantic World

contiguous, did not permit observation of one from another. Deserters crossed the straits by boats and improvised rafts from St. Jan. Boats also originated from Tortola; some even came by appointment to fetch a slave or group of slaves. In Tortola, Rothe observed, 'all classes receive them with open arms and emissaries await with tempting offers of money and free transportation to larger islands, and promises of high wages and little work.' For the years 1840–46, he reported desertion by 70 slaves.[79] Though the total seems insignificant, it was more than double the number of runaways from St. Thomas over the same period.[80] If Rothe was correct — and he admitted that no official records were kept — an important fact emerges. St. Jan's slave population declined from 1,970 in 1840 to 1,790 in 1846.[81] The 70 slaves therefore represented nearly 40 per cent of the decline over that period.[82]

As the 1840s began, the Danish West Indian government sought to close this route to freedom by using frigates on the naval station. Governor-General von Scholten's orders were apparently to shoot to kill, although his long-term objective, as expressed in a letter to Christian VIII, was to reduce the attractions of desertion by progressive amelioration of conditions for slaves.[83] In 1840, a slave woman attempting to reach Tortola by canoe was killed by naval fire. Two others in the party, a mother and child, were apprehended, but two escaped by swimming.[84] In Denmark, the newspaper *Fædrelandet* observed in righteous indignation that 'blood ought not to be shed to compensate for an inability to reconcile the slaves to their existence' and found a sinister significance in the recent erection of 'an enormous prison' in St. Croix.[85] Von Scholten and the authorities were for the moment impervious to such voices of humanitarian protest, but it was another matter when pursuit of slaves involved firing upon them in ill-defined territorial waters claimed by the British. An ensuing British protest led to an investigation in 1841 by a senior Danish naval officer, Hans Birch Dahlerup. Formal charges were brought against a Lieutenant Hedemann for the killing of the woman and violation of British waters. The investigation ended in a court martial in Copenhagen and two months' imprisonment for Hedemann — 'more to satisfy England and its then powerful abolitionist lobby,' Dahlerup concluded, 'than for the offence with which he was charged.'[86]

The year 1845 was a particularly successful one for slaves bidding for freedom in Tortola. The administration's preoccupation, if not

panic, was by then plain. Acting Governor-General Søbøtker, reported to the crown in tones of anguish a sequence of escapes. On October 26, six slaves — five men and a woman[87] — from plantations on St. Croix's north side, got hold of a fishing canoe and made it to Tortola, although police and fire corps went in immediate pursuit. The Tortolan authorities returned the boat but not the people. Of particular interest is the fact that the leadership of this escape was attributed to a seasoned maritime maroon who some years previously had deserted from Dutch Saba and had been recaptured and resold in St. Croix.[88]

Less than a month after this incident the most spectacular episode of *grand marronage* from St. Jan to Tortola occurred. On the night of November 15, 37 slaves, including six from one plantation, deserted from southside St. Jan in two English boats sent from Tortola for that purpose. The maroon patrol, such as it was, was based on the island's north side, closest to Tortola, leaving the south side unguarded. For some time planters in St. Jan had been allowed to get their supplies of salt from Tortola in boats from that island, but they were less than vigilant in this instance. No satisfaction was to be expected, Søbøtker felt, as the government of the British Leeward Islands was unlikely to make reparations and would take no action against the two Tortolan boatmen who were accessories. 'The established principle since emancipation,' he pointed out, 'was that no one who had helped an unfree person to gain freedom could be punished for it.' The best the frustrated Søbøtker could do was to issue stern warnings to plantation owners, increase night patrols by his inadequate militia, and make new regulations respecting planters' ownership of boats.[89]

Grand marronage by David West Indian slaves lasted from the beginning of colonization, when the slave population was exclusively African-born, until slavery's end in 1848, when it was largely creole. In the decade or so before that date, emancipation in the British West Indies, particularly in neighboring Tortola, stimulated desertions on a scale that, especially in St. Jan, threatened to destabilize the slave system. In the 1840s such desertions, though they may have robbed the slave population of its potentially most revolutionary leadership, nevertheless prefigured and arguably acted as a catalyst for the successful rebellion of 1848.

Later commentators, like earlier observers, rationalized *grand marronage* in a variety of ways, some self-serving, others perceptive. These included depravity, overwork, fear of punishment or impending trial, arbitrary owners, the attractions of a work-free Sunday on other islands, and scarcity of food.[90] Whenever the occasion arose, officals were given to asserting, in an access of obtuseness or arrogant self-satisfaction, that fugitives would willingly return if only they could enjoy more discretionary time.[91] One of the 37 who fled to Tortola in 1845 seized a boat and did indeed return to St. Jan early in 1846. The records do not disclose his reasons but do report him as having said that others were equally ready to return, 'which was not improbable,' the authorities smugly concluded, 'having regard to the prevailing destitution in Tortola.'[92] But there is no evidence that these escapees came back to St. Jan, nor did this one swallow make a summer. On the occasion of the 1759 slave conspiracy in St. Croix, the examining magistrate, Engebret Hesselberg, made the surprisingly enlightened observation that 'the desire for freedom is an inseparable part of the human condition'.[93] Oldendorp, no libertarian himself, concurred, although with less generosity of spirit. 'It is extraordinarily difficult,' he noted, 'to convince the . . . Negroes that the rights their masters exercise over them are their due rights. They follow their uncontrollable nature and consider every means of gaining their freedom justified. . . . [T]hey run away from their masters . . . and seek violent means of escaping from their service.'[94]

By running away as they had always done, and in the numbers they did to Tortola, slaves reinforced the truth of Hesselberg's observation. In the 1840s they began to press the issue of their freedom by bringing the metropolitan authorities urgently to consider concrete measures for emancipation. Their initiatives helped embolden liberal opinion in Denmark, already critical of absolute monarchy and colonial policy and favorably disposed to emancipation on economic as well as human-itarian grounds.[95] The newspaper *Fœdrelandet*, organ of the opposition, declared it 'impossible for all practical purposes to place limits on the longing for freedom'.[96]

Indeed, when a deserted slave spoke into the record, he gave poignant endorsement to *Fœdrelandet's* sentiments. Such a man was William F.A. Gilbert, the only escaped slave from the Danish West Indies from whom we have a personal written testament. We do not know when or how he reached Boston, Massachusetts, but it was from that city on August 12, 1847, a year before emancipation, that he addressed to Christian VIII an impassioned plea not only on his own behalf but for every member of his race who had ever been or was still oppressed by slavery:

To His Supreme Magistrate, King Christian VIII, Copenhagen, Denmark. Sir: I taken my pen in hand a runaway slave, to inform your excelcy of the evil of slavery. Sir Slavery is a bad thing and if any man will make a slave of a man after he is born free, i, should think it anoutrage becose i was born free of my Mother wom and after i was born the Monster, in the shape of a man, made a slave of me in your dominion now Sir i ask your excelcy in the name of God & his kingdom is it wright for God created man Kind equal and free so i have a writ to my freedom I have my freedom now but that is not all Sir. i want to see my Sisters & my Brothers and i now ask your excelcy if your excelcy will grant me a free pass to go and come when ever i fail dispose to go and come to Ile of St. Croix or Santacruce the west indies Sir i ask in arnist for that pass for the tears is now gushing from mine eyes as if someone had poar water on my head and it running down my Cheak. Sir i ask becose i have some hopes of geting it for i see there your Nation has a stablished Chirches and Schools for inlightning the Slave. that something the American has not done all though she is a republican my nam is Frederick Augustus Gilbert now i has another name thus

Wm F. A. Gilbert

Sir, when i see such good sines i cannot but ask for such a thing as liberty and freedom for it is Glorius. Sir i make very bold to write to a King but i cannot helpit for i have been a runaway slave i hope your excelcy will for give me if i is out in order Please to sind you answer to the Deinish Council in Boston

> His withered hands he hold to view
> With nerves once firmly strung,
> And scarcely can believe it true
> That ever he was yong,
> And as he thinks o'er all his ills,
> Disease, neglect, and scorn,
> Strange pity of himself he feels
> That slave is forlane
> William F. A. Gilbert.[97]

Notes

1. Useful introductory material on the Danish West Indies published in English can be found in Isaac Dookhan, *A History of the Virgin Islands of the United States* (Epping, 1974); Jens Larsen, *Virgin-Islands Story* (Philadelphia, 1950); and Waldemar Westergaard, *The Danish West Indies under Company Rule (1671–1754)* . . . (New York, 1917).
2. See John Macpherson, *Caribbean Lands: A Geography of the West Indies, (Kingston, Jamaica, 3rd edn, 1973), 123, and P. P. Sveistrup, 'Bidrag til de Tidligere Dansk-Vestindiske øers Økonomiske Historie, med ærligt*

Henblik paa Sukker-production og Sukkerhandel',
*National Økonomiske Tidsskrift for
Samfindssspørgsmaal Økonomi og Handel*, LXXX
(1942), 65, 87.

3. J. L. Carstens, 'En almindelig Beskrivelse óm Alle de
danske Amerikanske eller West-Indiske Eylande', H.
Nielsen (ed.), *Danske Magazin*, III, No. 8, Pts. 3 and 4
(1960-70), 260-61.

4. Svend E. Green-Pedersen, 'The Economic
Considerations behind the Danish Abolition of the
Negro Slave Trade', in Henry A. Gemery and Jan S.
Hogendorn (eds), *The Uncommon Market: Essays in
the Economic History of the Atlantic Slave Trade* (New
York, 1979), 407-08, and 'Slave Demography in the
Danish West Indies and the Abolition of the Danish
Slave Trade', in David Eltis and James Walvin (eds),
*The Abolition of the Atlantic Slave Trade: Origins and
Effects in Europe, Africa, and the Americas* (Madison,
Wis., 1981), 234; also in this volume.

5. Green-Pedersen, 'Slave Demography,' *loc. cit.*, 245.

6. N.A.T. Hall, 'The 1816 Freedman Petition in the
Danish West Indies: Its Background and
Consequences', *Boletín de Estudios Latinoamericanos
y del Caribe*, 29 (1980), 56.

7. N.A.T. Hall, 'Slavery in Three West Indian Towns:
Christiansted, Fredicksted and Charlotte Amalie in
the Late Eighteenth and Early Nineteenth Century', in
B. W. Higman (ed.), *Trade, Government and Society in
Caribbean History, 1700-1920: Essays Presented to
Douglas Hall* (Kingston, Jamaica, 1983), 18.

8. *Ibid.*, 23.

9. Green-Pedersen, 'Economic Considerations,' *loc. cit.*,
408.

10. Richard Price (ed.), *Maroon Societies: Rebel Slave
Communities in the Americas* (New York, 1973), 9.

11. *Ibid.*, 3.

12. That number is not to be taken at face value since West
made no distinction between *petit* and *grand
marronage*. West, *Beretning*, 'Mandtal Optaget for
1789'.

13. Oxholm's General Tabell, St. Croix, 1792, *Dokumenter
vedkommende Kommissionen for Negerhandelens
bedre Indretning og Ophævelse, samt Efterretninger
om Negerhandelen og Slaveriet i Vestindien, 1783-1806*,
General Toldkammer, Rigsarkiv.

14. *Recapitulation of the State of the Different Quarters of
the Island of St. Thomas, May 13, 1802*, Den Engelske
Okkupation 1801, 1807, General Toldkammer,
Rigsarkiv.

15. Westergaard, *op. cit.*, 121.

16. *Copies of Orders Issued during Governorships,
1672-1727*, Bancroft Papers, Z-A 1, 3, University of
California, Berkeley.

17. *Kongelig Secretaire Schwartkopp's Report*, October 13,
1786, *ibid.*, Z-A 1, 48.

18. In the case of St. Croix, contemplated legislation in 1783
against illegal felling of trees was justified on the basis
that 'since almost all the forests have been cut down,
illegal felling of trees is of greater importance than
previously' (*Udkast og Betænkning angaaende Neger
Loven med bilag 1783-1789*, No. 24, Pt. i, Article 48,
General Toldkammer, Rigsarkiv.

19. Carstens, 'En almindelig Beskrivelse', *op. cit.*, 225, 259.

20. N. A. T. Hall, 'Empire without Dominion: Denmark
and Her West Indian Colonies, 1671-1848', seminar
paper (University of the West Indies, Mona, 1983),
3-10.

21. Bro-Jørgensen, *Vore Gamle Tropekolonier*, 225.

22. Westergaard, *op. cit.*, 160.

23. *Ibid.*, 161.

24. Arturo Morales Carrión, *Albores Históricos del
Capitalismo en Puerto Rico* (Barcelona, 1972), 83.

25. Luis M. Diaz Soler, *Historia de la Esclavitud Negra en
Puerto Rico* (Rio Piedras, 1974), 233, 236.

26. Cayetano Coll y Toste (ed.), *Boletín Histórico de Puerto
Rico* (San Juan, 1914), I, 16, 20.

27. Fernández Méndez, *Historia Cultural de Puerto Rico,
1493-1968* (San Juan, 1971), 165.

28. Peter H. Wood, *Black Majority: Negroes in Colonial
South Carolina from 1670 through the Stono Rebellion*
(New York, 1974), 305-07.

29. Westergaard, *op. cit.*, 162. See also C.G.A. Oldendorp,
Geschichte der Mission der evangelischen Brüder
(Barby, 1777), I, 496, and N. A. T. Hall, 'Slave Laws of
the Danish Virgin Islands in the Later Eighteenth
Century', New York Academy of Sciences, *Annals*,
CCXCII (1977), 174-86.

30 Gov.-Gen. Walterstorff's Placat of November 21, 1791,
quoting earlier proclamations of 1742, 1744, 1750, and
1756, Bancroft Papers, Z-A 1, 52.

31. Oldendorp mentions amputations for which the
definitive slave code of 1733 made provision
(*Geschichte*, I, 396). But by the 1780s there were already
voices critical of the code's provisions as barbaric. See,
for example, Judge Colbiørnsen's Opinion, September
3, 1785, Miscellaneous Papers, *Udkast og Betænkning*,
General Toldkammer, Rigsarkiv, and General
Toldkammer Skrivelse to Danish West Indian
Government, Dec. 23, 1782, *Kommissions Forslag og
Anmærkning angaaende Negerloven*, Bind 1, 1785,
ibid.

32. 'Capital invested among the Spaniards that yeilds no
interest' (Haagensen, *Beskrivelse over Eylandet St.
Croix i America i Vestindien* [Copenhagen, 1758], 42).

33. *Ibid.*, 43.

34. Oldendorp, *Geschichte*, I, 396-97. Oldendorp did not
say whether he knew of any slaves who managed to
reach Puerto Rico or adjacent islands by swimming.

35. Gov.-Gen. Walterstorff's Placat, November 21, 1791,
Bancroft Papers, Z-A 1, 52.

36. *St. Croix Gazette*, March 12, 1811.

37. *Akter Vedkommende Slaveemancipation*, Frikulørte
1826, 1834, Dansk Vestindisk Regerings Deliberations
Protocoller, April 30, 1816, General Toldkammer,
Rigsarkiv.

38. Søbøtker to Christian VIII, December 13, 1845, Record
Group 55, Box 9, National Archives, Washington, D.C.

39. Haagensen, *Beskrivelse*, 43.

40. Oldendorp, *Geschichte*, I, 396-97; E. V. Lose, *Kort
Udsigt over den danskelutherske Missions Historie paa
St. Croix, St. Thomas og St. Jan* (Copenhagen, 1890),
22-23; Diaz Soler, *Historia de la Esclavitud*, 234-236;
Morales Carrión, *Albores Históricos*, 67; *Kommissions
Forslag*, Bind 2, fols. 74, 89, General Toldkammer,
Rigsarkiv.

41. Westergaard, *op. cit.*, 161. Diaz Soler is of the view that
the settlement of the claim under the 1767 convention
was facilitated by the demise of the Danish West India
Company, whose illicit trading with Puerto Rico had
always been an obstacle to negotiations (*op. cit.*, 234).

42. Clausen to de Muesos, July 4, 1775, Bancroft Papers,
Z-A 1, 43.

43. *St. Croix Gazette*, February 8, 1811.

44. *Ibid.*, April 9, 1811.

45. Von Scholten to Christian VIII, Jan. 13, 1841, in which
reference is also made to an unfiled letter of Nov. 18,
1840, *Originale Forestillinger fra Kommissionen
angaaende Negernes Stilling i Vestindien med
Resolutioner*, General Toldkammer, Rigsarkiv. See also
Christian VII to von Scholten, October 7, December 4,

1840, August 1, 1841, Privatarkiv 6795, Rigsarkiv.

46. C. Van Dockum, *Livserindringer* (Copenhagen, 1893), 74–77.

47. Andrés Ramos Mattei, *La Hacienda Azucarera: Su Crecimiento y Crisis en Puerto Rico (Siglo XIX)* (San Juan, 1981), 23–24. Demand for labor inspired the decree of 1849 establishing an obligatory work regimen for free labor in Puerto Rico. See *ibid.*, 24, and Labor Gomez Acevedo, *Organización y Reglamentación del Trabajo en el Puerto Rico del Siglo XIX* (San Juan, 1970), 449–53.

48. Etats Raad Laurbergs Erindringer, Jan. 12, 1784, *Kommissions Forslag*, Bind 2, fols. 10–11, General Toldkammer, Rigsarkiv, cf. *ibid.*, Bind 1, fol. 326.

49. It is possible that cane-field deserters were simply engaging in short-term absenteeism. The length of absence and the construction of shelter that made absence of that duration possible would suggest, more plausibly, an intention to remain at large and ultimately leave the island.

50. Hall, 'Slavery in Three West Indian Towns', in Higman (ed.), *Trade, Government and Society*, 19–20.

51. *Sankt Thomæ* Tidende, September 16, 1815.

52. *Ibid.*, March 5, 1822.

53. Hall, 'Slave Laws', *op. cit.*, 184.

54. Hall, 'Slavery in Three West Indian Towns', in Higman (ed.), *loc. cit.*, 27, 29, 30.

55. Clausen's Placat, 39, July 29, 1775, *Udkast og Betænkning . . . No. 27*, General Toldkammer, Rigsarkiv; de Maleville's *Anmærkning*, April 7, 1784, and de Maleville's *Betænkning*, October 19, 1787, *Kommissions Forslag*, Bind 2, fols. 33, 84, *ibid.*

56. Bentzon's Ordinance of September 11, 1817, *Forskellige Oplysninger*, V, fol. 315, General Toldkammer, Rigsarkiv.

57. Søbøtker's Proclamation of July 22, 1831, *ibid.*, VI, fol. 216.

58. A.S. Ørsted, 'Beholdes Herredømmet over en vestindisk Slave, naar han betræder dansk-europæisk Grund', *Arkiv for Retsvidenskaben og dens Anvendelse*, I (1824), 459–85.

59. *Sankt Thomæ Tidende*, Feb. 9, 1827.

60. *Ibid.*, March 9, 1819.

61. *Dansk Vestindisk Regerings Avis*, May 15, 1806.

62. *Sankt ThomæTidende*, March 9, 1833.

63. Green-Pedersen, 'Slave Demography', *loc. cit.*, 245. See also Alexander, *Om den moralske Forpligtelse*, 5–7.

64. Calendar of Records, High Court of Vice Admiralty, Jamaica, 1796, fol. 17. Jamaica Government Archives, Spanish Town. Freedmen sometimes also owned their own vessels. The brothers Jacob and August Dennerey jointly owned a boat in St. Thomas in 1820. See Hall, '1816 Petition', *Boletin de Estudios Lationoamericanos*, No. 29 (1980), 70.

65. General Toldkammer Skrivelse to Dansk Vestindisk Regering, November 23, 1793, and Dansk Cancelli to General Toldkammer, August 8, 1807, enclosure 4, October 29, 1805, *Akter Vedkommende Slaveemancipation*, Frikulørte 1826, 1834, General Toldkammer, Rigsarkiv. For further examples of boat legislation directed at St. Domingue/Haiti see N.A.T. Hall, 'Forslag til Ordning af Vestindisk Forfatningsforhold Angaaende Negerne med Mere', Bureau of Libraries, Museums and Archaeological Services-Department of Conservation and Cultural Affairs, Occasional Paper No. 5 (1979), 3, 7, n. 16.

66. Von Scholten's comments on G. W. Alexander's 'Anmærkninger til Kongen af Danmark m.h.t. de danske Øer' [n.d.], *Akter Vedkommende*

Slaveemancipation 1834–47, II, General Toldkammer, Rigsarkiv.

67. The scarcity of white labor was a continuous problem, especially for plantations, forcing von Scholten to pass deficiency legislation in the 1830s. See Hall, 'Empire without Dominion', 26.

68. *Royal Gazette*, Supplement, August 8–15, 1788.

69. *Jamaica Courant*, May 17, 1806.

70. *Royal Gazette.*, December 2–9, 1797.

71. Hall, 'Empire without Dominion', 18.

72. *Royal Gazette.*, November 7, 1792.

73. The total tonnage of shipping into St. Thomas, 1821–30, doubled that of the previous decade. There was an annual average of 2,890 vessels with a total tonnage of 177,441. See Westergaard, *op. cit.*, 252.

74. Hall, 'Slavery in Three West Indian Towns', *loc. cit.*, 30.

75. *Sankt Thomæ* Tidende, April 10, 1819.

76. The newspapers of the Leewards, Windwards, Barbados, and elsewhere in the eastern and southern Caribbean can be expected to be good sources for *marronage* from the Danish West Indies. It has not been possible at this writing to consult such sources.

77. Louis Rothe, 'Om Populations Forhold i de danske vestindiske Colonier og fornemlig paa St. Croix' [n.p.], *Neger Emancipation Efter Reskript af 1847*, General Toldkammer, Rigsarkiv.

78. Van Dockum, *Livserindringer*, 74–77.

79. Rothe, 'Om Populations Forhold' [n.p.], *Neger Emancipation Efter Reskript*, General Toldkammer, Rigsarkiv.

80. *Ibid.*

81. The figures for 1840 are derived from Alexander, *Om den moralske Forpligtelse*, 7. Those for 1846 are from Sveistrup, 'Bidrag', *National Økonomiske Tidsskrift*, LXXX (1942), 78–79.

82. Rothe did not make any attempt to quantify the effect of *grand marronage* from St. Jan, but he did state that *marronage* to Tortola would have a 'conclusive influence upon the structure of [St. Jan's] slave population' ('Om Populations Forhold' [n.p.], *Neger Emancipation Efter Reskript*, General Toldkammer, Rigsarkiv).

83. Von Scholten to Christian VIII, January 15, 1841, *Originale Forestillinger fra Kommissionen angaaende Negernes Stilling*, General Toldkammer, Rigsarkiv.

84. Alexander, *Om den moralske Forpligtelse*, 15.

85. *Fædrelandet*, December 15, 22, 1840.

86. Dahlerup, *Mit Livs Begivenheder* (Copenhagen, 1909), II, 270, 289, and 'Skizzer fra et kort Besøg paa vore vestindiske Øer i Sommeren 1841', *Nyt Archiv for Søvæsnet*, I (1842), 1.

87. Statistics on the sex distribution of deserters or groups of deserters are not abundant, but the available data do point to a heavy preponderance of males. For example, of the 86 deserters in St. Thomas in 1802 (see above, n. 14), 73 were male and 13 female. The 7 men and 1 woman in the incident in 1819 (see above, n. 75) represent a not dissimilar proportion. The party of 5 in 1840 (see above, n. 84), assuming the two escapees were men, appears to be almost evenly balanced. But that distribution, on the basis of other evidence, can be considered unusual.

88. Søbøtker to Christian VIII, November 11, 1845, No. 3, Copies of Letters Sent to the King, Record Group 55, Box 4, fols. 2–3, Natl. Archs.

89. For letters reporting the incident see November 28, December 13, 1845, January 27, 28, 1846, Nos. 4–7, *ibid.*

90. For examples see Gardelin's Placat, Sept. 5, 1733,

*Udkast og Bet*ænkning . . . No. 4, General
Toldkammer, Rigsarkiv; Walterstorff to General
Toldkammer, July 20, 1802, *Akter Vedkommende
Slaveemancipation*, Frikulørte, 1826, 1824, *ibid.*; and
von Scholten to Christian VIII, May 14, 1842, *Originale
Forestillinger fra Kommissionen, ibid.*; Søbøter to
Christian VIII, January 28, June 12, 1846, Nos. 7, 19,
Record Group 55, Box 9, Natl. Archs.; and Haagensen,
Beskrivelse, 35.

91. Von Scholten to Christian VIII, May 14, 1842, *Originale
Forestillinger fra Kommissionen*, General
Toldkammer, Rigsarkiv.

92. Søbøtker to Christian VIII, January 28, 1846, No. 7,
Record Group 55, Box 9, Natl. Archs.

93. 'Species Facti over den paa Eilandet St. Croix
Intenderede Neger Rebellion Forfattet efter Ordre af
Byfoged Engebret Hesselberg' [n.p.], *Udkast og
Bet*ænkning . . . No. 3, General Toldkammer,
Rigsarkiv.

94. Oldendorp, *Geschichte*, I, 394.

95. For a detailed discussion of opposition liberal and other
positions on the emancipation debate in Denmark see
Grethe Bentzen, 'Debatten om det Dansk Vestindisk
Negerslaveri 1833–1848 med sæligt Henslik paa de
igennem Tidsskrieft pessem og Stænderdebatterne
udtrykt Holdninger' (M.A. thesis, Aarhus University,
1976).

96. *Fædrelandet*, Jan. 5, 1941.

97. *Henlagte Sager*, Vestindisk Journal, No. 141, 1848,
General Toldkammer, Rigsarkiv.

69

Slave Resistance in Guadeloupe and Martinique, 1791–1848

BERNARD MOITT

The intensification of acts of resistance among slaves in Guadeloupe and Martinique in the late eighteenth and the first half of the nineteenth century was largely a response to local socio-political events in the French colonies. This was a period when slaves were engaged in constant political analysis of the forces surrounding them, not just the French Revolution. The Saint Domingue Revolution was the most important event, but other developments influenced the resistance of slaves. The arrival in the colonies of French civil commissioners on political missions and military personnel, whose activities were consistently monitored by slaves, was a constant source of tension and resistance. Likewise, the British occupation of Guadeloupe and Martinique was a basis of resistance which also served as a training ground for some slaves who later emerged as leaders in the armed struggle against the re-establishment of slavery. During the period outlined above, slaves also observed the planters' loss of political hegemony which had a bearing on the patterns of slave resistance.

Resistance of slavery in Guadeloupe and Martinique was multidimensional and included the circulation of revolutionary literature, concoction of plots, insurrections and armed resistance against external forces – the most prominent manifestation of the slaves' actions – as well as manslaughter, arson, acts of poisoning and labour strikes, all of which resulted in the deaths of hundreds of slaves, white colonists and French troops. The slaves were unsuccessful in overthrowing slavery, but an analysis of resistance from the 1790s to the abolition of slavery

in the French colonies in 1848 captures the mood, mentality and determination of the slaves to free themselves from bondage and define the value of their freedom.

The resistance of slaves in Martinique and Guadeloupe has not been well documented by scholars, whether writing in French or English, who have justifiably focused on Toussaint Louverture and the Saint Domingue Revolution. T.G. Stewart, C.L.R. James, Thomas Ott, Pierre Pluchon, Aimé Cesaire, David Geggus and Carolyn Fick[1] are among the many authors who have examined different aspects of the Saint Domingue Revolution. Only a few studies have been done on slave resistance in Guadeloupe and Martinique, none of them in English.[2] A major problem with the studies in French is that they do not give us an illuminating picture of the cleavages which existed in these two colonies. For example, the lines of allegiance among the different groupings – Blacks, *gens de couleur,* and Whites – are not revealed. Also, since resistance is presented as the resistance of slaves against the French authorities, the role of the planter class remains shrouded. In addition, these studies concentrate almost exclusively on the armed resistance of 1802. Led by slaves in Guadeloupe who fought the French army in their bid to stave off the re-establishment of slavery which had been abolished by the French National Assembly in 1794, the war in Guadeloupe did not last very long – a mere six months – but it was a struggle of immense social and political importance. No resistance on this scale took place in Martinique, which may explain why scholars have ignored the revolutionary activities of slaves in Martiniquan history. These problems are compounded by a general lack of documentation about local events which makes resistance in Guadeloupe and Martinique difficult to explore, and explains why studies which deal with it rely heavily of the works of two authors – Auguste Lacour and Oruno Lara.[3]

This paper is not meant to address all the gaps outlined above. It attempts to probe slave resistance in Guadeloupe and Martinique from the 1790s using the local political context of the period as a guide. However significant external factors may have been, the slaves in these colonies were conscious of their social reality which grew out of their day-to-day existence. This makes an analysis of their actions in a pan-Caribbean context all the more valuable. By so doing, we are certain to acquire a better understanding of the dynamics of resistance. Given its ideological impact on slaves in the Caribbean, the Saint Domingue revolt is of crucial importance to analyses of resistance from the 1790s. Although slaves in Martinique were also influenced by the struggles of their counterparts in Guadeloupe, Saint Domingue was the major catalyst.

In examining the background to the slave uprising in Saint Domingue which changed the political and ideological landscape in the Caribbean, C.L.R. James has rightly put great emphasis on the "colonial question." According to James, the "colonial question" for the bourgeoisie and National Assembly in Paris was a dilemma over the applicability of the "Declaration of the Rights of Man and Citizen" to the *gens de couleur* in the French colonies. Because of the social and racial hierarchy which characterised slave society and put Whites at the top, people of mixed ancestry in the middle and Blacks at the bottom, the *gens de couleur* were considered second class citizens and unequal before the law. The storming of the Bastille on July 14, 1789, and the subsequent dismantling of the French monarchy led to these rights of equality in France, but when the question of equality was raised for free coloureds, the "French bourgeoisie dodged the colonial question as long as it could".[4] This situation placed the *gens de couleur* in a precarious position, as they were seen as an intermediary group between Blacks and Whites whose political loyalty was difficult to establish.

The colonial question was all the more significant because of the numerical and economic strength of the *gens de couleur*. In 1791, they numbered 28,000 (compared to 40,000 Whites and about 500,000 slaves), constituted an important economic force in Saint Domingue and were served by distinguished leaders. As Fick notes, "they were richer, more numerous, and far more militant than elsewhere in the French West Indies."[5] Their wealth and agitation for political rights caused apprehension among white planters in Saint Domingue who believed that granting them rights meant the ruin of the colonies. As Fick explains,

if they allowed the free persons of color to vote and hold office, it would, they believed, open the way to, and encourage, insurrection among the slaves. It would be the end of white supremacy and of their fortunes.[6]

It is clear that, as James put it, "the bourgeoisie did not want the colonies ruined."[7]

Coloureds demanded the same rights as Whites from the French National Assembly, but the colonists in Paris, who owned plantations in the French Caribbean colonies, were against it and threatened the bourgeoisie with the spectre of a slave revolt. James argues convincingly that the maritime bourgeoisie feared for their investments and put the "Rights of Man" in their pockets whenever the colonial question came up.[8] Although there were periodic shifts in the position held by the National Assembly on the question of the *gens de couleur*, the belief that the Blacks should remain in bondage remained constant almost until the end of the century. The colonial question was thus a racial question,[9] and in spite of the many tenuous alliances between the *gens de couleur* and the slaves, the latter realised that freedom would not be granted; it had to be fought for. According to David Geggus, "the free coloureds acted like the slave owners they were and were careful not to have their cause confused with that of the black masses."[10] In this regard, Fick's evaluation of the position of the slaves in Saint Domingue around 1791 is also applicable to Guadeloupe and Martinique because it points to the importance of the French Revolution as a catalyst for revolt, but also recognises that the initiatives of the slaves, whose analysis of their social condition was grounded largely in the local scene, were an indispensable variable. For this reason, it is worth citing in full. She writes:

The slaves had depended neither upon France nor upon the success or failure of the mulatto struggle. They were organizing for something that did not figure in any of the political debates, either in France or in the colony. But for the past three years they had witnessed the events, the agitation, the revolutionary and counter-revolutionary ferment that was throwing the colony into disarray. When news of the French Revolution reached the colony, slaves heard talk of liberty and equality, and they interpreted these ideas in their own way. Domestics listened to their masters argue over independence, while they perfunctorily served them their meals and drinks. Some had even travelled to France with masters who could not do without their servants. They were exposed to new ideas, to the principles upon which the revolution was being built, and they carried the experience back with them. In the ports, newly arrived French soldiers brought news of the recent events in France and spoke to them with great enthusiasm. Sailors aboard the merchant ships did the same as they worked side by side with the slaves, loading and unloading cargo in the harbors.[11]

Hence, a series of plots and attempted uprisings in Martinique in the wake of the French Revolution suggest that slaves were knowledgeable about political events in France, but more importantly, that they observed cracks in the political hegemony of the planter class at home which resulted from these events. Thus, they struck while the debate over liberation weakened the planter class; at least, this may have been the perception. Though not well documented, these events are worth highlighting. One was the circulation of an anonymous letter in August, 1789, signed "by us Blacks" calling for freedom. At the end of the month, word of a slave insurrection in Saint-Pierre, then the capital, led to the sentencing of 20 slaves, eight of whom were put to death. Another plot was discovered in September, 1789, and a small scale revolt put down in October, a time when there was an increase in *marronage* and when the white bookkeeper of a plantation was murdered.[12]

The situation in Guadeloupe, where colonists feared for their well-being due to anti-slavery activity, was equally tense. In his reports filed in April, 1790, the Baron de Clugny – Governor of Guadeloupe – claimed that he had been occupied in putting down a slave insurrection on the island. He had been at the head of a detachment of 100 men in the parish of Capesterre where slaves had killed Whites. The local administrative council condemned the slave leaders to be hanged[13] and three months later, by which time the resistance had been crushed, the punishment

was carried out. By July, five of the slaves had already been executed.[14]

As the decade opened, slaves in Martinique continued to agitate for their liberty, causing fear on the part of the colonial administration. In January, 1791, a general slave revolt was averted at the last minute, but another took place on May 11 in Saint-Pierre. Writing to the Ministry of Marine and Colonies about the event, Belhaguey reported that he had called in the detachment of the *gens de couleur*, normally stationed at Morne Rouge, to provide security for the colonists.[15] It is important to underline that these events occurred before the slave uprising in Saint Domingue which began in August, 1791, and are an indication that slaves in Martinique pursued their own agenda. After 1791, their agenda remained the same, but they were increasingly motivated by the actions and achievements of the slaves in Saint Domingue.

In 1793, events in the French Caribbean colonies moved quickly and the political situation was characterised by confusion in the local administration in Guadeloupe and Martinique dating back to the previous year. In 1792, the Ministry of Marine and Colonies sent Lacrosse, an ambitious marine officer, to Martinique to help boost support for the French Republic. Having realised many of his objectives by early 1793, he took advantage of the political vacuum which existed to reward himself with several titles including that of Governor of Guadeloupe. Though pleased with Lacrosse's endeavours, Paris wanted to keep him in check and maintain control. To this end, the French government dispatched General Rochambeau to Guadeloupe in 1793 and gave him the title of Governor-General of the French Colonies and commander-in-chief of the armed forces of the Windward Islands. Upon his arrival in late January, Rochambeau proceeded to reshape the administration by redistributing political offices. In early February, he named General Collot governor of Guadeloupe, relegating Lacrosse to the position of provisional Governor and reserving the post of Governor of Martinique for himself – a move which Lacrosse contested. This situation led to a power struggle between Rochambeau and Lacrosse who was well liked in Guadeloupe, but who had to take orders from Rochambeau.[16] In the end, Rochambeau forced Lacrosse out of the region, but he returned, as we shall see, in 1801 on another administrative mission. In the meanwhile, Governor Collot rose in importance.

In April, 1793, two months after Collot took up his duties, slaves rose up in Trois-Riviéres (Guadeloupe) and killed 20 planters on the plantations Brindeau, Fougas and Mare et Roussel.[17] The slaves were captured, but the *Commission extraordinaire,* no doubt a patriot (Republican) who was in favour of overturning the old order in France and in the colonies, put them under his protection, which, until the British invasion and the return in numbers of the counter revolutionaries in 1794, saved the slaves from being prosecuted. The slaves were then arrested and "interned, two hundred of them, in the barracks of Fort Saint-Charles in Basse-Terre."[18]

There were other incidents of note in 1793, such as that in which twelve planters were executed in prison by an angry crowd in Pointe-à-Pitre on July 7.[19] Some French sources suggest that this may have been the result of a power struggle between patriots who used slaves to perpetuate their own cause, and royalists who wanted to maintain the old order.[20] But the uprising which occurred in Sainte-Anne in August, 1793, was more significant. The data are thin, but the scale of the revolt suggests that it had the potential of spreading. The revolt began on August 28, when Auguste – a free coloured – rallied 1,000 to 1,200 people, mostly slaves, whom he promised freedom if they revolted. They pillaged plantations in Sainte-Anne, seizing arms in the process. However, using the forces at his disposal, Governor Collot crushed them a day later and carried out a search of the plantations in the region aimed at capturing the rebels. Of those caught, 29 were shot, 10 were sentenced to hang and 5 received whippings.[21]

It is of particular interest that the revolt in Sainte-Anne occurred at a time when Sonthonax, one of three French civilian commissioners sent to Saint Domingue in 1792 to pacify the colony, was in the process of abolishing slavery there. Forced by internal upheaval to act quickly, Sonthonax began the manumission process in June, 1793, and proclaimed the abolition of slavery on August 29, 1793.[22] Future research may determine whether news of the manumission in Saint Domingue had reached slaves in Guadeloupe. The timing of the Sainte Anne revolt leaves such a possibility open, but the temptation to link both incidents without supporting data

must be avoided. In spite of the failure of the Sainte-Anne revolt, armed resistance remained an important dimension of slave resistance in Guadeloupe, as the struggles waged by the slaves during the British occupation of Guadeloupe and Martinique in 1794 demonstrate.

The British occupation occurred at a time when pressures from all quarters forced the French to yield on slavery. In essence, the protracted struggle for freedom in Saint Domingue and the contradictions in French policy which it revealed led the French National Convention to declare the abolition of slavery in the French colonies on February 4, 1794. In April, French commissioners Victor Hugues and Pierre Chrétien were scheduled to make the declaration to end slavery in the Caribbean colonies and to set up Provisional Councils to govern the islands. Before the commissioners arrived, however, the English, on whom the French had declared war in February 1793, seized the opportunity to occupy Martinique and Guadeloupe,[23] with the intention of perpetuating slavery and thereby thwarting the aspirations of the slaves.

The British subdued Martinique after initial fighting in which slaves took part, but met with stiff resistance in Guadeloupe which formed a strong, mixed colonial army – the result of changes in recruitment policies made necessary by the invasion. Made up of white planters, *gens de couleur* and slaves who enlisted with the prospect of liberation – usually obtained after eight years of service – this was not a standing army. In December 1792, the Colonial Assembly of Basse-Terre, where planters had great influence, created a special place in the colonial army for free *gens de couleur* – the *bataillion de volontaires libres de la Guadeloupe* – no doubt as a buffer against patriots and black slaves. In 1793, Governor Collot had only 144 men from the regiment of Guadeloupe and 27 from another regiment – the *régiment de Forez* – at his disposal.[24] The input of *gens de couleur,* and later, slaves who constituted this army of *sans-culottes,* was therefore crucial to the struggle against the British in 1794.

Hugues and Chrétien landed at Salines with a small expeditionary army of about 1,500 men who saw action almost immediately as fierce battles took place in the first days of the British occupation. In the initial stages, the expeditionary army suffered heavy casualties including

Chrétien and 100 soldiers and officers who were killed in the British attack on Fort Fleur d'Epée. The British forces also attacked Pointe-à-Pitre, Fort Mascot, and Berville. In the attempt to retake Fort Mascot, the expeditionary army lost 90 men. Another 200-300 were killed at Pointe-à-Pitre which the British bombarded from Saint-Jean hill to Baie-Mahault; others were killed in street combat with the British.[25] In spite of initial gains, the British were dislodged from Fort Fleur d'Epée and Pointe-à-Pitre by the end of 1794, but were still in a strong position to lay siege to Pointe-à-Pitre. This is the point at which Hugues broadened the colonial army to include mostly slaves freed by the 1794 abolition proclamation.[26]

Pélardy, an artillery captain, created a force of 3,000 black slaves in the days following the fall of Fort Fleur d'Epée.[27] Along with the remnants of the old colonial army, this army became the major fighting force against the British. In a letter to the *Comité de salut public,* Hugues praised the value of a mixed army, noting that he paid the Blacks the same as the French troops in the colonies and that the Blacks alone, without the Europeans, constituted a formidable army.[28] The struggle which this army waged was a struggle against slavery which the British wished to re-establish and it was successfully accomplished by the end of December, 1794.[29]

From 1794 to 1802, slaves in Guadeloupe lived in a tenuous state of freedom which has not received much scholarly attention, but a series of events following the war suggests that slaves were involved in a continual struggle. After 1794, most of the frigates operated by Frenchmen loyal to the king would not serve Guadeloupe and Victor Hugues had to organize an armed flotilla to supply the island.[30] In this situation, it is likely that slaves worked harder to cultivate provisions, given the emphasis on the production of sugar and the neglect of food crops. Hugues ruled with an iron hand and former slaves were still required to perform corveé labour. On June 18, 1795, for example, an *arrâté* designed to compel former slaves to return to their estates was introduced, forcing many to become maroons.[31] Also, French military authorities disarmed former slaves who had fought and thereafter imprisoned many.[32] And in 1799 when the French introduced constitutional changes in the form of a tripartite political system consisting of a *Captain-Genéral*, a colonial prefect and a high court judge to govern each colony, Hugues was replaced by Desfourneaux, who arrived in Basse-Terre in June. Most importantly, two former slaves who rose through the ranks of the colonial army and whose actions had great impact on slave resistance in the nineteenth century, also became actively involved, albeit in different camps, in the struggle over the re-establishment of slavery. Both came from similar backgrounds and had similar career experiences.

One was Magloire Pélage, a coloured slave from Martinique who, in 1794, fought with the French against the English there. He was deported and imprisoned by the English following the fall of Martinique, but returned to fight with Hugues' forces which attempted to recapture St Lucia from the British in 1795. From 1793 to 1795, Pélage moved from being a slave to becoming commander in the army. After another four years of distinguished service in France and the Caribbean, he returned to Guadeloupe in December, 1799,[33] where he became part of the provisional council – the *Conseil du gouvernement* of Guadeloupe – which swore allegiance to Napoleon Bonaparte, ruler of France. This has led the Guadeloupean scholar Henri Bangou to label Pélage a traitor.[34]

The other slave-soldier was Louis Delgrès, also a Martiniquan, who became a lieutenant in 1792 and served with distinction under General Rochambeau in the Martiniquan campaign during which he was captured by the British in February, 1794.[35] Like Pélage, he too was deported by the British, but came back to fight with Hugues' forces in the St. Lucia and St. Vincent campaigns of 1795 and 1796 respectively. Regarded as a brilliant soldier, Delgrès became an aid to General Lacrosse in Guadeloupe in October, 1801.[36]

Both Pélage and Delgrès came back to Guadeloupe at a time when the freedom which the former slaves had fought so hard to maintain was threatened by the politics of Bonaparte, who, by 1799, was determined to restore France's authority in the French Antillean colonies. In essence, this meant the restoration of slavery in Guadeloupe and Guyane (a French colony whose economic importance was not as significant as that of Guadeloupe, Martinique or Saint Domingue) and a redoubling of efforts to subdue Saint Domingue. The French sent Lacrosse back to the colonies in May, 1801, to help accomplish this task. Lacrosse, now Admiral, began his task by re-establishing slavery in Guyane that year. In March, 1802, under the Treaty of Amiens, Britain returned to France the island of Martinique and other French colonies the British had occupied since 1794. Since the French had decided to retain slavery in Martinique, they were certain, if they could, to do likewise in the other colonies. Thus, Guadeloupe became the logical target where French troops could salvage their honour.

On April 1, 1802, an expeditionary army led by Generals Antoine Richepance (commander-in-chief), Sérizat, Gobert and Dumoutier left France with two war ships, four frigates, four troop carriers and four small boats with 3,400 men.[37] They landed at Point-à-Pitre, the capital of Guadeloupe, on May 6, 1802, determined to execute Napoleon's orders to reimpose slavery. Richepance ordered that the forts be occupied and that black troops be assembled and disarmed at Stiwenson plain, north of Pointe-à-Pitre. Some black soldiers were also imprisoned in the holds of the French ships, but others including Louis Delgrès, Joseph Ignace and Palerme fled towards Basse-Terre to help organize the resistance. Bangou argues that it was the help which Pélage provided in executing Richepance's orders that gave the French the advantage over the rebels,[38] but there is no unanimity on this issue.

As the French had virtually no hope in winning the war against the slaves in Saint Domingue, whose extraordinary struggle for liberation has been well documented by French military personnel such as Antoine Métral,[39] Richepance spared no effort in making the Guadeloupean campaign a success. In this endeavour, Bonaparte's actions helped. On May 20, 1802, slavery and the slave trade were reimposed in French law.[40] There are indications that Bonaparte's decision stiffened the resolve of the slaves in Saint Domingue, however.[41] Given the swiftness with which he acted in dispatching troops, Bonaparte may have reasoned that a victory over the former slaves in Guadeloupe would have improved the morale of French forces fighting in Saint Domingue, and made the restitution of slavery easier. But slaves in Guadeloupe resisted fiercely.

In the revolutionary war fought by the former slaves in Guadeloupe in 1802, men and women participated in combat, though most women played important, supplementary roles. Women's roles, though neglected by scholars, were stressed by French observers. Former slave women along with men and children formed part of the forces of Louis Delgrès who led a slave army against General Richepance and the French forces. They were also part of the forces of Ignace and Palerme, Delgrès' commanders who led factions of the slave army after it separated to fight the French on several fronts in order to maximise its chances of success. Most of the fighting took place in Basse-Terre, the southern part of Guadeloupe which is separated from la Grande Terre, the northern part, by Pointe-à-Pitre, the capital. On May 12, 1802, one of the major battles fought under the slave commander Palerme took place at Dolé, an important post held by the rebels where white women and children whom the former slaves had rounded up on plantations were incarcerated.[42] The coloured woman Solitude, though pregnant, actively participated in battle at Dolé and has achieved legendary status as a result.[43]

While most of the former male slaves fought direct battles with the French, others fled, turning to *marronage*. Former women slaves generally demonstrated great zeal, however.[44] They served as messengers, transported ammunition, food and supplies, cared for the sick, acted as cover for men under fire and chanted revolutionary slogans which kept spirits high in the insurrectionary forces of Delgrès, Palerme and Ignace. On May 10 when the major battle of the war was fought, Whites in Basse-Terre, fearing massacre, barricaded themselves in their homes. The silence which characterised the city was, according to the Guadeloupean historian Auguste Lacour, broken only by "the gallop of horses ridden by officers carrying orders and the singing of the French National Anthem by females who transported bullets and other ammunition to artillery units."[45] Women transported ammunition in the fiercest of battles,[46] and used their bodies to shield men, thus risking their lives as much as men.

The chants of former women slaves during the war in Guadeloupe were a way of demonstrating commitment to the anti-slavery struggle and keeping spirits high. Chanting served to motivate the insurrectionary armies and rally the troops behind the rebels' ideology. Lacour highlighted this aspect of women's contribution when he wrote:

It was not their fault if their fathers, their sons, their mothers and their lovers were not endowed with super-human courage. When a bullet whistled above their heads or a bomb exploded near them, they sang loudly, holding hands while making their hellish rounds interrupted by the chant: "Vive la mort!" ("Long live death!")[47]

Mottoes such as "vive la mort!" and later, "Vivre libre ou mourir!" ("Freedom or death!") say little about the long term socio-political vision of the rebels, but aptly encapsulate their manner of thinking in 1802 when death was preferable to slavery.

As the French troops were far better equipped and more experienced in combat than the rebel army, casualties among the former slaves were high during the early stages of the war, but the French also suffered major losses. Delgrès' major artillery unit was set up on the left bank of the Rivière-des-Peres flanked by Fort Saint-Charles, a rebel stronghold. The French troops positioned themselves on the right bank which meant that both forces divided Basse-Terre into two. In spite of stiff resistance, the French troops crossed the river and engaged Delgrès' army. Though the rebels were able to retain some posts such as Dolé after inflicting heavy casualties on Richepance's forces, Delgrès was cognizant of the superior technology of the French. Military reports of the Ministry of Marine filed by the French Major-General of the army acknow-ledged the heroism and military capacity of the black troops who fought bravely and replaced the dead and wounded in order to maintain a steady fighting force of 3,000. They also noted that on May 11, 1802 the French suffered 120 casualties, dead and wounded.[48]

Delgrès' strategy of retreating to Fort Saint-Charles after engaging the French army was effective at first, but backfired as the fort became a target for French bombardment. As the fighting intensified, he and his army barricaded them-selves in the fort to which Richepance later laid siege. Richepance's appeals to Delgrès to surren-der and cease fighting the French Republic were rebuffed as was his offer to pardon should Del-grès surrender.

On May 22, Delgrès realised that his army had lost the battle against the French. Although he cites no hard evidence, Bangou's claim that the rebels lost because of the participation of 600 Blacks who were held prisoners by Richepance and whom Pélage persuaded, in the name of military discipline and French patriotism, to join the assault on Fort Saint-Charles where the flag of liberty and the Convention flew, is plausible in spite of French military superiority.[49] What-ever the case, on the evening of May 22, Delgrès abandoned the wounded in the fort and evacu-ated it by the Galion door with about 400 men, and a number of black women,[50] all of whom remained active in the resistance.

Some of the former slaves remained with Delgrès; others became part of the forces of Palerme and Ignace. On their way from Basse-Terre to Pointe-à-Pitre, Ignace's forces pursued a scorched earth policy, pillaged and scored in-itial successes against the French. Around May 24, Ignace staked out a position on the plantation Belle Plaine in the community Abymes, three kilometres north of Pointe-à-Pitre, but aban-doned it a day later for the fort at Baimbridge, on the outskirts of Pointe-à-Pitre.

Fort Baimbridge had very little artillery – two cannon – which left Ignace and his forces virtu-ally defenceless. They became easy targets for a section of the French army commanded by Gen-eral Gobert and, although they held out until the evening, they were massacred.[51] It is believed that Ignace was killed along with 675 members of his contingent, including his two sons, on May 25.[52] Fighting along with his father and the French forces, Pélage's son also lost his life in the battle of Baimbridge.[53] In addition to these casualties, most of 250 rebels taken prisoner by the French were executed (150 of them on Octo-ber 27 alone) at the *Place de Victoire* in Fouilole in Pointe-à-Pitre. The women who accompanied Palerme fared little better. Routed from Dolé, Palerme's compatriots fled into the forest.[54]

Delgrès knew the end was near and decided to take his last stand on the extensive plantation, Danglemont, where the battle of Matouba was fought on May 28, 1802. Matouba, like Dolé, was a fortified post in Goubéyre near the south-ern tip of Basse-Terre, an area whose geography provided natural cover. Since his forces were no match for the well-armed French, Delgrès re-solved to commit suicide and to take as many French troops with him as possible by setting fire to barrels of gunpowder he distributed to his troops. Gunpowder was spread along the ap-proaches to the main entrance of the plantation. Delgrès also placed gunpowder within firing range of his two defensive positions in the plantation Great House. Fire was to be set to the gunpowder as soon as the French penetrated the rebels' defences. Women did not flinch at the idea. In fact, Oruno Lara noted that they "were even more enthusiastic about dying"[55] than the men. According to the reports of the Commander-in-Chief of the French army and French prisoners who had escaped, after shouts of "Vivre libre ou mourir" Delgrès and about 500 men, women and children were killed in the explosion, although the number has usually been placed at 300 by General Richepance.[56] French casualties were put at 400.[57] Some rebels escaped into the surrounding forest and became maroons, but Delgrès' defeat brought organized resistance to an end. An arrêté of July 16, 1802, reimposed slavery in Guadeloupe.[58]

State repression of the black population, quick trials, deportations and summary executions of the male and female rebels who were caught, followed the crushing of the resistance and the re-establishment of slavery. A commission militaire headed by General Gobert and brigade chief Depotte was set up with branches in Basse-Terre and Pointe-à-Pitre to judge the accused. As a way of demonstrating continuity, dramatising the severity of revolting against slavery and intimidating the slaves, this tribunal ordered that the bodies of executed rebels be left to hang in public for 24 hours, a common practice during slavery.

Men and women who appeared before the military tribunal received the same sentences. The commission militaire sentenced Solitude, who had been captured among the insurgents, to death. Because she was pregnant, "the execution had to be postponed. She was executed on November 29, after her delivery."[59] Jacques Adlaïde-Merlande believes that the sentence could not be carried out until she had given birth.[60] This may well have been the case, but Gautier's explanation that the French army "awaited the birth of the child so that it would have a slave in due time!"[61] is also plausible.

The death penalty was also imposed on other women including Marthe-Rose (Toto), Delgrès' mistress who had been held up in Fort Saint-Charles with him and had experienced every facet of the resistance. A native of St. Lucia, one of the French islands occupied by the British in 1794, Marthe-Rose suffered a broken leg during the evacuation of the fort. She subsequently lost the use of one leg and had to be taken before the tribunal on a stretcher.[62] Accused by the tribunal in Basse-Terre of influencing Delgrès to resist and of inciting slave soldiers to kill white prisoners held in the fort, Marthe-Rose was hanged publicly. With the rope around her neck, she is said to have remarked to onlookers: "Having killed their king and left their country, these men have come to ours to bring trouble and confusion. May God judge them!"[63]

Christian Schnakenbourg has placed the number of slave casualties from the war of 1802 at 10,000. Of these, 7,000 died in combat or were executed afterwards, 3,000 were deported to Guyane and Senegal or imprisoned at Brest.[64] But the toll was likely higher as resistance stemming from the outcome of the war continued.

The restoration of slavery in Guadeloupe did not mean that slaves in Martinique, however inactive, accepted their condition. In October, 1822, slaves in Carbet rose up in an unsuccessful revolt which left two Whites killed and five wounded. Sixty two slaves were condemned to death of whom 19 were executed.[65] This was also a period when there was constant fear in Martinique that Haitian emissaries would enter the island secretly and incite the slaves to rebel. Although slaves in Martinique were independent in terms of interpreting and acting upon their social reality, planter fear of Haiti was deep, widespread and justified. After all, the Haitians were free in a sea of slavery. They were regarded by slaves in the region as models to emulate, in spite of the price they had paid for their freedom. The fear of Haiti was given legitimacy by events such as that which occurred in 1823 when a plot organized by free coloureds who intended to massacre Whites, burn Saint-Pierre and overthrow the government was discovered in Martinique. The free coloureds allegedly wrote to President Boyer of Haiti requesting soldiers. When news of the pending arrival of the French troops in Martinique broke, rebels postponed the revolt, moving the date from December 17, to December 24, 1823. It may well be that the rebels chose Christmas Eve, when security would normally have been slackened, thinking that it would give them a greater possibility of victory. The delay was fatal, however, in that it gave the authorities time to investigate the plot and disarm the rebels.[66]

The slaves made another attempt to overthrow slavery in February, 1831, when they rose up in Saint-Pierre. This was a period when, according to a police report, slaves had become unusually restless, insolent and insubordinate, setting revolutionary words to, and singing in public, *La Parisienne*, a patriotic tune composed in Paris in 1830 for the July Revolution. The lyrics to the slaves' version of this popular folk song were anti-colonist in tone. For "March against their cannons," the slaves substituted "March against the colonists."[67] Echoing an earlier period in Guadeloupe, they also wrote the inscription "la liberte ou la more [sic]" ("Freedom or death") on a French tricolour they removed from the Place Bertin – the main square – and placed it at the entrance of the Eglise du Mouillage on the evenings of February 5 and 6. From February 7, they set fires all over Saint-Pierre; on February 9 alone they torched eight plantations and eleven houses in the suburbs. According to an administrative report, the fire would have destroyed Saint-Pierre had colonists not moved so quickly to extinguish it.[68] The same evening some slaves armed with cutlasses came down from the hills to join others in a general insurrection against slavery and set fire to cane fields.[69] The white planter class was terrified and drew comparisons with the slave uprising in Saint Domingue. This may explain Governor Dumas de Champvallier's decision to declare a state of siege and call out the militia, the police force, other troops and the French marines. Massive force and superior arms were thus used to quell the rebellion on February 10, but it is noteworthy that the slaves gave in only after several had been killed, others injured and still others arrested.[70]

On May 2, 1831, a special session of the Assizes court convened to judge the accused – "two hundred and sixty slaves of both sexes"[71] which included the slave women Henriette, Pauline, Adèle and Hyacinthe.[72] Of these, 210 were set free for lack of evidence, but 21 of the 50 tried were condemned to death while the others received diverse penalties. It is conceivable that women were among the convicted not only because they participated in the revolt but because of the gender neutral punishments which were introduced following the defeat of the slaves. The Governor placed strict limits on the number of slaves authorized to be in designated areas. For Saint-Pierre, the numbers were

120 men and 60 women; for Fort-Royal, 50 males and 50 females.[73] As in the revolts in Saint Domingue and Guadeloupe, therefore, male and female slaves in Martinique joined forces to combat slavery, which proves that the struggle against slavery was gender blind.

The uprising in Saint-Pierre was still fresh in the minds of colonists in Martinique when news of a similar plot in Guadeloupe broke. In 1831, 19 slaves were arrested in Point-à-Pitre and Sainte Anne, brought before the Assizes court and charged with participating in an insurrection. As it was discovered soon after the Saint-Pierre uprising, colonists drew a direct relationship between the two,[74] although they had no proof to substantiate their claims.

The prospect of slave insurrections, which often began with arson and manslaughter, remained strong down to the end of slavery in Guadeloupe and Martinique. Such was the case in Martinique in the days leading up to the abolition of slavery. The French abolished slavery for the second and last time on April 27, 1848, but emancipation was not immediately proclaimed in the French Caribbean colonies. As word of the emancipation proclamation spread among the slaves, they grew restless, threatened colonists, launched mass actions and engaged in arson. On May 22, 1848, for example, a slave belonging to Léo Duchamp threatened him with a cutlass, upon which the latter called in the authorities who promptly arrested the slave. But other field slaves from neighbouring plantations got word of the incident, armed themselves and marched to Saint-Pierre where they demanded the release of their compatriot. The authorities held out at first, but Pory Papy, the Deputy Mayor, ordered the slave's release. White colonists saw this capitulation as a sign of weakness and lamented that rather than appeasing the slave population, it had the effect of encouraging them to make greater demands. It is likely, however, that as a coloured man, Pory Papy was sympathetic to the cause of liberty as free coloureds in Martinique had staged many revolts in their bid for liberty and suffered great humiliation from Whites even though they were legally free. He must also have realised that it was only a matter of time before the emancipation law would be implemented and probably acted to head off an explosive situation. However, the white colonists were correct in assuming that slaves would not be satisfied with less than full emancipation. Indeed, fear gripped the white community on the evening of May 22 when 20,000 slaves crowded into the streets, hurling insults at Whites and setting fires in Saint-Pierre.[75]

The slaves burnt 20 houses on the evening of May 22. In another arson attack, 35 people – white males and females and black women domestics – were killed in a house, allegedly the site of an arms depot. Among the dead were several members of the Désabays family. Désabays had helped to crush resistance movements in the early 1830s, and was, like de Sanois, the owner of the house, despised by the free coloureds and slaves as a consequence. As he was scheduled to testify on May 23 against Pory Papy, the fire was categorised as arson. One account of the incident claims that the fire started when Désabays fired upon one of the assailants who attempted to lay siege to the house, and that firemen were prevented from attacking the blaze by other rebels. Furthermore, the militia, fearing a mass slave revolt, took no action.[76]

Another account suggests that slaves were more deeply implicated in the incident, as the ammunition stores belonged to them. The presence of the slave women, who would likely have been aware of the ammunition and may even have deflected the attention of authorities away from males slaves, lends credence to this account.[77] What is worth stressing, however, is that the slaves accelerated the process of emancipation by their own actions. Indeed, aside from setting fires, slaves murdered Whites and burned plantations in several sections of Saint-Pierre. These events frightened the authorities and forced them to act. And act they did the following day, May 23, when Brigadier General Rostolan, the provisional governor of Martinique, yielded to the unanimous wish of the Provisional Municipal Council of Saint-Pierre and declared the abolition of slavery which was made official on June 4. In quite similar circumstances, the governor of Guadeloupe declared emancipation on May 28, five days after his counterpart in Martinique acted.

In spite of the impact which the events of May, 1848, had on French colonial authorities, emancipation was not achieved by any one means. In addition to armed resistance, arson and manslaughter, slaves in Guadeloupe and Martinique also resisted slavery by engaging in acts of poisoning and labour strikes. In the context of slave societies in the Caribbean, poison has been referred to as the "preferred means of inflicting death, because the crime was difficult to detect."[78] But this meant, as I have argued elsewhere,[79] that slaves were very vulnerable to accusations brought by slave owners when suspicious deaths of people and animals occurred. Slave owners in the French colonies were certainly paranoid about being poisoned, especially during periods of crises. They learned from their experiences in dealing with the slaves that they had to exercise caution during such times, but their continued dependence on a captive labour force to fulfil their needs made them vulnerable. This was the case in Guadeloupe in 1802 when women slaves, posing as nurses, poisoned French soldiers who suffered casualties and were hospitalised in Pointe-à-Pitre. In response, the military rounded up and shot the nurses after the resistance failed. Lacour used military statistics compiled by General Ménard to show that mortality at the hospital declined immediately after the executions from a high of seven to eight per day to a low of one.[80] These statistics appear to be convincing, but the nurses were also suspected of supporting disgruntled coloured soldiers and the decline in mortality may well have been exaggerated to justify their execution.

In Martinique, the use of poison appears to have become chronic by the 1820s, a time when many masters asked government authorities to execute or deport their slaves whom they suspected of engaging in acts of poison. In 1827, there were at least 25 slaves (mostly women) in the prison at Saint-Pierre awaiting trial for acts of poison.[81] That year, Sainson Sainville, a planter from Fort Royal, requested that several of his slaves whom he suspected of poisoning his animals be destroyed.[82] The archival data do not indicate whether his wishes were honoured, but poison remained a problem into the 1830s. Tomich cites a report of the de Tocqueville Commission of 1839 in which the governor of Martinique noted that "efforts at raising cattle were discouraged by poison and the planters of the colony took little interest in it." Tomich argues that the slaves used the threat of poison "to exert a degree of control over the labour process" whereby they attempted to establish quotas on production, control the duration and intensity of work, define a standard of acceptable treatment of overseers and drivers, and have some say in the process by which tasks were determined.[83]

There is no doubt that slaves were cognizant of the effects the threat of poison had on the planters' psyche, but to suggest, as Tomich does, that they dominated their owners as a result, is overstating the case. No aspect of resistance worked in isolation from others and whatever leverage slaves may have had, masters could still punish them with impunity. Indeed, the case studies which Victor Schoelcher compiled and documented show that some of the worst atrocities of slavery occurred in the 1840s.[84]

Slaves combined the use of poison with other acts of resistance, one of which was strike action that changes in the law in the 1830s and 1840s made possible. On April 30, 1833, a royal ordinance abolished mutilation and branding of slaves. In 1840, the French administration placed slaves under the jurisdiction of *Procureur Générals* – the chief legal officers – as a means of policing the slave system more effectively. Then came the Macau law of July 18, 1845. Promulgated under Baron de Macau, Minister of Marine and Colonies and former governor of Martinique, the law was designed to ameliorate slavery and deflect criticism from abolitionists. It contained elements of previous laws such as those regarding curbs on the disciplinary power of slave owners, and limits on the work day. In reality, the Macau law was no more effective than other laws, but it held out the prospect of compulsory manumission.[85]

On September 23, 1845, two days after it was promulgated in Martinique, slaves began to agitate for freedom, resorting to demonstrations on some plantations.[86] One such demonstration took place on the Leyritz plantation in Basse-Pointe on December 14, 1845. Tomich's account of this occurrence is as follows:

The *atelier*, (labour gang) composed of 250 slaves, simultaneously refused all night work. Their action practically brought manufacturing on the plantation to a halt and had potentially serious consequences for the state of order elsewhere. The slaves based their refusal on the claim that the Macau Law had abolished extraordinary work and night work. After several days of useless representation by the magistrates sent to the scene, a show of armed force was judged necessary to end the disorder that threatened to spread to the surrounding plantations. A detachment of

infantry was dispatched and quelled the disturbance without bloodshed. After having been dispersed, the slaves gradually returned in small bands and peaceably resumed work.[87]

As they awaited the implementation of the emancipation, slaves in Martinique advanced their struggle for liberation by refusing to work altogether. Pierre Dessalles had chronicled the experience of many planters who, in May 1848, entreated slaves to work in vain. Slaves also prevented planters from using wage labour. Dessalles' journal entry of May 18, 1848, indicates that one such planter, M. de La Guigneraye, hired 25 labourers after his slaves refused to work or leave the estate, as they believed that they would soon be the beneficiaries of land distribution. As the labourers were about to begin cutting the canes, the slaves emerged from their huts and threatened to chop them to pieces like the sugar cane de La Guigneraye had hired them to cut. As a result of this action, the labourers were forced to leave the estate.[88] Two days later, Dessalles wrote, "the blacks refuse to work on the plantations which means that this year's harvest cannot be completed and next year's will be in jeopardy."[89] Dessalles described the fear and helplessness of planters in the weeks leading up to emancipation when the prospect of liberty permeated the air. Like other colonists, he blamed the colonial government for not rallying behind them, and the free coloureds for inciting slaves. In reality, there was little the government could have done, as things remained in a state of limbo pending word from Paris. Dessalles' patronising view of slave motivation – common among white planters – also needs to be challenged, for despite the odd alliance with free coloureds, slaves generally fought their own battles. However difficult it may have been for them to accept, planters had to come to terms with the fact that by May 1848 the slaves had already crossed the threshold of liberty both psychologically and socially.

Resistance of slavery in the French Caribbean from the 1790s has often been seen as the collective effort of slaves in a particular colony, motivated largely by the political fallout of the French Revolution. While this Revolution played an important role in slave politics, however, the Saint Domingue Revolution of 1791 was of greater significance in the colonies, because of its magnitude and success. Slaves in

Martinique and Guadeloupe in particular emulated the efforts of slaves in Saint Domingue. But they were also influenced by events which occurred in their own colonies, as the proximity of these two islands facilitated communication.

As in Saint Domingue, slaves in these two colonies resisted slavery on many fronts. They engaged in armed resistance, arson, manslaughter, acts of poison, work slowdown and labour strikes. Individually, none of these acts of resistance brought down slavery, but all had an impact, which means that historians must look for convergence in analysing the actions of slaves. Much research remains to be done on some areas of resistance such as work slowdown and its relationship to changes in the law.

As we have seen, in spite of changes in the law and administrative efforts in the 1830s and 1840s to dress up the slave system and make it look more "humane," slave owners in Martinique and Guadeloupe acted in much the same way as they did in earlier times. They were able to do so because of white racial supremacy, despite the fact that Whites were not a homogeneous group. That slaves should never be seen to win over slave owners in areas which might threaten or erode the social fabric of slave society remained an important guiding principle. Nevertheless, slaves in Martinique and Guadeloupe resisted slavery down to 1848. The example set by the slaves in Saint Domingue never ceased to be a beacon for them despite their successive, albeit failed attempts to dismantle slavery. But slaves were realistic in dealing with their bondage; what could not be achieved today could be attempted tomorrow using different methods. The slaves in Martinique and Guadeloupe were thus inventive, innovative and resilient. These are the qualities which enabled them to constantly challenge the slave system and to survive it despite the odds.

Notes

1. T.G. Stewart, *The Haitian Revolution 1791-1804* (New York: Thomas Crowell, 1914); C.L.R. James, *The Black Jacobins: Toussaint Louverture and the San Domingo Revolution* (New York: Vintage, 1963); Thomas Ott, *The Haitian Revolution, 1789-1804* (Knoxville: University of Tennessee Press, 1972); Pierre Pluchon, *Toussaint Louverture, de l'esclavage au pouvoir* (Paris: Editions de l'école, 1979): Aimé Césaire, *Toussaint Louverture: la Révolution française et le problème colonial* (Paris: Présence Africaine, 1981); David Geggus, *Slavery, War and Revolution: The British Occupation of Saint-Domingue, 1793-1798* (Oxford: Clarendon Press, 1982); Carolyn Fick, *The Making of Haiti: The Saint Domingue Revolution from Below* (Knoxville: The University of Tennessee Press, 1990).

2. See Jacques Adélaïde-Merlande, *Delgrès ou la Guadeloupe en 1802* (Paris: Editions Karthala, 1986); André Nègre, *La rébellion de la Guadeloupe* (Paris: Editions Caribéennes, 1987); Henri Bangou, *La révolution et l esclavage à la Guadeloupe* (Paris: Messidor/Editions sociales, 1989).

3. Auguste Lacour, *Histoire de la Guadeloupe* 4 tomes, 1855 (Basse-Terre: Editions de diffusion de la culture antillaise, 1976); Oruno Lara, *La Guadeloupe dans l'histoire*, (Paris: l'Harmattan, 1979).

4. James, *The Black Jacobins*, 67.

5. Fick, *The Making of Haiti*, 78.

6. Ibid, 79.

7. James, *The Black Jacobins*, 68.

8. James, *The Black Jacobins*, 68.

9. Césaire, *Toussaint Louverture*, 171-190.

10. David Geggus, "The Haitian Revolution," in (eds.) Franklin Knight and Colin Palmer, *The Modern Caribbean* (Chapel Hill: University of North Carolina Press, 1989), 27.

11. Fick, *The Making of Haiti*, 85-86.

12. Christian Schnakenbourg, *Histoire de l'industrie sucrière en Guadeloupe* (Paris: l'Harmattan, 1980), 106.

13. Archives D'Outre-Mer (ADOM), Colonies, Guadeloupe C 7a 44 25, Correspondence générale, April 19, 1790.

14. Ibid, C 7a 44 49, Correspondence générale, July 20, 1790.

15. ADOM, Martinique, C 8A 98 F85, Fort Royal, June 15, 1791,

16. Nègre, *La rébellion*, 22-32; Bangou, *La révolution*, 55-56.

17. Roland Anduse, *Joseph Ignace: Le premier rebelle* (Paris: Editions Jasor, 1989), 86.

18. Bangou, *La révolution*, 58.

19. Ibid.

20. Ibid.

21. Anduse, *Joseph Ignace*, 86.

22. Ibid, 90-91.

23. Adélaïdé-Merlande, *Delgrès*, 5-10; Nègre, *La Rébellion*, 12-13.

24. Bangou, *La révolution*, 100-101.

25. Ibid, 101.

26. Ibid, 102.

27. Ibid, 103.

28. Ibid.

29. Adélaïdé-Merlande, *Delgrès*, 7.

30. Bangou, *La révolution*, 94.

31. Lucien Abénon, "L'ordre Révolutionaire en Guadeloupe: Travail et liberté, 1794-1802," in (eds.) Michel Martin and Alain Yacou, *De la révolution française aux réolutions créoles et négres* (Paris: Editions Caribéennes, 1989), 99-103.

32. Bangou, *La révolution*, 113-114.

33. Négre, *La rébellion*, 34-35; Bangou, *La révolution*, 116.

34. Bangou, *La révolution*, 121.

35. Négre, *La rébellion*, 444.

36. Ibid, 49.

37. Ibid, 114; Bangou, *La révolution*, 119.

38. Bangou, *La révolution*, 127. See also, Anduse, *Joseph Ignace*, 215- 216.

39. Antoine Métral, *Histoire de l'expédition des Français à Saint Domingue* (Paris: Fanjat aîne, 1825).

40. Lara, *La Guadeloupe*, 126.

41. Bangou, *La révolution*, 162-163.

42. Lacour, *Histoire*, 3, 311.

43. Lara, *La Guadeloupe*, 138.

44. Lacour, *Histoire*, 3, 275.

45. Ibid. 3, 271

46. Ibid. 3, 275.

47. Ibid.

48. Cited in Bangou, *La révolution*, 130.

49. Ibid, 133.

50. Lacour, *Histoire*, 3, 291; Bangou, *La révolution*, 134.

51. Roland Anduse, "Ignace, premier Rebelle Guadeloupeen," in Martin and Yacou, *De la révolution française*, 118.

52. Alfred Martineau and Louis-Phillippe May, *Trois siécles d'histoire antillaise: Martinique el Guadeloupe de 1635 á nos jours* (Paris: Société de l'histoire des colonies françaises, 1935), 218; Adélaïde-Merlande, *Delgrés*, 147; Bangou, *La révolution*, 135; Anduse, *Joseph Ignace*, 273.

53. Bangou, *La révolution*, 135.

54. Lacour, *Histoire*, 3, 331.

55. Lara, *La Guadeloupe*, 154.

56. Adélaïde-Merlande, *Delgrés*, 149; Lacour, *Histoire*, 3, 331; Martineau and May, *Trois Siécles*, 218; Germain Saint-Ruf, *L'épopée Delgrès* (Paris: L'Harmattan, 1988), 129.

57. Martineau and May, *Trois Siécles*, 218; Bangou, *La révolution*, 135.

58. Lacour, *Histoire* , 3, 325-354; Lara, *La Guadeloupe*, 157; Martineau and May, *Trois Siécles*, 218.

59. Lacour, *Histoire*, 3, 311.

60. Adélaïde-Merlande, *Delgrès*, 152.

61. Arlette Gautier, *Les Soeurs de Solitude* (Paris: Editions Caribéennes, 1985), 251.

62. Lacour, *Histoire*, 3, 398; Lara, *La Guadeloupe*, 174.

63. Lacour, *Histoire*, 3, 399; Négre, *La rébellion*, 150-151.

64. Schnakenbourg, *Histoire*, 108.

65. Ibid.

66. ADOM, Guadeloupe 51 429 February 10, 1824.

67. ADOM, Martinique 18 161, Extrait du Registre des procts verbaux, May 19, 1831; Maurice Niclas, *L'Affaire de la Grand'Anse* (Fort-de France, 1960), 18-19.

68. ADOM, Martinique 18 159, Extrait du registre des procès verbaux, September 10, 1831.

69. B. David, *Les origines de la population martiniquaise au fil des ans 1635- 1902* (Mémoire de la société d'histoire de la Martinique, 3, 1973), 103.

70. See note 68.

71. Nicolas, *L'Affaire*, 22.

72. ADOM, Martinique 18 162, 1831.

73. Nicolas, *L'Affaire*, 22.

74. Schnakenbourg, *Histoire*, 108.

75. Henri de Frémont and Léo Elisabeth, *La vie d'un colon à la Martinique au XlXe siécle: Pierre Dessalles, 1758-1857* 4 tomes (Courbevoire, 1986), 4, 40-41.

76. Ibid, 4, 41.

77. David, *Origines*, 105.

78. Gwendolyn Midlo Hall, *Social Control in Slave Plantation Societies* (Baltimore: Johns Hopkins University Press, 1971), 69.

79. Bernard Moitt, "Women and Resistance in the French Caribbean during Slavery," Forthcoming.

80. Lacour, *Histoire*, 3, 403-404.

81. ADOM, Martinique 42, 348, Directeur Général de l'intérieur, August 4, 1827.

82. ADOM, Martinique 42, 348, Directeur Général de l'intérieur au Gouverneur, Fort Royal, June 22, 1827.

83. Tomich, *Slavery*, 252.

84. Victor Schoelcher, *Histoire de l'esclavage pendant les deux dernières années*, 1847, 2 vols, (Pointe à Pitre: Desormeaux, 1976).

85. Schnakenbourg, *Histoire*, 98-100; Tomich, *Slavery*, 60-61.

86. Tomich, *Slavery*, 255-256.

87. Ibid.

88. de Frémont and Elisabeth, *La vie*, 4, 39.

89. Ibid, 4, 40.

SECTION FIFTEEN
The Haitian Revolution

In the second half of the eighteenth century, two revolutionary changes took place in the internal relations of Caribbean societies. First, the Spanish government was forced to liberalize its colonial economic policy. This allowed foreign merchants to trade freely in most of their colonial ports, especially Havana. This development marks the beginning of English capitalists' penetration of the Spanish colonies, and the establishments of their commercial supremacy in the region. Second, the slave rebellion in Saint Domingue led to anti-colonial revolution and the emergence in 1804 of the first black state in the New World, ending some 300 years of European political monopoly in the Caribbean. Rivalry in the Caribbean took on a different dimension. The slaves continued to fight their owners for freedom in other places; now they had a State as a symbol of success. It was the end of an era.

Since the beginning of the sixteenth century, Africans had been imported to work the mines and plantations of Europeans. By the end of the sixteenth century the Tainos (Arawaks), whose replacements they were, had been annihilated. The Kalinagos (Caribs) in the Lesser Antilles carried on the fight against Europeans, but they too were defeated by the end of the eighteenth century. Meanwhile, the Europeans fought each other over the trade in Blacks and the wealth which they generated in the colonies. Blacks were the pawns in the hands of the Europeans, and they were shifted between businesses and from colony to colony according to the trajectory profits of profit levels.

The revolutionaries, under the leadership of Toussaint L'Overture, overthrew the French planters between 1791 and 1795 and declared black liberty. In 1804 General Dessalines declared the republic. It was not given for twenty years official recognition by the French, or other imperial government, but the first black state seemed a permanent feature of the Caribbean world.

The revolutionaries, C.L.R. James' "Black Jacobins", seeking to protect their freedom and independence, defeated the French and the Spanish and resisted successfully an English attack. This was the beginning of a new era in Caribbean history. For the first time, blacks had state power to influence the development of the Caribbean.

Everywhere in the Atlantic, Blacks sought to emulate the Haitians' solution to slavery. Revolt reached a crescendo in the decades after it was understood that the revolution was irreversible. In Jamaica, Barbados, Martinique and elsewhere, the Haitians were applauded by Blacks and loathed by Whites. Freedom and slavery never rested comfortably alongside each other, and the Caribbean entered a period of unprecedented anti-slavery upheaval.

70

African Soldiers in the Haitian Revolution

JOHN K. THORNTON

The rebellious slaves of Haiti inflicted grievous military defeat on all who opposed them: the *colons* of the island and their militias, regular French regiments sent from Europe, a significant Spanish army from Santo Domingo, a British army with regular soldiers, and finally, a fully equipped French force fresh from Napoleon's victories in Europe led by the Emperor's own brother-in-law. For many who have recounted this story the victory is made all the more dramatic by the fact that the triumphant slaves, fresh from the debilitating labour of plantation agriculture in the tropics, were able to defeat experienced soldiers. As C.L.R. James put it: "The revolt is the only successful slave revolt in history . . . The transformation of slaves, trembling in hundreds before a single white man, into a people able to organise themselves and defeat the most powerful European nations of their day, is one of the great epics of revolutionary struggle and achievement." [1]

Historians seeking to explain this military achievement have not agreed on the reasons for the slaves' remarkable capacities in war. Some have emphasized the heroism of the slaves, and have seen their military performance as a reflection of broader themes connecting a love of liberty and desperate war, or have stressed the individual genius of slave leaders, especially Toussaint Louverture.[2] Still other historians find this interpretation too romantic in the real world of war. Enthusiasm ultimately could not overcome cold steel, and even Toussaint had no military experience other than that of a coachman. Instead they suggest the divisions among the various colonial powers, or the dissension

among the *colons* and between them and various factions of Frenchmen, hamstrung a war effort which should have easily defeated the slaves and returned them to the plantations. Most also stress the importance of the tropical climate and especially tropical diseases in decimating and debilitating European troops.[3] Varying assessments of the slaves' military capacity or that of their leaders were recently emphasized in Roger Buckley's criticism of David Geggus for having underestimated the military competence of both Toussaint Louverture and his soldiers.[4]

The crux of these differences often lies in the historians' understanding of the military capacity of the slaves. Most have assumed that the slaves had no military experience prior to the revolution, and rose from agricultural labour to military prowess in an amazingly short time. Romantics have tended to point to this rapid ascent as evidence either of the great capacities of revolutionary labourers or the brilliance of Toussaint Louverture, but others have found it incredible and sought non-military explanations.

However, it is probably a mistake to see the slaves as simply agricultural workers, like the peasants of Europe, and this is the crucial element in explaining the situation in Haiti. A majority of slaves, especially those who fought steadily in the revolution, were born in Africa, and were not just agricultural labourers with no experience in war.

In fact, a great many of the slaves had served in African armies prior to their enslavement and arrival in Haiti. Indeed, African military service had been the route by which many, if not most, of the recently arrived Africans became slaves in the first place, since so many people had been enslaved as a result of war. Under these circumstances, their military performance may not be as remarkable as historians have assumed. As ex-soldiers and veterans of African wars, they may have needed little more than the opportunity to serve again, in a rather different sort of war in America.

In order to understand the importance of the slaves' military background, one must first understand that a majority of the inhabitants of Saint Domingue in 1791 had been born in Africa and had arrived within ten years of the start of the revolution. Import statistics assembled by historians of slavery in Saint Domingue show this tendency clearly: 60-70 per cent of the adult slaves listed on inventories in the late 1780s and 1790s were African born.[5] Thus, a knowledge of the African background is essential in understanding anything that they did, and especially in knowing what skills or attitudes they had.

In addition to being African born, these slaves came overwhelmingly from just two areas of Africa: the Lower Guinea coast region of modern Bénin, Togo and Nigeria (also known as the "Slave Coast"), and the Angola coast area. Again the statistics of imports and inventories both converge to reveal this pattern which shaped the whole of the French slave trade. Indeed, French shippers were riding the crest of a great surge of exports from these two regions, a surge that was reflected in British shipping as well.[6] According to French shipping data, French ships transported over 224,000 slaves from Africa in the decade before the revolution, of which 116,000 (51%) came from the Angola coast, and 55,000 (25%) from Lower Guinea, making together over three-quarters of the total.[7]

Although one cannot discount the vagaries of European wars, blockades and demands in shaping the slave trade, the primary African cause of the surge seems to have been war. In Angola, this was the great civil war in the Kingdom of Kongo, which reached a high level of intensity in the period around 1780. In the Lower Guinea region it was the complex of wars between the Oyo Empire, the Kingdom of Dahomey and the smaller states of the coast, the Nago region and the Mahi country. In both Angola and Lower Guinea, slaves were taken in great military actions in which armies mobilised and fought in battles, thus resulting in a high percentage of the captives being prisoners of war, and veterans.

The Kongo civil wars can be said to have begun in the aftermath of the battle of Mbwila (29 October 1665), when the death of King António I without a clear heir left the country open for a succession struggle. The struggle was not resolved easily, since the various contenders were able to operate against each other from fairly secure bases, and within a few years the pretenders coalesced into two great family based groups, the Kimpanzu and the Kimulaza. The wars had a number of active episodes interspersed with periods of relative peace, such as that period which followed the nominal restoration of the kingdom under King Pedro IV (1696-1718),[8] in which a compromise between the two families was worked out, apparently coupled with an agreement to share power through selecting kings alternately from the two lines.[9] In spite of this, a new episode of war broke out in the 1760s: it began with an attempt on the part of Pedro V to seize power out of turn, and the successful attempt at resistance by Alvaro XI, who drove his rival from the capital of São Salvador and was crowned in 1764. However, Pedro V fled to a base at Mbamba Lubota and continued to bid for the throne.[10] This war went on with varying degrees of intensity, and eventually partisans of Pedro recaptured São Salvador around 1779, but José I, Alvaro XI's Kimulaza successor, drove them out in a large and bloody battle in September 1781.[11] Although a brief period of peace followed, it broke down after 1785 when José's brother and successor Alfonso V died under suspicious circumstances.[12] Squabbles broke out among his descendants and fighting recommenced, not really quieting down until Henrique I reestablished a shaky order in 1794.[13]

During this time, then, armies faced each other on a number of occasions, with the prisoners of war being sold in the outcome. Sometimes these armies were large: according to eyewitness testimony, some 30,000 troops stormed São Salvador under José I's command in 1781; the defenders must have also numbered in the tens of thousands.[14] Most of the slaves sold on the coast in those years were likely to have come from these engagements. They were carried from battlefields by the Vilis, a generic name for coast-based African merchants, to coastal ports ranging from Mbrize (Ambriz) in the south to Loango in the north.[15] Because the Vilis were not Christian, the Church, acting through Father de Castello de Vide who was the Apostolic Vicar in Kongo from 1780 to 1788, sought to persuade the kings of Kongo to expel the Vilis, or at least to make them sell slaves to Catholic (which actually meant Portuguese) Europeans.[16]

The European beneficiaries of this great surge were French merchants who fixed their operations along the coast north of the Zaire River, but regularly visited the Kongo coast as well. In the 1780s, French ships carried a total of over 116,000 slaves from this coast, mostly to Saint Domingue, while their closest competitors, the English, exported only 25,000.[17] This was also the period of the great growth of the slave population of Saint Domingue, and naturally enough the civil wars in Kongo really ended on the colony's coffee and sugar plantations.

At the same time as these people were carried from Angolan ports to Saint Domingue, however, French merchants were also capitalizing on another great war-driven export surge from Lower Guinea in West Africa, especially from the ports of Porto Novo and Whydah. The wars that led to the export of tens of thousands of people each year through Lower Guinea were quite different from those that drove the slave trade of the Angola region.

In late eighteenth century Lower Guinea, wars were interstate affairs rather than civil wars. Politically, there was a complex situation involving the expansion of two great powers, Dahomey and Oyo, their rivalries with each other, and the resistance of independent smaller states, both along the coast and farther in the interior, to their activities. We get an especially good picture of Dahomey's role in these various operations through a diary kept by Lionel Abson, the factor of Fort William, the English post at Whydah, from 1770 to 1803. Although his diary is no longer extant, it was used extensively by the Scottish sea captain Archibald Dalzel to write a detailed history of Dahomey in 1793.[18]

Dahomey is often seen as simply a slave-raiding state, conducting wars and terrorising its neighbours, while exporting people wholesale. Under such operations, the slaves exported through ports frequented by Dahomean merchants might well be simply peasants and not soldiers. In actual fact, however, Dahomey's

military activities, undoubtedly like those of its neighbours, were motivated by other concerns than just capturing slaves, and moreover, her neighbours possessed their own military systems.[19] Dahomey lost many of its wars, and saw its own citizens enslaved by its would-be victims, even as Dahomey also won wars. Moreover, smaller states, which probably had smaller armies, or at least smaller potential armies than Dahomey, often held their own as well as the larger ones might: in 1774, for example, Dahomey successfully attacked Little Popo, a small coastal state lying to its southwest and captured many slaves,[20] but a similar attack in 1775 on Serechi, Little Popo's eastern neighbour and an equally small state, was a military disaster.[21] Wars against the northern neighbours, the Mahi and Nago country, often ended in defeats, as in a campaign of 1775 or 1776, but might also bring victory as in 1777.[22] Under these military circumstances it is not surprising that the motives for war were likely to be political or diplomatic, sometimes even to the detriment of the slave trade. Before going on campaign against Mahi in 1777, Kpengla, Dahomey's king, said, "I want heads, not slaves," and in fact few slaves were taken.[23]

The political and diplomatic situation made wars in the Slave, Coast complicated. Far reaching alliances were sometimes assembled to conduct wars. In 1783 Dahomey joined Porto Novo and Sessu in an unsuccessful attack on Badagri, a state that lay east of Dahomey along the coast.[24] That attack failed, and in 1784, Dahomey joined a larger alliance led by the Empire of Oyo with Mahi, Port Novo, and the Nago to attack Badagri.[25] During much of this time Dahomey was only semi-independent, having to share some of the spoils of war with Oyo.

In the last analysis, what was significant about this period was the frequency of wars – Abson's diary lists a war every year of his stay, and Dahomey was not necessarily involved in all the wars in the area. In 1787, for example, Oyo invaded Mahi, and although Dahamey was not involved in the operation, many feared that the Oyo army would eventually attack Dahomey.[26] The operation was immensely successful; according to reports received at the coast, by the start of the rainy season of 1788, the Oyo army had "ravaged no less than fourteen districts; and burning and destroying multitudes of towns and villages."[27]No doubt its casualties contributed to the peak of imports from this area in Saint Domingue in 1787-89. The accounts of these and other wars in Dalzel and occasionally in other sources make it clear that all operations of Dahomey faced resistance from well organized and disciplined military forces, and the ebb and flow of war was largely due to the generalship, hardiness or sometimes luck of the various armies. Here, as in central Africa, soldiers must have been among the many exported slaves.

These soldiers, veterans of African wars, might well have had the military skills that made the revolution in Saint Domingue a success. The revolution was immensely complex, of course, with many episodes and differing histories in every region. In many areas, especially the revolutionary movements in the South and West Provinces, African military skills may not have been as important as elsewhere. For example, in the struggle between mulattoes and various white factions in the south and west, both of these elite groups armed their slaves, formed them into military units and used them to reach their own goals. The military experience of these slaves might have been important, but perhaps not decisive, since most of the organizational skills and even the tactical programmes came from the European background of these who organized the slaves. In time, these slaves may have used their military experience from their service in the early stages of the revolution for their own ends, as Carolyn Fick, who has analysed the movements in the South Province carefully, has argued.[28]

Where the African military background of the slaves counted for the most was in those areas, especially in the north, where slaves themselves led the revolution, both politically and militarily. But these areas, which eventually threw up the powerful armies of Toussaint Louverture and Dessalines, were the ones that eventually carried the revolution, and thus played an important role from a military standpoint. Even in the south and west, with its complex political manoeuvering between white and mulatto, there were slave led movements, such as those of Romaine la Prophetesse, Hyacinthe, or Armand and Maréchal whose revolt led to the founding of the "Kingdom of Platons."[29] Although all these movements were smaller in scale than the explo-

sion of the north, they still contributed to the shape of the revolution and its eventual outcome.

There can be little doubt that the early leaders of the northern revolt relied on the military skills of the slaves in the area to make the revolution's early success. Jean-François and Biassou, who had emerged as leaders in the north within a few weeks of the first outbreak of violence in August 1791, recognised the contribution of these slaves. In their correspondence with the Civil Commissioners,[30] the two leaders proposed ending the revolution and returning the rebel slaves to their plantations, in exchange for freedom for themselves and a number of their followers.[31] The only problem with the proposal was that Jean François and Biassou did not really control the army that they led. They complained in one of their letters about "blacks in bands" who gave trouble,[32] and they specified their situation when they noted that any action they took was "entirely dependent on the general will" exercised by the rebels which they did not control. The makers of this "general will" were slaves, "a multitude of *négres* from the coast [of Africa] who are scarcely able for the most part to say two words of French," but, and this was the important part, "in their homelands, however, had been accustomed to war [*à guerroyer*]".[33]

It was not surprising that Jean-François and the other early leaders of the rebellion were captives of this general will, because they did not possess much military training themselves. They and many of their colleagues were creole slaves, born in the New World, who held skilled or managerial positions in the plantation economy of Saint Domingue. Many documents and inquests from the time show that these elite creole leaders arranged the conspiracy that led to the initial explosion in August 1791.[34] If they could organize a conspiracy, however, they could not necessarily do the fighting to make the revolt a success. Such fighting required the kind of skill and discipline that could be found in veteran soldiers, and it was these veterans, from wars in Africa, who made up the "general will" of the revolt.

We cannot know exactly what transpired in the conspiratorial meetings that started the revolt, but it is unlikely that they organized military movements, set up units and made tactical decisions, especially when the early destructive rage of the rebels gave way to serious fighting with the colonial militia and the regular troops from Le Cap François. Two American observers, Captain Bickford and Mr. Harrington, who were in Saint Domingue throughout the early months, noted a distinct evolution in the rebels' behaviour as the fighting developed between August and early November 1791, when they left for Boston. In the early stages, the attacks were irregular and often confused, and the rebels were equipped mostly with the "instruments of their labour," but as time went on, they began to come in "regular bodies" and were now bearing muskets and swords.[35]

The two Americans, probably repeating the theories of the colonial military leaders, believed that this new found organization was attributable to the influence of mulattoes with military experience, runaway white soldiers and Spanish instigators who provided the necessary training in the short time between late August and late October.[36] Certainly, such elements were found in the rebel bands, manning artillery, for example,[37] or among black and mulatto members of the elite who had served in colonial militias, and even overseas. M. Gros, who spent several months in the camps of the rebels, also noted occasionally that mulattoes and free blacks held high office, although his account does not make it clear how important they were in organization of units or military tactics.[38] Given the very low opinion that the planter and governing class had of the slaves,[39] this theory seems to have been attractive and a good explanation for the surprising battlefield success that the slaves enjoyed.

In light of Jean François and Biassou's revelations, however, we should probably not place too much emphasis on the role of non-slaves in organizing the rebels or making their military success possible. In fact, the scattered documentation suggests that what contemporaries called "bands" formed quite spontaneously during August and perhaps September under individual leaders. Many of the band leaders were creoles, like Jean François, Jeannot or Biassou, but others, such as Sans Souci, mentioned as a leader by Gros, were slaves from Africa.[40] It was no doubt these bands, which were independently organized, that Jean François and Biassou complained could not be disciplined.[41]

To understand the nature of these bands, it might be appropriate to consider the way in which African armies were organized and fought, for their organizational and tactical principles were not identical to those of eighteenth century Europe, and seem to underlie those of the rebels. The art of war varied quite a bit in Angola or Kongo and in Lower Guinea, and we are much better informed about the manner of conducting war in Angola.

Portuguese soldiers who knew the African art of war in Angola often disparaged it, but as one militarily experienced observer, Elias Alexandre de Silva Corrêa, noted, it "had the same effect as that of Frederick the Great of Prussia." Indeed, Portuguese armies in Angola adopted most of the African tactical and organizational principles themselves, at least with their African troops.[42]

Kongolese armies, who probably contributed the most to Saint Domingue rebel bands, were generally recruited through fairly broad based drafts that took in a considerable portion of the adult male population. Smaller bodies of professional soldiers who served as personal guards for various members of the nobility were also noticeable, as we learn from the account of Castello de Vide for 1781.[43] Soldiers were typically equipped with muskets; Castello de Vide believed that all 30,000 troops that stormed São Salvador in 1781 were armed with "musket and ball."[44] As a matter of some significance for those who eventually were to end up in Saint Domingue, Kongolese forces, especially after the 1780s, were typically equipped with French muskets.[45] A mid-eighteenth century illustration in a guide to missionaries shows the army of the Prince Antonio Baretto da Silva of Sonyo, the coastal ruler, fallen out to greet an arriving priest, in which all carry muskets, and include a small cannon among their equipment,[46] and another illustration in the same collection shows that even the personal guard of one of the lesser district rulers was so equipped.[47] On the other hand, archery skills were not entirely lost: the missionary guide also shows that their own escorts carried bows, and as late as 1790 both Portuguese and Kongolese forces engaged in a battle near Encoge had some archers among their musketeers.[48]

In addition to muskets, however, Kongolese soldiers also carried swords for close order combat. Kongolese, like other Africans, eschewed the use of the bayonet in close fighting, and appear to have preferred to use personal weapons, especially swords and battle axes, in close fighting, as well as shields. A Portuguese commander, who fought against troops in southern Kongo in 1790, noted that they used muskets very well, and all carried as "arme blanche" (arma blanca in Portuguese) swords, lances and axes as well as "good shields."[49] The missionary guide's illustrations also show these close order weapons, especially in one case where the priest is depicted blessing the swords and shields of combatants before they depart to fight. These swords were either straight bladed weapons closely resembling those of Europe, or were more like scimitars.[50]

Kongolese tactical organization was very different from that of Europe. The differences were especially important because Kongolese forces often confronted European led armies in battle and in the years of war both sides had developed tactics that incorporated the two traditions. The Portuguese colony of Angola, located south of Kongo, had sought for many years to engross the trade of the area, and specifically to prevent northern Europeans from trading along the coast of Kongo or its northern neighbours. In 1759 they built a fort at Encoge in southern Kongo, and from time to time Portuguese forces based either at Encoge or at other points along the Kongo-Angolan frontier crossed into Kongo for shorter or longer campaigns.[51] These forces often engaged Kongolese armies, including those which would face each other in the battles of the civil wars around São Salvador. The upper Mbrize valley, stronghold of the Kimulaza, bordered on Encoge, while the coastal regions where the Kimpanzu had their strength bordered on areas where the Portuguese struck up the coast from Luanda. These African forces had learned to deal successfully with Portuguese armies and tactics in the years of struggle, driving out invaders in 1788, invading Angola and nearly reaching Luanda in 1790 and giving a good account in the indecisive "North Coast" war of 1790-91.[52] No doubt these tactics could help those who found themselves in Saint Domingue on the eve of the revolution.

A detailed description of Kongolese arms and tactics can be found in the report of the "North Coast War" led by the Portuguese commander Paulo Martins Pinheiro de Lacerda against the Kongolese Marquisate of Musulu in 1790-91, and in the diary of another campaign that he led through the same region and then to Encoge in 1793, though they reflect the "art of war" of at least the previous half century as well. Kongolese armies seem to:) have been organized in fairly small units that operated independently, "irregular bodies dispersed like our platoons." They were probably identified by unit flags: Castello de Vide mentions numerous war flags [bandeiras de guerra] flying over the Kongolese army of 1781,[53] Portuguese accounts make note of capturing enemy colours in the wars of 1790.[54]

These platoons struck at enemy advancing columns and sustained an engagement for a time before breaking off and retreating. In the 1793 campaign such engagements typically lasted from one to three hours.[55] In these encounters the Kongolese "fired without order" (probably meaning that they did not volley fire, but instead fired when ready), but with good effect. In the 1793 war it is clear they made use of cover, both from terrain and from woods and tall grass, in hiding their movements and directing their fire.[56] When they fled it was not possible to follow them.[57] The campaign diary of 1790 records numerous such sharp encounters between the Portuguese troops and the Kongolese: in the first three days of their advance the Portuguese force met four sharp and fairly sustained encounters with Kongolese forces,[58] in the entire campaign they fought nine "battles" of this sort, as well as three "shocks" [choques].

The "shocks" were much larger engagements involving massed Kongolese units. According to the Portuguese accounts, large bodies were assembled for shocks supported by artillery, sometimes they formed in extensive half moon formations which apparently sought partial envelopment of opposing forces, in other cases in columns of great depth along fronts of 15-20 soldiers, presumably where penetration was desired. At the engagement at Quincolo (11 December 1791) six of these columns were deployed.[59] In similar engagements with forces formed in columns at Bingue on the 29th and 30th October 1790, Portuguese forces were compelled, in the words of the official report, to "reform, not retreat"; although the commander claimed victory, his forces evacuated the area the next day and fell back some distance.[60] Another action by the army of Nambuangongo, in which an estimated 6,000 troops were deployed, drove the Portuguese from that area in a sustained battle on 3 July 1793.[61] In another action on 6

May 1794 near Nambuangongo a wounded prisoner gave the strength of one such column at 1,230 muskets; given its source it was probably based on real muster counts, and is indicative of the typical size of such larger units.[62]

In summary, the organization of Kongolese armies probably favoured small commands (the platoons) that could operate independently. Junior commanders undoubtedly had considerable leeway for decision making, though units might be quite cohesive, as indicated by the attachment to unit flags. Their tactics showed a penchant for skirmishing attacks rather than the heavy assaults favoured by Europeans in the same era. On the other hand, Kongolese armies had a higher command structure that could mass troops quickly, and soldiers were also accustomed forming effectively into larger units for major battles when the situation warranted it.

We possess a wealth of detailed information on the military culture of Kongo and its immediate neighbours in central Africa; unfortunately, we can say much less about the military systems of the Slave Coast. Only for Dahomey is there some information, and even there, military tactics and weapons are known from general descriptions, rather than from analysis of actual battlefield reports, as is possible in central Africa. Dahomey's armies included a fairly large professional force, recruited through a levy on male children who were then trained for war. This force was in turn supplemented in wartime by a general draft, although even in this case, it was the highly trained professional who did much of the fighting.[63] Much of the expense of maintaining military forces was borne by titled nobles, who were called up for war, although the state provided central armouries in which necessary weapons and supplies were deposited.[64] Although travellers focused their attention on Dahomey, some information on the coastal region suggests that military organization there resembled that of the near-by Gold Coast, in which larger militia armies, recruited, armed and equipped like those of Kongo, were more common outside of Dahomey.[65] In addition, however, mercenary armies raised from wealthier states like Great Popo might be added to the general levy in time of war.[66]

Certainly many seem to have been organized as the Dahomey army was: the same titles, for example, were borne by general officers in the army of Badagry in 1783-4, and co-ordinated attacks by three divisions against Dahomey's invading army suggest higher level organization as well.[67] Allada's army seems to have had different titles, but still comprised regular military units.[68] In the Mahi country, the division of the region into many small states seems to have prevented the development of large forces, though Mahi states were capable of raising large unified armies to defend themselves, or even to attack: according to Dalzel, 100 "caboceros" of Mahi states joined the Dahomey army in an attack on Weme in 1786.[69] The small state of Ape, said to have had an army of 800 when Dahomey attacked it in 1778, managed a heroic resistance, first cutting up the army of Allada, Dahomey's ally for the moment, then gallantly resisting the whole of the Dahomean army for an extended period.[70]

Dahomey and the coastal states seem to have had muskets and swords as their principal weapons, the muskets as a long range missile and the sword for close fighting. As elsewhere in Africa, people of the region were not interested in using bayonets and the tactics associated with them. The interior states, however, appear to have been less inclined to the use of muskets, perhaps because they lacked access to ready supplies.[71] Oyo in particular relied much more heavily on cavalry forces to carry the day for them, and had relatively few foot soldiers.[72] If there was a shortage of muskets in the interior, however, it does not seem to have affected the capacities of these peoples in war, for throughout the eighteenth century it was Oyo, not Dahomey, that was the pre-eminent military power of the region.

The cavalry of Oyo may well have affected how Dahomey's infantry armies fared (horses could not survive well in the climate of Dahomey, although a few could be found, and one of the king's officials bore the title "Inspector of Cavalry"[73]). According to descriptions, Dahomey's troops, unlike those of central Africa, and even other parts of west Africa, fought in close order using fire discipline quite similar to that of Europe.[74] Such tactics make sense in battlefield situations involving cavalry, since tightly formed units can resist cavalry charges much better than the "open order" of Kongo. It also then makes sense to develop fire discipline so that this mass of soldiers can keep up the highest rate of fire possible, since maneuver and especially retreat are difficult in tightly formed units. This is perhaps the reason that Dahomey had a complicated mechanism to effect tactical withdrawals, always with an eye to maintaining order, since the type of rapid and dispersed retreat that was characteristic of the Angolan wars would be a disaster in situations with cavalry, as the horsemen could easily ride down fleeing infantry. In Dahomey, one of the principal functions of the ready reserve, in fact, was to prevent the flight of the soldiers by ensuring that unauthorized battlefield deserters were killed immediately by the comrades in rear areas.[75]

European visitors, who admired Dahomey's tactical structure and military drill for being similar to their own, thus gave Dahomey high marks for discipline and the capabilities of its army were typically rated very high, a feature which has often been repeated by modern scholars. But the historical record does not show that Dahomey had a decisive advantage over its enemies, drill notwithstanding. It was unable to resist the Oyo cavalry throughout the eighteenth century, and was often unable to have its way against its neighbours who did not possess horses, or fight in close order tactics. A number of times, opponents succeeded in ambushing advancing Dahomean armies, or took advantage of terrain features to resist and even to cut up their opponents, as the armies of Badagri did in 1773-4[76] or Croo-too-hoon-too in 1788.[77] Even so, some, like the king of Ape in 1778,[78] or the general of Agoonah in 1781,[79] could still stand up to Dahomean armies in sustained battle.

It was from these disparate "arts of war" that the revolutionary African soldier of Saint Domingue was trained. Certainly knowing this African background helps us make sense of some of the military action of the rebels in the opening months of the Revolution.

One can easily see, in the formation of the bands mentioned in the early descriptions of the war, the small platoons of the Kongolese armies, each under an independent commander and accustomed to considerable tactical decision making, or perhaps those small units characteristic of locally organized Dahomean units, the state armies of the Mahi country or the coastal forces of the Slave Coast. Often they were based in small camps, like the one that formed among the slave quarters of one plantation belonging to Monsieur Robillard within a week of the outbreak of violence.[80] These camps were defended by artillery in places, and became the base of operations for the units within them.[81] In addition the pattern of attacks, with small scale harassing manoeuvres, short sustained battles and then rapid withdrawals are also reminiscent of the campaign diaries of the Portuguese field commanders in Angola. Félix Carteau, an early observer of the war in the north, noted that they harassed French forces "day and night." Usually, he commented, "they were repelled, but each time, they dispersed so quickly, so completely" in ditches, hedges and other areas of natural cover that real pursuit was impossible. However, rebel casualties were light in these attacks, so that "the next day they reappeared with great numbers of people."[82] "They never mass in the open," wrote another witness, or wait in line to charge, but advance dispersed, so that they appear to be "six times as numerous" as they really were. Yet they were disciplined, since they might advance with great clamour and then suddenly and simultaneously fall silent.[83]

Colonial troops who met these tactics sometimes reported at the time that they won all their engagements, as one enthusiastic French militiaman noted during the first week of fighting.[84] His diary reveals a number of these types of attacks, as for example one near Dondon on the 14th of September, 1791 where a strong body of rebels attacked the advancing French, but were repulsed, only to return shortly, reinforced for a renewed attack.[85] Another reaction to these tactics, reported by Captain Bickford and Mr. Harrington, noted that they began each engagement "with order and firmness, crying out 'Victory'" but they soon broke when hotly engaged, and once broken did not easily reform, at least according to the tactics of European trained soldiers.[86]

It was not long, however, before these observers also noted that the rebels had developed the sort of higher order tactics that was also characteristic of Kongolese forces, or those of the Slave Coast. Already on September 2, 1791, a very large force of rebels sought to take Le Cap François by storm. It was estimated at 4,000, although in such situations, these estimations might well be exaggerated.[87] A few days later, the plantation of Bréda was attacked by a force deployed in three columns,[88] a similar three column attack hit Port Marigot on September 14, while on September 19 the attacking force was now described as being in "three divisions" in an attack near Petit Anse.[89]

In addition to these tactical similarities to African wars, especially in Kongo, there were other indications of the African ethos of the fighters. Captain Bickford and Mr. Harrington, for example, noted that they marched, formed and attacked accompanied by the "music peculiar to negroes."[90] Religious preparation likewise hearkened back to Africa, for Pamphile Lacroix, using contemporary documents, noted that they began with the preparations of "wangas" or protective charms.[91]

Another eyewitness noted that sometimes when rebel forces advanced there was complete silence, so that the only thing that could be heard was the "incantations of their sorcerers."[92] In this regard they resembled even the Christian Kongolese, for troops fighting in the "North Coast" campaign against Pinheiro de Lacerda in 1791 were also exhorted by a traditional priestess.[93]

The Saint Domingue rebels seem to have developed an effective artillery quite quickly, although the connections between African artillery use and that in Saint Domingue must be considered speculative. Dozens of guns and other field pieces were reported as being used by the rebels in the early engagements, and they seem to have been well served, as for example, in the action of one battery which successfully drove off an armed boat through well aimed fire from 24-pounders.[94] Of the African armies, only the Kongolese seem to have made much use of artillery, though many of the slave coast states made use of artillery mounted on canoes[95] and apparently also in fortifications.[96] The Angolan campaign diary of 1793-94 shows not only a quite sophisticated use of guns, but considerable skill in fortifications employed by Africans, especially in the Marquisate of Kina.[97] But given the reports that various European deserters or mulattoes with military experience served in rebel ranks, especially in artillery, it might be best to assume that they rather than the Africans among whom they fought were responsible for the action.

On the other hand, it is harder to explain the speed with which rebel forces developed an effective cavalry by invoking training of renegade white colonists, mulattoes or Spaniards. A survey of rebel forces, probably exaggerated, suggested that they possessed six to eight hundred cavalry, "tolerably well armed" by August 27, 1791, less than a week after the outbreak of the rebellion.[98] These cavalry worked well with the infantry and gave them good support, as did a body of 150 in a hot engagement at Gallifet Plantation on 19 September.[99] Given that it is unlikely that many slaves would have learned equestrian skills as a part of their plantation labour, it seems likely that either all these horsemen were creoles and mulattoes (but they are not so described) or they had acquired the skill in Africa. It would take longer than a few weeks to make plantation labourers into cavalry that could stand up against European horsemen. Since there was virtually no cavalry in Angola, one can speculate that rebels originating from Oyo might have provided at least some of the trained horsemen (Senegalese, though a minority, also came from an equestrian culture). However, the evidence cannot provide a definite answer to this question.

The importance of African trained soldiers, and the development of bands organized quickly from African plantation workers, posed something of a problem for the creole leadership of the revolution. Their dilemma is clearly revealed in the letters of Jean-François and Biassou, who saw this uncontrollable host of fighters as a barrier to their making the kind of political settlement they hoped for. Creole goals and those of their African fellow combatants were not always the same, as was revealed by the early attempts to stop the fighting. As early as September 13, 1791, the leader of the insurgents near Le Cap François wished to abandon his followers and surrender, no doubt in exchange for personal freedom, but he was "detained among them by main force."[100] Soon after, the division between the leadership, with its goal of modified restoration of the plantation system and personal freedom, and the mass of the insurgents was made clear throughout the negotiations that followed the arrival of the Civil Commissioners towards the end of the year. Gros, a witness from the rebel camp, reported on the suspicion with which the rank and file fighters viewed their leaders, even as it was reflected in the letters of Jean-François and Biassou.[101]

It is not surprising, therefore, that creoles began to form and train their own military forces, typically using Spanish assistance (offered from early in the revolt) or colon renegades to assist them, and copying European military organization. By 1793, Jean-François and Biassou had gathered considerable personal forces around themselves, but it was ultimately Toussaint Louverture who developed this strategy to its height. After his defection to the Republic in 1793, Toussaint actively allied his small personal army to that of the French general Étienne Laveaux and then used Laveaux's resources to develop a regular army, organized in regiments and half brigades and fighting in typically European drill.[102] By 1796 one could meet armies of several thousand under Toussaint's command that marched in close order, held their ground under fire, and charged with the bayonet, like those forces who sought to storm St. Marc in June of that year, but were repulsed with heavy losses. [103]

These forces were to provide the backbone for Toussaint's rise to power and the base which kept him in control in Haiti. They did not replace the older bands that had formed under African leadership and using African soldiers and tactics in the early months of the revolution; the older tactical arrangements continued to co-exist effectively along with the new armies of the creole and mulatto leadership.[104] In fact, increasingly these forces were opposed to Toussaint and the creole leadership. On one occasion, for example, he was required to attack a Nago camp, while Macaya, one of his rivals and leader of a smaller band, raised his forces among Kongolese slaves, and by 1797 the forces loyal to creole generals (Toussaint and his southern rivals) were actively fighting the bands, no longer subject, as Jean-François and Biassou had been, to their "general will.[105]

African soldiers may well have provided the key element of the early success of the revolution. They might have enabled its survival when it was threatened by reinforced armies from Europe. Looking at the rebel slaves of Haiti as African veterans rather than as Haitian plantation workers may well prove to be the key that unlocks the mystery of the success of the largest slave revolt in history.

Notes

1. C. L. R. James, *The Black Jacobins: Toussaint L'Ouverture and the San Domingo Revolution* (London, 1938, 2d ed. New York, 1963), ix.

2. Prominent is James' classic study, *The Black Jacobins.*

3. For example, Thomas Ott, *The Haitian Revolution, 1789-1804* (Knoxville, 1972); David Geggus, *Slavery, War and Revolution: The British Occupation of Saint Domingue, 1793-1798* (Oxford, 1982).

4. Roger N. Buckley (ed.) *The Haitian Diary of Lieutenant Howard: York Hussars, 1796-1798* (Knoxville, 1985), 137-38, taking issue with statements in Geggus, 286-89.

5. David Geggus, "Sugar and Coffee Cultivation in Saint Domingue and the Shaping of the Slave Labor Force," in Ira Berlin and Philip Morgan (eds.) *Cultivation and Culture: Work Process and the Shaping of Afro-American Culture in the Americas* (forthcoming). My thanks to David Geggus for an advance copy of this article.

6. See the summaries of both plantation inventories and import statistics in David Geggus, "Sex Ratio, Age and Ethnicity in the Atlantic Slave Trade: data from French shipping and plantation records," *Journal of African History* 30 (1989): 23-44; David Richardson, "Slave Exports from West and West-Central Africa, 1700-1810: new estimates of volume and distribution," *Journal of African History* 30 (1989): 1-22.

7. Richardson, "New Estimates," 10-14. For another angle, based on shipping arriving in Saint Domingue, see Jean Fouchard, "The Slave Trade and the Peopling of Santo Domingo," in UNESCO, *The African Slave Trade from the Fifteenth to the Nineteenth Century* (Paris, 1979), 283-85.

8. For the background and early history of the civil wars, see John Thornton, *The Kingdom of Kongo: Civil War and Transition, 1641-1719* (Madison, 1983).

9. This process of alternating succession is described by an Italian priest, Cherubino da Savona, who resided in Kongo after 1760. It was probably not as neatly done or well kept as his retrospective account would have one believe: Cherubino da Savona, "Congo 1775. Breve ragguaglio del Regno di Congo e sue Missioni," fol. 41 in Carlo Toso (ed.) "Relazioni inedite di P. Cherubino Cassinis da Savona sul 'Regno del Congo e sue Missioni' *L'Italia Francescana* 75 (1974).

10. Da Savona, "Breve ragguaglio," fols. 41-41v.

11. The war and its aftermath are described by an eyewitness, Father Rafael de Castello de Vide, in Academia das Ciências de Lisboa, MS Vermelho 296, "Viagem do Congo do Missionario Fr. Raphael de Castello de Vide, hoje Bispo de S. Thomé," 118-22; MS of about 1800, recopying four letter reports of the period 1779-1788. The first of these reports survives in original form in the Arquivo Histórico Ultramarino (Lisbon), Angola, Caixa 64, doc. 62 [henceforward cited as AHU, Angola, Cx (Caixa), doc.] and was published in *Annes do Conselho Ul-*

tramarino, ser, 11 (1859-61): 62-80. I have cited the MS pagination.

12. ACL, MS Vermelho 296, Castello de Vide, "Viagem," 260.

13. ACL, MS Vermelho 296, Castello de Vide, "Viagem," 260-62; on the restoration of order by Henrique, see Raimondo da Dicomano, "Informação do Reino de Congo," fol. 108, MS of 1798 published from a Portuguese translation in the Biblioteca Nacional de Lisboa in António Brásio, "Informação do Reino do Congo de Frei Raimondo da Dicomano," *Studia* 34 (1972): 19-42. Analysis of the period, and publication of additional documents on the period 1792-4 can be found in the introduction and appendices of Carlo Toso's Italian translation, *L'informazione sul regno del Congo di Raimondo da Dicomano* (Rome, 1977).

14. ACL, MS Vermelho 296, Castello de Vide, "*Viagem*," 118-20.

15. For a general background, see Phyllis Martin, *The External Trade of the Loango Coast, 1576-1890* (Oxford, 1972). For an analysis of the slave trade and its impact on demography in this period, see John Thornton, "The Kongo Civil Wars, 1718-1844: Demography and History Revisited," Paper Presented at the Annual Convention of the Canadian African Studies Association, Montréal, 15-18 May 1992.

16. ACL, MS Vermelho 296, Castello de Vide, "Viagem," 284-94 for the context of the attempts to end the slave trade with Vilis, and Castello de Vide's futile efforts to carry it out.

17. Richardson, "New Estimates," table 5, 12 and 6, 14. Note that Portuguese shipping exported over 154,000 slaves from Angola in the same time period, but it is likely that their source was not the same as those of England and France, though there was some overlap in southern Kongo.

18. Archibald Dalzel, *The History of Dahomey: an inland kingdom of Africa: compiled from authentic memoirs* (London, 1793, reprinted with introduction by J. D. Fage, London, 1967). Abson's memoirs begin with the year 1774, on pp. 156 et seq. Abson was an exceptionally well informed observer, not only speaking Fon, the local language, fluently, and having married several Dahomean women, but he had frequent interviews with the king and other high officials. For periods before 1774, Dalzel was dependent on Robert Norris, *Memoirs of the Reign of Bossa Ahádée, King of Dahomey an inland country of Guiney* (London, 1789, reprinted London, 1968).

19. See, on this issue, especially Werner Peukert, *Der Atlantische Sklavenhandel von Dahomey, 1740-1797: Wirtschaftsanthropologie und Socialgeschichte* (Wiesbaden, 1978), a detailed critique of what he calls the "Atlantic model" of Dahomean history.

20. Norris, *Memoirs*, 130-32.

21. Dalzel, *History*, 163-65.

22. The attack is described on the basis of archival documentation by I. A. Akinjogbin, *Dahomey and its Neighbours, 1708-1818* (Cambridge, 1967), 165, as well as details in Dalzel, *History*, 165-67.

23. Dalzel, *History*, 166.

24. Ibid, 180.

25. Ibid, 182-90.

26. Ibid, 196.

27. Norris, *Memoirs*, 138-9.

28. Carolyn Fick, *The Making of Haiti: The Saint Domingue Revolution from Below, 1791-1804* (Knoxville, 1991), 133-34.

29. On these movements, see Fick, *Making of Haiti*, 127-29, 139-40, 141-53.

30. All this correspondence, 28 items in all, is found in Archives Nationales de France (henceforward AN), D-XXV, carton 1, dossier 4, [cited thus, AN D-XXV, 1, 4] "Lettres, addresses et pièces de correspondance des Commissaires Nationaux, avec les Chefs des Esclaves révoltés, December 1791.

31. For example, their plan as presented in AN D-XXV, 1, 4 no. 6, Jean-François and Biassou to Civil Commissioners, 12 October 1791; for a background on these events from the point of view of M. Gros, a European notary who served as their secretary, see M. Gros, *An Historick Recital of the Different Occurrences in the Camps of Grande-Riviere, Dondon, Sainte Suzanne and others from the 26th of October 1791 to the 24th of December of the Same Year* (Baltimore, n.d. [1793]; a French version was published the same year in Lille and then in Paris), 49-65.

32. AN D-XXV, 1, 4, no. 10, Jean-François and Biassou to Civil Commissioners, 17 December 1791.

33. AN D-XXV, 1, 4, no. 6, Jean-François and Biassou to Civil Commissioners, 12 October 1791.

34. The original document is examined in detail in Fick, *Making of Haiti*, 260-66.

35. Their report was published in the Boston *Independent Chronicle and Universal Advertiser*, 23, 1201 (3 November 1791) and then in the Philadelphia *General Advertiser*, no. 351 (14 November 1791).

36. Ibid. This position was more or less firmly stated in the official published report of the revolution which made use of numerous documents, some still extant, others no longer so, J. Ph. Garran-Coulon, *Rapport sur les troubles de Saint Domingue* (4 vols., Paris, AN V-VII [1797-99]) 2:256.

37. Letter of James Perkins, printed in Boston *Independent Chronicle*, 23, 1199 (20 October 1791), entry of 11 September 1791; Gros, *Historick Recital*, 23.

38. Gros, *Historick Recital*, 21, 23, 32.

39. This attitude was well represented by Governor Blanchelande's reports, especially AN D-XXV, 46, 431 and 433.

40. Gros, *Historick Recital*, 17-18.

41. AN D-XXV, 1, 4, no. 10, Jean-François and Biassou to Civil Commissioners, 17 December 1791.

42. Elias Alexandre da Silva Corrêa, *Historia de Angola* ([1798], mod. Ed. Manuel Múrias, 2 vols., Lisbon, 1937) 2: 57.

43. ACL MS Vermelho 296, Castello de Vide, "Viagem," 80, 93.

44. Ibid, 118.

45. AHU, Angola, Cx. 76, doc. 73, Letter to Manuel de Almada e Vasconcelos, 7 August 1791, fol. 1.

46. Biblioteca Civica di Torino, MS 457, published in full colour in Paolo Collo and Silvia Benso (eds.) *Sogno Bamba, Pemba Ovando e altre contrade dei Regni di Congo, Angola e adiacenti* (Milan, 1986), 144.

47. Ibid, 155.

48. AHU, Angola, Cx, 76, doc. 73, Letter to Manuel de Almeida e Vasconcellos, 7 August 1791, fol. iv.

49. "Noticia da campanha e paiz do Mosul, que conquistou o Sargento Mor Paulo Martins Pinheiro de Lacerda, 1790-91," printed in *Annaes Maritimos e Colonais* 3, 4 (1845): 129-30. Another detailed account of this campaign by the commander is found in his report in AHU, Angola, Caixa 76, doc. 28, 20 May 1791.

50. Collo and Benso (eds.) *Sogno*, 189.

51. For a general background to Portuguese policy, see Joseph C. Miller, *Way of Death: Merchant Capitalism and the Angolan Slave Trade, 1730-1830* (Madison, 1988), 581-630.

52. A summary is given in the account of the Barão de Mossamedes, AHU, Cx. 76, doc. 88, 20 September 1791, for details on the invasion of 1790, see doc. 73, letter to Manuel de Almeda e Vasconcelos, 7 August 1791, fol. 1.This document also describes a battle near Encoge at about the same time, fol. iv.

53. ACL, MS Vermelho 296, Castello de Vide, "Viagem," 93, 95.

54. AHU Angola, Cx. 76, doc. 34, Service Record of Felix Xavier Pinheiro de Lacerda, enclosure, report by Paulo Martins Pinheiro de Lacerda, n. d., early 1791.

55. Silva Corrêa, *História* 2: 182-83, which reproduces the diary, undoubtedly written by Paulo Martins Pinheiro de Lacerda.

56. Ibid, 181, 185, 188.

57. "Noticia da campanha," 132.

58. AHU Angola, Cx. 76, doc. 28, Paulo Marins Pinheiro de Lacerda report, 20 May 1791. See also note 54.

59. "Noticia da campanha," 131; the date is given in AHU, Angola, Cx. 76, doc. 34.

60. See note 58.

61. Silva Corrêa, *História* 2: 183-4.

62. Ibid, 241.

63. Robin Law, *The Slave Coast of West Africa, 1550-1750* (Oxford, 1992), 97-101, 270-72. Although Law's focus is on the period prior to 1750, much of his evidence relates to the later periods as well.

64. Vicente Ferreira Pires, *Viagem de África em o Reino de Dahomé* (1800) (mod. Ed. Clado Ribeiro de Lessa, São Paulo), 1957, 106.

65. On the Gold Coast, see Ray Kea, *Settlement, Trade and Polities on the Seventeenth Century Gold Coast* (Baltimore, 1982), 130-68; for the Slave Coast area, see Kea, "Firearms and Warfare on the Gold and Slave Coasts from the Sixteenth to the Nineteenth Centuries," *Journal of African History* 12 (1971).

66. Law, *Slave Coast*, 101, 229.

67. Dalzel, *History*, 180-2, 184-5.

68. Ibid, 168.

69. Ibid, 192.

70. Ibid, 167-69.

71. Ferreira Pires, *Viagem*, 105.

72. Robin Law, *The Oyo Empire, c. 1600-c. 1836: A West African Imperialism in the Era of the Atlantic Slave Trade* (Oxford, 1977), 193-98.

73. Ferreira Pires, *Viagem*, 46.

74. Ibid, 105; Law, *Slave Coast*, 269-72.

75. Ferreira Pires, *Viagem*, 101.

76. Dalzel, *History*, 184-5.

77. Ibid, 199.

78. Ibid, 167-6.

79. Ibid. 175-6

80. AN D-XXV 78, 772, "Declaration que fait M. Robillard, habitant du Plaine de Nord . . . 29 September 1791.

81. AN D-XXV 78, 772. Anon report, Le Cap, 27 September 1791.

82. F. C *** [Félix Carteau], *Soirées Bermudiennes, ou entretiens sur les événemens qui ont opéré la ruine de la partie française de l'ile St. Domingue* (Bordeaux, An X [1802]), 100.

83. Étienne Descourtiltz, *Histoire des désastres de Sainte Domingue* (Paris, An III [1795]), 192.

84. Diary of French militiaman, entry of 27 August 1791, printed in Philadelphia *General Advertiser* no. 321 (10 October 1791).

85. Diary, 14 September 1791 in Philadelphia *General Advertiser* no. 348 (10 November 1791).

86. "St. Domingo Disturbances,", Boston *Independent Chronicle and Universal Advertiser* no. 1199 (20 October 1791).

87. Diary of French militiaman, 2 September 1791, printed in Philadelphia *General Advertiser* no. 322 (11 October 1791).

88. Diary of French militiaman, 10 September 1791, printed in Philadelphia *General Advertiser* no. 322 (10 October 1791).

89. Diary of French militiaman, 14 September and 19 September 1791, printed in Philadelphia *General Advertiser* no. 348 (10 November 1791).

90. "San Domingo Disturbances," Boston *Independent Chronicle and Universal Advertiser* 23, no 1199 (20 October 1791).

91. Pamphile de Lacroix, *Mémoires pour servir à la revolution de Saint Domingue* (2 vols., Paris, 1819) 1: 94.

92. Descourtilz, "Histoire des désastres," 192.

93. Pinheiro de Lacerda, "Noticia da campanha e paiz do Mosul," 131.

94. Diary of French militiaman, 11 September 1791, printed in Philadelphia *General Advertiser* no. 322 (11 October 1791).

95. Dalzel, *History*, 169.

96. Ibid, 225.

97. Silva Corrêa, *Historia* 2:

98. Diary of French militiaman, 27 August 1791, printed in Philadelphia *General Advertiser* no. 321 (10 October 1791).

99. Diary of French militiaman, 19 September 1791, printed in Philadelphia *General Advertiser* no. 349 (10 November 1791).

100. Diary of French militiaman, 13 September 1791, printed in Philadelphia *General Advertiser* no. 322 (11 October 1791).

101. Gros, *Historick Recital*, 51-63.
102. See Toussaint's ambitious plan in his letter to Laveaux, 3 Thermidor, An III [1794], in Gerard M. Laurent (ed.) *Toussaint Louverture à travers sa Correspondance 1794-1798* (Madrid, 1953), 206-212.
103. The action is described in the journal of Lieutenant Howard, (ed. Buckley), *Haitian Journal*, 91-93.
104. See a number of engagements described by Lieutenant Howard, Ibid, 40, 48 and especially 80.

105. For more details and documentation on these developments, see John Thornton, " 'I Serve the King of Kongo': African Ideology in the Haitian Revolution," (Paper presented at the conference "Five Centuries of Achievement" St Augustine, Trinidad, January, 1992).

71

The San Domingo Masses Begin

C. L. R. JAMES

Eh! Eh! Bomba! Heu! Heu!
Canga, bafio té!
Canga, mouné de lé!
Canga, do ki la!
Canga, do ki la!
Canga, li!

The slaves worked on the land, and, like revolutionary peasants everywhere, they aimed at the extermination of their oppressors. But working and living together in gangs of hundreds on the huge sugar-factories which covered the North Plain of Haiti, they were closer to a modern proletariat than any group of workers in existence at the time, and the rising was, therefore, a thoroughly prepared and organized mass movement. By hard experience they had learnt that isolated efforts were doomed to failure, and in the early months of 1791 in and around Le Cap they were organizing for revolution. Voodoo was the medium of the conspiracy. In spite of all prohibitions, the slaves travelled miles to sing and dance and practise the rites and talk; and now, since the revolution, to hear the political news and make their plans. Boukman, a Papaloi or High Priest, a gigantic Negro, was the leader. He was headman of a plantation and followed the political situation both among the whites and among the Mulattoes. By the end of July 1791 the blacks in and around Le Cap were ready and waiting. The plan was conceived on a massive scale and they aimed at exterminating the whites and taking the colony for themselves. There were perhaps 12,000 slaves in Le Cap, 6,000 of them men. One night the slaves in the suburbs and outskirts of Le Cap were to fire the plantations. At this signal the slaves in the town would mas-

sacre the whites and the slaves on the plain would complete the destruction. They had travelled a long, long way since the grandiose poisoning schemes of Mackandal.

The plan did not succeed in its entirety. But it very nearly did, and the scope and organization of this revolt shows Boukman to be the first of that line of great leaders whom the slaves were to throw up in such profusion and rapidity during the years which followed. That so vast a conspiracy was not discovered until it had actually broken out is a testimony to their solidarity. In early August the slaves in Limbé, then and to the end of the revolution one of the storm-centres, rose prematurely and were crushed. This Limbé rising showed that it was dangerous to delay. Three days after, representatives from parishes all over the plain assembled to fix the day. Deputies on their way to Le Cap for the first session of the Colonial Assembly, to begin on August 25th, met throngs of slaves on the road who abused and even attacked them. On August 21st some prisoners were taken and de Blanchelande, the Governor, examined them himself the next day. He did not get much from them, but he understood vaguely that there was to be some sort of rising. He took precautions to safeguard the city from the slaves within and he ordered patrols to cover the outskirts. But these whites despised the slaves too much to believe them capable of organizing a mass movement on a grand scale. They could not get from the prisoners the names of the leaders, and what precautions could they take against the thousands of slaves on the hundreds of plantations? Some of the white rabble in Le Cap, always ready for loot and pillage, were revealed as being connected with a plot of some sort. De Blanchelande was more concerned about these than about the Negroes.

On the night of the 22nd a tropical storm raged, with lightning and gusts of wind and heavy showers of rain. Carrying torches to light their way, the leaders of the revolt met in an open space in the thick forests of the Morne Rouge, a mountain overlooking Le Cap. There Boukman gave the last instructions and, after Voodoo incantations and the sucking of the blood of a stuck pig, he stimulated his followers by a prayer spoken in creole, which, like so much spoken on such occasions, has remained. "The god who created the sun which gives us light, who rouses the waves and rules the storm, though hidden in the clouds, he watches us. He sees all that the white man does. The god of the white man inspires him with crime, but our god calls us to do good works. Our god who is good to us orders us to revenge our wrongs. He will direct our arms and aid us. Throw away the symbol of the god of the whites who has so often caused us to weep, and listen to the voice of liberty, which speaks in the hearts of us all."

The symbol of the god of the whites was the cross which, as Catholics, they wore round their necks.

That very night they began. The slaves on the Gallifet plantation were so well treated that "happy as the Negroes of Gallifet" was a slave proverb. Yet by a phenomenon noticed in all revolutions it was they who led the way. Each slave-gang murdered its masters and burnt the plantation to the ground. The precautions that de Blanchelande had taken saved Le Cap, but the preparation otherwise had been thorough and complete, and in a few days one-half of the famous North Plain was a flaming ruin. From Le Cap the whole horizon was a wall of fire. From this wall continually rose thick black volumes of smoke, through which came tongues of flames leaping to the very sky. For nearly three weeks the people of Le Cap could barely distinguish day from night, while a rain of burning cane straw, driven before the wind like flakes of snow, flew over the city and the shipping in the harbour, threatening both with destruction.

The slaves destroyed tirelessly. Like the peasants in the Jacquerie or the Luddite wreckers, they were seeking their salvation in the most obvious way, the destruction of what they knew was the cause of their sufferings; and if they destroyed much it was because they had suffered much. They knew that as long as these plantations stood their lot would be to labour on them until they dropped. The only thing was to destroy them. From their masters they had known rape, torture, degradation, and, at the slightest provocation, death. They returned in kind. For two centuries the higher civilization had shown them that power was used for wreaking your will on those whom you controlled. Now that they held power they did as they had been taught. In the frenzy of the first encounters they killed all, yet they spared the priests whom they feared and the surgeons who had been kind to them. They, whose women had undergone countless violations, violated all the women who fell into their hands, often on the bodies of their still bleeding husbands, fathers and brothers. "Vengeance! Vengeance!" was their war-cry, and one of them carried a white child on a pike as a standard.

And yet they were surprisingly moderate,[1] then and afterwards, far more humane than their masters had been or would ever be to them. They did not maintain this revengeful spirit for long. The cruelties of property and privilege are always more ferocious than the revenges of poverty and oppression. For the one aims at perpetuating resented injustice, the other is merely a momentary passion soon appeased. As the revolution gained territory they spared many of the men, women, and children whom they surprised on plantations. To prisoners of war alone they remained merciless. They tore out their flesh with red-hot pincers, they roasted them on slow fires, they sawed a carpenter between two of his boards. Yet in all the records of that time there is no single instance of such fiendish tortures as burying white men up to the neck and smearing the holes in their faces to attract insects, or blowing them up with a gunpowder, or any of the thousand and one bestialities to which they had been subjected. Compared with what their master had done to them in cold blood, what they did was negligible, and they were spurred on by the ferocity with which the whites in Le Cap treated all slave prisoners who fell into their hands.

As usual the strength of the mass movement dragged in its wake revolutionary sections of those classes nearest to it. Free blacks joined them. A planter of Port Magot had taught his black foreman to read and write, had made him free, had left him in his will 10,000 francs, had given to the foreman's mother land on which she had made a coffee plantation. But this black raised the slaves on the plantations of his master and his own mother, set them on fire, and joined the revolution, which gave him a high command. The Mulattoes hated the black slaves because they were slaves and because they were black. But when they actually saw the slaves taking action on such a grand scale, numbers of young Mulattoes from Le Cap and round about rushed to join the hitherto despised blacks and fight against the common enemy.

They were fortunate in that the troops in Le Cap were few, and de Blanchelande, afraid of the slaves and the white rabble in town, preferred to act on the defensive. One attack was made by the regulars, who drove the slaves before them, but de Blanchelande, yielding to the nervous fears awakened in the city, recalled the detachment. This left the revolution master of the country-side. Gaining courage the blacks extended their destruction over the plain. If they had had the slightest material interest in the plantations, they would not have destroyed so wantonly. But they had none. After a few weeks they stopped for a moment to organize themselves. It is at this period, one month after the revolt had begun, that Toussaint Bréda joined them, and made an un-obtrusive entrance into history.

It seems certain that he had been in secret communication with the leaders, but like so many men of better education than the rank and file, he lacked their boldness a the moment of action and waited to see how things would go. Meanwhile, hating destruction, he kept his master's slaves in order and prevented the revolutionary labourers from setting fire to the plantation. While all the other whites in the neighbourhood made a dash for Le Cap, Madame Bayou de Libertas remained on the plantation, protected by Toussaint. Bayou de Libertas himself was with a camp of planters not far off, on guard against the slaves, but came every day to the plantation. Toussaint, then as always master of himself and of all near to him, maintained this untenable situation for over a month. But as the insurrection grew, worn out by the strain of defending the property, his master and his mistress, and learning that Madame de Libertas' life was now in danger, he decided that the old life was over and a new one had begun. He told Madame de Libertas that the time had come for her to go to Le Cap, packed her and some valuables in a carriage and sent her off under the care of his brother, Paul. He sent his own wife and the two children of the household into a safe spot in Spanish San Domingo. Then he slowly made his way to the camp of the revolted slaves.

The man who so deliberately decided to join the revolution was 45 years of age, an advanced age for those times, grey already, and known to everyone as Old Toussaint. Out of the chaos in San Domingo that existed then and for years to follow, he would lay the foundations of a Negro State that lasts to this day. From the moment he joined the revolution he was a leader, and moved without serious rivalry to the first rank. We have clearly stated the vast impersonal forces at work in the crisis of San Domingo. But men make history, and Toussaint made the history that he made because he was the man he was.

He had had exceptional opportunities, and both in mind and body was far beyond the average slave. Slavery dulls the intellect and degrades the character of the slave. There was nothing of that dullness or degradation in Toussaint.

His post as steward of the livestock had given him experience in administration, authority, and intercourse with those who ran the plantation. Men who, by sheer ability and character, find themselves occupying positions usually reserved for persons of a different upbringing, education and class, usually perform those duties with exceptional care and devoted labour. In addition to this practical education, he had as we have seen, been able to read a little. He had read Caesar's Commentaries, which had given him some idea of politics and the military art and the connection between them. Having read and re-read the long volume by the Abbé Raynal on the East and West Indies, he had a thorough grounding in the economics and politics, not only of San Domingo, but of all the great empires of Europe which were engaged in colonial expansion and trade. Finally he had the exceptional experience of the last three years of the revolution in San Domingo. The plantation was only two miles from Le Cap, and his duties took him often into the town. The masses of the people learn much during a revolution, far more a man like Toussaint. His superb intellect had therefore had some opportunity of cultivating itself in general affairs at home and abroad: from the very beginning he manœuvred with an uncanny certainty not only between local parties in San Domingo but between the international forces at work.

An important thing for his future was that his character was quite unwarped. Since his childhood he had probably never been whipped as so many slaves had been whipped. He himself tells us that he and his wife were among the fortunate few who had acquired a modest competence and used to go hand in hand and very happy to work on the little plot of land which some of the slaves cultivated for themselves. Besides his knowledge and experience, through natural strength of character he had acquired a formidable mastery over himself, both mind and body. As a boy he was so frail and delicate that his parents had not expected him to live, and he was nicknamed "Little Stick". While still a child he determined to acquire not only knowledge but a strong body, and he strengthened himself by the severest exercises, so that by the time he was 12 he had surpassed all the boys of his age on the plantation in athletic feats. He could swim across a dangerous river, jump on a horse at full speed and do what he liked with it. When he was nearly 60 he was still the finest rider in San Domingo, habitually rode 125 miles a day, and sat his horse with such ease and grace that he was known as the Centaur of the Savannahs.

As a young man he had run after women. Then he decided to settle down. Refusing to live in the concubinage which was so widely prevalent among all classes in San Domingo, but particularly among the slaves, he married a woman who already had a son. She bore Toussaint one child, and he and his wife lived together in the greatest harmony and friendship, when he was master of all San Domingo just as in the days when he was an ordinary slave. For the life that so many lived in the colony, for the reputation that he had among the blacks and the opportunities that his position offered, this was an unusual thing for a man who had begun life as Toussaint had, and who, in the days of his greatness, was partial to the society of attractive women.

From childhood he had been taciturn, which singled him out among his countrymen, a talkative, argumentative people. He was very small, ugly and ill-shaped, but although his general expression was one of benevolence, he had eyes like steel and no one ever laughed in his presence. His comparative learning, his success in life, his character and personality gave him an immense prestige among all the Negroes who knew him, and he was a man of some consequence among the slaves long before the revolution. Knowing his superiority he never had the slightest doubt that his destiny was to be their leader, nor would those with whom he came in contact take long to recognise it.

Nothing could be imagined more calculated to revolt his orderly mind than the spectacle which the slave camp presented. Many men were entirely naked; others wore filthy rags made out of bits and pieces of silks and satins pillaged from the plantations. Their weapons were a few guns and pistols that they had seized, old rusty swords, agricultural implements, sticks pointed with iron, pieces of iron hoop, in fact anything they could lay their hands on. They were destitute of ammunition and the cavalry were mounted on old horses and mules worn down by fatigue. They were divided into two large bands – one under Biassou, the other under Jean François, while a third leader was Jeannot. Jean François was a native of San Domingo, good-looking, very intelligent, and of a proud spirit which had made him run away from his master and become a maroon long before the revolution. In addition to his exceptional intelligence he was very brave, very sober, and of a tenacity that never admitted defeat. Biassou was a fire-eater, always drunk, always ready for the fiercest and most dangerous exploits. He also had had a life more easy than usual, having belonged to a religious establishment, the Fathers of Charity, not far from Le Cap. Jeannot was the slave who had led the foolish expedition of the San Domingo whites in the early days of the revolution, when, dressed up in their military uniforms, they had looked around for an enemy on whom to practise.

Like their more educated white masters, the slaves hastened to deck themselves with all the trappings and titles of the military profession. The officers called themselves generals, colonels, marshals, commanders, and the leaders decorated themselves with scraps of uniforms, ribbons and orders which they found on the plantations or took from the enemy killed in battle. Biassou called himself a Brigadier. So did

Jeannot. Later Jean François entitled himself (in the fashion of European colonial governors to this day) Admiral, Generalissimo and Chevalier of the Order of St. Louis, while Biassou, after a quarrel with Jean François, assumed the title of "Viceroy of the Conquered Territories."

Yet, despite these absurdities, which served the same purpose of impressing their inferiors as the trappings, gold epaulettes and multifarious commands of twentieth century royalty, Jean François and Biassou were men born to command. Nothing but an iron discipline could have kept order among that heterogeneous body of men just released from slavery, and Biassou and Jean François imposed it with an iron hand. Jeannot was a cruel monster who used to drink the blood of his white victims and commit abominable cruelties. Jean François arrested him, tried him, and had him shot, a conspicuous difference from the behaviour of the white colonists in the case of Le Jeune. Jean François soon foresaw a long war and ordered the planting of provisions. Thus early the slave leaders were showing a sense of order, discipline and capacity to govern. Many emissaries of the royalist counter-revolution found their way to the slaves. The priests, in large numbers, remained among them. But even the Mulattoes failed to oust these black leaders, and Jean François and Biassou who were in command at the beginning of the revolution remained masters of their respective bands to the end. Toussaint joined the band of Biassou. On account of his knowledge of herbs Biassou appointed him Physician to the Armies of the King, and from the very beginning Toussaint was high up in his councils.

Masses roused to the revolutionary pitch need above all a clear and vigorous direction. But the first coup had failed and Jean François and Biassou, though they could keep order, had not the faintest idea what to do next. De Blanchelande sent them a proclamation demanding their submission. They refused, but in their reply called themselves the servants of God and the King, and naïvely invited the whites to take all their possessions and leave the island to those who had watered it with their sweat. To these bewildered political leaders Toussaint brought his superior knowledge and the political vices which usually accompany it.

The slaves had revolted because they wanted to be free. But no ruling class ever admits such things. The white cockades accused the Patriots and the Friends of the Negro of stirring up the revolt, while the red cockades accused the royalists and the counter-revolution in France. The small whites accused the Mulattoes and massacred them at sight in the streets.[2]

The Assembly took charge of the colony. It would not ask France for assistance, but sent envoys to the British at Jamaica, to the Spaniards, and to the United States. It did not fear the revolution. It was more afraid of the slaves in Le Cap, and the city rabble, always ready to foment anarchy for the chance of plunder. These small whites refused to fight unless they were given two-thirds of what they found on the plantations as booty. But the majority of the Mulattoes, anxious about their property, volunteered to serve and offered their wives and children as hostages in token of good faith. The Assembly (knowing nothing as yet of the September 24th reversal) promised not only to enforce the decree of May 15th but to extend it to all Mulattoes whether their parents were free or not. But this could only be done, said the Assembly, after the decree had reached the colony and when the troubles were over.

To deceive the Mulattoes the planters were trying tricks, but against the slaves they knew only one weapon – terror. The blacks had their stockades covered with the heads of white victims. The Colonial Assembly stuck the heads of Negroes on pikes placed all along the roads leading to Le Cap. When Boukman was killed (fighting bravely) the Assembly stuck up his head in Le Cap with a placard: "This is the head of Boukman, chief of the rebels." The whites built three scaffolds in Le Cap and broke 20 or 30 blacks on the wheel every day. With their usual disregard of the slave even as property they massacred all they met, even those on plantations which had not yet revolted. Masters denounced those who helped them to escape. Slaves presenting themselves to their masters seeking refuge from the devastation of the countryside or merely because they were afraid or tired of revolution, were killed at sight. The result was that all, timid as well as bold, soon understood that there was no hope except with the revolution, and they flocked to join its ranks. In a few weeks the insurgents had grown to nearly 100,000.

To help the slaves and confuse the white planters came news of a Mulatto revolution in the west. Early in August, a body of Mulattoes, weary of being persecuted and lynched by the small whites, now lording it as officials in the revolutionary Municipalities, crept out of Port-au-Prince and assembled at La Croix-des-Bouquets, a district about five miles from the capital. From all parts of the West Province the Mulattoes began to send contingents there, and with their education, not so widespread as among the whites, but immensely superior to the half-wild blacks, they at once found admirable leadership. The most famous of them was Rigaud, a genuine Mulatto, that is to say the son of a white and a black. He had had a good education at Bordeaux and then leaned the trade of a goldsmith. Unlike Toussaint, Jean François and Biassou, he was already a trained soldier. He had enlisted as a volunteer in the French Army which fought in the American War of Independence, became a non-commissioned officer and had also seen service in Guadeloupe. He hated the whites, not only for the indignities which he, an educated and widely-travelled soldier, had to suffer, but also because they were jealous of his goldsmith's business, in those days an important trade.

A very different type of man was Beauvais. He was a member of a Mulatto family which had long been free and rich. He also had been educated in France, had volunteered for service and fought as a non-commissioned officer in the American War of Independence. On his return home he had taken up teaching. He was not only a man of exceptional personal bravery. Tall, of a fine figure and distinguished presence, he was known as one of the handsomest men in San Domingo, and in that licentious age and country he was distinguished for the severity of his mode of life and the charm of his manners. His own people loved him and it would not be difficult for the whites (when in a corner) to forget his colour.

These were the two soldiers. The politician was Pinchinat, who had studied widely in France. In the first days of the revolution he came back to San Domingo to lead the Mulattoes. In 1791 he was already 60, a man loving play and loose living, and hating the whites with all the hatred of a vicious character. He was a most finished politician and well deserved the qualification of man of genius, given to him by Pamphile de Lacroix.[3] "What a man to write and to make treaties," another Mulatto leader would write of him, "he is unique."

Under such leaders, and trained to fight in the *maréchaussée*, the Mulattoes were a formidable force. For this reason the royalist counter-revolution in the west at once sought to make use of them.

Humus de Jumecourt, Commandant of the district of La Croix-des-Bouquets and Cul-de-sac, proposed an alliance guaranteeing them all their rights in return for support of the counter-revolution, or, as he would call it, the lawful government of the island. Pinchinat refused, but offered instead a united front against their common enemy, the Municipality of Port-au-Prince and the Provincial Assembly of the West. De Jumecourt agreed, and the royalist commandants and the rich whites of the West began to join the Mulattoes at La Croix-des-Bouquets. There were a few free blacks holding high command in this troop, so that despised blacks were now commanding whites. The Mulattoes also incorporated in their force a body of maroons, nicknamed "The Swiss" in imitation of the bodyguard of Louis XVI. Full of contempt for men of colour and hating them now for their persistent royalism, the Patriots attacked La Croix-des-Bouquets. They were heavily defeated, "The Swiss" fighting with great bravery. A few days later, the Mulattoes and the whites of the surrounding districts had a meeting at La Croix-des-Bouquets, where the Mulattoes and the whites the draft of a concordat embodying their demands for complete equality. The ninth and last clause consisted of four words: "If not, civil war." The whites accepted their demands immediately.

The Patriots of San Domingo were always ready to forget race prejudice in return for something solid. After he had been defeated in the field, Caradeu, leader of the Patriots, offered Beauvais Mulatto rights, in return for an agreement on independence without the intervention of the royalists.[4] Beauvais refused. By this time nearly all the rich planters had deserted the Patriots, and even the rich merchants in Port-au-Prince would have nothing to do with them. On October 19th a concordat embodying all the Mulatto demands was signed by all parties. The Provincial Assembly of the West was to be dissolved immediately, the white deputies from the West Province to the Colonial Assembly were to be recalled, two battalions of the National Guard were to be recruited among the Mulattoes, the memory of Ogé was to be rehabilitated, and the whole presented for the ratification of the National Assembly and the approval of the King. The leader of the whites extended the hand of friendship.

"We bring you finally words of peace; we come no longer to bargain with you, we come only to accord to you your demands, we come animated by the spirit of justice and peace to give you authentic recognition of your rights, to ask you to see in the white citizens only friends and brothers whom the colony in danger invites you, begs you, to unite with, in order to bring prompt assistance to our troubles. We accept entirely and without any reserve the concordat that you propose to us. Unfortunate circumstances of which you are doubtless aware made us hesitate for a moment. But our courage has broken all obstacles, and we have imposed silence on all mean prejudices, on the petty desire for domination. May the day on which the torch of reason has enlightened us all be forever memorable. May it be a day of forgetfulness for all errors, of pardon for all injuries. Let us henceforth be combatants only in zeal for the public welfare."[5] The "mean prejudices" and "the petty desire for domination"were the small whites who saw themselves being pushed into the background. But the news of the slave revolution in the North had sobered all who owned slaves, and they wanted peace.

All the 14 parishes of the West Province accepted the terms, and on the 24th of October the great ceremony of reconciliation took place in Port-au-Prince. The leaders of the whites and the leaders of the Mulattoes marched into Port-au-Prince arm in arm, with their troops marching behind, greeted by salvoes of artillery and mutual shouts of "Unity and Fidelity." In the general excitement a captain of the white National Guard jumped on a gun-carriage and proclaimed Caradeu Commander of the National Guard of the West Province. There was loud applause which was renewed when he named Beauvais second in command. Then all went to the Church to celebrate with a Te Deum as stipulated in the concordat. One more difficulty remained – "The Swiss." What was to be done with them? The whites argued that to send them back to the plantations would be bad for the slaves and it was

agreed to deport them to a deserted beach in Mexico.[6] Among the leaders, Rigaud and Pétion, Mulattoes, fought for "The Swiss"; Lambert, a free black supported the deportation. "The Swiss" out of the way, peace seemed assured, Mulatto rights guaranteed, and the counter-revolution well placed for action.

But in Le Cap the Assembly foamed with wrath at these goings-on in the west. The royalist commanders of the local forces, M. de Rouvrai and M. de Touzard, urged the Patriots in the North to grant Mulatto rights. "But, you will say, must we yield to the menaces of an inferior caste, admit it to civic rights, as a ransom for the evils which they cause us? . . . One day," said de Rouvrai, "the scornful laughs with which you greet the important truths which I dare to tell you will change into tears of blood . . . In the war of 1756 England wished to seize Cuba and Lord Albermarle was ordered to besiege Havana. He landed with 18,000 men; six months after he had only 1,800 . . .

"Where, I ask you, is the army capable of fulfilling our aim? . . . Have you any others than the Mulattoes? No. Well, why do you reject the help which they offer you . . .?

"I am not finished, I have some other truths to tell you, I shall tell them to you. France at this moment has her eyes fixed on San Domingo . . . It is impossible that the claims of the Mulattoes will not be listened to in France; if even they were unjust, they will be welcomed. The constitutional decree that you suppose irrevocable, that you regard as your palladium, will be inevitably modified . . ."

The Assembly promised to give the Mulattoes their rights, but after the troubles were over. True, there was a slave revolt. But they had appealed to France by now, and to give rights to Mulattoes who outnumbered them would be to hand over the colony, military and civil, to these bastard upstarts and their allies of the counter-revolution. They could see the results of that unholy alliance in the west. They had de Blanchelande, the Governor, in their power and they poured out their wrath on the concordat.

The west would not budge from their unity and repudiated the proclamations of the Assembly and the Governor. But six days after the ceremony of reconciliation, there arrived in the colony the decree of the 24th September, by which the Constituent had withdrawn all rights from the Mulattoes and once more put their fate in the hands of the white colonists. "Mean prejudices" and "the petty desire for domination" reared heads again, and the scarcely healed wounds re-opened. The intrigues of Barnave & Co. were coming home to roost.

The 21st November was fixed for the ratification of the concordat. Port-au-Prince was divided into four sections for the voting and three had already voted in favour of ratification. This for the small whites was ruin, and Pralotto and his band were on the look-out to create some cause for a breach. It came over a free Negro, a member of the Mulatto force, who was either insulted by or insulted some whites. He was immediately captured and hanged. Despite the moderation of the Mulattoes, fighting began in the streets. The Mulattoes, taken by surprise, retreated. Fire broke out in the city, for which they were made responsible. Pralotto and his followers massacred rich white citizens, Mulattoes, men, women and children; and plundered the wealthy quarter of the town, while the flames spread and burned two-thirds of Port-au-Prince to the ground, estimated at a loss of 50 million francs.

The Mulattoes had been very patient and forbearing, but now they seemed to go mad. Pinchinat, the man of proclamations, issued a ringing call for battle.

"Fly, my friends, to the siege of Port-au-Prince and let us plunge our bleeding arms, avengers of perjury and perfidy, into the breast of these monsters from Europe. Too much and too long have we served as sport for their passions and their insidious manœuvres; too much and too long have we groaned under this iron yoke. Let us destroy our tyrants, let us bury with them even the smallest vestige of our degradation, let us tear up by its deepest roots this upas tree of prejudice. Recruit some, persuade others, promise, menace, threaten, drag in your wake the decent white citizens. But above all, dear friends, unity, courage and speed. Bring arms, baggage, cannon, munitions of war, and provisions, and come at once to rally under the common standard. It is there that we all ought to perish, or take vengeance for God, Nature, law and humanity, so long outraged in these climates of horror."

Rigaud's brother wrote to his friends: "I fly to vengeance ... If my fate is not death on this expedition, I shall be back soon to join you....

Long live liberty, long live equality, long live love." Rich whites and royalist commandants followed the Mulattoes, but the Rigaud brothers, Beauvais, and Pinchinat (despite his treatment of "The Swiss") were genuine revolutionaries, putting liberty before property. In a frenzy of excitation and rage they summoned the slaves of the West Province and drew them into the revolution. In the advanced north the slaves were leading the Mulattoes, in the backward west the Mulattoes were leading the slaves. It does not need much wisdom to foresee the consequences.

In the south, whites and Mulattoes were on the point of forming a concordat on the model of the west. All terms had been agreed upon when Caradeu paid a visit to the south and intrigued so successfully that the unity agreement was broken. As soon as the news of the split in Port-au-Prince reached them, Mulattoes and whites each took to arms. The Mulattoes made themselves masters of Jacmel and other towns. In self-defense the whites in the South, outnumbered by the Mulattoes, raised the slaves.

In the north some Mulatto and white proprietors formed a concordat. The Assembly disallowed it and these Mulattoes joined the slaves.

The whites committed frightful atrocities against the Mulattoes. They killed a pregnant woman, cut the baby out and threw it into the flames. They burnt them alive, they inoculated them with small-pox. Naturally the Mulattoes retaliated in kind.

But here as everywhere the white planters began it, and exceeded all rivals in barbarism, being trained in violence and cruelty by their treatment of the slaves.

This was the San Domingo that the three Commissioners, Saint Leger, Mirbeck and Roume, were to restore to order when they landed at Le Cap on November 29th, 1791. They were welcomed by the Assembly and installed with an imposing ceremony. They issued a proclamation mendaciously announcing the near arrival of large bodies of troops. To their surprise and joy this seemed as if it would work a miracle.

Biassou, Jean François and the other Negro leaders, including Toussaint, after four months of insurrection, had come to a dead end. An insurrection must win victories, and the whites were content to hold the line of fortifications known as the Cordon of the West and prevent the insurrection penetrating into the West Province.

The former slaves could devastate the country around but that very devastation was making it impossible for them to exist. Famine began to kill them off. Frightened at what they considered their hopeless position, and afraid of being beaten into submission, Jean François and Biassou offered peace to the Commissioners in return for the liberty of a few hundred leaders. Jean François knew that it was a betrayal. "False principles," wrote this four-months-old labour leader, "will make these slaves very obstinate, they will say that they have been betrayed." But if the Commissioners granted liberty to those who were named they would co-operate with the King's troops and hunt down those who refused to submit. Jean François knew that the business would be difficult and dangerous and said as much, proof of the passion for liberty which filled the hearts of the blacks. But he was prepared to do all that he could to help, and to soothe his conscience wrote disloyally of his followers as a multitude of Negroes from Africa who did not know two words of French. In the long and cruel list of leaders betraying brave but ignorant masses this stands high, and Toussaint was in it up to the neck. Though working in a subordinate position he took the leading part in the negotiations, and the masterpiece of diplomatic correspondence which the envoys of the slaves presented at the bar of the Assembly showed the distance between the men who a few weeks before had asked the whites to leave the island and the already fully-fledged political maturity of Toussaint. To the end of his days he could hardly speak French, he literally could not write three words without the grossest errors in spelling and grammar. Years afterwards when he was master of San Domingo he wrote thus to Dessalines: Je vouss a vé parlé pour le forli berté avan theire . . . He meant to write: Je vous avais parlé du Fort Liberté avanthier. . . . He could never do better. But he dictated in the local bastard French or creole, and his secretaries wrote and re-wrote until he got the exact meaning he wanted.

The letter[8] begins by emphasizing that the King's proclamation has formally accepted the French constitution, and "very clearly and precisely" has asked for a spirit of "justice and moderation" to help in the restoration of a country which has suffered from the repeated shocks of a great revolution. This conciliatory spirit should cross the seas. "We pass now to the law relating to the colonies of September 28th, 1791. This law gives to the colonies the right of deciding on the status of the free men of colour and free blacks." Toussaint and the other traitors wanted not only freedom but political rights. But promises were not enough. They would defend the decisions of the Colonial Assembly "to the last drop of their blood," but these decisions must be "clothed with the requisite formalities." Followed a long apology for the evils which they had helped to afflict "on this rich and important colony." But they had not known of the new laws when they had written the first letter. "To-day when we are instructed in the new laws, to-day when we cannot doubt the approbation of the mother-country for all the Legislative Acts that you will decree, concerning the interior régime of the Colony, and the status of citizens, we shall not show ourselves refractory." After another long appeal to the Assembly to seize this opportunity to re-establish order promptly "in so important a colony," the letter touched on the difficult question of the slaves. "The laws which will be in force concerning the status of persons free and not free ought to be the same in the whole colony." This was obviously a finger pointing to the concordats in the West Province. "It would be even to your interest if you declared, by a decree bearing the sanction of the Governor, that it is your intention to concern yourselves with the lot of the slaves, knowing that they are the object of your solicitude." Inasmuch as the slaves had confidence in their chiefs, if the Assembly gave the job of pacification to these chiefs, the slaves would be satisfied, which would facilitate restoration of the "the equilibrium which has been broken." The conclusion was a protestation of good faith and desire for a speedy settlement. Freedom for the leaders, however, was "indispensable." The letter was signed by Jean François and Biassou, two others, and two commissioners *ad hoc*, one of whom was Toussaint. In its skilful use of both the moral and political connection between the mother-country and the colony, its dangling before the colonists the chance to restore the former prosperity "of this great and important colony," its firm but delicate insistence on political rights, duly certified by law, for the freed men, its luxuriance whenever it dealt with things that cost nothing such as peace, good-will, etc., the letter could have come from the pen of a man who had spent all his life in diplomacy. The writer, knowing the temper of the colonists, had even taken the trouble to suggest to them exactly how the slaves were to be bluffed back into bondage; no imperialist of today with three hundred years of traditional deception behind him could have garlanded his claws with fairer words; "the restoration of the broken equilibrium" as a phrase for slavery would not have disgraced the Mandates Commission of the League of Nations. Jean François had written that the thing was difficult but it could be done, and that they were not only prepared but able to do their Judas work the letter gave ample evidence. Political treachery is not a monopoly of the white race, and this abominable betrayal so soon after the insurrections shows that political leadership is a matter of programme, strategy and tactics, and not the colour of those who lead it, their oneness of origin with their people, nor the services they have rendered.

The high and mighty colonists refused. Treat with these brigands who had murdered and burnt and raped? Impossible. In vain the Commissioners protested. The colonists, supremely confident that they would without difficulty drive these revolted dogs back to their kennels, answered that they would grant pardon only to repentant criminals who returned to work. The message ended with the terse request to the envoys, "Get out!" The white colonists could not understand that Biassou was no longer a slave but a leader of 40,000 men. When he got this message he lost his temper and remembered the white prisoners. "I shall make them pay for the insolence of the Assembly which has dared to write to me with so little respect," and ordered them all to be killed. Toussaint, always a hater of unnecessary bloodshed, calmed his chief.

The disappointed Commissioners arranged an interview with Jean François. The Colonial Assembly accused them of plotting counter-revolution. The Commissioners invited them to send delegates.

At the appointed place and time Jean François appeared, leading his horse by the bridle. At the sight of him, M. Bullet, a colonist was so overpowered with rage that he struck him with a riding whip. Jean François, fiercely angry, fell back to his own band and peace hung on a thread. At this dangerous moment Saint-Leger had the quick-wittedness and courage to advance alone

among the hostile blacks and speak to them kindly. So moved were they at this unexpected behaviour that Jean François threw himself at the feet of the men from France. He reiterated his promise. For the freedom of 400 of the leaders and forgetfulness of the past he would lead the blacks back to slavery. The Commissioners asked him as a guarantee of good faith to return the white prisoners. He agreed and asked to return for his wife, a prisoner in Le Cap, whom the whites had not dared to execute for fear of reprisals. The interview ended amicably, Jean François assuring the Commissioners that he was "touched to see at last white men who showed humanity."

Next day he sent the promised prisoners to Le Cap. But the blacks had probably got to know that something was in the wind. The prisoners were under a strong escort, including Toussaint, which was scarcely sufficient to save them from the hostility of those they met on the way. The members of the delegation presented themselves at the bar of the Assembly. The president would not even speak to them but communicated with them only by note. "Continue to give proof of your repentance and say to those who send you, to address themselves to the Commissioners: it is only by their intercession that the Assembly can come to a decision on your fate." He wanted to impress on the blacks that the Commissioners were subordinate to the Assembly, and he succeeded. So disdainful was the Assembly that it would not include the negotiations in the minutes. Toussaint had plenary powers and in a vain attempt to break down the pride of the colonists he secretly reduced the number to be freed from 400 to 60.[9] The colonists would not hear of it. Then and only then did Toussaint come to an unalterable decision from which he never wavered and for which he died. Complete liberty for all, to be attained and held by their own strength. The most extreme revolutionaries are formed by circumstances. It is probable that, looking at the wild hordes of blacks who surrounded him, his heart sank at the prospect of the war and the barbarism which would follow freedom even if it were achieved. He was ready to go a long way to meet the colonists. He probably hoped for some attempt at better treatment. But having been driven to take his decision, as was his way, he never looked back. On his return he told his chiefs not to look to the Commissioners for anything.[10] They had only a faculty of intercession and their powers were subordinate to those of the Assembly. Biassou, who had demanded an interview, evaded it.

Henceforth it was war, and war needed trained soldiers. Toussaint dropped his post of Physician to the Armies of the King, and assuming the title of Brigadier-General started to train an army. Once only in his political life did he ever fail to meet an emergency with action bold and correct.

In the West Province Rigaud, Beauvais and Pinchinat were using as their agent in the gangs a young slave named Hyacinth. He was only 21 years of age, but he went from plantation to plantation claiming, as most leaders of agricultural revolts, that he was divinely inspired. We can judge the backwardness of the western slaves at the beginning of the revolution from the fact that both Hyacinth, and other men, Romaine the prophetess (*sic*), fortified their authority with divine attributes, while Jean François and Biassou in the north from the very beginning aimed at a social revolution. The blacks flocked to join the confederate army of Mulattoes and whites at La Croix-des- Bouquets, and on March 31st the battle betwen the Confederates and the Patriots of Port-au-Prince took place. The slaves were nearly all native-born Africans. Armed only with knives, picks, hoes, and sticks with iron points, they went into battle. Led by Hyacinth, they charged the bayonets of the Port-au-Prince volunteers and the French soldiers without fear or care for the volleys from Pralotto's cannon which tore their ranks: if they were killed they would wake again in Africa. Hyacinth, a bull's tail in his hand, ran from rank to rank crying that his talisman would chase death away. He charged at their head, passing unscathed through the bullets and the grape-shot. Under such leadership the Africans were irresistible. They clutched at the horses of the dragoons, and pulled off the riders. They put their arms down into the mouths of the cannon in order to pull out the bullets and called to their comrades "Come, come, we have them." The cannon were discharged, and blew them to pieces. But others swarmed over guns and gunners, threw their arms around them and silenced them. Nothing could stop their devotion, and after six hours the troops of Port-au-Prince retired in disorder. They had lost over a hundred soldiers, but nearly 2,000

slaves lay dead upon the field. The combined army then invested Port-au-Prince.

The whites were not only fighting with the Mulattoes, but were petitioning the Governor to prevent disturbers of the peace coming from the Colonial Assembly to disrupt the west. They sent him the concordats, they said they would stick to them whatever he said. They asked him to publish them, to send them to the King, to the Legislative in France, to the merchants of the great ports, to everybody.[11]

Whatever the reservations they had made when they formed this pact with the bastard Mulattoes, the whites were now eager to cement the alliance and Roume was overwhelmed by the number of these appeals. Revolution, says Karl Marx, is the locomotive of history. Here was a locomotive that had travelled at remarkable speed, for in April 1792, not yet three years after the fall of the Bastille, the white Patriots in Port-au-Prince were being besieged by a composite army of royalist commandants, white planters, brown-skinned Mulattoes, and black slaves, none of them constrained but all for the time being free and equal partners. No doubt most of the rich were only awaiting the restoration of "order" to put the slaves back in their places again, but the mere fact of the revolutionary association and the temporary equality meant that the old spell was broken and things would never be the same again.

The Colonial Assembly in addition to war with the slaves and war with the Mulattoes had started a fierce row with the Commissioners over precedence. In Le Cap the Patriots actually had the Governor under arrest for some time and were plotting to murder Mirbeck who sailed for home on February 30th. Saint-Leger had gone to Port-au-Prince. The Patriots there, spurred on by the Assembly in Le Cap, threatened to deport him, and he took refuge with the Confederates. Saint-Leger and Roume were now seriously alarmed, not at revolting slaves, but at the growth of the counter-revolution. In the same way as Barnave, the Lameths and their friends in France, white San Domingo was growing tired of the red cockade and beginning to look once more to the royal authority. The Confederate Army seemed all white cockade. But just at this time Pinchinat had a meeting with Saint-Leger, and what he told that gentleman made him fly post-haste to France. Roume also was due to leave three days after, but in a chance conversation he smelt a royalist plot and stayed to ward it off. The royalists indeed thought that San Domingo was now ripe for the picking. But they were mistaken. Pinchinat had played an astute game. The royalists had hoped to use the Mulattoes. Now they found that they had been used instead. As Beauvais told Roume afterwards, "We were never the dupes of the white cockades. We had to conquer our rights, we needed auxiliaries. If the Devil had presented himself we would have enrolled him. These gentlemen offered and we used them, while allowing them to believe that we were their dupes."

The decree of April 4th now came to clinch the victory of the Mulattoes and allow them openly to support the French Revolution – for a time.

The colonial question had frayed the nerves and exhausted the Constituent, all of whose members were excluded by law from the Legislative which met on October 1st. The new deputies were no better off as far as the colonial question was concerned for in addition to the Rights of Man for Mulattoes they now faced a slave revolt.

On the right were the Feuillants, or King's Party, led on the colonial question by Vaublanc, who approved the condition of slaves, even Mulattoes. The Left was stronger since the elections. But though they were over a hundred Jacobin deputies in the Legislative they were split; on the extreme Left were Robespierre and the Mountain, on the Right were the Brissotins, or followers of Brissot, better known in history as the Girondins. The Paris masses organized in the Commune were following the Jacobins. Robespierre and the Mountain would fight for Mulatto rights. So would Brissot, but Brissot's group was composed of Vergniaud, Guadet, and others, actual deputies of the maritime towns. The Girondins were so called after the Gironde province, whose chief town was Bordeaux. Vergniaud was deputy for Bordeaux and all the maritime towns were still firmly against the Rights of Man for Mulattoes.

What first frightened them was the way the news of the insurrection reached France. Paris heard of it from an English paper. The English Ambassador gave information about the seriousness of the uprising – he had got it from Jamaica through London. The *Moniteur*, day after day,

asked, why no news from de Blanchelande? On November 7th the *Moniteur* printed a copy of the letter the colonists had written to the Governor of Jamaica. Only on the 8th was a letter from de Blanchelande asking for troops read in the House. The maritime bourgeois began to look at these colonists with a different eye: the Mulattoes at least were faithful to France, and they were strong supporters of slavery.

The first question was for troops to quell the revolt. But in a revolution the revolution comes first. Right and Left wing of the Legislative wanted to know how many troops were to be sent and who would control them. The King was still head of the Army and Navy. The officers were royalist and centres of the counter-revolution. The King's Ministers and officials were still functioning, in Paris and in San Domingo. To put an army and a fleet into the hands of these people was to be putting weapons which, after the suppression of the insurrection, perhaps before, might be used against the revolution itself, and place the richest colony of France entirely in royalist hands. Jacobins and Feuillants fought it out day after day. But though it was a question of repressing a slave revolt, the Legislative, like the Constituent, would not tolerate the use of the word slave. When a deputy in the course of a speech happened to say "But the slaves are the property of the colonists...." there were the usual protests and demands that the speaker be called to order. The Legislative, more to the Left, was, perhaps for this reason, even more sensitive than the Constituent. The Colonial Commission, wishing as usual to have everything settled in the ministry, would not make any report. But the Friends of the Negro were far more powerful now, and Brissot gave warning. If the Commission did not present its report in ten days, he was going to open a debate on December 1st. During the interval delegates from the Colonial Assembly arrived in Paris, and on November 30th one of them, Millet, put the colonists' case. It is probable that never, in any parliamentary assembly, was so much impudent lying and dishonesty packed into any single speech.

Millet's description of slavery proved it to be the happiest form of society known in either ancient or modern times. "We live in peace, gentlemen, in the midst of our slaves. . . . . Let an intelligent and educated man compare the deplorable state of these men in Africa with the pleasant and easy life which they enjoy in the colonies. . . . . Sheltered by all the necessities of life, surrounded with an ease unknown in the greater part of the countries of Europe, secure in the enjoyment of their property, for they had property and it was sacred, cared for in their illnesses with an expense and an attention that you would seek in vain in the hospitals so boasted of in England, protected, respected in the infirmities of age; in peace with their children, and with their family . . . . . freed when they had rendered important services: such was the picture, true and not embellished, of the government of our Negroes, and this domestic government perfected itself particularly during the last ten years with a care of which you will find no model in Europe. The most sincere attachment bound the master to the slave; we slept in safety in the middle of these men who had become our children and many among us had neither locks nor bolts on our doors."

This was supposed to be the lot of the slaves up to 1787, the year before the Le Jeune case. Terror, to keep the slaves in subjection, attested in a thousand documents? No such thing. True, there were a small number of hard and ferocious masters. "But what was the lot of these wicked men? Branded by public opinion, looked upon with horror by all honest people, shut out from all society, without credit in their business, they lived in opprobrium and dishonour and died in misery and despair. . . . ''

What was it that changed this idyllic state of affairs? At this point enter the villain.

"However, gentlemen, a Society takes shape in the bosom of France and prepares from afar the destruction and the convulsions to which we are subjected. . . And far from being able to continue with our work, this society forced us to renounce it by sowing the spirit of insubordination among our slaves and anxiety among us."

Having hurled his bomb at the Friends of the Negro, Millet turned to the Assembly itself. He knew the tender spot. "Soon they say this Society will demand that the slave-trade be suppressed, that is to say, that the profits which can result from it for French commerce will be delivered to foreigners, for never will its romantic philosophy persuade all the powers of Europe that it is their duty to abandon the cultivation of the colonies and to leave the inhabitants of Africa a prey to the barbarity of their tyrants rather than to employ them elsewhere. Under kind masters they exploit a territory which would remain uncultivated without them, and of which the rich productions are, for the nation which possesses them, a great source of industry and of prosperity."

The Mulattoes? They and the whites had lived peaceably – nay happily. "The bonds of affection and of good feeling which existed between these two classes of men" would be strengthened by the just and humane laws a Colonial Assembly would pass. But here too the Friends of the Negro falsely represented the attitude of the whites as the pretensions of vanity and an endeavour to resist just claims.

But no man can keep it up for ever, least of all men trained in the French intellectual tradition. Before Millet concluded he suddenly let slip the elegant drapery and gave a glimpse of white San Domingo in all its bloated nakedness.

"These coarse men [the blacks] are incapable of knowing liberty and enjoying it with wisdom, and the imprudent law which would destroy their prejudices would be for them and for us a decree of death."

The Legislative listened in silence. This was no juggling with the word slavery – it was the thing itself, presented to the bourgeoisie for their endorsement through all eternity. Jaurès notes that there was no applause, none even of those disgusted interruptions with which the Legislative was wont to express its disapproval of the mere word slavery. When Millet was finished, the President invited the delegates to the honours of the session. But this was too much. One of the extreme Left jumped up in a rage. "What, Mr. President, you invite to the session men who have just outraged philosophy and liberty, men who have just insulted. . . . '' But the profits of the slave trade were too much for the Assembly and the Left itself had no heart for this business.

Next day Brissot took the floor, and on behalf of the Mulattoes made a masterly and celebrated speech. He showed the rich whites anxious to have peace and ready to give political rights to the Mulattoes; the Patriots, for the most part heavily indebted to France and bent on independence, jealous of the Mulattoes who did not owe, and determined to maintain the privilege of race, all the more dear to them in that it rested now on such insecure foundation.

"It is by this that we can explain the existence all at the same time in the heart of the same colonist, of hatred against the man of-colour who claims his rights, against the merchant who claims his debts, against a free Government which wishes that justice be done to all."

Once more the bourgeoisie battled over Mulatto rights. This time the contest lasted for weeks in and out of the House. Vaublanc took the place of the absent Barnave, but the Friends of the Negro had a new argument in the concordats between whites and Mulattoes, and the maritime bourgeois were now convinced that the only way to save the colony was to give the Mulattoes their rights: the negotiations of the Patriots with other countries had opened their eyes as to the real nature of these gentlemen. Vergniaud and Guadet were able to convince their patrons that the old policy was false. The great ship-owners, merchants and traders threw over the colonists. Barnave's group the Feuillants, formed the governing Ministry, but the revolution was taking courage again. The Feuillants were overthrown on March 10th and a Girondin ministry came in, with Roland at its head, but Madame Roland and Brissot as its leading spirits. On March 24th, by a large majority, the Legislative passed a decree, giving full political rights to the men of colour. Some tried to argue that the decisions of the Constituent were sacrosanct, but a deputy of the Left, to the accompaniment of great applause, challenged the theory that the Legislative was forever bound by the decrees of the Constituent and boldly asserted the sovereignty of the people over the rights of formal assemblies. Three new Commissioners were appointed with supreme powers and large forces to enforce the decree and restore order, and on April 4th the King's signature made the decree law.

But what of the slaves? The slaves had revolted for freedom. The revolt was to be suppressed. But at least there might be a promise of pardon, of kind treatment in the future. Not a word. Neither from Vaublanc on the Right nor Robespierre on the Left. Robespierre made an ass of himself by violently objecting to the word slavery, when proposed as a substitute for non-free. Brissot made a passing reference to them as being unfortunate, and that was all.

"The cause of the men of colour is then the cause of the patriots of the old Third Estate and finally of the people so long oppressed." So had spoken Brissot, and Brissot, representative of the Third Estate, was prepared to help the Third Estate of the Mulattoes and give the people, in France was well as in San Domingo, phrases. The French peasants were still clamouring for the Assembly to relieve them of the feudal dues. The Brissotins would not do it. They would not touch property, and the slaves were property. Blangetty, a deputy, proposed a motion for gradual enfranchisement. The Legislative would not even discuss it. On March 26th, two days after the decree in favour of the Mulattoes, Ducos dared to propose that every Mulatto child be free, "whatever the status of its mother." The Legislative in wrath voted the previous question, and Ducos was not even allowed to speak on his motion. The Friends of the Negro, good Liberals, were now in power and were as silent about slavery as any colonist. The slaves, ignorant of politics, had been right not to wait on these eloquent phrase-makers. Toussaint, that astute student of French politics, read and noted.

Toussaint alone among the black leaders, with freedom for all in his mind, was in those early months of 1792 organizing out of the thousands of ignorant and untrained blacks an army capable of fighting European troops. The insurgents had developed a method of attack based on their overwhelming numerical superiority. They did not rush forward in mass formation like fanatics. They placed themselves in groups, choosing wooded spots in such a way as to envelop their enemy, seeking to crush him by weight of numbers. They carried out these preliminary manœuvres in dead silence, while their priests (the black ones) chanted the wanga, and the women and children sang and danced in a frenzy. When these had reached the necessary height of excitement the fighters attacked. If they met with resistance they retired without exhausting themselves, but at the slightest hesitation in the defense they became extremely bold and, rushing up to the cannon, swarmed all over their opponents. At first they could not even use the guns they captured, and used to apply the match at the wrong end. It was from these men "unable to speak two words of French" that an army had to be made. Toussaint could have had thousands following him. It is characteristic of him that he began with a few hundred picked men, devoted to himself, who learnt the art of war with him from the beginning, as they fought side by side against the French troops and the colonists. In camp he drilled and trained them assiduously. By July 1792, he had no more than five hundred attached to himself, the best of the revolutionary troops. These and not the perorations in the Legislative would be decisive in the struggle for freedom. But nobody took much notice of Toussaint and his black followers. Feuillants and Jacobins in France, whites and Mulattoes in San Domingo, were still looking upon the slave revolt as a huge riot which would be put down in time, once the division between the slave-owners was closed.

Notes

1. This statement has been criticised. I stand by it. C.L.R.J.
2. Pamphile de Lacroix. *Mémories pour Servir à L'Histoire de la Révolution de Saint-Dominique.* 2 Vols. (Paris, 1819), Vol. 1, 91.
3. *Mémoires pour Servir . . .*Vol. 1, p.183.
4. Saintoyant, *La Colonisation Française pendant la Révolution (1789-1799)*, Paris, 1930, Vol. 1, p.59.
5. Quoted from L. Deschamps, *Les Colonies pendant la Revolution. (Paris, 1898),* 257-258
6. The captain of the boat took his money but dumped them in Jamaica. The English Governor in great anger shipped them back. The Colonial Assembly had them all murdered except about 20, whom they sent back to the West so as to prejudice the blacks against the Mulattoes.
7. For a well-documented summary of these atrocities, see V. Schoelcher, *Vie de Toussaint-L'Ouverture,* (Paris, 1899), chapt. VI.
8. Lacroix, *Mémoires pour Servir . . .*Vol. 1, pp. 148-152. For the full correspondence see *Les Archives Nationales,* DXXV, 1.
9. Toussaint in later years often said this. See Sannon, *Histoire de Toussaint-L'Ouverture.* Port-au-Prince, Haiti, 1933, Vol III, p. 18.
10. Lacroix, *Mémoires pour Servir . . .*Vol. 1, p. 157.
11. Memorandum from the *Commissaires Conciliateurs des Citoyens Blancs de l'Artibonite. Les Archives Nationales,* DXXV, 2. One of eight pieces collected by Roume and sent to France.

72

The Saint Domingue Slave Insurrection of 1791: A Socio-Political and Cultural Analysis

CAROLYN E. FICK

The Saint Domingue slave insurrection of August 1791 was by no means a spontaneous or unmediated event, and in the context of the anti-colonial and anti-slavery struggles of the late eighteenth and nineteenth-century Atlantic world in which it occurred, its importance is paramount. This article will attempt to provide closer insights into the political and military organization, the social composition of the leadership, and the cultural and ideological components of that momentous historical event.

One of the most prodigious and certainly one of the most respected writers on French Caribbean slavery was the late Gabriel Debien, who, in his monumental work, *Les esclaves aux Antilles françaises: XVIIe au XVIIIe siecle,* published in 1974, stated that no study had yet been made of the origins, the chronology, or the geographic development of the August 1791 Saint Domingue slave insurrection.[1] This article is a modest and, given the limited number of testimonies and eyewitness accounts, unfortunately only a partial attempt at providing a schematic record of what actually happened and how.[2] Specifically, the article will address controversial issues regarding the mode of organization and the political and cultural content of the slave gatherings that preceded the insurrection, as well as the logistics of its outbreak and of its subsequent geographic movement. It will attempt to identify the leaders and their relationship to the plantation regime and will examine the relationship of marronage (or the flight of slaves from the plantations under a variety of circumstances) to the organization and the unfolding of the insurrection, as well as to the character of the insurgency. Finally, it will begin to look at the developing cleavage – inevitable in all revolutions-between the behaviour of the leadership and the mentality and aspirations of the popular forces. It should be remembered, however, that the Saint Domingue revolution did not begin by slave rebellion. Rather, the slave insurrection of August 1791 broke out in the midst of a colonial revolt against the metropolis, whose political foundations themselves were being challenged. And so it was in an environment of revolutionary upheaval in France and of the consequent and ubiquitous breakdown of the ruling order in the colony, from 1788-89 onward, that the aspirations of the slaves found concrete expression and became both militarily and politically expedient.

As a significant portion of the colony's white planter elite had begun, in the name of free trade and local sovereignty, to rebel against the economic and political constraints of the crown's mercantile policy, Saint Domingue's free coloureds, in their turn, openly rebelled against colonial and metropolitan politics of white supremacy to obtain full civil equality. It was amid these upheavals that slaves of Saint Domingue were inauspiciously preparing to strike out on their own. Those in the colony's North Province had in fact been organizing themselves, with purpose and deliberation, for several weeks before that fateful night of 22nd August 1791, a date which marked the beginning of the end of one of the greatest wealth-producing colonies the world had ever known.

On Sundays during the month of August, slave representatives from the major plantations in the region had been meeting clandestinely to lay the plans for general insurrection, but it was on the night of the fourteenth, one week before the actual outbreak, that the final scheme was drawn up and the instructions given out. Numbering some two hundred in all, consisting of "two delegates each from all the plantations of Port-Margot, Limbé, Acul, Petite-Anse, Limonade, Plaine du Nord, Quartier-Morin, Morne-Rouge, etc., etc." covering the entire central region of the North Province, they were assembled to fix the date for the revolt that had been in the planning for some time.[3] They met on the Lenormand de Mézy plantation in Morne-Rouge, and all of the delegates were upper-strata slaves in whom the masters had placed their confidence, most of them slave foremen, or *commandeurs*, whose influence and authority over the field slaves were considerable. Upon a given signal, the plantations would be systematically and methodically set aflame and a general slave insurrection set afoot. To dissipate any hesitation or equivocation, a statement was read by an unknown mulatto or quadroon to the effect that the king and the National Assembly in France had decreed three free days per week for every slave, as well as the abolition of the whip as a form of punishment. They were told that it was the white masters and the colonial authorities who refused to consent and that royalist troops were on their way from France to execute the decree by force. The news was of course false, but it represented the nearest thing to freedom the slaves had ever known, and it served as a rallying point around which to galvanize the aspirations of the slaves, to solidify and channel these into open rebellion.

Although the majority of the delegates agreed in principle that they should await the arrival of these royalist troops, the slave representatives from some of the plantations in Limbé and Acul insisted upon instigating the war against the whites at whatever cost, with or without the troops. In the end, they nearly agreed to begin the revolt that very night, but then went back on this decision as they considered it inopportune to carry out, on the spot, a general insurrection for which the plans had been finalised only that evening. The majority of the slaves decided to wait, and the date was fixed for the 22nd.

The early leaders forming the core of this movement were Boukman Dutty, Jeannot Bullet, Jean-François, Georges Biassou. The first two, according to one source, were to take charge of the initial stages of the movement, while Jean-François and Biassou were to take over first and second command of the insurrection once under way. Toussaint Louverture, who was to emerge as supreme leader of the revolution years later, served, inauspiciously at this point, as the link between these leaders and the system, carefully dissimulating his actual participation.[4] Although he remained on the Bréda plantation where he served as coachman for the manager, Bayon De Libertas, he had been a free black, or *affranchi*, for well over a decade.[5] With a pass signed by the governor, Toussaint was thus permitted to circulate freely and to frequent other plantations; but he was also in communication with influential elements of the royalist faction who hoped to profit from, and who even helped stimulate, the brewing slave insurrection by invoking a common cause – the defense of the king who had, they rumoured, granted the slaves three free days per week. Once they had used the slave insurrection to defeat the rival colonial autonomist faction, known as the patriots, and once power was restored in royalist hands and the king securely on the throne of France, the blacks, they no doubt believed, could then be persuaded by their leaders to return to the plantations and be duped back into slavery. Undeniably, links between the slave leaders and certain royalists in the early stages were important, but for the latter to have assumed that the slave insurrection would, in the end, amount to little more than a traditional jacquerie was, in the context of impending revolution and imperial wars, a grave mistake.[6]

Of the leaders, it was Boukman who was to give the signal for the revolt. He had been a *commandeur* and later a coachman on the Clément plantation, among the first to go up in flames once the revolt began. While his experience as *commandeur* provided him with certain organizational and leadership qualities, the post as coachman no doubt enabled him to follow the ongoing political developments in the colony, as well as to facilitate communication links and establish contacts among the slaves of diverse plantations. Reputedly, Boukman was also a voodoo priest and, as such, exercised an undisputed influence and command over his followers, who knew him as "Zamba" Boukman. His authority was only enhanced by the overpowering impression projected by his gigantic size.[7]

Once the conspirators had reached agreement on the date, set for the 22nd, the accord was solemnized by a voodoo ceremony held in a thickly wooded area known as Bois-Caiman, not far from the Lenormand plantation.[8] According to one account, the ceremony was officiated by Boukman and a voodoo high priestess, an old negress "with strange eyes and bristly hair," just as terrifying as her counterpart.[9] Amidst raging streaks of lightning and violent bursts of thunder, as the account goes, accompanied by high winds and the torrential rains of the storm that had broken out that night, the high priestess raised her knife to kill a sacrificial pig, the blood of which was passed round for all to partake. As she began to invoke the deities, Boukman rose to deliver an impassioned oration to the assembled slaves. It was, in essence, a call to arms:

The Good Lord who created the sun which gives us light from above, who rouses the sea and makes the thunder roar – listen well, all of you – this God, hidden in the clouds, watches us. He sees all that the white man does. The god of the white man calls him to commit crimes; our god asks only good works of us. But this god who is so good orders revenge! He will direct our hands; he will aid us. Throw away the image of the god of the whites who thirst for our tears and listen to the voice of liberty which speaks in the hearts of all of us. [10]

Couté la liberté li palé nan coeur nous tous: "Listen to the voice of liberty which speaks in the hearts of all of us." It was a refrain that would later recur under Boukman's leadership during the early days of the insurrection as he would exhort the insurgent slaves under his command to attack. [11]

The story of this ceremony has long since passed into legend, rendering all the more difficult the separation of actual fact from the elaborate mythology that later developed around the event.[12] Contemporary evidence is sparse; in fact, there is no mention of it at all in the archival documents that recount the conspiracy and are based largely on the testimony of a few slaves. But then, given the imperative of utmost secrecy in voodoo ceremonies, it is hardly surprising that no detailed contemporaneous accounts exist. This hardly justifies, on the other hand, dismissing the various accounts that do exist as pure fabrication. In fact, certain nineteenth-century

Haitian family papers clearly identify one of the participants in the Bois-Caiman ceremony as Cecile Fatiman (that family member's own grandmother), a green-eyed mulatto woman with long silken black hair, the daughter of a Corsican prince and an African woman. She was herself a *mambo*, a voodoo high priestess.[13]

But in the absence of additional detailed documentation, many questions may still be raised concerning this event. Did all of the Morne-Rouge slave delegates participate in the Bois-Caiman ritual ceremony? Or conversely, were the participants in the Bois-Caiman ceremony the same individuals as those whose political views were expressed at the Morne Rouge assembly earlier that evening? Certainly Boukman, as one of the chief leaders of the revolt and orator who delivered the Bois-Caiman speech, would have been present at both. Here then, the often-assumed antipathy of elite creole slaves toward voodoo, and toward African-born slaves practising it, may be brought into question as well. All or nearly all of the slave delegates were from the upper ranks of slave society usually filled by creole slaves. Cécile Fatiman, though a creole mulattress, was nonetheless a *mambo*. But was she actually the officiating priestess described quite dissimilarly in the one account as "an old negress with strange eyes and bristly hair?" As to so many questions pertaining to clandestine slave practices and activities in Saint Domingue before and during the revolution, where hard evidence is lacking, the answers will necessarily remain conjectural ones. What we can safely say, however, is first, that the Bois-Caiman ceremony did occur following the Morne-Rouge assembly; second, that the oration delivered was authentically Boukman's and that the ceremony was, after all, a voodoo event.

Even more important, though, is the historical significance of the 14th August assemblies, and this can be viewed on both an ideological and a political level. First, the Morne-Rouge gathering was a thoroughly organized affair and constituted in every sense a revolutionary political assembly, where issues were discussed, points of view and differing strategies presented, where a final agreement was reached, and a call to arms issued. That agreement was then confirmed and solemnized during the ritual ceremony at Bois-Caiman by a blood pact (and the symbolic drinking of the blood is mentioned in the account of the contemporary writer, Antoine Dalmas) that committed the participants to utmost secrecy, solidarity, and a vow of revenge.[14] In this sense, voodoo provided a medium for the political organization of the slaves, as well as an ideological force, both of which contributed directly to the success of what became a virtual blitzkrieg attack on the plantations across the province.

Equally controversial in relation to the general framework and early stages of the conspiracy is the role of marronage, the desertion or running away of slaves from their plantations for diverse reasons and for varying lengths of time. Whether the August revolt was actually planned and organized in marronage, or by slaves in privileged positions within the plantation system, will no doubt remain a matter of dispute. What is probably closer to the truth is that the two elements worked hand in hand. Some evidence suggests that Jean-François was a maroon at the outset of the revolt and that Boukman was chronically maroon.[15] The report of the French civil commissioner, Roume, states that "for several weeks slave delegations had assembled on Sundays to work out together the plans for this destructive project."[16] As these slave delegations all came from different plantations throughout the North, from "Port-Margot, Limbé, Acul, Petite-Anse, Limonade, Plaine du Nord, Quartier-Morin, Morne-Rouge, etc. etc.," attendance at the meetings would have necessitated some sort of fairly regular small scale marronage, or at least numerous and frequent leaves of absence without permission, unless of course each and every one of them held a Sunday market pass.[17] Even so, such passes were notoriously forged by even minimally literate slaves.

On the other hand, it is known that Toussaint was in close communication with Jean-François, Biassou, and Boukman even though he remained on his plantation and did not officially join the ranks until nearly three months later. We also have the statement of a slave commandeur from the Desgrieux estate (referred to below) revealing that coachmen, domestics, and other trusted slaves of the surrounding plantations, in addition to the commandeurs, were involved in the conspiracy.[18] There is also the statement of an old Gallifet slave, Ignace, who was "distinguished from the other slaves by his exemption from any sort of work," who held the secret of the conspiracy for a long time and who had received instructions from a free black.[19] In fact, another of the core ringleaders was Jean-Baptiste Cap, a free black said to be possessed of substantial income and property.[20]

An incredibly vast network had been set afoot and facilitated by the interaction of several elements. These were African, as well as creole, and included the dynamics of marronage, as well as the subversive activities of commandeurs and of house slaves, and even a restricted segment of the free blacks, whose mobility and closer relationship to white society afforded them access to news, rumour, and information on the political situation in the colony. To separate any one element from the others, as if they are by nature mutually exclusive, will invariably leave the vital questions about the revolutionary organization and capacities of these black masses perpetually unanswered.

The 14th August conspiracy was an ingenious plan, and it would have been perfect were it not for the premature activities of a few slaves in the Limbé district, who either misunderstood the final instructions or who impatiently insisted, in spite of the accord, upon beginning the revolt before the designated date. On 16th August, two days after the Morne-Rouge affair, some slaves were caught setting fire to one of the buildings on the Chabaud estate, in which the bagasse, or straw residue of the sugar cane, was stored. One of them, armed with a sabre, was the commandeur from the Desgrieux plantation. A physical battle ensued and, though wounded, the slave was arrested, put into irons and interrogated. Upon questioning, he revealed that the commandeurs, coachmen, domestics, and other slaves whom the masters trusted from the neighbouring plantations had formed a conspiracy to burn the plantations and kill all the whites. He named as leaders a certain number of slaves from the Desgrieux plantation, four from the Flaville plantation in Acul, and Paul, a commandeur on the Blin plantation in Limbé.[21]

Upon confirming the declaration of the Desgrieux commandeur, the municipal authorities of Limbé issued a warning of the impending danger to the planters of the district and suggested to the manager of the Flaville estate that he apprehend those of his slaves who were denounced by name. Incredulous and unsuspecting, the Flaville manager convoked his slaves and offered his own head, in exchange, if the denunciations of the Desgrieux *commandeur* proved true. They all categorically denied any truth to the *commandeur's* statement, as did Paul Blin, who was also questioned and who also replied that the accusation brought against him was "false and slanderous," and that, filled with gratitude for the continual benevolence of his master, one would never see him involved in plots hatched against the whites or their property. A few days later (on the 20th) another conspirator, a mulatto slave, François, from the Chapotin estate was arrested and put to questioning for his part as accomplice to the arson committed at the Chabaud plantation. It was he who finally revealed the details of the Morne-Rouge assembly on the 14th. The following day the cook from the Desgrieux plantation was also to be arrested as one of the named conspirators, whereupon he managed to escape and went off to warn Paul Blin; together they joined the other ringleaders to prepare "the iron and the torch" for the execution of their dreadful projects. The general insurrection broke out on the following night as scheduled.

At ten o'clock, the slaves of the Flaville-Turpin estate in Acul, under the direction of one Auguste, deserted en masse to make their way to the Clément plantation, where they joined Boukman and combined their forces with the rest of the slaves there. Their numbers reinforced, they immediately set out to the Tremes estate; having narrowly missed the resident carpenter with their bullets, they took him prisoner and proceeded to the Noe plantation, where a dozen or so of these slaves had killed the refiner, his apprentice, as well as the manager. The only whites spared were the doctor and his wife, whose services they deemed might prove to be of great value to them.[22] By midnight the entire plantation was aflame, and the revolt had effectively begun.[23] The troops, by now consisting of the slaves from the Turpin-Flaville, Clément, and Noe plantations, returned with the three prisoners to the Clément estate, methodically assassinated M. Clément and his refiner, and left the prisoners there under guard. Armed with torches, guns, sabres, and whatever makeshift weapons they were able to contrive, they continued their devastation as they carried the revolt to the surrounding plantations. By six o'clock the next morning, both the Molines and Flaville plantations were totally destroyed, along with all of the white personnel; of all the plantations in the Acul district, only on two did some of the slaves refrain for the time being from participating in the revolt.[24]

From Acul, these slaves proceeded westward that same morning, the 23rd, toward the immediately adjacent Limbé district, augmenting their forces, by now close to two thousand,[25] as they moved from plantation to plantation and established military camps on each one as they took it over. One horrified colonist wrote at this point that "one can count as many rebel camps as there were plantations."[26] Making their way into Limbé via the Saint-Michel plantation, they were immediately joined by large numbers of slaves in the district where the premature beginning of this insurrection had been seen a week earlier. Within these few hours, the finest sugar plantations of Saint Domingue were literally devoured by flames. A resident merchant of Le Cap remarked how, "like the effect of epidemical disease," the example set by slaves on one plantation communicated itself throughout the quarter of Limbé, and "in a few hours that immensely rich and flourishing country exhibited one vast scene of horror and devastation."[27] Nor was there much tolerance in these crucial hours for slaves, and especially *commandeurs,* who hesitated or who offered opposition, for "wherever they have committed their ravages," the writer notes, "[the practice was] to seduce or oblige the Negroes on different plantations to join their party . . . Those who discovered a reluctance or [who] refused to follow and assist in their designs [if they could not escape] were cut to pieces."[28]

Continuing westward, the slaves attacked Port-Margot in the early evening of the 24th, hitting at least four plantations, and by the 25th, the entire plain of this district had been devastated. The slaves took care to destroy, as they did from the very beginning and would continue to do throughout the first weeks of the revolution, not only the cane fields, but the manufacturing installations, sugar mills, tools and other farm equipment, storage bins, slave quarters; in short, every material manifestation of their existence under slavery and its means of exploitation. Insufficiently armed and totally unprepared, the planters could do little to oppose the rebels, and nothing to stop the fires that lasted for three days. The residents of Port-Margot believed for a long time that their slaves had had no part in the revolt, "but almost all the *ateliers* in the lower quarter ended up participating in it."[29] Coordinating their forces with insurgent slaves of the plantations situated in the hills and mountainous region bordering on Limbé and Plaisance, they completed their near-total destruction of the parish, leaving only the central area intact.[30]

As these slaves attempted to penetrate Plaisance on the 25th, they met with armed resistance, the first they had encountered, from a group of inhabitants who managed to drive them back into the Limbé plain, whereupon they divided up and returned by two different routes the following day.[31] Having terrorised the inhabitants upon their re-entry, having pillaged and then burned dozens of plantations, they took possession of the Ravine Champagne, where they set up military outposts and fortified their troops. Here, they held out for over three weeks while the planters, disorganized and badly armed, having already suffered serious casualties, awaited aid from the neighbouring parishes. Yet whatever aid the whites managed to muster remained insufficient, for when strategically encircled or militarily overpowered, the slaves would disband and retreat into the mountains, only to attack again at different points with replenished and reorganized troops.[32]

At the very moment that these slaves were carrying out their depredations and defending their positions to the west of Acul, which appeared to have been the centre or hub from which the revolt would spread in all directions, slaves in the parishes to the east rose, torch in hand, with equal coordination and purpose. The movement of the revolt was indeed spreading like wildfire, and within these first few days, from the 22nd to the 25th, the plantations of the Petite-Anse, Quartier Morin and Plaine du Nord parishes surrounding Le Cap, as well as those of Limonade, all to the east of Acul, went up in flames as swiftly and as methodically as had those to the west.[33] The slaves on one of the Gallifet estates in Petite-Anse, however, had prematurely begun to revolt either on the 20th or the 21st by attempting to assassinate the manager, M. Mossut.[34] It is not surprising that it was on the smaller of the three Gallifet estates, on La Gossette, that this incident occurred. Of Gallifet's three sugar plantations, it was here that the slaves' conditions were harshest;[35] in fact, two years earlier, in

1789, 20 of these slaves had organized a "strike," or work stoppage, in the form of collective marronage, by remaining in the woods for two months in order to have the *commandeur* removed.[36] The account of the incidents from 20th to 24th August, presented by Antoine Dalmas, offers a small glimpse at some of the logistical difficulties involved in actually carrying through and strategically coordinating each part of the revolt. Particular circumstances over which the slaves had no control, such as the presence of key white personnel on the specified day, or other factors, like the degree of accord or dissidence between the *commandeur* and the slaves, or the role of the domestics, or simply the degree of impatience among the slaves, varied from one plantation to another.

For a reason that is unclear, the slaves at La Gossette had decided to begin before those in Limbé and Acul, and some 20 of them (perhaps some of the same that had deserted in protest in 1789) attempted to kill the manager during the night of his return from Le Cap on the 20th or 21st. It was also on the 20th and 21st that two of the key conspirators, the slave François and the Desgrieux cook, were arrested in Limbé, and while the latter got away, François was taken to Le Cap, put to the question, and revealed a major conspiracy. The La Gossette slaves, if they had received word of the arrests, may have deemed it unsafe to wait any longer. Whatever the case, their attempt on M. Mossut's life was unsuccessful, and the *procureur,* or plantation agent, M. Odeluc, along with several other whites from the main plantation, came to investigate. The *commandeur,* Blaise, who was the instigator of the assassination attempt, had already fled to warn the other leaders on the main plantation, La Grande Place, for when Odeluc returned there later that night, he found the gate wide open and the lock broken: "It was the work of the leader of the revolt who, seeing that the attempt at La Gossette had failed, ran with all his might to hold off the other conspirators." Several fires had, however, already broken out in the immediate area. The Gallifet slaves did not move until Boukman's band, or a section of it, arrived from Limbé on the 24th. Dalmas relates that, on the night of the 23rd, the rebel bands, "leaving the Plaine du Nord parish behind them," entered Petite-Anse and began their attack, not on the Gallifet, but on the Choiseuil plantation. From there they advanced on the Pères de la Charité, Bongars and Clericy plantations, killing the managers and setting the bagasse sheds ablaze, after which they entered the Quartier-Morin parish. Here, according to Dalmas, they met with some resistance from several *ateliers,* or slave gangs, who were opposed to the revolt, and then retreated en masse to La Gossette. It was here that Odeluc had concentrated the few forces of whites available who, upon sight of the band, fled, leaving Odeluc prey to his trusted coachman, Philibert. As Odeluc pleaded for his life and reminded Philibert that he had always been kind to him, the coachman replied: "That is true, but I have promised to kill you," and then did so.[37] By the 24th, the insurgents had already established themselves at Gallifet to form a major military camp.[38] Effectively, on the 24th, as two deputies who had hastily been dispatched by Governor Blanchelande to solicit military aid from the United States prepared to sail, "the village of Petite-Anse had [already] been destroyed, and the light of the flames was visible in the night in the town."[39]

Earlier that day, while the insurgents had begun to penetrate Quartier-Morin, a battalion of citizen-volunteers set out around noon to contain them. While Dalmas claimed, on the one hand, that the slaves of Quartier-Morin "displayed as much disdain and horror toward the rebels as they did zeal and attachment for their masters" and pushed them back,[40] a participant in the volunteer battalion provides quite a different picture. He writes, on the 24th:

Having arrived at the Quartier-Morin, which had yet received no injury, we saw the fire upon the plantation Choiseuil [the other one being in Petite-Anse], which is at the foot of Morin. We ran on towards the place, at the rate of three leagues in two hours. We were made to perform bad manoevres; our commander got drunk, and 5 or 600 negroes who were there got clear by flight. Arrived at the plantation we found the overseer killed, his body mangled, and marks of teeth on several parts. A few negroes remained with about 40 negro women; we killed 8 or 10 of the number and the remainder got off.[41]

The following day, the 25th, he writes that all, or nearly all, was ablaze in the parish.[42] On four plantations (perhaps those to which Dalmas referred) the slaves did not take part, but in less than two weeks they "who hitherto had remained quiet, yesterday [5th September] revolted, in the engagement at Petite-Anse, and joined the body of insurgents."[43]

What these two apparently contradictory accounts appear to indicate, then, is the dispersal of the insurgents into diverse bands that must have struck several places at once upon their entry into the parish on the 24th. At a few plantations, they were pushed back by slaves, while at others, such as Choiseuil, where they had amassed some five to six hundred cohorts, they obviously enjoyed the complicity of the *ateliers.* In fact, this seems to have been the general pattern of the revolt from the beginning, as the one or two thousand that they were on the first day split into bands to attack the designated plantations, automatically increasing their numbers as well as their strategic superiority. By midnight, the conflagration had already spread to neighbouring Limonade, and almost simultaneously, on the 25th, the Plaine du Nord parish was hit. In this latter parish, situated directly between Acul and Petite-Anse (and apparently circumvented on the 24th), rebel slaves arrived at the Robillard plantation and, joined by most of Robillard's *atelier,* began by assassinating the *commandeur* who refused to take part in the rebellion. What followed was a scene typical of those seen on plantation after plantation during these first days of insurrection. The rebels set fire to Robillard's three bagasse sheds, as well as the boiler house, the curing house, the mill house, and all of the cane fields. Thirteen of his boilers had been destroyed, along with the rest of the sugar manufacturing equipment, including the mill. In addition to Robillard's own house, they burned down the lodgings of the cooper, the carpenter, and the *commandeur* whom they had just killed. "In a word," wrote Robillard, "all that was left of my property was part of the shed for the hand trucks, which the brigands spared along with two large tables to take their meals. Everything, all the other buildings, all my furniture, as well, were totally consumed by flames." And once they had achieved their destruction, they set up a military camp, having spared their own quarters for the purpose.[44]

What appears to emerge from these accounts, then, is a brilliantly organized and strategically maneuvered plan of revolt that, had it succeeded in its entirety, conceivably would have enabled the slaves to take possession of the entire North Province very rapidly. For within three days, by the 25th, once all of the major parishes concentrated in the upper North Plain region had been

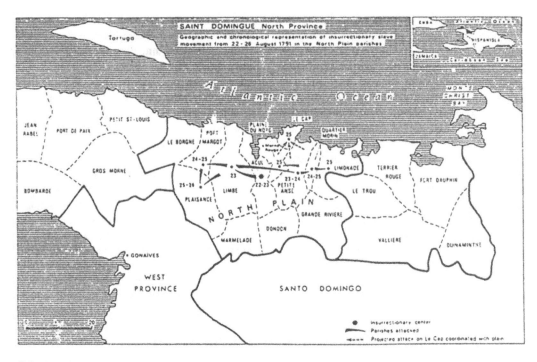

Saint Domingue, North Province: Geographic and chronological representation of insurrectionary slave movement, 22-26 August 1791 (Map by Lucien J. Goupil)

hit and communication links between them severed,[45] a junction was to take place between insurgent bands from these areas surrounding Le Cap and fellow rebels in the capital (See Map on next page).

The very first rumours of a plan to burn the capital were uncovered on the 22nd, immediately prior to the outbreak of violence in Acul and Limbé. Writing to the minister of the marine a little over a week after the insurrection began, Governor Blanchelande relates that, having been invited by the Provincial Assembly of the North on the 22nd to hear the declarations of various persons arrested the day before, "I was convinced that a conspiracy had been formed, in particular against the city of Le Cap, without being able to determine precisely whether it was fomented by whites, mulattos or free blacks, or, even yet, by the slaves."[46] Then, referring to the sequence of events, Blanchelande goes on to say, "There was some talk of setting fire, on the night of that day (the 22nd), to the plantations neighbouring around Le Cap; fire would then break out in this city and would serve as the signal to assassinate the whites."[47] As the revolt in Acul

grew awesome in dimensions, as *ateliers* from one plantation to another joined the revolt in succession, fear for the defense of Le Cap, whose inhabitants included some eight to ten thousand male slaves, caused Blanchelande to recall the detachment he had sent out early on the 23rd to aid the planters of Acul.[48] Le Cap was now the seat of colonial government and already sheltered a good number of whites who had managed to escape the vengeance of their slaves. Fears of a conspiracy were confirmed as, wrote Blanchelande, "we had successively discovered and continue daily to discover plots that prove that the revolt is combined between the slaves of the city and those of the plains; we have therefore established permanent surveillance to prevent the first sign of fire here in the city which would soon develop into a general conflagration."[49]

Other indications that the burning of Le Cap was an integral part of the original strategy are revealed in various letters of colonists and other residents writing at the moment the events were occurring. Mme de Rouvray, whose husband the marquis de Rouvray, had commanded a part of the military operations against the rebels, wrote to their son-in law of the insurrection that had just burst open. She relates that it was because of the impatience of the Desgrieux *atelier*, "more ferocious than the others," who began to revolt several days before the intended date, that the measures conceived by the others "to burn Le Cap, the plantations, and to massacre the whites all at the same time," were revealed. *The impetuous and premature activities of the Desgrieux slaves had apparently given the planters of the surrounding parishes enough time to become informed of the revolt but, though some of them managed to escape the carnage, nothing could save their plantations from the rebel torches.*[50]

From another resident we learn that after the first plantations had been set ablaze on the 24th and a score of whites assassinated, "the rebels dispersed and then came up to set fire to the city. They have been repelled and, in spite of their rage to advance on the city, we are certain their attempts will be in vain as it is guarded by the camp at Haut du Cap, which is the only point through which the rebels can penetrate the city."[51] According to another report, after the slaves had revolted on the Chabaud plantation in Limbé, "they advanced toward Le Cap, and most of the slaves on the plantations along the way joined them . . . The rebels marched without stopping and came within two miles of Le Cap; we believe they were that night already 1,500 strong."[52] A resident merchant of Le Cap also states that "on the 25th, the band from Limbé advanced into this neighbourhood."[53] Another writes on 26th August: "Since the 23rd every entrance to the city and every part of the neighbourhood has been guarded with the greatest care. For these two days past, a camp of 300 men has been formed in the upper part of the city. The negroes are at a distance of one league, and frequently approach in numbers to bid defiance. Many of them are killed by our cannon. They, notwithstanding, come up unarmed."[54]

Finally, confirmation that the conspiracy against Le Cap (coordinated with the revolt in the plains) had been scheduled for the 25th was obtained when, because of concentrated security around Le Cap, an attempt was made at the end of the month, on the 30th and 31st, to take the upper part of the city.[55] An anonymous observer, having kept a journal account of the disturbances, relates: "Yesterday [on the 30th] some

indications of a conspiracy had been discovered; several negroes have been taken and confined, some executed. It appears that the plot is to set fire to the city in 400 houses at once, to butcher the whites, and to take the city in the night by escalade. It appears that the revolted negroes have chiefs in town and who correspond with those in the plains."[56] Referring to this discovery on 30th-31st August of the renewed plot against Le Cap, another writes that "thousands of these scoundrels are going to fall under the iron hand of Justice."[57] One of them, sentenced to be broken on the wheel, was the free black, Jean-Baptiste Cap, an organizer and a key leader of the insurrection. In fact, as it was the practice of the insurgents to elect titular heads, a king and queen whom "they treated with great respect" in each quarter that they occupied, Jean-Bapiste Cap had been chosen as "King of Limbé and Port-Margot."[58] It was as he incited the slaves on one plantation, immediately outside the city of Le Cap to revolt that he was denounced by its *commandeur*, seized and interrogated, no doubt under severe physical duress.[59] From him the authorities learned that "on the night of the 25th [August] all the negroes in the plain were to attack the city in different parts at once."[60] He further declared that "in every workshop in the city there were negroes concerned in the plot."[61] For logistical reasons and because of tightened security around the capital, it seems the plan had been postponed to the end of August.

It was on this occasion, the first of three unsuccessful attempts to capture Le Cap,[62] that Boukman was cited as leading the band of insurgents, by now close to 15,000, that had come to lay siege to the capital.[63] The citing of Boukman is referred to in an account compiled from letters written by the nuns of the Communauté des Religieuses Filles de Notre-Dame du Cap-Français (an educational order for young girls in the colony) as they witnessed, from the window of their convent, the events that were occurring.[64] They spoke of a former pupil, a mulattress later known as the *princess Améthyste*, head of a company of Amazons; she had been initiated into the voodoo cult and had inveigled a good number of her companions to follow.[65] They would leave the convent at night to participate in ritual dances to an African chant, the words of which were inexplicable to the whites. The chant, in the Kikongo language as cited by the eighteenth-century writer, Moreau de Saint-Méry, went as follows:

Eh! eh! Bomba, heu! heu!
Canga bafio té
Canga mouné de lé
Canga do ki la
Canga li[66]

It might be translated in this way:

Eh! eh! Mbumba (rainbow spirit = serpent)
Tie up the Ba Fioti (a coastal African slave-trading
  people)
Tie up the whites (i.e. Europeans)
Tie up the witches
Tie them.[67]

In other words, the chant was an invocation to the rainbow serpent, Mbumba, who occupies a predominant place in the religious belief system of the ancient Kongo, for protection against the evil powers of the "whiteman," the "slavetraders," and the "witches," who, among other forces, may also be the Ba Fioti, dreaded for their believed powers of witchcraft.[68] The school mistresses noticed a certain agitation among the Negresses that increased particularly after they sang this round, adopted to the exclusion of all others. The reason for this agitation, as Père Adolphe Cabon remarks in his own comments on the narrative, became clear when "at the end of August 1791, Le Cap faced the uprising of Boukman, the fires on the plantations at the edge of the city, and the devastation of the plain. From the convent, the nuns saw the insurgents at the gates of Le Cap, heard their death cries, witnessed their dances; they felt the terror that had struck the soul of the whites upon hearing of the massacres and destruction that was carried out in the countryside."[69] The narrator of the account relates that the king of the voodoo cult had just declared war on the colonists; they were marching to the assault on the cities and had come to lay siege to Le Cap: "Amidst the rebels was Zamba Boukman inciting them to attack the barracks and the convent, which lodged a good number of young girls and other colonists." Then, in what amounts to a paraphrase of Boukman's Bois-Caiman oration, the writer notes how Boukman, "in his poetic improvisations, reminded the insurgents that the whites were damned by God because they were the oppressors of the slaves, whom they crushed without

pity, and [how] he ended each refrain with these words: *Couté la libertéli palé coeur nous tous.*"[70]

The relationship between voodoo and the insurrection, or the spirit of insurrection, is certainly not a gratuitous one, but nor is it, on the other hand, entirely intangible. The "Eh! Ee! Mbumba" voodoo invocation dated back to at least the mid-eighteenth century in colonial Saint Domingue, when, as part of the initiation ceremony for a neophyte, it was a call for protection against the dreaded forces of those who had enslaved them and, as such, a form of cultural and spiritual protest against the horrors of their New World environment. On the eve of the slave insurrection, however, in the midst of what would be a difficult and dangerous liberation struggle to actually rid themselves of their enslavers, the incantation certainly must have taken on a more specific, at more political if still fetishistic, meaning, for the individual rebel would now need, more than ever before, a great deal of protection and, perhaps even more, luck in the annihilative endeavours that lay ahead. Similarly, Boukman's Bois-Caiman oration – by no means a voodoo incantation in its strictest sense – may nonetheless have been an exhortation for the slaves to rely on the governing forces of the Supreme Being found within nearly all African animistic religions, as opposed to the "false" Christian god of the whites. In other words, they must draw from within themselves, from their own beliefs, and their belief in themselves, for success.

Though the colonists managed to spare Le Cap from destruction by the rebel armies, there was nothing they could do to save the plantations. One colonist wrote from Le Cap: "We had learned ... that a large attack was afoot, but how could we ever have known that there reigned among these men, so numerous and formerly so passive, such a concerted accord that everything was carried out exactly as was declared?"[71] Another wrote that "the revolt had been too sudden, too vast and too well-planned for it to seem possible to stop it or even to moderate its ravages."[72] The several frantic dispatches that were sent off to Jamaica, Cuba, Santo Domingo, and the United States for military aid were, with the single exception of a plea for assistance from a few American ships and crew at harbour, to no avail.[73] Finally, they accepted the offer of a body of mulattoes and free blacks in Le Cap to take up arms and assist the whites in fighting the slaves. Within eight days, the slaves had· devastated seven parishes and completely destroyed 184 sugar plantations throughout the northern province; in less than one month the count rose to over 200, to which would be added nearly 1200 coffee plantations.[74] An early estimate placed the loss in productive value for the sugar plantations alone, at nearly 40 million livres.[75] By September, all of the plantations within 50 miles on either side of Le Cap had been reduced to ashes and smoke; 23 of the 27 parishes were in ruins, and the other four would fall in a matter of days.[76]

If during the first few days of the revolt the slaves were roughly ten to fifteen hundred strong, perhaps even 2,000 by one account of 23rd August, their numbers continued to swell with astonishing rapidity as they were joined by masses of slaves that deserted or were otherwise swept from their plantations, one after another, throughout the countryside.[77] On 24th-25th August, by the time de Touzard, commander of the local militia, arrived at the Dufour and Latour plantations in Acul, where the slaves appeared to have concentrated a part of their forces just two days after the revolt began, their numbers here had already reached three to four thousand.[78] Indeed, according to a report of the 27th, "they are now reckoned ten thousand strong, divided into three armies, of whom seven or eight hundred are on horseback, and tolerably well armed; the remainder are almost without arms."[79] And though at first their losses were heavy by conventional standards, "their numbers," wrote one colonist, "unfortunately increase one hundred fold in proportion."[80] In less than two weeks, the original core of ten to fifteen hundred had increased over tenfold to fifteen, some claimed twenty, thousand, one-third of them fully equipped with rifles and ammunition pilfered from the plantations, the rest armed with sabres, knives, farm implements, and a whole host of other contrivances that served them as weapons. Fear and panic among the whites spread almost as rapidly as the insurrection itself, causing some to believe that there were, at this point, as many as forty or fifty thousand slaves in revolt, a number the rebels did, however, achieve by late September or early October, and the number may even have reached a near eighty thousand toward the end of November.[81] The total number

of slaves in the North Province was roughly 170,000.[82]

Here then, within the initial, lightning stage of the insurrection, within the first eight to ten days, were 15,000 slaves (a number that continued to multiply) who had deserted their plantations, by will or by force, or by the sheer thrust and compulsion of events purposefully set in motion by the activities of a revolutionary core. Had this phenomenon occurred anywhere else but revolutionary Saint Dominigue, it quite reasonably would have been called a maroon war, and under the pre-revolutionary colonial regime, the colonists characteristically would have designated these slave troops as marauding, ravaging maroon bands with their chosen leaders. But if the maroon wars that broke out in Jamaica and elsewhere had occurred in a context of revolution, had they assumed the same magnitude and degree of political complexity, the circuitous question of whether the slaves were maroons or revolutionary rebels, or some combination of both, would no doubt have played its role in the historiography of slave rebellion in these plantation societies as well. It should be sufficient to say, as the noted sociologist of slavery and slave rebellion, Orlando Patterson, has so lucidly pointed out, that all armed slave rebellion necessarily takes on a maroon dimension.[83] Here in Saint Domingue, the entire situation had radically changed; the past colonial context in which colonists could try to reassure themselves by seeing armed maroons and fugitive slaves as entities outside the plantation system – troublesome, to be sure, but not enough to threaten the foundations and institutional viability of slavery – had now fallen into a million pieces and reposed, literally, on little more than a pile of ashes.

In this whole process, caught up in the web of events that were taking place, many slaves became maroons by deserting their plantations, perhaps having killed the master, the overseer or even their own *commandeur*, perhaps having set fire to a cane field or a shed. Once maroon, they then found themselves in an irreversible position with little choice but to defend their lives with arms. The transformation of the fugitive slave or deserter into a hardened, armed rebel, fighting for freedom, is one that occurred, no doubt to varying degrees, within the consciousness of each individual slave; but equally, this transformation was accelerated by collective rebellion in a context of revolutionary social and political upheaval.

The example of some slaves on the Vaudreuil plantation in the Plaine du Nord parish, just prior to the outbreak, may provide a small glimpse into these very elusive circumstances. Situated at Morne Rouge, it was very near the Lenormand plantation where the 14th August conspiratorial gathering had first taken place.[84] Around the 20th, at about the same time as a few of the Limbé conspirators were being arrested and interrogated, and just before the revolt prematurely broke out at Gallifet's estates, the *commandeur* at Vaudreuil was caught setting fire to a part of the cane field. Apparently the slaves here were divided in their support for the insurrection that was to take place. Seeing the manager in battle with the *commandeur,* some of the slaves came to the aid of the manager and caught the *commandeur,* who, according to one letter, revealed that he had been influenced by a free mulatto; but then, according to another letter, 28 of the Vaudreuil slaves had also gone maroon. Three of them were captured in Limbé and revealed the conspiracy.[85]

Here one may ask whether the Vaudreuil maroons were actually involved in the revolt, as was the *commandeur,* or whether, having knowledge of the conspiracy, they ran away to flee the impending destruction. If the latter were the case, however, there would have been no need to flee since they would have had the support of the rest of the *atelier,* as well as the protection of the manager, whom these had just saved. More likely, they were in complicity with the *commandeur,* and, as he had just been apprehended with the aid of the other slaves, their own turn undoubtedly would be next. One may also find it significant that at least three of them ran away to Limbé, where the insurrection was to break out. Once having become maroons, though, it was now only a matter of days before the other 25 would be swept along into the larger body of insurgent slaves as a constituent part. It is perhaps at this conjuncture that slave deserters, who in ordinary times were called maroons or fugitives (and up to this point they still are by their unsuspecting masters), become, by the very nature of the circumstances, insurrectionaries, brigands, and rebels. They had in fact embarked on a collective struggle never before waged in

such a manner, or on such a scale, by colonial slaves anywhere, and their activities were now inscribed within an irreversible revolutionary situation. The real significance of their movement, in the early days as throughout the revolution, was the profound impact of self mobilization, of the popular organization and the obtrusive intervention of these slaves – on a revolutionary process already several years in motion.

During those first weeks of revolution, the slaves destroyed the whites and their property with much the same ruthlessness and cruelty as they had suffered for so many years at the hands of their masters. The scenes of horror and bloodshed on the plantations, as whites hopelessly tried to defend themselves or, at best, to flee from the unleashed terror and rage of their former slaves, were only too reminiscent of the brutality they had themselves endured under the plantation regime. Yet as atrocious as they were, these acts of vengeance were surprisingly moderate, in the opinion of one of the best known historians of that revolution, compared with those of cold-blooded, grotesque savagery and sadistically calculated torture committed by their oppressors throughout the past.[86] These were impassioned acts of revenge, of retribution, and were relatively shortlived.[87]

The uncontrolled explosions of vengeance and suppressed hatred that marked the beginning of the revolution constituted, however, only a temporary stage. Once expiated, these destructive energies were progressively channelled into military strategy, tactical manoevres, and political alliances as the slaves gained territory and began to stabilise their positions. They had no experience in the use of military weaponry, and though their losses in the early engagements; were heavy,[88] they learned quickly enough. A Le Cap resident who participated in the militia observed how, "in the beginning of the insurrection, the negroes made their attacks with much irregularity and confusion, and their weapons were mostly their instruments of labour, but . . . they now come on in regular bodies, and a considerable part of them are well armed with muskets, swords, etc., which they have taken and purchased."[89] In this respect, as well as in discipline, in the opinion of the militia recruit, they were growing more formidable.[90] When they repelled an attack by the whites on one of their outposts, they would make off with cannons and other equipment left behind with which to wage their struggle.

During these first months, the blacks continued to defend their positions across the province through tactical guerrilla warfare. They retreated into the hills when it was to their advantage, organized their forces for counterattacks, and often continued to burn and ravage the nearby plantations in reprisal. One general described their tactics and sense of military organization in this way:

> They established themselves nearly everywhere on the lower cliffs and on the slopes of high mountains to be within better range of their incursions into the plains, and to keep the rear well protected. For this, they always had behind them nearly inaccessible summits or gorges that they were perfectly familiar with. They established communication links between their positions in such a way that they were able mutually to come to each other's aid whenever we partially attacked them. They have surveillance posts and designated rendezvous positions.[91]

These were in fact maroon tactics, and they were utilised and refined in much the same way by maroons in colonies throughout the Caribbean, wherever their resistance had turned into protracted warfare.

What the slaves lacked in military hardware, they compensated for with ruse and ingenuity. They camouflaged traps, fabricated poisoned arrows, feigned cease-fires to lure the enemy into ambush, disguised tree trunks to look like cannons, and threw obstructions of one kind or another in the roads to hamper advancing troops; in short, any means they could invent to psychologically disorient, frighten, demoralise, or otherwise generally confuse the European units in order to defend their own positions.[92] On their flag was inscribed a motto calling for death to all whites. They marched to African martial music and would begin an engagement with considerable order and firmness, crying out victory. But they would retreat in what whites could only understand as "confused precipitation."[93] To disperse a prodigious body of slaves advancing on Le Cap, Blanchelande's troops had "fired three times, but without the least effect," as each man had devised for himself a kind of light mattress stuffed with cotton as a vest to prevent the bullets from penetrating, "and thus stood the fire without showing any signs of fear," as one observer noted.[94]

When caught by their pursuers, they could convincingly invoke past affective ties with whites during the old plantation days in a plea for pardon, as one slave who claimed to be the loving godson of his assailant's mother. Taken off-guard by these sentiments, the pursuer dismounted as the slave, meanwhile, had recharged his gun, shot and narrowly missed his opponent. Even then, he claimed he had not seen correctly and loved his godmother's son too much to kill him. But when contradicted by witnesses who had seen the entire incident, he admitted: "Master, I know that is true. It is the devil who gets inside of this body of mine." Though his fate was sealed as he was bound to a tree to be shot, he furiously reviled his captors through laughter, song, and joke, and jeered at them in mockery. He gave the signal for his own execution with neither fear nor complaint. In the end, the contents of his pockets revealed more about the mentality, the beliefs, the unatliculated ideals, and fighting spirit of the slaves than any grandiloquent declaration their leaders might make about emancipation and "liberty or death" to the colonial whites. In one of his pockets, the slave's captor relates, "we found pamphlets printed in France [claiming] the Rights of Man; in his vest pocket was a large packet of tinder and phosphate of lime. On his chest he had a little sack full of hair, herbs, bits of bone, which they call a fetish ... and it was, no doubt, because of this amulet, that our man had the intrepidity which the philosophers call Stoicism."[95]

The slaves were organized in bands, as European armies were organized in regiments, and although inter-band rivalry and divisions were not uncommon, the internal discipline of each band or camp was maintained with an iron hand by the individual leaders. In the camps, the least sign of insubordination or slightest evidence of uncertainty was often met with unimaginably harsh treatment and, on occasion, even death.[96] In the first weeks, their main camps were concentrated westwardly at Limbé, Morne-Rouge, and Gallifet in Petite-Anse. Following the Gallifet defeat in September, major strongholds had already formed, by October, in the eastward districts of Grande-Rivière and Dondon;[97] by November, Fort-Dauphin and Ouinaminthe at the eastern extremity of the province near the Spanish border, where participation of the free coloureds was particularly evident, were under rebel control.[98] It was under the military command of Jean-Baptiste Marc, a free black, seconded by Cézar, a recently emancipated free black, that they gained control of Ouinaminthe. Jean-Baptiste Marc, in particular, was described as one who ruled with the air of an army general (and who was also well known in Fort-Dauphin for thievery).[99] Through intrigue, skilful duplicity, and brilliant maneuvering, they had feigned desertion from the rebels and allied themselves with government forces under de Touzard, who graciously supplied them with as much military armament as they needed or requested, allowing them to hold complete control for over three months. De Touzard had nothing but praise for Cézar, whom he credited with having saved the entire district from the "brigands" and promised to write the Colonial Assembly to recommend that he receive a handsome recompense for his services. Cézar absconded to Dondon, having first taken the precaution of hiding three of the best cannons in the cane fields. Within two days, he was back fighting with his black comrades in the attack on Marmelade.[100] Shortly thereafter, Jean Baptiste Marc, having obtained replenished munitions to fight a few brigands, turned on the garrison and converged with rebel forces who took control of the district.[101]

The revolution had, in fact, produced hundreds of local leaders, for the most part obscure ones, slaves as well as free blacks like Jean Baptiste Marc or Cezar, who held military posts on the plantations, organized raids, and maneuvered with France's enemies, with royalists and Spaniards, for ammunition, military supplies, and protection. Certainly the most revered of the early leaders, however, was Boukman. It was in November, during an attack by the Cap regiment in the Acul plain, that he was killed, the first of the original leaders to fall, while defending a rebel post at Fond Bleu.[102] Upon his death, it was Jean-François and Biassou who were to coordinate the activities and assume the direction of the New World's first colonial liberation struggle of its kind: Jean-François now officially assumed the rank and responsibility of general, while Biassou, as lieutenant-general, was second in command, and Jeannot in charge of the black troops in the east.

As a political leader, Jean-François was ambitious; as a general, he was outwardly pompous and unabashedly flaunted his ego by decorating his uniform with an abundant assortment of medals and other impressive military trinkets, not the least among them being the Cross of Saint-Louis. Yet he was a man of exceptional intelligence for one who had spent the greater part of his life as a slave; he was highly respected and especially well liked by those mulattos and free blacks under his command, as well as the "better subjects" among the slaves.[103] Biassou was of a far more fiery disposition. He was, according to Haitian historian, Thomas Madiou, a fervent voodoo adept and kept himself surrounded by *houngans,* or voodoo priests, from whom he frequently sought advice.[104] He was impulsive and forever ready, at the first sign of personal insult or political deception on the part of his white enemies, to take revenge on the prisoners in his camp. He would have killed them all were it not for the judicious interventions of Jean-François or Toussaint, who at this stage served as Biassou's secretary and as physician of the black army.[105] Jeannot, as well as being commander in the east, had also received the title of judge, giving him undisputed authority over the life or death of his prisoners.[106] He was a man of insatiable vengeance who thrived on torturing the white prisoners in as barbaric a manner as that of those masters who, in the past, had known no bounds.[107] His tyranny did not stop here, but extended equally to the blacks under his command. Following a crushing defeat in Limbé by the combined forces under General Blanchelande, Jeannot immediately suspected treason, and Paul Blin was the victim. Knowing that he had earlier helped some white masters to escape, Jeannot had him burned alive on the pretext that he had removed the bullets from their cartridges.[108]

By November, the political situation in the colony had changed with the arrival of civil commissioners from France. Negotiations would soon be under way between the rebel leaders and the French representatives. Upon being informed of Jeannot's excesses, Jean-François, a man of humanity in spite of his arrogance, and possessing a sense of common decency, was revolted by such atrocities. He also realized that this executioner was a liability to the revolution; more than that, his uncontrolled barbarism could seriously jeopardize the imminent negotiations with the white authorities. The black general had him tried and gave him a military execution at about the same time that the whites, who had killed Boukman in battle, cut his head off and garishly exposed it on a stake at the public square in Le Cap with the inscription: "The head of Boukman, leader of the rebels." [109]

News of Boukman's death had in fact produced a profound effect in the rebel camps. There the slave leaders went into mourning and ordered solemn services to be held in honour of their deeply revered comrade. [110] But within the ranks of the slaves, the immediate reaction was quite different; their only wish was to assassinate, on the spot, every white prisoner to atone for their leader's death. Finally, they turned the event to their own advantage, extolled their abilities and successes on the battlefield, derided the whites for their cowardice, and celebrated with dance for three days. [111]

A far more serious differentiation between the mentality of the mass of slave rebels and that of their chief leaders, however, evidenced itself during the period of negotiations that had brought about a temporary cease-fire, as well as a set of demands formulated by Jean François and Biassou. It was under these circumstances that the first signs of division appeared between the aims of those who had become the official leaders of the revolution, and the aspirations of the black masses. Together they had practically annihilated an entire province; that they were fighting to free themselves can hardly be denied. But neither Jean-François nor Biassou, nor even Toussaint for that matter, knew what to do at this point. While Toussaint mediated and kept the peace within their camp, the difficult and unfortunate responsibility of officially representing the revolutionary slave masses in negotiation with French authorities fell to Jean-François.

The whole scope of the revolution, only three months under way but rapidly taking on wider and graver proportions, had gone far beyond his capacities as the political leader of a people engaged in revolutionary struggle. To negotiate the outright abolition of slavery would be absurd; no ruling class ever negotiates away the economic foundations of its own power. Jean-François knew this as well as anyone. When asked about the real causes of the insurrection by one of his white prisoners – it was M. Gros, a Le Cap lawyer who served as the general's personal secretary – Jean-François eventually answered, after brushing earlier questions aside, "that they

have not taken up arms to obtain a liberty which, even if the whites chose to grant it, would be for them nothing more than a fatal and venomous gift, but at least they hoped for an amelioration of their condition." [112]

Gros published an account of his captivity shortly thereafter, in which he relates somewhat differently that, while refusing to explain himself categorically, Jean-François nevertheless gave as his reply to this question:

It is not I who have installed myself as general over the slaves. Those who had the power to do so have invested me with this title: in taking up arms, I never claimed to be fighting for general emancipation which I know to be an illusory dream, as much in terms of France's need for the colonies as the danger involved in procuring for these uncivilised hordes a right that would become infinitely dangerous for them, and that would indubitably lead to the annihilation of the colony. [Moreover], if the owners had all stayed on their plantations, perhaps the revolution may never have occurred. [113]

But following this statement, the slave leader unleashed his animosity toward the plantation agents and the stewards, and wanted included as a fundamental article of their demands that these men should no longer exist in Saint Domingue. [114]

In spite of his personal respect for Gros, Jean-François was nevertheless speaking to the enemy. Moreover, he knew he would eventually have to answer to the French authorities for the tremendous devastation of property and lives by the rebels. It was now an impossible situation in which the one plausible alternative may have been precisely to blame it all on the royalists, while putting forward a reasonably limited set of demands for themselves. Under the circumstances, the best Jean-François could do was to demand, by dispatching a formal address to the Colonial Assembly with de Touzard as mediator, an unconditional amnesty for all slaves who had participated in the revolt, freedom for 50 of the leaders and several hundred of their officers, as well as an amelioration of conditions for the slaves (the abolition of the whip and the *cachot* as forms of punishment). In exchange for this, he promised to use his influence over the slaves to encourage them to return to their respective plantations and agreed to deliver the remaining prisoners, on the condition that his wife, who was held prisoner by the whites in Le Cap, also be released. Although personally opposed to these limited demands, Biassou finally agreed to subscribe to them, but demanded, as well, the release of his own family. To charge Jean-François with the deliberate and cold-blooded betrayal of his people at this stage in the revolution, however, may perhaps be too premature a judgment. The events of a revolution barely three months under way, but with rapidly broadening dimensions, hardly afforded him the political experience and fortitude of character necessary to see his way through at this point. Yet someone had to do something, and Jean-François was the only one in a position to do so.

Among the prominent leaders, it was now Biassou, the fiery and impassioned voodoo adept who, in his more impulsive moments, best incarnated the aspirations and mentality of the insurgent slaves. When they learned of the death of Boukman, they, as Biassou, had been enraged to the point of threatening to massacre all the white prisoners.[115] In the camps, the black troops and local officers, already irritated by the long delay in the Colonial Assembly's response to their leaders' address, were determined to continue the war when they learned that de Touzard, commander of the white troops at Fort Dauphin, had broken the temporary cease-fire to attack several of their camps. But they were under strict orders to refrain from all hostilities.[116] They became increasingly suspicious of the frequent contacts Jean-François and Biassou were having with various whites and swore they would exterminate all the whites, and even their own leaders, if these men dared to come to terms with the authorities.[117] Having gotten nowhere with the Colonial Assembly, the slave leaders had now turned to the newly arrived civil commissioners to be heard. The black troops soon learned of the impending negotiations and, near one camp, assembled themselves and "appeared ready to break by force any negotiation that would conduce their return to the plantations."[118] Of these slaves, Gros remarked that "it is useful to point out to those who are so good natured as to believe their slaves are being forcibly detained and that their [real] dispositions are peaceful ones, that, out of a hundred of these, generally speaking, if there are four whose intentions are good, it would be a lot; all of them, rather, breathe forth nothing but the total destruction of the whites."[119]

At the Gallifet camp in Grande-Rivière, the slave troops and especially their commander,

Jean-Baptiste Godard, openly affirmed that the French civil commissioners were representatives without any powers and without a mandate, that it was not the king who had sent them, and that if they proposed peace, it was to trick them into submission before killing them all off.[120] It was not the whole truth, but it was not too far from it. Some of them even began murmuring that it was all because of the mulattos that their leaders had entered into relations with the whites of Le Cap.[121] If a few of the white prisoners tried to convince these slaves that their revolt was pure folly, that the king had never granted them three free days per week, and that only the Colonial Assembly could legislate on such matters, they pretended not to listen and said that the government would give them what they wanted or they would continue the war to the bitter end. In their midst was a priest, Abbé la Porte, who tried to frighten them by describing the might and power of the combined forces of France, Spain and Britain, and all the other kingdoms of Europe that would unite to exterminate them if they did not give up their arms and go back to the plantations, but his words, as he said, went in at one ear and out at the other.[122]

By a proclamation of 28th September 1791, decreed by the National Assembly of France and sanctioned by the king, amnesty was granted to all free persons in Saint Domingue charged with "acts of revolution." Biassou received a copy of it and had it read to his troops who could not have cared less. They wanted war and *bout à blancs* – an end to the whites. Most of all, they wanted their three free days per week, and as for the other three days, they would see about those in due course.[123] At this point Toussaint rose, demanded that the proclamation be reread, and delivered such a moving speech in creole that the slaves' attitudes suddenly changed to the point where they were even willing to go back to their various plantations if that was what their leaders wanted.[124] Already Toussaint's qualities of leadership were beginning to take shape, and he knew more than anyone else what they really wanted. He had been discreetly involved in the 14th August affair from the very beginning and carefully observed all that went on before finally deciding in November to join with Biassou and Jean-François. Once the agreement was reached to surrender their prisoners, Toussaint accompanied them as escort to the bar of the Colonial Assembly.

But for the mass of armed slaves, this also meant their return to the plantations. They were now violently opposed to any settlement whatsoever with the whites, and, at the Tannerie camp along the way to the site designated for the exchange of prisoners, they besieged the delegation with sabres and threats of sending all their heads off to Le Cap, swearing vehemently against peace and against their own generals.[125] "We were convinced this time of a great truth," wrote Gros, "that the slave would never return to his duties but by constraint and by his partial destruction."[126] It was the uninstructed mass of slaves, and not their leaders, who saw so clearly what was at stake, regardless of the cost. And if the price they were ready to pay was high, it was no greater than the human suffering they had already endured.

The Colonial Assembly disdainfully refused to accede to any one of their leaders' demands (except for a nominal agreement on the release of Jean-François's wife), even after the number of requested emancipations was reduced by Toussaint himself from 400 to 60.[127] He returned to their camp and told the slaves what they already knew. There was nothing to be gained, neither from the civil commissioners nor from the Assembly. Jean-François convoked his council, and it was unanimously decided to continue the war, to finish what they had begun.[128]

In the course of their collective struggle against slavery, however, Jean-François eventually gave himself over to sheer political opportunism, shamelessly betraying the cause of a people he was initially supposed to have been leading. It would take yet another two years before Toussaint would emerge from the political background to provide clear, vigorous, and decisive direction to the profoundly felt aspirations of these slave masses who had killed their masters and burned the plantations to be free.

Notes

1. Gabriel Debien, *Les esclaves aux Antilles françaises: XVIIe au XVIIIe siecle* (Basse Terre: Société d'histoire de la Guadeloupe, 1974), 468.

2. The present essay, with some modifications, appeared previously in Carolyn E. Fick, *The Making of Haiti: The Saint Domingue Revolution from Below.*
Copyright © 1990 by the University of Tennessee Press. Used by permission.

3. Documents and discussion of the events up to and surrounding 22 August 1791 are presented in ibid., Appendix B, 260-66. Diverse elements in the above section of this article are taken from the documents contained therein. See also C. Fick, "The Black Masses in the San Domingo Revolution." Ph.D. Thesis. Concordia University, 1979.

4. Beaubrun Ardouin, *Etudes sur l'histoire d'Haiti*, 11 vols., ed. F. Dalencourt (Port-au-Prince, 1958), 1:51; also, Pauleus Sannon, *Histoire de Toussaint Louverture*, 3 vols., (Port-au-Prince: A Héraux, 1920), 1:88.

5. Jean Fouchard, Gabriel Debien and M.A. Menier, "Toussaint Louverture avant 1789," *Conjonction* 134 (Juin 1977): 65-80.

6. On the links between royalists and the slave insurrection, see Gérard Laurent, *Quand les chaines volent en eclats* (Port-au-Prince: Imp. Deschamps, 1979), 42-46.

7. In "Notice historique sur la Communauté des religieuses filles de Notre-Dame du Cap Français (Saint Domingue) fondée en 1733," *Lettre annuelle de l'Ordre de Notre Dame* (Bordeaux: Imp. B. Coussan et F. Constalet, 1889), 204. The word *Nzamba* is Congolese and means "elephant." See John K. Thornton, "I Serve the King of Congo: African Political Ideology and the Haitian revolution." Annual Conference of the African Studies Association of Canada. Toronto, 16-19 May 1991. In this light, *Zamba* may be both an affectionate and a respectful sobriquet for Boukman to whom references about his "colossal size" concern his head rather than his height. On this point, see D. Geggus, "Slave Resistance Studies and the Saint Domingue Revolution: Some Preliminary Considerations," Occasional Papers Series, no. 4 (Miami: Latin American and Caribbean Centre, Florida International University, 1983), 10. The writer of the "Notice historique" offers as a translation of *Zamba*: "professional poet" or "strolling musician" (*ménétrier*), 204. For additional speculation see Fick, *The Making of Haiti*, Ch. 4, n. 5.

8. The term *voodoo* is used here to reflect the overall composite realities of African religious cult practices in Saint Domiguean slave culture, as described in ibid., Ch. 1, n. 128 and Ch. 2, while further discussion of the role of voodoo in the Bois-Caiman ceremony and the preparations for the revolt is pursued in Appendix B, 264-266.

9. Sannon, *Histoire de Toussaint*, 1:89.

10. Translated by author from Sannon's French translation of the creole in ibid. Unless otherwise stated, all further translations from French are those of author. The very first citing of this speech at the Bois-Caiman assembly is found in Herald Dumsle's *Voyage dans le Nord d'Haiti* (les Cayes: Imp. du Gouvernement, 1824, 88), which was the source for its reproduction by Victor Schoelcher in *Colonies étrangères et Haiti* (2 vols. [Pointe-à-Pitre: Desormeaux, 1973], 2:99), written in 1843. The "Good Lord" or, in creole, "Bon Dié" invoked by Boukman may well characterise the notion of a distant supreme being

"hidden in the clouds" that is generally central to nearly all African cult religions.

11.   In "Notice historique," 204-5.

12.   Antoine Dalmas (*Histoire de la révolution de Saint Domingue*, 2 vols. [Paris: Mame Frères, 1814]), the first, if not the only directly contemporary historian to mention the Bois-Caiman ceremony (presumably writing in 1793), does not make reference to a priestess or to Boukman, as David Geggus rightly points out in his "Slave Resistance Studies," (18). Dalmas does, however mention the ritual killing of a sacrificial black pig (1: 117), a symbol of utter discretion, in the opinion of anthropologist Alfred Métraux, since it proves itself uninquisitive by seldom looking to the sky. *Voodoo in Haiti*, trans. Hugo Chartiris (New York: Schocken Books, 1972), 42-43. The black pig is usually associated with petro rites in Haitian voodoo. See also Geggus, "The Bois Caiman Ceremony," this issue.

13.   In Fouchard, Les marrons de la liberte, (Paris: Ecole, 1972), 528. First cited by Etienne Charlier in *Apercu sur la formation historique de la nation haitienne* (Port-au-Prince: Les Presses Libres, 1954), 49.

14.   Seen. 8 above.

15.   In Geggus, "Slave Resistance Studies," 10.

16.   AN, DXXV, 3, 31. Précis historique de la révolution de Saint Domingue, 9.

17.   On the significance of small-scale, or *petit* marronage and its potential for facilitating slave resistance, see Fick, *The Making of Haiti*, Ch. 2, n. 142. In a similar vein Robin Blackburn, in his recent book, *The Overthrow of Colonial Slavery* (London: Verso, 1988), writes that *petit* marronage ". . . would [nonetheless] produce a layer of slaves with outside knowledge, experience and contacts, yet a continuing presence within the plantations, a combination that could, under the right conditions, lead to plantation revolts." (Ch. 5, n. 13).

18.   AN, DXXV, 66, 667. L'Assemblée Coloniale de la partie française de Saint Domingue à l'Assemblée Nationale, 3 nov. 1791. (See n. 21 below).

19.   In Dalmas, *Histoire de la révolution*, 1: 116.

20.   "St. Domingo Disturbances," *Philadelphia Aurora*, 11 Oct. 1791. From a Journal kept there; entry for 4 Sept. 1791. (The first part of the Journal, ending with the entry for 31 Aug. 1791, is also published in Boston, *Independent Chronicle and Universal Advertiser*, 20 Oct. 1791.)

21.   AN, DXXV 56, 550. Discours fait à l'Assemblée Nationale le 30 novembre 1791 par MM. les commissaires de l'Assemblée de la partie française de Saint Domingue. (A rough draft of the beginning of this address, with corrections and marginal insertions, is found in AN DXXV 66,666. The completed address in proper manuscript form, is in DXXV 66, 667. It was delivered to the National Assembly in France on 30 November 1791 and exists in printed form in DXXV 56, 550. All future references to this document will use the latter archival reference.) In the original manuscript draft, the slave conspirator's name is clearly written throughout the document as Paul Belin, although in its printed form, the name is written first as Blin and later, in reference to a subsequent incident, as Belin. He is also sometimes referred to as the slave, Paul a Belin, presumably belonging to the Belin estate in Limbé. Extract of a letter from Capt Francais of 2 November received by the brig James, Capt. Row . . ., Boston, *Independent Chronicle and Universal Advertiser*, 8 Dec. 1791. Also AN, DXXV 78, 772. Liste des sucreries incendiees a Saint Domingue dont on a eu connaissance jusqu'au 30 septembre 1791, n.d. (oct. 1791?). The correct spelling of the name could possibly even be the latter of the two.

22.   AN, DXXV 78, 772. AA 148. La partie du Nord, paroisse de l'Acul. DXXV 78, 772. AA 183. Deposition dated le Cap, 27 Sept. 1791. DXXV 56,550. Discours.

23.   AN, DXXV 46, 432. Copies de différentes lettres sur les événements de Saint Domingue extraites de la gazette anglaise et transmises a Paris, Kingston. M. Tausias a M. Camuzat, Le Cap, 1 Sept. 1791.

24.   These were the Caignet and Busson plantations. AN, DXXV 78, 772. AA 183. Deposition, Le Cap, 25 Sept. 1791. DXXV 78, 772. AA 148. Partie du Nord. DXXV 78, 772. KK 175. La paroisse de l'Acul, signed by M. Caignet. The latter plantation was burned, in any event, at some point before the end of the following month. DXXV 78, 772. Liste des sucreries incendiées, n.d. (oct. 1791?). The *ateliers*, or slave gangs, leading the revolt in Acul were, according to Caignet, those of the Molines, Flaville, Plaigne, Sacanville and Pillat plantations. DXXV 78, 772. KK 175. La paroisse de l'Acul.

25.   "St. Domingo Disturbances," Boston, *Independent Chronicle and Universal Advertiser*, 20 Oct. 1791. Entry for 23 Aug. 1791.

26.   AN, DXXV 78, 772. KK 178. Renseignements sur la position actuelle du Limbé, Le Cap, 7 Oct. 1791.

27.   "A letter from James Perkins, Esq., resident at Cape François, 9 Sept. 1791," Boston, *Independent Chronicle and Universal Advertiser*, 20 Oct. 1791.

28.   Ibid.

29.   AN, DXXV 78, 772. KK 179. Paroisse de Port-Margot, signed by Traynier and Palmis, n.d. (Sept.-Oct 1791?).

30.   Ibid.

31.   AN, DXXV 78, 772. KK 161. Plaisance, signed by Manan, fils, Ch. Escot, A. Touvaudais, Le Cap, 27 Sept. 1791.

32.   Ibid. Also DXXV 47, 443. M. de Blanchelande a M. le président du Congrés de l'Amdrique, Le Cap, 24 aout 1791.

33.   "St. Domingo Disturbances," Boston, *Independent Chronicle and Universal Advertiser*, 20 Oct. 1791. Also, "Letters from James Perkins, Esq., resident at Cape François," in ibid.; DXXV 46, 432. Copies. M. de Blanchelande a M. Bertrand, Ministre de la Marine, Le Cap, 2 Sept. 1791. MM. Foäche, Pierre Morange et Hardivilliers du Cap en date du 25 sept. 1791 à MM. Foäche, frères, du Havre. Lettre de M. Nicoleau, habitant de Saint Domingue, Le Cap, 3 Sept. 1791. M. Tausias, Ndeociant du Cap et habitant de la plaine du Nord a Mme. Camuzat, 1 Sept. 1791.

34. Dalmas, *Histoire de la révolution,* 1:116-21. AN, DXXV 56, 550. Discours. See also, D. Geggus, "Les esclaves de la plaine du Nord a la veille de la Révolution française," RSHH 144 (sept. 1984): 25, 36. While Dalmas places the date of the incident on the twentieth, Geggus fixes it on the twenty-first.

35. See Geggus, "Les esclaves de la plaine," RSHH 14: 24-36.

36. Ibid., 32.

37. AN, DXXV 56, 550. Discours. Geggus, "Les esclaves; de la plaine," RSHH 144:36. Dalmas, on the other hand, attributes Odeluc's assassination to an unidentified slave, Mathurin, "the fiercest of them all." *Histoire de la revolution,* 1: 123.

38. Sannon, *Histoire de Toussaint,* 1:9 1.

39. "Insurrection of the Negroes in the West Indies," Boston, *Independent Chronicle and Universal Advertiser,* 22 Sept. 1791.

40. Dalmas, *Histoire de la révolution,* 1: 123-24.

41. "St. Domingo Disturbances," *Philadelphia Aurora,* 10-11 Oct. 1791. Entry for 24 Aug. 1791.

42. Ibid. Entry for 25 Aug. 1791.

43. Ibid. Entry for 6 Sept. 1791.

44. AN, DXXV 78, 772. Déclaration que fait M. Robillard habitant a la Plaine du Nord des désastres arrivés sur son habitation . . . "Le Cap, 29 sept. 1791. The details were related to Robillard by two mulattoes who later attacked the camp, killing four of Robillard's slaves and, to prevent the plantation being used again as a camp, burned the slaves' quarters.

45. AN, DXXV 46, 432. Copies. Tausias a Camuzat, Le Cap, 1 sept. 1791. DXXV 78, 772. AA 183. Deposition, Le Cap, 27 Sept. 1791.

46. AN, DXXV 46, 432. Copies. Blanchelande à Bertrand, Le Cap, 2 sept. 1791. M. de Rouvray claimed that Blanchelande had been warned of the plot as early as the 19th, but was too inept to crush it in its beginnings. M.E. McIntosh and B.C. Weber, eds., *Une correspondance familiale au temps des troubles de Saint Domingue* (Paris: Larose, 1957),41. M. de Rouvray to Ctesse de Lostanges, 6, 7 Dec. 1791.

47. AN, DXXV 46, 432. Copies. Blanchelande 4 Bertrand, le Cap, 2 sepL 1791.

48. Ibid. DXXV 78,77 AA 183. Deposition, le Cap, 27 Sept. 1791.

49. AN, DXXV 46, 432. Copies. Blanchelande a Bertrand, Le Cap, 2 sept 1791.

50. *Une correspondance familiale,* 29. Mme de Rouvray to Cte de Lostanges, Le Cap, 8 Sept. 1791.

51. AN, DXXV 46, 432. Copies. Lettre de M. Nicoleau, Le Cap, 3 Sept. 1791.

52. AN, DXXV 46, 432. Copies. Rapport de M. Bagnet. Extrait de la gazette anglaise transmise à Paris, Kingston, Ile Jamaique, 2 Sept. 1791.

53. "Letter from James Perkins," Boston, *Independent Chronicle and Universal Advertiser,* 20 Oct. 1791.

54. "St. Domingo Disturbances," *Philadelphia Aurora,* 10 Oct. 1791. Entry for 26 Aug. 1791.

55. Ibid, 10-11 Oct. 1791. Entries for 31 Aug. - 1 Sept. 1791.

56. Ibid. Entry for 31 Aug. 1791.

57. AN, DXXV 46, 432. Copies. Tausias à Camuzat, le Cap, 1 Sept, 1791.

58. "St. Domingo Disturbances," *Philadelphia Aurora,* 11 Oct. 1791. Entry for 5 Sept. 1791. Other evidence of this practice is revealed in various accounts of the subsequent engagements, in which blacks were taken prisoners: "The day before yesterday . . . we took the camp of Limbé . . .and took the King Jean-Louis and the Queen alive"; "The 16th October we captured one of his head men who calls himself King"; "We have in prison a priest who was taken at the capture of Gallifet, also the Queen of that quarter." Extract of a letter from Cape Français, 3 Nov. 1791, *Philadelphia Aurora,* 15 Dec. 1791; Extract of a letter from a gentleman in Cape Français, 1 Nov. 1791. Boston, *Independent Chronicle and Universal Advertiser,* 15 Dec. 1791, respectively. Boukman, of course, was also known and respected as a chief king.

59. "St. Domingo Disturbances," *Philadelphia Aurora,* 11 Oct. 1791. Entry for 1 Sept. 1791. For his loyalty to the whites in denouncing Jean-Baptiste Cap, the slave Jean, *commandeur* of the Chaperon de la Taste plantation, situated behind the Pères de l'Hôpital of the city, was granted freedom and a life pension of 300 livres per year. The owner received an indemnity for his slave from the colonial government. AN, DXXV 60, 595. Extrait des registres de l'Assemblée Générale de la partie française de Saint Domingue, 2 Sept. 1791.

60. "St Domingo Disturbances," *Philadelphia Aurora,* 11 Oct. 1791. Entry for 2 Sept. 1791.

61. Ibid.

62. A second attempt was made during September and a third at some point before early October. Boston, *Independent Chronicle and Universal Advertiser,* 13 Oct. 1791. Extract from the schooner Peggy, Capt. White, 6 Oct 1791.

63. AN, DXXV 46, 432. Permerle to his brother, les Cayes, 31 Aug. 1791. Here the writer states that "the 15,000 insurgent slaves had taken the route toward Le Cap." Another letter, dated 22 October, relates news that had arrived in France from a boat leaving the colony on 1 September: "There is a revolt of 15,000 slaves in Saint Domingue; they appeared at the city of Le Cap. The planters armed themselves and attacked. They killed some and dispersed the others." DXXV 46, 432. Extrait d'une lettre de Bordeaux datée du 22 octobre, envoyée.

64. The account is contained within a history of the Communaute (see n. 5 above) and, although compiled at a later date, is based nonetheless on the original correspondence of the nuns, as well as information related by other contemporary writers. So while some details may have somewhat gratuitously been attributed to the nuns by the reporter, the information is still based on fairly contemporaneous sources. See A. Cabon, "Une maison d'éducation à Saint Domingue: 'les religeuses du Cap'," RHAF 3 (déc. 1949): 417-19. Relevant passages of the text are translated from the original by author and presented in *The Making of Haiti,* Appendix B, 265-66; they are also

cited by J. Fouchard in *Les marrons du syllabaire* (Port-au-Prince: Imp. Deschamps), 39-40.

65. Upon the initiative of a nun, later to be known as Mere de Combolas, whose wish was granted when Le Cap was spared destruction from a British fleet threatening to attack in 1744, classes were opened for instruction to young black girls in the colony. Cabon, "Une maison," RHAF 3 (juin, 1949): 77-78. That a good number of these ended up in the voodoo cult toward the eve of the revolution reflects perhaps as much on the laxity of European mores in late eighteenth-century colonial society as the tenacity of African traditions and beliefs.

66. In M.E.L. Moreau de Saint-Mery, *Description topographique, physique, civil, politique et historique de la partie francaise de l'isle de Saint Domingue*, 3 vols. ([reprinted ed.] Paris: Société de l'histoire des colonies francaises, 1959), 1:67; also cited in Mgr. J. Cuvelier, *L'ancien royaume de Congo* (Brussels: Desclée de Brouwer, 1946), 290.

67. For this translation by anthropologist John M. Janzen and further interpretation of the chant see Fick, *The Making of Haiti*, 58, esp. nn. 58-61. On Mbumba as rainbow serpent, see also Georges Balandier, *Daily Life in the Kingdom of the Kongo: From the Sixteenth to the Eighteenth Century*, Trans. Helen Weaver (New York: Meridian Books, 1968), 248.

68. See n. 67 above.

69. Cabon, "Une maison," RHAF 3 (déc. 1949): 418-19.

70. See n. 45 above.

71. AN, DXXV 78, 772. AA 183. Deposition, Le Cap, 27 Sept. 1791.

72. AN, DXXV 56,550. Discours.

73. Boston, *Independent Chronicle and Universal Advertiser*, 20 Oct. 1791. *Philadelphia Aurora*, 10-11 Oct. 1791. AN, DXXV 46, 432. Copies. Blanchelande à Bertrand, Le Cap, 2 Sept. 1791.

74. Debien, *Les colons de Saint Domingue et la rivolution: essai sur le Club Massiac* (Paris: Armand Colon, 1953), 334. AN, DXXV 46, 432. Copies. Extrait d'une lettre du Cap français en date du 25 sept. 1791. Also, DXXV 80, 787. Liste des habitations sucreries incendiées (dans l'espace de quinze jours) dont less noms sont parvenus jusqua ce jour, Le Cap, 30 Sept. This list indicates 165 sugar plantations of the seven parishes hit during the first few days: Port-Margot, Limbe, Acul, Plaine du Nord, Petite-Anse, Quartier-Morin, and Limonade and estimates the loss in productive value at 39,800 *livres*. (It is a recapitulation of the same list as that cited in n. 21 above.) Another list, including the parishes of Dondon, Marmelade, Grande-Rivière, and Ste. Suzanne, and therefore drawn up somewhat later, lists 172 sugar, 1185 coffee, and 34 indigo plantations burned during the first month or two of the revolt, making a total of 1,391 plantations. DXXV, 63, 635. Liste des habitations incendiees, dépendance du Nord, n.d. (oct. 1791?). Obviously, figures vary from one source to another, making it nearly impossible to arrive at an exact count. Generally, however, colonists spoke of close to two hundred sugar plantations burned during the

first week, and over two hundred by at least mid-September.

75. See n. 74 above.

76. AN, DXXV 46, 432. Copies. M. l'Ambassadeur à MM. les colons de l'Hôtel Massiac, 4 nov. 1791. Letter from Kingston, 17 Sept. 1791. Lettre de M. Nicolcau, Le Cap, 3 sept. 1791. The four remaining districts, not including Le Cap, were Ouinaminthe, Fort-Dauphin (including Terrier-Rouge), le Trou, and Dondon.

77. AN, DXXV 46, 432. Copies. Tausias à Camuzat, Le Cap, 1 sept. 1791. See also Rapport de M. Bagnet, in ibid.; "St. Domingo Disturbances," *Philadelphia Aurora*, 10 Oct. 1791. Entry for 23 Aug. 1791.

78. AN, DXXV 78, 772. AA 183. Partie du Nord. DXXV 56, 550. Discours.

79. "St. Domingo Disturbances," *Philadelphia Aurora*, 10 Oct. 1791. Entry for 27 Aug. 1791.

80. AN, DXXV 78, 772. AA 183. Deposition, Le Cap, 27 Sept. 1791. The facility with which the slaves were able to recruit additional forces was also remarked by Mr. Henry, a merchant captain, in a letter to his brother from Le Cap, 27 Sept. 1791. DXXV 78, 772.

81. AN, DXXV 46, 432. Copies. Extrait d'une lettre de M. William Collann [?] à M. Thomas Collann [?] du Havre, en date du 28 octobre date de Londres. Lettre de M. Guilhem de Bordaux, propriétaire au Cap, 28 oct. 1791 (?). Lettre au Géneral Melville d'un officier d'artillerie en garrison a la Jamaque, Le Cap, 24 sept. 1791. Extrait d'une lettre du Cap Francais en date du 25 sept. 1791. See also J. Ph. Garran-Coulon, *Rapport sur les troubles de Saint Domingue*, 4 vols. Commission des Colonies (Paris: Imp. nationale, 1797-99), 2:215. Boston, *Independent Chronicle and Universal Advertiser*, 22 Sept., 13 Oct., 24 Nov. 1791. *Philadelphia Aurora*, 2 Oct, 14 Nov. 1791.

82. Cited in Arlette Gautier, *Les soeurs de Solitude: la condition feminine dans l'esclavage aux Antilles du XVIIe au XVXe siecle* (Paris: Editions Caraibéennes, 1985), 239.

83. In "Slavery and Slave Revolts: A Socio-historical Analysis of the First Maroon War: 1665-1740," *Maroon Societies: Rebel Slave Communities in the Americas*, ed. Richard Price (Garden City, New York: Anchor Press, 1973), 279.

84. Geggus, "Les esclaves de la plaine," RSHH 136:12.

85. AN, DXXV 46, 432. Lettre écrite par M. Testard à M. Cormier, contenant l'extrait de deux lettres qu'il a recues du Havre, Le Cap, 26 oct. 1791, cited in Fick, "The Black Masses in the San Domingo Revolution." Geggus also cites the second of these two letters: AN Arch. Col., CC9A. Extrait d'une lettre anonyme, 20 aout 1791, in "Les esclaves de la plaine," RSHH 136:12. Also see Fick, *The Making of Haiti*, Appendix B, n. 13.

86. C.L.R. James stated the case quite forcefully when he wrote that the crimes committed in the name of "property and privilege are always more ferocious than the revenges of poverty and oppression." *The Black Jacobins* [1938] 3d ed., London: Allison & Busby, 1980), 88 - 89. Eugene Genovese has also

gone to great lengths to defend this point in *From Rebellion to Revolution: Afro-American Slave Revolts in the Modern World* (Baton Rouge: Louisiana State University Press, 1979), 104-10.

87. The same may be said of the Haitian masses today as they are engaged in another struggle for liberation and for the basic principles of democracy and human dignity, indeed for the bare essentials of human survival. Any such violent expiation of repressed frustrations, hatred, and suffering as has occurred in the course of this struggle has been selective and relatively short-lived, compared with nearly thirty years of duvalierist repression and its aftermath.

88. While some estimates by colonists and other residents situate the number of insurgents killed at somewhere between three to four thousand in the first few months, others claim that in one of the attacks on Le Cap alone, they suffered 2,000 killed and 1,500 taken prisoner, of which every tenth man was decapitated; another states that in Port- Margot alone, from 1,200 to 1,500 were slain. The figures given out by the whites for these single encounters, if they are not grossly inflated, would, in contradiction, largely surpass the generally-cited overall figure of three to four thousand. One report of 13 September claims that, though upwards of 3,000 blacks had been killed, it would still require another 1,000 to 1,200 more killed before the slaves could be subdued. If, indeed, close to two thousand blacks were killed by white units at one single engagement, the reporter, then, would have been naively optimistic, for, by another report, although "about 3,000 insurgents have been killed, they are still strong and have fortified themselves in two or three different parts of the country." Extracts from the schooners Hardy, Peggy, 6 Oct. 1791; "Letter from James Perkins," Le Cap, 9 Sept. 1791, Boston, *Independent Chronicle and Universal Advertiser*, 13, 20 Oct. 1791. "St. Domingo Disturbances," Philadelphia Aurora, 11 Oct. (entry for 13 Sept.); 14 Nov. 1791. AN, DXXV 46, 432. Copies. Lettre écrite au Général Melville, Le Cap, 24 sept. 1791.

89. "St. Domingo Disturbances," *Philadelphia Aurora*, 14 Nov. 1791.

90. Ibid.

91. In G. Laurent, *Chaines*, 28. For a vivid example of maroon organization and fighting tactics during the Jamaican maroon wars, see the descriptions in Miltin C. McFarlane, *Cudjoe of Jamaica: Pioneer for Freedom in the New World* (Short Hills, NJ.: Ridley Enslow Publ., 1977), passim.

92. Laurent, *Chaines*, 29-31. Also, "St. Domingo Disturbances," *Philadelphia Aurora* 14 Nov. 1791.

93. Ibid. "Letter from James Perkins," Boston, *Independent Chronicle and Universal Advertiser*, 20 Oct. 1791.

94. Boston, *Independent Chronicle and Universal Advertiser*, 29 Sept. 1791.

95. In Althéa de Peuch Parham, trans. and ed., *My Odessey: Experiences of a Young Refugee from Two Revolutions, by a Creole of Saint Domingue* (Baton Rouge: Louisiana State Univ. Press, 1959),32-34.

96. AN, DXXV 56, 550. Discours.

97. AN, DXXV 46, 432. Copies d'une lettre de M. de Blanchelande au Ministre de la Marine, du Cap le 22 Oct. 1791.

98. AN, DXXV 20,198. Memoire fait par un habitant d'Ouinaminthe sur. . les événements arrivés a cette paroisse jusqu'au 15 janvier 1792, certifee par Alexandre la Fosse, Le Cap, 22 sept 1792. DXXV 65, 662. Faits et evenements relatifs a M. Wanderlinden, capitaine du régiment du Cap, lorsqu'il est venu au Fort Dauphin .... oct.-nov.1791.

99. AN, DXXV 20, 198. Memoire fait par un habitant d'Ouinaminthe. In addition to the command posts held at Ouinaminthe by Cézar and Jean- Baptiste Marc were those held by Noél, a black slave, and Jean-Simon, a free black. Their nominal general was Sieur Gérard.

100. Ibid.

101. Ibid. Also DXXV 65, 662. Faits et événements relatifs a M. Wanderlinden; and Parham, *My Odessey*, 69-71.

102. On the death of Boukman, see the letter of M. de Cambefort recounting the incident, cited in full in Fouchard, *Marrons de la liberte*, 530-32. Also Boston, *Independent Chronicle and Universal Advertiser*, 15 Dec. 1791. Sannon, *Histoire de Toussaint*, 1: 92-93; Dalmas, *Histoire de la revolution*, 1: 132.

103. BPL, Gros, *Isle de St. Domingue, Province du Nord. Précis historique . . .* (Paris, 1793), 17, 26.

104. *Histoire d'Haiti*, 3 vols., 2d ed., Département de l'Instruction Public (Port-au-Prince; Edmond Chenet, 1922), 1:105.

105. AN, DXXV 63, 635. Déclarations. Déclaration de M. Guillaume Moulient. BPI, Gros, Précis. 25-26. See also Lacroix, *Memoires*, 1: 153-54.

106. AN, DXXV 1, 2. Adresse a l'Assemblée Générale ... par MM. les citoyens de couleur de la Grande-Riviere, Sainte-Suzanne et autres quartiers ... n.d. (nov. 1791?).

107. BPI, Gros, *Précis*, 8-9.

108. Lacroix, *Memoires*, 1: 112-13. See also Dalmas, Histoire, 1: 216-17. Extract of a letter from Cape Francais of 2 Nov. ..., Boston, *Independent Chronicle and Universal Advertiser*, 8 Dec. 1791. Fick, The Making of Haiti, 108-9. (On Paul Blin's role in the organization of the 22 August outbreak see the chronology of events presented earlier in this article).

109. Sannon, Histoire de Toussaint, 1: 93.

110. BSL, Gros, *Précis*, 14. Madiou even states that Boukman was mourned by his companions for several months. *Histoire d'Haiti*, 1: 106.

111. BSL, Gros, *Précis*, 14.

112. AN, DXXV 46, 439. Journal rédigé par M. Gros. Entry for 17 Nov. 1791.

113. BPL, Gros, *Précis*, 17. It appears evident here Gros, writing from his Journal notes two years after his captivity, took a good deal of liberty to embellish Jean-François' words and feelings.

114. Ibid.

115. AN, DXXV 46, 439: Journal rédigé par M. Gros. Entry for 11 Nov. 1791. BPL, Gros, *Précis*, 14.

116. Ibid. 21.
117. Ibid. AN, DXXV 46, 439. Journal rédigé par M. Gros. Entry for 17 Nov., 5 Dec. 1791. DXXV 46, 439. No. 300. M. de Rouvray to M. de Blanchelande, 8 Jan. 1792.
118. BPL, Gros, *Précis*, 21.
119. Ibid. In his observations, Gros made a distinction, however, between the slaves of mountainous regions (where the somewhat less labour intensive coffee estates predominated) and those of the plains (where sugar production was concentrated); the former were far less ferocious than the latter, in Gros' opinion, and even seemed grieved over the fate of their masters.
120, AN, DXXV 60, 600, Extrait des registres. Suite de la déposition du Sieur Laroque, 21 janv. 1791.
121. BPL, Gros, *Précis*, 22.

122. AN, DXXV 79, 779. Extrait d'une lettre par M. Abbé de la Porte à M. l'Archevesque Thibaut, Valliére, 25 mars 1792.
123. The three free days per week had become a generalised demand throughout this early period; one exaggerated version of it even claimed that the slaves would be paid an average salary of three livres per day for the other three days. AN, DXXV 78, 772. Mr. Henry, capitaine du navire la Charlotte à son frère, Le Cap, 27 sept. 1791.
124. AN, DXXV 63, 635. Déclarations. Déclaration de M. Rene Guillemton. Déclaration de MM. René Cossait et. al.
125. BPL, Gros, *Précis*, 27.
126. Ibid.
127. Sannon, *Histoire de Toussaint*, 3: 18.
128. BPL, Gros, *Précis*, 28.

SECTION SIXTEEN

Rebel Women: Anti-Slavery Feminist Vanguard

If anti-slavery behaviour was endemic and not gender specific, then the question of women's role as carriers of anti-slavery ideas and agents of anti-slavery mobilization should not be considered exceptional or phenomenal. The political consciousness of women would warrant no particular examination since both men and women created the intellectual basis of the culture of resistance that characterized the slavery world. But the organizational forms of resistance took shapes that sometimes showed evidence of gender bias. These essays show that while the struggles of the slavery period were inherently collective in that they were conceived in the consciousness of slave communities, the gender relations of slavery determined actions in many ways. Logically then, the ideology of anti-slavery was not gender-free. Beckles, Mair and Moitt argue that groups of slaves, irrespective of sex or colour, figured prominently in various aspects of anti-slavery organization, and that the dominance of any one social group at any particular stage should be explained in terms of perceptions of organizational efficiency, the uneven distribution of knowledge and consciousness, as well as the politics of gender.

The system of slavery sought to degrade women and womanhood in ways which forced aspects of their resistance to assume specific forms. Maternity and fertility were placed at the core of strategies for slave plantation survival, and so women's resistance to the policies meant that their opposition to slavery was probably more broadly based. Furthermore, it can be argued that women's leadership of the resistance to slave owners' attempts to disintegrate the slave communities culturally and morally provided much of the organizational strength necessary for ideological and armed resistance. It is not an easy task, therefore, to separate the anti-slavery practices of slave women from those of the wider slave community. But it remains necessary to highlight resistance practices that were common among women in order to redress their rather low historiographic profile.

Neither the enslavers nor the slave communities considered women to be the less rebellious sex; slave owners were as fearful, suspicious and distrustful of women's potential activities as anti-slavery agents as they were of men's. They did not formulate, either implicitly or explicitly, any specific concepts of women within the culture of slave resistance. This thinking was expressed in legislative provisions for the control and discipline of slaves that made no concessions to women – except in cases of flogging in advanced pregnancy. But this specific provision emerged during the mid-eighteenth century when there was increasing emphasis on natural reproduction as an alternative form of securing a long-term labour supply.

In general, enslaved women and men were stripped and whipped, branded with hot irons, gibbeted, hanged or had limbs or joints amputated if convicted for acts of hostility to their owners and the white community at large. If anything, enslaved women, possibly on account of their closer interpersonal association with members of the white society, were likely to receive harsher and psychologically more damaging forms of punishment.

Women, then, were to be found in the vanguard of the anti-slavery movement. As non-violent protestors, as maroons, as leaders in areas of social culture, and as mothers, black women were critical to the forging of resistance strategies; their anti-slavery consciousness functioned at the core of slave communities' survivalist culture.

73

The Rebel Woman in the British West Indies During Slavery

LUCILLE MATHURIN MAIR

Introduction

Africans who were brought as slaves to the New World did not accept their condition meekly. They employed a variety of methods to express their resentment of the institution of slavery, and of the white masters who enslaved them. They employed quiet, subtle, almost negative methods of protest which today might be termed civil disobedience; for example, they pretended to be ill, and so avoided work. On the other hand, they sometimes went to the positive, violent extreme of armed rebellion. Historical studies have established fully the fact that black anti-slavery attitudes and actions were a strong and persistent feature of the West Indian past.

It is not so well established that women, who are often regarded as the submissive sex, also took an important part in forms of protest against slavery. Female slaves adopted some of the same techniques as men to defy the system: they frequently ran away from the plantation, on their own, or in mixed groups: and in addition they resisted in ways which were peculiar to them as women: for example they could, and did use periods of childbearing to do the minimum of work, and to extract the maximum of concessions from their masters.

Both types of female reaction against bondage will be discussed in the following pages.

1. The African Mother

It is not surprising that rebels were to be found among black women in the New World. For large numbers of Africans, including women, carried a fighting spirit with them across the Atlantic and into their life of slavery on British Caribbean plantations.

This was generally true of all enslaved Africans. Whether their native homes were in Sierra Leone, Nigeria, or the Congo, they were first and foremost human beings, who instinctively resented being reduced to the condition of mere property. It was particularly true of those Africans originating from that section of West Africa known as the Gold Coast, now Ghana, from where a very high proportion of slaves was exported. English slave traders shipped nearly half-a-million of them into the West Indies during the years 1690 to 1807.

The Gold Coast was famous for its internal wars in which the nations who inhabited the coastal forests battled with each other: they fought either to conquer their neighbours, or in order to free themselves of neighbours who had conquered them. It was a region of proud and militant people, not easily crushed.

Even when captured as prisoners of war, enslaved, and taken to the Caribbean they carried with them their reputation for courage and independence. The Governor of the Leeward Islands once described them as "all born heroes": Bryan Edwards, in his history of the West Indies, tells of the Koromantyn boys of the Gold Coast who boldly exposed their bosoms to the red-hot irons which West Indian slave owners used to brand their slaves: and this without sign of pain or fear.

Whites admired the Koromantyns, especially as they were not only brave but hard-working. At the same time whites feared them: they became associated in the planters' minds with the spirit of revolt. It is not a coincidence that two Caribbean colonies, Jamaica and Guyana, each of which had a long history of black protest, also had a high percentage of Gold Coast people in their slave population, amounting at times in the eighteenth century to as much as 39%.

Planters increasingly refused to buy Africans from this region of the continent, which in their opinion bred "troublesome" people. The Barbadian government, for example, after a time, made it illegal for Gold Coast blacks to enter the island. Jamaican imports from that area fell from 39% in the 1760s, 1770s and 1780s, to 8% in the last few years of the slave trade.

But there always remained in the slave population enough to keep resistance constantly alive.

Foremost among Gold Coast nations were the Ashantis who emerged as the leaders and conquerors of the region at the beginning of the eighteenth century. Probably a third of the Gold Coast Africans who were shipped to the West Indies were of Akan origin: as one might expect, they were often found among the ringleaders of slave resistance, both of passive, and in particular, of armed resistance.

The African mother-country not only gave to thousands of West Indian slaves this background of militancy and aggressiveness: it gave to thousands of black women a background of great self-respect and confidence.

Many countries of West Africa held, and still hold, a high opinion of the women, and especially of the mother. Among such nations the most vital event of a woman's life is bearing a child: this is of the greatest importance to her as an individual, and to the community as a whole. For without the great gift of children, the family, the tribe, the nation will die out. The mother and her child are therefore precious.

Societies which think so highly of mothers tend to produce women of authority. The traditional African marriage custom of polygyny, which permitted one man to have several wives, often gave the opportunity to the woman to control a good deal of her life and the lives of others. Each wife, with her children, occupied her own quarters in the family compound: the husband visited each in turn, but did not remain permanently with any: the oldest wife received more privileges and had more influence than other wives; but generally speaking each wife was the recognised ruler of her hut, and her household.

Among many West African societies, notably the Ashanti, there existed a matrilineal form of property inheritance by which the family's lands and goods were passed from one generation to another through the female members.

The woman's power extended beyond the family. African myth and history contained many examples of women who were dominant in public life. The Congolese chroniclers, for example, spoke of "the old mother of the tribe", Mpenba Nzinga, who directed the early mass migration of their ancestors which led to the founding of the Kingdom of Congo. The women of the royal household of Dahomey were in charge of the nation's taxes' and as a result, exercised national influence.

The Queen Mother of the Ashanti occupied an especially high position, which has survived until today. In the West African royal court the stool of the ruler, like the throne in the European palace, was the symbol of kingship. Among the Ashanti the Queen Mother's stool was for centuries superior to the king's (though not to the Golden Stool) and by ancient tradition she wielded great financial and political power in the royal household.

For nearly 200 years, thousands of young African girls and women entered the New World, the majority no younger than 14 and no older than 40. This age group was specified by slave traders and by planters who wanted as workers young adults at the peak of health. At that age they had already been through the African tribal ceremony, the *rite de passage* which marked the transition from youth to adulthood, from girlhood into womanhood. This meant that when Africans entered the Caribbean they were already educated and steeped in their national culture.

This culture contained, among much else a tradition of warrior nations and a history of proud and respected women. This sort of heritage produced rebels, and ensured that there would always be women among the rebels.

2. Equal under the whip

The life of the slave in the New World made it almost inevitable that women would strike out against their condition. For the greater period of slavery, West Indian planters had more African men than women as slaves on their estates. They needed physically strong workers for setting up plantations: in the larger areas of Jamaica and Guyana, this often meant breaking new ground in virgin land: after the estate was established, they needed sturdy workers to carry out the hard tasks required for growing cane and making sugar.

Male labour was physically more suited than female for the strenuous existence on sugar estates, where the majority of blacks was to be found in the West Indies during slavery. As a result traders carried on an average two African men to every one African woman to the New World, and this was often the ratio of men to women in the Caribbean colonies, particularly in the mid-eighteenth century. Jamaica, in 1789, had 30,000 more black men than women.

The woman, therefore, was in short supply in the slave population. She was therefore in great demand, as a partner for the man. And in spite of the degrading circumstances in which she lived as a slave, it must have strengthened her sense of her importance as a woman to be a member of a much-sought-after minority.

In the late eighteenth-century, the system of buying men and women in Africa, transporting them across the Middle Passage enchained in slave ships, and marketing them in the Caribbean, received heavy criticism from many influential persons and groups in Britain. The attack on the Slave Trade eventually produced its abolition in 1807. But slavery as a labour system continued, and the numbers of slaves were maintained, not by importation, but by the breeding of slave infants on the plantations.

The woman's sense of importance again became significant, for now she was valued as a mother of slave children, who in turn would grow into valuable workers for their masters. The woman's health became of more interest to the planter than it had been previously, she was granted special concessions, such as extra food and clothing allowances, she was urged in a number of ways to bear and rear children: after she had borne six children she became by law a privileged person, exempted from hard labour.

In the 1780s and 1790s, the Codrington estates in Barbados were a striking example of the prevailing policy by which plantation owners offered a variety of rewards to women to have as many children as possible. During this same period a Jamaican planter, William Ricketts, of Canaan estate in the parish of Westmoreland, wrote about the care and encouragement which he personally gave to the women who bore children: they received as badges of favour special coats which singled them out from the rest: the room for delivering babies was sited near his dwelling house: he had their young infants and children fed from his own table.

Such clear recognition of the black woman's vital role of mother indirectly helped to keep alive her awareness of herself as a woman. And it is essentially such awareness of oneself as a human being which makes the individual refuse to be reduced to the level of a non-human being in the way that slavery attempted.

Without intending to do so, the system of slavery organized men's and women's lives in a way which gave them a common cause. Slavery, in many essentials made men and women roughly equal in the eyes of the master. Legally they had identical status as chattels, as objects which could be owned. They were seen, not so much as men and women, but as units of labour. Their jobs on the plantation were distributed not according to sex, but according to age and health. In theory men were supposed to do the backbreaking tasks of the field and the factory; in fact, as long as women were young and fit, they were recruited into the same work force as men, and shared more or less the same labour.

Bryan Edwards wrote in 1801, about the organization of slave work in these words:

The Negroes are divided into three sets or classes, usually called gangs; the first consisting of the most healthy and robust of men and women, whose chief business it is, out of crop-time, to clear, hole and plant the ground; and in crop-time, to cut the canes, feed the mills, and attend the manufacture of sugar.

A Jamaican planter, Matthew Lewis, describes the manufacture of sugar on his Cornwall estate in 1815, and shows how women were involved in the operation of the factory:

The ripe canes are brought in bundles to the mill where the cleanest of the women are appointed, one to put them into the machine for grinding them, and another to draw them out after the juice has been extracted, when she throws them into the opening in the floor close to her, another band of negroes collects them below, when, under the name of trash they are carried away to serve for fuel.

When slaves caused offence, men and women alike received the same punishment in accordance with West Indian slave laws. One of the milder forms of punishment for small offences was the use of stocks. The hands and feet of the offending slave, man or woman, were fastened in a wooden frame, and remained confined in this position for periods of from three to six hours.

The most frequent form of punishment was flogging. Eye witnesses in one Caribbean colony after another, reported endless cases of the female slave being flogged by the estate overseer, or by the driver, himself a slave, who supervised the work gangs. The legal maximum limit of 39 strokes on any one day applied to the female, as to the male slave. Under the lash of his whip, men and women were equal.

For the most serious crimes, such as running away, men and women alike were either shipped out of the colony, or were put to death. Only one distinction was made in British West Indian slave laws between the penalties meted out to men and women: they ruled that if a pregnant woman were convicted of a crime punishable by execution, her sentence should be suspended until after the birth of her infant.

Since the system of slavery on West Indian plantations attempted to deprive men and women equally of their human status, made similar work demands on them, penalised them in almost identical ways, it is not surprising that as men reacted, so did women too react against slavery.

3. Unwilling to work

The most important thing which the master expected of the slave was his or her labour: the most damaging things which the slave could do to the master was to work slowly, to work badly, or not to work at all. Blacks, said the white slave owners, were born lazy, and only exerted themselves when driven to do so. When on the job, slaves did the absolute minimum of work: this was the main reason why slave owners insisted that they

had to use the whip. They claimed that the mere sound of a cow hide in the sugar fields was sometimes enough to make the slow-working slave gangs move faster at their canerow-digging or weeding, or cutting, or whatever task they were set to do. Without the frequent loud cracking of the whip, without the fear of its sting on their backs, slaves would do little or no work.

And yet even the whites who said this most often must have known otherwise. Slaves did enormous amounts of work when it was to their interest to work hard. They certainly shirked the masters' work whenever they could: but that was forced work; it was a different matter when they worked freely for themselves. All slaves, male and female, had allotted to them by law, a plot of land on which to grow food provisions in their own time. In the later years of slavery, colonial laws laid down the minimum time to which they were entitled for their own cultivation, twenty-six days in the year. Their long hours in the field and factory, which in crop-time could extend to as many as eighteen hours a day, left them little time or energy to work for themselves: often, too, these plots of land were several miles away in the backlands and hill slopes bordering the sugar valleys.

In spite of this, slaves found the time and the energy to work their plots. They not only fed themselves on the yams, plantains, dasheens and other vegetables which they grew, but they had crops left over and they sold their surplus in the local markets of Bridgetown, Castries, Falmouth, Kingston and other West Indian towns. Some reared poultry and small stock as well and they gradually became the main suppliers of foodstuffs for the white creole household.

In Jamaica in 1830, the value of ground provisions, nearly all of which were slave grown, was estimated to be worth £847,000. One eyewitness expressed it in these words before a committee of the British Parliament which investigated the lives of West Indian slaves in 1832:

(Slaves) are diligent and industrious in their provision grounds . . . they have generally a great way to go to market, and between planting their provisions, keeping their provision grounds clean, taking in their provisions, preparing them and taking them to market and selling them, their time is generally fully occupied.

The popular image of the "lazy" black did not fit into this context. It certainly did not fit the female slave who became a very prominent figure in this activity as "the higgler" woman, an important person in the Caribbean domestic economy. Having done her work on the estate, she tended her children, cultivated her plot, and walked sometimes ten miles and more to and from market at the weekend to sell her produce. The money she earned was her own to use as she wished: she bought clothes, she bought furniture for her hut, or she saved and bought her freedom and that of her children. This required determination and very hard work of which she was capable. If she failed to put that same amount of exertion in her master's canefield it was obviously because she chose not to.

Some slaves made it quite clear that they did not intend to work. In these instances when the whip failed to produce results, the master, in desperation, might take the offender before the slave court.

On the 27th October 1831, a female slave, ironically named "Industry" was brought up by her master before the magistrates of Port Royal, Jamaica, for "refusing to work and setting a bad example to other negroes on the property by her contumacious conduct." She was sentenced to two weeks' hard labour in the workhouse. There is no means of knowing whether her confinement was successful in reforming her habits.

It was more customary, however, for slaves to adopt more clever and subtle methods of avoiding work, and thereby undermining the operations of the plantation. They realised, for instance, that illness could be developed into a nearly foolproof technique for escaping the labour of the field, and they became accomplished actors and actresses in assuming the role of patient.

"On Wednesday" wrote Matthew Lewis, "there were about thirty invalids, of whom only four were cases at all serious; the rest had 'a lilly pain here, Massa', or 'a bad pain me know nowhere, Massa', and evidently only came to the hospital in order to sit idle, and chat away the time with their friends."

It was virtually impossible for the slaveowner to distinguish always the malingerer from the genuinely sick. He tended to think the worse, and to assume that the slave was lying and deceiving: often he was right.

Matthew Lewis describes the typical trials and tribulations of the slave owner in this respect:

"On Saturday morning there were no fewer than forty-five persons (not including children) in the hospital; which makes nearly a fifth of my whole gang. Of these, the medical people assured me that not above seven had anything whatever the matter with them; the rest were only feigning sickness out of mere idleness, and in order to sit doing nothing, while their companions were forced to perform their part of the estate-duty. And sure enough, on Sunday morning they all walked away from the hospital to amuse themselves, except about seven or eight: they will, perhaps, go to the field for a couple of days; and on Wednesday we may expect to have them all back again, complaining of pains, which (not existing) it is not possible to remove. Jenny (the girl whose hands were bitten) was told by the doctoress, that having been in the hospital all the week, she ought not, for very shame, to go out on Sunday. She answered, "She wanted to go to the mountains, and go she would." "Then", said the doctoress, "you must not come back again on Monday at least." "Yes" Jenny said, "she *should* come back;" and back this morning Jenny came. But as her wounds were almost completely well, she had tied packthread round them so as to cut deep into the flesh, had rubbed dirt into them, and, in short, had played such tricks as nearly to produce a mortification in one of her fingers."

Slaveowners repeatedly maintained that slaves went to the lengths of prolonging their illnesses, or worse yet, making themselves ill, so that they would be exempt from work. One favourite device which planters often described was that of allowing the tiny insect parasite, the chigoe, to lay its eggs in the toes, and so cause sore legs which could lay up the patient for a considerable time. Yaws was a dreadful contagious disease, requiring the strictest quarantine measures. But, so suspicious were masters of the slaves' schemes to shirk the work of the estate that they even accused their female slaves of deliberately causing this disease to spread among their children so that they could get time off to attend on them. One planter from the parish of St. Ann, Jamaica, wrote angrily in his diary, "I have this day seen an evident wish to get the children with yaws . . . under the idea that they will be permitted to sit down & mind their children, . . . I shall certainly allow no time of mine to be lost in their attendance . . ." Slaveowners were driven to desperation trying to outsmart the plans of slave malingerers. Matthew Lewis on one occasion, was reasonably successful: he decided to try his hand at curing his numerous slave "patients" who appeared to him to be merely having themselves a picnic in the hospital.

" . . . I directed the head-driver to announce, that the presents which I had brought from England should be distributed to-day, that the new-born children should be christened, and that the negroes might take possession of my house, and amuse themselves till twelve at night. The effect of my prescription was magical; two thirds of the sick were hale and hearty, at work in the field on Saturday morning, and to-day not a soul remained in the hospital except the four serious cases."

But it was not always easy or possible to catch out the slave invalid. Estate owners obviously exaggerated the extent to which slaves pretended illness. Slaves were so grossly overworked, ill-treated, and underfed that there was always a very high percentage who were either genuinely ill or in weak physical condition.

But what was certainly true was that this circumstance was exploited to the maximum by the slave, and particularly by the woman who was greatly assisted by nature in becoming a mistress of the art. In addition to sharing fully in the techniques employed by all slaves for "beating the system", she could, and did, for example, take fullest advantage of her menstrual processes for absenting herself from work.

Slave women's specialty was to prolong to the maximum, the period they spent as nursing mothers. A slave mother with a suckling infant was by law given extra food allowances and was customarily allowed to turn out to work an hour later, and to leave an hour earlier than other slaves: her baby accompanied her to the field, was tended under the trees by an elderly "nana", and she took regular intervals off from her labours to feed her infant. It became a practice throughout the West Indies for slave women to take an extraordinarily long time to wean their babies: breast feeding among blacks, as a number of witnesses testified to the British Parliamentary Committee on slavery in 1789, lasted "seldom less than Two Years, and many of them more." The planter in these circumstances could only note with concern the numbers of working hours lost by his female slaves: there was relatively little control he could exercise over the women who would not hesitate to employ nature's way of withholding her labour.

This became a factor of increasing importance to the West Indian economy. For by the 1830s women outnumbered men in the slave population, and so constituted the bulk of the estate labour force, particularly in the field tasks.

One of the crucial factors which eventually helped to put an end to black bondage in the British Caribbean in 1838 was the fact that slav-

ery, as a system of labour, became more and more expensive: it was expensive, because it was unproductive: it was impossible to get maximum work output from forced labour. An important element in this low productivity was the unwillingness of the slave woman to work for the master.

4. The Tongues of Women

"January 26 . . . It seems that this morning, the women, one and all, refused to carry away the *trash* (which is one of the easiest tasks that can be set), and without the slightest pretence: in consequence, the mill was obliged to be stopped; and when the driver on that station insisted on their doing their duty, a little fierce young devil of a Miss Whauncia flew at his throat, and endeavoured to strangle him: the agent was obliged to be called in, and, at length, this petticoat rebellion was subdued, and everything went on as usual." (M.G. Lewis: 1834 p. 139).

Matthew Lewis is here describing an incident which occurred on his estate, Cornwall, in Jamaica, in 1816. It was not peculiar to that estate, or that island. The black female spitfire was a plague in the life of drivers, overseers, and managers, who were often nearly driven to distraction by the quarrelsomeness of such women: their nuisance value did not in fact need even to take the form of physical violence.

The Governor of Trinidad in the 1820s, Sir Ralph Woodford, maintained that slave women were "the most prone to give offence." Another leading government official, the Commandant at Charuanas, who was responsible for the welfare and management of slaves, said in 1823 that it was a notorious fact that female slaves more often deserved punishment than male, for they used to great effect "that powerful instrument of attack and defence, their tongue." The Commandant was resisting the proposal made at the time by the British Government that the whip should be abolished as a form of punishment for slaves: he felt that only flogging could control their sharp tongues and hot tempers.

Barbados expressed similar views on the question of whether the gentler sex should be whipped. In a debate in their Council, also in 1823, it was pointed out that "even in civilised societies", like England, or France, female prisoners were corrected by flogging: why then should this not be the case in the West Indies, where "the black ladies," as it was said in Council "have rather a tendancy to the Amazonian cast of character?"

Like Barbados, like Trinidad, every other British Caribbean territory resisted furiously the attempt to cease flogging. Their colonists claimed that they would never otherwise be able to handle slaves, especially women.

Islands such as Barbados, Jamaica and the Bahamas, with independent Houses of Assembly controlled by slaveowners, obstinately refused to introduce laws to prevent women being flogged. It was only in Crown colonies, such as Trinidad and Guyana, over which the British Government had direct powers of legislation, that this humane reform was confirmed by law in 1824.

And in these territories, the colonists resented that they had been forced to adopt such measures against their will. The Trinidadians complained bitterly that the women, as a result, became unmanageable.

The Governor of Trinidad wrote to the Colonial Secretary in London on the subject, on the 10th February, 1825, and again in the following year. He pointed out the increasing difficulties which planters had in maintaining discipline on their estates: he referred to the "case of insolence and insubordination (which) frequently occur among the female slaves": between 1824 and 1826, nearly twice as many women as men - 1782 women as compared to 941 men - had to be punished. Confinement in the stocks seemed to be the most effective penalty left, but the problem then was that the planter would lose all that valuable labour time while the slave was in punishment. Smaller estate owners, in particular, suffered: they did not have the means "to repress the violence of turbulent women": for they could not afford to put them in the stocks: on the other hand it required "great patience to bear with the provoking tongues and noise of the women."

Some of the most trying cases of slave misbehaviour which Matthew Lewis dealt with during his two visits to Jamaica in 1812 and 1815 concerned such hot tempered "vixens" and "viragos". The very day after the incident with Whauncia, he had yet another "petticoat rebellion" and it took him a long lecturing to "the most obstinate and insolent of the women" before they could be persuaded to return to work.

Some of the records of West Indian magistrates' courts are revealing. During the years 1819 to 1835, 311 cases involving slaves came to trial in the parish of Port Royal in Jamaica: 150 of these cases concerned female slaves. The majority of women were accused and found guilty of either violent conduct, or the use of violent language towards other persons: 32 cases involved their conduct, 42 involved their language, which was described as either "indecent", "scandalous", "outrageous", "insulting", "abusive", or "threatening". When found guilty, the offender could be punished in a few instances by a warning, more often by a number of lashes, or by imprisonment.

Maria and Betty of Round Hill estate, for example, were tried on 4 April 1820 for behaving "rudely and contemptuously" to the overseer. Betty was sentenced to 4 months' confinement with hard labour; Maria, however, was given "a good character" and was admonished to behave better in future.

Clementina was an obstinate offender: she was found guilty by the magistrate on 20 August, 1832 for using abusive language to a free person and she was given 30 days' hard labour. When sentence was passed on her she used such "contemptuous language" in the court, that she was given an additional punishment of 30 lashes.

Numerous slave women in fact, showed little fear of their superiors, and did not hesitate to answer back.

One factor underlying their insolence was their knowledge that those same white overseers, and bookkeepers who were placed in command over them, found them attractive women, often took them as their housekeepers or common-law wives, and often also fathered their brown children. In these circumstances it was difficult to expect women to remain obedient and respectful to their white masters and mistresses. Their lack of respect came out clearly in the satirical songs which they made up: they even mocked at some white preachers whom they regarded as hypocrites, for while they claimed to be bent on saving the souls of black folks, they were winking at the young girls.

"Hi! de Buckra, hi!"
Massa W-f-e da come ober de sea
Wid him rougish heart and him tender look,
And while he palaver and preach him book
At the negro girl he'll winkie him yeye
"Hi! de Buckra, hi!"

Slave gangs very often sang these songs of mockery loudly and fearlessly as they worked in the fields: the white overseer stood by, hearing every word, not always sure whether he was the target or not, but helpless in any event to silence the singers.

Women were quick and loud in making complaints about their owners and overseers. Although few slaves could read, they were often well informed about the slave laws of the colony, and knew exactly what privilege and protection they were entitled to.

Domestic slaves in particular, many of whom were women, and lived at close range to the whites, listened carefully to the discussions of their masters and mistresses: planters spoke quite freely about slavery in their homes, at their dinner tables, in the presence of their house slaves, confident that blacks were too unintelligent to understand the conversation of whites.

Moreover, as the work of Christian missions developed in the nineteenth century, slaves, in their talks with missionaries, especially Baptist missionaries, learnt more and more about their legal status.

It was often, therefore, from the lips of whites, that blacks received information about their rights, as well as about the reform measures which were being proposed in England to improve their condition. This knowledge made them restless and impatient of any action which they felt was depriving them of their few legal rights. These rights varied slightly from colony to colony: generally they covered the minimum amount of clothing which all slaves should receive from masters, their food allowance, their working hours, the number of holidays due to them, the time off from work allowed to pregnant and nursing mothers, and so on. Laws also laid down the maximum amount of punishment a slave might receive, and further instituted courts or councils of protection to which the slave could appeal should the master break the law.

Slave women did not hesitate to appeal to these courts. When their complaints were regarded by the courts as sound, they received some redress for their wrongs. For example, in April 1823, eighteen slaves from Dallas Castle plantation in Port Royal, fifteen of whom were women, complained to the magistrate that they were severely and cruelly treated by the over-seer, Mr. John Stephens. Investigations were made by the court, and the overseer was found guilty of having inflicted more flogging on two female slaves, Elizabeth Craig, and Margaret Dallas, than was permitted under the twenty-seventh clause of the Consolidated Slave Law. Stephens was fined £20 for each offence by the court.

Another instance appears in the records of the slave court at Buff Bay in the parish of St. George in Jamaica in 1826. A number of slaves from Windsor Castle estate complained to the magistrate that the overseer, Saunders, treated them harshly. No one was found guilty, and the magistrate attempted to smooth over the differences between the parties. On the following day when the slaves turned out to work in the field, Saunders called out a number of those who had lodged the complaint against him and had them punished. Among them were some slave women, Eliza Oliver, Susan Irvine, Cardina Wilson and Harriet Buckmaster: they promptly went again to the court with their grievance, and the magistrate gave Saunders a severe reprimand, pointing out that it was quite improper to cause slaves to be afraid of appealing for justice.

Such incidents however, were rare: in the majority of cases, the slave was found to be in the wrong, and furthermore was punished for making a groundless complaint against the master. This is not surprising, as magistrates were themselves often slaveowners. In twenty-one cases of complaints in Port Royal in the 1820s which were lodged by women slaves against their owners, eighteen cases were thrown out as being "trifling", "groundless", "false", or "malicious", and the complainants were in a few instances discharged, the majority were punished.

A number of women from Orchard Plantation, Dido, Rosetta, Lizzy, Augusta and Tuba, were indignant that their masters had directed their children to be taken from them and weaned from the breast. The women claimed that their babies were too young to be left. When the magistrates investigated their complaint, they found that the infants were at least "a twelve months old each, the women were reprimanded and directed to proceed back to the property to work." A slave woman, Julia, complained that her owner gave her no food, and allowed her no grounds for her own cultivation: her complaint was found to be "frivolous", and the court decided that "in consequence of the delicate appearance of the woman, and her having a young child, their worships sentenced her only to twenty lashes publicly – then to be discharged."

Susanna Tucker, Camilla Eping and Mary McBeth, of Dallas Castle estate were each sentenced to three months' hard labour in the workhouse, when their complaint against the overseer was found to be groundless. The odds weighed so heavily against slaves in these proceedings, that it is remarkable that they continued to press the courts with their complaints. Nevertheless they did. In spite of the hopelessness of finding redress for their wrongs, in spite of the strong likelihood that rather than receiving justice, they would receive punishments for daring to lodge a complaint, women would not be silenced: they persisted in harassing the courts with their grievances.

They were obviously prepared to risk being flogged or imprisoned, for the satisfaction of knowing they had taken up the time of the magistrates, they had forced owners and overseers to appear in the court and answer for their actions: while these proceedings took place they themselves were naturally absent from work. Whether they won, or whether they lost their case, they had established their nuisance value.

By refusing to accept slavery like dumb animals, by regularly raising their voices, women in their way, forced their presence on the consciousness of many: this was the thin end of the wedge in undermining the system of slavery. For once the slave is seen and heard, as a human being, it becomes increasingly difficult to justify his or her existence as chattel.

5. Plotting and Conspiring

Women quietly schemed against the property and person of their masters and mistresses in a variety of ways. They perfected the means by which they could do damage without being found out.

Destruction of property by fire was a popular means of getting one's own back against the master. It was not always easy to know whether a canefield or an estate house was deliberately or accidentally burnt down! As most West Indian houses were built of wood, this form of sabotage could be widely used without fear of discovery.

Fires broke out regularly, and did extensive damage. A young slave girl Jemima was one of the few offenders who got caught. She appeared before the Port Royal slave court in 1819, accused of throwing fire on some wooden buildings: she was sentenced to three months' hard labour.

A much more serious matter was the fact that the house slave was well placed to plot harm as well against the person of the master. Whites were fully aware of this and lived under the constant fear that, for instance, a vindictive cook might use her position in the kitchen to poison those who enslaved her. It was widely claimed that Africans were experts in the various properties of herbs and bushes: their obeah men and women were supposed to be specially skilled in the use of magic and poison, and in the numerous possible ways of "setting evil" on people.

The proven cases of poisoning were actually fewer than one would expect, given the opportunities which the slave had. But the terrible fear of its happening which haunted the minds of whites was an important fact in undermining their sense of security: it is repeatedly referred to by contemporary writers.

The few cases which were recorded must have served to keep white terror alive. Barbados had instances in the eighteenth century of slaves being executed for attempting to poison their masters: they included one female slave.

A slave, Harriet, was tried in the parish of St. Dorothy in Jamaica, in 1817 for attempting to poison her master's coffee: she was sentenced to be hanged, but was subsequently pardoned and transported from the island.

A case such as the following, noted in 1824, would have kept the white community nervous. Ann Goodman was found guilty in the St. George slave court of "feloniously, wickedly, maliciously and knowingly" mixing and giving, or causing to be mixed and given some poisonous drug or drugs to a free woman of colour, one Mary Murray, with intent to cause her death. Powdered glass was also suggested as one of the things she attempted to give her victim. The jury felt that she was repentant and recommended her to the mercy of the court: in spite of this she was sentenced to death by hanging.

If in fact slaves did use poison widely, it was one of their most effective ways of striking at the master. Before modern medical knowledge brought many tropical diseases under control, many deaths were sudden, appeared mysterious, and were certainly never properly diagnosed. Illness or death by poisoning is not always easily detected. The relationships of slavery tend to aggravate feelings of fear on the one hand, rebellion on the other. It is highly significant that the master constantly feared that the slave's spirit of rebellion was strong enough to cause him or her to resort to the use of poison.

Plots during the period of slavery by blacks against white society frequently took the form of armed uprising, in which the plan was often to destroy white property by fire – there was one such scheme to burn Bridgetown down in the early eighteenth century, then to murder as many whites as possible, and either to take control of the colony, or to force the whites to improve the condition of the blacks. Such risings occurred constantly.

Women were much less prominent in this kind of conspiracy than men: they were no doubt squeamish about the cold-blooded killing which was involved. And indeed, cases occurred from time to time, when women who knew of the plans, revealed them in advance in order to save lives, or perhaps also to earn a reward.

A Jamaican plot of 1745 involved about 900 slaves who planned to destroy white society, but was betrayed to the authorities by a female slave, Deborah, when she realised that the child whom she nursed would most likely be among those to be murdered.

In 1768 a slave woman revealed to her owner a scheme to burn down Kingston. In Trelawney in 1798, when a determined group of runaway slaves launched a serious rebellion, under the leadership of the slave Kofi, Rebecca, a domestic in a white household, gave the warning in time for their masters and guests to arm themselves against their black attackers.

As a result of the well-known sympathies of women which could be regarded as treachery to the black cause, they were often excluded from the secret sessions at which these plots were hatched. Much of the planning for the famous Baptist War of 1831-2 in Jamaica, took place at religious meetings after the women had left.

But in spite of the strong male bias in such forms of protest, there are cases throughout slavery of women's active involvement in conspiracies. So that even in the plot which failed in eastern Jamaica in 1745, of eleven slaves found guilty and transported, one was a woman.

The slave woman, Venus, of the parish of St. George in 1824, along with eight men paid the penalty for her crimes. She was allegedly concerned "in a rebellious conspiracy to kill and murder the white inhabitants and to subvert and destroy the present government." She was sentenced to be transported for life.

In a wide cross section of Caribbean colonies, from Guyana, the Leeward Islands, the Virgin Islands, and especially Jamaica, Africans from the Gold Coast played a most prominent part in plots and revolts. They were nearly always to be found among the hard core of armed resistance. In view of their traditional respect for their women folk, originating in the African regard for the life-giving mother, it is not surprising that the woman from time to time featured as a symbolical, as well as an actual leader of conspiracy. An early Koromantyn slave conspiracy in the parish of Vere in Jamaica in the 1680s was supposed to have been led by a King, a Queen, and a chief captain, to whom the slave rebels paid full homage.

One of the major black uprisings of the era of slavery was planned to take place simultaneously throughout at least six parishes in Jamaica in 1760: it involved nearly all the island's Koromantyn slaves. Cubah, a female slave who belonged to a Jewess of Kingston was prominent among the plotters. She was crowned "Queen of Kingston" and was probably expected to perform the functions of a traditional West African Queen Mother. She presided in state under a canopy with a robe around her shoulders and a crown on her head. At the time when the plot was discovered, a wooden sword was also found, with a red feather stuck into the handle, symbolic no doubt, of the blow to be struck for freedom.

Cubah was captured, and shipped off the island, transported for life. She managed to sneak back into the island, and landed in the parish of Hanover. She was, however, subsequently caught and executed.

6. Runaways

As long as slavery existed, there were always slaves who defied the master by running away. From the very beginning of English occupation of the Caribbean islands in the seventeenth century, and before the intensive cultivation of the sugar belts in Barbados, the Leeward Islands and Jamaica, slaves ran away constantly. In Jamaica, for instance, it was estimated at one period during the 1660s that there were more fugitive blacks scattered throughout the island than there were on the estates.

As plantations developed in a more regimented way, runaways were fewer, relative to the slave population, but they were always there, right to the last days of slavery: in the early nineteenth century there may, in any one year, have been as many as 10,000 fugitive slaves at large in Jamaica.

Runaways attacked the system of bondage in one of the most outrageous ways possible. Under the laws of slavery, only the master had the right to say how, when, and where the slaves could come and go. From early in the seventeenth century, Barbados worked out a code of slave legislation which was adopted in other colonies: most important was the legislation which policed the movement of slaves. They were allowed a day off from work on Sundays, and could, on that day only, leave their estates; but if they did they were required to carry a ticket stating what hour their masters expected them back. Any slave found wandering away from his or her estate without such a ticket could be given "moderate whipping" by any white man who found them. One such group of slaves in Barbados in 1654 each received fifty lashes of the whip.

Such pass-laws existed in all the islands, and although they were not always strictly enforced they made clear that the slave had no freedom of movement. By shaking off the master's exclusive claim to control the movement of his human property, runaways were seriously questioning that master's claim, and as a result were regarded as among the most dangerous types of offenders against slavery: runaways created one of the most serious problems which the slaveholder had to face. Their treatment was therefore always severe, although more brutal in earlier than in later periods.

Tracking down escaped blacks was an important activity of slaveowners. Barbados in the seventeenth century kept a register of all slaves known to be missing, and regularly sent out search parties to scout the woods for them: whoever brought in a runaway, dead or alive received

a reward. Antigua at that time offered £2.10.0 for each live negro captive, £1 for a dead one. One Jamaican planter in 1686, among the equipment ordered for his estate, included two bloodhounds for hunting fugitive blacks.

Planters during this period were allowed to put "Iron Rings of great weight" on the ankles of captured runaways: they also fitted them round their necks with iron yokes which had hooks riveted to them, or they used "a spur in the mouth." In the eighteenth and nineteenth centuries, runaway slaves who got caught were punished by public whippings, and imprisonment with hard labour: if they persisted in escaping, they could be imprisoned for life or they could be shipped out of the colony.

The life of the runaway was a risky one. In a small island like Barbados, where hiding places were few and far between, runaways took to caves, and could venture out only at night in search of food. Although the penalties for harbouring runaways were almost as heavy as those meted out to runaways themselves, they were usually concealed by friends and relatives in the slave cabins on estates other than their own, or they got lost among the crowds of blacks in the towns. But in either case there was always the danger of being discovered, for nearly all slaves were branded on their flesh with the particular mark of the estate to which they belonged.

At the periods in West Indian history when runaways joined forces with militant black rebels, such as the Maroons of Jamaica, or became involved in armed revolt, their lives were at stake: they could be, and were frequently captured, and put to death.

Women were obviously at a great disadvantage in an adventure so full of physical dangers. It was difficult to face an outlaw's life with children, and this must have been a very big factor in keeping women tied to slavery. But in spite of this, women were always to be found among those slaves who "pulled foot". Early advertisements for missing slaves, in the seventeenth century in Jamaica, showed that for every two males who escaped from slavery, there was approximately one female, sometimes with young children and infants: they were regularly listed among the most "incorrigible" runaways – no punishment seemed severe enough to reform their determination to escape. Young or old, newly arrived African, or seasoned creole, alone or with their children, pregnant women even, they fled, for a week, a month, for years: they fled for a variety of individual reasons, but essentially their action was an attack on everything which slavery stood for.

Recently imported African women were always prominent among runaways. Not yet conditioned to slavery, they escaped at the earliest opportunity in search of a free life such as they had just left behind. Thirteen of the twentyone runaway slaves in the workhouse at Trelawney in Jamaica in 1791 were "new negroes". Families and friends often became separated on arrival in a Caribbean colony, and the first instinct was to go looking for the familiar faces.

Settled slaves, as well as creole slaves who were born in the West Indies, developed strong bonds of kinship and affection. A woman's husband might live on a neighbouring or distant estate: slaves constantly visited their relatives and friends in different parts of a colony. It happened often that a visitor outstayed his or her approved visiting time, and leave of absence became absence without leave.

Planters regularly sold their property, with some or all of their slaves: sometimes slaves were seized by their owner's creditors, in payment of debts. In these circumstances, rather than be separated from their friends and relatives, or rather than be handed over to a new owner, some slaves preferred to abscond. A slave might be threatened with punishment, and try to escape before the threat was carried out: so much so that many experienced slaveowners advised against warning in advance that he or she would be whipped. A sensitive slave, too, might take offence at something the master said or did, and expressed his or her hurt by disappearing.

Runaways included females of all ages. Sally, a child of six, was taken up at Passage Fort, in March 1780, running away from her owner to find her mother in Kingston. The Morant Bay workhouse in 1791, held among its runaways "a little hump-backed old woman, marked on both breasts A.M. speaks no English, owner and country unknown, 4 feet 6½ inches high." A surprisingly large proportion of women runaways were in fact described as "elderly", suggesting that not even years of bondage were sufficient to quell a really rebel spirit.

Numerous detailed descriptions of individual women who ran way, and who were advertised for by their owners, are very revealing. They indicate that often it was the woman who had some training such as a washer woman, a cook, a seamstress who obviously grudged giving all of her special abilities to an owner, and preferred to work for herself: "Esther, a creole negro woman, 37 years of age, a very good seamstress and washerwoman" who lived in Spanish Town, had apparently been in the habit of hiring herself out without her owner's consent, and doing private jobs on her own. She was well known in the towns of Port Royal and Kingston, and finally she ran away from Spanish Town in 1791. Nelly of the Chamba country in Africa, who still bore her tribal marks on her breast, was a baker by trade: she also in 1791 fled from her master.

Female runaways could be both bold and clever. Benny, alias Bennena, was fairly typical. She was a creole negro woman who ran away from her mistress in Kingston.

She is well known in St. Thomas-in-the-East where she has relations, and a husband in Garbrand-Hall, and is supposed to be harboured by them; she has been vending goods between Morantbay and Manchioneal and makes use of an old letter addressed to the subscriber, (ie her mistress) to protect herself from being taken up.

A runaway pair, like Mary Sadler and her son Will, must have been very conspicuous, but this clearly did not hinder them from attempting to make a break for freedom. She was "a creole sambo woman, has been marked MS on top, but is now defaced, on both shoulders, yet the place remains much darker than the general colour of her skin, she is 34 years of age, has a bushy head of hair, she dresses as a free woman, with long ear-rings, wears shoes and stockings and a high-crown hat, she was hired to one Jackson, a free man of colour who died in this town a short time ago and from him passed over to one Hodges, a free Quadroon man, with whom they said Mary Sadler lived as his wife."

"Also Will, alias Will Sadler, alias Will Waddell, son to the above Mary Saddler: he is 11 years of age, has a curly head of hair, of a light brown colour, is a little marked with the smallpox about his nose, he possesses a deal of drollery, very shrewd and likeable and can tell the hour of the day from the clock."

Female runaways were often described as "artful", and very skilled in deception, and whites were warned to be on their guard against them. One family of runaways consisted of

"Margaret, alias Amey, a black woman, slender make, large eye, prominent forehead and straight nose, and marked GH or MH," her daughter Eliza Arnold, "a slender black girl with very large eyes, and thin visage," and her son Richard McLeod, aged 18 years; they were described as "very plausible." They had run away from the parish of Hanover in western Jamaica and were supposed to be concealed "somewhere in the neighbourhood of Kingston where they probably will pass themselves as free people."

Women who absconded from their owners were not afraid to travel distances. "A stout creole negro woman, named Judy, 25 years of age, speaks good English" originated in the town of Falmouth in western Jamaica: in 1813 when she ran away she was seen in Kingston. Princess, a negro girl of about fifteen or sixteen years of the Mangola country, from Kingston, was supposed to be harboured on a sugar estate in St. Georges in the north.

Slaves would even seek freedom overseas: and this was the usual pattern in the smaller islands, where they would sneak away by rowboat. Puerto Rico was the destination of many runaways from the British Leeward and Virgin Islands. Haiti and Cuba were places of refuge for Jamaicans. Dr. Richard Martin of the north-coast parish of St. Mary lost eleven slaves in 1788: the group consisting of eight males and three females ("two wenches and a girl about seven years of age"), escaped in a canoe, spending six days at sea. Dr. Martin set out after them with a search party: he received news of them at the port of Trinidad in Cuba. There he found also " a great number of runaway negroes, known to be the property of several inhabitants of Jamaica." But the fugitives, were all protected by the Cuban authorities who claimed that these slaves had become converted to the Roman Catholic religion, and Cuban laws required that they should receive sanctuary. As a result none of these ex-slaves could be returned, to the fury of their former masters.

A remarkable fact about female runaways is their persistence. The punishments for running away were well known: these punishments got increasingly severe with each repeated offence. But women appeared over and over among those known as "incorrigible."

"French" Margaret, in 1825 was found guilty in a Jamaican court of running away: but the jury had the strong impression that she was not really incorrigible, they recommended her to the mercy of the court, and she got a relatively "light" sentence, six months' hard labour!

A more hardened sinner was not only imprisoned but publicly whipped: this was the punishment meted out to Harriet, in 1827, "a notorious, incorrigible runaway and evil disposed person" who received three months' hard labour and two dozen lashes on her bare back with a cat in the market place of Buff Bay. Even more incorrigible offenders like French Becky of Fort George Pen, Congo Nancy of Craig Mill Estate, and Sarah Henry, all of the parish of St. Georges in Jamaica, were regarded as beyond reform, and sentenced to imprisonment for life. Such were the consequences which women were prepared to face as they broke away from their lives of bondage, and ran.

7. Guerilla Women

"Bush, bush no have no law." These were the words which a slave once used to describe the life of freedom which rebels and runaways found when they "took to the bush."

Many British Caribbean colonies during slavery had lurking somewhere in their hinterland pockets of slaves who had escaped the plantations and led the lives of bush-rebels: it was not that they had no law but rather that they made their own.

The numbers of such black guerillas, and the length of time they stayed out, varied, depending very largely on the geography of the particular colony. In the relatively flat and intensively cultivated islands of Barbados and the Leeward Islands there was little land outside the estate, and very little forest undergrowth for concealing fugitive blacks. In spite of this, slaves in Barbados, St, Kitts, Nevis, Antigua, at various times found some hidden spots from the plantations where they attempted for even a short while to exist as free people. In Antigua for example, in the 1680s, the hilly south-west corner of the island round Boggy Peak, with its thick vegetation harboured a pocket of rebels who caused serious concern.

Guyana and Jamaica were, however, the guerilla countries par excellence. Both contained dense forests: in Guyana, the navigable rivers, with numerous secluded creeks, in Jamaica the deep mountain hollows, provided natural escape routes and hideouts for rebels: the Jamaican Blue Mountains and Cockpit Country, the Guyanese Berbice, Demerara, and Essequibo rivers throughout slavery were familiar to those slaves, men and women, who refused to be enslaved and created a free world for themselves in the bush.

Women played a most significant part in the lives of bush rebels, in particular those of Jamaica, the Maroons. At the time of the English occupation of the island in 1655, the ex-slaves of the Spanish colonists joined with their former masters against the newcomers, and were in the words of one contemporary "the best fighters on the Spanish side." When the Spanish resistance movement collapsed in 1660 and the remaining Spaniards took refuge in Cuba, it was the blacks who continued the guerilla warfare against the English.

These Jamaican freedom fighters were first organized in groups in Lluidas Vale, Los Vermejelos and Los Porus in what are now the parishes of St. Catherine and Clarendon. Their communities were not merely camps, but homes for families: rebel "polincks" as they were called, all contained women and children.

Maroon activity spread out during the late seventeenth and early eighteenth century into St. Elizabeth, Trelawney, St. Thomas, and Portland, retaining this family pattern; for example, Guys Town in the north eastern region of the Blue Mountains, an important Maroon centre, in the 1730s had more women and children, than armed men.

Some of those women were there reluctantly, for they had been kidnapped by Maroon men from the estates to which they belonged. This was not always a fortunate experience, and there were a few cases of women, who no doubt out of revenge for being taken by force, betrayed the hiding place of the rebels to the whites. This happened to at least two guerilla chiefs: one was Colonel Cudgoe, whose wife, previously stolen from her estate, revealed the numbers and whereabouts of her husband's group to the authorities in 1738. Ancouma, another black leader was murdered in his hut in the Portland forest in 1759 by his two wives, both of them whom he had originally kidnapped.

But the majority of Maroon women lived in the woods of choice: they had run away from their estates and voluntarily joined the rebel mountaineers: once established in these free villages they led a healthy outdoor life; were rid of the excessively hard regimented labour of the plantation, and often bore many children. By the end of the eighteenth century, there were actually more women than men in all Maroon towns, and always there was a high percentage of children, about a third of the free black population being boys and girls.

The leaders of the Jamaican Maroons, as well as the majority of the rebel communities, were Akan people: their place-names, such as Accompong, were Ashanti, so also were the names frequently found among their leaders, for example, Cudgoe, Quaco, Kofi. Their village organization, their strong beliefs in the magical gifts of their religious leaders, as well as a recognised position for the women in their society, were all aspects of their previous African experience which they reproduced in their rebel life.

These traditions helped to produce a well structured and disciplined community, which was essential for a life of continuous warfare.

The presence of women among the black guerillas was vital to the fighting effort. They had specific tasks to perform during campaigns, such as helping to carry off the spoil, or setting fire to a village which they might have to abandon.

Most importantly, however, women were the food providers. While the men fought the enemy and hunted the wild hogs in the woods for meat, the women worked on the provisions grounds, cultivating the same kinds of food crops which flourished in slave plots.

A reliable source of food supplies is essential to the survival of a resistance movement. An early black revel, Juan Lubola, had been a thorn in the flesh of the invading English: an important factor in his achievement was his two hundred acres of intensive cultivation of ground provisions near his headquarters at Lluidas Vale: it was in fact the largest food basket in Jamaica in the earliest years of the English occupation. In 1660 he abandoned his Spanish allies and went over to the English, transferring to them his fighting men, and his food supplies. It is not surprising that the Spanish were unable to hold out much longer, and the English completed their take-over.

The blacks who continued the struggle, like Juan Lubola, took great pains with their food grounds: the whites on their side, saw it as essential strategy that they should "starve out the rebels." One commander of a hunting party which went in 1732 after the Windward rebels in the Blue Mountains succeeded in capturing one of their major towns, Nanny Town, but made the mistake of sparing their "great plantain walk." He was most severely criticised for this by the Jamaican government, which saw such neglect as an act of treachery.

What made his crime even worse was that a Maroon woman warned him that her people intended to recapture their town and get back their cultivation: she declared that "it was better to be killed by the hands of the white man than die in the woods for want of provisions."

So said, so done. The Maroons surprised and recaptured their town, found their food supplies intact, were able to hold out again, and so prolonged the first Maroon war for another six years.

Without this essential division of labour with the women providing the sustenance of life through their agricultural efforts, while the men took on the enemy, a small group like the Maroons – never more than about two thousand persons – could never have achieved what they did, which was to hold the white community in fear, for nearly one hundred years after the English first entered the island.

The life of the rebel families was one of dangerous adventure. Their objectives up the end of the 1730s were twofold, to harass the whites, and to preserve their own free style of life: they therefore both attacked, and defended. Concealed among the trees they placed ambushes for the white raiding parties which set out regularly to flush them out of their hideouts: they themselves often fell victims to white ambushes. They became skilful at concealing the women and children in the most remote spots of the country.

But the women were often exposed to as much risk as the men. One particularly remarkable episode in Maroon history involved the women and children fully. By the 1730s, two main groups of Maroon rebels existed, the Leeward Maroons in the western parishes of Trelawney and St. James led by Captain Cudgoe, and the Windward Maroons of Portland and St. Thomas in the east. Both bands were increasing daily and the Jamaican government spent large sums of money in the attempt to repress them.

After yet a second attack and recapture of Nanny Town in 1734, a party of Windward Maroons in the parish of Portland decided to join forces with their fellow-rebels in the west. Three hundred men, women and children set out on what was one of the boldest hikes in Jamaican history. Their trek took them over one hundred miles across the island's central mountain ridge, through steep, thickly wooded country, much of it wild, virgin land. Throughout this whole adventure the British soldiers dogged their tracks in an attempt to scatter or destroy them. They reached their destination, nevertheless, only to find that the Leeward Maroons under Captain Cudgoe spurned their offer of an alliance, and they were eventually forced to retrace their steps over that same long dangerous march to the east. Again the English tried to stop them, but as an English commander stated at the time "their march was so silent and expeditious, that (they i.e. the English) did not succeed." This heroic episode says a great deal about the courage, the sense of discipline, and the physical hardiness, of not only the men, but of the women and children, who took part in this trek. Although it failed in its immediate aim, which was to unite the rebel movement, it was an important factor in causing the Jamaican government to decide that it was better to make peace with the formidable Maroons, than to attempt to fight them. And this they did, in 1739, thus ending the first Maroon war, and leaving the black guerillas to lead their independent lives in their free villages, away from plantation slavery.

The part played by the woman in the military struggle for black freedom was clearly recognised. Throughout the years of that first African resistance movement in Jamaica, the female guerilla, like the male, carried a price on her head. The government offered a reward of £20 for every rebel man, and £10 for every rebel woman taken dead or alive. The records tell repeatedly of the women and children, who with the men, were either killed or taken prisoners. Simon Booth, who seems to have earned his living by capturing rebel blacks, made a large catch after one of his raiding parties in 1729 in Clarendon. He received his reward for the three women he killed: in addition he had some live prizes of war:

". . . a negro woman belonging to Mr. Rippon who was out about seven years; one other negro woman, belonging to one Mr. Wright, said to be out above two years; the other an old negro woman of Colonel Suttons . . . besides seven children, the eldest not above seven years old."

8. Nanny – Rebel/Queen/Mother

Nanny of Nanny Town in the Blue Mountains was one of the most outstanding civic and military leaders in the history of black freedom movements in the New World. Posterity owes her the memorial of the first national heroine of the Jamaican people.

Official documents give relatively scanty, but highly significant information about her. It is recorded in the Journals of the Jamaica House of Assembly that she was an "obeah" woman, and that the largest and most formidable stronghold of the Portland Maroons was named after her. The establishment even accepted a claim made in 1733 by Cuffee "a very good party negro" that he had killed "Nanny" the rebel's old obeah woman, and they accordingly rewarded him. It is not easy to say precisely whether this was a genuine error, or whether it was deliberate misinformation. Nanny was very much alive, she survived the end of the first Maroon war in 1740 and received from the Government of Jamaica a grant of five hundred acres of land for herself and her people, a unique achievement for a black woman.

A good deal more than these few facts is known about this remarkable Ashanti chieftainess, largely through the strong oral traditions of her descendants who still occupy the towns which she established in the Portland mountains.

In Africa, nations have for centuries kept their history alive through their storytellers, who are often professional chroniclers charged with the vital responsibility of ensuring that each new generation knows its past. The arts of song, dance and drama have all been used to keep the historical narrative vivid in the minds of the community. Modern scholarship shows increasingly that the history of the folk memory is essentially as accurate as the history of the written page.

The Maroons of Jamaica, like many other Afro-Caribbean groups, carry their past in their heads, and can relate in detail events of historic significance to the growth of their community. The story of Nanny is one of the most faithfully preserved in the rich body of black Caribbean culture.

Nanny's time and place of birth, whether in Jamaica, or in Africa, is not clear. What is, however, certain, is that she was of Ashanti origin, and was a free woman who never personally experienced slavery. She was the sister of Cudgoe, the equally renowned Maroon leader; she was married to a Maroon of considerable prestige among their people, but a man of peace who played no active part in military affairs. She had no children of her own but was revered as the mother of her people. The community of old Nanny Town, covering over six hundred acres of land in the Back Rio Grande Valley, (strategically sited for its access to the coast), was probably founded in the 1690s, and was controlled by Nanny when the English first found it in the 1730s. It was a highly organized free community: under Nanny's leadership the position of women and children was greatly respected, their safety and dignity always receiving prior consideration during periods of fighting. After the first English attempt of 1730 to capture the town, "Grannie" Nanny had the women and children evacuated and settled in Girls' Town and Woman's Town in the John Crow Mountains on lands which subsequently became Moore Town. In the fierce encounters between blacks and whites which took place in those mountains throughout the years of the first Maroon war, Nanny's genius dominated the fighting strategies of the guerillas. She did not herself take part in the fighting, but blessed and directed the campaigns, with the Maroon horn, the Abeng, as her effective means of communication.

Her role was very much in the tradition of Ashanti priests/ priestesses and magicians who performed essential functions in African warfare. Such magico-religious leaders customarily advised on the best time for waging war, they gave warriors charms to protect them from injury, they participated with the military commanders in rituals designed to weaken the enemy.

Nanny became celebrated as a great worker of magic. In the words of a nineteenth century Maroon chief,

"Nanny had more science in fighting than even Cudgoe . . . After the signing of the treaty, Nanny say that she show them science. She told fifty soldiers to load their guns and then to fire on her. She folds back her hands between her legs and catches the fifty shots. This was called Nantucompong, Nanny takes her back to catch the balls."

Maroons believed strongly in these supernatural gifts. She was supposed also to keep a huge cauldron boiling, without the use of fire, at the foot of the precipice where Nanny Town stood; Maroon history has it that when curious soldiers and militiamen came close to inspect this freak of nature, they fell into the cauldron and were suffocated.

Of all the black resistance leaders of her time Nanny was foremost among those who resolved never to come to terms with the English. She infected her followers with this determination, and their aggressiveness became legendary. It was her people who made that epic trans-island trek in 1735 to join the Leeward Maroons. But they were too militant for the guerillas of the west who were moving towards a policy of peaceful co-existence with whites. Cudgoe, the Leeward chief accused the Windward Maroons of being cruel and insolent to the English, and he probably feared that they were too high-spirited and independent to accept his authority easily. Hence their eastward return march in 1737.

In that same year Nanny took a solemn pledge on the brow of Pumpkin Hill that she and her people would continue to fight the English raiding parties to the death. She greeted with bitterness the news in 1739 of Cudgoe's peace treaty with the English and ordered the execution of the white soldier who carried her the message. Reluctantly she accepted the peace terms for her own people, but it is significant that as the men signed the truce, the women stood by wearing defiantly round their ankles as ornaments the teeth of the white soldiers who had been killed in battle. After the conclusion of the truce, the Windward Maroons split into two groups, one went closer to the coast to Crawford Town with Quao as their chief, and the other to New Nanny Town (now Moore Town), under Nanny's leadership. On 5th August, 1740, her land patent was approved, duly granting to "the said Nanny and the people now residing with her, their heirs and assigns a certain parcel of land containing five hundred acres in the parish of Portland bounding South and East on King's land and West on Mr. John Stevenson . . ."

She continued to rule her people in peacetime, exercising a unifying influence for many years on the two Maroon groups of Portland. She died during the 1750s. But she is as alive today in the minds of Jamaican Maroons as she was when her heroic band of guerillas held the English to ransom in the eighteenth century. Visitors today still hesitate to explore that difficult mountain country where her descendants live. The legend persists that their rebel queenmother still keeps jealous watch over their liberties.

She lies buried on a hill in Moore Town under a great mound marked by river stones. The spot, called Bump Grave, is sacred ground. It remains as an enduring monument not only to the remarkable Nanny, but to the spirit of all of those black women of the New World, who actively or passively, singly or in groups, throughout the oppressions of slavery, played their many parts in reaffirming that woman, like man, is born free.

74

Persistent Rebels: Women and Anti-Slavery Activity

HILARY McD. BECKLES

Conceptual Framework

After informing his employer in 1796 of the diverse problems posed to management by a group of insubordinate and rebellious slave women on the Newton estate, Sampson Wood, the manager, stated that all the blacks, 'are a race of discontented beings'. Their dissatisfaction, he added, was only 'natural', as it was not possible to be contented with the condition of slavery. [1] With this statement Manager Wood touched unwittingly upon the then popular and revolutionary principle of political philosophy that liberty is the natural universal condition of man. Certainly, in his opinion it explained why the majority of slaves, on a daily basis, were so 'hard to be pleased'.[2] Slave owners in Barbados, and indeed throughout the region, however, would have rejected Wood's argument, and posited instead that, on the whole, their slaves were contented, or could be made so with better socio-economic treatment. But none would have argued, given the overwhelming evidence to the contrary, that resistance to slavery was not widespread, persistent and to be found in almost every area of slave life. It is upon the basis of this realization that some contemporary writers, and most modern historians, have argued that resistance, of both the violent and non-violent sort, was endemic to slave society in the West Indies.[3]

If anti-slavery behaviour was endemic, or natural, and not gender specific, then the question of women's role as carriers of anti-slavery ideas and agents of anti-slavery mobilization should not be considered as exceptional or phenomenal. The political consciousness of women warrants no particular examination since both men and women created the intellectual basis of the culture of resistance that characterized the slavery world. Only the organizational forms of resistance took shapes that sometimes showed evidence of a gender bias, but this had nothing to do with the perception of the need to resist which was uniform among all socially aware slaves. Orlando Patterson, Michael Craton, and Eugene Genovese, among others, have shown that the struggles of the slavery period were inherently collective, in that they were conceived in the consciousness of slave communities. Logically, then, the ideology of anti-slavery was also gender free.[4] Recently, Hilary Beckles and Barry Gaspar have argued that all groups of slaves irrespective of sex, colour, or work figured prominently in various aspects of anti-slavery organization over time, and that the dominance of any one group at any particular stage should be explained more in terms of perceptions of organizational efficiency and the uneven distribution of knowledge and consciousness than in terms of a gender division.[5]

In Barbados, and elsewhere, the system of slavery sought to degrade women and womanhood in ways which forced aspects of their resistance to assume specific forms. Maternity and fertility were placed at the core of strategies for slave plantation survival, and so women's resistance to these policies meant that their opposition to slavery was probably more broadly based. Furthermore, it can be argued that women's leadership of the resistance to slave owners' attempt to disintegrate the slave communities culturally and morally provided much of the organizational strength necessary for ideological and armed resistance. It is not an easy task, therefore, to separate the anti-slavery practices of slave women from those of the wider slave community. But it remains necessary to highlight resistance practices that were common among women in order to redress their rather low historiographic profile.

Neither slave owners nor the slave communities considered women to be the less rebellious sex; slave owners were as fearful, suspicious and distrustful of women's potential activities as anti-slavery agents as they were of men's. They did not formulate, either implicitly or explicitly, any specific concepts of women within the culture of slave resistance. This fact was expressed in that until the 1820s legislative provisions for the control and discipline of slaves made no concessions to women – except in not flogging women advanced in pregnancy. But this specific provision emerged during the mid-18th century when there was increasing emphasis on natural reproduction as an alternative form of long-term labour supply. It may, therefore, be argued that it had more to do, at least conceptually, with the protection of infant life and its capital worth, than with the restructuring of punishment policies to favour women. In general, both slave women and men were stripped and whipped, branded with hot irons, gibbeted, hanged or had limbs and joints amputated if convicted for acts of hostility to their masters and the white community at large. If anything, slave women, possibly on account of their closer interpersonal association with members of the white society, were likely to receive harsher and psychologically more damaging forms of punishment than men.

Patterns of Resistance

Many African women arrived in the West Indies with an anti-slavery consciousness already forced by activist resistance to capture and sale. For women already defined as slaves in their communities, it was enslavement outside familiar cultural barriers. The extreme brutalization

popularly associated with European slavers, and total alienation from kinship structures provided the basis of anti-slavery resistance. Also, some women were already accustomed to resisting certain forms of oppression in traditional societies, and acts of insurrection and defiance were part of their social behavioural patterns. Collective political behaviour, then, was not unfamiliar to West African women in the 17th and 18th centuries. The slave trade had the obvious effect of focusing and harnessing the political and social consciousness of these female agricultural cultivators for the purposes of survivalist activities.

There is now a small but growing body of literature on resistance activities at the point of capture, in the barracoons on the coast, and in the middle passage. Within this literature, women are attributed no lesser status than men in terms of functions. For instance, in a number of articles Okon E. Uya has argued that plantation resistance should be conceived as the culmination of a long process of anti-slavery struggle which had begun in Africa. The evidence – of which there is a significant amount in slave traders' journals – is, however, more extensive for middle passage revolts than for activities in West Africa.[6]

On slave ships the security was probably tighter than in the barracoons or on the plantations. Indeed, these vessels have been described quite aptly as 'floating prison[s]'. Each ship carried a number of guards armed with muskets and swords, while the captives were chained below deck. It was this constant vigilance that made revolts on board such remarkable achievements. Wish has analysed published data, dealing mostly with British slave ships for the 18th century, and found the incidence of mutiny and revolt to be slightly less than two per year.[7] In addition, Mannix has referred to at least 300 slave insurrections, including successful attempts by Africans to prevent ships leaving the coast.[8]

In 1694, Captain Phillips of the Royal Africa Company ship *Hannibal,* on collecting a 'cargo' from Whidaw for Barbados, commented on the Africans' attitudes and actions in opposition to enslavement in the New World. He stated:

The negroes are so wilful and loth to leave their own country, that they have often leap'd out of the canoes, boats and ships, into the sea, and kept under water till they were drowned to avoid being taken up and saved by our boats, which pursued them. They have a more dreadful apprehension of Barbados than we can have of hell ... we have likewise seen divers of them eaten by the sharks, of which a prodigious number kept about the ship in this place . . . We had about 12 negroes did wilfully drown themselves, and others starved themselves to death; for this belief that when they die they return home to their country and friends again.[9]

Slavers then, were forced to take measures to counter these resistance practices and beliefs. In 1725, the Royal Africa Company instructed Captain William Barry on the procedure necessary to reduce the number of Africans escaping ship: 'so soon as you begin to slave let your knetting be fix'd breast high fore and aft, and so keep them shackled and handbolted fearing their rising or leaping overboard; to prevent which, let always a constant and careful watch be appointed. . .'[10] Two years later, Captain Snelgrave outlined the technique used to counter the concept of slaves' spiritual return to their homeland. He stated that on one occasion his African captives revolted on ship, but after they were suppressed he cut off the head of one of the rebels and threw the parts overboard to let the others 'see that all who offended thus should be served in the same manner. For many of the Blacks believe that if they are put to death and not dismembered they shall return again to their own country after they are thrown overboard'.[11] In his 1694 report, Captain Phillips had stated that it was common to 'cut off the legs and arms of the most wilful to terrify the rest' during the passage.[12]

In spite of these measures, the evidence given by English slaver Captain John Newton indicates the frequency of middle passage revolt. He stated, in 1788, that ships under his command survived at least half-a-dozen insurrections by enchained men and women; and that during the passage the Africans were always 'upon the brink of mischief' and 'seldom a year passes ... but we hear of one or more' such risings.[13] Their motivations were generally the same irrespective of their origins: freedom to return to the world from which they had been involuntarily removed; fear of the unknown world beyond the ocean; suspicion that among the white men were cannibals in pursuit of black flesh; fear, especially among the women, that they were to be used for sexual purposes.

Often they revolted before ships left the coast. In 1704, for example, a revolt broke out on board

the *Eagle* while it lay in a river off the Gold Coast preparing for departure to Barbados. The ship already had some 400 men, children and women on board with only ten white men to secure them. The rebels killed some of their guards and managed to escape captivity. Snelgrave reported the suppression of a revolt by Coromantine women and men aboard the *Henry* in 1721, and the massacre of the white crew of the *Nancy* in 1767 off the coast of Old Calabar by some 232 rebelling women and men.[14] Many other cases of revolt in Africa went unreported by captains whose employers sometimes held them responsible for such managerial failure.

The rebellion aboard the *Thomas* in 1797 concerns more specifically the context of black women's enslavement in Barbados and the origins of resistance activity. As the ship was within a few days of Barbados, some of the women were released from their chains and brought above deck for exercise and extra food and water. These women, realizing that the musket chest was unlocked, managed to capture some guns and overpowered the crew. The men were released and the ship brought under control of these Africans, but the victory, pioneered by these courageous women, was short lived. Unable to navigate back to Africa, they drifted for 42 days before being spotted by a British warship, and were attacked, defeated and resold into slavery at Cape Nicola Mole by the commanding officer.[15]

On the slave plantations, the culture of anti-slavery resistance which permeated every aspect of life was forged and given social meaning by men and women who sought to attain a wide range of personal and collective goals. The objectives of females' resistance and the forms deployed varied over time and in accordance with their position within the structure of social relations. It would not be historically correct to argue that, although all women might have wanted legal freedom, their struggles were uniform and unrelated to social and material developments. Indeed, women showed a greater diversity than men in the pursuit of their goals, but this was largely due to their more complicated integration and overall functions within the slave system.

The typology in Table 74.1 illustrates the wide range of anti-slavery actions taken by black women in Barbados, and other colonies. In general, slaves pursued a range of objectives which varied in terms of the degree of freedom they encompassed. These goals were not thrust upon them, but arrived at by social analysis and the conceptualization of possibilities. Clear ideologies sometimes emerged from their actions, but generally, complex inductive methodologies are required to locate the thought processes and their rationality, behind their anti-slavery options. The heterogeneity of slave action was probably the most outstanding characteristic of anti-slavery resistance.

Table 74.1   Typology of Barbados slave resistance

Form	Objective
Violent Revolt	
armed combat individual/ collective	permanent self-liberation and abolition of slavery
Maroonage	
inter-plantation plantation-town inter-colony (overseas) plantation – internal frontier	temporary and permanent freedom from slavery
Non-violent Protest	
privileges benefits concessions rights autonomy	amelioration of slavery conditions
Constitutional Civil Rights Action	
manumission	legal freedom within slave society

Non-violent Resistance

At times, women offered their owners unswerving loyalty in return for protection and privileges; at others they ran away, committed murders, and supported revolutionary action. It is difficult to account for the kind of circumstances that influenced women to adopt particular strategies, but the shift in consciousness is important in accounting for the pattern and type

of resistance that slave communities offered at specific junctures. Whether the slave community adopted violent rebellion or a non-violent stance, women were visible participants. Not all women were made of heroic material, but some were, and these individuals stood out above others, even within slave owners' documentation.

Armed rebellions were the rarest form of resistance. The more ordinary day-to-day antislavery activities were of two basic kinds: first, actions designed to weaken the slave system, hastening its collapse, and resulting in the abandonment of slave labour; second, actions designed to improve the efficiency of the system so as to extract greater material, social and ideological rewards with the logical effect of rendering the quality of life more free than slave.[16] On the former type of action, the manager of Newton's estates said in 1796:

There are enough of them to turn the plantation upside down . . . many of them run, without reason, into the sickhouse, and sometimes take a day or two without leave, altho' they know, if they ask for it, they may have it, provided they are people of good character . . . and don't ask too frequently, nor come too many at a time.[17]

In 1816, in relation to the second type of action, William Dickson argued that the Barbadian slaves' rejection of collective armed violence as an antislavery measure during the 18th century was principally responsible for slave owners relaxing their techniques of control and granting extensive concessions to slaves that significantly ameliorated their social condition long before the end of the 18th century when imperial reform policies were in vogue.[18]

Field women's adoption of the strategy of labour withdrawal, interpreted as laziness by drivers and overseers, was considered a universal managerial problem. Some managers recognized that stripes administered to the backs of slave women by drivers were not always effective, and sought other means of dealing with these anti-productivists. In 1721, for example, Manager Smalridge of Codrington estate was instructed by his absentee employer to 'transport off the island' all lazy slaves who were a 'great discouragement to the industrious'. In 1725, he sold four 'lazy women' to a Virginian merchant, but the problem persisted.[19] Smalridge had difficulty in finding purchasers for these rebels, and so the estate had to continue with these 'dreadful idlers' who gave very little service. Other managers resorted to placing 'lazy' women in the stocks or in irons until their acceptance of hard labour returned. In a slave system in which women predominated, low levels of female labour productivity could hardly be tolerated. The driver's whip remained the most common antidote for this form of labour resistance.

Women also participated directly in leadership positions in collective bargaining in which field hands sought to negotiate improved conditions and terms of labour. Invariably, such actions meant opposition to overseers' work schedules and aspects of managerial policies. Slaves sometimes insisted upon changes before consenting to work at levels of production management considered acceptable. In June 1738, for example, a large field gang of women and men on Codrington plantation put down their tools, and marched off some 15 miles by foot into Bridgetown to lodge a complaint with, and make demands on, the plantation's attorney. As was common for many absentee-owned estates, attorneys were employed to handle legal and financial business and to assist managers with decisionmaking. In this instance, the slaves', petition contained the following demands: removal of the estate's book- keeper, an extension of their leisure time and a request that the estate should in future have no more than one white and one black overseer.[20] The use of slaves as overseers was not a feature of plantation management, though slave drivers answerable to white overseers were. 'The slaves were not persuaded to return to the estate until their case was heard in full. When it was, and they had departed, Manager Vaughan noted that they went:

Thro the country singing and dancing with drawn knives as great as if they had gain'd a conquest, which they continued in the plantation till I got home in the Evening, and when I got home still insisted upon their foregoing request. But they soon submitted and agreed to go to their work the next morning which they did do.[21]

But this challenge to managerial authority did not go unpunished. Vaughan informed his employer how, after he informed them that 'the Country would not submit to such Agreement', he secured the leaders of the delegation, two women and four men, and had them flogged and placed in confinement.

But in no form of anti-slavery action was the consciousness of women more evident than in their individual quest for improved conditions

and freedom. Narratives of individual women resisting the domination of the pro-slavery culture illustrate most clearly the nature of their experiences as well as the kinds of decisions they were forced to make. These decisions ranged from psychologically painful acts of infanticide to petitioning owners for manumission. There is as yet no concrete evidence that slave women practised what has become known as 'gynaecological resistance', although planters believed that the birth control techniques used were an attempt to reduce the flow of labour to the estates. But acts of infanticide are frequently cited in plantation records. For example, in 1796, Manager Wood of Newton estate stated that one of his slave women, Mary Thomas, became pregnant by the white book-keeper who did not consider her his favourite. The new-born child, he stated, was murdered by its mother with the assistance of her sister and mother. Wood concluded from this act that these three women 'are a vile set' who would stop at nothing.[22]

Mary Thomas was the great-niece of Old Doll, the retired housekeeper of the estate and a well-known matriarch of its principal slave family who launched a vigorous and partly successful pursuit of freedom between 1790 and 1815. Old Doll and her three daughters were treated as more 'free' than 'slave' by the former owner of the estate, Elizabeth Newton. In her old age Elizabeth passed the estate to her cousins John and Thomas Lane, with the provision, that Doll's family was to continue in their privileged position. Old Doll, however, found reason to believe that her family's freedom had been agreed by Elizabeth before she died, and that it was incumbent upon the new owners to ensure that this was honoured. What ensued, however, was an aggressive and sophisticated struggle between these women and the management which speaks of the tenacity of women and their vision of freedom.

Old Doll and her daughters were literate, and their quest for legal freedom involved not only their constant challenge to the authority of successive managers, but also letters written to their supposed owners in London. In 1795, for instance, Manager Wood was shocked when Dolly, one of the daughters, told him that 'she would rather starve with hunger than grind herself a pint of corn' as she and her family had been promised freedom and they were unaccustomed to arduous manual labour. Managers received their contempt and insubordination, but they presented themselves to their absentee owners with humility.[23]

Dolly's character and manner were forthright from the start. Manager Wood never appreciated her aggression and arrogance and had little time for her. Ideally, he would have liked to break her in the first field gang, but suspected that his employer might object. Dolly's letter to Thomas Lane reflects a rather business-like attitude towards the attainment of freedom by manumission.[24]

Barbados, November 26, 1807

Honoured Master,

I take the liberty of conveying these few lines to you hoping to find you my master and mistress and family well, and requesting the kind favour of you to be so good as to take the trouble to have my manumission executed for me. As you will find by Mr. Jackson's letter, my friend who has wrote to you on the subject, as I chose it sent to you from all your former kindness to me and my family, I would wish you to complete the business for your servant.

Hon'd Sir I remains
Your Humble Servant
Dolly Newton

In 1810, Dolly obtained her manumission and became a free woman.

Jenny, Dolly's sister, who preferred to use the surname 'Lane' rather than 'Newton', had obtained her freedom in 1807 at the age of 39. She too had written a letter to Thomas Lane some time in August 1804 requesting her manumission:[25]

My honoured Master,

I hope you will pardon the liberty your slave has taken in addressing herself to you on a subject which I hope may not give you the least displeasure or offence. When my valued and good Master Wood was about to leave this Country, I requested him to make a proposal to you in my behalf, which he most kindly promised to do, but as I understood he never had it in his power to make my request. I now with my Mistress Wood's approbation, venture to address myself to you which favour I have to ask good Master

is this. I have a friend who has been generous enough to promise me if I can obtain your consent will pay for my freedom but first I must implore you to take another good slave in my stead, or sell me, which ever you please to do, and you shall be most honestly paid if it should please you to sell me. I should never have thought of changing my situation if I could be assured of always living as I have done with my master and mistress Wood, but as you are at a distance and I don't know whose hands I may fall into, I hope you will not blame me for embracing this offer of my freedom. With all due obedience and submission I sign myself your humble slave,

Jenny Lane

But this was not the end of Jenny's anti-slavery strategy. It was now necessary to secure the freedom of her two sons, Robert and Henry. She had accumulated sufficient money as a free woman to purchase their freedom. Old Doll, the children's grandmother, had negotiated with Manager Wood for their release from field labour and for their apprenticeship as tradesmen; Robert was put to the joinery trade and Henry was taught tailoring. Now in 1813, at the age of 45 years, Jenny wrote jointly to John and Thomas Lane requesting the manumission of Robert, aged 26 years and Henry aged 24 .[26]

Barbados, March 4th, 1813

Honoured Sir/

I have taken the liberty to write to you, hope you will excuse me requesting the favour of your Goodness to oblige me with my two Mullato sons at Newton's; the Name of one is Robert a joiner by trade, but one of his arms is affected and no use to the estate; the other is William Henry a taylor by trade and a Poor constitution that I think is but little use to the estate. If I thought or knew they was any Great use, you may Depend I would not taken the liberty, but my having A little to Depend on and they poorly would wish to have them to own it, which I have named to General Haynes [plantation attorney], and I knows what
I say in this letter to be true.

I Remains your truly well wisher
and very humblest
Jane Lane

Both Robert and Henry were freed in 1819 at the ages of 32 and 30 years respectively. Jenny died the year before their manumission (1818) aged 50 years.

For Dolly and Jenny it had been a tiring struggle for legally recognized freedom. They had both worked as housekeepers and been threatened with field work by managers, for insubordination. By the manipulation of sexual relations with white plantation officers, both sought to remove themselves as far as possible from the brutal life-style associated with field labour. They also cultivated intimate social relations with wives of plantation personnel in order to ensure favoured treatment within the white household. By gaining some sympathy among these persons, they hoped to strengthen the case put to their owners for manumission. In both instances, plantation attorney Robert Haynes gave his support and encouraged the Lane brothers to send out the manumission papers. It was, however, their careful cultivation of social relations with whites that provided the platform for their petitioning approach for the attainment of freedom.

Elizabeth (Betsy) Newton, however, did not take the petitioning route to freedom which her two sisters took. She preferred more direct anti-slavery action. During the early 1790s, after a series of disputes between her family and management, she was removed from the house staff and sent to the fields. In her own statement, she was degraded and 'unmercifully' beaten, in addition to being threatened with the stocks. Claiming that the manager threatened her life, Elizabeth took flight and became a maroon, leaving behind her three children. [27]

Using money and contacts, Elizabeth went underground in Barbados for several months. When reports reached her that the manager had sworn to kill her if she was captured, she made arrangements to flee the island. But she had a carefully worked out plan: first she fled to the neighbouring island of St. Vincent, having made her way by offering money to the captain of a vessel. From there, she made similar arrangements and fled to London where, since Lord Mansfield's ruling in the Somerset case of 1722, former slaves were considered legally free on touching British soil.

Like her sister Jenny, Elizabeth, on gaining her freedom, soon set about obtaining freedom for her children. In London she settled with a Mr Miler, most likely a free black man, with whom she had a child. One Monday morning she appeared at the door of her former owners, John and Thomas Lane, to give an account of herself. First, she gave the reasons for her flight, and then explained that she wished to return to her children in Barbados, but only if they gave her a valid manumission paper so that she could go unmolested. Thomas Lane wrote of this encounter:

In short she pleaded strongly for her liberty, with her little girl in her arms . . . We cannot compel her to go back, she is free by setting her foot on English ground . . . Therefore, she is asking us to give her what she already has – Her Freedom, and what we cannot take away from her.[28]

Lane refused to comply with Elizabeth's wishes. But she was persistent, stating that she had received information that her sisters, who were then not yet freed, her mother, Old Doll, and her children were being brutalized by the estate manager.[29] She also claimed, like her sisters at a later date, that she was freed by Elizabeth Newton, her former owner and namesake, and therefore her children were born free – as the Slave Laws of Barbados provided that the status of infants at birth was the same as that of the mother. In 1801, she petitioned Lane for the manumission of her children in Barbados. The legal document stated:[30]

The case and petition of Elizabeth Ann Miler, a free Black woman from the island of Barbados, is currently and promptly recommended to Mr. Lane's humane attention and imperposition – Her four surviving children viz. John Scott, born Nov. 4th 1784, Elizabeth Ann, born Oct. 19th 1786, Nanny Doll Dorothy, born January 1790 and Anna Maria, born Nov. 8th 1791, all free born and living upon the Newton Estate in Christ Church, Barbados, were seized as slaves during the life of Mrs Newton by the then agent, William Yard, and are still detained as such by Mr Lane's agent, Mr. Wood; and have been at different times very severely treated. Elizabeth Ann Miler came over to England six years ago in hope of procuring an order from Mrs. Newton for their release, but upon her arrival learnt that Mrs. Newton had died just before. Elizabeth Ann Miler having therefore hitherto failed to accomplish the object which brought her to England, and being most desirous to return to her children in Barbados, most humbly solicited Mr. Lane's goodness and benevolence to grant her under his hand a certificate of her own freedom and an order upon his agent for the release of her children – for which compassion and kindness towards her she will never cease thro' life (as duty bound) in fervent gratitude to pray.

May 25th, 1801

Again, Lane did not comply. Elizabeth kept in touch by letter with her sisters and mother in Barbados, but she never succeeded in securing her children's freedom. She died in England before they were emancipated by the imperial legislation of 1833 and 1838.

Kill, Burn and Plunder

Women sometimes expressed their opposition to slavery by murdering those persons immediately associated with tyrannical authority. For slave women there was no recourse to civil law; when morality in social relationships broke down, there was nothing to protect them from the anti-social use of white power. Invariably, the circumstances under which women murdered white persons are not easily unravelled, but their context is closely related to concepts of self-defence and preservation of dignity. In 1768, for example, a black slave woman was convicted for the attempted murder of her master, a prominent member of the legislature, with whom she allegedly had a sexual relationship. She was sentenced to death. Her defence was not recorded as blacks could not give evidence against whites in courts.[31]

The convicted woman was popular and much loved within the slave community of the parish of St Peter where she and her master resided. The community considered her innocent of the charge, and organized a massive show of solidarity with her throughout the trial. Many slave women surrounded the courtroom, and attempted to visit her in prison. In spite of this show of opposition to the process of law, she was executed. But this was not the end of the female-led slave community protest. A proclamation issued by Governor Spry informed the public that the body of this 'negro woman, executed at Speigts [town] . . . had been attended to the grave with unusual pomp by numbers of negroes meeted together for that purpose'.[32] The slave women, in particular, were seen as using the burial ceremony to protest against the legally sanctioned victimization of black women. The gathering, noted the governor, was 'expressly invited and collected' and constituted an

open violation of the laws, a daring arraignment of the justice of the sentence by which she was executed, and a most outrageous insult to the person of a public magistrate and member of the Legislature whose life had been endangered by the horrid attempts of this wretch.[33]

Other recorded attempts by slave women to take the life of white persons were less dramatic though the motives of self-defence, revenge, and anger with owners were evident. In 1780, the management at Codrington estate spent more than £26 in legal fees in an unsuccessful attempt to prevent the capital punishment of 'a negro woman who was found an abettor in the murder of a white man'. Since the law provided that owners of slaves executed for felonies be compensated by the treasury, the estate received £45 for the murderess..[34] In 1774, a white overseer on a St Philip cotton estate was murdered by a group of slaves which included a woman. She was gibbeted and chained to the gallows until dead for public viewing.[35]

Occasionally the more vulnerable members of white households paid the penalty for offences committed by their parents upon slaves. Dickson reported the case of a young domestic slave girl who poisoned more than one of her mistress's children because she 'disliked the employment so'.[36] For these offences, he noted, the girl was hanged 'at the request of her humane mistress'. Slave owners, then, had reason to believe that black women would resort to any level of violent behaviour in order to express their anti-slavery sentiments. Many lived in fear of their lives, as evidence of whites being poisoned by women servants was reportedly substantial. Even the most loyal slave 'wenches' were not beyond the bounds of suspicion to slave owners alerted to the women's anti-slavery attitudes.

For those whose anger stopped short at killing their oppressors, it was easier to commit property-related crimes. In some cases, the objective was to ruin their owners financially, while in others, slaves sought to obtain capital to further their chances of obtaining freedom. Cases and motives were diverse, but slave owners considered the underlying trend to be the undermining of their power. In November 1815, for example, when Betty Phillis, a domestic·slave, ran away from Griffith's estate, she deliberately 'set fire to the bed and curtains' with the intention of 'burning the house to the ground'.[37] Such cases were common on plantations, as slaves would launch arsonist attacks upon their owners before taking flight as maroons.

Actions of a less damaging nature, such as the confiscation of property, were, however, commoner. In general, money realized from the disposal of inconspicuous articles was used to finance long-term and long-distance maroonage. This practice was particularly common among huckster slaves who sold goods on their owners' account, and who often vanished with goods and money proceeds. An example of this was the case of Nelly, the huckstress, who disappeared in October 1810. The notice placed in the *Barbados Mercury* for her recapture stated that she took with her £100 worth of dry goods – along with her child. In this case, as in many others, her owner was not prepared to take her back on account of her alleged dishonesty and cunning, but wanted the child returned. Finally, unable to achieve this end, her owner offered to accept £100 from anyone who captured, and was prepared to keep mother and child.[38]

Slave women, then, expressed their individual hostility to slavery and slave owners in multifarious ways. Often the specific circumstances of interpersonal relations with owners determined preferred options. But women were prepared to take whatever measures seemed necessary, from murder to confiscation of property. Murderers frequently hoped to go unrecognized, while attacks on property were commonly associated with flight.

Runaways

Maroonage was undoubtedly the most commonly reported anti-slavery action taken by women in Barbados. Those who did not themselves take flight frequently assisted others to do so. Also, the practice of harbouring fugitives was generally considered to be evidence of women's opposition to the slave owners' authority and the imposition of their own value system upon the social order. The small, densely populated island harboured a thriving maroon culture that slave owners could not eradicate. The vibrancy of this underworld of clandestine relationships enhanced the widespread and endemic nature of resistance by flight. The possibility of individual flight might have partially reduced the need for the collective, violent anti-slavery confrontation, but maroonage expressed certain philosophical characteristics found among slaves: their right to assert control over self; the supremacy of their social relationships over labour commitment to the workplace; and the power of their individuality to transcend the control mechanism of enslavement.[39]

Newspaper reports, plantation accounts, official documents, travellers' narratives and other historical data record the history of women as maroons. These data tell us a great deal about the life experiences and expectations of women as slaves; about their emotional relationships with family, sexual partners, and the slave communities in general. Moreover, they illustrate the organizational ingenuity and courage of women in the face of an oppressive and brutal social system. At times their flight was intended to be temporary, while at others they sought to sever permanently their relations with their owners. Sometimes the former (petit-maroonage) led to the latter (grand-maroonage) especially when slave control techniques were strict and punishments severe.

The pattern of maroonage activity was not complicated, though effective organization required skill, courage, and a large measure of good fortune. Options were limited. Slaves could attempt to disappear in the urban underground, or hide out on plantations, secure shelter in remote backlands, accessible though they were, or flee the island altogether. All these options were explored by slave women. Overseas flight was continuously attractive, and in some cases was the first resort. As the sugar culture absorbed the entirety of the island during the 18th century the internal frontier rapidly diminished, but in its limited form still sustained a sizeable number of fugitives.[40] It is, therefore, difficult to place any ranking of priority upon the various aspects of these options. For example, as towns grew larger their ability to sustain maroon life increased in direct proportion to the diminishing size of the internal frontier. British colonization of the Windwards in the second half of the 18th century, and of Trinidad and Guiana in the early 19th century, added, to the attractiveness of maritime maroonage. With Barbadian slave owners pioneering these settlements, slaves were likely to have relatives and friends from whom they could seek protection.

Women who fled their estates were generally dependent upon the collective support, tacit and active, of the wider slave community. The concealment of fugitives was a common social feature, symbolic of the slave communities' collective anti-slavery stance. Fugitives were fed, clothed, housed, and kept informed by their collaborators. Slave owners were fully aware that the frequency of maroonage and the unsatisfactory rate of recapture were the direct result of the collective assistance offered by slaves, both on the estates and in the towns, as well as those who worked in maritime-related activities. In this sense, successful maroonage expressed an aspect of communal black anti-slavery solidarity in the face of organized white power.

In 1731, slave owners sought to break up this solidarity by legislative action. On 11 November, an Act was passed which penalized all blacks who assisted runaways in their flight. It stated:

Whereas drivers, negroes and other slaves do often runaway and absent themselves from the service of their owners, and are wilfully entertained, harboured and concealed by other slaves to the great detriment of the owners of such runaway slaves, and to the grievous mischief of inhabitants . . . in general, be it therefore enacted . . . that if any negro or slave shall hereafter wilfully entertain, harbour or conceal any runaway slave and shall be thereof adjudged guilty by any Justice of the Peace, upon confession or proof, such negro or other slave shall receive one and twenty lashes on their bare backs; and for the second offence of the same nature . . . thirty and nine lashes . . ., and for the third offence . . ., shall receive thirty and nine lashes . . . and be branded in the right cheek with a hot iron, marked with the letter R, and shall be then punished at the discretion of the Justice, life and limb excepting.[41]

As with most laws, slaves continued to ignore this legislative provision. During the second half of the 18th and the early 19th century, the level of maroonage increased and law officials considered that effective harbouring was the source of encouragement.

It was common for women to conceal their fleeing friends, family and lovers and, as a result, advertisements for runaways invariably listed their social connections. For example, when Will ran away from his master in 1789, one of his two wives, who were undoubtedly visited by constables, was suspected of concealing him. Likewise, in 1783, it was suspected that Cudjoe was being harboured by his wife at Turner Hall estate in St Andrew. When Assey, a field woman, fled her estate in 1787, she was advertised as probably being concealed by her husband, a slave driver and father of her children, on a distant estate.[42] Slaves' determination to unify their

families and to express their social commitment to each other was a primary reason for maroonage and concealment. This assertion of their human needs above and beyond the interest of their owners was a central part of their search for self-definition and determination that constituted the basis of all acts of resistance.

The majority of field women escaped alone, and generally sought refuge on other plantations where they had supportive kin, but a significant proportion fled to towns. Advertisements in the local press were sometimes remarkably detailed on the biography and description of runaway women. In March 1829, Sarah Taylor forbade all persons from 'harbouring or employing' her three runaway women slaves, Molly, Betty, and Charlotte, otherwise 'the law will be enforced with the utmost rigour against all offenders'. [43] The following month, Henry Marshall placed the following, much more detailed notice in the *Barbados Globe*:

The subscriber will . . . reward . . . any person who will either apprehend and deliver to him or put in the slave prison, the slave Amelia, a yellow skin negro girl, about 16 years old, with a negro freckle under one of her eyes, an aperture in her top front teeth, and an excrescence behind each ear produced from their being pierced for rings. The girl was one of Cragg's people, and was bought in September last at the Marshall's sale, and came home for one day only; she then absented herself for three weeks, during which time she was harboured by her father Thomas Cragg . . . and her mother Harriett. She has again absented herself since 30th November last . . . and is supposed to be harboured by her father and his connections. [44]

Sarah, who ran away in June, was described by her owner as well known about the town as she has been for some time in the habit of selling dry goods.[45] Her owner, Mary Thompson, offered $4 for her lodgement in the 'slave prison'. Also in June, Mr E. S. White offered $6 reward for the capture of his 'negro woman name Sarah, rather stout, about middling stature, and with a mark under her chin'. He cautioned 'all the masters of vessels against taking her from the island', though he suspected her to be harboured in the town in Palmetto Street, Nelson Street or the Green Fields'. [46]

The Slave Code of 1688 provided for the issue of signed passes or testimonials to slaves by their owners as proof of the legitimacy of their off-plantation travel. Constables, and indeed any white person, were empowered to stop slaves in transit and demand to see their document. If this could not be produced then they were legally obliged to arrest them and convey them to the nearest place of detention. In this sense, the entire white community functioned under law as a collective police force. But from the beginning of the implementation of this provision the business of counterfeit passes flourished in the colony. Many slaves were literate, and forging documents was not difficult. Runaway slave women frequently possessed these counterfeits, and so constables were requested to inspect slaves' papers carefully. When Nancy Effey ran away from her estate in 1819 with her two mulatto children it was unlikely that she would have been successful without effective documents. As a result, her owner instructed constables to disregard any 'spurious papers' she may have produced. Nancy had a sister in Demerara, and was suspected of planning to reach that colony.[47] The owners of runaway Jane Francis advertised in 1817 that she might be in possession of forged papers which allowed her to 'pass as a free woman and in all probability will wish to quit the island'.[48] Likewise, in September 1831, the owner of Nancy Jane, a field woman, stated that she had 'a forge pass' with which she travels unmolested. She too was suspected of wanting to leave the island.[49]

Women with easily marketable skills stood a better chance of gaining employment even though their employers might suspect them of being runaways. Many whites in the urban areas appeared rather liberal on the matter of runaways and some were accused of condoning it. The loss of plantation skills resulting from runaways was considered by many urbanites as their gain, and many fugitive women found employment and shelter with sympathetic white households. Amelia, who escaped her estate in 1829, was able to evade constables and slave catchers because, according to her owner, 'she being a seamstress' would easily find employment in town.[50] Likewise, Sarah Rose, who absented herself on 15 April 1833, was at large for over a year when her owner placed a notice in the press stating that 'she has not only been harboured by slaves, but also by free thieves just as bad as herself'. He hoped that the 'notice will prove more successful than the former two', but he was not optimistic as he said she was clever enough to 'assume a different name', and 'being a pretty good seamstress is the easier concealed'.[51]

If runaway women dressed well and spoke 'good' English, their chances of passing as free women, or the trusted mistresses of white males, increased considerably. Constables were less inclined to question such women who were commonly found about Bridgetown. Advertisements, therefore, frequently made references to the language status of runaways. For example, when the 'negro wench' of Benjamin Pemberton took flight in 1746, his public notice stated that she 'speaks very good English' and was likely to pass as free. Also, when Chloe, an African-born woman, ran away in 1817, after going out on the pretence of selling glassware, the notice in the *Barbados Mercury* stated that though an African, she might pass as a Barbadian on account of her good English; the public was therefore warned not to be deceived by her speech. The converse was also true. In 1805, when Betsy, an African-born woman, ran away the public was informed that she 'can speak little or no English, having been purchased from a Guinea ship about ten months ago'. She was captured after being at large for two months.[52]

There were also the habitual runaways who, after being caught, were soon on the move again. These women seemed unperturbed by the consequences of recapture: the imprisonment, flogging, branding with hot irons, and other forms of torture. They possessed a determination and irrepressible anti-slavery consciousness which, when recognized by slave owners, it was hoped would not contaminate the entire slave community. One such woman was Quashebah, a field hand at Codrington estate during the last quarter of the 18th century. She was retrieved on five separate occasions by her manager - September and December 1775, January 1777, August 1778, and September 1784. This represents a maroonage career spanning some nine years. Largely in response to persistent rebels like Quashebah, the estate manager paid £1. 2s. 6d. for a 'silver mark' with the letters 'SOCIETY' to brand all captives, but this was rejected by the Bishops of London, the estate's owners.[53]

From an analysis of lists of runaways published in Barbados newspapers between 1805 and 1830, Gad Heuman made certain generalizations about maroonage. Lists were taken from the *Barbadian* and the *Barbados Mercury* for the years 1805, 1810, 1815, 1819, 1824 and 1830; he did not use the data found in the *Barbados*

Globe. In this 1984 survey, of the 368 slaves listed as having run away 133 were female (36.5%), 90.8% of whom were Creoles. The percentage of women is surprisingly low and might have something to do with the nature of the sample. That the overwhelming majority of runaways were Creoles is to be expected, as African-born slaves represented less than 10% of the slave population during this period. Of these females, 75% were under the age of 30 years, which suggests that runaways were generally young and aggressive slaves. More females ran away to country parts than to the towns, while some 90% of those slaves who ran to towns from estates were men. Women were also more reluctant than men to venture overseas, and so female maroonage was characterized by more limited, but careful organization.[54]

The failure rate among runaways in Barbados was high. Less than 20% were able to effect permanent maroonage. Most were captured within three months, though those who fled overseas were less likely to be returned.

Sometimes these 'maritime maroons' had to keep moving, travelling as far as Jamaica and the Virgin Islands in order to avoid the probes sent out by their former owners. Notices were placed in the newspapers in Demerara, St. Vincent and St. Lucia, where it was assumed that Barbadian maroons would make their first stop. Constables in those colonies made financial gains from the capture and return of the Barbadians; rewards were higher for 'maritime' than 'inland' runaways. When returned to Barbados, the captured slaves were lodged in the Bridgetown 'cages', constructed specifically for confining captured runaways until they were retrieved by their owners. According to Dickson, the term 'cage' was derived from the way they were constructed, with parallel, open bars made from hardwood.

The Bridgetown cages were the central depositories for captured runaways, not only from overseas, but also from towns and rural areas. Imprisoned women were not given preferential treatment, but were likely to be sexually and physically abused by slave catchers and the poor-white officers who served as security guards. Since the mid-17th century, when these institutions appeared, the Legislative Council had provided that captives be supplied with food and drink until retrieved by their owners. Their names were listed in newspapers on a weekly basis. Owners were required to pay the recapture fee and maintenance cost before collecting their fugitives. Sometimes, if slaves died in the cage, the treasury compensated their owners.

Bridgetown was served by more than one cage and between 1790 and 1816 the cages were frequently reported to be overcrowded with both men and women. They were generally described as unhealthy, dirty-looking structures, with grated doors and windows. Dickson described them as miserable receptacles, and, next to the plantation dungeons, the most poignant emblems of slavery. In them, he noted, runaways were confined to irons or in stocks. The main cage, sited on Broad Street, was a source of much public outcry on account of the stench and disease that the townspeople considered to emanate from it. Its centrality, however, also served the purpose of reminding thousands of slaves of the possible result of their flight.

Following the success of the Imperial Abolitionist Movement in enforcing important reform measures after 1800, and the outlawing of the slave trade in 1807, the anxieties of Barbados slaves increased in relation to the possibilities of freedom; this as was reflected in an upsurge in the incidence of maroonage. More slaves not only challenged what they considered to be the diminishing power of planter rule, but also appeared more confident in their perception of having an effective anti-slavery ally.[55] Every week more slaves were advertised as having absented themselves, and numbers in the cages rose continuously after 1810. Between mid-March and mid-June 1829, for example, 15 slave women[56] were lodged in the cages from a list of over 55 reported missing. In the closing five years of slavery the number of slaves reported as runaways and those listed as recaptured and lodged in the cages was more than twice that for the first five years of the 19th century. Between 1830 and 1833, the weekly additions to the cages averaged twelve, while for the period 1801 to 1804 it averaged five. The Slave Emancipation Act was passed in 1833, effective from 1 August 1834, but during the interim the incidence of maroonage rapidly increased. Large number of slaves were obviously unwilling to wait upon the imperial time agenda, but prepared to take freedom in their own way, as Table 74.2 illustrates.

Table 74.2   Number and sex of runaways in Barbados, 25 July to 21 November 1833

Date of Listing	No of Females	No of Males	Total	% Female	% Male
25 July	15	33	48	31.25	68.75
1 August	9	40	49	18.36	81.63
4 November	14	42	56	25.00	75.00
11 November	15	34	49	30.61	69.38
14 November	17	39	56	30.35	69.64
21 November	18	36	54	33.33	66.66

Source: The *Barbadian*, 25 July 1833, C.O. 33/4; *Barbados Globe*, 1 August to 21 November, C.O. 33/4.

Armed Revolt

Anti-slavery resistance in Barbados was rarely characterized by collective armed violence. The records point to two minor aborted plots in 1649 and 1701, two major aborted rebellions in 1675 and 1692 and one island-wide revolt in 1816. These records are silent on the leadership participation of women in the aborted plots, though not in the actual rebellions. According to Ligon, the 1649 event was betrayed by two men, while the 1675 affair was betrayed by a woman. In neither event do we know anything of the gender balance of the executed rebels. During the turmoil of the 1680s, however, when slave owners constantly feared slave insurrections, several women were tried and executed for insurrectionist behaviour.[57] The Minutes of Council for the period 1685-88, for example, list five women executed at law for rebellious activity, and refer to their owners, John Whetstone, John Mills, William Andrews, Michael Chamberlaine and Ann Newton receiving 5,000 lb. of sugar and £20, £23, £15 and £12 compensation respectively from the treasury.[58]

The political history of the slave community suggests that traditional African-based concepts of men as warriors and political leaders continued to influence the extent of women's involvement in armed struggle. Few women have been identified in the plantation data as soldiers or leaders in the post-rebellion order. In the 17th century, slaves sought to recreate African-style kingdoms, while in the late 18th and early 19th centuries they sought more to establish military dictatorships. Women were always present in the development of these anti-slavery programmes, but individuals such as Nanny of the Jamaican maroons did not surface in the Barbados process.[59]

In the 1816 rebellion, however, the only physical war that slaves initiated to gain their freedom, the anti-slavery revolutionary consciousness of women was widely reported. The rebellion, which began on the night of 14 April 1816, was crushed by the joint forces of local militia and imperial troops after four days of bloody combat in which one white was killed, dozens shot and injured, and hundreds of blacks killed and executed as captives.[60] In the immediate pre-rebellion period, reports from both the urban and rural areas indicated that the women's behaviour had grown unusually aggressive and insubordinate toward their owners, and that some were displaying overtly militant tendencies. Elizabeth Fenwick, for example, a Bridgetown inhabitant, stated that her female domestics were refusing to take orders, and to work, even when threatened with corporal punishment,[61] while Joseph Belgrave, a prominent sugar planter, reported after the rebellion that women were in the forefront of insurrectionist behaviour. He told the Assembly that two days before the rebellion broke out:

On his way to Bridgetown, at Carrington's he was attacked by a black woman there, who (to his face) abused him, and said he was one of the fellows who prevented the slaves having their freedom – that it had been sent out for them, and they would have it.[62]

The context of this statement lies in the apparently widespread view circulating among slaves that the Imperial 1814 Registration of

Slaves Bill, which the Assembly rejected, was indeed related to their emancipation. The slaves, therefore, had no choice but to attempt their self-liberation in the face of slave owners' objection to constitutional emancipation. [63]

Much evidence suggests that the revolutionary ideologue of the rebel slaves was Nanny Grigg, a Creole woman from Simmon's plantation. Jackey, the organizational force behind the rebellion, was the Creole head driver of Simmon's estate, Bussa, the African-born head driver at Bayley's estate being the overall political leader. The presence of Nanny Grigg at Simmon's might have accounted for its status as the organizational nucleus of the rebellion. She emerges from the data as a literate woman, most probably an old household slave, informed about the successful Haitian rebellion, and a believer in the military solution to ending slavery. [64] Robert, a slave from Simmon's giving evidence before the Assembly's investigative committee after the rebellion, stated that:

Sometime the last year, he heard the negroes were all to be freed on New Year's Day. That Nanny Grigg, a negro at Simmon's, who said she could read, was the first person who told the negroes at Simmon's so; and she said she had read it in the Newspapers, and that her Master was very uneasy at it; that she was always talking about it to the negroes, and told them that they were all damned fools to work, for that she would not, as freedom they were sure to get. That about a fortnight after New Year's Day, she said the negroes were to be freed on Easter Monday, and the only way to get it was to fight for it, otherwise they would not get it; and the way they were to do, was to set fire, as that was the way they did in St Domingo. [65]

This ideological position, attributed to Nanny Grigg by Robert, was considered the conceptual key to an understanding of the rebellion by the Assembly's commissioners. Nanny had succeeded in creating a militant core of slaves at Simmon's who were linked into similar groups throughout the island. These groups of militants included women who were prepared to take up arms for self-liberation. Throughout the colony also, women, especially the plantation field hands, were reported as anxious to receive information about imperial anti-slavery developments. For example, William Yard, a free black man, stated that prior to the rebellion

On his return from General Williams' to town, he saw, at Ayshford's plantation, the gang of negroes receiving their allowance; that one of them, a woman, asked him if he

had brought any good news for them, and could tell anything about their freedom? [66]

When the rebellion began, hundreds of these women threw their support behind the militant group motivated by Nanny Grigg's ideological forum. They fought, attacked property and were killed in the quest for freedom. Colonel Codd, commandant of the imperial troops, admitted that the militia in particular 'under the irritation of the moment and exasperated at the atrocity of the insurgents', used their arms 'indiscriminately' and slaughtered many of these captives. [67] Many women were interrogated and executed for rebellion, though the majority were given corporal punishment and sent back to their estates. The fate of Nanny Grigg is not known, but it is more than likely that she was executed.

Women, then, were to be found not only in the vanguard of the blacks' anti-slavery movement, but were central to the reproduction of anti-slavery ideologies. As non-violent protestors, as maroons, as the protectors of social culture and as mothers, black women were critical to the forging of resistance strategies; and their anti-slavery consciousness is the core of the slave communities' survivalist culture.

Notes

1. Sampson Wood to Thomas Lane, 1796, Newton Papers, M. 523/288.
2. Ibid.
3. See for an overview of slave resistance historiography, Hilary McD Beckles, "The 200 Years War: Slave Resistance in the British West Indies: an Overview of the Historiography." *Jamaica Historical Review, vol. 13.*(1982b), pp. 1-12. Michael Craton, *Testing the Chains: Resistance to Slavery in the British West Indies.*(Illinois University Press, Ithaca, 1982). and in Journal of Caribbean History, Vol. 13, 1980, pp. 1-21; also Hilary Beckles, *Black Rebellion in Barbados: The Struggle Against Slavery, 1627-1838* (Antilles, Bridgetown, 1984a), pp. 1-11.
4. Orlando Patterson, *The Sociology of Slavery: an Analysis of the Origins, Development and Structure of Negro Slave Society in Jamaica* (London University Press, London, 1967); Eugene Genovese, *From Rebellion to Revolution: Afro-American Slave Revolts in the Making of the Modern World* (Louisiana University Press, Baton Rouge, 1979), Michael Craton, in ' Proto-Peasant Revolts? The late Slave Rebellion in the British West Indies, 1816-1832', Past and Present, Vol. 85 1979, pp. 99-125.
5. Hilary Beckles, *Black Rebellion in Barbados: The Struggle Against Slavery, 1627-1838* (Antilles, Bridgetown, 1984a); Barry Gaspar, *Bondsmen and Rebels: a Study of Master-Slave Relations in*

Antigua; with Implications for Colonial British America (Johns Hopkins University Press, Baltimore, 1984).

6. See Okon E. Uya, in 'Slave Revolts in the Middle Passage: A Neglected Theme', *The Calibar Historical Journal*, Vol. 1, No. 1, 1976; H. Wish, in 'American Slave Insurrections before 1861', *Journal of Negro History*, Vol. 22, 1937.

7. H. Wish, Ibid.

8. Daniel Mannix and Malcolm Cowley (eds), *Black Cargoes: a History of the Atlantic Slave Trade* (Viking Press, New York,1962).

9. Elizabeth Donnan (ed.) *Documents Illustrative of the History of the Slave Trade to America*, 4 Vols. (Carnegie Institute, Washington D.C., 1930-35), Vol. 2, p. 403.

10. Instructions to William Barry from the Royal African Company, 7 October 1725, in Elizabeth Donnan (ed.) *Documents Illustrative of the History of the Slave Trade to America*, 1930-35 Vol. 2, pp. 327-8.

11. Cited in Donnan (ed.) *Documents Illustrative of the History of the Slave Trade to America*, 1930-35, Vol. 2, p. 359.

12. Ibid. p. 403.

13. See B. Martin and M. Spurrel (eds), *The Journal of a Slave Trader: John Newton, 1750-1754* (London, 1962), pp. 102-103.

14. See G. Williams, *History of the Liverpool Privateers and Letters of Marque with an Account of the Liverpool Slave trade* (London, 1897), p. 511.

15. Cited in Okon E. Uya, in *The Calibar Historical Journal*, Vol. 1, No. 1, 1976.

16. For a fuller discussion of this theme, see Hilary Beckles and Karl Watson, in 'Social Protest and Labour Bargaining: The Changing Nature of Slaves' Responses to Plantation Life in Eighteenth Century Barbados', *Slavery and Abolition*, 1987, Vol. 8, No.3.

17. Newton Papers, M. 523/288.

18. William Dickson, *The Mitigation of Slavery* (Negro University Press Reprint, Westport,1970), pp. 96-7, 8, 439-41.

19. J. Harry Bennett, *Bondsmen and Bishops: Slavery and Apprenticeship on the Codrington Plantations of Barbados*, 1710-1838 (University of California Press, Los Angeles, 1958), pp. 30-31.

20. See Beckles, *Black Rebellion in Barbados: The Struggle Against Slavery*, 1627-1838, p. 67; Monica Schuler, in 'Day to Day Resistance to Slavery in the Caribbean during the Eighteenth Century', *Association for the study of Africa and the West Indies* (A.S.A.W.I), Bulletin 6, December 1973, pp. 62-5. Also, Bennett, *Bondsmen and Bishops: Slavery and Apprenticeship on the Codrington Plantations of Barbados*, 1710-1838, p. 28.

21. Beckles, *Black Rebellion in Barbados: The Struggle Against Slavery*, 1627-1838, p.67

22. Wood to Lane, 1796, Newton Papers, M.532/288.

23. Ibid.

24. Dolly Newton to Thomas Lane, 26 November 1807, Newton Papers, M.523; see also Karl Watson, *The Civilised Island: Barbados, a Social History* (Bridgetown, 1979), p.143.

25. Jenny Lane to Thomas Lane, August 1804, Newton Papers, M. 523/579.

26. Jenny Lane to Thomas Lane, 4 March 1813, Newton Papers, M. 523/690.

27. Letters to Thomas Lane, Newton Papers, M. 523/973; also, Wood to Lane, 1796, M. 523/288.

28. From Lane's interview with Elizabeth, Newton Papers, M. 523/973, f. 1-2.

29. Thomas Lane to John Alleyne, 3 May 1796, Newton Papers, M. 523/967, f.9.

30. Elizabeth Newton to Thomas Lane, 25 May 1801, Newton Papers, M. 523/441.

31. Minutes of Council, 20 December 1768, Lucas MSS. Vol. 27, 7, f.157, Barbados Public Library.

32. Ibid.

33. Ibid.

34. Bennett, *Bondsmen and Bishops*, p. 26.

35. See Beckles *Black Rebellion in Barbados*, p. 69.

36. William Dickson, (1789) *Letters on Slavery* (Negro University Press Reprint, Westport, 1970), pp. 20, 36.

37. *Barbados Mercury* (BM) 28 November 1815.

38. BM, 9 October 1810.

39. See Hilary Beckles, in Gad Heuman (ed.), *Out of the House of Bondage: Runaways, Resistance, and Maroonage in Africa and the New World* (Frank Cass, London, 1986); also in *Slavery and Abolition*, Vol.6, No.3,1985, pp. 79-95. See also a collection of papers on maroonage by Richard Price, (ed.) *Maroon Societies: Rebel Slave Communities in America* (Johns Hopkins University Press, Baltimore, 1973); Bernard Marshall 'Maroonage in Slave Plantation Societies: A Case Study of Dominica, 1785-1815', *Caribbean Quarterly*, Vol. 22, 1976, pp. 26-32; Richard Hart, in 'The Formation of a Caribbean Working Class', *The Black Liberator*, Vol. 2, No. 2, 1973/74, pp. 131-48.

40. William Dickson (1815), *The Mitigation of Slavery* (Negro University Press Reprint, Westport, 1970), p. 440.

41. Richard Hall, *Acts Passed in the Island of Barbados from 1643 to 1762 Inclusive* (London,1764), pp. 286-7. See also, for reforms to these provisions in the 1825 Slave Consolidation Act, Parliamentary Papers,1826-27.

42. BM, 2 February 1789, 31 March 1783, 1 January 1787.

43. *Barbados Globe* (BG), 9 March 1829, C.O.33/1.

44. Ibid., 30 April 1829.

45. Ibid., 29 June 1829.

46. Ibid., 22 June 1829.

47. BM, 6 April 1819.

48. BM, 14 October 1817.

49. *Barbados Globe*, 22 September 1831.

50. Ibid., 30 April 1829.

51. Ibid., 4 September 1834.

52. *Barbados Gazette*, 5-18 November 1746, C.O. 28/27. BM, 4 March 1817, 5 October 1805.

53. See Beckles, *Black Rebellion in Barbados*, p. 76.

54. Gad Heuman, in Gad Heuman (ed.) *Out of the House of Bondage*, 1986.

55. See Beckles, in D. Richardson (ed.) *Abolition and Its Aftermath: the Historical Context* (Frank Cass, London, 1985), pp. 80-105.

56. See *Barbados Globe* and *Demerara Advocate*, 12 March to 20 June 1829, C.O. 33/1.

57. Jerome Handler 'Slave Revolts and Conspiracies in 17th Century Barbados', *New West Indian Guide*, Vol. 56, 1982, pp. 5-41; Beckles in *Journal of Caribbean History*, Vol. 18, No. 2, 1984, pp. 1-18.

58. Beckles, *Black Rebellion in Barbados*, p. 43.

59. A. Tulon in *Caribbean Quarterly*, XIX, 1973, pp. 20-73. See Craton, *Testing the Chains*, pp. 254-56.

60. Beckles 'The Slave Drivers' War: Bussa and the 1816 Barbados Slave Uprising', in *Boletin de Estudios Latinoamericanos y del Caribe*, No. 39, December 1985, pp. 85-109; also, 'On the Backs of Blacks: The Barbados Free Coloureds' Pursuit of Civil Rights and the 1816 Rebellion', in *Immigrants and Minorities*, Vol. 3, No. 2, July 1984, pp. 167-76.

61. See Beckles, *Black Rebellion in Barbados*, p. 68.

62. Report into the Late Insurrection[s], p. 39.

63. See Karl Watson, *The Civilised Island*, pp. 125-8; Michael Craton, *Testing the Chains*, pp. 255-7; Beckles *Black Rebellion in Barbados*, pp. 106-7.

64. See Beckles, in *Boletin de Estudios Latinoamericanos y del Caribe*, No. 39, December 1985, pp. 85-109.

65. Confession of Robert, Report into the Late Insurrection[s].

66. Evidence of William Yard, Ibid.

67. Colonel Codd to Governor Leith, 25 April 1816, C.O. 28/85; Beckles, *Black Rebellion in Barbados*, pp. 104-105.

75

Women, Work and Resistance in the French Caribbean During Slavery, 1700–1848

BERNARD MOITT

This article details and analyses the social condition of enslaved black women in the plantation societies of the French Caribbean from 1700 to 1848, when slavery was abolished in the French colonial empire. It focuses primarily on the organization of labour and its impact on slave women in Martinique, Guadeloupe, Saint-Domingue and French Guiana. It shows that gender was not a consideration in the allocation of most tasks; that women did proportionately more hard labour than men; and that the allocation of tasks conditioned women's responses to slavery, including resistance.

Research on slave women in the French Antilles is still in its infancy. Among other factors, the lack of good historical studies of the French colonies, itself the result of the paucity and unevenness of the data, especially for the *ancien regime,* is primary. This situation has led to an over-reliance on too few sources. For the seventeenth century, one of the few notable works we have is that of Jean-Baptiste (Père) Du Tertre[1] which provides an important window on the early lives of the slaves, though it falls into Lucien Abénon's category of works promoting exoticism.[2] The documentation for the eighteenth century is extensive in some cases, and includes valuable studies centred on slave law by Moreau de Saint-Méry and Lucien Petraud.[3] In general, however, the eighteenth-century works have focused heavily on Saint-Domingue, the most productive and richest colony in the Caribbean, indeed the world, in this period. Even so, gaining access to primary sources not in the French archives is difficult, and those which are housed in the archives are often in poor condition. In general, the quality of the data is spotty and often suspect. For most of the century, statistics are often widely divergent from source to source for any given year, and reveal mathematical errors. There is a lack of precision in the sources as well. Thus, Jean-Baptiste (Père) Labat's multi-volume work on slavery[4] remains indispensable because of its detailed, precise and valuable accounts of slave plantation life, including gender-specific labour. This is the case in spite of the fact that Labat, a priest and proprietor of Fond Saint Jacques plantation in Martinique was, in Gordon Lewis' words, 'the epitome of racial bigotry'.[5]

Were it not for the monumental contribution of Gabriel Debien, who spent much of his scholarly life working on slavery in Saint-Domingue, it would be much more difficult to reconstruct the lives of slave women in that colony. In addition to tapping traditional sources, Debien collected data from private archives and papers in the possession of families whose relatives owned plantations in the colony. Debien, a pioneer, did not focus on women, but it has been possible to extract a great deal of information about their lives from the rich historical legacy he has left us. Many of the studies on slavery in the French Antilles have been inspired by him, and the magnitude of his intellectual contribution is reflected in this article as well.

After 1804, when Saint-Domingue was already the independent Republic of Haiti, scholars began to concentrate on other colonies, especially Guadeloupe where resistance to slavery was more openly demonstrated than in Martinique and French Guiana. Many anti-slavery works appeared during this century, especially in the 1840s, as a counter to works promoting the view that slavery was beneficial and worth preserving. But, as with the historiography of earlier centuries, scholars have come to rely on too few sources.

In the twentieth century, French scholars have not been much concerned with research on slavery in the French Antilles, although important works by Debien and others have been produced.[6] Over the last decade or so, there has also been an increasing development of indigenous scholarship on slavery, no doubt due in part to the outlet provided by the publishing house Editions Caribéennes in Paris. Arlette Gautier's pioneering study on women and slavery in the French colonies[7] is an important beginning, though its treatment of gender is very general.

Women and Labour

Women on plantations in the French Antilles performed a variety of tasks, but they were mostly relegated to the fields where they outnumbered men in the gangs. Gender was not a consideration in the allocation of most tasks requiring hard labour, as women were required to do the same work as men. But some occupations like midwifery were the preserve of women, and were thus gender-specific. On the other hand, plantation owners allocated virtually all of the specialised tasks, most of which were artisanal, to men. Thus, as in Africa, slave men maintained their traditional spheres of influence as coopers, carpenters, masons and blacksmiths. But slave owners also gave certain non-specialised tasks to men, such as being driver of the first gang, sugar boiler, messenger and coachdriver. In this way, the allocation of tasks placed the burden of hard labour on women. Thus, though women were generally outnumbered by men for most of the slavery period, they performed proportionately more hard labour than men.

Women formed the greater numbers of slaves in the field gangs whose members performed the bulk of the arduous labour upon which the economic viability of the plantations depended. Only recently has this aspect of women's labour

been given the recognition it deserves. Indeed, much has been written about the economic prowess of Caribbean plantation economies during slavery, but only in the last decade or so has the historiography begun to reflect the significant role women played in the process.[8] This is hardly surprising. From the outset, the sugar plantation was associated with hard, intensive labour[9] and its failure to become a successful enterprise before it became entrenched in the Caribbean from the 1640s, has always been attributed to the lack of it. As black slave labour displaced white, European indentured labour throughout the Caribbean in the ensuing decades, sugar production became inextricably linked to slavery. After purchasing 12 slaves for 5,700 francs for the Fond Saint-Jacques plantation in Martinique in 1698, Père Labat assured his Superior General that it was 'absolutely necessary to have slaves unless we wish to discontinue the work of the sugar operations.'[10] Likewise, hard labour became synonymous with male labour. A primary reason is the preference expressed by Caribbean planters for male slaves as opposed to female slaves. Though not always respected by slavers, this preference nonetheless served to reinforce traditional and sexist views about women and labour on the plantations.

The preference implied that black women (perhaps women in general) were incapable of the hard labour upon which the fortunes of Caribbean planters depended in the seventeenth, eighteenth and nineteenth centuries. Similarly, it fostered the view that black men were naturally suited to the role of hewers of wood and drawers of water. Indeed, this view was articulated by Rose Price, owner of the Worthy Park plantation in Jamaica in a pamphlet he published in 1832. Aimed at members of the House of Commons where the abolition of British slavery was being debated, Price's pamphlet pronounced that the black man (and woman by inference) was 'destined by Providence to labour in a state of slavery, of some sort or other, till the curse of Adam is removed from the face of the earth, and from the brow of man in God's appointed time.'[11]

Field Labour

On sugar plantations in the Caribbean, labour, it is said, was allocated based on the planter's needs and the slave's capacity to work.[12] In reality, need was the primary factor; and need was blind to sexual differentiation. Thus, slave women on Caribbean plantations performed, with few exceptions, the same tasks as men from an early stage. The majority of slaves, males and females, worked in the fields, where labour was most intensive. They also worked in the manufacturing end of the sugar operation, since the plantation was an agro-industrial complex. Male slaves were the sugar boilers and distillers, but on some estates, women distillers were preferred. Planters also gave the job of mill-feeding to women, who also performed general labour around the sugar works.

Field slaves were at the bottom of the slave hierarchy where women and men laboured like beasts. Pere Labat observed that 'slaves performed the work of horses, transporting merchandise from one place to the other.'[13] Justin Girod-Chantrans, a Swiss traveller who visited Saint-Domingue in the eighteenth century, also captured the association between slaves and beasts of burden when he remarked that 'there is no domestic animal from which as much work is required as slaves and to which as little care is given.'[14] He also noted that the slave driver used his whip 'indiscriminately on animals and blacks'.[15] Girod-Chantrans brought out the realities of gender-neutral labour when he described a slave gang at work:

They were about a hundred men and women of different ages, all occupied in digging ditches in a cane-field, the majority of them naked or covered with rags. The sun shone down with fulforce on their heads. Sweat rolled-from all parts of their bodies. Their limbs, weighed down by the heat, fatigued with the weight of their picks and by the resistance of the clayey soil baked hard enough to break their implements, strained themselves to overcome every obstacle. A mournful silence reigned. Exhaustion was stamped on every face, but the hour of rest had not yet come. The pitiless eye of the manager patrolled the gang of several foremen armed with long whips moving periodically between them, giving stinging blows to all who, worn out by fatigue, were compelled to take a rest – men or women – young or old without distinction.[16]

The gang which Girod-Chantrans observed probably contained more women than men, given the pattern of task allocation. It was almost certainly the first gang, judging from the tasks in which its members were engaged. In the French Antilles, there were two or three field gangs on sugar plantations, depending on need. The first gang, the great gang, consisted of the strongest male and female slaves who performed the most

arduous tasks such as preparing the soil for planting, weeding, cutting canes and manufacturing sugar.[17] It was always led by a male slave driver. Less robust slaves, newly arrived slaves who had to be acclimatised, pregnant slaves and nursing mothers comprised the second gang which performed lighter and more varied tasks than those of the first gang, including the cultivation of food crops. On some sugar plantations weeding was the preoccupation of women in the second gang.[18] The third gang was made up of children between the ages of 8 and 13 years who picked weeds and gathered cane trash from around the mill. At age 13 or 14, young slaves moved up to the great gang.[19]

The driver of the third gang was a woman who normally served a dual purpose. She not only administered discipline but was able, according to Poyen de Saint-Marie, to care for younger slaves. Although the plantation did not pay much attention to the third gang, Poyen de Saint-Marie underlined its importance by stressing the tender care which he felt only women could provide because of their sex, and the knowledge which they were in a position to impart to young slaves. De Saint-Marie was inadvertently saying that the plantation depended on women to socialise young slaves into slavery. He writes:

The primary task of the female driver of the child gang must be the preservation of the children's health. She must monitor them constantly and prevent them from eating harmful substances. She must teach them how to perform their duties well . . . She must also instruct them to obey orders without question and to resist bickering among themselves. As nothing accounts more for laziness among blacks than chigoe infection, she must inspect, clean and remove chigoes from their feet daily. At a young age, children are very receptive. Thus, much depends on authority figures who mold them into either good or bad subjects. Those who execute their tasks well merit much from their masters. On the other hand, those who neglect their tasks and shatter the planters' confidence are guilty.[20]

Women outnumbered men in the field gangs, as the following examples from Saint-Domingue demonstrate. On the plantation Beaulieu, there were 141 slaves in 1768 of whom 87 were males and 54 females. But only 9 males worked in the fields as opposed to 20 females. Similarly, on the Galbaud du Fort plantation female slaves slightly outnumbered male slaves but performed almost all the field work. Of the 54 males on the plantation, only 9 were in the fields. But 44 of the 58 females were field workers.[21] Also, on the Fleuriau plantation in the late eighteenth century, 60 of the 80 slaves (that is, 75 per cent) working in the fields were women.[22]

The association between women and field work began with the rise of the slave plantation economies in the seventeenth century and lasted until emancipation in 1848. Thus the working lives of most slave women changed little over time. Plantation records which list the occupation of slaves confirm that most women worked in the fields while men monopolised the specialised tasks. Of the 83 active men on the Breda plantation in the North Plain of Saint-Domingue in 1785, just after the owner had increased the male work force, about half fell into the category of skilled workers. Thirty-six men worked in the fields, while 6 were inactive. On the contrary, 73 of the 78 active women were in the fields and 5 were inactive. Thus, 'Except for the [two] domestics, the 51-year-old nurse and the 53-year-old nurse maid – a position reserved for the aged – all the able-bodied women were field workers, even the 15 creole women among them'.[23]

A list of 218 state-owned slaves, mostly from Martinique, Guadeloupe and French Guiana, who were granted freedom en masse in 1847, contains mainly women field slaves. French grammar makes it possible to make this assertion as the slaves were listed by professions in the masculine and feminine. Moreover, there are instances of two and three generations of women slaves, all confined to field work. For example, Genviève, 52, of Martinique, is listed along with her three daughters, Marthe-Louise, 32, Augustine, 24, and Jeanne-Rose, 11, all field workers. While the women worked in the fields, Auge, 53, Genviève's husband, cracked the whip in his role as slave driver. Likewise, Célestre, 40, of Guadeloupe, was a field worker, while her husband Pierre-Louis, 58, was a slave driver. Another Guadeloupean woman slave, Séverine, 46, was also a field worker and her husband, Pierre-Noel, 51, was a sugar boiler.[24]

Given the rigours of slave life, it would be difficult to overlook the case of Félicie, 40, yet another field slave from Guadeloupe. She had eight children ranging in age from 1 to 15 years. Her 15-year-old daughter, Célaine, also worked in the fields, as did her other daughters Eugénie, 14, Angélina, 11, and Marie-Gabrielle, 9. Her only son Félix, 9, was a field slave as well, but the fields would have been the only place for him at that age. Her other children, aged 5 and under, were too young to work.

Many other such cases were common among women slaves from French Guiana like Mémée, 38, a field slave married to 38-year-old Wacoulé, also known as Emder, a slave driver. But there were also women slaves such as Marie-Rose the sixth, 79, who gave religious instruction to young slaves on the Gabrielle plantation.[25]

French scholars have acknowledged the numerical superiority of female over male slaves in the field gangs, but have generally accepted this labour division as the natural order of things. Like Michael Craton who has found it 'a curious society, as well as an inefficient agricultural economy, in which women for the most part were the labourers and men the specialist workers',[26] and Hilary Beckles who advances the argument that West African women were 'acculturised to agricultural tasks, more so than men, and might have been considered more adaptable, at least in the short run,'[27] they have adopted different positions on this issue. In the nineteenth century, André Lacharière expressed the opinion that such a labour division

will become more serious and will have a negative effect on reproduction. For this reason, there is no issue more important and worthy for the legislature to concentrate upon than on the increase by reproduction of the agricultural population whose maintenance is indispensable to the existence of the colonies.[28]

Lacharière inadvertently placed the continued existence of the French colonies in slave women's hands. Sexist as his comment may be, it strengthens the view that though slave women were primarily used as labour units, they were still expected to reproduce.

Victor Schoelcher, a philanthropist who sought to dramatise the plight of the slaves in the French colonies during the nineteenth century as a way of strengthening the argument for abolition, believed that slave 'women were perfectly suited to field work' and attributed the larger presence of women in the fields to the systematic promotion of young male slaves from field work to artisanal and other types of specialised labour, leaving the heavy tasks which required no skills to women. As he explained:

It is often the case in the field gangs that there are more women than men. This is how it can be explained. A plantation is, in itself, a small village. As it is usually established a considerable distance from major centres, it must provide all of its needs ... masons and blacksmiths as well as animal watchmen. All the apprentices who are destined to replace them are now in the field gangs (the [slave] driver included), and this diminishes the male population available for field work.[29]

This explanation has come down through time. Indeed, Gabriel Debien notes that there were always roofs rent by the wind, broken walls to repair, roads to improve and bridges to build. Planters aimed to get much of this work done after the canes had been cut, but the work often dragged on for many weeks due to interruptions by hurricanes and other problems.[30] On the plantations Boucassin and Vases in Saint-Domingue between 1774 and 1798, men did external work such as road repair, forced labour for the state on public works projects, and loaded barrels of sugar on to vessels. But whereas the ablest and strongest men were promoted in time to acquire enviable positions, becoming boilers, makers of animal-drawn carts and other specialists, women had few such distinctive positions which would have required an exemption from field labour. Debien holds the view that women

were better adapted than men to continuous work in the fields, perhaps because work outside the plantation and cane cutting – a task reserved for men – were considered to be the most demanding. As much as possible, it was seen as desirable for women to stay on the plantations ... They were never conscripted for forced labour required by the state. It may also be that women were easier to subjugate or were less subject to illness.[31]

Debien is suggesting that by virtue of their gender, women's mobility and occupational categories were restricted. This is more plausible than his assertion that men did more strenuous work. Cane-cutting, for example, was not a male occupation in all the colonies. Women also did corvée labour in some colonies, though it is not clear what type. A list of dead slaves from the sugar plantation Noël in Remire in French Guiana includes the slave woman Doué, who went to perform corvée labour on 12 April 1690 and contracted a fever which forced her to return two days later. On 28 April she gave birth prematurely to a stillborn boy.[32] This suggests that she was in an advanced state of pregnancy, but this did not exempt her from hard labour. Corvée labour usually involved public works projects such as the construction of forts and roads, and plantations had to send a proportion of their slaves, sometimes just the men. During corvée

planters did not feed slaves, so they had to manage how they could. Epidemics were therefore prevalent among corvée gangs, as was *marronage* or flight.

It should be emphasised that the structure of plantation society was sexist and that this sexism was reflected in the organization of labour. Thus the slave women's plight resulted largely from patriarchy and the sexist orientation of Caribbean slave plantation society which put them into structural slots that had no bearing on their abilities. This means that women were not permitted to move into roles traditionally ascribed to males. As Debien notes, 'At about the same age, there was no differential in the work performed by either sex', yet 'all their life, women remained in the fields'.[33]

After a field was cleared and prepared for planting sugar cane, field slaves, mostly women, planted cane cuttings using either the holing or trenching method, either of which was equally laborious. Using bills and cutlasses, women also cut canes, a long, back-breaking task which had to be done once the canes were ripe, irrespective of illness among the slaves, epidemics and the inevitable hurricanes. As cane-cutting had to be synchronised with other phases of the sugar operations, labour needs were at their maximum during the harvest and the pressure on women slaves was likely to be severe from January to about July each year. Indeed, Père Labat noted that it was customary to begin cutting canes on Saturdays so that the grinding process could begin at midnight on Mondays.[34] He assigned 25 slaves to cut canes on Fond Saint-Jacques, arguing that since it 'was the lightest of tasks, women do just as much of it as men'. This may well have been his reason for assigning mostly women to this task.[35] But during the harvest the sugar operations often ran for 24 hours and field slaves worked up to 18 hours per day[36] between the cane fields and the mill where the manufacturing process took place. The labour of first gang slaves was therefore heavily drawn upon to supplement mill labour and was rewarded with glasses of *tafia* (local rum) from the planters.

Mill-feeding

Sugar manufacturing involved the transformation of sugar cane juice into crystallised sugar through a process of heating. It required a number of mill workers, some of whom fed the canes into the sugar mills. In the French Antilles, mill-feeders were usually women. Much has been made of the role of the boiler who, in Richard Dunn's words, was 'the most valued laborer on the plantation staff'[37] in that he skilfully turned raw cane juice into sugar by means of a long, tedious and complicated process requiring sound judgement and an acute sense of timing. Simply put, if the planter had no sugar to sell, or if the sugar was of poor quality, revenue would decline. Though true, this argument minimises the contribution of women in the field and in sugar manufacturing.

In making sugar, Caribbean planters used three roller vertical mills powered by wind, water or animals. There was no technological advancement in this system, which, according to Christian Schnakenbourg, remained practically unmodified for close to two centuries after 1640.[38] This is not surprising as technological advancement is not usually encouraged in areas where labour is abundant, if not dispensable. Schnakenbourg has found that the vertical mills were highly inefficient, poor energy users and spun either too fast or too slowly.[39] The technology was the same, in all regions of the Caribbean as were the problems, especially those related to mill-feeding.

Père Labat has left a detailed description of mill-feeding which reveals a great deal about women's labour. On many estates in the French Antilles, four women usually worked at the mill, but most often the nature of the work really required five. Women's labour at the mill was particularly taxed when the canes from the fields arrived at the mill so rapidly that there was hardly time to clean the equipment – a necessary measure which ensured the smooth running of the operations. Women also had to labour more extensively when working with water-driven mills which ground the canes much faster than wind or animal-driven mills, or when the huts in which they stored bagasse (cane residue) to dry was far from the mill.

One woman transported bundles of canes brought close to the mill by animal-driven carts to the principal woman mill-feeder. If time permitted, she arranged them in piles to the left of the mill-feeder who then put them on the mill table in a feeding position. If she was pressed for time, she simply dumped the bundles and moved on to fetch others.

Among other things, the principal mill-feeder had to decide how much cane could safely be fed into the rollers. When the work piled up and she was in a hurry, she cut the two cords which held the bundles of cane together with a bill and pushed an entire load between the first two rollers.

The mill-feeder took greater risks when working with water-driven mills. The speed of the mills meant that she seldom had the time to untie the bundles of cane, and fed one untied bundle after another as a consequence. Labat believed that such a practice should have been discouraged as too many canes passing through the mill put enormous stress on it, forcing the rollers to expand in which case they extracted less juice. He insisted that mills be constantly and steadily fed, however.[40]

A third woman folded the residue (bagasse) and fed it back between the first and third rollers to extract the maximum juice. One, sometimes two, other women assembled the residue into bundles which they carried into a large shed to be stored, dried and used as firewood for the coppers. They gathered small pieces which could not be bundled in baskets made from *laines,* locally grown reeds, and dumped them near the mill as animal feed, especially for horses, cows and pigs.[41] When the storage huts were too far from the mill, the women were often too pressed to bundle the residue and resorted to dumping it as animal feed in order to rush back to the mill. This deprived the operations of valuable, highly combustible firewood and points up an important dimension of women's labour.

Planters considered mill-feeding not only women's work, but work which dishonoured male slaves. In fact, Labat used it as a form of punishment. He gave male slaves, whom he deemed slack or lazy, the work the second woman mill-feeder performed, a task normally given to the weakest woman slave employed at the mill.[42] This view minimises the hazards of mill-feeding, however.

The grinding process was fraught with danger. Apart from miscarriages and other misfortunes which women alone experienced, female slaves invariably suffered numerous accidents, many of which resulted in infirmity, while working at the mill. To be sure, the danger of being crushed by the rollers was very real. As soon as the canes touched the edge of the rollers they were drawn into the machinery rapidly. Finger tips which came into contact with the rollers produced deadly results, but the conditions under which slave women laboured at the mill made such accidents inevitable. Accidents were frequent at night when women were tired and drowsy after labouring in the fields all day. Labat's description of the accidents which resulted in the maiming and death of such slave women is a very graphic, but realistic picture of the dangers to which the slave system subjected them, year after year. For this reason, it is worth citing in full. He noted that accidents were:

certainly frequent among female slaves . . . particularly at night, when, exhausted by hard labour during the daytime, they fall asleep while passing the canes. Dragged towards the machinery which they follow involuntarily still clutching the canes in their hands, they thus become caught up in it and crushed before they can be rescued. This is particularly the case when the mill is water-driven where the movement is so rapid that it is physically impossible to stop it in time to save the lives of those whose fingers are already drawn in. On such occasions, the quickest remedy is to promptly sever the arm with a bill (which is why it makes sense to always keep one without the curved tip at the head of the table, sharp and ready to use if needed.) It is better to cut off the arm than to see a person passing through the rollers of a mill. This precaution has been very useful to us at Fond S[aint] Jacques where one of our women slaves was drawn into the mill. Fortunately for her, . . . a male slave was able to stop the mill in time to give us the opportunity to sever half of the mangled arm, and thus save the rest of her body.

A woman slave belonging to the Jesuits was not as fortunate. In attempting to pass something to the woman on the other side of the mill, her shirt sleeves became caught in the cogs, and her arm, followed by the rest of her body was drawn into the machinery in an instant, before she could be given help. Only the head does not pass; it separates from the neck and falls on the side where the body entered.[43]

Planters did not focus on these accidents, perhaps because they considered slaves indispensable for most of the slavery period, but it is highly probable that they occurred in all the French colonies. In 1699 the hand of a woman slave belonging to Sieur Gressier of Trois Riviéres in Guadeloupe became caught in the machinery. She attempted to free it by pulling at it with the other hand, but both became entangled. Hearing her cries, the sugar boiler on duty rushed to her assistance, pulling her arms away from the rollers. Another male slave wedged a piece of metal between the rotating cogs of the mill to stop it.

But the force of the water-driven mill cracked a cog, forcing out the piece of metal which then lodged between the spinning rollers. The pieces of shrapnel which this explosion produced were so forcefully ejected that they punctured the stomach and fractured the head of the slave who installed the wedge. Meanwhile, backed by the increased force of the water, the rollers drew the sugar boiler in along with the woman mill-feeder, both meeting their deaths in this way.[44]

Writing in 1845, Jean-Baptiste Rouvellat de Cussac mentioned that a woman slave on a plantation in Fort Royal in Guadeloupe had a hand crushed by the mill. In another incident, a 12-year-old girl was crushed by the rollers, and her head fell on the mill table. These occurrences which, according to him, occurred on other plantations,[45] indicate that working conditions around the mill remained horrendous and continued to take a toll on women's lives down to the end of slavery. Also, while Rouvellat de Cussac and others might have highlighted such cases to enhance the struggle for abolition, the use of young women slaves as mill-feeders suggests that they were moved into the first gang arbitrarily, without regard for age.

Some planters believed that slave women could avoid accidents at the mill if they took certain precautions. Women mill-feeders, especially the second mill-feeder, had to avoid standing on racks or other objects to gain a height advantage. Also, since slumber was the principal cause of accidents, planters had to ensure that women smoked and sang as they worked.[46] How this was to be achieved, it is not clear. Normally, the sugar boiler was considered the head of operations, but he was not necessarily in sight of the women. Planters put the emphasis on preventing women from slumbering, but the problem was fatigue and unsafe working conditions. Indeed, during the harvest the sugar mill operated around the clock. This was also the case in other areas such as Jamaica where women suffered similar accidents.[47]

Arlette Gautier may well be right in attributing the high incidences of infirmity among women to mill-feeding,[48] although she cites no evidence. Records from the Breda plantation in Saint-Domingue show a larger number of old women than men, but there was a higher level of infirmity among the women. There were also more women, mainly field slaves, than men who were considered old and worn-out though they had not yet reached the age of 60. Of 89 adult males in 1784, 9 were incapacitated; of 82 adult women, 15 were infirmed. What is particularly revealing about these statistics is that the Breda estate was considered better than most in terms of the treatment of slaves. For many years, Bayou de Libertas, Toussaint L'Ouverture's mentor who had a reputation for being fairer than others in working slaves, was the overseer.[49]

Rum Distillation

The distillation of local rum was another important labour activity performed by slave women in the French Antilles. Indeed, the Rochechouart plantation in Martinique had two women distillers.[50] This strong rum, which the slaves called *tafia* or *guldive*, was made at the *vinaigrerie*, a place which Labat correctly acknowledged should have been more appropriately called the *distillatoire*. Local usage of the word *vinaigrerie* had become so ingrained, however, that it remained in vogue. The fact is that women made rum, not vinegar. The label *vinaigrerie* may well have diminished, in the minds of many, the skills required to make this economic activity a success.

The reasons why planters preferred women distillers are cynical, if not patronising, however. They assumed that women were less apt to drink than men. Even so, they had no confidence in women's ability to abstain. Thus, according to Labat, they selected slave women 'considered loyal, and carefully monitored their reliability in an attempt to prevent them from yielding to the temptation of overindulgence, thereby risking insanity.' To guard against this possibility, and to deter them from stealing, Labat gave women distillers a jar of *tafia* each.[51] It would be interesting to find out whether this form of bribery was successful, since there was a local market for *tafia*.

The sale of *tafia* was an important part of a planter's revenue.[52] Besides being shipped abroad, it was sold in the colonies. In late seventeenth century Martinique it fetched 6 *sols* per jar, more in areas not engaged in sugar production, and at times when wines and liquor from France were either rare or scarce. With 120 slaves working steadily for 45 days per year, Labat calculated that the Fond Saint-Jacques plantation produced 60 barrels of *tafia*, of which at least 54 could be sold. It is no wonder that the distillery was off limits to unauthorised slaves.[53]

Women's labour in the distillery enabled planters to defray costs and shirk their responsibilities to slaves, an aspect of the women's contribution which has been overlooked by scholars. Indeed, some masters gave slaves a quantity of *tafia* per week in place of flour and meat, a clear violation of the *Code Noir*. Such slaves were sometimes forced 'to roam about on Sundays trying to trade their liquor for flour and other essentials. This they use as a pretext for arriving very late and tired for work on Mondays. Those who drink their supplies are forced to steal from their masters at the risk of being killed or imprisoned'.[54]

Besides distilling *tafia*, women also did a number of odd jobs around the mill and distillery, many of which required heavy lifting. Women transported cane syrup and scum from the mill to the woman distiller. Women also changed the hot coppers and lifted and loaded merchandise into small boats. They swept the sugar works, washed and cleaned the vertical rollers and washed the muslin used to strain the cane juice. The boiler had to ensure that the muslin was properly washed and dried by the sun, not by the heat generated by the hot coppers which destroyed the fabric. Planters gave the fabric to the slaves when it was worn and no longer useful to the boiler. The slaves used it as blankets for themselves and their children.[55]

Domestic Labour

Not all slave women were subjected to the harsh conditions characteristic of field-related work. The social reality of women in domestic labour must be seen from a different angle. Indeed, Pierre de Vassière viewed domestics as the fortunate lot,[56] but it is worth reiterating that, whether in the field or in the house, all black women were oppressed by slavery

When Moreau de Saint-Méry wrote that 'in Saint-Domingue everything takes on an air of opulence', he was referring to the multitude of slaves in the households of European slave-owners who apparently considered it a matter of dignity to have four times the required number of domestics.[57] He may as well have been talking about any of the Caribbean colonies during slavery. The number of domestics varied according to types of establishments and households, but there was a general tendency for slave-owners to have more servants than they needed. On the estates of rich sugar planters in Guadeloupe, domestics accounted for as much as 15 per cent of the slave force. In general, Guadeloupean planters also had a reputation for having many domestics, as most were not absentee planters[58] as was the case in Saint-Domingue. Also, slave-owners living in the towns usually had large numbers of domestics. Did they entertain more than other slave-owners? Perhaps they did.

Domestic slaves, male and female, performed a variety of tasks from as early as seven or eight years of age. This category of slaves included cooks, most of whom were males, servants, washerwomen and laundresses. But seamstresses, nurses, midwives and doctresses were domestics as well. For the most part, their work was lighter than that of field slaves and their life style was envied by the former. Of the domestics, cooks have received more attention than most, partly because they performed such a vital function. Indeed, the French placed a high premium on cooks, whose estimated value was higher than that of most other slaves, the median price in Guadeloupe being 2,600 livres in the period 1770-89. On 27 May 1783 M.L. Delagrange sold the slave cook Céladon for a record 8,000 livres. Another male cook, Gilles, owned by the merchant and militiaman E. Druault, was estimated at 4,500 livres in 1785.[59]

Scholarly interest in cooks must also be due to the fact that food was a powerful weapon in the hands of the slaves. No case illustrates this point more than that of the 55-year-old slave woman Magdeleine, head cook and surgeon on the plantation Caroline in French Guiana owned by Brémond and Favard. Around 1831, the owners incensed Magdeleine by replacing her son-in-law, the slave Mirtil, with Quenessou, a Frenchman, in the position of manager which he had occupied for many years. Through the skilful use of poison, Magdeleine made sure that neither Quenessou nor Rimal, another Frenchman who assumed the position after the former fell seriously ill, could occupy the post.[60] Thus control of the pharmacy and the kitchen put Magdeleine in a strategic position and her actions dramatise the relation between work and resistance.

Slave women, not men, cooked for the slave gangs and slave children who were left in their care while their mothers worked in the fields. The slaves called these women 'mama',[61] a designation Gautier believes is an African custom whereby men who were far from home and did not traditionally cook adopted a new mother who did the cooking for them.[62] 'Mamas' also did much of the preparatory work such as pounding manioc and transporting water. In Saint-Domingue, a group of women who pounded grain and did other domestic chores were persuaded by another group of women to become maroons in 1769[63]. As the flight of such a group would have undoubtedly dealt a severe blow to the plantation, the women may have been targeted because of the work they did. This case demonstrates that the allocation of tasks determined patterns of resistance among women.

Unlike cooks, most servants were women, both on the plantations and in private dwellings in urban centres. These were slaves who managed the household, and did the washing, using ropes, oranges and lemons for soap – as well as the cleaning and pressing. In 1785 Sr J. Vatable, militia major and merchant in Basse-Terre, had 13 slaves, among them a laundress, 2 male cooks, a woman servant and 2 washerwomen.[64] But servants also worked in commercial establishments. In 1779, L.F. Lemercier sold his sugar estate at Pérou in Abymes (Guadeloupe) for 450,000 livres and bought a large dwelling at Morne-à-L'Eau which he furnished with luxurious items such as porcelain, crystals, gilded mirrors, a cuckoo clock from Paris, ivory, marble and silverware. He established an inn and by 1782 he had 18 slaves[65] who had to polish the silver and clean the mirrors.

Though their presence was a sign of prestige, there were relatively few seamstresses among domestics, except in wealthy households.[66] Some were sent to France by their masters and creole wives to apprentice for several years. Upon their return, they made and repaired their mistresses' clothes and those of the slaves from cloth distributed by planters on Christmas Eve. They also altered ready-made clothes given to slaves.[67] Sewing for the slaves was probably a major part of the seamstress's job. Indeed, in 1778, Stanislas Foäche instructed his overseer, Paris, to keep the seamstress occupied sewing the yearly issue of clothing for the slaves. Foäche normally gave seamstresses the cloth in bulk, as it was easy to purchase. To avoid abuse, he recommended that Paris record the amount of cloth issued as some, considered '*mauvais sujets*' (bad numbers), sold some of it to buy liquor.[68]

There were also slave-owners who put young women to work as apprentices with the prospect of exploiting their labour. In a letter to his mother dated 6 August 1786, Raymund de Beaumont, who had arrived in Saint-Domingue in 1774 to seek work as a refiner and make a fortune, bought young slaves both as domestics and as an investment. To alleviate the economic hardships he faced, he told his mother that he had bought a boy and girl (10-11 years) whom he made into a valet and an apprentice seamstress. Of the girl he wrote, 'She shows great promise of becoming a first class seamstress, but she possesses every imaginable fault, among them stealing and a tendency towards *marronage*. De Beaumont found the going tough in Saint-Domingue, as salaries were low, irregularly paid and night work frequent. He was reduced to wearing his father's old clothing after the latter, a planter in Léogane, died. The fact that he purchased the slaves in spite of what he regarded as exorbitant prices, 2,500-2,700 livres, suggests that he considered the investment economically sound. Certainly, as slavery was coming to a close, a considerable number of women slaves between the ages of 17 and 24 were seamstresses, including several of 218 slaves freed by a royal ordinance in 1847.[69]

Women slave-owners often made hucksters out of female slaves who retailed items such as charcoal, fruits and vegetables. In the 1840s one such slave-owner in Saint-Pierre (Martinique) bought bulk goods and sent one of her women slaves to towns and villages to market them. According to Rouvellat de Cussac, 'This old woman had several such women slaves engaged in a profitable enterprise.' The severity of the punishment administered to slave women who did not live up to their mistresses' expectations may mean that the revenue which retail operations generated was important to them. Referring to the slave-owner above, de Cussac observed that it was 'hell for the slave who buys too dear or credits goods' as her 'old mistress would whip her with the *rigoise*,'[70] the thick thong of cowhide. Indeed, the notorious brothers, Charles and

Octave Jahan, of Martinique inflicted a vicious beating on the pregnant woman slave Rosette after she returned late from Saint-Pierre where she had been sent to sell charcoal.[71] As this was the second such beating in a matter of days, it is possible that Rosette consciously chose to defy her masters' wishes, a form of resistance which the relative independence of her work likely made possible. Certainly, the tone of the spirited testimony she gave in court against them points in this direction.

The other forms of domestic labour mentioned above relate to health care. In this area of work, nurses and midwives were central, as most plantations could only afford to engage a doctor periodically and in emergencies. Thus slaves looked after most of their own health care needs with the help of doctresses. That nine of them turned up in Vanony-Frisch's sample of Guadeloupean slaves[72] is certainly revealing, as not much attention has been paid to slave women and medicine.

Nurses staffed the plantation hospital or 'sickhouse' which Stanislas Foäche viewed as the most essential building.[73] Labat gave the nursing position to well-behaved and intelligent slave women who looked after the slaves diligently, made the hospital beds and permitted entry only to those authorised by the surgeon.[74] This position was seen as a sign of upward mobility on the Fleuriau plantation in Saint-Domingue. It was highly sought after but usually given to an older slave woman who had spent her formative years in the fields.[75] Overall, age was an important criterion. On the Breda plantation, the hospital nurse was 51 years old.[76]

Caring for sick slaves involved making tea, syrups and herbal remedies prescribed by the surgeons. Nurses also prepared special meals, paid regular visits to slaves convalescing in their own huts and ensured that they complied with the doctor's orders to exercise or return to work.[77] Nurses were women with authority. They treated simple cases of illness which saved the doctor time and the plantation money; they applied bandages and reported to the surgeon or planter the condition of the sick and the nightly events at the hospital. Slave women, in Foäche's words, were far more adept at diagnosing and treating the sick than male slaves. The importance he placed on good nurses is evident from the following comments:

A good nurse is a precious subject. She must also be intelligent as she must be able to distinguish between the early, advanced and late stages of fevers, and communicate them to the surgeon who cannot always monitor the sick. She must know how to dress wounds and use bandages in a multi-purpose way. She must be strong enough to resist the indiscreet demands of the sick and prevent their relatives and friends from bringing them things which may do them harm. If she performs her duties enthusiastically, treat her as well as you do the slave driver of the first gang. Next to him, she is the most useful slave on the plantation. If the plantation is large, give her a young, intelligent woman slave to assist and be trained by her. This is essential as the loss of a nurse can be devastating. The midwife can also assist the nurse when she is not busy. [78]

The multi-dimensional nature of domestic labour is brought out in Foäche's notes. The midwife, usually an older, prized slave woman who had put in a lifetime of service in the field gangs, and whose main duty was delivering babies, was expected to contribute to other spheres of domestic labour. This contribution was not always in the line of health care. Foäche instructed his overseer to have the cook or midwife on the Jean-Rabel estate learn how to make bread. Also, the nurse on the estate was once a cook and baker and 'like all intelligent people, she has succeeded in all the positions she has held. Fortunately, she is not old.'[79]

Given the high rates of infant mortality on slave plantations, the work of midwives was seen as crucial to the growth of the slave population. Masters believed that a good midwife could ensure more live births; that a hostile one was a danger to the expansion of the slave force. The instructions which Foäche gave to his manager in 1775 reveal both the barbarity to which women who could not produce a live child were subjected and the role of the midwife. For a live birth, Foäche ordered that the midwife be given 15 livres and the woman who delivered the baby, cloth. If the child died at birth, both women were to be whipped and the one who lost the child placed in iron collars until she became pregnant again.[80] But fear of such reprisals did not result in higher birth rates.

The foregoing case demonstrates that although domestic slaves received many perks such as money, better accommodation and larger allotments of rations, there were also drawbacks. The biggest drawback was instability. This was the case even among those who had served two generations in the same household. Such domestics were more likely to be sold when plantations changed hands and when planters left the colonies to return to France. The change was often so traumatic that it led them to become maroons.[81] Also, some female domestics had to remain single as a result of their ties to the master's household. The Jesuit priest Mongin, who lived in Martinique in the seventeenth century, also noted that some French slave-owners refused to consent to the marriage of their female slaves so as not to be deprived of their services, especially child care at night. [82] Clearly, all slaves were trapped by their condition, irrespective of the occupational categories and class distinctions to which they gave rise.

Conclusion

It is clear that gender was virtually obliterated under slavery since women, for the most part, were required to do the same work as men, in addition to work considered as women's work. Most slave women spent their lives in the fields, but others engaged in a range of domestic tasks which included not only household chores, but health care, retailing and sewing. Women performed a greater variety of tasks than men, and did proportionately more hard labour. Some aspects of women's work also put them at greater risk of infirmity and death than men, even in the case of gender-specific labour such as midwifery.

The psychological consequences of labouring in hazardous conditions or under threat of death may never be revealed, nor the social implications of a situation in which slave women did most of the hard work and men the whipping. But there are areas of women's labour which require more attention. Slave women who engaged in commerce and petty trading on their owners' behalf present good possibilities for future research. Also, there is hardly a mention of seamstresses in French historiography on slavery. Slave-owners expected many women domestics to fulfil a multiplicity of functions which makes the study of labour complex and challenging. As scholars rise to these challenges, we are certain to achieve a greater understanding of the social condition of slave women in Caribbean society.

Notes

1. Jean-Baptiste (Père) Du Tertre, *Histoire-générale des Antilles habitées par les Français*, 4 vols., 1671 reprint (Fort-de-France: Editions des horizons Caraïbe, 1973).
2. Lucien Abénon, *La Guadeloupe de 1671 à 1759*, 2 vols. (Paris: L'Harmattan, 1987), 1, p. 7.
3. M. Moreau de Saint-Méry, *Lois et Constitutions des Colonies Françaises de l'Amérique Sous le Vent, de 1550 à 1785*, 6 vols (Paris, 1785–90); Lucien Petraud, *L'Esclavage aux Antilles Françaises Avant 1789* (Paris: Hatchette, 1897).
4. Jean Baptiste (Père) Labat, Nouveau Voyage Aux Isles de l'Amerique, 6 vols. (Paris, 1722).
5. Gordon K. Lewis, *Main Currents in Caribbean Thought* (Baltimore: The Johns Hopkins University Press, 1983), p. 66.
6. See for example Gabriel Debien, *Les Esclaves aux Antilles Françaises, XVIIe-XVIIIe siècle* (Basse-Terre: Société d'histoire de la Guadeloupe, 1974); Antoine Gisler, *L'esclavage aux Antilles Françaises XVIIe-XIXe siècle* (Paris, Karthala, 1981); Gaston-Martin, *Histoire de l'esclavage Dans les Colonies Françaises* (Paris: Presses Universitaires de France, 1948).
7. Arlette Gautier, *Les Soeurs de Solitude: la Condition Féminine Dans l'esclavage aux Antilles du XVIIe au XIXe Siècle* (Paris: Editions Caribéennes, 1985).
8. See Gautier, *Les Soeurs de Solitude*; Barbara Bush, *Slave Women in Caribbean Society, 1650-1838* (Bloomington: Indiana University Press, 1990); Hilary Beckles, *Natural Rebels* (New Brunswick: Rutgers University Press, 1989); Marietta Morrissey, *Slave Women in the New World* (Lawrence: University of Kansas Press, 1989).
9. See N. Deerr, *A History of Sugar*, 2 vols (London: Chapman and Hull, 1949-50).
10. Labat, *Nouveau voyage*, 4, p. 110.
11. Rose Price, 'Pledges on Colonial Slavery, to Candidates for Seats in Parliament, Rightly Considered', cited in M. Craton and J. Walvin, *A Jamaican Plantation: The History of Worthy Park* (Toronto: University of Toronto Press, 1970), p. 191.
12. B. Higman, *Slave Population and Economy in Jamaica, 1807-1834* (Cambridge: Cambridge University Press, 1976), p. 1.
13. Labat, *Nouveau voyage*, 1, p. xxvii.
14. Justin Girod-Chantrans, *Voyage d'un Suisse dans différentes colonies d'Amérique*, 1785 reprint (Paris: Tallandier, 1980) p. 142.
15. Girod-Chantrans, *Voyage*, p. 139.
16. Ibid, *Voyage*, p. 131.
17. Debien, *Les escalves*, p. 135.
18. Ibid, pp. 137-38.
19. Ibid, p. 136.
20. M. Poyen de Saint-Marie, *De l'exploitation des Sucreries ou Conseil d'un Vieux Planteur aux Jeunes Agriculteurs des Colonies* (Basse-Terre: Imprimerie de la République, 1792) p. 14.
21. Debien, *Les esclaves*, p. 138; Bernard Moitt, 'Behind the Sugar Fortunes: Women, Labour and the Development of Caribbean Plantations during Slavery', in S. Chilungu and S. Niang, (eds.) *African Continuities* (Toronto: Terebi Publications, 1989) p. 412.
22. Jacques Cauna, *Au temps des Isles à Sucre* (Paris: Khartala, 1978), p. 114.
23. Gabriel Debien, 'Sucrerie Breda de la Plaine du Nord (1785)', *Notes d'histoire Coloniale # 100* (1966), p. 36.
24. Archives D'Outre-Mer (AD-M), Guadeloupe 107 (749), Bulletin des lois #1432.
25. AD-M, Guadeloupe 107 (749), Bulletin des lois.
26. Michael Craton, *Searching for the Invisible Man* (Cambridge, MA: Harvard University Press, 1978) p. 146.
27. Hilary Beckles, *Afro-Caribbean Women and Resistance to Slavery in Barbados* (London: Karnak House, 1988), p. 17.
28. André Lacharière, *De l'affranchissement des esclaves dans les colonies Françaises* (Paris: Eugène Renduel, 1836), p. 107.
29. Victor Schoelcher, *Des colonies françaises: abolition immédiate de l'esclavage* (Basse-Terre: Société d'histoire de la Guadeloupe, 1976) pp. 23-24.
30. Debien, *Les Esclaves*, p. 158.
31. Debien, 'Comptes, profits, esclaves et travaux de deux sucreries à Saint-Domingue (1774-1798)', *Notes d'histoire coloniale, # 6*, p. 22.
32. Debien, *Les Esclaves*, p. 161.
33. Debien, 'Comptes', p. 21.
34. Labat, *Nouveau Voyage*, 3, p. 175.
35. Ibid, III, p. 432.
36. Ibid, p. 210; Gautier, *Les Soeurs de Solitude*, p. 200.
37. Richard Dunn, *Sugar and Slaves*, (New York: Norton, 1973) p. 194.
38. Christian Schnakenbourg, *Histoire de l'industrie Sucrière en Guadeloupe aux XIXe et XXe siècles* (Paris: L'Harmattan, 1980), I, p. 36.
39. Schnakenbourg, *Histoire*, I, pp. 41-45.
40. Labat, *Nouveau*, 4, pp. 202-03.
41. Ibid, pp. 202-03
42. Ibid, p. 432.
43. Ibid, p. 206.
44. Ibid, p. 208.
45. Jean Baptiste Rouvellat de Cussac, *Situation des Esclaves des Colonies Françaises* (Paris, 1845), p. 43.
46. Labat, *Nouveau Voyage*, 3, p. 209.
47. Craton, *Searching*, p. 203; M. Lewis, *Journal of the West India Proprietor* (London: John Murray, 1834), p. 86.
48. Gautier, *Les Soeurs de Solitude*, pp. 200-201.
49. Debien, 'Sucrerie', p. 36.
50. See Debien, 'Destinée d'esclaves à la Martinique', *Bulletin de L'institut Français d'Afrique Noire*, 26, série B (1964), p. 41.
51. Labat, *Nouveau Voyage*, 3, p. 420.
52. Rum accounted for 10-33 per cent of plantation revenues, according to Stein. See Richard Stein, *The French Sugar Business in the Eighteenth Century* (Baton Rouge: Louisiana State University Press, 1988), p. 72.
53. Labat, *Nouveau Voyage*, 3, pp. 415-20

54. *Ibid*, p. 442. See also, Debien, *Les Esclaves*, p. 184; Anne-Marie Bruleaux *et al.*, *Deux siècles d'esclavage en Guyane Française* (Paris: L'Harmattan, 1986), p. 36.
55. Labat, *Nouveau Voyage*, 3, pp. 419-20.
56. Pierre de Vassière, *Saint-Domingue (1629-1789)* (Paris: Perrin, 1909), p. 168.
57. Moreau de Saint-Méry, *Description de la partie français de l'isle Saint-Domingue*, 3 tomes (Paris: Société d'histoire des colonies françaises, 1958), I, p. 33.
58. Nicole Vanony-Frisch, *Les Esclaves de la Guadeloupe à la fin de l'ancien Régime D'apres les Sources Notariales (1770-1789)*, extract from *Bulletin de al Société de la Guadeloupe*, Nos. 63-64 (1985), p. 89.
59. Frisch, *Les Esclaves*, p. 92.
60. A D-M, Guyane 129 P2 (11), 14 July 1831.
61. Labat, *Nouveau Voyage*, 4, 457; Gautier, *Les Soeurs de Solitude*, p. 204.
62. Gautier, *Les Soeurs de Solitude*, p. 204.
63. Jean Fouchard, *Les Marrons de la liberté* (Paris: Éditions de l'école, 1972) p. 289.
64. Vanony-Frisch, *Les Esclaves*, p. 89.
65. Ibid, *Les Esclaves*, p. 79.
66. Ibid, *Les Esclaves*, p. 94.
67. Debein, *Les Esclaves*, p. 90
68. Ibid, p. 93; Gabriel Debien, *Plantations et esclaves à Saint-Domingue* (Dakar: Publication de la section d'histoire, 1962), p. 123.
69. A D-M, Guadeloupe 107 (749).
70. De Cussac, *Situation*, p. 44.
71. *Gazette des Tribunaux*, 4 February 1846, in AD-M, Martinique 33, 286.
72. Vanony-Frisch, *Les Esclaves*, p. 89.
73. Debien, *Les Esclaves*, p. 331; Debien, *Plantations*, p. 126.
74. Labat, *Nouveau voyage*, 4, p. 190.
75. Cauna, *Au temps des isles*, p. 112.
76. Debien, 'Sucrerie', p. 36.
77. Poyen de Saint-Marie, *De l'exploitation*, pp. 49-50.
78. Debien, *Les Esclaves*, p. 330.
79. Ibid, p. 92.
80. Ibid, pp. 129-30.
81. Ibid, p. 93.
82. Mongin, *Bibliothèque de Carcassonne*, VII, pp. 93-94, cited in Gautier, *Les Soeurs de solitude*, p. 205.

SECTION SEVENTEEN
Capitalism, Ideology and Emancipation Processes

Emancipation from above by legislative intervention emerged in the nineteenth century as the dominant method of uprooting slave relations from colonial societies. It took nearly 100 years to complete the process. Though slaves launched a complex and relentless assault on the system of slavery over a period of 400 years, slave owners were able to assert their power so as to contain such actions. The Haitian revolution stands out as the grand exception to the generalization. In French Saint Domingue slaves were able to defeat the master class, and their imperial allies, declare the abolition of slavery, and establish the republic of Haiti. The slaves of Danish Saint Croix revolted on July 2 1848 and by so doing created the context in which Danish officials proclaimed emancipation. Such cases represent acts of self-liberation by revolutionary opposition to slave owners, and illustrate that slaves were first to implement emancipation schemes within the Caribbean.

As slave societies matured and became less creolized, their internal and external contradictions became increasingly problematic. Anti-slavery forces were not only internal, but by the end of the eighteenth century were supplemented from the culture of western civilization. In addi-tion, the rise of the industrial complex in the world economy posed certain difficulties for the decaying mercantile structures that had supported the slave systems of the region. Between 1794 [when the French Convention abolished slavery in French colonies] and the last quarter of the nineteenth century, the region's slave systems collapsed in a drawn-out programme of legislative emancipation.

Explanations for this progress are varied, and the essays in this section provide a sample of the arguments used by historians to account for the diverse nature and specific timing of imperial-sponsored emancipations. Considerable debate among historians has taken place in attempts to explain the relationships between Parliamentary legislative anti-slavery action, the development of industrial capitalism, and philosophical dis-courses about the nature of freedom. Anti-slav-ery movements in Europe targeted slave owners in their respective colonies, and in so doing generated important political dialogues that in-fluenced Parliamentary agendas. These essays speak to these issues, and illustrate the impor-tance of emancipationism to notions of Atlantic modernity.

76

The State of the Debate on the Role of Capitalism in the Ending of the Slave System

SELWYN CARRINGTON

The callousness of the trading interest beyond the sea to the distresses of the kidnapped servitors and the miseries of the slave trade, gradually roused a philanthropic sentiment, which was eventually to exercise a powerful influence on the condition of labour at home.

...Comparative little progress was made till the philanthropic agitation was reinforced by political and economic reasons for abandoning the trade as detrimental.

W. Cunningham, *The Growth of English Industry and Commerce in Modern Times* (Cambridge, 1907), p. 607.

No historical work in the twentieth century has elicited more controversy about the abolition of the slave trade and the final emancipation of slaves than Eric Williams' *Capitalism and Slavery*, 1944. Although almost 50 years have elapsed since the book first appeared, it has continued to send ripples throughout academic circles. Probably, this is because the themes of the work are as topical today as they were 150 years ago; it is certainly not because the academic world has reached a consensus on the scholarly and other achievements of the study. In fact, one historian, commenting on *Capitalism and Slavery*, points out that 'no history is timeless' and that, although the work has enjoyed 'enduring acclaim', it has also been severely criticised. Its methodological framework as well as its theoretical basis has 'begun to exhibit advancing age' in a world where modern technology has been applied to historical research. Yet he has warned historians, economists and other commentators to desist from writing the book's 'obituary' because 'Whenever in the past Williams' work has appeared irreparably discredited some new

academic physician has breathed fresh life into the old pages.'[1]

The attainment of freedom by the former slaves in 1834–38, like the abolition of the slave trade in 1807, must certainly be viewed as one of the truly momentous events in the annals of British history. Britain was the first industrial country to abolish the slave trade and then pass legislation in 1833 to emancipate the slaves in her colonies. The reasons for these decisions are less clear, and have led to a continuing lively debate among historians. As early as 1907, Cunningham had noted that three factors played important roles. In the first place, there was a 'philanthropic sentiment', but this had more impact on the condition of labour in Britain than on the slave trade or slavery in the colonies. While philanthropy played its part, however, it had to be reinforced by 'political and economic reasons' in order to achieve any success. This paper is an attempt to assess the economic reasons for abolition, and to investigate the state of the 'decline thesis'.

The Decline Thesis

Lowell J. Ragatz (1928) was the first modern historian to argue that the British West Indies were in decline after the 1750s because successive events conjoined to place great stress on the sugar plantation system at the end of the eighteenth century. Ragatz's *The Fall of the Planter Class in the British West Indies, 1763-1833* examines a series of events which occurred within the chronological period of his study and which in the long run led to the demise of the planter class. The decline of the British West Indies coincided with the rise of the movement for the abolition of the slave trade,

Journal of Caribbean History, 22, 1-2 (1988), pp. 20-41.

and Ragatz further observes that 'with the estate owners at the height of prosperity, the undermining of the old plantation system in the British West Indies was begun'.[2]

At first glance, one would immediately place Ragatz and Drescher in the same camp. On closer examination, however, it becomes clear that the time periods are different. While Ragatz sees West Indian prosperity, at least that of the old plantation system, as ending in the 1760s, Drescher has elected the post-1783 period as representing the height of West Indian economic prosperity.

While Ragatz had conceived of but had not developed the economic interpretation of abolition, he had intimated this position; but it was left to *Capitalism and Slavery* to establish the link between a declining British West Indian economy and the success of the movement in Britain to abolish the slave trade and to emancipate the slaves. It is clear that Williams had realised that, while the humanitarian movement was central to the process of abolition, it was in the words of William Cunningham, a 'philanthropic sentiment' until it 'was reinforced by political and economic reasons'. Williams had for the first time placed the British abolition 'in English works in economic history'.[3] He had challenged the traditional view of the role of the humanitarians and had subordinated it to the economic forces which had been largely overlooked by British scholars.

Pre-Williams Advocates

William Darity, Jr has recently examined the question of capitalism and slavery before the Williams thesis. He writes: 'Some British economic historians writing before Williams were struck equally by the ironies of British abolition. Williams could have turned to some British scholars themselves to make his case.'[4] However, Darity is worried by the absence of any mention of the works of William Cunningham, William E. H. Lecky and Samuel T. Coleridge. After offering several reasons for the omission of their work from Williams' study, Darity shows that the decline thesis, as it correlated to the abolition of the slave trade, was available in scholarship on English economic history during the Victorian period. However, he argues that it was Williams who brought a complexity and subtleness to an understanding of how the economic motives and patterns at work in British society conjoined to bring about the abolition movement.

Capitalism and Slavery successfully linked the rise of capitalism to the changes in the structure of the British imperial economic system which affected fundamentally the economic relationship between Britain and her colonies. This enabled Parliament to pass legislation affecting the economy of the colonies.

Cunningham's work established that there were several problems in the West Indian slave plantation economy in the late eighteenth century. It shows that the islands were no longer the props to British commerce, and it contends that the older colonies were finding it difficult to cope with the successful rivalry of St. Domingue, especially since British policy had created an invaluable trade between the United States and the French islands. It had restricted a free flow of goods and ships between the United States and British sugar colonies, and thus it triggered the existing latent problems which sent the sugar economy into a downward spiral.

Between 1775 and 1783, in addition to the decline of West Indian production, the trade between the local merchants and those in Spanish and Portuguese America fell off. By the end of the war, British merchants had established direct trade with the region, especially Brazil, and the new trade diverted a stream of commerce which had hitherto been very profitable to the West Indian merchants. Cunningham viewed this occurrence as 'a serious matter'. Furthermore, by the end of the eighteenth century, the decline in West Indian production and trade clearly indicated that 'there had always been something a little artificial in their . . . [British West Indian] prosperity'. Hence, it is clear to Cunningham that abolition resulted because there was 'the existence of deeper roots than the evangelical fervour for the movement to overturn the slave trade'.[5]

Darity supports Coleridge's assessment of Pitt's role in the humanitarian movement. He agrees that Pitt made no sincere effort to prohibit the slave trade to the newly conquered colonies and allowed the planters to accumulate slaves as a precautionary measure against the abolition of the trade. The advance of the sugar industry in the new colonies speeded up the decline of the old plantations and reduced the value of West Indian products as prices fell. The sugar dealers thus joined in support of the movement for the abolition of the slave trade. This action was certainly not based on humanitarian grounds or even evangelical fervour: it was intended to protect the interests of an important element of the British economy.

In addition, many abolitionists favoured the continuation of slavery. They believed that the existing slave population in the British West Indies could be sustained, even allowing growth, by improving the conditions and diet of the slaves. There also emerged during this period a commerce with Africa in order to secure raw material. This in Darity's opinion led to a new policy of exploiting Africans at home rather than in the West Indies. The Coleridge/Lecky assessment stresses the point that the abolition of the slave trade was not the consequence of humanitarianism. When it occurred, it did not result in any significant loss to the old plantation system. This view has been developed by Barbara Solow. Coleridge and Lecky were certain, in the view of Darity, that abolition did 'not evolve as an exclusive or necessary consequence of humanitarianism'.

William Darity therefore makes it evident that the main tenets of the Williams thesis are to be found in the writings of British economic historians in the late nineteenth and early twentieth century. Even Reginald Coupland had found little disagreement with the economic argument since it was under his supervision that the thesis was prepared, and he did acknowledge that he had neglected this aspect of the investigation. But, if Williams had neglected the works of British scholars, he certainly owed much to three other scholars — Lowell J. Ragatz, to C. L. R. James, (*The Black Jacobins*), and to German historian, Franz Hockstetter (*Die wirtschaftslichen und politischen Motu für der Abochuffung des brifischen Sklavenhandels*).[7]

Williams and His Support

Williams' provocative study, which examined the relationship between British economic growth and the West Indian plantation system, addressed the question of western capitalism and its dependence on the exploitation of labour through the slave trade and slavery. Williams argued that the British West Indies were pivotal to significant capital formation in Britain, which laid the foundation for the industrial revolution. It was not only the trade and the plantation system which maintained the West Indian hegemony. The West India interest, which attained its greatest success in 1763 when it forced Britain to retain Canada in preference to Guadeloupe, a major threat to the British sugar planters, had been severely weakened by the American War of Independence. Compounding this was the creation of the United States, which led to an irreversible economic decline from which there was only periodic recovery to the status quo ante-bellum; but there was certainly no growth.[8] Compounding the secular decline in the West Indian economy which gave rise to abolition, Williams argued that the short-run features of 'overproduction in 1833 demanded abolition'; and that 'overproduction in 1807 demanded emancipation'.[9] In his claim that overproduction gave rise to the abolition of the slave trade in 1807, Williams is again guilty of not citing his authorities effectively. He could have called upon further British support. Likewise, there is no indication that he was aware of the evidence which has been cited by Sheridan:

No less an authority than Lord Castlereagh can be cited to challenge Drescher's argument that the concept of overproduction did not enter into the decision for abolition. Writing to the governor of Jamaica on January 19, 1808, Castlereagh said that at a time when the world market was overstocked by the 'too great increase of colonial produce', an experiment for putting an end to the slave traffic had been undertaken...[10]

The American Revolution and Adam Smith

The beginning of the American War of Independence coincided with the publication of Adam Smith's *Wealth of Nations*. This work initiated a protracted debate over the issue of free trade, and postulated claims that Great Britain derived nothing but loss from the colonies. Hence the view of the West Indies changed from islands of great economic value to colonies that drained the British Treasury.[11] This negative view led to an atmosphere in which the very industries which depended on the West Indian trade found the sugar planters' monopoly of the home market irksome and influenced many in Britain to support the adoption of the principles of free trade while at the same time imposing mercantilist doctrines against the colonial trade with the United States.[12]

Compounding the problems of shortages and high costs of plantation supplies, the loss of credit from continental merchants, the drainage of cash from the islands, and the loss of a major consumer market for East Indian rum and other minor products, several internal factors making for decline were highlighted. For example, by the end of the eighteenth century, the islands suffered from outdated agricultural techniques, inability to maximise production, indebtedness, exhausted soil, and an inefficient labour force which made sugar production unprofitable. In his examination of the issue of the profitability of slavery at the end of the eighteenth and the beginning of the nineteenth century, William Dickson wrote:

it is a historical fact that Slaves could not be bought at the full value, without ultimate loss . . . excepting always, those few cases where the returns of their labour were uncommonly great, or where none of them died in seasoning, and they afterwards kept up or increased their numbers by births.[13]

By the time the official debate over the abolition of the slave trade began at the end of the 1780s, the downward spiral in the economy in the British West Indies had been established for over a decade.[14] The artificial nature of the plantation system of the British West Indian colonies was glaringly clear to financiers who saw better possibilities for investment in new areas more suited to sugar production.

The publication of *Capitalism and Slavery* was certainly overshadowed by war. Scholars were both cautious and muted in their appraisal, and there was also no unanimity among the critics. Many pointed to several economic factors which had plagued the sugar planters at the end of the eighteenth century, and they agreed that the economic decline of the West Indies had made it possible for the abolitionists to gain support for the termination of the slave trade. Yet these very scholars were not prepared to hand Williams all the kudos. They opposed his 'single mindedness' and his 'economic determinism' which had led him to establish the pre-eminence and the primacy of the economic forces at the expense of the humanitarians in the abolition movement.[15]

The next two decades of the history of the decline thesis could be accurately termed 'the calm before the storm'. The international scene changed dramatically. The Second World War ended; the United Nations Organization was created; black countries were emerging; racial segregation was being attacked; and television was highlighting the plight of blacks, the sons and daughters of slavery. Williams became the prime minister of a former sugar colony. The 'third world' had been created in the minds of people in the developed world; and historians and other scholars pondered over the theses, set in a compelling literary style of *Capitalism and Slavery*, which had become the guidebook for many scholars from developing societies which were struggling against capitalist exploitation by imperialist powers, and against the persisting plantation system.

Opponents to Williams — Pre-Drescherian

The reprint of *Capitalism and Slavery* in 1964 began the reassessment of the decline thesis. In conference papers, Roger Anstey and C. Duncan Rice concentrated on the claim by Williams that 'Britain's changing attitude to slavery and the slave trade was essentially a function of her changing economic situation and interest', and that this in part explains the abolition of the slave trade. Anstey also set out to reinterpret the claims against Pitt's conduct of the abolition movement and Lord Palmerston's policy on the suppression of the slave trade. It was his intention to resurrect the view that the movement for the abolition of slavery sprang from a new doctrine of Christianity associated with evangelical philosophy and the philanthropy of the Enlightenment which placed emphasis on the human soul and hence the individual.[16]

But Anstey, like his predecessors, was inconclusive on the Williams thesis. In the 1965 unpublished version of the conference paper, he wrote that 'much of Williams' general evidence is persuasive'. Yet in the published version he modified his initial statement: 'Williams' argument is to an extent persuasive'. Despite this minor alteration, Anstey willingly conceded:

It is difficult not to think that the radical change in the position of the British West Indies in the later eighteenth century did not affect English attitudes to the slave trade and slavery, whilst some of the figures Williams quotes are significant. For example, he shows that . . . the West Indies became relatively less important as a mart for British exports and that British sugar imports from Brazil, Cuba and Mauritius increased considerably whilst British Caribbean production remained stationary. Again . . . by 1807 the slave trade had become much less important to Liverpool, the British port most engaged in it.[17]

Having agreed with the principle of decline, Anstey was reluctant to follow Williams' lead and link it to the abolition of the slave trade. However, in the case of the passage of the Emancipation Act of 1833, Anstey contended that the Williams argument 'seems, *prima facie*, more convincing', and he concluded that by this time the British taxpayers were subsidising West Indian sugar on the European market in order to enable it to compete with foreign sugar. A decade later, Anstey, still conscious of the issue of decline, and turning to the relative economic importance of the slave trade, wrote: 'The Slave

Trade of the European nations with Western Africa was a commerce which reached its peak in the half century before British abolition.'[18] While, like David Richardson, Anstey undoubtedly favoured a link between abolition and evangelical Christianity in an effort to suppress the decline thesis, he had not lost sight of the fact that, in Parliament at the end of the eighteenth century, the humanitarians' cause was best served by James Stephen, who linked the West Indian condition to the question of abolition:

A more generalised but deep-rooted sense of the importance of the West Indies for British prosperity amongst the political nation, especially as represented in Parliament, was the critically important obstacle and it was this which made Stephen's discernment of how the cause of abolition would be linked to the chariot of national interest so important . . . [19]

Although only peripherally connected to the decline thesis, three articles published between 1973 and 1978 support the overall view of the profitability of the West Indian economy right down to the time of emancipation. J. R. Ward, whom Drescher has co-opted as an ally, employing as limited a methodology as W. A. Green and R. K. Aufhauser, contends however that West Indian profitability had fallen below the 40–55 per cent of the early years. According to Ward, profits declined throughout the eighteenth century to modest levels of approximately 10 per cent in the period 1744–55, 14 per cent in 1756–62, 9.3 per cent in 1763–75, 3.4 per cent in the war years, 1776–82, and 8.5 per cent in the decade 1783–93.[20] Other statistical information analysed by Carrington corroborates this trend. Profits fell from 12 per cent in the 1790s to 6 per cent in 1801–04 and to only 3 per cent for well-run estates by 1805–06.[21] All profits virtually disappeared by 1807 when the act abolishing the slave trade was passed.[22] A good example of this seemingly irreversible trend is the Worthy Park plantation during the 1780s, clearly identified by Michael Craton and James Walvin.[23]

On the question of declining profits and the negative image of the West Indian islands, no one makes the point more succinctly than David Brion Davis. He is very conscious, and rightly so, that 'opposition to slavery cannot be divorced from the vast economic changes that were intensifying social conflicts and heightening class consciousness', and that in Britain these changes contributed to a 'larger ideology' that ensured stability while initiating social change. By the end of the eighteenth century,

and even before the American Revolution, the West Indian sugar colonies were overvalued but only because 'sugar was a crucial symbol of national power'.[24] Davis writes:

The West Indies decline thus appeared all the more dramatic. Sugar and slaves were not a source of opulence, one discovered, but of debt, wasted soil, decayed properties and social depravity. . . . In the popular view there was thus a total dissociation between the old empire of plantation slavery and the new imperial search for raw materials and world markets. The emergence of the second empire involved a repudiation of the first. The second might depend on millions of involuntary labourers, but it was, by definition, a 'free world'.[25]

Not only was there 'decline and stagnation' of the British West Indian economy but, at the end of the eighteenth century, this reinforced and confirmed the contention 'that slave labour itself was inefficient, unprofitable and an impediment to economic growth'.[26] These were indeed the negative perceptions of the sugar economy which prevailed among capitalists at a time when the abolitionists were initiating their campaign against the slave trade.

Econocide and the Decline Thesis: Acclaim and Opposition

The most serious attack on the decline/abolition thesis of Eric Williams has been launched by Seymour Drescher in his *Econocide: British Slavery in the Era of Abolition* (1977). Countering the Ragatz/Williams position, Drescher challenged the claim that the West Indies had lost its relative position in British trade and in importance to the imperial power. He adopted the view that the economies of the sugar colonies were growing both in absolute and relative value which, after 1783, reached levels above those of any putative 'golden age' before the American Revolution. Unlike Anstey, Drescher argued that the slave trade was expanding at the turn of the nineteenth century and that Britain was altruistic in her economic policy because she abolished the trade when she stood to make significant profits. This interpretation has now been endorsed by David Brion Davis, and is repeatedly used, although not convincingly, by David Eltis in his recent monograph.[27] Because the American Revolution is considered a watershed period in the history of the West Indies, Drescher and his allies inadvisedly dismiss this event as having little or no negative impact on the economy of the sugar islands.[28]

Econocide, like *Capitalism and Slavery*, has had mixed reviews. Many hailed the work as having discredited the thesis of Eric Williams, and they concluded that Drescher's findings illustrate that decline followed abolition. Most of the reviewers who support the claims of Seymour Drescher are not themselves specialists in the area, and they are therefore emotionally following *Econocide's* assumptions. A few, like James Walvin and Philip D. Curtin, have had to overturn the positions they had adopted in highly acclaimed works. For example, Walvin had written of decline on a West Indian plantation in the 1780s as irreversible and symptomatic of a broader/general problem.[29] Curtin, who defended charges of biased research made by Joseph Inikori,[30] has succumbed to the Drescher mystique and admitted that his figures were wrong.[31]

Caribbeanists were less confused by Drescher's argument. Craton, while supporting many of his statistical offerings, concluded that the book was weakened by 'omissions and obscurities' and that 'his overall dynamics of abolition verges on the simplistic'. Craton disagrees that the slave trade was profitable and concludes that *Econocide* succeeded only in obscuring the debate.[32] Elsa Goveia pointed to several contradictions in Drescher's interpretation of the statistical evidence. Mary Turner and Richard Sheridan argue that the West Indian interest was concerned about over-production and the declining share of the British re-export trade.[33] Sheridan quoted Lord Castlereagh in contradicting Drescher's claim that there is no evidence that over-production gave rise to abolition in 1807. Walter Minchinton cited Lord Grenville's use of the over-production theme when moving for abolition in 1807.[34]

It was Minchinton who established that many of the claims of an advancing/increasing West Indian economy at the end of the eighteenth century made by Drescher have fallen short of their mark, and that the arguments are less compelling than were heralded by his supporters. Examining the same table which Drescher used to oppose the decline thesis, Minchinton observed:

Drescher has chosen his dates with care to support his argument but the full table enables a different interpretation to be presented. In his statement, Drescher made no reference to the period 1773–87 yet the peak quinquennium for the whole period 1713–1832 is 1778–82 (21.0 per cent) — a figure distorted by the American Revolution — and the position in 1803–12 is no more than a recovery to that level (20.8, 20.9).

Minchinton uses the table comprehensively to show that overall the British West Indies were in decline. Furthermore, he shows that the figures do not support the claim that the West Indies were more valuable to Britain in the period 1813–22 than the years 1773–87. On the basis of those figures, he concludes that 'Drescher has not done "brilliant demolition job". . . . If Drescher's case rests in the British West Indian share of total British trade . . . then the case is not proven. If these figures do not support the Ragatz-Williams doctrine of West Indian decline neither do they support the Drescher thesis of growth.'[35] Another interesting observation is that the upswings in British trade with the West Indies occurred during the years of war, and it is surprising that the trade figures for 1778–82 were better than those for 1803–07 or 1808–12, especially in light of the fact that during the former period the West Indian sugar economy was in shambles;[36] trade to the United States was prohibited; and the sugar economy depended totally on the British market.

Barbara Solow, in her assessment of the debate, stressed that the declining state of the West Indian economy had become an issue which had political consequences for abolition. Thus, she notes that by 1807 the act abolishing the slave trade had no negative impact on the British economy as would have been the case half a century earlier. Hence, 'abolition came when the economic development made it unimportant, not when it would have mattered a lot'.[37]

In the last five years, the debate over the Williams/decline thesis and the Drescher/non-decline interpretation has been intensified. Selwyn H. H. Carrington (the present author) produced one of the first full critiques of Drescher's arguments in his article, '."Econocide" — Myth or Reality — The Question of West Indian Decline, 1783–1806' (1984). Carrington set out to show that Drescher's work only confused the issue. Decline was evident during the American War of Independence, unlike the case during other eighteenth-century wars. What appeared to Drescher to be growth of the British West Indian economy during the French Revolutionary and Napoleonic Wars was a return to pre-1776 wartime conditions in the West Indies.[38] During the latter wars, increased prices resulting from the social and economic disruptions in the

French islands caused the value of West Indian goods to appreciate.[39] But even when prices rose, costs increased faster and led to diminished profits, as shown by J. R. Ward. Carrington utilised a staple analysis approach to arrive at a better understanding of the decline question. A crop by crop performance examination shows that, as with sugar, there was no overall increase in production in the older islands except in the case of cotton which expanded until about 1790 when United States production quickly overshadowed that of the islands. Evaluating Drescher's view of growing slave profits as a feature of British West Indian economy which was indicative of the viability of the slave system, Carrington denies that these profits reflect a healthy British West Indian economy. He shows that the number of slaves retained on the islands declined in the period after 1783.[40] More recently, Carrington has reassessed Drescher's claims and his use of the slave trade as an indicator of the continued value of the sugar colonies to Britain.[41]

New information provided by David Richardson shows that the total number of slaves imported into the sugar colonies declined as the profits of the planters dwindled. Richardson found a direct but lagged relationship between changes in Jamaican planters' gross receipts from sugar shipments to England between 1748 and 1775 and the number of slaves retained on the island. Richardson further argues that the peaks in slave imports into the British West Indies occurred in the 1720s–30s and in the years shortly before the American Revolution, and certainly not in the years cited by Drescher, although imports in some years were excessively high. During the years 1763–75, 'British vessels carried more slaves from Africa than in any previous or subsequent period of thirteen consecutive years.'[42]

William Darity has also turned his scholarship to an assessment of the Drescher hypothesis, and he 'takes a different line of defence of the Williams position', according to Walter Minchinton.[43] Darity argues that it is the interpreters of Williams' thesis who 'assume that his position hinges on the belief that the plantation system was in decline'. Darity's research establishes that the plantation system could have emerged as a 'millstone' around the neck of Britain, even though the islands were profitable in themselves. Hence, Darity shows that at the foundation of the thesis is indeed the belief that not only did the plantation system emerge as not valuable to furthering the interest of industrial capitalism, but also that there was a transition

of 'the thinking elements of Britain's governing elite away from principles of the mercantile system towards the *laissez-faire* principles of Adam Smith'.[44]

A most interesting observation is offered by David Brion Davis in his earlier interpretation of the state of the West Indian economy. Here, he agreed that American independence marked the end of one British empire with slavery as the major labour system, and the rise of the second British empire with an emphasis on capitalist exploitation which called for free or involuntary labour, and opposed to slavery. His vision was a declining West Indian economy lumbered by absenteeism, continued white depopulation, depleted soil, indebtedness, declining crop production levels and limited markets for slaves which established the illusion of slave labour as inefficient, wasteful, unprofitable and a retardation of economic growth.[45] This position seems very much in keeping with Darity's view that the West Indies could have still been profitable and have their supply of slaves removed by the British Parliament.

This was the view articulated by Adam Smith in his *The Wealth of Nations* where he sought to establish the groundwork for a free trade economy. Although Smith was technically incorrect, he identified two factors which countered the long-standing positions of the planter-historians. First, he credited the prosperity of the sugar colonies 'to the great riches of England, of which a part has overflowed' upon them. But, probably the more damaging claim was that 'Great Britain derived nothing but loss from the dominion which she assumes over her colonies'.[46] This latter claim, and certainly the loss of the American colonies, must have convinced the embattled conservative upper class that the future of Britain lay in a policy which favoured Englishmen at home. This was therefore not incongruent with the adoption of mercantilist restrictions on colonial trade with the United States on the one hand, and the movement to free trade on the other with the abolition of the slave trade in 1807.

Smith's polemical work has found support in the studies of modern economists who have attempted to discredit the Williams thesis. One of the best known works which adopts wholesale the Smithsonian concept of the colonies as a 'net loss' to Britain and as retarding the growth of the national economy is Robert Paul Thomas' article, 'The Sugar Colonies of the Old Empire: Profit or Loss for Great Britain'. Thomas employed a cost/benefit analysis to show that the British consumers paid more for colonial sugar under the mercantile system which gave preferential duties to the planters. Thomas' contention certainly enhances the idea that the West Indies were burdensome to British capitalists.[47] But Darity argues that this line of thinking does not detract from the Williams conclusion that British policy-makers became concerned about the colonial/mercantile system, but only after it had served its purpose in spurring British industrial growth and expansion in the eighteenth century.[48] Thomas' methodology has been criticised for being biased and too focused on 'consumer welfare'. It can also be argued that the successes of West Indian planters in securing protectionism made them appear in the end as burdensome to the metropole in their effort to maintain their self-interest.

Following the lead of Thomas, other writers have concentrated on the theme of the sugar colonies as a 'drain' on the British Treasury because of the monopolistic structures and the costs of administering and defending these colonies. Looking at the period 1768–72, Coelho concludes that the West Indian islands cost the British government an estimated £1.1 million annually. This work is basically a naive restatement of Adam Smith's criticism of the colonial-mercantile system.[49] One of its more serious flaws is the claim that the eighteenth century led to substantial net capital transfers to the colonies from Britain. Although these transfers did not occur, it was definitely good propaganda on the part of the free traders. It is a historical fact that the financial relationship between the planters and their merchant houses/factors in Britain, as it was emerging in the American colonies in the post-Seven Years War period, functioned on a credit/debit system.

A recent paper, highly critical of 'Drescherian history', was written by Cecil Gutzmore for the Hull Sesquicentennial in 1983. Drescher ignores this work in his 'The Decline Thesis of British Slavery since Econocide', which is his attempt to answer his critics. But the Gutzmore paper received a better fate at the hands of Minchinton, who notes that Gutzmore raises fundamental issues 'without dealing in detail with any of Drescher's arguments', and condemns Drescher as a 'bourgeois historian who . . . has misunderstood and misrepresented Williams'. According to Minchinton, Gutzmore accuses Drescher of 'empirical falsifications' which neither interrogate nor demolish the Williams-Ragatz decline thesis, and he 'dissents from the view that the "lengthy procession of British and other bourgeois scholars" have effectively "restored the claims of the British historical tradition in the matter of the humanitarian explanation of abolition and emancipation" '.[50]

Support for the overall concept of decline as a feature of abolition in slave economies can be found in an interesting article on comparative history. In this work, Gavin Wright draws attention to similarities between the British West Indies and the American South. For example, slavery contributed to industrialisation but showed a reluctance to expand. In the West Indies there was also evidence of stagnation and retardation; most sugar planters had little West Indian identity, and wealthy members of the West India interest did not reinvest in the colonies. As signs of a faltering economy, Wright suggests white depopulation as illustrated by ineffective deficiency laws; discouraged white immigration; increased reinvestments in other locations; and slave owners' interest in restricting imports as a way of raising prices and safeguarding their own investments. This was especially so in the older islands and was 'a factor in the success of the abolition movement'. Agreeing with Davis's earlier position, Wright contends that the birth of the movement for the abolition of the slave trade coincided with the destruction of the first British empire and the publication of *The Wealth of Nations*.

The 'Age of Adam Smith' in which growth was dominated by expansion of trade and commerce and by exploitation of the gains from trade and the market, gave way to the 'Age of Schumpeter' as entrepreneurship moved into search for innovation in technology and improvements in the process of production. The resemblance to Williams' conception is not hard to see. Slavery encouraged commerce by accelerating the production of exotic commodities in far-off places. As entrepreneurial energies moved into home-based production of manufactured goods, the sugar islands came to seem more remote and irrelevant to the important things in economic life, as indeed they were.[51]

Reborn Humanitarianism

Although it is certainly correct to link the decline thesis to the economic argument for abolition and emancipation, Williams also argued that mature capitalism had destroyed the very links which had fostered its growth. Wright compares this feature in the West Indies and the southern United States and reaches very much the same conclusion when he contends that, as the industrial revolution with its emphasis on domestic manufacturing took hold in Britain, the sugar islands and their slave economies seemed remote and irrelevant to economic growth in the metropole. David Eltis and Seymour Drescher remain opposed, preferring to base their interpretation of the period on speculative/'if' history.

Recent studies by Eltis and Drescher, although not primarily concerned with the decline thesis, uses the hypothesis formulated in *Econocide* to reaffirm the contention that the British had sacrificed a quicker rate of economic growth for 'the humanitarian cause' of abolition. Eltis accepts and expands Drescher's argument against the putative decline of slavery in his study which traces the relationship between slavery and industrial growth in Europe. Thus, he reconstructs the costs, profits and methods of the nineteenth-century Atlantic slave trade. The first part of the work which concerns us here is the section in which he restates many of Drescher's assumptions without himself, analysing and testing claims such as 'The Caribbean islands certainly experienced lower returns. But the long-run economic data testify to continuing vitality of the British West Indies well into the nineteenth century.' His evidence for this is Seymour Drescher's argument that the value and prospects of the slave trade and slavery to Britain were brighter 'when the British Parliament severed the umbilical link with Africa in 1807'. Reminiscent of Drescher, he therefore argues that it was British anti-slave policy that had destroyed the relative world position of the British plantations and resulted in the absolute decline of the sugar colonies. Eltis ignores the evidence that clearly indicates that the British West Indies were in decline at the end of the eighteenth century. This section conveys to the reader a morbid feeling as he examines the contention that had Britain not outlawed the slave trade and emancipated the slaves, her economic advance/growth would have been sustained at a much faster rate. This neoclassical analytic approach depends to a large extent on speculative analysis of an historical topic and on a *bourgeois* conceptualisation of the relationship between human labour and the market-place.[52] More importantly, however, this interpretation shows a limited knowledge of eighteenth-century West Indian history. It also illustrates a misreading of the British West Indian economic conditions by metropolitan historians in their effort to discredit Williams' *Capitalism and Slavery*.

Seymour Drescher's *Capitalism and Anti-Slavery* seems to be the brain-child of a reborn humanitarian who has moved away from the moral vision to the emergence and expression of a political culture which conjoined with other forces to sweep the Augean stables clean of slaves but to leave the stench. The work is very little concerned with denying the role of capitalism in the abolition of slavery. Instead, it seeks to show how Englishmen 'for the only time in their lives' could cut across class lines to abolish slavery because of political consciousness and activism. Then, they went to sleep because, as in the words of Lord Nelson at Trafalgar, 'Thank God [We] have done my [our] duty'. In some miraculous way, Drescher has been able to find the emergence of the British tradition of liberty in the anti-slavery movement one which was born of widespread literacy and political consciousness within the popular movement which witnessed mass petition campaigns against slavery between 1806 and 1838, never to reappear as far as blacks are concerned. Drescher's Britain differed significantly from Eltis'. The latter has shown in his work that throughout the early decades of the nineteenth century the British share in the slave trade increased despite the government's efforts at its suppression. Hence, in dissimilar ways, Drescher and Eltis trace/highlight, without acknowledging it as such, the development of British hypocrisy, which is nowhere more clearly expressed than in its attitude to race.

Capitalism and Anti-Slavery ignores many of the most serious criticisms levied against *Econocide*. However, Drescher acknowledges the economic decline of the British West Indies when he writes:

For more than three decades after 1807, the British planters were faced with a diminishing, mobile and more expensive work force. The British colonial system, which accounted for more than half of North Atlantic sugar in 1808, languished helplessly as its share of world production dropped throughout the first half of the nineteenth century.[53]

It is not clear whether Drescher's decline began in 1800, as the first half of 'the nineteenth century' would imply, or in the post-1807 period, as his thesis in *Econocide* indicates. But it was this diminishing importance of the islands and not his opposition to abolition, as claimed by Drescher, that led John Pinney of Nevis to write to his uncle:

Our situation is truly alarming. What with the shortness of our present crop and the low ebb of West Indian credit, united with our present unhappy contest. . . . Provisions and all plantations necessaries are so excessively dear, that the expense of supporting our slaves and keeping up our Estates in a proper condition, swallows up the greatest part of the produce. For these reasons, I want to contract my concerns here and fix a fund in England — not solely to depend upon estates subject to every calamity.[54]

Conclusion

This article has attempted an analysis of the major themes, issues and works on the question of decline. It has shown that the recent article by William Darity, Jr has undoubtedly established precedents for Williams' linking of the decline thesis with the increased movement for abolition and emancipation in the British West Indies. Caribbeanists who have supported the decline argument have analysed critically the performance of the islands' economies, demonstrating that these were in decline. Even anti-decline theorists, such as J. R. Ward, whose main research interest is profitability, demonstrate conclusively that profits had declined after the outbreak of the American Revolutionary War. The fact that profits recovered in the French Revolutionary War, representing a return to trends in these economies during wartime in the eighteenth century, has been neglected. These trends have been evaluated as growth. This is particularly the case in the approach of Seymour Drescher who has, however, joined forces with the decline theorists in the period after 1807. There is undoubtedly something amiss with the Drescherian perception of the abolition of the slave trade and its 'impact' on the economy of Britain. One cannot help but feel that Drescher's return to a school of historical thought which neither squares with history nor reflects British attitudes to race in the post-slavery period is an attempt to *whitewash* the issue, especially when at times the material used as evidence is misquoted.

The question of the role of 'mature capitalism' and its impact on the slave trade and slavery has basically been ignored by most critics of Eric Williams. Yet, it is one salient area which would undoubtedly shed light on the question of the relationship between advancing capitalism and slavery, and is clearly demonstrated by Gavin Wright. Cuban writers, in assessing the growth of capitalism in the Spanish sugar economy, have established that the adoption of capitalist principles was a factor in

the final abolition of slavery. Advancing industrialisation in Britain was certainly incompatible with a slave labour system in the productive areas because the raw material could be more advantageously and cheaply procured from satellite economies. The retention of mercantilist principles in some areas of the economy was also not incompatible with free trade in others. Self-interest was the hallmark of British policy makers, and since it became increasingly more common for Britain to legislate for the colonies after the American Revolution, the decision to abolish the slave system was initiated without the existence of a liberal political tradition towards blacks. It was simply the case of the mother country embarking on an economic policy initiated by political action to protect British self-interest. After 150 years, British economic interest continues to dictate its policy towards the question of freedom for blacks. Would British humanitarians lay claim to their 'traditional' place in the history of the struggle for freedom in South Africa?

Notes

1. William A. Green, 'Race and Slavery: Considerations on the Williams Thesis' in Barbara Solow and S. L. Engerman (eds), *British Capitalism and Caribbean Slavery. The Legacy of Eric Williams* (Cambridge, 1987), 25.
2. L. J. Ragatz, *The Fall of the Planter Class in the British Caribbean, 1763-1833* (New York, 1928), 240.
3. William Darity, Jr, 'The Williams Abolition Thesis Before Williams', *Slavery and Abolition*, Vol. 9: 1 (May 1988), 32-33.
4. *Ibid.*, 31. See D. Eltis, *Economic Growth and the Ending of the Atlantic Slave Trade* (New York, 1987).
5. Darity, *op. cit.*, 33-34. See S. H. H. Carrington, *The British West Indies during the American Revolution* (Holland, 1988), especially Chap. 7.
6. Darity, *op. cit.*, 37.
7. See Walter Minchinton, 'Abolition and Emancipation: British West Indies since 1975', unpublished Paper. I wish to thank Professor Minchinton for sending me a copy of this paper.
8. For a full examination, see Carrington, The British West Indies; 'The American Revolution and the British West Indies', *Journal of Interdisciplinary History*, 17:5 (1987), 823-50; 'Econocide — Myth or Reality; The Question of West Indian Decline, 1783-1806'. *Boletin de Estudios Latinamericanos y del Caribe* (1984), 36.
9. Eric Williams, *Capitalism and Slavery* (Chapel Hill, N.C, 1944), 152: Minchinton, *op. cit.*, 2.
10. Richard B. Sheridan, Review of *Econocide: British Slavery in the Era of Abolition* in *Journal of Economic History* 38:3 (1978), 765.
11. Barbara L. Solow, 'Caribbean Slavery and British Growth: The Eric Williams Hypothesis'. Unpublished Paper. See also Barbara Solow, 'Capitalism and Slavery in the Exceedingly Long Run', *Journal of Interdisciplinary History*, 17:4, 711-37, for a lengthy

discussion of the Williams hypothesis on the profitability of slavery and the slave trade to Britain.

12. Carrington, *The British West Indies*, Chap. XI.
13. William Dickson, *Mitigation of Slavery* (London, 1814), 198.
14. Carrington, 'Econocide — Myth or Reality?'; Carrington, *The British West Indies*, 164-81.
15. *Times Literary Supplement*, 26 May 1945, 250.
16. Richard Anstey, 'Capitalism and Slavery: A Critique'; C. Duncan Rice, 'Critique of the Eric Williams Thesis: The Anti-Slavery Interest and the Sugar Duties, 1841-1853' in *The Atlantic Slave Trade from West Africa* (University of Edinburgh, 1965).
17. Roger Anstey, *The Atlantic Slave Trade and British Abolition, 1760-1810* (London, 1975), 403.
18. *Ibid.*
19. *Ibid.*, 407. By this time Anstey had found an ally in Seymour Drescher, and he cited Drescher's work in support of his contention that the islands were still highly valuable to the imperial economy.
20. J. R. Ward, 'The Profitability of Sugar Planting in the British West Indies, 1650-1834', *Economic History Review*, 31:2 (1978), 197-213; See also W. A. Green, 'The Planter Class and British West Indian Sugar Production Before and After Emancipation'. *Economic History Review*, 26 (1973); R. K. Aufhauser, 'Profitability of Slavery in the British Caribbean', *Journal of Interdisciplinary History*, 5:1 (1974); S. Drescher, 'The Decline Thesis of British Slavery Since Econocide', *Slavery and Abolition*, 7:1 (1986).
21. Carrington, 'British West Indian Economic Decline and Abolition, 1775-1807; Revisiting *Econocide*', unpublished paper (September, 1987), 20; J. R. Ward, *British West Indian Slavery, 1750-1834: The Process of Amelioration* (Oxford, 1988), 49.
22. S. Drescher, '*Econocide: British Slavery in the Era of Abolition* (Pittsburg, 1977), 53.
23. Michael Craton and James Walvin, *A Jamaican Plantation: The History of Worthy Park, 1670-1970* (London, 1970), 118.
24. David Brion Davis, 'Reflections on Abolitionism and Ideological Hegemony', *The American Historical Review*, 92:4 (1987), 797-812.
25. David Brion Davis, *The Problem of Slavery in the Age of Revolution 1770-1823* (Ithaca, 1975), 62.
26. *Ibid.*, 61.
27. See Eltis, *Economic Growth*.
28. For an opposing view of the impact of the American Revolution on the British West Indian economy, see Carrington, *The British West Indies*.
29. Craton and Walvin, *op. cit.*, 118.
30. Joseph E. Inikori, 'Measuring the Atlantic Slave Trade: An Assessment of Curtin and Anstey'. *Journal of African History*, 17 (1976).
31. See Curtin's review of *Econocide in Journal of Interdisciplinary History*, 9:3 (1979), 539-41.
32. See Craton's review of *Econocide* in the *Canadian Journal of History*, 13:2 (1978).
33. For the viewpoint of the Caribbeanists, see *William and Mary Quarterly*, 3rd series, 35:4 (1978), *Peasant*

Studies, 8:4 (1978); *Journal of Economic History*, 38:3 (1978).
34. Walter Minchinton, 'Williams and Drescher: Abolition and Emancipation', *Slavery and Abolition*, 4:2 (1983), 91.
35. *Ibid.*, 86.
36. Carrington, *The British West Indies*.
37. See Barbara Solow's review of *Econocide* in the *Journal of Economic Literature*, 17 (1979).
38. One of the most significant studies which would have enabled Drescher to understand the fluctuations in the West Indian sugar economy in times of peace and war is Richard Pares' *War and Trade in the West Indies 1739-1763* (London, 1963).
39. Isaac Dookhan, 'War and Trade in the West Indies, 1763-1815. Preliminary Survey', *Journal of the College of the Virgin Islands*, 1 (1975).
40. Carrington, 'Econocide — Myth or Reality?', 36-45.
41. Carrington, 'British West India Economic Decline and Abolition, 1775-1807: Revisiting *Econocide*, unpublished paper (1987).
42. David Richardson, 'The Slave Trade, Sugar and British Economic Growth 1748 to 1776', *Journal of Interdisciplinary History*, 17:4 (1987), 742.
43. Minchinton, 'Abolition and Emancipation', 14.
44. William Darity, Jr, 'A General Equilibrium Model of the Eighteenth Century Atlantic Slave Trade: A Least-Likely Test for the Caribbean School'. *Research in Economic History*, 7, 289.
45. Davis Brion Davis, *Slavery and Human Progress* (New York, 1984), 335, n. 121, 178-79. In this work, Davis veers towards the position of Drescher without good reason or evidence.
46. Adam Smith (ed. E. Cannan), *An Inquiry into the Nature and Causes of the Wealth of Nations* (London, 1961), 362. See Abbé Raynal, *A Philosophical and Political History of the Settlement and Trade of the European Countries in the East and West Indies* (London, 1798), Vol. V, 106-07; E. Long, *History of Jamaica*, 3 vols (London, 1774); Bryan Edwards, *The History, Civil and Commercial of the British Colonies in the West Indies* (London, 1805), Vol. I.
47. Robert Paul Thomas, 'The Sugar of the Old Empire: Profit or Loss for Great Britain', *Economic History Review*, 2nd ser. 21 (1968), 30-45.
48. Darity, 'A General Equilibrium Model', 292.
49. P. R. Coelho, 'The Profitability of Imperialism: The British Experience in the West Indies, 1768-1771', *Explorations in Economic History*, 10 (1973).
50. Minchinton, 'Abolition and Emancipation', 11.
51. Gavin Wright, 'Capitalism and Slavery on the Islands: A Lesson from the Mainland', *Journal of Interdisciplinary History*, 17:4 (1987), 867-69.
52. Eltis, *Economic Growth*, Section I.
53. Seymour Drescher, *Capitalism and Anti-Slavery. British Mobilization in Comparative Perspective* (Oxford, 1986).
54. John Pinney to Simon Pretor, 12 June, 1977. Pinney Papers: Letter Book 2, p. 114. See Richard Pares. *A West India Fortune* (London, 1950), 93-94; Drescher, *Capitalism and Anti-Slavery*, 83.

77

The Antislavery Debate: Capitalism and Abolitionism as a Problem in Historical Interpretation

SEYMOUR DRESCHER

For more than a century after British slave emancipation in the 1830s the predominant interpretation held that chattel slavery had been terminated by a tide of humanitarian sentiment that overrode economic considerations. In 1944 in *Capitalism and Slavery* Eric Williams challenged this entire frame of reference by linking the rise and fall of slavery with two consecutive phases of capitalism, mercantile and industrial. For Williams, the turning point was the dramatic appearance of Adam Smith's *Inquiry into the Nature and Causes of the Wealth of Nations*, in 1776.[1] If subsequent scholarship has undermined many of the specific assertions of *Capitalism and Slavery,* Williams's insistence on the coincidence of antislavery and the industrial revolution has continued to attract scholarly curiosity. The hope of encompassing the development of abolitionism and the century of New World slave emancipations (1777-1888) within the ambit of economic development challenges the historical imagination.

However, a generation of research on the Atlantic economies during the century of emancipation has also made it increasingly clear that slavery was both economically competitive and compatible with non-slave counterparts throughout the world, even while it was being hobbled and destroyed in one political jurisdiction after another. The process increasingly appears to have been a series of "econocides," that is, the dismantling of economically viable systems of production, often near their peak of

significance to imperial polities or to the world market.[2]

If there was no necessary link between an economically declining chattel labour system and its legal abolition, how else might that relationship be understood? Over the past two decades a number of historians have proposed shifting the focus away from the productive performance or value of slave systems to the economic and ideological transformations within the "free labour" metropolises. Some have posited that the dynamism of economic growth at the metropolitan core led to assertions of the general superiority of free over slave labour in the colonial periphery. Others have argued that capitalist industrial transformation, specially in Britain, required a decisive change in free labour discipline, one widely resisted by workers still rooted in an older moral economy. In this context antislavery served to validate both ruling class leadership and the new relations of domination between capital and labour during the difficult birth of a new industrial order.[3] This complex hypothesis is the point of departure for *The Antislavery Debate.*

The Antislavery Debate is both more and less than its title implies. It is more in the sense that both the range of historical analogues and the theoretical arguments for establishing causal connections between one of the most elusive abstractions in the Western intellectual heritage (capitalism) and one of the most clearly bounded political processes in Western legal history (the termination of chattel rights in persons) are more broadly conceptualized than in any previous work on the subject. It is impossible to do full justice to the extended chains of reasoning which are brought to bear in the thrust and parry of critique and counter-critique among the principals. The three interlocutors freely invoke lengthy analogies, ranging from Marie Antoinette, Hank Aaron, Big Jim Farley, starving strangers in Bombay, and earthquake victims in Mexico, to putatively victorious vegetarians sometime during the next century. There are also briefer evocations of anti-labour union sentiment in Anglo-America, the Vietnam War, the Holocaust, the perils of Star Wars, and nuclear annihilation. Though hypothetical and counterfactual historical reasoning have already become a widely accepted medium of exchange in discussions of slavery and abolition, this volume sets a new standard in its ratio of synchronic and analogic reasoning to empirical or comparative historical analysis.

Moreover, the contributors also appeal to a cast of thinkers rarely called upon by historians of modern antislavery. In addition to rounding up the usual suspects – Aristotle, Smith, Hegel, Marx, and Mill – there is an awesome parade of allusions to Freud, Nietzsche, Halévy, Weber, Gramsci, Elias, Polanyi, among the illustrious dead, and a torrent of current scholarship previously untapped by the historiography of modern slavery. Indeed, erstwhile outsiders receive far more attention in this volume than does the accumulated historical scholarship of slavery and antislavery.

The The Antislavery Debate is also something less than its title implies. It might more accurately have been entitled The Davis Thesis or (given a sharp-edged internal dispute about the very nature of Davis's argument) The Davis "Thesis." Either way, this volume is not a debate by three independent researchers on a historical problem. John Ashworth and Thomas Haskell modestly but accurately describe themselves as "stowaways" on David Brion Davis's magisterial account of "the problem of slavery." They present a lively commentary on his description of the action, his identification of the relevant actors, and his selection and analysis of texts. Haskell and Ashworth reserve only the right relentlessly to unearth difficulties or ambiguities in the original account – or each other's commentaries. Moreover, they concentrate upon one

portion of one volume *(The Problem of Slavery in the Age of Revolution, 1770-1823)* of Davis's three penetrating books on the subject.[4] The The *Antislavery Debate* is also unusual in its format. It consists of four sections written at different times over seventeen years. Part One reprints three segments from Davis's *Age of Revolution* (1975). Part Two comprises four essays which first appeared in the *American Historical Review*. These include a lengthy two-part essay by Thomas Haskell (1985), a rebuttal by Davis, and an intervention by John Ashworth, plus a reply to Davis and Ashworth by Haskell (1987). Part Three closes the volume with two (1992) replies by Ashworth and Davis to Haskell's 1987 reply.

Two important bodies of significant material are thereby reduced or marginalized. Probably attempting to render the volume as self-contained as possible, the editor includes only one of the three chapters which Davis designated as the core of his *The Age of Revolution.* Thus one of the two chapters, on English abolitionism (including two-thirds of the analysis on that subject) is simply omitted.[5] On the other hand, the editor did include the *Age of Revolution*'s chapter on the Quakers, essential for the ensuing debate. In any event, the reader is offered no introductory warning about what was left out, nor any summary of other scholarly assessments of Davis's *Age of Revolution.* Readers may therefore be puzzled why Davis's first reply to Haskell (chapter six in this volume) actually devotes as much attention to "offstage" challenges as it does to Haskell's.[6]

This triangular debate, extending from the mid-1980s into the early 1990s, also creates internal difficulties. Since Davis focuses more on Haskell's comments than on Ashworth's, when the final curtain falls readers cannot be sure whether Davis silently accepted, or did not actually see, Ashworth's final essay which is directed as much at Davis as at Haskell.

While the three authors are far from agreed about what were the precise links between capitalism and antislavery, they all accept a common point of departure derived from Davis's first study, *The Problem of Slavery in Western Culture* (1966): In the mid-eighteenth century there was a profound and dramatic moral revolution in the West against its prior tolerance of slavery, and a new insight into the problem of slavery (3, 12, 188, 202-203, 298-299).[7] Davis's sequel

(Age Revolution) seeks to explain how economic, social, and political change, especially in Anglo-America, encouraged the historical development of that new moral attitude into a new collective movement, antislavery, and to account for its initial political victories during the "Age of Revolution" (1770-1823).

Davis's potent combination of two interpretative traditions, Marxian and Freudian, has long been recognized by both his critics and supporters as the *Age of Revolution*'s most stimulating intellectual contribution to the history of antislavery. In his core chapters on Anglo-America Davis valiantly steers a difficult course between the Scylla of exclusively intellectual history (for which he had been gently chided, in a review of his first book, by Moses Finley) and the Charybdis of economic determinism.[8] Briefly summarized, Davis found that late eighteenth century antislavery took a dramatic capitalist turn, one most visible in the "Quaker international." This Anglo-American mercantile and industrial capitalist vanguard pioneered the development of abolitionism into a broader social movement. It also simultaneously forged an ideological defense, albeit unconsciously, of the emergent capitalist industrial order. In the commercial cities of the newly independent United States Quaker elites helped to lead the attack on slavery and to devise new methods of labour discipline and urban social control. In Britain, where Quakers were more prominent among the capitalist vanguard than as members of the ruling political elite, they aligned their abolitionist and humanitarian efforts with those of other, more prestigious religious and political forces. This alliance bore fruit after two difficult decades in the abolition of the British slave trade (1806-1807).[9]

Davis also argues that the strength of abolitionism in early industrial Britain derived from its responsiveness to the needs of the dominant political elite, the new capitalist class and its modes of industrial discipline. The *Age of Revolution* explores this process via the "treacherous concept" of class ideology. In the British case abolitionists arguably focused attention on the intolerability of a distant evil in such a way that their vision of social reality and mode of argument justified the existing political structure and reflected the capitalists' needs in the emerging economy. Antislavery's key function in the so-

cial system as a whole was therefore to screen out, to camouflage, or to desensitize English society to the newer forms of labour exploitation and the less visible chains closer to home (70-76, 99-103).

While Davis noted in passing that antislavery could (and much later did) also catalyze radical social criticism and increase sensitivity to economic exploitation, in these core chapters of the *Age of Revolution* almost every abolitionist is identified as a conscious or unconscious apologist for the existing political hierarchy, for the free labour market, or for a new industrial discipline. Even those abolitionists usually considered radical by other historians were apparently not advocates of a freer, more egalitarian and less exploitive social future. Like the political economy of Adam Smith, British abolitionists reflected "the needs and values of the emerging capitalist order." They were essential, if unconscious, bearers of Smith's soothing message of natural harmony. In the generation before 1823, concludes Davis, antislavery succeeded in making "a sincere humanitarianism an integral part of class ideology, and thus of British culture (72)."[10]

The framework of explanation in these core chapters is overwhelmingly one of "class" and, via class, of national culture. The rhetorical linkage of economic development, class domination, ideological screening, humanitarianism, and nationalism are continuous. Davis also adds an element of lower class assent to this portrait of antislavery as a successful ideological device. In his theoretical discussion of ideology he refers to antislavery's "hegemonic" characteristic, whereby the dominant social classes also obtained the "spontaneous" (Davis's quotes) loyalty of subordinate groups (70).

Armed with this model at the opening of his chapters on England, Davis elaborately detailed the intellectual currents (political economy, utilitarianism, humanitarianism, and so on) which, with the aid of contemporary political and social developments, produced a triumphant convergence of abolitionism, political conservatism, and entrepreneurial capitalism. The conjuncture occurred between the mid 1790s and the early 1820s. Throughout this age of reaction abolitionism therefore functioned to reinforce hierarchical authority, to legitimate industrial capitalist values, and to redeem the established polity. Antislavery made the new chains of industrialization less visible and thereby legitimized the wage labour nexus of industrialism.[11]

Much of the exchange in *The Antislavery Debate* revolves around the significance of the capitalist market versus capitalist class tensions in explaining the origin, organization, and triumph of abolitionism. Haskell's critical point of departure proceeds from a desire to formulate the relationship between Western capitalism and antislavery more rigorously. For Haskell, antislavery is above all part of the "unprecedented wave of reform sentiment [that] swept through the societies of Western Europe and North America in the hundred years following 1750." Haskell is more interested in the origin and diffusion of that general humanitarian sentiment than in explaining the formation or triumph of abolitionism either as a class ideology or an instrument of hegemonic domination. His primary historical question is certainly not Davis's, that is, how antislavery unconsciously reinforced or legitimized capitalist or ruling class hegemony (70-71, 107).

Haskell is, in fact, unrelentingly sceptical about the utility of Freudian or quasi-Freudian attributions of individual or collective "self-deception" to the historical analysis of the relationship of capitalism to abolition. His lengthy argument rests upon the fundamental premise that, whether or not individual or collective self-deception exists as a general psychological phenomenon, it is impossible for the historian to bring concrete evidence to bear which will distinguish between unconscious intention and unintended consequences. He also challenges the utility of using the concept of "interest," whether individual or class, as a useful analytical category of motivation. The bottom line of his critique of the "Freudian" aspect of Davis's analysis is that any interpretation which relies on self-deception or unconscious intention (in this case, those of antislavery agitators) is almost impossible to test or verify. Ashworth also finds the argument from unconscious intention to be untenable. He also concludes that Davis's psychosocial hypothesis (that antislavery generally served a hegemonic function) is affirmed rather than being fully argued (116-121; 182).

As for the argument that antislavery served as a weapon in behalf of a hegemonic capitalist class, Haskell relies on Davis's own assertion that antislavery was not the conscious expression of a capitalist class interest. Without conscious motivation there can be no interest: "To say that a person is moved by class interest is to say that he *intends* to further the interest of his class, or it is to say nothing at all" (117, 182).

Haskell proposed a different linkage between capitalism and antislavery. For Haskell, capitalist expansion and especially its market system led to perceptual and cognitive changes which in turn expanded people's range of causal comprehension and moral responsibility. The positive feedback of market discipline changed social conventions. They encouraged increasing numbers of individuals to cross a cognitive and behavioural threshold into an active root-and-branch condemnation of slavery. Haskell's explanatory strategy is a self-consciously theoretical model in which social change is incrementally effected by and through individual agents. However, the model is not, as the volume's introduction speculates, an extension of the "Weberian project" in *The Protestant Ethic and the Spirit of Capitalism.* Haskell's causal explanation is rather Tawneyesque, flowing *from* the market *to* the "spirit" of antislavery, not *vice versa.* Indeed, Davis condemns Haskell's approach for being more akin to quasi-Marxian economic determinism than a Weberian affirmation of cultural autonomy (7, 140-156, 297-298).

In any event, as Ashworth points out, Haskell's dearth of historical evidence saps his argument at the first critical hurdle – "for example." Conceding that the market could, and did, have sympathy-reducing and slavery-expanding effects, Haskell supplies only one historical example of his model of the moral shift to antislavery, the Quaker John Woolman. Even in Haskell's own essay, that one example is balanced by a contradictory one – Daniel Defoe. Ashworth therefore challenges Haskell to generate a historical balance sheet of market economies and societies with antislavery as one test of his model's validity. Both Davis and Ashworth subsequently pile on any number of counterexamples. They enter in evidence commercial societies and entrepreneurial groups from medieval Italy to the United States South, all of which signally failed to cross the line from market-induced social conventions to antislavery (178-179, 186-187, 199, 231-234, 264, 291-293).

Haskell's general response is that he is not searching for the explanation of general societal change so much as a mechanism for inducing a threshold effect. In this case, the problem is to account for the emergence of individuals or groups who became sensitized to the intolerability of slavery. Even in terms of this narrow aim the reader is never told how one could empirically define the point at which the phenomenon occurred. Is it when one or two exemplars cross the threshold from tolerance to sharp antagonism, or does it require large numbers, or even an overwhelming majority? At the level of individual and even corporate hostility the threshold was crossed before the eighteenth century[12]

In any event Haskell's subsequent modesty seems to be at odds with his opening rhetorical salvo about the "unprecedented wave of humanitarian reform sentiment" that swept through the west after 1750. His long essay ends on the same cosmic note, with the evocation of a fundamental institutional reversal in western civilization, not the conversion of a sensitive unhappy few. In his final essay Haskell still hankers after something vaster than an explanation for the emergence of antislavery pioneers such as John Woolman, or even a thousand John Woolmans. Parrying a "Dutch" counterexample proffered by Davis, Haskell rhetorically asks "what else could account for the abandonment of slavery in the Dutch colonies, if not a pervasive sea change in moral perspective?" Haskell's metaphor remains oceanic (compare 107, 141, 149, 154-156, 159-160, 223-225, 233-234, 265-266).

The second major theoretical area of contention is the class centeredness and class interestedness of antislavery. Social history plays almost no role in the initial presentations, but all three interlocutors nevertheless assume that early antislavery activity was led and brought to fruition by the "dominant" economic and political classes in Anglo-America. In contrast to his position in the argument over unconscious intention and self-deception, Ashworth aligns himself with Davis and against Haskell's market model on this point. Indeed, while Davis progressively deemphasizes his initially stark tableau of British society in 1800 as a polarized world of capital and labour (a point to which we will return), Ashworth persists in reiterating that dichotomy. Analytically, Ashworth defines class interest as the economic, political, or ideological betterment "of the material conditions enjoyed by one class relative to another class" (280-281).

After lengthy and intellectually astute exchanges on both the difficulties of empirically measuring class interest and the relation of the concept of class to unconscious intention, social situation, and unanticipated historical outcomes, Davis and Ashworth remain convinced that antislavery implied class interest, if only in that abolitionists selectively and obsessively focused upon the evils of chattel slavery and thereby downplayed or legitimated the new evils of contemporary wage labour. Theoretically, the problem of ideological "selectivity," although not targeted as one of the keywords of the debate by the editor, is probably the central issue of *The Antislavery Debate.* To Haskell's rebuttal that abolitionists logically attacked the worst evil of their times, Davis and Ashworth reply that both slavery and wage labour could have been simultaneously attacked and were not. The asymmetry of selectivity is therefore logically attributable to some variant of class interest or to a "false consciousness" arising out of the abolitionists' class location and affiliation (4-6, 9, 117 note, 182, 184, 211-216, 247-253, 271-272, 274, 280, 293-294, 304-307) . [13]

One difficulty with this position resides in how convincingly the evidence for this "ideological" asymmetry has been presented, a matter not systematically addressed by the principals. Were attacks upon British slavery and the slave trade in the first two decades of the nineteenth century ideological legitimations of the social and political system as a whole? In *The Antislavery Debate,* the "ideological" evidence, in the form of contemporary texts against slavery, remains extremely thin. In his original presentation, Davis, while noting that his class-screening hypothesis is "a difficult thesis to substantiate," relies upon a few selected examples to make the British case. His primary text is an excerpt from the abolitionist James Stephen's *The Dangers of the Country,* containing a panegyric of English society. Davis also presents an extended analysis of "Charity," a poem by William Cowper (85-92). [14]

Unfortunately for its analytical clarity, the Stephen text does not rigorously conform to a distinctive prerequisite of ideological discourse laid out by Davis. Following Peter Berger, Davis emphasizes that ideology is quite distinct from deception and propaganda. But Stephen's *Dangers* was a propaganda tract, published precisely in order to sway the Parliamentary vote on abolition of the slave trade in 1807 (71).[15] Moreover, antislavery's supposedly conservative literary voice would have seemed far more radical and challenging to the political and social hierarchy had Davis chosen to include the fiery effusions of Blake alongside the quietistic, apolitical (and pre-abolitionist) poem of Cowper, or had he included the ironically subversive antislavery lectures and writings of Coleridge alongside the polemics of the Tory James Stephen.

Selectivity is therefore as problematic in the contemporary historiography of antislavery as it is in the antislavery texts of two centuries ago. To illustrate I need only place another document alongside that of Stephen's *Dangers*. A tract called *Christian Policy, the Salvation of the Empire* (1816) made Stephen's quoted panegyric seem pallid by comparison. The writer hailed "this nation, . . . the parent and nurse of liberty, civil and religious – the radiance of whose brightness has pierced all corners of the earth, extending a knowledge of the blessings of freedom: all the present enlightenment of mankind emanates from this spot, this England, as from divinity."

A few pages later, however, *Christian Policy* got to its real point, that slavery was but one British ruling-class crime among many:

Has it not been you, the oligarchy, the land-monopolists, of these realms, that have caused all the troubles, wars, and distractions in Europe and America for these last fifty years . . . ? Are not all the horrors of the colonies, of slavery, of men hunted down by bloodhounds – of the wars on the continent of America, scalping, burning, and hanging – of India, war, rapine, and famine – of Ireland, rebellion, executions, persecution, degradation, military coercion, and every species of oppression – of England, exactions, debt, taxation, deprivation, pauperism, bankruptcy, etc. to be attributed to you: that you might enjoy, by extension of wealth and power, secured to your families for ever in fields of blood?[16]

These words were written in the same city and during the same repressive and reactionary political period designated by Davis as the context for his hegemonic class thesis of antislavery.

Christian Policy was a manifesto by Thomas Evans, erstwhile secretary of the London Corresponding Society, and in 1816 leader of the Spenceans, one of the most radical sects in early nineteenth-century England. Evan's polemical and precise use of slavery as one outrage among many should be set alongside Stephen's polemi-

cal use of the slave trade as Britain's one evil in assessing Davis's designated key question: the social function of antislavery in the society as a whole. One must therefore agree with Ashworth's assessment that the emergence, the spread, or the ultimate success of antislavery cannot be explained in terms of "hegemony" as originally formulated in the *Age of Revolution* (289).

Nevertheless, there remains an important question about the precise relation of antislavery ideology to wage labour. For Davis, it is crucial that metropolitan abolitionism coincided with the emergence of more sinister forms of domestic exploitation and less visible chains of industrial bondage. Why, as Davis and Ashworth reiterate, did antislavery not focus upon "wage slavery" as well as overseas slavery? The ultimate "screening" or deflecting argument holds that antislavery writers either condemned slavery alone or actually lauded the relative condition of the wage labourer.[17]

One might again begin with the above text. Thomas Evans, who condemned slavery, did not specifically target wage labour, factory discipline, technological unemployment, industrialist oppressors, or any of the arsenal of "less visible" chains within his long list of upper class horrors. I would not, however, infer that Evans was thereby legitimizing the capitalist class or screening the national gaze from the new industrial order. Yet if we apply the same criterion of legitimation by silence, this is what Evans, like Stephen, would have been doing, despite (or indeed, perhaps because of) his diatribe against war, slavery, scalping, burning, hanging, rapine, famine, debt, taxation, pauperism and bankruptcy, all caused by the oligarchs of England. Evans's economic ideas were probably those of the local artisans and small masters among whom he lived and agitated.[18]

In the exploration of British political culture the juxtaposition of early nineteenth-century radicals and abolitionists in the *The Antislavery Debate* can lead to unanticipated findings. The most frequently invoked counterexample to abolitionist insensitivity towards free labourers is William Cobbett, who left no doubt about his detestation of canting "Saints" (Parliamentary Evangelicals) and their concern for overseas slaves. No Saint, however, could match Cobbett's marginalization of the social significance and the hardships of the manufacturing poor of Lancashire and Yorkshire at the time of slave trade abolition. During the winter of 1807-1808, Cobbett assured the textile workers that their jobs might vanish without harm to the nation and that their families might be pauperized, but the Poor Laws were assurance against outright starvation. What the manufacturing poor felt about Cobbett's perspective is unknown, but his cold comfort was demonstrably not inspired by any attachment to antislavery in any of its conservative or radical variants.[19]

Perhaps there is a plausible alternative explanation to the hypothesis that abolitionists screened out the evils of wage labour. The abolitionists of the 1790s and 1800s were not ignoring or displacing a nationwide ideological attack upon wage labour from radical or labour spokesmen. The analogy between slave and factory labour had existed prior to the rise of abolitionism and continued to emerge sporadically and regionally in times of economic conflict, especially after the passage of slave trade abolition. But at the national level the attack on antislavery hypocrisy came almost exclusively from slaveholders on the "right" rather than from the radical "left," to apply the then newly-coined terminology of the French Revolution.

From the outset, abolitionists had developed two stock responses to this slave-interested attack. The first was to delineate more precisely the specific conditions of the African slave-trade and colonial slavery: massacre; kidnapping; deportation in shackles; forced separation from kin, home, country; subjection to bulk sale; branding; gang labour; the discipline of the field whip; and so on. The second was to state very explicitly that the ills of the poor or workers of Europe did not justify slavery. They did not, as far as one knows, argue in reverse – that abolitionism implicitly justified the conditions of European labour. Indeed, in the very first major legal attack against black slavery in the British Empire, the bare subsistence living standards of English domestics were explicitly offered as a substantial reason for not adding coerced unpaid labour to the lot of black servants. Nor is it accidental that the pioneer opponent of slavery in England was also among the first to anticipate utopian agrarianism as a solution to slavery in Africa.[20]

Ironically, antislavery, rather than screening out metropolitan discontents, stimulated the popular discussion of domestic analogues to slavery: conscription, flogging, impressment, agricultural distress, imprisoned debtors, domestic service, parish apprenticeship, as well as abused schoolchildren, wives, tenants, animals, the Irish poor, the displaced Scots, and the politically disenfranchised. As in Evan's polemic, such popular denunciations tended to be scattered over a broad range of domestic ills and stress points. If one wishes to assert that all of those who spoke out against those variegated ills were also unintentionally validating wage labour by an embarrassment of discontents, then almost every group in early industrial Britain and every writer from Paine to Pitt was thereby displacing attention from wage labour. A screening thesis for wage labour that must simultaneously incorporate the "unselectivity" of general discourse and the "unselectivity" of abolitionist discourse in the period circa 1795-1823 is difficult to sustain (172, 178-179, 293).

Historians should be prepared to entertain a fine-grained analysis of the complex of attitudes towards overseas slavery and domestic labour among all classes. The world which gave birth to mass abolitionism was the same one in which Thomas Paine, a notoriously antislavery radical and advocate of the English poor, urged the freeing of the wage labour market as an amelioration from existing regulations and limitations. It was a world in which Manchester workers who signed abolitionist petitions in large numbers already believed in their right to decent wages as "free-born Englishmen." Antislavery added far less to either the legitimation or the delegitimation of the early industrial labour system than did the waves of prosperity and distress which flowed from the vertiginous political, military and economic developments of the age of revolution.[21]

Correspondingly, only after Waterloo, and especially after 1823, when the abolitionist elite became outspoken in its vindication of the British labour system, was this system most aggressively attacked by metropolitan labour reformers. The paradox seems readily explained. During the generation before 1815, when the slave trade was the focus of British abolitionism, the objective differences between enslaved and transported Africans and British workers were most obvious. After 1823, as abolitionists voluminously detailed the conditions of Caribbean slaves, some of the relative material advantages of the slaves over British workers were increasingly clear and widely known. British labour agitators then perceived an enormous polemical advantage in pursuing the comparison. Just when antislavery itself became most popular and radicalized, its ideology was most effectively turned against British industrialists – including many anti-slavery capitalists.[22]

Perhaps the most interesting development in *The Antislavery Debate* is that Davis's successive replies reflect his alertness to the growing historiography on non-elite forms of antislavery in Britain. In his rebuttals he increasingly turns his and the reader's attention toward the participation of groups marginalized in the English chapters of *The Age of Revolution*. One need only add that such groups, including artisans, were present and counted in British abolitionist politics during much of the period 1795-1823, as well as during earlier and later periods.

Second, while Davis's *Age of Revolution* conflates most forms of non-chattel labour as being globally legitimized by antislavery ideology, his closing essay in *The Antislavery Debate* emphasizes a crucial distinction between the historical perceptions of *"free* labour,"* on one hand and those of chattel slavery *and* "wage slavery" on the other. It was a distinction which "appealed to both artisans and workers of varying degrees of skill," and, one must add, to independent farmers and shopkeepers too (compare 95-103, 171-172, 178-179, 293, and especially 303-304).[23] These social groups and their aspirations were less visible in the English chapters of the *Age of Revolution*.[24]

The more completely the social base of antislavery is investigated, the less significant seem the hegemonic "screening" effects of antislavery ideology for British society. Ashworth and Davis occupy firm ground in continuing to insist that one must look closely at social position and group dynamics in analyzing antislavery texts, and in hypothesizing that individuals with different social affiliations probably accounted for differences in visions of antislavery. It must be made more explicit, however, that there was probably never, at *any* period, one ideological fit between capitalism and antislavery, nor one function of antislavery for British society as a whole.

The final unresolved question in *The Antislavery Debate* concerns antislavery's long-term impact. What difference did abolitionism actually make in the evolution of metropolitan Britain (or America), especially as regards the legitimation and maintenance of the "new industrial capitalist order" (308-309)[25]

Davis maintains that, regardless of the abolitionists' intentions, it legitimated and morally sustained that order. But can one articulate this as a sustainable hypothesis? As originally formulated it begged a counterfactual question, one not directly addressed by the participants themselves.

Can we sharpen the question of whether antislavery measurably delayed or distorted the discovery of the uglier side of the new capitalist industrial order and its manifold discontents? The few exemplary quotations deployed in *The Antislavery Debate* do not enable the participants to increase our confidence beyond the level originally attained by the *Age of Revolution*. Indeed, such a procedure rather freezes historians in an arbitrary battle of the texts. Is this text ideologically more representative than that text? There is perhaps a better way to verify or to invalidate the "screening" hypothesis. We might begin with comparative surveys of industrial stress. Did rising denunciation of, and collective action against, the ills of industrialization begin later, or proceed more slowly, within regions, religions, generations, genders, communities, classes, or polities where both intensified antislavery and intensified wage labour prevailed, than in similar areas and among similar groups lacking such a powerful antislavery concern? Or, did antislavery, more often than not, help sensitize and/or mobilize genders, generations, classes, religions, regions, and so on for industrial reform? Do we get different answers in the shorter or longer term? Any response to these questions is likely to require arguments more empirically grounded in social, political, and comparative history.

In fact, all three participants in *The Antislavery Debate* do seem to agree that one empirical investigation might resolve at least some of the outstanding issues about the impact of the market or of industrial capitalism on antislavery (or vice versa). Davis first raised the issue. Haskell and Ashworth then agreed that the Netherlands might work as a verifying case. Davis appropriately uses his final reply to show that the Netherlands, as a pioneer zone of intense mercantile capitalism, utterly failed to produce either a substantial antislavery moment, or an early end to slavery. The history of Dutch colonial slavery throws doubt on the hypothetical propensity of market capitalism to generate abolitionists. The market also did not encourage the Dutch polity to play a pioneering role in the history of slave emancipation. The Netherlands offers equally little encouragement for hypotheses which link abolitionism to industrial capitalism in general. And it is still less useful to those historians who affirm that antislavery was particularly attractive to the Western European bourgeoisie. The Netherlands turns out to be a killing field for most theoretical linkages between capitalism and antislavery to date (9-10, 178, 233-234, 264, 292-296).[26]

Where then, is one left at the end of this volume's formulations and reformulations of the relation of economic development to transformations in moral perception, collective action, and legislation? First, with the sense that its bright and resilient participants are extraordinarily adept at laying bare the weak links in their colleagues' arguments. *The Antislavery Debate* will make excellent fodder for rumination in historiography seminars. Under the counterexemplary and analytic pressure of Davis and Ashworth, Haskell reduces (or at least clarifies) the scope of his original world-historical quest to a search for significant threshold effects of convention in moral innovation. Ashworth potentially opens up a new front - the antebellum US North – for testing the thesis outside of Davis's original time-frame. Ashworth does not go much further in this volume than the introduction of American family ideology or the temperance movements as proxy variables for antislavery. By inference alone, however, one cannot get around Haskell's bottom line that the antislavery activity of reformers does not imply attitudes or even outcomes which legitimated or perpetuated the systematic oppression of capitalist domination.

Davis, whose *Age of Revolution* was the inspiration for most other post-Williams "class-ideological" interpretations of antislavery, has both reaffirmed and modified his original account. He reaffirms the correlation between "free" zone class conflicts and the expansion of antislavery. However, he has more clearly narrowed his hegemonic focus to one phase of in-

dustrial development in one country, and only for certain classes. He has also added enough new non-ruling or non-capitalist elements to his equation to soften the hard edge of his earlier emphasis on antislavery's role as a largely elite tool of social defense.

Shifts in the tone of an argument are important in a discursive discipline like history. One need only observe the way in which Davis deals with a traditional totem of antislavery debates. More than a century ago W. E. H. Lecky offered a now-famous hosanna to the English abolitionist crusade "as among the three or four perfectly virtuous acts recorded in the history of nations." Once a crown-jewel of Britain's triumphalist historiography, Lecky's phrase became, in recent decades, the archetypical example of a naive and filieopietistic historiography. Haskell unsurprisingly concurs in this assessment, since Davis's *Age of Revolution* also quoted Lecky's words in an ironic mode, as the once "unanswerable proof" that English humanitarianism had "outweighed English avarice and class interest." Davis now ends the *The Antislavery Debate* with a more ironic view of Lecky. He is more than just the ultimate example of triumphalist British antislavery:

I actually think that there is much truth in W. E. H. Lecky's often-quoted assertion "that the unwearied, unostentatious, and inglorious crusade of England against slavery may probably be regarded as among the three or four perfectly virtuous acts recorded in the history of nations." But in the 1990s it would be naive not to add that such a crusade inevitably helps to valorize and redeem the particular social order from which it springs. (309)

Thus does Davis close *The Antislavery Debate*. But where does the volume leave the capitalism and abolitionism debate? In some respects its dimensions have been significantly narrowed. The application of the hegemonic-ideological thesis has been very sharply bounded in both duration and space. Haskell's reply even expressed disappointment at Davis's easing away from what Haskell had presumed to be a powerful and global theory relating Western moral change to Western capitalism (204-205).

Davis, however, is not deterred from escalating this line of argument. In his final reply he rhetorically asks Haskell why all of the earlier stages of European capitalism, the "'commercial revolution' of the mid-tenth to the mid-fourteenth centuries or the spectacular expansion of trade and colonial settlement from the mid-fifteenth to the mid-seventeenth centuries" did not manage to produce any "synchronized development of humanitarianism or abolitionism." Nor did the fifteenth-century Mediterranean, nor did seventeenth-century England and Holland, nor did the early eighteenth-century trading centres of London, Bristol, and Liverpool (291-293).[27]

After such an extensive decoupling, the entire Haskellian arcade of a vast temporal transformation in Western Civilization à la Norbert Elias seems to lie in ruins. The potential links of English antislavery to C. B. Macpherson's "market society" of the seventeenth century and to other early modern bourgeois-social transformations are also frayed (143n, 191n). Even Adam Smith's invisible "long revolution" of Western European labour relations has no comfortable place in this historical retrospective.

So devastating a survey may risk toppling the very pillars of the original conceptual temple. Even when partly exempting industrial capitalism from his catalogue of commercial economies without antislavery, Davis alertly cautions the reader about the frequency of non-abolitionist industrialization and of non-industrial emancipations. After all, abolitionism became a powerful force in only three (or, very generously, four) countries: Britain, the United States, Brazil, and France. Abolitions without much abolitionism and before much industrialization were still the *rule,* not the exception, in the age of slave emancipation (296 and note).

How should we then view this final ironic and Samsonic twist to the once serenely reaffirmed "simple fact" of the coincidence of industrial capitalism and abolition? One way would be to rethink some of the central historiographical assumptions of the last half-century. Almost all recent historians of slavery have started with a dual "big bang" premise about antislavery and industrial growth: that is, there was an explosively rapid moral revaluation of slavery and an equally rapid transformation of British labour relations toward the end of the eighteenth century. This "dual revolution" became the frame of reference for explaining the triumph of antislavery.[28]

However, instead of positing an eighteenth-century reversal in attitudes toward slavery from acceptability to unacceptability, suppose we emphasize instead the more truly "unostentatious and inglorious" disappearance of chattel slavery in Northwestern Europe. It was a transformation

with Europe's long commercial expansion after the mid-ninth century. That development is more compatible with the stately pace of Elias's civilizing process, or of Adam Smith's millennial revolution of Western European labour. Wasn't that the fundamental Western transformation? What if we then conceptualize the Northern European acceptance of colonial overseas slavery as *exceptional* from its outset? Our long-term point of departure would be that slavery was not normative for countries North of the Pyrenees during the spectacular expansion of trade, conquest, and settlement in the three centuries after 1450.[29]

One would (ironically, of course) have to scrap Haskell's starting point and analytically separate modern European humanitarianism in general from overseas antislavery in particular. Above all we should never lose sight of the fact that economics more strongly supported New World plantation slavery than antislavery well into the nineteenth century. The historical problem now becomes geographically and morally simpler – it is one of explaining the separation between Northwestern Europe and the world beyond. Why did Western European rulers and citizens fail to reproduce their system of civil liberty abroad and to export metropolitan limits on labour and people to their overseas areas? The "fruits of distant merchant capitalism" are the simplest way of accounting for the political and cultural space allotted to the rising overseas slave system of circa 1450-1860.

What had to be overcome from the mid-eighteenth century onward was the greater leeway offered to capitalists overseas than to those at home. The eighteenth-century acceleration of British economic growth certainly seems to have enhanced the popular sense of the British polity's ability first to inhibit and finally to destroy its slave labour system. A class conflict model may also be applicable to this destruction process, but it requires a convincing correlation of the British abolitionist initiatives with moments and places of increasing tensions in industrial capitalism.[30]

Even the class analysis of British "free labour ideology" is still too structured by later lines of class cleavage rather than by the late eighteenth-century conflicts and coalitions which produced the breakthroughs to mass abolitionism and the abolition of the slave trade. Pioneering efforts in intellectual history and theories of cultural change suffer for lack of precise markers from social history. Without these markers one cannot relate antislavery to capitalist, or to any other major historical development. With them an elite-oriented class-based explanation risks splintering into cross-class and non-economic variables. But it is hard to see how the question can develop otherwise. In *The Antislavery Debate,* minimally armed with selected texts, the participants ascribe an overriding "class" ideology to all abolitionism or deny the significance of class perception altogether.

The capitalism and antislavery debate alerts us to the problematic nature of the original historiographical point of departure. One may tirelessly reiterate that "it is no accident that" the industrial revolution and antislavery reached critical mass together, or that the early British abolitionist victories coincided with one or another industrial crisis. But temporal coincidence is the weakest form of causal inference. It may tempt us down a long blind alley. *The Antislavery Debate* shows just how alluring has been the common sense assumption that antislavery cannot be "divorced from the vast economic changes of the late eighteenth century" (171, 289). The couple is certainly not yet living happily ever after. One may hazard the prediction that if the linkage is to remain fertile it must generate more empirical and comparative studies. Otherwise, theoretical sallies will only increase what Davis aptly terms the perils of ahistorical abstraction.

Notes

1. "Eric Williams: British Capitalism and British Slavery," *History and Theory* 26 (1987), 180-196; *British Capitalism and Caribbean Slavery: The Legacy of Eric Williams,* ed. Barbara L. Solow and Stanley L. Engerman (New York, 1987); Thomas C. Holt, "Explaining Abolition" (review essay), *Journal of Social History* 24 (1990), 371-378; and Michael Craton, "The Transition from Slavery to Free Wage Labour in the Caribbean, 1790-1890: A Survey with Particular Reference to Recent Scholarship," *Slavery and Abolition* 13 (1992), 37-67.

2. See, among others, Seymour Drescher, *Econocide: British Slavery in the Era of Abolition* (Pittsburgh, 1977); David Eltis, *Economic Growth and the Ending of the Transatlantic Slave Trade* (New York, 1987); Robert William Fogel and Stanley L. Engerman, *Time on the Cross,* 2 vols. [1974] (Boston, 1989); Robert W. Fogel, *et al., Without Consent or Contract: The Rise and Fall of American Negro Slavery,* 4 vols. (New York, 1989-1992); Selwyn H. H.

Carrington and Seymour Drescher, "Debate: Econocide and West Indian Decline, 1783-1806," *Boletín de Estudios Latinoamericanos y del Caribe* 36 (June, 1984), 13- 67; S. Drescher, "The Decline Thesis of British Slavery since Econocide," *Slavery and Abolition* 7 (1986), 3-24; John R. Ward, *British West Indian Slavery, 1750-1834: The Process of Amelioration* (Oxford, 1988); S. Drescher, "Brazilian Abolition in Comparative Perspective," in *Hispanic American Historical Review* 68 (1988), 429-460; Linda Colley, *Britons: Forging the Nation 1707-1837* (New Haven, 1992), 350-363.

3. Howard Temperley, "Capitalism, Slavery and Ideology," *Past and Present* 75 (1977), 44-118; Stanley Engerman and David Eltis, "Economic Aspects of the Abolition Debate," in *Antislavery, Religion and Reform: Essays in Memory of Roger Anstey,* ed. C. Bolt and S. Drescher (Hamden, Conn. 1980), 272-903; S. Drescher, *Capitalism and Antislavery: British Mobilization in Comparative Perspective* (London, 1986).

4. David Brion Davis, *The Problem of Slavery in Western Culture* (Ithaca, N.Y., 1966); *The Problem of Slavery in the Age of Revolution, 1770-1823* (Ithaca, N.Y., 1975) (hereafter, *Age of Revolution); Slavery and Human Progress* (New York, 1984); "Capitalism, Abolitionism, and Hegemony," in Solow and Engelman, *British Capitalism,* 209-227.

5. The omitted chapter is "The Preservation of English Liberty, II," 386-468. See also 478, 493-500.

6. Davis, "Reflections on Abolitionism and Ideology Hegemony" in *The Antislavery Debate,* 161-179 (chapter 6), esp. 165-174 (originally published in the *American Historical Review* 92 [October, 1987], 797-878, as part of the *AHR* "Forum on abolitionism, capitalism, and ideological hegemony.") Unfortunately all of the *AHR* essays were reprinted without alteration, so the participants' references to one another's works in the last 250 pages of this volume will not be useful to readers of *The Antislavery Debate.* The editor should have either also included the original pagination or have alerted readers that they will require the original version of Davis's *Age of Revolution,* and the 1985 and 1987 volumes of the *American Historical Review* to have ready access to the sources cited in *The Antislavery Debate* (henceforth *ASD).* I will attempt, wherever possible, to use the pagination of *ASD.*

7. See especially Davis, *Problem of Slavery in Western Culture,* "Epilogue," 483-493.

8. *Age of Revolution,* 564; on Finley's impact, see *ASD,* 299-300. For assessments of the thrust of Davis's "thesis" of capitalist abolition, see Eric Foner, "Abolitionism and the Labor Movement in Antebellum America," in *Anti-Slavery, Religion and Reform,* 254-272, esp. 267-269; Stanley L. Engerman and David Eltis, "Economic Aspects of the Abolition debate," *Ibid.,* 281-282; H. Temperley, "Anti-Slavery as a Form of Cultural Imperialism," Ibid., 339, 342; Seymour Drescher, "Cart Whip and Billy Roller: Antislavery and Reform Symbolism in Industrializing Britain," *Journal of Social History* 15 (September,

1981), 3-24; Betty Fladeland, *Abolitionist and Working-Class Problems in the Age of Industrialization* (London, 1984), 339-342; Robin Blackburn, *The Overthrow of Colonial Slavery, 1776-1848* (London, 1988), 26-27, 152; and Holt, "Explaining Abolition." Holt was concerned with Davis's *Slavery and Human Progress* for what he saw as its author's retreat from a capitalist-hegemonic mode of explanation in the *Age of Revolution.* See Holt, "Of Human Progress and Intellectual Apostasy," *Reviews in American History* 15 (March, 1987), 50-58. Holt upholds the applicability of the Davis thesis for a much broader "age of revolution," extending from 1780 to 1850. See Holt, *The Problem of Freedom: Race, Labour, and Politics in Jamaica and Britain, 1832-1938* (Baltimore and London, 1992), 24-33.

9. Davis's discussion of the United States in the *Age of Revolution* alludes to the compatibility of antislavery with Northern capitalist ideology by the end of the eighteenth Century.

10. See also *Age of Revolution,* 451-468.

11. See also Ibid., 14, 466-467.

12. In fact, Haskell's threshold of moral illegitimacy was crossed in Holland long before his century of mass humanitarianism (1750-1850). In the 1620s the Dutch West India Company's Directors, after consultation with theologians, "agreed that the trade in human beings was morally not justified and should therefore not be practiced by the company." Official avoidance, however, lasted no more than a decade. See Johannes Menne Postma, *The Dutch in the Atlantic Slave Trade, 1600- 815* (Cambridge, Eng., 1990), 11.

13. See Davis, *Age of Revolution,* 251-252, 349-350, 455-468. For a recent conclusion that most property owners who supported antislavery were not, consciously or subsconsciously, *primarily* impelled by a desire to shore up the basis of their wealth and power, see R. W. Fogel and S. L. Engerman, "Philanthropy at Bargain Prices: Notes on the Economics of Gradual Emancipation," in Fogel, *et al., Without Consent or Contract, Technical Papers,* 11, 587-605. The authors are struck by "how much of the rhetoric of the abolitionists was taken over by the critics of capitalism" (Ibid., 602).

14. On ideology, see 71; and Davis, *Age of Revolution,* Preface, 13. On *The Dangers* as propaganda, see Roger T. Anstey, *The Atlantic Slave Trade and British Abolition, 1769-1810* (London, 1975), 194-198. Davis also uses Stephen's *Crisis of the Sugar Colonies* (London, 1802) to illustrate Stephen's legitimation of English system of labour. To the extent that *The Danger's* exclusive focus on abolition "made an attack on Negro slavery serve as an all-redeeming atonement" (85-87), Stephen had already retreated to a less all-embracing position in his preface to the second edition (1807).

15. See also Davis, *Age of Revolution,* Preface, 13.

16. *Christian Policy* (London, 1816), 7, 23-24, quoted in Iain McCalman, *Radical Underworld: Prophets, Revolutionaries and Pornographers in London, 1795-1890* (Cambridge, Eng., 1988), 102. If Davis initially deflated assessments of the broad appeal of antislav-

ery to "working class leaders" (87n) in his reply to Haskell, however, he took note of a radical's comparison of the English poor to the West Indian slaves in 1817 (117). See also *The Horrors of Slavery and Other Writings by Robert Wedderburn,* ed. Iain McCalman (Edinburgh, 1991), 82, 114.

17. In addition to Davis's argument on 61-64, 92-103, and 169-171, see the summary of the whole argument in *Age of Revolution,* 459-468.

18. McCalman, *Radical Underworld,* 103.

19. On the use of Cobbett as the principal radical counterexample to abolitionists see 78n, 79, 86, 121n, 214; and Davis, *Age of Revolution,* 357, 359,367,409,450,467. For Cobbett's perspective in 1807-1808, see "Perish Commerce," in *Cobbett's Weekly Register* 12 (Nov. 28, 1807), 836; (Dec. 5, 1807), 875-877; 13 (Jan. 28, 1808), 107-109. Another scholar finds that Cobbett's humanitarian adversaries actually preceded him in developing new uses for the work/slave metaphor in the movement for factory reform. See Catherine Gallagher, *The Industrial Reformation of English Fiction: Social Discourse and Narrative Form, 1832-1867* (Chicago, 1985), 10-33. The most extensive Parliamentary comparison of slaves to factory operatives in the three decades before Waterloo was made by a West Indian spokesman; see *Hansard's Parliamentary Debates* 9 (1807), cols. 532-537.

20. See Thomas Clarkson, *An Essay on, the Slavery and Commerce of the Human Species, particularly the African* (London, 1786), 136-137. It was of great strategic comfort to the early abolitionists that all classes of the "principal manufacturing towns" of Manchester and Birmingham supported the abolitionist movement from the outset. See Clarkson, *Two Essays on the Impolicy of the African Slave Trade* (London, 1788), 117-118; and S. Drescher, *Capitalism and Antislavery: British Mobilization in Comparative Perspective,* chap. 4. Ashworth concludes that to equate class hegemony with cross-class agreement is to devalue considerably the term "hegemony" (286). Similarly, to infer that silence on wage labour is equal to the legitimation of all of its effects is to stretch the meaning of legitimation. When Clarkson wrote of the potential superiority of *"free labour"* over slavery his image of labour was linked to the ideal of self-cultivation (Clarkson, 5). (Clarkson was concerned with comparisons of slave and free labour within Africa.) For a strong abolitionist condemnation of some metropolitan conditions as "abominations" (coincidental with the publication of Stephen's *Dangers),* see Thomas Clarke, *Letter to Mr. Cobbett on his Opinions respecting the slave trade* (London, 1807), 22, 48, 73, 87. David Turley's *The Culture of English Antislavery* (London, 1991), 147, finds no unified attitude among early abolitionist activists concerning the regulation of the labour market. On early radicalism and antislavery, see Drescher, *Capitalism,* 258-259, citing, among others, Granville Sharp's *A Representation of the Dangerous Tendency of Tolerating Slavery* (London, 1769), 75. See also the discussion of Sharp's plan for the

colonization of Sierra Leone in Philip Curtin, *The Image of Africa: British Ideas and Action, 1780-1850* (Madison, Wisc., 1964), chap. 4, 99-101.

21.   *Life and Works of Thomas Paine* (New York, 1925), VII, *Rights of Man*, 78-79; Robert W. Malcolmson, "Workers' Combinations in Eighteenth-Century England," in *The Origins of Anglo-American Radicalism*, ed. Margaret Jacob and James Jacob (London, 1984), 153.

22.   See Drescher, "Cart Whip," 3-24, and Clarkson's *Argument that the Colonial Slaves are better off than the British Peasantry, answered from the Royal Jamaica Gazette* (Whitby, 1824). David Eltis's essay "Abolitionist Perceptions of Society After Slavery," in Slavery *and British Society, 1776-1846*, ed. James Walvin (London, 1982), 195-213, supports this periodization, perhaps unintentionally. All of his citations of abolitionist opinions vindicating free labour as superior date from 1823 or afterwards. Significantly, Eltis's suggested temporal context for understanding British comparisons of colonial and metropolitan labour is not late Georgian Britain (1760-1837), but early Victorian Britain. On the comparative living standards of British labourers and West Indian slaves, see Ward, *British West Indian Slavery*, 261-263, 286-288.

23.   Davis's first reply to Haskell claims that abolitionism "was always related to the need to legitimate free wage labour" (162). The meaning of "related" and "need" are very ambiguous, as both Haskell and Ashworth observe (202, 287). Davis's text might be taken to mean that capitalists or elites needed to valorize wage labour. Or, it might mean that antislavery, simply as an argument against slavery, implied the legitimation or vindication of wage labour. Davis's second reply rules out the second option: "I have never sought to claim that antislavery *had* to rest on the vindication of industrial wage labour; I argued only that in early industrial Britain it did serve such a function for a certain class" (293). The implicit argument from silence now seems to be ruled out. Absent such an argument, one must then demonstrate empirically where and when elite antislavery made the vindication of wage labour a prominent item in its agenda.

24   In his final reply, Davis notes that "the ideal of *free labour*," as "distinct from both chattel and 'wage slavery'," was especially important to artisans and skilled workers who faced and feared the disintegration of traditional work practices (304). However, this very situation faced artisans and skilled workers in early industrial England. Further up the social ladder, rather than deflecting concern from the newest forms of capitalist abuse, the same core area of popular antislavery and early industrialization produced simultaneous critics of both slavery and the factory system. Manchester's Dr. John Ferriar, in the vanguard of abolitionism, was also a pioneer in the exposure of working conditions in the cotton mills and of the living conditions of manufacturing operatives. Compare his *The Prince* of Angola, *a Tragedy altered from the play of Oroonoko* (Manchester,

1788), preface; and his *Medical Histories and Reflections* (1792). Another Manchester abolitionist, Dr. Thomas Percival, was one of Britain's earliest advocates of parliamentary regulation of cotton mills. Percival made his appeal during the height of the conservative repression of the mid-1790s. It would be difficult to identify prominent non-abolitionists of any political stripe who did so much to publicize the plight of the cotton operatives before the end of the eighteenth century. Until the whole range of attitudes towards slavery and free labour between 1795 and 1823 is more systematically analyzed, the relationship between antislavery and political culture as a whole will be impossible to assess.

25.   In *The Antislavery Debate* it is sometimes asserted that antislavery was attractive to the British social and governing elite because it gave them a major opportunity to legitimize both political authority and industrial capitalism. Participants also make a second, less ambitious assertion, that the elite legislated a popularly supported abolitionism because it was the most conservative and least risky of the salient reform movements during the generation after 1790. These are compatible but not identical questions. The first addresses the central assertion that abolitionism played a substantial role in assuring the success of industrialization without political or social upheaval. The second concerns the question of why one reform passed into law rather than another. Ashworth ultimately makes this important distinction. Compare 70, 163, 288-289, 304-305.

26.   See also S. Drescher, "The Long Goodbye: Dutch Capitalism and Antislavery" (forthcoming).

27.   On the recent debates over the connection between the ending of slavery and economic growth in Western Europe, see Adriaan Verhulst, "The Decline of Slavery and the Economic Expansion of the Early Middle Ages," *Past and Present* 133 (November, 1991), 195-203. If one includes the ending of serfdom as well as slavery, social conflict models of the European transition gain considerable plausibility.

28.   See, among others, Ellis, *Economic Growth*, 18-20; and Fogel, *Without Consent*, 201-202. Holt's *Problem of Freedom*, 3-4, 34-35, roots the ideological break in the late seventeenth century. He stresses the economic and political revolutions of the late eighteenth century as the culmination of earlier classical bourgeois liberal ideology.

29.   See Drescher, *Capitalism and Antislavery*, 12-24.

30.   See especially Temperley, "Capitalism," 101-105; Drescher, *Econocide*, 170-183; Eltis, *Econoinic Growth*, 3-28; Fogel and Engerman, *Time on the Cross*, chap. 6; Fogel, *Without Consent*, 1, 64-72, 84-107; Davis, *Slavery and Human Progress*, 234-240; and Davis, *Problem of Slavery in Western Culture*, rev. ed. (New York, 1988), 153-164. Unlike the more widespread phenomenon of slave uprisings, human and material resources were most intensively mobilized, both for and against slavery, within the Anglophone areas of the Atlantic world.

78

The Decline Thesis of British Slavery Since Econocide

SEYMOUR DRESCHER

Part One: The Decline Thesis and its Opponents

Appearing in 1944, *Capitalism and Slavery* was a comprehensive attempt to explain the rise and fall of British colonial slavery in relation to the evolution of European world capitalism.[1] In dealing with the final stages of slavery, Eric Williams developed a two-pronged argument linking its demise to changes in the British imperial economy. The first prong related to changes in the structure of economic relationships between the metropolis and the colonies. Down to the American Revolutionary War, concluded Williams, British slavery, including the Atlantic slave trade, was a growing and complementary element of the imperial economy. The slave system provided an ever-increasing amount of tropical staples, protected market for British manufactures, and a source of British metropolitan capital. In a number of ways, the slave economy thus helped to fuel the industrial revolution. Williams' second prong related to political economy, to an economic ideology designated as mercantilism. It sustained the multiple linkages of the system by assuming the need for a protected imperial zone in which British manufactures, trade and maritime skills could develop.

For Williams, the American War dramatically changed the economies and ideological relationship which had sustained the slave system. British colonial production, under increasing competition from its French counterpart, ceased to provide what was needed by the empire amply or cheaply enough. *In Capitalism and Slavery*, 1776 began the 'uninterrupted decline' of the British West Indies both as a producer of British staples, as a consumer of British industrial output and as a contributor to British capital. The very capitalism that had been nurtured by slavery now destroyed the fetter on its own further development. At precisely the same moment a new political economy was adumbrated, in Adam Smith's *Wealth of Nations*. It viewed protected colonial trade as a brake on the creation of national wealth. The demise of slavery was thus perfectly congruent with the rise of laissez-faire.[2]

At a less global level *Capitalism and Slavery* also provided a detailed set of rigorous economic motivations for the short-run successes and failures of British abolition. The failure of the British West Indies to recover its rate of profitability after the American war combined with the growth of alternative staple sources to set the stage for the rise of abolitionism in the 1780s. The St. Domingue revolution momentarily stemmed the tide, but colonial overproduction induced abolition of the slave trade in 1806–07 and emancipation in 1833. All of this was set against the background of a continuous decline in West Indian profits, the imperial significance of British slavery and its metropolitan economic supports. One by one those interests which had once supported slavery turned against it.[3] Each and every tightening of the noose could be explained by reference to the interplay of economic patterns and motives. *Capitalism and Slavery* also contained two interesting but basically post-scriptural chapters on the roles of the abolitionist 'Saints' and the colonial slaves but

*This essay was prepared during a fellowship at the Woodrow Wilson Center for Scholars. I wish to express my appreciation to the participants at the Bellaggio conference on British Capitalism and British Slavery in 1984 for their extensive comments, and to Stanley Engerman in particular for his advice.

Slavery and Abolition, Vol. 7, No. 1 (1986), pp. 3–23.

the main story was carried along the path of its putative economic determinants.

In the three decades following the appearance of *Capitalism and Slavery* a number of objections were raised to some of Williams' short-run interpretations. Its major structural elements, however, remained deeply entrenched in the historiography of British anti-slavery: the rise of abolitionism was closely correlated with the rise of laissez-faire and the decline of the British West Indies. One of these elements rested on a tradition of British imperial history which divided an 'old' mercantilist from a 'new' laissez-faire empire by the American Revolution. The other element rested on the work of a number of historians of the Caribbean, above all Lowell Ragatz's *Fall of the Planter Class in the British West Indies, 1763-1833*. The striking novelty of *Capitalism and Slavery* lay in Williams' vigorous fusion of these two historiographical streams.

In approaching the discussion of Williams' most famous work during the past decade one should begin by observing that the systematic discussion of *Capitalism and Slavery* is itself little more than a decade old. Apart from Roger Anstey's initial foray in the *Economic History Review* (1968),[4] *Capitalism and Slavery* was either praised in passing or summarily dismissed, both without extended analysis. It therefore percolated, rather than flowed, into historiographical discourse for reasons which would make an interesting study in its own right.[5] By the mid-seventies, the Williams decline theory was being described by some historians as the new orthodoxy.

A major challenge appeared with the publication of two works. In 1975 *The Atlantic Slave Trade and British Abolition*, by Roger Anstey, attacked some of Williams' short-run interpretations, especially the motives for British abolition in 1806-07. In *Econocide* (1977) I challenged both the long- and short-term premises of *Capitalism and Slavery*. With the same data used both by contemporary actors and by Williams to show the 'amazing value' of the British West Indies before 1775, I found no decline in the value of the British slave system until well after the abolition of the slave trade.[6] There was in other words a disjuncture between the dramatic rise of political abolitionism and the economic value of its target. *Econocide* also took sharp issue with the premise that there was a major shift in the political economy of the British Empire following the American Revolution. Here too, I found that the change required by the Williams thesis was not tangibly

operative until *at least* three-quarters of the age of British abolitionism (1788-1838) had expired, if then. The thrust of *Econocide's* attack was quite clear. If British slavery was economically expanding at the moment that its growth was decisively inhibited by political action, its economic decline was contingent upon, not determinative of, abolitionism. Economic decline may well have eased the later stages of destruction. Likewise, a structural change in imperial political economy could not have been determinant at the beginning or the middle of the abolition process. One might even question whether it was clearly so at the end, in 1833. Some of *Econocide's* subordinate arguments will be considered at the appropriate place. The basic point is that *Econocide* challenged the validity of these two givens in the explanation of British abolition. It neither precluded hypotheses based on indirect economic arguments nor urged a reversion to the old humanitarian narrative of the victory of the Saints.

Part Two: After *Econocide*
Defenders of the Decline Theory

In dealing with the Williams decline thesis since *Econocide* one initial difficulty presents itself. There have been few further extended discussions of the Williams thesis. In this sense the discussion of the critique of the Williams thesis has been almost as slow in getting off the ground as Williams' original critique of the 'Coupland' tradition. One extended essay on the status of the question was published by Stanley Engerman and David Eltis in 1980.[7] Another was produced by Cecil Gutzmore for the Hull Sesquicentennial in 1983.[8] A much lengthier critique of *Econocide*, by Selwyn Carrington, appeared, with an appended reply, in June 1984.[9] Otherwise the decline theory has been discussed more casually in books, essays, and introductions to other collective enterprises. For our purposes, one valuable vein of discussion can also be assayed — reviews and review essays on *Econocide*. To their authors my procedure might be viewed as sacrilege or, at the very least, as hitting well below the intellect. Scholars never expect to have what they say in reviews held against them. Yet the large number of reviews offer a very broad sampling of the general reaction to the issues raised by *Econocide*. There is already some precedent for using the reviews. Walter E. Minchinton's essay, 'Williams and Drescher: Abolition and Emancipation', in the September 1983 issue of

Slavery and Abolition, extensively quotes from the most critical ones. I will therefore use them to highlight typical reactions, including areas of agreement, disagreement, and ˙designated directions for future orientation.

One may logically begin with the decline theory. *Capitalism and Slavery* posited that the British Caribbean had attained an 'amazing value' for Britain on the eve of American independence. Its value depreciated from 1776 on. Williams' empirical demonstration was founded on the data of British overseas trade, drawn from official records from 1697 to 1773, as compiled by Sir Charles Whitworth.[10] It should be noted that Williams broadly and explicitly included both the African and foreign slave trades sectors in his accounting system.[11] He also compared the British Afro-Caribbean system with others. *Econocide's* first major step was to carry Williams' systemic analysis of 1697–1773 forward half a century, using the same database and 'filling in' the void in the Williams account for the period between the Declaration of Independence and Waterloo.[12]

The central indicator used by both *Capitalism and Slavery* and *Econocide* as a measure of value is conceptually important in another respect. It was the one measure most available to, and overwhelmingly used by, contemporaries in the political debate over abolition. Its use therefore avoids severe epistemiological problems which arise from employing measures of value which were either unclear to contemporaries or not central to their arguments. I must return to this problem below. *Econocide* portrayed the impact of the trade data graphically by superimposing the Williams 'rising' years (until the early seventies) with the putative 'decline' period thereafter (see figure 1).[13] One might easily perform similar operations in tabular form.

Table 1 shows the British West Indian percentage of British overseas trade using key pivotal years ranging from 1763 to 1783. In each case the period *after* exceeds the share of the period *before* the pivotal date, both for the medium and the long term. To judge from the general reception of *Econocide*, most scholars have accepted the idea that the systematic extension of the Williams database requires some revision of *Capitalism and Slavery's* argument in its classical format of '1776 and all that'.[14]

One statistical demolition did not of course end the discussion. One way of responding to any given data series is to extend it. Perhaps the Williams database doesn't work for the 50 years

Figure 1

British West Indian Trade, 1722–1822

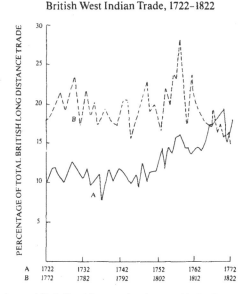

Source: Mitchell and Deane, Abstract, pp. 309–11, 'Overseas Trade'.

Table 1 British West Indian Shares of British Trade (Imports, Exports, and Re-exports) for Various 'Pivotal' years 1763–83

Years	%	Prior – equivalent period	
		Years	%
Pivot of 1763 (Ragatz)			
1763–92	18.30	1782–62	11.99
1763–97	18.24	1723–62	11.88
1763–1802	18.69	1718–92	11.90
1763–1807	19.08	1713–62	11.62
Pivot of 1776 (Williams)			
1777–1806	19.36	1737–76	14.50
1777–1811	19.82	1732–76	14.16
1777–1816	19.46	1727–76	13.96
1777–1821	18.97	1722–76	13.76
Pivot of Peace of Versailles			
1783–1807	19.42	1758–82	17.54
1783–1812	19.76	1753–82	17.04
1783–1817	19.36	1748–82	16.36
1783–1822	18.71	1743–82	15.82

Source: Mitchell and Deane, *Abstract of British Historical Statistics*, (Cambridge, 1962), pp. 309–11.

after 1763 or 1776, but what if we use Ragatz's 'falling planters' of 1763–1833 or Williams' 'rising free-traders' of 1776–1846?[15] Isn't decline visible toward the end? The answer is yes, but the point also strikes me as wide of the original mark. *Econocide's* own first table shows that by 1828–32 the British West Indies was relatively back where it had been in the mid-eighteenth century. (One might still be tempted to say that Britain's slave system had, at long last, declined only to the point where it was as valuable as in its Ragatzian 'golden age'.) Such a line of argument already grants the basic point of the original argument against the Williams thesis no matter how deeply or steeply the slave system declined after the abolition of the slave trade. It is clear that thereafter the limits to the value of anti-slavery were political rather than economic. It is also difficult to see how any scholar inclined toward economic determinism can take much comfort in the observation that the 'real' decline in West Indian fortunes was political.[16] The unique strength of *Capitalism and Slavery* resides in the affirmation of a conjuncture between economic and political change. No correlation, no thesis.

Econocide did not suppose that all political limitations on the slave system were ineffectual until the moment of emancipation. That seemed irrelevant. Lengthening the frame of reference to 1833 or even to 1983 does not alter the basic Williams hypothesis — that economic decline induced the abolitionist-capitalist attack in 1788-92, or the victory in 1806-07. The relationship between imperial economic policy in the final stages of abolition and apprenticeship may therefore be treated quite independently of the crucial policy decision to limit its further growth. Even beyond this the Williams scenario faces other difficulties which have not yet been faced by those who see the period 1823-46 as a saving remnant for *Capitalism and Slavery*. The final 'stage' of the Williams decline theory is based on the following argument. By 1833 a Parliament had been elected in Britain which, said Williams, 'was perfectly responsive to the needs and aspirations of British capitalists'.[17] Hence, British capitalism destroyed slavery as a first step in the destruction of the West Indian monopoly (p. 169). Yet the fact is that emancipation was not coordinated with a step against West Indian monopoly but with one which gave it a new lease of life.

If the protection of British slave sugar produced resentment after the Napoleonic wars, whether from East Indian or consumer interests, relief was clearly no priority in Parliament during the debates over emancipation and apprenticeship between 1823 and 1838. As late as 1841 the government was defeated in the Commons when it attempted to reduce the protection accorded to British colonial sugar. Therefore it seems that by 1833 either a Parliament had been elected which was

not 'perfectly responsive' to the aspirations of the capitalists, or the capitalists in 1833 did *not* aspire to anti-monopoly, or emancipation was not taken as a step toward the end of West Indian monopoly, or Parliament aspired more to destroy slavery than West Indian monopoly. From Williams' account I do not believe it is possible to sustain the sequence of his argument.

Alongside the role of the slave system as an imperial trading partner, *Capitalism and Slavery* stressed a second aspect of economic development — the putative profit decline of the West Indian planters. Here Williams challenged the economic viability of the British plantation system after the American Revolutionary War. He stressed not only the 'monopoly' character of the West Indies, 'but that it was so unprofitable that for this reason alone its destruction was inevitable'.[18] *Capitalism and Slavery* therefore argued for a sharp fall in Jamaica profits after 1774. Since the link between unprofitability and destruction is made so forcefully at the general level, recent scholars have rightly introduced more detailed and systematic analysis to this aspect of the Ragatz and Williams decline thesis.

It should be pointed out that there is a difference between the rate of plantation profits to the planters or African merchants, and the value of their system to the Empire. The happiness of the planters over their profit conditions was no more central to their utility to the metropolis than the happiness of the slaves over their working conditions.

In any event, the viability of slavery to the planters may have been less impaired by the abolition of the slave trade than was slavery's relative significance in the trade system. On this question J. R. Ward has done much to systematically demonstrate that the West Indian colonies as a whole were operating at a profit down to the eve of emancipation. His data seem to indicate that profit rates were as high or higher after the American War as before, and that, at least until 1820, an average return of 10 per cent was as characteristic of the period following as for the period before the American War, at least down to 1820. Ward also seems to agree that the Ragatzean picture of progressive decrepitude has to be modified.[19]

Econocide was also criticized for insufficient attention to the issue of shifting patterns of capital investment in the slave property of the British West Indies.[20] Using Caribbean slave population growth as an index of capital growth, it would appear that capital investment was increasing at a more rapid rate between

1790–1805 than between 1750–70. The capital value of the British slave empire more than doubled between 1785 and 1815 (including conquered areas). The £15 million sunk by British investors into Demerara alone between the British conquest in 1796 and its temporary return to the Dutch in 1802 served as a standing reminder to abolitionists concerning the prospects of slavery as a field for investment before the abolition of the slave trade.

Scholarly attention has also been recently focused on the significance of British slavery in accounting for the growth of British exports before and during the industrial revolution.[21] In this context François Crouzet estimates that the West Indies accounted for 18 per cent of the increase of British exports from 1700/01 to 1772/73. Until the end of the century the West Indies actually increased its share. Considering the three decades 1783/1812 as a whole the West Indies and Latin America (also served by the African slave trade) contributed more to Britain's cumulated additional exports (official values) than any area except the United States. Table 2 shows that the West Indies steadily maintained its relative role in British export growth until the abolition of the slave trade as other areas rose or fell dramatically. Africa's independent role fell as did that of North America and, most dramatically, the export trade east of the Cape of Good Hope.

These are measures which can be placed alongside the trade figures. For some supporters of a 1776 + decline theory, however, the use of trade figures to measure the long-range value of British slavery to the British imperial economy was spurious and beside the point. The same would apparently hold for both planter profits and capital accumulation rates. They were all amassed under protective barriers. For some reviewers, the central shift in the abolitionist victory lies not at all in the trade series but in a decisive shift of the *measurement* of value which presumably occurred under the aegis of a shifting political economy from mercantilism to laissez-faire. For Barbara Solow, as for Mary Turner and Elsa Goveia, *the* major long-run fact of British slave production is that the British consumer paid more for eighteenth-century British sugar than his or her continental counterpart paid for non-British, and especially French, sugar. Fundamentally, this is a cost-accounting argument, using the world market as the basic measure of value. If British importers were paying a higher price for their muscovado than was warranted by the world market the value of the sugar colonies was deceptive. Noel Deerr accounts for this in terms of a qualitative difference between British and French muscovado,[22] but the fact remains that for most of the eighteenth century British plantation sugar did not compete effectively on the continental market except in war years, when French sugars were bottled up by the British navy and privateers.

Whether or not it was Williams' principal line of attack, this point, acknowledged by *Econocide*, was part of an effort to resuscitate the decline thesis. This, says Barbara Solow, 'is the decline that matters'. Fair enough — let us give the price-competitive argument the attention it deserves. The single major problem

Table 2 British Percentage of Area Shares Contributions to Increased Exports, 1700–01 to 1804–06

Area	(Official values) 1700/01 to 1772/73 (1)	(Current values) 1784/86 to 1804/06 (2)	Manufacturing exports only 1784/86 to 1804/06 (3)
West Indies	18.2	21.1	22.3
Latin America		4.0	4.3
Africa	7.8	2.5	2.6
Ireland, etc	14.6	10.1	8.0
East Indies	13.5		
Asia (incl. China)		3.2	2.8
Europe	4.2	30.3	28.7
Continenal North America	41.8	28.3	30.7
Other		0.4	

Sources: Column 1, François Crouzet, 'Toward an Export Economy: British Exports during the Industrial Revolution', *Explorations in Economic History*, 17 (1980), 48–93, p. 72; columns 2 and 3, Ralph Davis, *The Industrial Revolution and British Overseas Trade* (Leicester, 1978), p. 89.

with the 'mercantilist sugar' argument is the same one that attaches generically to a whole set of parallel long-range indictments concerning the efficiency of the British slave system — absenteeism, indebtedness, white flight, demographic deficiency, soil exhaustion, etc. All of these 'disabilities' were identified on both sides of the ocean more than half a century before 1790 without inciting either to abolitionism or abolition.[23] So it is with French sugar. The condition did not, as Solow speculates, begin as early as the 1760s. It was definitively recognized at least as early as the 1730s, using, of course, the same import, export and re-export data used for the volume of trade measures in *Capitalism and Slavery* and *Econocide*. The planters and their friends complained of it, their North American enemies gloated over it, their own allies pled it every time there was an internal squabble over redistribution of mercantilist burdens — whether in the 1730s or the 1780s.

Without too much difficulty one could push the perception back still further. The comparative cheapness of foreign sugar was in fact emphasized by the West Indian planters as early as the Peace of Utrecht.[24] How then could such a hoary fact induce abolition? The neo-decliners claim that a new stimulus to recognition of this fact burst through in the 1780s and held fast thereafter. Why? Various 'candidate' catalysts are offered. Williams himself had offered booming St. Domingue after 1783. The American Revolution left the British sugar planters 'face to face with their French rivals'.[25] *Econocide* showed that the relationship remained 'back to back', as it had for half a century before. Each system served separate markets, and Jamaican sugar was actually expanding faster than that of St. Domingue on the eve of abolitionist take-off in the late eighties. *Econocide* therefore claimed that before 1790 'British planters did not seriously challenge their French rivals and that the metropolis did not seriously challenge the planter monopoly'. Therefore the British planters I concluded 'nestled comfortably in the arms' of their own protected market.[26] The neo-decliners disagree. Mary Turner's catalysts are the fall of the Bastille and the French Revolution. Solow's are Adam Smith in 1776 and Pitt's condemnation of the slave trade in 1791. All of these catalysts were followed (Solow's within a few hours) by Parliament's thumping *rejection* of abolition by a vote of almost two to one.

There is another more fundamental fact of sugar prices, however, which argues against the cheap sugar argument for abolition. Abolition scored its first symbolic victory in 1792, and its second substantive victory in 1806–07, after a decade in which world market sugar prices actually moved in favour of the British consumer.[27] It was precisely in 1791 that British sugar once again massively re-entered the continental market. (As for emancipation, Howard Temperley has also argued that, in the period prior to 1833, a large proportion of the West Indian crop was sold on the world market, which determined its price.[28]) The biggest price gap between the British and the world market reopened as a consequence, not a cause, of the advent of a free labour market after apprenticeship. Moreover, the market price economic interpretation of abolition must also account for the reason why planters' spokesmen were more open to laissez-faire on both the carrying and marketing of their sugar at the time of the abolition of the slave trade than was the British Parliament which controlled their destinies. In 1807 the British government served up the Orders-in-Council and protectionism all around. Economists might wish to do another estimate of the value of the Sugar colonies to Great Britain for the period 1790–1807 to see whether the abolitionists attacked and won during the precise period when, by cost-accounting criteria, the metropolis was a loss to the colonies, not vice versa. In the first decade of the nineteenth century, British per capita consumption of sugar was probably at its all-time peak for the entire era of British colonial slavery.

If a neo-classical cheap sugar model has difficulty enough in addressing the timing of abolitionism it gets into even more difficulty in accounting for the targets. If Smithian anti-monopoly sentiment was a source of antagonism to British slavery after 1788, why was the first target that segment of the slave economy (the African slave trade) which did so much of its business in successful competition in the world market? And why was abolitionism's second target (1805) the premier British *cotton* colony (Demerara) whose produce received absolutely no protection whatever in the metropolitan market? Neo-classical economism may wind up with as many facts to explain away as its Marxian predecessor.[29]

Finally, the classical approach must respond to the same epistemological problem as historians who regard trade figures as more central indicators (than planter profit) of value. Empirically, the trade figures were primarily used by contemporary policy makers in abolition debates. The abolitionists pointed to potential alternative sources of British trade, but until well after slave trade ended the abolitionists always had to point toward the bush rather than the hand. Over the course of the 50 years from 1783 to emancipation the abolitionists were always more speculative customer-counters than their opponents.

This approach to decline strikes me as deriving from a broader historical misconception. It assumes, with Williams, that there was a political swing away from mercantilism in the generation after the publication of *Wealth of Nations* and the Peace of Versailles. As P. J. Cain and A. G. Hopkins have argued, there was no widespread conversion to laissez-faire after 1776. There were merely sectoral adjustments for specific targets of opportunity within the old framework.[30] The French Wars gave added impetus to the arguments for strengthening the empire rather than lowering barriers to free competition. The burdens of war, not of the consumer, were the main concern of British governments in the decades before abolition. The ever-ascending proportion of the retail price of sugar determined by fixed rate duties amply demonstrates this. The great shift in the balance of economic power and priorities came during the 30 years after the fall of Napoleon. The Cain-Hopkins reassessment coincides with that of *Econocide* rather than with those theories requiring more of a laissez-faire 'spirit of '76'.

In addition to its neo-classical defenders, the decline thesis has also found new supporters within the mercantilist frame of reference which was less explicitly but in fact more frequently employed by *Capitalism and Slavery*. Given the stubborn persistence of the mercantilist perspective in Britain, indeed its reaffirmation less than two years before political abolition was placed on the parliamentary agenda, it has been re-argued that the very interests united by mercantilism before 1775 were instrumental in undermining the West India interest. Ragatz and Williams, now reinforced by Carrington, emphasize that in 1785 the British shipping interest decisively fought to limit the claims of the West Indians to trade with American carriers.[31] With major exceptions for 'emergencies', this prohibition remained in effect until the mid-twenties. The policy was particularly damaging to the planter interest in the mid-eighties and in 1805–08. The second structural pressure on the planters was the

metropolitan policy of heavy fixed duties upon sugar. Duties on imports rose during each conflict and were never substantially reduced before abolition.

Carrington argues that these facts demonstrate the decline of the planter class and, therefore, of British West Indian slavery. This by no means follows. The maintenance of the navigation laws clearly underlined the dependence of the British shipping interest on the West Indies. Within its mercantilist perspective the West Indian shipping interest thereafter supported the West Indies against abolitionists. After slave trade abolition the West Indies in fact supplied one of the few outlets for the re-deployment of former slave ships until the end of the continental blockade. Even more of former slave ships until the end of the continental blockade. Even more clearly, sugar duties were one of the fiscal mainstays of public revenue. No government considered risking a change during the course of, or immediately after, the French wars. Both the sugar revenues and the navigation system force us to recognize the important differences for the empire between the short-run prosperity of the planter and the value of the sugar colonies. This, again, is why trade figures strike me as a better indicator of the significance at the imperial level than profitability or prices. The mercantilist perspective, as *Econocide* emphasizes, did allow abolitionists, regardless of growth or decline, to move separately against the slave trade when they could convince Parliament that no unmanageable short-run damage would accrue to the slave colonies in the circumstances of 1806–07.

Both the neo-mercantilist and laissez-faire arguments assume an imperial or world-market context. Another strategic defence of the decline theory focuses on intracolonial comparisons. As one would expect, this frame of reference is most frequently invoked by historians of the West Indies. In defending *Capitalism and Slavery* these historians maintain that *Econocide* does not sufficiently emphasize differential development within the islands.[32] They point out that some old colonies, at least, had passed their peak. On similar grounds Carrington in his lengthy critique of *Econocide* has systematically attempted to revive the Ragatzian perspective in toto. His own analysis gives to the decline of the old islands primacy of position. Carrington goes even further. He imputes to *Econocide* the argument that 'the older islands (namely Barbados and the Leeward Islands) were not saturated as was generally believed but were developing with renewed strength'. Carrington considers that point critical to Drescher's study. In fact, *Econocide* explicitly argues exactly the opposite. Summarizing British Caribbean conditions in 1790, *Econocide* says: 'Taken as a whole, the slave colonies had exhausted neither their soil nor their potential. *Some, such as Barbados and the Leeward Islands, were considered to be at or past their optimum development. But this was only one segment of the islands'*[33] (italics added).

Econocide reiterates in its closing chapter for the period 1780–1833 as a whole, 'Metropolitan politicians would naturally think in imperial not regional terms. *Barbados had no special economic status as against Jamaica in 1788, and Jamaica had none vis-à-vis Trinidad in 1805 or Demarara in 1815.*' And, 'the dynamic of the colonial system was no more measured by the statistics of the seventeenth-century pioneers than were metropolitan trends by the statistics of Old Sarum.'[34] *Econocide* maintains that at *all* times from the end of the American war to Waterloo, and beyond, there were developing slave sectors. This was as visible to contemporaries as it should be to historians. Eric Williams' own favourite source for pre-1776, Sir Charles Whitworth, showed that as of 1790, Jamaica, Dominica and St. Vincent had clearly expanded beyond their pre-war peaks. Other official sources showed that Jamaica, St. Vincent and Trinidad were frontier *de jure* colonies as of 1802, to which one could add Demerara (*de facto*) in 1807 and Demerara, Mauritius and the Cape Colony (*de jure*) by 1815. Carrington's approach does indicate why many of the smaller islands were less apprehensive (but never to the point of advocacy) of abolition in 1807.

The method of reducing the decline theory of British slavery to the decline of some parts of British slavery does not, in fact, support Williams' turning point. Rather it undermines it and throws into question the very possibility of using such a theory in historical analysis. If, using Carrington's criteria, decline must be dated from the decline of the first slave area in an economic system, American slavery was declining almost before slavery crossed the Appalachians, when Pennsylvania legislated its gradual abolition. Using Carrington's criteria, the decline of slavery in Delaware after 1800 would mean that Southern slavery too was already in decline. In the West Indies Carrington's criteria dispose not only of *Econocide's* nineteenth-century turning point,

but of Williams' (1776) and Ragatz's (1763) as well. As Williams himself noted, 'as early as 1663, a mere twenty years after the rise of the sugar industry, Barbados was "decaying fast" and the complaints of soil exhaustion grew more numerous and more plaintive'.[35] This would, it is true, give economic decline a comfortable 150-year lead on abolition. It would, however, also mean that over 98 per cent of the slaves brought to America in British ships between 1620 and 1808 were boarded after the beginning of the decline of British slavery.[36] If, following Carrington, we use Deerr's 'old colony' sugar export figures rather than colonial complaints it still appears that Barbados reached its pre-abolition sugar peak in 1698, more than one hundred years before 1808. Nevis' pre-abolition peak was in 1710, Montserrat's in 1735.[37] Therefore, of the five little-old-islands possessed by Britain on the eve of the Seven Years' War, a majority were already long in decline. We would have to conclude that Ragatz was too late by a full generation and Williams by 40 years in identifying the turning point. A reduction of British slavery to its insular parts reduces the very idea of rise and fall, whether of Drescher, Williams, Ragatz, or most other historians of Atlantic slavery, to chaos.

Carrington also uses the crop by crop performance of the British West Indies between 1775 and 1806 to test and to reaffirm the decline theory against *Econocide*. I again take fundamental issue with his method of disaggregation. *Econocide* showed that the sugar islands were both dynamic and flexible in the face of new opportunities. As new opportunities opened up for sugar, the British colonies became the largest colonial producing area in the world. Far from being exclusively wedded to monoculture, British slavery became *increasingly* polycultural in the decades between the Treaty of Versailles and abolition of the slave trade.

British dependency on slave-grown imports clearly increased during the two decades prior to the abolition of the British slave trade. Table 3 shows that the primary slave products increased their relative contribution to total British imports. The fact that cotton and coffee gained on sugar does not alter the picture of the combined figures. Britain became more dependent not only upon the slave zone but upon the slave importing areas as well. If slave-based cotton production was entirely responsible for the increase in British exports between 1792 and 1806, half of that raw material was still dependent upon slave importing

Table 3 Slave-Grown share of British Imports, 1784–86 to 1814–16

Product	(1) Current value (£000)	(2) % Predominatly grown by slaves	(3) % of total British imports	(4) % grown in slave importing areas	(5) % of total British imports in same
			1784/86		
Sugar	2614	100	11.5	100	11.5
Coffee	158	88	0.6	88	0.6
Cotton	1817[a]	70	5.6	70	5.6
Total			17.7		17.7
All British imports	22761				
			1804/06		
Sugar	6879	97	12.0	97	12.0
Coffee	2458	99	4.4	99	4.4
Cotton	5628	89[a]	9.0	53[b]	5.4
Total			25.4		21.8
All British imports	55558				
			1814/16		
Sugar	11138	98	15.1	—	—
Coffee	2784	79	3.1	—	—
Cotton	8593	96	11.5	35	4.2
Total			29.7		4.2
All British imports	71796				
			1824/26		
Sugar	6722	93	9.4	—	—
Coffee	1022	87	1.3	—	—
Cotton	7452	86	9.7	18	2.0
Total			20.4		2.0
All British imports	66389				

[a] Estimates of contributing areas from *Econocide*, pp. 84–85.
[b] U.S. cotton production is excluded here from the slave-importing zone, although abolition was not effected until 1808. Column 2 represents the actual percentage in 1804/06.
Source: Ralph Davis, *The Industrial Revolution and British Overseas Trade* (Leicester, 1978), appendix on British imports.

economies. Even (prematurely) excluding the United States from the slave importing roster (column 3, 1804–06) does not alter the general picture (column 4). If one also added rice and tobacco to the slave-produced share of British imports the dependency on slavery would rise still higher, to 23 per cent in 1784/86, 27 per cent in 1804/06, and 32 per cent in 1814/16, according to Ralph Davis' figures.

Ralph Davis' post-*Econocide* figures on real trade values from 1794–96 to 1844–46 also show that while cotton and coffee accounted for only 28 per cent of the value of the 'big three' British slave staples in 1784–86, they accounted for more than 39 per cent in 1804–06.[38] On the eve of abolition slave production was tangibly

diversifying as well as expanding. All of this remains hidden if each crop is treated in isolation. Not only did coffee emerge as the new 'second' crop to sugar after the American war, but sugar culture itself underwent a 'green revolution'. The introduction of Otaheite cane in the last decade of the eighteenth century increased yields per acre. The British colonies were pioneers in this transformation.[39]

Carrington offers a final structural argument on behalf of the Williams decline dating. This concerns the slave trade itself as an indicator. While most recent scholarship has tended to accept the Anstey-Drescher claim that the British slave trade peaked only after the American War, in the 1790s, David

Richardson's findings seem to modify that claim.[40] His figures apparently indicate twin peaks, one just before the American War of Independence and a second only slightly higher, in the 1790s. By all counts the total American post-war volume exceeded any pre-war equivalent period. Most scholars also agree that the British trade was somewhat reduced by the Slave Carrying Act of 1799, further reduced by the abolition Act of 1806, and virtually annihilated by the Act of 1807. J. E. Inikori argues for a much higher 'hidden' trade than other scholars from 1800 to 1807.[41] *Econocide* was sceptical of the argument but emphasized that the impact of abolition would be magnified by Inikori's estimate.

Carrington disputes not the fact of expansion but its interpretation. He argues that the crucial point is not how *many* slaves were transported by British carriers but what percentage were re-exported from the old islands. 'One of the best indicators of West Indian prosperity during the eighteenth century', he claims, 'was the ability and readiness of the planters to purchase slaves. 'For most of the period up to 1775–76, the planters retained a majority of the slaves imported into the islands. After the American War, even if more slaves were imported into the islands than in the pre-1775 period, a larger number was also re-exported.'[42]

Jamaican data (the only island for which we have a full run of eighteenth-century re-exports) show that most of the years in which a majority of slaves was re-exported come from the period *prior* to 1775/76.[43] This misreading of the data brings us to the larger issue of Carrington's use of re-exports as an indicator of decline.

Carrington argues that the percentage of re-exports should be used as an indicator of decline. Elsewhere I have argued that, based on Jamaica's data series, there was no direct correlation between the rate of planter profits and the rate of re-exports. I also showed that post-1800 re-export figures could be quite deceptive since a substantial number were recycled to *de jure* British colonies. An even larger number went to *de facto* British planters. Further evidence against any positive correlation between the percentage of retained slave imports and planter prosperity may be observed from Carrington's own Bellaggio paper, 'The Economy of the British West Indies, 1775–1791: The Makings of the Williams/Drescher Controversy', Appendix V.[44] Ignoring for the moment the methodological difficulty in excluding slave import figures into the new frontier regions of

Table 4 Percentage of Received Slaves Re-exported from Jamaica by Five-Year Intervals, 1713–87

Period	% Re-exported	Period	% Re-exported
1713–17	50.2	1758–62	15.0
1718–22	40.1	1763–67	17.0
1723–27	43.9	1768–72	13.0
1728–32	44.5	1773–78	15.3
1733–37	43.6	1778–82	14.6
1738–42	15.5	1783–87	32.0
1742–47	24.0	Years over 50% re-exports:	
1748–52	22.1	1709, 1713, 1714, 1719, 1720,	
1753–57	12.1	1723, 1724, 1730, 1731, 1733	
		(peak 69.9%), *1786*	

Source: McKusker, 'The Rum Trade', pp. 615–16.

Trinidad and Demerara, one can easily observe that the planters retained the highest percentage of slaves just when their profits were *lowest*. From 1788 to 1798 planters enjoyed an almost uninterrupted period of high profits. Yet the lowest retention rates are clustered precisely in that period (with the exception of 1798). Correspondingly the years 1800–01 and 1805 were years of low or falling prices, yet they seem to be characterized by high retention rates. There are enough anomalies, even from this pattern, to cast doubt on the relevance of profits to re-exports altogether, but it is at least quite clear that the hypothesis of low profits–high re-exports and vice versa is not borne out.

Finally, I wish to draw attention to the untenability of the whole Carrington premise on even longer-term grounds. In Table 4, I carry the percentage of Jamaican re-exports back to the Treaty of Utrecht. The reader can easily observe that using percentages of re-exports as an indicator of decline places the nadir of the most dynamic old British colony in the 'Asiento' years at the beginning of the *eighteenth* century. As given, Carrington's re-exports theory, like his 'little-old-colony' theory, leads us to a Herodian slaughter of the innocents. It would simply destroy the development paradigms of most historians including Williams. If we accept Carrington's premises, we have truly entered an age of paradigms lost.

Ebb and Flow

In terms of the larger issues one can spend less time with the post-*Econocide* views which draw on *Capitalism and Slavery* to explain the ups and downs of abolitionist fortunes. Like the spatial and product segmentations just discussed, these tend to look to very short-run developments to explain political decisions. Scholars reflecting on these questions do not necessarily take issue with the broader findings of *Econocide* or defend those of *Capitalism and Slavery*. For the post-American War decade Carrington upholds Williams' short-run arguments to the letter. He asserts, with Williams, that the slave system failed to recover its 1774–75 level of profitability during the years between the Treaty of Versailles (1783) and the St. Domingue Revolution. I have again argued elsewhere that profits by and even before 1791 were well above their level of 1775.

Another post-war issue concerns the impact of the restrictions on American carriers to the British islands after 1783. Carrington maintains that shortages lasted until the St. Domingue uprising. I again take the opposite position. In this encounter Carrington sticks with the Ragatzian position *tout court* — that St. Domingue alone, and only momentarily, saved the tottering planters. Some historians slice the post-American War frame of reference even more finely. In an essay on Britain's policy towards St. Domingue, David Geggus focuses on the state of the West Indies just prior to the abolitionist breakthrough in 1788–91.[45] He nods in *Econocide's* direction by noting that production recovered pre-war levels by the mid-1780s. However, he faults the study for relying too heavily on the turbulent years after 1789 to make a case for the West Indies' recovery of its imperial position. If, however, Geggus had compared the '*non*-turbulent' pre-American War years (1771–1774) with only the equally non-turbulent post-war and pre-French revolutionary years (1784–1788), he would have found that the West Indies accounted for a higher percentage of British imports, exports and total trade in the second period than the first. *Econocide* characterized the 1780s as a period of West Indian recovery. As with the whole metropolitan export trade, it was only in the 1790s that recovery gave way to new growth.

Many historians, including Geggus and Carrington, point to annual downturns in production, profits, trade shares and the slave trade during the period 1783–1807. There is no objection to using these for carefully delimited comparisons. But decline theorists could hardly insist that annual or even quinquennial downturns in an economic sector are sufficient to categorize it as a declining trend. Otherwise, almost every major British trade in the Empire, metropolitan and colonial alike, was declining at some point between 1783 and 1806. Even the superstar of the post-1783 period, British cottons, staggered badly in the 1790s. Exceptional critics like Minchinton, who apply

such a rigorous criterion of cumulative trends to the British West Indian case, simply fail to note that by such a test no British trading zone in the world rose or fell continuously during every quinquennium of the century before Waterloo (see *Econocide*, table 2). Cyclical and politically induced fluctuations were bound to be part of any economic activity.

Some objections to *Econocide* consisted in quoting 'high authorities' on short-term issues to explain general motives. In *every* case to date this comes down to the pleasant pastime of 'pick your pundit'.[46] Arguing for Williams' overproduction thesis, one historian triumphantly cited a speech by the 'Leading Minister' in the Lords who in 1807 assured his House that abolition would save the planters from ruin. Hence concern about overproduction presumably predisposed the House to vote for abolition. The same historian neglects to observe that two weeks later the 'Leading Minister' of the other House assured *his* audience that abolition would lead to no decrease of production. The House then voted even more overwhelmingly for abolition. May we then conclude that the Commons was even more anxious about underproduction in 1807.

Aside from these possibilities, it is clear that the factors most important to Williams, a coalescence of antagonistic economic interests and a shift in political economy, simply have not been unearthed by further research as playing their allotted role in the decline and fall of slavery outlined by *Capitalism and Slavery*. This does not preclude incorporating negative short-term psychological effects of the American War on the West Indies on the slave interest. It does fundamentally challenge any account of abolition which incorporates either the decline of the West Indies or perceptions of the decline of the value of slavery to Britain during the generation after 1783. Just as Williams may have exaggerated the increasing importance of the West Indies to the imperial economy before 1775 so he appears, at the very least, to have exaggerated the diminution of its importance to Britain before emancipation. It is more likely that as in the case of American slavery two growing, if unequal, social systems faced each other, rather than a rising and a falling one.

Part Three: Alternatives to West Indian Decline

Thus far we have dealt with arguments tending to defend elements of the Williams thesis as given within the parameters of *Capitalism and Slavery*. Some approaches actually narrow the framework of discussion. It is now important to consider some of the alternatives to the Williams economic decline thesis.

We can begin at the extremes. On the one hand, one might conclude, with Roger Anstey, that the sapping of the Ragatz-Williams decline theory means that the case for explaining abolition in 'terms of fundamental economic change is seriously if not totally undermined'.[47] On the other hand, from the Marxist side, Cecil Gutzmore, in his survey of the 'bourgeois' critiques of *Capitalism and Slavery*, similarly assumes that the effect of these critiques is to return the state of the question 'to the rather narrow Christian (even Methodist) humanitarianism of those who originally erected the tradition'.[48] The pendulum presumably swings back from the pristine economic determinism of *Capitalism and Slavery* to the pure moralism of the Coupland school.

Neither the expectations of Anstey nor the fears of Gutzmore have prevailed. The outcome to date is illustrated by many of those who accepted the main critique of the Williams thesis as valid, yet immediately seek alternative explantation somehow grounded in fundamental economic development. Pieter Emmer's was a typical response to *Econocide*: Drescher's new interpretation, he concluded, 'has overturned most of the factual implication of the Williams thesis. But still . . . there remains something unassailable in this thesis concerning the connection between economics and abolition.'[49]

Econocide, some reviewers realized, did not at all dispute this. Philip Curtin noted that a staunch defender of a Marxian point of view could take a more roundabout approach, drawing a class struggle out of the religious ideology that pervaded British middle-class life in the eighteenth century. Alan Adamson, moving the argument toward the post-emancipation period, suggests that economic forces would be much more apparent in the struggle over the sugar duties. Richard Lopper also argues that a Marxist analysis can easily accommodate an abandonment of both the decline thesis and Williams' economic determinist reading of abolition.[50]

Embodied in many reactions, made as reservations or suggestions, are two fundamental propositions. The first of these might be called a historiographical gut feeling.

The response goes something like this: 'It is surely no accident that abolition coincided with the industrial revolution.' The second fundamental proposition, however, seems to derive from a recognition, sometimes wholehearted, sometimes grudging, that the abolition of slavery cannot be explained by direct extrapolation from pure economic motives or mechanisms any more than from pure moral consciousness. Most of the alternative approaches thus far lean toward an attempt to find a new ideological base for abolitionism. The attack on the Coupland school of pure ideas by the Williams school of impure interests begins with a search for convincingly impure ideas. The principal target of scholarly concern has become the anti-slavery 'ideology' — some combination of economic and non-economic ideas which called forth the abolitionist crusade and permitted it to triumph. There has also been a renewed search for an ideological combination which will include both the abolitionist spokesmen and the political economists of industrializing Britain.

Perhaps the most apt conclusion to this survey of the decline thesis since *Econocide* would be to emphasize the enduring heritage of *Capitalism and Slavery*, the book which constituted the object of its critique. As long as British slavery and abolition were regarded as *sui generis*, primarily as moral categories, they were more likely to be treated commemoratively than analytically. *Capitalism and Slavery* was therefore a classical demonstration of the value of even deliberately simplistic history. It would be no gain whatever to the historiography of slavery if apparent gaps in the causal chain forged by Williams fragmented slavery scholarship into clusters of specialists with no common framework. Williams cast his story in a global economic setting and that setting must, if anything, be remapped and resynthesized.

Williams' last and most enduring message was that abolition could not have triumphed independently of economic developments linked to industrialization. This simple hypothesis has already proved to be more fruitful than those offered by historians in the whole century before him. *Capitalism and Slavery* changed the way in which we view abolition precisely because it riveted attention on the context rather than on heroes. Historians are unlikely again to suspend disbelief in the existence of 'three or four perfectly virtuous pages in the history of nations'.

Notes

1. Eric Williams, *Capitalism and Slavery* (1944, rpt. 1966), hereafter *C&S*.
2. *Ibid.*, p. 120.
3. *Ibid.*, p. 154.
4. 2nd Ser. xxi, 307-20, No. 2 (1968). See also his 'A Re-interpretation of the Abolition of the British Slave Trade, 1806-07', *Economic History Review*, LXXXVII (1972), No. 343, 304-32.
5. Cf. Cecil Gutzmore, 'The Continuing Dispute over the Connections between the Capitalist Mode of Production and Chattel Slavery, presented at the Sesquecentennial of the Death of William Wilberforce and the Emancipation Act of 1833' (MSS), pp. 2-6.
6. *C&S*, pp. 52-54, 225-26, tables; *Econocide*, pp. 16-25.
7. 'Economic Aspects of the Abolition Debate' in Christine Bolt and Seymour Drescher (eds.), *Anti-Slavery, Religion, and Reform: Essays in Memory of Roger Anstey* (Folkestone, England; Hamden, Conn., 1980), pp. 272-73.
8. See note 4.
9. ' "Econocide" — Myth or Reality — The Question of West Indian Decline, 1783-1806' and the reply, 'Econocide, Capitalism and Slavery: A Commentary' in *Boletin de Estudios Latinoamericanos y del Caribe*, 36 (June 1984), 13-67.
10. See note 6.
11. *C&S*, p. 225, n. 16.
12. See note 5.
13. *Econocide*, p. 20, fig. 5.
14. Those reviews of *Econocide* which evidently accept the undermining of the Williams decline thesis are: W. J. Hausman, J. A. Casada, G. Heuman, L. J. Belliot, R. Anstey, D. Eltis, R. Lopper, J. Hogendorn, B. Hilton, J. Walvin, P. E. H. Hair, P. D. Curtin, R. Koch, I. R. Hancock, J. P. Greene, S. Daget, P. Emmer, J. A. Lesourd, Sv. E. Green-Pedersen. In the most novel portion of his essay on 'Williams and Drescher' in *Slavery and Abolition*, September, 1983, Vol. 4, No. 3, 81-105, Walter Minchinton dismisses the utility of official British trade statistics for measuring trends in the relative significance of global trade zones, including the British West Indies. On grounds that these figures used static official prices, Minchinton insists that they do 'not enable us to assess properly the importance of the British West Indies for Great Britain' (*ibid.*, p. 87). He does not, however, address the fact that the other economic historians of the same period consider it quite feasible to measure relative trade shares on the basis of the official data (see, for example, François Crouzet's 'Toward an export economy', cited in Table 2). More important, he overlooks the fact that Ralph Davis' *real* price data confirm the British West Indian trends at the end of the eighteenth century (see note 37, below). Minchinton also overlooks the fact that the official figures were those used exclusively by contemporary MPs and publicists in arguments about the value of the British West Indies (see *Econocide*, p. 231, note). (Incidentally, Minchinton's summary dismissal of the official data works directly against his own conclusion that *Capitalism and Slavery* remains a 'yardstick' for the study of abolition. If the official series cannot validate *Econocide*'s conclusions about the West Indies after 1775, how can the same data validate *Capitalism and Slavery*'s similar conclusions about the period before 1775?)
15. See, *inter alia*, Gutzmore, 'Continuing Dispute', pp. 16-17; Review of A. Adamson.
16. Review of M. Craton. The most systematic and elegant

elaboration to date of the implicit tension between abolition and the pattern of economic development yet written is David Eltis' 'Capitalism and Abolition: The Missed Opportunities of 1807-1865', typescript kindly circulated at the Bellaggio conference. It is a foretaste of Eltis' eagerly awaited two-volume synthesis on the nineteenth-century slave trade.
17. *C&S*, p. 134.
18. *Ibid.*, p. 135.
19. J. R. Ward, 'The Profitability of Sugar Planting in the British West Indies, 1650-1834', *Economic History Review*, 2nd ser., XXXI (1978); and his excellent unpublished sequel, 'The Profitability and Viability of British West Indian Plantation Slavery, 1807-1834'.
20. Review by M. Craton.
21. At the Bellaggio conference on British Slavery and British Capitalism, Barbara Solow placed special emphasis on the significance of the eighteenth-century export trade in British economic development. See the general discussion in John J. McKusker and Russel R. Menard, *The Economy of British America, 1607-1789* (Chapel Hill and London, 1985), 39-45.
22. See review essays by B. Solow and M. Turner; review by E. Goveia; Noel Deerr, *A History of Sugar*, 2 vols. (London, 1949-50), pp. 529-31.
23. *Econocide*, pp. 39-41.
24. See *Some Observations Showing the Dangers of Losing the Trade of the Slave Colonies, by a Planter* (1714), from the Huntington Library Collection, no. 146982.
25. *C&S*, p. 122.
26. *Econocide*, pp. 46-51.

Table: Re-exports of sugar compared to 'British'/foreign sugar ratios (1765-1818) (selected periods)

Period	% of British imports re-exported (cwt) (1)	London prices/foreign prices × 100 (per British cwt) (2)
1761-65	23.8	124 (a)
1771-75	4.5	144 (b)
1781-85	10.0	136 (c)
1791-95	24.5	—
1801-05	33.3	83 (d)
1814-18	31.8 (27.9)	88 (e)

Column 1: Parenthetical figure = British West Indian sugar only

Column 2: (a) = London compared with Amsterdam Muscovado; (b) = London compared with Nantes Muscovado; (c) = ditto, but Nantes prices for 1782-84 only; (d) = London/Amsterdam ratio, but Amsterdam prices 1801, 1804, 1806 only; (e) = London/Havana, ord. yellow.

Sources: Column 1: 1765-1805, *Econocide*, p. 80, 1814-1818 PP, 1847-48, LVIII; column 2: (a) and (b) London prices from R. Sheridan, *Sugar and Slavery: An Economic History of the British West Indies* (Baltimore, 1974), p. 497; Amsterdam prices, Deerr, *History*, p. 530; *ibid.*; (c) Nantes prices from Deerr, *ibid.*, British prices from *ibid.* Mean of range given by Deerr; (d) same as (c); (e) *RP* 1847-48 (44), p. 3 of *Report*.

27. See Deerr, *History*, p. 530, prices of sugar in London and Amsterdam, 1806. Just prior to the Commons debate of 1792, 5 January-5 March, British re-exports of sugar to Europe were running at about 300% of the rate of average re-exports for 1787-90. (calculated from

A Report from the Committee of Warehouses of the United East-India Company Relative to the Price of Sugar (London, 1792), p. 23). Below, I offer a table, but only suggestively, comparing the ratios of Britsh re-exports to 'British'/foreign sugar prices at points between 1765 and 1818. From the sources used, it is unclear whether different grades of sugar are being compared in the price series in different ports. In the re-export series it is also unclear how much 'foreign' sugar was beng re-exported, especially in the war years: 1761–63; 1781–83; 1793–95; 1801; 1804–05. Five-year intervals are chosen both because Parliament preferred these multi-year averages, and because quantities of foreign sugar, listed as 'retained' for consumption in one year might have been imported in prior years. (See, for example, *PP* 1847–48 LVIII Seasonal Paper No. 400: '*Return of Quantities of Sugar*', etc, p. 3, n. 1c.)

28. Temperley, 'Capitalism, Slavery and Ideology', *Past and Present*, No. 75 (May, 1977), 101.
29. *Econocide*, p. 53.
30. P. J. Cain and A. G. Hopkins, 'The Political Economy of British Expansion Overseas, 1750–1914', *Economic History Review*, 2nd ser., XXXIII, No. 4, (November 1980), 463–90. Referring to *Econocide*, Cain and Hopkins write: 'Contrary to a long-standing belief, the slave trade was not overthrown by powerful industrial interests cramped by colonial restrictions. Manufacturers were neither influential enough to overthrow the trade nor driven by economic logic to make the attempt' (p. 473, n.).
31. Carrington, 'Econocide/Myth'.
32. See reviews by Emmer, G. Heuman, and the essay by D. Geggus, 'The British Government and the Saint Domingue slave revolt, 1791–1793', *English Historical Review*, XCVI, No. 379 (April, 1981), 287.
33. *Econocide*, p. 64.
34. *Ibid.*, pp. 165–66.

35. C&S, p. 113.
36. P. Curtin, *The Slave Trade: A Census* (Madison, 1969), pp. 119, 216.
37. Deerr, *History of Sugar*, pp. 193–96.
38. R. Davis, *The Industrial Revolution and British Overseas Trade* (Leicester, 1979), pp. 89–125.
39. Deerr, *History of Sugar*, p. 21.
40. See for example P. E. Lovejoy, 'The Volume of the Atlantic Slave Trade: A Synthesis', *Journal of African History*, Vol. 23, No. 4, (1982), 473–501; James A. Rawley, *The Transatlantic Slave Trade: A History* (New York, 1981), p. 428; and D. Richardson, unpublished figures summarized in his Bellaggio conference paper 'The Slave Trade, Sugar, and British Economic Growth 1784–76.
41. J. E. Inikori, 'Measuring the Atlantic Slave Trade: An Assessment of Curtin and Anstey', *Journal of African History*, 17 (1976), 197–223; *Econocide*, pp. 211–13.
42. Carrington, 'Econocide/Myth', p. 42.
43. *Ibid.*, p. 43, figure XXIII: Slave imports into and exports from the B. W. I., 1783–1805.
44. J. J. McCusker, 'The Rum Trade and the Balance of Payments of the Thirteen Continental Colonies, 1660–1776', University of Pittsburgh, Ph.D. dissertation, 2 vols., 1970.
45. See note 32, above.
46. Another historian cited yet another leading Minister who assured the Governor of Jamaica in 1808 that abolition had been a practical response to overproduction. Yet only nine months earlier the same MP had opposed abolition as impractical on grounds of planter demand for slaves. is there any reason why one should prefer after-the-fact rationalizations to before-the-fact statements in determining motivations?
47. Anstey, *Atlantic Slave Trade*, pp. 51–52.
48. Gutzmore, 'Continuing Dispute', p. 26.
49. Emmer's review.
50. Reviews of Curtin, Adamson, and Lopper.

79

Victor Schoelcher and Emancipation in the French West Indies

ANDRE MIDAS

(Translated from the French by Mrs V. O. Aicalá)

The recent celebration of the centenary of the Revolution of 1848 in France, and of one of its most immediate and important consequences — the abolition of slavery — has revived interest in the action of the French abolitionists. Speeches were made, articles published and new editions of old texts appeared, on this occasion. Victor Schoelcher, the greatest of these gallant men who were called, not without a certain amount of irony, 'the philanthropists', received special mention, and his memory was revived throughout the nation by the transfer of his ashes to the Panthéon where illustrious Frenchmen are interred. Thus, a humanitarian enterprise of the highest order, involving men from various walks of life who differed fundamentally in their intellectual development, ideas and character, was commemorated. As was natural, this crusade aroused bitter controversies and unrelenting opposition in its time.

There is no doubt that Victor Schoelcher and the part that he played at a crucial turning point in colonial history are little known today in France, outside a small circle of scholars, and still less known in foreign lands. It is fair to add, however, that his name never ceased to be loaded with significance and fame in the minds of those whom he liberated and of later generations of their descendants. It is indeed difficult, outside of the French West Indies, to assess the importance of the position he held in those islands, almost the entire populations of which suddenly recovered their liberty. There are Schoelcher Streets, Schoelcher libraries and a Schoelcher High School in Martinique. A symbolic figure, a beacon for his fellowmen, an architect of justice, Schoelcher was all this in the eyes of sensitive and grateful human beings who worshipped him with mystic devotion and resigned themselves to his spiritual guidance with absolute confidence. They called him their father and, in his honour, they composed a very popular song, 'The Mountain is Green', a verse of which reads: 'Schoelcher must shine like a star in the East'. For many a year after his death, West Indian homes were decorated on the anniversary of his birth, with an improvised altar richly ornamented or more modest according to the financial resources available, where his portrait was displayed.[1] All the burning love of the West Indian soul and the shrewdness of a people who knew instinctively where homage was due were expressed in this pious gesture.

The outstanding part played by Schoelcher in the abolition of slavery cannot be exaggerated. Schoelcher was a man with a single idea, continually reiterated, sifted and strengthened, and fighting a single cause brought to a successful conclusion with implacable severity. Victor Schoelcher's history provides this point of interest, *viz.*, that he did not achieve that fierce strictness which he made his guiding principle, at the very start. At a certain stage of his evolution he said: 'It is no more possible to regulate slavery humanely than it is to regulate murder.' From then onwards that was his golden rule, and his goal — the immediate liberation of the slaves without compromise or equivocation.

Victor Schoelcher was a middle-class citizen in easy circumstances. His father, a porcelain merchant of the Rue Grange-Batelière in Paris, wished Victor to follow in his footsteps, the normal wish of a good father of a family, who is anxious to assure his child's future. The idea did not appeal to Victor Schoelcher who threw himself into a worldly life on leaving the Lycée Louis le Grand and frequented the literary circles. He engaged in politics, was active in the ranks of the liberals, and belonged to the Freemasonry. His father then sent him on a business trip to the United States and Mexico for the purpose of selling some merchandise. On his return, Victor Schoelcher published a series of articles entitled 'Letters about Mexico', in the *Revue de Paris*, from May to November, 1830. In these articles he recounted his first experience of slavery. In Cuba he saw the system functioning at close quarters, and his contact with 'ebony wood' (the name given to the slaves) certainly brought him a certain amount of disillusionment. He stressed the responsibilities of the masters who, under the slave system, possessed all rights. He was equally plain spoken, however, in dealing with the Negroes. 'I admit,' he said, 'that the Negroes, as they exist at present in slavery, constitute the most wretched, abject and immoral class that can be imagined.' Such were the conclusions of this young man of 26 years who treated the problem of slavery, with interest certainly, but without deep conviction and, above all, without passion. In his opinion, consideration must be given 'to the great task of emancipating the slaves'. It was necessary, however, to proceed with calm and caution and without undue haste: 'Leave it to the great healer, Time, to effect the cure,' were the words he used then.[2] The only measure on which he suggested immediate action was a rigorous suppression of the slave trade in order to dry up the very source of slavery.

When Victor Schoelcher's interest in the question of slavery, faint though it might be, first became apparent, it was clear that he shared generally the views of those who considered the problem before him. Prudent and moderate action was the course advocated by the Duc de Broglie who, for several years, had been working within the 'Society of Christian Morals' for the abolition of slavery. He, too, felt that the first step should be complete suppression of the slave trade and he discussed these views at great length, in a magnificent discourse delivered in the Chamber of Peers on March 28, 1822. Without any difficulty, he established the fact that traffic in slaves continued after the official abolition of the slave trade by France (Napoleon's Decree of March 29, 1815, confirmed by Louis XVIII on July 30 of the same year). His efforts in this direction were moderately successful. To the very end he gave no thought to immediate liberation and when, after three years, the Commission over which he presided published its report on the measures for effecting the emancipation of the slaves, the conclusions were very vague. De Broglie, who was responsible for them, offered two solutions: general emancipation at the end of ten years or partial and progressive emancipation. On July 7, 1845, de Broglie made another speech in the Chamber of Peers recommending the passage of certain draft bills providing for the re-purchase, education and welfare of the slaves, but not for their liberation. All the other contemporary defenders of the slaves showed a similar prudence and moderation in their views. Hypolite Passy, who presented a draft bill in connection with emancipation to the Chamber of Deputies on February 10, 1838, provided only for the freedom of children born to slave parents. Neither Lamartine, who made noble and moving speeches on the question of slavery, nor yet Montalembert, Remusat, Tocqueville and Wallon, who devoted their efforts and talents to the cause of the slaves, thought of immediate emancipation. The various petitions presented to the Chamber of Deputies on behalf of the slaves, the petition of the workers of Paris and Lyons in 1844, and the more representative one made by the whole nation in 1847, did not request any radical and immediate action. Ledru-Rollin, inspired and briefed by Schoelcher, was the first to demand the immediate abolition of slavery, from the gallery of the Chamber of Deputies in April, 1847.

After his first stand in 'Letters about Mexico', Victor Schoelcher, unlike his companions in the struggle, experienced a profound evolution in his way of thinking. In 1833 he published his first work entitled *De l'Esclavage des Noirs et de la Legislation Coloniale*. It is a violent, impassioned book, inspired by a great generosity, in which we find the origin of Victor Schoelcher's dedication of his life to the abolition of slavery. Why did he devote himself with such ardour to the cause of the slaves? He gave the reason in the very first lines of his foreword: it was idealism and natural generosity.[3]

Meanwhile he continued to display great clearsightedness and assessed the slaves without illusion.[4] Nevertheless, this man who, in 1842, became the uncompromising champion of immediate liberation of the Negroes,[5] was resolutely opposed to the idea nine years earlier.[6] About that time he published draft legislation couched in very general terms, in which the following statement occurs: 'It should be understood that slaves are men and, therefore, their masters should treat them as such.' This draft, comprising thirty articles altogether, springs undoubtedly from a generous inspiration, but seems hardly applicable at that period. Briefly, Schoelcher was in precisely the same position as the Duc de Broglie, with one voyage more (certainly a matter of importance), and several works, studies, conferences and political speeches less, to his credit.

What changed Schoelcher's outlook was the voyage which he made to the French West Indies in 1840.

Mr Périnelle, one of the most important proprietors in Martinique, was aboard the sailing ship that took Schoelcher to the West Indies. Quite willingly, this planter, who was well aware of Victor Schoelcher's convictions, secured him access to the different plantations on the island, thereby permitting him to gain direct experience of the functioning of the slave system. Victor Schoelcher revised his values in the light of facts. He irrevocably condemned the institution itself, being by then firmly convinced that it should be unconditionally abolished, and, at the same time, his opinion of both planters and slaves underwent a change. He did not think that all planters were fundamentally corrupt and, when he met slave owners who were humane and temperate (according to their own code of ethics), he said so loyally. Indeed, he emphasised that: 'They (the planters) fear one another and tremble before the tyranny of their own public opinion which drowns the voice of the good and the wise.' He saw instances where slaves did not seem unhappy, and cases where they enjoyed the rights of property, acquired by means of some form of regulation, and scrupulously respected by their masters. On the question of colour prejudice, he admitted that 'a great deal might be said in defence of the planters'. However, he also cited definite instances of extraordinary cruelty on the part of colonials who were acquitted of guilt by the colonial judiciary. The case of Brafin, estate owner at Rivière Salée in Martinique,[7] and that of Douillard-Mahaudière, a planter in Guadeloupe, men who tortured slaves and were acquitted by the courts, were eloquent examples of the complicated circumstances in which the slaves were caught.

Schoelcher's book, moving in its sincerity and its constant attention to facts in recounting events and allotting responsibility, drew the amply justified conclusion that slavery must be abolished without delay. Henceforward this was Schoelcher's opinion, which was strengthened still more by his voyages to Haiti, Egypt and Senegal.

Therein lies one of the dominant characteristics of Victor Schoelcher. He was not merely an abstract and 'ivory tower' idealist. When he cited the wretched condition of existence of the Negro slaves in support of his opinions, he was speaking of things he had seen in various countries and at different periods. In Cuba, he witnessed the sale of a slave in the public market and he described 'this unfortunate woman ... dirtily clad, cold and indifferent to her fate, surrounded by passers-by and purchasers ...' In his book on Les Colonies Françaises, he again described a sale of slaves by auction, which he witnessed in 1841, and he revived this scene in his Histoire de l'Esclavage au cours des Deux Dernières Années, published in 1847. He saw slaves whipped[8] and visited their prisons. He knew the 'commander's' power and all the degrading circumstances linked with slavery. He derived the force of his convictions and the ardour of his opinions, which he expressed both by spoken word and in writing, from a store of experience which he could bring to bear vigorously, against those metropolitan advocates of slavery who, like Granier de Cassagnac,[10] visited the West Indies in search of fresh arguments in support of their thesis. This direct contact, for which there is no substitute, was lamentably lacking in the other abolitionists of his time.

This argument did not escape the metropolitan advocates of slavery, the planters' friends and defenders. Seizing on an idea rashly expressed by Lamartine, the Parisian newspaper La Globe emphasised one of the weaknesses of the abolitionists' position. 'It is indeed true,' this paper said, 'that the philanthropists do not know, have never seen and probably will never see the men whose regeneration they seek. That is why their doctrines are misleading.' On the eve of emancipation in 1848, Schoelcher had already gained the friendship of the Negroes. He was in Africa at the outbreak of the Revolution of 1848. What was he doing there? He was continuing his research indefatigably, studying the African way of life and adding yet more documents to his file.

In the first half of the nineteenth century, Victor Schoelcher was, with the exception of

Thomas Clarkson in England, to whom he bears a marked resemblance, unquestionably the greatest European specialist on the question of slavery. This fact was appreciated in France where his republican friends made him a member of the government after his headlong return from Africa. He was entrusted with the task of solving the multiple problems which slavery posed. In a despatch to colonial territories, the new Minister of the Navy and the Colonies, François Arago, reminded all citizens that their first duty was 'to submit to the existing laws and authorities'. Would the republican régime continue the excuses and delaying policy of Louis Philippe's government, in so far as slavery was concerned? It is clear that Arago was uncertain. Moreover, the defenders of the planters in Paris, the Chambers of Commerce of the great seaports, who fully appreciated the gravity of the situation, devoted themselves with feverish activity to the task of lessening the significance of an eventual emancipation. Perrinon, a native of the West Indies, who was in Paris, was of the opinion that the interim government had not the right to abolish slavery, and concluded a letter addressed to the West Indians with these words: 'Patience, hope, unity, order and work, these are the things I recommend to all.'[12] The position was, therefore, unchanged and the liberation of the slaves seemed doubtful.

Schoelcher arrived in Paris on March 3, 1848, and conferred immediately with Arago. One of his first victories, according to Arago, in his *Memoirs*, was to persuade the new minister to end slavery and to present his colleagues with 'a decree of immediate emancipation'. Victor Schoelcher was appointed Under Secretary of State for the Navy and the Colonies. On March 4, the provisional government of the Republic, 'taking into consideration the fact that no French territory may countenance slavery', appointed a Commission responsible for preparing 'the order for immediate emancipation in all the colonies of the Republic, at its earliest convenience'. Victor Schoelcher, who, in the eyes of the government, personified the struggle against slavery which was nearing the end, was appointed President of this Commission. The Commission, composed of five members, one of whom was Perrinon, then a Major of the 'Marines', began its work immediately.

The planters and their representatives did not accept the event that was forecast, and took more and more steps to ward it off. The Council of Delegates from the Colonies (that is, from the planters) sent a letter to the Commission over which Schoelcher presided, on March 7, 1848, stating clearly that only the National Assembly was competent 'to pass two inseparable measures, Emancipation and Indemnity'. This letter went on to describe, in the blackest terms possible, the conditions that would result from a hasty liberation of the slaves: ruin of industries, decline of agriculture, impoverishment of society, ruin of trade with the colonies. The Chambers of Commerce of Marseilles, Nantes and Le Havre sent delegates to Paris to intercede with the Ministers.

Opinion was not unanimous even within the Commission. Certain members, like Mestro, Director of the Colonies, and Gatine, a lawyer, were concerned about the judicial aspect of the problem and the effects of abolition on the planters' right of ownership. Schoelcher maintained and won his point in the matter of immediate abolition. He used another argument very successfully, *viz.*, that any government that had the right of expropriation for public purposes might well exercise this right where moral issues were involved. Schoelcher also maintained forcefully that the newly liberated slaves should thenceforward be *citizens*. In opposition to Perrinon, who claimed that French slaves were inferior politically to English slaves, in opposition to Mestro and the delegates from Guadeloupe (Jabrun, Reizet), Réunion and Martinique, Schoelcher insisted that the liberated slaves enjoy the full rights of citizenship. Froidefont-Desfarges, the planters' delegate from Martinique, stated that 'the Negroes are big children equally incapable of recognising either their rights or their duties'. Schoelcher refused to believe this. He expressed his faith in the Negro race, and his decisions were adopted.

On April 27, 1848, the provisional government, acting on the Commission's proposals, abolished slavery in all the French colonies, and in the following year the National Assembly fixed the indemnity due to the planters at 126 million francs.[14]

Thus, within a few years, France repeated the action taken by England in 1833, when she decreed the abolition of slavery in her overseas possessions. The action of the English philanthropists was strongly supported by British commercial and industrial circles — cotton producers, shipowners, sugar refiners — and by the most important business centres, London, Manchester, Liverpool, etc. The monopoly of the British West Indies, and slavery on which this monopoly rested, offered no further interest from the economic standpoint, though both had contributed largely to the prosperity of the metropolitan country, particularly in the eighteenth century. In exchange for its exports, Great Britain received raw materials. The monopoly guaranteed to the British West Indies excluded foreign sugar from this trading arrangement and constituted an obstacle to British industry.[15] Great Britain, the workshop of the world, technologically ahead of its competitors in the world market, found the West Indian colonies doubly irksome in the early nineteenth century: they purchased insignificant quantities of British manufactures, whilst their monopoly of the British sugar market hampered the potentialities of British trade with such rival sugar producers as Cuba and Brazil.

The emancipation of the slaves in the French West Indies had its economic aspect also. Beet sugar production, first stimulated by Bonaparte and the Prussians as the answer to Britain's continental blockade, had, by 1848, become an established commercial fact. The French beet producers stressed the large white population involved in the cultivation and manufacture of beet sugar, their superior standard of living, and their greater importance to French capitalists.[16] They took the lead, therefore, in pressing for emancipation of the slaves in the French colonies — on humanitarian grounds, ostensibly, but in reality, for their own economic advantage.

There is some evidence that certain British abolitionists were closely identified with those economic vested interests which opposed the West Indian planters. As regards Schoelcher, however, there is no evidence to suggest that his conduct was even partially inspired by the defence of economic interests. Gaston Martin, whose *Histoire de l'Esclavage dans les Colonies Françaises*, published in 1948, is one of the most recent works on the question, makes no such inference. Augustin Cochin, in his *Abolition de l'Esclavage*, which appeared in 1861, makes no mention of such a possibility. However, Schoelcher's whole life, the struggle he kept up indefatigably, the nobility of feeling which appears in his writings, all these bear high testimony of his sincerity and disinterestedness.

His work accomplished, Schoelcher who had no further political ambitions, resigned his post as Under Secretary of State. His struggle for emancipation, however, had won him very great popularity among the newly liberated Negroes. In August, 1848, he was elected the people's representative both in Martinique and Guadeloupe, by 19,117 votes and 16,038 votes, respectively. He elected to be deputy for Guadeloupe.[17]

On December 2, 1851, Victor Schoelcher, a fervent republican, refused to accept Louis Napoleon Bonaparte's *coup d'état*. He joined the resistance group which was immediately formed and in which Victor Hugo was a notable figure. He flung himself into the defence of the barricades of Paris, where the deputy, Baudin, who became famous by his resistance to Bonaparte and sacrificed his life to his political convictions, was killed at his side. Then he went into voluntary exile to England where he spent eighteen years.

Schoelcher returned to France only in August, 1870, after the military disaster sustained by France at Sedan, and was appointed Colonel of the National Guard. At the elections, a few months later, he was appointed to the National Assembly by the Department of the Seine, French Guiana and Martinique. He chose to represent Martinique. He was next elected Senator for life.

The abolition of slavery in 1848 constituted an economic and social experiment of the greatest significance in the French West Indies. We have seen that the planters had predicted the worst disasters. Naturally, a period of transition and reorganisation of the system of labour was necessary. The government had recourse to immigration and two decrees, February 13, and March 27, 1852, provided for the introduction of European, African or Asiatic labour into the French colonies. Further, on July 1, 1861, the British and French Governments concluded an agreement providing for the recruitment of Indian labourers for the French West Indies. In the course of debates which took place in the Conseil Général of Martinique in December, 1884, as a result of which authorised immigration was suppressed, it was revealed that 25,509 Indian immigrants had been brought into Martinique by 55 convoys from 1853 to 1884, and that 13,271 of them still existed there.[18]

Schoelcher examined the problem in his work, *Polémique Coloniale*,[19] but gave somewhat different figures. 'From the commencement of immigration in 1854 to June 30, 1876,' he wrote, '31,640 Indians have been brought in (to Martinique). Of this number only 3,307 were repatriated when their contract expired; 17,890 are still living in the island; 10,443 are dead.' He drew the following conclusion: 'In 22 years, therefore, a third of these men have died more or less in their prime in a civilised country.' Did Indian immigration assist in the economic development of Martinique? Was it worth the cost? Schoelcher did not think so. He emphasised the fact that the Indians 'are of weak constitution', 'only fit for light work' and 'certainly figure in the debts on which interest at the rate of 10 and 12 per cent devours the best part of the revenue of the inhabitants'. Referring again to the figure in *The Yearbook of Martinique*, which fixes the number of workers 'employed in the different cultivations and sugar factories' at 57,000 in 1876, he estimated, further, that there were about 10,000 immigrants supplying regular agricultural labour. It was, therefore, on the 47,000 local workers that 'the largest part of the Colony's production depended'. Schoelcher concluded therefrom that the immigrants were far from being indispensable: 'We should do much better without them,' he added, 'for as fast as they disappeared we should see a certain number of native workers returning to the plantations, since the latter dislike being brought into contact with Indians whose introduction has been responsible for lowering wages'.

On his return to France, following the defeat of Sedan, Schoelcher renewed his close relations with the Caribbean islands. He was then able to determine the tangible results of his action in 1848. Towards the end of his life, he saw the birth and rise of the coloured generation, the descendants of the liberated slaves.

In 1880, Schoelcher reviewed the work accomplished, in the presence of men of colour from Martinique, Guadeloupe and Cochin China, who presented him with a work of art purchased with their subscriptions, as a mark of gratitude: 'What gigantic strides the emancipated class has made in such a short space of time!' he says, 'what immense moral and material progress it has made!' Then he stressed the fact that the population of African origin 'furnished this consoling testimony that, given equal education, all human races are equal'.

Indeed, he continued the bitter attack, which he had led against the planters who were bent on claiming their privileges as slave owners, on behalf of the coloured men who had so recently gained access to the social life of their territories. With an enthusiasm and ardour altogether youthful, Schoelcher rushed to the assistance of the young coloured class of Saint Pierre (Martinique) in the face of the fierce and bitter hostility of the old privileged class. It was inevitable that Schoelcher, in taking up this position again, should draw down on his head the fury of the planters of that period. By his very nature he must displease them. He did not believe in God, whom he confessed that he had sought unsuccessfully, and on March 23, 1882, before the French Senate, he had made a public declaration of atheism which caused scandal. Schoelcher was a republican. Further, the planters declared in their paper, *Les Antilles*: 'We do not like the Republic because in 1848 and 1870 it handed us over as a prey to Mr Schoelcher.'[20] The paper of Saint Pierre, *La Défense Coloniale*, in April, 1882, reprinted an article entitled 'The Atheist of Luxembourg' from the *Figaro* of Paris, in which Schoelcher was ridiculed. He was described as 'a tall, thin man, with pointed features, pointed and jutting ears'. Souquet-Basiège, who published a biased and controversial work on *Le Préjugé de Race aux Antilles Françaises*, denounced Victor Schoelcher as 'this embodiment of hatred, coldly proud, a sophist masquerading in the guise of a stickler for humanitarian doctrines.' The newspapers of Saint Pierre, in their opposition to Schoelcher, multiplied their attacks against him, accusing him of seeking the 'substitution' of one race for another, of having sworn 'Hannibal's oath against Martinique', and exciting rebellion and violation of property. 'Hatred of white people, their annihilation and disappearance, that is the programme, and Schoelcher has dictated it,' they said.[21]

When we read the two volumes of *Polémique Coloniale*,[22] a collection of attacks against Victor Schoelcher, and public refutations published by him and the newspapers published at Saint Pierre during this period, we cannot fail to be struck by the extreme violence of the controversy. The young generation, represented by brave and brilliant lawyers and journalists — Marius-Hurard, president of the local General Council and Martinique's deputy, Clavius-Marius, Césaire Lainé, Deproge, who also became one of Martinique's deputies — vigorously defended their newly won position in Martinique society. From Paris, Schoelcher watched events closely. In the eyes of young West Indians he was a wise Nestor, full of experience and aggressive courage. Nothing escaped him. He read the various colonial papers carefully and knew the strength of the forces mustered. Clearsighted, with abundant references always at his disposal, he answered untiringly the exasperated and often unjust criticisms which his adversaries levelled at him.

He contributed in Paris to *L'Homme Libre*, *L'Opinion Nationale*, *Le Rappel*, *XIXe Siècle*. These were so many forums from which he kept metropolitan public opinion informed of the position in the Colonies. He followed with interest the progress of the paper, *Les Colonies*, which Marius-Hurard founded in 1878 at Saint Pierre. On that occasion he wrote the following to him: 'I have received the first two numbers of your paper. I find it very good. . . . Fight colour prejudice whenever it appears. It is the greatest scourge of the French West Indies. Point out calmly, without irritation but firmly, all the evil that it causes in the present and all the dangers with which it is fraught for the future; as long as it survives there will be no peace or well-being for colonial society.'[23] Wherever he saw an instance of iniquity in the new social conditions of the French West Indies, he denounced it vigorously. He revolted against colour prejudice in all its many and frequent manifestations, quoted definite facts, dates and names.[24] He desired equality in education,[25] equality in justice.[26] To Mr Champvallier, who opposed representation for the colonies in a speech to the Chamber, because of the 'small number of voters at all colonial elections', Schoelcher replied that the colonies had always felt the urgent need in the past of defending their particular interests in the metropolitan assemblies. In support of his contention, he drew attention to the fact that, under Louis Philippe, the colonies 'hired the services of Mr Charles Dupin and Mr Jollivet at a cost of 20,000 francs per year, each, to plead their cause in the Chamber of Peers and in the Chamber of Deputies, respectively.'[27]

When Paul Leroy-Beaulieu, the distinguished French economist, expressed some doubt concerning the civic sense of the coloured population of Martinique and Guadeloupe in the re-issue of his work, *De la Colonisation chez les Peuples Modernes*, Schoelcher protested indignantly against his views.[28]

Schoelcher received letters from all quarters, informing him of the situation in the West Indies or asking his opinion, advice or intervention.[29] He never rested, and always went to the assistance of those whom he considered his *protégés*. The planters in the French West Indies, at least those among them whom Schoelcher called the 'Incorrigibles', knew the influence that he had acquired in France, and they wrote, not without bitterness: 'Mr Schoelcher is the perpetual minister of the colonies. He elaborates the programme every-one must follow, he it is who distributes blame

or praise, punishment or reward.'[30]

According to them, he exercised 'unlimited influence' on the Department of the Navy (which was also responsible for the Colonies). They charged that the Ministers were placed there for the sole purpose of initiating his *protégés*.

Commenting ironically on these accusations, Schoelcher stressed the point that, if any credence must be given to the painters of Saint Pierre, they, Admiral Pothuau, Admiral de Dompierre d'Hornoy, Admiral Montaignac, Admiral Fourichon, Admiral Jaureguiberry, Admiral Cloué, general officers 'holding political opinions that are opposed and different in character', have 'resigned the power into his hands'.

There was an obvious exaggeration in this charge which Schoelcher vigorously attacked. 'Behold!' he wrote, 'the ridiculous ideas spread by certain agitators shut up in St. Pierre, in their narrow circle, who neither see nor look at anything happening in the world, apart from their old prejudices and who detest anyone that does not share these.'

Schoelcher owed the enormous prestige which he enjoyed at the time to his unalterable fidelity to his ideal and to the uprightness of his life. His good faith was unassailable. This austere old man, robed in a long frock-coat, had voluntarily assumed certain responsibilities with regard to the slaves, and he intended to fulfil them to the end. At least he was not mistaken in the hopes that had constantly inspired his action. Events at the end of the century amply justified the daring risks he had taken.

Looking over the road traversed and the promise the future held, he jubilantly exclaimed: 'Bravo, "African savages", continue your self-enlightenment . . . and preserve your scorn for those who insult you. Your astounding progress speaks for itself.' This irony *à la* Montesquieu and this affection are both striking and moving.

His death, on December 26, 1893, brought dismay to the West Indies.

Notes

1. Robert Caddy, *Le Roman de Mayotte* (Fort de France, 1922).
2. *La Revue de Paris*, Vol. 20, No. 2, 1830.
3. *De l'Esclavage des Noirs et de la Législation Coloniale* (Paris, 1853).
4. *Ibid.*, p. 34.
5. *Des Colonies Françaises: Abolition Immédiate de l'Esclavage* (Paris, 1842).

6. *De l'Esclavage des Noirs*, p. 41.
7. *Des Colonies Françaises*, p. 34.
8. *Ibid.*, p. 84.
9. *Ibid.*, p. 84.
10. Granier de Cassagnac, *Voyage aux Antilles* (Paris, 1842).
11. Victor Schoelcher, *L'Immigration aux Colonies* (Paris, 1883), p. 67.
12. *Courrier de la Martinique*, 27 March 1848.
13. Gaston-Martin, *Histoire de l'Esclavage dans les Colonies Françaises* (Paris, 1948), p. 293.
14. *Ibid.*, p. 295.
15. Eric Williams, *Capitalism and Slavery* (Chapel Hill, N.C., 1944), p. 154.
16. See, for example, T. Lestiboudois, *Des Colonies Sucrières et des Sucreries Indigènes* (Lille, 1839), p. 11, 12, 17, 52-53; T. Dehay, *Les Colonies et la Métropole, le Sucre Exotique et le Sucre Indigène*, (Paris, 1839), pp. 29, 54, 183, 285.

17. *Biographie Impartiale des Représentants du Peuple à l'Assemblée Nationale* (Paris, 1848).
18. Eugène Revert, *La Martinique* (Paris, 1949), p. 241.
19. Victor Schoelcher, *Polémique Coloniale* (Paris, 1882), Vol. I, p. 241.
20. Victor Schoelcher, *Evènements des 18 et 19 Juillet* (Paris, 1882), p. 15.
21. *Ibid.*, p. 15.
22. *Polémique Coloniale*, Vol. I; Vol. II (Paris, 1886).
23. *Ibid.*, I, p. 281.
24. *Ibid.*, I, p. 281.
25. *Ibid.*, I, p. 66.
26. *Ibid.*
27. *Ibid.*, I, p. 13.
28. *Ibid.*, II, p. 119.
29. Victor Schoelcher, *Lettres Martiniquaises* (Paris, 1935).
30. *Evènements des 18 et 19 Juillet*, 9.

80

The Portrait of the Slave: Ideology and Aesthetics in the Cuban Antislavery Novel*

IVAN A. SCHULMAN

La primera taren que se impuso muestra literaturea. .
.[fue]. . .la preocupación social de orden ético . . .
Augusto Roa Bastos[1]

An Anticolonial Statement

The origins of the novel in Cuba are irrevocably linked to the internal contradictions and inconsistencies of the institution of slavery, the repressive policies of the colony, and the polar dynamics of Neoclassicism, Romanticism, Realism, *Costumbrismo* and Eclecticism. As a consequence, an exclusionary analysis of the early narratives, that is, their examination from either a purely literary, philosophic, socioeconomic or political perspective is bound to yield distorted and fragmentary results[2]; whereas a comprehensive methodology, even of the limited disciplinary scope provided in this study, will hopefully clarify some of the more perplexing genetic questions raised by their reading and provide a foundation for the further study of the special nature of their attitudes, concepts, perspectives, themes, language and style.

The first Cuban novels, largely historical, sentimental or antislavery in theme,[3] have attracted scant critical attention.[4] With respect to literary chronology, the antislavery narratives date from 1838, the period to which the first stirrings of the island's Romantic literature can be traced, and thus, there is a tendency to consider them products of the aesthetics of Romanticism. However, Cuban Romanticism must be examined in conjunction with other literary traditions, particularly, with a contemporary, intertwined, self-conscious, critical *costumbrista* expression whose significance, insofar as the antislavery novels are concerned, cannot be divorced from the history of the period. It seems to us especially significant, for example, that they first appeared in 1838, the year which, according to Ramiro Guerra, signalled the defeat, dispersal and, ultimately, the silence of the liberals and reformists of the island.[5] Their growing fears of personal reprisals for acts of opposition or even thoughts of disconformity in the face of ever more restrictive colonial edicts gave rise to a generational concern for human freedom[6] whose expression was sometimes veiled, at times distorted, in order to escape the vigilant eye of the viceroyal censors. Richard Henry Dana established the origins of this oppressive atmosphere even earlier – 1825 – from which time forward,

. . .vestiges of anything approaching to popular assemblies, juntas, a jury, independent tribunals, a right of voting, or a right to bear arms, have vanished from the island. The press is under censorship; and so are the theatres and operas. When "I Puritani" is played, the singers are required to substitute Lealtà for Libertà, and one singer was fined and imprisoned for recusancy; and Facciolo, the printer of a secretly circulated newspaper, advocating the cause of Cuban independence was garroted. The power of banishing, without a charge made, or a trial, or even a record, but on the mere will of the Captain-General, persons whose presence he thinks, or professes to think, prejudicial to the government, whatever their condition, rank, or office, has been frequently exercised and hangs at all hours over the head of every Cuban.[7]

This stifling milieu, a critical *costumbrista* tradition, the incipient polemic over Romantic aesthetics aired (1838) in *El Album* and the *Diario de la Habana*, dissatisfaction with the colonial regime on the part of the enlightened *criollas*, as well as their humanitarian concerns and economic anxieties over slavery, produced a narrative representing a counter-colonial statement in support of human liberty: the antislavery narrative which depicted the slave pitted against an inalterable fate in an unjust social order.[8]

A Collective Enterprise

If one views the archetypical thematic constructs of these novels in a vacuum, and misjudges, for example, their emotional tone or their striking distortion of the slave's character, it would be logical to identify them as nothing more than a product of Romanticism's early sway. To defend this facile, simplistic attribution, however, one would have to ignore the novel's economic, political, philosophic, moral and literary contexts.

To begin with, the antislavery novels, from both an aesthetic and ideological viewpoint, were largely the product of Domingo del Monte's literary *tertulias*. They were commissioned by him, owed their inspiration to his leadership, and, more often than not, were modified in response to his criticism. Anselmo Suárez y Romero, Felix Tanco y Bosmeniel, José Jacinto Milanés, José Antonio Echeverría, Juan Francisco Manzano, Ramón de Palma and Cirilo Villaverde were major writers of this generation, and devotees or disciples of Del Monte on whom they relied, to varying degrees, for guidance in the writing of their prose or poetry. Suárez y Romero, whose novel *Francisco* provides an abundant source of prototypical exemplification, in an 1839 letter to Del Monte, establishes *Francisco* as a commissioned work; begs his mentor to tell him frankly "the defects of my novel . . . to correct those errors which lend themselves to correction," and finally, invites his correspondent to "consider my novel yours and dispose of it as you wish".[9] Elsewhere he describes how Del Monte encouraged young writers with his patience, his firmness, his elegance and his firm criticism.[10]

On the basis of this as well as other testimonies, it is abundantly clear that we are dealing with a literature which, in large measure, represented a community of shared interests and talents. For this very reason, many of the antislavery novels of the early period must be viewed as works that reflect in a very conscious way the prevailing ideologies and aesthetics of the period, that is, those of Del Monte and José Antonio Saco, the pillars and catalysts of the educational and cultural development of this generation.[11]

Del Monte's Domination

Del Monte's influence in questions of literary sensibility was decisive. He was a defender of the cultural and linguistic unity of Cuba and Spain; a Neoclassic at heart, yet acquainted with Romantic literature; he espoused spiritual, moral, Christian values; and was one of the island's major disciples of Victor Cousin's Eclectic philosophy. Whenever possible he attempted to channel creative efforts in the direction of a didactic, moral literary expression closer to the canons of Neoclassical than to Romantic art. In 1838, he developed these very ideas in *El Album*, where he wrote of the poet's debt to society, underscoring his primary responsibility: He is a man before he is a poet, "and as such he will use all the sources of his talent to cooperate with all the other artists and philosophers of the century . . . to improve the conditions of his fellow man, spreading among them exact and wholesome ideas of morality and religion."[12] He asked for an almost militant spirit in the service of mankind, for otherwise literature would be, as Bentham claimed, a puerile and useless game.[13]

This insistence on a moral, elevating, social expression meshes with the strain of *costumbrista* literature, alluded to earlier, generating a socially-conscious aesthetic and ideology, too frequently neglected in evaluating the figure of the slave in the novel. It is more common to draw the conclusion reached by Portuondo that the amorous dialogues and constant tears in a novel such as *Francisco* belong to the purest traditions of the Romantic school.[14]

Literary Currents and Social Reform

One is tempted to question just how much in these novels is "pure Romantic tradition" and how much an artfully conceived, veiled counter-statement, an encoded reaction to the stifling, repressive environment in which these writers lived and wrote.[15] Del Monte himself, though a patrician of no mean privilege, suffered at the hands of the colonial censors who struck eight lines of antislavery sentiment from his *Romances cubanos*. Having experienced this painful blow, is it not conceivable that while in theory he preferred a novel based on reflected reality, that is, a tortured slave, he was prepared to accept the turning of "pure Romantic" conventions to the social purpose of evoking sympathy for the figure of an idealized protagonist, given the fact that only a nonrealistic portrait would be acceptable to the official censors or the conservative *criollas*? If one studies the slave's Rousseauean nobility, his pacific nature, his sometimes excessively passionate character, his pastoral, idealized romances; in short, if one studies such allegedly Romantic traits against the ideological, philosophic and political aspirations of Del Monte and his *contertulianos*, or traces the evolution of the slave's depiction against a chronological schema of the Cuban slave system's vicissitudes, insights that transcend the simplistic Romantic characterization come into focus. Moreover, with regard to the antithetical pull of Realism and Romanticism, it is important to keep in mind that the *costumbrista* tradition, as Portuondo suggests, was a "process of Romantic literature" which on the one hand represents "the satisfaction, the pleasure of painting oneself. . .and on the other. . . correcting certain social errors, certain customs, for the benefit of the same class."[16]

It is not surprising therefore, as Francisco González del Valle observed, that "young writers [of 1836-1840] wished to reform customs by placing the social evils of their time in bold relief," nor that " a moralizing tendency. . . dominated the youth even to the prejudice of art." It was "essential to improve customs, to awaken the sentiments of goodness and justice, and to that noble task the noble and generous souls who wished to see the slave trade and slavery abolished devoted themselves."[17]

González del Valle exaggerates in lumping abolition with suppression of the trade. For while early examples in support of abolitionism are to be found in Cuba's literature on slavery, even Francisco de Arango y Parreño's prudent 1816 "Ideas sobre los medios de establecer el libre

comercio de Cuba y de realizar un empréstido de veinte millones de pesos," frightened most in his period. So negative was the consensus of opinion on the question, that as late as 1841, El Lugareño wrote that the state of affairs in Cuba was so miserable "that not even in a rational way was it possible to speak [freely of abolition], because one is labelled an insurgent, or an abolitionist, which is worse than an insurrectionist."[18] Thus, up to 1860, and certainly until the conclusion of the Escalera affair, the aim of the antislavery writers, given their ties with the economic interests of the plantation owners, was a gradual, forward-looking and humanitarian policy of limiting the growth of slaves through the enforcement of the slave traffic treaties. Translated into artistic terms, this attitude suggested the advisability of encouraging a mild rather than a bold or rebellious antislavery narrative, one in which the slave might draw tears from the reader rather than cries of fear or horror.

For all of these reasons, the Del Monte group, in developing the budding antislavery works, chose to temper Realism with Romanticism.[19] They instilled in the novelists a concern for presenting reality faithfully; did not discourage idealized "exceptions"; but frowned upon the inflammatory, violent individualist tendencies of some of the European Romantic models.[20] Their ideal was the *negro racional*,[21] the *criada de razón*.[22] But, if the slave was idealized in the early period, his portrayal as a being superior to his reality was, as already indicated, a socially-determined exigency and not the mere result of a derivative Romantic characterization.

In this idealization process, "white" ideals were imposed on the slave by the novelists in the interest of presenting a victim of society, unlikely to alienate the conservative elements of the sacarocracy that staunchly defended the principle of the slave's tyrannization – *tiranizar o correr el riesgo de ser tiranizado*[23] – and the continuation of the illegal slave trade. The resultant pathetic being would, it was hoped, not only win converts to the *criollo's* humanitarian cause, but also court the mercy and justice of foreign readers, especially the English,[24] who, in turn, might bring pressure to bear on the Spanish crown to enforce the slave treaties. All in all, Del Monte and his followers hoped to use the literature of the first period to cure a social cancer, not through abolition, envisioned only in the second period, but by reversing or at least halting the growing imbalance of white to black population, which many feared could eventually bring a repetition of the Haitian rebellion in Cuba.

A Source of Poetry: A Generous Exception

For Del Monte and his disciples, the docile slave was also a source of poetic inspiration, an exotic *costumbrista* component of a national tradition, or, as Milanés puts it (1836), a "mine of our best poetry."[25] Yet, if this was so, perhaps we need to scrutinize more thoroughly the contradictions raised by this view on the one hand, and Del Monte's insistence on stark realism on the other. Or, is it simply a case, once again, of social caution overriding literary convictions to the extent that, as Varela and Giner suggested in 1834, "in no other matter should there be more prudence than in the manifestation of truth"?[26]

A close examination of some of the controversial issues raised by *Francisco* may shed light on these quandaries. We know for example, that Del Monte at one point was unhappy with Francisco's idealization and excessive docility.[27] Responding to this criticism, Suárez y Romero, in his correspondence with Del Monte, reports an exchange of ideas with Milanés, the implications of which, in our view, constitute the nucleus of the basis for understanding the philosophic ideological and literary complexities of slave's characterization:

I wrote Milanés what you criticized in my novel, and he answered me among other things, the following, which I transcribe – "So you should have painted Francisco evil to have painted him with truth?[28] Certainly slavery depraves the heart; but are we not counting on the temperate and pacific nature of the individual? Do we not see all the time slaves with a sweet nature who work tirelessly and contentedly without going beyond the circle of servile ideas in which they live? I do not believe you shortchanged on truth by painting Francisco of humble and melancholy disposition; for although his character is not very common, it exists and even its very exceptionality ought to excite a double interest in the work in which it shines."[29]

Suárez's transmittal of Milanés' ideas suggest an early critical reaction to Romanticism[30] among these writers, presumably in favour of Del Monte's espousal of Balzacian Realism. In addition, Milanés' reference to **counting** on the temperate nature of the slave, and to the notion of **exciting interest**, underscores the socially utilitarian aspect of the antislavery novel's char-

acteristics. And, finally, the question of exceptionality, which is especially pertinent, represents a notion that can be equated either with individuality or with an antithetic principle whose existence in these novels is too frequently identified with Romanticism. In explaining its presence, it might be useful to recall not only Cousin's precept that every idea has its double – the beautiful and the ugly, good and bad, true and false[31] – but also Del Monte's views on slavery, which surely must have swayed the thinking of his disciples. In his "Informe sobre el estado actual de la enseñanza primaria en la Isla de Cuba en 1836, su costo y mejoras de que es susceptible," he wrote the following: "A man who is born and brought up as a slave, regardless of his colour or race, precisely because of his station must be base, stupid, immoral . . . there are races such as the Ethiopian in which we find generous exceptions to this rule, but they are insufficient to change it, because to do so would upset the admirable order which Providence has placed in the governance of the world."[32]

This view of hierarchy, with its accompanying concepts of fixed station and loss of will, is reflected in *Francisco*. It is a view that justifies stasis, harmonizes with Neoclassic ideology and eschews violent movements towards change. It is illustrated in the passage of the novel where the slave, having been ordered by his mistress to cease and desist in his attempts to marry Dorotea, chooses not to "upset the admirable order" and avoids the use of "violent means to realize his request."[33] Elsewhere, and at a later date (1844) Del Monte wrote that he felt a natural, philosophic compassion for the slaves as for all other unfortunate beings, but that he did not wish to have slaves in his homeland, "and even less that these slaves be black, that is, of a branch so savage of the human race."[34]

At first glance, these ideas may seem at variance with Del Monte's Christian ethics, some of whose special characteristics vis-à-vis the slave Suárez y Romero echoes when he speaks of Francisco as a "phenomenon, an exception"[35] with "Christian resignation and meekness," instead of the ills and defects with which the institution of slavery should normally have endowed him. Reflecting upon his portrait of Francisco, Suárez laments the fact that he allowed his natural inclination for goodness and perfection to overwhelm his artistic inclination. The novelist, he declared, "must imitate nature . . . [and] not permit himself to be carried away on wings from the sugar mill to imaginary realms : . ."[36] The dynamics of the antithetical pull of Realism and Idealism, or Realism and Romanticism, is evident.

Yet, in any definitive evaluation of this matter, the question of the severity of Del Monte's criticism must be taken into account. If he was immovably critical, given what we know of the process of readings and corrections of these books, would the Del Monte *contertulianos* not have altered this manuscript; would Del Monte himself not have insisted on major modifications? If he did not, in addition to the reasons discussed above, perhaps he was swayed by the sentiments of Christian morality expressed in his "Moral religiosa" (1838), sentiments that in the final analysis we feel sure he placed above the "evil portrait" of the slave.

Christianity and Eclecticism

In this essay published in *El Plantel*, Del Monte wrote:

In our island the same influence [of the study of the Gospel] is felt, together with the precious remains of our religious faith, which we preserve in all its vigour. It will continue to gain terrain in pure souls of penetrating and cultivated understanding. On its complete triumph depends more than seems apparent, our individual domestic happiness, the tranquility of our souls and the happiness and social glory of our beloved country.[37]

Spiritualism may have triumphed over stark realities in the portrayal of the slave whose evangelic meekness must have seemed more appropriate to Del Monte, in the final analysis, in order to move the noble souls of the readers and provide spiritual remedies for domestic problems, including those of the slave society, through Christian "understanding." Thus, we return once more to the pivotal point of our thesis: the alternate or complementary influences in the portrayal of the slave, that is, factors from sources other than Romantic aesthetics which conceivably shaped the outline of the slave's portrait.

Among those factors not yet considered, there are other spiritual values that belong not to "religious faith," but to Cousin's Eclecticism whose ideas reached Cuba and were defended by Del Monte from 1830 forward,[38] that is, well in advance of the conception of the first antislavery narratives. Of Cousin's complex, evolving ideas, those that appear to have had a direct relationship with the characterization of the slave are (1) the French philosopher's emphasis upon psychology as a major point of departure of the Eclectic method; (2) the relationship of reason to the principles of substance and causality; (3) the existence of a free, intelligent, personal Supreme Being; and (4) a moral system that placed emphasis on both duty and liberty.[39]

Not all of Cuba's intellectuals subscribed to Cousin's philosophy. José de la Luz y Caballero was among its major detractors; Suárez y Romero, while familiar with its tenets, was more drawn to Locke and Condillac's sensualist doctrines.[40] Nonetheless, Eclecticism's mark on the antislavery novel is undeniable; it is evident in the importance granted to appropriate psychological portrayal,[41] the frequency with which the doctrine of causality appears, and the significance of the underlying concepts of liberty and duty to the theoretic foundation of these works.

Viewed in this light, philosophic questions bring us once again to a reconsideration of literary modes: the greater significance of Realism and *Costumbrismo*, rather than Romanticism, in the conception of the antislavery novel. To sum it up, it is our contention that Suárez y Romero, Tanco and Avellaneda chose the docile and submissive slave in order to call forth a sympathetic reaction to slavery's abuses from the more enlightened members of the community, who would probably have been offended by a rebellious protagonist. In so doing, they were moved by the principle of *excepción*, the concepts of duty and Christian spiritualism that tempered some of the more cruel aspects of Realism and set in motion a process of idealization in a literature whose theoretical foundation was intimately tied to progress and the Kantian sense of morality. For all of these reasons, the antislavery novelists were attracted to the Eclectic ideal that true morality led to political liberty; false morality to despotism and chaos.[42]

The Distortions of Censorship

The moderation and restraint we have already noted in these novels presided over the writers' vision of a more perfect order, partly because in their official attitudes[43] they favoured gradualism and reform, but largely because censorship required distortions which ultimately acquired the fixity of tradition. Of the censor's intimidation, Francisco González del Valle observed that "to combat the slave traffic, not to speak of slavery, was in those times [that is, 1836-1840], a crime, a crime more serious than plotting the independence of the island."[44] And Del Monte, in a letter (1838) sent to the editor of the Madrid periodical, *El Corres Nacional*, alludes to these same ideas while gingerly touching upon one of the less understood aspects of the black's portrayal, that is, his appearance in antislavery fiction in a frustrated love relationship (e.g., *Francisco, El negro Francisco, Sab*), a perspective erroneously identified on an absolute basis with Romanticism's influence. "I am sending you," wrote Del Monte,

... the first two numbers of El Album ... The censor is opposed to giving it a purely periodical form ... Do not be surprised if in these volumes love is the only subject, for to this narrow limit is reduced what the chained press of Havana produces. The author, on taking up his pen must compromise here, first with the royal censor, then with the sub-censor, a military officer of the Palace, a sort of vice-overseer, and finally, with the Captain-General. Consequently, it is impossible that after this triple filter of ideas, one will escape which is worth anything, especially if it is capable of offending, not only the spirit of the despotic institutions of the Colony, but the private opinion, no matter how narrow or uncouth, of each of these individuals.[45]

Thus, in the tension between "prudence" and truth, in the choice and development of novelistic themes, "prudence" won as the novelists bowed to both moderation – the docile slave; the theme of love; bland, socially limited references to social ills – and the exigencies of the official censors whose spectre constantly lurked in the background. That Del Monte's remarks were not exaggerated is borne out by the public example the Censor made of Avellaneda's novels *Sab* and *Dos mujeres* which, in 1844, were denied entrance at Customs in Santiago de Cuba by Hilario de Cisneros, the Censor Regio de la Imprenta. His decree of exclusion stated that the first "contained a doctrine subversive to the system of slavery in the island and contrary to morals and good customs, and the second ... was immersed in immoral doctrines ..."[46]

In such an oppressive environment, it is reasonable to assume writers refrained from creating plots in which the slavery question might be viewed by the authorities as a broad social issue,

and, by extension, an insurrectional tract. The plots of this narrative were thus reduced to the family unit, in preference to broader, social views. Its protagonists were types: Fernando, Rosalía, Doña Concepcíon, in *Petrona y Rosalía;* Francisco, Dorotea, Carlos, Señora Mindizábel in *Francisco*. The dynamics of these narratives centres about the conflict between pure (the slaves') and impure (the masters') love. This view of plot and character prevailed until the definitive edition of *Cecilia Valdés* (1882), which presented an entirely new concept of social literature.[47] But, until its appearance, the novelists wrote works in which facts were modified, truth distorted; and the male *amo* depicted as the sexual predator with designs on the noble, innocent slave.

The *amo's* depravity was "determined" not by any inherited flaw in character, but by his desultory upbringing, his lack of the fundamentals of modern education and the corrupt customs of Cuba's colonial society (adjective "slave" omitted). In Sab, Avellaneda presents some atypical social ills and polarities that are different from those of the *Francisco* and *Petrona y Rosalía* microcosms. There is, for example, no sexual violation; female social oppression is broached (a reflection of Avellaneda's personal experience), and the *amo—slave* antithesis yields a formula, for its time daring: the slave's soul (Sab's) is noble, altruistic and liberated; the patrician's (Enrique Otway's) is enslaved and mercantile. In spite of individual differences, however, there are enough characteristics in common, so that with respect to the violent passions and sexual crimes of these and other early Cuban novels, Mario Parajón sees in them a metaphoric social counter-statement, an "escape valve," so to speak, for the colonial asphyxia choking the artistic freedom of these writers. "The woman – he notes – became the compendium of all ideals when the concept of homeland [was] prohibited for those who wish[ed] to transform it and work in it."[48]

The Curse of Determinism

In a gradual process of transformation, the economic decline of the slave system, and the freer discussion of abolition strengthened the slavery novelists' early, cautious use of deterministic theories and resulted in a narrative whose events were viewed, not from the individual or family base, but from a much broader social perspective. Herein lies one of the major innovations of Villaverde's *Cecilia Valdés*: we are presented with a vivid, comprehensive picture of a corrupt society and witness the fatal consequences of maintaining an island under slavery and Spanish colonialism.

In examining the literature which leads to Villaverde's overarching view, it is not uncommon to find the novelists using the slave's will or the master's sins in fatalistically organized schemata which, in a veiled fashion, present a family's moral stain, presumably intended to suggest the notion that, given certain circumstances in a given society, fixed consequences would result under stasis. In a digression of his *El penitente*, Villaverde refers to this notion, and explains that "a stain as ugly as that which it is supposed, fell upon Isabel Cacanga with her birth and upon the birth of her daughter, always influences more or less in the fate of a family, and even blooms and propagates for many generations."[49] Given the frequency with which this concept of moral determinism surfaces in the antislavery novel, one is drawn to speculate that it was used to signal the unavoidable moral decline of Cuba, unless major social and political reforms were initiated.

Near the end of the slavery period, Francisco Calcagno openly referred to the stain of slavery[50] in the *Advertencia* (1883) to his novel, *Los crímenes de Concha* (1887). It would seem that he and other novelists were ultimately convinced that they needed to demonstrate that slavery was a cancer to which even whites would succumb. The sins of generations of Cubans – black and white – to which there is such abundant reference in these novels, are thus, in the final analysis, viewed as moral, social, and educational problems that concern all segments of society. Earlier Suárez y Romero said of Francisco's *ama* that she was "born and brought up among slaves, [and] could not elude entirely that pernicious influence."[51] Slavery's malignant growth was left unchecked, and ultimately it came to be an uncontrolled ailment that spread from family to society, from the individual to the collectivity.

As the antislavery novel moved toward its final period, the slave acquired ethnic veracity, psychological depth – especially in *El negro Francisco* (1875) – and a clear transition from a

humanitarian, reformist view toward an abolitionist stance. This, however, does not occur until 1860[52] when, according to Cepero Bonilla, the same *hacendados* who, as of 1836, fought the slave trade, now accepted the inevitability of slavery's extinction.

But abolition was not perceived either by hacendados or novelists as an immediate, sudden process, according to Calcagno. The sacarocracy whose misgivings the novelists reflected saw the need to solve the growing black problem, while avoiding a rebellion more disturbing or destructive than the exaggerated Escalera conspiracy. In addition, mechanization and industrialization had progressed sufficiently to produce a crisis in the sugar industry whose point of initiation Cepero Bonilla marks as 1870.[53] The landholders were worried about their role in society. In the face of these disturbing events, the novelists, responding to the sacarocracy's entrenched interests, accepted the inevitability of abolition, but recommended it be gradual so that the slave might be educated prior to becoming a free agent in Cuban society. Hence, Calcagno's gradualism, which was coupled with a new, franker view of the slave whose free circulation as a freed man acquired the status of general concern. No longer do we find the idealized *negro de excepción*. Instead Calcagno refers to the blacks as members of a vicious race,[54] (as Del Monte had previously in his essays). And, with this second-stage attitude toward the slave, we come full circle in the question of his characterization: he is now treated, as Del Monte originally wished, with more realism, and less idealism.

A Schema: Novel and History

In examining the antislavery novel in both its early and later periods, it is clear we cannot apply to this literature António Candido's precept that "literature evidences a certain time lag, and . . . the average production in a given moment is at that moment a tributary of the past."[55] Even if we use Cepero Bonilla's chronological outline of slavery's decline, the antislavery novel was not a literature expressing a past, but one whose Romantic strains were tempered by *Costumbrismo*, Realism and Eclecticism with the express purpose of creating a climate for the future of a complex, guilt-ridden, contradictory, morally corrupt society. This novel's clairvoyance is striking, even if in place of Cepero Bonilla's scheme we follow the more restrictive chronology of Cuba's slave system suggested by Pacheco.[56] In his view, the first visible signs of a crisis of values date from 1840. Even if we move the inception of decline from 1860[57] to 1840 (Cepero vs. Pacheco), the writers of the first generation of antislavery novels are in advance of their time. They do not recommend abolition, as does Calcagno later on, but they do set a mood, perhaps too lachrymose, and undertake a morally inspired social analysis, critical of a major economic institution in a period (1838-1841) in which prosperity still dominated the slave system. According to Cepero, this sense of prosperity was evident until 1860: "The form of labour was efficient until then, [he writes], but after that the regime reaches a crisis stage socially, politically and economically. This phenomenon was noticed by the perceptive investigators of Cuban problems a century ago."[58] He might have added it was the antislavery novelists who, guided by the ideas of Del Monte and Saco, first pointed out the gaping holes of a collapsing edifice, much before abolition became a public issue or even an openly expressible concept. Where, in this period, except in the early antislavery novels, is there an affirmation of the dignity of all men, or a humanitarian concern expressed with the poignancy of Avellaneda's Sab: "Is it possible [wrote the slave] the great master of this great human family established different laws for those born black and those born white?"[59]

Notes

* Part of this research was supported by a grant given in 1974 by the Joint Committee on Latin American Studies of the Social Science Research Council and the American Council of Learned Societies.

1.   1972. Las literaturas nacionales. Latinoamericana I(24). The Paraguayan novelist is referring to the social consciousness in all Latin American literature, which, of course, suggests the consanguinity of early political, social and cultural problems.

2.   For a particularly objectionable example see Remos y Rubio, Juan J. 1935. *Tendencias de la narración imaginativa en Cuba*. La Casa Montalvo Cárdenas. Havana, Cuba. Less superficial is the unpublished Ph.D. dissertation of Pedro Manuel Barreda. 1969. *La caracterización del protagonista negro en la novela cubana*. SUNY. Buffalo, New York, espe-

cially: 66–207. And, finally, of particular merit, though fragmentary, is the analysis of Luis Yero Pérez (with Ordenel Heredia Rojas). 1974. El tema de la esclavitud en la narrativa cubana. *Islas* 49 (Sept.–Dec.) 64-94.

3.   For the purpose of organizing our discussion in this paper, we have divided selected major antislavery novels into two groups:

First Period: The Early Novels

Date of composition

1838   Anselmo Suárez y Romero. 1947. *Francisco*. Dirección de Cultura, Havana, Cuba.

1838   Feliz Tanco y Bosmeniel. 1925. *Petrona y Rosalía*. Cuba Contemporánea XXXIX (Sept.-Dec.): 225-287.

1841   Gertrudis Gómez de Avellaneda. 1970. *Sab*. Anaya. Madrid, Spain.

1841   José Ramón Betancourt. 1885. Una feria de la Caridad en 183 . . . Imprenta de Luis Tesso Serra. Barcelona, Spain.

Second Period: The Later Novels

1875   Antonio Zambrana. 1875. *El negro Francisco*. Imprenta de la Librería del Mercurio. Santiago de Chile.

1839-1879   Cirilo Villaverde. 1964. *Cecilia Valdés, o la Loma del Ang—*, Las Américas Publishing Company. New York, New York.

1883   Francisco Calcagno. 1887. *Los crímenes de Concha*. Libreríe Imprenta de Elías F. Casona. Havana, Cuba.

4.   Chapters in literary histories or articles in periodicals. This paper is based on research that will form part of a book in Spanish on the Cuban antislavery novel.

5.   1971. *Manual de historia de Cuba*. :407. Instituto Cubano del Libro. Havana, Cuba.

6.   V. José Antonio Portuondo. 1969. *Bosquéjo histórico de las letras cubanas*. :21. Ministerio de Relaciones Exteriores. Havana, Cuba.

7.   1859. *To Cuba and Back, A Vacation Voyage*. : 233. Houghton, Mifflin. Boston, Mass.

8.   Portuondo, V., op. cit. :21.

9.   *Centón epistolario de Domingo Del Monte*. 1930. IV: 39 El Siglo XX. Havana, Cuba. This and all other translations from the Spanish into English are mine. In subsequent references to the seven volume *Centón*, we will use an abbreviated form (C.E.) followed by the volume and page.

10. In his prologue to *Obras de D. Ramón de Palma*, cited by Mario Cabrera Saque in his edition of *Francisco*. :18. 1947. Dirección de Cultura, Havana, Cuba.

11. Francisco de Arango y Parreño and José de la Luz y Caballero were also prominent intellectual leaders of this period. But neither constituted a major force in the intellectual development of these novelists. Luz and Del Monte engaged in a sharp polemic exchange over Eclecticism.

12. Cintio Vittier, Ed. 1968. Reproduced in *La crítica literaria y estética en el siglo XIX cubana*. I (125). Biblioteca Nacional José Marti. Havana, Cuba.

13. Ibid. :126.
14. *Bosquéjo*, op. cit. :24. However, he also points out the novel's realism: the description of the slave owner, the overseer, and the sugar plantation.
15. In analyzing Cuban colonial literature, one is frequently obliged to probe beneath the surface and question the more obvious solutions to textual problems. Consider for example, the subtle social implications of the *siboneista* movement, or the "escapism" of Julián del Casal.
16. 1972. Landaluze y el costumbrismo en Cuba. Revista de la Biblioteca Nacional Jan.-April: 52.
17. 1938. In his prologue to José Zacarías González del Valle: 5-6. *La vida literaria en Cuba* (1836-1840). Secretaría de Educación. Havana, Cuba.
18. Gaspar Betancourt Cisneros. C.E. V: 50.
19. Vittier, C., op cit. I: 35.
20. Victor Hugo's *Bug-Jargal*, with its violent slave revolt, was read by this generation. But it had no noticeable influence on the *delmontino* productions. In 1836, Tanco wrote Del Monte: "And what do you say about Bug-Jargal?" Enthused by this work, Tanco envisioned novels of "poetic truth," peopled with blacks and whites, filled with "infernal, diabolical" scenes (C.E. VII: 105). It is to be assumed Tanco and Del Monte did not see eye to eye on this subject. However, Hugo's novel, according to Mary Cruz, left its mark on *Sab*, the novel least connected with the Del Monte *tertulias*. v. Cruz's prologue to *Sab*. 1963: 4144. Instituto del Libro. Havana, Cuba.
21. V. Anastasio Orozco y Arango's letter to Del Monte (C.E. V: 11).
22. [Ivan A. Schulman, Ed. 1975: 57. *Autobiografía de un esclavo*. Guadarrama. Madrid, Spain.] The expression used by Juan Francisco Manzano to refer to his mother's superior attainments.
23. Feliz Varela and Thomas Gener, in a letter to Del Monte (1834), refer to this popular expression (C.E. II: 132).
24. Richard R. Madden, for example, after serving as Commissioner of the Mixed Tribunal was given a folder of antislavery literature by Del Monte to carry to England. It included Juan Francisco Manzano's *Autobiografía*; Rafael Matamoro's *Elegías cubanas*; Suárez y Romero's *Francisco*; and a poem by José Zacarías González del Valle. The Manzano work was published in a poor translation (done by Madden himself) in 1840.
25. C.E. III: 213.
26. C.E. II: 133.
27. V. Suárez y Romero's letter quoted below. At some point, however, its seems Del Monte must have been convinced of Suárez's point of view. Otherwise, he would surely have deleted the novel from the portfolio he gave Madden. Or, should we assume Suárez made modifications along the way following either Del Monte's or José Zacarías González del Valle's suggestions? The latter supposition would not be at variance with the complex genesis of this novel. Suárez y Romero refers to numerous esmiendas made by González del Valle in his Advertencia to *Francisco*, ed. cit. :3942.
28. José Zacarías González del Valle, in a letter to Suárez y Romero regarding *Petrona y Rosalía* complained of the opposite: "The author of *Petrona y Rosalía*, if he is guilty of anything, it is of following facts too closely, because I don't know who can doubt that in our society what he describes happens (*La vida literaria*. :64).
29. C.E. III: 198.
30. Vittier alludes to a critical and ironic reaction in these novels (*La crítica literaria* :35).
31. —— Janet. 1885. *Victor Cousin et son oeuvre*. :90. Calmann Levy. Paris, France.
32. 1929. *Escritos*. II: 43. Cultura. Havana, Cuba.
33. Ed. cit. :58.
34. *Escritos*. I: 201.
35. C.E. IV: 44.
36. C.E. IV. 45.
37. 1838. November, Entrega 3: 86.
38. José Augusto Escoto. 1916. Felix Manuel Tanco, adversario de José de la Luz y Caballero en la polémica sobre el eslectiscismo. Revista Histórica,Crítica y Bibliográfica de la Literatura I: 408–412; 408, n.l.
39. Ibid.: 409–410, n. 3.
40. Ibid.: 415, n. 9.
41. The adjective "appropriate" is especially significant in view of Del Monte's previously cited reaction to Francisco. In the same vein, see José Zacarías González del Valle's letter to Suárez y Romero: "Don't justify the mistress of the house, paint her as she is; but for the same reason, lower her, lighten the tints of goodness which are too heavy in your portrait so that there will be no contrast between her and the facts" (*La vida literaria*.: 66–67).
42. Janet, P., op. cit. :94–95.
43. Public, official attitudes are of major significance, since in spite of discrepancies – and there were many – between public and private opinion, the antislavery narratives were conceived as reformist, moralizing **public** documents.
44. Prólogo to José Zacarías González del Valle's *La vida literaria*. :8.
45. Escritos. I: 102–103.
46. 1941. Expediente donde se decreta la retención (y reembarque) de dos obras de Gertrudis Gómez de Avellaneda por contener doctrinas subversivas y contrarias a la moral. Boletín del Archivo Nacional XL: 103 ff.
47. In our book the antislavery novel, we will deal with details of this metamorphosis which are too complex to describe briefly here. Suffice it to say that some change in character development is evident by 1875. For Villaverde, the factors that produce this evolution are wider contact with foreign literature during his exile, a personal view of the consequences of slavery in the United States; the decline of the United States slave system; and, perhaps, the **antecedent** of *Uncle Tom's Cabin* (1852).
48. Cirilo Villaverde. 1962. *Prólogo. La joven de la flecha de oro*. :13. Comisión Nacional de la UNESCO. Havana, Cuba.
49. 1925: 39. La Burglesa. Havana, Cuba.

50.   1887: 30. Librería e Imprenta de Elías F. Casona. Havana, Cuba.
51.   *Francisco*, ed. cit. :50.
52.   Raúl Cepero Bonilla. 1960. *Azúcar y abolición.* : 29–30; 32. Echeverría. Havana, Cuba.
53.   Ibid.: 65. In a chapter entitled "La decadencia del sistema esclavista." Earlier, however, in Chapter III, he uses the 1860 decade (:29) as the dividing line of the growth and decline of the slave system. V. n. 57 below.
54.   *Los crímenes de Concha.* :29. He writes: "the race has a natural proclivity for indolence and vice . . . they are thieves . . . but, hasn't the law robbed them even of their dignity as men?"
55.   1972. *Literatura y subdesarrollo. América Latina en su literatura.* :343. Siglo XXI. Mexico.
56.   Francisco Pacheco. Dec. 1972. Aspectos del pensamiento esclavista en el siglo XIX. Unión XI: 162–178. Pacheco dates the crisis of values of the slave system as 1840–1860.
57.   We are using the earlier of the two dates given by Cepero, op. cit. V. n. 54.
58.   Op. cit. :29.
59.   Ed. cit. :220.

81

Explaining Abolition: Contradiction, Adaptation, and Challenge in Cuban Slave Society, 1860–86

REBECCA J. SCOTT

In the middle decades of the nineteenth century, as slavery was disappearing elsewhere in the New World, slave-based plantation production of sugar in Cuba reached remarkable heights of technological sophistication and output. In 1868 Cuba produced 720,250 metric tons of sugar, more than 40 per cent of the cane sugar reaching the world market in that year.[1] Yet just as production reached these levels, the abolition of slavery in Cuba was initiated, beginning a process of slave emancipation that was to last nearly 20 years. This concurrence of events raises the questions: What was the relationship between slavery and the development of sugar production? Why did emancipation in Cuba take place when and as it did?

My analysis of these questions takes a comparative perspective in two respects. First, it is partly in implicit comparison to other New World slave societies that the very late abolition of slavery in Cuba — 1886 — poses a problem of explanation. Second, and more important, an explicitly comparative analysis of the course of emancipation in distinct regions *within* Cuba can help to identify the forces that advanced, and those that retarded, emancipation, and thus can contribute to a fuller interpretation of the causes and nature of abolition.

The predominant explanations generally put forward for Cuban abolition invoke large-scale forces and internal contradictions. One argument, enunciated most fully by Cuban historian Manuel Moreno Fraginals, goes roughly as follows. There was a contradiction between slave-based production and necessary technological innovation. For the sugar industry to advance, it had to break free of this outmoded organization of production. Indeed, as the industry advanced, slavery itself decayed. Formal abolition was thus merely the de jure recognition of a de facto disintegration of slavery.[2] A complementary argument has been made about the attitudes of Cuban slave holders. Eugene Genovese compares planters in the United States with those in Cuba and concludes that major Cuban planters had only an economic attachment to the institution of slavery and were quite prepared to abandon it in order to advance and modernize.[3]

An alternative hypothesis, advanced by Arthur Corwin in his study of Spain and Cuba, sees abolition as part of a worldwide political and diplomatic campaign resulting from a basic ideological shift away from bound labor. Cuban abolition, in this view, results from Spanish colonial policies designed to end the institution of slavery, thus protecting the colonies from outside interference while bringing Spain in line with what were seen as more advanced and civilized modes of labor organization.[4]

The underlying explanatory problem posed is a challenging one, not so much because it has

This essay is part of a larger project that was funded by the Social Science Research Council, the Fulbright-Hays Program, and the Latin American Program of Princeton University. The author would like to thank David Davis, Seymour Drescher, Stanley Engerman, Albert Hirschman, Thoms Holt, Franklin Knight, Sidney Mintz, Magnus Mörner, David Murray, Stuart Schwartz, and Gavin Wright for their comments, and Manuel Moreno Fraginals for numerous discussions of the issue of slavery and abolition. This essay first appeared in *Comparative Studies in Society and History*, 26 (January 1984): 83–111. Parts in Rebecca Scott, *Slave Emancipation in Cuba: The Transition to Free Labor, 1860–1899*, to be published in 1985 by the Princeton University Press.

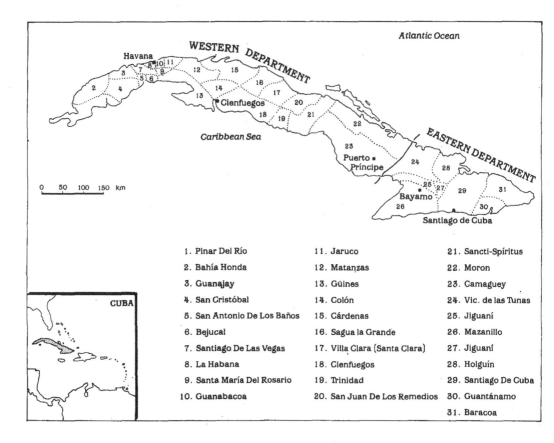

1. Pinar Del Río	11. Jaruco	21. Sancti-Spíritus
2. Bahía Honda	12. Matanzas	22. Moron
3. Guanajay	13. Güines	23. Camaguey
4. San Cristóbal	14. Colón	24. Vic. de las Tunas
5. San Antonio De Los Baños	15. Cárdenas	25. Jiguaní
6. Bejucal	16. Sagua la Grande	26. Mazanillo
7. Santiago De Las Vegas	17. Villa Clara (Santa Clara)	27. Jiguaní
8. La Habana	18. Cienfuegos	28. Holguín
9. Santa María Del Rosario	19. Trinidad	29. Santiago De Cuba
10. Guanabacoa	20. San Juan De Los Remedios	30. Guantánamo
		31. Baracoa

historiographical implications but because it obliges one to look at large-scale explanations and then at small-scale patterns of events and ask how well the explanations actually account for the patterns observed. The point is not simply to juxtapose the particularities or uniqueness of a given case against the large-scale explanation and conclude that one must reject simplifying generalities. Rather, it is to hypothesize appropriate links between the different levels at which the historical explanation might operate and then to determine whether the observed patterns of historical reality generally match the patterns anticipated from the explanation. For example, if it is the case that 'mechanization, the conversion of manufacture into large industry, unquestionably brings about the abolition of slavery'[5] then technologically advanced areas might be expected to shift toward free labor first, with the most advanced estates giving up the use of slave labor. If, on the other hand, abolition were the result of colonial policy, then emancipation might be expected to occur more or less evenly across provinces, closely tied chronologically to key legal changes.

The Chronology and Geography of Abolition

Let us begin with the background to abolition and the key events that marked the ending of slavery. In 1860 the island of Cuba was the world's largest producer of cane sugar and contained some 1,400 sugar mills. The majority of Cuban mills operated by steam power, and a minority (located primarily in the central province of Matanzas) also used advanced processing equipment.[6] The slave population was approximately 370,000, and by far the largest single occupation of slaves was that of sugar worker.[7] Production increased rapidly in the decade of the sixties, growing from 428,800 metric tons in 1860 to 720,250 tons in 1868.[8]

Despite the apparent prosperity and productivity of the sugar industry, problems were rising to the surface. The slave trade, illegal since 1817 according to a treaty between Spain and England, had nonetheless flourished as a vigorous contraband. But after a large upswing in slave imports in the latter part of the 1850s, the 1860s saw a rapid and permanent decline as British pressure and changing United States policy finally blocked off the trade.[9] Since the Cuban slave population did not fully reproduce itself, the work force would necessarily decline in size unless other steps were taken. One response to the labor supply problem was to import indentured Chinese workers, but this practice was halted by a treaty between Spain and China in the 1870s. Another was to institute a policy of what was referred to as 'good treatment', intended to encourage slave reproduction. This was to some extent successful, though not enough so as to maintain the size of the slave labor force.

The impact of these problems over the short term should not be exaggerated, however. Profits continued to be made in Cuban sugar production, and world prices for sugar remained relatively steady in the 1860s and early 1870s. Though planters had difficulties with agricultural credit, and resorted to extensive mortgaging, output continued to climb. Despite competition from beet sugar, Cuba's share of the world market in sugar remained about 25 per cent.[10] In the minds of larger planters, moreover, there were strong forces supporting both slavery and colonialism. Slavery was a form of labour organization that permitted the exaction of an extraordinary amount of labor from the men, women, and children who toiled under it. Planters were unsure whether free persons would willingly labor under the grueling regime prevalent in the cane fields and sugar-boiling houses of Cuba. At the same time, to most planters in the sugar areas Spanish colonialism was a known quantity, an extractive presence but a protective one, a bulwark against social disruption, and the ultimate guarantor of peace on the plantations.

It was in this environment that the rebellion of 1868, later to be called the Ten Years' War, broke out. Small-scale planters in the eastern end of the island, provoked by heavy new taxes and by a financial crisis in 1867, rose in rebellion against Spanish domination. The insurrection, begun by relatively conservative men, some sympathetic to the possibility of annexation to the United States, rapidly became more radical as its social base expanded. Though the rebellion was not successful, three results significant for the future of slavery emerged from the conflict.[11]

First, in order to gain the support of slaves and free blacks, the insurgents declared the qualified freedom of slaves under their control, a measure that quickly went beyond the limited aims of its initiators and undermined the social relations of slavery throughout the war zone.

Second, because the Spanish hoped to capture the apparent moral high ground and avoid appearing as retrograde defenders of slavery in the eyes of potential black recruits to the insurrection, as well as to potential international allies of the insurgents, Spain in 1870 adopted the Moret Law. This measure declared free all children born after 1868 and all slaves over the age of 60 and also promised some form of emancipation of the rest when Cuban deputies were seated in the Spanish parliament once the war was over. This was an extremely cautious form of gradual abolition and did not generally affect those of working age, but it did signal Spain's intention eventually to abolish the institution. Third, the 1878 peace treaty ending the Ten Years' War freed those slaves who had fought on either side. The Spanish government saw this policy as a necessary precondition for pacification — there would be little reason otherwise for slaves among the insurgents to lay down arms — but it was both controversial and disruptive.[12]

The following year, in 1879, the remaining slaves in the eastern provinces unexpectedly challenged their masters, refusing to work unless they were granted freedom *como los convenidos* — like those freed by the peace treaty. Eastern planters backed down, promising freedom in four years and wages during the interim. The Spanish government, already under pressure from abolitionists in Spain, backed down as well and declared both the end of slavery and the immediate transformation of slaves into 'apprentices' called *patrocinados*.[13] This intermediate status, under which former slaves were obliged to work for their former masters, was intended to last until 1888. Attacked by Spanish abolitionists and by the handful of Cuban abolitionists, and undermined by the behavior of masters and apprentices themselves, the interim arrangement was instead ended prematurely in 1886, finishing the legal process of abolition.

This, in effect, is the political sequence of events that comprised the abolition of slavery in Cuba. If we turn the search for underlying causes and mechanisms to examining the phenomenon regionally and demographically, however, it becomes clear that the process of emancipation, the actual achievement of legal freedom by slaves, followed a pattern quite different from abolition.

The rate of decay of slavery varied widely from province to province (Tables 1 and 2). Matanzas and Santa Clara, the major sugar provinces and the ones with most of the

Table 1   Slave and *Patrocinado* Population by Province, 1862–86

Province	1862	1867	1871	1877	1883	1885	1886
Pinar del Río	46,027	44,879	36,031	29,129	13,885	8,110	3,937
Havana	86,241	84,769	63,312	41,716	18,427	10,419	5,693
Matanzas	98,496	102,661	87,858	70,849	38,620	19,997	9,264
Santa Clara	72,116	68,680	56,535	42,049	23,260	12,987	5,648
Puerto Príncipe	14,807	14,889	7,167	2,290	246	153	101
Santiago de Cuba	50,863	47,410	36,717	13,061	5,128	1,715	738
Total	368,550	363,288	287,620	199,094	99,566	53,381	25,381

Source: See Appendix.

Table 2   Slave and *Patrocinado* Population Retained, Percentage by Province, 1862–86 (1862 = 100)

Province	1862	1867	1871	1877	1883	1885	1886
Pinar del Río	100	98	78	63	30	18	9
Havana	100	98	73	48	21	12	7
Matanzas	100	104	89	72	39	20	9
Santa Clara	100	95	78	58	32	18	8
Puerto Príncipe	100	101	48	15	2	1	1
Santiago de Cuba	100	93	72	26	10	3	1
Total	100	99	78	54	27	14	7

Source: See Appendix.

technically advanced mills, showed the greatest persistence of slavery into the early 1880s. Pinar del Río, in the west, where about one-third of the slaves in 1862 were living on tobacco farms and slightly over one-third on sugar plantations, showed a similar pattern. Havana, a province that contained the island's major urban area (about 25,000 slaves lived in the city of Havana in 1862) showed a substantially more rapid decline. By 1877 it held less than half of its 1862 slave population; by 1883, about one-fifth. The eastern provinces of Puerto Príncipe, a cattle area, and Santiago de Cuba, an area of some backward sugar mills and much small-scale farming and coffee growing, lost slave population very rapidly after 1867. These were the two provinces most involved in the Ten Years' War, which led to the destruction, both direct and indirect, of many plantations. Some had to cease operation for want of labor when their slaves fled; others were burned, which often resulted in de facto freedom for the slaves.

This pattern reveals that the course of emancipation was by no means uniform across the island, suggesting that the pace of achievement of freedom was determined by factors other than Spanish colonial policy. Moreover, the result of the unequal rates of emancipation was to concentrate slavery increasingly in the more technologically advanced sugar zones. In 1862 Matanzas and Santa Clara had 46 per cent of Cuba's slave population; by 1883 they had 62 per cent of the *patrocinados*. The freeing of slaves thus cannot be attributed solely to the requirements of the advanced sugar plantations, either, for as emancipation proceeded these plantations held proportionately more, not fewer, of Cuba's slaves.[14]

The chronology of the process is also significant. During the 1860s and 1870s, whatever the 'contradictions' facing the sugar industry, the major sugar areas were holding on to their slaves. In Matanzas in 1862 the slave population was around 98,500. About 20 per cent of those slaves would have been under the age of ten or over the age of 60, leaving approximately 78,800 between those ages.[15] In 1877 all slaves were by definition between the ages of nine and 59, as a result of the Moret Law, but about 70,850 slaves remained in Matanzas. The slave population of working age had indeed fallen in the intervening 15 years but only about 10 per cent, an amount plausibly attributable to deaths and a shift in the age structure, partially counteracted by some in-migration. There is no support in these figures for the idea of large-scale abandonment of slaves or of slavery by the owners of plantations in Matanzas.

There was significant decline, however, in the areas of backward technology and political unrest — Puerto Príncipe and Santiago de Cuba — where slaves and insurgents fought directly for an end to slavery. Decline was also marked in the province containing a large city, Havana, where lawsuits and self-purchase by slaves were facilitated by access to courts and by money earned through hiring out. Official tabulations of appeals by slaves for *coartación* (partial self-purchase) and freedom show disproportionate representation for the city of Havana.[16]

The strong persistence of slavery through the 1870s in major sugar areas suggests that the notion of an irreconcilable conflict between the existence of slavery and the technological advancement of plantations needs revision. Sugar production expanded in the 1860s and 1870s as planters with capital bought vacuum pans and other modern processing apparatus, increasing the output of sugar per unit of land planted. Additional workers appeared on estates. (The Chinese population of Cuba increased 35 per cent between 1862 and 1877, while the island's total population grew only slightly.) Some discharged Spanish soldiers and other Spanish immigrants also worked on the plantations. But the slave population, though diminishing, remained crucial. In enumerating the *dotaciones* (labor forces) of sugar estates, the 1877 agricultural census found 90,516 slaves working on the estates of their owners, 20,726 *alquilados y libres* (hired and free), and 14,597 Chinese. Slaves thus comprised at least 72 per cent of the *dotaciones*, and quite probably more, since the category *alquilados y libres* included not only hired laborers but rented slaves and some young and elderly former slaves who had been freed by the Moret Law and were not full-time workers.[17]

The regional and chronological pattern of persistence of the slave population suggests that the strategy of large planters was to maintain continued control over their slaves, even while expanding their labor force in other ways — to adapt, rather than repudiate, slavery. Thus the contradictions of Cuban slavery (of which the failure of the slave population to maintain its numbers was the most urgent) did not have to impel abolition as such. An observer sympathetic to Cuban planters noted dryly in 1873: 'The slave-owners in Cuba are convinced of the necessity of manumitting their slaves; but readily as they acknowledge the evils of the slave system, they are not persuaded of the wisdom of any measure by which it may be brought to an end.' He described planters' advocacy of a gradual substitution of free labor for the declining slave population, rather than support for actual suppression of the institution of slavery.[18]

The Plantation Work Force

The most distinctive characteristic of the plantation work force in the mid-1870s, then, was its diversity. Plantation slaves, rented slaves, indentured Asians, and black, white, and mulatto wage workers all labored on the estates. Plantation employers did not face a homogen-

eous supply of labor but rather a segmented labor force, with different forms and quantities of payment due different types of worker. Wages were paid by the day, the task, the month, the trimester, or the year; the amount paid varied widely; workers sometimes did and sometimes did not receive maintenance; compensation occurred in coin, bills, credit, goods, or shares.[19]

This is the situation that has been interpreted as chaotic, symptomatic of the internal collapse of slavery.[20] But one must examine carefully the argument that the diversity of forms of labor in the 1870s was indicative of a disintegration of Cuban slavery in the face of unavoidable contradictions.

The argument has several parts. One claim is, in a sense, definitional: that the slave who received a bonus, cultivated a provision ground, or was rewarded for learning a skill was in some sense no longer a true slave and that these developments were symptomatic of the disintegration of slavery. Although such concessions certainly affected slaves' lives, and in some cases hastened self-purchase, they had appeared in many slave systems long before abolition and do not, by definition or ortherwise, necessarily constitute disintegration. They were attempts to resolve a variety of problems within slavery, but they certainly did not need to lead to its demise.[21]

A second claim deals with the response of planters to the reduction in the slave trade. Aware that their supply of labor was being cut off, some Cuban planters had resolved to take better care of their existing slaves and to encourage reproduction. But, it has been argued, the policy of 'good treatment' inevitably led to a decline in the productivity of the slave work force because the proportion of the very young and the very old increased, eventually making the enterprise unprofitable. Moreno Fraginals's study of plantation records shows convincingly that the proportion of slaves of working age did decline on some Cuban estates through the first half of the nineteenth century.[22] But even if one accepts the argument that maintaining a self-reproducing slave labor force would eventually have undermined profitability for Cuban planters (in a way that it apparently did not, for example, in the American south), the question remains: Given the very late cessation of the contraband slave trade to Cuba, how far had this process actually proceeded on Cuban plantations by the time of abolition?

Though plantation lists for an adequately

representative range of estates in the 1870s have not survived, there is an extremely comprehensive source for one district: the manuscript returns of an 1875 slave count from Santa Isabel de las Lajas in the province of Santa Clara. Lajas was a prosperous area in the jurisdiction of Cienfuegos and contained both old and new plantations. In 1861 the district had a slave population of 1,930 and contained 17 *ingenios* (plantations, including fields and mill). In 1875, when the manuscript listing was drawn up, there were 15 *ingenios* and a slave population of 1,852.[23] The exceptional persistence of slavery in the region was no doubt due in part to the presence of estate owners, such as Tomás Terry and Agustín Goytisolo, who were both prosperous and tied to the slave trade. The district is thus not typical of the island as a whole, but analysis of its population reflects the labor situation facing large and small planters in an important sugar area in the mid-1870s.

Of the slaves on *ingenios* in Lajas in 1875, 58 per cent had been born in Cuba and 42 per cent in Africa; 61 per cent were male and 39 per cent female. It was a population that plainly had relied recently and heavily on imported slaves, probably during the boom in the contraband trade in the 1850s. The age structure of the plantation population is also quite striking, considering the date — just five years before the legal abolition of slavery and the establishment of apprenticeship. It was not an aged population: while 28 per cent were between the ages of 31 and 40, only 6 per cent were between the ages of 51 and 60, even though one might have expected this latter group to include some slaves over age 60 whose ages had been falsified by their masters to evade the Moret Law. Nor was there a high proportion of young slave children. Those born since September 1868 were technically free, and those between the ages of six and ten constituted only 7.5 per cent of the population. Even though those born since 1868 were still the responsibility of the plantation, the total burden was probably relatively small, for in some instances slave parents maintained their *liberto* children directly or later reimbursed the master for their maintenance. What is most significant is that the 16–40 age group, of prime working age, constituted fully 63 per cent of the plantation slave population and 66 per cent of the males (see Table 3 and Figure 1). One can contrast this with the situation in the coffee-producing municipality of Vassouras in Brazil, where the age 15–40 sector of the plantation population fell from a high of 62 per cent of the total labor force during 1830–49 to a low of 35

Figure 1   Age Pyramid for Slaves on *Ingenios* in Santa Isabel de las Lajas, 1875

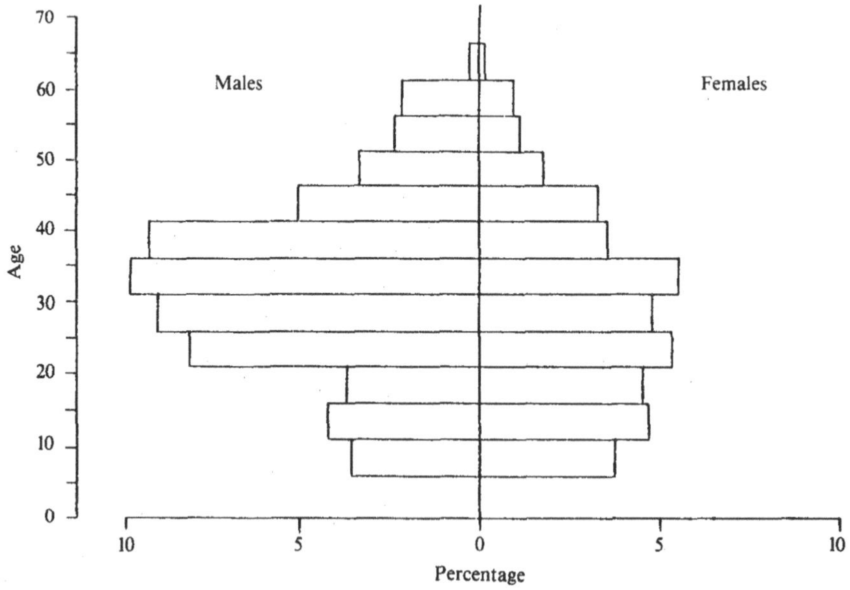

Source: See Table 3.

Table 3 Ages of Slaves in *Ingenios* in Santa Isabel de las Lajas, 1875

Ages	Males	Females	All slaves	Percentage of total
6–10[a]	49	51	100	7.5
11–15	56	61	117	8.8
16–20	51	58	109	8.2
21–25	108	69	177	13.3
26–30	120	64	184	13.8
31–35	132	72	204	15.3
36–40	124	46	170	12.8
41–45	69	44	113	8.5
46–50	45	24	69	5.2
51–55	31	15	46	3.5
56–60	29	10	39	2.9
61–65[a]	2	1	3	0.2
Total	816	515	1,331	100.0

Source: Archivo Nacional de Cuba, Misc. de Expedientes, leg. 3748, exp. B, Capitanía Pedánea de Santa Isabel de las Lajas, núm. 3, Padrón general de esclavos, 1875.

[a] All of those under age 6 or over age 60 should legally have been free under the Moret Law. Some of those age 6 were free.

per cent in the last eight years of slavery, thus bringing about a true age-related crisis of labor supply.[24]

The plantation population of Lajas was, at least potentially, a quite productive one. The Moret Law had so streamlined it that 100 per cent of the legally enslaved population was between the ages of 6 and 60, and between those limits the population was further weighted toward those of working age. The largest single groups consisted of males aged 31 through 40 and 21 through 30. Lajas plantations were not carrying a terrible burden of young and old slaves. Masters were not sustaining the full cost of reproduction of their work force. They were still operating with a carefully selected labor force built up primarily through purchase. The difficult future of slavery now that the trade had ended was apparent in the small number coming up through the ranks — there were less than half as many males aged 11 through 20 as aged 21 through 30 (see Table 3). But this problem would not be expected to make itself fully felt until some years later.

Though they were also using some Chinese laborers, free workers, and rented slaves, sugar plantations in Lajas remained heavily committed to slavery. Indeed, if one can trust the ambiguous figures from the 1877 agricultural census, the large Lajas plantations relied even more heavily on slave labor than the small. The Santa Catalina, Caracas, San Agustín, Amalia, and San Isidro estates, each with a work force of over 100, had a total of 701

slaves, 161 *alquilados y libres* (which could include *libertos* and rented slaves as well as free workers), and 89 Chinese. The smaller plantations of Sacramento, Dos Hermanas, Adelaida, Santa Elena, Maguaraya, and Destino together had 235 slaves and 105 *alquilados y libres*.[25]

Large planters in Lajas were not yet facing an internal collapse of slavery. Though the demographic structure of their slave populations indicated trouble in the long run, suggesting that free laborers would have to be attracted sooner or later, this fact motivated only a theoretical acceptance of an eventual transition, not a willingness to give up control over the existing work force. It is therefore not surprising that the *hacendados* of Cienfuegos, like those elsewhere in the western part of the island, held meetings during the 1870s to oppose immediate abolition.[26]

Slavery and Technology

A further element in the argument for the internal dissolution of slavery is the positing of an incompatability between slave labor and the needs of technology. This is often stated as a contradiction between slave labor, which is seen as brute labor, and advanced machinery, which is thought to require the motivations characteristic of free labor.[27] This argument also fits the image of a labor force whose quality was steadily deteriorating, based on the concept of slaves as instruments of production whose productivity depended simply on physical strength and whose value therefore dropped sharply once they were past their prime. The argument is coherent but not necessarily empirically correct. One needs to ask how slaves actually behaved and how they were viewed by planters.

It is suggestive that an owner of 300 slaves in Cuba, in a pamphlet addressed to the Spanish colonial minister in 1868, estimated the average value of male slaves aged 31–50 as *higher* than that of slaves aged 16–30, remarking that in the older group were those with skills, such as machinists, carpenters, masons, blacksmiths, and *paileros* (those who worked with boiling pans), among others.[28] Corroboration of this portrait would require an analysis of actual sale prices to determine the effect of various factors on the market value of slaves. But the statement does suggest that a slave work force with an age structure similar to that in Lajas was not necessarily experiencing sharply declining productivity and that planters did not invariably regard slaves as mere brute labor.

A more important challenge to the incompatability thesis is the direct evidence that slaves were used extensively in the large advanced mills. The *ingenio* España, for example, was one of the most advanced plantations in Cuba in the 1870s. Its work force in 1873 was composed of 530 slaves, 86 Asians, and just 19 whites. That is, the work force was more than 80 per cent slave, and 97 per cent unfree labor, if the Chinese were indentured, as is likely. The *ingenio* Álava, whose technological apparatus Moreno Fraginals has used to illustrate the industrial revolution on Cuban plantations, was operating in 1877 with 550 slaves and 71 Asians. It listed no free wage workers or rented slaves.[29] The Las Cañas plantation has been described as 'Cuba's most modern mill in 1850', in which, up to 1880, new machinery was being added 'in a continuous system of renovation'. Its work force in 1873 numbered 450 slaves, 230 Asians, and 27 whites. Again, the number of free white workers was very small, and they held the same jobs that they had always held on Cuban plantations: administrator, *mayordomo*, machinist, and so forth. On Las Cañas, the Asians do seem to have been treated differently from slaves and were concentrated in the processing sector.[30]

These examples do not really test the claim that technological advancement encouraged a shift to free labor — for that, one would need reliable statistics on the work forces of a large sample of Cuban plantations and detailed data on the internal division of labor. But these cases do suggest that major technological advances did not require the extensive use of fully free labor. In fact, the only substantial concession to the supposed necessity of a shift to free labor made on some major Cuban plantations in the 1870s involved the employment of Chinese. This was a limited step, for although the structure of incentives and motivations for the indentured Chinese, working on eight-year contracts bought and sold by planters, was somewhat different from that of slaves, it was not that of free wage workers.[31]

One could go further and argue that technological innovation is, under certain circumstances, quite compatible with a labor force that for one reason or another lacks motivation or elements of internalized industrial labor discipline. One economist has suggested that 'process-centered' industrial activities — of which sugar manufacture is a good example — which are often capital intensive, can be appropriate to a less socialized labor force because to some extent the machinery itself provides a pace and discipline to the work.[32] Although this hypothesis is not immediately adaptable to the circumstances of slavery, it does imply that the introduction of technology may cut both ways: advanced machinery can facilitate the labor and the pacing of labor of less experienced or less willing workers, even if at the same time it requires higher levels of skill and motivation for the performance of certain associated tasks.

Both slavery and indentured Asian labor did make labor costs in part a form of fixed capital, reducing the amount of capital immediately available from internal sources for investment in machinery. But the total available for further capital investment would depend on profitability and access to credit, which might in fact be facilitated by the purchase of slaves. Furthermore, individual planters often used rented slaves in order to mitigate the problem of fixed labor costs within the system of slavery. Rental permitted the shifting of the existing slave labor supply to areas of greatest profitability; it did not necessarily weaken slavery as an institution or loosen the bonds on slaves.[33]

Plantation records reveal the range of adaptations utilized on Cuban *ingenios* in the 1870s and convey a sense of the nature and tempo of change. The *ingenio* Angelita, for example, owned by J. A. Argudín and located in the jurisdiction of Cienfuegos, enumerated its work force several times between 1868 and 1877. On June 10, 1868, the plantation had 414 slaves; 20 'employees and workers of the estate', most of them white; and 35 *colonos*, in this case indentured Chinese laborers. By September 1868 the work force had increased with the addition of more Chinese workers, bringing their total to 74. In 1870 an epidemic of cholera hit, resulting in many deaths, and by September of that year the *dotación* consisted of 397 slaves and 58 Asians (see Table 4).

Another document lists the Angelita work force in January 1877, and an accompanying inventory confirms the impression that it was a mechanized plantation, complete with steam-powered grinding apparatus and vacuum pans, centrifuges, and the older Jamaica trains for processing. By this date the number of slaves had fallen to 247, although there were also 37 *libertos* over the age 60 and 29 children under age 8, clearly still part of the plantation population, who were not counted because of the Moret Law. The total comparable to the

Table 4 Work Force on the *Ingenios* Angelita, June 1868 and January 1877

1868		1877	
		Employees	
Administrator	1	Administrator	1
Doctor	1	*Mayordomo*	1
Overseer	1	Accountant	1
Mayordomos	2	Overseer	1
Machinest	1	Nurse (male)	1
Cattle handlers	2	Machinist	1
Carpenters	3	Carpenter	1
Distiller	1	Sugarmaster	1
[Illegible]	2	*Maestro de tacho*	1
Tachero		Plowmen	2
(works the *tacho*, or boiling pan)	1	Cattle handler	1
Sugarmasters	2	Overseer of the *batey* (mill area)	1
Mason	1	Supervisor of *colonos*	1
Montero	1	Mason	1
Asian, job unspecified	1	Barrel makers	2
		Overseer of the *potrero*	1
		Montero	1
		Messenger	1
		Head of the volunteers	1
		Movilizados (soldiers)	23
Total employees	20	Total employees	44
		Slaves	
Males	212	Males	126
Females	202	Females	121
Total slaves		Total slaves;	
(all ages)	414	(excludes 29 children	
		and 37 elderly)	247
		Chinese Laborers	
Total Chinese	35	Total Chinese	45
		Others	
		Free blacks (jobs unspecified)	8
		Rented slaves (owned by	
		administrator)	6
		Sharecroppers	
		(93 family members)	11
Total	469	Total	361
		(454 including families)	

Source: Archivo Nacional de Cuba, Misc. de Libros, núm. 11536, Libro Diario del Ingenio 'Angelita' de la propiedad de Sr. J. A. Argunín, 1868–71, pp. 1–13; Archivo Nacional de Cuba, Misc. de Libros, núm. 10789, Libro Diario del Ingenio Angelita Argudín, 1877, pp. 2, 3, 17, 18.

1870 figure of 397 slaves would thus be 313, a drop of 84 in six years. The work force also now included 8 free blacks, all apparently former slaves of Argudín, and 6 rented slaves. There were the usual 20 or so white employees, but also about 20 *movilizados*, soldiers presumably stationed on the plantation or released for employment there. A new category, *partidario* (sharecropper), had appeared by 1877 and included 11 heads of family and numerous family members. Forty-five *colonos asiáticos*

were employed at the time of the count, and at harvest time additional gangs of Asians were hired to cut cane (see Table 4).

Despite the increase in the complexity and variety of the work force on Angelita by 1877, the importance of the nucleus of 247 slaves between the ages of 9 and 59 remains apparent. The sharecroppers, though included in the plantation population, seem primarily to have been engaged in supplying food to the plantation rather than working in cane, though the evidence is not unequivocal. The increase in the number of free workers suggests that they were making inroads into some areas previously dominated by slaves, but it seems unlikely that either the temporary *movilizados* or the sharecroppers were performing any of the more technical tasks. Nor does it seem likely that all of the Asians worked in the more mechanized sectors, since this too was a fluctuating population, often rented out from the *depósito de cimarrones*, and prone to flight. In short, it seems that at Angelita it was not the introduction of technology but the death of slaves — and the necessity of replacing them — that initially brought the increased use of free labor.

After 1877 the decline in forced labor at Angelita accelerated. Asians persisted in fleeing, and replacements were not always available. Slaves became more likely to purchase their freedom. Although in the late 1860s such purchases were infrequent (just one man and his daughter obtained their freedom between June 1868 and September 1870), by the late 1870s they had become more common. In Feburary 1878 four women and two children freed themselves, apparently after having visited the *síndico* (protector of slaves) to have their prices set. In April, Secundina, a 30-year-old Creole, paid 750 pesos for herself and another 187 pesos to free her *liberto* children. That same month the slave Gervasia went to Cienfuegos to have her price set at 700 pesos, and in August her mother, Jacoba Lucumí, age 50, made a down payment of 500 pesos on that amount. As this was going on, the plantation began to increase the rewards given to slaves. At the beginning of the 1878 grinding season, tobacco, money, and bread were distributed.[34]

Reading through the daybook, one gets the sense that relations within the plantation were shifting as slaves, particularly women, found ways to buy their freedom and as the plantation increased the use of monetary incentives. Most of the money that slaves used for self-purchase probably came from their sales of pork and crops to the plantation, and such sales are frequently recorded. When the plantation accepted 700 pesos from a slave as payment for freedom, it was thus recouping some of what had been paid to that slave for goods produced, as well as recovering part of the investment in the slave. The master, unsurprisingly, might well come out ahead. But a circuit of money exchanges had been introduced — and not necessarily at the planter's initiative.

The records of other plantations in the 1870s show many of these same characteristics. Multiple forms of labor gathered around a slowly diminishing core of slave workers; 'gratuities' were paid to slaves more frequently; rent of slaves and the contracting of Asians provided considerable flexibility. None of these adaptations, however, suggests a repudiation of slavery, only a search for supplementary forms of labor and some modifications of the slave regime. Nor do the moves toward wages and compensation appear to be correlated closely with work on machinery — they are as likely to be payment simply for Sunday work or as a general incentive at the beginning of the harvest. Indeed, the repudiation of forced labor in the 1870s comes largely not from planters but from the slaves and Chinese indentured laborers themselves, through self-purchase and through flight.[35]

As late as 1879 most sugar planters appear to have remained strongly attached to the control that slavery gave them over their work force, though they were increasingly obliged by political circumstances to contemplate some shifts in its form. The Spanish government, however, had by 1879 come under pressure from domestic abolitionists, from rebels in Cuba, and from slaves in the east who refused to work. An apparent solution was to abolish the name of slavery, while keeping much of its substance.[36]

The *Patronato*

In February 1880 the Spanish parliament decreed the end of slavery and the beginning of apprenticeship, or *patronato*. All slaves were henceforth to be called *patrocinados* and remained obliged to work for their former masters until freed. Masters owed a stipend of 1–3 pesos monthly to their former slaves, and *patrocinados* could purchase their freedom for a specified and gradually diminishing amount. Limited rights were granted to *patrocinados*, such as the right to charge one's master with a violation of the regulations, with full freedom the reward if he were convicted. But masters also retained substantial prerogatives, including control over physical mobility, the setting of hours and conditions of labor, and, until 1883, the right to use corporal punishment. Beginning in 1885, one-quarter of the remaining *patrocinados* were to be freed each year, in descending order of age, under a complex system that was to conclude in 1888.

The previous discussion of the evolution of the nature and organization of labor in the 1870s suggests why planters might grudgingly accede to, though they did not initiate, such a gradualist solution. They wished to find substitutes for the diminishing slave work force, and nominal abolition might help attract new laborers, since European emigrants were believed to prefer non-slave societies. Both landowners and the government also wished if possible to defuse the emotional issue of abolition. At the same time, many planters sought to maintain the essentials of slavery and to keep their slaves on the plantation, which the *patronato*, in theory, would allow them to do.

The conservative nature of the law establishing the *patronato* meant that May 8, 1880, the date it went into effect, could come and go without an immediate impact on the plantations. Administrators shifted from paying irregular bonuses to paying stipends, increasing their need for cash but not severely disrupting the routine. Indeed, it appeared initially that a considerable degree of continuity was possible. For instance, while in the British West Indies masters had often withdrawn traditional indulgences from slaves when apprenticeship was established, on some Cuban plantations the old rhythm of holidays and rewards was maintained. On the *ingenio* Nueva Teresa, the New Year arrived just as the 1881–82 harvest was about to begin. On December 30 an ox was slaughtered, and the *dotación*, which included approximately 175 *patrocinados*, was given the day off. The following day, fresh meat, bread (a luxury), and salt were distributed, and *criollitos* were baptized in the *casa de vivienda* (plantation house). The first two days of January were also given as holidays; on the fourth and fifth the workers began to cut and haul cane; and at six o'clock on the morning of the sixth day the grinding began.[37]

Patronos may have felt it appropriate to observe these customs in order to maintain their own sense of legitimacy or to encourage productivity among the *patrocinados*. Since the government regulations were not being strictly enforced, masters may also have been less seized by a spirit of vengeance than their British West Indian counterparts. The usual rewards of the harvest could be maintained because the usual level of exploitation was being maintained. During the harvest of 1880–81 on Nueva Teresa, Sunday rest was ignored, and *patrocinados* received only one day of respite between March 17 and April 15. At the end of May, the harvest ended, and a cow was killed for the *dotación*, a calf for additional hired hands. Stipends for the *patrocinados*, due weeks earlier, were finally

paid. The withholding of stipends seems clearly to have been a means for maintaining work discipline, not a problem of cash flow; the man who regularly brought the money for stipends from Havana had arrived at the estate three weeks before.[38]

The law of 1880 nonetheless changed the rules of the game, and after a certain lag the impact began to be felt on plantations. By the 1882–83 harvest the administration on Nueva Teresa was becoming scrupulous about paying stipends on time. At the same time, *patrocinados* were beginning to obtain full freedom on their own by self-purchase. This was to have a complicated effect on the economics of running a plantation. On the one hand, working *patrocinados* who obtained their freedom would have to be paid wages or replaced by hired hands. On the other, the purchase of freedom of children, the aged, or the infirm could be a net financial gain to the estate. In any event, such purchases subsidized the wage bill: on the *ingenio* Nueva Teresa, deposits made for purchases of freedom covered almost 70 per cent of the amount paid in stipends during 1883–84, and between 1882 and 1886 approximately 80 *patrocinados* and *libertos* on the estate obtained full legal freedom through payment.[39]

On the *ingenio* Mapos in Sancti Spíritus, the number of working *patrocinados* initially fell only slightly. Early in 1882, however, a group of 35 *patrocinados* fled the estate to present their grievances to the local Junta de Patronato, the board established to oversee the enforcement of the 1880 law. They returned to the plantation, but a year later the effect of the challenge appeared when the estate's *patrocinado* population fell abruptly by almost one-quarter, as more than 60 *patrocinados* were freed by order of the junta, some on the grounds of age, others through self-purchase. The success of these initiatives, combined with the ever-lengthening period during which *patrocinados* could be accumulating funds, led to a steady stream of self-purchases after the harvest of 1883. By August 1884, Mapos retained only 135 of its original 277 *patrocinados*.[40]

The acceleration of emancipation throughout the island in the 1880s, well before the gradual freeings by age began, is evident in the figures gathered by the Juntas de Patronato. In the first year 6,000 *patrocinados* obtained full freedom; in the second 10,000; in the third 17,000; in the fourth 27,000 (see Table 5). Evidently many *patrocinados* learned to use the new situation to hasten their own emancipation. Some

Table 5   *Patrocinados* Legally Achieving Full Freedom, May 1881–May 1886, by Category and Year

Year (May to May)	Mutual accord	Renunciation by master	Indemnification by *Patrocinado*	Master's failure to Fulfill Article 4[a]	Other causes	By Article 8[b] (1885 and 1886 only)	Total[c]
1881–82	3,476	3,229	2,001	406	1,137	—	10,249
	(34)	(43)	(20)	(4)	(11)	—	(100)
1882–83	6,954	3,714	3,341	1,596	1,813	—	17,418
	(40)	(21)	(19)	(9)	(10)	—	(100)
1883–84	9,453	3,925	3,452	1,764	7,923	—	26,517
	(36)	(15)	(13)	(7)	(30)	—	(100)
1884–85	7,360	4,405	2,459	2,431	2,514	15,119	34,288
	(21)	(13)	(7)	(7)	(7)	(44)	(100)
1885–86	7,859	3,553	1,750	1,226	837	10,190	25,415
	(31)	(14)	(7)	(5)	(3)	(40)	(100)
Total	35,102	18,826	13,003	7,423	14,224	25,309	113,887
	(31)	(17)	(11)	(7)	(12)	(22)	(100)

Source: Archivo Histórico Nacional, Ultramar, leg. 4814, exp. 273 and exp. 289; *ibid.*, leg. 4926, exp. 144; Manuel Villanova, *Estadística de la abolición de la esclavitud* (Havana, 1885).

[a] Article 4 of the 1880 law listed the obligations of the *patrono*: to maintain his *patrocinados*, clothe them, assist them when ill, pay the specified monthly stipend, educate minors, and feed, clothe, and assist in illness the children of his *patrocinados*.

[b] Article 8 called for one in four of the *patrocinados* of each master to be freed in 1885, and one in three in 1886, in descending order of age. In the event that several *patrocinados* were of the same age, a lottery was to be held.

[c] Some rows do not add to 100 per cent because of rounding.

purchased their freedom; some brought charges against their masters; some found that they were unregistered and sued for freedom on those grounds. Even in rural Matanzas province more than 2,000 *patrocinados* successfully charged their masters with failure to fulfill the obligations of the 1880 law, and more than 3,000 others obtained their freedom through self-purchase between May 1881 and May 1886.[41]

Many masters tried to block such initiatives, through isolation, threats, or legal measures. The institution of the plantation store, for example, though a harbinger of controls that would be imposed on wage labor, helped for the moment to sustain the *patronato* system. In the 1880s local shopkeepers initiated a debate on the tax status of such stores, an occurrence interesting primarily for the attitudes it reveals among planters. Freely acknowledging that the main purpose of the stores was control, planters from several sugar areas made it clear that they wished to prevent their workers and particularly their *patrocinados* from setting foot off the plantation. They were not prepared to accept the physical mobility associated with fully free labor.[42]

Other masters, however, tried to come to some kind of agreement with *patrocinados* on the terms of freedom, which could include informal payment by the *patrocinado*, or an arrangement concerning future wages, resulting in emancipation by 'mutual accord'. Some masters actually renounced their rights over individual *patrocinados*, and a few of these were acclaimed in the liberal-press for their benevolence. Such manumissions, however, declined in relative importance after 1881–82, and renunciation was generally most frequent not in the sugar areas of Matanzas or Santa Clara but in the province of Havana. Freedom in Santa Clara or Matanzas was more likely to come through 'mutual accord', as masters exacted concessions in return (see Tables 5 and 6).[43]

By 1883 the total number of *patrocinados* on the island had fallen to about 99,600 (half of the number of slaves six years earlier) even though the gradual freeings by age had yet to begin. In an 1884 debate within the Consejo de Administración in Havana, two councillors argued that the *patronato* had led to the worst of both worlds, providing neither the stimulus of corporal punishment nor the fear of dismissal. They urged that the system be ended, claiming that there was a labor surplus and that, if freed, *patrocinados* would work for their former masters for low wages. The majority of the councillors rejected the argument for abolition of the *patronato*, however, and clung to the compulsion that it provided.[44]

A look at the municipality of Lajas may suggest why. Lajas recorded 1,852 slaves in 1875 and 1,137 *patrocinados* in 1883.[45] Approximately 100 slaves would probably have obtained their freedom in the interval on reaching age 60; thus other losses through

Table 6 *Patrocinados* Legally Achieving Full Freedom, May 1881–May 1886, Percentage by Province and Category

Terms of freedom	Number freed	Pinar del Río	Havana	Matanzas	Santa Clara	Puerto Príncipe	Santiago de Cuba
Mutual accord	35,102	9	10	43	32	0	6
Renunciation	18,826	15	36	19	19	1	10
Indemnification of service	13,003	16	16	27	24	0	17
Master's failure to fulfill Article 4	7,423	14	46	28	6	1	5
Other causes	14,224	13	21	31	23	1	11
Article 8 (1885 and 1886 only)	25,309	17	14	41	25	0	3
Total freed	113,887	13	20	34	25	1	8

Source: Same as Table 5.
Notes: Some rows do not add to 100 per cent because of rounding.

emancipation and death had been kept to only about one-third. For those in areas like Lajas, where the line had been held, extra-economic control over this nucleus of the labor force was still worth defending.

Simply retaining legal control over *patrocinados* was not enough, however. On the *ingenio* Nueva Teresa, for example, which in 1884 still held 150 *patrocinados*, it was necessary to use new incentives tied to productivity. In February 1884, apparently for the first time, the *patrocinado* Evaristo was paid 6 pesos as first prize for the quantity of cane hauled, and others received amounts in decreasing size for second through fifth prize. In March prizes were given to the first ten *patrocinados*, and again in April prizes appeared.[46] By the 1884–85 harvest, the picture at Nueva Teresa had changed still further, and the mobilization of labor began strongly to foreshadow post-abolition arrangements. About a dozen tenants brought cane and wood to the mill, drew supplies on credit, and in some cases hired laborers from the estate. Gangs of Chinese workers contracted to perform specific tasks, particularly in the *casa de calderas* (boiling house). Many *patrocinados* purchased their freedom, and some hired on as free workers at 18 pesos monthly for women and 20 pesos for men, plus rations. The work force was increasingly seasonal, with Chinese contract laborers providing much of the flexibility, whether they wanted to or not. The harvest of 1885 ended on August 16, and on September 4 the *cuadrilla* (gang) of Chinese found themselves 'expelled' by order of the administrator. Maintenance off season was no

longer the planter's responsibility.[47]

By 1885, the year the gradual freeings by age were to begin, the *patronato* was already in a state of decay. Only 53,381 *patrocinados* remained in the island, about half of the number two years before, and many fewer than had been anticipated in the original plan. In 1883–84, 26,517 *patrocinados* had obtained their freedom, 36 per cent through mutual accord, 15 percent through renunciation by the *patronato*, 13 per cent through formal self-purchase, 7 per cent through successfully charging their masters with violation of the laws, and 30 per cent through other means, probably including proof of non-registration. The process of emancipation had gained sufficient momentum that the interim institution could not possibly last. The financial crisis of 1884, brought on in part by a drop in sugar prices, may have further encouraged the abandonment of slavery, though renunciation still accounted for fewer than 15 per cent of the freeings in the island between 1884 and 1886 (see Table 5).

By the time of the harvest of 1885–86, the number of *patrocinados* on Nueva Teresa, for example had fallen to 50 or 60. The estate contracted out an increasing proportion of the cutting and hauling of cane, and paid by the cartload, while similarly contracting for wood. The contractors, generally white, took their pay in money and in sugar. Some of the estate's former slaves continued to be directly employed there at a monthly wage of 17–20 pesos, but not as many as had received their freedom. A Chinese contractor provided workers to serve in the field and at the centrifuges, and they were paid both by weight of sugar processed and by the month (at 40 pesos). Individual Chinese workers hired on at about 35 pesos and rations, as did gangs of wage workers of unspecified origin.[48]

On October 7, 1886, a royal decree, following a parliamentary resolution, abolished the *patronato*. When definitive abolition finally arrived, it merely confirmed an existing state of affairs. The number of *patrocinados* had fallen to about 25,000, and almost everyone, including the Planters' Association, was willing to see the *patronato* go.[49] The reality that the law ratified, however, had to a considerable extent been brought about in the immediately preceding years by the slaves and *patrocinados* themselves, both directly — through self-purchase, flight, and suits before the juntas — and indirectly — through the negotiation of agreements of mutual accord. Sheer abandonment of slavery by masters was not the main source of freedom for slaves and *patrocinados*.

Conclusions

At the beginning of this chapter it was suggested that a careful regional and chronological examination of the pattern of transition could help one to evaluate alternative explanations of the process of slave emancipation in Cuba. The evidence and arguments presented show that what is needed is a blending of elements from several hypotheses. The challenge is to make this blending coherent rather than eclectic and ad hoc.

It is true that Cuban slaveholders by the late 1870s had relatively little emotional attachment to the formal institution of slavery. Though some of their representatives continued to defend the institution as a benevolent one, the possibility of a controlled, gradual abolition did not put them up in arms.[50] The Moret Law had already in 1870 guaranteed the eventual demise of slavery by freeing the children of slaves, and demographic patterns were pushing in the same direction. There would not be enough slave workers to replenish the system; new sources and forms of labor had to be found.

This decay of the slave system during the 1870s must, however be interpreted with great care. Young and elderly slaves achieved formal freedom by decree; assertive slaves, particularly in cities and in the east, sometimes obtained their freedom through litigation or self-purchase; many slaves died or became free as a

result of war. The gaps thereby created were often filled with free workers. Mixed work forces were indeed common, but it does not appear, as has sometimes been argued, that the plantations invariably were driven to free labor either by the needs of the new technology or by a decline in the quality of the slave labor force caused by an excess of the young and the aged. Large plantations with available capital had often purchased Africans in the last years of the slave trade and still had substantial *dotaciones* of African and Creole slaves. An essential core of slaves of working age continued to be held in bondage in the major sugar areas, helping to maintain high levels of production during the 1870s despite the sharp drop in the total number of slaves.

If Cuba's planters by the end of the 1870s were no longer fully committed to the indefinite maintenance of an institution called slavery, they remained committed to many of the realities of slavery: its work rhythms, social relations, and power relations. They still extracted labor from substantial numbers of workers through extra-economic compulsion. This is why they wanted the control afforded by the *patronato* and why they generally did not engage in mass manumissions.

The *patronato*, however, contained contradictions of its own, particularly in the granting of limited rights and partial access to redress. The social relations of slavery are by their nature difficult to maintain. Alterations in the relative bargaining power and legal rights of masters and slaves may weaken those relations irreparably. In this sense, the passage of the 1880 law was not merely a reflection in law of an existing state of affairs. Mechanisms provided by the law, however inadvertently, emerged as significant for the actual process of emancipation. But it was the shifting interests and resources of apprentices and their masters, not the legislature's intentions, that determined the uses to which they were put.

What, then, remains of the internal contradiction argument? It does contain a key insight concerning the difficulty of achieving capital-intensive development with forced labor, the maintenance expense of which must be borne year-round. But even this contradiction, though perceived by some planters, did not push them to the abandonment of slavery. They sought instead to segment the labor force: to add flexibility through slave rentals, to add workers through immigration, and to maintain as much control as possible over their existing slaves. Their use of Chinese laborers, contract workers, convicts, and rented slaves is sometimes cited as proof that the slave system was dissolving in the 1870s. But one could just as easily see this as evidence of its resilience. That such mixtures of forms of labor were brought together *without* the abandonment of slavery is striking. And that the men who ran these mixed plantations continued to oppose abolition is further evidence of the gap between the seeming contradictions within slavery and the forces actually driving abolition forward.

It may have come as something of a surprise to planters that their strategy could not work indefinitely. But there is a sense in which these continued improvizations and innovations did undermine slavery. It is a social one, a kind of second-order contradiction. Free labor and indentured labor were *economically* complementary to slavery: indentured Chinese workers often dealt with the centrifuges while slaves handled other tasks; white woodcutters on contract relieved the plantation of direct responsibility for providing fuel; the employment of free workers during the harvest diminished the problem of year-round maintenance of all workers. But the use of these complementary forms of labor had indirect effects on the social structure necessary to sustain slavery. Plantation slavery as a social system depended to a large degree on isolation. The incorporation of free workers, beyond those supervisors and artisans rigidly and traditionally separated from the slave work force, broke some of that isolation. It made obvious to slaves the existence of alternatives, created new sources of information, and made possible new alliances — both of individuals and of groups. Such alliances could be a matter of a union between a slave woman and a Chinese man, both interested in freedom for their children; of communication between free black workers and those who remained enslaved; of assistance from a newly freed slave to other members of the family. These alliances and examples aided slaves in their efforts at challenge and self-purchase and, in extreme cases (as in the east during the Ten Years' War), encouraged flight and rebellion.

This should not imply that slavery in Cuba inherently was always socially brittle. But in this specific political context, when abolition was already on the agenda, when insurgency was a reality, and when there was division within the white population, innovations and adaptations carried serious risks.

The abolition of slavery in Cuba, then, should not be seen simply as an imposition from the metropolitan power nor as the result of an inevitable collapse of the system of bondage in the face of internal economic contradictions. The planters' desire to maintain a high degree of control over their work force meant that as a practical matter most of them inhibited, rather than facilitated, emancipation, up to the very last years of the 18-year process. Slaves and *patrocinados*, on the other hand, took advantage of the legal openings provided in the 1870 and 1880 legislation and in other ways resisted submitting to their masters' control. Their initiatives served in part as a countervailing force and tended to accelerate emancipation. Thus the actual course of emancipation can be fully perceived only through an understanding of the interaction of the groups involved. Emancipation was, throughout, a social process in which the struggle between master and slave, *patrono* and *patrocinado*, employer and worker, shaped the character, the timing, and the terms of the transition from slavery to free labor.

Although these internal dynamics may be the most interesting part of the story of Cuban abolition, one ought to return, at least momentarily, to the search for large-scale explanations and ask how one would begin to reconstruct an explanation from what remains of the original hypotheses about causation. This chapter therefore concludes with a few observations about three aspects of such a large-scale explanation: the importance of political pressures, the nature of slaveholder attitudes, and the relationship between slavery and technology. For each of these three aspects, what was initially proposed as a primary cause has emerged as a complicated kind of contributing factor, not in the simple sense of yet another in a great list of factors mechanically bringing about abolition but rather as a conditioning circumstance that determined the constraints under which the process of emancipation would operate.

First, there is no question but that international diplomacy and domestic political unrest narrowed the options of Cuban slaveholders. The ending of the transatlantic slave trade — an event explicable almost entirely in terms of forces external to Cuba, crucial among them British diplomacy and the outcome of the Civil War in the United States — set in motion a long-term problem of labor supply. As long as Cuba's slave population was not fully self-reproducing, then new labor forms would have to be found. And to the extent that the existence of slavery inhibited the free immigration that might provide such laborers, a powerful argument against slavery would continue to build, even before the actual demographic crisis of labor supply had made itself felt. At the same time, domestically, the existence of an anticolonial rebellion that took on abolition as a rallying cry, however opportunistically, changed the climate in which slavery existed. The insurrection opened new options, while creating new stresses.

What has become clear through an examination of the process of abolition is that both kinds of political forces — international and domestic — could to some extent be contained and that for most of the 18 years of gradual emancipation neither planters nor policy makers were prepared to deal with them by making substantial concessions. But these forces nonetheless conditioned the environment in which both slaves and slaveholders adopted strategies and sought to maintain or further their interests.

This brings us to a second general question involved in the search for large-scale explanations: the issue of slaveholder attitudes. It would be wrong to see modernizing Cuban planters as the prime movers behind abolition itself. The initiative simply did not come from them. Though most Cuban planters were not willing to give up slavery in pursuit of economic modernization, however, they were prepared to add free workers to their plantation work forces and to acquiesce in schemes of gradual emancipation, if these seemed to guarantee continuity of authority. Because they thought that they could control the inevitable through very gradual emancipation, they did not mount a last-ditch stand against it. They were to an extent wrong in the expectation that they could control the transition to free labor, and they were certainly wrong in thinking that they could fully control emancipation itself. But the fact that they were not utterly intransigent was a crucial circumstance as partial concessions grew beyond their intended dimensions.

Finally, on the issue of slavery and technology, there is a kind of irony in the post-emancipation history of the Cuban sugar industry. I have rejected the assumption that abolition was, or was even seen as, inherently necessary in order to adopt new technologies. Yet soon after abolition there was a rapid adoption of new modes of organization of production, including the extensive use of advanced processing equipment. The early 1890s saw a dramatic increase in capital investment in machinery, extensive consolidation of estates, and a great boom in sugar production. Several external factors having little to do with abolition stimulated this boom — including the fall in the prices of steel rails that made cane transport cheaper over long distances and shifts in the United States tariff policy that favored Cuban sugar. So the rapid development of central mills with very modern equipment, processing cane from several sources, cannot be fully attributed to the elimination of slavery. Even more important, the boom was by no means uniformly advantageous for former slaveholders. Many found their estates swallowed up in the new central mills and either lost their land entirely or became growers of cane rather than producers of sugar. It is not surprising that those who foresaw that abolition might be followed by such a change in their status would have opposed emancipation. But even those who stood to benefit from the development of central mills saw no reason for relinquishing any control over their workers along the way.[51]

The unfolding of emancipation and the development of post-emancipation society were processes so complex that one cannot infer from the post-emancipation experience of technological innovation and growth that a perceived need for such innovation actually motivated abolition. Moreover, as one moves away from the invocation of internal contradictions or diplomatic pressures as explanations for abolition, and shifts the focus to the dialectic of, on the one hand, stalling and improvization by slaveowners and, on the other, pressure and initiatives from slaves, gradual emancipation emerges as a form of social change largely controlled by planters and the state, but which nonetheless drew much of its character and timing from slaves and insurgents. Large-scale explanations and small-scale historical events can thus be linked in the case of Cuban abolition, but only by multiple threads of interaction and adaptation, woven together over time.

Appendix:
Notes on Census Data Used in Tables 1 and 2

The figures cited in Tables 1 and 2 are based on several official tabulations. Those for 1862 are from Cuba, Centro de Estadística, *Noticias estadísticas de la isla de Cuba en 1862* (Havana, 1864). I have derived provincial totals by aggregating the population figures for the 1862 *jurisdicciones* to match the provincial boundaries established in 1878. (For details on redistricting and the method of compilation, see Rebecca J. Scott, 'Slave Emancipation and the Transition to Free Labor in Cuba, 1868–1895' [Ph.D. dissertation, Princeton University, 1982], Chap. 4, note 2.) Returns from the 1867 slave count are neither reliable nor consistent and are included here only for the purpose of comparison. They can be found, divided by jurisdiction, in the 'Resumen general de los esclavos que segun el censo de 1867 . . . existían a la terminación de ese censo en las jurisdicciones que componían el territorio de la Isla', in the Archivo Histórico Nacional, Madrid, Sección de Ultramar (hereinafter AHN, Ultramar), legajo 4884, tomo 8, expediente 160. The 1871 figures are from the 'Resumen de los esclavos comprendidos en el padrón de 1871 . . .', in AHN, Ultramar, leg. 4882, tomo 4. The 1877 census has often been considered unreliable, but the article by Fe Iglesias García, 'El censo cubano de 1877 y sus diferentes versiones', *Santiago*, 34 (June 1979): 167–211, presents new evidence that in its final version the census was more accurate than previously imagined. I have used her totals for 1877. The figures for the 1880s are from AHN, Ultramar, leg. 4926, exp. 144, and leg. 4814, exp. 289, and are based on records of the provincial Juntas de Patronato.

Notes

1. Manuel Moreno Fraginals, *El ingenio: complejo económico social cubano del azúcar*, 3 vols (Havana, 1978), 3:37.
2. The thesis of the incompatability of slave labor and technology is argued by Moreno Fraginals in *El ingenio*, and he expresses it succinctly in several articles, including 'El esclavo y la mecanización de los ingenios,' *Bohemia* (June 13, 1969): 98–99, and 'Desgarramiento azucarero e integración nacional,' *Casa de las Américas*, 11 (September–October 1970): 6–22.
3. Eugene D. Genovese, *The World the Slaveholders Made: Two Essays in Interpretation* (New York, 1971). pp. 69–70.
4. Arthur F. Corwin, *Spain and the Abolition of Slavery in Cuba, 1817–1886* (Austin, 1967).
5. Moreno Fraginals, 'El esclavo y la mecanización de los ingenios', pp. 98–99.
6. Carlos Rebello, *Estados relativos a la producción azucarera de la isla de Cuba* (Havana, 1860).
7. Cuba, Centro de Estadística, *Noticias estadísticas de la isla de Cuba, en 1862* (Havana, 1864).
8. Moreno Fraginals, *El ingenio*, 3: 36–37.
9. David R. Murray, *Odious Commerce: Britain, Spain and the Abolition of the Cuban Slave Trade* (Cambridge, 1980).
10. Moreno Fraginals, *El ingenio*, 3: 36–37.
11. The best analyses of the Ten Years' War are to be found in Raúl Cepero Bonilla, *Azúcar y abolición* (Havana, 1948); Ramiro Guerra y Sánchez, *Guerra de los Diez Años* (Havana, 1950–52); and Franklin Knight, *Slave Society in Cuba during the Nineteenth Century* (Madison, 1970).
12. For a fuller analysis of the effects of the war on slavery, see Rebecca J. Scott, *Slave Emancipation in Cuba: The Transition to Free Labor, 1860–1899* (Princeton, 1985), Chap. 2.
13. For evidence on the events of 1879, see the opinion of José Bueno y Blanco in Archivo Histórico Nacional, Madrid, Sección de Ultramar (hereafter AHN, Ultramar) leg. 4882, tomo 5, 'Documentos de la Comisión . . . 1879', and AHN, Ultramar, leg. 4882, tomo 3, exp. 76, telegram from the Governor General to the Minister of Ultramar, September 11, 1879. José Martí vividly described the pressure on Spain from rebellious slaves in the east of Cuba and the double-edged response of abolition and increased military presence. See José Martí's speech given in Steck Hall, New York, January 24, 1880, printed in Hortensia Pichardo (ed.), *Documentos para la historia de Cuba*, 2 vols (Havana, 1976, 1977) 1: 424–49.
14. For these and other provincial totals, see Appendix.
15. The figure of 20 per cent was derived by using the age distribution of slaves in Cuba in the 1862 census. Of those listed, around 22 per cent were over age 60 or under age 10 (Cuba, *Noticias*). I have assumed that the proportion would be somewhat smaller in a plantation area, which would have a higher concentration of imported Africans. This estimate also coincides with the age pyramids derived by Moreno Fraginals from plantation accounts. Moreno Fraginals, *El ingenio*, 2: 90.
16. See Archivo Nacional de Cuba (hereafter ANC), Misc. de Expendientes, leg. 3814, exp. A. Expediente promovido pot este Gob° Gral para conocer las operaciones paracticadas en todas las Sindicaturas de la Isla durante el quinquenio de 1873 a 1877. Of the 3,359 *coartaciones* in the island, 1,413 were in the city of Havana.
17. For area planted in cane, see Rebello, *Estados*, and the *Revista de Agricultura* (Havana), 3 (March 31, 1879), 75. Population figures are from the 1862 census and from Fe Iglesias García, 'El censo cubano de 1877 y sus diferentes versiones', *Santiago* 34 (June 1979): 167–211. On the categories of workers in sugar, see the *Revista de Agricultura* cited above.
18. A. Gallenga, *The Pearl of the Antilles* (London, 1873), pp. 96, 105.
19. This picture emerges from censuses, account books, and observers' reports. See the 1877 agricultural census, the plantation records cited in notes 33–35 and F. de Zayas, 'Estudios de agricultura: II. El trabajador, el jornal', *Revista de Agricultura*, 1 (April 30, 1879): 83.
20. Moreno Fraginals puts foward this argument in 'Abolición o desintegración? Algunas preguntas en torno a un centenario', *Granma* (January 23, 1980), and in 'Plantations in the Caribbean: Cuba, Puerto Rico, and the Dominican Republic in the Late Nineteenth Century', in M. Fraginals, F. Moya Pons, S. Engerman (eds), *Between Slavery and Free Labor: The Spanish-speaking Caribbean in the Nineteenth Century* (Baltimore, 1985).
21. For an examination of the ways in which 'contradictions' within slavery are resolved, and in some cases give rise to new contradictions, see Sidney Mintz, 'Slavery and the Rise of Peasantries', in Michael Craton (ed.), *Roots and Branches: Current Directions*

in Slave Studies (Toronto, 1979), pp. 213–42. The point is that such things as bonuses and provision grounds may or may not signal disintegration, depending on the surrounding circumstances. In some cases, they may even strengthen slavery.

22. Moreno Fraginals, *El ingenio*, 2: 83–90. He states that the conscious policy of 'good treatment', aimed at creating a self-reproducing slave work force, was 'the most visible symptom of the dissolution of slavery' (p. 90).

23. See the 1862 census and Enrique Edo y Llop. *Memoria histórica de Cienfuegos y su jurisdicción* (Cienfuegos, 1888), appendix, pp. 5–6. The manuscript slave list is in ANC, Misc. de Expendientes, leg. 3748, exp. B, Capitanía Pedánea de Santa Isabel de las Lajas, núm, 3, Padrón general de esclavos, 1875.

24. Stanley J. Stein, *Vassouras: A Brazilian Coffee County, 1850–1900* (New York, 1974), p. 78.

25. See *Revista Económica*, 2 (June 7, 1878): 13. The Armantina and Manaca estates, excluded from the comparisons because their 1875 slave data are incomplete, had 122 slaves and 17 *alquilados y libres*.

26. Edo y Llop, *op. cit.*, p. 629. For evidence of planter hostility to abolition in the 1870s, see Corwin, *op. cit.*, Chap. 14.

27. In Cuba, this argument dates at least to Ramón de la Sagra in the mid-nineteenth century and is repeated by Moreno Fraginals. See *El ingenio*, 2: 30.

28. AHN, Ultramar, leg. 4759, exp. 85, 'Exposición del Excmo. Señor Cordede Vega Mar' (Madrid, 1868).

29. Fermín Rosillo y Alquier, *Noticias de dos ingenios y datos sobre la producción azucarera de la isla de Cuba* (Havana, 1873), describes the work force on España. For Álava, see the 1877 agricultural census in *Revista Económica*, 2 (June 7, 1878): 11.

30. The description of Las Cañas as 'Cuba's most modern mill' is from *El ingenio*, 1: 250. The figures on the work force are from Rosillo, *Noticias*. Observations on the treatment of the Chinese are from Juan Pérez de la Riva, 'Duvergier de Hauranne: un joven francés visita el ingenio Las Cañas en 1865', *Revista de la Biblioteca Nacional José Martí*, 56 (October–December 1965): 85–114.

31. On the Chinese in Cuba see Juan Pérez de la Riva, 'Demografía de los culíes chinos en Cuba (1853–1877)' and 'La situación legal del culí en Cuba', in his *El barracón y otros ensayos* (Havana, 1975), pp. 469–507, 209–45. See also Denise Helly, *Idéologie et ethnicité: les chinois Macao à China, 1847–1886* (Montreal, 1979). The question of whether the Chinese should, for the purposes of analysis, be considered wage workers is a difficult one. The extra-economic coercion to which they were subjected was so great, and so similar to that inflicted on slaves, that I am inclined to doubt the substance of their 'freeness'. If in Cuba they were seen as particularly suited for work with machinery, this may in part have reflected employers' high expectations of the Chinese relative to their low expectations of slaves. It may also have reflected actual differences in performance, but these differences could have had as

much to do with the cultural background of the Chinese and their anticipation of a future freedom as they did with any alleged juridicial freedom while under contract, a freedom often violated.

32. See Albert O. Hirschman. *The Strategy of Economic Development* (New Haven, 1958), ch. 8.

33. See, for example, the records of slave rentals on the Ingenio Delicias in ANC, Misc. de Libros, núm. 10802, Libro Diario del Ingenio Delicias, 1872–82.

34. Data on the work force at Angelita are from ANC, Misc. de Libros, núm. 11536, Libro Diario del Ingenio 'Angelita' de la propiedad de St. J. A. Argudín, 1868–71, and ANC, Misc. de Libros, núm. 10789, Libro Diario del Ingenio Angelita Argudín, 1877.

35. Other daybooks and slave lists for the 1870s include Archivo Provincial de Sancti Spíritus, Fondo Valle-Iznaga (hereafter APSS, Valle-Iznaga), leg. 27, Libro con la dotación de esclavos del ingenio La Crisis; ANC, Misc. de Libros, núm. 10806, Libro Diario al parecer de un ingenio, 1879–81; and ANC, Misc. de Libros, núm, 11245, Libro Mayor del Ingenio Nueva Teresa, 1872–85.

36. Fur a further discussion of the politics of abolition, see Corwin, *op. cit.*, and Knight, *op. cit.*

37. ANC, Misc. de Libros, núm. 10831, Libro Diario del Ingenio Nueva Teresa, 1880–86.

38. *Ibid.*

39. ANC, Misc. de Libros, núm. 11245, Libro Mayor del Ingenio Nueva Teresa, 1872–85.

40. APSS, Valle-Iznaga, leg. 24, Libro que contiene documentos del estado general de la finca Mapos.

41. For provincial figures on emancipation, see AHN, Ultramar, leg. 4814, exp. 273 and exp. 289; leg. 4926, exp. 144; and Manuel Villanova, *Estadística de la abolición de la esclavitud* (Havana, 1885).

42. For the debate, see AHN, Ultramar, leg. 4818, exp. 84, Sobre pago de contribuciones de las tiendas de los Ingenios.

43. For a more detailed discussion of the operation of the *patronato*, see Rebecca J. Scott, 'Gradual Abolition and the Dynamics of Slave Emancipation in Cuba, 1868–86', *Hispanic American Historical Review*, 63 (August 1983): 449–77.

44. AHN, Ultramar, leg. 4926, exp. 144, núm. 300, Informe del Consejo de Administración, August 8, 1884.

45. Edo y Llop, *op. cit.*, pp. 988–89.

46. ANC. Misc. de Libros, núm. 11245, Libro Mayor del Ingenio Nueva Teresa, 1872–85.

47. ANC, Misc. de Libros, núm. 10831, Libro Diario del Ingenio Nueva Teresa, 1880–86.

48. *Ibid.*

49. See AHN, Ultramar, leg. 4926, exp. 144, núm. 323, telegram from the Governor General of Cuba to the Minister of Ultramar, Havana, August 12, 1886.

50. For the debates in the Spanish parliament, see Spain, Cortes, 1879–80, *Discursos de la ley de abolición de la esclavitud en Cuba* (Madrid, 1879–80).

51. A good example of the later would be Francisco Feliciano Ibáñez, *Observaciones sobre la utilidad y conveniencia del establecimiento en esta isla de grandes ingenios centrales* (Havana, 1880).

SELECT BIBLIOGRAPHY

PREPARED WITH THE ASSISTANCE OF AHMED N. REID

The following lists contain a selection of published works, bibliographies and guides to sources that are intended to provide supplementary reading. These should be used along with the additional references that appear at the end of individual articles in the Reader.

BIBLIOGRAPHIES AND GUIDES TO SOURCES

Bobb-Semple, Leona. *Women in Jamaica: A Bibliography of Published and Unpublished Sources* (The Press, Univ. of the West Indies: Mona, 1997).

Brathwaite, Kamau. *Our Ancestral Heritage: A Bibliography of the Roots of Culture in The English-Speaking Caribbean* (Carifesta: Kingston, 1977).

Goveia, Elsa. *A Study of the Historiography of the British West Indies to the End of the Nineteenth Century* (Howard University Press: Washington, DC, 1980).

Green, William A. 'Caribbean Historiography 1600-1800', *Journal of Interdisciplinary History*, 7, 3 (1977), 509-530.

Handler, Jerome S. *A Guide to Source Materials for the Study of Barbados History, 1627-1834* (Carbondale & Edwardville: Illinois, 1971).

Higman, Barry W. 'Theory, Method and Technique in Caribbean Social History', *Journal of Caribbean History*, 20, 1 (1985).

Higman, Barry W. *Writing West Indian Histories* (Macmillan: London, 1999).

Ingram, K.E.N. (ed). *Sources for West Indian Studies* (Inter Documentation: Switzerland, 1983).

Marshall, Woodville K. 'A Review of Historical Writing on the Commonwealth Caribbean since ca 1940', *Social and Economic Studies*, 24, 3 (1975).

Miller, Joseph C. 'Slavery: Annual Bibliographical Supplement', *Slavery and Abolition*, 7, 3 (1986).

Miller, Joseph C. and Appleby, D. 'Slavery: Annual Bibliographical Supplement', *Slavery and Abolition*, 8, 3 (1987).

Miller, Joseph C. 'Slavery: Annual Bibliographical Supplement (1987)', *Slavery and Abolition*, 9, 2 (1988).

Miller, Joseph C. and Eisenach, E. 'Slavery: Annual Bibliographical Supplement', *Slavery and Abolition*, 14, 3 (1993).

Miller, Joseph C. and Holloran, J.R. 'Slavery: Annual Bibliographical Supplement (1996) *Slavery and Abolition*, 18, 3 (1997).

Miller, Joseph C. and Holloran, J.R. 'Slavery: Annual Bibliographical Supplement (1997)', *Slavery and Abolition*, 19, 3 (1998).

Oostindie, Gert J. 'Historiography on the Dutch Caribbean (1985): Catching Up?', *Journal of Caribbean History*, 21, 1 (1985).

Shepherd, Verene, 'Slavery and the Plantation System in the British Caribbean: The Example of Jamaica', *The Historian*, (1991) 9-12.

Williams, Eric. *British Historians and the West Indies* (PNM Publishing: Port of Spain, 1964).

GENERAL

Beckles, H. *Centering Woman: Gender Discourses in Caribbean Slave Society* (Ian Randle Publishers: Kingston, 1999).

Bisnauth, D. *A History of Religions in the Caribbean* (Kingston Publishers: Kingston, 1989).

Blackburn, R. *The Overthrow of Colonial Slavery, 1776-1848* (Verso Press: London, 1988).

Bolland, N. O. 'Slavery in Belize', *Journal of Belizean Affairs*, 6 (1978).

Bolland, N. O. *Struggles for Freedom: Essays on Slavery, Colonialism and Culture in the Caribbean and Central America (The Angelus Press Limited: Belize City, 1997).

Boucher, P. Cannibal Encounters: Europeans and Island Caribs, 1492-1763 (Johns Hopkins Univ. Press: Baltimore, 1992).

Brathwaite, K.. The Development of Creole Society in Jamaica 1770-1820 (Clarendon Press: Oxford, 1971).

Canny, N. (ed.). The Origins of Empire: British Overseas Enterprise to the Close of the Seventeenth Century (Oxford Univ. Press: Oxford, 1998).

Carey, B. The Maroon Story: The Authentic and Original History of the Maroons in the History of Jamaica, 1490-1880 (Agouti Press: Kingston, 1997).

Cohen, D. and Greene, J. Neither Slave Nor Free: The Freedmen of African Descent in the Slave Societies of the New World (Johns Hopkins Univ. Press: Baltimore, 1972).

Craton, M. Testing the Chains: Resistance to Slavery in the British West Indies (Cornell Univ. Press: Ithaca, 1982).

Craton, M. Empire, Enslavement and Freedom in the Caribbean (Ian Randle Publishers: Kingston 1997).

Curtin, P. D., The Atlantic Slave Trade: A Census (Univ. of Wisconsin Press: Madison, 1969).

Debien, G. Les Esclaves aux Antilles Francaises (Societe d' Histoire de la Martinique, 1974).

Debien, G. 'Les Esclaves des Plantations Mauger a Saint Domingue, 1763-1802' Extrait du Bulletin de la Societe' d' Histoire de la Guadeloupe, Nos. 43-44(1980).

Diaz Soler, L.J. Historia de la Esclavitud Negra en Puerto Rico (Universidad de Puerto Rico: Rio Piedras, 1965).

Dookhan, I. A History of the Virgin Islands 1652-1970 (Caribbean University Press: Barbados, 1975).

Drescher, S., Engerman, S.L. (eds.) A Historical Guide to World Slavery (Oxford Univ. Press: Oxford, 1998).

Dunn, R. Sugar and Slaves: The Rise of the Planter Class in the English West Indies, 1624-1713 (Univ.of North Carolina Press: Chapel Hill, 1972).

Forster, E. and Forster, R. (eds.) Sugar and Slavery, Family and Race: The Letters and Diary of Pierre Dessalles, Planter in Martinique, 1808-1856 (Johns Hopkins Univ. Press: Baltimore, 1996).

Fraginals, M., Pons F. M. and Engerman, S. L. Between Slavery and Free labour: The Spanish-Speaking Caribbean in the Nineteenth Century (Johns Hopkins Univ. Press: Baltimore, 1985).

Goveia, E. Slave Society in the British Leeward Islands at the end of the Eighteenth Century (Yale Univ. Press: New Haven, 1965).

Hall, D.G. In Miserable Slavery: Thomas Thistlewood in Jamaica, 1750-86 (Macmillan: London, 1989).

Higman, B. W. Slave Population and Economy in Jamaica, 1807-1834 (Cambridge Univ. Press: Cambridge, 1976).

Higman, B. W. Slave Populations of the British Caribbean, 1807-1834 (Johns Hopkins Univ. Press: Baltimore, 1984).

Higman, B. W. 'The Invention of Slave Society', Elsa Goveia Memorial Lecture, U.W.I, Mona, (1998).

Higman, B. W. Montpelier Jamaica: A Plantation Community in Slavery and Freedom, 1739-1912, (The Press University of the West Indies: Mona, 1998).

Hulme, P. Colonial Encounters: Europe and the Caribbean, 1492-1797 (Methuen: London, 1986).

Johnson, H. The Bahamas in Slavery and Freedom (Ian Randle Publishers: Kingston, 1991).

Klein, H. S. African Slavery in Latin America and the Caribbean (Oxford Univ. Press: Oxford, 1982).

Knight, F. W. Slave Society in Cuba During the Nineteenth Century (Univ. of Wisconsin Press: Madison,1970).

Knight, F. W. (ed.) The Slave Societies of the Caribbean (Macmillan: London, 1997).

Lewis, G. K. Main Currents in Caribbean Thought: The Historical Evolution of Caribbean Society in its Ideological Aspects 1492-1900 (Heinemann: Kingston,1983).

Leyburn, J. G. The Haitian People (Yale Univ. Press: New Haven, 1966).

Martinez-Alier, V. Cuba: Economia y Sociedad (Iberico: Paris, 1972).

Midgley, C. Gender and Imperialism (Manchester Univ. Press: Manchester, 1998).

Midgley, C. Women Against Slavery: The British Campaigns, 1780-1870 (Routledge: New York, 1992).

Midlo, H. G. Social Control in Plantation Societies: A Comparison of St. Domingue and Cuba (Johns Hopkins Univ. Press: Baltimore, 1971).

Mintz, S. Caribbean Transformations (Johns Hopkins Univ. Press: Baltimore, 1984).

Morrissey, M. Slave Women in the New World: Gender Stratification in the Caribbean (Univ. Press of Kansas: Kansas City, 1989).

Munford, C. J. 'Slavery in the French Caribbean 1625-1715: A Marxist Analysis', Journal of Black Studies, 17, 1 (1986).

Packwood, C. O. *Chained to the Rock: Slavery in Bermuda* (New York, 1975).

Patterson, O. *The Sociology of Slavery: An Analysis of the Development and Structure of The Negro Slave Society in Jamaica*. (MacGibbes and Kee: London, 1964).

Proesmans, Father R. 'Notes on the Slaves of the French', in *Aspects of Dominican History* (Rosseau: Dominica, 1972).

Saunders, G. *Slavery in the Bahamas, 1648-1838* (Nassau Gaurdian: Nassau, 1985).

Shepherd, V., Brereton, B. and Bailey, B. (eds.) *Engendering History: Caribbean Women in Historical Perspective* (Ian Randle Publishers: Kingston, 1995).

Shepherd, V. (ed.). *Slavery Without Sugar* (Special Issue of Plantation Society in the Americas, Fall 1998).

Sheridan, R. *Doctors and Slaves: A Medical and Demographic History of Slavery in the British West Indies, 1680-1834* (Cambridge Univ. Press: Cambridge, 1985).

Smith, J. E. *Slavery in Bermuda* (Vantage Press: New York, 1976).

Spingham, L. P. 'Slavery in the Danish West Indies', *American Scandinavian Review*, 45, 1 (1957).

Stein, R. *The French Sugar Business in the Eighteenth Century* (Louisiana State Univ. Press: Baton Rouge, 1988).

Thomas, H. *The Slave Trade: The Story of the Atlantic Slave Trade, 1440-1870* (Simon and Schuster: New York, 1997).

Turner, M. (ed.) *From Chattel Slaves to Wage Slaves* (Ian Randle Publishers: Kingston, 1995).

Van Lier, R. 'Negro Slavery in Suriname', *Caribbean Historical Review*, 3-4 (1957).

Walvin, J. *Questioning Slavery* (Routledge: New York, 1996).

Williams, E. *Capitalism and Slavery* (Univ. of North Carolina Press: Chapel Hill, 1994).

Williams, E. *From Columbus To Castro: The History of the Caribbean, 1492-1969*. (Deutsch: London, 1970).

SECTION 1.
THE ATLANTIC SLAVERY PROJECT

Andrews, K.R. and Canny, N. (eds.) *The Westward Enterprise: English Activities in Ireland, the Atlantic, and America, 1480-1650* (Wayne State Univ. Press: Detriot, 1979).

Andrews, K.R. *Trade, Plunder, and Settlement: Maritime Enterprise and Genesis of the British Empire, 1480-1630* (Cambridge Univ. Press: Cambridge, 1984).

Boxer, C.R. *The Portuguese Seaborne Empire, 1415-1825* (Penguin:London, 1965).

Bowle, J. *The Imperial Achievement: The Rise and Transformation of the British Empire* (Little, Brown: Boston,1979).

Canny, N. (ed). *The Origins of Empire: British Overseas Enterprise to the Close of the Seventeenth Century*, op. cit.

Cipolla, C. *Guns and Sails in the Early Phase of European Expansion, 1400-1700* (Collins: London, 1965).

Davis, R. *The Rise of the Atlantic Economies* (Weidenfeld and Nicholson: London, 1988).

Elliott, J. H. *Imperial Spain, 1469-1716* (Penguin: London, 1970).

Elliott, J. H. *The Old World and the New, 1492-1650* (Oxford Univ. Press: Oxford, 1970).

Fernandez-Armesto, F. *Before Columbus* (Univ. of Pennsylvania Press: Philadelphia, 1987).

Kamen, H. *European Society, 1500-1700* (Unwin Hyman: London, 1984).

McAlister, L. *Spain and Portugal in the New World, 1492-1700* (Univ. of Minnesota Press: Minneapolis, 1984).

Osterhammel, J. *Colonialism: A Theoretical Overview* (M Weiner: Princeton, 1996).

Palmer, C. *Africa in the Making of the Caribbean* (Methuen: London, 1981).

Parry, J. *Age of Reconaissance* (Weidenfeld and Nicholson: London, 1963).

Parry, J. *Europe and a Wider World, 1415-1715* (Hutchinsons Univ. Library: London, 1949).

Rice, E. F. *The Foundations of Early Modern Europe 1460-1559* (Weidenfeld and Nicholson: London, 1970).

Scammel, G. *The First Imperial Age: European Overseas Expansion 1400-1715* (Unwin Hyman: London, 1989).

Scammel, G. *The World Encompassed: The First European Maritime Empires 1800-1650* (Methuen: London,1981).

SECTION 2.
INDIGENOUS PEOPLES: CONQUEST, RESISTANCE AND REPRESENTATION

Beckles, H. 'The First Barbadians, 1540-1650: Amerindian Civilization', in H. Beckles, *A History of Barbados: From Amerindian Settlement to Nation-State* (Cambridge Univ. Press: Cambridge, 1990).

Beckles, H. *European Settlement and Rivalry 1492-1792: From Columbus to Toussaint* (Heinemann: Kingston, 1983).

Borome, J. A. 'Spain and Dominica, 1493-1647', in *Aspects of Dominican History* (Government Printing Office, Dominica, 1972).

Bosso, E. B. (ed.) *Carib-Speaking Indians: Culture, Society, and Language* (Univ. of Arizona Press: Tucson,1977).

Broomert, A. 'The Arawaks of Trinidad and Coastal Guiana, 1500-1650', *Journal of Caribbean History*, 19, 2 (1984).

Boucher, P. *Cannibal Encounters: Europeans and Island Caribs, 1492-1763*, op. cit.

Cook, S.F. and Borah, W. *Essays in Population History: Mexico and the Caribbean*, 2 vols.(Berkeley ,1971).

Craton, M. 'From Caribs to Black Caribs: The Amerindian Roots of Servile Resistance in the Caribbean', in G. Okihiro, *In Resistance: Studies in African, Caribbean and Afro-American History* (Univ. of Massachusetts: Amherst, 1986).

Craton, M. *Empire, Enslavement and Freedom in the Caribbean,*op. cit.

Davis, N. D. 'The Caribs of Guiana: As Enemies of the Spaniards and as Allies of The Dutch, 1733-1789', (Pamphlet, U.W.I., Mona, W.I.C.).

Denevan, W. M. (ed.), *The Native Population of the Americas in 1492* (Univ. of Wisconsin Press: Madison 1976).

Gonzales, N. L. *Sojourners of the Caribbean: Ethnogenesis and Ethnohistory of the Garifuna* (University of Illinois Press: Illinois, 1988).

Hulme, P. *Colonial Encounters: Europe and the Native Caribbean 1492-1797,*op cit.

Hulme, P. 'The Rhetoric of Description: The Amerindians of the Caribbean Within the Mode of European Discourse', *Caribbean Studies*, 23 (1990).

Jaenen, C. *Friend and Foe: Aspects of French-Amerindian Cultural Contact in the Sixteenth and Seventeenth Centuries* (Columbia Univ. Press: New York, 1976).

Jesse, C. 'The Spanish Cedula of December 23, 1511, on the Subject of the Caribs', *Caribbean Quarterly*, 9 (1963).

Marshall, B. 'The Black Carib-Native Resistance to British Penetration into the Windward Side of St. Vincent, 1763-1773', *Caribbean Quarterly*, 19 (1973).

Moore, R. B. 'Carib Cannibalism': A Study in Anthropological Stereotyping', *Caribbean Studies*, 13 (1973)

Newson, L. *Aboriginal and Spanish Colonial Trinidad: A Study in Culture Contact* (Academic Press: London, New York, 1976).

Osterhammel, J. *Colonialism: A Theoretical Overview*, op. cit.

Pennington, L. S. 'The Amerindian in English Promotional Literature', in K.R.Andrews and N.P. Canny (eds.), *The Westward Enterprise: English Activities in Ireland, the Atlantic, and America, 1480-1650*, op. cit.

Thompson, A. *Colonialism and Underdevelopment in Guyana, 1580-1803* (Carib Research and Publications Inc.: Bridgetown , Barbados, 1987).

Walker, D.J.R. *Columbus and the Golden World of the Island Arawaks: The Story of the First Americans and their Caribbean* (Ian Randle Publishers: Kingston, 1992).

Watts, D. *The West Indies: Patterns of Development, Culture and Environmental Change Since 1492 (Cambridge Univ. Press: Cambridge, 1987).*

SECTION 3.
IMPERIALISM, SERVITUDE AND COLONIAL SLAVERY

Andrews, K. *The Spanish Caribbean: Trade and Plunder, 1530-1630* (Yale Univ. Press: New Haven, 1978).

Beckles, H. 'English Colonization 1625-1644', in H. Beckles, *A History of Barbados: From Amerindian Settlement to Nation-State (Cambridge Univ. Press: Cambridge, 1990).*

Beckles, H. 'English Parliamentary Debate on "White Slavery" in Barbados, in H. Beckles, *White Servitude and Black Slavery* (Tennessee Univ. Press: Knoxville, 1989). 1659', Journal of Barbados Museum: and Historical Society, 36, 4, (1982).

Beckles, H. 'Sugar and White Servitude An Analysis of Indentured Labour during the Sugar Revolution of Barbados, 1643-1655' *Journal of Barbados Museum and Historical Society*, 35, 3 (1981).

Boxer, C. R. *The Portuguese Seaborne Empire, 1415-1825* (Hutchinson: London, 1969).

Boxer, C. R. *The Dutch: Seaborne Empire, 1600-1800* (Hutchinson: London, 1965).

Bridenbaugh, C. *No Peace Beyond the Line: The English in the Caribbean, 1624-1690* (Oxford Univ. Press: Oxford, 1972).

Cain, P. J. and Hopkins, A. G. *British Imperialism: Innovation and Expansion, 1688-1914* (Longman: Essex, 1993).

Craton, M. *Empire, Enslavement and Freedom in the Caribbean*, op. cit.

Crouse, N. *The French Struggles for the West Indies, 1665-1713* (Columbia Univ. Press: New York, 1943).

Curtin, P. 'The Black Experience of Colonialism and Imperialism', in S. W. Mintz (ed). *Slavery, Colonialism and Racism* (Norton: New York,1974).

Davis, R. *The Rise of the Atlantic Economies*, op. cit.

Elliot, J. H. *Spain and its World, 1500-1700: Selected Essays* (Yale Univ. Press: New Haven, 1989).

Elliot, J. H. 'The Seizure of Overseas Territories by the European Powers', in Hans Pohl (ed). *The European Discovery of the World and its Economic Effects on Pre-Industrial Society, 1500-1800 (F. Steiner: Stuttgart, 1990).*

Galenson, D. W. 'The Rise and Fall of Indentured Servitude in the Americas' in Robert Whaples and Dianne Betts, *Historical Perspectives in the American Economy: Selected Readings* (Cambridge Univ. Press: Cambridge, 1995).

Greenblatt, S. *New World Encounters* (Univ. of California Press: Berkeley, 1993).

McAlister, L. *Spain and Portugal in the New World, 1492-1700,* op. cit.

McFarlane, A. *The British in the Americas, 1480-1815* (Longman: Essex, 1994).

Muldoon, J. *The Americas in the Spanish World Order: The Justification for Conquest in The Seventeenth Century (Univ. of Pennsylvania Press: Philadelphia, 1994).*

Newton, A. *The European Activities in the West Indies, 1493-1688* (A. C. Black: London, 1933).

Osterhammel, J. *Colonialism: A Theoretical Overview,* op. cit.

Quinn, D. and Ryan, A.N. *England's Sea Empire, 1550-1642* (Allen and Unwin: London, 1983).

Scammel, G. *The First Imperial Age: European Overseas Expansion 1400-1715* , op cit.

Thompson, A. O. *Colonialism and Underdevelopment in Guyana, 1580-1803,* op. cit.

SECTION 4.
SLAVERY AND NEW ECONOMIC ORDERS

Beckles, H. 'The Economic Origins of Black Slavery in the British West Indies: A Tentative Analysis of the Barbados Model, 1643-1680', *Journal of Caribbean History,* 16 (1982).

Beckles, H. and Downes, A. 'An Economic Formalization of the Origins of Black Slavery in the British West Indies, 1624-1645', *Social and Economic Studies,* 34 (1985).

Beckles, H. 'Sugar and Slavery, 1644-1692', in H. Beckles, *A History of Barbados from Amerindian Settlement to Nation State,* op. cit.

Bryan, P. 'The Transition to Plantation Agriculture in the Dominican Republic, 1770-1844', *Journal of Caribbean History,* 10 & 11 (1970).

Chandler, A. D. 'The Expansion of Barbados', *Journal of the Barbados Museum and Historical Society,* 13 (1946).

Chardon, R. E. 'Sugar Plantations in the Dominican Republic, 1770-1844', *Geographical Review,* 74, 4 (1984).

Cripps, L. *The Spanish Caribbean from Columbus to Castro* (G.K. Hall: Boston, 1979).

Curet, J. 'About Slavery and the Order of Things: Puerto Rico, 1845-1873', in Fraginals, Pons and Engerman (eds.), *Between Slavery and Freedom,* op. cit.

Curtin, P. D. *The Atlantic Slave Trade,* op. cit.

Curtin, P. D. 'A Planting Economy', in Curtin, P.D. *Two Jamaicas: The Role of Ideas in A Tropical Colony 1830-1865 (Atheneum Press: New York, 1970).*

Curtin, P. D. 'The Sugar Revolution and the Settlement of the Caribbean', in Curtin, P.D. *The Rise and Fall of the Plantation Complex: Essays in Atlantic History* (Cambridge Univ. Press: Cambridge, 1990).

Dunn, R. *Sugar and Slaves, The Rise of the Planter Class in The English West Indies 1624-1713,* op. cit.

Galenson, D.W. 'The Atlantic Slave Trade and The Early Development of the English West Indies', in D.W. Galenson, *Traders, Planters and Slaves: Market Behaviour in Early English America* (Cambridge Univ. Press: Cambridge, 1986).

Galloway, J.H. 'The Atlantic Sugar Industry c. 1450-1680', in J.H. Galloway, *The Sugar Cane Industry: A Historical Geography From Its Origins to 1914* (Cambridge Univ. Press: Cambridge, 1989).

Galloway, J.H. 'The American Sugar Industry in the 18th century', in Galloway, *The Sugar Industry,* op. cit.

Goveia, E. *Slave Societies in the British Leeward Islands at the End of the Eighteenth Century,* op. cit.

Greenfield, S. 'Plantations, Sugarcane and Slavery', in M. Craton (ed.), *Roots and Branches: Current Directions in Slave Studies* (Pergamon Press: Toronto, 1979).

Higman, B.W. *Slave Populations of the British Caribbean 1807-1834,* op. cit.

Klein, H.S. 'Sugar and Slavery in the Caribbean in the 17th and 18th Centuries' in H.S. Klein, *African Slavery in Latin America and the Caribbean* (Oxford Univ. Press: Oxford, 1982).

Ratekin, M. 'The Early Sugar Industry in Espaniola', *Hispanic American Historical Review,* 34 (1954).

Scarano, F. A. 'Ponce: The Making of a Sugar Economy', in Francisco A. Scarano, *Sugar and Slavery in Puerto Rico: The Plantation Economy of Ponce* (Univ. of Wisconsin Press: Madison, 1984).

Sheridan. R. 'The Plantation Revolution and the Industrial Revolution, 1625-1775', *Caribbean Studies,* 9, 3 (1969).

Sheridan, R. *The Development of Plantations to 1750* (Caribbean University Press: Barbados, 1970).

Sheridan, R. *Sugar and Slavery: An Economic History of the British West Indies, 1624-1775* (Canoe Press: Kingston, 1994).

Stein, R. *The French Sugar Business in the Eighteenth Century*, op. cit.

Tomich, D. *Slavery in the Circuit of Sugar* (Johns Hopkins Univ. Press: Baltimore, 1990).

Watts, D. 'The Extension of the West Indian Sugar Estate Economy 1665-1833', in D. Watts, *The West Indies: Patterns of Development, Culture and Environmental Change Since 1492*, op. cit.

SECTION 5.
SLAVERY, FINANCE AND TRADE

Andrews, C. M. *British Committees, Commissions and Councils of Trade and Plantations, 1622-1675* (The Johns Hopkins Press: Baltimore, 1908).

Beer, G. L. *The Origins of the British Colonial System* (P. Smith: New York, 1933).

Boxer, C.R. *The Dutch Seaborne Empire, 1600-1800*, op. cit.

Claypole, W. A. and Buisserett, D. 'Trade Patterns in Early English Jamaica', *Journal of Caribbean History, 5 (1972).*

Craton, M. and Walvin, J. *A Jamaican Plantation: The History of Worthy Park, 1670-1970.* (University of Toronto Press: Toronto, 1970).

Dookhan, I. 'Era of Prosperity and Decline', in I. Dookhan, *A History of the Virgin Islands, 1672-1970*, op. cit.

Hagelberg, G.B. *Sugar in the Caribbean: Turning Sunshine into Money* (Woodrow Wilson International Center for Scholars, 1985).

Israel, J., *Dutch Primacy in World Trade, 1585-1740* (Oxford Univ. Press: Oxford, 1990).

Nelson, G. H. 'Contraband Trade Under the Asiento, 1730-1739', *American Historical Review*, 1 (1945).

Nettles, C. P. 'England and the Spanish American Trade, 1680-1715', *Journal of Modern History*, 111, 1 (1931).

Pares, R. *War and Trade in the West Indies* (Frank Cass: London, 1963).

Pares, R. *Yankees and Creoles: The Trade Between North America and the West Indies Before the American Revolution* (Archon Books: Hampden, Conn., 1968).

Pares, R. 'The London Sugar Market, 1740-1769', *Economic History Review*, 9 (1956/57).

Pares, R. 'Merchants and Planters', *Economic History Review*, 4 (1960).

Pitman, F. W. *The Development of the British West Indies* (Frank Cass: London, 1967).

Postma, J. *The Dutch in the Atlantic Slave Trade, 1600-1815* (Cambridge Univ.Press: Cambridge, 1990).

Sheridan, R.B. 'The Wealth of Jamaica in the Eighteenth Century: A rejoinder', *The Economic History Review*, 21, 1 (1968).

Thomas, D. *An Historical Account of the Rise and Growth of West India Colonies* (Arno Press: New York 1972).

Zahadieh, N. 'The Merchants of Port Royal, Jamaica and the Spanish Contraband Trade, 1655-1696', *William and Mary Quarterly*, 3rd Ser., 43 (1986).

Zahadieh, N. 'Trade, Plunder and Economic Development in Early English Jamaica, 1655-1689', *Economic History Review, 39* (1988).

SECTION 6.
THE WORK CULTURE OF THE ENSLAVED

Aimes, H. H.S. *A History of Slavery in Cuba, 1511 to 1868* (New York: G.P. Putnam's Sons, 1907).

Bolland, N. O. 'Slavery in Belize', *Journal of Belizean Affairs*, op. cit.

Braithwaite, K. 'Caribbean Women During the Period of Slavery', *Caribbean Contact* May 1984 (Pt 1), and June 1984 (Pt 2)

Bush, B. *Slave Women in Caribbean Society, 1650-1838* (Heinemann: Kingston,1990).

Craton, M. and Walvin, J. *A. Jamaica Plantation: The History of Worthy Park*, op. cit.

Craton, M. *Searching for the Invisible Man: Slaves and Plantation Life in Jamaica* (Harvard Univ. Press: Massachusets, 1978).

Debien, G. *Les Esclaves aux Antilles Francaise*, op. cit.

Debien, G. Les Esclaves des Plantations Mauger a Saint Domingue, 1763-1802', op cit.

Dunn, R. 'A Tale of Two Plantations: Slave Life at Mesopotamia in Jamaica and Mt. Airy in Virginia, 1799-1828', *William and Mary Quarterly*, 34 (1977).

Dunn, R. 'Dreadful Idlers in the Cane Fields: The Slave Labour Pattern on a Jamaican Sugar Estate, 1767-1831', *Journal of Interdisciplinary History*, 17 (1987).

Higman, B. W. *Slave Population and Economy in Jamaica, 1807-1834*, op. cit.

Higman, B. W. *Slave Populations of the British Caribbean, 1807-1834*, op. cit.

Knight, F. W. *Slave Society in Cuba During the Nineteenth Century*, op. cit..

Morrissey, M. *Slave Women in the New World: Gender Stratification in the Caribbean*, op. cit.

Munford, C. J. 'Slavery in the French Caribbean, 1625-1715: A Marxist Analysis', *Journal of Black Studies*, op. cit.

Packwood, C. O. *Chained to the Rock: Slavery in Bermuda*, op cit.

Pitman, F. W. 'Slavery on British West India Plantations in the Eighteenth Century', *Journal of Negro History*, 11, 4 (1926).

Proesmans, Father R. 'Notes on the Slaves of the French', in *Aspects of Dominican History*, op. cit.

Saunders, G. *Slavery in the Bahamas 1648-1838*, op. cit.

Smith, J. E. *Slavery in Bermuda*, op. cit.

Spingham, L. P. 'Slavery in the Danish West Indies', *American Scandinavian Review*, op. cit.

Van Lier, R. 'Negro Slavery in Suriname', *Caribbean Historical Review*, op. cit.

Ward, J. R. *British West Indian Slavery, 1750-1834: The Process of Amelioration*, (The Clarendon Press: Oxford, 1988)

SECTION 7. SLAVERY AND CAPITALIST GLOBALIZATION: THE FIRST PHASE

Beckles, H. 'Capitalism and Slavery: The Debate over Eric Williams', *Social and Economic Studies, vol.33, no.4 (1984).*

Carrington, S.H. *The West Indies During the American Revolution* (Foris Publications: Providence, USA, 1987).

Carrington, S.H. 'The American Revolution and the British West Indies Economy', *Journal of Interdisciplinary History*, 17, 4 (1987).

Carrington, S.H. 'Econocide: Myth or Reality?: Question of West Indian Decline, 1738-1806', *Boletin de Estudios Latinoamericanos y del Caribe*, 36 (1986).

Drescher, S. 'Capitalism and the Decline of Slavery', in V. Rubin and A. Tuden (eds.) *Comparative Perspectives in New World Plantation Societies* (New York Academy of Sciences: New York,1977).

Drescher, S. *Econocide: British Slavery in the Era of Abolition* (Univ. of Pittsburgh Press: Pittsburgh, 1977).

Drescher, S. '*Capitalism and Slavery* After Fifty Years', *Slavery and Abolition*, 18, 3 1997.

Dupuy, A. 'French Merchant Capital and Slavery in St. Dominique', *Latin American Perspectives*, 12, 3 (1985).

Engerman, S. L. 'The Atlantic Economy of the Eighteenth Century: Some Speculations on Economic Development in Britain, America, Africa and Elsewhere',

European Journal on Economic History, 24, 1 (1995).

Inikori, J. 'Slavery and the Rise of Capitalism' *Elsa Goveia Memorial Lecture*, Univ. of the West Indies, Mona (1993).

Morgan, K. 'Atlantic Trade and British Economic Growth in the Eighteenth Century' in P. Mathias and J. Davis (eds), *Nature of Industrialization, vol. 1x, International Trade and British Economic Growth from the Eighteenth Century to the Present* (Blackwell: Oxford, 1997).

Nettles, C. P. 'England and the Spanish American Trade, 1680-1715', *Journals of Modern History*, op. cit.

Pares, R. 'The London Sugar Market, 1740-1769', *Economic History Review*, op. cit.

Pares, R. *Yankees and Creoles: The Trade Between North America and the West Indies Before the American Revolution*, op.cit.

Richardson, D. 'The Slave Trade, Sugar, and British Economic Growth, 1748-1776', in P. Manning (ed) *Slave Trades, 1500-1800.*

Sheridan R. B. 'The West India Sugar Crisis and British Slave Emancipation 1830-1833', *Journal of Economic History*, 21, 4 (1961).

Solow, B. (ed). *Slavery and the Rise of the Atlantic System* (Cambridge Univ. Press: Cambridge, 1991).

Solow, B. and Engerman, S. (eds) *British Capitalism and Caribbean Slavery: The Legacy of Eric Williams*, (Cambridge Univ. Press: Cambridge, 1987).

Thomas, R. 'The Sugar Colonies of the Old Empire: Profit and Loss for Great Britain?', *Economic History Review*, 21 (1968).

Tomich, D. W. *Slavery in the Circuit of Sugar: Martinique and the World Economy, 1830-1948*, op. cit.

Ward, J. R. *British West Indian Slavery 1750-1834: The Process of Amelioration*, op. cit.

Williams, E. 'The Exclusive', in E. Williams, *From Columbus to Castro: The History of the Caribbean 1492-1969*, op cit.

SECTION 8. SLAVERY AND CAPITALIST GLOBALIZATION: THE SECOND PHASE

Bergad, L.W. 'The Economic Viability of Sugar Production Based on Slave Labor in Cuba, 1859-1878', *Latin American Research Review*, 24, 1 (1989).

Corwin, A. F. *Spain and the Abolition of Slavery in Cuba, 1818-1866* (Univ. of Texas Press: Austin, 1967).

Duncan, K. and Rutledge, I. (eds.), *Land and Labour in Latin America: Essays on the Development of Agrarian Capitalism in the Nineteenth and Twentieth Centuries* (Cambridge Univ. Press: Cambridge, 1977).

Gayer, A. D. *The Sugar Economy of Puerto Rico* (Colombia Univ. Press: New York, 1938).

Guerra y S. R. *Sugar and Society in the Caribbean and an Economic History of Cuban Agriculture* (Yale Univ. Press: New Haven, 1964).

Iglesias G. F. 'Changes in Cane Cultivation in Cuba 1860-1900', In Papers Presented at the Symposium on Caribbean Economic History, Univ. of the West Indies, Mona, November 7-9, 1986.

Iglesias G. F. 'The Development of Capitalism in Cuban Sugar Production, 1860-1900', in Moreno Fraginals, M., Moya Pons, F., and Engerman, S.L (eds.), *Between Slavery and Free Labour: The Spanish Speaking Caribbean in the Nineteenth Century*, op. cit.

Knight, F. W. 'Origins of Wealth and the Sugar Revolution in Cuba, 1750-1850', *Hispanic American Historical Review*, 57 (1977).

Moreno F. M. *The Sugarmill: The Socioeconomic Complex of Sugar in Cuba, 1760-1860* (Monthly Review Press, 1976).

Moreno F. M. *El Ingenio: Complejo Economico Social Cubano del Azucar* (Havana: Editorial de Ciencias Sociales, 1978).

Oostindie, G. 'Cuban Railroads, 1803-1868: Origins and Effects of Progressive Entrepreneurialism', *Caribbean Studies*, 20, 3&4, (1988).

Perez, L. A. *Cuba: Between Reform and Revolution* (Oxford Univ. Press: Oxford, 1988).

Scarano, F. A. *Sugar and Slavery in Puerto Rico: The Plantation Economy of Ponce, 1800-1850*, op cit.

Tornero, T. P. *Crecimiento economica y transformaciones sociales: esclavos, hacendados y comerciantes en la Cuba colonial, 1760-1840* (Ministerio de Trabajo y Seguridad Social: Madrid, 1996).

SECTION 9. RACE, CLASS, COLOUR AND THE POWER ORDER

Barker, A. J. *The African Link: British Attitudes to the Negro in the Era of the Atlantic Slave Trade, 1550-1807* (Frank Cass: London 1978).

Beckles, H. 'On the Backs of Blacks: The Barbados Free Coloureds' Pursuit of Civil Rights and the 1816 Rebellion', *Immigrants and Minorities*, 3, 2 (1984).

Beckles, H. 'Black Men in White Skins': The Formation of a White Proletariat in West Indian Slave Society', *The Journal of Imperial and Commonwealth History*, 15,1 (1986).

Beckles, H. 'Black Over White: The "Poor White" Problem in Barbados Slave Society', *Immigrants and Minorities*, 7, 1 (1998).

Beckles, H. 'Social and Political Control in the Slave Society', in F. Knight (ed) *The Slave Societies of the Caribbean* (Macmillan: London, 1997)..

Brathwaite, K. *The Development of Creole Society in Jamaica, 1770-1820*, op. cit.

Bush, B. 'White Ladies', Coloured 'Favourites' and Black 'Wenches': Some Considerations on Sex, Race and Class Factors in Social Relations in White Creole Society in the British Caribbean', *Slavery and Abolition*, 2 (1981).

Campbell, M. *The Dynamics of Change in a Slave Society: A Socio-Political History of The Free Coloureds in Jamaica, 1800-1865* (Sairleigh Dickinson University Press: New Jersey, 1976).

Cauna,, J. 'The Singularity of the Saint-Domingue Revolution: Marronage, Voodoo, and the Color Question', *Plantation Society in the Americas*, 3, 3 (1996).

Cohen, W. B. *The French Encounter with Africans: White Responses to Blacks, 1530-1880* (Indiana Univ. Press: Bloomington, 1980).

Cox, E. *Free Coloureds in the Slave Societies of St. Kitts and Grenada, 1763-1833* (Univ. of Tennessee Press: Knoxville, 1984).

Curtin, P. D. 'European Jamaica: The White and Coloureds Castes', in P.D. Curtin, *Two Jamaicas: The Role of Ideas in a Tropical Colony, 1830-1865* op.cit.

Edmondson, L. 'Trans-Atlantic Slavery and the Institutionalization of Race', *Caribbean Quarterly*, 22, 2and 3 (1976).

Engerman, S.L. and Genovese, E.D. (eds.) *Race and Slavery in the Western Hemisphere* (Princeton Univ. Press: Princeton, 1975).

Forster, E. and Forster, R. (eds.), *Sugar and Slavery, Family and Race: The Letters and Diary of Pierre Desalles, Planter in Martinique, 1808-1856*, op. cit.

Garrigus, J. D. 'Colour, Class, and Identity on the Eve of the Haitian Revolution: Saint Domingue's Free Coloured Elite as colons Americains', *Slavery and Abolition*, 17, 1 (1996).

Hall, D.G. 'Jamaica', in D. Cohen and J.P. Greene (eds.) *Neither Slave Nor Free*, op. cit.

Hall, N.A.T. 'Anna Heegaard- Enigma', *Caribbean Quarterly*, 22, 2 and 3 (1976).

Handler, J. *The Unappropriated People: Freedmen in the Slave Society of Barbados* (Johns Hopkins Univ. Press: Baltimore, 1974).

Heuman, G. 'White Over Brown Over Black: The Free Coloureds in Jamaican Society During and After Emancipation', *Journal of Caribbean History*, 14 (1981).

Heuman, G. *Between Black and White: Race, Politics and the Free Coloureds in Jamaica, 1792-1865* (Greenwood Press: Conn., 1981).

Heuman, G. 'Free Coloureds in Jamaican Slave Society', in G. Heuman. *Between Black and White, op. cit.*

Heuman, G. 'The Social Structure of The Slave Societies in the Caribbean', in Franklin Knight (ed.), *The Slave Societies of the Caribbean*, Vol. 3, op. cit.

Hoefte, R. 'Free Blacks and Coloureds in Plantation Suriname: The Struggle to Rise', *Slavery and Abolition*, 18, 2 (1997).

Lewis, G.K. 'The Eighteenth and Nineteenth Centuries: The Antislavery Ideology', in G.K. Lewis, op. cit.

Lokke, C.C. 'Malouet and the St. Domingue Mulatto Question in 1793', *Journal of Negro History*, 24, 4 (1939).

Martinez-Alier, V. Marriage, *Class and Colour in Nineteenth Century Cuba: A Study of Racial Attitudes and Sexual Values in a Slave Society* (Cambridge Univ. Press: Cambridge, 1974).

Midlo Hall, G. *Social Control in Plantation Societies: A Comparison of St. Domingue and Cuba*, op. cit.

Perontin-Dumon, A., 'Free Coloureds and Slaves in Revolutionary Guadeloupe:Politics and Political Consciousness', in Paquette, R.L. and Engerman, S.L (eds.), *The Lesser Antilles in the Age of European Expansion* (Univ. Press of Florida: Gainesville, 1996).

Puckrein, G. A. 'Race, Racism and the Imperial System', in G.A. Puckrein, *Little England: Plantation Society and Anglo-Barbadian Politics, 1607-1700* (New York Univ. Press: New York, 1984).

Shepherd, V. and Richards, G (eds.) 'Konversations in Kreole', *Caribbean Quarterly*, 44, 1&2, 1998).

Sio, A. 'Race, Colour and Miscegenation; The Free Coloureds of Jamaica and Barbados', *Caribbean Studies*, 26, 1 (1976).

Sio, A. 'Marginality and Free Coloured Identity in Caribbean Slave Society',*Slavery and Abolition: A Journal of Comparative Studies*, 8 (1987).

Smith, M.G. 'Some Aspects of Social Structure in the British Caribbean about 1820',*Social and Economic Studies*, 1 (1953).

Trouillot, M.R. 'Motion in the System: Coffee, Colour and Slavery in 18th Century St. Domingue', *Review* 5, 3 (1982).

Watson, K. *The Civilized Island: Barbados, A Social History* (K. Watson: Bridgetown, 1979).

SECTION 10. SEX, RACE AND THE GENDER ORDER

Beckles, H. *Centering Woman: Gender Discourses in Caribbean Slave Society*, op.cit.

Beckles, H. *Freeing Slavery: Gender Paradigms in the Social History of Caribbean Slavery*, (Elsa Goveia Memorial Lecture, UWI, Mona, 1997).

Beckles, H. *Natural Rebels: A Social History of Enslaved Black Women in Barbados*, op. cit.

Boa, S.M. 'Urban Free Black and Coloured Woman: Jamaica, 1760-1834 *Jamaica Historical Review*, 18 (1993).

Brathwaite, K. 'Caribbean Women During the Period of Slavery', *Caribbean Contact*, op. cit.

Brereton, B. *Gendered Testimony* (History Dept, Mona, 1994).

Burnard, T. 'Inheritance and Independence: Women's Status in Early Colonial Jamaica', *William and Mary Quarterly*, vol. 1 (1991).

Bush, B. 'White Ladies', Coloured 'Favourites' and Black 'Wenches': Some Considerations on Sex, Race and Class Factors in Social Relations in White Creole Society in the British Caribbean', *Slavery and Abolition*, op. cit.

Ferguson, M. (ed). *The History of Mary Prince: A West Indian Slave Related By Herself* (Pandora,1987).

Hall, D. *In Miserable Slavery: Thomas Thistlewood in Jamaica, 1750-86*, op. cit.

Kruse, D. 'Gender as a Historical Determinant: An Explanation', *Melbourne Historical Journal*, vol.17, (1985).

Midgley, C. *Gender and Imperialism*, op. cit.

Morrissey, M. *Slave Women in the New World: Gender Stratification in the Caribbean*, op. cit.

Morrissey, M. 'Women's Work, Family Formation, and Reproduction among Caribbean Slaves', *Review*, 9, 3 (1986).

Morton, P. (ed.), *Discovering the Women in Slavery* (Univ. of Georgia Press: Athens, 1996).

Reddock, R. 'Women and Slavery in the Caribbean: A Feminist Perspective', *Latin American Perspectives*, Issue 44, 12:1 (1985).

Terborg-Penn, S. Rushing, A. and Harley, S.(eds.), *Women in Africa and the African Diaspora* (Howard Univ. Press, 1989).

Shepherd, V. Brereton, B., Bailey, B. (eds.) *Engendering History: Caribbean Women In Historical Perspective*, op. cit.

Van der Spuy, P. 'Gender and Slavery: Towards a Feminist Revision', *South African Historical Journal*, 25 (1991).

SECTION 11. SUBALTERN SOCIAL AUTONOMY: SOCIAL AND ECONOMIC CULTURE

Beckles, H. 'Slaves and the Internal Market Economy of Barbados; A Perspective On Non-Violence Resistance', *Historia y Sociedad*, Ano 11, (1989).

Berlin, I. and Morgan, P. (eds.) *The Slaves' Economy: Independent Production by Slaves in the Americas* (Frank Cass: London, 1991).

Bisnauth, D. 'Africans and Africanism in the Caribbean', in D. Bisnauth *A History of Religions in the Caribbean* (Kingston 1989).

Braithwaite, K. *Folk Culture of the Slaves in Jamaica* (New Beacon Books: London, 1970).

Braithwaite, K. *The Development of Creole Society in Jamaica*, op. cit.

Carmichael, A. C. *Domestic Manners and Social Condition of the White, Colored, and Negro Population of the West Indies*, 2 vols. (London, 1833).

Dirks, R. 'Slaves Holidays', *Natural History*, 84,10 (1972).

Gaspar, D. B. 'Slavery, Amelioration and Sunday Markets in Antigua, 1823-31',*Slavery and Abolition*, 9,1 (1988).

Handler, J. 'An Archaeological Investigation of the Domestic Life of Plantation Slaves in Barbados', *Journal of the Barbados Museum and Historical Society*, 34, 2, (1972).

Higman, B. W. *Slave Populations of the British Caribbean, 1807-1834*, op. cit.

Jesse, C. 'Religion among the Early Slaves in the French Antilles', *Journal of Barbados Museum and Historical Society*, 28, 1 (1960).

Johnson, H. 'The Self-Hire System During Slavery', in *The Bahamas in Slavery and Freedom*, op. cit.

Johnson, H. 'The Emergence of a Peasantry During Slavery', in The Bahamas in Slavery and Freedom, op. cit.

Marshall, W. 'Provision Ground and Plantation Labour in Four Windward Islands: Competition for Resources during Slavery', *Slavery and Abolition*, vol. 12, 1 (1991).

Mintz, S. W. 'The Jamaica Internal Marketing Pattern', *Social and Economic Studies*, Vol. 4, No. 1 (1955).

Mintz, S. W. 'Caribbean Market Places and Caribbean History', *Nova Americano*, 1 (1978).

Mintz, S. and Hall, D. 'Economic Roles and Cultural Traditions' in Filomena Steady (ed.), *The Black Woman Cross-Culturally* (Schenkmann Publishing Co:Cambridge, Mass., 1981).

Patterson, O. *The Sociology of Slavery*, op. cit.

Schuler, M. 'Afro-American Slave Culture', in M. Craton (ed.), *Roots and Branches: Current Directions in Slave Studies*, op. cit.

Shepherd, V. 'Alternative Husbandry: Slaves and Free Labourers on Livestock Farms in Jamaica in the Eighteenth and Nineteenth Centuries', in Twaddle, M.(ed.), *The Wages of Slavery: From Chattel Slavery to Wage Labour in Africa, the Caribbean, and England* (Frank Cass: London, 1993).

Shepherd, V. 'Questioning Creole: Domestic Producers in Jamaica's Plantation Economy', *Caribbean Quarterly*, Vol.44, Nos.1&2 (1998).

Simmonds, L. 'Slave Higglering in Jamaica, 1780-1834', *Jamaica Journal* Vol. 20, No. 1 (1987).

Stephan, P. (ed.) *Slave Cultures and the Cultures of Slavery* (Univ. of Tennesse Press: Knoxville, 1995).

Tomich, D. 'Une Petite Guinee: Provision Ground and Plantation in Martinique, 1830-1848', *Slavery and Abolition*, vol.12, 1 (1991).

Turner, M. 'Slave Workers Subsistence and Labour Bargaining: Amity Hall, Jamaica, 1805-1832', *Slavery and Abolition*, op cit.

Turner, M. (ed.) *From Chattel Slaves to Wage Slaves* (Ian Randle Publishers: Kingston, 1995).

SECTION 12. A DEADLY BUSINESS: MORTALITY, HEALTH, NUTRITION AND THE CRISIS OF SOCIAL REPRODUCTION .

Butler, M. 'Mortality and Labour and the Codrington Estates, Barbados', *Journal of Caribbean History*, 19,1(1984).

Craton, M. 'Jamaican Slave Mortality: Fresh Light from Worthy Park, Longville and the Tharp Estates', *Journal of Caribbean History*, 3 (1971).

Craton, M. *Searching for the Invisible Man: Slaves and Plantation Life in Jamaica* op. cit.

Craton, M. 'Hobbesian or Panglossian?: The Two Extremes of Slave Conditions in the British Caribbean, 1739-1834', *William and Mary Quarterly*, 2nd Ser., 35, (1978).

Dunn, R. 'A Tale of Two Plantations: Slave Life at Mesopotamia in Jamaica and Mt. Airy in Virginia, 1799-1828', op. cit.

Dunn, R. 'Dreadful Idlers in the Cane Fields: The Slave Labour Pattern on a Jamaican Sugar Estate, 1767-1831', op. cit.

Engerman, S. L. 'Some Economic and Demographic Comparisons of Slavery in the United States and the British West Indies', *Economic History Review*, 2nd Ser., 29 (1976).

Galenson, D. ' Population Turnover in the English West Indies in the late 17th Century:A Comparative Perspective', *Journal of Economic History*, 42 (1982).

Green-Pedersen, S. E. 'Slave Demography in the Danish West Indies and the Abolition of the Danish Slave Trade', in D. Eltis and J. Walvin (eds.) *The Abolition of theAtlantic Slave Trade: Origins and Effects in Europe, Africa and the Americas* (Univ. of Wisconsin Press: Madison, 1981).

Higman, B. W. *Slave Population and the Economy in Jamaica*, op. cit.

Higman, B. W. 'Growth in Afro-Caribbean Slave Populations', *American Journal of Physical Anthropology*, 1 (1979).

Johansen, Hans C. 'Slave Demography of the Danish West Indian Islands', Scandinavian *Economic History Review*, 29, 1 (1981).

Kiple, K. *The Caribbean Slave: A Biological History* (Cambridge Univ. Press: Cambridge, 1984).

Klein, H. S. and Engerman S. L.. 'Fertility Differentials between Slaves in the United States and the British West Indies: A Note on Location Practices and Their Possible Implications', *William and Mary Quarterly*, Vol. 35, (1978).

Koplan, J.P. 'Slave Mortality in 19th Grenada', *Social Science History*, 7, 3 (1983).

Lamur, H. 'The Impact of Maroon Wars on Population Policy during Slavery in Suriname', *Journal of Caribbean History*, 23 (1990).

Lamur, H. 'Demography of Surinam Plantation Slaves in the Last Decade before Emancipation: The case of Catharina Sophia' In V. Rubin and A. Tuden (eds.), *Comparative Perspectives*, op. cit.

Lowenthal, D. and Clarke, C. ' Slave Breeding in Barbuda: The Past of a Negro Myth', In V. Rubin and A. Tuden (eds.), *Comparative Perspectives* op. cit.

Meredith, J. A. 'Plantation Slave Mortality in Trinidad', *Population*, 42, 2 (1988).

Meredith J. A. *The Plantation Slaves of Trinidad, 1783-1816: A Mathematical and Demographic Enquiry* (Cambridge Univ. Press: Cambridge, 1988).

Molen, P. 'Population and Social Patterns in Barbados in the early 18th Century', *William and Mary Quarterly*, 28 (1971).

Sheridan, R. B. 'Sweet Malefactor: The Social Cost of Slavery and Sugar in Jamaica and Cuba, 1807-1854', *Economic History Review*, 29 (1976).

Sheridan, R. B. 'Slave Demography in the British West Indies and the Abolition of the Slave Trade', in D. Ellis and J. Walvin (eds.), *The Abolition of the Atlantic Slave Trade*, op cit.

Sheridan, R. B. *Doctors and Slaves*, op. cit.

Sheridan, R. B. 'Mortality and the Medical Treatment of Slaves in the British West Indies', in Stanley Engerman and Eugene Genovese, *Race and Slavery in the Western Hemisphere: Qualitative Studies*, op cit.

Stark, D. 'Discovering the Invisible Puerto Rican Slave Family: Demographic Evidence From the Eighteenth Century', *Journal of Family History*, 21, 4 (1996).

Tomich, D. 'Caribbean Slavery and the Struggle over Reproduction', in Jane L. Collins and Martha Gimenez (eds.), *Work Without Wages: Comparative Studies of Domestic Labor and Self-Employment* (State Univ. of New York Press: New York,1990).

Ward, J. R. *British West Indian Slavery, 1750-1834: The Process Amelioration*, op. cit.

Wessman, J. 'The Demographic Structure of Slavery in Puerto Rico: Some Aspects of Agrarian Capitalism in the late 19th Century', *Journal of Latin American Studies*, 12, 2 (1980).

Wood, B. C. and Clayton, T.R. 'Slave Birth, Death and Diseases on Golden Grove Estate, Jamaica, 1765-1810', *Slavery and Abolition*, 6 (1985).

SECTION 13. REJECTING SLAVERY: BLACKS SPEAK BACK

Aptheker, H. (ed.) *A Documentary of the Negro People in the United States* (Citadel Press: New Jersey, 1955).

Beckles, H. and Shepherd, V. (eds.), *Slave Voices* (UNESCO Associated Schools Network Project, 1999).

Carmichael, A. C. *Domestic Manners and Social Condition of the White, Colored, and Negro Population of the West Indies, 2 vols.* op. cit.

Craton, M. *Empire, Enslavement and Freedom in the Caribbean*, op. cit.

Cuguano, O. *Thoughts and Sentiments on the Evil and Wicked Traffic of Slavery and the Commerce of the Human Species* (London, 1791).

Edwards, P. (ed.) *The Life of Olaudah Equiano, Gustavus Vassa, The African: Written by Himself* (Longmans: London, 1988).

Everett, S. *History of Slavery* (Grange Books: London 1996).

Ferguson. M. (ed.) *The History of Mary Prince: A West Indian Slave Related By Herself* op. cit.

Fick, C. *The Making of Haiti: The Saint Domingue Revolution from Below* (Univ. of Tennessee Press: Knoxville, 1990).

Hart, R. 'Slaves Who Abolished Slavery, vol.1.' *Blacks in Bondage* (ISER, U.W.I., 1980).

Hughs, L. *Thirty Years a Slave: From Bondage to Freedom* (South Side Co: Milwaukee, 1897).

MacArthur, B. *Historic Speeches* (Penguin: New York, 1995).

Manzano, J. F. *The Autobiography of a Slave* (Wayne State Univ. Press: Detriot, 1996)

Mellon, M.,. *Early American Views on Negro Slavery* (Mentor Books, 1969).

Stuckey, S. *Slave Culture: Nationalist Theory and the Foundations of Black America* (Oxford Univ. Press: Oxford, 1987).

Verteuil de, A. *Seven Slaves and Slavery, Trinidad, 1777-1838* (A. de Verteuil: Port of Spain, 1992).

Williams, C. *A Tour Through the Island of Jamaica From the Western to the Eastern End in the Year 1823*, (Hunt and Clarke: London, 1826).

SECTION 14. CARIBBEAN WARS: MARRONAGE AND REBELLION

Anderson, J. L. *Night of the Silent Drums: A Narrative of Slave Rebellion in the Virgin Islands* (Scribners: New York, 1975).

Beckles, H. 'Masters and Servants', in H. McD. Beckles, *White Servitude and Black Slavery in Barbados, 1627-1715*, op cit.

Beckles, H. 'The 200 Years War: Slave Resistance in the British West Indies: An Overview of the Historiography', *Jamaican Historical Review*, 12 (1982).

Beckles, H. 'Rebels Without Heroes: Slave Politics in Seventeenth Century Barbados', *Journal of Caribbean History*, 18, 2 (1984).

Beckles, H. *Black Rebellion in Barbados: The Struggle Against Slavery, 1627-1838* (Antilles Publications: Bridgetown, Barbados, 1984).

Beckles, H. 'The Slave Drivers' War: Bussa and the 1816 Barbados Slave Uprising', *Boletin de Estudios Latinoamericanos y del Caribe*, 39 (1985).

Beckles, H. 'From Land to Sea: Runaway Barbados Slaves and Servants 1630-1700', in G. Heuman (ed.), *Out of the House of Bondage: Runaways, Resistance and Marronage in Africa and the New World* (Frank Cass: London, 1986).

Beckles, H. and Watson , K. 'Social Protest and Labour Bargaining: The Changing Nature of Slaves' Responses to Plantation Life in Eighteenth Century Barbados', *Slavery and Abolition*, 8, 3 (1987).

Brathwaite, K. 'The Slave Rebellion in the Great River Valley of St. James, 1831/32', *Jamaican Historical Review*, 13 (1982).

Campbell, M. *The Maroons of Jamaica, 1655-1796: A History of Resistance,*
Collaboration and Betrayal (Bergin and Garvey: Granby, Massachusets, 1988).

Campbell, M. 'Marronage in Jamaica: Its Origins in the Seventeenth Century' in V. Rubin and A. Tuden (eds.), *Comparative Perspectives on Slavery in the New World Plantation Societies* (New York Academy of Sciences: New York, 1977).

Carey, B. *The Maroon Story: The Authentic and Original History of the Maroons in the History of Jamaica, 1490-1880*, op. cit.

Craton, M. 'Proto-Peasant Revolts? The Late Slave Rebellions in the British West Indies, 1816-1832', *Past and Present*, 85 (1979).

Craton, M. 'The Passion to Exist: Slave Rebellions in the British West Indies, 1650-1832', *Journal of Caribbean History*, 13 (1980).

Craton, M. *Testing the Chains*, op. cit.

Craton, M. 'We Shall Not Be Moved: Pompey's Slave Revolt in Exuma Island, Bahamas, 1830' *New West Indian Guide*, 57, 1-2 (1983).

Cripps, L. L. *The Spanish Caribbean from Columbus to Castro*, op. cit.

Curtin, P.D. 'The Jamaican Revolution', in P.D. Curtin, *Two Jamaicas*, op. cit.

Curtin, P.D. 'Revolution in the French Antilles', in P.D. Curtin, *The Rise and Fall of The Plantation Complex: Essays in Atlantic History*, op cit.

Debein, G. 'Le Marronage Aux Antilles Francaises au xvii siecle', *Caribbean Studies*, 6,3 (1966).

Degroot, S. 'Les Marrons de Saint Domingue en 1764', *Jamaican Historical Review*, 6 (1960).

Degroot, S. 'The Boni Maroon War, 1765-1793, Surinam and French Guiana', *Boletin De Estudios Latinoamericanos y del Caribe*, 18 (1975).

Dirks, R. *The Black Saturnalia: Conflict and its Ritual Expression on British West Indian Slave Plantations* (University Presses of Florida: Gainesville, 1987).

Gaspar, B. *Bondsmen and Rebels: A Study of Master-Slave Rebellions in Antigua: With Implications for Colonial British America* (Johns Hopkins Univ. Press: Baltimore, 1984).

Gaspar, D. B. 'The Antigua Slave Conspiracy of 1736: A Case Study of the Origins of Collective Resistance', *William and Mary Quarterly*, 3rd Ser., 33 (1978).

Gaspar, D. B. 'La Guerre des Bois: Revolution, War, and Slavery in Saint Lucia, 1793-1838', in D. B Gaspar and D. Geggus (eds) *A Turbulent Time: The Greater Caribbean in the Age of the Haitian and French Revolutions* (Indiana Univ. Press, 1997).

Geggus, D. 'Jamaica and the St. Domingue Slave Revolt, 1791-1793', *Americas*, 38, (1981).

Geggus, D. 'The Enigma of Jamaica: New Light on the Causes of Slave Rebellions',*William and Mary Quarterly*, 44 (1987).

Goveia, E. *Slave Society in the British Leeward Islands at the End of the 18th Century*, op. cit.

Handler, J. 'Escaping Slavery in a Caribbean Plantation Society: Marronage in Barbados, 1650s-1830s', *New West Indian Guide*, 71, 3-4 (1997).

Hartsinck, J. J. 'The Story of the Slave Rebellion in Berbice' (translated by W.E. Ruth), *Journal of the British Guiana Museum and Zoo*, 20-27 (1958).

Heuman, G. 'Runaway Slaves in 19th Century Barbados', in G. Heuman, *Out of the House of Bondage*, op. cit.

Lane, C.A. 'Concerning Jamaica's 1760 Slave Rebellions', *Jamaica Journal*, 7, 4 (1973).

Marshall, B. 'Marronage in Slave Plantation Societies: A Case Study of Dominica', *Caribbean Quarterly*, 22 (1796).

Marshall, B. 'Slave Resistance and White Reaction in the British Windward Islands, 1763-1833', *Caribbean Quarterly*, 28,3 (1982).

Patterson, O. *The Sociology of Slavery*, op. cit.

Patterson, O. 'Slavery and Slave Revolts: A Socio-historical Analysis of the First Maroon War', *Social and Economic Studies*, 19,3 (1970).

Patterson, O. 'The General Causes of Slave Revolts' in L. Foner and E. Genovese (eds), *Slavery in the New World* (Prentice Hall: New Jersey, 1969).

Paula, A. F. '1795: The Slave Insurrection on the Island of Curacao: Possible Connections Between the Curacao and Venezuela Revolts in 1795', *Cimarrons*, 2.

Price, R. *Maroon Societies: Rebel Slave Communities in the Americas* (Johns Hopkins Univ. Press: Baltimore, 1996).

Reynolds, C. R. 'Tacky and the Great Slave Rebellions of 1760', *Jamaica Journal*, 6,2 (1972).

Schuler, M. 'Ethnic Slave Rebellions in the Caribbean and the Guianas', *Journal of Social History*, 3 (1970).

Schuler, M. 'Day to Day Resistance to Slavery in the Caribbean in the 18th Century', *ASAWI Bulletin*, 1, iv (1973).

Scott, R. 'Insurrection and Slavery', in Rebecca Scott, Slave *Emancipation in Cuba: The Transition to Free Labour, 1860-1899* (Princeton Univ. Press: Princeton, 1985).

Sheridan, R. 'The Jamaican Slave Insurrection Scare of 1776 and the American Revolution', *Journal of Negro History*, 61, 3 (1976).

Smith, M.G. 'Some Aspects of Social Structure in the British Caribbean About 1870', in M.G. Smith, *The Plural Society of the British West Indies* (Univ. of California Press: Berkerley,1965).

Taylor, C. 'Planter Comment on Slave Revolts in Jamaica', *Slavery and Abolition*, 3,3 (1982).

Thompson, A. *Brethren of the Bush: A Study of the Runaways and Bush Negroes in Guyana* (Cave Hill, ISER, 1976).

Thompson, V. B. 'African Resistance to Slavery in the Americas', in V.B. Thompson, *The Making of the African Diaspora in the Americas, 1441-1900* (Longman: London, 1987).

Thompson, V. B. 'The Treatment of Slaves', in V.B. Thompson, *The Making of the African Diaspora*, op. cit.

Turner, M. 'The Bishop of Jamaica and Slave Insurrection in Jamaica', *Journal of Ecclesiastical History*, 26, 4 (1975).

SECTION 15. THE HAITIAN REVOLUTION

Beard, J. K. *The Life of Toussaint L'Ouverture, The Negro Patriot of Hayti: Comprising An Account of the Struggle for Liberty in the Island, and a Sketch of its History to the Present* (London, 1853).

Bryan, P. *The Haitian Revolution and its Effect* (Heinemann: Kingston, 1984).

Debs, R. *Written in Blood: The Story of the Haitian People, 1492-1995* (Univ. Press of America: Lanham, MD, 1996).

Dupuy, A. *Haiti in the World Economy. Class, Race and Underdevelopment since 1700.* (Westview Press: Colorado, 1989).

Fick, C. *The Making of Haiti: The Saint Domingue Revolution from Below* op. cit

Geggus, D. Slavery, War and Revolution: The British Occupation of Saint Domingue, 1793-1798 (Clarendon Press: Oxford, 1982).

Geggus, D. *The "Volte Face" of Toussaint L'Ouverture* (Paris: F Societe d' Histoire d' Outre Mer, 1978).

Geggus, D. 'Marronage, Voodoo, and the Saint Domingue Slave Revolt', in Patricia Galloway and Philip Boucher (eds.), *Proceedings of the 15th Meeting of the French Colonial Historical Society* (Univ. Press of America, 1992).

Geggus, D. 'Slavery, War and Revolution in the Greater Caribbean, 1789-1815', In D.B Gaspar and D. Geggus (eds.) *A Turbulent Time: The Greater Caribbean in the Age of the Haitian and French Revolutions* (Indiana Univ. Press: Bloomington, 1997).

Griffiths, A. *Black Patriot and Martyr: Toussaint of Haiti* (Julian Messner: New York, 1970).

James, C. L. R. *The Black Jacobins: Toussaint L'Ouverture and the San Domingo Revolution* (Vintage Books: London, 1963).

Jerome, Y. *Toussaint L'Ouverture* (Vantage Press: New York, 1978).

Lundahl, M. 'Toussaint L'Ouverture and the War Economy of Saint Domingue, 1796-1802, in *Slavery and Abolition*, Vol. 6, No. 2. (September 1985).

Ott, T. *The Haitian Revolution, 1789-1804* (Univ. of Tennessee Press: Knoxville, 1973).

Rainford, M. *An Historical Account of the Black Empire of Hayti* (Albion Press,1805).

Ros, M. *Night of Fire; The Black Napoleon and the Battle for Haiti* (Sarpedon Publishers: New York, 1994).

Stein, R. *Leger Felicite Sonthonax: The Lost Sentinel of the Republic* (Associated Univ. Presses:London, 1985).

Steward, T. *The Haitian Revolution, 1791 to 1804* (Russell and Russell: New York, 1914).

Stoddard, T. *The French Revolution in San Domingo* (Negro Univ. Press: Conn. 1970).

Syme, R. *Toussaint; The Black Liberator* (Marrow: New York, 1971).

Tabasuri, T. *A Theory of Revolution and a Case Study of the Haitian Revolution* (Univ. of Oklahoma Press: Oklahoma, 1981).

Trouillot, M. 'From Planters' Journal to Academia: The Haitian Revolution as Unthinkable History', *Journal of Caribbean History*, 25, 1-2 (1991).

Tyson, G. *Toussaint L'Ouverture* (Prentice Hall: New York, 1973).

SECTION 16. REBEL WOMEN ANTI-SLAVERY FEMINIST VANGUARD

Beckles, H. *Centering Woman: Gender Discourses in Caribbean Slave Society*, op. cit.

Beckles, H. *Natural Rebels: A Social History of Enslaved Black Women in Barbados*, op. cit.

Beckles, H. *Afro-Caribbean Women and Resistance to Slavery in Barbados* (Karnak House: London, 1988).

Brereton, B. *Gendered Testimony*, op. cit.

Bush, B. *Slave Women in Caribbean Society, 1650-1838*, op cit.

Bush, B. 'Defiance or Submission? The Role of the Slave Woman in Slave Resistance In the British Caribbean', *Immigrants and Minorities*, 1 (1982).

Bush, B. 'The Family Tree is Not Cut': Women and Cultural Resistance in Slave Family Life in the British Caribbean', in G. Okihiro (ed.), *In Resistance: Studies in African, Caribbean and Afro-American History*, op. cit.

Bush, B. 'Hard Labor: Women, Childbirth and Resistance in British Caribbean Slave Societies', in D.B Gaspar and D.C Hine (eds.) *More Than Chattel: Black Women and Slavery in the Americas* (Indiana Univ. Press: Bloomington, 1996).

Bush, B. 'Survival and Resistance: S lave Women and Coercive Labour Regimes in the British Caribbean, 1750-1838', in Manning, P (ed.), *Slave Trades, 1500-1800: Globalization of Forced Labour*, op. cit.

Dadzie, S. 'Searching for the Invisible Woman: Slavery and Resistance in Jamaica', *Race and Class*, 32, 2 (1990).

Gaspar, D.B. and Clark-Hine, D. (eds.), *More Than Chattel: Black Women and Slavery in the Americas*, op cit.

Kafka, J. 'Action, Reaction and Interaction: Slave Women in Resistance in the South of Saint Domingue, 1793-94', *Slavery and Abolition*, 18, 2 (1997).

Morrissey, M. *Slave Women in the New World: Gender Stratification in the Caribbean*, op. cit.

Reddock, R. *Women, Labour and Politics in Trinidad and Tobago: A History* (Zed Books: London, 1994).

Shepherd, V. Brereton, B. and Bailey, B. (eds.) *Engendering History: Caribbean Women in Historical Perspective*, op. cit.

Shepherd, V. (ed) *Women in Caribbean History* (Ian Randle Publishers: Kingston, 1999).

Silvestrini, B.G. 'Women and Resistance: Herstory in Contemporary Caribbean History', *Elsa Goveia Memorial Lecture*, (UWI, 1990).

SECTION 17
CAPITALISM, IDEOLOGY AND EMANCIPATION PROCESSES

Anstey, R. *The Atlantic Slave Trade and British Abolition, 1760- 1810* (Humanities Press: New Jersey, 1975).

Anstey, R. 'Parliamentary Reform Methodism and Anti-Slavery Politics, 1829-1833', *Slavery and Abolition*, 2 (1981).

Ashworth, J. 'Capitalism, Class and Antislavery', in T. Bender (ed). *The Antislavery Debate: Capitalism and Abolitionism as a Problem in Historical Interpretation* (Univ. of California Press: Berkeley, 1992).

Ashworth, J. 'The Relationship Between Capitalism and Humanitarianism', in T. Bender (ed). *The Antislavery Debate*, op. cit.

Bartlett, C. 'Britain and the Abolition of Slavery in Puerto Rico and Cuba', *Journal of Caribbean History*, 23, 1 (1990).

Blackburn, R. *The Overthrow of Colonial Slavery, 1776-1848*, op. cit.

Butler, M. 'Fair and Equitable Consideration: The Distribution of Slave Compensation in Jamaica and Barbados', *Journal of Caribbean History*, 22:1 and 2.

Butler, M. *The Economics of Emancipation* (Univ. of North Carolina Press: Chapel Hill, 1995).

Corwin, A, F. *Spain and the Abolition of Slavery in Cuba 1817-1866*, op. cit.

Craton, M. 'Emancipation from Below?: The Role of the British West Indian in the Emancipation Movement', in J. Hayward (ed.), *Out of Slavery: Abolition and After* (F. Cass: London, 1985).

Craton, M. 'Slave Culture, Resistance and the Achievement of Emancipation in the British West Indies, 1738-1828', in J. Walvin (ed.), *Slavery and British Abolition, 1776-1848* (MacMillan: London, 1982).

Darity, W. A. 'The Williams Abolition Thesis Before Williams', *Slavery and Abolition*, 9 (1988).

Diaz Soler, L. M. 'The Abolition of Slavery in Puerto Rico 1868-1878', *Caribbean Historical Review*, 2 (1951).

Drescher, S. 'Capitalism and the Decline of Slavery', in V. Rubin and A. Tuden (eds), *Comparative Perspectives on Slavery in New World Plantation Societies*, op. cit

Drescher, S. *Econocide: British Slavery in the Era of Abolition*, op. cit.

Drescher, S. 'The Decline Thesis of British Slavery Since Econocide', *Slavery and Abolition*, 7, 1 (1980).

Eltis, D. 'The Economic Impact of the Ending of the African Slave Trade to the Americas', *Social and Economic Studies*, 37, 1 and 2 (1988).

Eltis, D. and Walvin, J. *The Abolition of the Atlantic Slave Trade: Origins and Effects in Europe, Africa and the Americas,* op cit.

Emmer, P. 'The Abolitionist Movement Abroad in the Ending of Caribbean Slavery: The Case Of Surinam', *Caribbean Societies (ICS), 11: Collected Seminar Papers*, No. 34 (1985).

Engerman, S. L. 'Slavery and Emancipation in Comparative Perspectives: A Look at Some Recent Debates', *Journal of Economic History*, 46 (1986).

Hart, R. *Slaves Who Abolished Slavery* 11 (Institute of Social and Economic Research, Mona, 1985).

Holt, T. 'Explaining Abolition' *Journal of Social History*, 24, 2 (1990).

Knight, F. W. 'The Disintegration of the Caribbean Slave Systems', in F.W. Knight (ed.), *The Slave Societies of the Caribbean* (MacMillan: London, 1997).

Levy, C. 'Barbados: The Last Years of Slavery 1823-33', *Journal of Negro History*, 44, 4, (1959).

Nistal-Moret, B. 'Problems in the Social Structure of Slavery in Puerto Rico During the Process of Abolition, 1872', in Moreno Fraginals, M., Moya Pons, F and Engerman, S.L. (eds), *Between Slavery and Free Labour: The Spanish-Speaking Caribbean in the Nineteenth Century,* op. cit.

Ragatz, L. J. *The Fall of the Planter Class in the British West Indies, 1762-1833* (Octagon Books: New York, 1963).

Schuler, M. 'Plantation Labourers, The London Missionary Society and Emancipation in West Demerara, Guyana', *Journal of Caribbean History*, 22, 1 and 2 (1990).

Scott, R. 'Gradual Abolition and the Dynamics of Slave Emancipation in Cuba 1868-1886', *Hispanic American Historical Review* (1983).

Stein, R. 'The Revolution of 1789 and the Abolition of Slavery', *Canadian Journal of History*, 17, 3 (1982).

Tocqueville, A. *Report on the Abolition of Slavery in the French Colonies* (Negro Universities Press, 1970 rpt).

Turner, M. 'The Baptist War in Abolition', *Jamaican Historical Review*, 23 (1982).

Turner, M. *Slaves and Missionaries: The Disintegration of Jamaican Slave Society, 1787-1834* (University of Illinois Press: Urbana, 1982).

Ward, J. R. 'Emancipation and Planters', *Journal of Caribbean History*, 22, 1 and 2 (1990).

Williams, E. *Capitalism and Slavery*, op cit.

References to Chapter 2 (continued from page 31)

Lawrence A.W., *Trade Castles and Forts of West Africa*. London: Jonathan Cape. 1963

Livermore, H.V., "On the Conquest of Ceuta." *Luso-Brazilian Review* 2(I):3-13. 1965

Lobo, A. de Sousa Silva Costa, *História da Sociedade em Portugal no século XV*. Lisbon: Imprensa Nacional. 1903

Lovejoy, Paul, *Transformations in Slavery: A History of Slavery in Africa*. Cambridge: Cambridge University Press. 1983

Marchant, Alexander, *From Barter to Slavery. The Economic Relations of Portuguese and Indians in the Settlement of Brazil, 1500-1580*. Baltimore: Johns Hopkins University Press. 1942

Menses, Avelino de Freitas de, " A expansão ultramarina até a época de D. João ll: causas e vertentes." In *A viagem de Bartolomeu Dias e a problematica dos descobrimentos. Actas do seminário relaizado em Ponta Delgada, Angra do Heroísmo e Horta de 2 a 7 de maio de 1988*, pp. 79-114. Universiadade dos Açores/Centro de Estudos Gaspar Frutuoso. 1989

Miers, Suzanne, and Igor Kopytoff, "African 'Slavery' as an Institution of Marginality." In *Slavery in Africa. Historical and Anthropological Perspectives*, edited by Miers and Kopytoff, pp. 3-81. Madison: University of Wisconsin Press. 1977

Mota, Avelino Teixeira da, "Alguns aspectos da colonização e do comércio marítimo dos portugueses na Africa occidental nos seculos XV e XVI." Anais do Clube Militar Naval 101:680-81. 1976

Oliveira Marques, A.H. de, *Daily Life in Portugal in the Late Middle Ages*. Translated by S. S. Wyatt. Madison: University of Wisconsin Press. 1971

Os Açores e o Atlântico, séculos XIV-XVII,

——. Angra do Heroísmo: Insituto Histórico da Ilha Terceira. 1984

Pereira, Duarte Pacheco, "Book of Cosmography and Navigation." *Esmeraldo de Situ Orbis*. 2d ser., Written c. 1505/1508; translated into English and edited by George H.T. Kimble. London: Hakluyt Society. 1937

Perira, Isaías da Rosa, "Dois compromissos de irmandades de homens pretos." Arqueologia e historia 9 (4): 9-47. 1972

Peres, Damião, *Regimento das cazas das Indias e Mina*. Coimbra: Imprensa da Universidade. 1947

Perrone-Moisés, Beatriz, "A guerra justa em Portugal no século XVI." *Revista da Sociedade Brasileira de Pesquisa historica* 5:5-1. 1989-90

Pfandl, Ludwig (editor), "Itinerarium Hispanicum Hieronymi Monetarii, 1491-1495." *Revue Hispanique* 48 (113): 1-179. 1920

Phillips, Jr., William D., *Slavery from Roman Times to the Early Atlantic Trade*. Minneapolis: Univeristy of Minnesota Press.

Pina, Rui de, *Crónica de el-rei D. João II*. New edition with preface and notes by Alberto Martins de Carvalho. Coimbra: Atlântida. 1950

Randles, W.G. L., *L'ancien royaume du Congo des origines à la fin du XIXe siècle*. Paris, The Hague: Mouton. 1968

Resende, Garcia de, *Chronica del Rei dom João II*. n.d.

Ricard, Robert, Etudes sur l'histoire des Portugais au Maroc. Coimbra: Acta Universitatis Conimbrigensis. 1955

Rogers, Francis M., The Quest for Eastern Christians. Minneapolis: University of Minnesota Press. 1962

Russell, Peter, "Fontes documentais castelhanas para a história da expansão portuguesa na Guiné nos últimos anos de D. Afonso V." Do tempo e da história 4:5-33.

Russell-Wood, A.J.R., "Iberian Expansion and the Issue of Black Slavery: Changing Portuguese Attitudes, 1440-1770." American Historical Review 83(1):16-42. 1978

——. The Black Man in Slavery and Freedom in Colonial Brazil. London: MacMillan. Repr. 1993. 1982

——. "A Cause Célèbre of Colonial Brazil: António Fernades' Personal Struggle for Justice." Revista da Sociedade Brasileira de Pesquisa Histórica 4. Reprinted in A.J.R. Russell-Wood, Society and Government in Colonial Brazil, 1500-1822 (Variorum: Aldershot, 1992). 1987-88

——. "Prestige, Power, and Piety in Colonial Brazil: The Third Orders of Salvador." Hispanic American Historical Review 69 (1):61-89.

——. A World on the Move. The Portuguese in Africa, Asia and America, 1415-1808. Manchester: Carcamet Press; New York: St. Martin's Press. 1992

Ryder, A. F. C. Benin and the Europeans, 1485-1897. New York: Humanities Press. 1969

Saraiva, António José, *História da Cultural em Portugal*. 3 vols. Lisbon: Jornal do Foor. 1950

Saunders, A. C. de C. M. *A Social History of Black Slaves and Freedmen in Portugal, 1441-1555*. Cambridge: Cambridge University Press. 1982

Scammell, Geoffrey V. *The World Encompassed. The First European Maritime Empires, c. 800-1650*. Berkeley: University of California Press. 1981

Schwartz, Stuart B. "Indian Labor and New World Plantations: European Demands and Indian Response in Northeastern Brazil." *American Historical Review* 83 (1): 43-79. 1978

Serrão, Joaquim Veríssimo, *História de Portugal*. 3rd ed. Rev., vol 2. Lisbon: Editorial Verbo. 1977

Silva Horta, José da, "A representação do Africano na literatura de viagens do Sensgal à Serra Leoa (1453-1508)." *Mare Liberum* 2: 209-338. 1991

——. *The Travels of Leo of Rozmital through Germany, Flanders, England, France, Spain, Portugal, and Italy, 1465-1467*. Translated and edited by Malcolm Letts. Cambridge: Hakluyt Society. 1957

Thornton, John, *Africa and Africans in the Making of the Atlantic World, 1400-1680*. Cambridge: Cambridge University Press. 1992

Tinhorão, José Ramos, *Os negros em Portugal. Uma presença silenciosa*. Lisbon: Editorial Caminho. 1988

Van Sertima, Ivan, *They Came before Columbus*. New York: Random House. 1976

Verlinden, Charles, L'esclavage dans l'Europe médiévale. 2 vols. Bruges. 1955

Vieira, Alberto, O Comércio inter-insular nos séculos XV e XVI. Madeira, Acores e Canárias. Coimbra: Secretaria regional do turismo e cultura, Região autónoma da Madeira, Centro de Estudos de História do Atlântico. 1987

Vogt, John L., "The Lisbon Slave House and African Trade, 1486-1521." *Proceedings of the American Philosophical Society* 1179 (I): 10-11. 1973

Wright, John Kirtland, *The Geographical Lore of the Time of the Crusades*. New York: American Geographical Society.1925

Zurara, Gomes Eanes de, Crónica dos feitos de Guiné. Written ca. 1453/1460. Translated into French and edited by Léon Bourdon. Ifan-Dakar. Mémoires d l'Institut Français de l'Afrique Noire, no. 60. 1960

Lightning Source UK Ltd.
Milton Keynes UK
UKOW07f2301220915

259091UK00005B/215/P